THE
EXPOSITOR'S BIBLE COMMENTARY

ABRIDGED EDITION

New Testament

THE EXPOSITOR'S BIBLE COMMENTARY

ABRIDGED EDITION

New Testament

Kenneth L. Barker
John R. Kohlenberger III

GRAND RAPIDS, MICHIGAN 49530 USA

ZONDERVAN™

The Expositor's Bible Commentary—Abridged Edition: New Testament
Copyright © 1994 by the Zondervan Corporation

Formerly titled *Zondervan NIV Bible Commentary: Volume 2: New Testament*

Requests for information should be addressed to:

Zondervan, *Grand Rapids, Michigan 49530*

Library of Congress Cataloging-in-Publication Data

The Zondervan NIV Bible Commentary / Consulting editors, Kenneth L. Barker and
John R. Kohlenberger III
    p. cm.
An abridgment of The expositor's Bible commentary, retaining the interpretative material but missing the text of the NIV and the detailed scholarly notes and discussion.
Includes indexes.
Contents: v. 1. Old Testament — v. 2. New Testament.
    ISBN 0-310-57850-7 (v. 1) — ISBN 0-310-57840-X (v. 2)
    1. Bible—Commentaries.   I. Barker, Kenneth L.   II. Kohlenberger, John R.
III. Expositor's Bible commentary.
BS491.2.Z65   1994
220.7—dc20   94-6885

This edition ISBN 0-310-25497-3

All Scripture quotations, unless otherwise indicated, are taken from the *Holy Bible: New International Version*®. NIV®. Copyright © 1973, 1978, 1984 by International Bible Society. Used by permission of Zondervan. All rights reserved.

"NIV" and "New International Version" are registered in the United States Patent and Trademark Office by the International Bible Society.

All rights reserved. No part of this publication may be reproduced, stored in a retrieval system, or transmitted in any form or by any means—electronic, mechanical, photocopy, recording, or any other—except for brief quotations in printed reviews, without the prior permission of the publisher.

This edition is printed on acid-free paper.

Printed in the United States of America

---

07 08 09 10 /❖ DC/ 10 9 8 7

Contents

Acknowledgments vi
Preface vii
Pictures, Maps, and Charts viii
Abbreviations x

Matthew: D. A. Carson. 1
Mark: Walter W. Wessel 136
Luke: Walter L. Liefeld 206
John: Merrill C. Tenney 290
Acts: Richard N. Longenecker 376
Romans: Everett F. Harrison 519
1 Corinthians: W. Harold Mare 606
2 Corinthians: Murray H. Harris 658
Galatians: James Montgomery Boice 703
Ephesians: A. Skevington Wood 748
Philippians: Homer A. Kent, Jr. 787
Colossians: Curtis Vaughan 812
1 Thessalonians: Robert L. Thomas 843

2 Thessalonians: Robert L. Thomas 874
1 Timothy: Ralph Earle 889
2 Timothy: Ralph Earle 909
Titus: D. Edmond Hiebert 919
Philemon: Arthur A. Rupprecht 935
Hebrews: Leon Morris 940
James: Donald W. Burdick 1016
1 Peter: Edwin A. Blum 1040
2 Peter: Edwin A. Blum 1061
1 John: Glenn W. Barker 1077
2 John: Glenn W. Barker 1110
3 John: Glenn W. Barker 1114
Jude: Edwin A. Blum 1118
Revelation: Alan F. Johnson 1125

Index to Goodrick/Kohlenberger Numbers 1233

Acknowledgments

The publisher of the *Zondervan NIV Bible Commentary* wishes to thank the two editors who undertook the massive task of reducing eleven volumes of Bible commentaries into two: Richard Polcyn, who did the Old Testament, and Verlyn D. Verbrugge, who did the New Testament. Thanks also to Dr. Kenneth L. Barker and John R. Kohlenberger III, who offered invaluable assistance as consulting editors.

The publisher also deeply appreciates the assistance of Neal and Joel Bierling, who served as consultants for, and provided, most of the pictures used in this two-volume commentary. Unless otherwise noted, all pictures are theirs. Finally, thanks to the Bible Department of Zondervan Publishing House for allowing us to use many of the charts and maps from their best-selling study Bibles.

About the Editors

John R. Kolenberger III is the author or coeditor of more than three dozen biblical reference books and study Bibles, including *The Strongest Strong's Exhaustive Concordance of the Bible, NIV Interlinear Hebrew-English Old Testament, NRSV Concordance Unabridged, Greek-English Concordance to the New Testament, Hebrew-English Concordance to the Old Testament,* and the award-winning *NIV Exhaustive Concordance* and *NIV Bible Commentary.* He has taught at Multnomah Bible College and Western Seminary in Portland, Oregon.

Kenneth L. Barker (Ph.D., Dropsie College for Hebrew and Cognate Learning) is presently serving on the Committee for Bible Translation of the International Bible Society (the committee that oversees the New International Version of the Bible), is the general editor for the upcoming revised *NIV Study Bible,* and authored the commentary on "Zechariah" in *The Expositor's Bible Commentary.*

Preface

The NIV Bible Commentary has been in the making for a long time. In 1976 the first volume of *The Expositor's Bible Commentary* (Volume 10) was released, containing commentaries on Romans to Galatians, under the general editorship of Frank E. Gaebelein. The final volume in this series was published in 1992, with commentaries on Deuteronomy to 2 Samuel.

Contributors for *The Expositor's Bible Commentary* were solicited from among the best evangelical scholars on both sides of the Atlantic. Each expositor was committed to the divine inspiration, complete trustworthiness, and full authority of Scripture as God's Word. Each author's work aimed to provide preachers, teachers, and students of the Bible with insights into the Scriptures that were scholarly yet practical to everyday life. The full text of the New International Version of the Bible was printed along with the commentary section. The units of discussion were often followed by technical notes of interest mainly to scholars.

The Expositor's Bible Commentary has fulfilled its goal admirably, judging from the positive reviews it has received, the awards it has earned, and the tens of thousands of sets that have been purchased. It was felt that this excellent series could serve well as the basis for a two-volume commentary set designed primarily for lay persons. Consequently, the commentaries from Genesis to Revelation in the *Expositor's Bible Commentary* have now been abridged, retaining all the important interpretative material of the larger set but without the text of the NIV and the detailed scholarly notes and discussions.

This two-volume commentary has two additional features not found in the original set. First, both volumes are replete with maps, charts, tables, and pictures that are relevant to the passages under discussion. Secondly, throughout the commentary, where specific biblical words are discussed at some length, the Goodrick-Kohlenberger numbers (abbreviated GK) have been added. These numbers, which appeared first in *The NIV Exhaustive Concordance*, are based on the numbering system for each Hebrew, Aramaic, and Greek word in the Bible developed by Edward W. Goodrick and John R. Kohlenberger III (a numbering system similar but superior to the ever-popular Strong's numbering system). An index of the words that are referred to is found in the back of each volume.

It is the hope of the publisher that just as *The Expositor's Bible Commentary* has served so well the needs of pastors and teachers, this two-volume commentary will serve the needs of average lay persons in the church who want to learn more about the Bible in their personal study or prepare themselves to lead a Bible lesson in a small group study.

The Bible is the greatest and most beautiful book of all time, the primary source of law and morality, the fountain of divine wisdom, the infallible guide to life, and above all, the inspired witness to Jesus Christ. May this work fulfill its function of expounding the Scriptures with grace and clarity, so that its users may find that both Old and New Testaments do indeed lead us to our Lord Jesus Christ, who alone could say, "I have come that they may have life, and have it to the full" (John 10:10).

Pictures, Maps, and Charts

Pictures

Ancient Lamps	25
Site of the Sermon on the Mount	34
Site of John the Baptist's Preaching	55
Fishing Boat from the First Century A.D.	74
Roman Denarius	86
Palm Sunday Pilgrims	94
Whitewashed Tombs	105
Model of Ancient Jerusalem	128
Mount Hermon	169
Model of the Traditional Site of Golgotha	199
Site of Gabriel's Visit to Mary	213
Site Where Jesus Taught the Crowds	234
Rugged Terrain between Jerusalem and Jericho	250
Sycamore Tree	271
Mount of Olives and the Kidron Valley	279
Model of Herod's Temple	303
Jacob's Well	309
Model of the Pool of Bethesda	311
Solomon's Colonnade	332
Traditional Site of the Crucifixion	364
Caiaphas's Family Gravesite	404
Site of Stephen's Stoning	416
Outdoor Theater in Caesarea	451
Paphos, Cyprus	454
Ruins of the Temple of Zeus and Mars' Hill	477
Ruins of the Large Theater in Ephesus	489
Fragment of a Temple Mount Stone	496
Ruins of the Fortress at Antipatris	502
Mount Sinai	532
Ancient Ink Wells	556
Ruins of Corinth	620
Ruins of a Corinthian Temple	631
Mosaic Plate and Cup	639
Paul's Ephesian Prison	653
Ruins of Troas	668
The *Bema* of Corinth	677
Ruins of Capernaum Synagogue	716
Philippi's Central Square	799
Philippian Women	808
Site of Aphrodias	813
Restored Athenian Amphitheater	857
Roman Soldier	867
Leather Workers	887
A Scroll	902
The Roman Coliseum	915
Date Palm	965
Catacombs Painting	991
Bedouin Tents	996
The Mediterranean Sea	1020
Pilate's Cornerstone	1048

viii

Ruins of Ephesian Church	1111
Temple of Ephesian Goddess Artemis	1140
Pergamum's Altar to Zeus	1144
Hot and Lukewarm Pools at Pamukale	1153
John's Vision of the Attack of a Pregnant Woman	1182
Satan Worshipers' Scribbled 666	1194
Possible Site of the Battle of Armageddon	1203

Maps, Charts, Tables

Chart of the Herodian Family	12
Chart of the Miracles of Jesus	42
Chart of the Parables of Jesus	66
Chart of Passion Week	118
Chart of the Life of Christ	145–47
Map of the Decapolis and Beyond Jordan	156
Map of Jerusalem in the Time of Jesus	179
Map of Jesus' Ministry in Galilee	224
Map of Jesus' Ministry in Judea and Samaria	246
Chart of Jewish Sects	261
Chart on Resurrection Appearances	287
Table of Contrasts Between the Synoptics and John	296
Chart of John's Testimony to Jesus	323
Chart of the Work of the Holy Spirit	347–48
Map of the Countries Represented at Pentecost	390
Chart of the *Kerygma* of the Early Church	393
Chart of the Miracles of the Apostles	400
Map of Philip's and Peter's Missionary Journeys	426
Map of Roman Damascus	433
Map of Paul's First Missionary Journey	461
Map of Paul's Second Missionary Journey	469
Map of Paul's Third Missionary Journey	485
Map of Paul's Journey to Rome	511
Map of Rome in Paul's Time	520
Chart of Great Doctrines in Paul	549
Chart of Passages Indicating the Deity of Christ	570–71
Chart of Personal Gifts of the Holy Spirit	584
Map of Corinth in the Time of Paul	607
Map of Paul's Interaction with Corinth	659
Table of Jesus' Words Not Found in the Gospels	698
Chart of the Fruit of the Spirit	742
Map of Ephesus in Paul's Time	750
Chart of the Comparison of Ephesians and Colossians	758–59
Chart of the Ministry Gifts of the Holy Spirit	770–71
Map of Philippi in Paul's Time	789
Chart of the Colossian Heresy	823
Table of Songs in the New Testament	837
Map of Paul's Fourth Missionary Journey	892
Chart of Elder/Overseer and Deacon Qualifications	924
Chart of "Greater-Thans" in Hebrews	952
Chart on the Tabernacle Fulfilled in Christ	977
Chart of the Sayings of Jesus in James	1018
Map of Peter's Addresses	1041
Chart of Passages Indicating the Inspiration of Scripture	1069
Chart of John Compared with 1 John	1080–81
Chart of Biblical Evidence for the Trinity	1100
Table of Interpretations of Revelation	1129
Table of Theological Perspectives on Revelation	1129
Chart of the Relationship among Seals, Trumpets, and Bowls	1169
Chart of Millennial Views	1216

Abbreviations

Books of the Bible

Ge	Genesis	Ro	Romans
Ex	Exodus	1Co	1 Corinthians
Lev	Leviticus	2Co	2 Corinthians
Nu	Numbers	Gal	Galatians
Dt	Deuteronomy	Eph	Ephesians
Jos	Joshua	Php	Philippians
Jdg	Judges	Col	Colossians
Ru	Ruth	1Th	1 Thessalonians
1Sa	1 Samuel	2Th	2 Thessalonians
2Sa	2 Samuel	1Ti	1 Timothy
1Ki	1 Kings	2Ti	2 Timothy
2Ki	2 Kings	Tit	Titus
1Ch	1 Chronicles	Phm	Philemon
2Ch	2 Chronicles	Heb	Hebrews
Ezr	Ezra	Jas	James
Ne	Nehemiah	1Pe	1 Peter
Est	Esther	2Pe	2 Peter
Job	Job	1Jn	1 John
Ps	Psalms	2Jn	2 John
Pr	Proverbs	3Jn	3 John
Ecc	Ecclesiastes	Jude	Jude
SS	Song of Songs	Rev	Revelation
Isa	Isaiah		
Jer	Jeremiah		
La	Lamentations		
Eze	Ezekiel		
Da	Daniel		
Hos	Hosea		
Joel	Joel		
Am	Amos		
Ob	Obadiah		
Jnh	Jonah		
Mic	Micah		
Na	Nahum		
Hab	Habakkuk		
Zep	Zephaniah		
Hag	Haggai		
Zec	Zechariah		
Mal	Malachi		
Mt	Matthew		
Mk	Mark		
Lk	Luke		
Jn	John		
Ac	Acts		

Other Abbreviations

c.	about
cf.	compare
ch(s).	chapter(s)
EBC	Expositor's Bible Commentary
e.g.	for example
etc.	and so on
ff.	following verses
Gk.	Greek
GK	Goodrick/Kohlenberger number
Heb.	Hebrew
i.e.	that is
lit.	literally
NT	New Testament
OT	Old Testament
v(v).	verse(s)
ZPEB	Zondervan Pictorial Encyclopedia of the Bible

Matthew

INTRODUCTION

1. The Criticism of Matthew

Matthew, like Mark, Luke, and John, is a gospel, a unique literary form that has no true parallel in ancient writing (see the introduction to Mark, "Literary Form," for more on this topic). The earliest church fathers to mention the gospel of Matthew concur that the author was the disciple and apostle Matthew. Papias maintained that this apostle first wrote his gospel in Hebrew or Aramaic, and it was subsequently translated into Greek. Matthean priority was almost universally upheld; Mark was considered an abbreviation of Matthew and therefore somewhat inferior. For centuries Matthew held enormous influence and prestige in the church. With few exceptions these perspectives dominated gospel study till after the Reformation.

The consensus could not last. A. E. Lessing (1776, 1778) insisted that the only way to account for the parallels and seeming discrepancies among the Synoptic Gospels was to assume that they all derived independently from an Aramaic *Gospel of the Nazarenes*. The supposition of a "primal gospel," whether oral or literary, began to gain influence. Meanwhile J. J. Griesbach (1745–1812) argued for a two-source hypothesis, holding to the priority of both Matthew and Luke over Mark, which was taken to be a condensation of the other two.

In the latter half of the nineteenth century a new theory—the two-source theory—developed and, in various ways, still dominates. The gospels of Matthew and Luke were seen as to some extent dependent on Mark and Q (from the German word *Quelle*, meaning "source"; it designates the material that is common to Matthew and Luke but not in Mark). Streeter (in 1924) added M and L (material unique to Matthew and Luke respectively), creating a four-document theory. The form critics then assigned structure of each story in the Gospels to a particular *Sitz im Leben* ("life setting") in the church. The historical value of any pericope was then assessed against a number of criteria. The net result of this criticism was a stifling historical skepticism with respect to the material in the canonical gospels.

Following World War II, the age of redaction criticism began. Scholars sought to explain the differences in the Gospels as reflecting the theological agendas of the authors. This type of criticism offered one great advantage over form criticism: it saw the evangelists not as mere compilers of the church's oral traditions and organizers of stories preserved or created in various forms, but as theologians in their own right, shaping and adapting the material in order to make their own points.

Regarding Matthew, for example, the major redaction-critical studies have attempted to define the historical context in which the evangelist wrote and the community circumstances that called this gospel into being (as it was thought) between A.D. 80 and A.D. 100. Most pay little attention to the historical context of Jesus. Not all redaction critics interpret Matthew's reconstructed community the same way; indeed, the differences among them are often great. Moreover, several recent critics have argued that much more material in the Gospels (including Matthew's) is authentic than was recognized ten years ago.

Of all the theories regarding the origin and shape of the Gospels, redaction criticism seems the most firmly founded and offers the most possibility for interpretation to the reader. In God's providence we are able to compare the Synoptic Gospels with one another, and such study helps us better understand each of them. For example, Matthew's topical treatment of miracles (Mt 8–9), his chiastic arrangement of parables (ch. 13), and the differences he exhibits when closely compared with Mark help us identify his distinct emphases more precisely than would otherwise be possible. Thus no responsible modern commentary on the Synoptic Gospels can avoid using redaction criticism.

At the same time, any attempt to reconstruct a particular Christian community on the basis of comparisons made between Matthew and his supposed sources must be held tentatively at best. We must always remember the following: (1) What Matthew aims to write is a gospel telling us about Jesus, not a church circular addressing an independently known problem. (2) There is substantial evidence that the early church was interested in the historical Jesus and wanted to know what he taught and why. There is equally strong evidence that the Gospels constitute, at least in part, an essential element of the NT church's spreading ministry. (3) It is therefore methodologically wrong to read off some theme attributed by the evangelist to Jesus and conclude that what is actually being discussed is not the teaching of Jesus but an issue of A.D. 80. (4) Matthew's reasons for including or excluding this or that tradition, or for shaping his sources, must owe something to the circumstances he found himself in and the concerns of his own theology. But it is notoriously difficult to reconstruct such circumstances and commitments from a gospel about Jesus of Nazareth. Nor can we assume that all the changes in Matthew result from the theological agenda of Matthew's community. (5) Moreover, virtually all the themes isolated as reflections of A.D. 80 could in fact reflect interests of any decade from A.D. 30 to 100.

For more on the scholarly criticism of the Gospels, see EBC 1:437–58; 501–44.

In view of the weaknesses inherent in a radical use of redaction criticism and the uncertainties surrounding the two-source hypothesis, this commentary adopts a cautious stance. The two-source hypothesis is sufficiently credible that we do not hesitate to speak of Matthew's changes of, additions to, and omissions from Mark. In some instances it is apparent that Matthew used not only Mark but Q, probably other sources, and perhaps his own memory. Changes that Matthew has introduced may sometimes be motivated by other than theological concerns; but in any case the total content of any pericope in Matthew's gospel as a whole is a more reliable guide to determine distinct theological bent than the isolated change. The aim throughout has been to let Matthew speak as a theologian and historian independent of Mark, even if Mark was one of his most important sources.

2. Unity

The question of the unity of Matthew's gospel deals with how well the evangelist has integrated his material to form cohesive pericopes and a coherent whole. In sections very difficult to interpret (e.g., Mt 24), it is sometimes argued that the evangelist has sewn together diverse traditions that by nature are incapable of genuine coherence. Failing to understand the material, he simply passed it on without recognizing that some of his sources were mutually incompatible.

There are so many signs of high literary craftsmanship in this gospel that such skepticism is unjustified. It is more likely, not to say more humble, to suppose that in some instances we may not understand enough of the first-century setting to be able to grasp exactly what the text says.

3. Authorship

Nowhere does the first gospel name its author. The universal testimony of the early church beginning with Papias (c. A.D. 135) is that the apostle Matthew wrote it, and our earliest textual witnesses attribute it to him. If Papias is right, the theory of Matthew's authorship may receive gentle support from passages like 10:3, where on this theory the apostle refers to himself in a self-deprecating way not found in Mark or Luke.

Modern literary criticism offers many reasons for rejecting Matthew's authorship. For example, if the two-source hypothesis is correct, then (it is argued) it is unlikely that the eyewitness and apostle Matthew would depend so heavily on a document written by Mark, who was neither an apostle nor (for most events) an eyewitness. Others argue that the theology of the book and the Greek language it uses require a date later than the time of the apostle Matthew. Thus alternate proposals for the author of the first gospel have been made.

These arguments do not stand up under scrutiny. If Matthew, for example, thought Mark's account reliable and generally suited to his purposes (and he may also have known that Peter stood behind it; see introduction to Mark), there need be no objection to the view that an apostle depended on a nonapostolic document.

Furthermore, the charge that the Greek of the first gospel is too good to have come from a Galilean Jew overlooks the trilingual character of Galilee, the possibility that Matthew greatly improved his Greek as the church reached out to more and more Greek speakers (both Jews and Gentiles), and the suggestion that Matthew's training and vocation as a tax gatherer (9:9–13; 10:3) would have uniquely equipped him not only with the languages of Galilee but with an orderly mind and the habit of jotting down notes.

None of the arguments regarding Matthew's authorship is conclusive. Thus we cannot be entirely certain who the author of the first gospel is. But there are solid reasons in support of the early church's unanimous ascription of this book to Matthew, and on close inspection the objections do not appear substantial.

4. Date

During the first three centuries of the church, Matthew was the most highly revered and frequently quoted canonical gospel. The earliest extant documents referring to Matthew are the letters of Ignatius (c. A.D. 110–15). Thus the end of the first century or thereabouts is the latest date for the gospel of Matthew to have been written.

The earliest possible date is much more difficult to nail down because it depends on so many other disputed points, such as whether Luke used Matthew, Matthew used Mark or Mark used Matthew. Even so there are difficulties. For example, we do not know when Mark was written, though most estimates fall between A.D. 50 and 65 (see introduction to Mark). On this basis most critics think Matthew could not have been written until 75 or 80. But even if Mark is as late as 65, there is no reason based on literary dependence why Matthew could not be dated A.D. 66. As soon as a written source is circulated, it is available for copying. Furthermore, as suggested above, to suggest a date in the late first century on the basis of our knowledge of theological concerns and historical events between 80 and 100 is doubtful. In fact, a careful reading of Matthew suggests it was written well before the fall of Jerusalem. For example, Matthew records more warnings against Sadducees than all other NT writers combined; but after A.D. 70 the Sadducees no longer existed as a center of authority. This argues for a pre-70 date for this book.

5. Place of Composition and Destination

Most scholars take Antioch as the place of composition. Antioch was a Greek-speaking city with a substantial Jewish population; and the first clear evidence of anyone using the gospel of Matthew comes from Ignatius, bishop of Antioch at the beginning of the second century. This is as good a guess as any. Yet we must remember that Ignatius depends more on John's gospel and the Pauline letters than on Matthew, but this does not mean they were all written in Antioch.

We cannot be sure of the first gospel's place of composition. Still more uncertain is its destination. The usual assumption is that the evangelist wrote it to meet the needs of his own center—a not implausible view. But the evangelist may have been more itinerant than is usually assumed; and out of such a ministry he may have written his gospel to strengthen and inform a large number of followers and give them an evangelistic and apologetic tool. We simply do not know. The only reasonably certain conclusion is that the gospel was written somewhere in the Roman province of Syria.

6. Occasion and Purpose

Unlike many of Paul's letters or even John's gospel (20:30–31), Matthew writes nothing explicit about his purpose for his work. To some extent the gospel shows Matthew's purpose in the way it presents certain information about Jesus. But to go much beyond this and specify the kind of group(s) Matthew was addressing, the kind of problems they faced, and his own deep psychological and theological motivations, verges on speculation. Three restraints are necessary. (1) It is unwise to specify too precise an occasion and purpose, because the possibility of error and distortion increases as one becomes more and more specific. (2) It is unwise to specify only one purpose; reductionism cannot do justice to the diversity of Matthew's themes. (3) Great caution is needed in reconstructing the situation in the church of Matthew's time from material that speaks of the historical Jesus (see section 1). Matthew likely wrote his gospel to address his contemporaries, not just to satisfy someone's historical curiosity. But it does not necessarily follow that most of what he writes is a reflection of his own day rather than Jesus' day.

Nowhere are these restraints more important than in weighing recent discussion about the diverse emphases on evangelism in this gospel. On the one hand, the disciples are forbidden to preach to others than Jews (10:5–6); on the other, they are commanded to preach to all nations (28:18–20). Because of this bifurcation, some scholars have suggested that Matthew is preserving the traditions of two distinct communities—one that remained narrowly Jewish and the other that was more outward looking. Others think Matthew had to walk a tightrope between conflicting perspectives within his own community and therefore preserves both viewpoints—a sort of committee report that satisfied neither side. Such views of Matthew fail to recognize that the author himself makes distinctions between what Jesus demands during his earthly ministry and what he demands after his resurrection. Perhaps by mentioning the changed perspective effected by Jesus' resurrection, Matthew is encouraging Jewish Christians to evangelize beyond their own race. More generally, such reconstructions outstrip the evidence, fail to consider what other purposes Matthew may have had in mind, and frequently ignore the fact that he purports to talk about Jesus, not a Christian community in some particular decade of the first century.

At the broadest level we may say that Matthew's purpose is to demonstrate that (1) Jesus is the promised Messiah, the Son of David, the Son of God, the Son of Man, Immanuel; (2) many Jews, and especially the leaders, sinfully failed to perceive this during his ministry; (3) the messianic kingdom has already dawned, inaugurated by the life, ministry, death, resurrection, and exaltation of Jesus; (4) this messianic reign, characterized by obedience to Jesus and consummated by his return, is the fulfillment of OT prophetic hopes; (5) the church, the community of those, both Jew and Gentile, who bow unqualifiedly to Jesus' authority, constitutes the true locus of the people of God and the witness to the world of the "gospel of the kingdom"; (6) throughout this age Jesus' true disciples must overcome temptation, endure persecution from a hostile world, witness to the truth of the Gospel, and live in deeply rooted submission to Jesus' ethical demands.

Such a complex array of themes was doubtless designed to meet many needs: (1) to instruct and perhaps catechize; (2) to provide apologetic and evangelistic material, especially in winning Jews; (3) to encourage believers in their witness before a hostile world; and (4) to inspire deeper faith in Jesus the Messiah, along with a maturing understanding of his person, work, and unique place in the unfolding history of redemption.

7. Themes and Special Problems

We may consider Matthew's principal themes together with the special problems of this gospel, because so many of those themes have turned into foci for strenuous debate. To avoid needless repetition, the following paragraphs do not so much summarize the nine themes selected as sketch in the debate and then provide references to the places in the commentary where these things are discussed.

a. *Christology*. Matthew's view of Christ can, at least in part, be understood by an examination of the Christological titles he uses. These are rich and diverse. "Son of David" appears in the first verse, identifying Jesus as the promised Davidic Messiah; and then the title recurs, often on the lips of the needy and the ill, who anticipate relief from him who will bring in the Messianic Age (see comment on 9:27). Matthew uses *kyrios* ("Lord"; GK 3261) more often than Mark. While it is doubtful that anyone considered Jesus the divine Lord before his crucifixion, because *kyrios* is the most common LXX term for referring to God, the greater insight into Jesus' person and work afforded by the postresurrection perspective made the disciples see a deeper significance to their own use of *kyrios* than they could have intended at first. And, as we shall see, the term "Son of God" is also important in Matthew (see comments on 2:15; 3:17; 4:3; 8:29; 16:16; 17:5; 26:63).

b. *Prophecy and fulfillment*. One of Matthew's special characteristics is to show how Jesus fulfilled Scripture. Christians are prone to think of prophecy and fulfillment as something not very different from straightforward propositional prediction and fulfillment. A close reading of the NT reveals that prophecy is more complex than that (see comments on 2:15, 23; 27:9). Note also that a number of

Matthew's OT quotations are introduced by the word "fulfilled" (GK *4444*) and a text form rather more removed from the LXX than other OT quotations. Such problems have been extensively studied with very little agreement. Perspectives are given throughout the notes where applicable (e.g., see comments on 1:23; 2:15, 17–18, 23; 4:15–16; 5:17; et al.). Care in such formulations will help us perceive the deep ties that bind together the OT and NT.

c. *Law.* Few topics in the study of Matthew's gospel are more difficult than his attitude to the law and to the Pharisees and teachers of the law (see especially comments on 5:17–48). Doubtless we may link Matthew's treatment of the law with his handling of the OT prophecy. Matthew holds that Jesus taught that the law had a prophetic function pointing to himself. Its valid continuity lies in Jesus' own ministry, teaching, death, and resurrection. The unifying factor is Jesus himself, whose ministry and teaching stand with respect to the OT (including law) as fulfillment does to prophecy.

d. *Church.* The word *ekklesia* ("church"; GK *1711*) occurs twice in Matthew (16:18; 18:17). Certain things stand out on this issue. First, Matthew insists that Jesus predicted the continuation of his small group of disciples in a distinct community, a holy and messianic people, a "church" (see comment on 16:18). Second, Jesus insists that obeying the ethical demands of the kingdom, far from being optional to those who make up the church, must characterize their lives. Their allegiance proves false wherever they do not do what Jesus teaches (e.g., 7:21–23). Third, a certain discipline must be imposed on the community (see comments on 16:18–19; 18:15–18), though Matthew describes this discipline in principles rather than in details.

e. *Eschatology.* Matthew consistently distinguishes among four time periods: (1) the period of revelation and history previous to Jesus; (2) the inauguration of something new in his coming and ministry; (3) the period beginning with his exaltation—from which point all of God's sovereignty is mediated through him and his followers proclaim the Gospel of the kingdom to all nations; (4) the consummation and beyond.

f. *The Jewish leaders.* Two areas need clarification for understanding Matthew's treatment of the Jewish leaders. The first is the identification of the "Pharisees" (GK *5757*) at the time of Jesus. Two of their main contributions to society were to adapt the OT laws to the times and to lead first-century Judaism. The problem is that their minute regulations made ritual distinctions too difficult and morality too easy. The radical holiness demanded by the OT prophets became domesticated, preparing the way for Jesus' preaching that demanded a righteousness greater than that of the Pharisees (see comment on 5:20).

We hold that the Pharisees were a non-priestly group of uncertain origin, generally learned, committed to the oral law, and concerned with developing *Halakah* (rules of conduct based on deductions from the law). Most "teachers of the law" were Pharisees; and the Sanhedrin included men from their number (see comment on 21:23), though the leadership of the Sanhedrin belonged to the priestly Sadducees. Matthew also often links the Sadducees together with the Pharisees, not because the views of these two groups were similar, but because they were united in their opposition to Jesus.

The second area needing clarification is the way Matthew refers to Jewish leaders. It is universally agreed that Matthew is quite strongly anti-Pharisaic. His denunciations of these Jewish leaders are not racially motivated; they are prompted by the response of people to Jesus. The denunciations equally extend to professing believers whose lives betray the falseness of their profession (7:21–23; 22:11–14) and to unbelieving Jews; the governing motives are concern for the perseverance of the Christian community and for the authoritative proclamation of the "gospel of the kingdom" to "all nations," Jew and Gentile alike, to bring everyone to submission to Jesus Messiah.

g. *Mission.* It has long been recognized that the closing pericope (28:16–20) is fully intended to be the climax toward which the entire gospel moves. By tying together some of Matthew's most dominant themes, these verses give them a new depth that reaches back and sheds light on the entire gospel. For instance, the Great Commission is perceived to be the result of God's providential ordering of history (1:1–17) to bring to a fallen world a Messiah who would save his people from their sins (1:21); but the universal significance of Jesus' birth, hinted at in 1:1 and repeatedly raised in the flow of the narrative (e.g., see comments on 2:1–12; 4:14–16, 25; 8:5–13; et al.) is now confirmed by the concluding lines.

h. *Miracles.* The biblical writers do not see miracles as divine interventions in an ordered and closed universe. Rather, God as Lord of the universe and of history sustains everything that takes place under his sovereignty. Sometimes, however, he does extraordinary things. Biblical writers preferred to call these events "signs," "wonders," or "powers."

Miracles in Matthew share certain characteristics with those in the other Synoptics. Jesus' miracles are bound up with the in-breaking of the promised kingdom (8:16–17; 12:22–30). They are part of his messianic work (4:23; 11:4–6) and therefore the dual evidence of the dawning of the kingdom and of the status of Jesus the King Messiah.

Matthew's miracles are distinctive for the brevity with which they are reported. He condenses introductions and conclusions, omits secondary characters and the like (see comments on 8:1–4). He shifts the balance of event and implication a little in order to stress the latter.

i. *The disciples' understanding and faith.* Like Mark, Matthew portrays the disciples as failing to understand Jesus' teachings about his coming death and resurrection, primarily because of their unique place in salvation history. They were unprepared before the events to accept the notion of a crucified and resurrected Messiah. Their perspective radically changed after the triumph of Jesus' resurrection. Matthew's readers, whether in the first century or today, may profit from studying the disciples' experience as he records it. We should look back on this witness to the divine self-disclosure, observing God's wisdom and care as through his Son he progressively revealed himself and his purposes to redeem a fallen and rebellious race. By feeding our faith and understanding on the combined testimony of the earliest witnesses who tell how they arrived by a unique historical sequence at their faith and understanding, we shall learn to focus our attention, not on the disciples, but on their Lord.

8. Structure

Matthew was a skilled literary craftsman and gave his gospel structure, form, and rhythm. No outline, however, should be taken too seriously, as if it exhausts the complexity of the author's work.

The best way to view the book is to see it centering on five main discourses (each preceded by a narrative section): 5:1–7:29; 10:5–11:1; 13:1–53; 18:1–19:2; 24:1–25:46. Each discourse begins by placing Jesus in a specific context and ends with a formula found nowhere else in the gospel (see comment on 7:28–29) and with a transitional pericope pointing forward and backward. These five discourses are sufficiently well-defined that it is hard to believe Matthew did not plan them as such. In this scheme the birth narrative functions as a prologue anticipating the opening of the gospel. Matthew 26–28 constitutes an exceptional sixth narrative section with the corresponding teaching section being laid on the shoulders of the disciples (28:18–20).

EXPOSITION

I. Prologue: The Origin and Birth of Jesus the Christ (1:1–2:23)

A. The Genealogy of Jesus (1:1–17)

In each gospel Jesus' earthly ministry is preceded by an account of John the Baptist's ministry. This formal similarity does not extend to the prologues to the Gospels. In Matthew the prologue (1:1–2:23) introduces such themes as the son of David, the fulfillment of prophecy, the supernatural origin of Jesus the Messiah, and the Father's sovereign protection of his Son in order to bring him to Nazareth and accomplish the divine plan of salvation from sin.

1 The first words of Matthew may be translated as "a [coherent and unified] record of the origins of Jesus Christ," thus serving as an opening statement of the first two chapters.

The designation "Jesus Christ the son of David, the son of Abraham" resonates with biblical nuances. (For comments regarding "Jesus," see comment on 1:21.). "Christ" is roughly the Greek equivalent to "Messiah" or "Anointed" (see comment on Mk 8:29). In Jesus' day Palestine was rife with messianic expectation. Not all of it was coherent, and many Jews expected two different "Messiahs." But Matthew's linking of "Christ" and "son of David" leaves no doubt of what he is claiming for Jesus. In the Gospels "Christ" almost always appears as a title ("the Messiah"). But it was natural for Christians after the Resurrection to use "Christ" as a name (e.g., "Jesus Christ"), though it is doubtful whether the titular force ever entirely disappears. In Matthew, only in vv.1, 16, 18 can "Christ" be defended as designating a name as well as a title of Jesus.

"Son of David" is an important designation in Matthew. Not only does David become a turning point in the genealogy (1:6, 17), but the title recurs throughout the gospel (9:27; 12:23; 15:22; 20:30–31; 21:9, 15; 22:42, 45). God swore covenant love to David (Ps 89:29) and promised that one of his immediate descendants would establish the kingdom—even more, that David's kingdom and throne would endure forever (2Sa 7:12–16). Isaiah foresaw that a "son" would be given, a son with the most extravagant titles who would reign on David's throne (Isa 9:6–7). In Jesus' day at least some branches of popular Judaism understood "son of David" to be messianic. In the minds of the early Christians, the tree of David, hacked off so that only a stump remained, was sprouting a new branch (Isa 11:1).

Jesus is also "son of Abraham." The covenant with the Jewish people had first been made with Abraham (Ge 12:1–3; 17:7; 22:18). More important, Ge 22:18 had promised that through Abraham's offspring "all nations" would be blessed; so with this allusion to Abraham, Matthew is preparing his readers for the final words of this offspring from Abraham—the commission to make disciples of "all nations" (28:19).

2–17 Matthew's chief aims in including the genealogy are hinted at in the first verse—namely, to show that Jesus Messiah is truly in the kingly line of David, heir to the messianic promises, the one who brings divine blessings to all nations. Therefore the genealogy focuses on King David (1:6) on the one hand, yet on the other hand includes Gentile women. Many entries would touch the hearts and stir the memories of biblically literate readers, though the principal thrust of Matthew's genealogy ties together promise and fulfillment.

The names in the first two-thirds of the genealogy are taken from the LXX (1Ch 1–3, esp. 2:1–15; 3:5–24; cf. Ru 4:12–22). After Zerubbabel, Matthew relies on extrabiblical sources of which we know nothing. But there is good evidence that records were kept at least till the end of the first century.

More difficult is the question of the relation of Matthew's genealogy to Luke's, in particular the part from David on (for a description of the differences between Mt 1:2–17 and Lk 3:23–31, as well as attempts at a solution, see comments on Lk 3:23–38).

2 Of the twelve sons of Jacob, Judah is singled out, as his tribe bears the scepter (Ge 49:10; cf. Heb 7:14). The words "and his brothers" indicate that the Messiah emerges within the matrix of the covenant people (cf. the twelve tribes of Israel). Neither the half-siblings of Isaac nor the descendants of Jacob's brother, Esau, qualify as the covenant people in the OT.

3–5 Probably Perez and Zerah (v.3) are both mentioned because they are twins (Ge 38:27). Tamar, wife of Judah's son Er, is the first of four women mentioned in the genealogy (see comment on v.6). Little is known of the next five names in the genealogy. Amminadab is associated with the desert wanderings in the time of Moses (Nu 1:7). Therefore approximately four hundred years (Ge 15:13; Ex 12:40) are covered by the four generations from Perez to Amminadab. Doubtless several names have been omitted: the Greek verb translated "was the father of" (GK *1164*) does not require immediate relationship but often means "was the ancestor of." Similarly, the line between Amminadab and David is short: more names may have been omitted. For example, it is almost certain that the Rahab mentioned is the prostitute of Jos 2 and 5 (see comments on next verse) and was certainly not the biological mother of Boaz (see Ru 4:12, 18–22).

6 The word "King" with "David" would evoke profound nostalgia and arouse eschatological hope in first-century Jews. Matthew thus makes the royal theme explicit: King Messiah has appeared. David's royal authority, lost at the Exile, has now been regained and surpassed by "great David's greater son." David became the father of Solomon; but Solomon's mother "had been Uriah's wife" (cf. 2Sa 11:27; 12:4). Bathsheba thus becomes the fourth woman to be mentioned in this genealogy.

Inclusion of these four women in the Messiah's genealogy instead of an all-male listing, especially with the exclusion of names of such great matriarchs as Sarah, Rebekah, and Leah, shows that Matthew is conveying more than merely genealogical data. Tamar enticed her father-in-law into an incestuous relationship (Ge 38). The prostitute Rahab saved the spies and joined the Israelites (Jos 2, 5; cf. Heb 11:31; Jas 2:25). Ruth, Tamar, and Rahab were aliens. Bathsheba was taken into an adulterous union with David, who committed murder to cover it up. Matthew's peculiar way of referring to her, "Uriah's wife," may be an attempt to focus on the fact that Uriah was not an Israelite but a Hittite (2Sa 11:3; 23:39).

Several reasons have been suggested to explain the inclusion of these women, all of which are valid. (1) Some have pointed out that at least three were Gentiles. This goes well with the reference to Abraham (cf. on 1:1); the Jewish Messiah extends his blessings beyond Israel, even as Gentiles are included in his line. (2) Others have noted that three of the four were involved in gross sexual sin and that later in this same chapter Matthew introduces Jesus as the one who "will save his people from their sins" (1:21); this verse may imply a backward glance at some of the better-known sins of his own progenitors. (3) Still others hold that all four reveal something of the strange and unexpected workings of Providence in preparation for the Messiah and that as such they point to Mary's unexpected but providential conception of Jesus.

7–10 There is no obvious pattern to the kings mentioned here: wicked Rehoboam was the father of wicked Abijah, the father of the good king Asa. Asa was the father of another good king, Jehoshaphat, who sired the wicked king Joram. Good or evil, they were part of Messiah's line; for though grace does not run in the blood, God's providence cannot be deceived or outmaneuvered.

Three names have been omitted between Joram and Uzziah: Ahaziah, Joash, and Amaziah. The three omissions not only secure fourteen generations in this part of the genealogy (see comment on 1:17) but are dropped possibly because of their connection with Ahab and Jezebel, renowned for wickedness (2Ki 8:27), and because of their connection with wicked Athaliah (2Ki 8:26; 11:1–20). Manasseh (v.10), though notoriously evil, repented (2Ch 33:10–13), and he is included.

11 The Exile to Babylon marked the end of the reign of David's line, a momentous event in OT history. The locus of the people of God is thus traced from the patriarchs to the shame of the Exile, a theme to be developed later (see comment on 2:16–18).

12 The final list of "fourteen" (see comment on 1:17) begins with a further mention of the Exile. Jeconiah (Jehoiachin) was the father of Shealtiel. Matthew goes on to present Shealtiel as the father of Zerubbabel (cf. Ezr 3:2; 5:2), whereas 1Ch 3:19 presents Zerubbabel as the son of Pedaiah, a brother of Shealtiel. The best solution to this problem is the proposal of a levirate marriage (Dt 25:5–10; cf. Ge 38:8–9): Shealtiel died childless, and Pedaiah, his brother, married the widow (see also comment on Lk 3:23–31).

13–16 The nine names from Abiud to Jacob are otherwise unknown to us today. The wording in v.16 is precise. Joseph's royal line has been traced; Joseph is the husband of Mary; Mary is the mother of Jesus. The relationship between Joseph and Jesus is so far unstated. But this peculiar form of expression cries out for the explanation provided in the ensuing verses. Legally Jesus stands in line to the throne of David; physically he is born of a woman "found to be with child through the Holy Spirit" (1:18). Her son Jesus is the "Messiah" (see comment on v.1).

17 It was customary among Jewish writers to arrange genealogies according to some convenient scheme, possibly for mnemonic reasons. Matthew has grouped them according to fourteens, most likely a symbolic number. It is impossible to get the three fourteens without counting either David twice or Jeconiah twice.

Why "fourteen"? The simplest explanation—the one that best fits the context—observes that the numerical value of "David" in Hebrew is fourteen. That is, in the ancient world, letters served both to form words and to designate numbers. The numerical value of D+V+D is fourteen. By this symbolism Matthew stresses that the promised "son of David" (1:1), the Messiah, has come.

B. The Birth of Jesus (1:18–25)

Two matters call for initial remarks: the historicity of the Virgin Birth (more properly, virginal conception), and the theological emphases surrounding this theme in chs. 1–2 and its relation to the NT.

First, though many have questioned the historicity of the Virgin Birth, it is clear that both Matthew and Luke independently attest to its truth. Matthew's point in chs. 1–2 is surely that the Virgin Birth and attendant circumstances were most extraordinary, and that God was thoroughly involved in the event of bringing his Son into the world.

Second, the following theological considerations require mention. (1) The concept of "virginal conception" is thoroughly consistent with his "preexistence." Indeed, it is difficult to see how a divine being could become genuinely human without a birth of extraordinary means. (2) Undoubtedly during Jesus' lifetime, the disciples were not fully aware of Jesus' miraculous birth. Their understanding of Jesus naturally matured and deepened with time and further revelation, as did their thinking on other important topics. (3) Just because the Virgin Birth is not clearly outlined in the NT letters is no reason to claim it is a later creation of the church.

It is remarkable that the title "Son of God," important later in Matthew, is not found in chs. 1–2, though it may lurk behind 2:15. But these two chapters serve as a finely wrought prologue for every major theme in the gospel. We must therefore understand Matthew to be telling us that if Jesus is physically Mary's son and legally Joseph's son, at an even more fundamental level he is God's Son (cf 1:18, 20), and in this Matthew agrees with Luke's statement (Lk 1:35). The dual paternity, the one legal and the other divine, is unambiguous.

18 The word translated "birth" (GK *1161*; translated "genealogy" in v.1) refers to the beginnings of Jesus Messiah. A pledge to be married was legally binding. Only a divorce writ could break it, and infidelity at that stage was considered adultery (cf. Dt 22:23–24). Mary herself does not figure largely in Matthew.

"Before they came together" refers here to sexual intercourse, occurring at the formal marriage when the "wife" moved in with her "husband." Only then was this act proper. The phrase affirms that Mary's pregnancy was discovered while she was still betrothed, and the context presupposes that both Mary and Joseph had been chaste.

Mary's pregnancy came about through the Holy Spirit (even more prominent in Luke's birth narratives). The power of the Lord, manifest in the Holy Spirit who was expected to be active in the Messianic Age, miraculously brought about the conception.

19 Joseph did not know about the visit of an angel to Mary, but it eventually became obvious that she was pregnant. Because he was a righteous man, he could not in conscience marry Mary, who was now thought to be unfaithful. Such a marriage would have been a tacit admission of his own guilt. But because he was unwilling to expose her to the disgrace of public divorce, Joseph therefore chose a quieter form of divorce, before two witnesses, permitted by the law itself. It would leave both his righteousness (his conformity to the law) and his compassion intact.

20 Only when Joseph had made this decision did God intervene with a dream. Dreams as means of divine communication in the NT are concentrated in Matthew's prologue (1:20; 2:2, 13, 19, 22; elsewhere, possibly 27:19). An "angel of the Lord" calls to mind divine messengers in past ages (e.g., Ge 16:7–14; 22:11–18; Ex 3:2–4:16; et al.). The focus here is on God's gracious intervention and the messenger's private communication.

The angel's opening words, "Joseph son of David," tie this pericope to the preceding genealogy, maintain interest in the theme of the Davidic Messiah, and, from Joseph's perspective, alert him to the significance of the role he is to play. The prohibition, "Do not be afraid," confirms that Joseph had already decided on his course when God intervened. He was to "take" Mary home as his wife because Mary's pregnancy was the direct action of the Holy Spirit.

21 It was no doubt divine grace that solicited Mary's cooperation before the conception and Joseph's cooperation only after it. Here Joseph is drawn into the mystery of the Incarnation. In patriarchal times either a mother (Ge 4:25) or a father (Ge 4:26; 5:3) could name a child. According to Lk 1:31,

Mary was told Jesus' name; but Joseph was told both name and reason for it.

"Jesus" (GK 2652) is the Greek form of "Joshua," which means either "The LORD is salvation," or "The LORD saves." Mary's Son is the one who brings the Lord's promised eschatological salvation. Two Joshuas in the OT are used in the NT as types of Christ: Joshua, successor to Moses and the one who led the people into the Promised Land (cf. Heb 3–4), and Joshua the high priest, contemporary of Zerubbabel (Ezr 2:2; 3:2–9), "the Branch" who builds the temple of the Lord (Zec 6:11–13). But instead of referring to either of these, the angel explains the significance of the name by referring to Ps 130:8: "He [the LORD] himself will redeem Israel from all their sins."

There was much Jewish expectation of a Messiah who would redeem Israel from Roman tyranny and even purify his people. But no one expected that the Davidic Messiah would give his own life as a ransom (20:28) to save his people from their sins. The verb "save" (GK 5392) can refer to deliverance from physical danger (8:25), disease (9:21–22), or even death (24:22); but it focuses here on what is central, namely, salvation from sins. This verse therefore orients the reader to the fundamental purpose of Jesus' coming and the essential nature of the reign he inaugurates as King Messiah, heir of David's throne.

To Joseph "his people" (GK 3295) would be primarily the Jews, but Matthew has a broader view. He soon writes that both John the Baptist (3:9) and Jesus (8:11) picture Gentiles joining with the godly remnant to become disciples of the Messiah and members of "his people," i.e., "Messiah's people."

22 It is quite possible that the angel's comments continue through v.23 (cf. 26:56). After all, if Satan can cite Scripture (4:6–7), certainly it is not strange if a good angel does. Joseph needs to know at this stage that "all this took place to fulfill" Scripture. The last clause is phrased with exquisite care, literally, "the word spoken by the Lord through the prophet." The prepositions make a distinction between the mediate and the intermediate agent (see 2Pe 1:21).

Regarding the idea of prophecy and fulfillment, Matthew finds in the OT not only isolated predictions regarding the Messiah but also OT history and people as paradigms that, to those with eyes to see, point forward to the Messiah (see comment on 2:15).

23 This verse makes it quite clear that to Matthew, Mary is the virgin; Jesus is her son, Immanuel. But because of the quotation from Isa 7:14, complex issues are raised concerning Matthew's use of the OT.

The OT word for "virgin" used in Isa 7:14 is *almah* (GK 6625) and often means virgin (though sometimes a young woman of marriageable age). The LXX renders *almah* here as *parthenos* (GK 4221), which almost always means "virgin"—though even here there are exceptions, such as LXX of Ge 34:4. The overwhelming majority of occurrences of *parthenos*, however, in both biblical and nonbiblical Greek, require the rendering "virgin"; and the unambiguous context of Mt 1 (see vv.12, 16, 18, 20, 25) puts Matthew's intent beyond dispute.

The crucial question is how we are to understand Isa 7:14 in its relationship to Mt 1:23. Of critical concern is the fact that Isaiah uses v.14 to give a sign to King Ahaz about the Assyrian destruction of the kings of Israel and Syria (Aram), who were threatening Judah (see comment on Isa 7:14).

The most plausible view begins with a recognition that signs in the OT may function as a "present persuader" (e.g., Ex 4:8–9) or as "future confirmation" (e.g., Ex 3:12). Isa 7:14 falls in the latter case because Immanuel's birth comes too late to be a "present persuader." The "sign" (v.11; GK 253) points primarily to threat and foreboding. Ahaz has rejected the Lord's gracious offer (vv.10–12), and Isaiah responds in wrath (v.13). The "curds and honey" that Immanuel will eat (v.15) represent the only food left in the land on the day of wrath (vv.18–22). Immanuel's birth follows the coming events (it is a "future confirmation") and will take place when the Davidic dynasty has lost the throne.

Furthermore, some recent studies have demonstrated that Isa 7:1–9:7 must be read as a unit—i.e., 7:14 must not be treated in isolation. The promised Immanuel (7:14) will possess the land (8:8), thwart all opponents (8:10), and appear in Galilee of the Gentiles as a great light to those in the land of the shadow of death (9:1–2, quoted in Mt 4:12–16). He is the Child and Son called "Wonderful Counselor, Mighty God, Everlasting Father, Prince of Peace" in Isa 9:6, whose government and peace will never end as he reigns on David's throne forever (9:7).

According to this interpretation, Matthew has correctly understood Isaiah that the Immanuel figure of 7:14 is a messianic figure. And if this messianic figure's titles include "Mighty God" (9:6), there is reason to think that "Immanuel" refers to Jesus himself, that he is "God with us." Though "Immanuel" is not a name in the sense that "Jesus" is Messiah's name (1:21), in the OT Solomon was named "Jedidiah" ("Beloved of the Lord," 2Sa 12:25), even though he apparently was not called that. Similarly Immanuel is a "name" in the sense of title or description.

No greater blessing can be conceived than for God to dwell with his people (Isa 60:18–20; Eze 48:35; Rev 21:23). Jesus is the one called "God with us": the designation evokes Jn 1:14, 18. As if that were not enough, Jesus promises just before his ascension to be with us to the end of the age (Mt 28:20; cf. also 18:20).

24–25 When Joseph woke up (from his sleep, not his dream), he "took Mary home as his wife." Joseph's obedience and submission under these circumstances are scarcely less remarkable than Mary's (Lk 1:38). Matthew wants to make Jesus' virginal conception unambiguous, for he adds that Joseph had no sexual union with Mary until she gave birth to Jesus. The "until" clause most naturally means that Mary and Joseph enjoyed normal conjugal relations after Jesus' birth.

So the virgin-conceived Immanuel was born. And eight days later, when the time came for him to be circumcised (Lk 2:21), Joseph named him "Jesus."

C. The Visit of the Magi (2:1–12)

Few passages have received more diverse interpretations than this one. During the last hundred years or so, such diversity has sometimes sprung from a reluctance to accept either the supernatural details or the entire story as historically true and from an insistence that Matthew's real point is theological. The presupposed antithesis between theology and history is false. Matthew records history so as to bring out its theological significance and its relation to Scripture as prophecy-fulfillment; to establish God's providential and supernatural care of this virgin-born Son; to anticipate the hostilities, resentment, and suffering he would face; and to hint at the fact that Gentiles would be drawn into his reign. Matthew thus stresses early in his gospel that if Jesus had not been born in Bethlehem, this claim would have been challenged.

1 Bethlehem, the place near which Jacob buried Rachel (Ge 35:19) and Ruth met Boaz (Ru 1:22–2:6), was preeminently the town where David was born and reared. For Christians it has become the place where angelic hosts broke the silence and announced Messiah's birth (Lk 2:8–20).

Unlike Luke, Matthew offers no description of Jesus' birth or the shepherds' visit; he specifies the time of Jesus' birth as having occurred during the reign of King Herod the Great (see also Lk 1:5; ZPEB 3:126–38). Traditionally some have argued that Herod died in 4 B.C.; so Jesus must have been born before then. Though this has been challenged, most favor this date.

The "Magi" (GK *3407*) cannot be identified with precision. By NT times, the term loosely covered a wide variety of men interested in dreams, astrology, magic, books thought to contain mysterious references to the future, and the like. Apparently these men came to Bethlehem spurred on by astrological calculations. But they had probably built up their expectation of a kingly figure by working through assorted Jewish books.

2 The Magi saw a star "when it rose" (see NIV note). What they saw remains uncertain, and no single suggestion has gained support. Matthew uses language almost certainly alluding to Nu 24:17: "A star will come out of Jacob; a scepter will rise out of Israel." This oracle, spoken by Balaam, who came "from the eastern mountains" (Nu 23:7), was widely regarded as messianic.

Matthew's main purpose in this story is to contrast the eagerness of the Magi to worship Jesus, despite their limited knowledge, with the apathy of the Jewish leaders and the hostility of Herod's court—all of whom had the Scriptures to inform them. Formal knowledge of the Scriptures, Matthew implies, does not in itself lead to knowing who Jesus is.

The Magi's question indicates that Jesus was *born* king of the Jews. His kingly status was not conferred on him later on; it was his from birth. Jesus' participation in the

Davidic dynasty has already been established by the genealogy. The same title the Magi gave him was found over the cross (27:37).

"Worship" (GK 4686) probably means simply "do homage." Their own statement suggests homage paid to royalty rather than the worship of Deity. But Matthew, having already told of the virginal conception, doubtless expected his readers to discern that the Magi "worshiped" better than they knew.

3 In contrast with the Magi's desire to worship the King of the Jews, Herod was deeply troubled. In this "all Jerusalem" joined him, not because most of the people would have been sorry to see Herod replaced or because they were reluctant to see the coming of King Messiah, but because they well knew that any question like the Magi's would result in more cruelty from the ailing Herod, whose paranoia had already led him to murder his favorite wife and two sons.

4–5 All the chief priests and teachers of the law (i.e., those who served as leaders of the Jews) who were living in Jerusalem were quickly consulted. The majority of the teachers of the law were Pharisees; the priests were Sadducees. Since these two groups barely got along, Herod may have consulted each group separately. Herod's request of them implies that "the Christ" and "the king of the Jews" were recognized titles of the same expected

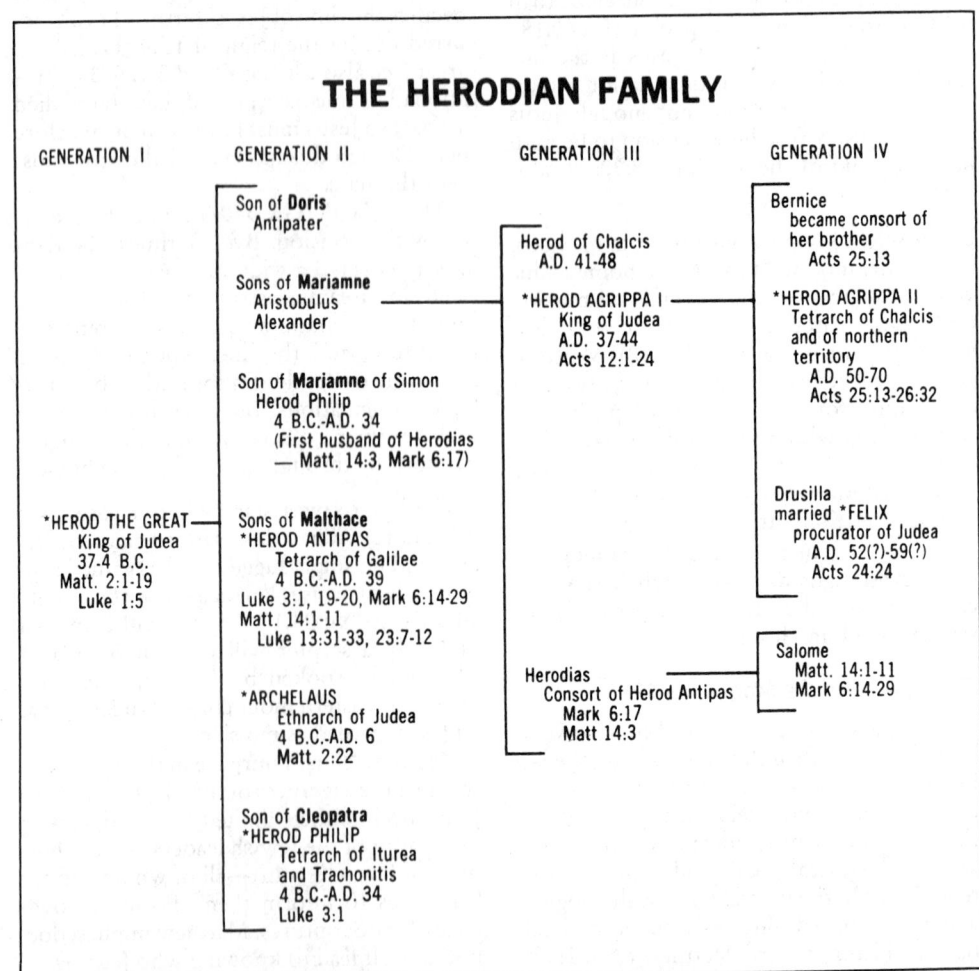

Several generations that descended from Herod the Great walk across the pages of the New Testament. Those mentioned are in capital letters, together with the relevant passages in Scripture. Courtesy Zondervan Publishing House.

person. The Jewish leaders answered the question by referring to what stands written in the OT, suggesting the authoritative and regulative force of the document referred to.

6 While expectation that the Messiah must come from Bethlehem occurs elsewhere, here it rests on Mic 5:2, to which are appended some words from 2Sa 5:2.

The addition of the shepherd language of 2Sa 5:2 makes it plain that the ruler in Mic 5:2 is none other than the one who fulfills the promises to David. Through these two OT texts, Matthew is hinting at a pair of contrasts (1) between the false shepherds of Israel who have provided sound answers but no leadership (cf. 23:2–7) and Jesus who is the true Shepherd of his people Israel, and (2) between a ruler like Herod and the one born to rule. Matthew also implies a contrast between the desires of the Gentile Magi to worship the Messiah and the apathy of the leaders who did not, apparently, take the trouble to go to Bethlehem.

7–10 The reason Herod wanted to learn, at his secret meeting with the Magi, the exact time the star appeared was that he had already schemed to kill the small boys of Bethlehem (cf. v.16). The entire story hangs together. Herod's hypocritical humility in v.8 deceived the Magi. Conscious of his success, Herod sent no escort with them. Herod could scarcely have been expected to foresee God's intervention (v.12).

Matthew does not say that the rising star the Magi had seen led them to Jerusalem. They went first to the capital city because they thought it the natural place for the King of the Jews to be born. But now the star reappeared ahead of them as they made their way to Bethlehem (it was not uncommon to travel at night). Taking this as confirming their purposes, the Magi were overjoyed. The Greek text does not imply that the star pointed out the house where Jesus was; it may simply have hovered over Bethlehem as the Magi approached it. They would then have found the exact house through discreet inquiry since (Lk 2:17–18) the shepherds who came to worship the newborn Jesus did not keep silent about what they saw.

11 This verse alludes to Ps 72:10–11 and Isa 60:6, passages that reinforce the emphasis on the Gentiles in this passage (cf. on v.6). Some time had elapsed since Jesus' birth (vv.7, 16), and the family was settled in a house. While the Magi saw both the child and his mother, their worship (cf. comment on v.2) was for him alone.

Bringing gifts was particularly important in the ancient East when approaching a superior (cf. Ge 43:11; 1Sa 9:7–8; 1Ki 10:2). Frankincense is a glittering, odorous gum obtained by making incisions in the bark of several trees; myrrh exudes from a tree found in Arabia and a few other places and was a much-valued spice and perfume used in embalming (Jn 19:39).

12 This second dream (cf. 1:20) mentions no angel. Perhaps Joseph and the Magi compared notes and saw their danger amid their fear and uncertainty; the dreams led them (vv.12–13) to flee. Which way the Magi went is unclear.

D. The Escape to Egypt (2:13–15)

13–14 The verb "had gone" (v.13) is the same as "returned" in the preceding verse, tying the two accounts together. This is the third dream in these two chapters, and for the second time an "angel of the Lord" is mentioned (cf. 1:20; 2:12). God was taking sovereign action to preserve his Messiah, his Son. Egypt was a natural place to which to flee. It was nearby, had a well-ordered Roman province outside Herod's jurisdiction, and had a population of about a million Jews. If Matthew was thinking of any particular OT parallel, probably Jacob and his family (Ge 46) fleeing the famine in Canaan was in his mind, since that is the trip that set the stage for the Exodus (cf. 2.15).

The angel's command was explicit. Joseph, Mary, and the Child must remain in Egypt, not only till Herod's death, but till given leave to return (cf. vv.19–20). The command was also urgent. Joseph left at once, setting out by night to begin the seventy-five mile journey to the border. The focus on God's protection of "the child" is unmistakable. Herod was going to try to kill him (v.13), and Joseph took "the child and his mother" (v.14—not the normal order) to Egypt.

15 The death of Herod brought relief to many. In Egypt, it made possible the return of the Child, Mary, and Joseph, who awaited a word from the Lord. Matthew goes on to point out that Jesus' exodus from Egypt fulfilled Scripture written long before.

The OT quotation almost certainly comes from Hos 11:1, which refers to Israel's exodus from Egypt. In what sense can Matthew mean that Jesus' return to the land of Israel "fulfilled" this text? Four observations clarify the issue.

(1) Jesus is often presented in the NT as the antitype of Israel, or better, the typological recapitulation of Israel. For example, Jesus' temptation after forty days of fasting recapitulated the forty years' trial of Israel (see comments on 4:1–11). Pharaoh had to let Israel go because Israel was the Lord's son (Ex 4:22–23). Thus it is only fitting that Jesus also come out of Egypt as God's Son, for already by this time he has been presented as the messianic "son of David" and, by the virginal conception, the Son of God (see also 3:17).

(2) The verb "to fulfill" (GK 4444) has broader significance than mere one-to-one prediction (see comments on 5:17). Not only in Matthew but elsewhere in the NT, the history and laws of the OT are perceived to have prophetic significance. Hebrews, for example, argues that the laws regarding the tabernacle and the sacrificial system were from the beginning designed to point toward the only Sacrifice that could really remove sin and toward the only Priest who could serve once and for all as the effective Mediator between God and humankind. "Fulfillment" must be understood against the background of such interlocking themes and their typological connections.

(3) It follows, therefore, that the NT writers do not think they are reading back into the OT things that are not already there germinally. Regarding v.15, Hos 11 pictures God's love for Israel. Although God threatens judgment and disaster, yet because he is God and not a man (11:9), he looks to a time when in compassion he will roar like a lion and his children will return to him (11:10–11). In short Hosea himself looks forward to a saving visitation by the Lord. The "son" language is part of this messianic matrix; insofar as that matrix points to Jesus the Messiah and insofar as Israel's history looks forward to one who sums it up, in that sense Hos 11:1 looks forward to Jesus the Messiah. The NT writers insist that the OT can be rightly interpreted only if the entire revelation is kept in perspective as it is historically unfolded (e.g., Gal 3:6–14).

(4) If this interpretation of Mt 2:15 is correct, it follows that for Matthew Jesus himself is the locus of true Israel. This does not necessarily mean that God has no further purpose for racial Israel; but it does mean that the position of God's people in the Messianic Age is determined by reference to Jesus, not race.

E. The Massacre of Bethlehem's Boys (2:16–18)

Few sections of Mt 1–2 have been as widely criticized as this one. But this story is in perfect harmony with what we know of Herod's character in his last years. That there is no other historical confirmation is not surprising. The death of a few children (perhaps a dozen or so; Bethlehem's total population was small) would hardly have been recorded in such violent times.

16 It probably did not take long to carry out Herod's barbarous order. Bethlehem was only five miles from Jerusalem. The Magi had set out in the same evening (v.9) and may have left that same night after their dream (v.12); the same would be true of Joseph with Jesus and Mary (vv.13–15). By the next evening Herod's patience would have been exhausted. The two-years age limit was to prevent Jesus' escape; at the time he was between six and twenty months old. Herod, aiming to eliminate a potential king, restricted the massacre to boys. Furious at being deceived, he raged against the Lord and his Anointed One (Ps 2:2). Yet this was no narrow escape. The One enthroned in heaven laughs and scoffs at the Herods of this world (Ps 2:4).

17–18 To Matthew, the massacre fulfills Jer 31:15. This text probably refers to the deportation of Judah and Benjamin in 587–586 B.C. Nebuzaradan, commander of Nebuchadnezzar's imperial guard, gathered the captives at Ramah before taking them into exile in Babylon (Jer 40:1–2). Ramah lay north of Jerusalem on the way to Bethel; Rachel's tomb was at Zelzah in the same vicinity (1Sa 10:2). Jeremiah 31:15 depicts Rachel as crying out from her tomb because her "children," her descendants, are being removed from the land and are no longer a nation.

MATTHEW 2

Why does Matthew refer to this OT passage? First, Jer 31:15 occurs in a setting of hope. Despite the tears, God says, the exiles will return; and now Matthew likewise suggests that, despite the tears of the Bethlehem mothers, there is hope because Messiah has escaped Herod and will ultimately reign.

But there may be a further reason, based on the differences between Matthew and the OT. Here Jesus does not, as in v.15, recapitulate an event from Israel's history. The Exile sent Israel into captivity and thereby called forth tears. But in Matthew the tears are not for him who goes into "exile" but because of the children who stay behind and are slaughtered. Why, then, refer to the Exile at all? If we look at the broader context of both Jeremiah and Matthew, Jer 31:9, 20 refers to Israel as God's dear son and goes on to introduce the new covenant (31:31–34) that the Lord will make with his people. Therefore the tears associated with Exile (31:15) will end. Matthew has already made the Exile a turning point in his thought (1:11–12), for at that time the Davidic line was dethroned. The tears of the Exile are now being "fulfilled"—i.e., the tears begun in Jeremiah's day are climaxed and ended by the tears of the mothers of Bethlehem. The heir to David's throne has come, the Exile is over, the true Son of God has arrived, and he will introduce the new covenant (26:28) that was promised by Jeremiah.

F. The Return to Nazareth (2:19–23)

19–21 This fourth dream and third mention of the "angel of the Lord" (v.19) continues the divine initiative in preserving and guiding the Child. Although the whole land was before Joseph and he apparently hoped to settle in Judea (perhaps in Bethlehem), he was forced to retire to despised Galilee.

22 Probably Joseph had expected Herod Antipas to reign over the entire kingdom; but Herod the Great made a late change in his will, dividing his kingdom into three parts. Archelaus, known for his ruthlessness, was

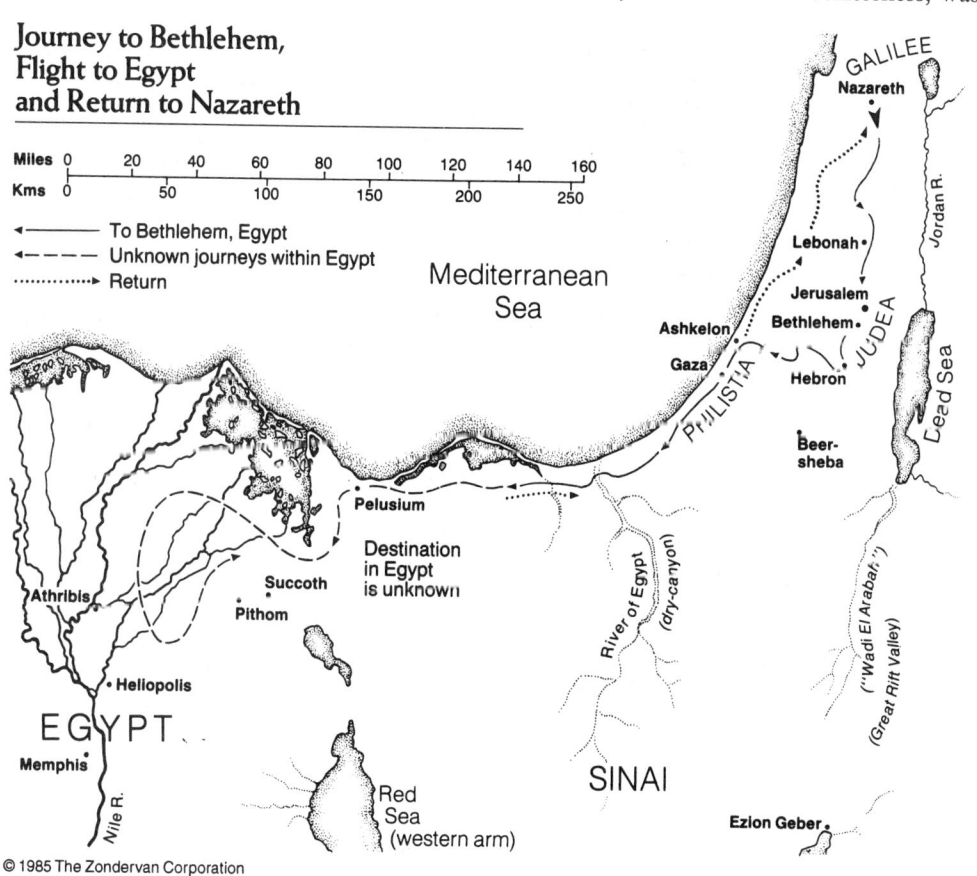

Journey to Bethlehem, Flight to Egypt and Return to Nazareth

© 1985 The Zondervan Corporation

15

given Judea, Samaria, and Idumea. Joseph, guided by the fifth and final dream, settled the family in Galilee.

23 The town Joseph chose was Nazareth, his former home and that of Mary (cf. 13:53–58; Lk 1:26–27; 2:39). This final quotation formula, like that of v.15, should probably be understood as taking place "in order to fulfill the prophets." Matthew's wording here suggests he had no specific OT quotation in mind; indeed, these words are found nowhere in the OT.

The interpretation of this verse has had numerous suggestions. The best one sees Matthew using "Nazarene" as an adjectival form meaning "from Nazareth," even though the Greek spelling is unusual. Nazareth was a despised place (Jn 7:42, 52), even to other Galileans (cf. Jn 1:46). Jesus grew up not in Bethlehem, with its Davidic overtones, but in Nazareth, with all the opprobrium of the sneer. When Christians were referred to in Acts as the "Nazarene sect" (24:5), the expression was meant to hurt. Matthew is therefore not saying that a particular OT prophet foretold that the Messiah would live in Nazareth; he is saying that the OT prophets foretold that the Messiah would be despised (cf. Pss 22:6–8, 13; 69:8, 20–21; Isa 11:1; 49:7; 53:2–3, 8; Da 9:26). The theme is repeatedly picked up by Matthew (e.g., Mt 8:20; 11:16–19; 15:7–8). In other words Matthew gives us the substance of several OT passages, not a direct quotation.

II. The Gospel of the Kingdom (3:1–7:29)

A. Narrative (3:1–4:25)

1. Foundational steps (3:1–4:11)

a. The ministry of John the Baptist (3:1–12)

All four Gospels preface the ministry of Jesus with that of John the Baptist. After four hundred silent years, God was speaking through a new prophet who called people to repentance and promised someone greater to come.

1 "John" had been a popular name among the Jews from the time of John Hyrcanus (died 106 B.C.). The John of this verse was soon designated "the Baptist," because baptism was so prominent in his ministry. He began his preaching in the "Desert of Judea," a vaguely defined area including the lower Jordan Valley north of the Dead Sea and the country immediately west of the Dead Sea. "Desert" had long had prophetic overtones (e.g., the Law had been given in the "desert"; cf. Ac 7:30, 36, 38).

2 John's preaching had two elements. The first was a call to "repent" (GK 3566). What is meant by this word is a radical transformation of the entire person, a fundamental turnaround involving mind and action and including overtones of grief; it results in "fruit in keeping with repentance." Of course, all this assumes that a person's actions are fundamentally off course and need radical change. John applies this repentance to the religious leaders of his day (3:7–8) with particular vehemence.

The second element in John's preaching was the nearness of the "kingdom of heaven," and this is given as the ground for repentance. Throughout the OT there was a rising expectation of a divine visitation that would establish justice, crush opposition, and renew the very universe.

The predominant meaning of "kingdom" (GK 993) in both the OT and NT is "reign": the term has dynamic force. In the first century there was little agreement among Jews as to what the messianic kingdom would be like. One popular assumption was that the Roman yoke would be shattered and there would be political peace and mounting prosperity for the people of God.

Except at 12:28; 19:24; 21:31, 43, Matthew always uses "kingdom of heaven" instead of "kingdom of God." His preferred expression certainly does not restrict God's reign to the heavens. The biblical goal is the manifest exercise of God's sovereignty, his "reign" on earth and among humans. There are enough parallels among the Synoptics to imply that "kingdom of God" and "kingdom of heaven" denote the same thing. The most common explanation why Matthew avoided "kingdom of God" was to remove unnecessary offense to Jews who often used circumlocutions like "heaven" to refer to God (e.g., Da 4:26). Matthew may also be subtly anticipating the extent of Christ's postresurrection authority: God's sovereignty *in heaven* and on earth is now mediated through him (28:18).

This kingdom, John preached, "is near" (GK 1581). The Messianic Age has now drawn near, the same message preached by

Jesus (4:17) and his disciples (10:7). According to Matthew, the kingdom came with Jesus and his preaching and miracles, it came with his death and resurrection, and it will come at the end of the age. The Baptist's terminology, though veiled, necessarily aroused enormous excitement (v.5). But assorted apocalyptic and political expectations would have produced a profound misunderstanding of the kingdom being preached (see comment on Mk 1:44). Therefore Jesus himself purposely used veiled terminology when treating themes like this. Moreover, just as the angel's announcement to Joseph declared Jesus' primary purpose to be to save his people from their sins (1:21), so the first announcement of the kingdom is associated with repentance and confession of sin (3:6)—these themes are constantly intertwined in Matthew.

3 Matthew goes on to identify John the Baptist in an eschatological, prophecy-and-fulfillment framework with the one of whom Isaiah spoke. In Isa 40:3 (cf. John's own application of this verse in Jn 1:23) the way of the Lord is being "made straight" (a metaphor using road building to refer to repentance); in Mt 3:3 it is the way of Jesus. This sort of identification of Jesus with the Lord is common in the NT (e.g., Ex 13:21 and 1Co 10:4; Isa 6:1 and Jn 12:41) and confirms the kingdom as being equally the kingdom of God and the kingdom of Jesus. The deity of Christ is clearly implicit in such texts.

4–5 Clothes of camel's hair and a leather belt were not only the clothes of poor people but established links with Elijah (2Ki 1:8; cf. Mal 4:5). "Locusts" are large grasshoppers, still eaten in the East. Both Elijah and John had stern ministries in which austere garb and diet confirmed their message and condemned the idolatry of physical and spiritual softness. John's impact was enormous (v.5), and his crowds came from a wide area.

6 Confession of sin was commanded in the law, not only as part of a priest's duties (Lev 16:21), but as an individual responsibility for wrongs done (Lev 5:5; 26:40; Nu 5:6–7). In Israel's better days this was carried out (Ne 9:2–3; Ps 32:5). In the NT (cf. Ac 19:18; 1Jn 1:9) confession is scarcely less important. Since John was urging people to prepare for Messiah's coming by repenting and being baptized, we may surmise that open renunciation of sin was a precondition of his baptism.

The Jordan River is fast flowing. No doubt John stationed himself at one of the fords as he prepared the way for the Lord.

7 Representatives of the Sanhedrin (composed of Pharisees, Sadducees, and the elders) came to examine what John was doing (cf. Jn 1:19, 24). The question with which the Baptist confronted them has this sense: "Who suggested to you that you would escape the coming wrath?" Thus John's rhetorical question takes on a sarcastic nuance: "Who warned you to flee the coming wrath and come for baptism—when in fact you show no signs of repentance?"

John the Baptist stands squarely in the prophetic tradition—a tradition in which the Day of the Lord points much more to darkness than to light for those who think they have no sin (Am 2:4–8; 6:1–7). "You brood of vipers!" also belongs to the prophetic tradition (cf. Isa 14:29; 30:6; cf. Mt 12:34).

8–9 The coming of God's reign either demands repentance (v.2) or brings judgment. Repentance must be genuine: if we wish to escape the coming wrath (v.7), our lifestyle must be in harmony with our oral repentance (v.8). Merely being descendants of Abraham is not enough (v.9). In the OT God repeatedly cut off many Israelites and saved only a remnant. Verse 9 not only rebukes the self-righteousness of the leaders but implies that participation in the kingdom results from grace and extends beyond racial frontiers (cf. 8:11).

10 The ax is "already" at the root of the trees (for the idiom, cf. Isa 10:33–34; Jer 46:22). Just as the kingdom is dawning already (v.2), so also is the judgment; the two are inseparable. To preach the kingdom is to preach repentance; any tree, regardless of its roots, that does not bring forth good fruit will be destroyed.

11 With the phrase "for repentance" (GK 3567), John wants to contrast his baptism with that of the one who comes after him, who is more powerful, for he will baptize with the Holy Spirit and fire. This is not the normal order: usually the one who follows is the disciple, the lesser one (cf. Mt 16:24; Jn 13:16; 15:20). But because John's particular ministry is to announce the eschatological figure, he cannot do other than precede him.

Just as John's purpose was to prepare a way for the Lord by calling people to repentance, so his baptism pointed to the one who would bring the eschatological baptism in spirit and fire. John's baptism was "essentially preparatory." Jesus' baptism inaugurated the Messianic Age.

"Baptism in the Holy Spirit" is not a specialized term in the NT (see Eze 36:25–27; 39:29; Joel 2:28); Matthew and Luke add "and fire." This probably symbolizes a purifying agent along with the Holy Spirit (cf. Isa 1:25; Zec 13:9; Mal 3:2–3). The preposition "with" is not repeated; it governs both "Holy Spirit" and "fire," suggesting a unified concept. John's water baptism relates to repentance; but the one whose way he is preparing will administer a Spirit-fire baptism that will purify and refine. In a time when many Jews felt the Holy Spirit had been withdrawn till the Messianic Age, this announcement could only have been greeted with excited anticipation.

12 Messiah's coming will separate grain from chaff. A winnowing fork tossed both into the air. The wind blew the chaff away; the heavier grain fell, to be gathered up from the ground, while the scattered chaff was swept up and burned. The "unquenchable fire" signifies eschatological judgment (cf. Isa 34:10; 66:24; Jer 7:20), i.e., hell (cf. 5:29).

b. The baptism of Jesus (3:13–17)

13–14 During the time John the Baptist was preaching to the crowds and baptizing them, Jesus came from Galilee also to be baptized.

Verses 14–15 are peculiar to this gospel. John tried to deter Jesus from his baptism, insisting that he stood in need of baptism by Jesus. Earlier John had difficulty baptizing the Pharisees and Sadducees because they were not worthy of his baptism. Now he has trouble baptizing Jesus. Why? John's baptism signified repentance and confession of sin. Whether John knew Jesus well, we do not know. It is, however, inconceivable that his parents had not told him of Mary's visit to Elizabeth some three decades earlier (Lk 1:39–45). At the very least John must have recognized that Jesus, to whom he was related, whose birth was more marvelous than his own, and whose knowledge of Scripture was prodigious even as a child (Lk 2:41–52), outstripped him. John the Baptist was a humble man; conscious of his own sin, he could detect no sin Jesus needed to repent of and confess. So John thought that Jesus should baptize him.

15 John's consent was won because Jesus told him, "It is proper for us to fulfill all righteousness." What does this mean? John's baptism, it will be remembered, had two foci: repentance and its eschatological significance of the kingdom being near. Jesus affirms, in effect, that it is God's will ("all righteousness"; GK *1466*) that John baptize him; and *both* John *and* Jesus "fulfill" that will by going through with it ("it is proper for us").

Within this framework we may recognize another theme. Jesus is seen as the Suffering Servant (Isa 42:1; cf. comment on Mt 3:17). But the Servant's first mark is obeying God: he "fulfills all righteousness" since he suffers and dies to accomplish redemption in obedience to the will of God. By his baptism Jesus affirms his determination to obey that will and to do his assigned work. Thus the "now" may be significant: Jesus is saying that John's objection to baptizing him is in principle valid. Yet he must "now," at this point in salvation history, baptize Jesus; for at this point Jesus must demonstrate his willingness to take on his servant role and identify himself with the sinful human race.

This interpretation assumes that Jesus knew of his Suffering-Servant role from the beginning of his ministry. This role was hinted at in 2:23; here it makes its first veiled appearance in Jesus' actions. The immediately following temptation narrative confirms it (4:1–11, see comments).

16 "As soon as" not only suggests that Jesus left the water immediately after his baptism but that the Spirit's witness was equally prompt. "He saw" most naturally refers to Jesus, not John, because Jesus is the focus of interest. But the voice was for John and possibly others, and it was stated in the third person.

"Heaven . . . opened" calls to mind OT visions (e.g. Isa 66:1; Eze 1:1). "The Spirit of God descending like a dove" simile could mean either that the manner of the Spirit's descent was like a dove's or that the Spirit appeared in a dove's form. Already in the OT, God promised that the Spirit would de-

17 The voice from heaven was God's own voice; it testified that God himself had broken silence and was again revealing himself to the human race—a clear sign of the dawning of the Messianic Age (cf. 17:5; Jn 12:28). The utterance from heaven reflects Isa 42:1, modified by Ps 2:7 (cf. Mt 12:18–21). The results are extraordinarily important.

(1) These words from heaven link Jesus with the Suffering Servant (cf. Isa 42:1) at the very beginning of his ministry and confirm our interpretation of v.15. (2) God refers to Jesus as "my Son"; implicitly the title "Son of God" is introduced and picked up immediately in the next chapter (4:3, 6). The reference to Ps 2:7 identifies Jesus as the royal, messianic Son of David. (3) Jesus has already been set forth as the true Israel to which actual Israel was pointing (see comment on 2:15); now the heavenly witness confirms the link. (4) At the same time the virginal conception suggests a more than titular or functional sonship: in this context there is the hint of an ontological sonship, made most explicit in the gospel of John.

These things are linked in the one utterance: at the very beginning of Jesus' public ministry, his Father presented him, in a veiled way, as the Davidic Messiah, the very Son of God, the representative of the people, and the Suffering Servant. Matthew will develop them further in his gospel.

c. The temptation of Jesus (4:1–11)

Both Matthew and Mark tie the temptations to Jesus' baptism. It is difficult to be certain exactly what happened or in what form Satan came to Jesus. Standing on a high mountain (v.8) would not itself provide a glimpse of "all the kingdoms of the world"; some supernatural vision is presupposed. But there is no reason to think the framework of the story is purely symbolic as opposed to visionary.

1 Jesus' three temptations tie into his baptism, not only by the references to sonship and the Spirit, but by the opening "Then." The same Spirit who engendered Jesus (1:20) and attested the Father's acknowledgment of his sonship (3:16–17) now leads him into the desert to be tempted by the devil. The "desert" (GK 2245) is not only the place associated with demonic activity (Isa 13:21; 34:14; Mt 12:43; Rev 18:2) but, in a context abounding with references to Dt 6–8, the place where Israel experienced her greatest early testings.

The "devil" (GK *1333*) is the chief opposer of God, the archenemy who leads all the spiritual hosts of darkness (cf. Ge 3; Jn 8:37–40; 2Co 11:3; 12:7; et al.). In a day of rising occultism and open Satanism, it is easier to believe the Bible's plain witness to him than twenty years ago.

That Jesus should be led "by the Spirit" to be tempted "by the devil" is no stranger than Job 1:6–2:7. "To tempt" (GK *4279*) can also mean "to test." Scripture "tempting" or "testing" can reveal or develop character (Ge 22:1; Ex 20:20; Jn 6:6; 2Co 13:5) as well as solicit to evil (1Co 7:5; 1Th 3:5; see comments on Lk 4:1–2). In Jesus' temptations God clearly intended to test him just as Israel was tested; Jesus' responses prove that he understood.

2 The parallels with historic Israel continue. Jesus' fast of forty days and nights reflected Israel's forty-year wandering (Dt 8:2). Both Israel's and Jesus' hunger taught a lesson (Dt 8:3); both spent time in the desert preparatory to their respective tasks. For both, God intended to prove their obedience and loyalty in preparation for their appointed work. The one "son" failed but pointed to the "Son" who would never fail (cf. comment on 2:15).

3–4 When the tempter came to Jesus, he did not challenge Jesus' sonship but assumed it and reflected on its meaning. Sonship of the living God, he suggested, surely means Jesus has the power and right to satisfy his own needs. Jesus' response is based solely on Scripture: "It is written" (followed by Dt 8:3). Everyone must recognize his or her utter dependence on God's word. Jesus' food is to do the will of his Father who sent him (Jn 4:34).

The point of each temptation must be determined by closely examining both temptation and Jesus' response. This first one was a temptation for Jesus to use his sonship in a way inconsistent with his God-ordained mission. Satan's aim was to entice Jesus to use powers that were rightly his but which he had voluntarily abandoned to carry out the Father's mission (cf. 26:53–54; 27:40).

Reclaiming them for himself would deny the self-abasement implicit in his mission and in the Father's will. Israel demanded its bread but died in the wilderness; Jesus denied himself bread, retained his righteousness, and lived by faithful submission to God's word.

5–7 The second temptation (Luke's third) is set in the "holy city," on the highest point of the temple complex (see comment on Lk 4:9–12). Satan quoted Ps 91:11–12 from the LXX, omitting the words "to guard you in all your ways." His deceit lay not in omitting a few words but in misapplying his quotation into a temptation that easily traps the devout mind by apparently giving approval to what might otherwise be thought sinful. According to this passage, the angels will lift anyone who trusts in God (preeminently Jesus) up in their hands. Jesus is thereby tempted to test his sonship against God's pledge to protect his own.

Jesus replied with Dt 6:16. His hesitation came because Scripture forbids putting God to the test (see Ex 17:2–7, where the Israelites "put the Lord to the test" by demanding water). So Jesus was tempted by Satan to test God; but Jesus recognized Satan's testing as a sort of manipulative bribery expressly forbidden in the Scriptures. For both Israel and Jesus, demanding miraculous protection as proof of God's care was wrong; the appropriate attitude is trust and obedience (Dt 6:17).

8–10 Satan offers the kingdoms of the world and their "splendor" without showing their sin. Jesus, however, came to remove sin. Here was a temptation to achieve power by taking a shortcut to fullest messianic authority, sidestepping the Cross and introducing idolatry (see comment on Lk 4:5–8).

Jesus recognized that Satan's suggestion entailed depriving God of his exclusive claim to worship: neither God's "son" Israel nor God's "Son" Jesus may swerve from undivided allegiance to God himself (cf. Ex 23:20–33; Dt 6:13). So Jesus responded with a third "it is written" and banished Satan from his presence. In other words, Jesus had in mind from the very beginning of his earthly ministry the combination of royal kingship and suffering servanthood attested at his baptism (see comments on 3:15, 17).

11 The devil temporarily left Jesus (cf. 16:23). Though the conflict has barely begun, the pattern of obedience and trust has been established. He had learned to resist the devil (cf. Jas 4:7). The angelic help is not some passing blessing but a sustained one. Jesus had refused to relieve his hunger by miraculously turning stones to bread; now he is fed supernaturally. He had refused to throw himself off the temple heights in the hope of angelic help; now angels feed him. He had refused to take a shortcut to inherit the kingdom of the world; now he fulfills Scripture by beginning his ministry and announcing the kingdom in Galilee of the Gentiles (vv.12–17).

2. Jesus' early Galilean ministry (4:12–25)

12 John the Baptist's imprisonment (likely in the fortress of Machaerus) appears to have prompted Jesus to return to Galilee. Though Jesus began his ministry in Judea concurrent with John the Baptist (see Jn 1:19–3:21), the Synoptics start with his ministry in Galilee after John's imprisonment. Why the Judean ministry is ignored is unknown, though perhaps it was because the imprisonment marked the end of the forerunner's ministry. Furthermore, especially for Matthew, Galilee is of profound significance because it heralds the fulfillment of prophecy (vv.14–16) and points to the Gospel's extension to "all nations" (28:19).

13 Jesus moved from Nazareth to Capernaum (cf. Lk 4:31), a village on the northwest shore of Lake Galilee. This village enjoyed a fishing industry that probably demanded the presence of a tax collector's booth (9:9). Here, too, was Peter's house (8:14). But Matthew is interested in pointing out Capernaum's location with reference to the ancient tribal allotments of Zebulun and Naphtali (see vv.15–16).

14–16 Jesus' move fulfilled Isa 9:1–2, a prophecy that is part of a large structure looking to Immanuel's coming (see comment on 1:23). The point of the quotation is clear enough. In despised Galilee, the place where people live in darkness without the religious and cultic advantages of Jerusalem and Judea, where the darkness is most dense, here the light has dawned. This was God's prophesied plan; from of old the Messiah was promised to "Galilee of the Gentiles," a foreshadowing of the commission to "all nations" (28:19). Moreover, if the messianic light dawns on the darkest places, then Messiah's salvation can only be a bestowal of grace; Jesus came to call, not the righteous, but sinners (9:13).

17 "From that time on" marks an important turning point because it ties something new to what has just preceded it. The burden of Jesus' preaching so far is, in itself, identical to that of John the Baptist: "Repent, for the kingdom of heaven is near" (see comments on 3:1–2). But John the Baptist had placed these words in an OT context that highlights his function as the forerunner who looks forward to the Messiah and his kingdom; when Jesus says the same words, they are linked (by "from that time") with an OT context that insists Jesus fulfills the promises of a light rising to shine on the Gentiles. With Jesus the kingdom has drawn so near that it has actually dawned. Therefore Jesus' hearers must repent—a demand made not only by the Baptist but by Jesus. The structure of the book thus sets up an implicit parallelism: Jesus is not so much a new Moses as a new Joshua, for as Moses did not enter the Promised Land but was succeeded by Joshua who did, so John the Baptist announced the kingdom and was followed by Jesus (Joshua) who leads his people into it (cf. comment on 1:21).

18–20 According to Jn 1:35–51 Peter and Andrew first followed Jesus at an earlier date, but then presumably took up fishing again. Perhaps this earlier event explains the speed with which they followed Jesus.

Simon was called "Peter" (meaning "rock"), but Matthew does not tell us how Peter received this name (cf. 16:18; Jn 1:42). Jesus called him and his brother Andrew to "follow me." This expression (along with several others) presupposes a physical "following" during Jesus' ministry. His "followers" were not just "hearers", they actually followed their Master around (as students then did) and became, as it were, trainees. There is a straight line from this commission to the Great Commission (28:18–20). Jesus' followers are indeed to catch other people.

21–22 James and John may have been making repairs after a night's fishing. Jesus took the initiative and "called" (GK 2813) them. In the Synoptics, unlike Paul's letters (e.g., Ro 8:30), Jesus' call is not necessarily effectual. But in this instance it was immediately obeyed.

23–25 This section summarizes Jesus' spreading of the news of the kingdom. Summaries are common to narrative literature; but the one before us, with its parallel in 9:35–38, has distinctive features. (1) It does not just summarize what has gone before but shows the geographical extent and varied activity of Jesus' ministry. (2) It therefore sets the stage for the particular discourses and stories that follow and implies that the material presented is but a representative sampling of what was available. (3) It is not a mere chronicle but conveys theological substance.

Jesus' ministry included teaching, preaching, and healing. Galilee, the district covered, is small (approximately seventy by forty miles), but it had a population of up to three million and over two hundred cities and villages. Jesus "went around doing good" (Ac 10:38). The sheer physical drain must have been enormous. Above all we must recognize that Jesus was an itinerant preacher and teacher who necessarily repeated approximately the same material again and again and faced the same problems, illnesses, and needs again and again.

On Jesus' teaching in a synagogue, see comment on Mk 1:21. The message Jesus preached was the "good news" (GK 2295) concerning the kingdom, whose nearness had already been announced (3:2; 4:17) and which is the central subject of the Sermon on the Mount (5–7). God was breaking into history with his saving reign in the person of his Son. The healings of various diseases among the people further attest the kingdom's presence and advance (cf. 11:2–6; Isa 35:5–6).

The geographical extent of "Syria" is uncertain. From the perspective of Jesus in Galilee, Syria was to the north. From the Roman viewpoint Syria was a Roman province embracing all Palestine, Galilee excepted, since it was under the independent administration of Herod Antipas at this time. The term "Syria" reflects the extent of the excitement aroused by Jesus' ministry; if the Roman use of the term is here presumed, it shows his effect on people far beyond the borders of Israel. Two of the areas specifically mentioned (Decapolis and the region across the Jordan) were primarily Gentile areas, a theme Matthew has already been emphasizing (see comments on 1:6).

Jesus healed various types of sick people. In the NT sickness may result directly from a particular sin (e.g., Jn 5:14; 1Co 11:30) or it may not (e.g., Jn 9:2–3). But both Scripture and Jewish tradition take sickness as resulting from living in a fallen world (cf. on 8:17); the Messianic Age would end such grief (Isa 11:1–5; 35:5–6). Therefore Jesus' miracles, dealing with every kind of ailment, not only heralded the kingdom but showed that God had pledged himself to deal with sin at a basic level (cf. 1:21; 8:17).

B. First Discourse: The Sermon on the Mount (5:1–7:29)

This commentary on the Sermon on the Mount proceeds with the assumption that Matthew presents the real, historical setting for this discourse, though it recognizes that these chapters are condensed notes rather than the entire sermon verbatim. Thus we find Matthew's idiom selected and presented in accord with his own concerns. Lk 6:20–49 is a separate report of the same occasion, with a somewhat different selection of material (for more on this, see EBC 8:122–26).

The unifying theme of the sermon is the kingdom of heaven. It envelopes the Beatitudes (5:3, 10) and appears in 5:17–20, which details the relation between the OT and the kingdom. It returns at the heart of the Lord's Prayer (6:10), climaxes the section on kingdom perspectives (6:33), and is presented as what must finally be entered (7:21–23). Matthew places the sermon immediately after two verses insisting that the primary content of Jesus' preaching was the Gospel of the kingdom (4:17, 23). It provides ethical guidelines for life in the kingdom, but does so within an explanation of the place of the contemporary setting within redemption history and Jesus' relation to the OT (5:17–20). The community forming around him, his "disciples," is not yet so cohesive and committed a group that exhortations to "enter" (7:13–14) are irrelevant. The glimpse of kingdom life (horizontally and vertically) in these chapters anticipates not only the love commandments (22:34–40) but also grace (5:3; 6:12; 7:7–11; cf. 21:28–46).

Matthew does not record any controversies with Jewish teachers as to the OT law's meaning prior to this Sermon. This means that the antitheses in 5:17–48 ("You have heard . . . but I tell") should not be read as tokens of confrontation but in the light of the fulfillment themes richly set out in chs.1–4 and made again explicit in 5:17–20: Jesus comes "to fulfill" the Law and the Prophets (i.e., the OT Scriptures). Therefore his announcements concerning the kingdom must be read against that background. Whatever controversies occupied Jesus' attention, the burden of his kingdom proclamation always made the kingdom the goal of the Scriptures, the long-expected messianic reign foretold by the Law and the Prophets alike.

1. The Setting (5:1–2)

1 The "crowds" are those referred to in 4:23–25. Here Jesus stands at the height of his popularity. Although his ministry touched the masses, he saw the need to teach his "disciples" closely, though this word must not be restricted to the Twelve, whom Matthew has yet to mention (10:1–4). Those who especially wanted to attach themselves to him, Jesus takes aside to instruct. As such, they are paradigms for believers of any age.

At this point in his ministry, Jesus could not escape the mounting crowds; and by the end of his sermon (7:28–29), he was surrounded by yet larger crowds. This suggests that his teaching covered several days, not just an hour or two. The place of retreat Jesus chose was in the hill country (see comment on Lk 6:17). He "sat down" to teach. Sitting was the accepted posture of synagogue or school teachers (Lk 4:20).

2 Literally, this verse translates, "he opened his mouth and taught them," found elsewhere in the NT (13:35; Ac 8:35; 10:34; 18:14) and reflecting OT roots (Job 3:1; 33:2; Da 10:16). It is used in solemn or revelatory contexts.

2. The kingdom of heaven: its norms and witness (5:3–16)

a. The norms of the kingdom (5:3–12)

The Beatitudes (from the Latin *beatus*, "blessed") find their roots in wisdom literature and especially the Psalms. The OT never bunch more than two beatitudes together (e.g., Ps 84:4–5).

3 The Greek word for "blessed" (GK *3421*) describes the person who is singularly favored by God and therefore in some sense "happy," though the word can also apply to God (1Ti 1:11; 6:15). The common factor between these two views is approval: humans "bless" God, approving and praising him; God "blesses" humans, approving them in gracious condescension. In the eschatological setting of Matthew, "blessed" refers to a promised eschatological blessing, specified by the second clause of each beatitude.

Because Luke has "poor" (GK 4777) rather than "poor in spirit," many have concluded that he preserves the true teaching of the historical Jesus—concern for the economically destitute—while Matthew has "spiritualized" it by adding "in spirit." But already in the OT, "the poor" has religious overtones, i.e., those who because of sustained economic privation and social distress have confidence only in God (e.g., Pss 40:17; 69:32–33; Isa 61:1). Poverty itself is not the chief thing; it can be turned to advantage only if it fosters humility before God. In other words, to be poor in spirit is not to lack courage but to acknowledge one's spiritual bankruptcy and one's need to depend on God alone.

The "kingdom of heaven" (see comment on 3:2) belongs to such people; it is they who enjoy Messiah's reign and his blessings. They joyfully accept his rule and participate in the life of the kingdom (7:14). While the rewards of vv.4–9 are future ("they will be comforted," "will inherit," etc.), the first and last are present ("for theirs is the kingdom of heaven"). Yet one must not make too much of this, for the present tense can function as a future; and the future tense can emphasize certainty. There is little doubt that here the kingdom idea is primarily future, made explicit in v.12. However, though the full blessedness of those described in these beatitudes awaits the consummated kingdom, they already share in the kingdom's blessedness so far as it has been inaugurated (see comment on 4:17).

4 The godly remnant of Jesus' day weeps because of the humiliation of Israel, but they understand that it comes from personal and corporate sins. Weeping for sins can be deeply poignant (Ezr 10:6; Ps 51:4; Da 9:19–20) and can cover a global as well as personal view of sin and our participation in it.

"Comfort, comfort my people" (Isa 40:1) is God's response to human sin. These first two beatitudes deliberately allude to the messianic blessing of Isa 61:1–3. But these blessings, already realized partially but fully only at the consummation (Rev 7:17), depend on a Messiah who has come to save his people from their sins (1:21; cf. also 11:28–30).

5 The word "meek" (GK 4558) generally suggests gentleness (cf. 11:29; Jas 3:13) and the self-control it entails. To be meek toward others implies freedom from malice and a vengeful spirit. Jesus exemplifies it best (11:29; 21:5). We may acknowledge our own spiritual bankruptcy (v.3) and mourn (v.4). But to respond with meekness when others tell us of our bankruptcy is far more difficult. Meekness therefore requires such a true view about ourselves as will express itself even in our attitude toward others.

And the meek—not the strong, aggressive, harsh, tyrannical—will inherit the earth. The verb "inherit" (GK 3099) often relates to entrance into the Promised Land (e.g., Dt 4:1; 16:20). But the specific OT allusion here is Ps 37:9, 11, 29—a psalm recognized as messianic in Jesus' day. Entrance into the Promised Land ultimately became a pointer toward entrance into the new heaven *and the new earth* ("earth" is the same word as "land"; cf. Isa 66:22; Rev 21:1), the consummation of the messianic kingdom.

6 "Hunger and thirst" vividly expresses desire (cf. Pss 42:2; 63:1). It is best to take "righteousness" (GK 1466) here as simultaneously personal righteousness and justice in the broadest sense. These people desire not only that they may wholly do God's will from the heart, but also that justice may be done everywhere. All unrighteousness grieves them and makes them homesick for the new heaven and earth—the home of righteousness (2Pe 3:13). What they taste now whets their appetites for more. Ultimately they will be satisfied without qualification only when the kingdom is consummated.

7 This beatitude is akin to Ps 18:25. Mercy embraces both forgiveness for the guilty and compassion for the suffering and needy. No particular object of the demanded mercy is specified, because mercy is to be a function of Jesus' disciples, not of a particular situation. This theme is common in Matthew (e.g., 6:12–15; 9:13). The reward is not mercy shown by others but by God. This does not mean that our mercy is the causal ground of God's mercy but its occasional ground (see comment on 6:14–15).

8 "Pure [GK *2754*] in heart" has two interrelated meanings. It means inner moral purity as opposed to merely external piety (cf. Dt 10:16; 1Sa 15:22; Ps 24:3–4; Mt 23:25–28); it also means singlemindedness, a heart free from deceit.

It is impossible to have one characteristic without the other. The one who is singleminded in commitment to the kingdom and its righteousness (6:33) will also be inwardly pure. Inward sham, deceit, and moral filth cannot coexist with sincere devotion to Christ. Either way, this beatitude excoriates hypocrisy (see comment on 6:1–18). The pure in heart will "see God"—now with the eyes of faith and finally in the dazzling brilliance of the beatific vision (cf. Heb 12:14; 1Jn 3:1–3; Rev 21:22–27).

9 Jesus' concern in this beatitude is not with the peaceful but with the "peacemakers." "Peace" (GK *1645*) is of constant concern in both OT and NT (e.g., Isa 52:7; Eph 2:11–22; Heb 12:14). The making of peace itself has messianic overtones (cf. "Prince of Peace" in Isa 9:6–7). Jesus does not limit the peacemaking to only one kind, and neither will his disciples. In the light of the Gospel, Jesus himself is the supreme peacemaker, making peace between God and us (Eph 2:15–17; Col 1:20) and among human beings. Our peacemaking will include the promulgation of that Gospel. It must also extend to seeking all kinds of reconciliation. Those who undertake this work are acknowledged as God's "sons" (GK *5626*). In the OT, Israel has the title "sons" (Dt 14:1; Hos 1:10). Now it belongs to the heirs of the kingdom who are especially equipped for peacemaking and so reflect something of the character of their heavenly Father.

10 It is no accident that Jesus should pass from peacemaking to persecution, for the world enjoys its cherished hates and prejudices so much that the peacemaker is not always welcome. Opposition is a normal mark of being a disciple of Jesus (cf. Jn 15:18–25; 2Ti 3:12; 1Pe 4:13–14). The reward of these persecuted people is the same as the reward of the poor in spirit: the kingdom of heaven (see comment on 5:3).

11–12 These two verses, switching from third person to second, apply the force of the last beatitude to Jesus' disciples. Verse 11 extends the persecution of v.10 to include insult, persecution, and slander. The reason for the persecution in this verse is "because of me." It so identifies the disciples of Jesus with the practice of Jesus' righteousness that there is no place for professed allegiance to Jesus that is not full of righteousness. Moreover, this is an implicit Christological claim, for the prophets to whom the disciples are likened were persecuted for their faithfulness to God and the disciples for their faithfulness to Jesus. Not Jesus but the disciples are likened to the prophets; Jesus places himself on a par with God.

The appropriate response of the disciples is rejoicing. They are to rejoice under persecution because their heavenly reward will be great at the consummation of the kingdom. Opposition is sure, for the disciples are aligning themselves with the OT prophets who were persecuted before them (e.g., 2Chr 24:21; Ne 9:26; Jer 20:2). The "reward" (GK *3635*) that Jesus promises is not earned or merited, but is entirely in keeping with the nature of the kingdom. Life lived under kingdom norms is inherently linked with the bliss of life in the consummated kingdom.

b. The witness of the kingdom (5:13–16)

13 In this verse and v.14, "You" is emphatic—"You, my followers and none others, are the salt of the earth." Salt was used in the ancient world to flavor foods and even in small doses as fertilizer. Above all, salt was used as a preservative. Rubbed into meat, a little salt would slow decay. Strictly speaking salt cannot lose its saltiness; sodium chloride is a stable compound. But most salt in the ancient world derived from salt marshes rather than by evaporation of salt water, and thus contained many impurities. The actual salt, being more soluble than the impurities, could be leached out, leaving a residue so dilute it was of little worth.

The question "How can it be made salty again?" is not meant to have an answer. The point is that if Jesus' disciples are to act as a preservative in the world by conforming to kingdom norms, they can discharge this function only by retaining their own virtue.

14–15 Though the Jews saw themselves as the light of the world (Ro 2:19), the true light is the Suffering Servant (Isa 42:6; 49:6), fulfilled in Jesus himself (Mt 4:16; cf. Jn 8:12; 1Jn 1:7).

Derivatively his disciples constitute the new light (cf. Eph 5:8–9; Php 2:15). In the OT as in the NT, light most frequently symbolizes purity as opposed to filth, truth as opposed to error, knowledge as opposed to ignorance, and divine revelation and presence as opposed to reprobation and abandonment by God.

The reference to the "city on a hill" is at one level fairly obvious. Often built of white limestone, ancient towns gleamed in the sun and could not easily be hidden. At night the inhabitants' oil lamps would shed some glow over the surrounding area. As such cities could not be hidden, so also it is unthinkable to light a lamp and hide it under a peck-measure. A lamp is put on a lampstand to illuminate all. The "city on a hill" saying may also refer to OT prophecies about the time when Jerusalem or the mountain of the Lord's house would be lifted up before the world and the nations would stream to it (e.g., Isa 2:2–5). Jesus' disciples constitute the true locus of the people of God and the means of witness to the world.

Ancient lamps found in archaeological digs in Palestine can still be filled with oil and lit.

16 Jesus drives the metaphor home. His disciples must show their "good works"—i.e., all righteousness, everything they are and do that reflects the mind and will of God. And others must see this light. It may provoke persecution (vv.10–12), but that is no reason for hiding the light by which others may come to glorify the Father. Witness includes not just words but deeds as well.

Thus the kingdom norms (vv.3–12) so work out in the lives of the kingdom's heirs as to produce the kingdom witness (vv.13–16). If salt (v.13) exercises the negative function of delaying decay and warns disciples of the danger of compromise and conformity to the world, then light (vv.14–16) speaks positively of illuminating a sin-darkened world and warns against a withdrawal from the world that does not lead others to glorify the Father in heaven.

3. The kingdom of heaven: its demands in relation to the OT (5:17–48)

a. Jesus and the kingdom as fulfillment of the OT (5:17–20)

The phrase "the Law and the Prophets" is repeated in 7:12. The two occurrences of this phrase mark the beginning and end of the body of Jesus' Sermon on the Mount and show that Jesus is taking pains to relate his teaching and place in the history of redemption to the OT Scriptures.

17 The formula "Do not think that" is a teaching device used by Jesus to clarify certain aspects of the kingdom and of his own mission and to set aside potential misunderstandings as to the nature of the kingdom (see also 10:34). Comparison with 10:34 shows that the antithesis may not be absolute. Few would want to argue that there is *no* sense in which Jesus came to bring peace (cf. comment on 5:9). Why then argue that there is *no* sense in which Jesus abolishes the law?

Jesus' mission was not "to abolish" (GK 2907; a term more frequently connected with the destruction of buildings [24:2; 26:61; 27:40]) "the Law or the Prophets," i.e., the Scriptures. The disjunctive "or" makes it clear that neither is to be abolished.

The nub of the problem lies in the verb "to fulfill" (GK 4444), for which a variety of interpretations have been offered. The best one says that Jesus fulfills the Law and the Prophets in that they point to him, and he is their fulfillment. Therefore we give "fulfill" exactly the same meaning as in the formula quotations, which in the prologue (chs. 1–2) have already laid great stress on the prophetic nature of the OT and the way it points to Jesus. Even OT events have this prophetic significance (see comment on 2:15). A little later Jesus insists that "all the Prophets and the Law prophesied" (11:13).

The manner of the prophetic foreshadowing varies. The Exodus, Matthew argues (2:15), foreshadows the calling out of Egypt of God's "son." The writer to the Hebrews argues that many cultic regulations of the OT pointed to Jesus and are now obsolete. In the light of the antitheses (vv.21–48), the passage before us insists that just as Jesus fulfilled OT prophecies by his person and actions, so he fulfilled OT law by his teaching. In no way does this "abolish" the OT as canon, any more than the obsolescence of the Levitical sacrificial system abolishes tabernacle ritual as canon. Instead, the OT's real and abiding authority must be understood through the person and teaching of him to whom it points and who so richly fulfills it.

The chief objection to this view is that the use of "to fulfill" in the fulfillment quotations is in the passive voice, whereas here the voice is active. But it is doubtful whether much can be made out of this distinction. Three conclusions are inevitable. (1) If the antitheses (vv.21–48) are understood in the light of this interpretation of vv.17–20, then Jesus is not primarily engaged there in extending, annulling, or intensifying OT law, but in showing the direction in which it points, on the basis of his own authority (to which, again, the OT points). (2) In vv.17–20 Jesus presents himself as the eschatological goal of the OT, and thereby its sole authoritative interpreter, the one through whom alone the OT finds its valid continuity and significance. (3) This approach eliminates the need to pit Matthew against Paul. Paul well understood that the Law and the Prophets pointed beyond themselves (e.g., Ro 3:21; Gal 3–4; cf. Ro 8:4) to Jesus, which is where, on the face of it, Matthew also intends the focus to be.

18 "I tell you the truth [*amen*; GK 297]" signals that the statement to follow is of the utmost importance; v.18 further explains and confirms the truth of v.17. The "jot" (KJV) refers to "the smallest letter" (NIV) of the Hebrew alphabet. "The least stroke of a pen" may refer to the small stroke that distinguishes several pairs of Hebrew letters. In any event Jesus here upholds the authority of the OT Scriptures right down to its individual letters. His is the highest possible view of the OT.

But vv.17–18 do not wrestle abstractly with OT authority but with the *nature*, *extent*, and *duration* of its validity and continuity. The *nature* of these has been set forth in v.17. The reference to "jot and tittle" (KJV) establishes its *extent* to the entire OT Scriptures, not just the Pentateuch or moral law. That leaves the *duration* of the OT's authority. The two "until" clauses answer this. The first—"until heaven and earth disappear"—simply means "until the end of the age." The second clause—"until everything is accomplished"—is more difficult, but "everything" is best understood as referring to everything in the OT, considered under its prophetic function. In other words, the entire divine purpose prophesied in Scripture must take place; not a single element will fail of its fulfillment (cf. 11:13). The OT reveals God's redemptive purposes and points to their fulfillment, their "accomplishment," in Jesus and the eschatological kingdom he is now introducing and will one day consummate.

19 The contrast between the least and the greatest in the kingdom probably supports gradation with kingdom ranks (as in 11:11; cf. 20:20–28; Lk 12:47–48). The one who breaks "one of the least of these commandments" is not excluded from the kingdom, but is very small or very unimportant in the kingdom. Distinctions are made not only according to the measure by which one keeps "the least of these commandments" but also according to the faithfulness with which one teaches them.

But what are "these commandments"? The expression most likely refers to the commandments of the OT Scriptures. The entire Law and the Prophets are not scrapped by Jesus' coming but fulfilled. Therefore the commandments of these Scriptures must be practiced. But the nature of the practicing has already been affected by vv.17–18. The law pointed forward to Jesus and his teaching; so it is properly obeyed by conforming to *his* word. As it points to him, so he, in fulfilling it, establishes the true direction to which it points and the way it is to be obeyed. Thus ranking in the kingdom turns on the degree of conformity to Jesus' teaching as that teaching fulfills OT revelation.

20 And that teaching, far from being more lenient, is nothing less than perfection (see comment on 5:48). The Pharisees and teachers of the law were among the most punctilious in the land. Jesus criticizes them because they domesticated the law and lost the radical demand for absolute holiness demanded by the Scriptures. What Jesus demands is the "righteousness" (GK *1466*) to which the law truly points, exemplified in the antitheses that follow (vv.21–48). The verb "surpasses" suggests that the new righteousness outstrips the old both qualitatively and quantitatively.

b. Application: the antitheses (5:21–48)

Verses 21–48 are often called the six antitheses because all six sections begin with some variation of "you have heard it said . . . but I say." By this phrase, Jesus is not criticizing the OT but the understanding of the OT many of his hearers adopted (cf. esp. vv.22, 43, where part of what was "heard" certainly does not come from the OT).

The contrast between what the people had heard and what Jesus taught is not based on distinctions like outer legalism versus inner commitment or false interpretation versus true. Rather, in every case Jesus contrasts the people's misunderstanding of the law with the true direction in which the law points, according to his own authority as the law's "fulfiller" (in the sense established in v.17). Thus if certain antitheses revoke at least the letter of the law, they do so not because they are thereby affirming the law's true spirit, but because Jesus insists that his teaching on these matters is the direction in which the law actually points.

21–22 Jesus' contemporaries had heard that the law given their ancestors forbade murder and that the murderer must be brought to "judgment." But Jesus insists—the "I" is emphatic in each of the six antitheses—that the law really points to his own teaching: the root of murder is anger, and anger is murderous in principle. One has not conformed to the better righteousness of the kingdom simply by refraining from homicide. The angry person will be subject to God's "judgment" (GK *3213*; for no human court tries cases of inner anger). To stoop to insult exposes one not merely to (God's) council but to the "fire of hell" (on this expression, see comment on Mk 9:43–48).

"Brother" (GK *81*) cannot in this case be limited to male siblings but to one's fellow believers. The Christian habit of calling one another "brother" and "sister" goes back to Jesus' instruction as part and parcel of his training them to address God as Father (6:9). Among Christians anger must be eliminated.

23–24 Jesus gives two illustrations exposing the seriousness of anger, the first in a setting of temple worship (vv.23–24) and the second in a judicial setting (vv.25–26). The first concerns a "brother"; the second an "adversary." Remarkably neither illustration deals with "your" anger but with "your" offense that has prompted the brother's or the adversary's rancor. We are more likely to remember when we ourselves have something against others than when we have done something to offend others. If we are truly concerned about our anger and hate, we should be no less concerned when we engender them in others.

The "altar" is the one in the inner court. There amid solemn worship, recollection of a brother with something against one should in Christ's disciples prompt immediate efforts to be reconciled. Only then is formal worship acceptable.

25–26 Jesus again urges haste to settle matters with an offended adversary while still "with him on the way" to court. In the ancient world debtors were jailed till the debts were paid. Jesus insists on immediate action: malicious anger is so evil—and God's judgment so certain (v.22)—that we must do all in our power to end it (cf. Eph 4:26–27).

27–28 The OT command not to commit adultery (Ex 20:14; Dt 5:18) is often treated in Jewish sources not so much as a function of purity as of theft: it was to steal another's wife. Jesus insisted that the seventh commandment points in another direction—toward purity that refuses even to lust after any woman. Insofar as a man looks at the woman with a view to enticing her to lust, he is committing adultery *with* her; i.e., he makes her an adulteress.

29–30 The radical treatment of parts of the body that cause one to sin has led some (notoriously the church father Origen) to castrate themselves. But that is not radical enough, since lust is not thereby removed. The "eye" is the member of the body most commonly blamed for leading us astray, especially in sexual sins (cf. Nu 15:39; Pr 21:4; et al.); the "right eye" refers to one's better eye. But why the "right hand" in a context dealing with lust? More likely it is a euphemism for the male sexual organ.

Cutting off or gouging out the offending part is a way of saying that Jesus' disciples must deal radically with sin. Imagination is a God-given gift; but if it is fed dirt by the eye, it will be dirty. All sin, not least sexual sin, begins with the imagination. Therefore what feeds the imagination is of maximum importance in the pursuit of kingdom righteousness (compare Php 4:8). The alternative is sin and hell, sin's reward.

31–32 This two-verse unit carries further the argument of the preceding section. The OT not only points toward insisting that lust is the moral equivalent of adultery (vv.27–30) but that divorce is as well. This arises out of the fact that the divorced woman will in most circumstances remarry (esp. in first-century Palestine, where this would probably be her only means of support). That new marriage, whether from the perspective of the divorcee or the one marrying her, is adulterous.

The OT passage to which Jesus refers is Dt. 24:1–4, whose thrust is that if a man divorces his wife because of "something indecent" (not further defined) in her, he must give her a certificate of divorce; and if she then becomes another man's wife and is divorced again, the first man cannot remarry her. This double restriction in the OT—the certificate and the prohibition of remarriage—discouraged hasty divorces. Here Jesus does not go into the force of "something indecent." Instead he insists that the law was pointing to the sanctity of marriage.

The natural way to take the "except" clause is that divorce is wrong because it generates adultery *except* in the case of fornication. In that case, where sexual sin has already been committed, nothing is laid down, though it appears that divorce is then implicitly permitted, even if not mandated (cf. further discussion at 19:3–12).

33–36 Jesus now cites an antithesis on a new theme. What the people have heard is not given as direct OT quotation but as a summary statement accurately condensing the burden of Ex 20:7; Lev 19:12; Nu 30:2; and Dt 5:11; 6:3; 22:21–33. The Mosaic law forbade irreverent oaths, light use of the Lord's name, and broken vows. Once the Lord's name was invoked, the vow to which it was attached became a debt that had to be paid to the Lord (see comments on 23:16–22).

If oaths designed to encourage truthfulness become occasions for clever lies and casuistical deceit, Jesus will abolish oaths (v.34). For the direction in which the OT points is the fundamental importance of thorough and consistent truthfulness. If one does not swear at all, one does not swear falsely. Jesus insists that whatever anyone swears by is related to God in some way, and therefore every oath is implicitly in God's name—heaven, earth, Jerusalem, even the hairs of the head are all under God's sway and ownership (v.36; see also 23:18–22).

37 The Greek might better be translated "But let your word be, 'Yes, Yes; No, No.'" The doubling is probably part of Jesus' rhetoric. This saying is not, however, a ban on any and all oaths. God himself "swears" in Scripture (e.g., Ge 9:9–11; Lk 1:68, 73; Heb 6:17), the earliest Christians took oaths (cf. Ro 1:9; 2Co 1:23; et al.), and Jesus himself testified under oath (Mt 26:63–64). It must be frankly admitted that here Jesus formally contravenes OT law: what it permits or commands (Dt. 6:13), he forbids. But if his interpretation of the direction in which the law points is authoritative, then his teaching fulfills it.

38–39a The OT prescription of the *lex talionis* (Ex 21:24; Lev 24:19–20; Dt 19:21) was not given to foster vengeance; the law explicitly forbade that (Lev 19:18). Rather, it was given, as the OT context shows, to provide the nation's judicial system with a ready formula of punishment, not least because it would decisively terminate vendettas. The trouble is that a law designed to limit retaliation and punish fairly could be appealed to as justification for vindictiveness.

Jesus' disciple is not to "resist [GK 468] an evil person." In the context of *lex talionis*, the most natural way of understanding the resistance is "do not resist in a court of law." This interpretation is required in the next example (v.40). As in vv.33–37, therefore, Jesus' teaching formally contradicts the OT law. But in the context of vv.17–20, what Jesus is saying is reasonably clear: the OT, including the *lex talionis*, points forward to Jesus and his teaching. But like the OT laws permitting divorce, enacted because of the hardness of human hearts (19:3–12), the *lex talionis* was instituted to curb evil because of the hardness of the heart.

As this legal principle is overtaken by that toward which it pointed, so also is this hardness of heart. The OT prophets foretold a time when there would be a change of heart among God's people, living under a new covenant (Jer 31:31–34; Eze 36:26). Not only would the sins of the people be forgiven (Jer 31:34; Eze 36:25), but obedience to God would spring from the heart (Jer 31:33; Eze 36:27) as the new age dawned. Thus Jesus' instruction on these matters is grounded in eschatology. In Jesus and the kingdom, the eschatological age that the Law and Prophets had prophesied (11:13) has arrived; the prophecies that curbed evil while pointing forward to the eschaton are now superseded by the new age and the new hearts it brings.

39b–42 Four illustrations clarify Jesus' point and drive it home. In the first, a man strikes another on the cheek—not only a painful blow, but a gross insult (cf. 2Co 11:20). If a right-handed person strikes someone's right cheek, presumably it is a slap by the back of the hand, probably considered more insulting than a slap by the open palm. Instead of seeking recompense at law under the *lex talionis*, Jesus' disciples will gladly endure the insult again.

Although under Mosaic law the outer cloak was an inalienable possession (Ex 22:26; Dt 24:13), Jesus' disciples, if sued for their tunics (an inner garment like our suit but worn next to the skin), far from seeking satisfaction, will gladly part with what they may legally keep.

The third example refers to the Roman practice of commandeering civilians to carry the luggage of military personnel a prescribed distance, one Roman "mile." Impressment, like a lawsuit, evoked outrage; but the attitude of Jesus' disciples under such circumstances must not be spiteful or vengeful but helpful—willing to go a second mile.

The final illustration requires not only interest-free loans (Ex 22:25; Lev 25:37; Dt 23:19) but a generous spirit (cf. Dt 15:7–11; Pss 37:26; 112:5). These last two illustrations confirm our interpretation of vv.38–39, that the entire pericope deals with the heart's attitude, the better righteousness. For there is actually no legal recourse to the oppression in the third illustration, and in the fourth no harm that might lead to retaliation has been done.

While these four vignettes have powerful shock value, they were not meant to be new legal prescriptions. Verse 42 does not commit Jesus' disciples to giving endless amounts of money to everyone who seeks a "soft touch." Verse 40 is clearly hyperbolic: no first-century Jew would go home wearing only a loincloth. Nor does this pericope deal with the validity of a state police force. Yet the illustrations must not be diluted by endless equivocations; the only limit to the believer's response in these situations is what love and the Scriptures impose.

43 The command "Love your neighbor" is found in Lev 19:18; no OT Scripture adds "and hate your enemies," though this seems to be the result of popular reasoning. Such reasoning seems to have said that if God commands love for "neighbor," then hatred for "enemies" is implicitly conceded and perhaps even authorized.

44–47 Jesus allowed no casuistry. The real direction indicated by the law is love, rich and costly, and extended even to enemies. Many take the verb and the noun "love" (GK 26 & 27) as always signifying self-giving regardless of emotion, but such an interpretation is unwarranted. The content of Christian love is not based on a presupposed definition but on Jesus' teaching and example. To love one's enemies, though it must result in activities such as doing them good (Lk 6:32–33) and praying for them (Mt 5:44), cannot justly be restricted to activities devoid of any concern, sentiment, or emotion. There is no reason to think the verb here in Matthew does not include emotion as well as action.

The specific "enemy" referred to here is one's persecutors. Jesus himself repeatedly warns his disciples of impending persecution (e.g., vv.10–12; 10:16–23; 24:9–13). If Matthew's first readers were being persecuted for their faith, that was doubtless one application they made.

Jesus' disciples have as their example God himself, who loves so indiscriminately that he sends sun and rain on both the righteous and the unrighteous. Yet we must not thereby conclude that God's love toward people is in all respects without distinction, and that therefore all will be saved (see 25:31-46). Theologians call this love of God his "common grace" (i.e., the gracious favor God bestows "commonly," without distinction, on everyone).

God's example provides the incentive for Jesus' disciples to be "sons of [their] Father" (v.45). Ultimately this clause points to the necessity of pursuing a certain kind of sonship patterned after the Father's own character. Jesus' disciples must live and love in a way superior to the patterns around them. Jesus goes on to point out that even the despised tax collectors (see comment on Mk 2:14) love those who love them; Christian love must go beyond what naturally takes place.

48 It is best to understand v.48 as the conclusion to all the antitheses. The OT background to this verse is Lev 19:2, with "holy" displaced by "perfect" (GK 5455). Here for the first time perfection is predicated of God.

In the light of the preceding verses (vv.17-47), Jesus is saying that the true direction in which the law has always pointed is not toward mere judicial restraints, concessions arising out of the hardness of human hearts, still less casuistical perversions, nor even the "law of love." No, it pointed rather to all the perfection of God, exemplified by the authoritative interpretation of the law bound up in the preceding antitheses. This perfection Jesus' disciples must emulate if they are truly followers of him who fulfills the Law and the Prophets (v.17).

4. Religious hypocrisy: its description and overthrow (6:1–18).

a. The principle (6:1)

1 Jesus, having told his disciples of the superior righteousness expected of them, now warns them of the danger of hypocrisy. "Your righteousness" recurs here (cf. comment on 5:20), though the focus has changed from "righteousness" in a purely positive sense to "righteousness" in a formal, external sense.

Jesus is primarily concerned with the motives behind righteous living. To attempt to live according to the righteousness explained in vv.21–48 out of an eagerness for human applause is to prostitute that righteousness. For this there will be no reward (see comment on 5:12) from the heavenly Father. There is no contradiction with 5:14–16, where disciples are told to let their light shine before men so that they may see their good deeds; there the motive is for others to praise the heavenly Father. To trade the goal of pleasing the Father for the trivial and idolatrous goal of pleasing people will never do.

This verse introduces the three chief acts of Jewish piety (cf. vv.2–18)—almsgiving, prayer, and fasting. In each act the logical structure is the same: (1) a warning not to do the act to be praised by human beings, (2) a guarantee that those who ignore this warning will get what they want but no more, (3) instruction on how to perform the act of piety secretly, and (4) the assurance that the Father who sees in secret will reward openly.

b. Three examples (6:2–18)

2 While some in Jesus' day believed almsgiving earned merit, ostentation rather than merit theology is the point here. Jesus assumes his disciples will give alms: "*When* you give to the needy," he says, not "*If* you give to the needy."

The reference to trumpet announcements is difficult. It seems most likely that Jesus is referring to a practice of proclaiming public fasts by the sounding of trumpets. At such times prayers for rain were recited in the streets (cf. v.5), and it was widely thought that almsgiving insured the efficacy of the fasts and prayers. But these occasions afforded golden opportunities for ostentation, and that is precisely what "hypocrites" (GK 5695) were guilty of.

The form of hypocrisy mentioned here seems to be that of those who deceive themselves into thinking they are acting for the best interests of God and others and deceive onlookers as well. The needy are unlikely to complain when they receive large gifts, and their gratitude may flatter and thus bolster a giver's self-delusion.

The Pharisees' great weakness was that they loved praise from others more than God's praise (cf. Jn 5:44; 12:43). Those who give out of this attitude receive their reward in full. They win human plaudits, and that is all they get (cf. Ps 17:14).

3–4 The way to avoid hypocrisy is not to cease giving but to do so with such secrecy that we scarcely know what we have given.

Jesus' disciples must themselves be so given to God (cf. 2Co 8:5) that their giving is prompted by obeying God and having compassion on other people. Then their Father, who sees what is done in secret (Heb 4:13), will reward them (a reward received both in time and in eternity).

5 In his second example, Jesus assumes that his disciples will pray, but he forbids the prayers of "hypocrites" (see comment on v.2). Prayer had a prominent place in Jewish life and led to countless rabbinic decisions. To Jesus, the critical element was not the location or position of the one praying, but the motives ("to be seen by man"). And again there is the same reward (cf. v.2).

6 If Jesus were forbidding all public prayer, then clearly the early church did not understand him (e.g., 18:19–20; Ac 1:24; 3:1; 4:24–30). The public versus private antithesis is a good test of one's motives; those who pray more in public than in private reveal that they are less interested in God's approval than in human praise. Not piety but a reputation for piety is their concern. Far better to deal radically with this hypocrisy (cf. 5:29–30) and pray in a private "room." The Father, who sees in secret, will reward such disciples.

7–8 Matthew 6:7–15 digresses from the three chief acts of Jewish piety. Yet the content of these verses is certainly relevant to the issue of prayer. Prayer is central to a believer's life. So Jesus gives further warnings and a positive example.

Jesus labels all those who pray repetitiously, Jew or Gentile, as pagan! He is not condemning prayer any more than he is condemning almsgiving (v.2) or fasting (v.16). Nor is he forbidding all long prayers or all repetition. He himself prayed at length (Lk 6:12), repeated himself in prayer (Mt 26:44), and told a parable to show his disciples that "they should always pray and not give up" (Lk 18:1). His point is that his disciples should avoid meaningless, repetitive prayers offered under the misconception that mere length will make prayers efficacious. Essentially such babble is thoroughly pagan, for pagan gods allegedly thrive on incantation and repetition. But the personal Father to whom believers pray does not require information about our needs (v.8).

9 What follows now is commonly called "the Lord's Prayer," not so much his own prayer (Jn 17 is just that) as the model he gave his disciples ("This is how [not what] you should pray"). The first three petitions are cast in terms of God's glory, the rest in terms of our good.

The fatherhood of God is not a central theme in the OT. Where "father" does occur with respect to God, it is commonly by way of analogy, not direct address (Dt 32:6; Ps 103:13; Isa 63:16; Mal 2:10). Not till Jesus is it characteristic to address God as "Father" (GK *4252*). Jesus himself addressed God as his own Father (Mk 14:36), and he teaches his disciples to do the same. Such an address to God could only appear familiar and presumptuous to opponents who were used to emphasizing God's transcendence.

Jesus' use of *Abba* ("Father" or "my Father"; Mk 14:36) was adopted by early Christians (Ro 8:15; Gal 4:6); and there is no evidence of anyone before Jesus using this term to address God. Throughout the prayer the reference is plural: "*Our* Father." In other words, Jesus teaches a prayer to be prayed in fellowship with other disciples (cf. 18:19), not in isolation (cf. Jn 20:17). We must pay attention to Jesus' use of pronouns with "Father." When forgiveness of sins is discussed, he speaks of "your Father" (6:14–15) and excludes himself. When he speaks of his unique sonship and authority, he speaks of "my Father" (e.g., 11:27) and excludes others. The "our Father" at the beginning of this model prayer is plural but does not include Jesus, since it is part of his instruction regarding how his disciples should pray.

This opening designation establishes the kind of God to whom prayer is offered. He is personal. That he is "our Father" establishes the relationship that exists between Jesus' disciples and God; in this sense he is not the Father of all people indiscriminately (see comment on 5:45). That he is "our Father *in heaven*" reminds us of his transcendence and sovereignty.

God's "name" is a reflection of who he is. Therefore to pray that God's name be "hallowed" (GK *39*) is not to pray that God may become holy but that he may be treated as holy (cf. Ex 20:8; Lev 19:2; 1Pe 1:15) and that his name should not be despised (Mal 1:6) by the thoughts and conduct of those who have been created in his image.

10 As God is eternally holy, so he eternally reigns in absolute sovereignty. God's "kingdom" or "reign" (see comment on 3:2; 4:17) can refer to that aspect of God's sovereignty under which there is life. That kingdom is breaking in under Christ's ministry, but it is not consummated till the end of the age (28:20). To pray "your kingdom come" is therefore both to ask that God's saving, royal rule be extended now as people bow in submission to him and to cry for the consummation of the kingdom.

To pray that God's "will" (GK *2525*), which is "good, pleasing and perfect" (Ro 12:2), be done on earth as in heaven is to use language broad enough to embrace three requests. (1) We pray that God's will may be done now on earth as it is now being accomplished in heaven. "Will" includes both God's righteous demands and his determination to bring about certain events in salvation history. So for that will to be "done" includes both moral obedience and the bringing to pass of certain events, such as the Cross. This prayer corresponds to asking for the present extension of the messianic kingdom. (2) We pray that God's will may ultimately be as *fully accomplished* on earth as it is now being accomplished in heaven. (3) We pray that God's will may ultimately be done on the earth *in the same way* as it is now being accomplished in heaven.

11 The last petitions explicitly request things for ourselves. The first is "bread" (GK *788*), a term used to cover all food (cf. Pr 30:8; Mk 3:20; Ac 6:1; 2Th 3:12; Jas 2:15); it may further suggest all of our physical human needs.

We must pray for our needs, not our greeds. It is for one day at a time, reflecting the precarious lifestyle of many first-century workers who were paid one day at a time and for whom a few days' illness could spell tragedy. "Daily" is a difficult word to translate, most likely meaning "for the coming day." Jesus thus instructs his disciples to pray: "Give us today our bread for the coming day." This may sound redundant to Western readers, but it is an urgent petition to those who lived from hand to mouth.

The idea of God "giving" the food in no way diminishes responsibility to work (see vv.25–34) but presupposes not only that Jesus' disciples live one day at a time (cf. v.34) but that all good things, even our ability to work and earn our food, come from God's hand (cf. Dt 8:18; 1Co 4:7; Jas 1:17). It is a lesson easily forgotten when wealth multiplies and absolute self-sufficiency is portrayed as a virtue.

12 In addition to physical provisions, we also need forgiveness of sin and deliverance from temptation. The word "debt" (GK *4052*) means "sin" or "transgression," here conceived as something owed God (cf. Lk 11:4).

Some have taken the second clause to mean that our forgiveness is the real cause of God's forgiveness, i.e., that God's forgiveness must be earned by our own. But we must distinguish between the concept of earning forgiveness (not taught here) and adopting an attitude that makes forgiveness possible. This thought is reinforced in vv.14–15 and 18:21–35 (see also comments on 5:5, 7).

13 The word used for "temptation" (GK *4280*) rarely if ever before the writing of the NT means "temptation" in the sense of "enticement to sin" (see comments on 4:1; Lk 4:1–2); rather, it means testing. But testing can have various purposes and diverse results (e.g., greater purity, growth in faith, but also sin); the word can thus slide over into the entirely negative sense of "temptation" (see especially Jas 1:13–14). In the light of Jas 1:13–14, the word used here cannot easily mean "temptation," for that would be to pray that God would not do what in fact he cannot do.

But if the word means "testing," we face another problem. The NT everywhere insists that believers will face testing or trials of many kinds and that they should face them with joy (Jas 1:2). Thus, to pray for grace and endurance in trial is understandable; but to pray not to be brought to testings is strange. Yet perhaps this is not so strange. The NT tells us that this age will be characterized by wars and rumors of wars (24:6) but does not find it incongruous to urge us to pray for those in authority so "that we may live peaceful and quiet lives" (1Ti 2:2). While Jesus told his disciples to rejoice when persecuted (5:10–12), he nevertheless exhorted them to flee from it (10:23) and even to pray that their flight should not be too severe (24:20).

"Deliver" (GK *4861*) can mean either "spare us from" or "deliver us out of." Both are spiritually relevant, and which way the verb is taken largely depends on how the preceding clause is understood. The words translated "the evil one" can either mean "evil" or refer specifically to the Devil. A reference to Satan is far more likely here for two reasons: (1) "deliver from" is an expression used predominantly of persons, and (2) Matthew's first mention of temptation (4:1–11) is unambiguously connected with the Devil. Thus the Lord's model prayer ends with a petition that, while implicitly recognizing our own helplessness before the Devil whom Jesus alone could vanquish (4:1–11), indicates trust in the heavenly Father for deliverance from the Devil's strength and wiles.

The doxology is theologically profound and contextually suitable, but it is best to leave out consideration of it as it is not part of Matthew's original work.

14–15 These verses reinforce the thought of the fifth petition (see comment on v.12). The repetition serves to stress the deep importance for the community of disciples to be a forgiving community if its prayers are to be effective (cf. Ps 66:18).

16 For fasting in the Bible, see comment on Mk 2:18 and ZPEB 2:501–4. In Jesus' day the Pharisees fasted twice a week (Lk 18:12). Some devout people, like Anna, fasted often (Lk 2:37). But such voluntary fasts provided marvelous opportunities for outward religious showmanship to gain a reputation for piety. The point is not that there was no genuine contrition but that these hypocrites were purposely drawing attention to themselves. They wanted the plaudits of other people and got them. And that's all they got.

17–18 Yet Jesus, far from banning fasting, assumes his disciples will fast as well as give alms and pray (vv.3, 6). What he condemns is ostentation in fasting. Moreover he forbids any sign at all that a fast has been undertaken, because the human heart is so mixed in its motives that the desire to seek God will be diluted by the desire for human praise, thus vitiating the fast.

Washing and anointing with oil (v.17) were merely normal steps in hygiene. The point of v.18 is not to draw attention to oneself, whether by somber mien or extravagant joy. Jesus desires reticence, not deception. And the Father, who sees in secret, will provide the reward (see comment on v.4).

5. Kingdom perspectives (6:19–34)

Having excoriated religious piety that is little more than ostentation, Jesus warns against the opposite sins of greed, materialism, and worry that stem from misplaced and worldly priorities. Instead, he demands unswerving loyalty to kingdom values (vv.19–24) and uncompromised trust (vv.25–34).

a. Metaphors for unswerving loyalty to kingdom values (6:19–24)

19 The prohibition of this verse could well be rendered "stop storing up treasures"; the time for a decisive break has come. The love of wealth is a great evil (1Ti 6:10), calling forth frequent warnings. For heirs of the kingdom to hoard riches in the last days (Jas 5:2–3) is particularly shortsighted. Yet as with many of Jesus' prohibitions in this sermon, it would be foolhardy so to absolutize this one that wealth itself becomes an evil. Elsewhere the Scriptures require a man to provide for his relatives (1Ti 5:8), commend work and provision for the future (Pr 6:6–8), and encourage us to enjoy the good things the Creator has given us (1Ti 4:3–4; 6:17). Jesus is concerned about selfishness; his disciples must not lay up treasures *for themselves*.

The "treasures on earth" might be clothing that could be attacked by moths. Fashions changed little, and garments could be passed on. They could also deteriorate. "Rust" refers not only to the corrosion of metals but to the destruction effected by rats, mildew, and the like. Less corruptible treasures could be stolen.

20–21 By contrast, treasures in heaven are forever exempt from decay and theft. They refer to whatever is of good and eternal significance that comes out of what is done on earth. Doing righteous deeds, suffering for Christ's sake, forgiving one another—all these have the promise of "reward" (see comments on 5:12; cf. 5:30, 46; 6:6, 15). Other deeds of kindness also store up treasures in heaven (10:42; 25:40), including willingness to share (1Ti 6:13–19).

Jesus' point is that the things most highly treasured occupy the "heart" (GK *2840*), the center of a personality that embraces mind, emotions, and will; thus the most cherished treasure subtly but infallibly controls one's whole direction and values.

22–23 Through the eye the body finds its way. The eye lets in light, and so the whole body is illuminated. But bad eyes let in no light, and the body is in darkness (v.23). The "light within you" is ironic; those with bad eyes, who walk in darkness, think they have light, but this light is in reality darkness. The darkness is all the more terrible for failure to recognize it for what it is (cf. Jn 9:41).

This fairly straightforward description has metaphorical implications. The "eye" can be equivalent to the "heart." The heart set on God so as to hold to his commands (Ps 119:10) is equivalent to the eye fastened on God's law (Ps 119:18, 148; cf. 119:36–37). Jesus similarly moves from "heart" (v.21) to "eye."

At the physical level the "whole body" is just that, a body, of which the eye is the part that provides "light." At the metaphorical level it represents the entire person who is plunged into moral darkness.

24 More basic than the choice between two treasures and two visions is the choice between two masters: God or Money. Both are portrayed, not as employers, but as slave-owners. Slavery involves ownership by one person and requires full-time service; a person cannot serve two slave-owners. Either God is served with a single-eyed devotion, or he is not served at all.

b. Uncompromised trust (6:25–34)

25 "Therefore," in the light of the alternatives set out (vv.19–24), Jesus instructs his disciples not to worry about the physical necessities, let alone the luxuries implied in the preceding verses. Far too often our entire existence focuses on such things. The argument goes from the greater to the lesser: if God has given us life and a body, both admittedly more important than food and clothing, will he not also give us the latter?

26 To worry about food and drink is to have learned nothing from the natural creation, which testifies to God's providence. The point is not that the disciples need not work—birds do not simply wait for God to drop food into their beaks—but that they need not fret. They may further strengthen their faith by remembering that God is in a special sense their Father and that they are worth far more than birds ("you" is emphatic). Here the argument is from the lesser to the greater.

27 Several options are available for translating this verse (see NIV note; see comment on Lk 12:25–26). Worry is more likely to shorten life than to prolong it, and ultimately such matters are in God's hands (cf. Lk 12:13–21). To trust him should be enough.

28–30 "Lilies of the field" (v.28) may be any of the wild flowers so abundant in Galilee. Jesus' point is a little different from the first illustration about birds; flowers neither toil nor spin. The point is not that Jesus' disciples may opt for laziness but that God's providence and care are so rich that he clothes the grass with wild flowers that are neither productive nor enduring. Even Solomon, the richest and most extravagant of Israel's monarchs, was not arrayed like one of these fields. Jesus closes with the thought that the root of anxiety is unbelief.

The hill where Jesus spoke the Sermon on the Mount is still covered with little flowers (possibily the lilies of 6:28) in the spring.

31–32 In the light of God's bountiful care, the questions posed in v.31 are unanswerable. Worse, they are essentially pagan. Jesus' disciples must live lives qualitatively different from those of people who have no trust in God's fatherly care and no fundamental goals beyond material things.

33 In view of vv.31–32, this verse makes it clear that Jesus' disciples are not simply to *refrain* from pursuing temporal things as their primary goal in order to differentiate themselves from pagans. Instead, they are to *replace* such pursuits with goals of far greater significance. To "seek first [God's] kingdom" (see comments on 3:2; 4:17) is to desire above all to enter into, submit to, and participate in spreading the news of the saving reign of God. It is to pursue the things already prayed for in the first three petitions of the Lord's Prayer (6:9–10).

To seek God's "righteousness" is not, in this context, to seek justification; rather, it is to pursue righteousness of life in full submission to the will of God, as prescribed by Jesus throughout this discourse (see comment on 6:1). For any other concern to dominate one's mind is to stoop to pagan fretting. Within such a framework of commitment, Jesus' disciples are assured that all the necessary things will be given them by their heavenly Father.

34 Worry over tomorrow's misfortunes is nonsensical, because today has enough to occupy our attention and because tomorrow's feared misfortunes may never happen. Furthermore, today's grace is sufficient only for today and should not be wasted on tomorrow. If tomorrow does bring new trouble, there will be new grace to meet it.

6. Balance and perfection (7:1–12)

a. The danger of being judgmental (7:1–5)

1 "Do not judge" (GK 3212) does not forbid all judging of any kind, for the moral distinctions drawn in the Sermon on the Mount require that decisive judgments be made. Jesus himself goes on to speak of some people as dogs and pigs (v.6) and to warn against false prophets (vv.15–20). Jesus' demand here is for his disciples not to be judgmental and censorious (see Ro 14:10–13). Those who judge like this will in turn be judged, not by other people (which would be of little consequence), but by God. Anyone who engages in such judgment usurps the place of God.

2 Using what was probably a proverbial saying, Jesus asserts that the judgmental person, by not being forgiving and loving, testifies to his own arrogance and impenitence, by which such individuals shut themselves out from God's forgiveness.

3–5 The "speck of sawdust" could be any bit of foreign matter. The "plank" is obviously colorful hyperbole. Jesus does not say it is wrong to help a fellow Christian remove the speck of dust in his eye, but it is wrong for a person with a "plank" in his eye to offer help. That is sheer hypocrisy (see comment on 6:2). But when a brother in a meek and self-judging spirit (cf. 1Co 11:31; Gal 6:1) removes the log in his own eye, he has the responsibility of helping his brother remove his speck (cf. 18:15–20).

b. The danger of being undiscerning (7:6)

6 The disciples, who have already been exhorted to love their enemies (5:43–47) and not to judge (v.1), might fail to consider the subtleties of the argument and become undiscerning simpletons. This verse guards against such a possibility.

"Pigs" and "dogs" serve together as a picture of what is vicious, unclean, and abominable (cf. 2Pe 2:22). The pigs trample the pearls under foot (perhaps out of animal disappointment that they are not morsels of food), and the dogs can be so disgusted that they turn on the giver. So the aphorism forbids proclaiming the "sacred" Gospel of the kingdom to certain persons designated as dogs and pigs. Rather than trampling the Gospel under foot, everything must be "sold" in pursuit of it (13:45–46).

This verse is not a directive against evangelizing the Gentiles, especially in a book full of various supports for this. "Dogs" and "pigs" refer to any persons who have given clear evidences of rejecting the Gospel with vicious scorn and hardened contempt.

c. Source and means of power (7:7–11)

7–8 Thus far the Sermon on the Mount lays down the righteousness, sincerity, humility, purity, and love expected of Jesus' followers; now it assures them such gifts are theirs if sought through prayer. In three imperatives ("ask," "seek," "knock") symmetrically repeated (v.8) and in the present tense to stress the persistence and sincerity required, Jesus assures his followers that, far from demanding the impossible, he is providing the means for the otherwise impossible. Far too often Christians do not have the marks of richly textured discipleship because they do not ask, or they ask with selfish motives (Jas 4:2-3). Like a human father, the heavenly Father seeks to teach his children courtesy, persistence, and diligence.

9–11 Using an argument similar in style to that in 6:25 (see comment), Jesus stresses that no parent would deceive a child asking for bread or fish by giving him a similar looking but inedible stone or a poisonous snake. His point is not merely the parents' willingness to give but their willingness to give good gifts—even though they themselves are evil. Jesus presupposes the sinfulness of human nature but implicitly acknowledges that that does not mean all human beings are as bad as they could be. How much more, then, will the heavenly Father, who is pure goodness without alloy, give good gifts to those who ask!

The blessings promised here as a result of prayer are not the blessings of common grace (see comment on 5:45) but of the kingdom. And though we must ask for them, it is not because God must be informed (6:8) but because this is the Father's way of training his family.

d. Balance and perfection (7:12)

12 The word "therefore" probably refers to the entire body of the sermon (5:17–7:12), for here there is a second reference to "the Law and the Prophets" (see comment on 5:17); Jesus stresses that he has taught about the true direction in which the OT law points, i.e., the Golden Rule. This rule sums up the Law and the Prophets (cf. Ro 13:9). In the context of fulfilling the Scriptures, it provides a handy summary of the righteousness to be displayed in the kingdom (cf. 5:20).

The verb translated "sums up" (lit., "is") might properly be translated "fulfills," as in Ac 2:16. In the deepest sense, therefore, the rule *is* the Law and the Prophets in the same way as the kingdom is the fulfillment of all that the Law and the Prophets foretold.

7. Conclusion: call to decision and commitment (7:13–27)

a. Two ways (7:13–14)

The Sermon on the Mount ends with four warnings, each offering paired contrasts: two ways (vv.13–14), two trees (vv.15–20), two claims (vv.21–23), and two builders (vv.24–27). They focus on eschatological judgment and so make it plain that the theme is still the kingdom of heaven. But if some will not enter it (vv.13–14, 21–23), the sole basis for such a tragedy is their response to Jesus' words.

13–14 The general picture here is clear enough: there are two gates, two roads, two crowds, two destinations. The "narrow" gate is clearly restrictive and does not permit entrance to what Jesus prohibits. The "wide" gate seems far more inviting. The "broad" road is spacious and accommodates the crowd and their baggage; the other road is "narrow" and restricting, because it is the way of persecution and opposition—a major theme in Matthew (see comment on 5:10–12; cf. Ac 14:22).

But the two roads are not ends in themselves. The narrow road leads to life, i.e., to the consummated kingdom (cf. vv.21–23); but the broad road leads to eternal death (cf. 25:34, 46; Jn 17:12; Ro 9:22; et al.). Democratic decisions do not determine truth and righteousness in the kingdom; the way that leads to life is exclusively by revelation.

It seems best to regard the gate as something entered in this life as one begins the path of discipleship. Entrance through the gate into the narrow way of persecution begins *now* but issues in the consummated kingdom at the other end of that way. In other words, even the beginning of this path to life is restrictive.

b. Two trees (7:15–20)

15 Jesus foresaw the continued existence of his newly formed community for a sustained period. He was doubtless steeped in the OT reports of earlier false prophets (Jer 6:13–15; 8:8–12; Eze 13; 22:27; Zep 3:4) and knew such people would infiltrate this new community. Warnings against false prophets are necessarily based on the conviction that not all prophets are true, that truth can be violated, and that the Gospel's enemies usually conceal their hostility and try to pass themselves off as fellow believers. At first glance they use orthodox language, show biblical piety, and are indistinguishable from true prophets (cf. 10:41). Thus it is vital to know how to distinguish sheep from wolves in sheep's clothing. Behind this saying is Jesus' view of himself as the true prophet (cf. 21:11, 46).

Neither the damage these false prophets do nor their brand of false teaching is stated; but the flow of the Sermon on the Mount as well as its OT background suggest that they do not acknowledge or teach the narrow way to life subject to persecution (vv.13–14; cf. Jer 8:11; Eze 13).

16–20 From a distance the little black berries on the buckthorn could be mistaken for grapes, and the flowers on certain thistles might deceive one into thinking figs were growing (v.16). But no one would be long deceived. So with people! One's "fruit" (GK 2843)—not just what one does, but all one says and does—will ultimately reveal what one is (cf. Jas 3:12). Living according to the kingdom can be feigned for a time, but what one is will eventually reveal itself in what one does. However guarded one's words, they will finally betray that person (cf. 12:33–37; Lk 6:45).

c. Two claims (7:21–23)

21–23 If vv.15–20 deal with false prophets, vv.21–23 deal with false followers. Their cry of "Lord, Lord" (v.21) reflects fervency. In Jesus' day it is doubtful whether "Lord" when used to address him meant more than "teacher" or "sir." But in the postresurrection period, it becomes an appellation of worship and a confession of Jesus' deity. Already here Jesus is implicitly claiming to be more than a mere teacher, since his name becomes the focus of kingdom activity; and he alone decrees who does or does not enter the kingdom (vv.22–23). Thus the warning and rebuke would take on added force when early Christians read the passage from their postresurrection perspective.

The determinative factor regarding who enters the kingdom is obedience to the Father's will (v.19; cf. 12:50). This is the first use of "*my* Father" in Matthew (cf. Lk 2:49; Jn 2:16); as such, it supports the truth that Jesus alone claims to be the authoritative Revealer of his Father's will.

"That day" is the Day of Judgment (cf. 25:31–46; 2Th 1:7–10; 2Ti 1:12; 4:8). The false claimants have prophesied in Jesus' name and by that name exorcised demons and performed miracles. There is no reason to judge their claims false; rather, their claims are insufficient.

Verse 23 presupposes an implicit Christology of the highest order. Jesus himself not only decides who enters the kingdom on the last day but also who will be banished from his presence. That he never knew these false claimants shows how close to spiritual reality one may come while knowing nothing of its fundamental reality (e.g., Judas Iscariot; cf. Heb 3:14; 1Jn 2:19).

d. Two builders (7:24–27)

24–27 Verses 21–23 contrast "saying" and "doing"; these verses contrast "hearing" and "doing" (cf. Jas 1:22–25). Moreover the will of the Father (v.21) now becomes definitive in what Jesus calls "these words of *mine*" (v.24): *his* teaching is definitive.

In the parable cited here, each house looks secure in good weather. But Palestine is known for torrential rains that can turn dry wadis into raging torrents. Only storms reveal the quality of the work of the two builders (cf. 13:21). The greatest storm is eschatological (cf. Isa 28:16–17; Eze 13:10–13), but Jesus' words about the two houses need not be thus restricted. The point is that the wise person builds to withstand anything.

What wisdom consists of is clear. A wise person represents those who put Jesus' words into practice; they too are building to withstand anything. Those who pretend to have faith, who have a merely intellectual commitment, or who enjoy Jesus in small doses are foolish builders. When the storms of life come, their structures fool no one, above all not God (cf. Eze 13:10–16).

The sermon ends with what has been implicit throughout it—the demand for radical submission to the exclusive lordship of Jesus, who fulfills the Law and the Prophets and warns the disobedient that the alternative to total obedience, true righteousness, and life in the kingdom is rebellion, a life that is self-centered, and eternal damnation.

8. Transitional conclusion: Jesus' authority (7:28–29)

28–29 This is the first of the five formulaic conclusions that terminate the discourses in this gospel (see also 11:1; 13:53; 19:1; 26:1). Matthew's formula is therefore a self-conscious stylistic device that establishes a structural turning point. In each case the conclusion prepares for the next section. Here mention of Jesus' authority leads into his authority in other spheres such as powerful and liberating miracles (8:1–17).

The crowds—probably a larger group than his disciples—are again pressing in on him (see comment on 5:1–2); they are amazed at both the content and the manner of his teaching, but such astonishment says nothing about their own commitment. Its cause is Jesus' "authority." In his authority Jesus differs from the "teachers of the law" (see comment on Mk 1:22).

The central point is this: Jesus' entire approach in the Sermon on the Mount is not only ethical but messianic. He is not an ordinary prophet who says, "Thus says the Lord!" Rather, he speaks in the first person and claims that his teaching fulfills the OT; that he determines who enters the messianic kingdom; that as the Divine Judge he pronounces banishment; that the true heirs of the kingdom will be persecuted for their allegiance to him; and that he alone fully knows the will of his Father.

III. The Kingdom Extended Under Jesus' Authority (8:1–11:1)

Several themes predominate in this section: faith, discipleship, the Gentile mission, and a diverse Christological pattern. At the same time these chapters prove that Jesus, whose mission in part was to preach, teach, and heal (4:23; 9:35), fulfilled the whole of it. Matthew has shown Jesus preaching the Gospel of the kingdom (4:17, 23) and teaching (chs. 5–7). Now he records some examples of his healing ministry.

A. Narrative (8:1–10:4)

1. Healing miracles (8:1–17)

a. A leper (8:1–4)

1 Jesus came down out of the hills (see on 5:1), where the Sermon on the Mount had been delivered; and the great crowds (4:23–25; 7:28–29) still pursued him.

2–3 Matthew now starts to elaborate on some specific miracles of Jesus, beginning with a leper (on leprosy, see comment on Mk 1:40). This man "knelt" (GK 4686) before Jesus, though this verb can also mean "worshiped." Clearly the former is meant in this historical setting. Yet as with the title "Lord" (see comment on 7:22–23), Christian readers of Matthew could not help concluding that this leper spoke and acted better than he knew. "If you are willing" reflects the leper's great faith, prompted by Jesus' healing activity throughout the district (4:24): he had no question about Jesus' healing power but feared only that he would be passed by. In affirming his willingness to heal, Jesus proved that his will is decisive. He already had the authority and power and only needed to decide and act. Jesus reached to touch the leper, probably because the leper did not dare come close to him.

By touching an unclean leper, Jesus would become ceremonially defiled himself (cf. Lev 13–14). But at Jesus' touch nothing remains defiled. Far from becoming unclean, Jesus makes the unclean clean. Both Jesus' word and touch (8:15; 9:20–21, 29; 14:36) are effective, possibly implying that authority is vested in his message as well as in his person.

4 Jesus' command for the leper to keep silent shows that Jesus is not presenting himself as a mere wonder-worker who can be pressured into messiahship by crowds whose messianic views are materialistic and political. His authority derives from God alone; he came to die, not to trounce the Romans. The people who disobeyed Jesus' injunctions to silence only made his mission more difficult.

Jesus commanded the cured man to follow the Mosaic prescriptions for lepers who claimed healing (cf. Lev 14). Why? Partly because Matthew wants to show that Jesus did submit himself to God's law. But the result is startling: the law achieves new relevance by pointing to Jesus. In conforming to the law, the cured leper becomes the occasion for the law to confirm Jesus' authority as the healer who needs but to will the deed for it to be done. Thus the supreme function of the "gift" Moses commanded is not as a guilt offering (Lev 14:10–18) but as a witness to others concerning Jesus.

b. The centurion's servant (8:5–13)

5 This is Matthew's second mention of Capernaum (cf. 4:13). In Jesus' day it was an important garrison town. No Roman legions were posted in Palestine, but there were auxiliaries under Herod Antipas, who had the right to levy troops. These were non-Jews, probably recruited from outside Galilee, perhaps from Lebanon and Syria. Centurions were the military backbone throughout the empire, maintaining discipline and executing orders. Matthew stresses this centurion's faith and race (vv.10–11).

6–7 On "Lord," see comment on 7:21–23. The servant of this centurion had a form of paralysis, though we do not know its precise nature. Jesus' response to the centurion's request for healing is likely a question: "Shall I [emphatic; i.e., I, a Jew] come and heal him?" (cf. 15:21–28). This response was based on Jesus' desire to find out exactly what the centurion was after and what degree of faith stood behind his ambiguous request (v.6).

8–9 Both here and in the story of the Canaanite woman (15:21–28), faith triumphs over the obstacle Jesus erects. The centurion's reply again opens with "Lord" (v.8), implying tenacity and deference. As John the Baptist felt unworthy to baptize Jesus, so this centurion felt unworthy to entertain him in his home. This feeling of unworthiness did not arise from an awareness that the centurion might render Jesus ceremonially defiled; rather, the man felt unworthy in the face of Jesus' authority. Here is someone who illustrates the truth of the first Beatitude (5:3).

The centurion's words presuppose an understanding of the Roman military system. All "authority" belonged to the emperor and was delegated. Therefore, because he was under the emperor's authority, when the centurion spoke, he spoke with the emperor's authority, and so his command was obeyed. A foot soldier who disobeyed would not be defying a mere centurion but the emperor, Rome itself, with all its imperial majesty and might. This self-understanding the centurion applied to Jesus. Precisely because Jesus was under God's authority, he was vested with God's authority, so that when Jesus spoke, God spoke. To defy Jesus was to defy God; and Jesus' word must therefore be vested with God's authority that is able to heal sickness. This analogy reveals an astonishing faith on the part of the centurion.

10 Jesus is astonished at the faith of the centurion and he addressed those following him (not necessarily his disciples; cf. 4:25; 8:1) with a solemn saying. Jesus commended the man's faith. The greatness of his faith did not rest in the mere fact that he believed Jesus could heal from a distance but in the degree to which he had penetrated the secret of Jesus' authority. That faith was the more surprising since the centurion was a Gentile and lacked the heritage of OT revelation to help him understand Jesus. But this Gentile penetrated more deeply into the nature of Jesus' person and authority than any Jew of his time. Matthew's words, therefore, underline the movement of the Gospel from the Jews to all people regardless of race—a movement prophesied in the OT, developed in Jesus' ministry (see comments on 1:1, 3–5; 2:1–12), and commanded by the Great Commission (28:18–20).

11–12 The picture in this follow-up saying of Jesus is that of the "messianic banquet," derived from such OT passages as Isa 25:6–9. Jesus here insists (contrary to most Jewish opinions) that many Gentiles will come from the four points of the compass and join the patriarchs at the banquet.

The "subjects of the kingdom" are the Jews, who see themselves as sons of Abraham (cf. 3:9–10), belonging to the kingdom by right. But Jesus reverses roles (cf. 21:43); and the sons of the kingdom are thrown aside, left out of the future messianic banquet, and consigned to darkness where there are tears and gnashing of teeth—elements common to descriptions of hell (i.e., *gehenna*; see comment on Mk 9:43–48).

Jesus goes on to describe the horror of the scene. Weeping suggests suffering and gnashing of teeth despair. The reversal is not absolute. The patriarchs themselves are Jews, as were the earliest disciples (Ro 11:1–5). But these verses affirm, in a way that could only shock Jesus' hearers, that the locus of the people of God would not always be the Jewish race. If these verses do not quite authorize the Gentile mission, they open the door to it and prepare for the Great Commission (28:18–20).

13 Regarding "just as," Jesus performed a miracle, not *in proportion to* the centurion's faith, nor *because of* the centurion's faith, but in content what was *expected by* the centurion's faith (cf. 15:28, where the emphasis is also on faith).

c. Peter's mother-in-law (8:14–15)

14–15 The main emphasis in this story is on Jesus' authority. Peter was married (1Co 9:5) and had moved with his brother Andrew from their home in Bethsaida (Jn 1:44) to Capernaum, possibly to remain near Jesus (Mt 4:13). His mother-in-law's fever may have been malarial; fever itself was considered a disease, not a symptom (cf. Jn 4:52; Acts 28:8). Jesus healed her with a touch, and she began to wait on him. Matthew mentions her service to make it clear that the miracle was effective and instantaneous (cf. v.26). Jesus' authority instantly accomplishes what he wills.

d. Many at evening (8:16–17)

16 Matthew mentions the evening to show the pace of Jesus' ministry. He focuses his attention on Jesus' power and on the scriptural witness to his person and ministry. He drives out "the spirits," evil beings that are often recognized in intertestamental literature as agents of disease (see comments on Mk 1:23–26, 34).

17 Matthew goes on to say that Isa 53:4 is being fulfilled in Jesus' healing ministry. What is the connection between these two? It is generally understood that when the NT quotes a brief OT passage, it often refers implicitly to the entire context of the quotation (which in this case is the entire "Servant Song" of Isa 52:13–53:12). Both Scripture and Jewish tradition understand that all sickness is caused, directly or indirectly, by sin (see comment on 4:24). But one main emphasis in the Servant Song is substitutionary atonement, whereby the servant bears the sicknesses of others through his suffering and death. Thus, Matthew suggests that *Jesus' healing ministry is itself a function of his substitutionary death,* by which he lays the foundation for destroying sickness.

That connection is supported by various collateral arguments. The prologue insists Jesus came to save his people from their sin, and this within the context of the coming of the kingdom. When Jesus began his ministry, he not only proclaimed the kingdom but healed the sick (see comment on 4:24). Healing and forgiveness are tied together, not only in a pericope like 9:1–8, but by the fact that the consummated kingdom, in which there is no sickness, is made possible by Jesus' death and the new covenant that his death enacted (26:27–29). Thus the healings during Jesus' ministry can be understood not only as the foretaste of the kingdom but also as the fruit of Jesus' death. In other words, for Matthew, Jesus' healing miracles pointed beyond themselves to the Cross.

Furthermore, the miracles in this chapter have been framed to emphasize Jesus' authority (see comment on vv. 8–9). This authority was never used to satisfy himself (cf. 4:1–10). He healed a despised leper (vv.1–4), a Gentile centurion's servant who was hopelessly ill (vv.5–13), and other sick people (vv.14–15), no matter how many (vv.16–17). Thus when he gave his life a ransom for many (20:28), it was nothing less than an extension of the same authority directed toward the good of others. Jesus' death reflected the intermingling of authority and servanthood already noted (e.g., 3:17) and now progressively developed.

It should be stated that this discussion cannot be used to justify healing on demand. This text and others clearly teach that there is healing in the Atonement; but there is also the promise of a resurrection body in the Atonement, even though believers do not inherit it until the Parousia. From the perspective of the NT writers, the Cross is the basis for all the benefits that accrue to believers; but this does not mean that all such benefits can be secured at the present time on demand, any more than we have the right and power to demand our resurrection bodies.

2. The cost of following Jesus (8:18–22)

18–19 Matthew now includes two brief stories that help show the nature of Jesus' ministry and the disciples he was seeking. Perhaps his imminent departure to the east side of the lake prompted certain people to beg him to include them in the circle of disciples going with him. Discipleship in the strict sense required close attachment to the master's person. All people, including "teachers of the law," divide around the absolute claims of Jesus and must be weighed according to their response to him.

20 Jesus' response shows that he identifies the teacher of the law as someone less than fully committed; he wanted to be a follower, not a full-fledged disciple. Jesus' reply was neither invitation nor rebuke but a pointed way of saying that true discipleship to the "Son of Man" is not comfortable and should not be undertaken without counting the cost (cf. Lk 14:25–33). In the immediate context of Jesus' ministry, the saying does not mean that Jesus was penniless but homeless; the nature of his mission kept him on the move and would keep his followers on the move.

The phrase "the Son of Man" could easily be replaced here by the word "I" (see comment on Mk 8:31). It occurs in a setting that stresses Jesus' humanity and may foreshadow his sufferings, a concept that was entirely incomprehensible to any Jew. Only after the Resurrection were the followers of Jesus able to understand the full message Jesus had in designating himself as "Son of Man."

21–22 If the scribe was too quick in promising, this "disciple" was too slow in performing. Palestinian piety, basing itself on the fifth commandment (Ex 20:12), expected sons to attend to the burial of their parents (cf. Ge 25:9; 35:29; 50:13). Jesus' reply used paradoxical language (as in 16:25): Let the (spiritually) dead bury the (physically) dead. These verses seem to be a powerful way of expressing the thought in 10:37—even closest family ties must not be set above allegiance to Jesus and the proclamation of the kingdom (Lk 9:60).

In actuality we may well question whether Jesus was really forbidding attendance at the father's funeral, any more than he was really advocating self-castration in 5:27–30. In this inquirer he detected insincerity, a qualified acceptance of Jesus' lordship. And that was not good enough. Commitment to Jesus must be without reservation. Such is the importance Jesus himself attached to his own person and mission.

3. Calming a storm (8:23–27)

Jesus' authority over nature is now displayed. He may have less shelter than the beasts and birds of nature, yet he is nature's master.

23–25 The narrative moves forward from v.18; the order to cross the lake to escape the crowd is now carried out. The "boat" here is doubtless a fishing boat, big enough for a dozen or more men and a good catch of fish, but not large, and without sails. The story that follows is primarily a miracle story with Christological implications (see comment on vv.26–27).

It is well known that violent squalls develop quickly on Lake Galilee. The surface is more than six hundred feet below sea level, and the rapidly rising hot air draws violent winds whose cold air churns up the water. Those among Jesus' contemporaries who really knew the OT would remember that in it God is presented as the one who controls and stills the seas (cf. Job 38:8–11; Pss 29:3–4, 10–11; 65:5–7; et al.).

26–27 That the disciples could cry to Jesus for help reveals that they believed, or hoped, he could do something. More than others they had witnessed his miracles and apparently believed he could rescue them. Jesus' calling them "you of little faith" is therefore not against skepticism of his ability, nor against the fear that the disciples might drown. Rather, Jesus rebukes their failure to see that the one so obviously raised up by God to accomplish the messianic work could not possibly have died in a storm while that work remained undone. They lacked faith, not so much in his ability to save them, as in Jesus the Messiah, whose life could not be lost in a storm, as if the elements were out of control and Jesus himself the pawn of chance. Jesus' sleep stems both from his exhaustion and from his awareness that his hour had not yet come.

The disciples expected Jesus to intervene. But just as a crowd expects a magician to do his trick, yet marvels when it is done, so the disciples are amazed when he stills the storm that there is a complete calm. What kind of man is this? Readers of this gospel know the answer he is the virgin-born Messiah who has come to redeem his people from their sins and whose mission is to fulfill God's redemptive purposes. But the disciples did not yet understand these things. They saw that his authority extended over nature and were thus helped in their faith. Yet they did not grasp the profundity of his rebuke. Indeed, wherever "little faith" is used in Matthew (see 6:30; 14:31; 16:8), it signifies the failure to see beyond the mere surface of things. Thus this section is deeply Christological: themes of faith and discipleship are of secondary importance and point to the "kind of man" Jesus is.

The Miracles of Jesus

Miracle	Matthew	Mark	Luke	John
Man with leprosy	8:2–4	1:40–42	5:12–13	
Roman centurion's servant	8:5–13		7:1–10	
Peter's mother-in-law	8:14–15	1:30–31	4:38–39	
Two men from Gadara	8:28–34	5:1–15	8:27–35	
Paralyzed man	9:2–7	2:3–12	5:18–25	
Woman with bleeding	9:20–22	5:25–29	8:43–48	
Two blind men	9:27–31			
Mute, demon-Possessed man	9:32–33			
Man with a shriveled hand	12:10–13	3:1–5	6:6–10	
Blind, mute, demon-possessed man	12:22		11:14	
Canaanite woman's daughter	15:21–28	7:24–30		
Boy with a demon	17:14–18	9:17–29	9:38–43	
Two blind men (including Bartimaeus)	20:29–34	10:46–52	18:35–43	
Deaf mute		7:31–37		
Possessed man in synagogue		1:23–26	4:33–35	
Blind man at Bethsaida		8:22–26		
Crippled woman			13:11–13	
Man with dropsy			14:1–4	
Ten men with leprosy			17:11–19	
The high priest's servant			22:50–51	
Official's son at Capernaum				4:46–54
Sick man at pool of Bethesda				5:1–9
Man born blind				9:1–7
Miracles showing power over nature				
Calming the storm	8:23–27	4:37–41	8:22–25	
Walking on water	14:25	6:48–51		6:19–21
Feeding of the 5000	14:15–21	6:35–44	9:12–17	6:5–13
Feeding of the 4000	15:32–38	8:1–9		
Coin in fish	17:24–27			
Fig tree withered	21:18–22	11:12–14, 20–25		
Large catch of fish			5:4–11	
Water turned into wine				2:1–11
Another large catch of fish				21:1–11
Miracles of raising the dead				
Jairus's daughter	9:18–19, 23–25	5:22–24, 38–42	8:41–42, 49–56	
Widow's son at Nain			7:11–15	
Lazarus				11:1–44

4. Further demonstration of Jesus' authority (8:28–9:8)

a. Exorcising two men (8:28–34)

28 The locale of this miracle seems to have been in the district controlled by the town of Gadara, near the village of Gerasa, which lay about midpoint on the lake's eastern shore (see comment on Mk 5:1). Jesus has withdrawn here, not for ministry, but to avoid the crowds (v.18). Yet there can be no rest as long as the hosts of darkness oppose him.

Matthew mentions two men in this story; Mark and Luke (8:26–37) only one. Presumably Matthew had independent knowledge of the second man. The violence of these demoniacs is more fully described by Mark and Luke.

29 The demons stand in contrast to the disciples of v.27, for they know who Jesus is. In spite of this knowledge, they remained demons; to know Jesus yet to hate him is demonic. The question the demoniacs hurled at Jesus could be either harsh or gentle, depending on context (2Sa 16:10; Mk 1:24; Jn 2:4). Here it is hateful and tinged with fear. The title "Son of God" is probably to be taken in its richest sense: the demons recognized Jesus not solely in terms of his power but also in terms of his person. He was the Messiah, God's Son (see comment on 3:17).

The second question shows that there will be a time for demonic hosts to be tortured and rejected forever (cf. Jude 6; Rev 20:10). As the question is phrased, it recognizes that Jesus is the one who will discharge that judicial function at the "appointed time" (GK 2789); therefore it confirms the fullest meaning of "Son of God." That Jesus was in any sense circumscribing their activity before the appointed time already shows that Jesus' casting out of demons was an eschatological function, a sign that the kingdom was dawning (cf. 12:28).

The significance of "here" means "here on earth, where we have been given some freedom to trouble people before the end." This presupposes that Jesus has come to the earth before the End. It is difficult to avoid the conclusion that Jesus' preexistence is presupposed.

30–31 The request for the demons to enter into the pigs came probably because of a hatred of God's creatures, and most certainly because of a desire to stir up animosity against Jesus. The Gospels elsewhere show that exorcised evil spirits sometimes expressed their rage by visible acts of violence or mischief (e.g., 17:14–20).

32–34 The question as to why Jesus would grant the demons their desire and let them destroy the herd of pigs, the livelihood of their owners, is part of larger questions as to why human beings are possessed or why disease, misfortune, or calamity overtake us—questions only to be answered within the context of a broad theodicy outside the scope of this commentary. But the context offers some hints. He who is master of nature (vv.23–27) is also its ultimate owner (vv.28–34; cf. Ps. 50:10). The "appointed time" for full destruction of the demons' power has not yet arrived. The pigs' stampede dramatically proves that the former demoniacs had indeed been freed. But in the light of vv.33–34, the loss of the herd becomes a way of exposing the real values of the people in the vicinity. They prefer pigs to persons, swine to the Savior.

This ending of this story bears significantly on its total meaning. It shows once more that Jesus' ministry is not restricted to the Jews but foreshadows the mission to the Gentiles; it also shows that opposition to Jesus is not exclusively Jewish. To this extent it confirms earlier exegesis (see comment on 8:11–12) that showed that opponents in Matthew are not elected on the basis of race but according to their response to Jesus.

b. Healing a paralytic and forgiving his sins (9:1–8)

1 It is unclear whether this verse ties in more closely with 8:28–34 or with 9:2–8. The problem is not just academic, for the preceding pericope is almost certainly chronologically later (cf. Mk 5:1–20) than this one (cf. Mk 2:2–12); and a break more easily fits between 9:1 and 9:2 than between 8:34 and 9:1. Begged to leave (8:34), Jesus embarked in the boat he had so recently left and returned to "his own town," namely, Capernaum (4:13), on the western shore of the lake.

2 Mark (2:3–12) and Luke (5:8–26) inform us that this paralytic was brought to Jesus by lowering him through the roof. Jesus "saw *their* faith"—presumably that of the paralytic and those carrying him—exemplified in their coming, though he spoke only to the paralytic. Jesus' statement to him implies a close link between sin and sickness (see comment on 8:17)—perhaps in this case a direct one (cf. Jn 5:14; 1Co 11:29–30). It implies that of paralysis and sin, sin is the more basic problem.

3 Some teachers of the law muttered among themselves that Jesus was blaspheming. It is God alone who can forgive sin (Isa 43:25; 44:22), since it is against him only that people commit sin (Ps 51:4). Though in Jesus' day the precise definition of blasphemy was hotly disputed, the consensus seems to be that using the divine name was an essential element. Here the teachers of the law, in their whispered consultation, expanded blasphemy to include Jesus' claim to do something only God could do.

4 Jesus had seen the faith of the paralytic and his friends; now he saw the evil thoughts of some of the teachers of the law. Such discernment may have been supernatural, though not necessarily so. Jesus' charge probed beyond their talk of blasphemy to what they were thinking in their hearts. And what they were thinking was untrue, unbelieving, and blind to what was being revealed before their eyes.

5–7 Jesus responded to this situation according to the perspective of the teachers of the law—namely, that to say "Get up and walk" is easier since only God can forgive sins. Jesus claimed to do the more difficult thing. Thus v.6 is ironical—"All right, I'll also do the lesser deed." Yet if Jesus had blasphemed in pronouncing forgiveness, how could he now perform a miracle (cf. Jn 9:31)? But so that they might know that he had authority to forgive sin, he proceeded to the easier task. The healing therefore showed that Jesus as "Son of Man" truly had authority to forgive sins. This is the authority of Immanuel, "God with us" (1:23), sent to "save his people from their sins" (1:21). To sum up, the healing not only cured the paralytic (v.7), it also assured him that his sins were forgiven and thus refuted the charge of blasphemy.

8 People *should* "fear" (GK 5828; NIV "filled with awe") the one who has the authority to forgive sins. Indeed, they should fear whenever they are confronted by an open manifestation of God (cf. 17:6; 28:5, 10). The onlookers here simply saw a man exercising the authority of God, but readers recognize him as "God with us." God's gracious reign has come "on earth" (v.6); the kingdom of David's Son, who came to save his people from their sins, has dawned.

5. Calling Matthew (9:9)

9 The locale is probably the outskirts of Capernaum. Matthew was sitting "at the tax collector's booth," a customs and excise booth at the border between the territories of Philip and Herod Antipas (see comments on Mk 2:14). Having demonstrated his authority to forgive sins (vv.1–8), Jesus now calls to himself a man whose occupation made him a pariah—a sinner and an associate of sinners (cf. 1Ti 1:15).

Since Jews not uncommonly had two or more names, the simple equation of Levi (see Mk 2:14) and Matthew (a name likely meaning "gift of God") is the most obvious course to take. Some suggest that Matthew's work as a tax collector assured his fluency in Aramaic and Greek and that his accuracy in keeping records fitted him for note taking and later writing his gospel.

6. Eating with sinners (9:10–13)

10–11 According to most scholars, this dinner at Matthew's house likely occurred much later than his call in v.9. Jesus had said that even a tax collector has his friends (5:46), and Matthew's dinner substantiates this. "Sinners" (GK 283) may include common folk who did not share all the scruples of the Pharisees. But certainly it groups together those who broke Pharisaic rules of conduct—harlots, tax collectors, and other disreputable people. Though eating with them entailed dangers of ceremonial defilement, Jesus and his disciples did so. The Pharisees' question, put not to Jesus but to his disciples, was less a request for information than a charge; and they contemptuously lumped together "tax collectors and sinners" under one article. Jesus became known as "a friend of tax collectors and 'sinners'" (Mt 11:19).

12–13 These verses again connect Jesus' healing ministry with his "healing" of sinners (see comment on 8:17). The sick need a doctor and Jesus heals them; likewise the sinful need mercy and forgiveness, and Jesus heals them. The Pharisees were not so healthy as they thought (cf. 7:1–5); more important, they did not understand the purpose of Jesus' mission. Expecting a Messiah who would crush the sinful and support the righteous, they had little place for one who accepted and transformed the sinner and dismissed the "righteous" as hypocrites. Jesus explained his mission in terms reminiscent of 1:21.

Jesus challenges the Pharisees to "go and learn" from Hos 6:6. Use of this formula may be slightly sarcastic—that those who prided themselves in their knowledge of and conformity to Scripture needed to "go and learn" what it means.

The Hebrew word for "mercy" (GK 2876) is close in meaning to "faithful covenant love," which, according to Hosea, is more important than "sacrifice" (an aspect of ritual worship). As applied to the Pharisees by Jesus, therefore, the Hosea quotation was not simply telling them that they should be more sympathetic to outcasts and less concerned about ceremonial purity, but that they were being aligned with the apostates of ancient Israel in that they too were preserving the shell while losing the heart of the matter, as exemplified by their attitude to tax collectors and sinners. On Jesus' final statement, see comment on Mk 2:17.

7. Fasting and dawning of the messianic joy (9:14–17)

14 Probably while they were at dinner, some of John the Baptist's disciples showed up with criticism (possibly with some Pharisees; cf. 2:18–22). The Baptist himself showed a noble freedom from jealousy when Jesus' ministry began to supersede his own (cf. esp. Jn 3:26–31). But some of John's disciples felt differently now that he was in prison (4:12); and because they kept up their leader's asceticism (11:18), not heeding his strong witness to Jesus, they saw an occasion for criticism about the conduct of Jesus' disciples.

15 For his response Jesus used three illustrations. The first, about the "guests of the bridegroom," picks up a metaphor from the Baptist, who saw himself as the "best man" and Jesus as the groom (Jn 3:29). This metaphor would therefore be more effective with the audience confronting Jesus—Jesus is the groom and the disciples his "guests," who are so overjoyed at being with him that for them to fast is inappropriate.

In exonerating his disciples' eating, Jesus used messianic-eschatological terms. In the OT the bridegroom metaphor was repeatedly applied to God (Isa 54:5–6; 62:4–5; Hos 2:16–20); and Jews sometimes used it of marriage in connection with Messiah's coming or with the messianic banquet (cf. Mt 22:2; 25:1; 2Co 11:2; Eph 5:22–32; Rev 19:7, 9; 21:2). Thus Jesus' answer was implicitly Christological: he himself is the messianic bridegroom, and the Messianic Age has dawned.

16–17 The next illustration is about a piece of unshrunk cloth tightly sewed to old and well-shrunk cloth in order to repair a tear; it will cause a bigger tear. The final one is also a "slice of life" in the ancient world. Skin bottles for carrying various fluids were made by killing the chosen animal, cutting off its head and feet, skinning the carcass, and sewing up the skin, fur side out, to seal off all orifices but one (usually the neck). The skin was tanned with special care to minimize disagreeable taste. In time the skin became hard and brittle. If new wine, still fermenting, were put into such an old skin, the buildup of fermenting gases would split the brittle container and ruin both bottle and wine. New wine was placed only in new wineskins, still pliable and elastic enough to accommodate the pressure.

These illustrations show that the new situation introduced by Jesus could not simply be patched onto old Judaism or poured into the old wineskins of Judaism. New forms would have to accompany the kingdom that Jesus was now inaugurating; to try to domesticate him and incorporate him into the matrix of established Jewish religion and piety would only succeed in ruining both Judaism and Jesus' teaching.

8. A resurrection and more healings 9:18–34)

Jesus performs three new kinds of miracles: raising the dead and healing the blind and mute. By these examples of spheres over which Jesus has authority, Matthew is preparing us for Jesus' defense to the disciples of John the Baptist (11:2–5): the blind receive sight, the lame walk, those who have leprosy are cured, the deaf hear (usually associated with muteness), and the dead are raised. Jesus' messianic credentials are thus grouped together.

a. Raising a girl and healing a woman (9:18–26)

18–19 Matthew tightly links this narrative to the dinner in his house. A synagogue ruler, hence a Jew and a man of considerable influence in the lives of the people, "knelt before" (GK *4686*) Jesus: the verb here suggests deep courtesy, a pleading homage before someone in a position to grant a favor. His daughter "has just died," and he requests Jesus to come and raise her. As usual, Jesus responded to faith, small or great, and got up from the table to leave.

20–22 The nature of the woman's hemorrhage is probably chronic bleeding from the womb, making her perpetually unclean (cf. Lev 15:25–33). Having heard of others who had been healed at Jesus' touch, this woman decided to touch even a tassel of Jesus' cloak. Moved in part by a superstitious view of Jesus, she struggled through the crowd, which, because of her "unclean" condition, she should have avoided.

Matthew's account is shorter than Mark's (Mk 5:22–43), keeping only what is of most interest to him. The woman was healed on touching Jesus' cloak. He turned to her and indicated that it was her faith that was effective, not the superstition mingled with it.

23–26 Flute players (v.23) were employed both on festive occasions (Rev 18:22) and at funerals. Matthew alone mentions them in the ruler's house, probably out of personal recollection. Jesus was about to reverse funeral symbolism of the finality of death (on funeral customs, see comments on Mk 5:38). His miracle not only brought a corpse to life but hope to despair.

The crowd mocked Jesus, not just because he had said, "The girl is not dead but asleep," but even more because they thought that this great healer had arrived too late. Now he was going too far; carried away by his own success, he would try his skill on a corpse and make a fool of himself. In such a situation Jesus' words became, in retrospect, all the more profound. Jesus touched the corpse; and the body, rather than defiling him, came to life. For Matthew the miracle showed that Jesus' authority as the Christ extended even over the dead.

b. Healing two blind men (9:27–31)

27–28 Apparently Jesus was returning from the ruler's house (v.23) either to his own house (4:13) or to that of Matthew (vv.10, 28). We should probably envisage a large crowd after the dramatic raising of the ruler's daughter. Attached to the crowd were two blind men who had faith enough to follow him indoors.

This is the first time Jesus is called "Son of David" (v.27), and there can be no doubt that the blind men were confessing Jesus as Messiah (see comment on 1:1). They may have been physically blind, but they really "saw" better than many others—further evidence that Jesus came to those who needed a doctor (vv.12–13). If Jesus were really the Messiah, they could expect to receive their sight (see Isa 35:5–6). So their need drove them to faith.

Jesus did not deal with the blind men until they were indoors. This may have been to dampen messianic expectations (see next comment) on a day marked by two highly public and dramatic miracles (v.26). It may also have been a device to increase their faith. The latter is suggested by his question (v.28), which accomplished two other things: (1) it revealed that their cries were not merely those of desperation but of faith; and (2) it showed that their faith was directed not to God alone but to Jesus' person and to his power and authority. Their title for Jesus was therefore right; he is truly the messianic Son of David.

29–31 Jesus' touching the blind men's eyes—perhaps no more than a compassionate gesture to encourage faith—was not the sole means of this healing: it also depended on Jesus' authoritative word. "According to your faith" means "since you believe, your request is granted" (cf. v.22). Jesus' stern warning not to tell anyone reveals his intense desire to avoid a falsely based acclaim that would not only impede but also endanger his true mission (see comment on 8:4). But the men whose faith brought them to Christ for healing did not stay with him to learn obedience. So the news spread throughout the region (cf. v.26).

c. Exorcising a mute man (9:32–34)

32–33 The man here may have been not only mute but a deaf mute. The NT frequently attributes various diseases to demonic activity;

but since the same ailment mentioned here appears elsewhere without any suggestion of demonic activity (e.g., Mk 7:32-33), the connection between the two here presupposes a real ability Jesus had to distinguish between natural and demonic causes. The crowd's amazement (v.33) climaxes the earlier excitement (vv.26, 31). Nothing has ever been seen like this in Israel—and, by implication, if not among God's chosen people, then nowhere. But the same amazement ominously sets the stage for the Pharisees' cynical response (v.34).

34 This is not the first intimation of direct opposition to Jesus in Matthew (vv.3, 11, 14, 24; cf. 5:10-12, 44). But the tide of opposition, which later brought Jesus to the cross, now becomes an essential part of the background to the next discourse.

9. Spreading the news of the kingdom (9:35-10:4)

a. Praying for workers (9:35-38)

As 4:23-25 prepares for the first discourse (chs. 5-7), so vv.35-38 provide a report and summary that prepares for the second (10:5-42). A new note is added; not only are we told again of the extensiveness of Jesus' labors, but we learn that the work was so great that many workers were needed. This leads to the commissioning of 10:1-4 and to the related discourse of 10:5-42.

35-36 Verse 35 summarizes the heart of Jesus' Galilean ministry and prepares us for the new phase of mission via the Twelve (see comment on 4:23). Like the Lord in the OT (cf. Eze 34), Jesus showed compassion on the shepherdless crowds and judgment on the false leaders. The "sheep" Jesus sees are bullied and oppressed; and in the face of such problems, they are "helpless," unable to rescue themselves or escape their tormentors. Parallels with the OT (e.g., 1Ki 22:17; 2Ch 18:16; Isa 53:6) remind us not only of the theme's rich background but also that the shepherd can refer either to God or to the Davidic Messiah whom God promised to send (cf. 2:6; 10:6, 16; 15:24; 25:31-46; 26:31).

37-38 The metaphor changes from sheep farming to harvest (v.37), as Jesus seeks to awaken similar compassion in his disciples. Later on the harvest is the end of the age (13:49) and the judgment it brings—a common symbol (cf. Isa 17:11; Joel 3:13). It is possible to see this verse as a warning to Israel that judgment time is near.

Jesus is speaking here to "his disciples," which many take to refer to the Twelve. More likely, this phrase designates a larger group exhorted to "ask" that the Lord of the harvest will thrust laborers into his "harvest field." By contrast the Twelve are immediately commissioned as workers (10:1-4). This interpretation best fits 10:1: Jesus "called his twelve disciples to him."

b. Commissioning the Twelve (10:1-4)

1 He whose word (chs. 5-7) and deed (chs. 8-9) were characterized by authority now delegates something of that authority to twelve men. This is the first time Matthew has explicitly mentioned the Twelve, though his language suggests that the Twelve became a recognized group somewhat earlier. This commission was also a stage in the training and preparation of those who, after Pentecost, would lead the earliest thrust of the fledgling church. Twelve were chosen, probably on an analogy to the twelve tribes of Israel (see comment on Mk 3:13).

The authority the Twelve received enabled them to heal "every kind of disease and sickness" (cf. 4:23; 9:35) and to drive out "evil spirits"—spirits in rebellion against God, hostile to humans, and capable of inflicting mental, moral, and physical harm. This is the first mention in Matthew of such spirits (see also 12:43).

2-4 For the first and only time in Matthew, the Twelve are called "apostles" (GK 693). "Apostle," as used in NT documents, has narrower and wider meanings. It can mean merely "messenger" (Jn 13:16), refer to Jesus ("the apostle and high priest whom we confess," Heb 3:1), or denote a group of "missionaries"—i.e., a group larger than the Twelve and Paul (Ro 16:7; 2Co 8:23). Nevertheless, the usual meaning is a narrow one, referring to special authoritative representatives chosen by Christ (cf. 1Co 9:1-5; 15:7; Gal 1:17, 19; et al.). Paul usually used the term to refer to the Twelve plus himself (by special dispensation, 1Co 15:8-10). For discussion of the twelve men mentioned here, see comment on Mk 3:16-19.

B. Second Discourse: Mission and Martyrdom (10:5–11:1)

1. Setting (10:5a)

5a Many scholars have suggested that this speech of Jesus is a compilation of Matthew from various sayings of Jesus (e.g., those found in Mk 6:8–11; 13:11–13; Lk 12:2–17, 51–53). However, careful study of the discourse shows a remarkable unity to it rather than a selective collation. Many of the alleged discrepancies are artificial. There is no conflict, for instance, between the ready harvest of 9:37–38 and the resistance in 10:16–22. "The blood of the martyrs is the seed of the church" is a valid principle; and many great awakenings, including the Whitefield and Wesleyan revivals, have shown afresh that the harvest is most plentiful when the workers reap in the teeth of opposition.

It is true that vv.17–23 go beyond the immediate mission of the Twelve and in at least two ways envision a mission to the Gentiles (in contrast to vv.5b–6). But these are not new themes (cf. 5:13–14; 7:13–14; 8:11–12). Therefore Jesus is here not only treating the short-term itinerary of his disciples but also using it as a paradigm for the longer mission stretching in the years ahead. The following exposition focuses on the meaning of the text as it stands.

2. The commission (10:5b–16)

5b–6 Jesus forbade the Twelve from taking the road to the Gentiles—presumably toward Tyre and Sidon in the north or the Decapolis in the east—and from visiting Samaritan towns in the south. They were to remain in Galilee, ministering to the people of Israel. Jews despised Samaritans, not only because they preserved a separate cult (cf. Jn 4:20), but also because they were a mixed race, made up partly of the poorest Jews who had been left in the land at the time of the Exile and partly of Gentile peoples transported into the territory and with whom the remaining Jews had intermingled, thereby succumbing to some syncretism (cf. 2Ki 17:24–28). The Twelve were to restrict themselves to "the lost sheep of Israel."

Why this restriction? Pragmatic considerations play a role. That Jesus felt it necessary to mention the Samaritans at all presupposes John 4. The disciples, happy in the exercise of their ability to perform miracles, might have been tempted to evangelize the Samaritans when they remembered Jesus' success there. Judging by Lk 9:52–56, however, the Twelve were still temperamentally ill-equipped to minister to Samaritans. And even after Pentecost, despite an explicit command from the risen Lord (Ac 1:8), the church moved only hesitantly toward the Samaritans (Ac 8).

The most important consideration, however, was not pragmatic but theological. Jesus stood at the nexus in salvation history where as a Jew and the Son of David he came in fulfillment of his people's history as their King and Redeemer. Yet his personal claims would offend so many of his own people that he would be rejected by all but a faithful remnant. Why increase the opposition by devoting time to Gentile ministry? His mission, as frequently noted above, was worldwide in its ultimate aim; and all along he had warned that being a Jew was not enough. But his own people must not be excluded because premature offense could be taken at such broad perspectives. Therefore Jesus restricted his own ministry primarily (15:24), though not exclusively (8:1–13; 15:21–39), to Jews. He himself was sent as their Messiah. The messianic people of God developed out of the Jewish remnant and eventually expanded to include Gentiles. The restriction of vv.5–6, therefore, depends on a particular understanding of salvation history that ultimately goes back to Jesus (see also Paul's statement in Ro 1:16 and his missionary practice as reflected in Ac 13:5, 44–48; 14:1; et al.).

7–8 The content of the disciples' message was much like that in 3:2; 4:17. "Repent" is not mentioned but is presupposed. The long-awaited kingdom was now "near" (see comment on 4:17), attested by miracles directed at demonism and at diseases.

Jesus expected the Twelve to be supported by those to whom they were to minister (cf. vv.9–13; 1Co 9:14), but they needed to understand that what they had received—the good news of the kingdom, Jesus' authority, and this commission—they had received "freely." Therefore it would be mercenary to charge others. The danger of profiteering is still among us (Mic 3:11; 2Co 2:17; 1Pe 5:2).

9–10 The imperative "Do not take along" (GK *3227*) more likely means "Do not procure" (as in Ac 1:18; 8:20; 22:28). Neither were they to provide their belt with money when they started out.

Matthew's account forbids "procuring" even sandals or a walking stick (see Mk 6:8). Presumably this account assumes that the disciples already have certain things (one cloak, sandals, a walking stick) and forbids them from "procuring" anything more. The disciples needed to learn the principle that "the worker is worth his keep" (cf. 1Co 9:14; 1Ti 5:17–18) and to shun luxury while learning to rely on God's providence through the hospitality of those who would take them in overnight, thus obviating the need for a second cloak.

11–15 To settle into the house of a "worthy" (GK 545) person implies that the disciples were not to shop around for the most comfortable quarters. In this place "worthy" refers to someone willing and able to receive an apostle of Jesus and the Gospel of the kingdom. As the disciples entered the house, they were to give it their "greeting," "Peace to this house" (Lk 10:5). But if the home turned out to be "unworthy," they were to let their greeting of peace return to them (v.13); i.e., they were not to stay. The Twelve were emissaries of Jesus. Those who received them received him (cf. v.40). Their greeting was of real value because of their relationship to him. Loss of their greeting was loss of their presence and therefore loss of Jesus.

What was true for the home applied equally to the town (v.14). A pious Jew, on leaving Gentile territory, might remove from his feet and clothes all dust of the pagan land now being left behind, thus dissociating himself from the pollution of those lands and the judgment in store for them. For the disciples to do this to Jewish homes and towns would be a symbolic way of saying that the emissaries of Messiah now viewed those places as pagan, polluted, and liable to severe judgment. Sodom and Gomorrah faced catastrophic destruction because of their sin (Ge 19) and became bywords of loathsome corruption (Isa 1:9; Mt 11:22–24; 2Pe 2:6; Jude 7). Although there is still worse to come for them on the Day of Judgment, there is even more awful judgment for those who reject the word and the messengers of the Messiah (cf. Heb 2:1–3).

Once again the Christological claim, though implicit, is unambiguous. As in 7:21–23, Jesus here insists that one's eternal destiny turns on relationship to him or even to his emissaries. At the same time, even in this early ministry, Jesus' apostles were to face the certainty of opposition. That opposition pointed to the greater suffering still to come (vv.17ff.) and also aligned the disciples of Jesus with the prophets of old (5:10–12) and with Jesus himself (10:24–25). Thus the disciples began to learn that the advance of the kingdom was divisive (vv.34–35) and would meet with violent opposition (see on 11:11–12).

16 Jesus pictured his disciples, defenseless in themselves, located in a dangerous environment. This is where he was sending them. The shepherd in this metaphor sends his sheep into the wolf pack (cf. 7:15; Jn 10:12; Ac 20:29). Therefore they must be "shrewd" (GK 5861; i.e., prudent) as serpents. But prudence can easily degenerate into cheap cunning unless it goes with simplicity. The disciples must therefore be innocent as well, toward both God and outsiders.

In this light the dove image becomes clear. Doves are retiring but not astute; they are easily ensnared by the fowler. So Jesus' disciples, in their mission as sheep among wolves, must be "shrewd," avoiding conflicts and attacks where possible; but they must also be "innocent," i.e., not so cautious, suspicious, and cunning that circumspection degenerates into fear or elusiveness. The balance is difficult, but not a little of Jesus' teaching combines such poles of meaning (see comments on 7:1–6).

3. Warnings of future sufferings (10:17–25)

a. The Spirit's help (10:17–20)

In this section Jesus envisages an extended time of witness in the midst of persecution—in short, a witnessing and suffering church.

17 Those who will hand the disciples over must be Jews, as the context is the synagogue; and so the persecution here envisaged is Jewish persecution of Christians (unlike v.18). The "local councils" (civic or synagogal) were charged with preserving the peace. That "flogging" is used for punishment, rather than the broader term "beating," implies that the opposition is not mob violence but the result of judicial action. Moreover, Jesus sees a time before the absolute separation of church and synagogue has taken place, for synagogue floggings were most easily inflicted on synagogue members.

18 As the witness would extend at some future time beyond Galilee and the Jewish race to Gentiles, so also would the opposition (cf. "governors" and "kings"). As in 8:4 and 24:14, the "witness" (GK *3457*) is not against people but to them; it becomes either the means by which they accept the truth or, when they reject it, a condemnation. The disciples would be harassed and persecuted, not on account of who they are but on account of who Christ is (see comment on 5:10–12).

19–20 The verb "arrest" (GK *4140*) is better translated as "hand over." The subject is ambiguous: people, opponents, or Jewish leaders could be "handing over" the disciples to the Gentile authorities. Later on this happened to Paul and other Christians, who at first witnessed to their faith with relative impunity under the Roman laws granting exemptions from emperor worship to Jews, but fell victim to increasing Roman wrath as the Jews progressively denied any link between themselves and Christians.

Confronting a high Roman official would be far more terrifying to believers than confronting a synagogue council. But if Jesus warned his disciples of dangers, he also promised them help: the Spirit would speak through them when the time came; so they should not fret about their response. This promise is neither a sop for lazy preachers nor equivalent to the promises given the Twelve in the farewell discourse (Jn 14–16) that the Spirit would recall to their memory all they had heard from Jesus (Jn 14:16, 26). It is a pledge to believers who have been brought before tribunals because of their witness.

Unlike Luke, Matthew does not often mention the Spirit. But from other passages in his gospel, it is clear that he associates the Spirit with the kingdom's dramatic coming (3:11; 12:28, 31) and the church's witness (28:18–20). That same Spirit, "the Spirit of your Father," would provide Jesus' followers with the help they needed under persecution when facing hostile officials.

b. Endurance (10:21-23)

21–22 It is not enough for Jesus' disciples to be opposed by Jewish and Gentile officialdom; they will be hounded and betrayed by their own family members (v.21; see further vv.34–39). Here Jesus alludes to Mic 7:6 (quoted in vv.35–36). "All men" (v.22) does not mean "all men without exception," for then there would be no converts, but "all men without distinction"—all people irrespective of race, color, or creed. That the good news of the kingdom of God and his righteousness should elicit such intense and widespread hostility is a sad commentary on "all men." The hatred erupts, Jesus says, either because one bears the name "Christian" (cf. 1Pe 4:14) or, more likely, "on account of me" (see comment on 5:10–12).

The one who exercises patient endurance will be saved; but he or she must stand firm "to the end." This phrase is ambiguous, meaning either "to the end of one's life" or "to the end of the age." This is not to say that only martyrs will be saved; but if the opposition one of Jesus' disciples faces calls for the sacrifice of life itself, commitment to him must be so strong that the sacrifice is willingly made. Otherwise there is no salvation. Thus from earliest times Christians have been crucified, burned, impaled, drowned, starved, racked—for no other reason than that they belonged to Christ.

23 This verse is among the most difficult in the NT. The coming of the Son of Man has been interpreted as Jesus catching up with the disciples after their mission, as the public identification of Jesus as the Messiah through his resurrection and Pentecost, and as the Second Coming of Jesus (often with the "church dispensation" being seen as not in Jesus' mind here).

The best interpretation, however, sees the "coming of the Son of Man" as his coming in judgment against the Jews, culminating in the sack of Jerusalem and the destruction of the temple. The coming of the Son of Man refers to the same event as the coming of the kingdom, even though the two expressions are conceptually complementary. Thus *the* coming of the Son of Man brings in the consummated kingdom (see comments on 24:30–31; 25:31). But the kingdom, as we have seen, comes in stages (see comments on 4:17; 12:28). In one sense Jesus was born a king (2:2); in another he has all authority as a result of his passion and resurrection (28:18); and in yet another his kingdom awaits the end. Mingled with this theme of the coming of the kingdom are Jesus' repeated warnings to the Jews concerning the disaster they are courting by failing to recognize and receive him. His warnings are unique because he himself is the judge and because the messianic reign is now dawning in both blessing and wrath (8:11–12; 21:31–32).

Against this background the coming of the Son of Man in v.23 marks that stage in the coming of the kingdom in which the judgment repeatedly foretold falls on the Jews. With it the temple cultus disappears, and the new wine necessarily takes to new wineskins (see comment on 9:16–17). The age of the kingdom comes into its own, precisely because so many of the structured foreshadowings of the OT, bound up with the cultus and nation, disappear (see comments on 5:17–48).

Above all this interpretation makes contextual sense of v.23. The connection is not with v.22 alone but with vv.17–22, which picture the suffering witness of the church in the post-Pentecost period during a time when many of Jesus' disciples are still bound up with the synagogue. During that period, Jesus says in v.23, his disciples must not use the opposition to justify quitting or bravado. Far from it. When they face persecution, they must take it as no more than a signal for strategic withdrawal to the next city where witness must continue, for the time is short. They will not have finished evangelizing the cities of Israel before the Son of Man comes in judgment on Israel.

c. Inspiration (10:24–25)

24–25 Here Jesus forbids the disciples from being surprised when they suffer persecution. If they follow him, they should expect no less. The statement reveals something of Jesus' perception of the nature of his own ministry and of the way the "gospel of the kingdom" will advance in the world.

The insult "Beelzebub" has an uncertain derivation. It is often seen as coming from a Hebrew term meaning "lord of the flies," a mocking takeoff on "Prince Baal." However, a better view is to see it as a straightforward translation of *oikodespotes* (GK 3867; "head of the house"). Beelzeboul (see NIV note) is recognized in the NT as the prince of the demons and identified with Satan (12:24–27; Mk 3:22–26; Lk 11:18–19). Thus the real head of the house, Jesus, who heads the household of God, is being willfully confused with the head of the house of demons. The charge is shockingly vile—the Messiah himself rejected as Satan! If so, why should his disciples expect less?

4. Prohibition of fear (10:26–31)

a. The emergence of truth (10:26–27)

26–27 Consideration of how disciples must expect to face persecution makes it necessary to say something about how to handle fear (vv.26–31) and about the high standards of discipleship such a perspective presupposes.

"Them" refers to the persecutors (v.23). The word "so" (i.e., "therefore") suggests that in view of a master who suffers ahead of his disciples (v.24), *therefore* do not fear, etc. The truth must emerge; the Gospel and its outworkings in the disciples may not now be visible to all, but nothing will remain hidden forever. And if the truth will emerge at the End, how wise to declare it fully and boldly now. Flat rooftops of Palestinian houses provided excellent places for speakers. In a sense the apostles were to have more of a public ministry than Jesus himself. He told them things in private, some of which they did not even understand till after the Resurrection. But they were to teach them fully and publicly.

b. The nonfinality of death (10:28)

28 The second reason for learning not to fear other people emerges from the fact that the worst they can do does not match the worst God can do. Though Satan may have great power (6:13; 24:22), only God can destroy soul and body in "hell" (see comment on Mk 9:42–49). If God be truly feared, none other need be. Unavoidable in this context is the thought that hell is a place of torment for the whole person: there will be a resurrection of the unjust as well as of the just.

c. Continuing providence (10:29–31)

29–31 The third reason for not being afraid is an a fortiori argument (see comment on 6:26–30): If God's providence is so all-embracing that not even a sparrow drops from the sky apart from the will of God, cannot that same God be trusted to extend his providence over Jesus' disciples? "Your Father" adds a piquant touch: this God of all providence is the disciples' Father. God's sovereignty is not limited only to life-and-death issues; even the hairs of our heads are counted. Jesus' third argument against fear is thus the opposite of what is commonly advanced. Some say that God cares about the big things but not about little details. But Jesus says that God's sovereignty over the tiniest detail should give us confidence that he also superintends the larger matters.

5. Characteristics of discipleship (10:32–39)

a. Acknowledging Jesus (10:32–33)

32–33 In Mk 8:38, Jesus addressed words similar to these to the crowds, though he used the phrase "Son of Man." Here, however, Jesus is addressing his disciples in an intimate gathering, and he does not hesitate to use "I" instead of "Son of Man." This was one of the things Jesus said clearly to his disciples in secret and which they would one day shout from the housetops (v.27).

Though addressed to the Twelve (vv.1–5), like much of vv.17–42, this saying looks beyond the apostles to disciples at large (cf. "whoever"). A necessary criterion for being a disciple of Jesus is to acknowledge him publicly (cf. Ro 1:16; 10:9). This will vary in boldness, fluency, wisdom, sensitivity, and frequency from believer to believer, but consistently to "disown" Christ results in being disowned by Christ. Jesus now speaks not of "your Father" (as in v.29) but of "my Father." In view is his special filial relationship with the Father, by which the final destiny of all humanity depends solely on his word (see comment on 7:21–23).

b. Recognizing the Gospel (10:34–36)

34–36 Since many Jews in Jesus' day thought the coming of Messiah would bring them political peace and material prosperity, so today many in the church think that Jesus' presence will bring them a kind of tranquility. But Jesus insists that his mission entails strife and division. Prince of Peace though he is (see comment on 5:9), the world will so violently reject him and his reign that men and women will divide over him (cf. Lk 12:49–53). Before the consummation of the kingdom, even the peace Jesus bequeaths his disciples will have its setting in the midst of a hostile world (Jn 14:27; 16:33; cf. Jas 4:4).

The repeated statement "I have come" shows Jesus' awareness of being the Messiah. Earlier he warned his disciples of the world's hatred of his followers, a hatred extending even to close relatives (vv.21–22); now he ties this perspective to an OT analogy (Mic 7:6). Micah described the sinfulness and rebellion in the days of King Ahaz; but insofar as Jesus' disciples by following him align themselves with the prophets (5:10–12), the situation in Micah's time pointed to the greater division at Messiah's coming. Even today the situation has not greatly eased. In the "liberal" West people who have become Christians have occasionally been disowned and disinherited by their families and have lost their jobs. And under totalitarian regimes of the right or the left there has been and still is untold suffering for Christ.

c. Preferring Jesus (10:37–39)

37–39 A man must love his wife, family, friends, and even his enemies (cf. 5:44), but he must love Jesus supremely. Moreover, Jesus demands death to self. "Taking one's cross" does not mean putting up with some awkward or tragic situation in one's life but painfully dying to self. In that sense every disciple of Jesus bears the same cross. After Jesus' death and resurrection, the emotional impact of these sayings must have been greatly heightened; but even before those events, the reference to crucifixion would vividly call to mind the shame and pain of such a sacrifice.

The appeal is not to gloom but to discipleship. There is a strong paradox here. Those who "lose" (GK 660) their "life," whether in actual martyrdom or disciplined self-denial, will "find" (GK 2351) it in the age to come. Those who "find" it now by living for themselves and refusing to submit to the demands of Christian discipleship will "lose" it in the age to come (cf. 16:25).

6. Encouragement: response to the disciples and to Jesus (10:40–42)

The foregoing teaching about what it means to be a disciple of Jesus has its darker side. This final section of the discourse is more encouraging—it reverts again to the ultimate tie between the treatment of Jesus and that of his followers (see comment on vv.24–25); it turns our eyes to the future (v.28) and shows us that God is indebted to no one.

40–42 As the discourse, viewed as a whole, moves from the Twelve to all believers, so also does its conclusion. Verse 40 probably refers primarily to the apostles, and vv.41–42 move through "prophets" and "righteous men" down to "these little ones" (GK 3625)—i.e., the least in the kingdom, seen as persecuted witnesses in the latter part of the discourse. The classes mentioned are not mutually exclusive, since "these little ones" surely includes the apostles, prophets, and righteous men; they are all "little ones" because they are all targets of the world's enmity. To give a cup of cold, freshly drawn water, the least that courtesy demands, to the least disciple just because he is a disciple will be rewarded. "Prophets" refers to those who speak for God and for those with whom Jesus' followers are aligned (cf. 5:10–12); "righteous men" is a generic category that refers to all those who are righteous in Christ Jesus (cf. 5:20), including the righteous people of earlier generations.

Verse 42 makes it clear that the sole reason for rewarding those who treat Jesus' disciples well is not because they are prophets or righteous people—they are in fact "little ones"—but because they are Jesus' disciples. The prophet's reward and the righteous man's reward are therefore not disparate but kingdom rewards (see comment on 5:12) that are the fruit of discipleship. To receive a prophet because he is a prophet (as in 1Ki 17:9–24; 2Ki 4:8–37) presupposes, in the context of v.40, that he is Christ's prophet; the same came be said about the "righteous man." Thus the person who receives a prophet receives Christ, his word, his ways, and his Gospel, and he or she expresses solidarity with the people of God (these "little ones") by receiving them for Jesus' sake (cf. 2Jn 10–11; 3Jn 8). Jesus promises that no such persons will lose their reward.

7. Transitional conclusion: expanding ministry (11:1)

1 For the significance of the formulas that end Jesus' discourses, see comment on 7:28–29. Attention returns to Jesus' ministry, for he did not send out the apostles in order to relieve himself of work but in order to expand the proclamation of the kingdom (9:35–10:4).

IV. Teaching and Preaching the Gospel of the Kingdom: Rising Opposition (11:2–13:53)

Thematically chs. 11–13 are held together by the rising tide of disappointment in and opposition to the kingdom of God that was resulting from Jesus' ministry. He was not turning out to be the kind of Messiah the people had expected. Even John the Baptist had doubts (11:2–19), and the Galilean cities that were sites of most of Jesus' miracles hardened themselves in unbelief (11:20–24). The nature of Jesus' person and ministry was "hidden" (11:25; GK 3221) from the wise, despite the most open and compassionate of invitations (11:28–30). Conflicts with Jewish leaders began to intensify (12:45), while people still misunderstood the most basic elements of Jesus' teaching and authority (12:46–50). But does this mean that he had been checkmated or that the kingdom had not come after all? Matthew 13 is the answer—the kingdom of God was continuing its advance even though it was often contested and ignored.

A. Narrative (11:2–12:50)

1. Jesus and John the Baptist (11:2–19)

a. John's question and Jesus' response (11:2–6)

2–3 Apparently John had been held in prison by Herod during Jesus' extensive Galilean ministry (see comment on 4:12), perhaps as long as a year. The one to whom he had pointed, the one who would come in blessing and judgment (3:11–12), had brought healing to many but, so it seemed, judgment to none—not even to those who had immorally and unlawfully confined the Baptist in a cruel prison.

John "heard ... what Christ was doing" (v.2). Matthew normally avoids using the name "Christ" (lit. here, "the Christ" or "the Messiah"). Why does he use it here? The entire gospel is written from the perspective of faith. The very first verse affirms Jesus as the Messiah, and the prologue (chs. 1–2) seeks to prove it. So at this point Matthew somewhat unusually refers to Jesus as "the Christ" in order to remind his readers who it was that John the Baptist was doubting. Though John doubted, from Matthew's perspective the time for doubt had passed. The phrase "what Christ was doing" (lit., "the works of

Christ") embraces a triple allusion, not only to Jesus' miracles (chs. 8–9), but also to his teaching (chs. 5–7) and growing mission (ch. 10).

As a result of these reports, John sent a pointed question by some of his disciples. John's question was whether Jesus was "the coming one" (v.3), exactly the same expression John himself used (see 3:11). John was asking Jesus whether he was the Messiah.

His question is understandable. Not only may he have become demoralized, like his namesake Elijah (cf. 1Ki 19), but he had preached in terms of imminent blessing *and* judgment. By contrast Jesus was preaching in veiled fulfillment terms and bringing much blessing but no real judgment; as a result the Baptist was having second thoughts.

4–6 Jesus' answer briefly summarized his own miracles and preaching, using the language of Isa 35:5–6; 61:1 (with possible further allusions to 26:19; 29:18–19). At one level the answer was straightforward: Isa 61:1 is an explicit messianic passage, and Isa 35:5–6, though it has no messianic figure, describes the return of God's people to Zion with accompanying blessings (e.g., restoration of sight). Jesus definitely claimed that his messianic visions were being fulfilled in the miracles he was performing, and that his preaching the Good News to the poor (see comment on 5:3) was fulfilling the messianic promises of Isa 61:1–2 (cf. Lk 4:17–21). The powers of darkness were being undermined; the kingdom was advancing (cf. v.12).

But there is a second, more subtle level to Jesus' response. All four Isaiah passages refer to judgment in their immediate context: e.g., "your God will come ... with vengeance; with divine retribution" (35:4); "the day of vengeance of our God" (Isa 61:2). Thus Jesus was allusively responding to the Baptist's question: the blessings promised for the end time have broken out and prove it is here, even though the judgments are delayed.

Verse 6 is then a gentle warning, applicable both to John and his disciples: "Blessed" (see comment on 5:3) is the one who does not find in Jesus and his ministry an obstacle to belief and therefore reject him. The miracles themselves were not irrefutable proof of who Jesus was (see comments on Mk 8:11–12); faith was still required to read the evidence against the background of Scripture and to hear in Jesus' claim the ring of truth.

b. Jesus' testimony to John (11:7–19)

(1). John in redemptive history (11:7–15)

John had often borne witness to Jesus; now Jesus bears witness to John. But, as we will see, the effect is to point back to himself as the sole figure who brings in the kingdom. Historically it was almost inevitable for Jesus to define the position of John the Baptist with respect to himself.

7–8 Jesus used this opportunity to speak to the crowd about John and to defend him. The rhetorical questions are a gently ironic way of eliminating obviously false answers in order to give the truth in vv.10–11. A "reed" (cane grass, found in abundance along the Jordan) swaying in the wind suggests a fickle person, tossed about in his judgment by the winds of public opinion or private misfortune. Certainly the people did not go out to witness such an ordinary spectacle. Nor did they go out into the desert to find a rich man dressed "in fine clothes" (see comment on 3:4–6). "Those who are ... in kings' palaces" is a sly cut at the man who was keeping John in prison.

Jesus was speaking in this way to disarm suspicion among the people that John's question (v.3) might betray signs of fickleness (v.7) or undisciplined weakness (v.8) in him. Not so, responds Jesus; the man the people went out to see was neither unstable nor faithless. His question arose not from personal weakness or failure but from misunderstanding about the nature of the Messiah, owing to John's place in salvation history (see comment on v.11).

9–11 What the people had flocked to the desert to see was a "prophet" (v.9), since it was commonly agreed that a true prophet had not appeared for centuries. Small wonder there was such excitement. Jesus confirms the crowd's judgment but goes beyond it—John was not only a prophet but more than a prophet. In what respect? Not only was he, like other OT prophets, a direct spokesman for God to call the nation to repentance, but he himself was also the subject of prophecy—the one who, according to Scripture, would announce the Day of the Lord (v.10).

MATTHEW 11

This is the traditional spot along the Jordan River where tradition says that John the Baptist preached and baptized.

The primary passage being cited is Mal 3:1 (see comment on Mk 1:2–3). The messenger of Mal 3:1 ("Elijah" in Mal 4:5–6) prepares the way for the great and dreadful Day of the Lord. John is that forerunner prophesied in the OT, and Jesus himself is that one who is now bringing in the Day of the Lord. Verse 10 ties v.9 and v.11 together. By citing Malachi, Jesus has shown in what way John the Baptist is greater than a prophet: he is greater in that he alone of all the prophets was the forerunner who prepared the way for the Lord Jesus and personally pointed him out (see Jn 1:19, 26–27; 3:25–30). This is what makes John the greatest born of women (v.11; i.e., the greatest human being).

Thus far the argument flows coherently. But who is the "least in the kingdom of heaven," and how is he greater than John the Baptist? For one thing, Jesus is implying that with John the Baptist, the kingdom had not yet come. Parallels between John's and Jesus' preaching are readily explained (see comment on 4:17), and v.12 can best be taken that way as well (see below).

In what way, then, is the least in the kingdom greater than John the Baptist? The answer must not be in terms of mere privilege (i.e., the least are greater because they see the kingdom actually inaugurated) but in terms of the greatness established for John. He was the greatest of the prophets because he pointed most unambiguously to Jesus. Nevertheless even the least in the kingdom is even greater because, living after the crucial revelatory and eschatological events have occurred, he or she points to Jesus still more unambiguously than John the Baptist.

This interpretation accomplishes three things. (1) It continues a defense of John by showing that his question owes its origin to his still-veiled place in the redemptive history now unfolding. (2) By contrast it continues the theme of discipleship whose essential function is to acknowledge Jesus before others (10:32–33) and establishes that function as the disciples' essential greatness. Even the least in the kingdom points to Jesus Christ more clearly than all his predecessors, including John. For they either live through the tumultuous events of the ministry, Passion, and beyond, after which things are much clearer; or they enter the kingdom after these events, with the same clear understanding. Thus the ground is being laid for the Great Commission: clear witness to Christ before others is not only a requirement of the kingdom (10:32–33) and a command of the resurrected Lord (28:18–20) but the true greatness of the disciple (11:11). (3) At the same time, by explaining John's greatness and his place in salvation history, this verse points back to the preeminence of Jesus himself.

12 This enigmatic saying has called forth a host of interpretations. The following interpretation does justice both to the context and to the language. "From the days of John the Baptist until now" means "from the time of the activity of John the Baptist." This expression does not say that John inaugurates the kingdom but only that during his time of ministry it was inaugurated and attacked. The expression assumes that the crucial period of his ministry during which the kingdom was inaugurated lies in the past. That kingdom has now begun, in however preliminary a way, with Jesus' preaching and powerful works during "the days of John the Baptist," and it is continuing. Thus there is

55

no reason why the Prophets and the Law should not prophesy "until John" in an inclusive sense (v.13).

The phrase "the kingdom of heaven has been forcefully advancing" suggests that the kingdom has come with holy power and magnificent energy that have been pushing back the frontiers of darkness. This is especially manifest in Jesus' miracles and ties in with Jesus' response to the Baptist (v.5). Some kind of compulsion even of people is presupposed elsewhere (Lk 14:23).

Regarding "and forceful men lay hold of it," Jesus seems to be suggesting that as the kingdom has been forcefully advancing, violent or rapacious people have been trying to plunder it. In other words, Jesus sets up the picture of a violent struggle being waged even as Jesus speaks. The kingdom inaugurated by Jesus has not swept all opposition away, as John expected (see comment on vv.2–4).

To summarize, simultaneous with the kingdom's advance have been the attacks of violent people on it. That is the very point John could not grasp. Now Jesus expressly affirms it. The statement is general because it does not refer to just one kind of opposition. It includes Herod's imprisonment of John, the attacks by Jewish leaders now intensifying (9:34; 12:22–24), and the materialism that craved a political Messiah and the prosperity he would bring but not his righteousness (11:20–24). Already Jesus warned his disciples of persecution and suffering (10:16–42); the opposition was rising and would get worse. Meanwhile, not the aggressive zealots will find rest for their souls, but the weary and burdened children to whom the Father revealed truth (vv.25–30).

13 In view of the preceding, "until John" means up to and including John. John the Baptist belongs to the last stage of the divine economy before the inauguration of the kingdom. The entire OT has a prophetic function, a function it maintained up until, and including, John the Baptist.

In the twin settings of Matthew's "fulfillment" theme (see comments on 2:15; 5:17–20) and the role of John the Baptist (11:10), it is understood that now, after John the Baptist, that which the Prophets and Law prophesied has come to pass—the kingdom has dawned and Messiah has come. This establishes the primary function of the OT in Matthew's gospel: it points to Jesus and the kingdom—this confirms our interpretation of 5:17–20. And from the time of the inauguration of the kingdom, the kingdom itself has been forcefully advancing.

14–15 The argument returns to vv.9–10, stating explicitly what Jesus said there: John the Baptist was the prophesied "Elijah" (v.14). This locates his place and function in the history of redemption and affirms again that what Jesus was doing was bringing in the Day of the Lord. The clause "if you are willing to accept it" does not cast doubt on the truth of the identification; but, like v.15, it acknowledges how difficult it was to grasp it, especially before the Cross and the Resurrection. The formula in v.15 is both a metaphorical description of and a challenge to spiritual sensitivity to the claims of the Gospel.

(2). The unsatisfied generation (11:16–19)

16–17 "Comparison" stands at the heart of Jesus' parables (see introductory comment on Mk 4). Here Jesus uses an analogy to show his view of his generation in connection with their general rejection of himself as Messiah (see comment on Lk 7:29–35). This identification of "this generation" (GK *1155*) is confirmed by the next pericope (vv.20–24).

18–19 "For" shows that Jesus now gives the reason why the behavior of "this generation" suggests the above comparison. John the Baptist lived ascetically, neither indulging in dinner parties (cf. 3:4) nor drinking alcohol (cf. Lk 1:15). Although he drew crowds (vv.7–8), yet the people as a whole rejected him, even charging him with demon possession. Jesus came eating and drinking (9:10–11) and was charged with gluttony, drunkenness, and bad associations. Like disgruntled children, "this generation" found it easier to whine their criticisms and voice their discontent than to "play the game" (see comment on Lk 7:29–35).

But the criticism runs at a still deeper level. If they had understood John, they would have understood Jesus, and vice versa; the thought has links with vv.7–15.

The closing proverb has provoked much debate because Luke has "all her children" (Lk 7:35) and Matthew "her actions." The proverb should be read in the light of the preceding parable: God's wisdom has been vindicated by the lifestyles of both John and Jesus, referred to in the previous verses. Wisdom in the OT is much concerned with right living. John and Jesus have both been criticized and rejected for the way they live. But wisdom, preeminently concerned about right living, has been vindicated by her actions: their respective lifestyles are both acknowledged.

2. The condemned and the accepted (11:20–30)

a. The condemned: woes on unrepentant cities (11:20–24)

The denunciation in the last section now becomes sharper. Structurally this section has e two series of warnings, each with the same sequence of warning, explanation, and comparison.

20 The verb "denounce" (GK 3943) is a strong verb, conveying indignation along with either insults (as in 5:11) or justifiable reproach. Jesus did not denounce these cities for vicious opposition but because, despite the fact that most of his miracles took place there—miracles that attested his messianic mission (vv.5–6)—they had not repented (see comments on 3:2; 4:17). The many miracles again remind us of the extent of Jesus' ministry and of the depth of responsibility imposed on those with more light.

21–22 The word translated "woe" (GK 4026) can mean doom or pity ("alas"); both are mingled here. Warnings have been given before; now woes are pronounced. Korazin may probably be identified with Kirbet Keraze, about two miles northwest of Capernaum. The Bethsaida in question was probably the home of Andrew, Peter, and Philip (Jn 1:44; 12:21) on the west side of Galilee. Tyre and Sidon were large Phoenician cities on the Mediterranean, not far away, and often denounced by OT prophets for their Baal worship (Isa 23; Eze 26–28; et al.). "Sackcloth" is a rough fabric made from the short hairs of camels and usually worn next to the skin to express grief or sorrow (2Sa 3:31; 1Ki 21:27; et al.).

Three theological propositions are presupposed by Jesus' insistence that on the Day of Judgment, things will go worse for the cities that have received so much more light than for the pagan cities. (1) The Judge has contingent knowledge; he knows what Tyre and Sidon would have done under such-and-such circumstances. (2) God does not owe revelation to anyone. (3) Punishment on the Day of Judgment takes into account opportunity. There are degrees of felicity in paradise and degrees of torment in hell (12:41; 23:13; cf. Lk 12:47–48), a point Paul well understood (Ro 1:20–2:16).

23–24 For Capernaum, see comment on 4:13. This city was not only Jesus' base (4:13), but he performed many specific miracles there (8:5–17; 9:2–8, 18–33). The favored city of Capernaum, like self-exalting Babylon (cf. Isa 14:15), will be brought down "to the depths" (i.e., Hades; GK 87; see comment on Mk 9:42–49). Hades must here be given rather sinister overtones. Capernaum's fate will be worse even than that of Sodom (see Ge 19). In the words "I tell you" (v.22), "you" is plural, probably implying the crowd (v.7), since the singular "you" is used for the city (vv.23–24).

b. The accepted (11:25–30)

If vv.20–24 describe those who are condemned, vv.25–30 describe those who are accepted.

25 "At that time" loosely joins this section with the immediate context. Matthew assumes that there has been some success in the mission of Jesus (and the disciples), but he draws a sharp antithesis between the recipients of such revelation and the "wise and learned" who, like the inhabitants of the cities just denounced, understand nothing.

Here Jesus addresses God as "Father" and "Lord of heaven and earth." These are particularly appropriate titles—the former indicating Jesus' sense of sonship (see comment on 6:9) and preparing for v.27, the latter recognizing God's sovereignty over the universe and preparing for vv.25–26. God is sovereign, free to conceal or reveal as he wills.

Many restrict the "wise and learned" to the Pharisees and teachers of the law, but the context implies something broader. Jesus has just finished pronouncing woes on "this generation" (v.16) and denouncing entire cities (vv.20–24). These are the ones from whom the real significance of Jesus' ministry is concealed. The contrast is between those who are self-sufficient and deem themselves wise and those who are dependent and love to be taught.

For revealing the riches of the good news of the kingdom to the one group and hiding it from the other, Jesus utters praise to his Father. We must not think of God's concealing and revealing as symmetrical activities arbitrarily exercised toward neutral human beings who are both innocent and helpless in the face of the divine decree. God is dealing with a race of sinners (cf. 1:21; 7:11) to whom he owes nothing. Thus to conceal "these things" is not an act of injustice but of judgment. The astonishing thing is that those who pride themselves in understanding divine things are judged, whereas those who understand nothing are taught. The predestination pattern is the counterpoint of grace.

26 Far from finding fault with his Father's revealing and concealing, Jesus delighted in it. Whatever pleases his Father pleases him. Jesus could simultaneously denounce the cities that did not repent and praise the God who does not reveal; for God's sovereignty in election is not mitigated by human stubbornness and sin, while human responsibility is in no way diminished by God's "good pleasure" that sovereignly reveals and conceals.

27 Like the term "Son of Man" (see comment on Mk 8:31), so with "Son of God," it appears that Jesus used this designation not firmly defined and open to several interpretations as part of his gradual self-disclosure—a revelation that could be fully grasped only after the Cross and Resurrection. Thus for Matthew there is no doubt of what Jesus is saying in v.27 because Matthew's "Son" or "Son of God" categories must be seen against the backdrop, not only of the prologue, but also of 3:17.

Verse 27 is a Christological claim of prime importance, fitting easily into the context. After vv.25-26, Jesus adds that he is the exclusive agent of the Father's revelation. The reciprocal knowledge of Son and Father, where the Father is God, presupposes a special sonship indeed. And this unique mutual knowledge guarantees that the revelation the Son gives is true. No mere mortal could honestly make the claim Jesus makes here. There is a self-enclosed world of Father and Son that is opened to others only by the revelation provided by the Son. The Son reveals the Father to those whom he, from time to time, wills (cf. Jn 3:35; 8:19; 10:15; 14:9). This text places enormous emphasis on Jesus' person and authority. What is made clear in this passage is that sonship and messiahship are not quite the same.

28 In the wake of v.27, the "me" of this verse is very important. Jesus invites to come to him, not "the wise and the learned" (v.25), but those who have become weary through heavy struggling and those who are overloaded like beasts of burden; and he (not the Father) will give them rest. There is an echo of Jer 31:25, where the Lord refreshes his people through the new covenant. It is impossible not to be reminded of the "heavy loads" the Pharisees put on people's shoulders (23:4). The "rest" (GK 399) is eschatological (cf. Rev 6:11; 14:13) but also a present reality—for the present world and the world to come.

29–30 The "yoke" (GK 2433), put on animals for pulling heavy loads, is a metaphor for the discipline of discipleship. If Jesus is not offering the yoke of the law, neither is he offering freedom from all constraints. The "yoke" is Jesus' yoke; discipleship must be *to him*. In view of v.27, the expression "learn from me" must mean "learn from the revelation that I alone impart."

The marvelous feature of this invitation is that out of his overwhelming authority (v.27) Jesus encourages the burdened to come to him because he is "gentle [GK 4558] and humble [GK 5424] in heart." Matthew stresses Jesus' gentleness (18:1–10; 19:13–15). Apparently the theme is connected with the messianic servant language (Isa 42:2–3; 53:1–2) that recurs in 12:15–21. Authoritative teacher that he is, Jesus approaches us with a true servant's gentleness.

The words "and you will find rest for your souls" (cf. v.28) are directly quoted from Jer 6:16. The entire verse is steeped in OT language; most likely this is a fulfillment passage, where Jesus is saying that "the ancient paths" and "the good way" of Jer 6:16 lie in taking on his yoke, because he is the one to whom the OT Scriptures point. The "rest" he promises is not only for the world to come but for this one as well. There is also irony here: Jesus offers real rest, while his opponents cannot do more than impose misguided standards of Sabbath rest (12:1ff.).

3. Sabbath conflicts (12:1–14)
a. Picking heads of grain (12:1–8)

Opposition to Jesus had already surfaced (9:3, 11, 14, 34; 10:25; 11:19). Now it erupts in a concrete issue that generates enough hatred to lead Jesus' enemies to contemplate murder (v.14).

1 The Jewish rules of conduct about the Sabbath were extremely detailed, though for many Jews of Jesus' day, the Sabbath was a joyful festival, a sign of the covenant, a reminder of divine creation in six days, and, provided the rules were obeyed, a means of gaining merit for Israel.

The point at issue in this section is burdensome Pharisaic regulations (cf. contrast to 11:28–30). The scene depicted here seems to be the disciples going on a Sabbath afternoon stroll within the permitted legal distance (a Sabbath day's journey); otherwise the Pharisees would not have been there. As they were doing so, they picked some grain along the path (see Dt 23:25).

2 The Pharisees' charge that the disciples were breaking the law was based, not on their picking grain in someone else's field, but on the fact that picking grain was one of thirty-nine kinds of work forbidden on the Sabbath under prevailing Jewish regulations. Though exceptions to these were granted in the case of temple service and where life was at stake, neither exception applied here.

3–4 The use of counterquestion and appeal to Scripture was common in rabbinic debates (cf. v.5; 19:4; 21:16, 42; 22:31). The account to which Jesus refers is from 1Sa 21:1–6. David entered the tabernacle at Nob, and he and his companions ate what should only have been eaten by the priests and did so after lying to the priest about their mission.

The argument takes a common rabbinical form, namely, the juxtaposition of two apparently contradictory statements from Scripture in order to draw a conclusion regarding regulations for conduct. On the one hand, David ate; on the other, it was unlawful for him to do so. Jesus' point is not simply that rules admit of exceptions but that the Scriptures themselves do not condemn David for his action; therefore the rigidity of the Pharisees' interpretation of the law is not in accord with Scripture itself, for they could not explain the incident of David.

How, then, does this apply to Jesus and his disciples? They were not desperate and famished, unlike David and his men. It is not even clear how they were breaking any OT law, where commandments about the Sabbath were aimed primarily at regular work. It seems that Jesus used the David incident not merely to question the Pharisees' view of the Sabbath; rather, he was questioning their approach to the law itself.

There is more. In the incident to which Jesus referred, regulations (even of the written law) were set aside for David "and his companions." Is there not therefore a case for setting aside regulations for Jesus and those with him? This analogy holds good only if Jesus is at least as special as David, and it is to this conclusion that the argument builds in the following verses.

5–6 Jesus' second appeal is from Nu 28:9–10. Formally speaking the Levitical priests "desecrate" the Sabbath every week, since the right worship of God in the temple required them to do some work (changing the consecrated bread [Lev 24:8] and offering the doubled burnt offering [Nu 28:9–10]). In reality, of course, the priests were guiltless; the law that established the Sabbath also established the right of the priests to "desecrate" it.

But how does this apply to Jesus and his disciples? The form of the argument is valid only if the "one greater than the temple" is truly greater. So the question is: Who (or what) is greater than the temple? The most likely answer is that the "something greater" is either Jesus himself (the more likely interpretation; cf. 26:61; Jn 2:20–21) or the kingdom. In fact, the two merge. If the kingdom, it is the kingdom Jesus is inaugurating; if Jesus, it is not only Jesus as a man but as Messiah, Son of David (vv.3–4), Son of Man (v.8), the one who ushers in the Messianic Age.

Jesus' argument, then, provides an instance from the law itself in which the Sabbath restrictions were superseded by the priests because their cultic responsibilities took precedence: the temple, as it were, was greater than the Sabbath. But now, Jesus claims, "something [NIV note] greater than the temple is here." And that, too, takes precedence over the Sabbath. This solution is entirely consistent with what we have seen as Jesus' attitude to the law in this gospel. The law points to him and finds its fulfillment in him (see comments on 5:17–48). Not only, then, have the Pharisees mishandled the law by their traditions (vv.3–4), but they have failed to perceive who Jesus is. The authority of the temple laws shielded the priests from guilt; the authority of Jesus shields his disciples from guilt.

7–8 Again (cf. v.3) Jesus rebuked the Pharisees for their failure to understand the Scriptures (cf. Jn 5:39), particularly Hos 6:6 (cf. 9:13). Jesus claims, in effect, that the Pharisees had not really grasped the significance of the law. The accusers stand accused; the disciples are explicitly declared "innocent," because the Son of Man is Lord of the Sabbath. This claim is implicitly messianic; it places the Son of Man in a position to handle the Sabbath law any way he wills, or to supersede it in the same way that the temple requirements superseded the normal Sabbath restrictions (see comment on vv. 5–6).

b. Healing a man with a shriveled hand (12:9–14)

In this incident, it is Jesus' activity that is in question, not that of his disciples; and his argument holds deeper implications. The first-century Jews discussed at length what was permitted in caring for the sick on the Sabbath. Jesus' attitude was more fundamental: it is lawful to do good on the Sabbath.

9–10 The action moves from the field to the synagogue. Matthew makes plain the malice in the Pharisees. The form of the their question in v.10 is general. The customary Jewish ruling was that healing was permitted on the Sabbath when life was in danger, which of course did not apply here.

11–13 For the third time in this gospel, Jesus' argument depends on a contrast between animals and people (cf. 6:26; 10:31) and presupposes the greater value of human beings based on their special creation: humans alone are made in the image of God (Ge 1–2). Jesus assumes that the Pharisees would not hesitate to lift an animal out of a pit on the Sabbath.

Jesus responds by arguing in a manner similar to vv.5–6. The question is simply one of doing good. Was the Sabbath a day for evil activity—like the intentions of the Pharisees in questioning him—or for the beneficent action, like the healing about to be done? His subsequent healing, like that in 9:1–8, comes after the shocking word and therefore serves to confirm that word. It also confirms Jesus' claim to lordship over the Sabbath, as his healing in 9:1–8 confirmed his authority to forgive sins.

14 The Pharisees now want to kill Jesus—not because of his ruling on the Sabbath, but because of the real issue involved here, Jesus' claim as Lord of the Sabbath. The Sabbath conflicts are merely the occasion of the plotting. Note that Sabbath disputes were not mentioned at Jesus' trials; in themselves they were never as much an issue as Jesus' claim to be Sabbath's Lord.

4. Jesus the prophesied Servant (12:15–21)

In this section, Matthew interprets Jesus' healing ministry in terms of the Lord's Suffering Servant (see also comment on 8:17). This section simultaneously contrasts the hatred of the Pharisees (v.14) with Jesus' tranquility (v.19) and gentleness (v.20) and prepares the way for themes in the rest of the chapter.

15–17 Jesus often withdrew when opposition became intense (cf. 4:12; 14:13; 15:21; 16:5); at least that was his custom until the appointed hour arrived (26:45). Thus his extensive ministry continued. Warnings to those healed to keep silent increased for the same reasons as before and with as little effect (cf. 8:4; 9:30). But Jesus' conduct under these pressures was nothing less than the fulfillment of the Scriptures. Though the Pharisees might plot to kill him (v.14), he would not quarrel or cry out (v.19). Matthew wants to separate himself from exclusively royal and militaristic interpretations of Messiah's role. He knows that the ministry of Jesus Messiah must also be understood as the fulfillment of the prophecies of the Suffering Servant.

18–21 This quotation from Isa 42:1–4 is the longest one in Matthew. Jesus is God's "chosen" (GK *1721*) or elect Servant, the one on whom God has poured out his Spirit with a specific mission in view. The words "the one I love" carry overtones of Mt 3:17; 17:5, because love and election are closely connected. God's "delight" (GK *2305*) in his servant and the mention of the Spirit God puts on him remind us of both Jesus' baptism and his transfiguration (3:16–17; 17:5).

This "servant" (GK *4090*) will proclaim "justice" (GK *3213*) to the nations—i.e., righteousness broadly conceived as the self-revelation of God's character for the good of the nations (cf. Isa 51:4), yet at the same time calling them to account. Concern for the Gentiles thus emerges again (cf. 1:1, 2:1–12; 3:9; 4:15–16; et al.) in anticipation of the Great Commission (28:18–20).

The servant "will not quarrel or cry out" or raise his voice in the streets (v.19). The picture is not one of utter silence (else how could he "proclaim" justice) but of gentleness and humility (11:29), and of quiet withdrawal (see comment on vv.15–17).

The double metaphor in the first two lines of v.20 breathes compassion: the servant does not advance his ministry with such callousness to the weak that he breaks the bruised reed or snuffs out the smoldering wick. This suggests, in the light of the last line of this verse, that he brings eschatological salvation to the "harassed and helpless" (9:36), the "weary and burdened" (11:28). What is pictured is a ministry so gentle and compassionate that the weak are not trampled on and crushed till the full righteousness of God triumphs. Small wonder that the Gentiles ("nations"; GK *1620*) would put their hope in his name (cf. Isa 11:10; Ro 15:12).

5. Confrontation with the Pharisees (12:22–45)

a. The setting and accusation (12:22–24)

22 The demon possession was the likely cause of this man's blindness and muteness (see comment on 9:32). The healing itself is told with admirable brevity, for it is not so much the miracle itself that captures the attention of Matthew but the confrontation with the Pharisees that follows.

23–24 The astonishment of the crowd prompted the question (v.23). Its form in Greek suggests the crowds were none too sure: "This couldn't be the Son of David [i.e., the Messiah], could it?" The Messiah was expected to perform miracles (cf. v.38), so the exorcism-healing stood in Jesus' favor. But perhaps his reticence, his nonregal sayings, and his servant ministry engendered doubt. On "Beelzebub" (v.24), see comment on 10:25.

b. Jesus' reply (12:25–37)

25–26 Knowing the thoughts of the Pharisees (v.26), Jesus points out that any kingdom, city, or household that develops internal strife will destroy itself; the same is true for Satan's "kingdom."

27 Jesus' argument here is ad hominem: he is saying "your sons" (either the Jews in general or people instructed by the Pharisees) cast out demons on occasion and their limited success must be due not to Beelzebub but to God's power. Jesus is even more successful and does even greater damage to Satan's kingdom. Surely, Jesus implies, this is also evidence of God's great power.

28 Jesus knows that his exorcisms, performed by the Spirit of God, prove that the kingdom age has already dawned. Of course, this also implies that Jesus is King Messiah without explicitly affirming it. This is one of only four places in Matthew where "kingdom of God" occurs instead of "kingdom of heaven" (see comment on 3:2).

29 Jesus now asks the Pharisees to look at this through a parable. Jewish expectation looked forward to the binding of Satan in the Messianic Age; under this metaphor Jesus is the one who ties up the strong man (Satan) and carries off his "possessions." The argument has thus advanced: if Jesus' exorcisms cannot be attributed to Satan (vv.25–26), then they reflect authority greater than that of Satan. By this greater power Jesus is binding "the strong man" and plundering his "house." So the kingdom of heaven is forcefully advancing (see comment on 11:12).

30 In our relationship to Jesus there can be no neutrality. Perhaps neutrality is possible and even wise regarding some issues and persons, but in life's great struggle (cf. vv.25–29), neutrality is impossible. The claims of the kingdom and the demands of Jesus are so exclusivistic that to be indifferent or apathetic to him is to be on the side of those who do not confess that he is the Messiah who brings in the kingdom of God (cf. 11:16–24). Jesus' claim implies a high Christology; he is the one who will harvest in the last days, a function that the OT regularly assigns to God.

31–32 "And so" ties the statements about blasphemy against the Spirit (v.31) to the preceding verse. But the transition cannot easily be readily grasped till vv.31–32 are understood. "Blasphemy" (GK *1060*) is extreme slander, equivalent to "speaking against" (cf. v.32). Blasphemy against God was viewed by Jews with utmost gravity (26:65); but here Jesus makes a sharp distinction between blasphemy against the Son of Man, which is forgivable, and blasphemy against the Spirit, which is not.

His statement is remarkable because one of the glories of the biblical faith is the great emphasis Scripture lays on the graciousness and wideness of God's forgiveness (e.g., Ps 130:3–4; Isa 1:18; Mic 7:19; 1Jn 1:7). Among the many interpretations of this difficult saying, the best treats it in its setting during Jesus' life. The Pharisees have been attributing to Satan the work of the Spirit and have been doing so, as Jesus makes plain, in such a way as to reveal that they speak, not out of ignorance or unbelief, but out of a conscious disputing of what should never be disputed.

The distinction between blasphemy against the Son of Man and blasphemy against the Spirit is that the first sin is rejection of the truth of the Gospel (for which there may be repentance and forgiveness), whereas the second sin is rejection of the same truth in full awareness that that is exactly what one is doing—willfully, thoughtfully, and self-consciously rejecting the work of the Spirit even though there can be no other explanation of Jesus' exorcisms than that. For such a sin there is no forgiveness, "either in this age or the age to come" (cf. 13:22; 25:46)—a dramatic way of saying "never" (as in Mk 3:29). This interpretation can also apply to Heb 6:4–6; 10:26–31; and possibly 1Jn 5:16.

If this interpretation is correct, the distinction between Son of Man and Spirit is relatively incidental. After all, blasphemy against the Spirit is also a rejection of Jesus' own claims. Jesus charges that those who perceive that his ministry is empowered by the Spirit and then, for whatever reason—whether from spite, jealousy, or arrogance—ascribe it to Satan, have put themselves beyond the pale.

The significance of the transitional words "And so" now becomes plain. Neutrality to Jesus is actually opposition to him (v.30); and therefore Jesus gives this warning regarding those who blaspheme against the Spirit, since the self-professedly neutral person may not recognize the inherent danger of his position.

33–35 Jesus tells his hearers to make a tree good or bad, knowing that its fruit will be correspondingly good or bad, because a tree is recognized by its fruit. Then Jesus drives the point home. "You brood of vipers" was most likely addressed to the Pharisees in the crowd. Verse 35 makes a tight connection with v.33: what a person truly is determines what that person says and does. Out of the "heart" (GK *2840*), the center of human personality, the "mouth speaks," revealing what is in the heart. How, then, can those who are evil say anything good? What is needed is a change of heart.

36–37 A person will be held accountable on the Day of Judgment for every seemingly insignificant word spoken insofar as it reveals what is in the heart. Every spoken word reflects the heart's overflow and is known to God. Therefore words are of critical importance (cf. Eph 5:3–4, 12; Col 3:17; Jas 1:19; 3:1–12).

c. Continued confrontation (12:38–42)

38 The Jewish leaders addressed Jesus respectfully ("Teacher") and asked for a "sign," not just for another miracle. A "sign" (GK *4956*) was usually some miraculous token to be fulfilled quickly or at once, in order to confirm a prophecy. The Jews were not asking for just another miracle, since they had already persuaded themselves that at least some of those Jesus had performed were of demonic agency (12:24); they were asking for a "sign" performed on command to remove what seemed to them to be the ambiguity of Jesus' miracles.

39–40 The Pharisees and teachers of the law, in Jesus' view, represented this "wicked and adulterous generation" (v.39; cf. 11:16–24). "Adultery" was frequently used by OT prophets to describe the spiritual prostitution and wanton apostasy of Israel (Isa 50:1; Jer 3:8; Eze 16:15, 32, 35–42; et al.). Jesus applies this metaphor to his contemporaries. Although Israel had abandoned idolatry after the exile, Jesus insists that she was still adulterous in heart. In the past God had graciously granted "signs" to strengthen the faith of the timid (e.g., Abraham [Ge 15]; Gideon [Jdg 6:17–24]). Here, however, Jesus says that signs are denied, because they are never to be performed on demand or as a sop to unbelief (cf. 1Co 1:22). The sign Jesus does offer, the "sign of Jonah," is not a sign at all as Jesus' opponents understood the word. It becomes a sign only for those with eyes to see.

But what is "the sign of Jonah"? "Of Jonah" must be construed as an explanatory phrase. It is a sign that Jonah himself *was*, not the sign given him or presented by him. This interpretation accepts the view that the Ninevites learned what had happened to Jonah and how he got to their city. Jonah himself thus served as a "sign" to them, for he appeared to them as one who had been delivered from certain death. As Jonah was three days and three nights in the belly of the fish, so the Son of Man will be buried three days and three nights in the earth. That is to say, Jesus' preaching will be attested by a deliverance like Jonah's, only greater; therefore, there will be greater condemnation for those who reject the significance of Jesus' deliverance. Note that this explanation rightly assumes that Jesus knew long in advance about his death, burial, and resurrection, and saw his life moving toward that climax (see 16:21).

Jonah spent "three days and three nights" in the fish (Jnh 1:17). But if the normal sequence of Passion Week is correct (see comments on Mk 14:1–2, 12), Jesus was in the tomb only about thirty-six hours. Since they included parts of three days, by Jewish reckoning Jesus was buried "three days" or, to put it another way, he rose "on the third day" (16:21). But this does not cover more than two nights. Some advocate a Wednesday crucifixion date; but though that allows for "three days and three nights," it runs into difficulty with "on the third day." According to Jewish tradition, a day and a night make an *onah*, and a part of an *onah* is as the whole. Thus, "three days and three nights" need mean no more than "three days" or the combination of any part of three days.

41 The first point of comparison between Jonah and Jesus is that they were both delivered from death—a deliverance that attested to the trustworthiness of their preaching. The second point of comparison is the different responses of the hearers. The people of Nineveh repented; but even though one greater than Jonah is here (i.e., Jesus), people are not repenting. The Ninevites will rise to bear witness against this generation on the Day of Judgment. Thus Jesus' "sign" did not meet the Jews' demand for a special token (see comment on v.38), yet it was the only one he would provide. For his own followers, his authority will be grounded in his death and resurrection. And as for those who do not believe, they will only prove themselves more wicked than the Ninevites.

42 The queen of the South was the queen of Sheba (1Ki 10:1–13), who came to Jerusalem because of reports of Solomon's wisdom. But Jesus is "one greater than Solomon"; he is the Messiah. Thus the queen of Sheba will rise at the Judgment to join the Ninevites in condemning the unbelieving generation of Jesus' time.

d. The return of the evil spirit (12:43–45)

This story about the unclean spirit who after being driven out returns with seven wicked spirits is set in the context of Jesus' veiled messianic claims. Those who through the kingdom power of God experience exorcisms must beware of neutrality toward Jesus the Messiah, for neutrality opens the door to demons even worse than the one driven out. Commitment to Jesus is essential.

43 When an evil spirit leaves a person, it goes "through arid places" in search of rest. This conforms to the view that demons have an affinity for such places. Ultimately, however, they seek another body in order to do even more harm.

44–45 Verse 44 is essentially a conditional clause to v.45: "If the demon on his arrival finds the house unoccupied [etc.]," it reenters the person with seven more demons. That person is now in a far worse condition than before. Jesus' final statement here closes off the main part of this section by referring again to "this wicked generation" (cf. 12:39) and by stressing the danger of neutrality to the claims of Jesus.

6. Doing the Father's will (12:46–50)

These verses are not so much a confrontation between Jesus and his family (cf. comments on Mk 3:31–35) as a statement about what it really means to be a disciple of Jesus and to be totally committed to him. The way for us to be as close to Jesus as his nearest and dearest kin is to do the will of his Father.

46–47 Jesus is presumably inside the house. The "brothers" mentioned here refer most naturally to sons of Mary and Joseph and thus to brothers of Jesus on his mother's side (contrary to the later dogma of the perpetual virginity of Mary).

48–50 Jesus' searching question and its remarkable answer in no way diminish his mother and brothers but simply give the priority to his Father and doing his will. Henceforth the disciples are the only "family" Jesus recognizes. Yet we do not *make ourselves* Jesus' close relatives by doing the will of his heavenly Father; rather, doing that will *identifies* us as his mother and sisters and brothers (cf. 7:21). The doing of God's will turns on obedience to Jesus and his teaching, for it was Jesus who preeminently revealed the will of the Father (cf. 11:27). These verses are full of Christological implications, but they also establish the basic importance of the community now beginning to form around him.

B. Third Discourse: The Parables of the Kingdom (13:1–53)

1. The setting (13:1–3a)

1 Matthew links the discourse on parables to the preceding controversies (either 12:38–50 or 12:22–37) and ends it with a formulaic conclusion (13:53), which implies that all these parables were given on this occasion. Jesus "sat by the lake," taking the normal position of a teacher (see comments on 5:1–2). During his ministry his chosen role was that of a teacher who taught others about the kingdom so that they might teach others (see comments on vv.51–52).

2 This is the only one of the five major discourses in Matthew that is addressed to the crowds in general. Therefore Matthew includes in it two major digressions (vv.10–23, 36–43) to explain to his disciples the significance of parables and to interpret two of them. While these digressions doubtless took place after the public discourse, Matthew moves them back as parentheses so that the significance of the parables will not be lost to the reader.

3a Jesus told the crowd "many things in parables." For a brief description of "parable," see introductory comment on Mk 4.

Regarding this chapter, if v.52 is seen as a parable, then the discourse can be broken down into two parts of four parables each (vv.3–33, 44–52). The first four are addressed to the crowds, the last four to the disciples. Of the first four parables, the first stands apart from the other three with a different introduction, separated by discussion about the purpose of the parables (vv.10–17) and the interpretation of the parable (vv.18–23). The other three have similar beginnings. The second half begins with three parables with the same opening and is separated from the fourth, which has a different beginning and an explanation, followed by the question and answer about the disciples' understanding of parables. Between these two sets of four are vv.34–43, which explore the function of parables and expound one of them. This structure is called "chiastic."

2. To the crowds (13:3b–33)

a. The parable of the soils (13:3b–9)

3b–7 The focus of this parable is not the sower but the soils. The farmer scatters the seed, which falls in various places. Paths run through and around the unfenced fields, which are too hard to receive the seed; it is eaten by birds. "Rocky places" are those in which the limestone bedrock lies close to the surface; there is little depth of soil. As the rainy season ends and the sun's heat increases, the shallow soil heats up quickly. The seeds sprout and promise to be the best of the crop. But the unrelenting summer heat demands that plants send deep roots down for water, and the bedrock prevents this, so they wither. Like grass on rooftops, the young plants wither before they can grow (Ps 129:6). Other seed falls into hedges of thorns that deprive the plants of needed sun and nourishment.

8–9 But some seed falls on good soil and produces crops of various yields, which are well within ordinary expectations. The same seed produces no crop, some crop, or much crop—all according to the soil's character. The final exhortation (cf. 11:15) warns Jesus' hearers and Matthew's readers that the parable needs careful interpretation.

b. Interlude and interpretation (13:10–23)

Matthew's treatment of the reason for parables (vv.10–17) includes more OT Scripture than Mk 4:10–12 or Lk 8:9–10 and is structured with great care. The disciples' question evokes Jesus' basic answer, which is then applied in greater detail first to "them" (vv.13–15) and then to "you" (the disciples; vv.16–18).

10 "The disciples" approached Jesus, apparently in private (cf. Mk 4:10). If this occurred at the end of the discourse, the plural "parables" would be well accounted for. The focus of Jesus' reply (vv.11–17) is on the fact that the revelation is given to some and not to others and why this is so.

11–12 Jesus' answer cannot legitimately be softened: at least one of the functions of parables is to conceal the truth, or at least *to present it in a veiled way*. In fact, it is entirely possible that the first word in Jesus' response (left untranslated in NIV) is "because." The disciples ask, "Why do you speak, etc.?" and Jesus replies, "*Because* the secrets of the kingdom have been given to the disciples but not to the others listening to me."

"The secrets [lit., "mysteries"; GK 3696] of the kingdom" are divine plans or decrees, often passed on in veiled language, known only to the elect and usually relating to events of the end time. For these secrets to be "given to" the disciples suggests that to them certain eschatological realities are being revealed. What is revealed is not who Jesus is, the nature of God, or the power of love (all of which have been suggested); rather, Jesus is revealing that the kingdom of God, especially as foreseen in Daniel, has in fact entered the world and is working, although secretly, among humankind (see comment on Mk 4:11–12).

The antithesis of v.12 is proverbial and repeated elsewhere (25:29; cf. Mk 4:25; Lk 8:18). It warns against taking spiritual blessings for granted and serves to increase gratitude and a sense of privilege among those who continue to enjoy them. What is lost in the second part of the antithesis is one's standing as the expected subject of the kingdom (cf. 8:11–12).

13 Jesus now explicitly applies his answer of vv.11–12 to those who are not disciples. Whereas Mark introduces this quote from Isaiah with "so that" (see comment on Mk 4:12), Matthew introduces it with "because," which means that Jesus speaks in parables because the people are spiritually insensitive. Though they "see," they do not *really* "see."

In other words, in v.11–12 Jesus acknowledges that he has chosen his disciples to understand his mysteries. Now in v.13, he gives the human reason behind his election process: spiritual dullness on the part of the crowd. Jesus affirms that what is taking place in his ministry is, on the one hand, the decreed will of God and the result of biblical prophecy and, on the other hand, a terrible rebellion and chronic unbelief. This places the responsibility for the divine rejection of those who fail to become disciples on their own shoulders while guaranteeing that none of what is taking place stands outside God's control and plan. The same sort of pairing has already been expressed in 11:25–30.

This sheds much light on the parables. It is naive to say Jesus spoke them so that everyone might more easily grasp the truth, and it is simplistic to say that the sole function of parables to outsiders was to condemn them. If Jesus simply wished to hide the truth from the outsiders, he need never have spoken to them. His concern for mission (9:35–38; 10:1–10; 28:16–20) excludes that idea. So he must preach without casting his pearls before pigs (7:6). He does so in parables—i.e., in such a way as to harden and reject those who are hard of heart and to enlighten his disciples. His disciples, it must be remembered, are not just the Twelve but those who were following him (see comment on 5:1–12) and who, it is hoped, go on to do the will of the Father (12:50) and do not end up blaspheming the Spirit (12:30–32). Thus the parables spoken to the crowds do not simply convey information, nor mask it, but present the claims of the inaugurated kingdom and so challenge the hearers.

For example, the parables of the soils not only says that the kingdom advances slowly and with varied responses to the proclamation of that kingdom but implicitly challenges hearers to ask themselves what kinds of soil they are. Those whose hearts are hardened and who lose what little they have do not participate in the messianic kingdom they have been looking for, and for them the parable is a sentence of doom. Those who have ears to hear, to whom more is given,

The Parables of Jesus

Parable	Matthew	Mark	Luke
Lamp under a bowl	5:14–15	4:21–22	
Wise and foolish builders	7:24–27		
New cloth on an old garment	9:16	2:21	
New wine in old wineskins	9:17	2:22	
Sower and the soils	13:3–8, 18–23	4:3–8, 14–20	
Weeds	13:24–30, 36–43		
Mustard seed	13:31–32	4:30–32	
Yeast	13:33		
Hidden treasure	13:44		
Valuable pearl	13:45–46		
Net	13:47–50		
Owner of a house	13:52		
Lost sheep	18:12–14		
Unmerciful servant	18:23–34		
Workers in the vineyard	20:1–16		
Two sons	21:28–32		
Tenants	21:33–44	12:1–11	20:9–18
Wedding banquet	22:2–14		
Fig tree	24:32–35	13:28–29	21:29–31
Faithful and wise servant	24:45–51		12:42–48
Ten virgins	25:1–13		
Talents (minas)	25:14–30		19:12–27
Sheep and goats	25:31–46		
Growing seed		4:26–29	
Watchful servants		13:35–37	12:35–40
Moneylender			7:41–43
Good Samaritan			10:30–37
Friend in need			11:5–8
Rich fool			12:16–21
Unfruitful fig tree			13:6–9
Lowest seat at the feast			14:7–14
Great banquet			14:16–24
Cost of discipleship			14:28–33
Lost coin			15:8–10
Lost (prodigal) son			15:11–32
Shrewd manager			16:1–8
Rich man and Lazarus			16:19–31
Master and his servant			17:7–10
Persistent widow			18:2–8
Pharisee and tax collector			18:10–14

perceive and experience the dawning of the Messianic Age; and for them the parable conveys the mysteries of the kingdom.

14–15 Matthew goes on to give a "fulfillment formula" passage from Isa 6:9–10. The Messiah who comes to reveal the Father (11:25–27) succeeds only in dulling what little spiritual sense many of the people have, for they do not want to turn and be healed. The context of Isa 6:9–10 reveals that their dullness will continue "until the cities lie ruined . . . and the fields ruined and ravaged . . . and the land is utterly forsaken. . ." (Isa 6:11–13). The reference is to the Exile; but the events surrounding it are seen as a paradigm, the classic case of rejection of God and resulting judgment, repeated in Jesus' generation on a new level and so fulfilling the words of the prophecy.

The part of v.15 beginning with "Otherwise" expresses God's judgment: the people have closed their eyes as the result of divine judicial action, otherwise they might see and turn, etc. The thought then becomes similar to 2Th 2:11. Neither Jesus nor Matthew would see anything incongruous in God's judicial hardening (see comment on v.13).

16–17 For "blessed," see comment on 5:3. The disciples were blessed by God and privileged above the crowd because they saw and heard what "many prophets and righteous men" (v.17; 10:40–42) longed to see but did not. The reference is to OT prophets and others who were righteous before God—people who looked forward to the coming of the kingdom. Here one cannot help but include Simeon (Lk 2:25–35) and Anna (Lk 2:36–38). Just as the crowd in Jesus' day stands in the line of the willfully blind in the OT (vv.14–15), so Jesus' disciples stand in the line of the prophets (as in 5:11–12). The fulfillment motif is operating, showing that the division taking place with the coming of the kingdom stands in succession to the divisions already spelled out in the Scriptures.

18 Jesus now asks his disciples to listen to an explanation of the parable of the soils. The general point is that the "message about the kingdom" (v.19) receives a varied reception among various people, and that during this time of difficulty and frustration there is an implied delay while the seed produces in some soils its various yields. The interpretation therefore demands that each person examine how he or she "hears" (GK 201) the message.

19 Matthew plunges right into the significance of the various soils. The first soil (that which is "along the path") refers to those who hear the message about the kingdom, but, like hardened paths, do not let the truth penetrate their hearts (see comment on 5:8). Before they really understand it, the evil one (cf. 6:13; 12:45) or Satan (cf. Mk 4:15) has snatched it away. Close study of birds as symbols in the OT and especially in the literature of later Judaism shows that birds regularly symbolize evil and even demons or Satan (Rev 18:2).

20–21 The person who receives the message of the kingdom in a thoughtless way may show immediate signs of life and promise to be the best of the crop: he or she receives the truth "with joy." But without real root, there is no fruit; and external pressures, trouble, and persecution (cf. 24:9, 21, 29), like sun beating on a rootless plant, soon reveal the shallowness of this soil. Just as quickly such people fall away. Such temporary disciples are always numerous in times of revival and were so in Jesus' ministry (cf. comments on 12:32).

22 The seeds among thorns represent those who do not hear the word "with joy" (v.20) and never permit the message about the kingdom to control them: life has too many other commitments that slowly choke the struggling plant, so that it never matures and bears fruit. The competing "thorns" are summed up under two headings—the worries of this life (see comments on 6:25–34) and devotion to wealth (cf. 6:19–24; 1Ti 6:9). Such concerns snuff out spiritual life. "Deceitfulness" suggests that one may not be aware of the choking that is going on. This warning is timeless.

23 By contrast with the negative results of the preceding verses, we now come to the person who hears the word and understands it (thus reverting to the categories of Isa 6:9–10 used in vv.13–15, 19). The interpretation, like the parable itself, ends positively. And we must not fail to notice that the soil that produces only a small crop is nevertheless called "good" (cf. 25:22–23).

c. The parable of the weeds (13:24–30)

The parable of the soils shows that the kingdom will produce an abundant crop in spite of hard hearts, competing pressures, and even failure. But one might ask whether Messiah's people should immediately separate the crop from the weeds. This next parable answers that question negatively: there will be a delay in separation until the harvest. This parable also explains how it is possible for the kingdom to be present in the world while not wiping out all opposition.

24 Jesus "told them" (i.e., the people, not the disciples; cf. vv.34, 36) another parable. The kingdom of heaven "is like" the situation of "a man who sowed good seed in his field." The Greek tense used here implies that the kingdom *has become* like the situation of this man. What Jesus argues is both that the kingdom has come (see 4:17; 12:28) and that the Parousia is still delayed.

25–27 "Sleeping" does not imply that the servants were neglectful but that the enemy was stealthy and malicious. What he sowed in the field was almost certainly bearded darnel, which is botanically close to wheat and difficult to distinguish from it when the plants are young. The roots of the two plants entangle themselves around each other; but when the heads of grain appear on the wheat, there is no doubt which plant is which. As the growing takes place, the servants tell their master or the head of the house (see comment on 10:25) about the weeds.

28–30 The owner blames an enemy, but forbids his servants from attempting to separate weed from wheat till the harvest. Then, as the workers reap the field, only the wheat will be gathered; the weeds, apparently so plentiful they must first be gathered up and burned, contaminate the wheat no longer. "Harvest" is a common metaphor for the final judgment (see comment on 9:37–38).

d. The parable of the mustard seed (13:31–32)

31–32 The mustard seed is "the smallest of all your seeds," but it becomes a large tree—large in comparison with the tiny seed and large enough for birds to perch in its branches. The image recalls OT passages that picture a great kingdom as a large tree with birds flocking to its branches (Eze 17:22–24; 31:3–14; Dan 4:7–23). The point Jesus is making is that there is a basic connection between the small beginnings taking place under his ministry and the kingdom in its future glory. Though the initial appearance of the kingdom may seem inconsequential (and here is where the emphasis is), the tiny seed leads to the mature plant.

e. The parable of the yeast (13:33)

33 The general thrust of this parable is the same as that of the mustard seed. The kingdom produces ultimate consequences out of all proportion to its insignificant beginnings.

If there is a distinction between this parable and the last one, it is that the mustard seed suggests extensive growth and the yeast intensive transformation. The yeast doesn't grow, it permeates; and its inevitable effect, despite the small quantity used, recalls 5:13. In both parables it is clear that at present the kingdom of heaven operates, but quietly and from small beginnings.

3. Pause (13:34–43)

a. Parables as fulfillment of prophecy (13:34–35)

34 The first verb ("spoke") refers to the specific situation of Jesus speaking parables at that time; the second verb ("did not say") implies that this was Jesus' constant custom. This section does not mean that he told nothing but parables; rather, Matthew stresses that parables were an essential part of Jesus' spoken ministry.

35 Again Matthew introduces a fulfillment passage, quoting from Ps 78:2. In what sense can Jesus' ministry in parables be said to be a fulfillment of Asaph's psalm? Note especially that Ps 78 repeats Israel's well-known history, none of which is "mysterious" or "hidden." But Matthew presents Jesus as uttering hidden "secrets" (see comment on v.11). The point of Ps 78 is that though the history of the Jews is well known, the psalmist selects certain historical events and brings them together in such a way as to bring out things that have been riddles and enigmas "from of old." The pattern of history is not self-evident; but the psalmist shows what it is really all about. He enlarges on God's might at the time of the Exodus and at other major turning points, a might exercised on behalf of his people. With these events the psalmist

juxtaposes the people's persistent rebellion, the result being a vivid portrayal of God's justice and mercy and the people's obtuseness, need, and privilege. The psalmist teaches all this by opening his mouth "in parables" (i.e., by comparing various things) and in so doing utters "things hidden from of old."

Jesus has adopted a similar pattern. He applies the second line of the quotation to himself as revealing things formerly hidden. This does not necessarily mean that he is teaching entirely new things any more than the psalmist was teaching new things. In both cases the patterns of redemptive history may be so stressed that when rightly interpreted they point toward new revelation—i.e., they are fulfilled (see comments on 2:15; 5:17–20). Jesus teaches these hitherto hidden things "in parables" (i.e., by comparing various things). The parables of this chapter are not exactly like the comparisons and wise sayings offered in Ps 78, yet the term "parable" can embrace both kinds of utterance.

But what are these "hidden things" (GK 3221) that Jesus is now revealing? They are the righteous acts of God in redemption taking place in his teaching, miracles, death, and resurrection. Matthew insists that the OT Scriptures prophesied these things. They are not novel. If in one sense they have not been known before, it is because they have not all been brought together in the same pattern before. Jesus' kingdom parables to the crowds bring together various pieces of previous revelation into new perspectives. Thus the Messiah is Son of David but also a Suffering Servant. Jesus is the royal King and Son of David foreseen in Scripture (21:4–11) but also the stricken Shepherd equally foreseen in Scripture (26:31). Who clearly foresaw that both streams would merge in one person?

Regarding the idea of fulfillment, Matthew understands that what the prophets say does not necessarily predict the future in simple predictive propositions; it may reveal hidden things. The entire OT Scripture, both Law and Prophets, comprehends certain patterns, types, predictions, and declarations, which cumulatively look forward to him who "fulfills" them (cf. comment on 11:13). As such, Ps 78 becomes part of the "Law and Prophets" that prophesy. If part of this sacred record interprets and brings new truth out of an earlier part, it establishes a pattern that looks to one who will interpret and bring new truth out of the whole. Jesus, Matthew claims, fulfills that role and is exercising it in his own parabolic teaching.

b. Interpretation of the parable of the weeds (13:36–43)

36 The house referred to is the one Jesus left in order to preach to the crowds (13:1) and was probably located in Capernaum. In Matthew's narrative the house provides the setting both for Jesus' private explanations (vv.37–43; cf. vv.10–23) and for the parables aimed at his disciples (vv.44–52). The disciples need explanations (cf. also 15:15–16). They are not distinguished from the crowds by their instant and intuitive understanding but by their persistence in seeking explanations (see comment on vv.10–13).

37–39 On "Son of Man," see comment on Mk 8:31. Jesus is the one who both sows the good seed and directs the harvest. One of the most significant details in the parables is the way key images that in the OT apply exclusively to God, or occasionally to God's Messiah, now stand for Jesus himself. These images include sower, director of the harvest, rock, shepherd, bridegroom, father, giver of forgiveness, vineyard owner, lord, and king.

"The field is the world" (not to be confused with the church). This brief statement presupposes a mission beyond Israel (cf. 10:16–18; 28:18–20) and confirms that the narrower command of 10:5–6 is related exclusively to the mission of the Twelve during the period of Jesus' earthly ministry (see comment on 10:5b–6).

In this parable and its interpretation, unlike the parable of the sower, the good seed stands for the "sons of the kingdom" (cf. comment on 5:9)—a healthy reminder that images can symbolize different things in different contexts. It refers to those who truly are the objects of messianic favor and participants in the messianic kingdom. For their sake the "weeds" are now preserved, and at the "harvest" for their sake the "weeds" will be destroyed. These weeds are "the sons of the evil one." The devil himself is the enemy (v.39); the harvest is the end of the age (see comment on 9:37); and the harvesters are angels (24:30–31; 25:31).

40–42 The identification of the actors is over, and the description of the action begins. As the weeds are "pulled up" and burned, so it is at the end. The kingdom we have known as the kingdom of heaven is also seen as the kingdom of the Son of Man, Jesus' kingdom (cf. 20:21; 25:31; cf. Da 2:35; Rev 11:15); his reign after the Resurrection extends to the farthest reaches of the universe (28:18). In that sense, "everything that causes sin and all who do evil" are weeded out of his kingdom (see 5:29; 7:23; cf. Zep 1:3) and, like the weeds, are thrown into the eternal fiery furnace (see comment on Mk 9:43–49), where there will be weeping and gnashing of teeth (see comment on Mt 8:12). What is clear is that Jesus ascribes to himself the role of eschatological Judge that the Lord assigns himself in the OT.

43 In contrast to the evildoers, "the righteous will shine like the sun in the kingdom of their Father" (an allusion to Da 12:3). These righteous people (see comments on 5:20, 45; 9:13; 10:41), once the light of the world (5:13–16), now radiate perfection and experience bliss in the consummation of their hopes.

The "kingdom of their Father" must not be set over against the kingdom of the Son of Man (v.41) on the supposed ground that the former alone is eternal, or that the Son of Man hands over the elect to him (1Co 15:24). The Son's postascension reign is a mediated reign. All God's kingly authority is given to Jesus (28:18) and mediated through him; and for all that time the kingdom can be called the kingdom of God or the kingdom of the Son of Man or, more generally, the kingdom of heaven.

4. To the disciples (13:44–52)

a. The parable of the hidden treasure (13:44)

The parables of the hidden treasure and the pearl are a pair; and pairing is not uncommon in Matthew (e.g., 5:14b–16; 6:26–30; 7:6; et al.), an excellent way of reinforcing a point. These two parables make the same general point but have significant individual emphases. They both deal with the superlative worth of the kingdom of heaven. Note, though, that the kingdom is not exclusively future here, but seen as already present (see comments on 4:17; 12:28).

44 The situation of the kingdom is like the situation of a treasure hidden in a field, which someone finds by chance. Under rabbinic law if a workman came on a treasure in a field and lifted it out, it would belong to his master, the field's owner; but here the man is careful not to lift the treasure out till he has bought the field. The focus of the parable, therefore, is on the value of the treasure, which is worth every sacrifice. When the man buys the field at such sacrifice, he possesses far more than the price paid (cf. 10:39). The kingdom of heaven is worth infinitely more than the cost of discipleship, and those who know where the treasure lies joyfully abandon everything else to secure it.

b. The parable of the expensive pearl (13:45–46)

45–46 The word "again" ties this parable closely to the preceding one. The connection is the supreme worth of the kingdom. But here we deal with a merchant whose business it is to seek pearls, and who chances on one of supreme value. Unlike the man in the last parable, he pays a full price. Although he is an expert in pearls, this single find so far surpasses any other pearl he has ever seen that he considers it a fair exchange for everything else he owns. Thus Jesus is saying that the person whose whole life has been bound up with "pearls"—the entire religious heritage of the Jews?—will, on comprehending the true value of the kingdom as Jesus presents it, gladly exchange all else to follow him.

c. The parable of the net (13:47–48)

47–48 Thematically and structurally, this parable is parallel to the parable of the weeds. But whereas the parable of the weeds focuses on the long period of the reign of God during which weeds coexist with wheat and the enemy has large powers, this parable simply describes the situation that exists when the Last Judgment takes place: the kingdom embraces "good" fish and "bad" fish, and only the final sweep of the net sorts them out.

d. Interlude and interpretation (13:49–51)

49–50 Jesus interprets the previous parable. Both the parable and its interpretation point to the Last Judgment (cf. vv.41–42). The focus here is on the state of the kingdom when the Judgment occurs. Though it includes both the righteous and the wicked, a thorough sorting out will certainly take place.

51 Jesus' question picks up the disciples' request for an explanation (v.36) but goes beyond it, since the question is introduced after three additional parables. "All these things" refers to the meaning of parables in general, to the meaning of unexplained parables, and to the "secrets of the kingdom" (v.11).

This is the only place in this chapter where the disciples themselves are explicitly said to understand, and they say it by themselves. Matthew portrays the disciples realistically. They certainly understood more than the crowds; on the other hand, they are shortly to be rebuked for their dullness (15:16).

e. The parable of the teacher of the law (13:52)

52 Interpretations of this difficult verse are legion. The problem in this parable is to discern the point of the comparison. There seem to be two comparisons. The emphasis in the first part is not that the teacher of the law has been instructed *about* the kingdom and therefore understands, but that he has become a disciple *of* the kingdom and therefore his allegiance has been transformed. Such a discipled person brings out of his storeroom (i.e., out of his heart, his very being) new things and old. We must not understand this saying to read (NIV) "new treasures as well as old," suggesting that new kingdom things have been added to the old Jewish ways. Rather, the Gospel of the kingdom, though new, takes precedence over the old revelation and is its fulfillment (cf. comments on 5:17–20). The new is not added to the old, but has renewed the old, which has thereby become new. Thus the OT promises of the Messiah and kingdom, as well as OT law and piety, have found their fulfillment in Jesus' person, teaching, and kingdom; and the teacher of the law who has become a disciple of the kingdom now brings out of himself deep understanding of these things and their transformed perspective affecting all life.

But there is a second point of comparison in the parable. The one who brings out these treasures is a "teacher of the law" (GK *1208*). He is not bringing forth things new and old for purely personal reasons *but in his capacity as teacher*. Jesus' disciples claim to have understood what he has been teaching. "Therefore," he responds, discipled teachers of the Scriptures must themselves bring out of their storeroom the treasures now theirs so as to teach others (cf. ch.10; 28:18–20).

5. Transitional conclusion (13:53)

53 Once again, this section of Matthew closes with a typical formula (see comment on 7:28–29). Jesus' movement from Capernaum to "his hometown" (vv.53–54) turns out to be a further fulfillment of vv.14–15: these people will be ever hearing but never understanding.

V. The Glory and the Shadow: Progressive Polarization (13:54–19:2)

A. Narrative (13:54–17:27)

The principal themes of these chapters are clear. There is a progressive polarization along several axes. As Jesus extends his ministry, the opposition sharpens (15:1–9; 16:1–14). When he reveals himself to his disciples, they perceive some truth clearly and entirely reject other truth (16:13–22; 17:1–13). As Jesus is increasingly opposed by Jewish leaders, so his own disciples become increasingly important (18:1–10). And rising less ambiguously now is the shadow of the Cross (16:21–22; 17:22–23).

1. Rejected at Nazareth (13:54–58)

Placing this story immediately after the discourse on parables extends the hostility and rejection of the scribes and Pharisees even to Jesus' hometown (cf. Mk 6:1–6).

54 Jesus' "hometown" is Nazareth (cf. 2:23; 4:13). That Jesus taught extensively in the synagogues is certain (cf. 4:23; 12:9), but he did not limit himself to this environment. The people who gathered in the synagogue wondered about the source of Jesus' authority. Do Jesus' wisdom and powers—his teaching and miracles, both evidences of his authority—reflect God's authority or something else (cf. 12:24)?

55–57a Obviously some of the questioners' motivation sprang from a serious desire to know whence Jesus derived his authority rather than from personal pique that a hometown boy had outstripped them. The questions are understandable. They knew Jesus had no special breeding or education. Whence, then, his wisdom and miracles? But by their questions the people merely condemned themselves; they could not doubt the fact of his wisdom and miracles, yet they rejected his claims. "They took offense at him" means they found in him obstacles to faith, even though the biggest obstacles were in their own hearts. On the question of Jesus' brothers and sisters, see comment on 12:46–50.

57b–58 The proverb in v.57b is true: most often a person is better received at home than anywhere else; but if one enjoys an elevated position, the reverse is true. Jesus did not do miracles there because of the people's "lack of faith." This was a source of profound grief and frustration for Jesus rather than something that stripped him of power (see comment on Mk 6:5–6).

2. Herod and Jesus (14:1–12)

a. Herod's understanding of Jesus (14:1–2)

1–2 It seems likely that this event took place after the mission of the Twelve (see Mk 6:7ff). Certainly the multiplication of Jesus' influence through his disciples would upset Herod, one of whose motives in imprisoning the Baptist had been to thwart any threat to political stability (on Herod, see comment on Mk 6:14).

Jesus' ministry was taking place largely within Herod's jurisdiction. His conclusion that this was John the Baptist risen from the dead is of great interest. It reflects an eclectic set of beliefs, such as the Pharisaic understanding of resurrection. During his ministry John had performed no miracles (Jn 10:41); therefore Herod ascribes the miracles in Jesus' ministry, not to John, but to John "risen from the dead." Herod's guilty conscience apparently combined with a superstitious view of miracles to generate this theory.

b. Background: Herod's execution of John the Baptist (14:3–12)

3–5 Herod Antipas's first wife was the daughter of Aretas (cf. 2Co 11:32), Arabian king of the Nabateans, whose land adjoined Perea. To divorce her in favor of Herodias was politically explosive. She was married to Herod Philip, Herod's half-brother. John probably did not denounce him for divorcing his former wife, an action probably judged allowable, but for incestuously marrying his half-brother's wife (Lev 18:16; 20:21); and John probably kept on repeating his rebuke. This political criticism coupled with John's messianic message (3:1–12) made him a dangerous man to Herod's security.

6–8 At Herod's birthday feast, Herodias's daughter by her former marriage, Salome, a girl between twelve and fourteen years old, danced before the king and his lords. The dance may have been very sensual. She pleased Herod Antipas enough for him to put on the airs of a lavish and powerful emperor; petty ruler though he was, he imitated the grandiloquence of ancient Persian monarchs (Est 5:3, 6; 7:2). Still young enough to ask her mother's advice, Salome's dancing became the means for accomplishing Herodias's darkest desire—the death of the man whose only offense had been telling the truth.

9–11 Though grieving because of his oath and his loss of face before his guests if he were to renege on his vow, Herod gave the order. Decapitation was contrary to Jewish law, which also forbade execution without trial. So John died, the last of the OT prophets (11:9, 13) who through persecution became models for Jesus' disciples (5:11–12).

12 The report of John's death and burial to Jesus draws John and Jesus together against the opposition and suggests a positive response to Jesus by John and his disciples following 11:2–6.

3. The feeding of the five thousand (14:13–21)

The feeding of the five thousand is found in all four Gospels. There is probably an implicit anticipation of the messianic banquet (see comment on 8:11); but the text focuses more on Jesus' compassion (v.14), on the responsibility of the disciples to minister to the crowds (v.16), and on this miracle of creation.

13–14 Verse 13 picks up the story from vv.1–2: When Jesus heard about Herod's response to his preaching and miracles, he decided to withdraw. He had done so previously to escape the animosity of the Pharisees (12:15); he now does so to avoid Antipas. But it was usually impossible for Jesus to escape the crowds even when it was possible for him to leave a place.

They ran "on foot" around the top of the lake, presumably crossing the upper Jordan at a ford two miles north of where the river enters Galilee. They saw where Jesus was going and set out after him; but arriving first, they were already there when he landed with his tired disciples.

15–17 It was now late afternoon. On the face of it, the conversation between Jesus and his disciples is straightforward. They wanted him to send the crowds to the small, unwalled hamlets for food. Jesus' words "you give them something to eat" were not easy to understand; but whatever they meant, the disciples did not understand them. Their answer in v.17 not only reveals limited vision but also an approach to the problem betraying a lack of both understanding and faith.

18–21 Jesus alone multiplies the loaves and fishes. He gives the orders, gives thanks, and breaks the loaves (vv.18–19). The actions—looking up to heaven, thanking God, and breaking the loaves—are normal for any head of a Jewish household in prayer (see comment on Mk 6:41).

The crowd was huge: fifteen or twenty thousand total, if there were five thousand "men," v.21. Yet all ate and were satisfied, and there were twelve baskets of leftovers. The "twelve basketfuls" may be significant (cf. twelve tribes and twelve apostles; 19:28). The best suggestion is that Messiah's supply is so lavish that even the scraps of his provision are enough to supply the needs of Israel, represented by the Twelve.

4. The walk on the water (14:22–33)

22 Jesus "made" (lit., "compelled"; GK *337*) the disciples go on ahead of him, probably because (1) he wanted to be alone to pray (v.23); (2) he wanted to escape the crowd with his disciples to get some rest (Mk 6:31–32); and (3) he may even have wanted to tame a messianic uproar (Jn 6:15).

23–24 On the phrase "on a mountainside," see comment on 5:1–2. The burden of Jesus' prayer is not revealed; but it is possible that the crowd's attempts to make him king (Jn 6:15) prompted him to seek his Father's face. The boat was out toward the middle of the lake, and the wind was likely coming out of the west as they were trying to run toward that shore.

25–27 The Romans divided the night from sunset to sunrise into four watches (reflected here). Jesus' approach to the boat therefore occurred between 3:00 A.M. and 6:00 A.M. The disciples were terrified, thinking they were seeing an apparition or ghost. "Take courage!" and "Don't be afraid" bracket the central reason for his calming exhortations: "It is I." Although the Greek words for "It is I" ("I am") can have no more force than that, any Christian after the Resurrection and Ascension would also detect echoes of "I Am," the decisive self-disclosure of God (Ex 3:14; Isa 51:12; cf. Jn 8:58). Once again we find Jesus revealing himself in a veiled way that will prove especially rich to Christians after his resurrection (see comment on 8:20).

28–31 How far Peter got is unclear, but at Jesus' command he walked on the water. But his outlook changed: when he saw the storm, he began to sink. It was not that he lost faith in himself, but that his faith in Jesus, strong enough to get him out of the boat and walking on the water, was not strong enough to stand up to the storm. Therefore Jesus calls him a man "of little faith" (GK *3899*; see comments on 6:30; 8:26), and his rhetorical question helps both Peter and the reader recognize that doubts and fears quickly disappear before a strict inquiry into their cause. Thus Peter here is both a good example and a bad example. His cry for help is natural, and Jesus' rescuing him is akin to God's salvation in the OT (Pss 18:16; 69:1–3; 144:7).

32–33 The climax of the story is not the stilling of the storm but the confession and worship of the disciples: "Truly you are the Son of God." This is the first time Jesus has been addressed by the disciples with this full title (cf. 16:16; 26:63; et al.). But it already lurks behind 3:17 ("my Son"), and the devil has used it of Jesus (see 4:3, 6). It is most likely abbreviated to "the Son" in Jesus' self-references in 11:25–27. Exactly what the disciples meant by this title is uncertain. They probably did not understand it in a genuine ontological sense (see comment on 3:17). They perhaps used the title in a messianic way, but still with superficial comprehension (see comment on 16:16). The final response of the disciples is to worship Jesus.

5. Transitional summary of constant and unavoidable ministry (14:34–36)

34–36 Gennesaret was the fertile plain on the northwest side of the lake. The crowds'

In 1987 a small fishing boat from Jesus' time was found at the bottom of the Sea of Galilee and brought up to the surface (protected here with polyurethane). Courtesy Israel Antiquities Authority

instant recognition of Jesus showed the extent of his ministry; again, word-of-mouth reports led to crowds (cf. 4:24). Like the woman with the hemorrhage (9:20–22), the people were satisfied if only they could touch the edge of his cloak (v.36); even that degree of faith brought thorough healing.

This little section does three things: (1) it again stresses the sweeping extent of Jesus' public ministry (cf. 4:23–25; 8:16; 9:35–36); (2) it shows that Jesus' ministry extended to all the people, though his close disciples had special access to him and his more intimate instruction; and (3) because the stricter groups (e.g., the Pharisees and Essenes) counted it an abomination to rub shoulders in a crowd—one never knew what ceremonial uncleanness one might contract—Jesus' unconcern about such things neatly sets the stage for the confrontation over clean and unclean in 15:1–20.

6. Jesus and the tradition of the elders (15:1–20)

Controversies become sharper and more theological as Matthew's narrative moves on. This controversy is of great importance in grasping Jesus' understanding of the law.

1 The Pharisees and teachers of the law mentioned here came from Jerusalem and were probably held in special esteem. But from Matthew's perspective, they were a quasi-official deputation (cf. Jn 1:19) and a source of Jesus' most virulent opposition.

2 The attack on Jesus again comes through the behavior of his disciples (see 9:14; cf. Mk 7:3–4). The "tradition of the elders" (cf. Gal 1:14; Col 2:18) refers to the great corpus of oral teaching that commented on the law and interpreted it in detailed rules of conduct, often recording the diverse opinions of competing rabbis. This tradition in Jesus' time was largely oral, but the Pharisees viewed it as having authority very nearly equal to the canon. It was codified about A.D. 135–200 to form the Mishnah.

3–6 Jesus' words are less a response than a counterattack. He made a fundamental distinction between the authority of "the command of God" (as found in Scripture) and Jewish tradition, and he insisted that the Pharisees and teachers of the law were guilty of breaking the former for the sake of the latter.

The two texts cited are Ex 20:12 and 21:17, and their point is clear enough. In a broad sense, Jesus expects children to take responsibility for their aging parents. Greed could keep a son from discharging this duty by simply declaring the goods or money that might have gone to support his parents *korban* (Corban, Mk 7:11), a gift devoted to God (cf. Lev 27:9, 16) and set aside for the temple treasury. Such a vow could be annulled in various ways. It would not mean that one could use the goods or money in question but that he could withhold it from his parents.

7–9 This is the first recorded instance of Jesus' calling the Pharisees and teachers of the law "hypocrites" (GK 5695; see comment on 6:2). His charge was that, while they made a show of devotion to God, their religious traditions took precedence over God's will. Jesus saw their hypocrisy as a fulfillment of Isa 29:13. Yet Isa 29:13 is addressed to men of Isaiah's day. What then did Jesus mean? There were three points of contact: (1) in each case those warned were Jews, (2) from Jerusalem, (3) with a religion characterized by externals that sometimes vitiated principle. The Jews of Jesus' day thought of themselves as preserving ancient traditions; but Jesus said that what they were actually preserving was the spirit of those whom Isaiah criticized long before. They had displaced the true religion of the heart with a religion of form. Therefore their worship was vain and their teachings their own, with nothing of God's authority behind them.

10–11 Jesus' sharpest barb against the Pharisees and teachers of the law had been private. Now he teaches the crowd the same things. These two verses also answer the Pharisees' question of v.2 directly, not just by countercharge (as in vv.3–9). What Jesus says, the disciples call a "parable" (v.15). In presenting it to the crowd, he exhorts them to understand; for the parable was not meant to be cryptic, though only few seemed to have grasped it at the time, and even the disciples had trouble with it (vv.15–16; see comments on 13:10–17, 34–35). The form of Jesus' argument is from principle (vv.10–11, 17–19) to specific application.

12–14 These verses reflect what took place after Jesus and his disciples had retired from the crowd and entered the house. The disciples' question shows that the Pharisees understood enough of Jesus' parable to take offense. The disciples wanted to have the parable explained (v.15); since they held the Pharisees in high regard, they wanted to be certain of exactly what Jesus had said that had offended them so badly. Jesus must disillusion his disciples as to the reliability of the Pharisees and teachers of the law as spiritual guides, as well as explain the parable.

Jesus uses two images. The first predicts the rooting up of any plant the heavenly Father has not planted. Israel often saw herself as a plant God had planted (Ps 1:3; Isa 60:21), and the prophets turned the image against them (Isa 5:1–7). Jesus is saying here that the Pharisees, the leaders of the Jewish people, are not truly part of God's planting. This shocking idea has already been hinted at in 3.9, 8:11–12 and will recur.

The second image may depend on a title some Jewish leaders apparently took on themselves. They had the law, they reasoned, and therefore they were fit to serve as "guides of the blind" (Ro 2:19). This Jesus disputes; in his view they were "blind guides of the blind" (NIV note) and "both will fall into a pit." Though the Pharisees and teachers of the law had the Scriptures and interpreted them in the synagogues, this does not mean that they really understood them. On the contrary, they were blind and failed to comprehend them (cf. 23:16–17). Jesus' denunciation presupposes that anyone who truly understands the "word of God" (v.6) will discern who he is and follow him (cf. Jn 5:39–40). The Pharisees did not follow Jesus; so they did not understand and follow the Scriptures.

15–16 Peter speaks on behalf of the other disciples. Their failure to understand shocks Jesus. Dullness might be understandable in others, but in the disciples? Thus, Jesus asks in effect, "Are you *still* without understanding?"

17–20 "What goes into a man's mouth" (v.11) is merely food, which passes through the body and is excreted (lit., "is cast into a latrine"). But "what comes out of a man's mouth" and makes him unclean comes from his "heart" (see comment on 12:34–35). In other words, what a person truly *is* affects what he or she says and does. True religion must deal with the inner nature of a person and not with mere externals. Matthew ends this section by coming back to the specific question that precipitated Jesus' comments.

Jesus' teaching here opens up a fresh approach to the question of the law. It discounts the Pharisees' oral tradition while defending the law (vv.3–6); yet it insists that real "cleanness" is of the heart, so discounting some of the law's formal requirements.

Like 5:21–48, Jesus insists that the true direction in which the OT law points is precisely what he teaches, what he is, and what he inaugurates. He has fulfilled the law; therefore whatever prescriptive force it continues to have is determined by its relationship to him. It is within this framework that Jesus' teaching here theologically anticipates passages such as Ro 14:14–18 and 1Co 10:31. What concerned Jesus most was to see people transformed and their hearts renewed (cf. 6:1–33; 12:34–35), because he came to save his people from their sins (1:21).

7. More healings (15:21–31)

a. The Canaanite woman (15:21–28)

This miracle records Jesus' withdrawal from the opposition of the Pharisees and teachers of the law (cf. 14:13) and contrasts their approach to the Messiah with that of this Gentile woman (see comments on Mk 7:24–30).

21–22 Jesus now entered pagan territory, where a woman came to him. Matthew's use of the old term "Canaanite" shows that he cannot forget her ancestry: a descendant of

Israel's ancient enemies comes to the Jewish Messiah for blessing. Her calling Jesus "Son of David" shows some recognition of Jesus as the Messiah who would heal the people (see comment on 9:27); "Lord" is ambiguous (see comment on 7:22–23).

23–24 Matthew's Jewish readers would be intensely interested in Jesus' doing a miracle to aid a Gentile, on Gentile territory. Jesus' silence does not quiet the woman; so his disciples beg him to stop her persistent cries, probably by meeting her request. Indeed only this interpretation makes sense, because v.24 gives a reason for Jesus' not helping her rather than for not sending her away.

Jesus' answer echoes 10:6, where the same language is used (see comment on 10:6). The phrase "the lost sheep of the house of Israel" means "the lost sheep *who are* the house of Israel"—i.e., all Israel, regarded as lost sheep. It appears, then, that Jesus wanted his disciples and the Canaanite woman to recognize that he was limiting his activities during his life on earth. The kingdom must first be offered to Jews.

25–26 The woman knelt before Jesus and cried, as only the mother of an afflicted child could, "Lord, help me!" Jesus made certain that she grasped the historic distinction between Jew and Gentile. Jesus' short aphorism supposes that the "children" are the people of Israel and the "dogs" are Gentiles. His concern is one of precedence: the children get fed *first*.

27–28 The woman's answer is masterly. Those two words "but even" reveal immense wisdom and faith. She does not argue that her needs make her an exception, or that she has a right to Israel's covenanted mercies, or that the mysterious ways of divine election and justice are unfair. She simply asks for help, hopeful that she may be allowed to receive a crumb from the kindness of the Lord. As Paul does in Ro 9–11, the woman preserves Israel's historical privilege over against all radical spiritualization of Christ's work; yet she perceives that grace is freely given to the Gentiles. A faith that simply seeks mercy is honored (v.28). Again Jesus speaks, this time with emotion; and the woman's daughter is healed "from that very hour."

b. The many (15:29–31)

Matthew now provides a summary of more extensive healings that take place in Gentile territory (the Decapolis). Lest anyone think the crumbs suggest a restricted blessing for Gentiles (15:21–28), Matthew records the blessing and then tells us of the feeding of four thousand Gentiles. The blessing meant for the Gentiles is beginning to dawn.

29–31 Mark 7:31 has Jesus traveling to the Decapolis on the southeastern side of the lake, still outside Herod's jurisdiction (cf. Mt 14:13), where he does many miracles. Matthew seems to assume the same location: (1) the clause "they praised the God of Israel" (v.31) could be naturally said only by Gentiles; (2) the remoteness of the place (v.33) suggests the eastern side of the lake; and (3) the number of "basketfuls of broken pieces" (v.37) left over avoids the symbolic "twelve" (cf. 14:20).

8. The feeding of the four thousand (15:32–39)

On the relationship of the story to the feeding of the five thousand, see comments on Mk 8:1–9. This feeding took place in Gentile territory (see comments on vv.29–31).

32–33 On Jesus' compassion, see comment on 9:36. It appears that Jesus' preaching and miracles so captivated the people (cf. v.31) that they refused to leave him till he hesitated to dismiss them, fearing that many of them would collapse for hunger on their way home (v.32). Some had come a long distance (Mk 8:3). The response of the disciples is not surprising. While they may have understood the feeding of the five thousand Jews as anticipating the messianic banquet, they were undoubtedly a long way from admitting that Gentiles could share in any anticipated messianic banquet. Furthermore, we must never lose sight of a human being's vast capacity for unbelief.

34–39 If the number of baskets of leftovers in 14:20 is symbolic, it is hard to see why the seven baskets here (v.37) are not symbolic. The number seven may be significant because it is *not* twelve and therefore not allusive to the twelve apostles or twelve tribes. As before, "those who ate" are all satisfied, and the men only are numbered. The whole crowd may have exceeded ten thousand.

The site of Magadan (v.39), where the following conflict with the Pharisees and Sadducees occurs, is unknown. If this occurred when Jesus and the disciples landed, it must have been on Jewish territory, probably on the western shores of Galilee.

9. Another demand for a sign (16:1–4)

Doubtless there were many requests for signs (see comment on 12:38–40). Jesus had barely returned to Jewish territory when the opposition of Jewish leaders again surfaced, prompting him to leave the area once more, to cross the lake, and to head far north to Caesarea Philippi (v.13). There in God's providence and in the heart of Gentile territory, Peter makes the great confession that Jesus is the Messiah (v.16).

1 The single article in the Greek for "the Pharisees and Sadducees" implies that they acted together. Perhaps they represent the Sanhedrin, which included both groups (cf. Ac 23:6); or else a common opponent transforms usual enemies into friends (cf. Lk 23:12; cf. Ps 2:2). These men came to Jesus to "test" him (see comment on 4:1), asking for "a sign [GK 4956] from heaven" (see comment on 12:38).

2–3 Jesus' point here is clear enough: the Pharisees and Sadducees can read the "signs" that predict weather, but they remain oblivious to the "signs of the times" already happening. These signs testify to Jesus and the kingdom now dawning (cf. 11:4–6; 12:28). The proof that they cannot discern the signs is simply that they ask for a sign (v.1)!

4 But if a definitive sign is demanded, none but the sign of Jonah will be given (see 12:38–42 for an exposition of the sign). Jesus then left his opponents and withdrew by boat to the other side of the lake (v.5). But his withdrawal is emotional and judicial as well as geographical.

10. The yeast of the Pharisees and Sadducees (16:5–12)

5–7 This is Jesus' last and most important withdrawal from Galilee before his final trip south (19:1). The setting for this conversation may be the boat in which Jesus and his disciples cross the lake. It reveals the contrasting attitudes of Jesus and his disciples; he is still thinking about the malignity of the Pharisees and Sadducees (vv.1–4), and the disciples are thinking about food (15:29–38) that they forgot to bring.

"Yeast" was a common symbol for evil and could therefore be applied to different kinds of wickedness (e.g., Lk 12:1; cf. Ex 34:25; Lev 2:11; 1Co 5:6–8), but always with the idea that a little of it could have a far-reaching and insidious effect. The disciples do not understand what Jesus is saying but find his words enigmatic and discuss them.

8–12 Because they were men of little faith (v.8; cf. 6:30; 8:26; 14:31), they came to an unimaginative conclusion. Jesus could not have been talking about bread because he had already shown his power to provide all the bread they needed. He had performed two "food" miracles, and there had been basketfuls of leftovers each time.

Jesus' charge against the disciples ran deep. He had already denounced the Pharisees and Sadducees for their particular "teaching" that demanded manipulative signs and for their unbelief in spite of the bountiful evidence already supplied. Now the disciples are perilously close to the same unbelief in Jesus' person and miracles. The miracles Jesus performs, unlike the signs the Pharisees demand, do not compel faith; but those with faith will perceive their significance.

Instead of explaining the meaning of his metaphor of the yeast, Jesus repeats it. Great teacher that he is, he is trying to train his disciples to think deeply about the revelation he is giving and is not content to keep on spoon-feeding them.

11. Peter's confession of Jesus and its aftermath (16:13–23)

a. The confession (16:13–20)

The Pharisees and Sadducees persistently refused to acknowledge Jesus as the Messiah (vv.1–4). Even the disciples struggled with questions of faith (vv.5–12), but increasingly they came to recognize him for who he was (see comment on 14:33). In this section, Peter recognizes Jesus as the Messiah by revelation, not by signs. That Jesus is the Messiah leads inexorably to his self-disclosure as the suffering Messiah (vv.21–23), a theme anticipated earlier (see comment on 8:17).

13 Caesarea Philippi was built by Herod Philip the tetrarch (cf. 2:20, 22), who enlarged a small town at the base of Mount Hermon. At that place, Jesus asks the disciples who he, the Son of Man (see comment on Mk 8:31), is.

14 Opinion on Jesus' identity was divided. Some thought he was John the Baptist risen from the dead—Herod Antipas's view (14:2). Those who thought he was Elijah saw him as forerunner to a Messiah still to come (see comment on 11:9–10). Only Matthew mentions Jeremiah, the largest of the major prophets in the Hebrew canon (cf. comment on 27:9). "One of the prophets" testifies to the diversity of eschatological expectations in Jesus' day, some of the people expecting a long series of prophetic forerunners. But no group was openly and thoughtfully confessing Jesus as Messiah.

15–16 The "you" is emphatic and plural (v.15). Therefore, at least in part, Peter serves as spokesman for the Twelve (as he often does: cf. 15:15–16; 19:25–28; 26:40). Peter confesses that Jesus is the Christ, i.e., the Messiah (see comment on 1:1).

The Synoptic Gospels show us that the disciples understand only by degrees (see comments on 14:33; 16:17). One of the marks of the gospel writers' fidelity to the historical development of the disciples' understanding of Christ lies precisely in this—that they show the disciples coming around to the same points again and again, each time with a deeper level of comprehension, but always with a mixture of apprehension.

17 Jesus calls Peter "blessed" (see comment on 5:3). Jesus is the "Son of the living God" (v.16); Peter is the "son of Jonah." Jesus' Father has revealed to Peter the truth he has just confessed. Indeed, no one knows the Son except the Father (11:27), who has now graciously revealed his identity to Peter. Such knowledge could not have originated in "flesh and blood"—a Jewish expression referring to a mortal human being (cf. 1Co 15:50).

On the other hand, we need not suppose that the idea that Jesus was Messiah entered the apostles' minds for the first time here (cf. 11:2–6). John's witness is surely sound: the disciples began following Jesus in the hope that he was the Messiah (Jn 1:41, 45, 49). But their understanding of the nature of his messiahship was hindered by their own expectations (see comments on v.22; Mk 1:44); and they did not come into a full "Christian" understanding until after Easter. This verse marks a crucial stage along that growth in understanding and faith. Partial as it was, Peter's firm grasp of the fact that Jesus is the Messiah set him apart from the uncertainty and confusion of the crowd and could only be the result of the Father's disclosure. Indeed, the depth of Peter's conviction was the very thing that simultaneously made talk of Jesus' suffering and death difficult to integrate and yet prevented more serious defection when the one confessed as Messiah went to his death on a Roman cross.

18 Peter was an accepted name in Jesus' day (see comment on 4:18; see also Jn 1:42), and Jesus makes a pun on the name. The word "Peter" (*petros*, meaning "rock"; GK 4377) is masculine, and in Jesus' follow-up statement he uses the feminine word *petra* (GK 4376). On the basis of this change, many have attempted to avoid identifying Peter as the rock on which Jesus builds his church. Yet if it were not for Protestant reactions against extremes of Roman Catholic interpretation, it is doubtful whether many would have taken "rock" to be anything or anyone other than Peter. If Jesus spoke Aramaic here, there is no distinction in "Cephas."

But none of this requires that conservative Roman Catholic views be endorsed. The text says nothing about Peter's successors, infallibility, or exclusive authority. What the NT does show is that Peter was the first to make this formal confession and that his prominence continued in the earliest years of the church (Ac 1–12). But he, with John, could be sent by other apostles (Ac 8:14); and he was held accountable for his actions by the Jerusalem church (Ac 11:1–18) and was rebuked by Paul (Gal 2:11–14). He was, in short, *primus inter pares* ("first among equals"); and on the foundation of such men (Eph 2:20), Jesus built his church. That is precisely why Jesus, toward the close of his earthly ministry, spent so much time with them. The honor was not earned but stemmed from divine revelation (v.17) and Jesus' building work (v.18).

The word "church" (*ekklesia*; GK *1711*) occurs only here and at 18:17 in the Gospels.

It is derived from the verb *ekkaleo* ("to call out") and refers to those who are "called out." In the NT *ekklesia* usually refers to a Christian congregation or to all God's people redeemed by Christ (in Ac 7:38, it refers to God's OT people). Acknowledged as Messiah, Jesus responds that he will build his *ekklesia*, his people, his church. Implicitly, then, this verse embraces a claim to messiahship, for a Messiah without a messianic people is unthinkable to any Jew. They are the people of the "new covenant" (26:28).

19 The promise about the "keys of the kingdom" goes beyond the days of Jesus' earthly ministry. What Jesus' disciples thought this meant at the time is uncertain. Perhaps they hoped that when Jesus established his earthly reign and defeated the Romans, they would hold major posts under his reign. In the postresurrection period, however, the nature of this inaugurated kingdom became progressively clearer.

The metaphor changes from "church" to "kingdom." The person with "the keys" (GK *3090*) has power to exclude or permit entrance (cf. Rev 9:1–6; 20:1–3). This is then linked with the idea of "binding" (GK *1313*) and "loosing" (GK *3395*). It is best to understand this concept by recognizing first that Peter, by proclaiming "the good news of the kingdom" (4:23), opens the kingdom to many and shuts it against many (e.g., Ac 2:14–39; 3:11–26). By this means the Lord adds to the church those who are being saved, or, otherwise put, Jesus builds his church (Mt 16:18). But the same Gospel proclamation alienates and excludes people, so we also find Peter shutting up the kingdom from some (Ac 4:11–12; 8:20–23). Peter is authoritative in binding and loosing only because heaven has acted first (cf. Ac 18:9–10). Those he ushers in or excludes have already been bound or loosed by God according to the Gospel already revealed, which Peter, by confessing Jesus as the Messiah, has most clearly grasped.

Does this promise apply to Peter only, to the apostolic band, or to the church at large? The disciples were called to be fishers of men (4:19), to be salt (5:13) and light (5:14–16), to preach the good news of the kingdom (10:6–42), and, after the Resurrection, to disciple the nations and teach them all that Jesus commanded (28:18–20). In one sense Peter stands with the other disciples as one who received the Great Commission (in v.20, Jesus warns *all* his disciples, not just Peter, to tell no one). In that sense the disciples stand as paradigms for all believers during this period of redemptive history. But this fact does not exclude a special role for Peter or the apostles (see comment on v.18). Peter was the foundation; he enjoyed this "salvation-historical primacy."

Confirmation that this is the way 16:19 is to be taken comes at 18:18. If the church has to exercise the ministry of the keys, if it must bind and loose, then clearly one aspect of that task will be the discipline of those who profess to constitute it. Thus the two passages are tightly joined: 18:18 is a special application of 16:19. If we may judge from Paul's ministry, this discipline is a special function of apostles, but also of elders and even of the whole church (1Co 5:1–13; 2Co 13:10; Tit 2:15; 3:10–11). The continuity of the church depends as much on discipline as on truth. Indeed, faithful promulgation of the latter both entails and presupposes the former.

20 Jesus' warning his disciples not to tell anyone that he was the Christ does not stem from personal reluctance to accept the title. Rather, it must be seen in the context that he steadily refused to make an explicit messianic claim and to bow to demands for a definitive sign (12:38–39; 16:4). The disciples are now charged with the same reticence. Having come to faith, they must go beyond the Master himself in the means and limitations of his self-disclosure (see comment on Mk 8:29–30).

b. The first passion prediction (16:21–23)

21 This is not the first time Jesus alludes to his death (see 9:15; 10:38; 12:40; cf. Jn 2:19; 3:14), but now he begins to discuss it openly with his disciples. The time for symbols and veiled language was largely over, now that they had recognized him as Messiah.

The prediction is remarkably detailed. Jesus must go to Jerusalem, though the "must" (GK *1256*) of Jesus' suffering lies not in unqualified determinism, nor in heroic determination (though some of both are present), but in willing submission to his Father's will. At Jerusalem, the killer of prophets (23:37), he will suffer many things (more details specified in 20:19) at the hands of the elders, chief priests, and teachers of the law—the three groups that largely constituted the Sanhedrin (see comment on 3:7). There he would be killed and rise again the third day (see comment on 12:40).

How much of Jesus' sayings about his death did the disciples understand before the event? The Gospel evidence points in two complementary directions. On the one hand, the disciples understood perfectly well; otherwise, for instance, Peter could not possibly have rebuked Jesus (v.22). On the other hand, they could not believe that Messiah would really be killed because their conceptions of the Messiah did not allow for a Suffering Servant. Therefore Peter dared to rebuke Jesus, and the disciples began to think Jesus' predictions of his sufferings must be in some way nonliteral (Mk 9:10; Lk 9:45; see comment on Mt 17:4).

22 Peter's rebuke reveals how little he understood the kind of messiahship Jesus had in mind. He used strong language: "Never, Lord! This shall never happen to you!" Peter's strong will and warm heart linked to his ignorance produced a shocking bit of arrogance. He confessed that Jesus was the Messiah and then spoke in a way implying that he knew more of God's will than the Messiah did himself.

23 Jesus then turned toward Peter to rebuke him. The rebuke is made up of three parts. (1) "Get behind me, Satan!" (cf. 4:10) means not that Peter should get out of Jesus' sight, but out of Jesus' way. (2) A few moments earlier Jesus had called Peter a rock. Now he calls him a different kind of "rock," a "stumbling block" (GK 4998). As Satan offered Jesus kingship without suffering (4:8–9), so Peter does the same, adopting current expectations of victorious messianic conquest. Jesus recognizes the same diabolical source behind the same temptation. The notion of a suffering Messiah, misunderstood by Peter so that he became a stumbling block to Jesus, itself becomes, after the Resurrection, a stumbling block to other Jews (1Co 1:23). (3) Peter was not thinking God's thoughts (i.e., that Jesus must go to Jerusalem and die, v.21), but human thoughts (i.e., that he must *not* go). In vv.13–17 Peter, unlike other people, did think God's thoughts because divine revelation was given him. Here, however, he has switched sides.

In summary of vv.13–23, Peter both did and did not understand the truth about Jesus. Along with the other disciples, he understood much more than the crowds; yet even so he did not reach full understanding until after the Resurrection. The juxtaposition of vv.13–20 and vv.21–23 clearly shows the (at best) qualified understanding of Jesus' disciples at this point in salvation history.

12. The way of discipleship (16:24–28)

This section does two things: (1) after the passion prediction in vv.21–23, it demands the disciples' willingness to deny themselves absolutely, a kind of death to self; (2) yet it assures us that the consummated kingdom will at last come.

24 Though addressed to Jesus' "disciples" (see comment on 5:1–2), the thought is expressed in widest terms—"if anyone." As in 10:33, Jesus speaks of "disowning" or "renouncing" oneself. The Jews renounced the Messiah (Ac 3:14); his followers renounce themselves (cf. Ro 14:7–9; 15:2–3). They "take up their cross" (see comment on 10:38). Though Jesus does not explicitly mention the mode of his death until a few days before it takes place (20:19), the impact of this saying must have multiplied after Golgotha. Death to self is not so much a prerequisite of discipleship to Jesus as a continuing characteristic of it.

25–26 For the sense of v.25, see comment on 10:39. Verse 26 furthers the argument by asking twin rhetorical questions, showing the folly of possessing all created abundance and wealth at the expense of one's "soul." The focus is eschatological, and the loss of one's soul is the eternal loss of one's life or self.

27 Not only Jesus' example, but the judgment he will exercise is an incentive to take up one's cross and follow him. The Son of Man (see comment on Mk 8:31) will come "in his Father's glory"—the same glory God his Father enjoys (cf. Mt 26:64; Jn 17:1–5)—along with his angels. At that time he will reward each person "according to what he has done "(cf. Ps 62:12; see comment on 5:12).

28 For the interpretation of this verse, see comments on 10:23 and Mk 9:1. It seems best to take this verse as having a general reference to the manifestation of Christ's kingly reign exhibited after the Resurrection in a host of ways, not the least of them being the rapid multiplication of disciples and the mission to the Gentiles. Some of those standing there would live to see Jesus' Gospel proclaimed throughout the Roman Empire and a rich "harvest" (cf. 9:37–38) of converts reaped for Jesus Messiah. This interpretation best suits the flexibility of the "kingdom" concept in the Synoptic Gospels (see comment on 3:2; 12:28) and the present context. Thus v.28 does not refer to the same thing as 10:23. At this point in salvation history it is the power of the kingdom working through Jesus' disciples that calls the church into being (see comments on 13:36–43).

13. The Transfiguration (17:1–13)

a. Jesus transfigured (17:1–8)

The narrative of the Transfiguration is clearly a major turning point in Jesus' self-disclosure; we must understand this story without allegorizing the passage.

1 The "six days" probably indicates the time it took to travel from Caesarea Philippi (16:13) to the high mountains (17:1); that is, the Transfiguration took place within a few days of the prediction that Jesus must go to Jerusalem and be killed. The two passages must therefore be read together. On the identity of the mountain, see comments on Mk 9:2; Lk 9:28. Those Jesus "took with him" were Peter, James, and John, the inner circle of the Twelve.

2 Moses' face shone because it reflected something of God's glory (Ex 34:29–30). But Jesus himself was "transfigured" (GK 3565), a word that suggests a change of inmost nature that may be outwardly visible (as here) or quite invisible (Ro 12:2; 2Co 3:18). That Jesus was transfigured "before them" implies that it was largely for their sakes. As they would come to realize, they were being privileged to glimpse something of his preincarnate glory (Jn 1:14; 17:5; Php 2:6–7) and anticipate his coming exaltation (2Pe 1:16–18; Rev 1:16). Their confession of Jesus as Messiah and his insistence that he would be a suffering Messiah (16:13–21; 17:9) were confirmed. Therefore they had reason to hope that they would yet see the Son of Man coming in his kingdom (16:28).

3 On the significance of the appearance of Moses and Elijah, see comments on Mk 9:4; Lk 9:30–31. While both Moses and Elijah experienced God's glory (Ex 31:18; 1Ki 19:8–13), the glory here is Jesus' personal glory, for it is he who is transfigured and who radiates the glory of the Deity.

4 Peter, sensing something of the greatness of what he, James, and John are seeing, suggests building three "tabernacles" ("shelters"; GK 5008). While the word looks back to the tabernacle in the wilderness, the forerunner of the temple, the idea of building "tabernacles" also reflects the Feast of Tabernacles, when Jews built shelters for themselves and lived in them for seven days (cf. Lev 23:42–43). That feast had eschatological overtones. So Peter may have been saying that in gratitude for witnessing Jesus' transfiguration and recognizing the imminent dawn of the Messianic Age, he would build three "tabernacles"—one for Jesus, one for Moses, and one for Elijah.

The rebuke that follows is administered solely because what Peter blurted out compromised Jesus' uniqueness. *Jesus* was transfigured; they must bear witness concerning *him* (see also comments on Mk 9:5; Lk 9:33).

5 The "cloud" (GK 3749) signifies the presence of God, as it did in the OT (Ex 13:21–22; 40:34–38): it was also associated with the future (Isa 4:5; Eze 30:3; Zep 1:15). Jesus is now succeeding Moses as the coming prophet (Dt. 18:15, 18) and is the messianic King whose kingdom is dawning. What the Voice from the cloud says is largely a repetition of 3:17, an apparent mingling of Ps 2:7 and Isa 42:1, stressing that Jesus is both Son and Suffering Servant. This is the high point of the story.

The additional words "Listen to him"—an allusion to Dt 18:15—confirm Jesus is the Prophet like Moses (cf. Ac 3:22–23; 7:37). Jesus is not another prophet of Moses' stature but the eschatological Prophet patterned on Moses as a type. Jesus so far outstrips him that when Moses is put next to him, people must "listen" to Jesus. The climax of biblical revelation is Jesus, the Son and Servant God loves and with whom God is well pleased.

6–8 The effect of the Transfiguration on the disciples reminds us of Daniel (Da 10:7–9). The visible glory of Deity brings terror, but Jesus calms his disciples' fears (cf. 14:26–27).

Matthew alone tells us that at the divine splendor the disciples "fell facedown to the ground," a prelude to their seeing no one "except Jesus." These words are pregnant with meaning: compared with God's revelation through Christ, all other revelations pale.

b. The place of Elijah (17:9–13)

9 This is Jesus' fifth and last command in Matthew for the disciples to be silent (see comment on 8:4). This time Jesus permits his disciples to tell everything after the Son of Man "has been raised from the dead." Jesus could scarcely have attached this permission to earlier warnings to keep silent (16:20), since he had not yet spoken clearly about his sufferings and death. Nevertheless the same salvation-historical change—first silence, then proclamation—occurs as early as 10:27.

Why did Jesus command silence here? (1) The story would only stir up superficial political messianism, already a menace (see comment on Mk 1:44). (2) The strongest evidence for Jesus' messiahship would be his resurrection, by which he "was declared with power to be the Son of God" (Ro 1:4). Premature self-disclosure in a direct fashion, without the supreme "sign of Jonah," the Resurrection (see comment on 12:40), would not only foster false expectations but would also quickly disillusion those who held them. Thus Jesus knew it was better to wait till after the Resurrection before allowing Peter, James, and John to tell what they had seen.

10 Elijah was expected to restore all things—to bring about a state of justice and true worship (Mal 4:5). If that were so, how could it be that Messiah would be killed in such a restored environment—killed, Jesus had told them only a week before, by elders, chief priests, and teachers of the law (16:21)? Their confusion is not merely chronological, though that may be involved; it is their inability to find a framework in which they can believe that the Messiah could die.

11–12 Jesus answers the concerns of his disciples. On the one hand, Elijah comes first and "will restore all things"; John's mission was a success (3:5–6; 14:5). On the other hand, "restore all things" must not be taken absolutely. The Baptist (Elijah) did fulfill his mission, but he was killed doing it. "In the same way the Son of Man is going to suffer at their hands." If the Baptist's restoration of "all things" did not prevent his own death, why should Messiah be any better received?

13 Matthew again rounds off a section by returning to the question first raised (see comment on 15:20); they now understand that John the Baptist is Elijah. It is not at all clear, however, that they have understood much more about the death and resurrection of the Son of Man, and it becomes obvious during the passion narrative that they have not understood (cf. esp. 26:50–56). This section, therefore, marks another step, but a small one, in the understanding of Jesus' disciples.

14. The healing of an epileptic boy (17:14–20)

14–16 When Jesus returned to the other nine disciples he is approached by a man with an epileptic son. "Epilepsy" in this instance is associated with demon possession (see comment on 8:28). The disciples had not been able to heal him.

The disciples' failures are a recurring theme throughout this section (14:16–21, 26–27, 28–31; 15:16, 23, 33; 16:5, 22: 17:4, 10–11). This failure in their healing ministry at first seems strange, since Jesus had clearly given them power to heal and exorcise demons (10:1, 8). Yet it is part of the pattern of the disciples' advance and failure. In other situations they had shown lack of faith (14:26–27, 31; 15:5, 8)—a reminder that their power to do kingdom miracles was not their own but, unlike magic, was entirely derivative and related to their own walk of faith.

17–18 Jesus' response is reminiscent of Dt 32:5, 20. He notes that unbelief is characteristic of "this generation" (GK *1155*)—a word that extends Jesus' excoriation beyond the disciples (cf. also 11:16; 12:39–42; 16:4; et al.). Juxtaposing "perverse" and "unbelieving" to this generation implies that the failure to believe stems from willful neglect or distortion of the evidence.

The rhetorical questions—"How long shall I stay with you? How long shall I put up with you?"—express not only Jesus' personal disappointment but also his consciousness of his heavenly origin and destiny. His disciples' perverse unbelief is actually painful to him; he must endure it. As for the miracle, Matthew describes it succinctly, leaving no doubt of Jesus' power to heal and exorcise demons (v.18). The boy is healed "from that moment."

19–20 The disciples who had tried and failed to drive out the demon (v.16) ask Jesus, in private (cf. also Mk 9:28), why they could not do the miracle. The reason, Jesus says, is because of their "little faith." The disciples had long been successful in doing miracles, and now they are surprised by their failure. But their faith is poor and shoddy. They are treating the authority given them (10:1, 8) like a gift of magic, a bestowed power that works *ex opere operato*. Poor faith is ineffectual (see also 6:30; 8:26; 14:31; 16:8). Removal of mountains was proverbial for overcoming great difficulties (cf. Isa 40:4; 49:11; 54:10; Mt 21:21–22; 1Co 13:2; et al.). Nothing would be impossible for them, and they could accomplish great works for the kingdom with sincere faith and prayer.

15. The second major passion prediction (17:22–23)

22–23 No sooner are all the disciples and Jesus together after the Transfiguration than Jesus for a second time takes up the theme he introduced to them earlier (see comments on 16:21–23). Jesus not only foresees the inevitability of his death but, precisely because he knows this to be the Father's will (26:39), recognizes it as an essential part of the divine plan. But that death issues in the Resurrection. On the word "betrayed" (GK *4140*), see comment on Mk 9:31. The disciples are beginning to absorb the announcement of Jesus' death, and it grieves them. But of his resurrection they have no comprehension.

16. The temple tax (17:24–27)

24 "The two-drachma tax" was probably not a civil tax in support of Rome (cf. 22:15–22) but a Jewish "tax" of half a shekel levied on every male Jew between the ages of twenty and fifty in support of the tabernacle (later, the temple) and its services (cf. Ex 30:11–16). In Jesus' day two drachmas equaled half a shekel.

25–26 Peter's defense of Jesus is misguided. Once they are alone in the house, Jesus takes the initiative and asks Peter a provocative question about a civil tax. It is best to see these two verses as a parable. The point is that, just as royal sons are exempt from the taxes imposed by their fathers, so too Jesus is exempt from the "tax" imposed by his Father. In other words Jesus acknowledges the temple tax to be an obligation to God; but since he is uniquely God's Son, he is exempt. The focus of the section is thus supremely Christological.

27 Exempt though he is, Jesus will pay the tax so as not to offend. Thus he sets an example later followed by Paul (1Co 8:13; 9:12, 22). The plural "we" and the four-drachma coin to pay for Jesus *and* Peter at first sight makes the above interpretation seem difficult. In what sense are we to suppose that Peter's reason for paying the tax is akin to Jesus'? Part of the explanation may lie in the freedom Jesus extends to his disciples: e.g., he alone is Lord of the Sabbath, and this has implications for his disciples (see comments on 12:1–8). More important, Jesus here implicitly frees his followers from the temple tax on the grounds that they, too, will belong to the category of "sons," though derivatively.

The miraculous way of paying the tax is something only Jesus could do; it therefore suggests that though Jesus as the unique Son is free from the law's demands, he not only submits to them but makes provision, as only he can, for the demands on his disciples (cf. Gal 4:4–5)—and this right after a passion prediction (17:22–23)! Perhaps, too, we are reminded again of Jesus' humility: he who so controls nature and its powers that he stills storms and multiplies food now reminds Peter of that power by this miracle, while nevertheless remaining so humble that he would not needlessly cause offense (cf. 11:28–30; 12:20). This lesson in humility for Peter and the other disciples is about to be explained in some detail (18:1–35).

B. Fourth Discourse: Life Under Kingdom Authority (18:1–19:2)

1. Setting (18:1–2)

1–2 This fourth discourse, like the previous three, is bracketed by remarks suggesting that it was delivered on the occasion specified (see comments on 5:1; 7:28–29). When Jesus speaks again of his suffering and death, the disciples' grief (17:23) proves short-lived; and they busy themselves with arguing about who is greatest in the kingdom. Jesus has already said that there will be distinctions in the kingdom (5:19); and recently three of them have been specially favored (17:1–3), while Peter has been repeatedly singled out (14:28–29; 15:15; 16:16–18). Perhaps these things set off the dispute, which continues in the ambition of James, John, and their mother in the period right before the Cross (20:20–23) and which embraces the jealousy of the other ten (20:24). Substantial misunderstanding of Jesus by his disciples (see comment on 5:1–2) is presupposed throughout Jesus' entire earthly ministry.

2. Humility and greatness (18:3–4)

3–4 Jesus responds by warning his disciples that they must turn from their present conduct and attitudes and "become like little children"; for unless they do, they will "never enter the kingdom of heaven" (the consummated kingdom is in view here). The child is held up as an ideal, not of innocence, purity, or faith, but of humility and unconcern for social status. Jesus advocates humility of mind (v.4), not childishness of thought (cf. 10:16). With such humility comes childlike trust. The person who truly "humbles himself [GK 5427] like this child is the greatest in the kingdom of heaven": the expression completes a link with v.1. The thought is not far removed from 5:3 and vitiates any thought that the kingdom can be gained by personal merit or violent force (see comment on 11:12). It is to "little children" (GK 4086) that the Lord of heaven and earth reveals his truth (cf. 11:25).

3. The heinousness of causing believers to sin (18:5–9)

5–6 This promise-warning couplet advances the thought by turning attention from the self-humiliation of the true disciple (vv.3–4) to the way others receive such "little ones" (GK 3625). The opening clauses of v.5 and v.6 are roughly parallel. The one who welcomes "a little child like this *in my name*" is not welcoming literal children but "children" defined in the previous verses—those who humble themselves to become like children and are Jesus' true disciples (cf. "who believe in me" in v.6). They are not welcomed because they are great, wise, or mighty, but because they come in Jesus' name (v.5). These "little ones" can stumble, even the greatest of them (14:28–31; 26:30–35); but whoever causes them to stumble stands in grave peril. The people most subject to Jesus' judgment here are people of the world (cf. v.7).

The person who "welcomes" (GK 1312) one of these "little ones" welcomes Jesus himself (cf. 10:42). Presupposed here is the world's animosity. Mere hospitality is not in view but hospitality given because of the "little ones'" link with Jesus; and it is probably presupposed that hospitality motivated in this way would be shown only if the benefactor were already well disposed toward Jesus, or at least moving in that direction. The antithetic alternative, causing the "little ones" to stumble, does not mean that the "little ones" are led into apostasy. Rather, they are rejected or ignored, which causes them to stumble in their discipleship. It may lead to serious sin; but, as in 10:40–42 and 25:31–46, the really grave aspect of the rejection is that it signifies a rejection of Jesus.

Because such estimates signal both a rejection of Jesus and a damaging of his people, drowning at sea before the evil is committed is much preferable to eschatological judgment, the eternal fire of hell (vv. 8–9) that awaits the perpetrators (see comments on Mk 9:42–49).

7 Jesus proclaims judgment on the "world" (GK 3180), understood as the source of all stumbling. Jesus pronounces this woe "because of the things that cause" the stumbling already referred to in v.6. Such things must come; but this inevitability does not mitigate the responsibility of the perpetrators. The necessity does not spring from divine compulsion but, like all things, falls nonetheless within the sphere of his sovereignty, so that he may use those very things to accomplish his plan and perfect his people (cf. 24:10–13; 1Co 11:19). Thus, on the one hand the disciples are not to think such opposition strange, for Jesus himself has declared it must occur; on the other hand they are assured that justice will be done in the end (cf. 26:24).

8–9 Jesus now abandons denunciation of the world's causing his disciples to stumble and tells his disciples they may prove to be not only victims but aggressors. Certain attitudes nurtured by them toward other believers could also be sinful; thus, instead of being enticed to sin by outsiders, they would cause their own stumbling. Perhaps the particular believer-to-believer attitude that most needs

4. The parable of the lost sheep (18:10–14)

10 This verse continues the note of humility struck at the discourse's beginning (vv.3–4) and the concern for "these little ones" (vv.5–9). Jesus is discussing here what will be normative when his passion and resurrection fully inaugurate the messianic community. Its members will be poor in spirit (5:3) and humble (18:3–4), and none will be admitted without these graces. If his disciples become like that, they will belong to the "little children"; if they look down on them, they will share in the woes (vv.8–9). The warning was not irrelevant: at least one disciple left Jesus.

Jesus says that those who believe in him must be treated with respect because "their angels in heaven" always see the face of the heavenly Father. These "angels" are best interpreted as the spirit of believers after death, and they always see the heavenly Father's face. Can the word "angel" (GK 34) be pressed into this interpretation? Yes, for Jesus teaches that God's people in the Resurrection "will be like the angels in heaven" as to marriage (22:30) and immortality (Lk 20:36).

12–13 Jesus now gives another reason not to despise these "little ones": the shepherd—the Father—is concerned for each sheep in his flock and seeks the one who strays. His concern for the one wandering sheep is so great that he rejoices more over its restoration than over the ninety-nine that do not stray. With a God like that, how dare anyone cause even one of these sheep to go astray?

14 Jesus drives the lesson home: the heavenly Father is unwilling for any of "these little ones" (see comment on vv.3–6) to be lost. If that is his will, why would anyone else seek to lead one of them astray? God loves each *individual* sheep, so that the flock as a whole may not lose a single one of its members. On God's preservation of his own, see comments on 12:32; 13:3–9, 18–23.

5. Treatment of a sinning brother (18:15–20)

15 Now the thought shifts. Jesus is looking at offenses within the messianic community from the opposite perspective—from the viewpoint of the brother against whom the sin is committed. The proper thing is to confront the brother privately and "show him his fault." The aim is not to score points over him but to win him over (GK *3045*; cf. 1Co 9:19–22; 1Pe 3:1), for all discipline, even this private kind, must begin with redemptive purposes (cf. Lk 17:3–4; 2Th 3:14–15; Jas 5:19–20). Jesus assumes that the individual who personally confronts a brother will do so with true humility (vv.3–4; cf. Gal 6:1): if it is hard to accept a rebuke, even a private one, it is harder still to administer one in loving humility. Behind this verse stands Lev 19:17.

16 If private confrontation does not work, the next step (backed by regulation regarding civil cases in Dt 19:15) is to take two or three witnesses. Jesus perceives a link joining his messianic community with ancient Israel. The function of the witnesses is likely to provide witnesses to the confrontation if the case were to go before the whole church. By the united testimony of two or three witnesses, every matter "may be established."

17 Refusal to submit to the considered judgment of Messiah's people means that they are to treat the offender as "a pagan or a tax collector." The flow of the argument and the NT parallels (e.g., Ro 16:17; 2Th 3:14) show that Jesus has excommunication in mind. Since "you" is singular, Jesus is suggesting that each member of the church is to abide by the corporate judgment and reminds the disciple of the individual responsibility each believer has toward the others (cf. v.15).

18 For discussion of this verse, see comments on 16:19.

19–20 These two verses should not in this setting be taken as a promise regarding any prayer on which two or three believers agree. Scripture is rich in prayer promises (21:22; Jn 14:13–14; 15:7–8, 16); but if this passage deals with prayer at all, it is restricted by the phrase "about anything" (lit., "about any judicial matter"). Perhaps Jesus is also saying that if two individuals in the church come to agreement concerning any claim they are pursuing (presumably on the basis of the church's judgment, v.18), it will be allowed or ratified by their heavenly Father. This is because God's will and purpose stand behind the binding and loosing of v.18 and also because (cf. "for," v.20) the presence of Jesus is assured with the two or three judges solemnly convened before the church and by the church to render a decision.

Here as elsewhere, Jesus takes God's place: he will be with the judges (cf. 28:20). Jesus implicitly points forward to a time when, as "God with us" (1:23), he will be spiritually present with the "two or three" and with all his followers; and he presupposes that this time will be of considerable duration (see comment on 24:1–3).

6. Forgiveness (18:21–35)

a. Repeated forgiveness (18:21–22)

21–22 The issue here is not the adjudication of the church, still less the absolute granting of forgiveness by the church (only God and Jesus can ultimately forgive sins), but personal forgiveness (cf. 6:14–15). In rabbinic discussion, the consensus was that a person might be forgiven a repeated sin three times; on the fourth, there was no forgiveness. Peter, thinking himself big-hearted, volunteers "seven times" in answer to his own question.

Jesus' response alludes to Ge 4:24: Lamech's revenge is transformed into a principle of forgiveness. Jesus is not saying that seventy-seven times is the upper limit, nor that the forgiveness is so unqualified that it vitiates the discipline and procedural step just taught (vv.15–20). Rather, he teaches that forgiveness of fellow members in his community of "little ones" (see comment on vv.5–6) cannot possibly be limited by frequency or quantity; for, as the ensuing parable shows (vv.23–35), all of them have been forgiven far more than they will ever forgive.

b. The parable of the unmerciful servant (18:23–35)

23 Since Jesus requires his followers to forgive, he goes on to tell a parable about the present kingdom. The reign of God establishes certain kinds of personal relationships, portrayed by this parable, whose point is spelled out in v.35. Jesus has just been discussing the question of *repeated, personal* forgiveness (vv.21–22) and the reasons for it. Those in the kingdom serve a great king who has invariably forgiven far more than they can ever forgive one another. Therefore failure to forgive excludes one from the kingdom, whose pattern is to forgive.

24–27 We glimpse some idea of the size of the indebtedness when we recall that David donated three thousand talents of gold and seven thousand talents of silver for the construction of the temple, and the princes provided five thousand talents of gold and ten thousand talents of silver (1Ch 29:4, 7). Such indebtedness could not possibly be covered by selling the family into slavery: top price for a slave fetched about one talent, and one-tenth that amount or less was more common. The practice of being sold for debt was sanctioned by the OT (Lev 25:39; 2Ki 4:1), though such slaves had to be freed in the year of Jubilee.

In this parable selling the slave and his family does not mean the debt is canceled but rather highlights the servant's desperate plight. With neither resources nor hope, he begs for time and promises to pay everything back (v.26)—an impossibility. So the master takes pity on him and cancels the indebtedness (v.27). The king mercifully then decides to look on the loss as a bad loan rather than embezzlement.

28–31 The servant's attitude is appalling. The amount owed him is not insignificant: though worth but a few dollars in terms of metal currency, it represented a hundred days' wages for a foot soldier or common laborer. Yet the amount is utterly trivial compared with what has already been forgiven him. The similarity of his fellow servant's plea (v.29) to his own (v.26) does not move this unforgiving man, and he has him thrown into a debtor's prison (v.30). Even an inexpensive slave sold for five hundred denarii, and it was illegal to sell a man for a sum greater than his debt. But the other servants

Thsse are the two sides of a Roman denarius coin, many of which have been found in Palestine.

(v.31), deeply distressed by the inequity, tell the master everything.

32–34 The king now calls the servant whom he had forgiven "wicked" (v.32) and, forgoing selling him, turns him over to the "torturers" (cf. vv.6, 8–9). He is to be tortured till he pays back all he owes (v.34), which he can never do.

35 Jesus sees no incongruity in the actions of a heavenly Father who forgives so bountifully and punishes so ruthlessly, and neither should we. Indeed, it is precisely because he is a God of such compassion and mercy that he cannot possibly accept as his those devoid of such compassion and mercy. This is not to say that the king's compassion can be earned: far from it, the servant was granted freedom only by virtue of the king's forgiveness. As in 6:12, 14–15, those who are forgiven must forgive, lest they show themselves incapable of receiving forgiveness.

7. Transitional conclusion: introduction to the Judean ministry (19:1–2)

1–2 As with Jesus' other discourses, Matthew concludes it with a formulaic saying (see comment on 7:28–29). Jesus "left" Galilee and began to make his way toward Jerusalem, most likely traveling by way of Perea, on the east side of the Jordan, thus avoiding Samaria.

The large crowds and the many healings show that Jesus did in Judea what he had already done in Galilee. But the summaries of his ministry in this gospel (cf. 4:23; 9:35; 14:14; 16:30), along with showing how busy Jesus was, clearly demonstrate that he engaged in both a word and a deed ministry, he was a prophet and a mighty healer.

VI. Opposition and Eschatology: The Triumph of Grace (19:3–26:5)

Certain themes in this section are crystallized. The opposition to Jesus becomes more heated and focused, and the stances of Jesus and the Jewish leaders become more irreconcilable. Jesus not only reveals more of himself and his mission to his disciples but centers more attention on the End, the consummation of the kingdom. Within these two poles, opposition and eschatology, the grace of God toward those under the kingdom becomes an increasingly dominant theme. Without ever using the word "grace," Matthew returns to this theme repeatedly (e.g., 19:21–22; 20:1–16). But grace does not mean there is no judgment (23:1–39). Rather, it means that despite the gross rejection of Jesus, the chronic unbelief of opponents, crowds, and disciples alike, and the judgment that threatens both within history and at the End, grace triumphs and calls out a messianic people who bow to Jesus' lordship and eagerly await his return.

A. Narrative (19:3–23:39)

1. Marriage and divorce (19:3–12)

3 This first section on divorce, always a burning issue in church and society, has produced much discussion among commentators.

Pharisees are often found in Matthew's gospel testing or opposing Jesus in some way (12:2, 14, 24; 15:1; 16:1; et al.). They hoped Jesus would say something to damage his reputation with the people or even seem to contradict Moses. Perhaps, too, they hoped that Jesus would say something that would entangle him in the Herod-Herodias affair so that he might meet the Baptist's fate (see 14:3–12).

The question whether it is right for a man to divorce his wife "for any and every reason" hides an enormous diversity of Jewish opinion. In Qumran community, divorce was judged illicit in all circumstances. Regarding mainstream Judaism, on any understanding of what Jesus says in the following verses, he did not agree completely with either the rabbinical school of Shammai or that of Hillel (see comments on v. 10; Mk 10:2).

The setting of the divorce question in this section is different from 5:31–32. There divorce is set in a discourse that gives the norms of the kingdom and the sanctity of marriage; here it is set in a theological disputation that raises the question of what divorces are allowed.

4–6 Jesus aligns himself with the prophet Malachi, who quotes the Lord as saying, "I hate divorce" (Mal 2:16), and also refers to the creation story. He cites Ge 1:27 and 2:24, implying that the two sexes should be united in marriage. The "one flesh" in every marriage between a man and a woman is a reenactment of and testimony to the very structure of humanity as God created it. Jesus concludes, then, that the husband and wife are no longer two but one, and that by God's doing (v.6). Divorce is therefore not only "unnatural" but rebellion against God.

Jesus' response sets forth two profound insights that must not be lost. (1) Although Jewish leaders tended to analyze adultery in terms, not of infidelity to one's spouse, but of taking someone else's wife, Jesus dealt with the sanctity of marriage by focusing on the God-ordained unity of the couple. (2) Jesus essentially appealed to the principle of Jewish exegesis: "The more original, the weightier." Since marriage is grounded in *creation*, in the way God has made us, then it cannot be reduced to a merely covenantal relationship that breaks down when the covenantal promises are broken. But the argument in this instance leaves unanswered the question of how the Mosaic law is to be taken; and therefore the stage is set for the Pharisees' next question.

7–8 The Pharisees refer to Dt 24:1–4, which they interpret to mean something like this: "If a man takes a wife ... and she does not find favor in his eyes ... he shall write a bill of divorce ... and shall send her away from his house." But the Hebrew more naturally means something like this: "If a man takes a wife ... and she does not find favor in his eyes ... and he writes a bill of divorce ... and he sends her away from his house ... and her second husband does the same thing, then her first husband must not marry her again." In other words, Moses did not *command* divorce but permitted it, and the text is less concerned with explaining the nature of that indecency than with prohibiting remarriage of the twice-divorced woman to her first husband. Divorce and remarriage are therefore presupposed by Moses: i.e., he "permitted" them (v.8).

Jesus goes on to say that Moses' concession reflected not the true creation ordinance but the hardness of human hearts. Divorce is not part of the Creator's perfect design. If Moses permitted it, he did so because sin can be so vile that divorce is to be preferred to continued "indecency." This is not to say that the person who, according to what Moses said, divorced his spouse was actually committing sin in so doing; rather, that divorce could even be considered testified that there was already sin in the marriage. Therefore any view of divorce and remarriage (taught in either OT or NT) that sees the problem only in terms of what may or may not be done has already overlooked a basic fact—divorce is *never* to be thought of as a God-ordained, morally neutral option but as evidence of sin, of hardness of heart.

9 Jesus gives what is called his famous "exception clause" here. What is the meaning of *porneia* (NIV "marital unfaithfulness"; KJV "fornication"; GK *4518*)? Some relate it to incest. Others have argued that it refers to premarital unchastity: if a man discovers his bride is not a virgin, he may divorce her. Still others hold that it means "adultery" here, no more and no less. Yet in Greek the normal word for adultery is *moicheia* (GK *3657*). Matthew has already used *moicheia* and *porneia* in the same context (15:19), suggesting some distinction between the words.

It must be admitted that the word *porneia* itself is very broad. Occasionally it can refer to a specific kind of sexual sin, but only because the specific sexual sin belongs to the larger category of sexual immorality. *Porneia* covers the entire range of sexual sins and should not be restricted unless the context requires it.

Consequently, what Jesus seems to be saying is that divorce and remarriage always involve evil; but as Moses permitted it because of the hardness of human hearts, so also does he—but now on the sole grounds of *porneia* (sexual sin of any sort). Admittedly, Jesus would appear to be abrogating something of the Mosaic prescription; for whatever the general "something indecent" refers to in Dt 24:1, it can hardly refer to adultery, for which the prescribed punishment was death. But *porneia* includes adultery as a sexual sin, even if not restricted to it. Jesus' judgments on the matter are therefore both lighter (no capital punishment for adultery) and heavier (the sole exception being some form of sexual sin) than Moses.

In some ways, Jesus is doing the same thing here as he did in the Sermon on the Mount (5:21–48). He points out the true direction in which the Old Testament points (19:4–8), even though formally it may be abrogating a Mosaic command. It should also be noted that because marriage is referred to in sexual terms in Ge 2:24, sexual promiscuity is therefore a de facto exception. It may not necessitate divorce; but permission for divorce and remarriage under such circumstances, far from being inconsistent with Jesus' thought, is in perfect harmony with it.

10 The disciples were puzzled by Jesus' response (v.10) though they were not astonished (cf. v.25). Jesus, though not forbidding *all* divorce and remarriage, has come close to the school of Shammai on the grounds for exceptions, while taking a far more conservative stance than Shammai on who may remarry (Shammai permitted remarriage when the divorce was not in accordance with its own rules of conduct). In the light of the position, tacitly adopted by most Jews, that marriage was a duty, the disciples rather cynically conclude that such strictures surely make marriage unattractive. This makes the appeal of marriage contingent on liberal divorce and remarriage rights—a stance that fails miserably to understand what Jesus has said about the creation ordinance.

11–12 "This word" refers to the disciples' question in v.10 rather than Jesus' statements in vv.4–9. Jesus responds that not everyone can live by such a verdict, i.e., abstinence from marriage. But some do, namely, those to whom it is given—those born eunuchs, those made eunuchs by others, and those who have made themselves eunuchs because of the kingdom of God (i.e., those who have renounced marriage in light of the disciples' remark, "it is better not to marry"). Neither Jesus nor the apostles see celibacy as an intrinsically holier state than marriage (cf. 1Ti 4:1–3; Heb 13:4), nor as a condition for the top levels of ministry (Mt 8:14; 1Co 9:5), but as a special calling granted for greater usefulness in the kingdom (see 1Co 7:32–35). Those who impose this discipline on themselves must remember Paul's conclusion: it is better to marry than to burn with passion (1Co 7:9).

2. Blessing little children (19:13–15)

13 Children in Jesus' day were often brought to rabbis and elders to be blessed, customarily by placing hands on them (cf. Ge 48:14). The disciples rebuked the parents and others who were bringing their children. Why? Perhaps they were annoyed that Jesus was being delayed on his journey to Jerusalem, or they felt they were being interrupted in their important discussion. Although children in Judaism of the time were deeply cherished, they were thought in some ways to be negligible members of society: their place was to learn, to be respectful, and to listen.

14–15 Jesus did not want the little children prevented from coming to him, because the kingdom of heaven belongs to those like them. Jesus receives them because they are an excellent object lesson in the kind of humility and faith he finds acceptable (see 18:1–9). Furthermore, having just given an important lesson on the sanctity of marriage and family (vv.3–12), Jesus continues this by saying something important about children.

3. Wealth and the kingdom (19:16–30)
a. The rich young man (19:16–22)

16–17 A certain man—identified by all three evangelists as rich, by Matthew (v.20) as young, and by Luke (18:18) as a ruler—asks Jesus what he must do to inherit "eternal life." According to Matthew's version, the word "good" (GK 19) stands alone rather than modifies teacher (see Mk 10:17).

Irrespective of what "good" refers to, the man approaches Jesus with a question showing how far he is from the humble faith that characterizes all who belong to the kingdom (vv.13–15). He wants to earn eternal life; and in the light of v.20, he apparently thinks there are good things he can do, beyond the demands of the law, by which he can assure his salvation. Many Jews believed that a specific act of goodness could win eternal life; and this young man, assuming this opinion is correct, seeks Jesus' view as to what that act might be. Jesus responds by calling into question the man's inadequate understanding of goodness. In the absolute sense of goodness required to gain eternal life, only God is good (cf. Pss 106:1; 118:1, 29; et al.). Jesus will not allow anything other than God's will to determine what is good. This man reveals by his questions that he wants something beyond God's will (v.20) and that he misconstrues the absoluteness of God's goodness.

"If you want to enter life, obey the commandments" (v.17) does not mean that eternal life is *earned* by keeping God's laws. Jesus tells this man what good things he must do to gain eternal life precisely because he perceives this questioner does not understand the teaching that without a certain purity, one cannot inherit the kingdom (cf. 1Co 6:9–10). But that is still far from telling him that by doing these things he will *earn* eternal life.

18–20 Jesus lists the sixth, seventh, eighth, ninth, and fifth commandments of Ex 20, in that order, and then adds, "Love your neighbor as yourself" (Lev 19:18). The man's impulsive reply is reflected by Paul (Php 3:6) on a certain understanding of the law; but the man's further words, "What do I still lack?" show his uncertainty and lack of assurance of ever being good enough for salvation, and they demonstrate his notion that certain "good works" are over and above the law.

21–22 Jesus answers the question in v.21. His basic thrust is not "Sell your possessions and give to the poor," but "Come, follow me." What Jesus suggests here is undivided loyalty and full-hearted obedience. This young man could not face that. He was willing to discipline himself to observe all the outward stipulations and even perform extra works; but because of his wealth, he had a divided heart. His money was competing with God; and what Jesus everywhere demands as a condition for eternal life is absolute, radical discipleship—the surrender of *self*.

Formally, of course, Jesus' demand goes beyond anything in OT law. Equally remarkable is the fact that the focus on *God's will* (vv.17–19) should culminate in following *Jesus*. The explanation of this is that Jesus is prophesied by the OT. The will of God, as revealed in Scripture, looks forward to the coming of Messiah (see comments on 2:15; 5:17–20; 11:11–13). Absolute allegiance to him, with the humility of a child, is essential to salvation. The condition Jesus now imposes not only reveals the man's attachment to money but shows that all his formal compliance with the law is worthless because none of it entails absolute self-surrender. What the man needs is the triumph of grace; for as the next verses show, for him entering the kingdom of heaven is impossible (v.26). God, with whom all things are possible, must work; the parable in 20:1–16 directly speaks to this issue. But the young man is deaf to it: he leaves because, if a choice must be made between money and Jesus, money wins (cf. 6:24).

b. Grace and reward in the kingdom (19:23–30)

23–24 Jesus is not saying that all poor people and none of the wealthy enter the kingdom of heaven. That would exclude Abraham, Isaac, and Jacob, to say nothing of David, Solomon, and Joseph of Arimathea. The point of Jesus' teaching lies elsewhere. Most Jews expected the rich to inherit eternal life, not because their wealth could buy their way in, but because their wealth testified to the blessing of the Lord on their lives. Jesus' view is different and more sobering. The proverbial saying of v.24 refers to the absolutely impossible; the camel was the biggest animal in Palestine.

25–26 "Saved" (GK 5392) is equivalent to entering the kingdom of God (v.24) or obtaining eternal life (v.16). The disciples, reflecting the common Jewish view of the rich, are astonished and ask that if rich people, blessed of God, cannot be saved, then who *can* be? Jesus agrees: "With man this [the salvation of anyone] is impossible, but with God all things are possible" (v.26; cf. Ge 18:14; Job 42:2; Lk 1:37).

27–28 Peter, impressed by "impossible" and speaking for his fellow disciples, thinks Jesus' words are unfair to the Twelve. His statement suggests that he and the others are still thinking in terms of deserving or earning God's favor. Jesus does not castigate his disciples for being mercenary: they have made sacrifices and deserve an answer. But his statement that the blessing to come (whether belonging exclusively to the Twelve at the consummation of the kingdom [v.28] or to all believers now [vv.29–30]) far surpasses any sacrifice they might make, implies that Jesus is giving a gentle rebuke.

The remarkable feature of this verse is that the Twelve will "sit on twelve thrones," sharing judgment with the Son of Man. That believers will at the consummation have a part in judging is not uncommon in the NT (Lk 22:30; 1Co 6:2). Jesus' emphasis here, however, seems to be that the Twelve will someday judge the physical nation of Israel, presumably for its general rejection of Jesus Messiah.

29–30 Jesus now extends his encouragement to all his self-sacrificing disciples. The promise is not literal (one cannot have one hundred mothers). God is no one's debtor: if one of Jesus' disciples has, for Jesus' sake, left, say, a father, such a person will find within the messianic community a hundred who will be as a father to him or her—in addition to inheriting eternal life (v.29).

The proverbial saying of v.30 is one Jesus repeated on various occasions. Here he illustrates it by a parable (20:1–16), climaxed by the proverb in reverse form (20:16) as a closing bracket. It indicates something of the reversals that often occur in the kingdom of God. It sets forth God's grace over against *all* notions that the rich, powerful, great, and prominent will continue so in the kingdom. Those who approach God in childlike trust (vv.13–15) will be received and advanced in the kingdom beyond those who, from the world's perspective, enjoy prominence now.

4. The parable of the workers (20:1–16)

From this parable, we learn how "the last" person can become "first" (19:30)—by free grace. The parable begins with a typical scene and introduces atypical elements to surprise the reader and make a powerful point about the kingdom of heaven.

1–2 The normal working day was ten hours or so, not counting breaks. The landowner in the parable finds his first set of workers at about 6 A.M. and agrees to pay each one a denarius—the normal wage for a foot soldier or day laborer.

3–7 There were twelve "hours" from dawn to sundown. The third hour (v.3) would be about 9:00 A.M., the sixth about 12:00 noon., and the eleventh about 5:00 P.M. The marketplace would be the central square, where all kinds of business was done and casual labor hired. The third-hour workers are promised "whatever is right"; and, trusting the landowner's integrity, they work on that basis. The last group were standing around because no one had hired them.

8–12 Laborers were customarily paid at the end of each day (cf. Lev 19:13). The foreman is told to pay each worker the standard day-laborer's wage. Who gets paid first is crucial: it is only because the last hired receive a full day's wage that those first hired expect to get more than they bargained for. They "grumble against" the owner because he has been generous to others and merely just to them. They have borne "the heat of the day" (v.12), either direct sunlight or hot wind, which could drive workers from the field; and, though fairly paid, they feel unfairly treated because others who worked much less received what they did.

13–15 The landowner insists, in a mild rebuke, that he is not cheating anyone. He has paid the agreed wage. Should he want to pay others more, that is his business. Provided he has been just in all his dealings, does he not have the right to do what he wants with his money? These rhetorical questions (vv.13b–15) show that God's great gifts, simply because they *are* God's, are distributed, not because they are earned, but because he is gracious. In the kingdom of God, the driving force is not merit and ability (as in the world) but grace.

16 Jesus makes a final statement that God's grace makes some who are last first (see also comment on 19:30).

5. Third major passion prediction (20:17–19)

See comments on 16:21–23; 17:9, 22–23. Here there is the first mention of the mode of Jesus' death and of the Gentiles' part in it (only the Romans could crucify people). These three verses may look back to the preceding parable by implying the grounds of God's grace—i.e., what his Son did on the cross. Also, just as 19:13–15 sets the stage for 19:16–30, so 20:17–19 sets it for 20:20–28. While Jesus faces crucifixion, his disciples, still blind to the nature of his messiahship, squabble over their places in the kingdom.

17 Before setting out for Jerusalem, doubtless to attend the festival, Jesus took the Twelve aside from the throngs of pilgrims choking the roads to Jerusalem at such times. Only the Twelve were even remotely ready to hear this passion prediction.

18–19 Jerusalem was the focal point of Jewish worship. We are going there, Jesus says, because there the Son of Man will be betrayed and crucified. He will be "condemned"—his death will result from legal proceedings (v.18). Mention of the Resurrection is brief (v.19) and apparently not understood (cf. Lk 18:34)—though in Matthew the disciples' misunderstanding is not spelled out as in Luke but exemplified by the succeeding story (vv.20–28).

6. Suffering and service (20:20–28)

Again the question of rank returns (cf. 18:1–5). Despite Jesus' repeated predictions of his passion, two disciples and their mother are still thinking about privilege, status, and power.

20 The mother of James and John, along with her sons, approaches Jesus to ask a favor, with the mother as speaker. That the mother should be the one to approach Jesus becomes the more plausible if she is Jesus' aunt on his mother's side—not certain, but not unlikely (cf. 27:56; Jn 19:25). The "kneeling down" is not "worship" of Deity but may imply homage to the one increasingly recognized as King Messiah (see comment on 2:2).

21 The "right hand" and "left hand" suggest proximity to the King's person and so a share in his prestige and power. Such positions increase as the King is esteemed and has absolute power (cf. Pss 16:11; 45:9; 110:1; et al.). The kingdom here is the reign of Messiah at the consummation. The link with 19:28—a verse that speaks of both "throne" and "glory"—is unmistakable. What the sons of Zebedee want and their mother asks for is that they might share in the authority and preeminence of Jesus Messiah when his kingdom is fully consummated—something they think to be near at hand without the Cross or any interadvent period.

22 Jesus' answer is not severe but mingles firmness with probing. It is often ignorance that seeks leadership, power, and glory; the brothers do not now what they are asking. To ask to reign with Jesus is to ask to suffer with him; and not only do they not know what they are asking for (cf. 10:37–39), they have as yet no clear perceptions of *Jesus'* sufferings. To ask for worldly wealth and honor is often to ask for anxiety, temptation, disappointment, and envy; and in the spiritual arena to ask for great usefulness and reward is often to ask for great suffering (cf. 2Co 11:23–33; Col 1:24; Rev 1:9). On the word "cup," see comments on Mk 10:38; 14:35–37.

23 Jesus answers them first on their own terms before speaking of his own death as a ransom (v.28). In a sense they can and will drink from his cup of suffering. James would become the first apostolic martyr (Ac 12:2); and John (if it is the same one) would suffer exile (Rev 1:9). Yet it is not Jesus' role but his Father's to determine who sits on his right hand and his left. Here, as elsewhere (11:27; 24:36; 28:18), Jesus makes it clear that his authority is a derived authority.

24–27 The indignation of the ten doubtless sprang less from humility than jealousy plus the fear that they might lose out. These verses demonstrate that interest in egalitarianism may mask a jealousy whose deepest wellsprings are not concern for justice but "enlightened self-interest." The disciples revert to the squabbling of an earlier period (Mk 9:33–37; cf. Mt 18:1). Jesus calls them together and draws a contrast between greatness among "Gentiles" and greatness among heirs of the kingdom. Power and authority characterized the Roman empire. Greatness among Jesus' disciples is based on service. Anyone who wants to be great must become the "servant." In the pagan world humility was regarded as a vice. Imagine a slave being given leadership! Jesus' ethics of the leadership and power in his community of disciples is revolutionary.

28 At this point Jesus presents himself—the Son of Man (see comment on Mk 8:31)—as the supreme example of service to others. The verse is clearly important to our understanding of Jesus' view of his death.

It is natural to take "did not come" as presupposing at least a hint of Jesus' preexistence, though the language does not require it. He came not to be served, like a king dependent on countless courtiers and attendants, but to "serve" (GK *1354*) others. The Son of Man had every right to expect to be served, but he served instead. Implicit is a self-conscious awareness of one who, because of his heavenly origin, possessed divine authority, but who humbled himself even to the point of undergoing an atoning death (cf. Php 2:6–9). The display of divine glory shines most brightly when it is set aside for the sake of redeeming humankind by a shameful death.

The Son of Man came "to give his life a ransom for many." The word "ransom" (GK *3389*) was most commonly used as the purchase price for freeing slaves; and there is good evidence that the notion of "purchase price" is always implied in the NT use of this word, even though there is never any mention of the one to whom the price is paid. The preposition "for" denotes substitution or exchange; Jesus took our place.

The "many" (GK 4498) underlines the immeasurable effects of Jesus' solitary death: the one dies, the many find their lives "ransomed, healed, restored, forgiven"—a great host no one can number. But it should be remembered that "many" can refer, in Jewish literature, to the elect community. This suggests Jesus' substitutionary death is payment for and results in the eschatological people of God. This well suits the "many" of Isa 52:13–53:12 (a passage that seems to underlie this verse). Matthew has earlier explicitly related the "Servant Passage" of Isaiah to Jesus (see comments on 12:15–21).

7. Healing two blind men (20:29–34)

This miracle pictures Jesus still serving and again links his healing ministry with his death (v.28; see comment on 8:17). Moreover it reminds us that the one going up to Jerusalem to give his life as a ransom for many is the Messiah, the Son of David, whose great power, used mercifully (v.30) and compassionately (v.34), is not used to save himself.

29 Jericho (see comment on Mk 10:46) was not only the home of Jesus' ancestor Rahab (1:5) but was also a day's journey from Jerusalem. The "large crowd" implies more than messianic excitement; it also reflects the multitudes of pilgrims from Galilee and elsewhere heading to Jerusalem for the feast.

30 The fact that Matthew refers to two blind men rather than one (cf. Mk 10:46–52; Lk 18:35–43) shows his personal knowledge of the events. There may have been many blind people in the Jericho area; for that region produced large quantities of balsam, believed to be beneficial for many eye defects. These two were sitting by the roadside, doubtless begging; and, hearing that Jesus was passing, cried out, "Lord, Son of David, have mercy on us!" On the relationship of the messianic "Son of David" to healing, see comment on 9:27.

31–34 Matthew's account is simple, stressing that Jesus mercifully healed the men despite the opposition of the crowds that, like the disciples (cf. 19:13–15), wanted to bask in his glory but not practice his compassion. After his healing, unlike 9:30 (see comment), there is no command to be silent. That point in Jesus' ministry has been reached when more public self-disclosure could not change the course of events. The two healed men joined the crowds following Jesus (v.34), pressing on to the Passover they expected and the Cross they did not.

8. Opening events of Passion Week (21:1–23:39)

a. The Triumphal Entry (21:1–11)

1–2 The Roman military road from Jericho to Jerusalem was about seventeen miles long and climbed three thousand feet. It passed through Bethany (where Jesus stayed six days before the Passover, Jn 12:1–10) and nearby Bethphage ("house of figs"), which lay on the southeast slope of the Mount of Olives, then crossed over the mount and the Kidron Valley and entered Jerusalem (v.1).

Jesus sent two disciples ahead to Bethphage to fetch the animals. The ride on a colt, because it was planned by Jesus, could only be an acted parable, a deliberate act of symbolic self-disclosure for those with eyes to see. Secrecy was being lifted.

3 The most natural way to take "Lord" here is Jesus' way of referring to himself. This step is not out of keeping with the authority he has already claimed for himself and fits this late period of his ministry, when he revealed himself with increasing clarity (see comment on Mk 11:3).

4–5 It is uncertain whether these are the words of Jesus or of Matthew (NIV chooses the latter). The quotation is from Zec 9:9. A donkey was sometimes ridden by rulers in times of peace (Jdg 5:10; 1Ki 1.33). Jews certainly understood Zec 9:9 to refer to the Messiah, often in terms of the Son of David. Therefore for those with eyes to see, Jesus was not only proclaiming his messiahship and his fulfillment of Scripture but showing the kind of peace-loving approach he was now making to the city.

Matthew alone of the four Gospels mentions *two* animals: a donkey and her colt (vv.2, 7). This reference is his way of highlighting what the other Synoptics affirm—the animal Jesus rode on was "a colt," thus fulfilling even this detail of Scripture. In the midst, then, of this excited crowd, an unbroken animal remains calm under the hands of the Messiah, who has nature in his control

Every year on Palm Sunday, Christian pilgrims make the journey from the Mount of Olives into Jerusalem carrying palm branches, reenacting Jesus' Triumphal Entry.

(8:23–27; 14:22–32). Thus the event points to the peace of the consummated kingdom (cf. Isa 11:1–10).

6–8 The two disciples returned from their errand (v.6) and put their outer garments on the beasts—both animals were in the procession (v.7). Jesus sat "on them" (probably the garments, not both animals). A "very large crowd" spread their cloaks on the road, acknowledging Jesus' kingship (cf. 2Ki 9:13). Still others "cut branches" and "spread them" on the road.

9 Crowds ahead and behind may be incidental confirmation of two other details. (1) John 12:12 speaks of crowds coming out of Jerusalem to meet Jesus. Apparently the Galilean pilgrims accompanying Jesus and the Jerusalem crowd coming out to meet him formed this procession of praise. (2) That the Jerusalem crowds knew he was approaching supports the stopover in Bethany (see comment on vv.1–2), which allows time for the news to spread. Messianic fervor was high, and perhaps this contributed to Jesus' desire to present himself as Prince of Peace.

The words of praise come primarily from Ps 118:25–26, a psalm that formed part of the "great Hallel" of the Passover. "Hosanna" (GK 6057) transliterates the Hebrew expression that originally was a cry for help: "Save!" In time it became an invocation of blessing and even an acclamation, the latter being the meaning here. "Son of David" is messianic and stresses the kingly role Messiah was to play. "He who comes in the name of the Lord" is cited by Jesus a little later (23:39; cf. 3:11; 11:3).

"Hosanna in the highest" is probably equivalent to "Glory to God in the highest" (Lk 2:14). The people praise God in the highest heavens for sending the Messiah and, if "Hosanna" retains some of its original force, also cry to him for deliverance.

10–11 Jesus probably entered Jerusalem through the north entrance to the outer court of the temple. As the city was stirred earlier (2:3), so here: news of Jesus' presence was inevitably disturbing. "Who is this?" does not mean that Jesus was virtually unknown in Jerusalem, but "Who really is this about whom there is so much excitement?" The answer of the crowds accurately reflects the historical setting: many of his contemporaries saw him as a prophet (cf. 16:14; 21:46) "from Nazareth in Galilee"—his hometown and primary field of ministry respectively. The phrase probably also connotes surprise that a prophet should come from so unlikely a place (see comment on 2:23; cf. Jn 1:45–46).

b. Jesus at the temple (21:12–17)

This is now the second time that Jesus cleanses the temple (see Jn 2:13–22). The Synoptics do not record the earlier one because they do not tell anything about Jesus' early Judean ministry. This second cleansing as Passover drew near soon led to violent reaction by the authorities.

12 Temple service required provision to be made for getting what was needed from the sacrifices—animals, wood, oil, etc.—especially for pilgrims from afar. The money changers converted the standard Greek and Roman currency into temple currency, in which the half-shekel temple tax had to be paid (cf. 17:24–27). But letting these things go on at the temple site transformed a place of solemn worship into a market where the hum of trade mingled with the bleating and cooing of animals and birds. Moreover, especially on the great feasts, opportunities for extortion abounded. Jesus drove the lot out.

13 Jesus here refers to Scripture, much as he did when confronted by the devil (4:1–10). His first words are from Isa 56:7. Isaiah looked forward to a time when the temple would be called a house of prayer. But now, at the dawn of the Messianic Age, Jesus finds a "den of robbers." The words come from Jer 7:11, which warns against the futility of superstitious reverence for the temple compounded with wickedness that dishonors it. This suggests that the Greek word for "robbers" (GK 3334) should be given its normal meaning of "nationalist rebel" (see comment on 27:16). The temple was meant to be a house of prayer, but they had made it "a nationalist stronghold." It was not fulfilling its God-ordained role as witness to the nations but had become, like the first temple, the premier symbol of a superstitious belief that God would protect and rally his people irrespective of their conformity to his will.

The Lord whom the people see now comes to his temple (cf. Mal 3:1). Purification of Jerusalem and the temple was part of Jewish messianic expectation. So for those with eyes to see, Jesus' action was one of self-disclosure and an implicit claim to his authority over the Holy Place. That the purification would entail destruction and building a new temple (Jn 2:19–22) none but Jesus could yet foresee.

14 This last mention of Jesus' healing ministry takes place probably within the temple precincts in the Court of the Gentiles. It was not uncommon for the chronically ill to beg at the approaches to the temple (Ac 3:2); but the only place where the lame, blind, deaf, or otherwise handicapped could go in the temple area was the Court of the Gentiles.

Most Jewish authorities forbade any person lame, blind, deaf, or mute from offering a sacrifice or appearing before the Lord in his temple. But Jesus heals them, thus showing that "one greater than the temple is here" (12:6). He himself cannot be contaminated, and he heals and makes clean those who come into contact with him. These two actions—cleansing the temple and the healing miracles—jointly declare his superiority over the temple and raise the question of the source of his authority (v.23).

15–16 The "chief priests and teachers of the law" express indignation, not so much at what he has done, as at the acclamation he is receiving for it. The children cry out, "Hosanna to the Son of David"; and if Jesus is prepared to accept such praise, then "the wonderful things" he is doing must have messianic significance.

When challenged, Jesus supports the children by quoting Ps 8:2, introducing it with his "have you never read." Jesus' answer is a masterstroke and simultaneously accomplishes three things. (1) It provides some kind of biblical basis for letting the children go on with their exuberant praise and thus stifles, for the moment, the objections of the temple leaders. (2) Thoughtful persons, reflecting on the incident later (especially after the Resurrection), perceive that Jesus was saying much more. The children's "Hosannas" are not being directed to God but to the Son of David, the Messiah. Jesus is therefore not only acknowledging his messiahship but justifying the praise of the children by applying to himself a passage of Scripture applicable only to God (Ps 8 was not considered a messianic psalm). (3) The quotation confirms that the humble perceive spiritual truths more readily than the sophisticated (cf. 19:13–15).

17 During the festivals Jerusalem was crowded. So Jesus spent his last nights at Bethany, at the house of Mary, Martha, and Lazarus (see comment on 21:9).

c. The fig tree (21:18–22)

On the chronology of this event, see comment on Mk 11:20–21. Cursing the fig tree is an acted parable related to cleansing the temple and conveying a message about Israel. But when the next day the disciples see how quickly the fig tree has withered, their initial—and shallow—response is to wonder how it was done; and this leads to Jesus' remarks on faith. So this single historical event teaches two theological lessons.

18–19 Somewhere on the road between Bethany and Jerusalem, Jesus approached a fig tree in the hope of allaying his hunger, but found only leaves (see comment on Mk 11:13). Fig leaves appear about the same time as the fruit or a little after. That it was not the season for figs (Mk 11:13) explains why Jesus went to this particular tree, which stood out because it was in leaf. Its leaves advertised that it was bearing, but the advertisement was false. Jesus, unable to satisfy his hunger, saw the opportunity of teaching a memorable object lesson and cursed the tree, not because it was not bearing fruit, but because it made a show of life that promised fruit, yet was bearing none.

What is the meaning of the cursing of the fig tree? Jesus is cursing those who make a show of bearing much fruit but are spiritually barren. That is, he is directing his attack against the hypocrites among the Jewish people, a constant target in all four Gospels, but especially in Matthew (e.g., 6:2, 5, 16; 7:5; 15:7; 22:18; and we now approach 23:1–39!). Thus this story falls in line with the cleansing of the temple, which criticizes those who used the temple to make a large profit and those who stifled the children's praises of Messiah. These, like this leafy fig tree, Jesus finds full of advertised piety without any fruit; and them he curses.

The cursing of the fig tree is not so far out of character for Jesus as some have claimed. The same Jesus exorcised demons so that two thousand pigs were drowned (8:28–34), drove the animals and money changers out of the temple precincts with a whip, and says not a little about the torments of hell. Perhaps the fact that the two punitive miracles—the pigs and the fig tree—are not directed against people should teach us something of Jesus' compassion. He who came to save his people from their sin and its consequences resorts to prophetic actions not directed against his people, in order to warn them of the binding power of the devil (the destruction of the pigs) and of God's enmity against all hypocritical piety (the cursing of the fig tree).

20–22 Verse 20 may be read as either a question or an exclamation. The substance of Jesus' response has already been given in 17:20 (see comment). Here, however, attention shifts from concern about the amount of faith to the opposition of faith to doubt. The miracle Jesus selects to teach the power of faith—throwing a mountain into the sea (v.21)—is no more than a hyperbolic example of a miracle.

Jesus used the fig tree to teach the power of *believing* prayer. But belief in the NT is never reduced to forcing oneself to "believe" what one does not really believe. Instead, it is related to genuine trust in God and obedience to and discernment of his will. Such faith reposes on the will of God who acts.

d. The question of authority (21:23–27)

This long section from 21:23–22:46 is characterized by a number of controversies with various Jewish leaders, along with several parables that must be interpreted in the light of such controversies. It was customary to stop well-known teachers and ask them questions (cf. 22:16, 23, 35), and the crowds delighted in these exchanges. Eventually Jesus turned primarily to the crowds and addressed them without excluding the Pharisees and teachers of the law (ch. 23); and then, as evening fell, he retired to the Mount of Olives and gave his last "discourse" to his disciples (chs. 24–25).

23 Jesus' teaching takes place in the "temple courts," probably in one of the porticos surrounding the Court of the Gentiles. The chief priests and the elders were both members of the Sanhedrin, described here in terms of their clerical status rather than their theological positions (e.g., Sadducees and Pharisees). They approached Jesus and challenged his authority to cleanse the temple, to do the miraculous healings, and perhaps to teach the

crowds. Their first question was therefore not narrowly theological but concerned Jesus' authority; yet their concern in asking who gave him this authority sprang less from a desire to identify him than from a desire to stifle and perhaps ensnare him.

24–26 Jesus' reply is masterly. He responds to their question with a question of his own (v.24), a common enough procedure in rabbinic debate. "John's baptism" is a way of referring to the Baptist's entire ministry. Jesus asks whether it was "from heaven, or from men." Jesus knows that if the religious authorities rightly answer it, they will already have the correct answer to their own question. If they respond, "From heaven," then they are morally bound to believe John—and John pointed to Jesus (see comment on 11:7–11); they will therefore have their answer about Jesus and his authority. If they respond, "From men" (v.26), they offer the wrong answer; but they will not dare utter it for fear of the people.

Far from avoiding the religious leaders' question, Jesus answers it so that the honest seeker of truth, unswayed by public opinion, will not fail to see who he is, while those interested only in snaring him with a captious question are blocked by a hurdle their own shallow pragmatism forbids them to cross. At the same time Jesus' question rather strongly hints to the rulers that their false step goes back to broader issues than Jesus' identity. If they cannot discern Jesus' authority, it is because their previous unbelief has blinded their minds to God's revelation.

27 The equivocation of the Jewish leaders gives Jesus a reason for refusing to answer their question. The Sanhedrin, of course, were required to check the credentials of those who spoke for God. Therefore, they raise the question of Jesus' authority; Jesus, however, raises the question of their competence to judge such an issue.

e. The parable of the two sons (21:28–32)

28 This is the first of three parables by which Jesus rebukes the Jewish leaders (vv.28–32, 33–46; 22:1–14). It is introduced without any preamble other than the question, "What do you think?" The normal way to take "first" and "second" in this context is "older" and "younger" son respectively.

29–31 In this parable, the older son says no, but repents and goes; the second son says yes, but does nothing. Who performs the Father's will? The first. The story is fairly straightforward. For the first time Jesus openly makes a solemn personal application of one of his parables to the Jewish leaders (v.31).

The shock value of Jesus' statement can only be appreciated when the low esteem in which tax collectors (see comment on Mk 2:14) were held, not to mention prostitutes, is taken into account. Jesus is saying that the scum of society, though they have said no to God, are repenting, performing the Father's will, and entering the kingdom; whereas the religious authorities have loudly said yes to God but never do what he says, and therefore they fail to enter. Their righteousness is not enough (cf. 5:20).

32 This verse links the parable to the preceding story, where the importance of believing John has already been established (vv.23–27). John preached God's will about what was right and pointed the way to the kingdom (11:12), which sinners are now entering (21:31). But he also pointed to Jesus and the kingdom's superior righteousness (cf. 3:2–3; 5:20). Yet the religious leaders did not believe John's witness, even after seeing society's vilest sinners repenting and believing him and his message.

f. The parable of the tenants (21:33–46)

On the face of it, this parable continues to make a statement against the Jewish religious authorities. The metaphorical equivalences are obvious: the landowner is God, the vineyard Israel, the tenants the leaders of the nation, the servants the prophets, and the son Jesus Messiah. That is, this parable has "allegorical" elements (see introductory comment on Mk 4).

33–34 This parable is probably addressed not only to Jewish rulers (v.2) but to the crowds in the temple courts (though not excluding the rulers; cf. Lk 20:9). "Another" links this parable with the last one. These verses clearly allude to Isa 5:1–7 and Ps 80:6–16; Jesus' parable is an old theme with new variations. The pains the landowner takes show his care for the vineyard. He builds a wall to keep out animals, a watchtower to guard against thieves and fire, and a winepress to squeeze the grapes right there. He is confident that his vineyard will bear fruit. The tenant farmers take care of the vineyard during the owner's absence and pay rent in kind. The "servants" are the owner's agents sent to collect some of his fruit.

35–37 The tenants mistreat some servants (cf. Jer 20:1–2), kill others (cf. 1Ki 18:4, 13; Jer 26:20–23), and stone others (cf. 2Ch 24:21–22; Mt 23:37). "Last of all" (v.37) the landowner sends his son—there is a note of pathos here—hoping the tenants will respect him. His forbearance with his wicked tenants (cf. Ro 2:4) eventually motivates the ultimate implacability of his wrath.

38–41 The action of the tenants is consistently callous. Precisely how it applies to Jesus is not entirely clear. True, their attitude was not, "This is the Messiah: come, let us kill him"; yet, in the light of the Scriptures, their rejection of him was no less culpable than if it had been that. Therefore, though all the parable's details may not be pressed, rejection of the son (v.39) by the leaders *is* the final straw that brings divine wrath on them.

Jesus elicits the self-condemning response (vv.40–41) of the hearers of the parable, thus concluding his teaching in this parable, instead of simply presenting it. Of course the conclusion remains his, regardless of how he gets it across.

42 Jesus' question in this verse, "Have you never read?" implies that the Scriptures point to him (Jn 5:39–40). The quotation is from Ps 118:22–23. "Stone" symbolism was important in the early church (Ac 4:11; Ro 9:33; 1Pe 2:6) to help Christians understand why Jesus was rejected by so many of his own people; and doubtless its effectiveness was enhanced by Jesus' use of it.

Jesus now turns to the image of a building. The "capstone" (lit., "head of the corner") is most probably the top stone of roof parapets, exterior staircases, and city walls. Psalm 118 concerns Israel. The nation was despised and threatened on all sides, but God made it the capstone. Jesus, who recapitulates Israel (see comment on 2:15) and is the true center of Israel, receives similar treatment from his opponents, but God vindicates him (cf. 23:39).

43–44 Jesus explains further the meaning of the parable. Up to this time the Jewish religious leaders were the principal means by which God exercised his reign over his people. But the leaders failed so badly in handling God's "vineyard" and rejecting God's Son that God was planning to give the responsibility to another people who would produce the kingdom's fruit (cf. 7:16–20). Strictly speaking, this verse does not speak of transferring the locus of the people of God from Jews to Gentiles, though it may hint at this; instead, it speaks of the ending of the role the Jewish religious leaders played in mediating God's authority.

A "capstone," if too low, could be tripped over by an unwary person, sending him over the parapet; if too insecurely fastened, leaning against it could dislodge it and send it crashing onto the head of some passerby. Jesus probably alludes to both Isa 8:14–15 and Da 2:35. This despised stone (v.42) is not only chosen by God and promoted to the premier place, it is also dangerous.

45–46 The two principal voices of authority in the Judaism of Jesus' day understood what this parable meant. The story ends with magnificent yet tragic irony (v.46). The religious leaders are told they will reject Jesus and be crushed (cf. v.44). But instead of taking the warning, they hunt for ways to arrest him, hindered only by fear of the people who accept Jesus as a prophet. Ironically, then, God foretells this very event; and these men, prompted by hatred, rush to bring it to pass.

g. The parable of the wedding banquet (22:1–14)

If the parable of the tenants exposes Israel's leaders' neglect of their covenanted duty, this one condemns the contempt with which Israel as a whole treated God's grace.

1–3 For "kingdom of heaven," see comment on 3:2. In this parable, the kingdom has already dawned; invitations to the banquet have gone out and are being refused. The son's wedding banquet doubtless hints at the messianic banquet; but this must not be pressed too hard, for when that final banquet comes, there will be no possibility of acceptance or refusal.

The king's son is clearly Messiah, not uncommonly represented as a bridegroom (9:15; 25:1; Jn 3:29; Eph 5:25–32; Rev 21:2, 9). Prospective guests to a major feast were invited in advance and then notified when the feast was ready, but at that time these guests persistently refuse.

4–5 The king not only graciously repeats his invitation but describes the feast's greatness in order to provide an incentive to attend it. Large wedding feasts went on for days in the ancient world; by v.13 the celebration is continuing at night. But those invited stay away for mundane and selfish reasons. They slight the king, whose invitation is both an honor and a command.

6–7 The scene turns violent. Some of those invited treat the king's messengers outrageously. Enraged, the king sends his army, destroys the murderers, and burns their city. In the light of 21:38–41 the violence of those invited and the response by the king are understandable.

8–10 The situation having gone beyond that at normal wedding banquets, these shocking developments make their points that much more effectively. The king sends his servant to the forks of the roads, where they would find many people. They extend the king's invitation to all and succeed in drawing in all kinds of people, "both good and bad." The superior righteousness (5:20) believers must attain to enter the kingdom is not merely rigorous obedience to law. After all, this gospel promises a Messiah who saves his people from their sins (1:21; 20:28).

11–13 Whether one is good or bad, there is an appropriate attire for this wedding feast. The guest without a special garment, though invited, did not prepare acceptably for the feast. His speechlessness proves he knows he is guilty, even though the king gently calls him "friend" (v.12; cf. 20:13). Thus, though the invitation is very broad, it does not follow that all who respond positively actually remain for the banquet. Some are cast out.

14 Jesus concludes with a pithy statement explaining the parable. Many are invited; but some refuse to come, and others who do come refuse to submit to the norms of the kingdom and are therefore rejected. Those who remain are called "chosen" (GK *1723*), a word implicitly denying that the reversals in the parable in any way catch God unawares or remove sovereign grace from his control. At the same time it is clear from all three parables (21:28–22:14) that not the beginning but the end is crucial.

h. Paying taxes to Caesar (22:15–22)

Jesus now has a series of confrontations with his enemies. In each one he is confronted in an attempt to show he is no better than any other rabbi, or an attempt to ensnare him in serious difficulties. Not only does Jesus respond with superlative wisdom, but he ends the exchanges by challenging his opponents with a question of his own that they cannot answer (vv.41–46)—another bit of veiled self-disclosure. All this probably takes place in the temple courts on Tuesday of Passion Week.

15–16a After Jesus spoke the three parables of warning to the Jewish leaders, the Pharisees went out from the temple courts where Jesus was preaching (21:23), were joined by the Herodians (see comment on Mk 12:13), and "laid plans to trap him in his words." "Trap" reveals the motive: this is no dispassionate inquiry into a proper attitude to the Roman overlord. Paying the poll tax was the most obvious sign of submission to Rome. Zealots claimed the poll tax was a God-dishonoring badge of slavery to the pagans. The trap, then, put Jesus into the position where he would either alienate a major part of the population or else lay himself open to a charge of treason.

16b–17 The title "Teacher" (GK *1437*) and the long preamble reflect flattery and pressure for Jesus to speak. If he does not reply after such an introduction, then he is not a man of integrity and is swayed by people. The question "Is it right?" is theological, as all legal questions inevitably were to a first-century Jew.

By NT times "Caesar," the family name of Julius Caesar, had become a title (cf. Lk 2:1; 3:1; Ac 17:7). The emperor at this time was Tiberius. The wording of the question, with its deft "or not," demands a yes or a no.

18–20 But Jesus will not be forced into a yes or no reply. He recognizes the duplicity of his opponents. Jesus chooses to answer them on his own terms and asks for the coin used for paying this tax. Such coins bore an image of the emperor's head, along with an offensive inscription ("Tiberius Caesar, son of the divine Augustus" on one side and "*pontifex maximus*"—which Jesus would understand as "high priest"—on the other), that would offend most Palestinian Jews. They hand

Jesus a denarius, and, as in 21:23–27, he asks his questioners a question—this time one they have to answer (v.20).

21–22 Superficially, Jesus' answer accords with Jewish teaching that people ought to pay taxes to their foreign overlords, since the great, even the pagan great, owe their position to God (cf. Pr 8:15; Da 2:21, 37–38). But Jesus' answer is more profound than that and can be fully understood only in the light of religion-state relations in first-century Rome. The Jews, with their theocratic heritage, were ill-equipped to formulate a theological rationale for paying tribute to foreign and pagan overlords, unless, like the Jews of the Exile, they interpreted their situation as one of divine judgment. But it was not only Jewish monotheism that linked religion and state. Paganism customarily insisted even more strongly on the unity of what we distinguish as civil and religious obligations. Indeed, some decades later Christians faced the wrath of Rome because they refused to participate in emperor worship—a refusal the state judged to be treason.

Seen in this light, Jesus' response is not some witty way of getting out of a predicament; rather, it shows his full awareness of a major development in redemption history. Jesus does *not* side with the Zealots or with any who expected his messiahship to bring instant political independence from Rome. The messianic community he determines to build (16:18) must render to whatever Caesar is in power whatever belongs to him, while never turning from its obligations to God. The lesson was learned by both Paul and Peter (Ro 13:1–7; 1Pe 2:13–17). Of course, Jesus' reply is not a legal statute resolving every issue. Where Caesar claims what is God's, the claims of God have priority (Ac 4:19; 5:29). Still, Jesus' pithy words not only answer his enemies but also lay down the basis for the proper relationship of his people to government. The profundity of his reply is amazing (v.22).

i. Marriage at the Resurrection (22:23–33)

The questioners' intent in this section is as malicious as in the last one. They hope to embroil Jesus in a theological debate where he must choose sides; but instead the exchange once again demonstrates his wisdom and authority.

23 This confrontation takes place in the same situation as the former one. Pharisees believed in a resurrection from the dead, basing their belief in part on Isa 26:19 and Da 12:2. But Sadducees did not believe in a resurrection: both body and soul, they held, perish at death (cf. Ac 23:8).

24–28 Like the Pharisees, the Sadducees approach Jesus with insincere respect ("Teacher"; cf. v.16). They begin by citing the Mosaic levirate law (Dt. 25:5–6), according to which, if a man dies without children, his younger brother must marry the widow and sire children who would legally be heirs of the deceased brother. Probably in Jesus' day the law was little observed.

Though the case brought by the Sadducees *could* have happened, it is most likely hypothetical, fabricated to confound Pharisees and others who believed in resurrection. Their question presupposes that resurrection life is an exact counterpart to earthly life; and if so, the resurrected woman must be guilty of incestuous marriages (see comment on 19:9) or arbitrarily designated the wife of one of the brothers. And if so, which one? Or—and this is the answer the Sadducees pressed for—the whole notion of resurrection is absurd.

29–30 In Jesus' mind the Sadducees were denying the clear teaching of Scripture on the subject (Isa 26:19; Da 12:2; cf. Job 19:25–27), assuming that if God raises the dead he must bring them back to an existence just like this one. In his response, Jesus insists that the Sadducees betrayed their ignorance of Scripture and of the power of God, who is capable of raising the dead to an existence quite unlike this present one. By God's power, the resurrection will bring about a change in sexual relationship; in this way we will be "like the angels in heaven." Jesus' use of angels contains a double thrust, since the Sadducees also denied their existence (cf. Ac 23:8).

31–32 Jesus now turns from the power of God to the word of Scripture (cf. v.29). He may have drawn the passage to which he appeals (Ex 3:6) from the Pentateuch, because the Sadducees prized the Pentateuch more highly than the rest of Scripture. "Have you not read?" (v.31) is a rebuke (see comment on 21:42).

If God *is* the God of Abraham, Isaac, and Jacob even while he was addressing Moses hundreds of years after the first three patriarchs died, then they must be alive to him. God is the eternal God of the covenant, a fact especially stressed wherever reference is made to the patriarchs (e.g., Ge 24:12, 27, 48; 26:24; 28:13). He always loves and blesses his people; therefore it is inconceivable that his blessings cease when his people die (cf. Pss 16:10–11; 17:15; 49:14–15; 73:23–26).

At first glance Ex 3:6 is sufficient to prove immortality but not resurrection. But the Sadducees denied the existence of spirits as thoroughly as they denied the existence of angels (Ac 23:8). Their concern was not to choose between immortality and resurrection but between death as finality and life beyond death, whatever its mode. Jesus' point is that God will raise the dead as the one who always keeps his promise to be their God.

33 Matthew does not tell us that the Sadducees are convinced but that the crowds are astonished at Jesus' authority and incisive insight into biblical truth (cf. 7:28–29; 13:54; 22:22).

j. The greatest commandments (22:34–40)

The rabbis of Jesus' day were much exercised to find summary statements of OT laws and establish their relative importance; and in all probability the question arose enough times in Jesus' ministry that he developed a fairly standard response to the question.

34 Matthew portrays this confrontation as owing something to the machinations of the Pharisees, who saw how Jesus had silenced the Sadducees.

35–36 An expert in the interpretation of Scripture, perhaps especially the Pentateuch, as well as a vast complex of Jewish traditions, "tested" Jesus, asking which is the greatest commandment. The Jews quite commonly drew distinctions among the laws of Scripture—great and small, light and heavy (cf. 23:23).

37–39 Jesus first quotes Dt 6:5 and then Lev 19:18. From the viewpoint of biblical anthropology, "heart" (GK *2840*), "soul" (GK *6034*), and "mind" (GK *1379*) are not mutually exclusive but overlapping categories, together demanding our love for God to come from our whole person, our every faculty and capacity. "First and greatest" means this command is primary because it is the greatest. The second also concerns love, this time toward one's "neighbor" (GK *4446*), which in Lk 10:29–37 expands to anyone who needs our help.

40 This verse is distinctive though enigmatic. How do all the Law and the Prophets "hang on" (GK *3203*) these two commandments?

First, the two commandments stand together. The first without the second is intrinsically impossible (cf. 1Jn 4:20), and the second cannot stand without the first—even theoretically—because disciplined altruism is not love. True love demands abandonment of self to God, and God alone is the adequate incentive for such abandonment.

Jesus also suggests that the basis of human love as beginning with the heart's sincere relationship with God is in keeping with the prophetic tradition of the OT (Dt 10:12; 1Sa 15:22; Isa 1:11–18; et al.). Sterile religion, no matter how disciplined, was never regarded as adequate.

The main point Jesus makes is the priority of love within the law. These two commandments are the greatest because all Scripture "hangs" on them; i.e., nothing in Scripture can cohere or be truly obeyed unless these two are observed. The entire biblical revelation demands heart religion marked by total allegiance to God, loving him and loving one's neighbor. Without these two commandments the Bible is sterile. This section therefore prepares the way for the denunciations of 23:1–36 and conforms fully to Jesus' teaching elsewhere.

k. The son of David (22:41–46)

After silencing the Jewish leaders, Jesus asks them a question. His purpose is not to win a debate but to elicit from them what the Scriptures themselves teach about the Messiah, thus helping people to recognize who he really is. The historical setting is the temple courts, where crowds and leaders mingled together and alternately listened to the teacher from Nazareth and fired questions at him (21:23–23:36). Matthew's details probably stem from his memory of the events.

41–42 Jesus' question focuses Christology, not on resurrection or taxes—the real issue that turned the authorities into his enemies.

The Messiah's identity according to the Scriptures must be determined. One way to do that is to ask whose son he is. The Pharisees gave the accepted reply: "the son of David" (cf. 2Sa 7:13-14; Isa 11:1, 10; Jer 23:5; see comments on 1:1; 9:27-28).

43-45 But this view, though not wrong, is too simple because, as Jesus points out, David called the Messiah his Lord. How then could Messiah be David's son? The force of Jesus' argument depends on his use of Ps 110, the most frequently quoted OT chapter in the NT. The Davidic authorship of the psalm is essential to his argument. The phrase "speaking by the Spirit" not only assumes that all Scripture is Spirit-inspired (cf. Ac 4:25; Heb 3:7; 9:8; 10:15, 2Pe 1:21) but here reinforces the truth of what David said.

How does Jesus use this psalm in his argument? We have already seen how Matthew portrays much prophecy and fulfillment as OT paradigms pointing forward to the Messiah, sometimes with the understanding of the OT writers, sometimes not (see comments on 2:15; 5:17; 8:16-17). David is regularly portrayed, even in the OT, as the model for the coming Anointed One; and David himself understood at least something of the messianic promise (2Sa 7:13-14).

The widely held, if not dominant, view of the Jewish community was that the coming Messiah would be the son of David. Jesus not only declares that view inadequate, but insists that the OT itself (e.g., Ps 110) tells us it is inadequate. But if Messiah is not David's son, *whose son is he?* The solution is given by the prologue to Matthew (chs. 1-2) and by the voice of God himself (3:17; 17:5): Jesus is the Son of God. Even the title "Son of Man" (see comment on Mk 8:31) offers a transcendent conception of messiahship. This does not mean, however, that Jesus (or Matthew) is *denying* that the Messiah is David's son. This gospel repeatedly recognizes that Jesus the Messiah is Son of David—by title (1:1; 9:27; et al.), by genealogy (1:2-16), and by portrayal of Jesus as King of the Jews (2:2; 27:11, 29; et al.). What Jesus does is to synthesize the concept of a human Messiah in David's line with the concept of a divine Messiah who transcends human limitations, even as Matthew elsewhere synthesizes kingship and the Suffering Servant. The OT itself looked forward to one who would be both the offshoot and the root of David (Isa 11:1, 10; cf. Rev 22:16).

46 Matthew uses the comment about the silence of Jesus' opponents in order to finish the entire section of confrontations (21:23-22:46). Many who were silenced were not saved; so Jesus' enemies went underground for a short time. Yet even their silence was a tribute. The teacher who never attended the right schools (Jn 7:15-18) confounds the greatest theologians in the land. And if his question (v.45) was unanswerable at this time, a young Pharisee, who may have been in Jerusalem at the time, was to answer it in due course (Ro 1:1-4; 9:5).

I. Warning to the crowd and the disciples (23:1-12)

Structurally, it is difficult to decide where this chapter belongs. It is not on a par with the five major discourses of Matthew, for it lacks the characteristic discourse ending (see comment on 7:28-29). From a thematic viewpoint, it is best perceived as the climax of the preceding confrontations.

The question "What do you think about Christ?" (v.42) stands at the heart of the Gospel. The failure of the Pharisees to recognize Jesus as the Messiah prophesied in Scripture is itself already an indictment, the more so since they "sit in Moses' seat" (see comment on v.2); and the woes that follow are therefore judicial and go some way toward explaining the prophesied destruction of Jerusalem in the Olivet Discourse (24:4-25:46). Thus the strong language Jesus uses here ("fools," "hypocrites," "blind guides," "son of hell") is the language of divine warning (cf. vv.37-39) and condemnation (cf. 7:21-23).

1 Perhaps a year earlier Jesus had begun to denounce the Pharisees (15:7). Subsequently he warned his disciples of the teaching of the Pharisees and Sadducees (16:5-12). Now his warning and denunciations are public. Matthew mentions both "crowds" and "disciples" because he sees that the essential thrust of Jesus' warnings is to compel people to follow either him, the Messiah as defined in 22:41-46, or the religious leaders. And those who do the latter will share their leaders' condemnation.

2–3 The "teachers of the law," most of whom were Pharisees in Matthew's time, were primarily responsible for teaching. They "sit in Moses' seat." Ancient synagogues had a stone seat at the front where the authoritative teacher sat. Moreover, "to sit on X's seat" often means "to succeed X" (1Ki 1:35, 46; 2Ki 15:12; Ps 132:12). This would imply that the "teachers of the law" were Moses' legal successors, possessing all his authority. Jesus goes on to assert they had astounding authority in all they taught, even if they did not live up to it.

4 This verse charges the leaders with putting "heavy loads" on "men's shoulders"—laying down irksome rules—and then refusing "to lift a finger" to help. This does not mean they were unwilling to obey burdensome rules themselves but that they refused to help those who collapsed under their rules. Thus the Pharisees are not like Jesus, whose burden is light and whose promises to give rest (11:28–30); by their teaching they are doing more harm than good.

This interpretation of this verse means that Jesus' words in vv.2–3a are an instance of biting irony, bordering on sarcasm. He is implying that the Jewish religious leaders have *presumed* to sit in Moses' seat. He therefore warns the crowds and his disciples in the sharpest way possible.

5–7 Jesus now illustrates some of the leaders' practices not to be copied (v.3b). He accuses them of being time-servers and applause-seekers (6:1–18). "Phylacteries" (v.5) were small leather or parchment boxes containing a piece of vellum inscribed with four texts from the law (Ex 13:2–10, 11–16; Dt 6:4–9; 11:13–21) and were worn on the arm or tied to the forehead (cf. Ex 13:9, 16; Dt 6:8; 11:18). To show their piety to the world, these leaders made large, showy phylacteries. The same ostentation affected the length of tassels, worn by all Jews (including Jesus, 9:20; 14:36) on the corners of the outer garment (cf. Nu 15:37–41; Dt 22:12).

Seeking a reputation for piety goes with seeking places of honor at great dinners or the most important seats—as close as possible to the law scrolls—in the synagogues. "Rabbi" means "my master" or "my teacher."

8–10 The "you" (v.8) is emphatic, and Jesus is probably speaking primarily to his disciples here, just as he later addresses the Pharisees directly (vv.13–36). A good preacher knows that forthright words about what is required of believers can be at the same time a powerful incentive to decision on the part of the sympathetic but uncommitted.

Unlike the religious authorities, Jesus' disciples are not to be called "Rabbi," for they have but one "Master" (or "Teacher"; GK *1437*; cf. 22:24), Jesus himself (cf. v.10). This verse not only proscribes self-exaltation in teaching divine things but rejects the authority of the religious teachers of Jesus' day. Such authority has been taken from them (see comment on 21:43). Among those who follow Jesus, a brotherly relationship (see comment on 5:22–24) is required.

Verse 9 moves from "Rabbi" or "Teacher" to "Father." "The fathers" became a common way of referring to earlier teachers of the law, especially the great masters; that practice may have stretched back to the days of the prophets (cf. 2Ki 2:12). The only one they should call "Father" (GK *4252*) is God himself. Jesus thus concludes this section by declaring that he himself is the only one qualified to sit in Moses' seat—to succeed him as authoritative Teacher of God's will and mind. Certainly we may conclude from this that the risen Christ is as displeased with those in his church who demand unquestioning submission to themselves and their opinions and confuse a reputation for showy piety with godly surrender to their teachings as he ever was with any Pharisee.

11–12 The substance of v.11 is in 20:26: Matthew often repeats Jesus' statements on humility. For instances of exalting oneself, see comments on 20:20–28; of humbling oneself, see comment on 18:4. The principle enunciated here reflects not natural law but kingdom law: the eschatological reward will humble the self-exalted and exalt the self-humbled (cf. Eze 21:26). What is commended are humility and service. The supreme example—the Messiah himself—makes this clear (20:26–28); for his astonishing humility and service to others were untainted by servility and were perfectly compatible with exercising the highest authority. Having done the greatest service, he has been most highly exalted.

m. Seven woes on the teachers of the law and the Pharisees (23:13–36)

Jesus now begins his seven woes against the Jewish leaders. They fit into a neat chiastic pattern:

A: First woe (v.13): failing to recognize Jesus as the Messiah
   B: Second woe (v.15): superficially zealous, yet doing more harm than good
      C: Third woe (vv.16–22): misguided use of the Scripture
         D: Fourth woe (vv.23–24): fundamental failure to discern the thrust of Scripture
      C:´ Fifth woe (vv.25–26): misguided use of the Scripture
   B:´ Sixth woe (vv.27–28): superficially zealous, yet doing more harm than good
A:´ Seventh woe (vv.29–32): heirs of those who failed to recognize the prophets

What stands out is the centrality of rightly understanding the Scriptures—a theme that is reflected in all the preceding controversies and is no less related to Jesus' rejection of the claims of the teachers of the law.

13 A "woe" (GK 4026) can be a compassionate "alas!" (24:19), a strong condemnation (11:21), or a combination of the two (18:17; 26:24). In this chapter condemnation predominates; but it is neither vindictive nor spiteful so much as judicial. Jesus the Messiah pronounces judgment.

The first woe assumes that the messianic reign ("the kingdom of heaven"; see comment on 3:2) has begun. The teachers of the law and the Pharisees are "hypocrites" (see comment on 6:2), since they claim to teach God's way but refuse to enter the messianic kingdom and hinder those who try to do so. The personal conduct of the Pharisees is not in view here, however, only entrance into the kingdom. Though proper conduct is essential, it does not admit anyone into the kingdom.

The last controversy (22:41–46) revealed the real failure—the teachers of the law and the Pharisees do not enter the kingdom because they refuse to recognize who Jesus is. When the crowds begin to marvel at Jesus and suggest he may be the Messiah, the authorities do all they can to dissuade them (cf. 9:33–34; 11:19; 12:23–24; 21:15). The "woe" pronounced on the authorities is therefore of a piece with 18:6–7.

15 Many scholars have convincingly argued that the first century A.D. until the Fall of Jerusalem marks the most remarkable period of Jewish missionary zeal and corresponding success. Even in the Christian mission, no one seems to have opposed Paul's or anyone else's outreach to Gentiles: rather, what was disputed was the basis of admitting them to the people of God.

How much of the Pharisees' activity was aimed at converting to their views those who had already become loose adherents of Judaism, we cannot know for certain. But whether they were winning raw pagans or sympathizers of Judaism, they were winning them to their own position. The converts in view, therefore, are not converts to Judaism but to Pharisaism. They would travel extensively to make one "convert" (GK 4670)—a word used in the NT only here and in Ac 2:11; 6:5; 13:43 and one that at this time probably refers to those who had been circumcised and had pledged to submit to the full rigors of Jewish law, including the oral traditions of the Pharisees.

Jesus did not criticize the *fact* of the Pharisees' extensive missionary effort but its *results:* the "converts" became twice as much a "son of hell" (see comment on Mk 9:42–49) as the scribes and Pharisees who won them. That is, their converts "out-Phariseed" the Pharisees. Psychologically this is entirely possible, as every teacher of converts knows. As for these converts, the Pharisees' teaching locked them into a theological frame that left no room for Jesus the Messiah and therefore no possibility of entering the messianic kingdom.

16–22 See comments on 5:33–37 and 15:14 for the background and thrust of these verses.

While it may be true that the rabbis fought the abuses of oaths and vows among the unlearned masses, the way they fought them was by differentiating between what was binding and what was not. In that sense, wittingly or unwittingly they encouraged evasive oaths and therefore lying. Jesus cut through these complexities by insisting that people must tell the truth. He charges the teachers of the law and the Pharisees with mishandling the Scriptures they claimed to defend.

23–24 The OT law on tithing (Dt 14:22–29) specifies grain, wine, and oil, though Lev 27:30 is more comprehensive. Certainly in the first century there was debate about how far the law of tithing should extend. The consensus was to include greens and garden herbs (v.23). Jesus does not condemn scrupulous observance in these things, but insists that to fuss over them while neglecting the "more important matters of the law" (cf. 22:34–40)—justice, mercy, and faithfulness— is to strain out a gnat but swallow a camel, both unclean creatures.

Several points deserve notice. (1) The "more important" (GK 987) matters do not refer to the "more difficult" but to the "more central" or "more decisive" matters versus "peripheral" ones. (2) In essence Jesus accuses the teachers of the law and the Pharisees of a massive distortion of God's will as revealed in Scripture. At a fundamental level, they fail to focus on the thrust of Scripture (cf. 9:9–13; 12:1–14). (3) The chiastic structure of the "woes" centers on this fourth one, where the *basic* failure of the Pharisaic teachers is laid bare (see comments on 23:13–26). Jesus holds readers of the OT responsible for discerning its purpose and recognizing its most important emphases (see comment on 22:40).

25–26 Jesus begins with the metaphor of the cup and dish (v.25a), reveals his nonmetaphorical concerns at the end of v.25, then returns to his metaphor in v.26, now that its real purpose has been exposed. The Pharisees have been occupied with external religion instead of that of the inner person (cf. v.23). Within themselves they remain "full of greed and self-indulgence." In the metaphor, cleaning the inside is basic and guarantees cleanliness of the outside.

27–28 During the month of Adar, just before Passover, it was customary to whitewash with lime graves or gravesites that might not be instantly identified as such, in order to warn pilgrims to avoid ritual uncleanness from contact with corpses and so prevent participation in the Passover. But in that case whitewashed tombs would not have been objects of beauty but of disgust: they were places to be shunned. Why does Jesus, then, call them "beautiful"? Most likely the graves were beautiful because of their structure (cf. v.29), not their whitewash. Thus Jesus' mention of whitewashing is a further thrust at the Pharisees' distinctive preoccupation with avoiding ritual defilement. They are sources of uncleanness just as much as the whitewashed graves are.

In the context of ch. 23, the point Jesus is making is not that the scribes and Pharisees were deliberate and self-conscious hypocrites, but that in their scrupulous regulations they appeared magnificently virtuous but were actually contaminating the people. The supreme irony is that their preoccupation with their law left them steeped in "wickedness."

29–30 By erecting monuments the religious leaders thought themselves morally and spiritually above their forebears who had persecuted the prophets whose monuments they

These contemporary "whitewashed tombs," on the Mount of Olives, overlook the city of Jerusalem.

were building. They believed that they would not have joined their ancestors in murdering the prophets—just as many Christians today naively think they would have responded better to Jesus than the disciples or than the crowds that cried, "Crucify him!"

31 But the distinction the Jews draw in v.30 Jesus now denies. Their own saying testifies against them. They speak fondly of their ancestors and so acknowledge themselves to be the sons (NIV, "descendents") of those who shed the blood of the prophets. But Jesus sees further irony here, based on the ambiguity of "fathers" and "sons." The Jews think in terms of their physical descent. Jesus responds by saying in effect that they are sons all right—more than they realize. They show their paternity by resembling the actions of their fathers. While piously claiming to be different, they are already plotting ways to put an end to Jesus (21:38–39, 46).

32 The conclusion is defiant and ironical. The idea behind "the measure of the sin" is that God can only tolerate so much sin; then, when the measure is "filled up" (GK *4444*) he must respond in wrath (cf. Ge 15:16; 1Th 2:14–16).

33 See comments on 3:7 and 12:34 for the epithets. The transition from the preceding verse is clear: if the teachers of the law and Pharisees are filling up the measure of the sin of their forefathers, how can they possibly escape the condemnation of hell (see comment on Mk 9:42–49)?

34 Because of the Jewish leaders' wicked reception of God's messengers, more messengers (i.e., Christian missionaries; cf. 5:10–12; 9:37–38; 28:18–20) will "therefore" be sent; and they will be treated the same way. This will fill up the full measure of iniquity, and judgment will fall. Regarding the word "crucify" (GK *5090*), perhaps we have an echo of 10:24–25: the servant is not above his master. If Jesus is to be crucified, his servants may expect the same.

35–36 The very messengers who were beaten and killed for calling the people to repentance in the mystery of providence fill up the measure of the people's sins (v.32)—namely, shedding righteous blood of God's emissaries from Abel to Zechariah (see comment on Lk 12:51). Verse 35 anticipates 27:24–25: Pilate tries to evade responsibility for crucifying Jesus, and the Jews clamor for that same dreadful responsibility because of their skepticism about who Jesus is.

All along in this chapter, the teachers of the law and the Pharisees have been Jesus' primary target. Now the reference is to "this generation," because the leaders represent the people, and the people, despite Jesus' warnings, do not abandon their leaders for Jesus Messiah. This sets the stage for the concluding lament over Jerusalem (vv.37–39).

n. Lament over Jerusalem (23:37–39)

The effect of this laments is twofold. First, it tinges all the preceding woes with compassion. There is a change of number from Jerusalem to people of Jerusalem: "you [sing.] who kill ... sent to you [sing.] ... your [sing.] children ... your [pl.] house ... you [pl.] will not see." The effect is to move from the abstraction of the city to the concrete reality of people. Jesus' woes in ch. 23 therefore go far beyond personal frustrations; they are divine judgments that, though wrathful, never call in question the reality of divine love (see comment on 5:44–45).

Second, the Christological implications are unavoidable, for Jesus, identifying himself with God, claims to be the one who has longed to gather and protect this rebellious nation. Phrased in such terms, Jesus' longing can only belong to Israel's Savior, not to one of her prophets.

37 Verses 37–39 preserve Jesus' last recorded public words to Israel. Jerusalem, the city of David, the city where God revealed himself in his temple, had become known as the city that killed the prophets and stoned those sent to her. Throughout his earthly ministry, Jesus longed to gather and shelter Jerusalem (by metonymy, all Jews) as a hen gathers her chicks (cf. Dt 32:11; Ps 91:4); for despite the woes, Jesus, like the "Sovereign LORD" in Eze 18:32, took "no pleasure in the death of anyone."

38 This verse may allude to both Jer 12:7 and 22:5. "Your house" (GK *3875*) in this context could refer to Jerusalem, to Israel, or to the temple in whose precincts Jesus was preaching (21:23; 24:1) and whose destruction was about to be predicted (24:2). Actually, all three are closely allied and rise and fall together. The "house" is left desolate either by God (as in Jer 12:7) or by Jesus, who is "Immanuel," "God with us" (1:23).

39 Here Jesus refers to his Parousia. When he returns, all will acknowledge him as Lord in the future consummation. The context strongly implies that the Parousia spells judgment (cf. 24:30–31; Php 2:9–11; Rev 1:7); but the quotation of Ps 118:26 here keeps open the way Jesus will be received—as a consuming Judge or a welcomed King. Jesus turns away, leaves the temple (24:1), and will not be seen again till the End.

B. Fifth Discourse: The Olivet Discourse (24:1–25:46)

Few chapters of the Bible have called forth more disagreement among interpreters than Mt 24 and its parallels in Mk 13 and Lk 21 (see comments on those chapters). The interpretation given here presupposes the authenticity of the discourse material in the Gospels and rejects the common notion that the "prophecy" of the Fall of Jerusalem must in reality be *ex eventu* (i.e., based on the event itself).

Our goal is to understand the most natural meaning of "the abomination that causes desolation" (v.15), the significance of "let the reader understand" (v.15), the reference to the "coming of the Son of Man" (vv. 27, 30), and the extent of "this generation" (v.34), limiting ourselves primarily to the text of Matthew.

As to overall approach, the view of Mt 24 finds clear breaks in the Olivet Discourse between the two topics discussed: the destruction of Jerusalem and the return of Jesus Christ. These breaks do not, however, occur at those places most commonly advocated by evangelical scholars.

In my understanding of the Olivet Discourse, the *disciples* think of Jerusalem's destruction and the eschatological end as a single complex web of events. This accounts for the form of their questions. Jesus warns that there will be delay *before* the End—a delay characterized by persecution and tribulation for his followers (vv.4–28), but with one particularly violent display of judgment in the Fall of Jerusalem (vv.15–21; Mk 13:14–20; Lk 21:20–24). Immediately after the days of that sustained persecution characterizing the interadvent period comes the Second Advent (vv.29–31). The warning in vv.32–35 describes the whole tribulation period, from the Ascension to the Second Advent. The tribulation period will certainly come, and the generation to which Jesus is speaking will experience all its features that point to the Lord's return. But the exact time of that return no one but the Father knows (vv.36–44). This structure works out in all three Synoptics (though with significant differences in emphasis), and the main themes developed have important ties with other NT books. The disciples' questions are answered, and the reader is exhorted both to look forward to the Lord's return and to live responsibly, faithfully, compassionately, and courageously while the Master is away (24:45–25:46).

1. Setting (24:1–3)

Matthew links the Olivet Discourse closely to the "woes" in chapter 23. This does not mean that chs. 24–25 continue a single discourse—the setting, audience, and principal themes all change. But Matthew does tie the prediction of desolation (23:37–39) to the destruction of the temple (24:1–2).

1 As Jesus departs from the temple (see comment on 23:39), his disciples call his attention to its various structures. They show that they have underestimated or even misunderstood the force of Jesus' denunciations in ch. 23. They still focus on the temple, on which Jesus has pronounced doom, since the true center of the relation between God and humankind has shifted to himself.

2 The question of Jesus in this verse anticipates a "yes" answer; of course the disciples see the buildings! Jesus' forecast of the destruction of the temple complex is unambiguous, cast in OT language (cf. Jer 26:6, 18; Mic 3:12) and repeated variously elsewhere (23:38; 26:61; Lk 23:28–31).

3 The Mount of Olives (see comment on 21:1) is an appropriate site for a discourse dealing with the Parousia (cf. Zec 14:4). The disciples ask Jesus several questions privately (i.e., without the crowds around) about the temple's destruction and the signs that will presage it and about the end of the age and Jesus' return.

"The end of the age" is used six times in the NT (13:39, 40, 49; 24:3; 28:20; Heb 9:26), five of which are in Matthew and look to final judgment and the consummation of all things. *Parousia* ("coming"; GK 4242) is found twenty-four times in the NT, four of which are in Mt 24 (vv.3, 27, 37, 39). The term can refer to "presence," "arrival," or "coming"—the first stage of "presence"—and need not have eschatological overtones (2Co 7:6; 10:10). Yet the word is often closely tied with Jesus' glorious "appearing" or "coming" at the end of human history.

2. The birth pains (24:4–28)

a. General description of the birth pains (24:4–14)

The things referred to in vv.5–7 are signs that Jesus is coming back, and they all will be manifest before the generation Jesus was addressing had died. But though these things show that the End is near, none of them stipulates how near; and the tenor of the warning is that the delay will be substantial and that during this period Jesus' disciples must not be deceived by false messiahs.

4–5 One of the greatest temptations in times of difficulty is to follow blindly any self-proclaimed savior who promises help (i.e., false christs). Those who "come in my name" claim to be Christ himself. They come as if they were he. Would-be deliverers have appeared in every age, not least the first century (Ac 5:36).

6–8 "Birth pains" (GK 6047) stems from such OT passages as Isa 13:8; 26:17; Jer 4:31; 6:24; Mic 4:9–10. By this time it was almost a special term for "the birthpangs of the Messiah," the period of distress preceding the messianic Age. Jesus' followers should not be alarmed by the types of events referred to here. "Such things must happen"; yet the End is still to come. Why *must* they happen? The reason may be hidden in God's providence, but it may also be that during this time of inaugurated reign before the messianic Age attains its splendor, conflict is inevitable, precisely because the kingdom is only inaugurated. The conflict extends not only to families (10:34–37), but to nations and even nature (cf. Ro 8:20–21; Col 1:16, 20).

The effect of these verses, then, is not to curb enthusiasm for the Lord's return but to warn against false claimants and an expectation of a premature return based on misconstrued signs.

9–13 During the "birth pains" (v.8) Jesus' disciples will be persecuted and killed. "You" quite clearly extends beyond the immediate disciples and includes all the followers Jesus will have. Persecution broke out early (cf. Ac 4:1–30; 7:59–8:3; 12:1–5; Rev. 2:10, 12) and kept on during the "birth pains," against a background of hatred by the whole world (cf. Ac 28:22). Persecution is a characteristic of this age (vv.9, 21, 29)—a time when many will "turn away" from the faith and hate each other.

There is a certain parallelism between v.10 and vv.11–12. Those who turn away from the faith are deceived by false prophets, and those who hate each other do so because wickedness abounds and the love of most grows cold; only those who endure—in love (v.12) and despite persecution (vv.9–11; cf. Rev. 2:10)—will be saved (v.13). They must "stand firm to the *end*"; individual responsibility persists to the end of one's life, but corporate responsibility to the final consummation. Thus, part of the effect of this "tribulation" is to purify the body of professed disciples: those who endure are saved (cf. Da 11:32, 34–35).

The reasons for falling away may differ. In 13:21 the cause is persecution or tribulation; in 24:10–12 it is false prophets. But even here false prophecy finds some of its appeal in the matrix of trouble and persecution (vv.4–9) from which it emerges; and Matthew cares little whether faith is lost owing to fear of physical violence or to deception effected by false prophets. The result is the same and is to be expected throughout this age.

14 But none of this means that the Gospel of the kingdom of heaven (see comment on 4:23) is not preached or that its saving message does not spread throughout the world. Despite persecution—and often because of it (Ac 8:1, 4)—the Good News is "preached as a testimony to all nations." This expression is itself neutral (see comment on 8:4), and the Gospel will bring either salvation or a curse, depending on how it is received. Thus the theme of Gentile mission is again made explicit (see comments on 1:1, 2:1–12; 4:15–16; 28:18–20).

b. The sharp pain: the fall of Jerusalem (24:15–21)

15 Having characterized the entire age during which the Gospel of the kingdom is preached as a time of distress, Jesus goes on to talk about one part of it where there will be particularly "great distress" (v.21), centered around "the abomination that causes desolation" (GK *1007* & *2247*).

This expression occurs four times in Daniel (8:13; 9:27; 11:31; 12:11). The third one clearly refers to the desecration under Antiochus Epiphanes (see comment on Da 11:31), who erected an altar to Zeus over the altar of burned offering, sacrificed a swine on it, and made the practice of Judaism a capital offense. The other references in Daniel are more disputed.

Jesus is identifying Da 9:27 and 12:11 with certain events about to take place; and the parenthetical "let the reader understand" is designed to draw the attention of the *reader of Daniel* to the passages' true meaning. This parenthetical aside comes from Jesus to draw the attention of his hearers who read Daniel to the importance of Daniel's words.

But to what event does Jesus make this text from Daniel refer? The obvious occasion, in general terms, is A.D. 70, though certain difficulties must be faced. For example, although "place" can refer to the city of Jerusalem, the normal meaning of "holy place" is the temple complex. But by the time the Romans had actually desecrated the temple in A.D. 70, it was too late for anyone in the city to flee.

In comparing the differences between this verse and Mk 13:14 and Lk 21:20, possibly Jesus said something ambiguous, such as Mark reports. Luke, writing for a Gentile audience less concerned with Daniel, emphasizes the aspect of warning. Matthew, believing the allusions to Daniel important for his Jewish audience because Jesus drew attention to them, makes explicit reference to "the abomination of desolation" and to "the holy place," since the setting up of the abomination in the holy place is the inevitable result of the pagan attack.

By the time the Roman military standards surrounded Jerusalem, the city had been defiled by the Zealot excesses that polluted the temple before A.D. 70 (including murder and the installation of a false high priest), when there was still time to flee. In any case, there is reasonably good tradition that Christians abandoned the city, perhaps in A.D. 68, about halfway through the siege of Jerusalem.

16–19 The instructions Jesus gives to his disciples about what to do in view of v.15 are so specific that they must be related to the Jewish War. The devastation would stretch far beyond the city; people all throughout the land of Judea should flee to the mountains and hide in caves. Most roofs were flat—pleasant places in the cool of the day. Verse 17 implies such haste that fugitives would not take time to run downstairs to take anything with them but would run from roof to roof to evacuate the city as quickly as possible. People in the fields would not have time to go home for their cloaks. It would be especially dreadful for pregnant women and nursing mothers.

20 Flight is obviously harder in winter. As for fleeing on the Sabbath, travel would become more difficult because few would help, and many would try to prevent traveling farther than a Sabbath day's journey. Jesus clearly expects these events to take place while the strict Sabbath law is in effect.

21 "For" introduces the reason for flight in vv.17–20: "great distress" (GK *3489* & *2568*) and unprecedented suffering (cf. Da 12:1; Rev 7:14). The savagery, slaughter, disease, and famine would be monstrous, "unequaled from the beginning of the world until now," and, according to Jesus, "never to be equaled again." There have been greater numbers of deaths—six million in the Nazi death camps, mostly Jews, and an estimated twenty million under Stalin—but never so high a percentage of a great city's population so thoroughly and painfully exterminated and enslaved as during the Fall of Jerusalem. From such distress Jesus' followers were to flee.

Jesus' comment in v.21 that such "great distress" is never to be equaled implies that it cannot refer to the Tribulation at the end of the age; for if what happens next is the Millennium or the new heaven and the new earth, it seems inane to say that such "great distress" will not take place again. At the same time, by these remarks Jesus finishes his description of Jerusalem.

c. Warnings against false messiahs during the birth pains (24:22–28)

22 Many problems in interpreting the Olivet Discourse relate to the assumption that "those days" here refers to the period described in vv.15–21 and v.29. But there are excellent reasons for concluding that vv.22–28 refer to the general period of distress introduced by vv.4–14 and that therefore "those days" refers to the entire period of which vv.15–21 are only one part. (1) The term "elect" (GK *1723*; in Matthew only at 22:14; 24:22, 24, 31; cf. 20:16) most naturally refers to *all* true believers, chosen by God; so it is reasonable to assume that it does so here. (2) Similarly, "no one" (lit. "all flesh") normally refers to all humankind and is more sweeping than "no one in Jerusalem." (3) The themes of the ensuing verses have already been taken up as characteristics of the entire age (vv.4–14), especially the warning against false christs (cf. vv.4–5). (4) It has already been shown that v.21 makes a suitable ending to vv.15–21.

If this interpretation is correct, then v.22 tells us that this age of evangelism and distress—wars, famines, persecution, hatred, false prophets—will become so bad that, if not checked, no one would survive. In a century that has seen two world wars and has had more Christian martyrs than in all the previous nineteen centuries put together, Jesus' prediction does not seem farfetched. But the age will not run its course; it will be cut short. Thus believers can look for God's sovereign, climactic intervention without predicting dates.

23–25 Empty-headed credulity is as great an enemy of true faith as chronic skepticism. Christian faith involves the sober responsibility of neither believing lies nor trusting impostors. As false christs and false prophets proliferate (v.24), so will their heralds (v.23). Jesus' disciples must not be deceived, even by spectacular signs and miracles. The impostor is perennial (Dt 13:1–4; Rev 13:13).

"If that were possible" refers to the intent of the deceivers: they intend to deceive, if possible, even the elect—though Jesus makes no comment on how ultimately successful such attacks will be. That Jesus tells these things in advance (v.25) not only warns and strengthens his followers (cf. Jn 16:4) but also authenticates him (cf. Dt 13:1–4; Jn 14:29).

26–27 It is pointless to look for Messiah's return in the desert or in inner rooms—whether in some desert monastic community or in some hidden, unrecognized enclave for insiders. Far from it! The coming of the Son of Man will be public and unquestionable, not confined to some little group of initiates. As the lightning comes out of the east but is everywhere visible, so also the coming of the Son of Man will be visible to all people everywhere.

28 Jesus quotes a proverb about a "vulture." The proverb itself is a difficult one. It is likely a colorful way of saying that things come to pass at just the right time; therefore, it applies here to the Parousia of the Son of Man which comes at just the right time. Concluding this broader section (vv.4–28) is this thought: Do not be too eager for Christ's coming, or you will be deceived by false claimants (vv.23, 26). When he comes, his coming will be unmistakable (v.27), in God's own time (v.28)—a time when the world will be ripe for divine judgment.

3. The coming of the Son of Man (24:29–31)

29 For general arguments that vv.29–31 refer to Jesus' Parousia, not the coming of the Son of Man in the events of A.D. 70, see comments on vv.1–3. The reference to "the distress of those days" goes back to vv.9, 22, not to the "great distress" of vv.15–21. Thus the celestial signs and the coming of the Son of Man do not immediately follow "the abomination that causes desolation" but "the distress of those days"—i.e., of the entire interadvent period of persecution and tribulation.

The cosmic portents (cf. esp. Isa 13:9–10; 34:4) are probably meant to be taken literally, because of the climactic nature of the Son of Man's final self-disclosure. Yet this is not certain, since in some political contexts similar expressions are used metaphorically (see comments on vv.1–13).

30 With regard to the "sign of the Son of Man," "sign" (GK *4956*) commonly meant "ensign" or "standard," a word regularly associated with the final gathering of the people of God (cf. v.31; Isa 11:12; 18:3; 27:13; 49:22; Jer 4:21; 6:1; 51:27). Therefore "sign" has two different meanings in this chapter (vv.3, 30)—a phenomenon common enough in the NT. Theologically this means that the kingdom is being consummated. The standard, the banner of the Son of Man, unfurls in the heavens, as he himself returns in splendor and power.

The event will prompt "all the nations of the earth" to mourn, an allusion to Zec 12:10–12; in Zechariah the reference is to the tribes of Israel in the land, and the mourning is that of repentance. But we must probe for a deeper link. What we discover is an implicit a fortiori argument. In Zec 12, the Lord enables the house of David and Judah to crush its enemies; and as a result the Jews weep, apparently in contrition for their past sins in light of God's merciful deliverance and salvation. But it is the Gentile enemies who are crushed. If, then, the Jews face judgment and mourning (Mt 24:15–21), even though not only Jerusalem but also *all nations* (v.9) have hated Jesus' disciples, *how much more* will all the nations of the earth, to whom the Gospel has been preached (v.14), also mourn at the Parousia, when the lost opportunities and the persecution of Jesus through persecuting his disciples are seen as they truly are!

The next allusion in v.30 is to Da 7:13–14. In Daniel "one like a son of man" approaches God to receive all authority, glory, and sovereign power—"an everlasting dominion that will not pass away." In the framework of NT eschatology, we may imagine Jesus the Son of Man receiving the kingdom through his resurrection and ascension, so that now all authority is his (28:18). Yet it is equally possible to think of him receiving the kingdom at the consummation, when his reign or kingdom becomes direct and immediate, uncontested and universal. Christ's approaching God the Father to receive the kingdom is combined with his returning to earth to set up the consummated kingdom. This interpretation goes well with its vivid context.

The Son of Man, whose standard has been unfurled, comes "on the clouds of heaven" (cf. 26:64; Rev 14:14–16). The clouds symbolize God's presence (see comment on 17:5): Immanuel ("God with us") comes "with power and great glory." The latter phrase not only ensures that the coming is universally witnessed and unmistakably plain (cf. vv.26–28, 30) but may allude to Isa 11:10: the nations will rally to "the Root of Jesse," and his place of rest will be (lit.) "the Glory."

31 The sound of a loud trumpet (cf. Isa 27:13; 1Co 15:52; 1Th 4:16) is a common eschatological figure. This verse is related to 13:41. For comments on "his elect," see v.22. The "four winds" represent the four points of the compass (Eze 37:9; Da 8:8; 11:4): the elect are gathered from all over (cf. 8:11), from every place under the sky, since that is how far the Gospel of the kingdom will have been preached (v.14). Although all nations of the earth will mourn, nevertheless the elect are drawn from them.

4. The significance of the birth pains (24:32–35)

32–33 The "lesson" (lit., "parable"; GK *4130*) of the fig tree (cf. 21:18–22) is based on the common observation that the twigs get tender before summer and arouse expectations of summer (v.32). It points to the relation between "all these things" and "it is near" (v.33). Though the antecedent of "it" is uncertain (the Parousia or Jesus), the nearness of the Second Advent is certainly in view. "All these things" is more problematic; most likely it refers to the distress of vv. 4–28—the tribulation that comes on believers throughout the period between Jesus' ascension and Parousia.

Having warned his disciples of the course of this age (vv.4–28) and told them of its climax in the Parousia (vv.29–31), Jesus now answers the part of his disciples' questions (v.3) dealing with timing. He makes two points. (1) "All these things" (vv.4–28) must happen; and then the Parousia is "near, right at the door"—"imminent." In other words the Parousia is the next major step in God's redemptive purposes. (2) This does not mean that the period of distress pinpoints the Parousia, for "no one knows about that day or hour" (vv.36–42).

34 "I tell you the truth" emphasizes the importance of what it introduces. "This generation" (GK *1155*; see comments on 11:16; 12:41–42; 23:36) can only with the greatest difficulty be made to mean anything other than the generation living when Jesus spoke. Yet it does not follow that Jesus mistakenly thought the Parousia would occur within his hearers' lifetime. If our interpretation of this chapter is right, all that v.34 demands is that the distress of vv.4–28, including Jerusalem's fall, happened within the lifetime of the generation then living. This does *not* mean that the distress must *end* within that time but only that "all these things" must happen within it.

35 The authority and eternal validity of Jesus' words are nothing less than the authority and eternal validity of God's words (Ps 119:89–90; Isa 40:6–8).

5. The day and hour unknown: the need to be prepared (24:36–41)

36 Many commentators read v.36 with the preceding paragraph; but it goes much better with the following verses, which constitute an exhortation to vigilance precisely because, the day and the hour being unknown to humanity, life goes on as it always has. In the Greek, v.37 begins with the word "for."

The gist of v.36 is clear enough. Jesus' disciples are morally bound to repress all desires to know what no one knows but the Father—not even angels or the Son. If the Son himself does not know the time of the Parousia, we too should respect that ignorance and leave things in the Father's hands. On Jesus' self-confessed ignorance here, see comment on Mk 13:32.

37–39 That the coming of the Son of Man takes place at an unknown time can only be true if in fact life seems to be going on pretty much as usual—just as in the days before the Flood. People continue to follow their ordinary pursuits (v.38). Despite the distress, persecutions, and upheavals (vv.4–28), life goes on: people eat, drink, and marry. In the human condition massive distress and normal life patterns coexist. For the believer the former point to the end; the latter warn of its unexpectedness.

40–41 These two vignettes stress the unexpectedness of the event *by means of* the sudden cleavage between two people. Two men are working in a field; one is taken, the other left. Two women work their hand mill—one normally operated by two women squatting opposite each other with the mill between them, each woman in turn pulling the stone around 180 degrees. The two are apt to be sisters, mother and daughter, or two household slaves. Yet no matter how close their relationship, at the Parousia one is taken, the other left (cf. 10:35–36).

6. Parabolic teaching: variations on watchfulness (24:42–25:46)

a. The homeowner and the thief (24:42–44)

Each of the five parables in 24:42–25:46 deals with some aspect of watchfulness. But watchfulness is not always passive: duties and responsibilities must be discharged by Jesus' followers (24:45–51), and foresight and wisdom are important (25:1–13). Responsible living under Jesus' directives is rewarded in the end (25:4–46).

42–44 The first parable teaches both the unexpectedness of the return of "your Lord" and the church's willingness to call Jesus "the Lord," a religious title hitherto reserved by the Jews for God himself (1Co 12:3; 2Th 2:2; see comments on 7:22–23; 8:21). It might be better to take "understand" (GK *1182*) as an indicative ("you know") rather than an imperative: the disciples know that an owner of a house would be awake and watching if he knew when a thief was coming. Since no one knows at what "watch" a thief might strike, constant vigilance is required. Similarly, we must also always be ready because in this one respect—the unexpectedness of his coming—the Son of Man resembles a thief.

b. The two servants (24:45–51)

The good servant is prepared for the Lord's return at any time, is faithful throughout his delay, and in the end is highly rewarded. The wicked servant is faithless in fulfilling responsibilities, abusive to fellow servants, and lax in waiting for the master's return; that servant ultimately earns the expected punishment.

45–47 The "servant" in this parable is the head over all the domestics. This, however, does not so much limit the application of the parable to leaders as establish that their responsibilities entail good personal relationships (v.49), requiring exemplary conduct and precluding harshness and lording it over others. The good servant is faithful and prudent, doing what is assigned him. When his master returns, he is "blessed" (see comment on 5:3) and promoted (v.47).

48–51 If the servant is wicked and lacks faithfulness and wisdom (v.45), he may convince himself that the master "is staying away a long time"—perhaps a subtle hint that the

Parousia could be considerably delayed (cf. 25:19). The wicked servant uses the delay to abuse his fellow servants and carouse (v.49). But the wicked servant, surprised and unprepared for his master's return, is put with the "hypocrites." His lot is with the punishment given those most constantly held up as vile in this gospel (6:2, 5, 16; 16:3; 23:13–29). The master "will cut him to pieces" (cf. 1Sa 15:33; Heb 11:37)—a most severe and awful punishment—and he joins the hypocrites in weeping and grinding of teeth (cf. 8:12).

c. The ten virgins (25:1–13)

This parable has several comparative features (for discussion of parable and allegory, see introductory comment on Mk 4). The idea of Messiah as a bridegroom springs from such OT passages as Isa 54:4–6; 62:4–5; Eze 16:7–34; Hos 2:19. There the Lord is portrayed as the "husband" of his people. We have noted how readily Jesus in his parables places himself in the Lord's place (see comment on 13:37–39). Moreover, both John the Baptist (Jn 3:27–30) and Jesus himself (Mt 9:15; Mk 2:19–20) have already made the equation that Jesus = Messiah = bridegroom.

The plot in this parable turns on the bridegroom's delay (cf. the previous parable) and the need for preparedness for the Son of Man. The foolish virgins do not *forget* to bring oil; rather, the delay of the bridegroom shows they did not bring enough. The delay of the Parousia requires certain types of behavior (24:45–51; 25:14–30), especially in light of the unexpectedness of Jesus' return. Thus the parable of the virgins fits well into this sequence of parables and agrees with what we know Jesus taught. The first parable (24:42–44) warned of the unexpectedness of Messiah's coming. The second (24:45–51) showed that more than passive watchfulness is required: there must be behavior acceptable to the master, the discharge of allotted responsibilities. This third parable (25:1–13) now stresses the need for preparedness in the face of an unexpectedly long delay.

1 At the time of the return of the Son of Man, this parable will become relevant; the kingdom of heaven will become like the story of the ten virgins.

The setting is fairly clear from what we know of the marriage customs of the day. Normally the bridegroom with some close friends left his home to go to the bride's home, where there were various ceremonies, followed by a procession through the streets—after nightfall—to his home. The ten virgins may be bridesmaids who have been assisting the bride; and they expect to meet the groom as he comes from the bride's house. Everyone in the procession was expected to carry his or her own torch. Those without a torch would be assumed to be party crashers or even brigands. The festivities, which could last several days, would formally get under way at the groom's house.

Jesus refers to ten (a favorite round number; e.g., Ru 4:2; Lk 19:13) maidens who were invited to the wedding. The "lamps" are here either small oil-fed lamps or, more plausibly, torches whose rags would need periodic dowsing with oil to keep them burning. In either case the prudent would bring along a flask with an additional oil supply.

2–5 The "wise" (GK 5861) are called such because they are prepared for the bridegroom's delayed coming. Both wise and "foolish" (GK 3704) wait and doze; no praise or blame attaches to either group for this. The sole distinction between the two groups is this: the wise bring not only oil in their lamps but an extra supply in separate jars, while the foolish bring either no extra oil or no oil at all. The wise are prepared for delay; the foolish expect to meet the groom, but are either utterly unprepared or unprepared if he is delayed. And the bridegroom is a long time coming (24:48; 25:19).

6–9 At midnight (a symbol of the end of time) "the cry rang out." All the virgins wake up and trim their lamps; but the lamps of the foolish virgins quickly go out. The wise virgins cannot help them; that is, the foresight and preparedness of the wise virgins cannot benefit the foolish virgins when the eschatological crisis dawns (vv.8–9). Preparedness can neither be transferred nor shared.

10–13 The bridegroom comes, the wise virgins enter, and the door is shut. The intense cries of the ill-prepared and foolish latecomers are of no avail. Because this parable concerns the consummation, the refusal to recognize or admit the foolish virgins must not be construed as calloused rejection of their lifelong desire to enter the kingdom. Far from it: it is the rejection of those who, despite appearances, never made preparation for the coming of the kingdom. The final verse reiterates the main theme of the parable mentioned: Be prepared! "Keep watch[ing]"!

d. The talents (25:14–30)

This parable goes beyond the first three (24:42–25:13) in that it expects the watchfulness of the servants to manifest itself during the master's absence, not only in preparedness and performance of duty, even if there is a long delay, but in an improvement of the allotted "talents" until the day of reckoning.

14 The introduction to this parable is somewhat abrupt; probably it is so tightly associated with the last one that it shares its introduction. Servants (lit., "slaves"; GK *1528*) in the ancient world could enjoy considerable responsibility and authority. The man going on a journey entrusts his cash assets to three of his slaves who are understood to be almost partners in his affairs and who may share some of his profits. The departure and the property are integral parts of the story and should not be allegorized to refer to the Ascension and the gifts of the Spirit.

15 Modern English uses the word "talent" for skills and mental powers God has entrusted to men; but in NT times the "talent" (GK *5419*) was a unit of exchange. Estimates of its value vary enormously for several reasons. (1) A talent could be of gold, silver, or copper, each with its own value. (2) The talent was first a measure according to weight, between 58 and 80 pounds, and then a unit of coinage, with a one common value assigned it (e.g., 6,000 denarii). (3) Modern inflation continues to change the value of a talent. Thus it is more sensible to compare the talent with modern currency in terms of earning power. If a talent was worth 6,000 denarii, then it would take a day laborer twenty years to earn so much. So the sums are vast. Moreover the talents are distributed according to the master's evaluation of his servants' capacities. The parable, therefore, lays intrinsic emphasis on the principle, "from the one who has been entrusted with much, much more will be asked" (Lk 12:28).

16–18 "At once" relates to the good servants' promptness to put the money to work by setting up some business and working with the capital to make it grow. They felt the responsibility of their assignment and went to work without delay. But one servant, unwilling to work or take risks, merely dug a hole and buried the money. This was safer than the deposit systems of the time.

19–23 The accounting begins "after a long time," the implication being that the consummation of the kingdom will be long delayed (24:48; 25:5). "Settled accounts" is a standard commercial term. The first servant, who doubled his five talents, is praised especially for his faithfulness and is given two things: increased responsibility and a share in his master's "joy." Jesus suggests by this that the consummated kingdom will provide glorious new responsibilities and holy delight (cf. Ro 8:17).

The second servant has likewise been faithful with what had been given him; he hears the same words as the first servant and receives increased responsibility to the limits of his capacity.

24–25 The third servant accuses his master of grasping, exploiting the labor of others, and putting the servant in an invidious position. Should he take the risk of trying to increase the one talent entrusted to him, he would see little of the profit. If he failed and lost everything, he would incur the master's wrath. Perhaps, too, he is piqued at having been given much less than the other two; so, in a rather spiteful act, he returns to his master what belongs to him, no more and no less.

What this servant overlooks is his responsibility to his master and his obligation to discharge his assigned duties. Such failure betrays his lack of love for his master, which he masks by blaming his master and excusing himself. Only the wicked servant blames his master. Grace never condones irresponsibility; even those given less are obligated to use and develop what they have.

26–27 The master condemns the servant on the basis of the servant's own words, which prove his guilt. If the master really was so harsh and greedy, should not the servant at least have put the money where it would have been relatively safe, earned interest, and required no work?

The OT forbade Israelites from charging interest against one another (Ex 22:25; Lev 25:35–37; Dt 23:19), but interest on money loaned to Gentiles was permitted (Dt 23:20). By NT times Jewish scholars already distinguished between "lending at interest" and "usury." It is wrong to assume that Jesus is here either supporting the Jewish tradition or setting aside the OT law. The question does not arise, for Jesus' parables are so flexible that he sometimes uses examples of evil to make a point about good (e.g., Lk 16:1–9; 18:1–8).

28–30 The talent entrusted to this wicked servant is taken from him, and the relationship between master and servant is severed. The talent is given to the man who now has ten talents, following the kingdom rule Jesus had already taught in 13:12. The wicked servant is "worthless," for to fail to do good and use what God has entrusted to us is grievous sin, which results not only in the loss of neglected resources but in rejection by the master, banishment from his presence, and tears and grinding of teeth.

The parable insists that the watchfulness that must mark all Jesus' disciples may not lead to passivity but to doing one's duty, to growing and developing the resources God entrusts to us, until "after a long time" (v.19) the master returns and settles accounts.

e. The sheep and the goats (25:31–46)

Strictly speaking, this passage is not a parable. Its only parabolic elements are the shepherd, the sheep, the goats, and the actual separation. It clearly functions in this discourse somewhat as 10:40–42 (with which it has some connections) does in the second discourse.

While the majority of scholars understand "the least of these brothers of mine" (vv.40, 45) to refer to all who are hungry, distressed, and needy, it seems more in keeping with Matthew to see the phrase as referring to Jesus' disciples (12:48–49; 28:10; cf. 23:8). The fate of the nations will be determined by how they respond to Jesus' followers, who are charged with spreading the Gospel and who do so in the face of hunger, thirst, illness, and imprisonment. Good deeds done to them, even the least of them, are not only works of compassion and morality but reflect where people stand in relation to the kingdom and to Jesus himself. Jesus identifies himself with the fate of his followers and makes compassion for them equivalent to compassion for himself.

31 Nowhere in this discourse does Jesus explicitly identify the "Son of Man" with himself. But since this epithet is used in answer to the question "What will be the sign of your coming?" (24:3), the inference is inescapable. There are clear allusions to Zec 14:5; but the role of eschatological Judge is, like many other things (see comment on 13:37–39), transferred without hesitation from the Lord to Jesus. The Son of Man will come "in his heavenly glory" (cf. 16:27; 24:30; 1Th 4:16; 2Th 1:8). He sits on his throne, not only as Judge, but as King (see v.34); for all of divine authority is mediated through him (28:18; cf. 1Co 15:25; Heb 12:2). (On the role of the angels, see 13:41–42; 24:31; 2Th 1:7–8; Rev 14:17–20.)

32–33 Presupposed is the fulfillment of 24:14. "All the nations" means "all peoples." As the Gospel of the kingdom is preached to Gentiles as well as Jews, so also must all stand before the King.

In the countryside sheep and goats mingled during the day. At night they were often separated: sheep tolerated the cool air, but goats had to be herded together for warmth. The right hand is the place of power and honor.

34–40 The change from "Son of Man" (see comment on Mk 8:31) to "King" (vv.31, 34) is not at all unnatural; for the Son of Man in Da 7:13–14 approaches the Ancient of Days to receive "a kingdom," and here that kingdom is consummated (see comment on 24:30). The kingship motif has long since been hinted at or, on occasion, made fairly explicit to certain persons (see 3:2; 4:17; 16:28; 19:28). Yet Jesus still associates his work with his Father, something he loves to do (10:32–33; 11:25–27; et al.). He addresses the sheep, "Come, you who are blessed *by my Father.*" They are "blessed" (GK *2328*) inasmuch as they now receive their inheritance (Ro 8:17; Rev 21:7), which presupposes a relationship with him. That inheritance is the kingdom (comments on 3:2; 4:17). This glorious inheritance, the consummated kingdom, was the Father's plan for them from the beginning.

The reason they are invited to take their inheritance is that they have served the King's "brothers" (cf. Isa 58:7). The reason for admission to the kingdom in this parable is more evidential than causative, as is suggested by the surprise of the righteous (vv.37–39). When he is questioned, the King replies that doing the deeds mentioned to the least of his brothers is equivalent to doing it to him (v.40), and by implication to refuse help to the King's brothers is sacrilege.

41–45 The condemnation is even more awful than in 7:23. The "goats" are cursed: they are banished from the King's presence and sent to the eternal fire. Hell is here described in categories familiar to Jews (see 3:12; 5:22; 18:8; Jude 7; Rev 20:10–15; see comment on Mk 9:42–49). The kingdom was prepared for the righteous (v.34); hell was prepared for the Devil and his angels but also serves as the doom of those guilty of the sins of omission of which Jesus here speaks—refusing to show compassion to King Messiah through helping the least of his brothers. There is no significance in the fact that the "goats" address Jesus as "Lord," for at this point there is no exception whatever to confessing Jesus as Lord (cf. Php 2:11).

More important is the surprise of the sheep (vv.37–39) and the goats (v.44), a major part of the parable, though rarely discussed. Three things can be said with confidence. (1) Neither the sheep nor the goats are surprised at the place the King assigns them but rather at the *reason* given for this—i.e., that they are admitted or excluded on the basis of how they treated Jesus. (2) The surprise of the righteous makes it impossible to think that works of righteousness win salvation. The sheep did not show love to gain a final reward, not did the goats fail to show it to flout final retribution. (3) The parable therefore presents a test eliminating the possibility of hypocrisy. If the goats had thought that their treatment of Jesus' "brothers" would gain them the kingdom, they would doubtless have treated them compassionately. But Jesus is interested in a righteousness of the whole person, a righteousness that comes from the heart. As people respond to his disciples and align themselves with their distress and afflictions, they align themselves with the Messiah who identifies himself with them. True disciples will love one another and serve the least brother with compassion; in so doing they unconsciously serve Christ. Those who have little sympathy for the Gospel of the kingdom will remain indifferent and, in so doing, reject King Messiah (cf. Ac 9:5).

We must not think that the Bible is unconcerned for the poor and the oppressed (Dt 15:11; Mt 22:37–40; 26:11; Gal 2:10), but that is not the center of interest here.

46 The same word "eternal" (GK *173*) modifies "punishment" and "life." This word refers to life or punishment in the age to come; it is "everlasting."

7. Transitional conclusion: fourth major passion prediction and the plot against Jesus (26:1–5)

1–2 For the other major passion predictions, see comments on 16:21; 17:22–23; 20:18–19. One last time Matthew uses the formula by which he brings all his discourses to a close (v.1; see comment on 7:28–29). In the narrative line of Matthew, this pericope is a masterpiece of irony. The Judge of the universe, King Messiah, the glorious Son of Man, is about to be judged.

The Passover began Thursday afternoon with the slaughter of the lamb. According to the tentative chronology, Jesus spoke these words on the Mount of Olives late Tuesday evening, which, by Jewish reckoning, would be the beginning of Wednesday (see comment on Mk 14:1–2, 12).

The "Son of Man" (see comment on Mk 8:31) is here both glorious and suffering: as often, the themes merge. The Passover is two days away; and it is during that festival that Jesus reveals for the first time that the Son of Man will be "handed over" (GK *4140*) to be crucified. Thus Jesus provides a framework for his disciples to interpret his death correctly after it happens—a framework alluded to a little more clearly in the institution of the Lord's Supper (vv.17–29).

3–5 Opposition to Jesus had been rising for some time (cf. 12:14; 21:45–46). God, however, is in control of these events. The leaders may plot; but if Jesus dies, he dies as a voluntary Passover sacrifice (vv.53–54; Jn 10:18).

Caiaphas is called the high priest in Matthew and John (11:49); Luke (Lk 3:2; Ac 4:6) specifies Annas. There is no real conflict. Annas was deposed by the secular authorities in A.D. 15 and replaced by Caiaphas, who lived and ruled till his death in A.D. 36. But since according to the OT the high priest was not to be replaced till after his death, the transfer of power was illegal. Doubtless some continued to call either man "high priest." Certainly

Annas, Caiaphas's father-in-law (Jn 18:13), continued to exercise great authority behind the scenes.

The combination of "assembled" and "plotted" in vv.3–4 strongly suggests an allusion to Ps 31:13 (cf. also Ps. 31:5; Lk 23:46). Earlier that day the leaders had wanted to arrest Jesus but dared not do so for fear of the people (21:46). Now they decide to do away with Jesus, recognizing that they must do this by stealth so as not to excite the crowds and start a riot (see comments on Mk 14:2, 10–11).

VII. The Passion and Resurrection of Jesus (26:6–28:20)

A. The Passion (26:6–27:66)

1. Anointed at Bethany (26:6–13)

This story begins the sixth narrative-and-teaching division of Matthew (26:6–28:20). with the teaching to be done by Jesus' disciples after his ascension (see 28:18–20 and the introduction, under "Structure"). From another viewpoint the Passion and Resurrection must, as in all the Gospels, be seen as the climax toward which the earlier narrative has been moving.

6–7 This is the second time Jesus was anointed, the first time being recorded in Lk 7:36–50 (on Bethany, see comment on 21:1-2). Matthew sets the scene in the home of "Simon the Leper," who was presumably cured—or else all there were violating Mosaic law. The action of the woman was not unprecedented: a distinguished rabbi might have been so honored. The evangelists stress the cost of the "perfume"; John suggests that it was worth approximately a year's salary for a working man (Jn 12:3). This perfume was possibly from the nard plant (native to India); it was extracted from the thin-necked alabaster flask by snapping off the neck.

8–9 With Judas as their spokesman (see Jn 12:4–5), the disciples fail to understand what is taking place, not only in the anointing, but also in who Jesus truly is and in the rush of redemptive events toward the Cross (see comments on 16:21–28; 17:22–23; 20:18–19). Doubtless there were thousands of poor people within a few miles of this anointing.

10–11 It is possible that Jesus' knowledge of the complaints is here supernatural; but perhaps they were whispered and came to Jesus' attention because they troubled the woman. Jesus begins his rebuke by accusing the disciples of "bothering" her. What they call waste, Jesus calls "a beautiful thing."

Jesus distinguishes between giving to the poor and the extravagance lavished on himself *on the grounds that he will not always be physically present to receive it* (cf. 28:20). His followers will always find poor people to help (cf. Dt 15:11). Implicitly, the distinction Jesus makes is a high Christological claim, for it not only shows that he foresees his impending departure but also that he himself, who is truly "gentle and humble in heart" (11:29), *deserves* this lavish outpouring of love and expense.

12–13 The anointing does not designate Jesus as Messiah but "prepares" him for his burial after dying the death of a criminal, for only in that circumstance would the customary anointing of the body be omitted. Jesus' defense of the woman does not necessarily mean that the woman understood what she was doing, though it allows this. Jesus may well be using the anointing to intimate again his impending crucifixion (cf. v.2). Jesus ends this incident by stating that the woman and her deed would be remembered wherever the Gospel of the kingdom is preached.

2. Judas's betrayal agreement (26:14–16)

All the Gospels speak of Judas's important role in Jesus' death but none explains what motives prompted his treachery. Like most human motives, his were mixed and doubtless included avarice and jealousy combined with profound disappointment that Jesus was not acting like the Messiah he had expected.

14–16 In Judas's view Jesus was acting less and less regal and more and more like a defeatist on his way to death. Judas may also have been smarting from Jesus' rebuke over the anointing of the woman as recorded in Jn 12:4–8. He therefore approaches the "chief priests" with an offer to hand Jesus over. They "counted out for him thirty silver coins," calling to mind Zec 11:12, to which Matthew will return in 27:3–10. In Zec 11, thirty pieces of silver is a paltry amount—the value of a slave accidentally gored to death by an ox (Ex 21:32). That Jesus is lightly esteemed is reflected not only in his betrayal

PASSION WEEK

1. ARRIVAL IN BETHANY   FRIDAY   Jn 12:1

Jesus arrived in Bethany six days before the Passover to spend some time with his friends, Mary, Martha and Lazarus. While here, Mary anointed his feet with costly perfume as an act of humility. This tender expression indicated Mary's devotion to Jesus and her willingness to serve him.

2. SABBATH — DAY OF REST   SATURDAY   Not mentioned in the Gospels

Since this day was the Sabbath, the Lord spent the day in traditional fashion with his friends.

3. THE TRIUMPHAL ENTRY   SUNDAY   Mt 21:1-11; Mk 11:1-11; Lk 19:28-44; Jn 12:12-19

On the first day of the week Jesus rode into Jerusalem on a donkey, fulfilling an ancient prophecy (Zec 9:9). The crowd welcomed him with "Hosanna" and the words of Ps 118:25-26, thus ascribing to him a Messianic title as the agent of the Lord, the coming King of Israel.

4. CLEARING OF THE TEMPLE   MONDAY   Mt 21:10-17; Mk 11:15-18; Lk 19:45-48

On this day he returned to the temple and found the court of the Gentiles full of traders and money changers making a large profit as they gave out Jewish coins in exchange for "pagan" money. Jesus drove them out and overturned their tables.

5. DAY OF CONTROVERSY AND PARABLES   TUESDAY   Mt 21:23–24:51; Mk 11:27–13:37; Lk 20:1–21:36

In Jerusalem - Jesus evaded the traps set by the priests.
On the Mount of Olives Overlooking Jerusalem - He taught in parables and warned the people against the Pharisees. He predicted the destruction of Herod's great temple and told his disciples about future events, including his own return.

6. DAY OF REST   WEDNESDAY   Not mentioned in the Gospels

The Scriptures do not mention this day, but the counting of the days (Mk 14:1; Jn 12:1) seems to indicate that there was another day concerning which the Gospels record nothing.

7. PASSOVER LAST SUPPER   THURSDAY   Mt 26:17-30; Mk 14:12-26; Lk 22:7-23; Jn 13:1-30

In an upper room Jesus prepared both himself and his disciples for his death. He gave the Passover meal a new meaning. The loaf of bread and cup of wine represented his body soon to be sacrificed and his blood soon to be shed. And so he instituted the "Lord's Supper." After singing a hymn they went to the Garden of Gethsemane, where Jesus prayed in agony, knowing what lay ahead for him.

8. CRUCIFIXION   FRIDAY   Mt 27:1-66; Mk 15:1-47; Lk 22:66–23:56; Jn 18:28–19:37

Following betrayal, arrest, desertion, false trials, denial, condemnation, beatings and mockery, Jesus was required to carry his cross to "The Place of the Skull," where he was crucified with two other prisoners.

9. IN THE TOMB   FRIDAY   Mt 27:57-61; Mk 15:42-47; Lk 23:50-56; Jn 19:38-42

Jesus' body was placed in the tomb before 6:00 P.M. Friday night, when the Sabbath began and all work stopped, and it lay in the tomb throughout the Sabbath.

10. RESURRECTION   SUNDAY   Mt 28:1-13; Mk 16:1-20; Lk 24:1-49; Jn 20:1-31

Early in the morning, women went to the tomb and found that the stone closing the tomb's entrance had been rolled back. An angel told them Jesus was alive and gave them a message. Jesus appeared to Mary Magdalene in the garden, to Peter, to two disciples on the road to Emmaus, and later that day to all the disciples but Thomas. His resurrection was established as a fact.

©1989 The Zondervan Corporation.

3. The Lord's Supper (26:17–30)

a. Preparations for the Passover (26:17–19)

17 Toward midafternoon of Thursday, 14 Nisan (see comment on Mk 14:1–2), the lambs (one per "household"—a convenient group of perhaps ten or twelve people) would be brought to the temple court where the priests sacrificed them. The priests took the blood and passed it in basins along a line till it was poured out at the foot of the altar. They also burned the lambs' fat on the altar of burnt offerings. The singing of the *Hallel* (Pss 113–18) accompanied these steps.

After sunset (i.e., now 15 Nisan), the "household" would gather in a home to eat the Passover lamb, which by this time would have been roasted with bitter herbs. The head of the household began the meal with the thanksgiving for that feast day and for the wine, praying over the first of four cups. A preliminary course of greens and bitter herbs was followed by the Passover *haggadah*—in which a boy would ask the meaning of all this, and the head of the household would explain the symbols in terms of the Exodus—and by the singing of the first part of the *Hallel* (Ps 113 or Pss 113–114). Though the precise order is disputed, apparently a second cup of wine introduced the main course, which was followed by a third cup, known as the "cup of blessing," accompanied by another prayer of thanksgiving. The participants then sang the rest of the *Hallel* (Pss 114–18 or 115–18) and probably drank a fourth cup of wine. Thus the preparations about which the disciples were asking were extensive.

18–19 The disciples (perhaps only two of them, Mk 14:13) are told to find an unnamed person, who would show them a room to prepare for Jesus' final Passover meal. His words "My appointed time is near" were probably purposely ambiguous. To the disciples and the owner of the house, they may have implied Jesus' timing for the Passover meal and prior arrangements for it. In the light of Easter, the words must refer to the now impending Crucifixion, the fulfillment of Jesus' mission.

The disciples do as Jesus has instructed them. He is quietly and consciously taking the necessary steps to complete his mission of tragedy and glory.

b. Prediction of the betrayal (26:20–25)

20–22 The Passover meal could not be eaten till after sundown; and for those living within Palestine, it had to be eaten inside Jerusalem or not at all. That is why we find Jesus reclining at a table in a room in the city "when evening came." Once the meal began Jesus solemnly says, "I tell you the truth, one of you will betray [GK *4140;* cf. 26:2] me." The disciples respond uniformly: one after another, as the enormity of the charge sinks in, each man asks, "Surely not I, Lord?"

23 Jesus' point in this verse is that the betrayer is a friend, someone close, someone sharing the common dish, thus heightening the enormity of the betrayal. If the main course, the roast lamb, was being eaten, the "bowl" would contain herbs and a fruit puree, which would be scooped out with bread.

24 For "woe," see comment on 23:13; for "Son of Man," see comment on Mk 8:31. Here the Son of Man is simultaneously the glorious messianic figure who receives a kingdom and the Suffering Servant. No single OT verse explains "as it is written of him"; but one may think of passages such as Isa 53:7–9; Da 9:26, or else suppose that an entire prophetic typology (see comment on 2:15; 5:17–20) is in view, such as the Passover lamb.

The divine necessity for the sacrifice of the Son of Man does not excuse or mitigate the crime of betrayal. Divine sovereignty and human responsibility are both involved in Judas's treason, the one effecting salvation and bringing redemption history to its fulfillment, the other answering the promptings of an evil heart (cf. Ac 2:22–23; 4:27–28). The one results in salvation from sin for Messiah's people (1:21), the other in personal and eternal ruin.

25 This exchange magnifies Judas's effrontery. Doubtless Judas felt he had to speak up; silence at this stage might have given him away to the others. In contrast to the other disciples (v.22), he uses "Rabbi," a title for a respected teacher. As in v.22, the form of the question anticipates a negative answer, but the expected answer bears no necessary relation to the real answer. Jesus' response is affirmative but depends somewhat on spoken intonation for its full force. It could be taken to mean "You have said it, not I" (cf. NIV note); yet in fact it is enough of an affirmative to give Judas a jolt without removing all ambiguity from the ears of the other disciples.

c. The words of institution (26:26–30)

26 Matthew now records a second thing that takes place "while they were eating" (cf. v.21). Jesus takes an unleavened loaf (cf. Ex 12:15; 13:3, 7; Dt 16:3), gives thanks (see comment on Mk 6:41), breaks it, distributes it, and says, "Take and eat; this is my body."

Few clauses of four words have evoked more debate than the last one. But three things must be said. (1) The words "this is my body" had no place in the Passover ritual; as an innovation, they must have had stunning effect, an effect that would grow with the increased understanding gained after Easter. (2) Both the breaking and the distributing are probably significant. The sacrificial overtones are clearer in vv.27–28, but the unambiguous sacrificial language connected with Jesus' blood requires that v.26 be interpreted in a similar way. (3) Much of the debate on the force of "is" is anachronistic. The verb itself has a wide semantic range and proves very little. But what must be remembered is that this is a Passover meal. The new rite Jesus institutes has links with redemption history. As the bread has just been broken, so will Jesus' body be broken; and just as the people of Israel associated their deliverance from Egypt with eating the paschal meal prescribed as a divine ordinance, so also Messiah's people are to associate Jesus' redemptive death with eating this bread by Jesus' authority.

27 Assuming this is a Passover meal, this "cup" is probably the third, the "cup of blessing." Jesus again gives thanks (see comment on Lk 22:19–20). The wine was likely fermented grape juice, though it was customary to dilute the wine with a double or triple quantity of water. Matthew records the command: "Drink from it, all of you."

28 This verse is rich in allusions. "Blood" (GK *135*) and "covenant" (GK *1347*) are found together in only two OT passages (Ex 24:8; Zec 9:11). Once again, we can penetrate near the heart of Jesus' own understanding of his relation to the OT (see comment on 5:17–20; 9:16–17; 11:9–13). Jesus understands the violent and sacrificial death he is about to undergo (i.e., his "blood") as the ratification of the covenant he is inaugurating with his people, even as Moses in Ex 24:8 ratified the "covenant" of Sinai by the shedding of blood. Jer 31:31–34, with the word "new" before "covenant," must also have been in Jesus' mind. The event through which Messiah saves his people from their sins (1:21) is his sacrificial death; and the resulting relation between God and the messianic community is definable in terms of covenant, an agreement with stipulations—promises of blessing and sustenance and threats of cursing, all brought here into legal force by the shedding of blood.

The words "which is poured out for many" could not fail to be understood as a reference to the Passover sacrifice in which so much blood had just been "poured out." They also connote other sacrificial implications (e.g., Lev 1–7; 16), especially significant since at least *Jesus'* crucifixion did entail much bloodshed. The phrase "for the forgiveness of sins" alludes to Jer 31:31–34; Jesus' sacrifice provides the real basis for forgiveness (cf. 1:21).

One more OT allusion is worth emphasizing. Jesus is probably also portraying himself as Isaiah's Suffering Servant. This is based on three things: (1) "my blood of the covenant" calls to mind that the servant is twice presented as "a covenant for the people" (Isa 42:6; 49:8)—i.e., he will reestablish the covenant; (2) "poured out" may well reflect Isa 53:12; and (3) "for many" recalls the work of the Servant in Isa 52:13–53:12 (see comment on 20:28).

29 Just as the first Passover looked forward not only to deliverance but also to settlement in the land, so also the Lord's Supper looks forward to deliverance and life in the consummated kingdom. The disciples will keep this celebration till Jesus comes (cf. 1Co 11:26); but Jesus will not participate in it with them until the consummation, when he will sit down with them at the messianic banquet (Isa 25:6; see comment on Mt 8:11) in his

Father's kingdom, which is equally Jesus' kingdom.

30 The "hymn" normally sung was the last part of the *Hallel* (Pss 114–18 or 115–18). It was sung antiphonally: Jesus as the leader would sing the lines, and his followers would respond with "Hallelujah!" Parts of it must have been deeply moving to the disciples when after the Resurrection they remembered that Jesus sang words pledging that he would keep his vows (Ps 116:12–13), ultimately triumph despite rejection (Ps 118), and call all nations to praise the Lord and his covenant love (Ps 117).

4. Prediction of abandonment and denial (26:31–35)

In laying out in advance much of the tragedy of the coming hours, this section shows that Jesus is not a blind victim of fate but a voluntary sacrifice; simultaneously he is preparing his disciples for their dark night of doubt.

31 "This very night" makes clear how soon the disciples' defection and Peter's denial will happen. The intimacy of the Last Supper is shortly to be replaced by disloyalty and cowardice. The disciples will find Jesus an obstacle to devotion and will forsake him. As the quotation from Zechariah makes clear, their falling away is related to the "striking" of the Shepherd. Jesus has repeatedly predicted his death and resurrection, but his disciples are still unable to grasp how such things could happen to the Messiah to whom they have been looking (16:21–23; 17:22–23).

Yet Jesus' words "for it is written" show that the disciples' defection, though tragic and irresponsible, does not fall outside God's sovereign plan. Zec 13:1–6 pictures a day when, owing to the prevailing apostasy, the Shepherd who is close to the Lord is cut down and the sheep scattered. In 13:8–9 most of the sheep perish; but one-third are left, after being refined, to become "my people"—those who will say, "The Lord is our God." If Jesus' quotation of Zechariah in the Gospels presupposes the full context of 13:7, then the disciples themselves join Israel, the sheep of God, in being scattered as the result of the "striking" of the Shepherd. Their falling away "this very night" continues to the Cross and beyond. But a purified remnant, a "third," will survive the refining and make up the people of God, "my people."

32 The prediction that the shepherd will be stricken and the sheep scattered might suggest that the disciples would return disconsolate to their homes in Galilee, leaving Jesus behind in a grave in Judea. But this new word promises that after Jesus has risen, he will arrive in Galilee before they get there: he will "go ahead of [them]."

33 Peter responds to Jesus' prediction about all the disciples falling away, not to Jesus' prediction of going to Galilee. Though Peter later followed Jesus into the courtyard, he initially joined the other disciples in fleeing (v.56); his later following was only "at a distance" (v.58), and then he denied Jesus. At the end of the day, all the sheep were scattered; all had fallen away.

34 Apparently it was usual for roosters in Palestine to crow about 12:30, 1:30, and 2:30 A.M., so the Romans gave the term "cockcrow" to the watch from 12:00 to 3:00 A.M. Despite Peter's claims of undeviating loyalty, Jesus says that Peter is within hours of "disowning" (GK 565; see also 16:4) him three times.

35 The language of Peter's protest shows that he does not really think that Jesus' death was likely; he still has visions of heroism. Nor is he alone in his brash protestations of loyalty—only quicker and more vehement than his peers.

5. Gethsemane (26:36–46)

Central in this section is the light shed on Jesus' perception of what he is about to do. The anguish in Gethsemane is not lightly to be passed over: three times Jesus prayed in deep emotional distress. He went to his death knowing that it was his Father's will that he face death completely alone (27:46) as the sacrificial Passover Lamb. As his death was unique, so also was his anguish; and our best response to it is hushed worship.

36–38 On "Gethsemane," see comment on Mk 14:32. Taking three of his disciples with him, Jesus now faces deep, inner distress. His words "My soul is overwhelmed with sorrow" reflect almost verbally the refrain of Pss 42–43. Jesus experiences a sorrow so deep it almost kills. Having revealed his deepest emotions and thus given his disciples the most compelling of reasons to do what he asks, he tells them to stay and "keep watch with me" while he goes a little farther on to pray alone. His words "with me" imply that he wanted them to keep awake and go on praying.

39 Jesus prays, prostrate in his intense anguish. He addresses God as "My Father" (see comment on 6:9). The "cup" (GK *4539*) refers not only to suffering and death but, as often in the OT (Ps 75:7–8; Isa 51:19, 22; Jer 25:15–16; et al.), also to God's wrath; it anticipates 27:46.

In one sense all things are possible with God (see comments on 19:26; Mk 14:36); in another some things are impossible. Thus Jesus prays that, if it be morally consistent with the Father's redeeming purpose that his "cup" be taken from him, that is what he deeply desires. But more deeply still, Jesus desires to do his Father's will. His deep commitment to his Father's will cannot be doubted. But in this crisis, the worst since 4:1–11, Jesus is tempted to seek an alternative to sin-bearing suffering as the route by which to fulfill his Father's redemptive purposes. He prays in agony; and though he is supernaturally strengthened (Lk 22:43), he learns only that the Cross is unavoidable if he is to obey his Father's will.

40–41 Jesus returns to his disciples—i.e., the inner three—and finds them sleeping. Jesus' question is addressed to Peter but is in the plural and therefore includes all three (see comment on 16:16). On "watch and pray," see comment on Mk 14:38.

It is doubtful that "so that you will not fall into temptation" means only "so that you will stay awake and not fall into the temptation to sleep." Rather, he tells them that only urgent prayer will save them from falling into the coming "temptation" (GK *4280*; see comments on 4:1; 6:13). Even in his own extremity, when he needs and seeks his Father's face, Jesus thinks of the impending but much lesser trial his followers will face. He speaks compassionately: "The spirit is willing, but the body is weak." Spiritual eagerness is often accompanied by carnal weakness—a danger amply experienced even by us today.

42–44 Jesus returns to pray "the same thing." As Jesus learned obedience (Heb 5:7–9), so he became the supreme model for his own teaching. In the first garden "Not your will but mine" changed Paradise to desert. Now "Not my will but yours" brings anguish to the man who prayed it but transforms the desert into the kingdom.

45–46 Jesus' words here form a gently ironic command. The hour of the Passion is near: it is too late to pray and gain strength for the temptations ahead. His disciples may as well sleep. He who is the resplendent, messianic King takes the path of suffering. Doubtless Jesus could see and hear the party approaching as it crossed the Kidron with torches and climbed up the path to Gethsemane. The sleepers for whom he would die have lost their opportunity to gain strength through prayer. By contrast Jesus has prayed in agony but now rises with poise and advances to meet his betrayer.

6. The arrest (26:47–56)

47 Judas Iscariot (see comment on 26:14–16) arrives with armed men. What he received payment for was probably information as to where Jesus could be arrested in a quiet setting with little danger of mob violence. He may have first led the "large crowd" to the Upper Room and, finding it empty, surmised where Jesus and his disciples had gone (cf. Jn 18:1–3). The "large crowd" was comprised of both temple police and a detachment of Roman soldiers. Especially during the feasts the Romans took extra pains to ensure public order, so a request for a small detachment from the cohort would not likely be turned down. Thus Pilate might have had some inkling of the plot from the beginning, and if he shared it with his wife, it might help explain her dream (27:19).

48–50 The need for pointing out the right man was especially acute, not only because it was dark, but because, in a time long before photography, the faces of even great celebrities would not be widely known. To identify Jesus, Judas chose the kiss, thereby turning it into a symbol of betrayal.

"Friend" is an open-hearted but not intimate greeting. The next words are either an imperative (as NIV), in which case Jesus has regained his poise and sovereignty, or a question (NIV note), which administers a rebuke steeped in the irony of professed ignorance that knows very well why Judas has come.

51–54 Peter's response is scarcely unexpected, especially in the light of his earlier protest of loyalty (vv.33–35). The crucial test of loyalty had arrived. He is magnificent and pathetic—magnificent because he rushes in to defend Jesus with characteristic courage and impetuousness, pathetic because his courage evaporates when Jesus undoes Peter's damage, forbids violence, and faces the Passion without resisting.

What of Jesus' response in v.52? The least we can say is that violence *in defense of Christ* is completely unjustified. Moreover, if Jesus wanted to use force, a simple request to his Father would bring twelve legions of angels to his assistance—perhaps one legion for Jesus and one for each of the Eleven. In addition, Jesus' stance regarding his own death is grounded on the fact the "Scriptures" must be fulfilled (see comments on vv.24, 31). Jesus is determined to obey his Father's will.

55–56 Every day for the preceding week, and presumably on earlier visits to the Holy City, Jesus had been teaching in the temple courts; yet the authorities had not arrested him. Why then do they seize him now as if he were a rebel (see comment on 27:16)? The implication is that there is no need to arrest him secretly and violently, except for reasons in their own minds that reveal more about themselves than about him. And then Jesus again referred to the fulfillment of prophetic Scripture.

All the disciples then fulfill one specific prophecy (v.31) and flee. Probably at this time Jesus is bound (Jn 18:12).

7. Jesus before the Sanhedrin (26:57–68)

In assessing blame for the crucifixion of Jesus, one must admit that, from a theological perspective every Christian is as guilty of putting Jesus on the cross as Caiaphas. Thoughtful believers will surely admit that their own guilt is the more basic of the two; for if we believe Matthew's witness, and Jesus could have escaped the clutches of Caiaphas (v.53), then what drove Jesus to the cross was his commitment to the Father's redemptive purposes.

Regarding the hour-by-hour procedure of Jesus' trial, see comment on Mk 14:53–65.

57–58 Well-to-do homes were often built in a square shape with an open, central courtyard. If Annas (cf. comment on v.3) lived in rooms on one wing of the court, then it is possible that he interviewed Jesus (Jn 18:14–16) in one wing while the Sanhedrin was assembling in another. Not much time would be required.

Peter followed Jesus "at a distance," midway between courage (v.51) and cowardice (v.70). He joined the servants (Jn 18:15–16) and temple police around the courtyard fire.

59–63a The Sanhedrin was composed of three groups: leading priests, teachers of the law, and elders. It had seventy members plus the high priest, but a mere twenty-three made a quorum. The "whole Sanhedrin" need not mean that everyone was present (cf. Lk 23:50–51). This group was looking "for false evidence" and obtained it from "false witnesses." Already convinced of Jesus' guilt, they went through the motions of securing evidence against him. When people hate, they readily accept false witness; and the Sanhedrin eventually heard and believed just what it wanted. Matthew knew that Jesus was not guilty, so he describes the evidence as "false."

The two men who came forward may or may not have been suborned. At least two witnesses were required in a capital case. Their witness had an element of truth but was evilly motivated, disregarding what Jesus meant in Jn 2:19–21 (see comment on these verses). Interpreted with crass literalism, Jesus' words might be taken as a threat to desecrate the temple, one of the pillars of Judaism. Desecration of sacred places was almost universally regarded as a capital offense in the ancient world, and in this Jews were not different from the pagans.

The high priest asks two questions in v.62. He probably hoped Jesus would incriminate himself. But, true to Isa 53:7, Jesus kept silent.

63b The high priest, frustrated by Jesus' silence, tried a bold stroke that cut to the central issue: Was Jesus the Messiah or was he not? The question had been raised before in one form or another (see comments on 12:38–42; 16:1–4). He boldly charged Jesus to answer "under oath by the living God."

The outcome is now inevitable. If Jesus refuses to answer, he breaks a legally imposed oath. If he denies he is the Messiah, the crisis is over—but so is his influence. If he affirms it, then, given the commitments of the court, Jesus must be false. After all, how could the true Messiah allow himself to be imprisoned and put in jeopardy? The Gospels' evidence suggests that the Sanhedrin was prepared to see Jesus' unequivocal claim to messiahship as meriting the death penalty, and their unbelief precluded them from allowing any other possibility.

64 The answer Jesus gives is affirmative, though reluctantly so (cf. comment on v.25). Certainly Caiaphas understood it as positive. Jesus' follow-up comment is a qualification, spoken because Caiaphas's understanding of "Messiah" and "Son of God" is fundamentally inadequate. Jesus is indeed the Messiah and so must answer affirmatively. But he is not quite the Messiah Caiaphas has in mind; so he must answer cautiously and with some explanation.

That explanation comes in allusions to two passages—Ps 110:1 (see comment on Mt 22:41–46) and Da 7:13 (see comment on Mk 8:31). Jesus is not to be primarily considered a political Messiah but as the one who, in receiving a kingdom, is exalted at God's right hand, the position of honor and power (cf. 16:27; 23:39; 24:30–31; 26:29). This is Jesus' climactic self-disclosure to the authorities, combining revelation with threat. He tells the members of the Sanhedrin that from then on they would not see him as he now stands before them but only in his capacity as undisputed King Messiah and sovereign Judge.

65–66 Rending garments was an expression of indignation or grief (cf. 2Ki 18:37; Ac 14:14). Whether the Sanhedrin thought Jesus was blaspheming because he claimed to be Messiah, because he put himself on the Mighty One's right hand, or because God had not especially attested who Jesus was is uncertain. The decision of the assembled members of the Sanhedrin appears to have been by acclamation. Jesus is "worthy" of the death penalty, mandated for "blasphemy" (GK *1059–1060*; cf. Lev 24:16).

67–68 The messianic claims of the accused do not impress the Sanhedrin, and the indignities to which Jesus is now subjected are probably meant to deride his false pretensions. The true Messiah would vanquish all foes. But this man is spit on, punched, slapped, blindfolded (Mk 14:65), and taunted, without displaying any power. For "prophesy," see comment on Mk 14:65.

8. Peter's denial of Jesus (26:69–75)

69–70 The remark of the servant girl to Peter reflects both an accusation and her curiosity, and "Jesus of Galilee" is the kind of derogatory remark one might expect from a Jerusalemite convinced of her geographical and cultural superiority. Peter denies her words "before them all," implying that several people were listening and that some may have joined in the questioning.

71–72 Peter "went out" to the gateway, apparently retiring from the brighter light of the fire into the darkness of the forecourt. There he denies another accusation, invoking a solemn curse on himself if he is lying and professing his truthfulness by appealing to something sacred (see comment on 5:33–34).

73–75 A little more time elapses. In any age accent in speaking varies with geography, and Peter's speech shows him to be a Galilean. That one of those present at Peter's denial said that his accent proved him to be a disciple of Jesus shows how much Jesus' ministry had been in Galilee and how relatively few of his disciples were from Judea. Having lied twice, Peter finds himself forced to lie again, this time with more oaths. Immediately the rooster crows, a bitter reminder of Jesus' words (v.34). He who thought he could stand has fallen terribly (cf. 1Co 10:12).

9. Formal decision of the Sanhedrin (27:1–2)

1 Whether this formal decision was reached as a final stage of the first meeting or at a separate meeting held either in Caiaphas's house or the temple precincts, we cannot say with certainty. Luke 22:66 implies a meeting in the council chamber.

The religious authorities decided just how to present their case to Pilate. If their own concern was Jesus' "blasphemy" (26:65), they were nevertheless more likely to get Pilate to sentence him to death by stressing the royal side of messiahship rather than blasphemy, since to Pilate that would suggest treason.

2 Jesus is led to Pontius Pilate, prefect appointed by Tiberius Caesar in A.D. 26. Prefects held the power of life and death, apart from appeal to Caesar (see comment on Lk 23:1–5). Extrabiblical sources portray Pilate as a cruel, imperious, and insensitive ruler who hated his Jewish subjects and took few pains to understand them. He stole money to build an aqueduct; and when the population of Jerusalem rioted in protest, he sent in soldiers who killed many. He defiled Jerusalem more than once (cf. Lk 13:1).

Both the Sanhedrin trial and the trial before Pilate were necessary for capital punishment. Without the Sanhedrin, Pilate would never have taken action against Jesus unless he had become convinced Jesus was a dangerous Zealot leader; without Pilate the Sanhedrin might whip up mob violence against Jesus, but it would not be a legally binding death sentence.

10. The death of Judas (27:3–10)

Matthew's prime interest in recording Judas's death is to continue the fulfillment theme—not only regarding Jesus' death but also regarding the major events surrounding his crucifixion as prophesied in Scripture.

3–4 Verse 3 looks back to 26:14–16, 20–25. Judas's "remorse" is not necessarily repentance. He recognizes not only that he is guilty of betrayal but that Jesus whom he has betrayed is "innocent." The Jewish leaders' callous response condemns them, for Judas's comments *should* have meant something to them. He betrayed innocent blood; they condemned innocent blood.

5–8 Exactly where Judas threw the money is uncertain. He then went out and hanged himself. The chief priests refuse to allow the blood money to supplement the funds of the "treasury" (cf. Dt 23:18). Matthew again points out the propensity of the Jewish leaders for ceremonial probity even in the face of gross injustice (cf. 12:9–14; 15:1–9; 23:23; 28:12–13).

With this probity in view, the chief priests decide to buy the potter's field to meet a public need. This field, used for burying foreigners, probably did not belong to "the potter" but was a well-known place, perhaps the place where potters had long obtained their clay. If depleted, it might have been offered for sale. Regarding the relationship of this passage to Ac 1:18–19, see comments in Acts.

9–10 Three aspects of this complex quotation need discussion.

(1) *The ascription to Jeremiah.* On the face of it, the quotation is a rough rendering of Zec 11:12–13. The only obvious allusions to Jeremiah are 18:2–6; 32:6–15—Jeremiah did visit a potter and buy a field. It is difficult to imagine why Matthew mentioned Jeremiah instead of Zechariah, even though Jeremiah is important in this gospel (cf. 2:17; 16:14).

We should first note that no extant version of Zec 11 refers to a field; thus Matthew's attributing the quotation to Jeremiah suggests we ought to look to that book. Jeremiah 19:1–13 is the obvious candidate, where Jeremiah is told to purchase a potter's jar and take some elders and priests to the Valley of Ben Hinnom. There he is to warn of the destruction of Jerusalem for her sin, illustrated by smashing the jar. A further linguistic link is "innocent blood" (Jer 19:4); and thematic links include renaming a locality associated with potters (19:1) with a name ("Valley of Slaughter") denoting violence (19:6). The place will henceforth be used as a burial ground (19:11), as a token of God's judgment. In other words, the quotation appears to refer to Jer 19:1–13, along with phraseology drawn mostly from Zec 11:12–13. Such fusing of sources under one "quotation" is not unknown elsewhere in Scripture (e.g., Mk 1:2–3). Jeremiah alone is mentioned, perhaps because he is the more important of the two prophets, and perhaps also because Jer 19 is more important as to prophecy and fulfillment.

(2) *Meaning.* How did Matthew understand the OT texts he was quoting? The question is not easy, because the two OT passages themselves can be variously explained. It appears that in Zec 11 the "buyers" (v.5) and the three shepherds (vv.5, 8, 17) apparently represent Israel's leaders, who are slaughtering the sheep. God commands Zechariah to shepherd the "flock marked for slaughter" (v.7), and he tries to clean up the leadership by sacking the false shepherds. But he discovers that not only is the leadership corrupt, but the flock detests him (v.8). Thus Zechariah comes to understand the Lord's decision to have no more pity on the people of the land (v.6).

Zechariah decides to resign (11:9–10), exposing the flock to ravages. Because he has broken the contract, he cannot claim his pay (presumably from the "buyers"); but they pay him off with thirty pieces of silver (v.12). But now the Lord tells Zechariah to throw this "handsome price at which they priced me" (probably ironical) to the potter in the "house of the LORD."

The parallel between Zec 11 and Mt 26–27 is not exact. In Zechariah the money is paid to the good shepherd; in Matthew it is paid to Judas and returned to the Jewish leaders. In Zechariah the money goes directly to the "potter" in the temple; in Matthew, after being thrown into the temple, it purchases "the potter's field." Nevertheless the central parallel is stunning: in both instances the Lord's shepherd is rejected by the people of Israel and valued at the price of a slave. And in both instances the money is flung into the temple and ends up purchasing something that pollutes and points to the destruction of the nation (see comments on 15:7–9; 21:42).

(3) *Fulfillment.* In the light of these relationships between the events surrounding Jesus' death and the two key OT passages that make up Matthew's quotation, what does the evangelist mean by saying that the prophecy "was fulfilled"? As in 2:17, the form of this introductory formula shrinks from making Judas's horrible crime the immediate result of the Lord's word, while nevertheless insisting that all has taken place in fulfillment of Scripture (cf. 1:22 with 2:17). What we find in Matthew, including vv.9–10, is not *identification* of the text *with* an event but *fulfillment* of the text *in* an event, based on a broad typology governing how both Jesus and Matthew read the OT (see comments on 2:15; 8:17; 13:35; 26:28, 54). Because of this typological model, Matthew can introduce the commonly noticed changes: e.g., the one on whom a price is set is no longer the prophet ("me," Zec 11:13), but Jesus.

11. Jesus before Pilate (27:11–26)

The setting for Jesus' trial before Pilate is uncertain. It might be the Tower of Antonia, on the northwest corner of the temple area; but more probably it is Herod's old palace on the west side of the city near the Jaffa gate.

11 For information on Pilate, see comment on vv.1–2. Pilate's question, "Are you the king of the Jews?" presupposes the background of Lk 23:2 and Jn 18:28–33 (for the Jews' charge against Jesus, see comment on Lk 23:10). In Roman trials the magistrate normally heard the charges first, questioned the defendant and listened to his defense, sometimes permitted several such exchanges, and then retired with his advisors to decide on a verdict, which was then promptly carried out. The first step led to this particular formulation of Pilate's question to Jesus. Jesus answers, as in 26:64, in an affirmative but qualified way. He is indeed the king of the Jews, but not exactly in the sense Pilate might think (see Jn 18:34–37).

Verse 11 is important theologically as well as historically. It stands behind the inscription on the cross and prepares the way for Christianity, which rests on the conviction that Jesus of Nazareth, who rose from the dead, is indeed the promised Messiah, the King of the Jews—basic themes in Matthew even in the prologue. The vindicated Lord is the crucified Messiah.

12–14 Persistent charges by "the chief priests and the elders" evoke only silence from Jesus. If Jesus had said nothing at all, Pilate would be bound to condemn him, since in the Roman system the defense depended heavily on the defendant's response. But Jesus *has* spoken (v.11). Now, surrounded by unbelief and conscious that the hour has come, he makes no reply. Thus he continues to fulfill Isa 53:7 (see comment on 26:63). Pilate's "great amazement" appears to be mingled with respect for Jesus and antipathy for the Jewish leaders, and so he takes tentative steps to release the prisoner.

15 In Roman law an imperial magistrate could acquit a prisoner not yet condemned or pardon one already condemned; but the gospel accounts make this a regular custom, apparently associated with Judea alone.

16 Perhaps Barabbas was the son of a famous rabbi (his name literally means "son of the father"; see comment on 23:9). Barabbas was probably an insurrectionist, and a well-known one. Revolts and bloodshed fostered by guerrilla action were common, and Barabbas had been caught. In the eyes of many of the people he would not be a "notorious" villain but a hero.

It may be that the two who were crucified with Jesus were co-rebels with Barabbas, for Mt 27:38 uses the same word for their offense as for Barabbas. The fact that three crosses had been prepared strongly suggests that Pilate had already ordered that preparations be made for the execution of the three rebels. If so, Jesus the Messiah actually took the place of the rebel Barabbas because the people preferred the political rebel and nationalist hero to the Son of God.

17–18 The "crowd" was the crowd of those trying to influence the selection of the prisoner who would receive amnesty (cf. Mk 15:8). Pilate sized up the real motivation of the Jewish leaders. They had no special loyalty to Rome; so if they were accusing Jesus of being a traitor to Rome, he must have been disturbing them for other reasons; and they were simply using Pilate to eliminate Jesus' challenge to them. Pilate, with his network of spies and informers, would be aware of how much popularity Jesus enjoyed among the people at large. He could hardly have been unaware of the upsurge of acclaim the previous Sunday (21:1–16). He thought to administer a reversal to Sanhedrin policy by using the paschal amnesty to encourage the crowd to free Jesus; therefore he offered them a choice: Barabbas or Jesus.

19 If Roman troops were involved in Jesus' arrest (see comment on 26:47), Pilate and perhaps his wife would have been informed. The interruption of Pilate's wife further stresses Jesus' innocence and gives the chief priests and elders a few moments to influence the crowd.

20–23 The leaders helped persuade the crowd. Historically, the crowd's response is comprehensible. They have come to demand Barabbas's release. Confronted with the choice of Barabbas or Jesus, both of whom were widely popular, their momentary faltering is resolved by their leaders. If the crowd must choose between Pilate's choice and the Sanhedrin's, especially if the Sanhedrin members are circulating stories of Jesus' "blasphemy," then there can be little doubt whom they will choose. Jews often confronted the Roman authorities with a large and noisy delegation, and now mob mentality begins to take over.

Tactically Pilate has blundered. Trying to save face he asks more questions. The first offers the hope of a milder sentence, and the second attests Jesus' innocence. But mob psychology prevails. The people prefer a murderous, nationalistic guerrilla leader over their Messiah, who exhorted them to love their enemies and said he would die as a ransom for many.

24 To the best of our knowledge, this hand washing was not a Roman custom. After living several years among the Jews he detested, Pilate picked up one of their own customs (Dt 21:6; cf. Ps 26:6) and contemptuously used it against them. Whatever his motives, Pilate had been trying to release Jesus. He sent him to Herod (Lk 23:6–12), suggested that the paschal amnesty be applied to him, proposed a compromise with a scourging (Lk 23:16), tried to turn the case back to Jewish authorities (Jn 19:6), remonstrated before pronouncing sentence (Jn 19:12–14), and here washes his hands. Matthew gives us only two of these steps.

Regardless of what Pilate thought, Matthew does not think the hand washing exonerated Pilate. He insists that Pilate's action was not prompted by desire for justice but by political and moral cowardice and fear of a mob. The Romans expected their magistrates to maintain peace, and a possible uproar would intimidate a governor. So when Pilate says, "It is your responsibility," Matthew intends his readers to remember the same words spoken by the chief priests and elders to Judas (v.4).

25 To Pilate's words, "all the people" answer, "Let his blood be on us and on our children!" The idiom is familiar (2Sa 1:6; 3:28; Ac 18:6; 20:26). In the narrative this is a swift retort to Pilate's taunt and mob pressure for him to pronounce the verdict.

But it clearly is more than that. How much more? Many say that by "all the people" Matthew is saying that *the Jews as a whole* reject Jesus. To them v.25 becomes a prophecy of the destruction of Jerusalem and the nation; and a new people of God, the church, would take over. There is some truth in this view, but it needs qualification. Matthew certainly knows that *all* the first disciples were Jews. Thus the gospel's denunciations of the Jews are not more severe than those of many OT prophets, and in both instances it is understood that a faithful remnant remains. So what Matthew actually says cannot be judged as a general anti-Semitic comment, certainly not any more than Jeremiah's prediction of the destruction of Jerusalem and the Exile can.

26 On flogging, see comment on Mk 15:15. Jesus' flogging took place before the verdict and so was not repeated after the verdict.

Pilate, after further entreaty (Jn 19:1–16), "handed him over to be crucified."

12. The soldiers' treatment of Jesus (27:27–31)

27 That the governor's troops are the ones involved in these shameful actions belies any suggestion that Matthew exculpates Pilate (see comment on v.24). The "Praetorium" is probably the old palace of Herod; the soldiers take Jesus into the palace courtyard, where they fulfill Jesus' predictions in 20:17–20.

28–31 Here we have humanity at its worst—a scene of vicious mockery. The Jews have mocked Jesus as Messiah (26:67–68); here the Roman soldiers ridicule him as king. Matthew's readers recognize that the soldiers speak more truly than they know, for Jesus is both King and Suffering Servant. The "robe" is probably the short red cloak worn by Roman military and civilian officials.

For a crown, the soldiers plait a wreath of thorns from palm spines or acanthus and crush it down on Jesus' head in imitation of the circlet on the coins of Tiberius Caesar. The staff they put in his hand stands for a royal scepter; and the mocking "Hail, King of the Jews!" corresponds to the Roman acclamation "Ave, Caesar!" and caps the flamboyant kneeling. Not content with the ridicule and the torture of the thorns, they spit on him and use the staff, the symbol of his kingly authority, to hit him on the head "again and again."

Jesus is then led away by an execution squad of four soldiers, dragging the crosspiece to which his hands would be nailed (Jn 19:17, 23).

13. The Crucifixion and mocking (27:32–44)

Crucifixion was unspeakably painful and degrading. Whether tied or nailed to the cross, the victim endured countless paroxysms as he pulled with his arms and pushed with his legs to keep his chest cavity open for breathing and then collapsed in exhaustion until the demand for oxygen demanded renewed paroxysms. The scourging, the loss of blood, and the shock from the pain all produced agony that could go on for days, ending at last by suffocation, cardiac arrest, or loss of blood. When there was reason to hasten death, the execution squad would smash the victim's legs. Death followed almost immediately, either from shock or from collapse that cut off breath. Beyond the pain was the shame. In ancient sources crucifixion was universally viewed with horror. In Roman law it was reserved only for the worst criminals and lowest classes. No Roman citizen could be crucified without a direct edict from Caesar.

Among Jews the horror of the cross was greater still because of Dt 21:23: "Anyone who is hung on a tree is under God's curse." In Israelite law this meant the corpse of a judicially executed criminal was hung up for public exposure that branded him as cursed by God. These words were also applied in Jesus' day to anyone crucified, and therefore the Jews' demand that Jesus be crucified rather than banished was aimed at arousing maximum public revulsion toward him. But in Christian perspective the curse on Jesus at the cross fulfills all OT sacrifices: it is a curse that removes the curse from believers—the fusion of divine, royal prerogative and Suffering Servant, the heart of the Gospel, the inauguration of a new humanity, the supreme model for Christian ethics, the ratification of the new covenant, and the power of God (1Co 1:23–24; Gal 3:13; Col 2:14; 1Pe 2:18–25). The dominant note of this section is the continuing mockery, but mockery that by an awful irony reveals more than the mocker thinks—for Jesus is indeed King of the Jews (v.37), the new meeting place with God (v.40), the Savior of humanity (v.42), the King of Israel (v.42), and the Son of God (v.43).

In Jerusalem this model of the ancient city is popular with tourists. In the foreground is the old palace of Herod (the Praetorium).

32 Executions normally took place outside the city walls (Lev 24:14; Nu 15:35–36; 1Ki 21:13; Ac 7:58), symbolizing still further rejection (cf. Heb 13:13). Jesus, weak as he was, managed to carry the crossbeam as far as the city gates (cf. Jn 19:17). There, as they were "going out" of the city, the soldiers forced Simon to assume the load. He came from Cyrene, an old Greek settlement on the coast of North Africa.

33–34 On "Golgotha," see comment on Mk 15:22. Mark says they offered Jesus wine mingled with myrrh, and he refused it; Matthew, that they offered him wine mingled with gall, and he tasted it and then refused it. It seems likely that this gesture was not one of compassion but of torment. Myrrh was used with wine to strengthen the drink, but it tastes bitter; so a large dose of it mingled with wine would make the latter undrinkable. Thus, when the drink was offered to Jesus, it was so bitter he refused it, and the soldiers were amused. Mark keeps the word "myrrh" to describe the content; Matthew uses "gall" to describe the taste and to provide a link with Ps 69:12. For another view of this element of the crucifixion, see comment on Mk 15:23.

35 Jesus was nailed to the crossbeam, which was then hoisted to its place on the upright. His feet were then nailed to the upright. The Romans crucified their victims naked, and their clothes customarily became the perquisite of the executioners; here they divided them—probably an inner and outer garment, a belt, and a pair of sandals—among themselves by casting lots, oblivious to the OT lament in Ps 22:18 that Jn 19.23–24 says was now fulfilled.

36 The soldiers kept watch to prevent rescue (men were known to have lived after being taken down from a cross).

37–38 The statement of the crime was often written on a white tablet in red or black letters and displayed on the cross. The charge against Jesus, written in Hebrew, Greek, and Latin (Jn 19:19–22), wrote more of the truth than Pilate knew. On the two "robbers," see comment on v.16.

39–40 Crucifixion was always carried out publicly as a warning to others. A public execution provided opportunity for those walking by to "hurl insults" at Jesus. Shaking their heads, and so calling to mind the derision in Pss 22:7; 109:25; Lam 2:15, the passers-by threw up the charge in Mt 26:60–61 (they had likely witnessed the proceedings of the Sanhedrin or had some report of them). The second taunt, "If you are the Son of God," not only harks back to the trial (26:63), but for Matthew recalls a dramatic parallel (4:3, 6). Through the passers-by Satan was still trying to get Jesus to evade the Father's will and avoid further suffering.

41–44 All the principal groups of the Sanhedrin do not address Jesus directly but speak of him in the third person, in a stage whisper meant for his ears. "He saved others" is probably an oblique reference to Jesus' supernatural healing ministry. "But he can't save himself" is cutting because it questions that same supernatural power. But there is level on level of meaning. For the Christian reader "save" (GK 5392) has full eschatological overtones. And although Jesus *could* have saved himself (26:53), he could *not* have saved himself if he was to save others.

The second of the three taunts, "He's the king of Israel!" substitutes the covenant term Israel for "the Jews" in Pilate's words (v.11) and is in fact the normal Palestinian form of Jesus' claim. The words "Let him come down from the cross, and we will believe in him" have several levels of meaning. They constitute a malicious barb directed at Jesus' helplessness, while having the effrontery to suggest that the leaders' failure to believe was his fault. The taunt piously promises faith if Jesus will but step down from the cross; but the reader knows that, in the mystery of providence, if Jesus were to step down, there would be no "blood of the covenant for the forgiveness of sins" (26:26–29), no ransom (20:28), no salvation from sin (1:21), no Gospel of the kingdom to be proclaimed to nations everywhere (28:18–20), and no fulfillment of Scripture.

In an unconscious allusion to Ps 22:8, the religious leaders launch their third taunt: "He trusts in God." They recognize that Jesus' claim to be the "Son of God" was at least a claim to messiahship. So assuming that God must crown every effort of Messiah with success, they conclude that Jesus' hopeless condition is proof enough of the vanity of his pretensions. Again their malice masks the ironic redemptive purposes of God. On the one hand, as Christian readers know, God will indeed vindicate his Son at the Resurrection. On the other hand, the leaders are right: Jesus is now facing his most severe test, the loss of his Father's presence, leading to the heart-rending cry of the following verses.

The other two crucified with him join in the abuse (but see Lk 23:39–43).

14. The death of Jesus (27:45–50)

45 The darkness that "came over all the land" from noon till 3:00 P.M. was a sign of judgment and/or tragedy (cf. Am 8:9–10). The judgment is therefore a judgment on the land and its people. But it is also a judgment on Jesus; for out of this darkness comes his cry of desolation. The cosmic blackness hints at the deep judgment that was taking place (20:28; 26:26–29; Gal 3:13).

46 In what language did Jesus utter his cry of desolation, taken from Ps 22:1? It was most likely in Aramaic; and at least some of the variants (cf. NIV note) stem from the difficulty of transliterating a Semitic language into Greek.

What does this psalm quotation signify? It is best to take the words at face value: Jesus is conscious of being abandoned by his Father. For one who knew the intimacy of 11:27, such abandonment must have been agony. If we ask in what ontological sense the Father and the Son are here divided, the answer must be that we do not know because we are not told.

47 According to 2Ki 2:1–12, Elijah did not die but was taken alive to heaven in a whirlwind. Some Jewish tradition, perhaps as old as the first century, held that he would come and rescue the righteous in their distress.

48–49 See comment on v.34; the allusion is again Ps 69:21. What is not clear is whether the offer of a drink here is meant as a gesture of mercy or as mockery; its purpose may have been to prolong life and agony, while with false piety the onlookers say they will wait for Elijah to rescue him.

50 This loud cry reminds us once more of Jesus' hideous agony. That "he gave up his spirit" suggests Jesus' sovereignty over the exact time of his own death. It was at this moment, when he was experiencing the abyss of his alienation from the Father and was being cruelly mocked by those he came to serve, that he chose to yield up his life a "ransom for many "(see comment on 20:28).

15. Immediate impact of the death (27:51–56)

51a On the tearing of the temple veil, see comment on Mk 15:38. In accordance with Matthew's fulfillment themes (cf. comments on 5:17–20; 11:11–13), the tearing of the veil signifies the obsolescence of the temple ritual and the law governing it (cf. Heb 9:1–14). Jesus himself is the New Temple, the meeting place of God and humankind (see comment on Jn 2:19–21); the old is obsolete. At the same time, the rent veil serves as a sign of the temple's impending destruction—a destruction conceived not as a brute fact but as a theological necessity.

51b–53 Matthew implies that the earthquake (v.51b), itself a symbol of judgment and theophanic glory, was the means of tearing the veil as well as opening the tombs.

But the resurrection of the "holy people" (GK *41*) remains difficult to understand. Perhaps the best explanation is to see a full stop after "broke open," so that the words that follow form a parenthesis in the flow of the narrative. The resurrection of "the holy people" then begins a new sentence that is linked only with Jesus' resurrection. Matthew does not intend his readers to think that these people were resurrected when Jesus died and then waited in their tombs till Easter Sunday before showing themselves. Instead, they were raised to life at the same time Jesus was. The language implies that these saints were certain well-known OT and intertestamental Jewish spiritual heroes and martyrs. If so, then Matthew is telling us that the resurrection of people who lived before Jesus Messiah is as dependent on Jesus' triumph as the resurrection of those who come after him.

54 "Son of God" is one of several major Christological titles in Matthew. But it is not certain what exactly the soldiers meant by "Son of God" (see comment on Mk 15:39). The darkness, the earthquake, and the cry of dereliction convinced the soldiers that this was no ordinary execution. The portents terrified them and probably led them to believe that these things testified to heaven's wrath at the perpetration of such a crime, in which the drawing on; so early on the first day of the week they "went to look at the tomb."

2–4 The clause introduced by "for" either suggests that the violent earthquake came with the "angel of the Lord" or was the means the angel used to open the tomb. The stone was rolled back, the seal broken, and the soldiers made helpless—not to let the risen Messiah escape, but to let the first witnesses in.

5–7 The angel speaks words that allay the women's fears. While the empty tomb by itself is capable of several explanations, this explanatory word of revelation narrows the potential interpretations down to one: Jesus had risen from the dead (v.6), a truth to be confirmed by personal appearances. Matthew also ties in the Resurrection with Jesus' promises—"as he said" (cf. 16:21; 17:23; 20:18–19). The women are invited to see the place where Jesus lay and commanded to go "quickly" to give his disciples the joyous message. Jesus had promised to go ahead of his disciples into Galilee (see comment on 26:32); the angel now reminds them of this.

2. First encounter with the risen Christ (28:8–10)

8–9 With mingled fear and joy, the women run to tell their news to the disciples, when "suddenly" (GK 2627 & 2779) Jesus meets them and greets them with a traditional greeting. The women clasp his feet and "worship" (or "kneel before"; GK 4686) him. The same verb occurs in the only other resurrection appearance (v.17) and encourages the view that the "kneeling" has instinctively become worship (see comment on 8:2).

10 Like the angel (v.5), Jesus stills the women's fears and gives them a similar commission. "My brothers" probably does not refer only to the Eleven but to all those attached to his cause who were then in Jerusalem, most of whom had followed him from Galilee to Jerusalem as his "disciples" (see comments on 5:1–2; 28:17).

Why does Matthew record a resurrection appearance in Galilee? The answer surely lies in the combination of two themes that have permeated the entire gospel. (1) The Messiah emerges from a despised area (see comment on 2:23) and first sheds his light on a despised people (see comment on 4:15–16), for the kingdom of heaven belongs to the poor in spirit (5:3). For this reason, too, the risen Jesus first appears to women whose value as witnesses among Jews is worthless. (2) "Galilee of the Gentiles" (4:15) is compatible with the growing theme of Gentile mission in this gospel (see comment on 1:1; 2:1–12, et al.) and prepares for the Great Commission (28:18–20).

3. First fraudulent denials of Jesus' resurrection (28:11–15)

Matthew simply intends this paragraph to be an explanation of the stolen-corpse theology and an apologetic against it. He may also be drawing out a startling contrast: the chief priests use bribe money to commission the soldiers to spread lies, while the resurrected Jesus uses the promise of his presence to commission his followers to spread the truth of the Gospel (vv.16–20).

11–14 The guards reported to the chief priests (see comment on 27:65–66) the earthquake, the angel, and the empty tomb. It is very difficult to believe that soldiers of Pilate would admit falling asleep; that would be tantamount to suicide. But temple police could more easily be bribed, even though it took "a large sum of money," and could more easily be protected from Pilate's anger. Once again the instinctive concern of the Jewish leaders relates to expedience and the people's reaction, not to the truth.

15 Matthew offers this section as the origin of the "widely circulated" Jewish explanation for the empty tomb, still common in the days of Justin Martyr.

C. The Risen Messiah and His Disciples (28:16–20)

1. Jesus in Galilee (28:16–17)

These final verses of this gospel recapitulate many of Matthew's themes, tying up several loose ends.

16 The Eleven do what Jesus says and go to Galilee, to a specific mountain "where Jesus had told them to go." This verse presupposes the arrangements implicit in 26:32; 28:7, 10. Associating the Great Commission (vv.18–20) with Galilee not only has nuances with Jesus' humble background and the theme of Gentile mission (see comment on v.10) but soldiers had participated. But this confession tells Matthew's readers that Jesus as the promised Messiah and unique Son of God is seen most clearly in his passion and death.

55–56 Along with the soldiers, certain women (generally not highly regarded in Jewish society) watched to the bitter end (see comment on Mk 15:40–41). They kept their distance (v.55), whether through timidity or modesty; and last at the cross, they were first at the tomb (28:1). Not only do they provide continuity to the narrative, but they prove that God has chosen the lowly and despised things of the world to shame the wise and strong (cf. 1Co 1:27–31).

16. The burial of Jesus (27:57–61)

Because of Dt 21:22–23, Jesus' body could not remain on the cross overnight. Romans customarily let bodies of crucified criminals hang in full view until they rotted away. If they were buried at all, it was only by express permission of the imperial magistrate. Such permission was usually granted to friends and relatives of the deceased who made application, but never in the case of high treason.

57 The approaching evening—about 6:00 P.M. at that time of year—would mark the end of Friday and the beginning of Sabbath. Matthew mentions that Joseph of Arimathea (see comments on Mk 15:42–43; Lk 23:50–54) was rich. This may direct attention to Isa 53:9–12: though Jesus was numbered with the transgressors, yet in his death he was with the rich. Joseph had become a disciple; he learned from Jesus and to some extent followed him, even if his discipleship was secret.

58–60 Joseph's initiative is remarkably courageous, and Pilate probably granted his request only because he was convinced that Jesus was not really guilty of high treason. Joseph had Nicodemus to assist him (cf. Jn 19:38–42). On the location of the tomb, see comment on Mk 15:46.

61 No mourning was permitted for those executed under Roman law. The women followed with broken but silent grief and watched the burial. That Jesus was actually buried became an integral part of Gospel proclamation (cf. 1Co 15:4)

17. The guard at the tomb (27:62–66)

This account of the guards at the tomb is needed in order to provide the background to 28:11–15.

62–64 On the Sabbath day, some members of the Sanhedrin paid a visit to Pilate, politely addressing him as "Sir" (GK *3261*). For discussion on the phrase "after three days," see comment on 12:40. The enemies of Jesus certainly do not *believe* Jesus' prediction; they are merely afraid of fraud. Their fears were really unfounded, because the disciples themselves disbelieved Jesus' words about rising again, not because they could not understand the plain words, but because they had no frame of reference capable of integrating a dying and rising Messiah into their own messianic expectations. The only thing they knew was the terrible fact that their Messiah had been crucified.

65–66 The NIV's rendering "Take a guard" is better read, "You have a guard of soldiers." That is, Pilate refuses to use his troops but tells the Jewish authorities that they have the temple police at their disposal; and he grants the leaders permission to use them. This explains why, after the Resurrection, the guards report to the chief priests, not to Pilate (28:11). Pilate's answer in v.65 must therefore be construed as cynical. He is saying, "You were afraid of this man when he was alive; now he is dead, and you are still afraid! By all means secure the tomb as tightly as possible, if you think that will help; but use your own police." So guards are posted and the stone sealed with cord and an official wax seal.

B. The Resurrection (28:1–15)

1. The empty tomb (28:1–7)

Because the Resurrection is central to Christian theology, few subjects have received more attention. Its theological implications are not treated at length by the evangelists; but the theme constantly recurs in Paul (e.g., Ro 4:24–25; 6:4; 8:34; 10:9; 1Co 15; 2Co 5:1–10, 15; Php 3:10–11; Col 2:12–13; 3:1–4; 1Th 4:14).

1 "After the Sabbath" is a general time indicator; i.e., the women would not walk far *during* the Sabbath; so they waited until *after* the Sabbath. But by then Saturday night was also suggests the continuation of Jesus' ministry in Galilee.

17 Doubt about Jesus' resurrection is expressed elsewhere (Lk 24:10–11; Jn 20:24–29), but only by those who have heard reports of Jesus' resurrection without actually seeing him. This verse is therefore unique. Two difficulties must be considered.

(1) Does "some" refer to "some of the Eleven" or to "some others" in addition to the Eleven? The question is partly decided by one's interpretation of v.10 (see comment). If the verb translated "worship" (GK *4686*) here means not merely "kneel" but "worship" (see comment on v.9), then the "eleven disciples" (v.16) and the "some" probably constitute two groups; for doubt about who Jesus is or about the reality of his resurrection does not seem appropriate for true worship.

(2) But why was there doubt at all? If others than the Eleven are the ones who doubt (lit., "hesitate"; GK *1491*), this does not solve the problem; it merely shifts it from the Eleven to other followers of Jesus.

Several solutions have been proposed, none of them convincing. Perhaps it is best to conclude that the move from unbelief and fear to faith and joy on the part of the larger group was for them a "hesitant" one. The Eleven, who according to the other gospels had already seen the risen Jesus at least twice, respond instantly with worship on the occasion of this new appearance, but some (others) "hesitated"—without further specification as to their subsequent belief or doubt. That is, Jesus' resurrection did not instantly transform people of little faith and faltering understanding into spiritual giants. Another thing (not dealt with by Matthew) was necessary, namely, the enduement of the Spirit at Pentecost.

2. The Great Commission (28:18–20)

18 "All" (GK *4246*) dominates vv.18–20 and ties these verses together: *all* authority, *all* nations, *all* things ("everything," NIV), *all* the days ("always," NIV). The authority of Jesus Messiah has already been heavily stressed in this gospel (e.g., 7:29; 10:1, 7–8; et al.). Therefore it is wrong to claim that the Resurrection conferred on Jesus an authority incomparably greater than what he enjoyed before his crucifixion. The truth is more subtle. After all, during his ministry his words, like God's words, cannot pass away (24:35); and he, like God, forgives sin (9:6). It is not Jesus' authority per se that becomes more absolute. Rather, the spheres in which he now exercises absolute authority are enlarged to include all heaven and earth, i.e., the entire universe. The Son becomes the one through whom *all* God's authority is mediated (cf. Php 2:5–11). It marks a turning point in redemptive history, for Messiah's "kingdom" has dawned in new power.

19 Two features tie the command in this verse to Jesus' universal authority. (1) The dawning of the new age of messianic authority impels his disciples forward to a universal ministry he himself never engaged in during the days of his flesh. His promotion to universal authority serves as an eschatological marker inaugurating the beginning of his universal mission. (2) Because of that authority, his followers may go in confidence that their Lord is in sovereign control of "everything in heaven and on earth" (cf. Ro 8:28).

The main emphasis in this verse is on the command to "make disciples" (GK *3411*; the rest of the verb forms are participles, though they function like imperatives). To disciple a person to Christ is to bring that person to accept Christ as his or her teacher. Disciples are those who hear, understand, and obey Jesus' teaching (12:46–50). This injunction is given at least to the Eleven, but to the Eleven in their own role as disciples. Therefore they are paradigms for all disciples to make others what they themselves are—disciples of Jesus Christ.

With the words "all nations," Matthew's gospel returns to the theme introduced in the very first verse (see comment on 1:1)—that the blessings promised to Abraham and through him to all peoples on earth (Ge 12:3) are now to be fulfilled in Jesus the Messiah. The expression is comprehensive, including Gentiles and Jews. The aim of Jesus' disciples, therefore, is to make disciples of all people everywhere, without distinction.

"Baptizing" and "teaching" (v.20) are not the *means* of making disciples, but they characterize it. Envisaged is that proclamation of the Gospel that will result in repentance and faith, for making disciples entails both preaching and response. The response expected of new disciples is baptism and instruction.

Those who become disciples are to be baptized "into" (see NIV note) the name of the Trinity. The preposition "into" strongly suggests a coming-into-relationship-with or a coming-under-the-Lordship-of Jesus (for comments about baptism, see comment on 3:6, 11, 13–17). Baptism is a sign both of entrance into Messiah's covenant community and of pledged submission to his lordship. The triple formula containing Father (or God), Son (or Christ), and Spirit occurs frequently in the NT (cf. 1Co 12:4–6; 2Co 13:14; Eph 4:4–6; 2Th 2:13–14; 1Pe 1:2; Rev 1:4–6). Thus it becomes difficult to deny the presence of Trinitarian thought in the NT documents, as confirmed by (1) the frequency of the God-Christ-Spirit formulas, (2) their context and use in the NT, and, (3) the recognition by NT writers that the attributes of the Lord of the OT may be comprehensively applied to Jesus.

20 Those who are discipled must be taught. The content of this instruction is everything Jesus commanded the first disciples. Three things stand out. (1) The focus is on *Jesus'* commands, not OT law. Jesus' words, like the words of Scripture, are more enduring than heaven and earth (24:35); and the peculiar expression "everything I have commanded you" is reminiscent of the authority of the Lord (Ex 29:35; Dt 1:3, 41; 7:11; 12:11, 14). This confirms our exegesis of 5:17–20. (2) Remarkably, Jesus does not foresee a time when any part of his teaching will be rightly judged needless, outmoded, superseded, or untrue: *everything* he has commanded must be passed on "to the very end of the age." (3) What the disciples teach is not mere dogma steeped in abstract theorizing but content to be *obeyed*.

The gospel ends with the promise of Jesus' comforting presence, which, if not made explicitly conditional on the disciples' obedience to the Great Commission, is at least closely tied to it. He who is introduced to us in the prologue as Immanuel, "God with us" (1:23), is still God with us every day, to the end of history as we know it, when the kingdom will be consummated.

Matthew's gospel ends with the expectation of continued mission and teaching. The five preceding sections each conclude with a block of *Jesus'* teaching (3:1–26:5); but the passion and resurrection of Jesus end with a commission *to his disciples* to carry on that same ministry, in the light of the Cross, the empty tomb, and the triumphant vindication and exaltation of the risen Lord. In this sense the gospel of Matthew is not a closed book till the consummation. The final chapter is being written in the mission and teaching of Jesus' disciples (cf. 2Ti 2:2).

The Old Testament in the New

NT Text	OT Text	Subject
Mt 1:23	Isa 7:14	The virgin birth
Mt 2:6	Mic 5:2	Birth in Bethlehem
Mt 2:15	Hos 11:1	My son from Egypt
Mt 2:18	Jer 31:15	Crying in Ramah
Mt 3:3	Isa 40:3	Voice in the wilderness
Mt 4:4	Dt 8:3	Not by bread alone
Mt 4:6	Ps 91:11–12	Protecting angels
Mt 4:7	Dt 6:16	Do not test God
Mt 4:10	Dt 6:13	Serve God alone
Mt 4:15–16	Isa 9:1–2	Galilee of the Gentiles
Mt 5:21	Ex 20:13; Dt 5:17	Sixth commandment
Mt 5:27	Ex 20:14; Dt 5:18	Seventh commandment
Mt 5:31	Dt 24:1	Certificate of divorce
Mt 5:38	Ex 21:24; Lev 24:20	Eye for eye
Mt 5:43	Lev 19:18	Love your neighbor as yourself
Mt 8:17	Isa 53:4	Taking our infirmities
Mt 9:13	Hos 6:6	Mercy, not sacrifice

The Old Testament in the New

NT Text	OT Text	Subject
Mt 10:35	Mic 7:6	A divided household
Mt 11:10	Mal 3:1	Messenger sent ahead
Mt 12:7	Hos 6:6	Mercy, not sacrifice
Mt 12:18–21	Isa 42:1–4	The servant of the Lord
Mt 12:40	Jnh 1:17	Three days and nights
Mt 13:14–15	Isa 6:9–10	Seeing but not perceiving
Mt 13:35	Ps 78:2	Speaking in parables
Mt 15:4	Ex 20:12; Dt 5:16	Fifth commandment
Mt 15:4	Ex 21:17; Lev 20:9	Cursing parents
Mt 15:8–9	Isa 29:13	Hypocritical worship
Mt 16:27	Pr 24:12	God's fair judgment
Mt 17:10–11	Mal 4:5–6	Elijah comes
Mt 18:16	Dt 10:15	Two or three witnesses
Mt 19:4	Ge 1:27; 5:2	Creation of humans
Mt 19:5	Ge 2:24	Institution of marriage
Mt 19:19	Lev 19:18	Love your neighbor as yourself
Mt 21:5	Zec 9:9	Palm Sunday
Mt 21:19	Ps 118:26	Blessed is he who comes
Mt 21:13	Isa 56:7	God's house of prayer
Mt 21:13	Jer 7:11	A den of robbers
Mt 21:16	Ps 8:2	Children praising God
Mt 21:42	Ps 118:22–23	Rejected cornerstone
Mt 22:24	Dt 25:5	A brother's widow
Mt 22:32	Ex 3:6	The living God
Mt 22:37	Dt 6:5	Love God
Mt 22:39	Lev 19:18	Love your neighbor as yourself
Mt 22:44	Ps 110:1	At God's right hand
Mt 23:39	Ps 118:26	Blessed is he who comes
Mt 24:15	Dan 9:27; 11:31	Abomination of desolation
Mt 24:29	Isa 13:10; 34:4	The end times
Mt 24:30	Dan 7:13–14	Coming Son of Man
Mt 26:31	Zec 13:7	Striking the shepherd
Mt 26:64	Dan 7:13–14	Coming Son of Man
Mt 27:9–10	Zec 11:13	Thirty pieces of silver
Mt 27:35	Ps 22:18	Dividing garments by lot
Mt 27:46	Ps 22:1	God-forsaken cry

Mark

INTRODUCTION

1. Purpose

The gospel of Mark is a succinct, unadorned yet vivid account of the ministry, suffering, death, and resurrection of Jesus. Mark tells the Good News about Jesus Christ so simply that a child can understand it. Nevertheless his gospel is far deeper than it looks. Therefore one ought to approach the study of this book humbly and with due recognition of the need for wisdom from almighty God and enlightenment from the Holy Spirit.

2. The Place of Mark's Gospel in Biblical Studies

The gospel of Mark was early relegated to a position inferior to that of the other gospels. In old manuscripts of the Gospels, it rarely occupies the first position. Few early Christian writers quoted from it. The first commentary on Mark of which we have any record is the one by Victor of Antioch in the fifth century. From the time of Victor till the rise of modern biblical criticism, little attention was paid to Mark's gospel. It is not difficult to explain this. Mark was not written by an apostle (as were Matthew and John); its language was rough and ungrammatical; and it was generally believed to be an abridgement of Matthew.

In the nineteenth century a dramatic change took place. Modern Bible scholars concluded that Mark was the first gospel to be written, containing the uninterpreted facts about Jesus of Nazareth, and that both Matthew and Luke used Mark as a major source for writing their gospels, expanding and interpreting the stories of Jesus as recorded in Mark.

Since Mark, with its emphasis on the humanity of Jesus, lent itself in such a remarkable way to the preconceived christological notions of the nineteenth-century liberal theologians, they warmly embraced this gospel.

In the early twentieth century however, scholars began pointing out the kerygmatic nature of the Markan material (i.e., it contains essentially preaching rather than historical materials). Wrede (1901) argued that Mark had a theological axe to grind. Before the Resurrection, believing in Jesus as the Messiah never occurred to anyone. When, however, people began to believe in him, there was an attempt to read it back into the accounts of Jesus. The messianic secret in Mark is such an attempt. Wrede's work, while not accepted, succeeded in undermining the assumption that Mark was a straightforward historical account of the life of Jesus.

Form critics (1919–54) sought to divide the gospel into units, maintaining that these circulated orally before they were written down and that in the oral period these units were shaped by the *Sitz im Leben* (life setting) of the early Christian community. The gospel writers were essentially scissors-and-paste men. The Gospels are therefore more the products of the community than of individual authors, and they record the history of the church more than the history of Jesus. This approach to the Gospels ruled out the possibility of an account of Jesus in any truly historical sense.

With the emergence of redaction criticism, a more positive and constructive approach to the Gospels began. Scholars turned attention to the editorial role of the gospel writers; their chief concern was how the Evangelists handled the tradition, both oral and written, that came into their hands and how they shaped each gospel in order to fulfill a particular theological purpose or set of purposes. Thus this approach recognized a third life setting in the production of the Gospels. Not only is there (1) the life setting of Jesus and (2) that of the early church, but there is also (3) that of the Evangelist himself. The insights of redaction criticism offer creative interpretive possibilities within a context of the historical reliability of Mark's gospel. This hermeneutical approach is reflected in this commentary. (On redaction criticism, cf. also EBC 1:448–49.)

3. Authorship

a. Early tradition

Although the gospel of Mark is anonymous, there is a strong and clear early tradition that Mark was its author and that he was closely associated with the apostle Peter, from whom he obtained his information about Jesus. The earliest reference is found in the church historian Eusebius, who quoted from a lost work written by Papias, bishop of Hierapolis, about A.D. 140. The Papias tradition suggests several important points about Mark's gospel: (1) behind Mark is the eyewitness account and apostolic authority of Peter; (2) Mark did not write his account about Jesus in chronological sequence; (3) nevertheless Mark was careful to record accurately what Peter said. It also fits well with the possibility of Mark being a redactor of the received tradition. If the tradition he received from Peter was in the form of disconnected homilies, Mark had much work to do in transforming Peter's preaching into a gospel. This would allow him the freedom to impress on the received tradition his own theological concerns with a view to the special needs of the community to which he addressed his gospel.

Another early tradition (A.D. 160–80), also connecting Mark to Peter, adds two more items of information: (1) Mark wrote his gospel after the death of Peter, and (2) he wrote it in Italy.

Irenaeus of Lyons (c. A.D. 180) and the Muratorian Canon (c. A.D. 200) agree with this tradition. Thus at least three different church centers are represented: Hierapolis, Rome, and Lyons. The tradition is repeated later by Tertullian of North Africa and Clement of Alexandria.

b. John Mark in the biblical tradition

It is generally agreed that the Mark who is identified as the author of the gospel is also the John Mark of the NT. He is first mentioned in connection with his mother, who lived in the house in Jerusalem that Peter went to on his release from prison (Ac 12:25). Mark accompanied Paul and Barnabas (his cousin, Col 4:10) when they returned to Antioch from Jerusalem after the famine visit (Ac 12:25). Mark next appears as a "helper" to Paul and Barnabas on their first missionary journey (13:5).

Unfortunately Mark did not last long as a missionary helper. At Perga, he deserted to return to Jerusalem (Ac 13:13). When Barnabas proposed taking Mark on the second journey, Paul flatly refused, a refusal that caused Barnabas to separate from Paul (15:36–39). Barnabas took Mark and sailed for Cyprus. Later, however, Mark was with Paul at Rome (Col 4:10; Phm 24). Apparently at this point Mark was beginning to win his way back into Paul's confidence. By the end of Paul's life, Mark was back in full favor (see 2Ti 4:11). Peter also witnesses to Mark's presence in Rome about this time (1Pe 5:13).

In addition to what has been mentioned thus far, two other considerations point to the Markan authorship. (1) It seems unlikely that the church would have deliberately ascribed the authorship of this gospel to a person of secondary importance like Mark, unless there were strong historical reasons for doing this. (2) It may be that Luke's interest in Mark as contained in Acts came in part because Luke knew he was the author of one of the major sources for his own gospel (cf. Lk 1:1–4).

4. Date

It is not possible to date Mark's gospel with precision. The early tradition is divided, some saying it was written after the death of Peter, others claiming Peter was still alive. Evidence within the gospel seems to support a date for the gospel after Peter's death in A.D. 64. Mark is very frank in pointing out the failures of Peter—a frankness more easily understood if Peter had already been martyred and had achieved a leading place in the affection of the early church. No recitation of his past failures could then threaten his high position. It could, however, be used to encourage and strengthen a suffering church, itself facing martyrdom.

The latest likely date for Mark is A.D. 70 since the gospel makes no reference to the destruction of Jerusalem that year. In fact Mark says nothing at all of the Jewish War (A.D. 66–70), which was climaxed by the destruction of the Holy City.

Thus, the best estimate for dating the gospel is the last half of the decade A.D. 60–70. This date embraces the period immediately following the great fire of A.D. 64, when intense persecution began to be directed against Christians in Rome. There are good reasons to believe that the gospel of Mark was written to meet this crisis in the Roman church (see below).

5. Origin and Destination

Early church tradition locates the writing of the gospel either in Italy in general or specifically in Rome. This is consistent with (1) the historical likelihood that Peter was in Rome toward the end of his life and probably was martyred there, and (2) the biblical evidence that Mark too was in Rome about the same time and was closely associated with Peter (cf. 2Ti 4:11; 1Pe 5:13, "Babylon" probably symbolizes Rome).

All indicators point to Roman or at least to Gentile readers as Mark's primary audience. He explains Jewish customs that would be unfamiliar to Gentile readers (7:2–4; 15:42); he translates Aramaic words (3:17; 5:41; 7:11, 34; 15:22); he used Latinisms and Latin loan words (e.g., the word for "penny" in 12:42 and the word "Praetorium" in 15:16—the large number of such words, especially in comparison with Matthew and Luke, seems to suggest such readership); he reveals a special interest in persecution and martyrdom (8:34–38; 13:9–13), subjects particularly relevant to Christians in Rome; and, finally, the immediate acceptance and widespread influence of his gospel (Matthew and Luke built their gospels on it) suggest a powerful church behind it. No church better fits the description than Rome.

6. Life Setting

Since Mark's gospel is associated with Rome, it is in the Christian community there that we must look for its occasion and purpose. There are two suggestions as to the life setting of the gospel.

a. The persecutions of the Roman church in A.D. 65–67

In A.D. 64 a devastating fire broke out in Rome. More than half the city was destroyed; and strong rumors persisted, despite all attempts to quash them, that the emperor Nero had himself deliberately set it. The Roman historian Tacitus wrote that Nero, to squelch the rumor, sought to blame the Christians for the fire and instigated massive persecution against them. If that is so, and Mark wrote at precisely that time, he intended his book to help guide and support his fellow Christians in this time of crisis.

The way Mark prepares his Christian readers for suffering is by placing before them the passion experience of Jesus. Jesus' way was a *via dolorosa*. The way of discipleship for Christians is the same—the way of the Cross. About one-third of Mark's gospel is devoted to the death of Jesus. And not only in the passion of Jesus is the theme of suffering found. Many explicit and veiled references occur elsewhere in the life of Jesus in Mark: in the temptation experience—he was in the wilderness with wild beasts (1:12–13); in the misunderstanding of his family (3:21, 31–35) and people generally (3:22, 30); in his statements about the cost of discipleship (8:34–38); and in his references to persecutions (10:30, 33–34, 45; 13:8, 11–13). To Mark, faithfulness and obedience as a follower by Jesus Christ inevitably lead to suffering and perhaps even death.

b. The emergence of heretical theological teachings

More recent studies of Mark's gospel have focused on its theology and particularly on its Christology. Scholars such as Ralph Martin suggest that after Paul's death, some Christians began to exalt the divine-man status of Jesus at the expense of his true humanity. Thus in Mark we find an emphasis on Jesus' true humanity, underscored by his sufferings. This possible setting for the gospel has much to commend it. It recognizes the Christological concerns of the author as well as his more directly pastoral concerns for the people to whom he is writing. It is entirely possible that both increased persecutions and false Christological ideas in the Roman church constituted the life setting that gave rise to the writing of this first gospel about Jesus Christ, the Son of God.

7. Literary Form

The nature of the literary form of Mark's writing has stimulated much discussion among NT scholars in recent years. Mark starts out with the statement, "The beginning of the gospel about Jesus Christ." But what *is* a gospel?

Perhaps it is best to state first what a gospel is not. It is not a biography (i.e., an organized historical account of a person, beginning with his background and family and continuing through each significant period of his life). Mark has no genealogy or birth narrative, and says nothing of Jesus' boyhood or adolescence. Mark starts right out, after quoting from the OT, with Jesus as a full-grown man.

Mark seems to have created the category "gospel" (GK 2295) to describe the literary form of his work, a work that contains preaching material about God's saving work in Jesus of Nazareth. Mark selects certain key points in Jesus' career and aims at a credible account of these historical events. At the same time the material is organized so as to stress certain subjects and motifs. The writing is not "objective" but confessional.

This means that though the material found in Mark's gospel is rooted in what happened in Palestine during the first century of our era, it also bears the stamp of the man God chose to put it into its final form. Mark conveys God's good news of salvation by emphasizing Jesus' saving ministry. He also writes as a theologian, arranging and interpreting the tradition to meet the needs of his hearers.

8. Language and Style

The vocabulary of Mark's gospel is rather limited. He uses 1,270 different words, of which 80 are peculiar to him among the NT writers.

He is fond of transliterating Latin words (at least ten of them) into Greek, and occasionally his Greek shows an underlying Latin construction or expression.

A more important influence on Mark's language is Aramaic (e.g., the use of parataxis in preference to subordinating clauses and the introduction of direct speech with the participle "saying"). It reads as if it might have come from those who spoke Aramaic as their mother tongue.

Although Mark's facility with the Greek language is clearly inferior to that of Luke and other NT writers, he manages to achieve a remarkably forceful, fresh, and vigorous style. He uses the historical present over 150 times, and the adverb "immediately" occurs 41 times. Thus he gives his readers the impression of listening to an on-the-spot report. Intimate details, such as one would expect from an eyewitness, abound: e.g., the reaction of the crowds (1:27; 2:12), the emotional responses of Jesus (1:41, 43; 3:5; 7:34), and the reactions of the disciples (9:5–6, 10; 10:24, 32).

Another important feature of Mark's style is his vigorous interaction with his readers. He accomplishes this by (1) directly addressing them (cf. 2:10; 7:19); (2) addressing his readers through the words of Jesus (cf. 13:37); and (3) rhetorical questions addressed to them (cf. 4:41). Mark wants his readers to be participants, not mere observers. He wants them to respond to what he tells them about Jesus by saying of him, "He is the Christ, the Son of God."

EXPOSITION

I. Prologue (1:1–13)

A. Preparing the Way (1:1–8)

1 The first verse seems to be a title. It may refer to the entire gospel or only to the ministry of John the Baptist.

Since in Ac 1:22 the starting point of the Good News is stated to be "from John's baptism" (cf. also Mt 11:12; Lk 16:16; Jn 1:6), Mark may have this in mind here. Another possibility, however, is that by using "beginning" Mark is imitating Ge 1:1 and wants his readers to realize that his book is a new beginning in which God reveals the Good News of Jesus Christ. Taken in this way, the first verse is not only a title for the entire book but a claim to its divine origin.

The word "gospel" comes from the old English "god-spel" ("good news") and translates accurately the Greek *euangelion* (GK 2295). In the NT the Good News is that God has provided salvation for everyone through the life, death, and resurrection of Jesus Christ. For Mark to convey this Good News, he has created a new literary genre—"a gospel."

This gospel is "about Jesus Christ." Mark intends to proclaim the gospel, already known and experienced by the Roman believers, by rooting it in the events of Jesus' life. There are indications that they had lost hold of these historical roots.

"Jesus" is the Greek form of the Hebrew "Joshua," which means "The LORD is salvation" or "salvation of the LORD," or "The LORD saves." This name was revealed by the angel to Joseph before Jesus was born and describes his mission of being Savior (Mt 1:21). "Christ" is the Greek word for "anointed" (see comments on 8:29 for a full discussion of the word). The last phrase, "the Son of God," is an important theme in Mark's gospel (cf. 1:11; 3:11; 5:7; 9:7; 12:6; 13:32; 14:36, 61; 15:39).

2–3 Mark cites the OT to show that any true understanding of the ministry of Jesus must be firmly grounded there. "It is written" underscores a strong belief in the unchanging authority of the Scriptures. The quotations that follow are from Mal 3:1 (though it differs in reading "your way" instead of "the way before me," allowing for a messianic interpretation of this passage) and Isa 40:3.

Mark brings together these OT texts in a striking way. He cites God's promise of a messenger "to guard you on the way and to bring you to the place I have prepared" (Ex 23:20), i.e., through the wilderness to the Promised Land. Isa 40:3 looks forward to the coming of another messenger "in the desert," who will go before the people of God in a second Exodus to prepare for the revelation of God's salvation in Christ.

4 Since Mark wants to highlight the saving facts of Jesus and their theological meaning for the Roman church, he does not include a nativity narrative. He immediately begins with the ministry of John the Baptist as the forerunner of the Messiah. This is precisely where Peter begins in his proclamation of the gospel in Ac 10:37.

John appeared suddenly, "baptizing in the desert region," the arid regions west of the Dead Sea. This general area was the abode of the Qumran sect. Though John likely came in contact with these people, it does not appear as if they exerted much influence on him, at least not as regards his baptismal practices or his great emphasis on ethical conduct and eschatological judgment.

John preached baptism as an indication that repentance either had already occurred or accompanied it. The end result is the forgiveness of sins. God's direct response to true repentance is forgiveness.

5 John's preaching caused great excitement, for many people kept going out to him. Although there is an element of hyperbole in Mark's report, it nevertheless implies that John's preaching aroused much interest and created a great stir. Jerusalem is at least twenty miles from the Jordan River and about four thousand feet above it. It was hard going down the rugged Judean hills to the Jordan and even harder coming back up. John preached the coming of the Messiah. This raised popular excitement to a fever pitch.

6 John is described as a typical "holy man" of the Near East. His clothing was woven of camel's hair and held in place by "a leather belt around his waist" (cf. 2Ki 1:8). His food consisted of locusts (cf. Lev 11:21–22) and wild honey.

7–8 In Mark's account John's message is brief, focusing on the coming of the Mighty One who will baptize with the Holy Spirit. So great is this Mighty One that John does not consider himself worthy even to untie his sandals for him. He contrasts his baptism with that of the Coming One: his baptism is water baptism, while that of the Coming One is Holy Spirit baptism. Again John emphasizes the superiority of the ministry of the Coming One to his own ministry. John's prophecy was fulfilled in a dramatic way at Pentecost (cf. Ac 1:5).

B. The Baptism and Temptation of Jesus (1:9–13)

9 Jesus probably began his public ministry about A.D. 27, when he was approximately thirty years old. Two events, however, immediately preceded the beginning of his ministry: his baptism by John and his temptation by the devil.

The baptism of Jesus by John must have been a problem to the early church. Why did Jesus submit himself to a baptism of repentance for the forgiveness of sins? Matthew recounts John's reluctance to baptize Jesus and Jesus' reply: "It is proper for us to do this to fulfill all righteousness" (Mt 3:14–15; see comment). Jesus had to identify himself with sinful humanity at the very outset of his ministry. This he did by submitting to baptism (cf. 2Co 5:21).

10 Mark seems to suggest that only Jesus saw "heaven being torn open and the Spirit descending," though he may have been so focusing on Jesus' experience that he says nothing of John's. Whatever else the descent of the Spirit on Jesus meant, it clearly indicated his anointing for ministry. Jesus himself claimed this anointing in the synagogue at Nazareth when he said, "The Spirit of the Lord is on me" (Lk 4:18).

11 God's response fuses the concept of the messianic King of the coronation Psalm (2:7) and that of the Lord's Servant of Isaiah (42:1). The main emphasis, however, is on the unique sonship of Jesus. Mark confesses Jesus as Son of God at the very outset of his gospel (1:1). Here God confesses Jesus as his Son and witnesses to his approval of his Son. He knows the unique mission he has given to his Son and states his confidence in him.

12 From his baptism Jesus goes "at once" (GK 2317, a characteristic of Mark) to his temptation. The humbling of Jesus by his identification with the failure and sin of humankind at the Baptism is continued by his subjection to the onslaughts of Satan. The same Holy Spirit who came on Jesus at his baptism drives him out into the desert.

13 Mark's account of the temptation is brief, recording no specific temptation and no victory over Satan. This emphasizes that Jesus' entire ministry was one continuous encounter with the devil and not limited to a few temptations in the desert. Indeed, in his gospel he vividly describes this continuing conflict.

The "forty days" recall the experiences of Moses (Ex 24:18) and Elijah (1Ki 19:8, 15) in the desert. Only Mark mentions the "wild animals"—a touch that heightens the fierceness of Jesus' entire temptation experience.

II. The Early Galilean Ministry (1:14–3:6)

A. Calling the First Disciples (1:14–20)

14–15 Jesus now begins his Galilean ministry. The opening of his public ministry is related to that of John the Baptist. Not until "after John was put in prison" (v. 14) and perhaps put to death did Jesus begin his ministry. John, the forerunner, had completed his God-appointed task. Mark may be hinting that just as John's ministry ended in death, so will the ministry of Jesus. The content of Jesus' preaching is "the good news of God." The Good News is both from God and about God. The gospel is the very best news ever to come to the hearing of humankind, because it contains the message of forgiveness, restoration, and new life in Christ Jesus (cf. 2Co 5:17).

Jesus witnesses to God's action for our salvation by saying, "The time has come." This is the decisive time for God's action. With the coming of Jesus, God was doing something special.

The concept of the "kingdom [GK 993] of God" is basic to the teaching of Jesus. It relates directly to the kingship of God described in the OT (e.g., Ex 15:18; Ps 29:10; Isa 43:15). The Lord's kingship is both a present reality (God is exercising his authority now) and a future hope (God will reign in the End, when he finally puts down all opposition to his reign).

The same tension between the kingdom of God as both present and future exists in the teaching of Jesus. Here Jesus proclaims, "The kingdom of God is near" (cf. Mt 12:28; Lk 11:20). In Jesus' actions God's rule has invaded this present world. But in other sayings the kingdom is spoken of as still future (e.g., Mt 8:11; 20:21). The solution to the dilemma of both a present and a future kingdom is not to be found in rejecting one or the other but in recognizing that both are true. The kingdom is present now, but there will be a full manifestation of it in the future.

In Mk 1:15 the kingdom is emphasized as having drawn near in the person of Jesus. The only appropriate response is repentance and faith. There is an urgency about the nearness of God's kingdom. Since it ushers in the End, it speaks of judgment.

16 Jesus must now gather around him a community whom he can teach so that they may become sharers in that message. He calls them in the midst of everyday life where they really live. God's reign does not operate in a void.

Jesus found Simon and his brother Andrew along the shore of the Sea of Galilee. (Much of Jesus' ministry took place near this lake.)

17–18 Mark says nothing of a previous encounter of these two disciples with Jesus (cf. Jn 1:35–42). Rather, Jesus called Simon and Andrew to the urgent task of rescuing people from the impending judgment that the coming of the kingdom in the person and work of Jesus presages. The urgency demands a response. "At once" the two fishermen left their nets and followed him (see comment on Mt 4:18–20).

19–20 The same call that was extended to Peter and Andrew was now extended to James and John, sons of Zebedee, and they too responded without any hesitation. In their case something of the price of discipleship is indicated by the breaking of family ties—the leaving of their father's business.

B. Jesus' First Healings—On a Sabbath (1:21–34)

21 The first Sabbath incident occurred in the synagogue in Capernaum. The synagogue originated in the Exile as the result of Jews meeting together for prayer and the study of the Torah. In NT times synagogues were found all over the Hellenistic world and were the center of Jewish religious and social life.

Capernaum was the home of Peter and became a kind of base of operations for Jesus' Galilean ministry. A Jewish custom permitted visiting teachers like Jesus to preach (based on the reading from the Law or Prophets) in the synagogue by invitation of its leaders.

22 While we are not told what Jesus said in the synagogue, the congregation reacted with amazement to his message. Jesus did not have to quote the authorities ("Rabbi so-and-so says such-and-such"); his authority came straight from God. His preaching stood in contrast to the teachers of the law, the scholars professionally trained in the interpretation and application of the law.

23 Suddenly the synagogue service was disrupted by the cry of a man "possessed by an evil spirit." Thus, early in his ministry Jesus came into conflict with Satan. This is significant, for Jesus came to destroy the power of the devil (1Jn 3:8). The NT accounts of demonism do not seem so bizarre as they once did. Reports of demon possession nowadays come not only from distant and remote mission fields but from the most sophisticated of our urban centers.

24 Although v.23 states that the man cried out, it was really the demon who had the man under his control who shouted. The "us" in his question shows that the demon was speaking for his fellow demons as well. They clearly seemed to recognize Jesus and his mission of judgment.

The utterance of the name of Jesus and his title "the Holy One of God" (cf. Lk 1:35) may have been an attempt by the demon to get control over Jesus, since it was widely believed that by uttering a person's name, one could gain magic power over him or her.

25–26 Jesus needed no magical formulas to exorcise the demon. He addressed it directly and ordered it, "Be quiet!" With this word of power the evil spirit convulsed the man "and came out of him with a shriek."

27–28 Mark again reports the reaction of the people (cf. v.22) as they asked themselves in amazement and alarm, "What is this?" Their answer stresses both the newness of Jesus' teaching and its authority. They had had no previous experience with this kind of teaching. Jesus' authority was inherent within himself; one command accomplished the exorcism of the demon. The inevitable result was that Jesus' fame began to spread "over the whole region of Galilee."

29–31 The eyewitness details of the next story suggest its origin with Peter, who, after all, had a special interest in what occurred. After Jesus left the synagogue, he went to the house of Simon and Andrew, where Peter's mother-in-law lay in bed with a fever. Jesus' healing of her is described simply, yet with interesting detail: "He went to her, took her hand and helped her up." The cure was instantaneous and complete, for she got out of bed and began to serve the needs of her guests.

32–34 The following day (since Sabbath ends at sundown), people could now bring, without breaking the law, their sick and demon-possessed to him. The exorcism of v.26 and the healing of v.31 were not isolated cases. Jesus extended his healing power to large numbers.

Again Jesus muzzled the demons, "because they knew who he was" (cf. Lk 4:46). His reluctance to have the demons reveal him as the Messiah is best explained by his desire to show by word and deed what kind of Messiah he was before he openly declared himself as the Messiah.

C. Leaving Capernaum (1:35–39)

35–37 Jesus, after a busy evening of healing and exorcisms, got up early the next morning and sought a quiet place to pray (cf. 6:46; 14:32–41). He was facing a crisis—the shallow and superficial response of the people who were only interested in what he could do to heal their physical afflictions. So he sought the strength that only communion and fellowship with the Father could provide.

The disciples did not understand Jesus or his need for communion with the Father, so they went to look for him. Apparently they thought Jesus would be pleased to know that everyone was looking for him (v.37). They did not understand that this popular and shallow reception of him was the very reason he withdrew to pray.

38–39 Jesus' reply shows that he feared his healings and exorcisms were hindrances to understanding who he really was. The people of Capernaum were interested in him only as popular miracle-worker. So Jesus suggested that they move on to other villages to preach. He knew that he came into the world primarily to proclaim God's Good News and all that was involved in discipleship and suffering. Healings and exorcisms had their place, but they were not to usurp this primary purpose. If Mark wrote his gospel to refute a christological heresy that placed too much emphasis on Jesus as a miracle-worker, the relevance of these verses is clear.

D. Healing a Leper (1:40–45)

40 This story serves to connect 1:21–29 and 2:1–3:6—two clearly identifiable units in Mark's gospel.

The word "leprosy" (GK 3320) was used in biblical times to designate a wide variety of serious skin diseases. It was not limited to what we know as leprosy (i.e., Hansen's disease). The law had specific requirements for a person with a skin disease (Lev 13:45–46). Instead of keeping his distance from Jesus, as the law demanded, the leper came directly to him and fell down on his knees to make his plea. Having no doubt that Jesus could heal him, he wondered only whether Jesus was willing. It is sometimes easier to believe in God's power than in his mercy.

41–42 "Filled with compassion" is probably better read as "being angered," a reading found in older, more reliable manuscripts. Why would Jesus be angry? The best answer is that Jesus recognized this foul disease as the work of the devil. His anger was focused neither on the man nor on the disease but on Satan whose work he came to destroy. This incident then becomes another example of the fierce conflict between Christ and Satan that plays such an important part in this gospel.

Jesus also expressed compassion. He reached out and touched the unclean leper, an act that, according to the Mosaic Law, incurred defilement. In doing so, Jesus demonstrated his decision to take our flesh upon himself so that he might cleanse us from sin. His touching of the leper not only resulted in his being cured but also revealed Jesus' attitude toward the ceremonial law. He boldly placed love and compassion over ritual and regulation.

43–44 "Sent him away" is from a word often used of driving out demons, and "with a strong warning" originally meant "to snort like a horse." In other words, an element of anger or indignation is contained in Jesus' warning. Why? Because Jesus knew that the man would disobey him. Jesus did not want to gain the reputation of just being another "miracle-worker," for this would thwart the essential spiritual purpose of his ministry by touching off a messianic insurrection. Instead, he instructed the leper to go to those whose job it was to rule whether he was clean or not and to offer sacrifices required by the Mosaic Law (Lev 14:2–31). "As a testimony to them" likely means as a testimony to the priest and the people of the reality of the cure.

45 The leper acted consistent with human nature. The prohibition against telling what had happened to him made him all the more eager to proclaim it everywhere. Jesus thus had to curtail his public ministry, avoiding the towns and choosing rather to stay in more isolated places. But even in his isolation, people managed to find him.

E. Conflict With the Religious Leaders (2:1–3:6)

Clearly 2:1–3:6 is a separate section in Mark's gospel. In it Jesus comes into conflict with the Jewish religious leadership in a series of five separate incidents. Mark brought these incidents together because they have a common theme: conflict with the religious authorities. Such stories were undoubtedly used by the church in its ongoing struggle with Judaism.

1. Healing a paralytic (2:1–12)

1–2 This passage shows the close relationship between the healing of the body and the forgiveness of sins. Jesus returns to Capernaum, a kind of base of operations for him in the northern part of the country, to the house of Peter and Andrew (cf. 1:29). His presence in town was soon discovered, so that even this place afforded him no privacy. The house filled with people, and the overflow was so great that the space outside the door was blocked. They no doubt wanted to see Jesus perform more miracles. But he was not working miracles inside the house; rather, he was preaching the gospel to the people.

3–4 To understand these verses, it is necessary to visualize the layout of a typical Palestinian peasant's house. It was usually a small, one-room structure with a flat roof, accessible by means of an outside stairway. The roof itself was usually made of wooden beams with thatch and compacted earth in order to shed the rain. Sometimes tiles were laid between the beams and the thatch.

The four men brought the paralytic to the house where Jesus was; but when they saw the size of the crowd, they realized it was impossible to enter by the door. So they carried the paralytic up the outside stairway to the roof, dug up the compacted thatch and earth, removed the tiles, and lowered the man through the now-exposed beams to the floor below.

5 Jesus recognized this ingenuity and persistence of the paralytic and his bearers as faith. But instead of healing the man of his lameness, Jesus forgave his sins. On the surface, this hardly seemed to be what the man needed. But Jesus was illustrating an OT claim that human suffering rests in separation from God. Thus forgivness is our deepest need.

6–7 Here the "teachers of the law" (cf. 1:22) become directly involved with Jesus. His statement about forgiveness gave them their opportunity to ensnare him on some theological point.

Their basic premise was that for anyone but God to claim to forgive sin was blasphemy. Since for them Jesus was not God, he was blaspheming. If they were right about who Jesus was, their reasoning was flawless. In Jewish teaching even the Messiah could not forgive sins. They failed to recognize who Jesus really was—the Son of God who does have authority to forgive sins.

8–9 The teachers of the law had not openly expressed their misgivings about Jesus' action, but Jesus knew their thoughts and challenged them with the question in v.9. As he meant his words, neither of the two was easier. To the teachers of the law, however, it was easier to make the statement about forgiveness because who could verify its fulfillment? But to say, "Get up and walk"—that could indeed be verified by an actual healing.

10–11 Jesus' statement in the first half of v.10 was addressed to the scribes. The words "he said to the paralytic" constitute a parenthesis to explain that the following words are addressed not to the teachers of the law but to the paralytic. Another possibility is to take the entire verse, with its early public use of the title "Son of Man," as addressed to Mark's readers (see comments on 8:31).

The subsequent healing verified the claim to grant forgiveness. As surely as actual healing followed Jesus' statement "Get up" (v.11), so actual forgiveness resulted from his "your sins are forgiven."

12 The man's cure was instantaneous; in full view of everyone there, he walked out. The crowd responded with amazement and gave praise to God for what had happened. Never before had they seen anything like this.

The emphasis in this story is not on Jesus' pity for a helpless cripple that moved him to heal, but on his power to forgive sins. In his act of forgiveness Jesus was also declaring the presence of God's kingdom among humans.

2. Eating with sinners (2:13–17)

13 This second conflict with the religious leaders is introduced by the story of the calling of Levi, the tax collector. The scene is the shore of the Sea of Galilee. Jesus' popularity with the crowds was still very evident.

MARK 2

The Life of Christ

CHILDHOOD

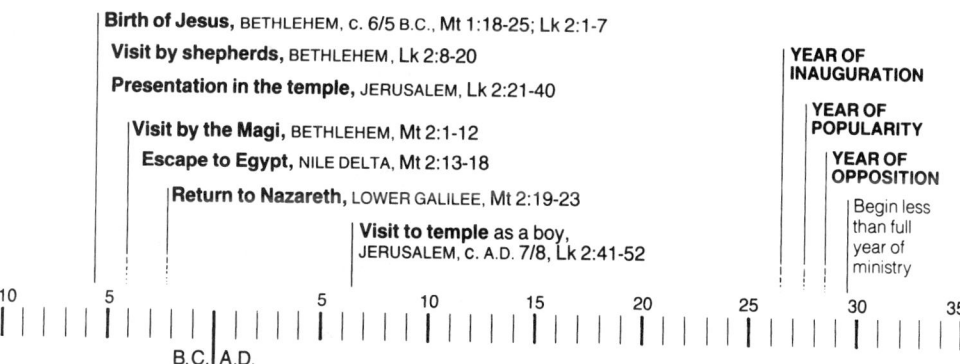

Dotted lines leading to the timeline
are meant to define sequence of events only.
Exact dates, even year dates, are generally unknown.

Jesus baptized
JORDAN RIVER
c. A.D. 26
Mt 3:13-17; Mk 1:9-11;
Lk 3:21-23; Jn 1:29-39

Jesus tempted by Satan
DESERT
Mt 4:1-11; Mk 1:12-13;
Lk 4:1-13

Jesus' first miracle
CANA
Jn 2:1-11

4 fishermen become Jesus' followers
SEA OF GALILEE
AT CAPERNAUM
A.D. 27
Mt 4:18-22; Mk 1:16-20;
Lk 5:1-11

Jesus heals Peter's mother-in-law
CAPERNAUM
Mt 8:14-17; Mk 1:29-34;
Lk 4:38-41

―――― YEAR OF INAUGURATION ―――― ―――― YEAR OF POPULARITY ――――

A.D. 27				28	
FALL	WINTER	SPRING	SUMMER	FALL	WINTER

Jesus' cleansing of the temple
A.D. 27
Jn 2:14-22

Jesus and Nicodemus
JERUSALEM
A.D. 27
Jn 3:1-21

Jesus talks to the Samaritan woman
SAMARIA
Jn 4:5-42

Jesus heals a nobleman's son
CANA
Jn 4:46-54

The people of Jesus' hometown try to kill him
NAZARETH
Lk 4:16-31

Jesus begins his first preaching trip through Galilee
Mt 4:23-25; Mk 1:35-39;
Lk 4:42-44

Matthew decides to follow Jesus
CAPERNAUM
Mt 9:9-13; Mk 2:13-17;
Lk 5:27-32

Jesus chooses the 12 disciples
A.D. 28
Mk 3:13-19; Lk 6:12-15

Jesus preaches the "Sermon on the Mount"
Mt 5:1-7:29; Lk 6:20-49

© 1985 The Zondervan Corporation

MARK 2

The Life of Christ (Continued)

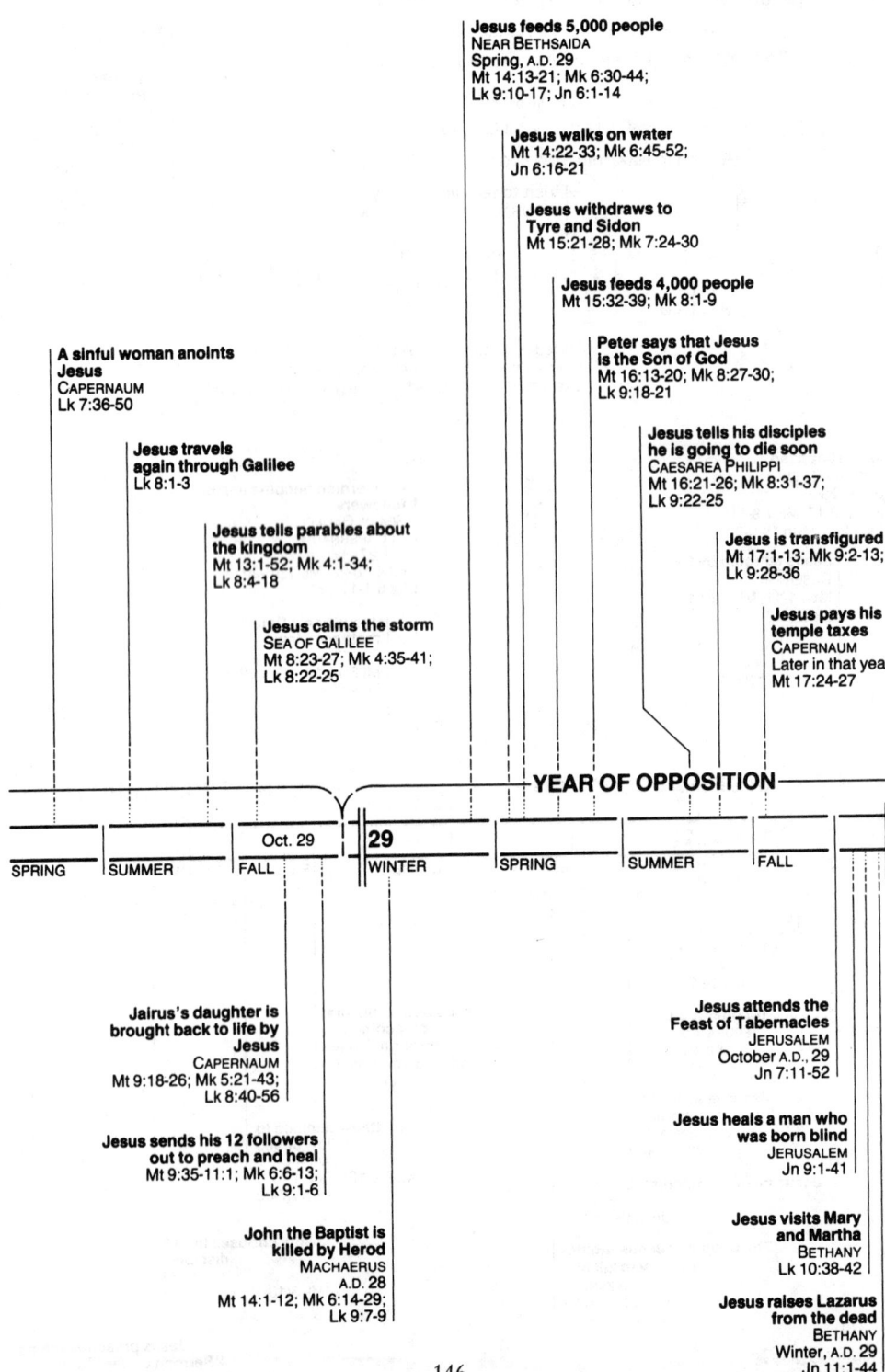

MARK 2

The Life of Christ (Continued)

Jesus begins his last trip to Jerusalem
A.D. 30
Lk 17:11

Jesus blesses the little children
ACROSS THE JORDAN
Mt 19:13-15; Mk 10:13-16; Lk 18:15-17

Jesus talks to the rich young man
ACROSS THE JORDAN
Mt 19:16-30; Mk 10:17-31; Lk 18:18-30

Jesus again tells about his death and resurrection
NEAR THE JORDAN
Mt 20:17-19; Mk 10:32-34; Lk 18:31-34

Jesus heals blind Bartimaeus
JERICHO
Mt 20:29-34; Mk 10:46-52; Lk 18:35-43

Jesus talks to Zacchaeus
JERICHO
Lk 19:1-10

Jesus returns to Bethany to visit Mary and Martha
BETHANY
Jn 11:55-12:1

THE LAST WEEK

The Triumphal Entry, JERUSALEM, Sunday
Mt 21:1-11; Mk 11:1-10; Lk 19:29-44; Jn 12:12-19

Jesus curses the fig tree
Monday Mt 21:18-19; Mk 11:12-14

Jesus cleanses the temple
Monday Mt 21:12-13; Mk 11:15-18

The authority of Jesus questioned
Tuesday Mt 21:23-27; Mk 11:27-33; Lk 20:1-8

Jesus teaches in the temple
Tuesday Mt 21:28-23:39; Mk 12:1-44; Lk 20:9-21:4

Jesus anointed, BETHANY, Tuesday
Mt 26:6-13; Mk 14:3-9; Jn 12:2-11

The plot against Jesus
Wednesday Mt 26:14-16; Mk 14:10-11; Lk 22:3-6

The Last Supper
Thursday Mt 26:17-29; Mk 14:12-25; Lk 22:7-20; Jn 13:1-38

Jesus comforts the disciples
Thursday Jn 14:1-16:33

Gethsemane, Thursday
Mt 26:36-46; Mk 14:32-42; Lk 22:40-46

Jesus' arrest and trial
Thursday night and Friday
Mt 26:47-27:26; Mk 14:43-15:15; Lk 22:47-23:25; Jn 18:2-19:16

Jesus' crucifixion and death, GOLGOTHA,
Friday Mt 27:27-56; Mk 15:16-41; Lk 23:26-49; Jn 19:17-30

The burial of Jesus, JOSEPH'S TOMB; Friday
Mt 27:57-66; Mk 15:42-47; Lk 23:50-56; Jn 19:31-42

30				A.D. 31		
WINTER	SPRING	SUMMER	FALL	WINTER	SPRING	SUMMER

AFTER THE RESURRECTION

The empty tomb, JERUSALEM, Sunday
Mt 28:1-10; Mk 16:1-8; Lk 24:1-12; Jn 20:1-10

Mary Magdalene sees Jesus in the garden, JERUSALEM, Sunday
Mk 16:9-11; Jn 20:11-18

Jesus appears to the two going to Emmaus, Sunday Mk 16:12-13; Lk 24:13-35

Jesus appears to 10 disciples, JERUSALEM, Sunday Mk 16:14; Lk 24:36-43; Jn 20:19-25

Jesus appears to the 11 disciples, JERUSALEM, One week later
Jn 20:26-31

Jesus talks with some of his disciples, SEA OF GALILEE, One week later
Jn 21:1-25

Jesus ascends to his Father in heaven, MT OF OLIVES, 40 days later
Mt 28:16-20; Mk 16:19-20; Lk 24:44-53

Dotted lines leading to the timeline are meant to define sequence of events only. Exact dates, even year dates, are generally unknown.

14 Jesus seems to be doing his teaching on this occasion as rabbis often did theirs—"as he walked along." If so, his teaching was interrupted by his encounter with Levi (i.e., Matthew; see Mt 9:9) at the tax collector's booth. He was employed by Herod Antipas, the tetrarch of Galilee, as a tax collector. Tax collectors were despised by the Jews because they were considered traitors and because they often were extortioners.

Jesus called Levi to follow him. There was much at stake for him in accepting Jesus' challenge, for there would be little possibility of his returning to his occupation. Tax collecting jobs were greatly sought after as a sure way to get rich quickly (see comment on Lk 3:12–13).

15–16 The dinner held in Levi's house was either his farewell party or a time for his friends to have an opportunity to meet Jesus. The tax collectors and "sinners" having dinner with Jesus suggests that he, not Levi, was the host! By calling sinners into his messianic kingdom, Jesus was showing that the basis of entering this kingdom was forgiveness.

"Sinners" (GK 283) denotes those people who refused to follow the Mosaic Law as interpreted by the Pharisees. Jesus' close association with despised tax collectors and "sinners" was too much for the "teachers of the law" to keep quiet about. These particular teachers were Pharisees (the successors of the pious Jews who joined forces with Mattathias and his sons during the Maccabean period; see comment on Lk 18:9–14; cf. EBC 1:192).

Although many of them were doubtless pious and godly men, those Jesus came into conflict with represented some of the worst elements of traditional religion: jealousy, hypocrisy, and religious formalism. Jesus' consorting with people who openly refused to keep the requirements of the law prompted them to ask why a supposedly observant Jew would associate with them.

17 No statement of Jesus in this gospel is more profound than this one. A doctor ministers not to healthy persons but to those who are sick. So Jesus came not to call the "righteous" (GK 1465; here meaning the self-righteous) but "sinners" (i.e., those who are alienated from God in their lives). Jesus' call is to salvation; and, in order to share in it, there must be a recognition of need. A self-righteous person is incapable of recognizing that need, but a sinner can.

3. A question about fasting (2:18–22)

18 In the law the only required fast was on the Day of Atonement (Lev 16:29, 31; 23:27–32), but after the Exile four other annual fasts were observed by Jews (Zec 7:5; 8:19). In NT times the stricter Pharisees fasted twice a week (Monday and Thursday; cf. Lk 18:12). The phrase "the disciples of the Pharisees" (used only here in the NT) probably refers to people who were influenced by the teachings and practice of the Pharisees. Both they and John the Baptist's disciples were fasting.

Why they were doing this, Mark does not say, but their fasting was a sign of true piety. Therefore, some unidentified people asked why Jesus' disciples did not give evidence of true religious piety by fasting.

19–20 Jesus answers in a parable emphasizing the joy that the presence of Jesus makes possible. Therefore fasting, as a sign of mourning, is not appropriate. To fast during a wedding, a time of great joy and festivity, would be unthinkable. Jesus is the bridegroom (v.19) and his disciples the guests. While he remains with them they will rejoice, not fast. However, he will not always be with them. When he is taken away, fasting will be appropriate. This is probably a veiled reference to his death (the word used implies a violent removal that causes sorrow).

21–22 The two parables in these verses were probably spoken on different occasions but both deal with a single theme. Obviously they bear on the question of fasting, but beyond that they also bear on the forms of Judaism generally. In ancient times wine was kept in goatskins. New skins were soft and pliable and would stretch when wine that had not yet completed fermentation was put in them. However, old wineskins that had been stretched would become brittle. The gas from the fermenting wine burst them open, destroying both wine and wineskins. Putting new wine into old wineskins and patching an old garment with a new cloth are just as inappropriate as fasting at a wedding feast. A wedding, new wine, and a new garment are all symbols of the newness that the coming of Jesus brings. That newness cannot be confined to the old forms of Judaism.

4. The Lord of the Sabbath (2:23–3:6)

The next two stories of conflict center on the keeping of the Sabbath, something far more important in Judaism than the question of fasting.

23–24 The main point at issue here was not the act of harvesting the heads of grain in fields that did not belong to them. Such activity as Jesus and his disciples were involved in was explicitly allowed in the law (Dt 23:25). What the Pharisees objected to was doing this reaping and threshing on the Sabbath.

25–26 Jesus met the accusation of the Pharisees with a counterquestion about the time when David and his companions were hungry and ate the consecrated bread (1Sa 21:1–6; cf. Ex 25:30; 35:13; 39:36; Lev 24:5–9). Although the action of David was contrary to the law, he was not condemned for it. Jesus does not claim that the Sabbath law has not been technically broken but that such violations under certain conditions are warranted.

27–28 The follow-up pronouncement is preceded by the phrase "Then he said to them" (cf. 4:2b, 11, 21, 24, 26; 6:10; 7:9; 8:21; 9:1), suggesting an independent saying of Jesus that is relevant to the subject at hand. To Jesus the Sabbath was not created for its own sake; it was a gift of God to the human race. Its purpose was not to put humans in a kind of straightjacket. Rather, it was for their good—to provide rest from labor and opportunity for worship.

Is v.28 a statement of Mark about Jesus or of Jesus about himself? If v.27 is a separate saying of Jesus inserted by Mark to climax the teaching of Jesus about the Sabbath, then it seems best to regard this verse as Mark's comment to the church (cf. 2:10). In any case, Jesus has authority to determine the use of the Sabbath.

3:1 In the final conflict story, Mark again gives no details of time or geographical location. The story takes place in a synagogue where there is a man with a "shriveled hand." Apparently some sort of paralysis is meant.

2 Mark does not specifically identify the opposition here, though he clearly means Pharisees and the teachers of the law (cf. Lk 6:7). Since Jesus had already raised suspicions in their mind because of his unorthodox actions, these men were present in the synagogue to spy on Jesus, "looking for a reason to accuse" him. They were convinced of his power to perform miracles, but were wondering if he would break rabbinic law that allowed healing on the Sabbath only if that life was actually in danger.

3–4 Jesus was fully aware of the designs of the opposition. Instead of acting carefully, he commanded the man to stand up and come to "center stage" so that all in the synagogue could see what he was going to do to him.

Jesus knew what was racing through the religious leaders' minds. So he asked them, "Which is lawful on the Sabbath: to do good or to do evil, to save life or to kill?" Perhaps Jesus meant that there is little difference between manslaughter and refusing to be concerned about relieving a distressed person. Or perhaps Jesus was indicting the Pharisees who were already plotting to kill him (v.6). The Pharisees were silent, refusing to debate the issue with Jesus.

5 Anger is rarely directly attributed to Jesus (cf. comment on 1:41). When he was angry, it was never the expression of injured self-concern. It was more like "righteous indignation"—what a good person feels in the presence of stark evil. Such anger was particularly appropriate to this situation, for Jesus saw the stubborn, unfeeling hearts of his enemies. He ordered the man to stretch out his hand; the man obeyed, and it was instantly and completely restored.

6 The healing resulted in further enmity against Jesus. The Pharisees, joined now by the Herodians (probably influential Jews who were friends and backers of the Herodian family), began to plot Jesus' death. The Herodians joined in opposition to Jesus because they feared he might be an unsettling political influence in Palestine.

III. The Later Galilean Ministry (3:7–6:13)

A summary statement (3:7–12) begins this new section of Mark's gospel, which ends with the sending out of the Twelve (6:6b–13). In between are two obvious sections: parables about the kingdom (4:1–34) and miracles of Jesus' power over hostile forces (4:35–5:43). In addition there are several units that deal with hostility and rejection (3:20–30, 31–35; 6:1–6a), and there is a brief account of the selection of the Twelve (3:13–19).

A. Withdrawal to the Lake (3:7–12)

7 Jesus withdrew, probably because he knew the authorities were out to get him (cf. Mt 12:15). Since the time had not yet come for a serious confrontation, he went to the Lake of Genessaret. This withdrawal, however, did not separate him from the crowds.

8 The crowds that came to Jesus were not only from the regions in the vicinity of Capernaum but also from the south (Jerusalem, Idumea), the east (across the Jordan including Perea and the Decapolis), and the northwest (Tyre and Sidon). The fact that the renown of Jesus reached the Jerusalem authorities, who sent their representatives up to Galilee to observe what was going on, suggests an advanced stage in the ministry of Jesus.

9–10 Only Mark includes the detail about the boat. Its purpose was, of course, to provide escape for Jesus in case the crowd began to get unruly. Great numbers of people were pressing forward just to touch Jesus in the hope that they might be healed. Once again, the crowd seems to have had little interest in Jesus other than as a miracle-worker. Despite this, he graciously healed many of them.

11–12 Again Jesus came into conflict with the demonic. The evil spirits recognized who Jesus was—even if the crowds did not. By crying out "You are the Son of God," they were trying to control him and neutralize his power (in Bible times, knowledge of a person's name conferred power over that person). "Son of God" is a true designation of who Jesus is. Jesus silenced the outcries of the demons because the time for the clear revelation of who he was had not yet come.

B. Selection of the Twelve (3:13–19)

13 Jesus withdrew to the hill country of Galilee and called twelve disciples to be his special followers. The designation of the Twelve suggests the foundation of a new Israel, after the original Israel had rejected their Messiah. The Twelve came to him without delay (cf. 1:18, 20; 2:14).

14–15 The purpose for which the Twelve were appointed was twofold: (1) they were to be brought into close association with the Son of God, live with him, travel with him, converse with him, and learn from him; (2) the training was not an end in itself—they were to be sent out to preach the Good News and to drive out demons. These last two elements are closely associated. The salvation Jesus brings involves the defeat of Satan and his demons.

16–19 There are three other lists of the apostles in the NT (Mt 10:2–4; Lk 6:14–16; Ac 1:13). The names of the Twelve as given in these lists naturally divide into four parts. Peter heads the three other names in the first section; Philip heads the second section; James the Son of Alphaeus (called "the Less" in Matthew) the third; the last section consists of the name of Judas Iscariot (except in Acts). Simon's nickname, "the rock" (Peter), was given him by Jesus (see comment on Mt 16:18).

James and John, the sons of Zebedee, were nicknamed "Sons of Thunder." This probably describes their disposition; it had something of the thunderstorm in it. Since Bartholomew is not a personal name but a patronymic, meaning "son of Talmai," this disciple probably had another name (Nathanael? cf. Jn 1:45). Matthew is doubtless to be identified with Levi (2:14). Thaddaeus is probably the Judas son of James of Luke's lists (Lk 6:16; Ac 1:13). Simon is called "the Zealot" (GK 2421; likely a reference to his membership in the party of the Zealots, a Jewish sect bent on the overthrow at all costs of the Roman control of Palestine). Judas's surname is given as Iscariot, probably meaning "the man from the place called Karioth." He is further identified as the man who betrayed Jesus.

It was a strange group of men our Lord chose as his disciples. Four of them were fishermen, one a hated tax collector, another a member of a radical and violent political party. Of six of them we know practically nothing. All were laymen; none was a preacher or expert in the Scriptures. Yet it was with these men that Jesus established his church and disseminated his Good News to the ends of the earth.

C. Jesus, His Family, and the Beelzebub Controversy (3:20–35)

The historicity of the incident of Jesus' family can scarcely be denied. The church would not have invented stories that put them into such bad light.

An important feature of this section is the insertion of one incident (the Beelzebub controversy) into another (the story of the relationship between Jesus and his family). This is a frequent device in Mark's gospel (cf. 5:21–43; 6:7–30; 11:12–25; 14:1–11). Mark uses this literary device to heighten the suspense and to allow for the passage of time. The association of these two incidents also suggests that Jesus' family members are not unlike the scribes in their attitude to Jesus.

20–21 Jesus was again being pressed by the crowds, demanding his undivided attention. When Jesus' family heard that he was so engrossed by his work that he failed even to care for his physical needs, they decided to go to him and "take charge of him," fearing that overwork had affected him mentally. They were planning to take him back to Nazareth.

Jesus' family was located in Nazareth, while Jesus himself was probably in Capernaum. To allow time for travel, Mark fills in the gap with the Beelzebub controversy.

22 The teachers of the law had come down from Jerusalem, indicating that the word about Jesus was spreading and causing concern in high places. Their analysis of Jesus' condition was "he is possessed by Beelzebub!" (i.e., "the prince of demons," or Satan; see comment on Mt 10:25). They accused Jesus and Satan of being in collusion with each other.

23–27 Jesus replied to the charge by making a comparison. His argument is as follows: I have just cast out demons. Now if I am doing this by Satan's power, then Satan is actually working against himself. But that would be absurd. Just as a house or a kingdom cannot stand if it is divided against itself or opposes itself, so Satan will bring about his own destruction by working against himself. In essence, Jesus was saying two things: (1) he cannot be in collusion with Satan; and (2) he is actually destroying Satan's work, which means he is more powerful than Satan.

By the parable of v. 27, Jesus implies that he is tying up Satan in order to deliver from bondage those under Satan's control. That was, after all, one of his main tasks (see comment on 1:23).

28–30 Jesus follows this story with a solemn pronouncement: forgiveness is available for all the sins and blasphemies of humans except for blasphemy against the Holy Spirit. What is that sin? Verse 30 suggests an explanation. Jesus had done what any unprejudiced person would have acknowledged as a good thing. He had freed an unfortunate man from the power and bondage of evil through the power of the Holy Spirit, but the teachers of the law ascribed it to the power of Satan. To call light darkness or good evil or Jesus' work satanic because of prejudice in one's heart is the worst sin of all.

The words of v.29 have caused great anxiety and pain in the history of the church. Many have wondered whether they have committed the "unpardonable sin." Surely what Jesus is speaking of here is not an isolated act but a settled condition of the soul—the result of a long history of repeated and willful acts of sin through hardness of heart (cf. 3:5). On the other hand, any who are troubled about this sin give evidence that they have not committed it. If the person involved cannot be forgiven, it is not so much that God refuses to forgive as it is the sinner who refuses to allow him.

31 Mark now returns to the family of Jesus. They did not enter the place where he was, but stood outside and sent someone in to call him. Since only Jesus' mother and brothers are mentioned, Joseph was probably no longer alive.

32–34 When Jesus was told that his mother and his brothers were looking for him, he responded by asking, "Who are my mother and my brothers?" Then with a sweep of his eyes over those seated in a circle around him (including his disciples), he identified his true family. Those who had responded to his call to be with him were spiritually far closer than blood relatives.

35 Jesus' true family includes all who obey the will of God. It can easily be imagined what this statement meant to the original readers of Mark's gospel. Though many had broken family relations and were being persecuted, they had an intimate relationship with the Son of God.

D. Parables About the Kingdom of God (4:1–34)

The gospel of Mark has only two sections of sustained teaching by Jesus: this passage and chapter 13. Chapter 4 contains four of Jesus' parables: the sower, the lamp, the secretly growing seed, and the mustard seed. Parables are the most striking feature in the teaching of Jesus. Although he did not invent this form of teaching (parables are found both in the OT and in the writings of the rabbis), he used it in a way and to a degree unmatched before his time or since.

Many parables are stories taken out of ordinary life, used to drive home a spiritual or moral truth. But they are not always stories. Sometimes they are brief similes, comparisons (e.g., Mt 15:15), analogies, or even proverbial sayings (e.g., Lk 4:23). The Greek word *parabole* (GK *4130*) includes all these meanings.

For centuries parables were interpreted allegorically; i.e., each element of the story was assigned a specific meaning. Thus Augustine found in the parable of the Good Samaritan references to Adam, Jerusalem, the Devil and his angels, the Law and the Prophets, and Christ and the church! Now we are more apt to look for the one main point that a parable teaches. Though some clearly have more than one point, the principle is generally valid.

Jesus' teaching in his parables is more than general religious truth. It is always related in a dynamic way to his message and mission. At the same time, like all Scripture, the parables contain truth relevant for God's people everywhere—throughout history.

1. Parable of the sower (4:1–9)

1–2 Jesus was teaching by the Lake of Galilee. The presence of the large crowd shows his popularity as a teacher. In fact, the crowd was so large that he found it convenient to use a small boat (cf. 3:9) pushed out from the shore as his lectern (actually he sat while teaching). What is contained in 4:1–34 is only part of Jesus' teaching in parables (v.2).

3–9 The parable of the sower begins and ends with a call for careful attention, suggesting that its meaning may not be self-evident. Alert minds are needed to comprehend its truth. The background of the parable is rural life in Palestine. Seed was sown in broadcast fashion (v.3). The sower deliberately sowed it on the path (v.4), in rocky places (v.5), and among the thorns (v.7) because sowing preceded plowing. However, if plowing was delayed for any time at all, the consequences Jesus mentioned inevitably resulted.

The great emphasis in the parable is on the act of sowing the seed (i.e., the kingdom of God breaking into the world through Jesus) rather than on the soils into which it is sown (i.e., the response to Jesus' preaching). Although difficulties face God's kingdom, it grows and ultimately produces an abundant harvest.

2. Secret of the kingdom of God (4:10–12)

10 The question about parables was directed toward their general purpose in Jesus' teaching. He had spoken other parables, and the disciples and other followers of Jesus were inquiring into their purpose. Jesus' teaching is not narrowly limited to the Twelve. He came to reveal the truth to all who were open to receive it.

11–12 These verses are among the most difficult in the entire gospel. It is important to look carefully at the terminology. The word translated "secret" (v.11) is *mysterion* (GK *3696*, occuring only here and in Mt 3:11; Lk 8:10 in the Gospels). Paul uses it frequently in his epistles (see also Rev 1:20; 10:7; 17:5, 7). It does not mean something only for the initiated few; rather, it emphasizes God's disclosure to humans of what was previously unknown. It is proclaimed to all, but only those who have faith really understand. Here in Mark the mystery is the disclosure that the kingdom of God has drawn near in the person of Jesus Christ.

This secret has been given to the disciples because they have responded in faith, but to those hardened by unbelief (cf. ch. 3), the entire significance of Jesus' person and mission lies "in parables" (i.e., "riddles").

12 Mark follows up this saying of Jesus with a quotation from Isa 6:9–10 (using the LXX, the Greek translation of the OT), introduced with "so that." He omits the strong statements of the first part of v.10 and changes the LXX's "and I heal them" to "and be forgiven." In doing this, Mark follows the Targum (an Aramaic paraphrase of the OT)—an indication of the authenticity of that statement.

Taken at face value, the statement seems to be saying that the purpose of parables is that unbelievers may not receive the truth and be converted. That this statement was thought to be difficult theologically may be seen in Matthew's change of *hina* ("in order that"; GK 2671) to *hoti* ("with the result that"; GK 4022) and in Luke's dropping of the *mēpote* ("otherwise") clause.

Several recent attempts have been made to weaken the telic force of *hina*. (1) It is held that *hina* is used in the text to introduce a result clause (like Matthew's *oti*). (2) Mark has mistranslated the original Aramaic word *de*; it means "who," not "in order that." Thus the text should read, "The secret of the kingdom of God has been given to you. But to those on the outside *who* are ever seeing but never perceiving . . . everything is said in parables" (emphasis mine). (3) The purpose idea is not authentic with Jesus but represents Mark's theology. (4) *Hina* is an introductory formula to the free translation of Isa. 6:9–10 and is almost equivalent to "in order that it might be fulfilled."

All of these attempts have their defects. Although (1) and (2) alleviate the problem of *hina*, they do not address that of "otherwise" which also suggests purpose. Solution (3) drives a wedge between Jesus and Mark, while (4), clearly the best choice of the four, founders on the fact that Mark elsewhere does not use *hina* with this meaning.

Perhaps the best way to understand v. 12 is that it simply teaches that one reason Jesus taught in parables was to conceal the truth to persistent unbelievers. Jesus' parables were not always clear. The disciples themselves had difficulty understanding them (cf. 7:17). So Jesus taught in parables (at least on some occasions) so that his enemies might not be able to comprehend the full significance of his words and bring false accusations or charges against him. He knew that in some cases understanding would result in more sin and not in accepting the truth. Then, too, God does on occasion harden some people in order to carry out his sovereign purposes (cf. Ro 11:25–32). Indirectly, Jesus is challenging us to penetrate beneath the surface of the story and to grasp its real meaning.

3. Interpretation of the parable of the sower (4:13–20)

Many modern scholars reject this passage as authentic because it allegorizes the parable, and they assume that Jesus never allegorized. But there is no evidence that Jesus never used allegory, nor is there anything in the interpretation of the parable that is contrary to the teachings of Jesus.

13 There is a slight rebuke in Jesus' statement. He implies that the meaning of the parable of the sower is clear and understandable. If the disciples could not understand this clear parable, how would they understand more obscure ones?

14 The "farmer" is Christ himself; and the "word" is the word of the kingdom (cf. Mt 13:19), i.e., the coming of the reign of God in the person and work of Jesus. Whereas in the parable itself the emphasis is on the sowing of the word, in the interpretation it is on the kind of reception Jesus' word receives. Note that Jesus had already received negative responses to his proclamation (chs. 2–3).

15–20 The seeds sown on the hard-beaten path indicate those who have a shallow reception of the word. Satan snatches it from them before it has had an opportunity to take root.

The seeds sown on rocky places picture another hindrance to proper reception of the word: persecution and trials. This word of Jesus must have been particularly relevant to the Roman church and probably sounded a warning to any who, because of persecution and trials, may have been thinking of defecting from the faith; such people have no root in themselves.

The third group of hearers seem to make good progress, but the word is choked out by daily worries that distract them, by wealth that gives a false sense of security, and by anything else that might prevent the sown word from being productive.

Some seed does fall on good soil and is productive. Such people are open and receptive to the word of the kingdom. The message gets through to them and issues forth in a productive life. The parable therefore emphasizes our responsibility to listen to and obey Christ's message to us.

4. Parables of the lamp and the measure (4:21–25)

21–23 In the parable of the lamp (the Greek has "*the* lamp"), the lamp represents Jesus who has come. As the purpose of the lamp is to be put on a lampstand and not under a bowl or a bed, so the present hiddenness of Jesus will not always be, and God intends that one day Jesus will be manifested in all his glory (at the Parousia). But now he is hidden. It is therefore of utmost importance for us to be careful hearers, i.e., to have spiritual perception.

24–25 The parable of the measure begins with an exhortation to spiritual perception. The more one listens to the word of Jesus with spiritual perception and appropriates it, the more the truth about Jesus will be revealed. Furthermore, the more one appropriates the truth now, the more one will receive in the future. On the other hand, whoever does not lay hold of the word now, even the little spiritual perception that person has will be taken away.

5. Parable of the secretly growing seed (4:26–29)

26–29 This parable emphasizes the mysterious power of the seed to produce a crop. All the farmer can do is plant the seed on suitable ground; he cannot make the seed grow, nor does he understand how it grows. But it does grow and produces grain. In the same way, the hidden and somewhat ambiguous kingdom of God will some day burst out in its full glory. The harvest spoken of is the eschatological judgment (cf. Joel 3:13).

6. Parable of the mustard seed (4:30–32)

30–32 This is the third and last of the parables about the seed sown. The mustard seed was proverbial for its smallness but when grown, it becomes a huge treelike shrub.

The main point of the parable is that the kingdom of God has insignificant and weak beginnings, but a day will come when it will be great and powerful. We should not judge the significance of the kingdom by the size of its beginning.

7. Summary statement on parables (4:33–34)

33–34 Mark ends this section with a statement about Jesus' use of parables (see introduction to 4:1–34). He wanted to help the crowd understand by means of a veiled confrontation with the truth, stimulating their thinking and awakening their spiritual perception. The crowd was not ready for a direct revelation of the truth. In contrast, when Jesus was alone with his disciples, he spoke more directly with them; but even they needed his explanation to understand.

E. Triumph Over Hostile Powers (4:35–5:43)

1. Calming the storm (4:35–41)

The calming of the storm on the Lake of Galilee is a classic example of a nature miracle. Miracles of this kind seem to present the greatest problem to people today. The NT, however, makes clear that Jesus Christ is not only Lord over his church but also Lord of all creation (Col 1:16–17). It is completely inadequate to explain this miracle of the sovereign Lord by coincidence or to relegate it to myth or imagination. If Jesus was, as he claimed to be, the strong Son of God, a miracle of this kind is not inconsistent with that claim.

35–36 Mark includes many details in the story: the time of day, the reference to Jesus "just as he was" (v.36), the "other boats," the position of Jesus in the boat, the cushion, the sharp rebuke made by the disciples, and their terror and bewilderment. These suggest the report of an eyewitness.

Evening had come, so Jesus decided to go over to the other side of the lake in the boat he had been teaching from (v.1), perhaps wanting to escape the crowd and renew his strength. He did not want to delay his departure by first going on shore.

37 The geographic location of the Sea of Galilee makes it particularly susceptible to sudden, violent storms. It is situated in a basin surrounded by mountains. Though at night and in the early morning the sea is usually calm, when storms come at those times, they are all the more treacherous. The storm mentioned here drove the waves into the boat so that it was being swamped.

38 Jesus, tired from a long day's teaching, was in the stern of the boat, asleep on a cushion. This cushion was apparently the only one on board, and Jesus used it as a pillow for his head. This is the only place in the Gospels where Jesus is said to have slept; but he did, of course, get tired and needed sleep like any other man. He must have been very tired to have slept through such a violent storm.

The disciples' rebuke of Jesus indicates that they did not know who he really was.

Such a rebuke of the Son of God was entirely inappropriate.

39–40 Jesus rebuked the wind and spoke to the waves, and a great calm came. The sovereign Lord spoke and his creation immediately responded. Jesus then rebuked his disciples for their lack of faith. He had expected them by this time to have demonstrated more mature faith in God's saving power, the power that they had seen present and active in the person of Jesus (see 7:18; 8:17–18, 21, 32–33; 9:19 for other rebukes of the disciples).

41 A feeling of awe came over the disciples as a result of Jesus' mighty act. Something about him was revealed to them on this occasion that they had not experience before. Their rhetorical question implied the answer, "He is the strong Son of God." It is not difficult to imagine what effect this story had on the members of the persecuted Roman church Mark wrote his gospel for. It assured them that the strong Son of God would go with them into the storm of opposition and trial.

2. Healing the demon-possessed man (5:1–20)

1 Jesus now demonstrates his power over the forces of evil by casting out demons from a possessed man. Like the previous story, it reveals that Jesus is truly divine. "Across the lake" means on the eastern side, an area where the population was largely Gentile (cf. the presence of a large herd of pigs, animals considered unclean by Jews). In the area where this story probably took place, there was a cliff along with some old tombs.

2 Jesus was immediately confronted by the possessed man, who had seen Jesus from a distance and came running to him (v.6). Since it was already evening (cf. 4:35) when they started across the lake, it was probably dark by now.

3–5 The possessed man lived in the tombs. Often in Palestine people were buried in natural caves or in tombs cut out of the limestone rock. It was a natural place for a demon-possessed man to dwell because of the popular belief that tombs were a favorite haunt of demons. Efforts had been made to control this wretched man, but without success.

6 The man fell on his knees in front of Jesus (an act of homage, not worship). The demon showed respect because he recognized that he was confronted with one greatly superior to him.

7–8 The demon's address to Jesus admitted that he was in the presence of one who threatened his very existence. He used Jesus' personal name and his title "Son of the Most High God." His intent was to gain control over Jesus (see comment on 1:24). Fearing that he would be exorcised, he pleaded exemption from torment. This may be a reference to eschatological punishment. Verse 8 seems to be an explanatory statement by Mark to make clear why the demon was acting so excitedly. Jesus had ordered him to come out of the man.

9 When Jesus asked the demoniac's name, he replied, "Legion." The significance of this name is not clear. Perhaps he had had an unfortunate experience with a Roman legion and this had caused his madness. Or perhaps the many demons in him combined to form one aggregate force, thus the name "Legion." The demons so fully possessed the man that he seemed to be unable to act apart from them.

10 The demons, speaking through the demoniac, requested not to be sent "out of the area" (see comment on Lk 8:31).

11–13 What caused the stampede of the pigs was the entrance of the demons into them. They were bent on destruction. Not having been able to destroy the man, they destroyed the pigs. Demons are emissaries of Satan, the Destroyer. Why the sovereign Lord allowed this destruction is uncertain, but perhaps he wanted to give tangible evidence to the man and to the people that the demons had actually left him.

14–15 The result of the stampede and destruction of the pigs was the flight of the herdsmen to tell everyone in the area what had happened (v.14). This brought the people to the scene of the miracle. When they arrived, they could scarcely believe their eyes! The violent, demon-possessed man was now sitting quietly, dressed and in his right mind.

Only the Son of God can deliver us from the tyranny of the devil.

Instead of rejoicing, the people were terrified to be in the presence of one with power to perform such a miracle.

16–17 The people decided it was time for Jesus to leave their region. In fact, out of fear, ignorance, and selfishness, they pleaded with him to leave. If the mighty force at work in Jesus could destroy an entire herd of pigs, might not this power strike again with even more serious consequences? Jesus complied with their request, for he does not stay where he is not wanted.

18–19 Jesus decided to return to the west side of the lake. The man who had been possessed wanted to go with him (v.18)—a perfectly natural reaction. He was eager for Jesus' company, for no one had ever shown him such love and compassion. But our Lord did not allow it. Instead he gave him the much more difficult task of returning home to his family to bear testimony to what Jesus in his mercy had done for him (v.19). This contrasts with Jesus' command to the leper in 1:44. Since the demoniac was in Gentile territory, there would be little danger that popular messianic ideas about him might be circulated. Jesus realized that this man could be trusted to convey to others the real truth about him.

20 The man obeyed without argument and began to bear testimony of what "Jesus had done for him." The Decapolis was a league of ten originally free Greek cities located (except Scythopolis) east of the Sea of Galilee and the Jordan River. These cities heard the testimony of the former demoniac and responded with amazement.

3. Jairus's daughter and the woman with a hemorrhage (5:21–43)

Mark probably brought together these two stories with the story of the healing of the demoniac because they all have to do with ritual uncleanness. According to Jewish

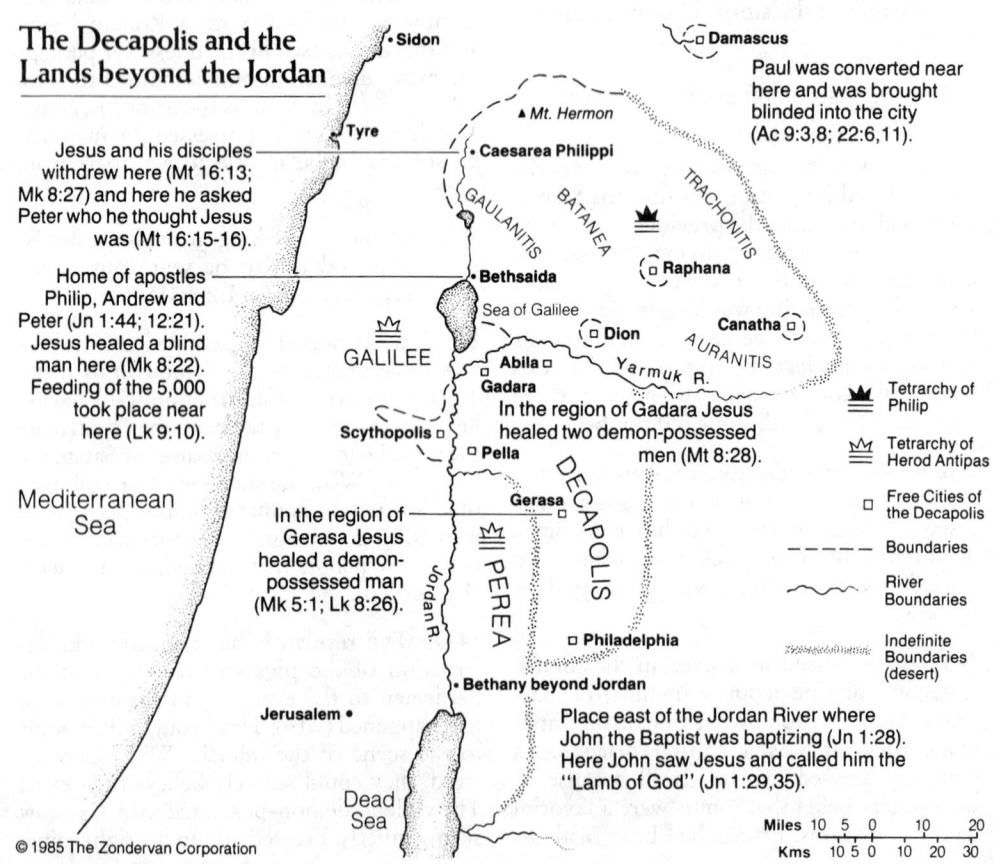

© 1985 The Zondervan Corporation

law contact with graves, blood, or death made one ceremonially unclean.

The account of the healing of the woman with a hemorrhage occurs within the story of the healing of Jairus's daughter. Once again, Mark sandwiches these two narratives to allow for the passage of time for Jairus's daughter to die or to heighten the suspense (see comment on 3:20–35). Both incidents read like eyewitness accounts.

21–24 On the west side of the lake again, Jesus was probably busy teaching when he was interrupted by the plea of someone who belonged to the Jewish group of "synagogue rulers" (GK *801*). These were laymen whose responsibilities were administrative, not priestly, and included such things as looking after the building and supervising the worship. Jairus's need was so urgent that he jettisoned all dignity and pride, fell at Jesus' feet, and begged for help. He had apparently heard about Jesus and believed that he could heal his child. Jesus gives no oral reply; rather, he set out with Jairus to go to the child, followed by a large crowd of curiosity seekers.

25–26 At this point Mark inserts the story of the healing of the woman with a hemorrhage. The precise nature of the woman's ailment is not stated. Probably some sort of uterine disease caused the bleeding that had persisted for twelve years. Mark includes vivid details: she had suffered much, had been treated by many doctors, and had spent all she had. But her condition had gotten worse.

27–29 The woman's hearing about Jesus' healings and her belief that he could help her led her to come to him. She possibly also shared the superstition, common in her day, that the power of a person was transmitted to his clothing (see comment on Lk 8:42–46). So she went into the crowd and, because of her ceremonial uncleanness, approached Jesus surreptitiously from the rear. The moment she touched him, her faith was rewarded. The bleeding stopped, and she felt a soundness in her body that assured her that she had been healed.

30–32 Jesus too was aware that something had happened to him. Healing energy had gone out of him for someone's benefit, and he insisted on knowing who it was. To his disciples his question seemed stupid in view of the crush of the crowd all about him. The harsh reply of the disciples may have been caused by their concern to get Jesus to Jairus's daughter where a real emergency existed. But Jesus' spiritual sensitivity told him that someone had touched his clothes; he wanted to find her, not to rebuke her but to make personal contact with her. She needed to know that it was her faith, not her superstitious belief, that had caused God to heal her.

33–34 The woman, though "trembling with fear," came forward, prostrated herself before Jesus, and told him everything. This must have taken great courage, especially since she was regarded as ceremonially unclean (Lev 15:19–30). Jesus made clear to her that it was her faith that had healed her (the word "healed" [GK *5392*] has both physical healing and theological salvation in mind; cf. 2:1–12).

The phrase "Go in peace" is a traditional Jewish formula of leave-taking (Heb. *shalom*; GK 8934; cf. Jdg 18:6; 1Sa 1:17). The woman was complete, being now in a right relationship with God (cf. Ro 5:1).

35–37 While Jesus was still speaking to the woman, "some men" brought Jairus the news not to bother Jesus anymore since his daughter was dead. But Jesus ignored the messengers and encouraged Jairus to keep on believing. This word of assurance must have been just what he needed. He in no way tried to dissuade Jesus from resuming his journey to the child's bedside. At this point Jesus decided to separate himself from the crowd following him (v.37). A momentous miracle was about to take place, and he wanted to have only a chosen few witness it.

38 When Jesus arrived at Jairus's house, a great commotion was taking place. Professional mourners had been secured and were already at work. Since Jairus occupied a prominent position in the Jewish community, the number of professional mourners was large. So along with members of his family, they were making a great uproar.

39–40 On entering the house, Jesus asked why they were making such a commotion since the child was not dead but only asleep. On the surface this statement is enigmatic. It could mean that she had slipped into a comatose state, from which he would awaken her. Or it could be Jesus' way of indicating that he proposed to bring her back from the dead. Since her death was not final, he spoke of it as sleep.

The mourners misunderstood Jesus' reference to sleeping to mean that she was not really dead. So they laughed at him. Jesus did not want any noisy crowd present when he performed this stupendous miracle; so he put the mourners out. Their lack of sensitivity disqualified them from being present at such a beautiful event. Only Jesus' three most intimate disciples and the mother and father were allowed to enter the room where the dead child lay.

41 Jesus stood by the side of the child, took her hand, and spoke the Aramaic words *"Talitha koum"* (translated by Mark for his Gentile readers). Aramaic was the language of Palestine in the first century A.D. and was probably the language Jesus and his disciples normally spoke. However, since they came from Galilee, an area surrounded by Gentile Decapolis and by Syrian Phoenicia, it seems likely that they also knew Greek and on occasion spoke Greek.

42-43 The twelve-year-old girl responded immediately to Jesus' words. She not only stood up, she began to walk around. The five witnesses to the miracle were completely amazed. Death is an enemy (cf. 1Co 15:25-26), but it must give way to the power of the kingdom present in Jesus, the Messiah.

Jesus gave two orders to the witnesses. First, they were not to reveal the facts about the miracle. Jesus revealed his messianic dignity to those who could be entrusted with it, but it was veiled to those (like the raucous mourners) who could not. Jesus' second order was that they should give the girl something to eat—beautiful evidence of his concern for ordinary human needs.

F. Rejection at Nazareth (6:1–6:6a)

1 Jesus now traveled to his hometown of Nazareth. Even though he was born in Bethlehem, his family lived in Nazareth and he had been brought up there (Mt 2:1, 23; Lk 2:1-7, 39-40). Jesus came here as a rabbi accompanied by his disciples.

2 On the Sabbath, Jesus went into the synagogue and began to teach (see comment on 1:21). This probably was the first time his fellow townsmen had actually heard Jesus teach, and many of them were amazed. But with some of them, there was an undercurrent of doubt as they wondered about the source of his teaching and his miracles. They were either from God or from Satan. Which?

3 The hostility of Jesus' townspeople toward him came out more clearly in the rhetorical questions in this verse. In essence they were asking: Isn't he just a common ordinary fellow who makes his living with his hands like the rest of us? How is it that he is parading as a rabbi and miracle-worker? The question "Isn't this Mary's son?" seems also to be derogatory since it was not customary among Jews to describe a man as the son of his mother; behind this question may be the rumor, circulated during Jesus' lifetime, that he was illegitimate (cf. Jn 4:41; 9:29).

The brothers and sisters of Jesus mentioned here were probably children born to Mary and Joseph. James was likely the oldest and was certainly the best known of Jesus' brothers. He was closely identified with the church in Jerusalem (Ac 12:17; 15:13; 1Co 15:7; Gal 1:19) and was probably the author of the epistle of James (Jas 1:1). Jude was probably the author of the book of Jude. We know nothing of Joseph and Simon.

The townspeople of Nazareth were offended at Jesus, and they refused to believe in him or his word.

4 Jesus responded to the doubts raised about the legitimacy of his teaching and his miracles by a proverb that has parallels in both Jewish and Greek literature. The people of Nazareth were incapable of appreciating who Jesus was because, like Jesus' own family, they identified him so closely with themselves.

5-6a Verse 5 is a bold statement in that it refers to something Jesus could not do. He did, of course, have the power to do miracles in Nazareth. His inability was related to the moral situation. In the climate of unbelief he chose not to exercise his miraculous power. One of the great emphases of Mark's gospel is that Jesus performs his miracles in response to faith.

Jesus expressed amazement at their lack of faith. Apparently he did not expect such a response from his own townspeople.

G. Sending Out the Twelve (6:6b–13)

6b Verse 6b probably belongs with vv. 7–13. As a result of the village ministry, Jesus decided to send out the Twelve, presumably to increase his own ministry through them.

7 Jesus had already been preparing his disciples for this mission. He had called them with his promise, "I will make you fishers of men" (1:17). He had withdrawn on several occasions to give them special attention (3:7, 13; 4:10), and they had witnessed his mighty acts and listened to his wise words. Now it was time for them to be sent out (cf. 3:14–15). The word used here for "sending" (GK 690) carries with it the idea of official representation; their message and deeds were to be an extension of his own. He sent them out "two by two," apparently a Jewish custom (cf. 11:1; 14:13; Ac 13:2), so that the truthfulness of their testimony about Jesus might be established "on the testimony of two or three witnesses" (Dt 17:6). The Twelve were given power over evil spirits. Mark especially highlights Jesus' power to exorcise demons.

8–9 Inherent in the commission of the Twelve was absolute trust in God to supply all their needs, including their physical needs. They were to take only what they had on their backs. The only exception was a staff. They were to take no food or money. Clothing was to be minimal. Sandals were allowed and only one tunic. Jesus probably made this last prohibition because he wanted the disciples to trust God for the provision of hospitality for each night (an extra tunic was used as a night covering in the open air).

Jesus undoubtedly expected them to preach the same message as he did (see 1:15). He also calls us to self-dedication to him and his message.

10–11 Jesus wanted to protect the good reputation of the disciples. Whenever they accepted the hospitality of a home, they were to stay there until they left that town, even if more comfortable or attractive lodgings were offered them.

Jesus also knew that the mission of the Twelve would not always be accepted. So he instructed them how to act in such circumstances. By shaking dust off their feet (a Jewish custom as one entered Jewish territory), they would declare the place to be heathen and would make it clear that those who rejected the message must now answer for themselves. The disciples' message, like that of Jesus, brings judgment as well as salvation. This always happens when the Gospel is preached.

12–13 Mark now describes the actual mission of the Twelve. It was clearly patterned after Jesus' own ministry: (1) preaching repentance, (2) driving out demons, and (3) healing the sick. By these activities they were demonstrating that the kingdom of God had come with power. At this point, their mission is a mere extension of the ministry of Jesus. Their independent mission did not occur until after Jesus' resurrection.

IV. Withdrawal From Galilee (6:14–8:30)

This fourth section of Mark's gospel finds Jesus withdrawing from the territory of Galilee for the primary purpose of further instructing his disciples. Though one incident of public teaching occurs in the section 7:1–23, the focus of his teaching was now on the Twelve.

A. Popular Views of Jesus' Identity (6:14–16)

14–15 The Herod mentioned here is Antipas (son of Herod the Great and Malthace), tetrarch of Galilee and Perea. Mark may be using the title of "King" here ironically or as a reflection of local custom. The "this" of v.14 likely refers to the mighty works of Jesus, multiplied by the works of the disciples, especially since the entire discussion focuses on the question of Jesus' identity.

What follows are popular views of who Jesus was. That some thought Jesus to be John the Baptist raised from the dead shows that they knew nothing of Jesus prior to his ministry in Galilee. John the Baptist did not perform miracles while he was alive, but apparently his resurrection status was thought to give him that power.

Another popular view identified Jesus with Elijah. John the Baptist had spoken of Jesus as "the Coming One"; to anyone who knew the OT it could be no one else but Elijah (cf. Mal 3:1; 4:5).

A third view was that "he is a prophet, like one of the prophets of long ago." This seems to be a lower estimate of Jesus than the previously mentioned one.

16 Herod's view—that Jesus was John the Baptist raised from the dead—arose not so much from what he had heard about Jesus as from the proddings of a guilty conscience, since Herod had been directly responsible for John's death. The mention of the death of John causes Mark to interrupt the account of the mission of the Twelve in order to tell the story of John's murder.

B. Death of John the Baptist (6:17-29)

17-18 Mark's gospel has two "passion narratives": the passion of John and the passion of the Messiah. Mark devotes fourteen verses to the death of John but only five to his ministry (1:4-8).

John the Baptist had been arrested by Herod, who put him in prison because he had denounced Herod's adulterous union with Herodias, his brother Philip's wife and his own niece. The Mosaic Law prohibited marriage to one's brother's wife while the brother was still alive (cf. Lev 18:16).

Josephus (a Jewish historian of the first century) emphasizes the political motives behind the action of Herod against John. In order to marry Herodias, Herod had to rid himself of the daughter of King Aretas IV, whose kingdom lay just to the east of Perea. The situation there was already sensitive, and John's preaching had the potential to cause real trouble. Mark, on the other hand, emphasizes the moral considerations; John did not hesitate to incur the wrath of Herod in his service to God.

19-20 Herodias was infuriated by John and wanted to kill him. She was thwarted in her design because Herod protected John (motivated by fear and a recognition of John's righteous and holy character).

21-23 Herodias finally got the opportunity she was waiting for. At a banquet for Herod's birthday, attended by military and political leaders, Herodias's daughter went before the guests to dance. Likely Herodias sent her into the banquet hall to dance as part of her scheme to get rid of John the Baptist.

The dance was probably a lewd one. Herod and his dinner guests were pleased with her performance—so much so that Herod offered her virtually anything she wanted as a reward.

24-25 The girl left the banquet hall to seek the advice of her mother. Herodias's quick reply betrayed the premeditated nature of her homicidal plan. Mark does not mention any surprise on the daughter's part when her mother made the request. In fact, when she went to convey the request for the head of John the Baptist, the daughter added two things: she wanted John's head "right now" and she wanted it "on a platter."

26-28 Herod was in a quandary, but "because of his oaths and his dinner guests," he could hardly refuse the girl. Reluctantly he ordered an executioner to be sent to the prison to decapitate John. John's head was brought to Herod, who presented it to Salome, who gave it to her mother.

29 Mark ends the shocking story with John's disciples coming for the body to give it proper burial. Herod no doubt thought that he was now finished with the righteous prophet. But this was not to be. The ministry of Jesus stirred up Herod's memories of John, and his fears returned.

C. Feeding the Five Thousand (6:30-44)

The story of the feeding of the five thousand with a simple meal of bread and fish stands in marked contrast to the elaborate banquet of Herod (see also later comments on this miracle in 6:52; 8:17-21).

30 Mark resumes the account of the mission of the Twelve. The disciples, here called "apostles" (GK 693; related to GK 690) returned to Jesus with a report on their apostolic work of preaching, casting out demons, and healing.

31-32 Their activities had created much interest. So many people were coming and going that the disciples had no time even to eat. Since the disciples were doubtless tired from their missionary activities and from the demands of the crowds, Jesus decided to seek rest for them in a quiet and solitary place.

Jesus may have had another reason for going to a deserted area in addition to seeking rest. It was in the desert that God had given rest to his ancient people after their Exodus from Egypt. Prophets such as Isaiah (63:14) and Jeremiah (31:2) saw the Israelites in the desert as a type of a second rest promised to the new people of God in a second exodus.

Jesus and his disciples fulfill this promise. Jesus, not the pillar and the cloud, is God's presence, and the Bread (instead of the manna) is God's provision of sustenance.

33–34 The best way for Jesus and his disciples to get away from the crowds was by boat, going to the northeast side of the lake. But the crowd saw it and followed by land. Somehow they managed to walk around the lake and arrive at the landing place ahead of the boat (v.33).

Jesus had every right to be annoyed with the crowd. They had prevented him and his disciples from having a much needed rest. But instead of being irritated, he responded compassionately and in love (v.34), seeing them as "sheep without a shepherd" (cf. Nu 27:17; Eze 34:5). These two OT passages associate the shepherd theme with the desert. Jesus, like Moses, was leading his people into the desert and, like David (cf. Eze 34:23, 25), was providing rest for them.

35–36 Jesus' disciples became concerned for the crowd. It was late in the day; and in that distant place, there was little possibility of obtaining food. Out of concern for the crowd, the disciples suggested Jesus dismiss the crowd to get food in the nearby towns.

37 Jesus, however, ordered the disciples to supply food. He uses the emphatic personal pronoun: "*You* give them something to eat" (emphasis mine). The disciples were startled. They could only think of the impossible amount of money it would take to feed a crowd like this one. Not even eight months' wages would buy enough bread for all to eat.

38 Jesus was not thinking of bread bought in the neighboring villages. Before proceeding with his approach to the problem, he asked his disciples what the present status of the supply was. They found it to be meager: five small rolls and two fish—a mere pittance in view of the number of people to be fed.

39–40 At Jesus' direction the disciples arranged the crowd into groups of hundreds and fifties in order to facilitate the distribution of the food. This arrangement helps calculate the total number of men at five thousand (v.44; cf. Mt 14:21). The arrangement may also suggest the teacher-student relationship or even recall the Mosaic camp in the desert (Ex 18:21, 25; Dt 1:15). Thus the people are like the new people of God and Jesus like a second Moses who transforms them into a new Israel.

41 Jesus did what any pious Jew would have done before eating—he prayed. The usual form of the prayer was a thanksgiving or eucharist: "Blessed art thou, O Lord our God, King of the Universe, who bringeth forth bread from the earth." As to how the miracle was performed, Mark does not give us so much as a hint. He simply says that Jesus broke the loaves, divided the fish, and gave them to the disciples to distribute among the people.

42–44 There can be no question but that Mark understood the actions of Jesus to have been miraculous. Not only were all the people fed and their hunger satisfied, but there was more left over at the end than there had been at the beginning—twelve small wicker baskets (see comment on Mt 14:21).

D. Walking on the Water (6:45–52)

45 Mark records no reaction of the crowd to the multiplication of the loaves and fish, but there must have been one. The hurried departure of the disciples to Bethsaida suggests that there was danger of a messianic uprising as a result of the miracle (cf. Jn 6:15). Jesus stayed to dismiss the crowd, no doubt to calm the people down.

46 Mark's mention of Jesus' praying is further evidence of the crisis nature of the situation. On three occasions in this gospel Jesus withdrew to pray, and each time some sort of crisis was involved (1:35; 6:46; 14:32–36). In each incident Jesus was tempted not to carry out God's mission for him—a mission that would ultimately bring suffering, rejection, and death. These crises increased in intensity, reaching their climax in the agony of Gethsemane.

47–48 The time of this incident was "evening," probably late at night. A boat in the middle of the Lake of Galilee could easily be seen at the time of the full moon.

Apparently the wind was blowing from the north or northeast and had blown the disciples off their course. They were facing a stiff headwind. Between 3–6 A.M. Jesus came to them "walking on the lake." The disciples in the boat thought that this ghostly figure was going to pass by them.

49–50 Although they did not recognize him at first, Jesus identified himself and calmed their fears with words of assurance: "Take courage! It is I. Don't be afraid."

51 When Jesus climbed into the boat, another miracle occurred as the wind ceased. The disciples were amazed as they realized unmistakenly some relationship between his getting into the boat and the calming of the wind.

E. Healings Near Gennesaret (6:53–56)

53–56 Jesus stayed with the disciples in the boat and crossed over with them to Gennesaret. Mark then summarizes the work of Jesus in Galilee before he withdrew to other regions (cf. 1:32–34 and 3:7–12). In this summary we see the widespread fame of Jesus as a healer. As a good Jew, he wore the fringes and tassels commanded by God (Nu 15:37–39; Dt 22:12). The faith of those who came to touch Jesus' clothes led to their healing (cf. 5:25–34).

F. Commands of God and Traditions of Men (7:1–13)

This incident is linked with the next section by the common theme of "cleanness." It is similar to the conflict stories found in 2:1–3:6 but functions here as an introduction to the extension of Jesus' ministry to the Gentiles (7:24–8:10).

1–2 Another delegation of fact-finding theologians came down from Jerusalem (cf. 3:22) to investigate the Galilean activities of Jesus. They discovered that Jesus' disciples did not wash their hands before eating. Their question was one of ceremonial purity versus ceremonial defilement, an important topic to devout Jews.

3–4 Mark felt it necessary to explain to his Gentile readers the Jewish custom of ceremonial handwashing, a custom based on the "tradition [GK *4142*] of the elders," a great mass of oral tradition that had arisen about the law. Its purpose was to regulate a person's life completely, and it was passed on from one generation to the next one as binding regulations.

Mark gives an example of the custom. After being in the marketplace and coming into contact with Gentiles or even nonobservant Jews, the Pharisees would wash themselves to ensure their ritual cleanness.

5–7 To the question of why his disciples acted as they did, Jesus answered by quoting Isa 29:13, preceded by his own comment: "Isaiah was right when he prophesied about you hypocrites." A "hypocrite" (GK *5695*) is someone whose worship is merely outward and not from the heart. Jesus did not mean that Isaiah had in mind the Pharisees and the teachers of the law when he originally wrote these words but that Isaiah's denunciation of the religious leaders of his day fitted those of Jesus' day. Their outward appearance of piety was a lie, because it was not accompanied by a life of total commitment to God. Jesus went on to equate neglect of true holiness with submission to rabbinic traditions made by humans.

8–9 Jesus then contrasted the "commands of God" with the "traditions of men." It is clear that the great body of Jewish tradition had failed to get to the heart of God's commands. It was supposed to fence in the law so that the people would not infringe on it. Actually, however, the tradition distorted and ossified the law (v.9) and even served as a means of getting around God's law.

10–13 Jesus cited a specific example of how the tradition could do this. He quoted (from LXX) Ex 20:12 and 21:16. In the latter the seriousness of failure to keep the fifth commandment is underscored—death is the penalty for anyone who curses his father or mother. But by means of the traditions of the Pharisees, the responsibility of children to their parents could be easily circumvented. A son need only declare that what he had intended to give his father and mother be considered "Corban," i.e., a gift devoted to God, and it could no longer be designated for his parents. By devoting the gift to God, a son did not necessarily promise it to the temple nor did he prevent its use for himself. What he did was to exclude legally his parents from benefiting from it (v.12). So the very purpose for which the fifth commandment had been given was being set aside ("nullified") by the tradition.

G. True Defilement (7:14–23)

The connection of these verses with what precedes is evident from Jesus' statement in v.15 that directly answers the question the Pharisees and teachers of the law had raised (v.5).

14–15 After speaking directly to the Pharisees and the teachers of the law, Jesus called the crowd around him because he wanted them to hear the crux of his teaching about what is clean. He prefaced his statement with a prophetic call to hear his words and then stated clearly what does and does not make a person unclean. What is external cannot defile a person. Food, for example, cannot do this—even if it is eaten with unwashed hands or declared unclean by kosher food laws. What really makes a person unclean comes from within, out of the heart and the will—what one thinks, says, desires, and does.

17–19 After leaving the crowd, Jesus entered a house and was teaching the disciples privately (cf. 9:28, 33; 10:10). Although the disciples had already spent considerable time with Jesus and belonged to the inner circle of his concern, they were slow to grasp the meaning of his teaching. Jesus expressed surprise that they still could not comprehend spiritual truth.

The reason nothing entering a person from the outside makes him or her "unclean" (GK 176) is because it enters into the stomach, not the heart (v.19). And the heart is the center of human personality that determines one's actions and inaction (cf. Pr 4:23; Isa 29:13).

In v.19b Mark explains for his readers the significance of Jesus' teaching about ceremonial purity. This statement relates to the situation in the Pauline mission churches about questions of clean and unclean foods (cf. Ac 10:9–16; 11:5–10; Ro 14:13ff.) and idol-meats (1Co 8–10). Mark is probably trying to publicize the charter of Gentile freedom by recording in the plainest terms possible Jesus' detachment from Jewish ceremonial laws and to spell out in clear tones the application of this principle to his readers.

20–23 The main force of this passage is the same as in v.15b: the source of uncleanness in anyone is the heart (Jer 17:9), for that is where the true issues of life lie. The list that follows has no parallel in any other known sayings of Jesus, but it is typically Jewish (cf. Ro 1:29–31; Gal 5:19–23). The list seems to move from overt sins to sinful attitudes or dispositions.

H. The Faith of the Syrophoenician Woman (7:24–30)

This incident seems to follow naturally the preceding incidents in which Jesus breaks with the Jewish oral law and particularly the law of ceremonial cleanness. Jews normally had no relationship with Gentiles because associations with them made them ritually unclean. Jesus now shows by example that those oral laws are invalid and deliberately associates himself with a Gentile woman. Mark also wants to emphasize the mission to the Gentiles. The Gospel of the kingdom is not limited to Israel, even though historically it came to her first (cf. v.27); the good news is for Mark's Gentile readers as it was for the Syrophoenician woman.

24 Jesus left where he was and traveled to Phoenicia (now Lebanon), in which the city of Tyre was located. Apparently Jesus did not go there for public ministry. He went into a house to get out of the public eye, perhaps to rest and to prepare himself spiritually for what he knew lay ahead of him. But once again (cf. 6:31–34) his hope for a time of quiet retirement was thwarted.

25–26 One of the persons who sought out Jesus was a Gentile woman. No doubt she had heard about his healing powers and came to him because her daughter was possessed by an evil spirit. By nationality the woman was a Syrophoenician (in those days Phoenicia belonged administratively to Syria).

27–28 Jesus probably conversed with this woman in Greek, not Aramaic. He replied by comparing the children of the household (the privileged position of Israel) and the little dogs that were kept as household pets (less privileged Gentiles). Israel was to have the first opportunity to hear the Gospel (cf. Ac 2–7); later would come the Gentiles' turn. So far as this woman was concerned, the "later" time had already come, because Jesus responded compassionately to her needs.

The reply of the woman was remarkable. She admitted her status but refused to believe she was thereby excluded from any benefits.

29-30 Jesus was pleased with the woman's reply. It revealed to him not only her wit but also her faith and humility, and he responded by declaring that her daughter had been healed (this is the only instance of healing at a distance found in Mark's gospel). The woman returned home and discovered the truth of what Jesus had said.

I. Healing a Deaf and Mute Man (7:31-37)

31 Mark includes this miracle in the Decapolis, a story unique to his gospel, because it connects with the previous story by giving an account of another healing on Gentile territory. The Decapolis (see comment on 5:20) was largely Gentile, but many Jews also lived there.

32 A man was brought to Jesus who was "deaf and could hardly talk" (perhaps a speech impediment). Mark must have had Isa 35:6 in mind, which is a poetical description of the messianic Age and where the same rare word for "mute" is used in the LXX. The people begged Jesus to lay his hands on the deaf mute, obviously wanting him to heal the man. "They begged" shows their concern for him, for the deaf mute could not make an intelligible request for himself. Jesus responded to their request.

33 In order to deal more personally with the mute, Jesus took him aside from the crowd. Here his actions seem to be done to help the man exercise faith—the fingers placed in his ears apparently indicate they were to be unblocked and the saliva on the tongue indicates it was going to be restored to normal use.

34-35 Jesus looked up to heaven in an attitude of prayer, thereby showing the man that God was the source of his power (cf. Jn 11:41; 17:1). Jesus' sigh should be seen as something that accompanied his inner communion with the Father.

Jesus' prayer consisted of only a single word—*Ephphatha* (an Aramaic word that Mark, as usual, explains). The effect of the command was instantaneous: the man's ears were opened, his tongue was loosed, and his speech impediment was gone.

36-37 Jesus again ordered the crowd not to divulge the miracle, but his command had no effect. The more he insisted on their not talking about it, the more they blazed the miracle abroad. His reason for enjoining silence here was probably the same as in 1:44 (see comment).

Also as a result of the healing the people were overwhelmed beyond measure. The statement "he has done everything well" reminds us of Ge 1:31: "God saw all that he made, and it was very good"; Mark goes on again to remind us of the messianic significance of this miracle by words that reflect Isa 35:5-6. Undoubtedly for Mark the significance of this miracle was the proclamation of the Gospel in the territory of the Gentiles, a sign of the messianic activity of Jesus.

J. Feeding the Four Thousand (8:1-10)

Interest in Mark as an author in his own right, not merely a scissors-and-paste editor of the tradition, has focused attention lately on the structural arrangement of his gospel. The section 8:1-30 reveals some important parallels with 6:31-7:37.

6:31-44	Feeding the Multitude	8:1-9
6:45-56	Crossing the Sea and Landing	8:10
7:1-23	Conflict With the Pharisees	8:11-13
7:24-30	Conversation About Bread	8:13-21
7:31-36	Healing	8:22-26
7:37	Confession of Faith	8:27-30

The motif that seems to be behind this arrangement of the tradition is spiritual understanding—or lack of it. Jesus sounds a call to spiritual understanding in 7:14-18, but the disciples fail to understand after each feeding miracle (6:52; 8:14-21). The miracles of healing—the opening of the ears of the deaf man (7:31-36) and the eyes of the blind man (8:22-26)—are symbolic of and prepare the way for the opening of the spiritual understanding of the disciples.

The striking similarity between this story and 6:34-44 raises the question whether there was one or two feedings of the multitude. The majority of scholars think there was only one and take 8:1-9 as a doublet of 6:34-44. Nonetheless there are strong reasons to support the view of two separate events. (1) The language in the two accounts has significant differences. (2) Jesus himself clearly refers to two feedings (8:18-21). (3) Verse 4 does not seem to be an insurmountable problem since it is presumptuous to assume that the disciples always expected Jesus to meet a crisis situation by performing a miracle.

(4) Mark clearly thought them to be two separate events.

1–3 Remaining in the Decapolis, Jesus taught a large crowd gathered there. After three days Jesus (not the disciples, as in 6:35–36) recognized the physical needs of the crowds. He was moved with compassion for them because they had not had anything to eat for three days, and he immediately dismissed the idea that the crowd should be sent away for food for fear they would collapse on the way.

4 The disciples' reply suggests they had completely forgotten the feeding of the five thousand. This is perhaps the strongest argument against the view that there were two separate feedings (would they have forgotten such an astounding event?). But the argument is not as strong as it appears. (1) A considerable period of time may have elapsed between the two events. (2) Even mature Christians (which the disciples were not), having experienced God's power and provision, have subsequently acted in unbelief. (3) The reluctance of Jesus to perform miracles must have so impressed itself on the disciples that they did not expect him to meet every crisis in that fashion. (4) The disciples responded by indicating the difficulty of finding enough food for such a huge crowd.

5–7 Only seven loaves (cf. 6:38) were available to feed the crowd of four thousand (v.9). The people were not ordered into groups, but simply were on the ground. Jesus gave thanks separately for the bread and the fish, and after each prayer the disciples distributed the food to the people.

8 As always Jesus' provision was sufficient. But it was not merely sufficient. Seven basketfuls of fragments were left over and collected by the disciples (cf. 6:43). The use of *spyris* (GK 5083) for "basket" here instead of *kophinos* (6:43; GK 3186) is striking and suggests two different occasions.

9–10 Jesus got into the boat with his disciples and headed to Dalmanutha (identity of this place is unknown).

K. Requesting a Sign From Heaven (8:11–13)

11 This paragraph seems quite separate from the one immediately preceding it. Mark probably placed it here to form a parallel in this section (8:1–30) with 7:1–23 in the previous section (6:31–7:37). Both incidents relate to conflict with the Pharisees.

The request for a sign by the Pharisees was not sincere; rather, it was to tempt Jesus. Jesus' temptation in the wilderness was not a once-for-all experience. The devil came back again and again to tempt him. Here the Pharisees were asking Jesus to provide indisputable outward compelling proof of divine authority, more proof than his miracles afforded. Jesus resolutely refused the request for such a sign because it arose out of unbelief.

12 Jesus responded to their request by sighing deeply, showing his grief and disappointment when faced with the unbelief of those who, because of their spiritual privileges, ought to have been more responsive to him. There is a note of impatience in his question of why the Jewish people were constantly asking for a sign. In truth, God would not give them any sign. Jesus' statement represents in Greek a shortened form of the Hebrew self-imprecation: "If I do such a thing, may I die."

For Mark and for Paul (cf. 1Co 1:18–2:6), the sign God gives is the ambiguity of the humiliated and crucified Lord (see also Mt 16:4; Lk 11:29–32). Faith can never find its grounds in spectacular signs. This teaching of Jesus was doubtless what the church in Rome needed to hear, especially if they had been too engrossed in an exalted-Lord Christology.

13 Having so emphatically made his point, Jesus left the Pharisees, got into the boat, and crossed over to the east side of the lake with his disciples (cf. v.14).

L. The Yeast of the Pharisees and Herod (8:14–21)

14 For some reason the disciples had forgotten to bring an adequate supply of bread with them for the trip across the lake. Their failure sets the stage for the teaching of our Lord. Some commentators see in the "one loaf" a symbolic reference to Jesus. The disciples have failed to see that the one loaf they had with them was none other than Jesus himself, and that was sufficient.

15 Jesus warned his disciples about the yeast of the Pharisees. Yeast is a symbol of evil; just as only a very small amount of it can leaven an entire loaf of bread, so evil has a permeating power. Here the yeast of the Pharisees clearly refers to their desire for a sign from God to validate the actions of Jesus (similarly, the yeast of Herod; see Lk 23:8). Jesus was appealing to his disciples to understand that the authority he possessed could not be proved by a sign. Only by faith could they recognize him as the bringer of God's salvation.

16 The meaning of v.16 turns on which reading is adopted. It seems best to translate it: "They discussed with one another why they had no bread." That is, the disciples were so concerned to find out who was to blame for not bringing more bread that they completely ignored Jesus' warning about the yeast of the Pharisees and of Herod. As elsewhere in Mark, the disciples lacked understanding.

17–21 Jesus rebuked his disciples for their lack of understanding. They were like those on the outside (cf. 4:11–12) who had eyes but did not see and ears but did not hear. They should not have been so concerned over the bread. They should have remembered how abundantly Jesus had provided for them on two occasions—so much so that on both occasions they had leftover bread to collect. He, the Provider, was with them in the boat. What else could they want or need?

M. Healing a Blind Man at Bethsaida (8:22–26)

22 This incident, recorded only in Mark, takes place at Bethsaida. "Some people" brought a blind man to Jesus for healing. The fact that the initiative seems to have come more from the people who brought him than from the man himself may account for the way Jesus dealt with him (cf. 7:32ff.).

23–24 Why did Jesus lead the blind man out of the village? Only on three occasions did Jesus withdraw from the people to heal: the raising of Jairus's daughter (5:35–43), where Jesus' motive is clearly to rid himself of the commotion caused by the professional mourners; the healing of the deaf mute (7:31–37), where Jesus wanted to establish a personal contact with the man to help his faith; and the present incident, where the motive seems to be the same as in the healing of the deaf mute.

Jesus performed a double action: he spit on the man's eyes and laid his hands on him. To Jesus' question "Do you see anything?" the answer of the blind man here in Mark is essentially "Yes, but not clearly" (v.24). Two things seem clear: (1) the man had probably not been born blind or else he would not have been able to identify trees as trees, and (2) the return of his sight was gradual. Jesus healed gradually in this case probably to prove that he had full liberty in how he healed and was not restricted to any fixed rule.

25–26 Jesus then ordered the man to go home directly without first going into the town of Bethsaida, perhaps because he did not want this man broadcasting his miraculous cure (cf. comment on 1:44).

The importance of this story for Mark is that it anticipates the opening of the eyes of understanding of the disciples. This is the second in a pair of incidents that only Mark records (the first one is 7:24–37) and that fulfill the OT messianic expectations of Isa 35:5–6. Mark uses both incidents to lead up to the full revelation of Jesus' messianic dignity to the disciples (8:27–30). Their eyes too were opened, not by human perception, but by the miracle of God's gracious revelation—which was as much a miracle as the opening of the blind man's eyes.

N. Recognizing Jesus as Messiah (8:27–30)

This incident is usually taken to mark the beginning of the second half of Mark's gospel. While it is true that 8:27–30 has a close connection with 8:31–9:1, its relationship to 8:22–26 is even closer. This may be seen by the remarkable parallelism in the two stories—a parallelism that may be set out like this:

8:22	Circumstances	8:27
8:23–24	Partial Sight—Partial Understanding	8:28
8:25	Sight—Understanding	8:29
8:26	Injunction to Silence	8:30

Where the parallelism breaks down is at the point of partial understanding (8:28), for this is a partial understanding on the part of the people, not the disciples. While Mark could have changed the story to force parallelism, that he did not do so supports the historicity of the account.

27 The first half of Mark's gospel mounts to a climax with the story of the disciples' recognition of Jesus' messiahship at Caesarea Philippi (at the foot of Mount Hermon). Jesus inquired of the disciples who people said he was, not simply to get information, but as preliminary to his second, more important question.

28 The answers that the disciples gave all reflect an inadequate view of Christ. John the Baptist, for example, had a preparatory role. He looked for another messenger far greater than himself (cf. 1:7–8; cf. also 6:14–15). "One of the prophets" reflects a lower view of Jesus, that he was merely one of many prophets who had come on the scene of Israel's history. It seems surprising that the disciples did not report that anyone called Jesus the Messiah, especially since the demons recognized who he was and said so publicly (1:24; 3:11; 5:7). But his messiahship was veiled from the crowd.

29–30 Jesus now directed the question at the disciples in an emphatic manner: "Who do you, my most intimate and trusted friends—in contrast to the other people who neither know me nor understand me—think I am?"

Peter, true to form, had a ready answer: "You are the Christ." He was the spokesman for the Twelve, and in his confession one of the themes of this gospel (cf. 1:1) is stated.

The Greek word *Christos* ("Christ"; GK 5986) translates the Hebrew *mashiach* ("Messiah"; 5431) and means the "Anointed One" of God. In the OT the word is used of anyone who was anointed with the holy oil, as, for example, the priests and kings of Israel (cf. Ex 29:7, 21; 1Sa 2:10, 10:1, 6; 16:13; 2Sa 1:14, 16). The word carries with it the idea of being chosen by God, consecrated to his service, and endued with his power to accomplish the task assigned. Toward the close of the OT period, the word "anointed one" assumed a special meaning, denoting the ideal king anointed and empowered by God to deliver his people and establish his righteous kingdom (Da 9:25–26). Jewish literature between the Testaments spoke of the coming rule as restoring David's kingdom to its former prosperity and greatness. The ideas that clustered around the title "Messiah" tended to be political and national in nature, which is why Jesus seldom used the term. Of its seven occurrences in Mark, only three of them are in sayings of Jesus (9:41; 12:35; 13:21); and in none of these does he use the title of himself (see also comment on Mt 1:1).

Because Jesus was reluctant to speak of himself as the Messiah does not mean that he did not believe himself to be the Messiah. In this passage (8:29) and in 14:60–62, he accepted it as used of him by others (cf. Jn 4:25–26). As Messiah, Jesus saw himself as the fulfillment of all those prophets, priests, and kings who were anointed in the OT; he was bringing into existence a new Israel.

Peter's confession revealed real insight into the nature of Christ's person and mission, but his concept of Jesus' messiahship was far from being perfect. He and the other disciples still had much to learn of Messiah's suffering, rejection, and death, as the immediately following incident reveals. He therefore told them to be quiet at this time about his role as Messiah. They still needed instruction about it before being given permission to proclaim it without restraint.

V. The Journey to Jerusalem (8:31–10:52)

A new section in Mark's gospel begins with 8:31. Its structure centers around three predictions Jesus makes of his passion (8:31; 9:31; 10:33–34). What had previously been veiled is now stated openly: the Son of Man must go up to Jerusalem, suffer and die, and on the third day be raised from the dead. This is the secret of Jesus' messiahship, and it is now revealed. Mark also stresses what this will mean for Jesus' followers. Throughout the section (cf. 8:34–38; 9:35; 10:29–30, 38–39) there are sayings about what true discipleship is, with the stress on suffering.

Another purpose of this middle section of Mark's gospel is to provide for Jesus' move from Galilee (where almost his entire ministry took place) to Jerusalem for the climactic events of his ministry. This section with its emphasis on the suffering of the Messiah and of those who follow him must have had special meaning for the persecuted Christians in Rome. Mark is reminding them that to follow Jesus is to follow the path of suffering and even death.

A. First Prediction of the Passion (8:31–33)

31 Having accepted Peter's ascription of his being "the Christ," Jesus now began to teach his disciples what messiahship really meant. Yet he did not refer to himself as Messiah but as the Son of Man, a theologically important title.

"Son of Man" occurs eighty-one times in the Gospels and, with the possible exceptions of Mk 2:10 and 28—where the title "Son of Man" seems to be part of Mark's editorial comments—only Jesus uses it about himself. Notice how in 8:38, Jesus parallels "of me" with "the Son of Man." Son of Man was the title Jesus preferred in referring to himself because, unlike "Messiah," it was not freighted with connotations that might prove harmful to his God-appointed mission (see comment on 1:43–44).

"Son of Man" occurs in the OT. In the Psalms it simply meant "human being" (cf. Pss 8:4; 80:17); and in Ezekiel, God addressed the prophet by this phrase. The most helpful text, however, is Da 7:13–14, which depicts the Son of Man as a heavenly figure who at the end time brings the kingdom to the oppressed on earth. This passage is especially reflected in the sayings of Jesus in Mark's gospel that speak of the coming of the Son of Man (8:38; 13:26; 14:62). The title has, however, been infused with additional meaning, especially in those passages that associate the Son of Man with suffering and death (8:31; 9:9; 12, 31; 10:33, 45; 14:21, 41). The combining of the motif of eschatological glory with that of suffering and death is what characterizes the Son-of-Man idea in the Synoptics.

The Son of Man "must" suffer. This necessity arises because of hostility from his enemies, because of the spiritual nature of Jesus' work (which did not allow him to use force), and because of God's revealed plan of redemption that required Jesus' death (see Isa 52:13–53:12).

Jesus predicted that the rejection of the Messiah would be by three groups: the elders (members of the Sanhedrin), the chief priests (members of the high priestly families), and the teachers of the law (professional scribes).

The death of the Son of Man would be followed by his vindication: after three days he would be raised from the dead. "After three days" occurs also in 9:31; 10:34. In Mt 16:21; 17:23; 20:19; Lk 9:22; 18:33, however, "on the third day" is used. The two expressions are identical in meaning. Contrary to English usage, in a Jewish context "after three days" can mean a period of less than seventy-two hours, as long as parts of three days are included.

Verse 31 is particularly important because it is the only explanation in Mark's gospel of "the messianic secret." Jesus did not want his messiahship to be disclosed because it involved suffering, rejection, and death. Popular expectations of messiahship would have hindered the accomplishment of his messianic mission.

32 The message got through to Peter, but he refused to accept it, for he followed the popular theological and political categories. A suffering Messiah? Unthinkable! The Messiah was a symbol of strength, not weakness. So Peter took Jesus aside and, amazingly, rebuked him (same word as used in 1:25; 3:12).

33 Jesus' words to Peter were not only severe, they were deliberately spoken in the presence of the other disciples, for they probably shared Peter's views and needed the same rebuke. Jesus recognized in Peter's attempt to dissuade him from going to the Cross the same temptation he had experienced from Satan at the outset of his ministry (cf. Mt 4:8–10). In both cases, Jesus rebuked the satanic option of using a different means to accomplish his mission.

B. Requirements of Discipleship (8:34–9:1)

The purpose of this section was to encourage and strengthen the Roman Christians, who were facing persecution and trials. Through sayings of Jesus, Mark is informing them that such experiences are normal in the life of discipleship.

34 Now Jesus addressed the crowd as well as his disciples. Two requirements of discipleship are (1) denial of self and (2) taking up one's cross and following Jesus. By denial of self, Jesus did not mean to deny oneself something, but to renounce self—to cease to make self the object of one's life and actions. God, not self, must be at the center of life. Cross bearing refers to the way of the cross. The picture is of a man, already condemned, required to carry his cross on the way to the place of execution, as Jesus was required to do (cf. Lk 23:26). Certainly the Christians in Rome were acquainted with this pattern. To bear the cross means suffering and possible death—a message especially relevant to the Roman Christians.

35 Sometimes Christians are faced with the alternatives of confessing Christ or denying him. Jesus warns that by denying him, one's physical life may be saved, but one's eternal life will be lost. Conversely, to lose one's physical life by remaining true to Christ assures one of salvation. Mark therefore sounded a warning to any who might be thinking of defecting under trial. "For me" stresses the absoluteness of Jesus' claim for allegiance, and "for the gospel" refers to the preaching of God's Good News for which people are to give their lives.

36–37 These two verses emphasize the incomparable worth of the "soul" (GK *6034*) that which survives human death). Once a person has forfeited his or her share in eternal life (in this context, by a denial of Jesus), even the whole world cannot buy back eternal life.

38 Jesus climaxes his warning section by referring to those who are ashamed of him and his words. In the End, at the Judgment (cf. 2Th 1:7), the Son of Man will be ashamed of any who are ashamed of him.

9:1 This verse is probably an independent saying Mark has placed here, used in order to make a transition between the Transfiguration (9:2–8), a momentary manifestation of the glory and power of the kingdom, and the Parousia (8:38), the full manifestation of it. On this understanding the Transfiguration anticipates and guarantees the Parousia. To "taste death," refers to experiencing death for the sake of Jesus. Before that happens to some of them, they will (temporarily) see God's kingdom come in power.

C. The Transfiguration (9:2–8)

The purpose of the Transfiguration is directed toward the disciples (observe the expressions "before them" [vv. 2, 4], "enveloped them" [v.7], and a voice addressing them [v.7]). Mark places the Transfiguration here as a confirmation of the difficult teaching Jesus had given the disciples about his suffering and death (cf. 8:31–38). Peter, James, and John—and through them the rest of the Twelve—were commanded to heed that disclosure of Jesus.

2 "After six days" suggests that the Transfiguration is historical, connected with the previous event (see comment on Lk 9:28). The

Mount Hermon, about forty miles northeast of the Sea of Galilee, is the highest mountain in this area of the world (9,000 feet above sea level). In winter it is often snowcapped.

revelation was given to Peter, James, and John, the inner circle of the disciples (cf. 5:37–42; 14:33–42). The "high mountain" is most likely Mount Hermon (over 9,000 feet high), located near Caesarea Philippi, where the event Mark has just recorded took place. The word "transfigured" (GK *3565*) describes Jesus' change into another form (see also Mt 17:2); the word is later used to denote the progressive change into the moral likeness of Christ (Ro 12:2; 2Co 3:18).

3 It is difficult to know exactly what happened at the Transfiguration. Jesus' clothes became "dazzling white." His appearnce was temporarily changed into that of a heavenly being (cf. Rev 1:13–14).

4 Why the appearance of Elijah and Moses? If what the disciples saw was a glimpse of Jesus' final state of glory, then Moses and Elijah's function is to announce the End. In Jewish expectation, Elijah clearly played that role (cf. Mal 4:5; Mk 9:11–12). But what of Moses? The possible reappearance of Moses just before the End developed later in Jewish thought. Or Moses and Elijah may have been at the scene as representatives of the Law and the Prophets—i.e., the OT, which was being fulfilled by Jesus.

5 True to form, Peter responded impulsively. His words show that he was greatly moved by the experience, yet did not understand it. He wanted to prolong it by erecting three shelters. But before Jesus could enter permanently into his glory and eternal rest he had to suffer and die. Peter again stumbled at the necessity of a suffering Messiah.

6 This endeavor to excuse Peter's inept remark shows Mark's sensitive concern for Peter. He was frightened and at a loss as to what to say. So he impulsively spoke, and what he said was not worth saying.

7–8 The OT background of v.7 lies in the passages where the cloud symbolized God's presence (Ex 16:10; 19:9, 24:15f.; 33:9; Lev 16:2; Nu 11:25); from it he spoke. At Jesus' baptism, the Voice had spoken to him (1:11); here the disciples were addressed. God assured them that in spite of Jesus' coming death, he loved his Son and accepted his mission.

"Listen" (GK *201*) must be given its full sense of obedience. The only true listening known in the Bible is obedient listening (cf. Jas 1:22–24).

D. The Coming of Elijah (9:9–13)

9 On the way down the mountain, Jesus gave the three disciples orders to keep their experience of the Transfiguration secret till after the resurrection of the Son of Man. To proclaim his full glory before the Cross would have been too much in keeping with current popular ideas of messiahship. First must come suffering and death. Then after the Resurrection (in itself a manifestation of the glory of the Son of Man), divulging the Transfiguration experience would be appropriate. In Mark's gospel on numbers of occasions, especially after Jesus performed a miracle, he commanded those involved to keep the matter quiet (cf. 1:34, 43–44; 3:11–12; 5:43, 7:36; 8:30; see comment on 1:44).

10 The disciples obeyed Jesus' injunction. But they were puzzled by his statement about the resurrection of the Son of Man. As Jews they were familiar with the idea of a general resurrection of the dead (cf. Da 12:1–3; Jn 11:24). But this special resurrection of the Son of Man baffled them, as their discussion of it showed.

11 Apparently the disciples did not feel free to ask Jesus what he meant by his "rising from the dead" (v.10). Instead they asked him about Elijah. No doubt the fact that three of them had seen Elijah at the Transfiguration reminded them that he would come before the Messiah and restore all things (Mal 4:5–6). Restoring all things involved, among other things, leading the people to repentance. Now if Elijah comes first and does his preparatory work, how is it that when the Son of Man comes he finds people so unprepared for him that they completely reject him and, indeed, kill him? They were still perplexed by the idea of a suffering Messiah.

12 Jesus' answer is that the teachers of the law were right about Elijah, but that it did not preclude the suffering of the Son of Man. The Scriptures, Jesus said, predict it (probably a reference to Isa 52:13–53:12).

13 Jesus went on to say that Elijah already had come in the person of John the Baptist. Though John is not named here, the reference to him is obvious; he had been imprisoned and put to death. "Just as it is written about him" refers to what the OT said about Elijah in his relationship to Ahab and Jezebel (cf. 1Ki 19:1–2), two people who foreshadow Herod and Herodias. The eschatological ministry of Elijah in no way does away with the necessity for the Son of Man to suffer and die.

E. Healing a Boy With an Evil Spirit (9:14–29)

14 This last exorcism story in Mark's gospel occurred when Jesus, Peter, James, and John rejoined the other disciples after the experience of the Transfiguration. The disciples were engaged in a debate with the teachers of the law who were monitoring the teaching and preaching of Jesus.

15 Why were the people so amazed when they saw Jesus? It may have been because he arrived at an opportune time for meeting a critical need. Or perhaps it was simply because Jesus' very presence provoked wonder.

16–18 Jesus' inquiry as to what the other disciples and the crowd were arguing about brought a reply from a man who had brought his demon-possessed and epileptic son for healing. Doubtless the disciples had fully expected to be able to exorcise the demon. Had that not been a part of their commission (cf. 3:15), and had they not already been successful at it (cf. 6:13)?

19 It seems best to restrict the meaning of "unbelieving generation" to the disciples. Thus the cry of Jesus reveals his bitter disappointment with them; in the crucial moment they had failed because of their lack of faith during Jesus' absence.

In the face of such unbelief, Jesus longed for his heavenly Father. He was weary with his disciples' spiritual obtuseness. But in teaching them, Jesus never gave up. Mark seems particularly anxious to show him persisting in instructing them (9:30–31; 14:28; 16:7).

20–22 Here Mark describes the deadly conflict between Jesus and the demonic powers. The demon immediately threw the boy, who had been sick since childhood and had experienced numerous vicious attacks, into a convulsion and made him fall on the ground and foam at the mouth. Pathetically the father asked Jesus for help. When he left home to bring his son to Jesus' disciples, he apparently believed the boy would be healed. Now he was not sure and said, "If you can do anything."

23–24 Jesus immediately fixed on the father's "if" clause. The question was not whether Jesus had the power to heal the boy but whether the father had faith to believe Jesus could. The father responded with a declaration of faith, but he recognized that his faith was far from perfect. It was still mixed with unbelief. So in a beautiful display of honesty, he asked Jesus to help him overcome his unbelief.

25 The crowd "running to the scene" was probably additional to the one already present (v.14). Jesus, wanting to avoid as much as possible further publicity, spoke to the demon before additional people arrived on the scene, ordering him to come out and stay out for good.

26–27 The demon's exorcism was accompanied by cries and convulsions. The effect on the boy was so severe that he seemed to the crowd to be dead. Completely exhausted and looking like a corpse, the boy responded to the touch of Jesus. Any confrontation of Jesus with Satan results in the victory of life over death.

28–29 Mark answers why the nine disciples were powerless to act in behalf of this boy. In private they asked Jesus about their failure, especially since they had been given authority over evil spirits (6:7) and had successfully cast out many demons before this incident (6:13). Jesus' answer suggests that they had taken for granted the power given them or had come to believe that it was inherent in themselves. So they no longer depended prayerfully on God for it, and their failure showed their lack of prayer.

F. Second Prediction of the Passion (9:30–32)

30–31 Jesus was now focusing his teaching ministry on the Twelve, and he sought seclusion to do this, so that the disciples could concentrate on what Jesus was saying to them. Jesus continued to teach them about his coming passion because they by no means had understood his first prediction. This second prediction included the new element of betrayal.

By translating the Greek verb used here as "betrayed" (GK *4140*), NIV opts for Judas as the implied subject of the action. The word literally means "to be delivered up" or "to be handed over." As early as Origen, it was interpreted to mean "delivered up by God," which is a better understanding of this verse. God took the initiative in providing salvation for the human race. His delivering up of Jesus was part of his plan for the world's redemption (cf. Ro 4:25; 8:32).

32 The disciples still did not understand. Mark does not soften this fact. Perhaps they were afraid of asking Jesus about what he had said because of their fear of facing a full disclosure of the suffering that lay ahead. Or they may have been fearful of being rebuked as Peter had been (8:33). Instead they chose to occupy themselves with arguing about who was the greatest among Jesus' disciples (cf. vv.33–34).

G. A Question About Greatness (9:33–37)

33–34 Jesus returned to Capernaum where his great Galilean ministry had begun (1:21) and where his headquarters in Galilee had been located. This time he did not linger there long, since his public ministry in the region had ended. He instructed his disciples privately, probably in the house belonging to Peter and Andrew (cf. 1:29).

The disciples must have been embarrassed and ashamed of their arguing among themselves about who was greatest because Jesus' question about it elicited only silence. And well might they have been ashamed. Instead of contemplating Jesus' passion and the suffering it would involve for both him and them, they had been occupied with self-centered arguments about greatness.

35 Jesus assumed the posture of a Jewish rabbi by sitting down (Mt 5:1; 13:1; Lk 5:3; Jn 8:2) and calling the Twelve to him. True greatness comes through service of others, as Jesus' own example demonstrated. This is a complete reversal of worldly values. How important this principle is can be seen by its repetition in the Gospels (cf. 10:31, 43–44; Mt 23:8–11; Lk 22:24–27; Jn 13:1–17). The kind of service Jesus was talking about here involved sacrifice.

36–37 To illustrate the principle in v.35, Jesus took a child, perhaps one from the family in whose house he was teaching, and first stood him by his side. Then Jesus took him into his arms (cf. 10:16). While all were watching, he indicated that true greatness entails caring about people—seemingly insignificant people like children—because Jesus himself was concerned about them. When one cares about such people, one is really "receiving" Jesus and God himself.

H. Driving Out Demons in Jesus' Name (9:38–42)

38 John's use of "we" shows that he was speaking for all the disciples. This is the only time Mark mentions John alone. The exorcist had been driving out demons in Jesus' name, i.e., with his authority. What irked the disciples was that, though he was not one of them, he was being successful at it! What made things even worse was that they doubtless remembered their own failure to exorcise the demon from the epileptic (cf. 9:14–18). The strange exorcist must have been a believer. Since he was not a part of the exclusive company of the Twelve, they took it on themselves to stop him.

39–40 Jesus did not have as restrictive a view of who could legitimately participate in his mission as his disciples did. The casting out of demons was done by God's power, and his power was not limited to the Twelve. So Jesus told his disciples not to stop the strange exorcist because such a man was not likely to speak badly of Jesus if he performed a miracle in his name (cf. Nu 11:26–29).

Casting out demons definitely demonstrated that the man was not against Jesus, and "whoever is not against us is for us." How does this relate to Mt 12:30, "he who is not with me is against me"? Jesus did not want to force people quickly into a decision about himself. He desired to give them plenty of time to decide, during which the principle in Mk 9:40 applies. But when the critical moment for decision arrives, then the principle laid down in Mt 12:30 takes over.

41 This verse seems to go best with v.37, before John's interruption. The giving of a cup of water is a very small act of hospitality. Yet if it is given to one who belongs to Christ, this act receives God's approval because it is the same as giving it to Christ.

42 This verse is probably better taken with what precedes it than with what follows. The warning points back to the disciples' attempt to prevent the unknown exorcist from doing his work in Jesus' name (v.38) or to prevent anyone from giving a cup of water in his name. "Little ones" refers to followers of Jesus, and "to sin" means to prevent them from acting in Jesus' name. The offense is so serious that it would have been better for one to be drowned than to commit it.

I. Demanding Requirements of Discipleship (9:43–50)

43–48 The main point of these verses is that it is so important to enter into eternal life that radical means must be taken to remove whatever can prevent it (i.e., sin). Here sin is connected with the physical self—the hand, foot, and eye. Jesus is not demanding the literal excision of our bodily members; he is rather demanding the cessation of the sinful activities of these members.

The word translated "hell" is *gehenna* (GK *1147*), a Greek form of the Hebrew words *ge hinnom* ("Valley of Hinnom"). This was the valley along the south side of the city of Jerusalem, which was used in OT times for human sacrifices to the pagan god Molech (cf. Jer 7:31; 19:5–6; 32:35). King Josiah put a stop to this dreadful practice (2Ki 23:10), and the Valley of Hinnom came to be used as a place where human excrement and rubbish were disposed of and burned. The fire of *gehenna* never went out, and the worms never died. So it came to be used symbolically of the place of divine punishment.

49 This is admittedly one of the most difficult verses in Mark; it has over a dozen different interpretations. Of these, two commend themselves, both taking their clue from the insertion by a copyist of the words, "and every sacrifice shall be salted with salt" (an allusion to Lev 2:13).

One interpretation sees the sacrificial salt as a symbol of the covenant relationship that the children of Israel had with God. For every disciple of Jesus, the salt of the covenant is the Divine Fire, the Holy Spirit (cf. Mt 3:11). Every follower of Christ, in other words, will receive the Holy Spirit.

The other interpretation sees in the fire the trials and persecutions of the disciples of Jesus. In the previous verses the various members of the body must be sacrificed, if need be, to enter into the kingdom of God. Here in v.49 the total self is in mind. Every true disciple is to be a total sacrifice to God (cf. Ro 12:1); and as salt always accompanied the temple sacrifices, so fire—i.e., persecution, trials, and suffering—will accompany the true disciple's sacrifices (cf. 10:30; 1Pe 1:7; 4:12). If this is Mark's meaning, this saying must have had special meaning for the persecuted Roman church. It helped them understand that the purifying fires of persecution were not to be thought of as foreign to their vocation as Christians, because "everyone will be salted with fire."

50 In this verse salt must be understood in a domestic setting and not in a religious or ritual one as in v.49. Salt played an important role in the ancient world. It was necessary to life, and was also used as a preservative to keep food from spoiling. But salt could lose its saltiness. Jesus was warning his disciples not to lose that characteristic in them that brought life to the world and prevented its decay, that is, not to lose their spirit of devotion and self-sacrifice (cf. v.49) to Jesus Christ and the Gospel. Jesus' disciples could only be at peace with one another where that kind of devotion instead of self-interest prevailed (cf. v.34).

J. Teaching on Divorce (10:1–12)

1 Jesus was moving closer and closer to the ancient city of Jerusalem where the final acts of the redemptive drama were to take place. He set his face to the accomplishment of his divine mission. Since 9:30 Jesus had been directing his teaching ministry toward his disciples, but now again he was among the crowds and teaching them.

2 The question posed by the Pharisees was not a sincere one. They were testing him, trying to catch him in some statement about a subject on which they themselves had no agreement, and then to use it against him. Jesus was in Herod Antipas's territory, the ruler who had put John the Baptist to death because John had denounced Antipas's marriage to Herodias. Perhaps the Pharisees hoped that Jesus, by his statements on marriage and divorce, would get himself into trouble with Antipas and would suffer the same cruel fate as John.

On the question of the lawfulness of divorce, there was general unanimity among the Jews: divorce was allowed. The real difference of opinion centered in the grounds for divorce as cited in Dt. 24:1. The crucial words are "something indecent" (GK 6872). What did that include? The school of Shammai, the stricter of the schools, understood these words to mean something morally indecent, in particular, adultery. The school of Hillel interpreted the words much more freely. Just about anything in a wife that a husband did not find to his liking was suitable grounds for divorce—even if she burned his food! So where did Jesus stand in this? That was their question.

3–4 Jesus, as he often did when in controversy with the Jewish religious leaders, countered with a question of his own. Moses was their authority—what did *he* say? Jesus knew they would appeal to Moses. They admitted that a man could divorce his wife, but only after giving her a certificate of divorce, making the transaction permanent and legal.

5–8 Jesus did not question the law. But his answer reaches back to first principles. Moses' permission to divorce was an accommodation to human weakness. It was an attempt to bring some sort of order in a society that disregarded God's standards. But that is not what God intended in marriage. His original design in creating man and woman was that marriage should be an unbroken lifelong union (Ge 2:18–24). Marriage was not a temporary convenience that could be terminated at will.

9 A husband and wife are to work together in marriage as a team of oxen yoked together. Behind the indissolubility of their marriage is the authority of God himself. Anyone who instigates a divorce is tearing apart an intimate union that God has created.

10–12 Mark records no response of the Pharisees to Jesus' teaching about divorce. Instead he moves directly to Jesus' private teaching of the Twelve, who wanted a clarification of the teaching Jesus had just given. Jesus gave them a straightforward answer: divorce and remarriage by husband or wife is adultery. Jesus did what the rabbis refused to do: he recognized that a man could commit adultery *against his wife*. In rabbinic Judaism a woman by infidelity could commit adultery against her husband; and a man, by having sexual relations with another man's wife, could commit adultery against that other man. But a man could never commit adultery against his wife. Jesus, by putting the husband under the same moral obligation as the wife, raised the status and dignity of women.

Furthermore, Jesus went on to recognize the right of a woman to divorce her husband (v.12), a right not recognized in Judaism. Matthew, writing for Jews, omits v.12; but Mark, writing for Romans, includes it.

K. Blessing the Children (10:13–16)

13 This story has lost all details of time and place. Mark may have placed it at this point because a story about children is a fitting sequel to Jesus' teaching about marriage.

Mark does not identify those who were bringing the children to Jesus. In the Greek the subject of the verb is indefinite—"they." NIV translates it "people"—probably mothers, fathers, and even brothers and sisters. Among Jews, it was customary to bring children to great men to have them blessed (cf. Ge 48:13–20). The children referred to here were small children (Jesus took them into his arms; cf. Lk 18:15). Why the disciples wanted to prevent the children from coming to Jesus is not stated. Perhaps they wanted to protect his privacy and shield him from needless interruptions. Though their motives may have been commendable, they again showed lack of spiritual sensitivity.

14 Jesus was "indignant" (GK 24) when he realized that the disciples thought children were unimportant and bothersome. Mark never softens the human emotions of Jesus, nor is he less than candid about the failings of the disciples. Jesus wanted children to come to him and not to be hindered in their coming. After all, children in their receptivity and dependence exemplify the characteristics of those who possess God's kingdom.

15 This verse reiterates and expands the statement in v.14. The kingdom of God is to be received as a little child receives something, that is, without self-consciousness and in dependence on the giver. The kingdom is both a gift to be received and a realm to enter.

16 Jesus took the small children in his arms (cf. 9:36) and blessed them—a striking act showing his love for them. Apparently they were fairly small children. This was the overflowing of Jesus' divine love for children. It was this experience that the disciples in their insensitivity were preventing the children from having and Jesus from giving. No wonder Jesus was indignant!

L. Riches and the Kingdom of God (10:17–31)

This section is made up of three parts. The most satisfactory division is (1) vv.17–22, which describe Jesus' encounter with a rich man; (2) vv.23–27, a logion on the difficulty of a rich person entering the kingdom of God; and (3) vv.28–31, Peter's statement about leaving all to follow Jesus and Jesus' reply to it. These were probably separate sayings brought together by Mark because of their common theme.

This teaching on the impossibility of wealth as a means of gaining the kingdom and on Jesus' call to commitment links Jesus' teaching about the importance of childlikeness and the third prediction of the passion.

17 Jesus was continuing on his journey to Jerusalem. A man ran up to him, probably a member of some official council or court (see Lk 18:18). Matthew says he was "young" (19:20). He fell on his knees before Jesus and addressed him by the revered title of "good teacher," thus expressing his high regard for Jesus. His question indicates that he was thinking in terms of Jewish works of righteousness. He wanted to *do* something to merit eternal life, whereas Jesus taught that eternal life (the kingdom of God) is a gift to be received (cf. v.15).

18 Jesus' reply seems unnecessarily abrupt. But we must remember that he was calling attention to the man's unthinking use of language. Jesus was saying, as it were, "Before you address me with such a title, you had better think soberly about what the implications are, and especially what they are for you."

19–20 Jesus answered by giving the man a condensed summary of the second section of the law (cf. Ex 20:12–17). It was a firm Jewish belief, based on OT teaching, that anyone who kept the law would live (Dt 30:15–16). So Jesus began there.

The young man answered confidently. From boyhood (probably age thirteen) he had kept all the commandments Jesus cited. At that age a Jewish boy became responsible to live by God's commands. The man spoke sincerely because to him keeping the law was a matter of external conformity (cf. Php 3:6). That the law required an inner obedience, which no one can comply with, apparently escaped him.

21 Recognizing the young man's sincerity, Jesus responded in love. The one thing that prevented him from having eternal life was the security of his wealth. Jesus put his finger on the sensitive place by commanding him to go, sell all he had, give to the poor, and as his final instruction, "Come, follow me." For this man there could be no following of Jesus before he went, sold everything he had, and gave it away. His wealth and all it meant to him of position, status, comfort, and security prevented him from entering into eternal life. There is no indication, however, that Jesus' prescription was meant to be binding on all Christians (cf. Lk 19:8–9). What Jesus does tell us is that we must not be attached to material things. Since eternal life is a gift of God and cannot be earned, no saving merit must be attached to the action of giving all to the poor.

22 Mark describes the reactions of the man in vivid detail. His face fell. To obey Jesus was too great a risk for him to take, so the security of wealth kept him out of the kingdom of God.

23–26 The failure of the rich man to respond to the challenge led to one of Jesus' most striking pronouncements. He addressed it to the disciples, and it underscores the difficulty of a rich person's entering the kingdom of God.

The amazement of the disciples at Jesus' words reflects their Jewish background, which placed great emphasis on the privileged position of the rich. To be wealthy was believed to be sure evidence of having the blessing of God. But with his penetrating spiritual insight, Jesus saw how wealth could hinder one from putting his trust and dependence in God.

The second half of v.24 may begin a new section, the last section ending with the amazement of the disciples. NIV considers it (along with vv.25–27) a part of the incident that begins with v.23. The fact that Jesus' disciples "were even more amazed" (v.26) looks back to their initial amazement in v.24 and supports the translators' decision.

Jesus supports his statement in v.23 by the proverb about the camel and needle that created even greater amazement on the part of the disciples. For the rich to enter the kingdom of God simply because of their wealth is indeed impossible. The proverb was not lost on the disciples. As their question "Who then can be saved?" shows, they completely understood it.

27 Jesus then pointed to the solution. His answer makes clear that salvation is totally the work of God. Apart from the grace of God, it is impossible for anyone to enter God's kingdom. Humanly speaking no one can be saved by his or her own efforts; but what we can never do for ourselves, God does for us. In this story the concepts of "eternal life," "salvation," and "entrance into the kingdom" are all used synonymously.

28 This verse begins what is probably a new incident that Mark places here because it fits the theme. In contrast to the rich man who failed to give up what he had and to follow Jesus, Peter was wondering what reward was in store for them (cf. Mt 19:27).

29–30 Instead of rebuking Peter, Jesus made a threefold promise: No one who forsakes home, loved ones, or lands for Jesus' sake and the Gospel's will fail (1) to receive back in this life a hundredfold what he or she has lost; (2) to suffer persecutions (only Mark includes this); and (3) to have eternal life in the age to come. The hundredfold return in this life must be understood in the context of the new community into which believers in Jesus come. There they find a multiplication of relationships, often closer and more spiritually meaningful than blood ties.

Jesus is also realistic about the Christian life. There will be persecutions, but through them the new relationships as members of the Christian community develop and flourish. Jesus goes on to promise eternal life in "the age to come." Everything that happens in the present is an earnest of that far richer fulfillment when there will no longer be any persecutions.

31 This saying of Jesus refers to the future when God will evaluate the lives of people and when human values will be reversed.

Those who have rank and position now will not have them, and those who do not have them now will have them then. This may be a kind of summary of Jesus' teaching in vv.17–31. In eternity the rich and the powerful will have the tables turned on them. Furthermore, Jesus emphasizes that discipleship entails suffering and service; it must be entered on because of love and commitment to Jesus, not because of what one hopes to get out of it either in this life or in the life to come.

M. Third Prediction of the Passion (10:32–34)

32 Jesus resumed his journey to Jerusalem, taking the lead (cf. Lk 9:51). Jerusalem is mentioned for the first time as his destination. The disciples were probably astonished because of the determination with which Jesus proceeded to his goal (cf. Isa 50:7). "Those who followed" were probably pilgrims on their way to the feast at Jerusalem. Jesus, as he so often does in Mark's gospel, separated the Twelve from the crowd for renewed instruction about his coming passion.

33–34 This is the third major prediction of the Passion (cf. 8:31; 9:31). It is more detailed and precise than the others, containing six details. Jesus is to be (1) betrayed; (2) sentenced to death; (3) handed over to the Gentiles; (4) mocked, spit on, and flogged; (5) executed; and (6) resurrected. To claim (as some do) that these verses are a post-resurrection church tradition put in the mouth of Jesus denies that Jesus, as the unique Son of God, could predict his passion in detail. That the events did not take place historically in the chronological sequence in which they are given in v.34 would tend to cast doubt on the thesis that the prediction was shaped by the passion narrative in chs. 14–16.

The climax of the passage is the prediction of the Resurrection. Mark does not record any response by the disciples to this startling statement. Luke (18:34), however, says, "The disciples did not understand any of this."

N. The Request of James and John (10:35–45)

Mark 10:35–45 parallels 9:30–37. Both contain discussions about true greatness, and both follow a prediction of Jesus' passion.

And in a woeful way both reveal how spiritually dense the disciples really were. It is not likely that the church created a story that cast such disrepute on the character of two of the best-known disciples.

35–37 The request made by James and John seems utterly preposterous. They vainly came to Jesus with a carte blanche request! When Jesus asked what that might be, their answer was that they might have the positions of highest honor in the messianic kingdom. The request reveals clearly that before the Crucifixion the disciples believed Jesus to be the Messiah; and since it was now clear that he was going up to Jerusalem, they expected his messianic glory to be revealed there. James and John wanted to be sure of a prominent place in this about-to-be-realized kingdom.

38 Jesus' answer is sharp and penetrating. The two disciples did not really know what they were asking. The way to privileged position in the messianic kingdom is not by grabbing for power but by relinquishing it through suffering and death. Jesus explained this to them by using the analogies of the cup and baptism. The cup, symbolizing trouble and suffering, is found in the OT (Ps 75:8; Isa 51:17; Jer 49:12; Eze 23:31–34 [see comment on 14:35–37]). Baptism is a symbol of a deluge of trouble (cf. Pss 18:16; 69:1–2).

39–40 With a confident "We can," the disciples answered Jesus' question about going through the suffering of his passion. How naive! James and John failed to understand what was involved in Jesus' sufferings, though they would indeed participate in them. But to grant them privileged positions in his kingdom was not within his authority. Jesus refused to usurp the authority of his Father.

41–44 Although Jesus had previously rebuked the spirit of ambition and jealousy among his disciples (cf. 9:35), it was still very much alive in them. The other ten were indignant with James and John. None of the disciples had yet in the least comprehended what Jesus had meant when he spoke of his passion. So Jesus had to give them another lesson in what greatness is. The Gentile rulers loved to be in charge. But this is not the way it should be among true followers of Jesus (v.43), where greatness is achieved by humble service (v.44). This is the great paradox of the kingdom of God.

45 The climax to this section (vv.35–45) comes in this verse. Even the Son of Man is not exempt from the rule of humble service in the kingdom. He is in fact par excellence the example of it, especially in his redemptive mission. He did not come as a potentate whose every personal whim was to be catered to by groveling servants, but he came as a servant, giving "his life as a ransom for many."

The word translated "ransom" (GK 3389) relates to "redemption" or "release" as a theological concept based on the experience of Israel's release from the slavery of Egypt. It may also contain an allusion to the Suffering Servant (see esp. Isa 53:6b).

The prepositional phrase "for many" is a clear indication of substitution. In his death, Jesus takes the place of the many. What should have happened to them happened to him instead. The expression "the many" (GK 4498) is not to be understood in the sense of "some but not all" but in the general sense of "many" as contrasted with the single life that is given for their ransom (cf. Isa 53:11–12).

O. Restoring Blind Bartimaeus's Sight (10:46–52)

46 This last of the healing miracles in Mark's gospel takes place near Jericho, a city located five miles west of the Jordan and about fifteen miles northeast of Jerusalem. There was an old Jericho and a new Jericho, built by Herod. It is possible that the miracle was done somewhere between the old Israelite city and the new city, for Luke records this miracle as Jesus went into the city and Mark, as he was leaving. Mark gives the name of the blind man—Bartimaeus ("son of Timai"). In the Middle East, a blind man sitting along the road begging is a common sight.

47–48 Bartimaeus must have heard of Jesus' reputation as a healer. When he discovered that Jesus was coming by, he seized the opportunity of approaching him. The title he used to address Jesus—"Son of David"—is messianic (cf. Isa 11:1, 10; Jer 23:5–6; Eze 34:23–24; cf. Mk 12:35). The pilgrims going up to Jerusalem for the Feast of Passover did not appreciate Bartimaeus's loud shouting and tried to silence him, but he shouted all the more.

Unlike the crowd, Jesus did not try to silence Bartimaeus. This implies that he did not reject the title "Son of David." Since Jesus was now close to the fulfillment of his messianic mission, it was no longer necessary to keep the secret (see comment on 1:43–44).

49–50 The loud cry stopped Jesus, and he called the beggar to him. The crowd then completely changed their attitude and encouraged the beggar. Bartimaeus's response was immediate. The cloak was his outer garment, which he had probably spread on the ground to receive the alms.

51–52 Before Jesus healed the beggar, he asked him a question to stimulate faith. Having done that, without any overt action or healing word on Jesus' part, he sent him away with the words "Go, . . . your faith has healed you." The cure was immediate, and the man joined the crowd going up to the feast.

The close of chapter 10 sets the stage for the climax of the story. The journey to Jerusalem has ended. Jesus is about to enter the Holy City where the last acts of the drama of redemption will take place. His opening the eyes of the blind man stands in sharp contrast to the blindness of the religious leaders he is about to encounter there.

IV. The Jerusalem Ministry (11:1–13:37)

At this point a new section in the gospel of Mark begins. Jesus arrived in Jerusalem, and the rest of his ministry took place within the confines of the city. Traditionally this period, beginning with the Triumphal Entry on Sunday and ending with the Crucifixion and Resurrection seven days later, has been designated the Passion Week. But if we had only Mark's gospel, it would be possible to allow for a Jerusalem ministry longer than one week. Some scholars do in fact argue for an entrance into Jerusalem in the fall of the year at the time of the Feast of Tabernacles, extending Jesus' final ministry in the city to about six months. However, in view of Jn 12:1 and 12:12–15, which closely associate Jesus' final visit to Jerusalem with the Passover, a week-long ministry is more probable.

The section 11:1–13:37 is essentially made up of three parts: (1) the initial events of the entrance into the city and the cleansing of the temple (11:1–19); (2) instructions to his disciples (11:20–25; 12:35–44; 13:1–37); and (3) conflict with the religious leaders (11:27–12:34).

A. The Triumphal Entry (11:1–11)

1–2 The approach to Jerusalem was through Bethany and Bethphage. Bethphage ("house of figs") was a village close to Jerusalem; Bethany, located on the eastern slope of the Mount of Olives, was about two miles from Jerusalem (cf. Jn 11:18). The Mount of Olives is directly east of the city, rising to an elevation of about twenty-six hundred feet.

Jesus sent two of his disciples, probably to Bethphage, to get a donkey colt (cf. Mt 21:2; Jn 12:15). Because of the prophecy of Zec 9:9, the donkey was considered the beast of the Messiah. Jesus stipulated that the colt must be an unused one. Such animals were regarded as especially suitable for sacred purposes (cf. Nu 19:2; Dt 21:3; 1Sa 6:7).

3 Jesus anticipated that the actions of the disciples might be questioned, so he instructed them how to answer when asked why they were taking the colt. By capitalizing "Lord" (GK 3261), NIV has interpreted the passage to mean that Jesus was referring to himself—the other option is to translate the Greek word used here as "owner.." Jesus probably was well known by this time in the area around Bethany, and his authority as "Lord" was recognized.

4–6 The disciples found the colt as Jesus had told them and carried out his orders to the letter. The people (the owners? see Lk 19:33) did not object to the disciples' taking the colt because apparently they knew Jesus and recognized his authority.

7–8 The action of the crowd was completely spontaneous. The outer garments on the back of the donkey made a kind of saddle for Jesus to ride on. When he mounted the colt, others in the crowd spread their garments on the road (an act of royal homage; cf. 2Ki 9:13) and spread branches before him (John mentions "palm branches," 12:13). These could easily have been cut from the fields located nearby. By sitting on a donkey and entering Jerusalem in fulfillment of Zec 9:9, Jesus was implicitly declaring himself to be the Messiah. His kingdom, however, was not a political one, but a spiritual one—one centered on peace. No one could charge Jesus with

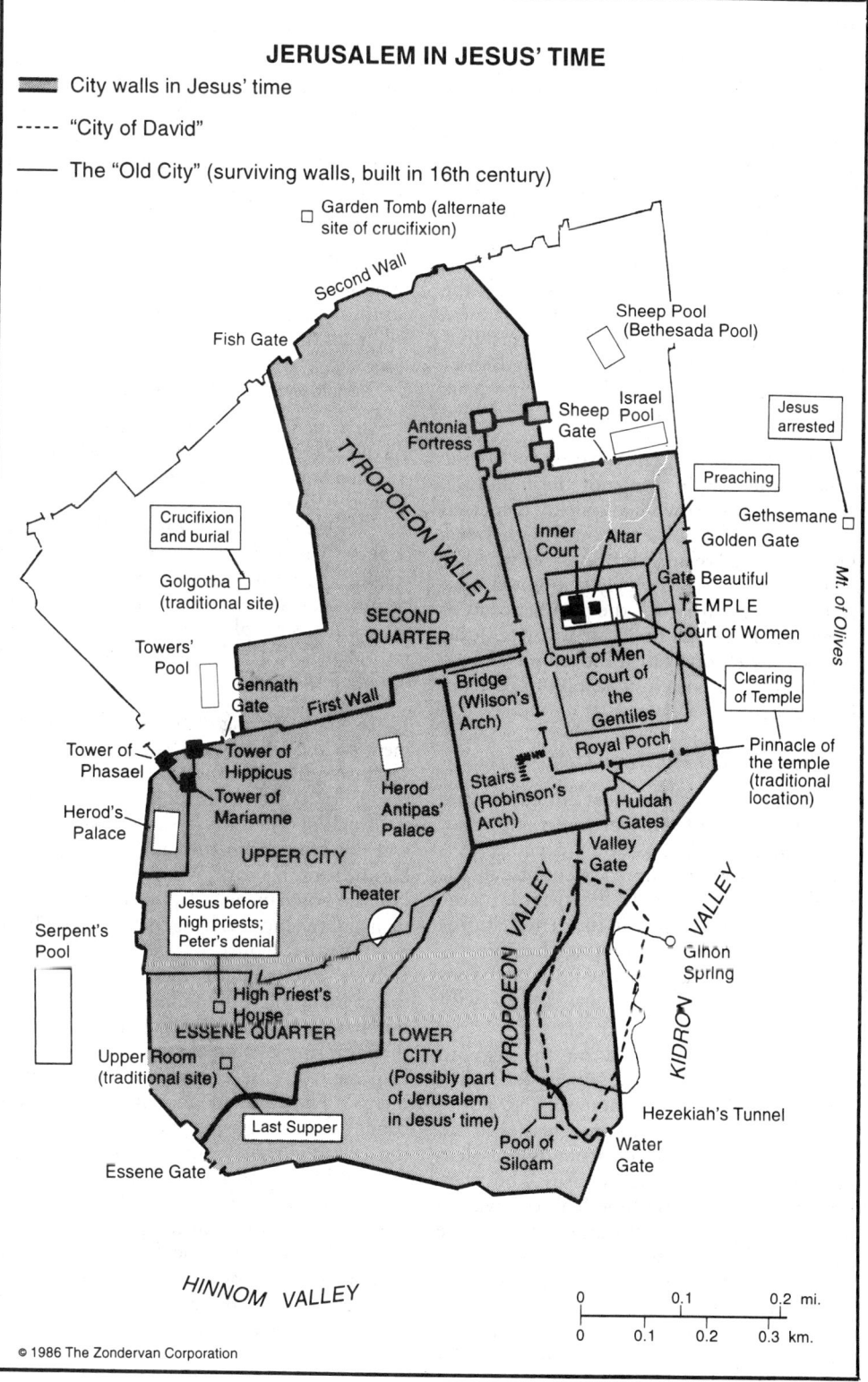

political activism by the manner in which he declared his messiahship.

9–10 "Hosanna" (GK 6057) literally means "save now," but it had become simply an exclamation of praise. "Blessed is he who comes in the name of the Lord" is an accurate quotation of Ps 118:26, one of the Hallel Psalms (Pss 113–18), which were used liturgically at the feasts of Tabernacles and Passover. This quotation was a customary religious greeting or blessing pronounced on pilgrims who had come to Jerusalem for the feast. Mark, however, seems to imply a messianic fulfillment of this passage in Jesus. In v. 10, the kingdom blessed is the "kingdom of our father David," clearly the messianic kingdom promised to David's son.

11 On entering the city Jesus went to the temple (the temple area, not the building). Apparently the crowd had quickly dispersed and only the disciples remained with Jesus. Jesus examined the institution to see whether it was fulfilling its divinely appointed mission, thus preparing for the prophetic act of cleansing. But since the hour was late, Jesus delayed his action against the temple and instead withdrew with his disciples to Bethany for the night.

B. The Unfruitful Fig Tree (11:12–14)

12–13 This is one of the most difficult stories in Mark's gospel to interpret. An important consideration is the position it occupies. It is one of Mark's interrupted accounts, in the middle of which stands the record of the cleansing of the temple, an incident that provides the clue for interpreting this miracle. Like the cleansing of the temple, the story of the unfruitful fig tree has to do with judgment.

The incident occurred on the way to Jerusalem from Bethany, where Jesus had spent the night. He was hungry; and, noticing a fig tree, he went to see whether it had any figs on it. Fig trees around Jerusalem usually leaf out in March or April, but they do not produce figs till June. This tree was no exception. It was in full leaf, but there were no figs on it "because it was not the season for figs." It is this phrase that makes the story such a problem. It seems best to consider it Mark's own insertion to explain to people not familiar with the characteristics of a fig tree why one fully leafed out would not have fruit on it.

14 Jesus addressed the tree directly and by his words performed a miracle of destruction (the only such miracle in the Gospels). It is best seen as an acted-out parable. Jesus' hunger provides the occasion for his use of this teaching device. The fig tree represents Israel (cf. Hos 9:10; Mic 7:1–4; Na 3:12; Zec 10:2). The tree is fully leafed out, and in such a state one would normally expect to find fruit. This symbolizes the hypocrisy and sham of the nation of Israel, which made her ripe for the judgment of God.

C. The Cleansing of the Temple (11:15–19)

All three synoptic writers have the cleansing of the temple at the end of Jesus' ministry (see also comment on Jn 2:13–14). It is sandwiched between the two incidents of the fig tree, an arrangement meant to link the accounts. The judgment symbolized by the cursing of the fig tree is initiated by Jesus' cleansing of the temple, and the cleansing of the temple is prophetic of the destruction of Jerusalem and the eschatological judgment (cf. Mk 13).

15–16 The cleansing of the temple, in fulfillment of Mal 3:1–3, was Jesus' next messianic act during the Passion Week after the Triumphal Entry. When he entered the temple area, the smell of the animals entered his nostrils; and the noise from the moneychangers' tables beat on his ears. Why were they there? For the convenience of pilgrims, the cattlemen and the moneychangers had set up business in the Court of the Gentiles. The animals were sold for sacrifices. It was far easier for a pilgrim coming to Jerusalem to purchase one that was guaranteed kosher than to bring an animal with him and have it inspected for meeting the kosher requirements. The Roman money the pilgrims brought to Jerusalem had to be changed into the Tyrian currency, since the annual temple tax had to be paid in that currency. Exorbitant prices were often charged for changing the currency. By overturning the tables of the moneychangers and the benches of those selling doves, Jesus was directly and forcefully challenging the authority of the high priest, because they were there by his authorization.

Jesus also put a stop to casual use of the temple by those who used it as a shortcut between the city and the Mount of Olives (v.16).

17 The first passage quoted by Jesus is Isa 56:7, a prediction that non-Jews who worship God would be allowed to worship in the temple. By allowing the Court of the Gentiles, the only place in the temple area where Gentiles could worship God, to become a noisy, smelly public market, the Jewish religious leaders were preventing Gentiles from exercising the spiritual privilege promised them. How could a Gentile pray amid all that noise and stench? The second quotation (from Jer 7:11) emphasizes that instead of allowing the temple to be what it was meant to be, a place of prayer, they had allowed it to become a robbers' den. This is to be understood both in terms of the Jews' dishonest dealing with the pilgrims and expecially in terms of using all their merchandising activities to rob the Gentiles of their rightful claim to worship Israel's God.

Jesus' concern that Gentiles receive equal privileges with Jews to worship God would have been particularly meaningful for Mark's predominantly Gentile readers.

18–19 The Pharisees and Herodians in Galilee had decided that Jesus must be put out of the way (cf. 3:6). Now the chief priests and teachers of the law came to the same decision. Jesus' action had challenged their authority and no doubt cost them a good deal of money. So they went into action against him, but not openly, because they feared what the response of the people might be. Since Jesus was so popular with the people as a teacher, the power and authority of the chief priests and teachers of the law could easily be broken.

Again Jesus and his disciples withdrew from Jerusalem and spent the night in Bethany, perhaps because Jerusalem was not safe for him.

D. The Withered Fig Tree and Sayings on Faith and Prayer (11:20–25)

The first three verses of this section form the second part of the story of the fig tree (11:12–14) that surrounds the account of the cleansing of the temple. (For the theological significance of this, see the introductory paragraph to the exposition of 11:15–19.)

20–21 The next morning, on returning to Jerusalem from Bethany, Jesus and his disciples passed the fig tree again (see comments on 11:12–14), now totally destroyed. Peter, remembering what Jesus had said, called his attention to the withered tree. Jesus did not in any way interpret the event. Yet the meaning is obvious: Jesus' predicted judgment on the temple would come to pass as surely as his prediction of the withering of the fig tree (cf. 13:1–2).

22 The sayings found in vv.22–25 occur elsewhere in the Synoptic Gospels in various contexts (Mt 6:13–14; 7:7; 17:20; 18:19; Lk 11:9; 17:6). Jesus used the incident of the fig tree to teach incidentally some lessons on faith and prayer. The source of the power for performing the miracle was God. He must be the object of our faith.

23 Since Jesus was standing on the Mount of Olives, from which the Dead Sea can be seen on a clear day, he may have been referring specifically to this mountain. Of course Jesus was speaking figuratively, saying that the greatest possible difficulties can be removed when a person has faith (cf. Jas 1:6).

24 There is a close connection between the kind of faith Jesus speaks of here and prayer. Prayer is the source of the power of such faith. A strong faith is a praying faith dependent on God's power and will.

25 The transition between v.24 and v.25 is abrupt, but there is a connection. To be effective prayer must be offered in faith—faith in the all-powerful God who works miracles. But it must be offered in the spirit of forgiveness. Faith and the willingness to forgive are the two conditions of efficacious prayer.

E. The Question About Jesus' Authority (11:27–33)

27–28 Jesus and his disciples came to Jerusalem and entered the temple area—the focal point of his ministry while in the city. On this occasion he received opposition from three elements of the Jewish religious establishment: chief priests, teachers of the law, and elders. These groups made up the Sanhedrin, the high court of the Jews. They directed a question to him about the source of his authority "for doing these things" (a reference to his cleansing the temple), hoping that his answer would bring him into disrepute with the people and thereby clear the way for their arresting him.

29–30 As Jesus often did, he answered a question by asking another one: whether John's mission (expressed by the word "baptism") was from God ("heaven") or from humans. The question was particularly appropriate for the situation. John had clearly testified to the divine source of Jesus' mission. If they recognized the divine authority of John's mission, they would be forced to recognize Jesus' mission also and his cleansing of the temple as the legitimate exercise of his authority.

31–33 This question of Jesus proved too much for them. Either alternative—"from heaven" or "from men"—would place them in a difficult position. An admission of John's divine authority would compel them to believe in Jesus; a denial would place them in an unfavorable position with the people who accepted John as a true prophet. So to save face they pleaded ignorance, which was tantamount to a refusal to answer Jesus' question. Jesus' reply was that he too would refuse to answer their question—at least directly. He had given them a veiled answer in his counterquestion (cf. v.30).

F. The Parable of the Tenants (12:1–12)

Like the parable of the sower (cf. 4:13–20), this one also has strong allegorical features. While it is true that most of Jesus' parables have but one point to make and the details have no separate significance, Jesus did use allegory on occasion.

The vineyard is Israel; the owner is God; the tenants are the Jewish leaders; the servants are the prophets; and the only son and heir is Jesus. Other details of the parable, such as the wall, winepress, and tower, have no separate significance.

1 Mark does not identify who Jesus' hearers were, though they were probably the chief priests, the teachers of the law, and the elders (cf. 11:27). The description in v.1 reflects the language of Isa 5:1–2, where the vineyard symbolizes Israel (cf. Ps 80:8–16; Isa 5:7; Jer 2:21). The details mentioned here are known to anyone who has traveled in Israel.

When the vineyard had been completely prepared, its owner rented it to tenants and went on a journey. This detail reflects a condition that actually prevailed in Galilee in Jesus' time, namely, that much of the land was in the hands of absentee landowners who contracted with tenants on a crop-sharing basis.

2–5 When harvest time came, the absentee landlord sent one of his servants to collect what was due him from the tenants. The payment was to be made in produce of the land according to a previously arranged percentage. The landlord sent three servants in succession to collect the payment, but the tenants repudiated the agreement. Instead they beat up the first two servants and killed the third. By referring to "many others," Jesus was forcing his listeners to think beyond the parable to the history of Israel and the rejection of the prophets, God's sent servants (cf. Jer 7:25–26; 25:4; Am 3:7; Zec 1:6).

6–8 The sending of the owner's own son underscores the serious view he took of the situation. He assumed that they would respect this son. (This statement should not be allegorized since God knew beforehand that Jesus would be rejected; cf. Isa 53:4; Ac 2:23.) The owner's expectations were thwarted, for the tenants' greed led to outrageous action (v.7). They saw the coming of the son as a golden opportunity for seizing the property; they may have inferred from the son's coming that the owner had died. If they did away with his son, the property would be ownerless and therefore available to the first claimants. There was no question in the minds of Jesus' hearers that he was the son in the parable (see their reaction in v.12).

9 Jesus then drew out the meaning of the parable with a question and proceeded to answer it himself. His answer underscores the seriousness of the action of the wicked tenants. Their punishment would be capital (cf. Isa 5:5–7), and the vineyard would be let to other tenants. The killing of the tenants may be a not-so-veiled prophecy of the destruction of Jerusalem, and the "others" to which the vineyard would be given those who believe in Jesus.

10–11 The quotation is from Ps 118:22–23, the same psalm from which the joyful Hosanna cry came (cf. 11:9). In the OT context the reference to "the stone" is probably to the construction of Solomon's temple. One of the stones was rejected but became the "capstone," the key stone in the entire building (but see NIV note).

In the original context the rejected stone symbolized the Davidic king or perhaps Israel, despised by the pagan nations but, after her return from Exile, exalted to the status of nationhood. Jesus applied the psalm to himself. His "stoneship" was a familiar theme in early Christianity (see 4:11; 1Pe 2:7). There is probably a veiled reference here to the death and resurrection of Christ.

12 The application of the parable was obvious, but again the religious leaders did not harm Jesus because they feared the crowd (cf. 11:18, 32). It was getting close to the time of the feast, and more and more pilgrims from Galilee were arriving in Jerusalem. Many of these knew Jesus either by personal contact or by reputation. The religious leaders knew it would be unwise to make their move now; "so they left him and went away."

G. The Question About Paying Taxes to Caesar (12:13–17)

13 Again Jesus came into conflict with the religious leaders (it was probably Wednesday now). The Herodians were as obnoxious to the Pharisees on political grounds as the Sadducees were on theological grounds. Yet the two groups united in their opposition to Jesus. Collaboration in wickedness, as well as goodness, has great power. Their purpose was to trip Jesus up in his words so that he would lose the support of the people, leaving the way open for them to destroy him.

14–15a The question was prefaced with an obvious and, indeed, obnoxious piece of flattery (v.14). Moreover, it was thoroughly insincere. Jews were required by the Romans to pay tribute money into the *fiscus*, the emperor's treasury. Some Jews (e.g., the Zealots) flatly refused to pay it, because it was for them an admission of the Roman right to rule. The Pharisees disliked paying it but did not actively oppose it, whereas the Herodians had no objections to it. The intent of this question was to force Jesus to a direct answer, identifying himself either with the Zealots or with the Herodians.

15b–16 Jesus was not about to fall into their trap; he called their question "hypocrisy." So he asked them for a Roman denarius. In showing one to Jesus, they had already answered their own question. By using Caesar's coinage they were tacitly acknowledging Caesar's authority and thus their obligation to pay the tax.

17 Jesus' answer avoided the trap. Caesar has a legitimate claim and so does God. Give to each his rightful claim, for obedience to God does not abolish obedience to the state. Jesus did not, however, say that the claims of God and those of Caesar are the same. For a more complete doctrine of the relationship of Christians to the state, this statement of Jesus must be coupled with Ro 13:1–7; 1Ti 2:1–6; and 1Pe 2:13–17.

The reply was not what they expected. It was simple yet profound, and "they were amazed at him." But because he did not give a direct yes-or-no answer, they felt they had enough to charge him with opposition to paying taxes (cf. Lk 23:2).

H. The Question of Marriage at the Resurrection (12:18–27)

18 Reliable information about the Sadducees (mentioned only here in Mark) is difficult to obtain because no documents that are clearly Sadducean have been preserved. The word "Sadducee" (GK 4881) is usually traced to Zadok, the high priest during the time of David.

In the time of Jesus, the Sadducees were small numerically but exerted great influence politically and religiously. They were not, however, popular among the masses. They represented the urban, wealthy, sophisticated class and were centered in Jerusalem. When Jerusalem was destroyed in A.D. 70, they disappeared from history.

Mark identifies the Sadducees as those "who say there is no resurrection." They held this position because they accepted as Scripture primarily the first five books of the Bible and rejected all beliefs and practices not found there. Since they claimed to be unable to find clear teaching about the Resurrection in the books of Moses, they rejected the doctrine. This set them against the Pharisees, who considered the oral tradition as authoritative as the written Scriptures.

19–23 The address by the Sadducees to Jesus is ironic; although they addressed him with the honorific title "Teacher," they did not intend to learn from him. The case cited arose out of a provision in the Mosaic Law (Dt 25:5–6), which required that if a man died without children, his brother had to marry his widow. The purpose of the law was to protect the widow and guarantee the continuance of the family line. The Saducees presented a hypothetical case in which one woman married seven brothers in turn, all of whom died childless. In the Resurrection whose wife of the seven would she be? The case is so ludicrous it may have been a well-known Saducean joke that was used for poking fun at the Pharisees' doctrine of the Resurrection.

24–25 In his answer Jesus accused the Saducees of ignorance of the Scriptures and the power of God. He then proceeded to take up the second accusation first. In the Resurrection there will be a new order of existence brought about by the power of God. Marriage will not exist as it does now, but all life will be like that of the angels. The basic characteristics of resurrection life will be service for and fellowship with God. The mention of angels in this context is significant because it served as a correction of another theological error of the Saducees (cf. Ac 23:8). Also, since in heaven there will be no more death, the need for marriage and the propagation of the human race will not exist.

26–27 Jesus then turned to the cause of the Saducees' erroneous thinking that he mentioned at first: ignorance of the teaching of the OT (cf. 2:25; 12:10). He directed them back to the story of Moses and the burning bush (v.26; Ex 3:6), a part of the OT that was considered particularly authoritative by the Saducees. The quotation may be understood as follows: Abraham, Isaac, and Jacob had long since died when God made the statement to Moses at the burning bush. Nevertheless, God said, "I *am* [not 'I was'] the God of Abraham, the God of Isaac, and the God of Jacob." Thus the patriarchs were still alive in Moses' time ; and if they were alive then, we may be sure that in the Resurrection God will raise up their bodies to share in the blessedness of eternal life. God is faithful to his covenant promises.

I. The Question Concerning the Great Commandment (12:28–34)

28 Mark seems to suggest that this next question was a sincere one. A teacher of the law had been impressed by Jesus' answer to the previous question and so ventured one of his own. The rabbis counted 613 individual statutes in the law, 365 negative and 248 positive. Attempts were made to differentiate between the "great" and "little" commandments. The rabbis also made attempts to formulate great principles from which the rest of the law could be deduced.

29–30 In answer to this question, Jesus quoted two passages from the OT (Dt 6:4–5 and Lev 19:18). The first of these is a confession of faith that is recited by pious Jews every morning and evening. It basically affirms two things: (1) the unity of God and (2) the covenant relationship of God with the Jewish people. God is to be loved completely and totally because he alone is God and because he has made a covenant of love with his people. In the covenant God gives himself totally in love to his people; therefore he expects his people to give themselves totally in love to him.

31 Jesus brought Lev 19:18 together with Dt 6:5 to show that love of "neighbor" (GK 4446) is a natural and logical outgrowth of love for God. These two commandments belong together; they cannot be separated. Thus, although the teacher of the law had asked for the one most important commandment, Jesus gave him two. Though the Jews had a narrow view of who was a "neighbor" (fellow Jews and proselytes), Jesus redefined the term to mean anyone whom we deal with (see Lk 10:25–37 and comments).

32–34 Mark records the favorable response of the teacher of the law. In repeating the commandment he omitted the divine name "the Lord" in keeping with the practice of pious Jews of avoiding the pronunciation of God's name. The phrase "and there is no other but him" is an interpretive addition from Dt 4:35, which underscores the uniqueness of Israel's God. The statement by the teacher of the law that love of God and neighbor are "more important than all burnt offerings and sacrifices" is in keeping with the teachings of the OT prophets (1Sa 15:22; Hos 6:6), though not necessarily in keeping with NT Judaism, which set law and sacrifices side by side with love.

What Jesus said was getting through to the teacher of the law and elicited the statement by our Lord that he was close to the kingdom of God—a statement no doubt meant to stimulate and challenge him to further thoughtful reflection and decisive action.

Jesus had so forcefully demonstrated his ability to answer questions meant to trap him and to turn such questions back on his accusers that they stopped asking questions. In the next section, Jesus, not the religious leaders, asked a question.

J. The Question About David's Son (12:35–37)

35 Jesus was still in the temple courts. Up to this point he was being asked questions. Now he took the initiative and asked in what sense the Messiah is the son of David.

36–37 Rather than waiting for an answer, Jesus provided it himself with a quotation from Ps 110:1. Both the Davidic authorship of this psalm is assumed and David's inspiration in writing it. "Speaking by the Holy Spirit" is a typical rabbinic formula to describe inspired utterance. In his reply, Jesus presupposed the psalm's messianic usage.

David called the Messiah "my Lord" (GK 3261) in this psalm. How could he at the same time be David's son and David's Lord? To Jesus, even though the Messiah was a descendant of David, he is also the Son of God and therefore senior in rank to David (see comments on Mt 22:41–45).

Mark goes on to say that the crowd was delighted to listen to Jesus. Apparently they enjoyed seeing the so-called experts stumped!

K. The Warning About the Teachers of the Law (12:38–40)

38–39 Jesus continued his teaching in the temple courts (cf. 12:35). While not all teachers of the law were frauds, many of them were using their position and influence in a cruel and greedy manner. Jesus condemned them for their religious show with long white linen robes that were fringed and reached almost to the ground. They also received special respect by the majority of the people, being addressed by the honorific titles "Rabbi," "Father," and "Master." In the synagogue they occupied the prominent bench in front of the ark that contained the sacred scrolls of the Law and the Prophets. They were often invited to banquets because of their prestige and were given special places of honor. What Jesus condemned was their seeking such honor for themselves instead of for God whom they professed to serve.

40 Since the teachers of the law were not allowed to be paid for their services, they were dependent on the gifts of patrons for their livelihood. Such a system was vulnerable to abuses. Wealthy widows especially were preyed on by the greedy and unscrupulous among these men. Jesus particularly condemned the hypocrisy of their long prayers that were used as a mask for their greed. Jesus promised punishment to all such people—a reference to God's judgment in the Last Day.

L. The Widow's Offering (12:41–44)

41–42 This is the final incident in Jesus' public ministry. This story contrasts the greed of the teachers of the law with the liberality of the widow. It also serves as a transition to the story of how Jesus gave his all for humankind. The setting is the court of the women, into which both men and women were allowed to come, and where the temple treasury was located. Jesus sat down on a bench where he could watch the people bring their offerings and put them in one of the thirteen trumpet-shaped boxes used for that purpose. It was not the rich with their large gifts who caught Jesus' attention but a poor widow. She placed in the box two of the smallest coins in circulation in Palestine. That Mark felt it necessary to explain the value of this Jewish coin by using a Latin coin only known in the west suggests strongly that he was writing to Romans.

43–44 The disciples were not sitting with Jesus, so he called them to him. The lesson he wanted to teach them was important enough for them to be there, both to see for themselves and to hear what he had to say. The widow's offering was more than all the others in proportion and in the spirit in which she gave.

M. The Olivet Discourse (13:1–37)

This is the longest connected discourse in Mark's gospel, but also the most difficult. The three major questions that present themselves in the study of Mk 13 are: (1) What is the origin of the passage? (2) What is its purpose in Mark's gospel? and (3) What is its meaning?

While some scholars have argued for an insertion into Mark of a separate, independent Jewish (or Jewish-Christian) apocalypse (called the "Little Apocalypse Theory"), there are no compelling reasons for not accepting the discourse as substantially from Jesus. Whether he spoke its contents on a single occasion is another matter. Mark may have brought into the discourse material he felt was on the same theme (observe that Mk 13:9b–12 is not found in Mt 24 but in Mt 10:17–21 in the missionary discourse to the Twelve). This shaping and arranging was within the original intent and meaning of Jesus' words.

Second, why did Jesus speak these words and why were they included in Mark's gospel? The discourse is patently apocalyptic in nature. This kind of literature was well known in the first century, especially to Jews. Daniel in the OT and the Revelation in the NT are examples of books that are apocalyptic in nature or have large apocalyptic sections. Such books are full of fantastic imagery, are highly symbolical, and purport to reveal information about the End. Mark's apocalypse is no exception. It has all the above characteristics, but in addition it has a distinctive hortatory character. There are nineteen imperatives in vv.5–37. This makes it abundantly clear that the main purpose of the discourse is not to satisfy curiosity about the future but to give practical, ethical teaching. Jesus was preparing his disciples—and beyond them the church—to live and witness in a hostile world.

Likewise, Mark uses this material to give an answer to his readers about Jesus' power as Lord of history and about his promise to be with them through the Holy Spirit.

Third, what does this chapter mean? That meaning is closely tied in with the two major predictions in it: the destruction of the city of Jerusalem in A.D. 70 and the end of the age. While various solutions to the relationship between these two have been proposed in regard to this passage, the best solution is to see in vv.5–23 a shift back and forth between an immediate and a remote future. Some of the events even seem to have a dual fulfillment, one in the destruction of the city and the other in the end time. This shift from close to remote prediction may be due in part to Mark's arrangement of sayings of Jesus spoken on different occasions.

1. Prophecy of the destruction of the temple (13:1–2)

1 As Jesus was leaving the temple, one of his disciples, on looking at the temple in all its grandeur, uttered an exclamation over its beauty and massiveness. This chapter in Mark's gospel is Jesus' response.

The temple area, including the temple building itself, had been rebuilt by Herod the Great. The courtyard had been greatly enlarged (to about four hundred by five hundred yards) in order to accommodate the large throngs of Jews who came to Jerusalem for the festivals. To accomplish this enlargement, a huge platform had to be erected to compensate for the sharp falling off of the land to the southeast. An enormous retaining wall was built to hold the platform in place. The massive stones used in the construction of this wall may still be seen today. At the southeast corner the temple platform towered two hundred feet above the Kidron Valley.

In addition to the temple building itself, on the platform stood porticoes and cloistered courts flanked by beautiful colonnades. The temple area covered approximately one-sixth of the area of the city of Jerusalem. It was an architectural wonder, and its size and location dominated the ancient city.

2 Jesus' reply was startling. Great though the temple buildings were, they would be completely destroyed. This prophecy was fulfilled in A.D. 70, when Jerusalem and the temple were destroyed by the Roman general Titus. All the buildings on the temple platform, including the temple itself to which the prophecy refers, were utterly destroyed. So completely were they destroyed that no trace of them remains today. Even their exact location on the temple mount is disputed.

2. The disciples' twofold question (13:3–4)

3–4 Between v.2 and v.3 the location shifts. Jesus was now on the Mount of Olives. With him were the four disciples who had been the first to be called by him (cf. 1:16–20). From the top of the Mount they could clearly see the Kidron Valley running below the eastern wall of the city, and especially the temple mount.

The question the four disciples asked Jesus privately not only goes back to his statement made as they were leaving the temple area (cf. v.2) but actually expands it. The disciples wanted to know when the things Jesus predicted would take place. But they also wanted to know what the sign would be that the predicted events were "all about to be fulfilled." The disciples thought that the destruction of the temple would come at the end of the age (cf. Mt 24:3). Thus they wanted a sign, some sure way by which they might know that the destruction of the temple was about to occur and that the end of the age was approaching. But Jesus refused to give them eschatological signs. Throughout his discourse he was more concerned to prepare them by exhortation and warning for the trials that lay ahead than to give them dates and signs.

3. Warnings against deceivers and false signs of the End (13:5–8)

5–6 The first word of the discourse proper is "Watch out" (GK *1063*), a word that recurs throughout the passage (vv.9, 23, 33, where it is translated as "be on your guard")—a clear indication that admonition is obviously one of Jesus' main concerns. He was warning against false claimants to messiahship. That Jesus said there would be many such false messiahs suggests that his statement should be understood broadly. Although before A.D. 70 few claimed to be the Messiah in the strictest sense, many claimed to have messianic authority. Furthermore, the reference may also look to the time preceding the End.

7–8 Wars and rumors of war must not be a cause for alarm, for these are within God's purposes. When they occur, they must not be mistaken as introducing the End; Jesus clearly states that the "end is still to come." What "end" he was talking about here is not clear, though he was likely referring to both the destruction of Jerusalem and the end of the age.

There will be other kinds of disturbances, too—international power struggles, earthquakes, and famine. These are indications of God's intervention in the historical process. Again, they must not be taken as marking the End. They are rather the beginnings of "birth pains" (the sufferings expected to occur in the period before the coming of the Messiah).

In Jewish thought the messianic kingdom would emerge after a period of intense suffering. The word "beginning" suggests that there will be many more sufferings.

4. Warnings of persecution and strife and a call to steadfastness (13:9–13)

9 Again Jesus warned his disciples to be on their guard, because persecutions of various kinds awaited them. The "local councils" (GK *5284*) to which they would be handed over are the religious courts, made up of the elders of the synagogues assembled for the purpose of exercising their disciplinary powers. From these courts, Jesus warned, they would be taken into the synagogues and publicly flogged. They would also be brought before secular authorities, most of whom were Gentiles. But persecution, whether by Jews or Gentiles, would be an opportunity for witness. This verse clearly anticipates fulfillment in the near future.

10 The word "must" (GK *1256*) underscores the will of God, who has decreed that the Gospel be preached to "all nations" (or "all Gentiles"). This is Jesus' mandate to his disciples and through them to his church. "First" probably means before the End. Jesus seems to be saying here, "Instead of looking for signs of the end, get busy and spread the 'good news'! All nations must hear before the End comes."

11 Jesus went on to predict that the disciples would be hauled into court and would there be cross-examined by the authorities. He promised them, in that situation, strength and resources beyond their own through the Holy Spirit. The Spirit would reveal to them on the spot the appropriate words to speak (cf. Jer 1:9; Ac 6:10; 7:55).

12–13 The breaking of ties of natural affection would be another trial the disciples would have to face (cf. Mic 7:2–6; Lk 12:51–53). Only a fanatical hatred of the Gospel could bring about unnatural behavior such as these verses describe. That hatred will not be limited to relatives, but "all men will hate you" (v.13).

Testing will be another feature of the last times. Not all will stand the test, but he who endures to the end of his or her life will be saved. Jesus is not here setting forth a doctrine of salvation by works. He is rather emphasizing that genuine faith will issue in Christian living that will endure trial and persecution (cf. 2Ti 2:12). This section with its warning and encouragements, must have had special relevance for the life situation of the Roman church.

Since some of these verses occur elsewhere in Matthew (see 10:17–22) and Luke (12:11–12; 21:12–17), Jesus probably gave these sayings on more than one occasion, or possibly Mark collated various sayings of Jesus from other contexts here because of their relevance.

5. The abomination that causes desolation and the necessity of flight (13:14–23)

14a This is one of the most difficult verses in Mark's gospel if not in the entire NT. The key phrase is "abomination that causes desolation," an expression derived from Daniel (cf. Da 9:27; 11:31; 12:11). The first word of the phrase, "abomination" (GK *1007*), suggests something repugnant to God, while "desolation" (GK *2247*) suggests that because of the abomination the temple is left deserted. The holy and pious worshipers vacate it.

The primary fulfillment of Daniel's prophecy of the "abomination that causes desolation" is usually found in the profanation of the altar of burnt offering in the temple of Jerusalem by a representative of Antiochus IV, Epiphanes, in 167 B.C. (cf. 1 Macc 1:54–59; 6:7). The fact that Jesus used the same expression here makes it clear that its fulfillment was not restricted to the events of the time of the Maccabees. What it does refer to has been hotly debated. Some refer it to events surrounding the fall of Jerusalem, such as the military standards of the Romans brought into the temple (cf. Lk 21:20). Others see this prophecy as being fulfilled in the end times by the Antichrist (cf. Mt 24:29–30; 2Th 2:3–10).

The best solution, however, is to understand the abomination that causes desolation as having a multiple fulfillment in (1) the Maccabean period, (2) the events of A.D. 66–70, and (3) the end times.

The exhortation to "let the reader understand" is probably Mark's editorial comment.

14b–18 It is difficult to consign the admonitions of these verses to the end times, for no one will be able to flee from the judgment of God in that day. The warnings, however, make good sense in the context of the approach of the Roman army before the fall of Jerusalem in A.D. 70. Two admonitions stress the urgency of the situation: (1) anyone on the roof of the house is not to go inside to get any belongings, and (2) anyone in the field is not to return to the house even to get an outer garment.

The outer garment was used at night to keep one warm; in the daytime it was taken off to allow more freedom of movement in working. Though the cloak would be especially useful in case of the necessity of fleeing to the mountains, where the night air is cold, the situation would be too urgent to allow one even to fetch it. A hurried flight to the mountains would be very hard for pregnant women and nursing mothers. And if the flight took place in winter it would be all the more difficult, since both the cold and rain-swollen wadis would present formidable hazards. These warnings and woes seem especially appropriate to what actually occurred at the time of the destruction of Jerusalem. The Christians in the city fled to the mountains—to Pella in Perea.

19–20 The primary temporal reference now shifts back to the End. The language here looks forward to the Great Tribulation that will precede the End. Mark uses language derived from Daniel's portrayal of the last days (Da 12:1; cf. Jer 30:7). Nowhere else does Scripture refer to the shortening of the time of tribulation. The "elect" (GK *1723*) are the people of God generally.

21–23 The section (vv.5–23) ends as it began, with a warning against false Christs. A crisis like that of the fall of the city would be sure to produce many false pretenders; so will the crisis of the approaching End. These pretenders will wield supernatural power great enough to perform "signs and miracles." Yet they will not be able to deceive God's people; that is not possible, for God will guard his elect. Mark closes with another exhortation to remain alert and on guard; we must do our own part to resist the temptations of the false prophets.

6. The coming of the Son of Man (13:24–27)

24–25 Verses 24–27 form a unit and relate to the End. They are set off from the previous verses by the strong adversative *alla* ("but"; GK 247). Whereas the preceding verses (5–23) point to both the destruction of Jerusalem and the end times, vv.24–27 speak only of the end times. "In those days" is a common OT expression having eschatological associations (cf. Jer 3:16, 18; 31:29; 33:15–16; Joel 3:1; Zec 8:23).

The coming of the Son of Man will be associated with celestial phenomena. The imagery and language are derived from the OT descriptions of the Day of the Lord (cf. Isa 13:10; 24:23; 34:4; Eze 32:7–8; Joel 2:10, 30–31; 3:15; Am 8:9). It is difficult to know whether the poetic language here is to be understood literally or figuratively. The repeated assertion in Scripture that the end times will be accompanied by cosmic disturbances seems to imply that there will be unprecedented celestial disturbances of some sort that are literal (cf. 2Pe 3:10). The fallen world will share the same fate of judgment as sinful humans. But out of it, a new world will be born.

26–27 The celestial drama reaches a climax when the Son of Man comes in the clouds with "great power and glory." Jesus describes his coming in these verses almost entirely in the words of Scripture. The reference here is to Da 7:13, the first time our Lord definitely connects the title "Son of Man" with the Daniel prophecy (cf. Mk 14:62; see comment on 8:31).

The major emphasis of these verses is on disclosure and triumph. Whereas the Son of Man has been veiled in his first coming, now he is revealed. People will see him for who he really is, and he will come in triumph with great power and glory. His chief concern at his coming will be to bring together his people so that they may be with him. Therefore he sends forth his angels to gather the elect from all over the world.

7. The lesson of the fig tree (13:28–31)

28 In Palestine most trees remain green throughout the year, but the fig tree is an exception. In the fall it loses its leaves; and when in the spring the sap rises in its branches and the tree begins to leaf out, summer cannot be far off. This parable is essentially an antidote to despair. In contrast to the sufferings and persecutions promised in the previous verses, here the prospect of the coming of the Son of Man is offered.

29 The chief problem in this verse is the identification of "these things." Do they refer to the events surrounding the fall of the city of Jerusalem or to the events immediately preceding the end of the age? If (as seems likely) that phrase relates to "all these things" in v.30, then Jesus appears to be referring to the former; those listening to him would experience these signs in a special way when Jerusalem fell.

The next phrase may be translated either "it is near" (NIV) or "he is near." Those who interpret vv.28–31 to relate to the events surrounding the fall of Jerusalem usually identify the "it" with the "abomination that causes desolation" (cf. v.14) or the fall of the city itself. If, on the other hand, vv.28–31 are descriptive of the End, then "he is near" would be a more fitting translation, though "it" (referring to the Parousia) would also be suitable. Luke (21:31) has for "it" (or "he") the "kingdom of God."

30 Jesus' words in this verse are not to be taken lightly. Their interpretation hinges on the meaning of the expressions "this generation" and "all these things." A multiplicity of interpretations have been given to "this generation"—humankind in general, the Jewish people, Christians, unbelievers. It seems best, however, to understand it to mean Jesus' own generation. "All these things" then refers to the signs found in vv.5–23.

At the same time, however, since the Incarnation, Crucifixion, Resurrection, Ascension, and Parousia all belong essentially together, and since only God's desire that everyone repent is holding back the last stage (cf. 2Pe 3:9–10), it has always been true that the Parousia is at hand for every "this" generation. This type of thinking may be difficult for contemporary people, but seems consistent with the biblical material.

31 The certitude and absolute reliability of Jesus' words (esp. in v.30) are far greater than the apparent continuance of the entire universe (implied by the words "heaven and earth"). It will someday pass away, but Jesus' words will always have validity (cf. Ps 102:25–27; Isa 40:6–8; 51:6).

8. The necessity of watchfulness (13:32–37)

Jesus' call for vigilance pervades this paragraph—"Be on guard! Be alert!" (v.33); "Therefore keep watch" (v.35); "do not let him find you sleeping" (v.36); and "Watch!" (v.37).

32 "That day" clearly refers to the Parousia, the great eschatological day that will bring to an end "those days" (vv.17, 19, 24). Of the days that precede the time of the End, certain signs have been given; but of "that day" neither the angels of heaven nor Jesus himself knows the time. Only the Father knows that time. And Jesus, at his ascension, clearly said that it was not for the disciples "to know the times or dates the Father has set by his own authority" (Ac 1:7). A map of the future would be a hindrance, not a help, to faith. Their responsibility—and ours—is to get busy and do his work without being concerned about date setting.

Jesus' ignorance of the day or hour of his return must be understood in terms of the NT teaching concerning the Incarnation. A genuine Incarnation involved such lack of knowledge. Jesus purposely laid aside temporarily the exercise of his omniscience as part of what was involved in his becoming a human being.

33–36 God's people must remain on guard because they do not know when God's appointed time is. The Parousia could occur at any time.

The parable here has in it some of the features of that of the talents (Mt 25:14–30) and the pounds (Lk 19:12–27). Christians have both a privilege and a responsibility, though the parable does not develop these elements. Jesus applies the parable to the disciples. Like a doorkeeper who must watch because he does not know when the owner will return, they too must be on guard. Evening, midnight, rooster crowing, and dawn are the names of the four watches of the night the Romans used. "Suddenly" emphasizes that the Parousia will happen suddenly.

37 The key word of the discourse, right from the beginning (v.5), was the imperative "Watch." Now at the end it is repeated once more, but this time it is no longer addressed only to the four disciples but to "everyone." In this way Jesus shows his concern not only for the disciples but for the whole community—all his followers for whom he was about to die—and his message is "Watch!"

VII. The Passion and Resurrection Narrative (14:1–16:8 [9–20])

The conflict of Jesus with the religious leaders, which in Mark's gospel begins as early as 3:1, reaches its climax in the passion narrative and is followed by the triumph of the Resurrection on Easter morning. Since these events constitute the heart of the Christian Gospel (cf. 1Co 15:1–4), they seem to have been the first part of the story of Jesus to be written down and circulated as a continuous whole. Mark likely has incorporated this narrative into his gospel with little editorial revision.

The importance of the passion and resurrection of our Lord for the early church is evidenced by the relatively large amount of space the narrative takes in each of the Gospels and especially in Mark. Out of Mark's 661 verses, 128 are devoted to the passion and resurrection story, and a total of 242 are devoted to Jesus' last week (from the Triumphal Entry to the Resurrection). These events formed the basis of the church's witness and worship—the lifeblood of early Christianity. The witnessing church proclaimed a crucified and living Savior, and the worshiping church reflected on the meaning of these events for its inner life.

This section in Mark's gospel plays on two basic themes: suffering and triumph. The suffering of Jesus is highlighted by (1) his betrayal and denial (by Judas, Peter, and all the disciples); (2) his trial before the Sanhedrin and Pilate, with its injustice and mockery; and (3) his crucifixion with its brutality and shame. The triumph of Jesus comes through his glorious resurrection on the third day after his crucifixion.

A. The Plot to Arrest Jesus (14:1–2)

1–2 These verses introduce the passion and resurrection narrative. Passover is the Jewish festival commemorating the occasion when the angel of the Lord passed over the homes of the Hebrews on the night he killed all the firstborn sons of the Egyptians (cf. Ex 12:13, 23, 27). The lambs used in the feast were slain on the fourteenth of Nisan (March/April), and the meal was eaten that evening between sundown and midnight. According to Jewish reckoning, that would be the fifteenth of Nisan, since the Jewish day began at sundown. The Feast of Unleavened Bread followed Passover and lasted seven days (cf. Ex 12:15–20; 23:15; 34:18; Dt 16:1–8). Since the Last Supper was probably a Passover meal and took place on Thursday night, this decision to arrest Jesus must have taken place on Wednesday of Passion Week. The phrase "only two days away" is better translated as "on the second day," i.e., "tomorrow."

For a long time the religious authorities had been looking for a way to get rid of Jesus (cf. 3:6; 11:18; 12:12). Now they renewed and intensified their efforts. But it was necessary for them to proceed with the utmost caution. Since Passover (like Tabernacles and Pentecost) was one of the pilgrim feasts, great throngs of people invaded the Holy City to celebrate it. The chief priests and teachers of the law realized that it would be too risky to move in on Jesus with such a highly excitable crowd present. The possibility of a riot was too great. It would be wiser to wait for a more propitious moment—perhaps after the pilgrims had left the city to go home. God's purposes were otherwise, and this part of their plan miscarried. Perhaps the unexpected help from one of Jesus' disciples (14:10–11) changed their minds, and they decided to go through with their wicked scheme despite the presence of the Passover pilgrims.

B. The Anointing at Bethany (14:3–9)

3 This is the second time Jesus was anointed by a woman (see Lk 7:36–50). In order to highlight the contrast, Mark places this incident about the love and devotion of Mary between the hatred of the religious leaders (vv.1–2) and the betrayal of Judas (vv.10–11).

The incident took place in the home of Simon the Leper at Bethany. The occasion for the dinner is not specified. Simon was probably a leper who had been healed. The retention of the name "the Leper" would suggest this—indeed he was probably healed by Jesus. Perhaps the dinner was an expression of gratitude for this. Mark does not identify the woman who anointed Jesus, but we know from John's gospel (12:3) that she was Mary, the sister of Martha and Lazarus. The "nard" (perfume) was made from the root of a plant found chiefly in India and was very expensive. Mary took the bottle and broke the neck of the jar so that she could pour the ointment profusely over Jesus' head.

4–5 Matthew writes that it was the disciples who reacted so indignantly (Mt 26:8), while John says it was Judas Iscariot (Jn 12:4–5). Judas probably expressed the most vigorous dissent because he was the treasurer of the Twelve. Their chief concern was mercenary. The perfume had a value of more than the average value of wages for three hundred days. The mention of the poor is natural because it was customary for the Jews to give gifts to the poor on the evening of the Passover. The insensitivity of Jesus' disciples to this beautiful expression of love and devotion is amazing, especially since they had often enjoyed the generous hospitality of Mary, Martha, and Lazarus while in Bethany.

6–8 Jesus rushed to Mary's defense. Her action of anointing Jesus with a bottle of expensive perfume was a beautiful expression of her love and devotion to him, and she should not be berated. In addition he would not be with them very long, and time for such expression of love while he was still here was running out. In contrast, opportunities for helping the poor would continue. (Jesus often expressed concern for the needs of the poor: cf. Mt 5:3; 6:2–4; 19:21; Lk 6:20, 36–38; 21:1–4; Jn 13:29.)

Mary's act was also interpreted by Jesus as an anointing of his body beforehand in preparation for his burial. Was Mary aware of this aspect of what she was doing? Probably not, but it is possible that she had a greater sensitivity to what was about to happen to Jesus than the Twelve did (cf. her attention to Jesus in Lk 10:34). Jesus' statement serves as yet another prediction of his passion.

9 This pronouncement is preceded by the solemn "I tell you the truth." In an indirect way Jesus was here predicting his resurrection, because the preaching of the Gospel presupposes the Resurrection. The central message of the Good News is Jesus' defeat of sin, death, and hell by his resurrection. And anywhere in the world that Good News is preached, Mary's act of love and devotion will be remembered.

C. The Betrayal Plan of Judas (14:10–11)

10–11 These verses are connected with vv.1–2. The chief priests and teachers of the law were looking for "some sly way to arrest Jesus" (v.1), and Judas "watched for an opportunity to hand him over." Judas is identified specifically as "one of the Twelve." He had all the advantages of being in the inner circle, yet he betrayed Jesus. Spiritual privilege in itself is not enough for salvation. There must be the response of faith and love.

Judas's offer to betray Jesus was readily accepted by the chief priests and teachers of the law because, being on the inside, he could choose the most opportune time to hand Jesus over to them. In that way they could avoid what they feared most, a riot of the people. It was undoubtedly the offer of Judas that changed their minds about not arresting Jesus during the feast. This was a golden opportunity, and they were not about to lose it! Money was involved in the deal—thirty silver coins (Mt 26:15; cf. Zec 11:12–13).

What motivated Judas? Many guesses have been made—jealousy, greed, disappointment with Jesus' mission, to name a few. None of the Evangelists answers the question specifically.

D. The Lord's Supper (14:12–26)

12 Ordinarily "the first day of the Feast of Unleavened Bread" would mean the fifteenth of Nisan, the day following Passover. But the added description of the day—"when it was customary to sacrifice the Passover lamb"—makes it clear that the fourteenth of Nisan is meant (see comment on 14:1–2). The entire eight-day celebration, including Passover, was sometimes referred to as the Feast of Unleavened Bread.

The day of the week was Thursday. Jesus and his disciples were probably in Bethany (cf. v.13). Since the Passover had to be eaten within the walls of the city, the disciples asked Jesus where in Jerusalem they were to go to make preparation. There was no time to lose because the Passover meal had to be eaten between sundown and midnight.

13–16 Jesus gave explicit instructions to two of his disciples (Peter and John; cf. Lk 22:8). The "man carrying a jar of water" would easily be identified because customarily women, not men, carried water jars. He was to lead them to the house where the owner had a guest room. Jewish custom required that if a person had a room available, he must give it to any pilgrims who asked to stay in it, in order that they might have a place to celebrate the Passover. Jesus had probably made previous arrangements with the owner of the house. The upstairs room had what was necessary for the celebration: table, couches, cushions, etc. The disciples were told to get the food and prepare it, which they did.

17 Jesus and his disciples had probably spent the day in Bethany. In the evening they returned to Jerusalem. Peter and John, after making preparations, had likely returned to Bethany, a distance of only a couple of miles, and then accompanied Jesus when he went into the city in the evening. Jesus and his disciples went to the room prepared by Peter and John. Since the Jewish day began at sundown, it was now Thursday night, the fifteenth of Nisan.

18 The Passover meal was originally eaten standing (Ex 12:11). But in Jesus' time it had become customary to eat it in a reclining position.

Jesus then disclosed that one of the Twelve would betray him. "One of you!" It came like a bolt of lightning. It was almost unbelievable. But Jesus must be speaking the truth!

Jesus further identified the betrayer as "one who is eating with me." To betray a friend after eating a meal with him was, and still is, regarded as the worst kind of treachery in the Middle East (Jesus may have had in mind Ps 41:9; cf. Jn 13:18).

19 The response of the disciples to Jesus' startling disclosure was one of sadness and self-distrust. One by one, including Judas (Mt 26:25), they asked Jesus, "Surely not I?" It was an honest question coming from most of them, prompted by fear and lack of confidence in their own spiritual and moral strength. With Judas it was hypocritical and an attempt to cover his intent; for him not to have asked the question with the other disciples would have made him liable to suspicion.

20 Jesus had already given two clues as to the identity of the betrayer: he was the one of the Twelve and he was eating with them. Now Jesus gave a third clue: the betrayer was the "one who dips bread in the bowl with me" (i.e., dipping a piece of unleavened bread in the Passover sauce). This clue did not specifically reveal the betrayer but emphasized again that it was one who enjoyed the closest relationship with Jesus.

21 Behind Judas's action a divine purpose was being carried out. What was about to happen to the Son of Man would not be a chance occurrence. In all this the Scriptures (undoubtedly Isa 53; see comment on 8:31) were being fulfilled. The woe pronounced on the betrayer emphasizes the personal responsibility of Judas in his wicked deed.

The NT records four accounts of the Lord's Supper (Mt 26:26–30; Mk 14:22–26; Lk 22:19–20; 1Co 11:23–25). Matthew's account closely follows Mark's, while those of Luke and Paul have certain agreements. All four include the taking of the bread, the thanksgiving or blessing, the breaking of the bread, the saying "This is my body," and the taking of the cup. Paul and Luke add Jesus' command to continue to celebrate the Supper.

22 The bread Jesus took was the unleavened bread of the Passover meal. He first gave thanks. After that blessing, Jesus divided the bread and gave it to his disciples with the words, "This is my body." Since this saying of Jesus was separated from the cup-saying by the eating of the main part of the meal, it is best to understand it as separate from that saying. The significant action of Jesus was the distribution of the bread, not its breaking. The bread represented his body, i.e., his abiding presence, promised to the disciples on the eve of his crucifixion; and the words become a pledge of the real presence of Jesus wherever and whenever his followers celebrate the Supper. The wine (used later) symbolized his blood about to be shed.

That Jesus did not mean that the bread became his body is clear; it remained ordinary bread. Jesus often used symbolic language to speak of himself (cf. Jn 8:12; 10:11; 14:6; 15:1). What Christ wants us to do in the supper is lovingly to remember his sacrifice, to embrace him by faith, and to anticipate his glorious return.

23–24 The cup Jesus referred to is the third cup of the Passover meal, which was drunk after the meal was eaten. Again Jesus gave thanks (the verb is *eucharisteo*; GK 2373), from which "Eucharist" is derived). The meaning of the cup, unlike that of the bread, is clearly placed in a sacrificial context. The phrase "my blood of the covenant" echoes Ex 24:8. "Covenant" (GK 1347) signifies the relationship of God's love for us and our response of obedience, a relationship brought into existence by Christ's blood. Jesus' death inaugurated a new covenant, a new era. Jeremiah had prophesied of just such a new day (Jer 31:31–34). The blood that establishes the covenant would be "poured out" (a clear reference to Christ's death) for the entire human race (cf. Isa 53:12).

25–26 Solemnly Jesus declared that this would be his last festal meal with them till the dawn of the messianic kingdom (for the idea of the messianic banquet, cf. Isa 25:6; Mt 8:11; Lk 22:29–30). The vow of Jesus consecrated him for his sacrificial death; but it also held out the promise of victory and salvation, for he would drink the festal cup anew, i.e., with a new redeemed community, in the kingdom of God (cf. Lk 14:15; Rev 3:20–21; 19:6–9).

Assuming the meal to have been a Passover meal, it ended with the singing of the second part of the Hallel (Pss 115–118).

E. The Prediction of Peter's Denial (14:27–31)

27–28 The predictions recorded here were probably spoken by Jesus as he walked with his disciples from the Upper Room to the Mount of Olives. The verb "fall away" (GK 4997) suggests not that the disciples will lose their faith in Jesus, but that their courage will fail and they will forsake him. When the Shepherd (Jesus) is struck by God, the sheep (the disciples) will be scattered (Zec 13:7). The prediction was fulfilled. The disciples were afraid of being identified with Jesus in his trial and death, and that caused them to forsake him. This was especially true of Peter, whose actions are often representative of the rest of the disciples.

After the death of the Shepherd, however, Jesus predicted a glorious resurrection and a reunion of Shepherd and sheep in Galilee.

29–31 Jesus' prediction of failure on the part of the disciples was too much for Peter to accept, and he told Jesus that. But Jesus' reply emphasized the absolute certainty of Peter's denial. Not only did he use the "I tell you the truth" formula, but he also used the emphatic "today—yes, tonight." The denial was not only certain, it was imminent; and it would be in spite of being warned twice by a rooster crowing.

Jesus' explicit description of Peter's forthcoming denial was not convincing to him. He insisted on his willingness even to die with Jesus rather than deny him. But Peter did not know how weak he really was—nor did the rest of the disciples, for they quickly chimed in with him to declare their allegiance (cf. 14:50, 71–72).

F. The Agony of Gethsemane (14:32–42)

The story of Jesus in Gethsemane reveals his humanity with astonishing fidelity.

32–34 Gethsemane was a garden located somewhere on the lower slopes of the Mount of Olives, in which there were olive trees and olive presses. It was one of Jesus' favorite spots (cf. Lk 22:39; Jn 18:2), no doubt often used by him and his disciples as a place to be alone. Here he faced one of his most crucial tests.

Leaving the rest of the disciples behind, Jesus took with him the three of the inner circle—Peter, James, and John. He must have felt his need for their presence in this time of crisis. The two verbs used in v.33 describe an intense and deep agony in Jesus. He wanted his disciples to know something of the depths of suffering he was about to experience for the redemption of the world. Then he withdrew to be alone with his Father. Jesus' command to them to keep watch meant either that they were to stay awake and so to share in his agony or that they were to be on the lookout for those Jesus knew were on their way to arrest him. John (18:2) says that Judas knew the place where Jesus was accustomed to pray.

35–36 Jesus did not die serenely; he was the Lamb of God bearing the penalty for the sins of all humankind. The wrath of God was turned loose on him. Only this can adequately explain what happened in Gethsemane. The burden and agony were so great he could not stand up. His prayer, uttered in a prone position, was addressed to "*Abba*, Father." The word "*Abba*," is the Aramaic familiar form for father—a word the Jews did not use to address God because they thought it disrespectful. Since Jesus was the unique Son of God and on the most intimate terms with him, it was natural for him to use it. Jesus believed that with God anything was possible and therefore prayed for the cup of God's wrath to be removed from him (cf. 10:38–39). In the OT "cup" (GK *4539*) is regularly used as a metaphor of punishment and judgment (cf. Isa 51:17; Jer 25:15–29; Rev 14:10; 16:19). Here it obviously refers to Jesus' death. Jesus desired the removal of the cup, but he willingly placed his will in submission to his Father's will.

37–38 Returning to his disciples, Jesus found them sleeping. They were doubtless very tired; the hour was late, probably past midnight, and they had experienced some exciting events during the long day. Nevertheless, it was a critical time, and they were expected to be awake. Jesus singled out Peter probably because he was the one who had boasted of his fidelity to Jesus (v.31), but he could not watch for even one hour.

The verbs "watch" and "pray" are both plural imperatives and are addressed to all three disciples, not just Peter. The conquest of temptation can only come through these two actions. The human spirit might be willing to do what is right, but the human body is weak (here its weakness refers to the inability of the disciples to stay awake).

39–40 Again, after having left his disciples to pray, Jesus returned to find them sleeping. When confronted by Jesus, they were speechless, probably because they were so embarrassed and ashamed. Even Peter had nothing to say on this occasion (cf. 9:6).

41 A third time Jesus left them to pray (cf. Mt 26:44) and on returning again found the disciples asleep. Once again Jesus expressed his hurt through a question. The next word (GK *600*) is difficult to translate. NIV renders it "Enough!" apparently meaning "enough of sleep," i.e., it was time for the disciples to wake up. It can also mean "the account is closed" (i.e., the end has come) or "it is settled" (i.e., it was now clear to Jesus that it was God's will for him to go to the cross). Both of these are supported by Jesus' next statement, that the time of his betrayal and death had come. The "sinners" into whose hands the Son of Man was to be betrayed were the satanic agents who were to bring about his death.

42 The disciples apparently were still lying on the ground; so when Jesus heard the approach of the arresting party, he told the disciples to get on their feet. Jesus did not flee from Judas but went to meet him.

This story of the disciples in Gethsemane must have had a powerful meaning for the persecuted Christians at Rome. It helped establish the spirit that should shape their own martyrdom—to depend on God, to watch, and to pray.

G. The Betrayal and Arrest (14:43–52)

43 The fact that Judas is described as "one of the Twelve" (cf. v.20) keeps this tragic element of the story. Judas was accompanied by a crowd sent from the three constituent groups of the Sanhedrin: chief priests, teachers of the law, and elders. This was not a motley crowd, but consisted of a detachment of soldiers and some official attendants of the Sanhedrin (Jn 18:3). They came armed with swords and clubs, apparently expecting to meet with resistance.

44–46 The prearranged means of identifying Jesus was for Judas to kiss him with a lingering kiss. Perhaps since it was dark the arresting party wanted to be sure not to arrest the wrong person. Rabbis customarily were greeted by their disciples with a kiss. Thus Judas's act would not be suspected for what it really was. Judas's instructions to the crowd were designed to assure the successful accomplishment of the arrest. They were to lead Jesus away securely—with no chance of escape. Once having become involved in the wicked affair, Judas did not want to make a fiasco of it.

47 John tells us that it was Peter who wielded the sword and that the servant's name was Malchus (Jn 18:10). Apparently Peter aimed at his head; but Malchus sidestepped, and Peter only caught his ear. Jesus' rebuke to Peter (Mt 26:52) and the restoration of the ear (Lk 22:51) are not recorded by Mark.

48–50 Jesus protested against the manner of his arrest. The crowd sent from the Sanhedrin had come after him with swords and clubs, as if he were a dangerous criminal or insurrectionist of some kind. He had been teaching every day in the temple courts. They could have arrested him there. Why then had they come at night? And why had they chosen to arrest him outside the city? The obvious answer is that they feared the people's reaction to Jesus' arrest.

The circumstances of Jesus' arrest were a fulfillment of Scripture (Isa 53:12, or perhaps Zec 13:7; cf. Mk 14:27). The disciples failed to stand by Jesus and left him completely alone.

51–52 Only Mark records this mysterious episode. The "young man" is not identified, but many argue is that he is Mark. Why else would he insert such a trivial detail in so solemn a story? Was this Mark's way of saying, "I was there too"?

Ordinarily men wore an undergarment, but this young man had only an outer garment, made of linen, an expensive material worn only by the rich. He fled naked. The forsakenness of Jesus was total; even this youth forsook him.

H. Jesus Before the Sanhedrin (14:53–65)

The trial of Jesus took place in two stages: a religious trial followed by a civil one. Each had three episodes. The religious trial included (1) the preliminary hearing before Annas, the former high priest (reported only in Jn 18:12–14, 19–23); (2) the trial before Caiaphas, the current high priest, and the Sanhedrin (Mk 14:53–65); and (3) the trial before the same group just after daybreak (Mk 15:1). The three episodes of the civil trial were (1) the trial before Pilate; (2) the trial before Herod Antipas (recorded only in Lk 23:6–12); and (3) the trial before Pilate continued and concluded.

53 After a preliminary hearing before Annas (cf. Jn 18:12–14, 19–23), Jesus was taken to Caiaphas (Mark never mentions his name), with the Sanhedrin (a maximum of seventy members) present. The meeting took place in the palace of Caiaphas in an upstairs room (cf. v.66). This must have been a large room to accommodate the Sanhedrin, though Mark's use of "all" does not necessarily mean all seventy were present. Certainly there were enough of them there to constitute a quorum. Since the Sanhedrin usually met in one of the market halls, the use of Caiaphas's house may have been to ensure secrecy.

54 This verse, interrupting the flow of the narrative, prepares us for the full account of Peter's denial (vv.66–72) and indicates that the trial and denial were concurrent. Peter followed at a distance because he was afraid, but he *did* follow. Apparently he could not bring himself to desert Jesus completely.

Eventually he arrived at the high priest's palace. John's gospel informs us that there was "another disciple" with Peter (see comment on Jn 18:15–16). The palace was built around an open courtyard that was entered through an archway (cf. v.68). Spring nights are cool in Jerusalem, so Peter sat with the guards and warmed himself before a charcoal fire (cf. Jn 18:18). From where he was sitting, he could see the upstairs room where the Sanhedrin was meeting to decide Jesus' fate.

55–56 Just how rigged the trial of Jesus was is made clear by these verses. Though it was late at night, many false witnesses were available. But a problem developed—the witnesses could not agree with one another! According to the OT law (Nu 35:30; Dt 17:6; 19:15), it was necessary in cases that required the death penalty to have two witnesses. These witnesses must, however, give consistent evidence. The smallest inconsistency was sufficient to discredit them. As is always true when witnesses testify falsely, there was no consistency in their testimony; this fact frustrated the court's wicked intent.

57–59 Soon a definite charge was made. Jesus had said he would destroy this "man-made temple" and build another "not made by man" in three days (compare Jn 2:19 with Mk 13:2). The charge, however, proved invalid because again the testimony of the witnesses was inconsistent.

60–61 The situation had become extremely tense. There were plenty of witnesses, but they could not pass the test of Dt 17:6. Finally, in exasperation, the high priest stood up in the Sanhedrin to interrogate Jesus himself. Caiaphas apparently wanted Jesus to respond to the charges made against him in the hope of provoking an incriminating answer. But Jesus refused to give him that opportunity.

The silence of Jesus to the first questions prompted the high priest to ask him another, based on the fact that the religious authorities either knew or suspected that Jesus regarded himself as the Messiah. "Son of God" was understood by the Jews of Jesus' time solely in a messianic sense; and since the Messiah in Jewish expectations was to be a man, the question of the high priest was about Jesus' claim to messiahship and had nothing to do with deity. The question proved to be a stroke of genius. Blasphemy was a capital crime. Perhaps Jesus' own testimony about himself could effect an accusation.

62 Jesus replied with a straightforward "I am." Note the sharp contrast to his deliberate avoidance of calling himself the Messiah or having others proclaim his messiahship up to this point in his ministry. He clearly did this not because he had no consciousness of being the Messiah. Rather, he avoided the messianic claim because of the false concepts of messiahship that were popular in his day and with which he did not want to be identified (see comment on 1:43–44). Now, however, the time of veiledness had passed. He was ready to state unequivocally his messiahship.

Jesus' affirmation of messiahship is followed by a Son-of-Man saying that brings together Da 7:13 and Ps 110:1. The two main ideas are the enthronement of the Son of Man and his eschatological coming. Jesus was looking to the future, beyond the Crucifixion and the Resurrection, to the Ascension, when he would take his place at the right hand of God—the place of authority—and to his Parousia, when he will come again in judgment (Rev 1:7).

63–64 The tearing of one's clothes was originally a sign of great grief (cf. Ge 37:29; 2Ki 18:37). The action of the high priest showed that he had just heard a blasphemous statement. Blasphemy was considered not only the overt and definite reviling of the name of God (cf. Lev 24:10–23) but also any affront to the majesty and authority of God (cf. Mk 2:7; 3:28–29; Jn 5:18; 10:33). Caiaphas understood Jesus' claim in the latter sense and therefore considered it blasphemy. All the members of the Sanhedrin concurred with his judgment and condemned Jesus "as worthy of death" (cf. Lk 24:14; Mk 10:33).

65 The decision that Jesus deserved the death penalty was the signal for the Sanhedrin to release their pent-up hostilities against him. Spitting and hitting were traditional means of expressing rejection and repudiation (cf. Nu 12:14; Dt 25:9; Job 30:10; Isa 50:6). The demand to "prophesy" meant for Jesus to say who hit him (see Mt 26:88; Lk 22:64). This was their way of trying to make a mockery of Jesus' messianic claims because a rabbinic interpretation of Isa 11:2–4 stated that the Messiah could judge by smell and did not need

I. Peter's Denial of Jesus (14:66–72)

66–68 While all the mockery and beating werehappening, Peter remained below in the courtyard, waiting to see what would happen to Jesus. The fact that Peter was there at all indicates that he loved Jesus and was concerned about him, but his love did not stand the test of fear. As Peter stood in the light of the fire, warming himself, a servant girl recognized him as part of a group whose leader was Jesus. Her contempt for Jesus is revealed in the order of the words she used to speak about him—"that Nazarene, Jesus." Peter denied the charge by a denial formula common in rabbinical law. Fearful of being identified and apprehended, Peter retreated into the archway that led into the street. He was now anxious for his own safety. Yet he still could not bring himself to abandon Jesus completely.

69–72 Peter's retreat to safety was short-lived. The servant girl saw him slip into the entryway and reiterated her contention—this time to the guards and others in the pay of the high priest. Peter's second denial was not convincing. Then, not the servant girl, but the others, apparently having their suspicions aroused by her and detecting Peter's Galilean accent (Jesus was known to have come from Galilee), accused him. Peter was now like a cornered animal. He called down curses on himself if he was lying and swore that he did not know Jesus at all. The first two times Peter had denied being identified *with Jesus*. The last time he denied *Jesus himself*.

The third denial was followed by the second crowing of the rooster and a look from Jesus (Lk 22:61). The first time the rooster crowed, Peter's conscience was not awakened. This time he remembered what Jesus had said about his denial of him, and he burst into tears.

Through this story, Mark was warning the persecuted church in Rome for whom he was writing. If denial of Jesus Christ was possible for an apostle—and one of the leaders of the apostles at that—then they must be constantly on guard lest they too deny Jesus. The end of the story also provided assurance that if anyone did fail Jesus under the duress of persecution, there was always a way open for repentance, forgiveness, and restoration (cf. 16:7).

J. The Trial Before Pilate (15:1–15)

1 What seems to be spoken of here is not another gathering of the Sanhedrin but the final stages of the meeting that had begun late the night before. They now made a resolution to accuse Jesus before the civil authority, not of blasphemy, but of high treason. The Roman government would not have considered blasphemy a punishable crime. It had to do with the Jewish religion, and this was of little or no concern to the Roman authorities. But high treason was a crime they could not overlook. Note the irony of the situation. Jesus, who disappointed the crowds for failing to lead a political revolution, was now being charged with that very crime.

The members of the Sanhedrin then led Jesus away and handed him over to Pilate. The official residence of the Roman governors of Judea was at Caesarea on the Mediterranean coast. Whenever they came to Jerusalem, they occupied the palace of Herod, where the trial of Jesus before Pilate took place (the Praetorium of v.16). Early in the morning, because that is when Pilate held trials, Jesus was led to Herod's palace. This explains why the Sanhedrin held their session late at night and very early in the morning.

2 Pilate's first question to Jesus—"Are you the king of the Jews?"—shows that the charges against Jesus had already been made known to him. According to Luke, the Sanhedrin brought before Pilate three charges against Jesus: (1) he is "subverting our nation"; (2) he "opposes payment of taxes to Caesar"; and (3) he "claims to be Christ, a king" (Lk 23:2). Pilate was primarily interested in the third accusation. Jesus' answer to Pilate's question in effect said, "Yes, I am the king of the Jews; but your concept of what that means and mine are poles apart."

3–5 The chief priests were now taking the lead in the attack against Jesus. Jesus, however, in his majestic serenity, refused to defend himself. His composure in the face of vicious accusations completely amazed Pilate.

6 The custom referred to here of releasing a prisoner at the Passover Feast is unknown outside the Gospels. Other documents confirm, however, that it was a Roman custom elsewhere and could well have been a custom in Palestine.

7–8 There apparently had been an uprising in the city of Jerusalem (cf. Lk 23:19), and one of the insurrectionists was a man named Barabbas (his first name may have been Jesus). He and his fellow insurrectionists had been thrown in prison for revolution and murder. Barabbas was probably a member of the sect of the Zealots, who deeply resented the Roman occupation of Palestine. The crowd apparently came to Pilate's tribunal for the primary purpose of asking for Barabbas's release. It was Pilate who deliberately faced them with the choice between Jesus and Barabbas.

9–10 The question of Pilate implies that the crowd had asked for the release of Jesus (perhaps Jesus Barabbas?). It is possible that Pilate mistook the crowd's request for releasing Jesus Barabbas as a request for releasing Jesus of Nazareth. Pilate, of course, used the title "king of the Jews" contemptuously (as in 15:2). He was too shrewd a politician to believe that the chief priests had handed Jesus over to him out of loyalty to Caesar! He reasoned, and rightly so, that they envied Jesus' popularity and influence with the people.

11 Pilate had attempted to deflect the purpose of the crowd and substitute the release of Jesus instead of Barabbas. This was a serious threat to the murderous purposes of the chief priests. They were not about to allow Jesus to slip through their fingers through some Passover Feast clemency custom. No other alternative was open to them but to urge the crowd to force Pilate to carry out their original request—the release of Jesus Barabbas, not Jesus of Nazareth.

12–14 Pilate's question is surprising (v.12). Apparently he held out other options than crucifixion for Jesus. If Barabbas was to be released, what should he do with Jesus? Was he suggesting the possibility of releasing Jesus too? Whatever was going through his mind, it is clear that he was reluctant to carry out the murderous intent of the chief priests. But his attempt to change the mind of the crowd failed. The chief priests had stirred them up to a frenzy. "Crucify him!" they shouted. And when Pilate, in a final attempt to save Jesus, asked, "Why? What crime has he committed?" the crowd, now a mob, ignored his question. They had reached a stage where they were beyond reason. No death for Jesus but crucifixion would satisfy them.

15 Pilate saw that he could not change the mind of the mob. He would have to go through with Jesus' crucifixion. According to historical sources, his previous handling of matters relating to the Jews' religion had not endeared him to the people. To risk alienating them in this crisis would be too dangerous for him politically. His wife's message may have made him think more deeply about Jesus than he might otherwise have done (Mt 27:19). So to protect his own interests and placate the priests and the people, he released Barabbas and ordered Jesus flogged.

Since flogging did not necessarily precede crucifixion, Pilate was probably still hoping he could dissuade the crowd from their demand for Jesus' crucifixion (cf. Jn 19:1–7). Flogging was no light punishment. The Romans first stripped the victim and tied his hands to a post above his head. The whip was made of several pieces of leather with pieces of bone and lead embedded near the ends. Two men, one on each side of the victim, usually did the flogging. The Jews mercifully limited flogging to a maximum of forty stripes; the Romans had no such limitation. It is not surprising that victims of Roman floggings seldom survived.

Even that did not satisfy the crowd, so Jesus was handed over by Pilate to be crucified. The use of the phrase "handed over" (GK *4140*) may be a deliberate attempt to identify Jesus with the Suffering Servant of Isa 53:6, 12, since these words are used there (in the LXX) of the Servant.

K. The Mocking of Jesus (15:16–20)

16 The scourging of Jesus took place out in front of the palace of Herod and in the presence of all the people. Afterward Jesus was taken by the soldiers into the "palace" ("the Praetorium"). "Praetorium" is a Latin loan word in Greek, here designating the Roman governor's official residence in Jerusalem (see comment on 15:1). The soldiers who led Jesus into the palace and then mocked and manhandled him were a part of the auxiliary troops Pilate had brought up to Jerusalem from Caesarea. They were non-Jews recruited from Palestine and other parts of the empire. Mark says the whole company took part in their perverted humor.

17–18 The soldiers thought it was a great joke that this gentle Jew claimed to be a king. So they took a purple robe, a symbol of royalty, and threw it across his shredded and bleeding back. The crown was made of some kind of prickly plant such as abounds in Palestine. This they pressed into his scalp. Again there must have been copious bleeding because the scalp is one of the most vascular areas of the body. They mocked him with a parody of "Hail, Emperor Caesar!"

19 The mocking was followed by further physical violence. The blows hitting his head from the staff drove the thorns more deeply into Jesus' scalp and caused even more profuse bleeding. They also kept spitting on him, and the climax came when they mockingly fell on their knees and paid homage to him. It is difficult to imagine a greater demonstration of insensitivity and cruelty.

20 At last, tiring of their sadism, the soldiers tore the robe from Jesus' back. The fabric had probably stuck to the clots of blood and serum in the wounds. Thus when it was callously ripped off him, it caused excruciating pain, just as when a bandage is carelessly removed. Jesus' own clothes were now put back on him.

In John's account Pilate makes one final appeal to the crowd by bringing the badly beaten Jesus out (see comments on Jn 19:4–5, 12–16). Perhaps he wanted to appeal to their sympathy. But Satan was controlling them. The scourging was not enough, so Pilate acquiesced to their bloodthirsty cries.

L. The Crucifixion (15:21–32)

21 Men condemned to die by crucifixion were customarily required to carry the heavy wooden crosspiece on which they were to be nailed to the place of execution. Jesus started out carrying his cross (Jn 19:17), but it proved too much for him. One can hardly imagine the pain caused by the rough heavy beam pressing into the lacerated skin and muscles of Jesus' shoulders. The scourging and loss of blood had so weakened him that

This model of old Jerusalem shows the traditional site of Golgotha, along a path outside the walls of the city.

he could not go on, so they randomly apprehended one Simon of Cyrene and forced him into service. Simon was no doubt a Jew and was on his way to the city of Jerusalem for the Passover celebration. Mark probably mentions Simon's two sons Alexander and Rufus because they were known to the Roman church (cf. Ro 16:13).

22 Both Roman and Jewish executions were customarily performed outside the city (cf. Jn 19:20). "Golgotha" is a slightly modified transliteration of the Aramaic word for skull, whereas the name "Calvary" is derived from *calva*, the Latin word for skull. How this site was named Golgotha is not known. The common conjecture is that the place looked like a skull. The traditional site is located inside the famous Church of the Holy Sepulchre, which is within the present walls of the city. Recent archaeological excavations tend to support the historicity of the traditional site by showing that it was once outside the city walls.

23 Someone offered Jesus wine mixed with myrrh when he arrived at the place of execution. It must have been needed to deaden the pain (see comment on Mt 27:33–34 for another explanation). Jesus refused the drink, choosing rather to experience the terrible sufferings of the Crucifixion with his senses intact.

24 Mark simply says, "And they crucified him." What incredible restraint! Especially when one considers that crucifixion was, as Cicero said, "the cruelest and most hideous punishment possible."

Death by crucifixion could come very slowly (see comment on Mt 27:32–44). If the victim was slow in dying, his legs would be broken by a club to hasten suffocation. Jesus had been so brutally beaten and lost so much blood that when the soldiers came to him to see whether they would have to break his legs, he was dead already (cf. Jn 19:31–33).

Jesus' clothes had been removed when he was nailed to the cross. They were now in the hands of the soldiers, who proceeded to while away their time by casting lots for them (cf. Ps 22:18).

25 Mark says that Jesus was crucified the third hour, i.e., 9:00 A.M. This conflicts with John's account, which says that the trial before Pilate was not quite over by the sixth hour, i.e., 12:00 noon, therefore implying that the Crucifixion took place later still.

Perhaps an early copyist has confused a Greek Γ—the letter that stands for three—with a F—the letter that stands for six. Or else v.25 may be a gloss; i.e., it was added by an early copyist. This is a possibility since both Matthew and Luke do not include this verse, and they ordinarily follow Mark's indications of time in the passion narrative (but see also comment on Jn 19:14–15).

26 A wooden board stating the specific charge against a condemned man was commonly fastened on the cross above his head. Over Jesus' head was placed the inscription "THE KING OF THE JEWS." The Gospels do not agree on the precise wording of the inscription, but they all assert that Jesus was crucified on the charge of claiming to be the King of the Jews. For the Romans, this was high treason.

27 The two criminals, probably insurrectionists (see comment on Mt 27:16), were crucified on either side of Jesus (cf. 15:7). They had probably been involved with Barabbas and had been sentenced at the same time as Jesus. His placement between the two criminals was probably to mock him as the insurrectionist par excellence.

29–30 The Crucifixion obviously took place in a public area, perhaps beside a thoroughfare where people were coming and going. As they passed by, they took the opportunity to vent their hostility on Jesus, using words that echo the OT (cf. Ps 22:7; La 2:15). They particularly remembered the charge made against him of destroying and rebuilding the temple (cf. 14:58), and they threw that into his teeth. Surely if he could destroy and rebuild the temple, he could save himself now!

31–32 The chief priests and teachers of the law were also there to add their mockery to that of those who passed by. This must have been especially difficult for Jesus to bear. As the spiritual leaders of the people, they should have championed Jesus' cause; instead, they had condemned him and demanded his crucifixion. Yet in their mockery, they unconsciously bore witness to his miraculous powers: "He saved others"—a reference to his healing miracles and perhaps the raising of Lazarus. Their statement "he can't save himself" is both false (he had the power to save himself) and true (if Jesus was to fulfill his messianic mission, he could not save himself).

The epithet "This Christ, this King of Israel" is full of derision. The religious leaders were mocking his claim to be the King of the people of God. And they tauntingly demanded a demonstration of his power—"come down from the cross, that we may see and believe." Jesus also had to bear the insults of the criminals who were crucified on either side of him (but see also Lk 23:39–43).

M. The Death of Jesus (15:33–41)

33 All three Synoptic Gospels report the darkness; none says what caused it. Perhaps it was dark clouds obscuring the sun or a black sirocco—a wind that comes in from the desert, not uncommon in Jerusalem in the month of April. Whatever its cause, it lasted for three hours (12:00 noon to 3:00 P.M.) and covered the entire land of Judah. There can be little doubt that Mark understood the darkness as God's supernatural act and associated it with his judgment.

34 This is the only one of Jesus' seven words from the cross Mark records (probably spoken in Hebrew). The meaning of the cry of agony "My God, my God, why have you forsaken me?" (Ps 22:1), lies beyond human comprehension. Some have felt that Jesus' cry of dereliction shows his utter agony in tasting for us the very essence of hell, which is separation from God. The cry undoubtedly reflects something of the depth of meaning of Paul's statement in 2Co 5:21: "God made him who had no sin to be sin for us."

35 The ignorant and heartless bystanders mistook the first words of Jesus' cry to be a cry for Elijah. Elijah, regarded as the forerunner and helper of the Messiah (see comments on 9:4, 11), was also regarded as a deliverer of those in trouble. So tauntingly they said, "Listen, he's calling Elijah."

36 Mark does not identify the person who went to get the wine vinegar, though most likely it was one of the soldiers. A sponge was filled with this wine vinegar, placed around the tip of a stick and held up to Jesus' lips so that he could suck the liquid from it. Apparently some of the bystanders wanted to prevent the soldier from giving the vinegar to Jesus (translating the first phrase as "Leave me alone"). He insisted on doing it, however, and then added his own taunt: "Let's see if Elijah comes to take him down."

37 After six hours of torture, Jesus cried out and died. Usually those who were crucified took much longer to die (cf. 15:44). The loud cry of Jesus is unusual because victims of crucifixion usually had no strength left, especially when near death. But Jesus' death was no ordinary one, nor was his shout the last gasp of a dying man. It was a shout of victory that anticipated the triumph of the Resurrection.

38 The curtain referred to was the one that separated the Holy Place from the Most Holy Place in the temple. It was torn from the top to the bottom. Mark must have regarded this as a supernatural act, though he does not assign theological significance to it (see Heb 9:1–14; 10:19–22). Since only the priests were permitted entrance into the Holy Place, this event probably became part of the tradition through the report of priests who were subsequently converted to Christianity (cf. Ac 6:7). Perhaps the experience of witnessing the tearing of the curtain in the temple prepared their hearts for receiving Jesus Christ as their Savior.

39 The Roman centurion in command of the detachment of soldiers at the cross had witnessed the scourging, mocking, spitting, crucifixion, and wagging of heads, and now he heard Jesus' last cry and watched him die. The soldier was deeply impressed. He had never seen anything like this before! He was deeply moved and drawn to the person of the Righteous Sufferer on the cross (cf. Lk 23:47). In view of Mark's opening affirmation of Jesus as "the Son of God" (1:1), the confession of the centurion at the climax of Jesus' passion takes on added significance. Whether or not the centurion realized the full import of his words, they were for Mark a profoundly true statement of the identity of the Man on the cross.

40–41 Women too were present at the Crucifixion, but they kept their distance. Mark identifies three of these women: Mary Magdalene, another Mary, and Salome. Mary Magdalene (i.e., Mary of Magdala) is mentioned only here in Mark (cf. Lk 8:2). The second Mary is designated as the "mother of James the younger and Joses." Although little is known about her, her sons were apparently well known in the early church. The third woman Mark mentions here is Salome, Zebedee's wife and the mother of James and John (cf. Mt 27:56). These three women had been with Jesus in Galilee and had served him there. They had come up to Jerusalem, along with many other women, especially to be with him and serve him.

N. The Burial of Jesus (15:42–47)

42–43 Preparation Day was the name given to the day before a festival or a Sabbath. Here it refers to the day before the Sabbath (as Mark explains for the benefit of his Gentile readers). It was now probably around 4:00 P.M., and there was not much time to take Jesus' body down from the cross. This is apparently what spurred Joseph of Arimathea into action.

Mark describes Joseph's request for the body of Jesus as a bold act, as indeed it was, because it would inevitably have identified him with Jesus and his followers. For a man in Joseph's position, a prominent member of the Sanhedrin, such an act could have serious consequences. But he was a pious man who had not consented in the decision and action of the council (Lk 23:51).

Ordinarily a relative or close friend would have requested the body, but apparently the mother of Jesus was so distraught that she was incapacitated; and all of Jesus' disciples but John had fled. There is no evidence that Jesus' brothers and sisters were in Jerusalem at the time of the Crucifixion.

44–45 Pilate was surprised to hear that Jesus had already died (see comment on 15:24). Only after he received confirmation of Jesus' death from the centurion was he willing to turn Jesus' body over to Joseph. For Pilate to release the body of a condemned criminal—especially one condemned of high treason—to someone other than a relative was highly unusual. It suggests that Pilate did not take seriously the charge of high treason against Jesus and had only pronounced sentence against him because of political expediency.

46 Mark does not mention anyone assisting Joseph in the actions described here. He must, however, have had help in removing the body from the cross, preparing it for burial, and carrying it to the place of burial in such a short time. Since he was rich (cf. Isa 53:9; Mt 27:51), he doubtless had servants to help him. Moreover, John says that Nicodemus helped Joseph and supplied some of the spices used in the preparation of the body for burial (Jn 19:39). After being properly prepared for burial (cf. Jn 19:40), it was placed in a new tomb, cut out of rock (cf. Mt 27:60; Jn 19:41).

The location of the tomb was in a garden very near the site of the Crucifixion (Jn 19:41), an area that has proven to be a cemetery during the first century A.D. Tombs cut out of the rock were closed by rolling a stone against the entrance.

47 The two Marys mention in v.40 as being witnesses of the Crucifixion were also present at Jesus' burial. Mark mentions this in anticipation of 16:1; the two women could identify the tomb on Sunday morning because they had been present at the burial.

O. The Resurrection (16:1–8)

The climax to Mark's gospel is the Resurrection. Without it the life and death of Jesus, though noble and admirable, are nonetheless overwhelmingly tragic events. With it Jesus was declared to be the Son of God with power (Ro 1:4), and the disciples were transformed from lethargic and defeated followers into the flaming witnesses of the book of Acts. The Good News about Jesus Christ is that God, by the resurrection of his Son Jesus, defeated sin, death, and hell. It was this message that lay at the heart of the apostolic preaching.

All four Gospels tell the story of the Resurrection and do so with the same dignity and restraint they use in telling the story of the Crucifixion. As the Crucifixion was a historical event—namely, something that actually happened at a specific time and place—so the tomb in which Jesus had been placed on Friday afternoon was actually found to be empty on the following Sunday morning. The explanation of this historical event, unavailable to us apart from divine revelation, was given by the young man (his white robe identifies him as an angelic being): "He has risen!" This word of revelation, the truth of the resurrection of Jesus, is the focal point in all four gospel accounts. Any claim that the Resurrection was a fabrication (cf. Mt 27:62–65) or a delusion is implicity denied.

1 When the Sabbath was over (about 6:00 P.M. Saturday evening), the three women mentioned at the Crucifixion (15:40), two of whom were also present at Jesus' burial (15:47), brought aromatic oils to anoint the body of Jesus. The anointing was not for the purpose of preserving the body (embalming was not practiced by the Jews) but was an act of love and devotion, probably meant to reduce the stench of the decomposing body. Palestine's hot climate causes corpses to decay rapidly.

2 Since it would have been too dark after the end of the Sabbath to go to the tomb, the women waited till Sunday morning, the period of time immediately after the sun rose.

3 As the women walked to the tomb, their chief concern was with the heavy stone they knew had been rolled in front of the opening of the tomb (cf. 15:46–47). Of the sealing of the tomb or the posting of the guard, they knew nothing (cf. Mt 27:62–66). Their concern with moving the stone was a real one because, no matter what kind of stone it was, it would have been difficult to move. A circular stone, though relatively easy to put in place since it was usually set in a sloped track, was very difficult to remove once established in place. It would either have to be rolled back up the incline or lifted out of the groove and then removed.

4–5 Mark makes no attempt to explain how the stone was removed. Once inside the tomb the women saw a young man dressed in a white robe; his dress suggests an angel (cf. Mt

28:2). No human eyes saw the resurrection, but angels, as witnesses of God's actions, could report what happened.

The reaction of the women to the angel was what one would expect: "They were alarmed."

6 The women's fright was calmed by words of reassurance: "Don't be alarmed." The angel knew whom they were seeking—Jesus of Nazareth. He then spoke the revelatory word, "He has risen!" and invited them to see the evidence of the empty tomb. An empty tomb, of course, invites the question, What happened to the body of Jesus? There had to be a word from God to interpret the meaning of the empty tomb, and the angel was God's gracious provision. The explanation is Resurrection! Across the centuries many other explanations have been proposed: the body of Jesus was stolen; the women came to the wrong tomb; Jesus did not actually die on the cross but walked out of the tomb; etc. Some of them have had success with skeptics. But the only adequate explanation is still what the angel said to the women who were at the tomb on the first Easter morning: "He has risen!"

7 "Go, tell his disciples and Peter" reveals how gracious was the provision God made for Peter's special need through the word of the angel. Peter is singled out because he had denied Jesus (14:66–72) and now needed reassurance that he was not excluded from the company of the disciples. Jesus had forgiven and restored him.

Jesus had predicted their regathering in Galilee (14:28). Why Galilee? Perhaps he wanted to meet not only with the disciples but also with the community of believers there to give them his last instructions before his ascension. Galilee would also be a fitting place for the launching of a Gentile mission.

8 The confrontation with the angel proved to be too much for the women. They fled "trembling and bewildered"—a natural and to-be-expected reaction. They were so frightened and confused that they were at first silent. After they had collected their wits, they did a lot of talking (cf. Mt 28:8; Lk 24:9).

If the gospel of Mark ends with 16:8, as some believe, Mark intentionally emphasizes the mystery and awesomeness of the Resurrection. The women were afraid because God's eschatological action in the resurrection of his Son had been revealed to them, an event Mark understood to be the climax of all God's saving acts and the inauguration of the time of the End.

P. The Longer Ending—The Appearances and Ascension of Jesus (16:9–20)

There are four sections of the Longer Ending: (1) the appearance to Mary Magdalene (vv.9–11); (2) the appearance to the two men (vv.12–13); (3) the appearance to the Eleven and the Great Commission (vv.14–18); and (4) the Ascension and session, and the disciples' response (vv.19–20). A discussion of the problem of the authenticity of this ending follows the commentary on vv.9–20.

9 The break in the continuity of the narrative seems to indicate that vv.9–20 were not originally a part of Mark's gospel but are rather a summary of post-resurrection appearances of Jesus composed independently. The Greek text of this verse has no subject (it is supplied for clarification by NIV), as if Jesus, not Mary, had just been mentioned. Also, since Mary Magdalene is mentioned for the fourth time (cf. 15:40, 47; 16:1), it is strange that the detail "out of whom he had driven seven demons" is for the first time mentioned here.

10–11 Mary carried out the command of the angel given in v.7. She found the disciples in a state of mourning (v.10)—but not for long. Her witness to them was that Jesus was alive, and she knew it to be so because she had seen him. The reluctance of the disciples to believe her is certainly understandable (v.11; cf. Mt 28:17; Lk 24:11). A resurrection is no ordinary event!

12–13 These verses are obviously a shortened account of the story of the two men on the way to Emmaus (cf. Lk 24:13–35). It adds nothing to Luke's account except the statement "but they did not believe them either" (v.13).

14 Again the account in Luke (24:36–44) is briefly summarized. The rebuke Jesus gave his disciples here is particularly severe—more severe, in fact, than any other rebuke elsewhere in the Gospels. One manuscript inserts a section here to tone down that rebuke.

15–16 In this rendition of the Great Commission (cf. Mt 28:18–20), the author gives an unusually wide scope for preaching (cf. 14:9). Belief and baptism are so closely associated that they are conceived of as virtually a single act. The inward reception (belief) is immediately followed by the external act or witness to that faith (baptism). The result is salvation. Refusal to believe results in judgment. One of the primary themes of this entire section (vv.9–20) is the importance of belief and the sinfulness of unbelief.

17–18 The promise of signs is not limited to the apostles, for they will accompany any who believe. The apostles' power to exorcise demons is to be shared by other believers. Speaking in tongues is not mentioned elsewhere in the Gospels and seems to reflect a post-Pentecost situation. Lk 10:19 speaks of trampling on snakes but not of picking them up with one's hands (v.18; cf. Ac 28:3–6). The drinking of poison without harm is unknown in the NT. Anointing the sick with oil is mentioned in 6:13, but no laying on of hands by the apostles occurs in the Gospels (cf. Ac 28:8).

19–20 "After the Lord Jesus had spoken to them" may refer to vv.15–18 or to some other occasion. The Ascension had been predicted by Jesus (cf. 14:7) and was witnessed by the apostles (cf. Ac 1:9); his sitting at God's right hand was a matter of faith but firmly believed and preached in the early church (cf. Ac 2:33–35; 7:56).

There is nothing like v.20 in any of the Gospels. It sounds more like a summary statement from the book of Acts of the activities of the apostles.

The Ending of the Gospel of Mark

The gospel of Mark has four different endings in the manuscript tradition, but only two have any significant claim to authenticity: (1) the ending that concludes the gospel with v.8 and (2) the so-called Longer Ending (vv.9–20).

1. External evidence

According to most contemporary scholars, the oldest and best attested manuscripts and versions, plus principles of textual criticism, tend in the direction of ending Mark with v.8. The external evidence seems to indicate that the Longer Ending was in circulation by the middle of the second century and was probably composed in the first half of the same century.

2. Internal evidence

a. *Vocabulary.* Of the 75 significant words in vv.9–20, 15 do not appear elsewhere in Mark and 11 others have a different meaning. In other words, more than a third of the words are non-Markan. The marked difference in vocabulary between 16:9–20 and the rest of Mark's gospel makes it difficult to believe that they both came from the same author.

b. *Style.* Here the argument against Markan authorship of vv.9–20 is even stronger. The connection between v.8 and vv.9–20 is abrupt and awkward. Verse 9 begins with the masculine nominative participle *anastas*, which demands for its antecedent "he," i.e., Jesus; but the subject of the last sentence of v.8 is the women, not Jesus. Mary Magdalene is referred to as if she had never been mentioned before; yet she appears three times in the crucifixion, burial, and resurrection narratives that immediately precede. The angel at the tomb spoke of a post-resurrection appearance in Galilee to the disciples, but Jesus' appearances in vv.9–20 are confined to Jerusalem and its immediate vicinity. All these factors weigh heavily against the Longer Ending.

3. Content

It is in the area of content that the most serious objections are found. The first has to do with the severe rebuke by Jesus of his disciples. Nothing like this is found in the rest of Mark's gospel (see commentary on v.14). The second relates to the "signs" of vv.17–18. Nowhere else do the Scriptures promise immunity from snakes and poisons, certainly not in the Gospels. It is doubtful that the Lord would have promised this unconditionally to all believers.

One final question arises: Did Mark actually intend to end his gospel at 16:8? Although some defend this view, it does not adequately explain (1) why the early church felt so strongly its lack of completion, witnessed by the insertion of both the Shorter and Longer endings; (2) why a book that purports to be the "good news about Jesus Christ" should end with the women being afraid; and (3) why it records no fulfillment of Jesus' promised resurrection appearances to Peter and the other disciples (cf. 16:7).

Thus the best solution seems to be that Mark did write an ending to his gospel but that it was lost in the early transmission of the text. The endings we now possess represent attempts by the church to supply what was obviously lacking.

The Old Testament in the New

NT Text	OT Text	Subject
Mk 1:2	Mal 3:1	Messenger sent ahead
Mk 1:3	Isa 40:3	Voice in the wilderness
Mk 4:12	Isa 6:9–10	Seeing but not perceiving
Mk 7:6–7	Isa 29:13	Hypocritical worship
Mk 7:10	Ex 20:12; Dt 5:16	Fifth commandment
Mk 7:10	Ex 21:17; Lev 20:9	Cursing parents
Mk 9:48	Isa 66:24	Unquenchable fire of hell
Mk 10:6	Ge 1:27	Creation of humans
Mk 10:7	Ge 2:24	Institution of marriage
Mk 11:9	Ps 118:25–26	Blessed is he who comes
Mk 11:17	Isa 56:7	God's house of prayer
Mk 11:17	Jer 7:11	A den of robbers
Mk 12:10–11	Ps 118:22–23	Rejected cornerstone
Mk 12:19	Dt 25:5	A brother's widow
Mk 12:26	Ex 3:6	The living God
Mk 12:29	Dt 6:4	Only one God
Mk 12:30, 33	Dt 6:5	Love God
Mk 12:31	Lev 19:18	Love your neighbor as yourself
Mk 12:32	Dt 4:35	No other God
Mk 12:36	Ps 110:1	At God's right hand
Mk 13:14	Dan 9:27; 11:31	Abomination of desolation
Mk 12:24–25	Isa 13:10; 34:4	The end times
Mk 13:26	Dan 7:13–14	Coming Son of Man
Mk 14:27	Zec 13:7	Striking the shepherd
Mk 14:62	Da 7:13–14	Coming Son of Man
Mk 15:34	Ps 22:1	God-forsaken cry

Luke

INTRODUCTION

Had modern methods of book publishing been available in the first century, the books of Luke and Acts might have been found standing side by side in paperback editions on a bookseller's shelf as two books from the same author. Possibly they would have been bound together in one hardback volume. One can picture Gentile readers going from adventure to adventure, delighting in the story of Paul's shipwreck and learning something of the Gospel of Jesus Christ through reading the various speeches. Likewise the gospel of Luke contains narratives and sayings of Jesus cast in a variety of literary forms. They, in turn, would have interested their friends in reading Luke-Acts.

1. Authorship

The present work is called a gospel (for comments on this literary form, see the Introduction to Mark, "Literary Form." It has traditionally been attributed to Luke.

The unique relation of Luke to Acts sets the authorship of Luke apart from the problem of the authorship of the other gospels. The following facts point to a common author for both works: (1) Both Luke and Acts are addressed to an individual named Theophilus (Lk 1:3; Ac 1:1); (2) Acts refers to a previous work (1:1), presumably the gospel of Luke; (3) certain stylistic and structural characteristics are common to both books and point to a single author; and (4) not only do the two volumes have a number of themes in common, but some of them receive distinctive emphases in this third gospel that are not found elsewhere in the NT.

The author of this gospel indicated that he was a second-generation Christian who was investigating the traditions about Jesus. As for the book of Acts, the author associated himself with Paul in the well-known "we passages" (Ac 16:10–17; 20:5–15; 21:1–18; 27:1–28:16). The use of the first person plural in the "we passages" certainly does not prove that Luke was the author of Acts, but it does accord with other data that we know about Luke. Paul himself mentioned Luke as a companion in Col 4:14; Phm 24; and 2Ti 4:11.

The tradition of the early church is consistent in attributing the third gospel to Luke. Already in A.D. 135 Marcion acknowledged Luke as the author of the third gospel. This tradition was continued in the Muratorian Canon (c. A.D. 180) and was affirmed by Irenaeus (A.D. 180) and successive writers.

Such passages indicate that Luke was a physician, that only he was with Paul during his final imprisonment, and that he was likely a Gentile (cf. Col 4:10–11). The tradition also informs us that Luke came from Antioch in Syria. This is generally accepted, not on its own authority, but because of Luke's involvement with the church in Antioch.

2. Purpose

Why did Luke write this two-volumed work? The answer must be based on a consideration of the prologue to the gospel (1:1–4), of the apparent purposes of Acts (see introduction to Acts), of the major themes and theology of the gospel of Luke (see that section below), and of its life situation.

Luke probably had several purposes in his writing. Certainly one clear purpose, evident in Lk 1:1–4, is evangelism. Central to both Luke and Acts are the theme and theology of salvation and the frequent proclamation of Good News. Luke supports the message about Jesus with eyewitness accounts (e.g., Lk 1:;, Ac 10:39) and proofs from prophecy (Ac 10:43), hoping to confirm the faith of Theophilus.

Luke seems concerned with recording the early history of Christianity as a means of forwarding the Christian movement. One likely goal he had in mind was to defend Christianity as a religion set in the Roman Empire. Jews had certain legal rights under the Roman Empire, and Luke may have written to demonstrate that Christianity should also have the same rights as Pharisaism and the other sects of Judaism. For example, at his trials Paul tried to identify himself with Judaism, especially with Pharisaism. He himself called Christianity a "sect" in Ac 24:14, a term used in the accusation against him in v.5.

3. Intended Readership

Any conclusions as to the readership of the gospel must be drawn primarily from the prologue (1:1–4) and secondarily from analyzing the gospel itself. As to the first, see the commentary on 1:1–4 for remarks about Theophilus. The previous section indicates that while Luke-Acts had an appeal to the non-Christian, Luke expected and desired it to be read by Christians, especially new converts. It is plausible that he had the God-fearers in mind—Gentiles at home in secular society, interested in Judaism, monotheistic by conviction, and accustomed to hearing the Jewish Scriptures read in the synagogue.

4. Literary Characteristics

Luke's Greek is some of the finest and richest in the NT, though it is combined with certain features of a Semitic style. This includes expressions characteristic of Hebrew, Aramaic, or both, and Septuagintisms. These characteristics occur more often in Lk 1 and 2 and in Ac 1–15 than in the rest of the books. There are fewer of these features in the "we passages."

What probably accounts for this style is that Luke was a Gentile who had a long exposure to Semitic idioms and unconsciously adopted a Septuagintal style, possibly through association with Paul. At times he may have been using a source with a tradition that went back to a Semitic original.

5. Method of Composition

The first written gospel in the NT form was probably Mark (see the introduction to Mark). Matthew apparently had access to Mark as well as other traditions that contained sayings of Jesus. These other traditions are referred to by scholars as "Q" (see the introduction to Matthew and "The Synoptic Gospels" in EBC 1:501–14). In addition to Mark and Q, Luke also seems to have had his own special sources(s), containing material not found in the other gospels (e.g., 1:5–2:52).

In Luke's use of his sources, he undoubtedly made various changes in style and emphasis, but we must take care not to assume that he changed or slanted material that was not true to those sources. There is no question but that each of the Gospels contributes a distinctive perspective on the life and teachings of the Lord Jesus. It is to the enrichment of our total understanding of the person and work of Christ that we thoroughly investigate these distinct contributions. But extreme caution is needed lest we superimpose on the gospel the supposed conditions of the church communities at the time Luke wrote and claim that he altered what Jesus actually taught.

6. History and Geography

On the historical value of Luke's writing, the data collected by W. M. Ramsay in his well-known works and by A. N. Sherwin-White demonstrate by and large that where Luke can be checked historically, his accuracy has been validated. Furthermore, as indicated earlier, Luke's theological intentions should not be taken as invalidating his historical accuracy. Just because Luke had a theological agenda does not necessarily mean that he wrote with deliberate errors.

The terminology of Luke's prologue (1:1–4) certainly implies careful historical research. While such a claim does not prove accuracy, Luke's honesty as a writer in distinguishing himself from the eyewitnesses and the care he took to provide an orderly, accurate account cannot be overlooked. Historians in the ancient world were, contrary to what many have thought, interested in accurate reporting. Even where there seem to be historical inaccuracies, solutions are available to the problems presented (discussed in the commentary).

7. Date

The dating of Luke depends largely on three factors: (1) the date of Mark and Luke's relationship to it, (2) the date of Acts, and (3) the reference to the destruction of Jerusalem in ch.21.

First, the date of Mark is, of course, relevant only if Luke used Mark as one of his sources. That probability is strong enough to assume here. With rare exceptions, scholars today hold that Mark was written by about A.D. 70, probably probably as early as A.D. 60 (see the introduction to Mark).

Second, the issues surrounding the date of Acts are more complex (see the introduction to Acts). Presumably Luke completed his gospel before writing Acts. The main considerations in the dating of Acts relate to the time of Paul's imprisonment and the date of the Neronian persecution. Acts 28:30 takes leave of Paul with a reference to his two-year imprisonment at Rome. This is generally agreed to have taken place around A.D. 60 to 62; this is the earliest possible date for Acts. The fact that there is no record in Acts of the subsequent persecution under Nero in A.D. 65 and of Paul's death at about that time suggests that Luke wrote Acts before these events. There is no hint of further hostilities between the Jews and the Romans or of the climax in A.D. 70. One might have expected Luke to cite the destruction of Jerusalem in his attempt to show the innocence of Christianity and the culpability of the Jewish rulers. On the ground of these historical matters alone, Acts can be dated anywhere between A.D. 61 and 65, probably around A.D. 63 or 64, and the gospel of Luke just prior to that.

The fact that Luke includes specific details of the destruction of Jerusalem (occuring in A.D. 70) in Jesus' prophecy recorded in Lk 21 does not prove that it must have been written after the event. After all, through both works Luke stresses the importance and centrality of Jerusalem. His gospel opens with a scene in the temple in Jerusalem; Jesus is constantly pressing toward Jerusalem; and Luke includes a lament of Jesus over the city (19:41–44). It is natural that he would pick up any tradition of Jesus' words about the fate of that city, even before the event occurred.

8. Themes and Theology

While we may never impose a theology on Luke, it is appropriate to discover from within the text itself certain emphases and themes that are characteristic of Luke-Acts. Particularly helpful in our analysis are (1) specific words that appear more frequently in Luke than in the other gospels; (2) Jesus' first preaching at Nazareth (4:16–21), providing a programmatic statement regarding his ministry; (3) coherence of certain themes (such as the messiahship of Jesus and the kingdom of God) within the gospel itself; and (4) the way in which the central part of Luke (9:51–18:14) has Jesus orienting his thinking and ministry toward Jerusalem, the city of destiny where he would die and rise again.

The following are some of the more significant topics in Luke.

a. Christology

The gospel opens with a series of birth narratives, alternating between Jesus and John the Baptist. Among other purposes, these narratives effect a contrast between the two figures. From the beginning it is apparent that Jesus is also the Son of God, born of a virgin (1:26–33). The atmosphere of chapters 1–2 is that of the OT. In them Jesus is presented in terms of messiahship (cf. 1:32b–33, 68–75). Simeon and Anna give testimony to the baby Jesus in the temple and announce that God's day of redemption has dawned, since the coming of the Savior means light to the Gentiles and glory to Israel (2:25–38). At the age of twelve, Jesus expresses his filial consciousness—his unique awareness that God is his Father (2:49).

There are hints throughout the gospel that Jesus came as a "prophet" (e.g., 4:24; 13:33; 24:19). Luke effectively focuses on the messiahship of Jesus (unlike Mark) by taking the reader directly from the question of Herod to the messianic act of feeding the five thousand (9:10–17) and then immediately to Peter's affirmation that Jesus is "the Christ of God" (9:20).

Unlike the other gospels, Luke's narrative concludes with the ascension of Jesus. This marks both the conclusion of the gospel and the beginning of Acts and is thus also pivotal in the two-volume work. Moreover, Luke makes mention of the Ascension in 9:51, at the beginning of the central section of his gospel.

b. Doxology

The prominence of the Resurrection and Ascension in Luke contributes to his "theology of glory." The descriptive term "glory" (*doxa*; GK *1518*) is also appropriate because there is a sense of doxology—i.e., of ascribing glory to God—throughout Luke's work. Those who observe or benefit from the healing power of Christ are filled with wonder and bring glory to God (e.g., Lk 5:25–26; Ac 3:8–10). Other examples of praising and blessing God in Luke are 1:46–55, 68–79; 2:13–14, 20, 28–32; 7:16; 10:21; 18:43; 19:37–38; 24:53.

c. Soteriology

If Luke has a theology of glory, this does not mean he lacks a theology of the Cross. While the Gospel as proclaimed in the first chapters of Acts does not feature the doctrine of the atonement as we find it in Paul, the Cross is central all the same. Even before the first passion prediction of Lk 9:22, there are foreshadowings of Jesus' sufferings (2:35; 5:35). Jesus is clearly moving toward the Cross in 13:33. His words instituting the Last Supper also give evidence of his understanding of the Cross (22:19–20).

d. Salvation

The central theme in Luke's writings is salvation, focusing on the person and the saving work of the Lord Jesus Christ. The verb "save" (GK 5392) occurs in 6:9; 7:50; 8:12, 36, 48, 50; 9:24; 13:23; 17:19; 18:26, 42; 19:10; 23:35, 37, 39; the noun "Savior" (GK 5400) in 1:47; 2:11; and the noun for "salvation" (GK 5401) in 1:69, 71, 77; 2:30; 3:6; 19:9. One of the key passages is 19:1–10, which concludes with the statement that the Son of Man "came to seek and to save what was lost." The entire gospel of Luke pictures Jesus as reaching out to the lost in forgiveness (see 7:36–50; 15:3–32). The Savior whom Luke presents is one who lived among people and cared about them. He lived among people; he was crucified and actually raised from the dead.

e. The Holy Spirit

The Holy Spirit receives considerable attention in Luke-Acts. It is through the overshadowing spirit and power of God that Mary conceives the one who will be called the Son of God (1.35). The same Spirit would fill John the Baptist (1:15) and his mother, Elizabeth (1:41). The Spirit was on Simeon, and through the Spirit he gave testimony to the Messiah (2:25–35). Jesus was full of the Spirit and was led by the Spirit at the time of his temptation (4:1). The great passage from Isaiah that Jesus quoted in the synagogue at Nazareth begins: "The Spirit of the Lord is on me" (4:18). Furthermore, Jesus promised the Holy Spirit both as an answer to prayer (11:13) and in anticipation of Pentecost (24:49; Ac 1:4). The Holy Spirit, of course, has a major place throughout Acts.

f. Prayer

Not only was prayer significant throughout Jesus' life and in the early church, but it seems to have been especially important in times of transition and crisis. Only Luke records that Jesus was praying at his baptism when the Holy Spirit descended on him (3:21). He prayed before choosing the twelve apostles (6:12) and just before being transfigured (9:29). Luke 11:1–13 and 18:1–8 contain his special teaching and parables on prayer (see also 5:16; 9:18; 11:1).

g. Sense of destiny

The word *dei* ("it is necessary"; GK 1256) is prominent in Luke and in Acts. Jesus "had to" be in his Father's house (2:49); he "must preach the good news of the kingdom of God," because that "is why I was sent" (4:43); he "must suffer" (9:22; cf. Mt 16:21; Mk 8:31); he must finish the way appointed to him, the way that culminated in the Cross (13:33); and it was necessary for the Son of Man to be betrayed and crucified, suffering first before entering his glory (24:7, 26, 44–47). In this way Jesus occupies the central place in salvation history, fulfilling the plan of God as prophesied in the OT (see 4:16–21; 26:25–27, 44; Ac 2:15–21; 4:11; et al.).

h. Eschatology

The continuity of the true people of God and the mission to the Gentiles are part of the plan of God that is a major theme in Luke. The opening chapters of Luke emphasize the messianic promises, especially through the songs of Mary (1:46–55) and Zechariah (1:68–79). The ultimate fulfillment of these still lies in the future. Luke, in common with the other Synoptic Gospels, contains teachings of Jesus about his return and about the glorification of the Son of Man. The author records Jesus' vivid warnings against coming judgment, an encouragement to watchfulness (e.g., 12:40), and the description of the coming of the Son of Man (17:22–37), but he also warns against misguided speculation (17:20–21). Faithfulness is needed during the time the Master is away (12:42–48; 19:11–27).

Along with this emphasis on the future is an emphasis on the present reality of God's work, using the word "today" eleven times: 2:11; 4:21; 5:26; 12:28; 13:32–33; 19:5–9; 22:34, 61; 23:43.

i. Discipleship and the Christian in the world

One topic common throughout Luke is his recording of Jesus' statements on wealth and poverty. A major question is whether Jesus required the sacrifice of material possessions for salvation or for discipleship, or whether he just presents it as an ideal for those who are especially devoted. The case of the rich ruler (18:18–30) is unique. Likewise those who want to be disciples should *yield* up all their possessions but not necessarily *disperse* them (see comment on 14:33). But if this is an ideal, it is an ideal strongly taught. Luke includes Jesus' woes as well as blessings (6:24–26), which speak strongly against the wealthy. He also addresses the matter of possessions in chapter 12 and in chapter 16. In addition Acts emphasizes the sacrificial giving of the early church (2:45; 3:6; 4:32–37; 5:1–11).

Luke also demonstrates the special concern Jesus had for social outcasts, such as women (8:1–3), Samaritans (10:30–37), those who were known as "sinners" (7:36–50), and tax collectors (19:1–10).

j. The word of God

This is a more important theme in Luke than is generally realized. The first appearance of *logos* ("word"; GK *3364*) is in 1:2: "servants of the word." Luke emphasizes the graciousness and effectiveness of Jesus' word in 4:22, 32, 36. The term is prominent in the parable of the sower (8:14–15). It is those who hear the word, retain it, and by persevering produce a crop who are truly related to Jesus. We also learn from Luke not only that the word of God in the OT is fulfilled in the life of Jesus, but also that Jesus' own words are fulfilled (e.g., 19:32: "just as he had told them"). Thus we have in the gospel of Luke the prophetic word, the authoritative word of Jesus, and the inspired words in the gospel itself.

EXPOSITION

I. Introduction (1:1–4)

The introduction to Luke is one long, carefully constructed sentence in the tradition of the finest historical works in Greek literature. It was customary among the great Greek and Hellenistic historians, including the first-century Jewish writer Josephus, to explain and justify their work in a preface. Their object was to assure the reader of their capability, thorough research, and reliability.

1 Luke begins by indicating that there was considerable interest in data about Jesus and his ministry prior to the present work. Luke does not say he himself actually reproduced material from any of the existing accounts, though that could be assumed from this and subsequent evidence. Nor does Luke speak adversely about his predecessors as if their attempts had failed. "To draw up an account" means to write a report or narrative, relating events in an orderly way.

The contents of this work are the things that have been "fulfilled among us." The word used here speaks of the accomplishment of the purposes of God in the life and ministry of Jesus.

2 In this verse Luke stresses the validity of the tradition of Jesus' words and deeds (an emphasis that occurs elsewhere in the NT; see 1Co 11:23; 15:3). Although the "eyewitnesses [GK *898*] and servants [GK *5677*]" may have included some of the "many" (v.1), they are mostly to be distinguished from them because they were prior to them. Witnesses are important to Luke to establish the validity of his information. The words "from the first" (probably meaning from the early days of Jesus' ministry) are tied grammatically to the word "eyewitnesses" (primarily the apostles, whose authority Luke upholds throughout Luke-Acts). These were not passive observers but "servants of the word." "Word" (GK *3364*) here means the message of the Gospel, especially as embodied in the words and deeds of Jesus. In Ac 1:1, Luke combines the words "do" and "teach" when he describes Jesus' ministry. In summary, v.2 makes a serious claim regarding careful historical research that has weighty implications for our estimate of the entire gospel.

3 Luke now describes his own work of investigation and writing. The word "everything" may partially explain how his work differed from that of the "many" (v.1) and also from that of Mark—namely, in its greater comprehensiveness. He plans to start from the beginning of Jesus' ministry and to record his research accurately and in an orderly manner.

We cannot determine from this preface alone whether Luke is referring to a chronological or to a thematic order.

The identity of Theophilus is unknown. The name ("friend of God") might be either a symbol or a substitute for the true name of Luke's addressee. Theophilus was, however, a proper name, and "most excellent" naturally suggests an actual person of some distinction. He may have been Luke's literary patron or publisher, after the custom of the times.

4 Though it is not clear whether Theophilus was a believer, he had doubtless received some instructions in the faith. He had learned of both the words and the deeds of Jesus. "Taught" (GK 2994) may refer to formal church teaching (Gal 6:6), but not necessarily. For some reason Theophilus needed assurance as to the truth of the things taught him. Possibly he was troubled by denials of the Resurrection and other historical foundations of the faith that incipient Gnostic speculation was challenging.

II. Birth and Childhood Narratives (1:5–2:52)

A. Anticipation of Two Births (1:5–56)

1. The Birth of John the Baptist foretold (1:5–25)

The birth and childhood narratives in Luke have no parallel in the other gospels. This section has several distinctive characteristics.

1. It has an atmosphere reminiscent of the OT, cast in a Semitic style. Luke is thereby connecting the OT and NT periods. He does not use the fulfillment formulas Matthew used but does show that OT predictions stand behind the events he describes, using the style and vocabulary of the LXX. He also takes pains to ground the Christian message in Jerusalem and in its temple.

2. To make a connection with the OT, Luke also uses a pattern of alternation, in which attention shifts back and forth between John the Baptist and Jesus. Luke clearly identifies John as a successor to the OT prophets. Through his alternating presentations, Luke links John and Jesus, whom Luke apparently also identifies as a prophet. Since he also sees in Jesus far more than a prophet, Luke's device of alternation goes beyond comparison to contrast, with Jesus presented as "Son of the Most High" and messianic Deliverer (1:32–33, 69, 76; 2:11, 30). The structure of the section then is (1) the announcement of John's coming birth, (2) the announcement of Jesus' coming birth, (3) Elizabeth's blessing of Mary, (4) Mary's praise to God, (5) John's birth (praised by his father Zechariah), and (6) Jesus' birth (praised by the angels in heaven and by saints in the temple).

3. The appearance of angels is likewise appropriate for an account that teaches that God has acted decisively in the history of his people to accomplish our salvation.

4. The theme of joy finds expression not only in the songs (1:48–55; 1:68–79, 2:14; 2:29–32) but also in the tone of the whole passage. The Gospel is always "good news of great joy" (2:10). At the same time, the passage realistically includes a reminder both of the pain of sin and of the cost of our deliverance (see 2:35).

5–6 As has already been said, the style of this section is different from the classical style of vv. 1–4. Likewise, the method of dating differs from that used later in 3:1, where Luke is interested in establishing a more precise point of historical reference. In this verse his only concern is to locate the events in the reign of Herod (king of Judea 37–4 B.C.).

Luke emphasizes the Jewish roots of Christianity by mentioning that, not only was Zechariah a priest, but his wife Elizabeth had also been born into the priestly line. They are a truly pious couple wholly devoted to God. Their childlessness clearly did not imply any sin.

7 To be childless brought sorrow and often shame. At her advanced age, Elizabeth could no longer entertain the hope of each Jewish woman to be the mother of the Messiah. While her situation and the subsequent intervention of God had its precedents in the OT (cf. Sarah, Ge 17:16–17; Hannah, 1Sa 1:5–11), no other woman had such a total reversal in fortune as to bear the forerunner of the Messiah.

8–9 The "division" (GK 2389) was one of twenty-four groups of priests divided by families and structured after the pattern of 1Ch 23 and 24 (cf. 1Ch 24:10 and Lk 1:5). The Exile had interrupted the original lines of descent; so the divisions were regrouped, most of them corresponding to the original in name only. Each of the twenty-four divisions served in the temple for one week, twice a year, as well as at the major festivals. An individual priest, however, could offer the incense at the daily sacrifice only once in his lifetime since there were so many priests. Therefore this was the climactic moment of Zechariah's priestly career, perhaps the most dramatic moment possible for the event described to have occurred. God was breaking into the ancient routine of Jewish ritual with the word of his decisive saving act.

10 Mention of the worshipers outside not only heightens the suspense but prepares the reader for vv.21–22. They were probably pious Jews who loved to be near the temple when sacrifices were offered.

11–12 The suddenness of the appearance of the angel in the Holy Place accords with other supernatural events in Luke (cf. 2:9, 13). Only a heavenly being had the right to appear in that place with the priest. Zechariah's startled and fearful reaction is not only a natural reaction to such an appearance but is also consistent with what the Gospels say about the response of the disciples and others to the presence of the supernatural (e.g., 1:38; 5:8–10).

13 This is the first indication of prayer on the part of Zechariah. The specific petition probably refers to both his lifelong prayer for a child (probably a son) and his just-offered prayer in the temple for the messianic redemption of Israel. Actually, the birth of his child was bound up with redemption in a way far beyond anything Zechariah expected. That the prayer included a petition for a son is substantiated by the further description of the child, beginning with his name "John" (meaning "The Lord [Yahweh] is gracious"). His being named before his birth stresses God's sovereignty in choosing him to be his servant.

14–15 The description of the child's mission has a counterpart in Gabriel's words to Mary (vv.32–33); this is part of the literary device that connects and compares the roles of Jesus and John.

The "joy" (v.14) so characteristic of the day of God's salvation and so prominent in Luke came first to the parents of the forerunner, then spread to many others (cf. v.16). Note the contrast between the promised joy and Zechariah's present fear (v.12). The child will be "great" (a word also used of Jesus in v.32) as the prophetic forerunner of the Messiah (v.15). Later some would find it hard to relinquish their devotion to John to follow Jesus. They would need to realize that while both were great, Jesus was the greater (3:16). "In the sight of the Lord" indicates divine choice and approval.

It is difficult to identify John with a particular religious group simply by this description or the description in Mk 1:6. Abstinence from wine suggests the Nazirite vow (Nu 6:1–12), but no mention is made of John's hair. Nazirites were to let their hair grow (Nu 6:5). Priests on duty were expected to abstain from strong drink (cf. Lev 10:8–9); this may identify John as a priestly figure calling the people to repentance. The Spirit's control of a person is contrasted with the control wine can have in a person (cf. Eph 5:18). In the life of Jesus, the Spirit's ministry will be even more prominent than in John's life.

16–17 The OT prophets were repeatedly concerned with turning the erring people back to God. In this work none was more prominent than Elijah on Mount Carmel (1Ki 18:20–40). Luke does not here identify John as a reincarnated Elijah but qualifies his statement with the words "in the spirit and power of Elijah" (v.17). Moreover Luke uses the language of Mal 4:5–6 (cf. Mal 3:1) to compare John's ministry with that of Elijah (see comment on 9:30).

"To turn the hearts of the fathers to their children" must be interpreted with reference to both the expanded form in Mal 4:6 and the next phrase in this verse. It probably means that when those who disobey heed wisdom and turn to the Lord, their Jewish ancestors would, if they knew of it, be pleased with them. In their OT context, the words "turn the hearts," etc., relate to averting divine wrath, a concept certainly basic in the ministry of John.

"People" (*laos*; GK *3295*) is a significant word in Luke and usually refers to Israel as the elect nation of God. This suggestion accords with Luke's interest in Jewish origins of Christianity. The "people prepared for the Lord" ultimately includes, however, not only these initial Jewish hearers but also the Gentiles.

18–20 Zechariah's question (v.18) seems innocent, but v.20 reveals that it was asked in doubt. In contrast Mary's question—"How can this be?" (v.34)—arises from faith (v.45). Mary simply inquired as to the way God would work; Zechariah questioned the truth of the revelation. "How can I be sure of this?" apparently was a request for a sign. Though we are told that Zechariah was devout (v.6), his quest for confirmation was perilously close to the attitude described in 11:29. The Gospel requires a response of faith, and Zechariah, of all people, should have believed without question. The narrative gains solemnity by mentioning that Gabriel stood "in the presence of God." The "good news" will come to fulfillment in spite of human unbelief, but Zechariah must nevertheless bear the sign of his doubt.

21–22 The element of suspense during the unusually long prayer-time contributes to the vividness of Luke's narrative. The worshipers, who had been praying outside, now understood without anyone telling them that Zechariah had seen a vision.

23–25 As with the announcement to Mary, the word concerning Zechariah and Elizabeth's promised son was given before his conception. It is characteristic of Luke to mention Elizabeth's grateful acknowledgment of the Lord's grace in removing the stigma of her childlessness.

2. The birth of Jesus foretold (1:26–38)

Luke continues in the same style in which he has described Zechariah's encounter with the angel of the Lord. The account of Jesus' nativity rests theologically on the angel Gabriel's announcement to Mary. Luke presents the theology of the Incarnation in a holy way, congruent with OT sacred history.

Several themes are intertwined in this passage: (1) the divine sonship of Jesus (vv.32, 35); (2) his messianic role and reign over the kingdom (vv.32–33); (3) God as the "Most High" (vv.32, 35; cf. v.76); (4) the power of the Holy Spirit (v.35); and (5) the grace of God (vv.29–30, 34–35, 38).

26 The mention of Elizabeth's "sixth month" (cf. v.24, 36) establishes a link between Jesus and the prophet John the Baptist. Nazareth was a small town off the main trade routes. Its insignificant size contrasts with Jerusalem, where Gabriel's previous appearance had taken place. Jn 1:46 records the negative Judean opinion of Nazareth. Likewise, the region of Galilee contrasts with Judea. Surrounded as they were by Gentiles, the Galileans were not necessarily irreligious but many were somewhat lax regarding strict Jewish traditions.

27 The young virgin Mary contrasts with the old priest Zechariah, who was past the time for having children. The word "virgin" (GK 4221) refers here to one who had not yet had sexual relations. Since betrothal often took place soon after puberty, Mary may have just entered her teens. This relationship was legally binding, but intercourse was not permitted until marriage. Only divorce or death could sever betrothal.

Luke calls Joseph "a descendant of David." Even though the genealogy in 3:23–37 is often taken as showing Mary's line, this is never stated as such (see comments). We

On the spot in Nazareth where it was believed that Gabriel visited the virgin Mary now stands the Church of the Annunciation.

should probably assume that Luke considers Jesus a legitimate member of the royal line by what we today might call the right of adoption. This has an important bearing on the promise in v.32b.

28 Here Luke establishes another contrast with the preceding narrative, for Zechariah had received no such greeting as Mary did. Mary is "highly favored" because she is the recipient of God's grace (cf. Eph 1:6). Mary has "found favor with God" (v.30), and she can therefore say, "My spirit rejoices in God my Savior" (v.47).

"The Lord is with you" recalls the way the angel of the Lord addressed Gideon to assure him of God's help in the assignment he was about to receive (Jdg 6:12).

29-30 Zechariah had been "gripped with fear" (v.12) at the very appearance of the angel, but it was the angel's greeting that "greatly troubled" Mary. He responded first by assuring her that she had indeed "found favor" with God (v.30; cf. Ge 6:8). God's grace, like his love, banishes fear of his presence (cf. 1Jn 4:17-18).

32-33 The striking term "Son of the Most High" (v.33; cf. vv.35, 76) leads to a clear messianic affirmation—the reference to the eternal throne and kingdom of David. Jesus' divine sonship is thus linked to his messiahship in accord with 2Sa 7:12-14 and Ps 2:7-9. In other words, Luke sees the messianic vocation as a function of God's Son, rather than seeing sonship as just an aspect of messiahship.

34 Unlike Zechariah, Mary does not ask for a confirmatory sign (cf. comment on v.18) but only for light on how God will accomplish this wonder. Her question does not relate to the remarkable person and work of her promised Son but arises from the fact that she has not had sexual relations with a man.

Because she was betrothed, we may assume that Mary fully expected to have normal marital relations later. It is difficult, therefore, to know why she saw a problem in Gabriel's prediction. Luke's condensed account seems to suggest that Mary assumed an immediate fulfillment before marriage (perhaps related to Isa 7:14).

35 Once again (cf. v.15) Luke mentions the Holy Spirit, as he does six more times in his first two chapters (1:41, 67, 80; 2:25, 26, 27). The word for "overshadow" (GK *2173*) carries the sense of the holy, powerful presence of God, as in the description of the cloud that covered the tabernacle (Ex 40:35). This word is used in all three accounts of the Transfiguration to describe the overshadowing of the cloud (Mt 17:5; Mk 9:7; Lk 9:34). Likewise, in each account the voice comes out of the cloud identifying Jesus as God's Son, a striking reminder of this verse where the life that results from the enveloping cloud is identified as "the Son of God."

The child is called "the holy one," both because of this connection with the Holy Spirit and because of Jesus' life of purity.

36-37 The angel cites the pregnancy of Elizabeth (v.36) as further evidence of God's marvelous power and concludes with the grand affirmation of v.37—surely one of the most reassuring statements in all Scripture.

38 Mary's exemplary attitude of servanthood recalls that of Hannah when she was praying for a son (1Sa 1:11). Her servanthood is not a cringing slavery but a submission to God that in OT times characterized genuine believers; it should also characterize believers today (cf. v.48). Mary's trusting submission at this point in her life may be compared with her attitude toward her Son later on (cf. Jn 2:5).

3. Mary's visit to Elizabeth (1:39-45)

At this point Luke deftly combines the two strands about Elizabeth and Mary; in it he stresses Jesus' superiority to John. Even so, the pattern of alternation continues, giving John his own important place as the prophet who goes before the Lord.

39-40 Mary apparently started on her journey as soon as possible (v.39). She probably traveled fifty to seventy miles from Nazareth to Zechariah's home in Judea, a major trip for Mary.

41-42 In this beautiful narrative, the stirring of the unborn child becomes a joyful prelude to Elizabeth's being filled by the Holy Spirit, who enlightened her about the identity of the child Mary was carrying.

43 Nowhere in the NT is Mary called "Mother of God." She was, however, the mother of Jesus the Messiah and Lord.

44–45 "Blessed" (GK *3421*) describes the happy situation of those whom God favors. Elizabeth gave the blessing Zechariah's muteness prevented him from giving (see vv.68–74). In her blessing Elizabeth called attention to Mary's faith and God's faithfulness.

4. Mary's song: The Magnificat (1:46–56)

This song, commonly known as the Magnificat, has several striking features. First, it is saturated with OT concepts and phrases (especially Hannah's prayer in 1Sa 2:1–10).

Second, it shows Mary's deep piety and knowledge of Scripture. Such familiarity with the OT was not at that time unusual for a pious Jewess like Mary. Moreover, it reflects qualities suitable to the mother of the Lord.

Third, though it reveals a God who vindicates the downtrodden and ministers to the hungry, it also strikes a revolutionary note. If Hannah spoke of the poor being raised to sit with nobles (1Sa 2:8), Mary sees the nobles toppled from their places of power (Lk 1:52). Luke conveys a strong social message to us, one that is rooted in the OT and that, with cultural adaptations, is of continued meaning.

Fourth, Mary's Magnificat markedly transcends Hannah's song through its messianic element and implies Mary's consciousness of her own exalted role as the kingdom dawns (v.48).

This song can be divided into four strophes: (1) vv.46–48 praise God for what he has done for Mary, (2) vv.49–50 mention certain attributes of God—power, holiness, and mercy; (3) vv.51–53 show God's sovereign action in reversing certain social conditions; and (4), finally, vv.54–55 recall God's mercy to Israel.

46–48 The excitement of Elizabeth, who actually shouted her benediction (v.42), gives way to a restraint that is no less joyful. After an opening ascription of greatness to God, Mary acknowledges her dependence on God, her Savior. Indirectly, she acknowledged herself as a sinner needing salvation. Her words are comparable to those of Habakkuk, who came through his trials rejoicing in God his Savior (Hab 3:18). Mary's "humble state" probably refers to her lowly social position; the word does not usually convey the idea of "humiliated." For the meaning of "servant," see comments on v.38; for that of "blessed," see v.45 and 6:20.

49–50 Mary is in awe of the "Mighty One" whose great power has been exercised in her life. God's "name" is, according to the common ancient meaning, his whole reputation or character. "Mercy" (GK *1799*) expresses an aspect of God's character sometimes overlooked when his power and holiness are stressed. "Fear" (GK *5828*) means here, as often in Scripture, a pious reverence.

51–55 The main verbs in the next two strophes are in the past tense. They probably recall the specific times in the OT when God acted (vv.51–52). We must not, however, overlook the fact that Mary's references to the acts of God relate to the coming of the Messiah. Indeed, they may actually be predictive (as in Isa 53:1–9), though general in content.

Mary recalls God's covenant (vv.54–55). The words translated "forever" are really the final, climactic words of the song.

56 Luke gives no hint whether Mary's stay of "about three months" ended before or continued after the birth of John (cf. vv. 26, 36, 39).

B. Birth Narratives (1:57–2:20)

1. The Birth of John the Baptist (1:57–66)

57–61 These verses give the impression that no one in the neighborhood knew of Elizabeth's pregnancy. On one level, the "joy" is over Elizabeth's emergence from the shadow of childlessness; on another, it accords with the messianic joy of vv.44, 46.

Circumcision on the eighth day (v.59) was in accord with Ge 17:9–14. Luke offers no explanation as to why the child had not been publicly named at birth (perhaps it was a Hellenistic custom to wait a week). In any event there was obviously a considerable audience for the naming at the circumcision. To choose a name after a baby's grandfather or father, especially if one of them was highly esteemed, was natural (v.61). The objection from Elizabeth (v.60) was against custom and was apparently discounted, probably because she was a woman.

62–63 Luke's description of Zechariah here suggests he may have been deaf as well as mute. The relatives and neighbors made signs to which he responded on a waxed writing tablet (v.63). The present tense in the statement "His name is John" has the ring of deliberate emphasis.

64–66 His time of disability over, Zechariah's first words were words of praise. Luke goes on to stress the widespread response to the events surrounding the birth of John, just as he later stresses the fame of Jesus (e.g., 2:52). A child whose birth was attended by such marvelous circumstances would surely have an unusual destiny (v.66).

2. Zechariah's song: The Benedictus (1:67–80)

This song of Zechariah has two main parts: (1) praise to God for messianic deliverance (vv.68–75), and (2) celebration of the significant role John the Baptist will have in this work of deliverance. In both sections there is a strong emphasis on salvation, national and personal, and on the covenant and preparation that are about to be realized in their fulfillment. God's faithfulness to his covenant occupies a central position theologically in the song (vv.72–73). Once again Luke makes the connection between the Christian Gospel and its OT roots. At the end, salvation is extended beyond Israel in language taken from Isa 60.

67 Zechariah the priest now prophesies. As the Holy Spirit had filled Elizabeth (v.41), he now fills Zechariah. His previous doubt and his discipline through loss of speech did not mean the end of his spiritual ministry. Likewise, when a believer today has submitted to God's discipline, he or she may go on in Christ's service.

68 The word "blessed" (GK 2329) can refer both to a human being on whom God has showered his goodness (as in vv.42, 45) and to God, to whom we return thanks for that goodness. "Israel" is paralleled by "his people" in vv.68, 77 (see comment on 1:17).

The action is centered in two verbs: "has come"(GK 2170) and "has redeemed" (GK 4472 & 3391). The first is used for God "visiting" people in grace or in judgment (Ex 4:31; Zec 10:3; Lk 7:16). Tragically, Jerusalem did not recognize the day when God came to her (19:44). The second verb speaks of a theme that runs throughout Scripture, with the Exodus being the great OT example of rescue from enemies and captivity. Luke 24:21 shows the expectation Jesus' followers had that he would do a similar work of freeing God's people. Luke, though committed to the universal application of the Gospel, includes these words of redemption that apply especially to Israel (see esp. v.69). Not only does this reflect his emphasis on the Jewish roots of Christianity, it also underlines the political aspects of redemption foremost in the minds of Zechariah's contemporaries.

69–70 "Horn" is a common OT metaphor for power because of the great strength of the horned animals of the Near East. The word "salvation" (GK 5401) describes the kind of strength Zechariah had in mind. The power of salvation resides in the Savior. Again, the messianic theme occurs—this time in an allusion to Ps 132:17, where, in fulfilling the Davidic covenant, God "will make a horn grow for David." Later in Luke's writing, the verb "raised up" will assume great importance in relation to the resurrection of Christ (24:6, 34; Ac 3:7, 15; 4:10).

The messianic motif is further emphasized by a reference to the "house of ... David." The mention of the "holy prophets of long ago" confirms the OT origin of and support for the messianic role of Jesus.

71–73 Zechariah cites three aspects of God's redeeming work: "salvation" (v.71), "mercy" (v.72), and the remembrance of God's "covenant." Mercy to the "fathers" seems to mean that God has not thwarted their hopes (cf. v.17). The "oath" (v.73) to Abraham in view here is recorded in Ge 22:16–18, where the Lord promised him both the subduing of his descendants' enemies and universal blessing as a result of his obedience. Therefore, the salvation in view here involves both political deliverance and spiritual blessing (cf. the next verses).

The words "covenant" and "oath" form the central point of the song, emphasizing the importance of God's covenant and his faithfulness to it. Not only does this serve as an important theme in Luke, but it also gives encouragement to us to trust the promises of God.

74–75 The fulfillment of God's promise does not mean passivity for Israel but a new opportunity for service—negatively, service "without fear" (v.74) and, positively, "in holiness and righteousness" (v.75; cf. Mal 3:3).

76–77 The second part of Zechariah's hymn begins with a direct word to his son. The role of John derives its significance and greatness from God's purpose and, even more, from the greatness of the Person he served. Before addressing the theme of salvation, Zechariah speaks of the "Most High" and "the Lord" whom John represents.

Zechariah's description of John in v.76 clearly links him with Elijah (cf. Isa 40:3; Mal 3:1; 4:5), dispelling any doubts about the recognition of this link in Luke. While Luke does not forthrightly say that John was the prophesied Elijah, he clearly affirms that John came "in the spirit and power of Elijah" (1:17; see comment). If Elijah could still appear in recognizable form, as he did at the Transfiguration, Luke may have hesitated to include in his gospel anything about his apparent identification with John.

The theme of "salvation" (GK *5401*) for God's people, expressed in political terms in v.71, now finds it spiritual identity through forgiveness. John will go on to preach "a baptism of repentance for the forgiveness of sins" (3:3).

78–79 NIV's "rising sun" (GK *424*) has a dynamic quality that suits a word used in the LXX to translate the word "branch" in Jer 23:5; Zec 3:8; 6:12. Thus it has a messianic aspect and fits well with the "come" of v.68 (see comment). Verse 79 uses beautiful language from Isa 60:1–3 to carry forward the imagery of light (the sun) and to offer hope of peace to those who were then outside the faithful remnant of Judaism (cf. Eph 2:12).

80 This brief description of John's boyhood reflects Luke's interest in human beings and is paralleled by a similar statement on Jesus' personal developments (2:40, 52). John's becoming "strong in spirit" means the development of his moral character (but cf. Eph 3:16, where similar language describes a strengthening by God's Spirit).

3. The birth of Jesus (2:1–7)

In comparison with the complex narrative in chapter 1, the actual birth narrative of Jesus is brief. In it Luke stresses three things: (1) the political situation (to explain why Jesus' birth took place in Bethlehem); (2) that Bethlehem was the town of David (to stress Jesus' messianic claim); (3) the humble circumstances of Jesus' birth.

1–3 Luke clearly intends to secure the historical and chronological moorings of Jesus' birth (approximately 4 B.C.). Ironically, it is precisely this that has led some to question Luke's accuracy.

The mention of Caesar Augustus may not only be for historical background but also to contrast the human with the divine decrees. A mere Galilean peasant travels to Bethlehem ostensibly at the decree of the Roman emperor. Actually, it is in fulfillment of the divine King's plan, which, as noted passim, is reflected in Luke's frequent reference to what "must" be done.

The first census (i.e., enrollment prior to taxation) known to have occurred under the governorship of Quirinius took place later (i.e., A.D. 6) than usually reckoned as the time of Jesus' birth (cf. Ac 5:37). Many have supposed that Luke confused this census of A.D. 6 with one he thinks was taken earlier, but which lacks historical support. The most satisfactory solutions that have been proposed follow.

1. Quirinius had a government assignment in Syria about 4 B.C. and conducted a census in his official capacity. Details of this census may have been common knowledge in Luke's time but are now lost to us (cf. "Quirinius," ZPEB, 5:5–6).

2. The word translated "first" can also mean "former" or "prior." This makes the meaning of v.2, "This census was *before* that made when Quirinius was governor."

It was customary to return to one's original home for such a census. Herod's name is not mentioned because, powerful as he was, he was only a client king under Rome and, like others, was subject to orders for a census.

4–7 Luke does not say how long in advance of Jesus' birth Joseph left for Bethlehem nor why he took Mary with him. It is possible that he used the emperor's order as a means of removing Mary from possible gossip and emotional stress in her own village. He had already accepted her as his wife (Mt 1:24), but apparently they continued in betrothal till after the birth. The text neither affirms nor denies the popular image of the couple arriving in Bethlehem just as the baby was about to be born. Luke simply states that the birth took place "while they were there" (v.6).

The word usually translated "inn" (GK 2906) may mean a room (e.g., the "guest room" used for the Last Supper as in 22:11), a billet for soldiers, or any place for lodging, which would include inns. It is not, however, the usual Greek word for an inn.

Luke states the simple fact that when Mary's time came, the only available place for the little family was one usually occupied by animals. It may have been a cave, as tradition suggests, or some part of a house or inn. Even today in many places around the world farm animals and their fodder are often kept in the same building as the family quarters. The eating trough, or "manger," was ideal for use as a crib. Luke does not seem to be portraying a dismal situation with an unfeeling innkeeper as villain. Rather, he is establishing a contrast between the proper rights of the Messiah in his own "town of David" and the very ordinary and humble circumstances of his birth. For "cloths," see comment on v.12.

4. The announcement to the shepherds (2:8–20)

8 There may be several reasons for the special role of the shepherds in the events of this unique night. Among the occupations, shepherding had a lowly place. Shepherds were considered untrustworthy and their work made them ceremonially unclean. Thus the most obvious implication is that the Gospel first came to the social outcasts of Jesus' day. This would accord with a recurring emphasis in Luke. It may also be significant that the Lord reminded David, who was to become Messiah's royal ancestor, that he was called from the shepherd's life (2Sa 7:8). Finally, in both OT and NT shepherds symbolize all the ordinary people who have joyfully received the Gospel and have become in various ways pastors to others. As to the time of year of the nativity, Luke provides no clue.

9 First a single angel (cf. 1:11, 26) appears. The shepherds' terror recalls that of Zechariah (1:12), though theirs is related to the visible manifestation of the glory of God. Again, as in 1:13 and 1:30, the angel speaks reassuringly.

10–11 The angel's announcement includes several of the most frequently used words in Luke's gospel: "bring . . . good news," "joy," "today," "Savior," and "Lord." This shows the tremendous importance of the angelic pronouncement. It is a bold proclamation of the Gospel at the very hour of Jesus' birth. The time has come for the fulfillment of the prophetic expectation of Messiah's coming.

12 Babies were snugly wrapped in long strips of cloth, giving them warmth, protection of extremities, and a sense of security in their newborn existence. The combination of a newborn baby's wrappings and the use of the manger for a crib would be a distinctive "sign" (Gk 4958). Perhaps they also imply that in spite of seeming rejection, symbolized by the manger, the baby was the special object of his mother's care (compare this story with Eze 16:1–5). On the other hand, the "sign" might be only the strange circumstance of the newborn child being in the manger at all.

13 "Suddenly" often describes the unexpected nature of God's acts, especially the eschatological events. Malachi had predicted the sudden coming of the Lord to his temple (Mal 3:1). Now the angels suddenly announce his arrival at Bethlehem. The Spirit's coming at Pentecost was sudden (Ac 2:2), as was the appearance of the Lord to Saul on the road to Damascus (Ac 9:3).

The "heavenly host" refers here to an army or band of angels (cf. 1Ki 22:19).

14 The doxology "Glory to God in the highest" is the climax of the story. Its two parts relate to heaven and to earth respectively. In Luke's account of the Triumphal Entry, the crowds say, "Peace in heaven and glory in the highest" (19:38). Verse 14b is best translated as in the NIV: "on earth peace to men on whom his favor rests." Luke emphasizes the work of Christ on earth (cf. 5:24).

The "peace" (GK 1645) here is that which the Messiah brings to those on whom God bestows his grace (cf. 1:79). Those whom Jesus healed or forgave on the basis of their faith could "go in peace" (7:50; 8:48). Those on whom God's "favor" rests are the "little children" (10:21) to whom God reveals truth according to his "good pleasure."

15–16 Luke does not say that the angels disappeared but that they went "into heaven." The realization of God's promise is expressed both here and in v.29. In other words, Luke combines the phenomena of ancient (v.15) and recent (v.29) prophetic words, thus emphasizing the connection between the old and new ages, the Jewish orientation of the Gospel and the reality of the heavenly in the earthly.

With a heightened sense of excitement and determination, the shepherds rushed off to the baby's side.

17–18 Then they "spread the word" and became the first evangelists of the Christian era. Luke's observation that those who heard them "were amazed" is the first of his many comments on the enthusiastic response to the messianic proclamation (see vv.33, 47; 4:22; 8:25; et al.).

19–20 In contrast to the overreaction of the people, Mary meditates on the meaning of it all (cf. v.51). Just as the seventy-two disciples later returned with joy after their preaching mission (10:17), so the shepherds returned "glorifying and praising God" (v.20). It is clear that in Luke this spirit of doxology is the proper response to the mighty words of God (cf. 5:25–26; 7:16; 13:13; et al.).

C. Jesus' Early Years (2:21–52)

1. Presentation of Jesus in the temple (2:21–40)

21–24 It is important to understand the sequence and background of these events. According to Jewish law a woman became ceremonially unclean on the birth of a child. On the eighth day a male child was circumcised (cf. 1:59; Ge 17:12), after which the mother was unclean an additional thirty-three days (Lev 12:1–5). At the conclusion of this period, the mother offered a sacrifice, either a lamb or, if she was poor, two doves or two young pigeons (Lev 12:6–8). In addition, the first son was to be presented to the Lord and then, so to speak, bought back with an offering (Nu 18:15). Luke, conflating the performance of these OT obligations into this single narrative, shows how Jesus was reared in conformity with them. His parents obeyed the Lord (1:31) in naming him. The offering of birds instead of a lamb shows that he was born into a poor family. Perhaps this helped him identify with the poor of the land (cf. 6:20).

25 In vv.25–38 Luke presents two pious figures who testify to the significance of Jesus. Once again Luke assures us of the credentials of Jesus as Messiah, taking care to show that each witness is an authentic representative of Judaism.

The first of these, Simeon, is simply described as "righteous and devout" (cf. 1:6). He could be described as one of the believing remnant of Judaism, looking forward to the Messianic Age in its spiritual aspect. It is appropriate that the Spirit, who is the Consoler (cf. Jn 14:16), was upon one who awaited the consolation—the time when God would end Israel's suffering with the Advent of the Messiah (cf. Isa 49:13; 57:18; 61:2).

26–28 The same Spirit had revealed to Simeon that the Messiah would come before he died. This may imply that he was an old man.

Mary and Joseph are referred to as Jesus' "parents" (v.27) and as "the child's father and mother" (v.33). Jesus would have been considered Joseph's own son, so Luke's terminology is not inconsistent. In the genealogy, however, the particulars of the relationship had to be made more explicit (3:23). Luke notes the providential timing in that the Spirit brings Simeon to the temple courts at the same time as the family's arrival. In this touching scene, Luke again shows the presence of Jesus, now in Simeon's arms, as an occasion of praise to God.

29–32 Simeon's psalm begins by emphasizing the fact that the Messiah has indeed come. "Dismiss" here means "allow to die"; peace is again stressed (cf. 2:14). On "as you promised," see comment on v.15.

Simeon does not say that he has seen the Messiah but rather that his eyes have seen God's salvation. To see Jesus is to see salvation embodied in him, a theme already noted as prominent in Luke (cf. 1:69, 71, 77; 19:9). Luke's concern for the universal application of the Gospel finds support in the words "in the sight of all people" (cf. Ps 98:3; Isa 52:10). In v.32, not only are Gentiles and Jews put in contrast, but the same light (Isa 49:6) that brings "revelation" to pagans (cf. 1:78–79) brings "glory" to Israel (cf. 1:77).

33–35 In spite of what they already know, Joseph and Mary are amazed (v.33; cf. comment on v.17) at Simeon's song. Moreover, Simeon adds a solemn note by predicting that because of the child "many in Israel" would be brought to moral decision, some to a point of collapse and others to what can well be called a resurrection (*anastasis;* GK *414;* NIV, "rising"). But there will be a cost to Jesus; he will be vulnerable to the hostility of unbelievers, who reject not only him but the whole of God's revelation (v.35; cf. Jn 5:45–47). This clash will inevitably wound Jesus' mother.

36–38 Luke's attention to the renewal of prophecy through Zechariah and Simeon at the coming of the Messianic Age continues with the introduction of Anna as a "prophetess." Prophetesses functioned in both OT and NT times (Ex 15:20; Jdg 4:4; 2Ki 22:14; Ac 2:17; 21:9). Apparently Anna could trace her genealogy; and, though the tribe of Asher was not outstanding (Ge 30:12–13; 35:26), Luke considered it important to show her true Jewishness. She was a familiar figure at the temple. Possibly she lived as a widow in one of the rooms surrounding the temple precinct. Once more Luke points out the providential timing. Anna, like Simeon, had been expecting the Messianic kingdom, and like the shepherds, she spread the news about Jesus.

39–40 Luke takes another opportunity to mention the fidelity of Jesus' parents to the Jewish law. He omits mention of the flight to Egypt (an event important to Matthew because it provided him with another example of fulfilled prophecy; see Mt 2:13–15). What is significant is that Jesus' parents were faithful to the Jewish law and that the child grew normally, the object of God's grace (v.40; cf. v.52).

2. The boy Jesus at the temple (2:41–52)

This section provides the only biblical account of Jesus' boyhood. The focal point is not his precocious wisdom, noteworthy as that was. Rather, Luke leads us to the real climax, Jesus' reference to God as "my Father" (v.49). This is the first recorded instance of Jesus' awareness that in a unique way he was the Son of God.

41–42 Luke takes yet another opportunity to emphasize the fidelity of Jesus' family to Judaism. Adults were supposed to attend the three major feasts in Jerusalem annually—Passover, Pentecost, and Tabernacles. For many this was impossible, but an effort was made to go at least to Passover. With puberty, a boy became a "son of the covenant," a custom continued in the present bar-mitzvah ceremony. It was considered helpful for a boy to attend the Jerusalem festivals for one or two years before becoming a son of the covenant so that he would realize what his new relationship involved.

43–47 At this intermediate age, Jesus might have been either with the women and children or with the men and older boys, the way the families were probably grouped. Each parent might have supposed he was with the other. After a day of travel Mary and Joseph missed Jesus; another day would have been required for the trip back, and on the next day ("after three days," v.46) the successful search was made.

The questions Jesus put to the teachers were probably not merely boyish inquiries but the kind of probing questions used in ancient academies and similar discussions. He also gave answers, some of which amazed the teachers.

48 Luke vividly describes the parents' emotions, the first of which is astonishment and awe (cf. v.33). His mother's natural concern then issues very humanly in a hint of scolding. Next she indicates their anxious pain as they hunted for him.

49–50 Jesus' answer, "Why were you searching for me?", pointedly prepares the hearer for a significant statement that is then understood as being theologically inevitable (cf. also 24:5–6). The importance of Jesus' use of the phrase "my Father," with its implied designation of himself as the unique Son of the Father, is heightened not only by the preceding question but by the subsequent statement of v.50, which underlines the awesome mystery of Jesus' statement of filial consciousness.

51 Luke hurries on to assure us also of Jesus' perfect humanity by noting his obedience to his parents. Once more Mary reflects inwardly on the significance of it all (cf. v.19; Ge 37:11).

52 Jesus' growth was entirely normal. His growth in wisdom does not detract from his deity, for Jesus willingly gave up the full use of his divine powers (Php 2:7). "Stature" likely refers to his personal development, i.e., maturity.

III. Preparation for Jesus' Ministry (3:1–4:13)

A. The Ministry of John the Baptist (3:1–20)

This narrative, like the foregoing, bears Palestinian Jewish characteristics in its language, themes, and setting. Verse 2 reflects the opening words of the OT prophets (e.g., Isa 1:1; Jer 1:1–3; Hos 1:1; Am 1:1). At this point in history, after a long silence, the prophetic word was again being heard.

1 The dating provided in this verse was useful to Luke's first-century readers to place the ministry of John. Since Luke was probably using the normal Roman method of reckoning, the date indicated would be from August, A.D. 28, to August, A.D. 29.

"Herod" is Herod Antipas, son of Herod the Great, who ruled Galilee and Perea 4 B.C.–A.D. 39 (cf. Lk 3:19–20; 13:31; 23:7). Philip, another son of Herod the Great, ruled a group of territories to the northeast of Palestine (4 B.C.–A.D. 33/34). Lysanias is unknown except through inscriptions. Pontius Pilate was governor of Judea A.D. 26–36.

2 The official high priesthood of Annas had ended in A.D. 15, but his influence was so great, especially during the high priesthood of his son-in-law Caiaphas (A.D. 18–36; cf. Jn 18:13), that his name is naturally mentioned along with that of Caiaphas. With the reference to the high priests, we move from the secular world to the religious and are ready for the introduction of the prophet John. He is in the desert, a place that held memories for the Jews as the locale of the post-Exodus wanderings of Israel. Luke's interest is not only in the coming of John, but in the message he brought from God.

3 Luke suggests that John had an itinerant ministry. Apparently he not only preached in the desert but followed the Dead Sea coast to the Jordan River and then a distance away from there. John's baptism was "of repentance" (GK 3567), that is, it required sorrow for sin and a moral change on the part of those being baptized (vv.8–14; see also 5:32; 15:7; 24:47 for Luke's use of this word). Repentance is an ancient prophetic theme (e.g., Eze 18:21, 30). The result of the repentance shown in baptism was forgiveness.

4–6 Luke found a clear prophecy of the ministry of John the Baptist in Isa 40:3. He includes more of the quotation than Matthew and Mark do. First he cites the extraordinary way in which, on the analogy of preparations made for a royal visitor, even the seemingly immovable must be removed to make way for the Lord (vv.4–5). What needs removal is the sin of the people.

Luke concludes the Isaiah quotation with words that aptly describe his own evangelistic and theological conviction: everyone will see God's salvation. Luke finds here (following the LXX version of Isa 40:5) a biblical basis for his own universal concern and his central theme of salvation.

7 The word "crowds" (GK 4063) represents an unidentified, assorted group of people who came out to the desert to see him (cf. Mt 3:7, where Matthew identifies them as Pharisees and Sadducees).

John's language is strong, as was that of OT prophets who preceded him. He refers to God's anger (cf. Ro 2:5; 1Th 1:10), not God's kingdom, as Jesus did (Lk 4:43). His question suggests that while their "coming out to be baptized by him" was the proper thing to do, their motives were in question.

8–9 The language is picturesque. Two images are presented. First, a tree that does not produce fruit should be chopped down and removed to make way for one that will (cf. 6:43–45; 13:6–9). The imagery may be intended to call to mind the figure of Israel as a fig tree or vine (cf. Isa 5:1–7). The second image, the ax "at the root," symbolizes an impending radical action, the destruction of the whole tree.

Mere physical descent from Abraham is not important (cf. Jn 8:31–43; Ro 9:6–8; Gal 3:6–9); God can create his own children out of stones, just as he can cause inanimate stones to praise his Son if humans remain silent (19:40). The threat of judgment is heightened through the imagery of fire, a theme reintroduced in the reference to Jesus' ministry (vv.16–17).

10–11 John's prophetic word of judgment elicits a response, first from the crowd in general, then from the unpopular and greedy tax collectors (v.12), and finally from the soldiers (v.14). The conversations, which are unique to Luke, provide opportunity for some clear statements about social justice and responsibility.

The crowd (v.7) is told to share clothing and food with the needy as evidence of repentance. The "tunic" was the short garment worn under the longer robe. One might have an extra tunic for warmth or as a change of clothes.

12–13 The "tax collectors" (v.12) were part of a despised system (cf. 5:27; 15:1). Of the three groups mentioned, they would have been considered most in need of repentance. The chief tax collectors, such as Zacchaeus (19:2), bid money for their position. Their profit came from collecting more than they paid the Romans. They then hired other tax collectors to work for them. Because their work and associations rendered them ritually unclean and because they regularly extorted money, they were alienated from Jewish society and linked with "sinners" (cf. Mk 2:15–16). While John shows social concern, he does not advocate overthrowing the system but rather reforming the abuses.

14 The "soldiers" were probably Jewish, assigned to internal affairs (cf. comment on 22:4). The very nature of their work gave them opportunity to commit the sins specified, for they could use threats of reprisal to extort money from the people. Here again John stresses ministering to the needs of others over against personal greed.

15–17 The question naturally arose whether such a radical prophet as John might be the Messiah (cf. Jn 1:19–25). John responds in several ways. The Messiah is "more powerful" than he is (v.16). The Messiah is worthy of such reverence that even the task of tying his sandals is more than John feels worthy of (cf. Jn 3:30).

The Messiah will baptize, not with water in a preparatory way, as John was doing, but actually "with the Holy Spirit and with fire" (v.16). That is, the coming of the Spirit is to have the effect of fire. John uses an agricultural image to explain this. When grain is tossed in the air with a "winnowing fork," the lighter and heavier elements are separated, with the heavier grain falling on the "threshing floor" and being stored for use. The "chaff," on the other hand, is burned up.

Fire is an ancient symbol of judgment, refinement, and purification (cf. Ge 19:26; Am 7:4; Mal 3:2). John is thus portraying the Holy Spirit as being active in saving, purifying, and judging. The Spirit had definitely, though not frequently, been associated with the Messiah (Isa 11:1–2), whose coming would mean also the availability of the Spirit's ministry.

18 That John not only "exhorted" the people but "preached the good news" (GK *2294*) shows that grace accompanied the warning to flee from judgment. It is noteworthy that Luke uses the word "people" (GK *3295*) here, a term usually reserved for a potentially responsive group. They apparently stayed on to hear more of John's message and heard the further proclamation of "good news."

19–20 "Herod" is Herod Antipas, mentioned in v.1. His wife, Herodias, had left his brother Philip to marry Herod. That marriage was one of his many sins, and the climactic sin "added" to this sordid series was his imprisonment of John (cf. the story of his death in 9:7–9). Luke underscores both the boldness of John and the sickness of the society he called to account. Verse 20 also indicates that John's ministry was completed before that of Jesus began.

B. The Baptism of Jesus (3:21–22)

21 As in the birth narratives, there is at Jesus' baptism a supernatural attestation. Many see in this event his "call" to his mission. His baptism comes as the climax of the baptism of "all the people."

Jesus was baptized, not because he was a sinner in need of repentance, but as a way of identifying himself with those he came to save (see comment on Mk 1:9). This is the first of several important events in Luke that took place when Jesus prayed (cf. esp. 6:12; 9:18, 29; 22:41). Luke's description of the opening of the heavens makes clear that Jesus had a true vision of the Deity (cf. Eze 1:1; Ac 7:56; 10:11).

22 God had appeared in OT times through various theophanies. Now the Spirit appears in bodily form as a dove. Luke does not say that anyone other than Jesus was aware of the Holy Spirit. Perhaps others present saw only a dove without realizing its significance. This was followed by a voice, designating Jesus as the unique Son of God. The words, like those heard at the Transfiguration (9:35; see comments), blend two OT christological passages (Ps 2:7; Isa 42:1). The concept of divine sonship in Jewish thought was not only applicable to angels (Job 1:6; 2:1) and to the nation of Israel and her kings (Ex 4:22; 2Sa 7:14; Hos 11:1), but it was also coming into use as a designation for the Messiah (cf. Lk 1:32). The words "love" (GK 28) and "well pleased" (Gk 2305) convey the idea of choice and special relationship. Jesus has now received his commission.

C. Jesus' Genealogy (3:23–38)

23–38 The age of Jesus is given in approximate terms. He might have been in his mid-thirties. "Thirty" might also indicate that, like the priests who began their service at that age, he was ready to devote himself to God's work.

Both Matthew and Luke recognize the importance of establishing a genealogy for Jesus, in accordance with the care given such matters in ancient Israel. In their handling of Jesus' genealogy, Matthew and Luke differ in several ways. (1) Matthew begins his gospel with the genealogy, thereby establishing an immediate connection with the OT and with Israel. Luke waits till the significant part of the ministry of John the Baptist is completed and Jesus stands alone as the designated Son of God. (2) Matthew begins with Abraham, stressing Jesus' Jewish ancestry; Luke, in reverse order, goes back to Adam, probably with the intention of stressing the identification of Jesus with the entire human race. (3) Matthew groups his names symmetrically; Luke simply lists them. (4) Both trace the lineage back through ancestral lines that diverge for a number of generations from each other, though both meet at the generation of David. (5) Matthew includes the names of several women (a feature one might have expected in Luke because of his understanding and respect for women).

The significance of the genealogy in Luke probably lies in the emphasis on Jesus as a member of the human race. He implicitly contrasts the obedient second Adam, the true Son of God, with the disobedient first Adam.

The differences outlined above, as well as some problems of detail, are perhaps best explained, at least in part, by the assumption that the legal line of Jesus is traced in Matthew, the actual line of descent in Luke. The widow of a childless man could marry his brother so that a child of the second marriage could legally be considered as the son of the deceased man in order to perpetuate his name. In a genealogy the child could be listed under his natural or his legal father. Joseph is listed as the son of Heli in Luke but as the son of Jacob in Matthew. On the levirate marriage theory, Heli and Jacob may have been half-brothers, with the same mother but fathers of different names. Perhaps Heli died and Jacob married his widow. Or alternately, it is possible that Jacob died without leaving any children of his own and thus his nephew, a son of his brother Heli (i.e., Joseph), became his heir.

D. The Temptation of Jesus (4:1–13)

This vivid narrative (vv. 1–13) contains an important blend of theological themes—the divine sonship and messiahship of Jesus, the warfare between Christ and Satan, OT theology, and principles of obedience to the divine Word.

1–2 Jesus is in the desert for a period of forty days. This probably parallels Israel's experience in the desert after the exodus; it may also allude to Moses' forty days without food on the mountain (Dt 9:9). The parallel with Israel becomes stronger if it is meant as a comparison between Israel as God's "son" (Ex 4:22–23; Hos 11:1), who failed when tested, and Jesus as his unique Son, who conquered temptation. God led Israel into the desert; likewise the Spirit led Jesus. In the former case, God tested his people; now God allows the devil to tempt his Son.

It is important here to distinguish between three kinds of tempting. (1) Satan tempts people, i.e., lures them to do evil. God never does this nor can he himself be tempted in this way (Jas 1:13). (2) People may tempt (test) God in the sense of provoking him through unreasonable demands contrary to faith. This is what Israel did in the desert (cf. v.12). (3) God tests (but does not tempt) his people, as he did in the desert (Ex 16:4; Dt 8:2).

In this temptation by the devil, the Lord Jesus shows the validity of what God had just said of him: "With you I am well pleased" (3:22).

In this section we see several contrasts. Israel failed God's test, while Jesus fully obeyed his Father. John also contrasts Jesus, who is both filled with and led by the Spirit (note Luke's emphasis on the Spirit), and the

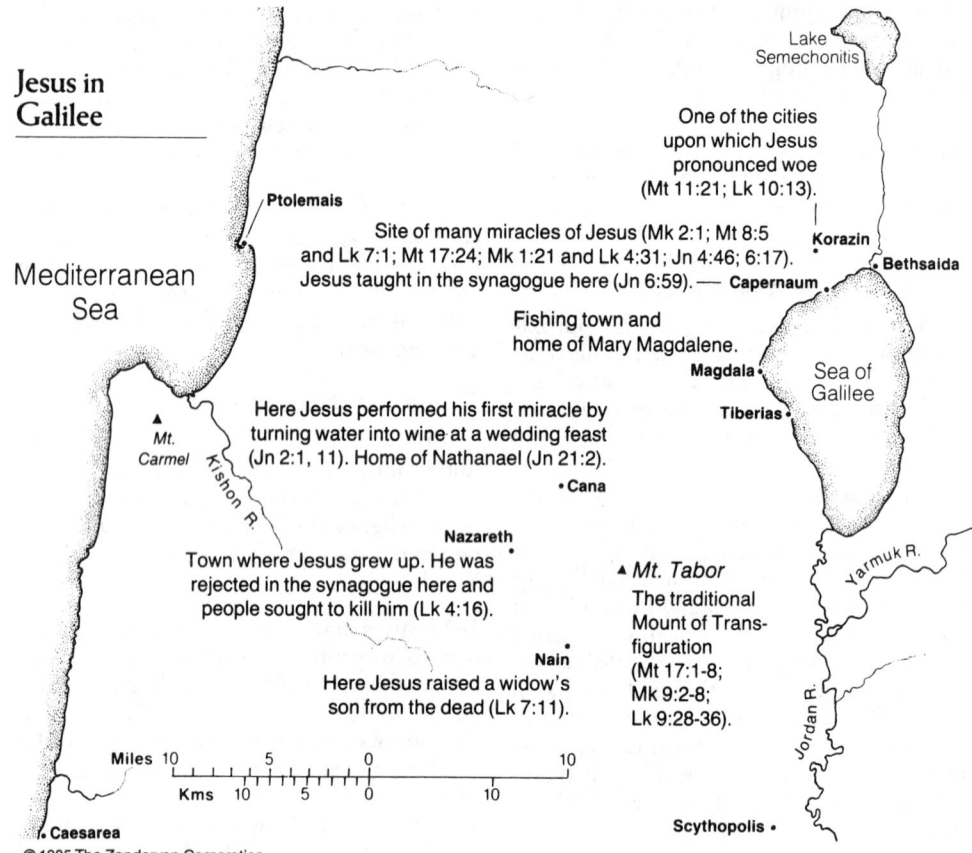

devil, who opposes both Christ and the Spirit. Finally, Luke implies a contrast between Jesus as "hungry," i.e., physically empty, and yet as "full of the Spirit." Our own experience is usually the reverse.

3–4 The "devil" (Gk *1333*) has several names in the Bible: notably the OT name "Satan" (e.g., 4:8; 10:18; 11:18). He opposes God and God's servants (1Ch 21:1; Job 1:6–12; 2:1–7; Zec 3:1–2). He may seem to be ubiquitous but is not omnipresent. Sometimes he works indirectly through the evil spirits who form his domain (cf. 11:14–20). The devil begins his temptation by picking up on the declaration of Jesus' sonship in 3:22.

The reference to bread is probably a temptation for Jesus to satisfy his own need and gratify himself. But since bread is not inherently evil (cf. 11:3), the main issue is not one of allurement to perverted self-gratification (as in Jas 1:14–15), but a challenge to act apart from faithful dependence on God.

Jesus' reply is brief, a partial quotation of Dt 8:2, where Moses was reminding Israel of God's testing of them for forty years. The next verse (Dt 8:3) specifically refers to hunger and the provision of manna, which the Lord gave Israel so that the people might know that humans need not merely bread but the sustaining word of God.

Thus, while he is being "tempted" (GK *4279*) by the devil, Jesus is also proving faithful to God, in contrast to Israel's response when they were "tested" by God in the desert. Jesus is dependent on God and obedient to his word.

5–8 The second temptation involves similar issues. In a vision, the devil takes Jesus to a "high place" and offers him the world. Once again, what the devil offered was legitimate in itself. The Messiah would one day rule all the world, possessing all "authority and splendor." In this temptation the devil claims to possess the world, a claim that Jesus neither challenges nor acknowledges.

Had Jesus accepted the devil's offer, our salvation would have been impossible. First, Jesus would have sinned by giving worship to the devil and thus could not have offered himself a perfect sacrifice for our sins. Second, Scripture teaches that the Messiah should first suffer and only then "enter his glory" (24:26). Had Jesus listened, he would have been avoiding the Cross.

By quoting Dt 6:13, Jesus responded as the perfect human being should respond, worshiping and serving God alone. Both of the OT texts Jesus quoted so far (vv.4, 8) are more than weapons against the devil; they apply to Jesus himself.

9–12 Luke records this temptation in the last rather than second place (cf. Mt 4:5–7). The essence of this temptation is that of presuming on God and displaying before others one's special favor with him. In this instance the devil quotes a passage of Scripture (Ps 91:11–12) out of context—the mere use of Bible words does not necessarily convey the will of God (v.10). The rabbinic tradition that the Messiah would appear on top of the temple may provide a background that accounts for the form of this temptation, even though the idea of jumping down from the temple is absent.

Again Jesus responds with Scripture (v.12), this time quoting Dt 6:16. Jesus applies the words to his own refusal to tempt God. That is, he will not repeat the sin that Israel committed in the desert by putting God to the test. To do that would be to provoke God in unbelief by making inappropriate demands for a divine sign to be used for display.

13 The devil leaves only temporarily until a more opportune time (cf. 22:53; 23:35, 37, 39).

IV. The Galilean Ministry (4:14–9:50)

A. Initial Phase (4:14–6:16)

1. First approach and rejection at Nazareth (4:14–30)

14–15 Once again, as Jesus enters a new phase of his experience, Luke mentions the special activity of the Holy Spirit. So far we have seen the Spirit's activity at Jesus' conception (1:35), baptism (3:22), and temptation (4:1). The "news" that spread about Jesus and the fact that "everyone praised him" are the first of several observations Luke makes about public response to Jesus' ministry (cf. vv.22, 28, 32, 36–37).

This passage (vv.16–30) has an important place in the Lukan presentation, for it marks the beginning of Luke's record of Jesus' ministry. The setting is Nazareth, the place of Jesus' childhood. A lengthy quotation from Isaiah (vv.18–19) issues in a proclamation of immediate fulfillment. Jesus also implies the selection of Gentiles for divine favor (vv.24–27). Since Luke places this event so early in Jesus' ministry (cf. Mk 6:1–6), he obviously considers it of prime importance (whether there were two "rejections at Nazareth" is impossible to say with certainty). Also, a pattern appears here that is unveiled more clearly later on in Luke-Acts: (1) the presentation of the Gospel to Jews in their synagogues, (2) rejection, and (3) turning to the wider Gentile world (cf. Ac 13:46).

16–17 Luke emphasizes that Jesus was in the town in which he grew up and stresses Jesus' Jewish piety by referring to his custom of synagogue attendance. This strengthens the contrast with his rejection. Jesus stood up to read the Scriptures; the passage chosen for that particular Sabbath was Isa 61:1–2, with the words "to release the oppressed" taken from Isa 58:6. The variation from the usual wording may simply reflect the interpretive translation in use at that time.

18–19 The quotation has significance both as our Lord's statement of his call to his saving ministry and as Luke's affirmation of this ministry as thematic in his gospel. Jesus identifies himself as the subject of Isaiah's prophetic word. Three elements are emphasized here. (1) Jesus is the bearer of the Spirit received at his baptism (3:22–23; cf. comment on 4:14). His ministry will be uniquely marked by the presence of the Spirit as prophetically foretold. (2) Jesus is an eschatological prophet, a role intertwined with that of John the Baptist as prophetic forerunner (see comments on 1:17 and 7:28). Jesus, not John, was *the* prophet predicted in Dt 18:18 (cf. Jn 1:19–24). Luke gives special attention to Jesus as a prophet in a number of ways (v.24; 7:16, 39; 13:33; 24:19; Ac 3:22; 7:37, 52). In the present passage, the prophetic mission described by Isaiah, a mission of proclamation of "good news," is accepted by Jesus. (3) The prophetic role of Jesus overlaps his role as Messiah. His ministry of deliverance for the oppressed is messianic in character. This assumption probably lay behind the doubts in John's mind when his release from prison was not forthcoming (7:18–19).

The "good news" (v.18; GK *2294*) Jesus was to proclaim recalls both the joyful announcement in 1:19 and the message of the angel in 2:10–11. It also builds on Isa 40:9; 41:27; 52:7. The "poor," like the "prisoners," the "blind," and the "oppressed," are not only the unfortunate of this world but those who have special need of dependence on God (cf. comment on 6:20). Luke 7:22 cites some ways Jesus fulfilled this mission.

The "year of the Lord's favor" is reminiscent of the Jubilee (one year in every fifty) when debts were forgiven and slaves set free (Lev 25:8–17). It defines the time in history when God in sovereign grace brings freedom from the guilt and effects of sin. The inclusion of this quotation is consistent with Luke's stress on the dawning of the new age of salvation.

The omission of the next phrase in Isa 61:2—"the day of vengeance of our God"—is also significant. Jesus' audience would suppose that the day of their salvation would be the day of judgment on their pagan enemies, but the delay of judgment means that this time of the Lord's favor benefits the Gentiles also. Jesus affirms (vv.24–27) that Gentiles are also recipients of God's grace, even when Jews were not so blessed.

20 We now have a description of the synagogue procedure. Jesus hands back the scroll to the "attendant," who had the sacred duty of handling the revered scroll. After this was replaced in its cabinet or ark, the reader took the customary sitting position for instructive comments on the passage. Luke begins to record the response of the congregation, which is at first intense attention and ultimately hostility. The phrase "eyes ... were fastened" denotes intense emotion (cf. Ac 1:10; 7:55).

21 The only comment of Jesus that Luke records is short but of the highest importance. He announces the fulfillment of the reading from Isaiah concerning the subject of the prophecy (Jesus) and the time of God's gracious work ("today"; GK *4958*).

The term "fulfilled" (GK *4444*) is not as prominent in Luke as it is in Matthew. Only here and in the Emmaus conversation (24:44) does Luke use the word in relation to the fulfillment of OT prophecy (see comment on 7:1). In other words, these two references to prophetic fulfillment stand out at the beginning and end of Jesus' public appearances, emphasizing the fulfillment of God's eternal purpose in Christ's ministry.

22 The audience appears to have responded first with a positive attitude to Jesus' words. They "were amazed," an expression that does not indicate clearly either favor or disfavor. The cause of their amazement was the kind and wise manner of Jesus' speech or of what he said about the grace of God (cf. Ac 14:3). Certainly Luke appreciates and conveys the gracious nature of Jesus' ministry. But at some point, here or shortly after, the hostility of the audience begins. Their question "Isn't this Joseph's son?" seems to express perplexity and irritation at this man who grew up in the home of a fellow Nazarene and is now making such impressive claims.

23 Jesus' response is not intended to reassure his audience but rather to draw out their subconscious attitudes. Since Jesus had already had a wide teaching ministry (4:15), his phrase "you will quote" probably expresses the reply he would expect the people to make in response to his message in the synagogue—namely, that they would challenge him to fulfill Isaiah's prophecy by doing miracles in the presence of those who heard him. Throughout his ministry Jesus would be challenged to do miraculous signs (e.g., 11:16, 29) to prove his claims.

24 "I tell you the truth" is used six times in Luke to introduce a solemn assertion. This expression shows the authority with which Jesus spoke and is clearly an authentic word of Jesus. This introductory formula appears often in Mark and even more frequently in Matthew. The statement so solemnly introduced anticipates Jesus' rejection. The word "accepted" (GK *1283*) is the same one used in v.19 to describe "the year of the Lord's favor." The double use of this word in this context may be intended to show that, though God desires to accept the people, they are not responding by accepting the prophet who tells them of God's grace. Jesus quotes a common adage that whoever achieves greatness is never fully trusted back home. But here its meaning is the deeper one that Jesus stands in the line of the prophets who were rejected by their own people.

25–27 Jesus does not state here that the prophets Elijah (v.26) and Elisha (v.27) went to Gentiles because they were rejected by the Jews; rather, they went because they were sent there by God. Jesus' audience, however, is becoming more and more enraged as they realize that they will receive no special favors from him and that he considers himself above home ties and tradition.

28–30 Nazareth lay among the ridges of the southern slopes of the Galilean hills. Jesus allowed the crowds to drive him out of the town (as he later did on going to the place of crucifixion). But it was not yet his time to die, and by some unexplained means he made his way out.

2. Driving out an evil spirit (4:31–37)

31–32 Luke has already mentioned Capernaum (v.23), a town on the northwest shore of the Sea of Galilee, as a center of miraculous activity in the ministry of Jesus. The expression "went down" reflects the descent necessary from the elevated situation of Nazareth to the coastal plain.

As was his custom, Jesus attended the synagogue (v.33) and began to teach there. The people listening to him, like those in Nazareth, were amazed, especially because this teacher, who in their eyes was not even a rabbi, taught with authority. The majority of rabbis would base their teaching on the chain of tradition, citing the opinions of their predecessors. Jesus' teaching, however, had authority inherent in his message (cf. v.36).

33–35 While Jesus was speaking, he was interrupted by a demon possessed man. Demon possession is too frequent and integral to the gospel narratives to minimize or, worse, to discard as Hellenistic superstition. The good news preached by Jesus (vv.18, 43) signaled an attack on the forces of evil. A holy war was being launched and the demons knew it. This war would be carried on by Jesus' disciples (9:1–2; 10:8–9, 17).

The "demon" (GK *1228*) is further described as an "evil [or unclean; GK *176*] spirit." An evil spirit is unclean in contrast to the holiness of God and may well cause both moral and physical filth in a possessed human (cf. ZPEB, 2:92–101). The possessed man shrieked, uttered an expression of surprise, and asked a questions that means, "What do we have to do with each other?" The demon, perhaps exemplifying James's comment that "the demons believe and shudder" (Jas 2:19), sensed the purpose of Jesus' presence. In keeping with the pattern in the Gospels, testimony to the truth about Christ comes from a number of different and unexpected sources. The term "the Holy One of God" contrasts strongly with the remark that this was an unclean demon.

Jesus responded sternly with a command to be silent. In this action we may see the beginning of a pattern of prohibiting the premature proclamation of his identity. Throughout the Gospels Jesus guards the fact of his messiahship, probably (1) to prevent a misinterpretation that would draw to him revolutionary-minded dissidents seeking a leader against Rome (see comment on Mk 1:44); (2) to allow his messianic works themselves to establish his authority among true believers (cf. Lk 7:18–23; see also comment on 5:14); and (3) possibly to avoid an inappropriate self-proclamation as Messiah (some studies suggest that the Jews felt that the true Messiah would allow others to proclaim him as such, rather than doing so himself).

What follows is not technically an exorcism, because Jesus does not use an incantation or invoke the authority of another. Instead he speaks a simple word of command on his own authority. Luke, always interested as a physician in the physical condition of people, observes that the demon came out violently but without hurting the man.

36–37 Once again Luke notes the amazement of the people—this time not only at his teaching and authority but also at his power. Luke's theme of the spread of the Gospel finds expression in the conclusion of the narrative.

3. Healing many (4:38–44)

38–39 Jesus' healing ministry continues in a more private setting, in the home of Peter's mother-in-law (this is the first time Peter is mentioned in this gospel). Both this passage and 1Co 9:5 inform us that Peter was married. A crisis of serious illness in the family gives occasion for Jesus to help. Jesus "rebukes" the impersonal fever, as he had earlier rebuked the demon; perhaps a personal evil force had caused the fever (cf. 13:16), or the fever is simply personified, or Luke is emphasizing the active force of Jesus' word. The woman immediately rises, and, doubtless in keeping with her character, begins to serve the group.

40–41 One of the most beautiful scenes in Scripture now follows. The crowds have apparently waited till evening, after the Sabbath was over. In the remaining hours of diminishing light, they perform the labor of love they could not do on the Sabbath, carrying the sick to Jesus. It is noteworthy that Jesus himself has not yet ventured out on the Sabbath to perform healings publicly (see 6:1–11). Luke carefully distinguishes between those who were just sick and those who were demon-possessed. This warns us not to assume that the gospel writers thought all disease was caused by demons. Luke mentions that Jesus laid his hands on the people who came to him, showing that Jesus was the source of the healing power and that he had a personal concern. The demons called Jesus "the Son of God" (see comment on v.34). Jesus' command for them to be silent is here amplified from v.35.

42–44 Shifting quickly from dusk to dawn, Luke portrays Jesus in a sharply contrasted setting. He is alone. Surprisingly, in view of his special attention to prayer (cf. 5:16), Luke does not tell us that Jesus is praying (cf. Mk 1:35). But Luke does strongly affirm why Jesus refused to linger at Capernaum. He felt an urgent need ("must"; GK *1256*) to preach the kingdom of God throughout all "the land of the Jews" (see NIV note). That is why God sent him into the world.

Here, then, Luke has provided representative incidents from the ministry of Jesus. It is the kind of activity summarized in Ac 10:38 as "doing good and healing all who were under the power of the devil."

4. Calling the first disciples (5:1–11)

In contrast to Mt 4:18–22 and Mk 1:16–20, Luke's account of the call of the disciples is much more complete, containing the unique encounter between Jesus and Peter. Luke also stresses the sovereignty and holiness of Jesus and mentions the total abandonment of the disciples' possessions as an act of discipleship (cf. 14:33). In all these gospels the climax is a call to "catch men," followed by the obedience of the disciples.

1–3 Luke begins this story mentioning the pressure of the crowds, as he occasionally does elsewhere (8:42, 45; 19:3). Their attention is on the "word of God" spoken by Jesus. The shore of the lake provided an excellent, acoustically serviceable amphitheater. Luke, being observant of detail, draws our attention to two boats, and then singles out Simon as the owner of one of them. Jesus gets into the boat and again teaches, his voice carrying across the water to the crowds.

4–5 The sharp contrast between the expert but unsuccessful fisherman and Jesus needs no comment. Jesus' command must have seemed unreasonable to them after their failure during the night. Peter, here called by his original name, Simon, demurs; but he does what Jesus says.

6–11 Luke now moves quickly to three focal points in his narrative. (1) He describes the gathering of the fish. The details of the breaking nets and loaded boats help give the narrative the ring of truth. (2) The miracle moves Peter, overcome by awe, to abase himself before Jesus. He is gripped not merely by a sense of his inferiority to the "Lord," but by his own sinfulness (in spite of his being a law-abiding Jew) (cf. Isa 6:5). Luke's reason for including this incident may be not only to portray the confrontation of human sinfulness with Jesus but also to show that to receive the saving grace of Christ a "sinful" person must repent. (3) Peter obeys Jesus in letting down the net, and Jesus follows this up by declaring that he will "catch men" from then on (v.10b). In view of Luke's emphasis on the kindness of God reaching out to embrace all humankind, this phrase signifies a beneficent ingathering of human fish. It presages the widening horizons of both Luke and Acts, culminating, in a sense, in Peter's vision symbolizing the reception of Gentiles into the church and his subsequent witness to the Gentile Cornelius (Ac 10:9–48, esp. vv.34–35).

The disciples then leave everything and follow Jesus, underscoring the condition of discipleship Jesus taught later on (14:33; cf. 18:22).

5. The man with leprosy (5:12–16)

12 Leprosy is a general term in Scripture for certain skin diseases. Though not necessarily equivalent to what we know as Hansen's disease (see ZPEB 2:138), they were repulsive and resulted in physical, social, and psychological isolation of their victims (cf. Lev 13, esp. v.45). Luke is once again careful to note the nature and extent of a disease ("covered with leprosy"). The assumption is that the man has some knowledge of Jesus' prior miracles. Just as Peter fell at Jesus' feet for shame at his sinfulness (v.8), this man falls face downward for shame at his uncleanness. The appellation "Lord" (GK 3261) doubtless has less meaning than on Peter's lips (v.8), meaning here little more than "Sir." The condition "if you are willing" may express a sense of unworthiness rather than doubt as to Jesus' ability or kindness.

13 The very act of touching is significant, especially since lepers were always kept at a distance. Perhaps our contemporary society, having rediscovered the significance of touching as a means of communicating concern, can identify with Jesus' kindness in touching the leper. Such contact also symbolized the transfer of healing power (cf. 8:44). Jesus' "I am willing" meets the man's need of reassurance; he was healed "immediately."

14 The command to silence follows Jesus' pattern (see comments on 4:35, 41). Jesus wanted first to do the works of the Messiah and to fulfill his basic mission of sacrificial suffering before being publicly proclaimed as Messiah.

For the cleansed leper to show himself to the priest was essential, both to observe the ritual prescribed in Lev 14 and to demonstrate the messianic act of healing "as a testimony to them" (see comments on 7:21–23).

15–16 If the command to silence is part of a pattern in the Gospels, so is the failure to obey it. The immediate effect of the healing is Jesus' increased popularity. Though this popularity leads others to come and be healed (v.15), Jesus is forced to withdraw to deserted areas in order to seek quiet. Once again Luke speaks of Jesus' habit of prayer (cf. comment on 3:21).

6. Healing a paralytic (5:17–26)

Jesus' activities inevitably brought him into confrontation with the religious authorities. The Gospels actually focus on several such occasions. Luke is especially concerned in his gospel and in Acts to clarify the original relationship between Christianity and Judaism and to show the reasons why the Gospel had to break out of the confines of Judaism. Here he stresses the authority of Jesus once more. In 4:32 Jesus' teaching was authoritative; 4:36 shows his authority over demons; 5:24 shows his authority to forgive sins.

17 Jesus was teaching over a period of some time, and this event occurred on one of those days. It seems that Jesus' reputation had aroused the attention of the Jewish religious authorities, who considered it important to hear what he was teaching. By doing this Luke lays stress on the crucial nature of the religious issues soon to be raised. This is his first mention of the "Pharisees and teachers of the law."

The "Pharisees" (GK 5757) had, earlier in their history, helped the Jews maintain the purity of their religion by teaching how the Mosaic Law and the traditions that grew up alongside it ought to be applied in daily life. Many of them became rigid, imbalanced, and hypocritical (see comments on 11:37–54).

The "teachers of the law" (GK 3791), most of whom were Pharisees, had expert knowledge of the details of the Jewish legal tradition and so would be expected to form an opinion about the correctness of Jesus' teaching.

Luke then turns from Jesus' teaching ministry to that of healing. These two elements, doctrine and healing power, serve as a climax to this narrative.

18–19 The friends of the paralytic were motivated by earnestness and faith. The typical flat roof could be reached by an outside stairway. Roofing materials were separable without being damaged.

20 Two declarations form the focal point of this narrative. The first is a declaration of forgiveness, the second an affirmation of Jesus' authority to make that declaration. The plural reference in the term "their faith" is to the faith of the four who brought the paralytic man, though we may assume from his subsequent forgiveness that he also believed. God responds to the intercession of others regarding a person in need. Those who brought the paralytic to Jesus believed that Jesus would save him, though the paralytic's salvation was an intensely personal matter between him and Jesus.

Jesus' declaration of the forgiveness of the paralytic's sin does not imply that sin was the immediate cause of his disease (see also Jn 9:2; 1Co 11:29–30).

21 In Jewish law conviction of blasphemy (an overt defilement of the divine name) was a capital crime penalized by stoning. Pharisees and teachers of the law were convinced that Jesus had crossed over the line.

22–23 Luke indicates that Jesus exercised extraordinary knowledge by having insight into one's inner thoughts. He placed his challengers in a hypothetical dilemma (v.23; cf. 6:9; 20:3–44). Obviously while Jesus' two options are in one sense equally easy to say (and equally impossible to do), in another sense it is easier to say that which cannot be proved or disproved: "Your sins are forgiven."

24 The structure of this sentence is broken by the redirecting of Jesus' comments from the leaders to the man. Thus a focus is maintained both on Jesus' running controversy with the religious leaders and on his ministry to the paralytic.

Here is the first appearance of the term "Son of Man" in Luke (see comment on Mk 8:31). It occurs in connection with the right to pronounce forgiveness rather than with the themes of suffering and glory that characterize its specific use in the other passages where it is used.

25–26 The healing validates the declaration of forgiveness. The command to the paralyzed man is impossible of fulfillment—except for the power of God. To respond took an act of obedience based on faith, and he stood up "immediately." The result is the glorification of God (see comment on 2:20), both by the man and by the crowd. The onlookers were also filled with awe at the powerful demonstration of God's word (cf. Ac 2:12). The final word is "today." Its use in this particular position, at the very end of the passage, strikingly recalls its occurrence as the first word said by Jesus after reading the Isaiah passage in Nazareth (4:21). By including it here Luke assures the reader that this indeed is the awaited eschatological "today."

7. Calling Levi (5:27–32)

The succession of people on whom the Lord bestows his favor continues. We have seen his grace to a demoniac, a leper, and a paralytic; and now we see it given to a tax collector. So Jesus liberates those suffering from malign spirits, physical handicap, and social disfavor. The antagonists, the Pharisees and teachers of the law (who were merely named in the preceding narrative), are again on the scene.

27–28 Levi (i.e., Matthew; see comment on Mt 9:9) was a tax collector (see comment on Lk 3:12); he obviously was treated by the Pharisees as a religious outcast.

The direct command of Jesus to follow him results in Levi's immediate and total obedience. Luke notes both the negative aspect (leaving everything) and the positive one (following Jesus) of what Levi did (see 9:23–25 for Jesus' comments on this pattern).

29–30 A banquet in the NT symbolizes joy and often hints at the eschatological banquet (see comments on Mk 14:25; Lk 13:28–30). Jesus is the guest of honor; but Levi does not limit the guest list to his new Christian friends, the disciples of Jesus. Instead of immediately cutting off his old associates, Levi invites them into his home, probably to bring them also into contact with Jesus. Luke mentions "others," who turn out to be "sinners," as far as the Pharisees are concerned. The joy of the participants is now opposed by the dour criticism of the religious leaders.

The complaint of the Pharisees is based on their dedication to upholding the purity of Jewish faith and life. Implicit in their teachings was strict adherence to both law and tradition, including necessary rites of purification and separation from all whose moral or ritual purity might be in question.

Their complaint against Jesus is specifically directed to his acceptance of these despised people sitting down in table fellowship with them. No act, apart from participation in the actual sinful deeds of the guests, could have broken the wall of separation more dramatically. Yet the Pharisees are not yet ready to argue with Jesus himself, so they direct their question to Jesus' disciples and also charge them with this unacceptable conduct.

31–32 Jesus not only originated certain proverbs and parables but also made wise use of current ones. So, citing a self-evident proverb of his day, he described his mission in terms that he would go on to amplify in the parables in chapter 15. Since no one is truly "righteous," Jesus used the word here either in a relative sense or with a touch of sarcasm. Jesus implies that the Pharisees only *thought* that they were righteous; his point is that they must first acknowledge themselves to be sinners before they can truly respond to the call "to repentance." With this word, Luke introduces a topic of major importance. While the Gospel of grace and forgiveness is for everyone (2:10), repentance is a prerequisite to its reception (cf. 18:11–14).

8. The question about fasting (5:33–39)

Levi's banquet leads to further questions about religious practices, particularly fasting and prayer. These practices were considered significant indications of religious devotion. Fasting was actually only prescribed for one day in the year but was practiced as a religious exercise at least twice a week by the Pharisees (cf. 18:12). In contrast to the two previous incidents (vv.21, 30), this time the leaders challenge Jesus directly.

33–35 By stating a fact about the disciples of John and of the Pharisees, the disciples are now criticized, not only for eating with sinners, but for having a lifestyle in contrast to proper religious decorum. Jesus' answer is indeed remarkable. The first part of the saying is clear. Jesus compares the situation to a wedding (cf. Eph 5:25–33; Rev 19:6–9), which naturally calls for joy. But to think at a wedding of the possibility of the groom's death is highly unusual. Jesus seems to anticipate already here his rejection and his death at the hands of his enemies.

36 The context provides opportunity for Jesus to state a basic principle in a series of parabolic figures. His mission involves a radical break with common religious practices. He teaches that he has not come merely to add devotional routines to those already practiced, for what he brings is not a patch but a whole new garment. Merely to "patch things up"—i.e., to have a dinner celebration in place of fasting —would fail for two reasons. (1) It would ruin the rest of the new garment from which it is taken. (2) Just one new patch will not help preserve the old garment but will in fact be conspicuously incongruous.

37–39 The second illustration suggests that Jesus' teaching is like fermenting wine, wine that seems to have almost inherent vigor and cannot be contained within an old rigid system, just as such wine cannot be contained in old wineskins that have lost elasticity. Jesus concludes by emphasizing that people tend to want the old and to reject the new, assuming (wrongly in this case) that the old is better.

9. Sabbath controversies (6:1–11)

The uneasy tension between Jesus and the Pharisees described in chapter 5 hardens into controversy over one of the main institutions of Judaism, the Sabbath.

Keeping the Sabbath provided an appropriate issue for debate because it (1) had roots both in the creation account and in the Ten Commandments, (2) involved every seventh day and consequently called for many decisions about what was permitted or forbidden on that day, and (3) afforded a public disclosure of one's observance or nonobservance of the day.

1–2 Luke centers attention on the disciples (v.1), though in accordance with custom their teacher was held responsible. To glean by hand in someone's field was permitted by law (Dt 23:25). But to do this and to rub the heads of grain was considered to be threshing. Jewish tradition forbad threshing on the Sabbath.

3–4 Jesus' response (v.3) centers in an analogy from Scripture (1Sa 21:1–6). He calls to mind an instance in which the infringement of a rule to meet human need received no condemnation. Note too that the Scriptural analogy and the present incident involve a Davidic figure and his companions. The point is that ceremonial rites must give way to a higher moral law.

5 Following this analogy, on which the Pharisees offer no comment, Jesus lays claim to unique authority and takes the argument of vv.3–4 a step further (see comment on Mk 2:27–28).

6–8 The second Sabbath controversy involves basically the same issue as the first—

human need versus ceremonial law. Jesus is teaching in the synagogue, and when he sees the man with the atrophied and useless hand, Jesus takes the initiative. As in 5:17, the "Pharisees and teachers of the law" (v.7) are present, scrutinizing Jesus' every action to find fault. Now, after the first Sabbath controversy, they think they have a case against him. Jesus is aware of their thoughts (v.8) and in the light of that knowledge performs the healing. He has the man stand in front of the people so that all will see what follows.

9 Jesus' question in this verse implies that if any illness is left unattended when healing can be provided, evil is done by default. Jesus is not breaking the Sabbath; he is using it to do good to a human being in need.

10–11 Here Jesus commanded the impossible. Presumably the man exercised obedience born of faith, and Jesus healed the withered hand completely. The response is violent; the opposition to Jesus mounts in a crescendo of fury more intense than that after the previous miracle. So now, near the very start of Jesus' ministry, a plot against him is beginning to form.

10. Choosing the twelve apostles (6:12–16)

12 Jesus spent an entire night in prayer, a sure indication that the circumstances were pressing: the preceding controversy, the resultant threatening atmosphere, and the selection to be made of the twelve apostles. How many of us Christians today have ever spent a whole night in prayer? In his prayer life, as in all else, the Lord Jesus stands far above even the best of us whose words about prayer need to be matched by the consistent practice of it.

13–16 The "disciples" (v.13; GK *3412*) up to this time were a group of followers interested in attaching themselves to Jesus the teacher. From among this group, Jesus chose the Twelve. Luke alone tells us in this context that Jesus gave them the designation "apostles." That Luke does this accords with his regard for apostolic authority (see comment on Mt 10:12).

Jesus probably chose twelve apostles to correspond with the number of tribes of Israel, thereby indicating that a new people of God was coming into existence (see comment on Mk 3:13; on the names of the Twelve, see comments on Mk 3:16–19).

B. Jesus' Great Sermon (6:17–49)

1. Blessings and woes (6:17–26)

Jesus' "Sermon on the Plain" here (and his similar "Sermon on the Mount" in Mt 5–7) was something like a "keynote" address. It was a basic affirmation of the kingdom message, beginning with beatitudes and ending with a parable about builders. Within this framework Matthew and Luke present samples or selections of Jesus' teachings that differ at points. Luke's version has five main points, discussed below.

17–19 The "level place" is probably a flat area or plateau on the "mountainside" mentioned in Mt 5:1. Luke mentions a "large crowd" of Jesus' disciples plus "a great number of people" who came to listen to Jesus. The people came to be healed and to have demons cast out (see comment on 4:40–41), as well as to listen to his teaching. Although Jesus directed his comments to the disciples (v.20), he was surely conscious of his larger audience.

20–23 Luke's version of the blessings (or "Beatitudes") is shorter than Matthew's and is different in some particulars; he also includes a negative form in the woes. Both blessings and woes are familiar forms in the OT (e.g., Ps 1; Isa 5:8–23). The entire theme of reversal of fortune has already been encountered in Lk 1:51–55. It is also implicit in the attention Luke gives to social and religious outcasts throughout his gospel.

"Blessed" (vv.20–22; GK *3421*), as elsewhere in the NT, refers to the religious joy that one receives from sharing in the salvation of the kingdom. The poor are those who are utterly dependent on God. They are the special recipients of the "good news" Jesus came to preach (4:18). Often the economically destitute sense their need of God more than others. To inherit the kingdom of God is the antithesis of poverty. Note the emphatic sense of assurance that the present tense gives: "yours *is*" (emphasis mine). Jesus suggests there are some aspects of the coming kingdom of God that are already present. In other words, the poor can rejoice even in the midst of their destitution because they are already able to partake of some of the kingdom blessings.

"Hunger" is presented in its reality without spiritualization (v.21; cf. Mt 5:6). Those who "weep" may be those who carry the burden not only of personal grief but of a hurting society. Both parts of v.21 stress the contrast between the situation "now" and the future blessing.

The idea of laughter is vividly carried forward in the next section on persecution (vv.22–26). Persecution is described in some detail, and "rejoice" and "leap for joy" stand out all the more (v.23). Note the progression from hate (v.22) to exclusion to insult to defamation of their name. Those who share the rejection of the "Son of Man" relive the experience of the prophets (cf. comments on 20:9–12).The promise of "reward in heaven" (v.23) does not suggest that the disciples are to work for some future gain but that there will be personal vindication for those who wait on God and appropriate recognition and blessing from the Lord.

24–26 The woes in both structure and content form a direct contrast to the blessings. This again follows the pattern of Mary's song in 1:53.

Jesus pronounces woe to the "rich," not simply because they are wealthy, but (1) because they have chosen present gratification over future blessing; (2) because rich people criticized in Luke disregard spiritual realities (e.g., 12:15–21); and (3) perhaps because, as was generally assumed, the wealthy became so at the expense of others (cf. Ja 2:6–7).

The word "all" in the clause "when all men speak well of you" (v.26) should be emphasized, lest we distort the basic concepts of honor and praise. False prophets plagued God's people in OT times; they were a threat in Jesus' day (Mt 7:15–23), in Paul's day (Ac 13:6; cf. 20:29–30), and on into the church age (cf. 1 Jn 4:1).

2. Love for enemies (6:27–36)

In place of the five antitheses of Mt 5:21–48, Luke selects one theme and enlarges on it. As might be expected from his basic concern for people, he chooses the theme of love. He does not present the teaching of Jesus over against the prevalent distortion of the OT (cf. Mt 5:43–44). Instead he conveys only the positive command.

27–31 "You who hear me" means those who are taking in what Jesus is saying. The word "love" must be understood in its classic Christian sense of *agape* (GK *27*), having a genuine concern for someone irrespective of his or her attractiveness or of the likelihood of any reciprocation in kind. Jesus spells out the specifics. In the first instance (v.28), apparently no physical harm has been done; so the response also is not physical but to "bless" and to "pray." The next situations involve action that must be met by some physical response. Being struck on the cheek probably refers to an insult slap or to a hand blow to the jaw. The injunction is directed to individuals who desire to live as "sons of the Most High" (v.35). Note too that Jesus is not advocating the suspension of normal civil judicial procedures.

"If someone takes your cloak" may refer to a street robbery, though the passage implies that the person has a need or thinks he does. The teaching of the passage as a whole relates not so much to passivity in the face of evil as to concern for another person. Inevitably, to refrain from doing evil often means suffering evil. This was the path of the Lord Jesus (cf. 1Pe 2:20–24), who prayed for his enemies (Lk 23:34) and died for them (Ro 5:10).

32–36 At this point we have a remarkable series of comparisons between the courtesies of believers and those of worldly people. Even "sinners" act decently to others when kindnesses are reciprocated.

Loving is augmented by doing good, which, in turn, is expressed in lending. "Expecting to be repaid in full" probably implies some kind of reciprocal treatment in return rather than the simple repayment of the loan. One should benefit the helpless as well as one's friends.

Believers are to be like what they really are, "sons of the Most High" (v.35), and as such will have recognition. Jesus is not teaching that one earns sonship (cf. Jn 1:12–13). Rather, the day will come when the world will recognize God's children (Ro 8:19, 23). "Be merciful" (v.36) singles out that area of life in which, given the preceding examples, one is likely to come short. The pattern for our kindness to others is God's kindness to us.

3. Judging others (6:37–42)

37–38 These verses further describe the kind of mercy expected of the Lord's disciples. "Do not judge" (GK *3212*) must not be understood as ruling out any ethical evaluation at all; rather, it is defined by the parallel "Do not condemn." Just as God will give a suitable reward to the merciful (vv.32–36), so v.37 implies that he will bring appropriate judgment on the unmerciful. Those who are generous, Jesus goes on to say, will be abundantly repaid for their kindness.

39–40 Assuming that v.39 and v.40 belong together, Jesus' thought in addressing the disciples runs like this: The disciple of a rabbi dedicates himself to his master's teachings and way of life. Thus he cannot be expected to be different from, or better than, his master. If the rabbi lacks a proper view of life, his student will also be misled. The criticism and hostility already apparent in the Pharisees (cf. 6:11) may unfortunately crop up in their disciples, but they must never find a place among Jesus' disciples.

41–42 The humorous illustration of the "speck" and the "plank" hits the mark with force when the person who casually calls the person he is criticizing "brother" suddenly hears himself being called "hypocrite" by the Lord.

4. A tree and its fruit (6:43–45)

43–45 The thought of v.40 continues—like teacher, like student; like tree, like fruit. Throughout the preceding section and this one, the idea is that of consistency between source and product.

5. The wise and foolish builders (6:46–49)

46–49 If Jesus' audience was relaxing in the assumption that the preceding teachings were directed only at the Pharisees and their followers, they could not dodge the direct force of this challenge. It is specifically directed to those who profess to follow Jesus as "Lord." It is not mere words, nor even generally ethical behavior or religious practice, that mark true believers, but whether they "do" what Jesus says (cf. Jas 1:22–25).

C. Ministry to Various Human Needs (7:1–9:17)

1. The faith of the centurion (7:1–10)

This incident marks a pivotal point in the progress of the word of the Lord from its original Jewish context to the Gentile world. The Jews' appreciation of a pious Gentile

This hill overlooking the Sea of Galilee, a popular place for tourists to Palestine, is considered to be one on which Jesus taught the crowds. During the spring, this hill is green and lush with wildflowers (see picture at Mt 6:25ff.); in the summer it is dry and dusty.

(the centurion) is an important theme in Luke, a book written partly to show the compatibility of early Christianity with Judaism. At the same time, Jesus compares the Gentile's faith more than favorably with that of the Jews, which serves Luke's desire to justify the prominence of Gentiles in the church.

This incident is paralleled by the conversion of Cornelius (Ac 10), which itself marks a historic transition from a purely Jewish church to one including Gentiles. Luke is careful to speak well of each centurion and his religious concern. Note too the progression of "faith" in Luke, from Mary (1:45) to the four Jewish men who brought the paralyzed man (5:20) to this Gentile (7:9).

1–5 The introductory words provide more than just a transition from the preceding sermon. They suggest another step in the mission Jesus came to fulfill (1:1); the word "finished" (GK *4444*) is the same word translated "fulfilled" in 4:21 (see comment). Matthew uses a different word for "finished" (GK *5464*) after a collection of Jesus' sayings (see Mt 7:28 and comment). "In the hearing of the people" echoes "you who hear me" (6:27).

On behalf of his seriously ill "servant," the centurion (who was probably in command of Jewish soldiers, not Roman ones) sent some of the leaders of the community to Jesus (v.3). Luke shows great interest in the character and importance of the centurion, more so than Matthew (Mt 8:5–13). In v.4 we learn why the village elders were willing to intercede for the centurion. They were genuinely indebted to him for his generosity (v.5).

6–8 It seems strange that at this point, having invited Jesus to come, the centurion now sends a second group of "friends" to express his sense of unworthiness and to stop Jesus short of entering. Indeed, one wonders why at this point the centurion did not simply come out and speak for himself (cf. Mt 8:5–6). Luke, however, apparently wishes to stress the humility of the man and possibly also his concern, on second thought, that Jesus might be criticized for entering a Gentile's house.

The focal point of the section is the centurion's concept of Jesus' authority (v.8). He compares Jesus' relationship to God with his own to his superiors. The position of responsibility implies "authority" to command others. Therefore he has faith that Jesus' authoritative "word" will accomplish the healing.

9–10 Jesus is not criticizing the faith he has found among Jews but rather says that not even in Israel has he found such faith as in this centurion. The Jews would be expected to have faith, considering their possession of God's revelation in their Scriptures (cf. Ro 3:1–2). "But not all the Israelites accepted the good news" (Ro 10:16). Their failure to respond to their privileges was ending in Jesus' day, and the response of the centurion stood out in welcome contrast.

2. Raising a widow's son (7:11–17)

Jesus is now about to perform the ultimate kind of miracle that will certify him as the Messiah and will be reported to John the Baptist ("the dead are raised," v.22). Luke also wants his readers to understand that while John the Baptist came in the spirit and power of Elijah, it is Jesus himself who is the great prophet of the end time. This miracle bears significant resemblance, as we shall note, to one performed by Elijah. Luke has already included a reference to the widow to whom Elijah ministered (4:25–26).

11 Nain lay a few miles to the southeast of Jesus' hometown, Nazareth. Luke typically notes the "large crowd" (e.g., 5:15, 29; 6:17; 8:4).

12–13 The cortege has already gone through the town and is on the way to the place of burial, customarily outside the town. The deceased was the "only son" of his mother. The compassion of the Lord Jesus goes out to the woman. As a widow without a man in her family, she would probably become destitute, unable in that society to earn a living. Our Lord's words are deeply human: "Don't cry," but only he could say that and at the same time remove the cause of the tears.

14–15 Jesus risked ritual defilement by touching the coffin. He then did what would seem useless—he spoke to a dead person. When the young man returned to life, Jesus "gave him back to his mother," words similar to those in 1Ki 17:23 regarding Elijah and the widow.

16–17 Once more Luke records the response of the people, noting that they "praised" (GK

1519) God (cf. 5:26; 18:43; 23:47; see comment on 2:20). They recognized in Jesus a prophet and echoed an OT expression: "God has come to help his people" (e.g., Ru 1:6). For the significance of "come," see comment on 1:68. Once again Luke emphasizes the spread of the "news" about Jesus.

3. Jesus and John the Baptist (7:18–35)

In Lk 3:16–17, John had described the one who would come as one who would baptize with the Holy Spirit and with fire. Then Jesus was baptized, receiving divine approval and anointing for his work. In 4:16–21 Jesus assumed the task prophesied in Isa 61:1–2. Now, after a cycle of teachings and healings, the validity of his messianic calling is once more under consideration; and John the Baptist is the other central figure.

18–20 The healings and presumably also the raising of the widow's son apparently have not sufficed to convince John of Jesus' messiahship. This reluctance seems strange, considering John's role in announcing the Coming One and in baptizing Jesus. There are several reasons why John needed further confirmation. He was in prison (3:20). This could lead to depression and, in turn, doubt. Further, he might wonder why, if the Messiah was to release prisoners (Isa 61:1) and if Jesus was the object of that prediction (Lk 4:18), he had not freed John. Also, though he had received reports of Jesus' ministry, John himself had apparently not witnessed spectacular messianic miracles such as he might have expected; nor had he heard Jesus claim outright that he was the Messiah. John still had "disciples" (vv.18, 20), but this need not mean he had been continuing a separate movement because of uncertainty about the Messiah.

21–23 Jesus responds by listing the messianic works that he has accomplished. It was understood in those days that the true Messiah would not proclaim himself such but would first do appropriate messianic works that would lead to public acknowledgment of his identity. The works Jesus cites echo not only Isa 61, but other passages from Isaiah (e.g., 35:5–6; 62:7). Jesus pronounces a blessing (v.23) on the person who accepts his credentials rather than being trapped because of a false evaluation of Jesus.

24–28 The topic now changes from the role of Jesus to that of John. Through some gently ironic questions that expect obviously negative answers, Jesus stresses the inflexibility and austerity of John. He calls John a "prophet" and adds the role of "messenger" from Mal 3:1. If John is the messenger, obviously this forcefully implies the significance of Jesus' own role.

Jesus now puts John into historical perspective. John came in advance of the kingdom, which has now become a reality (16:16). Great as John was (v.28), it is greater to participate in the kingdom than to announce it. We should not conclude from this, however, that John himself is excluded. Lk 13:28 says that all the prophets will be in the kingdom.

29–35 Attention now turns to the contrast between the response of the people (cf. comment on 1:17) and of their hostile leaders to John and Jesus. The tax collectors and the people stood ready to believe Jesus and thereby to "acknowledge that God's way was right." The issue is not only the role of Jesus and John but especially the entire counsel of God, whose "purpose for themselves" the "Pharisees and experts in the law" rejected.

John's baptism was one of the symbols they chose to reject. Their obdurate opposition to each of God's messengers is described as the fickleness of children, who become annoyed when others won't play their game. Jesus and John, when in confrontation with the Jewish leaders, refused to "play their game" and so are the object of their taunts. The people not only criticize but exaggerate the habits both of John (v.33), calling his asceticism demonic, and of Jesus (v.34), calling his normal habits of food and drink gluttony and drunkenness. The concluding saying probably means that those who respond to wisdom prove its rightness.

4. Anointed by a sinful woman (7:36–50)

The criticism Jesus has received (v.34) does not preclude Luke from setting down another example of Jesus' concern for sinners. The story contrasts a sinful woman (perhaps a prostitute) and a Pharisee (cf. Mt 26:6–13; Mk 14:3–9; Jn 12:1–8).

36–38 Since Jesus accepted an invitation from this Pharisee named Simon, Jesus cannot be accused of spurning the Pharisees socially.

The woman took advantage of the social customs that permitted needy people to visit such a banquet to receive some of the leftovers, but she came specifically to see Jesus, bringing a jar or little bottle of perfume. Since Jesus was reclining at the table according to custom (v.36), she prepared to pour the perfume on his feet, a humble act (cf. 3:16). A flow of tears preceded the outpouring of the perfume; so she wiped his feet lovingly with her hair and, perhaps impulsively, kissed them before using the perfume. Jesus allows her to proceed without shunning her.

39–43 In this masterly narrative, Luke now directs attention to the Pharisee, who in mulling over the matter reaches three conclusions: (1) If Jesus were a prophet, he would know what kind of woman was anointing his feet; (2) if he knew what kind of a woman she was, he would not let her do it; and (3) since he does let her anoint his feet, he is no prophet and should not be acknowledged as such. Jesus responds, however, by showing that he does have unique insight into the human heart, for he knows what the Pharisee is thinking. When Jesus tells Simon that he has something to say to him (v.40), Simon replies perfunctorily, "Tell me, teacher." Jesus then responds with a clear message in a brief parable. Simon is made to give the conclusion that will condemn him. His "I suppose" probably implies an uneasy reluctance.

44–50 Again the woman is the focal point of the narrative. Surprisingly, Jesus first contrasts her acts of devotion with a lack of special attention on Simon's part as host. The main point is reached swiftly. Jesus can declare that her sins (which he does not hesitate to say were "many," showing Simon he did have insight into the woman) have been forgiven, not because of her act of love (v.47), but because of her faith (v.50).

The episode ends with Jesus pronouncing the woman forgiven. Then he becomes the object of another discussion because he presumes to absolve her from her sins (v.49; cf. 5:21). The woman then receives Jesus' pronouncement of salvation—and a traditional benediction, "Go in peace" (though it now has a deeper meaning for her).

5. Parable of the sower (8:1–15)

1–3 The opening verses provide a summary of yet another preaching tour (cf. 4:44). Luke states Jesus' mission both in that passage and here as announcing the "good news of the kingdom of God." Luke is careful to mention "the Twelve" here, as they will serve as witnesses and authorities in the days following Jesus' ascension.

What is new is the mention of several women who not only accompany Jesus but share in his support. Jesus' relationship with them is morally pure. Some of these women had a great debt of love to Jesus, such as Mary Magdalene, who was an object of the grace and power of God in being released from seven demons. "Joanna the wife of Chuza" is otherwise unknown, but she was probably present at the Crucifixion (cf. 23:49, 55; 24:10), showing her faithfulness. She is the first person connected with the Herodian household to be mentioned in this gospel. These women were industrious and helped in the support not only of Jesus but of the Twelve (v.3).

4 Teaching by using parables was common among the rabbis of Jesus' day (see comment on Mk 4:1–34). The sequence in vv.4–15 is (1) the parable of the sower, (2) Jesus' reason for using parables, and (3) the interpretation of the parable of the sower. Each part deals with the mixed response Jesus was receiving from his audiences. Jesus explains the present parable and his reasons for using the parabolic form—both to warn those who neglect the word they hear and to encourage his disciples when that word is not fully accepted.

Luke begins with an observation on the size of the crowds and adds a comment about those who were coming to Jesus from "town after town." The effect is to help the reader visualize a large mixed group of people who represent the various types of "soil" in the parable.

5–8 This particular parable reflects a situation well known to the audience, and its details would have immediately been grasped by the hearers. The very fact that circumstances so familiar needed still further comment before the spiritual meaning was clear underlines the paradox presented in v.10—namely, that those who see and hear do not understand.

The focal point of the parable has been variously interpreted. In none of the Gospels is the sower the center of attention. Nor is particular stress laid on the seed, though it does represent the word of God (v.11); and the whole act of sowing the seed is proclaiming the Gospel of the kingdom.

What does catch attention is the variety of soils. The sower himself is not immediately concerned about the kind of soil. Since plowing followed sowing in Jesus' culture, the trampled ground where people crossed the field might later be plowed under with seed; so it is not excluded from the sowing. The same could be true of young thorn bushes (v.7). Furthermore, the rocky subsoil (v.6) might not be visible at the time of sowing. The low yield from the poor soil is overshadowed by the very large yield from the good soil (v.8)—an encouragement for Jesus' disciples to realize that the ultimate greatness of the kingdom will make all their efforts worthwhile.

9–10 Here in Luke the disciples' question refers only to this parable, not to Jesus' larger ministry (cf. Mt 13:10; Mk 4:10). Jesus refers to the "secrets" of the kingdom (the only time this word is used in the teachings of Jesus). Elsewhere in the NT "secret" (*mysterion*; GK 3696) refers to the purpose and plan of God, which he works out phase by phase in human history and through the church. The issues of the problem of evil, suffering, and the delay of vindication will be resolved when God finally reveals his "secret." The "mystery or "secret" is only revealed by God's sovereign grace to his people.

Regarding "others" (those outside the kingdom; see Mk 4:11), Jesus quotes from Isa 6:9 and utters a teaching in accord with the consistent principle in Scripture that those who fail to respond to a saving word from God will find that they are not only under judgment for rejecting what they have heard, but that they are unable to understand further truth (cf. Jn 3:17–19; 9:39–41; Ac 28:26–27; Ro 9:17–18). For such, the very parable that reveals truth to some hides it from them.

While "so that" (v.10) may be understood as indicating result, it more normally indicates purpose (see comment on Mk 4:12).

11–12 Jesus now returns to the parable, explaining why the proclaimed word of God fails to bring a uniform response of faith. Luke's inclusion of the clause "so that they may not believe and be saved" reflects his intense concern regarding salvation; the devil intends to do everything possible to keep us from salvation.

13–14 In the next two types of soils there is an initial response, though it is superficial. For some, "in the time of testing" they "fall away" (GK 923; a word related to "apostasy"), for they cannot endure adversity.

The third soil has to do, not with adversity, but with distractions of this world, like those Jesus warned against in 11:34–36; 12:22–32; 16:13. These distractions prohibit a person's faith from maturing. (That this matter of being fruitful is not simply a matter of the quality of one's Christian life but of whether one has life at all is suggested by Jesus' parallel teaching on wealth in Mt 6:19–34.) The unresponsive people described in this part of the parable apparently lack the necessary essentials to true saving faith.

15 Luke stresses the character of the individual by describing that person as "noble and good" (a Christian adaptation of an ancient Greek phrase). The word "heart" (GK 2840) means the spiritual, intellectual, and volitional center of a person's being, i.e., the whole person. This person is marked by singleness of purpose and is the kind of person who does persevere until an abundant crop is produced.

6. Parable of the lamp (8:16–18)

16–17 The theme of these verses is the same as that of vv.11–15—namely, that what is genuine can and will be tested for its authenticity. If what is "hidden" is evil, this saying affirms that God's judgment on those referred to in v.10 and in vv.12–15 will be just. Furthermore, God's truth, now partially hidden from those who reject it, will one day be publicly vindicated. The absurdity of lighting a lamp only to hide it reinforces the point.

18 Those who accept the message of the kingdom will also be given the knowledge of the "secret," but those who reject it will lose even the opportunity of hearing more teaching (cf. Mt 13:11).

7. Jesus' true family (8:19–21)

19–21 Luke turns at this point to the story of Jesus and his relationship to his family.

Jesus does not, of course, dishonor his family (vv.19–20) but honors those who obey God (v.21). Most Christians would probably say that we come closest to Jesus through prayer and reading the Bible. But with searching practicality Jesus says that the way to be close to him—even as close as his own family—is through being receptive to ("hearing") God's word and then doing it. Hours of praying and reading the Bible will not bring disobedient Christians as close to the Lord as doing his truth brings even the simplest believer.

8. Calming the storm (8:22–25)

Luke continues illustrating the powerful, authoritative word of Jesus (notice esp. 8:25, 29, 32, 54; cf. 4:36). Jesus exercises his power against natural forces, demons, illness, and death. Then he delegates this power to his disciples.

This story itself is noteworthy for its vividness and its portrayal of the Lord Jesus in complete control of himself and his environment. The climax comes not with the miracle itself but with the question of the disciples (v.25) concerning the identity of the Master. It is a nature miracle, marking the first time in Luke that Jesus applied his power to a non-living object. Jesus is affirming his sovereignty over storm and sea as God did in the Exodus.

22–23 Jesus' words "Let us go over to the other side of the lake" (v.22) should have assured the disciples that they would indeed complete their trip across the water. Luke mentions the fury of the wind three times (vv.23, 24, 25; see comment on Mk 4:37). Luke mentions earlier in the narrative than do Matthew and Mark that Jesus was asleep. This placement heightens the contrast between the turmoil of the storm and Jesus' peaceful rest.

24–25 The fear and unbelief of the disciples are in contrast not only to the calm of their Master but also to the endurance they themselves should have had in "the time of test" (cf. v.13). The double "Master, Master" expresses both respect and terror. The fear of being lost at sea is a common human fear and typical of helplessness in the immensity of life (cf. Ps 107:23–31).

The question of the disciples, "Who is this?" serves to show not only their amazement but also the slowness of their apprehension of the "Master's" true identity. This question not only marks the climax of this story but is a key question in Luke (see comment on 9:9).

9. Healing a demon-possessed man (8:26–39)

This narrative provides the strongest expression yet of the power of Jesus against the forces of evil. Luke provides a lively, forceful picture of the destructive effects of demon possession. If a raging sea is a threat, demonic force is much worse. Not only the power of the kingdom (11:20), but also the power of the Messiah to release the captives of the kingdom of darkness move against this demonic force. The very narrative that describes this power of Jesus grips the reader. First, there are several progressive levels of action, involving the demoniac, the demons, the swine, the townspeople, and finally the demoniac after his healing. Second, Luke by his literary skill has inserted part of the description of the demoniac's past life in between the lines of dialogue to heighten the readers' awareness of the man's helplessness under demoniac control.

26–29 "They sailed" connects this episode with the previous one, suggesting the accomplishment of the goal stated in v.22. If the purpose of the trip across the lake was to liberate the demoniac (no other activity is recorded in the region of the Gerasenes), it is possible to understand the storm at sea as the deliberate attempt of evil forces to prevent Jesus' arrival.

The miracle in this section took place in Gentile territory (see comment on Mk 5:1), a fact especially important to Luke as validating the Christian mission to Gentiles. Verse 27 implies that the man was right by the shore when Jesus arrived.

In vv.27 and 29 we have a classic description of demon possession. The symptoms of such possession are like those of certain psychic illnesses known today, but Luke does not confuse illness with demon possession (cf. 4:40–41). Certain effects of demon possession cited in this passage are (1) disregard for personal dignity (nakedness), (2) social isolation, (3) retreat to the simplest kind of shelter (caves, often containing tombs), (4) demons' recognition of Jesus' deity, (5) demonic control of speech, (6) shouting, and (7) extraordinary strength. The basic tragedy of the demoniac lay in his being controlled by powers totally antithetical to God and his kingdom.

The term "Most High God" is used here as a general term for deity apart from worship (contrast 1:32, 35, 76 with Ac 16:17). The words "fell at his feet" do not indicate worship: the plea "I beg you, don't torture me!" along with the dialogue in vv.30–31 make it clear that the man's words and actions are not his own. The "torture" is presumably that of being cast into the "Abyss" (cf. Rev 20:1–3).

30–31 Jesus was not actually an exorcist (see comment on 4:33–35). Therefore his asking the demoniac's name should not be interpreted as an attempt to control the demons through knowing their host's name. Moreover, it is not clear whether Jesus asked the name of the man or of the demons, though the response comes from the latter. "Legion" implies that there were many demons. As for "Abyss," see ZPEB 1:30–31 for a wide range of meanings.

32–39 When the demons entered the swine, they were carried into the lake. In ancient thought, the water of the sea or a large lake was one form of the Abyss, though that may not be Luke's intention here.

The episode of the pigs is integral to the present narrative in two ways. Theologically, it completes the cycle just described (see comment on 8:22–25). Psychologically, it is essential for understanding the complex response of the townspeople. The report of what happened to the swine first triggered the people's fear, which merged into overwhelming awe on seeing the former demoniac "dressed and in his right mind."

But what about the ethical aspect of the pigs' destruction? Obviously the good of the man was more important than that of the pigs. Moreover, the demons themselves insisted on entering the pigs; Jesus permitted them to do this but did not actively send them there. Inevitably the discussion moves from exegesis to theology and the problem of evil—why it exists and why God in his wisdom, power, and love permits evil in this world.

Once the demons are off the scene, attention centers on the man and Jesus. Now healed and a new man, the former demoniac is commissioned by Jesus, not to go with him as a disciple, but to be a witness where he lived. Jesus has different ways for different believers to serve him (cf. Jn 21:21–22).

10. Jesus' power to heal and restore life (8:40–56)

The third part of the section on Jesus' power is composed of two intertwined stories. In both, the power and compassion of Jesus are notably displayed. Also, in both we see the importance of faith. Another point of comparison may be that Jairus's daughter was twelve years old, while the woman had suffered a hemorrhage during the same period of time. Note also the tension created for Jesus and his disciples by the two pressing needs: prevention of impending death, and helping a pathetic woman whose illness had isolated her from normal life and relationships.

40–46 The "crowds" (see comment on 3:7), now an integral part of the narrative, cover the woman's furtive approach to Jesus. Luke does not specify the nature of the "bleeding" (v.43), which is usually taken to have been a gynecological problem. The restrictions imposed by Lev 15:25–33 and by Jewish custom would have radically affected the woman's life. But her primary problem was the discomfort and embarrassment of her prolonged malady.

More serious questions are raised by (1) the woman's touching his cloak as though magical power could be transferred, and (2) Jesus' awareness of the transfer of power apparently without knowledge of who had done this. As to the first, the intrusion of Hellenistic ideas and superstitions may indeed have influenced her action; but Jesus did not quench the "smoldering wick" (Mt 12:20) of her faith; instead, he fanned it into flame.

Regarding the second issue, Jesus' question need not imply ignorance of the woman's identity but only his intention of singling her out. Yet the dialogue suggests that he knew only the fact that power had been transferred. While at times Jesus chose to heal people who had not expressed any faith, the reverse seems to be true here—namely, that someone with faith in him drew on his power without his conscious selection of that person. God may have extended his healing power through his Son without Jesus' yet being aware of the woman's identity.

47–48 The woman had desired to go unnoticed, possibly because of the embarrassment of her illness or because of her audacity in breaking her ritual isolation to touch Jesus' cloak. Her public confession of faith seems to indicate why Jesus asked who touched him. Jesus prefaced his traditional words of benediction (v.48) by words of grace (see comment on 7:50).

49–50 The episode of the sick woman delayed Jesus until word of the death of Jairus's daughter reached him. Yet the woman's healing also paved the way for Jesus' words in v.50.

51–56 Occasionally Jesus selected Peter, James, and John alone to be with him—e.g., at the Transfiguration (9:28) and in Gethsemane (Mk 14:33). The secrecy involved and the command to silence fits in with Jesus' frequent desire to avoid publicity to prevent premature or misguided declarations of his messiahship from being made (see comment on Mk 1:44). Of course, it would be hard to keep silent about the girl's restoration to active life; but the use of the word "asleep" may suggest that the crowd assumed that she had, after all, only been in a coma. But the words "her spirit returned" plainly imply that the child actually was dead. The secrecy of this miracle is in contrast with the public nature of the raising of the young man from Nain (7:16–17).

11. Sending out the Twelve (9:1–6)

The differences among the various gospels on the instructions to the disciples may be the result of an intertwining of traditions; but Jesus may also have given similar instructions on different occasions. What is described in these "sending" passages in the Gospels is not appointment to a permanent office but commissioning for an immediate task. Such an appointment could therefore be repeated using words essentially similar, though varying in detail. The common theme in all such passages, including 3Jn 5–7, is that the servants of Christ should go forth, not seeking support from unbelievers but trusting God completely to supply their needs through his people.

1–2 The "Twelve" receive both the "power" (GK *1539*) and the "authority" (GK *2026*) to do works of the sort that Jesus has performed in the episodes Luke has thus far reported. Signs and wonders are important to Luke, especially as the validation of the Gospel by, among other means, the apostles' miraculous power as God's messengers. Since others were claiming supernatural power (cf. Ac 13:6–10; 19:13), it was necessary for Jesus' disciples to have both "authority" and "power." This principle appears in a different context in 5:24. The connection between casting out demons and the coming of the kingdom is not as clear there as in 11:20; but the double mention of the ministry of healing here in 9:1–2 suggests that relationship.

3 The instructions indicate the urgency of the task. The severely limited provisions Jesus allowed the Twelve to take with them may be intended to express their dependence on God alone for food, protection, and shelter. Without bread or money they would need to be given daily food.

4–5 The disciples should receive hospitality graciously. Hospitality was important as well as necessary in days of difficult travel conditions and poor accommodations at inns. The disciples were not to move about from house to house, a practice that might gain them more support but would insult their hosts.

They would also encounter those who refused them a welcome. As a solemn symbol of judgment, the disciples were to shake the dust of an unresponsive town off their feet (see comment on Mk 6:10–11).

6 Luke concludes this section with a summary of the mission of the Twelve, including another reference to preaching and healing. Their instructions had not included any limitation of scope; they went everywhere.

12. Herod's perplexity (9:7–9)

Jesus has come to the end of his great Galilean ministry. The subsequent events take place to the north and east of Galilee and culminate in the confession of Jesus' messiahship, followed by the first passion prediction (vv. 19–27; cf. Mk 6:30–8:26). Prior to the narrative about the feeding of the five thousand, Luke states that Herod "was perplexed" about Jesus. This is of great importance in the sequence of Luke's gospel because it introduces the question "Who then is this. . . ?" (v.9; cf. comment on 8:25).

This all-important question is picked up again in vv.18–20.

7–9 "All that was going on" probably refers to the activities of both Jesus and the disciples on their mission. Herod (see comment on 3:1) heard about Jesus' miracles (see Mk 6:14) and had his questions about him. The questions of Jesus' identity and also of the reappearance of a dead prophet are reintroduced in vv.18–19. John the Baptist is naturally on Herod's mind (and doubtless also on his conscience). Herod was not able to see Jesus (v.9) but had his curiosity satisfied when Pilate sent Jesus to him (23:8–11).

13. Feeding the five thousand (9:10–17)

The fact that this miracle is in all four gospels indicates its importance. Luke's account is sparse and straightforward.

10–11 The return of the disciples is the occasion for Jesus' withdrawal to Bethsaida (perhaps to rest, see Mk 6:31). This town was on the northeast side of the lake outside Herod's territory. But crowds followed him to that place, and Jesus "welcomed" all who came, telling them about the kingdom (cf. 4:43) and healing many.

12–13 Each of the Synoptics records both the disciples' unimaginative suggestion that the crowds be sent away to find their own food and Jesus' response, "You give them something to eat," putting the responsibility back on them. The loaves were a basic food, often eaten with fish from the Sea of Galilee.

14–17 The crowd was much greater than five thousand, since there were that many men, plus women and children (Mt 14:21). Luke briefly summarizes the miracle, showing the orderliness of the distribution, Jesus' thanks (providing a lasting example for Christians), and the adequacy of the food.

D. Climax of Jesus' Galilean Ministry (9:18–50)
1. Peter's confession of Christ (9:18–21)

Luke moves directly and naturally from the miracle of multiplying the loaves and fishes, which pointed to Jesus' messiahship, to Peter's confession of that messiahship. From there Luke moves directly to the transfiguration narrative through the natural transition of v.28.

Theologically, this is the most important statement that Luke has written thus far. It is the first time a disciple refers to Jesus as Messiah (cf. 2:11, 26; 3:15; 4:41). Immediately after Peter's great declaration, Jesus predicts his rejection, death, and resurrection (v.22), thus shedding light on the implications of his messiahship.

18–19 Regarding this episode, Luke omits a reference to Caesarea Philippi and inserts a reference to Jesus at prayer (v.18). Luke apparently disconnects Peter's confession from time and space in order to emphasize the link between the miraculous feeding and Jesus' intimate fellowship with God, as exemplified in his praying. This is one of the insights Luke gives us into Jesus' prayer life (cf. 3:21; 6:12; 11:1). Jesus asks for the opinion of the "crowds" as to who he is. The responses echo the rumors expressed in vv.7–8.

20 Peter called Jesus "the Christ" (see comment on Mk 8:29–30). The additional words "of God" in this verse emphasize Jesus' divine commission.

21 The command not to tell others (cf. comment on 8:51–56) probably stems from two circumstances: (1) the Jewish people, chafing under the domination of Rome, were all too ready to join a messianic revolutionary; and (2) there was apparently an understanding that one should not claim messiahship for himself but should first do the works of the Messiah and then be acclaimed as such by others (see comment on 7:21–23).

2. The suffering and glory of the Son of Man (9:22–27)

22 This statement is known as the first passion prediction. Although there had been foreshadowings of a dark fate for Jesus—Simeon's prediction (2:35) and Jesus' statement about the bridegroom (5:35)—here in Jesus' words is the first explicit recitation in Luke of the sequence of events at the close of his life. The entire following teaching on discipleship requires some basic understanding of the Passion and, indeed, of the Crucifixion, since Jesus mentions the Cross (v.23). The use of the term "Son of Man" in vv.22, 26 is understandable, assuming (1) that Jesus used it frequently, (2) that he used it especially in connection with his passion (see comment on Mk 8:31), and (3) that the occurrence of the term in Mt 16:14 is not editorial but reflects Jesus' actual use of it in his initial question to the disciples.

23 Those who want to be Jesus' disciples can only truly be said to "follow" (GK *199*) him when they have implemented a radical decision to "deny" (GK *766*) themselves. This verb functions as a polar opposite to the verb "confess" (GK *3933*) which has the sense of acknowledging a thing or a person. We should therefore on the one hand "confess" Christ, i.e., acknowledge him and identify ourselves with him, and, on the other hand, not set our desires and our will against the right Christ has to our lives. It does not mean cultivating a weak, nonassertive personality or merely denying ourselves certain pleasures; rather, it means we must live for Christ. The next words about the daily cross explain and intensify this principle. To take up the cross daily is to live each day, not for self, but for Christ.

24–26 These two statements (vv.24–25) show the futility of clinging to one's "life," because that, paradoxically, results in losing the very self one wants to preserve. In contrast, the person who invests his or her life for God finds that such a life is not lost after all. Jesus then goes on to emphasize his point. The world the disciple are willing to forfeit is to be succeeded by the new order when the Son of Man comes in glory (v.26). The one who seeks gain by letting the world's view of Christ make him or her ashamed of the Lord rightly draws a corresponding response from the glorified Son of Man.

27 This is a perplexing verse. "Some who are standing here" refers either to the disciples as a group as opposed to the crowd, or to some of the disciples as opposed to the rest of the disciples.

There have been a number of different proposals as to what specific experience Jesus had in mind when he said these words. He may have meant Pentecost, for the coming of the Spirit brought the dynamic of the kingdom. More likely, however, he meant the Transfiguration, which Luke is about to discuss. That event focuses even more sharply on the kingdom and is, among other things, a preview of the Parousia, which event is clearly connected with the reign of Christ (see comment on vv.28–36; see 2Pe 1:16–18).

If Jesus was referring to the Transfiguration here, then the "some" who would not die before seeing the kingdom were Peter, James, and John, who saw Jesus transfigured. Why Jesus said they would "not taste death" before participating in an event only days away is perplexing. But he may have chosen those words because most people despaired of seeing the glory of the kingdom in their lifetime.

3. The Transfiguration (9:28–36)

This glorious transformation of the appearance of Christ is the most significant event between his birth and passion. Both the transformation itself and the divine commentary expressed in the Voice from heaven declare Jesus Christ to be the beloved Son of God. Luke emphasizes a further dimension of the event—the suffering that lay ahead of God's chosen Servant (see comments on vv.30–31, 35). In addition to the main elements of the Transfiguration itself and the words from heaven, the narrative contains several motifs of deep significance: the eight-day interlude, the mountain, Moses and Elijah, Jesus' impending "departure," the shelters, and the cloud.

Two frames of reference, one past and one future, will help us understand these motifs. One is the Exodus of the people of Israel from Egypt with the events at Mount Sinai, especially Moses' experience on the mount (Ex 24). The other is the second coming of Christ, the "Parousia" (cf. v.26).

28 The Transfiguration occurred about a week after Peter's confession of Jesus. There may be a connection here with the amount of time Moses spent on Mount Sinai before God spoke to him (see Ex 24:15–16; Mk 9:2).

Peter, James, and John had been taken into Jesus' confidence elsewhere (8:5). Luke uses the definite article with "mountain." It may be Mount Meron, the highest mountain within Israel, northwest of the Sea of Galilee (see also comment on Mk 9:2). On the other hand, Luke may be using "mountain" symbolically. Symbolism is not infrequent in references to mountains, regardless of whether a historical mountain is referred to. If we think of the Exodus as a frame of reference, then Sinai is symbolically in mind; if the Parousia, then the Mount of Olives may be symbolized (Zec 14:4; Ac 1:10–12).

Once again Luke mentions that Jesus is at prayer.

29 Luke omits the actual word "transfigured," possibly to avoid a term that might have suggested Hellenistic ideas of an epiphany, the appearance of a god. Instead he describes the remarkable alteration of Jesus' face and the dazzling whiteness of his clothing.

30–31 Moses and Elijah also appear in this scene of supernatural glory, though Luke describes them as ordinary "men" (see comment on 24:4). Why these two? Moses had a mountaintop experience at Sinai; his face shone (Ex 34:30; 2Co 3:7); he was both a lawgiver and a prophet—indeed the prototype of Jesus (Dt 18:18). Elijah was not only a prophet but was also related to the law of Moses as symbolizing the one who would one day turn people's hearts back to the covenant (Mal 4:4–6). In other words, Moses is a typological figure who reminds us of the past (the Exodus), while Elijah is an eschatological figure who points to the future as a precursor of the Messiah. Each man was among the most highly respected OT figures; both had one distinctive thing in common—their strange departure from this world (see Dt 34:6; 2Ki 2:11). In summary, the presence of Moses and Elijah on the Mount of Transfiguration draws attention (1) to the place of Jesus in continuing the redemptive work of God from the Exodus to the future eschatological consummation; (2) to the appropriateness of Jesus' association with heavenly figures; and (3) to the superiority of Jesus over even these great and divinely favored heroes of Israel's past.

The conversation is about Jesus' "departure" (lit., his "exodus"; GK *2016*). It points to Jesus' death and recalls the redemptive work of God in the Exodus from Egypt. Jesus' coming death was one that he would deliberately accomplish. Luke portrays Jesus as moving unhurriedly toward the accomplishment of his goals. He specifies Jerusalem as the city of destiny for Jesus (see comments on 13:31–35).

32 The writers of the Gospels use fear and sleepiness to indicate the slowness of the disciples to understand and believe. They were far from alert during the conversation with Moses and Elijah about Jesus' approaching passion; and the spectacular scene aroused them thoroughly.

33 Peter's suggestion to make three shelters implies that he wanted to keep Moses and Elijah from leaving. But Luke points out that Peter's suggestion was highly inappropriate. The idea of three shelters is the main problem. These would have been temporary shelters, such as were used at the Feast of Tabernacles. Peter's proposal of three, presumably equal, shelters may have implied a leveling perspective, putting Jesus on a par with the others. More than that, it connotes an intention to perpetuate the situation as though there were no "departure" for Jesus to accomplish. He still failed to grasp the significance of the passion prediction of v.22 and its confirmation in v.31.

34 The cloud, like other elements in this narrative, can symbolize more than one thing, among them the cloud in the desert after the Exodus (Ex 13:21–22; 16:10; 24:16; 40:34–38). But clouds are also associated with the future coming of the Son of Man (Da 7:13; cf. Mk 14:62) and with the two prophets in Rev 11:12. There may be a possible reference to the Parousia here or to the cloud that will appear during a future time of rest under the Messiah (cf. Isa 4:5). But above all the cloud symbolizes the glorious presence of God (cf. Ex 19:16). Though the disciples enter the cloud, a sense of the transcendence of God is retained as the Voice comes "from" the cloud (v.35).

35 The Voice speaking from the cloud is the awesome Voice of God the Father himself. The message expressed by the Voice is so clear that any uncertainty about the meaning of some of the other aspects of this great scene become comparatively unimportant. The focus throughout the Transfiguration is on the supreme person and glory of the Lord Jesus Christ. And now he is expressly declared to be God's Son—a declaration similar to that spoken by the Voice at Jesus' baptism (cf. 3:22) and later just before his passion (Jn 12:28–30). It affirms that Jesus is the one who is sent by God and who has God's authority. These words spoken by the Voice on these three occasions affirm that Jesus is the Son of God, is obedient to him, and possesses divine authority for his mission. The words "this is my Son" recall Ps 2:7; "chosen" (GK *1721*) points us to Isa 42:1 and the concept of the Suffering Servant found in the broader context of Isaiah (esp. 52:13–53:12).

"Listen [GK 201] to him" is not only a command; it is a correction of the human tendency to substitute human opinion for divine revelation. The words also fulfill Dt 18:15, which predicts the coming of the prophet God would raise up and commands, "You must listen to him." Jesus alone is the True Prophet, the Chosen Servant, and the Son of God.

36 The scene ends with Jesus alone as the center of his disciples' attention. They remain silent about this event (see comment on Mk 9:9–10).

4. Healing a boy with an evil spirit (9:37–45)

This healing is another significant example of the power of God over demons. It also implies Jesus' strong censure of the disciples for not performing the exorcism.

37–42 "The next day" may imply that the Transfiguration happened at night. If so, then that great event would have been even more striking. The descent of Jesus and the disciples "from the mountain" meant a descent into the earthly world of illness, evil, and unbelief. A "large crowd" had gathered around a demon-possessed boy. The physical manifestations were similar to those of epilepsy and the boy experienced continual debilitating oppression. While three of the disciples were witnessing the Transfiguration, the others were helpless in the face of demonic power (v.40). Jesus rebuked the spirit and cast it out.

43a Luke concludes his account of the boy's healing by speaking of the greatness of God and the reaction of those who observed the healing. Elsewhere Luke speaks similarly of people giving God glory (5:25; 7:16).

43b–45 This repetition of the prediction of Jesus' passion (cf. comments on 9:22) might be considered as a separate section, had not Luke connected it closely with the preceding incident by the marveling of the crowd. The passion prediction serves to emphasize that Jesus' ultimate purpose went beyond such miracles. This time Jesus includes a reference to his betrayal. The people, however, failed to understand (cf. Mt 16:22), and they were not granted understanding of the meaning of Jesus' words. Luke does imply, however, that had they asked Jesus for help in understanding his words, they might have been given it.

5. Two cases of rivalry (9:46–50)

46–48 This passage naturally follows the preceding two verses. The disciples did not understand Jesus' role as the Suffering Servant and so could not grasp its implications for them as his disciples. They were still thinking of the Messiah only in terms of triumph, assuming, quite naturally, that their position was important. The issue was not whether there would be rank in the kingdom but the nature and qualifications of such rank (v.46). Jesus' reference to the "little child" refers to receiving for the sake of Christ a person who has no status. This is consistent with Jesus' (and Luke's) concern for neglected people. The meaning, then, is that instead of seeking status for ourselves (out of pride as an associate of the Messiah), we Christians should, as Jesus did, identify ourselves with those who have no status at all, welcoming them to join us in the kingdom. By ministering to a child one ministers, without realizing it, to Christ himself.

49 The next episode reveals the apostles' attitude of rivalry. The issue is not orthodoxy but association. The man referred to here had actually been "driving out demons" through Jesus' name.

50 This verse is proverbial in form. The man was not against Jesus. Apparently he had not yet joined the group of Jesus' disciples but was probably "on the way" to joining; he should be welcomed rather than repulsed.

V. Teaching and Travels Toward Jerusalem (9:51–19:44)

This extensive section has no counterpart in Matthew or Mark, though much of its material is found in other contexts in those gospels. Luke 9:51 implies that Jesus was setting out on a journey that one would expect to be described in the succeeding chapters. Yet these chapters say comparatively little about Jesus' traveling from one place to another, though we do occasionally find clues showing that Jesus is moving toward Jerusalem (e.g., 9:52; 10:38; 13:22, 32–33; 17:11; 19:28, 41). In 18:31, Luke notes Jesus' words: "We

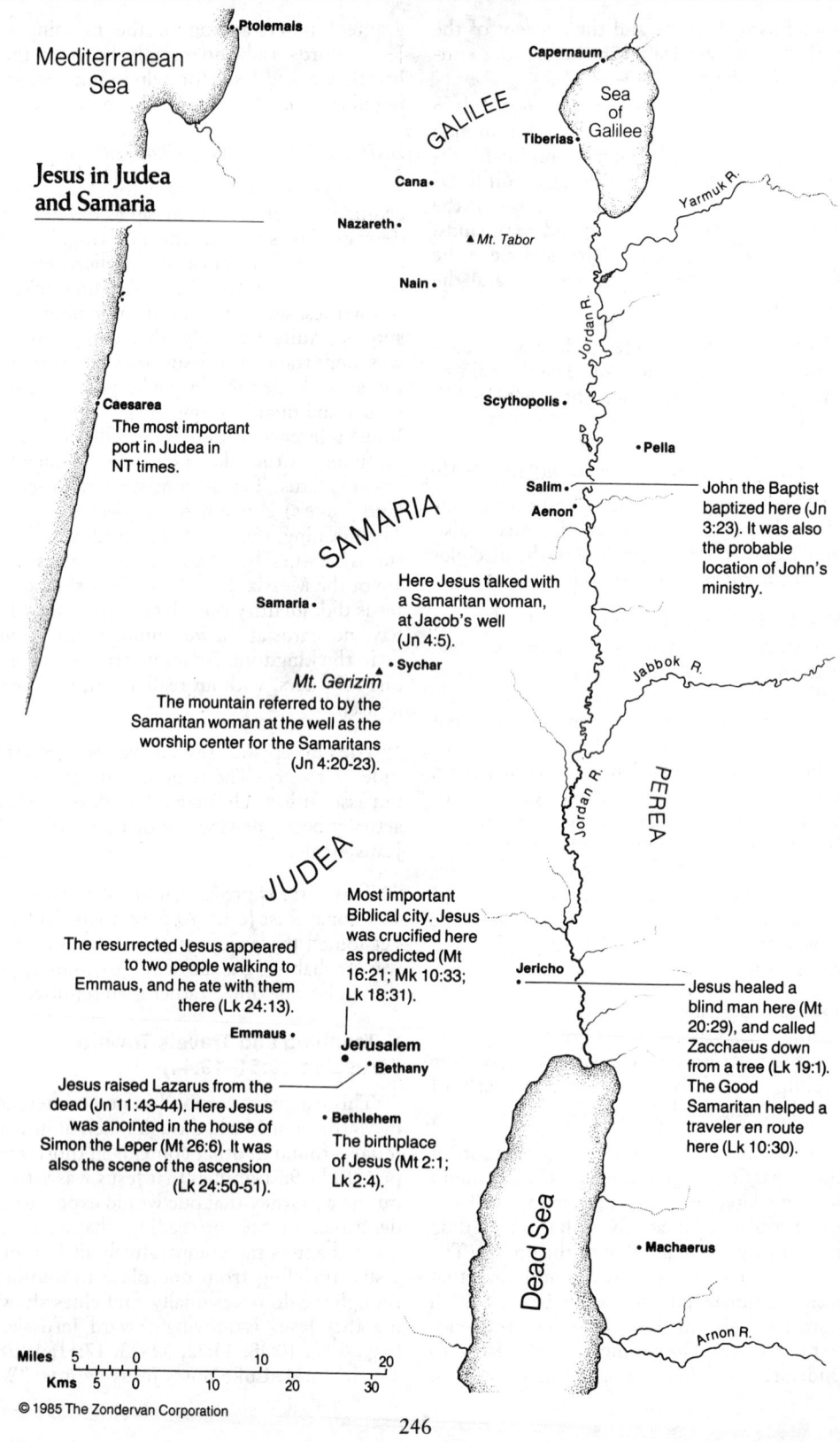

are going up to Jerusalem" (see 18:35; 19:1); he arrives near Jerusalem in 19:28–29. It is clear from all this that Jesus is now heading toward Jerusalem, not Galilee.

However, he did not make one continuous journey from Galilee to Jerusalem. Jesus' ministry has entered a new phase and has taken on some new characteristics. He follows routes that bring him away from Galilee and nearer to Jerusalem than his former itineraries did. During this period Jesus is no longer committed to the locale of his former ministry but is looking toward Jerusalem and the Cross. Much of his teaching at this time is directed to the disciples. Warnings to the rich and complacent are prominent, as well as words aimed at the Pharisees. On several occasions he actually visits Jerusalem, where he proclaims the truth about himself and enters into controversy with those who oppose his claim. Even at times when he may have traveled north again, his ultimate goal was Jerusalem. This also accords with the prominence of Jerusalem in the gospel of Luke (see comments on 13:33–34; 19:28, 41).

A. The New Direction in Jesus' Ministry (9:51–10:24)

1. Travel south through Samaria (9:51–56)

51 As just observed, there is now a major change in Jesus' orientation; he is heading to Jerusalem where he would die. At this significant turning point, Luke once again uses a word expressing fulfillment (unfortunately translated "approached" in NIV; GK 5230, a compound of GK 4444). God's plan is another step nearer fulfillment. The approaching goal is not only Christ's death and resurrection but especially his ascension (see introductory note on ch. 26). Now that Jesus faces the Cross, Luke mentions the exaltation that would follow his "exodus" (see v.31).

52 Jesus "sent messengers on ahead" (cf. 10:1–16), who were not told to preach but simply to "get things ready for him."

53–54 The residents of the Samaritan village reciprocated the hostile attitude of the Jews (cf. Jn 4:9). They were especially negative because they knew that Jesus was going to Jerusalem, which they refused to acknowledge as a valid center of worship (cf. Jn 4:20).

The history of the Samaritans is uncertain. Many hold that they were a mixed race since the fall of the northern kingdom of Israel. The king of Assyria deported the leaders of Israel, among them the religious teachers, and replaced them with foreigners (2Ki 17:6, 24–26). From that time on, the inhabitants of the northern kingdom received no further prophetic instruction, nor did they recognize God's revelation to the southern kingdom. The Samaritans were a fringe segment of the Jewish world for which Jesus, and Luke, had a concern (see 10:30–37; 17:11–19). James and John may have thought that Jesus would respond as Elijah had (v.54; 2Ki 1:9–12).

55–56 Jesus strongly disapproved the suggestion of James and John by rebuking them (cf. 4:35, 41; 8:24). If the Samaritans were consciously rejecting Christ by rejecting his disciples, one would have expected that Jesus' instruction in 9:5 would apply—a mild reaction compared to that of James and John. But Jesus' messengers were rejected merely because they were Jews going to Jerusalem.

2. The cost of following Jesus (9:57–62)

This is the second major treatment of discipleship in Luke (cf. v.23). The structure of this passage is noteworthy. The familiar "rule of three" is employed by Luke in recording three conversations. There is an interchange of order: in the first conversation the inquirer initiates the conversation and Jesus states the objection; in the second order this is reversed; in the third the man both initiates the dialogue and raises the objection, with Jesus adding a comment. Each dialogue contains some theological language: "Son of Man" (v.58), "proclaim the kingdom of God" (v.60), "service in the kingdom of God" (v.62). Discipleship is not simply following Jesus in one's lifestyle but is involvement in the important work of the kingdom.

57–58 Using the terminology of discipleship ("follow"), the first man amplifies it with a sweeping promise. Jesus' reply is in accord with his prior definition of discipleship in v.23 and constitutes a comment on the man's "wherever you go." Since most people do have homes, "Son of Man" must refer specifically to Jesus. The idea of the rejection—if not his actual suffering—of the Son of Man is implied in Jesus' words.

59–60 Since it was a religious, social, and family obligation to provide a decent funeral for one's father, Jesus' refusal to permit this is a striking example of the radical transfer of loyalty he demanded (see 14:25–27). "The dead" who are to perform the burial are usually thought to be the spiritually dead who do not follow Jesus but remain at home.

61–62 Although saying good-by is not at all the emotional equivalent of a funeral, it still represents a family duty that must be forsaken for service to Jesus. Some see here an allusion to the call of Elisha while plowing and his request to say good-by to his family (1Ki 19:19–21). It was important for an ancient plowman to concentrate on the furrow before him, guiding the light plow with his left hand while goading the oxen with the right. Looking away would result in a crooked furrow.

3. Sending out the seventy-two (10:1–24)

Luke's account of Jesus' commissioning of the seventy-two fits the immediate context well. It continues the procedure of sending messengers ahead during Jesus' journey (9:52). At the same time, the obedient response of the seventy-two provides a contrast to the three men (9:57–62) whose excuses disqualified them from discipleship. The instructions prescribed by Jesus were undoubtedly repeated frequently by Jesus and in the early church (see comments on 9:1–6).

1 The title "Lord" (GK *3261*) emphasized the serious dominical aspect of the instructions—namely, that they came from the Lord Jesus himself. Not only does the commissioning of the seventy-two lack any restriction to Jewish hearers (as in Mt 10:5–6), but the number of missionaries sent out parallels the number of nations thought to exist in the world (see Ge 10, LXX) and so suggests the deliberate inclusion of Gentiles.

Sending messengers "two by two" was common among the early Christians and the Jews (see comment on Mk 6:7). The seventy-two were to go everywhere Jesus was going. The extent of this mission underscores the mission of the church: to reach the plentiful harvest. It may also look toward the conclusion of the church's mission at Jesus' return (cf. Mt 10:23).

2–3 Although the harvest imagery in Scripture usually refers to God's intervention in history through gathering his people together (cf. Mt 13:37–43), here it applies to the urgent missionary task of the present age (cf. Mt 9:37–38; Jn 4:35). The imperative "go" anticipates the difficulties of the journey. Wolves are natural enemies of sheep. The disciples are like "lambs"—defenseless and dependent on God alone.

4 The limitations on what the seventy-two may take with them increase their vulnerability (see comment on 9:3). They must also be single-minded, even to the extent of not becoming involved in time-consuming greetings (cf. 2Ki 4:29).

5–6 Greetings are to be reserved for the hosts of the seventy-two. "Peace" (GK *1645*), so familiar in Jewish salutations, has a rich connotation here. If the host has a proper attitude toward God, he will receive the blessings of the kingdom (v.9). But this promised peace would leave those hosts who were not receptive to the kingdom's message.

7 Like the Twelve (9:4), the seventy-two are to remain with their original hosts. As the Lord's servants, they are deserving of support by the Lord's people (see 1Co 9:3–18; 1Ti 5:18; 3 Jn 5–8).

8–9 It is not clear whether the messengers feared being offered food prohibited to Jews. These words may have been preserved because of their appropriateness to later situations (cf. Ac 10:9–16; 1Co 10:27).

10–11 Rejecting the kingdom message has consequences: a Day of Judgment. Luke includes such warnings of it in 6:24–26; 12:46–48; 16:23–24; 21:22.

12 Sodom, destroyed along with Gomorrah (Ge 19:24–29), represents the consequences of ignoring God's warning to repent (cf. Mt 10:15; 11:20–24). "More bearable" probably relates not so much to the degree of punishment as to the degree of culpability. If Sodom cannot escape judgment, what hope does a city that rejects the Lord Jesus have?

13–14 Korazin and Bethsaida are located at the north end of the Sea of Galilee (see comment on Mt 11:21–22), where Jesus concentrated his ministry. The comparison with the Phoenician towns of Tyre and Sidon suggests utter rebellion against the Lord, for those two ancient pagan towns suffered drastic judgment for their proud opposition to God and his people (Isa 23:1–18; Jer 25:22; 47:4; et al.).

"Sackcloth," a coarse, black material, was worn as a sign of mourning or repentance (cf. 1Ki 21:27). "Ashes" could also symbolize repentance or contrition (e.g., Job 42:6).

15–16 Capernaum had the high privilege of hearing Jesus preach there frequently, but this privilege guaranteed neither its fame nor its survival. On the contrary, in language like that of Isaiah 14:12–15, Jesus graphically portrays Capernaum's fall. He goes on to iterate that reception or rejection of his messengers demonstrates one's attitude to the Lord himself (cf. Mt 25:31–46).

17 The messengers returned to Jesus filled with joy. The power of the kingdom was effective against demons just as it was in the ministry of Christ (11:20). Exorcism must be done in the name of Christ; that is, on his authority (contrast Ac 19:13–16).

18 This verse falls back on the taunt-song describing the fall of the king of Babylon (Isa 14:4–11). When the disciples exorcise demons, the forces of evil are shaken, symbolizing the defeat of Satan himself.

19 To have authority "to trample on snakes and scorpions" relates to the victorious work of Christ, who, according to the first promise of the Gospel in Ge 3:15, was to bruise the head of the Serpent, the devil. The ultimate implication of overcoming "all the power of the enemy" is to be victorious over the one through whose temptation sin entered into humanity.

20 This call to rejoicing in the supreme blessing of assurance of heaven is one of Jesus' great sayings, though the disciples may also rejoice in spiritual victories (cf. v.17). The idea of the names of God's faithful people being written down in heaven in a book is common in biblical writings (e.g., Ex 32:32–33; Ps 69:28; Da 12:1; Mal 3:16; Rev 20:12–15).

21–22 The emphasis on joy combines with another subject of Luke's special interest—the Holy Spirit in the life of Christ. These verses show (1) God's sovereignty in imparting revelation, (2) the relationship between the Father and the Son, and (3) the privilege the disciples had of participating in this instance of messianic revelation and salvation.

Jesus' words relate to the time in which the power of the kingdom is revealed. Jesus himself participates in the joy that characterizes the day of God's salvation, a theme established at the beginning of Luke's gospel (e.g., 1:44). He combines joy with thanksgiving on the occasion of God's mighty saving work. A remarkable thing stressed by Jesus is not that the wise do not understand God's revelation but that the simple do. The "children" are those whose open, trusting attitude makes them receptive to God's word.

The knowledge God gives is "committed" (GK *4140*) directly to the Son. This explains why Jesus spoke with authority (4:32) in contrast to the scribes (Mk 1:22), who received their ideas through tradition, passed on from rabbi to rabbi. Jesus' sayings confirm other teachings in the Synoptics and in John about the fatherhood of God and the unique sonship of Christ.

23–24 Jesus congratulates the disciples privately on participating in this revelation. The woes that Jesus pronounced earlier on those whose pride will be broken (vv.13–15) are balanced by the blessings of those granted salvation (cf. 1:52–55; 6:20–26).

B. Teachings (10:25–11:13)
1. Parable of the Good Samaritan (10:25–37)

This parable requires the utmost care in its interpretation. It must neither be overallegorized, as it was by the early church fathers, nor reduced to a simplistic meaning hardly worthy of Jesus' teaching. Above all, it must be understood in its context.

25 The expertise of the man in this incident lay in details of the Jewish religion. The fact that he wanted to "test" Jesus may, but does not necessarily, indicate hostility. He addressed Jesus as "teacher" and asked him about eternal life. Questions about achieving eternal life and about the essence of the law were common in Judaism; note his assumption of human responsibility in the attainment of eternal life. "Eternal life" here means the life of the kingdom.

26 Jesus' counterquestion does not constitute an affirmation of the assumption behind the question but directs the questioner back to the commandments of the OT, which are not only his special field but also the ultimate source of religious knowledge.

27 The expert on the law answers Jesus' question by quoting a commandment (cf. Mt 22:37-40). The answer is satisfactory so far as it goes, for it is based on the OT (Dt 6:5; Lev 19:18). The words "as yourself" will provide the crucial means of evaluating one's love of neighbor. The ultimate evaluation will have to be based on deeds, not words, as the parable shows.

28 Jesus affirms that the man has answered correctly. This does not mean that the inquirer has grasped the full meaning of the law, nor does it endorse the idea held by many Pharisees that by keeping the law a person can earn eternal life.

29 The only way to justify oneself is to limit the extent of the law's demand and consequently limit one's own responsibility (see comment on Mk 12:31). This maneuver not only fails but has an opposite effect. Jesus will change the man's very words ("Who is my neighbor?") from a passive to an active sense (v.36).

30 The characters of the story must have the same significance they had to the original hearers. The two religious persons act contrary to love, though not contrary to expectation. The priest, returning from Jerusalem, has been observing the Law, though studious readers will recognize the neglect of mercy (cf. Mic 6:8; Lk 6:36). Then a third character appears, but unexpectedly he is not just a layman (in contrast to the clerical characters) but a Samaritan (in contrast to the Jewish victim).

The distance from Jerusalem to Jericho is about seventeen miles, descending sharply toward the Jordan River just north of the Dead Sea. The road curved through rugged, rocky terrain where robbers could easily hide. It was considered especially dangerous.

31-32 Priests served in the temple; their highest duty was to offer sacrifices. Levites assisted in the maintenance of the temple services and order. We are not told why the priest and Levite refused to help, but the point of the story seems to require that the priest and the Levite have no legitimate excuse.

The terrain from Jerusalem to Jericho is rugged and isolated. In Bible times, robbers would hide in the hills and caves.

33-36 "Took pity" (GK *5072*) implies a deep feeling of sympathy, a striking response that stands in contrast not only to the attitude of the priest and the Levite, but also to the usual feelings of hostility between Jew and Samaritan. This pity is translated into sacrificial action. The Samaritan probably used pieces of his own clothing to make the bandages (v.34); he used his own wine as a disinfectant and his own oil as a soothing lotion. He put the man on "his own donkey" and paid the innkeeper out of his own pocket, with a promise to pay more if needed.

The NT parables aim to lead one to a decision; Jesus' question in v.36 forces the "expert in the law" to voice his decision. In his question, Jesus focuses on the person who loved, the Samaritan who made himself a neighbor. This reversal of the "expert's" question (v.29) provides in itself the key to the meaning of the parable and to Jesus' teaching on love. Love should not be limited by its object; its extent and quality are in the control of its subject. Furthermore, love is demonstrated in action, in this case in an act of mercy, and it may be costly. There is a striking reversal of roles here. The Jewish "expert" would have thought of the Jewish victim as a good person and the Samaritan as an evil one. To a Jew there was no such person as a "good" Samaritan.

37 The "expert" cannot avoid the thrust of the parable, though he apparently finds it impossible to say the word "Samaritan" in his reply. Jesus now refers back to the original question, "What must I do?" by saying, "Go and do likewise." God does not bestow the life of the kingdom on people who reject the command to love (see also 18:18–25). Such rejection shows that they have not truly recognized how much they need the love of God themselves (see 7:36–50).

2. The home of Martha and Mary (10:38–42)

In 8:1–3 Luke mentioned several women who traveled with Jesus and the disciples and contributed to their support. Now he tells about a woman who entered into discipleship. Once again Luke portrays the way Jesus transcended the prejudices of his day.

38–40 The unnamed "village" was undoubtedly Bethany (Jn 11:1), a town close to Jerusalem. Possibly Luke wants to reserve mention of Jesus' ministry in Jerusalem and its environs till later. The way Martha is mentioned seems to give her the role of hostess. It is Mary, however, who takes the place of a disciple by sitting at the feet of the teacher (v.39). It was unusual for a woman in first-century Judaism to be accepted by a teacher as a disciple. Notice that Jesus is called "Lord" throughout this passage. Martha, on the other hand, was "distracted" (v.40); she had to work alone rather than sit at Jesus' feet.

41–42 The Lord shows concern for Martha's anxiety, but the precise meaning of his saying (v.42) is difficult to ascertain. There is no explanation of "what is better," though the best interpretation is the kingdom of God. In comparison with the kingdom, household duties should have a radically diminishing demand on Martha. The word of the Lord has first claim, and for the disciple an attitude of learning and obedience should take first place.

The preceding narrative and parable establish the importance of priorities in the Christian life—i.e., heeding the commands to love God and one's neighbor. Martha must now learn to give the Lord and his word priority even over loving service. There are important human needs, whether of the victim in vv.30–35 or of Jesus himself. But what is *most* "needed" goes beyond even these.

3. Teaching on prayer (11:1–13)

The Lord's Prayer in Luke appears in connection with Jesus' own practice and teaching on prayer (see also comments on Mt 6:9–13). Luke offers a basic prayer to say what is characteristic of Jesus' teaching.

1–4 Once more Luke speaks of Jesus at prayer (cf. 3:21; 6:12; 9:28). His exemplary practice introduces the exemplary prayer. Since prayer inevitably expresses one's theology, the prayers of the Jewish sects in the first century were distinctive. This was true of John the Baptist (v.1). Jesus responds to the request from "one of the disciples" with a model that provides words his disciples can use with the confidence that they express Jesus' own teachings. The words "when you pray" (v.2) imply frequent repetition of the actual prayer.

The word "Father" (GK *4252*) expresses the essence of Jesus' message and the effect of his atoning work on our relationship with God. Through the use of this intimate but respectful term of address, the Son of God expresses his own unique relationship to God. Through his atoning death on the cross, the Savior has brought about reconciliation with God, making it possible for us to become his spiritual children through the new birth. While we cannot use the term "Father" (*Abba*) on an equal basis with Jesus, there is a sense in which both he and we may address God as such (Ro 8:14–17).

The petitions that follow are two kinds—the first two petitions relate to God, the last three to us. "Hallowed [GK *39*] be your name" is an ascription of worship basic to all prayer and is found in various forms in the OT (e.g., Ps 111:9) and in ancient Jewish prayers. It means "let your name be regarded as holy." It is not so much a petition as an act of worship; the speaker, by his words, exalts the holiness of God. God's people were told in the OT to keep his name holy (Lev 22:32; cf. Ps 79:9; Isa 29:33).

In the next petition, Jesus prays that the glory and reign of God may be realized soon; Jesus came to announce and bring in the kingdom. Though its consummation is still future, in his ministry the kingdom was inaugurated in power.

The three petitions that follow are closely connected with the "Father" and give a more distinctive character to the prayer as a whole.

The first of the three petitions relating to us is for "bread," representing food in general. The meaning of the word translated "daily" (GK *2157*) is obscure, so the context of the word becomes crucial. The petition can be paraphrased in the Greek word order as follows: "Our bread, the daily, keep giving to us each day." "Each day" is in an emphatic position at the end of the clause. The word "daily" may mean "for tomorrow," i.e., the next day. This would be appropriate if it were an evening prayer. It could also signify the eschatological bread, that is, God's abundant provision at the consummation of the kingdom. If that is the meaning, then Jesus asks us to pray for the provision of this aspect of the future feast in our own lives now. Finally, the word "daily" may also mean "sufficient." This meaning fits in with Luke's stress on depending on God for present needs. To trust God for sufficient food day by day was important to people in Jesus' time, for many were hired only a day at a time (cf. Mt 20:1–5). When the people of Israel were in the wilderness, they had to learn to trust God for manna day by day (Ex 16:4; Dt 8:6).

"Forgive us our sins" describes a petition that must be repeated as needed. Those who call God "Father" are believers, already justified and without guilt through the death of Christ. Therefore the forgiveness they must extend to others is not the basis of their salvation but a prerequisite for daily fellowship with the Father (see 1Jn 1:5-10). Conversely, one who does not forgive others may actually be revealing that he or she has not really known God's forgiveness (cf. Lk 7:47).

"Lead us not into temptation [GK *4280*] does not imply that God might otherwise entice us to do evil (see Ja 1:1-15). God does, however, allow his people to be tested as to their faithfulness (see comments on 4:1-12). Thus "testing" is a better translation than "temptation," though severe testing may be the occasion for one to sin. The request is clearly for the Father to keep his children from falling away in the hour of trial, with a possible allusion to the temptation and fidelity of Christ.

5–6 Jesus' teaching on prayer continues (vv.5-13) with a parable unique to Luke. The scene is that of a Palestinian home in which the family are all asleep in one room—perhaps the only room in the house—and probably all on one mat. The father could not get over to the door and slide back the heavy bolt that bars it without waking up his family. In such a situation no one would be happy to respond, especially in the middle of the night. Nevertheless the man does respond to his friend at the door. A host in first-century society would be expected to provide a welcome to a guest regardless of when he arrived.

7–8 The point of the parable depends partly on the context and partly on the meaning of the word "persistence" or "boldness" (NIV, NASB; GK *357*) or "importunity" (RSV, KJV). If it means the former, the parable would seem to teach that if we persist long enough, God will finally answer our prayers. But since the Bible refers frequently to God's eagerness to grant our requests, "boldness" is a more likely translation. This parable then presents a contrast to the way God answers prayer. If in human circumstances one will respond to a request, even though reluctantly, if pressed hard enough, surely God will answer and do so far more graciously (cf. 18:1–8).

9–10 In threefold poetic form, Jesus teaches that "everyone who asks"—not simply the persistent—will receive from God.

11–13 The bizarre examples in vv.11–12 reinforce the point that God will respond to our petitions only in kindness. There are two steps in the argument: (1) God is our heavenly Father (v.13) and will do no less for his children than would an earthly father; (2) God is perfect and will do "much more" than a sinful person would. While Mt 7:11 has the general term "good gifts," Luke specifically mentions the Holy Spirit, who was "promised" (cf. 24:49; Ac 1:4).

C. Growing Opposition (11:14–54)

1. Jesus and Beelzebub (11:14–28)

This event shows the real nature of the increasing opposition Jesus faced. The Beelzebub controversy leads to the sign of Jonah, continues with the woes against the unbelieving religious leaders, and concludes with a comment regarding Jesus' mother, together with a statement that obedience to God's word is more important than even the closest human ties to Jesus.

As in Matthew and Mark, this incident shows that Jesus' hearers must choose between good (Jesus, the Spirit, and God's kingdom) and evil (Satan and his demons).

The issue is nothing less than the source of Jesus' authority and power. This is especially important for Luke, who is deeply aware of the importance of the supernatural as a testimony that Jesus is the promised Messiah (cf. Ac 2:22, 43; 4:30; et al.). The climax of the passage comes in v.20 (see comment).

14–16 The setting of this account of the Beelzebub controversy is the healing of a deaf mute. Such a healing was among the signs of his messiahship that Jesus had reminded John the Baptist of (7:22). Once more (cf. 4:36 et al.) the crowds are amazed at Jesus' power over demons. The crowd is divided, however, between those who either oppose him outrightly by attributing his power to the head demon, "Beelzebub," a euphemism for Satan (see comment on Mt 10:25), or taunt him to give them an even more dramatic sign (which constitutes a "testing" or provocation; see comment on vv.29–30).

17–20 Jesus "knew their thoughts" (cf. 5:22; 7:39–47) and responded. The head of any army would hardly work with the enemy against his own troops. Moreover, if demons are exorcised by the power of their own leader, how do the Jews explain the power their own exorcists (cf. Ac 19:13–14) are supposed to have? Jesus' illustration shows the drastic antithesis between the powers of evil, darkness, and Satan on the one hand and the power of God, the Holy Spirit, and the kingdom of light (cf. Col 1:12–13) on the other hand. When the magicians in Egypt were unable to duplicate all the miracles Moses did before the Exodus, they said to Pharaoh, "This is the finger of God" (Ex 8:19). So here Jesus is affirming that the source of his power is "the finger of God" (v.20), i.e., God himself. If this is true, then Jesus' driving out demons is a messianic sign and the kingdom of God has arrived.

21–23 In the parable of the strong man guarding his own house, we have a principal reference to Jesus' tactics in his war against Satan. The ultimate and actual means of Jesus' victory is the Cross. The critical place in Jesus' ministry of his victory over Satan means that we also must take a stand for or against Jesus as the one who brings the kingdom (v.23). Whoever does not "gather" the sheep "scatters" them by default and thus works counter to Jesus (cf. Jn 10:11–13).

24–26 "Evil spirit" means "demon." In these verses a spiritual renewal has taken place, but without the indwelling of the Spirit and the power of Christ's kingdom (perhaps this refers to the work of the Jewish exorcists mentioned in v.19). The evil spirit wanders in the desert and seeks a human body. In order to repossess its previous abode, it enlists the aid of seven demons even worse than itself (contrast the "seven spirits" before the throne in Rev 1:4). The demons settle down there (the same verb is used in Eph 3:17 of Christ's full indwelling).

27–28 This saying provides another instance of Luke's identification of Jesus' sayings as the "word of God." It must not be taken as reflecting unfavorably on Mary.

2. The sign of Jonah (11:29–32)

In this passage Jesus responded to those who were prodding him for a "sign from heaven" beyond the miracles he performed (cf. Jn 2:11; 20:30). Some people resisted the testimony already obvious in his messianic works (cf. vv.14–16). The Synoptics oppose an inordinate demand for extraordinary miracles beyond those needed for a witness to Jesus' authority.

29–30 The "sign" Jesus provided to those who wanted one (cf. v.16) is the sign of Jonah himself, whose presence and brief message (cf. v.32), though more minimal compared with the preaching of Jesus, triggered immediate and widespread repentance. The preaching of Jesus carried its own authority, especially when affirmed by the power of God in miracles (e.g., 4:32, 36; see also Mt 12:40).

31–32 The inclusion of the Queen of Sheba (cf. 1Ki 10:1–13) fortifies the judgment on Jesus' generation, because she traveled a great distance to hear the wisdom of Solomon. A double contrast is implied in these two examples: (1) the response of the audience, and (2) the greatness of the preacher. The "one greater" (v.32) than Solomon and Jonah is, of course, Jesus.

3. The lamp of the body (11:33–36)

33 Hearing Jesus' message lays a responsibility on the hearer. The metaphors of light, signs, and judgment (cf. vv.29–32) are akin to what we have in John (e.g., 3:19–21; 9:39–41) and elsewhere in the NT (e.g., Ac 26:18; 2Co 6:14–15; Eph 5:5–14).

34–35 Good eyes admit light, bad ones do not. Jesus implies that the individual is responsible for receiving light. The eye is thus a "lamp," not in the sense that it emits light, but that through it the body receives light. The real source of light is outside the body; if we think we can generate our own light, we must beware lest that inner "light" prove to be darkness.

36 The body is only completely lighted when a lamp shines on it from the outside (cf. Eph 5:13–14a). That is, full illumination only comes when one is willing to receive light from the lamp of God's truth.

4. Six woes (11:37–54)

37–38 In a way typical of his use of material, Luke puts the major discourse in the setting of a dinner (cf. 14:1–24) that Jesus himself attended. Having accepted table fellowship with a Pharisee, Jesus offended his host by omitting the customary ritual washing prior to eating (cf. Mk 7:1–4). Luke gives us a concise selection of the indictments that Matthew records in Mt 23. These point up some of the most common of the sins that characterize strict religious persons: hypocrisy (vv.39–41), imbalance (v.42), ostentation (v.43), impossible demands (v.46), intolerance (vv.47–51), and exclusiveness (v.52).

39–44 In Jesus' estimation, the "Pharisees" (see comment on Mk 2:15–16) had lost the heart of their religion. In vv.41–42b Jesus offers a positive corrective that clearly shows he did not oppose strict attention to religious duties but rather the neglect of caring about people (cf. 10:25–37). Jesus implies that in their "greed and wickedness" (v.39) the Pharisees were depriving the poor of the very food and drink that were "inside" their own carefully washed dishes (v.40). Likewise (v.42) they apparently were tithing possessions that they should have shared with the needy. The vivid simile in v.44 is an example of Jesus' use of irony (see comments on Mt 23:23–24). Though the Pharisees avoided touching a grave for fear of ritual defilement, they themselves, through their own unrecognized corruption, were defiling those who came into contact with them.

45–46 Jesus now directs words against the "experts in the law," many of whom were Pharisees. Their religious legalism explains v.46. They could interpret the OT and the traditions built on it in such a way as to leave little room for personal moral decisions. As "experts," they could, of course, find ways of circumventing the rules themselves.

47–48 Some lavish tombs were built for royalty and others before and during the time of Christ. It was all very well for the experts in the law to build new tombs for prophets long since martyred by the experts' ancestors. Yet this very act ironically symbolized approval of their ancestors' crimes against God's messengers. They may even have been seeking to atone for the sins of their ancestors by the elaborate tombs.

49–51 These verses relate the grim truth behind the parable of the tenants (see comments on 20:9–19). God's "wisdom" (v.49) most likely refers to his sovereign wisdom that allows evil people to prosper and good ones to suffer. The Zechariah mentioned here may be either the one mentioned in 2Ch 24:20–25 or the minor prophet (Zec 1:1; see Mt 23:35), though we have no knowledge of the latter one being martyred.

52–54 Jesus directed his final woe against the experts in the law for their sin of taking away not just physical but eternal life, a dereliction of their most important duty. Those who should have opened the meaning of the OT with their "key" not only declined to use it themselves but prevented others from "entering." The implied subject of "knowledge" is probably the kingdom of God, which people were seeking to enter (cf. Mt 16:19).

Jesus' series of woes here made the violent hostility against him described in vv.53–54 inevitable. His opponents followed him out of the house and fired at him a barrage of difficult questions (v.53). Because he had challenged those who professed to be the expert biblical teachers, they were out to defend their reputation by discrediting his.

D. Teachings on Times of Crisis and Judgment (12:1–13:35)

1. Warnings and encouragements (12:1–12)

The crisis in Jesus' relationship with the teachers of the law at the end of chapter 11 gives rise to a series of strong statements about the eternal issues involved. Jesus' audience must choose sides. He gives promises and warnings, appropriate to each hearer's circumstance.

1–3 Again Luke notes the crowds, emphasizing the extremely large size of this one. Jesus addresses the disciples "first"; the crowds received his words later (vv.13–21, 54–59). The key word "hypocrisy" (GK 5694) was triggered by the charges in ch. 11. Jesus compares the insidious way this attitude can influence others to the action of "yeast." His next words about concealment and disclosure seem at first to be a warning that what hypocrites try to cover up will be revealed (v.2). But vv.3–4 have a positive thrust. Verse 3 is much like Mt 10:26–27, where the disciples are encouraged not to be afraid but to declare publicly what they have heard privately from Jesus (cf. 8:17; Mk 4:22).

4–7 "Friends" is an expression of confidence (Jn 15:14–15), one that is antithetical to the hostility of the Pharisees (v.4). Jesus does not guarantee protection from death but affirms that (1) God alone controls our final destiny, and people should "fear" him rather than those who can merely inflict physical death; and that (2) God is intimately aware of all that befalls us. "Hell" (mentioned only here in Luke) is clearly a place of torment (Mt 5:22; 18:8–9; see comment on Mk 9:43–48).

Sparrows and hairs are so insignificant that this kind of argument (from lesser to greater) points up the supreme worth of the disciples in God's eyes.

8–9 Jesus underscores the seriousness of the issues by referring to the ultimate issue—whether or not one sides with him. The cruciality of the present situation calls for its restatement (cf. 9:26). Jesus' third-person reference to the "Son of Man" (see comment on Mk 8:31) is consistent with his guarded use of titles. Not until his trial does he publicly combine the terms "Son of Man," "Son of God," and "Messiah" in an eschatological context (22:67–70). "Acknowledge" and "disown" are opposites. The reference is apparently to a future scene when the Lord Jesus, having achieved victory and honor, acknowledges those who have supported him and disowns those who repudiated him during the present age. He does this publicly before God the Father (see Mt 10:32–33) and the assembled angels.

10 Jesus' final warning relates to the "unpardonable sin." In Luke it occupies a climactic place in the continued buildup of hostility between Jesus and the teachers of the law. It is difficult, however, to determine its meaning without the contextual explanations in Mt 12:25–36; Mk 3:23–30.

Those passages make it clear that the blasphemy against the Holy Spirit is the attribution of the works of Jesus to the very prince of demons. According to Luke, therefore, if dishonoring the Son of Man is such a serious matter (vv.8–9), then total rejection of God by insinuating that his "holy" Spirit is "evil" is so much the worse. One may reject Christ and later, by God's grace, accept him; but there is no remedy for absolute and complete denial of the one holy God—Father, Son, and Holy Spirit. This is what "blaspheme" (GK 1059) seems to mean here.

11–12 The foregoing series of warnings and encouragements concludes with this striking contrast to the blasphemy against the Holy Spirit. Far from committing that sin of speaking against him, believers find that the Spirit speaks through them (cf. Mt 10:19–20; Lk 21:14–15). The circumstance in which the Spirit speaks through believers is not preaching but persecution; in that context preparation of an adequate defense is hardly possible.

2. Parable of the rich fool (12:13–21)

The change in topic seems abrupt, though a comparison with ch. 16 shows a similar placement of controversy with Pharisees alongside teaching about worldly wealth. There the words "the Pharisees, who loved money" (v.14) serve to link the two subjects. Chapters 12 and 16 have much in common. The topic of wealth is prominent in Luke's writing. Here Jesus turns a question into an opportunity for ministering to an individual's underlying need.

13–14 A person who recognized Jesus as a "teacher" would naturally expect him to have the ability to render a judgment in ethical matters. Rabbis were often consulted in this manner. Jesus' refusal to answer is not a denial of his right or ability to answer, nor of his concern for social and ethical matters.

Rather, he turns directly to an area in which others have no right to judge (cf. Mt 7:1)—namely, the question of motivation.

15 Jesus' audience is probably now the whole crowd, not just the two brothers. The issue revolves around the very nature of "life." Greed seeks worldly things, which must not be equated with true "living." In fact, material possessions become a substitute for the proper object of a person's search and worship—God. Therefore, "greed ... is idolatry" (Col 3:5).

16–21 Since this is a parable, Jesus can heighten certain elements that illustrate his point, even to the point of having God speak directly to the rich man. The man expresses in his words (vv.17–19) the attitude Jesus discerns not only in the inquirer but in others (cf. v.21). The word "fool" is used in the OT sense of one who rejects the knowledge and precepts of God as a basis for life. God addresses the man on his own pragmatic terms, dealing not with matters of the kingdom or of life beyond death but with the question of the disposition of his possessions. This underscores the fact that he will have to "leave it all" (cf. Ecc 2:18–19).

Verse 21, using the contrasting words "for himself" and "toward God," ends powerfully with the participle "rich" as the final word (see also Mt 6:19).

3. Anxiety over possessions (12:22–34)

This section is virtually identical to Mt 6:25–33. Both passages are connected with sayings against "storing up" things for oneself. The passage ends (v.34) with a saying about one's "treasure" (cf. Mt 6:21). What was implied in the warning parable of vv.16–20 is explicitly commanded here (note the "therefore" of v.22). Believers should not act like the "pagan world," represented by the rich fool of the parable.

22–23 After a brief address to the crowd in vv.13–21, Jesus again turns to his disciples (cf. v.1). Observe the parallelism between v.22 and v.23: a comment on food comes first in each verse, followed by one on clothing. Verse 23 provides the support for the exhortation in v.22: there is more to life than these. The exhortation "do not worry" stands alongside the implied "do not covet" in this passage and the preceding one (cf. v.15); both rich and poor can be guilty of these sins.

24–26 The thrust of the comparison "how much more valuable?" is similar to the argument from the lesser to the greater in vv.6–7. There the sparrows represent birds of little value. Here the ravens may represent birds that were considered unclean (Lev 11:13–20, esp. v.15) and therefore presumably unworthy of God's care. Jesus assures us that the God who cares for such birds surely will care for us. Verses 25–26 constitute still another argument from the lesser (adding minutes of life, or possible inches to height) to the greater (totality of life and its needs). If it is futile to worry about small matters we cannot control, it is even more futile to worry about the larger matters that lies further beyond our control.

27–28 Jesus gives two final examples of the lesser to greater argument. He contrasts (1) the grandeur of Solomon, who could afford the finest clothing, to common flowers, which can do nothing toward making clothes; and (2) the limited life-span of flowers to the (implied) eternal life that lies before the disciples. God's meticulous and lavish care for mere perishing flowers assures us of his unfailing care for his own people. In view of this, the disciples' "little faith" is all the more shameful.

29 Jesus repeats the prohibition against worry (cf. v.22), though a different verb is used (lit., it means "be in suspense" or "be up in the air").

30–31 Jesus now contrasts the pagan Gentiles with believers with regard to their relation to material possessions (cf. Mt 5:47; 6:7, 32). Pagans do not have the same relationship believers have with a loving, caring, providing heavenly Father. To know that he knows their needs is sufficient assurance for all believers. Secure in that knowledge, his disciples can turn all their attention to the kingdom Jesus commands them to seek.

32 "Do not be afraid" introduces another contrast. The "little flock," which now needs to be fed and defended, will one day inherit the kingdom, possessing its benefits and authority. The fatherhood of God and its connection with the giving of the kingdom are themes especially characteristic of Matthew.

This encouragement not to fear is appropriate in view of the hostility of the "experts in the law" who, instead of opening the way to the kingdom and its truth (11:52), stand in the way of those who seek it.

33 The injunction to "sell your possessions" concludes Jesus' exhortation on the "treasure" theme. It is difficult to know whether the reason for this exhortation is to benefit the poor or to rid the disciples of encumbering possessions. The contrast point of the passage, however, seems to be the total dependence of Jesus' disciples on God.

The word "all" is neither present nor implied before the word "possessions." As we have seen, the point of Jesus' teaching on treasures is that they are not to be hoarded for one's own selfish pleasure (cf. v.21; Mt 6:19). Nevertheless, the interpreter must be careful not to blunt Jesus' strong teaching regarding a life of abandonment and giving (cf. 6:27–36; 14:26, 33). One should live on such a modest level of subsistence that the only "purses" needed are those one needs for heavenly "treasure." By their nature, such purses are never moth-eaten nor stolen.

34 This verse shows the essential thrust of Jesus' teaching. It is not the *extent* but the *place* of one's possessions that is emphasized, because it is the direction of one's "heart," heavenward or earthward, that is important.

4. Readiness for the coming of the Son of Man (12:35–48)

Jesus goes on to contrast the attitude of the alert Christian to that of the pagans (v.30), who seek only the things of this present world. The word "watching" (v.37; GK *1213*) expresses the theme of this passage. The scene in vv.36–37 and the parable in v.39 point clearly to the necessity of being ready for the Son of Man (v.40). In this section Luke concentrates much of the Lord's teaching on the implications of his sudden return.

35–38 In Jesus' time, a person "dressed ready for service" tucked his flowing outer robe under his belt or sash. This was done to prepare for travel, fighting (Eph 6:14), or work (cf. 1Pe 1:13).

Jesus pictures servants waiting for their masters with burning lamps (cf. Mt 25:1–13). When the master does arrive, there is a striking reversal of roles as he dresses himself to serve and waits on the servants (but cf. also 17:7–10 and comments). If the return is late in the night or toward morning, the alertness of the servants is even more commendable.

39–40 The image now changes to one of burglary. Jesus seems to be using a recent incident known to his audience. Iit is unusual, but not impossible, for an evil character, such as a thief, to represent a good person (see also 18:1–8). It is the story as a whole, not the individual characters in it, that provides the comparison here. The focal point is the concluding exhortation to "be ready," because the time of the Son of Man's coming is unknown.

41–44 Peter responds, in his accustomed role as spokesman for the apostles, with a question about the extent of their responsibility. Jesus answers, as often, with a counterquestion. Although he says elsewhere that exhortations to "watch" apply to everyone (Mk 13:37), in this case the parable that follows (vv.42–46) shows that the apostles have a special responsibility. Jesus emphasizes the importance of faithfulness in doing the will of the master, especially for one who has others placed under his leadership.

45–46 These verses clearly imply that Jesus himself would not return immediately but that there would be an interval of waiting and serving (cf. 18:7; 19:12). The attitude of the manager in v.45 is contrary to that commanded in v.40, for he stops expecting the master's return and begins beating the servants under his care (cf. Ac 20:29–30, which warns against false leaders who ravage the congregation). "Cut in pieces" probably refers metaphorically to the person's being cut off from the sons of light and going to the place where unbelievers end up.

47–48 Jesus concludes this section by explaining God's principle of judgment. The servants here represent those who sin willingly and knowingly (cf. Nu 15:30–31; Ps 19:13) and those who sin unwittingly (cf. Nu 15:27–29; Ps 19:12). In both cases there is some definite personal responsibility and therefore judgment, because the servant should have made it his business to know his master's will. All have some knowledge of God (Ro 1:20), and God judges according to individual levels of responsibility (Ro 2:12–13). The closing statement (v.48) would apply especially to the apostles and church leaders throughout the successive centuries.

5. Division over Jesus (12:49–53)

49–50 The previous section leads into this paragraph about the personal crises Christ precipitates. It is difficult to determine the precise meaning of "fire" (v.49) because the word can signify either judgment or purification. The immediate context suggests judgment; while Jesus came to bring salvation rather than judgment (Lk 4:19; Jn 3:17), his coming also meant judgment (Jn 9:39). But it may also signify purification. John the Baptist promised that Jesus would "baptize ... with the Holy Spirit and fire" (see comments on 3:16). Since 3:16 links fire with the Holy Spirit, it is possible that this fire was to be "kindled" by the baptism of the Spirit (Ac 2:1–4), something that could only occur after his own "baptism" of death (v.50), the thought of which distressed him greatly.

51–53 Although the Messiah was to bring peace (cf. 2:14), this was not his only mission, nor, in the political sense, his immediate one. Isa 11:1–9 shows that even in the final period of peace, the Messiah, enabled by the Spirit, will exercise judgment. Already in his earthly ministry, there is a division. The expression "from now on" stresses the element of crisis, both immediately and at the Lord's return. During this time his disciples must be prepared for a break in their family relationships if others do not concur with their decision to follow Christ (vv.52–53; cf. 14:26). The wording of v.53 is probably from Mic 7:6).

6. Interpreting the times (12:54–59)

54–56 Jesus now turns from his disciples (v.22) to the crowd with a message on the element of crisis. The words "interpret this present time" imply a crisis by comparing the observation of changing weather with God's "time" of opportunity and responsibility (cf. also 19:41–44). The word "hypocrites" shows that the people Jesus was speaking to were not sincere in their professed inability to "interpret this present time."

57–59 Jesus now appeals to human judgment regarding a time of personal decision (cf. Mt 5:25–26). In human affairs one resolves a crisis situation wisely to avoid penalty. This is a secular illustration, and v.59 should be applied only in its basic application of reconciliation with God before the Day of Judgment.

7. A call to repentance (13:1–9)

At this point, a dialogue about the problem of human suffering and evil introduces a parable that, like Jesus' teaching in ch. 12, deals with crisis and judgment.

1–5 We cannot be certain as to the exact incident referred to in v.1. The social tension made revolutionary activity in those days possible at any time. Galileans were especially susceptible to revolt (see also comment on 1:26). Any attack by Pilate or any other governor against Jews who had come to offer sacrifices was horrendous whatever its reason. Jesus refuses to attribute tragedy or accident directly to one's sin as the Jews did (cf. Jn 9:1–3). On the contrary, he affirms the sinfulness of all people. Whereas the victims of the two calamities referred to in vv.1–5 perished physically, all who do not repent face spiritual death.

6–9 Once more Jesus alludes to Mic 7 (see comment on 12:53), this time to Mic 7:1, with its lament over unproductive fig trees. The symbolism applies to Israel (cf. Isa 5:1–7). Jesus' mention of both a fig tree and a vineyard makes the figure doubly clear. The tree is not immediately destroyed but is given an extra year of grace, even beyond the three years its owner had already waited. Israel, however, failed to recognize her season of opportunity.

8. Healing a woman on the Sabbath (13:10–17)

The Sabbath issue, a major cause of dissension earlier (6:1–11), now reappears. Jesus is again teaching in a synagogue. This incident, like the others in this chapter, shows that despite the failure of the religious leaders to acknowledge the time of God's working, the kingdom is still being manifested.

10–13 As Jesus was speaking, he suddenly became aware of a crippled woman. Any activity by a demon is ultimately Satan's responsibility (v.16; cf. comments on 11:14–20). Most important to Luke is the woman's instant healing and its direct attribution to God. This, of course, shows that Jesus was truly acting with God's authority. "Praised God" reflects Luke's special interest in the glory of God (cf. 5:26; see comments on 2:20; 7:16–17).

14–17 The controversy over Jesus' Sabbath activities now comes to the fore as the synagogue ruler speaks to the people on the ground of Ex 20:9–10. He avoids addressing Jesus directly. There was ample evidence of rabbinic precedent for helping animals in emergencies on the Sabbath. So Jesus used a lesser-to-greater argument to move from helping animals to helping human beings (cf. 12:6–7, 24–28). "A daughter of Abraham" means a Jewess. In keeping with Luke's purpose, this designation highlights the priority of the Jews in the program of the Gospel. As he often does, Luke gives us the crowd's reaction to Jesus' response (v.17; cf. 4:15, 22, 32, 36–37; 5:26).

9. Parables of the mustard seed and the yeast (13:18–21)

18–21 Luke uses two parables to add support to the account of the miraculous healing just described. In Jesus' teaching the "mustard seed" represents that which is tiny but effective (cf. 17:6; see ZPEB, 4:324–25), for the tree sprouting from that seed is large enough for birds to settle in its branches. The point of the parable is the power inherent in the seed. This power is implicit in the kingdom, as Jesus' healing of the woman has just demonstrated. Likewise the point of Jesus' simile of the yeast and the kingdom is not that yeast penetrates the dough but that it has the inherent power to do this (cf. also Mk 4:26–29).

10. Entering the kingdom (13:22–30)

22–23 Jesus' teaching now turns to personal responsibility. Luke first reminds us that Jesus is on his way to Jerusalem (see comments on (9:51 19:44; 19:28). Like the question on divorce (Mt 19:3), this one about whether few or many people will be saved (v.23) was occasioned by differing opinions among the rabbis.

24–27 Jesus' reply to the question posed to him emphasizes not "how many?" but "who?" The saved are those who seize their opportunity now (cf. 4:19). Once the time for decision has passed (v.25), attempts to enter into salvation afterward will be futile. The "narrow door" limits the opportunities a person has to enter (v.25); thus people should act now! Based on other Scripture references, the phrase "But he will reply" (v.27) indicates that the "owner" is Jesus, the Son of Man (cf. Mt 25:12, 31–46). The repetition of "I don't know you or where you come from" denotes total rejection. In other words, familiarity with Jesus will be of no benefit after the time to repent is past.

28–30 The contrast is heightened between those inside and those outside the door, i.e., outside the kingdom. Every Jew expected to sit with the patriarchs at the messianic banquet. The concept of such a feast in heaven as a celebration with the Messiah is alluded to throughout the OT (cf. 16:15). The tragedy would not only be that of looking at the patriarchs from the outside but also that of seeing Gentiles inside with them. Verse 30 clearly means the exclusion from future blessings of those who thought they were first in line for them. This exclusion will result in a terrifying sense of doom (cf. Mt 8:12; 22:13; 25:30).

11. Concern over Jerusalem (13:31–35)

This is the main passage in Luke in which Jesus expresses a strong sense of destiny in his final journey to Jerusalem. It marks a stage in Jesus' progress to Jerusalem and prepares the reader for the next chapter. Note the sense of divine purpose expressed by such characteristic Lukan words as "today" and "must."

31 Some Pharisees choose this time to warn Jesus of Herod's designs on his life. Luke attributes no evil motive to those who are warning Jesus; apparently these Pharisees have Jesus' safety at heart.

32–33 In Luke's last mention of him (9:7–9) Herod was troubled at the reports of Jesus' miracles. By having John the Baptist beheaded, Herod thought he had done away with prophetic opposition. But Jesus, far from being threatened by Herod, called him "that fox." Today foxes connote cleverness; in Jesus' day they also connoted insignificance (cf. Ne 4:3; SS 2:15). Jesus intended to continue his ministry and to manifest the power of the kingdom, but not indefinitely. That time was short. Since "today and tomorrow" are not literal days, the same goes for the "third day," which must have reminded Luke's readers of the day of Jesus' resurrection. The "goal" of v.32, however, undoubtedly meant his death (cf. the parallel expression "die [in] Jerusalem" in v.33).

The programmatic statement of Jesus' purpose and progress continues in v.33 with two additions: the specific reference to suffering ("die") and the word "must" (GK 1256). Luke strongly conveys Jesus' sense of purpose and necessity (see comment on 4:43). The way Jesus was traveling was leading him to the cross and on to glory (cf. v. 34; 11:50; Ac 7:52).

34–35 Luke draws the reader's attention to Jerusalem, that city of destiny, both as the place of our Lord's passion and as the pathetic, unwilling object of his love. The "house," perhaps specifically the temple, will now lose him till Ps 118:26 is fulfilled. The substance of this quotation is recorded by all four gospels in their account of the Triumphal Entry; but the words are said, not by the Jerusalemites, but by Jesus' supporters (19:37–38).

E. Further Teaching on Urgent Issues (14:1–18:30)

1. Jesus at a Pharisee's house (14:1–14)

Luke 14 incorporates several elements—healing, conversations, and a parable—all tied together in dinner-table conversation. The conversation revolves around the response and behavior of dinner guests. This leads into a discussion of the responses of would-be followers of Jesus and to a discussion on the cost of discipleship.

1–4 Since this is the fourth time Luke records a controversy over the Sabbath (v.1), it is obvious that this was a major issue between Jesus and the religious leaders (cf. 6:1–5, 6:11; 13:10–17). The host was one of the "ruling" Pharisees, possibly a member of the Sanhedrin. Luke pictures the Pharisees as watchdogs of the faith as they waited for some theological flaw to appear in Jesus' teaching (vv.1–3; cf. 5:17; 6:7). The man who enters the scene was possibly planted there to test Jesus. "Dropsy" (see ZPEB, 2:134) may have popularly been considered a curse for sin (Nu 5:11–27). As in 6:9, Jesus took the initiative with a question designed to shift the burden of proof to the opposition (v.3). During the silence of the "Pharisees and experts in the law," Jesus met the man's need. His condition could have waited another day, but Jesus was concerned to establish a principle. This may be why he dismissed the man without including him further in the conversation.

5–6 Jesus now turns to the Pharisees and draws them into his illustration (cf. 11:5, 11; 12:25; 14:28). "Immediately" stresses the urgency of meeting the need, a pointed reference back to the man with dropsy. The principle exampled in the case of a beast is fully in accord with the OT and rabbinic law. In the face of this, the silence of Jesus' opponents was no longer by choice but of necessity; they "had nothing to say."

7–11 Jesus continued to take the initiative (v.7). In his time the guests at a formal dinner reclined on couches, several on each one, leaning on their left elbows. The seating was according to status. The "head of the table" was the couch at one end with other couches extending from it and facing each other like the arms of a "U." The important places were those nearest the head couch position. If an important guest came late, someone might have to be displaced to make room for him. Jesus' practical advice illustrates the spiritual principle he stated in v.11 (cf. 18:9–14). In keeping with the Jewish custom of his day, Luke avoids direct reference to God by using the passive voice, though God is the one who does the humbling or exalting at the final judgment.

12–14 Having addressed the Pharisee's guests, Jesus turns to his host and speaks words resembling 6:32–36 (see comments). In view of one's ultimate reward from God, one should do good to those who cannot repay it, and without expecting a reward (cf. 6:35). Also, v.13 recalls Luke's report of Jesus' own concern for the poor and oppressed (cf. 4:18; 6:20–21).

2. Parable of the great banquet (14:15–24)

Jesus continues the figure of the banquet with a striking parable about the "feast in the kingdom of God" (v.15—the so-called eschatological banquet; see also comments on 13:28–30).

15 The concept of future celebration in the kingdom is certainly biblical. Jesus addressed the presumption by some present, perhaps

JEWISH SECTS

PHARISEES

Their roots can be traced to the second century B.C. — to the Hasidim.
1. Along with the Torah, they accepted as equally inspired and authoritative, all material contained within the oral tradition.
2. On free will and determination, they held to a mediating view that made it impossible for either free will or the sovereignty of God to cancel out the other.
3. They accepted a rather developed hierarchy of angels and demons.
4. They taught that there was a future for the dead.
5. They believed in the immortality of the soul and in reward and retribution after death.
6. They were champions of human equality.
7. The emphasis of their teaching was ethical rather than theological.

SADDUCEES

They probably had their beginning during the Hasmonean period (166-63 B.C.). Their demise occurred c. A.D. 70 with the fall of Jerusalem.
1. They denied that the oral law was authoritative and binding.
2. They interpreted Mosaic law more literally than did the Pharisees.
3. They were very exacting in Levitical purity.
4. They attributed all to free will.
5. They argued there is neither resurrection of the dead nor a future life.
6. They rejected a belief in angels and demons.
7. They rejected the idea of a spiritual world.
8. Only the books of Moses were canonical Scripture.

ESSENES

They probably originated among the Hasidim, along with the Pharisees, from whom they later separated (I Maccabees 2:42; 7:13). They were a group of very strict and zealous Jews who took part with the Maccabeans in a revolt against the Syrians, c. 165-155 B.C.
1. They followed a strict observance of the purity laws of the Torah.
2. They were notable for their communal ownership of property.
3. They had a strong sense of mutual responsibility.
4. Daily worship was an important feature along with a daily study of their sacred scriptures.
5. Solemn oaths of piety and obedience had to be taken.
6. Sacrifices were offered on holy days and during sacred seasons.
7. Marriage was not condemned in principle but was avoided.
8. They attributed all that happened to fate.

ZEALOTS

They originated during the reign of Herod the Great c. 6 B.C. and ceased to exist in A.D. 73 at Masada.
1. They opposed payment of tribute for taxes to a pagan emperor, saying that allegiance was due only to God.
2. They held a fierce loyalty to the Jewish traditions.
3. They were opposed to the use of the Greek language in Palestine.
4. They prophesied the coming of the time of salvation.

including the speaker in v.1, that they would inevitably participate.

16–17 The invited guests were waiting either for the second invitation (customary in fashionable circles) or else were being reminded that it was time to come.

18–20 The striking thing is that "all" of them declined. Their excuses are weak. One man "must" go to see a purchased field he probably had seen before he bought it. Contrast his urgent attention to material things with Jesus' healing a man on the Sabbath (vv.2–4). The second excuse is as worthless as the first; would anyone have bought oxen without examining them? In both instances materialism got in the way of honoring an invitation already extended and presumably accepted.

The third excuse has more validity in the light of Dt 24:5. Also, only men were invited to banquets. Yet marriage was not, especially in that society, an abrupt decision and could hardly have been an unexpected factor that intervened between the first and second invitations. With his superb narrative art, Jesus used these three excuses to show that just as a host may be snubbed, so God's gracious invitation may be flouted.

21–24 The host "became angry" because the rejections were a personal insult. The "streets" were those roads traveled by a wide variety of people, whereas the "alleys" were small lanes or side paths likely to harbor the loitering outcasts of society. Those brought from these places were precisely the same unfortunates Jesus had told his host to invite in v.13 (see comment). With room still available (v.22), the servant is to go outside the town and search even the "country lanes" (v.23). To "make them come in" is not compulsion but "an insistent hospitality."

Although Jesus does not interpret the parable, we may link it with 13:28–30 and find in it an allusion of the extension of the Gospel to the Gentiles. Those who had the benefit of the original invitation are the Jews with all their heritage and spiritual advantages (see Ro 9:4–5). "Not one" (v.24) refers to the parable and stresses the seriousness of the consequences of rejecting God's invitation.

3. The cost of being a disciple (14:25–35)

25–27 The serious tone of the preceding parable continues as attention now turns to those who profess allegiance to Jesus. Luke again points out Jesus' popularity (see comment on 4:15) and his continuing journey toward Jerusalem (see comment on 13:22). "Hate" (v.26; GK *3631*) is not an absolute but a relative term. To neglect social customs pertaining to family loyalties would probably have been interpreted as hate. Jesus is not contravening the commandment to honor one's father and mother. It is important to understand the ancient Near Eastern expression without blunting its force. (For the meaning of v.27, see comment on 9:23.)

28–32 Jesus uses two different circumstances to illustrate his basic point: discipleship requires a conscious advance commitment, made with a realistic estimate of the ultimate personal cost. The practical nature of the circumstances Jesus so vividly pictures underlines the fact that Christian discipleship is not some theoretical abstract ideal but hard reality.

33 This is clearly a crucial verse. But does it mean that it is impossible to retain any possessions at all if one wants to be a true disciple? In contrast to the cares of the rich young ruler (18:22), Jesus does not say a disciple should sell all his possessions and give everything away. His thought probably is that of a continual abandonment of things, yielding up the right of ownership or the desire to cling to things, rather than outright disposal of them. The disciple of Jesus may be given the use of things in trust, as a stewardship, but they are no longer his or her own. This understanding is therefore consistent with the command to use our possessions wisely (cf. 16:1–12).

34–35 This saying poses two questions: Why does it occur here? and, How does salt lose its saltiness? Its place here is due to the common element it shares with the preceding illustrations—the consistent quality of life that Jesus expects of his disciples. The reference to salt may be to adulteration either by impurities in the beds by the Dead Sea from which salt slabs were taken or by inert fillers introduced by unscrupulous dealers. The point is that tasteless salt is useless. Those who have ears are expected to apply this lesson to themselves.

4. Parables of joy (15:1–32)
a. The lost sheep (15:1–7)

This section begins what Manson has called the "Gospel of the Outcast." The large body of material in chapters 15–19 is unique to Luke and dramatically shows Jesus' concern for the social outcasts of his day. The twin parables (vv.3–7, 8–10), along with the longer one about the lost son (vv.11–32), depend for their interpretation on vv.1–2.

1 "Tax collectors" were among those ostracized because their work was considered dishonest or immoral (see comment on Mk 2:14). NIV appropriately puts "sinners" in quotation marks to show that this was not Luke's designation; it was the way others, i.e., the Pharisees, thought of them (see comments on 5:29–30). "All" signifies that a large proportion of "sinners" was usually among the crowds who came to hear Jesus.

2 In OT times it was taken for granted that God's people did not consort with sinners (cf. Ps 1), but the Pharisees extended this beyond the biblical intent. To go so far as to "welcome" them and especially to "eat" with them, implying table fellowship, was unthinkable to them. The parables that follow show that the return of "sinners" to God should be a cause for joy to the religious leaders, just as it was to God.

3–7 For the phrase "suppose one of you," see comment on 14:5. The situation Jesus describes was a common one. One hundred sheep was a normal-sized flock. A count was taken nightly. The "open country" was a safe place to leave the sheep, though they would have to be left in someone's care. The frightened, confused, and perhaps injured sheep would have to be carried.

Two things are striking. First, in the obvious analogy to the search for the sheep, Jesus takes the initiative in seeking out lost people—a major theme in Luke (cf. 19:10). Second, the climax of the story is not only the return of the sheep but the triumphant rejoicing in its rescue. Jesus is stressing, both by parable and by direct statement, that his seeking and receiving sinners pleases God. The future rejoicing (v.7) may include a future of gathering and feasting in God's kingdom (see comment on 13:24). There is none who is inherently righteous (cf. Ro 3:10); thus, the "righteous persons" referred to in v.7 are probably devout people (cf. 1:6) who have no gross, open sins to repent of.

b. The lost coin (15:8–10)

8–10 This parable is clearly linked to the preceding one. The "coins" are "drachmas," each worth about a day's wages (see NIV note). The mention of ten coins implies that they were all she had. "A lamp" was needed because the house would have had at best a few small windows or only a low doorway. She would "sweep" the hard earthen floor to find the coin by the sound of its clinking. As in v.6, the extent of the joy expressed is striking. Considering the neighborly feelings in a small village, such joy is understandable, especially if the coin represented a tenth of the woman's savings. Jesus' final comment reinforces that joy. This parable, like that of the lost sheep, justifies Jesus' welcome of sinners (v.2).

2. The lost son (15:11–32)

The great parable of the lost son speaks even more eloquently and vividly than its predecessors to the situation set forth in vv.1–2. The first part (vv.11–24) conveys the same sense of joy when the lost is found; in contrast, the second part deals with the sour attitude of the elder brother. Like the Pharisees, he could not comprehend the meaning of forgiveness. The positions of the two sons would be considered binary opposites; the lost son rises and the elder brother falls in moral state. The central figure, the father, remains constant in his love for both. By telling the story Jesus identifies himself with God in his loving attitude to the lost. He represents God in his mission, the accomplishment of which should elicit joy from those who share the Father's compassion.

11–12 The "share of the estate" that a younger son would receive on the death of the father would be one-third, because the older son received two-thirds, a "double portion" (Dt 21:17). If the property were given, as in this case, while the father lived, the heirs would have use of it (cf. v.31).

13–16 NIV captures the vivid wording of the account, including "squandered his wealth" and "wild living." The famine made employment and food even harder than usual to get. The "distant country" was apparently outside strictly Jewish territory, and the wayward son found himself with the demeaning job of feeding pigs, unclean animals for the Jews. He would even have eaten "pods," seeds of the carob tree used for pigs' food. He had fallen so low and had become so insignificant that "no one gave him anything."

17–20 "Came to his senses" seems to carry the Semitic idea of repentance. Certainly repentance lies at the heart of the words that the son prepared to tell his father. The motivation for his return was hunger, but it was specifically to his "father" that he wanted to return. He admitted that his sins were ultimately against God ("heaven"). The father in the story portrays the characteristics and attitudes of a loving heavenly Father, as Jesus' listeners would recognize (Ps 103:13). The son knew he had no right to return as a son, having taken and squandered his inheritance. He therefore planned to earn his room and board.

The description of his return and welcome is as vivid as that of his departure, with several beautiful touches. Jesus portrays the father as waiting for his son, perhaps daily searching the distant road hoping for his appearance. The father's "compassion" assumes some knowledge of the son's pitiable condition, perhaps from reports, and his warm embrace and kissing add to the impact of the story. Jesus used every literary means to heighten the contrast between the father's attitude and that of the elder brother.

21–24 The son's speech was never completed (v.21). Instead the father more than reversed the unspoken part about becoming a "hired man" (v.19). What he gave his son signified more than sonship: the robe was a ceremonial one such as a guest of honor would be given, the ring signified authority, and the sandals were those only a free man would wear. The calf was apparently being "fattened" for some special occasion. Note the parallel between "dead" and "alive" and "lost" and "found"—terms that also apply to one's state before and after conversion to Christ (Eph 2:1–5). As in the parables of the lost sheep and the lost coin, it was time to "celebrate."

25–32 It may seem strange that the older son was not there when the celebration began, but Jesus' parables are a fictional way of teaching enduring truth. Verse 28 contrasts sharply the older son with the father. The son became angry; but the father "went out," as he had for the younger brother, and "pleaded" rather than scolded. The older son's abrupt beginning—"Look!" (v.29)—betrays a disrespectful attitude toward his father. Likewise, "slaving" is hardly descriptive of a warm attitude to his father. "You never gave me," whether true or not, shows a long smoldering discontent. By saying "this son of yours," the elder brother avoids acknowledging that the prodigal is his own brother, a disclaimer the father corrects by the words "this brother of yours" (v.32). The older brother's charges include sharp criticism of both father and brother.

The father's response is nevertheless tender: "My son" is followed by words of affirmation, not weakness (v.31). "We had to celebrate" suggests that the elder brother should have joined in the celebration. The words "had to" introduce once more the necessity and urgency so prominent in Luke (see comment on 4:43).

5. Parable of the shrewd manager (16:1–18)

Chapter 16 follows the pattern characteristic of this part of Luke—namely, a combination of parables and sayings pointing again and again to the need for decision. In chapter 16, in spite of obvious diversity, one theme occurs several times: that of Jesus' teaching about material possessions—first in the parable of the shrewd manager, then in the comment about the Pharisees "who loved money" (v.14), and finally in the parable of the rich man and Lazarus.

The interpretation of the parable of the shrewd manager is notoriously difficult. Prior to any overall interpretation and application of it is a series of decisions regarding vv.8–13. Several interdependent questions face the expositor. (1) Is the "master" in v.8 the "master" in the parable (vv.3, 5) or the Lord Jesus (in Greek, *kyrios* [GK 3261] means "master" and "Lord")? (2) Why did the "master" commend a dishonest manager?—a question that becomes more acute if the "master" is the Lord Jesus. (3) Where does the parable end, before v.8, in the middle of v.8, or at the end of v.8? (4) Finally, are vv.10–12 and 13 part of the same unit or do they represent a separate tradition?

The most likely interpretation couples v.8a with the parable, so that the rich master in the story is the one who commends the dishonest steward. (1) This would not be an unusual secular use of the word *kyrios;* (2) the religious terminology of v.8b (e.g., "people of the light") seems to refer to real people (in contrast to the characters of the secular illustration) and therefore sounds like the beginning of Jesus' explanation; (3) v.8a seems to form a better conclusion to the parable than v.7.

But even if we are right that the "master" of v.8 is the one in the story, the Lord Jesus seems to agree with the commendation; so we are left with the second question in either case: Why was a dishonest manager commended? The answer on the surface is "because he had acted shrewdly" (v.8). But was his shrewd act not dishonest? The text does not say that the manager's action in writing off the debts was dishonest. Rather, the word "dishonest" may be referring back to his initial act of mishandling the master's funds. In other words, even one who had acted so dishonestly could do something commendable.

He had at last learned how one's worldly wealth can be wisely given away to do good. Some have suggested that the amount taken off the bills in vv.5–7 was not part of the debt owed the master but rather represented the interest the manager himself was charging. The bill to be repaid would be written in terms of the commodity rather than in monetary figures, with the interest hidden in the total. By law a master could not be held accountable for illegal acts of an employee. So the master in the parable was in a position to view the manager's activities objectively. If this explanation is correct, the manager's transaction was not illegal. In any event, the master would lose no money if the amount forfeited was simply the interest the manager would have personally gained. Furthermore, such a forgiveness of debts would probably have helped the master's own reputation. Therefore, the master admired the manager's shrewdness. For his part, the manager knew his job and reputation were gone because of his previous mishandling of funds. He needed friends; and, by foregoing the customary interest, he won friends among the creditors. Jesus then uses this story to show that the "people of the light" could also accomplish much by wisely giving up some of their "worldly wealth."

Some commentators see this parable as an exhortation to act decisively in time of eschatological crisis, just as the manager acted in his personal crisis. This interpretation, while possible, ignores the fact that the predominant issue here is the prudent use of material wealth.

Regarding vv.10–13, as they stand in the text, they provide an integrated sequence of teachings structured around the ideas of dishonesty and responsibility.

1–4 "Manager" is a broad term for an employee or agent who was entrusted with the management of funds or property. Mismanagement was possible because strict accounts were not always kept. When word came from others (v.2), he had to "give an account." The manager's plight (v.3) was that he had a respectable "desk job" but could do little else. His decision, therefore, is made with a view to his personal security after his dismissal.

5–8a As already noted, the bills may have been written in terms of commodities rather than cash, perhaps in order to hide the actual amount of interest. The amounts owed were large; the wheat is said to be equal to the yield of about one hundred acres. The actual value of the reduction in each case has been computed to equal about sixteen month's wages for a day laborer. The meaning of v.8a, as noted above, is not that a manager is commended for an act of dishonesty but that a dishonest manager is commended for an act of prudence.

8b–9 The contrast between those who belong to this age and those who belong to the light (v.8b) is a familiar one (cf. Eph 5:8; 1Th 5:5; 1Jn 1:5–7). Christians do not belong to this evil age, but they can nevertheless make responsible use of "worldly wealth" (v.9). The "friends" may not refer to any particular people but simply be part of the parable's imagery. Usually they have been understood as being poor people, for whom Jesus had a deep concern and to whom we are here urged to give alms (cf. 12:33). "Worldly wealth" should not be stored up for oneself (cf. 12:21), since one day it will be "gone."

10–13 The theme of stewardship is now discussed in terms of trustworthiness as over against dishonesty. "Worldly wealth" (v.11) appears for the second time (cf. v.9). The property here is "someone else's," presumably God's, in contrast to the parable's imagery in which the amount forgiven was the manager's own commission. Verse 13 (cf. Mt 6:24) is also appropriate to the context (the Greek word earlier translated "worldly wealth" is now translated "money"; GK 3440). Though one may *have* both God and money, we cannot *serve* them both.

14–15 Money links the next verses with the preceding. The charge that the Pharisees do not have a proper sense of values leads to the saying about the value of the kingdom and the law (vv.16–17). In turn, the reference to the permanence of the law becomes the occasion for a specific example of a contested moral standard, divorce and remarriage (v.18).

Regarding v.14, Jewish teachers in Hellenistic society were aware that philosophers often taught for fees. Rabbis in the first centuries of our era often had secular jobs. The Pharisees would not have been immune to desires for remuneration commensurate with their own sense of importance. Note Paul's desire not to be charged with greed (1Th 2:5; cf. 1Co 9:12). Self-justification (v.15) is a temptation for religious people (cf. Mt 5:20; 6:1).

16–17 The Pharisees had the truth of the "Law" of Moses (Genesis to Deuteronomy) and the "Prophets" (v.16, here representing the rest of the OT). They failed to respond not only to the good news of the kingdom but even to their own Scriptures (cf. Mk 7:8–9; see also comment on Lk 16:29; for the relationship of John the Baptist to the kingdom, see comment on 7:28).

The last part of v.16 is difficult to interpret (see comments on Mt 11:12–13). It seems best to see it as an expression of one's enthusiastic drive to enter the kingdom (cf. 13:24). In any case, it is clear that the Pharisees had missed what was really of value (v.15), while all around them were people whose values were in order and who were energetically seeking the kingdom (cf. Mt 13:44–46; for Lk 16:17, see comments on Mt 5:17–20).

18 This brief excerpt from Jesus' teaching on divorce and remarriage is included as an example of one aspect of the law that the Pharisees tended to minimize. The teaching is essentially the same as in Mt 5:32 (see comments), except that Luke (1) omits the phrase "except for marital unfaithfulness," (2) says that the remarried man commits adultery rather than that he causes his first wife to do so, and (3) includes a comment about a man who marries a divorced woman.

6. The rich man and Lazarus (16:19–31)

Despite not having an introduction as most parables do, this section is best seen as a parable. It is set in a series of encounters with the Pharisees (cf. 15:1–2; 16:14) and must be understood in that context. The Pharisees did not follow their own Scriptures, the "Law and the Prophets" (v.16); so they were no better than the rich man's brothers who "have Moses and the Prophets" (v.29). The Pharisees professed belief in a future life and in future judgment. They did not live in conformity with that belief, however, but in the pursuit of wealth (v.14), just like the rich man of the parable.

While the parable does contain a few doctrinal implications, the expositor must keep in mind that one cannot build a complete eschatology upon it. To do that will result in an anachronism, for Rev 20:14 places the throwing of death and Hades into the lake of fire at the end of history. What the story does emphasize about the last things is (1) the future reversal of the human condition (cf. 6:20–26), (2) the reality of future judgment based on one's decisions in this life, and (3) the futility of even a resurrection to persuade those who persist in rejecting God's revealed word.

19–20 This paragraph vividly pictures the earthly state of the two people and prepares us for the reversal in vv.22–24, though this is not in itself the main feature of the story. The fact that Jesus named the "beggar" (v.20) but not the "rich man" (v.19) suggests that the former was ultimately more important (characters in parables are not usually given names).

"Purple" (v.19) was a dyed cloth worn by the wealthy (cf. Mk 15:17, 20). In a vivid contrast to the rich man, Jesus depicts Lazarus as neglected and subjected to insult even by "the dogs" (v.20).

21–24 After his death, Lazarus is escorted by "the angels," in contrast to the rich man who is merely "buried" (v.22). "Abraham's side" may picture reclining at a banquet, like the "feast in the kingdom of God" at which Abraham will be present (13:28–29). If so, it may contrast with vv.20–21, where the rich man sits at the table while Lazarus longs for the scraps. Or else it is a symbol of reunion with Abraham and the other patriarchs at death. "Hell" is "Hades" (GK 87), the word used in the OT to translate "Sheol" (GK 8619), the realm of the dead. In the NT Hades is never used of the destiny of the believer; neither is it identified with Gehenna (see comment on Mk 9:43–48). In this story, Hades stands in contrast to the place and state of Lazarus's blessing.

25–26 By calling the rich man "son" (cf. 15:31), Abraham conveys something of the compassion God himself shows even to those who spurn him. In a masterly summary Jesus contrasts the previous states of the rich man and Lazarus with the "now" and "here" of their situations after death. Verse 26 shows the utter and unchangeable finality of their decision.

27–31 This unchangeability comes from a hardness not only toward Christ but also toward "Moses and the Prophets" (cf. Jn 5:46). Not even a spectacular "sign," like one returning from the dead, can change those whose hearts are set against God's word, as the response of many to the resurrection of Jesus was to show.

7. Sin, faith, duty (17:1–10)

As the heading indicates, this unit contains various brief teachings that Luke brings together. The common unifying theme is attitudes in the Christian community.

1–3a Jesus has been addressing the Pharisees since 16:14. Now he resumes his conversation with the disciples, warning them about "things that cause people to sin." "Woe" recalls 6:24–26. A "millstone" was a stone of sufficient weight to crush grain as it was being rotated in a mill. The "little ones" would seem to be either young or new believers (cf. Mt 18:1–6) or people whom the world takes little notice of. Since there is no antecedent for "these," it seems best to take it as referring to people who were actually standing there with Jesus.

3b–4 Both units of v.3b must be given equal weight. Rebuke of the sinner and forgiveness of the penitent are equally Christian duties. Verse 4 does not, of course, establish a specific number of times for forgiveness but rather shows the principle of being generous in forgiving others (cf. Mt 6:12). This is the only right response for those who have themselves been forgiven (cf. Mt 18:21–35).

5–6 The apostles may have felt that this kind of forgiveness would demand more faith than they had. The black mulberry tree grew quite large, to a height of some thirty-five feet, and would be difficult to uproot. The mustard seed is proverbially small, a suitable metaphor for the amount of faith needed to do the seemingly impossible (cf Mt 17:20; Mk 11:23). Jesus' answer to the request for additional faith seems to be that they should use the faith they had to petition God.

7–10 Luke here presents Jesus' teaching about the ideal of servanthood. The world's idea of success is to lord it over others; Jesus' way is the reverse—namely, servanthood—which is actually the way to true greatness. The circumstances that Jesus describes here were normal in that society and the point is obvious (cf. 12:35–37, where Jesus highlights God's grace by a reversal of this normal procedure). Through this parable Jesus emphasizes the proper servant attitude. He does not intend to demean servants but to make their duty clear.

8. Ten healed of leprosy (17:11–19)

This narrative stresses several characteristically Lukan themes. Jerusalem is the goal of Jesus' journey (cf. 9:51; 13:33); Jesus has mercy on social outcasts; he conforms to Jewish norms by requiring that the lepers go for the required priestly declaration of health (cf. Lev 14); faith and healing should bring praise to God (cf. 18:43; Ac 3:8–9); and the grace of God extends beyond Judaism, with Samaritans receiving special attention (cf. 10:25–37).

11–13 Though we do not know exactly where this miracle occurred, what Luke does consider important is Jesus' progress toward Jerusalem. The "village" lies somewhere in the border territory between Galilee and Samaria; so Jewish and Samaritan lepers share their common misery at its edge. The lepers maintain their proper distance, calling out to

Jesus and asking only for pity without specifying any request.

14–19 Jesus' command required obedience based on some faith in his healing ability (cf. Mt 12:13; Mk 3:5; Lk 6:10). On their way to the priests, the lepers are "cleansed." Jesus, however, uses the more comprehensive word "made well" (v.19; GK 5392) when he speaks to the Samaritan who returned to give thanks. The stress in this story is on the openly expressed gratitude of the Samaritan, who alone brought praise to God (vv.15–16).

9. The coming of the kingdom of God (17:20–37)

Luke contains two major discourses about the future, the present passage and 21:5–33 (see comments on that passage). Both have close parallels in Mt 24 and Mk 13. Luke 17 stresses God's acts directly from heaven (in contrast to the besieging armies of 21:20). Also the prohibition against lingering is stronger and more urgent here than in chapter 21.

The Pharisees' question about the kingdom initiates this new cycle of Jesus' teachings. This includes (1) a saying about the coming of the kingdom that is unique to Luke's gospel (vv.20–21), (2) the discourse on the coming of the Son of Man (vv.22–37), and (3) a parable of encouragement for those who wait for vindication when the Son of Man comes (18:1–8).

20–21 The time of the coming of the kingdom was important both to the Pharisees and to the Christians of Luke's day, though for different reasons (cf. 2Th 2:1–2; 2Pe 3:3–4 for concerns that Christians had). Jesus had already made it clear that the kingdom was already present (see 11:20); he will shortly indicate by a parable that the full expression of the kingdom does not take place in the immediate future (19:11–27). The present passage is therefore important as a further definition of the nature of the kingdom.

In answer to the question "When?" (v.20), Jesus says that the kingdom will not come as an observable process; that is, it will come suddenly. The NIV "within you" is a questionable translation, for Jesus would hardly tell Pharisees, most of whom (especially those who interrogated him) were unbelievers, that the kingdom was within them. The NIV margin ("among you") is surely right.

Luke's presentation of the kingdom in Jesus' teaching is dynamic rather than psychological (see 11:20). The idea behind "'Here it is' or 'There it is'" is that of the kingdom's authoritative presence. Jesus is thus saying that people are the subjects, not the timekeepers, of God's kingdom.

22–25 Jesus continues the emphasis on the suddenness of the kingdom's coming. "One of the days" probably refers to the initiation of the reign of the coming Son of Man (i.e., "his day" in v.24, or "the Day of the Lord"; cf. Am 8:11, 13 for similar interchange of "days" and "day"). When that day arrives, his coming will be obvious, "like the lightning"; thus rumors of seeing him in various places cannot be true.

The inclusion of the passion prediction (v.25) is natural in Luke, who stresses the order of suffering before glory (cf. 24:26, 46; Ac 17:3). "This generation" may obliquely refer back to the Pharisees. More broadly it refers to Jesus' contemporaries, elsewhere called by him "unbelieving and perverse" (9:41) and "wicked" (11:29).

26–29 Jesus' references to Noah and Lot serve to illustrate the suddenness of the revelation of the Son of Man. The words "eating, drinking," etc., describe the usual round of life's activities that were taking place when unexpected destruction came as a judgment during the time of Noah and Lot. God will similarly interrupt human affairs at the consummation of history, indeed, of the kingdom of God itself, when he reveals the Son of Man.

30–36 The sudden coming of the Son of Man leaves no time even for a quick gathering of possessions from one's home. This theme of imminency blends into a call for decision between eternal values and present possessions. Lot's wife, reluctant to leave her old life, looked back to Sodom (Ge 19:26). This leads to the saying in v.33 regarding discipleship (Mt 10:39), used here with a very concrete application.

The solemn words "I tell you" (v.34) introduce a warning that the return of the Lord reveals ultimate destinies. Even those closely associated (in bed and at work) are separated, one taken into fellowship with God, the other abandoned to judgment. The two illustrations reflect activities selected to show that the Son of Man could come at any time, day or night.

37 The Pharisees had asked "When?" (v.20); the disciples asked "Where?" For us Jesus' reply is somewhat obscure. The hovering "vultures" may symbolize judgment on the spiritually dead. Also they may merely represent the place of carnage.

10. Parable of the persistent widow (18:1–8)

1 This parable must be interpreted with reference to the theme of the return of our Lord in chapter 17, as v.8b makes clear. The story is not intended to apply to prayer in general, as though one needed to pester God for every need until he reluctantly responds (cf. 11:5–10). The theme is that of the vindication of God's misunderstood and suffering people. God's people in OT days needed to "wait" on God as he worked out justice with apparent slowness (see Ps 25:2–3). In the final days the martyrs wait for vindication (Rev 6:9–11). Meanwhile we wrestle with the problem of evil and with issues of theodicy. Under these circumstances we should "always pray and not give up."

2–3 The designation "unjust judge" is similar to the idiom in 16:8, "the dishonest manager." Therefore we should probably understand the judge to be a "man of the world," who, though crooked, prided himself on shrewd judicial decisions. The judge is typical of a local Gentile judge known throughout the Hellenistic world. Being easily accessible and having the authority to make quick decisions, he would naturally be besieged by people such as the widow of the story (v.3).

4–6 The words "wear me out" (lit., "to give a black eye to") probably relate to the common idiom in eastern countries, where to have one's face blackened means to suffer shame. In this parable the reputation of the one being petitioned is at stake. Therefore, though God is not compared to a crooked judge, there *is* a partial basis of comparison in that God will also guard his reputation and vindicate himself.

7 "Chosen ones" (GK *1723*) is a term used throughout Scripture to describe those who, at the end of history, are marked out as on the victorious side (Mt 24:31; Mk 13:27; Rev 17:14). The point of the verse is that God patiently listens to his chosen ones as they pray in their continuing distress, waiting for the proper time to act on their behalf.

8 Help is on the way, and the delay will prove shorter than it seems from our perspective. True believers who persistently wait with patient trust will seem few when the Son of Man comes (cf. vv.24–25).

11. Parable of the Pharisee and the tax collector (18:9–14)

In this parable we see the characteristics of recipients and rejecters of the kingdom most sharply defined. The Pharisee shows an attitude of pride and self-vindication (see Mt 23:5–7; Mk 7:6; Php 3:4–6). His words imply a contractual relationship with God whereby he would accept the Pharisee's merit in exchange for justification. Actually not only this parable but the two following stories (vv.15–17, 18–30) deal with conditions for entering the kingdom. Each stresses human inability.

9–12 Elements of this parable need little interpretation, only careful observation. The characters in this story represent extremes, but the sketches are true to life. The Pharisee follows custom in praying in the temple and in standing while praying. His prayer expresses the essence of Pharisaism—separation from others. This in itself was not reprehensible, because at the inception of Pharisaism there was a need for a distinctive group who would maintain a piety that stood in contrast to the encroaching pagan Hellenism (see comment on Mk 2:16). This initial good hardened into obnoxious self-righteousness on the part of many (not all) Pharisees (cf. Mt 23; Mk 7). Pharisees did tithe and fast (see comment on Mk 2:18), though fasting twice in the week was more than necessary and was only practiced by the most pious. The problem was that this Pharisee's prayer was a farce, being created only in himself; he mentioned God only in the beginning of his prayer.

13–14 The description speaks for itself. The tax collector (see comment on Mk 2:14) was one of the social outcasts so prominent in Luke as recipients of God's grace (e.g., 5:12, 27; 7:34, 37; 15:1–2; 16:20). Contrary to what people in Jesus' day would expect, he received immediate justification, granted by God in contrast to the self-justification that the Pharisee was futilely caught up in. Verse 14b states the principle that is further illustrated in vv.15–17.

12. The little children and Jesus (18:15–17)

15–17 Jesus' words about little children provide Luke's second example of the attitude essential for receiving God's grace. It is not age per se that is in view but childlike qualities such as trust, openness, and the absence of holier-than-thou attitudes. Jesus had compassion even on infants too young to understand the difference between right and wrong. In recent years we have begun to understand formally the importance of communication through touching.

13. The rich ruler (18:18–30)

Like the previous two stories, this one also illustrates the need for human receptiveness if one is to experience God's grace. Then, lest it be thought that this response lies within human power, Jesus points out that only by God's power is anyone saved (vv.25–27). The story thus emphasizes the responsibility and helplessness of humankind.

18 "Ruler" (only in Luke) is too broad a term to permit precise identification of the man's background (see comment on Mk 10:17). The appellation "Good teacher" is not a common one and calls for a comment by Jesus. "What must I do?" indicates a desire by this young man to discover if any deed has been overlooked in qualifying for eternal life.

19 Jesus replies by asking the ruler a question that has puzzled many. Perhaps he is subtly urging the ruler to see that if Jesus is good and if it is also true that only God is good, then there is a clear conclusion to be drawn as to his true identity. His more obvious purpose in this question is to establish a standard of goodness infinitely higher than the ruler supposes it to be (cf. Mt 5:20, 48).

20–21 Jesus now addresses this standard of righteousness. The first step is a summary of several of the Ten Commandments, omitting the first few that relate to God and the final one about covetousness. The man, like Paul (Php 3:6), has kept the letter of the law.

22 Jesus now moves to the heart of the tenth commandment by leading the ruler to face his attitude toward his possessions. Paul himself recognized his sinfulness when he became aware of the thrust of the command against covetousness (Ro 7:7–8). Jesus goes on to say what is still needed to produce righteous perfection. By the act of giving away his goods, the ruler would have shown himself rid of the sin of greed, and by following Jesus, he would have indicated his allegiance to God.

The command to sell everything (cf. 14:33) and give to the poor is difficult to interpret as well as to apply. This does not seem to be a universal requirement; it seems rather to be designed particularly for this man to shatter his covetousness. Such an act would also benefit others, as his wealth would be dispensed among poor people (cf. 6:30–31). Even this is insufficient, however, unless the ruler truly follows Jesus.

23–25 The ruler's sorrow over the decision about his wealth recalls the far deeper sorrow rich people who have incurred Jesus' "woe" will experience (6:24). Jesus' intense focus on the man as he spoke to him about the problem of wealth limits the application of v.24 to the kind of attitude the ruler had. The vivid hyperbole about the camel makes the point unforgettable (see comment on Mk 10:25).

26–30 If wealth is such a hindrance in respect to salvation, the situation for the rich seems hopeless. Jesus' reply about God's power (v.27) provides the assurance the audience needed and evokes an enthusiastic outburst from Peter, who feels that the disciples have done what the ruler did not do. Jesus acknowledges this by assuring his disciples who have left everything to follow him of abundant recompense, not only in the future age, but also in the present.

F. Final Approach to Jerusalem (18:31–19:44)

1. A further prediction of Jesus' passion (18:31–34)

31 Luke has already preserved various sayings that predict or foreshadow Jesus' death (5:35; 9:22, 44; 12:50; 13:32; 17:25). Once again Luke picks up words that stress the fulfillment of prophecy (cf. 2:25–38; 22:37; 24:27, 44).

LUKE 19

32–34 In this prediction, Jesus for the first time mentions the Gentiles as his executors. Luke attributes the ignorance of the disciples (a theme much emphasized by Mark) to what is apparently a supernatural withholding of understanding (v.34; 24:16).

2. Healing a blind beggar (18:35–43)

This incident shows that Jesus, who was on his way to the royal city of Jerusalem, was actually the "Son of David" (vv.38–39; cf. 1:32), i.e., the Messiah. It also allows Luke to point again to Jesus' concern for the needy and especially to show his healing of the blind as a messianic work (cf. 4:18). In addition, this miracle emphasizes the importance of faith (v.42) and the glory that God receives through the ministry of Jesus.

35–36 Jesus' final approach to Jerusalem is under way, moving from outside Jericho (v.35) to inside Jericho (19:1–10), and thence to the triumphal entry into Jerusalem, his city of destiny (19:11, 28). Luke refers to the crowds here (v.36) to explain how the blind beggar knew that something special was happening (v.37).

38–43 The description of the man's insistent calling draws attention to his faith, which was based on the messiahship of Jesus, the "Son of David." So does Jesus' question in v.41, which allows the man to voice his request. Only Luke speaks of the praise that both the man who had been blind and the people gave to God after the miracle (cf. 5:26; 17:18; Ac 2:47; 3:9).

3. Zacchaeus the tax collector (19:1–10)

This narrative contains what may well be considered the "key verse" of Luke—19:10. The incident contains several teachings. Luke emphasizes the universal appeal of the Gospel (vv.2–4); the ethical problem of wealth (v.2); the call of a "sinner" who was in social disfavor (v.7); the sense of God's present work (vv.5, 9); the feeling of urgency (v.5), of necessity (v.5), and of joy (v.6); restitution, with goods distributed to the poor (v.8); and, above all, salvation (vv.9–10).

1–4 Zacchaeus was a "chief tax collector," holding a higher office in the Roman tax system than Levi did (5:27–30). This system, under which an officer gained his income by extorting more money from the people than he had contracted to pay the Roman government, had evidently worked well for Zacchaeus. His location in the major customs center of Jericho was ideal. Observe the proximity of this story to that of the rich ruler, whose attitude toward wealth kept him from the Lord (18:27). Zacchaeus's desire to see Jesus was surpassed by the fact that Jesus wanted to see *him*.

5–6 Not only did he want to see Zacchaeus, Jesus had to stay with him ("must" in v.5); this type of divine necessity is stressed in Luke (see comment on 4:43). The reciprocity of the divine, sovereign call and the human response is striking (v.6; cf. v.10).

7 Earlier Luke gave us three parables Jesus used to answer the "Pharisees and teachers of the law" who opposed his eating with tax collectors and "sinners" (15:1–2). Now "all the people" complain that Jesus was consorting with a sinner (cf. 5:29–30). In each case table fellowship was involved—something that had a far deeper significance than our dinner parties (see comment on 5:29–30).

This sycamore tree in the city of Jericho is similar to the one that Zacchaeus climed in order to see Jesus pass by.

8 Zacchaeus's announcement sounds abrupt and is probably intended to seem so. After all, Luke (following Jesus) stresses the use of possessions as a major indicator of one's spiritual condition (cf. 14:33; 18:22). Restoring stolen funds "four times the amount" was far more than what the OT specified for restitution (Lev 5:16; Nu 5:7). His offer was unusually generous and was the sort of "fruit in keeping with repentance" earlier sought by John the Baptist (3:8).

9–10 Salvation did not "come to this house" because Zacchaeus finally did a good deed but because he was "a son of Abraham" (v.9), which probably means he was a believer and thus a spiritual descendant of Abraham (cf. Ro 4:11–17; Gal 3:6–9).

Verse 10 could well be considered the "key verse" of Luke, for it expresses the heart of Jesus' ministry as presented by Luke—both his work of salvation ("save"; GK 5392) and his quest for the lost. Luke has portrayed the "lost" (GK 660) throughout his gospel, from Jesus' own statements (e.g., 4:18–19) to the disdainful comments of the self-righteous (e.g., in 18:11). This whole incident is the epitome of the messianic mission described in Luke 4.

4. Parable of the ten minas (19:11–27)

This parable fulfills four important functions: (1) it clarifies the time of the appearance of the kingdom of God; (2) it realistically portrays the coming rejection and future return of the Lord; (3) it delineates the role of a disciple in the time between the Lord's departure and his return; and (4) it makes a unique contribution at this point in Luke's narrative.

11 This verse connects the parable of the ten minas with the pericope about Zacchaeus in two complementary ways. The emphasis on salvation *today* (v.9) does not mean that there is no future coming of the Son of Man and judgment. Second, the "Son of Man" in v.10 is related to the "kingdom of God" in v.11. The one who has the right to reign is precisely the same Son of Man who came to seek lost sheep (v.10).

This parable also furthers Jesus' teaching about the future in general, the present and future aspects of the kingdom, and the consummation of God's purposes in history. It teaches that Jesus predicted an interval of time between his ascension and return.

12–14 The historical background for the parable was the visit of Archelaus, son of Herod the Great, to Rome to secure permission to reign as a so-called client king over a Roman territory. This petition was opposed by a delegation of Archelaus's own subjects. Similarly, Jesus has gone to the heavenly seat of authority till the time for his return. In the meantime, he has been rejected by those who should serve him as his subjects (v.14).

The money each servant received was worth about three months' wages. Their responsibility was to "put this money to work" in business, in trading, or by investment.

15–19 Jesus singles out three of the ten servants as examples. The first two did well, one so well as to receive a special commendation for being "trustworthy." The test was "small," not because the amount itself was so small, but because of its relative insignificance in comparison to the cities awarded the trustworthy servants.

20–23 Our focus of attention should be on the last of the three examples. This servant allowed his fear of the nobleman's anger to prevent him from fulfilling his responsibility of putting the money given him to work (v.20). To be sure, its investment was risky. But he had been specifically charged to take the risk of investing the money. In his case conservatism was born of fear and was wrong.

24–27 The principle of taking from one who has little and giving to one who has much may strike us today as strange and unfair, though a person will probably want to have only a skilled investor entrusted with more money (v.25).

The nobleman's anger (vv.26–27) is not intended to attribute such behavior to Jesus himself. Rather, it does picture the kind of response one might have expected in Jesus' day, especially from the Herodians. It also reveals the seriousness of flouting the orders of the King whom God has appointed Judge.

5. The Triumphal Entry (19:28–44)

Luke does not mention Jesus' actual entry into Jerusalem—the Triumphal Entry. Instead, he shows us Jesus only as approaching

Jerusalem (v.11), and after the crowd's welcome he is still "approaching" Jerusalem (v.41).

The story comes to its climax, not in Jesus' entering Jerusalem, but in his lamenting over the city (vv.41–44). Therefore, while Jesus deserves a triumphal entry as "king" (v.38), Luke emphasizes that he is moving instead to the place of his rejection (see 13:33). From Matthew and Mark we learn that Jesus did enter the city (cf. Mt 21:10; Mk 11:11).

28–34 By linking Jesus' approach to the city with the parable of the ten minas by means of "After Jesus said this," Luke denies an immediate appearance of the kingdom and portrays the rejection of its ruler. Luke's mention of Bethphage and Bethany locates where Jesus went. Bethany was, of course, important as the home of Mary, Martha, and Lazarus. The Mount of Olives had a significant place in prophecy as the place of the coming Messiah's appearance (Zec 14:4). Luke also stresses the dependability of the prophetic word (v.32; cf. 2:15, 20, 29).

35–38 Luke shows us the humble king as he portrays Jesus riding on the colt. For the custom of spreading cloaks along the path, see 2Ki 9:13. The reference to praising God for Jesus' miracles is common throughout Luke (cf. comments on 5:25–26; 18:43). Luke stresses the messianic theme of this event with the word "king" (v.38). The word "comes" reminds us of the designation "the coming one" for the Messiah. Luke also gives us the words about peace and glory, reminiscent of the angels' proclamation at the Nativity (2:14).

39–40 This saying of Jesus is a fitting prelude to vv.41–45.

41–44 Jesus is still outside the city of Jerusalem as he utters this lament. Once more Luke focuses on Jesus' concern for the city (cf. 13:34) and adds his prediction of its destruction, a prediction not given in 13:34. The day of peace has finally arrived, but the city, whose very name means "peace," has failed to recognize it. For a further description of Jerusalem's fate, see 21:20–24. "God's coming" has here the sense of a "visitation" that brings good or ill—in this case, either salvation or judgment.

VI. Concluding Events (19:45–24:53)

A. Teaching in the Temple Area (19:45–21:38)

1. Jesus at the temple (19:45–48)

45–48 Jesus is now in the temple area, where he drives out those buying and selling (see Mt 21:12–13; Mk 11:15–17 for more vivid accounts). Luke mentions the importance of the temple as a house of prayer (prayer is an important theme in Luke). Verses 47–48 emphasize Jesus' teaching ministry (cf. comment on 20:1). This is appropriate because Luke has consistently portrayed Jesus as a teacher, especially since the beginning of the central section of the gospel (9:51–19:44). "The leaders among the people," along with the chief priests and teachers of the law, are trying to kill Jesus, though "the people" (GK 3295) as a whole are not hostile to him. On the contrary, they "hung on his words." Once again Luke distinguishes "people" from "crowd," thus demonstrating that Christianity is properly seen as a continuation of true Judaism (see comments on 1:17, 68; 2:29–32).

2. Jesus' authority questioned (20:1–8)

With this controversy Luke initiates a series of dialogues (20:1–21:3). They include the familiar form in which a question is answered by another question designed to catch the interrogators in their own inconsistency. The controversies are typical examples of the kind of challenges thrown at Jesus by the various opponents he had. These dialogues sharpen the issues so that the reader sees the hostility and the theological errors of the leaders of the people.

1–2 Jesus' authority is of paramount importance, and his work as teacher and prophet requires validation. It is therefore appropriate that the controversy section begins with this question about his authority as teacher and preacher. "One day" is indefinite. As in 19:47, Luke also emphasizes the people's (GK 3295) receptiveness to his teaching (cf. comment on 19:45–48).

3–8 The implication of Jesus' question is clear: Jesus refuses to give more light to those who refuse to accept the light they have (v.8) and make a decision concerning it (vv.5–7). They choose to stay on a worldly level of thinking. The word "heaven" (GK *4041*) is a surrogate for God in vv.3, 5.

3. Parable of the tenants (20:9–19)

The refusal of the leaders to accept Jesus' authority (vv.1–8) leads to this parable that not only clearly affirms that authority but also alludes to Jesus' death and his subsequent vindication. The parable draws its imagery from the Song of the Vineyard (Isa 5:1–7). This story tends more toward allegory than Jesus' parables usually do. The vineyard may be compared to Israel; the owner represents God; the son, Jesus; the tenants, the religious leaders charged with cultivating the religious life of Israel (as they acknowledge in v.19); and the servants correspond to the prophets.

9–12 The circumstances in this story were not such as to provoke a violent reaction. Only part of the fruit was requested, and in the early years of a vineyard's existence, the tenants would own little if anything.

13 The owner ponders what steps he should take. The expression "whom I love" (GK *28*) must be understood with respect to its meaning in ancient Near Eastern family relationships. As a synonym for "only and only," it defines the unique status of the person as a beloved only child (cf. Lk 7:12). The idea expressed here is the same as is used by Abraham and Isaac (Ge 22:2), by God at Jesus' baptism (3:22), and by God at the Transfiguration (Mt 17:15).

14–16 These verses contain the heart of the story. The vivid description of the son's murder and the father's vengeance (v.16; cf. 19:43–44) evoked from the people who heard the parable a strong "May this never be!" They sensed the horror of the story and its drastic application, even though they may have understood its details imperfectly.

17–19 Jesus follows up the people's exclamation by quoting from Ps 118:22 (cf. the quote in 19:38, from the same psalm). Not only will God vindicate his Son, who is the "stone" (v.17), but those who oppose him will meet destruction. This point is tacitly acknowledged in the reaction of the leaders (v.19). This carries forward the hostile scheming against Jesus referred to in 19:47.

4. Paying taxes to Caesar (20:20–26)

20–22 Luke's readers would certainly know about the various forms of heavy Roman taxation. These totaled over one-third of a person's income and included a poll tax, customs, and various indirect taxes.

23–26 The portrait on the coin represented submission to Rome. Jesus' statement may seem ordinary to us, as we have become so used to the saying. But it was an unexpected and telling response to the question. Jesus' questioners were sure his answer would alienate either the government officials or the pious people and zealots who opposed foreign domination. Actually Jesus appealed neither to those who preached revolution nor to the political compromisers. He stated a principle, not an accommodation or a compromise (cf. Ro 13:1–7). To give what the government requires is part of one's religious duty. In spite of Jesus' balanced position, he was later accused at his trial of promoting an insurrection against Rome.

5. The Resurrection and marriage (20:27–40)

27 This controversy section continues with still another group challenging Jesus. The Sadducees, who tended to be more conservative than the Pharisees, did not accept what they considered theological accretions to their beliefs. The OT has little specific to say about the future state of the individual after death. The Pharisees leaned toward a belief in resurrection that owed more to Greek ideas than to the OT. However, the Sadducees refused even to face the clear implications of OT teaching about the future state.

28–33 This hypothetical case of a woman who had successively had seven husbands rests on the Jewish law described in Dt 25:5–6. It provided for the remarriage of a widow to the brother of a husband who died childless, the purpose of the remarriage being to provide descendants to carry on the deceased husband's name. The Sadducees assumed that the idea of resurrection involves sexual reunion with one's earthly partner(s).

34–40 Jesus responded along these lines: It is not legitimate to project earthly conditions into the future state (vv.34–35). Eternal life is actually the life of the age to come (v.36). The believer already participates in that life (vv.37–38); but its full expression, involving the resurrection of the body, must wait till the new age has fully come.

Though in the coming age believers do not become angels (or gods), they do share certain characteristics of angels, such as marriage. The Greek syntax places the comment about angels nearer to "no longer die" than to "neither marry." This moves the emphasis from the issue of marriage to that of the nature of the Resurrection. God's children are children characterized by the Resurrection. Invoking, so to speak, the authority of Moses, whom the Sadducees revered, Jesus shows that Abraham, Isaac, and Jacob are also going to "rise." Therefore their existence does not lie only in the past but in the future as well; and God is called, in contemporary terms, their God.

Jesus' answer is approved by some of the teachers of the law, who are happy to see the Sadducees lose their argument. Jesus' wisdom has silenced all his questioners.

6. The sonship of Christ (20:41–47)

The opponents silenced, the controversy section concludes with a rhetorical question Jesus puts to his questioners—one that is designed to clarify from Scripture who the Christ is.

41–43 The term "Christ" is, of course, used here, not as a proper name, but as a title, "the Messiah" (see comment on Mk 8:29–30). The Messiah was commonly understood by the Jewish people to be a Son. If this is so, the question is why David calls his messianic descendant his "Lord" in Ps 110:1. Although the rabbis of the first Christian centuries did not interpret "to my Lord" as referring to the Messiah, that is the only meaning that makes sense here.

44 Jesus' question is not intended to suggest that there could not be a descendant of David who was also "Lord," but that the seemingly irreconcilable has meaning only if he is more than just a human descendant. Paul expressed the complete answer to the question in Ro 1:3–4, which says that Jesus was a descendant of David as to his human nature but declared Son of God by his resurrection.

45–47 Having responded with such authority to his opponents' controversial questions, Jesus now comments on those who sought to disprove his authority (cf. 11:37–52). Here he stresses their pride and ostentation, as well as accuses them of taking advantage of widows. Apparently they misused their responsibility as legal arbiters (see comment on 12:13).

7. The widow's offering (21:1–4)

1–4 The comment on how teachers of the law victimized widows (20:47) leads to a story on how a poor widow set an example of acceptable giving. The "temple treasury" was either a room in the temple or a "contribution box." The widow's "two very small copper coins" were each worth only a small fraction of a day's wage. Proportionate to her total financial worth, however, the woman's gift was far more valuable than the gifts of the wealthy.

8. Signs of the end of the age (21:5–38)

Jesus concludes his teaching ministry (apart from the Upper Room Discourse in Jn 14–16) with this discourse on the end times. It is immediately followed in Luke by the conspiracy by Judas.

Jesus' teachings in this discourse provide both a realistic warning about future events and a strong encouragement to persevere. They entail some notable difficulties of interpretation and literary analysis. But if the expositor concentrates on the series of exhortations in the discourse, then the supporting teachings along with the problems of interpretation will come into focus. These exhortations are ninefold.

1. Do not follow false leaders (v.8).
2. Do not be frightened by the awesome events associated with the end times (vv.9–11).
3. Do not worry about your legal defense when you are persecuted and face legal charges because of your Christian witness (vv.12–16).
4. When all turn against you, persevere and take a firm stand (vv.17–19).
5. Flee Jerusalem when it is besieged (vv.20–24).
6. When the final apocalyptic events (the portents in heaven and on earth) do take place, take heart at your coming redemption when the Son of Man returns (vv.25–28).
7. Recognize also that these things point to the approach of the kingdom of God (vv.29–31).

8. Be assured that throughout the apocalyptic period the Lord's words endure (vv.32–33).

9. Be watchful and pray so that you will come through all these things in a way the Son of Man will approve of (vv.34–36).

5–11 Warning against deception. The opening of the discourse resembles, with several exceptions, that in Mt 24 and Mk 13. Luke does not mention that Jesus himself was at the temple (though the mention of its architectural details and the "gifts" shows that Jesus and his disciples were on the premises, v.5). For the temple to be totally destroyed was unthinkable. Its sanctuary and surrounding structure were huge, solid, and glistening, a symbol of Jewish religion and Herodian splendor. The disciples do ask for a "sign" (v.7), not because they are doubting but because they need a clue as to when the end will come.

The word "deceived" (v.8; GK *4414*) was frequently used to describe the activities of heretics and false prophets (e.g., 2Jn 7; Rev 2:20). Certain frightening events (vv.9–11) are typically linked with the end times (e.g., Isa 13:10, 13; 34:4; Eze 14:21; 32:7–8; Hag 2:6; et al.). Jesus is teaching that, while such things are indeed to take place as history moves toward its climax, Christians should not be terrified by them (v.9). The reason is that wars, revolutions, and natural calamities are not a signal that the end of history is to come immediately.

12–19 Encouragement during persecution. In its content this section bears some similarity to Mk 13:9–13 and also the account of the sending out of the Twelve (Mt 10:17–22). (1) Luke omits the preaching of the Gospel to the Gentiles (Mt 10:18) and around the world (Mk 13:10). (2) He gives a promise of wisdom in time of persecution, though there is no reference to the Holy Spirit. (3) Unique to Luke is the phrase "not a hair of your head" (v.18). (4) Luke stresses that those who persevere, even if they lose physical life, will preserve spiritual life (v.19).

20–24 The destruction of Jerusalem. The reference to Jerusalem (v.20) need not be construed as a *vaticinium ex eventu* (a prophecy put in the mouth of Jesus after the event has occurred). If Luke were doing this, one would expect more precise details than the ones included here. The description of the siege of Jerusalem, a protracted event, contrasts with the sudden events in Luke's earlier apocalyptic passage (17:22–37). There the one on the roof will not even have time to reenter his house. But here those out in the country are warned not to try to get back into the city during the siege (v.21). The vivid description is painful to read. Jesus' predictions seem to incorporate two phases: (1) the events of A.D. 70 involving the temple and (2) those in the distant future, described in more apocalyptic terms. Since he has already elaborated on the latter (17:20–37), he can here concentrate on a prophetic oracle on Jerusalem.

In v.24, Luke again shows his interest in the Gentiles. This verse implies that an extended period of time is needed for its fulfillment—an idea consistent with Luke's twofold emphasis on a period of waiting along with an expectation of Christ's imminent return. It also implies an end to the period when Gentiles are prominent in God's plan (cf. Ro 11:11–27).

25–28 Future events. Jesus now speaks of apocalyptic signs of the end time. The "roaring ... of the sea" is reminiscent of Isa 17:12; in biblical prophecy the sea often symbolizes chaos or stands for a source of fear. Daniel 7:13 is the main OT source for v.27 and the NT concept of the glorified "Son of Man." "Power," "coming," and "glory" are terms appropriate to Christ as Son of Man and King (cf. Mt 16:27–28; Mk 9:1; Lk 9:26–27; 2Pe 1:16–17). This section concludes with Jesus' words of encouragement in expectation of redemption (v.28).

29–38 Assurances concerning these events. The illustration of the fig tree is clear. "Generation" (v.32; GK *1155*) can refer here to a span of time or to a class or race of people. In the former sense, it may mean the decades following Jesus' lifetime. If this whole passage therefore refers to the destruction of Jerusalem, the heavenly portents must be understood figuratively. But "generation" as a span of time may also refer to the period of time following the initial events of the end time. In that case, it indicates that once the sequence begins, it will be brought through to conclusion without delay.

The other major alternative, "generation" as a class or race of people, makes most sense if it is understood as meaning the Jewish people. The point then is that the Jewish people will be preserved throughout the ages until the consummation of history at Christ's return. (For a different approach, see comments on Mt 24:34.)

The conclusion of the discourse again emphasizes faithfulness, with warnings not only against carousing but against the "anxieties of life" (v.34; cf. 8:14; 12:22–26).

Luke ends the chapter by disclosing that Jesus taught in the temple by day but spent each night outside Jerusalem on the Mount of Olives (v.37). He is also careful to tell us, just as he did in his earlier narratives of Jesus' ministry (4:14–15, 22, 32, 37, 42; 5:19, 26, 29), just how popular Jesus was among the "people" (GK 3295), the responsive group who came to hear his teaching "early in the morning" (v.38; see comment on 19:45–48).

B. The Passion of Our Lord (22:1–23:56)

1. The agreement to betray Jesus (22:1–6)

Luke's passion narrative begins ominously with a description of Judas's plot. Luke says that "Satan entered Judas" (cf. Jn 13:27). In other words, Satanic opposition now starts to heighten.

1–2 The "Feast of Unleavened Bread," immediately following the Passover, lasted seven days (Ex 12:15–20). Earlier the Pharisees were prominent in opposing Jesus (cf. comment on 5:17). Now the "chief priests and teachers of the law" were taking the initiative against him. In that society the priests were not only religious leaders, but they also wielded great political power. The teachers of the law were involved undoubtedly because their legal expertise would be useful in building a case against Jesus. "The people," on the other hand, were a deterrent to the schemes of the leaders.

3–6 Luke mentions the presence of the "officers of the temple guard," whose soldiers probably captured Jesus (Jn 18:3). Municipalities had their own officers and so did the Jerusalem religious establishment. Luke also mentions that, in betraying Jesus, Judas sought to avoid the crowds.

2. The Last Supper (22:7–38)

7–13 Luke now sharpens his chronology, clearly stating it was the day of sacrifice—normally Nisan 14. The actual Passover meal was celebrated after sundown (i.e., Nisan 15; see comments on Mk 14:1–2, 12).

Jesus initiated plans for the Passover arrangements. His instructions guaranteed privacy, indeed, secrecy, perhaps to avoid his premature arrest. Verses 10–12 show his supernatural knowledge. The disciples were to follow a man carrying a water jar. Ordinarily only women carried jars; men used leather skins for water.

The "large upper room" was on the second story under a flat roof, accessible by an outside stairway. It was "furnished" with the couches for reclining at a Passover meal and with necessary utensils. The disciples found things "just as Jesus told them."

14–18 Luke forges a strong link between the Passover and the concept of redemption. This passage also exhibits the strong orientation to the future that characterizes Luke's gospel.

Both of Jesus' opening sentences are strongly worded: "I have eagerly desired" (lit., "with desire I have desired") and an emphatic future negative: "I will not eat" (cf. v.18). Together these sentences convey the depth of Jesus' feelings at this time and the immense significance of what is taking place. Jesus did partake of the meal when, as the host, he "took" the cup and the bread (vv.17, 19, 20). But he goes on to indicate that he will not eat the lamb (probably) till the coming of the kingdom.

Unlike the other accounts of the Last Supper, Luke mentions a cup before (v.17), as well as after (v.20), the bread. Luke has apparently combined his data from various sources to describe both the Passover setting of the supper (vv.7–18) and the institution of the Lord's Supper (vv.19–20). If so, the cup of v.17 may be the first of the traditional four cups taken during the Passover meal, and Jesus' comments come at the beginning of that meal (see comment on Mt 26:17). This cup was followed by part of the Passover meal and the singing of Pss 113 and 114. Alternately, the cup of v.17 may be the third cup, mentioned here in connection with the Passover setting and again in connection with its place in the Eucharist, on which Luke focuses (v.20).

Jesus' words in vv.14–18 are significant. The meal is a turning point. Jesus anticipated it; and he likewise anticipates the next genuine meal of its kind that he will eat sometime in the future when the longed-for kingdom finally comes, or, in Luke's characteristic vocabulary, "finds fulfillment." The believer in the present age observes the Lord's Supper "until he comes" (1Co 11:26).

19–20 The words of institution in these verses bear remarkable similarity to the rendition of Paul in 1Co 11:24–25. This supports the reliability of Luke's research (1:1–4). The suffering motif is consistent with Jesus' understanding of his mission as the Suffering Servant.

The "bread" was the thick unleavened bread used in the Passover. "Gave thanks" translates the verb *eucharisteo* (GK 2373), the source of the beautiful word "Eucharist," often used to signify the Lord's Supper. Luke alone has "given for you" in the saying over the bread, as well as "poured out for you" in the cup saying.

"In remembrance of me" directs our attention primarily to the person of Christ and not merely to the benefits we receive from taking the bread and cup. The final cup taken during the Passover signifies the "new Covenant" in Jesus' blood. The disciples would have been reminded in the Passover of the "blood of the covenant" (Ex 24:8), i.e., the blood used ceremonially to confirm the covenant. The new covenant (cf. Jer 31:31–34) carried with it assurance of forgiveness through Jesus' blood shed on the cross and the inner work of the Holy Spirit in motivating us and enabling us to fulfill our covenantal responsibility.

21–23 Because this saying follows the Last Supper, it is correct to assume that Judas was present at the institution of the Lord's Supper (cf. also Jn 13:21–27). By mentioning the "hand" of Judas (v.21), Luke draws attention to his participation in this special event, thus heightening the tragedy that one of Jesus' own disciples will betray him.

The use of "decreed" (GK 3988) emphasizes divine sovereignty, a theme dominant in Luke. Divine sovereignty is always balanced by human responsibility, so Jesus pronounces a "woe" on the betrayer (cf. Ac 2:23). Luke also records (v.23) both the disciples' concern and the secrecy that still surrounded Judas's treachery.

24–27 Their questions about this treachery leads immediately to the disciples' argument—shocking on this solemn occasion—about precedence (see also Mt 20:17–28; Mk 10:32–45). The word "considered" (GK 1506) in v.24 is well chosen since status has to do with self-perception and with how one desires to be perceived by others. Jesus replies by reminding the disciples of two objectionable characteristics of secular rulers. First, they "lord it over" others, an attitude Peter later warns elders of (1Pe 5:3). Second, they are given the title "Benefactor." In Mt 23:7, Jesus disapproved of a similar kind of status seeking. Actually he himself is the true "Benefactor" (a similar word is used of Jesus in Ac 10:38).

In v.26 "but you" is emphatic. Jesus makes two points about true greatness. First, one should not seek the veneration given aged people in ancient Near Eastern society but be content with the lower place younger people had. Second, one should not seek the position of the person sitting at a dinner table who had a higher social position than the waiter, who was often a slave. This illustration recalls the example of the Lord Jesus, who washed his disciples' feet as they reclined at the table of the Last Supper (Jn 13:12–17).

28–30 Verse 28 shows that Jesus' trials continued between his temptation by Satan (ch. 4) and the passion events. It also recognizes the faithfulness of the disciples during this time, though fidelity of one of them is about to be tested severely (v.31). This theme of testing and faithfulness is prominent in Luke, as we have seen. Jesus goes on to confer on his disciples a kingdom, just as he himself had received a kingdom (Jn 20:21). The picture here is not just that of a commission but of a conferral similar to a testament. The idea of a messianic banquet is reflected in v.30 (cf. 13:28–30 and comments). On the role of the Son of Man and the saints in judgment, see Dan 7:9–18.

31–34 Just after Jesus commended the disciples for their faithfulness and promised them a kingdom, he goes on to predict Peter's defection, which he attributes to the direct activity of Satan. The juxtaposition of these two sayings makes a strong contrast. The repetition of Simon's name adds weight to the warning. The metaphor of sifting implies separating what is desirable from what is undesirable. Here the thought is that Satan wants to prove that at least some of the disciples will fail under severe testing. The first occurrence of "you" in v.31 is in the plural, referring to all the disciples in contrast to Peter, who is addressed (v.32) by the singular "you."

Jesus' prayer that Simon's faith would not fail (v.32) has occasioned discussion over whether it was or was not answered. The phrase "may not fail" probably means "may not disappear completely" (as the sun in a total eclipse). If this is correct, then Jesus' prayer was certainly answered. Peter's denial, though serious and symptomatic of a low level of faith, did not mean that he had ceased, within himself, to believe in the Lord. Nevertheless his denial was so contrary to his former spiritual state that he would need to "return" to Christ. The whole experience, far from disqualifying Peter from Christian service, would actually result in a responsibility for him to strengthen his brothers. Peter's overconfident reply (v.33), which includes a reference to his willingness to die, is found among the four gospels only here and in Jn 13:37. Jesus then becomes specific and predicts Peter's denial.

35–38 This short passage is difficult to interpret, with two problems in particular: (1) the problem of Jesus' apparent support for using weapons, which is hard to reconcile with his words to Peter when the latter used the sword (Mt 26:52); and (2) the seeming reversal of the instructions Jesus gave the Twelve and the seventy-two on their missions (9:1–3; 10:1–3). Thus there is a question as to which principle regarding the use of force is normative for the church.

While some solve their problems by taking Jesus' words as ironical, this is not the best solution. Any approach to a solution must take into account the fact that later, when the disciples were armed with these swords, Jesus opposed their use (vv.49–51). Moreover, the tone of v.52 is nonmilitant. Verse 36 clearly refers back to 10:4, the sending of the seventy-two. In v.35 there seems to be an affirmation of the principle of nonmilitance in the question "Did you lack anything?" Yet a contrast is also clearly intended. What Jesus seems to be doing is making an exception for this time of crisis. Since he told them not to buy more swords than they had (v.38), and since two were hardly enough to defend the group, the swords may simply be a vivid symbol of impending crisis, not intended for actual use.

Verse 37a is one of several clear quotations of Isa 53 in the NT.

3. Prayer on the Mount of Olives (22:39–46)

In contrast to Matthew and Mark, Luke does not specify the location as being Gethsemane, and he alone includes at the beginning an exhortation to the disciples to ward off temptation by means of prayer.

39–42 Luke focuses his attention here on Jesus, who went to the Mount of Olives "as usual" (cf. 21:37). He did not change his habits to elude Judas.

Jesus begins with a general warning to his disciples not to fall into temptation. This is not surprising, for the themes of prayer and temptation are common in Luke (cf. v.46). Kneeling in prayer (v.41) was not customary in Jesus' time (standing was the normal posture). But this scene is one of intense emotional strain. Matthew and Mark say that Jesus fell to the ground (Mt 26:39; Mk 14:35). Luke, who throughout his gospel stresses Jesus' conscious fulfillment of the purposes of God, emphasizes Jesus' concern for the will of God.

Jesus uses the "cup" as a metaphor of his imminent passion (see comments on Mk 10:38; 14:35–36). In the OT the wrath of God expressed against sin was sometimes referred to by the metaphor of a cup (e.g., Ps 75:8; Isa 51:17; Jer 25:15–17).

This is a contemporary view of Mount of Olives, seen from the old city of Jerusalem. Between these two is the Kidron Valley.

43–44 Luke has already mentioned angels many times—in the Nativity narrative and elsewhere, e.g., 9:26; 12:8–9; 15:10; 16:22. So the appearance of an angel here in Gethsemane is not strange. Luke describes Jesus' agony in physical terms, as we might expect a physician to do. The sweating was apparently so profuse that it looked like blood dripping from a wound.

45–46 Luke does not dwell on the weakness of the disciples, nor does he describe in further detail Jesus' agony. He does explain the disciples' sleep as coming through exhaustion from sorrow. Jesus repeats the injunction for the disciples to pray lest they fall into temptation (see comment on Mt 26:41).

4. Jesus' Arrest (22:47–53)

47–48 While Jesus was still speaking to his disciples, Judas and the crowd make a sudden intrusion into the somber scene in Gethsemane. Note the word "crowd" (GK *4063*), often used in Luke to designate an unfeeling, perhaps even hostile, group of people. From the crowd attention moves to "the man who was called Judas." This designation is a dramatic way of isolating Judas—holding him off at a distance for a derogatory look and comment, i.e., "this Judas person." The betrayal was accomplished with a kiss in order to identify Jesus in the darkness of the night. But in the high drama of the actual situation, it was cruelly hypocritical.

49–51 (See comments on vv.33–38 for the background to this incident.) Jn 18:10 tells us that it was Peter who drew the sword; Luke alone tells us about Jesus' healing of the ear of the high priest's servant.

52–53 Verse 52 gives details regarding the makeup of the crowd—religious, political, and military leaders. These details suggest Luke's emphasis that it was not the believing Jews who brought about Jesus' crucifixion but their arrogant leaders. Jesus' comment shows the underhanded nature of their act. The word "hour" (GK *6052*) here designates a time of opportunity or destiny. The verb "reigns" represents the noun *exousia* ("power," "authority"; GK *2026*). Satan had previously offered Jesus *exousia* in the Temptation (4:6); but Jesus, who after obediently going to the cross would receive "all authority" (*exousia*) from the Father (Mt 28:18), was willing to have Satan exercise his authority for a time under God's plan of salvation.

5. Peter's denial (22:54–62)

Throughout this and the succeeding sections, dramatic tension mounts. A contributing feature is the simultaneous action taking place in the house of the high priest with Jesus (v.54) and in the courtyard with Peter (v.55). Luke separates the two sequences of events, enabling the reader to follow Peter's experience and then Jesus' trial separately. Luke does not tell us anything about a night session of the trial but allows for it in v.54 (cf. vv.63–65). The story of Peter's denial presents a sober and utterly real picture of the prominent apostle; and, along with vv.31–32, it offers a deep spiritual lesson about humility and spiritual conflict.

54–57 Jesus' first trial took place in the high priest's house (v.54)—possibly the house of Annas, father-in-law of the high priest Caiaphas (cf. Jn 18:13)—though this meeting seems also to have been a trial before the entire Sanhedrin (cf. comments on Mt 26:59; Mk 14:55).

Though he followed Jesus at a distance, Peter is the only disciple who, so far as we know, followed him at all. The fire in the courtyard was needed because the evenings are cool in springtime in Jerusalem. The denial had three phases. The first speaker was a servant girl. Who she was and what she said were relatively harmless and did not deserve a drastic response. Peter's response is called a denial. The word "deny" (GK *766*) is used in the NT as the polar opposite of the word "confess." We are to confess (i.e., acknowledge) Christ but deny ourselves (i.e., disown our private interests for the sake of Christ; cf. comment on 9:23). Peter here does the reverse. He denies Christ in order to serve his own interests.

58 After a brief time, someone else, a man this time, made another charge. In none of these dialogues does Jesus' name actually appear. The assumption is that the recent events in Jesus' life were already known to the group in the courtyard.

59–60 The third speaker then makes a definite assertion about Peter's association with Jesus. Luke does not record Peter's oath as Matthew and Mark do, but he does record

Peter's claim to ignorance about Jesus. At about this time, just as Jesus had predicted, the rooster crowed.

61–62 In telling how the Lord looked at Peter (v.61), Luke uses the same word John used (Jn 1:42) to describe the way Jesus looked at Peter when they first met. It was a look of love and concern. Peter's feelings (v.62) need no further comment.

6. The mocking of Jesus (22:63–65)

63–65 This incident of Jesus' being mocked and beaten is put in a position of sharp contrast between Jesus' sufferings and Peter's attempt to avoid any identification with Jesus. Also, the soldiers' hitting Jesus while he was blindfolded, taunting him about prophesying, contrasts with Luke's clear portrayal in his gospel of Jesus as a prophet.

7. Trial before the Jewish leaders (22:66–71)

The probable order of Jesus' trial appearances in all four gospels is (1) before Annas (John), (2) before Caiaphas and the Sanhedrin (Synoptics), (3) before Pilate (Synoptics, John), (4) before Herod Antipas (Luke), and (5) before Pilate (Luke). The charges before Caiaphas and the Sanhedrin were (1) threatening to destroy the temple and (2) blasphemy. The charges before Pilate were (1) subverting the Jewish nation, (2) opposing the payment of taxes to Caesar, (3) claiming to be king, and (4) sedition ("stirs up the people," 23:5).

66–69 Luke has already indicated that Jesus was arrested during the night (v.47) and has implied that he was confronted by the authorities while in the house of the high priest (v.54). Following that was an "official" trial early in the morning. Luke summarizes the crucial exchange between Jesus and the leaders and adds a time note that it was becoming day (v.66). Matthew and Mark refer to the same time of day when the religious authorities reached a decision (Mk 15:1). Luke's way of reporting the questioning separates the questions regarding messiahship and regarding the Son of God.

The word "Christ" (v.67) at this time had not yet become a proper name, so the question Jesus was asked is whether he was claiming to be the Messiah. Jesus answered by saying that they would not believe him even if he did answer them. He also said that if he were to question them, they would not answer (cf. 20:1–8).

Jesus continues with an assertion concerning the exaltation of the Son of Man (who must be identified with Jesus here or the saying is irrelevant); it vindicates Jesus and proves who he is. This saying in Luke stresses the fact that from that very time in Jesus' appearance before the council, he was to be exalted (note Luke's emphasis on "now," the present reality of events that have their main significance in the future). Luke is concerned with the present vindication of Jesus.

70–71 Standing independent of and subsequent to the question about messiahship is the question in v.70, which serves to emphasize that Jesus is himself the Son of God and is not merely called such as an honorific title because of his role as Messiah. Jesus' reply, while not a direct affirmation (cf. comments on Mt 26:25, 64), was taken as such, as v.71 shows. The nature of this reply is understandable in the light of Jesus' remarks in vv.67b–68.

8. Trial before Pilate and Herod (23:1–25)

The trial now moves into its Roman phase (see comment on 22:66–71). While there was doubtless more interrogation in front of Pilate than is reported here before he declared he found no basis for a charge against Jesus (v.4), it obviously did not take Pilate long to determine Jesus' innocence. The larger part of this section deals, not with the trial as such, but with the difficulty the Jewish authorities had in trying to convict an innocent man.

1–5 Verse 1 links the Jewish and Roman trials. The "whole assembly" is the Sanhedrin. Pilate was Roman governor (procurator) of the province of Judah. His official residence was at Caesarea, a magnificent city boasting Roman culture, where Pilate would no doubt have preferred to be at the time of Jesus' trial, were it not the Passover season (when special precautions were needed in Jerusalem against civil disturbances).

The Sanhedrin's accusation contains three distinct charges. The first (subverting the Jewish nation) would have been of concern to Pilate, who wanted no internal strife among the Jewish people. But it was not a matter for Roman jurisprudence. The second (opposing payment of taxes to Caesar) and third (claiming to be king) were more to the point. Luke has already shown (20:20–26) that the second charge was untrue. The third one became the key issue. Jesus' responses to the questions asked him by his Jewish interrogators had been understood as being clearly affirmative (22:66–71). It is also clear that the word Christ, or Messiah (v.2), was deliberately used to imply to Pilate that Jesus was a political activist and a threat to Roman sovereignty (note "king" in apposition to "Messiah").

In Luke's gospel, Pilate clearly declares Jesus' innocence (v.4). This point is especially important for Luke, who seeks throughout his gospel and Acts to vindicate Christianity through vindicating both Jesus and Paul in their appearances in court. The response from the Sanhedrin is clever. It implies seditious actions by saying that the people are being stirred up by Jesus' (unspecified) teaching.

6–12 Only Luke records Jesus' appearance before Herod; he had more interest in politics than Matthew or Mark (cf. 3:1; 9:7–9; 13:31). Herod had a more intimate experience with Jewish politics and religion than Pilate had. For a long time he had desired to learn more about Jesus (cf. 9:7–9). Like Pilate, Herod was probably in Jerusalem because of the Passover. (For Jesus' attitude toward him, see 13:31–33.) Herod's territory, as a local king under the authority of Rome, was Galilee and Perea. Verse 11 probably reflects a certain frustration on his part. He apparently had no legal accusation to make; so he vented his anger by echoing the hostility of the priests and teachers and by putting someone's fine clothes on him.

13–16 Once again Pilate protests Jesus' innocence, this time in front of the people as well. Luke seems to be making a significant point by mentioning their presence. Throughout his gospel, Luke has been careful to distinguish the "people" (GK *3295*) from the "crowd" (GK *4063*). The people appear again in v.27, following Jesus to the place of crucifixion, and then in v.35, watching Jesus die. Once more (24:19) Luke mentions them as witnesses of Jesus' mighty works. At their first mention in Acts, Luke refers to the "people" as approving the young Jerusalem church (2:47).

In order to placate the Jewish leaders Pilate (knowing Jesus' innocence) offered to scourge Jesus and then to release him. As a Roman official, he wanted to treat Jesus as fairly as possible. This would fit in with one of Luke's apparent goals in writing the gospel and Acts—namely, to show that Christianity deserved to be favorably treated by Rome.

18–22 Luke provides only a brief statement about Barabbas and his crimes. "For the third time" Pilate protests Jesus' innocence. Again, we see Luke's concern to vindicate Jesus (and Christianity) to his readers.

23–25 In vivid Greek, Luke brings the crowd's action to a climax. He shifts attention from Pilate to the people by ending the Greek sentence in v.23 not with the verb but with a reference to the shouting of the crowd.

Luke then proceeds directly to Pilate's action, who had acted in accord with the crowd's wishes. Having emphasized God's plan and will throughout his gospel, Luke now notes the human factor: Jesus is delivered to the "demand" of the crowd (cf. Ac 2:23).

9. The Crucifixion (23:26–43)

In their accounts of Jesus' crucifixion, the four gospels relate essentially the same series of events, but with varied selection of details and of Jesus' words. None of them portray the physical agony of crucifixion in the shocking details that might have been given. The stark facts are there but are presented with sober restraint. What was most important was the inner reality of Jesus' atoning death and his spiritual anguish in being identified with the sins of the world.

26 Jesus was required, like others condemned to crucifixion, to carry the cross-bar. The wood was heavy, and Jesus was weakened by the maltreatment. The soldiers could press civilians such as Simon into service. Cyrene is a port in North Africa.

27–31 As Jesus heads to Calvary, Luke records an incident that expresses Jesus' concern for the fate of Jerusalem (cf. 19:41–44; 21:20–24). Jewish women had always considered barrenness a misfortune and children a blessing. In the day of Jerusalem's destruction, however, women would have the horror of seeing their children suffer and would wish they could have been spared that agony. The words Jesus quotes from Hos 10:8 are a plea for protection, not for quick death. Fire spreads much more rapidly through a dry forest than through a wet one; so Jesus' words in v.31 warn of a future situation that is even worse than the events surrounding his crucifixion.

32–34 The presence of two criminals with Jesus emphasizes the humiliation of his execution and perhaps also his identification with sinners in his death as well as in his life. Luke's narrative is concise and effective in presenting the brutal facts. Nor is it surprising that he, who constantly portrayed Jesus both as offering God's grace and forgiveness to sinners (e.g., 7:40–43) and as praying, is the only one who records his prayer for the forgiveness of his executors (v.34; cf. Ac 7:60).

35 Luke's wording here suggests that the "people" (see comment on vv.13–16) are still passive rather than hostile, while everyone else, "even" the rulers, sneered. The word "saved" does not mean that the rulers believed in the claim of Jesus to forgive people but alludes to his reputation for restoring the sick and disturbed. For Christ as "the Chosen One," see comment on 9:35.

36–37 The taunts continue, this time from the soldiers. Although in the other gospels the offering of wine vinegar (v.36) seems to be an act of kindness (the drink being a thirst quencher carried by soldiers), Luke connects it with their mockery of Christ. It may have been a compassionate act done in the midst of taunts.

38 Luke's record of the superscription over the cross shows the issue as Pilate, Jesus' Roman judge, saw it. The word "this" is at the end of the sentence, conveying the emphatic idea: "The King of the Jews, this one!"

39–43 This conversation, unique to Luke's account, reinforces two characteristics of his gospel. One is the innocence of Jesus (v.41; see comments on vv.4, 22). The other is the immediate ("today") realization of God's saving grace through Christ (cf. comment on 4:21).

As elsewhere (cf. 5:1–11), Luke focuses on one person in a group. One of the criminals hurled insults at Jesus. The criminal's taunt, "Aren't you the Christ?" should probably be seen as sarcastic.

The other criminal recognizes that Jesus is no mere pretender and that he will reign as king. Jesus' response assures him that he need not wait for any future event but that he would have an immediate joyful experience of fellowship with Jesus "in paradise" (GK 4137). This Persian word, taken over into Greek, symbolizes a place of beauty and delight. It was used to refer to the Garden of Eden in Ge 2:8 (LXX) and to the future bliss that the garden symbolizes (Isa 51:3; cf. 2Co 12:4; Rev 2:7).

10. Jesus' death (23:44–49)

44–46 Luke refrains from giving a precise time but does imply by the word "now" that the preceding events had filled the morning. There was darkness from about noon to three o'clock. The whole "land" could refer to all the "land" of Israel or, possibly, to the local area only. Luke does not say what caused the sun's light to fail, nor does he say what significance should be given this fact. Certainly it emphasized the somberness of the event; it may also be linked with Jesus' experiencing God's judgment, for elsewhere the Scriptures link it with God's judgment (e.g., Am 5:8–10; Zep 1:4–15).

Luke states that the temple curtain was torn apart— doubtless the one separating the Holy Place from the inner Most Holy Place (Ex 26:31–33). Access to the most holy God is now open through the death of Christ (cf. Heb 10:19–22).

Normally a person in the last stages of crucifixion would not have the strength to speak beyond a weak groan, but Jesus is able to cry out with a "loud voice" (v.46) words from Ps 31:5. To the Christian reader who knows that Jesus' death was a voluntary act, they are beautifully appropriate. All four gospels describe Jesus' moment of death in terse, restrained words.

47–49 After Jesus' death, Luke calls on the centurion as a witness to Jesus' uniqueness. His words in his gospel emphasize, as in the trial scene, the innocence of Jesus (cf. comments on vv.4, 22). The crowd standing around was deeply affected, as were Jesus' own followers, who endured their inexpressible grief standing at a distance. Luke gave the names of some of these women from Galilee in 8:3.

11. Jesus' burial (23:50–56)

50–54 Luke assures his readers of the credentials of the man who offered to bury Jesus. Here again he presents someone qualified to affirm by word or action that Jesus was a just and innocent man; by inference, therefore, the claims of Christianity are valid. Joseph was a righteous Jew, "waiting for the kingdom of God" (v.51), and so joins others in Luke whose piety and expectation of the Messiah validate their testimony (e.g., Simeon and Anna, 2:25–38). He was a member of the Council (the Sanhedrin) but had disagreed with their decision against Jesus.

Joseph laid the body in a tomb "cut in the rock." We can still see such tombs today in rocky hillsides in Palestine. We learn in v.54 that it was Friday, and the Sabbath was about to begin at sundown.

55–56 Luke goes on to note the women's careful preparation of the spices in advance of Easter morning. The women did not do this on the Sabbath, even though Jewish tradition apparently would have allowed care for the dead on a Sabbath. In this way Luke stresses one more time the fidelity of Jesus and his followers to Jewish laws.

C. The Resurrection and Ascension (24:1–53)

1. The Resurrection (24:1–12)

Luke 24 not only presents the climactic event of the Resurrection, but it includes a recapitulation of the saving mission of Christ (vv.6–7, 19–27, 45–47). The Ascension, with which the chapter and the book conclude, is the final goal of Jesus' earthly ministry (cf. comment on 9:51). It also sets the scene for the church's ministry as recorded in Acts. The first section narrates events at the empty tomb; it contains elements that Luke uses to further his unique theological perspective.

1–3 All four gospels specify the first day of the week (v.1) as the day of the Resurrection. This became the day of Christian worship (cf. Ac 20:7). The change from the traditional and biblical Sabbath is in itself a strong evidence of the Resurrection because it shows the strength of the disciples' conviction about what happened on that day. Luke refers to the time of day by the general statement that it was "very early." When the women arrived at the tomb, they found the stone rolled away, and Luke specifically states that the body of the Lord was not there.

4–5 Once again, Luke describes someone pondering a remarkable event (e.g., 1:29, 66; 2:19). Luke speaks of "two men" in the tomb who address the women; this mention of two men seems consistent with his other references to witnesses to Jesus (cf. Simeon and Anna, 2:25–38; and esp. 24:48). Two witnesses are the minimum number required for validation (Dt 17:6; 19:15). That Luke understands that the two "men" were angels is evident from what he says of them in v.23 and from his description of their clothes as gleaming like lightning. Not only were the women frightened, but in their fear they bowed facedown to the ground (fear is a typical response in the presence of a supernatural visitation; e.g., 1:12; 2:9; 9:34). "The living" stresses the factual aspect of the Resurrection.

6–8 The angels show the meaning of the empty tomb by repeating the essence of the three passion predictions (9:22, 43–45; 18:31–33). They begin with the words "Remember how he told you," perhaps implying that what the women should have understood earlier the Resurrection has now clarified. The third prediction (18:31–33) was followed by a statement that the saying was obscure, hidden from them (18:34; cf. also 24:16). The Resurrection is the time for revelation and understanding (v.8). Luke centers the rest of his attention on Jesus' appearances in the vicinity of Jerusalem, the city of destiny in Luke (see comments on 13:32–35).

Luke's frequent use of "must" (GK *1256*) and other expressions of divine purpose have already been noted throughout this commentary (e.g., 2:49; 4:43; 19:5). It occurs in the first passion prediction (9:22), and in 13:33; 17:25; 22:37. Chapter 24 contains two more references to the inevitable sequence of Jesus' death and resurrection (vv.25–27, 44–46). Luke's stress on God's plan and providence continues throughout Acts.

9–12 At this point Luke reports the names of the women (cf. 8:1–3). While the witness of women was not acceptable in those days, nevertheless Luke records their testimony. The apostles, in their incredulity, were unable to comprehend the reality the women were trying to convey (v.11; see also vv.12, 22–24). This reluctance to believe has an important relation to the evidences for the Resurrection. The disciples were not expecting that event. Thus they cannot be called fit subjects for hallucination, as some would have them be.

The strips of linen in the tomb used in the burial of Jesus bear their silent but eloquent testimony to the absence of Jesus' body. Peter leaves, "wondering" to himself about this (cf. v.4).

2. On the Emmaus road (24:13–35)

The Emmaus story is a literary and spiritual jewel. It is at once a moving story, a testimony to the Resurrection, an explanation of the empty tomb, and an occasion for Luke to summarize several of his major themes.

13–16 The opening words of v.13 link this story with the entire Easter event. As two travelers are talking together, they experience the presence of Jesus; thus a valid witness is provided (see comment on vv.4–5). The words "of them" (v.13) do not clearly identify who the two are. They are not two of the Eleven (v.9; cf. v.33). Probably they are two of the followers of Jesus who had come to Jerusalem for the Passover. So they had been among the "disciples" who lauded Jesus on his triumphal entry to the city (19:39) and were now returning home.

The fact that this event occurs when the two disciples "were going" continues the travel theme prominent in Luke, especially in his unique central section (9:51–19:44). That section began as Jesus "resolutely set out" for Jerusalem (9:51); now these two are leaving that same city. Shortly after the earlier journey to Jerusalem began, a man had approached Jesus regarding discipleship "as they were walking" (9:57); after the Resurrection, Jesus approaches two disheartened followers as they are walking. Acts continues the theme of Jesus' disciples traveling, going from Jerusalem to Rome and ultimately to the ends of the earth as "witnesses" (1:8). As for the identity of Emmaus, this is uncertain, though it is a village near Jerusalem.

The two were talking about events surrounding Jesus' resurrection. Between the lines of their dialogue, Luke shows their bewilderment. Luke introduces Jesus into the story with the emphatic "Jesus himself" and comments that Jesus "walked along with" them. Their being kept "from recognizing him" (v.16) may be a "divine passive," i.e., a means of connoting that an action is actually the work of God.

17–18 Jesus, without them recognizing him, suddenly asks the two men a question about their conversation. It is striking that when Jesus addressed them, the two travelers stopped short and "stood still." Their attitude at that point was gloomy, perhaps even sullen. Only one of the two (Cleopas) is named, probably because he was known to at least some of Luke's readers.

19–24 What follows constitutes an affirmation about the person and work of Christ that is of great significance for our understanding of Jesus and of Luke's perception of him as recorded elsewhere (e.g., 4:14; Ac 19:38–39). The importance of the affirmation of the two disciples here in 24:19 must not in any way be underestimated. It is integral to Luke's theology and purpose.

"He was a prophet" recalls the passage in chapter 4 where Jesus clearly identified himself with the prophets (4:24). While in Luke's narrative Jesus is perceived as a prophet (e.g., 7:16), the Resurrection affirmed him to be much more, as the two on the Emmaus road are soon to learn.

The "chief priests and our rulers" (v.20) stand in contrast to the receptive "people" (v.19). It was they who "handed him over" for crucifixion. In v.21 the words "but we" provide still another contrast. Unlike the rulers, they "hoped" that Jesus would bring deliverance. The past tense used here is, under the present circumstances, a pathetic reminder of their inability to recognize Jesus or to believe the report of the empty tomb. Their expectation that he would "redeem Israel" recalls the words of Zechariah in 1:68 (cf. 2:38; 21:28). In view of v.46 and the passion predictions, the term "third day" had a significance to Luke's readers. What should have been the day of hope realized was for them the day of hope extinguished.

The final incomprehensible element in the travelers' report was the report of the empty tomb (v.22). The mention of "angels" shows that this is what Luke meant by "men" in v.4.

Verse 24 recalls v.12. The empty tomb without the appearance of Jesus himself was inadequate. It ironically becomes the last sad part of their confused response to Jesus' question, "What things?" (v.19).

25–27 Jesus himself now speaks, though still unrecognized. He, who in his transfiguration was superior to Moses and Elijah (9:28–36), now invokes Moses and the Prophets to substantiate the divine plan of his path from suffering to glory (v.27). The word "all" (v.25) is a warning not to treat the Scriptures selectively. Such selectivity could lead to the omission of the Messiah's suffering (v.26). But "the Christ" (Messiah) did "have to" suffer ("had to" or "must" is one of Luke's key ideas; cf. 2:49; 4:43; 9:22; 13:16, 33; 15:32; 18:1; 19:5; 21:9; 22:7, 37; 24: 7, 44). The future glory of the Christ (v.26) was mentioned in the context of the passion prediction, ascribed there to the "Son of Man" (9:26; cf. 21:27). Here it refers to the honor anticipated in the OT for the Messiah, including the Resurrection. Paul quoted the OT to prove the necessity of both the suffering and the resurrection of the Messiah (Ac 17:2–3).

For several reasons vv.25–27 are vitally important. With great clarity they show that the sufferings of Christ, as well as his glory, were predicted in the OT and that all the OT Scriptures are important. They also show that the way the writers of the NT used the OT had its origin, not in their own creativity, but in the postresurrection teachings of Jesus, of which this passage is a paradigm. The passage also exemplifies the role of the OT in Luke's own theology. Although he does not directly quote the OT Scriptures as many times as Matthew does, nevertheless he alludes frequently to the OT, demonstrating that what God has promised must take place and employing a "proof-from-prophecy" apologetic for the truth of the Gospel.

28–32 The invitation for Jesus to stay with the two follows the ancient custom of hospitality. As the afternoon drew on and suppertime approached, the stranger would need food and lodging. Jesus had "acted as if" he were going to continue his journey. Such a gesture would, like the invitation itself, be appropriate in the custom of those days. This polite action seems intended to draw out a very strong response from Cleopas and his companion, who indeed then "urged him strongly" to stay (v.29).

The recognition scene is one of the high points in this story. Once again we find a table scene characteristic in Luke (cf. 5:29; 7:36; 14:1, 7, 12, 15–16). What is remarkable is that Jesus took the role of the host and broke the bread, giving thanks (v.30). This recalls the feeding of the five thousand (9:10–17) as well as the Last Supper (22:19), though it was not a celebration of the latter.

As to whether it was through the actual breaking of bread or through divine intervention that the moment of truth came and the two disciples recognized Jesus, the answer must be that it was through both. Whether or not the two noticed the nail scars, Jesus acting as host led to the recognition. At the same time, the passive verb "were opened" implies divine action (v.31; cf. comment on v.16). God is the revealer of the risen Christ. Note the repetition of Jesus' opening "the Scriptures" (v.32) and later "their minds" (v.45).

The narrative ends abruptly as Jesus disappeared and Cleopas and his companion reflected on their feelings of intense inner warmth. The specific occasion of these feelings is the presence of the Lord and his expounding the OT.

33–35 The words "at once" continue the chronology of the resurrection day (cf. v.13). The reunion with the Eleven brought assurance to all, as the two disciples fulfilled their role as witnesses (vv.34–35). They especially spoke of recognizing Jesus when he broke bread with them (v.35).

3. The appearance to the disciples (24:36–49)

This is the third Easter narrative in Luke. In the first Jesus is not seen; in the second he appears to two disciples; this time he appears to the Eleven. The events Luke tells us of here provide the substance for his apologetic for Jesus' bodily resurrection in Ac 1:3–4 and Peter's witness to Cornelius (Ac 10:40–43). In this story it is not Jesus' resurrection as such that is being proved but the fact that the sudden visitor was indeed Jesus, present in a tangible body.

36 Once again Luke carefully connects the events after the Crucifixion chronologically (23:54, 56; 24:1, 9, 13, 33) with the words

Resurrection Appearances

EVENT	DATE	Matthew	Mark	Luke	John	Acts / I Corinthians
At the empty tomb outside Jerusalem	Early Sunday morning	28:1-10	16:1-8	24:1-12	20:1-9	
To Mary Magdalene at the tomb	Early Sunday morning		16:9-11		20:11-18	
To two travelers on the road to Emmaus	Sunday at midday			24:13-32		
To Peter in Jerusalem	During the day on Sunday			24:34		15:5
To the ten disciples in the upper room	Sunday evening		16:14	24:36-43	20:19-25	
To the eleven disciples in the upper room	One week later				20:26-31	15:5
To seven disciples fishing on the Sea of Galilee	One day at daybreak				21:1-23	
To the eleven disciples on the mountain in Galilee	Some time later	28:16-20	16:15-18			
To more than 500	Some time later					15:6
To James	Some time later					15:7
At the Ascension on the Mt. of Olives	Forty days after the resurrection			24:44-49		1:3-8

© 1985 The Zondervan Corporation

"While they were still talking about this." Suddenly Jesus himself "stood among them" (cf. Jn 20:19) and greeted them with a typical Semitic greeting, "Peace" (GK 1645; cf. *shalom*, GK 8934).

37-39 Luke's gospel opened with a terrified Zechariah in the unexpected presence of an angel (1:12). Now, near its end, Luke describes the fright of the disciples at the unexpected appearance of the risen Christ (v.37). One might have thought they would not respond this way, since they had just been hearing about Jesus' appearance on the Emmaus road. But whereas in that case Jesus had walked up to Cleopas and his companion as any traveler might, this time he appeared suddenly. Equally surprising to the reader are their doubts (v.38). These are significant for any who think that the disciples were expecting the Resurrection and therefore projected their hopes into a hallucination.

Jesus identified himself very emphatically (v.39): "It is I myself." The methods of crucifixion varied slightly, but Jesus apparently had nails in his hands and feet. Seeing and touching would convince the disciples. As in vv.3, 23, where Luke mentions the body of Jesus, here he again draws attention to the physical aspect of the Resurrection.

40-43 Verse 41a is a beautifully human touch. Jesus provides further evidence of his physical presence by eating (vv.42-43).

44-49 From time to time Luke has taken care to show that whatever the Lord has said unfailingly takes place (e.g., 2:20, 26; 19:32; 22:13, 37). That implication is perhaps present in the words "This is what I told you." Luke has a double emphasis in these verses, for not only had Jesus predicted the events that had happened, but the OT had also. The clause "while I was still with you" is a way of distinguishing between the days of Jesus' earthly ministry and his temporary postresurrection ministry before Ascension. "Law ... Prophets ... Psalms" expands

"Moses and all the Prophets" in v.27 by adding the Psalms as a major component of the OT, the third division called the Writings.

In v.31 the eyes of the two on the way to Emmaus were "opened." Now Jesus has "opened" the disciples' minds (v.45) to the "Scriptures." The formula "on the third day" (cf. v.7) goes back to the first passion prediction (9:22). Even the widespread preaching of repentance and forgiveness was predicted in the OT (cf. Ac 26:23). Such Scriptures as Isa 42:6; 60:3 may underlie v.47 here (cf. Ac 13:47). The fulfillment began in Ac 2:38: "Repent ... for the forgiveness of sins." Gentiles heard these words in Ac 10:43 and 17:30 (cf. Paul's commission, Ac 26:17–18). The idea of reaching the Gentiles is certainly prominent in Luke (see comment on 10:1). Also, the place of Jerusalem as the base of the mission accords with Luke's constant featuring of that city. Likewise Luke has stressed the place of "witnesses" (GK 3459) and will continue to do so in Acts (e.g., 1:8). Therefore, v.48 supports his emphasis. What the Father "promised" (v.49) is the Holy Spirit (Ac 1:4–5; 2:16–17), who is indeed the promised "power" (Ac 1:8). This "power from on high" has been known in Luke from the very beginning of his narrative, for the Son of God was conceived in Mary when the Holy Spirit came upon her and she was overshadowed by the "power of the Most High." Luke concludes where he began.

4. The Ascension (24:50–53)

The Ascension is more than the last event in Luke's narrative sequence or a postscript to the Resurrection. He had already mentioned it as Jesus' ultimate goal in his great journey toward Jerusalem (cf. comment on 9:51). The Ascension also has significance in the opening verses of Acts. The brevity of the account here at the close of Luke's gospel is not the measure of Luke's estimate of its importance. This brevity may also imply a telescoping of the entire closing narrative. Perhaps the author already had in mind an expanded version of the Ascension at the beginning of Acts. His words here, though few, are weighty with theological significance and very much in character with the entire book. Of the gospel authors, only Luke records the Ascension.

50–51 The vicinity of Bethany includes the Mount of Olives (Ac 1:12). Jesus' action in lifting up his hands and blessing the disciples (v.51) was priestly. The word "bless" (GK 2328) was significant at the opening of Luke. Zechariah the priest was rendered speechless in the temple, so that he was unable to pronounce the priestly blessing on the people when he came out (1:22). Such a blessing now concludes the book. Elizabeth blessed Mary and her child (1:42); Zechariah blessed God (NIV, "praising") when, on his declaration of John's name, his speech was restored (1:64); he then blessed (NIV, "praise") God again in his song (1:68); Simeon blessed (NIV, "praised") God in the temple on seeing Jesus (2:28) and then blessed his parents (2:34). This word does not appear again in Luke till Jesus blessed the bread at Emmaus (24:30). Luke then uses the word again in v.51 and in v.53. Thus he places Jesus clearly within the spiritual setting of the temple and priesthood. As the resurrected Messiah, Jesus has the authority to bless.

This imagery forms an important part of the letter to the Hebrews, which describes the high priestly intercession of Christ after his ascension into heaven (e.g., Heb 1:3, 4:14; 6:19–20; 7:23–25; cf. Ro 8:34; Eph 1:20). Jesus is also the Prophet of God, and we are again reminded of the prophet Elijah (who was "taken up" to heaven; 2Ki 2:11). Luke's conclusion, therefore, points to Jesus as prophet, priest, and Messiah.

52–53 Jesus is also the Son of God, and so his disciples "worshiped him" (v.52). This beautiful gospel closes with the theme of "joy" restated in v.52 and with the city of Jerusalem and its temple again presented as the true home of Christianity—the origin of the Christian Gospel and the Christian church (cf. introductory comment on 9:51–19:44; comments on 13:31–35; 19:41–44). Luke's theme of doxology reappears at the very end, as the disciples were last seen "blessing" (NIV, "praising"; GK 2328) God in response to Christ's blessing them (vv.50–51). This is both an appropriate conclusion to Luke's gospel and a reminder to us to live a life of praise as we wait for the return of the ascended Lord.

The Old Testament in the New

NT Text	OT Text	Subject
Lk 2:23	Ex 13:2, 12	Dedication of the firstborn
Lk 2:24	Lev 5:11; 12:8	Offering of the poor
Lk 3:4–6	Isa 40:3–5	Voice in the wilderness
Lk 4:4	Dt 8:3	Not by bread alone
Lk 4:8	Dt 6:13	Serve God alone
Lk 4:10–11	Ps 91:11–12	Protecting angels
Lk 4:12	Dt 6:16	Do not test God
Lk 1:18–19	Isa 61:1–2	God's Spirit on me
Lk 7:27	Mal 3:1	Messenger sent ahead
Lk 8:10	Isa 6:9–10	Seeing but not perceiving
Lk 10:27	Dt 6:5	Love God
Lk 10:27	Lev 19:18	Love your neighbor as yourself
Lk 12:53	Mic 7:6	A divided household
Lk 13:35	Ps 118:26	Blessed is he who comes
Lk 19:38	Ps 118:26	Blessed is he who comes
Lk 19:46	Isa 56:7	God's house of prayer
Lk 19:46	Jer 7:11	A den of robbers
Lk 20:17	Ps 118:22–23	Rejected cornerstone
Lk 20:28	Dt 25:5	A brother's widow
Lk 20:37	Ex 3:6	The living God
Lk 20:42–43	Ps 110:1	At God's right hand
Lk 21:27	Dan 7:13–14	Coming Son of Man
Lk 22:37	Isa 53:12	Numbered with transgressors
Lk 23:30	Hos 10:8	Hills falling on us
Lk 23:46	Ps 31:5	I commit my spirit

John

INTRODUCTION

1. Background

The gospel of John was probably the last of the Gospels to be written and circulated, though it definitely belongs to the first century. Its action took place between A.D. 27 and 36, when Pontius Pilate was removed from office by the order of Tiberius Caesar.

This gospel was probably written at a time when the church was composed of second- and third-generation Christians who needed more detailed instruction about Jesus and new defenses for the apologetic problems raised by apostasy within the church and growing opposition outside. The understanding of the person of Christ that had depended on the testimony of his contemporaries was becoming a philosophical and theological problem. Doctrinal variations had begun to appear, and some of the assertions of the basic Christian truths had been challenged. A new presentation was necessary to meet the questions of the changing times (see 20:31).

The gospel of John is, therefore, more theological and in some respects more cosmopolitan than the Synoptics. While it is not necessarily less Jewish, it has a wider appeal to growing Christian experience and to an enlarging Gentile constituency than the others. John presents Jesus as the Lord of the maturing and questioning believer.

This gospel contains little information about general historical events. It does refer to the ministry of John the Baptist (1:19–37; 3:22–36; 4:1); Herod's rebuilding of the temple (2:20); the high priesthood of Annas and Caiaphas (18:13–14); and the person of Pontius Pilate (18:28–19:16,38), prefect of Judea. The Roman domination of Palestine is implied but not featured. There is almost no direct allusion to current political affairs and no mention of the church by name. The author seems to be concerned less with time than with eternity.

2. Unity

The combination of intricacy and simplicity in the structure of the gospel of John conveys the unavoidable impression that it is the product of one mind. Its consistency of structure, distinctive vocabulary, uniformity of style, and directness of purpose can best be explained by ascribing it to a single author.

The main criterion of unity lies in the purpose of the work. It reads as a compact whole and is united by several distinct themes. The different topics it deals with—such as the "signs," the "I am's," the debates and personal interviews, and the discourses to the disciples—may not all appear in uniform sequence; nevertheless, there is complete unity in their teaching. All of them focus on the purpose expressed in the author's final note (20:30–31) and give the impression that they are just the sort of thing a friend of Jesus would remember about him.

3. Authorship

a. External evidence

The earliest tradition of the church ascribes the fourth gospel to John the son of Zebedee, one of the first of Jesus' disciples, and one who was closest to him. Irenaeus (c. 180) stated plainly that the disciple John had published a gospel when he lived in Ephesus. Irenaeus's testimony has been corroborated by other writers, such as Tatian (c. 150), who included it in his *Diatesseron*, a harmony of the Gospels; Theophilus of Antioch (c. 165); Clement of Alexandria (c. 220), who quoted from almost every chapter; and Tertullian (also c. 220). Likewise, Eusebius, the famous church historian of the fourth century, attributed the gospel to John.

b. Internal evidence

Internal evidence also testifies to likelihood of John as the single author of this gospel. The epilogue closes by focusing on "the disciple whom Jesus loved" as the witness and writer of the content of the gospel (21:20–24). The preceding chapters couple this disciple with Peter in the events on the morning of the Resurrection (20:2–8) and also identify him as the one Jesus committed his mother to at the Crucifixion (19:25–27). He was present at the Last Supper, where he reclined next to Jesus and was questioned by Peter (13:23–24).

Furthermore, the author was aware of the thinking of the disciples, and apparently he shared their interests and hopes. He reported the private discourses of Jesus at some length. He even shows knowledge of Jesus' inner consciousness, something that would have been possible only to a close associate (6:6, 61, 64; 13:1–3, 11; 18:4). Undoubtedly, therefore, he belonged to the Twelve, and he was probably a member of the inner circle. Obviously he was not Peter, nor is it likely that he was one of the others mentioned in the third person in the main body of the gospel (John himself is never mentioned by name). Nor could the author have been James, John's brother, for he was executed by Herod Agrippa I prior to A.D. 44 (Ac 12:2). Presumably, therefore, he was John, Peter's closest associate after the Resurrection (Ac 3:1–11; 4:13–20; Gal 2:9).

Second, this gospel was almost certainly written by a Jew. The author was acquainted with Jewish opinions and learning and with the details of Jewish customs. His vocabulary and general style are Semitic, even though the gospel was written in Greek. The OT is frequently quoted, and the necessity of prophetic fulfillment is emphasized (cf. 13:18; 15:25).

Furthermore, the author was a Palestinian Jew, not a member of the Diaspora. His knowledge of Palestinian topography was accurate. He distinguished between Bethany, the suburb of Jerusalem where Mary and Martha lived (11: 1), and "Bethany on the other side of the Jordan," where John the Baptist preached (1:28). Some of the sites he alluded to, such as Aenon (3:23) and Ephraim (11:54), are not described elsewhere; but, obviously, they were actual places well known to him. His description of the features of Jerusalem, such as the pool by the "Sheep Gate" (5:2), "the pool of Siloam" (9:7), the "Stone Pavement" (19:13), the place of execution called "Golgotha" (Aram. for "skull"; 19:17), the garden of Joseph where Jesus' body was buried (19:41), and the varied references to the temple (2:14–16 8:20; 10:23), shows that he was familiar with the city before its destruction. Archaeological investigations have confirmed the accuracy of many of the author's allusions, though complete data are presently unattainable.

A third deduction from the internal evidence of the gospel is that the author personally witnessed the events he described. He spoke easily and familiarly of the disciples and associates of Jesus (6:5–7; 12:21; 13:36; 14:5, 8, 22) and knew the background of those with whom Jesus had only casual contact, such as Nicodemus (3:1) or Annas (18:13). Small details appear frequently, such as the barley bread used at the feeding of the five thousand (6:9), the fragrance of the ointment Mary poured on Jesus (12:3), or the time at which Judas left the Last Supper (13:30). These are not the creation of literary imagination, but they are the natural touches that come from personal memory.

Although the author never names himself, it seems that his identity was well known to his contemporaries. Just why he or his colleagues who wrote the final chapter should have left the gospel anonymous is not clear—though, as a matter of fact, none of the Gospels mentions the name of its author. If it were written during a period of persecution, the writer possibly would have preferred to remain unidentified, though some of the recipients must have known who produced it.

4. Date

Much of Jerusalem was destroyed by the Roman suppression of the Jewish revolt of A.D. 66–70. As mentioned above, the detailed references in this gospel to many of the ancient landmarks indicate that the author was acquainted with them and that he must have been in Jerusalem before A.D. 70.

The date of the gospel has been variously estimated at almost any point between A.D. 45, shortly after the dispersion of Christians from Jerusalem following the persecution under Saul (Ac 8:1–4), and the middle of the second century. The explanation in ch. 21 concerning Jesus' words "If I want him to remain alive until I return, what is that to you?" (v.22) seemingly implies that "the disciple whom Jesus loved" must have attained a great age and must have been a contemporary of the second-generation church. Most conservative scholars suggest a date around 85 to 90, when the author had achieved advanced age but was still in full possession of his memory and active in ministry, though it may have been composed earlier.

5. Recipients

The intended recipients of John's gospel are not clearly identified. From the writer's habit of explaining Jewish usages, translating Jewish names, and locating Palestinian sites, it would seem that he was probably writing for a Gentile church outside Palestine. If the reading "believe" in John 20:31 is in the present tense, it would imply that the gospel was written to Christians who needed encouragement and deepening of their faith. If "believe" is in the aorist tense, it would suggest that the gospel was addressed, at least in part, to a pagan constituency to bring them to belief in Jesus as Christ and Son of God. The content of the gospel does not give overwhelming support to either possibility.

Probably it will not be too wrong to suggest that the gospel of John was written for Gentile Christians who had already acquired a basic knowledge of the life and works of Jesus but who needed further confirmation of their faith. By the use of personal reminiscences interpreted in the light of a long life of devotion to Christ and by numerous episodes that generally had not been used in the gospel tradition, John created a new and different approach to understanding Jesus' person.

If the Johannine letters (whose style is similar to this gospel) are any guide, the writer must have been a highly respected elder within the structure of the church. John considered himself responsible for its welfare and did not hesitate to assert his authority (2Jn 1, 4, 8; 3Jn 9–10). The doctrinal digressions implied by the counsel given in these letters indicate that the church was being imperiled, if not actually deceived, by false teachers who came in the guise of itinerant preachers. Many of these were followers of Cerinthus, a teacher who contended that Jesus was merely a human personality who was possessed by the Christ-spirit at his baptism and who relinquished this spirit on the cross. Contrary to this teaching, the gospel asserts that the Word became flesh (1:14) and that the descent of the Holy Spirit on Jesus at the baptism was the proof of his mission, not the origin of it (1:32–34). The Cross did not terminate his ministry; it simply marked the end of one stage of it. The Son returned to the Father in person; he did not cease to be the Son by death. The stress on sonship throughout the gospel conveys the idea that it was a live issue in the church; and that impression is strengthened by the warning in the first letter of John: "Such a man is the antichrist—he denies the Father and the Son. No one who denies the Son has the Father; whoever acknowledges the Son has the Father also" (1Jn 2:22–23).

6. Purpose

John wrote this gospel to meet the spiritual need of a church that had little background in the OT and that may have been endangered by the plausible contention of Cerinthus or men like him. John's intention is stated with perfect clarity: "These [signs] are written that you may believe that Jesus is the Christ, the Son of God, and that by believing you may have life in his name" (20:31). The total thesis of the gospel is belief in the Son who came from the Father.

The gospel gives an initial impression of discontinuity. Many of its episodes have little direct chronological or logical connection with one another. Nevertheless, they show a remarkable unity built on the one purpose of convincing the reader that Jesus was supernatural in his origin, powers, and goal. He was the *Logos* who had come into the world from another sphere (1:14). He performed miracles, or "signs," that illustrated his many-faceted powers, especially applied to human need. He died an unusual death, but he rose from the dead to send his disciples out on a universal mission. The last sentences of the gospel imply the promise of his return. An entirely new revelation of the plan and power of God is latent in this gospel (1:18).

7. Literary Form and Structure

The gospel of John is a narrative composed of various individual scenes from the career of Jesus; it is not a complete biography. The chronological gaps leave an impression of incompleteness for those expecting a complete chronicle of Jesus' career. Because the gospel has an apologetic or possibly polemic purpose, it utilizes only the episodes that will best illustrate its presentation of Jesus as the object of faith.

Throughout this gospel, certain personal interviews between Jesus and others are given at length. The author emphasizes dialogue and discourse between Jesus and his disciples. Miracles are few and are selected for individual illustrative purpose. The vocabulary is distinctive and is limited to major ideas such as those expressed by the words *believe, witness, love, abide, the Father, the Son, the Counselor, light, life, darkness, Word, glorify, true,* and others. Most of these are used metaphorically and represent the leading ideas of the gospel. It is almost impossible to read a single paragraph in the fourth gospel that does not identify itself as Johannine by at least one word or phrase.

The structure of this gospel may be analyzed from various viewpoints. The author uses at least five different approaches to his subject: (1) the central theme of "belief," (2) the phases of the ministry of Jesus, (3) a chronological sequence, (4) a geographic allocation of activity between Galilee and Jerusalem, and (5) the personal interviews.

a. Theme

The first of these criteria concerns the central theme of "belief." The varied episodes and teachings of the gospel all help develop this concept. The Prologue introduces the ministry of John the Baptist by stating that "he came as a witness . . . so that through him all men might believe" (1:7). The closing words of the main narrative that precedes the Epilogue (ch. 21) declare that "these [things] are written that you may believe that Jesus is the Christ, the Son of God" (20:31). The word "believe" (GK *4409*) appears ninety-eight times in the gospel. All the signs, teachings, and events in the gospel are used to stimulate faith in Christ and are so ordered that they mark growth in this faith on the part of his disciples. Growth was not always uniform, as Simon Peter's experience shows, and generally was countered by a growth of unbelief, as seen in the conduct of Jesus' enemies. The conflict between belief and unbelief, exemplified in the actions and utterances of the main characters, forms the plot.

The development of "belief "in John's work affords one key to its interpretation and marks its progressive evangelistic appeal. The following outline shows its general progress: (1) The Prologue: The Proposal for Belief (1:1–18); (2) The Presentation for Belief (1:19–4:54); (3) The Reactions of Belief and Unbelief (5:1–6:71); (4) The Crystallization of Belief and Unbelief (7:1–11:53); (5) The Crisis of Belief and Unbelief (11:54–12:50); (6) The Assurance for Belief (13:1–17:26); (7) The Rejection by Unbelief (18:1–19:42); (8) The Vindication of Belief (20:1–31); (9) Epilogue: The Dedication of Belief (21:1–25). In this scheme, the author is not so much concerned with a regular sequence of events as with the creation of a relationship. His main purpose is to involve his readers in an active faith in Jesus as the Christ, the Son of God.

b. Phases of ministry

The previous approach to the ministry of Jesus is topical rather than biographical. Nevertheless, the gospel is still strongly biographical. The phases of the ministry of Jesus follow a definite progression from the initial questioning of his authority down to its ultimate repudiation by his enemies. The outline used in this commentary notes five major divisions: (1) The Prologue, which states the basic preparation for understanding the ministry of Jesus (1:1–18); (2) the ministry of John the Baptist and the ministry of Jesus, which ultimately led to his rejection by the Jewish people (1:18–12:50); (3) the Farewell Discourse in the Upper Room, where Jesus prepares his disciples for his coming death (chs. 13–17); (4) the story of Jesus' death and resurrection, which is much shorter in John than in the Synoptic Gospels (chs. 18–20); and (5) the Epilogue, possibly added as a postscript to the main body of the gospel (ch. 21).

c. The chronological framework

The chronological framework of the gospel is loose. The segment from 1:19 to 2:11 represents the consecutive events of a few days, which are well marked by the phrase "the next day" (1:29, 35, 43), or some related expression. The major divisions of action following the initial sign (ch. 2) are indicated by the occurrences of feasts (2:13; 5:1; 6:4; 7:2, 14; 10:22; 12:1), though the chief reason for mentioning the feasts seems to be social, not chronological. Notwithstanding the difficulty of placing the events of this gospel in a fixed chronological order, it is still true that John seems to have had a knowledge of such an order and that he adhered to it, allowing for gaps at those places where he chose to be silent. The order of the last week begins with

John 12, "six days before the Passover" (12:1), and ends with Jesus' crucifixion just prior to Friday evening, the beginning of the Sabbath. The tomb was found to be empty on "the first day of the week" (20:1), and in the afternoon of the same day Jesus appeared to the disciples in the Upper Room (v.19).

d. Geographical structure

The gospel's structure by location does not seem to follow any particular design, except that it emphasizes Jesus' activity in Jerusalem. There are only three allusions to his ministry in Galilee—Capernaum in 2:12, Capernaum again in 4:43–54, and Bethsaida on the Sea of Galilee (6:1–15), followed by the address in the synagogue at Capernaum (vv.25–70)—plus a brief visit in Samaria (4:1–42) and in Ephraim (11:54). This emphasis on Jerusalem stands to reason, since John wants to show, against the background of his opposition, who Jesus was. Since opposition seemed to come largely from the leaders of the Jewish hierarchy whose headquarters were in Jerusalem, the main scene is laid where the sharpest theological debates occurred and where the closing scenes of Jesus' life took place. (On the relationship of this to the Synoptics, see the last section of this introduction.)

e. Personal interviews

One marked feature of John's gospel is the partiality to personal interviews. The Synoptics emphasize Jesus' public ministry as he talked to the crowds, though they do lay considerable emphasis on the training of the disciples. While John does on several occasions say that many believed in him in response to his public actions or appeals (2:23; 4:39; 7:31; 8:30; 10:42; 11:45; 12:11, 42), it records fewer of his general discourses. The personal interviews are rather widely distributed through the earlier part of the gospel: Nicodemus in Jerusalem (3:1–15), the woman of Samaria (4:1–26), the nobleman of Cana (4:43–53), the paralytic in Jerusalem (5:1–15), the blind man (9:1–38), and Mary and Martha in Bethany (11:17–40). These interviews represent different classes of society, occur at different times during Jesus' career, and have different occasions followed by varying appeals. All of them, however, whether implicitly or explicitly, illustrate the nature and consequences of belief. All of the interviews depict Jesus' personal concern for people.

The general interviews with groups are similar in content and teaching. In time and place they approximately parallel the individual interviews. "Many" listened to him in Jerusalem (2:23); "many of the Samaritans" received him willingly after his conversation with the woman (4:39); a crowd gathered to hear him in Capernaum after the feeding of the five thousand (6:24–40; see also 12:12, 17, 29–36). Likewise, John gives a great deal of attention to Jesus' personal ministry to the disciples: Andrew (1:40; 6:8), Peter (1:42; 6:68; et al.), Philip (1:43–44; 6:5; et al.), Nathanael (1:47–51; 21:2), Thomas (11:16; 14:5; 20:26–29), and Judas Iscariot (12:4–8; 13:26–30).

In contrast, John records interviews with hostile persons. At least six conflicts with "the Jews" are mentioned (2:18–20; 5:16–47; 6:41–59; 7:15–44; 8:31–58; 10:22–39). The title "The Jews" apparently is not given solely for the purpose of distinguishing their nationality from Samaritans or Gentiles but to identify Jesus' opponents (i.e., the Jewish leadership; cf. 7:13; 9:22; 20:19). Each of these instances indicates the progress of unbelief that leads to the climax of the Cross. The interview with Pilate is the only instance of a hostile individual confrontation in this gospel, and Pilate's hostility is due more to his political dilemma than to personal enmity.

These personal interviews, while not in themselves constituting a consistent basis for outlining the progressive development of the gospel, do illustrate it. Thus they serve much the same purpose as pictures in a book. The interviews clearly relate to the main theme and forcibly convey the revelation given through Christ and the effects of the power he exercised.

8. Theological Values

The gospel of John is predominantly theological. Although all four gospels present the person of Jesus from a theological viewpoint, John emphasizes it most strongly. His initial assertion in 1:1, 14, 18 declares that Jesus was no ordinary person; he was the incarnation of the eternal God, who chose that means of revealing himself perfectly to humankind. Throughout the gospel the essential deity of the Lord Jesus Christ is stressed.

A second theological aspect is the concept of atonement. Jesus was introduced by John the Baptist as the sacrificial "Lamb of God, who takes away the sin of the world" (1:29). Jesus told Nicodemus that "just as Moses lifted up the snake in the desert, so the Son of Man must be lifted up, that everyone who believes in him may have eternal life" (3:14–15). He spoke of his flesh, which he would "give for the life of the world" (6:51), and called himself "the good shepherd [who] lays down his life for the sheep" (10:11).

Another prominent theme is eternal life. Life in the sum of its total expression is a major subject of the Prologue (1:4). His gift to believers is eternal life (3:15–16; 10:10; 20:31), bestowed on those who commit themselves to him (3:36; 4:13; 5:21, 24; 8:12).

An important body of teaching on the person and functions of the Holy Spirit appears in Jesus' farewell discourse to the disciples (14:25–26; 15:26; 16:7–15). His intermediary relation between Christ and the believer and his functional relation to God, the believer, and the world are plainly defined.

Perhaps the greatest theological contribution of the gospel is a full discussion and demonstration of the nature of belief. Both by definition and by example its essence is described. Belief is equated with receiving (1:12), following (1:40), drinking (4:13), responding (4:51), eating (6:57), accepting (6:60, lit., "hear"), worship (9:38), obeying (11:39–41), and commitment (12:1–11). The lives of those who "believed" show both the method and result of their faith.

9. The Relation of John to the Synoptics

Since both the gospel of John and the three other gospels deal with narratives of the life of Jesus, the question of interrelationship naturally occurs. Matthew, Mark, and Luke distinctly resemble one another, not only in general subject and order of narrative but also in many instances of extended discourse. The text of John, on the other hand, differs radically in its form and content from the other gospels.

With respect to its general order, the gospel of John parallels the others. It begins with the ministry of John the Baptist, narrates the early contacts with disciples, contains accounts of Jesus' conflicts with the scribes and Pharisees, and places the feeding of the five thousand and the walking on the water at the turning point of his ministry. The story of the Passion Week begins with the entry into Jerusalem and terminates with the Crucifixion and the Resurrection.

On the other hand, John the Baptist's introduction of Jesus to his disciples is highlighted rather than his general preaching of repentance. Jesus' initial contact with the disciples is quite different from the calling of the first four disciples as reported elsewhere. The discourses of Jesus in John are mainly apologetic and theological rather than ethical and practical, as in the Sermon on the Mount. Only seven miracles are recounted, and of these only two duplicate those of the Synoptic Gospels. The chronological order is different, for John places a cleansing of the temple early in Jesus' ministry, whereas the Synoptics locate it in Passion Week. The events of the Last Supper, the betrayal, the hearing before Pilate, and the Crucifixion are reported quite differently from the other three gospels; and the Resurrection account has only slight resemblance to the others.

The best conclusion to be drawn is that John wrote independently of the others, not simply because he used different sources, but because he had a different purpose in organizing his material. He wrote as a first-hand witness making a special presentation of Jesus. John possessed knowledge of many facts of Jesus' life mentioned in the Synoptics, but he also knew much they did not record. He utilized this material in a different way and shaped it for a different purpose.

At the same time, there is a sense in which the fourth gospel complements the other three. It often seems to begin its narrative at a point where the others have stopped or to assume a knowledge they would supply. For example, in the account of the Last Supper John tells how the disciples reclined for the meal without the customary footwashing as they entered the room and how Jesus himself felt obligated to supply the lack of service (John 13:2–14). Luke tells us how on that occasion the disciples were bickering with one another for the highest place in the coming kingdom (Luke 22:24). If their attitude toward one another was rivalry for the best position in the coming rule of Jesus, it explains why no one was ready to wash the feet of the others.

Contrasts Between the Synoptics and John

The Synoptics	The Gospel of John
Chiefly concerned with Jesus' ministry in the north, around Galilee	Gives more coverage to Jesus' ministry in the south, around Judea
Much emphasis on the kingdom	More emphasis on the person of Jesus
Jesus as Son of David, Son of Man	Jesus especially as Son of God
Anticipation of the church and references to the infant church	Gospel of the maturing church
The earthly story	The heavenly meaning
Jesus' sayings generally short (e.g., parables)	More of the long discourses of Jesus
Comparatively little commentary by the gospel writers	Much commentary by John
Only one mention of a Passover	Mention of three, possibly four, Passovers

Adapted from Irving Jensen, *John* (Chicago: Moody, 1970), by permission.

The bulk of the teaching recorded in the first three gospels was delivered to crowds that gathered to hear his words of wisdom or to opponents who contended with him. The larger part of the teaching in the fourth gospel (e.g., chs. 14–17) was intended for the ears of his disciples only. But a short passage in Matthew and another in Luke (Mt 11:25–30; Lk 10:21–22) are similar in style to John's gospel. Although these two passages are brief, they are sufficient to show that Jesus could, and undoubtedly did, use both approaches in dealing with his contemporaries.

EXPOSITION

I. Prologue: Revelation of the Word (1:1–18)

A. The Preincarnate Word (1:1–5)

1 "In the beginning" recalls the opening words of Genesis 1:1: "In the beginning God created the heavens and the earth." The expression does not refer to a particular moment of time but assumes a timeless eternity. "Word" (*logos;* GK *3364*) has several meanings. Ordinarily it refers to a spoken word, with emphasis on the meaning conveyed. *Logos,* therefore, is an expression of personality in communication. Scripture also tells us that it is creative in its power: "By the word of the LORD were the heavens made, their starry host by the breath of his mouth" (Ps 33:6). To the Hebrew "the word of God" was the self-assertion of the divine personality; to the Greek the formula denoted the rational mind that ruled the universe. John is asserting that the "Word" is the source of all that is visible and antedates the totality of the material world.

The use of *logos* implies that John was endeavoring to bring out the full significance of the Incarnation to the Gentile world as well as to the Jewish people. While not adopting the Greek concept in its entirety, he indicates that Jesus had universal rather than local significance and that he spoke with ultimate authority. He was preexistent, involved in the act of creation, and therefore superior to all created beings. This presentation lifts Christ above the materialistic, pagan concept of deities just as the Incarnation brings the Hebrew concept of God into everyday life.

The preposition "with" (GK *4639*) in the phrase "the Word was with God" indicates both equality and distinction of identity along with association. The phrase can be rendered "face to face with." It therefore suggests personality and coexistence with the Creator, and yet is an expression of his creative being.

The three statements of v.1 bring out three different aspects of the nature of the Word. The first speaks of his preexistence, the second of his distinctiveness, and the third of his deity.

2 John succinctly reemphasizes the great truths of v.1. The Word's preexistence, distinctiveness, and deity are brought out in the statement "he was with God in the beginning."

3 The word "made" (GK *1181*) means "became" rather than "constructed." The visible universe with all its complexity owes its origin to the creative mind and power of God. Apart from his Word, existence is impossible (see also Col 1:16; Heb 1:2).

4 The term "life" (GK *2437*, occurring thirty-six times in John) is uniformly used throughout the gospel. Wherever it appears, it refers either to the principle of physical life or, more often, to spiritual life. Frequently it is coupled with the adjective "eternal" (GK *173*) to denote the quality and power of the believer's life. The life was embodied in Christ, who demonstrated perfectly what eternal life is by his career (cf. 14:6; 17:3). Christ is the "life" that is the "light of men." In him God's purpose and power are made available to human beings. He is their ultimate hope.

5 The metaphorical contrast between light and darkness as representing the powers of good and evil was common in John's day. A better translation of v.5b here is "The darkness did not overcome it" (see NIV note; cf. the use of this same verb in 12:35).

B. The Prophetic Announcement (1:6–8, 15)

6 In vv.6–8 the human agent for introducing the Word to people is presented. As the Word came to bring the heavenly light to humanity, so John came to speak from a human level and to awaken people to their need of God's revelation. This gospel stresses the function of John the Baptist rather than his origin or character (cf. Lk 1:5–24, 57–80). The author takes for granted that the reader knows the Baptist, and he emphasizes John's subordinate role (cf. Jn 3:22–30) and the fact that he was "sent"—a word that refers to the authority that commissioned him. John's function is defined in v.7.

7–8 "Witness" (GK *3456*) is distinctly a Johannine word. It is especially pertinent in this gospel, which attempts to establish by adequate testimony the claims of Jesus as the Son of God (see comment on 1:19). The preaching of John the Baptist was preparatory to the coming of the Christ (cf. Mt 3:11–12; Mk 1:1–8; Lk 1:17; 3:15–17). He told the crowds listening to him that he was only the forerunner of another who would confer on them the Holy Spirit and that they must repent, or change their attitude, in anticipation of meeting him. The author was careful to specify that John the Baptist was not the genuine light but that he came to attest it.

15 The author reverts to the witness of John the Baptist to explain further the Baptist's position as to Christ. The manifestation of Jesus came after John's appearance, but in importance Jesus took precedence over him. Jesus surpassed John because he was intrinsically greater.

C. The Reception of the Word (1:9–13)

9 Christ is the real or genuine light of humanity who was about to enter the world. His function would be to give the light of truth to all whom his ministry would affect, whether in greater or lesser degree.

10 "World" (GK *3180*) refers to the current organization or culture in which people live, whether applied to the natural environment (16:21) or to the present order as contrasted with the spiritual order (6:14; 9:39; 11:27; et al). Here it plainly refers to the total environment that the Word created (1:3). The second part of the verse places the emphasis on the ancient world of men and women who did not recognize him. There was no flash of awareness concerning his real person.

11 In the phrase "he came to that which was his own, but his own did not receive him," the former "own" (neuter in Greek) refers to things; and the phrase may mean "his own property" or "his own home" (as in 19:27). The latter "own" (masculine in Greek) refers to "his own people," the nation he belonged to. Jesus came to the place he had created and had a right to possess. Those who inhabited it turned him away in rejection.

12–13 Just as there is a sharp antithesis in vv.4–5 between darkness and light, so here is an equally direct contrast between rejection and reception. In spite of the many who rejected the Word, there were some who received him. This provides the initial definition of "believe" (GK *4409*) by equating it with "receive." When we receive a gift, we demonstrate our confidence in its reality and trustworthiness. We make it part of our own possessions. By being so received, Jesus gives to those who receive him a right to membership in the family of God.

"Become" indicates clearly that people are not the spiritual children of God by natural birth, for we cannot become what we already are. This verb implies a change of nature. "Not of natural descent" excludes a purely physical process; "nor of human decision" rules out the result of any biological urge; "or a husband's will" shows that this kind of birth is not merely the outcome of a legal marriage. The relation is spiritual, not biological. There is a connection with the concept of the new birth as elaborated in Jesus' conversation with Nicodemus (see comments on 3:3–8).

D. The Incarnation of the Word (1:14, 16–18)

14 Verse 14 marks the fourth statement about the Word. Note the contrast between vv.1 and 14. Verse 1 states that the Word "was," referring to his permanent condition or state, while v.14 states that the Word "became" flesh, involving a change in state. This is the basic statement of the Incarnation, for Christ entered into a new dimension of existence through the gateway of human birth and took up his residence among human beings. The verb translated "made his dwelling" (GK *5012*) means "to pitch a tent, to dwell temporarily." He left his usual place and accepted the conditions of human life and environment, with the attendant temporal limitations that all humans experience (cf. also 3:17; 6:38–42, 51; 7:29; 8:23; 9:5; 10:36; 16:28).

John's presentation of Christ as the Word is not primarily metaphysical but practical (cf. comment in v.1). As the preexistent Son of God, he was the Creator of the world and the Executor of the will of the Father. As the incarnate Son of God, he exercised in his human existence these same powers and revealed effectively the person of the Father. "We have seen his glory" implies a personal observation of a new reality. Probably there is an allusion to the Transfiguration (Mt 17:2–8; Mk 9:2–8; Lk 9:28–36). His incarnation was the full manifestation of grace and truth because it was the greatest possible expression of God's compassion for people and the most perfect way of conveying the truth to their understanding.

The "one and only [GK *3666*] Son" emphasizes the fact that Jesus is the unique Son of God; he has no equal and is able fully to reveal the Father. God's personal revelation of himself in Christ has no parallel elsewhere, nor has it ever been repeated.

16 Verse 15 has already been discussed as part of the section concerning John the Baptist. Verse 16 connects directly with v.14; it says that the Son was full of the grace and truth of the Father. The writer reminds his readers that they have already experienced that grace in increasing measure. When one supply of grace is exhausted, another is available.

17 The contrast between law and grace as methods of God's dealing with humans is expressed here as plainly as in the Pauline writings (see Ro 5:20–21; Eph 2:8). The law represented God's standard of righteousness; grace exhibited his attitude to human beings who found that they could not keep the law. Compare this verse with the words of Jesus in the Sermon on the Mount: "You have heard that it was said. . . . But I tell you" (Mt 5:21–22, 27–28, 33–34, 30–39, 43–44).

18 The noun "God" has no article in the Greek text, which indicates that the author is presenting God in his nature of being rather than as a person. "Deity" might be a more accurate rendering. The meaning is that no human has ever seen the essence of deity. God is invisible, not because he is unreal, but because physical eyes are incapable of detecting him. Deity as a being is known only through spiritual means that are able to receive its (his) communications. "God the one and only" is as strong an affirmation of the deity of Christ as is v.1.

"At the Father's side" is substantially the same expression as that used in 13:23 concerning "the disciple whom Jesus loved," who "was reclining next to him." It shows intimate association, which presupposes close fellowship. As the confidant of the Father, Jesus is uniquely qualified to act as the intermediary who can carry the knowledge of God to humans.

The phrase "has made him known" (GK *2007*) means to "explain" or "interpret." The being and nature of God, which cannot be perceived directly by ordinary senses, have been adequately presented to us by the Incarnation. The life and words of Jesus are more than an announcement; they are an explanation of God's attitude toward humans and of his purpose for them.

II. The Public Ministry of the Word (1:19–12:50)

Having introduced the figure of the incarnate Word by the Prologue, and having identified the forerunner by his name and by his mission, the author proceeds to present the ministry of the Word in some detail. Broadly, the book can be divided into two sections: the public and the private ministries of Christ. The former occupies the larger chronological section; the latter is brief and is closely related to the Passion, which concludes the narrative.

A. The Beginning Ministry (1:19–4:54)

1. The witness of John the Baptist (1:19–34)

19 The miracle of the Incarnation called for witnesses to substantiate its reality. First in order is that of John the Baptist. His preaching attracted such large crowds that the Jewish hierarchy in Jerusalem sent priests (the theological authorities of the nation) and Levites (those concerned with the ritual and service of the temple) to investigate him. John did not seem to fit into any category familiar to the Jewish authorities, and his unusual success demanded an explanation.

20 "Christ" (GK 5986) is the Greek equivalent of the Hebrew "Messiah," meaning "Anointed" (see comments on Mk 3:29–30). It was the title of the prophesied deliverer, who would bring renewal and political freedom to Israel (cf. 4:25). John the Baptist disclaimed the title because he was not the Messiah and because it had political implications that would have made him appear to the Romans as a potential insurrectionist.

21–22 The suggestion that John the Baptist might be identified with Elijah reflected the Jewish expectation that the return of Elijah would precede the advent of the Messiah (see Mal 4:5–6). Because John's rough exterior and ascetic tendencies corresponded to Elijah's type of personality (cf. Mk 6:14), some identified him with the stormy prophet who had challenged Ahab (1Ki 17–19). John rejected the suggestion and denied that he was Elijah raised from the dead.

Again they asked, "Are you the Prophet?" referring probably to God's word to Moses in Dt 18:15 (see also comment on 7:40, where some people thought Jesus might be the Prophet). When John disclaimed identity with all these persons, the delegation demanded in exasperation, "Who are you?"

23 The reference to Isaiah uses the figure of preparing a road for the king through open and uneven territory so that he may travel over a smooth highway. John the Baptist here called himself the "roadbuilder" for one greater than he who would follow him with a fuller revelation. Isaiah went on to say that "the glory of the LORD will be revealed, and all mankind together will see it" (Isa 40:5). This "glory" was revealed in the person of Jesus, of whom the writer of the gospel has already said, "We have seen his glory" (1:14).

24–25 The Pharisees represented the strict interpreters of the Law and were particularly interested in examining the credentials of any new religious teacher in Judaism. This gospel does not show unvarying hostility toward them. Nicodemus was a Pharisee and was apparently a sincere if unenlightened person (see 3:1–21). As a class, however, they were hostile toward Jesus because he did not observe traditional rules and because he openly rebuked their superficial and often hypocritical religiosity. These Pharisees challenged John's right to baptize.

26–27 John suggested that he did not profess to speak with ultimate authority. He was, after all, preaching repentance (Lk 3:3) and was calling for baptism as a confession of repentance in expectation of the greater person who was yet to appear. It seems likely that John's baptism followed the pattern of proselyte baptism, which required a renunciation of all evil, complete immersion in water, and then reclothing as a member of the holy community of law-keepers.

John drew his reference to untying the sandals of his successor from the practice of using the lowest slave of a household to remove the sandals and wash the feet of guests. John's witness, therefore, reflected the exalted nature of Jesus and placed the latter far above himself.

28 "Bethany on the other side of Jordan" was so named to distinguish it from the Bethany near Jerusalem (see 12:1). Its exact site is unknown.

29 The chronological scheme of this section is indicated by the reference to successive days: the first day, when the delegation from Jerusalem questioned John (1:19–28); the "next" (second) day, when John saw Jesus approaching (1:29–34); the "next" (third) day, when John pointed out Jesus to his disciples and when they visited him (1:35–42); and the "next" (fourth) day, when Jesus "decided to leave for Galilee" (1:43–50).

The witness of John the Baptist was positive as well as negative and focused on Jesus rather than on himself. Verses 29–34 contain his presentation of the person of Jesus. Two aspects stand out in the titles by which he introduced Jesus. "The Lamb [GK *303*] of God" reflects the sacrificial character of Christ's mission, probably alluding to Isa 53:7 (cf. v.36; Ac 8:32; 1Pe 1:19). The sacrifice of a lamb as a substitute or as an atonement for sin appears frequently in the OT, beginning with Abraham in Ge 22:2–8. In Lev 14:10–25, a lamb was prescribed as a guilt offering. The book of Revelation also refers to "the Lamb" (GK *768*; Rev 5:6–13; 6:1–3,5,7; et al.), though it employs this title as a triumphal title, memorializing the completion of Christ's sacrificial work. The title "Lamb of God" here in Jn 1:29 therefore refers to the atoning work of Christ, who by one final sacrifice of himself removed the guilt of our sins and opened the way to God. John the Baptist limited his own function to introducing Jesus and declared that only the latter could take away sin.

30 This verse is essentially a restatement of v.15, with one significant addition. John calls Jesus "a man who comes after me." The Greek word for "man" in the verse is the word for "male." It intimates the headship of Christ over his followers in the sense of the man-woman relationship in marriage.

31 The identity of the Messiah was unknown to John the Baptist. This does not mean that John did not know Jesus personally, for, after all, they were relatives (Lk 1:36). John's ministry was twofold: he was to lead his hearers to repentance (Mk 1:4) and to reveal the Messiah to Israel. Somehow John understood that the revelation of Messiah would take place in conjunction with his baptizing ministry; therefore, he remained faithful to his calling. However, even after Messiah had been revealed to Israel at the baptism of Jesus, John continued the other aspect of his ministry.

32–34 The second aspect of John's witness to Jesus (see comment on v.29) concerned the title "Son of God." This aspect was related to the work of the Holy Spirit, who both authenticated the mission of Jesus and was the seal of his work in individual lives. John announced that Jesus would impart the Holy Spirit to his followers. To "baptize with the Holy Spirit" means that just as the common experience of baptism in water signified repentance and confession of sin, so the indwelling of the Holy Spirit is the seal and dynamic of the new life. Repentance and confession are the conditions on which the believer receives the gift of the Spirit (cf. Ac 2:38; Gal 3:2; 5:16–25). The manifestation of the presence of the Spirit in Jesus' case was visible (see Lk 3:21–22), though this gospel records the Baptist's later reflection on that event.

John the Baptist's solemn avowal that he had seen the descent of the Spirit on Jesus and that he is "the Son of God" is the climax of his testimony. The significance of the title can be best understood in the light of 1:18 (see comment). John's emphatic declaration was the reason why the disciples left him to follow Jesus.

2. The first disciples (1:35–51)

35–36 The section immediately following John's testimony gives the response of Jesus' first disciples, who came to him largely because of John's influence. The whole section is tied together by a chronological framework (see comment on v.29), so that the entire episode of John's introduction of Jesus and the opening of his public ministry is treated as a unit. The previous section dealt with John's preparatory statement; this second one deals with the initial meeting between Jesus and his potential disciples; and the third one deals with the sign that demonstrated his power and confirmed their faith (2:1–11). The repeated allusion to the Lamb of God focused the attention of John's disciples on Jesus as the basis for the divine forgiveness of sin and for the assurance that their repentance would be accepted. It stirred their interest and prompted them to investigate who Jesus was.

37–39 As John's disciples followed him, Jesus turned to challenge their motives by asking, "What do you want?" He probed them to find out whether they were motivated by idle curiosity or by a real desire to know him. Their reply was not merely an inquiry for his address but a courteous request for an interview. "Rabbi" was a term of respect accorded Jewish teachers (cf. 1:49; 3:26). Jesus encouraged the two disciples to become acquainted with him and to spend time with him. "The tenth hour" probably means about four o'clock in the afternoon, since Jewish time was ordinarily reckoned from sunrise. They likely remained with Jesus overnight.

40 Of the two disciples who heard John, only Andrew is named; the other one may well have been John (the author) himself. Throughout the gospel he had an interest in Simon Peter. On this occasion he wanted to explain the origin of Simon's association with Jesus.

41 Andrew's testimony shows that the interview of the preceding hours was related to Jewish hopes and to Jesus' character. The statement "We have found the Messiah" does not necessarily imply an explicit claim by Jesus, but it does indicate that Andrew regarded Jesus as the candidate for that title. The expectation of a national deliverer was widespread in Judaism in the first third of the first century A.D. Probably all the disciples expected that Jesus would fulfill their hopes for an independent kingdom; those who joined him anticipated they would have political power (cf. Mk 10:28, 35–45).

42 The introduction of Peter to Jesus was brief but direct. The simple pronouncement Jesus made in this verse was really a diagnosis of Peter's personality. Simon, or Simeon (cf. Ac 15:14), was the name of Jacob's second oldest son (Ge 29:33), who, with his brother Levi (29:34), had ruthlessly avenged the violation of their sister by one of the Canaanite princes (34:25–31). The rash and impulsive character of Simeon was mirrored in Simon (cf. Jn 18:10). Jesus accepted Simon as he was but promised that he should become "Cephas," an Aramaic name, which, like the Greek "Peter," means "a rock."

43–45 Whereas the first disciples were introduced to Jesus by John the Baptist or by one of the other disciples, Jesus took the initiative in calling Philip. He, like Andrew and Peter, was a Galilean and quite likely a fisherman. The name Bethsaida, his hometown, means "house of fishing." Like Andrew, Philip found another person, Nathanael, and by his witness brought him to Jesus. The identity of Nathanael is uncertain. Some have equated him with Bartholomew, others with Matthew (see comment on Mk 3:16–19). This man seems to have been a student of the Law, for Philip appealed to him on the basis of the prediction in the Law and the Prophets. Jesus' phrase "under the fig tree" (v.48) was used in rabbinic literature to describe meditation on the Law.

46 Nathanael's response indicates that Nazareth did not enjoy a good reputation in Galilee. Perhaps Nathanael, who came from Bethsaida, looked down on Nazareth as a rival village, either poorer or morally worse than his own.

47–51 Jesus' comment on Nathanael suggests that the latter had been reading of Jacob's experience at Bethel (Ge 28:1–17). Jacob was filled with guile and had been forced to leave home because he had lied to his father and had swindled his brother. If under these circumstances Jacob was eligible for a revelation from God., would not Nathanael be even more worthy of such a blessing? Jesus said that Nathanael was free from "guile" (KJV) and then used the imagery of Jacob's dream to describe the greater revelation he would give to Nathanael. Jesus implied that he himself would be the medium of that revelation, and his order of the angels' procedure implies that they rose from earth to heaven with their inquiries and then returned to earth with the answers. His mission is to answer human need and to make sure that the answers are proclaimed. The term "Son of Man" is used here for the first time in John's gospel (see comments on Mk 8:31).

3. The first sign (2:1–11)

1 The wedding at Cana is linked to the preceding text by a chronological tie: "on the third day," a phrase that probably means "after three days." Cana was a village in the hills of Galilee. Its exact location is disputed, but the best site seems to be that of Khirbet Qana, about nine miles north of Nazareth.

2–3 A wedding is always a gala occasion, and in a village like Cana it would be a community celebration. "Refreshments" were provided for all guests. Of these, wine was very important. To fail in providing adequately for the guests would involve social disgrace. In the closely knit communities of Jesus' day, such an error would never be forgotten and would haunt the newly married couple all their lives. The situation prompted Mary's urgency when she informed Jesus of the emergency.

4–5 Jesus' reply to Mary was not so abrupt as it seems, for "woman" was a polite form of address (see also 19:26; 20:15). His statement probably means, "What business is that of ours?" Mary acknowledged that Jesus should act independently, and she confidently told the servants to follow his orders, fully expecting that he would take appropriate action. Jesus indicated that he was no longer under her authority but that he was living by a new pattern timed by the purpose of God. He would begin his miracles according to the purpose of his heavenly Father. The "time" (GK *6052*) refers to the first hour when he manifested the real reason for which he came (see 17:1).

6–7 The stone jars were large, containing about twenty gallons apiece. By the social rules of the day, all the guests were expected to wash their hands before eating, and a considerable amount of water would be needed for this. At the lowest estimate, 120 gallons of water would be available. If made into wine, it would supply approximately two thousand four-ounce glasses; and if, as was frequently customary, the wine was further diluted by three parts of water to one of wine, there would have been enough to last for several days.

8–10 The "master of the banquet" was not the host, but a headwaiter or toastmaster called in to take care of the distribution of food and drink at a large social occasion. He was astounded by the high quality of the wine, since generally a poorer quality was served once the taste of the guests became dulled.

11 The purpose of Jesus' first miracle after entering Galilee is not stated, but the nature of the miracle is very plain. Jesus had come to bring about conversion: water to wine, sinners to saints. And this latter miracle of transformation occurs in almost complete obscurity. Few know when or how it happens, but they know that it does happen.

The effect of this miracle is noteworthy. It marked the beginning of a ministry accompanied by supernatural power; and it proved so convincing to the new disciples that they "put their faith in him." That is, the deed helped confirm the conclusion they had drawn from their previous interviews with him: Jesus must be the Messiah.

4. The interlude at Capernaum (2:12)

12 This verse covers an unspecified period of time. Since the Synoptic Gospels seem to imply that he had an early ministry in Galilee, it may fit at this point. The allusion to Jesus' brothers probably refers to younger children of Joseph and Mary, born after Jesus (see Mt 1:24–25; Mk 6:3).

5. The cleansing of the temple (2:13–22)

13–14 About the time of the Passover, Jesus went up to Jerusalem from Galilee for the annual feast. The narrative poses a chronological puzzle, for the Synoptic Gospels unitedly attach Jesus' cleansing of the temple to his last visit to Jerusalem at the time of his death (see Mt 21:10–17; Mk 11:15–19; Lk 19:45–46). It is best to acknowledge that there were two such occasions, one of which was recorded by John and the other by the Synoptics, especially since there are some significant differences between this account and those in the Synoptics (see *EBC,* 8:44). It is not at all improbable that Jesus may have cleansed the temple twice, two Passovers apart, and that the second so enraged the hierarchy that their animosity toward him exploded into drastic action.

The sale of cattle and doves and the privilege of exchanging money were permitted in the temple court as a convenience for pilgrims who would need animals for sacrifice and temple shekels for their dues. Under the chief priests, however, the concessions had become merely a means of making money and had debased the temple into a commercial venture.

The temple from which Jesus cast out the money changers and the those selling animals had recently been lavishly remodelled by King Herod. This model, located in Jerusalem, is a reconstruction of what that temple must have looked like.

15–16 Jesus' action precipitated wild confusion. The animals would be bawling and running about aimlessly; the money changers would be scrambling for their coins in the dust and debris on the floor of the court; the officials would be arguing with Jesus about the rights of the case. Jesus' expression "my Father's house" reveals his feeling toward God. The merchandising of privilege was an insult to God and a desecration of the Father's house.

17 Jesus' vehemence revealed his inward passion for the Father and his jealous guardianship of the Father's interests. The Scripture brought to the disciples' minds is Ps 69:9, from which other passages have been applied to Christ (e.g., Ps 69:1–4 in Jn 15:25; Ps 69:21 in Jn 19:29).

18–21 The Jews' demand for a sign is quite in agreement with their general attitude toward Jesus during his lifetime (see Mt 12:38; 16:1; Mk 8:11; Lk 11:16). On this particular occasion, Jesus answered enigmatically, "Destroy this temple, and I will raise it in three days." His critics assumed that he was speaking of Herod's temple, which had been in process of construction for forty-six years and was still incomplete. Jesus, says the author, really meant the temple of his body, which he would raise up in three days' time.

22 The author's comment indicates that from the first of his ministry Jesus had the end of it in view. One can hardly escape the conviction that the fourth gospel depicts the career of Jesus as a voluntary progress toward a predetermined goal. The allusions to the destruction of the temple of his body (2:22), to the elevation on a cross (3:14; 12:32–33), to the giving of his flesh for the life of the world (6:51), to his burial (12:7), and to the announcement of his betrayal and death to his disciples (13:19, 21), attest to his consciousness of the fate that awaited him in Jerusalem. Though the disciples did not comprehend the situation during Jesus' career, the Resurrection placed the memory of his sayings in a new perspective.

6. The interview with Nicodemus (2:23–3:21)

a. Prelude (2:23–25)

These verses introduce three typical interviews in chs. 3 and 4: Nicodemus the Pharisee, the Samaritan woman, and the royal official at Cana (probably a Gentile). In other words, these three persons represented the Jews, the Samaritans, and the Gentiles—in short, the world he came to save.

23–24 Jesus had already begun performing miraculous works. These signs attracted the attention of the crowd and brought many to a stage of belief parallel to that of the disciples (2:11). They reasoned that since Jesus possessed such power, he must have the favor of God (cf. 9:30–33). Jesus, however, was not satisfied with a superficial faith. He did not trust himself to those who had professed belief only on the basis of his miracles.

25 Jesus had a thorough understanding of human nature. He could read people more accurately than a doctor can read physical symptoms in diagnosing an illness.

b. Nicodemus's visit (3:1–15)

1–2 Nicodemus is introduced as a man of the upper class, conservative in his beliefs, and definitely interested in Jesus' teaching. As a Pharisee he belonged to the strict religious sect of Judaism in contrast to the Sadducees, who were less rigid in their beliefs and were more politically minded. As a member of the "ruling council" or Sanhedrin, he was sensitive to the prevailing doctrinal trends of the time. His interest in Jesus had been prompted by the miracles he had witnessed, and he came for an interview to obtain more information. His approach shows that he was cautious, open-minded, and ready to receive a new revelation from God if he was sure of its genuineness.

The fact that he came by night does not necessarily mean that he was timid, though in the light of the later references to him in this gospel, he does not seem to have been aggressive in his discipleship (7:45–52; 19:38–42). His salutation was courteous, and he showed no sign of hostility.

3 Jesus' reply to Nicodemus's opening statement was cryptic and abrupt. He informed Nicodemus that no one could even see the kingdom of God without a spiritual rebirth. Birth is our mode of entrance into the world. To be "born again [GK 540]" (or "born from above," the preferable translation; see NIV note) means the transformation of a person so that he or she is able to enter another world and adapt to its conditions. To belong to the heavenly kingdom, one must be born into it.

4 Nicodemus's reply may be interpreted in two ways. At first sight he appears to be quite materialistic in his attitude, thinking that Jesus was advocating what was impossible—a second physical birth. On the other hand, perhaps he meant, "How can a man whose habits and ways of thinking have been fixed by age expect to change radically?" Physical rebirth is impossible, but is spiritual change any more feasible?

5 In response, Jesus repeated his solemn assertion and expanded on it with reference to water and Spirit. What did Jesus mean by "water" and "Spirit"? Since he wanted to clarify his teaching for Nicodemus, he would naturally use familiar terms. Furthermore, since his ministry came shortly after that of John the Baptist, Jesus was probably referring to John's preaching, which dealt with the baptism of *water* (signifying repentance) and with the coming messenger of God who would endow humans with the Holy *Spirit* (1:31–33). The new birth is conditioned on the repentance and confession of the individual in response to the appeal of God and by the transformation of life by the gift of the Holy Spirit.

6–8 Jesus asserted that the entrance into the kingdom of God that Nicodemus desired could not be achieved by legalism or outward conformity. It requires an inner change and is given only by the direct act of God. Just as the origin and the destination of the wind are unknown to the one who feels it, similarly the new life of one born of the Spirit is unexplainable by ordinary reasoning; and its outcome is unpredictable, though its actuality is undeniable.

9 Nicodemus's question "How can this be?" should not be interpreted as an exclamation expressing incredulity. Rather, it is a plea for direction. He wanted to know how this experience could become his. Nothing in the Judaism he knew offered anything like this. The answer of Jesus accords with the words of Ezekiel in Eze 36:25–28.

Proselytes to Judaism were washed completely, issued new clothing, and then received into the commonwealth of the people of God; but Israelites were regarded as sons of Abraham and children of God by covenant from birth. In effect, Jesus was telling Nicodemus that his descent from Abraham was not adequate ground for salvation. He would have to repent and begin a new life in the Spirit if he expected to enter the kingdom of God (cf. 8:37–44).

Jesus illustrated his point by a play on words applicable both in Hebrew and Greek. The word translated "spirit" also means "wind" (GK 4460). Verse 8 could be rendered "The Spirit breathes where he wills." NIV and other translations are undoubtedly correct in using "wind," for the allusion to sound in the second sentence would not make much sense in sequence with "spirit." Possibly Nicodemus called on Jesus at the time when the evening wind was blowing through the city, so that it was a ready illustration.

10 The Greek text uses the definite article with "teacher": "Are you *the* teacher of Israel?" (lit. tr.). Nicodemus's exact position in the theological circles of Israel is not defined, but the language suggests that he was an important person. Jesus implies that he should have been familiar with the teaching of the new birth. Evidently Jesus felt that since the OT contained this teaching in principle, those who read the Scriptures were responsible for knowing and believing the truth.

11 No doubt Nicodemus thought Jesus to be presumptuous when he said, "We speak of what we know." Jesus spoke with an air of authority (see comment on Mk 1:22). Jesus' use of "we" is unusual. Perhaps his disciples were present and he was including them. Or Jesus may have been speaking as the earthly representative of the godhead. Throughout the years God's "people" had rejected his instruction as ministered through the prophets and the Scriptures. And things were no different now.

12–13 The "earthly things" (GK 2103) Jesus alluded to were probably the phenomena he used for illustrations, such as the wind. If Nicodemus was unable to grasp the meaning of spiritual truth as conveyed by concrete analogy, how would he do so if it were couched in an abstract statement? No one had ever entered into heaven to experience its realities directly except Jesus himself, the Son of Man, who had come from heaven. Revelation, not discovery, is the basis for faith.

14–15 The reference to a story in the Pentateuch (Nu 21:4–9) would have been familiar to Nicodemus, for the Jewish scholars spent the larger part of each day in the study of Scripture and often memorized not only the Pentateuch but the entire OT. Although Jesus did not elaborate the details of this allusion, it has several aspects applicable to the present situation. (1) The ancient Israelites were guilty of disobedience and a grumbling and unthankful spirit. (2) They were under the condemnation of God and were being punished for their sin. (3) The object elevated before them was the emblem of their judgment. (4) They were unable to rescue themselves. (5) The poison of the serpents was deadly, and there was no antidote for it. (6) They were urged to *look* at the serpent in order to receive life.

Jesus insisted that he would be "lifted up" (GK 5738), a word used elsewhere for crucifixion (8:28; 12:32–33). He was summoning people to receive him as God's provision for the cure of sin and to place complete confidence in him for the future. Such confidence or belief would ensure partaking in the life of the age to come.

c. The author's comment (3:16–21)

16 Commentators are divided as to whether vv.16–21 are a direct continuation of the conversation between Jesus and Nicodemus or represent only the author's comment on Jesus' words. In either case, they express the most important message of the Gospel, emphasized elsewhere in many ways, that salvation is a gift received only by believing God for it. The nature of belief is implied in the illustration of Moses lifting up the serpent in the wilderness (v.14). It consists of accepting something, not doing something. The result of belief is that one is freed from condemnation, receives eternal life, and lives in a relation of total honesty with God.

"Eternal" (GK 173) refers not only to the duration of existence but also to the quality of life as contrasted with futility. Eternal life is a deepening and growing experience. It can never be exhausted in any measurable span of time, but it introduces a totally new quality of life. The verb "perish" (GK 660) depicts the opposite of salvation. It means to fail completely of fulfilling God's purpose and consequently to be excluded forever from his fellowship. Its use here clearly implies that those without God are hopelessly confused in purpose, alienated from him in their affections, and futile in their efforts.

The presentation of the good news of God's love offers only two options: to believe or to perish. Eternal life, which is accepted by believing, is a gift of God and brings with it the fullest blessings God can bestow. To perish does not mean to cease to exist; it means to experience utter failure, futility, and loss of all that makes existence worthwhile.

17–18 Notwithstanding this gloomy picture of "lost" or "perish," God's purpose toward humankind is positive; it is an attitude of love. He is not seeking an excuse to condemn human beings but is rather endeavoring to save them. His purpose in sending Jesus into the world was to show his love and to draw people to himself. If they are lost, it is because they have not committed themselves to God, the only source of life. Beginning at this point in this gospel, the contrast between belief and unbelief is increasingly exemplified. John has here defined the crux of belief and unbelief and has indicated the effects of each. The progress of both in the characters of those associated with Jesus becomes increasingly evident as the drama of this gospel unfolds.

19–21 The difference between believers and unbelievers does not lie in the guilt or innocence of either; it lies in the different attitudes they take toward the "light." Unbelievers shrink from the light because it exposes their sin; believers willingly come to the light so that their real motives may be revealed (see also 1Jn 1:8–9). Furthermore, darkness (defined as love of evil deeds) keeps people from responding to the light (1Jn 1:5). All of us are held accountable for our actions, and the choice is ours: evil deeds or truth.

7. Further testimony of John the Baptist (3:22–36)

22–24 This period of Jesus' ministry in Judea is not paralleled by any account in the Synoptic Gospels (cf. Mt 4:12–21; Mk 1:14). It occurred before the arrest and imprisonment of John the Baptist, for he and Jesus were preaching and baptizing simultaneously. Both were exercising a rural rather than urban ministry at this time. Jesus and his disciples remained in the Judean country; John was preaching farther north.

23 The exact location of Aenon is uncertain, though it is probably a site south of Bethshan, where there were numerous springs. In this region John would have been in the territory of the Greek city of Scythopolis, outside the domain of Herod Antipas.

25–26 The argument between a Jewish inquirer and the disciples of John indicates that there must have been confusion over the respective merits of Jesus and John. If both were baptizing, whose baptism was valid? By popular acclaim Jesus' influence was growing and John's was waning. John's interrogators felt that their friend and teacher had been eclipsed by Jesus' sudden popularity, and they wanted an explanation.

27–30 John showed no jealousy whatever; on the contrary, he reaffirmed his subordinate position (cf. 1:29–31). He would not claim for himself final authority but avowed that he had been sent in preparation for the Messiah. As the bridegroom is more important than the best man or "friend" of the bridegroom, so he would be content to act as an assistant to Jesus.

Just how far the simile of bride and bridegroom should be pressed here is questionable. Should the bride represent Israel, to whom the Messiah came, or the church? The imagery is applied to both (cf. Hos 2:19–20; Eph 5:32), but the focus of this passage is on the bridegroom, not the bride. The emphasis is on the relation of Jesus and John rather than on the relation of Jesus to Israel or to the church.

31–36 This paragraph, like vv.16–21, is likely the author's reflection on what he has just written. Its phraseology accords better with the style of vv.16–21 than with that of John the Baptist. John declares in no uncertain terms (1) that Jesus came from heaven and spoke with a higher authority than that of earth; (2) that he spoke from observation, not from theory; (3) that he spoke the words of God; (4) that the Father's love had caused him to endow the Son with complete authority to execute his purpose. These qualities made Jesus superior in every way to John the Baptist, though the latter had an important and divinely authorized message. John spoke as one "from the earth." The Son, however, was not merely the messenger of God; he was the revealed object of faith. Once again the dividing line is affirmed. The believer in the Son has eternal life; the unbeliever will never possess that life, for he is already under condemnation. The wrath of God remains on him.

This is the only passage in this gospel and John's letters in which "wrath" (GK 3973) is mentioned. This word does not mean a sudden gust of passion or a burst of temper. Rather, it is the settled displeasure of God against sin. God is neither easily angered nor vindictive. But by his very nature he is unalterably committed to opposing and judging all disobedience. The moral laws of the universe are as unvarying and unchangeable as its physical laws, and God cannot set aside either without violating his own nature.

8. The Samaritan ministry (4:1–42)

a. The woman at the well (4:1–26)

1–3 Jesus' early ministry in the region of Judea was gaining attention, especially by the Pharisees, who constituted the ruling religious class. The growth of any messianic movement could easily be interpreted as having political overtones, and Jesus did not want to become involved in any outward conflict with the state, whether Jewish or Roman. In order to avoid a direct clash, he left Judea and journeyed northward to Galilee.

4–5 The shortest route from Jerusalem to Galilee lay on the high road straight through Samaritan territory. Many Jews would not travel by that road, for they regarded any contact with Samaritans as defiling (on the Samaritans, see comment on Lk 9:53 54). By the time of Jesus a strong rivalry and hatred between Jews and Samaritans prevailed. The words "had to" translate an expression of necessity. As the Savior of all humanity, Jesus felt he had to confront the smoldering suspicion and enmity between Jews and Samaritans by ministering to his enemies.

Sychar was a small village near Shechem, about half a mile from Jacob's well, which is located in the modern Shechem or Nablus.

6 The well of Jacob lies at the foot of Mount Gerizim, the center of Samaritan worship. The "sixth hour" would probably have been about noon, reckoning from daybreak. It was an unusual time for a woman to come to a village well for water. Perhaps the Samaritan woman had a sudden need, or perhaps she did not care to meet the other women of the community, who may have shunned her because of her general character.

7–8 Undoubtedly the woman was surprised to find a man sitting by the well. Jesus' initial approach was a simple request for water, which would presuppose a favorable response. One would hardly refuse a drink of cold water to a thirsty traveler in the heat of the day. The request did have a surprising element, however, for no Jewish rabbi would have volunteered to carry on a public conversation with a woman, nor would he have deigned to drink from a Samaritan's cup, as she implied by her answer.

9–10 There was a trace of sarcasm in the woman's reply, as if she meant, "We Samaritans are the dirt under your feet until you want something; then we are good enough!" Jesus paid no attention to her flippancy or to her bitterness. He was more interested in winning the woman than in winning an argument. He appealed to her curiosity by the phrase "If you knew," implying that because of the nature of his person he could bestow on her a gift of God that would be greater than any ordinary water. His allusion was intended to lift her level of thinking from that of material need to spiritual realities.

11 The woman heard his words but missed his meaning. "Living water" meant to her fresh spring water such as the well supplied. She could not understand how he could provide this water without having any means of drawing it from the well (the well was over seventy-five feet deep).

12 The woman's reference to "our father Jacob" was perhaps designed to bolster the importance of the Samaritans in the eyes of a Jewish rabbi. She was well aware of the low esteem the Jews had of her people.

13–15 Jesus' second reply emphasized the contrast between the water in the well and what he intended to give. The material water would allay thirst only temporarily; the spiritual water would quench the inner thirst forever. The water in the well had to be drawn up with hard labor; the spiritual water would bubble up from within. Because of her non-spiritual perspective, the woman's interests were selfish.

16–17 Jesus' request to call her husband was both proper and strategic—proper because it was not regarded as good etiquette for a woman to talk with a man unless her husband were present; strategic because it placed her in a dilemma from which she could not free herself without admitting her need. She had no husband, and she would not want to confess her sexual irregularities to a stranger. The abruptness of her reply shows that she was at last emotionally touched.

18 Jesus shocked the woman when he lifted the curtain on her past life. The conversation had passed from the small-talk stage to the personal. Her evil deeds were being exposed by the light, but was she willing to acknowledge the truth?

19–20 Realizing his superhuman knowledge, the woman called him a prophet; but then she tried to divert him. Since his probing was becoming uncomfortably personal, she began to argue a religious issue. She raised the old controversy between Jews and Samaritans, whether worship should be offered on Mount Gerizim, at the foot of which they stood, or at Jerusalem, where Solomon's temple had been built.

The Samaritans founded their claim on the historic fact that when Moses instructed the people concerning the entrance into the Promised Land, he commanded that they set up an altar on Mount Ebal and that the tribes should be divided, half on Ebal and half on Gerizim. As the Levites read the Law, the people responded antiphonally (Dt 27:1–28:68). The Jews held that since Solomon had been commissioned to build the temple in Jerusalem, the center of worship should be located there. The controversy was endless, and Jesus did not intend to allow himself to be drawn into a futile discussion.

21–23 Jesus avoided the argument by elevating the issue above mere location. He made no concessions and intimated that the Samaritans' worship was confused: "You Samaritans worship what you do not know." Probably he was alluding to the error of the woman's ancestors, who had accepted a syncretism of foreign deities with the ancestral God of the Jewish faith. To Jesus, true worship is that of the spirit, which means that the worshiper must deal honestly and openly with God. She, on the contrary, had been furtive and unwilling to open her heart to God.

24 "God is spirit" carries one of the four noun descriptions of God found in the NT (the other three are "God is light" [1Jn 1:5]; "God is love" [1Jn 4:8, 16]; and "God is a consuming fire" [Heb 12:29]). Jesus was endeavoring to convey to the woman that God cannot be confined to one place nor conceived of as a material being. Only "the Word become flesh" (cf. 1:14) could represent him adequately.

25 Mystified by Jesus' words, the woman finally confessed her ignorance and at the same time expressed her longing for the Messiah. It was the one nebulous hope that she had of finding God, for she expected that the coming Messiah would explain the mysteries of life. There was a Samaritan tradition that the prophet predicted by Moses in Dt 18:15 would come to teach God's people all things. On this sincere though vague hope Jesus founded his appeal to her spiritual consciousness.

26 This is the one occasion when Jesus voluntarily declared his messiahship. In the Synoptic Gospels, normally he did not make such a public claim; on the contrary, he urged his disciples to silence (Mt 16:20; Mk 8:29–30; Lk 9:20–21). In Galilee, where there were many would-be messiahs and a constant unrest based on the messianic hope, such a claim would have been dangerous. In Samaria the concept would probably have been regarded more as religious than political and would have elicited a ready hearing for his teaching rather than a subversive revolt.

b. The return of the disciples (4:27–38)

27 The disciples had left Jesus at the well. He was tired, and there would have been no need for him to have accompanied them into the town to buy food. They were surprised to find him talking with a woman—an apparent violation of custom—but they respected him too highly to question his behavior.

28–29 As the disciples approached, the woman made her way back to Sychar to report the interview to her fellow villagers. She was so excited that she forgot her water pot. At the village she was bold enough to suggest

People can still pay a visit to Jacob's well today. Courtesy Bastiaan Van Elderen.

that perhaps the new person she had met might be the Messiah. "You don't suppose this could be the Messiah, do you?" would be a fair translation of her words.

30 The elders of Sychar would probably not accept theological information from a woman of her reputation, and she did not venture to make a dogmatic pronouncement. Nevertheless, her manner was so sincere and her invitation so urgent that they immediately proceeded to the well to investigate.

31–34 The disciples were mainly interested in Jesus' physical welfare. He must have been exhausted by the travel of the morning. They were amazed that he was not hungry and wondered whether somebody else had given him food. He tried to tell them that the satisfaction of completing the work the Father had entrusted to him was greater than any food he might have been given (cf. Dt 8:3; Mt 4:4).

35 "Four months more and then the harvest" is probably a quotation of a current proverb. Having once sowed the grain, all the farmer needed to do was wait for it to ripen. Jesus was pointing out that the spiritual harvest is always ready and must be reaped before it spoils. As he was speaking, the Samaritans were leaving the town and coming across the fields toward him (v.30), like grain ready for harvesting.

36–38 The disciples would not have to wait indefinitely for the result of their mission; the sowing and reaping could go on together. Jesus implied that they had already received a commission to reap for him and that they could benefit from the preparation he and the prophets had made. The reaping of people for the granary of God is not the task of any one group, nor is it confined to one era. Each reaps the benefit of its forerunners, and succeeding generations in turn gain from the accomplishments of their predecessors (see 1Co 3:6). Perhaps v.38 is an allusion to the preaching of John the Baptist, whose message of repentance had prepared the way for the disciples' preaching about Jesus.

c. The faith of the Samaritans (4:39–42)

39–42 These few verses indicate two necessary and interrelated bases for belief: (1) the testimony of others and (2) personal contact with Jesus. This woman's witness opened the way to him for the villagers. If he could penetrate the shell of her materialism and present a message that would transform her, the Samaritans also could believe that he might be the Messiah. That stage of belief was only introductory, however. The second stage was hearing him for themselves, and it brought them to the settled conviction expressed in "we know" (v.42). They had progressed from a faith built on the witness of another to a faith built on their own experience.

9. The interview with the nobleman (4:43–54)

43–44 The progress to Galilee is closely connected with the episode at Samaria. For the parenthesis of v.44, see Mt 13:57; Mk 6:4. Did Jesus intend to apply the principle stated in this verse to Judea or to Galilee? In the light of his comment to the nobleman in v.48, it seems likely that John was simply stating that Jesus had already been rebuffed in Galilee (cf. Lk 4:24–29) and that he was questioning the motives of the nobleman in the light of past experience. At this time the Galileans were somewhat more receptive because of the miracles they had witnessed at the Passover in Jerusalem. John says little in this gospel about Jesus' Galilean activities, though he shows knowledge of them (2:1–11; 4:43–54; 6:1–7:13).

45 The Galileans hoped Jesus would duplicate the signs they had witnessed in Jerusalem while they were attending the Passover. They were disappointed to discover that he had no intention of exhibiting his powers simply to satisfy their curiosity.

46 Jesus revisits Cana, where he had performed his first miracle (2:1–11). The royal official may have been a member of Herod's court and possibly a Gentile (see comment on 2:23–25). His son had been ill for some time and was not recovering from his sickness. Therefore, the father felt compelled to seek further aid.

47 The report that Jesus had healed people in Jerusalem must have reached this man's ears. Learning that Jesus had returned to Galilee, the official immediately sought Jesus out and strongly pleaded with him to heal his son, who was dangerously ill.

48 Jesus' reply seems like a heartless rejection. He seemed to insinuate that the official, like the rest of the Galileans, was merely attempting to elicit a miracle from him. On the other hand, Jesus' words may express a genuine hope. He desired a belief characterized by dedication rather than amazement, and as the second half of the episode shows, his aim was to inculcate a commitment rather than merely to perform a cure (cf. 20:30–31).

49 The genuine distress of the father is demonstrated by his words: "Sir, come down at once before my little boy dies!" (lit. tr.). The words used indicate that the case was desperate.

50 Jesus' response still seems somewhat impersonal and casual. By dismissing the official with the statement that his son was alive, Jesus created a dilemma of faith. If the father refused to return to Capernaum without taking Jesus with him, he would show that he did not believe Jesus' word and would consequently receive no benefit because of his distrust. On the other hand, if he followed Jesus' order, he would be returning to the dying boy without any outward assurance that the lad would recover. He was forced to make the difficult choice between insisting on evidence and thus showing disbelief or exercising faith without any tangible proof to encourage him. The official chose the second horn of the dilemma; he "took Jesus at his word" and set out on his return journey.

51–52 People are amazed by coincidences, but generally they do not attribute them to the direct activity of God. As the official went home, a miraculous report greeted him "while he was still on the way." There is an interesting progression in the description of the boy's condition. First the news came that "his boy was living." But more than that, the man was curious to know "the time when his son got better." Finally, he was told, "The fever left him yesterday at the seventh hour."

53–54 When the father considered the details of his meeting with Jesus and the good news concerning his son's recovery, he was convinced that more than coincidence was at work. The timing was miraculous, and the boy's recovery was more than circumstantial. "So he and all his household believed."

The notation in v.54 should probably be read in the light of John's footnote in v.44. The convincing character of the two signs recorded here and the forceful demonstration of God's response to faith afforded by the second provided cogent illustrations for the main theme of belief.

B. The Rise of Controversy (5:1–47)

1. The healing of the paralytic (5:1–15)

1 The words "some time later" mark a break in chronological sequence. Comparison with the Synoptic accounts shows that a measurable amount of time may have elapsed between the healing of the son of the royal official at Capernaum and the episode of the paralytic at the Pool of Bethesda. The reference to the feast does not define the time since the feast is unnamed.

2–4 Excavations have located this pool in the northwest corner of old Jerusalem. It was surrounded by a colonnade on all four sides and down the middle of the pool. People gathered at the water's edge, hoping to be cured of their ailments, when the water was agitated. The explanation of the moving of the water (v. 4; see NIV note) was probably added to the text of John later.

5–6 Jesus selected for his attention the person who seemed most needy. Confinement to a bed for thirty-eight years would leave the sufferer so weak that he would be unable to walk or even stand for any length of time. Jesus' question must have seemed rather naive to this invalid. Who would not want to be healed from utter helplessness? Yet the question also implies an appeal to the will, which the long years of discouragement may have paralyzed. Jesus thus was challenging the man's will to be cured.

7 The invalid's reply shows that he had lost his independent determination. He was waiting for somebody to assist him. Such efforts as he had been able to make had proved futile, and he was despairing of success.

8 The healing was not a response to a request, nor did it presuppose an expression of faith on the part of the man. Jesus asked him to do the impossible—to stand on his feet, pick up his bedroll, and go his way. Renewed by the miraculous influx of new power, the man responded at once and did so. Jesus supplied even the will to be cured!

9–10 The outcome of the miracle was twofold: the paralytic was healed and a controversy broke out. Since the healing took place on the Sabbath, it brought Jesus directly into conflict with the religious authorities, whose traditions regarding the Sabbath were more rigid than the Law itself. Jesus' healing on the Sabbath was one factor that brought him into disfavor with the religious leaders in Jerusalem (see also Mt 12:1–14; Mk 2:23–3:6; Lk 6:1–6; 13:10–16; 14:1–6; Jn 9:1–14).

11–12 The paralytic seems to have felt no particular gratitude to Jesus for his healing. He took no responsibility for the action on the Sabbath; and after Jesus had dealt with him the second time, he immediately informed the Jewish leaders who it was that had transgressed the Sabbath law. It seems unlikely that he would have been ignorant of the reason for their inquiry.

13 John indicates that on at least four occasions Jesus quietly withdrew from a scene of controversy. Each of these occurred after an argument with the Jews over his claims (see also 8:59; 10:39; 12:36). All these reinforce the concept of the fourth gospel that Jesus was immune to danger until the hour of his passion arrived (7:30; 8:20).

14–15 Jesus' interest in the man is implied in the word "found." Apparently Jesus searched for him out of a concern for his spiritual state as well as for his physical illness. The command to "stop sinning" presupposes the possibility that the man's affliction was caused by his own sin (but cf. comment on 9:2–3). There is no indication that this encounter strengthened the man's faith and attachment to Jesus; in fact, the contrary could easily be inferred. But he did confess Jesus as his healer.

2. Jesus' defense of his sonship (5:16–47)
a. The prerogatives of sonship (5:16–30)

16 This verse introduces the element of controversy between Jesus and his opponents. The immediate cause was his healing on the Sabbath, which they interpreted as a violation of the fourth commandment (Ex 20:8–11; see comment on Jn 5:9–10). Jesus contended that allaying human need was no violation of God's Law (cf. Lk 14:5).

17 Jesus' argument for healing on the Sabbath was that God does not suspend his activities on the Sabbath. The laws of nature take no holiday. But more important to the Jews, Jesus identified his activities with those of the Father; he claimed to be continuing the creative work of God.

18 The Jews were angry because of Jesus' violation of the Sabbath, but they were furious when he was so presumptuous as to claim equality with the Father. This claim of Jesus widened the breach between his critics and himself, for they understood that by it he was asserting his deity. His explanation shows

In this model of old Jerusalem, the Pool of Bethseda is in the middle of the picture, toward the right.

that he did not claim identity with the Father as one person, but he asserted his unity with the Father in a relationship that could be described as sonship. This sonship has many facets, as shown in vv.19–24.

19 The Son is dependent on the Father; he does not act apart from the Father's will and purpose. Throughout this gospel Jesus continually asserts that his work was to do the will of the Father (4:34; 5:30; 8:28; 12:50; 15:10). John presents Jesus as the Son, not as the slave, of God, yet as the perfect agent of the divine purpose and the complete revelation of the divine nature.

20 The Son is loved by the Father. Their relationship is that of a Father and a Son who are united by love. The Father has revealed to the Son the purpose and plan of his activity, much as the head of a family discusses with the others the plan he wishes to follow.

21 The Son is empowered by the Father. God is the source of life, who alone has power to reverse the processes of the material world and to bring life out of death. This supreme power he has conferred on the Son. Later Jesus demonstrates this power in the raising of Lazarus (11:41–44).

22–23 The Son has been entrusted with the power of judgment. He possesses equal dignity with the Father and shares with him judicial as well as executive authority. Conversely, since the Son is equal in authority, he can rightly claim equal honor with God.

24 The Son is the arbiter of destiny. The determination of this destiny is immediate, as the present tense in this verse implies. Eternal life becomes the possession of the believer at the moment of acceptance; the future judgment will only confirm what has already taken place.

25 The phrase "and has now come" may refer to the present era that will terminate in the return of Christ and the resurrection of the dead, or it may refer to the power Jesus had to raise the dead during his lifetime, as in the case of Lazarus. There is another sense in which our Lord's words are true. As the source of life, he was promising to those who were spiritually dead, like the woman at the well, a new and eternal life if they would listen to his voice.

26 We do not have inherent life within ourselves, for our life is derived from others. Again Jesus claimed deity by saying he was not dependent on another for life, just as the Father derived his life from no one. Jesus possesses inherent life, the power to create and the power to renew life that has been extinguished.

27 The title "Son of Man" has appeared twice previously in this gospel (1:51; 3:14). As the Son of Man Jesus is qualified to judge humanity because he belongs to it and can understand the needs and viewpoints of humans (cf. Heb 2:17).

28–29 This passage contains one of the few references to eschatology in John's gospel. No chronological distinction is drawn here between the resurrection of the righteous and that of the wicked, nor is any such distinction excluded. John says little about a program, but he does emphasize the fact that Jesus will be the door to the eternal world.

The double resurrection assumes that both the righteous and the wicked will receive bodies in the future life and that presumably each body will express the character of the person who is resurrected. Some commentators claim that the resurrection of v.25 is wholly spiritual while that of vv.29–30 is physical and future. There seems to be an unnecessary distinction here (see comment on v. 25), though these two verses are explicitly future. Obviously spiritual resurrection from being dead in transgressions and sins (Eph 2:1) must precede physical resurrection.

30 This verse marks a transition from self-affirmation to testimony. Jesus spoke with the confidence of being commissioned by the Father, not with the arrogance of self-assertion. Twenty-five times in this gospel he asserts that he has been sent by the Father, a reference to his commission for the ministry, which distinguishes him as the Son of God.

b. The witnesses to his authority (5:31–47)

31 Because the authority of Jesus was questioned by his critics, he summoned witnesses to vouch for him. "Witness" or "testimony," whether verb (GK *3455*) or noun (GK *3456*), is a common word in this gospel, occurring thirty-three times. This term is used to describe the attestation of Jesus' character and power. Jesus gives five specific sources of testimony about himself.

Jesus discounts his own witness here, admitting that it is "not valid" (because under Jewish law the self-testimony of any person was not accepted in court). On another occasion, however, he said, "Even if I testify on my own behalf, my testimony is valid, for I know where I came from and where I am going" (8:14). The apparent contradiction can be resolved because the statement in ch. 5 is based on legal grounds whereas that in ch. 8 is based on personal knowledge. In consideration of Jesus' essential truthfulness, his witness concerning himself is sound, though in legal process it would not be admitted.

32 "There is another who testifies in my favor" could refer either to the Father or to John the Baptist, both of whom are mentioned in the context. The latter is the more likely here, since the witness of John the Baptist follows immediately in v.33 and seems to be the elaboration of the statement in v.32.

33–35 "You have sent to John" is obviously a reference to the delegation sent from the Jewish rulers to John the Baptist when he was preaching in the Judean wilderness (1:19). The fact that they had already asked him for an explanation bound them to give proper consideration to his testimony. John himself had refused the title of Messiah but had predicted the coming of Jesus and had identified him at his appearance as the Lamb of God and the Messiah (1:29–36). Possibly by this time John had been imprisoned. Jesus' main point is that the Jews could not consistently accept John's preaching and reject Jesus.

36 Another witness is that of the works Jesus was doing, i.e., those deeds that revealed his divine nature. As the quality of one's deeds shows one's moral standards, skill, and personal competence, so Jesus' works marked him as superhuman in both his compassion and his power (cf. 3:19–21; 10:25; 14:11). Although Jesus never performed miracles for the purpose of drawing attention to himself, he regarded them as valid proofs of his claims.

The gospel lists seven of these works: (1) The turning of water into wine (2:1–11); (2) the healing of the official's son (4:43–54); (3) the healing of a paralytic (5:1–15); (4) the feeding of the multitude (6:1–14); (5) the walking on the water (6:16–21); (6) the cure of the blind man (9:1–41); and (7) the raising of Lazarus (11:1–44). Each of these miracles demonstrated Jesus' power in a different area of human experience. They are called "signs" (GK 4956) because they point to something beyond themselves. In most cases, these signs were followed by a confession of belief on the part of many of the spectators (2:11; 4:53; 6:66, 69; 9:38; 11:45).

37–38 The fourth witness is that of the Father. The allusion seems somewhat obscure, especially since Jesus disclaimed any visible or audible communication from God to the crowd in general. Nevertheless there were occasions on which a voice from heaven spoke, expressing approval of Jesus and affirming his Sonship (see Mt 3:17; 17:5; Mk 1:11; 9:7; Lk 3:22; 9:35; Jn 12:28). To a Jew, the voice from heaven would have meant the approval of God; yet this seems to have had little effect on the multitude. Jesus implies that his hearers had not apprehended the revelation of God because they had not believed him whom the Father had sent.

39–40 Jesus' final witness is the Scriptures. After the destruction of the temple of Solomon in 586 B.C., the Jewish scholars of the Exile substituted the study of the Law for the observance of the temple ritual and sacrifices. They pored over the OT, trying to extract the fullest possible meaning from its words, because they believed that the very study itself would bring them life. By so doing they missed the chief subject of the OT revelation. Jesus claimed the Law, the Prophets, and the Psalms (Writings) as witnesses to his person and claims (Lk 24:44). For example, they prefigured his sacrifice (Jn 3:14–15) and marked some of the events of the Passion (12:14–15; 18:9; 19:24, 28, 36). He rebuked his hearers for their inconsistency in studying the Scriptures so diligently while rejecting his claims.

41–42 The people were incapable of both interpreting and applying the Scriptures, for as students of the Scriptures they should have known that they spoke of him. Because the Jews did not give "praise" (or "glory"; GK 1518) to Jesus, it was evident that they were spiritually unable to make the connection between the Scriptures and the Savior. But this came as no surprise to Jesus.

43–44 Jesus expressed disappointment because the people would not accept his credentials, though they would accept the personal claims of others who acted solely on their own authority. Compare, for example, the choice of Barabbas over Jesus at the final trial (Lk 23:18–23). Verse 44 rebukes those students of the Scriptures who are more interested in establishing their competitive reputations for scholarship than in obeying the revelation of God so as to bring his approval.

45–47 Moses, who wrote the Law, was highly revered by the Jewish nation. They would not knowingly do anything contrary to his teaching. Their obedience to him was a source of pride. In fact, their very hope in securing God's favor and blessing lay in their relationship to Moses. Jesus told the people that the law of Moses would condemn them in their rejection of him because their failure to believe in him was essentially a rejection of Moses since Moses had prefigured him (cf. Lk 16:29–31).

C. The Beginning of Conflict (6:1–8:11)

Chapter 6 of John marks the watershed of Jesus' career. Up to this point his popularity had been increasing, in spite of the opposition of the leaders and the occasional grumbling of disaffected hearers or disciples. The interview with the disciples at Caesarea Philippi and the Transfiguration, which occurred shortly afterward, called for a new commitment on the part of the disciples and was followed by a new program on the part of Jesus. He openly declared to them that he would proceed to Jerusalem, where he would be delivered up to death (Mt 16:13–17:13; Mk 8:27–32; Lk 9:18–36). John does not narrate these incidents, but his account parallels them to some degree. The feeding of the multitude is identical, there is an allusion to his impending death (Jn 6:51), from that point the number of his disciples diminished (6:66), and the controversy with the Pharisees grew increasingly bitter.

1. The feeding of the five thousand (6:1–15)

1–4 This miracle of Jesus is the only one mentioned in all the Gospels. This fact alone should alert us to its significance. It took place in the spring shortly before the Passover (v.4). Jesus was well known because of the miracles ("signs") he had performed on sick people (see comment on 5:36). On the reasons why Jesus chose at this time to retreat to the north shore of the Sea of Galilee, see comments on Mt 14:13–14; Mk 6:31–32.

5–6 John's interest concentrates mainly on the relation of this occasion to the disciples. The crowd had come unbidden, prompted by curiosity and eagerness to share in Jesus' teaching and healing power. As the day declined, Jesus recognized that they were hungry. Desirous of involving the disciples in the responsibility for ministry, Jesus turned to Philip, asking, "Where shall we buy bread for these people to eat?" Jesus was not at a loss for a solution to the problem; he wished to educate the disciples by calling their attention to their responsibilities and by leading them to propose some plan of action.

7 Philip's reply shows that while he had a practical turn of mind, he was rather unimaginative. His calculation of "eight months' wages," however accurate, were futile, for he could only produce statistics to show what could not be done. No doubt none of the disciples would have enough money to purchase food for this crowd of approximately ten thousand persons, including women and children (Mt 14:21).

8–9 In contrast to Philip's pessimism, Andrew was more hopeful. He made the positive presentation of a boy's lunch: five small, flat barley cakes, made of the cheapest grain available, and the two small fish. But Andrew doubted the value of his own suggestion.

10 The action of Jesus reveals both his natural wisdom and supernatural power. His order to have the people sit down was necessary to stabilize the crowd so that there would not be a rush for the food. It also served to organize them in groups to facilitate serving.

11 The multiplication of the food was obviously not done with great fanfare. As the disciples distributed it, Jesus seems to have increased it by breaking it indefinitely until all were satisfied.

12–13 In spite of the miraculous power that effectively produced the ample supply, Jesus permitted no waste. Twelve large baskets full of remnants were salvaged—possibly one for each of the disciples—and carried back to Capernaum. The detail of collecting the remaining fragments of bread and fish may have been introduced to emphasize the ample sufficiency that Jesus provided, or it may indicate that he combined generosity with economy.

14 The miracle excited the wonder of the people and compelled them to recognize that Jesus was an unusual person. The allusion to "the Prophet" is probably a reflection of the promised prophet of Dt 18:15 (see comment on 7:40–41). Since Moses had provided food and water in the desert (Ex 16:11–36; 17:1–6; Nu 11:1–33; 20:2–11), the people likely expected that the Prophet like Moses would do likewise.

15 The desire of the multitude to make Jesus king marks both the height of his popularity and the moment of decision for him. They wanted someone to rule them who would feed them and guarantee their security; they had no comprehension of his spiritual mission or purpose. He, on the other hand, refused to become a political opportunist. He would not promote his kingdom by organizing a revolt against the existing political powers or by promising a dole to all who would join his banner.

2. The walking on the water (6:16–21)

16–17 "Evening" could be any time in the afternoon shortly before sunset. The disciples probably hoped to cover the short distance between Bethsaida and Capernaum while daylight lasted, but darkness had already fallen before they actually began to cross the lake. The fact that "Jesus had not yet joined them" may imply that they half-expected him to do so and waited until the last minute, hoping that he would come.

18 The Sea of Galilee is six hundred feet below sea level, in a cuplike depression among the hills. When the sun sets, the air cools; and as the cooler air from the west rushes down over the hillside, the resultant wind churns the lake. Since the disciples were rowing toward Capernaum, they were heading into the wind; consequently, they made little progress.

19–21 The disciples were still a considerable distance from the shore at Capernaum (cf. Mk 6:47). As they looked back, they were terrified to see a human form coming toward them across the water. Jesus calmed their fears by speaking to them. When they recognized his voice, they were willing to take him into the boat. As the multiplication of the loaves and fishes showed his power over matter, so the walking on the water revealed his divine power over the forces of nature. It was one more step in the education of the disciples' faith.

3. The address in the synagogue (6:22–59)

22–25 The people knew that the disciples had used the only boat that was available and that Jesus had not departed with the disciples. They were interested in seeing him again, but did not know where to find him. When boats became available (v.23), they went to Capernaum to look for Jesus (v.24). They were surprised to find Jesus with the disciples once again, so they asked, "When did you get here?" (v.25). Apparently Jesus' miracle of walking on the water was only for his disciples, for he did not tell the people how he had arrived at Capernaum.

26–27 Jesus was not flattered by the attention of the crowds, but immediately he began his instruction. The several answers he gave to their questions are mostly corrections of their opinions. The first was a reply to materialism, similar to the reply given to the woman at the well (see comments on 4:11–15). Jesus knew they were looking for him only because they ate; his reply was for them to search for "food that endures to eternal life," which he would give. That food is himself, as the later mystical utterance in v.54 states.

28–29 The second question implies both desire and a sense of self-sufficiency. The people seemed sure that if they wished to do so, they were capable of doing the works of God (i.e., works that God requires of those who seek to please him). To Jewish questioners, obtaining eternal life consisted in finding the right formula for performing works to please God. Jesus directed them to the gift of God that could be obtained only by faith in him (cf. 4:10), contradicting directly the presuppositions of his interrogators.

30–31 The third question about requesting a miraculous sign seems incredible. They seem to have forgotten that the Lord had just provided one in the feeding of the five thousand. The crowd went on to reveal their attempt to evaluate him by the ministry of Moses, who had provided manna for their ancestors in the desert.

32–33 Jesus informed the people that Moses had not given them the genuine spiritual bread. He did not mean that the manna had no food value; rather, it was not the means of sustaining spiritual life. Jesus himself claimed to be the only true source of spiritual nourishment (he may have had Dt 8:3 in mind here). As physical food is necessary for physical life, so spiritual food is necessary for spiritual life.

34–36 The request that Jesus should give the people the "bread [GK 788] of life" parallels the request of the Samaritan woman for the water of life (see comment on 4:15). Jesus had already startled the people by saying that Moses did not give them real bread from heaven. Now he shocked them a second time by announcing that *he* was the bread the Father had given. Jesus was claiming to be the only permanent satisfaction for the human desire for life. The attainment of this satisfaction hinges on belief. The definition of this term varies between the people's use of it (v.30) and Jesus' use (v.35). To them "belief" meant acceptance of his competence on the basis of miracles; to him it meant commitment, not on the basis of the miracles, but on trust in his person.

The assertion "I am the bread of life" is the first in a series of such declarations that are peculiar to this gospel (8:12; 10:7, 11; 11:25; 14:6; 15:1). Each represents a particular relationship of Jesus to the spiritual needs of humans: their light in darkness, their entrance into security and fellowship, their guide and protector in life, their hope in death, their certainty in perplexity, and their source of vitality for productiveness. He desired that people should receive him, not simply for what he might give them, but for what he might be to them. Jesus was talking about the bread that gives eternal life; but this was beyond their comprehension, just as the miracles Jesus had performed in their sight did not lead them to believe in him.

37 The Father has put everything under Jesus' control (cf. 5:19–27), including the people who are his. The paradox latent in this text has puzzled many. How can you be sure that the Father has really given you to Christ? In answer, Jesus made plain that human salvation is no surprise to God. He summons people to himself by his Word and by his Spirit. The invitation, however, is not restricted to any particular time or place, nor is it exclusively for any one nation, race, or culture. God will not refuse anyone. Nevertheless, a superficial attachment to God is not enough, for if the desire for salvation is not inspired by God, true salvation will not result.

38–40 Six times in this immediate context Jesus says that he "came down from heaven" (vv.33, 38, 41, 50, 51, 58). His claim to heavenly origin is unmistakable. Jesus also repeatedly affirmed that he had come to do his Father's will. That will is made clear here: Jesus will "lose none of all that he has given" him (v.39). Furthermore, Jesus' keeping ministry applies not only to this life, but also to the next. His constant allusion to the Father who gave him the believers, who sent him to give eternal life, and who draws believers to him indicates his close relationship with the Father—that of a Son who fulfills the Father's purpose (v.40). His prerogative of resurrection is the final proof of his authority.

41–42 "The Jews" in John usually represent those who are opposed to Jesus, especially those in leadership positions, not simply the people of Jewish origin (cf. 2:18, 20; 5:16). They might be called "the opposition party." Here they are probably local persons, for they show some acquaintance with Jesus' family. They took for granted that he was the son of Joseph and Mary, both well known to them. To them his claim of heavenly origin was incredible.

43–45 Jesus rebuked the people for their grumbling and told them that they would never come to him unless the Father initiated the action. He again spoke of the promise of resurrection for those who belonged to him (cf. v.39). Verse 45 indicates that God will do his drawing through the Scriptures and that those who are obedient to God's will as revealed in the Scriptures will come to Jesus.

46 Jesus' statement here is the foundation for the assertion in 1:18. Jesus claimed authoritative knowledge of God such as a son can claim concerning his own father.

47 As emphatically as he can, Jesus states that the one who believes in him "has everlasting life." The particular Greek construction used here indicates that the person's entire life is characterized by belief in Jesus.

48–50 Again Jesus says, "I am the bread of life" (cf. v.35). Previously, he linked this statement with the supplying of basic human needs. This time he links the statement to life itself. When the Jews ate the heavenly bread ("manna") in the desert, their physical needs were met. However, they eventually died (v.49). But Jesus said that he "is the bread that comes down from heaven, which a man may eat and not die" (v.50).

51 The key to a genuine experience with God lies in the sequence of statements in this verse. It is vested in the person of Christ, who descended from heaven to provide for humans what their nature requires. To eat of this bread means to appropriate Christ as one's life. It is a figure of speech for believing, for no one will eat what he or she cannot trust as edible. Eating a meal implies that it is wholesome, nourishing, and real. This verse also introduces the concept of Jesus' vicarious death, the sacrifice of his body for the sins of the world.

52–54 The last reaction of Jesus' opponents was prompted by the apparent impossibility of his statement. They took literally the figure of eating his flesh. Jesus responded by making himself perfectly clear. He repeated the statement with this added emphasis: "I tell you the truth." And with that, he added another aspect that was even more repulsive to the Jews: "Unless you eat the flesh of the Son of Man and *drink his blood*" (italics mine). If what Jesus said before was nonsense, this latter statement bordered on gross sin, for the law of Moses expressly forbade any drinking of blood (Lev 17:10–14).

Three times in vv.51–54 Jesus refers to the importance of eating his flesh and drinking his blood. His progression in thought is significant. First, Christ said he gives his flesh "for the life of the world" (v.51). Then he says whoever has not partaken of his flesh and blood has "no life" in him (v.53). And then whoever eats his flesh and drinks his blood does have "eternal life, and I will raise him up at the last day" (v.54). There could be no mistaking what he meant now.

55–57 Jesus now explains what he means by his flesh and blood. First of all, what he is talking about is as real to him as are the physical counterparts that his opponents had in mind. It is a real food and a real drink that produces a real life. To partake of the elements that Christ offers brings one into an abiding relationship with him. The reality of the Christ-imparted life has been attested to by the myriads of Christians throughout the age who have partaken of Christ's body and blood, in sweet communion with him. Jesus then likened the intimate relationship that believers sustain with him to the intimacy existing between the Father and himself.

58–59 Jesus climaxed his discourse by once more referring to the "bread that came down from heaven," the forefathers who ate it in the wilderness and died, and the promise of everlasting life to those who received him (see comments on vv.31–36). Jesus is far greater than Moses, for what he provides satisfies throughout all eternity. Ironically, this conversation took place at "the synagogue in Capernaum." What better place to promise eternal life than where people gather to seek that very thing through their religion!

4. The division among the disciples (6:60–71)

60 The enigmatic words of Jesus puzzled some of the disciples just as much as they did the mixed crowd. "Disciples" (GK 3412) here refers to the total group of adherents who had attached themselves to Jesus, however loosely, not solely to the Twelve. Any who could not understand him or were unwilling to trust him completely withdrew. They lacked the spiritual perception to grasp his meaning.

61 Jesus' inward knowledge of the disciples enabled him to detect their attitude (cf. 2:25). His questions revealed his surprise that they were mystified. If they could not understand the meaning of eating his flesh and drinking his blood, how would they be able to interpret his resurrection (implied) and his ascension? If they were bewildered by his language, how much more difficult would they find the final event that would lead to his return to God?

62 This reference to the Ascension is one of several in the gospel (3:13; 8:21; 14:3; 16:10; 17:11; 20:17), though the act itself is not recorded. The disciples had complained that the concept of Jesus' being the true bread that comes down from heaven was incomprehensible. He intimated here that if they witnessed his ascension, as he apparently expected, they would be even more astonished.

63 Jesus insists that the Holy Spirit is the one who imparts life to the believer; it is not transmitted by the process of physical eating. Jesus was saddened by the dullness of some of his disciples that prevented their truly believing in him.

64 Jesus' reference to those who did not believe is explained by his later allusion to Judas (v.70). Jesus had given ample opportunity for faith to all those who followed him; yet from the beginning his spiritual discernment made him aware of those whose faith was genuine and those whose attachment was only superficial.

65 Jesus strongly implied that faith is the result of God's enabling. Unbelief is natural to those who are selfish and alienated from God and who cannot accept the idea that he can do the impossible. The Holy Spirit must awaken a selfish heart and empower it to believe. This does not destroy the voluntary character of faith; it is rather in accord with the cry of the man who said to Jesus, "I do believe; help me overcome my unbelief" (Mk 9:24).

66 "Because of this [utterance]" (rather than "from this time") the attitude of the disciples had changed. Either it was too difficult to comprehend or it offended their sense of self-sufficiency.

67 Our Lord ever wishes to encourage faith that is weak, and he had a great deal of concern and love for his disciples. That is why he asked a question that expects a negative answer: "You do not want to leave too, do you?"

68 These words of Peter parallel those in the Great Confession given in Mt 16:16; Mk 8:29; Lk 9:20, spoken as the representative of the Twelve. He declared that nobody else had the life-giving message of Jesus and that there was no other source that would satisfy them. In spite of all his usual awkwardness, Simon's faith in Jesus was genuine, and he evidenced true spiritual sensitivity. His statement represents the spiritual discernment that the disciples had developed during their association with Jesus.

69 The emphatic use of the first personal plural pronoun implies a contrast between the Twelve and those who had deserted Jesus: "*We* believe" (italics mine). The Greek tense used here indicates that Peter is affirming that they have reached a final, firm conviction that Jesus is indeed "the Holy One [GK 41] of God." This term for Jesus closely resembles the expression "the Holy One of Israel" (see Isa 41:14; 43:3; 47:4; et al.).

70 Jesus indicated that his choice of the Twelve was conscious and deliberate; yet he included one whom he knew would be a traitor. Judas had no less opportunity than any of the others to know and serve Jesus; nor was he a victim of discrimination, for he was given a prominent place among them as treasurer of the group (12:6). Yet he chose to be dishonest in his financial administration and selfish in his attitude; he also chose to betray Christ.

71 This verse reads like a footnote. Although the Gospels never indulge in lengthy denunciation of Judas, almost invariably his name is followed by the phrase "who betrayed him [Jesus]" (see Mt 10:4; Mk 3:19; Lk 6:16; Jn 12:4). On "Iscariot," see comment on Mk 3:16–19.

5. The visit to Jerusalem (7:1–52)

a. The journey (7:1–13)

1 Although the writer evidently knew of Jesus' later Galilean ministry, he chose not to record it. He shows that Jesus did not return to Judea at once after the feeding of the multitude, because his life would be in danger. Ever since the healing of the paralytic in Jerusalem, his opponents had been attempting to kill him (5:18); and as time progressed, their hatred increased (7:19, 30, 32, 44; 8:59; 10:39; 11:8,53) until they finally accomplished his death. From this point the opposition to Jesus becomes increasingly prominent in this gospel.

2 The Feast of Tabernacles was celebrated in the autumn (Lev 23:33–36; Dt 16:13–14), beginning five days after the Day of Atonement (Yom Kippur) and lasting eight days. Each family constructed a temporary shelter of branches to live in for the period of the feast. This typified the years of wandering in the desert before the people entered the Promised Land. The feast itself was a joyful time of thanksgiving for the harvest they now enjoyed. It was one of the three annual feasts at which attendance was required of all Jewish men (Dt 16:16).

3–5 Because the gathering in Jerusalem brought together pilgrims from every section of Palestine, Jesus' brothers saw an excellent opportunity for him to acquire some publicity, especially since he seemed to have such miraculous powers. They advised him to join the crowds in Jerusalem so that he might enhance his reputation and gain more followers, though their suggestion may have been more sarcastic than serious, since they did not believe in him (v.5). In other words, they may have been suggesting he abandon the idealism of teaching multitudes in obscurity and of risking death.

6 Jesus' reply strongly resembles the one he gave his mother at the wedding in Cana of Galilee (2:4). He did not live by the chance of casual opportunity but by a divine calendar predetermined by the Father. For this reason the world did not understand his action, and the difference in standards created both misunderstanding and hostility.

7 Again Jesus asserted that he did not belong to this world. The world regarded him as an alien and an antagonist because he condemned its evil works (see also 15:18–21; 17:14, 16).

8–11 Jesus did not plan to go immediately to Jerusalem; he would wait until "the right time." His brothers may have intended to make a show of his arrival (cf. v.4), and Jesus wanted to avoid this. Therefore, his secret departure for Jerusalem was not an act of deception. It was an attempt to avoid unwelcome publicity. Jesus' enemies were watching for him, obviously for the purpose of arresting him (cf. v.1).

12–13 Public opinion was divided. The people who favored him were intimidated by the religious hierarchy, which was hostile toward Jesus. The atmosphere was tense, and Jesus did not wish to precipitate a crisis at this time.

b. The popular debate (7:14–36)

14 Jesus remained in seclusion until the feast was half completed and then appeared in the temple court to teach. His absence during the first half of the week had aroused the curiosity of the pilgrims who had expected that he would come in order to take advantage of the eager crowds (see comments on 6:14–15). But Jesus had passed the apex of his popular ministry, and many of his disciples had turned from him (6:66–67).

15 Even Jesus' critics admitted his acumen and learning. They could not comprehend how he could have acquired such knowledge without engaging in formal rabbinical study (cf. Mk 1:22).

16 Jesus insisted that his teaching did not originate with himself but came from God. As the perfect man and messenger of God, he gave all credit to the Father who had "sent" him (see comment on 5:30).

17–18 "If any one chooses to do God's will" means there must be a definite act of the human will in order to do God's will—a settled, determined purpose to fulfill it. Spiritual understanding is not produced solely by learning facts or procedures; rather, it depends on obedience to known truth. Obedience to God's known will develops discernment between falsehood and truth.

19 Jesus accepted the fact that Moses transmitted the Law to Israel and acknowledged the authority of that Law. He accused his opponents, who claimed to be champions of the Law, of failing to keep it. His charge that they were plotting to kill him should be interpreted in the light of Jesus' own teaching on the sixth commandment that the sin of hatred and anger is essentially murder (Mt 5:21–22; cf. Jn 7:44–45).

20 The response of the crowd to Jesus' accusation shows that the decision of the rulers had not been widely publicized. The people were bewildered by his statement. Curiously, the only allusions in John to demonic activity are accusations made against Jesus (8:48–52; 10:20; cf. Mt 9:34; Mk 3:22; Lk 11:5).

21–22 Jesus is not saying that he did only "one miracle," for he had performed several by this time; but these were of little interest to the "Jews." The reference to circumcision on the Sabbath shows that the issue of healing on the Sabbath (vv.23–24) was central to Jesus' controversy with the Jewish rulers. Thus, the "one miracle" refers to the healing of the paralyzed man at the Pool of Bethesda (5:1–18).

23–24 Circumcision was initiated by Abraham (Ge 17:9–14) and explicitly commanded in the law of Moses (Lev 12:3). Because it had to be observed on the eighth day after birth, it was allowable on the Sabbath. Jesus argued that if a rite symbolizing purification were permitted on one member of the body, why should he not be allowed to make the entire person whole and clean on the Sabbath? "Stop judging" implies that his enemies should cease making superficial pronouncements on his work and that they should evaluate it objectively.

25–27 The people were confused about the conflict between Jesus and the religious authorities. They wondered why he wasn't censored if he was such a threat to the nation. The reason the authorities did not promptly have him arrested was that they were uncertain of the sentiments of the people and that an arrest could cause an uprising that would most assuredly bring disciplinary action from the Romans (cf. Mt 26:3–5).

The people themselves were uncertain of Jesus' real identity. They knew the authorities sought to kill him, but their reluctance to act led the people to conclude that perhaps there was some validity to Jesus' messianic claim. What further confused them, however, was that they believed the Messiah would rise up out of total obscurity, that no one would "know where he is from." Such an attitude reflected an ignorance of the prophetic Scriptures (see Mic 5:2; Mt 2:5).

28–29 In the midst of all this confusion, Jesus replied positively. His first statement may be ironic—"So you know me and where I am from, do you?" The people must have been aware of his boyhood in Nazareth and no doubt considered him to be the son of Joseph and Mary (6:42). Jesus' reply was a renewed affirmation of his origin in God and his divine commission. His assertion evoked the dual response of belief and unbelief (cf. vv.41–44).

30 Jesus' enemies attempted to seize him, but they failed because the hour of crisis had not come. Not only did "the time" restrain him from sudden independent action (2:4), but it assured him of divine protection until the moment for action came (cf. Lk 22:53).

31 The response of many was belief, though it was hesitant. They did not affirm his messiahship but cautiously suggested that the Messiah would perform no more miracles than Jesus did. Consequently they tended to believe that he might be the promised leader they anticipated.

32 The favorable reaction of those who believed prompted the chief priests and Pharisees to action. To delay longer might result in more people turning to Jesus. The attempted arrest was official since the temple guards constituted the arresting party.

33–35 Jesus' reply to the action gave a hint of his coming death. The declaration that he would go where he could neither be followed nor found excited the curiosity of the crowd. They surmised that he expected to leave Palestine and to minister among the Dispersion and the Gentiles.

36 The perplexity of the crowd over Jesus' answer was echoed later by Simon Peter, who, upon hearing him speak similar words, said, "Lord, why can't I follow you now? I will lay down my life for you" (13:37). The crowd could not follow Jesus because of their ignorance of his true identity and purpose; Simon was incapable because he lacked the necessary courage.

c. The climactic appeal (7:37–44)

37 The climax of the controversy came "on the last and greatest day of the Feast" of Tabernacles. According to the law, the feast was held for seven days, followed by an eighth day of spiritual observance, including an offering to God (on this feast, see comments on Lev 23:33–44). Whether the "last day" was the seventh or the eighth day is not clear. If it refers to the eighth day, it makes the appeal of Jesus in this section all the more meaningful. He took the opportunity to make a public announcement concerning himself and his claims.

38 The celebration of the Feast of Tabernacles included a daily procession of priests from the temple to the Pool of Siloam, from which they drew water that was poured out as a libation at the altar, accompanied by a recitation of Isa 12:3: "With joy you will draw water from the wells of salvation." This offering of water memorialized God's provision for the thirsty people in the wilderness, but the water had been poured out and had left them unsatisfied. Now Jesus appeals to the individual: "Whoever believes in me." He was requiring an individual response of faith rather than a collective observance of a ritual. In the light of v.39, which connects the manifestation of the Spirit with the believer, it seems most likely that "from within him" refers to the believer, rather than to Christ.

If "as the Scripture has said" refers to a particular OT passage, it is impossible to locate it. The OT has numerous allusions to water, but none accords exactly with this utterance. Certainly Isa 12:3, quoted above, is a possibility; similar imagery with reference to "the pouring out" of the Holy Spirit occurs in Isa 32:15; 44:3; Eze 39:29; Joel 2:28–32. Jesus took the symbolism of the OT and applied it to the gift he intended to bestow on the disciples after his passion was completed (cf. Jn 14:16–17, 25–26; 15:26; 16:12–15).

39 John's statement shows that the passion of Christ was the important aspect of Jesus' revelation about the Holy Spirit, for it divided the era of law from that of the Spirit (1:17). The prophecy of Ezekiel (36:26–27) concurs with this.

This is the first use of "glorified" (GK *1519*) in John, a distinctly Johannine verb, occurring twenty-three times. Often it refers to establishing status or enhancing a reputation (8:54; 12:28; 13:32; 14:13; 15:8; 16:14; 17:1, 4, 5, 10; 21:19). In this particular context it refers to Jesus' death, which, despite all appearances, would be the entrance to glory for him (7:39; 11:4; 12:16, 23; 13:31; cf. Php 2:8–9).

40–41 "The Prophet" (GK *4737*) is presumably an allusion to the prediction of Moses that after him another prophet would appear who would command the attention of the people and who would bring them a further revelation from God (Dt 18:15). Moses explained that the prophet would not be accompanied by the frightening manifestations of Sinai, the great voice and the fire. He would rather be a fellow countryman, familiar to them, and one on their own level. Some regarded Jesus as this Prophet, hoping at the same time that he would lead them in a new Exodus and overcome their enemies; others suggested that he might be the Messiah.

42–44 The ignorance of the crowd in Jerusalem concerning Jesus is revealed by their uncertainty about his origin. On the basis of Scripture, they decided that Jesus could not be the Messiah since Mic 5:2 said the Messiah would come from Bethlehem and Jesus came from Nazareth. The confusion was such that no decision was made concerning his person and no action was taken to arrest him. Perhaps this is another illustration of Johannine irony, for Jesus *was* born in Bethlehem. The very passage that convinced his critics that he could not be the Messiah was one of the strongest to prove that he was.

d. The rejection by the leaders (7:45–52)

45 This text indicates that the chief priests and Pharisees had sent an arresting party, who failed in their mission. Since the high priest belonged to the Saducean party, the coalition of the Pharisees and Sadducees was significant. These two groups were strongly opposed to each other in doctrine (Ac 23:7), but their common animosity toward Jesus induced them to combine for action against him.

46 The report of the guards sent to arrest Jesus showed that he had a strong influence on all who listened to him. His teaching had so overawed them that they could not carry out their orders. Their statement to the Jewish leaders implied that Jesus must be more than an ordinary human being.

47–49 The Pharisees were irate when the guards returned without Jesus. Their question implied a negative answer: "No one of the Pharisees has believed in him, has he?" And their other statements reveal their religious snobbishness. They assumed that nobody could be right except themselves. If they did not believe in Jesus, he must be unreliable and his claims must be fraudulent.

50–51 Nicodemus reappears in the gospel at this point (cf. ch. 3). His tentative question, "Does our law condemn a man without first hearing him to find out what he is doing?" was not an open declaration of faith in Jesus. Rather, it was a protest raised on a legal technicality. Nicodemus may have felt that if he championed Jesus' cause unequivocally, he would lose his case; but if he raised a legitimate legal objection, he might prevent drastic action.

52 The scornful and snobbish reply "Are you from Galilee, too?" intimates that Nicodemus was taking the stand of the crude and ignorant Galileans who were gullible enough to trust in the wandering prophet, Jesus. The statement "a prophet does not come out of Galilee" seems inconsistent with the fact that some of the OT prophets, like Jonah, did originate from northern Israel.

6. The woman taken in adultery (7:53–8:11)

Although this narrative is included in the sequence of the outline, it can hardly have belonged to the original text of this gospel. It is absent from most of the oldest copies of the gospel that precede the sixth century and from the works of the earliest commentators. But this does not mean that it is unhistorical. Its coherence and spirit show that it was preserved from a very early time, and it accords well with the known character of Jesus.

7:53–8:1 Presumably an unknown group of people who had gathered in Jerusalem to listen to Jesus now dispersed, while Jesus went to the Mount of Olives, where he spent the night. This does not fit well with the preceding text because Jesus was not present at the meeting of the Sanhedrin mentioned in 7:45–52.

2–5 The present episode took place in the temple court at dawn. The entire affair had the appearance of trickery, a trap specially prepared to catch Jesus. The Sanhedrin forced their way into the center of the group and interrupted Jesus' teaching by bringing a woman before him. The guilt of the woman was indisputable; she had been "caught in the act of adultery," and Jesus did not challenge the charge. The dilemma that the scribes and Pharisees posed was this: According to the law, she should be put to death (see Lev 20:10; Dt 22:22–24). If, then, Jesus refused to confirm the death penalty, he could be charged with contradicting the law of God and would himself be liable to condemnation. If, on the other hand, he confirmed the verdict of the Pharisees, he would lose his reputation for compassion; and possibly he could have been reported to the Romans as inciting the Sanhedrin to independent exercise of the death penalty.

6–8 The Pharisees' question was emphatic: "You, there! What do you say?" Jesus made no reply but "bent down and started to write on the ground with his finger." It was, incidentally, the only occasion on record that refers to his writing; what he wrote is impossible to say. When his questioners kept pressing him for an answer, Jesus replied by putting the dilemma back on them. For this particular offense there would normally be no witnesses, since its nature would demand privacy. Either the witnesses became such by accident, which would be unusual; or they were present purposely to create the trap for Jesus, in which case they themselves were guilty; or they condoned the deed, and this would make them partners in it. Since Jewish law required the witnesses in any case of capital punishment to begin the stoning, each one of the accusers would either have to admit that he was guilty or else refrain from demanding the woman's death.

9 The accusers "began to go away one at a time, the older ones first." The older ones either had more sins for which they were answerable or else had more sense than to make an impossible profession of righteousness. Finally the woman was left alone.

10 Jesus' address to the woman was respectful (cf. 2:4; 20:13). Her accusers, more interested in destroying Jesus than in saving her, had made her the bait for a trap. Their vicious hatred of him was as bad as her immorality. His rebuke had prevented their pronouncing sentence on her; Jesus did not pronounce sentence either. But neither did he proclaim her to be innocent.

11 Jesus dismissed the woman by saying, "Go now and leave your life of sin." Meeting a man who was interested in saving rather than exploiting and in forgiving rather than condemning must have been a new experience for her. Jesus' attitude provided both the motivation and the assurance she needed. Forgiveness demands a clean break with sin. That Jesus refrained from condemning her was a guarantee that he would support her.

John's Testimony to Jesus

A. The Seven Miracles of Jesus

"Jesus did many other miraculous signs in the presence of his disciples which are not recorded in this book. But these are written that you may believe that Jesus is the Christ, the Son of God, and that by believing you may have life in his name." John 30:20–31

Turning water into wine at Cana	John 2:1–11
Healing the official's son at Capernaum	John 4:46–51
Healing the sick man at the pool of Bethesda	John 5:1–9
Feeding the five thousand in Galilee	John 6:5–13
Walking on the stormy Sea of Galilee	John 6:19–21
Healing the man born blind in Jerusalem	John 9:1–7
Raising Lazarus from the dead in Bethany	John 11:1–44

B. The Seven Great "I Am's of Jesus

"'You are not yet fifty years old,' the Jews said to him, 'and you have seen Abraham!' 'I tell you the truth,' Jesus answered, 'before Abraham was, I am!'" John 6:57–58

"I am the bread of life."	John 6:35, 48; cf. v.51
"I am the light of the world."	John 8:12; 9:5
"I am the gate for the sheep."	John 10:7, 9
"I am the good shepherd."	John 10:11, 14
"I am the resurrection and the life."	John 11:25
"I am the way and the truth and the life."	John 14:6
"I am the true vine."	John 15:1, 5

C. The Seven "Greater Than's" of Jesus

"To this John [the Baptist] replied. 'A man can receive only what is given him from heaven. . . . He [Jesus] must become greater; I must become less." John 3:27, 30

Jesus is greater than the angels.	John 1:51
Jesus is greater than Abraham.	John 8:56–58
Jesus is greater than Jacob.	John 4:11–14
Jesus is greater than Moses.	John 6:49–51
Jesus is greater than the law.	John 1:17; cf. 8:1–11
Jesus is greater than the Sabbath.	John 7:21–23; cf. 5:8–15; 9:14–33
Jesus is greater than the temple.	John 2:18–21

D. The Intensification of Controversy (8:12–59)

1. Teaching in the temple area (8:12–30)

12 Precisely at what time during Jesus' visit to Jerusalem this segment took place, John does not say. It may have been shortly after the close of the Feast of Tabernacles, while Jesus was still in the city. His claim to be the "light" (GK 5890) of the world is the second of the great "I am's" of Jesus (see comment on 6:34–36) and recalls 1:4–5. Perhaps Jesus drew his illustration from the Menorah that burned during the Feast. Jesus professes to be not only the inexhaustible source of spiritual nourishment, but also the genuine light by which truth and falsehood can be distinguished and by which direction can be established.

13–14 As usual, the Pharisees challenged Jesus' claims. Legally a testimony concerning oneself would be unacceptable because it would presumably be biased (see comment on 5:31). Here Jesus protested vigorously that his self-testimony is valid, for no one knew more about his own nature and experience than Jesus himself. He possessed knowledge concerning both where he came from and where he was going (see 13:3). The testimony about himself was therefore more accurate than that of his opponents, for they had no idea of either his origin or destiny (cf. 7:25–44).

15–18 Jesus argued further that the Pharisees were not qualified to render a verdict on the validity of his witness because they were using the wrong criterion of "human standards." He, on the other hand, is not measurable by such standards. He appealed to the rule of the OT law that prescribed two witnesses for an acceptable proposition (Dt 17:6). He would be qualified as one of the witnesses (for no human witness can authenticate a divine origin) and his Father, who sent him, as the other (cf. 5:23–21,37).

19 Whether the Pharisees' question here is a bewildered inquiry or an intentional insult is hard to determine, though in Eastern culture, to question a man's paternity is a definite slur on his legitimacy. It may be unwise to read into this question more hostility than is necessary (but see also v.41). Jesus was referring to God, and the Pharisees were unwilling to admit that he had so intimate a relation with God. Jesus asserted that the knowledge of the Father depended on knowing him. As the one whom the Father had sent (v.18), Jesus claimed to be an adequate and authoritative representative.

20 The second part of this verse is a footnote John adds that relates to the program of Jesus' life (see 2:4; 7:6, 30; 12:23, 27; 17:1). Jesus lived a protected life until his work was completed.

21–24 The following discourse marks the dual destiny of Jesus and his opponents: he would return to the Father, and they would die in their sins. Jesus claimed that he belonged to a totally different world from that of his questioners. To him the difference was natural; to them it was unnatural—something they could explain only by assuming that he belonged to the realm of the dead. But Jesus had come from the presence of God, and he asserted that only by faith could they attain his level. An insurmountable barrier separated them—unbelief (v.23). Not only did they repudiate his claims, they completely rejected his person.

25 The question asked by the Pharisees shows their exasperation with Jesus' hints and seemingly extravagant claims. The crowd had ventured many guesses about his identity (see 7:40–41). The longer his explanation, the less satisfying it seemed to be. Jesus avoided making a direct claim to deity, but he relied on his works and character to speak for themselves (see 5:36–38). They witnessed to the fact that he had come from another world, that he was different from humanity in general, and that he had a unique mission to fulfill.

26 Jesus certainly had enough accusations that he could have mustered to bring judgment on his accusers. The remainder of the verse implies that such judgment is tied to their unwillingness to acknowledge Jesus' relationship to the Father. Because he was speaking what the Father told him, the Father's judgment would come on them, too.

27–28 Jesus' questioners did not understand that he was speaking to them of God, so they missed the point of his peculiar relationship to the Father. He asserted that when they had lifted him up, they would recognize him for what he was. Jesus' reference to "lifted up" (GK 5738; see comment on 3:14) refers to the cross, but the verb also means "to exalt." It may carry an additional meaning: that Jesus would be glorified by the cross (see 12:23, 32). Another important phrase is Jesus' use of "I am" in "then you will know that I am." It occurs three times in this discourse (vv.24, 28, 58). It may be translated as in v.24, "I am [the one I claim to be]," referring to himself as the Son of Man. But it may also be related to God's revelation of himself to Moses as the "I AM" (Ex 3:14) and to Isaiah's theistic proclamations (Isa 41:4; 43:11–13; et al.). The Jews recognized "I AM" as a term for deity (cf. Mk 14:61–62). The term predicates self-existence and eternal being. Along with this claim to divine nature, Jesus reaffirmed his subordination to the Father as the bearer of his message. Both his nature and his message have come from God.

29 Four times in this discourse Jesus affirmed that he had been sent by the Father (vv. 16, 18, 26, 29). His message was not original; he was simply conveying the truth of the one who had sent him and was carrying out his orders. His whole purpose was to please the Father, and his utter devotion produced a life of complete holiness. This revelation forms a contrasting background to the slavery of sin that follows.

30 The validity of the belief referred to here seems questionable. The people's lack of perception and shallowness of commitment are reflected in the following paragraphs, which begin with proud resentment on the part of the Jews and conclude with an attempted stoning.

2. The discourse to professed believers (8:31–47)

31 Jesus now addressed those Jews who had expressed a measure of faith in him. He began his discourse with the assumption that they would proceed to a further commitment on the basis of his teaching, which would mark them as genuine disciples and lead them into a deeper experience of truth. Jesus did not, of course, wish to extinguish a smoldering wick of faith (cf. Mt 12:20), but he felt the necessity of making perfectly clear the conditions of discipleship.

32–33 The freedom Jesus spoke of was spiritual freedom from sin and its effects, as the following context shows. The Jews' response indicates that they were thinking of political freedom, since they spoke of being enslaved to persons (v.33). Their protest was ill-founded, for they were forgetting the slavery of Egypt, the oppressions at the time of the Judges, the Exile in Babylon, and the current Roman domination of their land. Because they were descendants of Abraham, with whom God had established a permanent covenant (Ge 12:1–3; 15:1–21; 17:1–14, 19; 22:15–18), they considered themselves exempt from any spiritual danger.

34 Jesus' reply dealt with the spiritual aspect of freedom. Sin enslaves because every act of disobedience to God creates an atmosphere of alienation and a trend to further disobedience that inevitably makes escape impossible. An act of sin can possibly be overcome, but the attitude and habit of sin are inescapable.

35–36 A slave has no security, for he can claim no family ties that entail an obligation toward him. The son of a family has permanent status within it. Jesus enlarged this analogy by stating that while *a* son is rightfully a partaker of family privileges, *the* Son can confer such privileges. The hope for real freedom does not lie in the ancestry of Abraham but in the action of Christ.

37–38 The contrast between the attitude of Abraham and that of his self-styled descendants was proof that they were falsely claiming him as their spiritual ancestor. They were murderous in intent and impervious to revelation. Jesus had brought a message from the Father, and, unlike Abraham, they would not receive it (cf. Lk 3:8). Jesus' contrast of what he had "seen" and what they had "heard" reinforces the concept of authority implicit in his repeated claim to have been "sent" by the Father (8:29). He spoke from firsthand knowledge; they were acting on misinformation. They had been misled by Satan himself.

39–41 Jesus insisted that the Jews were not the true children of Abraham. Their hatred of Jesus, refusal to listen to truth, and lack of simple faith belied their profession. The Jews' insistence that they were children of Abraham implied that they regarded their relationship to God as secure because of their lineal descent from the man with whom God had confirmed his covenant. While the covenant had not been abrogated, Jesus made it plain that his hearers needed to exercise individual faith to participate in it. His words give substance to his teaching on the new birth and are paralleled by Paul's explanation of Abraham's faith in Gal 3:1–29.

The Jews' insistence that they were true descendants of Abraham brought Jesus' flat denial of their spiritual claims, and he attributed their attitude to another source. Their protest, "We are not illegitimate children," may carry the implication of a sneer: "We are not illegitimate children—but you are!" While John does not speak directly of the virgin birth, there are hints in his gospel of a mystery surrounding his birth. In any case, the Jews were unwilling to listen to Jesus' claims; yet, at the same time, they were insisting that they came from God.

42 Jesus gave another evidence of the Jews' hypocrisy. If they truly loved God, they would evidence that love by showing love to his Son. Love for God is a family affair; it involves loving all whom the Father has sent, especially the Son, his most beloved representative.

43–44 The people might have been confused as to why they did not love Jesus if he was indeed sent from the Father. Jesus spoke to that point with a rhetorical question: "Why don't you know what I am saying?" Then he went on to give the reason: their family association was wrong; they belonged to their father, the devil. And because of this family tie, they were inclined to carry out their father's desire, just as Jesus carried out his Father's desire. The devil seeks to deprive life and distort truth. The Jews were merely demonstrating the truth of the adage, "Like father, like son."

45 "Truth" (GK *237*) is an abstract that is difficult for people to know and appreciate (cf. 18:38). Jesus told the Jews that because they were children of their father, they didn't know what truth was. They were living in a world of lies, distortion, and falseness.

46 Jesus' challenge "Can any of you prove me guilty of sin?" would have been impossible for anyone else to utter (cf. 8:7). No human being could risk making that challenge without many flaws in one's character being revealed. Had Jesus not been sinless, someone in the hostile crowd would eagerly have charged him with at least one sin.

47 Jesus closed the argument by repeating that the Jews refused to hear him because they did not belong to God. Their bitterness toward him and their obtuseness toward his teaching contradicted their spiritual claims.

3. The response of the unbelievers (8:48–59)

48 The hardened opposition to Jesus' claims appears in an accusation apparently leveled at him frequently that he was "a Samaritan and demon-possessed." The Samaritans held many beliefs in common with the Jews, for they also relied on the Pentateuch as the supreme authority for their faith. They differed, however, in their interpretation and were much more lax in their attitude toward other religious influences. Since Jesus did not agree with all the traditional interpretations of the Law, the Jews may have classed him with the Samaritans as a heretic. According to John, demon-possession was attributed to Jesus on three occasions (7:20; 8:52; 10:20). In this context it is the equivalent of calling a man crazy.

49–50 Jesus denied the allegations and placed the burden of proof back on his adversaries. His aim was to honor the Father; theirs, to bring Jesus into disgrace. He disclaimed all selfish desire for prestige and relegated the final evaluation of his works to the judgment of God.

51 With a solemn affirmation, Jesus declared that anyone who receives his message will not experience death. This is a negative version of the positive principle declared later by Jesus (see 10:10). It summarizes his mission, for he came "to destroy the devil's work" (1Jn 3:8) and to undo the penalty for sin that was pronounced in Eden (Ge 2:17). A fuller statement of this principle appears in Jesus' promise to Martha (Jn 11:25).

52 To receive eternal life by keeping Jesus' word seemed to the Jews the height of absurdity. They felt that their charge of demon-possession was confirmed. If their ancestor Abraham and the OT prophets as God's accredited messengers died, how could this obscure Galilean claim to have the power of life and death?

53 A better translation of this question would be, "You are not greater than our father Abraham, are you?" A negative answer is assumed. While Jesus' opponents frequently charged him with making himself divine (5:18; 10:33; 19:7), Jesus himself seldom asserted his deity, but preferred to live and act in such a way that others would observe his divine nature and confess it spontaneously (cf. Mt 16:13–17).

54 Again Jesus referred his defense to the Father, for God was responsible for Jesus' message and vindication. He reminded them that the God they claimed to be theirs was his own personal Father. Their relation to God was formal; his was familial.

55 By using two different Greek words for "know" (GK *1182* & *3857*) Jesus seems to be saying: "You have not really attained an experience of God; I have a full consciousness of him." Jesus could not deny his intimate knowledge of God without making himself a liar.

56 Jesus claimed that Abraham had a preview of his ministry and had rejoiced in it. This probably refers to the promise God gave to Abraham that his seed would become the channel of divine blessing to all the nations (Ge 12:3). By "my day" Jesus was likely referring to his redemptive work, which would summarize his career. Isaac represented to Abraham the "seed" through which God would fulfill his promise. The miraculous birth of Isaac, his unquestioning trust in his father, his willingness to become a sacrifice to fulfill the command of God, and his deliverance from certain death all seem to point forward to the coming incarnation, death, and resurrection of the promised Seed, Jesus (see Ge 22:1–18; Heb 11:17–19).

57 The Jews' retort that Jesus was "not yet fifty years old" affords an interesting sidelight on Jesus' age. Fifty years was the limit observers would assign to him on the basis of appearance. If, as many think, Jesus was born between 6 and 4 B.C., and if the Crucifixion took place in A.D. 33, Jesus would not have been older than his late thirties. Perhaps the tensions of his life had aged him prematurely, yet he was obviously less than fifty years of age (see also Lk 3:23).

58 The rejoinder of Jesus, "Before Abraham was born, I am" could only mean a claim to deity. "Was born" (or "came into being") implies the event of entering into a new state or condition of existence (the same verb is used in 1:14 to denote the Incarnation). "I am" (GK *1609* & *1639*) implies continuous existence, including existence when Abraham appeared. Jesus was, therefore, asserting that at the time of Abraham's birth, he existed (see also comments on 8:28 for a discussion of "I AM"). "I AM" was recognized by the Jews as a title of deity.

59 The crowd unmistakably understood Jesus' words as a blasphemous claim and immediately prepared to stone him. He did not protest their action as a mistake of judgment; he simply withdrew. How he managed to escape their wrath is not explained, though he had done so on previous occasions (7:30; cf. Lk 4:30).

E. The Manifestation of Opposition (9:1–11:57)

The widening rift between belief and unbelief, which had become clearly apparent at the time of the feeding of the five thousand and was accentuated at the Feast of Tabernacles, now became an open breach. Not only had many of Jesus' disciples abandoned his cause (6:66), but the religious authorities also were becoming actively hostile (7:32). The last few months of Jesus' life were filled with controversy and with attempts by the priests and scribes to trap him by his words or actions. Jesus, however, being fully aware of their designs, maintained his usual ministry and became bolder in his resistance.

1. The healing of the blind man (9:1–41)

a. The healing (9:1–12)

The cure of the blind man probably occurred shortly after the Feast of Tabernacles, while Jesus was still in Jerusalem. The episode is a unit by itself, used as an illustration of Jesus' utterance recorded in 8:12: "I am the light of the world. Whoever follows me will never walk in darkness, but will have the light of life." The healing was not only a sample of Jesus' ability to restore sight to a man who was congenitally blind; but it also represented, figuratively, and for the blind man, experientially the dawning of spiritual light. Furthermore, the healing brought new light to the disciples on one of the mysteries of life that had bewildered them.

1 Although Jesus had healed blind persons on other occasions (Mt 9:27–31; 12:22; 15:30; 21:14; et al.), this "sign" (GK *4958*) was an outstanding case because (1) the man had been born blind; (2) the sign was related to the issue of fate, raised by the disciples; and (3) it illustrates the origination and development of faith, a theme of this gospel. The encounter of Jesus and the blind man seems to have been a casual one. Since blind beggars had little opportunity for employment, they were dependent on charity for their sustenance.

2–3 The interest of the disciples was prompted by theological curiosity rather than compassion. For them the blind man was an unsolved riddle rather than a sufferer to be relieved. Their question was based on Ex 34:7, which the Jews construed to mean that if a person suffered from any ailment, it must have been because his parents or grandparents had committed some sin against God. To this they added the thought that perhaps he might have sinned before birth (either as an embryo or in a preexistent state); such a concept appears in the rabbinical writings. Jesus refused to accept either alternative. He looked on the man's plight as an opportunity to do God's work, not as a punishment or as a matter of irrational chance.

4–5 The growing pressure of hostility rising from unbelief warned Jesus that his time was short; the darkness would soon fall. As all the Gospels show, Jesus was working under the shadow of the coming cross (Mt 16:21; Mk 8:31; Lk 9:22). While he had the opportunity, he must let his light shine on the darkness around him by healing both bodies and minds. The use of "we" shows that he included his disciples in his ministry. They also would pass through perils and opposition, but they would have the support of the Father who had sent him. "I am the light of the world" repeats 8:12; the healing of the blind man illustrates the positive and practical application of that principle.

6–7 To make known his intention to the blind man, Jesus made clay from dust and spittle and placed it on the sightless eyes. The touch of a friendly hand would be reassuring. The weight of the clay would indicate to the blind man that something had been done to him, and it would induce obedience to Jesus' command. Certainly he would not want to continue sitting by the roadside with mud smeared over his eyes. Though his lifelong affliction may have made him apathetic, he now had at least one motive for obeying.

The Pool of Siloam was probably a considerable distance from the place where the blind man was. His trip must have been a venture of faith. Jesus had not even told him that he would be healed but had merely commanded him to wash. If the man had overheard Jesus' conversation with the disciples, he would have expected something to happen. Yet so extraordinary a miracle as giving sight to a man born blind would have seemed impossible.

8–9 The man's recovery of his sight created a genuine sensation. The effects of the miracle are described vividly by the responses of four groups or individuals: (1) the neighbors, (2) the Pharisees, (3) the parents, and (4) the man himself. The neighbors and acquaintances knew very well the man they had supported by their charity. To see him walking with normal sight was so incredible that they thought it must be a case of mistaken identity. He quickly settled the dispute by avowing that he was the man they had known.

10–12 The curiosity of the neighbors demanded an explanation. The man replied in matter-of-fact fashion, narrating the event just as it happened. His reply, however, indicates the first stage of faith: he accepted the fact. He made no attempt to evaluate Jesus' person but spoke of him simply as "the man they call Jesus."

b. The consequences (9:13–41)

13–15 The case was so mysterious that the neighbors took the man to the religious authorities, the Pharisees, who supposedly would be able to offer an explanation. Since the day on which the miracle was performed was a Sabbath, the Sabbath law was involved. The Pharisees inquired how the man received his sight, and he repeated the story he had given first to the neighbors.

There are both parallels and contrasts between the healing in ch. 9 and that in ch. 5. Both occurred at a public pool; both concerned apparently incurable cases; and both occurred on the Sabbath, which precipitated the question of the Sabbath law. In the previous instance, however, the man healed reported voluntarily to the Pharisees and identified Jesus afterward. In this instance the man had no knowledge of Jesus' whereabouts, nor did he report the matter to the authorities. Furthermore, Jesus implied that the former man had sinned and adjured him to cease doing so (5:14); of the man in this chapter he stated that his condition was not the result of sin (9:3).

16 The response of the Pharisees revealed reasoning from prejudice: "This man is not from God, for he does not keep the Sabbath." For the Pharisees there could be no other conclusion. Others, however, were hesitant and asked how a sinner could have the power to perform such miracles. The use of the plural "miraculous signs" suggests that they knew other miracles of Jesus comparable to this one. The contrast between these responses brings into focus an important principle of interpretation: Should Jesus be judged by an a priori application of the law or by an a posteriori consideration of his works?

The division among the Pharisees shows that there must have been at least a small minority who were not hostile to Jesus (perhaps including Nicodemus and Joseph of Arimathea). Their question, "How can a sinner do such miraculous signs?" sounds much like Nicodemus's opening words to Jesus in 3:2.

17 Again the man himself was questioned to help bring a decision in the dispute. His verdict was more definite than the preceding one: "He is a prophet." The prophets were agents of God, and in some instances they performed miracles (e.g, Elisha, 2Ki 2:19–22; 4:18–44; 5:1–14). If, then, Jesus had performed an indisputable miracle, it was indisputable evidence that he must have a divine commission. As an emissary of God, he could be empowered to heal on the Sabbath, if necessary.

18–23 The evidence was still insufficient to remove the objections of "the Jews" (a phrase here synonymous with "the Pharisees"). They proceeded to query whether the man really had been born blind; for if he had not been blind from birth, the miracle could be disputed. They also interrogated his parents, who, fearing excommunication from the synagogue, evaded the issue by stating that their son was an adult capable of answering for himself.

24 To the Jews there was only one solution. The Law forbade working on the Sabbath; Jesus had healed on the Sabbath; therefore, Jesus was a sinner. So they commanded the man to "give glory to God" for his healing.

25–27 The ensuing argument between the previously blind man and the Pharisees was a duel between an obvious fact and a legal syllogism. The fact of the healing was undeniable and was admitted by the blind man's opponents. Their incessant questioning exhausted his patience, and he indulged in some sarcasm by insinuating that their repeated inquiries showed an interest in becoming disciples of Jesus.

28–29 Such a response to learned rabbis on the part of an illiterate man was surely considered insulting. The Jews quickly retorted that they were abiding by the authority of Moses, whose law had been the standard of Israel's religion. Jesus they rejected as a vagrant prophet who did not keep the law.

30–33 Again the blind man pressed the pragmatic argument, and he also employed an argument of his own. Since, according to the assumption of the Jews, "God does not listen to sinners" (cf. Ps 66:18; Pr 28:9; Isa 1:15), how could Jesus have performed this miracle if he were under divine condemnation? Rather, the man reasoned, the healing should be ample evidence that Jesus came from God.

34 To this argument the Jews had no real answer, so they attacked the man by character assassination and made him feel unworthy to answer. Then they excommunicated him, thus isolating him from his family and friends and debarring him from employment (cf. v.22).

35–36 In contrast to the negative result of rejection is the positive result of Jesus' response. "Found" implies that Jesus looked for the man so that he might confirm his faith. The question "Do you believe in the Son of Man?" is a summons to commitment, demanding a personal decision in the face of opposition or rejection. Since the healing of the man occurred after Jesus' first interview, he would not have recognized Jesus by sight; and the question, couched in the third person, would not instantly identify the questioner as the object of faith.

37–38 When Jesus said that the "Son of Man" was the person speaking, the man instantly responded by worshiping Jesus. He was ready to believe on the one who had healed him. The progress in his spiritual understanding of Christ is marked by progressive descriptions: "The man they call Jesus" (v.11); "he is a prophet" (v.17); "from God" (v.33); "Son of Man" (v.35); and, lastly, "Lord" (v.38). This progression illustrates the man's movement from darkness to light, both physically and spiritually.

39–41 The negative result is illustrated by the Pharisees' response. Jesus' remark in v. 39 makes him the pivot on which human destiny turns. The Pharisees, assuming that they could "see" without his intervention, asked in resentment, "Are we blind too?" Jesus' reply indicated that if they had acknowledged blindness, they could be freed from sin; but since they were asserting that they could see when they were really blind, there was no remedy for them. Deliberate rejection of light means that "the light within . . . is darkness" (Mt 6:23).

2. The Good Shepherd discourse (10:1–21)

Chapter 10 opens a new topic, the discourse on the Good Shepherd. It is seemingly unrelated to the previous narrative, though the reference in v.21 to opening the eyes of the blind shows that the author connects it with the preceding text. This discourse in some respects resembles parables in the Synoptics (e.g., the parable of the lost sheep in Mt 18:12–14; Lk 15:3–7). The Johannine presentation, however, is not concentrated on one point but utilizes the allegory with a wider meaning. The teaching is based on the practice of shepherding, and several aspects are utilized to create a picture of the relation of Christ to his people.

1–2 Jesus introduces this section with a solemn affirmation ("I tell you the truth"), emphasizing the importance of the teaching that the allegory contains, particularly regarding the ministry of Jesus himself. The imagery of the first two paragraphs is based on the concept of the "sheep pen." It was usually a rough stone or mud-brick structure, only partially roofed, or a cave in the hills. It had a single opening through which the sheep passed when they came in for the night. The pen served to protect them against thieves, robbers, and wild beasts.

Thieves, who would have no right of access by the gate, used other means to gain entrance. The shepherd entered by the gate, the lawful method of entry. Jesus was contrasting himself with the false messiahs who by pretense or violence were attempting to gain control of the people. He came as the legitimate heir of the chosen seed and claimed to be the fulfillment of the OT revelation.

3 The "watchman" (GK *2601*) cannot be identified with any particular person; rather, the word illustrates Jesus' coming at the right time and in the right way. He alone has the right to spiritual leadership of his people, and the sheep listen to him. The Oriental shepherd usually named his sheep and could summon them by calling them.

4–6 A pen frequently held several flocks; and when the time came to go out in the morning pasture, each shepherd separated his sheep from the others by his peculiar call. Instead of driving them, he led them so that they followed him as a unit. Wherever they went, the shepherd preceded them, guiding them to adequate pasture and guarding against possible danger. The sheep refused to follow a stranger because his voice was unfamiliar. In fact, if a stranger should use the shepherd's call and imitate his tone, the flock would instantly detect the difference and would scatter in panic.

In view of the fact that shepherds and sheep were so common in Palestine, it seems incredible that Jesus' metaphor was not understood. His hearers, however, failed to comprehend his meaning because of their spiritual deadness. If they would not recognize his claims, they would not accept him as a shepherd; and their assumption that they were God's flock because they were descendants of Abraham (8:39) would eliminate the necessity of personal faith in Jesus for salvation.

7 The sudden shift of metaphor from shepherd to gate seems rather strange to us, but in reality it is not. When the sheep returned to the fold at night after a day of grazing, the shepherd stood in the doorway of the pen and inspected each one as it entered. He anointed any who were scratched or wounded and gave water to those who were thirsty. After all the sheep had been counted and brought into the pen, the shepherd lay down across the doorway so that no intruder—human being or beast—could enter without his knowledge. The shepherd became the door, the sole determiner of who entered the fold and who was excluded (cf. 14:6).

8 The "thieves and robbers" refer to the false messiahs and supposed deliverers of the people who had appeared in the period following the restoration from the Exile and especially in the century before Jesus' advent, or possibly to the religious leaders of the Jews. After the death of Herod the Great in 4 B.C., many factions were contending for the leadership of the nation and attempting by violence to throw off the Roman yoke. But Jesus' purpose was not political, as the emphasis of the discourse shows.

9–10 Jesus' main purpose was the salvation (health) of the sheep, which he defined as free access to pasture and fullness of life. Under his protection and by his gift they can experience the best life can offer. In the context of John's emphasis on eternal life, this statement takes on new significance. Jesus can give a whole new meaning to living because he provides full satisfaction and perfect guidance (cf. Eze 34:15).

11 The concept of a divine shepherd goes back to the OT (e.g., Ps 23; Jer 23:1–3; Eze 34:12, 15). To the disciples the figure would have been specially apt since shepherding was one of the major occupations in Palestine. It involved both a protective concern and a sacrificial attitude. This latter is expressed in the words "the good shepherd lays down his life for the sheep." This phrase, unique to the Johannine writings, means a voluntary sacrificial death (10:11, 17, 18; 13:37–38; 15:13; 1Jn 3:16). "Life" (GK *6034*) implies more than physical existence; it involves personality and is more frequently translated "soul." The good shepherd stands ready to sacrifice his total self for the sake of the sheep.

12–13 Jesus' statement about the hired hand indicates the differences between himself and the religious leaders of the day. The main concern of the hired hand is his pay (cf. 1Pe 5:2–3), not the welfare of the sheep. When the flock is attacked by a wolf, he deserts them, for he will not endanger himself for them. Without proper and courageous leadership, the sheep will be dispersed and easily become the victims of their enemies.

14–15 The reaffirmation "I am the good shepherd" is based on knowledge of the sheep. "Know" (GK *1182*) implies a relationship of trust and intimacy. The definitive analogy given here is drawn from Jesus' relation to the Father. The Shepherd is concerned for the sheep because they are his property and because he loves them individually.

16 The sheep "not of this sheep pen" probably refers to the Gentiles to whom Jesus sent his disciples (Mt 28:19; Lk 24:47; Ac 1:8) and whom he planned to include in his salvation. He also stresses this idea of unity in his farewell prayer (17:20).

17 The thrice-repeated allusion to laying down his life (10:11, 15, 17) gives the basis for Jesus' sacrifice as the means of our reconciliation both to God and to one another (see 1Jn 3:16).

18 Two important aspects of Jesus' death are clarified by his authority. (1) His death was wholly voluntary. His power was such that no human hand could have touched him had he not permitted it. The gospel has already made clear that Jesus avoided capture or execution (5:18; 7:44–45; 8:20, 59; cf. 10:39; 11:53–54). Only when he declared that "the hour has come" (12:23) was it possible for his enemies to arrest him. (2) Jesus had authority both to lay down his life and to take it up again. The death of Jesus was part of a plan to submit to death and then emerge from it victoriously alive. Anyone can lay down one's life, if that means simply the termination of physical existence; but only the Son of God could at will resume his existence. This entire plan was motivated by his love for the Father and his readiness to carry out his Father's purpose.

19–21 The reaction of the populace was divided. To Jesus' enemies, his claims seemed so exaggerated and so contradictory to the popular understanding of the unity of God that they could be attributed only to the irrational and blasphemous utterance of a demoniac (cf. 7:20; 8:48). On the other hand, many of the crowd regarded Jesus as thoroughly sane. After all, demoniacs do not cure the blind. The reference to the miracle narrated in ch. 9 shows that it must have left a strong impression in Jerusalem.

3. The debate in Solomon's Colonnade (10:22–42)

22–23 The Feast of Dedication, now known as Hanukkah, was established as a memorial to the purification and rededication of the temple by Judas Maccabeus in 165 B.C., after its profanation three years earlier by Antiochus IV Epiphanes. Antiochus, the king of Syria, had captured Jerusalem, plundered the temple treasury, and sacrificed a sow to Jupiter on the temple altar. His attempt to hellenize Judea resulted in the Maccabean revolt, which was successful in defeating the Syrian armies and liberating the Jewish people. Solomon's Colonnade (or Porch) was a long walkway covered by a roof supported on pillars on the east side of the temple, overlooking the Kidron Valley. Jesus used it as a center for informal teaching and preaching, since there were almost always some people present for worship at the temple.

24 The Jews encircled Jesus and demanded him to make a categorical statement of his identity, to dispel an illusion and/or to enlist their allegiance. Was he the Messiah or not? If so, they wanted him to fulfill his calling by achieving independence for the nation; if he was not the Messiah, they would look elsewhere. They could not escape the fact that his miracles exceeded the powers of any ordinary person and that his teachings carried an authority greater than that of the established religious leaders. On the other hand, he had not formally presented himself as the Messiah, nor had he evinced any political ambitions.

25–26 Jesus' reply placed the burden of proof on his questioners. He reminded them that his previous sayings and works should be sufficient to establish his messianic mission (cf. 5:16–47; 6:32–59; 7:14–30), but they were refusing that evidence. The reason they did not believe was that they were not his sheep. In saying that, Jesus implied that the main criterion of salvation is not descent from the chosen line, but whether or not people follow him. His immediate hearers refused to believe and thus cut themselves off from further revelation.

27–28 The sheep that are given by the Father to the Son belong to his flock and are characterized by obedience, recognition of the shepherd, and allegiance to him. They, in turn, are guaranteed eternal life and permanent protection. All the resources of God are committed to their preservation.

29 The gift of the Father to the Son is the "sheep" viewed collectively. He assures their destiny, for nobody can wrest them from his hand. Throughout the discourse, Jesus has been stressing his relationship with the Father, his intimate knowledge of the Father (v.15), the love of the Father for him (v.17), and his works done in the Father's name (v.25).

30 "I and the Father" preserves the separate individuality of the two Persons in the Godhead; the word "one" (GK *1651*) asserts unity of nature or equality (cf. 1Co 3:8). The Jews were quick to apprehend this statement and reacted by preparing to stone Jesus for blasphemy because he, a man, had asserted that he was one with God. For them Jesus' language did not mean simply agreement of thought or purpose but carried a metaphysical implication of deity.

31 The verb translated "picked up" literally means "to carry." It is doubtful whether there were any loose stones in the paved courtyard of Solomon's Colonnade. But not far off was the temple that was in the process of being built, and certainly stones would have been readily available there. Stoning was the punishment prescribed for blasphemy in the law of Moses (Lev 24:16), and the opponents of Jesus were preparing for just such an execution.

32 Jesus' question challenged the people's action on the ground that he had performed only helpful deeds. They should take stock of what he had done, and then they would see that stoning was incongruous with his actions.

33 The Jews replied that the issue was not the quality of his works but his blasphemous claim to be God. Had Jesus not meant to convey a claim to deity, he undoubtedly would have protested the action of the Jews by declaring that they had misunderstood him.

34–35 On the contrary, Jesus introduced an *a fortiori* argument from the Psalms to strengthen his statement. Psalm 82:6 represents God as addressing a group of beings whom he calls "gods" and "sons of the Most

Solomon's Colonnade is the large pillared, covered walkway that surrounded the courtyard of the temple on three side.

High." If, then, these terms can be applied to ordinary mortals or even angels, how could Jesus be accused of blasphemy when he applied them to himself, the One whom the Father set apart and sent into the world on a special mission? Jesus was not offering a false claim; he was merely asserting what he was by right.

The parenthetic statement "and the Scripture cannot be broken" illustrates the high regard Jesus had for the OT. Throughout this gospel the constant assumption is that Scripture is the revelation of God, setting the timing, content, and character of Jesus' ministry (see 1:45; 2:22; 3:14–15; 5:39; et al.). Such passages presuppose a confidence in the authority and trustworthiness of Scripture that is in keeping with Jesus' attitude.

36 Jesus unmistakably refers to himself as "God's Son [GK 5626]" To him it was not a strained assertion but a logical statement, for he was fully aware of his relation to the Father and to the responsibility the Father had committed to him. The accusation of blasphemy seems to be utterly unreasonable in the light of that relationship.

37–39 Jesus' appeal to his opponents summed up the attitude and method of his argument. He took his position, not on the basis of his personal authority, but on the attestation of his "miracles." If they showed that he was demonstrating divine compassion and exercising divine authority over people and matter, he was divinely accredited. Those miracles were peculiarly expressive of his nature and revealed his personality and mission. For those predisposed not to believe in him, he offered pragmatic proof of his special relationship with God: "The Father is in me, and I in the Father." The appeal failed; and once again "they tried to seize him, but he escaped their grasp."

40–42 Having eluded their attempt to capture him, Jesus retreated to Perea, on the east side of the Jordan, which was the domain of Herod Antipas and where the rulers in Jerusalem had no authority. There he would be comparatively safe from arrest. There also he found a better reception, for "many believed on him." The Jews' allusion to the testimony of John the Baptist indicates that his ministry had enduring influence, and they accepted Jesus on that basis. As in the case of the woman of Samaria, faith in Christ was preceded by the witness of another.

4. The miracle at Bethany (11:1–44)

a. The announcement of death (11:1–16)

The account of the raising of Lazarus is the climactic sign in the gospel of John. Each of Jesus' seven signs illustrates some particular aspect of his divine authority (cf. comment on 5:36), but this one exemplifies his power over the last and most irresistible enemy of humanity—death. For this reason it is given a prominent place in the gospel. It is also significant because it precipitated the decision of Jesus' enemies to do away with him. Furthermore, this episode contains a strong personal command to believe in Jesus in a crisis, when such belief would be most difficult. All that preceded in John is preparatory; all that follows it is the unfolding of a well-marked plot.

1–2 At this point Lazarus is introduced, though Mary and Martha are mentioned in Luke (10:38–42). Apparently Jesus was frequently a guest in their home when he visited Jerusalem (cf. Mk 11:11). Of Lazarus, however, nothing is known apart from John. The identification of Mary by the action recorded later in this gospel (12:1–10) is unusual, unless the author presupposed some knowledge of her action on the reader's part. John mentions it in order to identify Lazarus and to indicate Jesus' relations with the family.

3 Knowing Jesus' interest in them and the power of God to heal the sick, the sisters sent for him when Lazarus became ill. The malady must have been serious, for they were sufficiently alarmed to call Jesus back to the area where a price had been set on his head. The appeal was on the basis of love, and they felt confident that he would be prompt.

4–6 Jesus' reaction was optimistic and purposeful. He gave assurance to the disciples that Lazarus's illness would not terminate in death, and stated that Lazarus's illness would be an important aspect of his own glorification. Having said that, he deliberately stayed in Perea two more days. His action may have appeared to the disciples, and almost certainly to the sisters, as unfeeling and selfish. Since he had the power to heal Lazarus, why should he not reply instantly (cf. Lk 7:11–16; 8:41–42, 49–56)? Perhaps the disciples were not particularly puzzled, for their subsequent remarks indicated that they were well aware of the danger that threatened him in Jerusalem.

7–8 His proposal to the disciples that they should return to Judea was not welcomed with enthusiasm. They remembered the previous conflicts with the rulers and feared for Jesus' life, and possibly for their own as well.

9–10 Jesus countered the disciples' objection with this most enigmatic statement. That expression may have been a current proverb, perhaps similar to his remark in 9:4. In both instances, Jesus was thinking of his obligation to perform the work the Father had committed to him. Realizing that he was acting in accord with that purpose, Jesus resolutely decided to return to Jerusalem in spite of the peril. To digress from God's purpose is to walk in darkness; to remain in fellowship with God is to walk in the light (cf. 1Jn 1:6).

11–13 In order to explain his action, Jesus decided to educate his disciples by informing them that Lazarus was asleep and that he intended to wake him. Their interest and loyalty were plainly revealed by their willingness to listen to him and to move back into the area of danger if he so desired. The disciples, however, lacked imagination and took literally Jesus' announcement that Lazarus had fallen asleep. Assuming that "sleep" would mean that the fever had passed its crisis, they expressed their hope for Lazarus's recovery. But Jesus was using the word "sleep" (GK 5678) in a figurative sense, meaning "death." This does not mean that the dead are in a state of total unconsciousness, for Jesus' illustration of the rich man and the beggar predicates consciousness after death (Lk 16:19–31). It does show that Jesus looked on the death of Lazarus as a parenthesis after which there would be an awakening, not as a permanent removal from life.

14–15 Jesus' rejoinder to the disciples' comment made Lazarus's state unmistakable: "Lazarus is dead, and for your sake I am glad I was not there, so that you may believe." These words seem strange. Why should Jesus be glad that he was not present to save Lazarus from death or to comfort the sisters, and why should Lazarus's death bring any benefit to the disciples? Jesus considered this an opportunity for a supreme demonstration of power that would certify the Father's accreditation of him as the Son and confirm the faith of the sisters and the disciples. He was certain of the outcome.

16 Thomas's comment marks his first appearance in this book. John's gospel does not contain a complete list of the Twelve, though they are mentioned as a group on two occasions (6:67, 70–71; 20:24). Generally they are presented only as individuals and once in the Epilogue as a smaller group (21:1–2). Thomas appears four times: here, once in the discourse in the upper room (14:5), once after the Resurrection (20:24–29), and finally with the group described in the Epilogue (21:1). His attitude here is paradoxical: "Let us also go, that we may die with him [Jesus]." Thomas expected that Jesus would be seized and executed and that his disciples would suffer with him. Notwithstanding this unhappy prospect, Thomas's loyalty is revealed by his readiness to share Jesus' peril. The skepticism that he later evinced regarding the Resurrection was probably prompted by grief over Jesus' death rather than by disillusionment because of apparent failure.

b. The conversation with Martha and Mary (11:17–37)

17–18 The time between Lazarus's death and Jesus' arrival at Bethany was four days. Two full days had intervened between the arrival of the messengers and Jesus' departure for Bethany (v.6). The trip to Bethany would have taken at least a day, since Bethany was more than twenty miles distant from Jesus' refuge in Perea (10:40–42). So the death of Lazarus must have occurred not long after Jesus was first informed of his illness. After three days all hope of resuscitation from a coma would be abandoned; and in the hot Palestinian climate, decay would have begun.

19 The family at Bethany must have been well known in Jerusalem, since many "Jews" came to comfort Martha and Mary over the loss of Lazarus. A procession composed of relatives, friends, and sometimes hired mourners accompanied a body to the grave; and mourning usually lasted for several days afterward.

20 Martha, the more aggressive sister, went to meet Jesus, while quiet and contemplative

Mary stayed home. This portrayal of the sisters agrees with that found in Lk 10:38–42.

21–22 The words Martha addressed to Jesus express both a repressed reproach and a persistent faith. She was disappointed that Jesus had not responded to the first news of Lazarus's illness, but that did not lead her to break her relationship with him. Despite her remorse, she was confident that God would grant Jesus' desire in this matter.

23–26 Martha interpreted Jesus' promise (v.23) that her brother would rise again in terms of the expectation of a general resurrection. She may have taken his words as a conventional expression of comfort; he intended them to describe what he would do. In his reply, Jesus turned Martha's acceptance of a dogma into faith in his person. In what is surely one of his most majestic and comforting utterances, Jesus said that he embodied the vital power to bring the dead to life (vv.25–26). The one who believes in Christ has eternal life that transcends physical death. Those who live and believe will never die but will make an instant transition from the old life to the new life (cf. 1Th 4:16–17). On this basis, he asked her directly whether she believed.

27 Martha's commitment reveals a firm belief that Jesus was the Messiah, the Son of God, as preached by John the Baptist (1:34) and accepted by the disciples (1:49; 6:68), and the deliverer foretold by the prophets. Her language is emphatic.

29–30 Martha told Mary that Jesus was asking for her. To Mary, this was equivalent to a command to come. Her subsequent actions, though less assertive, reveal a trust in Jesus similar to Martha's. Jesus was waiting for her outside the town.

31 The Jews knew something was afoot when Mary left so hastily. Since they had come to mourn with the sisters, they thought it only fitting to follow her, supposing that she was going to the tomb.

32–35 Mary's greeting to Jesus was similar to Martha's. The response of Jesus to this calamity illustrates his human and divine natures. Up to this point he had been perfectly calm, assuring Martha that her brother would rise and asserting that he was the resurrection and the life. He was completely in command of the situation and challenged Martha's faith. But when Mary appeared, crushed with sorrow and accompanied by the waiting mourners, Jesus was moved with deep emotion.

His feeling is expressed by three words: "deeply moved" (GK *1839*), "troubled" (v.33; GK *5435*), and "wept" (v.35). The first of these connotes anger. Perhaps Jesus was expressing his resentment against the ravages of death that had entered the human world because of sin. The second word expresses agitation. That is, Jesus was not apathetic or unnerved by the prevailing mood of sorrow. Lazarus had been a beloved friend, and Jesus shared in the common feeling of grief over his death. Overcome by emotion, he spontaneously burst into tears.

36–37 Jesus' true humanity was emphasized by the response of the people at Lazarus's tomb. Some were impressed by Jesus' open show of emotion and took it as an evident token of his love for Lazarus. Others, perhaps not so lovingly, wondered why Jesus had not prevented Lazarus's death by one of his miracles. The reference to the healing of the blind man again (cf. 10:21) shows that it must have created a sensation in Jerusalem since it was remembered several months after it had occurred.

c. The raising of Lazarus (11:38–44)

38 The repetition of "deeply moved" from v.33 shows that Jesus was still under the same emotional tension that his first contact with the mourners had aroused. He planned to fulfill his prediction to the disciples that the outcome of Lazarus's death would be to the glory of God, as well as keep his promise to Martha that her brother would rise again. The burial place was a chamber cut in limestone rock and closed by a stone laid over the entrance.

39–40 Having challenged Martha's faith, Jesus now faced a challenge of his own. He ordered the covering stone to be removed. Martha's protest was natural, for it would seem improper to expose a decaying corpse. Such an act would demonstrate her faith and remove her uncertainty and hesitancy so that the glory of God might be revealed to her and all present. To Jesus the raising of Lazarus presented no problem.

41–42 When Martha met his condition, which was the last step of faith she could take, Jesus took the next step. He did not ask God to raise Lazarus; he thanked him for having already answered his prayer. So great was Jesus' faith in the Father that he assumed that this miracle, so necessary to his mission, was as good as done. His main reason for raising Lazarus was to convince the assembled people that he had been sent by the Father.

43–44 Having uttered this prayer, Jesus addressed the dead man. He had said on a previous occasion that a time would come when all who were in their graves would hear his voice (5:28). This occasion was a remarkable demonstration of that authority. The words spoken were brief and direct, and can be paraphrased, "Lazarus! This way out!" as if Jesus were directing someone lost in a gloomy dungeon. The creative power of God reversed the process of corruption and quickened the corpse into life. The effect was startling. The dead man appeared at the entrance to the tomb, still bound by his graveclothes. Jesus then ordered that he be released from the wrappings and returned to normal life. It was a supreme demonstration of the power of eternal life that triumphed over death, corruption, and hopelessness.

5. The decision to kill Jesus (11:45–57)

45–46 The response to the sign was twofold. "Many" of the Jews believed on the basis of the evidence they had seen, for the fact of Lazarus's restoration was incontrovertible. In contrast, others went to inform the religious leaders of Jesus' action, apparently as a gesture of disapproval. It seems unlikely that any of the believing Jews made up the delegation that went to the Pharisees.

47–48 As a result of Jesus' miracle in Bethany, a meeting of the Sanhedrin was called. The council expressed not only disapproval but also frustration. They anticipated that the miracles of Jesus would bring such a wave of popular support that the Romans, fearing a revolution, would intervene by seizing complete authority, thus displacing the Jewish government and destroying the national identity. Their fears revealed a complete misunderstanding of the motives of Jesus, who had no political ambitions whatever. He had already indicated by his refusal to be made king that he had no intention of organizing a revolt against Rome (cf. 6:15).

49–50 Caiaphas, the high priest, was the son-in-law of Annas, who is mentioned later in the account of Jesus' trial (18:12–14). Annas had been high priest from A.D. 7 to 14 and was succeeded by three of his sons and finally by Caiaphas from A.D. 18 to 36. The utterance of Caiaphas reveals his cynicism and duplicity. He was contemptuous of the indecisive attitude of the Pharisees and recommended the elimination of Jesus rather than risking the possibility of a long contest with Rome.

51–52 John takes Caiaphas's statement as a kind of double entendre, an unconscious and involuntary prophecy that Jesus would become the sacrifice for the nation so that it might not perish. The irony of the statement is paralleled by the record of the rulers' mockery of Jesus at the Crucifixion (see Mk 15:31). In both instances a sneering remark expressed an unintended truth. The statement of Caiaphas is applied by the author not only to the nation of Israel, but also to the "children of God" who have been scattered throughout the world. These words might apply to the Jews of the Dispersion. But in the light of the universalism of this gospel, they probably refer to the future ingathering of the Gentiles, who become the children of God when they acknowledge Jesus as Savior (1:12; 10:16).

53 The growing hostility of the Pharisaic party and of the Sadducean priesthood had developed into a settled decision to do away with Jesus. Although the hierarchy feared a popular uprising in his support, they were resolute that he should die.

54 For this reason Jesus left Bethany, where danger threatened him, and removed to Ephraim, a village north of Jerusalem. This town was on the edge of the Judean desert, into which Jesus could flee if necessary.

55–56 Just before the Passover, pilgrims from distant parts of the country began to assemble in Jerusalem. Ceremonial cleansing would take considerable time when a large crowd was involved, and the people wanted to be ready to participate in the sacred feast. Jesus had been present in Jerusalem at the Feasts of Tabernacles and Dedication and had been regularly engaged in teaching. Since the Passover would bring an even larger crowd to Jerusalem, the populace expected that Jesus would be there also. His previous visits had been accompanied by much controversy, and there had been several futile attempts to arrest or stone him (cf. 5:18; 7:30, 44; 8:20, 59; 10:38). On each occasion, however, he had eluded his enemies, for "his time had not come."

57 The high council of Judaism had issued a warrant for Jesus' arrest and had ordered that anyone who knew of his whereabouts should declare it. In the light of this situation, one can conclude that Judas was a messianist loyal to his nation and that his loyalty to the ruling priesthood took precedence over his personal loyalty to Jesus.

F. The Crisis of the Ministry (12:1–50)

Chapter 12 of John is devoted to the crisis of Jesus' ministry that preceded its conclusion. As previously noted, the hostility of the religious authorities had been increasing and had intensified because they had been unable to entangle Jesus in any compromising dilemma or defeat him in public debate. In spite of a decline in his popularity because he refused to become involved in a political coup (6:15) and because some of his teaching was obscure to his listeners (6:52–66), he still retained a loyal group of disciples; and a large segment of the populace still regarded him with awe. They hoped that he might still decide to use his miraculous powers on their behalf and establish a new political and economic order that would make Israel dominant among the nations.

For Jesus himself, the period was critical because the forces for and against him were crystallizing, and he had to make a decision as to which way he should turn. He had been living by a program that had been established by the Father and was outlined progressively by Scripture and experience. No doubt the temptation to deviate from it for considerations of power or safety was always with him (Lk 4:13). Now, as the moment for the fulfillment of the divine purpose approached, the tension increased.

1. The dinner at Bethany (12:1–11)

1–2 At this point Jesus' time schedule becomes more definite than previously in this gospel. Martha and Mary gave a dinner for Jesus. The notation that Lazarus was among the guests seems unnecessary at first reading. If the dinner was an expression of gratitude for the restoration of Lazarus (ch. 11), he would naturally be expected to attend it. Perhaps the writer is suggesting that after Lazarus's restoration to life he retired from any public appearance since he did not want to be an object of curiosity (cf. v.9). On this occasion he may have come out of seclusion to honor Jesus.

3 The anointing of Jesus' feet by Mary was not difficult because of the custom of reclining to eat instead of sitting at a table. Guests usually reclined on divans with their heads near the table. They leaned on cushions with one arm and ate with the other. Mary could easily have slipped from her couch, walked around the other couches, and poured the ointment on Jesus' feet.

Spices and ointments were quite costly because they had to be imported. Mary's offering was valued at approximately a year's wages for an ordinary working person. She presented it as an offering of love and gratitude, prompted by Jesus' restoration of her brother to the family circle. Wiping his feet with her hair was a gesture of utmost devotion and reverence. The penetrating fragrance of the ointment that filled the house told all present of her sacrificial gift.

4–6 Judas Iscariot reappears here (cf. 6:70–71, the only previous mention of him in this gospel). Jesus knew Judas's tendencies and was well aware of his coming defection. Whereas many of Jesus' disciples had deserted him (6:66), Judas remained to betray him. He was determined to make Jesus serve his purpose—by treachery if necessary.

Judas had been appointed treasurer of the band of disciples, but he had been using his office for his own enrichment. His remonstrance over Mary's gift revealed that he had a sharp sense of financial values and no appreciation of human values.

7–8 Mary seems to have been the only one who was sensitive to the impending death of Jesus and who was willing to give a material expression of her esteem for him. Jesus' reply shows his appreciation of her act of devotion. His words disclose also the current of his thought, for he was anticipating death. His comment on the poor was not a justification for tolerating unnecessary poverty; but it was a hint to Judas that if he were really concerned about the poor, he would never lack opportunity to aid them. Mary and Judas stand in sharp contrast to each other.

9–11 The response of the crowds to Jesus brought another crisis to his enemies. So many were becoming his followers that the priestly party was sure that their fears as expressed by Caiaphas were justified. Their resolution to destroy Jesus was strengthened, and in their wild madness of unbelief they even contemplated the possibility of removing Lazarus, since his restoration to life was an undeniable witness to Jesus' power.

2. The entry into Jerusalem (12:12–19)

12 This story is one that also appears in the Synoptic Gospels (Mt 21:1–11; Mk 11:1–10; Lk 19:28–40). John identifies two distinct multitudes: the larger one was composed of the "great crowd" of pilgrims who had come to Jerusalem for the Passover and were already there (v.12); the other one was those who were traveling with Jesus and had witnessed the raising of Lazarus (v.17).

13 If the former crowd came from Galilee, they would be well aware of Jesus' works there; a number of them had probably wished for a long time that he would declare himself as the expected Messiah. They applied to him the words of Ps 118:25–26, a song customarily sung by Passover pilgrims on their way to Jerusalem. These words ascribed to him a messianic title as the agent of the Lord, the coming king of Israel.

14–15 The entry into Jerusalem was Jesus' announcement that his hour had come and that he was ready for action, though not according to the expectation of the people. He did not come as a conqueror but as a messenger of peace. He rode on a common donkey, not a royal steed. John couples this entry with a prophecy of Zechariah (9:9), who announced that the king of Israel would appear in humility without pomp and ceremony. The pilgrims who had come to Jerusalem to attend the feast went out to greet Jesus; the other crowd gathered in his train. "Hosanna" is a Hebrew expression meaning literally "Save now!" (see comment on Mk 11:9). It may be interpreted as a plea for immediate action on the part of the king (cf. v.13).

"Daughter of Zion" is a personification of the city of Jerusalem; it occurs frequently in the OT, especially in the later prophets (Isa 1:8; 52:2; Jer 4:31; Mic 4:8; Zec 2:10; et al.).

16 This parenthetical statement by the author states that the disciples did not then understand the situation but that they later comprehended it (cf. 2:17, 22). His comments demonstrate that the gospel must have been written when he and the others had attained a spiritual perception they did not possess in the years of their travels with Jesus. The Passion and the Resurrection were keys in unlocking the mystery of Jesus' person.

17–18 The second group in this account consists of those who were following Jesus, some of whom had witnessed the raising of Lazarus in Bethany. These people continued to publicize Jesus' miracle and aroused the curiosity of many in the city. These, in turn, joined the crowd that was on the way to meet Jesus as he neared Jerusalem.

19 The convergence of the pilgrims from a distance with Jesus' enthusiastic supporters from Jerusalem made a popular following that caused the rulers to become apprehensive. They felt that their attempts to stop Jesus were too few and too late.

3. The response to the Greeks (12:20–36)

20 Another element that contributed to the crisis was the request of the Greeks to see Jesus. They were probably Gentile Greeks who had joined the Jewish pilgrims to Jerusalem—inquirers, possibly from Galilee or the Decapolis, who had become interested in the Jewish faith but had not become full proselytes.

21–22 Just why these Greeks approached Philip rather than one of the other disciples is not stated. Philip in turn referred them to Andrew, and both of them carried the request to Jesus himself.

23 Curiously enough, John never writes whether Jesus either gave these Greeks an audience or sent a reply back to them. Nevertheless, Jesus' action itself is an answer to their inquiry, because he announced openly that the great hour of his life had arrived. He felt the pressure of the Gentile world and realized that the time had come to open the way to God for the Gentiles and to fuse Jewish and Gentile believers into one body. To accomplish this objective, he had to sacrifice himself (cf. 10:16).

24 The likeness of the grain of wheat that is buried in the cold soil only to rise again multiplied for harvest is applicable to all believers in Christ. Until the seed is planted in the ground and dies, it bears no fruit; and if it is sacrificed, it produces a large crop. This also served as a metaphor for Jesus' own life's plan.

25 The man who attempts to preserve his life will lose it, while the man who readily sacrifices his life will keep it for eternal life. The two words translated "life" are different (GK *6034* & *2437*). The first is generally rendered "soul" and denotes the individual personality, with all its related experiences and achievements. The second is usually coupled with the adjective "eternal" in John and means the spiritual vitality that is the experience of God (17:3; cf. Mt 10:39; Mk 8:36; Lk 14:26).

The expression "who hates his life" is a hyperbolic expression which means that one is to base one's priorities on that which is outside oneself. In this instance, it is to make Christ the Master of one's life.

26 In this verse, Jesus explained what hating one's life means. The impending Cross would involve the disciples in the same way it would involve Jesus, and he was informing them that he was the model for them to follow (cf. his discourse on the Good Shepherd; 10:4). "Going ahead of them" implies that he does first what he asks them to do and that he confronts the dangers before they encounter them. Jesus went on to promise that wherever he might go, his servants would be privileged to accompany him and share his glory (cf. 17:24).

27–28a Turning from how the crisis would affect the disciples, Jesus revealed how it affected him. His dilemma here corresponds to what happened in Gethsemane as recorded in Mt 26:36–46; Mk 14:32–42; Lk 22:40–46. John reveals that that struggle, which he does not record, was the culmination of an earlier struggle. In these words spoken publicly in the period of crisis, Jesus indicates that he is breaking under the strain of the crisis; its dangers and irrationality are overwhelming him. Should he ask the Father to spare him from the cataclysm that was so rapidly approaching? Had he done so, he might have averted seeming disaster at the price of failing to achieve his redemptive purpose. But Jesus adhered boldly to his original purpose of completing the mission God had entrusted to him. His resolution was final. He wanted the Father's name to be glorified, no matter what the cost!

28b–30 The voice from heaven is the third and final instance recorded in the gospel narratives, and the only one in John (cf. the voice at his baptism, Mt 3:17; Mk 1:11; Lk 3:21–22; and at his transfiguration, Mt 17:5; Mk 9:7; Lk 9:35). On each occasion it was a public acknowledgment of the sonship and authority of Jesus and an endorsement of his work by the Father. John asserts unmistakably that the voice was a genuine, audible sound, though the crowd did not understand it. Jesus explained that the voice from heaven was intended to encourage the disciples and to inform the crowd, not to encourage him.

31 Jesus recognized and announced unmistakably that the final crisis had arrived. Both the disciples and the more sympathetic segment of the crowd were uncertain of what his fate would be (see 6:60–66; 7:25–27, 40–44; 10:19–24; 11:55–56). Now he declared that a decisive action must follow. God's purpose is to glorify him. The hour for judgment has come, and the prince of the world must be exposed for what he is. "Judgment" (GK *3213*) does not imply that the final day of judgment has come or that only now is retribution for sin exercised. Jesus conveyed the meaning that God, having now made his final revelation, must hold people responsible for their obedience or disobedience (cf. also Ac 17:30–31). The revelation of God in Christ is itself a disclosure of sin and a judgment on it.

"The prince of this world" can be none other than Satan (cf. 14:30; 16:11; similarly in 2Co 4:4; Eph 2:2; 6:12). The Cross and the Resurrection spelled Satan's defeat and marked the glorification of all Satan renounced and the reversal of all he sought to attain. Satan was motivated by self-will; Jesus, by the will of the Father. Satan's power brought destruction and death; Jesus' power imparted renewal and life. Though Satan is still active, his action is only the desperation of futility (cf. Rev 12:12).

32–33 The preposition "from" (GK *1666*) means "out from" rather than "away from." It connotes not only being lifted or suspended above the earth, as on a cross, but also being brought up out of the earth. Jesus had in mind not only the fact that he would be elevated on the cross but also that he would be exalted by the Resurrection (see also 3:14; 8:28; 12:32, 34). Elsewhere in the NT the verb "lifted up" does mean "exalt" (GK *5738*; see comment on 3:14). Thus, it lends itself well to the double meaning of the method of death as specifically stated here and the exaltation to spiritual sovereignty as described in apostolic preaching (Ac 2:33; 5:31; Php 2:9).

"All men" does not imply that everyone will ultimately be saved; instead, it means that Christ draws people to himself indiscriminately, without regard to nationality, race, or status. Jesus' utterance was prompted by the presence of the Greek Gentiles (v.20) and should be evaluated in that context. Note that there is a clear differentiation between believers and unbelievers, between the saved and the lost, in John's writings (cf. 1:11; 3:18, 36; 5:29; et al.; 1Jn 3:10, 15; 5:12).

34 The crowd was puzzled by Jesus' prediction of his death. According to their understanding, the Messiah would be a supernatural person who would inaugurate his final and eternal reign as God's Anointed, the Son of David. In the OT (expressed by the word "Law" here), God promised to David that his descendants would reign "forever" (2Sa 7:12–13, 16; cf. Ps 89:26–29, 35–36). The people were confused by Jesus' reference to the "Son of Man" and wanted to know who he was.

Although John 12:32 uses the first person pronoun "I" rather than "Son of Man," Jesus undoubtedly was speaking of himself by this title (see comment on Mk 8:31). The query of the crowd, "Who is this 'Son of Man'?" implies that his concept of its meaning was different from theirs. To them, the apocalyptic Son of Man (cf. Da 7:13–14) would not die. Jesus was enlarging the concept of "Son of Man" by applying it to the whole of his work: his true humanity, his suffering, his exaltation, and his judicial work.

35–36 Jesus spoke with urgency. The light would not always be available (cf. 9:4). If his hearers wished to walk with certainty, they should act at once, for after his departure they might find themselves in the darkness. "Put your trust" implies a persistent faith, not solely a momentary decision (cf. 14:1).

4. The response to unbelief (12:37–50)

Verses 37–50 are the author's explanation of the significance of his narrative up to this point. They focus on the conflict of belief and unbelief and include Jesus' final appeal for decision. The historical crisis must be resolved by immediate action that reveals either the belief or unbelief of those involved. The spiritual crisis that occurs when one confronts Christ is resolved through personal decision.

37–38 The author expresses surprise and regret that in spite of Jesus' numerous "signs" the people still obstinately refused to believe in him. Unbelief was rapidly approaching the climax attained in the rejection and crucifixion of Jesus. John connected this with the prophecy of Isaiah, thus plainly affirming that Jesus was the subject of the passage on the Suffering Servant (Isa 52:13–53:12; John quotes 53:1). Parts of this prophecy are quoted repeatedly in the NT (Mt 8:17; Lk 22:37; Ac 8:32–33; Ro 10:16; 15:21; 1Pe 2:22, 24–25), and it is an important basis for the doctrine of the Atonement. Prophecy repeatedly played a large part in apostolic preaching (e.g., Ac 2:17–35; 3:18, 21, 24).

39–40 Not only did prophecy describe unbelief, it also explained it. Why should the hearers of Jesus not believe in him when the signs so unmistakably accredited his claims? John quotes from Isa 6 (the story of Isaiah's commission) to show that unbelief is the result of the rejection of light, which act, by the sovereign law of God, gradually makes belief impossible. God warned the prophet in advance that his mission would not be successful, for the hearts of those who heard him would be hardened. John interprets this prophecy by its effect rather than by its intention. It was not God's desire to alienate his people; but without the offer of faith and repentance, they would never turn to him anyway. The cumulative effect of unbelief is a hardened attitude that becomes more impenetrable as time progresses.

41 The implication in this verse is startling. Isaiah 6 opens by Isaiah saying that he saw the Lord (Isa 6:1, 5). John now claims that

Isaiah saw Jesus and spoke of him. In other words, he identified Jesus with the Lord (Heb. "Yahweh"; GK 3378) of the OT.

42–43 John notes that many of the leaders believed (including probably Joseph of Arimathea and Nicodemus; cf. 19:38–39; Mk 15:43; Lk 23:50–51). Possibly John learned of this movement among the national leaders through his acquaintance with Nicodemus. Since the attitude of the council as a whole would call for the excommunication of any avowed believers in Jesus (Jn 9:22), these people remained silent.

44–46 Jesus equated belief in him with belief in God (cf. John 14:1; 1Jn 2:23). The Father and the Son are inseparable; though they are two personalities, they work as one being. Jesus spoke of the Father as the one who had sent him, and he claimed to be the light that illumines the darkness of those who are without God.

47–50 Judgment on unbelief is not arbitrary but inevitable. The message of Christ will become the condemnation in the last days of any who refuse it, since nobody who refused it can plead ignorance. Jesus' emphasis, however, is positive. His mission was intended to evoke belief and to rescue humans from darkness. The Father's sovereign purpose is to lift people out of helplessness and death and give them eternal life. Because Jesus speaks the message the Father commanded him to speak, he is the Word of God.

At this point John closes the account of Jesus' public ministry of teaching. Subsequently he taught only the disciples and prepared them for the final act of his life.

III. The Private Ministry of the Word (13:1–17:26)

A. The Last Supper (13:1–30)

1. The washing of feet (13:1–20)

1 The full Johannine account of the Passion begins at this point. John alludes to the nearness of the Passover as if to remind his reader that Jesus had been introduced by John the Baptist as the "Lamb of God, who takes away the sin of the world" (1:29). As the first Passover had been the turning point in the redemption of the people of God, so the Cross would be the opening of a new era for believers. John connects this with the manifestation of Jesus' love for "his own" (i.e., his disciples), a love that has no limits. Jesus had accepted the responsibility for them and was obliged to instruct and protect them (17:6–12).

2 Whether this meal was the actual Passover or not has been warmly debated. It seems to have occurred on the same night as the arrest and betrayal. If so, it was presumably Thursday night, and the Crucifixion occurred on Friday. John stated later (18:28) that the Jewish delegates could not enter Pilate's hall on Friday morning because they would be defiled and unable to eat the Passover. In that case, the Last Supper must have preceded the Passover by twenty-four hours. If, then, the Passover began on Friday night, the meal that took place on Thursday night would not have been the standard Passover Feast. The question is complicated by the fact, however, that the Synoptics imply that Jesus did intend to eat the Passover with his disciples (Mt 26:17–20; Mk 14:12–17; Lk 22:7–14). No mention is made of the Passover lamb, however.

Of all the suggestions regarding this problem, two are plausible. (1) Two calendars were in simultaneous use: one national group, using one calendar, ate the Passover on Thursday night whereas the other group, using the other calendar, ate the Passover on Friday night. (2) Jesus, having been repudiated by the priesthood and consequently considered apostate, would not have been allowed to obtain a lamb for sacrifice and would have been compelled to celebrate the feast at a different time. Whatever solution may be accepted, it seems clear that Jesus did celebrate the meal with his disciples on Thursday night, that the hearing before Pilate and the Crucifixion took place on Friday when the other Passover lambs were being sacrificed, and that his body was placed in the tomb before sunset late that afternoon.

The focus of action in this section lies in Jesus' washing the feet of the disciples. By this time, Judas had already determined to betray Jesus. His specific motive is not stated, and the impulse is attributed to satanic suggestion. In other words, the conflict was basically actuated by a rebellion against God. It is possible that Judas, realizing that Jesus' enemies were implacably hostile and were politically powerful, concluded that Jesus was doomed to lose in the struggle and so decided that he might as well gain immunity from sharing Jesus' fate. Furthermore, he could compensate himself by claiming the reward for betrayal. His act, however, was more serious than an incidental piece of treachery; he sold himself to the power of evil (cf. v.27).

3–5 John emphasizes the fact that Jesus was not the innocent victim of a plot, unaware of what was transpiring around him. Rather, he was fully aware of his authority, his divine origin, and his destiny. John says much more about the inner consciousness of Jesus than the Synoptics do, either because he was more observant or because Jesus confided in him.

The immediate situation was that they had come to the banquet room directly from the street. Ordinarily on such an occasion the host would have delegated a servant to the menial task of removing the sandals of the guests and washing their feet. Since the meeting was obviously intended to be secret, no servants were present. None of the disciples was ready to volunteer for such a task, for each would have considered it an admission of inferiority to all the others (cf. 1:27).

Sometime during the meal Jesus rose, removed his outer cloak, tied a towel around his waist, and began to perform the work of the servant who was not present. It was a voluntary humiliation that rebuked the pride of the disciples. Perhaps it accentuated the tension of the situation, because Luke notes that when the disciples entered the room, they were arguing about who among them would be the greatest in the kingdom of heaven (Lk 22:24).

6–8a The response of Simon Peter may have been representative of the common feeling that Jesus ought not to demean himself by washing their feet. He reveals both the impetuousness of his disposition and the high regard he had for Jesus.

8b Jesus' rejoinder expresses the necessity, not only for the cleansing of Peter's feet to make him socially acceptable for the dinner, but also for the cleansing of his personality to make him fit for the kingdom of God. The external washing was intended to be a picture of spiritual cleansing from evil.

9–10 Peter, mistaking Jesus' veiled figure for the literal act, expressed his devotion by asking for a bath. Separation from Jesus was abhorrent to him. Jesus reminded him that a person once bathed needed to wash only his feet. "You are clean, though not every one of you" gives the clue to the interpretation of this action. One of the disciples had consistently refused Jesus' spiritual ministration. The others, who had been loyal though sometimes slow to understand, needed only occasional correction.

11 This gospel emphasizes strongly the self-consciousness of Jesus concerning himself and his work. From the beginning of his ministry he had supernatural discernment of the potentialities of his disciples (1:42, 47–48, 51). He predicted his death and resurrection (2:19; 3:14; 6:51; 8:28; 10:18; 12:32). He claimed a peculiar relationship with God (5:19, 26; 10:38). Now, at the close of his ministry, the gospel emphasizes even more strongly his supernatural awareness of the significance of what was occurring. Jesus realized that the time had come to leave his disciples (13:1), that the Father had committed all action to his authority (v.3), that the betrayer was already at hand (vv.10–11), that the identity of the chosen believers was settled (v.18), that the outcome of the existing situation was fixed (v.19; cf. 18:4), and, finally, that the moment of consummation had come (v.21; cf. 19:28).

12–14 A second lesson Jesus wished to impart to the disciples by this act was one of love and humble service. His question, "Do you understand what I have done for you?" contrasts with his remonstrance of Peter in v.7. The discernment of the disciples developed slowly. It took them a long time to begin to comprehend the intensity of Jesus' love for them and the nature of his humility in dealing with them. "Teacher" and "Lord" are both titles of respect that placed Jesus on a level above the disciples. Jesus went on to emphasize the fact that his actions as their leader should set the pattern for dedicated living (see also Mt 10:24; Lk 6:40; Jn 15:20). The concept of the servant-master relationship appears frequently in Jesus' teaching.

15 The "example" does not necessarily imply the perpetuation of footwashing as an ordinance in the church. Rather, Jesus put his emphasis on the inner attitude of humble and voluntary service for others (see the fuller explanation of this in Php 2:4–8).

16–17 The recurrence of "sent" (GK *4287*) here is a reminder that Jesus was constantly conscious of being commissioned by the Father. Jesus included his disciples both in his commission and in his action of servanthood. The true nature of Christian living was serving one another. And for those who would be willing to take this role on themselves, Jesus said there would be blessings.

18 Jesus' reason for washing the disciples' feet was not solely good manners and sanitation. The imminence of the betrayal was pressing in on him, and the resultant anguish was tearing at his heart. He knew that the disciples would fail at the crucial moment, but he despaired of none except Judas. The psalm Jesus quoted is attributed to David, who was lamenting the defection of a trusted confidant (Ps 41:9). This likely refers to Ahithophel, who had been David's counselor and diplomatic advisor but deserted him in Absalom's rebellion (2Sa 15:12; 16:15–23; 17:4, 14, 23). Again this is an example of prophecy by parallelism.

19–20 Jesus was not merely asking for personal loyalty but for belief that he was the One sent by God (cf. 8:24, 28, 58). He wanted the disciples to commit themselves to his claims before other events would seemingly invalidate them and before the Resurrection would confirm them (cf. 2:22). He went on to say that accepting the messenger whom he sent was equivalent to receiving him and that receiving him involved also receiving God. The language implies a close connection between the disciple and the master and an equally close connection between Jesus and God.

2. The prediction of the betrayal (13:21–30)

21 Jesus was not surprised that Judas would betray him. He had announced it to the disciples at least a year earlier (6:70). Nevertheless, it "troubled" him immensely (the same verb is used of Jesus' agitation in 11:33 and 12:27). As "the hour" approached, the bitterness of the betrayal Jesus anticipated became known.

22 The announcement startled the disciples. Although Jesus had previously mentioned the betrayal, they had not taken it to heart. Now, realizing the hostility of the authorities in Jerusalem and knowing that Jesus' death might be imminent, the act that had seemed remote became an immediate possibility.

23–25 Peter signaled to the disciple who occupied the place next to Jesus and "whom Jesus loved" (presumably John), asking him to inquire who the traitor might be. His inquiry demonstrated not only a persistent trait of curiosity but also Peter's loyalty. He may have contemplated preventive action; for if he could know in advance who the person might be, he could intervene.

26 Jesus gave no specific identification. He simply indicated that the offender would be the one to whom he would give the special morsel he had dipped into the dish. For the host to select a tidbit from the main dish and give it to a guest would be a mark of courtesy and esteem. The disciples, seeing this, would conclude only that Jesus regarded Judas as a close friend. While Jesus' reply would answer the question for the beloved disciple, he could scarcely have communicated his knowledge to Peter at that moment without disturbing the peace of the group.

27a "Satan entered into him." This moment was Judas's last opportunity to renounce his treachery. If the other disciples were ignorant of Judas's intentions, he could change the course of his action without explanation, and none but Jesus would know. Once Judas left the room to seal his bargain with the priests, he would pass the point of no return.

27b–28 Conscious that the time had come for his sacrifice (13:1), Jesus wished Judas to get on with his plot and leave. Once he was gone, Jesus would be able to continue his intimate ministry with his disciples in the upper room.

29 The reference to making a purchase for the Passover may corroborate the view that this Last Supper was held on the night preceding the Passover (cf. comment on v.2). Jesus would hardly have waited until this moment to obtain a lamb if they were at the Passover at that moment; and the text says that the disciples didn't know the reason for Jesus' statement to Judas, which would hardly be the case if the lamb was missing.

30 The repetition of the phrase "As soon as Judas had taken the bread" (cf. v.27) indicates that Satan's control of Judas and Judas's departure from the group must have been simultaneous. As Judas left, it was dark outside. John's comment about "night" corresponds to Jesus' statement when Judas betrayed him: "This is your hour—when darkness reigns" (Lk 22:53). It also heightens the implication that Jesus' life was one of conflict. The opposition of darkness and light is announced in the Prologue (1:5) and is illustrated by the growing hostility between Jesus and his enemies. As the conflict becomes more marked, Jesus said it reflected the contrast between what he had seen with his Father and what they had heard from their father (8:38, 42–44). John notes the continuing progress of the spiritual conflict in 13:27; 14:30; 17:15.

B. The Last Discourse (13:31–16:33)

With the departure of Judas, Jesus commenced the long farewell discourse to his disciples. The dialogue comprising the first section (13:31–14:31) should not be broken at 14:1.

1. Questions and answers (13:31–14:31)

a. The new commandment (13:31–35)

31 The title "Son of Man" appears twelve times in the gospel of John, of which this is the last occurrence (see comment on Mk 8:31). As the "Son of Man," Jesus reveals divine truth (1:51); he has a supernatural origin (3:13; 6:62); his death by being "lifted up" achieves salvation for humans (3:14; 8:28; 12:34); he exercises the prerogative of final judgment (5:27); he provides spiritual nourishment (6:27); and he will be "glorified" (cf. 12:23), which John applies specifically to Jesus' death and resurrection (7:39; 10:16). In general, "Son of Man" is the title of the incarnate Christ who is the representative of humanity before God and the representative of deity in human life.

32 The Johannine use of "glorify" (GK *1519*) is peculiar. This word occurs five times in vv.31–32 in what seems to be unnecessary repetition. Intrinsically the word means "exaltation." But as Jesus used it, it relates to his death (see comment on 12:32–33). The Cross would become the supreme glory of God because the Son would completely obey the will of the Father. The meaning of "exalt" or "magnify" seems to fit better the last two uses in this verse. This dual dimension of "glorify" appears also in the prayer of ch. 17 (see comments on 17:4–5; see also Php 2:4–11). In this concept the Cross and the Resurrection are united as phases of a single redemptive event by which the purpose of God is completed and his righteousness vindicated.

33 "My children [GK *5448*]" is expressive of Jesus' love and concern for the Eleven, who must have seemed to him to be weak and immature (cf. John's use of the same term to introduce admonitions in 1Jn 2:1, 12, 28; 3:7, 18; 4:4; 5:21). Jesus recalled to their memory his words to the Jews: "Where I go, you cannot come" (8:21). To the disciples he was speaking of the fact that they were now unprepared to follow him, though they would rejoin him later (see 14:3). To the Jews he made no such promise; instead, he predicted that they would die in their sins.

34–35 The most important instruction that Jesus left for the Eleven was this fresh, "new commandment"— to love one another. If their motive in following him had been to obtain a high place in the messianic kingdom (1:40, 49), Jesus knew that the spirit of rivalry would disrupt their fellowship before they could accomplish his commission to them. The attitude of love would be the bond that would keep them united and would be the convincing demonstration that they had partaken of his own spirit and purpose. He had loved them without reservation and without limit (13:1–5) and expected them to do the same.

b. The question of Peter (13:36–14:4)

The structure of this dialogue offers a contrast between the attempt of Jesus to present some consecutive teaching in preparation for his departure and the nervous unrest of the disciples, who were disconcerted by the awareness of impending danger. As usual, Simon Peter was the first to speak.

36 Peter's question ("Where *are* you going?") expresses bewilderment and perhaps slight exasperation. Jesus had previously spoken publicly of going away (8:21). On that occasion his enemies were mystified and wondered whether he was contemplating suicide. Now, in the intimacy of his inner circle, the disciples are equally puzzled, though conceivably less critical. Jesus' promise, "You will follow later," implies that Peter had asked the question so that he might go with him. His affection for Jesus, though often expressed clumsily, was undeniably genuine.

37–38 Peter was impatient and avowed that he was ready to lay down his life. Jesus, who understood the situation as Peter did not and who knew Peter's inner weakness, was gently incredulous. His answer about Peter's denial reveals his estimate of this disciple. The crowing of the rooster was reckoned as the watch between twelve midnight and three o'clock in the morning, when the light of dawn began to glimmer on the eastern horizon. When Peter heard this word, he must have been completely baffled. He would not question Jesus' authority. Yet he was so sure of his own devotion that he could not imagine such a failure.

14:1 Furthermore, the other disciples must have been equally perturbed, for Jesus added, "Do not let your [plural] hearts be troubled." The way in which Jesus phrases this implies that they should "stop being troubled" (i.e., they should set their hearts at ease). He then urged them to maintain both their trust in God and in himself. Their uncertainty and discouragement had weakened them, and he wanted to strengthen them against complete collapse in the imminent tragedy.

2 In spite of the threatening circumstances, Jesus spoke with calm assurance of the divine provision for them and took for granted that they would have a place in the eternal world. Jesus never speculated about a future life; he spoke as one who was as familiar with eternity as one is with his hometown. The imagery of a dwelling place ("rooms") is taken from the oriental house in which the sons and daughters have apartments under the same roof as their parents. The purpose of his departure was to make ready the place where he could welcome them permanently. Certainly he would not go to prepare a room for his friends unless he expected that they would also eventually arrive.

3 "I will come back" is one of the few allusions in this gospel to Jesus' return. He was not speaking of a general resurrection but of his personal concern for his own disciples. Though he did not elaborate on the promise, the guarantee is unmistakable. His return is as certain as his departure, and he would take them with him to his Father's house.

4 Verses 1–4 not only contain Jesus' answer to Peter's question but also indicate Jesus' attempt to return to the theme of the discourse he had first begun. He assumed that they knew the way to their destination; all they would need to do would be to follow the road. His sheep would follow him and find "the house of the Lord" at the end of their journey (Ps 23:6; Jn 10:27–28).

c. The question of Thomas (14:5–7)

5 Thomas's abrupt question, like Peter's questions (13:6, 36–37), was characteristic of its proponent. Thomas was utterly honest, pessimistic, and uninhibited. He did not suppress his feelings but voiced his despair (cf. 11:16). He was confused by life and felt that its riddles were unsolvable. But he was not ready to accept a state of permanent bewilderment.

6 Jesus' reply is the ultimate foundation for a satisfactory philosophy of life. First, it is personal. He did not claim merely to know the way, the truth, and the life as a formula he could impart to the ignorant; but he actually claimed to *be* the answer to human problems. That is, Jesus' solution to perplexity is not a recipe; it is a relationship with him. Second, Jesus responded with an authoritative assertion as the master of life. He *is* the way to the Father because only he has an intimate knowledge of God, unmarred by sin. He *is* the truth because he has the perfect power of making life one coherent experience irrespective of its ups and downs. He *is* the life because he was not subject to death but made it subject to him. He died to demonstrate the power and continuity of his life. Because he is the way, the truth, and the life, he is the only means of reaching the Father (cf. 1:18). Jesus is the only authorized revelation of God in human form, and he is the only authorized representative of humanity to God.

7 The first part of this verse could be better rendered, "If you have attained an experiential realization of who I am, you will know my Father also." Jesus declared that he had adequately presented the Father in his own person (cf. Paul's teaching in Col 1:15). To the extent that the disciples had come to a satisfactory understanding of Jesus, they had a comprehension of the being of God.

d. The request of Philip (14:8–15)

8 If Thomas was a skeptic, Philip was a realist. Having determined in his thinking that the Father of whom Jesus spoke must be the Ultimate Absolute, Philip demanded that he and his associates might see him. Philip was also materialistic; abstractions meant little to him. Nevertheless he had a deep desire to experience God for himself. If he and the other disciples could only apprehend God with at least one of their senses, they would be satisfied. Perhaps Philip wanted to have an experience such as Jacob (Ge 32:24, 30), Samson's parents (Jdg 13:3–22), and Moses (Ex 34:4–8) had had.

9 Jesus was both pleased and saddened by Philip's request: pleased by his earnestness and saddened by his obtuseness. His union with the Father was so natural that he was astonished that Philip had not observed it. "I am in the Father, and . . . the Father is in me" (v.10) was his description of the relationship both in instructing the public and in his final prayer to the Father (cf. 10:38; 14:20; 17:21). For this reason he could say, "Anyone who has seen me has seen the Father." No material image or likeness can adequately depict God. Only a person can give knowledge of him since personality cannot be represented by an impersonal object.

10–11 Furthermore, if a personality must be employed to represent God, that personality cannot be less than God and do him justice, nor can it be so far above humanity that it cannot communicate God perfectly to humans. The way Jesus made known the character and reality of the Father was by his words and works. The truth of God filled Jesus' words; the power of God produced his works.

12 Jesus again slowly resumed the main current of his teaching. He wanted to impress on the disciples that he was not disbanding them in anticipation of his departure; rather, he was expecting them to continue his work and do even greater things than he had accomplished. Such an expectation seems impossible in the light of his character and power; yet, through the power of the Spirit whom Jesus sent after his ascension, there were more converts after the initial sermon of Peter at Pentecost than are recorded for Jesus during his entire career (see Ac 1:15; 2:41). The influence of the infant church covered the Roman world, whereas Jesus during his lifetime never traveled outside the boundaries of Palestine. Through the disciples Jesus multiplied his ministry after his departure.

13–15 The power of the disciples originated in prayer. Jesus could hardly have made more emphatic the declaration that whatever they should ask in his name, he would do. The phrase "in my name," however, is not a magical charm like an Aladdin's lamp. It was both a guarantee, like the endorsement on a check, and a limitation on the petition; for he would grant only such petitions as could be presented in a manner consistent with his character and purpose. In prayer we call on him to work out his purpose, not simply to gratify our whims. The answer is promised so that the Son may bring glory to the Father. The disciples' obedience to him will be the test of their love.

e. The promise of the Spirit (14:16–21)

16–17 With the preceding words, Jesus returned from the answer to Philip's question to the more general theme of preparation for his departure. His absence would make more difficult the realization of the person of the Father whom he represented. In his place, however, he promised to send the Holy Spirit, the "Counselor" (*parakletos*; GK 4156; lit., "a person summoned to one's aid"). The Spirit's function is to represent God to the believer as Jesus did in his incarnate state. The concept of the Holy Spirit was not new, for the Spirit of God had been active in the OT (see Ge 1:2; 6:3; Jdg 3:10; 13:24–25; 14:6, 19; 15:14; Zec 7:12). John the Baptist had predicted that Jesus would baptize with the Holy Spirit (Mt 3:11; Mk 1:8; Lk 3:16; Jn 1:33). In his discussion of the new birth, Jesus had already spoken to Nicodemus of the work of the Holy Spirit (Jn 3:5). The ministry of the Spirit, however, would be directed primarily to the disciples. He would direct their decisions, counsel them continually, and remain with them forever. The world would not understand the Spirit since it would not recognize him. His presence was already *with* the disciples insofar as they were under his influence. Later, after Jesus departed, he would *indwell* them. This indwelling of the Spirit is the specific privilege of the Christian believer (see 7:39).

The Work of the Holy Spirit

A. The Holy Spirit in Relation to Creation and Revelation

Task	References
1. Active in creation	Ge 1:2; Job 33:4
2. Imparts life to God's creatures	Ge 2:7; Job 33:4; Ps 104:30
3. Inspired the prophets and apostles	Nu 11:29; Isa 59:21; Mic 3:8; Zec 7:12; 2Ti 3:16; 2Pe 1:21
4. Speaks through the Word	2Sa 23:1–2; Ac 1:16–20; Eph 6:17; Heb 3:7–11; 9:8; 10:15

B. The Holy Spirit in Relation to Jesus Christ

Task	References
1. Jesus was conceived in Mary by the Spirit	Mt 1:18, 20–23; Lk 1:34–35
2. Was filled with the Spirit	Mt 3:16–17; Mk 1:12–13; Lk 3:21–22; Lk 4:1
3. Preached in the Spirit	Isa 11:2–4; 61:1–2; Lk 4:16–27
4. Performed miracles by the power of the Spirit	Isa 61:1; Mt 12:28; Lk 11:20; Ac 10:38
5. Will baptize believers in the Holy Spirit	Mt 3:11; Mk 1:8; Lk 3:16; Jn 1:33; Ac 1:4–5; 11:16
6. Promises the Holy Spirit	Jn 7:37–39; 14:16–18, 25–26; 15:26–27; 16:7–15
7. Is revealed to believers by the Spirit	Jn 16:13–15
8. Offered himself on the cross through the Spirit	Heb 9:14
9. Was raised from the dead by the Spirit	Ro 1:3–4; 8:11
10. Received the Spirit from the Father	Jn 16:5–14; Ac 2:33
11. Poured out the Spirit upon believers	Ac 2:33, 38–39
12. Is glorified by the Spirit	Jn 16:13–14
13. Spirit prays for his return	Rev 22:17

C. The Holy Spirit in Relation to the Church

Task	References
1. Dwells in the church as his temple	1Co 3:16; Eph 2:22; cf. Hag 2:5
2. Is poured out upon the church	Ac 1:5; 2:1–4, 16–21; cf. Isa 32:15; 44:3; Hos 6:3; Joel 2:23–32
3. Speaks to the church	Rev 2:7, 11, 17, 27; 3:6, 13, 22
4. Creates fellowship in the church	2Co 13:14; Php 2:1
5. Unites the church	1Co 12:13; Eph 4:4
6. Gives gifts to the church	Ro 12:6–8; Eph 4:11
7. Strengthens the church	Ac 4:30–33; 1Co 12:7–13; 14:1–33
8. Appoints leaders for the church	Ac 20:28; Eph 4:11
9. Works through Spirit-filled people	Ac 6:3, 5, 8; 8:6–12; 15:28, 32; cf. Nu 27:18; Jdg 6:34; 1Sa 16:13; Zec 4:6
10. Empowers preachers	1Co 2:4
11. Directs the missionary enterprise	Ac 8:29, 39; 13:2–4; 16:6–7; 20:23

C. The Holy Spirit in Relation to the Church (Continued)

Task	References
12. Guards the church against error	2Ti 1:14
13. Warns the church of apostasy	1Ti 4:1; cf. Ne 9:30
14. Equips the church for spiritual warfare	Eph 6:10–18
15. Glorifies Christ	Jn 16:13–15
16. Promotes righteousness	Ro 14:17; Eph 2:21–22; 3:16–21; 1Th 4:7–8

D. The Holy Spirit in Relation to Individual Believers

Task	References
1. Lives in every believer	Ro 8:11; 1Co 6:15–20; 2Co 3:3; Eph 1:13; Heb 6:4; 1Jn 3:24; 4:13
2. Convicts us of sin	Jn 16:7–11; Ac 2:37
3. Regenerates us	Jn 3:5–6; 14:17; 20:22; Ro 8:9; 2Co 3:6; Tit 3:5
4. Imparts God's love to us	Ro 5:5
5. Makes us realize God is our Father	Ro 8:14–16; Gal 4:6
6. Enables us to say "Jesus is Lord"	1Co 12:3
7. Reveals Christ to us	Jn 15:26; 16:14–15; 1Co 2:10–11
8. Reveals God's truth to us	Ne 9:20; Jn 14:16–17, 26; 16:13–14; 1Co 2:9–16
9. Enables us to distinguish truth from error	1Jn 4:1–3
10. Incorporates us into the church	1Co 12:13
11. Is given to all who ask	Lk 11:13
12. Baptizes us into Christ	Mt 3:11; Mk 1:8; Lk 3:16; Jn 1:33; Ac 1:4–5; 11:16; 1Co 12:13
13. Fills us	Lk 1:15, 41, 67; Ac 2:4; 4:8, 31; 6:3–5; 7:55; 11:24; 13:9, 52; Eph 5:18
14. Gives us power and boldness to witness	Lk 1:15–17; 24:47–49; Ac 1:8; 4:31; 6:9–10; 19:6; Ro 9:1–3
15. Gives us special gifts	Mk 16:17–18; 1Co 1:7; 12:7–11; 1Pe 4:10–11
16. Gives visions and prophecy	Joel 2:28–29; Ac 2:17–18; 10:9–22; 1Co 14:1–5, 21–25
17. Develops his fruit in us	Ro 14:17; 1Co 13; Gal 5:22–23; 1Th 1:6
18. Enables us to live a holy life	Ps 51:10–12; 143:10; Eze 11:19–20; 37:26; Ro 8:4–10; 15:16; Gal 5:16–18, 25; Php 2:12–13; 2Th 2:13; 1Pe 1:2
19. Frees us from the power of sin	Ro 8:2; Eph 3:16
20. Enables us to fight Satan with the Word	Eph 6:17
21. Enables us to speak in difficult moments	Mt 10:17–20; Mk 13:11; Lk 12:11–12
22. Gives us comfort and encouragement	Jn 14:17–18, 26–27; Ac 9:31
23. Helps us to pray	Ac 4:23–24; Ro 8:26; Eph 6:18; Jude 20
24. Enables us to worship	Jn 4:23–24; Ac 10:46; Eph 5:18–19; Php 3:3
25. Is our pledge of final redemption	2Co 1:22; 5:5; Eph 1:13–14
26. Makes us yearn for Christ's return	Ro 8:23; Rev 22:20
27. Gives life to our mortal bodies	Ro 8:11

18–19 Jesus' allusion to a return may refer to his reappearances after the Resurrection (chs. 20–21). But he did not remain visible for long, nor were there any public manifestations. The motive for these appearances was the need to reassure the disciples, who felt left as helpless orphans in an unfriendly world. Jesus knew that they, as spiritual children (13:33), would need the strong protection and guidance of a parent in order to survive. The resurrection of Jesus would also be the guarantee of life for the disciples. The eternal life that he would demonstrate is the same eternal life he promised to them.

20 The coming of the Spirit to indwell believers would bring the realization that the Father, Son, and Holy Spirit are united in purpose and operation and that there would be a new intimate relationship between them and believers (see also 15:26).

21 Jesus reiterated the statement of v.15 because of its importance. Love is the basis of our relationship with God. His love has been manifested in the gift of Jesus (1Jn 4:9–10), and our love for him is manifested in obedience (1Jn 5:3). Those who obey his commands and show their love for him will reap great benefits. The Father will love the obedient disciples, Jesus himself will love them, and Jesus will make himself known to them.

f. The question of Judas, not Iscariot (14:22–24)

22 The last question in this impromptu dialogue was posed by Judas (not Iscariot). Nothing is known of him beyond his name (cf. Lk 6:16; Ac 1:13), unless he can be identified with Thaddaeus (Mt 10:3; Mk 3:18). Judas could not understand how Jesus would appear to the disciples without being at the same time subject to public scrutiny. Either Jesus would be visible or he would not; for Judas there was no possibility of both.

23 In his reply, Jesus did not focus on his postresurrection appearances, but on the broader revelation that would come to them through obedience to his known teaching and through the work of the Holy Spirit. The reality of Jesus' and the Father's presence would be conditioned on obedience, an obedience that resulted from their love for God. Obedience is not, however, the condition of God's love for humans but the proof of their realization of his love and of their love for him.

24 Being obedient to Jesus' words extends beyond keeping the charges he personally delivered. Jesus equated his teaching with the Father's will. Thus, loving Jesus is demonstrated by one's obedience to the revealed will of God, the Bible.

g. Parting comfort (14:25–31)

25–26 Jesus now resumed his teaching on the Holy Spirit because Judas's question evoked it. Through the Spirit Jesus' presence would be perpetuated among them. The phrase "in my name [GK *3950*]" (cf. vv.13, 14) means that the Spirit would be Jesus' officially delegated representative to act in his behalf. Just as Jesus himself demonstrated the personality and character of God to others, so after his departure the Holy Spirit would make the living Christ real to his followers. The function of the Spirit is teaching. He instructs from within and recalls to the memory what Jesus taught. The Spirit will, therefore, impress the commandments of Jesus on the minds of his disciples and thus prompt them to obedience.

27 The peace Jesus spoke of could not be exemption from conflict and trial. Jesus himself had been "troubled" by the impending Crucifixion (12:27). The peace he spoke of here is the calmness of confidence in God. Jesus had this peace because he was sure of the Father's love and approval. He could therefore move forward to meet the crisis without fear or hesitation. The world can give only false peace, which mostly comes from the ignorance of peril or self-reliance. With his promise of peace, he repeated the words of comfort he had spoken in reply to Peter's earlier question (cf. v.1). The disciples must have continued to show their dismay as they contemplated Jesus' departure.

28 In concluding this discourse, Jesus reminded them that he was about to return to the Father and that he had forewarned them so that their faith might not be disrupted by his removal. The statement "the Father is greater than I" refers to position rather than essence; Jesus was speaking from the standpoint of his humanity (cf. 5:19). The numerous statements in this gospel that the Father had sent him confirm that Jesus was acting under authority and was obligated to fulfill the Father's commands.

29 Throughout the gospel the necessity of believing is emphasized (1:50; 3:12, 15–16; 4:21, 41; et al.). Jesus insisted that acceptance of his person is pivotal to spiritual experience. The particular form of "believe" used here by Jesus indicates the beginning of an action, not its continuation. After the previous statements that the disciples had believed (1:50; 2:11; 6:69), such a construction seems inconsistent. Nevertheless the final arrest and death that they would soon witness would undoubtedly shake their faith to its foundations, and Jesus wished to prepare them for the strain this crisis would place on them.

30–31 "The prince of this world" refers to Satan. Jesus was constantly aware of Satan's hostile presence and was preparing for his last attack. Satan first afflicted Jesus at his temptation (Mt 4:1–11; Mk 1:12; Lk 4:1–13). Luke, however, indicates that there would be other times when the devil would tempt Jesus (Lk 4:13). One of those times was certainly now. The betrayal by Judas, the frustration of human hopes, the disappointment of apparent failure, the agony of death—these would make him especially susceptible to suggestion or temptation. But Jesus did not fear Satan because Satan had no claim on him. There was nothing in his character or action that could be used against him. His obedience had been perfect, and he intended to complete the Father's purpose irrespective of what it might cost him.

At this point Jesus proposed leaving the upper room. Whether chs. 15–17 were spoken en route to Gethsemane or he and the disciples lingered while he finished the discussion is not plain; but in either case the words conclude the open dialogue.

2. The discourse on relations (15:1–27)

In this section of the Farewell Discourse, Jesus dealt with three relationships that involve the disciples: (1) their relationship with him, (2) their relationship with one another, and (3) their relationship with the world around them. Jesus knew his disciples would soon constitute a distinct community with a definite function, and he wished to prepare them for the change his departure would make in their manner of living. Viewed from the standpoint of the writer and his time, this section previews the church and its development in the postresurrection period.

a. The relation of the disciples to Christ (15:1–11)

The first of these relationships is primary, for the very existence of the group depends on the union of each individual with Christ. To illustrate it, Jesus uses the analogy (or parable) of the vine and vineyard, a common feature of Palestinian life that would have been familiar to the disciples. This symbolism has its precedent in the OT (e.g., Ps 80; Isa 5:1–2, 7).

1 Using the vine metaphor, Jesus expands its scope to all believers and individualizes its application. He stresses certain features. The first is that there is a genuine stock. One must plant the right kind of vine or tree in order to assure the proper quality of fruit, for no fruit can be better than the vine that produces it. Jesus said, "I am the true vine" (see comment on 6:34–36). Unless the believer is vitally connected with him, the quality of his fruitfulness will be unacceptable. There may be many branches, but if they are to bear the right kind of fruit, they must be a part of the real vine.

The second feature is that God the Father is the gardener. Success in raising any crop depends largely on the skill of the farmer or gardener. The relation of the believer to God is that of the vine to the owner of the vineyard. He tends it, waters it, and endeavors to protect it and cultivate it so that it will produce its maximum yield.

2 A third emphasis is on pruning. Two aspects are noted: the removal of dead wood and the trimming of live wood so that its potential for fruitbearing will be improved. Pruning is necessary for any vine. Dead wood is worse than fruitlessness, for dead wood can harbor disease and decay. An untrimmed vine will develop long rambling branches that produce little fruit because most of the strength of the vine is given to growing wood. The gardener is concerned that the vine be healthy and productive. This caring process is a picture of God's dealings with humans. He removes the dead wood from his church and disciplines the lives of believers so that they are directed into fruitful activity.

3 "Clean" (GK *2754*) recalls Jesus' statement to the disciples at the footwashing (13:10), where he singled out Judas as one who was not clean. "Clean" should not be equated with "perfect" but with sincere devotion that unites others to Jesus as branches are united to the vine. Judas was an example of a branch that was cut off.

The means by which pruning or cleaning is done is the Word of God. It condemns sin; it inspires holiness; it promotes growth. As Jesus applies the words God gave him to the lives of the disciples, they undergo a pruning process that removes evil from them and conditions them for further service.

4 Continued production depends on constant union with the source of fruitfulness. Branches that are severed from the parent stock may produce leaves temporarily, but inevitably they will wither because there is no source of life to sustain them; and they will never bear fruit. The effectiveness of believers depends on their receiving the constant flow of life from Christ.

5 Fruitbearing is not only possible but certain if the branch remains in union with the vine, though uniformity of quantity and quality is not promised. But if the life of Christ permeates a disciple, fruit will be inevitable.

6 Failure to maintain a vital connection brings its own penalty—rejection and uselessness. Since the Greek text literally reads "*the* branch," there may be a reference here to Judas Iscariot (cf. 17:12). In any case, Jesus intends to show that fruitfulness is normal for believers. An absolutely fruitless life is prima facie evidence that one is not a believer. Jesus leaves no place among his followers for fruitless disciples. The only option for such people is to be thrown away and burned.

7 The connection is maintained by obedience and prayer. To remain in Christ and to allow his words to remain in oneself means a conscious acceptance of the authority of his word and a constant contact with him by prayer. The prayer request itself must be related to a definite need and must be for an object Jesus himself would desire (see comment on 14:14). Jesus never promises to gratify every chance whim believers may have. But as long as they are seeking the Lord's will for their lives, Jesus promises to grant every request that will help accomplish this end.

8 The proof of discipleship is fruitbearing (see also Mt 7:20; Lk 6:43–44). Just as Jesus glorified God by his life, so his disciples will glorify God by theirs.

9–11 Love unites the disciples to Christ as branches are united to a vine. Two results stem from this relationship: obedience and joy. Obedience marks the cause of their fruitfulness; joy is its result. Jesus intends his disciples to be both spontaneous and happy rather than burdensome and boring. Obedience in carrying out his purpose guarantees success, for Jesus never plans failure for his disciples. Joy logically follows when the disciples realize that the life of Christ in them is bringing fruit—something they could never produce in their own strength.

b The relation of the disciples to one another (15:12–17)

12–13 Jesus repeats his command to "love each other" (cf. 13:34) because he knows that the future of the disciples' work among others depends on their attitude toward one another. His stress on love had been underscored earlier in this discourse (14:15, 21, 23, 28). Unity instead of rivalry, trust instead of suspicion, and obedience instead of self-assertion must rule the disciples' common labors. The measure of their love for one another is his love for them (cf. 13:34), which would soon be demonstrated by his forthcoming sacrifice (see also 1Jn 3:16).

14–15 Again Jesus defines friendship in terms of obedience. Christian friendship is more than a casual acquaintance; it is a partnership of mutual esteem and affection (14:21). Jesus elevates the disciples above mere tools and makes them partners in his work. A slave is never given a reason for the work assigned to him; he must perform it because he has no other choice. The friend, however, is a confidant who shares the knowledge of his superior's purpose and voluntarily adopts it as his own. Jesus declares that he has revealed to the disciples all that the Father has given to him. The disclosure of the mind of God concerning his career and theirs will give them assurance that they are engaged in the right task and that God will ultimately bring it to a successful conclusion.

16–17 The disciples had not followed Jesus by some chance impulse; they had been chosen. He had invited them to interview him (1:39), he had promised to reshape them to his requirements (v.42), and he had summoned them to follow him (v.43). His miracles had clinched their original faith (2:11), and he had solicitously pleaded with them not to forsake him when many had departed from him (6:66–67). At that time he said that he had chosen them (v.70). He claimed them as his special flock (10:27) and asserted that they would never perish (v.28). He now expects that they will fulfill his purpose for them and that their work will be enduring. For this reason he urges them to maintain the relationship of love for one another that will facilitate the fulfillment of his hopes. Again he emphasizes the need of prayer for the continuation of their mission (cf. 14:26). The effectiveness of prayer is linked to fruitbearing, which, in turn, is linked to obedience (vv.10, 14). He repeats the command to love one another, for in seeking to be obedient to the Lord and to be fruitful, it is possible to forget the brothers and sisters.

c. The relation of the disciples to the world (15:18–27)

18 The term "world" (GK *3180*) has several uses in John's writings: the universe as the object of creation (1:10), the materialistic order that allures humans from God (1Jn 2:15–16), and humankind in general as the object of God's love (3:16). Here it refers to the mass of unbelievers who are indifferent or hostile to God and his people. Jesus reminds the disciples that in spite of the fact that he has come on an errand of love, the world at large hates him, a fixed attitude that carries over to his disciples as well. The world assumes this attitude because it rejects all who do not conform to its lifestyle.

19–20 Jesus' choice of the disciples has set them apart for a different kind of life and for a different purpose. Therefore, the world will exclude them. Jesus' choice is also the guarantee that the lives of his disciples will have permanent value, but it does not guarantee immunity from attack. Jesus can promise them nothing more than what he himself had received (cf. 13:16).

21–22 There are two reasons for the obstinate attitude of the world. The first is ignorance: the world does not have a proper concept of God. Consequently, it cannot evaluate adequately the messenger whom he sent (cf. Ro 1:28). This ignorance is both intellectual and spiritual. The second reason is resentment of Jesus' claims and standards. By his life and words he rebukes human sin and condemns it. He uncovers the inner corruption and hypocrisy of people, and they react violently to the disclosure. He strips away all excuses and exposes their selfishness and rebellion against God.

23 The connection between Jesus and the Father appears as strongly in this passage as it did in the argument of ch. 5. He and the Father belong in the same category; neither can be accepted or rejected without the other.

24–25 The sin of Jesus' enemies was both deliberate and inexcusable. Accredited by the miracles that he had performed and the words he had spoken, he condemns them (cf. 9:30–33, 39–41). Consequently, their reaction against him cannot be attributed to ignorance of his words or to lack of evidence substantiating them. To further explain his position, Jesus quotes from Ps 69:4. The irony of this quotation is clear: those who posed as the champions of the Law were fulfilling the prophecy concerning the enemies of God's servant.

26–27 In response to this attitude of hatred, there must be a continuing witness to the love and grace of Christ. The last two verses of this chapter define the expected action of the disciples, who will maintain the testimony of Jesus after he has left the earth. He now completes the list of witnesses of 5:31–40 by adding the witness of the Holy Spirit, whose ministry he had already partially described (14:16–17, 26), and also the witness of the disciples themselves. They must "testify" concerning Christ.

"From the beginning" probably refers to the beginning of Jesus' public ministry. Later, when the disciples felt that it was necessary to choose a successor for Judas Iscariot, one requirement was that of having belonged to the company of disciples during his entire ministry (Ac 1:21–22). In order to witness to Jesus and his message, one must have complete experiential knowledge of his person. The coupling of the witness of the Spirit with that of the disciples defines their reciprocal relationship. Without the testify of the Spirit, the disciples' witness will be powerless; without the disciples' witness, the Spirit will be restricted in his means of expression.

3. The discourse on revelation (16:1–33)

a. The revelation of rejection (16:1–4)

1–2 In ch. 16, Jesus reveals to his disciples what they must know to prepare them for their coming mission. He links it with the preceding section of his final discourse by sharpening the warning he has already given them concerning the hatred of the world. He applies this revelation particularly to their local conditions and predicts that they will suffer excommunication from the synagogue and even death (cf. the blind man in 9:22, 34; Lazarus in 12:10). While Jesus was with the disciples, he could shelter and direct them. They must realize, however, that even his resurrection will not be sufficient to convince his enemies to remove the hatred that exists between them and Jesus' followers.

3 Jesus attributes the action of his foes to ignorance—not the ignorance of intellectual knowledge, but the lack of a personal experience of God and Christ (see comment on 15:21–22). Their attitude is determined by who they think Jesus is and by who they think God is, rather than by actual contact with either. So warped has that attitude become that their contact with Jesus has generated hate for both himself and the Father (15:24; cf. Mt 6:23).

4 It may well be that this particular utterance of Jesus was reported by John because of the pressing need for courage in the church of his day. The Apocalypse indicates a wide break between the church and the synagogue at the end of the first century (Rev 2:9; 3:9); those who professed faith in Jesus were completely disowned by their Jewish compatriots.

b. The revelation of the Holy Spirit (16:5–15)

The time has come for a new revelation. Previously Jesus had been with the disciples to counsel them and answer their questions. Now, in view of his imminent removal, they need someone to take his place. Thus he reveals to them the coming of the Holy Spirit, whom he has already mentioned in the general discourse (14:16–17, 26; 15:26).

5–6 The statement "none of you asks me, 'Where are you going?'" seems incongruous in the context of Peter's question in the earlier part of the discourse (13:36). At that point Peter's question was casual, and neither he nor the other disciples pressed the issue to ascertain what Jesus' plans really were. The same thing is true here. There is little concern about Jesus' future; they are interested mainly in their own future. They are sorrowful because they will lose him, so they make no inquiry about the reasons for his departure nor about the objectives he might wish to attain.

7 Jesus tells the disciples that his separation from them is in their best interest. As long as he is with them in person, his work is localized; once he leaves, it will be impossible to communicate with them equally at all times and in all places. The coming of the "Counselor" (see comment on 14:16–17), therefore, will equip them for a wider and more potent ministry.

8–9 Three major aspects of the ministry of the Holy Spirit are described in vv.8–15: (1) to the world—conviction of sin, righteousness, and judgment (vv.8–11); (2) to the disciples—direction and truth (vv.12–13); (3) to Jesus—revealing him more perfectly to and through those who represent him (vv.14–15).

(1) The key to this first aspect is the word "convict" (GK 1794). The word is a legal term that means to pronounce a judicial verdict by which the guilt of the culprit is defined and fixed. The Spirit not only accuses people of sin, he brings to them an inescapable sense of guilt so that they realize their shame and helplessness before God. This conviction applies to three particular areas: (a) sin, (b) righteousness, and (c) judgment.

(a) The Spirit is the prosecuting attorney who presents God's case against humanity. He creates an inescapable awareness of sin so that it cannot be dismissed with an excuse or evaded by taking refuge in the fact that "everybody is doing it." The Spirit's function is like that of Nathan the prophet, who said to David, "You are the man" (2Sa 12:7), and convicted him of his misdeeds. David acknowledged his sin in a state of complete penitence (2Sa 12:15; Ps 51:4).

The essence of sin is unbelief (v.9), which is not simply a difference of opinion; rather, it is a total rejection of God's messenger and message. A court can convict a person of murder, but only the Spirit can convict him or her of unbelief. Jesus insists that sin is fundamentally repudiation of his message and his mission.

10 (b) The second area in which the Spirit convicts people is "righteousness" (GK *1466*). He enforces the absolute standard of God's character, to which all thought and action must be compared. Apart from a standard of righteousness, there can be no sin; and there must be an awareness of the holiness of God before a person will realize his or her own deficiency—an infinite gap that humans cannot bridge. The first step toward salvation is the awareness that a divine mediatorship is necessary.

The connection between righteousness and Jesus' return to the Father is not immediately clear. It should probably be interpreted as meaning that his return to the right hand of God was a complete vindication of all he had done and consequently established him as the standard for all human righteousness. Apostolic preaching conveyed this concept (see Ac 3:14–15). Whereas righteousness had previously been defined by precepts, it now has been revealed in the incarnate Son, who exemplified it perfectly in all his relationships (cf. 1Jn 3:5).

11 (c) Judgment always occurs when an act or thought is evaluated by an absolute principle. When human sin is confronted by the righteousness of Christ, its condemnation is self-evident. In this context "judgment" (GK *3213*) refers to the condemnation of satanic self-will and rebellion through the obedience and love exhibited by Jesus toward the Father. The Cross utterly condemned and defeated the "prince of this world." Satan is already under judgment; the sentence is fixed and permanent. (For discussion of "the prince of this world," see comments on 14:30.)

12–13 (2) Jesus tells his disciples directly that his revelation to date is incomplete. They are not sufficiently mature to understand all he wishes to impart. A second function of the Holy Spirit, therefore, will be to "lead" (GK *3842*) them into the full comprehension of all he wants them to know. The Spirit will not present an independent message, differing from what they had already learned from him. Rather, they will be led further into the realization of his person and into the development of the principles he has already laid down. They will also be enlightened about coming events. In this promise lies the germinal authority of the apostolic writings, which transmit the revelation of Christ through his disciples by the work of the Holy Spirit.

14–15 (3) The third function of the Spirit is to "glorify"(GK *1519*) Christ. His chief purpose is not to make himself prominent but to magnify the person of Jesus. The Spirit interprets and applies the character and teaching of Jesus to the disciples and by so doing makes him central to their thinking and real in their lives.

c. The revelation of Jesus' reappearance (16:16–24)

16 Jesus' remark in this verse was obscure to his disciples and is still enigmatic to us. His prediction of disappearance refers to his death, but to what does the second appearance refer? It cannot refer to his coming in the person of the Holy Spirit because he has emphasized the distinction between himself and the Spirit and between their respective ministries. The disciples are confused by his language, both by the concept of his going to the Father and by the time element involved. The best solution seems to be that he was referring to the Resurrection, which would take place "a little while" after he had left them.

17–18 The two problems that vex the disciples are the prediction of disappearance and then reappearance after a short interval, and the concept of "going to the Father" (for the second one, see 14:28). The disciples have not yet established the mental perspective Jesus wishes them to have and are thinking only in terms of the present situation. They therefore hold a consultation among themselves about it; the discourse, in other words, does not proceed as an uninterrupted lecture. Apparently it is a casual conversation with periods of silence on Jesus' part.

19–22 The subsequent narrative develops the postresurrection period as a time in which the disciples' fears are quelled, their doubts dispelled, and their commission confirmed. Jesus compares their coming parting to the painful birth of a child, which, when fully accomplished, brings joy. The disciples are disappointed because the kingdom has not come; and they are distressed because of the calamity that is about to overtake Jesus. The "world" will rejoice that he has been removed and will pride itself in a victory, but the disciples will mourn the untimely loss of their leader. In Jesus' resurrection, however, the conditions will be reversed, and their lamentations will be transformed into joy because he will return to them.

23–24 The verb "ask" (GK *2263*) in the phrase "in that day you will no longer ask me anything" means "to ask a question" rather than "to request a favor." Jesus seems to mean that at his reappearance after the Resurrection the truth of his claims and the status of his person will be self-evident. At that time the disciples will no longer question him as one of their number but will present their petitions to the Father in his name (cf. 14:13) and will be eligible for the Father's response to their needs.

d. The revelation of the Father (16:25–33)

25 Jesus had used figurative or parabolic language to the disciples because of their spiritual immaturity. After the Resurrection, however, he will be at liberty to speak plainly about the Father. Little is said in the Gospels concerning the instruction Jesus imparted to the disciples during the forty days between his resurrection and his ascension. However, it is probable that during this period he gave them much of the teaching that was reflected in their later preaching and writing (see Ac 1:3).

26–27 It will be unnecessary for Jesus to make requests on their behalf, for they will be able to present their own petitions. The phrase "in my name [GK *3950*]" recurs frequently in this farewell discourse (14:13–14, 26; 16:23–24, 26) and indicates Jesus' sponsorship of the disciples. Their standing with God will depend on his merits. Because of his work and their relationship to him by faith, they will be able to approach the Father directly with their petitions.

28–30 Jesus' declaration that he has come from the Father and is about to return to the Father satisfies their inquiry. They feel that he is no longer talking in riddles. Their response to Jesus' straightforward declaration is a further confession of faith. Their questions have been occasioned by their bewilderment over his figurative language. The direct statement he has just made clarifies their understanding and eliminates the need for further questioning. In the light of that understanding they reaffirm their belief that he has come from God.

31–32 Jesus is skeptical of the firmness of the disciples' avowed belief, for he knows about their impending failure (already expressed about Simon Peter in 13:37; cf. Mt 26:33–35; Mk 14:29–31; Lk 22:33–34). "You will leave me all alone" reveals Jesus' disappointment and emotional tension. The sympathy and support of these men, imperfect as they are, means much to him. Nevertheless, his chief resource is the Father, whose purpose he has come to fulfill and by whose power he is able to execute it.

33 Jesus imparts to his disciples the information concerning his death and his provision for them that they might be calm and confident in the face of disillusionment and apparent disaster. "Peace" (GK *1645*) reiterates his statement in 14:27. Even in the hour of his greatest suffering he has an unshakable confidence in the victorious purpose of God. Jesus does not overlook the trial that will affect them as well as himself, for that is inevitable in a world alienated from God. He does, however, proclaim victory over it.

C. The Last Prayer (17:1–26)

The prayer of Jesus recorded in this chapter is not identical with the prayer in Gethsemane reported in the Synoptic Gospels (Mt 26:36–45; Mk 14:32–41; Lk 22:39–46). Its content is closely linked to that of the preceding chapters in John, especially those spoken in the upper room. The vocabulary, containing such familiar terms in John as "glory," "glorify," "sent," "believe," "world," and "love," connects its content with the same topics in preceding sections. And Jesus' concern for his disciples makes more lucid his attitude toward them on previous occasions. The prayer is intended to summarize in Jesus' own words his relationship with the Father and the relationship he wishes his disciples to maintain with him and the Father.

The prayer can be divided into three parts: (1) Jesus' prayer concerning himself (vv.1–5), (2) his prayer for the disciples (vv.6–19), and (3) his prayer for all believers present and future (vv.20–26). The prayer was spoken either just before the small company left the room where they had eaten together or as they were making their way out of the city to Gethsemane (see comment on 14:31).

1. The prayer concerning himself (17:1–5)

1 John records even the gesture of Jesus: "He lifted up his eyes" (lit. tr.). This was a typical Jewish gesture of prayer, whether offered to God or to idols (Ps 121:1; 123:1; Eze 33:25; Da 4:34; Jn 11:41). The prayer begins with the announcement "The time has come." Jesus' consciousness of living by a "calendar" has been manifest from the beginning of the gospel (see 2:4; 7:8; 7:30; 8:20); but now he acknowledges that the time of crisis has arrived (cf. 12:23; 13:1). This announcement enhances the significance of the prayer because it becomes Jesus' evaluation of the purpose of his life, death, resurrection, and ascension.

Jesus petitions the Father to glorify him. The word "glorify" (GK *1519*) should be applied to the total complex of these events as the climax of the Incarnation. The Son glorified the Father by revealing God's sovereignty over evil, his compassion for humans, and the finality of redemption for believers. His entire career was focused on fulfilling the Father's purpose and on delivering the Father's message (see also v.5).

2–3 The two sentences following the initial petition are parenthetical and explanatory. The first (v.2) indicates the scope of the authority Christ exercised in his incarnate state. He was empowered to impart eternal life to those who had been given to him. This gospel is replete with assertions that life is in Christ (see 1:4; 3:15–16; 4:14; 5:21, 26; 6:33, 54; 10:10; 11:25; 14:6). These words emphatically express the central purpose of Jesus: to glorify the Father by imparting life to humans.

The second sentence (v.3) defines the nature of eternal life. It is not described in chronological terms but by a relationship. Life is active involvement with environment. The highest kind of life is involvement with the highest kind of environment. A worm is content to live in soil; we need not only the wider environment of earth, sea, and sky but also contact with other human beings. For the complete fulfillment of our being, we must know God. This, said Jesus, constitutes eternal life. Not only is it endless, since the knowledge of God requires an eternity to develop fully, but qualitatively it must exist in an eternal dimension. As Jesus said further on in this prayer, eternal life will ultimately bring his disciples to a lasting association with him in his divine glory (v.24).

4–5 Although the final act of his career remains to be performed, Jesus asserts that he has completed his task. He takes for granted that the last step will be taken (cf. 12:27–28). Though aware that he has the option of refusing the Cross and so escaping death, he has resolved irrevocably to complete the work for which he has been sent. To all intents and purposes it is already done. In spite of many obstacles, Jesus never once faltered from doing the Father's will. He now has one main petition: that the Father will receive him back to the glory he relinquished to accomplish his task (see 1:18). This petition for a return to his pristine glory implies unmistakably his preexistence and equality with the Father, confirming 10:30.

2. The prayer concerning the disciples (17:6–19)

By far the largest part of Jesus' prayer relates to the disciples. He is much more concerned about them than about himself. He is sure of his own victory. The disciples, however, are a variable quantity; in themselves they are likely to fail, as he has already predicted (Mt 26:31; Jn 16:32). Nevertheless, he prays for them with confidence that they will be kept by the Father's power and presented for a future ministry. Jesus gives the reasons for his confidence in the next three verses.

6–8 The disciples have been given to Jesus by the Father. The gift was irrevocable and the Father was able to guarantee it. Jesus has no doubt of the final outcome. The disciples were obedient; they have accepted the message Jesus gave them. In spite of much misunderstanding on their part, those who were with Jesus in the upper room did not reject or doubt the truth he imparted to them, though they may not have comprehended it instantly (see 2:22; 20:9). They recognize that Jesus' message comes from God, and they accept him as a messenger of God (cf. 16:30). From the outset of his ministry, the disciples have received him as the Messiah, and their conviction of his messiahship has grown progressively during the period of association with him. Now as the supreme test of their faith is impending, Jesus prays that they might be preserved against the persecution that can separate them from him and from one another.

9 At this point, Jesus' intercession is confined to the Eleven who are present with him. He reminds the Father that these men are under his special care. As in his prayer at Lazarus's grave, Jesus takes for granted the concern of the Father for the immediate need and the provision he has already made in order to meet it.

10 This verse assumes Jesus' equality with the Father. Each has full title to the possessions of the other; they share the same interests and responsibilities. Jesus' words are a sample of the continued intercession that constitutes his present ministry (Ro 8:34).

11 Jesus asks for the continuation of the Father's protection of the disciples in the period of danger that lay ahead of them. The title "Holy Father" (like "Righteous Father" in v.25) is unique and occurs only in this prayer. The holiness of God contrasts with the selfishness and evil of the world that confronts the disciples. On the basis of the holiness of God's character, Jesus requests the Father to preserve his disciples. The verb "protect" (GK 5498) here has the sense of "preserve," with an implication of defense. "Name" (GK 3950) stands for the power of God manifested in his person (cf. 5:43; 10:25; 12:28; 17:6, 26), for a name represents authoritatively the person it describes.

The unity mentioned here is not simply a unity achieved by legislation. It is a unity of nature because it is comparable to that of the Son and the Father. The unity of the church must spring from the common life that is imparted to all believers by the new birth; and it is manifested in their common love for Christ and for one another as they face a hostile world. The unity of the Son and the Father is manifested in the deep love that each sustains for the other and by the perfect obedience of the Son to the Father and the perfect response of the Father to the Son.

12 Jesus' request for the protection of the disciples is occasioned by the prospect of his leaving the world. They will still remain in it, exposed to its temptations and hostility. In reviewing his care of them to date, he uses two different words: "protected" (see comment in v.11) and "kept them safe" (i.e., "guarded them against external attack"). Jesus has kept safely all the disciples except Judas, "the one doomed to destruction" (a phrase applied to the Antichrist in 2Th 2:3). This Semitic phrase denotes an abandoned character, one utterly lost and given over to evil. The language does not imply that Judas was a helpless victim who was destined to perdition against his will. Rather, it implies that, having made his decision, he had passed the point of no return; and, by so doing, he carried out what the Scriptures had indicated would happen (perhaps Ps 69:25; 109:6–8).

13 Jesus prays not only for the safety of the disciples but also that they may have joy in spite of the coming conflict (cf. 15:11; 16:22, 24). There will be nothing in the attitude of the world to promote their joy; but, as with Jesus, their awareness of the Father's approval and the consciousness of a task accomplished and the expectancy of glory will create true joy for them.

14 The very fact that the disciples received the message of God from Jesus differentiates them from the world at large. They have a different nature and a different affiliation. Such a radical contrast draws the hatred of the world, which always demands conformity to its viewpoint and practices. Having taken their stand with Jesus, they will be susceptible to the same rejection he experienced.

15–16 Jesus does not, however, ask that they be removed from a disagreeable and dangerous environment. Like him, they have a mission to discharge and must remain to fulfill it, however perilous it might be; but he does ask for protection for them from the evil one. The declaration that "they are not of the world" gives the negative aspect of the previous prayer that they may be one as Jesus and the Father are one. The disciples' unity binds them to Christ and at the same time separates them from the world. John stresses the separation that results from difference of nature (cf. 1Jn 2:19). The separation is inherent, not artificial.

17 "Sanctify" (GK 39) means "to set apart," usually for some specially good purpose or use; its derivative meaning thus becomes "dedicate" or "consecrate." Believers are so changed by the working of God's Word in their lives that they are separated from evil and to God. This new devotion, which results in separation from evil, produces purification of life and consecration to God's service. Since the Word of God is truth, it provides the unchanging standard for the course and character of life. The form of the expression "your word" raises the possibility that Jesus may be referring to himself. He has said that he is "the truth" (14:6); as the Logos of God he embodies truth in its totality.

18 "Sent" (GK 690, related to the word "apostle") implies equipment for a definite mission. Jesus unites the disciples with himself in the work he began and expects them to continue. Just as the Father has sent him with authority, so he gives them authority (cf. Mt 28:18–20); as he has come with a message of God's love and forgiveness, so they must proclaim the same; as he has come into danger and peril of death, so they will encounter the same problems; and as the Father has sent him to the victory of the Resurrection, so they can expect the same. His words include warning, commission, and encouragement.

19 In keeping with his words in v.17, Jesus does not intend to make himself more holy than he already is. Rather, he is devoting himself to God in the interest of his work for the disciples. His example of dedication to the will of the Father, demonstrated in his unswerving acceptance of the Cross, will be the standard for their sanctification.

The petitions of Jesus' prayer for the disciples define certain aspects of eternal life. The first is the authentic revelation of the Father in contrast to erroneous information or delusive myth. Jesus reinforces his claim to be the authorized revealer of the true God (v.6; cf. 1:18; 14:9–11). As his revelation was accepted, the disciples progressed to a knowledge of the Father and to a solid faith (v.8; cf. 16:25). This faith united them with Jesus so that they came under his protection and now experience security that eternal life imparts (v.12; cf. 10:29–29). Eternal life also implies sanctification—being set apart for the service of God.

3. The prayer concerning future believers (17:20–26)

20 The last section of Jesus' prayer shows that he expects the failure of the disciples to be only temporary. The entire tone of the farewell discourse is built on the assumption that after the Resurrection they will renew their faith and carry on a new ministry in the power of the Holy Spirit. The provisions and warnings in chs. 13–16 presuppose the continuation of Jesus' work through these men (cf. Mt 16:18). He expects the ministry of the Spirit in the disciples to result in adding more believers to their number. So his prayer includes all believers in all ages.

21 At this point, the burden of the prayer is for unity (cf. "one"; GK 1651). Jesus has already stressed the need for mutual love that will bind them together for their common task. Now, foreseeing the addition of many more who will increase the diversity of temperaments, backgrounds, and interests, he makes a special plea that all may be one. The standard is not an institutional but a personal unity.

Nor is he calling for uniformity, since he and the Father are distinct from each other and have different functions. He predicates that the unity will be one of nature; for he and the Father, while distinguishable in person, are one being. The new birth brings believers into the single family of God by spiritual generation (1:12–13; cf. 15:1–7; 1Co 12:12–13). The purpose of this unity is the maintenance of a convincing testimony before the world to the revelation of God in Christ and to his love for the disciples. Through the common witness and experience of the disciples, Jesus wishes to establish the fact of his divine origin and of the love of God for humankind.

22–23 The "glory" (GK 1518) the Father has given Jesus is the triumphant task of redeeming the human race to God (cf. Heb 2:9–10). By sharing in his calling, they participate in his glory and are united with him and with one another. God and humankind are together involved in bringing the new creation into being. The effect of this united testimony is a confirmation of the divine mission of Jesus and of God's love for believers.

24 The final aspect of eternal life relates to ultimate destiny. The final attainment is to be with Christ (cf. 14:3) and to observe his glory. The disciples have witnessed his incarnate life, which was a humiliation, voluntarily accepted for their sakes. Its process was epitomized by Jesus' action at the Last Supper, when he took the place of a servant to wash the disciples' feet (13:1–15). Now, on the eve of being "glorified," he desires the disciples to see him as he really is (see also 1Jn 3:2). "Before the creation of the world" is a further assertion of Christ's preexistence. This shows that the binding power of unity in the Triune God is love.

25–26 The entire prayer is based on the righteousness of God (see comment on v.11), who will vindicate the Son by glorifying him. Jesus' revelation of God is founded on personal knowledge and personal communion. The essence of the revelation lies in the love of God, which Jesus exhibits toward the disciples. His purpose is to perfect his union with them, that they in turn may know the Father. Jesus wants to include them in the inner fellowship of the Triune God.

IV. The Passion of the Word (18:1–20:31)

A. *The Arrest in Gethsemane (18:1–11)*

1–2 Jesus and the disciples left the room where they had convened, descended from the city, crossed the Kidron Valley, and made their way up the lower slope of the Mount of Olives, to the Garden of Gethsemane (the name assigned to the olive grove on the side of the mountain, meaning "oil press"). Jesus often used this place to meet with his disciples (cf. Lk 22:39). The city was filled with visitors at the Passover season and would have had little room for lodging within its walls. Neither Jesus nor the disciples were wealthy; so they probably camped outdoors during their visit to the temple for the Passover Week. Judas, probably having attempted to find Jesus at the house where he and the others ate the Last Supper, went to Gethsemane, expecting to locate him there.

3 The Greek word for "detachment of soldiers" technically denotes a tenth of a legion, or about six hundred men—probably the detachment of soldiers connected with the Castle of Antonia, the Roman barracks in Jerusalem (see also Mt 26:47; Mk 14:43; Lk 22:52). Possibly the hysterical alarm of the priests caused them to ask aid from Pilate in arresting Jesus, since the temple police had failed on a previous occasion (Jn 7:32, 45–47). The torches and the lanterns were needed, since the arrest took place at night and required a search in the darkness of the olive grove.

4–6 The author has emphasized Jesus' consciousness of surrounding circumstances and his own destiny (cf. Jn 6:64; 13: 1, 3, 11, 18). He was not taken unwillingly or by surprise. For a long time he had been aware of the plot against his life and, had he wished, he could have escaped (cf. 10:40; 11:54). Now "the time" had come (cf. 17:1). He did not wait to be apprehended but voluntarily confronted his enemies.

In the darkness of the garden they were not sure which man they wanted. So in answer to his question they replied, "Jesus of Nazareth." John omits the signal of Judas and mentions only Jesus' own statement for the identification. That reply startled the arresting party by its openness and readiness and possibly because it was like the claim he had made previously: "I am" (8:24, 28, 58). If it were intended as an assertion of deity, his calm demeanor and commanding presence temporarily unnerved his captors.

7–9 Jesus' chief intent seems not to have been to advance a claim but to shield the disciples. In a sense, he sacrificed himself for their safety. He had promised the Father that he would protect them (17:12), and he fulfilled his guarantee in the voluntary surrender of his life. The utterance in v.8 is a graphic illustration of the principle of substitutionary atonement that pervades this gospel (cf. 1:29; 3:14–16; 10:11, 15–18; 12:32; 17:19).

10 The action of Peter illustrates the curious combination of loyalty and obtuseness that characterized him. Realizing that Jesus was endangered, Peter was courageous enough to come to his defense and risk his own safety. To this extent he justified his boastful promise that if all others should forsake Jesus, he would not (13:37; cf. Mk 14:29–31). In his excitement, Peter began swinging his sword, cutting off the right ear of Malchus, probably the special deputy of the high priest. The recollection of this particular man's name suggests that this account in John rests on an eyewitness testimony.

11 Jesus' command to Peter declared his disapproval of Peter's sudden and violent intervention. Had Jesus desired defense, he could have summoned angelic aid (cf. Mt 26:52–53). "Shall I not drink the cup the Father has given me?" expresses both the necessity of his suffering and his absolute commitment to fulfilling his Father's purpose. The word "cup" connects this statement with the prayer in Gethsemane, which the other three gospels record (Mt 26:42; Mk 14:36; Lk 22:42). Though the writer must have known of Jesus' struggle, he recorded only the outcome. Jesus accepted the Father's will and calmly moved on to its fulfillment.

B. The Hearing Before Annas (18:12–14, 19–24)

12–14 With the willing surrender of Jesus, the arrest was complete. The "commander" was the officer in charge, possibly the executive of the Roman garrison in Jerusalem (cf. the use of the same term in Ac 22:24–28; 23:17, 19, 22). Jesus was taken at once to the residence of the high priest. Annas had served as high priest from A.D. 6 to 15, when he was deposed by the Roman procurator, Valerius Gratus. Four of Annas's sons were among those who succeeded him. His son-in-law, Caiaphas, held office from A.D. 18 until 36, during the time of Jesus' active ministry. Although others held the priestly office, Annas seems to have been the elder statesman and "the power behind the throne," particularly for Caiaphas. He was regarded with great respect by his contemporaries and must have been considered an expert in religious matters.

John's gospel alone takes note of Christ's appearance before Annas, which was probably a preliminary hearing to evaluate the case, prior to the main hearing that followed in the early hours of the morning before the members of the Jewish tribunal.

19–21 The questioning focused on Jesus' disciples and his teaching. The number and activity of the former would be important if the authorities suspected subversion, and the teaching would be scrutinized for possible revolutionary elements. This interrogation by Annas was unnecessary because Jesus had nothing to hide. He had so frequently and openly declared the principles of his kingdom that there would be many witnesses who could narrate in detail what he had taught.

22–24 Jesus' answer impressed one of the captors as disrespectful to the high priest, and he struck Jesus in the face. The act was illegal. No sentence had been passed, and a prisoner was not subject to abuse, especially when uncondemned. In spite of Jesus' protest, nothing was done; and he was sent bound to Caiaphas (possibly to another room in the same building). John writes nothing about the hearing before Caiaphas (see Mt 26:57–68; Mk 14:53–65; Lk 22:66–71).

C. The Denial by Peter (18:15–18, 25–27)

15–16 Peter and an unnamed disciple (possibly John, cf. 13:23–24; 20:2–3) had traced Jesus and his captors back from Gethsemane over the Kidron Valley to the residence of the high priest in Jerusalem. This anonymous disciple was known to the household of the high priest and readily obtained access for himself and Peter; there is evidence that John may have been distantly related to that family. Peter was in the "courtyard," standing with servants and retainers by a fire (v.18).

17 Apparently Peter's first statement of denial accompanied his admittance to the courtyard; the last occurred somewhat later, perhaps just as Jesus was about to be taken to the council chamber. While there are minor differences in all four accounts of the denial (see Mt 26:69–75; Mk 14:66–72; Lk 22:55–62), in general they agree. The first denial was a reply to a question asked by the girl who tended the gate and granted access to Peter and the other disciple. She recognized both the unnamed disciple and Peter as followers of Jesus.

18 Jerusalem is 2,600 feet above sea level, and on a spring night the air is chilly. The servants had lighted a charcoal fire, which would warm only those near it and would not give off a great deal of light. Peter must have edged toward it, hoping to absorb some warmth, yet not wishing to make himself visible. He certainly did not want to be recognized again!

25 The focus of attention on Peter is interrupted by the author's reversion to the interrogation of Jesus by the high priest (vv.19–24). Then Peter was asked a second time about his association with Jesus. Like the first question, this one called for a negative answer. Peter's answer drew him into a position he could not escape from, causing him to make an emphatic denial: "I am not."

26–27 The third question was raised by a relative of Malchus and was worded in such a way as to expect an affirmative answer. He was sure that he had seen Peter in the olive grove. As the questioning proceeded from suspicion to reasonable certainty, Peter became more nervous. With increasing vehemence he disavowed any connection with Jesus, and on this third occasion the rooster crowed (cf. 13:38). The author adds no further comment at this point, but the fact that he records the denial implies that it was a turning point in Peter's experience. It was a revelation of his own weakness that he could not escape. Peter's final response, however, was the opposite of Judas: Judas in his failure fell into despair; Peter returned to Christ.

D. The Trial Before Pilate (18:28–19:16)

This account of Jesus' trial before Pilate is the longest in the four gospels. Whereas the other three accounts deal largely with the legal charges, John's narrative places more importance on Jesus' concern with Pilate and on Pilate's shifting attitude. Its psychological portrait of Pilate is comparable to that of the Samaritan woman at the well of Sychar (ch. 4) or that of the blind man (ch. 9). The Johannine presentation makes it more of an interview than a trial.

28 John does not describe the early morning session of the council, with Caiaphas as presiding officer (see Mk 14:53–65 and comments). There Jesus was condemned to death; but because the high priest had no authority to execute a death sentence, it was necessary to transfer the case to the Roman prefect, Pontius Pilate, who was in Jerusalem during Passover Week in order to keep close control of the city. Jesus was moved to Pilate's residence about seven or eight o'clock. The Jewish delegation did not enter into the courtroom because entering a Gentile home or business room entailed seven days' defilement. Inasmuch as the Passover was imminent, they did not wish to be excluded from the feast for ceremonial uncleanness.

29–30 Pilate's initial question was the normal opening inquiry for a trial under Roman law: "What charges are you bringing against this man?" He would not automatically pronounce a sentence without knowing the alleged crime. The answer was elusive. The high priest no doubt knew that Jesus was not guilty of any crime under Roman law.

31 Pilate took much the same position Gallio later did at Paul's arrest in Corinth (Ac 18:12–16). An argument about the ceremonial requirements of Jewish law had no standing in a Roman court, and Pilate was ready to dismiss the case. The Jews' admission that they could not execute the prisoner was a confession of their intention. Pilate was shrewd enough to realize that their motive was not a sincere desire to remove a dangerous revolutionary (see Mt 27:18).

32 The introduction of Roman action at this point ensured death by crucifixion, if the Jews could persuade Pilate to render a verdict against Jesus. Jewish capital punishment was inflicted by stoning; but a Roman crucifixion would place Jesus under the curse of God (Dt 21:22–23; cf. Gal 3:13). His messianic claims would be discredited, and the rejection would be justified. The manner of death is explicitly connected with Jesus' own prophecy (Jn 3:14; 12:32–33). Ironically, the death that the Jewish hierarchy regarded as a final negation of Jesus' claims became the means of justification apart from the law (Gal 3:13).

33 Puzzled by the Jewish attitude, Pilate withdrew to the audience chamber within the building and summoned Jesus. His question to Jesus was emphatic: "Are *you* the king of the Jews?" (italics mine), as if he were asking for a straightforward answer because he did not trust the priests. Pilate may also have been expressing his surprise that Jesus did not look like a pretender to the vacant throne of Judaism. He had expected to meet a sullen or belligerent rebel and met instead the calm majesty of confident superiority. He could not reconcile the character of the prisoner with the charge brought against him.

34 Since he had shown sufficient interest in Jesus to confer with him personally, Jesus began to probe him to ascertain how sincere that interest might be. Was Pilate asking for information on his own initiative, or was he merely following a legal procedure at the instigation of the Jewish hierarchy?

35 Jesus' reply to Pilate's question irritated him, for he was accustomed to receiving answers to his questions, not challenges. His question expected a negative answer: "I am not a Jew, am I?" He insisted that he was merely endeavoring to find the key to the puzzling case the Jewish leaders had brought before him. He had not originated the accusation, but he wanted to know what Jesus had done to arouse their hatred.

36 Jesus asserted that his "kingdom" (GK 993) was not of this world because he had no military support and did not relate to any geographic locality. He did not, however, deny that "king" (GK 995) could be his proper title. He affirmed that his kingdom had a different origin and a different character from any that Pilate knew. Had he been an ordinary revolutionary, he would have offered armed resistance to those who took him captive.

37 Jesus' answer bewildered Pilate. Without attempting to argue about an abstraction that must have seemed irrational to him, Pilate came back to the central question: "So you are a king, then, aren't you?" (my translation). Jesus assented by confirming Pilate's conclusion. Then he declared that his purpose was to bear testimony to truth, and he intimated that anyone who was devoted to truth would listen to him. The obvious inference from his words was that he came into the world from another realm, that whoever did not listen to him would not be characterized by truth, and that if Pilate really wanted to know what truth was, he would give Jesus his earnest attention. As in Jesus' other interviews in this gospel, his focus was not on himself but on reaching the heart of the person he addressed. He appealed to Pilate, not for acquittal or mercy, but for recognition of truth.

The combined statement, "For this reason I was born, and for this I came into the world," can be linked with ch. 1 and reinforces Jesus' statement elsewhere in this gospel that he was fully aware of both his origin and destiny (cf. 8:14).

38 Pilate's reply, "What is truth?" is difficult to interpret. Was it facetious, scornful, impatient, despairing, or sincere? Even from the context it is not possible to be sure what he meant. Pilate's immediate response was to declare Jesus innocent of any crime that would have made him liable to punishment. He may have regarded him as a harmless philosopher or as an impractical dreamer. Certainly he did not look on Jesus as a dangerous subversive.

39 Aware, however, that there were political overtones in the situation that called for some sort of action, Pilate groped for a solution that would be satisfactory to all concerned. Although no other record of it can be found, there must have been the custom of releasing one prisoner at every Passover as a means of placating the Jewish population. Pilate seized on the opportunity to appeal to the masses and suggested that he would release Jesus if they demanded it. His proposal assumed that Jesus was popular with the general crowd, who did not always favor the hierarchy. Pilate may also have been indulging in finely honed sarcasm when he referred to Jesus as "the king of the Jews." If Jesus were not released, the people would be guilty of the death of the one they called their king.

40 Pilate miscalculated the attitude of the crowd at this point. They had been instructed by the priests to ask for the death of Jesus; so instead of his release, they demanded that of a brigand named Barabbas (a guerrilla "resistance fighter" who was being held for execution). In the eyes of the people, he was considered a champion of a free Israel and possibly something of a hero.

19:1 The flogging of Jesus (see comment on Mk 15:15) was the usual accompaniment of crucifixion. Evidently Pilate intended to make an appeal to the sympathy of the mob, hoping that by scourging Jesus, they would call for his release.

2–3 The legionnaires who had administered the scourging amused themselves by a crude joke. Knowing that Jesus was called "king of the Jews," they threw a scarlet cloak about his shoulders, twisted a crown from a thorny vine that grew in the vicinity, and mocked him with the salutation "Hail, king of the Jews!" as they slapped his face.

4–5 As the soldiers brought him out to the view of the crowd, Pilate, having once more declared Jesus' innocence, said, "Here is the man!" Pilate may have thought that the ironic spectacle of a king whose crown was thorns, whose robe a cast-off cloak, and whose status a prisoner would change their attitude. If so, he was speedily disillusioned.

6–7 The Jewish officials demanded crucifixion for no good reason that Pilate could determine. In disgust he told them to crucify him themselves, for no charge could be brought against him. Pilate obviously realized that the Sanhedrin could not execute the sentence; his apparent relegation of Jesus to them was an act of sarcasm. The Jews knew this and made a new approach to Pilate, claiming that by their law Jesus was worthy of death for blasphemy (cf. Lev 24:16), because he claimed to be the Son of God (see comments on 10:34–38).

8–9 To the Jews, Jesus' claim was the height of sacrilege. For Pilate, however, it had a different meaning. In pagan mythology the Olympian deities frequently consorted with men and women, and their semi-divine offspring, such as Hercules, had appeared on the earth and performed miraculous deeds. Hardened as he was, Pilate feared lest he should offend one of these visitors. Thus he questioned Jesus further, in an attempt to ascertain who Jesus was. If he really was a supernatural being, Pilate did not wish to be responsible for mistreating him, for that would make him liable to divine judgment. The silence of Jesus, like his silence in the presence of Herod (Lk 23:6–11), meant that he could accomplish nothing with a trifler. Pilate had already pronounced Jesus innocent; so the case resolved itself to the alternative of release or a gross perversion of justice.

10 Jesus' refusal to answer him angered Pilate, whose conceit and arrogance were shown by his question: "Don't you realize I have power either to free you or to crucify you?" He was insulted because Jesus had not shown him more deference. Pilate's assertion of authority seems almost ridiculous in contrast with the weakness and indecision he exhibited in this case. Jesus, who could view the situation in its true light, knew that though Pilate had the legal authority of which he boasted, he was really hampered by political pressures.

11 Jesus looked on Pilate as simply an instrument in God's purpose. The real guilt lay with those who had delivered Jesus to Pilate in the first place (i.e., Caiaphas and the Jewish hierarchy).

12 Jesus' penetrating analysis of the situation made Pilate more eager than ever to release him. But the popular pressure was too strong. The cry "If you let this man go, you are no friend of Caesar" carried the day. The phrase "a friend of Caesar" usually denoted a supporter or associate of the emperor, a member of the important inner circle. The cry was a veiled threat: if Pilate exonerated Jesus, the high priest would report to Rome that Pilate had refused to bring a rival pretender to justice and was perhaps plotting to establish a new political alliance of his own. Tiberius, the reigning emperor, was notoriously bitter and suspicious of rivals. If such a report were sent to him, he would instantly end Pilate's political career and probably his life.

13 Jesus' analysis of Pilate's situation accentuated the dilemma he found himself entangled in. If he condemned Jesus to satisfy the Jewish hierarchy, he would be making a travesty of Roman justice. If he released Jesus, he would add to his contention with the hierarchy and would endanger his already shaky political future. But the decision could no longer be deferred.

14–15 The time in view here depends on the method of reckoning "the sixth hour." If it were reckoned from midnight, it would be about six o'clock in the morning; if from sunrise, which accords better with John's general procedure, it would be about noon. But Mark states that the Crucifixion took place at "the third hour" (Mk 15:25). Perhaps Mark indicates that the trial came early and that the execution occurred at mid-morning, while John stresses the fact that it was accomplished before noon.

Pilate presented the bleeding, disheveled figure to the crowd with these words: "Here is your king." In their bitter irony, these words show Pilate's contempt for the Jews. As the people clamored for Jesus' crucifixion, Pilate scornfully asked, "Shall I crucify your king?" The reply of the chief priests is astonishing: "We have no king but Caesar." The official heads of the nation, who would gladly have welcomed independence, put themselves on record as subjects of the pagan emperor. Even allowing for the fact that the Sadducean priesthood was willing to compromise with the Romans for the sake of political advantage, nothing revealed their lack of spiritual principles so vividly as this act of betrayal. It was the final step in the process initially described in 1:11.

16 Realizing that the priests were implacable and that resisting them would only endanger his career, Pilate finally gave in and ordered the Crucifixion. Certain features of Pilate's examination of Jesus are significant. His behavior shows that he was apprehensive of trouble. He oscillated between public confrontation with the Jewish mob and private interrogation of Jesus. Seven times in this brief narrative the author says or implies that Pilate "went out" or "went in" (18:29, 33, 38; 19:1, 4, 9, 13). Beneath his arrogant manner, there was an uncertainty that came from the conflict between Pilate the Roman judge and Pilate the politician. He finally succumbed to expediency.

From the standpoint of Jesus, Pilate was a person in need; and Jesus gave him the opportunity of receiving truth if he would have it. Jesus made a greater effort to penetrate Pilate's mind than to defend himself. When Pilate asked, "What is truth?" (18:38), he was

At the place in Jerusalem where Jesus is traditionally considered to have been crucified stands the Church of the Holy Sepulchre.

near to the kingdom of God because incarnate truth was standing before him (14:6). Pilate sacrificed truth for what he thought was security and lost both.

E. The Crucifixion (19:17–27)

17 Under Pilate's orders, Jesus was turned over to an execution squad, which normally consisted of four legionnaires and a centurion (cf. v.23). A condemned person customarily wore a placard (v.20) giving his name and the nature of his crime and carried the transverse beam of his cross. The procession moved from Pilate's judgment seat to a place outside the city called Golgotha, "The Place of the Skull" (see comment on Mk 15:22).

18 Apart from this simple statement, the writer makes no attempt to describe the process of crucifixion, probably because it was well known to the readers and he did not want to dwell on the physical horror of the Cross. At the place of execution, the condemned man was affixed to the cross by nails driven through the hands or wrists and through the feet. Generally, a rope was tied around the chest knotted between the shoulders, and then tied to the wooden stake behind the body to prevent its falling forward as fatigue weakened the muscles. A peg was set in the upright stake to act as a supporting seat. The victim was stripped of his clothing and left shamefully naked, exposed to the mocking people, the heat of the sun by day, and the chill and dampness of night (on death by crucifixion, see comment on Mk 15:24). A crucified man might live as long as thirty-six hours, or even longer, in an increasing agony. Crucifixion was probably the most diabolical form of death ever invented. Paul, in writing of the humiliation of Christ, says, "He humbled himself and became obedient to [the point of] death—*even death on a cross*" (Php 2:8, italics mine), a statement that reveals his feeling toward death by this method.

John gives no details concerning the two others crucified with Jesus (see comments on Mt 27:16; Mk 15:27).

19–22 The placard (see comment on v.17) was written in three languages, in order to make the inscription plain to all: Aramaic, for the local inhabitants; Latin, for the officials; Greek, the lingua franca of the eastern Mediterranean world. Its content was Pilate's psychological revenge on the Jewish hierarchy for forcing his decision. It proclaimed loudly to all passersby that Rome had crucified the king of the Jews as a common criminal. Stung by the insult, the priests remonstrated, asking that Pilate make clear that it was only Jesus' claim to be king of the Jews. Having succeeded by his unjust compromise in removing any possible ground of accusation that he was derelict in his duty to the Roman state, Pilate resumed his haughty attitude and refused to change the wording. "What I have written, I have written" means essentially, "Take it and like it!"

23–24 Usually the clothing of a crucified man became the property of the executioners. Jesus' simple wardrobe was composed of five items: a turban or headdress; an outer robe; a sash or girdle, the folds of which would provide pockets; sandals; and a fairly long tunic woven in one piece, that was an undergarment. The first four were easily divided among the four legionnaires, but the fifth would be of no value if cut into four parts. Gambling was well-known in the Roman army, so the tunic was awarded to one of them at the cast of the dice. John's reason for mentioning this episode was its fulfillment of the prophecy of Ps 22. This psalm is a startling picture of the Crucifixion, which begins with Christ's fourth word from the cross: "My God, my God, why have you forsaken me?" (Mt 27:46; Mk 15:34). If Pilate's inscription shows that he exploited Jesus' crucifixion as a means of psychological vengeance, the gambling of the legionnaires shows their callous and mercenary attitude.

25–27 The harsh brutality of the scene is softened by the allusion to Jesus' care for his mother. Four women are mentioned here: Mary, the wife of Clopas; Mary Magdalene; Mary, the mother of Jesus; and his mother's sister, who was presumably Salome, the mother of James and John (cf. Mt 27:56; Mk 10:35; 15:40). The identity of Mary of Clopas is uncertain. Mary of Magdala (a town on the western side of the Sea of Galilee) appears in Luke's list of those who helped support Jesus by their contributions (Lk 8:2). Nothing in the NT implies that she was of loose moral character.

The anguish and terror of Jesus' mother at the Crucifixion must have been indescribable. His tender concern for her in the hour of his mortal agony illustrates his true humanity and compassion. On the assumption that John was "the disciple whom he loved," it could well be that Jesus consigned his mother to John's care because none of his brothers was present and because John was the nearest available relative. Apparently John removed Mary from the scene at once and took her to his home in Jerusalem. His temporary absence may account for the omission of some of the details found in the Synoptic Gospels, including Jesus' dialogue with the criminals who were crucified with him. Mary must have remained in Jerusalem for a time since she was present at the session of prayer that preceded Pentecost.

F. The Death of Jesus (19:28–37)

28 The phrases in John preceding Jesus' last request (his sixth word from the cross) show that he was consciously fulfilling the program the Father had set for him. "Knowing that all was now completed" accords with what he had said earlier in his prayer (17:4). Unerringly and methodically Jesus carried out the commission the Father had assigned to him. The phrase "I am thirsty" recalls Ps 69:21. Jesus' loss of blood, his nervous tension, and his exposure to the weather had generated a raging thirst.

29 The "vinegar" was probably the cheap sour wine that the legionnaires drank. Though it provided some refreshment, it was a strong astringent that could contract the throat muscles and prevent the condemned victim from crying out with pain. Just what is meant by "hyssop" is uncertain. The word may describe more than one plant. Perhaps it was the *Capparis sicula*, a plant that grows on the walls of Jerusalem (see ZPEB, 3:235). The thirst consummated Jesus' physical suffering. Having passed that stage, he had completed his work and was ready to end his mission.

30 The phrase "It is finished" (GK 5464) signifies the completion of Jesus' work and the establishment of a basis for faith. Nothing further needed to be done. His act was voluntary and confident, for he had discharged perfectly the Father's purpose and was triumphantly leaving the scene of his human struggle. This expression is almost certainly a shout of victory. John makes it the final report of Jesus to the Father, who would now exalt him to glory. Having said this, Jesus "laid his head to rest and dismissed his spirit" (lit. tr.). He retained consciousness and command of himself till the very end.

31–32 Jesus died on the day preceding the Sabbath, hence, on Friday, "the day of Preparation" (cf. Mk 15:42). The day began at sunset on Thursday and ended at sunset on Friday. The meal Jesus and his disciples ate must have been on Thursday night, which would actually fall on the Passover since the Jewish day began in the evening (see comments on Jn 13:2). The removal of bodies from the cross was a concession to Jewish religious scruples. The Romans usually left the bodies of criminals on their crosses as a warning to potential offenders, much as pirates in the eighteenth century were hung in chains so that passing ships might see their fate. The Jewish law forbade leaving hanged bodies on a gallows overnight (Dt 21:22–23; Jos 8:29). The soldiers broke the legs of the living victims to hasten death. The only way a crucified man could obtain a full breath of air was to raise himself by means of his legs to ease the tension on his arms and chest muscles. If his legs were broken, he could not possibly do so; and death would follow shortly because of lack of oxygen.

33 The execution squad was well acquainted with the signs of death. Consequently, not fracturing Jesus' legs shows that they considered him to be already dead. His swift death undoubtedly indicates a voluntary ending of his life because his work was ended (v.30; cf. Lk 23:46). He had said of himself that he could lay down his life that he might take it again (10:17).

34–37 One of the soldiers pierced Jesus' side with his spear, probably to see whether there would be any reaction. The flow of "blood and water" has been variously explained. Ordinarily dead bodies do not bleed because there is no action of the heart to produce arterial pressure. One suggestion is that since the body was erect, the flow was due to gravity and that the crassamentum (the heavy, red corpuscles) and the serum (the yellowish white aqueous part) of the blood had already begun to separate. Another is that either the stomach or the lungs contained water that flowed with the blood. The author places great importance on this fact, emphasizing that he had witnessed it for himself and that he was telling the truth. He connects the fact that no bones were broken with Ex 12:46; Ps 34:20 and the pierced side with Zec 12:10 (where that fact is related to the final manifestation of the Lord to Israel). Verses 35–37 are a footnote giving the author's viewpoint in the third person, a usage in keeping with his practice throughout the gospel.

G. The Burial of Jesus (19:38–42)

38 Burial in the Middle East usually takes place within twenty-four hours after death. Normally, the body of Jesus would have been flung into a common pit with the bodies of the two other victims, but two of his friends intervened. Jesus had no estate of his own from which to pay for a proper burial, and his relatives were either too poor or too afraid of the authorities to assume responsibility for it. Joseph of Arimathea stepped forward (see comments on Mk 15:42–43; Lk 23:50–54) and asked Pilate for permission to remove the body. His action was courageous, for his petition was a tacit admission that he was a friend of Jesus and consequently an associate in whatever supposed subversion Jesus might have advocated. He was now openly confessing his faith, for up to this time he had been a secret believer.

39 Nicodemus, another distinguished member of the Jewish aristocracy, shared the responsibility for receiving Jesus' body with Joseph. This marks his third appearance in the gospel (see 3:1–15; 7:45–52). Like Joseph, Nicodemus was a secret disciple whose faith grew slowly. As a member of the Sanhedrin, he had more at stake than the Galilean fishermen who had become followers of Jesus early in his career. His cooperation with Joseph in the burial shows that his faith had finally matured. Neither of these men appears in the Jewish records or traditions of the time, presumably because as traitors to Judaism, their names were erased from the records.

The mixture of spices that Nicodemus provided was a large quantity. Spices were generally imported and were very expensive. Myrrh is a gum exuded by a tree that grows in Arabia and is prized for its perfume. It was one of the gifts of the wise men to Jesus (Mt 2:11). Aloes are derived from the pulp in the leaves of a plant that belongs to the lily family. This spice is fragrant and bitter to the taste. Used with myrrh, it acts as a drying agent; and the fragrance would counteract the odor of decaying flesh. The quantity of one hundred Roman pounds (about 75 lbs.) reveals both Nicodemus's wealth and his appreciation of Jesus.

40 The burial of the body was hasty and had to be completed before sundown. The process is uncertain. The spices, being of somewhat gummy character, may have been laid in the folds of the cloth to provide a rigid casing for the body, or, more likely, they were ground and mixed with oil to form an ointment to rub on the body. "Strips of linen" refers to graveclothes, the sort that in the case of Lazarus were wrapped around him in such a way that he had to be released after he was raised (11:44–45).

41 The place of burial was a private garden, probably Joseph's own rock-hewn tomb (Mt 27:60). The privacy of this garden allowed the women to visit the tomb. No doubt they would have been hesitant to enter a public cemetery at any time—especially before daylight. The location was near the place of execution and was probably just outside the Second North Wall of the city.

42 The allusion to "the Jewish day of Preparation" creates the impression that the burial was hasty, though the amount of spices suggests that as far as Joseph and Nicodemus were concerned, it was final (though they may not have completed all they wished to do). The women observed the place of the entombment. Consequently they knew where to go in order to fulfill their desire for a part in the burial of Jesus.

H. The Resurrection (20:1–29)

If the narrative of John had ended with ch. 19, it would not have been exceptional; all human biographies end with death. The picture of Jesus would have been that of a man of exceptional character, who made extraordinary claims, and whose sincerity could not be reasonably doubted. Nevertheless, the main narrative would have been closed with a sense of frustration. His claims would have been negated, his aspirations would have been unrealized, and his teaching would have seemed too lofty to be true. The major difference between the life and teachings of Jesus and those of any other great religious leader lies in the fact that Jesus rose from the dead and the others did not, however persistent their influence may be.

In presenting the evidence for Jesus' resurrection, John deals more with its effect on human personality than with the material proofs that the Western mind would prefer. He assumes the fact and then shows how it influenced certain disciples in such a way that its reality becomes indisputable.

1. The witness of Peter and John (20:1–9)

1 "The first day of the week" was the day after the Sabbath. In the Jewish method of reckoning time, it began with sundown on Saturday and continued until sundown on Sunday. The text indicates that the visit of the women to the tomb occurred early on that Sunday morning. Only Mary Magdalene is mentioned by name, but others are listed in the Synoptic Gospels (Mt 28:1; Mk 16:1; Lk 24:10). Likely Mary Magdalene, noticing that the stone had been rolled away from the door of the tomb, ran to warn the disciples while the others investigated further.

2 Mary hastened to find Peter and "the other disciple, the one Jesus loved" (likely John), the leaders of the Twelve, and announced that the body was missing from the tomb: "They have taken the Lord." No identification is given for "they." Either the word is an impersonal plural or else, as is more likely, it is an oblique reference to the Jewish hierarchy who had designed Jesus' death. Obviously Mary thought the body had been secretly removed by Jesus' enemies.

3 The quick response of Peter and John shows that the disciples were not responsible for removing the body. Had they been aware of an official removal, or had some of their own number been involved in a conspiracy, they would not have been so concerned.

4–5 Both Peter and John "ran" to the tomb (cf. the women "running" in Mt 28:6). Their running shows they were activated by a powerful emotion, possibly either consternation, as in the case of Mary, or joy, as with the women. Peter, perhaps being the older and heavier of the two, was unable to maintain as swift a pace as his companion. John arrived first but did not venture to enter the tomb. Having seen that the graveclothes were still within, he probably concluded that the body was also there and so refrained from entering.

Either he felt that he should not enter the tomb out of respect for the dead, or he feared the ceremonial defilement of touching a corpse.

6–7 Peter, who by this time had arrived, had no such inhibitions and entered directly into the tomb. He also saw the graveclothes and observed that the headcloth was not lying with the other pieces but was rolled up in a place by itself. This means the headcloth still retained the shape that the contour of Jesus' head had given it and that it was still separated from the other wrappings by a space that suggested the distance between the neck of the deceased and the upper chest, where the wrappings of the body would have begun. Peter must have been wondering why the graveclothes were left in this position if the body had been stolen. A robber would not have left them in good order. He would have stripped the body completely, leaving the clothing in a disorderly heap; or he would have taken the body, graveclothes and all.

8 At this point, the "other disciple" summoned up courage to enter the tomb, perhaps wondering what had reduced Peter to silence. He saw the meaning of the empty graveclothes and "believed." The unique phenomenon of the graveclothes looking as if the body were in them when no body was there undoubtedly recalled Jesus' previous words (cf. 2:22; 11:25; 16:22).

9 The teaching of Scripture, however, was not yet clear to the disciples, and they required fuller explanation by Jesus (cf. Lk 24:25–27, 44–47). To what "Scripture" does this passage refer? There is a parallel in Jn 2:21, which asserts that the disciples understood Jesus' statement about raising the temple of his body in connection with Scripture. The gospel of John contains no specific text that might be interpreted as a prediction of the Resurrection. Perhaps Ps 16:10, quoted by Peter in Ac 2:24–31, is the "Scripture" being suggested.

For these two key disciples, the realization of the truth of the Resurrection began with material evidence, the significance of which dawned on them slowly. Their eagerness to visit the tomb showed their concern for Jesus. Had they dismissed him from their consciousness after his death, they would not have exerted themselves by running to Joseph's garden early in the morning. Their understanding, however, was slow in spite of Jesus' repeated predictions of his passion and resurrection.

2. The appearance to Mary Magdalene (20:10–18)

10 Puzzled but convinced that something unusual had occurred at the tomb, Peter and John returned to their lodgings in Jerusalem (possibly the "upper room") or perhaps to the same place that John took Mary at the time of the Crucifixion.

11 Mary Magdalene had returned to the tomb and stood outside, wailing for the loss of Jesus. On looking into the tomb, she saw two figures in white seated on the shelf where the body of Jesus had been lying, one at the foot and the other at the head. The tomb was a horizontal chamber cut through the soft limestone rock on which Jerusalem was built. Usually such tombs had a small antechamber into which the low entrance opened and from which the burial chambers radiated. This tomb seems to have been large enough to accommodate several living persons in addition to the burial cells.

12 No description is given of the angels, except that they were clothed in white (cf. Ac 1:10). When angels appear in the Bible, they are usually recognized by their powers rather than by any significant difference from human form. Mary did not respond to them in any unusual way, possibly because her eyes were clouded with tears or because she was preoccupied with the loss of Jesus' body.

13 The question the angels asked Mary brought from her only an expression of grief and frustration. The death of Jesus, which she had witnessed, was in itself distressing and unnerving; the disappearance of the body from the place of burial added apprehension and mystery to her grief. She had hoped for the sad consolation of completing the burial, and even that had now been taken from her.

14 As Mary turned back toward the outside of the tomb, she saw a person standing there whom she took for the keeper of the garden. She was aware of his presence, but paid scant attention to him because of her overwhelming concern for the body of Jesus.

15 The person addressed her first as a stranger, using the polite salutation "Woman" and asking the reason for her grief. From her lamentations one would conclude that she had lost some possession or some person. Thinking that Jesus was the keeper of the garden, she assumed that he would know she was looking for a body. So she requested that if he had removed it, he would tell her where she might find it that she might take it for final burial. Her words reveal her devotion. She never paused to consider how she would carry the corpse of a full-grown man or how she would explain her possession of it.

16 Only one thing was necessary to establish Jesus' identity—his uttering her name. One of the strange commonplaces of life is that the most penetrating utterance one can understand, no matter by whom spoken, is one's personal name. Furthermore, the way it is spoken often identifies the speaker. No gardener would ever have known her name, and no one else would pronounce it the way Jesus did. Turning again for a second look, she addressed him in Aramaic as "Rabboni" (a term by which one addressed a teacher). In this ecstatic moment of recognition, Mary must have prostrated herself before Jesus and clasped his feet, as the other women had done (see Mt 28:9).

17 In reply to her action, Jesus said, "Do not hold onto me." He was not refusing to be touched but was making clear that she did not need to detain him, for he had not yet ascended to the Father. He planned to remain with the disciples for a little while; she need not fear that he would vanish immediately. Ultimately he would return to God, and he urged her to tell the disciples that he would do so. The word "brothers" (GK 81) includes more than the members of his immediate family. It placed the disciples on a new plane of relationship with himself. Having passed through death and resurrection, Jesus had become the representative man, the Lord from heaven, who "is not ashamed to call them brothers" (Heb 2:11; cf. also Mk 3:33–34).

The way Jesus stated his destination is illuminating: "I am returning to my Father and your Father, to my God and your God." Nowhere in the Gospels did Jesus personally address God as "our Father" or "our God." The reason for the distinction in his word to Mary was not, of course, that there were two gods, but that her relationship with God was different from his. He is the eternal Son of the Father; she, as well as all the disciples, had become a member of the family by receiving him (cf. 1:12). Both relationships concerned only one God.

18 Mary's announcement to the disciples that she had seen the Lord was an additional confirmation of the belief that rested on inference from material evidence. The beloved disciple had believed, but he had not yet personally seen the risen Lord Jesus. Mary brought the witness of her experience to corroborate his deduction.

3. The appearance to the disciples (20:19–23)

19–20 The third episode came in the evening of the first day. John does not cite the appearances to Simon and to the travelers on the road to Emmaus (see Lk 24:13–35). This appearance came to the collective group in order to allay their fears. They had narrowly escaped arrest with Jesus in Gethsemane; they realized that as the disciples of one who was regarded as a dangerous agitator they would be under suspicion; and they were probably consulting together on how best to withdraw from the city without attracting the notice of the temple police or the Roman authorities. The doors were locked for fear that the Jews would send an arresting detachment for them as they had for Jesus.

The appearance of Jesus in the room resulted in both amazement and fear. The implication is clear that Jesus was not impeded by locked doors. The resurrection body has properties different from the body of flesh; yet it is not ethereal. There was a definite continuity between the physical body of Jesus' earthly career and the new body since his hands and side still showed the scars that identified him. His greeting of "Peace" and the assurance of his identity calmed their fears and demonstrated by unmistakable proof that he was alive. They were overjoyed, not only to see him again, but also to realize that he was undefeated by death and that his claims were validated.

21 The repetition of the common greeting "Peace" reassured the disciples of his real presence. Not only did his appearance renew their devotion and their hopes, but it also renewed their commission as disciples. Had there been no Resurrection, there would have been little motive for them to undertake a mission in his name. But since he had risen, the old commitment was even more compelling. "As the Father has sent me," he said, "I am sending you." He had come into the world to fulfill the Father's purpose—to speak his words, to do his works, and to lay down his life for the salvation of humans; now he expected them to continue his work in his absence by delivering his message (15:27), doing greater works than he had done (14:12), and giving their lives in his service. They would have all the privileges, all the protection, and all the responsibilities that he had during his ministry.

22–23 For this ministry Jesus provided the Holy Spirit and the commission to proclaim the forgiveness of sins. These are linked together for a new ministry. This was the initial announcement of which Pentecost was the historic fulfillment. The descent of the Spirit on the church at Pentecost brought the proclamation by Peter to his hearers: "Repent and be baptized, every one of you, in the name of Jesus Christ so that your sins may be forgiven" (Ac 2:38). The words of Jesus emphasize that the Holy Spirit is not bestowed on the church as an ornament but to empower an effective application of the work of Christ to the entire human race.

The commission to forgive sins is phrased in an unusual construction. Literally, it is: "Those whose sins you forgive have already been forgiven; those whose sins you do not forgive have not been forgiven" (similarly also Mt 16:19; see comments). God does not forgive people's sins because we decide to do so, nor does he withhold forgiveness because we will not grant it. We announce it; we do not create it. This is the essence of salvation. And all who proclaim the Gospel are in effect forgiving or not forgiving sins, depending on whether the hearer accepts or rejects the Lord Jesus as the Sin-Bearer.

4. The confession of Thomas (20:24–29)

24 Thomas is singled out for special treatment because his confession provides a climactic illustration of the triumph of belief. "Thomas" is Aramaic for "twin," of which Didymus is the Greek equivalent (cf. Jn 11:16; 21:2). In 11:16 and 14:5 Thomas appears as a loyal, outspoken, and rather pessimistic person who was uncertain of the future but closely attached to Jesus. Much the same picture emerges from this episode. He was absent from the gathering on the first day of the week, though he must have been in contact with the rest of the disciples afterwards.

25 In spite of the repeated assurances of his colleagues that Jesus had risen, Thomas was obstinate. So certain was he of the death of Jesus that he insisted he would not believe unless he could actually touch Jesus' body. Thomas would be satisfied by nothing less than material evidence. His incredulity is testimony to the fact that the resurrection appearances were not illusions induced by wishful thinking.

26 A week later, also on Sunday evening, Thomas was with the disciples, who had remained in Jerusalem. He must have recovered somewhat from the original shock of Jesus' death and was willing to rejoin his old associates. The reappearance of Jesus took place under the same conditions as the previous appearance, which the disciples had described to Thomas. Therefore, he could not charge them with having fabricated their report when Jesus greeted them in the same manner as before.

27 Jesus' appeal to Thomas shows that he knew what Thomas had said to his colleagues when they told him of the first appearance. Since Jesus had not been visibly present to hear his reaction to their report, Thomas must have been startled to hear Jesus quote his very words. Jesus did not immediately upbraid him for his doubts, but he challenged him to perform the test that he had suggested. Jesus' words can be translated "Stop becoming an unbeliever and become a believer." Jesus halted Thomas on the road to a despairing unbelief and offered him the positive evidence on which he could build an enduring faith.

28 Thomas was disposed to believe in Jesus by his personal attachment to him, as he demonstrated previously by his resolute adherence in impending danger (11:16). Now, having been challenged to make a personal test of Jesus' reality, Thomas expressed fullest faith in him. For a Jew to call another human associate "my Lord and my God" is incredible. The Jewish law was strictly monotheistic; so the deification of any man would be regarded as blasphemy (10:33). Thomas, in the light of the Resurrection, applied to Jesus *two* titles of deity.

29 Jesus' commendation of Thomas is extended to all others who, like Thomas, place a final faith in him but who, unlike Thomas, have no opportunity to see him in his postresurrection form. Thomas's declaration is the last assertion of personal faith recorded in this gospel. It marks the climax of the book because it presents Christ as the risen Lord, victorious over sin, sorrow, doubt, and death. It also presents the faith that accepts not only the truth of what Jesus said but also the actuality of who he is—the Son of God. In the experience of Thomas, the writer has shown how belief comes to maturity and how it changes the entire direction of an individual life.

I. Statement of Purpose (20:30–31)

30–31 The last two verses of this chapter are really the conclusion of the gospel. They summarize its strategy, subject, and purpose. The *strategy* is to use selected works of Jesus as "signs" (GK *4958*) that illustrate his character, demonstrate his power, and relate him to human need. Seven of these signs have been narrated, exclusive of the final sign, the Resurrection. Each one involved a human personality and showed how the power of Jesus can be applied to human emergencies. These signs were performed in the presence of the disciples so that they were attested by sympathetic and competent witnesses as well as by those who happened to be present at the time, whether friendly or hostile to Jesus. The criteria for selection seem to be magnitude, varied individual significance, and effect on both the disciples and the public.

The signs, however, are not of primary intrinsic importance. The chief *subject* of the gospel is the Lord Jesus Christ, whom the author desires to present as the Christ (Messiah or Anointed One; see comments on Mt 1:1; Mk 8:29–30), the Son of God. Jesus was given this title "Messiah" by the earliest disciples (1:41), but it seldom appears in this gospel (cf. 4:25–26); and Jesus did not use it concerning himself because of its political overtones. This title also represented the deliverer from sin promised in the Old Testament as the fulfillment of the covenants with the patriarchs and David, the one who would consummate God's purpose for the nation and the world. At that time the Jewish nation was still looking for the Messiah; John asserts that he had already come.

The title "Son of God" appears at intervals in the text of this gospel. John the Baptist introduced Jesus by this title (1:34); Nathanael applied it to him (1:49); and on several occasions Jesus applied it to himself (e.g., 5:25; 10:36; 11:4). This title would appeal to the Gentile world rather than to the Jew, for the Gentiles did not have the same reservations about it as the Jews did. The title does not, of course, imply biological descent like that of the Greco-Roman demigods; but the metaphor of sonship expresses the unity of nature, close fellowship, and unique intimacy between Jesus and the Father. To believe that Jesus is the Christ and the Son of God involves the total acceptance of the revelation of God that he offers, the acknowledgment of his divine authority, and the fulfillment of the commission he entrusted to his disciples.

The total *purpose* of this belief is eternal life, a new and enduring experience of God by the believer. This conclusion ties together the three persistent themes of the gospel: the "signs" that demonstrate Christ's nature and power; the response of "belief" that is exemplified in the crises and growth in the lives of the disciples; and the new "life" that is found in the relationship with Christ.

V. The Epilogue (21:1–25)

Chapter 21 of John is a postscript to the main development of the book. It is not irrelevant to the preceding text; in fact, it completes it by illustrating the result of belief. It reads like a reminiscence that the author might have added subsequent to the composition of the first part by dictation to an assistant or scribe. The language bears a strong likeness both to the Synoptics and to other sections of John. The miracle of the catch of fish resembles the initial episode related to the call of the disciples (Lk 5: 1–11); the action of Simon Peter is completely in character with other representations of his tendency toward impulsive speech or action (Mt 16:21–23; 26:33–35; John 13:36–38; et al.); the allusion to "sheep" follows the figure of 10:1–18; and v.19 uses phraseology concerning Peter that is applied to Jesus in 12:33. Apart from its relation to the themes and language of the main body of this gospel, it owes its origin to the need for dispelling a false legend that had become current concerning Jesus' supposed prediction that the author of John would not die before Jesus' return.

A. The Appearance at the Sea (21:1–14)

1 "Afterward" implies an indefinite lapse of time (cf.2:12; 3:22; et al.), but not always a long time. Since this event is categorized as Jesus' third appearance to the disciples after the Resurrection (v.14), it must have taken place between the beginning of the second week and the Ascension outside Jerusalem near Bethany (Lk 24:50–53; cf. Ac 1:1–12).

This appearance took place in Galilee. John is the only NT writer to use the name "Sea of Tiberias" for the Sea of Galilee (see Mt 4:18; 15:29; Mk 1:16; 7:31) or the Lake of Gennesaret (see Lk 5:1). John speaks once of the "Sea of Galilee" but qualifies it: "that is, the Sea of Tiberias" (6:1).

"Appeared" (GK 5746), translated by "happened" at its second occurrence in this verse, is a characteristic word in John. It was most frequently used to denote the self-revelation of Christ (1:31; 2:11; 9:3). It occurs three times in the epilogue (21:1 [twice], 14) in preparation for the final revelation of Jesus regarding the commissioning of Peter for his coming ministry. John also uses the term in his first letter, concerning both the incarnate Christ (1Jn 1:2; 3:5, 8; 4:9) and his return (2:28; 3:2). Not only was this occasion an appearance of Christ after his resurrection, but it was also a disclosure of his purpose for the disciples.

2 The seven disciples who were present include several previously named in this gospel: Simon Peter (1:40–42, 44; et al.); Thomas (11:16; 14:5–6; 20:24–29); Nathanael (1:45–50); the sons of Zebedee, who are not mentioned directly in this gospel; and two others, possibly Philip (1:43–46; et al.) and Andrew (1:40–42, 44; 6:8; 12:22). The reason for the disciples' return to Galilee may have been to escape scrutiny and criticism by the mob in Jerusalem or to obey the command of Jesus (Mt 28:7, 10; Mk 16:6). Or perhaps they were discouraged by Jesus' death and decided to return to their old occupation of fishing. The kingdom had not arrived, and they had to make a living.

3 The leadership of Simon Peter is apparent at this point, and the others assented to Peter's proposal; so they embarked in a boat that was available for a night of fishing (possibly Peter's; cf. "*the* boat"). Their enthusiasm ended in frustration, for no fish were caught.

4–5 Jesus appeared in the early morning, just as day was breaking. The fishermen no doubt were cold, wet with the dampness and spray of the lake, and discouraged by their lack of success. They failed to recognize Jesus, perhaps because they were preoccupied with their failure, or because they could not see him clearly through the morning mist on the lake. Jesus asked the disciples whether they had caught any fish. The construction of the question implies that he knew they had caught nothing. This was confirmed by their dispirited answer: "No."

6–7 By commanding them to cast the net on the right side of the ship, Jesus was either testing their faith by recommending a procedure the Galilean fishermen never used, or he could discern the presence of a school of fish from the more advantageous viewpoint of the shore. Whatever the reason for the suggestion, the disciples evidently felt that one more attempt at casting the net could be no more futile than their nightlong efforts had been; and it might be worthwhile. The resultant catch was so great that they could not load it into the boat. The similarities between this episode and the one recorded in Lk 5:1–11 prompted the disciples' recognition of Jesus. "The disciple whom Jesus loved" was the first one to recognize the mysterious stranger on the shore as none other than the Lord Jesus himself.

Peter's quick reaction revealed his real feeling toward Jesus. Grasping his outer cloak, which he had laid aside to give him more freedom in working, he wrapped it around himself and dived overboard. His eagerness to see Jesus was consistent with his former profession of loyalty, which he had intended to keep but had not. This was probably not the moment of reconciliation, however, for Luke states that Jesus had met Peter personally on the first day of the Resurrection (Lk 24:35), as well as at the locked-door episodes (Jn 20:19–29).

8 A net full of live fish swimming toward the depths rather than toward the shore would be difficult to manage. The disciples in the ship pulled the net into shallow water where they could disembark and then sort out the fish.

9–10 Jesus had breakfast ready for the disciples, but he suggested that they bring some of the fish they had caught. Earlier, in the miraculous feedings of the multitudes with the fish and the loaves (see 6:1–14), the Lord had taken what the disciples had provided, multiplied it, and used it to supply the needs of many. Here he showed that he would continue to multiply and bless their efforts. However, they were yet to be told what direction those efforts were to take.

11 Simon Peter returned to the boat and pulled the net to land. If he did this by himself, he must have possessed unusual strength. One hundred and fifty-three fish plus a wet net would probably weigh as much as three hundred pounds. The observation of the exact number of the fish and the fact that the net did not break reflect both an eyewitness account and a fisherman's perspective. John was impressed by the numerical size of the catch and the preservation of the net under the stress. These fish were probably sorted and distributed among the disciples.

12–14 When the catch had been safely brought to land and presumably sorted, Jesus invited the men to eat with him. Their attitude was peculiar. They desired to ask his identity, but they dared not do so because somehow they "knew" he was the Lord. He had appeared in their beloved Galilee and had repeated the same kind of miracle by which they first had been called to him. In spite of an apparent change in his outward appearance, the disciples' spiritual instinct confirmed his identity. His action in serving them with the bread and fish must have recalled the Last Supper, when he offered them bread and wine. There was, however, no sacramental overtone to this occasion.

The text states that this was Jesus' "third" appearance to the disciples as a group since his resurrection (see 20:19–23, 24–29).

B. The Reinstatement of Peter (21:15–23)

15–17 The chief reason for the narration of this episode seems to be to let Peter know that the Lord still loved him and had not cast him out (cf. 15:6). The three questions Jesus addressed to Peter stand in contrast to Peter's three denials. The disciples were no doubt aware of Peter's denial of Jesus, and the commission that Jesus renewed with him in their presence would reassure them of Peter's place among them. The wording of the first question, "Do you truly love me more than these?" contains an ambiguity. There are three possible solutions:

1. Do you love me more than these other men do?
2. Do you love me more than you love these men?
3. Do you love me more than these things—the boats, the fish, etc.?

In view of Peter's earlier boastful promise that whatever the others did he would not fail, the first option seems most likely.

The words translated "love" have also raised considerable debate. Two different terms are used: *agapao* (GK 26) is used in Jesus' first two questions and *phileo* (GK 5797) is used in Jesus' third question and in Peter's three replies. The former is the same word "love" that appears in 3:16; it is used of divine love and usually carries the connotation of will or purpose as well as that of affection. *Phileo* implies affinity, friendship, and fondness. Both words represent a high aspect of love, for both are used of God (3:16; 5:20) and of humans (14:21; 16:27) in this gospel. Some maintain that these words here are interchangeable. On the other hand, a good case can be made for a difference in Jesus' emphasis. There was less doubt concerning Peter's attachment to Jesus than there was concerning his will to love at all costs; and the change of term in Jesus' third question makes his probing of Peter even deeper. If the latter alternative is adopted, it explains better Peter's distress when questioned a third time, since Jesus would not only be challenging his love but would be implying that it was superficial.

Peter's affirmative answer to each question is substantially the same. The verb "know" (GK 1182) used in the first two responses is a word that implies the intellectual knowledge of a fact. In his third reply, however, Peter strengthened his statement by a word that denotes knowledge gained through experience.

Jesus' commands to Peter also contain fine distinctions:

1. "Feed [pasture] my lambs" (v.15).
2. "Take care of [shepherd] my sheep" (v.16).
3. "Feed [pasture] my sheep" (v.17).

The first and third imply only taking the sheep to pasture where they are fed; the second implies the total guardianship a shepherd exercises. This threefold injunction does not necessarily give Peter the sole responsibility for the oversight of Christ's followers; all of his spiritually mature disciples are called to be shepherds (cf. 1Pe 5:2). This challenge to Peter demanded a total renewal of his loyalty and reaffirmed his responsibilities.

18–19 The introduction of v.18 by "I tell you the truth" makes the statement of Jesus solemn and important. The author goes on to add an explanation of Jesus' enigmatic words. They predicted Peter's career: a new responsibility, a new danger, and violent death. Jesus placed Peter in a category with himself—a life spent for God and ultimately sacrificed to glorify God (cf. 12:27–32; 13:31). The command "Follow me" literally means "Keep on following me." Jesus showed Peter that if he were to fulfill his promise of loyalty, he would have to follow him to his own cross.

20–21 Peter's question concerning John reflects curiosity and possibly uneasiness. Peter had been given an important commission, but what would his friend be expected to do? Would he share equally in both the responsibilities and the perils of the same task?

22–23 Jesus' reply indicated that even if he intended that "the disciple whom Jesus loved" should outlive Peter, Peter's main concern should not be a comparison of his lot with that of his friend; rather, Peter's concern should be the fulfillment of Jesus' purpose. In Jesus' final comment, "*You* must follow me" (italics mine, reflecting the Greek), he was urging Peter to take his attention off his colleague and focus it on Jesus himself.

Jesus' reference to his return is one of the few clear references to the Second Coming in this gospel. The use here is hyperbolic, for it marks the utmost point to which the beloved disciple could survive and remain active. This utterance was remembered in the church and formed the basis of the rumor that Jesus had promised John that he would live until Jesus returned. As a matter of fact, Jesus had offered a supposition, not a promise. The author's explanation of Jesus' announcement may be taken as evidence that the disciple was still living at the time this gospel was written and that he was the source of its content.

C. The Colophon (21:24–25)

24 The epilogue contains a number of parenthetic statements that are likely the author's explanatory notes on the scene at the Sea of Galilee (vv.7, 12, 19, 20, 23). At the same time, they leave the impression that the account was written for a second generation of believers who were historically remote from the original events. This impression is corroborated by the last two verses, which are the endorsement of the narrative. Although v.24 is in the first person plural ("we know"), as if it were being certified by the testimony of a group, a different division on one word would make it a first person singular. In that case the author (or scribe) would be saying, "And I for my part know that his testimony is valid."

25 The tremendous content of Jesus' teaching and deeds is acknowledged again by the writer (cf. 20:30). This gospel must have been written at a period when Christian literature was beginning to multiply and the church was becoming conscious of it. The letters of Paul were collected and circulated before the turn of the century, and the Gospels or writings like them were already known in the church (cf. Lk 1:1). Though John admits that what he recorded is only a fraction of what Jesus said and did, the content of this gospel is one of the most valuable assets the church possesses.

The Old Testament in the New

NT Text	OT Text	Subject
Jn 1:23	Isa 40:3	Voice in the wilderness
Jn 2:17	Ps 69:9	Zeal for God's house
Jn 6:31	Ex 16:4; Ne 9:15; Ps 78:24–25	Bread from heaven
Jn 6:45	Isa 54:13	All are taught by God
Jn 10:34	Ps 82:6	You are gods
Jn 12:13	Ps 118:26	Blessed is he who comes
Jn 12:15	Zec 9:9	Palm Sunday
Jn 12:38	Isa 53:1	Unbelief of Israel
Jn 12:40	Isa 6:10	God blinds the eyes
Jn 13:18	Ps 41:9	A double-crossing friend
Jn 15:25	Ps 35:19; 69:4	Hated without a cause
Jn 19:24	Ps 22:18	Dividing garments by lot
Jn 19:36	Ex 12:46; Ps 34:20	No broken bones
Jn 19:37	Zec 12:10	Looking on one pierced

The Acts of the Apostles

INTRODUCTION

"The Acts of the Apostles" is the name given to the second part of a two-volume work traditionally identified as having been written by Luke, a companion of the apostle Paul. Originally the two volumes circulated together as two parts of one complete writing. But during the late first or early second century, the first volume became associated with the Gospels identified with Matthew, Mark, and John, thus forming the fourfold Gospel. Luke's second volume was left to go its own way. It was at this time, it seems, that the second volume received its present title, the word "Acts" evidently suggesting both movement in the advance of the Gospel and heroic exploits by the apostles. The reference to "the Apostles," however, is somewhat misleading, because the work deals almost exclusively with Peter and Paul and the persons and events associated with their ministries. Yet if we did not have Acts, we would know nothing of the earliest days of the Christian movement except for bits of data gathered from the letters of Paul or inferred by looking back from later developments. Acts is the third longest of the NT writings, being about one-tenth shorter than its companion volume Luke (the longest NT book) and almost exactly the length of Matthew. Together Luke-Acts comprises almost 30 percent of the material in the NT, exceeding both the Pauline and the Johannine writings in size.

1. Historical Writing in Antiquity

This book falls in line with ancient historical writing. The concern of classical Greek historians was not the mere chronicling of events, but the conviction that the actions and words of distinctive people in their respective periods represent more adequately the situation than any comments by the historian. That is, the "acts" of the subjects, understood in terms of both their actions and their words, were the building blocks for the historians and biographers of antiquity. What these historians and biographers were primarily interested in were illuminating vignettes that gave insight into the ethos of a period or of a person's character. One of the main ways in which to portray both these factors was through speeches, of which Acts has many. These speeches are, of course, not verbatim accounts but summaries of the original, more lengthy delivery (as poor Eutychus undoubtedly could testify! Ac 20:7–12).

Furthermore, in writing their histories the ancients frequently grouped their material in a topical manner, without always specifying chronological relationships. While the ancients were interested in what actually happened, it must also be insisted that history was written by the ancients for moral, ethical, and polemical purposes and not just to inform or entertain. This is true for Acts, for Luke certainly did not write for money, literary recognition, or only to add to human knowledge. He wrote, rather, as he tells us in the Prologue to his two-volume work, to proclaim the certainty of what his audience had been taught (Lk 1:1–4). In other words, Luke's Acts, like the historiography of the OT, traces the activity of God in various historical events as viewed from a particular perspective.

In the process of writing this history, the author of Acts has his own interests, theological viewpoint, and purposes in writing (see next section). And to a considerable extent these have affected his selection, arrangement, and shaping of the particular units of material that he incorporates, though that does not mean that his narrative must be viewed as historically suspect (see the introduction to Luke for comments on Luke's historical and geographical accuracy).

2. Luke's Purposes in Writing Acts

Basic to every evaluation of Acts is the question of the purpose or purposes of its author. Luke himself states that his purpose in writing his two-volume work was "so that you may know the certainty of the things you have been taught" (Lk 1:4). The "most excellent Theophilus" (Lk 1:3; cf. Ac 1:1) to whom Luke addressed his work seems to have been a man who, though receptive to the Gospel and perhaps even convinced by its claims, had many questions about Christianity as he knew it. From the way Luke writes to him, we may surmise that Theophilus was concerned about how the Christian faith related to Jesus' ministry, to Jews and the world of Judaism, to the lifestyle of certain scrupulous Jewish Christians, to the more universalistic outlook of Gentiles, and to the sanctions of Roman law. Also, he was undoubtedly interested in how the Gospel had been received and what success it had met in the various centers of influence known to him in the eastern part of the empire, from Jerusalem to Rome.

Certainly when receiving his first instruction in the Gospel, Theophilus had been told of Jesus' death and resurrection. But, judging from Luke's gospel, apparently the meaning and implications of that death and resurrection were not quite clear to him; and a number of references to persons and events associated with the ministry of Jesus baffled him. Likewise, the subsequent experiences of the early Christians seem to have been somewhat vague to him. The advent and activity of the Holy Spirit, the early ministries of the disciples, the conversion of Paul and his relation to the Jerusalem apostles, the nature and extent of Paul's ministry—and probably more—were all things that Theophilus had questions about. So Luke writes to deal with his friend's uncertainties and the queries of others like him who will read his account.

a. Kerygmatic purpose

Acts, therefore, like many another work, was probably written with multiple purposes in view. Primary among the reasons for its composition was undoubtedly a *kerygmatic purpose* (*kerygmatic* is from the Greek word *kerygma* [GK 3060], which means "preaching" or "proclamation"). It proclaims the continued confrontation of men and women by the Word of God through the church and shows (1) how that Gospel is related to the course of redemptive history, (2) how it is rooted in and interacts with secular history, (3) how it is universal in character, (4) how it has been freed from the Jewish law, and (5) how behind the proclamation of the Word of God stand the power and activity of the Holy Spirit.

In his first volume, Luke shows how men and women were confronted by the Word of God in the earthly ministry of Jesus (cf. Lk 5:1;8:11, 21; 11:28). In Acts, Luke seeks to show how men and women continue to be confronted by that same Word through the ministry of the church (cf. Ac 4:29, 31; 6:2, 4, 7; et al.). Luke's stress on the Word of God is rooted inextricably in the confessions of the earliest believers and the consciousness of Jesus himself. For Luke the message of salvation in Jesus proclaimed by the church is in direct continuity with the ministry and teaching of Jesus. That is why Luke wrote a sequel to his gospel, thus making explicit what was presupposed in the earliest Christian preaching.

Furthermore, this Word of God is firmly fixed in the context of world history. It began with the miraculous births that took place "in the time of Herod king of Judea" (Lk 1:5) and during the reign of Caesar Augustus, "while Quirinius was governor of Syria" (2:1–2; see also 3:1–2; 23:1–25). And it spread throughout the Roman world principally during the reign of the emperor Claudius (Ac 11:28; 18:2), when Gallio was proconsul of Achaia (18:12–17), when Felix and Festus ruled in Judea and Ananias was the high priest in Jerusalem (chs. 24–25), and between the times of the Jewish kings Herod Agrippa I (12:1–23) and Herod Agrippa II (25:13–26:32).

In addition, this Word regarding salvation in Jesus has permeated the Jewish homeland of Palestine-Syria and has been received with a measure of acceptance in the main centers of the eastern part of the Roman Empire, finally entering the capital city itself "without hindrance" (the final word of Luke's two-volume work). It is a universal message. It began in Jerusalem among Jews and spread "to the ends of the earth" (as promised by Jesus himself, Ac 1:8) to include all kinds of people. It is a message that by means of a process under the Spirit's direction, finally and inevitably freed itself from the shackles of Jewish legalism and a Jewish lifestyle. It is a Word of God that affected the lives of many through the power and activity of the Holy Spirit, that selfsame Spirit who came upon Jesus at his baptism and through whom he accomplished his mission.

b. Apologetic purpose

There is also inherent throughout the presentation of Acts an *apologetic purpose*. Its author seeks to demonstrate that Christianity is not a political threat to the empire, as its Jewish opponents asserted, but the culmination of Israel's hope and the true daughter of Jewish religion—and, therefore, should be treated by Roman authorities as a *religio licita* (a "legal religion") along with Judaism (see introduction to Luke). He notes, for example, that no Roman official in the first century ever accepted the charge that Christianity was an illegal new religion in the empire (cf. Lk 23:4, 14, 22; Ac 13:6–12; 16:35–39; 18:12–17; et al.).

c. Conciliatory purpose

A third purpose for writing Acts seems to have been a *conciliatory purpose* to the type of conflict depicted in 1Co 1:12. Acts presents the careers of Peter (chs. 1–12) and Paul (chs. 13–28) in strikingly parallel fashion (see introductory comments to 2:42–12:24). Likewise, Acts presents Paul as conceding primacy in the church to Peter and apostleship to the Twelve based on their earthly companionship with Jesus; whereas Peter and the Jerusalem authorities, in turn, concede to Paul another mode of apostolic authority and accept Peter's initiative in the law-free outreach to Gentiles.

d. Catechetical purpose

Finally, Luke may well have written Acts with a *catechetical purpose* in mind. Luke probably wrote his treatise to Theophilus with the expectation that it could also be used within various churches for instructional purposes, to show how Christianity moved out from its origins in Palestine to become a movement of God's Spirit in the Roman Empire. Thus Luke portrays in dramatic vignettes drawn from the early church's history the essence of early Christian preaching, the activity of the Holy Spirit in applying and spreading the message, the Gospel's power, its transforming quality, its type of adherents, their sacrifices and triumphs, and the ultimate entrance of the Christian proclamation into the city of Rome itself. Undoubtedly, such a catechetical purpose met a vital need among scattered congregations only recently formed—a need for instruction about the nature of the faith and the church's early history. Also, this instructional material helped draw believers together spiritually.

3. The Sources of Acts

It seems likely that, as with the gospel of Luke (see Lk 1:1–4), some basic source or sources, either written or oral, underlie the substructure of the first half of the book. The language of Ac 1–15 has a Semitic flavor, different from the Greek of the second half of the book. Many scholars have posited Aramaic writings as sources used by Luke.

As for possible source materials underlying the writing of Acts 16–28, attention has always been directed first of all to four passages in the narrative where the writer uses the pronoun "we"—16:10–17; 20:5–15; 21:1–18; 27:1–28:16. The most likely explanation for these passages is that the author of Acts had from time to time been a companion of Paul in his travels and discreetly indicated this by using "we" in those places in the narrative where he tells of events at which he had been present. The different styles in the speeches of Paul in chs. 13–28 suggest that Luke was using various sources for his accounts of Paul's sermons and defenses, even though Luke's thorough reworking of these sources prevents us from identifying or recreating them.

4. The Structure of Acts

The Acts of the Apostles was originally written as the second part of a two-volume work, and its inseparable relation to Luke's gospel must be kept in mind if we are to understand the work. The Prologue to the two-volume work (Lk 1:1–4) suggests, in fact, that the author's intention was to write "an account of the things that have been fulfilled among us"—things that stretched from the birth of John the Baptist to the entrance of the Good News into Rome. And his use of the emphatic verb "began" as he commences his second volume (Ac 1:1) sets up the parallel between "all that Jesus *began* to do and to teach [italics mine]" as recorded in his gospel and what he *continued* to do and to teach through his church as is shown in Acts.

Luke has taken pains to construct his second volume with an eye to the first; he sets up numerous parallels in the portrayal of events in the two volumes and repeatedly stresses features in the second that fulfill anticipations expressed in the first. The geographical movement of Jesus in the gospel from Galilee to Jerusalem, for example, is paralleled in Acts by the geographical advance of the Gospel from Jerusalem to Rome. The importance of the Holy Spirit in the birth narratives, in the Spirit's descent on Jesus at his baptism, and in the Spirit constantly undergirding his ministry (cf. Jesus' declaration of this fact found only in Luke 4:18–19) is paralleled in Acts by the Spirit's coming upon the disciples at Pentecost and the repeated emphasis upon the Spirit as the source of the church's power and progress.

On the other hand, Acts is not simply a parallel to the gospel, ending at Rome as the gospel ended at Jerusalem. If it were, it would be the less important part of Luke's two-volume work—something like a shadow of the original. But Acts is important in its own right as the logical and geographical completion of Jesus' journey to Jerusalem. The author presents the apostolic ministry as the necessary extension of the redemption effected by Christ. He views both the accomplishment of salvation and the spread of the Good News as inseparable units in the climactic activity of God's redemption of humankind—a truth probably picked up from Paul (cf. Ro 8:17; Php 3:10–11; Col 1:24). The Gospel had reached its culmination when it reached Rome, the capital of the Gentile world. And with that victory accomplished, Luke felt free to lay down his pen.

The structure for Acts as used in this commentary sees an introduction (1:1–2:41) and six panels, three for the Christian mission to the Jewish world (2:42–12:24) and three for the Christian mission to the Gentile world (12:25–28:31). Each of these panels concludes in a similar manner (see 6:7; 9:51; 12:24; 16:5; 19:20; 28:31).

5. Date of Composition

Various dates in the first and second century have been proposed for Luke's writing of his two-volume work. The best choice among those suggested is approximately A.D. 64. Acts contains a number of features that point to an earlier date than A.D. 70 for its composition. Chief among these is *the portrayal of the situation of the Jews.* They are represented as being both a spiritual and political power who had influence with the Roman courts and whose damaging testimony against the Christians must be countered. The Jews would likely not be depicted in this manner *after* their destruction as a nation in the war of A.D. 66–70. Nor would Luke have attempted in such a context to argue before a Gentile audience that Christianity should be accepted as a *religio licita* ("legal religion") because of its relation to Judaism. In the eyes of the Roman world Palestinian Judaism was largely defunct after A.D. 70, and Diaspora Judaism undoubtedly came under something of a cloud as a result. Luke's apologetic, however, is built upon the dual premises that (1) the Jewish leaders throughout the Diaspora and particularly the Jewish authorities at Jerusalem are at the time an important voice before Roman courts of law, even the imperial court at Rome; and (2) Judaism both in the Diaspora and at Jerusalem is accepted by Rome as a *religio licita.*

Likewise, *the estimation of Roman justice* implicit in Acts argues for its early composition. Acts expresses a generally hopeful outlook regarding Christianity's acceptance in the Gentile world and its recognition by Roman authorities. This could hardly have been the case after the Neronian persecution of Christians that began in A.D. 65 and resulted in the martyrdom of Paul and Peter, along with that of many other Christians (cf. 28:31, where Paul was able to preach "without hindrance" in Rome).

Finally, there is the surprising fact that *Acts reflects no knowledge of Paul's letters,* either in what is said or what is assumed on the part of its readers (cf. especially Paul's statements in 2Co 1–2; 11–12; Gal 1–2). This phenomenon may, of course, be interpreted as evidence for the personal aloofness and the chronological distance of the author of Acts from his hero. On the other hand, it may also suggest a very early date for Acts—namely, that it was before the significance of the Pauline correspondence was appreciated and before copies began to be distributed throughout the churches.

6. Authorship

Two observations from Acts itself must govern the discussion of its authorship. (1) Stylistically and structurally the gospel of Luke and the Acts of the Apostles are so closely related that they have to be assigned to the same author (see the introduction to Luke). (2) Luke-Acts claims to have been written by one who reports firsthand some of the events he records. In the Prologue (Lk 1:1–4) to his two-volume work, the author's use of the expression "among us" should probably be taken to imply his contemporary status with some of the events he purposes to narrate.

Furthermore, we have the evidence of the "we" sections in Acts (see above). Accepting the author as a traveling companion of Paul during some of his missionary journeys explains quite adequately two rather peculiar features about the plan of Acts: (1) the author devotes more than three-fifths of its space to Paul; (2) in the author's presentation of Paul, the first mission is narrated with great brevity while certain parts of the second and third missionary journeys, Paul's five defenses, and the journey to Rome are described in great detail. No writer who was altogether a stranger to apostolic times or working entirely from sources would have devoted so much space to the latter part of Paul's ministry. His work would have been more symmetrically planned.

Traditionally, the author of the third gospel has been identified as Luke, the companion of Paul mentioned in Col 4:14; Phm 24; 2Ti 4:11. Nor has tradition ever considered any author other than Luke. His authorship was accepted by Marcion (c. A.D. 135), was included in the Anti-Marcionite Prologue to the third gospel (c. A.D. 170), and was taken for granted by the compiler of the Muratorian Canon (c. A.D. 180–200). Furthermore, with Luke-Acts being originally one work in two volumes, which sometime during the last part of the first century or very early in the second began to circulate as two separate works, what is said regarding the one as to authorship must apply equally well to the other (see the introduction to Luke).

EXPOSITION

Introduction: The Constitutive Events of the Christian Mission (1:1–2:41)

The structural parallelism between Luke's gospel and his Acts is immediately seen in the comparative size of the two books and the time spans they cover. Each would have filled an almost equal-sized papyrus roll; each covers approximately thirty-three years. The parallelism is also evident in the plan and purpose of the opening chapters of each book. Luke 1:5–2:52 (after the Prologue of 1:1–4) is essentially a preparation for 3:1–4:13, and together these two sections constitute material introductory to the narrative of Jesus' ministry that begins with the pericope of 4:14–30. So, too, Ac 1:5–26 (after its preface of 1:1–4) serves to prepare for 2:1–41, and together these two chapters comprise an introduction to the ministry of the church that commences with the thesis paragraph 2:42–47 and continues by means of a series of illustrative vignettes beginning at 3:1.

A. A Resumptive Preface (1:1–5)

The Prologue to Luke-Acts is really Lk 1:1–4. Here, however, Luke begins his second book with what may be called a "resumptive preface," which serves to link the two books and anticipates the features he wants to stress as being constitutive for the Christian mission.

1 Luke calls his gospel "my former book." He uses the word *logos* (GK *3364*; usually translated "word" or "message" in the NT) in the technical sense of a section of a work that covers more than one papyrus roll. The subject of his first volume is "all that Jesus began to do and teach" up to his ascension. The word "began" stresses Luke's intent to show in Acts what Jesus *continued* to do and to teach through his church. And like the gospel, Acts is addressed to Theophilus (see comment on Lk 1:3).

2 Through a certain awkwardness in the Greek of this verse, Luke highlights four important introductory matters in approximately the same order in which he sets them out in his first two chapters and according to his priorities throughout Acts. Luke gives first place to Jesus' *mandate to witness*. The instructions he has in mind are undoubtedly those already set out in Lk 24:48–49 as the climax of Jesus' earthly teaching (quoted in slightly revised form in Ac 1:4-5 and developed in 1:6–8 as the theme of Acts). This mandate to witness was given to the *apostles*, who acted through the power of the *Holy Spirit*, whose coming was a direct result of our *Lord's ascension*.

3 Having stated the relation of his present book to its predecessor and shown his interest in the four factors named above, Luke turns back to the time before the Ascension. He recapitulates and expands upon certain features in Jesus' ministry crucial to the advance of the Gospel as he will present it in Acts. Like Paul in 1Co 15:5–7, his emphasis is on the living Christ, who "after his suffering... showed himself... alive" and demonstrated his resurrection by "many convincing proofs," such as the events in Lk 24:13ff. "Over a period of forty days" implies that during that time, the risen Lord showed himself at intervals, not continuously. When he did so, he "spoke about the kingdom of God."

The theme of "the kingdom [GK 993] of God" is a common one in the OT and NT. Primarily it refers to God's sovereign rule in human life and the affairs of history, and secondarily to the realm where that rule reigns. God's sovereignty is universal (cf. Ps 103:19). But it was specially manifested in the life of the nation of Israel and among Jesus' disciples; it is expressed progressively in the church and through the lives of Christians; and it will be fully revealed throughout eternity. In the Gospels the kingdom is presented as having been inaugurated in time and space by Jesus' presence and ministry (see comment on Mk 1:15). In Acts the phrase "the kingdom of God" usually appears as a convenient way of summarizing the early Christian proclamation (cf. 8:12; 19:8; 20:25; 28:23, 31). Jesus is explicitly identified as its subject (cf. 8:12; 28:23, 31).

We may infer that Jesus' teaching during the "forty days" dealt in essence with (1) the validation and nature of his messiahship, (2) the interpretation of the OT from the perspective of his resurrection, and (3) the responsibility of his disciples to bear witness to what had happened among them in fulfillment of Israel's hope (see Lk 24:25–27, 44–49). This is what Acts elaborates in the chapters that follow.

4 In vv. 4–5 Luke parallels his emphasis on the living Christ by stressing the coming and baptism of the Holy Spirit as essential to the advance of the Gospel. Luke gives us a specific occasion on which Jesus and his disciples ate together and he commanded them not to leave Jerusalem but to wait for the coming of the gift of the Holy Spirit, who had been promised by God the Father and spoken of by Jesus (repeated from Lk 24:49). This promise Jesus had made on behalf of the Father (see Jn 14:16–21, 26; 15:26–27; 16:7–15).

5 The statement appears to come from Mk 1:8 (see also Mt 3:11; Lk 3:16), where it is part of the message of John the Baptist. One could take v.5 as an explanatory comment on Luke's part, but its parallel in Ac 11:16, where it is given as the word of the Lord Jesus, suggests that here too it should be understood as being attributed to Jesus.

B. The Mandate to Witness (1:6–8)

Though vv.6–8 are usually treated either as the last part of the Preface (1:1–8) or as an introduction to the Ascension narrative (1:6–11), in reality they serve as the theme, setting the stage for all that follows in Acts: "You will be my witnesses in Jerusalem, and in all Judea and Samaria, and to the ends of the earth" (v.8). The concept of "witness" (GK *3459*) is so prominent in Acts (the word in its various forms appears some thirty-nine times) that everything else in the book, including the early preaching, should probably be seen as subsumed under it. So as Luke begins his second book, he highlights this witness theme and insists it comes from the mandate of Jesus himself.

6 The question the disciples asked reflects the embers of a once blazing hope for a political theocracy in which they would be leaders (cf. Mk 9:33–34; 10:35–41; Lk 22:24). Now the embers are fanned by Jesus' talk of the coming Holy Spirit. In Jewish expectations, the restoration of Israel's fortunes would be marked by the revived activity of God's Spirit, who had been withheld since the last of the prophets. But though his words about the Spirit's coming rekindled in the disciples their old nationalistic hopes, Jesus had something else in mind.

7 Jesus' answer to his disciples' misguided question is not a denial of any place for the nation of Israel in God's future purposes (cf. Ro 9–11, which speaks not only of a remnant within Israel responding to God but also of the nation of Israel still being involved in some way in God's redemptive program). Rather, it stresses the fact that the disciples were to revise their thinking about the divine program, leaving to God the matters that are his concern and taking up the things entrusted to them.

Jesus' insistence that "it is not for you to know" echoes his teaching in Mt 24:36 and Mk 13:32. The "times" (GK 5989) and "dates" (GK 2789) refer to the character of the ages preceding the final consummation of God's redemptive program and to the particular critical stages of these ages as they draw to a climax (cf. 1Th 5:1). These "the Father has set by his own authority"; they must not be the subject of speculation by believers—a teaching that, sadly, has been all too frequently disregarded.

8 The mandate to witness stands as the theme for the whole of Acts. It comes directly from Jesus himself—in fact, it is his final and conclusive word to his disciples before his ascension. All that follows in Acts is the result of Jesus' own intent and the fulfillment of his express word. This commission lays an obligation on all Christians and comes to us as a gift with a promise. It concerns a person, a power, and a program—the *person* of Jesus, on whose authority the church acts and who is the object of its witness; the *power* of the Holy Spirit, which is essential for the mission; and a *program* that begins at Jerusalem (cf. 2:42–8:3), moves out to "all Judea and Samaria" (cf. 8:4–12:24), and progresses until it finally reached the imperial capital city of Rome (12:25–28:31). The Christian church, according to Acts, is a missionary church that responds obediently to Jesus' commission, acts on Jesus' behalf in the extension of his ministry, focuses its proclamation of the kingdom of God in its witness to Jesus, is guided and empowered by the selfsame Spirit that directed and supported Jesus' ministry, and follows a program whose guidelines for outreach have been set by Jesus himself.

C. The Ascension (1:9–11)

Luke next speaks of the second constitutive factor of the Christian mission, the church's ascended Lord. The Greek of v.2 includes this as a fourth element in its listing of constitutive factors, but here Luke is proceeding more chronologically. So he speaks of the Ascension before mentioning the full complement of apostles and the coming of the Holy Spirit. The important thing about this account of the Ascension (cf. Lk 24:5–51) is the attention focused on (1) the fact of Jesus' ascension and entrance "into heaven" and (2) the angel's message that rebukes the disciples for their lack of understanding and assures them of their Lord's return. Luke's point is that the missionary activity of the early church rested not only on Jesus' mandate but also on his living presence in heaven and the sure promise of his return.

Many modern scholars have asserted that looking for Jesus' return paralyzes missionary activity and inhibits Christian social action by diverting attention away from present needs to the "sweet by and by." Luke, however, insists here that Christian mission must be based on the ascended and living Lord who directs his church from heaven and who will return to consummate what he has begun.

9 For Jesus' ascension Luke simply says that he "was taken up." He tells us very little else about it except that it occurred after Jesus had given his mandate to witness and while the disciples were watching. Not even the place where the Ascension occurred is mentioned in v.9, though in v.12 Luke says it took place on the Mount of Olives. More important for Luke than the description of the Ascension is its significance, and this he gives us in saying that "a cloud hid him from their sight."

The cloud undoubtedly symbolizes the shekinah (see comment on Ex 24:16–17), the visible manifestation of the divine presence and glory. Such a cloud hovered above the tabernacle in the wilderness as a visible token of the glory of God that dwelt within the tabernacle (cf. Ex 40:34); it also enveloped Jesus and three of his disciples on the Mount of Transfiguration as a visible sign of God's presence there and his approval of his Son (cf. Mk 9:7–11). Something similar is presented here: Jesus as the ascended Lord is enveloped by the shekinah cloud, the visible manifestation of God's presence, glory, and approval.

10–11 Luke describes the disciples as "looking intently up [a favorite word of Luke] into the sky as he was going." They were soon challenged by a double message from two angels "dressed in white." (1) The Jesus whom the disciples had known now had a heavenly existence (cf. the double use of the phrase "into heaven"). (2) The same Jesus they had known would return also enveloped in the cloud of the divine presence and glory (cf. Mt 24:30; 26:64; Mk 13:26; 14:62; Lk 21:27).

D. The Full Complement of Apostles 1:12-26)

Luke's third factor (cf. comment on 1:2) underlying the rise and expansion of the early Christian mission is the centrality of the apostles and their ministry. His interest in the apostles was evident already in Lk 6, where he adds that the disciples whom Jesus chose were also "designated apostles" (Lk 6:13). Now he resumes that interest, telling how under God's direction the apostolic band regained its full number after the defection of Judas Iscariot.

1. In the upper room (1:12–14)

12 The disciples had been instructed by Jesus to "stay in the city [of Jerusalem] until you have been clothed with power from on high" (Lk 24:49; cf. Ac 1:4) and to begin their ministry from that city (Lk 24:47; Ac 1:8). So they returned to Jerusalem from the Mount of Olives, a distance of "a Sabbath day's walk from the city" (about two-thirds of a mile).

13 Upper rooms in Palestinian cities were usually the choicest rooms because they were above the tumult of the crowded streets and beyond the prying eyes of passersby. For the wealthy, the upper room was the living room. Sometimes upper rooms were rented out. Often they served as places of assembly, study, and prayer. On their return to Jerusalem, the disciples "went upstairs to the room where they were staying," a room that presumably was well known to the early Christians—perhaps the room where Jesus and his disciples kept the Passover just before his crucifixion (Mk 14:12–16). Perhaps it was also the room where he appeared to some of them after he rose from the dead (Lk 24:33–43; cf. Jn 20:19, 26).

Luke has already listed the names of the Twelve in his gospel (6:14–16). Now he lists them again—though without Judas Iscariot, pointing out the incompleteness of the apostolic band and setting the stage for the account of its rectification through the choosing of Matthias. All this prepares for the coming of the Holy Spirit and the beginning of the apostolic ministry. In obedience to their Lord and in anticipation of what is to follow, the apostles have returned to Jerusalem—only they lack the full complement needed for their witness within Jewry.

14 In addition to the Eleven, also present in the upper room were "the women and Mary the mother of Jesus, and his brothers." They fill out the nucleus of the early church and in some way are to be included in the apostolic witness. The women Luke refers to are undoubtedly those mentioned in Lk 8:2–3; 23:49; 23:55–24:10, who followed Jesus throughout his ministry—even to his death—and contributed out of their personal incomes to support him and his followers. This mention of women fully accords with Luke's attitude toward women as portrayed in his gospel and the consciousness within the church of the implications of the Gospel proclamation.

The reference here to "Mary the mother of Jesus" continues Luke's interest in Mary begun in Lk 1, though this is the last occasion where she is recorded as being involved in the redemptive history of the NT. The reference to Jesus' "brothers" is particularly interesting because during his ministry they thought him to be "out of his mind" (Mk 3:21–35), perhaps even demon possessed, and because Jn 7:2–10 presupposes their disbelief. Paul, however, recounts an appearance of the risen Christ to James (cf. 1Co 15:7), and we may infer that Joses (or Joseph), Judas (or Jude), and Simon (cf. Mt 13:55–56; Mk 6:3) likewise came to believe in Jesus and attached themselves to the congregation of early Christians. These all are depicted as being assiduous in prayer (cf. Ac 2:42; 6:4). There must also have been others who were at various times assembled with these people, for 1:15 speaks of the total number of believers at the selection of Matthias as being "about a hundred and twenty."

2. Matthias chosen to replace Judas Iscariot (1:15–26)

15 In keeping with his character portrayal of Peter throughout his gospel, Luke here presents Peter as taking the lead among the apostles. The word "believers" here is usually "brothers" (GK *81*), a term that Luke frequently uses for Christian believers but also has just used for the blood "brothers" of Jesus.

16–17 The Greek literally reads "Men, brothers," a type of formal address found within first-century synagogues (cf. 2:29, 37; 7:2; 13:15, 26, 38; et al.). Peter's words in v.16, and again later in v.21, speak of the "necessity" (cf. "had to"; GK *1256*) of Scripture being fulfilled in relation to Judas's defection and the choice of another to replace him. Luke frequently stresses the compulsion inherent in the divine plan—a stress usually accompanied by an emphasis on human inability to comprehend God's workings. At times that divine necessity is explained in terms of the fulfillment of specific Scripture passages (as here; see also Lk 22:37; 24:26, 44), but more often that is not the case (e.g., Lk 2:49; 4:43; 9:22; et al.). This suggests that the concept of "divine necessity" is broader than just "the fulfillment of Scripture." We should therefore not say that the "necessity" here and in v.21 concerns only certain prophecies of Scripture. The understanding is rather (1) that God is doing something necessarily involved in his divine plan; (2) that the disciples' lack of comprehension of God's plan is profound, especially with respect to Judas; and (3) that an explicit way of understanding what has been going on under God's direction is through a Christian understanding of two psalms that speak of false companions and wicked men generally, and which by means of exegetical rules used in that day could be applied to the false disciple and wicked man par excellence, Judas Iscariot.

18–19 Luke now adds a parenthesis concerning the awful fate of Judas, presenting the tradition he has received (cf. v.6) and emphasizing the awfulness of Judas's fate, thus suggesting a basis for the disciples' perplexity in trying to comprehend the plan of God.

The difficulty of reconciling 1:18–19 with Mt 27:3–10 is well known and often considered the most intractable contradiction in the NT. The problem chiefly concerns how Judas died. But it also involves such questions as Who bought the field? and Why was it called "Field of Blood"? These latter matters are perhaps not too difficult. Probably the common explanation suffices: The chief priests bought the potter's field in Judas's name with the thirty silver coins belonging to him, and the local Jerusalemites (particularly Christians) nicknamed it "Field of Blood" because they felt it had been purchased with "blood money."

The major question as to how Judas died, however, is not so easily answered. Had he "hanged himself" (Mt 27:5)? Or was it that "he fell headlong, his body burst open and all his intestines spilled out" (Ac 1:18)? We shall probably never know the exact answer. But though the precise solution seems imponderable, the problem is not very different from many other differences among the evangelists in presenting the words and activity of Jesus. If, as seems likely, each writer wrote from the standpoint of his own theological purposes to the specific interests and appreciation of his audience, it is not too difficult to believe that in the context of Matthew's fulfillment theme it was sufficient for him and his readers to portray Judas's awful end with the terse expression "he hanged himself." But this would hardly suffice for Luke, Theophilus, and others in the Gentile world. Gentiles under Stoic influence generally looked on suicide as morally neutral. In order, therefore, to stress the awfulness of Judas's situation in a way that would grip his readers, Luke spelled out the gory details of Judas's suicide. He also highlights that what had happened to Judas was a divine necessity.

20 The OT passages Luke uses to support the divine necessity manifest in Judas's defection and replacement are Ps 69:25 and 109:8. These psalms speak of false companions and wicked men who have become enemies of God's righteous servant. They lament over his condition and give us his prayers for deliverance and his desire for retribution. Psalm 69 was applied variously within the early church to Jesus the Christ, the Servant of the Lord and Righteous Sufferer par excellence (v.9 is quoted in Jn 2:17 and Ro 15:3; vv. 22–23 in Ro 11:9–10). So here in v.20 we have another example of the Christian use of this block of messianic material, to which, using the commonly accepted exegetical principle of analogous subject, Peter added the ominous words of Ps 109:8 in order to defend the legitimacy of replacing a member of the apostolic band.

We need not insist that the early Christians believed that the primary reference of these two psalms was to Judas, as if no one could have understood them prior to the betrayal. What they seem to be saying, however, is that just as the psalmist's portrayals of "The Servant of the Lord and the Righteous

Sufferer" can on the basis of the Semitic concept of corporate solidarity be applied to God's Messiah, Jesus, the Servant and Righteous Sufferer, so the retribution spoken of as coming upon false companions and wicked men in general is especially applicable to Judas, who above all other men was false.

21–22 A twelvefold apostolic witness was required if early Jewish Christianity was to represent itself to the Jewish nation as the culmination of Israel's hope and the true people of Israel's Messiah (cf. Mt 19:28; Lk 22:30; Rev 21:10, 12, 14). The "remnant theology" of Late Judaism made it mandatory that any group that presented itself as "the righteous remnant" of the nation and had the responsibility of calling the nation to repentance and permeating it for God's glory, must represent itself as the true Israel, not only in its proclamation, but also in its symbolism. The Qumran community, for example, had twelve leaders heading up their community. Consequently, the early church found itself required to replace the defector Judas so as to have a full complement of twelve in its apostolic ranks.

For a candidate to succeed Judas among the apostles, Peter laid down two qualifications. The first was that the successor had to have familiar and unhindered association with Jesus from John's baptism to Jesus' ascension. Perhaps not all the Eleven themselves could claim association with Jesus from the days of John the Baptist (Jn 1:35–51 suggests that about half could). But they evidently wanted to make quite sure that there would be no deficiency on this first point. The second qualification was that of having been a witness to Christ's resurrection. From these two verses we may derive a strict definition of the term "apostle" (GK 693) and one that determines much of what Luke presents in the remainder of Acts (though, of course, Luke also uses the word "apostle" more broadly; cf. 14:14). An apostle was a guarantor of the Gospel tradition because he had been a companion of the earthly Jesus and a witness to the reality of his resurrection through an encounter with the risen Lord.

23 The eleven apostles together "proposed" two men: Joseph, who was called by Aramaic-speaking Jews "Barsabbas" and was also known by his Roman cognomen Justus, and Matthias. While more were perhaps considered (cf. v.21), only two had the necessary qualifications.

24–25 It was not enough to possess the qualifications that other apostles had. Judas's successor must also be appointed by the same Lord who appointed the Eleven. Likewise, though the church could not represent itself as the righteous remnant of Israel with one apostle lacking, it could hardly symbolize its consciousness as being the true Israel of God with one apostle too many. Therefore, prayer was offered to the Lord for his selection between the two candidates.

While it is not clear linguistically whether God the Father or Jesus is here being addressed in prayer by the vocative "Lord" (GK 3261), it is most natural to understand the same referent for the title here as in v.21: "the Lord Jesus." Furthermore, Luke seems to draw the parallel consciously by using the verb "to choose" for those selected by Jesus in 1:2 and for this replacement of Judas.

26 After determining qualifications and praying, they "cast lots, and the lot fell to Matthias." Determining God's will in this manner (likely by casting down marked objects) was common within Israel and the ancient world (cf. Pr 16:33). So by the appointment of Christ himself, the full complement of apostles was restored and the church was ready for the coming of the Holy Spirit and the beginning of its mission.

This pericope on the selection of Matthias has a number of significant implications. In the first place, it shows the necessity of a hermeneutical methodology that is able to distinguish between normative principles and culturally restricted practices in the progressive revelation of the Bible. We are exhorted as Christians to "search the Scriptures" and to "know what is the will of the Lord"—exhortations that are normative. But the early church's method for interpreting the OT (e.g., Ps 69) and the practice of casting lots in order to determine God's will need not bind believers today. Second, the pericope suggests that a Christian decision regarding vocation entails (1) evaluating personal qualifications, (2) earnest prayer, and (3) appointment by Christ himself—an appointment that may come in some culturally related fashion, but in a way clear to those who seek guidance.

In addition, it should be noted that it was Judas's defection and not simply the fact of his death that required his replacement. While the NT lays great stress on the apostolic message and faith and while Luke stresses the importance of the apostles themselves, this pericope gives no justification for the theological necessity of an apostolic succession of office, as is sometimes claimed for it. According to vv.21-22, the task of the twelve apostles was unique: to be guarantors of the Gospel tradition because of their companionship with Jesus in his earthly ministry and to be witnesses to the reality of his resurrection because they had seen the risen Christ. Such criteria cannot be transmitted from generation to generation. Thus when James the son of Zebedee was executed by Herod Agrippa I in A.D. 44 (cf. 12:1-2), the church took no action to replace him.

Finally, and contrary to an oft-heard claim that the apostles were wrong in selecting Matthias and should have awaited God's choice of Paul to fill the vacancy, it should be pointed out (1) that Paul had not been with Jesus during his earthly ministry—in fact, he acknowledges his dependence upon others with respect to the Gospel tradition (e.g., 1Co 15:3-5); (2) that the necessity of having exactly twelve apostles in the early church sprang largely from the need for Jewish Christians ministering within the Jewish nation to maintain this symbolic number, and, while Paul could appreciate this, he did not feel its necessity for his primarily Gentile ministry; and (3) that Paul himself recognized the special nature of his apostleship—namely, it was in line with that of the Twelve, but it also rested on a somewhat different base (cf. his reference to himself as an apostle "abnormally born" in 1Co 15:7-8). Paul's background, ministry, and call were in many ways different from those of the Twelve. Yet he insisted on the equality of his apostleship with that of the other apostles.

E. The Coming of the Holy Spirit (2:1-41)

Luke's fourth constitutive factor (see comment on 1:2) that undergirds the expansion of the early Christian mission is the coming of the Holy Spirit upon the assembled believers at Pentecost. To this the other three factors have pointed. And now Luke gives us an extended account of it that includes the baptism of the Spirit on the Day of Pentecost and Peter's sermon to the multitude and welds these separate incidents into a unified whole.

Matthew and Luke have preserved John the Baptist's distinction between his baptism with water and the baptism by the one who is to come, the "one more powerful" than he was (Mt 3:11; Lk 3:16). Luke goes on to connect the Baptist's prophecy of a baptism "with the Holy Spirit and with fire" with the miracle at Pentecost (Ac 1:5; 11:16). So Luke brings John's baptism of Jesus in the Jordan and the Spirit's baptism of assembled believers at Pentecost into a parallel in which each event is seen as the final constitutive factor for all that follows—for the ministry of Jesus in Luke's gospel and for the mission of the early church in Acts.

1. The miracle of Pentecost (2:1-13)

1 Luke describes the miracle of the coming of the Holy Spirit, with its accompanying signs, in four short verses, remarkable for their nuances. The miracle occurred on the festival known as Pentecost, which was celebrated on the fiftieth day after Passover (Lev 23:15-16; Dt 16:9-12). It was originally the Festival of the Firstfruits of the grain harvest (Ex 23:16; Lev 23:17-22; Nu 28:26-31); it was called the Feast of Weeks because it came after a period of seven weeks of harvesting that began with the offering of the first barley sheaf during the Passover celebration. By the time of the first century A.D., however, it was considered the anniversary of the giving of the law at Mount Sinai and was a time for the annual renewal of the Mosaic covenant; it was therefore looked upon as one of the three great pilgrim festivals of Judaism (along with Passover and Tabernacles).

Now no one who had been a companion of the apostle Paul could have failed to have been impressed by the fact that it was on the Jewish festival of Pentecost that the Spirit came so dramatically upon the early believers in Jerusalem. It is this significance that Luke emphasizes as he begins his Pentecost narrative; namely, that whereas Pentecost was for Judaism the day of the giving of the law, for Christians it is the day of the coming of the Holy Spirit. So for Luke the coming of the Spirit upon the early Christians at Pentecost is not only a parallel to the Spirit's coming upon Jesus at his baptism, it also shows that the mission of the Christian church, as was the ministry of Jesus, is dependent upon the Holy Spirit. And by his stress on Pentecost as the day when the miracle took place, he is also suggesting (1) that the Spirit's coming is in continuity with God's purposes in giving the law, and yet (2) that the Spirit's coming signals the essential difference between the Jewish faith and commitment to Jesus, for whereas the former is Torah-centered and Torah-directed, the latter is Christ-centered and Spirit-directed—all of which sounds very much like Paul.

As to just where the believers were when they experienced the coming of the Spirit, Luke is somewhat vague. His emphasis is on the "when"; all he tells us about "where" is that "they were all together in one place," in a "house" (v.2.). Most likely Luke is referring to the same upper room as in 1:12–26 as the setting for the miracle of the Spirit's coming and the place from where the disciples first went out to proclaim the Gospel.

2 There is, of course, nothing necessarily sensory about the Holy Spirit. Yet God in his providence often accompanies his Spirit's working by visible and audible signs—particularly at certain crises in redemptive history. This he does to assure his people of his presence. In vv.2–4 three signs of the Spirit's coming are reported to have appeared, each of them—wind, fire, and inspired speech—being considered in Jewish tradition as a sign of God's presence.

Wind as a sign of God's Spirit is rooted linguistically in the fact that both the Hebrew word *ruah* (GK 8120) and the Greek word *pneuma* (GK 4460) mean either "wind" or "spirit," depending on the context, and this allows a rather free association of the two ideas (cf. Jn 3:8). Ezekiel had prophesied of the wind as the breath of God blowing over the dry bones in the valley of his vision and filling them with new life (Eze 37:9–14), and it was this wind of God's Spirit that Judaism looked forward to as ushering in the final Messianic Age. Thus Luke tells us that one sign of the Spirit's coming upon the early followers of Jesus was "a sound like the blowing of a violent wind." Just why he emphasized the "sound" of the blowing of the "wind" is difficult to say. This sound "came from heaven" and "filled the whole house," symbolizing to all present the presence of God's Spirit among them in a way more intimate, personal, and powerful than they had ever before experienced.

3 Fire as a symbol of the divine presence was well known among first-century Jews (cf. the burning bush [Ex 3:2–5], the pillar of fire that guided Israel by night through the desert [Ex 13:21], the consuming fire on Mount Sinai [Ex 24:17], and the fire that hovered over the wilderness tabernacle [Ex 40:38]). John the Baptist explicitly linked the coming of the Spirit with fire (cf. Mt 3:11; Lk 3:16). The "tongues of fire" here are probably not to be equated with the "other tongues" of v.4 but should be taken as visible representations of the overshadowing presence of the Spirit of God.

Also significant is Luke's statement that these tokens of the Spirit's presence "separated and came to rest on each of them." This seems to suggest that, though under the old covenant the divine presence rested on Israel as a corporate entity and upon many of its leaders for special purposes, under the new covenant, as established by Jesus and inaugurated at Pentecost, the Spirit now rests upon each believer individually. In other words, though the corporate and individual aspects of redemption cannot actually be separated, the emphasis in the proclamation of redemption from Pentecost onward is on the personal relationship of God to the believer through the Spirit, with all corporate relationships resulting from this.

4 In OT times prophetic utterances were regularly associated with the Spirit's coming upon particular persons for special purposes (cf. Nu 11:26–29; 1Sa 10:6–12; et al.). In Judaism, however, the belief arose that with the passing of the last of the writing prophets in the early postexilic period, the spirit of prophecy had ceased in Israel, and God now spoke to his people only through the Torah as interpreted by the teachers. But Judaism also expected that with the coming of the Messianic Age there would be a special outpouring of God's Spirit, in fulfillment of Eze 37, and that prophecy would once again flourish. This is exactly what Luke portrays as having taken place at Pentecost among the followers of Jesus.

The "tongues" (GK *1185*) here are often identified with ecstatic utterances of the sort Paul discusses in 1Co 12–14. This identification is made largely (1) because in both instances the expression "other tongues" is used, and (2) because the verb translated "enabled" (or "gave utterance"; GK *1443* & *710*) is frequently used in the OT and other Greek literature in connection with ecstatics (cf. Mic 5:12; Zec 10:2). But the words spoken at Pentecost under the Spirit's direction were immediately recognized by those who heard them as being languages then current, while at Corinth no one could understand what was said until someone present received a gift of interpretation. And the above-mentioned verb appears in contexts that stress clarity of speech and understanding (see 2:14; 26:25). Therefore, the tongues in 2:4 are best understood as "languages" (see NIV note).

The coming of the Holy Spirit at Pentecost was of utmost significance both theologically and practically for the early church. Was Pentecost the birthday of the Christian church? A great deal depends upon what one means by the term "church" (GK *1711*) in the NT. One meaning is "the body of Christ" as the redeemed of all ages. For this meaning, it can hardly be said that the church had its beginning *only* at Pentecost. What Luke seems to be stressing is (1) that the relationship of the Spirit to the members of the body of Christ became much more intimate and personal at Pentecost, in fulfillment of Jesus' promise that the Spirit who "lives with you . . . will be in you" (Jn 14:17), and (2) that at Pentecost a new model of divine redemption was established as characteristic for life in the new covenant—one that, while incorporating both individual and corporate redemption, begins with the former in order to include the latter.

A second meaning of "church" is "an instrument of service" (distinguishable from the nation Israel) used by God for his redemptive purposes. It has been called by God to take up the mission formerly entrusted to Israel. In this sense, Luke is certainly presenting the coming of the Spirit at Pentecost as the church's birthday. Neither Jesus' ministry nor the mission of the early church would have been possible apart from the Spirit's empowering. So Luke emphasizes Jesus' explicit command to the disciples to stay in Jerusalem till they were empowered from on high by the Spirit (Lk 24:49; Ac 1:4–5, 8).

5–6 Certain "God-fearing Jews" who were residing in Jerusalem from many parts of the Diaspora, together with a number of Jews and proselytes who had returned to Jerusalem as pilgrims for the Pentecost festival, were "in bewilderment," "utterly amazed," and "perplexed" by the miraculous coming of the Spirit (vv.6–7, 12). Others, however, mocked (v.13). What drew the crowd and caused its bewilderment? Commentators differ as to whether it was the sound of the wind or the disciples' speaking in various languages. But if we break the sentence with some kind of punctuation after "crowd" rather than (as is usually done) after "bewilderment," we have two coordinate sentences with two separate yet complementary ideas: "When they heard this sound, a crowd came together. And they were bewildered because each one heard them speaking in his own language." On this reading, "this sound" refers back to the "sound" of v.2 and conjures up a picture of people rushing to the source of the noise to see what is going on. When they get there, they become bewildered on hearing Galileans speaking in their own native languages.

7–8 Galileans had difficulty pronouncing gutturals and had the habit of swallowing syllables when speaking; so they were looked down upon by the people of Jerusalem as being provincial (cf. Mk 14:70). Therefore, since the disciples who were speaking were Galileans, it bewildered those who heard because the disciples could not by themselves have learned so many different languages.

9–11 Why these fifteen countries and no others are named here and why they are cited in this order are questions without ready solutions. Presumably Luke is using a current literary convention to illustrate his more prosaic statement of v.5: "from every nation under heaven." The list includes both ancient kingdoms and current political entities, moving generally from east to west and in its middle section naming first the northern and then the southern lands.

The appearance of "Judea" in the listing is, admittedly, strange because (1) it hardly ranks being sandwiched between Mesopotamia to the east and Cappadocia to the north; and (2) it involves the curious anomaly of inhabitants of Judea being amazed to hear the apostles speak in their own language. Perhaps the most cogent solution involves viewing "Judea" here in a wider prophetic sense, wherein the reference is to "the land of the Jews" that was held to stretch from the Euphrates to the Egyptian border. This would explain its sequence in the list and the omission of Syria from the list, and it would allow for a variety of dialects different from the one that was native to Jerusalem. The inclusion of "Cretans and Arabs" probably refers to seafaring peoples and to Nabatean Arabs, whose kingdom traditionally extended from the Euphrates to the Red Sea.

Each area and country named had a considerable Jewish population within its borders. Some of these had returned to Jerusalem to take up residence there. One group, however, is singled out as being religious pilgrims to the city: Jews and proselytes to Judaism from Rome. Undoubtedly there were other festival pilgrims in the crowd (just as there must have been other Diaspora Jews in attendance who were residents of Jerusalem), but Luke's interest in Acts is in the Gospel reaching out even to Rome, the capital of the empire. So he singles out this pilgrim contingent for special mention. It may be that some of these "visitors" from Rome returned there and formed the nucleus of the church in that city.

12–13 The miraculous does not inevitably and uniformly convince. There must also be the preparation of the heart and the proclamation of the message if miracles are to accomplish their full purpose. This was true even for the miracle of the Spirit's coming at Pentecost. All of the "God-fearing Jews" (v 5) whose attention had been arrested by the signs at Pentecost and whose own religious heritage gave them at least some appreciation of them were amazed and asked, "What does this mean?" Others, however, being spiritually insensitive, only mocked, attributing such phenomena to drunkenness. All this prepares the reader for Peter's sermon, which is the initial proclamation of the Gospel message to a prepared people.

2. Peter's sermon at Pentecost (2:14–41)

Peter's sermon at Pentecost consists of (1) an explanation of the occurrence of the phenomena (vv.14–21), (2) a proclamation of the apostolic message in its most elemental form (vv.22–36), and (3) a call to repentance with a promise of blessing (vv.37–41). The sermon is headed by a brief introductory statement and followed by two summary sentences dealing with Peter's further preaching and the people's response. It was probably delivered in the outer court of the temple.

a. Explanation section (2:14–21)

14 The first section of Peter's sermon is addressed to the "fellow Jews" and "all ... [who are] in Jerusalem." Later on these two groups are combined under the captions "Men of Israel" (v.22) and "Brothers" (v.29), for it is natural for them to be classed together. But here Peter apparently wanted to include particularly those most bewildered by the multiplicity of the languages spoken, namely, the Diaspora contingent, who most appreciated the incongruity of the situation and wanted an explanation.

15 Peter begins negatively by arguing that the apostles could not be drunk, for it was only "nine in the morning." Unfortunately, this argument was more telling in antiquity than today.

16–21 Positively, Peter explains the phenomena taking place among the early Christians at Pentecost as fulfilling Joel 2:28–32. His use of the Joel passage employs a then-current method of OT interpretation that lays all emphasis on the fulfillment motif without attempting to exegete the details of the biblical prophecy it "interprets." The note of fulfillment is heightened by Peter's alteration of the OT's "afterwards" to "in the last days" and by his interruption of the quotation to insert the words "and they will prophesy" (v.18), thus highlighting the restoration of prophecy. The solemnity and importance of the words are emphasized by the addition of "God says" at the beginning (v.18).

The way Peter uses Joel 2:28–32 is of great significance for an appreciation of early Christian exegetical practices and doctrinal commitments and as a pattern for our own treatment of the OT. For Peter, we should note, what Joel said is what God says. And while what God said may have been somewhat enigmatic when first uttered, in the light of what has just happened it is clarified. Thus Peter can proclaim from the perspective of the Messiah's resurrection and living presence with his people (1) that "this" that he

ACTS 2

COUNTRIES OF PEOPLE MENTIONED AT PENTECOST

ASIA—Provinces of the Roman empire
Media—Provinces of the Parthian empire
Rome—Cities
CRETE—Island

(1) (2) (3) etc.—Numbers indicate sequence listed in Ac 2:9-11

© 1988 The Zondervan Corporation.

and the infant church were experiencing in the outpouring of God's Spirit "is that" prophesied by Joel, (2) that these are the long-awaited "last days" of God's redemptive program, and (3) that the validation of all this is the fact of the return of prophesying. By including the prophet Joel's call for response (v.21), Peter is also suggesting that a prophetic message of salvation and a call for repentance will go out from Jerusalem.

How Peter and the earliest followers of Jesus understood the more spectacular physical signs of Joel's prophecy (i.e., "blood and fire and billows of smoke"; "the sun will be turned to darkness and the moon to blood") has been debated (see EBC 1:103–26). What is important to note is that Peter quotes the entire prophecy in Joel 2:28–32 because of its traditional messianic significance and because of its final sentence ("And everyone who calls on the name of the Lord will be saved"), which leads logically into the proclamation section of his sermon.

b. Proclamation section (2:22–36)

Many scholars, beginning with C. H. Dodd, identify six themes that appear repeatedly in Peter's sermons in Acts 2–4:

1. The age of fulfillment has dawned.
2. This has come about through the ministry, death and resurrection of Jesus (a brief account is given, with proof from Scripture).
3. Jesus was raised from the dead and is now exalted at God's right hand.
4. The presence of the Holy Spirit is the sign of Christ's power and glory.
5. The Messianic Age will soon end in the return of Christ.
6. The preaching always ends by an appeal for repentance, the offer of forgiveness and of the Holy Spirit, and the promise of salvation to those who enter the elect community.

With the exception of the return of Christ (which appears in these early sermons only at 3:20–21), all these themes are in Peter's Pentecost sermon. The early church was interested in the life and character of Jesus. Its preaching about Jesus was principally functional in nature rather than philosophical and stressed ultimate causality more than secondary causes or means. Peter therefore proclaims our Lord as "Jesus of Nazareth," "a man accredited," "handed over," put "to death," and raised "from the dead." God was the true author of Jesus' miracles, the ultimate agent in Jesus' death, and the only cause for Jesus' resurrection. There is, to be sure, some allusion to means in the statement "and you, with the help of wicked men, put him to death by nailing him to the cross" (v.23b). Yet the primary emphasis here is focused on Jesus, including Peter's closing declaration (v.36) and his call to repentance (v.38).

22 Peter begins his proclamation section with an inclusive form of address: "Men of Israel," which he parallels with the synonymous vocative "Brothers" (v.29). His topic concerns "Jesus of Nazareth"—a common title used of Jesus throughout Luke's writings (cf. Lk 18:37; Ac 3:6; 4:10; et al.) and one by which early Christians themselves were at times called (cf. 24:5). The ministry of Jesus is characterized by "miracles, wonders and signs" that God did among the people through Jesus.

23 The death of Jesus is presented as resulting from the interplay of divine necessity and human freedom. Nowhere in the NT is the paradox of a Christian understanding of history put more sharply than in this earliest proclamation of the death of Jesus the Messiah: God's purpose and foreknowledge stand as the necessary factors behind whatever happens; yet whatever happens occurs through the instrumentality of wicked people expressing their own human freedom. It is a paradox without ready solution. To deny it, however, is to go counter to the plain teaching of Scripture in both the OT and NT and to ignore the testimony of personal experience. "With the help of wicked men" points to the Roman authorities in Palestine, who carried out what had been instigated by the Jewish authorities.

24 Here the resurrection of Jesus is attributed directly to God, apart from any human action or even Jesus himself—just as elsewhere in the NT it is so attributed in quotations from early Christian hymns and catechisms (e.g., 1Co 15:4; Php 2:9). The imagery is of "death pangs" and their awful clutches (cf. 2Sa 22:6; Pss 18:4–6; 116:3), from which God is "freeing" Jesus "because it was impossible for death to keep its hold on him."

25–35 Here Peter quotes from Ps 16:8–11 and Ps 110:1 in support of what he has just said about Jesus in v.24. Peter once again uses a principle of the interpretation of Scripture that was acceptable in his day, which said that the same words appearing in two separate passages can be brought together. Both quotations have "at my right hand" and thus are deliberately treated together (cf. v.33).

During this period, both Ps 16 and Ps 110 were considered by Jewish interpreters to be somewhat enigmatic and were therefore understood in various ways. There was no problem with the confidence expressed in Ps 16:8–9, 11, for it was appropriate for the psalmist to whom God's love had been pledged and who had experienced God's covenant-keeping lovingkindness. But how could the psalmist have expected God to keep him from the grave and from undergoing decay, as in v.10? And Ps 110 was even more difficult, for who is this "my Lord" to whom "the LORD" has said, "Sit at my right hand until I make your enemies a footstool for your feet" (v.34)? Some early rabbis linked the psalm with Abraham, others with David, and some even with Hezekiah; but there is no clearly attested messianic understanding of Ps 110 in rabbinic literature until about A.D. 260.

Nevertheless, Jesus is reported in all three Synoptic Gospels as having interpreted Ps 110:1 as a messianic passage and as applying it to himself (Mt 22:41–46; Mk 12:35–37; Lk 20:41–44). And it was probably Jesus' own treatment of this verse that (1) furnished the exegetical key for the early church's understanding of their risen Lord, (2) served as the pattern for their interpretation of similar enigmatic OT passages (e.g., Paul's combining 2Sa 7:6–16 with Ps 2:7 and Isa 55:3 with Ps 16:10 in his Antioch address of Ac 13:16–41), and (3) anchored all other passages as could be brought together on a "verbal analogy basis" (e.g., the passages listed in Heb 1:5–13).

Therefore working from Ps 110:1 as an accepted messianic passage and viewing Ps 16:8–11 as legitimately related to it, Peter proclaims that Ps 16:10 refers to Israel's promised Messiah and no other. Furthermore, Peter insists, David could not have been speaking about himself, for he did indeed die, was buried, and suffered decay—as the presence of his tomb in the city eloquently testifies (v.29). Nor did he ascend into heaven. Therefore, David must have been prophesying about the resurrection of the Messiah in Ps 16:10 and about his exaltation in Ps 110:1. And with God's raising of Jesus from the dead, these formerly enigmatic passages are clarified and the pouring out of the Spirit explained.

36 With the proclamation of Jesus as Lord and Messiah, Peter reaches the climax and conclusion of his sermon. The initial "therefore" shows that God's resurrection and exaltation of Jesus accredit him as humankind's Lord and Israel's Messiah. And Peter calls upon "all Israel" to know with certainty that "God has made this Jesus, whom you crucified, both Lord and Christ." Jesus was acknowledged and proclaimed Lord and Christ both after his resurrection and because of his resurrection. In Jewish thought, no one had a right to the title Messiah till he had accomplished the work of the Messiah. During his earthly ministry, as that ministry is portrayed in all the Gospels, Jesus was distinctly reluctant to accept the acclaim of Lord and Messiah, probably because his understanding of messiahship had to do with suffering and because his concept of lordship had to do with vindication and exaltation by God. But now that Jesus has accomplished his messianic mission in life and death and has been raised by God and exalted "at his right hand," the titles Lord and Christ are legitimately his. This theme of function and accomplishment as the basis for titular acclaim is a recurring note in the christological statements elsewhere in the NT (cf. Ro 1:4; Php 2:9–11; Heb 2:14; 1Jn 5:6). The resurrection of Jesus from the dead is God's open avowal that the messianic work has been accomplished and that Jesus now has the full right to assume the messianic title.

In the twelve instances in Acts where the word "Christ" (GK 5986; see comment on Mk 8:29–30) appears singly (2:31, 36; 3:18; 4:26; 8:5; 9:22; 17:3a, 26:23) and where "Christ" is in apposition to "Jesus" but still "used" singly (3:20; 5:42; 18:5, 28), it is used as a title, "Messiah." And in all these instances, it is addressed to a Jewish audience (only 8:5 and 26:23 are possible exceptions, though both the Samaritans and Agrippa II possessed something of a Jewish background and understanding). Apparently, therefore, the messiahship of Jesus was the distinctive feature of the church's witness within Jewish circles, signifying, as it does, his fulfillment of

Israel's hopes and his culmination of God's redemptive purposes.

The title "Lord" (GK *3261*) was also proclaimed christologically in Jewish circles, with evident intent to apply to Jesus all that was said of God in the OT (cf. the Christological use of Isa 45:23 in Php 2:10). But "Lord" came to have particular relevance to the church's witness to Gentiles just as "Messiah" was more relevant to the Jewish world. So in Acts Luke reports the proclamation of Jesus as "the Christ" before Jewish audiences both in Palestine and among the Diaspora, whereas Paul in his letters to Gentile churches generally uses Christ as a proper name and proclaims Christ Jesus as "the Lord."

c. A call to repentance and a promise of blessing (2:37–41)

37 Peter's preaching had been effective. The people were "cut to the heart" at the awful realization that in crucifying their long-awaited Messiah they had rejected their only hope of salvation. So with deep anguish they cried out, "Brothers, what shall we do?" The phrase "cut to the heart" may have been drawn from Ps 109:16, the same psalm Luke had earlier applied to Judas (see comment on 1:20). There it is a vivid phrase for those who stand with God's servant in opposing the wicked men: "those who have been cut to the heart" or those who are "the humble of heart" because they realize their need and are open to God's working.

The *Kerygma* of the Early Church

1. The promises by God made in the OT have now been fulfilled with the coming of Jesus the Messiah (Ac 2:30; 3:19, 24, 10:43; 26:6–7, 22; Ro 1:2–4; 1Ti 3:16; Heb 1:1–2; 1Pe 1:10–12; 2Pe 1:18–19).

2. Jesus was anointed by God at his baptism as Messiah (Ac 10:38).

3. Jesus began his ministry in Galilee after his baptism (Ac 10:37).

4. He conducted a beneficent ministry, doing good and performing mighty works by the power of God (Mk 10:45; Ac 2:22; 10:38)

5. The Messiah was crucified according to the purpose of God (Mk 10:45; Jn 3:16; Ac 2:23; 3:13–15, 18; 4:11; 10:39; 26:23; Ro 8:34; 1Co 1:17–18; 15:3; Gal 1:4; Heb 1:3; 1Pe 1:2, 19; 3:18; 1Jn 4:10).

6. He was raised from the dead and appeared to his disciples (Ac 2:24, 31–32; 3:15, 26; 10:40–41; 17:31; 26:23; Ro 8:34; 10:9; 1Co 15:4–7, 12ff.; 1Th 1:10; 1Ti 3:16; 1Pe 1:2, 21; 3:18, 21).

7. Jesus was exalted by God and given the name "Lord" (Ac 2:25–29, 33–36; 3:13; 10:36; Ro 8:34; 10:9; 1Ti 3:16; Heb 1:3; 1Pe 3:22).

8. He gave the Holy Spirit to form the new community of God (Ac 1:8; 2:14–18, 33, 38-39; 10:44–47; 1Pe 1:12).

9. He will come again for judgment and the restoration of all things (Ac 3:20–21; 10:42; 17:31; 1Co 15:20–28; 1Th 1:10).

10. All who hear the message should repent and be baptized (Ac 2:21, 38; 3:19; 10:43, 47–48; 17:30; 26:20; Ro 1:17; 10:9; 1Pe 3:21).

This schema served as the essential proclamation of the early church, though different authors of the NT may leave out a portion or vary in emphasis on particulars in the *kerygma*. Compare the entire gospel of Mark, which closely follows the Petrine aspect of the *kerygma*.

Taken from *Chronological and Background Charts of the New Testament* by Wayne House. Copyright© 1978 by The Zondervan Corporation. Used by permission.

38 Peter's answer to the people's anguished cry presents interpreters with a set of complex theological problems that are often looked upon only as grist for differing theological mills. But Peter's words came to his hearers as the best news they had ever heard—far better, indeed, than they could have hoped for. So today these words remain the best of good news and should be read as the proclamation of that news and not as just a set of theological problems.

Peter calls on his hearers to "repent" (GK 3566). This word implies a complete change of heart, beginning with the confession of sin. With this he couples the call to "be baptized," thus linking both repentance and baptism with the forgiveness of sins. So far this sounds familiar, for John the Baptist had proclaimed a "baptism of repentance for the forgiveness of sins" (Mk 1:4); and Jesus made repentance central in his preaching (cf. Mt 4:17; Mk 1:15) and baptized (cf. Jn 3:22, 26; 4:1–2). Judaism also had repentance at the core of its message and emphasized baptism (at least for proselytes). But while there is much that appears traditional in Peter's exhortation, there is also much that is new and distinctive—particularly in three ways.

In the first place, Peter calls on "every one" of his audience to repent and be baptized. Jews thought corporately and generally viewed the rite of baptism as appropriate only for proselytes (though some sects within Judaism baptized Jews). But like John the Baptist and probably Jesus, Peter calls for an individual response on the part of his hearers. So he set aside family and corporate relationships as having any final saving significance and stressed the response of the individual person—not, however, denying the necessity and value of corporate relationships, but placing them in a "new covenant" perspective.

Second, Peter identifies the repentance and baptism he is speaking of as being specifically Christian in that it is done "in the name of Jesus Christ." What that means, it seems, is that a person in repenting and being baptized calls upon the name of Jesus (cf. 22:16) and thereby avows his or her intention to be committed to and identified with Jesus.

A third feature in Peter's preaching at this point is the relation of the gift of the Holy Spirit to repentance and baptism. "The gift of the Holy Spirit" is another way of describing what the disciples had experienced in "the coming of the Holy Spirit," which Jesus called "the baptism of the Holy Spirit" (cf. 1:4–5, 8). We must distinguish between "the gift" (GK 1562) of the Holy Spirit and what Paul called "the gifts" (GK 5922; 1Co 12:1; 14:1) of that selfsame Spirit. "The gift" is the Spirit himself given to minister the saving benefits of Christ's redemption to the believer, while "the gifts" are those spiritual abilities the Spirit gives variously to believers "for the common good" and sovereignly, "just as he determines" (1Co 12:7, 11). Peter's promise of the "gift of the Holy Spirit" is a logical outcome of repentance and baptism. This primary gift includes a variety of spiritual gifts for the advancement of the Gospel and the welfare of God's people. But first of all, it has to do with what God's Spirit does for every Christian in applying and working out the benefits of Christ's redemptive work.

In trying to deal with the various elements in this passage, some interpreters have stressed the command to be baptized so as to link the forgiveness of sins exclusively with baptism. But it runs contrary to all biblical religion to assume that outward rites have any value apart from true repentance and an inward change. The Jewish mind, indeed, could not divorce inward spirituality from its outward expression. Wherever the Gospel was proclaimed in a Jewish milieu, the rite of baptism was taken for granted as being inevitably involved (cf. 2:41; 8:12 ,36–38; 9:18; 10:47–48; 18:8; 19:5; also Heb 10:22; 1Pe 3:18–21). But Peter's sermon in Solomon's Colonnade (cf. 3:12–26) stresses only repentance and turning to God "so that your sins may be wiped out" (v.19) and makes no mention of baptism. This shows that for Luke at least, and probably also for Peter, while baptism with water was the expected symbol for conversion, it was not an indispensable criterion for salvation.

A few commentators have set Peter's words in v.38 in opposition to those of John the Baptist in Mk 1:8 and those of Jesus in Ac 1:5, where the baptism of the Holy Spirit is distinguished from John's baptism and appears to supersede it. But neither the Baptist's prophecy nor Jesus' promise necessarily implies that the baptism of the Spirit would set aside water baptism. Certainly the early church did not take it that way. They continued to practice water baptism as the external symbol by which those who believed the Gospel, repented of their sins, and acknowledged Jesus as their Lord publicly bore witness to their new life, which had been received through the baptism of the Holy Spirit. In line, then, with the Baptist's prophecy and Jesus' promise, baptism with the Holy Spirit is distinguished from baptism with water. But baptism with the Holy Spirit did not replace baptism with water; rather, the latter was given a richer significance because of the saving work of Christ and the coming of the Spirit.

Again, some have observed that there is no mention in this passage, either in the report of Peter's preaching (vv.38–40) or in the summary of the people's response (v.41), of any speaking in tongues, as at Pentecost, or of laying on of hands, as in Samaria (8:17). From this various implications have been drawn. In a Jewish context, however, it would not have been surprising if both occurred; in fact, one is probably justified in being surprised had they not occurred. Nevertheless, that they are not mentioned implies (as with the omission of baptism in 3:19) that speaking in tongues and laying on of hands were not considered prerequisites for receiving the Spirit.

A more difficult problem arises when we try to correlate Peter's words here with the accounts of the Spirit's baptism in 8:15–17 (at Samaria), 10:44–46 (in the house of Cornelius), and 19:6 (at Ephesus). In v.38 the baptism of the Spirit is the logical outcome of repentance and water baptism; but in 8:15–17; 10:44–46; and 19:6 it appears to be temporally separated from conversion and water baptism—either following them (as at Samaria and Ephesus) or preceding them (as with Cornelius). Catholic sacramentalists take this as a biblical basis for separating baptism and confirmation; and Charismatics of various kinds see it as justification for a doctrine of the baptism of the Spirit as a second work of grace after conversion. But lest too much be made of this difference theologically, we ought first to attempt to understand the historical situation of vv.37–41 and to explain matters more circumstantially. Assuming for the moment that Luke shared Paul's view of the indissoluble connection between conversion, water baptism, and the baptism of the Holy Spirit (cf. Ro 8:9; 1Co 6:11), the following question may be asked: What if the Pentecost experience, particularly in regard to the sequence and temporal relations of conversion, water baptism, and Holy Spirit baptism, had been fully present in each of these latter three instances?

Take the Samaritans (8:4–8, 14–17), for example, who were converted through the instrumentality of Philip, one of the Hellenists expelled from Jerusalem at the time of Stephen's martyrdom. Samaritans had always been considered second-class citizens of Palestine by the Jerusalem Jews who kept them at arm's length. What if it had been the apostles residing at Jerusalem who had been the missioners to Samaria? Probably they would have been rebuffed, just as they were earlier when the Samaritans associated them with the city of Jerusalem (cf. Lk 9:51–56). But God providentially used Philip to bring them the Gospel—Philip, who had also (though for different reasons) been rebuffed at Jerusalem. The Samaritans received him and believed his message. But what if the Spirit had come upon them at their baptism by Philip? Undoubtedly what feelings some of the Christians at Jerusalem had against Philip and the Hellenists would have rubbed off on the Samaritan believers and they would have been doubly under suspicion. But God providentially withheld the gift of the Holy Spirit till Peter and John laid their hands on the Samaritans—Peter and John, two leading Jerusalem apostles who at that time would have been accepted by the new converts of Samaria. So in this first advance of the Gospel outside Jerusalem, God worked in ways conducive both to the reception of the Good News in Samaria and to the acceptance of these new converts at Jerusalem—ways that promoted both the outreach of the Gospel and the unity of the church.

Or take the conversion of Cornelius (10:34–48). What if, in Peter's ministry to this Gentile, the order of events Peter had set down after his sermon at Pentecost had occurred (2:38–39), namely, repentance, baptism, forgiveness of sins, reception of the gift of the Holy Spirit? Some at Jerusalem might have accused Peter of manipulating the occasion for his own ends (as his lengthy defense before the Jerusalem congregation in 11:1–18 takes pains to deny). But God in his providence gave the gift of his Spirit, coupled with such signs as would convince both Peter and his possible critics at Jerusalem, even *before*

Cornelius's baptism, so that all would attribute his conversion entirely to God rather than let their prejudices make Cornelius a second-class Christian. (Regarding 19:1–4, see comments on that passage.)

39 The "promise" (GK *2039*) of which Peter speaks includes both the forgiveness of sins and the gift of the Holy Spirit. Both are logically and indissolubly united in applying Christ's redemptive work to the believer, and they were only separated chronologically, it seems, for what could be called circumstantial reasons. The promise, Peter declares, is not only for his immediate hearers ("for you") but also for succeeding generations ("for your children") and for all in distant places ("for all who are far off"). It is a promise, Peter concludes, that is sure; for it has been given by God and rests upon the prophetic word of Joel 2:32: "And everyone who calls on the name of the Lord will be saved."

Two issues need to be discussed regarding the expression "for all who are far off." (1) Some prefer to see this as a temporal reference to future Jewish generations, paralleling the phrase "for your children." But the word "far off" (GK *3426*) in Greek is used exclusively as a spatial rather than as a temporal word in the NT. (2) Does it refer only to Diaspora Jews or also to Gentiles? The two OT passages alluded to here (Isa 57:19; Joel 2:32) are probably referring to Diaspora Jews. But this is one of those situations where a narrator like Luke has read into what the speaker said more than was originally there and so implied that the speaker spoke better than he knew. Peter himself was probably thinking of Jewish remnant theology, of God's call to a scattered but repentant Jewish remnant. But Luke's desire is to show how an originally Jewish gospel penetrated the Gentile world so extensively that it came to enter "without hindrance" (cf. 28:31) into the capital of the Roman Empire. Very likely, therefore, in recounting Peter's words here in Acts, Luke meant them to be read as having Gentiles in mind (see also 22:21).

40–41 Two summary statements conclude Luke's report of Peter's Pentecost sermon. (1) Peter spoke earnest, solemn words, connoted by the verbs "warned" and "pleaded." His characterization of this age as a "corrupt generation" has its parallel in Jesus' words (cf. Mt 16:4; 17:17) and in Paul's (cf. Php 2:15). What we have here is the vision of an evangelist—a vision that is all too often lost as the Gospel is acclimated to the world and the world to the church. The Jews generally looked on baptism as a rite only for Gentile converts (i.e., proselytes), not for one born a Jew, and it symbolized the break with one's Gentile past and the washing away of all defilement. So when Jews accepted baptism in the name of Jesus on hearing Peter's message, it was traumatic and significant for them in a way we in our mildly christianized culture have difficulty understanding. (2) Yet, as a result of Peter's preaching, "about" three thousand took the revolutionary step of baptism. Thus, the congregation of believers in Jesus came into being at Jerusalem—a congregation made up of the original 120 (1:15) and progressively augmented by about three thousand others.

Part I. The Christian Mission to the Jewish World (2:42–12:24)

Luke gives us the theme of Acts in Jesus' words: "You will be my witnesses in Jerusalem, and in all Judea and Samaria, and to the ends of the earth" (1:8). Behind them stands Dt 19:15, with its requirement that every matter be established by two or three witnesses. In his gospel Luke has frequently highlighted such matters as (1) the witness of the Scriptures coupled with the ministry of Jesus and the witness of the Spirit, (2) the pairings of the disciples in their journeys on behalf of Jesus (cf. 10:1), and (3) the two angels at the tomb. In his organization of the common tradition in his gospel, he set up a number of parallels between our Lord's ministry in Galilee (Lk 4:14–9:50) and his ministry in the regions of Perea and Judea (Lk 9:51–19:27). So in Acts Luke continues his pairings of apostolic men in their ministries (e.g., Peter and John in Ac 3:1, 3–4, 11; 4:13, 19; 8:14; Barnabas and Saul in 11:25–26; 12:25; 13:2; Paul and Barnabas in 13:43, 46, 50; 15:2, 12, 22, 35; Judas and Silas in 15:32; Barnabas and Mark in 15:39; Paul and Silas in 15:40; 16:19, 25; 17:4, 10; and Silas and Timothy in 17:14–15; 18:5). Luke also sets up a number of parallels between the ministry of Peter in the first half of his work and the ministry of Paul in the last half: both heal a lame man (3:2–8; 14:8–10); both do miracles at some distance (5:15; 19:12); both exorcise evil spirits (5:16; 16:18); both defeat sorcerers

(8:18–24; 13:6–11); both raise the dead (9:36–43; 20:9–12); both defend themselves against Jewish authorities (4:8–12; 5:27–32; 22:3–21; 23:1–6; 28:25–28); both receive heavenly visions (10:9–16; 16:9); both are involved in bestowing the Holy Spirit on new converts (8:14–17; 19:1–7); and both are miraculously released from prison (5:19; 12:7–11; 16:25–27). More important, both proclaim the same message and even use to some extent the same set of proof texts (e.g., Ps 16:10; cf. 2:27; 13:35).

It is, then, from Jesus' declaration about the apostles' witness (1:8) that Luke derives the framework for his narrative of Acts. First he portrays the mission of the Jerusalem apostles and their colleagues within the Jewish world; next he portrays the mission of Paul and his companions within the Gentile world. Luke presents this material in six blocks or panels—three of them are given to the mission to the Jews, three to the mission to the Gentiles.

Panel 1—The Earliest Days of the Church at Jerusalem (2:42–6:7)

Acts 2:42–6:7 describes the earliest days of the church at Jerusalem and covers the first three to five years of the new messianic movement (i.e., from A.D. 30 to the mid-thirties). Luke deals with the events of this period by means of a thesis paragraph followed by a series of vignettes that illustrate that paragraph. These portrayals of representative situations are drawn from many experiences within the early church and thus present his material succinctly. In this way he helps his readers feel the nature of what God was doing by his Spirit through the witness of the apostles.

A. A Thesis Paragraph on the State of the Early Church (2:42–47)

In addition to the six summary statements (6:7; 9:31; 12:24; 16:5; 19:20; 28:31) that conclude each of the six panels, Acts also has in its first panel three short summary-like paragraphs (2:42–47; 4:32–35; and 5:12–16). The latter two each introduce the block of material that immediately follows it, with the specific details in that material directly related to the respective introductory paragraph. But the first of the three paragraphs (2:42–47) is longer than the others and introduces the entire first panel of material. The rest of the first panel explicates, by means of a series of vignettes, the various points made in this first thesis paragraph.

42 Luke begins describing the early church by telling us that the believers in it were distinguished by their devotion to the apostles' teaching, to fellowship with one another, to "breaking of bread," and "to prayer." The verb translated "devoted" (GK *4674*) connotes a steadfast and single-minded fidelity to a certain course of action (cf. its use in 1:14 regarding devotion to prayer by the 120 in the upper room and in 6:4 regarding the apostles' resolve, in the context of the Hellenistic widows, to center their attention on prayer and the ministry of the word).

"The apostles' teaching [GK *1439*]" refers to a body of material considered authoritative because it was the message about Jesus of Nazareth proclaimed by accredited apostles. It undoubtedly included a compilation of the words of Jesus (cf. 20:35), some account of his earthly ministry, passion, and resurrection (cf. 2:22–24), and a declaration of what all this meant for humanity's redemption (cf. 1Co 15:3–5)—all of which was thought of in terms of a Christian "tradition" that could be passed on to others (cf. 1Co 11:2; 1Th 2:13; 2Th 2:15; 3:6). The number of references to teachers, teaching, and tradition within Acts and the letters to the churches (cf. Ro 6:17; 12:7; 16:17; 1Co 11:2; 14:26; 2Th 2:15; 3:6; Jas 3:1), and the frequent linking of prophets and teachers in the NT (cf. Ac 13:1; 1Co 12:28; 14:6; Eph 4:11), suggest that the creative role of prophecy in the early church was balanced by the conserving role of teaching. Undoubtedly the early congregation at Jerusalem, amid differences of perspective and along with a lively eschatological expectation, had a general "sense of center" provided by the teaching of the apostles.

Luke's reference to "*the* fellowship" (GK *3126*) implies that there was something distinctive in the gatherings of the early believers. With the influx of three thousand on the Day of Pentecost and with daily increases to their number after that (cf. 2:47), they must have had some externally recognizable identity. Perhaps in those early days others thought of them as a "Synagogue of Nazarenes" and gave them a place among other such groups within the mosaic of Judaism. But the Christian community was not just a sect of

Judaism, even though they continued to observe Jewish rites and customs and had no intention of breaking with the nation or its institutions. They held to the centrality of Jesus of Nazareth in the redemptive program of God and in their worship. Their proclamation of Jesus as Israel's promised Messiah and the Lord of the human race set them apart in Jerusalem as a distinguishable entity.

Just what is meant by "the breaking [GK 3082] of bread" in v.42 has been vigorously debated. Suggestions are a type of Jewish fellowship meal, a paschal commemoration of Christ's death, or an agape feast that emphasized the joy of communion with the risen Lord and of fellowship with one another. Here and in 20:7 Luke may well have had in mind the full Pauline understanding (1Co 10:16; 11:24), but elsewhere he uses this term for an ordinary meal (cf. Lk 24:30, 35; Ac 20:11; 27:35; likely also 2:46). Yet it is difficult to believe that Luke had in mind here only an ordinary meal, since he places the expression between two such religiously loaded terms as "the fellowship" and "prayer." Undoubtedly "the breaking of bread" was an occasion for joy, love, and praise because it was connected with Jesus. Probably it should also be understood as subtly connoting the passion of Christ, even though the full theology as described by Paul had not yet come into focus.

References to "prayer" (GK 4666) are frequent both in the summary statements and in the narrative of Acts (see 1:14, 24; 4:24–31; 6:4, 6; et al.). Just as Luke has set up in Luke-Acts the parallelism between the Spirit's work in relation to Jesus and the Spirit's work in the church, so he also sets up the parallelism between prayer in the life of Jesus and prayer in the life of the church. His use here of both the definite article and the plural in "the prayers" suggest formal prayers, probably both Jewish and Christian. The earliest believers not only viewed the old forms as filled with new content, but also in their enthusiasm they fashioned new vehicles for their praise.

43 Furthermore, Luke tells us that a lingering sense of awe rested on many who did not take their stand with the Christians and that miraculous things were done by the apostles. "Everyone," in contradistinction to "all the believers" of v.44, refers hyperbolically to nonbelievers in Jerusalem who knew of the events of Pentecost and were observing the life of the early congregation. In the expression "wonders and miraculous signs," Luke picks up the phraseology of Joel's prophecy (cf. 2:19) and of Peter's characterization of Jesus' ministry (cf. 2:22). Luke probably used it to suggest that the miracles that the apostles did give evidence of the presence of God with his people, just as throughout his ministry, Jesus performed miracles to show that God was with him. These miracles continued to happen during those early days.

44–45 Within the Christian congregation at Jerusalem, the believers' sense of spiritual unity expressed itself in communal living and sharing with the needy members of their group. While Acts implies that overt persecution of Christians came somewhat later, in certain instances economic and social sanctions were undoubtedly imposed on the early believers. Thus the communal life described in vv.44–45 should be understood, at least in part, as a response to these pressures. Such treatment of minority groups is not uncommon, as both ancient and contemporary history shows. The practice of holding possessions in community was a common feature of some Jewish sects of NT times (e.g., the group at Qumran). The sharing of the early Christians involved both what we would call their real estate ("possessions") and their personal possessions ("goods").

46–47a The favorite meeting place of the early believers was in the temple (cf. Lk 24:53), at the eastern edge of the outer court called Solomon's Colonnade (cf. 3:11; 5:12). There, in typically Semitic fashion, they carried on their discussions and offered praise to God. As Jews who were Christians and also Christians who were Jews, they not only considered Jerusalem to be their city but continued to regard the temple as their sanctuary and the Law as their law. Evidently they thought of themselves as the faithful remnant within Israel for whose sake all the institutions and customs of the nation existed. As such, their refocused eschatological hopes (cf. Mal 3:1) and all their desires to influence their own people were associated with the city of Jerusalem, the Jerusalem temple, and the Mosaic law.

But while they met formally for discussion and worship in the temple precincts, they ate their meals together in their own homes, doing so with gladness and sincerity of heart. They also found a large measure of favor among the people. In Luke's writings, "the people" (GK *3295*) usually refers to Israel as the elect nation to whom the message of redemption is initially directed and for whom (together with the Gentiles) it is ultimately intended (e.g., 3:9; 4:10; 5:13). Later in the narrative of Acts, the attitude of "the people" becomes more and more antagonistic to the Christian Gospel and its missioners. But in this first panel the response of the people (excluding their leaders) is largely favorable toward the early Christians and their manner of life. Luke shows that early Christianity was the fulfillment of all that is truly Jewish and that it directed its mission first to the Jewish world—themes stressed throughout this book.

47b Luke's thesis paragraph on the state of the early church at Jerusalem concludes with the triumphant note that as people were being saved, they were added to the growing number or Christians—a note that runs throughout this first panel but is not confined to it. Note that it is the Lord himself who adds to his church.

B. A Crippled Beggar Healed (3:1–26)

In 2:42–47, Luke has spoken of the early Christians' continued attendance at the temple, the wonders and miracles the apostles did, the awe that many of the Jews felt, and the apostles' teaching. Now he gives us a vignette illustrating these things. Much like the synoptic tradition that selected the healing of a leper as "Exhibit A" to represent the nature of Jesus' early ministry in Galilee (cf. Mk 1:40–45), or John's use of the healing of a Capernaum official's son for the same purpose (cf. Jn 4:46, 54), Luke now singles out this episode in the history of the early Jerusalem congregation to bring the reader into the picture. No doubt the episode at the time was well known and frequently recounted in the early church long before Luke wrote of it.

1. The healing (3:1–10)

1 The story of the healing of the crippled beggar begins with the straightforward statement that Peter and John went up to the temple at the time of prayer. That the apostles had been living in Jerusalem immediately after Jesus' ascension was in accord with his instructions that they stay in the city until the outpouring of the Holy Spirit (Lk 24:49; Ac 1:4) and begin their mission there (Ac 1:8; cf. Lk 24:47). But what kept these Galilean disciples in Jerusalem after Pentecost, and why did Jewish Christianity become centered in Jerusalem rather than Galilee? While there were Christians in Galilee who formed themselves into congregations there (cf. 9:31), the earliest extant Christian writings, the Pauline letters, take into account only the Jerusalem community and associate the Galilean apostles directly with that (cf. Gal 1:18–2:10; 1Th 2:14). In other words, as God's righteous remnant within Israel and as members of the Messiah's eschatological community, the apostles centered their activities in Jerusalem, the central city of Judaism. Along with that went their continued adherence to Israel's institutions and forms of worship.

Peter and John are presented as "going up to the temple at the time of prayer—at three in the afternoon." The stated times for prayer in Judaism were (1) early in the morning, in connection with the morning sacrifice; (2) at the ninth hour of the day (about three o'clock), in connection with the evening sacrifice; and (3) at sunset. The verb "going up" conveys a vivid visual impression of the apostles' movement toward Jerusalem. Going to the temple is always spoken of in terms of "going up"—principally out of reverential respect, though also because of location (Lk 18:10; Jn 7:14; Ac 11:2; cf. 15:2; 18:22).

2–3 The man is described as "crippled from birth" and having to be carried daily "to the temple gate called Beautiful" to beg for his living. Since almsgiving was classed in Judaism as a meritorious act, this man was placed at the gate so that those coming to the temple could gain merit by giving him a coin.

Just which gate is referred to as "Beautiful" is not easy to determine. Neither Josephus nor the Talmud refers to such a temple gate. We do not know whether it had to do with the outer court or one of the inner courts. Most scholars today believe it is the Nicanor Gate, which led from the eastern part of the outer court (Court of the Gentiles) into the first of the inner courts (Court of the Women).

4–6 In response to the beggar's request for money, Peter fixed his eyes on him and said,

"Look at us!" Thinking he had a benefactor, the beggar looked up expectantly. To his astonishment he heard the words: "In the name of Jesus Christ of Nazareth, walk." In Semitic thought, a "name" (GK 3950) does not just identify or distinguish a person; it expresses the very nature of his being. Hence the power of the person is present and available in the name of the person. Peter, therefore, does not just ask the risen Jesus to heal but pronounces over the crippled beggar the name of Jesus, thereby releasing the power of Jesus (cf. 3:16; 4:10). And the power of the risen Jesus, coupled with the man's response of faith (cf. 3:16), effects the healing.

7–10 The healing is described as an instantaneous one, accomplishing in a moment what God in his providence through the normal healing processes usually takes months to do. The effect on the man was traumatic; he began walking about and jumping and praising God. As for the people, they were "filled with wonder and amazement." What was taking place was but a token, to those who had eyes to see, of the presence of the Messianic Age, of which the prophet had long ago predicted: "Then will the lame leap like a deer" (Isa 35:6).

2. Peter's sermon in Solomon's Colonnade (3:11–26)

Peter's sermon in Solomon's Colonnade is in many ways similar to his sermon at Pentecost (2:14–41). Structurally, both move from proclamation to a call for repentance. The Pentecost sermon, however, is finished and polished, whereas this one is comparatively rough-hewn. Thematically, both focus on the denial and vindication of Jesus of Nazareth. But the Colonnade sermon expresses more of a remnant theology than the one at Pentecost. It shows a more generous attitude toward Israel, coupled with a greater stress on the nation's responsibility for the Messiah's death, than does the Pentecost sermon; and it makes explicit the necessity of receiving God's grace by faith. Christologically, Peter's sermon here (like his defense in 4:8–12) incorporates a number of archaic and primitive titles used of Jesus within early Jewish Christianity.

It seems strange, at first glance, that Luke would place two such similar sermons of Peter so close together. But his putting the Pentecost sermon in the introductory section of Acts was evidently meant to be a kind of paradigm of early apostolic preaching—a paradigm Luke seems to have polished for greater literary effectiveness. As for the Colonnade sermon, Luke seems to have included it as an example of how the early congregation in Jerusalem proclaimed the message of Jesus to the people of Israel as a whole. Probably the story and the sermon came to Luke from one of his sources as something of a self-contained unit (see the introduction to Acts), and he left it basically unchanged.

11 We are not given many of the "stage directions" for Peter's Colonnade sermon. What we are told, however, is significant: (1) the healed cripple "held on to" Peter and John so as not to let them get away; (2) "the people" came running to them in Solomon's Colonnade; and (3) they were "astonished" at what had happened. Solomon's Colonnade was a covered portico that ran the entire length of the eastern portion of the outer court of the

The Miracles of the Apostles

Miracle	Acts
Lame man cured (by Peter)	3:6–9
Death of Ananias and Sapphira	5:1–10
Saul's sight restored	9:17–18
Healing of Aeneas	9:33–35
Raising of Dorcas	9:36–41
Elymas blinded	13:8–11
Lame man cured (by Paul)	14:8–10
Demon cast out of a girl	16:16–18
Raising of Eutychus	20:9–10
Unharmed by viper	28:3–5
Healing of Publius's father	28:7–9

temple precincts, along and just inside the eastern wall of the temple (cf. 5:12; Jn 10:23).

12–16 The proclamation section of the sermon is an exposition on "the name of Jesus" (twice repeated in v.16). The sermon begins by denying that it was through the apostles' "own power or godliness" that the cripple was healed. Rather, "the God of Abraham, Isaac and Jacob" brought about this healing that glorified Jesus. Just as Peter earlier spoke of God as the true author of Jesus' miracles (cf. 2:22), so here he attributes solely to God such wonders as occurred in the apostles' ministries. And just as Jesus' miracles were done by God to accredit him before the people (cf. again 2:22), so miracles continued to be done through the apostles in order for God to glorify Jesus.

The sermon focuses on God's Servant, Jesus, whom Israel disowned and killed but God raised from the dead. It is through his name and the faith that comes through him that the healing of the crippled beggar occurred. In speaking of Jesus, Peter uses a number of early christological titles. (1) The sermon begins and ends by ascribing to Jesus the title "God's Servant" (vv.13, 26), which echoes the Servant theme of Isaiah 42–53 (cf. Isa 52:13). (2) Peter uses the theme of Moses as prophet (Dt 18:15, 18–19) and applies it to Jesus (vv.22–23). (3) He includes the titles "the Holy One" and "the Righteous One" (v.14) and the ascription "the author of life" (v.15). (4) And Peter stresses "the name of Jesus" as the powerful agent in the miracle (see comment on 3:4–6)—a significant fact since "the Name" was a pious Jewish surrogate for God and connoted his divine presence and power.

17 18 What strikes the reader immediately in the call-to-repentance section of Peter's sermon is its attitude toward Israel, which in its hopeful outlook is unmatched in the rest of the NT (except for certain features in Paul's discussion of Ro 9–11). In v.12 Peter addressed his audience as "Men of Israel" and in v.13 spoke of God as "the God of our fathers." And though he had emphasized Israel's part in crucifying Jesus (vv.13–15), he now magnanimously says that they had acted "in ignorance" and, somewhat surprisingly, includes their leaders in this. Then he mitigates their guilt still further by saying that God himself had willed it in order to fulfill the words of the prophets.

19–21 Even more positively, Peter goes on to say that if his hearers repent, their repentance will have a part in ushering in the great events of the end time. Evidently Luke wants us to understand Peter's call to repentance here as being set within the context of a remnant theology and as being quite unlike Stephen's attitude (cf. ch. 7). Not only so, but he also wants us to view the earliest proclamation of the Gospel in the Jewish world as a kind of intramural effort, with a self-conscious, righteous remnant issuing prophetic denunciations of Israel's part in the crucifixion of their Messiah and appealing to the people to turn to God in repentance for the remission of their sins.

The call to repentance itself is tersely stated. Then it is elaborated in words unique in the NT and reflective of Jewish remnant theology. "Repent, then, and turn to God," says Peter, "so that your sins may be wiped out"—and, further, so that there may be brought about the promised "times of refreshing" and so that with the coming of God's appointed Messiah, he may "restore everything" (the verbal form [GK 635] of the noun "restoration" [used here; GK 640] is often used in the LXX [Greek version of the OT] for the eschatological restoration of Israel; e.g., Jer 15:19; 16:15; Eze 16:55; Hos 11:11).

22–26 No group within Israel that considered itself to be God's righteous remnant in the inauguration of the final eschatological days could expect to win a hearing among Jews without attempting to define its position vis-à-vis Israel's great leaders of the past—particularly Abraham, Moses, and David. And that is precisely what Luke shows Peter doing as he concludes his call for repentance. Peter first refers to Moses, quoting his words in Dt 18:15, 18–19. This was a widely accepted messianic proof text of the time, one that emphasized the command to "listen to him" by the addition of the phrase "in everything he tells you." Peter's argument here, though not stated, is implicitly twofold: (1) true belief in Moses will lead to a belief in Jesus, and (2) belief in Jesus places one in true continuity with Moses.

In v.24 Peter defines Jesus' position with respect to David by alluding to Samuel and all the prophets who followed him and by insisting that they too "foretold these days." Now it is certainly difficult to find any prophecy of Samuel that could be applied to Jesus as explicitly as the words of Moses just quoted. But Samuel was the prophet who anointed David to be king and spoke of the establishment of his kingdom (cf. 1Sa 16:13; see also 13:14; 15:28; 28:17). Furthermore, Nathan's prophecy regarding the establishment of David's "offspring" as recorded in 2Sa 7:12–16 was accepted in certain quarters within Judaism as having messianic relevance and was taken by Christians as having been most completely fulfilled in Jesus (cf. 13:22–23, 34; Heb 1:5).

Finally, in v.25 Peter goes on to identify commitment to Jesus as Messiah with the promise God made to Abraham in Ge 22:18 and 26:4: "Through your offspring all nations on earth will be blessed." What exegetically ties this portion together with what has preceded it is the word "offspring," which appears in 2Sa 7:12 in reference to David's descendants and in Ge 22:18 and 26:4 in reference to the descendants of Abraham (see comments on 2:25–35 for this principle of Jewish interpretation of the OT). In this way, Peter proclaims that the promise to Abraham also has its ultimate fulfillment in Christ.

Peter's call to repentance in this sermon is an expression of the remnant theology of the earliest Christian believers at Jerusalem. He addresses his hearers as "heirs of the prophets and of the covenant." And he concludes with an offer of blessing that is extended first to individuals of the nation Israel (v.26; cf. Ro 1:16; 2:9–10). Luke wants his readers to appreciate something of how the earliest Christian preaching began within a Jewish milieu. From this he will go on to tell how this preaching developed through the various representative sermons that he later includes.

C. Peter and John Before the Sanhedrin (4:1–31)

As a direct outcome of the healing of the crippled beggar and as a further illustration of the thesis paragraph (2:42–47), Luke now presents a vignette concerning the arrest, trial, and witness of Peter and John. There is a connection of this arrest and trial with the second one in 5:17ff. Jewish law held that a person must be aware of the consequences of his crime before being punished for it. This meant that in noncapital cases the common people—as distinguished from those with rabbinic training, who, presumably, would know the law—had to be given a legal admonition before witnesses and could only be punished for an offense when they relapsed into a crime after due warning. Acts 4:1ff., therefore, presents the Sanhedrin as judging that the apostles were "unschooled, ordinary men" (v.13) and tells how they were given a legal warning not to speak anymore in the name of Jesus (v.17). But Acts 5:17ff. tells how the Sanhedrin reminded the apostles of its first warning (v.28) and turned them over to be flogged because they had persisted in their "sectarian" ways (v.40).

1. The arrest of Peter and John (4:1–7)

1 In vv.1–4 Luke both concludes the narrative of the crippled beggar's healing (by the phrase "while they were speaking") and introduces the first appearance of Peter and John before the Sanhedrin (cf. "the next day" in vv. 3, 5).

Luke shows that the early opposition against preaching the Gospel arose chiefly from priestly and Sadducean ranks—i.e., "the priests and the captain of the temple guard and the Sadducees." "The captain of the temple guard" was the commanding officer of the temple police force. He was considered inferior in rank only to the high priest and had the responsibility of maintaining order in the temple precincts (cf. 5:24, 26). The "Sadducees" (GK 4881) were descendants of the Hasmoneans, who looked to Mattathias, Judas, Jonathan, and Simon Maccabeus (168–134 B.C.) as having inaugurated the Messianic Age and saw themselves as perpetuating what their fathers had begun. As priests from the tribe of Levi, they claimed to represent ancient orthodoxy and were uninterested in innovations. Thus they opposed any developments in biblical law (i.e., the "Oral Law"), speculations about angels or demons, and the doctrine of the resurrection (cf. 23:8; Mk 12:18, 11). Likewise, they rejected what they considered to be vain hopes for God's heavenly intervention into the life of the nation and for a coming Messiah, since, as they believed, the age of God's promise had begun with the Maccabean heroes and was continuing on under their supervision. For them, the Messiah was an ideal, not a person, and the Messianic Age was a process, not a cataclysmic or even datable event. Furthermore, as political rulers and dominant landlords, to whom a grateful nation had turned over all political and economic powers during the time of the Maccabean supremacy, for entirely practical reasons they stressed cooperation with Rome and maintenance of the status quo. Most of the priests were of Sadducean persuasion; the temple police force was composed entirely of Levites; the captain of the temple guard was always a high-caste Sadducee, and so were each of the high priests.

2–3 The priests and Sadducees were "greatly disturbed" about two matters. First, the apostles were "teaching the people," an activity that those of the Sadducean ranks saw as a threat to the status quo. Like Jesus, Peter and John were rallying popular support and acting unofficially in such a way as to disrupt established authority—an authority vested in their hands. Second, Peter and John were annoying the Sadducees because they were "proclaiming in Jesus the resurrection of the dead." This probably means they were attempting to prove from the fact of Jesus' resurrection the doctrine of the resurrection (cf. 17:31–32; 23:6–8), which the Sadducees denied. So Peter and John were taken into custody by the temple guard and, since it was evening, put into prison until the Sanhedrin could be called together the next morning to judge their case.

4 Not everyone agreed with the Sadducees' view of the activities and message of the apostles. Later in Acts, Luke will speak of the general tolerance of the people, the moderation of the Pharisees, and the desire of Rome for peace in the land as each having a part in restraining the Sadducees from doing all they might have wanted to do to oppose the Gospel and its early missioners. Many who heard the message believed, with the result that the Jerusalem congregation grew to a total of about five thousand.

5 Though the Sadducees had among them the nation's titular rulers, they were actually a minority party and could govern only through the Sanhedrin. Thus on the next day, this seventy-member group, composed of "the rulers" or "the high priests" (cf. 23:5), the "elders," and the "teachers of the law" (most of whom were Pharisees) came together. The Sanhedrin ("council"; GK 5284) was the senate and supreme court of the nation, which had jurisdiction in all noncapital cases—though it also advised the Roman governors in capital cases—and in one case, namely, that of Gentiles trespassing beyond the posted barriers into the inner courts of the temple, could on its own sentence even a Roman citizen to death (see comment on 21:27–29). The high priest was president of the Sanhedrin. It met in a hall adjoining the southwest part of the temple area.

6 The early opposition to Christianity arose principally from among the Sadducees, for Luke stresses that the Sadducean element was especially well represented in this first trial of the apostles: "Annas the high priest was there, and so were Caiaphas, John, Alexander and the other men of the high priest's family" (see comment on Jn 18:12–14). Just who John and Alexander were, we do not know, though possibly the first was Annas's son Jonathan, who replaced Caiaphas in A.D. 36.

7 It was before such an assembly, which probably arranged itself in a semicircular fashion, that Peter and John were brought. The man who had been healed was also there (cf. v.14), though Luke does not say whether he had also been imprisoned or had been called in as a witness. The apostles were called on to account for their actions, and they used the occasion for an aggressive evangelistic witness.

2. Peter's defense and witness (4:8–12)

8 In a context of a prophetic description of national calamities and cosmic turmoil, Luke earlier quoted Jesus as saying: "But before all this, they will lay hands on you and persecute you. They will deliver you to synagogues and prisons, and you will be brought before kings and governors, and all on account of my name. But make up your mind not to worry beforehand how you will defend yourselves. For I will give you words and wisdom that none of your adversaries will be able to resist or contradict" (Lk 21:12–15). Undoubtedly Luke was thinking of many incidents of opposition to the Gospel message when he wrote down these words. Indeed, he records a number of such happenings in Acts. But certainly when he wrote about Peter's first defense before the Jewish Sanhedrin (and also about the apostles' second appearance

While constructing a road on the Mount of Olives (see picture on left), the Israelis recently found a gravesite that proved to be that of the family of Caiaphas (cf. 4:6). The drawing above depicts the front of the ossuary and the end, which has the inscription, "Joseph son of Caiaphas." Drawing by Rachel Bierling.

before the Sanhedrin in 5:17ff.), these words were ringing in his ears. For almost every item of Jesus' oracle is exemplified in Luke's account of Peter's situation, attitude, and message here in Acts, beginning with his being "filled with the Holy Spirit." Peter receives a special moment of inspiration that brings to a functional focus the person and ministry of God's Spirit.

9–10 Peter's defense focuses on the healing of the crippled man as being (1) "an act of kindness," which (2) was effected "by the name of Jesus Christ of Nazareth, whom you crucified but whom God raised from the dead." His message is specifically addressed to the "rulers and elders of the people," though it also has "everyone else in Israel" in mind.

11–12 The double use of the verb "to be saved" (GK 5392) to mean "restoration to health" physically and "preservation from eternal death" spiritually allows Peter to move easily from the healing of the cripple to the salvation of humankind and, therefore, from a defensive to an aggressive witness. And in his proclamation he uses two early Christological motifs.

The first is that of "the rejected stone," which has become "the capstone" of the building. In Judaism there was a frequent wordplay between the words for "stone" (Heb. 'eben; GK 74) and "son" (Heb. ben; GK 1201)—rooted generally in the OT (cf. Ex 28:9; Jos 4:6–8, 20–21; Isa 54:11–13; et al.)—which attained messianic expression in the combination of the stone and the Son of Man imagery in Da 2:34–35 and 7:13–14. It was for this reason, evidently, that Jesus concluded his parable of the vineyard and the rejected son (Mk 12:1–12) with the quotation of Ps 118:22–23: "The stone the builders rejected has become the capstone; the Lord has done this, and it is marvelous in our eyes." Peter picks up this motif here in his quotation of Ps 118:22, also building on the associations of "stone" and "son." While elsewhere in the NT (cf. Lk 20:18; Ro 9:33; 1Co 3:11; 1Pe 2:4–8) the ideas of a "foundation stone" and a "stumbling stone" were based respectively on Isa 28:16 and 8:14, here the thought is of Jesus as the rejected stone that becomes the capstone and completes the edifice.

The second early Christological motif in Peter's proclamation is "salvation" (GK 5401). In some Jewish documents of the first century, "God's Salvation" and "Salvation" appear as designations of the expected Davidic Messiah. Luke has already stressed this motif in Zechariah's hymn of praise (Lk 1:69, "a horn of salvation"), in Simeon's prayer (2:30, "your salvation"), and in his comments on the ministry of John the Baptist (3:6, "God's salvation"). Now in addressing the Sanhedrin, to whom such a messianic designation was doubtless well known, Peter proclaims, "Salvation is found in no one else [than in 'Jesus Christ of Nazareth, whom you crucified but whom God raised from the dead,' (v.10)], for there is no other name under heaven given to men by which we must be saved" (v.12). There is nothing of compromise or accommodation in Peter's preaching. As this magnificent declaration shows, he was wholly committed to the uniqueness of Jesus as the only Savior. Peter and the other apostles never watered down the fact that apart from Jesus there is no salvation for anyone.

3. The apostles warned and released (4:13–22)

13–14 While literacy was high among Jews of the first century, theological disputations required rabbinic training. Since the common people had not had such training, they were thought to be incapable of carrying on sustained theological discussion. But here were Peter and John, whom the Sanhedrin observed to be "unschooled, ordinary men," speaking fearlessly and confidently before the Jewish supreme court and senate. Their judges could not but wonder at such ordinary men having such a mastery of biblical argumentation. So they had to fall back on the only possible explanation—"these men had been with Jesus," who, despite his lack of rabbinic training, taught "as one who had authority" (Mk 1:22). Furthermore, just as Jesus' teaching was coupled with demonstrations of miraculous powers, which thus reinforced among the people the impression of authority (cf. Mk 1:23–28; 2:1–12; et al.), now Peter and John were beginning to do the same. There was no denying that the man *had* been healed. There he stood before them, physically regenerated at an age when regenerative cures do not occur of themselves (cf. v.22,). But even the miraculous is not self-authenticating apart from an openness of heart and mind; and the Sadducees' preoccupation with protecting their vested interests shut them off from really seeing the miracle that occurred.

15–17 Just how Luke knew what went on among the members of the Sanhedrin in closed session has often been debated, though we cannot know for sure. Perhaps Saul (Paul) was a member of the council at that time and he later told Luke. Or maybe Paul heard the gist of the discussion from his teacher Gamaliel and then told it to Luke. Or there may have been secret sympathizers of the apostles in the council who "leaked" to them what was said and from whom Luke picked it up. Most probable is the suggestion that the substance of the discussion was inferred from what was said to Peter and John when they were brought back to the meeting. What is certain about the council's response is that (1) they would have denied the miracle if they could, (2) they had no disposition to be convinced either by what had happened or by the apostles' arguments, and (3) they felt the need of stopping the apostles' activity and teaching and therefore proposed to take the measures allowed them by Jewish law.

18–20 The Sanhedrin decided to impose a ban on the apostles, both to warn them and to provide a legal basis for further action should such be needed (cf. 5:28; see initial comment on 4:1–31). So they called in the apostles and warned them "not to speak or teach at all in the name of Jesus." But the council had before it men whose lives had been transformed by association with Jesus, by God's having raised him from the dead, and by the coming of the Holy Spirit. As with the prophets of old, God's word was in the heart of Peter and John like a burning fire; and they could neither contain it nor be restrained from speaking it (cf. Jer 20:9). They had been witnesses of Jesus' earthly ministry and resurrection (cf. Ac 10:39–41) and had been commanded by their risen Lord to proclaim his name to the people (cf. 1:8; 10:42). When faced with this ban, their response was never in doubt; they would continue to speak about what they had seen and heard. Where the Jewish established authority stood in opposition to God's authority, thus becoming in effect demonic, the early believers knew where their priorities lay and judged all religious forms and functions from a Christocentric perspective.

21–22 The Sanhedrin had given its warning. And after stressing its nature and what would happen if it went unheeded, they let them go. The moderation of the people prevented them from doing more, for "all the people were praising God for what had happened." Yet a legal precedent had been set that would enable the council to take, if necessary, more drastic action in the future.

4. The church's praise and petition (4:23–31)

23-30 The church's response to the apostles' release was a spontaneous outburst of praise, psalmody, and petition. It begins (v.24) by addressing God as "Sovereign Lord" (GK *1305*), a common title in the Greek world for rulers and one that appears occasionally in Jewish circles as an address to God (cf. Lk 2:29; Rev 6:10). It is especially appropriate here in conjunction with the "servant" (GK *4090*) names used of David (v.25), Jesus (vv.27, 30), and believers themselves (v.29). Structurally, the church's response includes an ascription to God drawn from Hezekiah's prayer in Isa 37:16–20 (v.24b), a quotation of Ps 2:1–2 (vv.25–26), the reference to Jesus' passion in terms of the psalm just cited (vv.27–28), and a petition for divine enablement in the Christians' present circumstances (vv.29–30).

In the prayer of the church two matters of theological interest stand out. First, using a common Jewish method of interpreting the OT (cf. comments on 2:16), these Christians saw in Ps 2 the persons and groups involved in Jesus' crucifixion: "the kings of the earth" corresponds to King Herod, "the rulers" to the Roman governor Pontius Pilate, "the nations" to the Gentile authorities, and "the people" to "the people of Israel." Sometime just prior to the Christian period, Ps 2 was beginning to be used within some Jewish circles as a messianic psalm, and the early Jewish Christians knew of this usage, approved it, and applied it to Jesus of Nazareth (cf. also the use of Ps 2:7 in Ac 13:33; Heb 1:5; 5:5; and Ps 2:9 in Rev 2:27; 12:5; 19:15).

Second, in the church's prayer the sufferings of Christian believers are related directly to the sufferings of Christ and inferentially to the sufferings of God's righteous servants in the OT. This theme of the union of the sufferings of Christ and those of his own people is a theme that is developed in many ways throughout the NT (cf. esp. Mk 8–10; Ac 9:4–5; Ro 8:17; Col 1:24; 1Pe 2:20–25; 3:14–4:2; 4:12–13). It reaches its loftiest expression in Paul's metaphor of the body of Christ.

Most significant is the fact that these early Christians were not praying for relief from oppression or judgment on their oppressors but for enablement "to speak your word with great boldness" amid oppression and for God to act in mighty power "through the name of your holy servant Jesus" (v.30). Their concern was for God's word to go forth and for Christ's name to be glorified, leaving to God himself their own circumstances. With such prayer surely God is well pleased. Luke has evidently taken pains to give us this prayer so that it might serve as something of a pattern to be followed in our own praying.

31 As a sign of God's approval, Luke informs us that "the place where they were meeting was shaken" (cf. Ex 19:18; Isa 6:4) and "they were all filled with the Holy Spirit" (cf. comments on v.8). And with such motivation and divine enablement, their prayer was answered: they "spoke the word of God boldly" (i.e., with confidence).

D. Christian Concern Expressed in Sharing (4:32–5:11)

Going back to one of the themes of his thesis paragraph of 2:42–47, Luke now illustrates the nature and extent of the early believers' commitment to one another in social concern. This he does by a summary statement, then by an example of genuine Christian concern, and finally by an example of disastrous deceit. For Luke as well as for the early Christians, being filled with the Holy Spirit not only concerned proclaiming the Word of God but also sharing possessions with the needy because of believers' oneness in Christ.

1. Believers share their possessions (4:32–35)

In this section, v.32 speaks of a customary practice in the early church of believers retaining their personal possessions and property and sharing them among the believers; vv. 34–35 speak of an extraordinary response to special needs by some selling their property and possessions and distributing them to the needy. In other words, Luke here emphasizes that both continuous and extraordinary acts of Christian social concern were occurring in the early church, and he ties these acts into the apostolic proclamation of the Resurrection. Because of such acts and the recognition that they must always be an inextricable part of the Christian ministry, God's blessing rested upon the early church.

32 The whole congregation was united to one another in their allegiance to Jesus. This sense of oneness extended to sharing their personal possessions with others in need (cf. 2:45). Theologically, the early believers considered themselves the righteous remnant within Israel. So Dt 15:4 was undoubtedly in their mind, that if they wanted God to bless them, there should be no poor among them. Other Jewish groups that thought of themselves in terms of a remnant theology expressed their spiritual oneness by sharing their goods, and the Jerusalem church seems to have done likewise. Practically, they had many occasions for such sharing. With the economic situation in Palestine steadily deteriorating because of famine and political unrest, employment was limited—not only for Galileans and others who had left their fishing and farming for living in the city, but also for the regular residents of Jerusalem who now faced economic and social sanctions because of their new messianic faith. Experientially, the spiritual oneness the believers found to be a living reality through their common allegiance to Jesus must, they realized, be expressed in caring for the physical needs of their Christian brothers and sisters. Indeed, their integrity as a community of faith depended on their doing this.

Here, then, is Luke's illustration of his thesis statement in 2:44–45 regarding the way the believers practiced communal living. They were not monastics, for the Jerusalem apostles, the brothers of Jesus, and many of the other believers were married (cf. 5:1–11; 1Co 9:5). Nor did the believers form a closed society like Qumran. They lived in their own homes (cf. 2:46; 12:12) and had their own possessions as any household would. But they did not consider them private possessions to be held exclusively for their own use and enjoyment. Rather, they shared what they had and so expressed their corporate life.

33 Because of its juxtaposition with v.32, we must understand that the "great power" accompanying the apostles' witness "to the resurrection of the Lord Jesus" refers not just to rhetorical, homiletical, or even miraculous power but to the power of a new life in the believing community—a new life manifest in sharing possessions to meet the needs of others. It was this kind of power Jesus had in mind when he said, "All men will know that you are my disciples if you love one another" (Jn 13:35). In view of such a combination of social concern and proclamation of the Word, it is no wonder that Luke goes on to say, "And much grace was upon them all" (cf. Lk 2:40).

34–35 The acts Luke alludes to here were extraordinary and voluntary acts of Christian concern that were done "from time to time" in response to special needs among the believers, and they involved both sharing possessions and selling real estate. By separating these actions from those described in v.32, Luke suggests that they were exceptional and were not meant to be normative for the church. The church at Jerusalem—even in its earliest days—was neither a monastic nor semimonastic community. Nevertheless, such acts were highly regarded as expressions of a common social concern, though as with any noble deed they could be done either sincerely or hypocritically.

2. The generosity of Barnabas (4:36–37)

36 Luke uses the generosity of Barnabas as "Exhibit A" to illustrate the type of extraordinary social concern mentioned in v.34. Joseph was this man's Hebrew name, used at home, in the synagogue, and among Jews generally. To this the apostles added the descriptive nickname Barnabas, which means "Son of Encouragement," in order to distinguish him from others of the same name (cf. 1:23). His family came from Cyprus, and he may have had ancestral property there. John Mark was his cousin (cf. Col 4:10).

37 Barnabas is an important figure in Luke's account of the church's expansion from Jerusalem to Rome; he appears a number of times as a kind of hinge between the mission to the Jewish world and that to the Gentiles (cf. 9:27; 11:22–30; 13:1–14:28; 15:2–4, 12, 22, 36–41; see also 1Co 9:6). Here, however, he is introduced as one who sold a field and gave the money to the apostles for distribution among those in need. We are not told whether the property he sold was in Cyprus or Palestine. Nor are we told how the biblical prohibition against Levites owning real estate applied in Barnabas's case (cf. Nu 18:20; Dt 10:9); such a regulation seems not always to have been observed (cf. Jer 32:7–44). What we are told, however, is that Barnabas gave a practical demonstration of Christian social concern, undoubtedly under no compulsion of either precedent or rule (cf. 5:4).

3. The deceit of Ananias and Sapphira (5:1–11)

The case of Ananias and Sapphira is opposite that of Barnabas, though it was meant to look the same. No doubt the story circulated within the church as a warning of the awfulness of deceit, for at times of great enthusiasm such a warning is especially necessary. And though Luke has taken evident pleasure in reporting the progress of the Gospel and the vitality of faith during these early days of the church in Jerusalem, he does not omit this most distressing event. This situation must have lain heavily on the hearts of the early Christians, and it is a message that needs to be constantly kept in mind by Christians today.

1–2 The details of the conspiracy are concisely stated. A certain Christian man named Ananias (meaning "God is gracious" in Hebrew) and his wife, Sapphira (meaning "beautiful" in Aramaic), wanted to enjoy the acclaim of the church as Barnabas had, but without making a genuine sacrifice. So they too sold a piece of real estate and pretended to give the full price to the apostles for distribution to the needy, though they conspired to keep back part of the money for themselves. Luke's language here seems to draw a parallel between the sin of Achan just as the Israelites began their conquest of Canaan (see Jos 7) and the sin of Ananias and Sapphira as the church began its mission; both incidents come under the immediate and drastic judgment of God and teach the people a sobering lesson. This is very likely how the early church saw the incident as well.

3–4 Probably no account in Acts has provoked more wrath from critics than this one has. Commentators have complained about the difficulty of accepting the death of both husband and wife under such circumstances and have questioned Peter's ethics in not giving them an opportunity for repentance and in not telling Sapphira of her husband's death. Even more difficult for many is the way the story portrays Peter, who appears to be without the compassion or restraint of his Lord. Jesus' relations even with Judas, whose sin was a thousand times more odious, certainly were not on this level. But note that Peter did not view the action of Ananias and Sapphira as merely incidental. He spoke of it as inspired by Satan and as a lie to both the Holy Spirit and God. It was a case of deceit and was an affront, not just on the community level, but primarily before God. Deceit is spiritually disastrous—a sin, whatever its supposed justification, that sours every personal relationship. Where there is even the suspicion of conscious misrepresentation and deception, trust is completely violated.

Ananias and Sapphira were severely dealt with because their act of pretended piety (cf. v.4) was done voluntarily and because the greater freedom permitted in the church at Jerusalem made the individual Christian more responsible to be honest and more culpable when dishonest. In addition, the way Ananias and Sapphira attempted to reach their goals was so diametrically opposed to the whole thrust of the Gospel that to allow it to go unchallenged would have set the entire mission of the church off course. Like the act of Achan, this episode was pivotal in the life and mission of God's people, for the whole enterprise was threatened at its start. And while we may be thankful that judgment on deceit in the church is not now so swift and drastic, this incident stands as an indelible warning regarding the heinousness in God's sight of deception in spiritual and personal matters.

5 The psychological explanations of Ananias's sudden death attribute his fatal collapse to the shock and shame of being found out. The verb Luke uses for his death, however, appears in the NT only in contexts where someone is struck down by divine judgment (5:5, 10; 12:23). Whatever were the psychological and physical factors involved, Luke's emphasis is on God as the ultimate cause of Ananias's death. This is the light in which he means his readers to understand his further comment: "And great fear seized all who heard what had happened."

6 The expression "the young men" (cf. v.10) refers to certain younger men in the Christian community. Whether they covered Ananias with a shroud and carried him away or wrapped him up in some manner and then carried him away or simply picked him up from the floor and took him off for burial is impossible to say. It is understandable that burial in hot climates takes place soon after death. We have no explanation why Ananias was buried so quickly and his wife was not told about it.

7–11 "About three hours later" the tragic episode was repeated with Sapphira. Just as Ananias and his wife were united in their conspiracy, so they were united in the judgment that came upon them. It may seem redundant that Luke closes his account of Ananias and Sapphira's deception with the statement "Great fear seized the whole church and all who heard about these events." However, this is a vignette of warning; and in concluding it Luke wants to stress this note of reverent fear—as he expressly did in v.5 and implicitly does throughout his account.

This is the first time in Acts that the word "church" (GK *1711*) appears, though it is the regular word for both the church universal and local congregations elsewhere in the book (cf. 7:38; 8:1; 9:31; 11:22; 13:1; 14:23; 15:22, 41; 16:5; 19:32, 40; 20:28) and throughout the NT letters (cf. also Mt 16:18; 18:17).

E. The Apostles Again Before the Sanhedrin (5:12–42)

Luke now gives the second account of the apostles' arraignment before the Sanhedrin. Whether he clearly grasped or fully appreciated the rationale in Jewish jurisprudence for two such appearances is debatable (cf. introductory comments on 4:1–31). Nevertheless, in this account of the second appearance, he emphasizes the development of attitudes in these earliest days of the Christian mission in Jerusalem: the reverential fear on the part of the church and the people (cf. 5:5, 11), the deepening jealousy and antagonism of the Sadducees (cf. 5:17–33), the moderation of the Pharisees (5:33–40), and the increasing joy and confidence of the Christians (cf. 5:41–42). In so doing, Luke continues the elaboration of his thesis paragraph (2:42–47).

1. Miraculous signs and wonders (5:12–16)

This paragraph, like 2:42–47 and 4:32–35, is a Lukan summary introducing the material that follows. It includes some statements that reach back to what has been narrated before—principally vv.12–14, which recall the Christians' practice of meeting in Solomon's Colonnade, the reverential fear aroused by the awful end of Ananias and Sapphira, and the increasing number of people who believed. In the main, however, the paragraph introduces the story of the apostles' second appearance before the Sanhedrin by giving a reason for the Sadducees' jealousy and for their second inquisition of the apostles, namely, the continued success of the Christian mission at Jerusalem.

12a As with his summary paragraph of 4:32–35, Luke puts his thesis statement at the very beginning of his treatment. The Sadducees called the apostles to appear a second time before the Jewish Sanhedrin because, in defiance of the council's orders, they were continuing their ministry among the people, with "many miraculous signs and wonders" being performed.

12b–14 Luke now speaks resumptively of three groups of people and their response to the Sanhedrin's warning and to the fear engendered by Ananias and Sapphira's fate: (1) the Christians continued meeting together in Solomon's Colonnade; (2) the unbelieving Jews ("no one else") were reluctant to associate too closely with the Christians; and (3) some of the Jews ("the people") responded to and honored the Christians—in fact, many men and women from this group came to believe in the Lord and were added to the number of Christian believers. Thematically, the resumé serves to support the thesis statement of v.12a.

15–16 The material in these two verses is structurally much like that of 4:34–35, for in both cases there is a logical and linguistic connection with each thesis statement. In both instances special and extraordinary expressions of the respective thesis statements are detailed. Just as healing virtue had flowed from Jesus by touching in faith the edge of his cloak (cf. Mk 5:25–34,), so even Peter's shadow was used by God to effect a cure (cf. 19:11–12). And whereas the healing of the crippled beggar had originally aroused the Sadducees' antagonism, now, Luke tells us, such miracles were being repeated numerous times in the apostles' ministry. Thus crowds from the outlying districts around Jerusalem thronged the apostles. No wonder the Sadducees' jealousy erupted anew!

2. The arrest and trial of the apostles (5:17–33)

17–18 As in 4:1–31, Luke has the early opposition to Christianity arising principally from the Sadducees. Pharisees were undoubtedly present in the Sanhedrin (cf. comments on "the full assembly of the elders of Israel," v.21), but their presence in these earliest days of the church's existence (at least until ch. 7) is depicted as exerting a moderating influence on the antagonism of the Sadducees. Thus the high priest and members of the party of the Sadducees take official action a second time against the apostles by arresting them and putting them "in the public jail."

19–21a This is one of three "opening of the prison doors" stories in the book of Acts (cf. 12:6–11; 16:26–29). The "angel of the Lord" is the NT term for the OT "Angel of the LORD," which denotes God himself in his dealings with humans (cf. Ex 3:2, 4, 7; at al.). Here "angel" (GK *34*) denotes the presence or agency of God himself (cf. 8:26; 12:7, 23; cf. also Mt 1:20, 24; 2:13, 19; 28:2; Lk 1:11; 2:9). By divine intervention, then, the apostles were released from the public jail and told by God to go back to the temple and persist in preaching the message of new life to "the people" (i.e., the nation of Israel), in spite of the Sanhedrin's attempt to silence it. The focus of their message is on "this new life"—with "life" (GK *2437*) and "salvation" (GK *5401*) understood in the NT as synonymous. And since the apostles had been miraculously released and divinely commissioned, that is exactly what they began to do.

21b–27 Having (as they thought) confined the apostles in the public jail for the night, "the high priest and his associates" called together the members of the Sanhedrin in the morning in order to make some judgment and take some action about the disturbances the Christians were causing. Luke adds "the full assembly of the elders of Israel" here, probably to make clear that the Pharisees were well represented in the council at this time; though they may not have been at the first trial, they did become vocal through Gamaliel at the second one (cf. vv.34–40). So the Sanhedrin sent for their prisoners—but did not find them. "The captain of the temple guard and the chief priests were puzzled," probably concluding that the escape was aided by members of the temple guard. But when they heard that the apostles were teaching the people in the temple courts, "the captain" took command of his temple police and brought the apostles in before the council to be interrogated (v.26a). No violence was used in the arrest because the captain and his guard feared the reaction of the people (v.26b). This says something about the early Christians' response to Jesus' example of nonviolence and nonretaliation during his own arrest (cf. Mk 14:43–50), for they might have begun a riot and thus extricated themselves. It also continues the theme of "the favor of all the people" in 2:42–47.

28 As the apostles stood before the Sanhedrin, the high priest (the president) began the interrogation by reminding the apostles of the council's order for them to be silent, which obviously had not been complied with. It is uncertain whether Luke had in mind Annas or Caiaphas as leading the interrogation; while the latter was officially the high priest at the time, the former is assumed in the NT to be the real power behind the throne and continues to be called the high priest (cf. Lk 3:2; Jn 18:13–24). Formally, the high priest's interrogation contains no questions but only points up the apostles' refusal to obey the Sanhedrin's earlier order (i.e., a charge of "contempt of court"). He also objects to their insistence on blaming the council for Jesus' death (cf. 4:10). For the Sadducean leadership of the council, the uncontested charge of contempt of court was sufficient legal warrant for taking action against the apostles. With their vested interests, the Sadducees wanted only to preserve their own authority and put an end to the rising disturbance among the people. They evidently had no interest in determining the truth or falsity of the Christians' claims. Their hardened attitude is manifest in their refusal to mention the name of Jesus (compare v.28 with 4:18) and in their spitting out the epithet "this man" when they had to refer directly to him.

29–32 By saying "Peter and the other apostles replied," Luke suggests that Peter was the spokesman for the group of apostles on trial, with the others in some way indicating their agreement. Their response is hardly a reasoned defense but simply a reaffirmation of their position. As at the first trial (4:19), here they voice even more succinctly their noble principle, "We must obey God rather than men." Also as at the first trial, the focus is on Jesus. "By hanging him on a tree" is a locution for crucifixion that stems from Dt 21:22–23 (cf. Ac 10:39; 13:29; Gal 3:13 [quoting Dt 21:23]; 1Pe 2:24). The titles "Prince" and "Savior" are Christological ascriptions rooted in the confessions of the early church and particularly associated with the NT themes of exaltation and Lordship.

33 As far as the Sadducees were concerned, the charge of contempt of court was not only uncontested but repeated. On hearing the apostles reaffirm what to them could only be considered intolerable obstinacy, the Sadducees were furious and wanted to destroy them. While the Sanhedrin did not have authority under Roman jurisdiction to inflict capital punishment, undoubtedly they would have found some pretext for handing these men over to the Romans for such action—as they did with Jesus himself—had it not been for the intervention of the Pharisees, as represented particularly by Gamaliel.

3. Gamaliel's wise counsel of moderation (5:34–40)

The portrayal of Gamaliel's counsel is the high point of Luke's account of the apostles' second appearance before the Sanhedrin and the main reason why he included the whole vignette. His purpose here is to contrast the developed antagonism of the Sadducees with the moderation of Gamaliel as spokesman for the Pharisees.

34–35 The "Pharisees" (GK 5757) represent the continuation of the ancient Hasidim, that group of "pious ones" in Israel who, during the Seleucid oppressions, joined the Hasmoneans (the Maccabees; see comment on 4:1) in the struggle for religious freedom but later opposed the Maccabean rulers in their political and territorial claims. They came from diverse family, occupational, and economic backgrounds and gave themselves to studying the Law (Torah) in both its written and oral forms, to expounding the Law in terms of its contemporary relevance, and to preparing the people for the coming of the Messianic Age by means of education in Scripture and the oral tradition. The name "Pharisee" probably comes from the Aramaic verb meaning "to separate" (thus they are "the separated ones" or "holy ones dedicated entirely to God"). In the period before the fall of Jerusalem in A.D. 70, they were in the minority in the Sanhedrin. But their support by the people was so great that all matters of life and ceremony were guided by their interpretations, and Sadducean magistrates had to profess adherence to their principles in order to hold the formal allegiance of the populace.

Theologically, the Pharisees looked for a Messianic Age and a personal Messiah; they accepted a doctrine of the resurrection of the dead (though they understood such a doctrine to mean either the immortality of the soul or the resuscitation of the body); they believed in the presence and activity of angels and demons; they held in balance the tenets of God's eternal decrees and human freedom of will; and they tried to live a life of simple piety apart from needless wealth and luxury.

The first-century Pharisee Gamaliel I, who was either the son or grandson of the famous Hillel, was one of the most highly esteemed Pharisees. Here in Acts he is portrayed as having taken charge at a certain point in the council meeting and as having gained the acquiescence of those present—not through any vested authority but through personal forcefulness and respect for what he represented. And he addresses the council members with the traditional designation "Men of Israel" (cf. 2:22).

36–37 Many have seen a problem in Gamaliel's reference to the Jewish revolutionaries Theudas and Judas the Galilean in this speech. According to Josephus, the Jewish historian of the first century, Judas's rebellion occurred about A.D. 6 and Theudas's about A.D. 44, thus making Luke's chronology wrong (cf. "after him" in v.37). Furthermore, this scene before the Sanhedrin occurred about A.D. 34, well before the rebellion of Theudas. In answer to these problems, it seems most likely that the Theudas that Gamaliel referred to was one of the many insurgent leaders who arose in Palestine at the time of Herod the Great's death in 4 B.C., *not* the Theudas who led the Jewish uprising of A.D. 44. Our problem with these verses, therefore, may result just as much from our own ignorance of the situation as from what we believe we know as based on Josephus.

38–39 It has frequently been claimed that the words of Gamaliel here are "a historical mistake," for they are not in character with what we know of Pharisaism. But Josephus himself informs us that whereas the Sadducees were rather boorish in their behavior, the Pharisees were affectionate, interested in harmonious relations among the Jews, and often lenient in matters of punishment. Many of them were content to allow history to be the final judge of whether something was of God or not.

Of course, later on in Acts (cf. 8:1, 3; 9:1–2), Saul of Tarsus, who was trained under Gamaliel I (cf. 22:3), takes a very different attitude toward the Christians, joining with the Sadducees and obtaining the high priest's authorization to track them down and imprison them. But between Gamaliel's advice in Ac 5 and Saul's action in Ac 8–9, there arose from the depths of Christian conviction what the Pharisees as well as the Sadducees could only have considered to be a threat of Jewish apostasy. Before Gamaliel's counsel of moderation, the central issues of the church's proclamation had been the messiahship, lordship, and saviorhood of Jesus of Nazareth—his heaven-ordained death, his victorious resurrection, and his present status as exalted Redeemer. To the Sadducees who instigated the early suppressions, such teaching not only upset orderly rule but, more important, impinged upon their authority. To the more noble of the Pharisees, however, the Jerusalem Christians were yet within the scope of Judaism and not to be treated as heretics. The divine claims for Jesus as yet lay in the subconsciousness of the church, and those who were his followers showed no tendency to relax their observance of the Mosaic law because of their new beliefs.

Between Gamaliel's advice and Saul's action, however, there arose within Christian preaching something that could only be viewed within Jerusalem as a real threat of Jewish apostasy. In Ac 6–7 Stephen began to apply the doctrines of Jesus' messiahship and lordship to traditional Jewish views regarding the land, the law, and the temple. Moreover, he is seen as beginning to reach conclusions that related to the primacy of Jesus' messiahship and lordship and the secondary nature of Jewish views about the land, the law, and the temple (see comments on ch. 7). For Stephen this was a dangerous path to tread, particularly in Jerusalem—a path even the apostles seemed unwilling to take at that time. Stephen's message was indeed Jewish apostasy. Had Rabbi Gamaliel the Elder faced this feature of Christian proclamation in the second Sanhedrin trial of the Jerusalem apostles, his attitude would undoubtedly have been different.

40 Gamaliel's wise counsel here prevailed to some extent among his Sanhedrin colleagues and held back the worst of Sadducean intentions, though it did not entirely divert their wrath. Thus the apostles were flogged (probably with the severe beating of thirty-nine stripes), were warned that the ban against teaching in the name of Jesus was still in effect, and were then released.

4. The apostles' rejoicing and continued ministry (5:41–42)

Luke ends his account of the apostles' second appearance before the Sanhedrin with a brief summary that speaks of their rejoicing and continued ministry. It is a statement that has nuances of defiance, confidence, and victory; and in many ways it gathers together all Luke has set forth from 2:42 on.

41 Luke stresses the fact that just as the apostles performed miracles through the power of the name of Jesus (cf. 3:6) and proclaimed that name before the people and the council (cf. 3:16; 4:10, 12), so they rejoiced when "counted worthy of suffering disgrace for the Name."

42 Furthermore, Luke tells us that "they never stopped teaching and proclaiming the good news that Jesus is the Christ." In this somewhat formal statement, which comes close to concluding our author's whole first panel of material, there is both a correlation with the thesis paragraph of Acts (2:42–47)—explicitly in the phrases "in the temple courts and from house to house" (cf. 2:46), though also inferentially in the note of continuance that is sounded—and an anticipation of the final words of Luke's sixth panel at the very end of Acts: "boldly and without hindrance" (28:31).

F. The Hellenists' Presence and Problem in the Church (6:1–6)

In this last section before the beginning of the second panel of Part I of Acts (the second panel focuses on three individuals—Stephen, Philip, and Saul of Tarsus—and their ministry among the Greek-speaking Jews, i.e., the Hellenists), Luke finds it necessary to tell his readers something about this Hellenist element in the church. He might have started his second panel with discussing the presence of the Hellenistic Christians in Jerusalem, for that would have provided a good thematic introduction for the panel. To have done so, however, would have separated them from their roots in the early church and would have damaged his theme of continuity amid diversity and development. Thus he chose to include the portrayal of the Hellenists in the Jerusalem congregation in his first panel and before the summary statement (6:7) that concludes that panel.

1 This verse is not only one of the most important in Acts, it is also one of the most complicated and discussed verses in the entire book. What one concludes regarding the identity of "the Grecian Jews," their relation to "the Aramaic-speaking community," and their circumstances within the church largely affects how one understands the material in Luke's second panel (6:8–9:31) and the whole course of events within the Jerusalem church. It is important, therefore, to understand as precisely as possible what Luke says *and* implies in describing "the Grecian Jews" (i.e, the Hellenists) within the early church, a group he introduces by the phrases "in those days" and "when the number of disciples was increasing."

As for differentiating the Hellenists from the believers of Hebrew background, scholars have made various suggestions: the Hellenists are (1) Greek-speaking Jews of the Diaspora who settled in Jerusalem among the native-born and Aramaic-speaking populace, (2) Jewish proselytes from a Gentile background, (3) Jews who were related in some manner to the Essene movement in Palestine, (4) the Samaritans, and (5) Jews (whether by birth or as proselytes) who spoke only Greek and no Semitic language such as Hebrew or Aramaic. Of these choices, the last one seems the best. It hurdles the difficulty of how Paul could call himself a Hebraic Jew even though he was from the Diaspora (Php 3:5), it provides an explanation as to why Hellenistic synagogues were required in Jerusalem, and it offers an insight into the problem of why two of the seven men chosen in 6:5 (Stephen and Philip) appear almost immediately thereafter as evangelists within their own circle when they had actually been appointed to supervise more mundane concerns.

Probably, therefore, "the Grecian Jews" in Acts 6 were originally Hellenized Jews who had come from the Diaspora but who were now living in Jerusalem and had come under some suspicion (by reason of their place of birth, their speech, or both) of being more Grecian than Hebraic in their attitudes and outlook. Many of them, no doubt, had originally returned to the homeland out of religious ardor and today would be called Zionists. Perhaps they tended to group together because of their similar backgrounds and common language, as the many Hellenistic synagogues in Jerusalem would seem to indicate. Since coming to Jerusalem, they had become Christians. But since attitudes and prejudices formed before conversion are often carried over into Christian life—too often the unworthy more than the worthy ones—some of the problems between the Hebraic Jews and the Hellenistic Jews in the church must be related back to such earlier differences and prejudices.

In 6:1–6, Luke tells us that the Hellenists' "widows were being overlooked in the daily distribution of food." Judaism had a system for the distribution of food and supplies to the poor, both to the wandering pauper and to those living in Jerusalem itself. The early Christian community at Jerusalem likewise expressed its spiritual unity in communal sharing of possessions and in charitable acts (cf. 2:44–45; 4:32–5:11). Apparently with the "increasing" number of believers and with the passing of time, the number of Hellenistic widows dependent on relief from the church became disproportionately large. Many pious Jews of the Diaspora had moved to Jerusalem in their later years in order to be buried near it, and their widows would have had no relatives near at hand to care for them as would the widows of the longtime residents. Nor as they became Christians would the "poor baskets" of the national system of relief be readily available to them. So the problem facing the church became acute.

The issue about the distribution of food may not have been all that disrupted the fellowship. It is likely that it was only the symptom of a larger tension between the two groups, opening up earlier prejudices. If the Hellenists spoke mostly in Greek, they may have required separate meetings within the Christian community, and these too could have brought back old resentments.

2–4 The apostles' response in this matter was to call the Christians together and suggest a solution. It is significant that the apostles were not prepared simply to ignore the problem; they seem to have realized that spiritual and material concerns are so intimately related in Christian experience that one always affects the other for better or worse. Similarly, there was no attempt to assign blame or to act in any paternalistic fashion. Rather, they suggested that seven men "full of the Spirit and wisdom" be chosen from among the congregation (perhaps only from among the Hellenists) who could take responsibility in the affair. The apostles would give their attention exclusively "to prayer and the ministry of the word."

The reference to the apostles as "the Twelve" occurs only here in Acts (cf. 1Co 15:5), though earlier Luke has spoken of "the Eleven" in such an absolute and corporate manner (cf. Lk 24:9, 33; Ac 2:14). Likewise, the references to Christians as "the disciples" here and in v.1 are the first instances of this usage in Acts, though in the remainder of the book it occurs fairly often. In using both these terms, Luke has gone back to the language of the earliest Christians and tried to make idiomatic use of it. The words "full of the Spirit and wisdom" evidently refer to guidance by the Holy Spirit and skill in administration and business, which, singly and together, are so necessary in Christian service. While Christian ministers wish such qualities were more characteristic of their own boards and councils, it is only fair to say that boards and councils often wish their ministers were given more "to prayer and the ministry of the word"! A pattern is set here for both lay leaders and clergy, and God's work will move ahead more efficiently if it is followed carefully.

5–6 The apostles made a proposal, but the church, the community of God's Spirit, made the decision. The apostles therefore laid their hands on the Seven and appointed them to be responsible for the daily distribution of food. The laying on of hands recalls Moses' commissioning of Joshua in Nu 27:18–23, where through this act some of Moses' authority was conferred on Joshua. That is evidently what the laying on of hands was meant to symbolize here, with the apostles delegating their authority to the seven selected by the church (cf. also 8:17; 9:17; 13:3; 19:6).

All seven men have Greek names; one of them is singled out as having been a Gentile convert to Judaism (i.e., a "proselyte"). But it is impossible to be sure simply from the names whether all seven were Hellenists, for at that time many Palestinian Jews also had Greek names. Nevertheless, the fact that Luke gives only Greek names suggests that all seven were in fact from the Hellenistic group within the church. Furthermore, Luke does not directly call these seven by the ecclesiastical title "deacon" (*diakonos*; GK *1356*), even though he uses the cognate noun *diakonia* ("distribution"; GK *1355*) in v.1 and the verb *diakoneo* ("wait on"; GK *1354*) in v.2 for what they were to do. Yet the ministry to which the seven were appointed was functionally equivalent to what Paul covered in the title "deacon" (cf. 1Ti 3:8–13); in the NT ministry was a function long before it became an office.

Acts 6:1–6 is particularly instructive as something of a pattern for church life today. In the first place, the early church took seriously the combination of spiritual and material concerns in carrying out its God-given ministry. In doing so, it stressed prayer and the proclamation of the Word, but never to the exclusion of helping the poor and correcting injustices. And even when the church found it necessary to divide internal responsibilities and assign different functions, the early believers saw these as varying aspects of one total ministry.

Second, the early church seems to have been prepared to adjust its procedures, alter its organizational structure, and develop new posts of responsibility in response to existing needs and for the sake of the ongoing proclamation of the Word of God. Throughout the years various so-called restorationist movements in the church have attempted to reach back and recapture the explicit forms and practices of the earliest Christians and have tried to reproduce them as far as possible in their pristine forms, believing that in doing so they are more truly biblical than other church groups. But Luke's narrative here suggests that to be fully biblical is to be constantly engaged in adapting traditional methods and structures to meet existing situations, both for the sake of the welfare of the whole church and for the outreach of the Gospel.

Finally, Luke's account suggests certain restraining attitudes that could well be incorporated into contemporary churchmanship. Among these are (1) refusing to get involved in the practice of assigning blame where things have gone wrong, preferring rather to expend the energies of God's people on correcting injustices, praying, and proclaiming the Word, and (2) refusing to become paternalistic in solving problems, which implies a willingness to turn the necessary authority for working out solutions over to others—even, as was possibly the case here, to those who feel the problem most acutely and may therefore be best able to solve it.

G. A Summary Statement (6:7)

7 Luke concludes his first panel of material on the earliest days of the church in Jerusalem with this summary statement, which is very much in line with his thesis paragraph (2:42–47) and his summary paragraphs (4:32–35; 5:12–16) that head their respective units of material. His focus in this first panel has been on the advances of the Gospel and the responses of the people. Therefore he concludes by saying that "the word of God spread" and "the number of disciples in Jerusalem increased rapidly."

Before he leaves his first panel of material, however, Luke—almost, it seems, as an afterthought—inserts the comment that "a large number of priests became obedient to the faith." At first glance this is, to say the least, somewhat perplexing because, in view of 4:1ff. and 5:17ff., it seems extremely difficult to believe that priests in any numbers would have become Christians. Nevertheless, there were perhaps as many as eight thousand "ordinary" priests and ten thousand Levites, divided into twenty-four weekly courses, serving at the Jerusalem temple during the period of a year, whose social position was distinctly inferior to that of the high priestly families and whose piety in many cases could well have inclined them to an acceptance of the Christian message. Luke indicates that a great number of persons calling themselves priests became believers in Jesus and were numbered with the Christians in the Jerusalem church.

Panel 2—Critical Events in the Lives of Three Pivotal Figures (6:8–9:31)

Luke now turns to three key events in the advance of the Gospel beyond its strictly Jewish confines: the martyrdom of Stephen, the early ministries of Philip, and the conversion of Saul of Tarsus. Luke's presentation is largely biographical. This is the type of material that would have circulated widely among the dispossessed Hellenistic Christians, including Stephen's argument before the Sanhedrin. Furthermore, Luke may have heard Philip and Paul speak together about these matters either during Paul's stay for "a number of days" at Philip's home in Caesarea (cf. 21:8–10) or during Paul's imprisonment at Caesarea (cf. 25:27).

No doubt Stephen's martyrdom was imprinted on Philip's memory, and accounts of his defense had probably become the *raison d'être* for the Hellenists' continued ministry. Likewise, Philip must have made a lasting impression on Luke as an important figure in the advance of the Christian mission, just as he was an important person in the Christian community at Caesarea (cf. 8:40; 21:8–9). And Paul was of such immense significance for Luke's narrative that an account of his conversion was inevitable—particularly because of its miraculous circumstances.

Just when the events of Luke's second panel took place depends largely on the dates for Paul's conversion and ministry. Since Stephen's death occurred before the conversion of Saul of Tarsus (cf. 7:58; 8:1), and since Luke presents Philip's ministries in Samaria and to the Ethiopian eunuch as following on the heels of the persecution that arose with Stephen's martyrdom, the accounts of these two Hellenistic spokesmen are historically tied to the conversion of Saul. For the chronological issues associated with Paul, see the comments on 9:1-30 and other succeeding passages. As for this second panel, it is sufficient to say that the events Luke presents in it took place somewhere in the mid-thirties, possibly as early as A.D. 33 or as late as A.D. 37.

A. The Martyrdom of Stephen (6:8–8:3)

1. Opposition to Stephen's ministry 6:8–7:1)

8 Stephen has earlier been described as being "full of the Spirit and wisdom" (6:3) and "full of faith and of the Holy Spirit" (6:5). Now

Luke says he was "full of God's grace and power." The three descriptions are complementary. The word "grace" was previously used by Luke to characterize both Jesus (Lk 4:22) and the early church (Ac 4:33) and connotes "spiritual charm" or "winsomeness." "Power" has already appeared in Acts in conjunction with "wonders and signs" (2:22) and "grace" (4:33) and connotes divine power expressed in mighty works.

Like Jesus and the apostles (cf. 2:22, 43; 5:12), Stephen is portrayed as having done "great wonders and miraculous signs among the people." Just what these were, Luke does not say, though we are undoubtedly to think of them as being of the same nature as those done by Jesus and the apostles. Nor does Luke tell us just when these manifestations of divine power began in Stephen's ministry. Perhaps they were a direct result of the laying on of the apostles' hands (cf. 6:6).

9–10 Stephen soon began preaching among his Hellenistic compatriots. Many commentators have found this to be a major problem in the narrative because Stephen was appointed to supervise relief for the poor, not to perform the apostolic function of preaching. But if we posit (1) the continuation, to some extent, of old tensions between Hebraic Jews and Hellenistic Jews in the Jerusalem church and (2) occasional separate meetings for the Aramaic-speaking and Greek-speaking believers (cf. comments on 6:1), several difficulties in the historical reconstruction of this period are partially explained. While not minimizing the importance of the apostles to the whole church, we can say that in some way Stephen, Philip, and perhaps others of the appointed seven may well have been to the Hellenistic Christians what the apostles were to the those born in Palestine. Philip seems to have performed such a function later on at Caesarea. And in the early church, where ministry was a function long before it became an office, such preaching was evidently looked upon with approval.

Opposition to Stephen arose from certain members within the Hellenistic community. Opinion differs widely as to just how many Hellenistic synagogues are in view in v.9. Many have insisted that there are five, though more likely the singular form of "synagogue" in the passage and the epexegetical nature of the last four designations posit only one syn-

Outside this Jerusalem gate (called Stephen's Gate or Lion's Gate) is the traditional place where Stephen's stoning is remembered.

agogue, the synagogue of the Freedmen, made up of Jews from Cyrene, Alexandria, Cilicia, and Asia (cf. NIV text). The word "Freedmen" probably refers to Jewish freedmen and the sons of such freedmen.

We have no account of the content of Stephen's preaching that so antagonized his Hellenistic compatriots. Luke labels the accusations against him (vv.11–14) as false—though, to judge by his response of ch. 7, they seem to have been false more in nuance and degree than in kind. From the accusations and from his defense, it is clear that Stephen had begun to apply his Christian convictions regarding the centrality of Jesus of Nazareth as the Messiah in God's redemptive program to such issues as the significance of the land, the law, and the temple for Jewish Christians. This, however, was a dangerous path to tread, particularly for Hellenistic Jewish Christians! It was one that the apostles themselves seem to have been unwilling to explore. And it was a path that Jews who had lately returned to Jerusalem from the Diaspora would view with reticence.

Having originally immigrated to their homeland out of a desire to be more faithful Jews, and having come under some suspicion of an inbred liberalism by the native-born populace, the Hellenistic Jewish community in Jerusalem undoubtedly had a vested interest in keeping deviations among its members to a minimum, or else exposing them as outside its own commitments, lest its synagogues fall under further suspicion. Thus the Hellenistic members of the Synagogue of the Freedmen were probably quite eager to bait Stephen in order to root out such a threat from their midst—though it is evident from the record that Stephen welcomed the challenge. But as Luke tells us, "they could not stand up against his wisdom or the Spirit by which he spoke." This fulfills Jesus' promise of the gift of "words and wisdom" in the time of persecution (cf. Lk 21:15).

11–14 Four things are said about certain members of the synagogue of the Freedman: (1) "they secretly persuaded some men to say" that Stephen had spoken "blasphemy" (GK *1060*); (2) "they stirred up the people and the elders and the teachers of the law" on their trumped-up charge against Stephen; (3) "they seized Stephen and brought him before the Sanhedrin"; and (4) "they produced false witnesses" at his trial.

The rumors had to do with Stephen's being "against Moses and against God"— "against Moses" because his arguments appeared to challenge the eternal validity of the Mosaic law, and "against God" because he appeared to be setting aside that which was taken to be the foundation and focus of national worship—the Jerusalem temple. In so doing, the rumors struck at the heart of both Pharisaic and Sadducean interests. In the first century, "blasphemy" was broadly interpreted along the lines of Nu 15:30: "Anyone who sins defiantly, whether native-born or alien, blasphemes the LORD, and that person must be cut off from his people."

The testimony of witnesses who repeated what they had heard a defendant say was part of Jewish court procedure in a trial for blasphemy. But the testimony against Stephen (v.14), according to Luke, was false (cf. the testimony against Jesus, Mt 26:61; Mk 14:58). Its falseness lay not so much in its wholesale fabrication but in its subtle and deadly misrepresentation of what was intended. Undoubtedly, Stephen spoke regarding a recasting of Jewish life in terms of the supremacy of Jesus the Messiah and expressed in his manner and message something of the subsidiary significance of the Jerusalem temple and the Mosaic law, as did Jesus before him (e.g., Mk 2:23–28; 3:1–6; 7:14–15; 10:5–9; cf. Jn 2:19–22). But that is not the same as advocating the destruction of the temple or the changing of the law—though on such matters we must allow Stephen to speak for himself in Acts 7.

6:15–7:1 The members of the council "looked intently" at Stephen as he was brought before them and saw one whose appearance was "like the face of an angel." Luke probably wants us to understand that Stephen, being filled with the Holy Spirit (6:3, 5) and possessing a genuine spiritual winsomeness (6:8), radiated a presence marked by confidence, serenity, and courage. And with the question of the high priest—"Are these charges true?"—the stage is set for Stephen's defense.

2. Stephen's defense before the Sanhedrin (7:2–53)

The defense of Stephen before the Sanhedrin is hardly a defense in the sense of an explanation or apology calculated to win an acquittal. Rather, it is a proclamation of the Christian message in terms of the popular Judaism of the day and an indictment of the Jewish leaders for their failure to recognize Jesus of Nazareth as their Messiah or to appreciate the salvation provided in him. Before the fall of Jerusalem in A.D. 70, the three great pillars in the religious faith of the vast majority of Jews were the land, the law, and the temple. It is this type of thought that Stephen confronts here, as the writer of Hebrews also did later.

a. On the land (7:2–36)

Declarations of faith within a Jewish milieu were often tied into a recital of God's intervention in the life of Israel, for God is the God who is known by his redemptive activity on behalf of his people in history. So by beginning his defense with a resumé of Israel's history, Stephen is speaking in accord with Jewish form. But while Jewish in form, the content of his address runs counter to much of the popular piety of the day. He argues that God's significant activity has usually taken place outside the confines of Palestine, that wherever God meets his people can be called "holy ground," that God is the God who calls his own to move forward in their religious experience, and that therefore dwelling in the land of promise requires a pilgrim lifestyle in which the land may be appreciated but never venerated.

In the OT the important concepts of "rest" (GK 4957) and "remnant" (GK 8642) are frequently associated closely with the land. For example, Dt 12:9–10 reads: "You have not yet reached the resting place [GK 4957] and the inheritance the LORD your God is giving you. But you will cross the Jordan and settle in the land the LORD your God is giving you as an inheritance, and he will give you rest from all your enemies around you so that you will live in safety" (cf. Dt 3:20; Jos 1:13; Joel 2:32b; Mic 4:6–7). Facing much the same problem and with much the same purpose as the writer of Hebrews (cf. Heb 4:1–13; 11:8–16), though with a difference of method and structure in his argument, Stephen argues against a veneration of the Holy Land that leaves no room for God's further saving activity in Jesus of Nazareth, Israel's Messiah. Stephen is not renouncing Israel's possession of the land; he makes no attempt to deny or avoid mentioning God's promise that Abraham's descendants would inherit Palestine. He is rather delivering a polemic against a veneration of the land that misses God's further redemptive work. And while his message relates to his time and situation, it also has great relevance for us. For we Christians today are constantly tempted to assert that our nation and our possessions are God-given rather than to confess our dependence on a God who is not limited by anything he has bestowed and to affirm our readiness to move forward with him at all cost.

2–8 Stephen begins by addressing the council in a somewhat formal yet fraternal manner: "Men, brothers and fathers" (cf. 22:1). Then he launches into his message, taking up first the situation of Abraham. "The God of glory," Stephen says, "appeared to our father Abraham *while he was still in Mesopotamia, before he lived in Haran* [italics mine]." God's word to him was to move forward into the possession of a land that was promised to him and his descendants. But though he entered into his promised inheritance, he did not live in it as if living in it was the consummation of God's purposes for him. Rather, he cherished as most important the covenantal and personal relationship that God had established with him, whatever his place of residence—a relationship of which circumcision was the God-given sign.

There are a number of difficulties as to chronological sequence, historical numbers, and the use of biblical quotations in Stephen's address that have led to the most strenuous exercise of ingenuity on the part of commentators in their attempts to reconcile them. Four of these difficulties appear in vv.2–8. Verse 3 quotes the words of God to Abraham given in Ge 12:1 and implies by its juxtaposition with v.2 that this message came to Abraham when he was still in Mesopotamia, whereas the context of Ge 12:1 suggests that it came to him in Haran. Verse 4 says that he left Haran after the death of his father, whereas the chronological data of Ge 11:26–12:4 suggest that Terah's death took place after Abraham's departure from Haran. Verse 5 uses the words of Dt 2:5 as a suitable description of Abraham's situation in Palestine, whereas their OT context relates to God's prohibition to Israel not to dwell in Mount Seir because it had been given to Esau. And v.6 speaks of 400 years of slavery in Egypt, whereas Ex 12:40 says 430.

We need not, however, get so disturbed over such things as, on the one hand, to pounce on them to disprove a "high view" of biblical inspiration or, on the other hand, to attempt to harmonize them so as to support such a view. These matters are paralleled in other popular writings of the day, whether overtly Hellenistic or simply more nonconformist in the broadest sense of that term. The Jewish philosopher Philo, for example, explained Abraham's departure from Ur of the Chaldees by referring to Ge 12:1, even though he elsewhere wrote that Ge 12:1–5 is in the context of leaving Haran. The Jewish historian Josephus spoke of Abraham's being seventy-five years old when he left Chaldea (contra Ge 12:4, which says he was seventy-five when he left Haran). Likewise, Philo placed the departure of Abraham from Haran after his father's death. And undoubtedly the round figure of four hundred years for Israel's slavery in Egypt—a figure that stems from the statement credited to God in Ge

15:13—was used in popular expressions of religious piety in first-century Judaism.

There is a remarkable psychological or emotional truth in Luke's report of Stephen's address. With his life at stake, Stephen was speaking under intense emotion and with God-given eloquence. With remarkable verisimilitude Luke shows him using commonly understood language in vivid terms and with burning eloquence as he refers to Israel's history. Stephen's speech was not a scholarly historical survey; it was a powerful portrayal of God's dealing with Israel, and it mounted inexorably to a climax that unmasked the obstinacy and disobedience of Israel and of their leaders in Stephen's time. Church history knows of few, if any, greater displays of moral courage than Stephen showed in this speech. And to dissect it on precisionist grounds shows lack of understanding of its basic truth.

9–16 Stephen's address next turns to the sons of Jacob, or "the twelve patriarchs" as they were known more popularly. Here Stephen's point is that God was with Joseph and his brothers in *Egypt* (the name itself is repeated six times in vv. 9–16), even though the only portion of the Holy Land that they possessed was the family tomb in Palestine, to which their bones were brought back later for final burial.

This section has two further difficulties of the type noted in vv.2–6: (1) v. 14 gives the number seventy-five as the total number who originally went down to Egypt, whereas Ge 46:27 sets the figure at seventy, and (2) v.16 confuses Abraham's tomb at Hebron, in the cave of Machpelah, which he bought from Ephron the Hittite (cf. Ge 23:3–20) and wherein Abraham, Isaac, and Jacob were buried (cf. Ge 49:29–33; 50:13), with the burial plot purchased by Jacob at Shechem from the sons of Hamor (Ge 33:19), wherein Joseph and his descendants were buried (cf. Jos 24:32). Again, these are but further examples of the conflations and inexactitudes of Jewish popular religion, which, it seems, Luke simply recorded from his sources in his attempt to be faithful to what Stephen actually said in his portrayal. And again, they can in large measure be paralleled elsewhere.

17–36 Still on the subject of "the land," Stephen recounts the life of Moses. Incorporated into this section, largely by way of anticipation, is a Moses-rejection theme in vv.23–29 and 35, which will later be highlighted in vv.39–43 and then driven home in the scathing indictment of vv.51–53. But here Stephen's primary emphasis is on God's providential and redemptive action for his people apart from and outside the land of Palestine, of which Stephen's hearers made so much: (1) God's raising up of the deliverer Moses *in Egypt* (vv.17–22); (2) his provision for the rejected Moses *in Midian* (v.29); (3) his commissioning of Moses *in the desert near Mount Sinai*—the place God himself identified as being "holy ground," for wherever God meets with his people is holy ground though it possesses no sanctity of its own (vv.30–34); and (4) Moses' resultant action in delivering God's people and doing "wonders and miraculous signs" for forty years *in Egypt, at the Red Sea, and in the desert*. This narration of events in Moses' life is not given just to introduce the Second Moses theme that follows in vv.37–43, though it certainly does that. Its primary purpose seems rather to be that of making the vital point, contrary to the popular piety of the day in its veneration of "the Holy Land," that no place on earth—even though given as an inheritance by God himself—can be claimed to possess such sanctity or be esteemed in such a way as to preempt God's further working on behalf of his people. By this method Stephen was attempting to clear the way for the proclamation of the centrality of Jesus in the nation's worship, life, and thought.

b. On the law (7:37–43)

Involved inevitably with the Jews' exaltation of the law were veneration of Moses the Law-giver and idealization of Israel's days in the desert. All parties within Judaism of the first century A.D.—whether Sadducees, Pharisees, Essenes, Zealots, Apocalypticists, Hellenists, Samaritans, or the so-called People of the Land—were united in this veneration and idealization. So in meeting the accusation that he was speaking blasphemous words "against Moses" (6:11) and "against the law" (6:13), Stephen argues two points clearly and a third inferentially: (1) Moses himself spoke of God's later raising up "a prophet like me" from among his people and for his people, which means therefore that Israel cannot limit the revelation and redemption of God to Moses' precepts (vv.37–38); (2) Moses had been rejected by his own people, even though he was God's appointed redeemer—which parallels the way Jesus of Nazareth was treated and explains why the majority within the nation refused him, even though he was God's promised Messiah (vv.39–40); and (3) even though Moses was with them and they had the living words of the law and the sacrificial system, the people fell gross idolatry and actually opposed God (vv.41–43).

37–38 Tension is now beginning to build up in Stephen's speech. Starting from the rather placid historical narrative of vv.2–34 and moving to the more strident conclusion in vv.35–36, the speech peaks with a passionate treatment of the Moses testimonium passage in Dt 18:15 and of the significance of Moses himself there. This probably reflects a method of interpreting Scripture common to nonconformist Jews in general (cf. comments on 2:16) and points to the crux of Stephen's argument.

Stephen in no way disparages Moses. Indeed, in referring to Moses as being "in the congregation in the wilderness, with our fathers and with the angel who spoke to him on Mount Sinai," he was speaking in a complimentary way. Likewise, Moses received "living words" that he passed on—an expression that implies the opposite of any disparagement of the Mosaic law. But Stephen's point is that in Dt 18:15 Moses pointed beyond himself and beyond the instruction that came through him to another whom God would raise up in the future and to whom Israel must give heed; therefore, Israel cannot limit divine revelation and redemption to the confines of the Mosaic law.

In the first century A.D., Judaism was generally looking for a Messiah who would in some way be "like Moses." Numerous contemporary Jewish documents suggested a parallel between Israel's first redeemer Moses and Israel's expected Messiah-Redeemer, who would be like Moses. Stephen's argument from Dt 18:15–18, therefore, was generally in accord with Jewish eschatological expectations. And he evidently used it, as Peter did before him (cf. 3:22–23), expecting it to be convincing.

39–40 But while Peter and Stephen agree in seeing Christological significance in Dt 18:15–18 and in considering it an important testimonium passage for a Jewish audience, their attitudes toward Israel are very different. For Peter, his hearers are the sons of the prophets who should hear the new Moses (cf. 3:22–26); whereas for Stephen, his hearers are the sons of those who rejected Moses and killed the prophets (cf. 7:35–40, 51–53). In vv.39–40 Stephen specifies his rejection-of-Moses theme by picking up the awful words of Nu 14:3, "Their hearts turned back to Egypt" (v.39) and citing almost verbatim the people's defiance of Ex 32:1: "Make us gods who will go before us. As for this fellow Moses who led us out of Egypt—we don't know what has happened to him!" (v.40).

The Jewish Talmud also speaks of the people's rebellion in making the golden calf and generally views it as Israel's first, ultimate, and most heinous sin. But there is a decided difference between the way they treat the people's rebellion and the way Stephen does. The rabbis do not take this episode as the people's rejection of Moses, but emphasize Moses' successful intercession for Israel. Stephen, however, lays all his emphasis on Israel's rejection of their deliverer, implicitly drawing the parallel between their treatment of Moses and their treatment of Jesus—a parallel he will broaden and drive home in his scathing indictment of vv.51–53.

41–43 Stephen emphasizes that the golden calf incident was the time when the Israelites "brought sacrifices to it and held a celebration in honor of what their hands had made." So detestable to God was this episode in Israel's experience in the desert that Stephen calls it a time when "God turned away and gave them over to the worship of the heavenly bodies" (cf. Ro 1:24, 26, 28 for the expression "God gave them over"). The inescapable inference from Stephen's words is that Israel's shameful behavior and God's drastic response to it find their counterparts in the nation's rejection of Jesus.

To support his assertion that Israel's idolatry caused God to give them over to the worship of heavenly bodies, Stephen quotes Am 5:25–27 (following closely the Greek translation of the OT). In applying this passage, Stephen emphasizes that rejection of God's activity in the eschatological day of salvation brings God's judgment, despite all the sacrifices and offerings that may be offered, just as Israel's idolatry of the golden calf eventuated in Israel's exile "beyond Babylon."

c. On the temple (7:44–50)

Stephen has met the accusation of blasphemy against the law by reassessing Moses' place in redemptive history and by countercharging his accusers with both rejecting the one Moses spoke of and turning to idolatry in their refusal of Jesus the Messiah. Stephen now proceeds to meet the charge of blasphemy against the temple in the same way. In form, this section of the address recalls the more placid manner of vv.2–34. In tone and content, however, it carries on the strident and passionate appeal of vv.35–43, which amounts to a vigorous denunciation of the Jerusalem temple and the type of mentality that would hold to it as the apex of revealed religion.

44–46 Stephen's assessment of Israel's worship experience lays all the emphasis on the tabernacle, which he eulogistically calls "the tabernacle of Testimony." It was with our forefathers, he says, during that period in the desert, which so many consider exemplary. It was made according to the exact pattern God gave Moses and was central in the life of the nation during the conquest of Canaan under the leadership of Joshua. And it was the focus of national worship through the time of David, who found favor in God's sight. So significant was it in Israel's experience, in fact, that David asked to be allowed to provide a permanent type of "dwelling place" for God in Jerusalem. (Here Ps 132:5 is quoted and 2Sa 6:17; 1Ch 15:1 are alluded to.)

Like the writer to the Hebrews (cf. Heb 8:2, 5; 9.1–5, 11, 24), and probably like many other nonconformist Jews of his time, Stephen seems to have viewed the epitome of Jewish worship in terms of the tabernacle, not the temple. This was likely because he felt the mobility of the tabernacle was a restraint on the status quo mentality that had grown up around the temple. Furthermore, also like the writer to the Hebrews, Stephen attempts to lift his compatriots' vision to something far superior to even the wilderness tabernacle—namely, to the dwelling of God with humans in Jesus of Nazareth and as expressed through the new covenant.

47 "But it was Solomon," Stephen tersely says, "who built the house for him." This brevity shows something of Stephen's pejorative attitude toward the temple. And his contrast between the tabernacle (vv. 44–46) and the temple (v.47) expresses his disapproval. Probably Stephen had in mind 2Sa 7:5–16 (cf. 1Ch 17:4–14). There God spoke through the prophet Nathan of his satisfaction with his "nomadic" situation and declined David's offer to build a house for his divine presence; but he went on to announce that David's son would build such a house and promised to build a "house" (lineage) for David. Certainly 2Sa 7:5–16 was a foundational passage for much of early Christian thought (cf. Lk 1:32–33, alluding to 2Sa 7:12–16; Ac 13:17–22 to 7:6–16; Heb 1:5b to 7:14; and, possibly, 2 Cor 6:18 to 7:14). Obviously Stephen did not consider Solomon's temple to be the final fulfillment of God's words to David in 2Sa 7. Probably he understood the announcement of a temple to be a concession on God's part and laid greater emphasis on the promise of the establishment of David's seed and kingdom (cf. 2Sa 7:12–16).

48–50 Stephen reaches the climax of his anti-temple polemic by insisting that "the Most High does not live in houses made by men"—a concept he supports by citing Isa 66:1–2a. Judaism never taught that God actually lived in the temple or was confined to its environs but spoke of his "Name" and presence as being there. In practice, however, this concept was often denied. This would especially appear so to Stephen, when further divine activity in Jesus Christ was refused out-of-hand by the people in their preference for God's past revelation and redemption as symbolized in the existence of the temple.

As a Hellenist, Stephen seems to have had a tendency to view things in a more "spiritual" manner than most Jews (i.e., in more inward and nonmaterial terms)—a tendency with both good and bad features. As a Christian, he could have been aware of the contrast in the early oral instruction of converts between what is "made with hands" and what is "not made with hands" (cf. esp. Mk 14:58; Heb 8:2; 9:24). But whatever its source, Stephen's main assertion is that neither the tabernacle nor the temple was intended to be such an institutionalized feature in Israel's religion as to prohibit God's further redemptive activity or to halt the advance of God's plan for his people. The response Stephen wants from his hearers was what God declared as his desire for his people in Isa 66:2b (this text follows the passage Stephen cites): "This is the one I esteem: he who is humble and contrite in spirit, and trembles at my word." To those who desired to localize God's presence and confine his working, however, Stephen repeated the denunciation of Isa 66:1–2a, leaving the appeal in Isa 66:2b to be inferred.

d. The indictment (7:51–53)

The most striking feature of Stephen's speech and the one that sets it off most sharply from Peter's temple sermon of Ac 3 is its strong polemical stance toward Israel. As Stephen recounts the history of Israel, he sees a litany of sin, rebellion, and rejection of God's purposes and emphasizes the unworthiness and continual rebelliousness of the Jews. Some have supposed that the suddenness and harshness of the indictment were occasioned by an angry outburst in the court, to which vv.51–53 are a kind of "kneejerk" response. But there is little reason to assume that to be the case. Stephen's address has led naturally up to the invective; and after his quotation of Isa 66:1–2a, there was really nothing to add.

51 Stephen's description of his accusers is loaded with pejorative theological nuances. The phrase "stiff-necked" was fixed in Israel's memory as God's own characterization of the nation when it rebelled against Moses and worshiped the golden calf (cf. Ex 33:5; Dt 9:13). And the expression "with uncircumcised hearts and ears" recalls God's judgment on the apostates among his people as being "uncircumcised in heart" (cf. Lev 26:41; Dt 10:16; Jer 4:4; 9:26). And now, says Stephen, speaking like a prophet of old, God's indictment rests upon you just as it did on your idolatrous and apostate ancestors.

52 Israel's persecution and killing of her prophets is a recurrent theme in Jewish literature. The OT not only speaks of the sufferings of individual prophets but also has a number of general statements about how the nation had persecuted and killed the prophets of God (cf. 2Ch 36:15–16; Ne 9:26; Jer 2:30). Various writings from this period of Judaism elaborated on this theme, particularly as a result of the idealization of martyrdom that arose in Maccabean times. Even the Talmud speaks frequently about Israel's persecuting and killing her prophets. All such statements, though, were for the council well-learned lessons from the past. Stephen's accusation, however, was that they had learned nothing from the past since an even more horrendous crime had been committed in the present—the betrayal and murder of "the Righteous One"—by the very ones who were so smug about Israel's past failures.

53 Stephen's address began with the fraternal greeting "Men, brothers and fathers." It affirmed throughout his deep respect for such distinctly Jewish phenomena as the Abrahamic covenant (vv.3–8), circumcision (v.8), and the tabernacle (vv.44–46). He repeatedly referred to "our father Abraham" and "our fathers" in such a way as to stress his ready acceptance of his Israelite heritage (vv.2, 11–12, 15, 19, 39, 44–45). Yet his repeated use of the second person plural pronoun in vv.51–53 shows his desire to disassociate himself from the nation in its recurrent refusal of God throughout its history. Consequently, taking the offensive, Stephen drives home his point: "*Your* fathers always resisted the Holy Spirit. . . . *Your* fathers persecuted the prophets. . . . *You* received the law put into effect through angels, but *you* have not obeyed it." Perhaps he jabbed with a finger at his accusers—though even a blind man would have felt his verbal blows.

3. The stoning of Stephen (7:54–8:1a)

54 To interpret Stephen's address as an absolute renunciation of the land, the law, or the sacrificial system is an exaggeration. Indeed, Stephen saw worship in terms of the tabernacle, not the temple, to be the ideal of Israel's worship. But that is not to say he rejected the worship of the temple, particularly as it continued the pattern of worship instituted by God in giving the tabernacle. Nor can it be said that Stephen was proclaiming a law-free and universal Gospel or suggesting the futility of a Christian mission to Israel. Instead, his desire, it seems, was to raise a prophetic voice *within* Israel, pleading with his hearers to make Jesus, not their traditional holy things, the center of their worship and thought. Certainly Stephen was more daring than the Jerusalem apostles, more ready to explore the logical consequences of commitment to Jesus than they were, and more ready to attribute Israel's rejection of its Messiah to a perpetual callousness of heart.

Nonetheless, Stephen's message was, for his hearers, flagrant apostasy—in both its content and its tone. While his purpose was to denounce the status quo mentality that had grown up around the land, the law, and the temple, thereby clearing a path for a positive response to Jesus as Israel's Messiah, this was undoubtedly taken as a frontal attack against the Jewish religion in its official and popular forms. And in the council's eyes, its assumed prophetic stance together with its obnoxious liberal spirit must have represented the worst of both Jewish Hellenism and the beginning Christian movement. So, Luke tells us, "they were furious and gnashed their teeth at him."

55–56 While the content and tone of his address infuriated the council, Stephen's follow-up solemn pronouncement raised again the specter of blasphemy and brought his hearers to a frenzied pitch: "Look, I see heaven open and the Son of Man standing at the right hand of God." Only a few years before, Jesus had stood before this same tribunal and had been condemned for answering affirmatively the high priest's question as to his being Israel's Messiah and for saying of himself: "And you will see the Son of Man sitting at the right hand of the Mighty One and coming on the clouds of heaven" (Mk 14:62). Now Stephen was saying, in effect, that his vision confirmed Jesus' claim and condemned the council for having rejected him. Unless the council members were prepared to repent and admit their awful error, they had no option but to find Stephen also guilty of blasphemy. Had he been judged only an impertinent apostate (cf. 5:40), the thirty-nine lashes of Jewish punishment would have been appropriate. But to be openly blasphemous before the council as well was a matter demanding death.

Luke's description of Stephen as "full of the Holy Spirit" is in line with his characterizations of him in 6:3, 5, 8, 15. The identification of Jesus as "the Son of Man" is used outside the Gospels only here and at Rev 1:13; 14:14 (also at Heb 2:6, though as a locution for a human being in line with Ps 8:4). In the Gospels except for Lk 24:7; Jn 12:34, Jesus alone used "Son of Man" in referring to himself (see comment on Mk 8:31). The title was generally not attributed to Jesus by the church between the time when his sufferings were completed and when he would assume his full glory. Here, however, an anticipation of Christ's full glory is set within a martyr context (as also at Rev 1:13; 14:14), and, therefore, "Son of Man" is fully appropriate.

In Stephen's vision the juxtaposition of "the glory [GK *1518*] of God" and the name of Jesus—together with his saying that he sees "heaven open and the Son of Man standing at the right hand of God"—is Christologically significant. The OT viewed "the glory of God" as the revelation of the nature of God or even as the divine mode of being itself. By bringing together "the glory of God" and the name of Jesus, therefore, Luke suggests that Jesus manifested the divine nature and the divine mode of being. Likewise, inasmuch as God dwells in the highest heaven, the open heaven with Christ at God's right hand suggests something about his work as providing access into the very presence of God.

Stephen's reference to Jesus "standing" at the right hand of God, which differs from the "sitting" of Ps 110:1 (the passage alluded to here), has been variously understood. Most commentators have interpreted the "standing" to suggest Jesus' welcome of his martyred follower, who, like the repentant criminal of Lk 23:43, was received into heaven the moment he died. Dispensational commentators have taken Stephen's reference to Jesus' "standing" as supporting their view that the distinctive redemptive message for this age was not proclaimed till the Pauline gospel; and, therefore, in the transitional period between Israel and the church, Jesus is represented as not yet having taken his seat at God's right hand. Still others speak of Jesus as "standing" in order to enter his messianic office on earth or depict him as "standing" in line with the common representation of angels standing in the presence of God.

Regardless of what position one takes, we should emphasize the idea of "witness" as being connoted in Jesus' "standing." Stephen has been acknowledging Christ before the council, and now he sees Christ acknowledging his servant before God (cf. Mt 10:32). The proper posture for a witness is standing. Stephen has been condemned by an earthly court and appeals for vindication to a heavenly court.

57–58 There is a progression in Luke's portrayals of the trial scenes of 4:1ff., 5:17ff., and here, with the first ending in threatenings (4:17, 21), the second with flogging (5:40), and the third with stoning (7:58–60). Moreover, the historical interplay of divergent ideological factors gave rise to Judaism's united stance against the Hellenists.

The message of Stephen, it seems, served as a kind of catalyst to unite Sadducees, Pharisees, and the common people against the early Christians. Had Gamaliel been confronted by this type of Christian preaching earlier, his attitude as reported in 5:34–39 would surely have been different. The Pharisees could tolerate Palestinian Jewish believers in Jesus because their messianic beliefs, though undoubtedly judged terribly misguided, effected no change in their practice of the Mosaic law: the Pharisaic and priestly devotees of the new movement continued their scrupulous observance of the law, and the Hebraic Christians continued to live in accordance with at least its minimal requirements. But the Hellenistic Christians, who had probably entered Palestine avowing their desire to become stricter in their religious practice, were now beginning to question the centrality of Israel's traditional forms of religious expression and to propagate within Jerusalem itself a type of religious liberalism that, from a Pharisaic perspective, would eventually undercut the basis for the Jewish religion itself. They might have been able to do little about such liberalism as it existed throughout the Diaspora and in certain quarters within Palestine. But they were determined to preserve the Holy City from further contamination by such outside elements and thus, as they saw it, best prepare the way for the coming of the Messianic Age.

It is not easy to determine whether the stoning of Stephen was only the result of mob action or whether it was carried out by the Sanhedrin in excess of its jurisdiction. The reference to "the witnesses" in v.58, whose grisly duty it was to knock the offender down and throw the first stones, suggests an official execution. If, as we believe, Stephen's martyrdom occurred sometime in the mid-thirties and during the final years of Pilate's governorship over Judea (A.D. 26–36), and if, as we have argued, the Pharisees were not prepared to come to his defense in the council, conditions may well have been at a stage where the Sanhedrin felt free to overstep its legal authority. Pontius Pilate normally resided at Caesarea, and the later years of his governorship were beset by increasing troubles that tended to divert his attention.

"The witnesses," Luke tells us, in preparing for their onerous work of knocking Stephen down and throwing the first stones, "laid their clothes at the feet of a young man named Saul." This suggests that Saul had some official part in the execution. "Young man" generally refers to someone from about twenty-four to forty years old. Some have argued from the action of the witnesses and from Saul's age that he was a member of the Jewish Sanhedrin at the time (see comment on 8:1a), though he may also have been exercising only delegated authority.

59–60 As Stephen was being stoned, he cried out, "Lord Jesus, receive my spirit," and, "Lord, do not hold this sin against them." The cries are reminiscent of Jesus' own words from the cross in Lk 23:34, 46, though the parallelism of sequence and wording is not exact. While it is probably going too far to say that Luke meant Stephen's execution to be a reenactment of the first great martyrdom, that of Jesus, the parallelism here is certainly not just inadvertent; and it was probably included to show that the same spirit of commitment and forgiveness that characterized Jesus' life and death was true of his earliest followers. The expression "fall asleep" (GK *3121*) is a common biblical way of referring to the death of God's own (cf. Jn 11:11; Ac 13:36; 1Co 7:39; 11:30; 2Pe 3:4), and the word "sleep" suggests something as to the nature of personal existence during that period of time theologians call "the intermediate state."

8:1a Again, as in 7:58, Luke makes the point that Saul was present at Stephen's death and approved of it. Because the verb "to give approval" (GK *5306*) is also used in 26:10, some have taken the reference here to be to Saul's official vote as a member of the Sanhedrin. But that is not necessarily implied. All Luke wants to do here is provide a transition in his account of the developing Christian mission,

4. The immediate aftermath (8:1b–3)

1b Taken in the broader context of Luke's presentation, we should probably understand the persecution recorded here as directed primarily against the Hellenistic Christians of Jerusalem rather than chiefly against the whole church. A certain stigma must also have fallen on the native-born and more scrupulous Jewish Christians, and they probably became as inconspicuous as possible in the countryside and towns around Jerusalem. The Hellenistic Jews of the city had already been able to disassociate themselves from the Hellenistic Jewish Christians among them. Probably the Jewish leaders made a somewhat similar distinction between the Hellenistic and the more Hebraic Christians within the Jerusalem church, though not nearly so sharply. We are told by Luke in a somewhat sweeping statement that "all" the Christians of Jerusalem "except the apostles were scattered throughout Judea and Samaria." Apparently, however, only the Hellenistic believers felt it inadvisable to return.

As a result of the persecution that began with the martyrdom of Stephen, the Gospel was carried beyond the confines of Jerusalem, in initial fulfillment of Jesus' directive in 1:8. From this time onward, the Jerusalem church seems to have been largely, if not entirely, devoid of Hellenistic believers. With the martyrdom of Stephen, the Christians of Jerusalem learned the bitter lesson that to espouse a changed relationship to the land, the law, and the temple was (1) to give up the peace of the church and (2) to abandon the Christian mission to Israel. The issues and events connected with Stephen's death and the expulsion of those who shared his concerns would stand as a warning to the Jerusalem congregation throughout its brief and turbulent history and would exert mental pressure upon Christians in the city to be more circumspect in their future activities within Judea.

2–3 Luke has already used "godly men" to describe the Jews at Pentecost who were receptive to the working of God's Spirit (2:5). He has also used the adjective "devout" of the aged Simeon in the temple (cf. Lk 2:25), and he will use it of Ananias of Damascus (cf. Ac 22:12). Therefore, when Luke says that "godly men buried Stephen," he apparently means that certain devout Jews who were open to his Christian message volunteered to ask for Stephen's body and bury him, much as Joseph of Arimathea did for Jesus (cf. Lk 23:50–53). Luke also tells us that those who buried Stephen "mourned deeply for him," which may well be Luke's way of suggesting their repentance toward God as well as their sorrow for Stephen.

Saul, who had had some official capacity at Stephen's stoning, now began a campaign to destroy the church (cf. also 9:1–30; 22:1–21; 26:2–23).

B. The Early Ministries of Philip (8:4–40)

The accounts of Philip's ministries in Samaria and to the Ethiopian minister of finance are placed in Acts between the Hellenists' expulsion from Jerusalem and the outreach of the Gospel to Gentiles—an outreach prepared for in Saul's conversion and first effected through the preaching of Peter to Cornelius. Luke uses these accounts of Philip's ministries as a kind of bridge in depicting the advance of the church. Each account represents a further development in proclaiming the Gospel within a Jewish milieu: the first, an outreach to a dispossessed group within Palestine who were often considered by Jerusalem Jews as "half-breeds," both racially and religiously; the second, an outreach to a proselyte or near-proselyte from another land.

1. The evangelization of Samaria (8:4–25)

Historically, the movement of the Gospel into Samaria following directly on the heels of the persecution of Hellenistic Jewish Christians in Jerusalem makes a great deal of sense. Doubtless a feeling of kinship was established between the formerly dispossessed Samaritans (see comment on Lk 9:53–54) and the recently dispossessed Christian Hellenists because of Stephen's opposition to the mentality of mainstream Judaism and its veneration of the Jerusalem temple—an opposition that would have facilitated a favorable response to Philip and his message in Samaria.

4 Luke records the mission to Samaria as inaugurated by Philip and carried on by Peter and John as "Exhibit A" for his thesis that "those who had been scattered preached the word wherever they went." Luke does this because in the mission to Samaria he sees in retrospect a significant advance in the outreach of the Gospel.

5 Philip, the second of the seven enumerated in 6:5 (cf. 21:8) and one of the Hellenistic believers expelled from Jerusalem in the persecution directed against Hellenistic Christians, traveled to the north and proclaimed "the Christ" to Samaritans. The text is uncertain as to which city of Samaria he preached in, for every direction from Jerusalem is "down." Luke was evidently not interested in giving a precise geographical identification for that city.

6–8 In the highly fluid and syncretistic atmosphere of first-century Palestine a number of parallels of outlook and ideology existed between various nonconformist groups generally looked upon as being Jewish. Stephen, the covenanters of Qumran, and the Samaritans, for example, all had an antitemple polemic, which, at least superficially, could have drawn them together (though, in actuality, their positions were each based on quite different rationales). In addition, as the antagonism of Jerusalem Jews was focused upon the Hellenistic Christians, these lately dispossessed Jewish believers undoubtedly found something of a welcome among the Samaritans, who had felt themselves the objects of a similar animosity for so long.

In Philip's preaching of Jesus as the Christ (vv.5, 12), he undoubtedly used Dt 18:15, 18–19 as a major testimonium passage in his preaching, just as Peter and Stephen had done (3:22; 7:37). With the Pentateuch as their Scriptures, and looking for the coming of a Mosaic Messiah, the Samaritans were open to Philip's message. Furthermore, God backed up his preaching by many "miraculous signs," with many demoniacs, paralytics, and cripples healed. Thus Luke summarizes the response of these Samaritans to Philip's ministry by saying, "So there was great joy in that city."

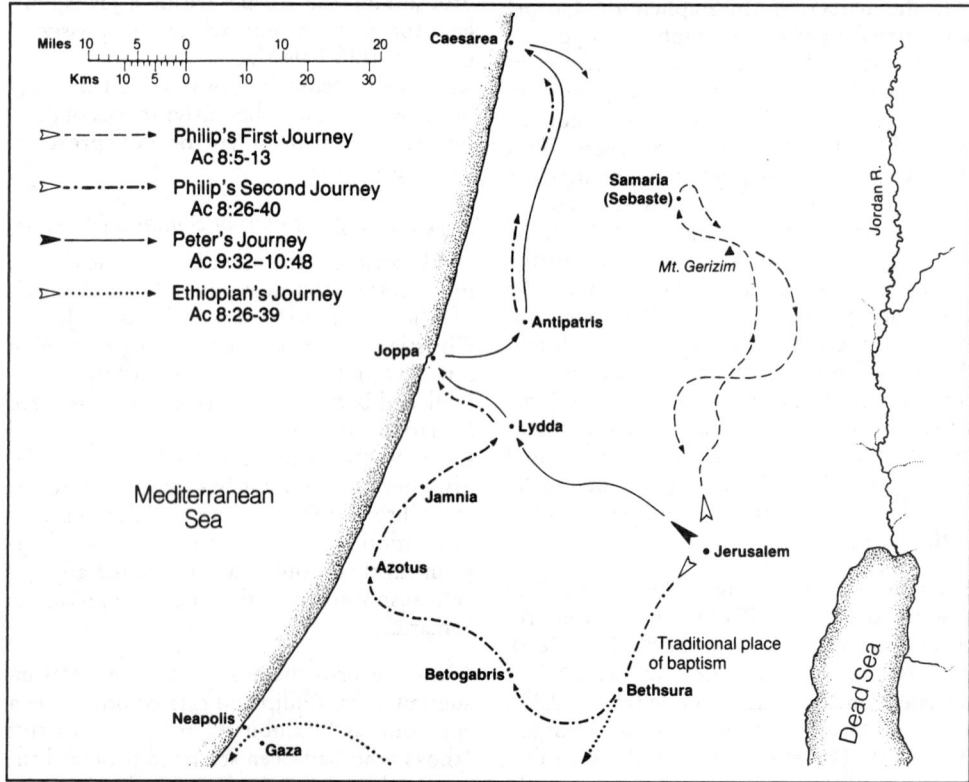

©1989 The Zondervan Corporation.

9–13 Simon the sorcerer, or Simon Magus as he is called in postapostolic Christian writings, was a leading heretic in the early church. Justin Martyr (died c. 165), who was himself a Samaritan, says that nearly all his countrymen revered Simon as the highest god, and many legends grew up around him. Just exactly how Simon of Ac 8 is related to Simon Magus of later legend is not clear. Luke's statement about the Samaritans' veneration of Simon (they said, "The man is the divine power known as the Great Power") seems to support the identification of these two. Likewise, what exactly is meant by the title "the Great Power" (v.10) is uncertain; it may mean that Simon was acclaimed to be God Almighty. At any rate, he claimed to be some exceedingly great person and supported his claim by many acts of magic.

Nevertheless, as the Gospel advanced into Samaria, Simon believed and was baptized. His conversion must have greatly impressed the Samaritans, and their evangelist Philip must have long remembered it. But Simon himself, to judge by the narrative that follows, was more interested in the great acts of power accompanying Philip's preaching than God's reign in his life or the proclamation of Jesus' messiahship. Simon's belief in Jesus seems to have been like that spoken of in Jn 2:23–25—i.e., based only on miraculous signs and thus inferior to true commitment to Jesus.

14 For the early church the evangelization of Samaria was not just a matter of an evangelist's proclamation and people's response. It also involved the acceptance of these new converts by the mother church in Jerusalem. So Luke takes pains to point out here (see also his account of Cornelius's conversion in 10:1–11:18) that the Jerusalem church sought to satisfy itself as to the genuineness of Philip's converts and that they did this by sending Peter and John to Samaria. Along with his thesis about development and advance in the outreach of the Gospel, Luke is also interested in establishing lines of continuity and highlighting aspects of essential unity within the church. Therefore, in his account of Philip's mission in Samaria, he tells also of the visit of Peter and John. Instead of minimizing Philip's success in Samaria, as some have proposed, it is more likely that Luke wants us to understand Peter and John's ministry in Samaria as confirming and extending Philip's ministry.

Just as in Ro 15:26 and 2Co 9:2, where a whole province is regarded as acting in a Christian manner when represented by only one or two congregations located there, so Luke here speaks sweepingly of the Jerusalem church hearing "that Samaria had accepted the word of God," even though in v.25 he refers to further evangelistic activity in other Samaritan villages.

15–17 When Peter and John arrived, they prayed for the Samaritan converts, laid their hands on them, and "they received the Holy Spirit." Before this, Luke tells us, "The Holy Spirit had not yet come upon any of them; they had simply been baptized into the name of the Lord Jesus." We are not told just how the coming of the Holy Spirit upon these new converts was expressed in their lives, but the context suggests that his presence was attended by such external signs as marked his coming on the earliest Christians at Pentecost—probably by some form of glossolalia. On the temporal separation of the baptism of the Spirit from commitment to Jesus and water baptism, see comment on 2:38. In effect, in this first advance of the Gospel outside the confines of Jerusalem, God worked in ways that were conducive not only to the reception of the Good News in Samaria but also to the acceptance of these new converts by believers at Jerusalem.

18–24 Simon's response to the presence of God's Spirit and the evidences of God's power is one of those tragic stories that accompany every advance of the Gospel. Whenever and wherever God is at work among people, there are not only genuine responses but also counterfeit ones. Simon "believed" and "was baptized," Luke has reported. Evidently Simon was included among those on whom Peter and John laid their hands. But the NT frequently reports incidents and events from a phenomenal perspective without always giving the divine or heavenly perspective. For this reason the verb "believe" (GK *4409*) is used in the NT to cover a wide range of responses to God and to Christ (e.g., Jn 2:23; Jas 2:19). Neither baptism nor the laying on of hands conveys any status or power of itself, though Simon with his shallow spiritual perception thought they could.

Simon's offer to pay for the ability to confer the Holy Spirit through the laying on of hands evoked Peter's consignment of Simon and his money to hell. Simon regarded the bestowal of the Spirit as a specially effective bit of magic, and he had no idea of the spiritual issues at stake. Peter's analysis of the situation, however, is that Simon's heart was "not right before God" because it was still "full of bitterness and captive to sin." So Peter urges him, "Repent of this wickedness and pray to the Lord. Perhaps he will forgive you for having such a thought in your heart." But Simon, preoccupied with external consequences and physical effects, asks only and rather lamely, "Pray to the Lord for me so that nothing you have said may happen to me." Luke expresses a sobering truth here: It is all too often possible to make a counterfeit response to the presence and activity of God's Spirit.

25 Luke closes his account of the evangelization of Samaria with a transitional sentence that tells us that on the apostles' return journey to Jerusalem, further evangelization of Samaria took place. The "they" of this verse refers primarily to Peter and John, but it may also refer to Philip for part of the journey, as they evangelized together in the southern regions of Samaria.

2. An Ethiopian eunuch converted (8:26–40)

This account of Philip's ministry to a high-ranking Ethiopian government official represents a further step in the advance of the Gospel from its strictly Jewish confines to a full-fledged Gentile mission. Though a Gentile, the official was probably a Jewish proselyte or near-proselyte (a so-called Proselyte of the Gate) and was therefore viewed by Luke as still within a Jewish religious milieu. He had been to Jerusalem to worship, was studying the prophecy of Isaiah, and was open to further instruction from a Jew. Here was a notable instance of providential working that carried the development of the Gospel proclamation even beyond Samaria.

26 Luke does not tell us just where Philip was when he received his divine directive to go south to the road from Jerusalem to Gaza. He highlights instead the fact that Philip's ministry to the Ethiopian eunuch was especially arranged by God and providentially worked out in all its details.

When Luke desires to stress the special presence and activity of God in his narrative, he frequently uses the expression "the angel of the Lord" (cf. Lk 1:11; 2:6; Ac 12:7, 23) for the more normal reference to "the Spirit of the Lord." Here Luke begins in just such a way and with such a purpose, telling us that "an angel of the Lord" began the action by giving instructions to Philip—and also sustains it throughout, though the more usual "the Spirit" and "the Spirit of the Lord" are used in vv.29, 39. Gaza was the southernmost of the five chief Philistine cities in southwest Palestine and the last settlement before the desert waste stretching away to Egypt. The fifty-mile journey from Jerusalem to Gaza trailed off at its southwestern terminus into patches of desert.

27–28 It is difficult to determine from the text itself how Luke wanted his readers to understand the Ethiopian eunuch's relation to Judaism. It is also uncertain how first-century Judaism would have viewed a eunuch coming to worship at Jerusalem. While Dt 23:1 explicitly stipulates that no emasculated male could be included within the Jewish religious community, Isa 56:3–5 speaks of eunuchs being accepted by the God of boundless lovingkindness. Nor is it clear what the Ethiopian's physical condition was, for the word "eunuch" (GK *2336*) frequently appears in the LXX and in secular Greek writings as a euphemism for high military and political officials, without necessarily suggesting emasculation. Therefore, we are probably justified in taking this eunuch as a governmental officer in an Oriental kingdom and in emphasizing two facts when considering his relation to Judaism: (1) he had been on a religious pilgrimage to Jerusalem, and (2) he was returning with a copy of the prophecy of Isaiah in his possession, which would have been difficult for a non-Jew to get.

The ancient kingdom of Ethiopia lay between Aswan and Khartoum. It was ruled by a queen mother who had the dynastic title Candace and ruled on behalf of her son the king, since the king was regarded as the child of the sun and therefore too holy to become involved in the secular functions of the state. The minister of finance in the Ethiopian government had become either a full proselyte or a Proselyte of the Gate and had gone to Jerusalem to worship at one of the Jewish festivals. He was now returning home reading Isaiah; possibly Isa 56:3–5, the passage that refers to God's lovingkindness to eunuchs, first caught his attention and caused him to return to Isaiah again and again. But whatever got him into Isaiah's prophecy, the interpretation of the Servant passage of Isa 52:13–53:12 troubled him.

29–30 Having been directed to the desert road on the way to Gaza, Philip is again directed by the Spirit to the carriage that the Ethiopian minister of finance is traveling in. As Philip approaches, he hears the man reading aloud from Isaiah (the normal practice in the ancient world). So while running along beside the Ethiopian's carriage, Philip asks, "Do you understand what you are reading?"

31–34 The Ethiopian, being open to instruction from a Jew, invites Philip into his carriage to explain Isa 53:7–8 to him. His problem, it seems, concerns the references to suffering and humiliation: "Who is the prophet talking about, himself or someone else?" Perhaps he had heard an official explanation of this passage at Jerusalem, but he still had questions about its meaning.

While in Judaism at this time the concept of God's Servant carried messianic connotations in certain contexts and among certain groups, there is no evidence that anyone in pre-Christian Judaism ever thought of the Messiah in terms of a Suffering Servant. What rabbinic interpretations are available relate the suffering either to the nation Israel (at 52:14; 53:2, 4, 10) or to the wicked Gentile nations (at 53:3, 7–9, 11). Though it is true that the certain Jewish elements were in the process of forming the concept of a suffering Messiah (such as at Qumran), a doctrine of a suffering Messiah was generally considered unthinkable.

35 At a time when only what Christians call the OT was Scripture, what better book was there to use in proclaiming the nature of divine redemption than Isaiah, and what better passage could be found than Isa 52:13–53:12? Thus Philip began with the very passage the Ethiopian was reading and proclaimed to him "the good news about Jesus," explaining from Isa 53:7–8 and its context a suffering messianology. Matthew and John applied Isa 53 to Jesus' ministry of healing (cf. Mt 8:17 on Isa 53:4; Jn 12:38 on Isa 53:1), but Luke portrays Jesus quoting Isa 53 as being fulfilled in his passion (Lk 22:37 quotes Isa 53:12). Luke, therefore, sets up a parallel between Jesus' use of Isa 53 and Philip's preaching based on this chapter and implies in that parallel that the latter was dependent on the former (cf. also 1Pe 2:22–25 on Isa 53:4–6, 9, 12). After beginning his preaching about Jesus with Isa 53, Philip probably went on to include other passages from that early Christian block of testimonium material that has been dubbed "Scriptures of the Servant of the Lord and the Righteous Sufferer" (i.e., Isa 42:1–44:5; 49:1–13; 50:4–11; and Pss 22, 34, 69, 118).

36–38 The eunuch responded to Philip by asking for baptism. As a Jewish proselyte or near-proselyte, he probably knew that water baptism was the expected external symbol for a Gentile's repentance and conversion to the religion of Israel. Therefore, it would have been quite natural for him to view baptism as the appropriate expression for his commitment to Jesus, whom he had come to accept as the fulfillment of Israel's hope and promised Messiah. Or perhaps Philip closed his exposition with an appeal similar to Peter's at Pentecost (cf. 2:38) and his own in Samaria (cf. 8:12). However the subject of baptism arose, Philip baptized the eunuch. That is the climax Luke has been building up to.

39–40 The account of the Ethiopian's conversion ends as it began—with a stress on the special presence of God and his direct intervention. We are told that the Spirit of the Lord "suddenly took" Philip from the scene. This verb connotes both a forceful and sudden action by the Spirit and a lack of resistance from Philip.

With our Western interest in cause-and-effect relations and our modern understanding of historiography, we would like to know more about what exactly happened between the eunuch and Philip and about their subsequent lives. Irenaeus writes that the eunuch became a missionary to the Ethiopians, though we have no way of knowing whether this is true. All that Luke tells us about the eunuch is that his conversion was a significant episode in the advance of the Gospel and that he "went on his way rejoicing." Likewise, all Luke tells us about Philip is that his early ministries in Samaria and to the eunuch were important features in the development of the Christian mission from its strictly Jewish confines to its Gentile outreach. He refers to further evangelistic activity on the part of Philip in the maritime plain of Palestine and to a final ministry at Caesarea. Later he mentions Philip and his four prophetess daughters at Caesarea in connection with Paul's last visit to Jerusalem (cf. 21:8–9). Beyond these meager references, Luke tells us nothing because he is interested in the advances of the Gospel proclamation and not in what happened after that.

C. The Conversion of Saul of Tarsus (9:1–30)

There are three accounts of Paul's conversion in Acts: the first here in ch. 9 and two more in Paul's defenses in chs. 22 and 26. Luke uses such repetitions to indicate that something is extremely important.

The major charge Paul faced in his life was his willingness to carry the Gospel directly to Gentiles, refusing to be confined to a mission to the Jews. All three accounts stress that Christ himself brought about this change in the strategy of divine redemption. It was not a strategy Paul thought up or a program given to him by another; it was a compelling call that came directly from Christ himself, and he had no choice but to obey. Luke, therefore, climaxes his portrayals of three pivotal figures in the advance of the Gospel to the Gentile world (the theme of this panel) by recording the conversion of Saul of Tarsus, emphasizing the supernatural nature of the call and the miraculous circumstances of the conversion. With these emphases, though with inevitable variations in detail, Paul himself was in full agreement (cf. Gal 1:1–24).

1. The Christ encounter on the Damascus road (9:1–9)

1–2 The account of Saul's conversion opens with the picture of him "still breathing out murderous threats against the Lord's disciples" (cf. 8:3). Even after the death of Stephen and the expulsion of the Hellenistic Christians from Jerusalem, Saul felt it was necessary to continue the persecution in places outside the Sanhedrin's jurisdiction.

The past generation of commentators, particularly those of the English-speaking world, often read into such passages as Ro 7:14–25, Gal 1:13–14, Php 3:4–6 and the portrayals of Ac 9, 22, and 26 a mental and spiritual struggle on the part of Saul that was, either consciously or unconsciously, fighting fervently against the logic of the early Christians' preaching, the dynamic quality of their lives, and their fortitude under oppression. Therefore his "breathing out murderous threats" was taken as his attempt to slay externally the dragons of doubt he could not silence within his own heart. But the day of the psychological interpretation of Paul's conversion experience appears to be over, and deservedly so. Indeed, Luke connects historically the martyrdom of Stephen, the persecution of the Hellenistic Jewish Christians, and the conversion of Saul. But the argument for a logical connection is not as certain.

It is, of course, impossible to speak with certainty about what was going on in Saul's subconscious mind at the time, for psychoanalysis two millennia later is hardly a fruitful exercise. His own references as a Christian to this earlier time in his life do not require us to view him as struggling with uncertainty, doubt, and guilt before becoming a Christian. They rather suggest that humanly speaking, he was immune to the Christian proclamation and immensely satisfied with his own ancestral faith. While he looked forward to the full realization of the hope of Israel, Paul seems from his reminiscences of those earlier days to have been thoroughly satisfied with the revelation of God that was given through Moses and to have counted it his chief delight to worship God through those revealed forms. Nor need we suppose that the logic of the early Christian preachers greatly affected Paul. His later references to "the offense of the cross" show that for him the cross was the great stumbling block to any acknowledgment of Jesus of Nazareth as Israel's Messiah—a stumbling block no amount of logic or verbal gymnastics could remove (cf. 1Co 1:23; Gal 5:11).

It is probable that Saul took up his brutal task of persecution with full knowledge of the earnestness of his opponents, the stamina of the martyrs, and the agony he would necessarily cause. Fanaticism was not so foreign to Palestine in his day as to leave him unaware of these things, and it is quite possible that he was prepared for the emotional strain involved in persecuting those he believed to be dangerous schismatics within Israel.

More important, however, in days when the rabbis viewed the keeping of the Mosaic law as the vitally important prerequisite for the coming of the Messianic Age, Paul could validate his actions against the Christians by reference to such godly precedents as (1) Moses' slaying of the immoral Israelites at Baal Peor (cf. Nu 25:1–5); (2) Phinehas's slaying of the Israelite man and Midianite woman in the plains of Moab (cf. Nu 25:6–15); and (3) the actions of the Maccabees and the Hasidim in rooting out apostasy among the people. With such precedents and parallels, coupled with the rising tide of messianic expectation within Israel, Saul could very well have felt justified in mounting a further persecution against the Christians. Probably he felt that the nation must be faithful in its obedience to the law and kept from schism or going astray if their messianic hopes were to be fulfilled. In his task, he doubtless expected to receive God's commendation.

The Sadducean high priests of Jerusalem were, it seems, recognized by Rome as the titular rulers of their people in most internal matters; and evidently they retained the right of extradition in strictly religious situations. Therefore Saul, seeking the return of Jewish Christians, went to the high priest and asked him for written permission to take any Christian men and women as prisoners to Jerusalem (cf. 22:5; 26:12).

Damascus was a large and thriving commercial center at the foot of the Anti-Lebanon mountain range. Since 64 B.C. it had been part of the Roman province of Syria and was granted certain civic rights by Rome as one of the ten cities of eastern Syria and the Transjordan called the Decapolis (cf. Mk 5:20, 7:31). It had a large Jewish population. It was to this city that Saul went with the authority of the Jewish Sanhedrin, seeking to return to Jerusalem Christians who had fled the city—chiefly the Hellenistic Jewish Christians—in order to contain the spread of Christianity.

While we have spoken repeatedly of the early believers in Jesus as Christians, the term "Christian" was first coined at Antioch of Syria (see comment on 11:26). Before then and during the early existence of the church, those who accepted Jesus' messiahship and claimed him as their Lord called themselves those of "the Way" (see also 19:9, 23; 22:4; 24:14, 22), while their opponents spoke of them as members of "the sect of the Nazarenes" (cf. 24:5, 14; 28:22). The origin of "the Way" (GK *3847*) as a term for Christians is uncertain, though it surely had something to do with the early believers' consciousness of walking in the true path of God's salvation and moving forward to accomplish his purposes. In the vignette of 9:1–30, it is synonymous with such self-designations as "the disciples of the Lord" (vv.2, 10, 19), "saints" (v.13), "all who call on your [Jesus'] name" (v.14), and "brothers" (vv.17, 30).

3–6 As he approached Damascus, Saul saw a light from heaven and heard a voice from heaven. In 9:3 the light is described as simply "a light from heaven," while both 22:6 and 26:13 emphasize its brightness. Likewise, in 9:4 Luke reports that Saul heard the voice and in v.7 that his companions also heard the voice, whereas both 22:9 and 26:14 state that only Saul heard the voice. Since the Greek noun used here (GK *5889*) means both "sound" in the sense of any tone or voice and "articulated speech" in the sense of language, undoubtedly while the whole group traveling to Damascus heard the sound from heaven, only Saul understood the spoken words.

As Saul fell to the ground, the voice from heaven intoned his name in solemn repetition: "Saul, Saul." It was common in antiquity for a person in a formal setting to be addressed by the repetition of his name (cf. Ge 22:11; 46:2; Ex 3:4; Lk 10:41; et al.). Saul understood the voice to be a message from God himself, for to the rabbis to hear a voice from heaven connoted a rebuke or a word of instruction from God. Therefore when the voice went on to ask the question "Why do you persecute *me?*" Saul was without doubt thoroughly confused. He was not persecuting God! Rather, he was defending God and his laws!

Some have translated Saul's reply in v.5 as "Who are you, sir?" since the Greek title *kyrios* (GK *3261*) was used in the ancient world not only as an ascription of worshipful acclaim but also as a form of polite address and since the context indicates that Saul did not know whom he was speaking to. But he did know that he had been struck down by a light from heaven and had been addressed by a voice from heaven, both of which signaled the divine presence. So his use of the term "Lord" was probably meant in a worshipful manner—even though he was thoroughly confused as to how he could be rebuked by God for doing his will and service. Unable even to articulate his confusion, though realizing the need for some response in the presence of the divine, he cries out in stumbling fashion, "Who are you, Lord?"

In what must have been for Saul almost total disbelief, he hears the following reply: "I am Jesus, whom you are persecuting." Then in a manner that throws him entirely upon the guidance of Jesus, apart from anything he could do or work out for himself, the voice continues: "Now get up and go into the city, and you will be told what you must do." Such a confrontation and such a rebuke must have been traumatic for Saul. Time would be needed to heal his emotions and work out the implications of his experience, and both Acts and Paul's later Christian letters reveal something of the process of development throughout the rest of his life. But in this supreme revelational encounter, Saul received a new perspective on divine redemption, a new agenda for his life, and the embryonic elements of his new Christian theology.

Once Saul had been encountered by Christ on the Damascus road, a number of realizations must have begun to press in upon his consciousness—each of which was to receive further explication in his thought and life as time went on. First, Saul began to understand that despite his zeal and his sense of doing God's will, his previous life and activities in Judaism lay under God's rebuke. A voice from heaven had corrected him, and there was nothing more to be said.

Second, Saul could not escape the fact that the Jesus whose followers he had been persecuting was alive, exalted, and in some manner to be associated with God the Father, whom Israel worshiped. He, therefore, had to revise his whole estimate of the life, teaching, and death of the Nazarene because God had beyond any question vindicated him. Thus he came to agree with the Christians that Jesus' death on the cross, rather than discrediting him as an impostor, fulfilled prophecy and was really God's provision for the sin of humankind and that Jesus' resurrection confirmed him as being the nation's Messiah and the world's Lord.

Third, Saul came to appreciate that if Jesus is the nation's Messiah and the fulfillment of Israel's ancient hope, then traditional eschatology, rather than merely dwelling on the future, must be restructured to emphasize the realized and inaugurated factors associated with Jesus of Nazareth and focus on the personal and transcendent dimensions instead of just the historical.

Fourth, in the question "Why do you persecute me?" Saul came to realize something of the organic and indissoluble unity that exists between Christ and his own. For although he believed he was only persecuting the followers of Jesus, the heavenly interpretation of his action was that he was persecuting the risen Christ himself.

Fifth (though hardly final), Saul came to understand that he had a mission to carry out for Christ. Its details, to be sure, were first given in general terms by Ananias of Damascus (vv.15–16) and only later set forth more fully by various visions and providential circumstances (cf. comments on chs. 13–28). But though it was not till later that Saul understood that his mission involved the equality of both Jews and Gentiles before God and the legitimacy of a direct approach to the Gentile world, it was his constant habit to relate his Gentile commission firmly and directly to his encounter with Christ on the Damascus road.

7–9 The effect on Saul's traveling companions of his encounter with Christ was dramatic. Acts 26 says that they fell to the ground at the flash of heavenly light. Here we are told that after getting up they "stood there speechless." Evidently they were able to regain a semblance of composure and thus lead Saul into Damascus. For Saul, however, for whom the spoken message was even more traumatic than the light, the experience was overpowering. Physically, as his system reacted to the emotional shock, he became blind for three days, during which time he neither ate nor drank while waiting for further instructions.

2. Ananias's ministry to Saul (9:10–19a)

10–16 Ananias was a Jew of Damascus and a believer in Jesus. Here (v.10) he is called a "disciple" and is presented as one who immediately recognizes the Lord Christ, who speaks to him in a vision, while in 22:12 he is called "a devout observer of the law and highly respected by all the Jews." From his

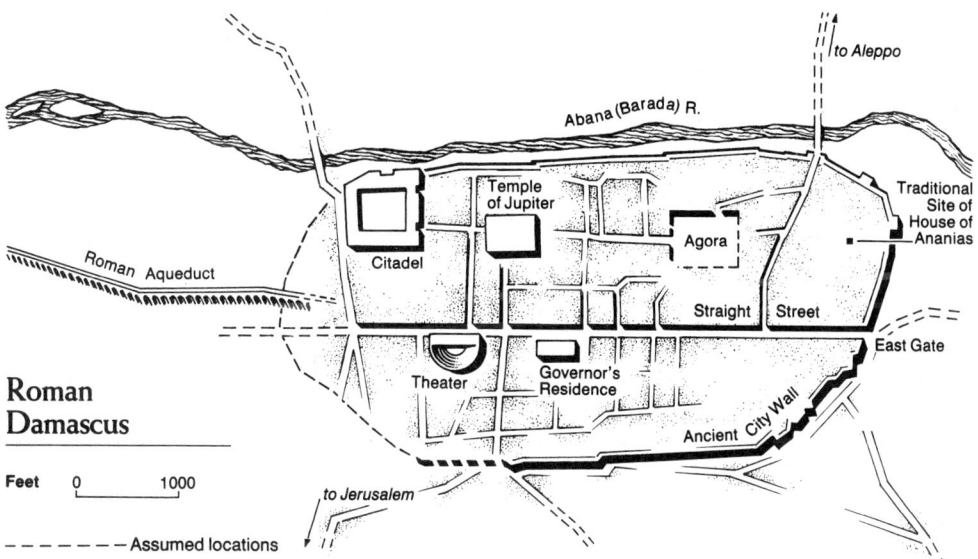

Roman Damascus

Damascus represented much more to Saul, the strict Pharisee, than another stop on his campaign of repression. It was the hub of a vast commercial network with far-flung lines of caravan trade reaching into north Syria, Mesopotamia, Anatolia, Persia and Arabia. If the new "Way" of Christianity flourished in Damascus, it would quickly reach all these places. From the viewpoint of the Sanhedrin and of Saul, the arch-persecutor, it had to be stopped in Damascus.

The city itself was a veritable oasis, situated in a plain watered by the Biblical rivers Abana and Pharpar.

© 1985 The Zondervan Corporation

Roman architecture overlaid the Hellenistic town plan with a great temple to Jupiter and a mile-long colonnaded street, the "Straight Street" of Ac 9:11. The city gates and a section of the town wall may still be seen today, as well as the lengthy bazaar that runs along the line of the ancient street.

The dominant political figure at the time of Paul's escape from Damascus (2 Co 11:32-33) was Aretas IV, king of the Nabateans (9 B.C.-A.D. 40), though normally the Decapolis cities were attached to the province of Syria and were thus under the influence of Rome.

statement that he had heard reports about Saul's persecutions in Jerusalem (v.13), it may be inferred that he was not one of the Hellenistic Christians who had formerly lived in Jerusalem but that he lived in Damascus. We are not told anything about how he became a Christian.

The Lord Jesus directed Ananias: "Go to the house of Judas on Straight Street and ask for a man from Tarsus named Saul, for he is praying." Straight Street was an east-west street and is still one of the main thoroughfares of Damascus. Jesus' words identified Saul as one who was praying. For Luke, his hero Paul was a man of prayer (cf. 16:25; 20:36; 22:17), as was Jesus in his earthly ministry (cf. Lk 3:21; 6:12; 9:18, 28; 11:1; 22:41). Probably in the religious experience of Paul, his devotion to prayer was the most important link between his life as a Pharisee and as a Christian.

It takes no great imaginative power to appreciate the reasons for Ananias's hesitation in going at once to meet Saul. Even the prophets of old had doubts about the appropriateness of what they understood to be God's will, particularly when it seemed so contrary to what might be expected. But Luke lays emphasis on Ananias's hesitancy, not just to humanize his narrative, but also to impress on his readers the magnitude of the change in Saul's life and to highlight the heaven-ordained nature of his later Christian mission: (1) instead of a persecutor, he is Christ's "chosen instrument"; (2) instead of a concern for Israel alone, his mission is "to carry my [Jesus'] name before the Gentiles and their kings and before the people of Israel"; and (3) instead of prominence and glory, it is necessary for him "to suffer for my [Jesus'] name." In highlighting these three features, Luke has, in effect, given a theological précis of all he will portray historically in chs. 13–28—a précis that also summarizes the self-consciousness of Paul himself as reflected in his own letters.

17–19a Ananias was obedient to his Lord and followed the directions given in the vision. He was undoubtedly comforted by knowing that Saul too had been given a vision about his coming (v.12), though he must have proceeded with some trepidation. Going to the house of Judas on Straight Street, he entered, laid his hands on Saul, and greeted him with the fraternal greeting "brother"—believing, it seems, that whomever Jesus had accepted was his brother. He spoke about Jesus, who had appeared to Saul on the Damascus Road, and about the restoration of Saul's sight and his being filled with the Holy Spirit. And "immediately," Luke tells us, "something like scales fell from Saul's eyes, and he could see again. He got up and was baptized, and after taking some food, he regained his strength."

We would like to know more about the persons and details of this event, but this is all Luke records. What he says, however, is significant. As the Gospel advanced to the Gentiles, the main missioner was converted to Christ and given his commission in a manner that fully showed the heaven-ordained nature of his conversion and call—a manner that did not make him dependent on the Jerusalem church for either his conversion or call, yet brought him into essential unity with all those who are Christ's.

3. Saul's conversion evidenced in Damascus (9:19b–25)

It may seem strange for Luke to include in his account of Saul's conversion a sketchy report of his preaching Christ in Damascus and his unceremonious exit from the city. But Luke wants to emphasize the unprecedented nature of Saul's about-face and the genuineness of his conversion. In clarifying his purpose, Luke (1) presents Saul as proclaiming Jesus as both "Son of God" and "Messiah," (2) depicts his hearers as being so astonished that they had to ask themselves if this was indeed the same man who had been persecuting Christians, and (3) highlights the fact that the persecution he once headed was now directed against him.

19b–22 Luke's references here to what Saul did immediately after his conversion is difficult to fit in with Paul's own account of his conversion and the immediately subsequent events (see Gal 1:15–24). But these differences help substantiate Lukan authorship of Acts. Certainly no later admirer of Paul would have disregarded Paul's most important autobiographical statement about his conversion and commission and given a portrayal that can be taken as ambiguous and contradictory. But if, as seems likely, the letter to the Galatians was written before Luke himself joined Paul's missionary team, then it may very well have been the case that Luke was unfamiliar with the specific contents of Paul's earlier Galatian letter.

Of more importance, however, is the fact that the purposes of Paul in Gal 1:15–24 and Luke here are different, with these purposes affecting both the selection and shaping of each writer's presentation. Thus in his desire to assert the revelational nature of his Gentile ministry, Paul emphasized in Galatians that he was not dependent upon "any man" (Gal 1:16) for his distinctive gospel, and particularly not upon the Jerusalem apostles. Luke, however, while also interested in depicting the heaven-ordained nature of Paul's conversion and commission, is concerned here to stress the genuineness of Saul's conversion and call. This he does by speaking of the new convert's distinctly Christian proclamation in the synagogues of Damascus and his persecution by the Jews of the city because of his preaching (neither of these is ruled out by Gal 1:15–24).

A likely historical reconstruction is as follows: (1) Saul's conversion and commission (9:1–19a); (2) his preaching in the synagogues of Damascus for a time immediately following his conversion (9:19b–22); (3) his prolonged residence in Arabia (Gal 1:17); (4) his return to Damascus (9:23–25); and (5) his first visit to Jerusalem as a Christian some three years after his conversion, with his subsequent travel to Caesarea, Syria, and Cilicia (9:26–30; Gal 1:18–24).

The content of Saul's preaching in the Damascus synagogues focused on Jesus: "Jesus is the Son of God" (v.20) and "Jesus is the Christ" (v.22), i.e., the "Messiah." That Saul could preach such a message immediately after his conversion is not impossible because the certainty of Jesus' messiahship was deeply implanted in his soul by his experience on the Damascus road. And while he had much to understand about the implications of commitment to Jesus as Israel's Messiah, he was certainly in a position to proclaim Jesus' messianic status with conviction and enthusiasm.

Nor is it surprising that Saul also spoke of Jesus as "the Son of God," though this is the only occurrence in Acts of this Christological title. In a number of NT passages the titles "Messiah" and "Son of God" are brought together (cf. Mt 16:16; 26:63; Lk 4:41; Jn 11:27; 20:31), for the Anointed One par excellence expressed uniquely that loving obedience inherent in the Hebraic understanding of sonship. That is how Paul used the titles "Son" and "Son of God" some fifteen times later in his own letters (e.g., Ro 1:3–4, 9; 1Co 1:9; 2Co 1:19; Gal 1:16; et al.).

Those who heard Saul preach, Luke says, were "astonished" and "baffled." But with his interest in advance and growth (cf. Lk 2:52), Luke also says that "Saul grew more and more powerful," suggesting both a growth in his understanding of the meaning of commitment to Jesus as Messiah and Son of God and an increasing ability to demonstrate the validity of his proclamation.

23–25 Luke's expression "after many days had gone by" probably means three years later (see Gal 1:18). Paul himself refers to his escape from Damascus in 2Co 11:32–33. Both Luke and Paul clearly state that Saul's preaching stirred such opposition that plans were laid to kill him. The persecutor became the persecuted, but rather ingeniously, he was able to elude his opponents' designs.

Acts uses "disciple" (GK *3412*) almost exclusively to denote the members of the Christian community (e.g., 6:1–2, 7; 9:19; 11:26; 13:52). The one exception to the normal usage in Acts is here in v.25, where this word is translated and used of "followers" of Saul; it suggests that his proclamation of Jesus had a favorable response among at least some. One of these converts, it seems, had a home situated on the city wall, from whose window Saul was let down in a basket outside the wall, thus eluding his opponents. From there, he evidently made his way directly to Jerusalem.

4. Saul's reception at Jerusalem (9:26–30)

As in the narrative concerning the evangelization of Samaria (8:4–25) and the later accounts of the conversion of Cornelius (10:1–11:18) and the founding of the church at Antioch of Syria (11:19–30)—in which not only are features of advance and development stressed but also continuity with the mother church at Jerusalem—Luke ends his account of the conversion of Saul of Tarsus by telling of his reception by the Christians at Jerusalem. As in Luke's depiction of Saul's preaching in Damascus (vv.19b–25), here the material, when compared with Paul's own account in Gal 1:18–24 of his first visit to Jerusalem as a Christian, entails a number of problems relating to historical correlations—probably for much the same reasons as in vv.19b–25, though heightened here by Paul's purpose in Galatians to stress his lack of dependence upon the Jerusalem church whereas Luke's purpose is to trace out lines of continuity.

26–28 Saul's arrival at Jerusalem as a Christian was three years after his conversion (Gal 1:18). Being *persona non grata* among his former associates and suspected by Christians, he probably stayed at his sister's home in the city (cf. 23:16). We can understand why his reception by his former colleagues might have been less than welcome. But that the apostles and other Christians in Jerusalem were leery of him does raise questions. Certainly they must have heard of his conversion and his preaching in Damascus. Yet, it seems, they never knew him personally, either as a persecutor or as a Christian; and stories about his motives and activities during a three-year period might well have become distorted. Many might, in fact, have asked why, if Saul had really become a Christian, he remained aloof from the Twelve and the Jerusalem congregation for such a long time. We may wish, and might even have expected, that there had been more openness toward Saul the convert on the part of the Jerusalem Christians. History, however, has shown that minority movements under persecution frequently become defensive and suspicious of news that sounds too good.

It was Barnabas, Luke says, who was willing to risk accepting Saul as a genuine believer and who built a bridge of trust between him and the Jerusalem apostles. This is certainly in character with what is said about him elsewhere in Acts (cf. 4:36–37; 11:22–30; 13:1–14:28; 15:2–4, 12, 22). In presenting Saul to the apostles, Barnabas told what Saul had seen and heard on the road and that he was now preaching "in the name of Jesus" in

Damascus itself—thus summarizing Luke's account of Saul's conversion and explicitly using his activity in Damascus to support the genuineness of his conversion. So with Barnabas's help, Saul and the Jerusalem apostles were brought into fellowship.

In light of Paul's own insistence in Gal 1:18-20 that he saw only Peter and James on this first Jerusalem visit, Luke's use of the term "apostles" must be considered a generalizing plural to be taken more broadly than "the Twelve." Likewise, in view of Paul's statement in Gal 1:18 that he stayed with Peter for fifteen days, Luke's claim that he "stayed with them and moved about freely in Jerusalem" must be seen as somewhat overstated. Probably we are not far wrong in reconstructing the situation as follows: Saul resided with his sister's family on his first visit to Jerusalem as a Christian; through the aid of Barnabas he came to visit with Peter for fifteen days and to meet James as well; broadly speaking, his reception by the Christians he met was cordial, though there undoubtedly still existed some fears about him within the Christian congregation.

29-30 At Jerusalem Saul took up a ministry to Jews in the Hellenistic synagogues there. It was a ministry that had been neglected, it appears, since Stephen's death and the expulsion of the Hellenistic Jewish Christians. But it was one that Saul may have felt himself particularly suited to, coming as he did from Tarsus in Cilicia and having probably carried on such a ministry at Damascus. In so doing, however, he soon faced the same opposition Stephen had faced, and he seems to have gotten into the same difficulty Stephen did. The Jerusalem church apparently did not care to go through again the same kind of thing that followed Stephen's preaching. So when they realized what was taking place in Saul's newly begun ministry in Jerusalem, "they took him down to Caesarea and sent him off to Tarsus." Saul took it as by divine approval, for in his defense in Ac 22 he speaks of having received a vision in the Jerusalem temple that not only confirmed his apostleship to the Gentiles but also warned him to flee Jerusalem (22:17-21).

Saul is not mentioned in the period between these experiences in Jerusalem and his ministry at Antioch (11:25-30), though from his words in Gal 1:21-24 it seems fairly certain that he continued his witness to Diaspora Jews in Caesarea and his hometown of Tarsus. The cordiality of the Christians in Caesarea at the end of his third missionary journey may imply that Saul had an earlier association with Philip and the believers there. Many of the hardships and trials he enumerates in 2Co 11:23-27 may stem from situations in Caesarea and Tarsus during those days, and perhaps also the ecstatic experience of 2Co 12:1-4.

D. A Summary Statement (9:31)

31 Luke's second panel of material on the martyrdom of Stephen, the early ministries of Philip, and the conversion of Saul ends with a summary statement that speaks of the church throughout Judea, Galilee, and Samaria (an expression for all of the Jewish homeland of Palestine) enjoying a time of peace after the turbulence resulting from what happened to these three pivotal figures. Here also he insists that the church in the homeland, instead of being torn apart, "was strengthened; and encouraged by the Holy Spirit, it grew in numbers, living in the fear of the Lord."

Panel 3—Advances of the Gospel in Palestine-Syria (9:32–12:24)

In his portrayal of the gradual widening of the Christian mission from its strictly Jewish beginnings to its ultimate Gentile outreach, Luke presents in this third panel three episodes of the Gospel's advance: (1) the ministry of Peter in the maritime plain of Palestine (9:32-43), (2) the conversion of a Roman centurion and his friends at Caesarea (10:1–11:18), and (3) the founding of the church at Antioch of Syria (11:19-30). Two notes are sounded in these episodes of advance. (1) The Gospel was now spreading into areas more distant from Jerusalem than before. (2) The second, and undoubtedly the more important, has to do with the attitude of the converts and that of the missioners. Then, before moving on to speak of the distinctive advances of the Gospel within the Gentile world through the ministry of his hero Paul, Luke again returns to an account of the circumstances at Jerusalem and gives two vignettes of God's continued working on behalf of his people there (12:1-23). Luke seems to be trying to make the point that though his interest is in tracing the movement of the early Christian mission from Jerusalem to Rome, his readers are not to assume that God was finished with Jerusalem Christianity or that his divine activity within the Jewish world had come to an end—a point all too often ignored by Christians since then. Finally, Luke summarizes the material in this third panel with the following statement: "But the word of God continued to increase and spread" (12:24).

A. The Ministry of Peter in the Maritime Plain of Palestine (9:32–43)

Luke's rationale for the inclusion of Peter's miracles at Lydda and Joppa has often been debated. Most likely he had two goals in mind. (1) The vignettes of the healing of Aeneas and the raising of Dorcas shift the focus of Luke's narrative from Jerusalem to the west country of Palestine, thereby setting the stage for the conversion of Cornelius at Caesarea. (2) Luke may also be suggesting that with Peter's ministry in the maritime plain, the evangelization of Palestine was completed and it was therefore time to look farther afield.

1. Aeneas healed at Lydda (9:32–35)

32 Lydda was located twenty-five miles northwest of Jerusalem, at the crucial intersection of the highways from Egypt to Syria and from coastal Joppa to Jerusalem. At this time Peter was engaged in an itinerant ministry in the western part of Palestine, somewhat like his earlier preaching in Samaria (cf. 8:25). In the course of his travels, he visited "the saints" in the important commercial center of Lydda. However they came to commit themselves to Jesus as God's Messiah, Peter viewed them as within the sphere of his ministry—even though many of them were probably less scrupulous in keeping the Mosaic law than Jews of the capital city.

33 At Lydda Peter came upon Aeneas, a paralytic who had been bedridden for eight years. Luke does not say that Aeneas was a Jew nationally or a Christian by profession, though presumably he was both. It would hardly have been consistent with Luke's purpose to show Peter ministering to a Gentile before his encounter with Cornelius, and the "there" of the sentence has as its antecedent the community of saints at Lydda and not just the city itself.

34–35 Peter's words, "Jesus Christ heals you. Get up and take care of your mat," express in Greek the idea that "this moment Jesus Christ heals you." Aeneas responded immediately to Peter's command. News of his healing spread throughout Lydda and northward into the Plain of Sharon (the largest of the maritime plains of northern Palestine, stretching from Joppa to Mount Carmel). Rather hyperbolically Luke says that "all those who lived in Lydda and Sharon saw him and turned to the Lord." So, Luke tells us, there was a further widening of the Christian mission within the Jewish nation, preparing the way geographically and ideologically for the accounts of Peter's ministry at Joppa in 9:36–43 and at Caesarea in 10:1–48.

2. Dorcas raised at Joppa (9:36–43)

36–39 Joppa (modern Jaffa) was the ancient seaport for Jerusalem. Situated on the coast thirty-five miles northwest of the capital city and ten miles beyond Lydda, it possesses the only natural harbor on the Mediterranean between Egypt and Ptolemais (see 2Ch 2:16; Jnh 1:3). Its rival in NT times was Caesarea, thirty miles to the north, which Herod the Great, because the people of Joppa hated him, built into a magnificent new port city and provincial capital. At Joppa lived a woman called Tabitha (Heb.) or Dorcas (Gk.); both names mean "gazelle." She was a "disciple" and "was always doing good and helping the poor," particularly destitute widows. When she died, the Christians at Joppa sent this message to Peter at Lydda: "Please come at once." Luke does not say what they expected from him or asked him to do. But since (1) Tabitha's body was washed but not anointed for burial and (2) her good deeds were told to Peter when he arrived, they apparently wanted him to restore her to life. Having heard of Aeneas's healing, they seem to have thought it merely a slight extension of divine power to raise the dead.

40–42 Peter had been instrumental in a number of physical healings (cf. 3:1–10; 5:12–16; 9:32–35) and even pronounced the death sentence on Ananias and Sapphira (cf. 5:1–11). Yet raising people from the dead was hardly a common feature of his ministry. Nevertheless, knowing himself to be an apostle of Jesus empowered by the Holy Spirit—and probably remembering his Lord's raising of

Jairus's daughter (cf. Mk 5:21–24, 35–43)—Peter responded to the urgent call. As he had seen Jesus do in the case of Jairus's daughter, he ordered the mourners out of the room, prayed, and then spoke these words: "Tabitha, get up" (cf. Mk 5:41). When she opened her eyes and sat up, he took her by the hand, helped her to her feet, and presented her alive to the Christians who stood by. It was an exceptional exhibit of God's mercy and the Spirit's power, and "many people believed in the Lord."

43 This verse serves as a geographical and ideological hinge between the accounts of Peter's miracles in the maritime plain and the account of Cornelius's conversion at Caesarea. Instead of returning ten miles to Lydda, Peter remained at Joppa "for some time" (cf. 8:11), where the messengers from Cornelius later found him. Of greater significance, however, is the fact that Peter stayed there with a man called Simon, a tanner who was presumably working in his own home. Luke's stress on this feature of Peter's lifestyle provides a preface to 10:1–11:18.

B. The Conversion of Cornelius at Caesarea (10:1–11:18)

With the range of the Christian mission steadily broadening, the time had come for the Gospel to cross the barrier that separated Jews from Gentiles and to be presented directly to Gentiles. Thus Luke takes up the story of the conversion of Cornelius, the importance of which in his eyes can be judged in part by the space he devotes to it—sixty-six verses in all.

Four matters in the account of Cornelius's conversion receive special emphasis and in turn provide insight into Luke's purpose for presenting this material. (1) The early church resisted the idea of Gentiles being either directly evangelized or accepted into the Christian fellowship apart from any relationship to Judaism (cf. 10:14, 28; 11:2–3, 8). (2) God himself was the one who introduced the Gentiles into the church and miraculously showed his approval (cf. 10:3, 11–16, 19–20, 22b, 30–33, 44–46; 11:5–10, 13, 15–17). (3) Peter, the leader of the Jerusalem apostles, not Paul, was the human instrument in opening the door to the Gentiles (cf. 10:23, 34–43, 47–48; 11:15–17). (4) The Jerusalem church subsequently accepted a Gentile's conversion to Jesus the Messiah, apart from any allegiance to Judaism, for God had so obviously validated it (cf. 11:18).

1. Cornelius's vision (10:1–8)

1 Caesarea is in the center of the coastal Plain of Sharon in northern Palestine, on the shores of the Mediterranean, some sixty-five miles northwest of Jerusalem. It was named in honor of Augustus Caesar (cf. Lk 2:1). Herod the Great made the harbor into a magnificent seaport and the village into his provincial capital. He deepened the harbor, built a breakwater against the southern gales, constructed an imposing city with an amphitheater and a temple in honor of Rome and Augustus, brought in fresh water through an aqueduct that ran over stately brick arches, and established a garrison of soldiers to protect not only the harbor and city but also the fresh water supply.

The name Cornelius was common in the Roman world from 82 B.C. onwards, when Cornelius Sulla liberated ten thousand slaves, all of whom took their patron's name as they established themselves in Roman society. Probably, therefore, the Cornelius of this story was a descendant of one of these freedmen. He is identified as a centurion of the Italian cohort, i.e., a noncommissioned officer who had worked his way up through the ranks to take command of a group of soldiers within a Roman legion. A cohort numbered anywhere from three hundred to six hundred men in size, being officially always the latter.

2 Cornelius was "devout [GK 2356] and God-fearing"—characteristics also attributed to his entire household (a "household" included both one's immediate family and one's personal servants). Perhaps we are to understand by "God-fearing" that Cornelius was a near-proselyte to Judaism or a so-called Proselyte of the Gate (cf. comments on 8:27–28), though more likely it simply means something like "a religious man," especially in view of Luke's addition of "devout" and "righteous" in v.22. From his report of Peter's use of this expression for Cornelius in v.35 ("men from every nation who fear him [God] and do what is right"), it seems that Cornelius was a Gentile who, having realized the bankruptcy of paganism, sought to worship a monotheistic God, practice a form of prayer, and lead a moral life, apart from any necessary association with Judaism. It was, then, to such a spiritually minded Gentile, Luke tells us, that God first reached out his hand in the advance of the Christian mission.

3–4 "One day about three in the afternoon," an angel of God appeared to Cornelius in a vision and called him by name. The time element here emphasizes that the vision happened in broad daylight. In response, Cornelius "stared in fear" and could only blurt out the words "What is it, Lord?" While the Greek title *kyrios* ("Lord"; GK *3261*) was used in antiquity for everything from polite address to worshipful acclamation (see comment on 9:3–6), Cornelius undoubtedly meant it in some sense of worshipful acclaim—even though he might not have had any firm idea of whom he was addressing (cf. 9:5). In his consternation he heard the reassuring words that his prayers and alms had arisen as a memorial before God (cf. Lev 2:2; Php 4:18; Heb 13:15–16), a biblical and traditional way of saying that he was commended before God and that God was attentive to his situation.

5–6 Cornelius was told to send to Joppa for Simon Peter. The surname Peter distinguishes the apostle from his host Simon the tanner, whose house was by the sea. No indication is given as to why Peter was to be summoned. Instead, the emphasis is on the fact that Cornelius was prepared to respond to God.

7–8 Cornelius's response was immediate. Calling two of his household servants and one of his soldiers and telling them what had occurred and what he had been told to do, he sent them to Joppa to bring back Peter. The servants were probably two of those already mentioned in v.2 as part of Cornelius's household; and the soldier is identified as being also "devout," one to whom the full characterization of v.2 (also vv.22 and 35) also applied.

2. Peter's vision (10:9–16)

9–13 Though Peter was not by training or inclination an overly scrupulous Jew, and though as a Christian his inherited prejudices were wearing thin, he was not prepared to go so far as to minister directly to Gentiles. A special revelation was necessary for that, and Luke now tells how God took the initiative in overcoming Peter's reluctance.

The revelation came to him on the day following Cornelius's vision, as the three from Caesarea were approaching Joppa. About noon Peter went to the roof of the tanner's house to pray, apparently looking not only for solitude but also for shade under an awning and a cooling breeze from the sea. While in prayer, Peter became very hungry and, it seems, somewhat drowsy. As he was waiting for food, he fell into a trance and saw a vision (cf. 10:17, 19; 11:5) of "something like a large sheet being let down to earth by its four corners," on which were "all kinds of four-footed animals, as well as reptiles of the earth and birds of the air." Then he heard a voice say, "Get up, Peter. Kill and eat." Psychologically, the details of the vision may be explained in terms of (1) Peter's increasing perplexity about Jewish-Gentile relations within various Christian congregations of the maritime plain, (2) the flapping awning over him (or perhaps, the full sail of a boat out on the sea), and (3) his gnawing hunger. God frequently reveals himself not only in but also by means of our human situations. And Peter took what the voice said as a message from God—a message in the form of an almost inscrutable riddle, but one soon to be clarified by both word and event.

14 Peter's shock and repugnance are expressed in his words: "Surely not, Lord"—a response like that of the prophet Ezekiel when called upon by God to eat unclean food among the Gentiles (Eze 4:14). While not overly scrupulous, Peter nonetheless had always observed the basic dietary restrictions of Lev 11, which distinguished clean and unclean animals. And while clean animals were represented in the sheet, Peter was scandalized by the unholy mixture of clean and unclean and by the fact that no distinctions were made in the command to "kill and eat." Indeed, it was a command given him by one he acclaimed as "Lord"—perhaps recognizable to him as the voice of Jesus. But that did not leave him any less repelled by the idea.

15–16 The voice told Peter, "Do not call anything impure that God has made clean." The particular application had to do with nullifying Jewish dietary laws for Christians in accord with Jesus' remarks on the subject in Mk 7:17–23. But Peter was soon to learn that the range of the vision's message extended much more widely, touching directly on Jewish-Gentile relations as he had known them and on those relations in ways he could never have anticipated. Three times this interchange took place, and three times the message was indelibly impressed on Peter's subconscious. Luke then says, "The sheet was taken back to heaven."

3. Messengers from Cornelius arrive at Joppa (10:17–23a)

17–18 While Peter was recovering from the shock of the vision and its message, the men from Cornelius had found the tanner's house. It had immediate access from the street through a gateway or vestibule. Thus at the gate the messengers shouted out their inquiry for anyone within earshot to hear: "Is Simon who is known as Peter staying here?"

19–20 But on the roof of the tanner's house, Peter was still so deep in thought about the vision that even their shouting and calling out his name failed to rouse him. Rather, the Spirit told him of the messengers' presence and then urged him to go with them. "For I have sent them," he said. A question naturally arises about the relation of the "angel of God" that appeared to Cornelius (10:3–6, 22, 30; 11:13), "the voice" that spoke to Peter (10:13–15; 11:7–9), and "the Spirit" who urges him to go with the messengers from Cornelius. But the question, though legitimate, is almost unanswerable because it is by the Holy Spirit that the ascended Christ manifests his presence to his own. That is, we cannot draw any sharp lines between the angel of God, the Holy Spirit, and the ascended Christ (cf. also 8:26, 29, 39; 16:6–7). It appears in even such closely reasoned didactic statements on the relation of Christ and the Spirit as Ro 8:9–11 and 2Co 3:17–18.

21–23a In response to the Spirit's urging, and probably by means of an outside stairway, Peter went down to meet the messengers. After he identified himself and asked why they had come, they told him of their master, Cornelius, of the angel's visitation, and of their mission to bring Peter back so that he might tell their master what he had to say. In their response they characterized Cornelius as not only "a righteous and God-fearing man" (cf. comments on 10:2) but also as one whose personal qualities were witnessed to "by all the Jewish people." Then Peter, in obedience to the command of the vision, received these Gentiles into the house as his guests, acting (no doubt with the tanner's permission) more as a host than a lodger.

4. Peter's reception by Cornelius (10:23b–33)

23b–24 The conversation in the tanner's house that evening must have been a lively one, with many of the Joppa believers joining in the discussion of the strange visions. Six of the Joppa believers accompanied Peter to Caesarea the next day (cf. 11:12), a wise action in view of the questions that would later be raised at Jerusalem. So the party of ten set out for Caesarea. It apparently took them longer to cover the thirty miles than the messengers had taken earlier because they did not get to Caesarea till the following day. Cornelius was expecting them and had drawn together a group of relatives and close friends to hear Peter.

25–26 As Peter was brought into the centurion's home past the gatehouse and then into the courtyard, Cornelius came from his living quarters to meet him. He fell at Peter's feet and offered him "reverence" (GK 4686)—doubtless an expression of his belief that there was something supernatural about Peter. But Peter, not only unaccustomed to such honors but brought up to consider them blasphemous, ordered him to stand up and assured him: "I am only a man myself" (cf. 14:14–15; Rev 19:10; 22:8–9).

27–29 In Cornelius's living quarters Peter found a large group waiting to hear what he had to say. Perhaps self-consciously, he began by saying that Jewish law prohibited a Jew from associating with Gentiles. Admittedly, this was an ideal representation of the Jewish position, for Jewish ethical law contained a number of provisions for Jewish-Gentile business partnerships. But such contacts made a Jew ceremonially unclean, as did entering Gentiles' buildings or touching their possessions. Above all, it was forbidden to accept the hospitality of Gentiles and eat with them, particularly because Gentiles did not tithe. But, Peter said, God had taught him in a vision not to call anyone impure or unclean; so now he was associating with them without traditional scruples. Then he asked, "May I ask why you sent for me?"

30–33 Cornelius told all about his vision, described how he sent for Peter, and invited him to relate "everything the Lord has commanded you to tell us." Few preachers have ever had a more receptive audience than Peter had on this occasion.

5. Peter's sermon in Cornelius's house (10:34–43)

Peter's sermon in Cornelius's house is a précis of the apostolic kerygma. It is similar structurally and in content to his earlier sermons in 2:14–40 and 3:11–26, though it contains more information about Jesus' precrucifixion ministry than those two sermons (cf. also 4:8–12; 5:29–32). Peter told more about Jesus' earthly ministry because a Gentile audience, even though knowing something about Jesus of Nazareth from living in Palestine, would require more details of Jesus' life and work than a Palestinian Jewish audience would.

34–35 The sermon is prefaced by the words, "Opening his mouth, Peter said" (lit. tr.). This is one way to introduce a weighty utterance (cf. Mt 5:2; 13:35; Ac 8:35); and in Luke's eyes, what Peter was about to say was indeed momentous in sweeping away centuries of racial prejudice. It begins by Peter's statement that God does not show racial "favoritism" (cf. Ro 2:11; Eph 6:9; Col 3:25; Jas 2:1; 1Pe 1:17) "but accepts men from every nation who fear him and do what is right." While some consciousness of this may be implicit in Israel's history and at times may have been expressed by her prophets (cf. Am 9:7; Mic 6:8), it was only by means of a revelational clarification of what had earlier been considered highly enigmatic (a "mystery"; cf. Eph 3:4–6) that Peter came to appreciate the racial challenge of the Gospel.

36 The Greek of vv.36–38 is syntactically awkward, probably stemming from Peter himself as he spoke before his Gentile audience in somewhat "broken" Greek. The apostle captions his sermon as "the message God sent to the people of Israel, telling the good news of peace through Jesus Christ, who is Lord of all." This caption contains three emphases that set the tone for what follows. (1) It is a divine revelation, a message from God. (2) Peter emphasizes the proclamation of the Gospel "to the people of Israel," its immediate recipients. (3) His third emphasis relates the bringing of that Gospel to the Gentile world in terms comprehensible to Gentiles, characterized by the expression "Lord of all" (both Jews and Gentiles). This phrase was a pagan title for deity, but it was rebaptized by the early Christians to become an appropriate christological title (cf. Col 1:15–20).

37–41 Peter begins his sermon with a resumé of Jesus' life and work during his earthly ministry. Though Peter assumes that his hearers already know something about this ministry through living in Palestine, he proceeds to summarize it in greater detail than anywhere else in his recorded preaching. In scope and emphasis, the account is much like the portrayal of Jesus' ministry in Mark's gospel. It begins with John the Baptist, moves on to Jesus' anointing with the Holy Spirit, refers to Jesus' many acts of divine power in Galilee, alludes to his continued ministry throughout Palestine and in Jerusalem, stresses his crucifixion, and concludes with a declaration of his resurrection and its verification by his appearances to chosen followers.

As it stands before us, the sermon is only a summary of what Peter actually said at the time. Originally it may have contained a number of examples of Jesus' acts of kindness and healing, such as those recorded in the Synoptic Gospels. In addition, as a summary of what Peter said, it shows several interests of Luke who put the sermon into its present form: (1) the influence of Isa 61:1 in v.38, an OT passage Luke highlighted in his theme paragraph of Lk 4:14–30 at the start of his two volume writing; (2) the importance of the apostolic witness in establishing the Christian tradition (see vv.39–41); (3) Luke's interest in Jesus' postresurrection eating and drinking with his disciples (cf. Lk 24:41–43; Ac 1:4) as a convincing proof of his physical presence.

42–43 Peter ends his sermon by stating that the risen Christ has commanded his apostles to preach "to the people" and to testify about his divine appointment as "judge of the living and the dead." The word "people" probably refers to "the Jewish people." And until then the early church knew no other mission. But then Peter went on to speak of the OT prophets testifying about this risen Lord and saying that "everyone who believes in him receives forgiveness of sins through his name." It was this reference to "everyone who believes in him" that seems to have broken through the traditional barrier between Jews and Gentiles (see next comment).

6. Gentiles receive the Holy Spirit (10:44–48)

44 As Peter was "speaking these words, the Holy Spirit came on all who heard the message." Most likely "these words" refer back to "everyone who believes in him receives forgiveness of sins through his name." Luke suggests that it was this phrase that struck like a thunderbolt into the consciousness of the assembled Gentiles, releasing their pent-up emotions and emboldening them to think that they could believe and so receive the blessings promised to Israel. With their reception of that inclusive message, the Holy Spirit came upon the Gentile congregation gathered there, just as he had come upon the disciples at Pentecost.

45–46 The six Jewish believers who were there with Peter were astonished at what they saw and heard. For in accepting these Gentiles and bestowing his Holy Spirit on them, God had providentially attested his action by the same sign of tongues as at Pentecost. This gift at Pentecost should probably be understood as distinguishable languages, because the tongues were immediately recognized as dialects then current (cf. comment on 2:4). Here, however, an outburst of foreign languages would have fallen on untuned ears and failed to be convincing. So we should probably view "the tongues" (GK 1185) here as being the ecstatic utterances that Paul later describes in 1Co 12–14. Undoubtedly the sign of tongues was given primarily for the sake of the Jewish believers right there in Cornelius's house. But it was also given for Jerusalem believers, who would later hear of what happened, so that all would see the conversion of these Gentiles as being entirely of God and none would revert to their old prejudices and relegate these new converts to the role of second-class Christians.

47–48 Peter may not have been much of an abstract thinker. But to his great credit he was ready to follow the divine initiative, if only he could be sure that God was really at work. So, convinced by God and consistent with his conviction about the logical connections between Christian conversion, water baptism, and the baptism of the Holy Spirit (cf. comments on 2:38), Peter calls for the Gentiles who have received the baptism of the Spirit to be baptized with water "in the name of Jesus Christ." While Acts 2 and 8 indicate that water baptism does not take the place of the Spirit's baptism but that the two go hand-in-hand with conversion, so vv.47–48 speak of the baptism of the Holy Spirit not as supplanting baptism with water but rather as being the spiritual reality to which water baptism testifies. Thus the baptism of these Gentile converts pointed to a new spiritual reality in their lives. But it also had immense significance for Peter and his six companions. For in baptizing these Gentiles, Peter and those with him confessed that God in his sovereignty does bring Gentiles directly into relationship with Jesus Christ, apart from any prior relationship with Judaism. Peter may have remained uncertain as to just how Cornelius's new-found faith should be expressed in worship and service and how it would be related to the Roman social order and to Judaism. But now that God had broken down the traditional barriers between them, Peter was content to stay with them in Caesarea "for a few days."

7. The response of the Jerusalem church (11:1–18)

The conversion of Cornelius was a landmark in the history of the Gospel's advance from its strictly Jewish beginnings to its penetration of the Roman Empire. True, it did not settle any of the issues relating to Jewish-Gentile relations within the church, nor did Jewish believers take it as a precedent for a direct outreach to Gentiles. But it did show that the sovereign God was not confined to the traditional forms of Judaism and that he could bring a Gentile directly into relationship with himself through Jesus Christ, apart from any prior commitment to distinctive Jewish beliefs or lifestyle. Cornelius's conversion is important to Luke not only because of the Gospel's advance but also because of the response of the Christians in Jerusalem to it. Amid his thesis of development and advance, Luke is interested in emphasizing lines of continuity and areas of agreement within the early church. So he takes pains to point out here, as in his account of the conversion of the Samaritans (cf. 8:14–25), that the leadership of the Jerusalem church accepted the validity of Cornelius's conversion. And that acceptance was of as great importance in validating a later Gentile mission as the event itself.

1–3 News of Peter's direct approach to Gentiles at Caesarea and his acceptance of them apart from the strictures of Judaism reached Jerusalem and the believers there before Peter himself did. This news caused great alarm both within the church and among the Jewish populace generally. The Hellenistic believers had stirred up much antagonism by their liberal attitudes toward the tenets of Jewish popular piety (cf. 6:8–7:56). The immediate consequences were the martyrdom of Stephen and the expulsion of the believers from areas under Sanhedrin control (cf. 7:57–8:3). Now if it were really true that Peter, the leading member of the apostolic band, had gone further in disregarding the traditional laws of Judaism in favor of a direct association with Gentiles, what goodwill still remained toward believers in Jerusalem would be quickly dissipated. The practical implications for the existence and the mission of the Christian church in Jerusalem were grave, and such practical considerations undoubtedly led to principial questions. Peter's return to Jerusalem, therefore, was like lighting a match in highly combustible air. "The circumcised believers" (i.e, "Jewish Christians") immediately confronted Peter and charged, "You went into the house of uncircumcised men and ate with them." This charge, while traditionally worded, was tantamount to saying that Peter had set aside Christianity's Jewish features and thereby seriously endangered its relation with the nation.

4–17 Peter defended his actions by recounting his experiences at Joppa and Caesarea, with an emphasis on (1) the divine initiative in all that transpired and (2) his inability to withstand God. Thus he recounts the details of the vision that came to him at Joppa (vv.5–10), of his reception by Cornelius (vv.11–14), and of the Spirit's coming upon the group gathered in Cornelius's house (vv.15–17). It was the Lord, insisted Peter, who gave him the vision and who explained its meaning. It was the Spirit who told him to have "no hesitation" to go with the messengers to Caesarea and enter Cornelius's house. And it was God who took the initiative by baptizing Cornelius and his companions with the Holy Spirit. Therefore, concluded Peter, "Who was I to think that I could oppose God?"

By giving a second witness to this story of the Gospel reaching out to Gentiles (cf. introductory comments on 2:42–12:24), likely taken from a different source than ch. 10, Luke is providing greater support for his theme of the legitimacy of a mission to Gentiles.

18 On hearing about Peter's experiences, the Christians at Jerusalem "remained silent" and "praised God." This probably means that his critics, at least for the moment, were silenced, while those more receptive to God's working acknowledged that Peter was right and credited God rather than human ingenuity for what had happened. In view of what Peter reported, the Jerusalem church could come to no other conclusion than that "God has even granted the Gentiles repentance unto life."

This was a response of momentous importance by the church at Jerusalem, and Luke meant his readers to appreciate it as being as significant in validating a later Gentile mission as Cornelius's conversion itself. But while of vital significance for the acceptance of Gentiles, it said nothing about the many related questions that soon were bound to arise. For example, what lifestyle was appropriate for Gentiles coming to Christ directly out of paganism? How should they relate themselves as Christians to Jewish Christians and to Jews, both of whom followed a Jewish lifestyle? And how should the Jerusalem church relate itself in practice to these new Gentile believers that it had in theory accepted? These are matters the Jerusalem church did not address itself to in ch. 11. Yet such matters were logically involved in its response and were to be taken up again later (cf. 15:1–35).

And just as there were ideological issues left unresolved in the response of the church in ch. 11, so there are also a number of historical matters about which Luke gives us no information, though we would like very much to know. For example, whatever happened to

Cornelius and his fellow Gentile Christians after Peter left them? Did they join with Philip and his converts in Caesarea (cf. 8:40) to form a worshiping community there? Or did they somehow inaugurate a distinctive form of Gentile Christian worship? Or, being doubtless all associated in one way or another with the Roman army and the Roman administration in Palestine, were these Gentile believers in Jesus transferred to other posts in the empire by Rome, either through due course or because of their recent alignment with a minority group within Palestine? Luke does not tell us.

Neither does Luke tell us how such a response affected the Jerusalem church itself. Did it lose some goodwill among its Jewish compatriots because it accepted Cornelius? Were there believers within its ranks who felt badly about this decision and who expressed their dissatisfaction—now or later—in ways disruptive for a further Gentile outreach? Was this one reason why the church soon found it appropriate to have as its leader the Pharisaically trained and legally scrupulous James the Just rather than one or more of the apostles (cf. comments on 12:2)? Again, Luke does not tell us, though some of these matters will come to the fore later in Acts.

C. The Church at Antioch of Syria (11:19–30)

Antioch of Syria was founded about 300 B.C. by Seleucus I Nicator, who named it after either his father or his son, both of whom bore the name Antiochus. It was situated on the Orontes River about three hundred miles north of Jerusalem and twenty miles east of the Mediterranean, at the joining of the Lebanon and Taurus mountain ranges where the Orontes breaks through and flows down to the sea. To distinguish it from some fifteen other Asiatic cities built by Seleucus and also named Antioch, it was frequently called "Antioch-on-the-Orontes." During the first Christian century, it was, after Rome and Alexandria, the third largest city in the empire, having a population of more than 500,000. It was a melting pot of Western and Eastern cultures, where Greek and Roman traditions mingled with Semitic, Arab, and Persian influences. The Jewish population is estimated to have been about one-seventh of the total population and had vested rights to follow its own laws within its three or more settlements in and around the city. During the reign of Caligula (A.D. 37–41), however, many Jews were killed; and during the tumultuous period of the middle and late 60s, Jewish acceptance and prosperity in Antioch came to an end.

In Christian history, apart from Jerusalem, no other city of the Roman Empire played as large a part in the early life and fortunes of the church as Antioch of Syria. It was the birthplace of foreign missions (13:2) and the home base for Paul's outreach to the eastern half of the empire. It was the place where those of "the Way" (9:2) were first called "Christians" (11:26) and where the question as to the necessity for Gentile converts to submit to the rite of circumcision first arose (15:1–2; cf. Gal 2:11–21). It had among its earliest teachers such illustrious persons as Barnabas, Paul, and Peter (cf. Gal 2:11–13). In the light of its great importance for the early church, it is surprising that Luke's account of the founding of the church at Syrian Antioch and of the progress of the Gospel there is so compressed.

1. The founding of the church (11:19–26)

19 Luke opens his account of the Gospel's proclamation at Antioch of Syria with the same words with which he began the story of the mission to Samaria in 8:4—a fact that suggests he wants to reach behind his accounts of Peter's ministries at Lydda, Joppa, and Caesarea and start a new strand of history that began with the death of Stephen. From such an opening we should probably understand that the Hellenistic Christians' outreach to Phoenicia, Cyprus, and Antioch was (1) logically parallel to that in Samaria, rather than a continuation of Peter's outreach at Lydda, Joppa, and Caesarea, and (2) chronologically parallel, at least in its early stages, to the accounts in 8:4–11:18. Phoenicia, Cyprus, and Antioch had large Jewish populations; and Syria, like Babylonia, was often considered an integral part of the Jewish homeland because of the many scrupulous Jews living there. Thus since this mission to the north was carried on within areas roughly considered to be Jewish terrain, was mounted by Hellenistic Jewish believers in Jesus, and was directed, at least at first, "only to Jews," Luke presents it here as still being part of the Christian witness to the Jewish world, even though the account speaks of a time when the categories "Jew" and "Gentile" were beginning to break down.

20–21 At Antioch, some of the Hellenistic Jewish Christians "began to speak to Greeks also." Did Luke have in mind Gentiles who had no affiliation whatever with Judaism, or did he have in mind Gentiles who had some kind of relationship with Judaism—perhaps "Proselytes of the Gate," or something like that? Usually Luke speaks of such near-proselytes as "God-fearers" (GK 4936; cf. 13:50; 16:14; 17:4, 17; 18:7). Yet judging by his evident purpose in Acts to present Paul as the first to inaugurate a deliberate policy of a direct approach to Gentiles, one should probably not view these Greeks apart from some contact with Judaism. Peter's activity in Caesarea was indeed a direct approach to Gentiles, but it set no precedent and established no policy for such an outreach. With the merging of cultures and blurring of distinctives that was taking place in Antioch generally, perhaps even Judaism itself faced some problems in drawing a sharp line between Gentiles who had some minimal relationship with the synagogue and those who were considered near-proselytes.

Whatever their exact status, it seems fair to say that Luke did not look on the Greeks in v.20 as simply Gentiles unaffected by the influence of Judaism and that he did not view the Hellenistic Christians' approach to them as preempting the uniqueness of Paul's later Gentile policy. All we are told about the identity of the Jewish-Christian missioners to Antioch is that they were from Cyprus and Cyrene. Perhaps Simeon Niger and Lucius of Cyrene were two of them (cf. 13:1), though Barnabas of Cyprus was not. But Luke does say that the missioners' proclamation of "the good news about the Lord Jesus" led to a significant response, so that "a great number of people believed and turned to the Lord." And since among that "great number" were both Jews and Gentiles, the Antioch church took on a decidedly different complexion from that of other early Christian congregations spoken of thus far. It was a mixed body of Jews and uncircumcised Gentiles meeting together for worship and fellowship in common allegiance to Jesus of Nazareth (cf. Gal 2:12).

22–24 News of the situation at Antioch was of definite concern to believers in Jerusalem. With the conversion of Samaritans, the conversion of some Gentiles in Caesarea, and now the report of a mixed congregation in Syrian Antioch, many in Jerusalem were doubtless fearful that the Christian mission was moving ahead so rapidly as to be out of control. The Jerusalem church, therefore, as in the case of the Samaritan conversions, decided to send a delegate to Antioch, probably in order to regularize whatever had gone awry and report back to the mother church. The man chosen for this task was Barnabas, a Jew from Cyprus who had gained an outstanding reputation for piety and generosity among the believers at Jerusalem (cf. 4:36–37). In all likelihood, Barnabas's position as both a Diaspora and "Zionistic" Jew and his piety and generosity qualified him in the eyes of the Jerusalem church for this mission to Antioch. In addition, the high esteem in which he was held made it certain that both his counsel and his report would be received with all seriousness.

The Jerusalem church could hardly have selected a better delegate. His generous spirit was gladdened by what he saw of the grace of God at work among the believers at Antioch, and, true to his nickname "Son of Encouragement" (cf. 4:36), he "encouraged them all to remain true to the Lord with all their hearts." Here was a crisis point in the history of the early church, for much depended on Barnabas's reaction, counsel, and report—not only at Antioch itself, but also at Jerusalem and in the later advance of the Gospel through Paul's missions. With evident feeling, therefore, Luke says of him, "He was a good man, full of the Holy Spirit and faith." And as a result of his response, the work that was started at Antioch was enabled to go on, with many being brought to Christ.

25–26 Sometime after reaching Antioch, Barnabas went to Tarsus to find Saul to help him in the ministry back in Syria. We have no record of what Saul was doing between the time when he left Jerusalem and when Barnabas found him in Tarsus, though he was probably ministering to Gentiles (see comments on 9:30). Barnabas was the one who had supported Saul when there was suspicion at Jerusalem about his conversion (cf. 9:27). And now, knowing of Saul's God-given commission to minister to the Gentiles, recalling his testimony at Jerusalem, and needing help for the work among the Gentiles, Barnabas involved Saul in the ministry at Antioch where they served together "for a whole year" and taught "a great crowd of people."

In joining Barnabas at Antioch, Saul may have thought he was carrying out the mandate received at his conversion to take the message of the risen Christ to Gentiles. Most likely, however, the Antioch mission in those days was confined to the synagogue, so that there was little thought of the propriety of appealing more widely and directly to Gentiles. All the early believers at Antioch, whether Jews or Gentiles, may well have been related in some way to the synagogue. Thus in the eyes of many Jewish Christians, the conversion of Gentiles who had to some extent come under the ministry of Judaism before they believed in Jesus would not have been thought exceptional.

But others within the city—evidently the nonbelievers, who were more perceptive in this matter than the church itself—nicknamed this group of Jewish and Gentile believers "Christians" (GK 5985; i.e., "Christ followers," or "those of the household of Christ"). They saw that the ministry to Gentiles and the fellowship of Jews with Gentiles went beyond the bounds of what was usually permitted within Judaism. They also voiced an insight that the Christians themselves only saw clearly later on: Christianity is no mere variant of Judaism. The new name doubtless helped develop the self-consciousness of the early Christians, despite its having first been given in derision. Later the early Christians accepted it and used it of themselves (cf. 26:28; 1Pe 4:16) along with their earlier self-designation of "the Way" (see comment on 9:2; cf. 19:9, 23). But the use of the name "Christian" posed two great problems for the church. For one thing, Christians began to risk losing the protection that Rome gave to a *religio licita* (i.e., a legal religion; cf. "Luke's Purposes in Writing Acts" in the introduction to Acts), which they had enjoyed when considered only a sect within Judaism. Furthermore, being now in some way differentiated from Judaism, Christians were faced with how to understand their continuity with the hope of Israel and the promises of the Jewish Scriptures. As we shall see, these problems were to loom large as the Christian mission moved onto Gentile soil.

2. The famine relief for Jerusalem (11:27-30)

27-28 Here Luke uses the connective "in those days" just as he did at 1:15 and 6:1, to link parts of his narrative. Now he tells of certain "prophets" who "came down from Jerusalem to Antioch." Among them was Agabus, with his dire prediction of impending famine in Jerusalem (cf. 21:10). The Jews believed that with the last of the writing prophets, the spirit of prophecy had ceased in Israel; but the coming Messianic Age would bring an outpouring of God's Spirit, and prophecy would again flourish. The early Christians, having experienced the inauguration of the Messianic Age, not only proclaimed Jesus to be the Mosaic eschatological prophet (cf. 3:22; 7:37) but also saw prophecy as a living phenomenon within the church (cf. also 13:1; 15:32; 21:9-10) and ranked it among God's gifts to his people next to that of being an apostle (cf. 1Co 12:28; Eph 4:11).

Agabus's prediction was of a "severe famine" affecting "the entire Roman world," which took place, Luke notes, during the reign of the emperor Claudius (A.D. 41-54). Although there is no record of a single famine that ravaged the whole empire in the time of Claudius, various Roman historians referred to a series of bad harvests and famine conditions during his reign. One of them, the Jewish historian Josephus, refers to famine relief sent from northern Mesopotamia to Jerusalem.

29-30 Similarly, the Christians at Antioch, in response to Agabus's prophecy, decided to provide help for their fellow believers at Jerusalem, whose plight as a minority group within the nation would be particularly difficult at such a time. We are not given any details as to how the relief was collected, how it was administered, or when it was delivered. All we know from the text is that it was an expression of Christian concern by the Antioch church "for the brothers living in Judea" and was taken by Barnabas and Saul "to the elders" (i.e., the leaders) of the Jerusalem church.

The "famine visit" of Barnabas and Saul to Jerusalem of 11:27-30 should probably be dated about A.D. 46. That date, even though tentative and general, presents commentators with their first real date for working out a Pauline chronology (cf. comments on the reign of Herod Agrippa I at 12:1–23, the Edict of Claudius at 18:2, and Gallio's proconsulate at 18:12). But as to how we are to reconcile this date with what Paul tells us in his letters and how we are to fit it into an overall chronology depends largely on the answer to the conundrum of the relation of Paul's two Jerusalem visits mentioned in Galatians to his three Jerusalem visits reported in Acts. While most accept the correlation of Gal 1:18–20 with Ac 9:26–29 and count that as the first visit, many feel that Gal 2:1–10 should be identified with the Jerusalem Council of Ac 15. But this appears to make Ac 11:27–30 either a fabrication on Luke's part or a doublet of the Ac 15 material placed here by Luke for his own purposes.

The issues are complex and have far-reaching consequences. (See comments on Ac 15 in the context of 12:25–16:5.) Here it is sufficient to say that the simplest solution, one that provides the most satisfactory and convincing reconstruction and leaves the fewest loose ends, is that Gal 2:1–10 corresponds to the famine visit of Ac 11:27–30. On such an understanding, and taking the temporal conjunctions "then" of Gal 1:18 and 2:1 as referring back to Saul's conversion (A.D. 33, allowing some flexibility in rounding off the years), his first visit to Jerusalem can be dated about 36, and his famine visit some fourteen years after his conversion about 46. On such a basis, the reference in Gal 2:2 to Saul's having gone to Jerusalem "in response to a revelation" should probably be related to Agabus's prophecy of Ac 11:28.

D. Divine Intervention on Behalf of the Jerusalem Church (12:1–23)

With its acceptance of the conversion of "half-Jews" in Samaria, a Gentile centurion and his friends at Caesarea, and Gentiles who were only loosely associated with the synagogue at Antioch of Syria, the Jerusalem church was straining the forms and commitments of Judaism almost to the breaking point. There is hardly any further room for expansion within the traditions of Judaism, and soon the Christian mission would break out of those limits to embrace a direct mission to the Gentile world. In fact, the preparation for this had begun with Saul's conversion and with his early attempts to carry on a Christian ministry, even though not till later would he formally espouse and explicitly carry out a direct mission to Gentiles.

But before Luke turns to his portrayal of the Christian mission to the Gentile world, he takes the opportunity of presenting two further glimpses of God's working on behalf of the believers at Jerusalem. Just as his mentor Paul, while arguing for the legitimacy of a direct outreach to Gentiles, continued to characterize Jewish Christianity as "the church of God" (Gal 1:13; cf. 1Th 2:14) and to respect God's ongoing activity within the Jewish world (cf. Ro 9–11), so Luke seems desirous of making the point that, though he is about to portray the advances of the Gospel within the Gentile world, it should not be assumed that God was finished with Jerusalem Christianity or that his activity within the Jewish world was finished. Luke has portrayed the Christian mission to the Jewish world that had its center at Jerusalem. Now he prepares to present the Christian mission to the Gentiles as a kind of ellipse emanating from that same center.

Before doing so, however, Luke gives us two further vignettes relating to God's intervention on behalf of the Jerusalem church so that his readers might more fully appreciate the fact that while the Christian mission within the Jewish world and the Christian mission to the Gentiles differed, in many ways they possessed a common focus, had many similarities, and were complementary. Divine activity on behalf of the Gentiles, Luke appears to be insisting, does not mean divine inactivity on behalf of Jewish Christians or unconcern for Jews—which is a heresy that has often afflicted Gentile Christians and resulted in horrendous calamities.

1. The deliverance of Peter (12:1–19a)

1–4 The narrative of Peter's miraculous deliverance from prison and death really begins at v.5. The narrative is introduced as having taken place "about this time," which refers to the events of the famine visit to Jerusalem of 11:27–30. But if the famine visit occurred about A.D. 46 and Herod Agrippa I died in A.D. 44 (as will be seen below), 11:27–30 and the material of 12:1–23 are chronologically reversed. Yet we must remember that ancient historians frequently grouped their materials without always being concerned about chronology (see introduction). So Luke, having begun his account of Christianity in Antioch by speaking of the founding of the church, tied into that narrative a further vignette about the famine relief Antiochean believers sent to Jerusalem. As a result, his full account of the church at Antioch (11:19–30) reaches back behind Peter's ministries at Lydda, Joppa, and Caesarea at its start (cf. 11:19) and goes beyond the accounts of Peter's deliverance and Herod Agrippa I's death at its close (the events of ch. 12 coming between those of 11:19–26 and 11:27–30). Luke seems to have wanted to close his portrayals of the Christian mission within the Jewish world (2:42–12:24) with two vignettes having to do with God's continued activity on behalf of the Jerusalem church.

The Herod of Ac 12 is Agrippa I (born in 10 B.C.), the grandson of Herod the Great and the son of Aristobulus. After his father's execution in 7 B.C., he was sent with his mother Bernice to Rome, where he grew up on intimate terms with the imperial family. In his youth he was something of a playboy, and in A.D. 23 he went so heavily into debt that he had to flee to Idumea to escape his creditors. Later he received asylum at Tiberias and a pension from his uncle Herod Antipas, with whom, however, he eventually quarreled. In 36 he returned to Rome but offended the emperor Tiberius and was imprisoned. At the death of Tiberius in 37, he was released by the new emperor Caligula and received from him the northernmost Palestinian tetrarchies of Philip and Lysanius (cf. Lk 3:1) and the title of king. When Herod Antipas was banished in 39, Agrippa received his tetrarchy as well. And at the death of Caligula in 41, Claudius, who succeeded Caligula and was Agrippa's friend from youth, added Judea and Samaria to his territory, thus reconstituting for him the entire kingdom of his grandfather Herod the Great, over which he ruled till his death in 44.

Knowing how profoundly the masses hated his family, Herod Agrippa I took every opportunity during his administration in Palestine to win their affection. When in Rome he was a cosmopolitan Roman. But when in Jerusalem, he acted the part of an observant Jew. In A.D. 40 Agrippa cajoled Caligula not to carry out his insane plan of erecting a statue to himself as a god in the Jerusalem temple and intervened on behalf of the Jews in Alexandria for their more humane treatment. When Judea came under his jurisdiction, he moved the seat of government from Caesarea to Jerusalem. This established the holy city in Jewish eyes as the political capital of the country. He also began to rebuild the city's northern wall and fortifications, thus enhancing both its security and its prestige. Many Jews viewed these days as the inauguration of a better era—perhaps even the Messianic Age. Agrippa himself, however, seems to have been primarily interested in a successful reign through the cooperation of loyal subjects, and his expressions of concern for the people and their religion were probably more pragmatically based than sincere.

Agrippa's policy was preserving the Roman peace through preserving the status quo. He supported the majority within the land and ruthlessly suppressed minorities when they became disruptive. He viewed Jewish Christians as divisive and felt their activities could only disturb the people and inflame antagonisms. So he arrested some of the believers in Jesus and had James, one of Jesus' original disciples, beheaded by the sword (a form of execution supported by Jewish tradition). Finding that this pleased the Jewish leaders, he then took Peter during Passover Week and imprisoned him till he could bring him out for public trial after the Jewish holy days. While in prison, the apostle was guarded by "four squads of four soldiers each," with two soldiers chained to him on either side and two standing guard at the inner entrance to the prison (cf. v.6). Evidently Agrippa planned to make of Peter a spectacle and warning at a forthcoming show trial. And he did not want to be embarrassed by Peter's escape.

5 Peter was likely imprisoned somewhere within the Fortress of Antonia, which overlooked the temple area to the north and had entrances to both the temple courts and the city. More important to Luke, for whom prayer is the natural atmosphere of God's people and the normal context for divine activity (cf. 1:14, 24; 2:42; 4:24–31; 6:4, 6; 9:40; et al.), is the fact that "the church was earnestly praying to God for him [Peter]."

6–9 On the night before Agrippa's show trial, "an angel of the Lord" appeared in the apostle's cell and began to take charge of affairs. The "angel of the Lord" signifies God himself in his dealings with people (cf. Ex 3:2, 7;

Mt 1:20, 24; Lk 1:11; 2:9; Ac 5:19; 8:26; 12:23; et al.). The angel awoke Peter, and as he stirred, the chains by which he was bound fell from his wrists. Then the angel, like a parent with a child awakened from sound sleep, carefully instructed the groggy apostle to get dressed. Then he ordered Peter to follow him, and they left the cell. But Peter, too sleepy to grasp the reality of what was happening, thought he was dreaming.

Herod Agrippa I had planned to try Peter as the leader of the divisive minority in Palestine that identified itself with the crucified Jesus of Nazareth and then execute him as a warning to other followers of Jesus to stop their activities. Usually a prisoner was chained to only one guard, but in view of Agrippa's intentions, the guard was doubled. The Christians in Jerusalem understood Agrippa's intentions because he had earlier imprisoned some of them and killed James the son of Zebedee. Neither Peter nor his fellow believers were in any doubt about what the king had in mind. It was a crisis of great magnitude for the life of the early Christian community at Jerusalem. But while God does not promise deliverance from persecution and death, at crucial times he often steps in to act for the honor of his name and the benefit of his people. This was what now happened. Peter's deliverance must be ascribed entirely to God, for it was in no way due to the apostle's own efforts or those of the Christian community—apart, of course, from their prayers.

10–11 Passing the two guards at the inner entrance to the prison, Peter and the angel came to the main iron gate, which opened automatically as they approached. Then the angel left Peter a block away from the prison. For Peter, standing there alone in the street and brought to his senses by the cool night air, there was no doubt that "the Lord sent his angel and rescued me [Peter] from Herod's clutches and from everything the Jewish people were anticipating."

12 Realizing where he was and the danger he faced if Herod's soldiers should find him there, Peter went to one of the meeting places of the early Jerusalem Christians, the home of Mary, John Mark's mother. A number of people were praying there. Luke's identification of Mary by her son implies that her son's name was better known to his readers than hers. It also suggests that the John Mark referred to here was the one who was with Paul and Barnabas on a portion of the first missionary journey (Ac 13:5, 13)—namely, a cousin of Barnabas and the likely writer of the second gospel (cf. Ac 15:37–39; Col 4:10; Phm 24; 1Pe 5:13).

13–16 Mary's house must have been of some size, with a vestibule opening onto the street, a courtyard, and rear living quarters—not only were "many people gathered" there, but Peter was knocking at the door of the vestibule, and Rhoda the servant girl was rushing back and forth for joy. The unfolding scene is one of confusion and joyful humor, which must have led to hilarity every time it was repeated among the early believers. There was Peter's knocking, becoming more and more urgent as he beat on the door; Rhoda's losing her wits for joy and forgetting to open the door; the Christians' refusal to believe it was Peter, even though they had just been praying for him; their belittling of Rhoda and of her insistence she had heard Peter's voice at the door; Rhoda's frantic persistence; and their utter astonishment when they finally opened the door and let him in.

17 On entering, Peter "motioned with his hand for them to be quiet." This was not the time for celebration. After all, Herod's soldiers would soon be prowling on the streets to look for him. Peter had to get moving to escape being recaptured. So he gave them a quick summary of "how the Lord had brought him out of prison" and instructed them to tell James and the other brothers what had happened. And with that, Luke tells us, Peter left "for another place."

The James mentioned here is, of course, James the Lord's brother, not James the brother of John and son of Zebedee who was earlier beheaded by Herod Agrippa I (cf. v.2). Undoubtedly Peter was the leader of the first Christian community at Jerusalem, as the early chapters of Acts presuppose. But from the mid-thirties through the mid-forties James seems also to have exercised administrative leadership along with Peter and the apostles (cf. Gal 1:19; 2:9), and he presided at the Jerusalem Council of A.D. 49 (cf. 15:13–21). Later still Luke refers to him as head of the Jerusalem church (cf. 21:18). He was likely martyred in 62. Luke does not state how or why the shift in leadership of the church from Peter to James came about, nor what qualified James for such a position. Apparently it had to do with (1) external pressures on the Jerusalem congregation to demonstrate its Jewishness, and (2) the need within the church for someone who could lead the growing number of scrupulously minded converts drawn from Pharisaic and priestly backgrounds (cf. comments on 6:7).

After the expulsion of the Hellenists, both the Jews and the Jewish Christians in Jerusalem felt the need for the community of believers in Jesus to demonstrate more actively their continued respect for the traditions of Israel. Peter and his fellow apostles would hardly have been the best ones to head such an endeavor—in fact, Peter's association with the Samaritans and Cornelius may have made him particularly suspect in certain quarters. It is, therefore, not improbable the Jerusalem church found it advantageous to be represented in its leadership by one whose legal as well as spiritual qualifications were above reproach. Such a person was James, the Lord's brother, who seems to have been a devout Pharisee and who was not only physically related to Jesus but also had seen the risen Jesus (1Co 15:7).

Furthermore, the missionary activities of Peter and the apostles would require some kind of arrangement for the continuance of administrative authority at Jerusalem. That the apostles considered themselves to be something other than ecclesiastical functionaries has already been shown in Ac 6:2–6. And it is not too difficult to imagine that with the dispersion of the Hellenists and the Seven who were appointed to supervise the distribution of food within the community, the church turned to James for administrative leadership—not only, to demonstrate its Jewishness, but also to free the apostles for their "ministry of the word" (cf. 1Co 9:5).

The mention of "another place" to which Peter went after his miraculous deliverance has led to various suggestions. Roman Catholics have frequently suggested Rome, though most now agree it is unlikely. If 12:1–19 precedes 9:32–11:18 chronologically (see comments on 12:1), this other place may refer to the maritime plain of Palestine, with its cities of Lydda, Joppa, and Caesarea. But such a region was still within Herod Agrippa's jurisdiction. More likely Antioch of Syria is the place Luke had in mind—a place where Peter had fellowship with a mixed body of Jewish and Gentile believers till "certain men came from James," and where he suffered the rebuke of Paul (cf. Gal 2:11–21). Later on Peter appears at Jerusalem in connection with the Jerusalem Council (cf. 15:7–11, 14), though presumably only in transit.

18–19a In Roman law, a guard who allowed his prisoner to escape was subject to the same penalty the escaped prisoner would have suffered. No wonder that in the morning when Peter's escape was discovered, "there was a great commotion among the soldiers." When Herod heard of Peter's escape, he instituted a search and cross-examined the guards. Frustrated by his lack of success, he ordered the guards to be taken out to execution.

2. The death of Herod Agrippa I (12b:19–23)

Peter had been miraculously delivered from prison and death, but the tyrant Herod Agrippa was still at large, continuing his oppression of the church. Therefore Luke gives us a second scene in his account of God's intervention on behalf of the Jerusalem church. He does this not only to show how far-reaching this intervention was but also to reinforce by a second witness the theme of God's continued interest in Jewish Christianity (cf. the introductory comments on 2:42–12:24).

19b–20 The situation Luke describes in these verses is not entirely clear. Caesarea, with its excellent man-made harbor (see comments on 10:1), was still nominally the provincial capital of Palestine. Though we have no other record of conflict between Herod and Tyre and Sidon, Herod became enraged with the people of these two cities; and they, in turn, sent a delegation to ask for peace, using in some way the good offices of Blastus, King Agrippa's personal servant, for their purposes. Agrippa appears to have left Jerusalem for Caesarea shortly after the Jewish Passover, perhaps because of frustration over Peter's escape.

21–23 Luke's account of Agrippa's death is paralleled by a story in Josephus, the Jewish historian of the first century. Both accounts differ from each other in significant ways, but they are so similar in outline that we may

In this outdoor theater in Caesarea, the Lord struck down King Herod. The person is standing where Herod's throne would have been placed.

assume that we know in general how Herod Agrippa I died in A.D. 44. Both Luke and Josephus attribute his death to the king's impiety and God's judgment. Moreover, Luke sees it as part of God's activity on behalf of the Jerusalem church. Luke's reference to worms suggests an infection by intestinal roundworms, which grow as long as ten to sixteen inches and feed on the nutrient fluids in the intestines. Bunches of roundworms can obstruct the intestines, causing severe pain, copious vomiting of worms, and death.

E. A Summary Statement (12:24)

24 Luke's third panel on the Christian mission within the Jewish world ends with a summary statement comparable to the summaries that conclude the two preceding panels (cf. 6:7; 9:31). In its context, v.24 contrasts the progress of the Gospel to the awful end of the church's persecutor Herod Agrippa I. More broadly, it implies that though in the remainder of Acts Luke's attention will be focused on the advances of the Gospel to Gentiles, within the Jewish world "the word of God continued to increase and spread." In other words, God was still at work on behalf of the Jerusalem church and its ministry and was still concerned for his ancient people Israel.

Part II. The Christian Mission to the Gentile World (12:25–28:31)

In the Nazareth pericope (Lk 4:14–30), Luke set the main themes for all that follows in Luke-Acts. Two features of particular relevance stand out in those verses. (1) Luke presents Jesus' reading of Isa 61 as ending in mid-sentence at Isa 61:2a, thereby emphasizing grace ("to proclaim the year of the Lord's favor") without sounding the note of judgment ("and the day of vengeance of our God"). The omission of the judgment theme underscores the fact that the period of the Gospel is a time characterized by grace, when the offer of deliverance is freely extended. To such a message of salvation, the residents of Nazareth responded positively. They failed to see any other implication in a message of free grace than God's messianic blessings poured out on Israel. So they spoke well of Jesus and commented favorably about his "gracious words" (Lk 4:22). (2) Next, Luke shows Jesus as indicating that the blessings of the Messianic Age were not intended for Israel alone but were for Gentiles as well—with the blessings of God's grace extending even to a Phoenician widow and a Syrian leper. Here was a repudiation of the Jewish concept of exclusive election. Jesus' townsmen were furious, drove Jesus out of the synagogue, and tried to kill him.

Jesus' own earthly ministry was, of course, limited almost entirely to Jews. Luke's gospel depicts only one healing of a centurion's servant (7:1–10) and two brief contacts with Samaritans (9:52–55; 17:11–19). Moreover, it even omits the story about the Syro-Phoenician woman of Mk 7:24–30 (cf. Mt 15:21–28), though it contains several intimations of a later inclusion of Gentiles (cf. Lk 2:30–32; 3:6; 11:31; 13:29; 14:16–24). Also, in the first half of Acts, Luke has presented the Jerusalem church's ministry as focused primarily on the Jewish world, with such outreaches as Samaria, Caesarea, and Syrian Antioch being understood in some ways as exceptional. In effect, then, Luke has reserved for Paul the mission to the Gentiles that Jesus saw as inherent in Isa 61. Now as Luke turns to a portrayal of how the Gospel advanced among the Gentiles, he also concludes his two-volume work by explicating Jesus' promise of the universal extension of God's grace. This he does (1) by building on what Jesus accomplished in his earthly ministry, death, and resurrection, as presented in his gospel, and (2) by paralleling in its Gentile advances many features of the extension of God's grace within the Jewish world, as presented in the first half of Acts.

Panel 4—The First Missionary Journey and the Jerusalem Council (12:25–16:5)

Luke's fourth panel, the first of his three on the Christian mission to the Gentile world, embodies both Paul's first missionary journey and the Jerusalem Council. It concludes by telling how believers in Syria, Cilicia, and Galatia received the decisions of the council. Luke presents his material more thematically than geographically. Therefore, before closing with the summary in 16:5, he draws together several matters: (1) a report of events on the first missionary journey that led up to the Jerusalem Council; (2) an account of the debate and decisions reached at the council; and (3) a précis of how those decisions were received in areas of Gentile outreach.

In his first missionary journey, Paul began a radically new policy for proclaiming the Gospel and making converts: namely, he approaches the Gentile world apart from any prior commitments to Judaism on the part of the converts or any Jewish stance on the part of the missioners; on their part, the Gentile Christians express their faith in Jesus apart from a Jewish lifestyle and distinctive Jewish practices (cf. 14:27b; 15:3). For the early church with its Jewish roots, such a policy was revolutionary. It had enormous significance and many implications for the Christian movement that required a full discussion and decision at the Jerusalem Council.

A. The Missioners Sent Out (12:25–13:3)

25 This verse reaches back behind the events of ch. 12 to connect 13:1–3 with the account of the Antioch church in 11:19–30. Luke uses it as a kind of bridge statement before turning to the missionary journey itself. Thus he shifts his readers' attention from Jerusalem to Antioch of Syria and tells of John Mark's return with his cousin Barnabas (Col 4:10) and with Saul from Jerusalem to Antioch.

13:1 At Antioch there were five "prophets and teachers" in the church. The Greek suggests that Barnabas, Simeon, and Lucius were prophets, and Manaen and Saul were teachers—with prophecy here understood to include "forthtelling" as well as "foretelling" and teaching having to do with showing OT relationships and implications.

We know Barnabas was a Levite from Cyprus who resided in Jerusalem and became a leading figure in the Jerusalem church (4:36–37; 9:27; 11:22–30). He was, as Luke tells us, "a good man, full of the Holy Spirit and faith" (11:24) and undoubtedly served as a channel for the truth of the Gospel direct from the Jerusalem congregation. Simeon Niger (meaning "black") may have come from Africa; he was possibly the Simon from Cyrene of Lk 23:26. As for Lucius and Manaen, we know nothing certain apart from this verse. Lucius of Cyrene was frequently identified in the postapostolic period with Luke the evangelist and author of Acts; but this is not likely, for Luke refrains from identifying himself with Paul's missionary journeys, except through the occasional use of the pronoun "we." Manaen is identified as one "who had been brought up with" (GK 5343; lit., a "foster brother" or "intimate friend") Herod the Tetrarch. This suggests that he had been raised as an adopted brother or close companion of Herod Antipas. As for Saul, we know him from 7:58–8:3; 9:1–30; and 11:25–30.

2–3 While Barnabas and Saul were carrying out their activities at Antioch, the Holy Spirit directed that they should be set apart for a special ministry. Luke does not tell us how the Spirit made his will known, though it was probably through a revelation given to one of the believers. Neither does he tell us the nature of the special ministry the two were set apart for, though from what follows it is obvious that we are meant to understand that it was to be a mission to Gentiles. The whole congregation, together with its leaders, was involved in attesting the validity of the revelation received, laid hands on the missioners, and sent them out (cf. 14:27, where the missioners reported back to the whole church). Ultimately, though, Luke insists that Barnabas and Saul were "sent on their way by the Holy Spirit" (v.4).

B. The Mission on Cyprus and John Mark's Departure (13:4–13)

The first major outreach of the Gospel from Antioch soon encountered the false prophet Bar-Jesus in Cyprus, just as the first major outreach from Jerusalem ran afoul of Simon the sorcerer in Samaria (cf. 8:9–24). By the manner in which he narrates both events, Luke apparently wanted his readers to see the parallel. Moreover, not only does Luke seem to have been interested in this parallel between these two episodes, he was also interested in showing how great a step forward the mission on Cyprus really was—with its revolutionary implications for the Christian mission to Gentiles and its radical effect on the missioners themselves.

4 Luke now begins the account of the missioners' outreach to Cyprus, Pamphylia, and the southern portion of Galatia. While the church confirms in its own experience the divine will, identifies itself with God's purposes and those whom he has called for specific tasks, and releases them from their duties for wider service (cf. v.3), it is God who by his Spirit is in charge of events and sends out his missioners. Thus, being "sent on their way by the Holy Spirit," they went down to Seleucia on the Mediterranean and sailed from there to the island of Cyprus. Just why they thought of going to Cyprus first in carrying out their mandate we don't know. But Barnabas was from Cyprus (4:36); and knowing generally the will of God, he and Saul were ready to move from the known to the unknown.

Seleucia was the port city of Antioch of Syria, some sixteen miles west of Antioch and four or five miles northeast of the mouth of the Orontes River. It was founded by Seleucus I Nicator, the first king of the Seleucid dynasty, about 300 B.C. in conjunction with the founding of Antioch. Cyprus was an island of great importance from very early times, being situated on the shipping lanes between Syria, Asia Minor, and Greece. In 57 B.C. it was annexed by Rome from Egypt and in 55 B.C. incorporated into the province of Cilicia. In 27 B.C. it became a separate province governed on behalf of the emperor Augustus by an imperial legate. In 22 B.C. Augustus relinquished its control to the senate, and, like other senatorial provinces, it was administered by a proconsul.

5 Leaving the mainland of Syria, the missionary party sailed to Salamis on the eastern coast of Cyprus, about 130 miles from Seleucia. Salamis was the most important city of the island and the administrative center for its eastern half, though the provincial capital was 90 miles southwest at Paphos. The population of Cyprus was dominantly Greek, but many Jews lived there as well. Thus Barnabas and Saul began their mission in the synagogues of the city, and John Mark was with them as their helper.

6–11 From Salamis, Barnabas and Saul traveled throughout the island of Cyprus, continuing to preach within the Jewish synagogues to both Jews and "God-fearing" Gentiles. But when they reached Paphos—or, more exactly, New Paphos, the Roman provincial capital seven miles northwest of the old Phoenician city of Paphos—their ministry definitely changed. At Paphos the Roman proconsul Sergius Paulus asked them to present their message before him. This was probably meant to be an official inquiry into the nature of what the missioners were proclaiming in the synagogues so that the proconsul might know how to deal with charges already laid against these wandering Jewish evangelists and head off any further disruptions within the Jewish communities. The invitation could not have been refused. But neither the proconsul nor the missioners could have anticipated what actually happened at the inquiry.

Luke describes Sergius Paulus as a man of discernment, which he proved to be in accepting the Christian message. Within his court at Paphos was a certain Jewish sorcerer and false prophet named Bar-Jesus. In assuming himself as the Jewish spokesman in opposition to these Christian evangelists, this man probably wanted to enhance his own reputation. While sorcery and magic were officially banned in Judaism, there were still Jews who practiced it, both under the guise of Jewish orthodoxy and as renegades (cf. Lk 11:19; Ac 19:13–16). Bar-Jesus is also called Elymas (a name meaning "sorcerer," "magician," "fortune-teller").

In all of Saul's activities thus far, nothing had happened to suggest that he was anything but "a Hebrew born of Hebrew parents" (cf. Php 3:5). He was interested in an outreach to Gentiles but made no special appeal to them directly. Nor did he approach them as being on an equal footing with Jews or apart from the synagogue. Though his preaching aroused strong feelings within certain Jewish communities, it engendered no more ill will than had been directed against the other apostles before him. Here in the hall of the proconsul, however, Saul was in new surroundings as he presented his message before a leading member of the Roman world, a world of which he himself was a member. As a Jew, he proudly bore the name of Israel's first king, Saul. As a Roman citizen (cf. 16:37–38; 25:10–12), he undoubtedly had two Roman names, a praenomen and a nomen, though neither is used of him in the NT. But as a Jew of the Diaspora, who must necessarily rub shoulders with the Gentile world at large, he also bore the Greek name Paul, which became his cognomen in the empire and was used in Gentile contexts. So at this point in his narrative Luke speaks of "Saul, who was also called Paul," and hereafter refers to him only by this name.

As the Gospel was being proclaimed to Sergius Paulus, Bar-Jesus tried to divert the proconsul from the faith. But Paul turned on the sorcerer and pronounced a curse upon him. In highly biblical language, he denounced Bar-Jesus as "a child of the devil," "an enemy of everything that is right," one "full of all kinds of deceit and trickery," always "perverting the right ways of the Lord," and pronounced a curse of temporary blindness on him. "Immediately," Luke tells us, "mist and darkness came over him, and he groped about, seeking someone to lead him by the hand."

12 The nature of the proconsul's response has often been debated, chiefly because the text says nothing about his being baptized when he believed. But the statement that Sergius Paulus believed can hardly be taken with any less significance than Luke's use of the same word in 14:1; 17:34; and 19:18, where baptism is also not mentioned yet where we might well assume it was performed.

The conversion of Sergius Paulus was, in fact, a turning point in Paul's whole ministry and inaugurated a new policy in the mission to Gentiles—namely, the legitimacy of a direct approach to and full acceptance of Gentiles apart from any distinctive Jewish stance. This is what Luke clearly sets forth as the great innovative development of this first missionary journey (14:27; 15:3). Earlier Cornelius had been converted apart from any prior commitment to Judaism, and the Jerusalem church had accepted his conversion to Christ. But the Jerusalem church never took Cornelius's conversion as a precedent for the Christian mission and apparently preferred not to dwell on its ramifications. Paul, however, whose mandate was to Gentiles, saw in the conversion of Sergius Paulus further aspects of what a mission to Gentiles involved and was prepared to take this conversion as a precedent fraught with far-reaching implications for his ministry. It is significant that from this point on, except for 14:14; 15:12; and 15:25 (situations where Barnabas was more prominent), Luke always emphasizes Paul's leadership by listing him first when naming the missionaries.

13 Verse 13 has puzzled many commentators. Pamphylia was a geographically small and economically poor province on the southern coast of Asia Minor, with the mountains of Lycia to the west, the foothills of Pisidia to the north, and the Taurus range to the east. It contained a mixed population and seems to have been as open to the Gospel as any other province. Yet Luke gives us no account of evangelization in Perga or its environs at this time, though he expressly states later that the missioners "preached the word in Perga" on their return to Syrian Antioch (14:25). And it was at Perga that John Mark left the group to return to Jerusalem.

The usual explanation for the missioners' initially bypassing Perga and moving on to Antioch of Pisidia is that Paul may have been ill with a case of malaria and that this forced redirecting the mission to gain the higher ground to the north. As for John Mark's departure, it is usually explained as a combination of homesickness, the rigors of travel, dissatisfaction with Paul's assuming leadership over Mark's cousin Barnabas, and unhappiness at leaving Cyprus so soon. But discussion among the missioners after Paphos and during their stay at Perga may very

In Paphos on Cyprus is a church associated with Paul. Legend has it that Paul was tied to one of these pillars and beaten.

well have focused on the implications of Sergius Paulus's conversion for their ministry. And it can plausibly be argued that (1) the lack of preaching in Perga at this time was due primarily to uncertainty within the missionary party itself about the validity of a direct approach to and full acceptance of Gentiles, and (2) John Mark left because he disagreed with Paul and was concerned about the effect the news of a direct Christian mission to Gentiles would have in Jerusalem. His return to the Christian community in Jerusalem may originally have stirred the "Judaizers" in the church to action. In any case, Paul's strong opposition to Mark in 15:37–39 suggests that his departure on this first missionary journey was for reasons more than merely personal.

C. At Antioch of Pisidia (13:14–52)

At Pisidian Antioch the typical pattern of the Pauline ministry was established: an initial proclamation in the synagogue to Jews and Gentile adherents and then, when refused an audience in the synagogue, a direct ministry to Gentiles. This pattern is reproduced in every city visited by Paul with a sizable Jewish population—except Athens. As he later declares in Romans, there is no difference between Jews and Gentiles in condemnation (Ro 2:1–3:20) or in access to God (Ro 3:21–31); so his ministry at Pisidian Antioch began to express this equality. While the synagogues were appropriate for beginning his ministry in the various cities, offering as they did an audience of both Jews and Gentiles theologically prepared for his message, they were not the exclusive sphere of Paul's activity. Since Jews and Gentiles stood before God on an equal footing, they could be appealed to separately if need be.

This understanding of the validity of a direct approach to Gentiles and their full acceptance as Christians is what Paul speaks of as "my gospel" (Ro 16:25; cf. Gal 1:11–2:10). It was a gospel not different in content from the earliest gospel (1Co 15:1–11) but a gospel distinct in strategy and broader in scope. The nature of Paul's ministry had been given to him by revelation (see Eph 3:2–6); by providential action at the beginning of his first missionary journey, its specifics were spelled out.

1. A welcome extended at Antioch (13:14–15)

14a Pisidian Antioch was founded by Seleucus I Nicator about 281 B.C. (see comment on 11:19–30). It was situated a hundred miles north of Perga on a lake-studded plateau some thirty-six hundred feet above sea level. The foothills between Perga and Pisidian Antioch largely ruled out any extensive east-west traffic until one reached the plateau area, but following the river valleys one could move northward from the Pamphylia area. On the plateau Antioch stood astride the Via Sebaste, the Roman road from Ephesus to the Euphrates. The city had been incorporated into the expanded Roman province of Galatia in 25 B.C. by Augustus, who at that time imported into it some three thousand army veterans and their families from Italy and gave it the title of Colonia Caesarea. Antioch was the most important city of southern Galatia and included a rich amalgam of Greek, Roman, Oriental, and Phrygian traditions. Acts tells us that it also had a sizable Jewish population.

14b–15 Arriving at Pisidian Antioch, Paul and Barnabas entered the synagogue on the Sabbath. A typical first-century synagogue service would have included the *shema* (see comments on Dt 6:4–5), the liturgy of "The Eighteen Benedictions," a reading from the Law, a reading from one of the prophets, a free address given by any competent Jew in attendance, and a closing blessing. The leader of the synagogue, usually one of the elders of the congregation, took charge of the building and made arrangements for the services (Lk 8:41, 49). This office was sometimes held for life and passed on within a family. Perhaps Paul's dress proclaimed him a Pharisee and thereby opened the way for an invitation to speak.

2. Paul's synagogue sermon at Antioch (13:16–41)

Three missionary sermons of Paul are presented in Acts: the first here before the synagogue at Antioch of Pisidia, the second to Lystrans assembled outside the city gates (14:15–17), and the third before the Council of Ares at Athens (17:22–31). Each sermon as we have it is only a précis of what was said, for the longest in its present form takes no more than three minutes to deliver and the shortest can be read in thirty seconds or less. But there is enough in each account to suggest that whereas Paul preached the same gospel wherever he went, he altered the form of his message according to the circumstances he encountered.

16 When Jesus addressed the congregation at Nazareth, he read the lesson standing and then sat down to speak (cf. Lk 4:16, 20). Luke, however, portrays Paul as "standing" to address the synagogue worshipers at Pisidian Antioch. Paul's speech at Pisidian Antioch was probably an exhortation not arising from the passages read that day from the Law or the Prophets. In Paul's audience were both Jews and "God-fearing" Gentiles. So he addressed both groups: "Men of Israel and you Gentiles who worship God." With a gesture of his hand and with his words, he invited them to listen to him.

17–22 Paul's exhortation begins with a review of Israel's history that emphasizes the pattern of God's redemptive activity from Abraham to David. It is an approach in line with Jewish interests and practices and can be paralleled by Stephen's defense before the Sanhedrin, by the argument of the Letter to the Hebrews, and by the underlying structure of Matthew's gospel.

Highlighted is a four-point confessional summary that for Jews epitomized the essence of their faith: (1) God is the God of the people of Israel; (2) he chose the patriarchs for himself; (3) he redeemed his people from Egypt, leading them through the desert; and (4) he gave them the land of Palestine as an inheritance. To such a confessional recital, Jews often added God's choice of David to be king and the promises made to him and his descendants (cf. Pss 78:67–72; 89:3–4, 19–37). Paul proclaims these great confessional truths of Israel's faith, which speak of God's redemptive concern for his people and undergird the Christian message.

Of importance also is the fact that underlying Paul's treatment of David is 2Sa 7:6–16, the passage that speaks of David's descendant as God's "son." By anchoring Israel's kerygma in the messianically relevant "son" passage of 2Sa 7, Paul has begun to build a textual bridge for the Christian kerygma, which he will root in the messianic "son" passage of Ps 2:7. And by drawing these two passages together, he will draw together Israel's confession and the church's confession, thereby demonstrating both continuity and fulfillment.

23 Paul's Christian proclamation begins by announcing that God has brought forth the messianic Deliverer from David's line in the person of Jesus. The promise Paul alludes to is in Isa 11:1–16, a messianic passage of special importance for Judaism because it speaks of the Messiah's descent from David, of his righteous rule, of his victories, and of the establishment of his kingdom.

24–25 The announcement of Jesus as the Messiah is put in the usual form of the apostolic proclamation, beginning with John the Baptist and his ministry (cf. Mk 1:2–8). John's preaching and baptism of repentance paved the way for the public ministry of Jesus. John was the forerunner of the Messiah, as he himself confessed (cf. Lk 3:15–18).

26–31 As Paul comes to the heart of his sermon, he appeals respectfully and urgently to both the Jews and the God-fearing Gentiles for a hearing. Then he presents a four-point Christian confession like that in 1Co 15:3–5: (1) Jesus was crucified; (2) they "laid him in a tomb"; (3) "God raised him from the dead"; and (4) "for many days he was seen by those who had traveled with him from Galilee to Jerusalem," who are "now his witnesses to our people." Also significant is the clear note of fulfillment explicitly sounded in v.27 and implied throughout the whole presentation.

32–37 To support this four-point confession and to demonstrate the fulfillment of what God has promised, Paul cites three OT passages fraught with messianic meaning for Christians and also for some Jews. The first is Ps 2:7, which Paul uses to bind together Judaism's confession and Christianity's confession by juxtaposing it with 2Sa 7:6–16 (the text underlying vv.17–22). Both 2Sa 7:14 and Ps 2:7 portray God as speaking of his "son." Linking passages on the basis of their verbal analogies was common in Judaism (see comment on 2:25–35). In doing this Paul does two things: (1) he brings these two "son" passages together as the substructure of his argument in this synagogue, and (2) he joins OT redemptive history and the history of Jesus, understanding both as having messianic significance.

Paul then quotes Isa 55:3 and Ps 16:10, joining his OT passages again on the interpretative principle of verbal similarities between "the holy blessings" and "the Holy One." The messianic treatment of Ps 16:10 stems from the earliest Christian preaching at Pentecost (cf. 2:27).

38–41 Paul now uses the simple appellation "Men, brothers" (cf. vv.16, 26) as he applies his message and calls the people to repentance. Through Jesus, Paul declares, are "forgiveness of sins" and justification for "everyone who believes." What we have here are his distinctive themes of "forgiveness [GK 912] of sins," "justification" (GK 1467; cf. 1466), and "faith" (GK 4409; cf. 4411)—themes that resound in his first address in Acts just as they do throughout his extant letters.

The call to repentance is cast in terms of Hab 1:5. In effect, Paul concludes by warning the congregation that Habakkuk's words apply to all who reject God's working in Jesus' ministry and who refuse Jesus as the divinely appointed Messiah.

3. Varying responses to the sermon (13:42–45)

42–43 Those who heard Paul's sermon requested Paul and Barnabas "to speak further about these things on the next Sabbath." More than likely the synagogue authorities took a less favorable view of the sermon. But "many of the Jews and devout converts to Judaism" were interested and after the service followed the apostles to hear more. And "some" of those who did this were "persuaded" (NIV "urged") by the apostles "to continue in the grace of God"—which, to judge by Paul's usual understanding of grace, must connote continuance in the Good News about salvation through Jesus.

44–45 "Almost the whole city," Luke says rather hyperbolically, gathered on the following Sabbath to hear "the word of the Lord"—an expression suggesting the Christological content of Paul's preaching. But "when the Jews saw the crowds," their initial interest turned to antagonism. Not only was the synagogue being flooded by Gentiles as though it were a common theater or town hall, but, even more, it became clear that Paul and Barnabas were ready to speak directly to Gentiles without first relating them in some way to Judaism. The majority of the Jews, including their leaders, were apparently unwilling to countenance a salvation as open to Gentiles as it was to Jews. So in their opposition "they blasphemed" (NIV: "talked abusively"; GK 1059), because from Luke's perspective opposition to the Gospel is directed not so much against the messengers as against the content of the message—Jesus himself (cf. 26:11).

4. To the Jews first, but also to the Gentiles (13:46–52)

46–47 In response to the Jews' abuse and blasphemy, Paul and Barnabas asserted their new policy—"To the Jews first, but also to the Gentiles"—a policy that had begun with the conversion of Sergius Paulus and had evidently been discussed by the missioners on the way from Paphos to Pisidian Antioch (see comment on v.13). There is evidence from the fifth century Latin commentator Jerome that this policy of preaching first to Jews and then to Gentiles, though initiated on Paul's first missionary journey and not in Jerusalem, was acknowledged very early even among certain Jewish Christians at Jerusalem.

As Paul and Barnabas saw it, the Jews of Pisidian Antioch in their exclusiveness had rejected the very thing they were looking for—"eternal life." Now, however, the Gospel must be directed to the Gentiles, for included in its mandate is the promise of Isa 49:6, that God's servant will be "a light for the Gentiles" and a bringer of salvation" to the ends of the earth" (cf. Lk 2:28–32). It was, of course, Jesus of Nazareth who was uniquely God's Servant and who was at work through his Spirit in the church, completing what he had begun and also making the missioners God's servants and inheritors of the promise in Isa 49:6.

48–49 Many of the Gentiles responded with thanks for the apostles' ministry and with openness to their message. "All who were appointed [GK 5435] for eternal life believed" suggests that belief in Christ is not just a matter of one's faith but primarily involves divine appointment. And through the conversion of many of the Gentiles, who brought the message of salvation to others, "the word of the Lord spread through the whole region." This spreading of the word, along with the apostles' own outreach to the cities named in chs. 13 and 14, probably led to the agitation of the so-called Judaizers that resulted in the problem Paul dealt with in Galatians.

50 Unable to confine the ministry of Paul and Barnabas to the synagogue, the Jews stirred up trouble against them and brought pressure on the city's magistrates through their "God-fearing" wives. Since Luke speaks of the persecution as expulsion rather than mob action, it probably took the form of a charge that Christianity, being disowned by the local Jewish community, was not a *religio licita* in Rome's eyes and therefore must be considered a disturbance to the Pax Romana. Later in Acts, Luke will show how the agitation against the Gospel usually arose from within the Jewish community, not from the Roman authorities, and that the charge was that Paul was preaching an illegal religion (cf. 16:20–21; 17:7; 18:13)—a charge Luke insists was unfounded. This is part of the fabric of why he wrote Acts (see Introduction: Luke's Purposes in Writing Acts).

51–52 Having been expelled from Pisidian Antioch, Paul and Barnabas "shook the dust from their feet in protest against them"—a Jewish gesture of scorn and disassociation, which was directed at the city's magistrates and the Jewish leaders. Then they went southeast on the Via Sebaste, heading for Iconium some eighty miles away. The new "disciples" left behind at Pisidian Antioch, far from being discouraged at this turn of events, were "filled with joy and with the Holy Spirit."

D. At Iconium, Lystra, and Derbe and the Return to Antioch (14:1–28)

The Via Sebaste, the great Roman road from Ephesus to the Euphrates, became two roads at Pisidian Antioch. One went north through mountainous terrain to the Roman colony of Comana about 122 miles away. The other moved southeast across rolling country, past the snow-capped peaks of Sultan Dag, to the important Greek city of Iconium, some eighty miles distant from Antioch, and from there to the Roman colony of Lystra. As Paul and Barnabas left Pisidian Antioch, therefore, they were faced with a choice as to the future direction of their mission. Choosing the southeastern route, they headed off to what would become a ministry to people of three very different types of cities in the southern portion of the Roman province of Galatia.

1. The ministry at Iconium (14:1–7)

1–2 Iconium, an ancient Phrygian town, had been transformed by the Greeks into a city-state. Situated in the heart of the high and healthy plateau of south-central Asia Minor, it was surrounded by fertile plains and verdant forests, with mountains to its north and east. With Augustus's reorganization of provinces in 25 B.C., Iconium became part of Galatia. But while Rome chose Antioch of Pisidia and Lystra as bastions of its authority in the area, Iconium remained largely Greek in temper and somewhat resistant to Roman influence. Greek was the language of its public documents, and during the NT period it attempted to retain the ethos of the old city-state. The name "Iconium" is probably Phrygian, but a myth was invented to give it a Greek meaning. According to the myth, Prometheus and Athena recreated humankind in the area after a devastating flood by making images of people from the mud and breathing life into them. The Greek for "image" is *eikon*, hence the name Iconium.

Entering Iconium, Paul and Barnabas went to the Jewish synagogue, following the same pattern as they had at Pisidian Antioch. As they proclaimed the Gospel, a great number of both Jews and Gentiles believed. Opposition to the Gospel soon arose, but since this city was governed by Greek jurisprudence, this opposition did not follow the same pattern as in Antioch. Paul and Barnabas were able to stay there for some time.

3 Luke tells us that the apostles ministered for a "considerable time" in the city and preached boldly "for the Lord," with God confirming "the message of his grace" by "miraculous signs and wonders." The mention of "the Lord" undoubtedly refers to Jesus the Lord, thus showing the Christocentric nature of the missioners' preaching. And the couplet "miraculous signs and wonders" (cf. 15:12) places the ministry of Paul and Barnabas directly in line with that of Jesus (cf. 2:22) and the early church (cf. 2:43; 4:30; 5:12; 6:8; 7:36) in fulfillment of prophecy (cf. 2:19). Later when writing his Galatian converts (assuming a "South Galatian" origin for the letter), Paul appeals to these mighty works performed by the Spirit as evidence that the Gospel as he preached it and as they received it was fully approved by God (cf. Gal 3:4–5).

4–5 There was a division among "the people" (GK *4436*) of the city regarding the apostles and their message, some siding with the Jews and others with the apostles. Interpreted broadly, "the people" denotes no more than the populace of the city, though it may denote an assembly of prominent citizens that met to conduct the business of a Greek city-state. While no official action seems to have been taken against them, there was a "plot" brewing among some of the Gentiles and Jews to mistreat and stone them.

Significant here is Luke's lumping Barnabas together with Paul in the phrase "with the apostles" (GK *693*), While Barnabas was neither one of the Twelve nor a claimant to any special revelation, he was probably one of the 120 (cf. 1:15) and may have been a witness of Jesus' resurrection. Yet as with most titles of the NT, Luke, like Paul himself (cf. 2Co 8:23; Gal 1:19; Php 2:25), not only used "apostle" in the restricted sense of a small group of highly honored believers who had a special function within the church but also in the broader sense of messengers of the Gospel.

6–7 The opposition to the ministry of Paul and Barnabas must have grown to sizable proportions, for they took it seriously enough to leave Iconium and travel to Lystra and Derbe. By referring to Lystra and Derbe as "Lycaonian cities," Luke implies that Iconium belonged to a different region from Lystra and Derbe. All three, of course, were part of the Roman province of Galatia. But in the administration of so large a province, the Romans subdivided Galatia into various regions, four of which have come down to us by name: Isauria, Pisidia, Phrygia, and Lycaonia. In fleeing to Lystra and Derbe, therefore, Paul and Barnabas were leaving one political region to start afresh in another. Thus in the Lycaonian region they continued preaching the Gospel, both in the cities of Lystra and Derbe and in the surrounding countryside.

2. The ministry at Lystra (14:8–20)

8–10 Lystra was an ancient Lycaonian village whose origins are unknown. Caesar Augustus turned it into a Roman colony in 6 B.C., and, by bringing army veterans and their families into it, made it the most eastern of the fortified cities of Galatia. Jews also lived there (16:1–3), but their influence seems to have been minimal. The Via Sebaste joined this city with Iconium (see comment on 14:1–28).

That Paul began the ministry at Lystra by preaching to a crowd may imply that no synagogue was available for him to preach in. While he was speaking, Paul saw "a man crippled in his feet, who was lame from birth and had never walked" and who was listening to him attentively. Seeing "that he had faith to be healed," Paul commanded him to stand up, and the man jumped up and walked about. Luke undoubtedly wanted his readers to recognize the parallel between the healing of this crippled man and the healing of another one by Peter (cf. 3:1–8). But the sequel to the healing of the crippled man here differs significantly from that of Peter's miracle.

11–13 The healing amazed and excited the crowd, and they shouted out in Lycaonian: "The gods have come down to us in human form!" (cf. 28:6). Barnabas they identified as Zeus, the chief of the Greek pantheon, probably because of his more dignified bearing. Paul they identified as Hermes, Zeus's son by Maia and the spokesman for the gods, since "he was the chief speaker." Archaeological findings have confirmed that both Zeus and Hermes were worshiped in Lycaonian Galatia.

Approximately half a century before Paul's first missionary journey, the Roman poet Ovid retold an ancient legend that may have been well known in southern Galatia and helps explain the wildly emotional response of the people to Paul and Barnabas. According to the legend, Zeus and Hermes once came to "the Phrygian hill country" disguised as mortals seeking lodging. Though they asked at a thousand homes, none took them in. Finally, at a humble cottage of straw and reeds, an elderly couple, Philemon and Baucis, freely welcomed them with a banquet that strained their poor resources. In appreciation, the gods transformed the cottage into a temple with a golden roof and marble columns. Philemon and Baucis they appointed priest and priestess of the temple, who, instead of dying, became an oak and a linden tree. As for the inhospitable people, the gods destroyed their houses. Seeing the healing of the crippled man and remembering the legend, the people of Lystra believed that Zeus and Hermes had returned, and they wanted to pay them homage lest they again incur the gods' wrath.

That the people shouted in Lycaonian explains why the apostles were so slow to understand what was afoot until the preparations to honor them as gods were well advanced. But when the priest of Zeus joined the crowd and began to do them homage, Paul and Barnabas realized what was about to happen. We can visualize the priest of Zeus bringing out sacrificial oxen draped in woolen "wreaths" and preparing to sacrifice at an altar that stood in front of the Temple of Zeus, hard by the city gates. And as the idolatrous worship proceeded, Paul and Barnabas began to see that they were the object of it.

14–18 When they finally realized what was going on, Paul and Barnabas tore their clothes in horror at such blasphemy and rushed out into the crowd—shouting their objections and trying to make the people understand them. There is no reason to think that the majority of the Lystrans knew anything of Jewish history or of the Jewish Scriptures, or that they had been vitally affected by Athenian philosophies. Culturally, they were probably peasants living in the hinterland of Greco-Roman civilization, with all of the lack of advantages of people in their situation. Such is the context of Paul's second missionary sermon. By far the briefest of the three (cf. 13:16–41; 17:22–31), its brevity reflects its confused setting.

Negatively, Paul's sermon at Lystra has to do with the futility of idolatry; positively, it is a proclamation of the one true and living God. Its language, particularly in its denunciation of paganism, is biblical. But its argument is suited to its hearers. And despite the brevity with which Luke reports it, two features stand out in the development of Paul's argument. First, his demonstration of the interest and goodness of God is drawn neither from Scripture (as at Pisidian Antioch) nor from philosophy (as later at Athens) but from nature: "He has shown kindness by giving you rain from heaven and crops in their seasons; he provides you with plenty of food...." It is an approach to theism that peasants would understand.

Second, Paul preached that "in the past, he [God] let all nations go their own way," which suggests that at Lystra Paul preached about a progressive unfolding of divine redemption. While the sermon does not explicitly refer to salvation through Christ, it is hard to believe that it was not meant to point to Jesus Christ and his work as the divine climax of history. "We too are only men, human like you," Paul and Barnabas insisted. But, they went on to say, "we are bringing you good news"—the best news possible—of the unity and character of the one true God and of redemption through the person and work of Jesus his Son. Yet for most of the Lystrans, the message fell on deaf ears, and they tried to carry on the sacrifices in honor of the visitors.

19–20 Later on certain Jews from Pisidian Antioch and Iconium, disaffected with Paul and Barnabas, came to Lystra to spread their views. Complaining first among the Jewish residents of the city, they managed to gain a hearing with the people. The fickle Lystrans, thinking that if the apostles were not gods they were impostors, stoned Paul and dragged him outside the city for dead. But with the aid of those who had accepted the Gospel, he revived; and, with great courage, he returned that evening to the city where he had almost been killed. The next day, Paul and Barnabas left for the border town of Derbe.

Some months later, when Paul wrote the believers in Galatia (again, we assume a "South Galatian" destination for the letter), he closed by saying, "Finally, let no one cause me trouble, for I bear on my body the marks of Jesus" (Gal 6:17). Some of the marks may well have been scars caused by the stoning at Lystra. And when still later he wrote the Corinthians of his being stoned (2Co 11:25), it was Lystra he had in mind (cf. also 2Ti 3:11).

3. The ministry at Derbe and the return to Antioch (14:21–28)

21a Derbe was situated in the southeastern part of the Lycaonian region of Galatia, about sixty miles southeast of Lystra. In 25 B.C. Augustus incorporated it into the province of Galatia, making it a provincial border town on the eastern edge of the southern Galatian plateau. Luke's account of the ministry at Derbe is brief. All he says is that the apostles "preached the good news" there and "won a large number of disciples." Luke spends more time talking about the larger and more influential churches in Antioch and Iconium, though the congregations in the smaller and more rural towns seem to have contributed more young men as candidates for the missionary endeavor (e.g., Timothy from Lystra [16:1–3; 20:4]; Gaius from Derbe [20:4])—a pattern not altogether different from today, where the larger churches often capture the headlines and the smaller congregations provide much of the personnel.

21b–23 Having preached at Derbe, Paul and Barnabas returned to Lystra, Iconium, and Pisidian Antioch. Why they did not push instead further east through the passes of the Taurus range into Cilicia, Luke does not tell us. Perhaps Cilicia was considered already evangelized through Paul's earlier efforts (cf. comment on 9:30); this would also explain why the apostles began their missionary outreach on Cyprus and not in Cilicia (cf. 13:4). Undoubtedly their concern for the new converts in the Galatian cities led them to return by the same road. In returning to Lystra, Iconium, and Pisidian Antioch, they probably confined their ministries to those already converted, and thus did not stir up any further opposition (cf. 16:6; 18:23; 20:3–6).

While returning through the Galatian cities, Paul and Barnabas tried to strengthen their converts personally and corporately. They encouraged them to remain in the faith, telling them that many persecutions must necessarily be the lot of Christians in order to enter into the kingdom of God—that is, that the same pattern of suffering and glory exemplified in Jesus' life must be theirs as well if they are to know the full measure of the reign of God in their lives (cf. Mk 8:31–10:52; Ro 8:17; Php 3:10–11; Col 1:24). And "they appointed elders for them in each church," thus leaving them with suitable spiritual guides and an embryonic ecclesiastical administration. In the early Gentile churches (as also undoubtedly at Jerusalem), the terms "elders" (GK 4565) and "bishops" (or "overseers"; GK 2176) were used somewhat interchangeably and functionally rather than as titles (cf. 20:17, 28).

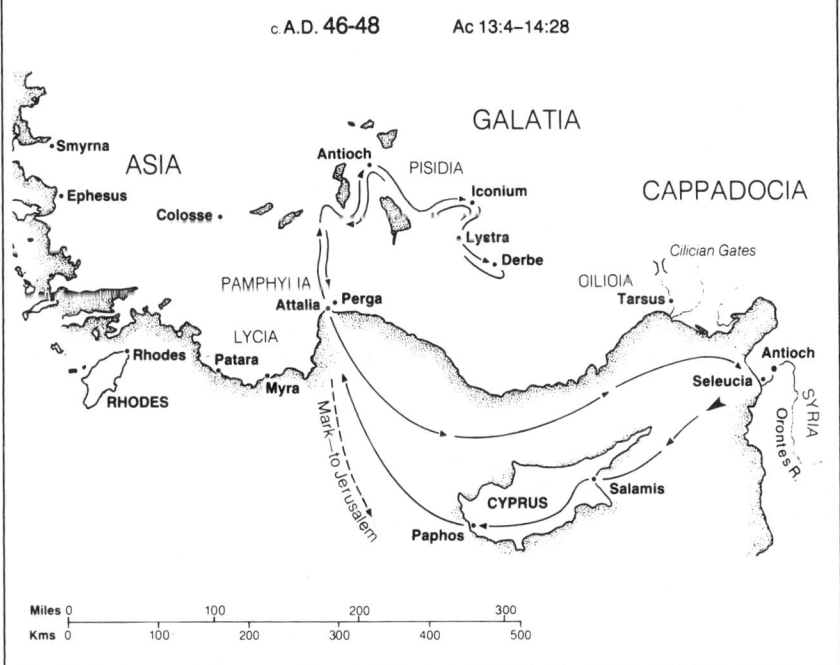

© 1989 The Zondervan Corporation.

24-25 Directly south of Phrygia was the region of Pisidia and south of that the province of Pamphylia. In Pamphylia the apostles preached at Perga, the chief city of the province, thus beginning the kind of witness in Perga they had been unable to begin on their first visit (cf. comment on 13:13). Of its results we know nothing, nor do we know the nature of their visit to the port of Attalia, some eight miles further south on the Mediterranean coast, from where they embarked on a boat for the voyage back to Syria.

26-28 On returning to Antioch of Syria and to the congregation that had sent them out, Paul and Barnabas "reported all that God had done through them and how he had opened the door of faith to the Gentiles." They had gone out under divine ordination, and their report stressed the fact that God himself had brought about the new policy for evangelizing the Gentiles, which was inaugurated at Paphos and followed throughout the cities of southern Galatia—a claim that was called into question by some believers in Jerusalem and was soon to be tested at the Jerusalem Council. So having returned from a missionary journey that occupied the best part of a year, the apostles remained at Syrian Antioch, ministering in the church there for approximately another year.

E. The Jerusalem Council (15:1–29)

The convening of the council of apostles and Christian leaders at Jerusalem in approximately A.D. 49 was an event of greatest importance for the early church. That Gentiles were to share in the promises to Israel is a recurring theme of the OT (cf. Ge 22:18; 26:4; 28:14; Isa 49:6; 55:5–7; Zep 3:9–10; Zec 8:22). It was the underlying presupposition for Jewish proselytizing and was implicit in the sermons of Peter at Pentecost (Ac 2:39) and in the house of Cornelius (10:35). But the correlative conviction of Judaism was that Israel was God's appointed agent for the administration of these blessings—that only through the nation and its institutions could Gentiles ever have a part in God's redemption and share in his favor. There seems to have been no expectation on the part of Christians at Jerusalem that this program would be materially altered, though they did insist that in these "last days" God was at work in and through Jewish Christians as the faithful remnant within the nation.

In the experience of the church, all Gentiles—with one exception—who had come to acknowledge Jesus as Messiah had been either full proselytes or near proselytes ("Godfearers"). Only Cornelius's conversion did not fit into the pattern (cf. 10:1–11:18). But this event was viewed as exceptional and not an occasion for changing policy. The practice of preaching directly to Gentiles begun by Paul in his mission on Cyprus and throughout southern Asia Minor, however, was a matter of far-reaching concern at Jerusalem, especially in view of the tensions that arose within Palestine after the death of Herod Agrippa I in A.D. 44.

As the faithful remnant, the Jerusalem church naturally expected the Christian mission to proceed along lines God laid down long ago. It could point to the fact that, with few exceptions, commitment to Jesus as Israel's Messiah did not make Jews less Jewish. Indeed, it sometimes brought Gentiles who were only loosely associated with the synagogues into greater conformity with Jewish ethics. The Christian movement had always insisted on its integral relation to the religion and nation of Israel, even though this relation contained some unresolved ambiguities and was defined in various ways within the movement. But Paul's new policy for reaching Gentiles, despite his claim of the authority of revelation and of providence for it, seemed to many Jewish Christians to undercut the basis of the ministry of the Jerusalem church. It seemed to give the lie to the stance of Jerusalem Christianity—particularly if condoned by believers of Jerusalem.

A word should be said here about Pauline chronology (for full discussion, see EBC 9:440–42; also 10:417–20), particularly the thorny question of the relation of Paul's "second visit" to Jerusalem (Gal 2:1–10) to the Jerusalem Council (Ac 15). The literary and historical issues are complex (cf. comments on 11:29–30). But one point drawn from the polemic in Galatians needs to be made here: Paul's silence in Galatians as to the decision of the Jerusalem Council forces the irreconcilable dilemma of saying either (1) that Luke's account in Ac 15 of a decision reached in Paul's favor at Jerusalem is pure fabrication or (2) that Galatians was written before the Jerusalem Council. It is the opinion of this commentary that the second option is the more likely.

Accepting Galatians, then, as having been written before the Jerusalem Council, we have some idea from Paul himself concerning repercussions in Jerusalem in regard to his Gentile ministry, both as it was carried on in the synagogues at Antioch of Syria and as it was further developed in Cyprus and southern Asia Minor. On his second visit to Jerusalem after his conversion (cf. 11:27–30 and comments on 11:29–30), the issue came to a head in the case of the uncircumcised Titus who accompanied Paul and Barnabas to Jerusalem. In spite of pressures and some uncertainty, the Jerusalem apostles stood with Paul on the validity of a Gentile mission and the inappropriateness of making circumcision a requirement for Gentiles—though probably neither Paul nor they at that time saw a massive direct ministry to Gentiles in the offing. Paul's account of the Antioch episode in Gal 2:11–21 clearly shows that the Gentile ministry was causing repercussions at Jerusalem and that the Jerusalem congregation was exerting pressure. The passage also suggests that the rationale for separating Jewish and Gentile believers was based on expediency rather than on principle. And it was this issue of expediency versus theological principle that required clarification in the early church and lent urgency to the Jerusalem Council.

1. The delegation from Syrian Antioch (15:1–4)

1 The immediate occasion for the Jerusalem Council was the visit to Syrian Antioch of some Jewish Christians from Jerusalem and their teaching that on principle, circumcision was essential to salvation. These became known as "Judaizers," and their comrades were promoting similar teaching among Paul's converts in Galatia. They may have been incited by the return of John Mark and his unfavorable report (cf. comment on 13:13). Both James and Peter (cf. Gal 2:9) were interested in minimizing conflicts between Judaism and Jewish Christianity. Yet neither was prepared to sacrifice the principles of the Gospel to expediency when the implications of doing this became plain. Undoubtedly the Judaizers thought of themselves as acting conscientiously and on sound theological principles (cf. comment on v.5 below). But as Paul saw it, they sought "a good impression outwardly ... to avoid being persecuted for the cross of Christ" (Gal 6:12).

2 With the issues highlighted by the "sharp dispute and debate" that followed, Paul and Barnabas were appointed, along with certain others from the Antioch congregation, to go up to Jerusalem to meet with "the apostles and elders" about the matter. It was probably the entire congregation at Antioch and its leaders that appointed these men to discuss the issue (cf. 13:3). Antioch Christians were desirous for the relation between the Jerusalem church's policy of cautious expediency and the Judaizers' argument founded on theological principle to be clarified. The Jerusalem Christians, for their part, undoubtedly welcomed an opportunity to air their concerns—particularly the impasse created for them by Paul and Barnabas through their Gentile policy. For while there may have been general agreement on the validity of evangelizing Gentiles (cf. Gal 2:7–10), recent events opened that agreement for reconsideration.

3–4 As the delegation from Antioch journeyed to Jerusalem, they told the believers in Phoenicia and Samaria the news of "the conversion of the Gentiles." The Phoenician and Samaritan Christians, being themselves converts of the Hellenists' mission after Stephen's martyrdom (cf. 8:4–25; 11:19), probably took a broader view than that which prevailed at Jerusalem and rejoiced at the news. Believers at Jerusalem also were interested, but their interest by no means involved whole-hearted approval.

2. The nature and course of the debate (15:5–12)

5 In the ensuing debate among believers in general and in the council itself, some Christian Pharisees, in support of the Judaizers, insisted that it was necessary for Gentile Christians to "be circumcised and required to obey the law of Moses." And by this necessity they meant that these things were not only expedient but required by the revealed will of God. In their thinking, they read that the prophets spoke of the salvation of the Gentiles as an event of the last days (cf. Isa 2:2; 11:10; 25:8–9; Zec 8:23) through the witness of a restored Israel (cf. Isa 2:3; 60:2–3; Zec

8:23). Thus they could hardly oppose reaching Gentiles through the ministry of the church. But they felt that the outreach to Gentiles should come from within their group and follow a proselyte model, not come from outside their group and be apart from the law. After all, in the last days, all nations were to flow to the house of the Lord at Jerusalem (cf. Isa 2:2–3; 25:6–8; 56:7; 60:3–22; Zec 8:21–23), not depart from it.

6 While Luke says only that the apostles and elders met to consider these questions, his mention of "the whole assembly" in v.12 and "the whole church" in v.22 shows that other members of the congregation were also present. The discussion was undoubtedly heated, but Luke centers on its Pauline aspect.

7–11 Peter was no longer the chief figure of the Jerusalem church, for James had now assumed that role (cf. comment on 12:17). But Peter was dominant in the Jewish Christian mission and responsible to the Jerusalem church. And it is as a missionary, not an administrator, that he spoke up and reminded the council that God had chosen to have the Gentiles hear the Gospel from him and accept it. He argued that since God had established such a precedent within the Jewish Christian mission some ten years earlier—though it had not been recognized by the church as such—God has already indicated his approval of a direct Gentile outreach. Thus Paul's approach to the Gentiles could not be branded as a deviation from the divine will. Peter had evidently completely recovered from his temporary lapse at Syrian Antioch. Now he saw matters more clearly and was ready to agree with Paul's position that there is "no difference" between Jews and Gentiles and that the Mosaic law was a "yoke."

12 Luke's reference to the silence of the assembly after Peter spoke implies that the turning point had come. Though resisted at Jerusalem for almost a decade, the precedent of Cornelius's conversion had opened the way for Barnabas and Paul's report of God's validation of their missionary policy through "miraculous signs and wonders." It was a report not of their successes but of how God had acted, and its implication was that by his acts God had revealed his will. Barnabas is mentioned first here (cf. v.25), probably because he enjoyed greater confidence at Jerusalem.

3. The summing up by James (15:13–21)

13 James, the Lord's brother, presided at the Jerusalem Council (cf. comment on 12:17). He was ascetic and scrupulous in keeping the law. The Judaizers within the church looked to him for support, knowing both his legal qualifications and his personal qualities. But while rigorous and scrupulous in his personal practice of the faith, James was more broad-minded than many of his followers. After calling the council to order by using the formal mode of address "Men, brothers," he went on to sum up the emerging view of the council in a way that linked it to what had already been said.

14 In summing up, James made no reference to Paul and Barnabas's report, probably more for political reasons than any of principle. After all, it was the work of Paul and Barnabas that was on trial, and James wanted to win his entire audience to the position he believed to be right without causing needless offense. Therefore, he began by reminding the council of Peter's testimony and went on to show how he felt about the question at issue by speaking of believing Gentiles as a "people" (GK *3295*) whom God had taken "for himself"—thus (1) applying to Gentile Christians a designation formerly used of Israel alone, and (2) agreeing with Peter that in the conversion of Cornelius God himself had taken the initiative for a direct Gentile ministry.

15–17 James's major contribution to the decision of the council was to shift the discussion of the conversion of Gentiles from a proselyte model to an eschatological one. Isaiah had expected Gentile converts to come to Jerusalem to learn God's ways so that they might walk in them. But Isaiah also spoke of the Gentiles' persistence as nations whose salvation did not destroy their national identities (cf. Isa 2:4; 25:6–7). Likewise, Am 9:11–12 (in the LXX version) spoke of "the remnant of people" in the last days when "David's fallen tent" would be rebuilt as being "all the Gentiles who bear my name" and whose continuance as Gentiles was understood. In the end times, James is saying, God's people will consist of two concentric groups. At their core will be restored Israel (i.e., David's rebuilt tent); gathered around them will be a group of Gentiles (i.e., "the remnant of people") who will share in the messianic blessings but will persist as Gentiles without necessarily becoming Jewish proselytes. It is this understanding of Amos's message, James insisted, that Peter's testimony has affirmed, the result being that the conversion of Gentiles in the last days should be seen not as proselytizing but in an eschatological context.

18 The interpretation of v.18 is notoriously difficult. Many (such as NIV) understand the clause as part of a conflated biblical citation that extends from v.16 through v.18, probably alluding to Isa 45:21. It seems better, however, to interpret the words here as a comment by James to this effect: We cannot be in opposition to the express will of God, as evidenced by Peter's testimony and the prophets' words—but only God himself knows for certain how everything fits together and is to be fully understood!

19 On the basic issue that brought the members of the first ecumenical council together—that of the necessity of relating Gentiles to Judaism in the Christian mission—James refused to side with the Judaizers. He may not have been prepared to endorse openly all the details of Paul's Gentile policy. Certainly there is no indication that he expected the Jerusalem church to do that. But he could not be in opposition to the express will of God, and therefore his advice was that Jewish Christianity should not take any stance against the promotion of the Gentile mission. In so concluding, he swept aside the obstacles that had arisen to Paul's Gentile mission among believers at Jerusalem and left it free for further advances within the empire.

20–21 On the practical question that troubled many Christians in Jerusalem and that originally gave rise to the Judaizers' assertion—namely, the question of fellowship between Jews and Gentiles in the church and of tolerance for the scruples of others—James's advice was that a letter be written to the Gentile Christians. This letter should request them to abstain "from food polluted by idols, from sexual immorality, from the meat of strangled animals and from blood." These prohibitions have often been viewed as a compromise between two warring parties, which nullified the effect of James's earlier words and made the decision of the Jerusalem Council unacceptable to Paul. But in reality they should be viewed not as dealing with the principal issue of the council but as meeting certain practical concerns. They were not primarily theological but more sociological in nature—concessions to the scruples of others for the sake of harmony within the church and the continuance of the Jewish Christian mission. Therefore James added the rationale of v.21, suggesting that since Jewish communities are found in every city, their scruples are to be respected by Gentile believers.

To sum up, we may say that two types of "necessary" questions were raised at the Jerusalem Council. The first had to do with the theological necessity of circumcision and the Jewish law for salvation, and that was rejected. The second had to do with the practical necessity of Gentile Christians to abstain from certain practices for the sake of Jewish-Gentile fellowship in the church and the Jewish Christian mission throughout the Diaspora, and that was approved.

4. The decision and letter of the Council (15:22–29)

22 With James's judgment "the apostles and elders, with the whole church," agreed, deciding to send their decision back to Antioch of Syria not only by Paul and Barnabas but also by two leaders of the Jerusalem congregation, Judas Barsabbas and Silas, whose presence would assure reception of the decision and who could interpret the feelings of the council from a Jerusalem perspective. It seems clear that within the Jerusalem church, the congregation was involved in the deliberations of its leaders.

When one considers the situation of the Jerusalem church in A.D. 49, the decision reached by the Jerusalem Christians must be considered one of the boldest and most magnanimous in the annals of church history. While still attempting to minister exclusively to the Jewish nation, the council refused to impede the progress of that other branch of the Christian mission whose success meant further difficulty for them from within their own nation. Undoubtedly there was some uncertainty among the council's leaders about details of the decision. Certainly they reached it only after much agonizing. Likewise, there probably remained in the Jerusalem church a recalcitrant group that continued to predict ominous consequences. But the decision was made and the malcontents silenced—at least for a time.

The effects of the council's decision were far-reaching. (1) It freed the Gospel from any necessary entanglement with Judaism and Israelite institutions, though without renouncing the legitimacy of continued Christian activity within them. Thus both Paul's mission to the Gentiles and the various Jewish Christian missions were enabled to progress side-by-side without conflict. (2) Attitudes to Paul within Jewish Christianity were clarified. While some of the Jewish believers probably became even more opposed to Paul, others (e.g., John Mark, see vv.37–39) seem to have become more reconciled to him. Also, some felt happier in a Gentile ministry than at Jerusalem (e.g., Silas; see v.40). (3) The decision of the council had the effect of permanently antagonizing many Jews. From this time onward, the Christian mission within the nation—particularly in and around Jerusalem—faced rough sledding (cf. Ro 11:28). When coupled with the zealotism within the nation during the next two decades, this antagonism proved fatal to the life and ministry of the Jerusalem church.

23–29 With Judas, Silas, Paul, and Barnabas, who were going to Antioch, the Jerusalem church sent a letter, recorded here in Ac 15. The placing of "brothers" in apposition to "the apostles and elders" in the salutation is unusual. But it should probably be understood as reflecting a form of expression used within the Jerusalem congregation, similar to "Men, brothers" (cf. 1:16; 2:29, 37; 15:7, 13; et al.). Likewise, the address "to the Gentile believers in Antioch, Syria and Cilicia" is surprising, for though Paul refers to spending some time in Syria and Cilicia, Luke has not spoken of any mission outside Antioch in these areas. Yet vv.36, 41 assume that churches were established in these areas with Paul's assistance. And 16:4 shows that the content of the letter from the council was meant not only for congregations in the areas listed in 15:23 but that it applied to Gentile believers generally (cf. 15:19; 21:25).

The body of the letter encapsulates the problem confronted by the churches because of the Judaizers' claims and the Jerusalem Council's reaction to them, commending to the churches Barnabas and Paul (cf. comments on 14:14 and 15:12 for this order of their names) and the Jerusalem emissaries Judas and Silas. On the fundamental matter of the theological necessity of circumcision and a Jewish lifestyle for Gentile Christians, the letter rebukes the Judaizers for going beyond their authority and assures the churches that there are no such requirements for salvation. On the practical issues of fellowship between Jewish and Gentile believers in the churches and of preventing needless offense to Jews throughout the empire, the letter asks Gentile Christians to abstain from the four prohibitions mentioned in v.20. The letter closed in a way typical of many contemporary nonliterary papyri.

F. The Reception of the Council's Decision and of the Letter (15:30–16:4)

Luke describes the aftermath of the Jerusalem Council in three vignettes that all relate to the reception of the council's decision and letter in three localities of earlier Gentile outreach: Antioch of Syria (15:30–35), Syria and Cilicia (15:36–41), and the southern part of Galatia (16:1–4). Other items of information are also included, as Luke uses these final scenes of his fourth panel of material to prepare for the extensive outreach of the Gospel through Paul's second and third missionary journeys.

1. At Antioch of Syria (15:30–35)

30–32 At Antioch of Syria the delegation on returning from Jerusalem "gathered the church together and delivered the letter," with Judas and Silas saying "much to encourage and strengthen the brothers." And the believers, Luke tells us, "were glad." Having gained a decided victory in the principal matter of circumcision, Paul and the existing Gentile churches were prepared to accept the four decrees as a modus operandi for reducing friction between two groups of people drawn from two different ways of life. Such an attitude is quite in accord with what Paul himself wrote later in 1Co 9:19–23.

33–35 After some time, Judas and Silas returned to Jerusalem with the commendation of the Antioch believers. Paul and Barnabas, however, remained at Syrian Antioch and joined others in carrying on the ministry there. Later Paul appears to have sent for Silas to accompany him on his missionary journeys (v.40).

2. Disagreement and two missionary teams (15:36–41)

36 Luke now presents Paul as taking the initiative for another missionary journey. To Paul, of course, it was not intended as a new outreach but only a revisiting of believers converted on the first missionary journey. Nevertheless, God was to bring a second missionary journey out of it. This section provides something of a bridge between the completion of the advances reported in panel 4 and the beginning of those reported in panel 5.

37–39 John Mark, Barnabas's cousin (cf. Col 4:10), probably became convinced of the appropriateness of Paul's Gentile policy by the action of the Jerusalem Council, despite earlier qualms about it (see comment on 13:13). Barnabas had evidently called him back to Syrian Antioch to minister in the church there. Barnabas's earlier involvement in the dispute at Antioch showed that his natural sympathies lay principally with Jewish Christians (cf. Gal 2:13), and it was also natural for him to want to take Mark with them in revisiting the churches. Paul, however, for what seem to have been reasons of principle rather than personal ones, did not want to have so unreliable a man with them day after day. The scar tissue of the wounds Paul suffered in establishing his missionary policy was still too tender for him to look favorably on Mark's being with them—particularly if, as we have assumed, Mark was in some way responsible for inciting the Judaizers to action.

The fact that Luke does not gloss over the quarrel between Paul and Barnabas shows his honesty. Yet far from letting the disagreement harm the outreach of the Gospel, God providentially used it to double the missionary force, with Barnabas taking Mark and returning to Cyprus (cf. 13:4–12). Acts tells us nothing more about the mission to Cyprus or the missioners there, though Paul later refers in cordial terms to both Barnabas (cf. 1Co 9:6) and John Mark (cf. Col 4:10; 2Ti 4:11; Phm 24).

40–41 Paul's selection of Silas (or "Silvanus," as he is referred to more formally by his Latinized name in 2Co 1:19; 1Th 1:1; 2Th 1:1; 1Pe 5:12) to accompany him on his return visit to the churches was wise. He had evidently come to appreciate Silas in their contacts at Jerusalem and Syrian Antioch and concluded that he would make a congenial colleague. More than that, Silas was a leader in the Jerusalem congregation (15:22) and was explicitly identified in the Jerusalem letter as one who could speak with authority on the attitude of the Jerusalem church (v.27). He was also, it seems, a Roman citizen who could claim, if need be, the privileges of such citizenship along with Paul (16:37). This was not true of Barnabas. Likewise, Silas was a prophet (15:32), who appears to have been fluent in Greek (15:22, 32) and a helpful amanuensis (1Th 1:1; 2Th 1:1; 1Pe 5:12). Thus Paul and Silas set out with the blessing of the Antioch congregation. The churches in Syria and Cilicia that they revisited and strengthened were presumably founded through the efforts of Paul (15:23, 36). Because of that, they would be receptive to the decision and letter of the Jerusalem Council.

3. Paul adds Timothy to the team in Galatia (16:1–4)

1–2 Pushing on through the Cilician Gates in the Taurus mountains, Paul and Silas came to the Galatian border town of Derbe and then moved on to Lystra. At Lystra he found a young man who was highly spoken of by believers in both Lystra and the neighboring city of Iconium. The Jewish community at Lystra seems to have been small and without influence (cf. comments on 14:8–10). Probably for that reason Timothy's mother, a Jewess, was allowed to marry a Greek. Timothy, however, had never been circumcised. In Jewish law, a child takes the religion of its mother; so Timothy should have been circumcised and raised a Jew. But in Greek law the father dominates in the home. Apparently the Jewish community at Lystra was too weak or lax to interfere with Greek custom. In 2Ti 1:5 Paul speaks of the sincere Jewish faith of Timothy's grandmother Lois and of his mother, Eunice, and 2Ti 3:15 speaks of Timothy's early instruction in the Hebrew Scriptures. Here Eunice is identified as a Jewess as well as a Christian believer, who had probably been converted during the first visit of Paul and Barnabas to Lystra. The Greek implies that her husband was now dead. From Paul's reference to Timothy in 1Co 4:17 as his "son," we may assume that Timothy's conversion to Christ also dates from the proclamation of the Gospel on that first missionary journey.

3–4 Why, after all the discussion in Jerusalem, would Paul circumcise Timothy? Some commentators even question whether Paul actually did this. But while Paul stoutly resisted any imposition of circumcision and the Jewish law upon his Gentile converts (e.g., Titus; see Gal 2:1–5), he himself continued to live as an observant Jew and urged his converts to express their Christian faith through the cultural forms they had inherited (cf. 1Co 7:17–24). As for Timothy, because of his Jewish mother, he was a Jew in the eyes of the Jewish world. Therefore, it was both proper and expedient for Paul to circumcise him. As Paul saw it, being a good Christian did not mean being a bad Jew. Rather, it meant being a fulfilled Jew. Paul had no desire to flout Jewish scruples in his endeavor to bring both Jews and Gentiles to salvation in Christ. Similarly, there is no reason to think he would have refused to deliver the decision of the Jerusalem Council to his Galatian converts and every reason to believe he would—particularly if he had written Galatians to them earlier and was now able to say that the Jerusalem leaders supported his position.

G. A Summary Statement (16:5)

5 This summary statement, concluding a crucial phase of Luke's narrative, is comparable to the summary statements of 6:7; 9:31; 12:24 that culminate their respective panels (cf. also 19:20 and 28:31 later). It stresses the strengthening and growth of the churches as a result of Paul's missionary policy and the response of the Jerusalem church to it.

Panel 5—Wide Outreach Through Two Missionary Journeys (16:6–19:20)

Panel 5 presents the wide outreach of the Christian mission through two further missionary journeys of Paul in the eastern part of the empire. Having described the gradual extension of the Gospel to new groups of people and through a new missionary policy, Luke now shows its entrance into new areas. Notable in this panel are Luke's emphases upon (1) God's direction in and supervision of the Gospel's outreach, (2) Christianity's right to be considered a *religio licita* (see Introduction: Luke's Purposes in Writing Acts), and (3) Paul's circumstantial preaching in terms of proclamation and persuasion. Also of interest is the fact that the missionary outreach was confined to the major cities of the Aegean coastline connected by the main Roman roads, and that at the beginning of this panel we have our first "we" section (16:10–17; cf. 20:5–15; 21:1–18; 27:1–28:16). Temporal references in the panel are fairly general, and even when datable—e.g., the Edict of Claudius (18:2) and Gallio's proconsulate (18:12)—they leave some margin for dispute. Generally, however, the material given here covers the years A.D. 49–56, with the journey into Macedonia and Achaia taking place about 49–52 and the one centered in Ephesus during 53–56.

A. Providential Direction for the Mission (16:6–10)

6 The missionary journeys of Paul reveal an extraordinary combination of strategic planning and sensitivity to the guidance of the Holy Spirit in working out the details of the main goals. This is especially noticeable here. Having revisited the churches at Derbe, Lystra, Iconium, and Pisidian Antioch, Paul evidently expected to follow the Via Sebaste westward to the important coastal city and capital of the Roman province of Asia, Ephesus. But he was "kept by the Holy Spirit" from entering Asia and so continued to travel throughout "the region of Phrygia and Galatia." There is some uncertainty as to what Luke meant by this region. Some think that Paul journeyed into northern Galatia, but there is no linguistic support here for a so-called North Galatian theory. Rather, the juxtaposition of "Phrygia" and "Galatia" must be understood either (1) politically, meaning not the entire province of Galatia but only its Phrygic region, or, possibly, (2) ethnologically and popularly, meaning a district adjoining the region of Phrygia in the southern portion of the Roman province of Galatia where both Phrygian and Celtic dialects could be heard.

The heightening of terminology in vv.6–10 from "the Holy Spirit" to "the Spirit of Jesus" to "God" is not just stylistic but an unconscious expression of the early church's embryonic trinitarian faith. All three terms refer to God by his Spirit giving direction to the mission. But just how the Holy Spirit revealed his will we are not told. Perhaps in one or more instances Silas had a part, for he was a prophet (15:32).

7–8 Mysia was a region in northwest Asia Minor that lacked precise boundaries because it never was an independent political entity. It was generally considered to be bounded by the Aegean Sea on the west; the Hellespont (or Dardanelles), Propontis (or Sea of Marmara), and Bithynia along its northern extremities from west to east; Galatia on the east and southeast; Phrygia to the south; and the area of Lydia to the southwest. It included the historic Aegean seaport of Troas and the site of ancient Troy some ten miles inland.

As Paul's party moved northwest along the borders of Mysian territory, they decided to go on into the Thracian area of Bithynia in order to evangelize the strategic cities and important Black Sea ports there, all of which were interconnected by an elaborate Roman road system. But, Luke tells us, "the Spirit of Jesus would not allow them to" (v.7). Later, Christians in Bithynia were included in the salutation of 1Pe 1:1. But Paul was not directed by God to evangelize there. Instead, the missionary party turned westward again, traveling through Mysia till they reached Troas on the Aegean coast.

9–10 Troas became an important Greek port about 300 B.C. and was named Alexandria Troas. After the break-up of Alexander the Great's short-lived empire, Troas was ruled for a time by the Seleucids from Syrian Antioch, but it soon became an independent city-state. At the mouth of the Dardanelles, it was the pivotal port between the land masses of Europe and Asia Minor and the great waterways of the Aegean and Black Seas.

At Troas Paul received a vision of a Macedonian asking for help. He took this as a divine call to evangelize Macedonia. Many

PAUL'S SECOND MISSIONARY JOURNEY

c. A.D. 49-52   Ac 15:39–18:22

© 1989 The Zondervan Corporation.

commentators have suggested that Paul met Luke at Troas, perhaps initially for medical reasons, and that Luke impressed upon him during their conversations the need for the preaching of the Gospel in Macedonia—an encounter God used in a vision to direct Paul and his colleagues to Macedonia. Whatever secondary means God may have used, Paul and his party responded to it at once by making preparations to leave for Macedonia. Such preparations would have required finding passage on a ship sailing for Neapolis.

Authentic turning points in history are few. But surely among them that of the Macedonian vision ranks high. Because of Paul's obedience at this point, the Gospel went westward; and ultimately Europe and the Western world were evangelized. Christian response to the call of God is never a trivial thing. Indeed, as in this instance, great issues and untold blessings may depend on it.

It is at Troas that the first of the "we" sections of Acts appears (16:10–17). Because (1) this "we" section stops at Philippi, (2) the second "we" section (20:5–15) begins when the missionaries revisit Philippi after the third missionary journey, and (3) the ministry at Philippi receives the greatest attention (thirty verses) in this fifth panel, we may reasonably suppose the narrator implied in "we" was Luke and that he was a resident of Philippi who traveled from Troas to Philippi with Paul and Silas.

B. At Philippi (16:11–40)

Luke devotes more space to Paul's mission in Philippi than he does to any other city on his second and third missionary journeys—and he does this despite the brief stay there. To judge from the "we" sections that end in 16:10–17 and begin again in 20:5–15, it may be that Luke had some part in the founding and growth of the church there.

1. Arrival in the city (16:11–12)

11 Samothrace is an island in the northeastern part of the Aegean Sea, lying between Troas and Philippi. It is the most conspicuous landmark in the North Aegean, for its mountains reach up 5,577 feet. It was a stopover for ships plying their trade in the North Aegean. Neapolis on the northern coast of the Aegean was the port for Philippi, which lay ten miles farther inland. Neapolis was on the Via Egnatia, which ran east to Byzantium and west to Philippi, then to Thessalonica, and finally across the Balkan peninsula to the Adriatic coast.

Since Luke was on board, we have a port-by-port description of the voyage, with specific mention of the time it took—as we do in the other "we" sections (see comment on 16:6–19:20). The wind at this crossing must have favored the travelers, for it took only two days to sail the 156 miles to Neapolis, though the trip in the other direction after the third missionary journey took five days (cf. 20:5).

12 Philippi was situated on a plain bounded by Mount Pangaeus to the north and northeast, with the rivers Strymon and Nestos on either side. Its fame in earlier days came from its fertile plain and gold in the mountains to the north. Philip II of Macedon recognized the city's importance, and in 356 B.C. he established a large Greek colony there. With the subjugation of the Macedonians by Rome in 167 B.C., Philippi became part of the Roman Empire. In 146 B.C. it was included within the reorganized province of Macedonia, whose capital was at Thessalonica. In 42 B.C., the city was designated a Roman colony, meaning that its government was responsible directly to the emperor and not to the provincial administration. Philippi's importance during the NT period, therefore, resulted from its agriculture, its strategic commercial location on both sea and land routes, its still functioning gold mines, and its status as a Roman colony. In addition, it had a famous school of medicine with graduates throughout the then-known world.

Luke's reference to Philippi as "the leading [or first] city of that district of Macedonia" is somewhat confusing. Actually, Amphipolis, the early district capital between 167 and 146 B.C., and Thessalonica, the provincial capital after that, had a more valid claim to that title. Luke's designation of Philippi in this manner probably expresses his pride in his city (though the expression might also mean that is was the leading city only in that particular part of Macedonia).

2. The conversion of Lydia (16:13–15)

13 In Jewish law, a synagogue congregation could be formed only if there were at least ten male heads of households. Failing this, a place of prayer under the open sky and near a river or the sea was to be arranged for. Philippi apparently did not have the quorum and so was without a synagogue. On the Sabbath, therefore, Paul and his companions walked outside the city in search of a Jewish place of prayer, probably heading toward the Gangites River about a mile and a half west of the city. There they found some women gathered for informal worship (see comment on 13:14b–15). The most they could hope for was to hear from a traveling Jewish teacher an exposition or exhortation from Scripture and receive a blessing. Paul and his companions sat down with these women and began to speak to them.

14–15 One of the women was from Thyatira, a city of western Asia Minor. It had been part of the ancient kingdom of Lydia before its incorporation into the Roman province of Asia; hence the woman was called Lydia (or, perhaps, "the Lydian lady"). Thyatira was famous for making purple dyes and for dyeing clothes—industries that were mostly carried on by women at home. Lydia had come to Philippi to carry on her trade. She was a "God-fearer," having doubtless received instruction at a synagogue in her native Thyatira. She was likely either a widow or unmarried, and some of the women gathered for worship were relatives and servants living in her home. As she listened, God opened her heart to the Christian message and "she and the members of her household were baptized." Then she urged the missionary party to stay at her home, which they did.

From such small beginnings the church at Philippi began. To judge from his letter to the Philippians, it was one of Paul's most-loved congregations. Luke, as suggested above, was probably involved in the establishment and growth of this church. Soon, it seems, Lydia's home became the center for Christian outreach and worship in Philippi (cf. 16:40).

3. The demon-possessed girl (16:16–18)

16 One day on their way to the Jewish place of prayer, the missionaries were met by a slave girl possessed by a demonic spirit. Undoubtedly all who knew the girl regarded her as neither fraudulent nor insane but one who could foretell the future. By her fortune-telling, she earned her masters much money.

17–18 As the girl followed Paul and his companions around, she kept on screaming out: "These men are servants of the Most High God, who are telling you the way to be saved" (cf. Mk 1:24; 3:11; 5:7; Lk 4:34, 41; 8:28). This acknowledgment is stated in terms acceptable to the Jewish world and readily understandable to Gentiles. The title "Most High God," while originally a Phoenician ascription for deity, was used by the Hebrews for the Lord their God (cf. Nu 24:16; Ps 78:35; Isa 14:14; et al.) and by the Greeks for Zeus. And the announcement of "salvation"—while for Paul and the Jews referring to deliverance from sin—would have connoted for Gentiles release from the powers governing the fate of humans and of the material world. It was, therefore, cast in terms Gentiles could understand but Paul could build on.

But while the demon-inspired words provided some free publicity for the missionaries and helped gather an audience, when it continued for many days, it became a nuisance. The demon's words were getting more of a hearing than the proclamation of the Gospel! So Paul commanded the evil spirit "in the name of Jesus Christ" to come out of the girl, and the demon left her. Presumably, having been delivered by the power of God, she became a Christian and a church member.

4. Paul and Silas in prison (16:19–34)

19–21 What Paul did for the slave girl was not appreciated by her masters. In exorcising the demon, he had exorcised their source of income. Because of interference with what they claimed as their property rights, and with callous disregard for the girl's welfare, they seized Paul and Silas and dragged them into the marketplace to face the city's authorities. The charge laid was that Paul and Silas were advocating a *religio illicita* and thus disturbing the Pax Romana. But the charge, spoken in terms that appealed to the latent anti-Semitism of the people ("these men are Jews") and their racial pride ("us Romans"), ignited the flames of bigotry and prevented any dispassionate discussion of the issues.

Many have asked why only Paul and Silas were singled out for persecution, with Timothy and Luke left free. Of course, Paul and Silas were the leaders of the missionary party and therefore most open to attack. But we must also remember that Paul and Silas were Jews and probably looked very much like Jews. Timothy and Luke, however, being respectively half-Jewish and fully Gentile (cf. Col 4:14, where Luke is grouped by Paul with his Gentile friends), probably looked Greek in both their features and their dress and therefore were left alone. Anti-Semitism lay very near the surface throughout the Roman Empire. Here it seems to have taken over not only in laying the charge but also in identifying the defendants.

22–24 As a Roman colony, Philippi had a form of government that was independent of the provincial administration headquartered in Thessalonica. There were two chief "magistrates" (vv.20, 22, 35–36, 38), who had "officers" (vv. 35, 38) serving under them to carry out their orders. Jailers commonly were retired army veterans, who could be expected to follow orders and use their military skills as required.

Incited to anti-Semitic fury by the slave girl's owners, the crowd turned on Paul and Silas. The magistrates had them stripped and severely flogged as disturbers of the peace and then ordered them to be jailed. The jailer put them into the innermost cell, fastening their feet in stocks. Though both Paul and Silas were Roman citizens and politically exempt from such treatment (cf. comments on v.37), the frenzy of the mob and the rough justice of the colonial magistrates overrode whatever protestations they may have made. Later when writing to the Christians at Corinth, Paul looked back on this experience as one of the afflictions he suffered as a servant of Christ (2Co 11:23, 25).

25–28 One would expect that after such brutal treatment, Paul and Silas would be bemoaning their plight. Certainly they were suffering pain and shock from the flogging. But about midnight, while Paul and Silas were "praying and singing hymns to God," God suddenly vindicated his servants by sending an earthquake that shook the prison, opened its doors, and loosened the chains of all the prisoners. When the awakened jailer saw the doors open, he surmised the worst. In Roman law a guard who allowed his prisoner to escape was liable to the same penalty the prisoner would have suffered. Thus the jailer drew his sword to kill himself, believing the prisoners had all escaped. But Paul saw him in the doorway and shouted out from within the prison, "Don't harm yourself! We are all here!"

29–30 Since it was midnight, the jailer called for torches to dispel the darkness of the prison. Rushing in, he fell trembling before Paul and Silas, doubtless taking them to be some kind of divine messengers. If he had not heard the shouts of the demon-possessed slave girl (v.17), he undoubtedly had heard from others what she was saying. And now what had happened confirmed her words about Paul and Silas. So he cried out, "Lords [*kyrioi*; GK *3261*; NIV "sirs"; a word that certainly carries a note of adoration here], what must I do to be saved?" His question showed recognition of his spiritual need and opened the way for Paul and Silas to give him the Good News about Jesus Christ.

31–34 What Paul and Silas gave the Philippian jailer was the same Christ-centered Gospel that had been proclaimed since Pentecost: "Believe in the Lord Jesus, and you will be saved—you and your household" (cf. 2:38–39; 3:19–26; 4:12; et al.). But since it was all new to the jailer, the missionaries took time to explain to him and the others of his household "the word of the Lord." To judge by their actions, the jailer and his family believed in Christ and received the Holy Spirit. The jailer washed the wounds of Paul and Silas, probably at a well in the prison courtyard, and there too he and all his family were baptized. Then he brought the missionaries into his home and fed them. "And the whole family," Luke tells us, "was filled with joy, because they had come to believe in God."

5. Paul and Silas leave the city (16:35–40)

35–36 In the morning the magistrates sent the officers to the prison with an order to release the two vagabond Jews. They had probably only wanted to teach them a lesson about the peril of disturbing the peace in a Roman colony and felt that a public flogging and a night in the city's jail would be sufficient to do that. So they ordered the jailer to release Paul and Silas.

37 Paul, however, refused to be dealt with so summarily. Claiming the rights of Roman citizenship for himself and Silas, he demanded that they be shown the courtesy due a citizen and be escorted out of the prison by the magistrates themselves. According to Roman law, a Roman citizen could travel anywhere within Roman territory under the protection of Rome. He was not subject to local legislation unless he consented, and he could appeal to be tried by Rome, not by local authorities, when in difficulty.

Evidence regarding the exercise of this right of appeal is scanty. We do not know, for example, how a citizen who made the claim "I am a Roman" supported his claim then and there. Most of our information regarding these rights comes from Acts itself (cf. 22:25–29; 25:9–12; 26:32; 27:1; 28:16). Nevertheless, it does seem that the law protected a Roman citizen against arbitrary flogging without a trial.

Paul took pride in his Roman citizenship and valued it highly (22:25–28)—a feeling that was doubtless shared by Silas. Just why they didn't assert their rights earlier we can only conjecture. Perhaps the uproar of the mob and the hubbub of the beating kept their protestations from being heard. But now they claimed their rights as Roman citizens—probably not only for their own sakes but also to provide some measure of protection for the few believers meeting at Lydia's home.

38–39 To beat and imprison a Roman citizen without a trial was a serious offense. So when the magistrates heard that Paul and Silas were citizens, they came to apologize for their illegal actions and to escort them out of prison. Then in order to avoid any further embarrassment or opposition from the crowd, they asked Paul and Silas to leave Philippi. Here was one case where Roman officials took action against the Gospel and its messengers. As such, it seems to run counter to Luke's apologetic purpose in Acts (cf. Introduction: Luke's Purposes in Writing Acts). But his point is that the magistrates initially acted in ignorance; and when they came to understand matters more fully, they apologized and did what they could to avoid repetition of the blunder.

40 After leaving the prison, Paul and Silas met with the small body of Christians at the house of Lydia and encouraged them in their new faith. Then they left with Timothy to go westward toward Thessalonica. Apparently, Luke stayed behind at Philippi, for only later (20:5) does the second "we" section begin—again at Philippi. By that time the little congregation that had begun so modestly had grown in size and spirituality; for in the letter Paul later wrote them, he speaks of their "overseers and deacons" (Php 1:1), counsels them as believers growing in maturity, and commends them for their continuing concern for him (cf. Php 2:25–30; 4:10–19).

C. At Thessalonica (17:1–9)

1 Thirty-three miles southwest of Philippi was Amphipolis, at one time the capital of the northern district of Macedonia. Situated on the east bank of the Strymon River, it straddled the Via Egnatia. But though it was larger and more important than Philippi, Paul and his companions "passed through" it. As they continued west-southwest, they also passed through Apollonia some twenty-seven miles beyond Amphipolis. Their desire was to reach Thessalonica, the capital of Macedonia and its largest and most prosperous city, lying another forty miles southwest of Apollonia.

Thessalonica (modern Salonika) was strategically located on the Thermaic Gulf. Straddling the Via Egnatia, it linked the rich agricultural plains of the Macedonian interior with the land and sea routes to the east. When Rome conquered Macedonia in 167 B.C., Thessalonica became the capital of the second of the four administrative districts of the province. With the reorganization of Macedonia into one province in 142 B.C, it became the capital. It was declared a free city in 42 B.C.

As a large commercial and government city of perhaps two hundred thousand, Thessalonica naturally attracted diverse groups of people, including a substantial Jewish contingent (1Th 2:14–16). Paul seems to have looked on it as the strategic center for the spread of the Gospel throughout the Balkan peninsula (1Th 1:7 8). Therefore Paul and Silas—though doubtless in some pain from their recent beating and time in the stocks—pushed on resolutely the hundred miles from Philippi to Thessalonica.

2–3 In portraying the extension of the Gospel to the main cities bordering the Aegean Sea, Luke lays special emphasis on the fact that Paul's preaching consisted of both proclamation and persuasion—interlocking elements of the one act of preaching. He had struck such a note earlier (cf. 13:43), and it will continue to be heard in 17:17; 18:4, 19; 19:8–10; 20:9; 24:25; 26:28; 28:23.

At Thessalonica the missionaries, true to their policy of "to the Jews first, but also to the Gentiles" (cf. comments on 13:46–52), sought out the local synagogue, sure of finding there a prepared audience of both Jews and "God-fearing" Gentiles. During the span of three Sabbath days Paul carefully reasoned from Scripture, attempting to prove that the Messiah had to suffer, die, and rise from the dead. Then he went on to declare: "This Jesus I am proclaiming to you is the Christ." In other words, the preaching of Paul at Thessalonica was a "proclaimed witness"—i.e., a witness to the facts that Jesus of Nazareth is the Christ, that his suffering and resurrection were in accord with the Scriptures, and that through his earthly ministry and living presence men and women can experience the reign of God in their lives. At times miracles accompanied the proclamation.

4 "Some of the Jews were persuaded," but the greater number of those who responded positively to Paul's preaching in the Thessalonian synagogue were "God-fearing" Greeks and "prominent women" (i.e., women of high standing in the city who were the wives of the principal citizens). The Jason mentioned in v.5 as Paul's host was probably one of the Jewish converts; Aristarchus and Secundus, identified as Thessalonians in 20:4, may have also been converted at this time.

5–7 Just as at Antioch, Iconium, and Lystra, the Jews who did not believe the Gospel were incensed at the Gentiles' response to Paul's preaching and with his direct approach to them. So they stirred up a riot. Their plan was to bring Paul and Silas before "the crowd" and "the city officials" on a charge of disturbing the Pax Romana by preaching a *religio illicita* and by advocating another king in opposition to Caesar. But when they could not find the missionaries at Jason's house—evidently because Jason and some others who believed their message had hidden them—they dragged Jason and some other Christian brothers before the politarchs.

As a free city, Thessalonica had its governing assembly of citizens, which is probably what Luke had in mind by the use of the term "crowd" (*demos*; GK *1322*) in v.5. The magistrates of Thessalonica were called "politarchs," a title applied almost exclusively to Macedonian cities. From five inscriptions referring to Thessalonica, it appears that a body of five politarchs ruled the city during the first century A.D.

Certainly the assembly of citizens and the politarchs at Thessalonica would have known of the troubles within the Jewish community at Rome in connection with Christianity and of Claudius's edict of A.D. 49–50 for all Jews to leave that city (see comment on 18:2). Probably the Jewish opponents of the missionaries played upon the fear that such a situation might be duplicated at Thessalonica, unless Paul and Silas were expelled. In addition, from their charge that the missionaries proclaimed "another king" (v.7), it may be inferred that they tried to use Paul's mention of "the kingdom of God" (cf. 14:22; 19:8; 20:25; 28:23, 31) to arouse suspicion that he was involved in anti-imperial sedition. Indeed, it may be for this reason that Paul avoided the use of "kingdom" and "king" in his letters to his converts, lest Gentile imperial authorities misconstrue them to connote opposition to empire and emperor.

8–9 The charges against Paul and Silas and their companions naturally alarmed the Thessalonian politarchs. But apparently they found the evidence for the charges scanty; after all, Paul and Silas could not be found. Therefore, they took what they thought to be a moderate and reasonable course of action. They made Jason and those with him post a bond, assuring them that there would be no further trouble. This probably meant that Paul and Silas had to leave Thessalonica and that their friends promised they would not come back, at least during the term of office of the present politarchs.

When writing his Thessalonian converts a few months later, Paul speaks of many times desiring to visit them again but of being unable to because "Satan stopped us" (1Th 2:18). Likely Paul had in mind that posted bond, and therefore his hands were tied. But though he was unable to return, that did not stop either the spread of the Gospel or the opposition of the Jews (cf. 1Th 1:2–10). Amid all their persecutions and difficulties, the Christians of Thessalonica maintained their faith and witness in a manner that filled Paul with joy (cf. 1Th 3:6–10).

D. At Berea (17:10–15)

10 The bail bond Jason and his friends posted would have been forfeited were Paul and Silas to be found in their homes. So the brothers sent them, together with Timothy, on to Berea, some fifty miles southwest of Thessalonica by way of Pella. A city in the foothills of the Olympian range south of the Macedonian plain, Berea was of little importance historically or politically, though it had a large population in NT times. It also was south of the Via Egnatia, but with access to the eastern coastal road that ran down to Achaia and Athens. On arriving there, Paul and his companions went as usual to the synagogue to proclaim the Good News of salvation in Jesus the Christ.

11–12 Luke gives the Jews at Berea undying fame by characterizing them as being "more noble" (GK *2302*) than the Thessalonian Jews because they tested the truth of Paul's message by the touchstone of Scripture rather than judging it by political and cultural considerations. So they examined the Scriptures daily to see whether what Paul proclaimed was really true, and many believed. Among them was probably Sopater son of Pyrrhus (see 20:4; cf. Ro 16:21). Included among the Berean believers were not only "a number of prominent Greek women" but also "many Greek men"—that is, not just converts from among Gentile "God-fearers," but also converts who had been pagan Gentiles.

13–15 The Thessalonian Jews, on hearing that "the word of God" was being preached at Berea, sent a delegation there to stir up the same opposition as at Thessalonica. Evidently the Berean Christians recognized that not only was Paul not safe at Thessalonica but he was not safe anywhere else in the region, because the Thessalonian Jews had the ear of the provincial authorities. So the Bereans acted immediately as if they were taking Paul to a coastal town to sail for some other country. Having thrown their opponents off the track, they escorted Paul down to the province of Achaia and into Athens, apparently to stay there with some of their relatives. Silas and Timothy remained in Berea since they were not in such danger as Paul. But when those accompanying Paul to Athens returned to Berea, they brought a message from Paul for Silas and Timothy to join him as soon as possible—doubtless because he saw that Athens was another strategic center for proclaiming the Gospel and wanted Silas and Timothy with him.

The movements of Silas and Timothy after Paul left them at Berea are rather difficult to trace, because Luke was not always concerned with details of the minor characters in his narrative and because Paul's references to their activities are somewhat incidental and allusive. But in accord with Paul's instructions, Silas and Timothy rejoined Paul at Athens (1Th 3:1). Then Timothy was sent back to Thessalonica (1Th 3:2). Silas, however, seems to have gone back to Macedonia (cf. 18:5—probably to Philippi, where he received from the young congregation there a gift of money for the support of the missionaries; see Php 4:15). In the meantime, Paul moved from Athens to Corinth (Ac 18:1) and was rejoined there by Silas and Timothy (18:5; 1Th 3:6).

E. At Athens (17:16–34)

Paul's coming to Athens appears to have been intended primarily to escape persecution in Macedonia; preaching in Athens was not part of his original plan. Presumably, when called to Macedonia (16:6–10), he had planned to follow the Via Egnatia all the way to Dyrrhachium, then cross the Adriatic to Italy, and so to Rome. When writing the Christians at Rome some six or seven years later, Paul speaks of having often planned to visit them but being unable to do so (Ro 1:13; 15:22–23). Provincial action in Macedonia appears to have thwarted his plans for a continued mission in Macedonia, and news of Claudius's expulsion of the Jewish community in Rome (A.D. 49–50; see Ac 18:2) would have caused him to change his plans.

But now in Athens, Paul saw rampant idolatry all around him; this compelled him to present the claims of Christ to Jews and "God-fearing" Gentiles in the synagogue on the Sabbath and to whoever would listen in the marketplace on weekdays. As with Jeremiah (cf. Jer 20:9), "the word of God" burned within Paul like a fire in his bones, and he could not keep silent.

1. Inauguration of a ministry (17:16–21)

16 Athens is five miles inland from its port of Piraeus, which is on an arm of the Aegean Sea stretching fifty miles between Attica and the Peloponnesus. It is situated on a narrow plain between Mount Parnes to the north, Mount

Pentelicus to the east, and Mount Hymettus to the southeast. When the Persians tried to conquer Greece in the fifth century B.C., Athens played a prominent part in resisting them. It reached its zenith under Pericles (495–429 B.C.); and during the last fifteen years of his life, the Parthenon, numerous temples, and other splendid buildings were built. Literature, philosophy, science, and rhetoric flourished; and Athens attracted intellectuals from all over the world. Politically it became a democracy.

Culturally and intellectually, Athens remained supreme for centuries, with such figures as Socrates, Plato, Aristotle, Epicurus, and Zeno living there. In 338 B.C. Philip II of Macedonia conquered Athens, but the conquest only served to spread Athenian culture and learning into Asia and Egypt through his son, Alexander the Great. Even when the Romans conquered Athens in 146 B.C., it continued as the cultural and intellectual center of the world. Rome also left the city free politically.

When Paul came to Athens, its population probably numbered no more than ten thousand. Yet it had a glorious past on which it continued to live. Its temples and statuary were related to the worship of the Greek pantheon, and its culture was pagan. Therefore Paul, with his Jewish abhorrence of idolatry, could not but find the culture of Athens spiritually repulsive.

17 In spite of not wanting to begin a mission in Athens until Silas and Timothy came from Macedonia, Paul could not keep from proclaiming the Good News about Jesus the Messiah when he attended the synagogue on the Sabbath. There he "reasoned" (GK *1363*) with the Jews and God-fearing Gentiles. He also presented Jesus in the marketplace (the agora, i.e., the forum of the city and the center of Athenian life) every day to all who would listen.

18 Athens was the home of the rival Epicurean and Stoic schools of philosophy. Epicurus (342–270 B.C.) held that pleasure was the chief goal of life, with the pleasure most worth enjoying being a life of tranquillity free from pain, disturbing passions, superstitious fears, and anxiety about death. He did not deny the existence of gods but argued in deistic fashion that they took no interest in the lives of people. Zeno (340–265 B.C.) was the founder of Stoicism. His teaching centered on living harmoniously with nature and emphasized one's rational abilities and individual self-sufficiency. Theologically, he was essentially pantheistic and thought of God as "the World-soul."

Epicureanism and Stoicism represented the popular Gentile alternatives for dealing with the plight of humanity and for coming to terms with life apart from the biblical revelation and God's work in Jesus Christ. When the followers of Epicurus and Zeno heard Paul speaking in the agora, they began to dispute with him. Some in their pride declared him to be a "babbler" (i.e., a ne'er-do-well; GK *5066*). Others, however, thought Paul was advocating foreign gods, probably mistaking *Anastasis* ("resurrection"; GK *414*) as the goddess consort of a god named Jesus.

19–20 The Areopagus (meaning "Council of Ares"; GK *740*) reaches back to legendary antiquity. Presumably it first met at Athens on the Hill of Ares, northwest of the Acropolis, for murder trials. Early descriptions of processions in ancient Greek city-states, however, depict the Areopagus of the cities as always heading the column of dignitaries, which suggests that the "Court" or "Council of Ares" was the senate or city council of a Greek city-state. In Roman times it was still the chief judicial body of the city and exercised jurisdiction in such matters as religion and education.

It was before this council that the followers of Epicurus and Zeno brought Paul—probably half in jest and half in derision, and certainly not seeking an impartial inquiry after truth. The city fathers, however, took their task seriously because the fame of Athens rested on its intellectual ferment and on the interplay of competing philosophies. So we should doubtless understand Paul's appearance before the Athenian Council of Ares as being for the purpose of explaining his message before those in control of affairs in the city so that he might either receive the freedom of the city to preach or be censored and silenced.

21 Luke's comment about the Athenians "doing nothing but talking about and listening to the latest ideas" is paralleled in the evaluation of his fellow Athenians by Cleon, a fifth-century B.C. politician and general, and by Demosthenes (384–322 B.C.).

2. Paul's address before the Council of Ares (17:22–31)

22–23 Paul does not begin his address by referring to Jewish history or by quoting the Jewish Scriptures, as he did in the synagogue of Pisidian Antioch (cf. 13:16–41). He knew it would be futile to refer to a history no one knew or argue from fulfillment of prophecy no one accepted as authoritative. Nor does he develop his argument from the God who gives rain and crops and provides food, as he did at Lystra (cf. 14:15–17). Instead, he took for his point of contact an altar he had seen in the city with the inscription "To an Unknown God." The presence of such altars is attested by other Greek writers, so it is not surprising that Paul came across such an altar in the city.

As with the other speeches in Acts, this one is a précis by Luke, in which he summarizes the basic content of what Paul said. Luke gives us another illustration of how Paul began on common ground with his hearers and sought to lead them from it to accept the work and person of Jesus as the apex of God's redemptive work for humanity.

24–28 The substance of the Athenian address concerns the nature of God and the responsibility of human beings to God. Contrary to all pantheistic and polytheistic notions, God is the one, Paul says, who has created the world and everything in it; he is the Lord of heaven and earth (cf. Ge 14:19, 22). He does not live in temples "made by hands," nor is he dependent for his existence upon anything he has created. Rather, he is the source of life and breath and everything else humanity possesses. While Paul's argument can be paralleled at some points by the paganism of his day, its content is decidedly biblical (cf. 1Ki 8:27; Isa 66:1–2).

Contrary to the Athenians' boast that they had originated from the soil of their Attic homeland and therefore were not like other people, Paul affirms the oneness of humankind in their creation by the one God and their descent from a common ancestor. And contrary to the "deism" that permeated the philosophies of the day, he proclaimed that this God has determined specific times for humans and "the exact places where they should live," so that they would seek him and find him.

In support of this teaching about humankind, Paul quotes two maxims from Greek poets. The first ("For in him we live and move and have our being") comes from the Cretan poet Epimenides (c. 600 B.C.); the second ("for we are his offspring"), from the Cilician poet Aratus (c. 315–240 B.C.). By such maxims, Paul is not suggesting that God is to be thought of in terms of the Zeus of Greek polytheism or Stoic pantheism. He is rather arguing that the poets his hearers recognized as authorities have to some extent corroborated his message. In his search for a measure of common ground with his hearers, he is, so to speak, disinfecting and rebaptizing the poets' words for his own purposes. But despite its form, Paul's address was thoroughly biblical and Christian in its content.

29–31 The climax of the address focuses on the progressive unfolding of redemption and

The picture on the left shows the ruins of the temple of Zeus in Athens, with the Acropolis in the background. In the foreground of the other picture is Mars' Hill, from where, perhaps, Paul delivered his address to the Council of Ares.

the apex of that redemption in Jesus Christ. Since we are God's "offspring" (GK *1169*)—not in a pantheistic sense but in the biblical sense of being created in God's image—we should not, Paul insists, think of deity in terms of gold, silver, or stone. All that idolatrous ignorance was overlooked by God in the past (cf. 14:16; Ro 3:25) because God has always been more interested in repentance than judgment. Nevertheless, in the person and work of Jesus, God has acted in such a manner as to make idolatry particularly heinous. To reject Jesus, therefore, is to reject the personal and vicarious intervention of God on behalf of humankind and to open oneself up God's future judgment meted out by the very one rejected in the present. And God himself has authenticated all this by raising Jesus from the dead.

3. The response to Paul's address (17:32–34)

32 While the resurrection of Jesus from the dead was the convincing proof to the early Christians and Paul that "God was reconciling the world to himself in Christ" (2Co 5:19), to the majority of Athenians it was the height of folly. The tragic poet Aeschylus (525–456 B.C.), for example, made the god Apollo say, "When the dust has soaked up a man's blood, once he is dead, there is no resurrection." If Paul had talked about the immortality of the soul, he would have gained the assent of most of his audience except the Epicureans. Instead, outright scorn was the response of many of his hearers. Others, probably with more politeness than curiosity or conviction, suggested that they would like to hear Paul on the subject at another time.

33–34 Paul obviously failed to convince the council of the truth of his message, and he evidently failed as well to gain the right to propagate his views. He could tell from this first meeting that sentiment was against him. Some, of course, did believe, for God always has his few in even the most difficult of situations. Among them were Dionysius, who was himself a member of the Council of Ares, and a woman named Damaris. But because no action had been taken to approve Paul's right to continue teaching in the city, his hands were legally tied. With a vast territory yet to be entered and a great number of people yet to be reached, Paul decided to move on. We hear of no church at Athens in the apostolic age; and when Paul speaks of "the first converts in Achaia," it is to "the household of Stephanas" in Corinth that he refers (1Co 16:15).

Many have claimed that Paul's failure at Athens stemmed largely from a change in his style of preaching and that later on at Corinth he repudiated it (cf. 1Co 1:18–2:5). He spoke, they charge, about providence and being "in God" but forgot the message of grace and being "in Christ"; about creation and appealed to the Greek poets but did not refer to redemption or revelation; about world history but not salvation history; about resurrection but not the cross. We should remember, however, that going to Athens was not part of Paul's original missionary strategy. Nor should we minimize the working of God's Spirit or Paul's message because only a few responded. Still, the outreach of the Gospel at Athens in overall terms must be judged a failure. But the reason for this lay more in the attitude of the Athenians themselves than in Paul's approach or in what he said.

F. At Corinth (18:1–17)

Paul's coming to Corinth was "in weakness and fear, and with much trembling" (1Co 2:3). Though he was directed through a vision to minister in Macedonia (cf. Ac 16:9–10), the mission there had not gone at all as he had expected. Nor had his initial attempt in Achaia provided him with any reason to hope for a change in his fortunes. So he must have traveled from Athens to Corinth in a dejected mood, wondering what worse could happen and why God had allowed matters to fall out so badly. Also, he was almost sick with anxiety over the state of the Thessalonian converts whom he had been forced to leave with the threat of persecution hanging over them (cf. 1Th 2:17–3:5). All this drove Paul into depression. He was only human, and he found that his emotions affected his spiritual well-being and his work. Perhaps at this time he prayed repeatedly for deliverance from his "thorn in the flesh," to which the Lord responded, "My grace is sufficient for you, for my power is made perfect in weakness" (cf. 2Co 12:7–10).

At Corinth the exact situation is difficult to ascertain, mainly because in his letters to the Corinthians Paul provides so much allusive material about his relations with them, while Luke gives so little in Acts. One reason for this problem is the wide difference of purpose between Paul and Luke in their written materials: Paul's concern was pastoral and Luke's apologetic. Luke's main interest here in Ac 18 is the proceedings before Gallio (vv.12–17), in order (1) to demonstrate that one of the wisest of the Roman proconsuls had declared Christianity to be a *religio licita* and (2) to warn that if Rome began to persecute the church, it would be acting contrary to Gallio, a ruler renowned for his urbanity and wit.

1. Arrival at Corinth (18:1–4)

1 Corinth was on a plateau overlooking the isthmus connecting central Greece to the north with the Peloponnesus to the south. It was built on the north side of the Acrocorinth, an acropolis rising precipitously to 1,886 feet and providing an almost impregnable fortress for the city. To the east was the port of Cenchrea leading out to the Aegean Sea, and to the west, the port of Lechaeum opening to the Adriatic. Smaller ships were actually dragged over wooden rollers across the isthmus for the three and one-half miles between Cenchrea and Lechaeum in order to avoid the long and dangerous trip around the southern tip of the Peloponnesus; cargoes of larger ships were carried overland from port to port.

Because of its strategic land and sea location, Corinth had become a prosperous city-state in the eighth century B.C., reaching its zenith during the seventh and sixth centuries with a population of approximately two hundred thousand free men and five hundred thousand slaves. In 338 B.C. the city was captured by Philip II of Macedon, who made it the center of his Hellenic League, and after Alexander the Great died, it became a leading member of the Achaian League of Greek city-states. In 196 B.C. Corinth was captured by the Romans and declared a free city. In 146 B.C., however, it was destroyed as retribution for the leading part it played in the revolt of the Achaian League against Rome. Julius Caesar decreed in 46 B.C. that it should be rebuilt; in 27 B.C. it became the capital of the Roman province of Achaia.

The population of Corinth in NT times was probably over two hundred thousand, made up of local Greeks, freedmen from Italy, Roman army veterans, businessmen and governmental officials, and Orientals from the Levant—including a large number of Jews. Thanks to its commercial advantages, the city greatly prospered. But along with its wealth and luxury, there was immorality of every kind. Beginning with the fifth century B.C., the verb "to corinthianize" meant to be sexually immoral. Corinth was also the center for the worship of the goddess Aphrodite, whose temple at one time boasted of a thousand sacred prostitutes and crowned the Acrocorinth. Many other pagan shrines, such as those built to Melicertes (the god of sailors), Apollo, and Asclepius (the god of healing), were also located there.

2–3 Entering this large and thriving city, Paul probably asked a passerby where he could find a master tentmaker or leather worker to seek a job from so that he could support himself. On his missionary journeys Paul earned his living in this occupation (cf. 20:34; 1Co 9:1–18; 2Co 11:7–12). So he came in contact with the Jewish Christian couple Aquila and Priscilla, with whom he lived and worked, presumably alongside other journeymen.

Aquila was a native of Pontus, a region in northern Asia Minor on the south shore of the Black Sea. Priscilla is the diminutive of the more formal name Prisca. Since Priscilla is often listed before her husband (18:18–19, 26; Ro 16:3; 2Ti 4:19), we may conclude that she came from a higher social class than her husband or was in some way considered more important. Perhaps Aquila was a former Jewish slave who became a freedman in Rome and married a Jewess connected with the Roman family Prisca, which possessed citizenship rights. Together they owned a tentmaking and leather-working firm, with branches of the business at Rome, Corinth, and Ephesus (see texts listed above).

Lately Aquila and Priscilla had been forced to leave Rome because of the Edict of Claudius, an expulsion order proclaimed during the ninth year of Emperor Claudius's reign (i.e., January 25, A.D. 49 to January 24, 50). It was directed against the Jews in Rome to put down the riots arising within the Jewish community there "at the instigation of Chrestus" (according to the Roman historian Suetonius). Many take this to be a reference to Christ (Gk. *Christos*), where the dispute in the Jewish community was between those who accepted his messiahship and those did not. We do not know whether Aquila and Priscilla had any part in the riots—either as agitators or victims.

4 While working with Aquila and Priscilla, Paul attended the local synagogue every Sabbath. There, Luke tells us, "he reasoned" (GK *1363*) with those gathered, "trying to persuade" both Jews and Gentiles. But his ministry during those weeks seems to have been relatively unobtrusive, probably conforming to the kind of witness Aquila and Priscilla were already carrying on among the Jews.

2. An eighteen-month ministry (18:5–11)

5 The coming of Silas and Timothy to Corinth altered the situation for Paul. They brought good news about the Christians at Thessalonica (cf. 1Th 3:6) and a gift of money from the congregation at Philippi (cf. 2Co 11:9; Php 4:14–15). The news from Thessalonica was better than Paul dared expect, and it greatly comforted and encouraged him (cf. 1Th 3:7–10)—though it also told of a slanderous campaign started against him outside the congregation (1Th 2:3–6) and of some perplexity within it concerning the return of Christ (1Th 4:13–5:11). The money from Philippi was especially welcome at this time, for Paul was now able to devote himself "exclusively to preaching." His purpose was to proclaim the Good News to the Jews of the synagogue that Jesus is "the Christ."

In response to the report from Thessalonica, Paul wrote 1 Thessalonians, in which are interwoven (1) commendation for growth, zeal, and fidelity; (2) encouragement in the face of local persecution; (3) defense of his motives against hostile attack; (4) instruction regarding holiness of life; (5) instruction about the coming of the Lord; and (6) exhortation to steadfastness and patience. Some weeks later, on learning of continued confusion at Thessalonica regarding the return of Christ and the believer's relation to it, he wrote 2 Thessalonians. In that second letter, while acknowledging that the church lives in eager expectation of the Lord's return, Paul insists that imminency must not be construed to mean immediacy but is rather the basis for dogged persistence in doing right.

6–7 The ministry at Corinth followed the pattern set at Pisidian Antioch (cf. 13:46–52): initial proclamation in the synagogue, rejection by the majority of Jews, and then a direct outreach to Gentiles. In solemn biblical style (cf. Ne 5:13), Paul "shook out his clothes"—an act symbolizing repudiation of the Jews' opposition, exempting himself from further responsibility for them (cf. 13:51), and protesting against what he considered the Jews' "blasphemy" (NIV, "became abusive"; GK *1059*; cf. 13:45; 26:11). So leaving the synagogue, he went next door to the house of Titius Justus, a "God-fearing" Gentile who was receiving instruction at the synagogue. He invited Paul to make his home the headquarters for his work in Corinth, presumably because he believed Paul's message. The house of Titius Justus therefore became the first meeting place of the Corinthian church. The first name of this person may have been Gaius, for in Ro 16:23 Paul says that he and the whole church at Corinth enjoyed Gaius's hospitality. In 1Co 1:14 Paul also speaks of a Gaius whom he personally baptized as he began his Christian ministry in Corinth.

8 One of the first to accept Paul's message at Corinth was Crispus, the leader of the synagogue, who, together with his whole household, "believed in the Lord." He was certainly one of the most prominent believers, and his conversion must have made a great impact and led to other conversions. Paul lists him first in 1Co 1:14–16 among the few that he had baptized.

9–10 Paul had come to Corinth in a dejected mood, burdened by the problems in Macedonia and his dismissal at Athens. Of course, he had been encouraged by the reports and the gift brought by Silas and Timothy, and he was beginning to witness a significant response to his ministry. But a pattern had developed in his Galatian and Macedonian journeys of a promising start, followed by opposition strong enough to force him to leave. Undoubtedly he was beginning to wonder whether this pattern would be repeated at Corinth. So one night God graciously gave Paul a vision in which "the Lord" (GK *3261*; evidently Jesus, as in 23:11) encouraged him not to be afraid but to keep on, assured him of his presence and of suffering no harm, and told him that many "people" in the city were to be Christ's own. Here was one of those critical periods in Paul's life when he received a vision strengthening him for what lay ahead (see also 23:11; 27:23–24). In this case, it was confirmed by the ensuing Gallio incident.

11 With such a promising start and encouraged by the vision, Paul continued to minister at Corinth for a total of eighteen months, during which time he taught the message about salvation in Jesus. This period probably stretched from the fall of A.D. 50 to the spring of 52, as can be determined from the story about Gallio (vv.12–17).

3. Before the proconsul Gallio (18:12–17)

12–13 The promise given Paul in the vision was that he would be protected from harm at Corinth, not that he would be free from difficulties or attack. As more and more people responded to Paul's preaching, his Jewish opponents attacked him and laid a charge against him. This occurred, Luke says, "while Gallio was proconsul of Achaia." From what we know of Roman history, Luke is amazingly accurate in the words he uses to designate the various governing officials of Roman provinces.

Gallio was the son of Marcus Annaeus Seneca, the distinguished Spanish rhetorician (50 B.C.–A.D. 40). He was born in Cordova at the beginning of the Christian Era and named Marcus Annaeus Novatus. On coming to Rome with his father during the reign of Claudius (A.D. 41–54), he was adopted by the Roman rhetorician Lucius Junius Gallio, and thereafter bore the name of his adoptive father. He was renowned for his personal charm. An inscription at Delphi mentions Gallio as being proconsul of Achaia during the period of Claudius's twenty-sixth acclamation as imperator—that is, during the first seven months of A.D. 52. Proconsuls entered office in the senatorial provinces on July 1, and therefore Gallio became proconsul of Achaia on July 1, 51, but only for a brief period of time.

Paul seems to have been preaching in Corinth for eight or nine months before Gallio came to Achaia as proconsul (i.e., from the fall of 50 to July 1, 51). When he took office, the Jews decided to try out the new proconsul. They brought Paul before him on a charge that he was preaching a *religio illicita* and therefore acting contrary to Roman law.

14–16 The word "law" (GK 3795) in v.13 is somewhat ambiguous. Undoubtedly when it was first used by Paul's antagonists in their synagogue, it referred to God's law against which they were convinced Paul was speaking. But at the proconsul's forum, they meant "law" to be understood as Roman law, which they charged Paul was breaking. Gallio, however, after hearing their charges, was not at all convinced that this was true. For him the squabble was an intramural one about "a word [NIV, words; GK 3364] and names and their own law"—which doubtless means a squabble concerning "a message," "names" (having to do with an expected Messiah), and particular interpretations of the Jewish law. Gallio's responsibility was to judge civil and criminal cases, not to become an arbitrator of religious disputes. What Paul was preaching, in his view, was simply a variety of Judaism that did not happen to suit the leaders of the Jewish community at Corinth but which was not for that reason to be declared *religio illicita*. Thus he did not need to hear Paul's defense but ejected the plaintiffs from the forum as not having a case worth being heard by a proconsul.

The importance of Gallio's decision was profound. Luke highlights it in his account of Paul's ministry at Corinth and makes it the apex of all that took place on Paul's second missionary journey. No Roman authority had yet repudiated Christianity's claim to share in the *religio licita* status of Judaism—neither in Macedonia nor in Athens. If Gallio had accepted the Jewish charge and found Paul guilty of the alleged offense, provincial governors everywhere would have had a precedent, and Paul's ministry would have been severely restricted. As it was, Gallio's refusal to act in the matter was tantamount to the recognition of Christianity as a *religio licita*; and the decision of so eminent a Roman proconsul would carry weight wherever the issue arose again. Later, in the sixties, Rome's policy toward both Judaism and Christianity changed. But for the coming decade, the Christian message could be proclaimed in the provinces of the empire without fear of coming into conflict with Roman law.

17 Taking their cue from the snub that Gallio gave the leaders of the Jewish community, the crowd at the forum—in an outbreak of the anti-Semitism that always lay near the surface in the Greco-Roman world—took Sosthenes, the synagogue ruler, and beat him. Gallio, however, turned a blind eye to what was going on, evidently because he wanted to teach a lesson to those who would waste his time with such trivialities.

G. An Interlude (18:18–28)

The ministry at Corinth proceeded without any legal hindrance and with considerable success for some nine months after Gallio's decision. In the spring of 52, however, Paul left Corinth to return to Jerusalem and then to Syrian Antioch—primarily to complete a vow at Jerusalem he had taken earlier. In vv.18–23 Luke briefly summarizes Paul's route. And in vv.24–28 he uses this interlude in his portrayal of the advance of the Good News to introduce Apollos (cf. 1Co 3:5–9; 4:6–7; 16:12).

1. Paul's return to Palestine-Syria (18:18–23)

18 Paul now decided to leave Corinth, sail for Jerusalem, and then go on to Syrian Antioch. As he set out, he had his hair cut "because of a vow he had taken." Paul had apparently earlier taken a Nazirite vow that had now ended; such a vow had to be fulfilled at Jerusalem, where the hair would be presented to God and sacrifices offered. For one who thought of himself as a Jewish Christian (2Co 11:22; cf. Ro 9–11) and who at the conclusion of three missionary journeys to the Gentile world could still insist that he was "a Pharisee, the son of a Pharisee" (Ac 23:6; cf. 26:5), such an action should not be thought strange. As a Gentile writing to Gentiles, however, Luke felt no need to explain this distinctly Jewish practice.

19 Boarding a ship at Cenchrea, Paul crossed to Ephesus, the major commercial center and capital of the Roman province of Asia. With him were Aquila and Priscilla, his hosts at Corinth, who were either transferring their business from Corinth to Ephesus or leaving their Corinthian operation in charge of a manager in order to open a new branch at Ephesus. What happened to Silas and Timothy during this time, we do not know. They may have remained at Corinth to carry on the ministry there. Or perhaps they went with Paul to Jerusalem, then to Antioch in Syria, and back to Ephesus.

On arriving at Ephesus, Aquila and Priscilla set up their business in the city. There they were to remain for four or five years, hosting a congregation of believers in their home and sending their greetings back to their Corinthian friends in one of Paul's letters (cf. 1Co 16:19). They were probably there during Demetrius's riot (cf. 19:23–41), even risking their lives to protect Paul (cf. Ro 16:4). Sometime after Claudius's death in A.D. 54, they returned to Rome (cf. Ro 16:3). Paul, having wanted earlier to minister at Ephesus (cf. 16:6), went to the synagogue and "reasoned" with the Jews gathered there. Though it was not the Sabbath, he knew he could find an audience in the synagogue and probably desired to "test the waters" in anticipation of his later return.

20–21 In the synagogue at Ephesus, Paul found a receptive audience. But though they encouraged him to stay, he seems to have felt that fulfilling his vow at Jerusalem took priority over everything else. Nevertheless, he promised to return, if it were in the will of God. And with a heart lightened by the prospect of a future ministry at Ephesus, he sailed for Jerusalem.

22 Paul probably booked passage for Caesarea, the port city of Jerusalem since the time of Herod the Great (cf. comments on 10:1). From Caesarea, he "went up" to Jerusalem, some sixty-five miles southeast. While the name "Jerusalem" does not appear in the text, it is certainly implied by the expressions "went up" and "went down," and also by the absolute use of the term "the church." At Jerusalem, then, he met with the mother church. In addition, he undoubtedly entered into a thirty-day program of purification for his Nazirite vow, after which he presented his shorn hair to God in thanksgiving and offered sacrifices. Then he "went down" to Antioch of Syria, some three hundred miles north, reporting to and ministering within the church that originally commissioned him to reach the Gentiles (13:1–4).

23 Paul remained at Syrian Antioch probably from the summer of 52 through the spring of 53. Then, on what was to be his third missionary journey, he set out for Ephesus some fifteen hundred miles to the west, revisiting the churches throughout "the region of Galatia and Phrygia" and "strengthening all the disciples." Once again, Luke is probably referring to the Phrygian region of Galatia or some district in southern Galatia where both Phrygian and Celtic dialects could be heard (cf. comments on 16:6). He strengthened the Christian disciples in the areas surrounding Pisidian Antioch, Iconium, Lystra, and Derbe.

2. Apollos at Ephesus and Corinth (18:24–28)

24–26 Between the time of Paul's stopover at Ephesus (18:19–21) and his return to the city on his third missionary journey (19:1ff.), Apollos came to Ephesus. A native of Alexandria, he was a highly educated man and possessed a thorough knowledge of the Jewish Scriptures. Somewhere and somehow he had received instruction about Jesus, and to that extent he knew the Gospel "accurately" and "spoke with great fervor" concerning Jesus. When Priscilla and Aquila heard Apollos in the synagogue, they recognized some deficiencies in his understanding of the Christian message. So they invited him to their home and explained "the way of God" to him "more accurately."

Apollos's knowledge of Jesus seems to have come through disciples of John the Baptist, perhaps when he was in Alexandria. Presumably he knew that Jesus of Nazareth was the Messiah and knew something of Jesus' earthly ministry, but that is all. When instructed further by Priscilla and Aquila, Apollos readily accepted all God had done in the death and resurrection of Jesus and in sending the Holy Spirit at Pentecost.

27–28 A number of people who identified themselves in some way with the Gospel were at Ephesus before Paul began to minister there—people like Priscilla and Aquila who understood clearly, like Apollos whose understanding was growing, or like those mentioned in 19:1–7, 13–16, whose faith was to some extent deviant. When Apollos desired to visit Achaia, apparently on behalf of the Gospel, the Christians of Ephesus encouraged him and sent along a letter of commendation, probably written by Priscilla and Aquila, to the believers at Corinth. There he vigorously debated with the Jews and showed from the OT that Jesus was the Messiah. People in the Corinthian church obviously thought highly of him, as Paul also did later (see 1Co 1–4).

H. At Ephesus (19:1–19)

The third missionary journey of Paul was chiefly devoted to an extended ministry at Ephesus, the city he apparently hoped to reach at the start of his second journey. On his brief visit there less than a year before, it had shown a real response to the Gospel (18:19–21). Luke's account of the ministry at Ephesus is abbreviated, with a short summary of only five verses (vv.8–12) sandwiched between two striking vignettes of a deviant kind of faith (vv.1–7, 13–19). In all, Paul's Ephesian ministry lasted about three years, from A.D. 53 through 56.

1. Twelve men without the Spirit (19:1–7)

1 Ephesus was on the western coast of Asia Minor, at the mouth of the Cayster River and between the Koressos mountain range and the Aegean Sea. It was founded in the twelfth or eleventh century B.C. by Ionian colonists from Athens as a gateway to the vast resources of the Asian steppes. In 334 B.C. Alexander the Great captured it at the start of his "drive to the East." From Alexander's death to 133 B.C. it was ruled by the Pergamum kings. With the inevitability of a Roman takeover, Attalus III, the last of these kings, willed the city to Rome at his death; and Ephesus was made the capital of the newly formed Roman province of Asia.

Ephesus relied upon two important assets for its wealth and vitality. The first was its position as a center of trade, linking the Greco-Roman world with the rich hinterland of western Asia Minor. But because of excessive lumbering, charcoal burning, and overgrazing the land, topsoils slipped into streams, streams were turned into marshes, and storm waters raced to the sea laden with silt that choked the river's mouth. The Pergamum kings promoted the maintenance of the harbor facilities at Ephesus, and Rome followed suit. But it was a losing battle against the unchecked erosion of the hinterland. In Paul's day, the zenith of Ephesus's commercial power was long since past.

The second factor the life of Ephesus depended on was the worship of Artemis, the multibreasted goddess of fertility whose temple was one of the Seven Wonders of the ancient world. King Croesus of nearby Lydia (reigned 564–546 B.C.) had built the first temple to Artemis one and a half miles northeast of Ephesus. It was rebuilt on the same site in the fourth century B.C. after a fire, its size being almost four times that of the Parthenon at Athens. With the decline of its commerce, the prosperity of Ephesus became more and more dependent on the tourist and pilgrim trade associated with the temple and cult of Artemis. Around it swarmed all sorts of tradesmen and hucksters who made their living by supplying visitors with food and lodging, dedicatory offerings, and souvenirs. The temple of Artemis was also a major treasury and bank of the ancient world, where merchants, kings, and even cities made deposits, and where their money could be kept safe under the protection of deity. At the time of Paul's arrival, the people of Ephesus were becoming conscious of the precariousness of their position as a commercial and political center of Asia.

After revisiting the churches of Galatia (cf. 18:23), Paul "took the road through the interior" and came to Ephesus. He arrived after Apollos had left for Corinth, entering the city probably in the summer of 53. There he found "about twelve men" (v.7) who professed to be Christian "disciples," but in whom Paul discerned something amiss.

2–3 The question Paul put to the twelve, "Did you receive the Holy Spirit when you believed," suggests two things: (1) that he assumed they were truly Christians, since they professed to believe; and (2) that he held that true faith and the reception of the Holy Spirit always went together. These two assumptions caused Paul some difficulty when he met these twelve men, for something in their life indicated that one or the other assumption was wrong. When they answered his question by saying, "We have not even heard that there is a Holy Spirit," he knew the second assumption was not in error. So he asked further about the first one and found that they claimed to have been baptized only with "John's baptism."

The account is extremely difficult to interpret, principally because it is so brief. Probably these twelve men thought of John the Baptist as the height of God's revelation—perhaps even as the Messiah himself (cf. Jn 1:19–34; 2:22–36, which counters such thinking). Presumably a John-the-Baptist sect existed within Jewish Christian circles in Asia in the first century (cf. Eph 4:5). As in any such group, some (such as Apollos; see Ac 18:24–26) would have appreciated John the Baptist and yet looked forward to the greater fulfillment of which he spoke; others (such as the twelve men here whom Paul met in Ephesus) would have stayed in their devotion to the Baptist himself without any real commitment to Jesus.

4–7 Despite their being known as disciples, Paul preached Jesus to the men as he would to any Jew. "John's baptism," he said, "was a baptism of repentance" that pointed beyond itself and the Baptist to "the one coming after him"—that is, to Jesus. So on their acceptance of Jesus as the focus of Christian faith, they were baptized "into the name of the Lord Jesus." Then Paul laid his hands on them, and they received the Holy Spirit and evidenced the same signs of the Spirit's presence as the first believers did at Pentecost—namely, tongues and prophecy. Doubtless in Paul's mind they were not rebaptized but baptized into Christ once and for all.

2. A summary of the apostle's ministry (19:8–12)

8–10 The ministry of Paul at Ephesus lasted approximately three years (cf. 20:31). It is remarkable how concisely Luke summarizes this extensive period—though perhaps not so remarkable if we may assume from the absence of the pronoun "we" that Luke was not himself an eyewitness of the events here narrated. The conciseness of the passage is particularly notable when compared with Luke's expansive, anecdotal treatments of the ministry at Philippi (cf. 16:10ff.) and the return journey to Jerusalem (cf. 20:5ff.), where he was an eyewitness.

In the synagogue at Ephesus, Paul argued "persuasively about the kingdom of God." He was speaking to those who had earlier received him favorably (cf. 18:19–21), and the three-month hearing they gave him was one of the longest he had in any synagogue. When opposition to "the Way" arose within the synagogue, he withdrew and continued to minister for two more years at the lecture hall of Tyrannus. This was probably the hall of a local philosopher named Tyrannus ("Tyrant") or one rented out to traveling philosophers by a landlord of that name. Since it is

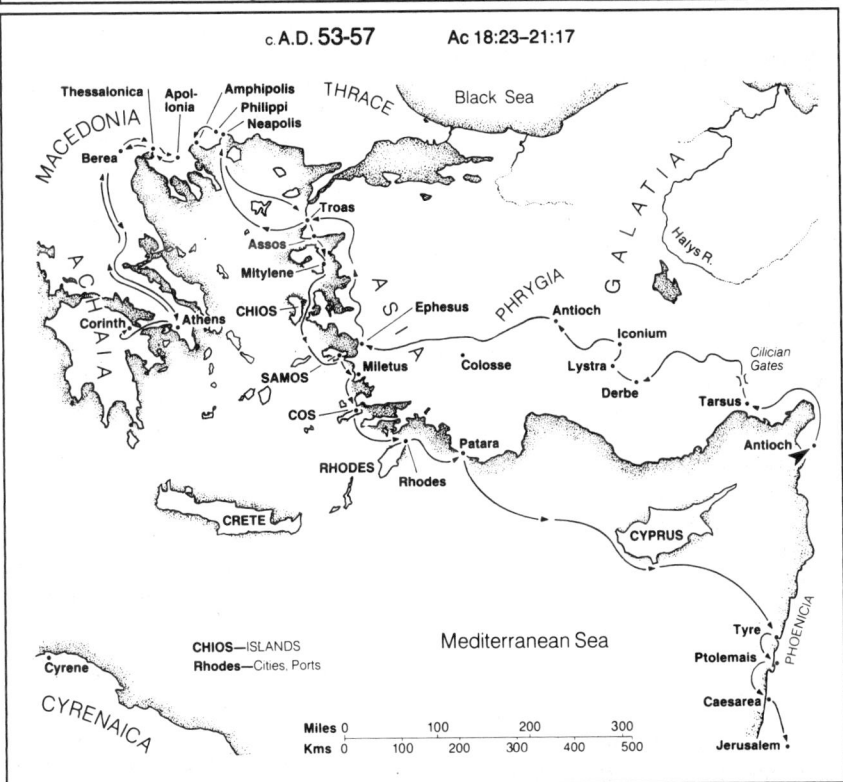

PAUL'S THIRD MISSIONARY JOURNEY
c. A.D. 53–57   Ac 18:23–21:17

© 1989 The Zondervan Corporation.

difficult to think of any parent naming his or her child "Tyrant," the name must have been a nickname.

As for the rent for the hall, perhaps Priscilla and Aquila shared it or the growing congregation underwrote it. For two years Paul had daily discussions about the claims of Christ; during that time the Gospel radiated out from Ephesus through Paul's converts so that the entire province of Asia heard the word of the Lord, with the result that many churches in the outlying cities and villages were founded (cf. Col 1:7; 2:1; 4:16; Rev 2–3). Then after sending Timothy and Erastus as his envoys to Macedonia and Achaia, Paul stayed for a while longer at Ephesus (cf. 19:21–22).

While there, Paul wrote the Corinthian church a letter on the subject of separation from the ungodly (cf. 1Co 5:9–10)—a letter either not now extant or partially preserved (as often suggested) in 2Co 6:14–7:1. In reply he received a letter from certain members of the Corinthian church (cf. 1Co 7:1) seeking his advice on matters concerning marital problems at Corinth, food previously dedicated to idols, the decorum of women in worship, the observance of the Lord's Supper, spiritual gifts, and (possibly) the nature and significance of the resurrection. At about the same time he also had some visitors from Corinth, whom he identifies as "Chloe's household" (1Co 1:11), who told of deep and bitter divisions within the church. And from rumors widely circulating (cf. 1Co 5:1), he knew that some of the Corinthian believers were manifesting blatant immorality and pursuing litigations in the public law courts. To deal with these matters, the apostle wrote a second pastoral letter—1 Corinthians.

The problems at Corinth seem to have involved opposition to Paul's authority and criticism of his doctrine, and he was forced to make a "painful visit" to the city in an attempt to settle matters within the church (cf. 2Co 2:1; 12:14; 13:1). This visit to Corinth from Ephesus is extremely difficult to place historically because Luke's summary of events during this time is so brief and Paul's references so allusive. It was not entirely successful, however, for Paul continued to rebuke the Corinthians. His opponents even taunted him, it seems, with being humble in their presence but bold when away (cf. 2Co 10:1).

11–12 From his Corinthian correspondence we learn that Paul, while at Ephesus, had his difficulties, which arose chiefly from conditions at Corinth. But Luke does not mention them or refer to any further difficulties at Ephesus beyond his general reference to Jewish opposition (v.9) and the Demetrius incident (vv.23–41). Instead, he rounds off his summary of Paul's Ephesian ministry by speaking of "extraordinary miracles" taking place directly through Paul and through such personal garments as Paul's sweat-cloths and work-aprons being taken to the sick and demon possessed. Luke seems to have had in mind two types of "extraordinary miracles": (1) direct healings through the laying on of Paul's hands, and (2) indirect healings through the application of Paul's clothing. It is certainly strange to read of healings occurring through sweat-cloths and work-aprons. But Ephesus was the home of all sorts of magic and superstition, and the phrase "Ephesian writings" was common in antiquity for documents containing spells and magical formulae. So Paul was likely just meeting his audiences at a point of common ground in order to impress them and lead them on to the Good News of salvation in Christ. The virtue, of course, lay not in the materials themselves but in the power of God and the faith of the recipients.

Luke's interest throughout this chapter is in emphasizing the supernatural power of the Gospel. Therefore he has highlighted these "extraordinary miracles." Also, he doubtless included reference to miracles done through Paul's clothing in order to set up a further parallel with the ministries of Jesus and Peter, where healings took place by touching Jesus' cloak (Lk 8:44) and through Peter's shadow (Ac 5:15).

3. The seven sons of Sceva (19:13–19)

13–16 The use of magical names in incantations to exorcise evil spirits was common in the ancient world, and it seems to have been especially prominent at Ephesus. In addition, Jewish practitioners of magic were highly esteemed in antiquity, for they were believed to have command of particularly effective spells. The great reluctance of the Jews to pronounce the divine name was known among the ancients and often misinterpreted according to magical principles. Moreover, those connected with the Jewish priesthood would have enjoyed great prestige in magical circles since they were the most likely ones to know the true pronunciation of the Ineffable Name.

Some Jewish exorcists, on coming into contact with Paul and his preaching about Jesus, attempted to make magical use of this new name. Luke identifies them as "seven sons of Sceva, a Jewish chief priest." Perhaps they did belong to one of the high priestly families of Jerusalem, though the title "Jewish chief priest" was more likely a self-designation manufactured to impress their clients and is reported by Luke without evaluation. Perhaps they even professed to accept Paul's message and to be committed to Jesus personally themselves, much as Simon of Samaria did (cf. 8:9–24). But their main goal was for the benefits they could derive for their magical arts from the power of the name of Jesus, and so they simply continued in their old ways with a new twist.

When, however, they tried to use this more powerful name in their exorcisms, Sceva's sons found they were dealing with realities far beyond their ability to cope. The demon they were trying to exorcise turned violently on them, and they fled from the house naked and bleeding. The name of Jesus, like an unfamiliar weapon misused, exploded in their hands; and they were taught a lesson about the danger of using the name of Jesus in their dabbling in the supernatural.

17–19 News of what happened spread quickly throughout Ephesus. All who heard were overcome by reverential fear and held the name of Jesus in high honor. Negatively, they learned not to misuse the name of Jesus or treat it lightly, for it is a powerful name. Positively, many Christians renounced their secret acts of magic and several magicians were converted. Openly demonstrating the change in their lives, they brought their magical scrolls together and burned these expensive items in the presence of the gathered congregation.

I. A Summary Statement (19:20)

20 The advances of the Gospel into Macedonia, Achaia, and Asia did not come about without great difficulty and repeated discouragements. At times, in fact, matters looked very bleak (cf. 1Co 2:3). But God also gave Paul an open door and a successful ministry in places such as Corinth and Ephesus.

Paul's second and third missionary journeys read like a slice of life. Having shown in his earlier panels the gradual widening of the Gospel to new groups of people and the establishment of a new missionary policy to the Gentiles, Luke in Panel 5 presents for his readers a graphic account of the Gospel's entrance into entirely new regions. It is the story of the church's dedicated service under the guidance and power of the Holy Spirit in proclaiming the Good News to those who desperately needed to hear it. Through both the hardships and the blessings, God was at work. In looking back on those days, Luke simply says, "In this way the word of the Lord spread widely and grew in power."

Panel 6—To Jerusalem and Thence to Rome (19:21–28:31)

The last panel in Acts presents Paul's somewhat circuitous journey to Jerusalem, his arrest and defenses, his imprisonment and defenses in Caesarea, his voyage to Rome, and his ministry at Rome. The panel is introduced by the programmatic statement of 19:21–22 and concludes with the summary statement of 28:31. Three features immediately strike the reader in this sixth panel: (1) the disproportionate length of the panel, including one-third of the total material of Acts; (2) the prominence given the speeches of Paul in his defense; and (3) the dominance of the "we" sections in the narrative portions (cf. 20:5–15; 21:1–18; 27:1–28:16). The length seems to be related to Luke's apologetic purpose, particularly in Paul's five defenses, and to the eyewitness character of the narrative (i.e., a predominance of "we" sections) with its inevitable elaboration of details (see introductory comment on 16:11–40). The events narrated here span the time from approximately 56 through 62.

A. A Programmatic Statement (19:21–22)

21 "After all this had happened" (lit., "fulfilled"; GK *4444*; tr. "finished" in 12:25) refers to the events of the first, second, and third missionary journeys of Paul, as recorded in Panels 4 and 5 (12:25–19:20). For Luke the fulfillment of the Gentile mission came (1) in the inauguration of the new missionary policy for reaching Gentiles that was established on the first missionary journey and confirmed at the Jerusalem Council (i.e., Panel 4), and (2) in the extensive outreach to the Gentile world that took place during the second and third missionary journeys (i.e., Panel 5). All that took place earlier (i.e., Panels 1–3) was for Luke a preparation for the Gentile mission; and all that happened afterwards (i.e., Panel 6), its aftermath and extension into Rome.

With the eastern part of the empire evangelized (cf. Ro 15:23), Paul decided to return to Jerusalem and then go on to Rome. On the way he planned to revisit the churches of Macedonia and Achaia, ministering to them and gathering from them a collection for the Jewish Christians of Jerusalem (cf. 1Co 16:1–4). Thereupon he hoped to take up a Gentile mission in the western part of the empire, using the Roman congregation as the base for that western outreach just as the church at Syrian Antioch had been his base for evangelizing the eastern part of the empire (cf. Ro 15:24–29). Now, however, he had to return to Jerusalem, knowing full well that serious difficulties could befall him there (cf. Ro 15:30–32). In all these plans, Paul was under the direction of the Holy Spirit (implied in the NIV word "decided"; lit., "placed in the Spirit").

22 Before going to Jerusalem, Paul sent Timothy and Erastus into Macedonia while he remained "in the province of Asia" somewhat longer—which probably means that he stayed on at Ephesus. Luke has not mentioned Timothy since 18:5, but he was with Paul at Ephesus and served during Paul's Ephesian ministry as his emissary to Corinth (cf. 1Co 4:17; 16:10–11). This is the first time we hear of Erastus (cf. 2Ti 4:20). As for Silas, though Luke speaks of him repeatedly in describing the second missionary journey, he makes no reference to him in the rest of Acts. Another companion of Paul not mentioned by Luke is Titus, who was extensively involved at various times during the Gentile mission (cf. 2Co 2:13; 7:6, 13–14; 8:6, 16, 23; 12:18; Gal 2:1, 3; 2Ti 4:10; Tit 1:4).

B. The Journey to Jerusalem (19:23–21:16)

1. The riot at Ephesus (19:23–41)

Before Paul left Ephesus, a riot threatened his life and could have put an end to the outreach of the Gospel in Asia. The situation was undoubtedly more dangerous than Luke's account suggests. For in what may well be allusions to this riot, Paul said later that he had "despaired even of life" in the face of "a deadly peril" in Asia (2Co 1:8–11; cf. 1Co 15:32), and that Priscilla and Aquila had "risked their lives" for him (Ro 16:4). Luke's purpose in presenting this vignette is clearly apologetic, in line with his argument for the *religio licita* status of Christianity (cf. Panel 5 [16:6–19:20]) and in anticipation of the themes stressed in Paul's speeches of defense (Panel 6, esp. chs. 22–26). Politically, Luke's report of the friendliness of the "officials of the province" toward Paul and of the city clerk's intervention on his behalf is the best defense imaginable against the charge that Paul and Christianity threatened the official life of the empire.

23 This event of the riot most likely took place at the end of Paul's Ephesian ministry. What happened here was not simply against Paul personally but threatened primarily the continued outreach of the Gospel.

24–27 Artemis of Ephesus, depicted as a grotesque, multibreasted woman, was believed to have been fashioned in heaven and to have fallen from the sky (cf. v.35). Probably she was originally a meteorite that resembled a multibreasted woman and became the object of worship. Her temple had become the primary basis for Ephesus's wealth and continued prosperity (cf. comment on 19:1).

Paul's preaching had turned many away from the idolatry of the Artemis cult, with the result that the economy of Ephesus was being affected. One profitable business was the making of "silver shrines of Artemis," probably silver statuettes of Artemis to be used as souvenirs, votive offerings, and amulets. When the Gospel began to touch their income, the silversmiths, led by their guild master Demetrius, instigated a disturbance they hoped would turn the people against the missionaries and stir up greater devotion for the goddess Artemis—and greater profits for them.

28–29 The silversmiths began shouting out the ceremonial chant: "Great is Artemis of the Ephesians!" hoping thereby to stir up the city on a pretext of religious devotion. A magnificent boulevard ran through the heart of Ephesus, lined with fine buildings and columned porticoes. Into this boulevard Demetrius and his fellow craftsmen most likely poured, sweeping along with them in noisy procession all the residents and visitors within earshot. Their destination was the large open-air theater on the eastern side of the city, large enough to seat twenty-four thousand people. On their way, the crowd laid hold of Gaius and Aristarchus, two traveling companions of Paul from Derbe and Thessalonica respectively (cf. 20:4; 27:2), and dragged them along into the theater. There, much to the delight of Demetrius and his fellow silversmiths, the procession became a fanatical mob.

30–31 The riot faced Paul with an extremely serious situation. He wanted to appear before the assembly, doubtless believing that because of his Roman citizenship and his earlier successful appearances before government officials, he could quiet the mob, free his companions, and turn the whole affair to the advantage of the Gospel. But his Ephesian converts would not let him enter the theater, and even some of "the officials of the province" (lit., "Asiarchs"; GK *825*) who were his friends sent an urgent message for him not to go there. The Asiarchs were members of the noblest and wealthiest families of the province of Asia and were bound together in a league for promoting the cult of the emperor. While they did not have political authority, they served Rome's interests by securing loyalty to Roman rule. That some of these men were friendly to Paul and gave him advice in such an explosive situation suggests that imperial policy at this time was not hostile to Christianity. This fits in with Luke's apologetic purpose.

32 The crowd had been worked up into a frenzy; most didn't even know why they were there. What united them was a common resentment against those who paid no honor to the goddess Artemis.

33–34 The Jewish community at Ephesus was large and enjoyed a number of special exemptions granted by past provincial proconsuls. Yet it also suffered from the latent anti-Semitism that always lay beneath the surface of Greco-Roman society. In an endeavor to disassociate themselves from the Christians in such an explosive situation, the Jews sent one of their number, Alexander, to the podium. To the idolatrous mob, however, Jews were as insufferable as Christians on the point at issue in the riot because both worshiped an invisible deity and rejected idols. So Alexander was shouted down with the chant "Great is Artemis of the Ephesians." This shouting kept on for about two hours.

35–40 The "city clerk" of Ephesus was the chief executive officer of the assembly. He came to his position from within the assembly and was not appointed by Rome. As the most important native official of the city, he was responsible for disturbances within it. He argued with the crowd that a riot would hardly enhance the prestige of the city in the eyes of Rome, and therefore any complaint raised by Demetrius and his guild of silversmiths should be brought before the legally constituted authorities. Gaius and Aristarchus, standing before them, were neither robbers of temples nor blasphemers of other gods (common accusations in antiquity made against Jews generally, including Jewish Christians). Anything further that could not be brought before the courts and the proconsuls could be presented "in a legal assembly." Otherwise, he concluded, the city would risk losing its favorable status because of a riot for which there was no reason.

41 The city clerk then dismissed the crowd. Luke highlights his arguments because they are important elements in his apologetic motif in Acts, which he emphasizes further in the accounts of Paul's five speeches in his own defense later in this panel.

2. A return visit to Macedonia and Achaia (20:1–6)

This report of Paul's return visit to Macedonia and Achaia is the briefest account of an extended ministry in all of Acts—even more so than the summary of the ministry at Ephesus (cf. 19:8–12). Nevertheless, it can be filled out to some extent by certain personal references and historical allusions in 2 Corinthians and Romans, which were written during this time.

1 Leaving Ephesus, Paul moved north either by land or by ship to Troas. There he hoped to find Titus, whom he had earlier sent to Corinth to deal with and report on the situation in the church there. Not finding him and being disturbed about conditions at Corinth, he went on to Macedonia without any further preaching in either Troas itself or the surrounding region (cf. 2Co 2:12–13). As at Athens and Corinth when his concern for the

The large theater in Ephesus in which the riot of ch. 19 took place still stands, though in ruins. Excavations at Ephesus have uncovered statues of the multibreasted goddess Artemis, probably similar to the ones made and sold by Demetrius and the other silversmiths.

Christians at Thessalonica prevented him from giving full attention to an evangelistic outreach (cf. introductory comments on 18:1–17), so at Troas Paul seems to have been consumed with concern about the Christians at Corinth and was unable to launch out into any new missionary venture.

2 In Macedonia (probably at Philippi) Paul met Titus, who brought him reassuring news about the church at Corinth (cf. 2Co 7:5–16). In response to the triumphs and continuing problems that Titus told him about, Paul sent back to the church the letter known as 2 Corinthians.

Just how long Paul stayed in Macedonia we do not know. Luke's words seem to suggest a fairly prolonged period. It was probably during this time that the Gospel entered the province of Illyricum in the northwest corner of the Balkan peninsula (Ro 15:19; cf. also 2Ti 4:10, where Titus is mentioned as returning to Dalmatia, the southern district of the province of Illyricum). Perhaps Paul himself traveled across the Balkan peninsula on the Via Egnatia to the city of Dyrrhachium. It is probable that this ministry in Macedonia lasted for a year or more, from the summer of 56 through the latter part of 57.

One activity that especially concerned Paul at this time was collecting money for the relief of impoverished believers at Jerusalem. He instructed the churches in Galatia, Asia, Macedonia, and Achaia about this (cf. Ro 15:25–32; 1Co 16:1–4; 2Co 8–9). The collection was an act of love like that undertaken by the church at Syrian Antioch earlier (cf. 11:27–30). More than that, Paul viewed it as a symbol of unity that would help his Gentile converts realize their debt to the mother church in Jerusalem and give Jewish Christians an appreciation of the vitality of faith in the Gentile churches.

3 After spending some time in Macedonia, Paul went to Corinth, where he stayed for three months, probably during the winter of 57–58. While there, and before his final trip to Jerusalem, Paul wrote his letter to the church at Rome (cf. Ro 15:17–33). The Greek world in the eastern part of the empire had been evangelized (cf. Ro 15:19, 23), and he desired to transfer his ministry to the Latin world, as far west as Spain (cf. Ro 15:24). He anticipated using the Roman church as his base of operations, much as he had previously used the church at Antioch in Syria. But first he needed to go to Jerusalem if the collection from the Gentile Christians was to have the meaning he wanted it to have (cf. Ro 15:25–32). So, instead of going to Rome at this time and in preparation for his future visit—and also to expound the righteousness of God—Paul sent a formal letter to the Christians at Rome (the longest and most systematic of his writings).

At the end of three months in Corinth, Paul sought to sail for Palestine-Syria, doubtless intending to reach Jerusalem in time for the great pilgrim festival of Passover. But a plot to kill him at sea was uncovered, and he decided to travel overland through Macedonia. Robbery was common on the ancient roads, and with Paul carrying a substantial amount of money collected from the Gentile churches, he undoubtedly wanted to get to Jerusalem as quickly and safely as possible. Nevertheless, he felt it best to spend time on the longer land route, preferring its possible dangers to the known perils of the sea voyage; so he began to retrace his steps through Macedonia.

4 Gathered at Corinth for the return journey to Jerusalem with Paul were representatives from the churches: Sopater of Berea, Aristarchus and Secundus of Thessalonica, Gaius of Derbe, Timothy of Lystra, and Tychicus and Trophimus from Asia. With the change in travel plans, they then accompanied him (together with Silas and perhaps others) into Macedonia. Almost all the main centers of the Gentile mission were represented, with the notable exception of Corinth. The lack of mention of this church may suggest continued strained relations within the church there. Luke, who appears to have joined the group at Philippi (cf. v.5), may have represented that church.

5–6 Having been unable to get to Jerusalem for Passover, Paul remained at Philippi to celebrate it and the week-long Feast of Unleavened Bread. He sent his Gentile companions ahead to Troas and stayed on at Philippi, apparently with Silas and Timothy. Then after the Feast of Unleavened Bread, the missionaries—accompanied by Luke (note the "we" section of vv.5–15)—went down to Neapolis, the port city of Philippi, and crossed the Aegean to Troas. It was evidently a difficult crossing because it took five days instead of two days as earlier (16:11).

3. The raising of Eutychus (20:7–12)

From 20:5 through the end of Acts (28:31), Luke's narrative gives considerable attention to ports of call, stopovers, and time spent on Paul's travels. The use of "we" (20:5–15; 21:1–18; 28:16) shows its eyewitness character.

7 Though Paul himself had not undertaken a mission at Troas (cf. 2Co 2:12–13), the Gospel had radiated out from many centers of influence in Galatia, Asia, Macedonia, and Achaia to penetrate the Gentile world of the eastern part of the Roman Empire. Thus at Troas Paul and his colleagues found a group of believers and met with them "to break bread" and to give instruction regarding the Christian life. The mention of their meeting "on the first day of the week" is the earliest unambiguous evidence we have for Christians gathering together for worship on that day (cf. Jn 20:19, 26; 1Co 16:2; Rev 1:10). The Christians met in the evening, which was probably the most convenient time because of the necessity of working during the day. They met to celebrate the Lord's Supper (cf. 1Co 10:16–17; 11:17–34; see comment on 2:42). Paul "spoke to" the believers till midnight.

8–9 "As Paul talked on and on," Eutychus went to sleep and fell to his death. He may simply have been bored by Paul's long discussion, though Luke's reference to the many torch lamps in the room suggests that lack of oxygen and the hypnotic effect of flickering flames caused Eutychus's drowsiness. But whatever its cause, his fall brought the meeting to a sudden and shocking halt. They dashed down and found him dead.

10–11 Of course, Paul also ran down. In an action reminiscent of Elijah and Elisha (cf. 1Ki 17:21; 2Ki 4:34–35), he "threw himself on the young man and put his arms around him," restoring Eutychus to life. Then they returned to their third-story room, had a midnight snack, and listened to Paul until dawn.

12 There is no hint that Paul took the incident as a rebuke for long-windedness. Nor were the people troubled by the meeting's length. They were eager to learn and only had Paul with them a short time. It was an evening of great significance for the church at Troas: Paul had taught them, they had fellowshiped together in the Lord's Supper, and they had witnessed a dramatic sign of God's presence and power. No wonder Luke says that they "were greatly comforted."

4. From Troas to Miletus (20:13–16)

13 Leaving Troas, Paul's companions took passage on a coastal vessel that was to stop at various ports along the western coast of Asia Minor. Paul, however, waited a while longer at Troas; then, while the boat went around Cape Lectum, he took the direct route to Assos on the Roman coastal road and got there in time to join his colleagues on board. He may have wanted to avoid the northeastern winds that blew around Cape Lectum or may just have wanted to be alone with God on the walk to Assos.

14–15 Assos was on the Roman coastal road and faced south toward the island of Lesbos. The boat went on to Mitylene, a splendid port on the southeast coast of Lesbos and the chief city of this largest of the islands of western Asia Minor. From there they went to Kios; then they passed through the channel separating Kios from the mainland of Asia Minor to come to Samos, an island directly west of Ephesus. So the boat arrived at Miletus, the ancient port at the mouth of the Meander River, some thirty miles south of Ephesus.

16 Paul had to miss the Passover at Jerusalem (cf. comments on vv.3, 5, 6). But he wanted, if at all possible, to get to Jerusalem for Pentecost, the fiftieth day after Passover (cf. comment on 2.1). He had previously decided not to take a boat that stopped at Ephesus, for he evidently preferred to forego the emotional strain of another parting with the entire Ephesian church and to avoid (possibly) some local danger.

5. Paul's farewell address to the Ephesian elders (20:17–38)

Paul's farewell address to the Ephesian elders is the nearest approximation in Acts to the Pauline letters. Its general content recalls how in his letters Paul encouraged, warned, and exhorted his converts. Moreover, its theological themes and vocabulary are distinctly Pauline. In his three missionary sermons (13:16–41; 14:15–17; 17:22–31) and five defenses (chs.22–26), Paul addressed non-Christian audiences. But here he was speaking to Christians. It is significant that, in a situation similar to those he faced in many of his letters, this farewell to the Ephesian elders reads like a miniature letter of his. This becomes all the more significant when we recognize that nowhere else in Acts is there any evidence for a close knowledge of Paul's letters.

The address is constructed in a way familiar to readers of Paul's letters. Its body has three parts, which deal with (1) Paul's past ministry at Ephesus (vv.18–21), (2) Paul's present plans in going to Jerusalem (vv.22–24), and (3) the future of Paul himself and of the church at Ephesus (vv.25–31). It concludes with a blessing (v.32) and then adds further words of exhortation that point the hearers to Paul's example and the teachings of Jesus (vv.33–35). Heading each section is a formula: "you know" at v.18; "and now behold" at v.22; "and now behold I know" at v.25; and "and now" at v.32 (pers. tr.).

17 At Miletus the coastal boat docked for a number of days to load and unload cargo. So Paul took the opportunity of sending for the elders of the Ephesian church to join him at Miletus. The road back to Ephesus around the gulf was considerably longer than the thirty miles directly between Ephesus and Miletus. It would have taken some time to engage a messenger to summon the elders, who could hardly have made the return trip as quickly as a single runner. Doubtless, therefore, elders arrived at Miletus, at the earliest, on the third day of Paul's stay there.

18–21 Paul's address to the Ephesian elders begins with an apologia that closely parallels 1Th 2:1–12. As at Thessalonica, evidently Paul's Ephesian opponents had been prejudicing his converts against him in his absence; he therefore found it necessary to defend his conduct and teaching by appealing to his hearers' knowledge of him. The opposition at Ephesus seems to have been chiefly Jewish and to have insisted that full acceptance with God could come only through a fully developed Judaism. Therefore Paul had to declare that he had faithfully preached what was helpful to them, focusing on repentance to God and faith in the Lord Jesus—a content wholly sufficient for salvation (cf. Ro 10:9–10; 2Co 5:20–6:2; cf. Ac 26:20–23).

22–24 The second section of Paul's address concerns his plans to go to Jerusalem. Many have claimed a discrepancy between his being "compelled by the Spirit" to go to Jerusalem (vv.22–24) and his later being warned by the Spirit not to go to Jerusalem in 21:4, 10–14. But Luke opened Panel 6 of Acts with the statement that Paul's decision to go to Jerusalem was "by the Spirit" (cf. comment on 19:21), and nothing here is incompatible with that programmatic statement. Both compulsion and warning were evidently involved in the Spirit's direction, with both being impressed upon Paul by the Spirit at various times as he journeyed—probably through Christian prophets he met along the way. Nothing would keep him from completing his ministry of testifying to the grace of God throughout the eastern part of the empire by taking to the Jerusalem believers the money sent by Gentile believers in Galatia, Macedonia, Achaia, and Asia (see comment on 20:2).

25–27 In the third section of his address, Paul began by speaking of his own future expectations after visiting Jerusalem. He told the Ephesian elders that neither they nor any of those he had ministered to in the eastern part of the empire would ever see him again, for he was intending to leave his ministry there and, after visiting Jerusalem, move on to the western part of the empire with Rome as his base (Ro 15:23–29). He said he felt free from any further responsibility in the East because he had done all that he could in proclaiming "the whole will of God." At it turned out, however, it seems that Paul was able to return later to Ephesus (see 2Ti 4:9–13). Luke thus probably wrote this book before Paul's release and further ministry.

28–31 The third section of Paul's address continues with an exhortation to the Ephesian elders in light of what Paul sees will soon take place in the church. He warns regarding persecution from outside and apostasy within (cf. later evidence in 1Ti 1:19–20; 4:1–5; 2Ti 1:15; 2:17–18; 3:1–9; Rev 2:1–7). So he gives the elders the solemn imperative of v.28.

Theologically, much in Luke's précis of this address reflects Paul's thought at this stage in his life, as these are revealed in the letters he wrote at Ephesus (1 Corinthians), in Macedonia (2 Corinthians), and at Corinth (Romans) immediately prior to this time. Paul's use of the word "church" (GK *1711*) in v.28 is a case in point. While in the salutations of Galatians and 1 and 2 Thessalonians he used "church" in a local sense (Gal 1:1; 1Th 1:1; 2Th 2:1), in addressing the Corinthians he used the word more universally: "To the church of God in Corinth" (1Co 1:2; 2Co 1:1). And thereafter in his writings "church" always appears in a universal sense (cf. esp. Ephesians and Colossians). Other phrases of Paul are his identification of God with Jesus in the phrase about God's obtaining the church for himself "with his own blood" (cf. Ro 9:5) and the reference to the blood of Jesus as instrumental in our redemption (Ro 3:25; 5:9; cf. Eph 1:7; 2:13; Col 1:20).

32 Paul concluded his address with a blessing, committing them "to God and to the word of his grace." Though Paul had to leave them, God was with them and so was his word—the word of grace that was able to build them up, give them an inheritance, and sanctify them. Again, the expressions used in Luke's summary of Paul's blessing comprise a catena of Pauline terms: "grace" (GK *5921*, which appears in almost all his salutations and benedictions); "build up" (GK *3868*; cf. 1Co 8:1; 10:23; 14:4, 17; 1Th 5:11); "inheritance" (GK *3100*; cf. Ro 8:17; Gal 3:18; Eph 1:14; 5:5; Col 3:24); and "sanctified" (GK *39*; cf. Ro 15:16; 1Co 1:2; 6:11; 7:14; Eph 5:26; 1Th 5:23).

33–35 Following his blessing, Paul adds a few words of exhortation (as in his letters), urging the elders of the Ephesian church to care for the needs of God's people without thought of material reward. He asks them to follow his example (cf. Php 3:17) and calls on them to remember the words of Jesus applicable here: "It is more blessed to give than to receive." Paul often related his ethical exhortations to the teachings of Jesus (cf. Ro 12–14; 1Th 4:1–12) and the personal example of Jesus (cf. Php 2:5–11), so he does that here. The specific words attributed to Jesus here do not appear in any of the Gospels. But they can be approximately paralleled by Lk 6:38.

36–38 When Paul had finished speaking, he knelt down with the Ephesian elders and prayed with them. On the basis of the parallels between this farewell address and Paul's letters, the substance of what he prayed for can be found in such places as Eph 1:15–23; Php 1:3–11; Col 1:3–14; and 1Th 1:2–3; 3:11–13; 5:23–24. After a deeply affectionate and sorrowful farewell with tears on both sides, Paul and his traveling companions boarded the ship.

6. On to Jerusalem (21:1–16)

The narrative of Paul's journey to Jerusalem is of literary and historical significance because it comprises the third of Luke's four "we" sections (21:1–18; cf. 16:10–17; 20:5–15; 27:1–28:16). This section is theologically significant because Luke seems to describe Paul's trip to Jerusalem in terms of Jesus' going up to Jerusalem to die. Luke knows, of course, that Paul did not die at Jerusalem. Yet he seems to sketch out Paul's journey to Jerusalem in terms that roughly parallel that of Jesus: (1) a similar plot by the Jews; (2) a handing over to the Gentiles (v.11); (3) a triple prediction on the way of coming suffering (20:22–24; 21:4, 10–11; cf. Luke 9:22, 44; 18:31–34); (4) a steadfast resolution (v.13); and (5) a holy resignation to God's will (v.14). As Luke has reserved for Paul the mission to the Gentiles, which Jesus saw as inherent in the Servant theology of Isa 61 (cf. Lk 4:16–21; see introductory comments on 12:25–28:31), so he describes Paul's journey to Jerusalem in terms reminiscent of the Suffering Servant.

1–2 After the emotional farewell, Paul and his party (including Luke) continued by boat to Cos. The next day they sailed to Rhodes, the capital of the large Dodecanese island of Rhodes just twelve miles off the mainland of Asia Minor. The next stop was Patara, a Lycian city on the southwest coast of Asia Minor with a fine harbor. There Paul and his party boarded a large merchant ship bound nonstop for Tyre, for they desired to travel quickly.

3–4 Paul and company sailed the four hundred miles from Patara to Tyre, the famous Phoenician seaport of Syria. A church had been established at Tyre through the witness of the Christian Hellenists forced to leave Jerusalem at the time of Stephen's martyrdom (cf. 11:19). While the ship was unloading, Paul had fellowship with the believers there for a week, who tried to dissuade him "through the Spirit" from going on to Jerusalem. This phrase most likely means that the Spirit's message, given through a Christian prophet, was the occasion for the believers' concern because they knew what lay in store for him (cf. vv.10–15).

5–7 After a scene reminiscent of the parting with the Ephesian elders (cf. 20:36–37), Paul and his companions sailed from Tyre. The ship went on to Ptolemais, another ancient Phoenician seaport south of Tyre. There it made harbor for a day, undoubtedly again to unload cargo. Once more Paul met with the believers of the city. Probably Christianity at Ptolemais also stemmed from the witness of the Hellenistic Christians (cf. 11:19).

8–9 Paul and his party came to Caesarea, the magnificent harbor and city built by Herod the Great as the port of Jerusalem and the Roman provincial capital of Judea (cf. comment on 10:1). There they stayed with Philip the evangelist, one of the seven who had been appointed in the early days of the Jerusalem church to take care of the daily distribution of food (cf. 6:1–6). He had evangelized in Samaria and the maritime plain of Palestine (cf. 8:4–40), after which he apparently settled at Caesarea for some twenty years. Paul stayed at his home for "a number of days." For a man in a hurry to get to Jerusalem, this delay of several days may seem strange. But he wanted to be in Jerusalem on the Day of Pentecost (cf. 20:16)—not just get there as early as possible. So Paul's stay in Caesarea was probably a deliberate matter of timing.

Luke speaks of Philip's four unmarried daughters as prophetesses, yet says nothing about what they prophesied. Perhaps these prophesying maidens and their father gave Luke source material for Luke and Acts—for example, on Philip's mission in Samaria and to the Ethiopian eunuch.

10–14 While Paul was at Caesarea, the Jerusalemite prophet Agabus (cf. 11:27–28) came there. With the belt that held Paul's outer cloak together, he tied his own feet and hands in an act of prophetic symbolism (cf. 1Ki 11:29–39; Isa 20:2–6; Eze 4:1–5:17) and announced that Paul would be bound by the Jews and handed over to the Gentiles. In response to this dramatic prophecy, the Caesarean believers—together with Paul's own traveling companions—begged him not to go. But Paul's determination to go to Jerusalem came from an inward spiritual constraint that could not be set aside (cf. 19:21; 20:22), for he was increasingly convinced that he must present the gift from the churches personally for it to be understood as the symbol of unity he intended it to be (cf. 1Co 16:4 with Ro 15:31). Paul well knew that his reception at Jerusalem might be less than cordial (cf. Ro 15:30–32).

15–16 Paul and his colleagues, accompanied by some Caesarean Christians, took the road up to Jerusalem, some sixty-five miles away to the southeast. They brought Paul to the home of Mnason, a Cypriot and an early follower of Jesus. Not everyone in the Jerusalem church would have been prepared to have Paul and his company of Gentile converts as house guests during Pentecost. But the Caesarean Christians knew their man.

C. Various Events and Paul's Defenses at Jerusalem (21:17–23:22)

1. Arrival at Jerusalem (21:17–26)

17–18 With these two verses, the third "we" section of Acts concludes, though Luke may have remained in Palestine for a longer time than vv.17–18 imply. Paul is now the focus of the narrative—particularly in his discussion with the leaders of the Jerusalem church, his arrest in the temple precincts, and his five speeches of defense at Jerusalem and Caesarea—and so Luke speaks only of him.

It was probably at Mnason's house that the believers gathered to receive Paul and his party "warmly." Then on the next day, as Luke says, they called on James, the resident leader of the Jerusalem church (cf. comments on 12:17; 15:13). Sharing with him in the administration of the church was a body of elders, who were also there to meet Paul and his colleagues.

19 On this occasion Paul "reported in detail what God had done among the Gentiles through his ministry." Undoubtedly he also presented the collection from the Gentile churches to James and the elders, for that was his chief motive for going to Jerusalem (see comments on vv.10–14). Nowhere in Acts (except later at 24:17) does Luke mention this collection, probably because he did not know how to explain to his Gentile readers (1) its significance as being much more than a way of currying favor and (2) Paul's fears that the Jerusalem Christians might not accept it.

To understand Paul's fears, we must realize that the Jerusalem church was increasingly being caught between its allegiance to the nation and its fraternal relation to Paul's Gentile mission. To accept the contribution from the Gentile churches was to be identified further with that mission and to drive another wedge between themselves and their compatriots. True, they had accepted such a contribution earlier (cf. 11:27–30) and had declared their fraternity with Paul in previous meetings (cf. Gal 2:6–10; Ac 15:13–29). But with the rising tide of Jewish nationalism and a growing body of scrupulous believers in the Jerusalem church, Jewish Christian solidarity with the Gentile mission was becoming more and more difficult to affirm if the Jerusalem church's relations with the nation were to be maintained and opportunities for an outreach to Israel kept open. Undoubtedly Paul recognized the increased tensions at Jerusalem. No wonder he feared that James and the elders, for the sake of their Jewish relations and mission, might feel themselves constrained to reject the contribution (Ro 15:31), thus severing, in effect, the connection between the Pauline churches and the Jerusalem church.

20–24 James and the elders responded to Paul's report and the gift from the churches by praising God. Yet they also urged Paul to join with four Jewish Christians who were fulfilling their Nazirite vows and to pay for their required offerings. In effect, they were saying to Paul, "We can accept this gift from the churches and so identify ourselves openly with your Gentile mission, if you will join with these men and identify yourself openly with the nation." Thus they were protecting themselves against Jewish recriminations while at the same time affirming their connection with Paul and his mission. And, as they saw it, they were providing Paul with a way of protecting himself against a slanderous accusation floating about that he was teaching Jews to apostatize from Judaism. In view of his having come earlier to Jerusalem in more placid circumstances to fulfill a Nazirite vow of his own (cf. 18:18–22), Paul would not have viewed such a suggestion as particularly onerous. It doubtless seemed to all concerned a particularly happy solution to the vexing problems that both Paul and the Jerusalem church were facing.

25 James and the elders reminded Paul of the fourfold Jerusalem decree (see comment on 15:20–21) of the early Christians' agreed-on basis for fellowship between Jewish and Gentile believers. Having urged Paul to follow their proposed course of action, the leaders of the Jerusalem church went on to assure him that this in no way rescinded their earlier decision to impose nothing further on Gentile converts than these four injunctions given for the sake of harmony within the church and in order not to impede the progress of the Jewish Christian mission.

26 Coming from abroad, Paul would have had to regain ceremonial purity by a seven-day ritual of purification before he could be present at the absolution ceremony of the four Jewish Christians in the Jerusalem temple. In keeping with this ritual, therefore, Paul reported to the priest at the start of his seven days of purification, informing him that he was providing the funds for the offerings of the four impoverished men who had taken Nazirite vows; he undoubtedly returned to the temple at regular prescribed intervals during the week (the third and seventh days) for the appropriate rites.

2. Arrest in the temple (21:27–36)

27–29 The strategy of Paul's taking a vow and paying for the Nazirite offerings hardly proved successful—probably nothing could have conciliated those whose minds were already prejudiced against him. Jews from Asia who had come to Jerusalem for Pentecost determined to take more effective action against him than they had at Ephesus. So toward the end of Paul's seven-day purification (possibly when he came to receive the water of atonement on the seventh day), they instigated a riot under the pretense that he had brought Trophimus, a Gentile representative from Ephesus, beyond the barrier that separated the Court of the Gentiles from the temple courts reserved for Jews alone. Archaeologists have found inscriptions at this point of the temple that read: "No foreigner is to enter within the balustrade and embankment around the sanctuary. Whoever is caught will have himself to blame for his death which follows." Roman authorities supported Jewish scruples about this matter and ratified the death penalty for any Gentile—even a Roman citizen—caught going beyond the balustrade.

The charge against Paul resulted from the fact that he and Trophimus were seen together in the city, which led to the assumption that they went together into the Holy Place in the temple. Paul would hardly have done this, however, since his purpose at this time was to appease Jewish susceptibilities.

30 "The whole city," Luke tells us in natural hyperbole, "was aroused." The crime Paul was alleged to have committed was a capital one and could easily ignite the fanatical zeal of the many pilgrims in Jerusalem. So they seized Paul in one of the inner courts of the temple and dragged him out to the Court of the Gentiles. Then the temple police who patrolled the area and stood guard at the gates leading into the inner courts closed the gates to prevent the inner courts from being defiled by the tumult and possible bloodshed.

31–32 Word of the riot came to the commander of the Roman garrison stationed in the Fortress of Antonia, a building built by Herod the Great to the north of the temple precincts where it could overlook the temple area to the south and the city to the north and west. With some soldiers and centurions, he rushed into the mob and prevented the people from beating Paul further. While the temple police were drawn from the ranks of the Levites (cf. comments on 4:1), the commander of the fortress was a Roman military officer, whose responsibility was to keep peace in the city. He represented Rome's interests and was to intervene in the affairs of the people on behalf of those interests.

33–36 The commander formally arrested Paul and ordered him bound with two chains. Undoubtedly he considered him a criminal and was prepared to treat him as one. But when he asked the mob about his crime, he got no clear answer. Therefore he ordered him to be taken into the fortress where he could be questioned directly and where a confession could be extracted from him. But the mob still pressed hard after their quarry, so hard that the soldiers had to drag Paul up the steps to the fortress. All the while the mob was crying out, "Away with him!" (i.e., "Kill him!" cf. Lk 23:18; Ac 22:22).

This fragment was one of several stones set on the Temple Mount warning Gentiles not to proceed any further. Paul was accused of taking a Gentile past this point. Courtesy Andre Lemaire.

3. Paul's defense before the people (21:37–22:22)

The account of Paul's defense before the people consists of three parts: (1) Paul's request to address the people (21:37–40), (2) his speech in defense (22:1–21), and (3) the people's response (22:22). In this first of Paul's five defenses, Luke's apologetic interests come to the fore in highlighting the nonpolitical character of Christianity (contrary to other messianic movements of the day, cf. 21:38) and in presenting Paul's command to preach to the Gentiles as being the major reason for Jewish opposition to the Gospel (cf. 22:10–22).

37–38 At the head of the stone stairway leading into the Fortress of Antonia, Paul asked for permission to say something to Claudius Lysias, the commander (cf. 23:26). The commander was startled to hear his charge speaking in fluent Greek and surmised that perhaps the prisoner was the Egyptian Jew who three years earlier had appeared in Jerusalem claiming to be a prophet and had led a large band of followers into the wilderness and then to the Mount of Olives in preparation for the messianic overthrow of Jerusalem. Most people had considered him a charlatan, and Felix and his soldiers had driven him off.

39–40 But Paul assured the commander that he was not the Egyptian revolutionary; rather, he was from Tarsus. The epithet "no ordinary city," by which Paul referred to Tarsus, was used by various cities to publicize their greatness; Paul was proud of the city of his birth. The Roman commander, probably impressed by Paul's courteous composure under such trying circumstances and also hoping to gain some insight into the cause of the riot, gave him permission.

Paul then began his speech to the crowd "in Aramaic" (or "in Hebrew"; see NIV note). Though probably frustrating for the commander, this was appreciated by the crowd and elicited for him a temporary measure of goodwill.

22:1–2 Paul opens his defense with the formal Jewish address "Men, brothers" (cf. 7:2). Many commentators have objected that this speech does not fit the occasion, for it makes no mention of the people's charge that Paul had defiled the temple by taking Trophimus, a Gentile, into its inner courts (cf. 21:28b–29). In reality, however, this speech deals eloquently with the major charge against him—that of being a Jewish apostate (cf. 21:28a)—by setting in a Jewish context all that had happened in his Christian life and by insisting that what others might consider apostasy really came to him as a revelation from heaven. Indeed, the speech parallels much of what Luke has already given us about Paul's conversion in 9:1–19 and what he will give us again in 26:2–23. Such repetition impresses something of exceptional importance indelibly on his readers' minds (cf. introductory comment on 9:1–30). Yet the variations in each of these three accounts correspond to their respective contexts and purposes.

3 The triad of birth, upbringing, and training was a conventional way in antiquity of describing a man's youth. What Paul is here saying is, "I am a Jew, 'born' in Tarsus of Cilicia, 'brought up' in this city at the feet of Gamaliel, and 'instructed' in the strict manner of the law of our fathers." That is, his Jewishness cannot be disputed (cf. 2Co 11:22; Php 3:5), and he insists that with such a background he was as zealous for all that Judaism stands for as any of those in the crowd before him (cf. Gal 1:14).

4–5 As evidence of his zeal for God and the Jewish religion, Paul cites his earlier persecution of Christians (cf. comments on 9:1–2). The ascription "this Way" picks up what was the earliest self-designation of the first believers in Jesus at Jerusalem—namely, "those of the Way" (cf. comment on 9:2).

6–9 This description of Christ's encounter with Paul on the road to Damascus, except for stylistic differences, closely parallels the one in 9:3–6 (cf. comments there). As in Acts 9, he maintains that his conversion to Jesus as God's Messiah was the result of a heavenly confrontation and that it was not something Paul originated subjectively or others imposed on him. It was, indeed, "Jesus of Nazareth" who confronted him, and this places his messianology in the matrix of the Jewish homeland. But it was the risen and ascended Jesus of Nazareth, the heavenly Christ, who rebuked him and turned him about spiritually; this alone explains his new understanding of life and his new outlook on all things Jewish.

10–11 In response to the heavenly confrontation and as a good Jew who thought first in terms of how he should act in obedience to divine revelation, Paul's question was "What shall I do, Lord?" He was told to go into Damascus, where the divine will would be revealed to him. So in his blindness he was led into Damascus by his companions to await instructions as to God's purposes for him.

12–16 At Damascus Paul was visited by Ananias, God's messenger to bring about renewal of Paul's sight and to announce God's purpose for him as a witness "to all men." The Jewish matrix of Paul's commission is highlighted by the description of Ananias as "a devout observer of the law and highly respected by all the Jews living there" (v.12); and the Jewish flavor of the episode is strengthened by the expression "the God of our fathers" and the messianic title "the Righteous One" (v.14; cf. 3:14). The words "Brother Saul, receive your sight" (v.13) summarize the fuller statement reported in 9:17. What was important in the present circumstance was not to reproduce the exact words of Ananias but to emphasize that the commission Paul received from the risen Christ was communicated by a pious Jew who spoke in distinctly Jewish terms. Later on, when Paul defended himself before Agrippa II (ch. 26), there was no need for this particular emphasis; therefore, the substance of what Ananias said in the name of the Lord Jesus is there included in the words spoken by the heavenly voice on the Damascus Road (cf. 26:16–18). Having thus delivered the Lord's message, Ananias called on Paul to respond: "Get up, be baptized and wash your sins away, calling on his name" (v.16); cf. 2:38).

17–21 Paul's commission at Damascus to be God's witness "to all men" was reaffirmed and amplified in a vision he received as he was praying in the temple, which most likely occurred on Paul's return to Jerusalem three years after his conversion (cf. 9:26–29; Gal 1:18–19). At that time, Luke tells us, Paul faced opposition from the Hellenistic Jews of the city, who viewed him as a renegade and sought to kill him (cf. 9:29). At a period in his life when he most needed divine direction and support, the same heavenly personage he met on the road to Damascus, the risen and exalted Jesus, directed him to "leave Jerusalem immediately, because they will not accept your testimony about me" (v.18). More important, the same exalted Jesus also ordered him: "Go, I will send you far away to the Gentiles" (v.21). Jerusalem, therefore, Paul says, was his intended place of witness, and the temple was God's place of revelation. Nevertheless, his testimony was refused in the city, and by revelation his earlier commission "to all men" was to have explicit reference to Gentiles, those who are "far away" (GK *3426*; cf. comments on 2:39).

22 During most of Paul's defense, the crowd listened with a certain respect, for he had spoken mostly of Israel's messianic hope and had done so in a thoroughly Jewish context. Even his identification of Jesus with his people's messianology and with the Revealer from heaven, while straining the credibility of many in the crowd, could have been tolerated by a people given more to orthopraxis (authorized practice) than orthodoxy (correct thought). When, however, Paul spoke of being directed by divine revelation to leave Jerusalem and go far away to Gentiles who had no relation to Judaism, that was "the last straw." In effect, Paul was saying that Gentiles could be approached directly with God's message of salvation without first being related to the nation and its institutions. This was tantamount to placing Jews and Gentiles on an equal footing before God, and for Judaism that was the height of apostasy indeed! Paul was thus shouted down, and the crowd called for his death.

4. Paul claims his Roman citizenship (22:23–29)

23–24 The garrison commander, puzzled why they were rioting and probably unable to understand Paul's Aramaic, decided to find out the truth of the matter by scourging Paul (see comment on Mk 15:15). His earlier friendliness toward Paul soured, and the brutal part of his nature and job came to the fore. By this time Paul had already received thirty-nine lashes at the hands of Jewish authorities five times and beatings with rods by the order of Roman magistrates three times (cf. 2Co 11:24–25; see comments on 9:30; 11:25; 16:22–24). But this type of flogging was far more brutal than these others. Here Paul was at the brink of the kind of unjust punishment Christ endured when Pilate, in a travesty of justice, had him flogged after declaring him innocent (Mk 15:15; Jn 18:38–19:1).

25 Roman citizens were exempt from examination under torture. In such trials there first had to be a formulation of charges and penalties, then a formal accusation laid, and then a hearing before a Roman magistrate and his advisory cabinet. Therefore, as the soldiers "stretched him [Paul] out to flog him," he said to the centurion in charge, "Is it legal for you to flog a Roman citizen who hasn't even been found guilty?"

26–28 At this time, Roman citizenship (GK *4486*; also *4871*) was a highly prized right conferred only on those of high social or governmental standing, those who had done some exceptional service for Rome, or those able to bribe some imperial or provincial administrator to have their names included on a list of candidates. In the second and third centuries A.D., the use of bribery became increasingly common, but earlier it accounted for only a small minority of citizens. The names of new citizens were recorded on one of the thirty-five tribal lists at Rome and on their local municipal register. Succeeding generations of a citizen's family possessed at birth a registration of their Roman status and were registered as citizens on the taxation tables of their respective cities.

No article of apparel distinguished a Roman citizen from the rest of the people except the toga, which only Roman citizens could wear. But even at Rome the toga was unpopular because of its cumbersomeness and was worn only on state occasions. Papers validating citizenship were kept in family archives and not usually carried on one's person. The verbal claim to Roman citizenship was accepted at face value; penalties for falsifying documents and making false claims of citizenship were exceedingly stiff.

We do not know how and when Paul's family acquired Roman citizenship. Most likely one of Paul's ancestors received it for valuable services rendered to a Roman administrator or general in either the Gischala region of northern Palestine or at Tarsus. When Paul claimed his Roman citizenship, the centurion immediately stopped the proceedings and reported to the commander: "This man is a Roman citizen" (v.26). This brought the commander immediately to question Paul, who convinced him that he was indeed a Roman citizen (v.27). His own citizenship, the commander said, was purchased by a large sum of money—probably, since his name was Claudius Lysias (23:26), during the reign of Claudius through paying a member of Claudius's court. Paul's response, "But I was born a citizen" (v.28), implies his high estimate of his citizenship.

29 That Paul was a Roman citizen put the situation in a different light (cf. 16:37–39). Examination under torture, while suitable for ordinary people in the empire, had to be abandoned; some other way of determining the nature of the charge had to be found. Undoubtedly the commander shuddered as he realized how close he had come to perpetrating a serious offense against a Roman citizen.

5. Paul's defense before the Sanhedrin (22:30–23:11)

The irregular structure of Luke's account of Paul's defense before the Sanhedrin evidently reflects the tumultuous character of the session itself. Three matters pertaining to Luke's apologetic purpose come to the fore: (1) Christianity is rooted in the Jewish doctrine of the resurrection of the dead (cf. 23:6); (2) the debate Paul was engaged in regarding Christianity's claims must be viewed as first of all a Jewish intramural affair (cf. 23:7–10); and (3) the ongoing proclamation of the Gospel in the Gentile world stems from a divine mandate (cf. 23:11).

30 Still unsuccessful in ascertaining why the people were so angry at Paul, the commander ordered the Jewish Sanhedrin (cf. comment on 4:5) to come together to interrogate his captive. As a Roman citizen, Paul had a right to know the nature of the charges against him and the penalties involved before formal accusations were laid. The commander also needed to know these things in order to decide what else should be done. Perhaps he had talked with Paul after releasing him from his chains (cf. 21:33). Since this was a religious matter, he decided to have it clarified before the highest judicial body of Judaism. As a Roman military commander, he had no right to participate in the Sanhedrin's deliberations. But as the Roman official charged with keeping peace in Jerusalem, he could order the Sanhedrin to meet to determine the cause of the riot.

23:1 Paul began his defense by addressing the members of the Sanhedrin as "Men, brothers" (see comment on 22:1–2). Then he asserted, "I have fulfilled my duty to God in all good conscience to this day"—a bold claim but not without parallel on Paul's part in other situations (cf. 20:18–21, 26–27; 24:16, Ro 15:19b, 23; Php 3:6b; 2Ti 4:7).

2 This so enraged the high priest Ananias that, in violation of the law, he ordered those near Paul to strike him on the mouth. Ananias served as high priest from A.D. 48–58 (or 59) and was known for his avarice and liberal use of violence. As a brutal and scheming man, he was hated by Jewish nationalists for his pro-Roman policies.

3 Indignant at the affront, Paul lashed out at Ananias and accused him of breaking the Jewish law, which safeguarded the rights of defendants and presumed them innocent until proved guilty. Paul was not yet charged with a crime, let alone tried and found guilty.

Anyone who behaved as Ananias did, Paul knew, was bound to come under God's judgment. Paul's words were more prophetic than he realized, for Ananias's final days were lived as a hunted animal and ended at the hands of his own people.

Paul's retort to Ananias' order seems quite out of character for a follower of the one who "when they hurled their insults at him, he did not retaliate; when he suffered, he made no threats" (1Pe 2:23). Paul momentarily lost his composure—as evidently Ananias hoped he would—and put himself at a disadvantage before the council. We cannot excuse this sudden burst of anger, though we must not view it self-righteously. We are made of the same stuff as Paul, and his provocation was greater than most of us will ever face. Paul himself realized his wrong and quickly acknowledged it.

4–5 At regular meetings of the Sanhedrin, the high priest presided and would have been identifiable for that reason. But this was not a regular meeting, and the high priest may not have occupied his usual place or worn his robes of office. Also, since Paul had visited Jerusalem only sporadically during the past twenty years, and since the high priest's office had passed from one to another within certain priestly families (cf. comment on Jn 18:12–14), Paul presumably did now know who the high priest was in A.D. 58. Nor, in fact, would he have known any of the current high priestly claimants by sight. All he could do when told he was speaking to the high priest was apologize—though more to the office than to the man—and acknowledge by citing Scripture (Ex 22:28) that, while he did not accept the view that the OT law provided the supreme direction for life (cf. 1Co 2:15; 9:20–21), he had no intention of being guided by Christ and his Spirit to act contrary to the law or do less than the law commanded.

6 Ananias's interruption changed the entire course of the meeting, but not as he had expected. Instead of being cowed into submission, Paul began again (note the resumptive use of the formal address used in v.1). This time he took the offensive. "I am a Pharisee, the son of a Pharisee," he declared. "I stand on trial because of my hope in the resurrection of the dead" (cf. 24:21; 26:6–8; 28:20b). Pharisaism in Paul's day was not as stereotyped as it later became under rabbinic development. He still considered himself a Pharisee because of his personal observance of the law and his belief in the resurrection, even though he did not separate himself from Gentiles. The phrase "the resurrection of the dead" seems to have been used by Paul and by Luke to refer to the whole doctrine of resurrection as that doctrine was validated and amplified by the resurrection of Jesus (cf. 17:32 in the context of 17:31).

7–10 Paul's declaration served to divide the council, with Sadducees on the one side (cf. comment on 4:1) and Pharisees on the other (cf. comment on 5:34). Some of the Pharisees saw in the inquisition of Paul an attempt by the Sadducees to discredit Pharisaism and its theology, and they rose to his defense. The Sadducees, however, kept pressing their objections, and the debate soon got out of hand. So violent, in fact, did it become that the commander had to bring in soldiers and rescue Paul. Once more the commander was frustrated in his effort to learn exactly why the Jews were so adamantly opposed to his prisoner.

11 Paul had feared such a reception at Jerusalem (cf. 20:22–23; 21:13; Ro 15:31), and now his worst fears were being realized. He had planned to go to Rome (see comment on 19:21). But developments at Jerusalem were building up to a point where it appeared his life could come to an end in the city through any number of circumstances beyond his control. Undoubtedly he was despondent as he awaited the next turn of events in his cell in the fortress. But "the following night," the risen and exalted Jesus appeared to Paul—as he had done at other critical moments in his ministry (cf. 18:9–10; 22:17–21)—and encouraged him by his presence. "Take courage!" he said, and he assured Paul that he would yet testify in Rome as he had done in Jerusalem. This assurance must have meant much to Paul in the ensuing months.

6. A plot to kill Paul (23:12–22)

12–15 Failing in their earlier plot to kill Paul in the temple precincts, more than forty fanatical Jews (probably many of them Asian Jews who had instigated the earlier plot, cf. 21:27–29) resolved to do away with him by ambushing him in the narrow streets of Jerusalem. For this they needed a pretext to lure him out of the fortress. So they arranged with "the chief priest and elders" to ask for Paul's return before the Sanhedrin for further questioning. They pledged to kill him as he was being brought from the Fortress of Antonia to the hall of the Sanhedrin (cf. comment on 4:5). To show their determination, they vowed not to eat or drink until they had accomplished their purpose. The conspirators' plan, though violating both the letter and the spirit of Jewish law pertaining to the Sanhedrin, was in keeping with the character of the high priest Ananias (cf. comment on 23:2).

16–17 We know nothing about Paul's sister and his nephew (this is the only reference anywhere to Paul's relatives), nor do we know how the young man learned of the plot. With his uncle in mortal danger, Paul's nephew could not stand by without warning him. After all, in Judaism the saving and preservation of life takes precedence over everything else. As a Roman citizen under protective custody, Paul could receive visitors—among them his nephew. On hearing the warning, Paul asked one of the centurions to take his nephew to the commander.

18–22 The seriousness with which the commander took the warning about the plot shows that he knew Ananias was the kind of man who could support such action and realized that Jewish feeling against Paul was strong enough to nurture it.

D. Imprisonment and Defenses at Caesarea (23:23–26:32)

1. Imprisonment at Caesarea (23:23–35)

23–25 Since the commander could not risk having a Roman citizen assassinated while in his custody, he took steps to transfer Paul to the jurisdiction of Felix, the governor of the province of Judea. He wanted to get Paul to Caesarea, the provincial capital (cf. comment on 10:1), as quickly as possible and before the conspirators got wind of it. So he ordered two centurions to ready two hundred infantry and seventy cavalry, together with two hundred "spearmen" (more likely, the word used here means "additional mounts and pack animals"), leaving for Caesarea at nine that evening. In addition, he ordered that "mounts" be provided for Paul—probably not only a horse for Paul but also another one for either riding or carrying his baggage, or both.

The purpose of the detachment was security and speed—the first being provided by the two hundred infantry and the second by the seventy cavalry with their two hundred extra mounts and pack animals, many of which may also have been used to carry the infantry during the night. If the garrison at Jerusalem consisted of about six hundred men and the word "spearmen" refers not to infantry but to additional mounts and pack animals, then the commander considered the plot against Paul serious enough to commit almost half the garrison at the Fortress of Antonia to escort Paul, with most of them due to return in a day or two (cf. v.32).

In saying that the commander wrote a letter "as follows" (lit., "of this type"), Luke suggests that what follows is only the general purport of the letter. He would hardly have been in a position to read the correspondence between a Roman commander and a Roman provincial governor. What he knew of the letter probably came from Paul, who himself would only have known about its contents as the governor used it in the initial questioning of his prisoner.

26 A letter beginning with a salutation that (1) named the sender, (2) named the recipient, and (3) sent greetings was the standard form for a letter of antiquity and is common to every letter of the NT, except Hebrews and 1 John.

For the first time in Acts, the commander's name is given. He was evidently a freeborn Greek who had worked his way up through the ranks of the Roman army and at some time paid an official of Claudius's government to receive Roman citizenship (cf. comment on 22:28). At that time his Greek name Lysias became his Roman cognomen, and he then took the nomen Claudius in honor of the emperor. Felix was the governor of the Roman province of Judea from A.D. 52–59 (see comments on 24:1). The title "Excellency" (GK 3196) here denotes an honorific title for highly placed officials in the Roman government (cf. 24:3; 26:25).

27–30 The body of the letter summarizes the events from the riot in the temple precincts to the commander's discovery of a plot against Paul's life. Paul may very well have smiled to himself when he heard how Lysias stretched the truth to his own benefit in claiming to have rescued Paul from the mob because "I had learned that he is a Roman citizen," omitting any reference to the proposed flogging. The most important part of the letter, that concerning Lysias's evaluation of the Jewish opposition to Paul, was clear: "I found that the accusation had to do with questions about their law, but there was no charge against him that deserved death or imprisonment" (v.29). That was of great significance not only for Paul's fortunes but also for Luke's apologetic purpose.

31–32 The soldiers carried out their orders and brought Paul during the night to Antipatris, a town built by Herod the Great in honor of his father Antipater. Having left Jerusalem at nine in the evening (cf. v.23), the detachment lost no time in covering the distance by morning. When the conspirators were left far behind and ambush was less likely, the infantry turned back to Jerusalem and the cavalry took Paul to Caesarea, some forty miles distant.

33–35 At Caesarea, the prisoner and Lysias's letter were turned over to Felix, the governor. On reading the letter, he questioned Paul on the basis of its contents. Had Paul been from one of the client kingdoms in Syria or Asia Minor, Felix would probably have wanted to consult the ruler of the kingdom. But on learning that Paul was from the Roman province of Cilicia, he felt competent as a provincial governor to hear the case himself, when Paul's accusers arrived from Jerusalem. In the meantime, Paul was kept under guard in the palace Herod the Great built for himself at Caesarea. It now served as the governor's headquarters and also had cells for prisoners.

2. Paul's defense before Felix (24:1–27)

In his account of Paul's defense before Felix, Luke gives almost equal space to (1) the Jewish charges against Paul (vv.1–9), (2) Paul's reply to these charges (vv.10–21), and (3) Felix's response (vv.22–27). He wants to show that despite the devious skill of the Jewish charges and the notorious cruelty and corruptibility of Felix, no other conclusions can be drawn from Paul's appearance before him than that (1) Christianity had nothing to do with political sedition and (2) Jewish opposition to Christianity sprang from the

Paul was removed from Jerusalem and spent a night in the fortress at Antipatris (v.31), the ruins of which are shown here.

Christian claim to legitimate fulfillment of the hopes of Judaism.

1 "Five days later" evidently means five days from Paul's arrest in the temple (cf. Paul's remark that "no more than twelve days ago I went up to Jerusalem to worship," v.11). With the notations of time and of place ("Caesarea"), the names of Paul's adversaries ("the high priest Ananias . . . with some of the elders and a lawyer named Tertullus"), and the identification of the judge ("the governor," i.e., Felix), the stage is set for Paul's defense. Ananias characteristically decided to prosecute Paul as quickly as possible (cf. comment on 23:2). To present his trumped-up charges as effectively as possible, he employed a lawyer named Tertullus. This man was probably a Hellenistic Jew who had expertise in affairs of the empire and had manifested strong allegiance to Judaism.

The governor, Antonius Felix, was born a slave and freed by Antonia, the mother of the emperor Claudius. He was a brother of Pallas, who was also a freedman of Antonia and became a good friend of the young prince Claudius. Through the influence of Pallas, Felix was appointed in A.D. 48 to a subordinate government post in Samaria. In 52 Claudius appointed him governor of Judea. History tells us that he was a master of cruelty and lust. During his governorship, insurrections and anarchy increased throughout Palestine. Try as he would to put down the uprisings and regain control, his brutal methods only alienated the Jewish population more and led to further disturbances. Despite his low birth, Felix had a succession of three wives—the third being Drusilla, the youngest daughter of Agrippa I, who had been unhappy as the wife of Azizus, king of Emesa; Felix desired her because of her beauty and persuaded her to leave Azizus for him. The relationship between these two seems to have been based upon greed, lust, and expectations of grandeur.

2–4 Tertullus began the case for the prosecution with the customary flattery for the judge in words chosen for his purpose. Many Jews would have been shocked to hear the high priest's mouthpiece attributing "a long period of peace" and "reforms" to Felix's administration; and few would have joined in any expression of "profound gratitude" for the governor's frequent displays of ferocity, cruelty, and greed. But Tertullus knew how to appeal to Felix's vanity. It was also customary to promise brevity, though such is human nature that the promise was rarely kept.

5–9 The three charges laid against Paul (v.5) are probably only a précis of the entire case. Tertullus obviously intended to create the impression of political sedition against Rome in his first two charges (disturbing the peace among the Jews; being a ringleader of the Nazarenes) and to argue the right for Judaism to impose the death penalty in his third charge (attempting to desecrate the temple; cf. comment on 21:28–29). During his reign over Judea, Felix had repeatedly crucified the leaders of various uprisings and had killed many of their followers for disturbing the Pax Romana. Tertullus's endeavor, as supported by the high priest and the Jewish elders with him, was to put Paul on the same level as these brigands, with the hope that in his insensitivity to the issues, Felix would act in his usual manner simply on the basis of their testimony. As in Jesus' trial before Pilate, their accusations were framed principally in terms of political sedition (cf. Lk 23:2, 5), though all along their main grievance was religious.

10 Invited to respond, Paul also began with a complimentary statement—but a briefer and truer one. Felix had been in contact with the Jewish nation in Palestine for over a decade, first in Samaria and then as governor over the entire province of Judea. Therefore Paul was pleased to make his defense before one who was in a position to know the situation as it was and to understand his words in their context.

11–13 In refuting the charges against him, Paul dealt with each in turn. First, it was "no more than twelve days ago" that he came to Jerusalem, not for political agitation but for worship. In such a short time, he implied, there would hardly have been sufficient opportunity to foment a revolt. Second, his accusers could hardly charge him with being a ringleader of any sedition, for he was alone when they arrested him in the temple and they could not cite any time when he was stirring up a crowd anywhere in the city (v.12). Third, their claim that he desecrated the temple was unproved because it was entirely without foundation (v.13).

14–16 The real reason Ananias and the Jewish elders opposed him, Paul insisted, was religious. He was "a follower of the Way," a Jewish group that agreed with the basic doctrines of Judaism. And while he differed from Ananias and the elders in his acceptance of "the Way," his conscience in the matter was "clear before God and man" (cf. 23:1).

Paul's statements about having "the same hope in God as these men" and accepting "a resurrection of both the righteous and the wicked" have led to much comment since Ananias himself would not have accepted the doctrine of a resurrection (cf. comment on 4:1 regarding Sadducean beliefs) and Paul in his letters speaks only of a resurrection of the righteous (cf. 1Co 15:12–58; 1Th 4:13–5:11; 2Th 2:1–12). But evidently some Pharisees were among the elders who had come down to Caesarea with Ananias (cf. v.1). And though Sadducees did not accept the hope of a resurrection, Paul as a Pharisee was probably sufficiently self-confident to believe that it was the Pharisaic hope that characterized—or, at least, should characterize—all true representations of the Jewish faith. Furthermore, while Paul in his letters speaks only of a resurrection of the righteous (as also did our Lord in Lk 14:14; 20:35–36), this is probably because such treatment is pastoral in nature and deals only with the righteous.

17 Reconstructing for Felix what happened in Jerusalem, Paul spoke of coming to Jerusalem "to bring my people gifts for the poor and to present offerings" (cf. v.11). This is the only time Luke mentions the collection for the poor at Jerusalem, which was so dear to Paul's own heart (cf. Ro 15:25–27, 31; 1Co 16:1–4). Some have objected that for Paul to say that the gift was "for my nation" adds a note of insincerity, for certainly Paul's efforts were directed toward relieving the plight of poor believers in the Jerusalem church and not of Jews in general. Yet Paul brought the gift not only for the relief of Christians and as a symbol of unity between believers but also with a view to the conversion of the entire nation. By aiding that branch of the church whose mission it was to call the nation to its Messiah, he was indirectly engaged in a mission to his own nation (cf. Ro 11:13b–14).

18–21 Continuing the summary of what took place at Jerusalem, Paul spoke of his arrest in the temple (v.18) and his arraignment before the Sanhedrin (v.20). But, he insisted, he made no attempt to create a disturbance; rather, he was taken by the crowd while worshiping in a ceremonially clean condition. If the Asian Jews who instigated the riot had any serious charge against him, they should have been present to accuse him before the governor. Roman law imposed heavy penalties upon accusers who abandoned their charges, and the disappearance of accusers often meant the withdrawal of a charge. Their absence, therefore, suggested that they had nothing against him that would stand up in a Roman court of law. Nor did the Sanhedrin, Paul went on, find any crime in him—except that he believed in the resurrection of the dead. Therefore, Paul declared, he was on trial because of his belief in "the resurrection of the dead" (v.21).

22–23 Felix seems to have summed up the situation accurately. After a decade in Palestine (cf. comment on v.1), he was "well acquainted with the Way" (v.22). While certainly not a Christian, he could see that the Jewish charges against Paul were entirely religious in nature—even though presented in the guise of political sedition. He therefore sought to preserve the Pax Romana within his jurisdiction simply by removing the possibility of confrontation between the disputants and by delaying judicial procedure. So Paul was placed under protective custody in the palace of Herod the Great, and Ananias was given the deceptive promise of a decision being reached when the commander Lysias came down to Caesarea and presented his testimony (which he had already given in his letter, cf. 23:25–30). As a Roman citizen, Paul was allowed some freedom and permitted visits from friends to care for his needs. But both he and Ananias seem to have realized that Felix had no intention of bringing the case to a decision in the near future; and they evidently, each for his own reasons, decided to await the appointment of a new provincial governor (anticipated soon) before pressing for a resolution.

24–26 Added to the description of Felix's response is this vignette about the interaction between the Roman governor, his Jewish wife, and the Christian apostle, which elaborates further the nature of Felix's response and highlights one aspect of Paul's continued, though restricted, ministry while under protective custody at Caesarea. Drusilla apparently still had some qualms of conscience about her marriage to Felix and therefore took the opportunity to send for Paul in order to hear his message.

Paul spoke to Felix and his wife about the necessity of "faith in Christ Jesus" (v.24). He also made it plain that this involved an ethical life, for he spoke of "righteousness, self-control and the judgment to come" (v.25)—three subjects Felix and Drusilla particularly needed to learn about! Felix ordered him to stop, for he became afraid in the presence of such preaching. Apparently Drusilla was offended by what she considered Paul's moralistic ranting, for Luke makes no mention of her having listened to him again. Felix's corruption led him to call Paul often before him in hope of getting a bribe for his release. He must have believed that Paul had access to some money—perhaps through a large number of Christian friends who visited him (cf. 24:23; 27:3).

27 After two years Festus replaced Felix as governor of Judea. According to Josephus, Felix's downfall came through an outbreak of hostilities between Jews and Greeks at Caesarea, with both claiming dominant civil rights in the city. Using the Syrian troops under his command, Felix's intervention retaliated on the Jews. Many were killed, taken prisoner, or plundered of their wealth; and a delegation of Jews went to Rome to complain. Felix was recalled to Rome and replaced by Festus in A.D. 60.

During those two years, Paul remained in Herod's palace at Caesarea—with Felix undoubtedly rationalizing his imprisonment as a protection for Paul and a favor to the Jews. It must have been an extremely tedious time for Paul. Luke, however, probably made full use of these two years to investigate "everything from the beginning" about Christianity (cf. Lk 1:3). And while we cannot say whether he at this time produced either a preliminary draft of his gospel or any portion of Acts, it is probable that he became quite familiar with (1) the traditions comprising Mark's gospel, (2) other materials having to do with the story of Jesus that he would also incorporate into his gospel, (3) accounts circulating in Palestine of events in the early church that he would include in the first half of Acts, and (4) recollections and interpretations of Paul as to his activities before Luke joined him.

3. Paul's defense before Festus (25:1–12)

Luke's account of Paul's defense before Festus is the briefest of his five defenses. Most of it parallels in summary fashion Paul's appearance before Felix. The new element is Paul's appeal to Caesar, setting the stage for his journey to Rome. Luke's apologetic purpose here is to show that only when Roman administrators were largely ignorant of the facts of the case were concessions made to Jewish opposition that could prove disastrous for the Christian movement.

1 For the Jewish population of Palestine, Porcius Festus was a welcome successor to Felix. Nothing is known of him before he assumed the governorship of Judea. Nor can the time of his nomination for the post or his arrival in Palestine be precisely fixed, though it was probably sometime in A.D. 60. He inherited all the troubles and tensions that were mounting during Felix's maladministration, which culminated in the disaster of 66–70. His term of office was cut short by his death in 62.

The situation in Palestine demanded immediate action to bring together opposing factions within the Jewish nation. Therefore on arriving in Palestine, Festus took only three days to settle in at Caesarea before going up to Jerusalem to meet with the leaders of the nation.

2 The high priest at Jerusalem when Festus took office was Ishmael, appointed by Herod Agrippa II to succeed Ananias during the final days of Felix's governorship. Ananias, however, continued to exercise a dominant role in Jerusalem affairs right up to his death in 66 at the hands of Jewish nationalists. This is probably why Luke speaks of "the chief priests" and not just the high priest as appearing with the elders before Festus when he came to Jerusalem (cf. 4:23; 9:14; 22:30; 23:14; 25:15).

3 Counting on the new governor's inexperience, the Jewish authorities urged Festus to transfer Paul's case to Jerusalem for trial. They were hoping to ambush and murder him on the way (cf. 23:12–15). Perhaps also they hoped that with such a change of venue, if their plans for an ambush were again frustrated, they could arrange to have Paul tried before the Sanhedrin on the single charge of profaning the temple—for which they had the right to impose the death penalty (see comment on 21:27–29).

4–5 Unwittingly, Festus overturned their plans by inviting the Jewish leaders to return with him to Caesarea and press charges against Paul there. Evidently he desired to carry out only such business as was absolutely necessary on his first visit to Jerusalem and preferred to preside over any extended trial back at Caesarea—particularly since the prisoner was already there.

6–8 Festus convened court and ordered Paul brought before him, thus reopening the whole case against him, and the Jewish accusers restated their charges (cf. 24:5–6). But again they produced no witnesses, nor could they prove their charges. As for Paul, he stoutly continued to insist on his innocence (v.8). So the impasse remained.

9 Festus was at a loss to know what to make of the Jewish charges and Paul's denials (cf. vv.18–20a). Yet the Sanhedrin plainly wanted the case transferred to Jerusalem for trial; and as the new governor of Judea, Festus saw no reason why he could not concede the Jews this. He seems not to have fully appreciated what lay behind their request and apparently thought it would be politically wise to gain their goodwill by a change of venue.

10–11 Paul knew that to return to Jerusalem would place him in serious jeopardy. It would likely involve being turned over to the Sanhedrin; for once he was in Jerusalem, the Jewish authorities would pressure Festus to have Paul turned over to them for trial on the charge of profaning the temple. "I am now standing before Caesar's court, where I ought to be tried," he asserted. But being unsure as to just what action Festus might take in the matter if left at that, Paul went on to claim one final right he had as a Roman citizen: "I appeal to Caesar!"

Roman law at this time protected Roman citizens by their right of appealing to the emperor. Such appeals could only be made in cases that went beyond the normal jurisdiction of a governor—particularly where the threat of violent coercion or capital punishment by provincial administrators was present. It may seem somewhat strange that Paul should have preferred to appeal to the emperor Nero (A.D. 54–68), the persecutor of Christians at Rome, rather than continue to entrust his case to Festus, whether at Caesarea or Jerusalem. But the early years of Nero's rule, under the influence of the Stoic philosopher Seneca and the prefect of the praetorian guard Afranius Burrus, were looked upon as something of a Golden Age. There was little in A.D. 60 that warned of Nero's character and relations with Christianity during the last five years of his life.

12 Festus's discussion with his advisors was probably not whether an appeal to Caesar should be allowed. Rather, he had to determine (1) whether the charges against his prisoner fell into the category of normal provincial jurisdiction or went beyond that jurisdiction, and (2) whether it was either just or feasible to acquit the prisoner and make the appeal unnecessary. Since the charges against Paul concerned political sedition, which in Roman law could be punished by death, and profanation of the Jerusalem temple, which in Jewish law called for death, Festus had no choice but to acknowledge the extraordinary character of the charge and accept Paul's appeal. But Festus still had the legal right to pronounce an acquittal after the act of appeal. Yet politically no newly arrived governor would have dreamt of antagonizing the leaders of the people he sought to govern by acquitting one against whom they were so vehemently opposed. It was more a political than legal decision Festus had to make, and he was probably only too glad to have this way out of a very sticky situation. So he agreed to the appeal.

4. Festus consults with Herod Agrippa II (25:13–22)

Though ridding himself of one problem, Festus now took on another: What would he write in his report to the imperial court at Rome about the charges against Paul and the issues in the case? Undoubtedly, Luke had no direct knowledge of what was said in private between a Roman governor and the king of a neighboring principality. But the gist of what was discussed would certainly have been evident from their resultant actions, and Luke here fleshes out the details of that conversation in order to prepare the way for Paul's last great defense before Herod Agrippa II.

13 Marcus Julius Agrippa II (A.D. 27–100) was the son of Herod Agrippa I (see comment on 12:1). He was brought up at Rome in the court of Claudius and, like his father, was a favorite of the emperor. At his father's death in 44 (see 12:21–23), he was only seventeen years old—too young to rule over his father's domains. Therefore Palestine became a Roman province administered by a provincial governor. In 50, Claudius appointed Agrippa II king of Chalcis, a petty kingdom to the northeast of Judea. In 53 Claudius gave him the tetrarchy of Philip in exchange for the kingdom of Chalcis, which he gave to Agrippa's uncle Herod. And in 56 Nero added to his kingdom the Galilean cities of Tarichea and Tiberias with their surrounding lands and the Perean city of Julias with fourteen other villages. As ruler of the adjoining kingdom to the north, Herod Agrippa II came to pay his respects to Festus, the new governor of Judea.

With Agrippa II was Bernice (properly Berenice), his sister one year younger than himself. She had been engaged to Marcus, a nephew of the philosopher Philo. Then she married her uncle Herod, king of Chalcis, but at his death in A.D. 48, she came to live with her brother Agrippa. Rumors of their incestuous relationship flourished in both Rome and Palestine.

14 Though Agrippa II did not rule over Judea, he had been appointed by Claudius to be "the curator of the temple," with power to depose and appoint the high priest and with the responsibility of preserving the temple's treasury and priestly vestments. He developed an interest in the Jewish religion and was, in fact, looked upon by Rome as an authority. Thus Festus broached the subject of Paul's case when Agrippa visited him.

15–21 Festus told Agrippa how the Jewish leaders confronted him with Paul's case when he first went to Jerusalem and that they had asked for Paul's death (v.15), but he acted in accordance with Roman law in demanding that charges be properly laid and the defendant allowed his day in court (v.16). Furthermore, he insisted, he acted with due dispatch, for on the day after he and the Jewish leaders returned to Caesarea, he convened court in order to try the case (v.17). To his surprise he found that the charges did not concern real offenses punishable under Roman law but theological differences of a Jewish intramural nature (vv.18–19a) and a debate "about a dead man named Jesus who Paul claimed was alive" (v.19b). With a shrug of his shoulders, Festus confessed his total inadequacy to deal with them (v.20a). In an endeavor to resolve the impasse, Festus told Agrippa he was prepared to accede to the Sanhedrin's request for a change of venue to Jerusalem (v.20b). But Paul objected and appealed to Caesar, an appeal Festus had granted (v.21). Now then, what was he to write in sending Paul on to the imperial court regarding the charges against the prisoner and the issues of the case?

22 This stirred Agrippa's interest so that instead of merely giving his advice, he had an intense personal desire to hear Paul himself. Festus was only too happy to arrange a meeting for the very next day. Paul's meeting with Herod Agrippa II has often been paralleled with that of Jesus before Herod Antipas in Lk 23:6–12. Not only was each arraigned by a Roman governor, but each was brought before a Jewish king who wanted very much to meet him (Lk 23:8). Paul's time with Agrippa II, however, turned out far more harmoniously than that of Jesus before Antipas.

5. Paul's defense before Herod Agrippa II (25:23–26:32)

Paul's defense before Herod Agrippa II was for Luke the most important of the five defenses. It is the longest and most carefully constructed of the five. Perhaps Luke was even in the audience chamber through the courtesy of an officer of the guard.

All the attention in the account is focused on Paul himself and the Gospel, not on the charges brought forward by the Jews, and certainly not on any rumored incest between Agrippa and Bernice. Inherent in Luke's account are at least three apologetic themes: (1) Paul's relations with the Roman government in Judea did not end in dissonance but with an acknowledgment of his innocence (cf. 25:25; 26:31); (2) even though the Jewish high priests and Sanhedrin opposed Paul, the Jewish king who in Rome's eyes outranked them agreed with a verdict of innocence (cf. 26:32); and (3) Paul's innocence was demonstrated not only before Roman and Jewish rulers but also publicly before "the high ranking officers and the leading men of the city" (25:23).

Yet Paul's speech before Agrippa II is not just a personal defense of himself. It is also a positive presentation of the Gospel with an evangelistic appeal: (1) according to the OT prophets, the Christ would suffer, rise from the dead, and proclaim light to both Jews and Gentiles (26:23); (2) what God did in and through Jesus the Christ was done openly, "not done in a corner" (v.26); (3) believing the prophets leads one to accept redemption in Christ (v.27); (4) Paul's prayer for all who hear is that they "may become what I am, except for these chains" (v.29). After this climactic speech of Paul, all that remains for Luke is to sketch out the apostle's journey to Rome and his ministry there, thus completing the geographical framework of Luke's presentation and concluding it on a note of triumph (cf. 28:31)

23 Luke describes Agrippa and Bernice as entering the audience chamber of Herod the Great's Caesarean palace "with great pomp," accompanied by a procession of "high ranking officers and the leading men of the city." The Romans always knew how to process well. The sight of Agrippa's royal robes, Bernice's finery, and the military and civil dignitaries decked out in their official attire doubtless overwhelmed those unaccustomed to such displays. Paul the prisoner was then brought in. But though the situation asserted the importance of Roman officialdom and the inferiority of the man who stood before it, Luke's inspired insight penetrated the trappings and saw that the situation was really reversed. And his evaluation has prevailed in history.

24–27 Festus opened the proceedings by turning the dignitaries' attention to Paul with the words "You see this man!" After saying that he could not substantiate the charges against Paul, he told them how Paul had appealed to Caesar. Then, asking for help with what he would have to write in sending Paul to the imperial court, Festus turned the inquiry over to King Agrippa.

A number of subtle touches in these verses are particularly appropriate for the situation. The title *Sebastos* ("Emperor," v.25; GK *4935*), found only here and in v.21 in the NT, is the Greek equivalent of Augustus (a title first conferred on Octavian by the Senate in 27 B.C. to denote one who is lifted above other mortals). The addition of *Kyrios* ("Lord" or "His Majesty"; GK *3261*) to the imperial title began in the time of Nero (A.D. 54–68). Despite its associations with deity in the eastern realms of the empire, the growth of the imperial cult, and the pretensions to divinity of such emperors as Nero and Domitian, *Kyrios* did not by itself signal to Romans the idea of deity but rather connoted that of majesty. Likewise, Festus's statement (v.27) that he thought it "unreasonable" to send on a prisoner with unspecified charges against him is typical of the face-saving language used among officials, for the failure to specify charges was a dereliction of duty.

26:1 At Agrippa's invitation to speak for himself, Paul, though manacled by chains (v.29), motioned with his hand for attention (cf. 21:40) and began speaking. While we have only a summary of his speech, it is the longest of Paul's five defenses, undoubtedly reflecting the relative length of the address. Since Agrippa was considered an authority on the Jewish religion, he might have been expected to listen closely to Paul's lengthy explanation of the relation of his message and ministry to the hope of Israel.

2–3 This was just the kind of situation Paul had longed for during two bleak years in prison—namely, a knowledgeable judge and a not inherently antagonistic audience before whom he could not only make his defense but also proclaim his message. Therefore he began with unusual fervor, expressing appreciation for the opportunity of speaking, complimenting the judge, and asking for patience in hearing him out. Since Festus had already said that Paul had not committed a capital crime (cf.25:25), Paul chose to defend himself only against the charge that he had transgressed against Judaism.

4–8 It was not in spite of his Jewish heritage but because of it, Paul insisted, that he believed and proclaimed what he did. So he began the body of his address by drawing together his Pharisaic background and his Christian commitment, arguing that the Jewish hope and the Christian message are inseparably related. His life had been spent among his people in his own country and in Jerusalem (v.4; cf. 22:3). He had lived as a Pharisee, "the strictest sect" of the Jewish religion (v.5; cf. Php 3:5–6). It was because of the Jewish hope in the resurrection of the dead that he was being tried (v.6). Ironically, the charges against him were brought, of all people, by the Jews themselves. Yet why should any of his audience think it "incredible that God raises the dead" (v.8), particularly when God had validated the truth of the resurrection by raising Jesus from the dead (cf. comment on 23:6)?

9–11 Paul went on to acknowledge that he too at one time thought that Christian preaching about the resurrection of Jesus was incredible. Pharisee though he was, he too had denounced belief in Jesus' resurrection and had persecuted those who claimed to have seen him alive after his crucifixion. He put Christians in prison, agreed with the death penalty for their "blasphemy" (cf. 8:1), and went through the synagogues seeking to punish them for apostasy and to get them to recant. This he did not only in Jerusalem but also in cities outside Judea.

12–14 While Paul was trying to stamp out nascent Christianity, the encounter that changed his life took place. That Paul's account of his Damascus Road conversion appears three times in Acts (chs. 9; 22; 26) undoubtedly shows how important this event was not only for Paul but also for Luke (cf. introductory comments on 9:1–30). It is in this third account that Luke's purpose to proclaim the Gospel of Christ in Luke-Acts reaches its climax. Each account fits its own special context in Paul's life and in Luke's purpose. Here there is an intensification and explication of the details that is not found in the earlier accounts: (1) the heavenly light was "brighter than the sun" (cf. 9:3; 22:6); (2) it blazed around both "me and my companions" (cf. 9:3; 22:6); (3) "we all fell to the ground" (cf. 9:4; 22:7); and (4) the voice from heaven spoke "in Aramaic" (or "in Hebrew"; see NIV note).

Likewise in v.14b we have the only place in the three accounts where "It is hard for you to kick against the goads" is included (cf. 9:5; KJV). This was a well-known Greek expression for opposition to deity; Paul used it here to show his Greek-oriented audience the implications of the question "Saul, Saul, why do you persecute me?" Lest he be misunderstood as proclaiming only a Galilean prophet he had formerly opposed, he was pointing out what was obvious to any Jew: correction by a voice from heaven meant opposition to God himself.

15–18 On the other hand, this third account leaves out certain features of the other two: (1) the heavenly speaker identifies himself only as Jesus (cf. 22:8); (2) there is no mention of Ananias (cf. 9:10–19; 22:12–16); (3) there is no mention of Paul's blindness and subsequent healing (cf. 9:8–9; 18–19; 22:11, 13). There was, however, no need here to refer to Jesus "of Nazareth" or to the devout Jew Ananias (cf. comment on 22:12–16). Nor was it necessary for Paul to refer to his blindness and healing, which might have been confusing to a pagan audience. Rather, in his address before Agrippa and the others, Paul merged the words of Christ as spoken on the road to Damascus (cf. 9:5–6; 22:8,10), as given through Ananias of Damascus (cf. 22:14–15), and as received in a vision at Jerusalem (cf. 22:18–21). In other words, while not emphasizing details of time or human aid, Paul did emphasize the lordship of Christ and the divine commission Christ gave him.

The words of the risen Jesus calling Paul to his mission (vv.16–17) recall the commissioning of the prophets Ezekiel and Jeremiah (Eze 2:1, 3; Jer 1:7–8), and the commission itself (v.18) echoes that of the Servant of the Lord in Isa 42:6b–7. Indeed, Paul's mission was a prophetic one that perpetuated the commission originally given to God's Righteous Servant, Jesus Christ. And Christians today, as God's servants and prophets, are called to the same kind of ministry.

19–21 Having been confronted by the risen and glorified Jesus, Paul henceforth knew but one Master and found it impossible to resist his commands. So he told Agrippa how he began preaching about Jesus in Damascus and continued to do so in Jerusalem (cf. 9:20–30). The words "and in all Judea" are grammatically strange and conflict with the evidence of Ac 9:20–30 and Gal 1:18–24 that Paul did *not* preach the Gospel throughout "all the region of Judea." Perhaps this phrase was an early gloss that entered the text through a false reading of Ro 15:19. And Paul also preached to the Gentiles a message of repentance and conversion. It was because of his preaching to Gentiles, he insisted, that the Jews were so aggressively opposed to him.

22–23 Nevertheless, in fulfillment of Christ's promise (v.17), God had stood by Paul, protecting him and enabling him to proclaim "to small and great alike" a message thoroughly in accord with Israel's faith and in harmony with all that the prophets and Moses said would happen: "that the Christ would suffer and, as the first to rise from the dead, would proclaim light to his own people and to the Gentiles." The proclamation of both a suffering Messiah and the resurrection of Jesus were distinctive teachings in early Christianity. To these foundation tenets of the early faith, Paul, by revelation (cf. Gal 1:11–12; Eph 3:1–6), added the legitimacy of a direct outreach to Gentiles, a development brought about by God himself as the true intent of Israelite religion.

24 At this point Festus broke into Paul's address, unable to endure it any longer. He may not have been speaking for the Jews, to whom a suffering Messiah and a direct ministry to Gentiles were outrageous. But no sensible Roman could believe in the resurrection of a man from the dead—and even if he did privately accept such a strange view, he would not allow it to interfere with his practical living or bring him into danger of death. Paul, Festus concluded, was so learned in his Jewish traditions that he had become utterly impractical. Such talk was the height of insanity.

25–27 But what Festus declared to be madness Paul insisted was "true and reasonable." Then he turned to Agrippa for support. The ministry of Jesus was widely known in Palestine, and Agrippa would have heard of it. Jesus' death and resurrection were amply attested, and the Christian Gospel had now been proclaimed for three decades. Certainly the king knew of these things, because they had been done openly. And certainly the king believed the prophets—a belief, as Paul saw it, that inevitably brought one to Christ. So the prisoner became the questioner, as Paul boldly said, "King Agrippa, do you believe the prophets? I know you do."

28 Paul's direct question embarrassed Agrippa. He had his reputation to maintain before Festus and the other dignitaries. Whatever he may have thought about Paul's message personally, he was too worldly-wise to commit himself in public to what others thought was madness. So he parried Paul's question with his own clever, though rather inane, one: "Do you think that in such a short time you can persuade me to be a Christian?" The KJV's translation of this reply, "Almost thou persuadest me to be a Christian," has become one of the famous quotations in history. It has inspired countless sermons and even a gospel hymn. Nevertheless, "almost" is not what Agrippa said.

29 Addressing the king with extreme politeness and taking up Agrippa's own word "short time," Paul replied, "Short time or long—I pray God that not only you but all who are listening to me today may become what I am." Undoubtedly he spoke with evangelistic fervor, directing his appeal not only to the king but also to the other dignitaries. Then in a lighter vein, recognizing the apparent incongruity of appealing for their acceptance of spiritual freedom while he himself stood chained before them, he raised his hands and added, "except for these chains."

30–32 Paul had had the last word, and his light touch at the end of his response evidently broke up the meeting. With it Agrippa dismissed the proceedings and with Festus and Bernice strode out of the audience chamber to discuss the situation. Agrippa had presumably heard enough to instruct Festus what he should write in his report to Rome. Their conclusion was that Paul had done nothing that in Rome's eyes merited death or imprisonment, and Agrippa was heard to comment, "This man could have been set free, if he had not appealed to Caesar." This comment should not be taken to mean that a provincial governor could not free a prisoner after an appeal to Caesar (see comment on 25:12). In this situation, however, Paul's status was not a question of law only but also of politics. With these words, Luke concludes his apologetic motif in Acts and vindicates both Paul and Christianity from any suspicion of sedition.

E. The Journey to Rome (27:1–28:15)

One would like to know many things about Paul's two-year imprisonment at Caesarea. For instance, how was the apostle supported during this time (cf. comment on 24:26)? How cordial were Paul's relations with the Jerusalem Christians and their leaders? How about his contacts with the Caesarean believers or with other groups of Christians in the area? What were Timothy and Luke doing? What happened to Silas and to those who represented the Gentile churches during Paul's last visit to Jerusalem (cf. 20:4)? Such matters, however, were evidently not of interest to Luke or to Paul in his letters. In an endeavor to fill these gaps in Luke's account of Paul's stay in Caesarea, some have proposed that several of Paul's letters (notably Ephesians, Colossians, Philemon) were written while he was in prison in Caesarea. But more likely they were composed during his subsequent Roman imprisonment.

Luke's account of Paul's voyage to Rome stands out as one of the most vivid pieces of descriptive writing in the whole Bible. Its details regarding first-century seamanship are exceptionally precise and its portrayal of conditions on the eastern Mediterranean remarkably accurate. What stands out is his portrayal of Paul as a man of powerful personality, who commanded respect in various situations. Most of all, he was an apostle of Jesus Christ, who had been promised divine protection and assurance that he would reach Rome (cf. 23:11), and, as elsewhere in Acts, Paul was one through whom God by his Spirit worked in an extraordinary fashion (cf. 19:11–12; 20:10–12).

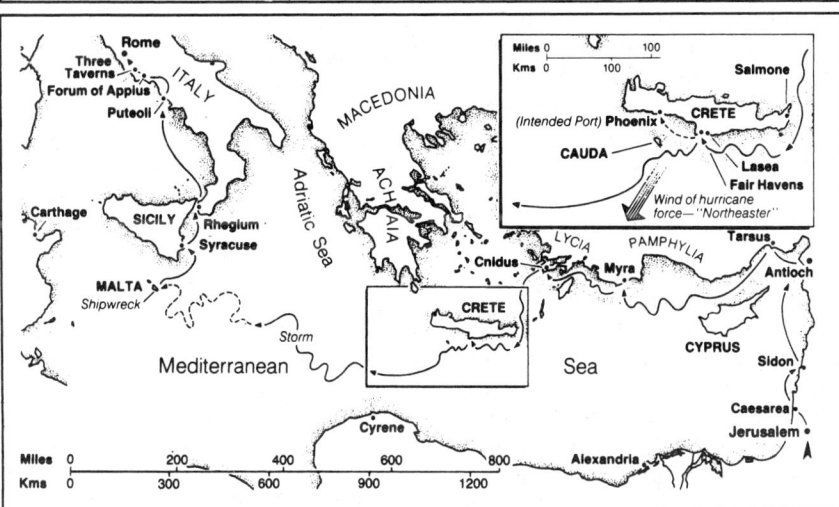

PAUL'S JOURNEY TO ROME

1. From Palestine to Crete (27:1–12)

1 The account of Paul's journey to Rome is the longest of Luke's four "we" sections (27:1–28:16; cf. 16:10–17; 20:5–15; 21:1–18). The vividness and precision of the narrative confirm what the use of "we" implies—that it is an eyewitness report. The centurion Julius, assigned to take Paul to Rome, was a member of "the Imperial Regiment." The soldiers who performed the police and escort services in Paul's day were the *speculatores*, a special body of imperial guards who were particularly prominent in times of military intrigue. They did not belong to any division of a Roman army legion; instead, they formed a special unit of their own.

2 The port of embarkation was undoubtedly Caesarea. The boat they boarded was a coastal vessel from the city of Adramyttium in Mysia. Embarking with Paul were Luke (cf. "we") and Aristarchus, who were possibly entered on the passenger list as Paul's personal doctor and servant, respectively. As a Roman citizen who had appealed to the emperor, Paul would naturally have had a more favored position than the other prisoners; and the centurion would have recognized his superiority as a gentleman with attendants. That Aristarchus is included in Col 4:10 and Phm 24 as sending greetings from Rome (assuming a Roman origin for these letters) suggests that he traveled with Paul all the way to Rome and remained with him during his imprisonment there.

3 At Sidon, the ancient Phoenician port some seventy miles north of Caesarea, the boat took on cargo. Here Paul was permitted to visit the Christians of the city, who, like those at Tyre (cf. comment on 21:4), had probably become believers through the witness of Christian Hellenists forced to leave Jerusalem at the time of Stephen's martyrdom (cf. 11:19). The centurion Julius had probably been advised by Festus to be lenient with Paul, and doubtless Paul had already made a good impression on him. Yet a soldier would have been always with him during his visit.

4 5 From Sidon, the boat sailed northwest toward Cyprus, staying close to the long east coast of the island because of the westerly winds that blow from spring through fall on the eastern Mediterranean. Two and one half years earlier Paul and his companions had sailed with that westerly wind from Patara to Tyre and had passed Cyprus on the south (see 21:3). Now, however, their voyage was considerably slower as their boat had to run against the winds, and they tried to stay in the lee of sheltering land masses. Crossing the open sea between Cyprus and Cilicia, the vessel worked its way westward to Myra in Lycia, on the southwest coast of Asia Minor, helped along by local land breezes and a westward current that runs along that coast.

6 Myra was the most illustrious city in Lycia, with distinguished public buildings, a large theater, and many evidences of wealth. It became the natural port of call for grain ships bound for Rome from Egypt, and in commercial importance it overshadowed its rival Patara to the west. There Julius arranged with the owner of a larger Alexandrian grain ship to take the soldiers and prisoners on board for the longer voyage to Italy.

7–8 Leaving Myra, the grain ship moved slowly along the peninsula that thrusts seaward between the islands of Cos and Rhodes to the port of Cnidus, at the southwestern tip of Asia Minor. Cnidus was the last port of call before sailing west across the Aegean for the Greek mainland. But the northern winds that blow down the length of the Aegean at this time of year pushed the ship off course and forced the pilot to seek protection along the southern coast of Crete, the 160-mile-long island southeast of Greece. Passing Cape Salmone on the eastern tip of Crete, the ship entered the small bay of Fair Havens.

9–10 Navigation in this part of the Mediterranean was always dangerous after Sept. 14 and was considered impossible after Nov. 11. The ship had lost valuable time since leaving Myra, and it was obvious that there was no hope of reaching Italy before winter. "The Fast" (i.e., Yom Kippur or "Day of Atonement"), the chief festival of Judaism celebrated on the tenth of the lunar month Tishri (between the latter part of September and the first part of October), was already past. So Paul warned that disaster would befall them if they tried to go further.

11–12 But the pilot and the ship's owner preferred not to winter in the small, open bay of Fair Havens, being reluctant to seek quarters for themselves and their passengers in the small town of Lasea. They hoped to winter instead at the larger and safer port of Phoenix, forty miles west of Fair Havens. Between these two ports, however, the south coast of Crete turns suddenly to the north and exposes a ship to the northern gales before it regains the protection of the coast just before Phoenix. The centurion agreed with the pilot and the ship's owner that it would, if at all possible, be best to winter at Phoenix.

2. Storm and shipwreck (27:13–44)

13–15 Shortly after the decision to winter at Phoenix was made, a gentle southern breeze began to blow; and it appeared that they would have no trouble in crossing the Gulf of Messara that began west of Cape Matala on the southern coast of Crete. But no sooner had they rounded the cape and entered the gulf than they were caught in a hurricane coming from Mount Ida to the north. Sailors called this wind the Euroquilo (lit., "northeaster"). Before it they were helpless.

16–17 Driven southwest some twenty-three miles to the small island of Cauda, the ship managed to gain the lee of the island. The sailors pulled in the dinghy, which was full of water, reinforced the ship with ropes to keep it from breaking up (exactly how these ropes were positioned is not known, though most argue that ropes were passed under the ship and secured above the deck), and put out the sea anchor to keep the ship from running onto the sandbars of Syrtis, off the African coast.

18–20 For fourteen days and nights (cf. v.27), the ship was in the grip of the northeaster. The crew tried to lighten the ship by throwing overboard all the deck cargo (v.18), then by disposing of the ship's tackle (v.19). In the darkness of the storm they could not take their bearings from the sun or stars. All hope of being saved had vanished.

21–26 Undoubtedly Paul shared the general pessimism on board ship (cf. the inclusive use of "we" in v.20). But one night toward the close of the fourteen-day storm, "an angel of God" stood by him and reassured him with a message of comfort for this time of crisis (cf. 23:11). The next morning when Paul shared this vision with his companions on shipboard, he was human enough to (in effect) say "I told you so" to those who had not taken his advice at Fair Havens. He added that in his opinion they would not be saved without running aground on some island.

27–29 During the fourteenth night after leaving Crete, it was clear—probably from the running swell and the roar of surf—that they were near a shore. Soundings indicated shallower water. To keep the ship from being wrecked against the rocks of an unknown coast in the darkness, they dropped four anchors and waited for dawn. Luke tells us that they were in the Adriatic Sea (the name used in ancient times for all parts of the Mediterranean between Greece, Italy, and Africa).

30–32 Contrary to the best tradition of the sea, the sailors schemed to save themselves by lowering the dinghy (cf. vv.16–17) under cover of lowering some more anchors from the bow. But Paul saw through the ruse, doubtless realizing that no sailor would drop anchors from the bow under such conditions. He knew that to try to make shore in the morning without a full crew would be disastrous. So Paul warned Julius that all would be lost if the sailors deserted the ship. Though he had not listened to Paul earlier (cf. vv.11–12), Julius took his advice here and ordered his men to cut the lines holding the dinghy and let it fall away.

33–38 The storm had been so fierce that preparing food had been impossible. Once again, Paul's great qualities of leadership came to the fore. Urging all on board to eat, he took some bread, gave thanks to God, and ate it. The others on board also ate. Then, strengthened by the food, they threw the cargo of grain overboard to give the ship a shallower draft as they beached her. Only at v.37 does Luke tell us how many were on board. Probably in distributing the food, they had to know the exact number, and Luke himself may have helped supervise the distribution.

39–41 With a profusion of nautical detail that makes this chapter unique, Luke tells how the ship was beached amid the pounding surf on a sandbar some distance from land and began to break apart. From then on it was every man for himself.

42–44 Roman military law decreed that a guard who allowed his prisoner to escape could expect the same penalty the escaped prisoner would have suffered (cf. comments on 12:18–19a; 16:25–28). Thus the soldiers wanted to kill the prisoners, lest they escape while getting to land. Julius, however, determined to protect Paul, prevented this and ordered all to get to land either by swimming or by holding on to pieces of the wreckage. So God in his providence brought them all safely to shore, as he had promised Paul he would (cf. v.24). Many, like Luke, undoubtedly saw the relation between the promise and their safety and in their own ways praised the God Paul served.

3. Ashore at Malta (28:1–10)

1 Malta is an island about 18 miles long and 8 miles wide, lying 58 miles south of Sicily and 180 miles north and east of the African coast. It had been colonized about 1000 B.C. by Phoenicians, but was captured by Rome in 218 B.C (though it was given much local autonomy). Augustus established a Roman governor on the island and settled a number of army veterans and their families there. In Paul's day the island was known for its prosperity and residential architecture, and its native population spoke a Phoenician dialect, though many probably knew some Latin and Greek.

2–4 The islanders showed kindness to "us all" (i.e., the 276 survivors) by building a fire, which was just what was needed in the cold and rain. When Paul was bitten by a viper, the islanders concluded he was a murderer whom Justice had at last caught up with since he had not died at sea. The Greek goddess Dike (i.e., "Justice"; GK *1472*), or her Phoenician counterpart, was apparently venerated by the Maltese.

5–6 Seeing that Paul was unaffected by the snakebite, the islanders decided that he must be a god—or, perhaps, a favorite of the gods. Nothing is said about Paul's rebuking the islanders as he had rebuked the people at Lystra (cf. 14:15–18), for evidently they made no attempt to worship Paul. Luke gives us such a vividly detailed account of the incident because he wants his readers to appreciate that Paul was not only a heaven-directed man with a God-given message but also a heaven-protected man. The powerful account of the storm and shipwreck has shown this, and now this vignette stresses it once more.

7–9 Though Paul spent three months (cf. v.11) on Malta, Luke gives us only one more incident from his stay there—the healing of Publius's father. This account is much like that of Peter and the crippled beggar (cf. 3:1ff.) in purpose, though not in length. Luke likely included it to illustrate the continuing power of Paul's ministry despite his being in Malta as a prisoner. No matter what the circumstances are, the true servant of Christ is, like Paul, never off duty for his Lord.

As the Roman governor of Malta and as an act of official courtesy, Publius brought the survivors of the wreck to his estate and entertained them for three days while their respective situations were sorted out and arrangements made for their lodgings over the winter. Luke's reference to the governor only by his praenomen may reflect a friendly relationship that developed between Publius, Paul, and Luke during those three months.

The malady that the father of Publius was suffering from may have been Malta fever, which in 1887 was traced to the milk of Maltese goats. Cases of Malta fever are long-lasting—an average of four months, but in some cases lasting two or three years. Luke uses the plural "fevers" here, probably implying the way it affects its victims with intermittent attacks.

After Paul had healed Publius's father through prayer and laying on of hands, "the rest of the sick on the island" came to him and were healed. Paul's ministry to those he met consisted in both proclaiming the Good News of Christ Jesus and healing them physically. Luke's inclusion of this vignette prepares for the climax of his book—Paul's entrance into Rome and the triumphant note of the Good News being preached "without hindrance" (see comment on v.31).

10 As a result of Paul's ministry during his months on Malta, the islanders honored him and his party in many ways. Paul was no god, as they had soon learned. But he was a messenger of the one true God, with good news of life and wholeness in Jesus Christ. In carrying out his God-given commission, Paul gave of himself unstintingly on behalf of people. That they appreciated his ministry is evidenced by their giving him and his colleagues supplies for the rest of their journey.

Luke suggests that Paul may have looked on his stay in Malta as a high point in his ministry—a time of blessing when God worked in marvelous ways, despite the shipwreck and his being still a prisoner. God seems to have been refreshing Paul's spirit after the two relatively bleak years at Caesarea and the disastrous time at sea, and he was preparing him for his witness in Rome.

4. Arrival at Rome (28:11–16)

11 "After three months" (probably about mid-February), the centurion Julius arranged for another ship to take his contingent of prisoners and soldiers for the last leg of their voyage to Italy. It was another Alexandrian vessel, probably another grain ship (cf. comment on v. 13) from Egypt that had harbored at Malta before winter set in. Ships, like inns, took their names from their figureheads; and this one had the painted carving at its prow of Castor and Pollux, who in Greek mythology were transformed by Zeus into twin gods represented by the constellation Gemini. Their cult was especially widespread in Egypt, and the Gemini were considered by sailors a sign of good fortune in a storm. For an Alexandrian ship, the figurehead was an appropriate one.

12 Sailing north-northeast, the ship reached the harbor of Syracuse, on the east coast of Sicily. There it remained for three days, probably awaiting better wind conditions and loading and unloading cargo.

13 From Syracuse the ship "set sail" for Rhegium, an important harbor at the toe of Italy and on the Italian side of the Strait of Messina. Docking there to await a more favorable breeze, they sailed the next day when a southerly wind began to blow and made the 180 miles up the coast of Italy to Puteoli in only two days. Puteoli was a resort city on the Bay of Naples, the port city of Neapolis (modern Naples) and the principal port of southern Italy. There many grain ships from Egypt docked, and there Julius and his contingent disembarked with Paul and his party.

14 There are two rather surprising statements in this verse. First, at Puteoli Paul and his companions "found some brothers who invited us to spend a week with them." It was not, of course, unusual for Christians to be found in such an important city as Puteoli, especially since there was a Jewish colony there. What is surprising, however is that prisoner Paul was at liberty to seek out the Christians of the city and accept their invitation to spend seven days in fellowship with them. For some reason Julius found it necessary to stay at Puteoli for a week, and during that time he allowed Paul the freedom (though undoubtedly accompanied by a guard) to seek out his fellow believers and enjoy their hospitality (cf. 27:3). As Luke presses toward the end of his story, his account becomes more and more concise.

A second surprising feature of v.14 is its forthright conclusion: "And so we came to Rome." It is not surprising that they came to Rome, for that had for some time been the goal of Paul's journey and Luke's narrative. But that the mention of their arrival appears here before v.15 and not as the opening statement of v.16 is indeed surprising. The best explanation is that it reflects Luke's eagerness to get to the climax of his story and that this eagerness led him to anticipate their arrival at Rome even though he had to go back in v.15 and include another detail of the last stage of the journey.

15 Paul and company took the Via Domitiana from Puteoli to Neapolis, turning northwest to travel to Rome on the Via Appia—that oldest, straightest, and most perfectly made of all the Roman roads. During the seven-day stopover at Puteoli, news of Paul's arrival in Italy had reached Rome. So a number of Christians there set out to meet him and escort him to Rome. Some of them got as far as the Forum of Appius, one of the "halting stations" built every ten to fifteen miles along the entire length of the Roman road system. It was forty-three miles from Rome, and a market-town had grown up around it. Others only got as far as the Three Taverns Inn, another halting station about thirty-three miles from Rome. Paul's gratitude to God for the delegation that met him must have been unusually fervent, for Luke makes special mention of it. In his letters, Paul often urges his readers to be thankful, and here he illustrates his own advice.

16 At Rome, Paul was allowed to live in private quarters, though a soldier guarded him at all times. The chain he wore (v.20) was probably attached to his wrists. Yet in Luke's eyes Paul entered Rome in triumph. Through his coming the Gospel penetrated official circles in the capital of the empire, and God used his detention there for two years to spread the proclamation of the kingdom of God and the Lord Jesus Christ throughout the city (cf. vv.30–31).

With this verse, the last "we" section in Acts closes. To judge by Paul's greetings in Col 4:10–14 and Phm 23–24 (assuming a Roman origin for these letters), Luke and Aristarchus remained with Paul through most—if not all—of his detention at Rome, being joined from time to time by such friends as Epaphras, John Mark, Demas, and Jesus (surnamed Justus).

F. Rome at Last (28:17–30)

At last, Paul's great desire to visit the capital of the empire (cf. Ro 15:22–24, 28–29) was fulfilled. Despite his manacles, guard, and house arrest, he was free to receive visitors. Among them, Luke tells us, were (1) the leading Jews of the city, whom he asked to visit him when he first arrived (vv. 17–28) and (2) others, evidently both Jews and Gentiles, who came to his quarters at various times during his two-year detention (v.30).

1. Meetings with the Jewish leaders (28:17–28)

17–20 Three days after arriving at Rome, Paul invited the leaders of the Jewish community to meet with him in his own quarters. He wanted to learn what they had heard from Jerusalem about him and to find out their attitude toward him. Through their contacts in the imperial court and with their money, they could, if they desired, support the charges against him. Since they undoubtedly knew something about his case, he wanted to defend himself before them. Also, he hoped the occasion would be an opportunity for proclaiming the message about Jesus the Messiah and that some would respond to it.

Paul began with the typical salutation used at Jewish formal gatherings (cf. comment on 23:1). The first word of his address, "I," clearly shows that Paul was about to deliver a personal defense. He had done nothing, he insisted, against the Jewish people or against the customs of the fathers (v.17). The Roman authorities had in fact judged that he had not committed any capital crime and were willing to release him (vv.17b–18). But objections from Jerusalem forced him to appeal to Caesar—not to accuse his own people but to save his life (v.19). The point of contention between him and his accusers at Jerusalem had to do with the messianic hope of Israel, which Paul believed was fulfilled in Jesus of Nazareth and they did not. Therefore he concluded: "It is because of the hope of Israel that I am bound with this chain" (v.20; cf. 23:6; 24:21; 26:6–8).

21–22 The immediate response of the Roman Jewish leaders to Paul's address is surprising. Apparently they did not want to get involved. They disclaimed having gotten any letters about him from the authorities at Jerusalem and said they had heard nothing, officially or unofficially, against him from any Jew who had come to them from Judea (v.21). Yet Christianity had been known within the Jewish community at Rome for some time (cf. comments on 2:10; 18:2). Certainly the Jewish leaders at Rome knew a great deal about Christianity generally and at least something about Paul, and their claim to know only "that people everywhere are talking against this sect" (v.22) seems much too "diplomatic" in light of their knowledge.

It is, however, in the light of their recent experience that we should judge the Jewish leaders' response to Paul's words. Having been expelled from Rome in 49 or 50 because of riots about Christianity in their community (cf. 18:2), and having only recently returned to their city after Claudius's death in 54, they were simply not prepared in 61 to become involved in Paul's case one way or another. They doubtless had their own opinions about it. But (1) the Jerusalem authorities had not requested them to get involved; (2) Paul was a Roman citizen who had had essentially favorable hearings before Felix, Festus, and Agrippa II; and (3) his case was now to be tried before Caesar himself. So they wanted to have as little as possible to do with Paul and Christianity. But they did say that they were willing at some future time to hear his views on "this sect."

23–24 So they arranged a second meeting, and an even larger delegation came to Paul's quarters. Luke tells us only that it lasted "from morning till evening" and that Paul proclaimed "the kingdom of God" (cf. comment on 1:3), focusing on Jesus, to whom the Law and the Prophets bore witness (v.23; cf. v.31). For the content of what he said, we should probably think of his sermon in the synagogue at Pisidian Antioch (13:17–41) and the letter sent to the Romans. As for his method, he "tried to convince them," which implies that Paul combined proclamation with persuasion (cf. comment on 17:2–4) and that there was a good deal of impassioned debate. The day-long session proved profitable, for "some were convinced by what he said"—though, sadly, "others would not believe" (v.24).

25–28 The points at which many of the Jewish leaders disagreed with Paul and left the session, Luke says, were two. (1) Paul attempted to prove the obduracy of Israel from Scripture on the ground that Isaiah, in Isa 6:9–10, had foretold the Jews' rejection of Jesus as Messiah (cf. the use of this passage in Mt 13:13–15; Lk 8:10; also Mk 4:12; Jn 12:40, though not with quite the same thrust). Paul had elaborated on this issue in Ro 9–11. (2) He quoted prophecy here not just to explain Israel's stubbornness but to set the stage for his second point: because of Israel's hardened attitude the message of "God's salvation" had been sent directly to Gentiles, who would respond positively.

A revolutionary new policy for proclaiming the Gospel and making converts had been providentially worked out during Paul's first missionary journey and at the Jerusalem Council (cf. 12:25–16:5 and comments). That policy was then carried out through two more missionary journeys extending into Macedonia, Achaia, and Asia (cf. 16:6–19:20). This policy advocated the proclamation of the Gospel "first for the Jew, then for the Gentile" (Ro 1:16; cf. Ac 13:46–52). Luke has carefully shown how everything that happened in the ministry of the early Jerusalem church essentially looked forward to the inauguration of this policy and how it lay at the heart of Paul's missionary purpose. Now having traced the story of the advance of the Gospel to Rome, Luke reports how that same pattern was followed at Rome. His account of the Gospel's advance from Jerusalem to Rome in terms of the distinctive policy of first the Jew, then the Gentile comes to a fitting conclusion with the quotation of Isa 6:9–10.

2. Continued ministry for two years (28:30)

30 Luke does not give us details about Paul's two years in Rome because he is not writing Paul's biography. But during the storm at sea, the angel of the Lord had assured Paul that he would stand trial before Caesar (cf. 27:24). Therefore, it seems proper to assume that Luke intended his readers to infer that Paul's case, whatever its outcome, did come before the imperial court.

With Acts ending so abruptly, we must look elsewhere for information about Paul's Roman imprisonment and its aftermath. Accepting the Prison Letters as having been written during this time, we may surmise that Paul fully expected to stand before Caesar's court and that, while we cannot not be certain about the outcome, he did expect to be released (cf. Php 1:19–26; Phm 22). We may date such a release around 63. Accepting the Pastoral Letters as genuine, after Paul's release from this imprisonment, he continued evangelizing the eastern portion of the empire (at least in lands surrounding the Aegean Sea)—perhaps even fulfilling his desire to visit Spain (Ro 15:23–24). And since 2Ti 4:6–18 speaks of a second trial in a tone of resignation, we may conclude that Paul was rearrested about 67 and, according to tradition, beheaded at Rome by order of Nero.

G. A Summary Statement (28:31)

31 This summary statement has often been viewed as only an amplification of v.30, indicating the nature of Paul's ministry during his two years of detention at Rome. But to judge by Luke's practice in the other five summary statements in Acts (6:7; 9:31; 12:24; 16:5; 19:20), we should take it as the summary statement for the whole of Panel 6 (19:21–28:31). In all of his prison experiences at Jerusalem, Caesarea, and Rome, Luke is saying, Paul "boldly ... preached the kingdom of God and taught about the Lord Jesus Christ." And he did this "without hindrance" (GK *219*)—the last word in the Greek text of Acts, which thus closes this work on a victorious note. This word shows the tolerance of Rome at that time toward Christianity—a tolerance Luke was passionately promoting throughout these last chapters and hoped would continue.

In seeming to leave his book unfinished, Luke was implying that the apostolic proclamation of the Gospel in the first century began a story that will continue until the consummation of the kingdom in Christ (Ac 1:11).

The Old Testament in the New

NT Text	OT Text	Subject
Ac 1:20	Ps 69:25	Judgment on Judas
Ac 1:20	Ps 109:8	Replacement for Judas
Ac 2:17–21	Joel 2:28–32	God's Spirit poured out
Ac 2:25–28, 31	Ps 16:8–11	Resurrection of Christ
Ac 2:34–35	Ps 110:1	At God's right hand
Ac 3:22–23	Dt 18:15, 18–19	The prophet
Ac 3:25	Ge 22:18; 26:4	Nations blessed in Abraham
Ac 4:11	Ps 118:22	Rejected cornerstone
Ac 4:24	Ex 20:11; Ps 146:6	God the creator
Ac 4:25–26	Ps 2:1–2	Kings against the Lord
Ac 7:3	Ge 12:1	Call of Abraham
Ac 7:6–7	Ge 15:13–14	Prophecy to Abraham
Ac 7:18	Ex 1:8	King who did not know Joseph
Ac 7:27–28, 35	Ex 2:14	Moses in Egypt
Ac 7:32	Ex 3:6	The living God
Ac 7:33	Ex 3:5	Moses at the burning bush
Ac 7:34	Ex 3:7–8, 10	God promises to deliver Israel
Ac 7:37	Dt 18:15	The prophet
Ac 7:40	Ex 32:1, 23	Asking for idols
Ac 7:42–43	Am 5:25–27	Sin and judgment

The Old Testament in the New

NT Text	OT Text	Subject
Ac 7:49–50	Isa 66:1–2	No temple contains God
Ac 8:32–33	Isa 53:7–8	Jesus as the dying lamb
Ac 13:33	Ps 2:7	You are my Son
Ac 13:34	Isa 55:3	Blessings of David
Ac 13:35	Ps 16:10	Resurrection of Christ
Ac 13:41	Hab 1:5	Judgment for sin
Ac 13:47	Isa 49:6	Salvation of the Gentiles
Ac 14:15	Ex 20:11; Ps 146:6	God the creator
Ac 15:16–17	Am 9:11–12	Restoration for everyone
Ac 23:5	Ex 22:28	Cursing rulers
Ac 28:26–27	Isa 6:9–10	Seeing but not perceiving

Romans

INTRODUCTION

1. Background

By common consent, Romans is the greatest of Paul's letters, and the Roman church became one of the major centers of Christendom. However, next to nothing is known about the founding and early history of this church. Paul does not deal with these issues in the course of his letter, nor does Luke provide any help beyond mentioning that Aquila and Priscilla, with whom Paul lived and labored at Corinth, had recently come from Italy (Ac 18:2). He says nothing about Paul's witnessing to them, so the presumption is that they were already believers. The expulsion of Jews from Rome by order of the emperor Claudius was dictated by "disturbances at the instigation of Chrestus [Christ?]" (A.D. 49; see comment on Ac 18:2). It is likely that by the fifth decade of the first century the Christian faith had gained a foothold in the capital of the empire, and by A.D. 57 (when Paul wrote this letter), it was famous far and wide for its faith (1:8).

2. Authorship, Date, and Place of Origin

From the post-apostolic church to the present, with almost no exception, this letter has been credited to Paul. If the claim of the apostle to have written the Galatian and Corinthian letters is accepted, there is no reasonable basis for denying that he wrote Romans, since it echoes much of what is in the earlier writings, yet not slavishly. A few examples must suffice: the doctrine of justification by faith (Ro 3:20–22; Gal 2: 16); the church as the body of Christ appointed to represent and serve him through a variety of spiritual gifts (Ro 12:3–8; 1Co 12:12–27); the collection for the poor saints at Jerusalem (Ro 15:25–28; 2Co 8–9). Understandably, Paul makes fewer references to himself and to his readers in Romans than in these three other letters, since he had not founded the Roman church and guided its struggles to maturity as he had the others.

Fixed dates for the span of Paul's labors are few, but one of them is the summer of A.D. 51, when Gallio arrived in Corinth to serve as proconsul of Achaia (see comment on Ac 18:12–13). After this the apostle stayed in the city "some time" (18:18). Possibly in the spring of 52 he went to Caesarea and Jerusalem, stopping at Antioch on the way back and probably spending the winter of 52 there. Presumably, his return to Ephesus was in the spring of 53, marking the beginning of a three-year ministry there (20:31). At the end of 56 he spent three months in Corinth (20:3), starting his final trip to Jerusalem in the spring of 57. When he wrote Romans the fund for the Jerusalem church seems to have been finally completed (Ro 15:26ff.). This suggests a date in early 57 for the writing of the letter.

Corinth is the most likely place of composition, since Phoebe of nearby Cenchrea was apparently entrusted with the carrying of the letter (Ro 16:1–2). The mention of Gaius as Paul's host (16:23) confirms this conclusion, Gaius having been one of the most prominent of converts during the apostle's mission at Corinth (1Co 1:14).

3. Destination

The titles of the Pauline Epistles are not part of the text, so the superscription "The Letter of Paul to the Romans" cannot be attributed to the apostle but must be taken as reflecting the understanding of the church as a whole sometime during the second century. Yet, since the intended readers are located at Rome by the writer (Ro 1:7, 15), all doubt about the destination would seem to be removed. A few scholars argue that Paul also sent a copy of this letter to Ephesus, especially since some manuscripts do not have ch. 16 included. They claim that the people mentioned in the closing chapter were living at Ephesus rather than at Rome. Attractive though this view is, it has not been universally received, because a good case can be made for a Roman destination for ch. 16.

ROMANS

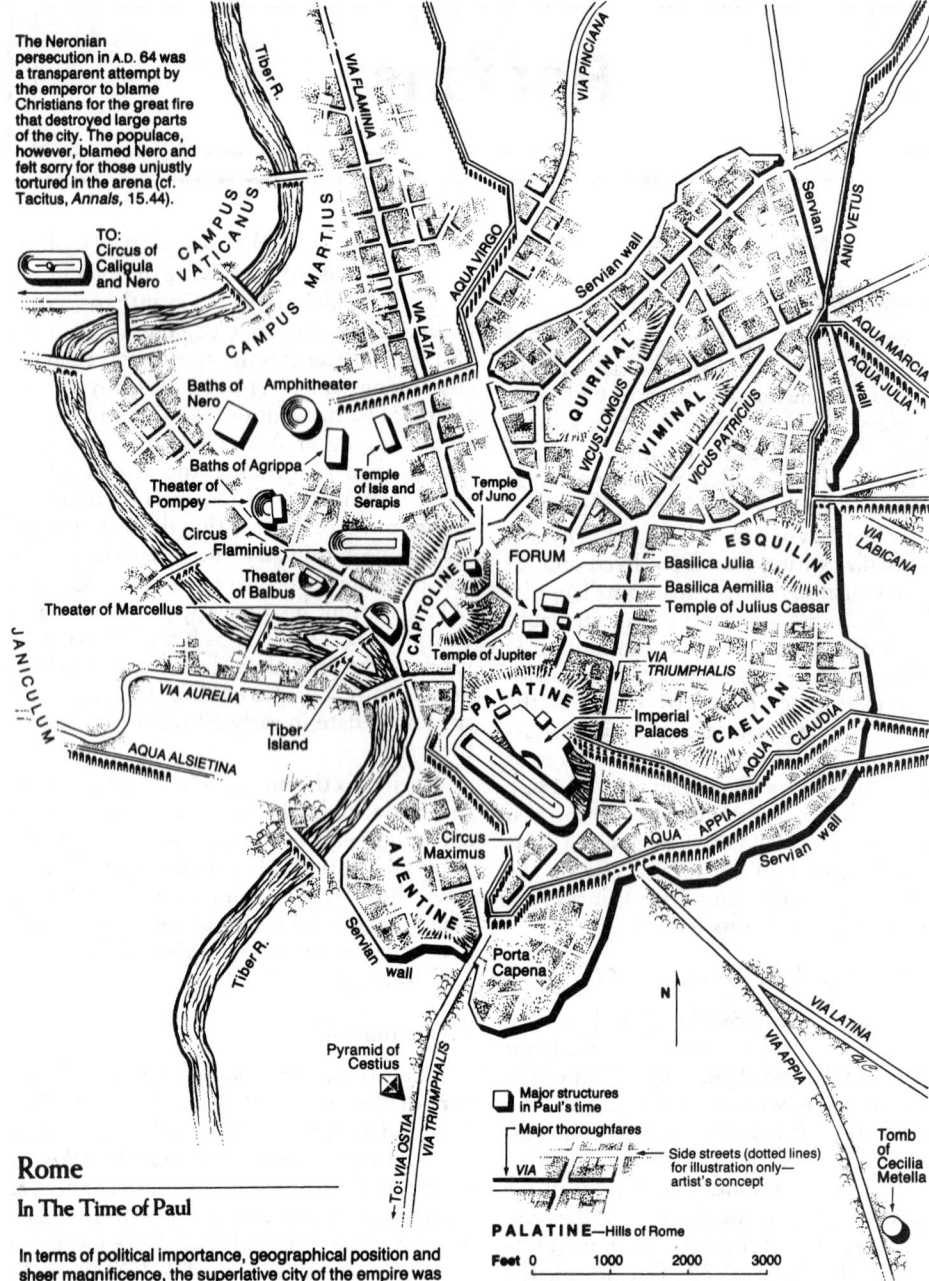

The Neronian persecution in A.D. 64 was a transparent attempt by the emperor to blame Christians for the great fire that destroyed large parts of the city. The populace, however, blamed Nero and felt sorry for those unjustly tortured in the arena (cf. Tacitus, *Annals*, 15.44).

PALATINE—Hills of Rome

Rome
In The Time of Paul

In terms of political importance, geographical position and sheer magnificence, the superlative city of the empire was Rome, the capital.

Located on a series of jutting foothills and low-lying eminences (the "seven hills") east of a bend in the Tiber River some 18 miles from the Mediterranean, Rome was celebrated for its impressive public buildings, aqueducts, baths, theaters and thoroughfares, many of which led from distant provinces. The city of the first Christian century had spread far beyond its fourth-century B.C. "Servian" walls and lay unwalled, secure in its greatness.

The most prominent features were the Capitoline hill, with temples to Jupiter and Juno, and the nearby Palatine, adorned with imperial palaces, including Nero's "Golden House." Both hills overlooked the Roman Forum, the hub of the entire empire.

© 1985 The Zondervan Corporation

Alternatively described as the glorious crowning achievement of mankind and as the sewer of the universe where all the scum from every corner of the empire gathered, Rome had reasons for both civic pride in its architecture and shame for staggering urban social problems not unlike those of cities today.

The apostle Paul entered the city from the south on the Via Appia. He first lived under house arrest and then, after a period of freedom, as a condemned prisoner in the Mamertime dungeon near the Forum. Remarkably, Paul was able to proclaim the gospel among all classes of people, from the palace to the prison. According to tradition, he was executed at a spot on the Ostian Way outside Rome in A.D. 68.

4. Occasion and Purpose

These two items are so closely related as to warrant considering them together. When Paul's Ephesian ministry had continued for more than two years, with tremendous impact on the city and province, he sensed that it would soon be time for him to move to another field of labor. It may be that for some time he had been looking westward toward Rome (see "many years" in Ro 15:23). Now the conviction grew that he must begin to plan for work in the West (Ac 19:21). He had already preached the Gospel in the strategic centers of population in the East, and his restless spirit yearned to reach out to places where Christ was not known. Thus he planned to go through Rome to Spain to plant the Gospel there (Ro 15:22–24).

The question naturally arises, Why did this plan dictate the writing of a letter such as Romans? Why not send a note by Phoebe simply to inform the church that he would be coming to them in a short time? Two things should be said about this.

First, since Paul hoped to go beyond Rome even as far as Spain, he evidently expected to have in the Roman church a base of missionary operation comparable to Antioch in the East. If this was to be realized, he needed to share with the church a rather complete exposition of the Gospel he had been preaching for over twenty years. By putting this exposition in writing and sending it ahead, he would give the Christian community in Rome an opportunity to digest the message and be ready to share in the extension of the Gospel to the West.

Another factor may have entered in. The very passage that sets forth his plan and purpose is followed by one requesting prayer for his safety and success as he went on to Judea prior to leaving for Rome. Particularly ominous is his expressed need to be rescued from unbelievers in Judea (Ro 15:31). The plot by Jews at Corinth against his life (Ac 20:3) may already have been made and become an omen of future events. Possibly at this point intimations from the Holy Spirit began to warn him about the imprisonment and afflictions that awaited him (Ac 20:23). What if he should not live to declare the Gospel in the West? Then he must write a letter so systematic and comprehensive that the church would be able intelligently to continue his work, proclaiming the very Gospel he was spelling out for them, taking it in his stead to the farthest reaches of the empire. For all he knew at the time, this letter might be in a sense his last will and testament, a precious deposit bequeathed to the church and through it to the community of the faithful everywhere.

Furthermore, we should not overlook the distinct possibility that in addition to its evangelistic function, Romans may have been designed to meet needs within the congregation of Rome, for, alongside its kerygmatic materials, it abounds in teaching. The degree to which Paul was familiar with conditions within the church at Rome may be debatable, but it is probable that he knew a good deal about them. Beginning at least from the time of his contact with Priscilla and Aquila at Corinth, he doubtless had a fairly continuous stream of information about the church, especially during his stay at Ephesus, since travel to and from Rome was relatively easy. The number of people listed in ch. 16 suggests many sources of information.

Yet for Paul to exhibit an intimate knowledge of conditions in the church and to attempt to deal with these problems too directly and pointedly would be unseemly in view of his personal detachment from the Roman situation. The most one can say is that the broad and general statements contained in Romans would compel the Christians at Rome to wonder at the unexpected discernment of an apostle who had never set foot in their city. Especially pertinent in this connection is the tension between Jew and Gentile within the church, two groups that may be approximately identified with the weak and the strong in 15:1–8. Then there is a warning not to be lifted up with pride because of Israel's being set aside (11:20–21), followed by a reminder that this setting aside is temporary (11:25–26). The very fact that Jew and Gentile (rather than humankind in general) are given so much prominence in the main theme of the letter (1:16) and in the section that demonstrates the need for salvation (1:18–3:20) argues for the impact on the apostle of this tension at the time of writing.

5. Theological Values

Romans satisfies the craving of the human spirit for a comprehensive exposition of the great truths of salvation set out in logical fashion, supported and illumined by OT

Scripture. The systematic element includes due attention to doctrine and life—in that order, because right relations must be established with God before one can live so as to please him and mediate his blessings to others.

The question as to what is most central to Paul's theology has been long debated. Some have said that it is justification by faith. Others have insisted that the life "in Christ" is the secret, for it lifts one out of the rigidity and barrenness of legal terminology, disclosing the positive and dynamic relationship the believer may have with God's Son. Fortunately, we do not have to choose between these two, because both are important in Paul's presentation. Without justification there can be no life in Christ (5:18), and such life in turn confirms the reality of justification.

Salvation is the basic theme of Romans (cf. 1:16)—a salvation presented in terms of the righteousness of God, which, when received by faith, results in life (1:17). It is helpful to realize that salvation, righteousness, and life are eschatological terms. The apostle talks about salvation with a future reference (13:11). Righteousness, too, in the absolute sense, belongs only to the perfected state. Again, life comes to fullness of meaning only in terms of the future (6:22; cf. Mk 10:29–30). Yet all these future realities are to be entered into and enjoyed during the earthly pilgrimage of the saints. Salvation is a present reality (10:10), as are righteousness (4:3–5) and life (6:23; 8:2). In the last analysis, only the grace of God permits us to participate now in that which properly belongs to the future.

Though Romans does not give special instruction about the Trinity, it clearly delineates the respective responsibilities of the members of the Godhead. The Gospel is called "the gospel of God" at the very beginning (1:1), before it is called "the gospel of his Son" (1:9). God's righteousness must be reckoned with, both by sinner and by saint, for it is the basis of judgment as well as of salvation. The Son of God is held up to view also from the first, because the Gospel centers in him (1:3). He is the one through whom the grace of God is mediated to sinful humanity in justification, reconciliation, and redemption. The man Christ Jesus is set over against the first Adam as the one who has succeeded in undoing the ruin brought about by the Fall (5:12–21) and who now sustains and preserves all who put their trust in him (5:10). The Spirit's role is to nurture the new creation life of the children of God by providing assurance of their sonship (8:16), their release from bondage to sin (8:2–4), their effectiveness in prayer (8:26–27), and their experience of the love of God (5:5) and of other joys of spiritual life (14:17), crowned by a confident hope that the bliss of the better state that is to come will be realized (8:23; 15:13). The Spirit also provides the dynamic for Christian service (15:19).

It is not possible, however, to claim for Romans a complete coverage of doctrine. Though salvation is central, its climax in terms of the coming of the Lord is not unfolded to any extent (13:11), though the glorification of the saints is included (8:18–19, 23). Furthermore, though the word "church" appears five times in ch. 16, it is not a theme for definitive instruction per se. Too much can be made of this seeming incompleteness, however, for in chs. 9–11 Paul is deeply concerned about the composition of the church and about how Jew and Gentile relate to it in the divine plan. Again, any attempt to deal with the concept of "covenant" is lacking, for the two references (9:4; 11:27) say nothing about the new covenant in Christ (contrast 2Co 3; Gal 3–4). That there should be no mention of the Lord's Supper may seem strange, especially since baptism is mentioned (6:4). But in Romans Paul is not concerned with ecclesiology, at least not in the sense of giving it specific treatment. Despite these omissions, it remains true that nowhere else in Scripture is the subject of salvation dealt with in such breadth and thoroughness.

In the so-called practical section of the Epistle (chs. 12–15), the effect of these great truths is set forth in terms of transformed conduct. Christians have a life to live in this world as well as a faith to hold and a fellowship to enjoy. Paul was pastor as well as preacher. In Romans, as in his other letters, his theological teaching was given not merely for the sake of information, but to build up and encourage the people of God.

6. Special Problem

Only one problem will be dealt with here—a question of whether the believers in Rome were mainly Gentile or Jewish Christians. At the outset, Paul considers his readers Gentiles (1:13), and this should be decisive unless contrary evidence of the strongest sort can be adduced. Such evidence is sometimes given in 4:1, where the apostle speaks of Abraham as "our forefather," and in 7:1ff., where he treats the law (presumably Mosaic) and says that his readers know it.

Neither of these constitutes compelling evidence, however. As to the former item, Paul also alludes to Israel's history in speaking of "our forefathers" in 1Co 10:1, in a letter intended for a Gentile church. Paul was careful to teach the spiritual kinship that existed between the Israel of the past and the people of God in the Christian dispensation. In the case of Abraham, this is spelled out clearly when he calls Abraham "the father of all who believe but have not been circumcised" (Ro 4:11). As to the familiarity of Roman Christians with the Mosaic law, Paul feels perfectly free to quote the law and other portions of the Hebrew Scriptures even when writing to predominantly Gentile churches—e.g., Galatians and Corinthians. Many Gentile converts to the Gospel had previously attended the synagogue as God-fearers and there had heard the OT read and expounded.

There remains, however, the awkward fact that the apostle devotes chs. 9–11 to the nation of Israel. The failure of this people as a whole to turn to Jesus as the Messiah was a source of deep grief to him. One may well ask, Was he not writing a section of this length to inform and comfort a Jewish Christian church that may have been struggling with this issue? Not necessarily, for one can ask a counter question: Isn't it possible that Paul was using this section to warn Gentile believers not to take their position for granted and to lapse into a false security (11:13ff.)?

Going back to the solid fact that Paul addresses the church as Gentile in character (1:13), chs. 9–11 might indeed have a special purpose for that type of audience. These people could certainly learn much from the passage—namely, the obvious advantages God had given the Jew, his own sovereignty in setting them apart as his chosen people, his righteousness in cutting them off from national privilege, and his faithfulness to covenant commitments to be seen when the nation by repentance and faith would be restored. On reading this, Gentile believers would inevitably feel an impulse to pray for and witness to Israel. When these considerations are added to the generous use of the OT in the development of the theme of Romans, it becomes clear that Paul is concerned lest Gentile Christianity should lose sight of its heritage in OT history and revelation.

EXPOSITION

I. Introduction (1:1–15)

A. Salutation (1:1–7)

1 As in all his letters, Paul uses his Roman name (cf. Ac 13:6–12). His relation to Christ is primary, so to express his attachment to his Lord he uses the term "servant" (GK *1528*). In Israel the citizenry regarded themselves as servants of their king. This same word is used of Christ in relation to the Father (Php 2:7). By beginning in this fashion, Paul is putting himself on the same plane as his readers; he does not seek to dominate them.

The word "apostle" (GK *693*) sets forth his authority as Christ's appointee—his right not only to preach the Gospel (believers in general can do that) but to found and supervise churches and to discipline them if necessary. But this authority carries with it responsibility, for he must give account of the conduct of his mission (1Co 4:1–4).

Paul has been "set apart" ever since his conversion (Ac 9:15; Gal 1:12) for the Gospel of God. As a Pharisee he had been set apart to a life of strict observance of Jewish law and custom. Now his life's work is to further the Gospel, the Good News that God has for all humanity.

2 Before the historic events providing the basis for the gospel message unfolded, God "promised" the Good News in the prophetic Scriptures. Promise means more than prophecy, because it commits the Almighty to make good his word, whereas a prophecy can be merely an advance announcement of something that will happen. The concept of promise permeates this letter (4:13–25; 9:4; 15:8). The reference to "the Holy Scriptures" prepares the reader for rather copious use of the OT, beginning with 1:17.

3–4 The Gospel centers in God's Son, who had this status before he took on a "human nature" and who, in becoming human, became not only an Israelite (9:5) but a son of

David (Mt 1:1; Lk 1:32; Ac 13:22–23; 2Ti 2:8), a qualification he needed as Messiah (Isa 11:1). By beginning with the sonship, Paul guards against a heretical adoptionist Christology. The period of Christ's earthly life and ministry was followed by another phase—that which resulted from his resurrection. "With power" most likely belongs not with "declared" but with "Son of God," indicating the new quality of life Jesus had after his resurrection (Php 3:10; Col 1:29).

"Spirit of holiness" is an expression that means "Holy Spirit." There may be a suggestion here that Jesus, anointed and sustained by the Holy Spirit in the days of his flesh, was acknowledged by the fact of resurrection to have successfully endured the tests and trials of his earthly life. By resurrection he has become a life-giving spirit (1Co 15:45).

Appropriately, Jesus Christ is now described as "our Lord" (GK *3261*). Though this title was fitting during his earthly ministry, it attained more frequent use and greater meaning following the resurrection (Ac 2:36; 10:36; Ro 10:9). It is notable that in this initial statement about the Gospel nothing is said concerning the redeeming work of Christ, which is reserved for later consideration (3:21–26; 4:25; 5:6–21). It was the infinite worth of the Son that made his saving work possible.

5–7 Now the apostle returns to his responsibility to proclaim the Good News (cf. v.1). Two problems present themselves here, and they are somewhat related. Who is indicated by "we," and how should one understand the phrase "all the Gentiles"? Clearly, in using "we," Paul cannot be including his readers, because they did not possess apostleship. Could he be referring to other apostles, of whom the Roman believers must have heard? This is a possibility. The problem is complicated by the mention of the intended sphere of labor—"among all the Gentiles." This wording tends to limit the "we" to Paul as a literary plural, since the Gentiles constituted his special field of labor (cf. 15:16, 18, where the word "obey" corresponds to the word "obedience" in this passage). On the other hand, "all the Gentiles" can equally be rendered, "all the nations" or "all peoples" (cf. Mt 28:19). This would favor the wider reference of "we" to all the apostles, since Israel would be included as one of the peoples. It is difficult to decide this question.

The desired response to the gospel message is "obedience that comes from faith" (see 15:18; 16:26 on obedience and 1:16–17; 10:17 on faith). Paul's readers were not called, as he was, to apostleship; they were called "to belong to Jesus Christ" and to be "saints" (GK *41*), the common term designating believers. This term has almost the same force as the expression Paul uses for himself—"set apart" (v.1). It carries the aroma of holiness to which every child of God is called (6:19, 22).

Finally the apostle is ready to extend a greeting to his readers—"grace and peace." Ordinary letters of that period usually contained a single word meaning "greeting" (cf. Jas 1:1). Paul, however, is partial to terms with theological import. He desires his readers to have a continuing and deepening experience of spiritual blessing that only God can bestow. Father and Son are the joint benefactors. People may long for grace and peace, but only God can grant such gifts. The rich meaning of these terms will emerge as Paul uses them in the body of his work.

B. Paul and the Church at Rome (1:8–15)

8–10 The salutation has been unusually long; but instead of moving on immediately to his main theme, the apostle still lingers over introductory matters. Doubtless he felt the need to get acquainted, so to speak, by unburdening his own heart about what his readers meant to him. It is a shining example of his pastoral concern mingled with his gracious sensitivity.

First of all, Paul customarily expresses his thanks to God for his readers. His thanksgiving for the Roman believers is based on their faith (cf. Eph 1:15–16; Col 1:3–4; 1Th 1:3).

Not without reason Paul had become known in Christendom as the apostle of faith. To him, faith was the basic Christian virtue, and he was eager to commend it wherever he saw it. Here his commendation is exceedingly generous, even hyperbolic. The whole world has heard of their faith (cf. 1Th 1:8). Paul's thanksgiving is followed by a statement concerning his prayer—both intercession for them and a special plea that his hope of coming to them would be realized, provided it is God's will.

But why should Paul find it necessary to summon God as his witness that he had been faithful in praying for the Roman believers? He only does this when the thing he is claiming is difficult to believe. Here there are two reasons. Since he claims to have been praying repeatedly, it seems almost too much to expect of a man who did not know most of these people. Furthermore, as he would tell his readers later (15:25), he was about to leave for Jerusalem, and this could give the appearance that he was not putting the Roman believers first in his plans.

11–13 The apostle confesses to a great desire to see his readers, not simply in order to know them personally, but especially to minister to them. By "spiritual gift" (GK 5992) we should probably not understand some "charismatic" gift as in 1Co 12, since Paul does not specify any particular gift and avoids the plural. Moreover, his own prominence in this contemplated gift hardly makes room for the specialized gifts of the Spirit (cf. 1Co 1:7). But no sooner has this sentiment been expressed than it is halfway recalled, being revised because it seems to suggest that a blessing will flow only one way, from Paul to the church. So he alters his language to make room for mutual encouragement and upbuilding. Seeing faith at work in one individual after another adds zest to Christian fellowship. Paul himself needed this.

As he had prayed constantly for the Romans, so he had planned many times to visit them, but the plan often had to be set aside. Presumably his work in the East had involved him so completely that he did not see his way clear to break away for the projected trip to Rome.

His hope to have "a harvest" among his readers should not be interpreted narrowly as though he is hinting that some in their ranks are not genuinely saved. His use of the word "Gentiles" instead of "churches" may be a pointer for us, hinting that "among you" is a reference to the community rather than to the church specifically, and that the fruit he envisions is the reaching of the unsaved. This would not, of course, exclude fruit-bearing in the sense of developing the saints in character (Gal 5:22–23).

14–15 Paul looks forward to his visit, but he also considers it an obligation. Why? He has already laid the groundwork for such a statement by acknowledging that he is Christ's servant (v.1), who has been given a charge with taking the Gospel to all peoples (v.5). The phrase "Greeks and non-Greeks [Gk. *barbaroi*; GK 975]" refers to all non-Jewish members of the human race (cf. "Gentiles" in v.13), dividing them into two categories. It is probable that *barbaroi* refers mostly to the people in the territory west of Rome, where he hoped to go, though he would undoubtedly find representatives of both groups also in Rome.

The "wise" are not to be equated with the Greeks, for this would mean that non-Greeks are being dubbed "foolish," which would be unwarranted. Rather, Paul seems to have in mind what he wrote in 1Co 1:18–31 (see comments). The wise are perishing in the midst of their worldly wisdom, and the foolish in their abject simplicity. Both need the Gospel.

How heartwarming is the apostle's attitude toward his obligation! Instead of considering it a burden he must bear, a duty he must carry out, he is "eager" to fulfill it. While success in preaching demands the finest intellectual and formal preparation, it also requires great zeal.

II. Theme: The Gospel As the Revelation of the Righteousness of God (1:16–17)

16 Having confessed his fervent desire to preach the Gospel at Rome, Paul goes on to give a reason for his zeal. He has no sense of reserve about his mission. He is ready to challenge the philosophies and religions in Rome that vie for the attention of people, because he knows from his experience in the East that God's power at work in the proclamation of the Good News is able to transform lives. "Power" (GK 1539) stresses not how the Gospel operates but what its intrinsic efficacy is. It offers something not found anywhere else—a righteousness from God (see below).

Power is linked closely with salvation. Judaism was prone to think of the law as power, but this is not affirmed in Scripture. As for salvation, the OT is clear that whether it is conceived of physically as deliverance (Ex 14:13) or spiritually (Ps 51:12), it comes from the Lord. This is maintained in the NT as well in Paul's affirmation in this verse. So the apostle permits himself to say that if he himself saves anyone (1Co 9:22), it is only in the sense that he is Christ's representative who is able to point out the way of salvation to his fellow human beings.

"Salvation" (GK 5401) is a broad concept. Its basic meaning is soundness or wholeness. It promises the restoration of all that sin has marred or destroyed, and it unites in itself the particular aspects of truth suggested by justification, reconciliation, sanctification, propitiation, redemption, and glorification. But its efficacy depends on one's willingness to receive the message. "Everyone who believes" will benefit equally. This sweeping declaration ties in with the previous statement (concerning Greeks and non-Greeks) and now includes both the Jew and the Gentile. The Jew receives "first" consideration. This does not mean that every Jew must be evangelized before the Gospel can be presented to Gentiles. But it does mean that God, after having dealt in a special way with the Jew in OT days and having followed this by sending his Son to the lost sheep of the house of Israel (Mt 15:24), could not pass by this people. To them was given the first opportunity to receive the Lord Jesus, both during his ministry (Jn 1:11) and in the Christian era (Ac 1:8; 3:26). Paul himself followed this pattern (Ac 13:45–46; 28:25, 28). It is a case of historical priority, not essential priority, for the Jews who are first to hear the Gospel are also the first to be judged for their sins (2:9).

17 The apostle now explains his statement (cf. "for") that the Gospel means salvation for those who receive it by faith: it discloses "a righteousness [GK 1466] from God." Paul is dependent here on the OT (Isa 46:12–13; 61:10), which emphasizes that God is righteous in the way he acts—an idea foreign to Greek thought. Clearly, the character of God is involved in the sense that what he does and provides is fully in keeping with his righteous nature (cf. 3:26). But just as clearly, this expression also includes the activity of God. The Gospel would not be the good news if it simply disclosed God's righteousness, and such a message would scarcely demand faith. But if salvation as God provides it is fully in keeping with his righteous character, then it has integrity.

We should compare Paul's statement here with Php 3:9, where he contrasts his pre-Christian state, in which he had a righteousness based on obeying the law, with his present situation, in which he rests on a righteousness which is from God, based on faith. In summary, God's righteousness in this context stresses divine provision. What this entails will be unfolded in due course.

Somewhat baffling is the twofold reference to faith—lit. "from faith to faith" (cf. NIV "by faith from first to last"). These two prepositional phrases relate directly to God's righteousness, indicating how that righteousness is to be received (cf. Paul's restatement of this idea in 3:21–22). Having said that, we must inquire into the distinctives of the two phrases involving "faith" (GK 4411). Among the numerous suggestions are these: from the faith of the preacher to the faith of the hearer; from OT faith to NT faith (cf. the following quotation); entirely from faith; and from God's faithfulness to human faith. It is best to see the first phrase ("from faith") as indicating the basis on which God grants justification (3:26; 5:1; Gal 2:16) or righteousness (9:30; 10:6). The really troublesome element here is the second phrase ("to faith"). It is intended to remind believers that justifying faith is only the beginning of the Christian life; that same attitude must govern them in their continuing experience as children of God (this is how NIV understands the phrase).

What about "The righteous will live by faith"? Should it be translated this way or "The one who is just by virtue of faith shall live"? Since the apostle quotes the same passage in Gal 3:11 to show that one is not justified by law but rather by faith, it is probable that he intends the reference in the same way here. Also, since the quotation is used at the very beginning of Romans, Paul's main concern here is not how justified sinners should live (chs. 6–8), but how they can be considered just or righteous in the sight of God. Ethical righteousness depends on a right relationship to God, so the latter merits priority of treatment.

Why did not Paul then change the order to read, "The one who is righteous by faith will live?" Apparently he did not want to disturb the form of a familiar quotation, even though he changed its emphasis from the OT. The liberty involved in using an OT quotation somewhat differently from its original setting is necessitated by the progress of revelation. It was a practice used in Judaism before Paul's time, as we know from the Dead Sea Scrolls, and it was also used by other

III. The Need for Salvation: The Plight of Humanity (1:18–3:20)

Instead of plunging at once into an exposition of the Gospel, Paul launches into a lengthy exposure of human sinfulness. This is sound procedure, for until people are persuaded of their lost condition they are not likely to be concerned about deliverance. So Paul undertakes to demonstrate in the human situation a grievous lack of the righteousness God requires.

A. In the Pagan World (1:18–32)

18 At the outset it is important to observe the correlation between righteousness and wrath. Both are represented as *being* revealed from God. Just as full salvation awaits the future (see comment on 1:16) but also belongs to the present and is appropriated by faith (1:17), similarly wrath, while an eschatological concept, is viewed here as belonging to the present age. It is "being revealed" (GK 636). This means that the unfolding of history involves a disclosure of God's wrath against sin, seen in the terrible corruption and perversion of human life. This does not mean that the price of sin is to be reckoned only in terms of the present operation of wrath, for there is a day of judgment awaiting the sinner (2:5). But the divine verdict is already in some measure anticipated. Paul regards the degrading depths of sin among pagans as a present judgment from God (cf. vv. 24, 26, 28).

This wrath of God is being revealed "from heaven." This phrase as used in the Gospels means "from God." Some scholars object to the idea of the wrath of God, but such objection is often molded by human experience of anger as passion or desire for revenge. God's wrath, however, is not temperamental; rather, it is righteous (cf. 13:4–5).

The object God's wrath is twofold—"all the godlessness and wickedness of men." Paul explicates the first term in vv.19–27 and the second in vv.28–32. "Godlessness" (GK 813) means a lack of reverence, an impiety that arrays people against God, not simply in terms of neglect but also of rebellion. "Wickedness" (GK 94) means injustice, relating to the vitiating of a person's conduct toward other human beings. The two together serve to denote the failure of humankind in terms of the requirements of the two tablets of the Decalogue. No distinction is made here between Jews and Gentiles, since "men" includes the entire human race. These are the very areas in which the prophets found fault with Israel. But as the thought unfolds here, the culprit appears much more sharply in terms of Gentiles than of Jews.

They "suppress the truth by their wickedness." That is, whenever the truth about God (cf. v.25) starts to assert itself and makes them feel guilty, they suppress it—either by further immoralities or by denial. Suppression of the truth implies a knowledge of the truth, and what this involves is explained in the sequel.

19–20 The creation bears clear witness to its Maker, and the evidence is "plain" to people. Here Paul enters upon a discussion of what is usually designated natural revelation in distinction from the special revelation that comes through the Scriptures. Four characteristics are noted. (1) It is a clear testimony set before human eyes. (2) The word "understood" (GK 3783) suggests that the revelation does not stop with perception, but is expected to include reflection, the drawing of a conclusion about the Creator. (3) It is a constant testimony, maintained "since the creation of the world" (cf. Ac 14:17). (4) It is a limited testimony in that it reflects God in certain aspects only—namely, "his eternal power and divine nature." One has to look elsewhere for the disclosure of his love and grace—i.e., to Scripture and especially to God's revelation in his Son (Jn 1:14). Natural revelation is sufficient to make human beings responsible (they are left "without excuse"), but is not by itself sufficient to accomplish their salvation.

21–23 Despite the knowledge of God conveyed to them through the creation, people failed to act on it. They "neither glorified him as God nor gave thanks to him" (two obligations embracing one's entire duty toward God). Those who refuse to let God have the place of preeminence that is rightfully his will put something or someone else in God's place.

"Their thinking became futile." This phrase suggests that mythology and idolatry grew out of an insistent need by people to recognize some power in the universe greater than themselves, coupled with their refusal to give God the place of supremacy. It is highly suggestive that the verb "to become futile" yields a noun form that was used for idols (Ac 14:15). Idols are unreal and unprofitable, and their service can only lead to futility and further estrangement from the true and living God (cf. Da 5:23).

This abandonment of God in favor of inferior objects of worship is traced in a descending scale. "Mortal man" is the first substitution; the Creator is forsaken in preference for the being created in his image. Scripture shows us such deification of humankind in the case of Nebuchadnezzar (see Da 2:38; 3:1). In Paul's day the cult of Caesar had spread throughout the empire. In modern times the western world has outgrown crass idolatry, but humanism has subtly injected the worship of humanity without the physical trappings. God is quietly ruled out and the human spirit is placed on the throne.

The next stage is worship of the animal kingdom. Paul alludes to Ps 106:19–20 here, using a text that refers to Israel's sin in making the golden calf at Horeb and bowing down to this molten image. Although Paul is dealing with a characteristic sin of paganism, he resorts to OT history for an illustration. God did not and could not condone idolatry in the people he had chosen. His judgment fell heavily when there was no repentance, eventually deporting them from the land he had given them.

24–25 The opening word "therefore" carries the reader all the way back to the mention of the revelation of God's wrath, taking in also what lies between. The false worship just pictured is God's judgment for abandoning the true worship. Human religion in its various cultic forms is a species of punishment for spurning the revelation God has given of himself in nature. In many cases it is a means of keeping people so occupied that they never arrive at a confrontation with the true God.

"God gave them over" becomes a refrain (vv.24, 26, 28). The same expression is used of God's judgment on Israel for idolatry (Ac 7:42). In our passage the reference is principally to Gentiles. We are not told how this giving over was implemented, but most likely we are to think of it in negative terms—i.e., that God simply took his hands off and let willful rejection of himself produce its ugly results in human life.

At this point a problem surfaces. How is it that we have a reference to sexual immorality in v.24 and again in vv.26–27? Is this a case of repetition? No, the immorality lies in different areas. The earlier reference is to cultic prostitution, the latter to immoral relations in ordinary life. Paul was no stranger to the matter he discusses here. Writing from Corinth, where the temple of Aphrodite was fabled to have once housed hundreds of cult prostitutes, he must have been keenly aware of how this scourge affected the moral life of that city so adversely. How true is the observation that "their foolish hearts were darkened."

"They exchanged the truth of God for a lie" (lit. "the lie"). This is *the* lie above all others—the contention that something or someone is to be venerated in place of the true God. According to Paul elsewhere, history will repeat itself in that when the man of lawlessness is revealed and demands to be worshiped, people will follow him and reap ruin because they have refused the truth and have believed the lie (2Th 2:3–12). There, too, God gives them over to strong delusion (v.11).

Paul's indictment here is that by a wretched exchange human beings came to worship and serve "created things rather than the Creator." They have wholly rid themselves of God by substituting other objects in his place. This should be sufficient to banish the notion that the practice of idolatry is simply using a man-made image in order to worship God (cf. Hos 14:3). Contemplating this abysmal betrayal, the apostle cannot resist an outburst to counteract it. The Creator "is forever praised." God's glory remains, even though unacknowledged by many of his creatures.

26–27 For the second time the sad refrain is sounded—"God gave them over"—this time to immorality, with emphasis on perversion in sexual relations. What is the connection between the idolatry and immorality? By inventing their own deities, people were free to follow their own sinful passions, for they had no outside God to give account to. Moreover, the heathen went so far as to project their own license onto their gods, who in many cases were extremely immoral. Paul's use of "exchanged" is suggestive. The first exchange, that of the truth for the lie (v.25), is followed by another—the upsetting of the normal course of nature in sexual relations. Instead of using the ordinary terms for men and women, Paul substitutes "males" and "females." The irony is that this sort of bestiality finds no counterpart in the animal kingdom. Sexual perversion is the unique contrivance of the human species.

In bringing this discussion to a close, the apostle uses the expression "received ... the due penalty," which denotes the idea of recompense, a punishment in keeping with the offense. Sexual deviation contains in itself a punishment for the abandonment of God and his ways. This need not demand the conclusion that every homosexual follows the practice in deliberate rebellion against God's prescribed order. What is true historically and theologically is in measure true, however, experientially. The "gay" facade is a thin veil for deep-seated frustration. The folly of homosexuality is proclaimed in its inability to reproduce the human species in keeping with the divine commandment (Ge 1:28). To sum up, what people do with God has much to do with their personal character and lifestyle. Throughout the passage they are represented as actively choosing a religion and a lifestyle; they are not being taken captive against their will.

28–32 Paul now explains the word "wickedness" in v.18. This section describes the havoc wrought in human relations because of suppressing the knowledge of God. In the original there is a wordplay—when people *disapproved* of retaining God in their knowledge, God in turn gave them over to a "depraved" (lit. "*disapproved*"; GK 99) mind, which led them in turn to commit all kinds of sin. It is God's function to judge, but people have usurped that prerogative in order to sit in judgment on him and dismiss him from their lives. Paul's theme here accords with our Lord's appraisal, who traced the wellspring of sinful acts to the inner life rather than to environmental factors (Mk 7:20–23). The depraved mind is explained in terms of what it approves and plans—to do what even the popular moral consciousness regards as wrong.

Scholars have found it difficult to detect any satisfactory classification in the long list of offenses included here, which only confirms the fact that sin is irrational in itself and disorderly in its effects. It can be pointed out, however, that the initial group contains broad, generic descriptions of sin. The first of these, "wickedness," is the antithesis of righteousness, denoting the absence of what is just. It necessitates the creation of laws to counteract its disruptiveness, lest society itself be rendered impossible. "Evil" denotes what is evil not in the sense of calamity, but with full ethical overtones, signifying what is sinister and vile (cf. the devil, who is called "the evil one"). "Greed" indicates the relentless urge to acquire more (cf. Col 3:5). "Depravity" is a term describing a condition of moral evil, emphasizing its internal and resident character.

Among the final twelve descriptions, "God-haters" stands out, since it alone is related directly to an attitude toward the Almighty. But it is not isolated. The hatred that vents itself on God readily finds objects of hatred among his creatures. When human beings start worshiping themselves, insolent pride is the inevitable attitude assumed toward their fellow human beings. Some of the descriptions Paul uses here are not found again in his writings or elsewhere in the NT, but four of them occur in 2Ti 3:2–3, in predictions of the state of society in the last days.

The final item in the indictment is climactic (v.32). It is prefaced by the reminder that people have not lacked a sufficient knowledge of God's "righteous decree" or requirement (cf. 2:26; 8:4). If the knowledge of his power and deity (v.20) was sufficient to obligate them to worship God, the knowledge of his righteousness, innate in their very humanity, was sufficient to remind them that the price of disobedience was death. Yet they were not deterred from their sinful ways by this realization. In fact, they were guilty of the crowning offense of applauding those who practiced all kinds of wickedness. Instead of repenting of their own misdeeds and seeking to deter others, they promoted wrongdoing by encouraging it in their fellow human beings, in a defiant revolt against a righteous God.

Two final questions need to be raised about vv.18–32. Since the use of the past tense predominates in this section, are we to conclude that Paul has in view some epoch in the past when sin manifested itself with special intensity? This is unlikely, for he occasionally moves to the present tense. The conclusion is that the description fits his own time as well as earlier ages. If this were not so, the passage could scarcely deserve a place in the development of his theme.

Another problem is raised by the sweeping nature of the charge made in this portion of the letter. Are we to think Paul is accusing every pagan of this total list of offenses? Such a conclusion is unwarranted. While sinful people are capable of committing all of them, no one is necessarily guilty of each one.

B. Principles of Judgment (2:1–16)

In turning to this section, one can recognize considerable resemblance to 1:18-32. Human inadequacy in the light of divine standards continues to characterize the discussion (compare 2:1, "no excuse," with 1:20, "without excuse"). The indictment is stated first in broad terms, with no indication whether the people in view are Jews or Gentiles (cf. 1:18; 2:1), but as the picture unfolds, the Jew takes shape before our eyes just as the Gentile has come into focus in the previous section. In both portions, general terms for sin are followed by specific accusations (compare 1:18 and 1:23, 26–32 with 2:1–16 and 2:17–29).

1–4 Paul changes his style here as he enters into dialogue with an imagined questioner who has absorbed what was said up to this point and who shows by his attitude that he is in hearty agreement with the exposure of Gentile wickedness. That Paul had experienced such encounters in his missionary preaching is hardly open to doubt.

A Jewish listener, heartily endorsing the verdict rendered concerning the Gentiles, fails to realize his own plight. True judgment rests on the ability to discern the facts in a given case. If one is able to see the sin and hopelessness of the Gentile, one should logically be able to see himself or herself as being in the same predicament. But such people are so taken up with the faults of others that they often do not consider their own failures (cf. Mt 7:2–5). The charge that those who pass judgment do the same things they see in others is enlarged in 2:17–24. The allegation "you ... do the same things" stings, for the word "do" is the term used in 1:32 for the practices of the sinful Gentile.

Paul repeats himself in v.2. As he moves to state the first of his principles of divine judgment, he carries the observer with him. Surely this person will agree ("we know") that when God pronounces judgment on those who make a practice of indulging in sin, his judgment is based on truth. By this Paul simply means that God's judgment is reached on the basis of reality, not on appearances. He then asks (v.3): "Do you think you will escape God's judgment?" Two words are emphatic here, "think" and "you." Paul is reading the inmost thoughts of the Jew, whom he understands thoroughly from his own pre-Christian experience.

Paul carries the probing deeper still (v.4) by suggesting that people ignore and despise the fact that God, to be true to himself, must bring sin into judgment. There is even a scornful attitude toward God's patience with his people Israel, as though that forbearance confirmed their security, if not signaled weakness on God's part. "When the sentence for a crime is not quickly carried out, the hearts of the people are filled with schemes to do wrong" (Ecc 8:11). God's kindness toward Israel, noted here, is noted again in Ro 11:22.

In this passage "tolerance" and "patience" seem to be explanatory of "kindness," which is repeated as the governing thought. "Tolerance" (GK 496) has the idea of self-restraint. "Patience" (GK 3429) is literally "long-spiritedness." The intent of the kindness is to give opportunity for "repentance" (cf. 2Pe 3:9, 15), a term that occurs only here in Romans, though it must have been often on Paul's lips in preaching (Ac 20:21).

5–11 The apostle speaks plainly in order to startle Jews out of their lethargy of self-deception. What the nation is doing by its stubbornness and impenitence is to invite retribution, which is slowly but surely building up a reservoir of divine wrath that will be crushing when it breaks over the guilty in the day of reckoning. Then the judgment will be revealed to all, in contrast to the indirect working of God's wrath in the present scene (cf. ch. 1). At that time a second principle of divine judgment will become apparent, emphasizing performance: "to each person according to what he has done" (lit., "according to his works"). What Paul has in mind here is the final reckoning (cf. the word "day"). National judgment may fit into a temporal scheme, but personal judgment belongs to the frontier of the ages to come.

In amplifying this second principle of judgment Paul makes room for only two broad classes—those who persist in doing good and those who follow an evil course (vv.7–10). The first group, pictured as seeking glory, honor, and immortality, are promised eternal life. What can the apostle mean by his breathtaking assertion about attaining "eternal life"? At the very least, it is safe to say that he is not contradicting what he says later about the impossibility of having salvation by means of the works of the law (3:20). In fact, the statement of v.7, rightly understood, teaches the opposite. The reward of eternal life belongs to those whose good deeds result from their hope in God. Paul is simply portraying the motivation and the tenor of the life of faith that will culminate in eternal fellowship with God. The good works that believers perform do not bring them salvation, but they attest to the salvation they have received by faith (6:22; Eph 2:8–10).

On the other side of the ledger is a pattern of evil defined in terms of self-seeking and rejection of the truth, leading to divine wrath in terms of trouble and distress. The statement "who reject the truth and follow evil" echoes 1:18. Destiny does not depend on whether one is Jew or Gentile. The Jew is mentioned first simply because of God's prior dealing with that nation in history. Mention of the two divisions of humankind leads naturally to the pronouncement of Paul's third principle: God's judgment is impartial; he "does not show favoritism" (v.11). This is the truth that Peter learned in the Cornelius incident (Ac 10:34). Paul's explanation of what it involves belongs to the following paragraph.

12–15 The principle of impartiality has to face a problem as soon as the two groups, Jews and Gentiles, are considered together, for God has not dealt with them in similar fashion. The Jews have received a revelation of God in Scripture that has been denied the Gentile. But in this section Paul shows that Gentiles do have a law, and this suffices as a basis for judgment. Before discussing this law, however, Paul sees in it no power to save, for "all who sin apart from the law will also perish apart from the law." Gentiles do not perish for the reason that they lack the law which Jews possess, but because they sin. In speaking of Jews, Paul says they "will be judged" by the law, but this does not imply exoneration, for no Jew has succeeded in keeping the law.

The expression "all who sin under the law" could strike a Jewish reader as incongruous, but Paul is linking sin with law deliberately in order to prepare the way for his next statement—that the righteous are not those who "hear the law" (cf. Jas 1:22–24). Rather, doers of the law are the ones who will be "declared righteous" (v.13; GK *1467*). This is the first occurrence in Romans of the important expression "be declared righteous." Full treatment of this matter must wait until ch. 3, though the full theological significance of this word should be retained here.

Paul's purpose is to undercut the position of those Jews who are counting on their (limited) obedience to the law for acceptance with God. To Paul, one's compliance would have to be perfect if one were to be declared righteous by an absolutely righteous God (cf. Lk 10:28; contrast Lk 8:12). By analogy, Gentiles are in essentially the same position, seeing that they also are not without law (cf. vv.14–15). The future tense in "will be declared righteous" favors the conclusion that final judgment is in view. Paul is not raising false hopes here; on the contrary, he is dashing them. Only after the flimsy edifice of humanly contrived righteousness has been leveled will the apostle be ready to put in its place the sturdy foundation of the justification provided by God in Christ.

The word "indeed" in v.14 demonstrates that Paul intends to counter the boastfulness of the Jews by a discussion of the Gentile situation, to which he now turns. He seems anxious to avoid the impression that he is discussing the Gentiles in their entirety (he says "Gentiles," not "the Gentiles"). He is thinking of them in individual terms, not as masses. He goes on to recognize that there are Gentiles who, despite their apparent disadvantage in not possessing the Mosaic law, "do by nature" what the law requires.

What are these things? Presumably, they are not matters peculiar to the law of Moses, but moral and ethical requirements widely recognized and honored in people generally. It was a commonplace of rabbinic teaching that Abraham kept the laws of Sinai long before they were given. Paul states that such people as he has in mind are "a law for themselves." He is not talking about laws invented in their own self-interest; rather, they are laws that come from the law that is written on their hearts. We must not confuse this statement with God's promise in Jer 31:33 of the law written in the heart, for if that were the case, Gentiles would have the law in a more intimate way than Jews did. Rather, Paul is insisting that the basic requirements of the law are stamped on human hearts. Presumably, he can say this because human beings are made in the image of God. All people, for example, when they quarrel, instinctively try to determine who is in the right and who is in the wrong. Similarly, despite the great differences in laws and customs among peoples around the world, what unites them in a common humanity is the recognition that some things are right and others are wrong.

An additional element that belongs to the equipment of the Gentiles is "their conscience," which "[bears] witness" (v.15; GK 5210). The word used here has the idea of bearing witness *with*; so one must ask, With what? Only one answer seems possible: with the requirements of the law written on the heart. The two function together. While in the Greek OT the word "conscience" never appears, the operation of a conscience is recognized in such passages as Ge 42:21 and 2Sa 24:10.

Paul's fairly frequent use of the term "conscience" (GK 5287) indicates his indebtedness to his Greek environment and his desire of capitalizing on a concept familiar to his Gentile churches. In his thinking, the function of conscience in Gentiles is parallel to the function of the law for Jews. The way conscience operates is described as a process of accusation or defense by the thoughts of a person, the inner life being pictured as a kind of debating forum, so that at times one finds oneself exonerated at the bar of conscience, at other times convicted of wrong.

16 "This will take place on the day when God will judge men's secrets" (v.16). What does "this" refer to? Does Paul mean that only at the judgment will conscience be engaged in the manner he has just indicated? This would seem to be a severe limitation. Perhaps, therefore, it is best to see vv.14–15 as a parenthesis, so that what takes place on the day of judgment is the declaration of righteousness (or otherwise) referred to in v.13 (cf. NIV).

God's judgment will include "men's secrets" (cf. 1Co 4:5). This is the only court able to assess them. Many an act that seems entirely praiseworthy to those who observe it may actually be wrongly motivated; and contrariwise, some things that seem to us to merit stern disapproval may pass muster in this supreme court because the intention behind the deed was praiseworthy. The Jews theoretically admitted judgment and certainly welcomed it in the case of the Gentiles, while trying to shield themselves behind their privileged position. Non-Jews admitted the reality of judgment implicitly by the very process of reasoning that either accused or excused their conduct. What they did not know was the item included here—that God will judge "through Jesus Christ" (Jn 5:27; Ac 17:31). Paul concludes this section by noting that these principles of judgment are consistent with the Gospel that he preached.

C. Specific Guilt of the Jew (2:17–3:8)

Two main developments are discernible in this section. In 2:17–29 the advantage of the Jews in terms of their possession of the law and the distinctive mark of circumcision is offset by their boastfulness and fruitlessness. In 3:1–8 a new factor is introduced: Israel failed to respond to God in terms of trust and obedience, justifying the visitation of his wrath upon them.

The law of God is naturally associated with his revelation given to Moses on Mount Sinai (see also 2Co 3; Gal 4:42–31).

17–20 Paul now begins to dialogue with a representative Jew, and his razor-sharp irony is superb for its deftness. He first builds up the Jew, citing his various distinctives and appearing to appreciate them (vv.17–20), only to swing abruptly into a frontal assault by exposing the inconsistency between his claims and his conduct (vv.21–24). Jews were characterized by their reliance on the law, given by God through Moses. Such reliance came as the result of a relationship with God enjoyed by no other people. In Paul's time some of the leaders of Judaism were making such extravagant statements about the law as to put it virtually in the place of God. Many Jews were trying to keep the law for its own sake, to honor the law rather than its Giver. This tendency became even more developed after the fall of Jerusalem, when the law became the rallying point for a nation that had lost its holy city and its temple.

Paul concedes that the use of the law brings knowledge of God's will and a recognition of its superior teaching. But this is not all, for Jews think that this advantage had made them superior to Gentiles. We can paraphrase Paul's statement to his Jewish opponent: "You come to Gentiles and propose yourself as a guide for their blindness (when, as a matter of fact, as I have already shown, they have a light and a law as well as you). You come to the Gentiles as though they were dumb and childish, giving you the whip hand, which you thoroughly relish. To you they are mere infants, knowing next to nothing." By employing terms actually used by the Jews for the Gentiles, one after the other, not once suggesting that the Gentile has anything to his credit, but invariably magnifying the Jew, Paul has succeeded in exposing Jewish pride and boasting as utterly ridiculous.

21–24 Abruptly the shadow-boxing turns aggressive and the blows become lethal as the Jew is confronted by the disparity between what he teaches others as the will of God and his own manner of life. The thrust loses nothing of its forthrightness by being posed in a series of questions, for the effect is to turn the complacent Jew back on himself to search his own soul.

The indictment is summarized by the general charge of breaking the very law the Jew boasts of (v.23). In fact, the failure is so notorious that even non-Jews notice the discrepancy. At this point Paul introduces a quotation from Isa 52:5. God has been obliged to chasten his disobedient people by permitting them to go into captivity, where their captors make sport of their God who was apparently unable to prevent their deportation (cf. Eze 36:20–21). But there also the fault lay not with God but with his people who had refused to take his law seriously.

25–27 If the law was the major distinctive of the Jews, a close second was circumcision. As with the law, so with circumcision, the nation was guilty of placing unwarranted confidence in this rite. Many held the view that only circumcised children shared in the world to come. In dividing people into two classes, circumcised and uncircumcised, the Jews were in effect indicating those who were saved and those who were not.

But Paul contends that circumcision and observing the law cannot be separated. If one has the symbol of Judaism and lacks the substance, of what value is the symbol? If a Gentile should show success in observing the law, the lack of circumcision is surely not so important as to discount his spiritual attainment (cf. 2:14). In fact, says Paul, one can go a step further (v.27) and say that the circumcised Jew may find himself on a lower plane than the despised Gentile, because if the latter obeys the law that the former takes for granted, then the Gentile will "condemn" (GK *3212*) him. This does not involve the bringing of any charge, but is a specialized use of the word "condemn" to indicate the effect created by one who surpasses another despite his inferior status or limited advantage (cf. Mt 8:11 12; 12:41).

28–29 That this portion is intended as a conclusion to the discussion of both the law and circumcision is evident, for both are mentioned, though the law is referred to in terms of "letter" (cf. v.27). There was plenty of background for Paul's appeal for circumcision of the heart (e.g., Dt 30:6; Jer 4:4; 9:25–26). A real Jew is one who has circumcision of the heart, accomplished "by the Spirit, not by the written code" (cf. 2Co 3:6). How striking this is! The law is part of the Scripture that the Spirit has inspired, yet there is no hint here that the true Jew is one in whom the Spirit has made the teaching of the law dynamic. By avoiding any such suggestion,

Paul prepares the way for his treatment of the law in ch. 7.

He goes on to note that a Jew transformed by the Spirit would really be living up to the name he bears ("Jew" comes from Judah, meaning "praise"). He would be praiseworthy in the eyes of God, fulfilling what the law requires but cannot produce (cf. 8:3–4). Paul writes, of course, as a Christian, as one who has suffered much for his faith from his countrymen. But the closing verses of the chapter show that for all the bluntness of his references to the Jew he is not motivated by a desire to belittle his nation. Rather, he seeks their highest good (cf. 9:1–3; 10:1).

3:1–4 Paul continues with the subject of the guilt of the Jew, but now with an emphasis on the element of unbelief and on a sophisticated claim of immunity from divine judgment. His opening question reflects a devastating attack: What advantage is there in being a circumcised Jew? Paul implies that there are many such advantages, but he proceeds no further than the first one. The reader is kept waiting a long time for any resumption, but eventually the full list is provided (9:4–5).

For present consideration, the chosen advantage is that this nation has been "entrusted with the very words of God." The Greek word for "words" (lit., "oracles"; GK *3359*) was used especially for divine utterances. To be "entrusted" (GK *4409*) with these divine oracles obviously meant more than being the recipient of them, and even more than being their custodian and transmitter. What God expected were faith and obedience.

Precisely at this point the Jews failed (v.3). Paul has already dealt sufficiently with Jewish failure in terms of the law, but here he deals with it in terms of God's revealed purpose. He is considerate in saying that "some did not have faith" (cf. 1Co 10:1–10). Actually, of the exodus generation only two men pleased God and were permitted to enter the Promised Land. Paul is here recognizing the concept of the faithful remnant in Israel.

We should understand "God's faithfulness" in terms of the covenant aspect of God's dealings with Israel. There are really two sides to this faithfulness, the one positive, the other negative (cf. a similar duality in "the righteousness of God"; 1:17–18). Here the negative aspect is before us, as evident from the mention of "his wrath" (v.5). This is in harmony with a frequent emphasis in the prophets. When Israel fractured the Sinaitic covenant, God's very faithfulness compelled him to judge his people by sending them into captivity. The positive aspect will appear in Paul's sustained discussion of God's dealings with Israel (chs. 9–11).

As might be expected, Paul vigorously rejects any suggestion that God could fail in terms of his faithfulness (v.4). The concept of his fidelity is carried forward by the use of a closely related term. He is "true" to his covenant promises because he is true in himself. If one had to choose between the reliability of God and of humankind, one would have to agree with the psalmist who declared in his disillusionment concerning his fellow human beings, "Every man [is] a liar" (Ps 116:11). Even David, one of the best men in Israel's history, a man after God's own heart (1Sa 13:14), proved a disappointment. After being chastened for his sin and his refusal to confess it for a long time, he was ready to admit that God was in the right and he was in the wrong (Ps 51:4).

5–8 The supposition that human wrong could serve to display the righteousness of God was probably suggested to Paul in his quoting of Ps 51. Is it not possible (so the question goes) that since human failure can bring out more sharply the righteousness of God, the Almighty ought to be grateful for this service and soften the judgment that would otherwise be due the offender? The question is one a Jew might well resort to in line with the thought that God would go easy on his covenant people. So Paul speaks for a supposed interlocutor. The mention of wrath ties in with 2:8–9.

Paul's explanatory statement, "I am using a human argument," is due to his having permitted himself to use the word "unjust" of God, even though it is not his own assertion. If God were unjust, says Paul, he would not be qualified to judge the world. He makes no attempt to establish God's qualifications, since the readers have no doubt about this point.

Once more the apostle entertains a possible objection (vv.7–8). The thought is closely related to what has been stated in v.4. Speaking again for an objector, Paul voices the hoary adage that the end justifies the means. He has evidently had to cope with this in his own ministry, and he will be dealing with it again in a different context (6:1). Here he is content to turn the tables on the objector. Those who claim that their falsehood, which throws into sharp relief the truthfulness of God, promotes his glory and should therefore relieve the sinner of condemnation, should ponder the apostolic verdict—their "condemnation is deserved."

D. Summary (3:9–20)

9 Paul now identifies himself with the Jews, of whom he has been speaking. He asks whether they, with their moral and spiritual fitness, have an edge over Gentiles. His answer, "Not at all," registers an emphatic denial. Paul then backs up that denial of Jewish superiority by reminding his readers of the charge he has been bringing, "that Jews and Gentiles alike are all under sin." To be under sin is to be under its sway and condemnation. Up to this point in his discussion of sin, Paul does not charge the Jew with the death of Christ (cf. 1Th 2:15), nor does he charge the Gentile with this crime (cf. Ac 4:27–28). Perhaps this is because few Jews and still fewer Gentiles were involved in effecting the actual death of the Lord Jesus. Paul is basing his case on a much wider sampling of human character and conduct.

10–18 However, there is another argument waiting to be brought into play to seal the verdict. It is the testimony of Scripture. Writing to those who were for the most part Gentiles, Paul does not set down Scripture first and then work from that as a base for exposition, rather, he uses a minimum of references to the OT to substantiate what he has already established. Leaving a string of OT references to the conclusion of the argument is calculated to increase the respect of the Gentiles for Scripture as being able to depict the human condition accurately and faithfully. Both Jews and early Christians often drew up collections of Scripture passages relating to various topics as proof texts for instruction or argumentation.

The present list serves a double purpose: (1) to affirm the universality of sin in the human family, and (2) to assert its ramifications in every facet of human existence. "There is no one righteous, not even one." The language is devastatingly clear and sharp. No exception is allowed. Again, it can be put positively: "All have turned away," which seems to echo the thought of ch. 1 that people had an opportunity to know God but discarded him to their own detriment and confusion. Paul wants the full impact to register. He does not turn aside to answer the objection that the OT does speak of the righteous as a class of people over against the wicked (Ps 1) or as individuals (Job 1:8). From the standpoint of the divine righteousness, they all fall short, as Paul has affirmed of both Jews and Gentiles.

The latter half of the OT list, beginning with v.13, reflects the second emphasis mentioned above. As far as relationship with God is concerned, the rupturing power of sin has been noted (vv.11–12). But what effect does sin have on the sinner? The effect is total, because one's entire being is vitiated. Paul selects texts that refer to various members of the body: the throat, the tongue, and the lips (v.13); the mouth (v.14); the feet (v.15); and the eyes (v.18). This list affirms what theologians speak of as total depravity, i.e., not that humans in their natural state are as bad as they can possibly be, but rather that their entire beings are adversely affected by sin. Human relations also suffer, because society can be no better than those who constitute it. Some of the obvious effects—conflict and bloodshed—are specified (vv.15–17).

The chain of Scriptures closes by giving the root difficulty: "There is no fear of God before their eyes" (v.18). This is the same observation gleaned from the study of ch. 1. Being out of step with God causes conflict and chaos in human relations.

19–20 In these closing statements of the indictment, the apostle may be reading the mind of a Jew who questions the legitimacy of appealing to the type of passages used in vv.10–18, on the grounds that humankind in general is in view and at best includes only those Jews who by their very godlessness do not represent the nation as a whole. But the stubborn fact is that "whatever the law says, it says to those who are under the law" (v.19). The first reference to "law" (GK 3795) here must refer to the law in the general sense of the OT revelation (cf. 1Co 14:21); note that the string of quotations in vv.10–18 derives from various parts of the OT. The second reference, "under the law," is more literally "in the law"; the thought is not so much that the Jews are under the law's authority and dominion in the legal sense as that they are involved in Scripture, which has relevance to them at every point. The legislative aspect of the law is involved only by virtue of its being a part of Scripture.

"So that every mouth may be silenced." When human achievement is measured against what God requires, there is no place for pride or boasting but only for silence that lends consent to the verdict of guilty. In various biblical scenes of judgment, the silence of those who are being judged is a notable feature (e.g., Rev 20:11–14). Questions may be raised for the sake of clarification of the reason for the verdict (Mt 25:41–46), but when the explanation is given, no appeal is attempted. The Judge of all the earth does right (Ge 18:25).

In making these statements (v.19) the apostle has been concerned primarily with Jews because Scripture has been at issue. Suddenly he makes a statement involving the entire human race, which he pictures as "accountable to God." This may seem puzzling. How can Jewish failure in terms of what Scripture requires lead to the conclusion that all humanity is included? Two possibilities come to mind. One is that the Jewish nation is regarded as a test case for all peoples. If given the same privileges enjoyed by Israel, the rest would likewise have failed. A more likely explanation is that the failure of Gentiles is so patent that it is not a debatable subject; it can be taken for granted as already established (1:18–32). Once it has been determined that the record of the Jew is no better, then judgment is universally warranted. The final word to the Jews (v.20) is designed to rob them of any fancied support in the law of Moses. Justification before God cannot be attained by trying to observe the law, however much one may take satisfaction in that. As Jesus pointed out, no one had succeeded in keeping the law (Jn 7:19).

For the first time in Romans we encounter the expression "observing the law" (lit., "works of law"; cf. v.28), which has such prominence in Galatians (2:16; 3:2, 5, 10). That "no one will be declared righteous in his sight" is a quotation from Ps 143:2. The practical result of working seriously with the law is to "become conscious of sin" (cf. 5:20; 7:7–11). How startling it is to contemplate the fact that the best revelation the human race has apart from Christ only deepens one's awareness of failure. The law loudly proclaims one's need for the Gospel of Christ.

IV. Justification: The Imputation of Righteousness (3:21–5:21)

A. The Description of Justification (3:21–26)

To help his readers follow his train of thought, the apostle reverts to the term he used in stating the theme of the letter in 1:17—God's righteousness. He repeats also the necessity for faith (cf. 1:16) and then summarizes the material from 1:19–3:20 by the reminder that there is no difference between Jew and Gentile insofar as all have sinned. Having done this, he goes on to give a rich exposition of salvation through the use of various theological terms, with principal attention given to justification.

21 God's "righteousness" (i.e., his method of bringing people into right relation to himself; GK *1466*) is "apart from law." This stands to reason, for Paul has been declaring that the law operates in quite another sphere, making those who live under it conscious of their sin (v.20). God's righteousness "has been made known"; the Greek tense used here draws attention to the appearing of Jesus Christ in history (cf. 2Ti 1:10) and especially to the fulfillment of God's saving purpose in him. Yet even before the Savior appeared, this method of making people right with himself was operating in principle, as "the Law and the Prophets"—a summary term for the OT—testify. This observation prepares the reader for the recital of God's dealings with Abraham and David in the following chapter.

22 God's righteousness becomes operative in human life "through faith in Jesus Christ." This statement is more explicit than the initial mention of faith in connection with the Gospel (1:16–17), since it specifies Jesus Christ as the necessary object of faith. A problem lies beneath the surface, however, in that a literal translation is "through faith of Jesus Christ." This raises the possibility that our Lord's own faith, or more precisely, his faithfulness in fulfilling his mission, is the thought intended (note 3:3, where *pistis* ["faith"; GK *4411*] is translated "faithfulness"). However, Mk 11:22 makes it clear that the *pistis* of God can also mean faith in God, as the situation there requires. What should settle the matter here in v.22 is the precedent in Gal 2:16, where we find the identical phrase "through faith of Jesus Christ," followed by the explanatory statement "we believed in Christ Jesus."

Incidentally, it is never said that people are saved *on account of* their faith in Christ, as if our faith makes a contribution to our salvation. On the contrary, faith is simply that which appropriates God's gift; it adds nothing to it. And the way of salvation is the same for everyone, for "there is no difference" (cf. 3:9).

23 The reason all must come to God through faith in Christ is that "all have sinned and fall short of [or 'lack,' cf. Mk 10:21] the glory of God." This "glory" (GK *1518*) cannot refer to God's final glory (cf. 5:2), since even believers, for whom the sin problem has been solved, lack the future glory now. Rather, glory must be associated with the divine presence and the privilege that the human race originally had of direct communion with God. This ever-present deprivation is depicted in the restriction of God's glory to the holy of holies in the tabernacle and in the denial of the right of access to that glory except through the high priest once a year. God's glory is the majesty of his holy person. To be cut off from this fellowship is the great loss occasioned by sin.

24 One might think that Paul is committing himself to a doctrine of universal salvation—that all who have sinned are justified. That impression is certainly incorrect. The problem can be handled in either of two ways. Either the last statement in v.22 and all of v.23 should be regarded as semi-parenthetical (joining this verse with "all who believe"), or else Paul intends us to read it this way: "Since all have sinned, all must be justified—if they are to be saved—by God's free grace."

The concept of "justification" (GK *1466*) is the leading doctrinal contribution of Romans. How to be just or righteous in God's sight is the age-old problem of humanity (Job 9:2; 10:14). To get at the meaning of the doctrine, some attention must be given to terminology. The Greek verb used here ("are justified"; GK *1467*) is a forensic term (i.e., the language of the law court); in both OT and NT it means "to acquit" (Ex 23:7; Dt 25:1). But the idea of "acquittal" expresses only a part of the range of the word, for there is a positive side that is even more prominent in the NT—"to consider, or declare to be, righteous." God not only acquits believers, but he declares them to be righteous in his sight.

In the background is the important consideration, strongly emphasized by Paul, that the believer is "in Christ," a truth that he unfolds in greater detail later in his discussion (see 8:1; cf. 1Co 1:30; 2Co 5:21). His doctrine of justification and its link with being in Christ is perhaps best stated in Php 3:8–9: "that I may gain Christ and be found in him, not having a righteousness of my own that comes from the law, but that which is through faith in Christ." To be justified, in other words, includes the truth that God sees sinners in terms of their relation to his perfect Son.

Though justification has much in common with forgiveness, the two terms ought not to be regarded as interchangeable, for even though forgiveness of sins can be stated in comprehensive fashion (Eph 1:7; 4:32), one's continuing need for forgiveness (cf. Jn 1:8–9) sets it somewhat apart from justification, which is a once-for-all declaration of God on behalf of the believing sinner.

Sinners are justified "freely" (GK *1562*), i.e., as a gift. The same word is used in Jn 15:25, where it bears a somewhat different but not unrelated meaning—"without reason." God finds no reason, no basis, in sinners for declaring them righteous. He must find the cause in himself. This truth goes naturally with the observation that justification is offered by God's grace. If "freely" is the manner in which justification operates and if grace is its basis, "the redemption that came by Christ Jesus" is the means a gracious God employed to achieve this boon for humankind. The benefit that redemption brings in this life, according to Eph 1:7, is forgiveness of sins, and this is applicable in our passage. Another aspect, belonging to the future, is the redemption of the body, which will consummate our salvation (8:23; Eph 4:30).

25 "God presented him as a sacrifice of atonement." The emphasis on faith in this verse suggests that the force of "presented" is in the proclamation of the Gospel that makes

Christ's saving work central—a proclamation emphasizing that Christ, under God, has become "a sacrifice of atonement." This phrase renders the Greek *hilasterion* (GK 2663). In LXX the first occurrence of this word is in Ex 25:17, where it refers to the lid on the ark of the covenant ("atonement cover"; KJV "mercy seat"). The only other occurrence of this word in the NT (Heb 9:5) also alludes to this atonement cover. Does Ro 3:25 have the same frame of reference? Perhaps not, for Hebrews is filled with references to the sanctuary and its ritual, whereas Romans is not. But the contrast should not be overdrawn (cf. Ro 12:1). And although the ark of the covenant was withheld from public view and access, Heb 9 emphasizes that the death of Christ opened up what had formerly been concealed and was inaccessible to the people. The word "presented" here in Romans is a signpost suggesting a similar concept here. God's atonement has been set up before the eyes of the entire world. Christ has become the meeting place of God and humankind where the mercy of God is available because of the sacrifice of the Son.

The idea of atonement also relates to the context of Romans up to this point. The first main section of the book (1:18–3:20) is permeated with the concept of the divine wrath (cf. 1:18; 2:5, 8; 3:5), along with an emphasis on judgment. It would be strange for Paul to state the remedy for human sin and unrighteousness without indicating that this wrath of God has been satisfactorily met by his own provision. There is no other term in 3:21–26 that can convey this idea besides *hilasterion*.

The phrase "through faith in his blood" (v.25) poses a problem. This translation suggests that the believer's faith is to be placed in the blood of Christ, and the sequence of terms favors this. However, Paul nowhere else calls for faith in a thing rather than in a person. Thus an alternative suggestion is to place a comma after "faith," separating the clauses and making both of them dependent on *hilasterion*.

The remainder of v.25 deals with the necessity of Christ's propitiation in terms of God's "justice" (GK *1466*; the same word in the original as "righteousness"). God's character needs justification for him to pass over "sins committed beforehand"—i.e., in the ages prior to the cross. His "forbearance" (GK *496*) must not be thought of as sentimentality or weakness but as an indication that meeting the demands of his righteous character would be accomplished in due season. This happened at the cross. The full penalty for sin was not exacted earlier, in line with God's forbearance.

26 Now the bearing of the cross on God's dealings with the human race "at the present time" is unfolded. It amounts to a declaration that God is at once just in himself and justifying in his activity on behalf of humankind.

B. The Availability of Justification Through Faith Alone (3:27–31)

27–30 The opening words here suggest that this paragraph is designed especially for Jews, for even though boasting is not confined to them, it has already been noticed as a distinct tendency in their case (2:17, 23). On what established principle is boasting excluded? God has ordained faith as the sole condition for receiving salvation; that is what provides no basis for boasting, for in the last analysis faith, like the salvation it embraces, is God's gift (Eph 2:8). While Paul could speak of the righteousness he sought through observing the law as his own righteousness (Php 3:9), he cannot so speak of the righteousness he has in Christ. Once again he insists that justification takes place by faith apart from observing the law. Does this statement contradict 2:13? No, for everything depends on the right motive. To glory over one's achievement ruins the whole enterprise: it becomes an affront to God, and its value is gone (see Gal 3:12).

Again Paul moves to catch the eye of his Jewish readers by appealing to their awareness that God is one (vv.29–30). Jews, surrounded by pagan idolatry, proudly repeated the monotheistic confession of Dt 6:4. Paul now turns it to good account. Logically, if God is one and if he alone is God, then we can expect him to employ only one method to bring humanity to himself. Faith is therefore the condition for receiving salvation on the part of Jew and Gentile alike (v.30). Neither has any advantage over the other. The Gentile must come "by that same faith" required of the Jew (cf. 1:16; Gal. 2:15–16).

31 The final verse of the chapter has elicited many interpretations, attesting its difficulty.

The correct view is the one that most closely accords with the foregoing material.

Paul has twice mentioned that observing the "law" (GK 3795; vv.27–28) does not enter at all into justification, which is by faith apart from works of the law. May we draw the conclusion, then, that the law is useless? By no means, the apostle would answer, for the operation of faith really upholds or establishes the law; i.e., the Gospel vindicates the law. The law has fulfilled a vital role by bringing an awareness of sin (v.20). Breaking the law made the redeeming work of Christ at the cross necessary (vv.24–25). Those who see that the cross was a divine necessity will never feel that they can make themselves approved by God by fulfilling the law's demands. If that were possible, Christ would have died in vain. Since the death of Christ was performed in accordance with God's righteousness (v.26), this means that the demands of the law have not been set aside in God's plan of salvation.

One other interpretation of v.31 should be noted briefly, that this verse provides a transition to ch. 4, where Abraham's justification is explained. On this view "law" simply means Scripture, or more specifically, the Pentateuch (cf. "the Law" in v.21). While such an interpretation is possible, the word "law" does not have an article with it as it does in v.21. Further, it is doubtful that the material of the following chapter can be said to uphold the law.

C. The Illustration of Justification From the Old Testament (4:1–25)

The fact that in the Gospel a righteousness from God is *revealed* (1:17) could suggest that justification is a new thing, peculiar to the Christian era. To discover that it was already present in the OT serves to engender confidence in the basic unity of the Bible. This chapter is devoted almost exclusively to Abraham and God's dealings with him. The NT writers turn to Abraham almost instinctively when discussing faith (Heb 11; Jas 2). If Paul can establish as true that the father of the nation of Israel was justified by faith rather than by works, he will have scored heavily, especially with his Jewish readers.

1. The case of Abraham (4:1–5)

1–5 Paul now asks what Abraham had "discovered" about getting into right relation to God. In calling Abraham "our forefather," he is not addressing Jewish believers only, because he makes the point in this chapter that Gentile believers also have a stake in Abraham (v.16). In his answer, Paul picks up the matter of boasting from 3:27, but denies that it is possible to boast of works "before God." Abraham was not guilty of pharisaic folly. To show that his close relation to God was not based on works, a simple appeal to Scripture (Ge 15:6) is sufficient: "Abraham believed God, and it was credited to him as righteousness" (v.3). That appeal was necessary because Judaism even before Paul's day placed great emphasis on Abraham's piety and grounded his justification in his obedience. But Paul selects a text that emphasizes Abraham's faith and mentions nothing about his obedience.

At the time referred to in the Ge 15:6 quotation, Abraham was in the promised land but had as yet no progeny. Reminding God of this fact, he protested that "a slave born in my house will be my heir" (Ge 15:3), i.e., that he would have to adopt Eliezer his servant to be his heir. As time went on and Sarah did not bear a son, Abraham saw no prospect other than this. But God directed him to look up into the heavens and count the stars, promising that his descendants would be as numerous. Abraham accepted this promise, relying on God to fulfill it. This was the basis on which God pronounced him righteous.

The nature of Abraham's faith described here was essentially the same as that of the NT believer despite the difference in time. That is, Abraham trusted in a promise that looked forward to Christ (Jn 8:56; Gal 3:16), even though at this time it may not have been clear to the patriarch. Christians, on the other hand, look back to what God has provided in Christ. When God saw Abraham's faith, he credited it to him "as righteousness," which means that faith itself is not righteousness.

Paul goes on to contrast faith with works (vv.4–5), noting that work yields wages that must be treated as an obligation for an employer, whereas faith means that the one who exercises it receives a righteous standing from God simply as a "gift" (lit., "grace"; GK 5921). So grace is pitted against obligation and faith against works (cf. 11:6).

How far grace goes beyond justice is seen in the statement that God "justifies the wicked" (or ungodly). Not only does God justify people apart from works but he does so contrary to what they deserve. OT law required a judge to condemn the wicked and to justify the righteous (Dt 25:1), but where God is both Judge and Savior, the wicked have an opportunity denied to them in human reckoning. The prophetic word anticipated this result through the work of the coming Servant of God (Isa 53:5–6, 11).

2. The case of David (4:6–8)

6–8 Though the case of David is not strictly parallel to that of Abraham and is treated only briefly, it is clear from the phrase "the same thing" that the overall theme remains the same. What strikes one as peculiar, however, is the apparent lack of harmony between the quote from Ps 32 and what Paul announces as its meaning. While Paul indicates that Ps 32:1–2 concerns the reckoning of righteousness apart from works, the passage itself contains neither of these terms. Instead, it speaks about offenses that have been forgiven and about sins that have been covered. But when we compare v.6 with vv.7–8, one Greek word stands out as common to both: the word translated "credit" in v.6 and "count" (GK 3357) in v.8. In fact, this word dominates the early part of the chapter, occurring in vv.3, 4, 5, 6, 8, 9, 10, 11.

Paul's training as a Pharisee shows through here, since it is evident that he is utilizing a principle of rabbinic interpretation known as the principle of analogy. This means that in situations where the same word occurs in two passages of Scripture, the sense in one may be carried over to explain the meaning in the other. In the case of Abraham, righteousness was credited to him, apart from works, on the basis of faith. In the case of David, obviously no good work is involved; rather, sin has been committed. So the far-reaching nature of justification is seen to still greater advantage.

One may add that since David was actually already a justified man, known as the man after God's own heart, in his case we learn the truth that sin in the life of a believer does not cancel justification. God's gifts are irrevocable (11:29). At the same time, God showed his displeasure regarding David's sin, severely chastening him until the sin had been fully confessed, and even afterward, his sins produced havoc in his family (see 2Sa 12–21). Yet God did not withdraw his favor and support but guided him through these family crises. In contrast to Abraham, David lived under the regimen of the Mosaic law. Though the law is not mentioned, the text says that David "speaks of the blessedness of the man to whom God credits righteousness apart from works" (v.6). Paul may be suggesting here that after David sinned, he could not rectify his situation by means of works. He was completely dependent on God's mercy of forgiveness.

3. The promise to Abraham—apart from circumcision (4:9–12)

9–12 The issue discussed here is the importance of *time*: the time of God's declaration of righteousness on behalf of Abraham in relation to the time of his circumcision. By using the term "blessedness" (GK 3422) from the opening of Ps 32 Paul moves from David back to Abraham. Are the uncircumcised able to share in the blessedness mentioned by David? To the Jews, such blessedness was properly confined to the circumcised. Paul dissents, arguing skillfully that this benefit was enjoyed by Abraham, and Abraham received it when he was still uncircumcised! To all intents and purposes, he was like one of the Gentiles. This opens the door to the extension of the blessedness of justification to the Gentiles.

Paul is still using the above-mentioned method of analogy regarding "credited." As Ge 15:6 had been explained with the aid of Ps 32:1–2, now the apostle reverses direction and explains Ps 32 with the aid of Ge 15. Since Abraham was not circumcised until fourteen years after being pronounced righteous, circumcision was therefore really a sign of what he previously had. It was a testimony to his justifying "faith" (GK 4411) and was not something in which to take any pride (cf. 2:25–29). Circumcision was delayed to teach the future believing Gentiles that they too can claim Abraham as their father. It could even be said that Gentiles have first claim on the patriarch, who was just like them when justified. Jews stand rebuffed for their pride and exclusiveness (cf. Ac 15:11; Gal 2:16). The people referred to in v.12 are Jews who are not only circumcised but, more important, are believers who share the faith Abraham had before he was circumcised.

4. The promise to Abraham—apart from the law (4:13–17)

13–17 The thought moves on to consider that Abraham's justification was apart from any law or legal considerations. Paul speaks of a promise received by "Abraham and his offspring" that "he should be heir of the world." Nothing so precise can be detected in the text of Genesis. So what does Paul mean? The theme of the chapter has not changed; it is still that vast influence of this man of faith on succeeding generations and peoples. The word "world" (GK *3180*), therefore, denotes the multitude of those in future generations who will follow Abraham in terms of his faith as his rightful heirs. He will be their father in the sense that he is the father of their faith, since by that means they will be justified (cf. Ge 12:3; 22:18).

But we must return to Paul's main thrust, that the promise is not conditioned "through law." The thought is not developed in quite the same way as in Gal 3:17–18 (see comments). Here Paul makes the point that if inheriting the promise comes to those "who live by law," then faith is emptied of value and the promise has effectively been put out of operation. As soon as a promise is hedged about with conditional elements, it loses its value. Particularly is this true if these conditions are the law, with its inflexible character. As Paul puts it, "The law brings wrath." In other words, if God's promise had been conditioned by keeping the law, the human inability to observe the law with complete fidelity would have occasioned disobedience and consequently the operation of God's wrath, resulting in forfeiture of what was promised. In summary, the need to keep the law as a condition for receiving the promise would have two disastrous effects. It would pit the God of grace over against the God of judgment (an intolerable impasse), and it would make the realization of the promise impossible for us, since no one has been able fully to keep the law (see vv.14–15).

The promise, however, belongs to the realm of faith and grace (v.16). By mentioning faith first, Paul seems to put grace in a secondary position, but it cannot have been his intent to make grace depend on faith (cf. Eph 2:8). Rather, faith is put forward here to reaffirm v.13, after vv.14–15 have ruled out law—hence its prominence in the sentence. The only ground for certainty in relation to the promise is grace (as opposed to attempted legal obedience). This certainty (cf. the word "guaranteed" in v.16) is intended to apply to faith as well as to grace. In other words, the ultimate guarantee must be God and his faithfulness.

"Those who are of the law" are not excluded from Abraham's offspring. This means that the Israelites who happened to live during the Mosaic era were not excluded from the blessing of the Abrahamic covenant, provided they had faith. The above expression cannot refer to legal obedience, for then Paul would be contradicting himself. And the blessing of Abraham is also for those who, though not belonging to the Mosaic epoch, yet share the faith of the patriarch. Both Jews and Gentiles, then, are in the statement "He is father of us *all.*" This is followed by an appeal to the prediction that Abraham would be a father of many nations (Ge 17:5), a statement that cannot refer exclusively to the twelve tribes of Israel, since they constituted but one nation. Only God could foresee the course of history that was to include the coming of Christ, his finished work, his command to evangelize all nations (Mt 28:19–20), and the response of faith to the Gospel around the world.

God is described by two terms. (1) He is one "who gives life to the dead." It is perhaps natural to think of such an expression in terms of resurrection (vv.24–25), but hardly with reference to receiving Isaac back, as it were, from the dead, when Abraham was ready to offer him to God (a subject pursued in Heb 11:19 but not mentioned here). The thought seems to move rather along the line of making it possible for Abraham and Sarah to have offspring despite their deadness as producers of offspring (cf. v. 19, where the word "dead" occurs twice). (2) This conclusion is favored when we read that God is the one who "calls things that are not as though they were." The word "calls" (GK *2813*) in this case means to "summon" or "call into being," a word that may be used for God's creative activity. That is, Isaac was real in the thought and purpose of God before he was begotten.

5. Abraham's faith as the standard for every believer (4:18–25)

18–22 The final value of Abraham in respect to justification is that his faith becomes the standard for all believers. "Against all hope," this man believed. In view of his "deadened" condition (and that of Sarah likewise) because of advanced age, the situation seemed past hope. Nevertheless, he believed the promise of God that offspring would be given. "In hope" (GK *1828*) takes account of the great change that came over his outlook because of the pledge God gave him. After making the original promise (Ge 15:5), God waited until it was physically impossible for this couple to have children. Then he repeated his pledge (Ge 17:5). Abraham's act of faith was essentially the same as on the previous occasion, but meanwhile circumstances had made the fulfillment of the promise impossible apart from supernatural intervention. He was shut up to God and was able to rest his faith in God alone.

He "faced the fact" of his physical condition and that of Sarah and "did not waver through unbelief." The refusal to waver answers to the refusal to weaken in faith. Abraham apparently suffered a momentary hesitancy (Ge 17:17), but it passed and was not held against him. That he really trusted God for the fulfillment of the promise is seen in his readiness to proceed with circumcision for himself and his household before Isaac was conceived (Ge 17:23–27). This act in itself could be construed as giving "glory to God," an expression of trust in the power of the Almighty to make good his promise. Moreover, it was an open testimony to others of his trust in God's faithfulness to his word.

As far as Abraham was concerned, he was not taking a chance. He was "fully persuaded" that God's power would match his promise. This man of God was called on to believe in a special divine intervention—not after it occurred, as the Jews were challenged to do concerning the resurrection of Jesus (Ac 2–5), but before. His faith is the more commendable because it was exercised in the face of apparent lack of necessity. Would not Ishmael do as the desired progeny? He had been born to Abraham through Hagar in the interval between the original promise (Ge 15) and its renewal (Ge 17). Abraham was willing to rest in the wisdom as well as in the will of God. Verse 22 probably refers to the original statement of Abraham's justification, emphasizing that his ability to meet the renewed promise of God by unwavering faith was strictly in line with the faith that brought justification at an earlier point (v.3).

23–25 Having dealt with Abraham's situation, the apostle turns finally to applying God's dealings with the patriarch to the readers of this letter. This procedure accords with his observation that "everything that was written in the past was written to teach us, so that through endurance and the encouragement of the Scriptures we might have hope" (15:4). There are differences between Abraham's case and the position of the readers. Yet the basic similarity in God's dealings with both is unmistakable. Both believe in God as the one who acts in their behalf; both receive justification. Of course, the mention of the resurrected Jesus (v.24) is an element that could not belong to the OT as history, but the intended parallel with Abraham's experience is fairly evident. The same God who raised Jesus our Lord from the dead quickened the "dead" body of Abraham so as to make parenthood possible.

Death and resurrection were the portion of the Savior (v.25). One can hardly fail to notice the carefully balanced character of this final statement, relating as it does the death of Jesus to our sins and his resurrection to our justification. Beyond question, the statement owes much to Isa 53, where the Servant is pictured as delivered up on account of the sins of the many (v.12). Moreover, the resurrection, though not stated in so many words, is implied in 53:10, 12. Perhaps this statement is one that Paul has taken over from Christian tradition (cf. 1Co 15:3–4). In any case, this passage shows the early tendency to phrase redemptive truth in brief, creedlike formulations.

The chief difficulty for interpretation lies in the preposition "for" that is common to both clauses. In itself our word "for" is ambiguous. It can mean "because of" or "with a view to." In this case, however, "delivered over to death for our sins" is best seen to mean "because our sins were committed" and that on account of them Jesus had to die if salvation were to be procured. Similarly, "raised to life for our justification" means that Jesus was raised because our justification was accomplished in his death (cf. "justified by his blood," 5:9). It may be helpful to recognize that justification, considered objectively and from the standpoint of God's provision, was indeed accomplished in the death of Christ (5:9) and therefore did not require the resurrection to complete it. Subjectively, however, the resurrection of Christ was essential for the exercise of faith, since his continuance under the power of death would create serious doubts about the efficacy of his sacrifice on the cross. To believe in a Christ who died for our sins is only half the Gospel (cf. 6:3–4). Furthermore, justification is not simply a forensic transaction, important as that aspect is, but involves also a living relationship with God through the living Jesus Christ (5:18).

D. The Benefits of Justification (5:1–11)

The discussion of justification now goes beyond the exposition of what it is in itself, for that has been sufficiently covered. We hear no more of the law or of fancied merit built up through obedience to it. Justification is now viewed in the light of the wealth of blessings it conveys to the child of God. This section demonstrates beyond any doubt that justification is a central teaching with Paul.

Some contend that Paul is already dealing with sanctification in this chapter, pointing to the strong emphasis on experience in vv.2–5. The elements mentioned there obviously have an important bearing on Christian life, but the overall emphasis still remains on justification (vv.9, 16), along with reconciliation as seen against the background of enmity occasioned by sin (vv.10–11). Perhaps even more decisive is Paul's use of prepositions, a small but significant indicator. The emphasis in ch. 5 is on what has been done for believers *through* Christ and his saving work, whereas in ch. 6 Paul deals with what has happened to believers together *with* Christ and what they enjoy *in* Christ. The word "sanctification" (or "holiness") does not appear until 6:19, 22.

1–2 "Therefore" suggests that the whole argument from 3:21–4:25 is the background for what is now set forth. Paul is assuming the reality of justification by faith for himself and his readers ("we have been justified").

The first of the blessings conveyed by justification is "peace" (GK *1645*). We have encountered the word in the salutation (1:7) and in an eschatological setting (2:10). Here, however, the milieu is the estrangement between God and humankind because of sin. Peace relates back to Paul's emphasis on divine wrath in 1:18–3:20 (cf. "wrath" in v.9 and "enemies" in v.10). Peace in this setting means the believer's harmony with God rather than a subjective state within his or her consciousness.

That the objective meaning is to be adopted here is put beyond all doubt by Paul's assertion that the kind of peace he is referring to is peace *"with God."* Since this particular boon is placed first among the benefits of justification, it shows how central the wrath of God is to Paul's exposition of the plight of people that God has moved to remedy, a plight that could be dealt with only through the mediation of our Lord Jesus Christ (see also Eph 2:14; Col 1:20 for similar comments on peace).

The second benefit is "access" (v.2). Here also faith is mentioned as the essential instrument. The word rendered "access" (GK *4643*) can mean either "approach" or "introduction"; the latter meaning seems the more appropriate here. We must think of the Father in his exaltation and glory as the one being approached, with the Lord Jesus introducing us as those who belong to him and so to the Father (see also Eph 2:17–18; 3:12ff.).

The "grace in which we now stand" sums up the privilege of the saints in this present time, enjoying every spiritual blessing in Christ, and the possession of this grace gives warrant for the hope that we will share the glory of God (v.2). In this prospect believers exult. Grace gives a foothold in the door that one day will swing wide to permit the enjoyment of the glorious presence of the Almighty, a privilege to be enjoyed forevermore. Worth noting is the close relationship between faith and hope. As with Abraham (4:18), so with the believer in this age, the two virtues have much in common (cf. Heb 11:1; 1Pe 1:21).

3–5 The word "rejoice," used to characterize the hope of the Christian for participating in the glory yet to be revealed (v.2), now carries over to another area, different both in nature and in time—that of "sufferings." Peace with God does not necessarily bring peace with other people. The actual conditions of life, especially for believers in the midst of a hostile society, are not easy or pleasant, but the knowledge of acceptance with God, of grace constantly supplied, and of the prospect of future glory enables believers to exult in the face of sufferings. The usual setting for the term "sufferings" is external suffering such as persecution, though it is used occasionally for distress resulting from external events affecting the human spirit.

At this point Paul does not give full treatment on the subject of suffering, since he refers to it here simply as one link in a chain of events that benefit the Christian. Elsewhere Paul stresses that our sufferings are an extension of the sufferings experienced by Christ in the days of his flesh, rightly to be experienced now by those who make up his body (Php 3:10; Col 1:24). Believers rejoice when by their suffering they can show their love and loyalty to the Savior (Ac 5:41).

Suffering has value in that it produces "perseverance" (GK 5705) or "steadfast endurance." Believers do not take the pressure of tribulation passively by abjectly giving in to it; rather, they resist it, like Christ who "endured" the cross and thus triumphed over suffering. One of the distinctives of the Christian faith is that believers are taught to glory and rejoice in the midst of suffering rather than to sigh and submit to it as an inevitable evil.

Such perseverance develops "character" (GK 1509). Job sensed its worth, saying in the midst of his troubles, "When he has tried me, I shall come forth as gold" (Job 23:10 RSV). The word "character" indicates tested value. The newborn child of God is precious in his sight, but the tested and proven saint means even more to him because such a one is a living demonstration of the character-developing power of the Gospel. When we stand in the presence of God, all material possessions will have been left behind, but all that we have gained by way of spiritual advance will be retained.

This helps to explain Paul's statement that character produces "hope" (GK 1828), the climax of the items beginning with "sufferings." Just prior to that (vv.1–2) Paul had described hope from the standpoint of another series—faith, peace, access, grace, and then hope of the glory of God. In other words, just as our present access to God gives hope of sharing the divine glory, so with our sufferings. They help to produce character, and approved Christian character finds its ultimate resting place in the presence of God, not in a grave. By the tutelage of suffering the Lord is fitting us for his eternal fellowship.

Paul then makes it plain that this hope is not just a pious wish, for it does not put one to shame. It does not disappoint, because it is coupled with the love of God (v.5). Human love may bring disappointment and frustration, but not the love of God. Subjective desire is supported by an objective divine gift guaranteeing the realization of an eternal fellowship with God.

This passage concludes with a statement about the importance of the believer's possession of the Holy Spirit as a certification concerning the future aspects of his salvation, a theme developed more fully in ch. 8. But even in the limited treatment given the Spirit here we see something that specially characterizes the Spirit. By him God's love is "poured out" (GK 1772) in our hearts. This verb speaks of the inexhaustible abundance of the supply of God's love through the Spirit. All the blessings found in Christ are mediated to God's people by the Spirit. Looking back over the paragraph, we see that the thought has advanced from faith to hope and from hope to love (the same order as in 1Co 13:13).

6–8 Having dwelt on the powerful influence of the divine love ministered to the hearts of believers by the Spirit, Paul goes on to explore the depths of that love, finding it in the cross of Christ. The demonstration of God's love in Christ came "at just the right time" (cf. Gal 4:4). The law had operated for centuries and had served to expose the weakness and inability of people to measure up to the divine standard of righteousness (cf. Ro 3:20; 4:15). No further testing was needed. It was the right time for the Messiah to come into the world.

"Powerless" (GK 822) is the translation of a word that commonly means "weak" or "sickly," but here it has a somewhat specialized force of the inability for us to work out any righteousness for ourselves. A still more uncomplimentary description of those who needed the intervention of Christ's death on their behalf is "ungodly" (GK 815; cf. 4:5).

A third word descriptive of those for whom Christ died is "sinners" (GK 283). The verb "to sin" (GK 279) has been used in 3:23 to summarize the human predicament traced in the opening chapters. We need to see how

Paul prepares the way for the impact of this term by contrasting it with both "righteous" (GK 1465) and "good" (GK 19). He puts aside for the moment the technical theological force of the word "righteous" in the sense of "justified" and uses it as it is used in ordinary parlance. Likewise, he ignores the fact that in 3:12 he has quoted "There is no one who does good" from Ps 14:3, and then proceeds to use "good" as we do when recognizing kindness and benevolence in one another. In other words, Paul is illustrating a point from ordinary life. It is a rare thing, he says, to find a person ready to die for an upright person, but conceivably it would be easier to find one willing to die for a good person. Evidently the "good man" stands on a higher plane than the "righteous man."

Now Paul is ready to proceed to his main point. It was for "sinners" that Christ died—for people who were neither "righteous" nor "good." The stark contrast is between the tremendous worth of the life laid down and the unworthiness of those who stand to benefit from it. Behind the death of Christ for sinners is the love of God (v.8): God loved; Christ died. Paul does not attempt to deal with the Savior's reaction or motivation. He leaves much to Christian awareness of the intimate bond between Father and Son—the whole truth about God being in Christ (2Co 5:19) and Christ being motivated by love for the lost (Jn 15:12–13). What he puts in the foreground is the love of God for the unsaved, and this Paul underscores by designating it as God's "own love." It is distinctive, unexpected, unheard of (cf. Jn 3:16).

Four times in these three verses the expression "die for" occurs, and in each instance Paul uses the Greek preposition *hyper* ("on behalf of"; GK 5642). This word expresses the substitutionary character of the sacrifice of Christ plus the additional element of action on behalf of another in line with the loving empathy of God in Christ.

9–11 Whereas the preceding paragraph dealt with the depth of the love of God as seen in the cross, the present section moves on to declare the height of that love, namely, its refusal to stop short of effecting final and everlasting salvation in which the enmity created by sin has been completely overcome.

Once again Paul assumes an achieved justification (cf. v.1), repeating the means whereby it was accomplished ("by his [Christ's] blood"). Then he turns to face the far-reaching effects of this justification on our future. We were reconciled when we were enemies. Surely, then, since God no longer looks on us as enemies subject to his wrath, he will maintain the status quo and not suffer us to lapse back into an unreconciled position and, furthermore, will carry us on to the full end of our salvation. The agency of Christ continues to be crucial, only now with this difference, that, whereas our justification was achieved by his death, our preservation is secured by his life. This is a clear reference to Christ's postresurrection life rather than to his life in the days of his flesh. Here Paul conjoins justification and salvation as he did when he stated the theme of this letter (1:16–17).

The pivotal word for the right understanding of vv.10–11 is "enemies" (GK 2398), the fourth term Paul has used for those in the unsaved state (see vv.6–8 for the others). Does Paul use "enemies" in an active sense, meaning those who experience enmity toward God (cf. 8:7), or in the passive sense, meaning those who are reckoned as enemies by God? Several reasons dictate that the latter is the intended force of the word. (1) That the word is capable of conveying this meaning is evident from 11:28, where the people of Israel are spoken of as enemies in the reckoning of God and yet loved by him. The enmity there is judicial. (2) The mention of "God's wrath" in v.9 points to the conclusion that the "enemies" are the objects of his wrath. (3) The whole tenor of the argument leads one to the same conclusion. Paul reasons from the greater to the lesser. If God loved us when he considered us his enemies, now that he has made provision for us at such infinite cost, he will certainly all the more see us through to the final goal of our salvation. (4) Paul not only states that we have been reconciled (v.10) but that we have received the reconciliation (v.11). He avoids saying that we have done anything to effect the reconciliation. God provided it through the death of his Son. The appropriate response is exultation (cf. vv.2–3).

E. The Universal Applicability of Justification (5:12–21)

This most difficult portion of the letter, packed with close reasoning and theological terminology, stands at the very heart of the development of Paul's thought. He has presented all people as sinners and Christ as the one who has died to redeem them. Now he delves into the question: How does it come about that every human being—with no exception but Jesus Christ—is in fact a sinner? In answer, he goes all the way back to the first man Adam to affirm that what he did has affected the whole of humankind, involving everyone in sin and death. But over against this record of disaster and loss he puts the countermeasures taken on behalf of the human race by another man, Jesus Christ, of whom all are potential beneficiaries.

12 The one man through whom sin entered the world is not immediately named (see v.14). The same procedure of talking about a man before he is named is followed with Christ (v.15). Except for two nontheological references (Lk 3:38; Jude 14), every mention of Adam in the NT comes from the pen of Paul. In 1Ti 2:14 he makes the point that Adam, unlike Eve, was not deceived, but sinned deliberately. In 1Co 15:17, 56, as here in Romans, Paul institutes a comparison between the first and the last Adam, but confines his treatment to the issue of death and resurrection, whereas here both sin and death are named immediately and are woven into the texture of the argument throughout. In that earlier letter Paul made the significant statement, "For as in Adam all die, so in Christ all will be made alive" (1Co 15:22), in line with Ro 5:12. In the only previous mention of death in Romans (1:32) exclusive of the death of Christ (5:10), Paul referred to the inevitable connection between sin and death. Here in v.12 he pictures sin and death as entering the world through one man, with the result that death permeated the whole of humankind. It was the opening in the dike that led to the inundation, the poison that entered at one point and penetrated every unit of a person's corporate life.

If Paul had stopped with the observation that death came to all human beings because all have sinned, we would be left with the impression that all sinned and deserved death because they followed the example of Adam. But subsequent statements in the passage make it abundantly clear that the connection between Adam's sin and death and what has befallen the human race is far closer than that. Paul can say that the many died because of "the trespass of the one man" (v.15). Clearly the gist of his teaching is that just as humankind has become involved in sin and death through Adam, it has the remedy of righteousness and life only in another man, in Jesus Christ.

What, then, is the precise relation of Adam in his fall to those who come after him? Paul does not comment on that issue in this verse, though he later states that all sinned in the first man (v.19). Why does he not say so here? Was it his sudden breaking off to follow another line of thought in vv.13–14 that prevented the full statement? Or was it his reluctance to gloss over human responsibility, which he had already established in terms of universal sin and guilt (3:23)? Experience demonstrates that despite the inheritance of a sinful nature from Adam, people are convicted of guilt for the sins resulting from it that they commit themselves. Conscience is a factor in human life, and the Holy Spirit does convict of sin (Jn 16:8). Perhaps, then, as some hold, while the emphasis on original sin is primary in the light of the passage as a whole, there is a hint that personal choice and sin are not entirely excluded (cf. "many trespasses" in v.16).

That we could have sinned in Adam may seem strange and unnatural to the Western mind. Nevertheless, it is congenial to biblical teaching on the solidarity of humankind. When Adam sinned, the human race sinned because it was in him. To put it boldly, Adam was the race. What he did, his descendants, who were still in him, did also. This principle is also utilized in Heb 7:9–10: "One might even say that Levi, who collects the tenth, paid the tenth through Abraham, because when Melchizedek met Abraham, Levi was still in the body of his ancestor."

If one is still troubled by the seeming injustice of being born with a sinful nature because of what the father of the human race did and of being held accountable for sins resulting from that disability, one should weigh carefully the significance of the reconciliation statement of Paul: "that God was reconciling the world to himself in Christ, not counting men's sins against them" (2Co 5:19). The sins committed, that owe their original impetus to the sin of the first man, are not reckoned against those who have committed them if they put their trust in

Christ crucified and risen. God takes their sins and gives them his righteousness. Would we not agree that this is more than a fair exchange?

13–14 The dash at the end of v.12 (NIV) is intended to indicate that the comparison that Paul launched with his "just as" is not carried through. In view of what follows, the complete statement would have run something like this: "Just as sin entered the world through one man, and death through sin, and in this way death came to all men, because all sinned, so righteousness entered the world by one man, and life through righteousness" (cf. v.18, which sums up vv.15–17). Throughout the passage the thought is so tremendous that it proves intractable from the standpoint of expressing it in orderly sequence. The thought outruns the structural capacity of language.

Judging from the use of "for" at the beginning of v.13, these next two verses are intended to support and explicate v.12. From Adam to Moses the law was not yet given, so sin was not present in the sense of transgression. The human race did not have a charge from God similar to that which Adam had and violated. But the very fact that death was regnant during this period is proof that there was sin to account for death, seeing that death is the consequence of sin. The sin in view here was the sin of Adam, which involved all his descendants. Death in this case means physical death, which suggests that the same is true in v.12. This agrees with Paul's treatment of the subject of death in 1Co 15 (see especially v.22).

Adam is described as "a pattern of the one to come." "Pattern" translates the word *typos* (GK 5596), often rendered "type." It may seem strange that Adam should be designated as a type of Christ when the two are so dissimilar in themselves and in their effect on humankind. But there is justification for the parallel. The resemblance is that Adam and Christ each communicated to those whom he represented that which belonged to him ("sin" and "righteousness" respectively). In other words, what each did involved others. "The one to come" is to be taken from the perspective of Adam and his time; it has no reference to the second coming of Christ (cf. Mt 11:3).

15–17 In this section Christ's effect on the human race is seen as totally different from that of Adam—and vastly superior. Any hint of parallelism suggested by "pattern" is replaced by the element of contrast. True, there is one similarity: the work of Adam and that of Christ relate to "the many." It will readily be seen by comparing v.15 with v.12 that "the many" is the same as "all men" (compare "death came to all men" with "the many died"). This use of "the many" (cf. Isa 53:11–12; Mk 10:45) underscores the importance of Adam and Christ respectively. What one did, in each case, affected not one but many.

The contrast between Adam and Christ is particularly noted in the expression "how much more" (vv.15,17). The force of this seems to be bound up with the recurring use of "grace" (GK 5921) and "gift" (GK 5922), suggesting that the work of Christ not merely canceled the effects of Adam's transgression so as to put human beings back into a state of innocence under a probation such as their progenitor faced, but in fact gives them far more than they lost in Adam, more indeed than Adam ever had. The gift, prompted by grace, includes righteousness (v.17) and life (v.18), which is later defined as eternal life (v.21). Paul further observes that in Adam's case, a single sin was involved, one that was sufficient to bring universal condemnation, but in the work of Christ a provision is found for the many acts of sin that have resulted in the lives of his descendants (v.16).

Whereas up to this point Paul's train of thought has been concerned with developing the concept of sin taken over from v.12, now it turns to its companion factor, death (v.17), also mentioned in v.12. The point of this "much more" appears to be that in Christ not only is the hold of death, established by Adam's sin, effectively broken, but because of Christ's redeeming work the believer is able to look forward to reigning in life through Christ. This, of course, implies participation in the resurrection (cf. ch. 6). Believers will have a share in the Lord's kingdom and glory.

18–19 At this point, Paul provides something of a conclusion to v.12 (see comment on vv.13–14), but in such a way as to take account of the intervening material. The word "consequently" shows his intent to summarize. Paul carefully balances the clauses. One trespass brought condemnation for all humanity and one act of righteousness brought justification for all. Adam's sin is labeled "trespass" (GK *4183*), indicating that it was deliberate breaking of a command (cf. v.14). The reference is clearly to his violation of the divine restriction laid down in Ge 2:16–17, resulting in condemnation for the entire human race. His act involved others directly; it did not merely set a bad example. Over against Adam's act, Paul put another of an entirely different character—an "act [or better, 'work'] of righteousness [GK *1468*]." The same Greek word occurs at the end of v.16, where it is rendered "justification." The whole scope of the ministry of our Lord is in view. He came "to fulfill all righteousness" (Mt 3:15). The word "justification" is set over against "condemnation" (GK *2890*), but something is added, namely, the observation that justification is more than the antithesis of condemnation, more than the setting aside of an adverse verdict due to sin, and more than the imputation of divine righteousness. It is the passport to life, the sharing of the life of God (cf. v.21).

Another term for Adam's failure occurs in v.19, "disobedience" (GK *4157*). This accents the voluntary character of his sin. Matching it is the "obedience" (GK *5633*) of Christ, a concept that was highly meaningful to Paul (see Php 2:5–11). The interpretation of that passage in Philippians should be along the lines of a latent comparison between Adam and Christ. Instead of grasping after equality with God, as Adam had done, the Lord Jesus humbled himself and became obedient even to the point of accepting death on a cross.

The result of Christ's obedience is that "the many will be made righteous." Does this refer to righteous character? Possibly so, if the future tense points to the glorious time when imputed righteousness becomes righteousness possessed in unblemished fullness. But "will be made righteous" may simply be the equivalent of "will become righteous" in the forensic sense (cf. 2Co 5:21), in which case the future tense embraces all who in this age are granted justification (most of whom are future to Paul's time).

Does the sweeping language used here suggest that all humankind will be brought within the circle of justification, so that no one will be lost? Some have thought so. But if the doctrine of universalism were being taught here, Paul would be contradicting himself, for he has already pictured people as perishing because of sin (2:12; cf. 1Co 1:18). Furthermore, his entire presentation of salvation has emphasized the fact that justification is granted only on the basis of faith. We must conclude, therefore, that only insofar as "the many" are found in Christ can they qualify as belonging to the righteous.

20–21 At the conclusion of the chapter, Adam as a figure fades from view. Yet his influence is still present in the mention of sin and death. Paul now introduces another factor—the Mosaic law—to show its bearing on the great issues of sin and righteousness. There is scarcely a subject treated by Paul in Romans that does not call for some consideration of the law. The closest affinity to the thought in v.20 is found in 3:20, "Through the law we become conscious of sin" (see also ch. 7).

The apostle is not maintaining that the purpose of God's giving of the law is exclusively "that the trespass might increase," because he allows that the law is a revelation of the will of God and therefore has a positive benefit (7:12). The law also serves to restrain evil in the world (implied in 6:15; stated in 1Ti 1:9–11). Paul says the law "was added," suggesting that it was something temporary, designed to disclose the transgression aspect of sin and so prepare the way for the coming of Christ (see Gal 3:19). In the Sermon on the Mount, it appears that Jesus sought to apply the law in precisely this way, to awaken a sense of sin in those who fancied they were keeping the law tolerably well but had underestimated its searching demands and the sinfulness of their own hearts (Mt 5:17–48).

Lest someone raise a charge against the Almighty that to make possible an increase in sin is not to his credit, Paul insists that only where sin is seen in its maximum expression can divine grace truly be appreciated. "Grace increased all the more." The apostle waxes almost ecstatic as he revels in the superlative excellence of the divine overruling that makes sin serve a gracious purpose.

With great effect Paul brings the leading concepts of the passage together in the final statement (v.21). "Sin reigned in death" picks up vv.12, 14; "grace" looks back to vv.15, 17; "reign" reflects vv.14, 17; "righteousness"

Great Doctrines in Paul

The apostle Paul has often been called the first great Christian theologian. His writings have shaped Christian doctrine from the time that he wrote his letters. The following chart lists many of the great doctrines of the church and the main passages in Paul that explore these doctrines. There are, of course, many other passages in Paul, not listed here, that touch on these doctrines, and there are many other passages of the Bible, not written by Paul, that also explore these teachings. The ones listed here are the main ones of Paul.

The Inspiration of Scripture	Gal 1:11–12; 2Ti 3:14–17
Divine Election	Ro 8:29–30; 9:6–33; Eph 1:3–14
God's Plan for Israel	Ro 11:1–32
The Universality of Human Sinfulness	Ro 1:18–3:20; 3:23; Tit 3:3
Victory Over Sin and Satan	Ro 6:11–7:6; 8:31–39; Eph 6:10–18
The Twofold Nature of Jesus Christ	Ro 1:3–4; Php 2:5–11
The Sacrificial Atonement of Christ	Ro 3:25–26; 5:6–10; Gal 3:10–14
Reconciliation Between Human Beings and God	Ro 5:10–11; 2Co 5:16–21; Col 1:19–23
Christ as the Second Adam	Ro 5:12–21; 1Co 15:20–22, 42–49
The Supreme Lordship of Jesus Christ	Ro 10:9–13; Eph 1:15–23; Php 2:9–11; Col 1:15–20; 2:6–15
The Old and New Covenant	2Co 3:1–18; Gal 3:15–4:7; 4:21–31
Justification by God's Grace through Faith	Ro 1:16–17; 3:21–4:25; Gal 2:16–3:14; Eph 2:1–10; Php 3:7–11; 1Ti 1:12–16; Tit 3:4–8
Life Through the Holy Spirit	Ro 8:1–17, 26–27; Gal 5:16–26
The Christian's Life of Love	Ro 12:9–21; 13:8–10; 1Co 13; Gal 5:13–15; Col 3:12–14
The Gifts of the Holy Spirit	Ro 12:3–8; 1Co 12:1–11, 27–31; 14:1–40; Eph 4:7–12
Marriage in Christ	1Co 7:1–40; Eph 5:22–33; Col 3:18–19
Christian Freedom	Ro 14:1–15:13; 1Co 8:1–13; 10:23–33; Gal 5:1–12; Col 3:16–23
Unity in the Church	1Co 1:10–17; Eph 2:11–21; 4:1–16
Baptism	Ro 6:1–10; 1Co 12:12–13; Col 2:11–12
Lord's Supper	1Co 10:14–22; 11:17–34
Death for Believers	2Co 5:1–8; Php 1:19–26
The Resurrection	1Co 15; Php 3:20–21
The End of History	1Co 15:23–29; 2Co 5:10; 1Th 5:1–11; 2Th 1:5–2:12; 2Ti 3:1–9
The Second Coming of Jesus Christ	1Co 15:51–57; Php 3:20–21; 1Th 4:13–18; Tit 2:11–14

life" completes and crowns the allusion to "life" in vv.17–18. Sin and death are virtually personified throughout. Sin poses as absolute monarch, reigning through death as its vicar; but in the end it is exposed as a pretender and is obliged to yield the palm to another whose reign is wholly absolute and totally different, being as much a blessing as the other is a curse.

V. Sanctification: The Impartation of Righteousness (6:1–8:39)

Up to this point the letter has answered such questions as these: Why do we need salvation? What has God done to effect it? How can we appropriate it? The answers have come in terms of sin, condemnation, the gift of Christ, faith, and justification. Is there need for anything more? Yes, there is. For the saved cannot safely be turned over to their own wisdom and their own devices, seeing that they have not yet reached the perfect state. They must still contend with sin and must depend on divine resources. God's plan of salvation does not stop with justification but continues on in sanctification. A diagram may help to clarify the relationship between the two.

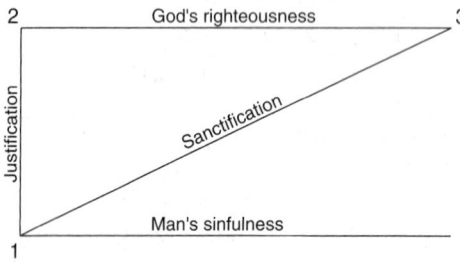

Point 1 marks conversion, or, if we think objectively rather than subjectively, regeneration. It is here that justification takes place. The line from 1 to 2 is not to be thought of as a process but as a change of position effected by God—his declaration of righteousness on behalf of condemned sinners. Justification by faith means that people are lifted once for all to the level of God's righteousness. Their standing before him is complete and perfect, because Christ has been made their righteousness (1Co 1:30; cf. 2Co 5:21). At no time in this life or in the life to come will their status in terms of righteousness be any greater (the line from 2 to 3).

But God is concerned not only with believers' status but also with their state, their actual condition. No sooner has he justified a person than he begins a process of growth that we know as sanctification. It is represented by the diagonal line between 1 and 3. This is a *process*, to be sure, but it should be observed that the term "sanctification" as used in Scripture is also a *position*, a setting apart by God that is basic to any progress in the Christian life. Consider, for example, Paul's description of the Corinthian believers as (already) "sanctified" (1Co 1:2), in spite of a seeming contradiction to the unholy state of many of them as evidenced by their many shortcomings. We can understand this by Paul's observation about what happened at their conversion: "You were washed, you were sanctified, you were justified in the name of the Lord Jesus and by the Spirit of our God" (1Co 6:11). Mention of their sanctification is given priority over their justification, which reverses the expected order. This is the initial or *positional* sanctification, which is basic to any improvement in their manner of life (cf. 1Pe 1:2). This aspect of sanctification cannot be distinguished from justification in respect to time. But sanctification as a *process* is naturally dependent on and subsequent to justification.

Point 3 is the juncture at which the process of sanctification reaches its consummation, when the saints experience complete sanctification because their sinful natures have been left behind and their lives are fully conformed to the divine standard as seen in God's Son (8:29). This occurs at death (Heb 12:23) or at the return of Christ in the case of the saints who are alive at that time (1Jn 3:2). Then for the first time the believers' actual state in terms of righteousness will conform to the status conferred on them at their justification (Gal 5:5).

A. The Believer's Union With Christ in Death and in Resurrection Life (6:1–14)

Paul now refers to the various epochal experiences that Christ passed through—namely, death, burial, and resurrection. Viewed from the standpoint of his substitutionary sacrifice for sin, these events do not involve our participation, though our salvation depends on them. Our Lord was alone in enduring the cross, in being buried, and in being raised from the dead. But his redeeming work is not only substitutionary; it is also representative. "One died for all, and therefore all died" (2Co 5:14). So Christians are viewed as being identified with Christ in his death, burial, and resurrection. And as truly as he, having borne our sin, is now removed from any claim of sin against him—because he died to sin and rose again—we also by virtue of being joined to him are delivered from any claim of sin to control us. This line of thought is what Paul proceeds to develop in the passage before us. It is evident that God has a plan for dealing with the *power* of sin as well as with its *guilt*. The way has been prepared for this emphasis by the presentation of the solidarity between Christ and the redeemed in 5:12–21.

1. The statement of the fact (6:1–10)

1–2 Paul begins his discussion by raising an objection and answering it—an objection that grows out of his presentation of justification, especially the teaching that where sin increased, grace increased all the more (5:20). The query is to this effect: "Are we not able, or even obliged, by the logic of justification, to continue on in sin, now that we are Christians, in order to give divine grace as much opportunity as possible to display itself? The more we sin, the more God's grace will be required to meet the situation; this will in turn contribute the more to his glory."

The apostle shows his horror at such a suggestion: "By no means!" (see also his repudiation of a similar suggestion in 3:8). It is likely that as Paul taught justification by faith, objections of this sort were raised from time to time by those who feared that his teaching would open the door to libertinism by encouraging indifference to the ethical demands of the law. If so, his answer is forged in years of reflection under divine guidance.

His answer is crisp: "We died to sin; how can we live in it any longer?" He does not say that sin is dead to the Christian; ch. 7 is a sufficient refutation of any such notion. Rather, we died to sin. Nor does Paul here explain when or how we died to sin; instead, his emphasis lies on the logical impossibility of a Christian continuing in a life dominated by sin. Death to sin is not something hoped for by the believer; it is something that has already taken place. It is a simple fact basic to the living of the Christian life.

3–4 The explanation of how this death to sin occurred follows immediately (vv.3–4): by being "baptized into Christ Jesus." What is being described is a spiritual reality of the deepest import—not a mere ceremony, not even a sacrament. The metaphor of baptism is clearly used by Paul in a relational sense elsewhere, as in the Israelites being baptized into Moses when they crossed the Red Sea (1Co 10:2). They became united to him as never before, recognizing his leadership and their dependence on him. Union with Christ means union with him in his death. It is significant that although Jesus emphasized discipleship throughout his ministry, he never spoke of union with himself until he was on the verge of going to the cross (Jn 14–16). He had earlier spoken of his death under the figure of baptism (Lk 12:50).

Baptism illustrates this vital union with Christ in his death, though baptism does not accomplish it. Apparently, Paul pictures burial with Christ, however momentarily, in the submergence of the body under the baptismal waters. The importance of burial is that it attests the reality of death (1Co 15:3–4). It expresses with finality the end of the old life governed by relationship with Adam. It also expresses the impossibility of a new life apart from divine action. The God who raised Jesus Christ from the dead has likewise imparted life to those who are his. The expression to "live a new life" is literally "to walk in newness of life," the walk being the evidence of the new type of life granted to the child of God. This is a distinctive type of life realized only by one united to Christ (cf. 2Co 5:17), so that Christ is its dynamic. In this connection the question arises, Why should the resurrection of Christ be described as accomplished "through the glory of the Father?" It is because "glory" here has the meaning of power, as in the resurrection of Lazarus (Jn 11:40).

The latter half of v.4 has a noticeably balanced structure ("just as Christ ... we too"), recalling the pattern in 5:12, 18, 21. This suggests that the principle of solidarity advanced in 5:12–21 is still thought of as operating here in the significance of baptism. There is no explicit statement that in baptism we were raised with Christ as well as made to share in his death. Resurrection is seen rather as an effect that logically follows from the identification with Christ in his death (but see Col

2:12, where resurrection is verbally connected with baptism).

5–7 In v.5 we encounter a problem concerning resurrection. Is Paul referring to the future bodily resurrection of the saints? Many expositors think so, pointing both to the future tense of the verb ("we will . . . be") and to the fact that Christ's resurrection was indeed a bodily one. But a future tense can indicate what must logically or inevitably occur (cf. Gal 6:5, which has a future tense). Furthermore, Paul does not say that just as Christ was raised, so we too shall be raised. Instead, he connects the resurrection of Christ with the possibility of a new life in the present for those who are his. In addition, the "for" at the beginning of v.6 shows that what follows is intended to relate closely to the mention of resurrection at the end of v.5. Yet one looks in vain for anything in v.6 that relates to future bodily resurrection. Instead, Paul returns to the matter of participation in Christ's death and its bearing on freedom from the bondage of sin. Consequently, the resurrection in v.5 has to do with spiritual resurrection—raised with Christ (see also Eph 2:6; Col 2:12; 3:1).

The certainty of our present participation in this new resurrection life is grounded on the truth that "we have been united with him in his death." Clearly this union is not something gradually arrived at through a process of sanctification. Rather it is something established by God that becomes the very basis of our sanctification in Christ.

The problem of sin continues to dominate the thought of this section, and Paul returns to this theme by insisting that "our old self was crucified with him" (v.6). While the relation to v.5 is close, the language now becomes sharper and more realistic—e.g., "united with him in his death" becomes "crucified with him" (cf. Gal 2:20). Our spiritual history began at the cross. We were there in the sense that we were joined to him who actually suffered on it. The time element should not disturb us, because if we sinned in Adam, it is equally possible to die to sin with Christ.

But what was it that was crucified? "Our old self" is literally "our old man" (GK *4094 & 476*; see also Eph 4:22; Col 3:9). In Eph 4:22, however, the putting off of the old self is a matter of exhortation. In some sense, then, the old man has been crucified; in another sense, it may still claim attention. Since "man" has been used of Adam (5:12, 17, 19), it is possible that what has been crucified with Christ is our place in Adam, our position in the old creation, which is under the sway of sin and death. For Christians, the old self is gone; they belong to the new creation order (2Co 5:17).

The purpose behind the crucifixion of "our old self" is that sin should be rendered powerless so far as we are concerned. But the expression "body of sin" is a phrase that needs clarification. The term "body" (GK *5393*) glances at the fact of Christ's crucifixion, which he endured in the body. Our body can become the instrument of sin, thus negating the truth of crucifixion with Christ. So "body of sin" seems to mean human body insofar as it may become the vehicle of sin. Its previous slavery to the dictates of sin is broken. This annulling of the power of sin is based on a recognized principle—that death settles all claims. Our union with Christ in his death, designed to deal with sin once for all, means that we are free from the hold of sin. Its mastery has been broken (v.7).

8–10 Union with Christ continues to be the theme here, but attention shifts from its effect on the problem of sin to a consideration of its bearing on the problem of death. Consequently, resurrection comes into focus. Though there is considerable similarity with the close of v.4, the note of futurity ("we will also live with him") makes it apparent that future bodily resurrection is now in view. For a brief time, death as the executor of sin held the Savior, but not for long. Since he was not guilty of personal sin, death had no right to hold him indefinitely (Ac 2:24). Likewise, it had no right to call him again to the experience of death. Once having been raised from the dead, our Lord is alive for ever and ever (Rev 1:18).

It was important for Paul to emphasize this truth, for believers must have full confidence that the captain of their salvation will never again come under the power of sin and death. If they lack that assurance, the teaching about union with Christ will be of little help to them. "He died to sin once for all." In his risen life our Lord is set free to resume his face-to-face fellowship with God (Jn 1:1) and his preoccupation with the consummation of God's eternal purpose. In this respect he presents a pattern for believers in their expectation of the future and also in their motivation for life in the present time (2Co 5:15).

2. The appeal based on the fact (6:11–14)

11–14 In this section Paul uses the key word "count" or "reckon" (GK *3357*; the same term used so often in ch. 4 in connection with righteousness). Reckoning does not create the fact of union with Christ but makes it operative in one's life. The charge to count ourselves dead to sin but alive to God in Christ Jesus is in the present tense, indicating a necessity to keep up the process if we are to avoid reactivating the body of sin. Christians are dead and alive at the same time (Gal 2:20)—dead to sin and self but alive to God. They must give no more response to sin than the dead can give. On the other hand, all the potential that redeemed life affords should be channeled Godward.

Since Paul lays considerable stress on the importance of this process of reckoning, we should inquire about its value—especially in view of the objection that such a process smacks of attempting to convince oneself of something unrealistic in terms of actual experience. The justification for the use of this terminology is at least threefold. (1) This is a command freighted with apostolic authority. God is speaking through his servant, and what God commands must be efficacious. (2) The command is psychologically sound, for what we think tends to be carried out in our actions. (3) This process must not be undertaken in a mechanical fashion, as though there were some sort of magic in going through the motions. We must really desire to have freedom from sin and to live responsibly to God. To that end we must avail ourselves of the means of grace, particularly the diligent use of Scripture and faithfulness in prayer.

This element of willing cooperation receives emphasis in v.12. The implication is that sin has been reigning. Believers must do their part by refusing obedience any longer to sin's enticements. If the body is kept dead, it will have no ear for the subtle suggestions of evil. Paul's description here of the body as "mortal" reminds us that despite the glorious asset of being united to Christ, we are still living in a frail instrument subject to the ultimate call of death.

Turning from the body as a whole to its separate members, Paul admonishes his readers not to hand these over to sin (the old master). But this is only half of our obligation. On the positive side, we must offer our total selves to God with our separate bodily capacities "as instruments of righteousness."

Paul concludes this portion of text with an encouragement and an incentive. He promises the Roman Christians that if they will do as he has enjoined, sin will not be their master; then he adds, "because you are not under law, but under grace" (v.14). Why should law be injected here? Surely because under law sin increases (5:20; cf. 1Co 15:56). The law lords it over its subjects, condemning and bringing them into virtual slavery. But under grace there is liberty to live in accord with a higher principle—the resurrection life of the Lord himself.

It is worthy of attention that Christians are said to be *under* grace. Usually grace indicates a principle of divine operation, a moving out in kindness and love to lift the sinful person to God. Here it appears as a disciplinary power, in line with the apostle's effort to show that grace is not license (6:1ff.; see also Paul's reminder that God's grace has appeared for the salvation of all, training us to live sober, upright, and godly lives; Tit 2:11–12).

B. Union With Christ Viewed As Enslavement to Righteousness (6:15–23)

15–17 Paul has just affirmed, "You are not under law." Now he shows that this does not mean that believers are free from the demands of living according to righteousness. It would be strange if those who are under grace should evidence a manner of life inferior to the standard held by those who are under law. As a matter of fact, believers must face the fact that their salvation actually means a change of bondage. As they once served sin, they are now committed to lives of practical righteousness.

At first glance, the opening question seems to repeat v.1. The difference, however, lies in the tense of the verb. In v.1 the question was "Shall we go on sinning so that grace may increase?" Now the question is "Shall we sin [in any given case, or sin at all] because we are not under law but under grace?" Law is supposed to be a restraining influence. But if we move out from under that umbrella, will we not be exposing ourselves to the danger of committing sin even more than in our previous situation?

In answer, Paul appeals first of all to a fact familiar to all—whatever one submits to becomes his or her master (cf. Jn 8:34). To commit sin, then, puts one into bondage to sin, and the sequel is death (cf. 5:12; 8:13). The other option is a life of obedience resulting in righteousness (cf. 5:19). Paul is happy to acknowledge that his readers have renounced the service of sin and are now wholeheartedly obeying Christian teaching (v. 17). Let us take special note of the way he puts the matter: "you wholeheartedly obeyed the form of teaching to which you were committed." By virtue of becoming Christians, believers had obligated themselves to obey what we might call the law of Christ (Gal 6:2). Even though Paul had not founded the Roman church, he was confident that the Christians there had been taught the standard teaching of the apostles (see Ac 2:42). Just as the Gospel itself had certain ingredients (such as Christ's death, burial, and resurrection, as in vv.1–5; 1Co 15:3–4), so the teaching about the lifestyle of believers, derived from what Jesus and the apostles taught, was standard throughout the church. This is the point being made in the use of the word "form" (GK 5596).

18 The term that most adequately describes the standard Christian instruction about lifestyle is "righteousness" (GK 1466). Here Paul arrives at the full answer to the question raised in v.15. There is no middle ground to a believer's service to righteousness, no place where Christians are free to set their own standards and go their own way. So it is idle to object that on becoming a believer one is simply exchanging one form of slavery for another. There is no alternative. Let no one say, however, that the two bondages are on the same plane. The one is rigorous and relentless, leading to death; the other is joyous and satisfying, leading to life and peace.

19–20 Reviewing his own remarks, Paul grants that he has spoken "in human terms" (v.19). This is a kind of apology (see comments on 3:5) for having described the Christian life in terms of slavery to righteousness. Paul's reason for this reference to slavery is "because you are weak in your natural selves." The nature of the weakness, while not expressed, likely relates to one's moral fiber. After all, Christians have just come from lives characterized by slavery to "impurity" and "ever-increasing wickedness." The readiness and zeal with which they once served sin now become the basis for a challenge. Surely the new master is worthy of at least equal loyalty and devotion! That new master is not described in personal terms but in personified terms of righteousness and holiness—a lifestyle demanding one's complete attention.

21–22 The pre-Christian state is undesirable, for it yields no benefit. In fact, it leaves behind memories that produce shame (v.21). On the other hand, the Christian state of freedom from servitude to sin and the corresponding commitment to serve God produce a harvest of holiness, at the end of which is eternal life (cf. Gal 6:8). Paul is not denying the present possession of eternal life (see v.23), but is simply presenting eternal life as the inevitable conclusion of the process of sanctification (see chart at the beginning of the chapter; also Mk 10:29–30).

23 In a fitting conclusion, Paul puts God (and his mastery) over against sin, gift over against wages, eternal life over against death—crowning it all with the acknowledgment that the mediation of Christ Jesus our Lord accounts for the shift from one camp to the other.

C. Union With Christ Viewed As Deliverance From Law (7:1–6)

Sin and death in their correlation have occupied Paul to a great degree from 5:12 on, with an occasional reference to a third element, the law. In ch. 6 he sought to explain that the believer's crucifixion with Christ has brought freedom from enslavement to sin's dominion. Since the law has served to promote sin (5:20), it is expedient now to show that Christ's death, which involved the death of those who are his, effected release from the law also. At the same time Paul is careful to indicate that this emancipation from the law is in order to permit a new attachment, namely, to the risen Lord and his Spirit, so that from this union might flow a fruitfulness of life unattainable under the law. Deliverance from the law does not open the door to irresponsible and sinful conduct.

1 The readers are described as those who know "the law." The fact that "law" (GK 3795) here does not have a definite article in the Greek suggests that Paul is primarily interested not in the specifics of the Mosaic law but in its essential character as law, as that which has binding force. In this opening statement, the principle is laid down that law imposes a lifelong obligation on a person.

Already in this initial statement we have a clue for determining the thought that Paul is about to develop. The law has authority over a person only during his or her lifetime. Since the believer has died with Christ (ch. 6), one can anticipate the conclusion—that whatever authority the law continues to exercise over others, for believers that power has been abrogated. The law remains, of course, an entity that expresses the will of God. The life under grace does not belittle the ethical demands of the law.

2–3 To illustrate the binding character of the law, Paul uses the case of a woman who is married to a husband and remains bound by law in that relationship as long as her husband is living. During this time she is not free to seek another attachment; that may be done only in the event that the husband dies. Particularly in Jewish life this was the actual legal status of the wife, for she could not divorce her husband; divorce was a privilege granted only to the man. If the husband died, she was then released from "the law of marriage."

4–6 Paul now applies this illustration. But the reader is apt to be somewhat disturbed about a measure of inconsistency in the way it is applied. In the case under consideration three essential statements are made: a woman is married to a man; the man dies; then the woman is free to be married to another. In the application three statements likewise can be readily inferred: the readers have had a binding relation to the law; they have died to the law; and they are now free to be joined to another, even the risen Lord. The parallel breaks down at the second item, for the law, which is the assumed master or husband in the application, is not represented as dying; rather, the readers are said to have died to the law. Paul avoids saying that the law died (something that is never affirmed in Scripture). The only thing he is concerned with is continuing the emphasis already made in ch. 6, that death ends obligation. Paul was no doubt aware of the incongruity between illustration and application, but counted on the understanding of his readers to see that he was seeking merely to underscore the truth that death with Christ brought to an end the sway of the law over those who are in him and ushered in a new, superior relationship.

Death to the law is said to have occurred "through the body of Christ" (v.4). This is a reference to the personal body of the Savior in his crucifixion. Through their being crucified with Christ (6:6), believers became dead both to the law and to sin.

Death to the law occurred so that believers "might belong to another." To belong to Christ involves participation not only in his death but also in his resurrection. Severance from obligation to serve the law is only part of the truth. We are married, as it were, to the risen Lord, with a view to bearing fruit to God. Perhaps an analogy is intended here—as a marriage produces progeny, so the believer's union with Christ results in spiritual fruit (cf. Jn 15:1ff.). In Gal 5:22–23, bearing fruit is attributed to the Spirit, in contrast to the output of the flesh and of the law. Since Paul speaks of the Spirit in Ro 7:6, the parallel with Gal 5 is close.

In the pre-Christian state there was fruit of a sort, but it was corrupt and perishable, emanating from the sinful nature and produced by the sinful passions as these were aroused by the law (v.5). The phrase "controlled by our sinful nature" is an attempt to render the Greek phrase "in the flesh." Paul has used "flesh" (GK 4922) in several senses thus far: (1) the "human nature" of Jesus Christ (1:3); (2) the "physical" body (2:28), (3) humankind—"no one" in 3:20 is literally, "not all flesh"; and (4) moral, or possibly intellectual, weakness ("natural selves" in 6:19). Now he adds a fifth: the so-called "ethical" meaning of flesh, which is his most common use of the word and denotes the old sinful nature. It is this sense of the word that pervades chs. 7–8, together with a final use in 13:14. In noting here in v.5 that the "sinful passions" are aroused by the law, Paul is anticipating his fuller discussion in vv.7–13 about the manner in which the law promotes sin.

Release from the law has, as its objective, service to God "in the new way of the Spirit," in contrast to "the old way of the written code" (cf. 2Co 3:6). The written code, which refers specifically to the OT law, has no power to give life and to produce a service acceptable to God. Only a person can beget human life, and only a divine person can impart spiritual life, which is then fostered and nurtured by the Spirit. The word "new" (GK 2786) has in it not so much the idea of newness in time as freshness and superiority. This is the only mention of "the Spirit" in the chapter. It anticipates ch. 8 with its unfolding of the wealth of blessing to be experienced in this relationship.

D. The Relationship Between Law and Sin (7:7–25)

Paul must now clarify his thoughts, especially his statements that believers have died to sin (6:2) and to the law (7:4). Are these so similar as to be in some sense equated? The explanation has been touched on briefly in 7:5, but Paul now expands it. In essence, the solution of the problem is this: the law cannot be identified as sinful simply because it provides awareness of sin (cf. 3:20). Can one say of an X-ray machine that revealed a disease that the machine is diseased? That would be utter nonsense.

As Paul elsewhere appealed to the experience of his converts to support Christian truth (Gal 3:1–5; 4:1–7), so he now appeals to his own experience (Ro 7:7–13). This personal reference then broadens into a more general picture of the soul-struggle of those who try to serve God by obeying the law but find themselves checkmated by the operation of sin within themselves (vv.14–25).

Paul sharpens his observation that consciousness of sin is produced by the law through a specific example. He seizes on the tenth commandment, "Do not covet." His use of this commandment helps define the meaning of law in vv.1–6, the law from which believers have been released. What he has in mind includes the moral law. While students of Scripture find it convenient at times to distinguish between the ceremonial law and the moral law, Paul regards the law as a unit. To those who may be disturbed by the thought that the divine standard for one's life is abandoned by maintaining release from the law, Paul will reply in due course that no such danger exists (8:4).

7 "Sin" (GK 281) is an oft-repeated word in this paragraph. It does not refer here to an act of sin, but to the sin principle, to that mighty force that a human being cannot tame, but which lurks dormant or relatively inactive in a person's life, is then brought to the fore by prohibition, and proceeds to rise up and slay its victim. Sin, then, has essentially the same meaning here as in 5:12ff.

The subject in hand is the awareness of sin in a personal, existential sense—an awareness created by the law's demands. To come to grips with this the apostle selects an item from the Decalogue, the tenth commandment. Possibly he chose that one because he saw something basic here, for "to covet" means "to desire." If one gives rein to wrong desire, it can lead to lying, stealing, killing, and all the other things prohibited in the commandments. In analyzing sin, one must go behind the outward act to the inner person, where desire clutches at the imagination and then puts the spurs to the will.

8 In the background is the Genesis story of the temptation and the Fall. Eve was faced with a commandment—a prohibition. When desire was stirred through the subtle suggestion of the serpent, a certain rebelliousness came into play that is the heart of sin—a preference for one's own will over against the expressed will of God. The warning "Don't" to a small child may turn out to be a call for action that had not even been contemplated by the child. A sure way to lose blossoms from the garden is to post a sign that says, "Don't pick the flowers." Prohibition furnishes a springboard from which sin is all too ready to take off.

"For apart from law, sin is dead." It appears from a comparison of "dead" with "sprang to life" in v.9 that the word "dead" is intended to be taken in a relative sense,

Writing flourished in the ancient world; even marriage contracts were written down (cf. 7:1–3). These ink wells were found at Qumran. Courtesy Israel Antiquities Authority.

namely, quiescent, dormant, inactive. This statement appears to be an axiom, a broad and general principle.

9–11 Paul's statement that he was once alive apart from the law should be taken in a relative sense, for there was actually no time in his life before his conversion when he was unrelated to the law. He was the son of a Pharisee (Ac 23:6) and lived in strictest conformity to the regulations of his sect (Ac 26:5). What he means is that there was a time when he was living in a state of blissful indifference to the intensely searching demands that the law made on the inner self. He was careless and self-deceived as to his own righteousness (see Php 3:6). Before and at the time of his conversion, his struggle was intellectual rather than moral. He was convinced that Jesus could not be the Messiah, for God had permitted him to die as a criminal. His conversion, however, meant a complete reversal in this matter. He felt within himself the sentence of death ("I died"), becoming bogged down in hopelessness and despair in contrast to the blithe self-confidence he had before.

The commandment not to covet, like the others, "was intended to bring life." Its design and ideal were to promote observance that would lead to divine blessing and consequent human happiness (see Lev 18:5). The practical difficulty, of course, is that a sinful person fails to do the will of God as set forth in the commandments.

In v.11 sin is strongly personified, being represented as acting as a person would act. The language is reminiscent of the Fall, with sin taking the place of the tempter and provoking a deception that led to death (spiritual death occurred then; physical death would follow later). The word "deceive" (Gk 1987) occurs here in a strong form indicating utter deception (see 2Co 11:3; 1Ti 2:14). Sin within him led Paul to do the very thing the commandment forbade, thus bringing him under condemnation as a lawbreaker (cf. 2Co 3:6).

12 It is time for the apostle to give a decisive answer to the question he raised in v.7: "Is the law sin?" So far from being identifiable with sin, the law is holy, as are the individual commandments (such as the command not to covet). The law is "holy" because it comes from a holy God and searches out sin. It is "righteous" because it lays just requirements on people and because it forbids and condemns sin. It is "good" because its aim is life (v.10). The misuse of the law at the hands of sin has not altered its own essential character.

13 Having detached the law from any wrongful association with sin, Paul must still treat the problem of its relation to death, the other great enemy of the human race. Continuing to present the case in personal terms, he protests that the responsibility for incurring death must be assigned to sin rather than to the law. By using the law to bring death, sin shows how "utterly sinful" it is. At the same time, the law, which seemed to be victimized by being taken over by sin, emerges as having gained an important objective. It has exposed sin for the evil thing it is.

From this point on to the end of the chapter, the personal emphasis continues, and with increased intensity. The powerful forces of law and sin are depicted as producing a struggle that ends in a confession of despair, relieved only by the awareness that in Jesus Christ there is deliverance. Paul does not shrink from putting himself prominently in this arena of conflict if only his doing so will help others (cf. 1Co 4:6).

A shift of emphasis is discernible on moving from vv.7–13 to vv.14–25. In the former section Paul has shown that the fault lay not with the commandment of God but with sin in its use of the commandment. In the latter section he will maintain that the responsible party, ultimately speaking, is not "I" but the sin that dwells within.

14–20 At the outset Paul wants it understood that he is not depreciating the law, for it is "spiritual" (GK 4461)—that is, emanating from God (vv.22, 25), who is Spirit (Jn 4:24). The law reflects the character of God. Godly people recognize this fact ("we know").

"But I am unspiritual." What a stark contrast! The word "unspiritual" is literally "fleshly" (see comment on 7:4–6), what I am in myself. I am not subject to the law and therefore I am in rebellion against God, since the law is from him. (The problems as to whether Paul speaks individually or universally here and as a saved or an unsaved man will be dealt with at the close of this chapter.)

Then Paul moves on to a second description more wretched than the first: "sold as a slave to sin." This strikes the keynote of what follows, down to the anguished cry, "Who will rescue me...?" (v.24). The slavery extends to the totality of his being. It numbs and blinds him, for he confesses that he does not know what he is doing (v.15). This is a graphic picture, one of a slave going through certain motions under the authority of a master. Whatever obedience there seems to be is really not a matter of volition, but something almost mechanical. Paul feels forced to carry out what he does not want to do, what he really hates, whereas what he would like to do never seems to materialize (v.15).

The failure to do what he desires must not be attributed to a wrong attitude toward the law, such as indifference or defiance, since he concurs in the verdict that the law is praiseworthy (v.16). Rather, doing things contrary to the law must be traced to the power of sin working within him (v.17). Paul is not attempting to escape responsibility, but is putting his finger on the real culprit—indwelling sin. The invader has managed to secure more than a foothold; he roams the place, considering it his home. In putting the matter like this, Paul has moved from a consideration of outward acts to an emphasis on the unwanted tenancy of sin. With this alien master in control, no matter how strongly he wants to do the good, he finds himself checkmated. He cannot carry it out (v.18). Verse 19 is a virtual repetition of v.15; v.20 of v.17.

21–25 Paul now summarizes what has gone before. "So I find this law at work." So far, "law" (GK 3795) meant the law of Moses, but here it has a specialized meaning—that of "principle" (cf. 3:27; 8:2). This usage makes it necessary, when speaking once more of the Mosaic law, to call it "God's law" (v.22). In Paul's inner being the divine law is welcome and brings delight, but that which manifests itself in the bodily members (what may be called the outward self) is the law (i.e., principle) of sin. There is a state of war, and he finds himself a captive (cf. the slave figure in v.14) to the imperious operation of sin. The agony of this unhappy condition comes out in the cry "What a wretched man I am!" It is a powerful and moving cry, recalling the words of Isaiah when he became aware of his sin (Isa 6:5). Since Paul is unable to help himself he must look elsewhere.

In answering this cry of desperation, the apostle does not say, "What will rescue me?" but "Who...?" There is deliverance, provided by God through Jesus Christ, for his sinlessness and triumph over evil assure him that deliverance is possible.

The final statement of the chapter (v.25b) is another summary. Coming as it does after the cry of thanksgiving for deliverance through Christ, it seems strange that there should be a reversion to the state of tension described earlier. What could possibly account for this strange concluding statement? Apparently Paul wanted to state once more the essence of the struggle he had depicted in order to prepare the reader to appreciate the grand exposition of one's deliverance in terms of Christ and the Spirit in the next chapter.

Before moving on to that portion, we must return to the overall problems of interpretation in ch. 7. First of all, is Paul giving a truly autobiographical sketch, or is the "I" a vehicle to present a human being in his or her extremity, a means to universalize the experience treated here? It is difficult to decide, as both are possible explanations. Perhaps the personal and the universal are intended to mingle here.

The more strenuously debated issue is the question of interpretation of the material itself, especially vv.14–25. Are we to regard the state pictured here as that of the unsaved person or of the Christian? The case for the unsaved condition is as follows: (1) It was the prevailing view among the Greek Fathers of the early church. (2) Such expressions as "sold as a slave to sin" and "unspiritual" seem more fitting as a description of the unsaved than of genuine believers. After all, the main message of ch. 6 is that Christians are free from sin. How can Paul then say they are sold as slaves to sin (v.14)? (3) If the "now" of 8:1 means what it seems to mean, Paul is passing from a consideration of the unsaved to the saved condition. (4) The absence of the Holy Spirit from the discussion and even of Christ (until the very close) is hard to understand if a redeemed experience is under review.

The other interpretation holds that a Christian is being depicted, despite his wretchedness. The case for that position is as follows: (1) This was the conclusion of Augustine and of the Reformed interpreters. (2) Paul changes from the past tense in vv.7–

13 to the present tense in vv.14–25. Presumably, then, the former section relates to Paul's pre-Christian experience and the rest of the chapter to his postconversion experience. (3) Paul's description of his pre-Christian life in Php 3:6 as a blameless condition in terms of the law does not jibe with his wretchedness in the passage before us. (4) The progress of thought in Romans needs to be taken into consideration. Paul has passed beyond his description of the unsaved state and is now giving attention to sanctification and its problems; so the theme is really relevant only to believers. (5) That a conflict of the sort described here can and does characterize the Christian life is apparent elsewhere in Paul (see Gal 5:17). (6) The power of self-diagnosis at the penetrating level found here (vv.22–23) is beyond the capacity of an unbeliever. (7) A person desiring holiness of life, as pictured here, could only be a believer, for the unsaved person does not long for God but is hostile toward him. (8) The last verse of ch. 7 acknowledges deliverance in Christ, yet goes on to state the very problem sketched in vv.14–24 as though it continues to be a problem for one who knows the Lord.

The wide difference between these two views puts the general reader in a dilemma. Which view is correct? Which has the better of the argument?

Another and more satisfying approach is possible—namely, that the experience pictured here is not wholly autobiographical but is deliberately presented in such a way as to demonstrate what the situation would indeed be if someone who is faced with the demands of the law and the power of sin in his life were to try to solve his problem independently of the power of Christ and the enablement of the Spirit. That is, Paul is hypothetically describing what life under the law would be like if it was seen according to the logic of its nature.

A parallel use of this methodology may be detected in Ecclesiastes. The writer knows God personally, but purposely and deliberately views life from the standpoint of his natural self in order to expose it as meaningless, empty of lasting value. Romans 7 performs a service by calling into question certain popular notions that lack biblical foundation: that the soul's struggle is essentially against specific sins or habits; that human nature is essentially good (cf. v.18); that sanctification is by means of the law; that if one will only determine to do the right, he or she will be able to do it. These are some of the misconceptions that must be removed, and they might not have been removed had the apostle proceeded directly from ch. 6 to ch. 8. Without ch. 7 we would not be able to appreciate to the full the truths presented in the next chapter.

E. The Blessings of Life in the Spirit (8:1–39)

It is altogether too narrow a view to see this section only as the antidote to the wretched state pictured in ch. 7. Actually the chapter gathers up various strands of thought from the entire discussion of both justification and sanctification and ties them together with the crowning knot of glorification. Like ch. 5, it presents the blessings of the justified life, grounded in the removal of condemnation. Like ch. 6, it stresses freedom from the bondage of sin and ultimately from the bondage of death. Like ch. 7, it deals with the problem of the flesh (or sinful human nature), finding the solution in the liberating and productive ministry of the Spirit. The chapter begins with instruction, rises to consolation, and culminates in jubilation. This is high and holy ground indeed for the Christian pilgrim to tread.

1. Liberation by the Spirit from the law of sin and death (8:1–11)

1–2 We are hardly prepared by the contents of ch. 7 for the glorious pronouncement that there is no condemnation at all for those who are in Christ Jesus, and we find it hard to associate the "therefore" with anything in the immediately preceding context. The connection must thus be sought in the entire sweep of the thought as developed from ch. 3 on. The natural antithesis to condemnation is justification. Justification is such a basic truth to Paul that he brings it even into his discussion of the Christian life (8:33–34; cf. 8:10). It is the basis and starting point for sanctification. Believers must be assured of acceptance with God before they can grow in grace and conformity to Christ.

Furthermore, the construction of vv.2–4 carries us beyond the thought of freedom from condemnation to the application of the redeeming work of Christ by the Spirit to the believer's life in such a way that the dominion of sin is broken and the reign of godliness assured. The noun "condemnation" has its counterpart in the verb "condemned" (v.3), which is followed immediately, not by a statement about the legal standing of believers, but by one concerning their manner of life (v.4). Thus, there is both a forensic and a practical force in "no condemnation."

Verse 2 immediately picks up this practical, dynamic aspect by concentrating on the freedom from the imperious rule of sin and death, a freedom now available to believers through the operation of the Spirit. The word "law" is used figuratively here in the sense of "principle" (cf. 7:21, 23). Clearly it would be impossible for Paul to refer to the law of Moses as "the law of sin and death," even though it provokes sin (7:7–8) and produces death (7:9–11; 2Co 3:6–7); the Mosaic law in itself is holy (7:12). In the present passage, therefore, "law" indicates the certainty and regularity of operation that characterizes sin (which leads to death) and the Spirit (which leads to life). "Life" (GK 2437) emphasizes both supernaturalness and spontaneity—hence the superiority of the Spirit's operation over that of sin. The Spirit gives us freedom from the enslaving power of sin.

3–4 But how was this freedom gained (v.3)? The opening statement about the powerlessness of the law because of the weakness of the sinful nature to which its commands are addressed is an obvious reminder of the major thrust of ch. 7. The law makes demands and condemns when those demands are not met, but it cannot overcome sin. This inability of the law required the personal action of God in Christ. He sent "his own Son." This mission could not be entrusted to anyone else or anyone less than his Son. While the preexistence of the Son is not formally taught here, it is implied (cf. Jn 3:17; 7:33; 17:18; 20:21). When vv.2–3 are taken together, they bear a close resemblance to Gal 4:4–6, where Father, Son, and Spirit are pictured as involved in the mission of Christ.

The Son was sent "in the likeness of sinful man" ("man" is literally "flesh"; GK 4922). Observe with what care Paul states the incarnation. He does not say "in sinful flesh," lest the Son's sinlessness be compromised, nor "in the likeness of flesh," which would convey a docetic idea and thereby deny the reality of the humanity of our Lord. Paul's terminology here fully agrees with Php 2:7: "being made in human likeness."

What about the work of Christ? The purpose of his coming was "to be a sin offering" (lit., "for sin"). Christ's mission was to deal effectively with sin, making possible among his people the type of life presented in the following verse. Included in that mission was the expiation of sin, which he accomplished through his sacrifice on the cross (cf. 2Co 5:21).

"So he condemned sin in sinful man" ("sinful man" is literally "flesh"). It is possible that "in the flesh" is intended to be correlated with "through the flesh" at the beginning of the verse, in which case the NIV translation is justified. However, since "flesh" can be used of Christ apart from any sinful connotation (e.g., "physical body" in Col 1:22), it is also possible to refer the phrase to our Savior rather than to sinful humanity; in that case, Paul is saying that God condemned sin in the same sort of (human) nature that, in everyone else, is dominated by sin. This brings the teaching in line with 6:5–11.

The purpose of the incarnation, so far as the believer's life is concerned, is stated in v.4 in such a way as to indicate that the apostle has not allowed the agonizing struggle of ch. 7 to fade from view. There the law was pictured as faultless in itself, but agonizingly elusive for those who try to keep it in their own strength. The self-satisfied will minimize the law's demands by magnifying their own achievement, whereas the conscientious will end up in despair. In God's plan, however, the law must be honored not simply in lip service or in desire but in reality. Its righteous requirements must be fully met. This can be done only by living according to the divine aid of the Spirit rather than according to the sinful human nature (cf. "Spirit of life" in v.2).

One should observe the balance in this passage between the divine and human elements in the Christian life. Paul recognizes that believers are not robots, but persons accountable for their redeemed lives. At the same time Paul pictures the requirement of the law as fulfilled (passive) *in* believers, not *by* them, as though to remind them that the redeemed do not possess spiritual power that they can control and utilize on their own. Rather, the Spirit is always channeling that power and never releases it to those in whom he lives for them to use independently of him. The power to keep the law resides in the Spirit.

It would be a mistake, however, to ground the Christian "walk" solely on the enabling ministry of the Spirit. The close connection with v.3 demands that we include the saving work of Christ (cf. 6:4, where Paul has observed that identification with the Savior in his death and resurrection has this very objective, that "we too may live [lit., walk; GK 4344] a new life").

5–8 At this point Paul launches upon a fairly extended statement contrasting the terms "sinful nature" (lit., "flesh") and "Spirit," which he has used in v.4. Both terms are difficult because they can have more than one meaning (for "flesh," see comment on 7:4–6). To be in the flesh, as the word is used here, is to be in the unregenerate state. To "be [NIV live] according to" the flesh (v.5) is to have the sinful nature as the regulating principle of one's life. To "walk [NIV live] according to" the flesh (v.4) is to carry out in conduct those things dictated by the sinful human nature.

Less complicated is the use of "Spirit" (*pneuma*; GK 4460), but even here there is some question as to whether or not this word as used in contrast to "flesh" perhaps refers to the (redeemed) human spirit. This much is clear: in the passage under consideration *pneuma* does not mean "spirit" simply as an element in the constitution of a person (cf. 1Co 5:3). The problem is to determine whether *pneuma* in this passage means the divine life-principle (the new spiritual nature communicated to the believer) or whether it means the Spirit of God.

Two considerations strongly favor the view that this is a reference to the Holy Spirit. (1) This chapter has begun with an obvious allusion to the divine Spirit (v.2), so that unless there is clear indication to the contrary, one should expect this to be the intended meaning of *pneuma* in the verses that follow. (2) In stating the ground of Christian victory over sin, the apostle would likely assign the basis of that victory to the highest source possible rather than to a lower, intermediate factor.

The statements in vv.5–8 about the sinful nature refer to the unregenerate person, especially judging by the care with which Paul excludes his readers in v.9. This is not sufficient ground, however, for claiming that the Christian has nothing to do with the sinful flesh. The warning of 8:12ff. would be meaningless if that were the case. But for the moment Paul wishes to expose the flesh in its stark reality as totally alien to God and his holy purposes. He insists that there is a correspondence between one's essential being and what interests that person. The fleshly are occupied with fleshly things, whereas those who possess the Spirit and are controlled by him are concerned with the things of the Spirit (see also 1Co 2:14). The expression "have their minds set on" denotes far more than a mental process, for it also includes one's inner desires (cf. Php 2:5ff.; Col 3:2).

The same root word appears again (v.6), only in the noun form: "The mind of sinful man is death." The unsaved are cut off from God, and this amounts to death in the sense of separation from God. Those who are spiritual, on the contrary, enjoy life from God (cf. v.2) and the peace such life affords (cf. 14:17). The dead state of the natural man, both present and future, is then traced to the inveterate hostility to God that characterizes "flesh," a hostility that manifests itself in opposition to the law of God. Such people refuse to obey it and thereby are in rebellion against God. In summary, Paul names four characteristics of the sinful unregenerate person: hostility toward God, insubordination to his law, failure to please God, and death. It is no wonder that when Jesus spoke to Nicodemus of "the flesh," he went on to declare, "You must be born again" (Jn 3:7).

9–11 Turning now to his readers, Paul reminds them of the basic difference between themselves and those he has been describing. As believers, they have, in the Spirit, an antidote for the sinful human nature ("the flesh"; see comment on 7:4–6). Furthermore, the Spirit of God "lives" in them (the word "if" here presupposes the truth of the statement). Previously (v.2) the Spirit has been called "the Spirit of life" because of his regenerating and renewing power; here he is "the Spirit of God" and "the Spirit of Christ," indicating that he carries out the purposes of God and applies the fruits of Christ's redemptive mission to the lives of believers (cf. Gal 4:6).

No one who lacks the Spirit belongs to Christ. Everyone who trusts Christ has the Spirit (Eph 1:13). The title "Spirit of Christ" is made meaningful by the deliberate way in which Paul says essentially the same thing about both the Spirit and Christ in relation to believers: the Spirit lives in you (v.9) and Christ is in you (v.10). The presence and fullness of Christ are realized in a Christian's life by means of the indwelling Spirit (Eph 3:16–17).

Paul's observation (v.10) about those in whom Christ lives—"your body is dead because of sin, yet your spirit is alive because of righteousness"—has proved difficult for interpreters. The NIV and most leading modern translations make "spirit" refer to the spirit of the Christian rather than to the Spirit of Christ. But it seems preferable to see *pneuma* ("spirit"; see comment on vv.5–8) here as referring to "the Spirit of God," for three reasons. (1) It is unlikely that Paul, having consistently referred to *pneuma* as the Spirit of God, would give this word a different frame of reference in this one instance. His use of the word "body" here, not the word "spirit," refers to the entire human person. He maintains that sin necessitated our dying with Christ. (2) The phrase about the *pneuma* being alive because of righteousness relates back to "the Spirit of life" at the beginning of the chapter (v.2). (3) The first part of v.11 refers to the living presence of the Spirit in believers; Paul seems there to be repeating what he said at the end of v.10 in order to present a further observation—namely, that the same Spirit will provide resurrection life in due season. The close of v.10 teaches, therefore, that the Spirit who is life in himself brings life to those in whom he lives only because they have already been granted God's righteousness (through their justification).

In v.11 the Spirit is given yet another title: "the Spirit of him [i.e., God; cf. 4:24] who raised Jesus from the dead." The Spirit's future work on behalf of the saints will be to "give life" to their mortal bodies. This accords with Paul's description of the glorified bodies of believers as "spiritual" (1Co 15:44). The life bestowed by the Spirit in that coming day is beyond the power of death or any other agency to vitiate or destroy. It is the very life of God, blessedly spiritual and indestructibly eternal.

2. Additional ministries of the Spirit (8:12–27)

12–13 The apostle turns now from instruction to exhortation, from what God has done through Christ and the Spirit to what the believer is expected to do by way of response. But even with a strong emphasis on human responsibility, the desired lifestyle can be accomplished only "by the Spirit." The special ministry described here is *mortification* (putting the sinful nature to death). It is the message of 6:11–14 all over again, except for the reminder that no one can hope to deal effectively with the sinful nature simply by determination alone. The Holy Spirit is needed, and he is the Spirit of power.

"Obligation" (GK *4053*) is the keynote. Only the negative side is stated; the positive side—that we are debtors to the Spirit and must put on the Lord Jesus (13:14)—must be inferred. If we do not have an obligation to live in terms of the sinful nature, the conclusion must be that we are obligated to live and serve God in terms of the Spirit. It is important to grasp the import of v.12, because it teaches beyond all question that believers still have the sinful nature within themselves, despite having been crucified with Christ. The "flesh" (see comment on 7:4–6) has not been eradicated, but we are obliged not "to live according to it" (see comment on 8:3–4). Sanctification is not a luxury but a necessity. Since the solicitations of the fleshly nature are constant, we must continually put to death (that is the force of the verb) the deeds of the body. And since the Spirit is the Spirit of life, he cannot do otherwise than oppose the flesh and its desires, which lead to death.

14–17 The Spirit's ministry set forth in these verses may be thought of as his *attestation*, in which he confirms for believers the reality of their position as children of God based on adoption into the heavenly family. Though this ministry is mentioned after that of mortification, it is basic to it, because those who want to be successful in contending against the flesh must be assured that they have been claimed by God and equipped with his infinite resources. Later (v.23) Paul will move on to set forth another aspect of adoption that belongs to the future.

The relation of the Spirit to the children of God is presented as being much like that of a shepherd to his sheep. They are "led" by him as their guide and protector. In Gal 3:24 Paul pictures the law as leading people to Christ. Once this goal is achieved, the law must hand over the guiding role to the Spirit, who guides into the truth (Jn 16:13) and, as in the present passage, into holiness. Unlike sin, which may at first only gently seduce, then deceitfully begin to drive as a hard taskmaster, the Spirit relies on persuasion rather than force. In fact, Paul goes to some pains to avoid misunderstanding on this very point, assuring us that the Spirit's leadership does not involve a new bondage in which fear ruled one's life (cf. Heb 2:15). The new title given to the Spirit, namely, "the Spirit of sonship" (lit., "Spirit of adoption") emphasizes the vast gulf between slavery and family relationship. By the Spirit believers cry, "Abba, Father" (cf. Gal 4:6). The two terms are equivalents, the first being the Aramaic word Jesus used in prayer (Mk 14:36).

The term "adoption" (GK 5625) bears a relationship to justification in that (1) it is declarative and forensic (i.e., it is a legal term); (2) it bestows an objective standing; (3) it is a pronouncement that is not repeated but has permanent validity; (4) it rests on the loving purpose and grace of God (Eph 1:5).

Paul's readers are called "sons" (v.15) and "children" (v.16), without any appreciable distinction. Both are family terms. "Children" emphasizes family relationship based on regeneration, while "sons" stresses the legal standing. In v.16 (cf. Gal 4:6) the Spirit bears witness together with the redeemed spirit in people to the reality of that membership in the family of heaven, i.e., to the actuality of salvation through Christ. Hebrew law prescribed that at the mouth of two or three witnesses every matter was to be established (Dt 17:6; cf. Mt 18:16). Similarly, there are two witnesses to one's salvation, the individual person in his or her inmost being and the Holy Spirit, who confirms the believer's realization to having been made God's child through faith in Christ.

A comparison of vv.15 and 16 brings out an important truth concerning the assurance of salvation. We sometimes come to the point of doubting our salvation because our sanctification has proceeded so slowly and so lamely. The Spirit, however, does not base his assuring testimony on progress or the lack of it in the Christian life. He does not lead us to cry, "I am God's child." Rather, he leads us to call upon God as Father—to look away from ourselves to him who established the relationship.

A final truth about adoption is that it involves an inheritance (v.17). In line with current legal provisions that enabled even a slave, once adopted, to inherit his master's possessions, Paul teaches that the Christian follows a similar course: a slave (to sin), a child, then an heir (vv.15–17; cf. Gal 4:6–7). How unexpected and how breathtaking is the gracious provision of God! The marvel increases with the news that we are co-heirs with Christ. Sharing his sufferings may be looked at as simply the cost of discipleship. Yet it has a brighter aspect, because it is the prelude to partaking with him of the coming glory (cf. 1Pe 4:13).

18–22 Before passing to the final ministry of the Spirit (vv.26–27), Paul lingers over the concept of future glory in relation to present suffering. His presentation may be seen as an expansion of what he had already written to the Corinthians (2Co 4:17). Weighed in the scales of lasting values, the sufferings endured in this life are light indeed, compared with the splendor of the life to come—a life undisturbed by anything hostile or hurtful. Scripture does not tell us much of what that glory will be, but it assures us that it will be. The glory will be revealed "in us" (or possibly "to us").

Instead of considering the future simply from the standpoint of the redeemed, Paul enlarges the perspective to include the whole "creation" (GK 3232), which is here personified as longing for the time when the children of God will enjoy the consummation because creation's own deliverance from the frustration imposed on it by the Fall cannot come until that time. This accords with the superior place given humankind in the creation (Ge 1:26–28; Ps 8:5–8). "Eager expectation" is a picturesque term describing a person leaning forward out of intense interest and desire, usually used in Scripture regarding one's attitude toward the Lord's coming (e.g., Gal 5:5; Php 3:20; Heb 9:28).

The one who subjected the creation to frustration is not named. The most natural interpretation is that God, at the time sin entered the world, did the subjecting. The creation is pictured as not willingly enduring the subjection, yet as having hope for something better—liberation from its "bondage to decay." The apostle is concerned with the creation only as it relates to humanity. How gracious of God to retain for believers the habitat they have long been accustomed to, only so changed and beautified as to harmonize with their own glorified state.

Verse 23 implies that the expression "whole creation" (v.22) excludes the people of God. Its "groaning" looks back to its subjection to frustration (v.20), whereas the "pains of childbirth" anticipate the age of renewal. In other words, the same sufferings are at once a result and a prophecy. Christ too spoke of the renewing of the world as a "rebirth" (Mt 19:28).

23 The parallel Paul has been drawing between the saints and the material creation is true in at least two respects—groaning (cf. 2Co 5:2) and eagerly awaiting the new age (Ro 8:23). Perhaps a third element of comparison is intended: "the redemption of our bodies," answering to the transformation of the earth. But in one respect no parallel can be made. Only the people of God have "the firstfruits of the Spirit" (v.23).

The concept of "firstfruits" (GK 569) is prominent in the OT, where the Israelites were expected to bring the first ripened elements of grain, fruit, etc., to the Lord as an offering (Ex 23:19; Ne 10:35). By doing so the offerer acknowledged that all produce was the provision of God and was really his. Implicit also in the ritual was the assurance from the divine side that the general harvest to be enjoyed by the offerer would providentially follow. As applied to our passage, the concept seems somewhat out of place, for if the Spirit is truly a person, how can any more of him be given in the future than has been given at conversion? We should rather understand the gift of the Spirit to believers at the inception of Christian life as God's pledge of the completion of the process of salvation, here stated as "adoption as sons, the redemption of our bodies." These bodies were earlier described by Paul as spiritual bodies (1Co 15:44). The future bodily resurrection of believers will be the full harvest of redemption.

In this connection we encounter "adoption" for the second time (see comment on vv.14–17). The saints who already have an adoption and are sealed by the Spirit for the day of redemption (Eph 1:13–14; 4:30) will receive their second and final adoption. Between the two events stretches the course of sanctification, and at the final adoption the children of God will be fully conformed to the likeness of God's Son (v.29; cf. 1Jn 3:2). Their bodies will be like the body of him who has provided redemption from sin and death (Php 3:20–21). This is the Spirit's work of *glorification*.

24–25 In keeping with the eager waiting of those who long for their complete salvation (v.23) is the emphasis on hope (vv.24–25; cf. also 5:4). The Christian pilgrims are on the road to glory, assured that the promises of the word and the spiritual energy provided for their "walk" are not illusory. As they see the dark tunnel of death ahead of them, they are confident that beyond it the road leads on to their ultimate destination, even though it remains unseen. Because an element of our salvation—the redemption of the body—is held in reserve, we have hope. If all were ours now, there would be no place for this experience. Since the object of our hope is not yet realized, "we wait for it patiently" (or "with endurance," if the hardships and sufferings that remain to be faced are in view).

26–27 At length Paul arrives at the final ministry of the Spirit mentioned in this chapter, his work of *intercession*. "In the same way" seems to link this ministry with hope. Both help to sustain believers amid the burdens and disappointments of life. The word "weakness" (GK 819) is a general expression for the Christian's limitations while still in the human body. Paul had long before discovered his weakness and along with it the compensating factor of the power of God (2Co 12:9–10). He admits that we often do not know our real needs as God sees them, nor do we know the needs of others. Going deeper, we do not know the will of God respecting these things. In the last analysis, it is God's will that determines how our prayers will be answered.

Standing over against this severe limitation is the gladdening information that "the Spirit helps us." The culmination of the Spirit's activity on our behalf is the declaration that he intercedes "for the saints" (intercessory prayer means prayer for others). Prayer activity on the part of believers goes on in the background and is overshadowed played by the Spirit of God. Elsewhere (Eph 6:18) this is called praying in the Spirit.

Verse 27 is needed to clarify something referred to in v.26, i.e., the inexpressible groanings. How can such prayer, if it be called prayer at all, be answered? Are not such prayers unintelligible? Not for God! He is no stranger to the intent of the Spirit. He knows what the inexpressible meaning is, because the petitions that the Spirit voices are strictly in accord with the will of God. It is a mistake to associate the inexpressible groanings with glossolalia.

3. The security and permanence of the life of the redeemed (8:28–39)

God's provision for his own is spelled out in exalted and fervent language—reaching back into the past to include his eternal purpose and its implementation in the love and sacrifice of Christ, moving into the present to proclaim God's keeping power, and sweeping down the years to defy any power to separate the saints from the abiding love of God in Christ.

28–30 Verse 28 begins with the notion that God works for the good of believers. This thought is connected with the foregoing section in that we now have a broad, general statement after a more specific one relating to the work of the Spirit as intercessor.

What is the meaning of "all things"? It most likely refers to those things that, while themselves adverse, are turned to good account by the sovereign God working on our behalf. This line of thought agrees with 5:3–5 as well as with the mention of sufferings and opposition in the present chapter. The "good" (GK *19*) is not defined, but should be sought in the intended conformity to God's Son.

The beneficiaries are those who on the human side "love God" and on the divine side are "called according to his purpose." Paul seldom refers to love for God on the part of the saints (1Co 2:9; 8:3). Nor does he introduce it here as the ground for the benefit he has been describing, for it is simply a response to the divine love and grace. The "called" (GK *3105*) are not those who are merely invited to respond to the proclamation of the Gospel; they are called according to God's (electing) purpose.

This calling is further explained in terms of foreknowledge ("foreknew"; GK *4589*) and predestination (v.29). The former term does not indicate advance awareness of someone; it refers to God's choice, his electing decision (see especially 1Pe 1:20). God's calling is not a haphazard thing, nor is it something cold and formal. It is filled with the warmth of love, as in the Hebrew word "to know" (GK *3359*; see Ge 18:19; Am 3:2). Though foreknowledge is not mentioned in Dt 7:6–8, that passage illumines the concept. God's sovereign choice precludes any possibility of human merit entering into the decision (cf. Eph 1:4). Observe also that we are called according to God's purpose, not according to his foreknowledge; hence foreknowledge must be included in the electing purpose.

If "predestined" (GK *4633*) stood by itself without any amplification, one might conclude that only an action by God is involved whereby one is chosen to salvation. But the remainder of the sentence indicates otherwise, pointing to much more than deliverance from sin and death. The background is adoption, but now presented not as in v.15 (where it is related to the Father and the Spirit) but as related to the Son. Paul presents two aspects of this conformity. By a sharing in the sufferings of Christ (Php 3:10) that is based on having the mind of Christ (Php 2:5–8), the believer is gradually being made into his likeness. This is the essence of sanctification. Its second and final aspect is conformity of the body to that of the risen Lord, to be realized at the resurrection (Php 3:21), which is the culmination of a growth in likeness to Christ based on the Spirit's work in the believer (2Co 3:18).

From these passages we learn that fellowship with Christ in his sufferings is the prelude to sharing with him in his glory. God sent his Son in our likeness (v.3) that we might eventually be like him. This makes understandable and legitimate the use of "brothers" as a description of believers in relation to the Son. The likeness will be complete except for the fact that glorified humanity never, of course, becomes deity.

Verse 30 states the various steps involved in the realization of the divine purpose: the call (cf. v.28), justification, and glorification. The marvel is that the final item is stated as though it had already occurred. This is what we might call a prophetic perfect (cf. Isa 53, where the work of the Servant of the Lord is spoken of as though his sacrifice had already been made).

Why is sanctification not mentioned in this verse? It is probably left out deliberately because sanctification is the one area in which human cooperation is essential. God never appeals to us to be called or justified or glorified, but there are numerous appeals to cooperate with him in the realization of the life of holiness.

31–36 From this point on to the end of the chapter Paul expounds the impregnable position of the believer. The key lies in the sentence "If God is for us, who can be against us?" (v.31). God has not given empty promises. He has acted, and what he has done in Christ and by the Spirit constitutes all the proof we need that the glorification will be ours in due season. This is precisely the point of v.32. God's activity has cost him dearly—he did not spare "his own Son," Jesus, who endured the cross. In all of this God was with him (2Co 5:19). Moreover, the Son was not an unwilling victim pressed into sacrificial service. "God gave him up" (GK *4140*) expresses the Father's participation, but the same verb is used of the Son's involvement (Gal 2:20). With the cross before us as the mighty demonstration of God's grace in giving his dearest to help the neediest, it naturally follows that the same grace will not withhold anything from those who are his (see 2Pe 1:3).

Paul does not deny that Christians face foes and hardships. Yet his challenging question stands: "If God is for us, who can be against us?" Amplifying it, he proceeds to ask a series of questions and then to provide answers. First, "Who will bring any charge against those whom God has chosen?" (v.33). No one can successfully press charges, no matter how hard he may try. Satan is busy doing just that (Rev 12:10), no doubt pointing out the discrepancy between the profession of believers and their "walk," but he gets nowhere with his pretended zeal for righteousness. Ultimately, as David perceived (Ps 51:4), all sin is committed against God. Logically, therefore, God is the only one who can bring charges against us. This, Paul is saying, God refuses to do, because he is for us, not against us.

The second question, "Who is he that condemns?" (v.34), finds its answer in Christ. He will never renounce the efficacy of his own work on our behalf. Paul packs four aspects of that work into one great sentence (v.34b). (1) Christ died and thereby secured the removal of sin's guilt; (2) he was raised to life and is able to bestow life on those who trust him for their salvation (Jn 11:25; 14:19); (3) he was exalted to God's right hand, with all power given to him both in heaven, so as to represent us there, and on earth, where he is more than a match for our adversaries; and (4) he intercedes for us at the throne of grace, whatever our needs may be (Heb 4:4–16; 7:25).

A third question is "Who shall separate us from the love of Christ?" (v.35). Can there be a contradiction between Christ's love for his own and his allowing suffering to overtake them? Severance from his love is no more thinkable than that the Father ceased to love his Son when he allowed him to endure the agonies of the cross, apparently forsaken. Christ predicted trouble for his people who are left in the world, but told them to be of good cheer because he had overcome the world (Jn 16:33). The quotation from Ps 44:22 (v.36) reminds believers that suffering has always been the lot of the godly. Whereas the people of God in the OT were often perplexed about the reason for their trials, the saints of NT times can trace their sufferings back to identification with Christ and rejoice that they are counted worthy to suffer for his name (cf. Ac 5:41).

37–39 Here Paul bursts into a magnificent piece of eloquence. This passage, like 1Co 3:21–23, is notable for largeness of conception and majesty of expression: "No, in all these things we are more than conquerors through him who loved us" (v.37). That is, we win the supreme victory through Christ, who loved us. By saying "loved us," Paul does not intend to restrict Christ's love to the past; he rather is emphasizing the historic demonstration of this love that gives assurance of its continuance under all circumstances. "Death" cannot separate the believer from that love (cf. 2Co 5:8; Php 1:21), nor can "life," with all its allurements and dangers and trials.

Surprisingly, Paul includes "angels" here (v.38). Since he uses other terms for hostile supernatural powers, the angels should be understood as good ones. Perhaps he means that no angel will ever seek to come between Christ's love and the object of that love. "Demons" are evil spirits, such as those often mentioned in the Gospels. Being agents and underlings of the devil, they would delight to separate Christians from Christ, but they cannot do so.

Time is equally powerless to do this, whether it be "the present" with its temptations and sufferings or "the future" with its uncertainties. "Powers" probably refers to hostile spiritual intelligences who, though conquered by Christ (Eph 1:21), are nevertheless permitted to carry on spiritual warfare against the saints of God (Eph 6:12).

Nor can space come between us and the love of Christ (v.39). If there are other possibilities, Paul is sure they are all equally impotent. For he declares that there is nothing in all creation that can drive a wedge between the love of the Savior and his redeemed people. After all, the creation itself is his handiwork and cannot thwart the will of the Creator. God is love, and that love has been manifested in the redemption of humankind.

VI. The Problem of Israel: God's Righteousness Vindicated (9:1–11:36)

This section contains "unfinished business." Although Paul has insisted on the priority of the Jew (1:16) and has noted in part their advantages (3:1ff.), he has also been obliged to expose their failure and guilt, despite their being the chosen people of God. Those who have been under divine tutelage for centuries in preparation for the coming of the Messiah have failed to receive him. Has the purpose of God been frustrated? What does the future hold for this people? The problem faced here was underscored in Paul's own ministry. He had been faithful in going to the Jew first, but in place after place he had been rebuffed by Jewish unbelief. Was his earlier statement about the power of the Gospel (1:16) too hasty or too optimistic? Or were his own labors among his people inadequate? Paul could not subscribe to either conclusion. He had to face the problem from the standpoint of God's purposes and ways.

Jew and Gentile (or circumcised and uncircumcised) are distinguished in the first four chapters. In chs. 5–8 the Jew/Gentile tension drops out of sight, only to be renewed in chs. 9–11 and brought under searching examination. Notable is a shift in terminology. Although "Jew" occurs twice in this section, Paul prefers "Israel," using it ten times here and nowhere else in the letter. The reason for the change will be noted later.

In line with the nature of the problem Paul is dealing with, he frequently mentions God in chs. 9–11 (26 times). References to Christ are limited (7 times), and the Holy Spirit has no place except in 9:1. For all its distinctiveness, this section does not lose continuity with the foregoing material. "Salvation," "save," "righteousness," "believe," and "faith" are all prominent (cf. 1:16–17, the theme of this letter). There is also a tie-in with the end of ch. 8: election, which is treated on an individual basis in 8:28–30, 33, is now viewed from the national perspective of Israel. Adoption is common to both portions (8:15; 9:4), as is the concept of "call" or "calling" (8:28-30; 5 times in ch. 9).

Another feature is the liberal use of OT quotations, partly to emphasize the sovereignty of God and his covenant faithfulness and partly to substantiate the apostle's exposure of Israel's failure. Unfaithfulness to God in OT times has its parallel in rejection of his Son in recent times. Israel according to the flesh has not materially changed.

A survey of the movement of thought in these chapters warrants the conclusion that Paul, who has written so penetratingly on the justification of sinners, now turns to write on the justification (vindication) of God himself (cf. 3:3–4). He reminds us that the Almighty is free and sovereign in what he does (ch. 9). Then he turns the discussion to the Jews' mistake in trying to establish their own righteousness before God in terms of meritorious obedience to law instead of responding to the Gospel of Christ by faith. They have not lacked opportunity to hear (ch. 10). So God did not set Israel aside arbitrarily. This matches the great section on condemnation at the beginning of this letter.

In ch. 11 Paul introduces further considerations. One is that Israel's rejection was not complete, for there was a believing remnant in Paul's day. Also, the rejection is not final, for a mass conversion of Israel will occur. In addition, Paul weaves in the observation that during the time of Israel's hardening God continues his work of grace by saving a host of Gentiles. In the end, God is found faithful to his covenant promises in spite of the unfaithfulness of Israel. This final, grand achievement embracing both Jew and Gentile leads Paul to conclude with a worshipful note of praise for this unfathomable divine wisdom. It is a testimony to the divine mercy (11:32) which, along with God's righteousness, provides the insight needed to appreciate his ways.

A. Paul's Sorrow Over Israel's Condition (9:1–5)

1–3 The apostle begins on a personal note, expressing, like the prophets of old, the burden of his soul over the condition of the Jews. Since he has left Judaism behind, this sorrow might be interpreted as somewhat less than sincere. Hence the solemn introduction in which he summons two witnesses—his union with Christ who is the truth (cf. Eph 4:21) and his conscience as aided by the Holy Spirit (cf. 8:16). As though that were not enough, he declares himself ready to accept severance from Christ (cf. 8:39) if that would avail to bring his countrymen into the fold of the Savior (cf. Ex 32:32). Paul could not, of course, actually become anathema from Christ (cf. ch. 8). Yet if it were possible, he would gladly make the sacrifice. This readiness takes on poignancy in light of Paul's having suffered the loss of all things in order to gain Christ (Php 3:8). So he would be facing a double loss.

Paul's longing for the salvation of his people comes out in the way he speaks of them—"my brothers" (cf. Ac 2:29; 3:17; 22:1; 28:17). To avoid misunderstanding, he qualifies this by noting that the bond is one of "race" rather than of a common faith in Christ.

4–5 Paul goes on to cite the spiritual heritage of his nation that he shares with them. He avoids the term "Jews" in v.4, for that term ordinarily stresses the racial, political, and ritualistic aspects of his nation. By referring to his countrymen as "the people of Israel," he is emphasizing that they are the covenant people of God, different from every other people on earth.

It is only when the distinctives of Israel are spelled out that the full implication of the word can be appreciated. Probably Paul has in mind his implied promise to enlarge on the advantages of his people (3:2). In the forefront in v.4 he puts "the adoption as sons." Though this specific word is not used in the OT, the idea is certainly present (see Dt 14:1–2; also Ex 4:22; Hos 11:1). This explains Israel's enjoyment of the glory of God's presence, symbolized by the pillar of cloud that settled over the sanctuary in the wilderness and filled the temple at its dedication.

"The covenants" (GK *1347*) are either the arrangements God entered into with Abraham, with the nation of Israel at Sinai, and with David, and with Israel and Judah in the new covenant (Jer 31:31-34)or else those arranged with Abraham (Ge 15), then renewed with Isaac (Ge 17) and with Jacob (Ge 28). The word "covenant" used here implies divine initiative.

"The receiving of the law" refers, of course, to what was communicated through Moses to the children of Israel at Sinai. In Paul's time the nation tended to look on this as its most prized possession (2:17), the most precious portion of the OT. A closely related item is "the temple worship" (i.e., the laws concerning sacrifices as prescribed in the law). "The promises" have a close relationship to the covenants (cf. Eph 2:12) and represent various aspects of the messianic salvation promised in the OT.

The importance of "the patriarchs" (v.5) can be seen in 11:28. They are the men to whom the promises were given prior to the giving of the law. God was pleased to announce himself as the God of Abraham, Isaac, and Jacob (Ex 3:15). In "from them is traced the human ancestry of Christ" (v.5), "them" refers to the people of Israel (v.4) rather than to the patriarchs, for there were many generations between them and the advent of the Messiah (cf. Mt 1:1–17; Lk 3:23–38). A subtle distinction is to be noted between "theirs" and "from them." Israel cannot lay claim to Christ in the same way they can claim the patriarchs, even though he entered the human family through the Israelite gate (cf. 1:3). Christ is much more than the patriarchs. In his earthly origin he does belong to one nation, but by virtue of his heavenly origin and mission he cannot be claimed exclusively by any segment of the race, seeing he is "God over all." In this final affirmation, Paul attests to the divine nature of Christ.

Looking back over vv.1–5, one is bound to conclude from the combination of Paul's sorrow and the extended enumeration of Israel's privileges that the subject of his nation's spiritual condition constantly weighed on him. His statement of the advantages of Israel anticipates the fuller discussion of her election and serves to accent the element of tragedy in her current state. A double purpose is served by the culminating statement concerning the Messiah: it not only underscores the blindness of Israel but is also calculated to keep believing Gentiles from gloating over Israel's fall (11:20), seeing that Israel has been the channel by which God gave Christ to the world.

B. God's Choice of Israel Based on Election, Not on Natural Generation or Works of Merit (9:6–13)

6–9 The atmosphere of tragedy is qualified by Paul's forthright denial that the course of events has taken God by surprise. If there is failure, it must be attributed to human beings, not to God and his declared purpose. He points out that God's saving purpose does not include all who belong to Israel in the biological sense (cf. his distinction in the term "Jew" in 2:28–29). Though unnamed, Ishmael is apparently in view, in contrast to Isaac; Paul's contrast is between merely being a physical descendant of Abraham and enjoying God's call to spiritual destiny—belonging to the godly line of descent that culminated in the Messiah himself (Gal 3:16). Ishmael was born by natural processes, and God bestowed on him material blessings simply because he belonged to Abraham (Ge 17:20; 21:13). Isaac was unique in that he was the child who was promised. God's purpose was centered in him before he was born. In fact, apart from divine enablement to the parents, Isaac would never have been born (cf. 4:18–21).

10–13 "Not only that" (v.10). Something more needs to be said, for any Jew could point out that the nation of Israel looked back to their origin in Isaac rather than in Ishmael. It was only natural that the son of Sarah should be chosen rather than the son of Hagar the bondwoman. So Paul feels impelled to cite the case of the twin brothers, both of them sons of Isaac and Rebekah. According to ordinary human expectation, they should stand on equal terms before God in his dealings with them. But it was not so. Natural generation from Isaac, the promised seed of Abraham, did not assure them of the same place in God's plan. God made a distinction between them before they were born—before their characters had been shaped or any deeds had been performed that might form a basis for evaluation. The freedom and sovereignty of God were thus safeguarded. He deliberately disturbed the normal pattern of the culture into which the children were born by decreeing that the elder should serve the younger.

By quoting Mal 1:2–3 here, Paul lifts the discussion from what might appear to be a purely personal one to the plane of corporate, national life. God's love for Jacob and his hatred for Esau should not be construed as temperamental. Malachi is appealing to the course of history as fulfilling the purpose of God declared long before. Hatred in the ordinary sense will not fit the situation, since God bestowed many blessings on Esau and his descendants. The "hatred" is simply a way of saying that Esau was not the object of God's electing purpose (cf. the use of "hate" in Lk 14:26). The value of using these two brothers is to make clear that in election God does not wait until individuals or nations are developed and then make a choice on the basis of character or achievement. If he did so, this would make a mockery of the concept of election, because it would locate the basis in a human being rather than in God. God's love for Jacob, then, must be coupled with election rather than explained by some worthiness found in him (cf. Dt 7:6–8).

C. God's Freedom to Act in His Own Sovereign Right (9:14–29)

14–18 God's dealings with Jacob and Esau might be challenged as arbitrary, on the ground that Esau was the object of injustice. To demonstrate that this is not God's character, Paul goes further into the history of Israel, focusing on the golden calf incident at Sinai. There the people sinned grievously. If God had acted simply in justice, he could have blotted out his people. Instead, he recalled Moses to the mountain and for a second time gave him the Ten Commandments, yet not until he had proclaimed to him, "I will have mercy on whom I will have mercy" (Ex 33:19). And lest that mercy be construed as depending on human "desire or effort," Paul denies any such qualification (v.16). "Mercy" (GK *1796* & *1799*), like grace, stands over against human worth and effort

Passages Indicating the Deity of Christ

Many passages in both the OT and NT help to demonstrate that Jesus Christ is fully God—a teaching often denied by sectarian groups and cults. This chart compiles the major passages that support this important Christian doctrine.

In the Old Testament	
God's Son is to rule on the throne at God's right hand, equal in power with the Father	Pss 2:7–12; 110:1–2
The promised Messiah will be "Immanuel" (i.e., "God with us")	Isa 7:14 (cf. Mt 1:23)
The promised Messiah will be "Mighty God," ruling eternally	Isa 9:6–7
The ruler born in Bethlehem has origin from all eternity	Mic 5:2
The righteous Branch of David is called "The LORD Our Righteousness"	Jer 23:5–5; 33:15–16
The one who will appear in the temple is "the Lord"	Mal 3:1
Self-Affirmations of Jesus	
His is "Lord" of the Sabbath, having created it	Mt 12:8; Mk 2:28; Lk 6:5
He is the "I am" of Ex 3:14	Jn 8:57–58
He is one with the Father	Jn 10:30
He is the judge of the living and the dead	Mt 25:31–32; Jn 5:22, 27 (cf. Ps 98:9)
He deserve the same honor as the Father	Jn 5:23
He made himself equal with God	Jn 5:16–18; 10:33
He, like God, is everywhere present	Mt 28:20
He, like God, is all-powerful	Mt 28:18
He, like God, is all-knowing	Jn 1:47–50 (cf. 2:22–23)
He has the authority, which belongs only to God, to forgive sins	Mt 9:2–7; Mk 2:5–12; Lk 5:20–25
Believing in him and believing in God are the same	Jn 14:1
To know him is to know the Father, and vice versa	Mt 11:27; Lk 10:22
He is the only way to the Father, and to see him is to see the Father	Jn 14:6–10
Other Testimonies in the Gospels and in Acts	
Jesus is the eternal Word of God	Jn 1;1
Jesus was present at the time of creation	Jn 1:2–3
Jesus is the One and Only God	Jn 1:18
Thomas confessed Jesus as "My Lord and my God"	Jn 20:28
Evil spirits recognized Jesus as "the Holy One of God" (an OT term used for God)	Mk 1:24 (cf. Isa 6:3; 30:15)

Passages Indicating the Deity of Christ (cont.)

Other Testimonies in the Gospels and in Acts (cont.)	
Jesus is "Lord" (the same Greek word as translates "Yahweh" ("LORD") in the LXX	Ac 2:36; 10:36
Jesus is "the Holy and Righteous One"	Ac 3:14 (cf. Isa 6:3; 30:15; Jer 23:6)
Jesus is the coming Judge	Ac 10:42; 17:31 (cf. Ps 98:9)
The Testimony of Paul	
Jesus is "God over all"	Ro 9:5
Jesus is in very nature God and equal with God	Php 2:6
Jesus is Lord (the same Greek word as translates "Yahweh" ("LORD") in the LXX	Ro 10:9; 1Co 2:8; Php 2:11; Col 2:6
Jesus is the fullness of the Deity	Col 1:19; 2:9
Jesus was present at the time of creation	Col 1:16
There is only one God and Lord	1Co 8:5–6; Eph 4:5–6
Jesus is "our great God and Savior"	Tit 2:13 (cf. 1Ti 4:10; 2Ti 1:10)
The Testimony of the Other New Testament Letters	
The Son is "the exact representation of God"	Heb 1:3
The Son is God	Heb 1:8
God commands the angels to worship the Son, an act that belongs only to God	Heb 1:6 (cf. Mt 4:10; Rev 19:10; 22:8–9)
Jesus, like God, is unchanging	Heb 13:8 (cf. Mal 3:6)
Jesus is "our God and Savior"	2Pe 1:1
Jesus is "our Lord and Savior"	2Pe 1:11; 2:20; 3:18
Jesus Christ is "the Righteous One"	1Jn 2:1 (cf. Jer 23:5)
To acknowledge the Son is to acknowledge the Father	1Jn 2:23
The Son Jesus Christ is "the true God"	1Jn 5:20
The Testimony in Revelation	
Jesus is "the Alpha and Omega," "the First and the Last" (a term ascribed to God in the OT)	Rev 1:8; 2:8; 21:6; 22:13 (cf. Isa 44:6; 48:12)
Jesus is "the Almighty"	Rev 1:8
Jesus is "the Living One"	Rev 1:18 (cf. Jos 3:10; Pss 42:2; 84:2)
Jesus holds the key of David (ascribed in the OT to God)	Rev 3:7 (cf. Isa 22:22)
Jesus is "Lord of Lords"	Rev 17:14; 19:16
Jesus received worship from people, an act that belongs only to God	Rev 5:11–14 (cf. 19:10; 22:8–9)

whenever salvation is concerned. It is free, because God is not bound to show mercy to any.

Paul's thought moves from Moses to Pharaoh, the king of Egypt at the time of the Exodus—i.e., from the leader of Israel to their oppressor (v.17). The Scripture is represented as speaking, a vivid reminder that it is God's word. "I raised you up" does not refer to Pharaoh's emergence in history, but to God's providence in sparing him up to that time. Pharaoh deserved death for his oppression and insolence, but his life would not be taken during the series of plagues, so that the full extent of his hardness of heart might be evident and the glory of God in the deliverance of his people enhanced (cf. Jos 9:9). The fame of this Pharaoh actually depended on the mercy of God in sparing him. God can be glorified both through those who oppose him (cf. Ps 76:10) and through those who trust and serve him.

In his conclusion to the Pharaoh episode (v.18), Paul does not record those texts that say that Pharaoh hardened his own heart in unbelief and rebellion, because the apostle is emphasizing the freedom of God's action in all cases. God's hardening of Pharaoh's heart can profitably be related to the principle laid down in ch. 1: in dealing with those who reject the revelation of himself in nature and history (and in Pharaoh's case, also in miracles), God abandons them to still greater excess of sin and its consequences.

19–26 As he continues the review of God's sovereign activity, Paul presents another problem. If God acts unilaterally, according to his own will and purpose, does this not remove all basis for judgment, since no one can resist the divine will? Why, then, should a person be blamed? In reply, Paul first points out the inappropriateness of creatures talking back to God (v.20), as though they had sufficient wisdom to judge the Almighty. The illustration of the potter and the clay (v.21) shows how ridiculous this is (cf. also Isa 29:16; Jer 18:6). The apostle insists on the right of the potter to make whatever type of vessel he chooses. Those made for "noble purposes" are valuable for their beauty and decorative function, while those made for "common use" are not admired, though they are actually more essential to the household than the other ones. Pharaoh was useful in fulfilling God's purpose. Apart from this, he would not even have appeared on the pages of sacred history.

In v.22 the crucial problem is the correct interpretation of "prepared for destruction." Is Paul teaching a double predestination—i.e., that God chooses some people to experience his mercy and others to experience his wrath? This is improbable, because he avoids involving God in this case, whereas God is involved in showing mercy to the objects of his mercy (v.23). Furthermore, God's patience in bearing with the objects of his wrath suggests a readiness to receive such people on condition of repentance (cf. 2:3–4; 2Pe 3:9). So "prepared for destruction" designates a ripeness of sinfulness that points to judgment unless such people turn to God, yet God is not made responsible for their sinful condition. The preparation for destruction is the work of human beings, who allow themselves to deteriorate in spite of knowledge and conscience.

Presumably, and in view of what follows, when Paul speaks of "the objects of his [God's] wrath" (v.22), he is thinking of those in Israel who have remained obdurate in opposing the Gospel, yet are still the objects of the divine longsuffering. In contrast to them are "the objects of his mercy" (v.23) in whom God wills to show the riches of his glory. These include both Jews and Gentiles (v.24), in line with the previous teaching (1:16; 2:10–11; 3:22) and with the prophetic announcement. Through the prophet Hosea God declared his freedom to call others to be his people (v.25). Strictly, this passage from Hos 2:23 refers to the reversal in Israel's status from being called "not my people" (Hos 1:9) to being restored, but both Ro 9:25 and 1Pe 2:10 apply it to include Gentiles. The Gentiles, who are not actually a people but masses of humanity, are called by the grace of God to a distinctive role—that of being the people of God. This was happening in Paul's day.

The second quotation is from Hos 1:10 (omitting the first half of the verse, which refers to the prophesied increase in the number of the people of Israel). Here too the background is the Lo-ammi prophecy of Hos 1:9, which is seen to be revoked when Israel will once again be called "sons of the living God." In light of Peter's use of Hos 2:23 to apply to Gentiles (1Pe 2:10), Paul's intimation of a similar application would be understandable. It is just possible, however, that he does not intend Hos 1:10 to apply to Gentiles but rather to Jews, in which case he may be giving a hint of something developed in ch. 11—the influx of Gentiles during Israel's temporary rejection, followed by the turning of Israel to the Lord in great numbers (11:25–27).

27–29 As Paul used Scripture to show that God's purpose is to extend his mercy to Gentiles, so now he uses Scripture again to make clear that the election of Israel does not preclude her reduction through chastening judgments; yet in the sparing of the remnant his mercy and faithfulness are to be seen. Both passages quoted here are from Isaiah. The former anticipates the depletion of the nation by reason of the Assyrian invasion under Sennacherib. Without softening his decree and without delay, God would permit the judgment to fall; Jacob would be reduced to a remnant (Isa 10:22). The remainder of the sentence, however, underscores the divine mercy—"the remnant will be saved." The Hebrew text has "will return" (i.e., after deportation). But Paul sees the promise of a greater deliverance, for he says, "will be saved." Even as he wrote, there was a remnant of Israel found in the church. In view of the nation's rejection of Jesus as Israel's Messiah, Messianic Jews should be grateful for the minority of Jews who have embraced the Gospel of Christ (Paul returns to this theme in 11:5). If God's judgment had been unsparing, the nation would have become as truly wiped out as Sodom and Gomorrah (v.29). But the divine judgment is tempered by unfailing mercy, of which the remnant is the eloquent proof.

D. Israel's Failure to Attain Righteousness Due to Reliance on Works Rather Than Faith (9:30–10:21)

30–33 Paul now introduces a contrast between Gentiles and Israel, emphasizing that what has come to the former by the exercise of faith has been denied the latter by their insistence on seeking righteousness on the basis of works.

There is no blanket inclusion of all Gentiles; only those are included who meet the description laid down here—that of not pursuing righteousness in the manner followed by the children of Israel. Paul uses the figure of a foot race. The paradox here is sharp—Gentiles who are unconcerned about acquiring righteousness actually get the prize, even though they are not competing in the race with the Jews. The prize is justification by faith. It is a pitiful picture of the nation of Israel struggling intensely to perfect their religious life and coming up empty-handed. Gentile success is attributed to their avoidance of the false approach of the Jew and their willingness to receive righteousness as a gift. Hardly a passage in the NT is stronger than this one in its exposure of the futility of works as a means of justification.

Verse 31 presents a difficulty: "But Israel, who pursued a law of righteousness, has not attained it." What is the "it"? The Greek has the word "law" here. Yet the reader looks for a repetition of the word "righteousness." Perhaps we can translate, "has not attained to such a law" (i.e., the law of righteousness in the sense of righteousness gained by means of the law). Israel confusedly identified their own works, in which they took pride, with the absolute standard the law requires. Their whole effort was not grounded in faith but in works designed to gain acceptance (v.32).

"They stumbled over the stumbling stone" (v.32). The analogy of the race continues to influence Paul's thought. Absorbed in their own efforts, the Israelites did not recognize in Christ the stone of their prophetic Scripture and they fell headlong over him. By failing to receive him, they denied their own election of which he was the fulfillment and crown. Paul's quotation of Isa 8:14; 28:16 here demonstrates that the Lord Jesus himself, though provided as a foundation stone for faith and life, was actually to become for Israel a stumbling stone. This became especially true with respect to his cross (cf. 1Co 1:23). The misdirection of Israel's thinking became painfully clear in that the preaching of the cross, the event that was at once the quintessence of her sin and the sole hope of her salvation, left her defiant in her self-righteousness.

10:1–4 The chapter division does not mark a break in the thought, for such key words as "righteousness," "law," and "faith" continue to appear, especially in the beginning of the chapter. Paul has spoken pointedly about Israel's failure, but not censoriously. He feels deeply for his countrymen. He knows their plight because their condition was his own condition prior to his conversion. His desire for their salvation is reflected both in his going to the Jews first (Ac 13:46; 18:5–6; cf. Ro 1:16) and in his praying to God on their behalf.

Paradoxically, it is Israel's zeal for God that constitutes their greatest barrier (v.2). The apostle knows whereof he speaks, for his zeal on behalf of Judaism had been notorious (Ac 22:3; Gal 1:14). That zeal so preoccupied him that he considered Jesus and his followers as traitors to the faith of his fathers. But he persecuted in ignorance (1Ti 1:13). So here he diagnoses the zeal of Israel as lacking in "knowledge," as ignoring "the righteousness that comes from God" (cf. 1:17). In trying to establish their own righteous standing before God, the Jews have refused submission to God's righteousness. They have attempted to achieve a standing in righteousness by imagining success in meeting the demands of the law of Moses. Paul knew whereof he spoke, for he had been where they were. It was a great day for him when he gave up his cherished righteousness, based on obeying the law, in exchange for the righteousness that comes from God and depends on faith (Php 3:9).

Israel's covenant relation to God and reliance on observing the law do not add up to salvation (Jn 14:6; Ac 4:12). For this reason Paul points to Christ and his righteousness as Israel's great need (v.4). The proof that Israel was out of line with respect to God's will lies in the fact that when he sent his Son as the one who brought salvation in full accord with his righteousness, the nation rejected him. The same kind of revolution in thinking that was necessary for Paul was required for his people.

Considerable debate has centered on the interpretation of v.4, especially on the intended meaning of the word translated "end" (*telos*; GK 5465). Just as in English we speak of "the end of the matter" and we use the expression "to the end that"— meaning either "conclusion" or "purpose"—the same dual possibility lies in the Greek word *telos*. The second meaning has some plausibility here, because the statement "Christ is the end of the law" fits in with Paul's teaching about the law as that which brings people to Christ (Gal 3:24). Favorable to the first meaning ("Christ terminated the law") is the fact that the law had a certain course to run (Lk 16:16; Gal 3:19, 23; cf. Mt 5:17) in the economy of God. Both concepts seem to fit rather well in our passage. The decisive factor that favors "termination" rather than "purpose" as the main idea, however, is the contrast in 9:30–33 between the law and God's righteousness. Though the law is righteous in its requirements, it fails as an instrument of justification (cf. 8:3–4). Paul's contention regarding the Jews (v.3) is not the incompleteness of their position, which needed the coming of Christ to perfect it, but the absolute wrongness of that position, because it entailed an effort to establish righteousness by human effort rather than by accepting a divine gift.

Paul adds a certain qualification to the statement about Christ as the end of the law for righteousness: he is that "for everyone who believes." This implies that the law still applies to those who do not believe and that they still feel its power.

5–8 The thread of the discourse in the next section (vv.5–13) continues the emphasis on "everyone who believes." This is developed in two ways: first, by showing that the principle of faith is amply set forth in the OT—in fact, in the pages of Moses—and then by expressly indicating, in line with 1:16, that "everyone" includes Gentiles as well as Jews.

Paul deals first with the negative side of the attainment of righteousness by citing a passage (Lev 18:5) that calls for obedience and performance of the will of God as contained in his statutes and ordinances. The one who complies will live. Paul had already dealt with Lev 18:5 in Gal 3:12. In both letters the emphasis in this verse falls on *doing* if one expects to gain life (cf. 2:13). The dark side of the picture is that a curse rests on anyone who fails to meet the law's demands. The upshot of the matter is that the course being pursued by Israel—the attempt to gain righteousness for themselves by keeping the law (v.3)—cannot bring life because of human weakness and imperfection. It can only lead to self-deception and pride.

Next Paul addresses himself to the positive approach, for which purpose he makes use of another passage from Moses (Dt 30:11–14), this one designed to describe "the righteousness that is by faith." At first sight, this passage seems inappropriate, since neither "righteousness" nor "faith" can be found here, and there is heavy emphasis on doing, as in Lev 18:5. But the context helps us, for the passage presupposes a heart attitude of loving obedience (Dt 30:6–10) rather than a legalistic attempt to attain righteousness. The whole burden of the passage is to discourage the idea that doing God's will means to aspire after something that is too difficult and out of reach. Actually, if life is attuned to God, his will is as near as the mouth and heart (the mouth as the organ that repeats the word of God and turns it back to him in prayer and praise; the heart as the source of desire to please him).

Paul then applies the reference to heaven (v.6) in order to emphasize certain aspects of the Gospel. There is no need to try to ascend to heaven to gain spiritual knowledge or acceptance, for Christ has come from heaven to proclaim and effect salvation for the world. In v.7 Paul substitutes "the deep" ("the abyss") for "the sea" in Dt 30, changing the figure from one of distance to one of depth—thus making the contrast with heaven sharper. This affords opportunity to think of Christ as going down into death as a prelude to resurrection. Apparently lost to us by death, he has been returned to us by resurrection. This means that our grasp of the righteousness of God, with his Son as the object of our faith, is not difficult. Everything is of him. Our part is to believe. The saving message lies at hand, waiting to be received.

9–10 Building on the Deuteronomy passage, especially its use of "mouth" and "heart," Paul goes on to speak directly of the content of the Christian Gospel and its availability to Jew and Gentile alike. "The word of faith" (the gospel message) is something to "confess" as well as to "believe" (cf. 2Co 4:13–14). To "confess" (GK 3933) means to say the same thing as other believers say regarding their faith. This was done within the Christian group especially by new converts in connection with their baptism; when it was done "before men" (Mt 10:32) it had an evangelizing function. The priority of confession over believing is simply due to Paul's preservation of the "mouth" and "heart" in Dt 30:14. The influence of the OT passage is also evident in that, whereas it provided a point of contact for citing the resurrection of our Lord (vv.7,9), there was nothing to provide a basis for mention of the saving death of Christ (contrast 1Co 15:3–4). The concentration on the resurrection is understandable also when it is recognized that the creedal statement before us pertains to the person of Christ rather than to his redeeming work. "Jesus is Lord [GK 3261]" was the earliest declaration of faith fashioned by the church (Ac 2:36; 1Co 12:3). It stressed the objective lordship of Christ, the very cornerstone for faith. Paul links his lordship with the resurrection, which in turn validated our Lord's saving death.

11–13 Scripture indicates how faith can be transforming for one's life, replacing fear and hesitation with bold confidence that rests on the sure promises of God. For this purpose Paul uses Isa 28:16 (cf. the close of 9:33). This belief and its blessing are open to Jew and Gentile alike. Whatever "difference" there may be in the two groups in some respects, there is no difference when it comes to the need for Christ and the availability of his salvation (cf. 3:22). The source of their spiritual life is found in "the same Lord," whose blessings (notably salvation) are richly bestowed on them without partiality. In support of this, Paul cites Joel 2:32 (cf. Peter's use of this verse in Ac 2:21). This calling on the Lord is the echo within the human heart of the call of God himself according to his gracious purpose (8:28–30). God will hear the cry of any who call upon him for salvation. When v.13 is compared with v.9, it becomes evident that the Lord of Joel 2:32 is being identified with the Lord Jesus Christ.

14–15 Paul now turns from the responsibility of the seeker after salvation to emphasize the role that believers have in God's plan for reaching the lost. Calling on the Lord is meaningless apart from some assurance that he is worthy of confidence and trust, that he has something to offer guilty sinners. Calling on the Lord continues to be a mark of the believer, not simply the first step in the direction of establishing relationship to him (cf. 1Co 1:2).

Paul then proceeds to the second consideration in his closely reasoned argument—that faith depends on knowledge. One must hear the Gospel before he or she can be expected either to receive it or to reject it. The message of the Gospel has to be communicated by word of mouth to the hearing of others.

The third step is the necessity that someone proclaim the message. We are saved to serve, and the paramount element in that service is to bear witness to the saving power of Christ.

"And how can they preach unless they are sent?" (v.15) rounds out Paul's series of questions. No answers are given, for the logic is so airtight that no one could properly question the essential role of each step in the process. To be "sent" (GK 690) suggests at least two things: that one operates under a higher authority and that one's message does not originate with oneself but is given by the sending authority. The OT prophets had been sent in these two respects. So was the Lord Jesus (Jn 3:34; 7:16). The apostles also received their commission from the risen Lord (Jn 20:21; cf. Ro 1:1). All Christians are sent in these two respects in their witness-bearing capacity. The task was too big for just a handful of people (see Ac 8:4; 11:19). The sending out of missionaries by a sponsoring group of believers (Ac 13:3) is likewise included here.

Once again (v.15) Paul corroborates his words by the sayings of the prophets, this time using Isa 52:7, which heralds the favor of the Lord to the city of Jerusalem that had lain desolate during the Babylonian captivity. The tidings are good; the proclamation is one of peace. If the message to returning Israel in the former day was good news, how much more the promise of eternal salvation in God's Son!

16–17 But here an element of tragedy enters. The good news of physical restoration may have been welcome to Israel, but the spiritual salvation God promised to provide through his Servant and did provide in the fullness of time has met with unbelief. What a change of atmosphere from Paul's quotation of Isa 52:7 in v.15 to his quotation of Isa 53:1 in v.16! The prophet foresaw a repudiation of the message about salvation through a suffering Servant. History has sustained prophecy (1Co 1:23).

Paul sums up by saying that faith depends on hearing and understanding the message. "And the message is heard through the word of Christ." This can mean either "the word about Christ" or "the word proclaimed by Christ" (the former is more likely).

18–19 In his indictment of Israel, Paul is prepared to investigate any possibility that would offer an excuse for the nation's failure. Could it be, he asks, that they did not hear the Gospel? He could have appealed to widespread missionary activity, but he is content to cite Scripture, so that Israel may stand condemned by the testimony of God rather than by that of other people. In making use of Ps 19:4 (v.18), Paul sees a parallel between the diffusion of light and darkness every day and night, of which no one can be ignorant, and the proclamation of the Gospel in the areas where Jews made their home. This was essentially the Mediterranean basin, where Paul and his helpers had been laboring for some years. His countrymen could not claim lack of opportunity to hear the Gospel (cf. Ac 17:6; 21:28).

There remains the possibility, however, that in spite of hearing the message, Israel has not understood it (v.19). So in all fairness this should be considered. But the form in which Paul asks his question makes this highly unlikely. It is true that at Pentecost Peter spoke of the ignorance of his countrymen as explaining the crucifixion. But as time went on, fewer and fewer Jews in proportion to the total population of the nation responded to the Gospel. A hardened attitude was setting in. The precedent of the Jews who did respond to the Gospel, instead of moving their fellow Jews, only embittered them. Then, as the Gospel spread abroad and was received by Gentiles in ever greater numbers, this served to antagonize them still further.

It is over against this situation that Paul quotes Dt 32:21b, a part of Moses' song to Israel in which he chides the congregation for perversity and (in Dt 32:21a, not quoted here) voices the complaint of God that the people had provoked him to jealousy by their idolatry. This in turn prompts God to resort to something that is calculated to make Israel jealous. It will be done through "a nation that has no understanding." This must be understood of Gentile response to God and his word in such a way as to surpass the response of Israel—exactly what was happening during Paul's day. Those who lacked special revelation and the moral and religious training God provided for Israel have proved more responsive than the chosen people.

20–21 The quotation from Isa 65:1 clearly supports what has been declared in the previous passage (Dt 32:21). Paul sees in the OT an anticipation of what has come to pass in his day. The pagan world, occupied with its own pursuits, was in the main not seeking after God (cf. 9:30), but now they were. Paradoxically, God had been continually seeking and reaching out to his people Israel with a plea that they return to him in loving obedience, only to be rebuffed. Consequently, the spiritual condition of Israel did not come from a lack of opportunity to hear the Gospel or a lack of understanding of its content, but must be traced to a continuous pattern of a stubborn and rebellious spirit.

E. Israel Not Entirely Rejected; There Is a Remnant of Believers (11:1–10)

Thus far, Paul has treated the problem of Israel from two standpoints. In ch. 9 he emphasized the sovereignty of God in choosing this people for himself in a special sense. In ch. 10 he dealt with Israel's failure to respond to God's righteousness, ending with the verdict that they are "a disobedient and obstinate people" (10:21). These two presentations involve a serious tension. Will Israel's sin and stubbornness defeat the purpose of God, or will God find a way to deal effectively with the situation so as to safeguard his purpose? To this question Paul now turns. His answer will dip into Israel's past, encompass her present, and reveal her future.

1–6 Preparation for this section has been made, especially in 9:27–29, where the OT teaching concerning the remnant is summarized by quotations from Isaiah. That teaching involved both judgment and mercy—judgment on the nation as a whole for its infidelity and wickedness, and mercy on those who are permitted to escape the judgment and form the nucleus for a fresh start under the blessing of God.

The opening question, "Did God reject his people?" (based on Ps 94:14) requires that we keep in mind what was made clear early in the discussion—that "not all who are descended from Israel are Israel" (9:6). That the bulk of the nation proved disobedient (both in OT days and at the opening of the gospel period) does not mean rejection of "his people." Paul has in mind the remnant, as the ensuing paragraph demonstrates.

Why does Paul now inject himself into the discussion as a bona-fide Israelite (cf. Php 3:5)? He not only is certifying that he is able to handle the subject with fairness to Israel, but, sensing his prominence in the purpose of God, he cites himself as sufficient evidence to refute the charge that God had rejected Israel.

For God to reject his people would require repudiation of his deliberate, unilateral choice of Israel (for the meaning of "foreknew" in v.3, see comment on 8:29). The inference is that God could not do such a thing (v.2). But instead of dealing in abstractions, Paul turns to the OT for confirmation, to the time of Elijah. If ever there was a period of flagrant apostasy, it was during the reign of Ahab, when Jezebel promoted Baal worship throughout the land. The situation was so bad that Elijah, in his loneliness, cried to God against the killing of prophets and destruction of altars. He went so far as to assert that he was the only one left and that he was being hunted down so as to complete the destruction of God's servants (1Ki 19:10). Paul, likewise persecuted by his own countrymen, may have felt a special kinship with Elijah, and this also may help to account for his mention of himself in v.1.

The important thing is the contrast between the assertion of Elijah—"I am the only one left"—and God's reply: "I have reserved for myself seven thousand who have not bowed the knee to Baal" (v.4). If in that dark hour such a goodly company of the faithful existed, this is sufficient evidence that God does not permit his own at any time to disappear completely. The sparing of the remnant is inseparably related to the choice of the remnant.

This parallel between the days of Elijah and Paul's own time suggests that when he wrote, the vast majority of Israel were resisting the Gospel and that, therefore, despite their claim of loyalty to God and the law, they had failed to move forward in terms of the climactic revelation in his Son. Those who had turned to Christ were only a remnant (v.5).

But the matter of numbers is not crucial. What is important is the reminder that irrespective of its size, the remnant is "chosen by grace." This element is brought out in the quotation "I have reserved for myself seven thousand" (v.4). It is also evident, though not expressed, that the existence of the church, far from being contrary to the will of God, is actually the present channel of the operation of his "grace" (GK *5921*). Having mentioned grace at the end of v.5, the apostle cannot pass by the opportunity to contrast grace with works (v.6). They are mutually exclusive as the means of establishing one's relationship to God (cf. Eph 2:8–9).

7–10 Here Paul sets forth in the case of Israel according to the flesh the tragic consequences of persisting in the pattern of "works." Once again he cannot overlook Israel's "earnestly" seeking to get from God what they prized (see comment on 10:3). But the elect obtained righteousness not by works but by depending on divine grace. While this was true in the past, Paul's main emphasis is the present situation (cf. v.5). In distinction from the elect, Israel as a whole has become hardened. The comparison between present and past, already made on the favorable side between the current remnant according to the election of grace and the 7,000 in Elijah's time, is now projected to cover the dark aspects of the situation.

The failure of the bulk of Israel to attain divine righteousness and their being hardened are in line with OT history. Paul throws the weight of Scripture behind his presentation; by so doing he avoids having to speak on his own as bluntly and severely as the Word of God does. The first quotation weaves together Dt 29:4 and Isa 29:10 so as to provide illustrations from two periods. In Deuteronomy, it is the testimony of the *eyes* that is stressed: the people had seen the wonders of the Exodus and God's miracles in the wilderness, but from these experiences they did not derive a heart of loving trust in God. In Isaiah, the background is the faithful testimony of the prophets; yet the people shut their *ears* to the voice of God through these spokesmen. As a consequence, God sent them a "spirit of stupor." That involved a judicial punishment for their failure to use God-given faculties to perceive his manifested power and to glorify him (see Jn 12:39–40).

Before leaving v.7, something should be said on the word "hardened" (GK *4800*), especially since it is not the same word as the term used in 9:18. It is a strong word, suggesting petrification and permanent bluntness and insensibility in the intelligence.

David's word of imprecation in Ps 69:22–23 follows (vv.9–10). David suffered reproach and torment from his enemies, who were also viewed as the enemies of the Lord. Apparently their feasts were times for special outbreaks of blasphemy. David prays that the Lord will make their table their snare so as to entrap them. Then he prays for the darkening of the eyes that have looked with complacency and even glee at the sufferings of the one whom God has permitted to be smitten (cf. Jn 2:17; 15:25; Ac 1:20, which also quote Ps 69). One problem arises regarding the final word of the quotation, "forever." It is best to understand this word as "continually," for in the following section, Israel's obduracy and rejection are not treated as lasting indefinitely, but as giving way to a great ingathering of repentant Israel.

F. Israel's Temporary Rejection and the Salvation of Gentiles (11:11–24)

Paul now turns from the remnant to consider Israel as a whole, insisting that her rejection is not final and that during the period when the nation continues to resist the divine plan centered in the Messiah, God is active in bringing salvation to the Gentiles. The figure of the olive tree emphasizes that Gentile salvation is dependent on Israel's covenant relationship to God; Gentiles have to be grafted into the olive tree. The purpose of this Gentile influx into the church is not merely to magnify the grace of God toward outsiders, but to evoke envy on the part of Israel as a factor in leading to her ultimate return to God as a people. This in turn prepares the way for the climax in vv.25–27.

11–12 A dark picture of Israel has been painted both from the OT and from present observation. This leads naturally to an inquiry: Is this hardening a hopeless situation? Are they doomed to stumble so as to fall and rise no more? "Not at all!" The stumbling is admitted; an irreparable fall is not. This is a broad hint of the future salvation of Israel that Paul goes on to affirm. Those who stumbled are "the others" of v.7, those not included in the believing remnant. The language recalls the indirect reference to the Messiah in 9:32–33 as the stumbling stone.

God is bringing good out of apparent evil. Israel's stumbling has opened the way for Gentile salvation on such a scale as to make Israel envious (cf. Ac 13:42–47). That envy, though it may involve bitterness, will ultimately contribute to drawing the nation to her Messiah. The longer the process goes on, the more unbearable the pressure on Israel becomes. Her transgression "means riches for the world."

A word should be said about "loss" (v.12; GK 2488). This is a military figure. An army loses a battle because of heavy casualties. In other words, as surely as Israel's defeat (identified with her stumbling) has brought the riches of God's grace to the Gentiles on a large scale, so the conversion of Israel to her Messiah (v.26) will bring even greater blessing to the world. The word "fullness" (GK 4445) refers to that conversion, meaning the full complement in contrast to the remnant. It will mark an end to the state of hardening that now characterizes the nation.

13–16 This paragraph follows naturally from the preceding, because Paul now applies to his own position and ministry the truth he has stated. He wants the Gentiles in the Roman church to catch the full import of what he is saying. They have looked on him as "the apostle to the Gentiles." Very well, but they must not suppose that he has lost sight of the need to witness to Israel. His work among Gentiles is not simply as an end in itself but is a means of reaching his countrymen (cf. v.11). The salvation of the Gentiles is for the sake of God's election of Israel, of whom Paul hopes thereby to save "some" (cf. 1Co 9:22). The word "some" suggests that he does not expect his efforts will bring about the actual eschatological turning of the nation to the crucified and risen Son of God, when "all Israel will be saved" (cf. v.26). This belongs to the indefinite future. But if God could turn him around, a proud Jew who bitterly set himself against Jesus as the Christ, surely through him others can be won. These others are the "firstfruits" (the "remnant"; cf. v.5), who contain in themselves the promise of the ultimate harvest of a nation of believers (v.16).

There is some difficulty in ascertaining the meaning of "life from the dead" (v.15). In order to retain the balance of the sentence, this expression must pertain to the world (cf. the structure of v.12). Perhaps Paul is suggesting the promise of a worldwide quickening and deepening of spiritual life when Israel is restored to divine fellowship. She will become a tonic to the nations that are to be saved.

There is a difficulty in understanding the final statement: "if the root is holy, so are the branches." Paul uses "root" in anticipation of his use of this word in the following verses to refer to the historic Israel, especially to its patriarchal foundation (see vv.17–24; cf. the use of "building" in 1Co 3:10 anticipating 3:11–15). Israel's future restoration conforms with the holy character impressed on them at its beginning.

17–24 Paul now expands the figures of root and branches by setting forth the allegory of the olive tree. Actually, there are two trees, the cultivated olive and the wild olive. Israel is the cultivated olive, the Gentiles the wild olive. The breaking off of some of the branches of the former and the grafting in of some of the branches of the latter represent the present partial rejection of Israel and the corresponding reception of the Gentiles. From this presentation two lessons are drawn. (1) Paul warns the Gentile Christians of the danger of repeating the sin of the Jews—boasting of their privileged position (vv.18–21). (2) Even more important, if God, by cutting off the branches of the natural olive, has made room for Gentile believers, how much easier will it be for him to restore the natural branches to their place in the cultivated olive (vv.23–24)! So the groundwork is laid for the next stage in the argument. God is not only able to do this; he will do it (vv.25–27)

By stating that only some of the branches have been broken off (v.17), Paul inserts a reminder of the fact that Israel's rejection is not complete (cf. v.5). The "others" are the Jewish Christians who rub shoulders with Gentile believers in the church. Both depend on the "olive root," the patriarchal base established by God's covenant (cf 4:11–12). This calls to mind Eph 2:11–22, where Paul writes that the Gentiles, once aliens and foreigners, are now "fellow citizens with God's people and members of God's household." The two have been made one in Christ.

"Do not boast over those branches" (v.18)—i.e., the broken-off branches of vv.17, 19. The temptation to boast must have been considerable, a kind of anti-Semitism that magnified the sin of the nation Israel in rejecting the Lord Jesus and saw in Jewish persecution of the church a sure token of an irreparable rift between the nation and her God. But Israel's plight is not to be traced to a change of attitude on the part of God toward her. It is due simply to her unbelief, a condition noted earlier (3:3). The reason Gentile believers have a standing with God is that they have responded to the Gospel in faith, the very thing that Israel has failed to do. The current Gentile prominence in the church was made possible by the rejection of the Gospel on the part of the nation of Israel as a whole. Let Gentile Christians beware. Their predominance in the Christian community may not last!

"Kindness and sternness" (v.22) are aspects of the divine nature, the latter experienced by Israel in her present condition, the former being the portion of Gentile believers. But the positions can be reversed, and if this occurs, it will not be due to any fickleness in God, but to the nature of the human response. Once Israel's unbelief is put away, God is prepared to graft her branches in again (v.23).

Paul's concluding observation (v.24) has a double value. It helps to explain the curious circumstance that his illustration of the olive tree does not follow the pattern of grafting ordinarily found in the ancient Mediterranean world but is in fact the reverse of it. Paul grants that his allegory is "contrary to nature." Normally, a tame olive branch was grafted into the stem of a wild olive tree. Furthermore, one would not expect that the natural branches, after being broken off, will ever be grafted in again. Paul's argument is that if the hard thing, the thing contrary to nature—i.e., the grafting of wild branches into the cultivated olive—has been accomplished, one should not find it difficult to believe that God will restore the broken-off branches of the cultivated olive to their former position. Since in tree culture this would be impossible because of the deadness of the branches after they were removed, Paul is indeed talking "contrary to nature." But he rests his case not on nature but on God's being "able" to do it. With God nothing is impossible. The branches that will be grafted in are not of course identical with those that were broken off, but they are the same in two respects: their Israelite heritage and the attitude of unbelief they have maintained in the past. Then both Jews and Gentiles will share together the blessings of God's grace in Christ.

G. Israel's Future Salvation (11:25–32)

This is the crowning feature of the discussion, the outcome of everything that chs. 9–11 have been pointing to. The same mercy that has overtaken the Gentiles who were formerly disobedient will finally overtake the now disobedient Israel.

25 Now Paul speaks of a "mystery" (GK 3696), lest his readers imagine that either he or they are capable of understanding the course of Israel's history simply by observation and insight. The term "mystery" refers to the activity of God in salvation history, once hidden (16:25), but now made known to his people by revelation. The content of this mystery embraces Israel's present hardening—which is "in part" because the believing remnant constitutes an exception and because the hardening is limited in duration, lasting only "until the full number of the Gentiles has come in." But it also embraces the salvation of "all Israel" that follows.

26–27 The expression, "all Israel," when taken in the light of the context, is the climax of this entire section. It must be understood to mean the nation Israel as a whole, in contrast to the present situation when only a remnant has trusted Christ for salvation. The language does not require us to hold that when this final ingathering of Israel occurs, every living Israelite will be included, but only that Israel as a nation will be saved.

Not all interpreters agree, however, on this meaning of "all Israel." Some insist that it means the entire company of the redeemed, both Jew and Gentile. But "Israel" has not been used of Gentiles at all in these chapters, and it is doubtful that such is the case here. Paul has used "Israel" for the nation or the godly portion of it (cf. 9:6). To be sure, Gentiles are included in the seed of Abraham (4:11–12), and this concept is applicable to the church at the present time. But he is speaking here of something to be fulfilled in the future. Clearly "all Israel" stands over against "part" of Israel by way of contrast.

Does our passage throw light on the time when Israel's national conversion is to be expected? Not in terms of "that day or hour" (Mt 24:36), but rather in terms of the time when the full number of the Gentiles has come in (v.25). The "so" (v.26) is apparently intended to correlate with "until" (v.25), thereby acquiring temporal force, such as "when that has happened."

The declaration concerning the future of Israel is now confirmed by citing Isa 59:20–21 and 27:9. While there are problems of exact correspondence with these OT passages, Paul's use of them implies that Israel's conversion will occur at Messiah's return, when he will come out of Zion, i.e., from the heavenly Jerusalem (cf. Gal 4:26; Heb 12:22). It is hard to account for the wholesale conversion of Israel in any other way, since the activity of the Spirit of God has not produced any such mass movement of Israel during the course of this age. Paul possibly sensed a certain parallel between his own conversion and the future conversion of his people as a whole. Christ revealed himself to him directly, sweeping away his rationalizations and his self-righteousness; someday he will do the same for the nation.

The effect on Israel is not couched in terms of material prosperity or martial invincibility, but purely in spiritual terms, in the forsaking of godlessness and the removal of sins by the Lord God. The reference to covenant suggests that Jer 31:31–34 was also in Paul's mind.

28–29 Even though the condition of the Israelites is presently considered by God as those who are enemies for the sake of the Gentiles, yet all the time, when viewed from the standpoint of their national election, they are loved by God for the sake of the fathers (cf. v.16). God's promises are irrevocable, and time will prove it. "God's gifts" are doubtless the special privileges of Israel mentioned in 9:4–5. These bear witness to the reality of the calling—the summons of Israel to a unique place in the purpose of God.

30–32 God's purpose must be implemented if it is to be effective. His mercy is the needed factor. Paul is addressing his Gentile readers here. In fact, the "you" is emphatic, as though to remind Gentile believers (who might be prone to think it strange that God has a glorious future in store for Israel) that they themselves were formerly disobedient toward God. It was Jewish disobedience in regard to the Gospel that opened the gates of mercy for them.

Again, to warn the Gentiles against being inflated over their present position in grace, Paul reminds his readers (v.31) that it was the very mercy received by the Gentiles that made the Jews more firm in their disobedience. Yet God has not given up on his chosen people, but keeps in view his plan for their salvation and extends his mercy. The second "now" in v.31 is somewhat perplexing in the light of the eschatological emphasis in vv.26–27. It may refer to the present salvation of the remnant, or it may include the future along with the present and so anticipate the ultimate salvation of the nation. The conclusion of the whole matter is that God has magnified his mercy by the very fact of disobedience, binding all people over to it (cf. 3:9) that he might have mercy on all. So disobedience does not have the last word (cf. Gal 3:22).

H. Praise to God for His Wisdom and His Ways (11:33–36)

33–36 In view of the assurance generated by v.32, it is no wonder that Paul, despite his burden for the Israel of his day, is able to lift his heart in adoring praise to God. We are reminded of Isa 55, where the ungodly and sinful are urged to return to the Lord and find mercy, for God's thoughts and ways are not human but are infinitely higher and better. Instead of being vindictive, God is gracious. His plans defy the penetration of the human mind and his ways surpass the ability of any person to trace them out. The Lord has not been obliged to lean upon another person for advice (v.34). He has not had to depend on human assistance that would make him indebted to people (v.35). He is the source, the means, and the goal of all things (v.36).

While this exalted and moving ascription of praise has in view God's plans and operations in the history of salvation affecting both Jews and Gentiles, the closing verse applies also to the individual life that pleases God. For the life of every believer has its source in God, lives by his resources, and returns to him when its course has been run. To God be the glory!

VII. Our Spiritual Service: The Practice of Righteousness (12:1–15:13)

A distinct break in the train of thought occurs as Paul moves from 11:36 to 12:1. His theological exposition centering around the problem as to how sinful humanity can be put into a right relationship with God is over. But more must be said, because after we have been made right with our Maker, we need to know what difference this makes in our relations with other people, what God expects of us, and how we should apply our new resources to all the situations. This last main section of Romans is designed to meet these needs (cf. Eph 4:1). It is notable that the key word "righteousness," which until now has dominated the book, occurs only once in the closing chapters (14:17; see comment). Paul's exhortations include both commands and prohibitions and are spread over various areas of application: Christian conduct toward fellow believers, toward society (especially in meeting hostile reactions), and toward the state.

A. The Appeal for Dedication of the Believer (12:1–2)

This introductory portion is a prelude to the discussion of specific duties of believers. It sets forth the fundamental obligations we must meet before being prepared to face the challenge of living as believers in this world.

1 "Therefore" establishes a connection with the entire foregoing presentation in this letter. It particularly relates to 6:13, 19, as a comparison of the terminology will show. The apostle begins by urging his readers instead of simply instructing them ("urge" lies between commanding and beseeching). "Mercy" (GK 3880) denotes that quality in God that moved him to deliver sinners from their state of sin and misery and therefore underlies his saving activity in Christ. It serves here as the leverage for the appeal that follows. Whereas the heathen are prone to sacrifice in order to obtain mercy, biblical faith teaches that the divine mercy provides the basis for a life of sacrifice as the fitting response.

Since the milieu of thought is so similar to ch. 6, it is natural to conclude that "bodies" (GK 5393) here include both the person (the volition of the one making the dedication) and the bodily powers that are thus set apart for God's use. In Greek thought the body was considered the receptacle containing the soul, but this was not the Hebraic concept, which viewed the human being as a unit.

Thus Paul is not urging the dedication of the body as an entity distinct from the inner self; rather, he views the body as the vehicle that implements the desires and choices of the redeemed spirit. Through the body we serve God.

The words "offer" and "sacrifices" are cultic terms (cf. 15:16). Before a priest in Israel could minister on behalf of others, he had to present himself in a consecrated state and the sacrifices he offered were to be without blemish (Mal 1:8–13). "Holy" (GK 41) is a reminder of that necessity for the Christian, not in terms of rite or ritual but as renouncing the sins of the old life and being committed to a life of obedience to the divine will (cf. 6:19). The body is not evil in itself; if it were, God would not ask that it be offered to him. As an instrument, it is capable of expressing either sin or righteousness. If we do the latter, then we give an offering "pleasing to God." The word "living" may glance by way of contrast to the animal sacrifices of the OT, which, when offered, no longer possessed life. But it is also a reminder that spiritual life, received from God in the new birth, is the presupposition of a sacrifice acceptable to him. Christian sacrifice has in view a total life of service to God. In Israel the whole burnt offering ascended to God and could never be reclaimed. It belonged to God.

Next, the living sacrifice is equated with "spiritual worship." While the exact sense is difficult to determine, the main idea is that the sacrifice we render to God is intelligent and deliberate, in contrast to the sacrifices of the Jewish worship in which the animals had no part in determining what was to be done with them. "Worship" (GK 3301) is perhaps too narrow a translation, for in the strict sense worship is adoration of God, which does not fit well with the concept of "bodies." The term "service" (KJV) has an advantage, since it covers the entire range of a Christian's life and activity (cf. Dt 10:12). Serving God is the proper sequel to worship.

2 The dedicated life is also the transformed life. Whereas v.1 called for a decisive commitment, v.2 deals with the maintenance of that commitment. We must be continually vigilant lest our original decision to serve God is vitiated or weakened. The threat comes from "this world" (GK 172), whose ways and thoughts can so easily impinge on the child of

God. Believers have been delivered from this present evil age (Gal 1:4), which has Satan for its god (2Co 4:4), and they live by the powers of the age to come (Heb 6:5). But their heavenly calling includes residence in this world, among sinful people, where they must show forth the praises of him who called them out of darkness into God's marvelous light (1Pe 2:9). They are in the world for witness, not for conformity to that which is a passing phenomenon (1Co 7:31).

Complementary to the refusal to be conformed to the pattern of this world is the command to be "transformed" (GK *3565*). These two processes of renunciation and renewal are going on all the time. Our pattern is Christ, who refused Satan's solicitations in his temptation and was transfigured in his acceptance of the path that led to Calvary (Mk 9:2–3). As his mission could be summarized in the affirmation that he had come to do the Father's will (Jn 6:38), so the Christian's service can be reduced to this simple description. But we must "test and approve," refusing the norms of conduct employed by the sinful world and reaffirming for ourselves spiritual norms befitting the redeemed. Aiding this process is "the renewing of your mind"; i.e., believers must keep going back in their thoughts to their original commitment and reaffirm its necessity and legitimacy in the light of God's grace extended to them. In this activity the working of the Holy Spirit is important (cf. Tit 3:5). Believers are not viewed as ignorant of God's will, but as needing to avoid blurring its outline by failure to renew the mind continually (cf. Eph 5:8–10). Dedication leads to discernment and discernment to delight in God's will. An intimate connection between certifying the will of God and making oneself a living sacrifice is demonstrated by the use of "pleasing" in each case (cf. Php 4:18; Heb 13:16).

B. Varied Ministries in the Church, the Body of Christ (12:3–8)

3 The will of God (v.2) is identical for all believers in respect to holiness of life and completeness of dedication. But what that will involves for each one with respect to special service in the church may be considerably diverse. Since God also calls for individual application in a Christian's life, the apostle must remind his readers of his authority to expound this subject even though he is unknown to most of them and their gifts are unknown to him (cf. 1:5; Gal 2:9; Eph 3:7). But this reminder is not intended to erect a barrier between himself and them, because what he has by way of authority and teaching ability is traced to divine grace, the same grace that has bestowed spiritual gifts on them.

In addressing himself deliberately to "every one of you," Paul grants that every believer has some spiritual gift (cf. v.6; 1Pe 4:10). But his primary goal in getting their attention in this regard is to drive home the necessity of appropriating and using their gifts with utmost humility. After all, God did not have to spread his gifts around so lavishly. Paul recognizes the danger that the possession of a particular gift can easily result in pride (v.3; cf. his experience with the Corinthian church, 1Co 12:14–31; 13:4; 14:12, 20). He equates humility with "sober judgment," in contrast to thinking of oneself more highly than one should (cf. also v.16). Obviously, there is less danger of a person's depreciating himself than of exaggerating one's own importance.

Is there some gauge that will enable a person to estimate his or her position with respect to spiritual gifts? Paul answers in the affirmative, pointing to "the measure of faith." "Faith" (GK *4411*) here, as elsewhere in Paul, is that which a Christian exercises; it is subjective rather than objective. One's faith should provide the basis for a true estimation of oneself, since it reveals that each believer is dependent on the saving mercy of God. That, in turn, ought to induce humility.

4–5 To offset the danger of individualistic thinking with its resulting danger of pride, Paul refers to the human body—an illustration familiar from his earlier use of it in 1Co 12:12ff. Three truths are set forth: the unity of the body; the diversity of its members, with corresponding diversity in function; and the mutuality of the various members—"each member belongs to all the others." The third item calls attention to the need of the various parts of the body for each other. None can work independently. Furthermore, each member profits from what the other members contribute to the whole. Reflection on these truths reduces preoccupation with one's own gift and makes room for appreciation of other people and their gifts.

Personal Gifts of the Holy Spirit

Gift	Definition	General References	Specific Examples
Message of wisdom	An utterance from the Holy Spirit applying God's Word or wisdom to a specific situation	Ac 6:3; 1Co 12:8; 13:2, 9, 12	Stephen: Ac 6:10 James: Ac 15:13–21
Message of knowledge	An utterance from the Holy Spirit revealing knowledge about people, circumstances or Biblical truth	Ac 10:47-48; 13:2; 15:7–11; 1Co 12:8; 13:2, 9, 12; 14:25	Peter: Ac 5:9–10
Faith	Supernatural faith imparted by the Holy Spirit, enabling a Christian to believe God for the miraculous	Mt 21:21–22; Mk 9:23–24; 11:22–24; Lk 17:6; Ac 3:1–8; 6:5–8; 1Co 12:9; 13:2; Jas 5:14–15	A centurion: Mt 8:5–10 A sick woman: Mt 9:20–22 Two blind men: Mt 9:27–29 A Canaanite woman: Mt 15:22–28 A sinful woman: Lk 9:36–50 A leper: Lk 17:11–19
Healing and miraculous powers	Restoring someone to physical health or altering the course of nature by divinely supernatural means	Mt 4:23–24; 8:16; 9:35; 10:1, 8; Mk 1:32–34; 6:13; 16:18; Lk 4:40–41; 9:1–2; Jn 6:2; 14:12; Ac 4:30; 5:15–16; 19:11–12; Ro 15:19; 1Co 12:9, 28, 30; 2 Co 12:12; Gal 3:5	Jesus: see chart on THE MIRACLES OF JESUS Apostles: see chart on THE MIRACLES OF THE APOSTLES
Prophecy	A special temporary ability to bring a word, warning, exhortation or revelation from God under the impulse of the Holy Spirit	Lk 12:12; Ac 2:17–18; 1Co 12:10; 13:9; 14:1–33; Eph 4:11; 1Th 5:20–21; 2Pe 1:20–21; 1Jn 4:1–3	Elizabeth: Lk 1:40–45 Mary: Lk 1:46–55 Zechariah: Lk 1:67–79 Peter: Ac 2:14–40; 4:8–12 Twelve men from Ephesus: Ac 19:6 Four daughters of Philip: Ac 21:9 Agabus: Ac 11:27–28; 21:10–11
Distinguishing between spirits	Special ability to judge whether prophecies and utterances are from the Holy Spirit	1Co 12:10; 14:29	Peter: Ac 8:18–24 Paul: Ac 13:8–12; 16:16–18
Speaking in tongues	Expressing oneself at the level of one's spirit under the direct influence of the Holy Spirit in a language he or she has not learned and does not know	1Co 12:10, 28, 30; 13:1; 14:1–40	Disciples: Ac 2:4–11 Cornelius and his family: Ac 10:44–45; 11:17 Ephesian believers: Ac 19:2–7 Paul: 1Co 14:6, 15, 18
Interpretation of tongues	Special ability to interpret what is spoken in tongues	1Co 12:10, 30; 14:5, 13, 26–28	

6–8 "We have different gifts [GK 5922]." Paul is not referring to gifts in the natural realm, but to those functions made possible by a specific enablement of the Holy Spirit granted to believers (though, of course, such a gift may build on one's natural gift). The variety in gifts should be understood from the standpoint of the needs of the Christian community, which are many, as well as from the desirability of giving every believer a share in ministry. With his eye still on the danger of pride, Paul reminds his readers that these new capacities for service are not native to those who exercise them but come from divine grace (cf. also 1Co 12:6; Eph 4:7; 1Pe 4:10).

Although Paul has spoken of different gifts, he does not proceed to give an exhaustive list (cf. 1Co 12:27–28). Rather, he emphasizes the need for exercising the gifts and for exercising them in the right way—"in proportion to [one's] faith." He uses this specific expression only in connection with prophesying, but there is no reason to suppose it is not intended to apply to the other items as well. What is meant by this phrase (v.6)? The most satisfactory explanation is that "faith" retains the subjective force it has in v.3 and that the whole phrase has the same thrust as "measure of faith" there. A prophet is not to be governed by emotions (1Co 14:32) or by love of speaking (1Co 14:30) but by dependence on the Spirit of God.

Paul does not define "prophesying" (GK 4735) here, but if we are to judge from the earlier reference to it in 1Co 14:3, 31, the nature of that gift is primarily the communication of revealed truth that both convicts and builds up the hearers. This gift is prominent in the other listings of gifts (1Co 12:28; Eph 4.11), where prophets are second only to apostles. That Paul says nothing of apostles in this passage may be a hint that no apostle, Peter included, had anything to do with the founding of the Roman church.

"Serving" is a broad term. The Greek word *diakonia* (GK 1355) is sometimes used of the ministry of the word to unbelievers (Ac 6:4; 2Co 5:18), but the gifts in this passage seem intentionally restricted in their exercise in the body of Christ. Despite its place between prophesying and teaching, the narrower meaning of service as ministration to the material needs of believers is probable here (such as that provided by deacons). It may be compared to the gift of "those able to help others" (1Co 12:28).

The gift of "teaching" (Gk *1436*) is mentioned next. It differs from prophesying in that it was not characterized by ecstatic utterance as the vehicle for revelation given by the Spirit (cf. 1Co 14:6, where it is paired with knowledge). Probably the aim in teaching was to give help in the area of Christian living rather than formal instruction in doctrine, even though it must be granted that the latter is needed as a foundation for the former. Paul himself gives a notable example of teaching in vv.9–21. His considerable use of the OT in this section suggests that early Christian teachers were largely dependent on it for their instruction.

"Encouraging" (*paraklesis*; GK 4155) has a variety of meanings; only the context can indicate whether to render it "encouragement" (Ac 15:31), "exhortation" (1Ti 4:13), or "comfort." Assuredly some encouragement could be included, but exhortation seems to be the dominant meaning here.

"Contributing to the needs of others" has to do with spontaneous private benevolence (cf. 1Jn 3:17–18). This is not intended as a repetition of serving (v.7), thus favoring the view that the latter activity belongs to the public distribution of aid by the church to its needy. The only doubt concerning this interpretation resides in the word "generously," which KJV rightly translates as "simplicity" (i.e., with singleness of heart, free of mixed motives). That wrong motivation can enter into giving is shown by the account of the sin of Ananias and Sapphira in Ac 5.

"Leadership" (GK *4613*) translates a word that means to stand before others, so the idea of governing derives readily from it (cf. 1Th 5:12; 1Ti 3:4–5; 5:17). This gift should be carried out "diligently." Even in church life some people are tempted to enjoy the office rather than use it as an avenue for service.

"Showing mercy" (GK *1796*) does not pertain to the area of forgiveness or sparing judgment. Rather, it has to do with ministering to the sick and needy. This is to be done in a cheerful, spontaneous manner that convey blessing rather than engender self-pity.

C. Principles Governing Christian Conduct (12:9–21)

Paul presupposes the dedicated life, which enables one to discover and demonstrate the will of God. Relationship to fellow Christians is treated first (vv.9–13), then the stance to be assumed toward those who are outside the church (vv.14–21).

9–10 "Love" (GK 27) is primary, but if it is not sincere, it is not real love but only pretense. In 1 Corinthians Paul paused in his discussion of spiritual gifts to inject a chapter on love (1Co 13); thus it is fitting that he should follow his presentation of spiritual gifts here in Romans with the same emphasis. The whole conduct of believers should be bathed in love. Failure to love our fellow Christians casts doubt on our professed love for God (1Jn 4:19–21).

Love readily suggests purity. The two are found together in God, who is of too pure eyes to behold evil (Hab 1:13) and cannot be tempted by it (Jas 1:13). Hatred of evil therefore readily follows love. To "cling to what is good" (v.9) is to be wedded to it. Total commitment leaves neither time nor inclination to court evil.

In v.10, the apostle puts love in a living context. It must be shown to people, not lavished on a principle. He uses a special term here denoting "brotherly love" (GK 5789). "Devoted" is appropriate, since it customarily denotes the family tie. Believers are members of the family of God.

"Honor one another above yourselves" (v.10). To "honor" (GK 5507) is to accord recognition and show appreciation. This is based not on some personal attractiveness or usefulness but rather on the fact that every Christian has Christ in the heart and can express him through one's own individuality. We honor God when we recognize his transforming work in our lives. If the according of such honor seems to diminish the recognition of what God has done in our own lives, the problem is readily solved by the example of the Son's exalting of God the Father despite the Son's equality with him (Jn 10:30; Php 2:4–6).

11–12 Paul now momentarily directs our attention to the Lord and our service to him before returning to the horizontal relationship within the body of Christ (v.13). After converts have experienced the initial glow and ardor of Christian life there is often danger of slipping back into a deadening spiritual inertia. To counter this, the apostle urges diligent endeavor fed by fervency of spirit. The lack of such fire brought down a rebuke from the Lord on the Laodicean church (Rev 3:15–16). The Lord calls us to serve him with our best. Such service arouses hope in us, tinged with joy, of seeing Jesus in his glory and of being united with him (1Pe 1:7–8). This hope sustains us as his servants, enabling us to be "patient in affliction" (cf. 5:3–4). At this point, Paul's mention of prayer is natural, since it is our great resource when we are under stress and strain.

13 Even under persecution we should not allow ourselves to be so preoccupied with our own troubles that we become insensitive to the needs of other believers. To share our earthly goods with others is never more meaningful than when people are hard pressed to find sufficient supplies for themselves. When this sharing takes place under one's own roof, it is labeled "hospitality" (lit., "love for strangers"; GK 5810). The word "practice" is strong (lit., "pursue"; GK 1503), calling for an undiminished ardor in extending this courtesy to traveling believers. The Lord had encouraged his disciples to depend on such kindness during their mission (Mt 10:11). Without hospitality, the spread of the Gospel during the days of the early church would have been greatly impeded. With it, the "church in the house" became a reality (16:23; cf.16:5). What sanctified this practice above all was the realization that in receiving and entertaining travelers, those who opened their doors and their hearts were receiving and entertaining Christ (Mt 10:40; 25:40).

14–16 The material in these verses seems to describe a Christian's relations to one's neighbors and friends (including believers), preceded by one reference to their opponents (v.14, anticipating vv.17ff.).

Paul's injunction to bless persecutors rather than curse them undoubtedly goes back to our Lord's teaching (Mt 5:44; Lk 6:28). The teaching was incarnated in the Savior himself and became clearly manifested during his trial and his suffering on the cross. Persecution can take various forms, stretching from verbal abuse and social ostracism to the use of violence resulting in death. Some form of persecution was so common in the experience of the early church that Paul can assume as a matter of course that his readers will suffer it. If such treatment is not encountered in our society, we can at least cultivate the readiness to meet it and so fulfill the injunction in spirit. To bless one's persecutors involves praying for their forgiveness and for a change of outlook regarding the Christian faith. It can be done only by the grace of Christ.

One charge follows another without any apparent connection as Paul calls on his readers to share one another's joys and sorrows (v.15; cf. 1Co 12:26). It has often been noted that it is easier to fulfill the second half of this command than the first, because our natural inclination is to feel genuine sympathy for those in sorrow, but to share their joy may present difficulty if another's achievement or good fortune is viewed with envy. In general, people have less need for fellowship in times of joy than in times of grief, for if loneliness is added to sorrow, the trial is compounded.

Living "in harmony with one another" (v.16; cf. Php 2:2) dispels discord in the church. As a means to attaining this harmony, Paul stresses the necessity of rejecting the temptation to think superior thoughts about oneself and of coming down off the perch of isolation and mingling with people "of low position" or of a humble frame of mind. And lest one consent to do this while still retaining heady notions of one's own superiority, Paul puts in a final thrust: "Don't be conceited" (v.16). Conceit has no place in the life ruled by love (1Co 13:4).

17–21 Paul takes his stand alongside believers by giving them explicit counsel about how to face the hostile world. "Do not repay evil for evil" (v.17), for to do so would be to follow the inclination of the sinful human nature. The remainder of v.17 means that believers are constantly under the scrutiny of unsaved people as well as of fellow Christians, and they must be careful that their conduct does not betray the high standards of the Gospel (cf. Col 4:5; 1Ti 3:7). Each situation that holds prospect for a witness to the world should be weighed so that the action taken will not bring unfavorable reflection on the Gospel.

The charge to "live at peace with everyone" is hedged about with two qualifying statements. "If it be possible" suggests that there are instances in human relations when the strongest desire for concord will not avail. If disharmony and conflict should come, however, we should accept the responsibility for resolving it. Believers may not be able to persuade the other party, but they can at least refuse to be the instigator of trouble. God wants us to be peacemakers (Mt 5:9).

This peace-loving attitude may be costly, however, because some will want to take advantage of it, figuring that Christian principles will not permit the wronged party to retaliate. In such a case, what is to be done? The path of duty is clear: We are not to take vengeance, for vengeance trespasses on the province of God, the great Judge of all. We must "leave room for God's wrath" (v.19), trusting that he will take care of the situation. He will not be too lenient or too severe. Here Paul quotes Dt 32:35, whose context indicates that the Lord will intervene to vindicate his people when their enemies abuse them and gloat over them.

Paul does not suggest that God's wrath will be visited on the wrongdoer immediately. On the contrary, the hope is that those who have perpetrated the wrong will have a change of heart, will be convicted of their sin, and will be won over by the refusal of the Christian to retaliate (v.20). Here again Paul lets the OT speak for him (Pr 25:21–22). "Burning coals" are best understood as the burning pangs of shame and guilt. There is, of course, no definite promise at this point that offenders will be converted. By going the second mile and showing unexpected kindness, believers may also spare their companions from having the same experience. In that measure, society has benefited.

Guidance on the problem of coping with evil reaches its climax in the final admonition: "Do not be overcome by evil, but overcome evil with good" (v.21). Being overcome by evil means to give in to the temptation to meet evil with evil, to retaliate. To overcome evil with good has been illustrated in v.20. The world's philosophy leads people to expect retaliation when they have wronged another. To receive kindness, to see love when it seems uncalled for, can melt the hardest heart.

D. The Duty of Submission to Civil Authority (13:1–7)

This is the most notable passage in the NT on Christian civic responsibility. It probably reflects the famous saying of Jesus: "Give to Caesar what is Caesar's, and to God what is

God's" (Mt 22:21). That Paul lived in conformity with his own teaching is apparent from his relation to various rulers as recorded in Acts. Because he realized that this subject had a definite bearing on the spread of the Gospel (cf. 1Ti 2:1–7), he saw its relevance to the theme of salvation and included it here in Romans. These verses are an expansion and special application of the teaching about good and evil (12:17, 21) and living "at peace with everyone" (12:18). The word "wrath" (GK 3973) in 12:19 seems to anticipate the same Greek word in 13:5 (translated "punishment" in NIV).

More important, however, is the broader connection in terms of thought. (1) There is the natural connection with 12:1–2, where the foundation is laid for Christian service in its various ramifications. The believer's relation to the state is one of those areas. (2) Another possible connection is with chs. 9–11; Paul may be intent on warning the Roman church, which contained some Christian Jews as well as Gentile believers who sympathized with them over the plight of their nation, not to identify with any revolutionary movement advocating rebellion against Rome. As is well known, Jews had been expelled from Rome by Claudius (see comment on Ac 18:2), and it is possible that the Jews who later returned to Rome (including some Christian Jews) were hostile toward the state because of the way Claudius had treated them. These needed to be mollified.

1 The teaching in this section is addressed to "everyone," i.e., every believer. What Paul requires is to "submit" (GK 5718) to those who ruled from Rome. Submission means placing oneself under someone else. Paul seems to avoid using the stronger word "obey" (cf. also v.5), probably because believers may find it impossible to comply with every demand of the government. A circumstance may arise in which they must choose between obeying God and obeying people (Ac 5:29). But even then they must be submissive in that, if their Christian convictions do not permit their compliance, they will accept the consequences of such refusal.

Paul makes a sweeping statement when he says, "There is no authority except that which God has established." This is true even of Satan: what authority he exercises has been given him by God (cf. Lk 4:6). The name of Christ does not appear anywhere in the passage, probably because Paul's concern is not with redemption or the life of the church as such, but with one's relation to the state. While Christians have citizenship in heaven (Php 3:20), they are not excused from responsibility to acknowledge the state as possessing authority from God to govern them. They hold a dual citizenship.

2 Those who refuse submission are rebelling against what God has ordained. While it is true that "the world" can be set over against God (1Jn 2:16), this cannot be said of the state, despite the fact that individual governments may at times be anti-God in their stance. Those who rebel "will bring judgment on themselves." This judgment refers to that which is administered through human channels and in the sphere of human affairs (cf. Jesus' words in Mt 26:52). For example, the Jewish revolt against Rome that began within a decade after Paul wrote led to the sack of Jerusalem and the dispersion of the nation.

3–4 These verses constitute the most difficult portion of the passage, for they seem to take no account of the possibility that government may be tyrannical and may reward evil and suppress good. A few years after Paul wrote these words, Nero launched a persecution against the church at Rome; multitudes lost their lives, and not because of doing evil. Later emperors also lashed out against Christians. It should be noted, however, that the empire did not persecute Christians for their good works or even for their faith, but rather because they felt the Christians' refusal to honor Roman gods threatened stability in the empire.

There are two ways to deal with this problem. (1) Paul is presenting the norm here, i.e., the ideal for government, which is certainly that of punishing evil and rewarding or encouraging good. If this is the correct interpretation, then we can understand why Paul warns against rebellion and makes no allowance for revolutionary activity. This interpretation does allow for revolution in cases where rights are denied and liberties taken away, since the state has ceased to fulfill its God-appointed function. At the very least, when justice collapses, the Christian community is obliged to voice its criticism of the state's failure and deviation from the divinely ordained pattern. (2) The other possibility is to introduce the principle of 8:28, whereby God finds ways to bring good out of apparent evil, so that even in the event that the state should turn against the people of God in a way that could rightly be termed evil, he will bring good out of it in the long run.

Paul terms the state "God's servant [GK 1356]" to extend commendation to the one who does good and, conversely, to punish the wrongdoer. This implies considerable knowledge on the part of the governing authority as to the nature of right and wrong, a knowledge not dependent on awareness of the teaching of Scripture but granted to human beings in general as rational creatures (cf. 2:14–15). While "God's servant" is an honorable title, it contains a reminder that the state is not God and that its function is to administer justice for him in areas where it is competent to do so. The state must not be thought of as infallible in its decisions. Yet this does not entitle persons to flout the state's authority when decisions are not to their liking.

The warning to believers to avoid evil carries with it the admonition that if this warning is neglected, "fear" will be in order because the authority has the power to use the sword. This warning relates to public acts that threaten the well-being and security of the state, not to individual crimes that might warrant capital punishment. That is, Paul is warning believers against becoming involved in activity that could be construed by the Roman government as encouraging revolution or injury to the state. To engage in subversive activity invites speedy retribution.

5 In bringing this portion of the discussion to a close, Paul advances two reasons why Christians must submit to the state. One is the threat of punishment if one does not put oneself in subjection. Paul appeals here to personal advantage, to the instinct of self-preservation. To defy the state could mean death. The other reason is "conscience" (GK 5287), which is more difficult to determine. Most likely this word denotes a personal awareness that the ultimate foundation of all of life is God. In other words, Christians, by virtue of divine revelation, can have a clearer understanding of the position of the governing authority than an official of the government is likely to have (cf. 1Pe 2:19). Let that knowledge guide them in their attitudes and decisions.

6–7 Building on his allusion to conscience, the apostle explains the payment of taxes. The more clearly a person recognizes that the governing authority is God's servant, the greater appears the reasonableness of providing support by taxes. While the person in authority may be unworthy, the institution is not; and without financial undergirding, government cannot function. For the third time Paul speaks of rulers as God's servants, but this time he uses a different word, one that means workers for the people or public ministers. Their work is carried on under God's scrutiny and fulfills his will. These public servants give full time to governing; therefore they have no time to earn a living by other means (cf. Lk 10:7).

There is deliberate repetition in the sense that the paying of taxes is assumed (v.6), then enjoined (v.7). But the word Paul uses in v.7 literally means "give back" (GK 625; the same word Jesus used in Mk 12:17), suggesting that what is paid to the government in the form of taxes presupposes value received.

The various items mentioned in v.7 are all classified as obligations. Since the Christian ethic demands clearing whatever one owes another (cf. v.8), no basis is left for debate. The very language that is used supports the imperative form of the communication. The word "taxes" means tribute paid to a foreign ruler. "Revenue" pertains to indirect taxation in the form of toll or customs duties. "Respect" refers either to that which one gives to God (cf. "fear" in 1Pe 2:17) or to the veneration that is due to the highest persons in the government. "Honor" is the respect due any who hold a public office.

E. The Comprehensive Obligation of Love (13:8–10)

Although Paul has previously put in an urgent call for love (12:9–10), he now returns to this theme, knowing that he cannot stress too much this essential ingredient of all Christian service. The connection of the present paragraph with the foregoing section is his use of the word "debt" (GK 4053), which comes from the same root as "owe" (GK 4051) in v.7. Christians owe submission and honor to the civil authorities, but they owe all people much more.

8 "Let no debt remain outstanding." While it is appropriate for a believer to incur debt, to be perpetually in debt is not a good testimony, and to refuse to make good one's obligations is outrageous. But there is an exception to the rule: the "continuing debt to love one another." One can never say that he or she has completely discharged it. Paul has in mind here love for all other people; its sweep is universal (cf. also Gal 6:10; 1Th 3:12).

In saying that the one who loves has fulfilled the law, Paul presents a truth that parallels his statement in 8:4 about the righteous requirement of the law being fulfilled in those who live in accordance with the Spirit. The connecting link between these two passages is provided by Gal 5:22–23, where first place in the enumeration of the fruit of the Spirit is given to love and the list is followed by the observation that against such fruit there is no law. So the Spirit produces in believers a love to which the law can offer no objection, since love fulfills what the law requires.

9 When we want to know what the law of love requires, we naturally think of those precepts that pertain to human relationships, since love for one's neighbor is at issue, not love for God. Consequently, Paul lifts from the second tablet of the law certain precepts that call for the preservation of the sacredness of the family, the holding of human life inviolable, and the recognition of property rights, concluding with the key item that is involved in the other three, the control of one's desires (cf. 7:7). These and other demands of the law are summed up in the positive command, "Love your neighbor as yourself."

Once again Paul follows the Lord Jesus in summarizing the horizontal bearing of the law with Lev 19:18 (Mt 22:39). Jesus rebuked the narrow nationalistic interpretation of the word "neighbor" (GK *4446*) in the parable of the good Samaritan. This word in Greek is derived from "one who is near." Both the priest and the Levite found their nearness to the stricken man a source of embarrassment (Lk 10:31–32), but the Samaritan saw in that same circumstance an opportunity to help a fellow human being. In the light of human need, the barrier between Jew and Samaritan dissolved. Love provides its own imperative.

10 "Love does no harm to its neighbor." This is an understatement, for love does positive good. But the negative form is suitable here, because it is intended to fit in with the prohibitions from the law (v.9). By concluding with the observation that love is the fulfillment of the law, Paul returns to the same thought he began with (v.8).

What, then, is the relationship between love and law? In Christ the two concepts that seem to have so little in common come together. To love others with the love that Christ exhibited is his new commandment (Jn 13:34). And if this love is present, it will make possible the keeping of all his other commandments (Jn 14:15). Love promotes obedience, and the two together constitute the law of Christ (Gal 6:2).

F. The Purifying Power of Hope (13:11–14)

Though this passage contains no explicit mention of either hope or love, both are surely involved. Paul is loath to let go of the theme of love. So, with a final word about it, "And do this," he is ready to plunge into a delineation of the critical nature of the time that intervenes before the Lord's return. It is as though he is saying, "Show love while you can, and meanwhile keep girded with hope and sobriety for the consummation." While love identifies Christians with others in their need, hope puts a gulf between them and the world. They refuse to be conformed to an age that is satisfied with earthly things (cf. Php 3:18–21). Paul summons us to self-discipline rather than profligate living.

11 Paul sounds a call for alertness. The era between the Christ's first and second coming is critical, because the promise of his return hovers over believers. They must not be lulled to sleep by indulgence in pleasure or be influenced by the specious word of those who suggest that the Lord delays his coming or may not return at all. Paul does not know how near the day of the Lord's appearing is, but he is content to advance the reminder that "our salvation is nearer now than when we first believed." To be sure, salvation is already both an achieved fact for the believer (Eph 2:8) and a continuing fact (1Co 15:2; 1Pe 1:5), but it has also its future and final phase (cf. Php 3:20; 1Pe 1:9). Only at the return of the Savior will our salvation be complete. Believers are not like a child looking for a clock to strike the hour because something is due to happen then. They are content to know that with every passing moment the end is that much closer to realization.

12–13 Paul's line of thought here resembles 1Th 5:1–11. Even as darkness is symbolic of evil and sin, light fittingly depicts those who have passed through the experience of salvation. Paul pictures Christians as those who anticipate the day by rising early. The night clothes are the works of darkness, the deeds that belong to the old life. The garments to which they transfer, however, are unusual. They are likened to armor as in 1Th 5:8. To walk through this world as children of light involves a warfare with the powers of darkness (cf. Eph 6:12–13). Even though the final day has not yet arrived, believers belong to the day (1Th 5:8), anticipating the glory that will then be revealed (2Co 3:18; 4:4).

This forms the basis for the plea, "Let us behave decently, as in the daytime." Christians must live as though that final day had actually arrived, bringing with it the personal presence of Christ. There should be no place for the type of conduct that characterizes unsaved people, especially in the night seasons. Paul describes this manner of life in three couplets, the first on intemperance, the second on sexual misconduct, and the third on contention and quarreling. Here we learn the double lesson that one sin leads to another and that committing the sin does not bring inner rest but rather dissatisfaction that betrays itself by finding fault with others.

14 In conclusion, the apostle returns to his figure of putting on clothing (cf. v.12), but now the garment is personalized: they must put on the Lord Jesus Christ. They must consciously accept the lordship of the Master. But how can Paul say this when believers have already put on Christ at conversion and baptism (Gal 3:27)? There is always room for decisive renewal, for fresh advance.

Paul allows no room for a spirit of complacency, as though a life of godliness automatically follows faith. The redeemed must always be attuned to the Savior. They must exercise ceaseless vigilance lest the flesh prevail. They must not give thought to how the desires of the old nature can be satisfied (cf. ch. 6). Union with Christ must be accompanied by a constant reckoning of oneself as dead to sin and alive to God and his holy will.

G. Questions of Conscience Wherein Christians Differ (14:1–15:13)

It is uncertain to what extent Paul possessed definite information about the internal affairs of the Roman church. Consequently, it is difficult to know whether his approach to the problem of the "weak" (GK *820* & *822*) and the "strong" (GK *1543*) is dictated by awareness of the precise nature of the problem in Rome or whether he is writing out of his own experience with other churches, especially the Corinthian congregation (1Co 8:1–11:1). There definitely are similarities, such as the danger that by their conduct the strong will cause the weak to stumble, and the corresponding danger that the weak will sit in judgment on the strong. But the differences are numerous: the treatment in Romans is briefer and couched in more general terms; there is no mention in Romans of idols or food offered to idols; the word "conscience" does not appear; the strong are not described as those who have knowledge. On the other hand, 1 Corinthians does not refer to vegetarians or to those who insist on observing a certain day in contrast to others who look on all days as being alike.

The weaker brethren at Rome should probably be identified with the Jewish element in the church, those who had avoided certain foods because of the dietary laws of the OT. Information may have reached Paul that with the return of Jewish Christians to Rome after the death of Emperor Claudius in A.D. 54, tension had developed in the church with the Gentile element that had been able to enjoy freedom for several years without challenge.

Judging from his discussion in 1 Corinthians, Paul would place himself among the strong. Yet he was careful not to become an occasion of stumbling to a weaker brother. He had words of warning and words of encouragement to both groups. His primary concern was to promote unity in the church (15:5).

1. Brethren must refrain from judging one another (14:1–12)

1–4 The word "eat" characterizes this section. Diet practices differ, and these differences can easily become a basis of disagreement. Paul terms overscrupulous believers as those who are "weak in faith," meaning that the faith of such persons is not strong enough to enable them to perceive the full liberty they have in Christ. They are plagued by doubt as to whether it is right for them to eat certain foods (cf. v.23). The injunction to those who do not share this weakness is to "accept" them warmly (v.1) and not to pass judgment on them. Weak Christians must not be made to feel inferior or unwanted.

The specialized use of "faith" (GK *4411*) becomes clearer when Paul gives it a definite context (v.2). One person, obviously strong in faith, feels he can eat anything. Paul would concur that he has this freedom (1Ti 4:3–4). Another person, weak in his faith, confines his diet to vegetables. The motive for doing so is a personal matter, and for that reason Paul does not make it an issue. He is solely concerned with specific practice and the reaction of the strong to this practice. The omnivorous man is apt to "look down" on the weak brother, an attitude that is not conducive to full fellowship. The weak brother may retaliate by condemning the one who has no inhibitions about his food. If so, the latter needs to reflect on the fact that God has accepted this man (v.3), so why should he himself not do so?

To reinforce the rebuke, Paul cites the relationship of a servant to his master (v.4). In ordinary life, it would be unseemly for anyone to attempt to interfere in a case involving the servant's actions. Thus the strong certainly may enjoy their freedom in Christ. This assurance is grounded not so much on the discretion of the strong as on the power of Christ to sustain him.

5–8 Here the recurring phrase is "to the Lord," indicating that whether one be thought of as "weak" or "strong," the important thing is that each one conduct his or her life in the consciousness of God's presence, because God's approval is more significant than the approval or disapproval of fellow Christians. Eating is still in view, but alongside it Paul places a second topic—the holding of certain days as sacred.

Does this refer to Sabbath observance or to special days for feasting or fasting? The answer is not easily determined. Since the early church in Jerusalem almost certainly observed the Sabbath and did not want to offend non-Christian Jews, and since the Roman church presumably had a good-sized minority of Jews, it is not impossible that Paul has the Sabbath in mind. But the close contextual association with eating suggests that Paul has in mind a special day set apart for observance as a time for feasting or for fasting. The important thing is that one should "be fully convinced in his own mind" as to the rightfulness of his observance. More important still is the certitude of the individuals involved that their motivation is their desire to honor the Lord in what they are doing. It is possible for the observant and the nonobservant to do this, as illustrated by the giving of thanks at mealtime (cf. 1Ti 4:5). The one partaking can give thanks for the meat before him, while the one abstaining from meat can give God thanks for his vegetables. The latter should be able to do this without resentment toward his brother who enjoys richer fare.

In vv.7–8 Paul is not expressing a maxim applicable to all people; rather, he is speaking of believers. Christians do not live to themselves because they live to the Lord. This attachment, which is also an obligation, does not cease with death but carries forward into the next life (Php 1:20). Paul has already affirmed that death cannot separate Christians from the love of God in Christ (8:38–39; cf. 2Co 5:9). Their death is to be viewed as an enlarged opportunity to show forth the praises of the Lord. Relationship to him is the key to life on either side of the grave.

9–12 Both groups will have to answer to God in the coming day. It is premature to pass judgment on one another (cf. 1Co 4:5), since Christ will assume that responsibility. He gave his life, laying it down in obedience to the will of God and thereby purchasing the church by his blood (Ac 20:28). But he is also "Lord" by virtue of his resurrection, an event that established his claim to deity, to Saviorhood, and to universal dominion. He is in fact the Lord of both the dead and the living.

Against this background the apostle returns in v.10 to direct address, first to the weak brother, then to the strong. The former is prone to judge, the latter to depreciate or even scorn. Both attitudes are virtually the same, because they involve improper judgment. The true judge is God, and his time for judging is coming, making human judgment not only premature but also a usurpation of

God's role. Notable is the ease with which Paul passes from the Lord (v.9) to God (v.10). The two are inseparable in their operations. In fact, God's judgment seat (v.10) can be identified with the judgment seat of Christ (2Co 5:10). The same phenomenon occurs in the quotation in v.11, which combines Isa 49:18 and 45:23 (cf. Php 2:10–11). In Paul's summary of the situation in v.12, the note of judgment is retained, but the emphasis falls on the fact that each person must give a personal account of himself or herself to God (cf. Gal 6:5).

2. Brethren must avoid offending one another (14:13–23)

Paul's appeal in this section for the most part is directed to strong Christians, who are warned that their example may have a disastrous effect on those who are weak by leading them to do what their spiritual development disapproves of. The discussion proceeds along the same line as before—what Christians should include in their diet.

13–15 The opening statement gives the gist of what has been already said. Both parties have been guilty of passing judgment on one another. Then, by a neat use of language, Paul employs the same verb "judge" (GK *3212*) in a somewhat different sense ("make up your mind"). He calls for a course of action that will not hurt fellow believers, a decision once for all to avoid whatever might impede anyone's progress in the faith or cause another person to fall. Strong believers must not put a "stumbling block" in the way of the weak. A "stumbling block" (GK *4682*) is literally something against which one may strike one's foot, causing that person to stumble or even fall. An "obstacle" (GK *4998*) presents the picture of a trap designed to ensnare a victim (cf. its use in Mt 16:23). In v.13 it could be taken as a stern warning against deliberately enticing fellow believers to do what for them would be sinful (cf. v.23). Even if such an act were motivated by the desire to get them out of the "weak" category, it would still be wrong.

Paul himself is convinced of something that the weak believer does not share, namely, that "no food is unclean in itself" (v.14; cf. also 1Ti 4:4). He is most likely thinking of what Jesus said in Mk 7:15–23. But not everyone has been enlightened on this issue, and those who are convinced that some foods are unclean (in terms of the Levitical food laws), for them such foods remain unclean. Until they are convinced otherwise, they would violate their conscience if they partook.

Moreover, even if the strong do not try to convince the weak to change their habits, the practices of the strong can be a stumbling block to the weak, causing distress of soul. Such distress may contain a hint of something tragic, a sorrow of heart induced by following the example of the strong, only to find their consciences ablaze with rebuke and their lives out of fellowship with the Lord. In such a situation, love is not operating.

Paul's basis of approach to the strong has changed from granting them their position of liberty to an appeal to love, which may call for sacrifice. If such sacrifice is refused, then the strong must face the responsibility for bringing spiritual ruin on the weak. A selfish insistence on freedom may tear down and destroy, but love, when it is exercised, will invariably build up (1Co 8:1).

16–18 In v.16, the "good" must be understood as the liberty to eat, since all foods are regarded as clean. This liberty, however, if resented because it has been flaunted in the face of the weak, can be regarded as an evil thing on account of its unloving misuse.

Then, with pastoral insight, Paul lifts the entire discussion to a higher level than mere eating and drinking (v.17). His readers, all of them, are the loyal subjects of Christ in the kingdom of God. In that sphere the real concerns are not externals such as diet but the spiritual realities motivating life and shaping conduct. Surely the strong will agree that if their insistence on Christian liberty endangers the spiritual development of the church as a whole, they should be willing to forgo that liberty (cf. 1Co 9:12–23). In this context "righteousness" (GK *1466*) does not mean justification but right conduct to which the believer is called to obey the will of God (cf. 6:13, 16, 18). This conclusion is supported by the fact that "joy" is an experiential term. "Peace" here means the peace of God (Php 4:7; see comment on v.19). Mention of "the Holy Spirit" is understandable, because joy and peace are included in the fruit he produces in the believer's life (see Gal 5:22–23). Paul then links these matters to the believer's service of Christ. The manifestation of the fruit of the Spirit is acceptable not only to God who provides it, but also to those who see it in operation and experience its blessings.

19–21 The entire church is urged to pursue "peace" (harmony between the two groups; GK *1645*), which alone can provide the atmosphere in which "mutual edification [GK *3869*]" can take place (cf. the importance of edification in 1Co 14:5, 12, 26). Mutual edification implies that the strong, despite their tendency to look down on the weak, may actually learn something from them. Perhaps they will come to appreciate loyalty to a tender conscience and begin to search their own hearts to discover that they have cared more about maintaining their position than about loving the weaker Christians. Through the fresh manifestation of love by the strong, the weak will be lifted in spirit and renewed in faith and life.

Paul then reinforces his point about edification by warning of the reverse process (v.20). To "destroy" (GK *2907*) the work of God is to tear it down, making it impossible for the church to function as the instrument of God's purpose. It is disheartening to realize that such colossal loss could be occasioned by a difference of opinion over food! Although all food can properly be regarded as clean and proper to eat, the wrong lies in causing someone to stumble by one's eating.

The "better" or more noble course is to do without meat under such circumstances and to refrain from drinking wine, if that would be a stumbling block to anyone. For the first time in the discussion wine is mentioned, suggesting that a measure of asceticism may be in view here.

22–23 Although the language of the opening statement of this section is general (cf. vv.1–2), in all probability Paul is directing his counsel in v.22 chiefly to the strong, since they are the ones who must be warned to act on their confidence privately, where God is their witness. To exercise their freedom in public would grieve the weak and raise a barrier between them. The strong are "blessed" in their private enjoyment of freedom, because they are free from doubt and no one who might be scandalized is looking on. They are therefore not faced with the danger of causing the weak to condemn themselves by approving something their conscience will not endorse.

Then in v.23 Paul addresses the weak. "Faith" here must be understood in the same way it was used at the beginning of the chapter (see comment on vv.1–4)—not as saving faith, but as a reference to the confidence one has to make free use of what God has created and set apart for the good of humanity. In keeping with this, "condemned" does not refer to God's action of excluding a person from salvation, but it means that the person stands condemned by his or her own act as being wrong. To act in contradiction to one's conscience or to the known will of God inevitably brings an experience of guilt. When believers refuse to move in a certain direction because they feel that step is out of line with God's will, they receive strength by their refusal, so that it is much easier on other occasions to move on the basis of faith.

3. The unity of the strong and the weak in Christ (15:1–13)

Two fairly distinct motifs run through this portion. In vv.1–6 the appeal to both the strong and the weak is grounded on the example of Christ, who did not please himself but gladly accepted whatever self-denial his mission required. In vv.7–13 Christ is again the key. He has accepted both Jew and Gentile in accordance with the purpose of God. To refuse to accept each other is to resist that purpose in its practical outworking.

1 As Paul draws the discussion on Christian liberty to a close, he openly aligns himself with the strong. They are the ones who hold the key to the solution of the problem. If they are interested simply in maintaining their own position, the gulf between the two groups will not be narrowed and the weak will continue to be critical and resentful. But if the strong reach out the hand of fellowship and support, this will be a bridge. So to the strong belongs the obligation of taking the initiative. The word "bear" (GK *1002*) is the same word used in Galatians where believers are to fulfill the law of Christ by bearing each other's burdens (Gal 6:2). Let the strong, then, bear the burden of the scrupulousness of the weaker Christians. But if they do this in a spirit of mere resignation or with the notion that this condescension marks them as superior Christians, it will fail.

Rather, they must do it in love—the key to fulfilling the law of Christ. They must resist the inclination to please themselves, for that is the antithesis of love.

2 Indeed, refusal to live a self-pleasing life should characterize every believer, whether strong or weak, and should extend beyond the narrow circle of like-minded people to all with whom we come in contact (i.e., our neighbors). Our chief concern must always be to contribute to the spiritual good of others, in order to edify the church and to win as many as possible to the Lord (1Co 9:19–23).

3 For the first time in this letter Paul holds Christ before his readers as an example. Christ was also faced with whether he should please himself and go his own way. His concluding affirmation was: "I always do what pleases him" (Jn 8:29), even though the cost was heavy: "The insults of those who insult you [God] have fallen on me" (quoting Ps 69:9). In spite of reproach and insult, our Lord remained faithful in his ministry to help those about him. Paul's readers must likewise seek the good of others even if they are misunderstood or maligned in doing so.

4 Having cited Ps 69, a portion evidently regarded in the early church as messianic (see comment on Ro 11:7–10), the apostle then refers to the Scriptures in a more general way as useful for the instruction of NT believers—in fact, it was deliberately written for their edification. The very phenomenon of quoting from the OT speaks loudly of the dependence of the church on the course of redemption history. The example of Christ was also bound to influence the church to revere and use the OT. In many cases, Gentiles were already familiar with the OT in the synagogue (Ac 13:44–48) before they heard the Gospel and put their trust in the Lord Jesus. The use of the Scriptures promotes "endurance" and supplies "encouragement." Both may be learned by precept and example from these records of the past. These two elements are intimately connected with "hope," for the endurance is worthwhile if it takes place on a course that leads to a glorious future, and the encouragement provides exactly that assurance.

5–6 Endurance and encouragement are ultimately God's gift, though they are mediated through the Scriptures. They tend, however, to be individually appropriated, some realizing them to a greater degree than others. So Paul prays for a "spirit of unity" that will minimize individual differences as all fix their attention on Christ as the pattern for their own lives (cf. v.3). This does not mean that all believers must see eye-to-eye on everything, but that the more Christ fills the spiritual vision, the greater will be the cohesiveness of the church. Though this unity will help the church in its witness to the world, Paul is more interested here in its effect on the worship of the people of God—"with one heart and mouth" glorifying the God and Father whom Jesus so beautifully glorified on earth.

7 As he moves forward to the conclusion of his treatment of the strong and the weak, Paul summarizes what he has already stated. "Accept one another" picks up the emphasis of 14:1, where the same verb occurs, but here the charge is directed to both groups rather than to the strong alone. Then, in line with 15:3, 5, he again brings in the example of Christ and states that bringing praise to God is the grand objective (cf. v.6).

8–12 From the three elements that constitute v.7 Paul now singles out the second—Christ's example of accepting all who make up his body—and proceeds to enlarge on it, first in relation to the Jewish Christians (v.8) and then in relation to the Gentiles (vv.9–12). In both these directions Christ has fulfilled the OT.

"Christ has become a servant of the Jews" (v.8). This brief statement epitomizes the earthly ministry of our Lord, who announced that he was sent only to the lost sheep of the house of Israel (Mt 15:24) and restricted the activity of his disciples during those days to their own nation (Mt 10:5–6). The word "servant" (GK 1356) reminds us how far Jesus went to minister to the needs of Israel (cf. Mk 10:45). This dedicated limitation of ministry to his own people was in the interest of "God's truth" in the sense of God's fidelity to his word, especially his promises made to the patriarchs (cf. Ro 9:4–5). This statement served to remind the Gentile element in the church (the strong) that God had given priority to Israel (cf. 1:16–17; chs. 9–11) and that they should be concerned not to slight or depreciate the Jewish element.

Once that point has been made, however, Paul brings out the truth that all the time

God's purpose was not exclusively directed toward the nation of Israel (cf. Ge 12:3), since the Scriptures portray the Gentiles as embraced in the saving mercy of God and responding to it. Consequently, the Jewish believers of Paul's time should not think it contradictory for God to lavish his grace on the nations through the Gospel. There is an element of progression in Paul's quotations from the OT in vv.9–12. The first (Ps 18:49) pictures David as rejoicing in God for his triumphs in the midst of the nations that have become subject to him. In the second (Dt 32:43, in the LXX), the position of the Gentiles is elevated to participation with Israel in the praise of the Lord. The third and fourth quotations no longer picture the Gentiles in relation to Israel but in their own right, praising the Lord (Ps 117:1) and hoping in him whom God has raised up to rule over the nations (Isa 11:10).

13 As he had done at the close of the first section in this chapter (v.5), Paul again expresses his desire that God will meet the needs of his readers. Although the subject of the last things has little formal place in Romans, its subjective counterpart, "hope" (GK *1828*), is mentioned more often than in any other of his letters, especially here (vv.4, 12–13).

The expression "the God of hope" (v.13) means the God who inspires hope in his children. He can be counted on to fulfill what yet remains to be accomplished for them (5:2; 13:11). Likewise, in the more immediate future and with the help of Paul's letter, they can confidently look to God for the working out of their problems, including the one Paul has been discussing. Hope does not operate apart from trust; in fact, it is the forward-looking aspect of faith (Gal 5:5; 1Pe 1:21). Paul expects a rich, abounding experience of hope along with an overflowing of love (Php 1:9; 1Th 3:12; 4:10), of pleasing God (1Th 4:1), and of thanksgiving (Col 2:7). Believers can count on God to enable them to increase in the manifestation of Christian graces "by the power of the Holy Spirit" who lives in them and fills the inner life.

VIII. Conclusion (15:14–16:27)

A. Paul's Past Labors, Present Program, and Future Plans (15:14–33)

The remainder of this chapter contains a prominence of personal matters that Paul feels will be of interest to the believers at Rome (cf. 1:8–15). Here and in ch. 1, however, his own affairs are invariably regarded as important only as they relate to the Gospel of Christ, of which he is such a committed minister.

14–16 Paul now reflects on the character of his readers and what he can expect his letter to accomplish for them. Since he had earlier acknowledged their strong faith (1:8), it is now in order to add some other things he has picked up about them from various sources, including people mentioned in the closing chapter.

The first item is "goodness" (GK *20*). Having just written about the Holy Spirit, Paul undoubtedly has in mind the moral excellence that is the fruit of the Spirit (Gal 5:22). This quality is needed to carry out the recommendations mentioned in 14:1–15:13. Desiring to do the right thing for someone else is essential, but it must be coupled with "knowledge" of what is rightly expected. Paul goes so far as to call his readers "complete" in this area and therefore "competent to instruct one another." Such language shows his confidence that the Roman church, which had been in existence for at least a decade, had been well taught (cf. 6:17). The word "instruct" (GK *3805*) reflects more than merely imparting information; "inculcate" comes close to expressing its force (a word translated "counsel" in Col 3:16; "warn" in 1Th 5:14). In the absence of resident pastors, believers were expected to exercise such a ministry among themselves.

Though he was not the founder of the Roman church, Paul has been outspoken, and he proceeds to explain this lest he be thought tyrannical or perhaps tedious in going over what they already knew. He is simply doing his duty, fulfilling the commission God in his grace has granted him as a minister of Christ (vv.15–16). Furthermore, his boldness has been in evidence "on some points" (v.15) but has not pervaded the letter as a whole. Since he here emphasizes his call to go to the Gentiles, one may assume that most of his readers were Gentiles (cf. 1:13). They are his special offering, a sacrifice acceptable to God (cf. Isa 66:18–20). His own function as a priest pertains directly to proclaiming the Gospel and winning Gentiles to Christ.

It remains for the Romans to make their own personal commitment to God (12:1). Their acceptability to God comes not only from their reception of the Gospel of Christ but also from the ministry of the Holy Spirit that sets them apart to God as the people of his possession (cf. 1Co 6:11). This initial sanctification makes possible the progressive spiritual development that spans the two great foci of justification and final redemption (1Co 1:30).

17–19 Paul refuses to boast in his special ministry to the Gentiles. He restricts his glorying to Christ Jesus (cf. Gal 6:13–14), the one he serves as a minister (cf. v.16). This relationship means not only that the glory goes to the Savior, but also that as Christ's minister Paul must depend on him for everything he has accomplished. He is only the instrument by which God brings Gentiles to obey Christ (cf. 1:5). His ministry has consisted both of word and deed ("what I have said and done," v.18). His word ministry (which permeates this letter) he simply calls "the gospel of Christ" (v.19); he goes on to give more details about his deed ministry.

"Signs and miracles" (v.19) served to accredit the messenger of God and validate the message he brought. It was so in the ministry of Jesus (Ac 2:22) and of the original apostles (Ac 5:12). Paul is able to certify the same for himself (cf. 2Co 12:12). A "sign" (GK 4956) is a visible token of an invisible reality that is spiritually significant. The same act may also be a "wonder" (GK 5469), something that appeals to the senses and is recognized as a phenomenon that needs explanation. In the OT, God's presence and power were indicated through such means, especially at the time of the Exodus and during the wilderness sojourn. However, "the power of the Spirit" was required to persuade people to make the connection between the miracles and the message and so believe.

How well has Paul fulfilled his task in proclaiming the Gospel as a minister of Christ? He now affords his readers a glimpse into his activity over many years (v.19b), not by citing the number of churches founded, of converts won or of sufferings endured, but by drawing a great arc reaching from Jerusalem to Illyricum (a Roman province northwest of Macedonia). Luke's account of Paul's final visit to Macedonia and Achaia before going up to Jerusalem for the last time is brief (Ac 20:1–2). Yet it is possible that Paul visited Illyricum before settling down at Corinth for the winter (see comments on Ac 20:1–2).

The statement "I have fully proclaimed the gospel of Christ" means not that he had preached in every community between Jerusalem and Illyricum but that he had faithfully preached the message in the major cities along the way, leaving to his converts the task of evangelizing surrounding districts (cf. 1Th 1:8). His ministry in Jerusalem had been brief and met with great resistance (see Ac 9:28–29). But the very fact that it was attempted at all displayed his determination to fulfill that part of his commission that included Israel (Ac 9:15). His habit of visiting the synagogues wherever he went points in the same direction.

20–22 From this brief outline of his missionary activity, the apostle turns to the drive that kept him ceaselessly at his task. He had a godly "ambition" to preach the Gospel where Christ was not known. Such an item was not contained in his call to service except by implication in connection with reaching the Gentiles, so it represents his own desire to blaze an uncharted trail for the Gospel no matter how great the cost to himself. He longed to preach "in the regions beyond" (2Co 10:16). Somewhat parallel is his insistence on preaching the Gospel without charge, supporting himself by the labor of his hands (1Co 9:18).

Paul had not been able to visit Rome because he had been fully occupied elsewhere. For example, conditions in the Corinthian church detained him a long time, so that he did not feel free to move on to another area. His dislike of building "on someone else's foundation" did not come from an overweening sense of self-importance that could be satisfied only when he could claim the credit for what was accomplished. Actually, he preferred to work with companions, and he was always appreciative of the service rendered by his helpers (cf. 1Co 3:5–9). But he was impelled by the love of Christ to reach as many as possible (2Co 5:14–15). He felt deeply his obligation to confront everyone with the good news (Ro 1:14). This is confirmed by the quotation in v.21 of Isa 52:15.

23–24 Only by taking into account the restless pioneer spirit of Paul can we understand how he could claim to have "no more place ... to work" in the regions where he had been laboring. Plenty of communities had been left unvisited and several groups of believers could have profited from a visit, but his eyes were now on the western horizon (see Ac 19:21). His mention of "many years" suggests his desire to go to Rome had been born even earlier, though not crystallized into resolve until the successes at Ephesus showed him that a move to more needy fields was in order. Others could carry on after he had laid the foundation.

Now a still more remote objective than Rome comes into view: Spain (v.24), the frontier of the empire on the west. Thus his stay in Rome will be limited. Though Paul looks forward to fellowship with the believers there (cf. 1:11–12), he hopes to go beyond. Openly, he announces his hope that the Roman church will assist him in making the Spanish campaign a reality. This sharing will naturally include their prayers on his behalf, their financial cooperation, and possibly some helpers to go with him. If Paul were ever to reach Spain, he would no doubt feel that he had realized in his own ministry a measure of fulfillment of the Lord's Great Commission (Mt 28:18–20; Ac 1:8). Whether Paul actually reached Spain is not certain.

25–29 The contemplated trip to Spain by way of Rome will have to be postponed, however, until another mission is accomplished, namely, his impending visit to Jerusalem. So three geographical points lie commingled in the mind of the apostle: Rome as the goal of much praying, hoping, and planning; Jerusalem as the necessary stop on the way; and Spain as the ultimate objective. Obviously the journey to Jerusalem was critical in his thinking; otherwise, the lure of the West might take precedence over everything else. So Paul explains just how important this trip to the mother church is, so that his readers will understand that he is not dilatory about visiting them.

The principal reason, no doubt, for remaining in the East so long is the situation necessitating this final trip to Jerusalem. Paul's churches were made up mainly of Gentile converts. While the Jewish-Christian element in the church had an interest in the growing work among the Gentiles (Ac 11:21–22; 15:4), some were concerned that these Gentiles were not being required to accept circumcision in accordance with the OT provision for receiving proselytes into Israel (Ex 12:48) and were not keeping the various OT laws, such as avoiding unclean foods (Ac 15:1, 5). A further concern was the rapid growth of the Gentile churches, while growth in Jerusalem and Judea had diminished because of persecution and other factors. Jewish believers might be outnumbered before long.

As the leading apostle to the Gentiles, Paul found this situation troubling. What could be done to cement relations between the Jewish and Gentile elements in the church? He felt that the answer might well lie in a great demonstration of love and desire for unity on the part of his churches toward the mother church in Jerusalem, using a gift of assistance to the poor Christians there similar to what Barnabas and Paul had brought years before from the Antioch church (Ac 11:27–30). The gratitude of the recipients was real and lived on in the memory of Paul. Perhaps on the quick trip Paul made to Jerusalem as reported in Ac 18:22 he conferred with the leaders of the church there about this plan. At an earlier period he had expressed eagerness to help the leaders at Jerusalem in ministering to their needy (Gal 2:10). Shortly thereafter he began to inform his congregations of the plan and their responsibility to participate in it (1Co 16:1; cf. 2Co 8–9). Soon after writing to the Romans, he prepared for the trip to Jerusalem, accompanied by representatives of the various churches bearing the offerings that had been collected over a period of time (Ac 20:3–4).

According to v.27, this contribution could be looked at from two standpoints: as a lovegift ("they were pleased to do it") and as an obligation ("they owe it to them"). The latter statement is then explained. Had it not been for the generosity of the Jerusalem church in sharing their spiritual blessings (the Gospel), the Gentiles would still be in pagan darkness. So it was not such a great thing that they should reciprocate by sharing their "material blessings" (v.27). Paul here mentions only those of Macedonia and Achaia as taking part in the contribution, perhaps because he was in Achaia at the time of writing and had recently passed through Macedonia (2Co 8–9). From 1Co 16:1 and Ac 20:4, though, it is clear that believers in Asia Minor participated also.

Evidently Paul looked forward to a great feeling of relief when he would convey the monetary offering into the custody of the Jerusalem church. It would mark the completion of an enterprise that had taken several years. He saw this gift as a "fruit" (v.28), probably meaning that the generosity of the Jerusalem church in dispersing the seed of the Gospel to the Gentiles would now be rewarded, the offering being the fruit of their willingness to share their spiritual blessings.

The completion of the service at Jerusalem would free Paul to make good on his announced purpose to visit the saints at Rome. He looked forward to it as a time when the blessing of Christ would be poured out on all. It would be a time of mutual enrichment in the Lord (cf. Ac 28:15 for the account of his reception by the Christians in Rome).

30–33 At the time of writing, Paul was aware of stubborn Jewish opposition to him and his work. The attempt on his life when he was about to leave for Jerusalem (Ac 20:3) clearly shows that his apprehension was justified. He had experienced deadly peril before and knew that prayer was the great resource in such hazardous times (2Co 1:10–11). So he requests prayer now, the kind involving wrestling before the throne of grace that the evil designs of other people may be thwarted (cf. Eph 6:18–20). He strengthens his request by presenting it in the name of the one whom all believers adore—the Lord Jesus Christ—and by adding, "by the love of the Spirit," i.e., by the love that the Spirit has (cf. 5:5). We should never think impersonally of the Spirit, as if he denotes the power of God. Paul clearly affirmed the Spirit's deity, personality, and equality with Father and Son (2Co 13:14)

The request for prayer includes two immediate objectives. One was deliverance from nonbelieving Jews in Judea. This group had forced his departure from the city at an earlier date (Ac 9:29–30), and there was no reason to think they had mellowed. The other objective concerned the attitude of the Jerusalem church to the above-mentioned offering. Evidently the opposition of the Pharisaic party in the church (Ac 15:5) had not ceased, despite the decision of the council (Ac 15:19–29). This opposition was nourished by false rumors concerning his activities (Ac 21:20–21). It would be a terrible blow to the unity of the church if the love-gift from the Gentile congregations was spurned or accepted with only casual thanks. The body of Christ could be torn apart.

These two items are intimately related to the successful realization of Paul's hope of reaching Rome safely, coming with joy because of the goodness of God in prospering his way and finding refreshment in the fellowship of the saints (v.32). Yet he knew that all this was conditioned on God's will (cf. 1:10). As it turned out, he did reach Rome, but not as a free man. Yet that very circumstance enabled him to demonstrate the all-sufficient grace and power of Christ (Php 1:12–14; cf. 2Ti 4:17). However strife-torn may be his lot in the immediate future, he wishes for his friends the benediction of the God of peace (v.33; cf. v.13).

B. The Commendation of Phoebe (16:1–2)

1–2 Paul hoped to come soon to the believers at Rome (15:32), but he must first go to Jerusalem (15:25). But another believer, Phoebe, was about to leave for the imperial city, so Paul took this opportunity to commend her to the church. It was customary for believers who traveled from place to place to carry with them letters of commendation (2Co 3:1). This woman belonged to the church at Cenchrea, located some seven miles from Corinth and serving as the seaport of the city (cf. Ac 18:18). It was one of the Achaian communities to which the Gospel spread from Corinth during and after Paul's original ministry in that city (2Co 1:1).

Phoebe is called a "servant" (GK *1356*) of this church. The same word can be rendered "deaconess." Men were serving as deacons about this time (Php 1:1), and before long women were being referred to in a way that suggests they held such an office in the church (1Ti 3:11). But Paul is not stressing office but service (cf. v.2). Phoebe apparently stopped at Corinth on her way to Rome. From what is said about her, it seems likely that Paul sent his letter in her care. She was accustomed to serve, so this would be in character for her. Many had reason to thank God for her assistance in the past, Paul among them. Possibly, like Lydia, she was a Christian businesswoman and would need help in connection with her visit to the great metropolis.

C. Warning Concerning Schismatics, Personal Greetings, and Doxology (16:3–27)

Certain preliminary observations are in order before plunging into these greetings to individuals. It has seemed strange to some scholars that Paul would know so many people in the imperial city, seeing that he had never been there. But presumably he had met them or at least heard of them elsewhere. Travel was facilitated by peaceful conditions in the empire, by the fine network of Roman roads connecting the principal centers, and by available shipping during sailing season.

But why so many names here? A clue is provided by Paul's letter to the Colossians, which also contains greetings to a church he did not personally establish. Paul is taking advantage of all the ties he has with this congregation that he hopes to visit in the near future. To send greetings to specific individuals in churches where he knew virtually the entire congregation would expose Paul to the charge of favoritism. But the congregation at Rome was not such a church.

Since his letter to the Philippians was in all probability written from Rome, the greetings he sends from those of Caesar's household (Php 4:22) to the believers at Philippi may well have been from slaves and freedmen serving in the imperial establishment. That this is so seems evident from the fact that many of the names in Ro 16 appear also in burial inscriptions of households of emperors of that period, notably those of Claudius and Nero (the reigning emperor when Paul wrote).

3–5 First to be greeted are Priscilla and her husband, Aquila. Paul's friendship with them went back several years to his mission at Corinth, when they gave him hospitality, encouragement, and cooperation in the Lord's work (Ac 18:2). Their usefulness is confirmed by his taking them with him to Ephesus on leaving Corinth (Ac 18:18). When he left for Jerusalem, they remained there to lay the groundwork for his long ministry there (Ac 18:19) and were used of God in the life of Apollos (Ac 18:24–28). It was during the mission at Ephesus (Ac 19) that these "fellow workers" proved their mettle and personal devotion to Paul. They "risked their lives for me" (v.4). Probably the reference is to the dangerous riot that broke out, endangering the apostle's life (Ac 19:28–31; cf. 1Co 16:9; 2Co 1:8–10).

Their presence with Paul at Ephesus just prior to the riot is confirmed by 1Co 16:19; cf. v.8). At that time they had a church in their house, so it is not surprising to find that the same is true of their situation in Rome. Their return to the imperial city fits in with their earlier residence there (Ac 18:2). Paul likely encouraged them to return, so that they could prepare for his arrival by acquainting the church with his work and by helping in his plans for the future (cf. Ac 19:21). Priscilla and Aquila represent a splendid image of Christian married life. Since several women are mentioned in this chapter, it is well to note that there was a married woman whom Paul encouraged to labor in the Gospel along with her husband. Paul's habit of naming Priscilla first testifies to her great gifts and usefulness in the kingdom of God.

Epenetus is the next to be greeted (v.5). It is understandable that Paul should speak of him as "my dear friend," since this man was the first convert (lit. "firstfruits" [GK 569], suggesting that many more were to follow) to Christ during his mission in the province of Asia, of which Ephesus was the leading city. He naturally held a special place in Paul's heart.

6–15 Mary is a Semitic name borne by several women in the NT. Paul indicates his precise knowledge of her, testifying to her hard work for the saints, but without any hint as to the nature of the work. Emphasis falls rather on her willingness to grow weary in serving them.

Andronicus and Junias (v.7) are Latin and Greek names respectively. Three things out of the four said about them create difficulty for the interpreter. (1) What does "relatives" (GK 5150) mean? The identical word is found in 9:3, where it means fellow Israelite. It may be best to conclude that this word connotes "those who are also Christians." To take the word in the ordinary sense of "relative" is difficult, since Paul gives the impression that he suffered the loss of all things for Christ's sake (Php 3:7), which would include kindred. Added to this is the improbability of his having three kinfolk in Rome (cf. v.11) and three more in Corinth (v.21). (2) Paul adds that these "have been in prison with me." Since Paul was imprisoned many times (2Co 11:23), the expression in this case is doubtless intended to be taken literally, even though we have no idea when it occurred. (3) The pair are further described as "outstanding among the apostles." The word "apostle" (GK 693) can hardly mean "messenger" here (cf. Php 2:25), and it goes without saying that Andronicus and Junias do not belong in the circle of the Twelve. What is left is the recognition that occasionally the word is used somewhat broadly to include leaders in Christian work (cf. 1Th 2:7). Evidently their conversion to the faith occurred in the early years of the history of the church, so they have had ample time to distinguish themselves as leaders.

Paul confesses to a warm personal attachment to Ampliatus (v.8), demonstrating the reality and depth of Christian friendship that developed between him and others who remain obscure to us. Paul was a man who gave himself to the people among whom he served and to those who worked alongside him.

Urbanus (v.9) had helped Paul at some time in the past and assisted others also in the work of the Lord ("our fellow worker"). Regarding Stachys, Paul contents himself with indicating, as with Ampliatus, a very close bond of affection.

Apelles (v.10) was a fairly common name, but this man has an uncommon pedigree, for he is one who is "tested and approved in Christ." This was Paul's desire for Timothy (2Ti 2:15) and for himself (1Co 9:27). The "household of Aristobulus" are Christian slaves either of a certain grandson of Herod the Great who lived in Rome or of some unknown person.

Herodion (v.11) was a Hebrew Christian (cf. the word "relative" again, as in v.7). The household of Narcissus were probably the Christian slaves of a well-known wealthy freedman.

Similar in name, Tryphena and Tryphosa (v.12) were likely sisters. It was not uncommon then, as now, to give daughters names with a certain resemblance. Since their names mean "dainty" and "delicate," their Christian convictions led them to put aside any tendency to live a life of ease. They are given an accolade for being hard workers in the Lord's cause. To these two women Paul adds another, probably a single woman: Persis, a "dear friend" of Paul. He knew enough about her efforts to commend her as having worked "very hard" in the Lord.

A person bearing the name of Rufus is mentioned in Mk 15:21 as one of the sons of Simon, the man who was compelled to bear the cross of Jesus. On the supposition that Mark's gospel was composed at Rome, all is clear: Mark refers to Rufus because he is well known to local readers as a member of their church. He is "chosen in the Lord," probably used here to connote the idea of "noble" or "eminent." The incident involving his father may have brought him a certain fame among believers at Rome. Paul cannot think of Rufus without thinking of his mother. Though she remains unnamed, she was special in the eyes of the apostle, because she evidently perceived his loneliness after the loss of his family when he became a Christian (Php 3:8) and resolved to mother him. Where this occurred remains unknown, but her presence in Rome made him look forward with special anticipation to his visit.

In vv.14–15 two groups of believers are mentioned without accompanying descriptions or commendations. For both groups, a greeting is extended to the believers associated with them. This appears to indicate a house church in both cases. Rome was a large place, making it probable that there were circles of believers in several sections of the city. They would certainly maintain communication and, when necessity dictated, could arrange to meet together.

16 The admonition to share a holy kiss may well be intended in this case to seal the fellowship of the saints when the letter has been read to them (cf. 1Co 16:20; 2Co 13:12; 1Th 5:26). The reminder that it is a "holy" kiss guards it against erotic associations. It was a token of the love of Christ mutually shared and of the peace and harmony he had brought into their lives. In order to encourage warm relations among churches and among the individuals within them, Paul takes the liberty of extending the greetings of the churches he has founded in the East.

In summary, two observations concerning the greetings should be made, especially since the church at Rome eventually became the strongest in all Christendom. (1) Several of these names appear in inscriptions at Rome in reference to slaves of the imperial household. If many of Paul's acquaintances were actually slaves, this may seem a rather inauspicious beginning for an influential church. But slaves in Roman times were often people of education and outstanding ability. Frequently they were able to gain their freedom and play a larger role in society. The very fact that at Rome believers were found in the service of the emperor (Php 4:22) augurs well for the growth of the church in subsequent days. Yet it should be remembered that God's grace, not human nobility, is the important thing (cf. 1Co 1:26-31).

(2) Prominent in this list are women. They occupied various stations—a wife, a single woman, and a mother—and all are represented as performing a valuable service for the Lord. Evidently Paul esteemed them highly for their work's sake. It is certainly wrong to label Paul, on the basis of 1Co 14:34 and 1Ti 2:11-15, as a misogynist.

17-18 Before Paul ends his letter, he includes a warning concerning schismatics. Is it possible to identify these troublemakers? Perhaps it glances back at the problem of the strong and the weak already discussed in 14:1-15:13 (cf. the word "obstacles" here in v.17 and in 14:13). However, the general tone of vv.17-20 is so much sharper than the earlier one, so that any relationship is dubious. The sort of people the apostle singles out here do not seem to have come yet on the Roman scene but posed a threat of doing so. Paul does not specify the particular doctrines of these interlopers, but he is quite pointed in identifying their motives and tactics, which suggests that his warning is based on his missionary experience that had often brought him into contact with false teachers who tried to build their own work on the foundation he had laid (Ac 20:29-30; Php 3:18-19). Some of them may even have kept track of Paul's movements and, being aware of his plan to visit Rome, were hoping to arrive there before him. If they could gain a foothold in this influential church, it would be a notable success.

Paul's command to the believers in Rome is to "watch out" (GK 5023). Alertness to the danger is the main consideration, because failure to be on guard could result in being deceived. Whatever they did, their activity could affect the whole church. As an antidote to their corrupting influence, the apostle points them to "the teaching you have learned." This is hardly to be identified solely with the contents of this letter, but is more particularly intended to refer to the instruction they have already received in the basics of the faith (cf. 6:17). This should serve as the touchstone enabling them to discern error. But such counsel is not enough. As a practical measure, they must "keep away from them," giving them no opportunity for inroads into the congregation.

Paul uses the term "such people" (v.18) rather than "these people," an important distinction that confirms the opinion already given that he does not have in mind a group he could name or identify precisely, but a class he has become all too familiar with in his travels. They may talk about the Lord but they do not serve him. Rather, they serve "their own appetites' (cf. Php 3:18-19; 1Ti 6:3-5). With their smooth talk and flattery intended to deceive, they brand themselves as sophists and charlatans. Those they aim to reach are the "naive," the simpleminded folk so innocent of ulterior motives.

19 Despite the warning, Paul affirms his confidence that his readers will be able to handle the situation (cf. 15:14). This assurance is based chiefly on their "obedience" (cf. 1:5; 6:16), which is so well known in the church at large as to make it almost inconceivable that there will be a failure in the matter under discussion. An appeal to one's record always puts a person on his mettle. So Paul strikes a balance: on the one hand, he rejoices as he thinks of the good name of this congregation; on the other hand, he wants to make sure that they are discerning, able to spot trouble and avoid falling into it.

20 Perhaps the mention of "what is evil" leads Paul to think of the instigator of evil (Satan) and of the One who had blocked the devil's efforts and will thwart his hoped-for triumph. God is the God of peace (cf. 15:33; Php 4:9; 1Th 5:23), who is concerned to preserve harmony among his people and protect them from divisive influences. He is able to defeat the adversary who delights to sow discord among Christians. The word "crush" suggests that Paul has in mind the "promise" of Ge 3:15.

The benediction, as usual, magnifies the grace of our Lord Jesus. The odd feature, however, is that it does not conclude the letter. It appears as if Paul allowed his companions to send greetings after he had written this benediction.

21–23 Paul usually had coworkers and friends around him. This occasion is no exception, and they take this opportunity to send greetings. Timothy, named first, had been Paul's helper on the mission to Macedonia and Achaia (Ac 17–18) and his assistant in handling problems in the Corinthian church (1Co 4:17; 16:10).

The next three persons named are called "relatives," raising the same problem of interpretation faced in vv.7, 11 (see comment). There is a possibility that Lucius is an alternate form for Luke (but see Col 4:14), who does seem to have been with Paul at Corinth (Ac 20:5). Jason could be the individual who entertained Paul and his two helpers at Thessalonica (Ac 17:5), though this too is uncertain (especially since he is not mentioned in Ac 20:4). Sosipater could be the Sopater mentioned in Ac 20:4; his home was in Berea.

At this point (v.22) Tertius, Paul's amanuensis (the one who wrote down the letter at Paul's dictation; cf. 2Th 3:17), asks for the privilege of adding his personal greeting. We may be sure Paul carefully chose believers to write down his letters rather than public secretaries. We also may be sure that people like Tertius would undertake that task as work for the Lord.

Resuming his closing remarks, Paul again takes up the pen and passes on the greeting of Gaius, with whom he had been staying while he wintered at Corinth (v.23). Gaius seems to have been one of the early converts in Paul's mission to the city (1Co 1:14), and the very fact that Paul made an exception in his case by personally baptizing him suggests that his conversion was a notable event due to his prominence. This mention of Gaius as Paul's host helps confirm that Paul was writing from Corinth.

Erastus (v.23) also, a notable figure because of his public office, sends a greeting. Archaeologists have found an inscription in Corinth that bears the name of this public official (cf. also Ac 19:22). Nothing more is known of Quartus than what is stated here. He was probably a member of the Corinthian church and may have had some contact with the congregation in Rome.

25–27 Since Paul has already given his usual benediction of grace (v.20) found at the close of all his letters, we must seek some other explanation for the doxology here. Since Paul allowed other greetings after that benediction (vv.21–23), he probably wanted to write another concluding thought—a magnificent doxology (an ascription of praise to God) that draws into itself words and concepts found in his earlier letters and gives special emphasis to the leading matters discussed in the preceding chapters. This one is lengthy, so much so that the final verse is separated from the rest by a dash in order to indicate a resumption of the thought with which the passage begins and to bring it to a proper conclusion.

The opening words in v. 25 express confidence in God's ability to do what is needful for the readers (cf. Eph 3:20; Jude 24). In the introduction (1:11) Paul had written that he was looking forward to his ministry at Rome as a means of strengthening the congregation. Here he acknowledges that ultimately only God can bring that result. As an instrument for establishing the saints, nothing can compare with the Gospel. Paul is not being egotistical or possessive in calling it "my gospel" (cf. 2:16; 2Ti 2:8). Doubtless the possessive pronoun points up the fact that in Paul's case it came by direct revelation (1:1; cf. Gal 1:12), though it was confirmed as to its historical content by leaders of the Jerusalem church (1Co 15:1–11). Another term for the Gospel is "the proclamation of Jesus Christ," i.e., the preaching that has Jesus Christ as its message (cf. 1:2–3; cf. 1Co 1:21; 2:4; 15:14).

"Proclamation" follows upon "revelation," and both stand in contrast to "the mystery hidden" (see also 1Co 2:7–10). Paul has his usual meaning to "mystery" here (GK 3696; contrast 11:25). What was hidden in God's purpose ultimately becomes revealed and is the property of all his people. The mystery was hidden "for long ages past," i.e., for "eternity past" (cf. 2Ti 1:9; Tit 1:2), by "the eternal God" (v.26), but has now been "revealed" and "made known through the prophetic writings." This probably refers to the OT, even though that material was not necessarily understood as referring to Christ (see Lk 24:25–27, 44–45), and even the OT prophets themselves were puzzled by the messianic element in their own predictions (1Pe 1:10–12). No doubt Paul is taking a backward glance at what he had set down at the beginning of the letter concerning the Gospel as promised by God through his prophets in the Holy Scriptures (1:2).

"The command of the eternal God" points to the Great Commission, which includes all the nations as embraced in the divine purpose (Mt 28:19). This emphasis recalls what Paul said about his own commission (1:1, 5; cf. Col 1:25–27; Tit 1:3). He had a special concern to reach Gentiles (11:13).

In the final verse, God is described under two terms. "Only" (cf. 1Ti 1:17) recalls the line of thought in 3:29–30; he is God of both the Jew and the Gentile. "Wise" (GK 5055) invites the reader to recall the outburst of praise to God in his wisdom (11:33) that brought to a close Paul's long review of God's dealings with Israel in relation to his purpose for the Gentiles. Wisdom is also allied to the hidden/revealed tension noted in v.25, as we gather also from 1Co 2:6–7. So the God whose eternal purpose has been described as hidden and then manifested in the Gospel of his Son, draws to himself through his Son the praise that will engross the saints through all the ages to come. The silence that for so long held the divine mystery has given way to vocal and unending praise. To God be glory forever!

The Old Testament in the New

NT Text	OT Text	Subject
Ro 1:17	Hab 2:4	The righteous live by faith
Ro 2:6	Ps 62:12; Pr 24:12	God's fair judgment
Ro 2:24	Isa 52:5; Eze 36:22	God's name cursed among Gentiles
Ro 3:4	Ps 51:4	God's righteous judgment
Ro 3:10–18	Ps 5:9; 10:7; 14:1–3; 36:1; 53:1–3; 140:3; Ecc 7:20; Isa 59:7–8	Sin of humanity
Ro 4:3, 9	Ge 15:6	Faith of Abraham
Ro 4:7–8	Ps 32:1–2	Blessings of forgiveness
Ro 4:17	Ge 17:5	Abraham as a father of many
Ro 4:18	Ge 15:5	Offspring of Abraham
Ro 4:22	Ge 15:6	Faith of Abraham
Ro 7:7	Ex 20:17; Dt 5:21	Tenth commandment
Ro 8:36	Ps 44:22	Sheep for the slaughter
Ro 9:7	Ge 21:12	God's choice of Isaac
Ro 9:9	Ge 18:10, 14	Promise for Sarah
Ro 9:12	Ge 25:23	God's choice of Jacob
Ro 9:13	Mal 1:2–3	Love for Jacob, not Esau
Ro 9:15	Ex 33:19	Mercy of God
Ro 9:17	Ex 9:16	Purpose of Moses
Ro 9:20	Isa 29:16; 45:9	Potter and clay
Ro 9:25–26	Hos 1:10; 2:23	Now God's people
Ro 9:27–29	Isa 1:9; 10:22–23	The remnant
Ro 9:32–33	Isa 8:14	A stone on which people stumble
Ro 9:33	Isa 28:16	Trust in the cornerstone
Ro 10:5	Lev 18:5	Living by the law
Ro 10:6	Dt 30:12	The word not in heaven
Ro 10:7	Dt 30:13	The word not in the deep
Ro 10:8	Dt 30:14	The word near you
Ro 10:11	Isa 28:16	Trust in the cornerstone
Ro 10:13	Joel 2:32	Salvation in the Lord
Ro 10:15	Isa 52:7	Beautiful feet
Ro 10:16	Isa 53:1	Unbelief of Israel

The Old Testament in the New

NT Text	OT Text	Subject
Ro 10:18	Ps 19:4	General revelation
Ro 10:19	Dt 32:21	Making Israel envious
Ro 10:20	Isa 65:1	Salvation of the Gentiles
Ro 10:21	Isa 65:2	Obstinate Israel
Ro 11:3–4	1 Ki 19:10, 14, 18	A saved remnant
Ro 11:8	Dt 29:4	A misunderstanding mind
Ro 11:8	Isa 29:10	God seals the eyes
Ro 11:9–10	Ps 69:22–23	Judgment on enemies
Ro 11:26–27	Isa 59:20–21	Deliverer from Zion
Ro 11:27	Isa 27:9	Full removal of sin
Ro 11:34	Isa 40:13	The mind of the Lord
Ro 11:35	Job 41:11	God owns all
Ro 12:19	Dt 32:35	God avenges sin
Ro 12:20–21	Pr 25:21–22	Treating one's enemies
Ro 13:9	Ex 20:13; Dt 5:17	Sixth commandment
Ro 13:9	Ex 20:14; Dt 5:18	Seventh commandment
Ro 13:9	Ex 20:15; Dt 5:19	Eighth commandment
Ro 13:9	Ex 20:17; Dt 5:21	Tenth commandment
Ro 13:9	Lev 19:18	Love your neighbor as yourself
Ro 14:11	Isa 45:23	Every knee shall bow
Ro 15:3	Ps 69:9	Insults on Christ
Ro 15:9	2Sa 22:50; Ps 18:49	Praise among the nations
Ro 15:10	Dt 32:43	Rejoice, O nations
Ro 15:11	Ps 117:1	Nations praising God
Ro 15:12	Isa 11:10	The root of Jesse
Ro 15:21	Isa 52:15	Gentiles hear the gospel

1 Corinthians

INTRODUCTION

1. Background

The ancient city of Corinth was located on the isthmus between Attica to the northeast and the Greek Peloponnesus to the south; it had controlling access to two seas—the Aegean to the east and the Ionian to the west. Its eastern port was Cenchrea, located on the Saronic Gulf (Ac 18:18; Ro 16:1), while its western harbor was at Lechaeum on the Corinthian Gulf. This proximity to the seas and its nearness to Athens, only forty-five miles to the northeast, gave Corinth a position of strategic commercial importance and military defense. It lay below the steep north side of the 1,800-foot high fortress rock, the Acrocorinth with its temple of Aphrodite. Thus located, the city received shipping from every major city on the Mediterranean. Instead of going around the south end of the Peloponnesus, ships often docked at the Isthmus and transported their cargoes by land vehicles from one sea to another; or if the ships were small, they were dragged the five miles across the isthmus. Today there is a canal running through the narrowest part of the isthmus near Corinth.

Corinth was a prosperous city. At the peak of its power and influence it probably had a free population of 200,000, plus half a million slaves in its navy and in its many colonies.

Julius Caesar had reestablished Corinth in 46 B.C. He populated it with Roman war veterans and freedmen. In the reign of Augustus (27 B.C.–A.D. 14) and his successors, the city was built on the pattern of a Roman city, with all remaining buildings reclaimed and new ones added in and around the old marketplace (the *agora*). It became the capital of the Roman province of Achaia (cf. Ac 18:1–2), which included all the Peloponnesus and most of the rest of Greece and Macedonia.

The celebration of the Isthmian games at the temple of Poseidon made a considerable contribution to Hellenic life. This temple was located about seven miles east of Corinth, not far from the eastern end of the isthmus. But with the games came an emphasis on luxury and profligacy, because the sanctuary of Poseidon was given over to the worship of the Corinthian Aphrodite, whose temple on the Acrocorinth was once purported to have had more than 1,000 female prostitutes in the pre-Roman era. The Greek language developed a verb, *korinthiazomai*, which meant "to live like a Corinthian in the practice of sexual immorality."

Paul probably came to this important but immoral city in the fall of A.D. 50, after preaching the Gospel to the highly intellectual Athenians. He ministered there a year and a half (Ac 18:11) before he was brought by the Jews into court before the proconsul Gallio (v. 12). That these were the dates of Paul's stay at the city is established by comparing the reference to Gallio with a Gallio, proconsul of Achaia, mentioned on an inscription of the Emperor Claudius at Delphi, dated between January and August, A.D. 52. This Gallio took office on July 1, A.D. 51, and Paul had arrived in Corinth about a year earlier. Shortly after this court appearance, Paul left Corinth for Syria (v.18).

In the Corinthian church were both Jews and Gentiles (see 1Co 1). Some Gentile members had Latin names (e.g., Gaius, Fortunatus, Crispus, Justus, and Achaicus: 1:14; 16:17); so did some Jews (e.g., Aquila and Priscilla, Ac 18:1–4; Crispus, the ruler of the synagogue, v.8). No doubt the greater part of the church was composed of native Greeks (cf. 1Co 1:20–24; 12:2).

The existence of a synagogue in Corinth (Ac 18:4–8) is confirmed by an inscribed lintel block with enough of the words remaining to make out the reading "Synagogue of the Hebrews." The miserable nature of the inscription, which has no ornamentation, fits the social position of the Jewish people at Corinth with whom Paul was dealing (see 1Co 1:26).

1 CORINTHIANS

Archaeologists have identified other buildings of the ancient city. An ornamented triumphal gateway, located at the south end of the Lechaeum Road, led into the *agora*. Around the market were a good many shops, numbers of which had individual wells, suggesting that much wine was made and drunk in the city (cf. Paul's warning in 1Co 6:10). Located near the center of the marketplace was the *bema*, the judicial bench or tribunal platform. This was a speakers' platform, and officials addressed audiences assembled there. It was to this place that the antagonistic Jews brought Paul before Gallio (Ac 18:12–17).

Besides its many temples and shrines, the city had two theaters to the north and west, one of which could seat 18,000 people. In a paved street at the east side of this theater was found a reused paving block with this inscription: "Erastus, the aedile [commissioner of public works], bore the expense of this pavement." This Erastus may well have been the one who became Paul's fellow worker (see Ac 19:22; Ro 16:23).

Besides his initial stay in Corinth as recorded in Ac 18, Paul's contact with the Corinthians can be outlined as follows (see map on Paul's interaction with the church at Corinth in the introduction to 2 Corinthians): At Ephesus (Ac 19) he apparently wrote the "previous letter" (1Co 5:9—now lost to us). Besides hearing of the Corinthians' seeming misunderstanding of that letter, Paul had reports from Chloe's household of disorders in the church there (1:11). He may also have received a delegation from Corinth (16:17) who presented him with questions from the congregation (cf. 7:1). As a result, he wrote 1 Corinthians. Paul then heard other unfavorable reports from the church and paid them a "painful visit" (2Co 2:1). This visit was no doubt necessary because the church had failed to act on Paul's advice given in 1 Corinthians. Upon his return to Ephesus, he sent the church a "sorrowful letter" (2Co 2:4; 7:8–9), probably carried by Titus. From Ephesus Paul went to Macedonia, where he received from Titus an encouraging report (2Co 7:5–7). So he wrote

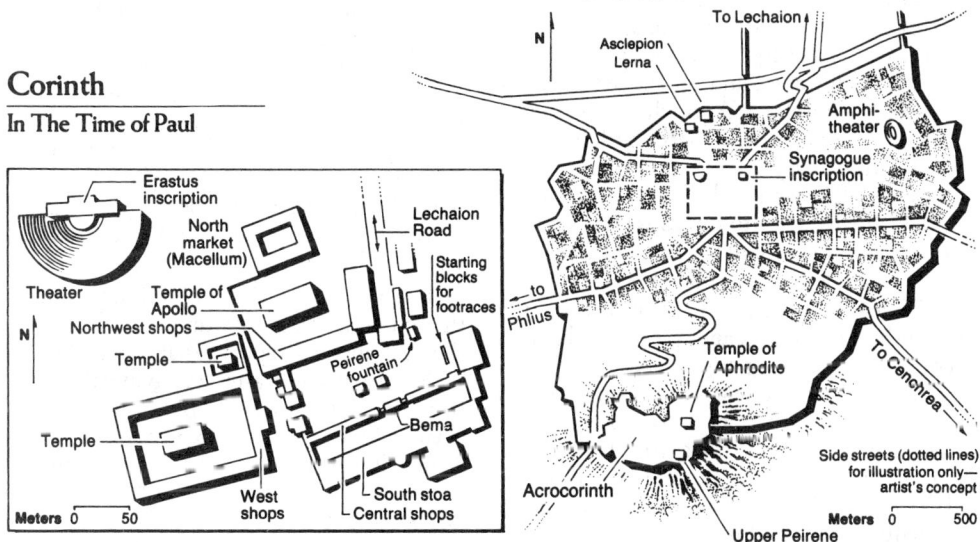

Corinth
In The Time of Paul

The city of Corinth, perched like a one-eyed Titan astride the narrow isthmus connecting the Greek mainland with the Peloponnese, was one of the dominant commercial centers of the Hellenic world as early as the eighth century B.C.

No city in Greece was more favorably situated for land and sea trade. With a high, strong citadel at its back, it lay between the Saronic Gulf and the Ionian Sea and ports at Lechaion and Cenchrea. A *diolkos*, or stone tramway for the overland transport of ships, linked the two seas. Crowning the Acrocorinth was the temple of Aphrodite, served, according to Strabo, by more than 1,000 pagan priestess-prostitutes.

© 1985 The Zondervan Corporation

By the time the gospel reached Corinth in the spring of A.D. 52, the city had a proud history of leadership in the Achaian League, and a spirit of revived Hellenism under Roman domination following the destruction of the city by Mummius in 146 B.C.

Paul's lengthy stay in Corinth brought him directly in contact with the major monuments of the *agora*, many of which still survive. The fountain-house of the spring *Peirene*, the temple of Apollo, the *macellum* or meat market (I Co 10:25) and the theater, the *bema* (Ac 18:12), and the unimpressive synagogue all played a part in the experience of the apostle. An inscription from the theater names the city official Erastus, probably the friend of Paul mentioned in Ro 16:23.

2 Corinthians, expressing his gratitude for the improvement. Later he spent the winter in Corinth (Ac 20:2–3) before departing for Jerusalem with the contribution for the poor among the Christians of Palestine. On the basis of this analysis of the events, we may conclude that Paul wrote the Corinthians four letters (two of which have been lost) and that he paid the church three visits.

2. Authorship, Date, Place of Origin, and Destination

Few doubt that Paul was the author of this letter. Not only does the letter itself clearly state this (1:1), but evidence from early church fathers universally confirms it. There is no question, therefore, of the canonicity of this letter; it was accepted almost immediately as God's word. Paul himself makes the strong statement in 14:37, "If anybody thinks he is a prophet or spiritually gifted, let him acknowledge that what I am writing to you is the Lord's command."

Obviously, the letter was written some time subsequent to Paul's first visit to Corinth from A.D. 50–52. Following his departure from the city, he sailed from Cenchrea, stopped at Ephesus briefly, visited the Jerusalem churches, and journeyed north to his home church at Antioch in Syria (Ac 18:18–23). After a stay there, he left on his third missionary journey, visiting the churches of Galatia and Phrygia (Ac 18:23), until he finally came to Ephesus (19:1), where he preached and taught for almost three years (19:10; 20:31)—from A.D. 53–56.

While at Ephesus, Paul heard of the Corinthians' troubles and questions through reports from Chloe's house (1Co 1: 11) and possibly through a delegation from Corinth (16:17). At this point he wrote this letter—toward the end of his stay there. (1) Paul specifically says he is writing from Ephesus (1Co 16:8–9, 19). (2) The letter was written subsequent to Apollos's stay at the city (Ac 18:26, 27; 1Co 1:12) and after Timothy and Erastus had been sent by Paul from Ephesus to Macedonia (Ac 19:22) and Timothy had been sent on to Corinth (1Co 4:17). (3) The letter was written in late spring, because in 1Co 16:8 Paul intimates that it is a relatively short time to Pentecost, after which he intended to leave Ephesus. The time of writing is certainly before winter, for he plans to spend the winter with them (16:6). This all adds up to A.D. 56, about five years after his initial departure from Corinth in the fall of A.D. 51.

It is not fully clear who carried the letter to Corinth, but most likely Stephanas, Fortunatus, and Achaicus did, who according to 16:17, had arrived from Corinth and were with Paul. Since in 16:18 the apostle says that the Corinthian Christians should show respect for these men, it is logical to conclude that they were returning to Corinth with the letter.

3. Occasion and Purpose

First Corinthians is a source book of answers to church problems in the past and today. After the introductory material, Paul answers the theological and practical problems raised through the report from members of the household of Chloe (1Co 1:11)—reports about divisions, incest, adultery, Christians taking fellow Christians to court, and the misuse of Christian liberty (chs. 1–6). Following this, a letter came from the church (7:1), posing a number of questions and requiring Paul's answer—questions about marriage, eating meat offered to heathen idols, disorderly public worship, spiritual gifts, and the resurrection (chs. 7–15). Finally, Paul wanted the Corinthians to participate in the offering he was taking for the Christians in Jerusalem (16:1–4). These things, together with Paul's desire to send greetings to Corinth, were sufficient occasion for him to write the letter.

It may well be that Paul did not compose the whole letter at one time. He first wrote the response to reports that came through Chloe; then later, after receiving the letter from the Corinthians (7:1), he wrote the rest. That is likely why the expression and tone change in various parts of 1 Corinthians.

4. Theological Values

Several theological emphases stand out in 1 Corinthians, related to the daily living of Christians as well as to the corporate testimony of the worshiping church. For example, in ch. 15 Paul sets forth valid reasons for believing in the bodily resurrection of Christ and relates this to Christ's second coming. In ch. 11 the doctrine of the Lord's Supper is effectively taught, along with the admonition for Christians to take it seriously.

In chs. 5 and 6 Paul speaks forcefully against the incident of incest and adultery in the church and condemns all sexual immorality. Also in ch. 6 the thorny problem of believers' taking other believers into secular court is faced and Christian arbitration suggested. The practical problem of whether Christians should marry and how they should conduct themselves in a married or unmarried state is adequately discussed in ch. 7. Christian liberty versus the responsibility of believers to their fellow Christians is clearly explained in chs. 8 and 10. In the area of ecclesiology, the subjects of Christian gifts and their use for the church, as well as orderly conduct in church services, are fully expounded in chs. 12–14.

EXPOSITION

I. Greetings (1:1–3)

1 Characteristically, Paul begins by naming himself and by identifying his position as an apostle of Jesus Christ. He stresses his apostleship because his authority has been challenged (cf. 1:12; 9:1–27). He makes it clear that he is an apostle by divine calling through God's sovereign will (cf. Ac 9:15). The word "apostle" (GK 693) means "a sent one" and connotes a commissioned envoy.

Paul links Sosthenes to himself as a Christian brother; he was evidently one of the apostle's special helpers and was presumably well known to the Corinthian church. It is possible that he was at one time a leader of the Corinthian synagogue (Ac 18:17). If so, he must have been subsequently converted and gone off to help Paul in his Ephesian ministry.

2 The believers in Corinth are designated as the "church [*ekklesia*; GK 1711] of God" (cf. also Ac 20:28; 2Co 1:1), a phrase that has OT associations, as in the expression "assembly [or congregation] of the Lord" (Nu 16:3; 20:4, Dt 23:1; 1Ch 28:8) and the "assembly of Israel" (Lev 16:17; Dt 31:30). For Paul, this church at Corinth was considered a part of the universal "church of God"; note his reference to Palestinian churches as also being a part of that same body (1Co 15:9; cf. 10:31–32). The apostle may have found it particularly useful in Corinth to distinguish the church from the secular *ekklesia* (assembly) of Greek cities, which was the gathering of the citizenry in a city-state to discuss and decide on matters of public interest (cf. Ac 19:39).

The Corinthian Christians are described as "sanctified" (GK 39), i.e., set apart and in a holy position before God because of their spiritual union with Jesus Christ. Paul goes on to emphasize that they are called to live as God's holy people. They are on an equal footing with the people of God everywhere, who also call on the name of Jesus Christ as Savior and Lord (cf. Ac 9:14, 21). The unity of believers in Christ is shown by Paul's emphatic words in v.2, "their Lord and ours."

3 This verse is identical to Ro 1:7b; 2Co 1:2; Gal 1:3; Eph 1:2; and Phm 1:3. Though carrying a sense of greeting, "grace and peace" also refer to the truth of redemption purchased by Christ. It was of God's grace that the Corinthian believers were saved (2Co 8:9; Eph 2:8–9), just as all Christians are saved, and through this redemption Jesus Christ purchased peace with God for the sinner (Eph 2:14; cf. Ro 5:1). This grace and peace are from God our Father, who planned redemption, and from Christ, who purchased it on the cross for the justification of his people.

II. Paul's Thanksgiving for God's Work in the Lives of the Saints (1:4–9)

4–6 As is characteristic of Paul in his other letters (cf. Ro 1:8; Php 1:3–7; Col 1:3–8; et al.), he begins by thanking God for those whom he is addressing. He realizes that God has given them his grace through their union with Christ, enriching their lives by their ability to speak about God and by their knowledge of him (v.5). He is thankful that the testimony he gave them was confirmed in their lives. The form of the verb "I thank" (GK 2373) indicates that Paul regularly interceded for the believers at Corinth as well as those wherever he preached the Gospel (cf. Eph 1:16; Php 1:3; et al.).

Greeks naturally put emphasis on knowledge and wisdom (cf. 1:18–25), and they certainly were good at expressing their thoughts. However, God had so enriched the lives of these Christians in Corinth in spiritual perception and expression that they had been given increased ability in speaking. The extent of their enrichment is seen in the use of the adjective "all" with both "speaking" and "knowledge" (v.5). These two terms are interrelated, for Paul uses a single preposition "in" to unite them. He is convinced that this was a real work of God's grace because he saw his witness about Christ established in their lives at the time of their conversion and had heard about it since then.

The reference to "knowledge" (GK *1194*) in v.5 should not be construed to mean that the Corinthians possessed some hidden mystical knowledge by which they could, without the cross of Christ, somehow reach God and be saved (cf. Php 3:8, 10). While it is true that in the later heresy known as Gnosticism some thought they could do this, Paul is speaking about concrete knowledge based on the reality of Christ's person and his death on the cross.

7–8 Now Paul addresses himself to the Corinthians' need for present and future Christian living. He introduces the thought by "therefore": "Therefore you do not lack any spiritual gift." The potential lack indicated by the Greek verb does not necessarily refer to the lack of special gifts mentioned in chs. 12–14, because there Paul indicates that each Christian is not to exercise every gift (12:27–31). Rather, he seems to be referring more generally to God's grace actively counteracting the sins and faults so prevalent in the Corinthian congregation. Paul expresses confidence that God will keep them strong and will present his people blameless before him at Christ's return, for which they are eagerly waiting.

It is not clear in v.8 whom "he" refers to—God the Father or Christ. Christ is the nearer antecedent (v.7), but in the light of the reference to God's faithfulness in v.9, it is best taken as referring to the Father. Through his power and strengthening, Christians will certainly be blameless when Christ comes again.

9 Before concluding this section of thanksgiving, Paul assures the Corinthians of God's faithfulness. As God called them initially into fellowship with Christ, so he is "faithful" (GK *4412*) in completing the work, granting them every grace and gift for daily life (cf. Php 1:6). Observe the apostle's fivefold repetition of the name of Jesus Christ in this brief section. All of salvation—past, present, and future—is based on Christ's redemptive work. And he is coming again!

III. The Problem of Divisions in the Church (1:10–17)

10 In the light of information given him about divisions in the church, Paul strongly exhorts the Christians both positively and negatively. He begins by charging them to have a united testimony, then adds his plea for inward harmony in mind and confession about Christ. Between these two positive exhortations Paul introduces the solemn purpose: "that there may be no divisions" in the Christian community. The word "divisions" (GK *5388*) graphically conveys the idea of the dissensions that were rending the church. He makes this exhortation through the authority of Jesus Christ, whose name they revere.

11–12 Paul had received word about the divisions (which he here calls "quarrels") in the Corinthian church from members of a certain Chloe's house. Presumably, all of those quarrelling were Christians and were members of the church. They were divided into at least four factions, each one having its own emphasis, following its own leader, and acting in antagonism to the other three. How frequently local church congregations today are likewise divided into cliques!

At Corinth the four groups centered around four prominent leaders. First, there were those who claimed to be special adherents of Paul, possibly because of his emphasis on the ministry to the Gentiles, a ministry with which many of them were connected. Then there were those following Apollos, enamored of that learned and eloquent preacher from Alexandria (Ac 18:24; 19:1; Tit 3:13). The followers of Cephas (Peter's Aramaic name; cf. Jn 1:42) were no doubt impressed by this apostle's emphasis on the Jews. Possibly they connected him with the Judaizers. The mention of the "Christ" party suggests that some Corinthians claimed special relationship to Christ (2Co 10:7) or placed a special emphasis on him—an emphasis they felt the followers of Paul, Apollos, and Cephas had neglected or did not have.

13 Paul quickly destroys the validity of such distinctions by insisting that Christians are all one in Christ. "Is Christ divided?" he asks. He shows the foolishness of even raising the question by asking two other questions that imply a negative answer: he, Paul, was not crucified for them, nor were they baptized in his name. The same could be said also of Apollos and Peter.

14–16 The mention of baptism leads Paul to comment that the Corinthian believers had no reason to depend on the efficacy of baptism by him as a sanctifying grace, because he had baptized so few—Crispus, Gaius, and the household of Stephanus, these being the only ones he could remember as having been baptized by him. Crispus probably was at one time the head of the Corinthian synagogue (Ac 18:8), and Gaius was probably the Gaius mentioned as Paul's host in Ro 16:23. Stephanus was one of those whom Paul calls the "first converts in Achaia"; he, with Fortunatus and Achaicus, was with Paul at Ephesus (1Co 16:15, 17). The whole household (i.e., the family members and the servants) of this prominent man had been baptized by Paul.

17 Why Paul did not baptize more during his stay at Corinth we are not told. He does go on to state that his essential work was not baptizing but preaching the Gospel (Ac 26:17–18). That is, baptism was of secondary importance. This, then, gives him an opportunity to talk about the thrust of his preaching ministry. His method was to preach not "with words of human wisdom [GK *5053*]," i.e., not with the cleverness of human argumentation (such as the methods used by philosophers like Plato and Aristotle). If he were to depend on human argument, the heart of the message of the cross would be emptied of its essential meaning.

IV. The Wisdom of God—the Preaching of Christ Crucified (1:18–2:16)

A. Christ, the Power and Wisdom of God (1:18–31)

In this section Paul emphasizes that salvation is in Christ and not in human wisdom. Because Christ, the power and wisdom of God, is the source of our salvation, we have no basis for boasting.

18–20 These verses flow logically from the proposition of v.17 that Paul did not come preaching with human wisdom. In his avoidance of human ostentation, he realizes that the straightforward presentation of the message of the cross produces two effects. It is foolishness to those who are on the way to being lost, but the power of God to those who are being saved (cf. Ro 1:16). In his emphasis that God's power for salvation is in the cross, Paul introduces an OT quotation from Isa 29:14 to show that God dismisses human wisdom as a means of salvation. In the Isaiah context, the Lord deplores the man-made precepts and mouthing of words for salvation (Isa 29:13) and declares that he will set aside human wisdom and understanding as a means of finding favor with him. This thought Paul now adapts to his argument.

Having established God's rejection of human striving for salvation through wisdom, the apostle now asks just where in fact "the wise man" (possibly an allusion to the Greeks; cf. v.22b) can be found who was able to do what the message of the cross of Christ had done. The "scholar" (GK *1208*; translated "teacher of the law" elsewhere) was the Jewish professional who was skilled in interpreting the law. For the saved Jews in the Corinthian congregation this idea would be relevant. "The philosopher of this age" (v.20) was the man who wanted to dispute every issue and solve it by human reason. The designation could fit both Greek and Jew. The question Paul asks at the end of v.20 is introduced with a word that anticipates a positive response.

21–22 To Paul, in God's all-wise purpose human beings with all their philosophical and religious wisdom and searching "did not come to know God." This is not to deny the truth that people have a certain knowledge of God through the natural creation (cf. Ro 1:18–20). But Paul says it was God's good purpose to save those who believe by the seemingly foolish process of preaching the cross (cf. v.18).

In explaining the world's seeking God through wisdom, Paul states that the Jews seek for "miraculous signs" (GK *4956*) and the Greeks seek "wisdom" (GK *5053*), and that through these means they hope to find the answers to the questions about God and life. The Jews were seeking signs to identify the Messiah and the apocalyptic deliverance they hoped God would bring them (cf. Mk 8:11; Jn 6:30). But Jesus had said that they would be given only "the sign of the prophet

Jonah" (Mt 12:39–40), pointing to his death as Messiah. The "Greeks" are primarily the native Greeks of Corinth, though in a broader sense that word also refers to the whole non-Jewish world (cf. Col 3:11; see also Paul's use of "Gentiles" instead of "Greeks" in v.23).

23 Paul's task is to preach Christ crucified. He uses the form of the verb "crucified" that implies that Christ's death has a continuous vicarious effect (cf. Gal 2:20). To the unsaved Jews, however, this message of a crucified Christ was a "stumbling block" (GK *4998*), an offense, for they expected a political deliverer. To the nonJewish world the cross was "foolishness" (GK *3702*)—criminals died on crosses, so how could the cross provide any moral philosophical standard to help them toward salvation? Furthermore, the Greeks and Romans looked on one crucified as the lowest of criminals, so how could such a one be considered a savior? The sophisticated Greeks would also have had difficulty in conceiving of how a god, being spirit, could become incarnate and thus provide a god-man atonement for sin.

24–25 In contrast, Paul states that God has his chosen ones, the "called" (GK *3105*), from both the Jews and Gentiles. Paul has preached to such people about God's effective power to save them and his wise plan through Christ to bring this about. He then uses a kind of paradoxical hyperbole to present the greatness of God's wisdom: God has foolishness, God has weakness! What Paul means is that God's smallest, least significant thought is more worthwhile than the wisest plans of all humankind. And God's seemingly insignificant expression of his creative and providential power, such as the coming of the dew or the unfolding of a leaf, is greater and more effective than the mightiest thoughts and acts of people. God has complete control and fully accomplishes his purposes, while the power, acts, and thoughts of human beings are in comparison as nothing.

26–27 Having contrasted God's strength and human weakness, Paul now speaks about the circumstances under which God has called his people. The word "called" stresses his dynamic drawing of his people to himself (Ro 11:29; Eph 1:18). Not many of them were of the intellectual-philosopher class (i.e., wise according to human standards), nor of the politically powerful, nor of the upper level of society. By these three terms, Paul has given the sweep of all that humans count as socially, politically, and intellectually important.

Instead, God has chosen from the world those who seem foolish, weak, and helpless so that he might put to shame the wise and powerful by showing how temporary and insignificant to salvation their achievements are. In his grace he has showered his mercy on them and made them strong and wise in Christ.

28–29 Paul continues by stating that God has chosen those of the lower levels of society. First he mentions the slave class and the despised. These terms were particularly appropriate for the situation at Corinth because there were so many slaves there. Also among those God has called, Paul lists "the things that are not"—i.e., "the nonexistent," those who seem to the world to be nonentities. God has done this so that he might show those who seem to be important ("the things that are") that they can accomplish nothing for their own salvation because their wisdom, power, and importance are ineffective for this. As a result, no one may boast in God's presence that salvation has been gained by his or her own effort.

30–31 Instead of boasting, redeemed people must realize that salvation is all of God's grace: it is because of his effective plan that they are in saving union with Christ (cf. Jn 15:1–7; Ro 5:12–21). This saving relationship is a true one because Christ has been made for us wisdom from God, so that through him we have come to know God (Jn 1:18; 14:6–9) and are made "wise for salvation" (2Ti 3:14–17). Paul shifts from "you" to "we" to make certain the readers understand that all Christians, including himself, have this vital union with Christ.

Paul adds other effects or results of our union with Christ: he is righteousness, sanctification, and redemption for us. These concepts are best seen as explanatory of God's wise plan that is effective in the substitutionary atonement. Christ has become our righteousness, having our sin on himself (2Co 5:21). He has become our sanctification, having made possible our growth in grace in the

Christian life (Ro 8:9–10; Eph 2:8–10; 2Pe 3:18). He is our redemption—the one by whom we have been delivered from sin (Ro 3:24), the devil, hell, and the grave (1Co 15:55–57).

Because of God's gracious provision of salvation in this way, all praise must go to the Lord. To strengthen this conclusion, Paul appeals to the authority of an OT quotation (Jer 9:24), using it in condensed form. In OT times as in NT times, it was the duty of saved people to glory in the Lord for his great salvation.

B. Paul Preaches Christ in the Power of God (2:1–5)

Paul now returns to the manner of his own preaching introduced in 1:17. He argues that since salvation is attained not through human wisdom or might but only through the cross, he came to Corinth in dependence on the Holy Spirit and simply preached Christ and the efficacy of his death.

1 In alluding to his visit to Corinth, Paul is thinking of the initial trip recorded in Ac 18:1–18, when the Corinthians first heard the message of salvation and believed. He did not depend on overpowering oratory or philosophical argument. He rather came preaching the "mystery" (GK *3696* [see NIV note]; NIV text reads GK *3457*, "testimony") of God—the message not fully understood by them before, but now explained by him and illuminated by the Holy Spirit (2:10–14).

2 Paul came with the sole purpose of centering his attention on the truth concerning Jesus Christ—on the fact and meaning of his crucifixion. The "for" introducing this verse confirms the statement in v.1 about his simple proclamation of the cross. It was not sufficient for Paul to tell about Jesus and his life; he had also to tell about his death for sinners (cf. Ac 10:37–43). Christ died on a Roman cross at Jerusalem, and his death was effective then and is effective now to bring forgiveness to sinners (Gal 2:16).

3 Paul adds, in effect, "I came preaching, simply as a frail insufficient human being; I came with fear and a great deal of trembling as I realized the importance of preaching the eternal gospel." In writing somewhat later to the Christians at Philippi, he encouraged them to live their lives in a similar humble attitude, though with complete reliance on God (Php 2:12–13).

4 So Paul's message and preaching conform to his own personal attitude—he did not present his message in a way that depended on overpowering them with wise and persuasive arguments. Though he came in this unostentatious way, yet he came in a display of spiritual power because of the Holy Spirit. This is the first time in this letter that Paul mentions the Spirit's ministry.

5 Paul intends that the Corinthians' faith might not be a superficial, misdirected belief coming from human wisdom, but a real Christian faith generated by the power of God, who also worked in Paul as he preached (v.4). "The faith" (GK *4411*) spoken of here is not just the act of believing but the substance of their belief based on the person and work of Christ. We must have the word of God as well as the power of God through the Spirit.

C. Wisdom of Christ Revealed by the Holy Spirit (2:6–16)

Paul now makes clear that his presentation of God's eternal plan of salvation (v.7) is based, through the Holy Spirit, on the wisdom of God revealed to Paul and to others, a wisdom to be understood by those who are God's people.

6 In case some think that the Gospel is devoid of wisdom, Paul states that it involves a higher wisdom discernible by those who are spiritually mature. Though some understand "the mature" (GK *5455*) as referring to those far advanced in spiritual understanding compared with infants in Christ (cf. 3:1), the context favors the conclusion that the spiritually mature were the saved—those enlightened by the Holy Spirit—in contrast to the unsaved. This latter view is supported by Paul's argument that it is the unsaved who think the Gospel is foolish (1:21–23) and that the unsaved do not receive the things of the Spirit of God (2:14). This wisdom, Paul says, does not come from this age of time and space and certainly not from the rulers of this age (i.e., those who are of highest importance in the world), because such people crucified the Lord of glory (v.8). These rulers with their wisdom will end up in futility.

7 Describing God's wisdom further, Paul states that it is a wisdom that is contained in a mystery ("God's secret wisdom") not fully revealed, but one that God had planned before the beginning of the ages. This plan originated in God's mind, and though outlined in the OT, it is not as fully explained and understood there as it is in the NT. Moreover, God conceived of this plan of redemption in relation to the final glory of Christians when they will share with Christ the glory of God (Ro 8:17–18).

8 None of the earthly rulers understood such redemption relating to wisdom. By "rulers" Paul means the Sadducees, Pharisees, teachers of the law, and Herod Antipas, as well as the Romans represented by Pilate and his soldiers (Ac 4:25–28). Otherwise, they would not have crucified "the Lord of glory" (cf. "King of glory" in Ps. 24:7–10; "God of glory" in Ps 29:3; Ac 7:2). This phrase describes Christ's divinity, and Paul brings it together with Christ's human nature (he was crucified in a real body on a hard, real cross), leading to the conclusion that the Son of God, incarnate in a human being, died on the cross (cf. Ac 20:28).

9 However, Paul goes on to say, the "hidden" (GK *648*) wisdom he has been preaching is the wisdom referred to in the OT. It was set forth in the promises God had prepared and laid up for his people—for those who love him. It is these promises that people like the rulers of this world still do not see and have not even thought of obeying. That God has prepared these things for us Christians implies that we will sometime know and share in these promised blessings (Ro 8:18–25), which, Paul hastens to say, have been revealed to God's people by the Spirit (v.10).

The expression "it is written" (v.9), often used to cite OT Scripture (cf. Mt 4:4; Mk 11:17; Ro 1:17, et al.), may mean here "to use the language of Scripture" or "to speak generally from Scripture" (cf. Jn 1:45), without meaning that the passage is formally cited. The first two lines of the quotation and the last line loosely refer to Isa 64:4, whereas the third line may merely be a thought from the OT generally as summarized by Paul (but cf. Isa 65:17). Verse 9 does not make a complete sentence in Greek (see the dash at the end of the verse), but Paul, in giving more than one OT thought, is not attempting strictly to weave them into his sentence structure.

10 Paul now begins to stress the work of the Holy Spirit in revealing the wisdom of God. God has revealed "to us" (i.e., to Paul, the other apostles, and their associates) the spiritual wisdom that the unsaved rulers of this world did not understand. "Revealed" (GK *636*) is a strong term, usually used in the NT to indicate divine revelation of certain supernatural secrets (Mt 16:17; Lk 10:22) or an eschatological sense of the revelation connected with certain persons and events (Ro 8:18; 1Co 3:13). Throughout vv.10–16 it is Paul who speaks. mostly in the first person plural, strengthening the interpretation that he is referring primarily to divine revelation given to apostles. Later in 3:1–3 Paul returns to addressing the Corinthians as "you." But what is true primarily of Paul and the other apostles, is true secondarily for all Christians—the Holy Spirit helps them to interpret Scripture.

The latter part of this verse amplifies the first part by showing the extent ("all things") and depth ("the deep things of God") of the Holy Spirit's revelation of God's wisdom and truth. The Holy Spirit infallibly guided the writers of Scripture (2Pe 1:21) and continually works effectively in the lives of believers (Eph 1:17–19; 3:16–19).

11–12 "For" introduces an illustration that shows that the spiritual wisdom and truths of God can be understood only through the Holy Spirit, just as human wisdom needs the human spirit to understand it. The conclusion is that only the Holy Spirit can reveal God's wisdom and truth to humankind. The concept of "spirit" (GK *4460*) in this verse involves a real personality who thinks and acts; it is not an impersonal force.

By way of application, Paul states that it is the Spirit of God they have received. This is in contrast to some other kind of spirit through which some might try to know God's wisdom and truth—whether the spirit of the wisdom of this world (1:20; 2:6; 3:19) or another kind of spirit (cf. 1Jn 4:2–6). The purpose of the Holy Spirit's special work of revelation (v.10) is that "we may understand what [i.e., the truths] God has freely given us."

13 Paul now reverts to the nature of his own ministry (cf. vv.4–5). He and other associates do not speak "in words taught . . . by human wisdom but in words taught by the Spirit," as they express spiritual truths in words conveying the real spiritual truth. Again, the contrast is between human wisdom and wisdom from God.

14 In using the generic term "man" (GK 476), the apostle now shows he is speaking of the unsaved in general, governed as they are only by their "soulish-human" nature; they do not accept enlightenment and truths from the Spirit of God. Therefore such persons consider those truths to be foolish. Paul states it even more strongly when he says that "the man without the Spirit" cannot understand these truths because they can be discerned and understood only with the guidance of the Spirit.

The verb translated "discerned" in v.14 is the same verb translated "make judgments" and "subject to man's judgments" in v.15 (GK 373). The idea of this verb involves making intelligent spiritual decisions following the examination (cf. 4:3).

15 In contrast to the unregenerate, persons who are guided by the Spirit draw discerning conclusions about all kinds of spiritual things, but such spiritual people are not subject to spiritual judgments by those who are without the Spirit (v.14). Elsewhere Paul teaches Christians the appropriateness of making judgments concerning the spiritual condition and actions of other Christians (see 5:9–12; 12:3; Gal 1:8.)

16 This verse confirms the thought of v.15 by quoting the LXX of Isa 40:13. The quotation in the form of a question casts doubt on the possibility of knowing God's wisdom, but the final statement gives reassurance that Christians do know it. This explains v.15b — the person who has God's Spirit is not subject to judgments by one who does not have the Spirit.

Paul introduces the "mind [GK 3808] of Christ" terminology in order to relate it to the OT expression he has just quoted—"the mind of the Lord." The verse implies that we and all God's people can understand spiritual truths and spiritual wisdom in a way similar to the way the Lord knows them. This verse is the climax of Paul's argument about his preaching of God's "foolishness" (the cross of Christ) without ostentation. Let the philosophers of Greece (cf. Ac 17:18, 32) and the Jews in their sign-seeking jeer and mock. They cannot really judge the message of Paul, who has the mind of Christ, because they do not have the Spirit of God and cannot judge spiritual truths.

V. Servants of Christ (3:1–4:21)

A. Workers With God—False Estimate Corrected (3:1–23)

In this passage Paul speaks to the Corinthians about the lack of spiritual discernment he has been discussing in ch. 2. This lack is seen in their misconceptions about those who are fellow workers with God. The corrective is given in his later statements about the importance of working correctly for the Lord (3:10–17) and not depending on humans or on human wisdom (3:18–23).

1. Spiritual immaturity and divisiveness (3:1–9)

1 As in 2:1, Paul calls the Corinthians "brothers" (GK 81) before reprimanding them for their spiritual immaturity. Not only had he not preached to them with persuasive words (2:1–5), but here he states he could not even speak to them as to those with spiritual maturity. They were acting immaturely as people controlled by the fleshly prejudices and viewpoints of the unsaved. Part of what he means is shown by his reference in vv.4–5 to the party contentions he had discussed in 1:10–17. The word "spiritual" (GK 4461) must be interpreted differently in 3:1 from its meaning in 2:14–15, where Paul uses it to denote the saved person in contrast to the unsaved. Here he combines it with "worldly" and "infants," so that "spiritual" refers to believers who are spiritually mature Christians.

2 Paul now amplifies the reference in v.1 to infants by explaining that when he first came, he fed the Corinthian Christians spiritual milk—i.e., the elementary salvation truths of the Gospel. He could not teach them deeper doctrines ("solid food") because they could not spiritually digest them. And their immaturity is continuing.

3–4 The word "worldly" (lit. "fleshly"; GK 4920) further indicates that these Christians are showing characteristics of spiritual immaturity. "For" prepares for Paul's illustrations of this worldliness—the "jealousy" and "quarreling" that plague the Christian community. His questions are stated in a way that expects a positive answer. The Corinthians, if honest with themselves, should admit their failing here. They are living the way the ordinary sinful people live—in selfishness, pride, and envy.

Implied here is an allusion to their divisions (see 1:10–17). Paul's example of himself and Apollos who shared in the ministry at Corinth (Ac 18:1–28) was needed to show the Corinthians that they had a distorted view of the Lord's work. Whenever they thought of God's work in terms of belonging to or following a particular Christian worker, they were simply acting on the human level and taking sides, just as the world does.

5 Paul now answers the question of how Paul and Apollos should be viewed. They are simply servants, as are any other workers. No Christian worker is ever to be idolized. Indeed, those who are idolized can become instruments for fragmenting the work of God. Believers must realize that Christian workers are simply God's agents through whom people believe in Christ. By "believe" (GK *4409*) Paul not only means the initial trust in Christ (Ro 3:22–24) but, as v.6 shows, the planting, watering, and God-given increase—the whole process of growth in the Christian life to maturity (2Pe 3:18).

6–9 Paul bluntly states, "I planted the seed," and quickly adds, "Apollos watered it, but God made it grow." In vv.7–9 he draws some conclusions from his basic premise. (1) Since they are merely God's servants, they cannot themselves produce any spiritual results. Only God can do that (cf. Jn 3:5). (2) The servants with their various functions are really one, being united in God's work. (3) Though they are one in the work, yet they are individually subordinate to God and responsible to him who will reward them according to their faithful labor. (4) All is from God, and the church is his work (v.9). He uses people of different talents and temperaments to help him cause the church to grow.

Christians are the spiritual "field" in which God's servants are working. In speaking of their being God's cultivated field and of Paul and Apollos and others as God's workers in the field, the apostle brings to the minds of the Corinthians the farming going on in the plain below the city. There the land was plowed, the crops reaped, the grapevines tended, and the grapes gathered (cf. also Eph 2:20–22; 1Pe 2:5).

2. Building on Christ the foundation (3:10–17)

Paul closed v.9 by changing from the picture of a field to that of a "building" (GK *3869*). He now discusses how God's servants can build the church of Christ. The foundation laid down through the preaching of the cross of Christ (1:18) is always the same—Jesus Christ. The Christian workers bring to it their labor and the spiritual materials they use to build the church upon Jesus Christ. At the end (i.e., the second coming of Christ), the payday comes, when the right kind of work will be rewarded and the wrong kind will be destroyed. This section ends with a declaration that Christians are the temple of God and a warning that no one is to destroy this temple, for such people will themselves be destroyed.

10–11 Paul views his skill as an expert builder (cf. Pr 8:30) as being possible only through God's grace. He knew God's plan for the building of his church (Eph 3:7–10) and had laid the doctrinal "foundation" (GK *2529*) of "Jesus Christ and him crucified" (2:2; cf. Isa 28:16; Ac 4:11; Eph 2:20; 1Pe 2:6). He acknowledges that others, such as Apollos, also build on this same foundation. Then, shifting from the worker to the work, Paul gives a warning: All builders—Paul, Apollos, and whoever works for God—must be careful how they build. Any defects in their work will be their own fault. Christ cannot be blamed for it.

12–15 Paul turns his attention to the kind of materials Christian workers are using: the materials of preaching the cross for salvation, building up believers (cf. 1:18), and living a Christian life that is commensurate with that preaching (2:2–4). The purity and depth of such Christian teaching and a life corresponding to it are crucial, for that kind of building material will stand the test of fire on the day of the Lord's judgment.

Since valuable metals and precious stones were used to adorn ancient temples (cf. Rev 21:18–21), Paul could have taken his imagery from Herod's temple in Jerusalem (Mt 24:1–

2) or from the beautiful public and religious buildings in Athens (Ac 17:23) and Corinth. Such imagery would be sufficient to convey the thought of pure doctrine. The frames of ordinary houses and buildings were built of wood; hay or dried-grass, mixed with mud, was used for the walls; and roofs were thatched with straw or stalks. So the kind of insipid teaching and life represented by these lesser things will also have to face the test of the pure fire of God's justice and judgment, when it will be consumed.

"The Day" (GK 2465) is "the day of the Lord" (1Th 5:2–9), the day of the second coming of Christ (cf. 2Th 2:2). The "quality" of each one's work refers to the kinds of materials of doctrine and life that are used. The fire is the fire of God's judgment. Fire in Scripture is used figuratively in two ways: as a purifying agent (Mt 3:11; Mk 9:49) and as that which consumes (Mt 3:12; 2Th 1:7–8; Heb 12:29). So it is a fitting symbol here for God's judgment, as he tests the quality of the Christian's work.

Those Christians whose works stand the test of fire (cf. 1Pe 1:7) will be rewarded (cf. Mt 25:14–30; Lk 19:11–27). Those whose works are consumed by the fire will themselves escape the flames (as if they were jumping out of the burning wooden structure they had built) and be saved, but without any works of praise to present to Christ.

16–17 The "temple" (GK 3724) is reminiscent of the OT tabernacle and temple as well as the holy sanctuary built by Herod. As Jesus spoke of his earthly body as the "temple" (Jn 2:19–21), so his redeemed people, indwelt by the Spirit of God (1Co 6:19), can be called individually and collectively God's temple.

Paul challenges the church with the fact that they together (the word "you" is plural) are the spiritual temple of God, because the Spirit of God dwells in them (Eph 2:22; 1Pe 2:5). Therefore those who build this temple in a shoddy way deserve the destruction of their doctrine and false testimony as described in v.15. Implicit in this is a warning against any false teachers coming in among the believers.

More pointedly, Paul states that anyone who actually destroys or tends to destroy God's temple will be destroyed by God (cf. Lev 15:31). The reason is clear: God's temple is "sacred" (GK 41), i.e., set apart to holiness (Isa 28:16; Rev 3:12). In his justice and holiness, God cannot allow any part of his holy work to be damaged without bringing retribution. Here is a fitting warning to every Christian minister and worker.

3. Complete dependence on God, not other people (3:18–23)

18–20 Paul now returns to the subject of "wisdom" (GK 5055) and warns the believers not to be deceived into thinking that the wisdom of this human age is sufficient for obtaining salvation and for building up the church of God. Rather, if any Christians think themselves to be wise by this world's standards, they must renounce dependence on that wisdom in order to really receive God's wisdom (v.18).

To prove this, Paul again mentions the truth of 1:18–25—the seeming foolishness of the preaching of the cross is really God's true wisdom for salvation. Directly and forcefully he declares that the wisdom of this world is foolishness in God's sight, and he uses two OT Scriptures to support this. The first is a free rendering of Job 5:12–13, which he applies in a special sense to God. The graphic word "catches" vividly portrays the idea that humans in their craftiness are no match for God—they set up their schemes of salvation against God's, but he catches them up short. His second quotation is Ps 94:11 (from the LXX), showing that the Lord knows all the futile thoughts of the so-called wise men—nothing that enters their minds is beyond his understanding. All that is not in tune with God's thoughts is vain.

21–22 The conclusion is that no Christian should be "boasting" (GK 3016) or glorying in human wisdom and attainments—not even in those of Paul or Apollos. Why not? Because all things—yes, all the blessings of God in the whole universe—belong to the redeemed church. So the ministry of Paul, Apollos, Cephas (Peter), and any other Christian worker belongs to God's people. Also the world itself, the processes of living and dying, the present and the future—all must be viewed in relationship to God's purposes and plans for his redeemed people. So Paul can say, "All things are yours." Everything is for the believers' benefit and belongs to them.

23 All things are not, however, centered in believers, for all things actually and finally belong to God. They belong to Christians only as they themselves belong to God through the mediatorship of Jesus Christ, the Son of God. Christ and the Father are one (Jn 1:1; 10:30), yet Christ was sent by the Father into the world (Jn 10:36; 17:18) to effect our redemption so that we may "inherit the kingdom" (Jas 2:5).

B. Servants of Christ: the Ministry of the Apostles (4:1–21)

1. Faithful servants (4:1–5)

These verses follow up the preceding discussion about Christian workers. Here Paul adds that such servants of Christ must also be considered stewards of God—those to whom a trust has been committed, a trust they are to be faithful to.

1 Everyone should count Paul and other Christian workers as "servants" (GK 5677) of Christ, fully responsible to him and not to the Corinthians. The phrase "those entrusted with" (GK 3874) means "house stewards" and refers to a position often held by a slave (e.g., Joseph, Ge 39:2–19) entrusted with managing the affairs of a household. "The secret things [GK 3696] of God" indicates the mysteries of salvation God has revealed in his Word (Ro 16:25; Eph 1:9; 3:3–4; 1Ti 3:16)—things one cannot discover by human wisdom (cf. 2:1). These truths of the cross have been entrusted to Christian workers to be carefully used and guarded. As subordinate servants of Christ, they have no right of authority over those truths, but must minister them in Christ's name to God's people.

2–4 Paul now examines the character of those who are handling God's truth: they, including himself, must first of all show themselves faithful. Since he is the Lord's servant and steward, it is to the Lord that he owes responsibility, and it is the Lord who "judges" (GK 373) him for the quality of his service. Human judgment has little value; even self-evaluation is unreliable. Christ is Lord of the conscience and the one who can evaluate it properly.

5 The apostle leaps forward to the return of Christ when all Christians will have their works examined at the judgment seat of Christ (2Co 5:10). Because of this, he charges the Corinthians not to judge his faithfulness, for this can be done truthfully only by the Lord when he returns. Therefore, knowing that the Corinthians are already judging him and others, he says to them in effect, "Curb your habit of judging."

"What is hidden in darkness" are the acts and motives concealed in the inner recesses of a person's mind and heart. In Hebrew poetic style (cf. Ps 18:10), Paul says the Lord will "expose the motives of men's hearts" as an explanation of his statement, "He will bring to light what is hidden in darkness." Thus, at the second coming of Christ, those who have been faithful in their work for the Lord will receive praise from him (cf. 3:8; also the parables in Mt 25:14–23; Lk 19:12–19). As the final judging must be done by God, so one's final praise will come from him.

2. The proud Corinthians and the despised servants (4:6–13)

Paul describes the difference between himself and Apollos and some of the other Christian leaders. The Corinthians, he says, were proud and claimed to be spiritually rich. On the other hand, Paul and Apollos were considered weak and were despised and persecuted.

6 What Paul has said about not judging or misjudging Apollos or himself he wants understood as applying to the Corinthians' attitude toward all of God's people; they should not take pride in some and despise others. In referring to this misconception on their part, the apostle may be alluding to the real leaders of the factious parties for whom the other names—Paul, Apollos, Peter, and Christ—had been substituted. Or he may be simply referring to some who were responsible for stirring up this misconception about how God's ministers should be viewed.

In the expression "I have applied these things to myself and Apollos," Paul says he is teaching the Corinthians by personal illustration that ministers are only examples, rather than merely teaching them by abstract principles.

The saying "Do not go beyond what is written" contains the familiar phrase often used to introduce OT quotations. Paul is advising the Corinthians not to go beyond any written doctrine in the OT. The last clause in v.6, like the preceding clause, is one of result and fits into the context as follows: If they learn not to go beyond the teaching of the Scripture about how they should treat God's teachers and all of God's people, then the result will be that they will not be conceited in taking a stand for one teacher or person over against another.

7–8 Some Christians evidently were boasting because of their talents, positions, and parties. So Paul puts the rhetorical question to them: "What do you have that you did not receive?" The obvious answer is that they received everything from God and had no right to boast. He therefore derides their conceit by a series of dramatic boasts of theirs: they, so they think, have all they need; they are rich and are reigning like kings, even without any help from Paul. The Corinthians evidently thought they had reached full maturity and were ruling and reigning rather than walking humbly with God.

9 Continuing the irony, Paul replies that in his opinion, God has not placed the apostles in a reigning position such as the Corinthians think they themselves are in. The irony is that the Corinthians were trying to reign as "kings," while their spiritual fathers and examples were far from reigning. Actually, Paul goes on to explain that God has publicly displayed the apostles (using this term in the widest sense to include not only Peter and himself but also Apollos and perhaps other prominent Christian workers; cf. Ac 14:14; Ro 16:7) as humble, despised men—men worthy of death. He pictures those of the apostolic band as condemned to death and led forth by a conqueror. The word "spectacle" (GK 2519) alludes to the figure of condemned men tortured and exposed to the wild animals in the colosseum. They are despised before both the whole world and the angelic hosts.

10 Paul makes a series of contrasts between the proud Corinthians and the "dishonored" apostles—all from the warped viewpoint of the Corinthians. What a contrast: the apostles—foolish, weak, and dishonored; the Corinthians—wise, strong, and honored!

11–13 To set the record straight, Paul describes in detail the hardships he and his fellow Christian workers have suffered throughout their ministry. He first emphasizes the physical deprivations they were suffering: hunger, thirst, lack of clothing, rough treatment, and homelessness. To remind the Corinthians again that he has no desire to be a physical burden to them, he injects the statement, "We work hard with our own hands." He continues by mentioning mainly the verbal abuse he and his friends took and their response to it. They were frequently reviled, but they called on God to bless their revilers! When persecuted, they endure it; and when slandered, they answer kindly. Climaxing this moving passage, Paul states that he and his fellow workers have become like the scum of the earth.

3. The challenge to be God's humble servants also (4:14–21)

Paul concludes this section (4:1–21) with a challenge for the Corinthian Christians to be spiritually humble; to this end he has sent Timothy to help them, and he himself will also come later.

14–17 Paul's seeming harshness in writing this to the Corinthians was not to "shame" (GK 1956) them but to warn them of the seriousness and perverseness of their actions and their pride. He grants that they have countless guides or guardians but denies that they have spiritual fathers to advise them. This reference to "guardians" (GK 4080) calls attention to the distinction between himself, their spiritual father, and their other leaders. In the ancient Roman Empire, "guardians" were slaves who escorted boys to and from school and were in charge of their general conduct. So, in a sense, they could be called instructors (cf. Gal 3:24). But he, Paul, has begotten them in Christ (i.e., by Christ's atoning work) through the Gospel and is therefore their spiritual father. So he feels he has a right to advise them, specifically to ask them to become imitators of him (cf. 1Co 11:1; Gal 4:12; Php 3:17; 1Th 1:6; 2Th 3:9). He has sent Timothy to them to help them in their progress. Timothy, too, was Paul's beloved child, "begotten" through the Gospel, and faithful in the Lord—i.e., in his service for Christ.

Though Paul mentions having sent Timothy, the latter was evidently not the messenger who brought the 1 Corinthians letter. He is not mentioned in the greetings at the beginning or at the end of this letter, suggesting that he was not with Paul in Ephesus at the time Paul wrote this letter. Further, Ac 19:22 states that Paul had sent Timothy from Ephesus to Macedonia, and 1Co 16:10 implies that he was to continue on to Corinth and was still on his way. It is more likely that Stephanus, Fortunatus, and Achaicus, who are indicated as being from Corinth and who are said to be with Paul (16:17), were the bearers of the letter (see the introduction). Paul expects that when Timothy arrives at Corinth he will cause the saints there to reflect on all Paul's work and actions, and that they correspond to his teaching in all the churches. As should be true of every Christian, Paul practiced what he preached.

18–21 Now concerning his own proposed trip to Corinth, Paul addresses some in the church who had acted arrogantly as though he were not going to come and did not dare to do so. These were the false teachers who were trying to undermine his authority (cf. 9:1–3; 2Co 12:12) by saying he was unstable (2Co 1:17) and weak and that his message was of no importance (2Co 10:10).

Paul replies that, the Lord willing, he will come without delay and will then find out the real power of the arrogant persons who are doing all the talking against him (v.19). "But" emphasizes the contrast: Talk is cheap! What real power do these people have to promote their unscriptural and derogatory ideas? Paul uses the expression "kingdom [GK 993] of God" here in the present spiritual sense of God reigning over his people and demonstrating his power in their lives. He is talking about the life that comes from Christ (2Co 5:17)—the new birth and its power (cf. Jn 3:3–8).

Paul climaxes his thought with the question, "What do you prefer?" He poses two alternatives: to come "with punishment, or in love and with a gentle spirit" (i.e., in a manner expressing gentleness). So Paul has answered their charge that he is afraid.

VI. Paul's Answer to Further Reported Problems in the Church (5:1–6:20)

A. Paul's Condemnation of Sexual Immorality—Incest (5:1–13)

The sin of sexual immorality and the church's indifference to it is the second major evil in the Corinthian congregation that Paul mentions. Corinth was noted for its loose

The ruins of the central square in old Corinth are still highly visible. Courtesy Bastiaan Van Elderen.

and licentious living (see the introduction), a situation duplicated in the prevailing lack of moral standards in contemporary society. In this chapter Paul condemns the sin of incest and rebukes the church for its arrogance in this matter and its failure to excommunicate the violator—something Paul insists on (vv. 1–5). The purity he describes is symbolized in the removal of yeast in the celebration of the OT Passover, which is fulfilled in Christ, "our Passover lamb" (vv.6–8). He closes with instructions that the church should guard its own membership against sexually immoral persons, but should not try to Christianize unbelievers by forcing biblical standards on them (vv.9–13).

1 The Greek word *porneia* (GK *4518*) used in this verse is accurately translated "sexual immorality." Paul has heard a widespread report that a particular man of their congregation had married his stepmother (the NT expression "to have a woman" means "to marry" her; cf. Mt 14:4; 1Co 7:2, 29). Such a sin of incest, Paul says, is not even practiced among non-Christians. It was also strictly forbidden according to Lev 18:8 and Dt 22:30 and carried with it a curse (Dt 27:20). Rabbinic law, however, seems to have allowed a marriage when a proselyte married his stepmother, since his becoming a proselyte broke all bonds of relationship. It is possible that some in the Corinthian church who had come from the synagogue may have known of this allowance. Though as a Pharisee (cf. Php 3:5) Paul knew the system of Jewish law with its varying interpretations, he applies the OT law and its teaching on marriage strictly.

2–3 Paul again alludes to the pride of the Corinthians. This time it was a pride that, rather than causing them to mourn over the shocking sin, allowed them to tolerate such a sinner in their midst. Paul presses his judgment of the case by saying that he is with them in spirit and has already passed judgment on the offending person.

4–5 Though the local congregation itself is to gather and discipline the offender, Paul reminds them of his apostolic authority over them by saying, "I am with you in spirit." But he does not overassert his authority, because he recognizes that the decision is to be made "in the name [GK *3950*] of our Lord Jesus" (i.e., by the authority of Jesus, for his name carries authority), and that it is to be done with "the power [GK *1539*] of our Lord Jesus." These two expressions amplify each other: church discipline must be exercised carefully on the authority of Jesus' name, and the verdict given is accompanied by the spiritual power of the Lord.

By saying, "Hand this man over to Satan, so that his sinful nature [or body] may be destroyed," Paul includes both the man's excommunication (cf. v.2) and some form of physical suffering, even as far as death (cf. 1Ti 1:20). The word *sarx* (lit., "flesh"; GK *4922*) can mean the "sinful nature," but since "flesh" in this verse stands in contrast to "spirit" (GK *4460*), the reference seems to be to the human body. That Satan has power to afflict the body is evident from frequent NT references to the effects of demon possession (cf. Mt 9:32–33; Lk 9:39–42) and to satanic activity in causing affliction or limitation (2Co 12:7; 1Th 2:18). This bodily punishment by Satan, Paul hopes, will have the effect of causing the man to repent so that his spirit (i.e., his person) may be saved at the second coming of Christ.

Although Paul teaches church excommunication here, he does not say that the man should divorce his stepmother. This accords with the scriptural teaching that marriage is an indissoluble bond (Ge 2:24). He does imply that by repenting the man's spirit will be saved. Some interpreters see in 2Co 2:6–7 and 7:9–12 a reference to this man, that he did repent. If true, such an interpretation implies that the man was to be allowed to come back into fellowship in spite of his incestuous marriage.

6–8 Paul illustrates Christian holiness and discipline by the OT teaching that no yeast was allowed in the bread eaten at the Passover feast. Yeast in Scripture generally conveys the idea of evil or sin (cf. Mt 16:6). If the church allowed such sin as that described here to go undisciplined, it would affect the attitude of the entire Christian community toward sin by working its way "through the whole batch of dough." The church must get rid of the old yeast—"the sin that so easily entangles" (Heb 12:1)—by getting rid of the sinner; it must thus become an unleavened batch of dough, a new creation in Christ, who has been sacrificed as our Passover lamb.

Christ, "our Passover lamb" (GK *4247*), died at the time of the Jewish Passover celebration (see the discussion of this issue in comments on Jn 13:2). The Passover, which began when the lambs were sacrificed, is called the first day of the Feast of Unleavened Bread (Mk 14:12). So Paul concludes in v.8, "Let us keep the Festival"—that is, let us live the Christian life in holy consecration to God (cf. Ro 12:2; 1Pe 2:5). This means, he says, that we are to live not with the old yeast of malice and wickedness, but on the basis of the unleavened principles of sincerity and truth. Therefore, such sins as incestuous marriages cannot be tolerated or left undisciplined in the church.

9 Though the letter here referred to could possibly be a reference to the preceding part of the present letter, it is more natural to conclude that Paul had written a previous letter that we do not possess. Paul now comments on a subject discussed in that former letter—that of not associating with sexually immoral people (those committing any type of sexual sins, including incest), a point the Corinthians had not fully understood. The social milieu in Corinth was notoriously immoral and if the Corinthians took the command in the previous letter too literally, as they seem to have done, they would have had to break contact with even some family members, business associates, and social acquaintances.

10 Paul proceeds to correct their misunderstanding. By referring to other categories of sinners besides the sexually immoral, he shows that his earlier reference to the sexually immoral meant only that such people should not continue as a part of the church community. If Paul had meant that contact or even acquaintance with all sinners was to cease, then Christians could not live at all in human society.

By the words "not at all," Paul limits the extent of his command. He is talking about the sexually immoral of the secular world system, who are not to be included as a part of the church community. The "greedy" (GK *4431*) persons here are literally the ones "who must have more" (cf. Ro 1:29; Eph 4:19; Col 3:5). Greed is a serious sin, and Paul touches on aspects of it in 6:7–8. The word translated "swindler" (GK *774*) really means one who steals by violence.

11 Having explained that he did not mean Christians are to be totally dissociated from the world, Paul hastens to add that the church community should not "associate" (GK *5264*) with such flagrant sinners as those enumerated, even if they carry the name "brother" (i.e., are part of the Christian fellowship). They should not eat together. In sharing in a common meal, Christians show their union with one another. This eating is probably not the Lord's Supper, but any meal, including the Christian *agape* (love feast). This kind of association should still be avoided, for otherwise believers raise questions about the validity of their own Christian profession. To the list of sinners in v.10 Paul now adds the slanderer and the drunkard (cf. 6:10; 11:21; Eph 5:18; 1Th 5:7).

12–13 Though it is logical and necessary for the church to exercise spiritual discipline over members within its fellowship (the question asked in v.12 implies a positive answer), the church has no business judging and seeking to discipline those outside the church's communion, i.e., unsaved society. Paul concludes by insisting that the wicked man who had married his stepmother must be put out of the church. This he commands by quoting somewhat loosely from Dt 22:24 (a context of adultery) and Dt 24:7 (a context of stealing).

B. Christian Morality Applied to Legal and Sexual Matters (6:1–20)

1. Christian morality in legal matters (6:1–11)

Continuing in the area of moral and ethical practice, Paul now discusses the apparently common practice of the Corinthians of settling noncriminal property cases before non-Christian judges or arbitrators. He refers to the Roman law courts, where Roman law was strictly administered in accordance with Roman standards. "What about God's standards?" Paul asks. They as a Christian community should have been deciding such cases among themselves. In Christian love they should have "turned the other cheek" (cf. Mt 5:39) and suffered wrong and loss of material goods (v.7) rather than go to court over such matters.

1–2 In speaking of Christians taking other Christians to court, Paul does not specify any criminal cases, for he teaches elsewhere that these, along with any punitive penalties, must be handled by the state (Ro 13:1–7). The legal "cases" (GK *3215*) referred to here, therefore, include different kinds of property cases (v.7). The decisions to be made by Christians are ministerial and declarative (cf. Mt 16:18–19; 18:18–20; Jn 20:19–23), not punitive. By "dare" (GK *5528*), Paul strongly admonishes rather than commands Christians to take their legal grievances for settlement before qualified Christians. In this way, he allows for the possibility that under some circumstances Christians might take cases to the secular civil court.

Paul writes here in the light of Roman law, which allowed Jews to apply their own law in property matters; and Christians, who were not yet distinguished as a separate class, must have had the same privilege. But since Jewish and Christian communities appealed to Roman law for the right to try their own property cases, certainly it would be right to take some cases before the civil court. By analogy, Paul himself, who had received his Roman citizenship according to Roman law, appealed to the civil courts—to the Roman commander (Ac 22:25–29), to the governor (Ac 23:27; 24:10–21), and to the emperor (Ac 25:4–12)—to establish his right to a proper trial and proper treatment as a Roman citizen (Ac 16:37–39). In modern life this biblical principle allows for church cases to be brought into civil courts to determine the extent of the rights of the congregation—as, for example, their right to own and retain their own church property. What concerned Paul was that the Corinthians were failing to exercise their prerogative in settling such cases themselves.

The "saints" (GK 41) are those who are holy—those consecrated and set apart for God; the same word is translated "God's people" in v.2. They are in sharp contrast with the "ungodly" (GK 96) or the unsaved. In saying that God's people will judge the world, Paul is writing eschatologically. At the second coming of Christ, God's people, who are coheirs with Christ (Ro 8:17), will reign and judge the world with him in his millennial kingdom (2Ti 2:12; Rev 20:4; cf. Da 7:22; Mt 19:28).

3 To make his argument even stronger for the validity and competence of Christians to settle cases at Corinth, Paul teaches that Christians will even judge angels, though he does not specify any details (v.3). He probably means that Christians, when ruling in the future with Christ, will have a part in judging the devil and the fallen angels at the Second Coming (cf. Rev. 19:19–20; 20:10). Alternatively, Paul may mean that Christians will preside with Christ over the angelic host (cf. Mt 19:28, where Jesus speaks about sitting "on twelve thrones, judging the twelve tribes," i.e., presiding over them).

4 The main verb "appoint" (GK 2767) is probably an imperative with a sarcastic tone. What Paul is saying is this: "If you must have disputes about these mundane matters when you are destined to judge men and angels, well then go ahead and get the least esteemed members of the congregation to take care of these little matters!" Such an interpretation fits in with Paul's other ironic remarks to the Corinthians (see 4;8).

5–6 Paul now argues positively that if it is really necessary for such disputes to be handled, they should find a Christian wise enough to take care of them, rather than have Christians oppose each other in secular litigation. They should be ashamed of themselves in the way they are acting.

7–8 In climaxing his argument, Paul feels that the very existence of legal cases among the Corinthians shows a malicious attitude and spiritual failure. Instead of being involved in all these disputes and harming and cheating their fellow Christians, they should be willing to suffer wrong.

9–10 Paul concludes that in practicing such acts of wickedness toward others, they had better realize that the wicked will not inherit "the kingdom" (GK 993) of God (cf. Jn 3:3–5). They are in a dangerous frame of mind—they must remember that if they act wickedly in this way, they are no better than those who will not inherit heaven. To the list of sinners already mentioned in 5:10–11 Paul points out specific kinds of sexually immoral people: the adulterers, the male prostitutes, homosexuals (in Ro 1:26 he also mentions lesbians), and thieves. In the light of this comparison, the Corinthians should have seen how unchristian and sinful their actions were toward one another.

11 Some of the Corinthians at one time participated in such sins. In describing their conversion, the apostle lists three transactions that occurred at the time when the Lord saved them: they were "washed" (GK 666), i.e., they were spiritually cleansed by God in submitting themselves to baptism (cf. Mt 28:19); they were "sanctified" (GK 39), an expression either amplifying the concept "washed" (cf. Tit 3:5–6) or meaning that they had been set apart as God's people (cf. 1Pe 2:9); and they were "justified" (GK 1467), showing God's act as judge in declaring sinners righteous because of Christ (Ro 3:23–26; 5:1) and in qualifying them for his cleansing. All this, Paul says, was done by God for them on the authority of the Lord Jesus Christ and by the regenerating power of the Holy Spirit.

2. Christian morality in sexual matters (6:12–20)

Every action we contemplate should be tested by two questions: "Is it beneficial?" and "Will it overpower and enslave me and so have a detrimental effect on the church and my testimony for Christ?" The main thrust of these verses argues against sexual immorality and for glorifying God in our bodies.

12–13 Undoubtedly there were some Christians in Corinth who, without examining the Scriptures and its implications, claimed that it was permissible for them to do anything they desired. In making such claims to unrestricted freedom, they evidently argued that since the physical activity of eating and digesting food did not have any bearing on Christian morals and one's inner spiritual life, other physical activities such as promiscuous sex did not touch on either morals or spiritual life.

Paul grants that food and the stomach are temporal and transitory and, in God's providence, will disappear—but he denies that what affects the body is unimportant; this denial especially includes the undisciplined and unscriptural use of the body in sexual practices (v.13b). So he denies the parallel between eating and digesting food as a natural process and practicing sexual immorality as a natural process. Of course, he is not denying that sex in wedlock is natural and wholesome (7:3–5; cf. also Heb 13:4).

The apostle sets the stage for discussing the horrors of sexual immorality and the contrasting holy use of the Christian's body by stating that as they evaluate their right to do "all things," Christians should ask themselves four questions: (1) Is the thing contemplated beneficial to me? (2) Will the practice in question overpower and dominate me, and will the result affect others? (3) Will the practice support the truth that the body is "for the Lord," who created it and intended it to be used for his glory? (4) Will it support the truth that "the Lord is for the body"—i.e., the Lord has redeemed my body (vv.19–20)? Thus the Christian must have no part with sexual immorality, because the body is not meant for sexual license (v.13b; cf. Ge 2:24) but for the Lord.

14 Paul goes on to state God's interest in the Christian's body. As God raised the body of Jesus from the tomb, so he will raise the bodies of his people from the grave through his power. The phrase "through the power of God" is probably to be taken with both parts of the sentence: the power of God was used to raise the Lord, and it will also be used to raise his people.

15–17 A further argument that the Christian's body is for the Lord is that God's people are members of his mystical body (cf. 1Co 12:27). So Christians may not unite their bodies with that of a prostitute. They should understand that sexual relations involve more than a physical act—they join the two persons together (v.16; quoting from Ge 2:24; cf. Mt 19:5). Since Christians have been joined in union to the Lord, they dare not form another union with a prostitute.

Verse 17 states the case even more strongly: while the one who cleaves to a prostitute is one body with her, the one who cleaves to the Lord is united to him spiritually. In saying this, Paul is not making the union of normal marriage mutually exclusive of the union of God with his people. He teaches in Eph 5:21–32 that the human marriage union is valid and is to be viewed in the light of the Christian's higher union with the Lord. What Paul argues against here is that unholy union with a prostitute is a wicked perversion of the divinely established marriage union.

18 Those who commit sexual immorality sin against their own body—that is, by weakening and perverting the very life process, as well as human character. In contrast, other sins are "outside the body." From such sins Christians should be continually fleeing.

19–20 Now Paul talks positively about how Christians should view their bodies. (1) They should consider that their bodies, including their whole personality, form "the temple" (GK *3724*)—the sacred dwelling place—of God, the Holy Spirit. (2) Christians have received the Spirit from God to help them against sin. (3) They have no right to pervert and misuse their bodies, for they are not their own master but have been purchased by God at a price (v.20). That price, though not mentioned here, is the blood of Jesus Christ (Eph 1:7; 1Pe 1:18–19; et al.). The picture is of a slave (Ro 6:17; cf. 1Co 7:23) being purchased from the horrible system of slavery. Christians have been freed from being overpowered by sin (Ro 6:17–18) and Satan (Col 1:13) and are enslaved to Christ (Ro 1:1) and to righteousness (Ro 6:18).

The conclusion of the matter is that Christians must glorify God in their bodies. Since Paul has been writing about individuals and since the individual Christian is indwelt by the Holy Spirit, it is best to understand v.19 to mean that each individual Christian's body is a temple of the Holy Spirit (contrast 3:16–17).

VII. Paul's Answers to Questions Raised by the Church (7:1–14:40)

Paul now begins to answer questions the Corinthians had raised in a letter to him (7:1). He begins by using the Greek words *peri de* ("now concerning"); he uses this same introductory phrase elsewhere in this section as he takes up other questions of the Corinthians—about the unmarried (7:25), food sacrificed to idols (8:1), and spiritual gifts (12:1). It is not certain whether his instruction in 16:1–4 regarding giving for the need of the saints was in answer to their written question, since it is separated by ch. 15 from the main section dealing with these questions (7:1–14:40). But since the same introductory phrase occurs in 16:1, it is reasonable to conclude that this issue is a postscript answer to another of their questions (see comment on 16:1–4).

A. Instructions Concerning Marriage (7:1–40)

The Corinthians had written a letter to Paul, asking at least two questions concerning the subject that is the topic of this entire chapter. The first was whether a Christian should get married at all (7:1), and the second was whether virgins should get married (7:25). Evidently there were those in Corinth who, as Jewish believers relying on Ge 2:24, were advocating marriage. Others were no doubt arguing for the unmarried state. Besides answering these questions, Paul deals with an additional point, that a Christian should live according to God's calling, whether married or single (7:17–24).

1. Christian obligations in marriage (7:1–16)

1 As to the question from the Corinthian church on the pros and cons of being married, Paul may seem to agree completely with those who argued for a celibate life—in contrast to Ge 2:18, "It is not good for the man to be alone," and the usual Jewish view in favor of the married state. But Paul's statement of 7:1 is not to be taken absolutely; it is his suggestion specifically for Corinth because of some present crisis there (v. 26; cf. vv.29, 35). Part of this crisis may have been connected with possible persecution they might have to suffer for the Lord.

It is difficult to hold, as some do, that Paul here is teaching against marriage because he felt the second coming of Christ was near. If that were his position, he would naturally have argued against marriage in his other letters also. But in Eph 5 and 1Ti 3 he speaks in favor of marriage. Further, in 1Ti 4:1–3 Paul states that "forbidding to marry" is one of the signs of the approaching end-time apostasy, and in Heb 13:4 it is said that "marriage should be honored." It is true that distresses and crises are connected with both the first and second comings of Christ (cf. Mt 24:3–14; 1Pe 1:10–12). But reference to "crises" (7:26) need not be pressed to mean that the Corinthian Christians should not get married because the Lord was to come shortly.

For an alternate view, see the NIV note.

2–4 Having said that it would be good under the present circumstances not to get married, Paul hastens to add that the general rules for marriage should apply. The reason, especially true at Corinth, is the prevalence of sexual immorality, into which they also might be tempted to fall. Since the temptation might affect either sex, Paul specifies that each man should have his own wife and each woman her own husband.

So that no abnormal situations in the Christian marital status might develop, leading to sexual immorality (v.5), the apostle gives instruction regarding normal sexual behavior and attitudes that the Christian man and woman should have (vv.3–6); in doing so he argues against a forced asceticism. Christians should have normal sexual relations, and Paul strengthens his argument by stating that the bodies of the marriage partners belong to each other (cf. 6:16). Having stated the principle in v.4, Paul adds the command that husbands and wives may withhold these normal marital rights from each other by mutual consent, but only for a specified purpose (so that they may spend time in prayer) and for a specified period of time (v.5). In this way, as those who are united to Christ (6:17), they may exercise their rights and privileges in communing with God. But when this separate time of prayer is over, the married pair are to come together again, lest Satan, the enemy of Christians (1Pe 5:8), tempt one or the other partner with sexual immorality through possible lack of sexual self-control. Paul recognizes the strong but normal sexual drive in the human being (cf. Ge 1:28), but also knows that it can be used wrongly to displease God.

5–7 The present tense of the verb "deprive" (GK *691*) in the prohibition in v.5 indicates that some at Corinth were practicing a kind of celibacy within marriage. This sentence may be translated, "Stop depriving one another." Through the word "time" (GK 2789), the apostle impresses on Christians that a time limitation should apply for marriage partners to agree to be parted from one another.

In Paul's comment that "this" comes not by direct command (i.e., from the Lord) but by permission or concession, it is not clear what the "this" refers to. Perhaps it is best to understand it as referring to v.2, indicating that though marriage is desirable and is according to God's creation plan, it is not mandatory. That this is Paul's meaning is evident from v.7, where he says he really wishes everyone was single like him. However, he recognizes that God gives each one his or her own gracious "gift" (*charisma*; GK 5922). Some are given the desire or the inclination to be married, and some have the power to refrain from marriage.

8–9 Paul now gives advice to those who are single, whom he classifies as the unmarried and the widows. It is good or advisable for them to remain in their single state for the reasons spelled out in vv.26, 32–35. However, in another situation Paul counsels the younger widows to marry (1Ti 5:14). He then adds a postscript. If the situation is such that these persons cannot control their sexual desires, they should marry. It is, after all, better to get married than be inflamed with sexual desire, which is hard to control outside of marriage.

10–11 Paul's next major concern relates to Christians and divorce. What he states in v.10 "to the married" is by "command"—not his own, but the command of the Lord. He has just stated that for the unmarried to remain so is a "good" thing if a person can control his or her sexual desires. But for a married couple to stay together is not just "good"—it is commanded by the Lord.

How specifically Paul is citing the words of Jesus depends on whether he had access to the notes of one of the gospel writers or to one of the Gospels themselves. He could have had access to such notes when he visited the Jerusalem area earlier in his ministry (cf. Ac 9:26–28; 11:30; 15:1–2). That such material, as well as any accurate oral tradition regarding Jesus, was available is seen from a statement given by Luke, Paul's close companion (see Lk 1:1–4). Furthermore, the formula for the Lord's Supper in 1Co 11:23–26 is clear evidence that Paul acquired accurate information from an oral or written source concerning Jesus' teaching.

The burden of Christ's command was that the married were not to be divorced (Mt 5:32; 19:3–9; Lk 16:18)—a principle Paul summarizes from both sides of the marriage partnership: the woman is not to separate herself from her husband, and the husband must not divorce his wife (v.11). Such separations seem to have occurred at Corinth, for Paul says, "If she does [separate], she must remain unmarried, or else be reconciled to her husband." The stress in this passage on maintaining the marriage bond unbroken definitely strengthens the second of these options, that separated marriage partners become reconciled.

12–16 Paul now adds instructions beyond those given by the Lord Jesus—instructions having to do with mixed marriages, where one partner has, since marriage, become a Christian. Paul addresses himself to this problem by saying, "To the rest [to the others with marital questions] I say this...."

According to the way Paul writes, there were mixed marriages in the Christian community in this pagan city. Since he preached in Corinth for over a year and a half (Ac 18:11, 18), with many turning to the Lord, we may conclude that while he was still with them some marriages became mixed marriages. Had he at that time given them advice about this? Doubtless he had. But the problem then was probably not so acute for the unbelieving partner when the other partner was a new Christian. The unbelieving one may have thought this stand for Christ was a passing fad or a superstition. As time went on, however, the condition in these Corinthian homes was becoming more serious. In spite of Paul's teaching about Christian living and the sanctity of the home (cf. Eph 4–6), the unbelieving partners in some instances were threatening to leave their Christian husbands or wives. So Paul was confronted with the question, "What should the Christian marriage partners do?"

We should note first, in the light of 2Co 6:14–7:1 (cf. Ezr 10:10), that Paul would not have allowed an already-professing Christian to marry an unbeliever. But on the question of what should be done by a husband or wife who has turned to the Lord after marriage,

Paul is decisive. If the unbelieving partner is content or willing to live with the Christian, then the Christian must not divorce the partner—for the sake, Paul implies, of the marriage bond God has ordained.

Rather (v.14), the Christian partner should think of the truth that the Lord can use him or her as a godly, holy influence in such a mixed family relationship and in helping that family to be consecrated to God. The word "sanctified" (GK 39) does not refer to moral purity—Paul is certainly not teaching that the unbelieving partner is made morally pure through a believing spouse. What the word emphasizes is a relationship to God, a claim of God on the person and family to be set apart for him (cf. Ac 20:32; 26:18). The tense of the verb stresses that the unbeliever who is in a Christian family has already become and continues to be a part of a family unit upon which God has his claim and which he will use for his service. The same is true of children born in such a family. They are "holy" (GK 41) and not "unclean" (GK 176)—i.e., not spiritually separated from God, as is the case in unbelieving families. The Bible's teaching elsewhere about Christian parents and their covenant children set apart for God is also relevant to this passage. Consider Ge 17:1–14, where the children of God's people of the OT were included among God's covenant people, and Ac 2:38–39, where God's promise applied to the children of all believers (cf. Eph 2:12–13). Covenant children are to be counted a part of God's people and should be nurtured in the Christian faith and in the fear of the Lord (Eph 6:4).

Dealing with the actual situation at Corinth, Paul realizes that in some instances the unbelieving marriage partner will not stay. So he teaches that in such an event (v.15), the believer must let the unbelieving partner go. Paul adds two reasons: First, in this case the believer is not "bound" (GK 1530), for the unbeliever by willful desertion (the other legitimate reason for divorce besides sexual immorality; Mt 19:9) has broken the marriage contract. Second, God has called his people to live in peace, which would not be possible if the unbelieving partner were forced to live with the believer.

The force of v.16 tempers any tendency to foster or encourage a rupture in the marriage. For Paul is teaching that the believer must try to keep the mixed marriage together in the hope that the testimony of the believer will be used by God in his providence to bring the unbeliever to Christ.

2. Christian obligation to live according to God's call (7:17–24)

In extending the principle that God has called his people to live in peace (v.15), Paul now teaches that Christians should live contentedly in any station of life in which God has placed them. They should live obediently to God with full confidence in his sovereign purpose whether married or unmarried, Jew or Gentile, slave or free. Paul is not in favor of the subjugation or elevation of certain segments of society, but he wants individual Christians to realize and accept God's sovereign purpose in saving and keeping them regardless of the level of society they are in. Paul is more afraid of the spirit of anarchy and rebellion (cf. Ro 12:3; 13:1–7; 1Co 12:4–11; 2Co 10:13) than of social inequality.

It may well be that Paul's teaching that all Christians are equal (Gal 3:28), that all things material should be viewed as relatively insignificant in the light of eternal realities (2Co 4:18), and that the second coming of Christ will bring in a new order of divine rule (1Co 15:23–28) had made the Christians restless and somewhat discontented with their lot in life. Their place in life is what God has "assigned" (v.17; GK 3532) and called them to. God's people can and must live as Christians, whatever social, economic, and religious level of society they are in. Their conditions do not affect their relationship and service to Jesus Christ.

17 Paul now expands his thought of the Christian's call to other areas besides that of marital status. Christians should live for the Lord wherever they are. This, Paul says, is the principle that he orders to be followed in all the churches (cf. Eph 5:21–6:9; Col 3:18–4:1)—a principle that transcends all boundaries.

18–20 The apostle's first application of this principle is to the religio-national distinctions related to being Jews or Gentiles, being circumcised or uncircumcised. In a Gentile situation like that in Corinth, some Christian Jews may have tried to obliterate the OT covenant mark of circumcision. On the other hand, Judaizers tried to force circumcision on the Gentile Christians (cf. Ac 15:1-5; Gal 3:1-3; 5:1). Paul argues that this outward sign of circumcision with its stress on the Jew versus the Gentile now has no significance. If a person was a circumcised Jew when he was saved, he should not become uncircumcised. If he was an uncircumcised Gentile, he should not be circumcised. Circumcision and uncircumcision now make no difference (Ro 2:25, 29; Gal 5:6), but keeping God's command is essential (cf. Jn 14:15). By repetition, Paul emphasizes this principle in v.20. One should not seek to change his or her station in life.

21-22 Paul's other illustration relates to slavery. The key phrase in this passage is "Don't let it trouble [GK 3508] you" (v.21). Paul is not speaking against human betterment or social service, but he is stressing that Christians in Corinth should live for the Lord without anxiety in their present situation. If they were slaves when they became Christians, they should live on as Christians even while remaining slaves. He adds a parenthetical comment that "if you can gain your freedom, then do so." However, the Bible teaches that Christianity does not guarantee material or social betterment but makes it a matter of individual responsibility (cf. Ps 73; Ac 11:29; 20:35).

Verse 22 refers to v.21. Paul is saying, "If you were a slave when God called you, don't let it trouble you—you are the Lord's freedman. If you were free when called, remember you are Christ's slave." The spiritual antithesis is striking. The Lord has freed us from the penalty of sin (2Co 5:21) and from Satan and his kingdom (Col 1:13) and bound us as "slaves" to himself (Ro 1:1).

23-24 Paul points up the priority of Christ's authority over Christians. In all earthly service they must realize that their obedience and service are to Christ, not to other people. The reason is that God bought us with the price of Christ's blood (5:7; 1Pe 1:18-19). Thus, because on this higher level we are slaves to Christ, we are not to become mere slaves of other people. We serve faithfully in our earthly position, but we serve as slaves of Christ (cf. Eph 6:5-9, Col 3:24; 1Ti 6:2). In v.24 Paul repeats the command of vv.17, 20 but adds the phrase "before God," as though he is saying, "God is looking on and is there with you to help you."

3. Instructions concerning virgins (7:25-40)

Now Paul turns to the second main question: What about "virgins" (GK 4221) and marriage? In this section he discusses the advisability in the present situation of remaining in an unmarried state (vv.25-35). Then he advises that they do what they think is right for the virgin who is unmarried, whether it is by initiating marriage or by remaining single (vv.36-38). He concludes with a statement regarding the married woman's responsibilities to her husband and regarding her freedom to be married again in the Lord if her husband dies. However, Paul thinks she would be happier if she remained unmarried (vv.39-40).

Regarding vv.25-35, Paul maintains that "because of the present crisis" (GK 340), it is better for a man or woman to remain in their present state, whether married or single (v.26). He advises this because the time to do the work of the Lord is so short (v.29); and anyway the material conditions of this world are changing and disappearing (v.31). Paul also introduces certain corrective statements lest the Corinthians draw false conclusions from the main principle. In saying that they should stay married, he insists that marriage itself is not a matter of right or wrong (v.28). He also argues that the real problem they face in their present world situation is the proper expenditure of their time and energies. He is desirous that they devote their energies to the service of the Lord, and this they can do better if they are unmarried (vv.32-34). But he hastens to add that he does not mean to hamper them in such a way as to keep them from marrying—he only wants to help them. His advice, he implies, is not an argument for the superiority of celibacy or the obligatory nature of it (v.35).

25 Paul is not now relying directly on a command from the Lord—i.e., from Jesus—as he was, for example, in Ac 20:35. Rather, he is giving his own opinion on the matter at hand, but his opinion must be taken seriously because by the Lord's mercy he is trustworthy. In other words, his command is not any less inspired than one from Jesus.

26-27 Each person should remain as he or she now is "because of the present crisis" (see comments on vv.1, 29-31). In other words, remain married if you are married; single if you are single.

28 Paul hastens to make it plain that there is nothing sinful in marriage, whether entered into by a widow, a widower, or a virgin. His main motive in dissuading the unmarried from marriage is to spare them the hardship and suffering in physical life that accompany times of trouble and persecution.

29–31 The apostle explains that the time for doing the Lord's work is short and is coming to an end. This is not necessarily a reference to the second coming of Christ, for Paul may have been anticipating severe persecutions and a resulting curtailment of freedom to witness. So for the time remaining Paul admonishes them not to be overwhelmed by the social and material problems of the world but to live for the Lord. By "those who have wives should live as if they had none" (v.29) he means, "Live for the Lord in marriage." If life brings sadness, live beyond it and do not be bound by it. If things are joyous, do not be engrossed in them. Those who are blessed with material possessions should not cling to them, as though they were to have them always. The reason for this challenge is that the material things (this is the meaning of "the present form" in v.31) of this world are changing and disappearing (cf. Col 3:12–14).

32–35 Paul goes on to argue that if they want marriage, they must realize that it brings extra cares, and he wants them to be free from concern. Married persons, whether men or women, have their attentions centered on the desires and needs of their spouses (vv.33–34). In saying that the unmarried woman or virgin is concerned with how she may please the Lord (v.34), Paul implies that the married person is apt to neglect this Christian duty. Since the apostle upholds the right and privilege of marriage even for himself (9:3–5), he must here be advising against marriage because of particular abuses and tensions at Corinth. He is giving this advice for their own benefit, not to restrain them or put them in a noose. Rather, he wants them to live properly in complete and undivided devotion to the Lord.

36 Paul now turns to teaching about virgins of marriageable age, insisting that they must be treated honorably, whether they become married or not. Who is meant by "he" in this verse, the father of the virgin or the man who is engaged to her? Both have been suggested, for in ancient times a father arranged for his daughter's marriage. But more likely "he" refers to the man who is considering the possibility of marrying his fiancée. Paul is teaching that if the situation in Corinth seems to be unfair to a particular virgin and especially if she is passing her prime marriageable years, then the fiancé should go ahead and marry her. There is no sin in their getting married.

37–38 In contrast, the man who feels no need to get married has done the right thing too. The words "who is under no compulsion" refer to outward pressure to marry, such as might come from some prior engagement contract or the pressure of a master on a slave. Paul favors the man who does not marry.

39–40 In climaxing the discussion, Paul states that marriage is a life-long contract. If a woman marries, she is to cleave to her husband till he dies (Ge 2:24). But when he dies, she is free to marry anyone she chooses, so long as he is a Christian. But, Paul says, the woman will be happier—freer from hardship and care—if she remains unmarried. This is his judgment for the Corinthian situation. When he says, rather modestly, "And I think that I have the Spirit of God," he means that in writing this he also is inspired by the Holy Spirit as were the other writers of Scripture. It is possible that some in Corinth were claiming inspiration; if so, Paul is contrasting himself with them in a veiled way.

B. Instructions Concerning Christian Freedom: Its Privileges and Responsibilities (8:1–11:1)

This section focuses on the next question the delegation from Corinth put to Paul: "What about eating food offered in heathen sacrifices to idols?" Paul's answer leads to a discussion of the larger question of how believers should use their Christian liberty. He lays down the principle that love for one's brother or sister in Christ should be the motivating factor in contemplating one's Christian liberty (8:1–13). Then he gives a personal example of how he was ready to forego the exercise of his own rights as an apostle for the sake of God's people (9:1–18). He argues that though he was under obligation to no one, he showed his self-restraint and love by placing himself on the cultural and social level of everyone so that he might reach some for Christ (9:19–27). By way of warning, he speaks of the lack of self-restraint by the OT Israelites, who actually embraced the idolatry they toyed with (10:1–13). So God's people must avoid participation in idol feasts and "flee from idolatry," because they belong to the Lord and have their own feast with him, the Lord's Supper (10:14–22). Paul's conclusion is this: Live your testimony with loving concern for your fellow believers, but do not make an issue of meat sold in the market. Eat it as a gift from God. Do this, except when the point is explicitly made that the meat was offered in sacrifice to an idol. For you would in such a case seem to be participating in this religious heathen practice. Refrain, then, for your weaker brother's sake and for your own peace of mind. Above all, do everything for the glory of God (10:23–11:1).

1. Eating meat sacrificed to idols (8:1–13)

a. Knowledge and love contrasted (8:1–3)

1 With the phrase "Now about," Paul turns to another question asked by the Corinthian delegation (cf. introductory comment on 7:1–14:40). The importance of the question of "foods offered in sacrifice to idols" becomes evident when one realizes how thoroughly idolatry and pagan sacrifices permeated all levels of Greek and Roman society. In Corinth itself, there were no less than sixteen temples and shrines, some of which had dining rooms in them.

Indeed, people could hardly escape contact with the pagan practices and their influence. The meat offered on the heathen altars was usually divided into three portions: one portion was burned up, a second given to the priest, and the third given to the offerer. If the priest did not use his portion, it was taken to the meat market. Thus a considerable amount of sacrificed meat ended up in the public market, on the tables of pagan neighbors and friends, or at the pagan festivals. With such idolatry and other pagan practices dominating the life and culture of Corinth, no wonder Paul was so concerned how Christians exercised their freedom to eat meat sold in butcher shops after it had been offered to some idol and consecrated in pagan worship in the city. They faced questions such as these: Was the meat spiritually contaminated? Did the pagan god actually have an effect on the meat? Even if one did not think so, what would one's participation do to a fellow Christian who might have scruples about this? Though Christians today do not have to deal with this particular problem, they too must face questions of how to conduct themselves in a non-Christian society.

In v.1 Paul concedes that all Christians know—at least theoretically—the real meaning about the meat sacrificed to idols. But, he implies, there is something more—some may really feel that there is something wrong with that meat (v.7). So he adds that the mere knowledge that there is nothing wrong with it inflates one to a level of false security and indifference. As a result, in dealing with this issue, love is necessary. Love takes one beyond himself to aid another; it builds up.

2 Paul warns against dependence on simply knowing something, since a person never knows all that ought to be known about a subject. Such an attitude exhibits a complete dependence on one's own self-sufficient knowledge and illustrates what Paul means by saying, "Knowledge puffs up [GK 5881]."

3 With the essential ingredient of love, knowledge is tempered and made the right kind of discerning and compassionate knowledge exhibited when one loves God. In loving God, a person shows that he is known by God—that God recognizes him as his own and that he had the right kind of knowledge, because he is exercising it in love to his fellow Christians and to God.

b. The meaning of eating meat sacrificed to idols (8:4–6)

4 The word translated "food" (GK 1111) is sometimes translated "meat," since the subject involves altar sacrifices and the meat market. The main thing to remember in connection with such meat is that the idol before which it was sacrificed and the god it represents are actually nothing—i.e., nothing as to personal reality and power. There is only one true God in the entire universe (cf. Dt 6:4–9; 1Ki 18:39; Isa 45:5).

5–6 Paul grants for argument that there are "so-called gods" in heaven and earth, such as those the pagans recognized in Greek and Roman mythology. He also mentions the many "gods" and "lords" who are called

When Paul came to Corinth, he found a city filled with idolatry. These are the ruins of one of the pagan temples at which its residents worshiped. Courtesy Bastiaan Van Elderen.

such in Scripture (cf. Dt 10:17; Ps 136:2–3) and who in the widest sense represent rulers in the universe who are subordinate to God (Col 1:16). Paul is therefore teaching that the "so-called gods" of the pagans are unreal and that the real "gods" and "lords," whatever they may be, are all subordinate to the one supreme God whom alone we recognize. To Paul, there is only "one God, the Father," and "one Lord, Jesus Christ." The Father is the source of all creation, and Jesus Christ is the dynamic One through whom creation came into existence. As for Christians, they live for God, the source of all, and have the power for living through Jesus Christ. So why, implies Paul, should we be concerned with idols or meat sacrificed to idols?

c. Freedom to be exercised with care (8:7–13)

7 The knowledge Paul speaks of here is the previously mentioned knowledge regarding an idol and the existence and position of the "so-called gods." Some may not fully realize the significance of these truths, because in their former unsaved state they had become so accustomed to idols and to the sacrificed meat that when they now eat such meat, they think of it only as something sacrificed to the idol, rather than as food provided by God. Their moral awareness—their conscience—is weak, being unable to discriminate in these matters, and so is defiled.

8 This next statement has a twofold thrust. First, as in v.1, we should know that there is nothing inherently wrong with sacrificial meat and that in itself food neither enhances nor minimizes our standing before God. Second, since the eating of meat is of no spiritual importance, the Corinthians should realize that to eat sacrificial meat is not a practice to be avoided or to be insisted on for maintaining Christian liberty.

9–12 Though Christians have the authority to act as Paul has just described, they must "be careful" (GK 1063) lest through the exercise of this authority they somehow cause the weak (in conscience) to stumble in living their Christian lives. By "stumbling block" (GK 4682) is meant causing the weak believer not only to have a sense of guilt (v.7), but to go beyond this into sin (v.13) by compromising with pagan idolatry.

So Paul depicts for the Corinthians what may well have been an actual scene (v.10): Suppose a brother who is weak in conscience sees you, who understand that an idol is nothing, reclining at table to eat in an idol temple; won't he also be encouraged to eat and so do what his conscience forbids him to do? When you do such a thing, you are using your freedom and knowledge to bring your weak brother down the path toward spiritual weakness and destruction. Paul does not mean ultimate spiritual destruction, for he calls this man a "brother, for whom Christ died." The stress is on weakening the faith and ruining the Christian life of a fellow believer.

Speaking to the strong brother (v.12), Paul says in effect, "If you cause the weak brother to stumble into sin, you yourselves are sinning in a twofold way: (1) against your brother and (2) against Christ, by wounding the conscience of those who belong to him." The plurals in this verse imply that Paul has in mind a sizeable group at Corinth who were both the offenders and the offended.

13 In closing the discussion, the apostle includes himself. He may be indicating that when he was in Corinth, he had had to face this question and had, for the sake of the Christians there, refrained from eating meat that had been sacrificed to idols. So he ends with the personal declaration: "Therefore, if what I eat causes my brother to fall into sin, I will never eat meat again, so that I will not cause him to fall" (v.13)—a noble resolve that stands as an enduring principle for Christian living.

2. Paul: on giving up his rights as an apostle (9:1–18)

a. Rights of an apostle (9:1–12a)

1–2 Paul's reference to the spiritual freedom we have in Christ, coupled with his claim of apostleship, leads him to expand the theme of Christian freedom and apply it in a wider context than that of sacrificial meat. His illustration is particularly pertinent because it involves himself and his important rights as an apostle and Christian worker. The four rhetorical questions in v.1 (all anticipating a positive answer) relate to freedom and apostleship, the last three specifically relating to his apostleship. Paul contends that he is an "apostle" (GK *693*) and then states one of the criteria for an apostle: he had seen the Lord (Ac 1:21–22; 9:3–9). (Another evidence of apostleship is working signs and wonders [2Co 12:12], which Paul had done in Corinth.) Paul then contends that his apostleship had produced spiritual work "in the Lord"—the Corinthians were the fruit of his work. He expected them to accept him as an apostle—though others did not—because they were really the seal that stamped his apostleship as genuine.

3–6 Paul now begins to defend himself against those who have criticized his apostleship on the ground that he had not exercised all the rights one might expect an apostle to use. He brings up certain rights that he and others, such as Barnabas, had the authority to exercise. The first one, "the right to food and drink," means, in the context, daily provisions at the expense of the church (cf. vv.9–11). Next he claims the right to have a wife join him in his missionary travels. In referring to the "rest of the apostles" (v.5), Paul is not saying that all were necessarily married, but that at least a larger part were. The phrase "brothers of the Lord" should be taken at face value—physical brothers (i.e., half-brothers), children of both Joseph and Mary after Jesus was born (Mt 1:18–25; 12:46; 13:55; Ac 1:14; Gal 1:19).

In v.6 Paul raises the practical question of his and Barnabas's right to be supported financially in the ministry. It was Paul's practice to support himself materially by tentmaking (Ac 18:2–3; 1Co 4:12) in order not to be a burden to the church. Some apparently misunderstood this to mean that he was not on a par with other apostles and Christian workers who depended on the church to support them. In not denying that principle, Paul asserts, by way of a rhetorical question, that he has a right to be supported.

7–10 These verses present illustrations supporting the proposition that God's servants have the right to be supported with food and drink and other necessities of life as they labor in their work. Verse 7 gives illustrations from common experiences in ancient life: the soldier supported at public or royal expense; the vineyard keeper, who eats of the grapes he gathers; the shepherd, who drinks milk from his flock. But as an additional argument, Paul cites the authority of Scripture, "Do not muzzle an ox when it is treading out the grain" (Dt 25:4). This merciful command covered the practice in ancient times of oxen pulling the threshing sledge over the grain or treading it out with their feet (Isa 28:28; 41:15; Hos 10:11). They were allowed to eat as they did their work. The reason for the command, Paul says, is not just God's care for the cattle (cf. Mt 6:26–29), but because by it he wants to teach us a lesson about God's care for us (v.10). This is evident, too, in the provision for the farmer: When a plowman and thresher do their work, they do so expecting that through God's blessing they will share in the crop.

11–12a The same principles of the worker's sharing in the results of his crop are now applied to God's spiritual work. Those who have sown the spiritual seed at Corinth with its resultant harvest can expect to have their material needs supplied from that harvest. Certainly, if the Corinthians have supported other Christian workers, should they not also support Paul and his companions, who have sown spiritual seed among them?

This basic principle is true today. The Christian worker who sows the spiritual seed of the Gospel has a right to be supported materially by those who benefit from the Gospel.

b. Rights not used (9:12b–18)

12b The apostle now announces that he will not exercise this or any other "right" (GK 2026) that is his because he and his companions do not want to hinder the advance of the Gospel.

13–14 To emphasize further the reason and importance for his self-restraint in exercising this right of being supported, Paul turns to a religious illustration that was applicable both in OT biblical worship and in pagan temples. The question in v.13 expects a yes answer. His illustration has a particularly telling relation to the Corinthians with their former connections with pagan worship. Paul's language is pointed: When people serve in a temple or are offering sacrifices at the altar, they eat of the temple offerings as part of their payment for their work.

Paul then applies what he has just said. The principle of giving material support to those who serve in the temple must be applied also to ministers of the Gospel. The Lord Jesus himself commanded that those who preach the Gospel should be supported by those who believe the Gospel (see Mt 10:10; Lk 10:8).

15–16 In spite of all this evidence, Paul again states that he has not used these privileges. Nor is he writing this to get them to start supporting him, for he wants to be able to face his opponents at Corinth with the boast that he is unselfishly serving them and the Lord in the Gospel. If one considers only his preaching, that gives Paul no reason for boasting, since the Lord has laid on him the necessity of preaching (Ac 26:16–18). In further explanation, he cries out that God's judgment would descend on him if he did not preach.

17–18 It is true that there is reward or pay in preaching, but only if done without pay. Paul states the alternatives. If he preaches freely, voluntarily, he has a reward; if for pay, he is merely fulfilling the commission entrusted to him (Ac 26:16). His reward is the boasting he can make before them that he is preaching to them without charge and not making use of his rights as a gospel minister. Paul wants to prove to the Corinthians the genuineness of his ministry.

3. Paul: subjection of self for others and to meet God's approval (9:19–27)

19 Going beyond his right to financial support, the apostle now discusses other areas of life in which he has forfeited his right to freedom in order to win more to Christ. His statement is a strong one: "I am free from all men, but I have enslaved myself to all."

20 In discussing his self-sacrificing concern in vv.20–23, Paul mentions three groups—the Jews, the Gentiles, and those whose consciences are weak. For the Jews' sake Paul became like a Jew. That is, when necessary and regarding indifferent matters, he conformed to the practice of Jewish law (cf. Ac 16:3; 18:18; 21:20–26) to win the Jews. "Those under the law" need not be taken as a separate group such as proselytes to Judaism, but as reference again to Jews. In the parenthetical phrase "though I myself am not under the law," Paul means that in his freedom he was not obligated to practice such Jewish laws.

21 For the Gentiles "without the law," those who did not have any written revelation from God (Ro 2:12), Paul says he became like one not having the law—and took his place in their culture in order to reach them (cf. Gal 2:11–21). But he hastens to correct any misunderstanding: he counts himself still under God's law, and even more, under Christ's law.

22–23 Those with a "weak" (GK 822) conscience (cf. 8:9–12) he also wants to be sure to win. With them he becomes "weak"—that is, he refrains from exercising his Christian freedom and acts as they do regarding these indifferent things. He has forfeited his freedom for the sake of all, that by all these means some may be saved. He does this for the sake of the Gospel, that he might share in the blessings of the Gospel personally and see others come to Christ.

24–27 By way of practical application, Paul now gives a strong exhortation for Christian self-denial, using himself as an example and employing athletic figures familiar to the Corinthians at their own Isthmian athletic games, hosted every other year by the people of Corinth. The particular events he refers to are running and boxing.

Paul assumes their common knowledge of the foot race in the stadium (v.25). Every one of the Corinthians believers should run as these runners do, with an all-out effort to get the prize. "Strict training" refers to the athlete's self-control in diet and his rigorous bodily discipline. Paul observes that the athletes train vigorously for a "corruptible crown"—a laurel or celery wreath that would soon wither away. But the Christian's crown, eternal life and fellowship with God, will last forever (Rev 2:10).

Paul says of himself that he does not contend like an undisciplined runner or boxer. Rather, he aims his blows against his own body, beating it black and blue. The picture is graphic: the ancient boxers devastatingly punishing one another with knuckles bound with leather thongs. So by pummeling his body, Paul enslaves it in order to gain the Christian prize.

In the Greek games, there was a herald who announced the rules of the contest; but Paul is not only a Christian herald (i.e, preacher), he is also one who plays in the game. That is, he not only preached the Gospel but he also lived by the Gospel's rules. True Christians, while confident of God's sovereign grace, are nevertheless conscious of their own battle against sin. They do not want to be "disqualified [i.e., tested and disapproved] for the prize."

4. Warning: Israel's lack of self-restraint (10:1–13)

Paul now presents several examples of the sins of Israel during the time of Moses as a basis for warning the Corinthians. Though the Israelites had the covenant blessings and were miraculously delivered and sustained, yet most of them died in the wilderness because of disobedience and unbelief.

1–5 The word "for" connects these verses with the argument in chs. 8–9. Having challenged the Christians in Corinth to self-discipline, Paul now looks back to Israel, who were in the race described in 9:24–27. "I do not want you to be ignorant" is a phrase used by Paul to introduce an important truth (cf. Ro 1:13; 1Th 4:13).

First, Paul stresses the miraculous passage of the Israelites through the Red Sea. "Under the cloud" indicates that they were under God's sure guidance (Ex 13:21–22; Nu 9:15–23; 14:14; Dt 1:33; Ps 78:14). That "they were all baptized into Moses in the cloud and in the sea" simply means they were initiated and inaugurated into union with God and also with Moses and his leadership (cf. the expression "baptized into Christ" in Ro 6:3–4; Gal 3:27); the thought is a spiritual one (v.3). The cloud represented God in his shekinah glory; the sea, God's redemption and leadership.

In the desert they were provided with food and drink. Paul calls these provisions "spiritual" (vv.3–4; GK *4461*), meaning that these physical objects were a means of grace to God's people. They pointed forward to Christ, the true bread and drink to come (cf. Jn 6:30–65). In other words, the entire nation shared in the blessings and the privileges of God's grace.

In spite of all these blessings, however, God was not pleased with most of them (v.5; cf. Heb 3:17–19). He saw in them a heart of unbelief (vv.6–10) and scattered their corpses over the desert. Only Caleb and Joshua entered Canaan and won the prize.

6 All these experiences of the Israelites serve as examples for us to think about, lest we who also have received the covenant blessings should displease God by lusting after evil things as Israel did.

7–10 Paul then cites several OT incidents of what that lusting involved and warns against following the example of the Israelites. Many of them became idolaters, as the story about the worship of the golden calf indicates (Ex 32:1–6). Israel ate a sacrificial meal in dedication to the calf and then got up to dance in ceremonial revelry (Ex 32:6), just as the pagans danced before their gods. This may look back to Paul's discussion in ch.8 about eating meat sacrificed to idols.

Paul's next allusion is to Israel's joining herself to Baal of Peor (Nu 25:1–9), an act involving both spiritual and sexual unfaithfulness. This god of the Moabites was worshiped through the prostitution of virgins; idolatry and sexual immorality were joined together, and Paul warns against such acts (v.8). The NT says 23,000 died, whereas the OT reports 24,000 (Nu 25:9). Paul is speaking about how many died in that one day; he does not include others who were killed subsequently, among them being the leaders in the rebellion, whom God ordered Moses to hang (Nu 25:4).

Paul's next example (v.9) is the murmuring of Israel against the Lord for bringing them out of Egypt, for which they were severely punished (Nu 21:6). With the use of the plural pronoun "we," Paul includes himself in cautioning the Corinthians against complaining like the Israelites and against testing the Lord to see what he will do.

The final example (v.10) relates to Israel's grumbling against the Lord at Kadesh Barnea (Nu 14:2) and their desire to have died in Egypt or in the desert. The "destroying angel" (GK *3904*) was the angel of God (cf. Ex 12:23), whom Paul indicates was sent to bring the plague spoken of in Nu 14:37. The incident referred to may also be the destruction of Korah, Dathan, and Abiram (Nu 16:30).

11–13 Paul now applies these examples for the Corinthians. They have been written down to warn us, he says. His warning amounts to this: "Do not be smug in your firm stand for Christ. Keep alert lest you fall." "The fulfillment [GK *5465*] of the ages [GK *172*]" is the entire stretch of time between the coming of Jesus and the end of the world.

Verse 13 is one of the most helpful verses in the NT and presents the great antidote to falling into sin through temptation. "Temptation" (GK *4280*) is not itself sinful. God allows it as a way of purifying us (Jas 1:12), but the devil uses it to entice us into sin (cf. Mt 4:1). The temptations that come to the Christian are those all human beings face—they are unavoidable. But, says Paul, God is right there with us to keep us from being overwhelmed by the temptation. He will provide a way out, not in order to avoid the temptation, but to meet it successfully and to stand firm under it.

5. Warning: attendance at pagan sacrifices means fellowship with idolatry (10:14–22)

Paul now applies the example of Israel's idolatry to the problem of ch. 8—eating meat sacrificed to idols. There is the danger of going a step beyond just eating sacrificed meat—i.e., joining the pagans in the sacrificial feasts in their pagan temples. To do this would be wrong and sinful. Paul illustrates this by showing that participation in the Lord's Supper signifies that the believer is in a sharing relationship with the Savior. So participation in idol feasts in pagan temples means sharing in the pagan worship, and such participation is forbidden. This is the mistake Israel made. Christians today must discern how the illustration applies to their own lives.

14–15 The apostle's terse injunction, "Flee [GK *5771*] from idolatry," applies not only to the weak who through eating might be led into idolatry but also to those with a strong conscience who, by leading the weak into sin, are also guilty. Paul asks the Corinthians to use good sense and to determine the truth of what he says.

16–17 The cup of blessing or thanksgiving used in the Lord's Supper brings us spiritually into participation in the blood of Christ and into fellowship with him. The same is true of the bread, whereby we become one body with him. The "cup of blessing" was a technical term for the third cup drunk at the Jewish Passover (see comment on Lk 22:14–18), the time when the Lord's Supper was instituted (Mt 26:17–30; Mk 14:12–26; Lk 22:7–23; Jn 13:21–30). That "participation [GK *3126*] in the blood of Christ" is meant to be a memorial symbol of fellowship with Christ rather than a literal drinking of his blood is clear from the fact that (1) Christ had not yet died when he instituted this supper, and (2) this participation is in remembering him, not in drinking him (1Co 11:25).

18–20 Here Paul compares the OT sacrifices with pagan offerings. When the people of Israel sacrificed at the altar and ate part of the sacrifice (Lev 7:15; 8:31; Dt 12:17–18), they participated in and became a part of the sacrificial system and worship of God. The apostle does not mean that the meat sacrificed to an idol or the idol itself is anything, but he does insist that when the pagans sacrifice, they do so to demons, and he does not want the Corinthians to share in worship having to do with demons. One cannot do both—participate in Christ and in demons.

21 To make it clearer, Paul speaks of "the Lord's table"—a term that the Corinthian converts from paganism would readily associate with "tables" used for pagan idol meals. Here is an example of an invitation from an ancient pagan letter: "Chairemon invites you to a meal at the table of the lord Serapis in the Serapeum, tomorrow the fifteenth from nine o'clock onwards." To Paul, a Christian cannot at the same time participate in the meal at the table of the pagan god and the table of the Lord.

22 The conclusion is that if we as Christians share in pagan idolatry, we will "stir up" the Lord's jealousy and thus incite him to action in his hatred of sin and for mixed allegiance (cf. Dt 32:21; Ps 78:58). And surely, Paul says, we are not stronger than God and cannot overcome or subdue his jealousy and anger against sin if we share in pagan practices.

6. Freedom, but within limits: do all to the glory of God (10:23–11:1)

Returning specifically to the thought of ch. 8 that eating meat sacrificed to idols is essentially a matter of indifference, Paul now adds that it can be harmful. He lays down three principles: (1) Though Christians have the right to do all things, such as eating sacrificial meat, it may not be beneficial to them. (2) Such practices of liberty may not in fact build up a fellow Christian. (3) In summary, Christians are not merely to seek their own good but to promote the good of their fellow Christians and the glory of God.

23–30 Meat eaten at an idol feast is associated with pagan worship and is contaminated, Paul claims. But meat sold in the public meat market has lost its religious significance and is all right to eat, as long as one remembers that meat and all things come from the Lord (v.26; the OT quotation from Ps 24:1 was used as a Jewish blessing at mealtimes). The Greek word for "meat market" (GK *3425*) mentioned on an inscription found in Corinth; this establishment could be the very one Paul is referring to, where meat previously offered in sacrifice to idols was sold.

In approving of a believer joining an unbeliever at the latter's house for dinner (v.27), the apostle is thinking of the believer's giving the unbeliever a quiet, appreciative testimony. If, however, at the dinner someone (probably a fellow Christian; cf. v.29a) points out that the meat was offered to an idol, then the believer should refrain from eating the meat. The reason for this is that he does not want his Christian freedom condemned through another man's conscience (v.29). Paul asks why he should be condemned for partaking of something in the meal he could thank God for. So the strong brother has the power to protect his "right" to eat by choosing not to eat meat in such cases.

31–33 These verses introduce a positive and more ultimate perspective. It is not just the other brother who should be in view, but God as the creator and giver of all things. Paul relates this ultimate concept to one's attitude toward the weak brother. The "glory [GK *1518*] of God" must be the Christian's objective in everything (Col 3:17; 1Pe 4:11). But Paul says that doing all for the glory of God means thinking of the good of others, both Christians and non- Christians (v.32). By "the church of God" Paul means to include the brother with the weak conscience (cf. Ro 14:13, 21). So we find encompassed by these verses the two great commandments—love God and love your neighbor (Mt 22:37–39). Paul seeks to benefit others, not himself. His ultimate objective in all his conduct is that people might be saved—not superficially but fully and to the glory of God.

11:1 This verse belongs to the previous discussion. The command given has a continual relevance, "Follow my example" (lit., "Ever become imitators [GK *3629*] of me"). Paul is calling the Corinthians to the unity that had been disrupted (ch. 1). He can do this because he himself is an imitator of Christ (Gal 2:20)—the same Christ who had dealt gently with Paul in all his prejudices (Ac 26:12–18).

C. Worship in the Church (11:2–14:40)

This entire section deals with problems connected with church worship—matters concerning the veiling of women (11:2–16), observing the Lord's Supper (11:17–34), and the granting and use of spiritual gifts (12:1–14:40).

1. Propriety in worship: covering of women's heads (11:2–16)

2–3 Since Paul does not begin this section the way he did 7:1, 25 and later 12:1 (see introductory comment on 7:1–14:40), he is likely taking up the subject on his own rather than answering another question that had come in their letter to him (7:1).

Verses 3–16 have evoked considerable difference of opinion about the nature of the head covering and about the place of women both in public worship and in their relationship to men. The head covering has been interpreted as either a veil or shawl, or else hair—either long or short. As to the use of veils, women in the ancient Orient were veiled in public or among strangers, but otherwise they were unveiled. Rebecca, for example, was unveiled till she met Isaac (Ge 24:65). Painting on ancient pottery, however, shows Greek women in public without head coverings. In Corinth the women may well have gone to public meetings without veils. But the question is whether Paul is talking about the use of veils in public worship or about women letting their long hair hang loose—a sign of mourning or of the shame of an accused adulteress—rather than having it "put up."

4–6 Whichever view is held as to the nature of the head covering, the same basic principles emerge from the passage. In vv.3–10 Paul emphasizes the order of authority and administration in the divine structure of things. As every man is to be under Christ's authority and Christ is under God's authority, so the woman is under her husband's authority. (Paul does not mean by this analogy that subordination in each case is of the same completeness.) Therefore, the woman should not demonstrate her authority by having her head uncovered, as the man did when he was praying and prophesying. Evidently at Corinth women were coming to church with their heads improperly covered, thus causing disorder and disrespect in the services. Paul is not necessarily giving his opinion on the propriety of women praying or prophesying in the church, which he later observes was being done (cf. 14:34), though some feel that since he mentions women praying and prophesying here, he approves of the practice. Paul's point is that if a woman is in the public worship with her head uncovered, it is as if she had her head shaved (v.5). He insists that if the woman in fact does have her head uncovered, she should have her hair cut; on the other hand, since it is shameful for a woman to have her hair cut or her head shaved, then, of course, she should have her head properly covered (v.6).

7–9 In stating that a man should not have his head covered in church, Paul argues that this follows from the principle that man was prior to woman and is the "image" (GK 1635) and "glory" (GK 1518) of God—meaning that he is to be subject to and represent God in authority. The woman, however, is the glory of the man—i.e., she is to be subject to man and to represent him in authority. Although God created Adam and Eve and gave both dominion over the creation (Ge 1:26), Paul argues for man's exercise of authority over woman on the basis of man's prior creation to woman. The argument goes like this: Woman was made from man's body and she was made for man's sake and not the reverse (Ge 2:7).

Although it was not proper for a first-century Jewish man to cover his head for prayer (a custom originally meant to indicate sorrow), yet the act seems to have been innovatively tried in the Jewish synagogues of Paul's time.

10 The woman has a certain authority in that by having her head properly covered in worship, she shows respect for God's ministering angels who are in attendance and serve God's people (Heb 1:14). Perhaps angels are mentioned in this discussion about the place of women in the church to remind Christians that angels are present at the time of worship and that they are interested in the salvation of God's people (1Pe 1:10–12; cf. Gal 3:10) and sensitive to the conduct of Christians at worship. So the angels would recognize the breach of decorum if Christian women did not have proper head coverings and the long hair distinguishing them as women—the "sign of authority [GK 2026] on her head" (v.10), which symbolized her husband's authority over her.

11–12 But lest he be misunderstood as wanting to demote women, Paul now argues that men and women are equal in the Lord and mutually dependent.

13–15 The final point in the passage is that man is to be distinguished from woman. Thus the Corinthians are to see that women should not pray with their heads uncovered as men do. They are reminded that in ordinary life men with short hair are distinguished from women with long hair. If a man has long hair like a woman's, he is disgraced, but with long hair a woman gains glory in her position of subordination to man. Also long hair is actually given to her as a natural veil.

16 Finally, Paul states that he and the churches follow the principle that in worship men come with short hair and women with long, and that the man exercises the position of authority (v.16). This, he implies, should deter those who would want to be contentious about the matter. In using "we" (meaning the apostles), Paul teaches that the Corinthians must take his statements given in vv.2–16 as having apostolic authority, and not as pious advice.

Summary of vv.2-16 The instructions given by Paul relating to the place of women in the church were addressed to the cultural milieu of the Corinthian believers in the first century A.D. Corinth was a pagan Greek city out of which God was calling a church of his redeemed. Apparently some Greek women in the Corinthian church were coming to worship services without a veil on. Also other women may have been going to church with hair disheveled and hanging loose (a sign of mourning or the shame of adultery). So disorder and unrest had begun to mar the services.

The apostle Paul, of course, wanted to correct any such improprieties in that church. But his teaching in these verses goes far beyond the cultural conditions affecting the Corinthian church. Indeed, it was applicable also to other first-century churches (v.16b) and it is applicable to God's people at any time. The principles Paul presents here that are to govern the church and individual Christians in their life and conduct are as follows:

(1) Christians should live as individuals and in corporate worship in the light of the perfect unity and interrelatedness of the persons of the Godhead. The Father and the Son are perfectly united (Jn 10:30), and yet there is a difference administratively: God is the head of Christ (1Co 11:3). So Christians are one, but they too have to be administratively subordinate to one another.

(2) Christians must remember that God first created man, then woman (Ge 2:21–23), and placed the man as administrative head over the woman and the woman as his helper-companion (Ge 2:18). So in the Christian community, the man is to conduct himself as a man (1Co 11:4) and as the head of the woman (v.3), while the woman is to conduct herself as a woman with dignity, without doing anything that would bring dishonor to her (v.5).

(3) Since Christians live in the Christian community of the home and the church, they must remember that God has established the man and the woman as equal human beings (v.12). So in the Christian community believers should treat one another with mutual respect and admiration as they realize each other's God-given special functions and positions.

(4) Christian men and women should remember that, though God has made them equal human beings, yet he has made them distinct sexes. That distinction is not to be blurred in their realization that they are mutually dependent (v.11)—the man on the woman and the woman on the man. It is also to be observed in their physical appearance (vv.13–15), so that in worship the woman can be recognized as woman and the man as man.

(5) God is a God of order. This means order in worship and peaceful decorum in the church (v.16). Therefore Christian men and women should conduct themselves in a respectful, orderly way not only in worship but also in daily life.

2. The Lord's Supper (11:17–34)

In dealing with the Lord's Supper, Paul discusses three matters: first, the problem of believers making a mockery of the Supper because of abuses practiced at the *agape* (GK 27; cf. Jude 12)—the love feast or dinner accompanying the Supper (vv.17–22); second, the necessity of taking the Lord's Supper seriously through rehearsing its institution as given by the Lord (vv.23–26); and third, the warning about partaking of the Supper unworthily (vv.27–34).

17–19 Regarding the meal that evidently preceded the communion service, the apostle condemns the conduct of the believers as harmful and degrading to the communion (see v.20). Their actions at the common *agape* meal were betraying their divisions, including class distinctions between the rich and the poor. Though he might discount part of what he heard, Paul felt he had to believe some of it. Knowing human nature, he assumes some such divisions are inevitable even among Christians, so that those who act worthy of God's approval might be evident.

20 "It is not the Lord's Supper you eat" may be interpreted in two ways—either by supplying the word "it" as in NIV, or by taking the verb "is" to mean "can," thus rendering it, "You cannot eat [or celebrate] the Lord's Supper." Either translation fits the context. What Paul means is that in acting the way he is about to describe, they were not approaching the Lord's Supper in the right manner but were nullifying its spiritual meaning.

21–22 The Christian common meal (*agape* feast) apparently followed the pattern of public sacred feasting among the Jews and Greeks. The food was brought together for all to share (a sort of "potluck" supper), with the rich bringing more and the poor less. As Paul describes it, however, cliques were established and the food was divided inequitably. The rich took their "lion's" share and became gluttons, and the poor remained hungry. So they were bringing contempt on the church of God and humiliating the poor.

23–24 The chief reason why Paul cannot commend their actions is that they do not agree with the spirit of the Lord's Supper as he had received it. Using technical words, Paul writes that he "received" (GK *4161*) from the Lord and "passed on" (GK *4140*) to them the Christian tradition of the Lord's Supper. That most likely means that he received the Lord's words of the institution of the Supper through its being passed on by others, just as he then passed them on to the Corinthians—i.e., through a process of repetition (cf. 15:3–4). Observe the similarity of Paul's words about the Supper with Mt 26:26–29; Mk 14:22–25; Lk 22:14–20.

Since the Supper was celebrated in connection with the Passover (cf. Mt 26:17–29; Lk 22:7–20), we assume that the bread that was available was unleavened. Jesus gave thanks, as was the Jewish practice at a meal. The breaking of the bread was symbolic of Christ's bruised body (Isa 53:5), "given for you" (Lk 22:19). The word "this" most naturally means in the context "this bread" that Christ was holding in his hand as a symbol to represent his body; the bread was not Christ's body itself (cf. somewhat similar figures in John 10:7; 1 Cor 10:4).

25–26 That the Lord's Supper was connected with the Passover meal is clear in the phrase "after the supper," meaning, as the Synoptic Gospels show, "after the Passover Supper." This cup was the third of the Passover cups (see comment on Lk 22:14–18). The word "cup" (GK *4539*), used metonymously for its contents, symbolizes the covenant in Jesus' blood (Lk 22:20). The covenant idea is that of God's sealing his agreement of salvation with his people through Christ's blood. It is a new covenant in being the fulfillment of the covenant promises of God in the OT exemplified in the sacrificial system (cf. Eph 2:12; Heb 8–10). In the ceremony Jesus does not say how often the communion was to be held but indicates that it is to be periodic—"whenever you eat . . . and drink"—and it is to be continued to his second coming. The statement "you proclaim" involves the personal application of the meaning of the Lord's death in the believer's testimony.

27 Participating "in an unworthy manner" (GK *397*) entails coming to the table in an

This mosaic plate and cup, symbols of the Lord's Supper, are replicas of those found at ancient church sites.

irreverent and sinful way and so sinning against the body and blood of Christ. This is what some of the Corinthians had been doing (vv.20–22). Of course, any other sinful approach to the table would be unworthy also. The apostle does not teach, however, that in eating and drinking the elements Christians are physically eating of Christ (see comment on vv. 23–24).

28–30 Now Paul shows how to guard against unworthy partaking of the Lord's Supper. "To examine [oneself]" (GK *1507*) is to put oneself to the test as to the attitude of one's heart, outward conduct, and understanding of the true nature and purpose of the Supper. The Supper is a means of spiritual grace. By self-examination believers guard against eating and drinking to their own judgment through not recognizing the importance of this Supper that commemorates the death of Christ. This judgment is not God's eternal judgment but some temporal judgment such as sickness and death.

31–32 The purpose of self-examination is to come to the table prepared in heart. Paul's teaching justifies the wholesome practice of some churches in having a communion preparatory service that affords opportunity for such self-examination. Here he quickly adds that even when a Christian is judged by the Lord, this judgment is not punitive to destruction, but a form of fatherly discipline (Heb 12:5) to bring God's child to repentance, so that he or she will not be finally and totally judged with the unsaved world (Rev 20:12–15).

33–34 Paul now deals positively with the *agape* meal. In eating it, the Corinthians should show respect for their fellow believers' physical as well as spiritual needs by waiting for each other and eating together. If they come only to satisfy their physical craving and not for communion with the Lord and his people, then they should eat their meal at home, for otherwise God will judge them in some way.

Paul's final comment suggests that there were other irregularities regarding worship and the Lord's Supper, but they were not sufficiently urgent for him to deal with at this time.

3. The use of spiritual gifts (12:1–14:40)

This long section on "spiritual gifts" (*charismata*; GK *5922*) may be divided into several sections. The first emphasizes the source of the gifts, the Holy Spirit (12:1–11); the second, the diversity of the gifts in their unity (12:12–31a); the third, the necessary ingredient of love in the exercise of all gifts (12:31b–13:13); the fourth, a discussion of the priority of prophecy over tongues, with rules for the exercise of each (14:1–25); and finally, the teaching that all church worship must be done decently and in order (14:26–40).

a. The Holy Spirit, the source of spiritual gifts (12:1–11)

1 "Now about" suggests that this section is an answer to another question asked by the Corinthians in their letter (see introductory comment on 7:1–14:40).

2–3 In saying that they had been "led astray to mute idols," Paul implies that the Corinthians had experienced the effects of evil spirits in their former pagan worship. In contrast, he now stresses the twofold test of the presence of the Holy Spirit in a believer's life. Negatively, no person by the Spirit can curse Jesus; and positively, only by the Spirit can a person openly testify that Jesus is Lord (v.3). Lord (*kyrios*; GK *3261*) was used in the LXX (Greek translation of the OT) to translate Yahweh ("LORD" in NIV). In this context Paul recognizes the deity of Jesus and of the Holy Spirit in the phrases "Jesus is Lord" and "Spirit of God."

4–6 By using the words "service" (GK *1355*) and "working" (GK *1920*), Paul indicates that such spiritual gifts were useful in serving the Christian community. Here he teaches that the Trinity is involved in administration of these gifts: the Spirit; the Lord; God (cf. 2Co 13:14; Eph 4:3–6).

7–10 Paul goes on to declare that many spiritual gifts are given by the Spirit for the total good or profit of his church. Different gifts are given to different people—not all have the same gift (cf. 12:29–30). The gifts given to each person are clearly intended to be used for the common good.

The gifts listed begin with the most important one—the ability to express the message of God's wisdom in the Gospel of Christ. The second is the ability to communicate with knowledge of God's way of salvation by the Spirit. The gift of "faith" (GK 4411) does not refer to one's initial trust in Christ for salvation but to deeper expressions of faith, such as undergoing hardships and martyrdom; hence it can be rendered "faithfulness."

The next two gifts—the outwardly demonstrable ones of healings and miracles—belong together and were particularly applicable to the ministry of Paul and the other apostles (Ac 19:11–12; 28:7–9; 2Co 12:12). The mention of the gift of prophecy anticipates ch. 14 and seems to include an ability to give insights into, and to convey the deeper meanings of, God's redemptive program in his Word. It is to be distinguished from the inspiration of the Holy Spirit (2Ti 3:16) given the apostles and their associates to prophesy in setting forth God's truth in Scripture. Paul separates the apostles' office from that of prophets in 12:28, where the prophetic office is listed between that of the apostles and the teachers and does not include in it, in this period of church development, the miracle-working function listed separately in 12:29.

By the gift of distinguishing between spirits (v.10b), Paul must be indicating a distinct ability beyond that which the apostle John calls on Christians in general to exercise (1Jn 4:1). The ability to speak in different kinds of "tongues" (GK 1185) has been taken to mean speaking in ecstatic, humanly unintelligible utterances, possibly similar to the ecstatic speech exhibited in pagan Greek Dionysiac expressions. In the light of Ac 2:4ff., however, where it is said that the Holy Spirit gave the Christians on Pentecost the ability to speak with different languages, we are safe to say that the ability mentioned here is the ability to speak unlearned languages.

Many have attempted to differentiate between the tongues-speaking at Pentecost in Ac 2 and that in 1Co 12–14. A list of these differences, together with responses, is as follows:

1. At Pentecost the disciples spoke to people (Ac 2:6) but at Corinth the speaking was to God (1Co. 14:2, 9). Reply: In Corinth, though the speaking in tongues was to God, it was also a speaking to people when there was speaking in the church service through someone who interpreted (14:26–27).

2. At Pentecost tongues were a sign or credential to believers but at Corinth to unbelievers (1Co 14:22). Reply: At Pentecost, at the time when the people heard the tongues they were unbelievers (Ac 2:12–13); it was only when they heard the message in Peter's sermon that many of them believed (Ac 2:41).

3. At Pentecost the unbelievers were filled with awe and marveled (Ac 2:7–8), but at Corinth the unbelievers thought the Christians were mad (1Co 14:23). Reply: In Acts 2 the unbelievers also were bewildered (v.6); they were amazed and perplexed (v.12), and some even thought the believers were intoxicated and they made fun of them (v.13).

4. At Pentecost there was harmony (Ac 2:1), at Corinth confusion (1Co 14:23). Reply: This contrast must not be pressed to imply a difference in the nature of the tongues spoken; it only reveals the generally disorderly conduct of the Corinthian congregation seen in their party spirit (1:10–17) and in their reprehensible conduct at the Lord's Supper (11:17–34).

The foregoing points suggest that there is no significant difference in the nature of tongues between Ac 2 and 1Co 12–14. The only concrete evidence we have as to the nature of the tongues-speaking in the early church is found in Ac 2, where it is a speaking in foreign languages that were understood by those who listened. Since in this initial instance the speaking in foreign tongues was done by the apostles and their close companions, it is logical to conclude that as the apostles were involved in the subsequent scriptural examples of tongues-speaking (Ac 10:44–46; 19:1–7; 1Co 12–14), these situations should also be understood as speaking in a foreign language.

In v.10d Paul hastens to add that such speaking in tongues should be accompanied by interpretation or translation by someone with that ability, a subject expanded in ch. 14. That Paul is simply giving a sampling of gifts is evident from his expansion of the list in 12:27–30 and in Ro 12:3–8.

11 Paul concludes that regardless of what spiritual gift each person has, the Holy Spirit has sovereignly distributed them to produce his own spiritual results. Therefore, no one should despise another person's gift, a gift given by the Spirit for the good of all (v.7). This theme the apostle develops in vv.12–26. The Spirit mentioned here is set forth as one who is sovereignly God (he wills to give the gifts) and personally active (he "works" all these gifts in the lives of his people).

b. Unity in the diversity of gifts in the body of Christ (12:12–26)

12–13 Paul now illustrates the diversity and unity of the spiritual gifts by the example of the human body. It is made up of many parts, all of them important, and yet the whole body functions as a unit. By the words "So it is with Christ," he means so it is with Christ's "body" (GK *5393*), the church. That the invisible church is an organic whole is seen in that every believer, regardless of racial and religious connection (Jew or Greek) or social standing (slave or freedman), has been united by the one Spirit into one spiritual body in baptism. The figure is now reversed—all the believers have drunk one Spirit; i.e., each one has received the same Holy Spirit (cf. 1Co 6:19; Eph 5:18–20). Paul is here emphasizing spiritual baptism and the communion of spiritual food and drink (cf. Jn 7:37–39; Ro 6:4; 1Co 10:3–4). It is not the local church alone that Paul is speaking of here, but the church universal.

14–20 Paul now emphasizes the necessity of having diversity in a body for it to operate as one. Each part (such as the eye or the ear) must be willing to perform its own function and not seek to function in a role for which it was not made. The whole body cannot be a single part, or it would not be a functioning body. So it is with the church. Members with one gift should not repudiate that gift and complain that they do not have some other gift. The apostles were to function as apostles, the elders as elders (1Pe 5:5), the deacons as deacons (Ac 6:1–6), etc.

The logic of v.17 is compelling: no body can function as all seeing, all hearing, or all smelling. So for the church to function properly, it must have different gifts and offices. In vv.18–20 Paul brings the believers back to the sovereign purposes of God. It is God who has organized the human body in the way he wants it, and it is the same with the church; according to his will, its many parts should function as one body—the body of Christ.

21–26 Here the emphasis is on the mutual dependence and concern of the various members of the body. As the organs of the human body—such as the eye, hand, head, and feet—need each other, so the members of the church with their various functions need each other. Moreover, the least attractive and inconspicuous parts of the body are important and should be treated with respect (vv.22–23). So also the inconspicuous members of the church are essential—those who pray, those who work with their hands and bring their meager tithes into the church, etc. As the humbler parts of the body are given special attention by covering them with appropriate clothing and, as in the case of the digestive organs, providing them with food, so the inconspicuous members of the church—the poor, the despised, the less prominent—are to be cherished and nurtured.

The "But" in the middle of v.24 brings the argument back to God's sovereign purposes. He has brought the members of the body together in perfect harmony. By saying that God "has given greater honor to the parts that lacked it," Paul means that through implanting modesty and self-respect in our hearts, God has caused us to protect our unpresentable parts (such as the sex organs) from exploitation by properly covering them. All this concern for the body is for the purpose of enabling it to operate in unity, so that all its parts will mutually respond to each other's needs—e.g., the brain sending nerve signals to the hand. The word "division" (GK *5388*) in v.25 reminds the Corinthians of the discussion in 1:10–17. As it is with the body, so with the church (v.26). What happens to one part affects the well-being of the whole.

c. Offices and gifts in the one body of Christ, his church (12:27–31a)

As he speaks about that spiritual unity of the body of Christ, Paul declares that each Christian has his or her function as a part of that body. He illustrates this by a selective list of church offices and spiritual gifts (cf. Ro 12:3–8; Eph 4:11).

27 Paul has the entire Christian church in mind with the phrase, "the body of Christ." The plural "apostles" confirms that here there is a wider reference than to Corinth alone.

28 It is the sovereign God alone who dispenses offices and gifts to his church. The order of the gifts here is instructive. The first three—apostles, prophets, and teachers—are in the same order as in Eph 4:11 (cf. Ro 12:6–7) and, as placed first, must be considered of greatest importance; these are classes of persons ruling in the church. The next gifts are set off from the first three by "then" and range in order from miracles to the ability to speak in different kinds of tongues, which, being mentioned last, seem to be of least importance. The office of apostle was all-encompassing, including the gifts of prophecy, teaching, miracles, and the rest. But the prophetic gift (cf. Ac 11:24; 13:1; 15:32; 21:10) did not include apostolicity, though it did include teaching. The teacher class did not compare with that of apostles or prophets. The rest of the list includes gifts given various members of the church—gifts that, while of lesser significance, are yet of importance.

Those having the gift of being "able to help others" are persons gifted in helping the church officers deal with the poor and sick. Those with "administration" have ability to govern and manage affairs in the church.

29–30 By these rhetorical questions, all of which imply "no" for an answer, Paul stresses the principle of divine selectivity. Not all believers function in each of the ways listed. God selects individuals and gives them their specific gifts (v.28). Paul ends v.30 with the gift of interpretation of tongues, because he will comment on this in ch. 14. As in v.28, "tongues" comes last in his list.

31a Having mentioned tongues and their interpretation, Paul urges Christians to seek the better gifts—not that of speaking in tongues, which the Corinthians apparently wanted to have more fully. The possession of specific gifts, says Paul, is not so important as the way in which the gifts are exercised.

d. The supreme position of love in the ministry of the church (12:31b–13:13)

This supremely beautiful chapter speaks first of the superiority and necessity of love—gifts are nothing without love (12:31b–13:3). It then describes the essential character of Christian love (vv.4–7) and tells of the enduring nature of love (vv.9–12). Finally, it proclaims love to be greater even than faith and hope (v.13).

12:31b–13:1-3 Verse 31b introduces ch. 13. Love is the most excellent way for Christians to use their spiritual gifts. The word "love" (*agape* GK *27*) is used in the NT of the deep and abiding affection of God and Christ for each other (Jn 15:10; 17:26) and for us (1Jn 4:9). It is also used of Christians in their relationship with one another (e.g., Jn 13:34–35). Christians are to love, because they belong to God, and "God is love" (1Jn 4:8).

In referring to tongues and prophecy (13:1–3), Paul is apparently trying to counteract the excessive emphasis the Corinthians were evidently placing on these gifts to the detriment of love for Christ and for their fellow believers. "Tongues of men and of angels" are obviously the languages humans and angels use. (On occasion, angels spoke to people in human language; e.g., Lk 1:13–20, 26–38.) It was in the temple worship that the "resounding gong" and "clanging cymbal" were struck (2Sa 6:5; 1Ch 13:8; Ps 150:5). Also prophecy, understanding mysteries and knowledge, and possessing dynamic faith are nothing apart from love. Both "mysteries" (GK *3696*) and "knowledge" (GK *1194*) mean the deep, secret things to be discovered about God's redemptive works. "Faith" (GK *4411*) refers to special acts of faith (e.g., performing miracles), as the reference to the moving of mountains shows (cf. Mt 21:21). Moreover, Paul says that giving all one's material wealth to the poor can be done without love and that one can even be martyred or submit voluntarily to torture without a sense of love for others.

4–7 Christian love is now described positively and negatively. Its positive characteristics are patience (slow to become resentful), kindness, delight in the truth, and a protective, trusting, hopeful, and persevering attitude. Verses 4b–6a state love's characteristics negatively. "Is not rude" may refer obliquely to the disorderly conduct at worship (11:2–16; 14). Love "keeps no record of wrongs"; indeed, for love to keep a record of wrongs violates its nature. Love does not rejoice in evil, in which it has no part; but it does "rejoice with" the truth, with which it does have a part.

Furthermore, love covers the faults of others rather than delighting in them (v.7). It is trusting, optimistic, and willing to endure persecution (cf. Ro 5:3-4). In short, it "perseveres" (GK *5702*).

8-12 Love is permanent, in contrast with prophecies, tongues, and knowledge—all of which will cease to exist because they will cease to be needed. The reason these three will cease is that they are imperfect and partial (vv.9-10) compared to perfect knowledge and prophetic understanding in heaven. Paul does not say when they will cease. Some think he meant that the need for miraculous gifts would cease to exist at the end of the apostolic period. This view is based in part on the implications of the meaning of the term "perfection" (GK *5455*) in v.10, which is taken to refer here to the completion of the canon at the end of the first century A.D. With this view, the term "prophecies" (GK *4735*) in v.8 is taken narrowly as referring to direct, inspired revelatory communication from the Holy Spirit. This cessation would apply also to tongues and to the special gift of knowledge (vv.8-9).

There is something attractive about this view as an argument against the position that the gifts of vv.8-10 continued beyond the apostolic period; however, it is difficult to prove the cessation of these gifts at the end of the first century A.D. by taking "perfection" (*teleion*) to refer to a completion of the canon at that time, since that idea is totally extraneous to the context. On the other hand, in a number of contexts the Greek words related to *teleion*, such as *telos* ("end"; GK *5465*) and *teleo* ("to bring to an end"; GK *5464*) are used in relation to the second coming of Christ. This is true in both 1:8; 15:24 and in non-Pauline writing (cf. Jas 5:11; Rev 20:5, 7; 21:6; 22:13). Therefore, it seems more appropriate to understand *teleion* in v.10 to mean that "perfection" is to come about at the Second Coming, or, if before, when the Christian dies and is taken to be with the Lord (2Co 5:1-10).

All things considered, one can argue for the cessation of the gifts of prophecy, tongues, and the special gift of knowledge on the basis of the larger context of Paul's writings and on the basis of the grammar of vv.9,13, rather than on the meaning of a specific word. According to Paul, prophecies, tongues, and knowledge will pass away soon. His view seems to be that this passing away will occur when the important office of apostle with its requirement of men having seen the Lord and having been a witness to his resurrection (Gal 1:14-24) is no longer exercised. But "now" faith, hope, and love continue to remain.

Paul's illustration of a child's thoughts and speech, real but inadequately conceived and expressed in comparison with those of mature persons (v.11), aptly conveys the difference between the Christian's present understanding and expression of spiritual things and the perfect understanding and expression he or she will have in heaven (v.12). The metaphor is that of the imperfect reflection seen in a polished metal mirror (cf. Jas 1:23) of the ancient world in contrast with seeing the Lord face to face (cf. Ge 32:30; Nu 12:8; 2Co 3:18). Paul's thought in 12b may be expanded as follows: Now through the Word of God, I know in part; then, in the presence of the Lord, I will know fully—to the full extent that a redeemed finite human being can know and in a way similar in kind to the way the Lord in his infinite wisdom fully and infinitely knows me. The Corinthians, Paul implies, must not boast now of their gifts (cf. 13:4), for those gifts are nothing compared to what is in store for the Christians in heaven.

13 The words "and now" introduce Paul's conclusion; namely, "and now, there are faith, hope, and love—they, to be sure, remain now and forever." By faith and hope remaining in eternity Paul means that trust in the Lord begun in this life will continue forever and that hope in the Lord begun now (Ro 8:24- 25) will expand and issue into an eternal expectation of his perfect plan for our eternal existence with him (cf. Rev 22:3-5). Love is the greatest of these three graces because through faith love unites Christians personally to God (1Jn 4:10, 19) and through God's love (Ro 5:5) we are enabled to love one another (Jn 13:34-35). Love is communicating grace and identifies us as children of God (Jn 13:34-35; 1Jn 4:8; et al.).

e. The priority of prophecy over tongues and rules for the exercise of both (14:1-25)

This significant chapter deals with two important subjects: (1) the relative value and use of prophecy and speaking in tongues (vv.1-25) and (2) orderly conduct in public worship (vv.26-40).

1 CORINTHIANS 14

Having established in ch. 13 that prophecy, tongues, and all spiritual gifts must be exercised in love, Paul now argues that prophesying is to be preferred over speaking in tongues since the former, because it is understood, edifies the church; whereas, without an interpreter, the latter does not. Because of Paul's stress on the need for interpretation (vv.5, 13), the implication is that the Corinthians, in their desire to speak in tongues and their pride in it alone, had neglected this essential matter.

1 In making his transition from the beautiful thirteenth chapter (14:1a), Paul uses a strong verb—"pursue" ("follow the way of" in NIV; GK *1503*; cf. Php 3:12, 14)—as he charges the Corinthians to seek love. This verb is stronger than the following one ("eagerly desire"; GK *2420*), which he applies to seeking spiritual gifts. So love must have the priority; after that the gift of prophecy must particularly be sought.

2 Paul now begins to show why tongues are not to be preferred. In speaking in tongues, the speaker is talking only to God (cf. Ro 8:26) in a language unknown to other people. "Mysteries" (GK *3696*) refers to the deep truths of God's salvation (cf. Ac 2:11). "By [or, with] the spirit" does not refer to the Holy Spirit, who is not mentioned in the context, but to the person's own spirit (vv.14–15).

3–4 Paul describes the advantages of prophesying (GK *4736*). Prophecy edifies the church, whereas by speaking in tongues, one builds oneself up in seeking spiritual fellowship with God. There is no mention here that the speaker understands the tongues; not until later does Paul discuss the problem of understanding and insist that the gift of interpretation should be sought by speakers in tongues (vv.13–15). "Encouragement" and "comfort" are aspects of the edifying or strengthening that comes from prophesying.

5 Paul emphatically restates v.1b: Speak in tongues, you Corinthians, yes; but more than that, I want you to prophesy, because this gift brings understanding and strengthening to the church. However, if there is an interpretation of the tongue, then speaking in tongues can strengthen the church.

6 At this point Paul draws a conclusion. Since tongues without interpretation do not edify, what good would it do the Corinthians if Paul came speaking in tongues unless the message he brought were understandable? The four kinds of messages he lists may be put into two categories: (1) supernatural revelation (cf. Gal 2:2) and prophecy, and (2) natural tools of communication—knowledge and teaching (cf. 1Co 12:8–10). The conditions are stated here as possible, not factual. Paul is not saying that he will come to them speaking in tongues, but only that *if* he were to do so, it would be futile unless he brought an understandable message.

7–9 Paul now gives some vivid illustrations. The flute and the harp were well-known and valued musical instruments in Greece, and the Jews would be acquainted with the music of temple worship. But music is nothing more than senseless sounds without systematic differences in pitch, tone, and time. Everyone in Corinth would understand the necessity of the trumpet's call to battle (cf. Nu 10:9; Jos 6:4, 9). Applying the illustrations, Paul says that it is not the mere sound of speaking that is important, but whether the sounds can be understood by the hearers.

10–12 Paul's reference to the "languages in the world" and the "foreigner" substantiates the conclusion that in his discussion of tongues he has in mind known foreign languages, which convey meaning by their systematic distinction of sounds. The "meaning" (lit., "power"; GK *1539*) of a language refers to its "power" to convey meaning. In v.12 Paul applies these things to the Corinthians. They should major in gifts that will strengthen the church.

13–14 With the possibility before them of a non-understood tongue, Paul now argues that its interpretation must be sought. He urges this not only so that those who hear but do not understand may know the meaning, but also that the speaker himself may be benefited by getting an intellectual as well as a spiritual blessing from the exercise. The expression "my mind is unfruitful" means that the mind does not intelligently share in the blessing of the person's spirit. The mind is that faculty in a person that is involved in conscious, meaningful reasoning. Paul desires the Corinthians to have a complete blessing here, both in their spirits and in their minds.

15–17 Praying and singing in the spirit and mind (v.15) are involved in praising and giving thanks to God (v.16), all of which are to be a coherent part of Christian worship (Eph 5:18–19). "Those who do not understand" are Christians who do not understand the tongue without an interpretation, or inquirers about Christianity who do not understand the language. Such people, too, are important, Paul implies, for they also ought to be able to say "Amen" (cf. 1Ch 16:36; Ne 5:13; 2Co 1:20; Eph 3:21) to the thanksgiving conveyed in the strange language. But how can they do that and mean it, when they do not understand what they have heard? Paul grants that the tongue may in itself be conveying thanksgiving to God, but it was important for Christians without that gift to understand it (v.17).

18–19 Having said that he has the ability to speak in foreign tongues more than all of them (an ability he could properly use), Paul hastens to add he would rather speak a few words in a language the church knows so that they might grow spiritually.

20–25 In this section Paul first calls on the Corinthians to think maturely, as "adults" (GK *5455*) in Christ, rather than be controlled by evil motives in their appraisal of tongues. He then implies that prophecy is superior to speaking in tongues because though tongues, as in Ac 2, can be impressive to the unbelievers in showing that God is present and can lead them to face the claims of Christ, yet prophecy can be more effective in bringing the unbeliever to conviction of sin. This was true of Peter's sermon following the speaking in tongues at Pentecost (Ac 2:14–37). To illustrate his point that there is no special mark of divine blessing to have people in the congregation who can speak in a language not understood, Paul cites Isa 28:11–12, his point being that if Israel would not hear the Lord through the prophets, they certainly would not hear when he spoke in foreign languages to them through foreign people. So, Paul is saying, why put so much stress on tongues?

Paul concludes (v.22) that tongues can be and are a sign of something miraculous, an indication of God's presence to unbelievers (cf. Ac 2). Believers do not need that sign, for they already have the indwelling Holy Spirit (Ro 8:9–11; 1Co 6:19). But this is not all. Too much emphasis should not be placed on tongues even for unbelievers, for excessive use of this gift will have an adverse effect on them, and they will think that the Christians are out of their minds (v.23). Furthermore, everyone needs the blessing of prophecy that can bring unbelievers visiting the church under conviction of sin (vv.24–25). Those who "do not understand" seem to be unbelievers who have begun to show interest in the Gospel—inquirers. The effect of Christian prophecy on such people is threefold: They will be convicted of sin (cf. Jn 16:8); they will be called to take account of their sins and examine their sinful condition; and they will have their sinful heart and past laid open to inspection (cf. Jn 4:16–19). The entire church through its prophetic message has, in God's providence, a part in bringing unbelievers to this place of conviction. They will then recognize that God really is present and is dealing with them.

f. Orderly conduct in Christian worship (14:26–40)

In this final section on conduct in church worship, Paul insists that all the parts of worship should be conducive to instruction and edification. Tongues, prophecy, and other gifts were to be practiced under strict regulation (vv.26–33a). Also, for the sake of decorum in the churches, women were not to speak in public worship (vv.33b–36). Paul declares that what he is writing is the Lord's instruction (vv.37–38). He concludes by encouraging the Corinthian Christians to seek to prophesy and not to prohibit people from speaking in tongues, provided the whole of the worship service is decorous and orderly (vv.39–40).

Paul is not so much addressing his remarks here to particular individuals as to the entire church. All his imperatives are in the present tense, indicating that the church must keep a constant supervision over all these aspects of its worship.

26–28 Verse 26 gives us a short outline of the elements of worship in Corinth: a hymn, instruction, revelation, a tongue, an interpretation. Some of this is reminiscent of Jewish worship (cf. Mt 26:30; Lk 4:16–30). Paul again stresses here the unity and diversification of gifts in the church. One person has this ability, another that one; but all gifts must be used to build up the church (cf. vv.3–5). As for tongues, they must be regulated, with only two or three speaking, one at a time and with someone interpreting (v.27). The phrase "in turn" (v.31) suggests that the speaker in tongues is not the one doing the interpreting, though on some occasions it is conceivable that he may himself have done so (v.13). Without an interpreter, there was to be no public tongues-speaking in the church. Thus the one speaking in tongues had the responsibility of finding out first if an interpreter was present. If not, the speaker must be silent in the worship service and speak only to himself and God (v.28). Perhaps this means that if no interpreter was on hand, one should do tongues-speaking at home.

29–33a As for regulating prophesying in church, only a limited number—not over three—should speak, lest so much be said as to cause confusion. The mention of revelation (v.30) suggests that the prophecy in mind involved a revelation, a special deep teaching, which, however, was distinct from the kind of revelation of inspired Scripture (2Ti 3:14–17). Such teaching should be heard even from one who had not been on his feet to speak. In some way the person with this revelation was a spokesman for God in giving some edifying message to the church. The "spirits of the prophets" (v.32) are the spirits of those who were guided by the Holy Spirit in using this special gift. And these prophetic utterances were subject to being checked by other prophets for accuracy and orthodoxy. All this would lead to the peace and order of which God is the author (v.33). Paul was afraid of unregulated worship that might lead to disorderly conduct and belie the God of peace who had called them to be orderly.

33b–36 Paul now turns to the role of women in public worship, the implication being that men were to lead in worship. Paul indicates that his instruction for Corinth was followed in all the churches, thus emphasizing the universality of the Christian community. All the churches were composed of "saints" (those set apart for God), and should be governed by the same principle of orderly conduct.

The command seems absolute: Women were not to do any public speaking in the church. This restriction was not to be construed as demoting women, since the expressions "be in submission" (GK 5718) and "their own husbands" are to be interpreted as simply consistent with God's order of administration (cf. 11:7–8; Eph 5:21–33). "The Law says" must refer to the law as set forth in such places as Ge 3:16; 1Co 11:3; Eph 5:22; 1Ti 1:12; Tit 2:5. A woman's request for knowledge was not to be denied, since she was a human being equal to the man. Her questions could be answered at home rather than by asking her husband in the public service and so possibly interrupting the sermon.

The word "woman" (GK 1222) has the general meaning of an adult female, but it also means "wife." Paul uses the word here in the general sense when he states that "women should remain silent in the churches." That he assumes there were many married women in the congregation is evident from his reference to "their husbands" (v.35). He does not address himself to the question of where unmarried women (cf. 7:8, 36ff.) were to get their questions answered. We may assume, however, that they were to talk in private with other qualified persons, such as Christian widows (7:8), their pastor (cf. Timothy as a pastor, 1Ti 5:1–2), or elders who were "able to teach" (1Ti. 3:2). At any rate, a woman's femininity must not be disgraced by her trying to take a man's role in the church.

But what about the seeming contradiction between these verses and 11:5ff., where Paul speaks of women praying and prophesying? The explanation may be that in ch. 11 Paul does not say that women were doing the sort of things in public worship that are discussed in ch. 14.

Paul's rhetorical questions (v.36) are ironical and suggest that the Corinthians had their own separate customs regarding the role of women in public worship and were tending to act independently of Paul's other churches. They were presuming to act as though they had originated the Word of God (i.e., the Gospel) and as if they could depart from Paul's commands and do as they pleased in these matters of church order.

37–38 Paul now steps delicately. He had given strict commands but wants to soften their impact. He asks for those who have the gift of prophecy and are spiritually gifted to authenticate the fact that his commands are from the Lord (v.37). But immediately Paul returns to his strict injunction (v.38). The tone is abrupt, the meaning is clear: anyone who ignores it will be ignored by Paul and the churches, or possibly even the Lord, and so be considered an unbeliever (1:18).

39–40 These closing verses revert to prophecy and tongues. Paul urges the Corinthians to keep on desiring to prophesy and not to prohibit people from speaking in tongues. But Christian worship must be marked by good order.

Summary At this point a summary of the place of speaking in tongues in the apostolic community of the first century A.D. and also a discussion of tongues in the post-apostolic period and the relevance of tongues in the twentieth-century church are in order. (1) In Paul's discussion of this and other gifts in chs. 12–14, he emphasizes priority of love over tongues and other gifts (ch. 13).

(2) In the list of offices (those of apostles, prophets and teachers) and gifts for the church (12:27–31a), the office-gifts are listed first, with other gifts following, the last being "tongues." This implies that Paul gives priority to office-gifts over the others. Furthermore, among the office-gifts, that of apostles, who were unique in having seen the Lord, ceased to exist in the first century A.D.

(3) In his treatment of tongues and prophecy in ch. 14, Paul again shows his preference for prophecy over tongues, since the former was the gift that brought edification to the church (vv.1–5). He minimizes the importance of the gift of tongues (v.19).

(4) In his discussion in ch. 12 regarding the diversity of gifts and their functions in the church, the body of Christ, Paul uses the analogy of the human body with its various parts functioning in unique and distinct ways without each one trying to usurp the function of another part. So he shows that the gifts, including tongues, were not to be sought for the sake of the gifts, nor was everyone to seek to have the same gift, such as tongues.

(5) God does not have to work by miraculous means in order to accomplish his purposes; he usually uses ordinary natural means—e.g., in the production of crops, he uses the sun, the rain, and the nutrients of the ground, as well as the hard work of people in farming the land. In connection with "spiritual gifts," it is significant that in 12:5–11 not all of the gifts mentioned are miraculous; in fact, gifts of wisdom and knowledge (v.8) are mentioned before the miraculous ones, including tongues. It is not essential that everyone have a miraculous gift (see 12:29–30).

(6) On the basis of the phenomenon of foreign languages spoken of in Ac 2:5–12, we have argued that the tongues referred to in 14:13–15, 20–25 were also foreign-language tongues—not ecstatic utterances, gibberish, or nonunderstandable erratic variations of consonants and vowels with indiscriminate modulation of pitch, speed, and volume.

(7) The essential offices for building up the body of Christ, the church, are, according to Paul (Eph 4:11–16), those of apostles, prophets, evangelists, and pastors-teachers. He says nothing there about the necessity of miraculous gifts either in evangelism (Eph 4:11) or in the teaching-edifying ministry of the church (vv.12–16).

(8) The other NT passages in which Christian worship patterns are set forth do not include miraculous gifts and functions. This is true not only for worship in the developing church under Paul's ministry as portrayed in the last half of Acts and in the letters, but also in the worship of the OT and early NT periods involving predominantly Jewish Christians. These important elements of worship were: the reading of Scripture and expounding it with understanding (Ne 8:1–8; Lk 4:16–30; Ac 2:17–36); prayer (1Ki 8:10–61; Ac 14:23; 16:25); singing (1Ch 25; Ac 16:25; Eph 5:19); Christian fellowship (2Ki 23:1–3; Ac 2:42); and Christian ceremonies or sacraments (as the Passover in Ex 12 and the Lord's Supper in Ac 2:42; 20:7; 1Co 11:17–32). Miraculous gifts, including tongues, are absent from these contexts, the conclusion being that they were not to be a necessary part of the general worship patterns of the church.

(9) Miraculous activity, including speaking in a tongue, did come in biblical times from other sources than the Lord. Witness such activity induced by evil spirits and satanic forces—the Gerasene demon-possessed man (Lk 8:26–39) and the spirit-possessed girl (Ac 16:16–18). Psychological factors were involved in the superhuman strength and tongue-speaking activity of the Gerasene demon-possessed man, for upon his deliverance from the demons, he was found to be in

his "right mind" (Lk 8:35). Therefore caution and balance are needed in relation to such miraculous activities as speaking in tongues. We must also recognize that other gifts were similarly perverted by Satan. The OT speaks more than once of false prophets, as does the NT. The Bible speaks of false pastors (e.g., Zec 11:17; Jn 10:12–13) and frequently warns against false teachers. Yet no one would insist that either prophecy in its valid sense of speaking out for God to the people or the pastoral-teaching ministry is no longer valid. Misuse of a gift does not invalidate the gift itself. However, because of their intimate psychological nature, "tongues" must be viewed with special caution and not be overstressed.

(10) Directly after the first-century apostolic period, legitimate miraculous gifts, such as tongues, practically ceased. There is little evidence for miracle-working in the post-apostolic church; not until the fourth century did claims to miracles become abundant. Furthermore, the writings of the Apostolic Fathers contain no clear and certain allusions to miracle-working or any other supernatural gifts.

Why was there a preponderance of miraculous gifts, including tongues, at the time of the ministries of Jesus Christ and his apostles? After all, miraculous gifts do not appear as a part of God's working among the believers in many parts of the biblical record. Abraham, Isaac, Jacob, and the twelve patriarchs did not possess or use miraculous gifts, nor did David, Isaiah, Jeremiah, and others. However, when certain prophets of God needed particular support and verification, then God performed great miracles through them, as with Moses and Joshua (Ex 12–40; Jos 1–7) and Elijah and Elisha (1Ki 17–2Ki 13). Likewise, during Jesus' ministry and that of his apostles, God verified their message and work by performing mighty miracles through them, including the speaking in tongues on Pentecost. Then miracles ceased when the need for the particular witness ended and the writing of the Scriptures was complete.

As to the relevance of tongues-speaking in the church today, we may observe, in addition to the foregoing discussion, that the requirements Paul gives for the important offices of elder and deacon (1Ti 3:1–13; Tit 1:5–9) say nothing about the necessity that the bearers of these offices have such gifts (cf. also Eph 4:11–13). Also, the instructions given Christians as to how they are to live together in the various units of society (Eph 5:21–6:9; Col 3:18–4:1; 1Pe 2:13–3:7; 5:1–7, et al.) say nothing about the exercise of these kinds of gifts.

In conclusion, this writer believes that the best answer to the question of the relevance of the gift of tongues today is found in the principle that God used this and other miraculous gifts in OT and apostolic times to authenticate the messengers of his word, and that the present-day Christian should not seek such gifts. This is not to say that the churches collectively and individually should not pray that if it is God's will, the sick may be healed by his power, or that the church should not pray for deeper illumination in understanding God's inerrant written Word.

Having said this, this writer realizes that many Christians of orthodox and evangelical commitment hold that the gift of tongues as set forth in Acts and 1Co 12–14 is relevant today. Some of them no doubt recognize that speaking in tongues is the least of the gifts, as suggested in 12:28–30 (where Paul placed it last in the list) or in 14:5, 18–20, 22–24 (where he subordinates it to prophecy). But they would insist that the gift is not completely ruled out for this modern era, since Paul declares, "Do not forbid speaking in tongues" (14:39).

Moreover, some Christians who accept the present validity of tongues maintain that contemporary conditions point to the end times and are the reason for a resurgence of tongues. Also, they emphasize that any practice of tongues-speaking today must be done in accordance with the guidelines of 14:26–40. Perhaps most would say that tongues-speaking may best be practiced in private (especially when there is no interpreter), where one can speak in a tongue to God alone (14:2, 8).

These present-day advocates of tongues would undoubtedly agree that this gift, as well as any of the other gifts, should not be considered an end in itself but must be exercised in love (13:1–3)—not as a spiritual ornament to be seen or as a test of spiritual attainment. Rather, they would say, it must be used as an instrument for the service and glorification of God.

VIII. The Resurrection of Christ and of the Christian (15:1–58)

This is the classic chapter on the resurrection. In it Paul argues the whole subject of the resurrection from the dead—a teaching that some in the church at Corinth had been questioning (see v.12).

How he had heard about this denial he does not say. But the question gives him an opportunity to bring again before the church the doctrine of the bodily resurrection of Christ, which, along with the death of Christ, he had faithfully communicated to them (vv.1–3). He validates the historical reality of Christ's resurrection by citing eyewitnesses, including himself (vv.4–11). He argues the validity of the resurrection of believers from the fact of the resurrection of Christ (vv.12–19) and then shows that Christ's having been raised and becoming the firstfruits of the believing dead guarantees the sequence of events at the second coming of Christ (vv.20–28). He refers to the futility of certain practices of baptism for the dead (vv.29–30) if the dead are not actually raised. He also asks why Christians should suffer for Christ if there is no resurrection and calls on the Corinthians to give up these doubts and witness to their faith in a risen Christ (vv.29–34). Finally, in a passage of great eloquence, Paul discusses the nature of the resurrection body and the victory over death that God will give us through our Lord Jesus Christ (vv.35–58).

A. The Resurrection of Christ (15:1–11)

1–2 Paul begins by reminding the Corinthian Christians that the resurrection is an integral part of the Gospel he had preached and they had received and believed (see comment on 11:23). The "if" clause in v.2 implies that Paul believes they are really holding firmly to the Word of God and are therefore saved. So the sentence "Otherwise, you have believed in vain" means that the Gospel assures them of salvation unless the supposed faith they had was actually empty and worthless.

3–8 "Of first importance" stresses the centrality of the doctrines cited to the Gospel. Paul gives two kinds of witness to the historic events of Christ's death and resurrection: the OT Scriptures and the testimony of eyewitnesses. He does not quote specific OT passages but must have had in mind such texts as Isa 53:5–6 and Ps 16:8–11. He mentions Christ's burial to show the genuineness of his death and resurrection. Paul feels no compulsion to cite any eyewitnesses of Christ's death, because its factuality was commonly accepted. The resurrection was a different matter, however. If Christianity was to be believed, valid eyewitnesses must be cited to attest this historical event and set to rest doubts about the resurrection of the dead.

That "Christ died for our sins" (v.3) implies that Christ was sinless. That he was raised agrees with the Scripture in Ps 16:10 (cf. Ac 2:25–32); so also does Paul's statement about the third day, which may be based on Jesus' words in Mt 12:40 that relate his three days in the tomb to Jonah's three days inside the fish (Jnh 1:17). According to Jewish reckoning, "three days" would include part of Friday, all of Saturday, and part of Sunday.

Part of the message Paul passed on to the Corinthians was eyewitness reports of the resurrection of Christ, some of whom Paul names. It is natural for him to include Cephas (Peter) and the apostles (possibly referring to the meeting recorded in Lk 24:36ff. and Jn 20:19ff.). "The Twelve" is a designation of the apostles as a group and is not to be pressed numerically, since Judas was no longer there and on one occasion Thomas (Jn 20:24) was not with them. The apostolic witness was of vital importance for the Corinthians, and Paul doubtless included the witness of the 500 especially to impress doubting believers with the sheer number of eyewitnesses of the event. Some of them may have been known to the Corinthians. This appearance of Christ to so many at one time may have taken place in Galilee, where the eleven and many more went to meet the risen Lord (Mt 28:10, 16). "Fallen asleep" (GK *3121*) is an early Christian expression for dying (cf. Ac 7:60; 1Co 11:30).

The James mentioned in v.7 certainly is not one of the two apostles of that name—James the son of Zebedee and James the son of Alphaeus (Mt 10:2–4), since the whole group of apostles is mentioned next and would include these two. Instead, it must be the Lord's half-brother (Mt 13:55), who had, with his brothers, joined the apostolic band (Ac 1:14) and eventually became prominent in the Jerusalem church (Ac 15:13). We do not know when this appearance took place. Since Paul had mentioned "the Twelve" in v.5, "all the apostles" (v.7) must be used more loosely to include others who met with the apostolic band (cf. Ac 1:13–15). All this evidence (vv.5–8) was received by Paul from the eyewitnesses themselves (cf. Gal. 1:18–19) and possibly from some of the gospel writers.

Paul includes himself as the last witness (v.8). He describes himself as one born of a miscarriage, thus conveying his feeling that he was not a "normal" member of the apostolic group, but one who had been snatched out of his sin and rebellion by the glorified Christ (Ac 9:3–6).

9–11 Paul reflects on his own unworthiness and on God's matchless redeeming grace. Though he taught that all are unworthy before God (Ro 3:10–18), he felt himself particularly unworthy because he had persecuted the church. He calls it "the church of God"; therefore, in persecuting it, he felt he had been persecuting God. With true humility, he attributes all his hard work for the cause of Christ solely to God's amazing grace (v.10). Then, with great emphasis, he declares that all—both he and the other apostles—preached the same Gospel with the same stress on the resurrection, and this is the message the Corinthians believed.

B. The Validity of the Resurrection of the Dead (15:12–19)

12–16 Paul now presents his major proposition. Some at Corinth had argued that there was no resurrection of the dead. He replies that this is absolutely contrary to the proclamation that Christ has been raised. The particular verb form he uses (in vv.4, 12–14, 16–17, 20) emphasizes the present reality of that historic fact (cf. Gal 2:20). The conditional sentences throughout this section use a construction that assumes a fact: "If it is preached [as it is] that Christ has been raised . . ." (v.12; also in vv.13–14, 16–17, 19).

Having questioned the contention of some that the dead do not rise (v.12), the apostle states a series of conclusions flowing from the contention that the dead do not rise: (1) There is no resurrection of Christ (v.13); (2) preaching that he has been raised is then empty and meaningless (v.14a); (3) their resultant faith in Christ is also meaningless (v.14b); and (4) his own testimony about Christ's resurrection is false, because it claims God did something he really did not do (v.15). Verse 16 closes this set of conclusions by reiterating the statement of v.13.

17–19 Paul draws additional hypothetical conclusions from the thesis that Christ has not risen from the dead: (1) Faith is not only vain or meaningless (v.14), it is also fruitless (v.17); (2) believers still carry the guilt of their sins and are not justified (v.17b; cf. the converse in Ro 5:1); (3) there is no hope for those who have died in Christ—they have perished (v.18); (4) therefore putting up with persecutions and hardships is futile; and finally, (5) we are most to be pitied among men (v.19).

C. Christ the Guarantee of the Resurrection From the Dead (15:20–28)

20 The "but . . . indeed" is an emphatic and conclusive way of introducing some vitally important affirmations. Certainly, Paul implies, none of the Corinthian believers would deny that an integral part of the Gospel is the resurrection of Christ (15:1–4). Therefore, they must now accept the sequel—Christ guarantees the resurrection of the Christian dead, as the word "firstfruits" (GK 569) teaches. By "firstfruits" Paul brings to bear the rich imagery of the OT. The "firstfruits"—the first sheaf of the harvest offered to the Lord (Lev 23:10–11, 17, 20)—was not only prior to the main harvest but was also an assurance that the rest of the harvest was coming. So with Christ. He preceded his people in his bodily resurrection and he is also the guarantee of their resurrection at his second coming.

21–22 These verses are similar to Paul's two-category contrast in Ro 5:12–21. The man who brought death is Adam, and the one who will bring about the resurrection of the dead is Christ (cf. also 1Co 15:45). All who are represented in Adam—i.e., the whole human race—died. All who are in Christ—i.e., God's redeemed people—will be made alive at the resurrection (cf. Jn 5:25).

23 The expression "each in his own turn" stresses the different times involved: Christ the "firstfruits" was made alive three days after his death; the other group, those who belong to Christ, will be made alive "when he comes" (*parousia*; GK 4242). This term refers here to Christ's second coming at the rapture (cf. Mt 24:27; 1Th 4:13–17).

24–27 Paul continues with the idea of time-sequences (cf. "then"). At the time of Christ's second coming and the resurrection of the blessed dead (cf. Rev 20:4–6), then in order will come the process of his handing over the kingdom to God. This will include his conquest of all earthly and all spiritual powers and enemies (cf. Col 1:16). The picture is total, including the physical kingdoms of this world. This future total conquest of the rulers of this world is further suggested in v.25. Christ must continue his reign (i.e., his millennial reign; Rev 20:4–6) until all his enemies are conquered. The expression "under his feet" (an allusion to Ps 110:1; cf. Mt 22:44) is an OT figure for total conquest. The mention of Zion in Ps 110:2 suggests further that his enemies include those who attack Palestine (Rev 16:12–16) and Jerusalem (Rev 20:7–10) at the time of the millennial reign of Christ. Finally, death, the last enemy, is destroyed (v.26) at the close of the second-coming events at the great judgment (Rev 20:2–15). This results in the consummation of Christ's conquest of his enemies and all other things, as implied by the prophetic statement about "man" and particularly about the incarnate Christ in Ps 8:6 (quoted in v.27).

Some think the reference to "the end" (GK 5465) in vv.24–27 refers to the absolute end of this world, at which time believers will be raised. They hold that what follows "then" in v.24 is identical with what follows the "then" in v.23. According to this view, the end in v.24 is the final end, and it is not preceded by a literal thousand-year reign in which Christ puts his enemies under his feet. But this interpretation changes radically Paul's idea of events following each other in temporal sequence, to an abrupt "then the end will come," where there is no more sequence. This seems arbitrary, and it does not take adequate account of the fuller teaching on this subject in Rev 20:4–10—a passage that posits a reign of Christ and a time when this earth will have peace and rejuvenation before its final destruction (Rev 21:1). In Ro 8:18–25 it is stated that the whole creation (including the earth) will be delivered from "its bondage to decay" and will be delivered from decay at the time of the "glorious freedom" of the children of God. All of this occurs, according to Rev 20–21, before the destruction of the present heavens and earth. God's dealings with this present heaven and earth are described in Rev 21:1, not as a rejuvenation, but as a total destruction of what is called the "first" heaven and earth; a "new" heaven and a "new" earth (an earth in which there is "no longer any sea") take the place of the old ones (cf. 2Pe 3:10–13).

28 Verse 27 makes clear that in the "all things" God the Father is not made subject to Christ. On the other hand, v.28 suggests that the Son in a certain sense will be made subject to God the Father. That this does not mean inferiority of person or nature is shown by the future tense of the verb: "the Son himself will be made subject." If there were inherent inferiority, the present tense would be expected—i.e., "he is ever subjected to the Father." But the future aspect of Christ's subjection to the Father must rather be viewed in the light of the administrative process in which the world is brought from its sin and disorder into order by the power of the Son, who died and was raised and who then, in the economy of the Godhead, turns it all over to God the Father, the supreme administrative head. All this is to be done so that God will be recognized by all as sovereign, and he—the triune God—will be supreme (cf. Rev 22:3–5).

D. Implications of Denying the Resurrection From the Dead (15:29–34)

29 Paul now returns to his argument for the resurrection of the dead. There is a special difficulty in understanding v.29 because we do not know the background of the words "baptized for the dead." There are many interpretations, but it is difficult to find a satisfactory one. The present tense of "baptize" suggests that the practice of baptizing for the dead was current and evidently well known to the Corinthians. Most views center around the idea that Paul is referring to the practice of living believers being baptized for deceased believers who had died unbaptized or perhaps for deceased relatives who had never become believers. At any rate, Paul simply mentions the superstitious custom without approving it and uses it to fortify his argument that there is a resurrection from the dead.

30–32 Another argument for the resurrection is that if it is not true, then suffering and hardship for the sake of Christ are useless. By "endangering ourselves every hour," Paul seems to be alluding to peril looming up in his ministry in Ephesus (cf. Ac 19; 2Co 1:3–10), where he was when he wrote this letter. He is in danger of death every day (v.31). He seals this assertion with the oath that this is as true as the fact that he glories over them and over their union with Christ.

Paul's reference to fighting with wild beasts in Ephesus (v.32) may be taken literally or figuratively. But since from Ac 19 we see no evidence of such punishment and since it was questionable whether a Roman citizen would be subjected to such treatment, it is best to take the words metaphorically—the human enemies he fought with at Ephesus were like wild beasts. Paul's main point is: why go through all this suffering if there is no hope of resurrection? To prove his point, he first quotes Isa 22:13 (possibly for the benefit of the Jewish believers at Corinth). Without eternal hope through the resurrection, people have nothing to turn to but gratification of their appetites.

33 Turning to Greek literature, Paul supports his position by quoting a piece of practical worldly wisdom from the Greek poet Menander, relevant to the situation in the Corinthian church. The "bad company" points to those who were teaching that there is no resurrection and so were a threat to the testimony of the church.

34 Paul calls for the Corinthians to stop sinning in denying the resurrection of the dead and, by implication, the resurrection of Christ—a denial that leads to loose living. There were some in the church who did not know God or the precious doctrine of the resurrection. They were in a shameful condition, Paul says, because they were espousing such a denial of the truth.

E. The Resurrection Body: Its Nature and Change (15:35–58)

With incomparable logic, Paul's argument mounts toward its magnificent climax. First, he discusses the nature of the resurrection body (vv.35–49). Then he describes the transformation the body must undergo before death is conquered and the believer lives with God eternally (vv.50–58).

35–49 Paul now answers the question some believers were asking: since a resurrection "body" (GK *5393*) would be like the sinful mortal body we now have, how can the resurrection of such a body occur? Paul calls such questions foolish, and in replying to them he uses analogies from the physical life and world. His first analogy is the seed analogy (v.37), which teaches that through "dying" (decaying in the ground), a seed gives birth by God's power to a new and different "body," though one related to the seed it came from.

A second analogy involves the body of flesh that various forms of animal life have—the different kinds of flesh for humans, animals, birds, and fish (v.39).

A third analogy relates to inanimate objects of creation (vv.40–41), in connection with which Paul again uses "body." These also differ. The "heavenly bodies," such as the sun, moon, and stars, differ from "the earthly bodies," and their "splendor" differs from "the splendor of the earthly bodies." Moreover, the heavenly bodies themselves differ from one another in splendor and brilliance. So, Paul is arguing, God is able to take similar physical material and organize it differently to accomplish his purposes.

In vv.42–44a the apostle applies these analogies to the truth of the resurrection of the body. God can take the mortal body,

According to legend, Paul was incarcerated in a prison in Ephesus, located in the mountain in the background of the picture.

perishable (Gal. 6:8), dishonored, humiliated because of sin (Php 3:20–21), and weak (Mk 14:38)—a natural body like those of the animal world—and bring that body that "is sown" in death (cf. Jn 12:24) into a different order of life in a spiritual body. Such a body will indeed have immortality (2Ti 1:10), glory (Php 3:21), and power. It will have a spiritual way of functioning similar to the way heavenly bodies function in contradistinction to earthly bodies. This spiritual body is an imperishable yet utterly real body—one of a different order and having different functions from the earthly body; it is a body given by God himself—a body glorified with eternal life.

Verses 44b–49 develop the distinction between the natural body and the spiritual body by bringing in two categories—one of Adam and his descendants and the other of Christ, the last Adam, and his redeemed ones. By "natural body" Paul means one such as Adam had when he was made of the dust of the ground and given the breath of life (cf. Ge 2:7). By "spiritual body" the apostle means an imperishable body that has received eternal life from Christ, the life-giving Spirit (cf. Jn 5:26)—a body that will be changed, without either corruption or mortality, in order to live with God eternally (Php 3:21), just as Christ in his resurrected and glorified human body (Lk 24:36–43) went to heaven to be with the Father (cf. Acts 1:11; 2:33). There is, indeed, a real sense in which the accounts of the post-resurrection appearances of Christ in Lk 24; Jn 20–21; and Acts 1:1–9 shed light on the nature of the resurrection body (see also 2Co 5:1–10; 1Jn 3:2).

50–58 Paul now comes to the conclusion of his argument for the resurrection. God's people must have more than the natural body to inherit the eternal kingdom of God. "Flesh and blood" (GK *4922* & *135*) refers to the mortal body—our present humanity, which Christ fully shared through his incarnation (Heb 2:14). This mortal body is perishable and cannot inherit that which is imperishable. So the unsaved cannot be in heaven at all, and the saved must have their bodies changed.

By using "mystery" (GK *3696*) in reference to the resurrection body, Paul implies that there are various things about that body that the Corinthians did not understand, and about which he wants to inform them. (1) Not all Christians will "fall asleep," for some will be alive when Christ returns (1Th 4:15). (2) All Christians will receive changed bodies when Christ comes back and summons his people at the sound of the last trumpet (cf. Rev 11:15). Theologians call this "the rapture" (1Th 4:13–17). (3) The change will occur instantaneously and completely for all Christians, whether living or dead. (4) The change will occur from one kind of body to another. The "perishable" (GK *5785*) bodies (i.e., those in Christ whose bodies are decaying in the grave) will be given "imperishable" ones. The "mortal" (GK *2570*) bodies (i.e., those in Christ living in mortal bodies at the time of Christ's return) will be given "changed" (GK *248*) immortal bodies—ones that will not die. When this occurs (v.54), the triumphant words in Isa 25:8 and Hos 13:14 will become a reality for God's people. (5) With strong emphasis on the words "victory" (GK *3777*) and "sting" (GK *3034*), Paul reaches the climax of this song of triumph in vv.56–57. If it were not for sin, death would have no sting. It is the law of God with its stringent moral demands that strengthens the power of sin by showing us how sinful we are, and thus condemns us. But death does not have the final victory! Hear the glorious closing exclamation (v.57): "Thanks be to God! He gives us the victory through our Lord Jesus Christ." Yes, victory, even over death and the grave, has been won through our Lord, who died and rose and is coming again.

Following this glorious outburst of eloquence, Paul concludes with a practical, down-to-earth exhortation (v.58). It is almost as if he is saying to the Corinthian Christians and indeed to all of us: "Now, my brothers and sisters, in the light of these sublime truths, be steadfast in doing the Lord's work, knowing that he will reward you at his coming."

IX. The Collection for God's People, Requests, and Final Greetings (16:1–24)

A. The Collection for God's People (16:1–4)

1–4 This section begins with "Now about," the same phrase as was used in 7:1 and 12:1 (see introductory comment on 7:1–14:40). The Corinthians had evidently asked about the "collection" (GK *3356*) to be taken up for

God's people at Jerusalem (v.3). Paul must have spoken to them earlier about it, as he also did later (cf. 2Co 8–9). This offering for the poor in Jerusalem was much on his mind during his third missionary journey (cf. Ro 15:26). That he mentions the Galatian churches here implies that this collection was to be a widespread and extensive effort with the Corinthian Christians contributing along with those from other lands. Why some of the Christians in Jerusalem were poor (Ro 15:26) at this time (c. A.D. 55–56) he does not say. It may have been in part because of the famine referred to in Ac 11:29 (c. A.D. 49). Some maintain that the poverty resulted from the Jerusalem Christians' being overgenerous in giving away their property and goods (cf. Ac 2:44–45; 4:34–35).

Paul teaches that the collection was to be set aside by each individual (and family) on the first day of the week (i.e., Sunday). While we are not told specifically that it was to be collected at church, the reference to Sunday suggests that the Christians were to bring their offerings to church on that day, since that was the day they assembled for worship (Ac 20:7; cf. Rev 1:10). Giving was to be proportionate; all were to participate, whether rich or poor; and the money was to be regularly set aside. The offering was to be planned for and saved up ahead of time instead of being hurriedly and ineffectively collected when Paul visited them. It was to be properly handled by messengers approved by the Corinthians themselves, who, bearing letters of recommendation to the church at Jerusalem, carried the gift. Paul eventually made provision for approved messengers to avoid any suspicion of wrongdoing with the funds (cf. 2Co 8:16–21).

In v.4 Paul does not explain why he may be going to Jerusalem, but he probably is thinking that some missionary business to be conducted there (cf. Ac 21:17–19) might compel him to do so. Or he may be thinking that he would like to be in Jerusalem when the gift was delivered. At any rate, he says that if he should go, the approved messengers would accompany him.

B. Personal Requests (16:5–18)

These requests revolve around Paul's travel plans (since he expects to leave Ephesus) and around his friends—Timothy, Apollos and others who have helped him, and the Corinthians.

5–9 The projected journey through Macedonia fits the record of Paul's travel in Ac 19:21 and 20:1–2, which shows that after following that route, he ended up spending three months in Greece—most likely in Corinth. This intention of spending the winter with them (1Co 16:6) relates to the "three months" mentioned in Ac 20:3. "To help him on his journey" must mean endorsing Paul's intended trip and encouraging him, perhaps with fresh supplies and equipment. Paul did not seem to want to burden them by asking directly for money (cf. 1Co 9:7–12).

His work, Paul feels, is not yet finished at Ephesus (vv.8–9), because a great door (cf. "door" in Ac 14:27; 2Co 2:12; Col 4:3) of opportunity stands open for him there. We are not told just who the opponents at Ephesus were, but according to Ac 19:23–27 they included the pagan craftsmen engaged in making miniature silver shrines of Artemis. The reference to Pentecost means that Paul expected to stay at Ephesus until well into spring, then go during the summer to Macedonia (including Philippi), and finally spend the winter in Corinth. The following spring, by Pentecost time, the apostle was at Jerusalem (Ac 20:16; cf. 20:6, which states that Paul sailed from Philippi after the Feast of Unleavened Bread, about forty-two days before Pentecost).

10–11 The reference to Timothy's coming must be connected with Ac 19:22, where Paul sent Timothy (and Erastus) into Macedonia. Therefore, at the time Paul wrote this, Timothy was traveling and was expected to arrive in Corinth (1Co 4:17). Because Paul remembered that the Corinthians had acted so harshly toward himself (4:1, 8–13), he was afraid that they would treat the timid Timothy (1Ti 4:12; 2Ti 1:7) coldly.

Paul's young helper, Timothy, had been with him for several years (Ac 16:1–3) and (as the Corinthians must have known) was doing effective work. When Timothy's work for the Lord was finished at Corinth, Paul expected the Corinthians to send him back with all his needs supplied and with their blessing. The brothers coming back with Timothy may have included Erastus (Ac 19:22), who was a Corinthian believer (Ro 16:23).

12 The way Paul brings up the matter of Apollos—"Now about" (cf. introductory comment on 7:1–14:40; also comment on 16:1)—suggests that the Corinthians had asked about him and had perhaps suggested that he visit them. The text implies that Apollos was working independently of Paul, for Paul could only strongly urge him to go. Apollos was apparently with Paul when the Corinthians made their inquiry, but because of the past tense of the verb "was willing," when Paul actually wrote 1 Corinthians Apollos was apparently no longer with him.

13–14 Paul now includes several apt exhortations, as he generally does at the end of his letters (Ro 16:17–19; 1Th 5:12–22; et al.). His reference to "the faith" reminds one of the discussion of the faith in 15:14, 17. In a dramatic way, he encourages them to "be men [and women] of courage" (GK *437*).

15–18 The reference to "the household [GK *3864*] of Stephanas" was evidently prompted by the Corinthians' lack of respect for them; by personal experience the apostle knew full well that the Corinthians were capable of disrespect. There is no conflict with Ac 17:34 in the statement in v.15 that those "in the household of Stephanas" were the first converts in Achaia, for Ac 17:34 speaks only of individuals like Dionysius, Damaris, and "a number of others" at Athens; here, however, a whole household (including the family and slaves) is in view. He urges the Corinthians to submit to the household of Stephanas and others like them because that entire family was committed to serving God's people.

Fortunatus and Achaicus—mentioned here for the first time (v.17)—were, along with Stephanas, probably the ones who brought the letter referred to in 1Co 7:1 to the apostle. That this delegation had "supplied what was lacking" may be taken to mean that their coming had encouraged Paul by showing him that the Corinthians were at least willing to ask his advice. So they "refreshed his spirit" and the spirit of the Corinthians also (v.18) in that they were willing to go to Paul. Or perhaps Paul means that the Corinthians will be refreshed when the three men get back home and tell of their visit to him.

C. Final Greetings (16:19–24)

19–20 Characteristically Paul concludes with a series of final greetings. First, he wants the Corinthians to know that the churches of Asia are interested in them and send greetings. The term "Asia" is used by Paul for the Roman province of Asia located in what is now western Turkey. By "churches" Paul may be implying the existence of more than one church group in Ephesus and the existence of other churches in the area, such as at Colosse, Laodicea, and Hierapolis (Col 4:13–16; also Rev 2–3). The word of the Lord had spread all over the province (Ac 19:10). It was natural for Aquila and Priscilla to send greetings, since they had been of such help in founding the Corinthian church (Ac 18:2). They had left Corinth with Paul (Ac 18:18) and evidently were with him at Ephesus. While they were there, a church met in their house, which was also true at Rome (v.19; cf. Ro 16:3–5). To "greet" (GK *832*) one "in the Lord" was to greet a person as a professed believer. When the Corinthians receive this letter and read it in church, Paul encourages them to give one another a "kiss" (GK *5799*). The holy kiss (see also Ro 16:16; 2Co 13:12; 1Th 5:26) was apparently a public practice among early believers to show their Christian affection and unity in the faith. The kiss of respect and friendship was customary in the ancient East. Such a greeting may have been practiced in the synagogue by first-century Jews—a practice in which men would have kissed men and women women. If this custom was taken over by the early Christian church, it is unlikely that in the worship services the church would have practiced kissing between the sexes.

21–24 Paul is now ready to take the pen to append a greeting and sign the letter, as was his practice (Col 4:18; Phm 19). This was a mark of the letter's authenticity (2Th 3:17). Up to this point, he had dictated the letter to an amanuensis (secretary).

Then, in view of the problems existing at Corinth, Paul felt the need to add a strong warning: "a curse be on him" (v.22). A curse (*anathema*; GK *353*; cf. 12:3; Ro 9:3; Gal 1:8) meant that the person involved was to be delivered over or "devoted to the divine displeasure" as being under the wrath and curse of God. Paul's use of this curse is not at variance with Jesus' words in Mt 5:34, because there Jesus qualifies what he means by saying in effect: "Do not take oaths on the basis of any of God's created things—the heavens, the earth, or Jerusalem." Here Paul is bringing God himself to witness and is saying he who does not love and obey God is under God's wrath. Having spoken so strongly, Paul then turns to the future hope and cries out, *"Marana tha"*—Aramaic words that came to be used in the early church and that can best be translated "Our Lord, come!"

Paul ends with his usual shorter benediction (Gal 6:18; Eph 6:21; et al.; cf. 2Co 13:14 for its enlarged trinitarian form). In concluding with an expression of his own love for all the believers (v.21), Paul wants the whole Corinthian church to know that, in spite of the stern way in which he has had to rebuke them, he really loves them.

The Old Testament in the New

NT Text	OT Text	Subject
1Co 1:19	Isa 29:14	Worldly wisdom perishes
1Co 1:31	Jer 9:24	Boasting in the Lord
1Co 2:9	Isa 64:4	What no eye has seen
1Co 2:16	Isa 40:13	The mind of the Lord
1Co 3:19	Job 5:13	God and the crafty
1Co 3:20	Ps 94:11	God knows human thoughts
1Co 5:13	Dt 17:7	Purge out evil
1Co 6:16	Ge 2:24	Institution of marriage
1Co 9:9	Dt 25:4	Not muzzling an ox
1Co 10:7	Ex 32:6	Sin of idolatry
1Co 10:26	Ps 24:1	The earth is the Lord's
1Co 14:21	Isa 28:11–12	Through strange tongues
1Co 15:27	Ps 8:6	Everything subject to Christ
1Co 15:32	Isa 22:13	Tomorrow we die
1Co 15:45	Ge 2:7	Creation of Adam
1Co 15:54	Isa 25:8	Death is swallowed up
1Co 15:55	Hos 13:14	Victory over death

2 Corinthians

INTRODUCTION

1. Historical Background

Probably no part of Paul's life is more difficult to reconstruct accurately than the thirty or so months he spent in and around Ephesus (perhaps from the fall of A.D. 53 to the spring of A.D. 56). It was a stormy period, particularly toward its close. There were many evangelistic opportunities (Ac 19:8–10; 20:20–21, 31; 1Co 16:9) and many healings and conversions (Ac 19:11, 18–20). There was also widespread opposition owing to Paul's conspicuous success (Ac 19:9, 13–16; 1Co 4:9–13; 15:30–32; 2Co 4:8–9; 6:4–5, 8–10). Whether or not the Demetrius riot (Ac 19:23–41) actually precipitated his withdrawal from Ephesus, it must have climaxed the hostility directed against him by the devotees of Artemis, not to speak of the Jewish opposition he encountered in the city (Ac 20:19).

A chronological list of the events that took place between the writing of 1 and 2 Corinthians will be helpful, though no such reconstruction of events commands universal agreement.

1. After they received 1 Corinthians, the Christians at Corinth probably rectified most of the practical abuses for which Paul had censured them in his letter. For example, he says nothing further in 2 Corinthians about abuse of the Lord's Supper (1Co 11:11–34) or about litigation among Christians (1Co 6:1–8).

2. In spite of this and because of the arrival of Judaizing intruders from Palestine (2Co 11:4, 22), conditions in the church at Corinth deteriorated, necessitating Paul's "painful visit" (see 2Co 2:1; 12:14, 21; 13:1–2; see sec. 5, below).

3. At some time after this visit, Paul (or his representative) was openly insulted at Corinth by a spokesman of the anti-Pauline clique (2Cor 2:5–8, 10; 7:12).

4. Titus was sent from Ephesus to Corinth with the "severe letter," in which Paul called for the punishment of the wrongdoer (2Co 2:3–4, 6, 9; 7:8, 12; see sec. 5, below). In addition, Paul instructed Titus to organize the collection for the saints at Jerusalem (2Co 8:6a), which had gone by default since the Palestinian interlopers had arrived and had begun to derive their support from the church (cf. 2 Cor 11:7–12, 20; 12:14). Titus was to meet Paul in Troas, or, failing that, in Macedonia (perhaps Philippi; 2Co 2:12–13; 7:5–6).

5. Paul left Ephesus shortly after the Demetrius riot (Ac 19:23–20:1), began evangelism in Troas (2Co 2:12–13), and then suffered his "affliction in Asia" (2Co 1:8–11).

6. Paul traveled to Macedonia (2Co 2:13; 7:5) and engaged in pastoral activity (Ac 20:1–2) while organizing the collection in the Macedonian churches (2Co 8:1–4; 9:2; see sec. 5, below).

7. Titus arrived in Macedonia with his welcome report of the Corinthians' responsiveness to the "severe letter" (2Co 7:5–16).

8. Paul wrote 2 Corinthians 1–9 during further pastoral work in Macedonia and pioneer evangelism along the Egnatian Road and probably in Illyricum (see comments on Ro 15:19–21).

9. On returning to Macedonia and hearing of fresh problems at Corinth, Paul wrote 2Co 10–13 and sent the whole letter to Corinth.

10. Paul spent three months in Greece (primarily Corinth) (Ac 20:2–3), during which time he wrote Romans.

2. Unity

Many scholars have questioned whether 2 Corinthians is a single composition because of four problem areas in the letter as it presently stands: 2:14–7:4; 6:14–7:1; chs. 8–9; and chs. 10–13. The last section has generated the most debate and the largest number of theories (see discussion of this issue in EBC 10:304–6). Suffice it to say that this commentary adopts the position of the unity of 2 Corinthians, though we do sympathize with

PAUL'S INTERACTION WITH CORINTH

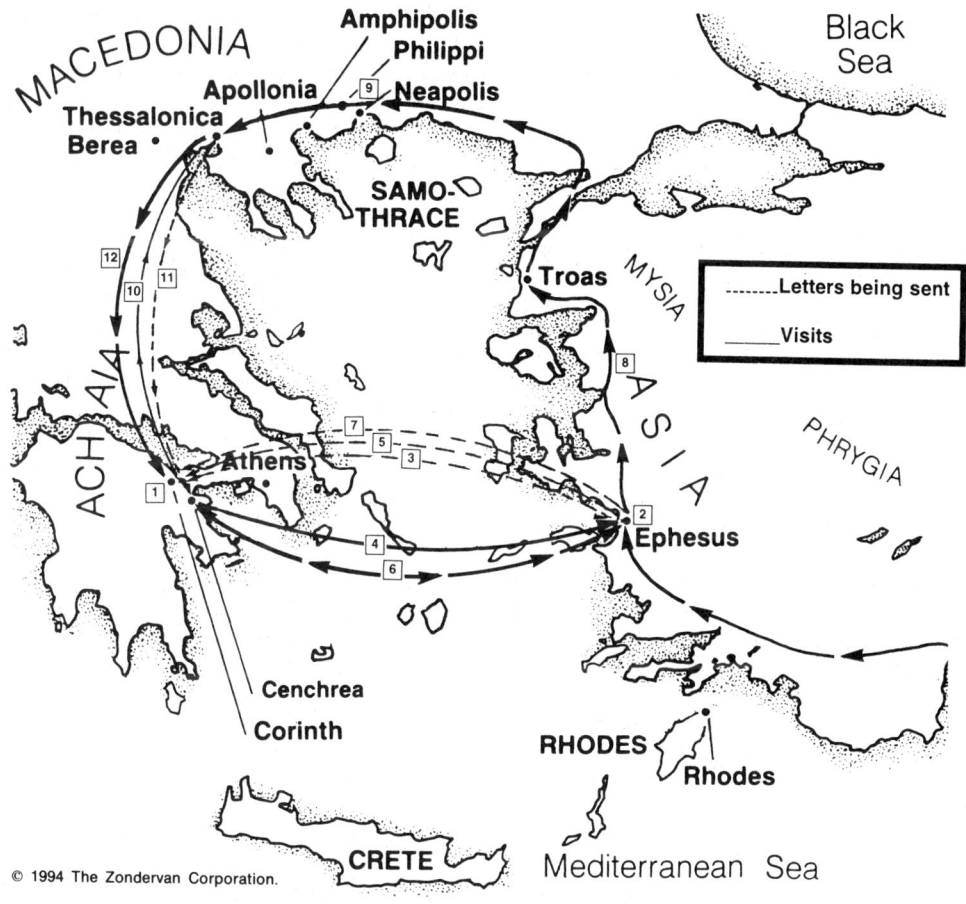

© 1994 The Zondervan Corporation.

1. A.D. 50–52: Paul establishes the church at Corinth (Acts 18:1-18).
2. 53–56: Paul establishes the church at Ephesus (Acts 19:1-22).
3. 54: Paul hears about immorality at Corinth and writes a brief letter (see 1Co 5:9).
4. 54: People from Chloe's household (1Co 1:11) and later Stephanas, Fortunatus, and Achaicus (1Co 16:17) visit Paul in Ephesus; one of these groups brings a letter (1Co 7:1).
5. 55: Paul writes 1 Corinthians and sends it to Corinth — perhaps with Stephanas, Fortunatus, and Achaicus.
6. 55: Paul hears about further problems in Corinth and pays a brief, painful visit to the church (2Co 2:1; cf. 12:14; 13:2).
7. 55: Paul sends off a third letter to Corinth, called the "severe letter" (2Co 2:3-4, 9; 7:8, 12). He sends it with Titus, who is also told to organize the collection in Corinth (2Co 8:6).
8. 56: Paul leaves Ephesus and has opportunity to evangelize Troas, but he does not do so (2Co 2:12-13).
9. 56: Paul crosses over into Macedonia and begins evangelistic work there (Acts 20:1-2; 2Co 2:13; 7:5).
10. 56: Titus meets Paul in Macedonia (Thessalonica or Philippi?) and reports on his successful stay in Corinth (2Co 7:6-16).
11. 56: Paul writes 2 Corinthians 1-9, and after hearing of further problems, also writes chapters 10-13; he sends the whole letter to Corinth, with Titus (2Co 8:16-24).
12. 56: Paul arrives in Corinth and spends the winter there (Acts 20:3).

those who hold that 2Co 10–13 is a later letter than 2Co 1–9.

3. Authorship and Date

Unlike some other Pauline Epistles, 2 Corinthians has rarely been called into question with regard to its authenticity. The author twice identifies himself as Paul (1:1; 10:1). Certainly no one imitating Paul's style would portray the apostle as in danger of losing his authority at Corinth or struggling to preserve the Corinthians from apostasy. Already early in the second century Polycarp quoted this letter (c. A.D. 105), as did Irenaeus, Clement of Alexandria, and Tertullian at a later time. Marcion (c. A.D. 140) considered it a Pauline letter, and it is included in the Muratorian canon (late second century A.D.).

The dates of 1 and 2 Corinthians are linked together. Paul wrote 1 Corinthians in the spring (cf. reference to "Pentecost" in 1Co 16:8), probably in A.D. 55. Second Corinthians was written from Macedonia, probably in the fall (see 7:5; 8:1; 9:2–4), shortly before Paul spent three winter months in Corinth (Ac 20:3). While these two letters could have been written in the same year (i.e., six months apart), it seems more likely that eighteen months intervened between them. Adequate time must be allowed for Paul to engage in pioneer evangelism all the way into Illyricum (cf. Ro 15:19), a campaign that must have occurred between his Ephesian residence (Ac 19) and his arrival in Greece (Ac 20:2). It is difficult to fit into a six-month period all the travel between Ephesus and Corinth and all the events at Corinth that took place between the writing of 1 and 2 Corinthians (see sec. 1 above).

In our opinion, therefore, 1 Corinthians was written in the spring of A.D. 55, while the sending of 2 Corinthians may be placed in the fall of A.D. 56. If 2Co 10–13 is a separate letter after 2Co 1–9, these last four chapters also date from the fall of A.D. 56, while the first nine chapters may have been sent at any time between the fall of A.D. 55 and early fall A.D. 56.

4. Occasion and Purpose

The outline of events given above suggests that the immediate circumstances prompting Paul to send 2 Corinthians were twofold: (1) the arrival of his pastoral assistant Titus, who brought welcome news of the favorable response of the majority of the Corinthians to the "severe letter" (see 7:6–16), and (2) the arrival of fresh, disturbing news concerning Corinth. An interval between the arrival of Titus and the sending of 2 Corinthians seems indicated by 7:8. Paul had several overriding purposes in writing. He wished (1) to express his great relief and delight at the Corinthians' positive response to his "severe letter" that had been delivered and reinforced by Titus (2:6, 9, 12–14; 7:5–16); (2) to exhort the Corinthians to complete their promised collection for the saints at Jerusalem before his next visit (8:6–7, 10–11; 9:3–5); (3) to prepare them for that forthcoming visit by having them engage in self-examination and self-judgment (12:14; 13:1, 5, 11)—so that they could discover the proper criteria for distinguishing between rival apostles (chs. 10–13), and so that Paul could be spared the pain of having to exercise discipline (10:2, 5–6, 11; 11:3; 12:19–21; 13:10).

Was 2 Corinthians successful where 1 Corinthians had been only partially so? Apparently it was, because Paul made the promised visit (Ac 20:2–3) and during this three-month stay in "Greece" (primarily Corinth, in the winter of A.D. 56–57) he wrote his letter to the Romans, which gives no hint of trouble at Corinth. Also Ro 15:26 shows that the Corinthians did complete their collection for their fellow believers at Jerusalem.

5. Special Problems

a. The "painful (or intermediate) visit"

In spite of Luke's silence in Acts, there are several passages in 2 Corinthians showing that Paul had visited Corinth twice before his final visit, the second one being "painful" (GK *1877 & 3383*). (1) Paul is planning his third visit to Corinth (12:14; 13:1–2). (2) In 2:1 and 12:21, Paul specifies that one of the two earlier visits was painful. This can hardly have been his first visit to Corinth when he founded the church, in spite of the opposition he encountered at that time (Ac 18:6, 9–10, 12–17). Since 1 Corinthians gives no hint about a second, difficult visit, this visit likely took place after 1 Corinthians and before the "severe letter," because in writing 2 Corinthians Paul is dependent on Titus for his information about the outcome of the "severe letter"; he had not himself visited the church after the sending of the "severe letter."

At some stage after the Corinthian believers received 1 Corinthians, therefore, conditions within the church deteriorated. Possibly a cleavage developed over the implementing of Paul's injunction of 1Co 5:2, 5, 13 about the incestuous man. Perhaps an ultra-loyal group of Paulinists (cf. 1Co 1:12; 2Co 2:6–7) confronted the influential anti-Pauline clique of Judaizing intruders from Palestine and their Corinthian adherents in a bid for control of the uncommitted and vacillating majority. In any case, Paul received adverse news, perhaps from Timothy, that induced him to hurry to Corinth to reinforce the effect of 1 Corinthians and prevent any further undermining of his authority at Corinth.

Little is known about what happened during this visit. Certainly Paul would have explained the reasons for the change in his travel plans (see the comments on 1:15–17), for the Corinthians were expecting him to arrive from Macedonia (cf. 1Co 16:5–6), not from Ephesus. Apparently he rebuked those guilty of immorality ("those who sinned earlier," 2Co 12:21; 13:2), but refrained from exercising summary discipline, choosing rather to issue a warning: "If I come again, I will not spare you" (cf. 13:2). Also he seems to have been humiliated by the Corinthians' failure to champion his cause against the false apostles (cf. 12:21).

As a sequel to this brief visit, Paul or his representative was personally insulted by some individual at Corinth in an open act of defiance by which all the Corinthians were to some extent pained—if not at the actual time, at least later on (2:5–11; 7:12). So Paul sent Titus to Corinth after considerable persuasion (7:14) as his personal envoy to deliver the "severe letter" (see next section) and to organize the collection (8:6a).

b. The "severe letter"

Clearly the general aim of the "severe letter" was to arouse the church to discipline "the one who did the wrong" (7:12; cf. 2:6, 9). But 2 Corinthians contains four additional statements of Paul's purpose in writing: (1) to spare the Corinthians and himself another painful visit (1:23–2:4); (2) to demonstrate his affection for the Corinthians (2:4); (3) to put to the test the Corinthians' obedience to apostolic authority (2:9); and (4) to make them aware before God of their genuine concern and affection for him as their spiritual father (7:12; cf. 1Co 4:15).

Titus, who took the letter to Corinth, related to Paul its outcome (7:6–16). The Corinthians as a whole had felt concern and remorse over their behavior during the "painful visit." They now longed to see Paul again to assure him of their change of attitude. They had zealously punished the offender whose scandalous action had provoked their indignation. But now some Corinthians were in danger of being merciless in their punishment; so Paul needed to stay their hand and encourage them to forgive the offender who had repented (2:6–8).

When Titus gave his report, Paul's initial reaction was to regret that he had caused such pain, but upon reflection, his opinion had altered: "I do not regret it" (7:8). The infliction of pain, though unavoidable, had proved remedial; in fact, God had inspired their grief and had prevented the letter from causing them any permanent injury (7:9–11a).

While some scholars identify this severe letter with 1 Corinthians and many with 2Co 10–13, neither of these seems to fit the description given by Paul in ch. 7. Consequently, it seems most likely that this letter has been lost. It was an intensely personal letter, quite brief, and addressed to a specific unedifying situation, so that its nonpreservation is not a matter of surprise.

c. The collection for the poor at Jerusalem

From A.D. 52 to 57 a considerable proportion of Paul's time and energy was devoted to organizing a collection among his Gentile churches for "the poor among the saints in Jerusalem" (Ro 15:26). There is general agreement that Ac 20:4 contains a list of the appointed delegates from certain Gentile churches who were Paul's traveling companions on his final visit to Jerusalem when he was delivering the collection (see comment on Ac 20:4). The offering was intended for the Jewish Christians at Jerusalem, who were going through difficult times. Several factors account for their poverty: (1) After their conversion to Christianity, many Jews in Jerusalem would have been ostracized socially and economically. (2) The community sharing described in Ac 2:44–45 and 4:32, 34–35 undoubtedly would have aggravated their poverty. (3) Persistent food shortages in Palestine because of overpopulation culminated in the famine of A.D. 46 in the time of Emperor Claudius (Ac 11:27–30). (4) As the mother church of Christendom, the Jerusalem church was obliged to support a proportionately large number of teachers and probably to provide hospitality for frequent Christian visitors to the holy city. (5) Jews in Palestine were subject to a twofold taxation the crippled them—Jewish and Roman.

Why did Paul to take up this offering? Several motives can be mentioned here. (1) Most important, it was an expression of brotherly love (Ro 12:13; 13:8; Gal 6:10), a tangible expression of the interdependence of the members of the body of Christ (1Co 12:25–26) that would honor Christ (2Co 8:19) and help effect equality of provision (2Co 8:13–15). (2) It symbolized the unity of Jews and Gentiles in Christ (Eph 2:11–22) and may have been designed to win over those Jewish Christians who were still suspicious of Gentile missions (cf. Ac 11:2–3). (3) It dramatized in material terms the spiritual indebtedness of Gentile believers to the church at Jerusalem (Ro 15:19, 27; cf. 1Co 9:11). (4) It marked the culmination of Paul's ministry in the eastern Mediterranean; he planned to turn westward after visiting Rome (Ro 15:24, 28). (5) It was a visible sign of Paul's fulfillment of a promise (2Co 8:19; Gal 2:10) and perhaps a way of partially compensating for his earlier persecution of the Jerusalem saints (Ac 8:3; 9:1; 26:10–11; 1Co 15:9; Gal 1:13; 1Ti 1:13).

In spite of Paul's misgivings about the potential success of the enterprise (Ro 15:31), the offering was evidently gratefully received on his arrival in Jerusalem (see Ac 21:17).

d. Paul's opponents at Corinth

Regarding the problem of Paul's opponents at Corinth, three basic questions clamor for solution. First, who were they? Everyone acknowledges that Paul's adversaries were Jews (cf. 11:22). But were they Judaizers? If a Judaizer is defined as one who insists on circumcision as a prerequisite for salvation (cf. Ac 15:1), they were not Judaizers, for 2 Corinthians lacks any trace of a dispute over circumcision. But if a Judaizer is a person who tries to impose Jewish practices on Gentiles as conditions either for salvation or for the enjoyment of Christian fellowship, then the opposition to Paul may appropriately be labeled Judaizing. Most likely in their attempt to reproduce Jerusalem in Corinth or to claim Corinth for Jerusalem, they sought to impose on the Corinthians the provisions of the Apostolic Decree, especially its food regulations (Ac 15:20, 29).

Second, what was the relation between Paul's antagonists at Corinth and the church of Jerusalem, particularly the three "pillars" (Gal 2:9) or the Twelve? In our opinion, they were self-appointed agents from Judea who appealed to the authority of the Twelve, especially Peter, in defense of their Judaizing program. (1) That these persons were from Palestine is based on the term "Hebrews" in 11:22 (cf. Php 3:5), which refers to Jews of Palestinian descent. (2) We should draw a distinction between the "super-apostles" of 11:5; 12:11 and the "false apostles" of 11:13. The former expression represents Paul's ironical description of the exalted view of the Twelve held by the "false apostles" who appealed to them, whereas "false apostles" describes the Palestinian intruders who laid claim to apostleship and preached "another gospel" (11:4). (3) We know that some persons from Judea had already invoked the authority of the Twelve without their authorization (Ac 15:24; cf. Gal 2:4). (4) We also know that one clique at Corinth had already set a precedent for appealing to Jerusalem by using the name of Peter (1Co 1:12).

Finally, what message did these Jewish missionaries teach? There can be no doubt that their primary aim was to undermine and destroy Paul's apostolic authority. They were hoping to bring about Paul's downfall, at least in Corinth, and to establish their own credentials as authentic servants of Christ.

Several of their charges against Paul can be inferred from what he writes in this letter. Paul was a double-minded worldling who acted capriciously (1:17–18; 10:2–4) and lorded it over his converts (1:24; 7:2). He carried no letters of commendation (3:1; 10:13–14) because he commended himself (4:2, 5; 5:12; 6:4; 10:12, 18; 12:11; cf. 1Co 9:1–3; 14:18; 15:10b) as would a madman (5:13; 11:1, 16-19; 12:6, 11) or impostor (6:8). Just as his gospel was obscure (4:3; 6:2–3), so also the letters he wrote were unintelligible or devious (1:13), written with the perverse aim of condemning and destroying (7:2–3; 10:8; 13:10) and causing pain (2:2, 4–5; 7:8). He was impressive at a distance but weak and contemptible when he attempted to make a personal appearance (10:1–2, 9–11; 11:6; 13:3–4, 9). His refusal to accept remuneration from the Corinthians proved that he cared little for them and that he was aware of being a counterfeit apostle, not the mouthpiece of Christ (11:5, 7–11, 13; 12:11–15; 13:3a, 6). On the other hand, he was exploiting the willingness of a church to support him by having his agents organize a collection, ostensibly for the saints at Jerusalem but in reality for himself (12:16–18).

Paul's opponents also apparently made claims about themselves, as may be inferred from his reply (4:5). Proof of their genuine apostolicity could be found, they claimed, in their polished eloquence and erudite knowledge (11:6), their visions and revelations (5:13; 12:1, 7), their healing miracles (12:12), their possession of commendatory letters (3:1), their willingness to accept remuneration (11:12; cf. 1Co 9:5–7, 11–12), their pure Palestinian origin (11:22), their being disciples of Jesus (5:16; 10:7), their high estimate of Moses (3:7–16) and Abraham (11:22), and their preaching of the true Gospel of Jesus (11:4). Little wonder that the impressionable Corinthians were swayed by the vaunted self-sufficiency (3:5) of these rival claimants to apostleship.

6. Theological Values

Traditionally, Paul's two letters to Timothy and one to Titus are called "the Pastoral letters." But 2 Corinthians has a strong claim to be recognized as Paul's most important pastoral letter, because it contains "applied" pastoral teachings. Paul, the pastor, has penned a profound, though brief, autobiography. In it we can see beautiful examples of the tenderness of a spiritual shepherd sensitive to the needs of his flock (1:24; 2:6–7; 6:1; 10:2; 13:5, 10) as well as the pleading of a spiritual father jealous of his children's affection, purity, and unity (6:11–13; 11:2–3; 13:11).

This letter also contains the classic discussions of the theology of Christian suffering (1:3–11; 4:7–18; 6:3–10; 12:1–10), the role of a minister of the new covenant (2:14–17; 4:1–5; 5:16–21; 11:28–29; 12:14–15), the relation between the old and new covenants (3:7–18), the theology of death and resurrection (4:7–5:10), and the principles and practice of Christian stewardship (chs. 8–9).

EXPOSITION

I. Paul's Explanation of His Conduct and Apostolic Ministry (1:1–7:16)

A. Introduction (1:1–11)

1. Salutation (1:1–2)

1 In most of his letters, Paul begins by referring to himself as "an apostle" (GK 693) of Christ Jesus. Although he was not one of the twelve chosen by Christ (Mk 3:14–19), he claimed equality with them (see 2Co 11:5; 12:11; Gal 2:6) on the basis of the special revelation of Christ God gave him at the time of his conversion (1Co 9:1; Gal 1:15–16). Like them, he had been commissioned "by the will of God" to be a "chosen instrument" of God (Ac 9 15).

Paul's delight in speaking of a fellow Christian as "our brother" (GK 81) may be traced to Ananias's generous and reassuring use of that term ("Brother Saul," Ac 9:17) at a time when the believers in Damascus had every reason to regard Saul as the archenemy of the church (Ac 9:1–2, 13–14). The mention of Timothy (not Sosthenes, as in 1Co 1:1) as a cosender of the letter may be intended to reinstate this timid young man (1Ti 4:12; 2Ti 1:7; 2:1) in the eyes of the Corinthians, possibly after his failure or limited success as Paul's representative at Corinth (see 1Co 4:17; 16:10–11). Titus had replaced Timothy as Paul's chief envoy to Corinth by the time this letter was written.

Paul refers to the principal addressees not as "the church of Corinth" but as "the church of God in Corinth"—the local representatives of God's universal church. Linked with them are "the saints throughout Achaia," i.e., believers in such places as Athens (cf. Ac 17:34) and Cenchrea (Ro 16:1).

2 This characteristically Pauline salutation combines and elevates the traditional Greek and Hebrew greetings. *Chairein* (the common Greek greeting) becomes *charis* ("grace," i.e., God's unsought and unmerited favor; GK 5921)—a word that occurs in every opening greeting of Paul. The word "peace" (GK 1645) reflects the Hebrew *shalom* (GK 8934)—the peace that comes to humanity from God (cf. Php 4:7) as a result of salvation (Ro 5:1).

2. Gratitude for divine comfort (1:3–7)

The paragraph embodies the chief emphasis of chs. 1–7: "comfort in the midst of affliction."

3–4 Paul generally follows his salutation with thanksgiving for the divine grace evident in the lives of his converts and a summary of his prayers for them. Here, however, he offers praise to God for consoling and encouraging him, while later (v.11) he solicits their prayers for himself. This atypical preoccupation with his own circumstances shows the distressing nature of the experience in Asia from which he had so recently been delivered (vv.8–10). He highlights the aspects of God's character he had come to value in deeper measure as a result of personal need and divine response, namely, God's limitless compassion (cf. Ps 145:9; Mic 7:19) and never-failing comfort (cf. Isa 40:1; 51:3, 12; 66:13).

Paul sees his suffering not merely as personally beneficial, driving him to trust God alone (v.9; 12:7), but also as directly benefiting those he ministered to: "God ... comforts [GK *4151*] us ... so that we can comfort...." To experience God's help, consolation, and encouragement in the midst of all one's affliction is to become indebted and equipped to communicate the divine comfort to others in any kind of affliction or distress.

5 This verse supplies the reason why suffering equips Christians to mediate God's comfort. Whenever Christ's sufferings were multiplied in Paul's life, God's comfort was also multiplied through the ministry of Christ. The greater the suffering, the greater the comfort and the greater the ability to share with others the divine sympathy. "The sufferings of Christ" (cf. Gal 6:17) cannot refer to the atoning passion of Christ that Paul regarded as a historical fact, a completed event (Ro 5:8–10; 6:10). Rather, they include sufferings that befall the "man in Christ" (12:2) engaged in his service (cf. 4:11–12). They are Christ's sufferings not simply because they are similar to his but because they contribute to the fulfillment of the suffering destined for the body of Christ (Ac 14:22; Col 1:24) or because Christ continues to identify himself with his afflicted church (cf. Ac 9:4–5).

6–7 Verse 6a restates and applies v.4b. Paul's affliction and endurance of his trials ultimately benefited the Corinthians in that he was now equipped to administer divine encouragement to them when they were afflicted and to ensure their preservation when they underwent trials (cf. Eph 3:13; 2Ti 2:10). Paul then makes explicit (v.6b) the divine comfort he received in the midst of affliction. Whether he suffered affliction or received comfort, the advantage remained the same for the Corinthians (cf. 4:8–12, 15). They too would know an inner revitalization, an infusion of divine strength that would enable them to endure patiently the same type of trial that confronted Paul (cf. 1Pe 5:9).

Since Paul realized that to share Christ's sufferings always involved the experience of God's comfort through that suffering, his hope that the Corinthians would be triumphant in their time of trial was securely grounded (v.7).

3. Deliverance from a deadly peril (1:8–11)

8 Paul proceeds to describe the particular hardship in which he received divine comfort and empowering. It overtook Paul "in the province of Asia" (i.e., probably some part of the province other than Ephesus; cf. Ac 19:22), possibly Troas (2:12–13). That it had occurred recently—certainly after 1 Corinthians was written—seems indicated by the vividness of Paul's description of the divine deliverance. While the Corinthians may already have known about Paul's trial, he now informs them of its overwhelming and unique character. He had been through such a devastating hardship that he was forced to renounce all hope of survival.

9 In his estimation Paul had received a death sentence (the word used can refer to an official verdict) from which there was no reprieve. But in the wake of this trying experience there followed a further experience that, by God's intervention, was tantamount to resurrection. All this undermined Paul's self-confidence (see 1Co 15:31; 2Co 12:9–10) and compelled his utter dependence on a God who raises the dead (cf. Ro 4:17) and therefore can rescue the dying from the grip of death (cf. Php 2:27, 30).

10–11 "The Father of compassion" (GK *3880*) had delivered Paul from his deadly peril (cf. vv.3–4). But since such perils were likely to recur, continuing divine intervention on his behalf was necessary if death was to be robbed of its prey. Immediately Paul qualifies his bold assertion, "and he will deliver us" (cf. 2Ti 4:18), by adding, "On him we have set our hope that he will continue to deliver us." He could not presume on "the gracious favor" of protection or deliverance from danger and death; this came from "the God of all comfort" (v.3) "in answer to the prayers of many," and it would prompt still further thanksgiving.

Of the various proposed identifications of Paul's affliction in Asia, five deserve mention: (1) his fighting with "wild beasts in Ephesus" (1Co 15:32); (2) his suffering the "thirty-nine stripes" (2Co 11:24); (3) the riot at Ephesus instigated by Demetrius, the silversmith (Ac 19:23–41), or an unsuccessful attempt by the populace, after the Ephesian uproar, to lynch the apostle; (4) a particular persecution encountered in Ephesus or elsewhere (cf. Ac 20:19; 1Co 16:9) shortly before his departure for Troas; and (5) a prostrating attack of a recurrent malady. The last-mentioned view seems favored by (1) the allusion in v.10 to Job 33:30; (2) the fact that a Jew could regard sickness as death and healing as a return to life (cf.Hos 6:1–2); (3) the present tenses of vv.4–6; and (4) the twice-repeated "he will deliver" in v.10.

B. Paul's Conduct Explained (1:12–2:13)

1. Characteristics of his conduct (1:12–14)

12–14 Before defending himself against the specific charges of vacillation and domineering leveled against him by his opponents (1:15–2:4), Paul deals with two more general accusations: that he had acted shamelessly and insincerely in his relations with the Corinthians (cf. v.12a), and that in his letters he had shown worldly shrewdness and had been evasive by writing one thing but meaning another (cf. vv.12b–13a).

These baseless charges Paul answers in the only way possible for him—by appealing to the testimony of his own conscience and the Corinthians' knowledge of his conduct. He thus claims that in both church and world his conduct had been characterized by God-given purity of intention and openness and had been governed by "God's grace" (v.12; GK 5921). Then he asserts that in none of his correspondence—the Corinthians had already received at least three letters from him—did his meaning become apparent only by "reading between the lines." Rather, his meaning lay on the surface and could be understood simply by reading (v.13a). Paul concludes by reminding his converts at Corinth that they had already begun to appreciate his motives and intentions, especially through the recent visit of Titus (see 7:6–16). He expresses the hope that they would reach the full assurance that he could give them as much cause for pride now (cf. 5:12) as they would give him pride "in the day of the Lord Jesus" (cf. 1Co 15:31; Php 4:1; 1Th 2:19–20).

2. Charge of fickleness answered (1:15–22)

15–17 In 1Co 16:3–8 and in these three verses are found the outlines of two different itineraries relating to Paul and Corinth. Plan A had been: Ephesus-Macedonia-Corinth-Jerusalem (possibly). But now in 2Co 1 we find Plan B: Ephesus-Corinth-Macedonia-Corinth-Judea (now definitely). If, as is probable, Plan A discloses Paul's original intention, Plan B, made after the writing of 1 Corinthians, introduces two modifications of that previous itinerary: Paul now planned to visit Corinth twice—before and after his activity in Macedonia—and he definitely intended to travel to Judea with the collection.

But not only did Paul have to explain these changes. His actual itinerary (see the introduction) seems to have been: Ephesus-Corinth (i.e., the "painful visit")-Ephesus-Troas (2:12–13)-Macedonia (7:5)—the place of writing. In other words, neither Plan A nor Plan B was carried out as intended. It may be said that after the "painful visit" Paul reverted to Plan A (see Ac 20:1–3, 16). In other words, to Plan A Paul seems to have said, "Yes-No-Yes"; to Plan B, "Yes-No." He had apparently provided his opponents with a convenient handle for a charge of fickleness!

His detractors were shrewd enough to convert the charge into one of capricious vacillation. His arbitrary changing of travel plans, they urged, was motivated purely by self-interest, with no concern for broken promises or for needs at Corinth. He made his plans on mere impulse like a worldly man, according to the mood of the moment, so that he could say, "Yes, yes" one day and "No, no" the next day, with the result that he seemed to be saying both "Yes" and "No" in the same breath.

18 Paul is so distressed by this charge and so convinced of his innocence that he solemnly invokes the unquestionable trustworthiness of God (1Co 1:9; cf. 11:10) as guaranteeing and testifying to the consistency of his message to the Corinthians. Neither in proclaiming the good news to them nor in telling them of his travel plans was his language a blending of "Yes" and "No." How could the messenger of a faithful God vacillate between a reassuring "Yes" and a disconcerting "No" or deliver a message that was not an emphatic "Yes"?

19–20 Paul now elaborates this last point. The message originally proclaimed at Corinth (Ac 18:5) by the threefold testimony (cf. 13:1; Dt 19:15) of Paul, Silas, and Timothy centered in none other than God's Son, in whom inconsistency and indecision have no place. So Paul contrasts the humanity of the messengers and the divinity of the Person who was the essence of their message. Indeed, in and through him the divine "Yes" has come into effect as a permanent reality (v.19), because all God's promises (cf. 7:1; Ro 9:4; 15:8), whatever their number, find their fulfillment in him (v.20a). "They are 'Yes' in Christ," since he forms the climax and summation of the divine self-revelation. That is why, in their corporate worship offered to God through Christ, Christians joyfully utter the "Yes" or "Amen" of agreement (cf. Rev 1:7; 3:14; 22:20). Such a response enhances God's glory (v.20b).

The Corinthians' "Amen" (GK *297*) to the Gospel declaration itself validated the apostolic preaching (cf. 1Co 1:6; 2Co 3:2–3; 13:5–6). With his consistency confirmed here, was it likely that Paul would act in a worldly manner in relatively trivial affairs? How could they distrust the apostle who himself had taught them to affirm the trustworthiness of God by repeating the "Amen"?

21–22 Paul's final defense of himself against the charge of indecision (v.17a) points to the constant activity of God in producing stability in Paul *and* in the Corinthians—in those who have been brought into intimate and dynamic relation with Christ, God's secure and permanent "Yes." Each of the four verbs in these two verses has God as its subject. The first ("makes ... stand firm"; GK *1011*) is a legal term denoting a seller's guaranteeing of the validity of a purchase; God continually strengthens believers in their faith in Christ and progressively enriches their knowledge of Christ. The other three ("anointed," GK *5987*; "set his seal of ownership," GK *5381*; and "put [GK *1433*] his Spirit") indicate what took place at the time of their conversion and baptism. God commissioned believers for his service by consecrating them as his "anointed ones" and imparting those gifts necessary for their task. God "set his seal of ownership on us" by putting "his Spirit in our hearts as a deposit, guaranteeing what is to come." Believers are "branded" as God's property, the reality of their faith is attested, and their status is guaranteed "for the day of redemption" (Eph 4:30).

3. A cancelled painful visit (1:23–2:4)

Allied to the charge that Paul had arbitrarily altered his travel plans regarding Corinth according to the mood of the moment, there was in all probability the accusation that by doing so he had shown himself to be a spiritual dictator who tried to dominate his converts and did not hesitate to cause them pain.

1:23–2:1 In answering this charge, Paul solemnly invokes his faithful God (cf. 1:18) as his own witness to the truth of statements like these: "The reason I postponed my intended visit to Corinth was to spare you a second painful visit (1:23b; 2:1). So far from being unstable in my desires, I have the settled purpose of promoting your highest good and joy (1:24) and of saving you unnecessary pain or sorrow." That is, Paul wanted to spare the Corinthians and himself further pain by not returning to Corinth from Ephesus after the so-called "painful visit." "I made up my mind" (2:1) refers to a decision Paul made at Ephesus after hearing of the insult hurled at him or one of his deputies at Corinth by "the one who did wrong" of 7:1 (see comment on 2:5–8). He resolved to pay the Corinthians a visit by this letter (2:3–4; 7:8, 12) rather than by another personal visit that might have proved mutually painful.

For Paul to speak of "sparing" (GK *5767*) the Corinthians (v.23) implied that he might have punished them. He therefore proceeds in 1:24, which is parenthetical, to reject the inference—probably also an actual Corinthian charge—that he was some tyrannical overlord, seeking to intimidate and domineer in matters of faith and conduct. An apostle was obligated to serve his converts, not dominate them. It was his privilege to work with them to secure their "joy in the faith" (Php 1:25), not to lord it over them by causing them unnecessary pain.

2 Paul acknowledges that his decision not to revisit Corinth had been partially determined by his awareness that to inflict needless pain on the Corinthians at that time would have effectively dried up the only source of his own happiness. His joy was intimately connected with theirs (1:24). To cause them pain meant he would experience pain himself, a pain that could be relieved and then converted into gladness only by their repentance (see 7:8–10).

3–4 In place of a second painful visit to Corinth, Paul wrote the Corinthians a letter that has come to be known as the "severe letter" (see the introduction). By this letter he wanted to avoid being pained by them when he finally did pay another personal visit (v.3a). It was incongruous to Paul that his converts, who ought to have been a constant source of joy to him (1Th 2:19–20), should cause such distress to their spiritual father. Yet in writing that letter, he had had the buoyant assurance that whatever made him glad would give all of them pleasure too, for they were all one in joy, as in sorrow (v.3b).

In v.4a Paul describes the origin and circumstances of this sorrowful letter. It was born "out of great distress and anguish" and had been produced "with many tears." Since such expressions can hardly be true of 1 Corinthians as a whole, this letter (cf. also 7:8, 12) must be identified with a letter no longer extant, sent to Corinth after 1 Corinthians and after his "painful visit" (see the introduction). A second purpose (cf. vv.3, 9; 7:12) behind this letter is stated in v.4b. Although it actually proved painful to its recipients (7:8), its aim was not vindictive or even vindicative. On the contrary, it sought to convince the Corinthians of the intensity of Paul's affectionate concern for them.

4. Forgiveness for the offender (2:5–11)

In 1:23–2:4, Paul has spoken about feeling pain, causing pain, and avoiding further pain. All three aspects recur in this paragraph with reference to a certain wrongdoer at Corinth. Particularly apparent here is Paul's sensitivity as a pastor: He avoids naming the culprit (vv.5–8); he recognizes that Christian discipline is not simply retributive but also remedial (vv.6–7); he understands the feelings and psychological needs of the penitent wrongdoer (vv.6–8); he appeals to his own conduct as an example for the Corinthians to follow (v.10); and he is aware of the divisive operation of Satan within the Christian community (v.11).

5–6 The man referred to in these verses is almost certainly *not* the man guilty of incest (1Co 5; see comment on vv.10–11). Rather, after Paul's painful visit some powerful insult had been directed against him or one of his representatives by a visitor to Corinth or by a Corinthian, who perhaps headed the opposition against Paul at Corinth and objected in particular to his disciplinary methods. The apostle here discounts the sorrow caused him by the unfortunate episode.

On the basis of Titus's report about the Corinthian reaction to the severe letter (see 7:7–11), Paul counsels the church to terminate the discipline they had inflicted on the man in question. Whether a formal gathering of the church had been held and specific disciplinary measures had been decided on is impossible to say. The words rendered "the majority" (GK *4498*) may simply mean "the main body," referring generally to the membership. But what was the view of the implied minority? In light of v.7a, it seems likely that they were a pro-Pauline clique, the "ultra-Paulinists," who regarded the penalty as insufficient.

7–9 Instead of continuing or increasing the punishment, the Corinthians ought to rescue the man from inordinate grief and complete his reformation by forgiving and encouraging him and by publicly reaffirming their love for him. This would serve to assure the wrongdoer that God had, in fact, forgiven him (cf. "binding" and "loosing" in Mt 16:19; 18:18; Jn 20:23). Such a positive Corinthian response to this plea would afford Paul further evidence of the church's willingness to acknowledge his divinely given authority. By reproving the offender after hearing the "severe letter," they had already stood the test and proved their loyalty to the apostle in all respects (cf. 7:11–12). Now by ending the punishment, they would be doing the same.

10–11 Paul here aligns himself with the Corinthian decision to forgive the person in question—a decision he trusts they will make after receiving the present letter. But he hastens to add that he has already forgiven the man—if, in fact, there was anything to forgive. Clearly it was Paul, not the Corinthians, who had taken the initiative in this matter of forgiveness.

Verse 10 affords perhaps the clearest evidence that the offense was basically a personal act of effrontery against Paul rather than some act of immorality in the church. There was need for Paul's personal forgiveness, although, in deference to the penitent offender's feelings, he discounts the personal pain he himself experienced (v.5) and deliberately understates the seriousness of the offense (v.10) lest anyone imagine that he considered himself virtuous in granting forgiveness so readily.

The circumstances and purpose of Paul's forgiveness are then defined. First, forgiveness was granted "in the sight of Christ," i.e., as Christ looked on as a witness and approved—the One who taught that willingness to forgive one's brother was a precondition for receiving divine forgiveness (Mt 5:12, 14–15; 18:23–35; cf. Eph 4:32; Col 3:13). Moreover, forgiveness was granted for the welfare of the Corinthians ("for your sake"), i.e., to preserve their unity and to relieve them of their patent embarrassment at not having acted against the offender before Paul wrote to them. Verse 11 states an additional but related purpose: to avoid being outwitted by the master strategist, Satan, who hoped to create discord within the church at Corinth, either between the church at large and a dissident minority or between the repentant wrongdoer and his fellow Christians. To withhold forgiveness when the man was repentant was to play into Satan's hands, who already had gained one advantage when the man sinned. There is a point at which punishment can become purely vindictive (cf. v.6) and suffering a penalty can drive one to despair (v.7; Col 3:21). While Christian discipline does include punishment administered in love, it is not simply retributive or punitive; it is also remedial or reformatory (cf. 1Co 5:5; 11:32; 2Co 7:9–10; 13:10). It aims at reinstatement after repentance, through forgiveness and reconciliation.

5. Restlessness at Troas (2:12–13)

12–13 This is the final section in Paul's explanation of his recent conduct (see the introduction for more on the historical events). Titus had been dispatched to Corinth with the "letter of tears" while Paul continued work in and around Ephesus (cf. Ac 19:22b). His departure for Troas, mentioned here, was probably precipitated by the Demetrius riot (Ac 19:23–41). Evidently Paul had already planned to leave the city, for when he sent Titus to Corinth, he had arranged to meet him at Troas, or, failing that, probably at Philippi.

We may safely assume that Paul actually preached in Troas, though v.12 speaks only of his intent. He would recognize an open "door" of opportunity (note Ac 16:6–10) only after grasping the evangelistic opportunities initially afforded by the Lord. But evangelism was curtailed because of Paul's restless spirit (perhaps seen as a device used by Satan, cf. v.11). This disquiet (7:5–6) was caused by several factors: (1) the disheartening opposition at Ephesus, forcing his premature departure; (2) persistent uncertainty and fears concerning the situation at Corinth (7:5b); (3) Titus's nonarrival; and (4) concern for the safety of Titus in travel (note 7:6b–7a), particularly if he was carrying the completed Corinthian collection.

The city of Troas, the ruins of which are seen here, played a significant role in the life of the apostle Paul. On his second missionary journey he received a vision here of a man from Macedonia, beckoning him to evangelize their area (Ac 16:8–10). Now on his third journey, he once again landed in Troas, though he only stayed a short while.

C. Major Digression—The Apostolic Ministry Described (2:14–7:4)

1. The grandeur and superiority of the apostolic ministry (2:14–4:6)

a. The privilege of apostolic service (2:14–17)

14 Here begins the so-called "great digression," brought about by Paul's remembering his happy reunion with Titus in Macedonia, who brought encouraging news from Corinth that relieved his fretful tension (7:5–16). In the favorable Corinthian reaction to the "letter of tears" as reported by Titus, Paul saw God's vindication of his apostleship and a triumph of God's grace in the hearts of the Corinthians.

Paul likens the irresistible advance of the Gospel, in spite of temporary frustration, to a Roman "triumph" (GK 2581), in which a victorious general, along with his proud soldiers, led in triumphal procession the wretched prisoners of war who were exposed to public ridicule. Not all the details of this picture can be pressed. The apostles, as well as Christians in general, may be either exultant soldiers who share in the benefits of Christ's victory (cf. Ro 8:37) or willing captives who count it a privilege to be part of God's "triumph" (cf. Ro 1:1; Col 1:10). The metaphor is certainly suggestive: Christ undertook a battle not rightly his; we share in a triumph not rightly ours. The reference to the diffusion of fragrance may be carrying on the imagery, for sacrifices were offered when the procession reached the temple of Jupiter and perfumes may have been sprinkled or incense burned along the processional route. Through the apostles, God was spreading far and wide the fragrant knowledge of himself that can be gained through knowing Christ (Col 2:2–3).

15–16a As faithful preachers and followers of Christ, the apostles themselves formed a sweet "aroma" (GK 2380) of Christ rising up to God as a pleasing "fragrance" (GK 4011; cf. Lev 1:9, 13, 17; Nu 15:7). To the extent that they diffused the fragrance of Christ, they were that fragrance or aroma. Irrespective of the human response to the Gospel, its proclamation delights God's heart, because it centers on the Son whom he loves.

Behind Paul's thought in both these verses may be the rabbinic concept of the Law as simultaneously life-giving and death-dealing. Just as the Torah had a beneficial effect on those who received and obeyed it and a lethal effect on those who rejected it, so the proclaimers of Christ are at the same time a "life-giving perfume" to those who believe the Gospel and so are being saved, and a "death-dealing drug" to those who repudiate it and so are perishing (cf. 1Co 1:18, 23–24).

16b–17 To Paul's urgent question "Who is equal to such a task [of preaching the Gospel of Christ or being the aroma of Christ]?" the answer may be either, "We apostles are, for we are not peddlers of an adulterated message," or "No one is, if a person depends on his or her own resources." The latter reply is supported by 3:4–6; the former by 3:1.

By the phrase "unlike so many," Paul may be referring to the numerous wandering teachers and philosophers of the first century (see comment on 11:8) who expected payment for what they claimed was "the word of God," or, more likely, to the group of Judaizing opponents at Corinth who converted preaching into a means of personal gain. In contrast, Paul appeals to the sincerity of his motives and the purity of the message as shown by his divine commission ("like men sent from God"; cf. Gal 1:1, 12, 15–16), his sense of divine dependence and responsibility ("we speak before God"), and his divine authority and power ("in Christ"). The principle is clear: As those who dispense the life-giving remedy for sin, preachers must avoid diluting or adulterating the medicine of life, the word of God.

b. The results of the ministry (3:1–3)

1 Behind each of the two questions in this verse, both of which expect the answer "no," stands an actual or expected charge against Paul. Since he had just spoken of the distinctive role of apostles (2:14–16) and of his own divine commission and authority (2:17; cf. 1:12; 1Co 4:15–16; 11:1; 14:18; 15:10), some of the Corinthians might say, "Paul, once again you are indulging in your notorious habit of self-commendation." Furthermore, some of "the many" who were profiting from preaching (2:17) had undoubtedly been making a charge like this: "Since Jerusalem is the starting point of Christianity, anyone working outside that city must be able to give proof of his apostolic commission by letters of recommendation from the believers there. We brought you Corinthians such commendatory letters, and you yourselves have supplied us with such when we have visited other places. Why should you regard Paul as an exception? Does not his unconcern about letters of recommendation prove he is an intruder and impostor?"

Paul is not here disparaging the use of letters "of recommendation" (GK 5364). He himself had sought epistolary credentials from the high priest at Jerusalem before setting out for the synagogues of Damascus (Ac 9:2; 22:5), and their use within the Christian world was established (see Ac 15:22, 25–27; 18:27). Paul himself wrote what amounted to commendatory letters (Ro 16:1–2; 1Co 16:3, 10–11; 2Co 8:16–24).

His opponents apparently carried letters as their credentials, probably not from the three Jerusalem "pillars" (Gal 2:9) or the Twelve, but from the Pharisaic wing of the Jerusalem church, who regarded the scrupulous observance of the Mosaic law as essential for salvation (Ac 15:5) and were unable to distinguish between the law-abiding conduct of the Twelve and legalistic teaching.

2–3 The latter of the two questions posed in v.1 Paul now answers explicitly. He insists that for him to carry commendatory letters to Corinth would be completely superfluous. The most complimentary letter he could possibly possess had already been written (cf. 1Co 9:2). Their very lives as men and women "in Christ," the result of the grace of Christ operative in his apostolic ministry, were an eloquent letter that all could read. To bring another letter would amount to a personal insult to the Corinthians.

The letter imagery is further developed and explained. This letter was not a human document recorded in ink on papyrus. Nor was it a divine composition, such as the Decalogue, engraved on inanimate tablets of stone (Ex 31:18; 32:15–16). Rather, the letter was authored by Christ, was "written by the Spirit of the living God," and was indelibly inscribed on living tablets, sensitive human hearts (Jer 31:33; 32:38; Eze 11:19; 36:26). Proof of Paul's genuineness was to be found not in written characters but in human characters.

So Paul delivers a powerful rebuttal to his opponents. His commendatory letter had been written before theirs; it was indelible; it was widely circulated, not confidential or unpublished; and its author was Christ, not a partisan group within the Jerusalem church.

c. Competence for service (3:4–6)

4–5 Paul's confidence before God in claiming that the Corinthians were a letter written by Christ that validated his apostolic credentials came through Christ (v.1). It was not the product of a pious wish or imagination. Still speaking of this confidence before God, he disowns any ability to form a competent judgment on the results of his own ministry or any personal right to lay claim to the results of what was in reality God's work. Paul's confidence came through Christ and his competence came from God.

6 Paul realized that being divinely commissioned required being divinely equipped. His equipment to be a minister of a new covenant was given at his Damascus call when he was named a "chosen instrument" of God and filled with his Spirit (Ac 9:15, 17–19). There follows a contrast between two basic characteristics of the old and new covenants. The basis of the old covenant between the Lord and Israel was a lifeless, written code, "the book of the covenant" (Ex 24:7). The basis of the new covenant between God and the church is a dynamic, pervasive Spirit. The written code (or "letter"; GK 1207) pronounced a sentence of death (see Ro 7:9–11; Gal 3:10), but the Spirit brings a transformation of life (Ro 7:6; 8:3). Though the new covenant was ratified by the shedding of Christ's blood (Heb 13:20) and is symbolized in the communion cup (Lk 22:20; 1Co 11:25), it becomes operative only through the indwelling Spirit who imparts new life. Where "the letter" was powerless, the Spirit is powerful in producing holiness of life, enabling a person fully to meet the righteous requirements of the law (Ro 8:4). This is what makes the new covenant "new" (GK 2785) and the old covenant (3:14) "old" (see Heb 8:6–13).

d. The surpassing glory of the new covenant (3:7–11)

Thus far in this chapter, Paul has progressed from the idea of commendatory letters written on human hearts by the Spirit to his reflection on the new covenant promised by God through Jeremiah, under which the law would be written on human hearts (Jer 31:31–34). This now prompts him to compare the old and new economies. Each involved a distinctive ministry that was accompanied by "glory" (GK *1518*), but so superior was the glory of the new covenant that the glory of the old covenant faded into insignificance.

7–9 In the remainder of the chapter Paul provides a commentary on selected points of the narrative in Ex 34:29–35. When Moses descended from Mount Sinai with the two tablets on which were written the Ten Commandments, his face shone so brightly that "the Israelites could not look steadily" at him. Well then, argues Paul, if such glory attended the giving of the law under the administration that brought death and condemns people, how much more glorious will be the ministry of the Spirit that brings righteousness! What was a distinctive and positive feature of the old order must also characterize the new economy, but in greater measure. The new covenant has surpassing glory inasmuch as it is a more adequate revelation of God's character.

10–11 The comparison in glory between the covenants advances one step further. So pronounced is the contrast between the two dispensations that what once was rightly considered resplendent now appears scarcely resplendent at all (v.10). The greater light obscures the lesser light, just as the sun obscures the moon. The old covenant belonged in fact to a vanishing order, which began to fade immediately after its inception—the glory on Moses' face began to fade as soon as he left the divine presence. On the other hand, a covenant destined to be permanent (cf. Heb 13:20) must be invested with a far greater glory.

e. Veiling and unveiling (3:12–18)

12–13 As participants in the new covenant, Paul and his fellow apostles and fellow preachers had the certain hope that it was a permanent, irrevocable covenant, never to be superseded and never to be surpassed in splendor. This accounted for their boldness and confidence in preaching. They had nothing to conceal but every reason for fearless candor (v.12).

This idea of openness prompts Paul to continue his commentary on Ex 34:29–35. This OT passage suggested to him that after each encounter between Moses and the Lord in the tent of meeting, when Moses returned to the people of Israel to tell them what he had been commanded, they were dazzled by the radiance of his face and he put on his "veil" (GK *2820*). Only in the tabernacle did he keep the veil on. Although the OT does not explicitly state that the radiance on the face of Moses gradually faded and then disappeared, Paul suggests that the reason for Moses' veiling was not so much to prevent the Israelites from being dazzled by its brightness (cf. Ex 34:30–31) as it was to prevent them from continuing to gaze in amazement until his face totally lost the brilliance of the reflected glory (cf. v.7). He was attempting to teach them, Paul implies, that the newly established order was destined to be eclipsed and pass away.

Alternatively, the purpose of Moses' veiling may have been to deny the Israelites the privilege of looking right on to the end of the fading glory. It was an acted parable condemning them, emphasizing that their sins had made them unable and unworthy to behold even temporary glory without interruption. Others suggest that Moses wished to avoid the personal embarrassment of having the people realize that the splendor of his face was fading.

14–15 Moses' laudable attempt was, however, unsuccessful; instead of recognizing the significance of Moses' veiled face, the Israelites became dulled in their powers of perception. Paul finds evidence of this spiritual insensitivity in the fact that down to his own day, when the old covenant (or the OT) was read in the synagogue, the ability of the Jews to recognize the impermanence of the Mosaic order was impaired. A "veil" (GK *2820*) covers their hearts comparable to the veil that covered Moses' face. Paul could call it the "same" veil because in both cases a veil prevented vision, or because it was identical to the veil of ignorance about the transitory nature of the Mosaic economy. To Paul, this veil remained unlifted in the case of unbelieving Jews, because only as they came to Christ was the veil set aside.

16 The verse restates and amplifies v.11, that only in Christ is the veil set aside. Whenever a person turns to the Lord and finds in him the end or fulfillment of the law (Ro 10:4), the Lord completely removes the veil from that person's heart. No longer is one's spiritual perception impaired. Such people recognize that the dispensation of grace has superseded the dispensation of the law (cf. Jn 1:17). They are a "new creation" in Christ (5:17).

17 This verse explains v.16. There are three possible interpretations. (1) "The Lord" (Yahweh; GK 3378) mentioned in Ex 34:34, to whom the Jew must now turn for the removal of the veil, is none other than the life-giving Spirit of the living God (cf. vv.3, 6, 8). Thus Paul is describing the Spirit here, not Christ, and he is describing his function, not his identity. (2) Another view finds a functional equivalence between Christ (identified as "the Lord") and the Spirit: in v.14 it is Christ who removes the veil; in v.16 it is the Spirit. (3) Again, some believe Christ is being identified as "the life-giving Spirit," as in 1Co 15:45.

Paul's point in v.17b is that the Spirit's presence brings liberation, not bondage (Ro 8:15). Not only does he remove the veil; he also sets a person free from bondage to sin, to death, and to the law as a means of acquiring righteousness.

18 In vv.4–6 Paul was speaking primarily of his apostolic ministry. Now, as he draws his conclusion concerning the superiority of the new covenant against the background of his commentary on Ex 34, he refers to Christian experience in general. Under the new covenant, not just one person, but all Christians behold and then reflect the glory of the Lord. Moreover, unlike the Jews, who still read the law with veiled hearts, Christians, with unveiled faces, behold in the mirror of the Gospel the glory of the Lord, who is Christ. Again, the glory is displayed not outwardly on the face but inwardly in the character. Finally, so far from losing its intensity or luster, as did Moses' glory, the glory experienced under the new covenant progressively increases until the Christian finally acquires a "glorious body" like that of the risen Christ (Php 3:21).

Paul concludes by noting that the progressive transformation of the Christian's character is the work of the Lord who is the Spirit (cf. v.17a). After conversion to the Spirit of God (v.16), there is liberation through the Spirit (v.17b) and transformation by the Spirit (v.18).

f. The light brought by the Gospel (4:1–6)

1 Paul now resumes the theme of 3:6—divine appointment and provision to be a minister of a new covenant. He had no reason to lose heart (cf. Gal 6:9), for God in his mercy had granted him a privilege exceeding the ministry of Moses (cf. 1Ti 1:12–16). He had been called not to communicate the law but to dispense grace. Paul regarded this divine commission to serve under the new covenant as more than compensating for all the trials he endured for being true to his calling (vv.7–12, 17; cf. Ro 8:18), including the malicious charges of his Corinthian opponents (v.2).

2 To the thought of refusing to grow disheartened Paul will return presently (v.16). Now he expands his brief self-defense of 2:17. Evidently he had been accused of deceitful behavior (cf. 7:2; 12:16) and of willfully adulterating the Gospel (perhaps by not insisting on Gentile compliance with the Mosaic law). These charges he emphatically rejects. The openness marking the new covenant had always been reflected in his conduct. He had never been secretive or deceptive, nor had he ever dishonestly manipulated the message of God entrusted to him.

In any self-defense, self-commendation must play some part. But Paul's particular self-commendation was distinctive. He commended himself, not by self-vindication at every point, but simply by openly declaring the truth of the Gospel. He appealed not to a partisan spirit or the prejudices of other people but "to every man's conscience [GK 5287]." In his self-commendation, God was an onlooker.

3–4 Paul's Gospel, some had claimed, was designed only for a spiritually minded elite; what he said was obscure and what he did was underhanded (v.2). For the sake of argument, Paul concedes his critics' point. Even if his Gospel is veiled in the case of some people, it is not his doing, he insists, because he sets forth the truth plainly (v.2). Any veiling (cf. 3:14–15) comes from the unbelief of "those who are perishing" (cf. 1Co 1:18; 2Co 2:15), whose minds have been blinded by the god of "the present evil age" (Gal 1:4)—i.e.,

Satan, who wishes to prevent people from seeing the light of the Gospel that focuses on Christ's glory as the image of God. Paul's reference to Christ as "the image [GK 1635] of God" means that Christ is the visible and perfect representation of the invisible God (Col 1:15; cf. Jn 1:18). Christ is one with God the Father by nature, but distinct from him in person.

5 Though Paul might have been forced to commend himself to everyone's conscience (v.2; cf. 1:12; 6:4), he never advertised or preached himself. The essence of his Gospel was the proclamation of "Jesus Christ as Lord" (Ro 10:9; 1Co 12:3; Col 2:6), a message faithfully delivered by him and eagerly embraced by the Corinthians. Paul saw himself related to his converts, not as a spiritual overlord (1:24) but as a willing servant. In this he followed in the footsteps of "the Lord of glory" (1Co 2:8), who himself had adopted the status and role of a servant (Php 2:7; cf. Ro 15:8).

6 Paul now states the reason why he preached Christ and served the Corinthians. It was because God had dispelled his darkness by illuminating his heart and had given him a knowledge of Christ he wished to share (cf. Ac 9:15; 26:16, 18; Gal 1:15–16). In this second creation, as in the first, darkness is dispersed and light is created by divine intervention. In the first case it was a personal word: "Let there be light" (cf. Ge 1:2–3); in the second creation it was a personal act: "God shone in our hearts" (cf. 1Pe 2:9).

This is an unmistakable allusion to Paul's Damascus encounter with the risen Christ when God "was pleased to reveal his Son" to him (Gal 1:15–16). Each of the three accounts of Paul's conversion mentions the noonday light from heaven, brighter than the sun, and emphasizes the revelatory nature of the experience (Ac 9:3–9; 22:6–10; 26:13–18). In the unveiled face of Christ (cf. 2Co 3:7, 13, 18) Paul saw God's glory.

2. The suffering and glory of the apostolic ministry (4:7–5:10)

a. The trials and rewards of apostolic service (4:7–15)

No person was ever more aware of the paradoxical nature of Christianity than Paul. And perhaps none of his letters contains more paradoxes than 2 Corinthians, of which vv.7–12 are typical.

7 Here is the first paradox—the difference between the indescribable value of the Gospel "treasure" (GK 2565) and the apparent worthlessness of the Gospel's ministers, whom Paul terms "jars of clay" (GK 5007 & 4017). Behind this contrast Paul sees a divine purpose—that people may recognize that "this all-surpassing power" is God's alone. His power finds its full scope in human weakness (12:9).

8–9 Then follows a series of four vivid antitheses that illustrate both the weakness of Paul in discharging his commission and the power of God in preserving his life and his spirit. Each metaphor may reflect gladiatorial or military combat. Paul was "hard pressed on every side," but not completely cornered and never driven to surrender. He was "at a loss, but never totally at a loss" (an attempt to retain the word-play of the Greek between "perplexed" and "despair"). He was hounded by the foe, but not left to his mercy. He was knocked to the ground, but not permanently grounded.

10–11 Verse 10 summarizes the four preceding contrasts in the paradox. In the phrase "the death [or dying; GK 3740] of Jesus," Paul sums up his experience of being "hard pressed," "perplexed," "persecuted," and "struck down" during his ministry. On the other hand, the phrase "the life [GK 2437] of Jesus" expresses the Lord's saving him from being "crushed," "in despair," "abandoned," and "destroyed," all of which prefigures the Christian's final deliverance from mortality at the resurrection. This idea of "life in the midst of death" is, of course, closely related to the main theme of chs. 1–7—"comfort in the midst of affliction."

But the meaning of the arresting phrase "the death of Jesus" is also explained by what follows, for v.11a amplifies v.10a. What Paul carried around in his body was nothing other than his being always "given over to death [GK 2505] for Jesus' sake." He faced perilous hazards every hour and death every day (cf. 1Co 15:30–31; also 4:9). This interpretation is preferable to understanding this phrase as a reference to the Christian's once-for-all baptismal identification with Christ in his death (Ro 6:3–5), to one's daily mortification of the sinful nature (Gal 5:24), or to the gradual weakening of one's physical powers while serving Christ.

Both verses stress that the death and the life of Jesus were simultaneously evident in Paul's experience (cf. 1:4–5). For him it was not a matter of life after death, or even of life through death, but of life in the midst of death. Paul's repeated deliverances from death evidenced the resurrecting power of God (1:9–10); otherwise stated, the resurrection life of Jesus was operative in his "mortal body" (cf. Php 3:10).

12 With a bold stroke, Paul relates this theme of life in the midst of death to his earlier statements in ch. 1 about vicarious suffering (1:3–7). There he had said in effect: "I suffer for Christ; God comforts me; I comfort you during your suffering." Here his thought seems to be: "I suffer exposure to physical death for your sakes [cf. v.15a]; you enjoy more of the risen life of Christ as a consequence." He apparently saw not only a causal but also a proportional relation between his "death" and the "life" of the Corinthian believers. The deeper his experience of the trials and sufferings of the apostolic life, the richer their experience of the joys and privileges of Christian existence (cf. Col 1:24; 2Ti 2:10). The "middle term" between his experience and theirs was the divine comfort that, having received, he could then dispense (cf. 1:4). This rich theology of suffering was forged on the anvil of his own experience of "the sufferings of Christ" (1:5).

13–14 But what enabled Paul faithfully to discharge his ministry (3:6; 4:1, 5), even though it involved suffering? It was (1) his sharing the psalmist's conviction that faith cannot remain silent and (2) his own Christian conviction that Christ's resurrection guarantees the resurrection of all believers.

Regarding the first reason, Paul quotes Ps 116:10a (from the LXX): "I believed; therefore I have spoken." The psalmist recounts a divine deliverance from a desperate illness and its accompanying despondency (vv.1–11) and then considers how he might most fittingly render his devotion to the Lord (vv.12–19). In a real sense, then, the psalmist's expression of thanksgiving arose from his vindicated trust in God: "I held firm to my faith and was vindicated; therefore I have spoken." Similarly, Paul, for his part, could not remain silent about the Gospel he believed: "Woe to me if I do not preach the gospel" (1Co 9:16).

A second reason Paul proclaimed the good news with the utmost confidence (cf. 3:12) was a firm conviction of his personal resurrection and his being presented along with all believers before the presence of God or Christ (cf. 11:2; Eph 5:27; Col 1:22). Our being raised "with Jesus" (cf. 1Th 4:14) means that the resurrected Christ forms the prototype and ground of our resurrection. His resurrection from the dead is the firstfruits of the Easter harvest; ours is the full ingathering (1Co 15:23).

15 This verse concludes a section of Paul's thought, for in v.16 he repeats the phrase "we do not lose heart" (GK *1591*) from v.1. Rather movingly, he reminds his converts that he endures all his afflictions with resilience, not to promote his own good but for their benefit (cf. 4:5), and ultimately for God's glory. As God's grace expanded in their hearts and through them reached ever-increasing numbers, so too the volume of thanksgiving to God for the receipt of illumination (cf. 4:6) was increasing and promoting the glory of God.

b. Glory through suffering (4:16–18)

16 Paul has supplied several reasons for refusing to grow discouraged in spite of seemingly overwhelming odds: (1) his divine commission as a minister of a new and superior covenant (4:1), (2) the prospect of sharing Christ's triumphant resurrection from the dead (4:14), and (3) his immediate task of promoting the Corinthians' spiritual welfare and the glory of God (4:15). But he was realistic enough to recognize that his toil and suffering had taken their toll on him physically. For this, however, there was splendid compensation. Matching the progressive weakening of his physical powers was the daily renewal of his spiritual powers. It was as though the more he expended himself for the Gospel's sake (cf. 12:15), the greater his spiritual resilience (cf. Eph 3:16).

17 Paul then supplies a surprising definition of daily spiritual renewal. It is a constant production of solid, lasting glory (lit., "an eternal weight of glory"), out of all proportion to the slight, present affliction that causes physical weakness (v.16); this eternal glory "far outweighs" any "light and momentary troubles" that are being presently experienced (cf. Ro 8:18). Again, as in vv.12, 16, the idea of proportion seems to be present: the greater the affliction Paul suffered, the greater the glory produced for him.

18 But this production of glory was by no means automatic. Only as attention was focused on what was unseen did suffering lead to glory. Behind the contrast between "what is seen" and "what is unseen" is the Pauline tension between the "already" and the "not yet" (cf. Ro 8:24–25; 1Co 13:12), the contrast between what is now seen by mortals and what is as yet hidden from mortal gaze. Paul affirms that his affections are set "on things above" (Col 3:1–2), on lasting realities as yet unseen, on the age to come that is present in promises and blessings still to be fully realized.

This preoccupation with the realm "where Christ is seated at the right hand of God" (Col 3:1) was not the result of an arbitrary choice; it was an informed decision. Paul was profoundly aware that the present age is transient (cf. 1Co 7:31), whereas the age to come is destined to last for ever; his afflictions therefore were temporary but his reward eternal.

c. Confidence in the face of death (5:1–10)

No passage in 2 Corinthians has prompted more discussion than this one. Paul's message here relates directly to ch. 4, where he pointed out that even in the midst of affliction, perplexity, and persecution, there was, through divine consolation, the hope of glory (4:8–9, 13–14, 17); and that even in the presence of the ravages of mortality and death, there was, through divine intervention, the operation of life (4:10–12, 16). Paul continues this twofold theme by specifying the sources of divine comfort afforded the believer who faces the possibility of imminent death. Basically they are three: (1) the certainty of the future possession of a spiritual body (v.1), (2) the present possession of the Spirit as the pledge of ultimate transformation (vv.4b–5), and (3) the knowledge that death begins a walk in the realm of sight (v.7) and involves departure to Christ's immediate presence where personal fellowship with him is enjoyed (v.8).

1 Apparently for the first time in his apostolic career Paul reckons seriously with the possibility, even probability, of his death before the return of Christ. Previously, to judge by 1Th 4:15, 17 and 1Co 15:51, he had expected to be among those Christians living when Christ returned. But now, as a result of his recent devastating encounter with death in Asia (1:8–11), he realized that he could die before the Parousia.

As a Cilician leatherworker whose duties included tentmaking, Paul naturally likened his present body to an "earthly tent" (GK *2103 & 5011*; cf. vv.2, 4) that might at any moment be dismantled or destroyed. This would simply mark the termination of the process of weakness and decay already at work in his body (4:16). But this possibility did not daunt him, for he was the assured recipient of a permanent heavenly house—a spiritual body provided by God.

2–4 These verses belong together, since v.4 expands v.2, while v.3 is parenthetical. One reason for Paul's assurance of his future acquisition of a resurrection body was the raising up of the temple of Christ's body (Mk 14:58; Jn 2:19–22), alluded to by the phrase "not built by human hands" in v.1. An additional reason was the experience of Spirit-inspired groaning (vv.2, 4; GK *5100*; cf. Ro 8:23). Paul's sighing did not stem from a desire to become permanently disembodied but from an intense longing to take up residence in his "heavenly dwelling."

The passage does not define the precise nature of the "groaning," but the immediate context and Paul's thought elsewhere (Ro 8:19–23; Php 3:20–21) suggest it was his sense of frustration with the limitations and disabilities of mortal existence, knowing as he did that he was destined to possess a spiritual body perfectly adapted to the ecology of heaven. Paul sought liberation only from the imperfection of present embodiment (i.e., from "bondage to decay," Ro 8:21), not from any and every form of corporeality. After all, Paul taught that the Christian will have a "spiritual body" (1Co 15:35–49).

But not all at Corinth shared Paul's view of the Christian's destiny. Some were teaching that one's resurrection lay in the past (see 1Co 15:12), accomplished spiritually and corporately for all believers at the resurrection of Christ or else personally experienced at the moment of baptism (cf. 2Ti 2:17–18); to them there was no future, bodily resurrection but only a disembodied immortality. To such people Paul asserts, "We do not wish to be unclothed but to be clothed with our heavenly dwelling." This background also affords a satisfying interpretation of v.3, where Paul seems to be repudiating the teaching that the Christian looks forward to a vague immortality: "when we are clothed, we will not be found naked [as some of you would like us to believe]."

Another possible interpretation of vv.2–4a sees Paul expressing his own eager desire to avoid the unpleasantness or pain of a disembodied intermediate state between his own death and his receipt of a new body at the coming of Christ. He shrinks from the denudation of death and longs to put on his heavenly dwelling over his preserved earthly tent through the return of Christ before his death, though he is uncertain whether this will happen.

Verse 4b states the purpose and actual result of the receipt of the heavenly dwelling—the swallowing up of the mortal body by the revivifying action of the indwelling Spirit of life (Ro 8:2, 11; 2Co 3:6, 18). This transformation forms the climax of the incessant process of inward renewal (4:16b). In other words, 5:4b is related to 4:16b as 5:1a is related to 4:16a. For Paul, resurrection consummates rather than inaugurates the process of spiritual re-creation.

5 The "very purpose" for which God had "made" (or "prepared"; GK 2981) the believer is defined by v.4b as the transformation of the mortal body. God has given believers the Spirit as the pledge of that coming transformation—"a deposit, guaranteeing what is to come." The Greek word lying behind this paraphrase (GK 775) meant either (1) a pledge or guarantee, differing in kind from the final payment but rendering it obligatory, or (2) a down payment that required further payments but gave the payee a legal claim to the goods in question. Clearly not all these elements apply to Paul's use of the word, for redemption is not a process of reciprocal bargaining ratified by some contractually binding agreement but is the result of the grace of God, who bestows on believers his Spirit as an unsolicited gift. But how can the Spirit be God's pledge of the Christian's final inheritance (Eph 1:13–14; cf. 4:30)? No doubt through his present work of empowering the Christian's daily re-creation (2Co 3:18; 4:16; Eph 3:16), the Spirit guarantees his future completion of that work (cf. Php 1:6).

6–8 With the assured hope of receiving a glorified body (v.1) and with the pledge of his transformation in the presence and activity of the Spirit within him (v.5), Paul was always confident, even in the face of death. However, he continues, because we realize that we are absent from the Lord's presence as long as this body forms our residence, we really prefer to leave our home in this body and take up residence in the presence of the Lord.

Just as the repeated verb "we groan" shows vv.2 and 4 to be related, so "we are confident" relates vv.6 and 8, with v.7 being parenthetical (cf. v.3). But v.8 does not simply repeat v.6; it stands in antithetical parallelism to it. The corollary of "residence in the body = absence from the Lord" (v.6) is "absence from the body = residence with the Lord" (v.8). In other words, as soon as a person dies (v.8a), residence in the presence of the Lord begins (v.8b).

What is involved in being "at home with the Lord"? To be sure, it denotes a change of location. But the preposition translated "with" (GK 4639) also implies an active fellowship between two persons (cf. its use in Mk 6:3). Being "at home with the Lord" supersedes earthly experience where believers simply know the Lord (cf. Php 3:10); it is a higher form of the intimate fellowship with Christ than what we experience on earth (cf. Php 1:23; 1Th 4:17).

In v.7 Paul corrects a possible misinterpretation of v.6. If the clause "we are away from the Lord" (v.6) is interpreted in an absolute sense, present fellowship with Christ would appear illusory and being in the physical body would hinder spirituality. Since both deductions are totally false, Paul qualifies his statement by observing that "we do in fact still walk in the realm of faith, not of sight." To the believer the Lord is present, not to sight but to faith. Any spatial separation is temporary, not final.

9–10 Verse 9 follows vv.1–8 in much the same way as an ethical imperative frequently follows a doctrinal indicative in Paul's letters ("You are . . . ; therefore be!"; see comment on Ro 12:1). After stating profound doctrinal facts (vv.1–8), Paul shows their implications for present behavior (v.9). His constant ambition to please Christ (v.9) resulted directly from his awareness that death would terminate his relative exile from Christ and would inaugurate his walking in the realm of sight in the presence of the Lord (vv.6–8). Entertaining the hope of intimate communion with Christ after death (v.8) naturally prompts the desire to gain acceptance in his eyes especially before death (cf. Gal 1:10; Php 1:20; Col 1:10; 1Th 4:1), through "things done while in the body."

In v.10 we find a second and secondary reason for Paul's eager striving to win Christ's approval: his accountability to Christ (v.10) requires his compulsory attendance before the "judgment seat" (GK 1037) of Christ. From 1Co 4:5 we know that this not only requires us to appear in the court of heaven (cf. Ro 14:10), but also involves both the divine illumination of what has been hidden by darkness and the exposure of one's secret aims and motives. The person thus scrutinized will then receive an equitable and full recompense.

Of whom is this attendance required? While it is true that all people are accountable to God their maker and judge (Ro 2:1–11), Paul is here thinking primarily, if not exclusively, of each Christian's obligation to "give an account of himself of God" (Ro 14:12). Appearance before Christ's tribunal is the privilege of Christians. His judgment is concerned with the assessment of works and, indirectly, of character, not with the determination of one's eternal destiny. Judgment on the basis of works is not opposed to justification on the basis of faith. Delivered from "observing the law" (Ro 3:28), Christians are presently committed to "work produced by faith" (1Th 1:3). Not all verdicts on the Judgment Day, however, will be comforting (see comment on 1Co 3:15).

3. The function and exercise of the apostolic ministry (5:11–6:10)

a. Motivation for service (5:11–15)

11 "The fear [GK 5832] of the Lord" here is not personal piety nor the terror that the omnipotent Lord arouses in the hearts of people (e.g., Ge 35:5), but the reverential awe Paul had for Christ as his divine assessor and future judge (v. 10). Aware of his personal accountability, Paul strove to persuade other people of the truth of the Gospel, which included both exposition of Scripture about Jesus and his kingdom and discussion about practical life, and the truth concerning himself (i.e., that his motives were pure and sincere [cf. 1:12] and that his apostolic credentials and conduct were sound [cf. 3:1–6; 4:1–6]). Whether or not those to whom Paul addressed his appeal recognized his claims as true, God recognized him for what he was. Yet Paul realized it was necessary for the Corinthians to come to a proper understanding of his apostolic status and conduct.

12 Paul insists that these assertions about himself in relation to God and other people should not be interpreted as a further attempt at self-commendation (cf. 3:1). But he does want his converts to have the necessary ammunition with which to defend his apostleship. They ought, he implies, to have had sufficient pride in him to have undertaken this defense on their own initiative (cf. 12:11) with their weapons in hand—namely, their personal knowledge of his devoted service as an apostle. However, he reluctantly supplies them with additional weaponry by reminding them of the testimony of their individual consciences.

Paul describes the opposition as those who prided themselves on outward appearances. No doubt they made superficial claims to superiority over him—such as their relation to the Jesus of history (cf. 5:16) and to Palestinian orthodoxy (cf. 11:22) or to their greater number of visions and revelations (cf. 12:1–7). Paul was content to take his stand on

The *bema* (judgment seat) of the city of old Corinth is still visible (Paul adopts this word for "the judgment seat of Christ" in v.10). Courtesy Bastiaan Van Elderen.

what was not outwardly evident or fully provable, i.e., what was "in the heart."

13 Whatever the background to this difficult verse, its general message seems clear. Paul disowns self-interest as a motive for any of his actions; all is for God's glory (1Co 10:31; 2Co 1:15). Of this the Corinthians can be justly proud (v. 12). This interpretation accords well with his following appeal to Christ (v.14) and his definition of the purpose of Christ's death (v.15)—that believers should lead a life that is not centered on self but on Christ.

Verse 13a has been explained in several ways: (1) Paul's critics had accused him of being "out of his mind" (cf. Mk 3:21), perhaps because of his allegedly esoteric teaching (cf. Ac 26:24), his ecstatic experiences, or his indefatigable zeal in his work. To this charge he replies, "That is for God to judge." (2) Paul is referring to his experience of speaking in tongues or having visions (cf. Ac 22:17–21; 1Co 14:18, 23). If this is the charge, his answer is, "That is a matter between God and me." (3) Sometimes the Corinthians had viewed Paul as having been carried away by excessive emotion. To this charge he affirms, "It led to the glory to God." (4) Paul had been criticized for his self-commendation, which appeared to be sheer lunacy (cf. 11:1, 16–21). To this charge he replies, "It is in defense of God's cause."

14–15 Why was a life of self-pleasing impossible for Paul? Because of the supreme example of his Lord in dying for all. "The love Christ showed for us compels us to love and serve him and you [cf. v.13b], because when he died, sin's penalty was paid and we died to ourselves, while through his resurrection we live to please him [cf. v.9] by serving you." Thus Paul has now isolated two motives for Christian service: knowledge of accountability to Christ (v.11) and awareness of Christ's example of self-sacrificing devotion (v.14); in other words, Christ as Savior and as Judge.

Ever since his conversion, Paul felt he had no other choice but to expend himself in the service of others for Christ's sake (4:11–12; 12:15). In addition he had two convictions about the death of Christ. The first was that since one man died on behalf of and in the place of all, all had undergone death (v.14b). What is this latter death? Either the death deservedly theirs because of sin (cf. Ro 6:23) or the death to sin and self that is involved in Christian living (cf. Ro 6:11–13). In neither case was the death a physical death like Christ's; rather, it was a *potential* "death" of all human beings. Paul is not suggesting that, irrespective of one's response and attitude, everyone knows forgiveness of sins or experiences selfless living. There is universalism in the scope of redemption in that no one is excluded from God's offer of salvation; but there is a particularity in the application of redemption, since not everyone appropriates the benefits afforded by this salvation.

Paul's second conviction was this: Dying with Christ should lead to living for Christ. He is not speaking of every person without exception but only of "those who live" in union with the resurrected Christ. While all people died potentially when the Man who represented them died, not all were raised when he rose. But for those who rose with Christ to walk "in newness of life" (Ro 6:4; Col 3:1–2), slavery to sin and self has ended while devotion to Christ and his church has begun (cf. Ro 6:6, 11). The outcome of Christian self-denial is a Christ-centered life filled with concern for others.

b. The message of reconciliation (5:16–6:2)

16 Paul now introduces the first of two consequences of Christ's death and his own living for Christ. Since his conversion ("from now on"), when he gained the twofold conviction about his own death (v.14) and life (v.15), Paul had ceased to make superficial personal judgments based on external appearances (v.12). It was now his custom to view others, not in terms of nationality but in terms of spiritual status. The Jew-Gentile division was less important for him than the Christian-unbeliever distinction (Ro 2:28–29; 1Co 5:12–13; Gal 3:28; 6:10; et al.); Gentile believers were his brothers "in Christ" while his unbelieving compatriots were "without Christ."

Similarly, his sincere yet superficial preconversion estimate of Jesus as a misguided messianic pretender whose followers must be extirpated (Ac 9:1–2; 26:9–11) he now repudiated as being totally erroneous, for he had come to recognize him as the divinely appointed Messiah whose death had brought life (vv.14–15).

17 Paul's second stated consequence of the death and resurrection of Christ (vv.14–15) is that whenever a person becomes part of the body of Christ by faith, there is a new act of "creation" (GK *3232*) on God's part. One set of conditions or relationships has passed out of existence and another set has come to stay. Paul clearly emphasizes the discontinuity between the two orders (cf. Ro 12:2; Eph 4:23; Tit 3:5) and the "newness" of the person in Christ, although he does acknowledge the coexistence of the present age and the age to come (e.g., 1Co 10:11; Gal 1:4).

18–19 "All this is from God" looks back to the new attitudes of v.16 and the new creation of v.17. God is as surely the author of the second creation as he was of the first (cf. 4:6).

At this point Paul passes from the subjective to the objective aspects of the atonement as he talks about "reconciliation" (GK *2903*). Elsewhere he shows that reconciliation is the divine act by which, on the basis of the death of Christ, God's holy displeasure against sinners was appeased, the enmity between God and humankind was removed, and human beings were restored to proper relations with God (Ro 5:10–11; Col 1:20–22). Reconciliation is a total and objective removal of hostility.

Here Paul makes it clear that God was the reconciler, that humankind was what God reconciled to himself (but cf. Col 1:20), that Christ was God's agent in effecting reconciliation, that the reconciliation has been accomplished, and that reconciliation involved the nonimputation of trespasses (i.e., forgiveness and the accompanying imputation of righteousness; see comment on Ro 3:24). Those to whom God has committed the ministry of reconciliation (cf. 4:7) are primarily Paul and his fellow ambassadors. Nevertheless, a reference to all believers cannot be excluded (cf. v.18a, "God . . . reconciled us," including the Corinthians).

20 As proclaimers of the good tidings about reconciliation, the apostles were acting on Christ's behalf as messengers and representatives duly appointed by him. Furthermore, it was as if God were issuing a personal and direct invitation through them to their hearers to enter into the benefits of the reconciliation already achieved by Christ. "We implore you on Christ's behalf: Be reconciled to God" summarizes that message of reconciliation.

This appeal issued in Christ's name is the God-designed link between the objective work of reconciliation and its subjective appropriation by the sinner. From this viewpoint reconciliation is a continuing process as well as an accomplished fact. Yet there is a real sense in which reconciliation was effected before its results are subjectively felt (see Ro 5:11).

21 Thus far Paul has been content to give the broadest outlines of the drama of reconciliation, stating merely the relationship between the principal actors. Now he explains, so far as human language and imagery permit, the "how" of reconciliation. The fifteen Greek words defy final exegetical explanation, dealing as they do with the heart of the atonement. Perhaps the best way to understand the first section of the verse, particularly the second use of "sin" (GK *281*), is to recognize that Christ, treated as if he were a sinner, became the object of God's wrath and bore the penalty and guilt of sin. So complete was the identification of the sinless Christ with the sin of the sinner, including its dire guilt and its dread consequence of separation from God, that Paul could say profoundly, "God made him . . . to be sin for us."

Paul's declaration of Christ's sinlessness may be compared with other affirmations in Scripture: Heb 4:15; 7:26; 1Pe 2:22 (quoting Isa 53:9); 1Jn 3:5. Just as "the righteousness of God" is extrinsic to us, so the sin with which Christ totally identified himself was extrinsic to him. He never had a sinful attitude or did a sinful act.

The glorious purpose of the Father's act in making Christ "to be sin" was that believers should "become the righteousness [GK *1466*] of God" in Christ. This is a bold restatement of the nature of justification. Not only do believers receive from God a right standing before him on the basis of faith in Jesus (Php 3:9), but "in Christ" believers in some sense actually share the righteousness that characterizes God himself (cf. 1Co 1:30).

6:1 If God "[made] his appeal" (GK *4151*) to people through Paul (5:20), there was a sense in which Paul was a fellow worker with God (cf. 1Co 3:9). As such he was concerned to plead God's cause with unbelievers and believers alike. Hence this urging (GK *4151*), addressed to the whole body of Christians at Corinth, "not to receive God's grace in vain."

This latter phrase may mean one of two things: (1) Paul does not want the Corinthians to show by their present lives that they had received God's grace to no purpose. (2) Paul does not want the Corinthians to spurn the grace of God, which was being perpetually offered to them. How could they fail to profit from that grace? By refusing to purify themselves from everything that contaminated body and spirit (7:1; 12:20–21), by allowing a chasm to develop between faith and conduct, or by embracing a different gospel (11:4), one based on observing the law as the ground of acceptance before God.

2 To emphasize the seriousness and urgency of his appeal and to highlight the privilege of the present and the danger of procrastination, Paul quotes Isa 49:8 and then applies the passage to the age of grace. In its original context this quotation belongs to a section of Isaiah where the Lord directly addresses his Servant who has been "despised and abhorred by the nation" (Isa 49:7), promising him vindication before people in due time and calling on him to carry out the work of restoration after the return from exile. Paul uses the quotation to establish that the gospel era ("now") is "the day of salvation," when God's favor is shown to humankind. How unthinkable that such grace should be received in vain (v.1)!

c. The hardships of apostolic service (6:3–10)

3 Since v.2 is grammatically a parenthesis, v.3 is closely connected to v.1 and 5:20. As was fitting for an ambassador for Christ, Paul tried to put "no stumbling block [GK 4683] in anyone's path" lest the ministry should incur discredit. That various accusations were being leveled against Paul was inevitable, given the success of his ministry and the jealousy of others. His concern was that such charges be totally without foundation, that no "minister of reconciliation" be guilty of inconsistent or dishonest conduct, and that no handle be given adversaries who wished to ridicule or malign the Gospel. The life of the Christian minister is the most eloquent advertisement for the Gospel.

4–5 Paul proceeds to itemize his hardships (cf. 1Co 4:9–13; 2Co 4:8–9; 11:23–29) as he seeks to commend and defend his ministry as a servant of God and to provide the Corinthians with further material they might use in his defense (cf. 5:12). Paul's commendation was a matter of actions, not words.

After a reference to the "great endurance" that marked all his service and suffering (cf. 12:12), Paul lists nine afflictions, which fall into three groups. (1) General trials: "troubles" are oppressive experiences; "hardships" refer to unrelieved adverse circumstances; "distresses" are frustrating tight corners (cf. 4:8). (2) Sufferings directly inflicted by others: "beatings, imprisonments and riots." (3) Self-inflicted hardships: "hard work" includes the arduous task of incessant preaching and the toil of manual labor (cf. 1Th 2:9; 2Th 3:7–8); "sleepless nights" means voluntary abstention from sleep (cf. Ac 20:7–11); "hunger" probably refers to voluntary fastings (cf. 11:27).

6–7 From mention of outward circumstances (vv.4b–5) Paul moves on to specify the inward qualities he sought to display (v.6) and the spiritual equipment he relied on (v.7) while discharging his apostolic commission.

"Purity" refers to both moral uprightness and singleness of purpose. "Understanding" is not simply pastoral insight but also knowledge of the Christian faith and sensitivity to God's will (cf. 1Pe 3:7). By "patience" Paul means the endurance of insult or injury without anger or retaliation. "Kindness" is the generous and sympathetic disposition that acts in love. Paul's reference to the person of the Holy Spirit here emphasizes the Spirit as the source of all spiritual graces. That is, "the Holy Spirit" probably denotes the gifts or graces of the Holy Spirit.

After a reference to his proclamation of the truth "in the power of God" (cf. 1Co 2:1–5), Paul introduces a military metaphor that he had used earlier (1Th 5:8) and would develop later (Ro 6:13; Eph 6:11–17). "Weapons of righteousness" means either weapons supplied by God (Eph 6:10–11) as a result of justification or weapons that consist of personal integrity. Weapons "in the right hand and in the left" may allude to "the sword of the Spirit" and "the shield of faith" that form part of the Christian's armor (Eph 6:16–17).

8–10 Behind these verses probably lie a number of actual allegations that Paul's opponents made against him (cf. Ro 3:8; 1Co 4:13). In some quarters, Paul had probably become an object of disrepute and slander (v.8). He was thought a "nobody" who relied on deceit to become a "somebody" (vv.8b–9a), an irresponsible person who, needlessly courting danger and death, suffered for his trouble (v.9b–c), and a morose individual lacking the power that wealth affords (v.10).

"Glory and dishonor, bad report and good report" (v.8) may epitomize the two types of response to Paul's preaching, or they may contrast the opinion of others (dishonor, bad report) with the reward of God (glory, good report). In the contrasts that follow (vv.8c–10) the paradoxical character of Paul's apostolic ministry is emphasized. If in fact various charges had been made against him, he takes the accusation, lets it stand or invests it with his own meaning, and supplies an opposing complement to form a series of antitheses that point to the vicissitudes and tension of living as a persecuted "ambassador for Christ" (5:20).

4. The openness and joy of the apostolic ministry (6:11–7:4)

a. A plea for generous affection (6:11–13)

11–13 Paul did not customarily address his readers by name, doing so only when his emotions had been deeply stirred—as at the bewitchment of the Galatians (Gal 3:1), at the generosity of the Philippians (Php 4:15), or here, at the remarkable candor of his defense and the intensity of his affection for the Corinthians. Behind his freedom of speech (cf. 3:12; 4:2) was a warmly receptive attitude of heart. "If there are any feelings of constriction or restraint in our relationship," he continues, "they are on your side, not mine. I appeal to you as my spiritual children [cf. 1Co 4:14–15]: in fair exchange for my unrestricted affection, give me yours, too." Although Paul's desire was for complete reciprocity in family relationships, he was acutely aware that affection could only be given, not taken.

b. Minor digression–call to holiness 6:14–7:1)

14–16a Paul has just appealed to the Corinthians for mutual openness in affection and in speech. His own heart is open wide to them, but both he and they know why they cannot reciprocate as fully as they ought. Some of them have an uneasy conscience about their continuing pagan associations. The apparent abruptness of v.14a after v.13 may be explained: (1) by this mutual knowledge; (2) by Paul's "coming to the point" immediately, as he sets forth the truth plainly (4:2) or speaks the truth in love (Eph 4:15); and (3) perhaps by a brief dictation pause.

Paul begins with a concise summary of his message in this brief digression (6:14–7:1), which repeats the main point of 1Co 10:1–22, his warning to the Corinthians of the danger of idolatry (note 1Co 10:14: "Flee from idolatry"). "Do not be yoked together with unbelievers" clearly is not an injunction against any and all association with unbelievers (cf. 1Co 5:9–10; 10:27). Paul actually encouraged the Christian partner in a mixed marriage to maintain the relationship as long as possible (1Co 7:12–16). Rather, this is a prohibition against *forming* close attachments with non-Christians, using an agricultural metaphor about yoking (cf. Dt 22:10; also Lev 19:19). Although precisely what constituted a "diverse yoke" for the Corinthians remains unstated, it clearly involved compromise with heathendom, such as contracting mixed marriages (cf. Dt 7:1–3), initiating litigation before unbelievers in cases involving believers (1Co 6:1–8), or forming any relationship with unbelievers that would compromise Christian standards or jeopardize consistency of Christian witness. Paul is content to state a general principle that needs specific application under the Spirit's guidance.

Five rhetorical questions follow (vv.14–16a), each of which presupposes a negative answer. They stress the incompatibility of Christianity and heathenism, the incongruity of intimate relationships or fellowship between believers and unbelievers (cf. 1Co 10:21). After two comparisons of abstract nouns ("righteousness" and "light" with "wickedness" and "darkness"), there follow two personal comparisons—"Christ" and the "believer" with "Belial" and the "unbeliever." The final contrast (v.16a) climaxes the series and prompts what follows (vv.16b–18).

16b–c The chief reason why believers must not enter any compromising relationship with unbelievers (v.14a) is that they belong exclusively to God. Corporately they form "the temple [or sanctuary; GK *3724*] of the living God" (cf. 1Co 3:16–17; Eph 2:22; see also 1Co 6:19). To establish this last point (v.16b) Paul quotes or alludes to several OT passages: Lev 26:11a, 12, (cf. Ex 25:8; 29:45a;

1Ki 6:13; Eze 37:27a) and Ex 6:7 (cf. Jer 32:38).

17 Paul's next quotation (Isa 52:11) stresses God's demand for purity of life and separation from evil. In Isaiah, the call was for separation (or departure) from Babylon with its pagan idolatry. In Paul, the call is for separation from unbelievers with their pagan way of life. This verse may not be used to defend separation from believers on the ground of doctrinal differences.

"And I will receive you" stems from Eze 20:34, 41. God's acceptance and approval of his people is dependent on their obedience to his commands. Separation from the world leads to fellowship with God (cf. Jas 4:4).

18 The next mosaic of OT texts comes from 2Sa 7:14a, 27, with the reference to "daughters" possibly coming from Isa 43:6. What God promised to Solomon through David and to Israel through Solomon (cf. Jer 31:9) finds its fulfillment in what God is to the community of believers through Christ (Gal 3:26; 4:6). If Christians corporately are the temple of the living God (v.16), individually they are his sons and daughters.

7:1 In his chain of OT quotations Paul has stressed both the privilege of being a temple of God (v.16) and the benefits of compliance with the divine will (vv.17d–18). As recipients of such promises of fellowship with God, all Christians should avoid every source of possible defilement in any aspect of their lives. "Body and spirit" here denotes a Christian in his or her total personality in relations with other people and with God (cf. 1Co 7:34).

Paul is probably implying that the Corinthians have become defiled, perhaps by occasionally sharing meals at idol-shrines or by continuing to attend festivals or ceremonies in pagan temples (cf. 1Co 8:10; 10:14–22), or even by maintaining membership in a local pagan cult. If they make a clean break with pagan life in any and every form, they will be bringing their holiness nearer completion by this proof of their reverence for God.

c. Paul's pride and joy (7:2–4)

2–4 After this brief digression (6:14–7:1) Paul renews his appeal (cf. 6:13) for the Corinthians' full affection. He knows of nothing in his past conduct or instruction that can cause them to doubt his sincerity or lose confidence in him. Paul had been accused of bringing about the moral and financial ruin of innocent victims at Corinth by callously exploiting them (v.2), and apparently some at Corinth were inclined to believe these charges. As before (cf. 1Co 4:4; 2Co 4:2; 5:11; 6:3), Paul can do no more in reply than appeal to his clear conscience and the Corinthians' knowledge of his conduct and insist that the charges are groundless.

But to mention the charges did not imply that the Corinthians really believed them, nor was Paul trying to blame them for anything (v.3a). He reminds them (cf. 6:11) that they occupy a permanent and secure place in his love and concern. The leveling of charges, the arrival of death, the trials of life—none of these could divorce them from his affection (v.3b).

The situation at Corinth was not perfect and probably never would be. But Paul had grounds for great confidence and pride in his converts. In spite of all his frustrations and in the midst of all his affliction, he was filled with comfort and overflowing with joy (v.4; cf. 6:10). The reason? The safe arrival of Titus in Macedonia with encouraging news about Corinth (vv.5–7).

D. Paul's Reconciliation With the Corinthians (7:5–16)

1. Comfort in Macedonia (7:5–7)

5 At this point Paul resumes the account of his movements broken off at 2:13. Although he expected to meet Titus when he (Paul) arrived in Macedonia, his hopes were frustrated just as they had been at Troas (2:12–13). His body (Gk. *sarx*, "flesh"; GK *4922*) had no rest. In 2:13 he had said that his "mind" (Gk. *pneuma*, "spirit"; GK *4460*) had experienced no rest at Troas. If a distinction is to be drawn between the *pneuma* of 2:13 and the *sarx* of 7:5, terms often contrasted in Paul's writing (e.g., Gal 5:16–24), the former denotes Paul in his spiritual sensitivity; the latter, Paul in his physical suffering. But more likely the terms as used here are virtually synonymous.

"Fears within" alludes to Paul's persistent apprehension about Titus's reception at Corinth, his safety in travel, and the Corinthian response to the "severe letter." "Conflicts on the outside" may point to violent quarrelling that focused on Paul or to persecution that may have happened to him in Macedonia.

6–7 It probably seemed to Paul that from the human point of view his whole future as apostle to the Gentiles was related to the Corinthians' reaction to his assertion of authority in the letter delivered by Titus. And now the nonarrival of Titus tended to confirm his worst fears (see comment on 2:12–13).

God used three means to dispense comfort to the "downcast" (GK *5424*) apostle: the actual arrival of Titus, Titus's positive experience at Corinth, and the reassuring news he brought concerning the Corinthians' attitude toward Paul—their great "affection" for him, their "deep sorrow" over their disloyal behavior, and their "ardent concern" to defend Paul's cause and to follow his directions in disciplining the guilty party.

2. The severe letter and its effect (7:8–13a)

8–10 "My letter" refers to the so-called "severe letter," one that is no longer extant but was written after 1 Corinthians and Paul's "sorrowful visit" and was delivered by Titus (see comments in the introduction, sec. 5). From the report of Titus Paul had learned for the first time that his letter had caused the Corinthians considerable distress, at least for a period (v.8). As a spiritual father who disliked causing pain for whatever reason, his first reaction was to regret that he had written so stern a letter. But some later time, possibly after Paul had had time to reflect on the whole episode, his initial regret had disappeared when he realized that the temporary pain suffered by the Corinthians had produced sincere "repentance" (GK *3567*). Of what had the Corinthians repented? Probably their failure to defend Paul before his detractor (cf. v.12). Thus Paul could now say that he did not regret the letter; it had caused no permanent harm. The inference is clear: the imposition of discipline or the suffering of pain that does not, under God, lead to repentance, can cause irreparable harm.

Verse 10 describes two ways of reacting to pain or sorrow. God's way ("godly sorrow") invariably produces a change of heart; this repentance "leads to salvation" and therefore gives no cause for regret. Sorrow borne in a worldly way, on the other hand, does not lead to repentance but has the deadly effect of producing resentment or bitterness. What makes suffering remedial is not the actual experience of it but one's reaction to it.

11 A splendid example of the beneficial outcome of "godly sorrow" was the positive response of the Corinthians to Paul's letter that had for a time pained them. It could have compounded trouble at Corinth and caused widespread resentment against Paul, if it had not been received in a spirit of humility and with a willingness to follow God's will. As it was, it produced in them seriousness of purpose, "eagerness" to clear themselves from blame, "indignation" at the scandalous action of the person who denigrated Paul, "alarm" over their behavior and its effects, "affection" for Paul, "concern" lest he should visit them with a rod (1Co 4:21: cf. 2Co 7:15; 13:2), and a "readiness to see justice done" by the punishment of the offender (cf. 2:6).

The second sentence in this verse probably means that by their favorable response to the "severe letter" the Corinthians had proved themselves "to be innocent."

12–13a Paul's principal aim in writing the "severe letter" was for the Corinthians to recognize "before God" how devoted to their spiritual father they really were (cf. 2:9) and to ensure their future loyalty to Paul. This statement of his aim was likely influenced by his knowledge of the letter's outcome. At the time he actually wrote that letter he was unsure of Corinthian loyalty and hence was restless (2:12–13; 7:5). But since God had prevented the letter from making the Corinthians resentful (v.9b), Paul was encouraged (v.13a).

Paul also hints at two subsidiary aims in this letter: the punishment of the guilty party (cf. 2:6, 9) and the vindication of "the injured party." The offender was probably not the man guilty of incest (see comments on 2:5–6, 10–11), but an anti-Pauline intruder in the church; the injured party was likely Paul himself.

3. The relief of Titus (7:13b–16)

13b–14 Through the "godly sorrow" of the Corinthians, Titus was as relieved and encouraged as Paul. He apparently had little occasion before his visit to Corinth as bearer of the "severe letter" to form an independent judgment about the Corinthians; so he was dependent on Paul's glowing recommendation. This would suggest that this visit was his first one (though he may have had a brief earlier visit to organize the collection; see 1Co 16:1–2; see comment on 2Co 8:6–7). Titus seems to have ventured on this visit with some trepidation. But now that the visit was over, "his spirit has been refreshed."

Paul's relief stemmed from the fact that his generous assurances to Titus about the Corinthians had not proved unfounded and therefore embarrassing to him (v.11). On the contrary, just as his own truthfulness had been vindicated at Corinth (cf. 1:18–20), so also his boasting about them had now proved fully justified.

15–16 The Corinthian Christians had originally received Titus "with fear and trembling," afraid (cf. v.11) that they would fail to meet their obligations toward an envoy from Paul. But they had all readily complied with demands Titus had made of them. As Titus recalled their obedience and respectful deference to him, his affection grew all the warmer (v.15). This gave Paul good reason for complete confidence in the Corinthians (v.16) and a secure base from which to propose the completion of the collection (chs. 8–9).

II. The Collection for the Saints at Jerusalem (8:1–9:15)

For a summary of the historical background and theological significance of the collection, see the introduction.

This was not the first time the Corinthians had heard of the collection for the poor at Jerusalem, for in 1Co 16:1–4 Paul gave them certain information and directions about the project that they had probably requested in their earlier letter (see comment on 1Co 16:1–4). Whether they had acted on Paul's instructions is uncertain. But in all probability progress on the collection soon stopped, particularly as the result of (1) the unfortunate incident alluded to in 2:5–11; 7:12 and its aftermath, and (2) the malevolent influence of the intruders from Palestine, who at least for a period gained their support from some Corinthian sympathizers (cf. 11:7–12, 20; 12:13–16). But when Paul sent Titus to deliver and reinforce the effect of the "severe letter," he probably told him to attempt to revive the flagging collection if the church responded favorably to the letter (cf. 8:6a). Now, with firm evidence from Titus of their loyalty to him (7:6–16), Paul can discuss the project again and press for its completion.

A. The Need for Generosity (8:1–15)

1. The generosity of the Macedonians (8:1–5)

1–2 Tactfully, Paul begins with an example, not a plea. Although they were facing a severe ordeal involving persecution (cf. 1Th 1:6; 2:14), the Macedonian churches (e.g., those at Philippi, Thessalonica, and Berea) had contributed generously. As Paul expresses it, their "rich generosity" resulted from "overflowing joy" (v.2). Their "extreme poverty" no more impeded their generosity than their tribulation diminished their joy. This liberal giving by destitute Christians to fellow believers not personally known to them Paul traces to the influence of God's "grace" (*charis*; GK *5921*; this word occurs 10 times in chs. 8–9, with varying meanings). The apostle was not concerned about the actual size of the gift but about the attitude of the givers (cf. Ro 12:8) and the relation between the size of the gift and the resources of the givers (cf. Mk 12:41–44).

3–5 In describing the nature of the Macedonians' generosity, Paul makes several observations. First, they gave far more generously than their slender means and adverse circumstances permitted. Their eagerness to contribute led them to surpass all expectations.

Second, acting on their own initiative, they "urgently pleaded" with Paul for the "privilege of sharing" (Gk. *koinonia*, "fellowship"; GK *3126*) in the collection. Since 1Co 16:1 mentions only "the Galatian churches," not the Macedonian churches, and since 1Co 16:5 makes no reference to the collection, it seems likely that the collection in Macedonia began after the spring of A.D. 55. One reason for Paul's sending Timothy and Erastus into Macedonia (Ac 19:22) may have been to introduce the collection project there, though Paul was reluctant to encourage the poor Macedonians to contribute (v.2).

A third reason why the Macedonians exceeded Paul's expectations was that they did not restrict their contribution to financial aid. Rather, they dedicated themselves to Christ first and then also to Paul for the performance of any service in connection with the collection. They recognized that dedication to Christ involved dedication to his servants. All was part of God's will.

2. A plea for liberal giving (8:6-12)

6-7 The sterling example of the Macedonians encouraged Paul to ask Titus to make arrangements for the completion of the offering among the Corinthians. After all, unlike the Macedonians, they were not facing persecution, nor were they in desperate financial straits. How willingly they ought to contribute! Earlier Titus had "made a beginning" on the collection, though when this occurred is not clear. It may have been when he delivered the "severe letter," or at an even earlier time.

Titus had already brought to a successful completion an "act of grace" among them—likely his task as Paul's special envoy to Corinth to deliver the "severe letter" and to carry out its measures. But in Paul's judgment something more than another letter was needed to make sure the Corinthians now completed their offering. Thus Paul wants Titus to pay another visit.

A special visit from Titus, however, would not in itself guarantee the success of the collection. So Paul appeals to the Corinthians' desire to exhibit every sign of spirituality (cf. 1Co 1:5, 7; 12:31; 14:37). By using the word *charis* ("grace"; cf. comment on vv.1-2) of this virtue of giving, he makes it clear that generosity stands alongside faith, speech, knowledge, and love as an expression of divine grace in a person (v.7).

8 Although vested with full apostolic authority (10:8; 13:10), Paul declined to issue directives, preferring rather to request, suggest (cf. v.10), encourage, or appeal (cf. 1Co 7:6; 2Co 8:6, 10, 17). Spontaneity and warmth would be absent from the Corinthians' giving if coercion were present. But he did see in the enthusiastic generosity of the Macedonian churches a convenient standard for assessing the genuineness of the Corinthians' professed love for him and for all believers, as well as a compelling incentive to arouse them to action.

9 In encouraging the Corinthians to bring their contribution to a satisfactory completion (v.6), Paul has thus far appealed to the example of the Macedonians (vv.1-5, 8), to their own promising beginning (v.6), and to their desire for spiritual excellence (v.7). Now he turns to the example of Christ, in whom Paul saw the supreme example of one who showed eagerness and generosity in giving as a demonstration of love. If the sacrificial giving of the Macedonians did not stimulate emulation, the example of Christ's selflessness certainly would. Paul typically buttresses ethical injunctions with doctrine (e.g., Ro 15:2-3; Eph 5:2; Col 3:9-10).

Christ "became poor" by the act of incarnation that followed his preincarnate renunciation of heavenly glory (cf. Php 2:6-8). That glory is depicted as wealth, in contrast to the lowliness of earthly existence, which amounts to "poverty." Through his voluntary surrender of glory, others derived spiritual wealth (Eph 1:3). Unlike the Macedonians, who gave when they were poor (v.2), Christ gave when he was incalculably rich. In their present circumstances the Corinthians fitted somewhere between these extremes. Like the Macedonians (v.5), Christ gave himself. The Corinthians would do well to emulate these examples.

10-11 Again Paul emphasizes that he is not giving orders but offering advice (cf. v.8a), though an imperative follows in v.11! It is clear from 1Co 7:25, 40, however, that such a considered opinion came from one who regarded himself as worthy of trust. The apostle hints at several reasons why it was "best" for the Corinthians to bring their contribution to a speedy completion. (1) Considerable time had elapsed since they had expressed an "eager willingness" to help. (2 Since their enthusiastic intention had already been partially translated into action, it was incumbent on them, having put their hands to the plow, not to look back but to bring the project to a successful completion. (3) They thus enjoyed a twofold precedence over the Macedonians—both in deciding to contribute and then in beginning to collect money. But now the Macedonians themselves had completed their offering! (4) The Macedonians had contributed "even beyond their ability" (v.3); now the Corinthians were being asked to contribute "according to [their] means."

12 The phrase "according to your means" at the end of v.11 is now explained. Provided a gift is willingly given, its acceptability is determined solely on the basis of what a person might possess, not on the basis of what one does not own. God assesses the "value" of a monetary gift not in terms of the actual amount given, but by comparing what is given with the total financial resources of the giver (see Mk 12:41–44). No one is expected to give "according to what he does not have."

3. The aim of equality (8:13–15)

13–14 Perhaps one reason the collection project had been languishing at Corinth was an objection like this: "As if we had no financial problems of our own, Paul is imposing fresh burdens on us so that others can become free of burdens." Christian giving, Paul insists, does not aim at an exchange of financial burdens but rather at an equal sharing of them and an equal supply of the necessities of life. The rich are not called upon to give so lavishly that they become poor and the poor become rich. That would simply prolong inequality. But those who enjoy a greater share of material benefits are called upon to make certain that those who have a smaller share through no fault of their own are not in want.

If v.13 alludes to an equal sharing of burdens that will lead to equality of supply, then v.14 speaks of mutual sacrifice that will maintain equality. Paul here is not predicting economic plenty in Jerusalem and economic dearth in Corinth. But he saw that with the uncertainty of economic conditions in the first century, it was not inconceivable for the Jerusalem Christians some day to become the donors of financial aid and the Corinthian Christians the recipients. On the other hand, since chronic poverty existed in Jerusalem, perhaps Paul means that the Jerusalem believers would dispense nothing other than what they had already supplied to Gentile churches—namely, the spiritual blessings of the Gospel (cf. Ro 15:27).

15 Paul now illustrates this principle of equality of supply from the account of God's provision of manna to the Israelites in the wilderness (Ex 16:13–36; esp. v.18). Although some gathered more than others and some less, the needs of all were met. Miraculously there was equal provision, with neither surplus nor deficiency. But Paul's illustration also points to a contrast. The equality the Israelites miraculously experienced in the wilderness was enforced; the equality Christians are themselves to create in the church and the world is voluntary.

B. The Mission of Titus and His Companions (8:16–9:5)

1. The delegates and their credentials (8:16–24)

This section amounts to a "letter of commendation" (cf. 3:1) from Paul to the church at Corinth, giving the credentials of the three appointed delegates and encouraging the Corinthians to welcome them warmly.

16–17 Although Titus's affection for the Corinthians naturally developed as a result of his positive interaction with them (7:13–15), Paul could trace Titus's keen interest in their welfare to the providential working of God (v.16). Nothing could be more reassuring to the Corinthians than to know that the devotion and concern for them shared by Paul and Titus were simply a reflection of God's own affection for them—and it was concern for them, not for their money (cf. 12:14). Paul goes on to describe the intensity of Titus's concern. It was true that Paul had "urged" him (v.6; cf. "appeal" here; GK *4155*) to arrange for the collection to be completed, but this invitation merely confirmed Titus's eager willingness; in reality he was going "on his own initiative."

18–19 The unidentified Christian brother whom Paul was sending with Titus had a double qualification. He was well known and highly praised in all the (Macedonian?) churches "for his service to the gospel" (probably a good administrator, maybe also an evangelist or teacher). Also, he had been selected and commissioned by an unspecified number of churches to travel with Paul on behalf of the collection. Paul adds a phrase to explain why he personally was supervising the administration of the collection. He sought to promote not his own glory but the Lord's and to prove his "eagerness to help" (cf. Gal 2:10).

20–21 Experience in Corinth had taught Paul that he must anticipate suspicions or accusations of his detractors and take the necessary precautions (e.g., 11:9, 12). As the prime mover behind the Jerusalem collection that he expected to be sizable (cf. "this liberal gift"), he was particularly susceptible to malicious charges that the whole project was designed to bribe the Jerusalem church fully to support his ministry or that he was quietly retaining a commission for himself. This explains, for example, his original uncertainty as to whether he would accompany the churches' delegates to Jerusalem (1Co 16:3–4; but cf. 2Co 1:16; Ro 15:25), his insistence that the Corinthians appoint their own accredited representatives (1Co 16:3), and his sending to Corinth (before he arrived!) two delegates along with his personal representative, Titus (vv.18–19, 22–23).

Paul was not one who sought human praise (Gal 1:10), but he recognized that the progress of the Gospel was hindered if its ministers for any reason acquired a reputation for dishonest dealings (cf. 1Co 9:12; 2Co 4:2; 6:3). Verse 21 is virtually a quotation of Pr 3:4 (in LXX).

22 The second anonymous representative who would travel to Corinth with Titus is identified simply as "our brother," i.e, a brother in Christ (see comment on 1:1). On many previous occasions Paul had proved this man's zeal, which in the present matter was all the greater "because of his great confidence" that this mission to Corinth would prove highly successful.

Why are the two "brothers" who would accompany Titus not identified? Either because both would be personally introduced by Titus when the present letter was first read at Corinth, or because both delegates, as renowned appointees of the Macedonian churches, were already well known at Corinth.

Why were three delegates chosen? Evidently Paul was more susceptible to misrepresentation at Corinth than in most of the other churches he had founded, so added precautions were necessary. To have sent one personal representative would have been to lay himself open to slanderous gossip (cf. 12:16–18), while two independent envoys would be able to testify to his honest intentions and conduct (cf. Dt 17:6; 19:15). Furthermore, it is not impossible that Paul wished to exert subtle pressure on the Corinthians (cf. 9:4), knowing as he did the somewhat erratic progress of the collection at Corinth thus far, the propensity of the Corinthians for disorderliness (cf. 1Co 14:33, 40), and the disturbing effect of the parasitical intruders from Palestine.

23 As he sums up the credentials of the three delegates, Paul draws a distinction between Titus, his "partner" and personally appointed representative, and the two "representatives of the churches." Titus, like Timothy (Ro 16:21), is described as Paul's "fellow worker." If anyone should raise questions about the two others, says Paul, three facts are relevant: they are "brothers" in Christ; they are the appointees and envoys of the Macedonian churches; by their life and service they are a credit (Gk. *doxa*, "glory"; GK *1518*) to Christ.

24 Paul's short "letter of commendation" (vv.16–24) concludes with a warm appeal. The Corinthians were to give evidence of their love for Christ and for the members of his body (cf. v.8) by extending to the three delegates warm hospitality and by cooperating with their efforts to supervise the final arrangements for the collection. Also, they were to vindicate Paul's confident boasting about them (cf. 7:14) by contributing eagerly, promptly, and generously (cf. vv.7, 20). All was to be done openly, so that all the churches contributing to the collection could see it.

2. The need for readiness (9:1–5)

1 Having completed his letter of commendation, Paul resumes his discussion of the collection and states why he was convinced that his pride in the Corinthians and his boasting about them (8:21) would not prove to have been misguided.

2 In 8:10 (cf. 8:6) Paul dated the beginning of the collection at Corinth as "last year." Here he uses the same phrase to speak of his current boast to the Macedonians: since last year the Christians in Achaia, certainly including the Corinthians, were ready to give. But since Paul was writing here because of the presumed reluctance of the Corinthians to give, how can Paul now say that he used the example of their "readiness" in his effort to have the Macedonians contribute quickly and liberally?

In answer, we must draw a careful distinction between the Corinthians' ready desire to give and the actual fact of having completed the collection. This verse concentrates only on the former aspect, their enthusiastic eagerness to help out (cf. 8:11). From vv.3–5 it is clear that they had not yet been giving liberally. The relation, then, between chs. 8 and 9 is this: The Corinthian enthusiasm for participating in the collection (cf. 8:10–11) served as an example worthy of emulation by the Macedonians for their own contribution (9:2). Now, however, because the Macedonians had now successfully completed what they had enthusiastically begun under the stimulus of the Corinthian example (8:1–5), their exemplary action formed a basis for Paul's appeal to the Corinthians to complete their contribution (8:6, 10–11).

3–4 Although Paul knew that the Corinthians were so eager to help that further written reminders about the collection were superfluous (vv.1–2), he was sending a personal reminder in the form of the "brothers" (cf. 8:16–24). Paul wanted to avoid two situations. One was that his repeated and confident boast to the Macedonians about the Corinthians' "eagerness" and readiness (v.2) would turn out to be without foundation upon his arrival. The other was that when delegates from the Macedonian churches arrived at Corinth with Paul on his forthcoming visit (12:11: 13:1–2), the Corinthians would be still unprepared and this would lead to his (and their own) embarrassment.

5 To make certain that neither of these predicaments arose, Paul "thought it necessary to urge the brothers" to prepare for his coming to Corinth by supervising final arrangements for the collection there. He reminds the Corinthians of their earlier commitment ("the generous gift you had promised"). By a prompt response when the brothers arrived, they would be fulfilling an obligation they had voluntarily assumed and would ensure that the gift was not "grudgingly given."

Twice in this verse the Corinthian contribution is called a "generous gift" (Gk. *eulogia*, "blessing": GK *2330*), a biblical word that refers either to an act of blessing or consecration or to some concrete benefit given by God or a human being. Here the latter meaning is more appropriate—"a benefit bestowed" by the Corinthian believers on the Jerusalem saints. But other ideas are also suggested. (1) The Corinthian contribution would be an act that produced the blessing of thanksgiving to God; cf. vv.11–13). (2) Paul hoped that the "collection" (Gk. *logeia*, 1Co 16:1) at Corinth would be a "first-rate collection" (*eu-logia*). (3) Since "blessing" implies generosity, the word may denote "a generous gift" (NIV).

C. The Results of Generosity (9:6–15)

1. The enrichment of the giver (9:6–11)

6–7 To emphasize the rewards of generous giving (v.5), Paul cites what appears to be a proverb (v.6): "scanty sowing, scanty harvest; plentiful sowing, plentiful harvest." No exact parallel to this maxim is extant, though a similar sentiment is expressed in several places (e.g., Pr 11:24–25; 19:17; 22:8–9; Lk 6:38; Gal 6:7). The image of the harvest naturally suggests the freedom of the sower to plant as much seed as he chooses—whether "sparingly" or "generously." Similarly, each person is responsible first to decide "in his heart" what he should give (cf. Ac 11:29; 1Co 16:2) and then to give what he has decided (v.7). Giving should result from inward resolve, not from impulsive or casual decision. Once the amount to be given has been determined, says Paul, the gift should be given cheerfully, since a cheerful giver always receives God's approval (cf. Pr 22:8 in LXX).

8–9 God shows his approval of the cheerful giver (v.7b) in his provision of spiritual grace and material prosperity ("*all* grace") that enable this person constantly and generously to dispense both spiritual and material benefits. As regularly as the resources of a cheerful giver are taxed by one's generous giving, they are replenished by divine grace. This gives that individual "all that you need," in dependence on an all-sufficient God (cf. Mal 3:10).

At this point Paul quotes Ps 112 to illustrate the generosity of "the man who fears the LORD" (112:1) and the positive results of one's giving. From "the wealth and riches . . . in his house" (112:3a), this God-fearing person freely distributes gifts to the poor (112:9a). As a result, such benevolent acts of piety will never be forgotten but rather will have permanent beneficial effects in this life and will gain one an eternal reward (112:9b).

10–11 In v.6 Paul observed that the person who sows sparingly will reap a meager harvest. Now he develops the imagery of sowing and reaping to reinforce the point that generosity pays handsome dividends. He argues from God's bounty in nature to his even greater liberality in grace. The crops of the generous person are always full and his harvests rich. If God supplies us with the seed needed to produce a harvest of grain, and thus food (cf. Isa 55:10), he certainly will supply and multiply all the resources needed to produce a full harvest of good deeds ("your righteousness"; cf. Hos 10:12).

Verse 11a restates v.8. God continues to enrich benevolent people so that they can go on enriching others by their generosity (cf. 1:4). The greater the giving, the greater the enrichment. The greater the enrichment, the greater the resources to give. Paul then adds a statement (v.11b) that he will develop in vv.12–15. The Jerusalem saints, as the grateful recipients of the liberal gift administered by Paul and his colleagues, would express their thanks to God, the source of all good gifts (cf. Jas 1:17).

2. The offering of thanks to God (9:12–15)

12–13 The believers at Corinth are now reminded of the encouraging results that will stem from their generous gift. Not only does "this service" of giving enrich the donor (vv.6–11) and help supply the needs of the recipients (v.12a), but above all, it promotes the glory of God by prompting "many expressions of thanks" to him. The saints at Jerusalem, as well as other Christians who heard of the collection, would praise God because this act of Christian service had proved the reality and vigor of the Corinthians' faith (v.13a), which may have come under suspicion at Jerusalem through reports of certain irregularities in their church. Then there would be two items for thanksgiving: (1) the Corinthians' obedience to the dictates of the Gospel that accompanied their "confession of the gospel of Christ"; (2) their sacrificial liberality demonstrated in sharing material benefits with the Jerusalem church and therefore in one sense with all Christians (cf. 1Co 12:26). Praise is offered less for the gift itself than for the spiritual virtues of the donors expressed in the gift.

14 As to further results of generosity, Paul is convinced the giving will be reciprocal. The Jerusalem believers will receive material benefits and in return will dispense the spiritual blessing of intercession for the Corinthians. As they pray, they will recall "the surpassing grace" (Gk. *charis*; see comment on 8:1–2) imparted to the Corinthians by God and evident in their liberality; as a result, their hearts will be warmed toward those at Corinth and they will long to see them and enjoy a closer relation with them.

15 This doxology is a final appeal to the lofty grandeur of divine giving (cf. 8:9; 9:8, 10–11). Since the gift here is said to be given by God and is beyond adequate human description, it can hardly refer to the Corinthian contribution or even the boon of Jewish-Gentile reconciliation in Christ alluded to in v.14a; rather, it must refer to the surpassing grace that God imparts (v.14b), especially the Father's gift of the Son (cf. Ro 8:32).

Were Paul's appeals to the Corinthians in these two chapters successful? The apostle paid his third visit to Corinth as planned (12:14; 13:1), spending three months (the winter of A.D. 56–57) in Greece (Ac 20:2–3), during which he wrote Romans (see Ro 16:23; 1Co 1:14). In Ro 15:26–27 he writes that the believers in Macedonia *and Achaia* eagerly made "a contribution for the poor among the saints in Jerusalem." Evidently in the five or so months between the writing of 2 Corinthians and Romans, the believers at Corinth had responded to Paul's appeals. Why then does Acts not refer to any delegate from Achaia (see comment on Ac 20:4)? Perhaps Titus was their representative, a man who for some reason is nowhere mentioned in Acts.

III. Paul's Vindication of His Apostolic Authority (10:1–13:14)

A. The Exercise of Apostolic Rights and Authority (10:1–11:15)

1. The potency of apostolic authority (10:1–11)

No commentator denies that an abrupt change of tone occurs at this point in the letter. Defenders of the unity of 2 Corinthians explain the change in various ways, some of which are the following: (1) Paul pauses in dictation and hears more disturbing news; (2) like chs. 1–7, chs. 10–13 are tempered polemic, with not a few tender expressions of affection (e.g., 11:2–3; 12:14–15a); (3) Paul intentionally reserves his criticism until after his commendation; (4) after consolidating his apostolic authority (chs. 1–7), Paul then exercises it (chs. 10–13); (5) the contrast between chs. 1–9 and chs. 10–13 has been overdrawn—all 2 Corinthians is polemical in tone; (6) Paul now addresses a different audience—in chs. 1–9 Paul addresses the whole church, in chs. 10–13 the intruders and their partisans; (7) on other occasions Paul is given to abrupt changes of mood (e.g., 1Co 4:8).

1–2 There is no evidence that Paul now addresses only a segment of the Corinthian church—those favorably disposed toward his adversaries from Palestine. On the contrary, throughout these next four chapters Paul regularly identifies the views of certain unnamed people (e.g., 10:7, 10–12; 11:4, 12–13, 15, 20–23; 13:2) who formed a recognizable subversive element at Corinth, thus alerting the entire church (cf. 12:19; 13:11–13) to the danger of becoming spiritually infected.

Paul had been accused of being courageous at a distance, shooting his epistolary arrows (e.g., the "severe letter"), but subservient and weak when personally present (cf. v.10; 1Co 2:3). This charge Paul ironically repeats in v.1b as a prelude to an appeal to all the Corinthians regarding a vocal minority ("some people"), who persisted in thinking that worldly standards and motives governed all his conduct and that he relied on human powers and methods in his ministry (cf. 1:17; 2:17; 3:5; 4:2; 7:2).

What Paul wished to avoid on his forthcoming visit was a display of boldness—boldness when present, not absent! Yet he is ready to exercise his apostolic authority, whatever the outcome, if the Corinthians do not repudiate his opponents and mend their ways (cf. 12:20–21; 13:11). His "meekness and gentleness" as a true servant of Christ (cf. Mt 11:29) should not be confused with timidity (cf. 13:10; 1Co 4:21).

3–4 Paul draws a clear distinction between existence "in the world" and worldly conduct and techniques. He does not deny his human weakness, yet he affirms that spiritual warfare demands spiritual weapons (vv.3–4a; cf. Eph 6:11–17). A successful campaign can be waged in the spiritual realm only as worldly weapons are abandoned and total reliance is placed on spiritual weapons, which can demolish apparently impregnable fortresses where evil is entrenched (v.4b).

5 What are these fortified positions that crumble before the weapons of the Spirit? Fanciful human sophistry and intellectual pretensions, otherwise called "the wisdom of this world" (1Co 3:19). The phrase "every pretension" refers to any human act or attitude that forms an obstacle to the emancipating knowledge of God contained in the Gospel of Christ and that keeps people in bondage to sin. Closely related is the expression "every thought," which means every human device that temporarily frustrates the divine plan; they must be forcibly reduced to obedience to Christ. Paul presents the picture of a military operation in enemy territory that seeks to thwart every single hostile plan of battle, so that there will be universal allegiance to Christ.

6 If circumstances forced Paul to turn from "meekness and gentleness" to a stern assertion of his authority, his plan of action has two stages. (1) He must bring the Corinthians' obedience to completion (cf. 2:9; 7:15), achieved only when they dissociate themselves from his opponents, fully recognize his apostolic authority, and make a total break with idolatry (6:14–7:1). (2) There is the (as yet undefined) punishment of "every act of disobedience" performed by his adversaries from Palestine or by any remaining insubordinate Corinthians.

In other words, Paul must secure a firm base in the Corinthian church before he will risk a face-to-face confrontation with those who still oppose him. Unless a church as a whole is willing to support spiritual discipline, that discipline will remain largely ineffective. Another important principle emerges when vv.5 and 6 are compared: Obedience to Christ entails submission to his appointed representatives.

7 Paul's opponents were not unaware that the most successful way to undermine his effectiveness was to cast doubt on the genuineness of his apostleship. If his converts could be persuaded that he lacked apostolic credentials, they would cease to believe his teaching.

In response, Paul does not discourage the testing of credentials (cf. 13:2–3) but casts doubt on the adequacy of the criteria the Corinthians were using. They were impressed by externals (cf. 5:12), with "the surface of things"—the confident claim of being an authorized apostle, commendatory letters (3:1), an authoritarian manner (11:20), spectacular visions (cf. 12:1–7), rhetorical skills (11:6), and "pure" Jewishness (11:22). Paul argues that the right to make a subjective claim based on personal conviction cannot fairly be granted his opponents and yet denied him; later in this section he will mention more objective criteria for testing apostolic credentials. In all this, his motive was not personal vindication but the desire to defend the Corinthian church from the danger of apostasy (cf. 11:2–3).

8 If the need for self-defense in the face of opposition compelled Paul to "boast [GK *3016*] somewhat freely" about his apostolic authority, he was confident that he would not be embarrassed by a charge of exaggeration or deception, for the facts themselves spoke eloquently in his favor. Everyone knew that his service at Corinth had resulted in the upbuilding of the Corinthian church in faith and in harmony, while the presence of the false apostles had produced friction and division (cf. 1Co 3:17). He stresses the divine origin of his authority (cf. 3:5–6; 13:10) and its employment for the common good (1Co 12:7).

9–11 However legitimately Paul may have boasted about his God-given authority, he decides to refrain from expanding his simple claim in v.8 lest he appear to be frightening the Corinthians into submission by "weighty and forceful" letters (vv.9–10a). He has no desire to give substance to the charge that he is bold and impressive only when absent (cf. v.1). Those who compare unfavorably what they believe to be his epistolary boldness, "unimpressive" presence, or contemptible rhetoric (v.10) are reminded that when present with them he will act in precise accord with his letters (cf. 13:2, 10).

It is not difficult to understand the origin of the malicious accusation against Paul reported in v.10. Each of his earlier letters to Corinth had been "forceful." In fact, to judge by their contents, they seemed to be growing more forceful each time! Moreover, unlike his opponents (11:20), Paul avoided self-assertiveness and admitted the inferiority of his rhetorical skills (1Co 1:17; 2:1–5; 2Co 11:6). What he firmly resists, however, is the inference drawn from the claim about his personality and his manner of speaking—namely, that he is " 'timid' when face to face" (v.1).

2. Legitimate spheres of activity and boasting (10:12–18)

Behind Paul's continuing self-defense in this section lies an indirect attack on the intruders from Palestine. From his firm denials ("we do not," vv.12, 16; "we... will not," v.13; "we are not," v.14; et al.) we may deduce the content of his charges against his rivals (not, as elsewhere, the content of accusations made against him). Only in v.12b does Paul make a direct charge: the false apostles have trespassed on his legitimate area of authority at Corinth in defiance of the agreement of Gal 2:1–10. In addition, in their unrestrained self-commendation, his opponents are falsely claiming credit for work he has done in Corinth.

12 In one aspect of his conduct, Paul admits his timidity (cf. v.1). He lacked the boldness and temerity to compare himself with those who indulged in self-praise. Writing ironically, he asserts that in their folly his opponents were establishing their own conduct as normative and then finding great satisfaction in always measuring up to the standard. The implication is clear. If the Corinthians try to assess Paul's credentials against the artificial and subjective criteria established by his detractors, they will be just as foolish.

13–14 Unlike his adversaries, Paul refuses to boast of what has occurred beyond the limits of his own ministry as the apostle to the Gentiles (Ac 9:15; Gal 2:9). In boasting about his special "field" at Corinth and appealing by implication to the existence of the Corinthian church as a vindication of his apostleship (cf. 3:2–3), he is not overstepping his limits, since historically his God-ordained field included Corinth. In fact, he had been the first to reach the Corinthians with the Gospel of Christ (v.14b; cf. 1Co 3:6, 10).

It was the activity of the false apostles from Palestine at Corinth that encroached on Paul's legitimate "field" because it violated the concordat of Gal 2:1–10, which predated their arrival at Corinth (see comments in the introduction, sec. 5). Even if these opponents had no relationship with the Jerusalem church, they must have been aware of the agreement of Gal 2, particularly that the Jerusalem apostles recognized that Paul had been entrusted with special responsibility for propagating the Gospel among the Gentiles or uncircumcised (Gal 2:7–9). True, their presence at Corinth was not technically an infringement on any precisely defined apostolic "treaty," but it amounted at least to a repudiation of the spirit of this agreement concerning apostolic "division of labor," for they were not in Corinth to aid Paul (as Apollos had been, 1Co 3:5–6) but to supplant him.

15–16 Twice here Paul indirectly chides his opponents for priding themselves on work already done by others. They probably boasted that the spiritual vitality of the Corinthians was directly attributable to them. Paul, however, so far from boasting of "work already done" (v.15), made it his policy to avoid preaching the Gospel where Christ had already been named lest he build on another man's foundation (Ro 15:18–21).

As their spiritual father (1Co 4:15), he hoped that the growth of their faith would result in the enlargement of his influence among them and the improvement of their estimation of him. Then and only then could he contemplate fulfilling his eager desire to visit the Christians at Rome (Ac 19:21; Ro 1:11; 15:24) and to advance westward to Spain (Ro 15:24, 28). Paul felt he could not pursue pioneer evangelism in the western Mediterranean when his converts in the eastern Mediterranean were unsettled and in danger of apostasy (11:3). In this sense, Paul's future was in the Corinthians' hands. Consolidation had to precede advance; in other words, any evangelistic expansion would be the joyful outcome of his total acceptance at Corinth.

17–18 As in 1Co 1:31, Paul cites Jer 9:24. Boasting is illegitimate, whether it be of one's own accomplishments or status or of another person's achievements as though they were one's own (v.16). For Christians, only boasting "in the Lord" is legitimate—i.e., boasting of what Jesus Christ has done for them (Gal 6:14) or through them (Ro 15:18; cf. Ac 11:27), or of what they can do through him. So far from being an evidence or guarantee of divine approval, self-commendation (such as Paul's adversaries practiced) disqualifies them. Only those who boast in the Lord and so give God his due glory enjoy the Lord's commendation at his tribunal (cf. 5:9).

3. Paul's jealousy for the Corinthians (11:1–6)

1 Paul has firmly stated that self-praise is inadmissible and worthless (cf. 3:1; 5:12; 10:12), but he realizes that the present situation demands it if his converts at Corinth are to be preserved intact for Christ (v.2). His antagonists were indulging in self-praise (5:12; 10:7, 12–18) and the Corinthians were evidently sympathetic to that. Consequently his hand was forced (12:11); he must indulge in foolish boasting in order to win the Corinthians' attention and gain a fair hearing. Reluctantly, he decides to employ his opponents' methods; but unlike theirs, his motive is not personal gain but the Corinthians' welfare (v.2). He goes on to supply three grounds for his appeal to the Corinthians to bear with him: (1) his divine jealousy for them especially when they were endangered (vv.2–3); (2) their willingness to put up with rivals who presented an adulterated message (v.4); and (3) his claim not to be in the least inferior to the "super-apostles" (v.5).

2 With a "jealousy" (GK *2419*) that sprang from God and was like God's own jealousy for his people (e.g., Hos 2:19–20; 4:12; 6:4; 11:8), Paul was jealous for his converts' undivided loyalty to Christ in the interval between their conversion (= betrothal to Christ) and their glorification (= presentation to Christ). He pictures himself as the father of the bride (cf. 1Co 4:15; 2Co 12:14), whose ultimate goal was to present "the church of God in Corinth" (1:1) as a pure virgin to her husband at his appearance (cf. 4:14; Eph 5:27; 1Jn 3:2–3). Human jealousy is a vice, but to share divine jealousy is a virtue. There is a place for a spiritual father's passionate concern for the exclusive and pure devotion to Christ of his spiritual children (11:29).

3 Prompting Paul's jealousy for Corinthian fidelity was his fear, based on disturbing evidence (v.4), that their minds and affections might be corrupted so that they would lose their single-minded faithfulness to Christ. He recognized the false apostles as Satan's agents (v.15), capable of repeating at Corinth what Satan had successfully achieved in the garden of Eden (Ge 3:13; 1Ti 2:14). The danger was intellectual deception leading to apostasy.

4 Paul's fear had a foundation in fact; the "if" as used here denotes an actual, not a hypothetical, situation (i.e., "if, as has happened, someone comes"). In justifying his plea for the Corinthians' tolerance of his enforced boasting (v.1), Paul ironically appeals to the ready welcome they gave visitors who came proclaiming a message other than the Gospel that they had embraced and that had brought them salvation. Surely they ought to show their father in the faith the same degree of tolerance they showed a newcomer preaching a different faith!

It is impossible to reconstruct the precise content of what these false apostles said; it is also uncertain whether "spirit" here alludes to the Holy Spirit or to a spirit of fear and slavery (Ro 8:15; 2Ti 1:7). What seems clear, however, is that the willingness of the Corinthian believers to entertain the eloquent preacher of an adulterated gospel (cf. Gal 1:6–9) that added human merit to divine grace illustrated their tendency to look "only on the surface of things" (10:7; cf. 1Co 1:17; 2:1, 4–5; 2Co 10:10).

5 The third justification for the request of v.1 now appears (see comment). Still engaging in his "senseless" but pardonable self-praise, Paul maintains that he is in no way inferior to the "super-apostles." This expression is either the description of the Twelve used by Paul's opponents and here (as in 12:11; see comment) quoted by Paul, or the apostle's ironical description of the exalted view of the Twelve held by the "false apostles." In this verse, Paul claims to be in no respect inferior to the original apostles (see 1Co 9:1; 15:5–8, 10) with whom he was being unfavorably compared and whose authority his adversaries illegitimately invoked in support of their Judaizing program at Corinth.

6 Paul rates himself by the criteria used by the Corinthians to assess the credentials of apostles or visiting missionaries. With regard to his lack of professional training and skill in rhetoric, Paul is willing to admit his deficiency (cf. 10:10) and perhaps even his inferiority to the "false apostles." But in his judgment his expertise in knowledge, which he had made perfectly clear to the Corinthians, more than compensated for this deficiency.

4. Financial dependence and independence (11:7–12)

7–8 Itinerant teachers of the Hellenistic age commonly gained their financial support by charging a fee for their instruction. Traveling teachers who were concerned about their reputation, however, would often work at a trade. Under the influence of example set by Jesus in his instructions to the Twelve (Lk 9:3–4; 10:4, 7), early Christianity adopted a third method of support: a preacher accepted gifts from the community (something Paul refused to do; see 1Co 9:3–18). But the believers at Corinth had been influenced by the pseudo-apostles into thinking that such acceptance of remuneration for teaching was a criterion of true apostolicity. Their thought seemed to be: "If it is the apostles' right to get their living by preaching the Gospel, why did Paul refuse to accept support for preaching unless he considered himself inferior?"

In his defense, notable for its powerful irony, Paul makes two points. (1) He had committed no offense simply by waiving his apostolic right to support (1Co 9:12, 15, 18); rather, he did not want anyone to charge him with peddling God's word for profit (2:17). (2) His purpose in "humbling" himself in the Corinthians' eyes by doing manual labor while ministering to them (see Ac 18:3) was to "elevate" them above their inherited idolatry and vicious past (cf. 4:12; 8:9), just as his "robbing" other churches of money they could not really spare was motivated solely by his desire to serve the Corinthians more effectively (v.8).

9 During his initial visit to Corinth, Paul had at first supported himself by plying his trade as a "leather-worker" (Ac 18:3), but on the arrival of Silas and Timothy from Macedonia, "he began to devote himself entirely to preaching" (Ac 18:5), presumably because "brothers who came from Macedonia" brought monetary gifts from Philippi (Php 4:15) and possibly Thessalonica (cf. 1Th 3:6). Providentially the gift arrived just when his resources had failed and he had begun to feel need. Even in this extremity he had not been a burden to anyone in Corinth. Financial independence would continue to be his policy.

10–12 This policy, which enabled Paul to boast that he was preaching the Gospel free of charge (v.7; cf. 1Co 9:18), he refused to abandon (cf. 1Co 9:15). It was Christ's truth he was speaking when he affirmed that he would not bow to pressure from his opponents anywhere in Achaia regarding this issue (v.10).

But why did Paul not accept money for preaching? Two conflicting explanations are mentioned here. (1) Some had malevolently asserted that it was evidence of Paul's lack of affection for the Corinthians. He dismisses this by appealing to God's knowledge of his heart (v.11). (2) Like the wandering preachers of the day, the intruders at Corinth had apparently received remuneration for their instruction. Since they regarded themselves as in some sense apostles, they probably felt fully within their rights that they could accept or even demand wages as a validation of their apostleship. But Paul's stance was an acute embarrassment to them, for they could not boast as he did about preaching a message gratuitously. Thus Paul hoped to deprive his opponents of the opportunity of boasting that they were working at Corinth on precisely the same terms he had been. His financial independence would highlight his rivals' financial dependence and cause the Corinthians to rethink their attitude toward him.

5. False apostles (11:13–15)

13–15 Paul does not contest the right of his adversaries to support but rather lays against them a single all-embracing charge. Those who vainly sought equality with him were in fact "false apostles," apostolic pretenders who passed themselves off as righteous servants of Christ (cf. 11:23) while in reality they were agents of Satan. Like this archdeceiver (Jn 8:44), whose habit was to masquerade "as a shining angel," they relied on disguise and deceit in carrying out their nefarious schemes (cf. vv.3–4). The destiny of these men would accord with the actual deeds they performed (cf. 5:10; Php 3:19), not the outward appearance they adopted (cf. 5:12). As preachers of "a different gospel" (v.4), they stood under the anathema of Gal 1:8–9.

When referring to the "super-apostles" (cf. 11:5; 12:11), Paul shows remarkable restraint; he is not their inferior in any respect. But he does not hesitate to attack ruthlessly the "false apostles," the Judaizing intruders from Jerusalem. Regarding the former Paul is defensive and mildly ironical; regarding the latter he is polemical and intensely serious. The solution to the problem of the Palestinian opponents was outright condemnation, since as minions of Satan they were trying to impose certain elements of Jewish teaching and practice on Gentile Christians as prerequisites for salvation.

B. Boasting "As a Fool" (11:16–12:13)

1. Justification for foolish boasting (11:16–21a)

16 After digressing to defend his policy about financial support (vv.7–12) and describing the true identity of his opponents (vv. 13–15), Paul now resumes from vv.1–6 the theme of boasting like "a fool" (GK *933*). He has decided to boast like his opponents, since he knows the Corinthians' determination to compare him with his rivals and their vulnerability to those who commend themselves. From 11:16–12:13, therefore, he engages in ad hominem argumentation, boasting about things that are not "boastworthy" and answering fools according to their folly (Pr 26:5). There was a danger, however, that some Corinthians might not see or wish to see that Paul was simply playing a part, so he tells them so and solicits their indulgence as he does "a little boasting."

17–18 These two verses are likely a sort of parenthesis. Under normal circumstances, Paul claims, his conduct and words as a servant of Christ and of the Corinthians (4:5; 11:23) would have been marked by "the meekness and gentleness of Christ" (10:1), not the "self-confident boasting" of the fool (v.17). This was not the example of Christ, but he felt he had to follow the example of his opponents in order to win over the Corinthians, who had driven him to this desperate measure of self-exaltation.

Although hesitant to talk "as a fool," Paul partially overcomes his reluctance when he recalls that his converts have grown accustomed to self-advertisement—people boasting "in the way the world does" of personal privileges and achievements (as Paul himself is about to do; vv.22ff.).

19–21a Probably no verses in the letter are more scathingly ironical than these. Not only do the Corinthians humor fools; they do so "gladly," because the folly of the fool serves to highlight the wisdom of the "wise." Their tolerance seems to have no limits. They put up not only with the speech of fools but also with the despotism of tyrants. The intruding aliens had reduced them to slavery by robbing the Corinthians of their liberty in Christ and by seeking to reimpose the Mosaic law (cf. Gal 2:4; 5:1). They had exploited them by greedily devouring any and all maintenance offered them (cf. Mk 12:40). They had entrapped them with tantalizing bait (cf. Lk 5:5); they had put on airs of superiority and had gravely insulted and humiliated them.

None of Paul's readers would have failed to catch his message with its indictment of their inconsistency. Claiming to be followers of a meek, gentle Christ (10:1; cf. Mt 11:29), they were impressed by the aggressiveness and authoritarianism of false apostles (v.13); yet they were unimpressed by Paul's "weak" considerateness as a genuine "apostle of Christ Jesus" (1:1; 10:1, 10). Paul has to confess with shame (though really with biting irony) that his character had been too weak and his disposition too mild to use the tactics of the opposition (v.21a)!

2. Paul's heritage and trials (11:21b–29)

21b–22 Paul has already made several efforts to begin sustained boasting (see 10:8; 11:1, 16). Now he finally brings himself to this distasteful task. No bold claim made by his rivals will go unmatched (v.21b). So to the first three claims mentioned, he responds with the simple, disarming word, "so am I."

By "Hebrews" is meant Jews of Palestinian descent, especially those whose native tongue was Aramaic or Hebrew and whose intellectual and cultural heritage was within Palestinian rather than Diaspora Judaism. Whether he himself was brought up in Tarsus or in Jerusalem, Paul was a Hebrew of Hebrew parentage (Php 3:5). As an "Israelite" he was a member of God's people Israel. As a descendant of Abraham who had been "circumcised on the eighth day" (Php 3:5), Paul was an heir to the covenants based on God's promise (Eph 2:12). All in all, with regard to descent, citizenship, and heritage, he was the equal of his rivals.

23–25 When Paul turns from the matter of his nationality to that of achievement (vv.23–29), he lays claim to superiority over his rivals and begins to speak as a madman (v.23). Although he compares himself with both the "super-apostles" and the "false apostles," in the former case the comparison is negative ("I am not in the least inferior," 11:5; 12:11); in the latter case it is positive ("more," "much harder," "more frequently," "more severely," v.23).

In the light of v.13, it might seem unlikely for Paul to call his opponents "servants of Christ." But the question "Are they. . . ?" means "Do they claim to be. . . ?" He concedes his opponents' estimate of themselves only for the sake of the comparison that follows. As he begins his list of "accomplishments," he does not list triumphs but apparent defeats and refers not to strengths but "weaknesses" (cf. 11:30; 12:5, 9–10). This accords with his view that lowliness and weakness as seen in Christian service provide the only incontestable vindication of apostleship.

If we compare this list of Paul's sufferings (cf. 1Co 4:9–13; 2Co 4:8–12; 6:4–5) with the account of his experiences given in Acts, it immediately becomes clear how incomplete Luke's record is. Since Paul wrote this letter during his stay in Macedonia at Ac 20:2a, only the events recorded before this verse relate to the comparison. To be sure, Luke gives ample proof of Paul's hard work (v.23) and records his stoning at Lystra (v.25; Ac 14:19). But he mentions only one imprisonment (cf. v.23) before Ac 20—that at Philippi (Ac 16:23–40)—and only one of his three beatings with rods (v.25), also at Philippi (Ac 16:22–23). The other imprisonments and Gentile beatings, the Jewish whippings, the shipwrecks, are not recorded in Acts. Paul's life was even more colorful than Acts would lead the reader to believe!

26–27 From specific hardships (vv.24–25) Paul turns to the dangers he confronted (v.26) and the privations he endured (v.27; cf. 6:5). In speaking of "danger from rivers" and "danger from bandits," he could be thinking especially of crossing the Taurus range between Perga in Pamphylia and Antioch in Phrygia near Pisidia (Ac 13:14; 14:24), a journey made hazardous by the mountain torrents and the predatory Pisidian highlanders. Acts records several examples of early Jewish plots against Paul's life (e.g., Ac 9:23, 29; 14:19; 18:12) but only two incidents involving "danger from Gentiles" (Ac 16:16–40; 19:23–41). "Danger from false brothers" may point to Paul's being betrayed to local authorities by counterfeit Christians and the resulting reprisals.

Paul's "sleepless nights" could refer to insomnia because of physical discomfort or illness, but the phrase more likely alludes to voluntary sleeplessness from pressure of work. And Paul may have undertaken some of his voluntary fasts because of his determination not to accept support from the Corinthians (1Co 9:12, 15, 18; 2Co 11:7–12).

28–29 None of the afflictions mentioned in vv.23–27 was a continuous experience. Paul's crowning trial and privilege was, however, incessant—the daily pressure of his anxious "concern" (GK *3533*) for all the churches (cf. Ac 20:18–21, 28–31). If his trials at Corinth were any indication, the total burden he always bore must have been well-nigh oppressive. But as a faithful "under-shepherd," he shared the constant burden of the chief shepherd with regard to all the sheep.

This total identification of shepherd with sheep, or of a spiritual father with his children in the faith, is illustrated in v.29. Paul was at one with all his converts (cf. 1Co 12:26), sympathizing with their weakness in faith, conduct, or conscience (cf. 1Co 8:7–13; 9:22). It is difficult to know what Paul means when he says, "I inwardly burn." The view that best suits the context is that he felt so ablaze with compassion for a person who was "led into sin" that he shared that person's deep remorse.

3. Escape from Damascus (11:30–33)

30–31 For a moment Paul pauses to reflect on what he has just written. Both he and his opponents might boast, but his boasting was distinctive, since, paradoxically, he prided himself on evidences of his weakness that became evidences of God's surpassing power in supporting and delivering him (cf. 1:8–10; 4:7, 10–11; 12:5, 9–10).

Because he had been so precise in describing his afflictions and perils, he realized that the record sounded not only incredible but also out of keeping for an apostle and that his rivals might easily dismiss it as gross exaggeration. Hence Paul's appeal to the divine omniscience (cf. 1:18; 11:10–11; also Ro 9:1; Gal 1:20; 1Ti 2:1) to confirm the trustworthiness of his word.

32–33 After the solemn invocation of v.31, the account of a nocturnal escape from Damascus might seem trivial and out of place. Why he mentions it here is not altogether clear; he is most likely recalling the first attempt on his life, one that was a significant reversal from his former life as persecutor (Ac 9:1–2). This episode forms a suitable backdrop for what follows: an embarrassing descent to escape the hands of people and then an exhilarating ascent into the presence of God (12:2–4).

Aretas IV, the father-in-law of Herod Antipas, ruled over the kingdom of the Nabataean Arabs from c. 9 B.C. to A.D. 40. Why did he or the governor in Damascus want to arrest Paul? Probably because Aretas had been offended by Paul's evangelistic activity in his kingdom (Gal 1:17). It is unlikely that Paul's sojourn in Arabia was simply a spiritual retreat, for Luke mentions that immediately after Paul's conversion he began to dispute in the synagogues of Damascus (Ac 9:20; see also Gal 1:22–23).

Luke's account of Paul's escape (Ac 9:23–25) reveals that the Jews were watching the gates in order to kill Paul; yet here we are told that the governor under King Aretas was guarding the city in order to arrest Paul. What was the relation between the Jews and the governor? Since it seems likely that Damascus was still under Roman rule, the governor was probably the head of a semi-autonomous colony of Nabataeans in Damascus. According to this view, a coalition of Jews and Nabataeans, acting through the governor, was trying to arrest and kill Paul. But it is possible that the Jews were watching for Paul inside the walls and the Nabataeans outside. What stands out, of course, is his providential deliverance.

4. A vision and its aftermath (12:1–10)

1 Once again Paul stresses that in this matter of boasting he has had no choice (see comments on 11:1–6). He feels forced to break a fourteen-year silence (v.2) and boast about a vision the Lord had given him. This will not edify the church or gain anything for him personally, but the Corinthians will see that he was not outmatched by his rivals in an important area of their boasting.

If Paul intended to distinguish between "visions" (GK *3965*) and "revelations" (GK *637*), then a vision is always seen, whereas a revelation may be either seen or perceived in some other way; i.e., all visions are also revelations, but not all revelations come through visions. From Acts it is clear that Paul frequently had visions (Acts 9:12; 16:9–10; 18:9–10; 22:17–21; 23:11; et al.).

2–4 None of the visions recorded in Acts can be identified with the one related here, since it occurred fourteen years before the time of writing—i.e., during the ten so-called "silent years" (A.D. 35–45) that Paul spent in Syria and Cilicia (Gal 1:21).

Paul's expression "a man in Christ" refers to himself. How do we know? (1) He knew the exact time the revelation took place (v.2) and that its content was beyond words, even if it were permissible to try to communicate it (v.4). (2) The revelation was directly related to the receipt of a "thorn," which was given to Paul (v.7). (3) Paul would not likely feel embarrassment (cf. v.1) about boasting on another person's behalf (cf. v.5a). (4) For Paul to relate a remarkable experience that happened to someone unknown to the Corinthians would scarcely fit the context.

The scene of the vision was the "hidden Paradise" of Jewish thought—the abode of the righteous dead that is here located within the third heaven. If Paul was quite certain of the location of the vision, he was uncertain about whether the experience happened to him in his body or apart from it (vv.2b, 3b). Consciousness of God totally eclipsed any awareness of the physical world of space and time.

What Paul heard (and saw?), human words were inadequate to relate (v.4b). Furthermore, he was not permitted to try to share the content of the revelation, perhaps because it had been designed for him alone, to fortify him for future service and sufferings (Ac 9:16; Ro 8:18). Glimpses the NT does give of the coming glory are intended to strengthen faith and promote holiness (cf. 2Pe 3:10–14; 1Jn 3:2–3), not satisfy curiosity.

5–6 The remarkable contrast between Paul and the certain "man in Christ" (v.2) comes into even sharper relief in v.5 and naturally prompts the question: If Paul is speaking of himself in vv.2–4, why does he speak about his experience in the third person? (1) He was clearly embarrassed at needing to boast at all (v.1). (2) He wished to avoid suggesting that he was in any sense a special kind of Christian. The revelation was given him as "a man in Christ"; the initiative had been not his but God's. (3) Although Paul recognized the honor involved in being the recipient of a vision, he wanted to dispel any idea that it added to his personal status or importance.

Concerning himself as a man in Christ who had received a special revelation, Paul was prepared to boast if circumstances demanded it. But concerning himself as a man of action and accomplishment, he refused to boast at all. Only experiences that showed his "weakness" (GK *819*) he considered suitable material for any personal boasting (v.5). If, however, anyone asserted that Paul had not done anything worth boasting about, he adds a word of defense (v.6). If he were to boast of his strengths or things that were not inexpressible, he would *not* appear as some fool who was priding himself on imagined glories. Rather, he would be speaking truth. He had every reason to boast, but he refrains because he wanted the Corinthians' estimate of himself to be based on their recollection of his personal credentials (cf. 5:11b; 12:12). All this suggests that his rivals may have been boasting about imaginary visions or about exploits.

7 Others might be tempted, "because of these surpassingly great revelations" (v.7) accorded to Paul, to form an estimate of him that outstripped the evidence (v.6b). But he himself was in no such danger. For to keep him from becoming conceited there "was given" him a thorn in his flesh. Two inferences are fair. (1) The agent in the passive verb "was given" is God; he had given the "thorn" to Paul to achieve a beneficial purpose—the prevention of spiritual conceit (v.8). (2) The thorn was given immediately or shortly after the vision described in vv.2–4.

The efforts to identify Paul's "thorn" are legion. But paucity of information and the obscurity of Paul's language have frustrated all attempts to solve this problem. As it is, countless believers have been helped by this reference to his "thorn" to cope with "thorns" of their own.

It is remarkable that Paul could regard his affliction as given by God and yet be "a messenger of Satan." This may support the view that the affliction was some type of physical malady, for a recurrent and tormenting illness could be considered "a messenger of Satan" (cf. 1Co 5:5; 11:30; also Lk 13:16). Furthermore, a severe illness could bring Paul within the shadow of death (cf. 2Co 1:8–9) or hinder the advance of the Gospel. Be that as it may, behind all machinations of Satan, Paul discerned the overarching providence of a God who perpetually created good out of evil.

8 The "thorn" proved so tormenting to Paul that on three separate occasions he begged the Lord (Jesus) to remove it. In the NT, formal or liturgical prayer was customarily offered through Christ to the Father in the Spirit (Eph 2:18), but on occasion an individual (Ac 7:59) or a group (Ac 1:24) invoked the Lord Jesus directly.

9–10 The answer to Paul's prayer did not take the form he had expected. The thorn remained, but so did his recollection of the divine reply. In the distress inflicted at various times by his ailment, God promised that Paul would never lack sufficient grace to overcome it (cf. Ro 8:35–37). This grace of Christ (13:11) was adequate for him precisely because divine power finds its full scope and strength only in human weakness—the greater the Christian's acknowledged weakness, the more evident Christ's enabling strength (cf. Eph 3:16; Php 4:13). The cross of Christ forms the supreme example of "power-in-weakness" (see 13:4).

With this spiritual lesson well learned, Paul indicates he would prefer to boast about the sorts of things that exposed his weakness rather than to pray for the removal of the thorn. It was not, however, in the weaknesses themselves that Paul took delight but in the opportunity that such sufferings endured "for Christ's sake" afforded him for Christ's power to be effective in his life.

5. Proof of apostleship (12:11–13)

11 His boasting as a fool now virtually over, Paul again reiterates that it had been by coercion. It was not really the foolish boasting of his opponents that had driven him to boast but the folly of the Corinthians in heeding the boasting of his opponents. If any Christian community was qualified to write Paul's testimonial, it was the Corinthian church. Yet they had remained silent, forcing Paul to speak up. His action had been excusable, but not theirs.

They had every good reason to commend him, for, as they well knew, he was "not in the least inferior to the 'super-apostles'" at Jerusalem (see comment on 11:5). "Even though I am nothing" is either an ironical citation of his opponents' opinion of him or a serious disavowal of any personal merit that could have made him worthy of apostleship (cf. 1Co 15:8–10).

Words of Jesus Not Found in the Gospels

Passage	Description
Acts 1:4–5, 7–8	Jesus' words to his disciples shortly before his ascension
Acts 9:4–5; 22:7–8, 10, 18, 21; 26:14–18	Jesus' words to Paul at the time of his conversion
Acts 9:11–12, 15–16	Jesus' words to Ananias at the time of Paul's conversion
Acts 11:7, 9	Jesus' words to Peter in Joppa
Acts 11:16	Peter recalls Jesus' words about John the Baptist
Acts 18:9–10	Words of encouragement to Paul in Corinth
Acts 20:35	Saying of Jesus: "It is more blessed to give than to receive."
Acts 23:11	Words of encouragement to Paul imprisoned in Jerusalem
1Co 11:24–25	Record of Jesus' words about the Lord's Supper in the Upper Room
2Co 12:9	Jesus' words regarding Paul's thorn in the flesh
Rev 1:8, 11–12, 17–20	Jesus' words to John in exile on Patmos
Rev 2:1—3:22	Jesus' message to the seven church in Asia Minor
Rev 4:1	Jesus invites John to see visions of the last things.
Rev 16:15	Jesus' promise to return "like a thief"
Rev 22:7, 12–16, 20	Jesus' promise, "I am coming soon!"

12 Paul gently reminds his converts of certain characteristics of his ministry at Corinth that proved he was a genuine apostle. "Signs, wonders and miracles" (GK *4956, 5469, & 1539*) does not describe three types of miracles but considers them from three aspects—their ability to authenticate the message, evoke awe, and display divine power. These, of course, were not the only marks of apostleship, for there was also faithfulness to the apostolic message (11:4) and conduct consonant with the example of Christ (10:1; 13:14), especially "great perseverance" in the face of opposition (for Corinth, cf. Ac 18:6, 9–10, 12–16). By using the passive voice in "were done," Paul disowns any credit for the supernatural signs accompanying his ministry.

13 Again indulging in gentle irony, Paul observes that the only respect in which the marks of an apostle were not evident in the apostolic church of Corinth was that of support. He never was a financial burden to them—an injustice for which he playfully pleads forgiveness! As in 1Co 9:1–18 and 2Co 11:5–12, Paul has moved naturally from a consideration of the signs of apostleship (vv.11–12) to the issue of apostolic rights, particularly support from the church or churches being served.

C. The Planned Third Visit (12:14–13:10)

1. A promise not to be burdensome (12:14–18)

14–15 The apostle announces that his third visit to Corinth is imminent and that his policy regarding support will not be altered. He is determined always to be financially independent of the Corinthians (cf. 1Co 9:15; 2Co 11:9, 12); they will have to continue bearing the "injury" he is inflicting on them (cf. v.13)! His affections were set on the Corinthians themselves (cf. 6:11–12; 7:2–3), not on their money. He craved their reciprocated love (6:13; 12:15b), their Christian maturity (cf. 1Co 3:1–4; Col 1:28–29), and their exclusive devotion to Christ (11:2–3).

In defense of this refusal to accept support, Paul appeals to the self-evident truth that it is not the responsibility of children to save up and provide for their parents, but only parents for children. The principle, however, is not universally applicable, for Paul had earlier defended the right of apostles to be supported by their spiritual children (1Co 9:3–11), and he later asserted, "If anyone does not provide for his relatives, and especially for his immediate family, he has denied the faith and is worse than an unbeliever" (1Ti 5:8).

Far from coveting the Corinthians' property, Paul planned to use all his own resources to achieve their highest good; he would spare nothing in his efforts to win their affection for Christ (cf. Ac 20:24). Yet he looked for a fair exchange (cf. 6:13): "If I love you more [intensely], will you love me less?" There may be an actual comparison here. If Paul's love for the Corinthians exceeded the love of a father for his children, how could they love him less than children love their father? In other words, Paul is seeking a response of filial love to his paternal affection (cf. 11:11).

16–18 Whether or not the Corinthians loved Paul the less for his intense love for them, all had to agree that he himself had not proved a financial strain on the church. Yet the rumor had circulated at Corinth that because Paul was unscrupulous by nature, he was exploiting the church's generosity and trying to gain surreptitiously through his agents what he had declined to accept personally. What Paul almost certainly has in mind here is the collection for the poor at Jerusalem, which some charged was a convenient way to fulfill his covert wish to live at the church's expense.

Since Paul knew the charge had been maliciously made and was couched in general terms, he refutes it first by indirectly appealing to the Corinthians to adduce specific evidence (v.17) and then by referring to a particular occasion on which his chief agent had been sent to Corinth on a mission involving finance (v.18a). If Titus was guiltless, so too was Paul, for all their conduct had been governed by the same principles (v.18b). Which visit of Titus does Paul refer to? Either the visit alluded to in 8:6a, when he commenced the collection, or the visit mentioned in 8:16–24 when he completed the collection.

2. Fears about the unrepentant (12:19–21)

19 Paul repudiates the suggestion, which might readily have occurred to any Corinthian, that he had all along been seeking to defend his conduct and reputation before a panel of Corinthian judges. It was to God, not to them, that Paul felt he was ultimately accountable (cf. Ro 14:10; 1Co 4:3–5; 2Co 5:10), so that self-defense before human beings was never his primary concern. He had been speaking as a man "in Christ" whose words and motives were open before God (cf. 2:17; 5:11). His aim in all his relations with the Corinthians was not personal vindication but their spiritual edification.

20–21 Paul expresses a threefold apprehension that the present letter might not be wholly successful and that the Corinthians, by harboring Judaizing intruders and persisting in sin, would contribute to weakening, not consolidating, their church fellowship. (1) Paul was concerned about the outcome of his impending visit to the Corinthians (v.20a). Would they be mutually disappointed and embarrassed—Paul by the church's questioning of his apostleship and their refusal to break with sins of the spirit (v.20b) and of the flesh (v.21b), and the Corinthians by Paul's vigorous exercise of church discipline (cf. 1Co 4:21; 5:3–5)?

(2) The apostle is fearful that the sins that seemed endemic to Corinth (cf. 1Co 1:11–12, 31; 3:3; 4:6; 5:2, 11; 8:1; 11:18; 14:33, 40) should still be rife as a consequence of the unrest and disorder created by the Palestinian intruders (v.20b).

(3) Finally, Paul fears a repetition of humiliation under God's hand that he had experienced on his second visit—i.e., the "painful visit" (2:1). Any future humiliation would stem from his acute disappointment at the Corinthians' preference for domineering false apostles (11:20) and their supercilious attitude toward him (cf. 1Co 4:18–19), as well as from his grief over those who had consistently rejected his call to holiness and were continuing unrepentant in their earlier gross sexual sins.

3. Warning of impending discipline (13:1–4)

1–2 After expressing his personal fears about the forthcoming third visit (12:20–21), Paul issues two direct warnings relative to this issue: "Every matter must be established by the testimony of two or three witnesses" (v.1), and "On my return I will not spare those who sinned earlier or any of the others" (v.2).

What are the "two or three witnesses"? Some believe Paul is referring to his three comings to Corinth (two actual, one promised) as three separate witnesses at whose testimony justice would certainly fall on the dissidents at Corinth. Another possible view sees a reference to the threefold warning that Paul would not spare the Corinthians: the first was either 1Co 4:21 or the warning given on the "painful visit"; the second is the warning given here; and the final one is the proposed third visit. In any case, the general import is clear: "Sufficient warning has been given; punishment is imminent."

"Those who sinned earlier" are the immoral persons of 12:21b who did not repent during Paul's "painful visit" and were evidently still indulging in their sexual sins. "The others" are probably those Corinthians who had been adversely influenced by the false apostles and were arrogantly fomenting unrest within the church (12:20b). Both groups receive their final warning here. If they remained unrepentant, he would be harsh in his use of authority (cf. v.10; cf. 1Co 5:5).

3 It seemed as if in their immaturity the Corinthians were unimpressed by Christlike gentleness and meekness (10:1) but were overawed by arbitrary displays of power (11:20). In their misguided judgment, Paul's gentle demeanor raised doubts about his claim to apostolic authority; he had to give them some proof that Christ in his resurrection power was speaking through him. His reply was that, though he had previously been "weak" in the Corinthian estimation (10:1, 10), his impending severity would provide sufficient proof that he was a spokesman of Christ and that Christ was powerful among them. The Corinthians had in effect challenged Christ, who would not disappoint them as he exhibited his resurrection power through his apostle.

4 The relationship between Christ and Paul with regard to weakness and power is now clarified. Jesus Christ was crucified because of "weakness" (GK *819*); this weakness was not physical frailty or moral impotence, but the "weakness" of nonretaliation and the "weakness" of obedience to God. Christ's "weakness" in assuming the poverty of earthly existence (8:9) and in humbling himself and becoming obedient even to death on a cross (Php 2:8) was, however, the most perfect evidence of strength. But that "weakness" of Christ is past. Now he lives a resurrection life sustained by God's power, "the Spirit of holiness" (Ro 1:4).

As a result of being in Christ, Paul shared in the weakness of his crucified Master (cf. 12:7–10). As a result of his fellowship with Christ, he shared in the mighty power of his risen Lord, a power imparted by God. From a human standpoint, the nonassertiveness that had marked Paul's conduct on his second visit to Corinth (cf. 10:1, 10) was simply weakness. But on his forthcoming visit, God's power would be vigorously displayed through him in his dealings with the Corinthians.

4. A plea for self-examination (13:5–10)

5–6 Rather than demanding proof that Christ was speaking through Paul (v.3), the Corinthians ought to be examining themselves. Paul asks in effect: "Don't you know yourselves sufficiently well to recognize that Christ Jesus lives within each of you [cf. Ro 8:9] and that therefore you are in the faith?" Although for the sake of emphasis he adds "unless, of course, you fail the test," he does not really believe the Corinthians are counterfeit, and he knows that no Corinthian is likely to form such a conclusion about himself or herself.

To Paul, the Corinthians' belief in the genuineness of their faith carried with it the proof of the genuineness of Paul's apostleship and Gospel, for he had become their father in Christ Jesus (1Co 4:15). As men and women in Christ they themselves formed the verification of his credentials (cf. 2Co 3:2–3). Only if they doubted their own salvation should they doubt Paul's claim to be a true "apostle of Christ Jesus" (1:1). If they did not fail the test, then neither did he.

7 Once again (cf. 3:1; 5:12; 12:19) Paul anticipates and answers the objection that he had been commending or defending himself. His chief desire and his prayer to God were not for his vindication (though he was concerned about this, v.6) but for their avoidance of wrongdoing, including especially the refusal to repent of sin (12:20–21) and to repudiate the visitors from Palestine. It would be better that the Corinthians did what they knew to be good and right, even if this were to place Paul seemingly in the wrong, than that they should do something wrong. Paul did not expect to be shown up as counterfeit, but even such a price would be worth paying if it guaranteed that the Corinthians would do good (cf. Ro 9:3).

8 This verse, which reads like a proverb, bears one of two meanings in this context. (1) Paul's concern was that truth, especially the truth of the Gospel (cf. 4:2; 6:7), should prevail at all costs—even if it were to involve his exposure as a false apostle and counterfeit Christian (vv.6–7). (2) Paul did not need to exercise his apostolic authority where "truth" already existed, but was able and willing, if necessary, to act decisively to establish "truth," i.e., to restore the Corinthians to wholeness (v.9b).

9–10 Paul's sole concern was to further and consolidate the truth of the Gospel (cf. 1Co 9:16). Thus he was happy whenever his converts gave evidence of robust and mature Christian character. If the Corinthians were strong in Christ, he would not have to use his apostolic authority harshly but could come to them in the "weakness" of a "gentle spirit" (1Co 4:21). Such "weakness" as a result of "strength" on their part would make him rejoice. In fact, his prayer was precisely for the restoration of the Corinthians to spiritual strength and wholeness (cf. v.11; 1Co 1:10; Gal 6:1).

If 12:20–21 expresses Paul's fears about what he would find at Corinth on his arrival, 13:10 indicates his hope in this regard. But even here a veiled warning is registered. While the Lord had not invested Paul with apostolic authority primarily for the negative work of tearing down, if destruction had to be done before the positive task of construction, it would be reluctantly undertaken—and with the same authority (cf. 10:8).

Was Paul's final visit to Corinth actually an unpleasant one? Though direct evidence is lacking, we have several indications that it was not unsuccessful. (1) During the visit (which lasted three months; cf. Ac 20:2–3) he wrote the Epistle to the Romans. This letter betrays some apprehension for the future (Ro 15:30–31) but none for the present. (2) Paul would hardly have planned to visit Rome and then do pioneer evangelism in the west (Ro 15:24, 28), if the church in the city from which he was writing was in a state of disorder and disloyalty (cf. comments on 2Co 10:15–16). (3) It is clear from Ro 15:26–27 that the Corinthians heeded Paul's appeal in 2Co 8–9 and completed their collection for the saints at Jerusalem. Twice Paul notes that they "were pleased" to contribute, scarcely an appropriate description unless the church in Corinth was in harmony with the promoter of the collection. (4) The very preservation of this letter argues in favor of the success of the visit promised in it.

D. Conclusion (13:11–14)

11 Paul closes with several general instructions. He wants the Corinthian believers to strive to achieve that perfection for which Paul himself was praying (v.9b). They are to heed his "appeals"—for a break with all idolatry (6:14–7:1), for warm hospitality to be shown the three delegates, for a generous and prompt contribution to the Jerusalem relief fund (chs. 8–9), and for a changed attitude toward him (chs. 10–13). They are also to agree in the Lord (cf. 1Co 1:10; Php 4:2) and live in peace without divided loyalties (11:2–3; 12:20).

The second part of this verse has two possible senses. If Paul is stressing love and peace as characteristics of God (cf. Ro 5:8; 1Co 14:33), the meaning will be: "[If you] aim for perfection, etc., then the God of love and peace will be with you" (cf. Php 4:9). But if love and peace are here viewed as God's gifts (cf. Php 4:7), Paul is indicating the divine resources that will enable the Corinthians to follow his injunctions.

12 Evidently the early church invested the kiss, a common form of salutation in the Orient, with a special and sacred significance (cf. Ro 16:16; 1Co 16:20; 1Th 5:26; 1Pe 5:14). It expressed union and fellowship within the one family of God, and perhaps it was also a sign of mutual forgiveness and reconciliation that was exchanged before the Lord's Supper was celebrated (cf. 1Co 16:20b, 22).

13 The "saints" referred to may well be the Philippians, but they could be the Thessalonians or Bereans, depending on the place where Paul was when he wrote this letter. Like the holy kiss, this epistolary greeting expressed unity within the one body of Christ.

14 Paul grounds his pastoral appeal for unity of spirit and for the rejection of discord (vv.11–12) in the theological doctrine of the Trinity. The "grace" (GK *5921*) of Christ banishes self-assertiveness and self-seeking, the "love" (GK *27*) of God puts jealousy and anger to flight, while the "fellowship" (GK *3126*) created by the Spirit leaves no room for quarreling and factions (cf. 12:21).

This embryonic Trinitarian formulation is noteworthy for the unusual order of Son, Father, and Holy Spirit. It is through the grace shown by Christ (8:9) in living and dying for humankind that God demonstrates his love (Ro 5:8) and the Spirit creates fellowship (Eph 4:3). This order also reflects Christian experience.

The Old Testament in the New

NT Text	OT Text	Subject
2Co 3013	Ex 34:33, 35	Veil of Moses
2Co 4:6	Ge 1:3	Creation of light
2Co 4:13	Ps 116:10	Faith and speech
2Co 6:2	Isa 49:8	God's day of salvation
2Co 6:16	Lev 26:11–12; Eze 37:27	God living with us
2Co 6:16	Jer 32:38	God and his people
2Co 6:17	Eze 20:41	Separate from the world
2Co 6:17	Isa 52:11	Touch no unclean thing
2Co 6:18	2Sa 7:14	Father and son
2Co 8:15	Ex 16:18	God provides enough
2Co 9:9	Ps 112:9	Gifts for the poor
2Co 10:17	Jer 9:24	Boasting in the Lord
2Co 13:1	Dt 19:15	Two or three witnesses

Galatians

INTRODUCTION

Not many books have made such a lasting impression on human minds as Paul's letter to the Galatians, nor have many done so much to shape the history of the Western world. This letter has been called the "Magna Carta of Christian liberty," for it maintains that only through the grace of God received through faith in Jesus Christ can a person escape the curse of sin and of the law and live a new life, not in bondage or license, but in a genuine freedom of mind and spirit through the power of God. This theme was the cornerstone of the Protestant Reformation. Luther especially loved Galatians, and in his hands it became a mighty weapon in the Reformation arsenal. The thesis of Galatians is no less important for our time.

1. The Historical Setting and Content of Galatians

In the decade or so surrounding the year A.D. 50, the infant church was drifting almost unnoticeably toward its first great doctrinal crisis. When the Gospel was being preached primarily to Jews by Jews, the development of the church progressed smoothly. But as the ambassadors of Christ pushed out into largely Gentile communities and the Gospel began to take root there, questions arose regarding a Christian's relationship to the law of Moses and to Judaism as a system. Was the church to open her doors wide to all comers, regardless of their relationship to the particularized traditions of Judaism? Or was she to be only an extension of Judaism to the Gentiles? In more particular terms, was it necessary for a Gentile believer to observe the law of Moses in order to become a Christian? Must a Gentile be circumcised?

Galatians is a record of the form this struggle took in one area of Asia Minor. But it is also a reflection of the way in which the issue was being debated and handled in Jerusalem and at Antioch in Syria. Acts supplements this information. Was it right for Gentile and Jewish Christians to have mutual fellowship by eating together? For a time, debate seemed to move in a direction destructive of Christian unity and of the survival of the Gospel of grace, but Paul almost singlehandedly withstood this trend and turned the tide. At Jerusalem the question was taken up formally in council, and Paul's approach was upheld (Ac 15:1–29).

As the apostle to the Gentiles, Paul deliberately did not bring up questions of conformity to Jewish law when presenting the Gospel in non-Jewish communities. He had followed this practice in Galatia on both occasions when he had preached there (cf. 4:13). To him, salvation is never to be achieved by conformity to rules and regulations, even if God-given, for law condemns. Consequently, salvation for sinners must come in another way—through Jesus Christ, who died for sin. Now God offers righteousness freely to all who put their trust in him.

Paul had taught this Gospel to the Galatians, and it had been well received. He had been detained in Galatia unexpectedly because of a repulsive illness, but instead of rebuffing him, the Galatians actually embraced both him and the Gospel willingly (4:13–15). These former pagans (4:8) were baptized (3:27) and received the Holy Spirit, who began to work miracles among them (3:5). After establishing churches in Galatia, Paul moved on.

Some time later, however, Paul received word that the Galatian believers were on the point of departing from the faith they had previously received so openly. Conservative Jewish teachers who were legalizers had arrived from Jerusalem claiming to be from James, the Lord's brother, and had begun to teach that Paul was wrong in his doctrine. They contended that Gentiles had to obey the law of Moses to be saved. To the grace of Christ must be added circumcision.

Paul was immediately filled with righteous indignation. He saw in a moment that if their views prevailed, grace and the cross of Jesus Christ would be emptied of all value

(5:2–4). Moreover, Christianity would soon lose its distinctive character and become little more than a minor sect of Judaism. Thus Paul wrote this letter to reprove legalism and regain the Galatian churches.

It is evident that Paul had heard of three distinct charges made by his Jewish opponents. (1) One was directed against Paul personally. He had been called by Christ as an apostle and had preached those doctrines that Christ had revealed to him. Now enemies were saying that he was not a genuine apostle and that the Gospel he preached had not been revealed by God. Paul had not lived with Jesus when Jesus was here on earth, as had the "true" apostles. He was not one of the Twelve. Actually, they asserted, he was merely an evangelist who, after he had received some knowledge of Christianity, turned to his own devices and, in order to please the Gentiles, taught an easy gospel opposed to that of the apostolic model (1:10). They said that Paul must teach as the disciples taught or be rejected.

Paul answers these accusations by retelling the story of his life, particularly as it was related to the other apostles (chs. 1–2). (a) His apostolic teaching is not dependent on other human authorities, for it came directly from God. (b) His authority had been acknowledged by the other apostles on each occasion on which they had come into contact. (c) He had proved his worth by remaining firm at Antioch when others, including even Peter and Barnabas, had wavered. Paul was therefore able to assert his own authority as an apostle without diminishing either the authority or reputation of those who were apostles before him.

(2) Another charge, closely related to the first, was that his Gospel was not the true gospel. Obviously, if Paul was a "false" apostle, his teaching could not be true teaching. He taught that the law could be set aside, but this was wrong, the legalizers said. God's law is eternal and it can never be set aside. All who have ever been saved have been saved by keeping the law. Moreover, it is perfectly evident from all that is known of the life of Jesus that Jesus himself kept the law. Who, then, was Paul to dismiss the requirements of the law for salvation?

Paul answers this charge by showing that the issue is not one of who does or does not keep the law, but rather of the true basis on which God reckons a sinful person righteous. At this point of his letter (chs. 3–4) Paul appeals both to the personal experience of the Galatians and to Scripture, showing, primarily from the case of Abraham, that God accounts a person righteous on the basis of faith rather than works. This imputed righteousness does not come from either the law or circumcision, for God had declared Abraham righteous on the basis of faith years before either was given.

(3) The opponents of Paul also charged that the Gospel he preached led to loose living. By stressing the law, Judaism had stressed morality. Jews looked down on Gentile sin and excesses. But what would happen if the law should be taken away? Clearly, lawlessness and immorality would increase, the legalizers argued.

Paul replies that this is not true (chs. 5–6). Christianity does not lead believers away from the law into nothingness. Rather, it leads them to Jesus Christ, who, in the person of the Holy Spirit, comes to live within them and furnishes them with a new nature that alone is capable of doing what God desires. The change is internal. So it is from within rather than without that the Holy Spirit produces the fruit that is "love, joy, peace, patience, kindness, goodness, faithfulness, gentleness, and self-control" (5:22–23). Life in the Spirit is free from either legalism or license. It is true freedom—a freedom to serve God fully.

2. Who Were the Galatians?

There would seem to be few difficulties in relating a book with such a clear message to its time. But this is not true of Galatians. In fact, from the historian's point of view, few NT books contain so many problems. We do not know for certain when the letter was written, where it was written, or even (which is a more serious problem) to whom it was written. Each of these questions has been the subject of intense scholarly debate.

The word "Galatians" has two basic meanings. It has an ethnic meaning. The first people who became known as Galatians came from the barbarian tribe known in France as the Gauls, some of whom had invaded Macedonia and later northern Asia Minor (third century B.C.). Their region became known as Galatia; its principal cities were Ancyra, Pessinus, and Tavium.

The second meaning is a political one. The Romans conquered the Galatians in 189 B.C., though they were permitted to maintain much of their independence and to be governed in part by their own princes. This system worked so well that in 25 B.C., their territory was incorporated into a much larger Roman province to which the old ethnic name, Galatia, was extended. This province contained the districts of Lycaonia and Isauria as well as portions of Pisidia and Phrygia. In particular, the cities of Pisidian Antioch, Iconium, Derbe and Lystra—cities Paul visited on his first missionary journey—belonged to it.

To the Christians in which of these two areas did Paul write? Or, to state the question another way, in what sense does Paul use the name "Galatia"? Until the eighteenth century, no commentator ever seriously disputed the idea that Paul's letter was written to Christians living in northern (ethnic) Galatia, even though Acts does not record Paul's having founded churches in this area (but cf. Ac 16:6; 18:23). In the last century, however, beginning with William Ramsay, scholars questioned whether Paul ever visited northern Galatia at all and argued that he wrote this letter to Christians in the southern area of the Roman province, i.e., to Christians living in those cities Paul had visited on his first missionary journey. A number of impressive arguments were raised in support of this position (the south Galatia theory).

1. According to Acts, Paul did have a missionary journey in southern Galatia. Since he tended to go where there were major cities and since ethnic Galatia had few such cities, it seems unlikely that Paul did mission work there. Furthermore, during his second missionary journey, after revisiting churches in southern Galatia, Paul, Silas, and Timothy headed north but were forbidden by the Holy Spirit to preach either in Asia to the south or Bithynia to the north (Ac 16:6–7). Thus they ended up in Troas, where they encountered an open door before them into Greece. On this journey they would have had to take a most unlikely detour of about three hundred miles over rugged terrain to get to ethnic Galatia and preach there. If Paul did in fact establish a series of important churches in north Galatia, it would be unusual for Luke to neglect to say so.

2. Paul in his letters tends to use provincial, not ethnic, names—e.g., Macedonia (2Co 8:1), Asia (1Co 16:19), and Achaia (2Co 1:1). He also speaks of Judea, Syria, and Cilicia, but never of Lycaonia, Pisidia, Mysia, and Lydia (which are not names of Roman provinces). Thus the presumption that he is using the political rather than the ethnic meaning for Galatia is strong.

3. We know of no churches at all in northern Asia Minor at this early date, either mentioned in the NT or outside it, and what information we do have seems to point to the establishing of churches much later than Paul's time. By contrast, we do have a record of the founding of the strong, important churches of the southern region, into which all that Paul tells us about his initial preaching to the Galatians fits nicely.

4. It is more natural to suppose that the legalistic party would have pursued Paul first in the southern region of Galatia, where Paul had early established churches, than that they bypassed these bastions of "Paulinism" in order to push north to less important strongholds. We know from Acts that Paul did meet with Jewish opposition in southern Galatia. It seems most natural, therefore, that the legalists would first go there if Jews in any sizeable number were turning from Judaism to Christianity.

5. In writing to the Galatians, Paul mentions Barnabas several times without bothering to explain who he is (2:1, 9, 13), so presumably he is known to the Galatians. Since Barnabas accompanied Paul only on the first missionary journey, to southern Galatia, nothing but an identification of the Galatians with Christians in the cities of the south seems possible.

6. Paul argues that he did not give place to the legalizers at the council in Jerusalem even for an hour, so that "the truth of the gospel might *remain* with you [i.e., with the Galatians]." In other words, Paul must already have preached to the Galatians by the time of the conference, i.e., on his first missionary journey, which involved southern (but not northern) Galatia.

While the south Galatia theory has captured the attention of a majority of scholars today (and that is the position adopted in this commentary), there still are those who hold to a north Galatia theory. Their arguments are as follows:

1. Luke never refers to those living in the cities of Derbe, Lystra, Iconium, and Pisidian Antioch as Galatians when he describes Paul's work there. It is strange to think that he is not, therefore, still using geographical terminology when he refers to Paul passing through Galatia in Ac 16:6–7.

2. Paul assumes in his letter that all, or at least most, of the Galatians are Gentiles. This does not seem to fit conditions in the south, which had a large Jewish population. Moreover, if the churches of Galatia contained many Jews, it is hard to see how a *later* drifting into Judaism by Paul's converts could have occurred, particularly in a manner that seems to have surprised him. The issue of a Christian's relationship to the law of Moses would certainly have had to be faced from the start.

3. Paul's account of his work in Galatia does not tally with what Luke tells us of Paul's work in Derbe, Lystra, Iconium, and Antioch; for example, there is no reference to his illness (Gal 4:13). So Paul must be speaking of another area.

In spite of these arguments, the weight of probability now lies on the side of the south Galatia hypothesis.

3. The Jerusalem Council

Another problem is which visit to Jerusalem Paul is referring to in 2:1–10. In Acts, Luke records three visits of Paul to Jerusalem prior to his final visit in Ac 21:17ff.: a visit shortly after his conversion (Ac 9:26–30), a "famine visit" (Ac 11:27–30), and a visit for the church council that decided the issue of Gentile adherence to the law (Ac 15). Paul, however, records only two visits to Jerusalem, the second of which seems to fit better with Luke's third visit than with the second. Consequently we must either identify Paul's second visit with Luke's second (with obvious difficulties involved) or with Luke's third—and then explain why Paul neglected to mention the second in writing to the Galatians. On the surface this neglect is difficult to understand, simply because Paul seems to be chronicling all contacts with the Jerusalem apostles in order to refute the charges of the legalizers.

In the opinion of this writer, the case for identifying the Jerusalem visit of Gal 2:1–10 with the council meeting of Ac 15 is strongest, above all because of the striking coincidence of circumstances. In both accounts, communications take place between Jerusalem and Antioch. The false brethren have their headquarters in the first city but cause trouble in the second. Also, in both accounts, Paul and Barnabas apparently go to Jerusalem from Antioch and return to Antioch after the council. The participants at the council are the same: the legalizers who are causing the trouble, Paul and Barnabas who represent the church at Antioch, and the Jerusalem apostles, primarily Peter and James. The subject of dispute is the same. Finally, the results are essentially the same, for in each case, the victory goes to Paul.

There are, however, obvious difficulties in linking Gal 2 with Ac 15. First, there are apparent discrepancies. Acts gives the impression that Paul and Barnabas presented their case publicly before an assembled council of apostles and elders, but Galatians tells of a private meeting in which the dispute seems to be resolved between a small group of those who were considered leaders. Galatians says Titus accompanied Paul and Barnabas to Jerusalem, while Acts does not mention Titus. Finally, in Galatians Paul writes that he and Barnabas went up to Jerusalem by revelation, whereas in Acts Luke indicates that they were delegated by the leaders of the church in Antioch.

Although discrepancies should not be passed over lightly, it is not difficult to see how they may be resolved. Every great public meeting is accompanied by private meetings. Titus is not mentioned by Luke because he did not become an issue, which is precisely the point Paul makes in Galatians (Gal 2:3). And concerning how Paul was sent to Jerusalem, a "revelation" is simply an alternate way of telling what happened, since the church at Antioch undoubtedly prayed about who their representatives should be and believed that they were responding to God in commissioning Paul and Barnabas.

More serious is the failure of Paul to mention the decrees of the council. Wouldn't he have appealed to the council if, at the time of writing Galatians, he held such a trump card in his hand? Not necessarily. First, the decrees were not as significant as this line of arguing implies. They were addressed to "the Gentiles in Antioch and Syria and Cilicia" to start with, not to Gentiles throughout the whole Roman world. Second, the decrees were a compromise. They freed the Gentiles from adherence to the law, but they added certain restrictions for conscience' sake. Paul could very well have agreed with the decrees at the time they were devised but later, when writing to the Galatians, considered the restrictions a dangerous concession likely to be misunderstood. Finally, in quoting the decrees Paul would seem to be conceding the very thing his enemies were insisting on—i.e., the authority of the Jerusalem apostles as greater than his own. In any case, Paul shows that the other apostles did agree with him regarding circumcision and actually supported him.

But if Gal 2:1–10 refers to the council of Ac 15, why does Paul not mention the famine visit of Ac 11? It is impossible to say exactly why, but there may be an explanation in the historical circumstances. The time of the famine visit was a time of turmoil and political agitation against the apostles, in which James the son of Zebedee was killed by Herod and Peter was imprisoned (Ac 12). Because of that, it seems likely that every Christian of any rank had fled the city. In fact, Luke mentions that the money for famine relief was delivered into the hands of "the elders," not the apostles. Furthermore, that dangerous time was not an opportune occasion for discussing so momentous an issue as Gentile adherence to the law and to circumcision.

Finally, one should note that Paul's main goal in Galatians is not giving a full account of all his activities but answering specific criticisms directed against him by the legalizers. The first criticism is that he got his Gospel from others; Paul answers this by showing that in the early years he was not influenced by the Jerusalem apostles at all—either before, during, or after his conversion (see ch. 1). On the other hand, Paul was not preaching something different from the Gospel preached by the other apostles, as the legalists had also maintained (see ch. 2). Neither of these issues was relevant in the famine visit.

4. Date and Authorship

Adopting the south Galatia theory and the identity of Gal 2:1–10 and Ac 15, the earliest the letter could have been written is A.D. 49 (the date for the council in Jerusalem). Since Paul does not appear to be in prison while writing this letter, the latest date it could have been written is A.D. 58, when he was arrested in Jerusalem. Within these limits there are roughly eight or nine years in which Paul made two missionary journeys and during which the letter could have been written. This range can be narrowed somewhat by assuming that Paul had visited the Galatians twice before writing to them, once on the first missionary journey and once as he was setting out on the second (cf. Gal 4:13); in that case, Galatians must have been written after Paul's arrival at Corinth on his second journey (A.D. 50).

Galatians has almost universally been accepted as a genuine letter of Paul. He is mentioned as the author in 1:1 and in 5:2, and the entire letter from beginning to end breathes such an intensely personal autobiographical tone that only a genuine historical situation involving the true founder of the Gentile mission within the church accounts for it. Since very early in the history of the church, Galatians was included in canonical lists as a letter of Paul.

EXPOSITION

Introduction (1:1–10)

A. Salutation (1:1–5)

Most ancient letters, Paul's included, opened with a salutation containing the author's name, the name of those to whom he is writing, and an expression of good wishes. But Paul's opening remarks also generally breathe something of the content and tone of the letter or, at the very least, employ explicitly Christian terms as greetings. Galatians follows this pattern, beginning with the writer's name, the name of the recipients, and a wish for grace and peace on their behalf. But there are a brevity and vigor of expression that immediately plunge the reader into the heart of the letter, reflecting Paul's concern. Most surprisingly, there is no expression of praise for these churches, a normal procedure in his other letters. In these few verses the three major themes of the letter—the source of his authority, the doctrine of grace, and the promise of full deliverance from sin's power—are tied together in a way that relates all to the sovereign and gracious will of God.

1 By adding the word "apostle" (GK 693) Paul at once highlights his claim to be commissioned by Jesus to preach the Gospel with authority and to plant Christianity. It was this commission that was being challenged by the Galatian legalizers. Greek-speaking Jews had used the word "apostle" for authorized representatives. With the coming of Christ, Christians applied it to those commissioned by Christ as authoritative bearers of the Gospel.

It would seem from Ac 1:21–26 that two major prerequisites for being an apostle were: (1) to have been an eyewitness of Christ's ministry from the time of the baptism by John up to and including the resurrection, and (2) to have been chosen for the office by the risen Lord. At first the number of those so commissioned was twelve (Matthias was chosen to replace Judas), but there is no indication either in Acts or elsewhere that the number was always so limited. Paul obviously claimed to have fulfilled the conditions as the result of his Damascus experience; and Luke, who clearly endorses Paul's claim, also speaks of Barnabas as having this office (cf. also James, the Lord's brother, implied in 1Co 15:7; Silas and Timothy in 1Th 2:7, cf. 1:1).

The difficulty that Paul's enemies saw was not in the number twelve, but rather that Paul did not meet the proper conditions. They could claim that he had never met Jesus, and he had certainly had not been an eyewitness of Christ's ministry. They could claim too that he had never received a commission, at least not like the formal and official action when Matthias was chosen. Paul answered by entirely overlooking the matter of his not being an eyewitness of Christ's earthly ministry, though undoubtedly he considered his Damascus experience to be the equivalent of this, and by denying that his status required a human decision. Instead, Paul claimed that his apostleship came to him directly from and through God the Father and the Lord Jesus Christ in his experience on the Damascus road. His reference to the resurrection stresses the important point that it was the risen and glorified Lord of the church who commissioned him.

2 From Paul's normal habit of including the names of his fellow missionaries at the beginning of his letters, it would appear that "the brothers" mentioned here are his fellow missionaries, though their actual identity cannot be known for sure. The interesting point is that Paul does not name these fellow missionaries, as he does elsewhere, not wanting to give the impression that his Gospel requires additional support. It was, after all, received directly from God. At the same time, he wishes to remind the Galatians that the Gospel that had been preached to them, far from being a Pauline oddity, is actually the received doctrine of all the Christian church and its missionaries.

3 Paul's nearly standard formula of Christian blessing and greeting seems particularly appropriate at the start of this letter. Normally, Paul alters the traditional Greek greeting (*chairein*) to the important Christian word "grace" (*charis*; GK 5921). This is always striking, but it is doubly striking here, inasmuch as it occurs in a letter to churches where the sufficiency of salvation by grace was being questioned and perhaps even denied. In the same way, "peace" (*eirene*; GK 1645), the Greek equivalent of the Hebrew greeting *shalom* (GK 8934), is appropriate, for it denotes that state of favor and well-being into which people are brought by Christ's death on the cross and in which they are kept by God's persevering grace. To choose law, as the Galatians were doing, is to fall from grace. To live by works is to lose the peace with God that was purchased for believers by Christ's atonement (cf. Ro 5:1).

Paul characteristically joins the names of the Father and Son together in the statement that they are the source of grace and peace (cf. Jn 17:21). But inverting the order, as he does here (from v.1 to v.3), heightens the effect.

4 To the doctrines of the Christian faith already stated in germinal form—the source of authority in religion, the person and character of God, the divinity of Christ, the resurrection, grace, and peace—Paul now adds a statement affirming the substitutionary death of the Lord Jesus Christ and its outcome in delivering humankind from sin. All this, he asserts, is according to the "will" (GK 2525) of the Father. It is hard to imagine a statement better calculated to oppose any intrusion of human will or merits in the matter of attaining salvation. This phrase, unique here in Paul's greetings, is undoubtedly added for the sake of the erring Christians in Galatia.

Salvation that began in the eternal will of God (cf. Ro 9:16) led to the coming of the Lord Jesus Christ, who died as a substitute for sinners. Paul then articulates the goal of his death: to "rescue us from the present evil age." The word "rescue" (GK 1975) implies a "rescue from the power of." Thus, it strikes the keynote of the latter, ethical section of the letter, beginning in ch. 5. Believers are not rescued out of the present evil world (though that will also be true eventually), but from the power of evil and the values of the present world-system through the power of the risen Christ within the Christian.

5 Paul does not usually include a doxology at the beginning of a letter, but the doxology here serves an important purpose. It sets the Gospel, centering in the preeminence of the Lord Jesus Christ and his work, above any human criticism or praise. The fact that the glory of God and the giving of glory to God will last forever contrasts markedly with "the present evil age," which is passing away (cf. 1Co 7:31; Eph 2:2–7).

B. The Reason for the Letter (1:6–9)

At this point Paul would normally introduce an expression of praise for the Christians of the church to which he is writing. Instead, there is an abrupt and indignant cry of astonishment at what seems to be happening among the Galatians. Paul had delivered to them the one Gospel of salvation by grace through faith in Jesus Christ, and they had received it. But now, according to reports that had come to him, he has reason to believe that the Christians of Galatia are turning from this Gospel to embrace something that was no gospel at all, but only legalism. Paul pronounces a judgment upon any who would pervert this one Gospel of salvation by grace.

6 The agitation Paul feels is shown by the tone and vocabulary of these verses. But his words also show why he is so stirred. (1) The Galatians are "deserting" (GK 3572) the one who had called them to faith in Christ Jesus. The Greek word used here can be used of military revolt as well as of a change of attitude. Their revolt was not the result of outside influences, but something they were freely doing to themselves. The only ray of hope is that they were still in the process of deserting and could possibly be reclaimed.

(2) There is a tragic personal element in the way Paul describes their desertion. They are not just departing from an idea or a movement but from a person, from God the Father who had called them to faith. Embracing legalism means rejecting God, because it means substituting a human being for God in one's life. It is noteworthy that once again Paul reiterates the true nature of the Gospel: (a) it is of God, who does the calling, and (b) it is of "grace" rather than of merit.

(3) Paul is also agitated because the Galatians were deserting God and the Christian faith "so quickly," that is, so soon after their conversion.

(4) By embracing legalism the Galatians have actually turned their back on the Gospel in order to embrace "a different gospel," which, however, does not even deserve to be called by that name.

7 Paul now wants to explain or correct his phrase, "a different gospel." If left without any comment, that phrase might suggest that there are various gospels from which a Christian may choose. This is the opposite of what Paul is saying. So he adds that actually there cannot be another Gospel besides the one that describes God's way of salvation in Christ. The Gospel is one, and any system of salvation that varies from it is counterfeit.

For the first time now Paul mentions the false teachers, though not by name, presumably because he does not want anyone to think his remarks were originating from a dislike of certain personalities rather than from concern for the truth. He objects to two aspects of the conduct of these teachers: (1) they were perverting the Gospel, and (2) they were troubling the church. These two always go together.

8 The logical objection to the message Paul had been preaching is that it was not actually *the* Gospel, but only the gospel of Paul. If that is so, then the Galatians must evaluate the source of the teaching they had received, taking into account that the legalizers were the official representatives of the Jerusalem apostles, while Paul was not. Paul wards off this accusation, arguing that ultimately the human source does not matter, nor would it matter even if the source were an "angelic" one. Satan can disguise himself as "an angel of light," as can his ministers (2Co 11:14–15). So the Galatians must learn to evaluate their teachers, and they must learn that any attempt to alter the true Gospel is culpable and that any who go about teaching another gospel will be condemned.

Paul vehemently denounces those who teach another gospel, using the strong word *anathema* (GK *356*), a word semantically related to the Hebrew word *herem* (GK 3051) and used of that which is devoted to God, usually for destruction. In spiritual terms it means "damnation." Paul is not venting his anger here, for he is impartial in his judgment and mentions no names. He even includes himself in the ban, should he do otherwise in his preaching than he has done thus far. Moreover, he is universal in his judgment; his words include "anybody" who should so teach.

How can it be otherwise? If the Gospel Paul preaches is true, then both the glory of Jesus Christ and the salvation of the human race are at stake. If people can be saved by works, Christ has died in vain (Gal 2:21); the cross is emptied of meaning. If people are taught a false gospel, they are being led from the one thing that can turn them away from destruction (cf. Mt 18:6).

9 No doubt Paul repeats the *anathema* primarily for the sake of emphasis. But the restatement involves three alterations that tie it more closely to the situation in Galatia: (1) "The one we preached" is changed to "what you accepted"; (2) the element of improbability is lessened—"we or an angel from heaven" being changed to "anybody"; and (3) the thought of future possibility—"if we ... should preach"—is replaced by present supposition.

C. Transition (1:10)

10 Before Paul moves to state his first important thesis (vv.11–12), he makes a brief transition. He had been accused of being a people-pleaser by his enemies, who no doubt also implied that he was such at the expense of the truth (cf. 2Co 10; Gal 6:12). Would his enemies dare to say this now, Paul asks, after he has written so sharply? Do people-pleasers pronounce *anathemas* against those who teach false gospels?

It is important to point out that Paul's words cannot be used to justify the belligerent and fault-finding attitude so often found among religious crusaders. For one thing, Paul did strive to please people sometimes (1Co 9:19–22), though not where the Gospel was at stake; he is merely saying here that he did not please people *as opposed to* pleasing God. Furthermore, the word "now" gives a limited sense to this verse, as if he were saying: "Have I made myself clear enough about Christ's Gospel? Can anyone *now* charge that I seek to please people in presenting it?"

The incongruity of charging Paul with being a people-pleaser is strengthened by the following sentence, in which Paul mentions being "a servant of Christ." Jesus had said, "No one can serve two masters" (Mt 6:24). Thus, when faced with the necessity of making a choice, Paul would choose to stand with Christ, not with other people. The choice of the word "servant" (lit., "slave"; GK *1528*) is interesting because this letter is about freedom. It is an early indication of the paradoxical teaching that real freedom is to be found in bondage—bondage to Christ.

I. Paul's Defense of His Apostleship (1:11–2:21)

A. Thesis: Paul's Gospel Received Directly From God (1:11–12)

With these two verses the reader comes to Paul's first important thesis. He has spoken of the Gospel (vv.6–9), stating clearly that there is only one Gospel. But certain questions might be asked: "Why should your Gospel be normative, Paul? Why not another gospel? Or if it is true that there can be only one gospel, why should not some entirely different teaching be normative?" In his answer, Paul stresses the divine origin of his teaching, having been received by him directly from God. Throughout the rest of chs. 1–2 Paul defends this thesis by appealing to his own religious experience.

11 The verb introducing this verse means "to make clear," "to certify" (GK *1192*), and has the effect of suggesting that a somewhat formal statement will follow, as indeed it does. Just as v.1 advanced Paul's claim to apostleship by denying alleged inadequate sources for that apostleship and affirming the true one, so this section denies inadequate sources for the gospel, while affirming that what Paul preached came directly from God by revelation.

Paul goes on to deny three possible sources for his teaching. First, it was not "something that man made up." This is patently true, for the centrality of a cross and a resurrection do not figure in man-made religion. People seem always to prefer what flatters them and affirms human goodness, not what judges them.

12 Paul also denies that his teaching was received "from any man." This is a different denial from that in v.11, for both "from" and "receive" (GK *4161*) refer to the transmission of established religious teaching from one person to another. Paul uses the verb in this sense in 1Co 15:1, 3 to indicate that the basic facts of Christ's life—his death, burial, and resurrection—were received by him and passed on intact to his hearers. Important as this type of transmission may be, however, this was simply not the way Paul received his message.

Finally, Paul adds that he was not "taught" (GK *1438*) the Gospel either. Instruction was not the channel through which he came to the truth. This may be the way the vast majority of Christians receive the Gospel, including the Galatians, since Paul had himself instructed them. But it was not the way Paul himself had received the truth.

He now asserts the positive side of his thesis, saying that the Gospel came to him by "revelation" (GK *637*), an unexpected unfolding of what had been a secret—a distinctive experience paralleled only by that of those who were apostles before him. The Gospel that was revealed to Paul is unique, precisely because its source was not Paul but God himself. And Christians value it properly only when they make it an integral part of their lives and share it with others.

B. Paul's Personal History (1:13–24)

1. Paul's early years and conversion (1:13–17)

Paul has written that his Gospel did not have its source in a human being. But how could he prove this to the Galatian churches? The answer is by appeal to his personal history. Hence, in the remainder of the chapter Paul shows that the conditions of his life before his conversion, at his conversion, and within a reasonable period after his conversion were not such that he could have received the Gospel from others, particularly the Jerusalem apostles. On the contrary, the very isolation of his life at this period shows that the Gospel must have come to him directly from God, as he has just indicated.

13 The first part of this cumulative argument concerns Paul's former life in Judaism, before his conversion to Christianity. At this point, so far was he from coming under Christian influences that he actually was opposing the church and persecuting it.

The Judaism Paul practiced was an all-inclusive way of life, consuming his entire existence before his conversion. This brief reference to his former life is augmented by his lengthier descriptions elsewhere (see comments on Php 3:4–6). "You have heard" suggests that these facts were known to the Galatians long before any question had been raised about Paul's teaching.

Two aspects of his former life are specifically brought forward in his review of it here: he persecuted the church (v.13), and he advanced in the traditions of Judaism well beyond those of his own age among his countrymen (v.14). In both of these aspects Paul was fanatical, demonstrating his fanaticism against the church by the violence of his persecution and by his actual endeavor to "destroy" (GK *4514*) it (cf. v.23; Ac 8:1–4; 9:1–2, 13–14; 22:4–5).

14 The zeal that later fired Paul in his missionary efforts existed before his conversion, for it was part of his personality. Before his Damascus experience this zeal was devoted to advancing as a Pharisee in Judaism. This he did beyond his own contemporaries. He undoubtedly spent much time memorizing the Torah and the rabbinical traditions. With such a background no one could claim that Paul did not know Judaism or the OT. Nor could anyone claim that during this period he had subtly received his instruction in Christianity from others.

15–16 No one with such a personality and with such zealous persecution of the church is about to be converted by another person or by human testimony. Only God himself could accomplish such a conversion. This is precisely what happened to Paul. Thus, Paul begins to speak of his conversion, stressing that God did it entirely apart from any human agent. The reference is to Paul's experience on the road to Damascus (see Ac 9:1–19;

22:1–16; 26:9–18). The contrast in subjects between vv.13–14 and vv.15–16 is interesting. In the first section Paul himself is the subject (cf. "I"). In the second section, "God" is the subject, and his grace is emphasized.

There are three things Paul says God did for him. (1) God set him apart "from birth." Paul's words parallel Jeremiah's description of his own calling (Jer 1:5) and may consciously reflect it. Paul emphasizes God's grace in electing him to salvation and to the apostleship. (2) God called Paul "by his grace." This is a reference to his conversion, the moment in which Paul became aware of God's work in him. (3) God "reveal[ed] his Son in [Paul]" (v.16). This phrase probably refers to the sudden realization of what God had done in Paul's life by placing the life of the Lord Jesus Christ within Paul. God did this in order that he might become the apostle to the Gentiles.

God's revelation of Jesus in Paul was essentially an inner revelation concerning who Jesus was and what his life, death, and resurrection meant. This became so much a part of him, even at this early stage of his Christian experience, that he immediately began to make the revelation of Christ known to others. What grace this demonstrates! Paul, the chief opponent of Christianity in the apostolic era, now turned preacher of what he once tried to destroy! Was this change accomplished by a human being? No! Hence, even in his conversion (as in the period before his conversion) Paul could not have received the Gospel that he preached from other people.

17 Finally, Paul did not receive his message from any person after his conversion. He insists that he did not consult anyone, particularly the Jerusalem apostles, but went instead into Arabia (probably occurring between Ac 9:22 and 23). Most likely that time was spent in thinking and studying. Not until three years later (v.18) did he go up to Jerusalem and meet Peter.

2. Paul's early years as a Christian (1:18–24)

18 The "three years" mentioned here are hard to define. It may have been three full years or only one full year plus parts of two others. Nor does Paul's wording here indicate the point from which the three years or parts of three years are to be reckoned. Was it from the time of his conversion or his return to Damascus? Most likely it was the former (i.e., his conversion), in which case this visit to Jerusalem would have been about A.D. 35 (cf. 9:26–29).

What is certain is the general drift of Paul's argument. He has been stressing that none of the apostles was in touch with him in order to impart the Gospel to him before, during, or immediately following his conversion. Now he is adding that a considerable length of time passed before he even met one of the Twelve in Jerusalem. What is more, even then he stayed no more than a fortnight and met only Peter and James.

Why did Paul go to meet Peter? No doubt they talked about Christ, and Paul used the occasion to enrich his already firm grasp of the Gospel by the stories Peter could tell of the life and actual teachings of Jesus. Paul undoubtedly valued knowing these things. But the wording of the text in Galatians suggests that Paul's main purpose for this trip was to "get acquainted" (GK 2707) with Peter. The word used here suggests the telling of a story. Paul would have told his story, Peter his. So these two leading apostles became acquainted and encouraged each other in their forthcoming work. For the point of Paul's argument, it is important to note that this was a private visit and not one designed to secure the support of any human authorities.

19 Perhaps Paul's legalizing opponents would take advantage of this admission of a visit to Peter to attempt to show that Paul was dependent on the Jerusalem apostles after all. Well, let them! Paul will even admit that he also saw James, the brother of the Lord (see comment on Mk 6:3), who later played an important part in the Jerusalem Council. A reading of Ac 9:26–29 might suggest that Paul was introduced to all the apostles by Barnabas, but he is affirming that, in point of fact, he met only two.

20 Paul swears (cf. Ro 9:1; 2Co 1:23; 11:31; 1Th 2:5; 1Ti 2:7) that this account of his relationship with the Twelve is accurate. He takes this solemn oath probably in order to answer a specific charge of misrepresentation made against him. That Paul is answering specific charges should be remembered throughout these first two chapters. Each historical event he mentions relates to a specific argument raised by Paul's opponents. It is important to realize that Paul is not trying to provide a full chronology of his life.

21 Strict chronology is certainly not the main concern in this verse; if it were, the correct order of the areas Paul visited would be Cilicia and then Syria (see Ac 9:30; 11:25–26). Actually, he is merely indicating that in the next period of his life he worked, not in Jerusalem and Judea, where one could argue he was under the authority of the other apostles, but far away in the regions of Syria and Cilicia where he was on his own. Tarsus, Paul's hometown, was in Cilicia. Barnabas went there to get Paul when he needed his help for the work in Antioch (Ac 11:25), the capital of Syria. There Paul carried on a long and fruitful ministry.

22 Because Paul had worked so long in relative obscurity in the north and had paid no new visits to Jerusalem, he was "personally unknown" to Christians in Judea. Only after many years did Paul begin his famed missionary journeys in response to the call of the Holy Spirit through the Christians at Antioch.

23–24 The word "only" (v.23) suggests that after his conversion, Paul dropped so completely from sight that he was almost forgotten. The only report heard was that the one who long ago had persecuted the church was now preaching the Gospel. Once again Paul stresses his isolation from everything going on in Jerusalem. Would that there were more such contentment among Christians today—the contentment to be unknown! There would be, if this were the goal—to have God glorified (v.24). Too often those in prominent places within the church seek their own glory in Christian service rather than the glory of God.

C. Paul's Relationship to the Other Apostles (2:1–21)

1. The council at Jerusalem (2:1–5)

Chapter 2 begins a different unit of Paul's argument. There is a connection, of course, for he is still speaking of his apostolic authority. But now he wants to demonstrate the essential unity between himself and the other apostles, whereas ch. 1 focused on his independence from them. There are four main differences between the first ten verses of this chapter and those preceding it: (1) There is a new subject—not the source of Paul's Gospel, but the nature of the Gospel as centered in the issue of circumcision for Gentiles; (2) there is a new aspect of Paul's relationship to the Twelve—not independence from them, but harmony and cooperation; (3) there is a new period of Paul's ministry and of early church history; and (4) there is a new conclusion—namely, that in the essential content of the Gospel and of the plan for missionary activity, Paul and the Twelve were one.

This is the first point historically at which Paul came into sharp conflict with the heresy that was troubling the Galatian churches. What was to be done about this distinct point of view? Was it a minor matter to be passed over quickly? Was it an issue on which to seek compromise? Should a battle be fought? Apparently few besides Paul and perhaps Barnabas recognized the full importance of the issue at the time. So it is to Paul's steadfastness in conflict that Christians everywhere owe, humanly speaking, the continuation of the full Gospel of grace.

1 The "fourteen years" are most likely to be reckoned from the end of the three years mentioned in 1:18. Paul's main point is not how long after his conversion he made this visit to Jerusalem, but how long after last seeing the apostles he went up to see them again. Besides, Paul undoubtedly thought of the years of labor in Syria and Cilicia as a set period of his ministry, and his point is that these years were broken only by the trouble from the legalizers and by the revelation that he had to go up to Jerusalem to argue the cause of Gentile liberty. The council in Jerusalem, therefore, likely took place in A.D. 49 (see comment on 1:18).

Barnabas and Titus accompanied Paul, though Luke does not mention the presence of Titus in his account of the council. The presence of Titus is best explained by Paul's desire for a test case (see vv.3–5).

2 Luke says that Paul and Barnabas went up to Jerusalem as the result of a decision by the believers at Antioch (Ac 15:2). Yet there is no real contradiction between this account and Paul's statement about going up "in response to a revelation." Either the church at Antioch prayed about what should be done and then commissioned Paul and Barnabas in response to what they believed God told them to do, or else the revelation was a parallel and confirming one to Paul. Undoubtedly, Paul mentions the matter of revelation only to emphasize once again that at no time was he at the call of the other apostles. On the contrary, his movements as well as his Gospel are to be attributed directly to the revealed will of God.

The discussion of Paul's experiences in Jerusalem goes as far as v.10, but the essence of the matter and its outcome are already suggested in the second half of this verse. Paul spoke privately to those who were the apparent leaders of the Jerusalem church, wishing to avoid public remarks or a decision that would seriously affect the work he was doing among the Gentiles. If the doctrine of grace were not boldly and clearly upheld, terrible consequences for the church's missionary outreach would ensue. What happened at the council, then? Obviously, Paul's point was upheld, for the present tense of the verb "to preach" shows that the Gospel preached by Paul in his early years was still being preached by him at the time of his writing.

3–5 In the context of relating his contacts with the apostolic leaders at Jerusalem Paul now introduces an instance in which he claims to have defended the purity of the Gospel from the encroachments of those who would have mixed aspects of the Mosaic law with grace as the way of salvation. This incident was the attempt of the Jewish legalists to force the rite of circumcision on Titus. The outcome of the struggle, as Paul said, was a successful defense of the Gospel.

These verses have generated a significant amount of discussion, both because the words "This matter arose" in v.4 are not in the original Greek (and thus v.5 is needed to complete the sentence of v.4 if the words are not added) and because some manuscripts omit the words "not" and "to them" in v.5 (this makes the passage say that Paul did in fact yield for a moment). Furthermore, one must face the question whether Paul is referring in v.5 to the apostles or to the false brothers of v.4.

It is the contention of this writer that the NIV has by and large correctly interpreted Paul's thought here. In other words, v.4 is related to the thought of pressure being applied to Paul by the leaders at Jerusalem in deference to the false brothers, yet it was successfully resisted by Paul in defense of Gentile liberty.

Historically the picture one gets is this. The apostles at Jerusalem were wavering on neutral ground, tending to advise compliance to the law on Paul's part, but they finally came out for Paul by declaring openly for freedom from the law. This wavering attitude is suggested in the following verses, both in the attitude of reserve Paul seems to have encountered at Jerusalem (vv.6, 9) and in the related wavering of Peter at Antioch (vv.11–14). Moreover, this fits in with what is most clear in this passage, namely, that the conflict was primarily between the false brothers and Paul and that in the end (whether wavering before that time or not) the apostles stood solidly with Paul and Barnabas.

The term "false brothers" (used here and in 2Co 11:26) defines those who are not in fact Christians, though they pretend to be so. Paul's reference to these men "infiltrating" and "spying" entails a military metaphor and suggests the subversive and militant nature of the evil that Paul was fighting. In Paul's mind, the desire of the legalizers "to make us slaves" occurred in a manner similar to those who would take a city by stealth or force in order to place the inhabitants in chains.

Defending the Gospel that Paul had received from God was not done for any personal or selfish reasons, but "so that the truth of the gospel might remain" with believers (v.5). The word "truth" (GK 237) stands in marked contrast to the falseness mentioned in the preceding verse. Therefore, it must mean "the true gospel" as opposed to "the false gospel" being taught by the false brothers. The issue at stake here is an either-or issue: either the true Gospel in its entirety, or that which is no gospel at all! The importance of this issue made Paul adamant in his relationship to all others, Christians and non-Christians; it should make all who know the Lord Jesus Christ and who love the Gospel equally adamant in their thought, speech, and writings.

2. Paul and the pillar apostles (2:6–10)

6 As in v.4, the construction is again broken, with the result that the first few words (followed by an interjection concerning God's refusal to judge by appearances) are left hanging. Undoubtedly, Paul intended to revert to the subject of v.2 in order to point out that, having laid before the pillar apostles the Gospel he had been preaching, they found it to be in accordance with the truth. But Paul's thought is interrupted, and he hastens to add that whatever the historical advantages of the original apostles might have been in that they knew the historical Jesus, this was not important either to him or to God—and they added nothing to his message.

Three times in this chapter (vv.2, 6, 9) Paul refers to the three major figures at Jerusalem in an unusual way. The persons in question are James, Peter, and John (v.9), described as "those who seemed to be leaders," "those who seemed to be important," and "those reputed to be pillars." Why this unusual and perhaps even deferential way of referring to them? Though not all commentators agree, it does seem as if Paul is making a real (though balanced) note of disparagement of these three apostles. The very repetition of the phrase seems ominous, in the same way as Antony's repetition of the word "honorable" concerning Brutus in his eulogy at Julius Caesar's funeral in Shakespeare's play makes the conspirators seem dishonorable. Furthermore, each occurrence of the phrase seems to grow stronger with each repetition. Third, the story of Peter's conduct at Antioch in vv.11–14 lends credence to the feeling that Paul is disappointed with the conduct of those who should have been leaders in this great crisis of faith and doctrine but who failed to take the lead.

In other words, the delicate situation lying behind these verses explains the movement of Paul's thought. Paul is torn between a desire to stress the basic unity that did exist between himself and the Twelve and the need to be honest in indicating that, so far as he was concerned, the apostles did not perform well in the crisis. Thus, his initial allusion to the apostles in v.2 seems to him on second thought to be too vague. He breaks in with the Titus incident, but again not indicating clearly enough that it was the apostles who for the sake of harmony were urging that Titus be circumcised. Finally, Paul picks up the matter of the apostles again (v.6) and eventually names them (v.9), this time indicating that those who were reported to be "pillars" almost failed to do the work of supporting the Gospel.

Paul has therefore done the following: (1) recognized the position and authority of the Jerusalem apostles without diminishing his own authority in the slightest; (2) indicated, in opposition to the exaggerated claims about them made by the legalizers, that the apostles were men after all and hence not always perfect in their conduct; (3) decisively separated the Gospel and policies of the Twelve, for all their weaknesses, from the Gospel and policies of the legalizers; and (4) taken note of the fact that he and the Twelve, rather than the legalizers and the Twelve, stood together. Eventually, he will even show that the agreement between himself and the Twelve was cordial both in relation to their respective spheres of ministry (cf. v.9, "James, Peter and John . . . gave me and Barnabas the right hand of fellowship") and in regard to the special obligation of the Gentiles toward the Jerusalem poor (cf. v.10, "the very thing I was eager to do").

So far as the Gospel Paul preached was concerned, the Jerusalem conference had two results. Negatively, the Twelve "added nothing" to Paul; his Gospel was complete because it was received by revelation. Positively, the "pillars" recognized that all of them had been entrusted with the same Gospel and that they differed only in respect to the different fields they had been assigned to preach it in.

7–8 The phrase "they saw" implies a change of mind by the Twelve as a result of Paul and Barnabas's having reported on all that God had done through them among the Gentiles (cf. Ac 15:4). At first they were skeptical and uncertain, but later they came to stand with Paul on the issue of circumcision (cf. NIV text note). And just as the Gospel is one Gospel, no matter to whom it is preached, so also the commissioning and enabling of those who preach it are one—the reason being that the one who commissioned and empowered both Peter and Paul is God.

9 The exact use and order of the names of the leading apostles in this verse should not escape notice. First, the order obviously corresponds to the relative positions and work of James and Peter as recorded in Acts. Peter was a great missionary. Hence, when Paul is speaking of the ministry to the Jews, Peter is prominent (vv.7–8). But in dealing with a particular and official act of the Jerusalem church, James (who apparently presided at

James, Peter, and John are called "pillars" of the church. Pillars were used in ancient building techniques to support the superstructure. Here are the ruins of the synagogue in Capernaum, the town from which Peter and John came (see Mk 1:14–34).

the council) is mentioned in the first position, with the names of Peter and John following.

10 Paul had already shown a concern for the poor at the time of the famine visit when he traveled to Jerusalem with Barnabas as a representative of the church at Antioch (Ac 11:27–30). At the time of the council he was reminded of this good work and encouraged to pursue it. Out of this request, with which he was in great sympathy, arose the collection from among the Gentile churches that occupied so large a part in Paul's later thought and writings (cf. Ac 24:17; Ro 15:26; 1Co 16:1–4; 2Co 8–9). The change from the plural first person ("we") to the singular ("I") may reflect Paul and Barnabas's parting company by the time the collection was actually taken up (see Ac 15:36–40).

3. Peter comes to Antioch (2:11–14)

The account of the Jerusalem Council is followed immediately by another historical incident, the last in Paul's series, in which he dramatically supports his claim to possess an authority equal to and independent of the other apostles. In the opening part of this chapter, Paul has demonstrated his essential unity with those who were apostles before him. Now he shows that he stood so firmly grounded in the Gospel that he opposed even Peter, contradicting him publicly when Peter's conduct at Antioch threatened to compromise that Gospel.

For some reason, Peter had left the Jewish community at Jerusalem and had gone to the Gentile city of Antioch in Syria. There he discovered a community of Jewish and Gentile Christians living together and, in particular, eating together in apparent disregard of Jewish dietary customs. This was probably against the practice then prevailing in Jerusalem even after the council, but God had already shown Peter what he was to do in such situations (see Ac 10:15). So Peter joined with other Jews for some time in eating with his Gentile brothers. In this decision, he went beyond the letter of the decrees of the council, for though the council had acknowledged the right of freedom from the law for Gentiles, it had nevertheless retained the observance of the law for Jews. Now Peter was declaring that the Jew as well as the Gentile was free from Mosaic legislation.

After a time, some influential Jews arrived in Antioch from Jerusalem, claiming to represent James. They were the legalists, and Peter's practice shocked them. Not only was his conduct not required by the Jerusalem agreement, they might have argued, it was actually contrary to it. These persons brought such pressure to bear on Peter that he gradually detached himself from the Gentile fellowship and began to eat with Jews only. Moreover, his conduct drew others away with him, so that when Paul returned to Antioch from wherever he had gone, he found a church divided and the Gentiles under an unwarranted pressure either to accept the division or to conform to the legalistic standards of Judaism as the means of avoiding it.

What did Paul do? Since the schism was public, Paul confronted Peter publicly, charging him with inconsistency and stating once again that observing the law has no place in God's plan of salvation. From this response, the Galatians could realize that Paul was not a self-appointed apostle, nor even a worker appointed and approved by the Twelve. He was rather a full apostle in his own right, who could therefore speak with full authority—even, if necessary, in opposition to another apostle.

11 It is not known exactly when Peter came to Antioch, but the flow of events suggests that it was after the council. The Antioch incident reflects an entirely new situation from the council. There was a new issue (foods rather than circumcision), a new area of the faith (Christian living rather than the basis of salvation), and a new subject (Jewish liberty rather than the freedom of Gentile Christians). This dispute could have followed naturally upon the compromise reached at the council.

12 Here is the reason why Peter stood condemned. He was not simply making an honest mistake. The Peter who had received a vision prior to going to the house of Cornelius (Ac 10) and who had defended Paul at the council (Ac 15:7–11) was not fooled by the arguments of the legalizers. Instead, he had gradually given in to the pressure exerted by the legalizers. In other words, Peter played the hypocrite.

13 Unfortunately, conduct such as Peter's is not inconsequential, neither in his day nor now, for he was a pillar apostle. Thus one is not surprised to read that other Jews, including Barnabas, were led away by his hypocrisy. If Peter had been a lesser man or less prominent, the defection would have seemed less serious. The greater one's position or responsibility, the more important one's actions become.

14 Paul has already shown that he opposed Peter to his face because he was wrong (v.11), but we are not to think that he did this because he loved exposing error or, even less, because he loved an argument or wanted to enhance his own prestige. Paul's real concern was for the truth of the Gospel, and he acted out of the very concern that Peter lacked.

This is the second time that Paul has spoken of "the truth of the gospel" (vv.5, 14)—the good news that men and women are not accepted with God because of anything they have done or can do but solely on the basis of God's grace shown in the death and resurrection of Jesus Christ. Moreover, on the basis of this death all who believe are to be accepted equally. Peter's conduct compromised this principle, for it implied that there could be a superiority in some Christians based on race or traditions. It is not enough merely to understand and accept the Gospel, as Peter did, nor even to defend it, as he did at Jerusalem. A Christian must also practice the Gospel consistently, allowing it to regulate all areas of conduct.

4. Justification by faith alone (2:15–21)

The verses that conclude this chapter contain capsule statements of some of the most significant truths of Christianity. In particular, Paul clearly states the doctrine of "justification" (GK *1467–1470*) by grace through faith and defends it over against the traditional objection that justification by faith leads to lawlessness. This message is central to the letter, to his Gospel, and indeed to Christianity generally. This statement flows out of the situation at Antioch and anticipates the fuller argument of the same doctrine in chs. 3–4.

15 It is impossible to say precisely where Paul's remarks to Peter on the occasion of Peter's hypocrisy at Antioch leave off and Paul's direct remarks to the Christians of Galatia begin. Some commentators end the direct quotation at v.14; others, like the NIV, carry it to the end of the chapter. Paul seems to be gradually moving away from commenting on the situation at Antioch, but he does it so naturally that he himself was unconcerned with the transition. In v.14, he speaks of "you" (meaning Peter) and in v.15 "we" (meaning himself, Peter, and other Jews), undoubtedly with the situation at Antioch in mind. Later he is probably thinking of the broader situation that faced the Gentile churches.

The argument in v.15 is addressed to those who are "Jews by birth," i.e., those who possessed the advantages of a privileged birth and a revealed religion (cf. Ro 3:1–2; 9:4–5). But such great advantages are inadequate for achieving a state of righteousness before God; even Jews must be saved through faith. It is folly, therefore, to attempt to reestablish Judaism as a base for Christianity. The phrase "Gentile sinners," used seriously by legalistic Jews, has an ironic ring in Paul's mouth.

16 This is one of the most important verses in the letter. It contains the first mention of the words "justify" and "law" (GK *3795*), and is also the first place in which "faith" (GK *4411*) is brought forward as the indispensable channel of salvation.

"Justify" (GK *1467*) is a forensic term borrowed from the law courts. It means "to declare righteous or innocent"; the opposite is "to condemn" or "to pronounce guilty." Such a term involves an objective standard, and since righteousness is understood to be the unique characteristic of God, that standard must be the divine standard. In themselves, all persons fall short of this standard (Ro 3:23), but in Christ, God declares all who believe as righteous, imputing divine righteousness to them apart from human merit. In justification, the guilty are pardoned, acquitted, and reinstated as God's children and as fellow heirs with Jesus Christ.

This experience does not happen automatically to everyone. God justifies as he unites a man or woman to Christ, a union that takes place only through the channel of human faith. Faith is the means, not the source, of justification. Faith is trust. It begins with knowledge, so it is not blind. It builds on facts, so it is not speculation. It stakes its life on the outcome, so it is not impractical. Faith is trusting Christ and proving his promises. The expression in the middle of v.16 (lit., "we have believed *into* Christ") implies an act of personal commitment, running to him for refuge and seeking mercy.

It is also implied in this commitment that a person will turn one's back on the only other possibility—the attempt to be justified by works done in obedience to formal statutes from whatever source. Paul's emphasis here is not on the Jewish law (there is no article in Greek with the word "law"), though it includes it, but rather on any system of attempting to please God by good deeds.

The threefold repetition of the doctrine of justification by faith in this one verse is important, because it shows the importance the apostle gives to the doctrine. Besides, the three phrases increase in emphasis. The first is general: "A man is not justified by observing . . . law, but by faith in Jesus Christ." "A man" is anyone. The second phrase is particular and personal. "We, too, have put our faith in Christ Jesus that we may be justified by faith in Christ and not by observing . . . law." This phrase involves Paul himself, as well as all who stand with him in the faith. The final statement is universal: "By observing the law no one will be justified." The words are literally "all flesh," i.e., all humankind without exception. This final statement quotes Ps 143:2 (cf. Ro 3:20), adding the stamp of biblical principle.

17 In Paul's day, as today, arguments were directed against this way of salvation. So in this verse and the following ones Paul begins to answer these objections, first noting the main argument of his opponents and then revealing the argument by which he refutes theirs.

There have been many interpretations of this verse, because the wording contains several ambiguities. Is Paul speaking hypothetically or is he referring to actual experience? He obviously denies the conclusion that Christ is the minister of sin, but does he also deny that "we ourselves . . . are found sinners" (KJV)? In what sense is sin mentioned?

The best interpretation—one that reflects Paul's thought elsewhere (Ro 6–8) and best explains the following verses—is that Paul refers to the standard antinomian objection to the doctrine of justification by faith, namely, that eliminating the law entirely encourages godless living. The argument goes, "Your doctrine of justification by faith is dangerous, for by eliminating the law you also eliminate one's sense of moral responsibility. If people can be accounted righteous simply by believing that Christ died for them, why then should they bother to keep the law or live by any standard of morality? There is no need to be good. The result of your doctrine is that people will believe in Christ but thereafter do as they desire." Paul's reply is abrupt: "Absolutely not!" The form of his expression suggests that he was aware of the possibility that Christians can (and do) sin. But this is not the result of the doctrine of justification by faith, and therefore Christ is not responsible for it. Such a thought is abhorrent. If there is sin, as Paul acknowledges indirectly in the next verse, human beings themselves are responsible.

Why is it that Paul can reply so vigorously to the objection that his Gospel promotes lawlessness, especially since he seems to admit that those who have been justified by faith do sin? His answer is that the objection totally misunderstands the nature of one's justification. In the eyes of legalizers, justification by faith is nothing more than a legal fiction by which men and women are accounted righteous when in fact they are not. But justification is not a legal fiction. It is true that people are accepted by God as righteous when they are not, but this takes place only because God has first joined them to Christ and this in its turn implies a real transformation. They are "in Christ," says Paul. Consequently, they are "a new creation" (2Co 5:17; Gal 6:15). Obviously, to return to the old way of life after such a change is inconceivable.

18 The interpretation of this verse is not difficult in the light of the interpretation of v.17 given above. The legalizers had accused Paul of encouraging sin because his doctrine overthrows the law for God's grace. This Paul denied. Nevertheless, he replies, sin could be encouraged if having once come to God by faith in Jesus Christ the one coming should then return to law as a basis for the relationship. This is an argument *e contrario*. It refers to a situation precisely like that one into which Peter had fallen—he turned back to Jewish practices and ended up sinning against the Gentiles. In view of the following verses, Paul is likely thinking of the great sinfulness of turning from the Savior (whom the law anticipated) to mere ordinances (for a similar argument, see Heb 6:4–6).

19 The "we" of v.17 (which included both Paul and Peter) has changed to the "I" of v.18. This personal form of expression continues as Paul begins to unfold the full nature of the justification that is his because of his being "in Christ." In this verse "I" is emphatic by being in the first position in the sentence. It contrasts with the similar position given to "in Christ," which (in the Greek text) begins v.20.

Paul has argued that if he should return to law after having come to God through faith in Christ, he would make himself a transgressor. But this is not what he does. On the contrary, the opposite is true, for in coming to God in Christ he died to the law so completely that he could not possibly return to it. The law cannot bring life, for no one has ever fulfilled it. Law brings death, for by it all stand condemned. Nevertheless, the law does perform a good function, for in the very act of destroying all hope for salvation by human works, the law actually opens the way to discovering new life in God (for a more complete explanation of these issues, see comments on Ro 5:20; 7:1–13).

20 This same point Paul now repeats in greater detail, with the name of Christ prominent. He has died to law so that he might live for God, but this is true only because he has been joined by the Father to the Lord Jesus Christ. Jesus died; so did Paul. Jesus rose again; so did Paul. The resurrection life he is now living he is living through the presence of the Lord Jesus within him. By having died and come to life in Christ the believer actually participates in Christ's death and resurrection, conceived on the basis of the mystical union of the believer with the Lord (cf. Ro 6:4–8; Col 2:12–14, 20, 3:1–4).

What does it mean to be "in Christ"? It means to be so united to Christ that all the experiences of Christ become the Christian's experiences. Thus, his death for sin was the believer's death; his resurrection was (in one sense) the believer's resurrection; his ascension was the believer's ascension, so that the believer is (again in one sense) seated with Christ "in the heavenly realms" (Eph 2:6). When one died with Christ, one's "old self" (cf. Eph 4:25) died with Christ. This was arranged by God so that Christ, rather than the old Paul, might live in him.

True, Paul is still living. But he adds that the life he lives now is lived "by faith." It is a different life from the life in which he was striving to be justified by law. In another sense, it is not Paul who is living at all, but rather Christ who lives in him.

21 This last sentence of ch. 2 is introduced abruptly and from a new point of view. In the preceding verses Paul has answered the objections of his critics. Now he objects to their doctrine, showing that if they are right, then Christ has died in vain. The heart of Christianity lies in the grace of God and in the death of Jesus Christ. To insist on justification by works undermines the foundation of Christianity by nullifying God's grace.

Paul's logic is incontrovertible. Yet many still pursue the fallacious logic of the legalizers. They suppose that to earn their salvation is somehow praiseworthy and noble, when actually it is vainglorious and ignoble. True nobility (and humility) is to accept what God offers.

II. Paul's Defense of the Gospel (3:1–4:31)

A. The Doctrinal Issue: Faith or Works (3:1–5)

The apostle has been defending the Gospel of grace from the very beginning of this letter, but until now he has done so from the viewpoint of his own experience and calling. These had been challenged. So he has been insisting that God rather than another human being called him and gave him his message. In speaking of his own experiences, however, Paul has gradually worked around to talking about the Gospel itself, and this has brought him to the place where he is now set for a theological—or, better, a scriptural—defense of the Gospel. So he returns to the Galatians themselves and to the point at which the doctrine of justification through faith bore down upon their own experience.

1–2 This is the first time since 1:11 that Paul addresses the Galatians. Now it is by the impersonal term "Galatians" rather than by the word "brothers," and it sets a sober tone for the formal argument to follow.

Paul cites three things that are inexplicable in regard to the Galatians' conduct. (1) Their conduct is irrational or "foolish" (GK 485), a word that suggests the actions of one who can think but fails to use those powers of perception (cf. Lk 24:25; Ro 1:14; 1Ti 6:9; Tit 3:3). This term was suggested to Paul by the trend of his thought at the end of the previous chapter—namely, that a doctrine of salvation by works foolishly denies the necessity for grace and declares the death of Jesus Christ unnecessary. A doctrine leading to such a conclusion is irrational. Yet this is what the Galatians were on the verge of embracing. How can such nonsense be explained? Paul suggests facetiously that perhaps they have been placed under a spell by some magician.

(2) Paul cannot understand what is happening because the true Gospel had been so clearly preached to them. Undoubtedly, he is referring to his own preaching, arguing that the Gospel had been made as clear by him as if he had posted it on a public bulletin board. The heart of the Gospel that Paul preached is—and always must be—"Christ crucified" (cf. 1Co 2:2).

(3) The conduct of the Galatians is inexplicable because it was so totally contrary to their initial experiences of Christianity. How did they begin? This is what Paul would like to hear from them, and he is not interested in hearing anything other than the basic answer to this basic question. Did they receive the Holy Spirit by living up to some formal statutes? Or did they enter into the Christian life simply by believing and receiving what they heard concerning the death of the Lord Jesus Christ?

3 Paul presupposes their answer, which is obviously that they became Christians only through believing what they heard. The conclusion follows that, having begun by faith, they must continue in faith. It cannot be otherwise, because the two ways—faith versus works—are in conflict. Paul emphasizes this conflict by three sets of comparisons: (1) works versus hearing, (2) law versus faith, and (3) Spirit versus flesh. The last antithesis will come to prominence in the ethical section (5:13–26).

4 There is some ambiguity in the question "Have you suffered so much for nothing?" It may imply actual suffering, as is suggested in NIV. Or it may refer simply to the Galatians' previous spiritual experiences: "Have all your great experiences been in vain?" (NEB). Both views make sense in interpreting the letter as a whole, but the latter seems to fit the immediate context better. In this case, the experiences of the Galatians are further amplified by the reminder in v.5 that God was working miracles in their midst through the power of his Holy Spirit.

5 Nothing must be allowed to obscure the point Paul is making, so once more he voices the test question of v.2, but his emphasis now is on God's point of view, asking on what basis God is working miracles among them right up to the present. Paul anticipates here the end of the argument, for it is evident that blessing in the Christian life comes just as it began—through faith, and not as the result of any human attainments.

B. The Doctrinal Argument (3:6–4:7)

Many outlines have been given of these next verses. A helpful outline is to be found in the very antithesis that Paul develops in this section. Is a person justified by "observing law" or by believing what one has heard? With this question in mind, Paul begins to discuss the alternatives—dealing first with faith, then with law, then with faith, then with law, and so on. The following diagram suggests the flow of the argument.

The Test Question:

Believing what was heard	"observing the law"
The true Gospel	The legalizers' "gospel"
3:6-9 Faith ("Abraham")	3:10-14 Law (the "curse")
3:15-18 Faith ("covenant")	3:19-22 Law ("trangressions")
3:23-29 Faith ("heirs")	4:1-7 Law ("bondage")

1. Children of Abraham (3:6–9)

Paul turns to the first section of the alternating argument. The issue is scriptural, for he is concerned to show that not only the experience of the Galatians but also the words of the OT support his teaching that the means of entering into salvation is faith. Abraham is his example.

Paul's statements presuppose a knowledge of Abraham by the Galatians, and it is not difficult to imagine how the Christians of Galatia had learned it. If Paul had preached among the Galatians for any length of time, he would undoubtedly have taught Christian doctrine in part on the basis of Abraham's life. Furthermore, if (as we argued in the introduction) the churches of Galatia were the churches of the south, there was undoubtedly a large Jewish population in the area with which Christians must at least have had some contact and with whose history they must have been familiar. Most significant, however, is the probability that the obligation to become "children" of Abraham through circumcision formed the central argument of the legalizers' teaching. This argument would have focused on Ge 12 and 17; they would have claimed that no one could be blessed by God who was not part of the company to whom God's promises were made, and one entered this company solely through circumcision. These arguments Paul encounters head on, for he shows that even Abraham was blessed through faith, not circumcision.

6 Paul begins his argument by linking his OT example to the Galatians' spiritual experience, showing that what they had known to be true in their own lives (salvation by faith alone) was also true for others and is confirmed by Scripture.

To appeal to Abraham is more than to appeal to just any historical example, because Abraham was the acknowledged father and prototype of Israel. He was the man God started with. He had come from a pagan ancestry beyond the river Euphrates (Jos 24:1–2), but God had called him and had made a covenant with him. From Abraham the Jewish people came, and all Jews looked back to him as their spiritual father and example. How, then, did Abraham receive God's blessing? How was he justified? Paul answers by a quotation of Ge 15:6, noting that Abraham "believed God, and it was credited to him as righteousness."

What does Paul mean by faith being imputed to Abraham as "righteousness" (GK *1466*)? The answer depends on the definition of "righteousness." This may be either a forensic term (denoting a right standing before the law) or a term denoting a right relationship (in this case to God). If the latter definition is taken, Paul's point is that Abraham's trusting attitude toward God was accepted by God as righteousness. But if the forensic use predominates, then it must be God's own personal righteousness that was imputed to Abraham in place of his own, which was inadequate. If there were nothing else to go on than Ge 15:6, the second of these two uses might be preferable. But in view of Paul's development of the doctrine elsewhere, the first must be adopted. It is only by thinking of God's righteousness actually being credited to our account that Paul can say (2Co 5:21): "God made him [Christ] who had no sin to be sin for us, so that in him we might become the righteousness of God." These two views are not in opposition, of course, for justification does bring one into a right relationship with God out of which ethical changes follow. The changes result from one's being placed "in Christ," as Paul has shown (2:20).

7 One example does not make a case, however. So Paul continues his argument with a sentence linking the situation of Abraham to the present. He means, "Since Abraham was saved by faith, his true children are, therefore, even now, those who are saved by faith, as he was." The background is undoubtedly the claim of the Judaizers that one became a genuine child of Abraham by circumcision and subsequent obedience to the law. This verse is an important one for linking the two covenants, that of the OT and that of the NT, for Paul stresses that Abraham's faith was of the same kind as Christian faith.

8 Paul now continues to use Scripture as evidence of what he has already concluded in v.7. His quotation from Ge 12:3 makes two points: (1) that the blessing promised to Abraham was from the beginning intended to include the Gentiles as well as the Jews, and (2) that the Gospel promise preceded everything else in God's dealings with his people, including the giving of the law (cf. v.17).

The unusual way the OT is cited here makes this an important verse in assessing the value given the OT by Paul and other NT writers. The Scriptures are personified here; they "foresaw that God would justify the Gentiles by faith, and announced the gospel in advance to Abraham." Paul views the Scriptures as if they were God speaking (cf. also Ro 9:17). Such verses highlight an absolute identification of Scripture with the words of God in the minds of the NT writers and are important biblical support for the historical Christian belief in the total inspiration of the Bible.

9 The reader is now at the peak of the first section of Paul's argument. It is a throwback to the question of v.5: Who are the ones who enter into spiritual blessing? The answer is: Those characterized by the approach of faith are blessed along with Abraham, who had faith. Since the blessing of Abraham is declared to have been intended for the Gentiles also, how could the Gentiles be blessed except by faith?

2. The law's curse (3:10–14)

Having established his doctrine of justification by faith positively, Paul now turns to its negative counterpart: the impossibility of being justified by law. Significantly, he rests his case on statements from the law itself, contending that those who wish to live by the law are bound by their own principles to these statements. Three points follow: (1) Those living under the principle of law are under the law's curse, for the law pronounces a curse upon all who fail to keep the law in its entirety; (2) no one is justified by law, since the law itself teaches that people are justified by faith; and (3) no mixture of these principles is possible, for they are mutually exclusive. To this argument Paul adds a reference to the twofold benefit of the work of Christ: redemption from the curse that the law has imposed on everybody and a blessing by which the promise of the Spirit made to Abraham is fulfilled for all who believe on Christ as Savior.

10 In the first four verses of Paul's formal argument (vv.6–9) he has cited two OT texts: Ge 15:6 and Ge 12:3. In vv.10–12 he quotes the OT three more times, in each case demonstrating that an attempt to live by law, rather than producing a blessing, actually brings a curse from God. Why? First of all, because the law demands perfection, as Dt 27:26 declares. The law is not a collection of stray and miscellaneous parts, some of which may be conveniently disregarded. It is a whole and must be kept in all its parts if it is to be considered kept at all. A curse is attached to any failure to keep it, no matter how small. Since all fail, all are under that curse and consequently under God's wrath (cf. Ro 3:23). That is, the law condemns a person and points human beings in their desperation to their need for a Savior (Ro 3:20–21).

11 One must not think that the law did nothing but condemn during all the centuries between the giving of the law through Moses and the coming of Jesus. On the contrary, the law itself showed the way of salvation. Paul proves this by a quotation of Hab 2:4—"The righteous will live by faith," one of the few OT verses in which faith is presented as the means of salvation. Paul does not misrepresent Habakkuk's meaning here, for if, as seems likely, "the righteous" in Hab 2:4 means those who are standing in a right relationship to God rather than those who are literally righteous before the law, then Habakkuk's view is essentially in accord with Paul's position here. One stands in a right relationship to God and lives before him by faith.

12 But perhaps both are needed, both faith and law? Not so, says Paul. For faith excludes law, and law by its very nature excludes faith. He quotes Lev 18:5 (part of the law) to support this position. Mentally we are to supply "the law says that" after "on the contrary."

13 If these principles are true and if they support the topic sentence of v.10, then the condition of humankind under law is obviously hopeless. If there is to be hope, it must come from a different direction entirely. Abruptly, therefore, Paul introduces the work of Christ through which the curse of the law has been exhausted and in whom all who believe find salvation.

This is the first time Christ has been mentioned since the opening verse of the chapter, but now both he and his work are prominent. Christ is the only possible means of redemption. Since the "curse" of v.10 implies the idea of divine disapproval of the entire human race, the "us" in "Christ redeemed us" refers to both Jews and Gentiles. Paul goes on to show that the purpose of Christ's death was that the blessing given to Abraham might come upon both Jew and Gentile.

To "redeem" (GK *1973*) means "to buy out of slavery" by paying a price. Christ paid this price by dying (cf. Ac 20:28; 1Pe 1:18–19). An alternate way of saying the same thing is to say that Christ became "a curse for us," which Paul does. In what sense did Jesus do this? Paul's quotation from Dt 21:23—"Cursed is everyone who is hanged on a tree"—suggests that Jesus passed under the law's curse in a technical way by virtue of the particular means by which he was executed. Thus, having violated the law in one part—through no fault of his own—he became technically guilty of all of it and bore the punishment of God's wrath for every violation of the law by every person. But the curse of the law was not merely a technical thing; it was real. Jesus bore this real curse on our behalf when he died in our place. This can be understood in part both through the illustration of OT sacrifices (cf. the scapegoat taking away the curse of sin in Lev 16:5ff.) and in Christ's cry of dereliction from the cross—"My God, my God, why have you forsaken me?" (Mt 27:46).

14 Paul concludes this section of the argument with a twofold statement of the purpose for which Jesus Christ redeemed us through his death: first, that the blessing of Abraham (i.e., justification, as in vv.8–9) might come to Gentiles as well as Jews, and second, that all might together receive the gift of the Holy Spirit. These two purposes are coordinate; i.e., they express the same reality from two perspectives. Both return to the point from which Paul's argument started—namely, that the blessing of Abraham, seen today in the reception of the Holy Spirit, is received through faith and through faith only.

3. The seed of Abraham (3:15–18)

At the close of the preceding section Paul introduced the idea of God's promise to Abraham. Now he picks up this idea once more and develops it in relation to the giving of the law. This is the beginning of the second unit of his alternating answer to the question of v.2: "Did you receive the Spirit by observing the law or by believing what you heard?" (see diagram above).

Paul's opponents were undoubtedly not ready to admit that Abraham was justified by faith in God's promise. But even if he were, they might argue, still the giving of the law at a later time changed the basis for a person's entrance into salvation. Anticipating this objection, Paul draws on the acknowledged character of human wills and covenants so as to show that no new development could change the promise made to Abraham.

15 "Brothers" introduces a change of tone on the part of the apostle, in contrast to the somewhat distant and formal beginning of ch. 3 (cf. 4:31; 6:1). It is as though he now invites the erring Galatians to reason along with him as he uses an analogy from everyday life. Paul is borrowing an illustration from human relationships (so also at Ro 3:5; 6:19; 7:1–3; 1Co 9:8).

Commentators have found difficulty in Paul's use of the word "covenant" (GK *1347*) here because the word can mean either "agreement" or "will." But is it necessary to choose between the two meanings? Perhaps not. In English one has to choose between them simply because there are two separate words. But in the Greek language, it is possible to use both ideas. That this is the case here seems to be supported by: (1) Paul's custom of playing on words elsewhere (e.g., Gal 5:12), (2) the same double meaning in Heb 9:15–20, and (3) the particular nature of the "covenant" made by God with Abraham. Paul is alluding to the promise of a universal blessing both to Jew and to Gentile through Abraham's "seed" (Ge 12:2–3), which he conceives as the offer of justification to every human being through Christ. But if this is so, Paul certainly also has in mind God's formal unilateral enactment of the covenant by the ceremony recorded in Ge 15.

In Abraham's day an oath was sometimes confirmed by a ceremony in which animals were cut into two parts along the backbone and placed in two rows, the rows facing each other across a space marked off between them. The parties to the oath walked together into the space between the parts and spoke their promises there. This oath would be especially sacred because of the shed blood. But the ceremony in Ge 15 had this exception: In the case of God's covenant with Abraham, God alone passed between the pieces of the slain animals, thereby signifying that he alone stood behind the promises (cf. also Heb 6:13–15). It did not depend on any condition to be fulfilled by Abraham.

The idea of a will is not far removed from this type of covenant, except in the matter of the death of the testator, which obviously cannot apply to God. Paul's point is simply that the promise of justification through faith first made to Abraham is permanent. If a human will or agreement cannot be added to or annulled, how much less can the solemn promises made to Abraham and his seed be altered later by the living God!

16 This verse appears to be a parenthesis. But showing the scope of the promises made to Abraham is essential to Paul's argument. If those promises were made only to Abraham and his immediate descendants, they might well be considered fulfilled even before the giving of the law; the law would then inaugurate a new era in God's dealings with humankind. But the promises were not fulfilled in the period before the giving of the law, Paul argues. They were embodied in the coming Redeemer through whom the fullness of blessing was to come. That Redeemer was Christ. Consequently, God's blessing of justification by grace through faith spans the ages; and the law, whatever else one might think of it, served only an interim function. Paul's essential point is that the promises made to Abraham must be in effect eternally.

When Paul speaks of "seed" in the singular as opposed to "seeds," he poses a problem for commentators, especially since the singular form has a collective significance and often denotes more than one person. The nearest English equivalent is the word "offspring." What is the explanation? Obviously, Paul knew as well as anybody that "seed" generally referred to many persons (cf. Ro 4:16–18; 9:6–8). But he is simply pointing out that the singular word "seed" (rather than a plural word like "children" or "descendants") is appropriate, inasmuch as Israel had always believed that the ultimate messianic blessing would come through a single individual.

17 The 430 years comes from the LXX of Ex 12:40, defining the period between Abraham and Moses rather than (cf. the Hebrew text) the period during which the Israelites were slaves in Egypt. The difference is of no consequence for Paul's argument, however, because his point depends only on the historical sequence. If God had been blessing Abraham and his posterity through the way of promise for 430 years and if he was to do the same for all humanity through Christ, how could the giving of the law annul this promise? It could not, as even the human analogy of covenants and wills shows. Therefore, the law cannot add to, nor subtract from, God's first and only way of salvation.

18 This verse adds an objective as well as temporal reason why the giving of the law cannot change the promise. Promise and law are antithetical by nature. They can be neither mingled together nor combined (cf. also v.12). In the last phrase the words "to Abraham" are emphasized, thereby once again driving all discussion of how men and women enter into a right relationship with God to its original source. The word "gave" (GK *5919*) is important, because it emphasizes that salvation is both a free gift and is permanent. Whatever may be said about the law, this much is certain: God saved Abraham through promise, not law, and the original way of salvation is still operative.

4. Law versus covenant (3:19–22)

Paul has proved, at least to his own satisfaction and perhaps even to that of the Galatians, that the only way of salvation is by means of the promise received through faith. But the legalizers might object that the approach he has taken has actually proved too much. If the way of salvation is by promise and the law brings a curse, it would seem to follow (1) that the law has no purpose at all in the scheme of salvation, or (2) that it is actually opposed to it. This would be an intolerable conclusion for most, particularly those Jews whose lives had been dominated by the law for centuries. Paul answers these charges by denying both conclusions and by establishing God's true purpose in giving the law: it was given not to save people but to reveal their sin, it was temporary, and it was inferior to the promise because, unlike the promise, it was given through a mediator.

19 To the question "What, then, was the purpose of the law?" Paul provides as his first answer that the law was added "because of transgressions" (GK *4126*). That is, the law was given to make the transgressions known, perhaps even to encourage them or to provoke them to a new intensity (see also Ro 3:20; 4:15). Though sin was in the world before God gave the law, sin was not always known as such; it was the law that revealed sin as sin. Hence, it may be said that it is the law that turns sin into transgression—transgression of law—and even accentuates it (Ro 5:20). In this act, law performs the function of showing one's need of a Savior.

The second half of this verse carries the thought further by showing that the giving of the law was temporary ("until the Seed to whom the promise referred had come") and inferior (because it was "put into effect through angels by a mediator"). Here the mediator is doubtless Moses who, as an agent of a mediated revelation, is brought forward in contrast to Abraham, to whom God made promises directly. The role of angels in the giving of the law is suggested in Dt 33:2 and Ps 68:17 and is referred to explicitly in Ac 7:53 and Heb 2:2.

20 This verse is probably the most obscure verse in Galatians, if not in the entire NT. The difficulty lies in the abrupt, aphoristic character of the verse and in its relationship to Paul's context. The most important interpretations fall into three categories:

(1) Those that take Paul's reference to a "mediator" in a general sense. According to this approach, Paul is introducing a general principle in support of the point made at the end of the preceding verse. Mediators always act between parties. Hence, since Moses was a mediator of the law, it follows that he acted between God and the people and that the law thereby came indirectly. The last phrase suggests that in giving the promise to Abraham (see vv.15–18) God acted directly and unilaterally.

(2) Those that take the reference to a "mediator" as a specific reference to Moses, the mediator in the previous verse. This approach can obviously lead to an interpretation similar to that given above. However, it can also lead to other views, such one in which Moses is contrasted with Christ as one who was unable to be a mediator of "a perfectly united body."

(3) Those that refer "the mediator" to Christ (cf. 1Ti 2:5). This view does not relate well to the context. If it is right, Paul would be acknowledging that even in Christianity there is a mediator, Christ; but he would be adding that since Christ is God as well as human, in Christ God is still dealing with people directly.

Whatever the details of the interpretation, the general thought seems to be that the promise must be considered superior to the law because the law is bilateral. That is, it was mediated, and ; humankind was a party to it. The promise, on the other hand, is unilateral; humankind is not a party to it. This thought reinforces what Paul has said earlier about the unconditional and unilateral nature of the promises.

21 The second apparent conclusion the legalizers might take from Paul's doctrine of justification is that the law becomes evil because it opposes grace as the true means of salvation. But this does not follow, Paul replies. It is an abhorrent idea, for it suggests a conflict within the nature of God, who gave both the law and the promise. True, the law increases transgressions (Ro 5:20) and it can even kill (Ro 7:7–11). Still, the law is not bad; it is good—so good that if a person could do what the law requires, that person would find life (Lev 18:5; cf. Gal 3:12).

22 Because it is impossible to find life through law, however, the law fulfills its actual function by shutting all people up within the bounds of acknowledged sin. It condemns them, with the result that they turn from trying to please God through legalism and instead receive the promise of God through faith in Jesus Christ. In the first part of this verse Paul summarizes the major truths of Ro 1:18–3:20, that the law shows that all have sinned and need a Savior. The second half of the verse reminds us that there is indeed a Savior and that it had always been God's purpose to save a great company through faith in him. Seen from this angle, even the law flowed from God's grace, because it prepared people to receive the Lord Jesus Christ when he came.

5. Heirs with Abraham (3:23–29)

The closing section of ch. 3 begins the third unit of Paul's alternating answer to the question of v.2 (see diagram above). It follows directly on what Paul has said regarding the true purpose of the law. Still, a change has taken place. Before, he has been concerned with the law's true purpose, which is to lead people to Christ. Now, though he begins with this point, he moves on to the idea of a change of status for those who have passed from being under the bondage of the law to being sons and daughters in Christ. Before, we were prisoners, shut up under the law. Now we are sons and daughters, reconciled to God and made one with each another and with all who throughout history have been justified on the basis of God's promise.

23 The proper understanding of the phrase "before this faith came" is found in the fact that the definite article occurs before the word "faith." By "this faith" Paul means "the Christian faith," that faith he has just spoken of in v.22—faith in Jesus Christ as Savior (cf. 1Ti 4: 1 for a similar usage). This faith is like the faith exercised by Abraham, but it is different in that it relates to the explicit revelation of Christ in time and to the distinct Christian doctrines concerning him. Faith waited for this complete revelation. Paul's point is that the law was intended to function only during this 1,500-year period of anticipation.

While the law was here, however, it did serve a purpose: to hold us prisoner, locking us up until Christ should be revealed (cf. v.22). Paul is thinking here that the law, like a jailer, has kept people locked up and therefore out of trouble until Christ, the liberator, should come to set them free.

24 The phrase "put in charge" is the Greek noun *paidagogos* (GK *4080*), which means "a child-custodian" or "child-attendant." The pedagogue was a slave employed by wealthy Greeks or Romans to have responsibility for one of the children of the family. He had charge of the child from about ages six to sixteen and was responsible for watching over his behavior wherever he went and for conducting him to and from school. Paul's point is that this responsibility ceased when the child entered into the fullness of his position as a son, becoming an acknowledged adult by the formal rite of adoption by his father (see on 4:1–7). The reference "to Christ" is temporal; it means "until we come of age at the time of the revelation of our full sonship through Christ's coming." The final phrase (lit., "in order that by faith we might be justified") gives the ultimate objective of the law in its role of pedagogue. The emphasis is on justification rather than faith, for Paul has already shown that faith is the only means to salvation.

25 The two most important points of the previous verses are repeated for emphasis: first, the time element—we were under the law as pedagogue until the faith should come; second, the reference to the fully revealed faith of Christianity. Paul is here thinking historically, stressing that the reign of law has ended for those believers who now through the coming of Jesus have become mature sons and daughters of God.

26 But what are the actual results of this passage from the reign of law to grace through faith in Jesus Christ? In the final verses of the chapter Paul lists three of them.

First, through faith in Christ all who believe become "sons of God"—i.e., they have passed through spiritual infancy into full maturity as justified persons. In view of Paul's previous reference to the pedagogue, the mention of full-grown "sons" is particularly appropriate. Still we must not think of this as a matter of growth alone. To be true children of God means to be justified by faith in Christ and to have therefore passed into a new and right relationship to God. Before, they were under law, but now they are under grace. In this verse emphasis falls on the word "all." All are included in these statements, the Galatians particularly.

27 This new relationship is not something that happens automatically to everyone. Not everyone is a child of God in the sense that Paul speaks of here. In fact, one can become a son or daughter only through union by faith with Christ Jesus.

Baptism signifies this transforming identification with Christ, so Paul refers to it here. Paul is not suggesting here that baptism now replaces circumcision as a saving sacrament. No one is saved by baptism. Indeed, Paul mentions baptism only once in the paragraph, but faith five times. Rather, baptism is an outward sign of the union that already exists through faith. To be "clothed with Christ" means to become like Christ.

28 The second result of passing from law to grace through faith in Jesus Christ is that all who believe become one with each other so that there is now "neither Jew nor Greek, slave nor free, male nor female," but all are "one in Christ Jesus." In what sense is this true? Clearly, it does not mean that differences of nationality, status, and sex cease to exist. A Jew remains a Jew; a Gentile, a Gentile. Instead, having become one with God as his sons and daughters, Christians now belong to each other in such a way that distinctions that had divided them lose significance.

Race is the first example. In Paul's day there was a deep division between the two, not only nationally but also religiously. Gentiles were uncircumcised and therefore not children of Abraham. They did not have the law or the ceremonies; they were not of the covenant. This barrier Paul now claims to have been broken down in Christ (cf. Eph 2:11–18). Today this principle must be extended to deny the significance of all racial barriers. In Christ there must be neither black nor white, Caucasian nor Oriental, nor any other such distinction.

Social status is a second example ("slave nor free"). Again, this is not meant to deny that in actual fact there are social distinctions among people. It is merely meant to affirm that for those who are united to Christ these things do not matter. On this pattern the ideal church should be composed of members from all spectra of society: wealthy and poor, educated and uneducated, straight and long-hair, management and labor, and so on. When Christians treat each other as true brothers and sisters in Christ regardless of their social standing, then the power of such distinctions is broken and a basis is laid for social change.

There is also the example of sex, for Paul declares that there is neither "male nor female." It is hard to imagine how badly women were treated in antiquity, even in Judaism, and how difficult it is to find any statement about the equality of the sexes, however weak, in any ancient texts except those of Christianity. Paul reverses this. Indeed, in this statement we have one factor in the gradual elevation and honoring of women that has been known in Christian lands.

When Paul concludes this breakdown of the distinctions that are superseded by Christianity, he speaks of the fact that all who are in Christ are "one," one unified personality as the living body of Christ. In this body all are truly one with one another. The only permissible distinctions are those of function (cf. 1Co 12).

29 The third result of passing from law to grace through faith in Jesus Christ is that all who believe become one with those who have been saved by faith throughout the long history of salvation. Thus, by union with Christ, believers become "Abraham's seed, and heirs according to the promise." Here that which Paul had previously declared to be Christ's—the inheritance of the promise made to Abraham (3:16)—he now applies to the entire Christian church by virtue of its actually being Christ's body. The verse carries the thought back to the beginning of the chapter.

The use of the word "seed" without the article is of great importance, for it keeps the necessity of a union with Christ constantly before the Galatians. The prize the legalizers had been holding before the eyes of the Galatian Christians in their hope to win them to the ceremonial aspects of Judaism was the possibility of becoming part of the physical seed of Abraham. Paul now replies that what the legalizers were offering through circumcision was actually already theirs in Christ. He is *the* seed to whom the promises were made. Believers enter into the promises by entering into him and become spiritual seed to God as well.

6. Heirs of God (4:1–7)

Paul gives his final contrast between God's people before Christ's coming and the position they enjoy now. The difference between these verses and 3:23–29 is in emphasis. Paul has been stressing the temporal nature of the change. At this point he dwells on their status, moving from being slaves to becoming sons and daughters of their heavenly Father. This development flows from the thought of the pedagogue in vv.23–29.

1–2 The moment of growing up was a definite one in antiquity, and it involved matters of great religious and legal importance. For instance, in Judaism a boy passed from adolescence to manhood shortly after his twelfth birthday, at which time he became "a son of the law." In the Greek world the minor came of age at about eighteen, but there was the same emphasis on an entering into full responsibility as an adult. Roman law also had a time for the coming of age of a son, but the age when this took place does not seem to have been firmly fixed; the father apparently had discretion in setting the time of his son's maturity. It seems likely that Paul is referring primarily to the Roman custom as he observed a child "under guardians and trustees until the time set by his father." At that time the child was formally adopted by the father as his acknowledged son and heir and received special adult clothes.

When the child was a minor in the eyes of the law, his status was no different from that of a slave, even though he was the future owner of a vast estate. He could make no decisions, he had no freedom. But at the time set by his father, the child entered into his responsibility and freedom. The application of the illustration is obvious as Paul applies it to the inferior condition of people under law, both minors and slaves, and to the new freedom and responsibility that come to them in Christ.

3 Paul now applies the illustration as already indicated. Before Christ came we were children and slaves, slaves to the "basic principles" or "elemental spirits" (GK 5122) of the world (cf. v.9).

There has been much debate about what Paul means by this word here. Of the three major interpretations, the best one sees it as referring to the basic elements that the ancient world saw as making up the world—earth, fire, air, and water. These elements had been associated from the dawn of civilization with the gods. In Paul's time it seems that this exceedingly early view had been expanded so that the elements also referred to the sun, moon, stars, and planets—all of them associated with gods or goddesses and, because they regulated the progression of the calendar (cf. "days and months and seasons and years" in vv.9–10), also associated with the great pagan festivals honoring the gods. In Paul's mind these gods were demons (cf. "those who by nature are not gods" in v.8). Hence, he would be thinking of a demonic bondage in which the Galatians had indeed been held prior to the proclamation of the Gospel (cf. Ro 8:38–39; Eph 6:10–12). Thus, this whole issue takes on a cosmic and spiritual significance. The ultimate contrast to freedom in Christ is bondage to Satan and the evil spirits.

4–5 But God has set believers free! These are wonderful words, because they show that the entry of the Christian message is at the same time the turning point of history. Apart from these words, life offers no future hope for anyone. We are lost, without hope and without God (cf. Eph 2:12). But God has intervened in a way that brings an effective and complete salvation.

Paul goes on to spell out what God has done. First, he "sent his Son." From the historical point of view, the fact that "the time had fully come" suggests several factors. It was a time when the Roman peace extended over most of the civilized earth and when travel and commerce were therefore possible in a way that had formerly been impossible. Great roads linked the empire of the Caesars, and its diverse regions were linked far more significantly by the all-pervasive language of the Greeks. Add the fact that the world was sunk in a moral abyss so low that even the pagans cried out against it and that spiritual hunger was everywhere evident, and one has a perfect time for the coming of Christ and for the early expansion of the Christian Gospel. Viewed theologically, however, it may also be said that the time was full because God himself had filled it with meaning.

Specifically, God sent his Son "to redeem" those who were under the law's bondage and to provide the basis by which God is able "to adopt" them as sons and daughters. Redemption is mentioned here for the first time since 3:13 and is particularly appropriate in view of the imagery Paul is using. Redemption means "to buy out of slavery" (cf. comment on 3:13). People were slaves either to the law, as Jews, or to the "basic principles of the world," as Gentiles. Christ paid the price of their redemption and set them free. Moreover, it is through him that human beings have the adoption. That is, they move not only from bondage into freedom; they also move into the household of God, where all are free and are "heirs of God and co-heirs with Christ" (Ro 8:17). Observe the subtle link between the central ideas of this verse and the phrase "weak and miserable principles" in v.9. The opposing powers are "weak" because they cannot redeem and "miserable" (or "poor") because they cannot provide the adoption.

And who is the one through whom this great salvation comes? It is striking how much of the important Christian teaching about Jesus is revealed here. He is divine, for he is God's "Son." This speaks of an ontological relationship existing from eternity (Php 2:5–11; Col 1:15). He is human, for he was "born of a woman." He was "under law"; i.e., he was born into Israel and thus within God's historical stream of salvation. Paul may even be alluding here to the virgin birth.

6 Paul has already pointed out the first great redemptive act of God in history: God sent his Son. Here he adds the second act: "Because you are sons, God sent the Spirit of his Son into our hearts, the Spirit who calls out, *'Abba*, Father.'" In other words, to the other doctrines of the faith already spilling over from vv.4–5 Paul now adds Trinitarian teaching, for he is telling us that salvation consists in its fullness of acts by God the Father in sending both God the Son and God the Holy Spirit. Moreover, this salvation is both objective and subjective. God the Father sent the Son in order that believers might have the *position* of sons and daughters, and he sent his Spirit so that they might have the *experience* of the same reality. We should notice that the gift of God's Spirit is not something the children of God are to strive after as if, having been given salvation, they must now work to realize it or achieve it on a higher level. The Spirit is the gift of God to all believers because they are sons and daughters.

How do Christians experience what is theirs objectively? Paul suggests that this is primarily through the reality of God's presence made known to them in prayer. Before, they were alienated from God, who indeed did not even hear them. Now, being made members of his family, Christians are permitted and even urged to cry, "Father." "*Abba*" is the Aramaic word for "Father," suggesting an intimate relationship with God. "Father" was the word Jesus habitually used in his prayers to God (e.g., Mt 11:25; Mk 14:36; Jn 11:41; 17:1, 5, 21, 24–25) and which he passed on to those who through him became God's children (Mt 6:9).

7 This verse sums up all that Paul has said previously. Formerly slaves, Christians are now both children of God and heirs. It is connected with the previous verse in that the Spirit teaches us about our relationship with God as Father. The change from the plural of v.6 to the singular of v.7 brings the argument home to the individual reader. Each reader should therefore ask, "Do I know the reality of such an internal witness by God's Spirit? Am I assured of these things?"

C. Paul's Appeal to the Galatians (4:8–31)

1. A return to bondage (4:8–11)

At this point the formal argument for salvation by grace rather than by works is finished, but Paul seems unwilling to end the discussion without a direct and, indeed, lengthy appeal to the Galatians. He reminds his converts of their former bondage in paganism and expresses his astonishment that they could even consider a return to such slavery. In view of this possibility, he expresses concern that his labors among them may have been to no purpose.

8–9 For the third time (cf. 3:23ff.; 4:1ff.) Paul speaks of the former enslaved state of the Galatians. His reason this time is to establish the folly of their proposed action of returning to the law's bondage. In their former state of bondage and immaturity, they did not know the true God and worshiped instead those who were "no gods" (cf. Ro 1:18–23)—a clear reference to the idols of paganism.

Their former bondage was, of course, a matter of ignorance. But that they should voluntarily return to this bondage after having been delivered from such ignorance by God himself—this is astonishing and, indeed, totally incomprehensible. In essence, what Paul is saying here is this: "But how can it be that, on the one hand, having formerly been in ignorance of God and therefore enslaved to those who are not gods and, on the other hand, having come to know God or (which is more to the point) being known by him, you are now returning anew to those weak and bankrupt elements which once controlled you?"

There are three causes for Paul's astonishment: (1) the Galatians were going back to what they had already been through—i.e., not to a new error but to an old one; (2) they were turning from reality (the true God) to nonreality (non-gods); and (3) this was done after they had actually come to "know" (GK 1182) God in an intimate and personal way.

Paul understands total spiritual depravity and the electing grace of God in such a manner that he does not want to leave the impression that it is possible for anyone to come to know God by his or her own efforts. The truth of the matter is that God comes to know us. We come to know him only because we are first "known [GK 1182] by God"—i.e., through Christ a Christian has become an object of God's personal recognition and favor.

We have already seen why the elemental spirits or principles the Galatians were in the process of turning to are "weak and miserable" (lit., "powerless and bankrupt"); they are weak because they are unable to set people free, as Christ has done by redeeming them. They are bankrupt because they have no wealth by which they can provide an inheritance.

10 The Judaizers were probably not intentionally trying to enslave the Galatians, and it is even more probable that the Galatians did not regard their current drift toward legalism as a return to slavery. Yet that is precisely what it was, as Paul reminds them.

In the context of the struggle in Galatia, there is little doubt that the observances the Galatians were succumbing to were Jewish observances. "Days" refers to sabbath days and feasts that fell on specified dates; "months" refers to celebrations tied to the recurring monthly cycle; "seasons" refers to seasonal events, such as the feasts of Tabernacles, Passover, etc.; "years" most naturally refers to the recurring years of Jubilee. What is most significant, however, is not that Paul opposed these Jewish special days, in that observing them was but one step removed from a full Jewish legalism, but that he regards them in exactly the same light as the pagan festivals—i.e., as controlled by and interacting with demonic spirits (see comment on v.3).

This does not, of course, mean that Paul attributed the origin of the law, which includes the religious feasts, to Satan. Far from it. The law is good and comes from God (cf. Ro 7:12). Nevertheless, even the law, when distorted into a way of trying to earn salvation, can be used by Satan to increase human bondage. That Paul, the Jew, would even consider the Jewish observances in the same context as the pagan festivals shows the intensity of his estimate of the deadly character of legalism.

11 Can his readers have missed that point? If so, it comes to them once again as the same Paul who speaks elsewhere of the fact that nothing can ever separate Christians from the redeeming love of God (Ro 8:35–39) and who expresses confidence that the work begun in the Christian by God will be continued till the day of Christ (Php 1:6) now expresses the fear that his labor in bringing the Gospel to the people of Galatia might be wasted. This is not, to be sure, the same thing as saying that a Christian can lose salvation. Indeed, even the Galatians have not gone that far; they have only begun to observe the feasts and have not yet been circumcised (5:2). Nevertheless, they are wavering, and their wavering is inexplicable and inexcusable. It can only be that they are "nearsighted and blind" and have "forgotten" that they were cleansed from old sins (see 2Pe 1:9).

2. Their past and present relationships (4:12–20)

If the reader is inclined to think Paul has been impersonal in dealing with the problems at Galatia, the present passage should remove any suspicion. It is true that Paul has dealt with the issues facing the Galatians as doctrinal ones and has even been somewhat distant in addressing his converts, at best calling them "brothers" (cf. 1:11; 3:15). Now, however, all this changes, and his deep pastoral concern for the Galatians surfaces as he intensifies his appeal to them by again calling them "brothers" and then "dear children." Moreover, he bases his appeal on their past and present relationship to one another; first, their past relationship to him (vv. 12–16), and second, his past and present relationship to them (vv.17–20). He contrasts the former with their present actions; the latter he contrasts with the actions of the Judaizers.

12 The opening words of this verse are somewhat puzzling, for there is not enough said to know precisely what Paul is referring to. Most likely he is asking the Galatians to enter into the Christian freedom he knows, with the reminder that he had identified himself with them in order to preach the Gospel to them (cf. 1Co 9:20–22). That is, when Paul went to the Galatians, he did not stand on any special dignity or insist that the Galatians first come to him by becoming Jews. He became like them, in order to win them to Christ.

This is a principle of great importance for all who are trying to win other people for Christ. Our *goal* must be to make them like us, while the *means* to that end is to make ourselves like them. Witnessing involves doctrine, but it also involves the most personal involvement of the witness with those to whom he or she is witnessing.

13 "You have done me no wrong" (v.12) really belongs with vv. 13–15, verses describing Paul's original reception by the Galatians. They had received him graciously and with compassion (see v.14). And this was all the more remarkable since he had not been at his best when among them. He had been sick. In fact, illness had brought about his visit to Galatia in the first place. While many attempts have been made to identify the precise nature of Paul's illness (e.g., malaria, the physical abuse and resulting weakness he had suffered at Lystra [Ac 14:19], his "thorn in the flesh" [2Co 12:7], or bad eyesight), the only thing we can say with certainty is that some form of unpleasant sickness lay behind Paul's first visit to the Galatians and that, though they could have despised him because of it, they did not but, instead, received him favorably.

14 They actually received him as "an angel of God," i.e., "as if I were Christ Jesus himself." It is noteworthy that though Paul was well aware that he, like the Galatians, was a sinner, and though he had been careful when among them not to allow any conduct on their part that suggested worship of Paul (see Ac 14:8–18), nevertheless he does not suggest here that their respect for him as a messenger of God was in error. On the contrary, they were quite right to receive him in this manner. For he came among them as the approved messenger of the Lord Jesus Christ.

Today there are no apostles. But to the degree that ministers and teachers of the Word of God do teach the Word, to that same degree should they be received as the Galatians received the apostle Paul. Ministers should not be received and evaluated on the basis of their personal appearance, intellectual attainments, or winsome manner, but as to whether or not they are indeed God's messengers bearing the word of Christ.

15–16 In spite of their initial attitude toward Paul, their opinion of him had changed. The joy (lit., "blessedness," GK *3422*) they experienced as a result of his preaching had vanished, and they were now apparently regarding him as their enemy. If one thinks that Paul possibly suffered from bad eyesight (cf. 6:11), then the expression "you would have torn out your eyes and given them to me" refers to actual conversations they had at the time.

Why had Paul become their enemy? The only possible explanation is that he had become an offense to them through telling them the truth. Unfortunately, this is often the case for those who are faithful to Christ's teaching.

17 Paul can appeal, not only to the former attitude of the Galatians or to the contrast between that and their actions in the present (vv.12–16), but also to his own attitude toward them. That attitude was guileless and in marked contrast to that of those who had since been attempting to woo the Galatians into legalism.

Paul notices two things about the actions of the legalizers: their zeal and their motives. Being "zealous" (GK 2420) is not bad in itself. This word can have two meanings: "to envy" and "to be deeply concerned for someone to the point of courting their favor"; both are implied here. Certainly Paul had been zealous with a godly jealousy (cf. 2Co 11:2) for the Galatians as he worked among them, and he encourages them to be zealous in regard to the Gospel. Zeal placed at the service of Christ is a fine characteristic. In the case of the legalizers, however, this zeal was misdirected, for it was a zeal for their own cause and glorification, and it was alienating the Galatians from both Paul and Christ.

There is here an interesting throwback to a previous verse. When Paul says that the Judaizers "want . . . to alienate you" (lit., "lock you up"), he is probably thinking of the function of the law in "locking" people up under sin (3:23). The locking up was the same action, but the purposes were different. The law served a proper function in locking people up as sinners so that they might find salvation in Christ. The legalizers, however, were trying to lock the Galatians up under law so that they might be separated from Christ and from Paul and serve their teachers. They must take note, for if that happens, the roles will be reversed, and the Galatians will find that they must court the legalizers. Failure to maintain Christian liberty always leads to ecclesiastical as well as other forms of bondage.

18 Though there are several possible meanings of this verse depending on who is exercising such zeal, it is best to refer the zeal to the Galatians, which Paul wishes was as intense now in pursuit of the right thing as it was when he was with them. This verse, then, makes a transition that, though somewhat abrupt, leads on to the thought of Paul's having been with them in the past and of his wish to be with them once again if possible (v.20).

19 Paul now comes to his main point about the actions and motives of the legalizers: his own attitude to the Galatians was quite different. He had not come to them in order to build up his own personal following, as the false teachers had. He had come to help them—to see that they were born again and to labor for them until Christ himself should be formed in them. In calling the Galatians his "dear children" and in speaking of his labor "pains" on their behalf, Paul pictures himself as a mother who went through the pains of childbirth when they converted to Christ; he is now in labor again as the result of their apparent defection. He wants them to know that his present pastoral concern matches his evangelistic fervor; indeed, neither has diminished because of the Galatians' listening to the legalizers.

20 We do not know why Paul was unable to visit Galatia again at this time, but if he could, he says he would change his "tone." This does not mean that he would change his teaching or have fewer expectations of them, but his approach would be different. He could ask questions. He could find out why they were in the process of turning from freedom to bondage, and so he would no longer be perplexed. Perhaps he could even speak to them differently as he continued to recall them to the Gospel.

3. An appeal from allegory (4:21–31)

Commentators are sometimes embarrassed because Paul's doctrinal argument in the central two chapters of Galatians concludes with an allegory based on what many consider an unjustified use of an OT story. But such embarrassment is unnecessary, as is the thought that the allegory was somewhat of an afterthought for Paul, who had, in fact, actually concluded his argument early in the fourth chapter. In one sense, the formal argument did conclude there; vv. 8–31 are mostly an appeal to the Galatians to remain in that freedom to which God has called them.

However, one may also argue that Paul has deliberately saved this argument for his capstone. The advantages are these: (1) The allegory allows Paul to end on a final citation of the law and, in particular, on a passage involving Abraham, who has been his primary example. (2) It allows him to use a method of argument which, we may assume, had been used by the legalizers, thus turning their own style of exegesis against them. (3) It illustrates and reviews all his main points—the radical opposition between the principle of law and the principle of faith, the fact that life under law is a life of bondage and the life of faith is freedom, and that the life of faith is a result of the supernatural working of God by means of the Holy Spirit. (4) The story contains an emotional overtone suited both to a wrap-up of the formal argument and to a final personal appeal. (5) It gives Paul a base upon which to suggest what he had undoubtedly thought but had apparently been reluctant to say previously—that the Galatians should obey God by casting out the legalizers (v.30). Therefore, the allegory effectively ties together the doctrinal section of the letter and the appeal based on it, and it leads into chs. 5–6, the ethical section.

Paul introduces the facts of the story itself (vv.21–23), develops the allegory (vv.24–27), and then applies the allegory to the Galatians and indeed to all believers (vv.28–31). The latter section speaks of the supernatural basis of the new life in Christ, the inevitability of persecution for those who stand by the Gospel, and the need to so stand.

21 Paul has already appealed to statements of the law to show that the law brings a curse to those who desire to be under it (3:10–14). But that was both indirect and negative. Now he appeals directly and demands that those desiring to be under law hear what the law actually says and retreat from their folly. He does not yet consider that the Galatians have actually rejected the Gospel, only that they are desiring to reject it for law.

22 For the final time Paul turn to Abraham, upon whom the legalizers had undoubtedly based a large part of their argument. Jews derived much satisfaction from their physical descent from Abraham and in many cases considered the promises and blessings of God to be theirs because of it (see comment on 3:6; see also Mt 3:6; Jn 8:31–41). The present passage deals with the same issue, only Paul's method of attack is slightly different from that of John the Baptist and Jesus. Instead of denying outright their descent from Abraham, Paul simply reminds his opponents that Abraham had two sons (Ishmael and Isaac) and asks, in effect, which of these two children the legalizers take after.

23 There were two main differences between these sons. (1) They were born of different mothers (v.22); one was a free woman, the other a slave. This, according to ancient law, also affected the sons' status. (2) In the manner of their conception, Ishmael's was entirely by natural means (Abraham was elderly at the time, but still the conception was natural), whereas Isaac's was by means of a miracle (by this time Abraham had passed the age at which it was normally possible to engender children and Sarah was long past the age of conceiving them). Isaac was brought into being "as a result of a promise" from God.

This contrast lends itself well to the distinction Paul is trying to make between natural or man-made religion and supernatural or God-made religion. The religion of works and law corresponds to the natural birth of Ishmael; the religion of the Spirit, which is Christianity, corresponds to the supernatural birth of Isaac.

24–26 This basic distinction between the two sons and in the manner of their conception and birth Paul now carries out in more complete spiritual terms, using the historical account as an allegory. This does not mean that Paul's exegesis is fanciful, as some have implied, but only that he uses the story for the sake of its major principle, which he then quite properly applies to the struggle between Judaism and Christianity. The best way to understand the allegory is to carry it through in parallel columns.

Hagar, the slave woman	*Sarah, the free woman*
Ishmael, a natural birth	*Isaac, a supernatural birth*
The old covenant	*The new covenant*
Earthly Jerusalem	*Heavenly Jerusalem*
Judaism	*Christianity*

In this arrangement Hagar, the slave woman, stands for the old covenant enacted at Mount Sinai, while her son, Ishmael, stands for Judaism with her center at earthly Jerusalem. On the other hand, Sarah, the free woman, stands for the new covenant enacted on Calvary through the blood of the Lord Jesus Christ, and her son, Isaac, stands for all who have become part of the church of the heavenly Jerusalem through faith in Christ's sacrifice. On the most superficial level, Isaac and Ishmael were alike in that both were sons of Abraham. But on a more fundamental level they were entirely different. In the same way, Paul argues, it is not enough merely to claim Abraham as one's father (cf. Ro 9:6–9). The question is: Who is our mother and in what way were we born? If Hagar is our mother, then we were born of purely human means and are still slaves. If our mother is Sarah, then the birth was by promise, and we are free.

It is significant that when Paul contrasts "the present city of Jerusalem" with "the Jerusalem that is above" he mixes two metaphors so as to enrich his meaning. Strictly speaking, the phrase "the present city of Jerusalem" should be matched with "the Jerusalem that is to come," and the phrase "the Jerusalem that is above" should be matched with "earthly Jerusalem." These connotations are more or less evident. But by not actually saying "the Jerusalem that is to come," Paul suggests that while it is true that there is a Jerusalem to come (Rev 21:2), this Jerusalem is also now present in those born again by God's Spirit.

27 There is no evidence that the verse Paul now quotes (Isa 54:1) was ever associated with the story of Hagar and Sarah and their children; nevertheless, it is highly appropriate. This verse is a prophecy of Jerusalem's restoration following the years of exile and involves the thought that the blessing of the latter years will be greater than that enjoyed formerly. The pre-exilic Jerusalem and the post-exilic Jerusalem correspond, then, to Paul's distinction between the earthly and heavenly Jerusalems, and the promise to the blessings of God to Israel under the old covenant as contrasted with the greater blessings to the church under the new covenant. The element common to these verses is the supernatural intervention of God in order to establish Christianity. The new element is the suggestion, soon to be fulfilled, that the numbers of Christians will outnumber those within Judaism.

28–29 In the third section of this treatment of the Hagar and Sarah story, Paul applies the allegory to all Christians, pointing out that because they are like Isaac, who had a supernatural birth, rather than like Ishmael, their experiences will be consistently similar to that of the younger son.

In the first place, they must expect persecution from their brother. Paul is referring to Ge 21:8–13, when, at the weaning of Isaac (he was about two years old and his half-brother Ishmael about seventeen), Ishmael began "mocking" Isaac. Thus Sarah asked that Hagar and her son be sent away. So it is today, says Paul. True Christians will be persecuted (cf. Mt 5:10–12; Php 1:29; 1Th 3:1–4; 2Ti 3:12; 1Pe 4:12–13). And the remarkable thing is that this will not always be by the world but indeed more often by their half-brothers—the unbelieving but religious people in the nominal church. This is the lesson of history. It was the Jews who killed the prophets, not the Gentiles. It was the Pharisees and other religious leaders who opposed Jesus and instigated his execution, which was carried out by the Romans. Paul's fiercest opponents were the fanatically religious Judaizers. Today the greatest enemies of the believing church are found among the members of the unbelieving church, the greatest opposition emanating from the pulpits and church hierarchies.

30 Second, the Christians at Galatia must recognize the incompatibility of man-made and God-made religion and respond by casting out the legalizers. Those born after the flesh (v.29) will never share in the inheritance God has reserved for his true children, born after the Spirit. Therefore, Christians must reject both legalism and those who teach it. Taking a story from Genesis that the Jews undoubtedly interpreted as a statement of God's rejection of the Gentiles and applying it instead to the exclusion of unbelieving Jews from Christianity probably infuriated Paul's opponents, but his point was well taken. God does not look on physical descent but on spiritual affinity. The true sons of Abraham are those who are born of the Spirit.

31 Of such are the Galatians. The "therefore" of this verse sums up the whole allegory and indeed the entire section of Paul's doctrinal argument. The shift to the first person ("we") once again includes both Paul himself and all who embrace the true Gospel.

III. The Call to Godly Living (5:1–6:10)

A. Summary and Transition (5:1)

Paul has already reached two important goals in his appeal to the Galatians. He has defended his apostleship, including a defense of his right to preach the Gospel with or without the support of other human authorities (1:11–2:21), and he has defended the Gospel itself, showing that it is by grace alone, apart from human works, and that the Christian is freed from the curse of the law and brought into a right relationship with God (3:1–4:31). But Paul must make one more point before he concludes his letter: that the liberty into which believers are called is not a liberty that leads to license, as his opponents charged, but rather a liberty that leads to mature responsibility and holiness before God through the power of the indwelling Holy Spirit. This theme dominates his last two chapters.

1 Before plunging into this third section of his letter, Paul interjects a verse that both summarizes all that has gone before and serves as a transition to what follows. It is, in fact, the key verse of the entire letter. Because of the nature of the true Gospel and of the work of Christ on their behalf, believers must now turn away from anything that smacks of legalism and instead rest in Christ's triumphant work for them and live in the power of the Spirit. The first part of this verse aptly sums up the message of chs. 3–4, while the second part leads into the ethical section. Paul appeals for an obstinate perseverance in freedom as the only proper response to any attempt to bring Christians once more under legalism.

Since the Jews of Paul's time spoke of taking the yoke of the law upon themselves, Paul probably alludes to such an expression here. To the Jews taking up the law's yoke was the essence of religion; to Paul it was assuming the yoke of slavery. He may also be remembering Jesus' reference to Christians taking his yoke upon them (Mt 11:29–30), but his yoke was "easy" and "light."

B. The Danger of Falling From Grace (5:2–12)

The reader may think that in the opening verses of ch. 5 Paul reverts back to a theme he has already covered and so departs from his purpose to move on to the ethical section. But such reasoning misses an important point—that even the ethical life must begin by recognizing that the foundation of God's dealings with us is grace through faith rather than obedience to the law. "Do you wish to lead a holy life?" Paul seems to be asking. "Then begin with the principles of faith and shun legalism. Holiness will never come as the result of insisting on adherence to either man-made or even God-made regulations." He makes this point twice here: first, from the viewpoint of those who, like the Galatians, seem about to fall into legalism (vv.2–6) and, second, by referring to those who teach such false doctrines (vv.7–12).

2 Paul wants the Galatians to take careful note that if they allow themselves to be circumcised (the verb tense used here implies that they had not yet taken this step but were considering it), then Jesus Christ will profit them absolutely nothing. Circumcision was, of course, the particular form of legalism that was a problem in Paul's day; the choice was between Christ and no circumcision at all, or circumcision and no Christ at all.

This explains why Paul is so categorical in condemning the practice of circumcision for the Galatians. It is not that circumcision in itself is so important. In fact, Paul himself had once circumcised Timothy (Ac 16:3), and he would soon declare that "neither circumcision nor uncircumcision has any value" (v.6). Rather, what Paul condemns is the *theology* of circumcision, which makes works necessary for salvation and seeks to establish conformity to some external standards of behavior as a mark of spirituality.

Ones's motivation is the important thing. Paul was in no sense condemning those Jewish Christians who had been circumcised. His advice to such people is given in 1Co 7:17–20: circumcised Christians should remain circumcised; uncircumcised Christians should remain uncircumcised. Particular forms of legalism are not themselves the important issues; the critical issue is works versus grace, or, as we will soon see, spirit versus flesh. Paul's concern was that nothing should cloud perception of this central Christian doctrine.

3 Paul has already stated that to fall into circumcision is to lose the value of Christ's death both for salvation and for living the Christian life. Now he adds another reason why the Galatians should remain firm in the freedom Christ has given them: to choose circumcision is to choose legalism, which in turn involves taking on the burden of the entire law—something that the legalizers had probably not warned the Galatians about.

4 Paul again states his points, this time dropping the hypothetical "if" for the strong assertion that those who want to be justified by law have been alienated from Christ and have fallen away from grace. Christ is of no value to them and the burden of keeping the whole law is theirs.

What does "You have fallen away from grace" mean? Does it mean, as some claim, that salvation can be lost if a Christian falls into sins? Not at all. There is a sense in which to sin is to fall into grace, if one is repentant. But to fall from grace, as seen by this context, is to fall into legalism. Or to put it another way, to choose legalism is to relinquish grace as the principle by which one desires to be related to God.

5 The essence of that message of the Gospel is now brought forward in the last full statement of the principle of justification by faith in this letter. Up to this point Paul has been talking only of the Galatians (cf. the pronoun "you"), warning them about what they seemed to be doing. Now he changes to "we," emphasizing something like this: "But, on the other hand, we Christians do not choose legalism; rather, we wait in faith through the Spirit for the full realization of God's righteousness."

Each phrase in this verse is important and has already been defined. "By faith": this key word stands in contrast to human effort, as all should be aware from the arguments of chs. 3–4. "We eagerly await": Christians wait for the full realization of their salvation. They do not *work* for it; they *wait* for it. "Through the Spirit": this is a reminder of the electing grace of God in salvation. "The righteousness for which we hope": this does not refer to that imputed righteousness the believer has in the present through faith in Christ's death, but rather (in line with the ethical section to follow) to that actual righteousness in which believers grow and to which they will be perfectly conformed in glory. In the Bible, "hope" (GK *1827* & *1828*) refers to that which, though certain, is not yet fully realized.

6 Paul makes two final points as he wraps up the first half of this section. In doing so, he comes close to giving a full and beautiful definition of true Christianity. (1) As hard as Paul has been on circumcision and as much as it would serve his purpose to downgrade it in preference to uncircumcision, he nevertheless acknowledges that neither circumcision nor uncircumcision in themselves counts for anything. This is further evidence that his concern is theological and not ceremonial (cf. a similar point made about eating meat offered to idols in 1Co 8:8).

(2) True faith, having an ethical side, works itself out "through love." This is what matters—this kind of faith! True, we are saved through faith rather than by works; but faith is no mere intellectual conviction, as if Christians can do as they wish as long as they believe the right doctrines. This is a horrible idea, as Paul writes elsewhere (Ro 6:1–2). To believe is to place one's personal confidence in Christ, who loves us and gave himself for us. Therefore, Christians must respond in a genuine and self-denying love for others.

In vv.5–6 the three great terms "faith" (GK *4411*), "hope" (GK *1828*), and "love" (GK *27*) appear together (cf. 1Co 13; Col 1:4–5; 1Th 1:3; et al.).

7 Up to here in this section Paul has been contrasting those who desire to add circumcision to Christianity and true believers who trust Christ alone. Now the contrast changes to a false teacher or teachers, designated as "the one who is throwing you into confusion" (v.10), versus "I" (i.e., Paul, who is teaching correctly).

Paul was fond of using athletic imagery to describe the Christian life, often including himself as a competitor (1Co 9:24–27; Gal 2:2; Php 3:13–14; 2Ti 4:7). To him life is a race, demanding adherence to rules and discipline if the race is to be completed successfully and a prize obtained. Here he applies the imagery to his converts. The Galatians had begun the race well. They had both assented to certain truths and adopted a Christian lifestyle. In other words, theirs was both a head and a heart religion. This is the full meaning of the phrase "obeying the truth." In spite of this good beginning, however, something had obviously gone wrong. Someone had hindered them by setting up an obstacle in front of them. In Paul's analogy, this probably refers to the illegal interference of a runner who cuts in ahead of another and thereby disadvantages that runner. Thus, the situation at Galatia was one in which the Galatians had already ceased, in some measure, to obey the plain truth of the Gospel.

8 But what should be said regarding the false teacher(s)? Much indeed. In three succinct statements Paul traces the origin, results, and end of such doctrine. (1) Somewhat understating the case, Paul says that the origin of the doctrine of salvation by works does not lie in "the one who calls you" (i.e., God; cf. 1:6). Rather, it proceeds from that which is hostile to God's grace. Though Paul does not say that it originates with Satan, that may well be the case.

9 (2) As the present results of such teaching, Paul asserts that it spreads. It is permeating, insidious, and therefore dangerous. No doubt Paul is quoting a proverb at this point (cf. 1Co 5:6). False teaching, like yeast, grows and affects everything it touches. Therefore, this alone would justify Paul's alarm at the state of affairs in the Galatian churches.

10 (3) Even though evil spreads, God will not permit it to triumph ultimately. In fact, its end is the opposite. Paul concludes with an optimistic expression of his confidence that the Galatians will return to a right mind and that the false teacher(s) will suffer God's judgment. What does "no other view" refer to? Does it mean "no other view" than the true Gospel? Than their first opinions formed as the result of Paul's teaching? Or than what Paul has just said regarding the origin and danger of the legalizers' teaching? The answer is not given. Any of the three is possible, and indeed Paul may have all of them in mind.

11 Two personal remarks conclude the section. The first presents a difficulty. What does Paul mean by saying, "If I am still preaching circumcision"? This cannot refer to his pre-Christian days only, for there would be no point to the criticism in that case. Furthermore, Paul links his alleged preaching to times in which he was persecuted as a Christian. But could anyone have actually made that claim about Paul? The most likely explanation is simply that Paul's words are a reply to an accusation that he did preach circumcision when it suited him, however unfounded or unlikely that accusation was. That accusation could have originated from views such as those expressed in 1Co 7:18 or from Paul's circumcision of Timothy (Ac 16:3).

The "offense [GK *4998*] of the cross" is an important concept in Paul and is an important reference in this context. Paul suggests that the preaching of the cross is so offensive to the natural mind that it arouses fierce opposition. But why should Paul link his refusal to approve circumcision for Gentiles to the offense of the cross? Obviously, for the same reason that he opposed it or any other human effort generally. All these things—feasts, circumcision, ceremonies, legal observances, or anything symbolizing external religion—are part of a system that seeks to attain standing before God through merit. In contrast, the cross proclaims our complete ruin in sin, so that nothing we do or can do can save us, and thus it also proclaims our radical need for God's grace. The natural self does not understand such teaching (1Co 2:14) and, in fact, hates it, because it strips away any pretense of spiritual achievement.

12 The second of Paul's personal remarks concerns the legalizers. It is his wish, expressed somewhat obliquely, that they would not stop with circumcision in their zeal for ordinances but rather would go on to castration. Sacral castration was known to citizens of the ancient pagan world. But for Paul to compare the ancient Jewish rite of circumcision to pagan practices even in this way is startling. Not only does it put the efforts of the Judaizers to have the Gentiles circumcised on the same level as abhorred pagan practices, but it actually links this desire to that which in Judaism disbarred one from the congregation of the Lord (Dt 23:1).

To many in our day Paul's expression sounds coarse and his wish reprehensible. But we may be sure that Paul did not speak out of a malicious spirit or in ill temper. He spoke out of a concern for the Gospel of grace and for God's truth. We too should wish that false teachers stop afflicting our churches.

C. Life in the Spirit (5:13–26)

Paul has already spoken of freedom several times in this letter (2:4; 4:26, 31; 5:1)—one of his central themes. But up to here, he has not defined it, at least not in practical terms dealing with the ethical life. Now he does so, showing not only what the true nature of Christian freedom is but also that only through the Spirit and by the Spirit's power can Christians live for God and not fulfill the desires of their sinful nature. Negatively, freedom in Christ is not license. Positively, it is service both to God and to other people and expresses itself in the great Christian virtues. This latter point is emphasized by two contrasting catalogs of the works of the sinful human nature versus the fruit of the Spirit.

One reason why Paul adds this section to his letter is to show what he means by "faith expressing itself through love" (v.6). A second reason is apparently to counter developing strife and divisiveness in the churches of Galatia, for the verses speak of a "biting," "devouring," and "destroying" of each other. The greatest reason, however, is undoubtedly Paul's desire to complete his portrait of true Christianity by showing that the freedom we have been called to in Christ is a responsible freedom that leads to holiness of life. Called to freedom? Yes! But this is a freedom to serve God and others as love dictates! Paul has in mind the fear within Judaism that a faith without law would not be sufficiently strong to resist the ethical debauchery of paganism.

1. Liberty is not license (5:13–18)

13 Like v.1, this verse is transitional and marks a new beginning. "You" is emphatic, showing that Paul is building on the confidence expressed earlier as to what side the Galatians are on (v.10). He echoes here the original challenge of v.1, but follows it up this time with a warning not to allow this freedom to become an excuse for sinful self-indulgence. Here the contrast is between indulgence and the serving of one another in love.

Christians must not allow their freedom in Christ to become a beachhead for the armies of indulgence to gain a foothold ("indulge," GK *929*; cf. 2Co 11:12) in their lives. Paul's reference to "the sinful nature" (*sarx*; GK *4922*) means all that a person is and is capable of doing as a sinful human being apart from the unmerited intervention of God's Spirit (see comment on v.16).

It is ironical that, having urged the Galatians not to become slaves to law, Paul should now encourage them to become slaves of one another, for that is what "serve" (GK *1526*) means. It is a paradox, but the paradox is instructive. The Galatians are to be slaves of one another, though this slavery is not at all like the first. In fact—this is the paradox—it is the Christian form of being free. Slavery to sin is involuntary and terrible; a person is born into sin (Ps 51:5) and cannot escape it (Ro 7:18). Slavery to law, which comes by choice, is foolish and burdensome. On the other hand, slavery to one another is voluntary and a source of deep joy. It is possible only because Christians are delivered through the presence and power of the Holy Spirit from the necessity of serving sin in their lives.

14 Throughout his letter Paul has been arguing against law and in defense of the Gospel of pure grace. Now, in a most striking fashion, he returns to law and seems to speak favorably of it, stressing that when Christians love and serve others, the law is fulfilled. There is a play on two meanings of the Greek word translated "summed up" (GK *4444*). On the one hand, it refers to the fact that the law can aptly be summarized by Lev 19:18 (a common rabbinic opinion, also endorsed by Jesus in Mt 22:39; Lk 10:25–28). On the other hand, the word can mean "fulfilled" (cf. Ro 13:8); in this sense Paul is suggesting that it is actually out of the new life of love made possible within the Christian community through the Spirit that the law finds fulfillment.

This use of the word "law" (GK *3795*) is most instructive, because it shows that in spite of all Paul has said, there remains a sense in which the requirements of the law are a proper concern for Christians. This does not mean that the Christian is to make progress in holiness by once again setting up a system of rules and regulations. But the essential ends of the law will be met in those who, being called by God and being filled with the Spirit, allow God to produce the Spirit's fruit within them. Faith in Christ is the bond that forms the basis for the fulfillment of God's holy will in one's life.

15 It is not hard to imagine the kind of strife that may have been present in the Galatian churches, either strife parallel to that of the Corinthians (1Co 1:10–12; 3:1–4) or strife arising directly out of the conflict with the legalizers. Paul does not say precisely what it was, but intense strife was definitely going on among the Galatians.

16 What is the solution to such biting, devouring, and destroying that is all too common among Christian assemblies? The answer, Paul says, is to "live by the Spirit." Then, and only then, will one cease to gratify the desires of the flesh. It is the Spirit alone who can keep the believer truly free.

The contrast between *sarx* ("flesh"; NIV "sinful nature"; GK 4922), on the one hand, and *pneuma* ("spirit"; GK 4460), on the other, is one of the characteristic themes in NT, and particularly Pauline, theology. It is as important, for instance, as the contrast between the observance of the law and the hearing of faith that has thus far dominated the letter. Although *sarx* can mean the whole person as conditioned by a bodily existence and by natural desires, in Christian vocabulary (especially in Paul), it came to mean a human being as fallen, whose desires even at best originate from sin and are stained by it. Thus, *sarx* came to mean all the evil that one is capable of apart from the intervention of God's grace in one's life; i.e., it is synonymous with "the natural man," "the old nature," or "the sinful nature." *Sarx* also contains thoughts of human limitation, both intellectually and morally (Ro 7:18). Thus, that which is flesh is incapable of knowing God apart from special revelation and the redemption that removes the barrier of sin (cf. 1Co 2:14).

The other term is *pneuma*, usually translated "spirit." Its earliest meaning is "wind," "air," "breath," or "life." Later it came to refer to the incorporeal part of a person, which (like breath) leaves at death. These meanings do occur in the NT. But the main emphasis is always on "spirit" as the Spirit of God or related to the Spirit of God. Indeed, it is because God breathes his spirit or breath into a person that that person has breath (cf. Ge 2:7). The incorporeal part of a human being has God-consciousness. In distinctly religious terminology, the Spirit of God takes up residence in Christians to enable them to understand spiritual things (1Co 2:14), receive Christ as Savior and Lord, call God "Father" (Ro 8:15; Gal 4:6), and develop a Christian personality. The Spirit is thus the presence of God in a person, through whom fellowship with God is made possible and power given for winning the warfare against sin in the soul.

The Spirit is not natural to a human being in one's fallen state. But this does not mean that by the gift of the Spirit a redeemed person escapes the need to struggle against sin. The Spirit simply makes victory possible—and that only to the degree that the believer "lives by the Spirit" or "walks" in him.

17 A characteristic of the contrast between *sarx* and *pneuma* is that the two principles are in deep and irreconcilable conflict. In the sense in which Paul uses the words, the sinful nature does no good and does not desire good, whereas the spirit does no evil and, indeed, opposes anything that does not please God (see Ro 7 for a fuller discussion of this same principle).

The last clause of this verse probably means that the sinful nature keeps a person from doing the good he or she desires (see Ro 7:15–16). Some have maintained that there is no conflict within the Christian because the old nature governed by the "flesh" has supposedly been eradicated. But this is not true. Naturally, the sinful nature is to become increasingly subdued as the Christian learns by grace to walk in the Spirit, but it is never eliminated in this life. So the Christian is never released from the necessity of consciously choosing to go in God's way and to depend on his grace.

18 The final verse of this section is best taken as a summary in which Paul reminds the Galatians that, though he is now talking of the need to live a godly life, he is not thereby reverting to legalism. Life by the Spirit is neither legalism nor license—nor a middle way between them. It is a life of faith and love that allows a person to be led by the Spirit.

2. The works of the sinful nature (5:19–21)

That *pneuma* and *sarx* (see comment on v.16) are in conflict is now illustrated by contrasting lists of the works of the sinful nature and of the fruit of the Spirit. At the same time, the lists are more than a mere proof of what he has written earlier. For by raising these particulars of conduct, he also provides a checklist for measuring the conduct of those who consider themselves spiritual. If one's conduct is characterized by the traits in the first list, then he or she is either not a believer or else a believer who is not being led by God's Spirit.

19 When Paul says that the "acts of the sinful nature" are obvious, he does not mean that they are all committed publicly where they may be seen. Some are, some are not. Instead, he means that it is obvious to all that such acts originate with the sinful nature, not with the nature given believers by God. Here the full scope of the word *sarx* ("flesh") becomes evident, for the list not only contains the so-called "fleshly" sins, but it also contains sins that emanate from every part of human nature.

Four divisions of sin are obvious in his list: (1) three violations of sexual morality; (2) two sins from the religious realm; (3) eight sins pertaining to conduct in regard to other human beings—i.e., social sins; and (4) two typically pagan sins.

(1) The first three words cover sexual sins. They are obviously intended to be somewhat comprehensive and inclusive. "Sexual immorality" or "fornication" (*porneia;* GK 4518) is the broadest term, denoting any immoral sexual intercourse or relationship. In starting with this vice, Paul begins with what was acknowledged to be the most open and shameless vice of the Greek and Roman world. "Impurity" (GK 174) refers to a person who was either morally or ceremonially unclean. Paul uses it almost exclusively of moral impurity. "Debauchery" (GK 816; cf. also 2Co 12:21) is an open and shameless contempt of what is proper. In this regard it is a fitting term for what is probably intended to be a climax of several evils.

20 (2) Paul goes on to list two sins of religion: "idolatry" (GK 1630), the worship of the creature rather than the Creator (Ro 1:21–25), and "witchcraft" (GK 5758), a secret tampering with and at times a worship of the powers of evil. These two terms are arranged in an ascending horror of evil and indicate that the works of the sinful nature include offenses against God as well as against ourselves or our neighbors.

(3) Neighbors are in view in the third section of Paul's list, since it includes much of what would today be called social offenses. Most of the words are self-explanatory. "Hatred" (GK 2397) means "enmities," such as those between classes, nations, and individuals. It is these enmities that have been broken down for those who are in Christ (Gal 3:28; Eph 2:14–16). "Discord" (GK 2251) is the natural outcome of hatred both in the world and in the church. Four out of six of Paul's uses of the word are connected with church life. "Jealousy" (GK 2419) and "fits of rage" (GK 2596) can denote both good and bad qualities. There is a godly jealousy or zeal (see comment on 4:17) as well as righteous anger. When either originates from selfish motives and hurt pride, however, it is evil and harms others. "Selfish ambition" (GK 2249) may be translated in many ways: contention, strife, selfishness, rivalry, intrigues. Its basic meaning is a selfish and self-aggrandizing approach to work. "Dissensions" (GK 1496) and "factions" (GK 146) denote a state of affairs in which people are divided and feuds flourish.

21 "Envy" (GK 5784) is so closely related to "jealousy" that it is hard to tell the difference between them, except for the fact that this attitude is always bad. This third set of words shows the sinful nature to be responsible for the breakdown in interpersonal relationships seen in all strata of society.

(4) The final grouping is concerned with sins of alcohol: "drunkenness" (GK 3494) and "orgies" (GK 3269). They denote pleasures that have degenerated into debauchery. There are more items that could be mentioned, for when Paul adds "and the like," he indicates that the list is not exhaustive.

Paul adds a solemn warning, saying that those who habitually practice such things will never inherit God's kingdom. This does not mean that if Christians fall into an isolated lapse into sin through getting drunk or some such thing, they thereby lose their salvation. Rather, Paul is referring to a habitual continuation in sins of the sinful nature, and his point is that those who continually practice such sins give evidence of having never received God's Spirit. When he says that he warned the Galatians of this previously (presumably when he was among them), he reveals that his preaching was never what one might call mere evangelism but that it always contained a strong dose of the standard of morality expected from Christians.

The reference to the "kingdom [GK 993] of God" introduces an entirely new and large subject, one that is an important and complex idea in the New Testament (see comment on

Mk 1:15). Here, however, Paul is doubtless thinking of God's kingdom only in an eschatological sense. The phrase "will not inherit" carries the thought back to Paul's words about Abraham in ch. 3. His point is that those who keep on living in the sinful nature give evidence that they are not Abraham's seed and therefore will not inherit salvation.

3. The fruit of the Spirit (5:22–26)

Paul continues his contrast between the natural productions of the sinful nature and Spirit that he had begun in v.19. Here, however, he speaks of the "fruit" (GK 2843) of the Spirit (using both a new term and the singular form) in contrast to the "acts" (v.19; GK 2240) or works of which the sinful nature is capable. The term "acts" already has definite overtones in this letter. It refers to what a human being can do, which, in the case of the works of the law (2:16; 3:2, 5, 10), has already been shown to be inadequate. The fruit of the Spirit, on the other hand, suggests that which is a natural product of the Spirit, made possible by the living relationship between the Christian and God through Christ (cf. 2:20; Jn 15:1–17). The singular form stresses that these qualities are a unity, like a bunch of grapes instead of separate pieces of fruit, and also that they should all be found in all Christians. In this they differ from the "gifts" of the Spirit, which are given one by one to different people as the church has need (1Co 12).

The nine virtues that are the Spirit's fruit hardly need classification, though they seem to fall into three categories of three each. The first three comprise general Christian habits of mind; their primary direction is Godward. The second set primarily concerns Christians in their relationship to others and are social virtues. The last three concern Christians as they are to be in themselves.

22 It is appropriate that "love" (*agape*; GK 26) should head the list of the Spirit's fruit, for "God is love" (1Jn 4:8), and the greatest of Christian qualities is love (1Co 13:13). In biblical texts it is the association of *agape* with God that gives the word its distinctive character. Divine love is unmerited (Ro 5:8), great (Eph 2:4), transforming (Ro 5:5), and unchangeable (Ro 8:35–39). It is this love that sent Christ to die for sinners and that perseveres with them in spite of their willfulness and desire to sin. Now because the Spirit of Christ is living within them, believers must show love both to other Christians and to the world. By this, people will know that Christians are indeed Christ's disciples (Jn 13:35).

"Joy" (GK 5915) is the virtue in the Christian life corresponding to happiness in the secular world. On the surface they seem related. But happiness depends on circumstances, whereas joy does not. In the NT a form of the word "joy" becomes a typical Christian greeting (Mt 28:9; Lk 1:28; Ac 15:23; 2Co 13: 11; Jas 1:1). Joy is particularly full when what was lost spiritually is found (Lk 15:6–7, 9–10, 32).

The second of the two most popular Christian greetings is "peace" (GK 1645; see comment on 1:3). Above all, peace is God's gift to us, achieved by him at the cross of Christ. It is peace with God (Ro 5:1) and expresses itself both in peace of mind (Php 4:6–7) and in a practical peace between all those who know God. This latter peace should be seen in the home (1Co 7:12–16), between Jew and Gentile (Eph 2:14–17), within the church (Eph 4:3; Col 3:15), and indeed in all relationships of believers with other people (Ro 12:18; Heb 12:14). Moreover, Christians are to strive for it (1Pe 3: 11). The importance of this word is evident in that it occurs in every NT book and eighty times altogether.

"Patience" (GK 3429) is the quality of putting up with others, even when one is severely tried. The importance of patience is evidenced by its frequently being used to describe the character of God, as in the great text from Joel: "Return to the LORD your God, for he is gracious and compassionate, *slow to anger*, and abounding in love, and he relents from sending calamity" (Joel 2:13).

"Kindness" (GK 5983) is the divine kindness out of which God acts toward humankind. It is what the OT means when it declares that "God is good," as it so frequently does. Christians should show kindness by behaving toward others as God has behaved toward them.

"Goodness" (GK 20) is hard to define. Though it is related to "kindness," it differs from it in being a more active term. The primary idea seems to be generosity that springs from kindness.

The last three virtues are concerned with Christians primarily as they are to be in themselves. They are to be characterized by "faithfulness" (GK *4411*), a word that also means "faith," but undoubtedly here means that which makes a person one on whom others can rely—i.e., trustworthiness or reliability. This word describes a faithful servant (Lk 16:10–12), including servants of the Gospel and of Christ (1Ti 1:12; 2Ti 2:2). It describes the character of those who will die for their confession of Christ (Rev 2:10; 3:14). It goes without saying that it is also descriptive of the character of Christ, the faithful witness (Rev 1:5), and of God the Father, who always acts faithfully toward his people (1Co 1:9; 10:13; 1Th 5:24; 2Th 3:3).

23 "Gentleness" (GK *4559*) describes those who are so much in control of themselves that they are always angry at the right time and never angry at the wrong time—e.g., Moses, who is praised for being the gentlest or meekest man on earth (Nu 12:3). This is the spirit in which discipline must be applied and faults corrected (Gal 6:1). It is also the virtue for meeting opposition (2Ti 2:25) and for giving a Christian witness (1Pe 3:15–16).

"Self-control" (GK *1602*) is the quality that gives victory over sinful desires and is therefore closely related to chastity both in mind and conduct. This quality enables a person to live and walk in this world without getting one's garments spotted by the world.

These are the qualities of the life that has been claimed by Jesus Christ and is led by the Spirit. "Against such things there is no law" (v.23b). The last clause is most likely an understatement used for rhetorical effect. The law, as Paul has said, was given to restrain evil; but these qualities do not need to be restrained. Hence, no law opposes them. There may also be a sense in which Paul is suggesting that the law cannot be against those who live in this manner because by being so led, they are in principle fulfilling all that the law requires.

The Fruit of the Spirit

The aspects of the fruit of the Spirit advocated by Paul in Galatians 5:22–23 occur not only here but also elsewhere in the Scriptures. Most of the attributes are those by which God himself lives.

Aspect	GK number	Definition	Attribute of God	Attribute for Christians
love	26	sacrificial, unmerited deeds to help a needy person	Ex 34:6; Jn 3:16; Ro 5:8; 1Jn 4:8, 16	Jn 13:34–35; Ro 12:9–10; 1Pe 1:22; 1Jn 4:7, 11–12, 21
joy	5915	an inner happiness not dependent on outward circumstances	Ps 104:31; Isa 62:5; Lk 15:7, 10	Dt 12:7, 12, 18; Ps 64:10; Isa 25:9; Php 4:4; 1Pe 1:8
peace	1645	harmony in all relationships	Isa 9:6–7; Eze 34:25; Jn 14:27; Heb 13:20	Isa 26:3; Ro 5:1; 12:18; 14:17; Eph 2:14–17
patience	3429	putting up with others, even when one is severely tried	Ro 9:22; 1Ti 1:16; 1Pe 3:20; 2Pe 3:9, 15	Eph 4:2; Col 1:11; Heb 6:12; Jas 5:7–8, 10
kindness	5983	doing thoughtful deeds for others	Ro 2:4; 11:22; Eph 2:7; Tit 3:4	1Co 13:4; Eph 4:32; Col 3:12
goodness	20	showing generosity to others	Ne 9:25, 35; Ps 31:19; Mk 10:18	Ro 15:14; Eph 5:9; 2Th 1:11
faithfulness	4411	trustworthiness and reliability	Ps 33:4; 1Co 1:9; 10:13; Heb 10:23; 1Jn 1:9	Lk 16:10–12; 2Th 1:4; 2Ti 4:7; Tit 2:10
gentleness	4559	meekness and humility	Zec 9:9; Mt 11:29	Isa 66:2; Mt 5:5; Eph 4:2; Col 3:12
self-control	1602	victory over sinful desires		Pr 16:32; Tit 1:8; 2:12; 1Pe 5:8–9; 2Pe 1:6

24 It should be evident by this time that the warfare between the sinful nature and the Spirit is both intense and unremitting. The qualities of each are fundamentally opposite, and those who feel caught in this warfare cannot do the good they would like to do. How, then, is victory to be achieved? What must believers do to triumph? In the final verses of this chapter Paul gives two answers.

First, he reminds his readers that when they came to Christ, they repented fully of the works of the sinful nature and indeed turned their backs on them forever. This act they must sustain. In speaking of this radical repentance, Paul uses the vivid image of crucifixion, though in a different way from such passages as Ro 6:6 and Gal 2:20. In those instances, the verb is in the passive voice ("was crucified," "have been crucified"), and the reference is to what has been done for believers as a result of Christ's death. But in this passage the verb is in the active voice ("have crucified") and points rather to what believers have themselves done and must continue to do. The proper term to describe this act is repentance. Thus believers have already repented of their former way of life to the degree of actually having executed the old nature. This does not mean that the battle is thereby over, however. As in an actual crucifixion, life lingers even though the criminal has been nailed to the cross. Nevertheless, believers must regard the decisive act as having been done. They are not to seek to remove from the cross what has once been nailed there.

25 The second answer is Paul's reminder that since believers have been made alive by the Spirit, they must also walk by the Spirit. The Spirit leads; they must follow. Indeed, they are to get in line with him or keep in step with him.

26 It is hard to tell whether this verse belongs with the preceding section or with what follows. Certainly, it is the first of a number of specific actions that should characterize those who are being led by the Spirit. On the other hand, it is also a return to the theme of v.15 and, therefore, a summation. This verse probably refers to a situation Paul knew to be existing in Galatia and hence is a direct attempt to discourage pride and dampen party spirit. Walking by the Spirit is the ultimate solution to such evils.

D. Two Practical Exhortations (6:1–10)

1. Bearing one another's burdens (6:1–5)

In the closing verses of ch. 5, Paul contrasted the works of the sinful nature and the fruit of the Spirit, concluding that Christians must live Spirit-led lives. But what does it mean to live a life characterized by love, joy, peace, patience, and the other virtues? To those who might prefer a mystical experience or a flight of fancy, it comes as a shock to find Paul returning at once to the most down-to-earth subjects—personal relationships (vv.1–5) and the use of money (vv.6–10)—and to find him measuring spirituality by action in these areas. Christians need to learn that it is in concrete situations, rather than in emotional highs, that the reality of the Holy Spirit in their lives is demonstrated.

1 The first situation is one that, more than any other, reveals the real character and spiritual maturity of a believer. Paul imagines a hypothetical situation—which is, however, not at all infrequent—in which one believer unexpectedly learns that another believer is trapped in some sin. What should one do? Does love mean that one should overlook the sin and refuse to face the facts? Or should one expose the sin openly and so gain a reputation for superior holiness? To Paul, a Spirit-led person should not proceed in either of these ways; he then goes on to describe the proper course of action.

First, Christians should restore the person who has fallen into sin. The verb used here is a medical term used for setting a fractured bone; what is wrong in the life of the fallen Christian must be set straight. It is not to be neglected or exposed openly.

Second, the work of restoration must be done by those who are "spiritual" (GK 4461). This word cuts two ways. It is obviously related to Paul's use of it at the end of ch. 5, as if to say, "Do you consider yourself to be a spiritual instead of a carnal Christian? Well, then, here is a good test. Restoring an erring Christian is exactly the kind of thing that spiritual Christians do." But Paul is also reminding his readers that only those who are genuinely led by the Spirit have the maturity to deal with sin in others. Every Christian should desire such maturity.

Third, the restoration should be made "gently" (cf. 5:22), being aware that no one is immune to temptation and that everyone can fall. Such an attitude avoids unkind gossip, prevents more serious backsliding, advances the good of the Church, and glorifies the name of Christ.

2 The second practical example of spirituality is the bearing of one another's burdens. Paul refers to helping other Christians—sharing their load—whenever temptations oppress them or life depresses them. Here Paul deliberately returns to the thought of love being the fulfillment of the law, for the "law of Christ" is the new commandment (Jn 13:34) fulfilled in part by such actions. The burdens we do impose on ourselves should be the burdens of mutual sympathy.

3 Two errors might keep believers from fulfilling this role of mutual sympathy. The first is conceit, i.e., Christians thinking themselves to be more important than they are. The implication seems to be that if Christians neglect or refuse to bear another's burdens, it is because they think themselves above it. But this is to be self-deceived, for, measured by God's standards, no one amounts to anything. A positive statement of the same principle occurs in Ro 12:3.

4 The second error that might keep believers from bearing the burdens of another Christian is to be always comparing themselves and their own works with others. This can be harmful both in a positive sense ("I am doing better than they are") and in a negative sense ("I am unable to do anything; everyone else is much better"). To counter both these forms of the error, Paul suggests that each believer has a task from the Lord and is responsible only to the Lord for doing it. To use others as a norm for one's activities is a kind of escape. When Christians have their eyes on God rather than on other Christians, then in their own eyes they will at best be unprofitable servants (Lk 17:10) and God himself will receive glory (2Co 10:12–18).

5 In other words, the duty of each Christian is to carry his or her own load. There is no contradiction between this verse and v.2, for different words are used for what one is to bear. The word in v.2 (GK 983) means "heavy burdens"—those that are more than one person should carry. The word in this verse (GK 5845) denotes a person's "pack." Each Christian has his or her own work to do, so let each one take pride in how they do it.

2. The use of money (6:6–10)

The second area to which Paul seeks to apply the life of the Spirit in a practical way is the use of money; indeed, few things more clearly disclose the priorities of the heart than this. While many commentators hesitate to relate this entire section to the use of money, and while it is true that the section as a whole goes beyond that topic, at least three factors indicate that Paul was thinking primarily of money. First, the phrase "do good to all" (v.10) is certainly a euphemism for giving alms, so that a concern for financial matters never entirely leaves Paul's mind. Second, v.7 is a proverb that Paul used on at least one other occasion to encourage generous giving (2Co 9:6). Finally, giving was important to Paul at this time, for the collection for the Jerusalem poor was part of his policy and the admonition to proceed with it was fresh in his mind as a result of the Jerusalem council (Gal 2:10). This passage may even be alluding to the collection.

Three uses of money are mentioned: (1) the support of the teacher in a Christian congregation, (2) the use of money to build up the life of the Spirit rather than to feed the flesh, and (3) the spending of money to help others, particularly Christians. The principle that ties all three points together is that enunciated in the proverb: reaping is in proportion to sowing.

6 The reference to the one "who receives instruction" probably does not imply a fully developed catechetical system, but it does point to a class of paid teachers at a surprisingly early date. Paul's own policy was to preach the Gospel without receiving money, preferring to earn his living as a leatherworker. But this was in pioneer work. As soon as possible he seems to have established a more fixed structure. So here, as elsewhere (1Co 9:11, 14; 1Ti 5:17–18; cf. Lk 10:7), he asserts that a worker is worthy of his pay.

To support the Lord's servants is not, however, a grim duty. Instead, Paul speaks of it as mutual sharing. As the teacher shares the good things of the word, so the congregation is to share all good things with the teacher (cf. Ro 15:27).

7 The special advice of v.6 is now enlarged to benevolence in general, and the principle that ties everything together is stated: "A man reaps what he sows." This is an immutable law of God, which the phrase "God cannot be mocked" emphasizes. Consequently, though people may fool themselves (by sowing little but expecting much), they cannot fool God, and the results of their poor sowing will be manifest.

8 The principle of sowing and reaping is especially true of Christian living. Those who spend their money on what gratifies their fleshly nature will reap a fleshly harvest. And since the flesh is mortal and will one day pass away, the harvest will pass away also. On the other hand, those who use their money to promote spiritual causes and to feed their spiritual nature will have a bountiful harvest. While the primary application of this principle is to money, it also applies more broadly. For example, if congregations refuse to support ministers and so forfeit good teaching, preferring to spend their money on themselves, the results will be corruption. But if, on the other hand, they support good teachers, a spiritual harvest will result. The principle also applies to the use of time, the use of the mind, etc.

9 The great hindrance to good sowing is weariness that results in discouragement and eventually in giving up. Four months elapse between planting and harvest (Jn 4:35); and, while it is true that in spiritual sowing the results may occasionally come sooner, more often they take much longer. The best reason for resisting weariness and giving up is that if the necessary preparation is done, the harvest is certain.

One cannot help feeling that Paul may be talking to himself as he thinks of the extensive but thus far unrewarding efforts he had expended on the churches of Galatia. The change to the first person plural supports this supposition.

10 Finally, Paul speaks broadly about the obligation to do good to all people, returning again primarily to the thought of giving money. But suppose a Christian is limited in his resources? In that case, says Paul, he or she should give primarily to Christian causes, knowing that if they are not supported by Christians, they will not be supported at all. One with unlimited funds should give to every valid charity that comes along.

Two parts of this verse are of special interest. (1) Paul speaks of the "family of believers." This really means those who have become related to us by believing in Christ and points to a relationship transcending all others. Giving should not be unduly restricted by denominational or party loyalty. (2) Paul mentions "opportunity" (GK *2789*; also translated "time" in v.9). This word denotes "the proper time" for anything; consequently a time that occurs only once before it is lost forever. No one can hope to reap a harvest before the time appointed for it by God (v.9). But if one does not seize the time appointed for sowing, he or she will never reap a harvest.

3. Conclusion (6:11–18)

The apostle has said nearly everything he wishes to say, and the letter is drawing to a close. He now takes the pen from the hand of his writing secretary and adds a summary in his own handwriting. It contains a fresh warning against the legalizers, a restatement of the basic principle that Christianity is internal and supernatural rather than external and human (as the legalizers were trying to make it), a final reference to his own suffering for the cause of Christ, and a benediction. The somewhat abrupt ending has the effect of leaving the great issue of the letter—faith or works—sharply before the Galatians.

11 There can be little doubt that Paul took the pen in his own hand at this point and that he did so for at least two purposes: (1) to authenticate the letter, as he seems also to have done on other occasions (cf. 1Co 16:21; Col 4:18; 2Th 3:17), and (2) to emphasize his main points. There is less agreement about the meaning of the words "large letters," though most now see this as referring to the size of his letters. But why write in large letters? It is generally assumed that Paul increased the size of his letters for emphasis, much as in contemporary printing a paragraph is italicized or set in boldface. Another possibility is that Paul's large letters were due to poor eyesight (cf. 4:15; perhaps also his "thorn in the flesh" in 2Co 12:7).

12 For the last time Paul speaks of the legalizers, this time warning the Galatians about what they were attempting to do and why they were doing it. The object of their legalism is "to make a good impression outwardly." The Greek for this phrase is richer than any single English translation can make it. For one thing, the verb translated "to make a good impression" carries overtones of insincerity; they were not what they seemed. The word "outwardly" is literally, "in flesh" (*sarx*; see comment on 5:16); it refers to people whom the legalizers wanted to impress, and to circumcision, which had become the touchstone of their religion. In contrast to this, Christianity consists in those who, as a result of his grace, have become new creatures (vv.14–15) desiring to please God.

But why did the legalizers persevere so strongly in their error if, indeed, as Paul claims, it is an error? There are two reasons. First, they desired to escape the persecution that is attached to Christ's cross. The cross on which the Son of God died presents three disquieting and humiliating doctrines: (1) human beings are sinners; (2) their sin brings them under the curse of God, which Christ bore; and (3) nothing they can do can earn salvation, for if this were possible, the cross would have been unnecessary. These doctrines humble people. Consequently, they hate the cross and actively persecute those who proclaim it.

13 Second, the legalizers persevered in their error because they desired to boast that they had been able to win over the Galatians to Judaism. There were two things wrong with this. (1) It was an attempt to win others to that which was itself bankrupt; for not even those who were circumcised (i.e., Jews) were able to keep the law. (2) It was based on pride; the legalizers wanted to boast in the "flesh" of the Galatians (i.e., in the number of circumcisions). They were trophy hunters and wanted to be able to report on mass "conversions" in Galatia. The humbling parallel would be in the tendency to take pride in counting the number of "decisions for Christ" or "baptisms" today.

14 Over against all such improper and sinful boasting, Paul sets an entirely different boasting of his own—a boasting "in the cross of our Lord Jesus Christ." So important is this cause of boasting that, says Paul, it is inconceivable that he could boast in anything else. It is striking how much of the Gospel is involved in this statement. The cross speaks of the atonement necessitated by human sin (see comment on v.12). The full name of the Savior speaks of the significance of his person and the role he played (lit., "God who saves, the Messiah"). Finally, the pronoun "our" speaks of the personal aspects of Christ's redemption, for it becomes "ours" through the response of faith.

The legalizers had a motive for their actions. Well, so did Paul—only his motive was not that of a fear of persecution or of a desire to boast in statistics; rather, he boasted in the cross of Christ because of what the cross had accomplished in his life. As Paul looks back on his life he realizes that before his conversion he was exactly like the legalizers. Once he, too, was ruled by externals and gloried in human attainment (Php 3:3–6). But when he met Jesus, all this passed for him, so much so that he is able even to apply the bold image of crucifixion to it. The world with its selfish attitudes was crucified to him and he to the world. In its place came Christ alone—Christ, who is everything.

15 The summary is brief. Neither circumcision nor uncircumcision counts for anything as a means of salvation (cf. 5:6; 1Co 7:19). The only thing that counts is to be born again, to become a new creation. This comes about not by observing the law in any form but by receiving the truth of the Gospel.

16 Has anyone yet missed the point? If so, Paul will state it once again in even starker language—"Peace and mercy to all who follow this rule, even to the Israel of God" (cf. the blessings of Pss 125:5; 128:6). This statement makes three points: (1) the peace and mercy of God are given only to those who adhere to this Gospel; (2) all who believe the Gospel have an obligation to continue walking in it; and (3) these, and these only, are the true Israel. "Rule" here clearly refers to the heart of the Gospel just enunciated, though it may also be applied to the "canon" of Scripture and to the whole of Christian doctrine. There can be no peace or mercy for the church when those responsible for following this "rule" depart from it.

17–18 Paul's last words are a request and a benediction. The request is that henceforth he be not troubled with the kind of problem that had erupted in the Galatian churches. He does not want them to trouble him any longer by giving way to the legalistic heresies, for he has suffered enough already. It would be far better if the churches he founded at such cost would assume their own share of suffering, above all by resisting the kind of teaching that the legalizers upheld and therefore, if necessary, by enduring whatever persecution might follow.

The "marks [GK *5116*] of Jesus" refer to the scars Paul bore on his body as the result of the persecutions he had endured for the sake of his Lord (cf. 2Co 6:2–6; 11:23–30). These marks revealed his relationship to Christ, just as the marks of a slave revealed his ownership. These genuine and honorable marks in the body contrast strikingly with the ritualistic mark of circumcision the legalizers wished to impose on the Galatians.

Paul ends the letter as he had begun it, upon the single and glorious note of God's grace, expressing the wish that this grace might abide with the spirits of the Galatians. The church will always know great days when whatever external marks there might be (v.17) are not an effort to impress God ritualistically but are a natural result of true Christian service.

The Old Testament in the New

OT Text	NT Text	Subject
Gal 3:6	Ge 15:6	Faith of Abraham
Gal 3:8	Ge 12:3; 18:18	Gospel to Abraham
Gal 3:10	Dt 27:26	Curse of the law
Gal 3:11	Hab 2:4	The righteous live by faith
Gal 3:12	Lev 18:5	Living by the law
Gal 3:13	Dt 21:23	Curse of the cross
Gal 3:16	Ge 13:15; 24:7	Offspring of Abraham
Gal 4:27	Isa 54:1	Joy of the barren woman
Gal 4:30	Ge 21:10	Expulsion of Ishmael
Gal 5:14	Lev 19:18	Love your neighbor as yourself

Ephesians

INTRODUCTION

1. Authorship

The letter to the Ephesians was accepted as the work of the apostle Paul until about the beginning of the 1800s, when his authorship came under suspicion. Such denials have persisted to the present day among a considerable body of scholars. But a strong case can still be made for the traditional view.

First, Ephesians clearly claims to have been written by Paul. The writer begins by identifying himself and proceeds in typically Pauline fashion to ascribe his apostolic authority to the will of God (1:1; cf. 2Co 1:1; Gal 1:1; Col 1:1). Paul's name also reappears later (3:1). The writer often uses the first person singular, and the self-portrait that emerges from these passages corresponds with what we know about Paul from other sources.

The structure of Ephesians is in line with the rest of Paul's correspondence. We can trace the same sequence of salutation, thanksgiving, doctrinal exposition, moral appeal, final courtesies, and benediction. Particularly striking is the author's treatment of ethics as an extension of theology, so typical of Paul. Furthermore, the language used is sufficiently similar to that of the other letters of Paul to substantiate his authorship.

Furthermore, the doctrinal stance of this letter is characteristically Pauline. While it is true that fresh emphases appear (particularly in the doctrine of the church), the reader gains the overall impression of continuity with Pauline thought. These familiar themes recur: God's gracious sovereignty (1:3, 9, 11, 12; 2:4–7), the centrality of Christ's work of reconciliation on the cross (1:7; 2:13–18), the resurrection and exaltation of Christ (1:20–22), and the distinctive ministry of the Holy Spirit (2:18, 22; 3:5, 16; 4:1–4, 30; 5:18; 6:18). While there are differences in his treatment of these themes, these developments are consistent with Paul's other letters. In other words, in Ephesians Paul seeks to relate the great doctrines he has previously handled to the concept of the church as the body of Christ through which the purpose of God is fulfilled.

Regarding external evidence, Ephesians was widely circulated and accepted as one of Paul's letters by the middle of the second century. It was listed in the canon of Marcion (c. A.D. 140) and in the Muratorian Canon (c. A.D. 180). That is, this letter was unhesitatingly assigned to Paul from the time when the NT corpus began to be recognized in the mid-second century.

2. Destination

a. The problem

To whom was this letter addressed? The title "To the Ephesians" was supplied at least as early as the middle of the second century and appears on all subsequent Greek manuscripts. It was almost everywhere acknowledged as directed to the Christians in Ephesus; the only exception is Marcion, who referred to it as the Epistle to the Laodiceans.

But uncertainty as to the destination of Ephesians and the originality of the title arises from a textual problem in 1:1. The definitive place name "in Ephesus" is omitted from some of the oldest and most reliable manuscripts. If "in Ephesus" did in fact appear in the original text, then reasons would have to be sought to explain its omission in the earlier manuscripts.

Furthermore, an examination of the letter itself serves to deepen the suspicions aroused by the textual dilemma. Paul does not appear to be acquainted with his readers personally, or at least not with all of them. He has only heard of their faith and love (1:15), and they have only heard of the stewardship of God's grace entrusted to him (3:2). Paul seems only to be able to assume that they have been taught the truth about Jesus (4:21). Yet Paul had remained in Ephesus for no less than three years. Could he have written like this to the Christians there?

There is little trace of local coloring in the letter. Timothy, for example, was with Paul when he wrote Colossians and Philemon (Col 1:1; Phm 1), two letters written about the same time. Timothy was well known in Ephesus (Ac 19:22), yet he is not mentioned in Ephesians. Moreover, there are no personal greetings, nor is a single word of familiarity or affection to be found. Even the benediction is in the third person and not the second, as in every other instance in Paul's letters (6:23–24). These considerations compel us to subscribe to the general consensus today, which considers it most unlikely that the Ephesian church was exclusively or immediately addressed.

b. Possible solution

Various solutions have been proposed to the lack of "in Ephesus" in 1:1. Of these, the best is to see this letter as a circular letter. On this view Ephesians is a letter intended to be read by Christians living in the Roman province of Asia, of which Ephesus was the capital. It was not addressed to any particular local congregation, but to all. From Ephesus it was circulated throughout the churches of Asia, no doubt by means of a courier (possibly Tychicus; cf. 6:21; Col 4:7). An alternate acceptable view is that at some stage copies of this letter were sent to other churches with the original destination erased, so that the church could fit in its own name. A few manuscripts omit "in Rome" from Ro 1:7, giving rise to a similar conjecture that this letter was also used for more a general distribution.

3. Background

The foundation of the Ephesian church was laid by the apostle Paul on his return from his second missionary journey. On his route from Greece to Syria, the apostle paid a visit to Ephesus, accompanied by Priscilla and Aquila, whom he left behind in the city (Ac 18:18–21). It was only a brief stopover, for he was hurrying on to Jerusalem. He found time, however, to engage in dialogue with the Jewish leaders in the local synagogue. He so impressed them that they begged him to remain. He was unable to change his plans, though he promised to return if that was God's will for him.

Clearly this proved to be so, for he included Ephesus in his itinerary on his next missionary tour and actually extended his stay to a period of approximately three years, probably from A.D. 54 to 57 (Ac 19:8, 10, 21–22). Evidently the apostle realized the strategic potential of the metropolis, situated on the main highway between east and west. Ephesus was surrounded by 230 independent communities within the Roman province of Asia. If the Christian faith were firmly established in the capital city, it could be spread from the hub to the rim.

While in Ephesus, Paul began by resuming his previous confrontation with the Jews, but he soon aroused opposition. He took his converts with him and transferred to the lecture hall of Tyrannus, where he held daily conferences over a period of two years (Ac 19:9). From Ephesus, all the residents of provincial Asia, Jews and Greeks alike, heard the word of the Lord (Ac 19:10). Those who came into the capital on business or for pleasure could not fail to hear of what was happening. Some apparently became Christians and then went back to their own towns to communicate the gospel. The places in Asia explicitly named in the NT include the seven churches referred to in Rev 2–3, together with Troas, Assos, Adramyttium, Miletus, Trogyllium, and Hierapolis.

This remarkable expansion led to and was temporarily halted by the disturbance described in Ac 19:23–41, when Demetrius the silversmith rallied his fellow trade-unionists to riot against the Christian movement. Paul was already on the point of departure, and this was the signal for his withdrawal. On his last voyage to Syria, he landed at Miletus and there took leave of the Ephesian elders, committing the oversight of the flock to them in a solemn and moving charge (Ac 20:18–35). Paul was never to visit Ephesus again. Yet it is altogether credible that he would wish to write a circular letter to the church in Ephesus and to all the Christian communities established during the Ephesian mission.

4. Place of Origin and Date

Paul wrote Ephesians from prison (3:1; 4:1; 6:20). Since Tychicus was the bearer of this letter (6:21), as well as of Colossians (Col 4:7) and presumably of Philemon also (cf. Phm 24), it may be deduced that these three documents belong to the same time and place. But where was Paul imprisoned? Three possibilities present themselves: Rome

(Ac 28:30), Ephesus (cf. 1Co 15:32; 2Co 1:8–10), and Caesarea (Ac 24:23)—see introduction to Philippians. Of these, the best (and the traditional) choice is Rome.

Paul was placed under house arrest in Rome for two years (Ac 28:30). The conditions of his free confinement allowed him scope to proclaim the gospel (Ac 28:16–17, 23, 31; Eph 6:18–20; Php 1:12–18; Col 4:2–4), and from prison he wrote Ephesians, Philippians, Colossians, and Philemon. A Roman imprisonment accords well with the personal references in each of these letters. The mention of the palace guard and the emperor's household in Php 1:13 and 4:22 favors it. The fact that Paul is conscious that he might have to face a sentence of death also confirms a location in Rome (Php 1:19–26; 2:17, 23). Aristarchus is associated with Paul's greetings in Col 4:10, and we are told in Ac 27:2 that he accompanied Paul on the journey to Rome. The presence of Luke (Col 4:14) during the Roman imprisonment is attested by Ac 28:14, 16.

The date of Ephesians is tied up with the question of its place of origin, and, of course, its authorship. If we are correct in our analysis of those two matters, then the letter was written sometime around A.D. 60, perhaps as late as 63. Almost certainly Ephesians was written shortly after both Colossians and Philemon.

5. Occasion and Purpose

While Paul was under house detention in Rome, he enjoyed certain privileges, such as the freedom to receive a constant stream of visitors. Representatives of the Jewish community came to inquire about Christianity (Ac 28:22–23), and some of Paul's intimate friends were with him (e.g., Luke, Aristarchus, and Timothy). From time to time he received messengers from churches that he had started, one of whom was Epaphras (see Col 1:7; 4:12; Phm 23). This man seems to have been instrumental in evangelizing the Lycus Valley region during the Ephesian mission and founded churches in Colosse, Hierapo-

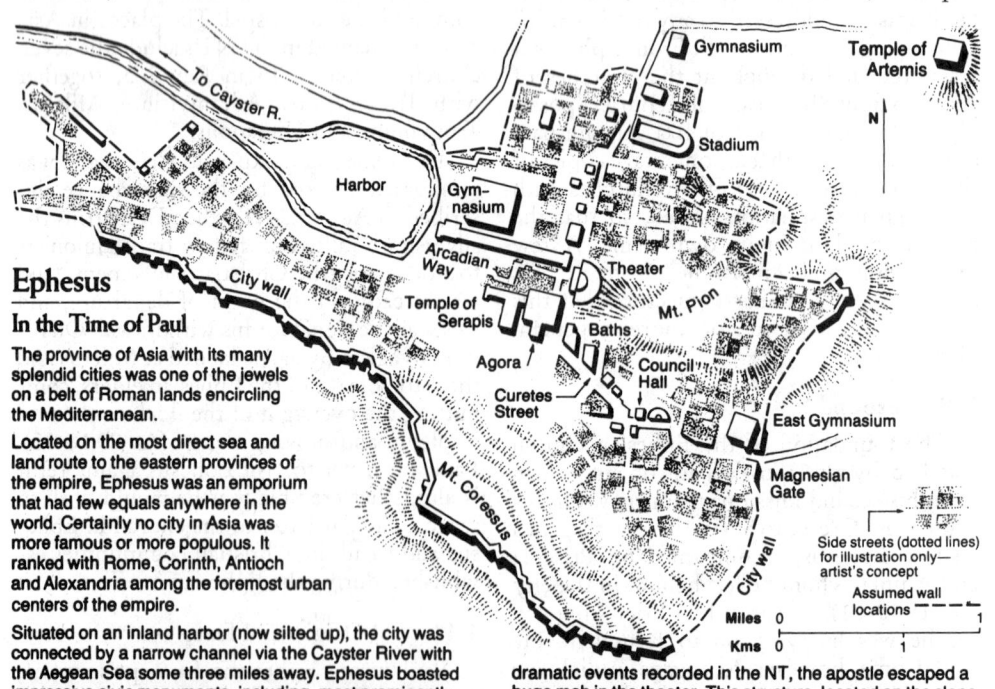

Ephesus
In the Time of Paul

The province of Asia with its many splendid cities was one of the jewels on a belt of Roman lands encircling the Mediterranean.

Located on the most direct sea and land route to the eastern provinces of the empire, Ephesus was an emporium that had few equals anywhere in the world. Certainly no city in Asia was more famous or more populous. It ranked with Rome, Corinth, Antioch and Alexandria among the foremost urban centers of the empire.

Situated on an inland harbor (now silted up), the city was connected by a narrow channel via the Cayster River with the Aegean Sea some three miles away. Ephesus boasted impressive civic monuments, including, most prominently, the temple of Artemis (Diana), one of the seven wonders of the ancient world. Coins of the city proudly displayed the slogan *Neokoros*, "temple-warden."

Here in Ephesus Paul preached to large crowds of people. The silversmiths complained that he had influenced large numbers of people here in Ephesus and in practically the whole province of Asia (Ac 19:26). In one of the most dramatic events recorded in the NT, the apostle escaped a huge mob in the theater. This structure, located on the slope of Mt. Pion at the end of the Arcadian Way, could seat 25,000 people!

Other places doubtless familiar to the apostle were the Commerical Agora, the Magnesian Gate, the Town Hall or "Council House," and the Street of the Curetes.
The location of the lecture hall of Tyrannus, where Paul taught, is unknown.

© 1985 The Zondervan Corporation

lis, and Laodicea. Epaphras came to Paul in Rome to bring a progress report about these congregations. There was much to rejoice about, but he also told Paul about a virulent heresy that was threatening Christians in Colosse and perhaps others (see introduction to Colossians).

Tychicus, another friend of Paul and a native of Ephesus, was also with Paul at this time. He was about to leave for the province of Asia, and Paul took advantage of using him as a courier for Colossians. Also, Onesimus (a fugitive slave from Colosse) had been befriended by Paul at this time and had confessed Christ. He had defrauded his master Philemon, and Paul was anxious that he be pardoned and possibly released for Christian service. Paul therefore decided to send Onesimus along with Tychicus (see introduction to Philemon).

But before Tychicus and Onesimus left, Paul finished a third letter to take along—one that he sent to Ephesus and to all the churches founded as a result of his mission throughout Asia. As befits a letter intended for more general circulation, Paul did not deal with particular issues (as in Colossians). His aim was not to combat error and expose false teaching. Rather, it was more detached and therefore more exalted. He rose above the smoke of battle and captured a vision of God's sovereign plan that transcends the bitterness of controversy and the necessity for the church militant to fight incessantly for its very existence. Consequently, he treated his doctrinal themes more broadly in terms of the fellowship of Christians in Christ's body, the church, and the reconciliation of the entire universe to him. Yet Paul's objective was not purely inspirational. He sought to relate his vision to the practical demands of Christians living in a hostile society.

6. Theological Values

Ephesians is above all a hymn of unity. Paul's conception of oneness in Christ extends beyond the church to include all creation. God's ultimate purpose is "to bring all things in heaven and on earth together under one head, even Christ" (1:10). Yet our Lord has been appointed as "head over everything for the church, which is his body, the fullness of him who fills everything in every way" (1:22–23). The corporate aspect of Christ's Saviorhood and Lordship, adumbrated in other letters and particularly in Colossians, is here expounded more thoroughly.

Unity was a topic of general interest in the first century A.D. The Stoic philosophers recognized an orderliness in the universe which they attributed to the cosmic Reason or Logos. The fact that much of the Mediterranean world was politically unified under the imperial government led to the vision of a universal commonwealth. At the same time the mystery cults, which were gaining in popularity as conventional religion declined, offered a certain sense of oneness in the common quest for deliverance from demonic forces and the achievement of personal integration.

In Ephesians Paul was able to demonstrate that this almost obsessive search for unity finds its ultimate goal only in Christ. It is he who represents the coordinating principle of all life. The ideal of world citizenship, cherished by the philosophers, is realized in the universal church. Human beings can be liberated from bondage to the principalities and powers that threaten their welfare only as they share the triumph Christ gained over them at the Cross (1:21; 2:2; 3:10–11; 6:12–13; cf. Col 2:15). Thus the distinctive theology of Ephesians is no academic abstraction. It was tuned to the contemporary mood of Paul's day, and in a deeply divided world today it still conveys a relevant word from God.

EXPOSITION

Salutation (1:1–2)

1 As in his other letters, Paul adopts the conventional form of address used in letters of the period. Usually a writer identified himself, named the prospective recipients, and added some expressions of greeting. Paul freely expanded or contracted these three items as circumstances required.

Each phrase of this salutation can be paralleled in other Pauline letters. Paul usually refers to his apostleship at the opening of his letters. "Apostle" (GK 693) is a comprehensive term for one who bears the NT message. It was applied first to the original disciples (Mt 10:2; Ac 1:2) and then to other Christian missionaries (Ac 14:14; Ro 16:7). Paul claimed that, like that of the Twelve, his commission came directly from Christ (Ac

26:16–18; 1Co 9:1). This title stresses the authority of the sender and the accountability of the one sent. Paul alludes to "the will of God," not in order to draw attention to his own status but to reflect his awareness that his mission did not arise from any qualifications he himself might possess.

Paul regularly addresses "the saints" (GK *41*) in the church to which he writes. This word is the normal NT designation for Christians; it denotes inward, personal consecration to God. As in Col 1:2, he describes them as "faithful ... in Christ.""Faithful" (GK *4412*) combines the ideas of trust and fidelity. This exercise of faith with its matching faithfulness is possible only "in Christ Jesus." On the particular question whether "in Ephesus" belongs in this letter, see the introduction.

2 "Grace" (GK *5921*) and "peace" (GK *1645*) reflect the standard greetings in Greek and Hebrew (cf. Ro 1:7b). Paul prefers to replace the Greek *chaire* ("rejoice") by *charis* ("grace") as embodying the essence of the gospel. For "peace" (Heb. *shalom*; Gk 8934), see Ezr 4:17; 5:7; 7:12; Da 4:1; 6:25, et al. Paul associates "the Lord Jesus Christ" with "God our Father" as the originator of these blessings. The name of Christ appears in each of the three clauses in this opening salutation. What follows in the body of Ephesians has to do with the relationship between "the saints" and their living Lord.

II. Doctrine: The Implications of Christian Faith (1:3–3:21)

A. An Act of Praise (1:3–14)

As in previous Pauline letters, the first part of Ephesians is doctrinal and the second part practical. In this case, however, the whole doctrinal section (1:3–3:21) is a thanksgiving expressed in the language of worship and prayer.

3 The focus of praise in vv.3–14 is what God has done in Christ. Christian faith and life have their center in God's Son, and the letter therefore opens with an expression of gratitude for all that is found in him. It is cast in the form of a Jewish blessing. Its structure is poetic and is ruled by parallelism, though scholars are not agreed as to how its stanzas are to be grouped.

"Praise be to" (or "blessed be"; GK *2329*) is used exclusively of God (Father or Son) in the NT to indicate the One who alone is worthy of worship. "Father of our Lord Jesus Christ" is a distinctively Christian addition arising out of a unique relationship. God who is to be blessed has already blessed all his people in Christ through the saving events of his life, death, and resurrection. A blessing in the OT denotes the bestowal of good; it is often material and invariably specific. God's blessings for us in Christ are more exclusively spiritual but nonetheless definite. These benefits are "spiritual" (GK *4461*) in nature because they are communicated to us through the Holy Spirit, whose function is to transfer to believers all that God has achieved in Christ. They have already been secured "in the heavenly realms" (cf. 1:20: 2:6; 3:10; 6:12) where Christ now reigns, having triumphed over "the spiritual forces of evil" (6:12) that threatened to usurp control. Their value is measured by the price that was paid to obtain them when on the cross the Son of God fought satanic opponents and disarmed them (Col 2:15).

4 Paul now traces the spiritual blessings of v.3 to their ultimate source in the eternal purpose of God. Christians have been selected in Christ prior to the work of creation. The verb "chose" (GK *1721*) is the usual one employed in LXX in connection with God's choice of Israel. Before the foundations of the world were laid, God had determined that all who believed on his Son should be saved.

Election in Christ has a moral aim in view: to be "holy" (GK *41*) and "blameless" (GK *320*). "Holy" means to be set apart for God in order to reflect his purity; "blameless" means "free from blemish," like the sacrificial animals presented on the altar in the old dispensation. The latter word is applied to Christ himself (Heb 9:14), to the ideal church (Eph 5:27), and to Christians at the end of the age (2Pe 3:14; Jude 24) and also now (Php 2:15).

5 The NIV takes "in love" (v.4) as starting a new sentence, thus emphasizing the loving nature of predestination. Any interpretation of this mysterious doctrine that detracts from the love of God is rightly suspect. It has to do with those who through Christ are to be received into God's family by adoption. Under

Roman law, an adopted son enjoyed the same status and privileges as a real son. Christ is God's Son "by nature"; believers are so by adoption and grace, yet they are co-heirs with him (Ro 8:17). The basis of this gracious action is in the character of God himself—his "pleasure" (GK 2306) and "will" (GK 2525).

6 The ultimate aim throughout the divine plan of redemption is that the recognition of God's merciful dealings with people should evoke unlimited praise. The "grace" (GK 5921) that evokes such praise finds its richest outlet in God's love-gift to us—his Son. It is the objective grace of God that is in view, indicating his favorable regard, rather than the further ethical effect of that grace in making us gracious.

The Son is referred to as the one the Father loves. "Beloved" is a title applied in LXX to Israel in its special role as God's chosen race, along with "Servant" and "Elect." Because of his filial obedience, Jesus gained the Father's approval.

7–8 Paul proceeds to list some of the blessings that flow from the matchless grace of God. It may be that an early Christian confession of faith underlies this text. These blessings are all "in Christ"; he is not only their source but also their sphere (cf. Col 1:14). They are enjoyed by the believer in the present.

"Redemption" (GK 667) has to do with the emancipation either of slaves or of prisoners. The term implies the payment of a ransom price, a factor frequently reflected in its usage. Here it is specified as being "through his blood" (cf. Col 1:20). The price paid for our redemption from bondage to sin was costly beyond measure; it was the very lifeblood of Christ himself, poured out in his death on the Cross. What was foreshadowed in the Levitical system of sacrifices was realized at the Cross when the Son of God laid down his life in death and ransomed us from sin.

"Forgiveness" (GK 912) means loosing a person from what binds him or her; it stems from a verb meaning "to send away" (GK 918). When God deals with our sin, it is dispatched into the wilderness like the scapegoat (Lev 16:20–22). Here, however, the reference is not to "sin" (GK 281), as in Col 1:14, but to "sins" (GK 4183). The first term denotes a sinful condition; the second, sinful acts or deviations from the right path. Forgiveness deals with both. The magnanimity of God displayed in redemption and remission of sins is in proportion to "the riches of God's grace" (a Pauline expression that also occurs in 1:18; 2:4, 7; 3:8, 16).

These riches of grace have been "lavished" (GK 4355) on us; God always gives generously. Paul then enumerates further blessings: every kind of "wisdom" (GK 5053; i.e., knowledge which sees things as they really are) and "understanding" (GK 5860; i.e., discernment that leads to right action).

9–10 What God has thus revealed is the mystery concerning his will. "Mystery" (GK 3696) is a recurring term in this letter (3:3–4, 9; 5:32; 6:19). Here, as in the rest of the NT, it simply means a truth once hidden but now made known (Ro 11:25; Col 1:26; cf. Mt 13:11, 35). For many Jews in Paul's day, the secret plan of God would become apparent at the end of the age. In the NT the unlocking of that mystery has now taken place by virtue of Christ's appearance in the flesh, and there is no need to wait till the last day. This affirmation may be intended to counteract the incipient Gnosticism appearing in Asia Minor (see introduction to Colossians). "Us" covers all believers (cf. "we" in vv.11–12).

All this is in accordance with God's "pleasure" (as in v.5), which has been set out in Christ (cf. v.11; Ro 1:13; 3:25). From all eternity, the Father cherished in his own mind a plan "to be put into effect" (GK 3873) in Christ (cf. 3:9). This has now been revealed to the church through Paul. In the rest of Ephesians the content of the plan is more fully elaborated. Here the apostle restricts himself to a brief summary.

This plan takes place when the messianic age is inaugurated. Salvation history is regarded as unfolding in a series of "times" (GK 2789) that reach their climax in the advent of Christ (Gal 4:4). The Christian era has still to run its course, however, and not until its close will God's eternal purpose come to full fruition (Ac 1:6). Then universal reconciliation will be achieved; God will "bring ... together under one head" (GK 368) everything in heaven and on earth under Christ (cf. 1Co 15:24–28; Php 2:10–11). This recognition of Christ's preeminence will ensure that the original harmony of the universe is restored (Ro 8:18–21). Christ's mission extends beyond the human race and assumes cosmic dimensions.

11 Paul now passes on to a further consideration—namely, that Christians have been "chosen [as heirs]" (GK *3103*). Israel was regarded as the Lord's inheritance and portion. The church, the new Israel, now enters into the same privilege (Ro 8:17; Gal 3:29; Col 1:12). This apportionment stems from the divine foreordination (cf. vv.4–5). It is no accident that God has allotted to his new people in Christ the inheritance designed for those who recognize the Savior. But we must not think that Christians have somehow usurped Jewish privileges. Before time began, God marked out those in Christ to be co-heirs with his Son. Whatever he decides is put into effect, for he is the one who ensures that everything is worked out in line with his own will (cf. v.5).

12 So far, what Paul has written applies to Jews and Gentiles alike, united in the one body of Christ. Now he refers in turn to one class (v.12) and then to the other (vv.13–14). The "first to hope [GK *4598*] in Christ" (lit., "the Christ" or "the Messiah") were Jews who recognized Jesus as their Messiah prior to the conversion of the Gentiles. This expectation of God's coming deliverer was distinctive to the Jews; the Gentiles had not entertained any such prospect (2:12). Paul earlier showed that the adoption of Christians as God's children furthers the praise of his glorious grace (v.6). Here he says that their participation in the divine inheritance will have a similar effect. The "glory," or revealed character, of God will shine out through them and evoke praise from the whole universe (3:10).

13 "You also," in contrast to "we," clearly identifies the Gentile Christians in Ephesus (cf. 2:19). They are only addressed in this specific manner in order to remind them that they are fully incorporated into the body of Christ. Jews can no longer cling to their former prerogatives; Gentiles are equal partners and in every respect share the inheritance. In the Christian community there are no second-class citizens.

It is the hearing of faith that brings salvation. The Ephesians had embraced "the word of truth"—i.e., the teaching that told them the truth because it was derived from the God of truth (4:21). The truth they needed to know was that they as Gentiles had a place in God's redemptive plan (2Co 6:7; Col 1:5; Jas 1:18). This was good news indeed, and through accepting it they were liberated from bondage to sin.

Hearing, faith, and salvation were immediately followed by the sealing of the Holy Spirit. At the moment they believed, the Ephesian Christians received the stamp of the Spirit (cf. Ac 19:2). Paul does not have water baptism primarily in mind here, but rather what water baptism symbolizes—the effusion of the Holy Spirit himself. He is made available to believers according to the promises recorded in the OT and confirmed by Jesus. The Holy Spirit is at once the one promised and the one in whom the promises are fulfilled.

A "seal" (GK *5381* & *5382*) had various uses, all of which are instructive as applied to the Holy Spirit. It was affixed to a document to guarantee its genuineness. It was attached to goods in transit to indicate ownership and ensure protection. It also represented a designation of office in the state service.

14 Paul adds a further analogy: The Holy Spirit is a "deposit" (GK *775*; cf. 2Co 1:22; 5:5). This word is borrowed from the commercial world and means a deposit or first installment in hire purchase. It is a token payment assuring the vendor that the full amount will eventually follow. Paul regards the Holy Spirit as the first installment of the Christian's inheritance. At the end of the age God will redeem his pledge and open the treasuries of heaven to all who are his in Christ. Meanwhile, the Spirit gives us the assurance that these things will one day be ours.

B. A Prayer of Intercession (1:15–23)

The Christian "blessing" in vv.3–14 has intervened between the opening salutation and the thanksgiving that normally follows it in Paul's letters. Although Paul uses the customary formula of gratitude in v.16, this section becomes a prayer of intercession from v.17 onward.

15 Paul's thanksgiving for the spiritual progress of the Ephesian Christians arises out of what he has just written in vv.13–14. News had been brought to him in Rome about the continuing "faith" and "love" displayed by those whom he now addresses (cf. Phm 5). Faith finds its focus in Christ and expresses itself in love to others (Gal 5:6). We need not assume that the reference in this verse is to their initial experience of Christ and that Paul therefore did not know them personally. On the other hand, if Ephesians is a circular letter, there may well have been some readers who were not actually known to him.

16 Paul assures the Ephesians of his unremitting remembrance of them in his prayers—both thankfulness and intercession. He had already taken on similar responsibilities in relation to other churches. "Remembering" (lit., "making mention") implies that those for whom Paul prayed were actually named before God.

17 The apostle addresses his constant prayer on their behalf to God, the only one who is capable of answering it (v.3). "Glorious Father" is a typical expression that points both to God's essential being and to what proceeds from it in mercy (v.7). Paul prays that his readers may be fully endowed with the Holy Spirit. God has already made provision for this, but it was necessary that they themselves should be quickened with the spiritual powers of wisdom and vision. "Revelation" (GK 637) refers here to the insight and discernment that the Spirit brings into the mysteries of divine truth (1Co 2:14, 16). All this is so that they may get to "know" God more completely.

18–19 Paul now employs an unusual and figurative expression ("the eyes of your heart") to denote an inner awareness, provided by the Holy Spirit, that realizes everything that God has made available to them. The "heart" (GK 2840) is the seat of thought and moral judgment as well as of feeling. Three items are selected for particular attention. (1) Calling ("called"; GK 3104) is regarded here as a pledge of "hope." This call has already taken place (2Ti 1:9) and yet represents an ongoing calling (1Th 2:12; 5:24); it looks to the future, since it is attached to the "blessed hope" (Tit 2:13) of eternal glory.

(2) Paul wants his readers to appreciate that they will inherit all the "riches" of God himself (cf. vv.11, 14). Old Israel was promised an inheritance on earth; new Israel is given an inheritance in heaven. The everlasting Canaan-rest of glory is assured all the saints, and God's faithfulness will be vindicated.

(3) Paul wants his readers to recognize the "incomparably great power" of God. The word "incomparably" (GK 5650) suggests an unimaginable divine potency that is directed toward all who believe. Paul then proceeds to collect all the synonyms he can lay hands on as he describes how the "power" (GK 1539) of God functions according to the "working" (GK 1918; cf. 3:7; 4:16) of the "strength" (GK 3197; cf. 6:10) of his might (GK 2709; cf. 6:10; a word used of bodily strength and muscular force).

20 Having piled up the vocabulary of divine power, Paul shows where it was most impressively exerted—in the resurrection of Christ and his subsequent exaltation to the place of authority. Paul has no hesitation in ascribing the resurrection of Jesus to the Father in accordance with other Scriptures. Yet Father and Son are so at one in this, as in all things, that our Lord could also claim in Jn 10:19 that he had authority both to relinquish his life and to resume it again.

Paul links with Christ's resurrection his ascension and his sitting down at God's right hand in heaven. God not only raised his Son from the grave but exalted him to the seat of power. Paul alludes here to Ps 110:1; the exaltation of the king of Israel as the Lord's anointed found its ultimate application in Christ's exaltation. Although spatial imagery is involved, we must not think of God's right hand as a place but as a symbol of authority. Similarly, the "heavenly realms" are not to be identified with outer space (cf. v.3).

21 "Far above" (cf. 1:10; Heb 9:5) is not a dimensional expression but simply indicates the superiority of Christ. "Rule" (GK 794), "authority" (GK 2026), "power" (see v.19), and "dominion" (GK 3262) no doubt reflect various degrees of angels in the Jewish hierarchy. They are not to be classified in a graded series, nor should we ask whether the ranks are arranged in ascending or descending order. Angels were thought to control human destiny, but Paul sees Christ as controlling them with absolute authority because he is infinitely superior.

Paul then proceeds to use a comprehensive phrase ("every title that can be given") to include not only those names known now by people living on earth but also those that will be used in "the [age] to come." The familiar contrast between the present era and the coming messianic age was adopted by writers in the early church who nevertheless recognized that for those in Christ the last days had already begun.

22 The apostle winds up this opening chapter by underlining the exaltation of Christ. The verb "placed . . . under" (GK 5718) refers not only to the supremacy of Christ but also to the subjection of all things to him (cf. 1Co 15:27). Psalm 8:6 (cf. Heb 2:8) is clearly in Paul's mind. The psalmist affirms humanity's dominion on earth; here Paul claims that Christ, as God's new man, has universal dominion. Human beings have largely forfeited their status through sin, but through Christ they are restored to their proper dignity. So far from constituting a threat to the realization of true humanity, the Christian gospel provides the only means by which it can be attained. Only at the end of the age will the consummation take place, when death itself will be finally overcome; yet even now the Christian becomes a new creation in Christ Jesus (2Co 5:17).

We might have expected the apostle to explain (cf. Col 1:15–20) that, as head over everything, Christ is head of his body, the company of believers. But that is not how he puts it. Instead, he says that Christ in his exaltation over the universe is God's gift bestowed on the church. In other words, the head of the church is also the head of all things. The church can thus overcome all opposition because of the absolute Lordship of Christ.

23 The church is described as Christ's body (Col 1:18). It is so not only in symbol but in fact (cf. 4:4, 12, 16; 5:30). The church is not an institution but an organism. It exists and functions only by reason of its vital relationship with the risen Lord as its Head. This picture of the church as a body deriving life and power from its Head is developed only in Ephesians and Colossians. In Paul's earlier letters the church is regarded as a body because its members are coordinated in a common function (see Ro 12:4–5; 1Co 10:17; 12:22–27; but cf. 1Co 11:3).

The church is further described as "the fullness of him who fills everything in every way." The precise significance of these enigmatic words has been widely discussed. "Fullness" (GK 4445) here suggests two things: (1) that which is filled with Christ; i.e., the church contains the fullness of Christ; (2) that which is filled by Christ; i.e., the church is filled by Christ not only with his own life and presence but also with the gifts and blessings he bestows. As his body, the church manifests Christ to the world, but it can do so only as he fills it with himself (Col 3:19) and with all his gifts of grace (Eph 4:7, 11; cf. 1Co 12:1–11). But this Christ also fills the whole universe. He is at once immanent within the church and transcendent over it, as he is both within and above the cosmos. This carefully balanced statement of Christ's role was designed to encourage the church militant here on earth.

C. Life from Death (2:1–10)

Ephesians 2 elaborates ch. 1. In vv.1–10 the theme of redemption (1:7) is developed in terms of God's raising of humanity from the death of sin to the new life in Christ (a theme that permeates Romans). From v.11 on, the theme of reconciliation (1:10, 22–23) applies to the relationship between Jews and Gentiles in the church. Throughout the chapter Paul contrasts humanity prior to the revelation of faith with humanity under faith.

1 "As for you" resumes the second person of 1:13, 15–18 and anticipates v.11 ("you who are Gentiles by birth"). However, as v.3 makes clear, the Jews are in no better condition, for the sinful human nature is shared by all alike (cf. Ro 2:1–3:20). Redemption has made it possible for human beings to be brought from death to life (v.5). Without God, people are spiritually dead (Col 2:13) and utterly unable to meet the requirements of the divine law (Ro 7:9). Paul is not speaking here about physical death nor only about the sinner's ultimate fate in the second death. What is meant is a real and present death. The most vital part of a person's personality—the spirit—is dead to the most important factor in life—God.

"Transgressions" (GK 4183) are lapses, while "sins" (GK 281) are shortcomings. This repetition simply serves to underscore the multiplicity of ways in which our spiritual death is evidenced.

2 Verses 2–4 are a typical Pauline digression. The mention of "transgressions and sins" in v.1 leads the apostle to supply a fuller account than he had intended of the Ephesians' former way of life. As a result, he does not pick up the thread of his original sentence until v.5.

To "live" (lit., "walk about"; GK *4344*) is the customary word used in the Greek OT for one's manner of life. This use is carried over into the NT and is prominent in Paul's writings (cf. 2:10; 4:17; 5:2). The Ephesians' former walk-about, Paul adds, was in accordance with "the ways [lit., "age"; GK *172*] of this world [GK *3180*]" (cf. these same two words in 1Co 3:18–19). The terms represent the same idea from the standpoints of time and space respectively. The word "age" may even represent the devil (cf. 1 Cor 2:8).

In any case, the evil one is certainly identified in the two clauses that follow. He is the "ruler" (GK *807*) of a realm said to be "of the air." Taken literally, this would signify the atmosphere around the earth, which, according to ancient cosmology, was the abode of demons. Paul may be adopting that term as a figure of speech to suggest Satan's dominion. Satan is also the unholy "spirit" (1Co 2:12) who apes the operations of his divine counterpart by being constantly "at work" (the same basic word as used of the Holy Spirit in Eph 1:19–20, implying a mutual rivalry). "Those who are disobedient" discloses the fact that rebellion against God and refusal to believe in him are inherent in humankind (Eph 5:16).

3 "Among them" refers to the "disobedient" rather than to "transgressions and sins" (v.1). So far Paul has been depicting the former lifestyle of Gentile Christians. Now he admits that Jewish believers were no better, for they too once "lived" an earth-bound life in the grip of sin. Nor does he exclude himself from this general indictment (cf. "all of us"), despite his claim to have been technically blameless under the law (Php 3:6; but cf. Ro 7:7–11).

The past life of Jewish Christians, like that of the Gentiles, was dominated by the appeal of fallen nature. The "sinful nature" (lit., "flesh"; GK *4922*) is not merely the body but the whole person orientated away from God and toward one's own selfish concerns. Human beings have a multiplicity of sinful urges. "Thoughts" refers not to the mind itself but to the projects it entertains with uncontrolled abandon. The natural human being is altogether at the mercy of the tyrant self and its rash impulses.

Because of all this, the Jewish converts were just as much in danger of God's "wrath" and judgment as anyone. "By nature" (GK *5882*) contrasts with "by grace" in vv.5, 8. Those who prefer to stand on their own and refuse to accept what God has done for them in Christ are self-condemned.

4 Over against humanity's churlish rejection of God, Paul sets God's gracious acceptance of human beings in Christ. Though he cannot approve of sin if he is to remain righteous, God is not hostile toward those he has created. He loves them and has made possible their reconciliation to himself. Had he decided to destroy his refractory children, he would have been entirely justified, and nothing could have averted the catastrophe (Hos 13:9). Instead, love led to "mercy" (GK *1799*)—God's compassion for the helpless, issuing in action for their relief. There is an inexhaustible treasury of such mercy in the loving heart of God.

5 The main verb of this extended sentence in the Greek does not emerge until this verse (see comment on v.1). Paul's main point is that God "made us alive with [GK *5188*] Christ" (cf. Col 2:15). This is the first of three verbs that describe what God has done in Christ for every Christian (the other two are in v.6). For those who were spiritually dead in transgressions, God gave new life together "with Christ." This is not the language of mysticism but of fact. The life Christians now possess is an effect of which Christ's resurrection was the cause.

Christ's revivification was by an act of God's power (cf. 1:19–20); the regeneration of believers is by an act of God's "grace" (GK *5921*; a bold, definitive assertion that is reiterated in v.8). Salvation is viewed retrospectively. The Ephesians are now in the position of having been saved.

6 In addition to making us alive with Christ (v.5), God has "raised us up" with him (GK *5283*; cf. Col 2:12) and has "seated us with" (GK *5154*) him on his throne "in the heavenly realms." Jesus actually left the tomb in which he had been laid and appeared to his disciples; forty days later, he ascended into heaven (Ac 1:6–11) and sat down at the right hand of the Father (1:20–21). Both these

Comparison of Ephesians and Colossians

Paul wrote both Ephesians and Colossians about the same time, from prison in Rome. There are an amazing number of similarities in content between these two books.

Theme	Ephesians	Colossians
Paul's greeting	1:1–2	1:1–2
Holy and without blemish in God's sight	1:4; 5:27	1:22
Redemption through Christ's blood	1:7	1:14, 20
Wisdom, knowledge, and understanding from God	1:8, 17	1:9–10
Knowledge of God's will	1:9	1:9
All things (re)created through Christ	1:10	1:16
Paul heard about faith and gave thanks	1:15–16	1:3–4
Paul's continual prayer for Ephesians/Colossians	1:16	1:9
The believer's hope	1:18	1:5, 27
An inheritance for the saints	1:18	3:24
Strengthened by God's power	1:19; 3:16; 6:10	1:11
Christ's power over rule, authority, and dominion	1:21	1:13, 16; 2:10, 15
Christ as the head of his body, the church	1:22; 4:15–16	1:18, 24
Christ as God's fullness	1:23; 3:19	1:19; 2:9
Christ fills all things	1:23	3:11
Apart from Christ people are dead in sin	2:13	2:13; 3:7
God made us alive in Christ and in his resurrection	2:5–6	2:12–13
Reconciliation through Christ's blood	2:13	1:20
Christians called to peace	2:14–15	3:15
Christ abolished the law and its regulations	2:14–15	2:14
Being built up in Christ	2:20–22	2:7
Paul's call by God's grace to reveal God's mystery	3:2–4	1:25–27; 2:2
God's grace at work in Paul	3:7, 20	1:29
God's mystery hidden for centuries	3:9	1:26
Rooted in Christ and his love	3:17	2:7
Humility, gentleness, patience, and love	4:20, 31; 5:1	3:12–14

events have their counterpart in the experience of believers. Not only do they anticipate resurrection and glorification at the end of the age; they are matched by a present realization of the risen life in Christ and of our participation with him in his ascended majesty (Col 3:1–4).

7 All this was done by God in Christ with a single end in view: to demonstrate in successive ages "the incomparable riches of his grace" (cf. 1:7, 18; 2:4, 7; 3:8, 16). This was God's publicity program for the whole of history—and beyond. He planned a continuing exhibition of his favor toward humankind to cover all the centuries between the ascension and the return of Christ, and after that through all eternity (cf. Jude 25). This dimension implies that it will be for the benefit of angels as well as human beings. "Kindness" (GK 5983) is love in tender action, which God showed to humans when it was most needed (Ro 5:8).

8 Paul again reminds his readers (cf. v.5) that they owe their salvation entirely to the undeserved favor of God. "Grace" is the objective, operative, and instrumental cause of salvation. Paul expands v.5 by adding that the medium that apprehends salvationis "faith" (GK 4411), which is also its necessary condition. Faith, however, is not something a person can produce; it is simply a trustful response that is itself evoked by the Holy Spirit.

Lest faith should be in any way misinterpreted as our contributing in any way to our own salvation, Paul immediately adds a rider to explain that nothing is of our own doing; rather, everything is the "gift of God." The

Theme	Ephesians	Colossians
Encouragement to unity	4:3	3:14
Becoming mature/perfect in Christ	4:13	1:28
Obtaining fullness in Christ	4:13	2:10
Growth in Christ	4:16	2:19
Apart from Christ, alienation from God	4:18	1:21
Impurity and lust in unbelievers	4:19	3:5
Putting off the old self and putting on the new	4:22–24	3:9–10
Putting off falsehood and lies and speaking the truth	4:25	3:9
Putting away filthy language	4:29; 5:4	3:8
Speaking in order to help others	4:29	4:6
Getting rid of anger, malice, and slander	4:30	3:8
Being forgiving	4:31	3:13
Believers should allow no one to deceive them	5:6	2:4, 8
God's coming wrath	5:6	3:6
Doing what pleases the Lord	5:10	3:20
Walking carefully and making the most of every opportunity	5:15	4:5
Singing psalms, hymns, and spiritual songs	5:19	3:16
Giving thanks to God the Father	5:20	3:17
Instructions for wives	5:22	3:18
Instructions for husbands	5:25	3:19
Instructions for children	6:1	3:20
Instructions for fathers	6:4	3:21
Instructions for slaves	6:5–8	3:22–25
Instructions for masters	6:9–10	4:1
Praying and keeping watch	6:18	4:2
Praying for Paul, the missionary	6:19–20	4:3–4
Tychicus as Paul's messenger	6:21–22	4:7–8
Closing benediction	6:24	4:18

entire process of salvation comes from nothing that we have done (cf. Ro 10:17).

9 Paul firmly excludes *every* possibility of self-achieved salvation by adding to his emphasis in v.8, "not by works." The apostle does not specify these "works" (GK 2240) as those related to the law, since he is not thinking only of Jewish Christians. Any kind of human self-effort is comprehensively ruled out by this terse expression. The reason is immediately attached: it is to prevent the slightest self-congratulation. If salvation is by the sheer unmerited favor of God, boasting is altogether out of place.

10 This verse is the outcome of the whole process. It shows what salvation is intended for: to produce the good works that attest its reality. While works play no part at all in securing salvation, Christians will prove their faith by works. Here Paul shows himself at one with James (see Jas 2:14–26).

We are God's "workmanship"—his work of art, his new creation. "Created" (GK 3231; also in OT, 1343) is a verb used exclusively of God and denotes the creative energy he exerts. The creation takes place "in Christ Jesus" (cf. vv.6–7). The life of goodness that regeneration produces has been prepared for believers to "do" from all eternity. Here is a further reason why Christians have nothing left to boast about. Even the good they now do has its source in God, who has made it possible.

D. Jews and Gentiles Reconciled (2:11–22)

In vv.1–10 Paul considered the moral condition of the Gentiles before their conversion to Christianity. Now he reminds them of their previous deprivation in terms of their religious status as estimated from a Jewish point of view.

11 "Therefore" refers back not simply to v.10 but to the entire paragraph (vv.1–10), which presents a single sentence in the Greek text. Second-generation Gentile Christians, such as those now emerging, were apt to forget their former disadvantages. They had been and indeed still were "the Gentiles": the article specifies the underprivileged group to which they belonged. They were non-Jews or pagans so far as their physical descent was concerned. The rest of the verse elaborates on the distinction by citing the contemptuous nickname attached to them by the Jews: "uncircumcised." Paul does not himself use it in a derogatory manner: he simply reports its use. As a Jew, however, he points out that the self-styled circumcisionists have nothing to boast about, since an external man-made mark in itself holds no spiritual significance. Real circumcision is of the heart (Gal 5:6). Physical circumcision used to be a token of the covenant, but its function ceased when redemption was accomplished in Christ.

12 The apostle goes on to urge the Ephesians to recall what they once were in their heathen state. Four successive phrases depict their debit as compared with the Jews (cf. Ro 9:4–5). (1) They were "separate from Christ"—they had no expectation of a Messiah to light up their darkness. They knew nothing at all about him. (2) They had no rights of "citizenship" (GK *4486*) in his kingdom by reason of their birth. This word contrasts with the more intimate expression "members of God's household" in v.19; it signifies a commonwealth or state. (3) The Gentiles were not entitled to the benefits accruing to the covenantal community. In this respect, they were in the position of "foreigners," who could not claim the prerogatives of nationals. (4) As a consequence, they lived in a world devoid of "hope" (1Th 4:13) and "God." This does not imply that they were forsaken by God, but that, since they were ignorant of him (Gal 4:8), they did not believe in him.

13 Quickly and eagerly Paul turns from the tragedy of the Gentiles' former desolation to the joy of their reconciliation in Christ. "But now" stands in sharp antithesis to v.12. They are no longer "separate from Christ" (v.12) but "in Christ Jesus." He is the sphere of their new possibilities. The historical name "Jesus" is added at this point to suggest that he is not only the anticipated Messiah of the Jews but the Savior of all (see comment on Mt 1:21). Those who trust in him possess a present salvation as well as a future hope.

"Far away" and "near" are words that describe the position of Gentiles and Jews (the original reference in Hebrew related to distance from Jerusalem). God's word of peace to both groups is recorded in Isa 57:19 and is fulfilled through the sacrifice of Christ on Calvary (cf. 1:7; 2:15–17).

14 Christ and no one else has solved the problem of our relationship with God and with other people. He draws people to God and to each other in his own person. It is not simply the message he proclaimed or even the message proclaimed about him that effects this reconciliation. It is himself (cf. Mic 5:5). That is, Paul announces that Christ is "peace" as well as "life" (Col 3:4) and "hope" (Col 1:27). The "I am" sayings recorded in the Fourth Gospel provided a foundation for such assertions.

Christ is both peace and peacemaker. He actually brought about the reconciliation of Jew and Gentile when he died on the cross. There he made both into one (cf. vv.15–16). Paul thinks of two parts being united as one whole. Then he personalizes it and speaks of "two" men being recreated as "one new man." Christ has thus removed "the hostility" that existed between these deeply divided groups. The battlement created by hatred has been broken down forever.

This hostility Paul describes as a "barrier" (GK *5850*), a word that means simply a "fence" or "railing." It recalls the common rabbinic idea of the law as a fence dividing the Jews by their observance of it from all other races and thus arousing hostility. There may be a further allusion to Ps 80:12, where the word also occurs. The breaking down of the protecting wall that surrounded Israel the vine prepares the way for God's strong man (Ps 80:17).

The second word describing hostility is "dividing wall" (GK *3546*); it is a much rarer word and literally means a "middle wall." Josephus used this term (as well as the previous one) to refer to the balustrade in the Jerusalem temple separating the court of the Gentiles from the temple proper. On it was an inscription that read: "No foreigner may enter within the barricade which surrounds the sanctuary and enclosure. Anyone who is caught doing so will have himself to blame for his ensuing death." When Jerusalem fell in A.D. 70, this partition was demolished along with the temple itself. But Paul saw it as already destroyed by Christ at the cross. Ironically enough, he himself had been wrongfully accused of taking an Asian Gentile, Trophimus, past this checkpoint (Ac 21:29).

15 The barrier between Jews and Gentiles was overthrown when Christ effectively disposed of the old law with its meticulously defined sanctions enshrined in its innumerable decrees. Paul does accept that in itself the law is right and good, but he insists that the unregenerate are incapable of complying with its legal demands (Ro 3:19–31; 7:7–12; 8:2–4). "Abolishing" (GK 2934) is a favorite Pauline verb not easy to translate. Literally it means "to make ineffective or powerless." In Lk 13:7 it refers to ground exhausted by a barren tree; it also sometimes meant "to bring to a standstill or to put out of action." Eventually it signified "to invalidate, nullify, quash." Paul is thinking of the abolishing of the totality of the law considered as a moral burden.

It was in his crucified flesh that our Lord accomplished the annulment of the law (cf. v.17), so that he might "create in himself" the new humanity of which he as the second Adam is the Head. The Christian is no hybrid but a new creation (v.10).

16 "To reconcile" (GK 639) is a uniquely Pauline verb (cf. Col 1:20, 22) that involves the idea of restoration to a primitive unity (Eph 1:10). The purpose of Christ's death was not simply that Jews and Gentiles should be reconciled to each other (v.15), but that both of them together should be reconciled to God. "This one body" is neither the crucified body nor the glorified body of Christ. Rather, it suggests that in addition to Jews and Gentiles, a third type of person has now appeared—Christians. This phrase therefore refers to the church (cf. 1:23; 3:6) as the place of peace (cf. Col 3:15). This reconciliation has been brought about "through the cross"; by it the death blow was dealt to the longstanding antipathy between Jew and Gentile and between human beings and God.

17 Another factor in the reconciliation is now added: the preaching of peace. When did Christ come to bring the good news of peace, so that Gentiles far away as well as Jews near at hand could hear it? Clearly it was not during his earthly ministry prior to the cross. Was it after the resurrection and before his ascension? No, it was by the Spirit and through the apostles, as the missionary program of the infant church was inaugurated in obedience to the Great Commission (Mt 28:19–20). Paul suggests that the once-alienated Gentiles are now accorded priority, even though the gospel was taken first to the Jews (cf. Ro 1:16).

18 It is solely through Christ that both Jews and Gentiles now have their "access" (GK 4643) to God the Father. This word was sometimes used to designate the official in an oriental court who conducted visitors into the king's presence. Is this approach to the Father ensured "by one Spirit" (i.e., the Holy Spirit; cf. 1Co 12:13) or "in one spirit" (i.e., the unity in the body of Christ created by the Holy Spirit)? While a case can be made for either, it is best to follow the NIV in referring it to the Holy Spirit, making the trinitarian implications of this verse obvious.

19 Paul now draws a conclusion from vv.14–18 and expands on v.13. Two technical terms commonly denoting inferiority of status are contrasted with "fellow citizens." "Foreigners" (GK 3828) refers in particular to short-term transients; "aliens" (GK 4230) to those who had settled in a country of their choice. These latter were sojourners who received protection and legal status by paying a small tax, though they had no intrinsic rights. Such had been the position of the Gentiles in relation to the kingdom of God before the coming of Christ. But now they enjoy all the privileges of God's new people. They are united with the saints of the past (1:18) as well as with contemporary Christians (cf. vv.21–22). In addition, the Gentiles are "members of God's household"; this phrase describes theocracy in its domestic aspect.

20 "Built" (GK 2224) allows Paul to develop a favorite metaphor of his. When the Gentiles became Christians, they were placed on a firm foundation. In 1Co 3:11 Paul calls Christ himself the foundation. Here, however, the apostles and prophets constitute the foundation as those who were closely associated with Christ in the establishment of the church. They were the witnesses of his resurrection appearances and the preachers of the good news. Filled with and guided by the Spirit, they had a unique role in establishing the church.

Apostles and prophets head the list of leaders in the church set out in Eph 4:11 (cf. 1Co 12:28–30). The apostles included Paul himself (cf. comment on 1:1). The prophets were those of the new Israel, not the old. Christ is the "the chief cornerstone" (GK 214). This word refers to the capstone or binding stone that holds the whole structure together. It covered a right angle joining two walls. Often the royal name was inscribed on it. In the East it was considered even more important than the foundation.

21 Paul expounds on the significance of the building. The function of the cornerstone (v.20) is precisely defined by "joined together" (GK 5274; cf. 4:16), a verb embracing the complicated process of masonry by which stones are fitted together.

Paul refers to "whole building" rather than to each separate building. It has no article in the Greek, implying that the work is still in progress—i.e., "all building that is being done." "Rises" strengthens the insistence on continuing progress and organic growth. The word used for "temple" (GK 3724) denotes not the entire holy precinct, but the inner shrine. This metaphor is applied in the NT to both the individual and the church (cf. 1Co 3:16–17; 6:19; 2Co 6:16). Without doubt, Paul had the Jewish temple in mind, but he may also have had in mind the famous temple of Artemis at Ephesus, which was one of the seven wonders of the world. Paul's mission in Ephesus had brought him into head-on collision with the cult of the goddess (Ac 19:23–41).

22 "In him" continues the theme of v.21 (cf. 1:11–12) and "you too" links with v.13. Once again Paul emphasizes continued building. The aim of this entire process is that the church should become God's "dwelling" (GK 2999), a frequent term in LXX to denote the divine resting place either on earth or in heaven. Formerly, God's earthly abode was thought to be on Mount Zion and in the Jerusalem temple. Now he makes his home in the church. All this is achieved not only *by* but also *in* the Spirit.

E. Grace and Apostleship (3:1–13)

Paul continues the prayer that he began in the opening chapter and has never really abandoned, despite asides and digressions. Once again, however, there is an interruption, for no sooner has he announced in v.1 that it is for the sake of the Gentiles that he finds himself under house arrest than he is diverted from his main theme (resumed in v.14) as he explains how his ministry as the apostle to the nations was given to him. What prompts this parenthesis in vv.2–13 is the mention of his imprisonment in v.1. He hastens to assure the Ephesians that his present circumstances are not to be regarded as a hindrance to his apostolate (v.13).

1 "For this reason" (repeated in v.14) connects immediately with 2:22, but Paul recalls 2:11–22 and perhaps what lies even further back than that. "I, Paul" is left suspended without a verb until v.14, where it is at last supplied—"I kneel." Having identified himself by name, Paul is reminded of his captivity in Rome. He refuses to regard himself as a victim either of the Jews or of the Roman emperor; rather, he is "the prisoner of Christ Jesus." He insists that his imprisonment is a mark of his apostleship.

Furthermore, it was his championship of the Gentile cause that had brought about his arrest in Jerusalem (Ac 21:21, 28). It was on account of an Ephesian convert, Trophimus, that he had eventually run afoul of the Jewish mob. "You Gentiles" follows on from Eph 2:11.

2 Paul elaborates on his ministry as a preacher to the Gentiles. He assumes that his readers are aware of his special commission, having heard about it either from Paul himself when he was with them or by report from others.

Paul refers to his ministry as an "administration [GK 3873] of God's grace." The term usually means stewardship or task (Col 1:25). Here and in 1:9, however, it means the implementation of a strategy. Paul is not referring here to saving grace as in 2:5, 8, but to what enabled him to fulfill his calling as a missionary to the Gentiles (cf. vv.7–8; 4:7–13). Despite his personal unworthiness as one who had persecuted the church, Paul was God's chosen instrument to carry his name before the Gentiles as well as to Israel (Ac 9:15).

Furthermore, Paul recognizes that the extension of gospel privileges to the Gentiles is itself an act of grace (Ac 11:23), a grace given him for their benefit.

3 The nature of this administration of grace now becomes clear. It has to do with the "mystery" or secret plan (see comment on 1:9) by which God determined to incorporate the Gentiles into the one body of the church (2:16) as equal partners with Israel (3:6). This was disclosed by means of direct "revelation" or spiritual enlightenment (1:18). No doubt Paul's reference here is to his experience on the Damascus road when he was commissioned as the apostle to the Gentiles. He adds that he has already dealt with this subject of the "mystery" in passing, presumably in the previous part of his letter (e.g., 2:11–22 or even 1:9–10). "Briefly" means in a few words or a short space.

4 As they reread the earlier portions of the letter, the Ephesians will be able to judge for themselves whether Paul has really grasped the essence of God's secret plan. "Understand" (GK *3783*) is to receive into the mind or perceive; an element of intellectual discrimination is implied. "Insight" (GK *5304*) results from the revelation (v.3) and represents the profound comprehension God grants his own. In Col 1:27, the "mystery" is Christ's residence in or among believers, giving them an expectation of future glory. Here it has to do with the inclusion of the Gentiles as those who now inherit such promises (cf. vv.3, 6).

5 Although God's blessing intended for Gentiles through the people of God was revealed in the OT from Ge 12:3 onward, it was not proclaimed so fully or so extensively as now under the new dispensation. In particular, OT saints did not clearly realize that the old theocracy would be superseded by the body of Christ composed of Jews and Gentiles forming "one new man" (2:15). "Men" in this verse is literally "the sons of men," a Hebraic phrase that means human beings in general, in contrast with "sons of Israel"— the normal designation of Jews. These people now form God's new community.

This further disclosure was made to the whole church of Christ (1:8–10, 17–18) through the "apostles and prophets" (2:20), of whom Paul was one. Indeed, he was the first to receive this truth that was not immediately recognized by the rest. The apostles and prophets are designated as "holy" because they were set apart for the special task of proclaiming Christ. Paul is not arrogantly assuming moral superiority here (cf. v.8), but displays a serene and modest objectivity.

The instrument of revelation, as always, is the Holy Spirit. There may well be a subtly ambiguous allusion here, as elsewhere in the NT (cf. Ro 1:4), to the interplay between the Holy Spirit and the human spirit (Eph 1:17; cf. 2:22; 5:18). This is particularly relevant in the context of revelation.

6 The content of the mystery is now stated, summarizing 2:11–22. It is that through the proclamation of the gospel, the Gentiles are received into the fellowship of Christ on an equal footing with Hebrew Christians. Paul describes this fellowship with three terms, each having the word "together." (1) The Gentiles now "are heirs together [GK *5169*] with Israel." In Ro 8:17 Paul speaks of believers being "co-heirs with Christ." Here, as in Gal 3:29 and 4:7, he stresses that in Christ Gentiles are co-inheritors of the kingdom along with the Jews. This is how far the new witness of Jew and Gentile stretches.

(2) They are "members together of one body" (GK *5362*) and hence enjoy a corporate relationship. Paul seems to have coined this term to meet the unique situation created by the gospel, for it is found only here in the NT and is afterward exclusive to Christian writers. No other society is comparable with the church, since Christ is its Head (Eph 4:15; 5:23; Col 1:18).

(3) Because of Christ, they are "sharers together" (GK *5212*) in the covenant promises originally made with Jews (cf. the contrast with 2:12). This union of Jews and Gentiles in one body is a logical consequence of the central doctrine of the gospel that God accepts all who believe.

7 Paul explains how he himself was enlisted in the service "of this gospel," not through any ambition or qualification of his own but solely through the gift and calling of God (v.2; cf. Col 1:23, 25). The important word here is "servant" (GK *1356*). The NT rejects titles of high office and focuses on a word altogether unassociated with prestige. "Servant" designates a table waiter who is always at the bidding of his customers. In the NT, it denotes one who lives and works in the service of Christ and the church.

Paul again stresses that his apostolic function came from God (cf. vv.2, 8) and adds that it came "through the working of his power." He recognizes that the dramatic intervention which transformed him from an enemy into a friend of Christ was nothing less than an act of divine omnipotence. Now his apostleship reflects God's power at work in the church (1:19–20).

8 "Given me" forms a link with v.7 (cf. v.2). "Less than the least" is a unique combination of comparative and superlative. Literally it is "more least." Perhaps there is a playful allusion here to Paul's own name (v.1), meaning "little." In 2Co 12:11 Paul acknowledges that in himself he is a nobody, while at the same time recognizing that God has made him a somebody. Such humility is an essential qualification for effective service.

Paul's God-given commission is "to preach [lit., to announce the good news; GK 2294] to the Gentiles." In doing so, he is continuing Christ's own ministry (see 2:17, where the same verb is used). "Unsearchable" is that which cannot be traced out; the accent lies on the boundless treasury of riches in Christ.

9 Paul was called to "make plain" (GK *5894*) to everyone the outworking of this mystery of God (see comments on vv.3–5). That is, he was to shed a flood of light on what had earlier been hidden, so that no one would need to be in the dark anymore. This mystery (v.6), now available to all, was for long ages consciously concealed in the mind of God so that not even angelic intelligences knew it (cf. v.10; Col 1:26). This was in accordance with God's deliberate policy. It was formed before time began (1Co 2:7), but the concealment dated from the inception of the ages (Ro 16:25). In his capacity as the universal Creator, God thus determined what his strategy would be, and the inference is that the world was brought into being with the realization of this purpose in view (1:9–10). "God, who created all things" may be directed against heretical teachers in Asia who anticipated the Gnostic dichotomy between creation and redemption, ascribing the former to subordinate agencies (see the introduction to Colossians).

10 The ultimate goal of both creation and redemption is the manifestation of the divine "wisdom" (GK *5053*). This wisdom displayed in creation and embodied in Christ is a many-splendored thing, iridescent with constantly unfolding beauties. What had been screened from the angelic hierarchy (cf. 1:21) is now to be declared through the body of Christ on earth (2:6–7). The ecclesiological implications of such a verse as this are staggering indeed (cf. 1Pe 1:12). Through the mirror of the church, the angels of heaven see the glory of God.

11 Again Paul reverts to God's overall "purpose" (GK *4606*) recognizable through all his dealings (1:11). This purpose is "eternal," suggesting not only the infinite length but also the complexity of God's age-long purpose (Heb 1:1). In v.9 the "ages past" appear to begin in time and end with Christ. This purpose God "accomplished in Christ Jesus our Lord." Paul has more than its conception and predetermination in mind here; he is also deeply concerned with its historical realization.

12 A practical conclusion is drawn from these considerations. The centrality of Christ has a bearing on the devotional life of believers. In Christ and on the ground of faith in him we can enter God's presence (2:18) without the inhibitions that might arise from any sort of self-reliance and self-consciousness. "Freedom" (GK *4244*) is liberty of speech, a word that is normally used in relation to people (cf. 6:20), but here in relation to God. Such openness of speech leads to confidence before God, because he graciously accepts those who come to him through Christ. In turn, after enjoying such freedom of access to God, the Christian acquires a new boldness before other people (6:19).

13 Paul rounds off his account (begun in v.2) of the administration of God's grace that has been entrusted to him. He makes a request, arising from what he had said in v.1 about his imprisonment. There he had made it clear that what he endured was for the sake of the Gentiles. Now he repeats the assertion that his sufferings are for them, but he begs them not to lose heart because of his predicament. After all, he has learned to take his share of Christ's continuing passion (Col 1:24). Those sufferings are the price to be paid so that blessing may come to the Gentiles. Paul saw his trials as their glory, and they must learn to look at them like that too.

F. Knowledge and Fullness (3:14–21)

This section contains Paul's actual prayer. After his parenthesis in vv.2–13, he resumes his prayer, comprising three major petitions (vv.16–17a; 17b–19a; 19b), the first two of which lead into the next, with the last preparing for the closing doxology (vv.20–21). This prayer has a trinitarian outline, in which the apostle asks that his readers may possess the strength of the Spirit (v.16), the indwelling of Christ (v.17), and the fullness of God (v.19).

14 "For this reason" is repeated from v.1 as Paul proceeds along the line he had digressed from in vv.2–13. Because the Gentile Christians are now incorporated into the body of Christ, he prays that they may appropriate their spiritual privileges to the full. Paul says he "kneels." Standing was the more normal posture among the Jews but kneeling was not unknown (cf. Da 6:10). It symbolizes submissiveness, solemnity, and adoration. Paul turns in prayer "before the Father." The word for "before" indicates an intimate relationship; he addresses God as Father because through the redemptive act of Christ access is now made possible to him through the Spirit (2:18).

15 The Father is the One after whom "the whole family" is named. Paul confines the concept of family here to believers. This is altogether in keeping with the context and the inference drawn from 2:18–19 (cf. 2:20, 22; 3:6). This family of God is not confined to earth but embraces heaven as well. This may simply refer to the church triumphant, but could include the angelic hosts, described in rabbinic literature as "the higher family."

16 Paul now sets out the content of his prayer in three items: vv.16–17a; 17b–19a; 19b. As in 1:17–18, the prayer is concerned with the appropriation of God's provision in Christ through the Spirit. The divine resources that make this possible are described as "his glorious riches" (see comments on "glory" in 1:6, 17; "riches" in 2:4, 7; cf. Ro 9:23). Paul asks God to endow his readers with spiritual blessings on this lavish scale.

Earlier Paul used three terms to indicate aspects of God's power (see comment on 1:19). Now he reverts to them in the context of what is made available to the believer. The verbal form "strengthen" is the opposite of "be discouraged" in v.13. The Holy Spirit is the agent of this enablement, which is continually being provided to us (cf. Php 1:19). "Inner being" contrasts with the outward person that is wasting away (2Co 4:16), whereas the new self is daily renewed (Col 3:10).

17 The result will be that Christ takes up his residence in the hearts of believers. As the Christian keeps trusting (i.e., "through faith"), Christ continues to indwell. No static condition is in view here but a maintained experience. The "heart" is the focus of mind, feeling, and will; it stands for the whole personality.

"In love" properly belongs with "being rooted and established." Love will result from Christ's indwelling presence. Paul mixes biological and architectural metaphors (1Co 3:9), conjuring up two pictures. One is of a tree with deep roots in the soil of love (Col 2:7); the other is of a building with strong foundations laid on the rock of love (Col 1:23; 1Pe 5:10). Jesus himself spoke about trees and buildings (Mt 7:15–20, 24–27).

18 What Paul is praying for is not an isolated experience unique to Christians in Ephesus, but something that is shared by all God's people. In a letter so concerned with the church and its unity, we would not expect the corporate aspect of spiritual experience to be overlooked. The verb "may have power" (related to "mighty" in 1:19) suggests a relationship between divine empowerment and personal enlightenment; "grasp" here means "to perceive" or "comprehend."

The four dimensions Paul now presents as the object of such perception are closely linked with the knowledge of Christ's love. That love, exemplified in Christ's magnanimity to the Gentiles, is too large to be confined by any geometrical measurements. It is "wide" enough to reach the whole world and beyond (1:9–10, 20). It is "long" enough to stretch from eternity to eternity (1:4–6, 18; 3:9). It is "high" enough to raise both Gentiles and Jews to heavenly places in Christ Jesus (1:13; 2:6). It is "deep" enough to rescue people from sin's degradation and even from the grip of Satan himself (2:1–5; 6:11–12). The love of Christ is the love he has for the church as a united body (5:25, 29–30) and for those who trust in him as individuals (3:17).

19 Paul recognizes, however, that he is attempting to measure the immeasurable and so paradoxically prays that the Ephesian Christians may in fact come to know a love that is ultimately unknowable (cf. 1:19; 2:7; 1Co 8:1; Php 4:7). It is cast into a totally different realm where the normal faculties of rational apprehension are incapable of functioning.

The final item in Paul's prayer is introduced in v.19b, though some regard it simply as a consequence of knowing Christ's love. It seems preferable to treat it as the climax of Paul's intercession. He makes the bold request that his readers may be filled up to "the measure of all the fullness of God," meaning the fullness that God requires. The fulfillment that God intends for us is the maturity that is measured by the full stature of Christ (4:13).

20 The doxology is plainly the climax of the first half of Ephesians; it may be regarded as the climax of the whole letter, which rises to a spiritual peak at this point and then concentrates on practical outworkings in chs. 4–6. If chs. 1–3 are couched in the form of a traditional Jewish blessing (see comment on 1:3) and indeed contain echoes of some synagogue prayers, this parallelism extends to the doxology and Amen (cf. Ro 11:33–36).

The apostle has repeatedly insisted that the end of redemption is the glory of God (1:6, 12, 14, 18; 2:7; 3:10, 16). In the doxology he rehearses themes already touched on—the abundance of God's gift (1:18, 19; 2:7; 3:19), the power made available to the Christian (1:19; 3:7, 16, 18), and the indissoluble link between Christ and the church (1:22–23; 3:10). "Immeasurably more" (GK *5655*) appears only here and in 1Th 3:10; 5:13. God's capacity to meet his people's spiritual needs far exceeds anything they can either request in prayer or conceive by way of anticipation (Php 4:7). It is actualized through "his power," which continually operates within the lives of believers.

21 This liturgical ascription of glory is a recognition rather than an augmentation of what belongs to God alone. The close juxtaposition of "the church" (put first!) and "Jesus Christ" is arresting. For Paul, body and members form a single entity. The honor of Jesus is in the hands of his church. Paul closes by combining two common liturgical expressions (cf. Da 7:18), producing a stronger phrase than usual to describe eternity. Once again, the fact that the church is included here is remarkable. In Christ, the Bride will live forever (1Th 4:17; Rev 22:17), to which the response of all God's people must be "Amen" (i.e., "Yes indeed, Lord").

III. Practice: The Application to Christian Life (4:1–6:20)

A. The Unity of the Church (4:1–16)

The opening of ch. 4 marks the principal transition of the entire letter. As in his other writings, Paul turns from doctrinal concerns to practical ones. It must not be imagined, however, that the break is complete. Theology continues to be interwoven with the moral exhortations that make up the bulk of chs. 4–6. Nor does the liturgical style, so apparent in chs. 1–3, disappear altogether. The predominant hortatory element may reflect the content and method of Paul's sermons, set here in a context of praise and worship. Significantly, the first item on his agenda is the need for Christians to live together in love and unity.

1 Does the retrospective "then" connect only with 3:20–21 or with what precedes those verses? It is most probable that Paul has in mind certain references in chs. 1–3 to spiritual privileges and the Christian's calling (3:6, 12, 14–19; cf. 1:18; 4:4).

It is "as a prisoner for the Lord" (cf. 3:1; 6:20) that Paul makes his appeal. The verb "urge" (GK *4151*) here means "to exhort." He urges the Ephesians to lead the sort of life that matches their Christian vocation. "Worthy" (GK *547*; lit., "bringing up the other beam of the scales") suggests that there must be a balance between one's profession and one's practice. So Paul provides a criterion by which possible courses of action can be weighed. Christians will always seek to do what is most in keeping with their "calling." By definition this is a calling they have received, not one they have acquired by self-effort. Those who share such a divine call constitute the church (*ekklesia*; GK *1711*), the "called-out company" of those who are in Christ.

2 The apostle now specifies four graces that evidence this essential proportion between calling and character: humility, gentleness, patience, and forbearance. These are all qualities necessary for good relations with others in the Christian community and beyond. "Humble" (GK 5425) occurs five times in Paul and only once elsewhere in the NT. In classical Greek this word was a derogatory term suggesting low-mindedness and groveling servility. The adjective was redeemed by the gospel to represent a distinctively Christian virtue and stands over against the admired high-mindedness of the heathen. Linked with being humble is being "gentle" (GK 4559) or considerate. The element of restraint is included so that it denotes controlled strength and not supine weakness.

Being "patient" (GK 3429) is a characteristic of God himself. It can mean steadfastness in the endurance of suffering, but more often in the NT it describes reluctance to avenge wrongs. It is to be displayed to other Christians and to everyone else (Ro 12:10, 18). Being patient finds its expression in "bearing with [lit., holding up] one another" (GK 462; cf. Col 3:18). Christians must put up with each other's faults and idiosyncracies, knowing that all of us have our own. "Love" (GK 27) is a recurring theme in Ephesians. The four graces Paul recommends here are all aspects of love and are exemplified to perfection in Christ (Php 2:2, 5).

3 The absence of these qualities may jeopardize Christian unity. That is why Paul presses his readers to exert all their powers to maintain the oneness in Christ that binds all believers to each other because they are bound by him and to him. "Make every effort" (GK 5079) suggests difficulty and a resolute determination to overcome it. It is assumed that unity between Christians already exists as given in Christ (2:13–18) by the Spirit. The "one Spirit" (v.4) is the agent of unity. Through the Spirit, Christians can attain a profound oneness. "Peace" (see comment on 1:2) is the clasp that ensures that this God-given unity will not fall apart.

4 The reasons why those who belong to Christ should be eager to preserve their unity are now supplied in a crescendo of nouns. In three groups of three items each, Paul's thought ascends from the realization of unity in the Spirit to the focus of unity in the Son and thence to the source of unity in the Father.

"One body" depicts the church as a single visible community. It is not simply a mystical concept; its unity is recognizable in that Jews and Gentiles are now seen to be reconciled in Christ (2:14–18). Christians are all members of the same body.

"One Spirit" indwells this body of Christ. By him the body lives and moves (1Co 12:13). The Spirit is its soul; apart from him it cannot exist. The same Spirit fell on the Jews at Pentecost and on the Gentiles in the house of Cornelius. This Spirit who has already spanned this widest of all gulfs will bring together all other diverse groups within the church.

The Holy Spirit, the pledge of our inheritance (1:14), is also the guarantor of the "one hope" (GK 1828) to which we are called (1:18; 2:12). This is not the hope that stems from the calling but the hope that belongs to the call (v.1). It is, of course, the hope of sharing Christ's glory at the end of the age (1Jn 3:2), a hope shared by both Jewish and Gentile Christians.

5 The second trio of unities is related to the "one Lord" or master to whom all Christians owe their allegiance. The three expressions may well be intended to convey a single idea, i.e., one Lord in whom we all believe and in whose name we are baptized. Certainly Christ is central. He is the sole Head of his body, the church. The pagan world spawned many lords; Christianity has only one whose claim is absolute. That is why believers cannot call anyone else Lord, even to escape death.

"One faith" in the one Lord unites all true believers. Faith here is personal commitment to Christ, though it is not purely subjective. It involves a recognition of who he is as Son of God and Savior of humankind.

"One baptism [GK 967]" is the external seal of incorporation into the body of Christ. Falling as it does in the second triad (related to Christ) and not in the first (related to the Spirit), it appears to indicate water baptism and not primarily the baptism with the Spirit of which water baptism is the sign. Baptism is the sacrament of unity. In the Christian church baptisms are not multiplied as with the Jews (Heb 6:2). There are not even two baptisms—one of John and one of Jesus.

There is "one baptism," symbolizing identification with Christ in his death and resurrection, sealing with the Spirit, and incorporation into the body of Christ, so that all Christians become one in Christ Jesus (1:13; 2:5–6; 3:15). Baptism provides the evidence that all Christians, without discrimination as to color, race, sex, age, or class, share the grace of Christ.

6 The last in the ascending scale is the "Father." He is not associated with other unities like the one Spirit and the one Lord. He stands alone. There is only "one God," not many as in pagan culture (1Co 8:5–6). He is the "Father of all," with particular reference to his redemptive paternity, though his creative fatherhood is not entirely ruled out in view of what follows. The triple note mentioned here divides up his modes of action. If the first "all" is exclusively personal, the rest are not necessarily so. God reigns "over" all in his transcendent sovereignty; he works "through" all in his creative activity; he dwells "in" all by reason of his immanent pervasiveness.

The trinitarian structure of vv.4–6 bears out the assumption that here we have an incipient creed. It was on the basis of such biblical passages that the historic affirmations of faith were developed.

7 The apostle has been considering the church as a totality. Now he focuses on the individual ("each one of us"). Within the body of Christ each member enjoys a share of God's grace. As in 3:2, it is equipping rather than saving "grace" (GK *5921*) that Paul describes. This word denotes the grace provided for and manifested in the gift. The distribution of grace, and so the distribution of grace-gifts, is in Christ's own hands and apportioned as he decides.

8 Paul supplies biblical proof of the foregoing by a quotation from Ps 68:18. "It says" is not the apostle's usual formula to introduce Scripture, and some expositors infer "he" (i.e., God, see NIV note) as the subject. Which is assumed is immaterial, because for Paul Scripture cannot be separated from its Author.

The quotation itself, though undoubtedly biblical, is not without its difficulties, since Paul does not cite either the Hebrew or Greek OT. His major change is from "received gifts for men" to "gave gifts to men." Attempts have been made to account for the apparent discrepancy by conjecturing that Paul was quoting from memory and that his recollection was imperfect. With more plausibility some have claimed that, under the inspiration of the Spirit, Paul felt free to amplify the meaning of the Psalm, since the "giving" is implicit in the "receiving for." But it seems most probable that the apostle was drawing on an ancient oral tradition reflected in the Aramaic Targum on Psalms and in the Syriac version of the OT, both of which read, "Thou hast given gifts to men."

9 Ascension presupposes a prior descent, and Paul describes this as being made into "the lower, earthly regions." The rendering of the NIV understands this phrase as referring to the incarnation of our Lord. It was from the earth that he ascended into heaven, and it had been to the earth that he came (Jn 3:13). Others link this verse with the belief that Christ descended to the underworld during the interval between his death and resurrection (see 1Pe 3:19–20; 4:6). The obscure expression in this verse may also simply signify death and burial.

10 The apostle affirms the identity of the incarnate Savior with the ascended Savior. His exaltation is "higher than all the heavens." The Jews calculated seven heavens, but for Paul, higher than all of them is the rightful throne of Christ, to whom all things are one day to be subjugated (1:10; cf. 1Co 15:28). No one else is qualified thus to "fill the whole universe." This is more than the fulfillment of prophetic predictions concerning Christ's cosmic role or the accomplishment of every task entrusted to him by the Father. It is his filling all things with his presence.

11 The apostle now resumes the train of thought inaugurated in v.7 but interrupted by his excursus on the ascent and descent of Christ in vv.8–10. This diversion was necessary in order to stress that none other than the exalted Lord is the one who has endowed his church with gifts by grace, so that it may indeed be his body in the world (1:23; 4:4). Paul does not go on to list the grace-gifts, however, but only those who receive them. After "each one of us" in v.7 we might have expected him to include all the members of Christ's body (as in 1Co 12:4–11). Instead, we read only of those who are appointed to leadership, whose ministry is exercised for the sake of the whole community (vv.12–13).

"Apostles" and "prophets" have already been paired as providing a foundation for the Christian temple (see comment on 2:20). "Evangelists" (GK 2296) were missionaries who pioneered outreach in areas where the faith had not as yet been proclaimed (e.g., Philip in Ac 21:8; cf. 8:6–40; Timothy in 2Ti 4:5). With "pastors and teachers," Paul turns from itinerant to local ministry. These are grouped together, suggesting that the two roles were regarded as complementary and often coordinated in the same person. "Pastors" (or "shepherds"; GK 4478) probably included presbyters and bishops; they were entrusted with the nurture, protection, and supervision of the flock. "Teachers" (GK 1437) are linked with prophets in Ac 13:1 and follow them in the list in 1Co 12:28.

12 The aim of the ministries mentioned in v.11 is now disclosed: to equip all God's people for service. "To prepare" (GK 2938) is "to put right." In the NT this verb is used for the mending of nets (Mt 4:21) and the restoration of the lapsed (Gal 6:1). It may also signify the realization of purpose and the completion of what is already good as far as it goes (1Co 1:10; 1Th 3:10). Such preparation is needed to inspire God's people to do the work "of service" (GK 1355). Service is what unites all the members of Christ's body from the apostles to the most apparently insignificant disciple (1Co 12:22). Christ himself set the example (Mk 10:45; Lk 22:27). It is by this means that the body of Christ will be consolidated (cf. Eph 2:21).

13 The ultimate end in view is the attainment of completeness in Christ. "We all" clearly includes all believers, but not all people (3:9). In v.3 "the unity of the Spirit" is a gift to be guarded; here "unity in the faith" is a goal to be reached. Such a realization of unity will arise from an increasing knowledge of Christ as the Son of God in corporate as well as in personal experience.

In this way the church comes of age; it becomes "mature" (that is, "a perfect, full-grown man"). The singular is employed because the church as a whole is seen as "one new man" in Christ (2:15). Individualism is a mark of immaturity. This perfection or completeness is proportionate to the fullness of Christ himself. "Whole measure" or "perfection" can denote age (Mt 6:27; Jn 9:21) and may well be used here in this sense, since the context has to do with becoming adult. The meaning would be "attain to the measure of mature age" proper for Christians, who have left infancy behind (v.14). But the phrase may also refer to spiritual attainment (cf. Lk 2:52). "Fullness" (see comment on 1:23) is here related to Christ. Just as Christians may be "filled to the measure of all the fullness of God" (3:19), so together they are to aspire to "the full measure of perfection found in Christ."

14 The metaphor of maturity is carried over from v.13. There must be no symptoms of arrested development among believers, who are to abandon childish attitudes and act their age (1Co 13:11). Paul switches metaphors as he depicts the features of spiritual infantilism. Its victims will be tossed to and fro like a cork in a surging sea (Jas 1:6) and whirled around by every chance gust of fashionable false teaching, which creates dizziness in the mind. The source of this dangerous teaching is to be traced in the cleverness of people who craftily seek to lead us astray. "Cunning" is cheating at dice and so, by extension, trickery of every kind. "Craftiness" is unscrupulousness that stops at nothing. Error is organized with a deliberate policy to undermine the truth of God. Paul may well be thinking of emergent Gnosticism (see Col 2:8).

15 Paul contrasts the deception of heresy with the integrity of the gospel. The church cannot allow falsehood to go uncorrected, yet the truth must always be vindicated in the accents of love. This fundamental concern for the truth is the secret of maturity in the church. It is into Christ as the Head that the body grows up.

16 Christ is at once the One into whom all Christians grow and out of whom the church consolidates itself in love. This process depends on the interrelationship of the various parts of the body. The whole is continually being integrated and kept firm by each separate ligament. The precision with which these medical terms are employed makes us wonder whether Paul checked the details with Luke. It is only when each part is working properly that the body receives the support it

Ministry Gifts of the Holy Spirit

Gift	Definition	General References	Specific Examples
Apostle (Specific)	Those specifically commissioned by the resurrected Lord to establish the church and the original message of the gospel	Ac 4:33–37; 5:12, 18–42; 6:6; 8:14, 18; 9:27; 11:1; 15:1–6, 22–23; 16:4; 1Co 9:5, 12:28–29; Gal 1:17; Eph 2:20; 4:11; Jude 17	12 apostles: Mt 10:2; Mk 3:14; Lk 6:13; Ac 1:15–26; Rev 21:14 Paul: Ro 1:1; 11:13; 1Co 1:1; 9:1–2; 15:9–10; 2Co 1:1; Gal 1:1; 1Ti 2:7 Peter: 1Pe 1:1; 2Pe 1:1
Apostle (General)	Any messenger commissioned as a missionary or for other special responsibilities	Ac 13:1–3; 1Co 12:28–29; Eph 4:11	Barnabas: Ac 14:4, 14 Andronicus and Junias: Ro 16:7 Titus and others: 2Co 8:23 Epaphroditus: Php 2:25 James, Jesus' brother: Gal 1:19
Prophet	Those who spoke under the inspiration of the Holy Spirit, bringing a message from God to the church, and whose main motivation and concern were with the spiritual life and purity of the church	Ro 12:6; 1Co 12:10; 14:1–33; Eph 4:11; 1Th 5:20–21; 1Ti 1:18; 1Pe 4:11; 1Jn 4:1–3	Peter: Ac 2:14–40; 3:12–26; 4:8–12; 10:34–44 Paul: Ac 13:1, 16–41 Various people: Ac 13:1 Judas and Silas: Ac 15:32 John: Rev 1:1, 3; 10:8–11; 11:18
Evangelist	Those gifted by God to proclaim the gospel to the unsaved	Eph 4:11	Philip: Ac 8:5–8, 26–40; 21:8 Paul: Ac 26:16–18
Pastor (Elder or Overseer)	Those chosen and gifted to oversee the church and care for its spiritual needs	Ac 14:23; 15:1–6, 22–23; 16:4; 20:17–38; Ro 12:8; Eph 4:11–12; Php 1:1; 1Ti 3:1–7; 5:17–20; Tit 1:5–9; Heb 13:17; 1Pe 5:1–5	Timothy: 1Ti 1:1–4; 4:12–16; 2Ti 1:1–6; 4:2, 5 Titus: Tit 1:4–5 Peter: 1Pe 5:1 John: 1Jn 2:1, 12–14 Gaius: 3Jn 1–7
Teacher	Those gifted to clarify and explain God's Word in order to build up the church	Ro 12:7; Eph 4:11–12; Col 3:16; 1Ti 3:2, 5:17; 2Ti 2:2, 2	Paul: Ac 15:35; 20:20; 28:31; Ro 12:19–21; 13:8–10; 1Co 4:17; 1Ti 1:5; 4:16; 2Ti 1:11 Barnabas: Ac 15:35 Apollos: Ac 18:25–28 Timothy: 1Co 4:17; 1Ti 1:3–5; 4:11–13; 6:2; 2Ti 4:2 Titus: Tit 2:1–3, 9–10
Deacon	Those chosen and gifted to render practical assistance to members of the church	Ac 6:1–6; Ro 12:7; Php 1:1; 1Ti 3:8–13; 1Pe 4:11	Seven deacons: Ac 6:5 Phoebe: Ro 16:1–2
Helper	Those gifted for a variety of helpful deeds	1Co 12:28	Paul: Ac 20:35 Lydia: Ac 16:14–15 Gaius: 3Jn 5–8

Ministry Gifts of the Holy Spirit (Continued)

Gift	Definition	General References	Specific Examples
Administrator	Those gifted to guide and oversee the various activities of the church	Ro 12:8; 1Co 14:3; 1Th 5:11, 14–22; Heb 10:24–25	Barnabas: Ac 11:23–24; 14:22 Paul: Ac 14:22; 16:40; 20:1; Ro 8:26–39; 12:1–2; 2Co 6:14–7:1; Gal 5:16–26 Judas and Silas: Ac 15:32; 16:40 Timothy: 1Th 3:2; 2Ti 4:2 Titus: Tit 2:6, 13 Peter: 1Pe 5:1–2 John: 1Jn 2:15–17; 3:1–3
Giver	Those gifted to give freely of their resources to the needs of God's people	Ac 2:44–45; 4:34–35; 11:29–30; 1Co 16:1–4; 2Co 8–9; Eph 4:28; 1Ti 6:17–19; Heb 13:16; 1Jn 3:16–18	Barnabas: Ac 4:36–37 Christians in Macedonia: Ro 15:26–27; 2Co 8:1–5 Christians in Achaia: Ro 15:26–27; 2Co 9:2
Comforter	Those gifted to give comfort by acts of mercy to people in distress	Ro 12:8; 2Co 1:3–7	Paul: 2Co 1:4 Hebrew Christians: Heb 10:34 Various Christians: Col 4:10–11 Dorcas: Ac 9:36–39

needs and will be able to grow as God intended it.

B. The Changed Life (4:17–24)

The practical section of this letter opened with an appeal to maintain Christian unity. Paul substantiated it by enlarging on the way in which the body of Christ is being built up. Now, before dealing with specific moral injunctions, he reminds his readers about the kind of life they once lived and the need to make a clean break with the past (cf. 2:1–3, 11–13).

17 "So" resumes the exhortation in v.3. In a solemn declaration the apostle strongly implores the Ephesians to abandon all their former practices, because both he and they are "in the Lord." In other letters Paul has not been slow to remind Hebrew Christians that they must not cling to Jewish legal practices. In similar vein he now urges Gentiles not to fall back into their old self-indulgent habits. Such permissive behavior springs from an aimless and futile attitude to life that cuts the nerve of moral endeavor.

18 This reprehensible attitude is traced to its source. Such people are impeded by a mental fog that blots out the divine light. They are cut off from contact with God (2:12) and the life he alone can impart. Such a condition arises in turn from deep-seated "ignorance." Although inborn (cf. 2:2–3), it was not irreversible and might have been removed had they followed such light as came to them. Instead, they steeled their hearts against the truth until they grew altogether impervious to its impact. "Hardening" (GK *4801*) describes a state of petrifaction. It is used medically to denote the callus formed when a bone has been fractured and reset. Such a callus is even harder than the bone itself. This dreadful situation has affected the hearts of the pagans. Their whole personality is incapable of appreciating what God offers.

19 People like these have "lost all sensitivity." They can no longer respond to moral stimuli. Their consciences are so atrophied that sin registers no stab of pain. They have abandoned themselves to every sort of vice. From Ro 1:24–28 we learn that in such circumstances God leaves sinners to endure the full consequences of their tragic decision. "Sensuality" is license in the physical aspect of one's being, especially sexual excesses. This fearful self-abandonment leads to all kinds of filthy practices, which are so absorbing as almost to become a total preoccupation.

All this is pursued "with a continual lust" (GK 4432). This term is not necessarily associated with sexual misconduct, though the context here suggests it. It means the determination to gratify self-interest at all costs, regardless of the rights of others.

20 "You" stands in contrast to the insensitive, passion-dominated pagans who exist only to satisfy their lower nature. That was not how the Gentile converts in Ephesus came to "know Christ" for themselves. The expression implies more than receiving catechetical instruction; it means to learn in such a way as to become a devotee or disciple. It was Christ they thus came to know—God's anointed Son, no longer the prerogative of the Jews but shared by the Gentiles.

21 Paul now adds a note of certainty. In the preaching of the word Christ himself was present (2:17), and so those who heard were introduced to him and accepted him. They were also "taught in [Christ]." That is, as disciples remaining in him (Jn 15:4, 9–10), they received further instruction in the "truth" (GK 237), which is "in Jesus." Paul does not often employ the historical name "Jesus"; when he does, it is invariably connected with our Lord's death and resurrection. The truth in Jesus, then, has to do with the fact that the man from Nazareth was shown by his rising again to be the Son of God and the Savior of the world.

22 Paul now gives the content of the teaching his readers received. Their previous lifestyle was to be discarded completely. They must forsake their old behavioral haunts and indeed lay aside the costume of their unregenerate selves. The metaphor of doffing and donning garments is common in Scripture. There may also be an allusion here to the fact that baptismal candidates changed into white robes.

The old self is subject to an internal process of continuous disintegration. Moral degeneration has set in and the road to perdition lies ahead. "Deceitful desires" translates a phrase in which the treacherous duplicity of sin is almost personified.

23 In a contrasting positive statement, Paul reminds the Ephesians that instead of being subject to progressive deterioration, they were to be perpetually renovated in mind and spirit. "To be made new" (GK *391*) possibly involves an element of restoration, since the image of God, impaired by the Fall, is fully reinstated in the new creation. As over against the futile thinking of the unregenerate Gentiles (v.17), Christian converts are to undergo a radical reorientation of their mental outlook. This can only take place under the influence of the Holy Spirit, acting on the human spirit as it affects the realm of thought.

24 The "new self" (3:16) assumed by the believer is the direct opposite of the worthless "old self" (v.22). It is not the former nature refurbished but a totally new creation (2:10; cf. 2Co 5:17). This is said to be "like God," as Adam was at first (Ge 1:27; 5:1). God is both the author and the pattern of this changed life (see also Col 3:10). The characteristics of the divine image are "righteousness and holiness." These are qualities in God that are reproduced in his genuine worshipers: his love of right and his aversion to sin. In the NT "righteousness" (GK *1466*) often stands for the uprightness of those who are made right with God. "Holiness" (GK *4009*) here is not the usual Greek word, but one that means "free from contamination" (also in Lk 1:25).

C. Christian Behavior Patterns (4:25–5:2)

In vv.17–24 the apostle contrasted the old life with the new without descending to particulars. Now he embarks on a series of detailed warnings against what "deceitful desires" (v.22) may produce. "Therefore" in v.25 makes the connection between principle and practice.

25 The first item included in the putting off of the "old self" (v.22) is "falsehood" (cf. Col 3:8–9). This is not lying in the abstract but "*the* lying"—falsehood in all its forms as over against "the truth that is in Jesus" (v.21) and "true righteousness and holiness" (v.24). All that belongs to "deceitful scheming" (v.14) and "deceitful desires" (v.22) must be left behind, for it has no place in the community of Christ. Because our Lord is himself the truth (Jn 14:6), his body must reflect the truth. Because each member belongs to the rest, the fellowship of the church must be

marked by a refreshing openness; any kind of deception is a sin against the Spirit. The reference to the "body" makes it clear that fellow Christians are in view but, of course, the injunction has a universal application.

26 A quotation from Ps 4:4 introduces the next admonition: "In your anger do not sin." The meaning is, "Do not let your anger be mixed with sin." There is such a thing as righteous indignation, for anger is ascribed to God and to Jesus. Thus it is also legitimate for Christians to express anger. But it can easily degenerate into bitterness—hence, the appended prohibition. Under the Mosaic law all sureties were to be returned and all wages paid before sunset (Dt 24:13, 15). A Christian's exasperation or provocation, however justifiable, must not be allowed to simmer overnight.

27 If this advice is followed, the devil will be afforded no leeway. He will have no room to move. Instead, we must leave a place for the wrath of God, because vindication is his prerogative (Ro 12:19).

28 In this warning against breaking the commandment against theft, Paul is thinking of some convert who had been in the habit of stealing before he became a Christian. Stealing covers every kind of misappropriation. For the new self in Christ all this must stop. Christians should not be afraid to exert themselves to the point of exhaustion in manual labor (1Co 4:12; 1Th 4:11). Hands that used to pilfer the property of others must now be hardened like Paul's in honest toil (Ac 20:34–35). As a result believers should be in a position to help those worse off than they are. "To share" (GK *3556*) means to distribute personally rather than through some agent or official.

29 Not only will Christians do "the good" (v.28); they will also speak "what is helpful." No unhealthy language will pass through their lips. "Unwholesome" is that which is itself rotten and disseminates rottenness. When joined with "talk" (GK *3364*), it may signify not simply bad language but malicious gossip and slander; anything that injures others and sparks dissension is covered by this expression. Christians, however, will only say what is calculated to build up the church (Eph 2:21–22; 4:12, 16) by encouraging its members. This is to be done whenever the need arises, so that those who hear may receive a blessing. The ultimate source of all blessing is God himself. The channel may be human, and so even the everyday conversation of Christians may become a means of grace to others.

30 "And" indicates that, while there are various ways of bringing sorrow to the Holy Spirit, it is doing so through "unwholesome talk" (v.29) that Paul is rebuking here. Since the Spirit lives within Christians, their experience of his fullness will have its effect, among other things, in speech (5:18–19). Any kind of careless, unbecoming talk pains the Spirit, since it is incompatible with the holiness he conveys to those who belong to Christ. The moving anthropomorphism implicit in "grieve," combined with the full-length title "the Holy Spirit of God," serves to underline the gravity of the prohibition.

The clause beginning with "with whom" provides the basis for this prohibition. The Holy Spirit has sealed believers (1:13–14) for the final "day of redemption" (GK *667*). This word involves the payment of a ransom (see comment on 1:7–9): Christ's death on the cross has purchased not only present but final liberation.

31 A condensed series of imperatives winds up this section about the Christian's attitude to one's neighbor. This verse is negative; v.32 is positive and leads into the next chapter. "Get rid of" (GK *149*) is "let it be removed" and thus "have no more to do with it." Every trace of these blemishes is to be forsaken. "Bitterness" (*4394*; cf. Col 3:19) is the opposite not only of sweetness but of kindness. It is the spite that harbors resentment and keeps a score of wrongs (1Co 13:5). "Rage" (GK *2596*) is what flows from bitterness in an outburst of uncontrolled passion and frustration. "Anger" (GK *3973*) describes the wrath of God in 5:6 and of people in v.26. It signifies an unjustifiable human emotion that manifests itself in noisy assertiveness and abuse (cf. Col 3:8). The poisonous source of all these regrettable reassertions of the "old self" (v.22) is "malice" (GK *2798*).

32 Having put aside these malicious traits, Christians will instead display kindness, compassion, and forgiveness. "Be" is really "become," for Paul realizes that his readers have not yet attained "the full measure of perfection found in Christ" (v.13). To be "kind" (GK *5982*) is to show a sweet and generous disposition. "Compassionate" is a rare word, related to the intestines. The ancients located the seat of the emotions in the internal organs—liver, kidneys, and larger viscera.

Mutual forgiveness is a further mark of true Christian fellowship (Col 3:13); it requires a give and take. Paul sets forth the strongest possible motive: Christians must forgive one another because all of them have already been forgiven by God in Christ, when he became "the atoning sacrifice... for the sins of the whole world" (1Jn 2:2). "As" further implies that our forgiveness of others is to be like God's forgiveness of us. It must flow from ungrudging love (cf. Mt 18:23–35).

5:1 The apostle carries these injunctions over from the previous chapter and closes this section on Christian behavior patterns at v.2. "Be" ("become") confirms the close relation between this verse and the last where the same expression has been employed. Here it introduces a staggering conception: Paul invites his readers to imitate God! What follows elucidates his meaning. A child will show himself to be a true child by wanting to grow up like his father. In the same way, God's precious children will be eager to copy him, as he enables them. This was the teaching of Jesus himself.

2 God is love (1Jn 4:8), and the life that is like the life of God will be a life of love. Love is the essential of the Christian character. Paul has repeatedly emphasized love in this letter (1:4, 15; 2:4; 3:17–19; 4:2, 15–16). The model of love is Christ himself. Because he laid down his life for us, we are to love others to the point of sacrifice (cf. Jn 13:14; 15:12–13).

Paul borrows two technical terms in Jewish sacrificial vocabulary without differentiation. "Offering" (GK *4714*) is the word used in the LXX for the "grain offering" (GK 4966). On the cross, Christ presented himself to God as an offering; Paul adds that it was "fragrant"—a phrase that occurs in a sacrificial context over forty times in the Pentateuch. This metaphor suggests that our Lord's self-sacrifice was pleasing to his Father and was thus accepted as a means of reconciliation. "Sacrifice" (GK *2602*) indicates that the victim was slain; Paul has spoken of Christ's death on the cross (2:16) and his sacrificial shedding of blood (1:7; 2:13). Because it is identified with Christ in his death, the Christian's life will likewise prove an acceptable sacrifice to God.

D. Light in the Lord (5:3–20)

Paul has epitomized the Christian behavior pattern as "a life of love" (v.2). Now he turns to another theme: "Live as children of light" (v.8). But they can be "light in the Lord" only because Christ is the world's true light (v.14).

3 The apostle begins by speaking about the effect of light in a life of purity. He resumes the prohibitive character of 4:26–31, taking it further by declaring that such aberrations should not only be avoided but not so much as mentioned (v.12), since they are altogether unsuitable for those who belong to the consecrated community of God.

"Sexual immorality" (GK *4518*) was tolerated in the permissive pagan society of Paul's day (Ro 1:24–32). "Impurity" (GK *174*) has already been mentioned in 4:19 as a characteristic of secularized existence, along with "greed" (GK *4432*). In Col 3:5 this word is conceived of as idolatry (cf. v.5), because it makes a god of what it seeks to possess.

4 Paul has already warned against "unwholesome talk" (4:29) because of the harm it does to those who are compelled to hear it. Now he attacks it from another angle, because it is unseemly for Christians and usurps the place of praise. "Obscenity" is broadly equivalent to "filthy language" (Col 3:8); "foolish talk" is stupid chatter or silly twaddle. Along with "coarse joking," these things must be repudiated. Instead, the Christian's mouth should be continually filled with thanks to God (2:7; 5:18; Col 2:7; 3:15).

5 The apostle warns his readers about the serious consequences of immorality. They must surely be aware that there is no room in the kingdom of God for those who blatantly continue in sensual sin. The three categories of v.3 are singled out again, with the rider that the greedy make an idol of their possessions. No such person has any place reserved in the eschatological kingdom. The "inheritance" (GK *3100*) is a present title to a future position (1:14, 18); it cannot be acquired by the disobedient (v.6). In Col 1:13 Paul refers to "the kingdom of the Son" whom the Father loves (cf. Eph 1:6). But since it is God who "placed all things under his feet" (1:22), the kingdom is his as well as Christ's.

6 There were those then as there are now who protest that Christian standards are too demanding and that people must be allowed to live as they like (1Co 15:32). In the name of a spurious freedom, they attempt to bring converts into bondage to sin once again. The Ephesians must not to fooled by such futile arguments (4:17). They are promoted by the arch-deceiver himself (2:2). Paul's indictment includes all the propagandists of permissiveness.

It is on account of "such things"—the sins mentioned above rather than the deceptive teaching that encourages them—that divine retribution is already on its way. It will keep on coming till in the end it deals with the offenders.

7 An unambiguous admonition rounds off the paragraph begun at v.3. Christians are not to get mixed up with those who have excluded themselves from the kingdom by their impurity. The word "partners" (GK 5212) is the same one used in 3:6 to describe how Gentiles now share in the messianic promise.

8 Paul enlarges on the contrast between darkness and light. As in 2:1–3 and 3:17–24, he reminds his readers of what they once were. One word suffices by way of summary—"darkness." Not only did they live in darkness: they *were* darkness (cf. 4:18). But now they have been rescued from the dominion of darkness and inherit the kingdom of light (Col 1:12–13). They not only live in the light: they *are* light. This is possible only in union with Christ, who is himself the light (cf. Jn 8:12). Henceforth believers must behave as those who live in the light.

9 A parenthesis explains the command at the end of v.8. Light is known by its effects. When the light of Christ shines in the lives of believers it produces benevolence, fairness, and integrity. These three qualities counteract the dark influence of malice (4:31), injustice, and falsehood (4:25). "Goodness" is the achievement of moral excellence combined with a generous spirit. "Righteousness" was understood by the Greeks as giving all their due. "Truth" stands for genuineness and honesty; it is not only something to be said but something to be done (see comment on 4:25; cf. 1Jn 1:6; 3:18). A life lived in the light is found not only in all these qualities held in balance, but in every aspect of each.

10 The exhortation in v.8 is further supplemented by an instruction to "find out what pleases the Lord" (cf. v.17). "To find out" (GK *1507*) has to do with the testing of metals and so can mean to discover by examination, to verify, or to approve. Those who live as "children of light" (v.8) will be continually trying to ascertain what the will of God is in every situation so that all they do may satisfy him.

11 Another exhortation is added to that in v.8. Christians are not to be involved in "the fruitless deeds of darkness." Paul is not advocating pharisaical separatism, for the "deeds" must be shunned, not the doers. Followers of Christ will go where their master went and meet those their master met. But though they do not withdraw from the world, they refuse to adopt its standards or fall in with its ways. They are concerned to produce "the fruit of the light" (v.9).

Far from participating in these practices, believers should "expose" (GK *1794*) them. When the object of "expose" is a person, the verb means "to convince or reprove"; this is the distinctive work of the Spirit. But when the object is impersonal, the verb may signify "to bring to light or expose." This exposure is not effected by what is actually said by way of rebuke (cf. vv. 3, 12), but simply by letting the light of Christ shine through and show them up.

12 Paul reiterates the insistence of v.3 that the abominable things pagan profligates do under cover of secrecy must not be breathed among Christians. Sometimes sin can be publicized by a reaction against it. What has been done in the dark is best kept dark. Paul goes so far as to say that the shamefulness of these ugly vices may rub off on Christians if they are continually talking about them, even if it is to disapprove of them.

13 Paul appeals to the effect of light in the natural world. It penetrates wherever it shines, so that everything is lit up by it. In the same way, whenever the light of Christ appears, it shows up sin for what it is. Evil can no longer masquerade as anything else. Hidden wickedness thus revealed can no longer be obscured by darkness. It is also possible here to see a reference to the transformation brought about by light, so that the exposure and reproval of sin by the light of Christ lead to salvation, as it did for the Ephesians themselves (v.8).

14 The same introductory formula as in 4:8 prefaces a poetical quotation. The lines form a metrical triplet in a rhythm that was specially associated with religious initiation chants. This may well supply a clue in tracing their origin. They are not a direct quotation of OT Scripture (though they contain echoes of Isa 60:1 and possibly Isa 9:2; 26:19; 51:17; 52:1). Most likely this section is an early baptismal hymn based on Isa 60:1. Paul is soon to mention hymns in the context of worship (v.19), so that this may well have been a liturgical chant addressed to those about to be baptized (cf. 1Ti 3:16).

The exhortations "wake up" (GK *1586*) and "rise [GK *482*] from the dead" place the hymn firmly in the context of resurrection—possibly written for Easter day. The connection between resurrection and baptism is so close that there is no need to restrict the intention. Moreover, in the early church, baptism was described as an enlightenment (cf. Heb 6:4; 10:32). The verb translated "shine" (GK *2213*) is applied to the rising of a heavenly body. Christ, as the morning star, has already risen and sheds his light on all who are raised to newness of life in him.

15 Further exhortations follow, backing up v.11. Because of their illumination, believers will pay scrupulous attention to their personal behavior (v.8b), in order that they may lead an irreproachable life. The metaphorical contrast between light and darkness is now replaced by that between wisdom and folly. Christians must no longer act like simpletons, since God's own wisdom is always available to them (1:8–9; 3:10).

16 Christians should be "making the most [GK *1973*] of every opportunity." What is meant is simply to make the best possible use of all circumstances like prudent merchants and not waste opportunities as they present themselves. "The days are evil" in a moral sense, not necessarily by reason of hardship and distress, though this may accompany these sinful times.

17 "Therefore" resumes the thought of v.15 with its exhortation to be wise. "Foolish" (GK *933*) here is a stronger word than "unwise" in v.15, alluding to stupid imprudence or senseless folly in action. To "understand" is to give the mind to something so as to get hold of or grasp it. The object of this determined attempt at apprehension is the Lord's will (v.10). Paul recognizes the divine will as the regulative principle of the Christian life (1:1, 5, 9). Here he refers to the will of the Lord (i.e., of Jesus Christ), perhaps because Christ left us an example.

18 A specific instance of the foregoing generalization follows. Quoting Pr 23:30, Paul warns against the folly of overindulgence in strong drink. Drunkenness was all too common in the pagan world, and cautions in the NT show that it presented a serious temptation to Christians. The danger of drunkenness (Gal 5:21) lies not only in itself but in what it may induce. "Debauchery" (GK *861*) in the NT means the type of wild living that characterized the prodigal son (Lk 15:13). In classical Greek it signified extravagant squandering both of money and of the physical appetites. Christians will avoid all such excess.

Instead of continuing in drunkenness, believers must go on being "filled with the Spirit." That is a surprising alternative. We might have expected the apostle to plead for abstinence as over against intemperance. But he takes a more startling and positive line. He urges his readers to draw on the reinvigorating resources of the Holy Spirit. The Spirit produces a genuine exhilaration others vainly seek from alcohol. On the day of Pentecost the effect of such an experience was mistaken for drunkenness (Ac 2:13). "With the Spirit" is actually "in spirit"; the Greek text does not indicate whether the Holy Spirit is intended. However, it seems probable that Paul intended the Spirit, in view of the many other scriptural references to being filled with the Spirit.

The theological implications of "be filled" (GK *4444*) are crucial for a biblical doctrine of the Holy Spirit. The imperative makes it clear that this is a command for all Christians. The Greek present tense used here rules out any once-for-all reception of the Spirit but points to a continuous replenishment (lit., "go on being filled"). Nor does it appear that Paul is urging his readers to enter into a new experience. Rather, he is inviting them to go on as they have already begun. Finally, the verb is passive: "Let yourselves be filled with the Spirit." This is not a manufactured experience, though it can be rejected (cf. Gal 3:2, 5). There may, therefore, be successive fillings of the Spirit; indeed, the Christian life should be an uninterrupted filling. What this verse will *not* substantiate is the claim that after becoming a Christian, a single, additional, definitive filling is essential for completion.

19 The outcome of being filled with the Spirit is described in vv.19–20 in a series of four participles that virtually amount to imperatives. Each of these expressions of the Spirit's fullness has to do with praise. The verb "to speak" (GK *3281*) is not confined to normal conversation but covers utterance of any kind and so is perfectly applicable to the medium of psalms, hymns, and songs. Such communication is with "one another." "Psalms" seems to refer to the OT Psalter, which was integrated with Christian worship from the first. Christian hymns exalted the name of Christ (v.19) or God (v.20). Such canticles appear in the NT itself (as at v.14). "Spiritual songs" may be so designated either to differentiate them from secular compositions or to represent spontaneous singing in the Spirit. Paul is describing the heart's inner melody that keeps in tune with audible praise. If it is offered "to the Lord," it does not need to be heard by others.

20 The perpetual accompaniment of all these outlets of the Spirit in the Christian life is "giving thanks." The context is not restricted to that of the church's liturgy (cf. "always"), for such gratitude to God should cover every circumstance. It is to be addressed to God the Father—the Father of our Lord and Savior Jesus Christ (1:3, 17), who is also "our God and Father" (Gal 1:4)—in the name of the Son as the one who fully reveals him.

E. Christian Relationships: Marriage (5:21–33)

The basic principle of Christian submissiveness (v.21) that governs the community life of the church applies also to social relationships. Paul selects the most conspicuous of these and shows how they are transformed when controlled by a prior obedience to Christ. In 5:22–33 he deals with wives and husbands; in 6:1–4, with children and parents; and in 6:5–9, with slaves and masters (cf. Col 3:18–4:1 for a close parallel). The gospel places such relationships as these on a revolutionary new footing, since all are subjected to the lordship of Christ.

21 Does this verse represent the conclusion of the previous section or the start of a new one? While grammatically it may be attached to v.20, its content coincides more naturally with what follows. The verb "to submit" (GK *5718*) occurs twenty-three times in Paul and denotes subordination to those considered worthy of respect, either because of their inherent qualities or more often because of the position they hold. Christians are to submit to civil authorities, to church leaders, to parents, and to masters. The whole structure of society as ordered by God depends on the readiness of its members to recognize these sanctions. Without them anarchy prevails.

The Christian, however, observes them not merely for their own sake, or even because they are imposed by God, but out of "reverence" for Christ (cf. v.17). Moreover, within the fellowship of the church (Paul has this more prominently in mind than the community at large), submission to others is reciprocal ("to one another"). No one is to coerce another, for all voluntarily accept the discipline. Hence, any delusions of superiority are banished.

22 "Submit" is assumed here from the previous verse, since no verb appears. The fact confirms that v.21 fits more with what follows than with what precedes. It is to their own husbands that wives are to be subject (Col 3:18). The legally binding exclusiveness of the marriage relationship is thus underlined. "As to the Lord" suggests that in obeying her husband, the Christian wife is obeying the Lord who has sanctioned the marriage contract. It should be noted that Paul is speaking here about Christian marriage. He is not implying that women are inferior to men or that all women should be subject to men. The subjection, moreover, is voluntary, not forced. The Christian wife who promises to submit does so because her vow is "as to the Lord."

23 The marriage relationship is now set out as being a reflection of the relationship between Christ and his church. This raises it to an unimaginably lofty level. In 1Co 11:12 Paul had already marked out a hierarchy in which God is seen as the head of Christ, Christ as the head of the man, and the man as the head of the woman. Here he looks at it from another angle. If the head of the woman is the man and the head of the church is Christ (Eph 1:22; 4:12, 16), then it is permissible to draw an analogy between the wife's relationship to her husband and the church's relation to Christ. Marriage is thus interpreted in the sublimest terms; it is compared with the marriage of the Lamb to his bride.

Unless we take the next comment as an aside that bears no relation to the analogy Paul is presenting, it must be assumed that there is an intended parallelism. It remains true, of course, that Christ is the Savior of his body, the church, in a unique manner. The word "Savior" is never used in the NT except of Christ or God. But having recognized and safeguarded that vital truth, we may legitimately pursue the analogy and assume that Paul regards the husband, even if to an infinitely lesser degree, as the protector of his wife (cf. vv.28–29).

24 "Now" continues the same line of argument rather than reversing it. That is, Paul is pursuing a further likeness between the husband-wife relationship and the Christ-church relationship. Here the verb "submit" stands unambiguously in the text and does not have to be supplied (cf. v.22). The church as the bride of Christ readily acknowledges his authority and seeks to please him in every respect. When marriage is seen in the light of this higher relationship between Christ and his body, the wife finds no difficulty in submitting to her husband, for he too has obligations to her in the Lord (vv.25–33).

25 Paul turns to the reciprocal duties of the husband. Greco-Roman society held that wives had obligations to their husbands, but not vice versa. Christianity introduced a revolutionary approach to marriage that equalized the rights of wives and husbands and established the institution on a much firmer foundation than ever before. The word that sums up the role of the wife is "submit" (vv.22, 24); the word that does the same for the husband is "love" (GK 26). This is the highest and distinctively Christian word for loving. As over against words for "sexual passion" and "family affection," Paul chooses a verb that insists that the love of a Christian man for his wife must be a response to and an expression of the love of God in Christ extended to the church (cf. vv.1–2; see also Col 3:19).

The apostle again draws a comparison between the marriage relationship and the relationship of Christ and the church (cf. vv.22–24), this time emphasizing our Lord's sacrifice. On the cross Jesus gave himself up for the church, his bride. The analogy is all the more telling, since the word for "church" is feminine. This aspect of the atonement does not have much prominence in the NT. While Paul elsewhere declared that Christ laid down his life "for our sins" (Ro 4:25; Gal 1:4), or "for me" (Gal 2:20), or "for us all" (Ro 8:32), now he affirms that our Lord's sacrificial death was "for her," i.e., for the church.

26 In vv.26–27 Paul explains more fully the aim of Christ's atonement for the church. It was "to make her holy" and "to present her to himself as a radiant church" (v.27). "To make holy" (GK 39) is to set apart; by his death on the cross, Christ intended to separate for himself a people for his own possession. From the beginning the church has been called out in this way, but the ethical demands of such privilege require a response in every age.

If the church is to attain the actual holiness that alone befits her status as the bride of Christ, then "cleansing" (GK 2751) is essential. A need for such cleansing before the church begins to be holy clearly indicates that Paul's concept of holiness involves an immediate subjective change. While cleansing may assume a logical priority, however, the process is really simultaneous.

This essential cleansing is effected "by the washing [GK 3373] of water," which is said to be accompanied by a spoken word. The term "washing" emphasizes the action of bathing, not the bath itself. Beyond doubt the reference here is to baptism, thus being equivalent to "the washing of rebirth" in Tit 3:5. There is, however, no hint of any mechanical view of the sacrament, as if the mere application of water could in itself bring about the purification it symbolizes. Nowhere does the NT countenance baptismal regeneration in an *ex opere operato* sense.

What is "the word" that accompanies baptism? It is likely the formula used at the moment of baptism. In principle, this word was trinitarian in shape (Mt 28:19), but on occasion it simply invoked the all-sufficient name of Jesus. Possibly the candidate for baptism confessed faith in Christ and called on the Savior's name as he or she was being baptized.

27 The ultimate aim in view when Christ gave himself up for the church (v.25) was that at the end of the age he might be able to "present" her to himself in unsullied splendor as a bride adorned for her husband (Rev 21:2). The verb "present" (GK 4225) is used of the presentation of Christ in the temple (Lk 2:22). Paul himself applies it to the presentation of the church as a pure virgin to Christ her husband (2Co 11:2). Normally it was the friend of the bridegroom (Jn 3:29) who handed over the bride. But Christ dispenses with all intermediaries, and he alone introduces the bride to the bridegroom, who paradoxically is himself. As used here, this verb becomes almost equivalent to "make" or "render." The eschatological church is transformed by Christ so as to be made "all glorious" (Ps 45:13). No ugly spots or lines of age disfigure the appearance of the bride. The church becomes what it was intended to be—"holy and blameless" (cf. 1:4). All this is possible only because Christ is the Savior of his body (v.23).

28 Paul returns to his analogy and declares that just as Christ loves the church, so husbands ought to love their wives as being one flesh with themselves. Christ loves the church—not simply as if it were his body, but because it is in fact his body. Husbands therefore are to love their wives, not simply as they love their own bodies, but as being one body with themselves, as indeed they are. Lest the staggering implication of what he has affirmed should fail to register with his readers, Paul puts it in another way to avoid ambiguity. So intimate is the relationship between man and wife that they are fused into a single entity. For a man to love his wife is to love himself. She is not to be treated as a piece of property, as was the custom in Paul's day. She is to be regarded as an extension of a man's own personality and so part of himself.

29 The apostle appeals to a self-evident fact. It will hardly be denied that no one ever hates his or her own body (Ge 2:23; Eph 5:30–31). Rather, one devotes oneself to looking after it and provides for it in every way, supplying it with food to promote its development and maintain its health. Everyone cares for his or her own body and cherishes it. This is how Christ loves his body, the church (v.25), argues Paul. He appeals to the same principle when addressing husbands as he did when addressing wives. Just as wives are to submit to their husbands as the church submits to Christ, so husbands are to love their wives as Christ loves the church.

30 The reason why Christ thus cares for the church is now made clear. It is because Christians are living parts of his body. In 4:25 Paul has dealt with the relationship of the members to one another individually. Here he is concerned with their relationship to the whole. Earlier in the letter he has spoken about the church as a body whose head is Christ (1:22–23; 4:12, 16). Here he stresses the closeness of the Christian's communion with Christ as a part of himself, just as the branches are part of the vine.

31 Paul introduces Ge 2:24 at this point to substantiate his argument from Scripture, just as Jesus himself did (cf. Mk 10:7). "For this reason" is not a preface to the quotation but part of it. When Adam recognized that Eve was part of himself (Ge 2:23), the next verse adds: "For this reason a man will leave his father and mother and be united to his wife, and they will become one flesh." That is, the marriage tie takes precedence over every other human relationship and for this reason is to be regarded as inviolable. At the same time, what is basically a divine ordinance is graciously designed for mutual satisfaction and delight. "United" means closely joined and, taken in conjunction with the reference to "one flesh," can refer only to sexual intercourse, which is thus hallowed by the approval of God himself. It is because of this exalted biblical view of marital relations that the church has taken its stand on the indissolubility of the marital bond and the impermissibility of polygamy, adultery, or divorce.

32 This is a mystery of far-reaching importance. But what is meant by "mystery" here? Already we have seen that for Paul in this letter "mystery" means a secret of revelation made known through a special dispensation of grace (3:2–3). Usually it embraces the total sweep of God's purposes in Christ (1:9; 3:3–4, 9; 6:19), but it may also refer to some specific truth within that wider revelation (cf. Ro 11:25; 1Co 15:51). With regard to Ge 2:24, the more profound truth now revealed is that in order for Christ, the husband, to win his bride, the church, he had to sacrifice himself for her on the cross (v.25).

Paul does not add the words "but I am talking about Christ and the church" as if he has been diverted from his theme. Rather, he is saying that so far as he is concerned, he refers the mystery to the relation between Christ and the church—a mystery into which he himself had been given unusual insight because of the revelation entrusted to him.

33 The final word in this section is a practical one. Whether or not Paul's readers have fully understood his allusions to the "profound mystery" (v.32), they should at least get hold of the essential instructions he has been endeavoring to convey. Paul addresses every husband individually (lit., "you each, one by one"). Each one is to go on loving his wife as his very self (vv.25, 28–29). For her part, the wife is to give her husband the respect that is due him in the Lord (v.22)—a respect that is conditioned by and expressive of reverence for Christ. It also assumes that the husband will so love his wife as to be worthy of such deference.

F. Christian Relationships: Parenthood (6:1–4)

After dealing with husband-wife relationships, Paul considers the relationship between parents and children. He has the Christian family in mind; he assumes that both partners and their offspring recognize the lordship of Christ (vv.1, 4). He envisages no clash of loyalties in which God has to be obeyed rather than other people.

1 Paul addresses "children" directly, taking it for granted that they will be present in the congregations where the letter is being read. They belong to the total Christian family, the church. As in the previous paragraph on wives (5:22), the less-privileged and subordinate group in society of that time is given priority of treatment (cf. also slaves in vv.5–9). Social distinctions, rigidly observed in the Roman empire and even in Judaism, are transformed by the gospel so that those previously dispossessed acquire new rights.

Obedience by children consists in listening to the advice given by parents, an obligation supported by many passages in both OT and NT. In Col 3:20, Paul adds that this obedience is to be comprehensive in its scope. Isaac's willingness to be offered as a sacrifice is a model of such submission. Disobedience to parents is a symptom of a disintegrating social structure (cf. 2Ti 3:2), and Christian families have a responsibility not to contribute to the collapse of an ordered community. Both parents are mentioned, though in v.4 only fathers are given instructions as to reciprocal behavior. As head of the family, the husband acts representatively for his wife (as mother) as well as on his own behalf.

All this is "in the Lord," as are the other relationships (cf. 5:21–22; 6:5–9). Children are invited not simply to copy the example of Jesus when he was subject to his parents (Lk 2:51), but to realize that both they and their parents are under the authority of the living Christ. This is said to be the "right" thing for them to do, for such obedience "pleases the Lord" (Col 3:20). Obedience to parents is part of the divine law. Children need to recognize that some things have to be accepted even though at the time they themselves cannot understand them.

2 The fifth commandment is quoted as confirmation of v.1 (Ex 20:12; Dt 5:16). Paul appeals to what the children had already learned, for their Christian education began with the Decalogue. To "honor" (GK 5506) is more than to obey; it means to respect and esteem.

This is said to be "the first commandment with a promise." If we connect "first" and "promise," a difficulty arises because the fifth commandment is not the first of the ten to which a promise is attached. The second commandment against making idols also contains one. We should therefore separate "with a promise" from "first" and insert a comma after "commandment." But in what sense can this commandment be regarded as "the first"? It seems most likely that "first" here means first in importance. The rabbis regarded this commandment as the weightiest of all. Perhaps Paul meant to convey the fact that this is the most important commandment for children. Another likely explanation is to note the absence of the article before "first," suggesting that this is a primary commandment, i.e., one of foremost significance.

3 The promise attached to the fifth commandment in Dt 5:16 is not in itself appropriate to the church, so Paul stops short of the final clause, which speaks about the specific land God has given his people. What was originally a specific assurance to the Jews about Canaan becomes a generalization for Christians. The prospect of longevity is not held out elsewhere in the NT as part of the Christian hope, and commentators have tended to spiritualize the application by linking it with eternal life. "On the earth" rules out that interpretation. It is more likely that Paul wished to emphasize that by obeying their parents, children will live to prove that their true welfare depends on God (Dt 5:10).

4 The child-parent relationship is not one-sided. A standard feature of Paul's treatment of these domestic categories is that the stronger have obligations to the weaker. The gospel introduced a fresh element into parental responsibility by insisting that the feelings of the child must be taken into consideration. In a society where the father's authority was absolute, this was revolutionary.

Paul addresses "fathers" as the heads of their families, though the term could mean "parents." Above all else, he warns them against goading their children into a state of perpetual resentment (cf. 4:26). He is not thinking of extreme instances like disinheritance, but the everyday tensions of family life. Fathers must not make unreasonable demands. Otherwise children, being overcorrected, may lose heart (cf. Col 3:21). Children should be treated with tenderness.

Children are a heritage from the Lord (Ps 127:4); they are to be reared for him. The verb "bring up" (GK *1763*) has to do in the first place with bodily nourishment (5:29) and then with education in its entirety. Paul mentions two aspects of such domestic education. "Training" (GK *4082*) in the Greco-Roman world meant strict discipline; what Paul is referring to here is training in righteousness. "Instruction" (GK *3804*) is correction by word of mouth. Remonstration and reproof are implied, but also advice and encouragement. What we have here is the beginning of Christian education in the home.

G. Christian Relationships: Employment (6:5–9)

The apostle deals finally with the relationship between slaves and masters. He is still concerned with the Christian household, for the majority of slaves were employed in the home. It is estimated that there were over sixty million of them in the Roman empire—about one-third of the total population—and more and more were becoming Christians. Most of them would be in pagan employment, though a few may have had Christian masters, like Onesimus (a slave of Philemon).

The fact that Paul has more to say to slaves than to masters (cf. Col 3:22–4:1) may reflect the social structure of these Asian churches. He addresses them on an equality with their masters and assumes that they have a Christian vocation. In a society that regarded slaves as no more than living tools, this was a sufficiently radical change of attitude. It did not immediately lead to emancipation but clearly paved the way. It is significant that, whereas marriage and the family are presented as divine ordinances, no such claim is made for the institution of slavery.

5 Slaves are to obey their masters whether they are good or bad. They are only "earthly" masters. The Christian slave has a heavenly Lord to whom he owes supreme allegiance. Because of this overriding relationship slaves can bear the burden of their servitude with equanimity, for in reality, they are free in the Lord.

"Respect and fear" must not be confused with craven servility but represent a sense of one's shortcomings and a desire not to make any mistake. "Sincerity" (GK *605*) is the opposite of duplicity in thought or action. It implies openness and concentration of purpose, especially in the context of generosity. The Christian slave has one goal before him: to obey his human master as an expression of his commitment to the divine Lord.

6 Christian slaves were not merely to render eye-service by working hard when their master is watching them. They were under more temptation in this respect than paid workers, for they had nothing to gain materially from diligence. All the more reason, then, for Christian slaves to do their job well for its own sake and for Christ's sake. Paul may also be suggesting that Christian slaves should do more than what lies immediately before them. By showing some initiative, they would be acting as free agents and so transcend their social status.

Slaves should not be out simply to win favor with people. Rather, they should seek to please God as they seek to "obey Christ" (v.5) and to function as "slaves of Christ." The double reference to Christ is all the more relevant in the light of our Lord's own servanthood. He himself took the form of a slave and performed the menial task of washing his disciples' feet (Jn 13:1-11). As servants of the one who became the servant of humanity, Christian slaves will enthusiastically embrace the known will of God in this respect.

7 Such service must be rendered with genuine goodwill. Among papyrus letters found in Egypt was a will dated A.D. 157, in which the testator freed five slaves "because of their goodwill and affection." If even pagan slaves could display such qualities, how much more should Christians do so, without expecting their freedom as a reward. "As if" implies no fiction: they actually do serve the Lord rather than mere human beings.

8 Even though Christian slaves will not bank on any material reward, they can be assured of eternal gain (cf. Col 3:24). This is something they fully appreciate because of the catechetical instruction they have been given; it is from the Lord himself that each one will receive back the equivalent of whatever good he or she has done. This principle applies to both the slave and the master. The future tense looks forward to the final judgment when this compensation will be awarded. Like Jesus, Paul does not shrink from referring to rewards (Mt 5:12; Lk 14:12-14), for they are all of grace. They are undeserved, since a Christian's goodness is simply what God has enabled that person to do.

9 The idea that "everyone" will be rewarded for whatever good he or she has done provides a transition to dealing with the duties of "masters." The church did not include in its membership many people of higher social rank, and presumably the number of slave-owners in a local congregation was not large. But there must have been some who were masters, or it would have been pointless for Paul to address them. In fact, Paul wrote a personal letter to Philemon at Colosse about reinstating his fugitive slave, Onesimus.

The golden rule is extended to this most controversial of all relationships within the society of the day. Masters were to treat their slaves as they themselves expected to be treated. Though they gave the orders, they were to do so as themselves being under the authority of a heavenly Master. The common factor is that both were seeking to do the will of God (v.6). Masters must therefore refrain from browbeating their slaves by the threat of severe reprisals for unsatisfactory work. Vicious cruelty was rife among pagan slave-owners. Since their victims had no legal redress, they could be kicked around at will. Christian masters were to show themselves different by not cracking the whip but treating their slaves kindly and fairly.

Christian masters as well as Christian slaves (v.8) know that they all serve a heavenly Lord to whom they equally belong. With him no "favoritism" (GK *4721*) exists. This word means literally to look to see who someone is before deciding how to treat that person. God has no "teacher's pets." Slaves are as precious in his sight as masters, and more is expected from those who are entrusted with greater responsibilities.

H. Into Battle (6:10–20)

This ringing passage sounds a call to arms. What Paul writes here concerning Christian warfare is the external counterpart of his emphasis on the inward growth and edification of the church (4:12, 16). The body of Christ must be united and built up so as to be ready for the inevitable encounter with evil, and each believer needs to be prepared for the fight. This passage may represent a kind of baptismal charge. Its text is "Be on your guard; stand firm in the faith; be men of courage; be strong" (1Co 16:13). It is taken for granted that the victory is already assured through what Christ accomplished by his death and resurrection (Eph 1:20–23). Christ the Lord is the mighty victor who routed all the hosts of wickedness. The Christian is identified with the deliverer in his conquest (Ro 13:14).

10 Paul now begins his final instructions in this letter. His addressees are to let themselves be strengthened in Christ himself (Php

4:13). Even though victory is secure, it has to be won through battle. All the resources that the Christian soldier needs are drawn from Christ and "his mighty power." Three of the four words for power in Eph 1:19 (see comment) are brought together again here. Paul's readers will recall that this is the same power that raised Jesus from the dead (1:20) and brought them to life when they were dead in trespasses and sins (2:1). Its adequacy cannot possibly be in doubt.

11 The call to "put on" (GK *1907*) God's armor recalls a similar appeal in 1Th 5:8. This accoutrement is provided by God and modeled on what he wears himself (Isa 11:5; 59:17). It is a complete outfit ("full armor," also v.13). The soldier must be protected from head to foot, and his armor is made up of all the various pieces, both defensive and offensive.

"Stand" is a key word in this passage (cf. vv.13–14). It is a military term for holding on to one's position. The equipment enables the soldier to ward off the attacks of the enemy and to make a stand against him. Before any offensive can be launched, one must first of all maintain his own ground. The fourfold use of "against" stresses the determined hostility confronting the Christian soldier. The commander-in-chief of the opposing forces is the devil himself, the sworn enemy of the church. He is a master of ingenious stratagems and his tactics must not be allowed to catch us unawares. These stratagems probably reflect his deliberate attempts to destroy the unity of Christ's body (3:14–22; 4:1–16, 21) through the invasion of false doctrine and the fomenting of dissension (4:2, 21, 31–32; 5:6).

12 In military strategy one must never underestimate the strength of the enemy. Paul is certainly not guilty of such fatal misjudgment but gives a realistic report of its potential. The "struggle" (lit., "wrestling") is not merely against human foes but a war to the death against supernatural forces.

Four aspects of the corporate menace are presented here. The particular terms used are in themselves morally neutral, though in Paul they invariably indicate something sinister (1:21; 3:11). "Rulers" (GK *794*) are "cosmic powers." Until the end of this age these demonic forces, already defeated by Christ on the cross (4:9), exercise a certain limited authority (here "authorities"; GK *2026*) in temporarily opposing the purposes of God. The title "powers" (GK *3179*) denotes those who aspire to world control. It was attached to savior gods in the ethnic religions and identified with the sun. The expression "the spiritual forces of wickedness" suggests the heavenly bodies, which were regarded as the abode of demons who held human lives in their grip. Pagans had no option but to resign themselves to an unalterable destiny. But Christians can fight against such malign influences. "The heavenly realms" probably denotes the unseen world in general, including both good and evil forces.

13 Because the warfare in which Christians are engaged is on the scale described in v.12, the command to take advantage of the "full armor of God" is reiterated from v.11. The verb, though translated "put on," is a different one from that in v.11; here it means "take up, assume" (GK *377*). Thus, when the battle is at its fiercest, the soldiers of Christ will still be able to hold their line even against the most determined attack (i.e., "the day of evil"). When the emergency is over, it will be found that not an inch of territory has been yielded. Christians will "have done everything," not only in preparing for the conflict but also in pursuing it.

14 The exhortation to "stand" repeats the emphasis in vv.11, 13 on the need for immovable steadfastness in the face of a ruthless foe. In v.13 Paul talked about standing firm in the midst of battle. Now he writes at greater length about standing ready in anticipation of it.

The several items of the soldier's armor appear in the order in which they would be put on. Together they comprise "the whole armor" worn before taking the field. First, the "belt" tied tightly around the waist indicated that the soldier was prepared for action. A soldier slackened his belt only when he went off duty. It served to gather in the short tunic and helped keep the breastplate in place when the latter was fitted on. From it hung the scabbard in which the sword was sheathed (v.17).

In Isa 11:5 the Messiah is depicted as wearing the belt of righteousness around his waist and faithfulness as the sash around his body. Here "truth" (GK *237*) is said to be the soldier's belt. "Truth" is to be interpreted both objectively as the truth of the gospel (1:13; 4:15) and subjectively as truth in one's inward being. Because Christians have accepted the truth of revelation and are now indwelt by the risen Lord, who is himself the truth, their lives have truth as its basis, and they display the consistency of character that springs from it.

The "breastplate" covered the body from the neck to the thighs. Usually it was made of bronze, though more affluent officers wore a coat of chain mail. The front piece was strictly the breastplate, but a back piece was commonly worn as well. In Isa 59:17 we are told that Yahweh himself put on righteousness like a breastplate. "Righteousness" (GK *1466*) stands for uprightness and integrity of character—a moral rectitude and reputation for fair dealing that results directly from the appropriation of Christ's righteousness (see comment on 5:9). Christians should not seek protection in any works of their own but only in what Christ has done for them and in them.

15 Once the breastplate has been fitted into position, the soldier puts on his strong army boots; these ensured a good grip. The military successes both of Alexander the Great and of Julius Caesar were due in large measure to their armies being well shod and thus able to undertake long marches at incredible speed over rough terrain. What does "readiness" suggest (GK *2288*)? It signifies a prepared foundation; that is, "the gospel of peace" with God through which believers have already been reconciled to God (2:17) affords them a sure foothold in the spiritual campaign in which they are engaged.

16 "In addition to all this," the Christian soldier is to "take up the shield of faith." The shield is the large oblong or oval scutum that the Roman soldier held in front of him for protection. It consisted of two layers of wood glued together, covered with linen and hide, and bound with iron. Soldiers often fought side by side with a solid wall of shields. But even a single-handed combatant found himself sufficiently protected.

For the Christian this protective shield is "faith" (GK *4411*). We should regard faith here both as our faith in action and as the objective content of faith. Believing cannot be divorced from what is believed, and no rigid line should be drawn between these two aspects. Here only does Paul indicate the effect of a particular piece of armor. With such a shield believers can extinguish all the incendiary devices flung by the devil (v.11). In ancient warfare cane darts were sometimes tipped with tow, dipped in pitch, and then ignited. The Christian's shield effectively counteracts such diabolical missiles not merely by arresting or deflecting them, but by actually quenching the flames to prevent them from spreading.

17 Two more items remain. The "helmet" covered the head. It was made of bronze with leather attachments. In Isa 59:17 the Lord wears "the helmet of salvation" along with the "breastplate of righteousness." Christians share that divine equipment. The verb "take" reflects that the helmet and sword were usually handed to a soldier by his armorbearer. This verb is appropriate to the "givenness" of salvation. In 1Th 5:8 the helmet is identified with the hope of full salvation; this may well be the inference here (Eph 1:18).

The final weapon is the "sword," the short two-edged cut-and-thrust sword wielded by the heavily armed legionary. The "sword of the Spirit" is the Christian's only weapon of offense—meaning either the sword that is supplied by the Spirit or that is used by the Spirit. "The word of God" is the divine utterance or speech. In Isa 11:4 the Messiah is portrayed as one who strikes the ruthless with the rod of his mouth (i.e., by the authoritative impact of what he says).

But what specifically is this utterance of God? Some suggestions are the recorded words of Scripture in the OT, the remembered sayings of Jesus, or apostolic sayings that were incorporated into the NT. Others regard it as words given by the Spirit to meet the critical need of the moment (cf. Mk 13:11), or as prayer in which the Spirit speaks through the Christian (v.18). The best interpretation is probably the most obvious; it refers to those words that the Spirit has inspired so that Christians may use them to drive away Satan. It is significant that in Matthew's temptation narrative Jesus himself (quoting Dt 8:3) refers to "every word that comes from the mouth of God" (Mt 4:4) and employs relevant Scriptures to defeat the devil's stratagems.

18 This verse effectively rounds off the preceding verses. It commands believers with their full armor on to "be alert" by praying. "On all occasions" suggests that they will be in constant prayer in preparation for the battle as well as in the engagement itself. But it is in the critical hour of encounter that such support is most required (cf. "the day of evil" in v.13). "In the Spirit" means in communion with the Spirit or in the power of the Spirit. "Prayers" represents the approach to God in general and "requests" a special form of such prayers (supplication). Every avenue of such praying is to be thoroughly explored.

19 In other letters Paul asks his readers to remember him in their prayers. He recognizes his own dependency upon their intercessions despite his apostolic calling. He knows that only through what God himself supplies can he hope to fulfill his appointed ministry. So he invites his readers to pray that the gift of ready speech may be bestowed on him. To "open [one's] mouth" is a common phrase for making a public address or a long defense.

"Fearlessly" (GK *4244*, repeated in a verbal form in v.20) is attached to "make known." As a favorite word of Paul, it means frankness and uninhibited openness of speech. Being "an ambassador in chains" (v.20), the apostle no doubt is thinking especially of his upcoming appearance before the imperial authorities—perhaps even the emperor himself—when he would have the opportunity to reveal the secret of the gospel. He had been chosen to carry the name of Jesus "before the Gentiles and their kings" (Ac 9:15), and this defense in Rome was to be the climax of his distinctive ministry. Meanwhile, as he awaited his trial, he wanted to make the most of every occasion that could be capitalized in the interests of the kingdom (cf. Ac 28:31).

20 Because of his faithfulness in preaching the Good News, Paul has been placed under house arrest. He is an ambassador on behalf of Christ, and yet paradoxically he is in chains. Ambassadors normally enjoyed diplomatic immunity, but Paul would be compelled to appear in the imperial court as a prisoner. Instead of wearing a golden chain of office he would be shackled to his guard (Ac 28:20; 2Ti 1:16). Once again, Paul says that he is counting on the prayers of the church so that he might speak out boldly "the mystery of the gospel" (v.19). "As I should" (Col 4:4) is not only "as it is incumbent upon me" but "in the way I ought."

IV. Conclusion (6:21–24)

21 This is almost a word-for-word parallel with Col 4:7–8. Nowhere is the connection between these two captivity letters closer than here. Paul had just completed Colossians, and Ephesians had been hurriedly concluded so that Tychicus could act as bearer of both letters. Since at this point he had exactly the same information to convey as to the Colossians, it is understandable that he employed the same terms.

Tychicus was the apostle's personal representative to the churches in Colosse (Col 4:7–9), Ephesus, and, assuming Ephesians to be a circular letter, other Asian churches. Later we find him with Paul again and named along with Artemas as a possible relief for Titus in Crete (Tit 3:12). Soon afterward he was dispatched to Ephesus (2Ti 4:12). The fact that he was entrusted with these important commissions reflects his reliability. Paul describes Tychicus as a loyal Christian servant and a brother dearly loved, not only by Paul but by all who knew him. He would pass on news Paul did not have time to include at the end of his letter, so that the readers may be brought up to date with details about his affairs and what he was doing.

22 Paul had only one aim in view as he commissioned Tychicus to visit the churches in and around Ephesus. It was to let them know what was happening in relation to him and to encourage them. They could easily become discouraged because of his sufferings on their behalf (3:13). Thus it would comfort them to learn that Paul was being well treated and was free to preach to those who visited him (Ac 28:17–31).

23 Ephesians finishes with a truly apostolic benediction, but one different in form from others in Paul's writings. Couched in the third person, not in the second, it has two parts instead of one. "Grace," which usually comes first, stands last. The three blessings that figure most prominently throughout Ephesians—peace, love, and faith—occupy the first half of the benediction. This is more than a farewell greeting; it is a prayer for reconciliation. Paul longs to see the whole brotherhood of believers in Ephesus and its environs—Jews and Gentiles alike—at "peace" with each other in the one body of Christ (3:15, 19; 4:3). This will only be brought about through mutual "love" (1:15; 3:17–18; 4:2, 16) combined with "faith," from which it is derived (1:15: 3:17; Gal 5:6). The ultimate source of these three essential features of Christian community life is God himself. The name of Christ the Son is associated with that of God the Father in perfect equality.

24 "Grace" is the hallmark of all Paul's benedictions. It is a recurring theme throughout Ephesians (1:2, 7; 2:5, 7–8; 3:2, 8; 4:7). Paul uses the article here ("*the* grace"), perhaps in order to emphasize that this grace is from "the Lord Jesus Christ" (2Co 13:13; Gal 6:18; Php 4:23) or to refer to the grace he has already written so much about in this letter.

"All who love our Lord Jesus Christ" means all believers (cf. Ac 5:14; 1Ti 4:12), for love is a necessary corollary of belief. Those who fail to love the Lord are anathematized in 1Co 16:22 as having no place in the church. Finally, Paul invokes grace on all who love our Lord Jesus Christ "with an undying love." That is the last and sealing word of the letter. The adjective in this phrase means "imperishable" or "unfading" and seems to indicate that Christian love will never die. An alternate meaning to this phrase signifies that lovers of the Lord are guaranteed, and indeed already enjoy, eternal life and immortality (cf. 1:13). As Christians put on the "new self" (4:24), they are recreated and assigned a seat in the heavenly realms (2:6).

This letter began with an ascription of praise "to the God and Father of our Lord Jesus Christ, who has blessed us in the heavenly realms with every spiritual blessing in Christ" (1:3). On this interpretation, it ends with a benediction invoking God's grace on all who love our Lord Jesus Christ in incorruption, because they are sealed with the Holy Spirit for the day of redemption (1:13–14; 4:30).

The Old Testament in the New

NT Text	OT Text	Subject
Eph 1:22	Ps 8:6	Everything subject to Christ
Eph 4:8	Ps 68:18	Ascension and gifts
Eph 4:25	Zec 8:16	Speaking the truth
Eph 4:26	Ps 4:4	Anger and sin
Eph 5:31	Ge 2:24	Institution of marriage
Eph 6:2–3	Ex 20:12; Dt 5:16	Fifth commandment

Philippians

INTRODUCTION

1. Background

Philippi was located in Macedonia about ten miles inland from the Aegean Sea. The original settlement was called Krenides, but in 356 B.C. the name was changed by Philip II, king of Macedonia, when he enlarged the city with many new inhabitants and considerable construction.

During the era of Roman rule, Philippi became a military colony in 42 B.C.; in 27 B.C., its status was again changed so that it received autonomous government, immunity from tribute, and treatment of its residents as if they actually lived in Italy. It was therefore one of the leading cities in the district of Macedonia (cf. Ac 16:12). The Via Egnatia, the main highway from Asia to the west, passed through Philippi and ran alongside the forum of the city. Near the city was the river Gangites.

The church at Philippi was founded in A.D. 50 in the course of Paul's second missionary journey (Ac 16). While the apostle was in Troas, he was instructed in a vision to proceed into Macedonia, and Philippi became the first European city in which he preached. Apparently the Jewish population in Philippi was small, for there was no synagogue. The missionary party, consisting of Paul, Silas, Timothy, and Luke, met first with some women at a Jewish place of prayer by the river bank outside the city. The first convert was Lydia, a "God-fearer" (a term denoting a Gentile who had become a partial adherent to Judaism), who responded to Paul by receiving Christian baptism and opening her home to the missionary party. Other significant incidents were the exorcism of the demon from a slave girl and the conversion of the jailer and his family. These early converts were a most diverse and unlikely group with which to found a local church, but the grace of God overcame their differences.

When the apostolic party moved on, Luke may have been left behind to guide the new work (the use of "we" in the narrative of Acts is dropped until 20:5–6, when Paul returns to Philippi). The new church did not forget its founder, however, for gifts were sent to Paul on several occasions (Php 4:15–16).

Paul made a second visit to Philippi in A.D. 55–56 on his third missionary journey (Ac 20:1–6). He must have passed through the city twice: on his outward trip toward Corinth and again on his return when he was on the way to Jerusalem. Luke apparently rejoined the party at that time. This visit to Jerusalem culminated in Paul's arrest and eventual imprisonment in Rome (Ac 21–28), which in turn brought about the occasion for this letter.

2. Authorship and Unity

That the apostle Paul wrote this letter to the Philippians is virtually unquestioned. The straightforward claim of the letter (1:1) is supported by the reference to Paul's acquaintances, the reflection of known circumstances in his life, and the many indications of Pauline thought. Even those who have questioned the unity of Philippians have usually concluded that Paul was the author of its various parts.

The case for a composite document has not commended itself to the majority of scholars. The rather abrupt break in tone and subject matter at 3:1 could have been due to the receiving of new information from Philippi as Paul was writing the letter or to an interval of several hours or even days between the several parts. The word "finally" in the middle of the letter (3:1) may simply mean "in addition."

3. Date and Place of Origin

Inasmuch as Paul was a prisoner at the time that Philippians was written (1:7, 13, 16), identification of this imprisonment would make possible the fixing of the date and place of origin of the letter. Three possibilities must be considered: Caesarea, Rome, and Ephesus.

1. *Caesarea.* Paul was a prisoner in Caesarea for two years (A.D. 57–59) and his friends had access to him (Ac 24:23, 27). The fugitive slave Onesimus could have fled there (this assumes that Colossians and Philemon came out of the same imprisonment as Philippians). The "praetorium" (1:13; NIV, "palace guard") could be understood of Herod's palace at Caesarea (Ac 23:35). Furthermore, the polemic against Jewish teachers (3:1–16) fits well the period of Jewish-Gentile controversy.

This theory has not been widely adopted, however, because there is not much evidence favoring it. Paul expected prompt release (2:24), but there was little reason for such optimism while he was at Caesarea, and this prospect was no longer possible after he had appealed to Caesar.

2. *Rome.* The traditional view places the writing of Philippians during Paul's first imprisonment in Rome during A.D. 59–61 (Ac 28:30). This is the most natural understanding of "palace guard" (1:13) and "Caesar's household" (4:22). Paul's trial was evidently going on during the writing, and its outcome could bring either life or death. Apparently there could be no appeal from its verdict (1:19–24). His circumstances reflected in the letter fit the Roman imprisonment better than the one at Caesarea, since he had freedom to arrange itineration for his associates and opportunity to carry on considerable correspondence. This view is the one that is most widely held; it will be assumed in this commentary.

3. *Ephesus.* The case for the origination of this letter at Ephesus would place its writing in A.D. 53–55 during Paul's stay in Ephesus (Ac 19). While Acts mentions no imprisonment of Paul there, hints of it are found in Ro 16:4, 7; 1Co 15:32; 2Co 1:8–10; 11:23. But this is by no means established, for it demands treating the passages in Corinthians with wooden literalness rather than as the dramatic figures they are.

The letter to the Philippians presupposes several time-consuming journeys between Philippi and Paul's location. Consequently, some scholars hold that an Ephesus origin is more likely than one at Rome. As many as six trips may have occurred (requiring at least one month each between Philippi and Rome, but only one week between Philippi and Ephesus): (1) News of Paul's plight reaches Philippi; (2) Epaphroditus travels with a gift to Paul; (3) news of Epaphroditus's illness reaches Philippi; (4) the report of the Philippians' concern reaches Epaphroditus; (5) a trip was made by Timothy to Philippi; and (6) a return trip by Timothy to Paul was contemplated. Nevertheless, several factors weaken the force of this argument in favor of Ephesus. Not all of these trips necessarily originated after Paul was put in prison. Furthermore, two years in Rome would have provided sufficient time for these trips.

The Ephesus theory is also weakened by the fact that at Ephesus Paul could have appealed to Caesar as he did at Caesarea (contra 1:20, 23–24). Philippians also says nothing about the collection—a project Paul was engaged in while at Ephesus. Thus, the Ephesus theory does not seem to have sufficient foundation to dislodge the traditional view of Rome as the place of origin. It does seem, however, to be separated from the other prison letters (Ephesians, Colossians, and Philemon), because it was carried by a different messenger and reflects circumstances apparently somewhat later than those relating to the other three. A date of A.D. 61 is suggested.

4. Occasion and Purpose

The Philippian church sent Epaphroditus to Paul with a gift from their congregation (4:18) and with instructions to minister to his needs through personal service (2:25). He also must have brought news of the progress and problems of the church. In the performance of his responsibilities, Epaphroditus became gravely ill, and the Philippians heard about it. For some reason, this latter circumstance greatly distressed Epaphroditus. Paul was therefore sending him back; his request that the church receive him with all joy and hold him in high regard (2:29) implies that some misunderstanding had occurred. He assures the church that Epaphroditus had been a real fellow soldier in the Lord's work (2:25), that his illness had been extremely serious (2:27–30), and that he was worthy of a hero's welcome (2:29).

The mention of the Philippians' gift (4:10–20) should not be regarded as Paul's first acknowledgment of their help. Too much time had elapsed since Epaphroditus's arrival for this to be a reasonable inference, nor would this mention have been delayed to the end if

Philippi In the Time of Paul

The Roman colony of Philippi (*Colonia Augusta Julia Philippensis*) was an important city in Macedonia, located on the main highway leading from the eastern provinces to Rome. This road, the Via Egnatia, bisected the city's forum and was the chief cause of its prosperity and political importance. Ten miles distant on the coast was Neapolis, the place where Paul landed after sailing from Troas, in response to the Macedonian vision.

As a prominent city of the gold-producing region of Macedonia, Philippi had a proud history. Named originally after Philip II, the father of Alexander the Great, the city was later honored with the name of Julius Caesar and Augustus. Many Italian settlers from the legions swelled the ranks of citizens and made Philippi vigorous and polyglot. It grew from a small settlement to a city of dignity and privilege. Among its highest honors was the *ius Italicum*, by which it enjoyed rights legally equivalent to those of Italian cities.

Ruins of the theater, the acropolis, the forum, the baths, and the western commemorative arch mentioned as the "gate" of the city in Ac 16:13 have been found. A little farther beyond the arch at the Gangites River is the place where Paul addressed some God-fearing women and where Lydia was converted.

© 1985 The Zondervan Corporation

---

it had been the occasion for Paul's writing the letter. Because of the several contacts between Philippi and Rome before this time, Paul had undoubtedly sent his initial thanks promptly. We may account for the additional mention of the gift as the apostle's grateful recollection of a very generous contribution.

Of all the letters Paul wrote to churches, this one stands out as being the most personal. No sharp rebukes of the congregation mar its joyful spirit, and no disturbing problems threaten the progress of the church. The warnings are of a cautionary and preventive nature. The frequent emphasis on Christ explains the underlying relationship of Paul to his readers.

EXPOSITION

Introduction (1:1-11)

A. Greeting (1:1-2)

1 "Paul and Timothy" are associated in the greeting, not because they were co-authors, but because Timothy was a well-known Christian leader, especially at Philippi, and was now with Paul. Paul alone was the author (see the singular verb and pronouns in 1:3-4 and the discussion in 2:19-23). Timothy had been present at the founding of the church at Philippi (Ac 16:1-12) and on several subsequent occasions (Ac 19:22; 20:3-6). Perhaps he served as Paul's amanuensis for the letter.

Both Paul and Timothy are designated as "servants [GK 1528] of Christ Jesus." This word is not a technical reference to a specific office, but emphasizes submission and dependence on their Lord and characterizes their willing service for Christ.

The addressees are "all the saints in Christ Jesus" who resided in the Macedonian city of Philippi. All believers are "saints" (GK 41) through their spiritual union with Christ, a fact Paul often expressed by the phrase "in Christ Jesus" (Ro 8:1-2; Eph 2:6, 10, 13; 3:6) or "in Christ" (Ro 12:5; 2Co 5:17). "Saints" here emphasizes not their personal holiness, though their conduct should correspond increasingly to their standing, but the objective status believers possess because the merits of Christ are imputed to them.

Though "overseers and deacons" were the two orders of officers in the local NT churches (1Ti 3:1-3), Philippians is the only letter to mention them in its greeting. The church at Philippi was organized, and this greeting endorses the officers' authority. "Overseers" (GK 2176) denotes the chief administrative officers in a local church; the term is interchangeable with "elders" (cf. Tit 1:5, 7). "Deacons" (GK 1356) were secondary officers in the church, charged with various temporal concerns (see comments on Ac 6:1-7). Because Epaphroditus had previously been sent with a monetary gift (Php 2:25), the deacons were equally involved in the project of aiding Paul (1:14–16).

2 The familiar blessing, "grace and peace," combines Greek and Hebrew expressions but transforms them into a thoroughly Christian greeting. God's "grace" (GK 5921) is his favor, needed by us in countless ways and bestowed without regard to merit. "Peace" (GK 1645) refers not to the cessation of hostilities between sinners and God (Ro 5:1), but to the inner assurance and tranquility that God ministers to the hearts of believers and that keeps them spiritually confident and content even in the midst of turmoil (4:7). The source of these blessings is "God our Father and the Lord Jesus Christ." To Paul, Jesus the Messiah is the divine Lord, ascended to the Father's right hand and equal to him in authority and honor. Just as Christ and the Father joined in the sending of the Holy Spirit (Jn 14:26; 15:26), so they jointly convey these blessings.

B. Thanksgiving (1:3–8)

3–4 Paul begins his letter by thanking God for his readers—a pattern followed in all his letters except Galatians. With the Philippians Paul had a warm relationship, and this tone is established at the outset of the letter. By stating his thanks to "my God," the author reveals his personal devotion. This was no stereotyped formula, but the natural outflow from the heart of a deeply spiritual man. The thanksgiving was prompted by the joyous memory Paul had of his Philippian friends. "Joy" (a word used five times in this letter, with "rejoice" occurring seven times) permeated his prayers even while he prayed for their needs.

5 What caused Paul the deepest satisfaction was the Philippians' "partnership [GK 3126] in the gospel." This term denotes participation or fellowship and expresses a two-sided relation. It includes the believer's participation in the life of God (1Co 1:9; 1Jn 1:3) and also the sharing of a common faith. Thus it assumes the existence of a brotherly relationship among believers (2Co 8:4; Gal 2:9; 1Jn 1:7). Their partnership certainly involved the Philippians' recent gift, but that was only one expression of it. Paul was filled with joy over the frequent evidences of their sharing in the work of the Gospel. These had been shown to him "from the first day" he had preached the Gospel in Philippi about ten years before. At that time he had experienced the hospitality of Lydia (Ac 16:15) and the jailer and his family (Ac 16:33–34). Later he had received gifts sent to him at Thessalonica (Php 4:16) and at Corinth (2Co 11:9), as well as the more recent one brought by Epaphroditus.

6 Of course, it was God who had produced their transformed lives by the work of regeneration. Even though Paul rejoiced in the Philippians' generous gift and their evidences of spiritual growth, his confidence did not rest ultimately on them but on God, who would preserve them and enable them to reach the goal. The "good work" refers to the salvation begun at their conversion. God not only initiates this salvation, but continues it and guarantees its consummation at the glorious coming of Jesus Christ, which will vindicate both the Lord and his people. Nothing in this life or after death can prevent the successful accomplishment of God's good work in every Christian.

"The day of Christ Jesus" is a phrase occurring six times in the NT (1Co 1:8; 5:5; 2Co 1:14; Php 1:6, 10; 2:16). This expression is similar to the "day of the Lord" (1Th 5:2) and the OT "day of the LORD" (Am 5:18–20). It will be the time when Christ returns for his church, salvation is finally completed, everyone's works are examined, and believers are rewarded.

7 Paul was right in regarding the Philippians so highly, because in a sense they had become partners in his imprisonment and his current legal obligations. To say they were in his "heart" (GK 2840) denotes not an emotional response on his part, but the essence of his inner consciousness and personality.

The reference to Paul's imprisonment belongs with the following rather than the preceding words, as giving evidence of the Philippians' partnership in God's grace. Even when it might have been dangerous to identify themselves openly with Paul, they had treated his misfortunes as their own and had come to his assistance with their gifts. "Defending and confirming the gospel" is legal terminology. "Defending" (GK 665) is used elsewhere in the NT of a legal defense (Ac 22:1; 25:16; 2Ti 1:16), and "confirming" (GK 1012) was a legal technical term (Heb 6:16) for guaranteeing or furnishing security. So

Paul is probably thinking of his approaching hearing in which he must give a defense of the Gospel he preached and in which he hoped also to offer clear proofs of its truth and validity. In Paul's view, all Christians were on trial with him, for the outcome could ultimately affect them all. The Philippians' assistance by their warm fellowship was a clear reminder that they felt the same way.

8 Only God could truly vouch for Paul's feelings about his Philippian friends, because they ran so deep. These yearnings for this church were prompted by the "affection of Christ Jesus," with whom Paul was in vital union. The indwelling Christ was producing the fruit of love in Paul by the Holy Spirit, enabling him to yearn for their welfare with the compassion of his Lord.

C. Prayer (1:9–11)

9 Paul's genuine thanks for the fellowship of the Philippian saints caused him to pray for their continued spiritual progress. Concern for others should express itself first in prayer, as one recognizes the importance of the divine factor in any lasting spiritual growth. The basic petition of Paul's prayer is that his readers' love might "abound more and more." "Love" (GK 27) is an aspect of the fruit of the Spirit (Gal 5:22), enabling all other spiritual virtues to be exercised properly (1Co 13:1–3). Without it no Christian is spiritually complete (Col 3:14). There is no reason to limit this to love for God, for each other, or for Paul. It is unrestricted and refers to any continuing demonstration of this spiritual fruit in any and all ways.

Love must be intelligent and morally discerning, however, in order to be genuine. It is based on knowledge, the intellectual perception that recognizes principles from the Word of God as illuminated by the Holy Spirit. Such spiritual knowledge enables believers to love what God commands. "Depth of insight" stresses moral perception and the practical application of knowledge to the myriad circumstances of life. Spiritual knowledge is thus no abstraction but is intended to be applied to life.

10 The atmosphere in which their love should operate requires the Philippians continually "to discern what is best." Some things are clearly good or bad. In others the demarcation is not so readily visible. In Christian conduct and the exercise of love, such factors as one's influence on others and the effect on oneself must be considered (1Co 10:32). The question should not only be "Is it harmful?" but "Is it helpful?" (1Co 10:23).

The goal in view is the "day of Christ," in which all believers must stand before the Lord and give an account of their deeds (2Co 5:10). This sobering and joyous prospect should have a purifying effect on their lives (1Jn 3:3).

11 The conduct that receives Christ's commendation is "the fruit of righteousness"—i.e., transformed lives as proof that God works in believers. Paul desires that when his readers stand before Christ, their lives will have been filled with the right kind of fruit. He is not talking about mere human uprightness measured by outward conformity to law (3:9). He is rather speaking of the spiritual fruit that comes from Jesus Christ, produced in them by the Holy Spirit (Gal 5:22). Consequently, all the glory and praise belong not to believers but to God, for he has redeemed them by the work of his Son and has implanted within them his Spirit to produce the fruit of righteousness (cf. Eph 1:6, 12, 14).

I. The Situation of Paul in Rome (1:12–26)

A. Paul's Circumstances Had Advanced the Gospel in Rome (1:12–18)

12 "I want you to know" typically introduces an important assertion and may imply that misunderstanding has arisen over a matter. In this instance, the significance of Paul's immediate situation was the important matter. On the assumption that the letter was written from a Roman imprisonment, Paul is saying that his recent circumstances had not been detrimental but advantageous to the Gospel. This event does not seem to refer to his imprisonment as such, about which the Philippians had been informed, but to more recent developments. Perhaps Paul had been moved from his hired house (Ac 28:30) to some place more accessible to the trial scene. This could easily have been interpreted as bad news, but it had "really served to advance the gospel." Paul does not imply that his case had been settled, nor that any official action favoring Christianity had been taken.

Nevertheless, his immediate circumstances should be viewed as a plus for the Gospel.

13 There were at least two ways in which the Gospel had been advanced through Paul's circumstances. The first was that it had been made clear throughout "the whole palace guard" that Paul's imprisonment was "for Christ." During the first century, prisoners sent to Rome in cases of appeal were entrusted to the care of praetorian guards. As these guards were assigned in succession to Paul, it soon became clear to them that he was no ordinary captive. The words "for Christ" are connected with "clear" in the Greek text; thus Paul was claiming that his relationship to Christ had been made clear to his guards.

Paul's bold testimony to the Gospel of Christ in spite of his imprisonment had also been borne "to everyone else" who came to his quarters, including members of the Jewish community (Ac 28:17ff.), at least one Gentile (Phm 10), and many Christian coworkers. Instead of falling into self-pity, he took every opportunity to make the Gospel known.

14 The second way the Gospel had been advanced was that Paul's circumstances had emboldened other Christians in Rome. One might suppose that his imprisonment would have dampened any evangelizing efforts and have caused believers in Rome to "go underground." Or if Paul had become depressed by these new developments, the others too would have lost enthusiasm for the Gospel. But exactly the opposite was true. They drew courage from Paul's example, laid their fears aside, and became more bold in proclaiming God's word. The present tense shows it was no momentary enthusiasm that quickly passed but was still the situation as Paul wrote his letter.

15 Not all of these newly encouraged "preachers" in Rome, however, were responding with the highest of motives. Some were proclaiming the message of Christ "out of envy and rivalry." In the light of vv.16–17, it is clear that their wrong spirit was directed against Paul. It is not difficult to imagine that even those jealous of Paul could well have been intimidated at first by his imprisonment and have kept quiet to protect themselves.

Who were these disappointing preachers? Some have identified them as the Judaizers of 3:1–16. But one can hardly imagine Paul commending such people for speaking "the word of God" (v.14) and "preach[ing] Christ" (vv.17–18) and then later denouncing them so strenuously (3:2). Furthermore, in Paul's view, Judaizers preached another gospel (Gal 1:6–9). More likely, Paul was referring to a part of the group mentioned in 1:14. They were doctrinally orthodox, but at the same time mean and selfish, using the occasion of Paul's confinement to promote themselves. Envious of Paul, they stirred up discord within the Christian community (see comment on v.17).

Others, to their credit, were moved by feelings of goodwill for Paul. Their renewed vigor in proclaiming Christ was a true joining with Paul in the great enterprise of the Gospel.

16 These nobler preachers recognized the apostle's sincerity and unselfishness. They realized that his present circumstances were part of a larger divine program and that he had never deviated from it. He had been "put here" not by his own miscalculations, nor by chance, but by the operation of God's sovereignty "for the defense of the gospel." By ways that could never have been humanly foreseen, God had accomplished within the short space of thirty years the spreading of the Gospel of Jesus Christ from its humble beginnings in obscure Judea to its defense before Caesar at the center of the Empire. No doubt it was with some sense of awe that Paul evaluated his situation in this manner. Recognition of the nature of Paul's imprisonment caused many stalwart Christians to respond out of love for him, to step into the breach, and to take their stand with him, eager to ensure that the Gospel did not fail to be proclaimed while Paul was in prison.

17 The former group of preachers (v.15a) were guilty of insincerity, particularly toward Paul. That they preached Christ and that Paul found no fault with the content of their message shows that their problem was not doctrinal but personal. They were self-seeking opportunists, promoting themselves at Paul's expense. Perhaps they had enjoyed some prominence in the church before he arrived, but had been eclipsed since he came to the city. By taking advantage of Paul's imprisonment, they may have hoped to recover their former popularity. They may have supposed that he would bitterly resent their success (just as they did his) and his imprisonment would become all the more galling to him. If so, they failed to reckon with the greatness of the man.

18 Paul's conclusion, "But what does it matter?" reveals his sense of values. The importance of the Gospel and its proclamation so outweighed any personal considerations that he would not cloud the issue by insisting on settling personal grievances. He was convinced that "Christ is preached" even by these preachers whose motives were suspect. To preach Christ meant to proclaim the good news of salvation provided freely by God's grace through the redemptive work of Christ and received by faith.

As long as the antagonism was only personal, Paul could rejoice that the greater purpose of disseminating the Gospel was being served. Even when some of the preaching arose out of "false motives," utilized to camouflage attacks on Paul, the apostle took the magnanimous view that affronts to himself could be ignored, and he could rejoice in the advance of the Gospel.

B. Paul's Circumstances Would Turn Out for Salvation (1:19–26)

19 Paul moves to the second encouraging aspect of his present situation in Rome—the prospect for his "deliverance" (GK 5401). Is this a reference to deliverance from his present imprisonment? It is true that Paul expressed confidence of release (1:25; 2:24), but the immediate context puts the "deliverance" as somewhat apart from physical life or death (1:21), and the inner struggle described in 1:22–24 makes it questionable whether he would have stated the anticipated result of his Roman trial with this sort of certainty. Thus "deliverance" has the sense of spiritual salvation. Paul viewed salvation as having several aspects—past (Eph 2:8), present (Php 2:12), and future (Ro 13:11). Here the present and future aspects are fused into one as the apostle looks to the unfolding of his Christian life and his ultimate hope of standing unashamed both before human judges and before his Lord (cf. v.20). He viewed his salvation as being accomplished by two means: the effective prayers of the Philippians on his behalf, and the support furnished by the Holy Spirit ("the Spirit of Jesus Christ"). These two are interrelated, inasmuch as Paul would have regarded the Philippians' prayers as being answered by the Spirit's increased activity on his behalf.

20 If "deliverance" has the above-mentioned sense, then Paul is saying that regardless of the outcome of his immediate physical circumstances, he has every reason to "eagerly expect" and "hope" for spiritual victory. These two words (nouns in the Greek text) are grammatically joined by a single article so as to indicate a single concept.

While waiting for the settlement of his case, Paul had a well-founded hope that he would "in no way be ashamed." This is a broad statement referring first to his appearance before the authorities for the final disposition of his case. There may also be overtones of his ultimate appearance before Christ, because he speaks of the possibility of death and of the advantage of being with Christ. He is confident that he will continue to maintain the sort of courage characteristic of his ministry in the past.

The expression "sufficient courage [GK 4244]" conveys the thought of openness, courage, boldness, or confidence, whether toward God or people. Prominent are instances in which this quality is viewed in relation to speech. Paul may be thinking in terms of his coming testimony before his imperial judges. It would not be as easy to give a courageous witness in those circumstances, apart from the help of the Holy Spirit.

Paul wants Christ "to be exalted," regardless of whether (physical) "life" or "death" would be the verdict on his "body." The passive voice of the verb "to be exalted" suggests that Paul was not relying on his own courage but on the action of the Holy Spirit, who would produce this result in response to the prayers of Paul and the Philippians (v.19).

21 "For to me" stresses that Paul's own faith was unshaken, regardless of the circumstances. No adverse decision from the court nor the alarm of his friends could alter his firm belief about his present or his future. "To live is Christ." The very essence of Paul's present life was Christ and all that this entailed. Paul's identification with Christ in a vital spiritual union (Gal 2:20) resulted in far-reaching practical implications. Christ had become for him the motive of his actions, the goal of his life and ministry, and the source of his strength. "To die" after such a life could only mean "gain." Not only would Paul's death be the gateway to Christ's presence (v.23), but the act itself of dying at the hands of Rome was no tragedy in his eyes. Such a death would bear added witness to the power of the Gospel.

22 If, however, he continued to live as a result of a favorable disposition of his case in Rome, he would have continuing opportunity to labor fruitfully in the cause of Christ. For Paul this never meant an easy life. His labors in establishing churches and nurturing them toward maturity were characterized by frequent opposition, physical hardships, and much spiritual anguish (cf. 2Co 11:23–29). Yet he looked on his apostolic ministry as a challenge to be grasped and as fruit to be harvested.

Paul did not know which option he would "choose" (GK *145*) if he could. This word is used of the election of believers by God (2Th 2:13) and of Moses' choice in aligning himself with his own people (Heb 11:25). It does not mean that Paul could actually choose his fate, but it refers to his personal preference. The verb "know" (GK *1192*) means "to make known" in all other NT occurrences, and it seems to have this sense here. Thus, the meaning is, "I cannot tell [you]" or "I cannot declare [to you]." Paul was so positively committed to the will of God that both life and death held certain attractions. If the choice were left to him, he would not be able to tell what he would decide. How fortunate that God does not force us to make such choices!

23 As Paul thought of his prospects, he felt himself in a dilemma ("I am torn"; GK *5309*), though in his case either alternative (continued life or sudden death inflicted by Rome) was a good one. The verb used here is sometimes used of diseases that control their victims. Here the idea of distress seems to be present (cf. Lk 4:38).

From his view of what would be most advantageous to him, Paul desired to leave this life and "be with Christ." Death for him would not be a catastrophe. Paul's expression here indicates that he did not foresee a soul-sleep while awaiting the resurrection, nor any purgatory. As he had already explained to the Corinthians, absence from the body means immediate presence with the Lord (2Co 5:8). This was undoubtedly "better by far," because it would bring him rest from his labors (Rev 14:13) and the joy of eternal fellowship in the very presence of the Lord whom he loved.

24 Yet the apostle also recognized another standpoint from which his future might be viewed. By remaining alive he would offer a certain advantage to his Philippian readers. He does not state specifically what this advantage was, but the obvious reference is to the ministry he might still perform for them.

25 With his situation in the Lord's hands (1:19–24), Paul was confident that what occurred would bring glory to God, regardless of how it turned out. That confidence now prompted him to say, "I know that I will remain." This probably represents Paul's personal conviction based on what seemed to be most probable in the light of all the factors. The need of many for his apostolic ministry outweighed his own need to be with Christ immediately. Furthermore, he must have known that the case against him was not strong (Ac 23:29; 25:25; 26:31–32), and thus his hope of release was well-founded. Evidence from the pastoral letters, confirmed by early historical testimony, indicates that Paul was released from this first Roman imprisonment and began to travel, including a trip through Macedonia (and presumably Philippi), before being reimprisoned and suffering a martyr's death.

Paul's continued ministry among the Philippians would be aimed at advancing their spiritual growth and deepening their joy in the Christian faith. Believers should not be static in their faith but should grow in understanding of spiritual truth. This will increase their joy as they enter more fully into the understanding of their privileges and prospects in Christ.

26 The "joy" (lit., "boasting"; GK *3017*) in Paul's thought here is that as the Philippians experienced the progress and joy that Paul's labors among them would produce (v.25), they would have new and greater reasons for overflowing with joy. Their ultimate reason for glorying would be found "in Christ Jesus," of course, but its immediate occasion would be "on account of me." His ministry among them would enable them to see more clearly the riches of their salvation in Christ.

II. First Series of Exhortations (1:27–2:18)

A. Exhortation to Unity and Courage in View of External Foes (1:27–30)

27 As citizens of a spiritual realm, the Philippians should stand firm in one spirit. This should be true "whatever happens" to Paul, for the responsibility for their spiritual growth rests ultimately with them and their appropriation of the riches in Christ (see v.26). Whether Paul would be released and thus enabled to visit them in person, or be forced to remain away from them and learn of their progress through the reports of others, his exhortation is the same. They must conduct their lives in a manner appropriate to the Gospel of Christ.

In this connection, Paul uses a verb that meant literally "to live as a citizen" for "conduct yourselves" (GK *4488*). This was an apt term for a letter written to a church in a city whose inhabitants were proud of their status as Roman citizens (Ac 16:12, 20–21). The earliest members of the Philippian church would have remembered that Paul had used his own Roman citizenship to bring about a speedy and dignified release from imprisonment there (Ac 16:36–40). Out of this cultural background the readers were challenged to live as those who had a higher and vastly more significant citizenship (Php 3:20).

Paul then urges his readers to "stand firm in one spirit [GK *4460*]." True unity can only be produced by the Holy Spirit, though the emphasis in this verse on the inner result, not the source. They should contend together in the faith "as one man" (lit., "soul"; GK *6034*). It is doubtful whether Paul was trying to draw sharp psychological distinctions between "spirit" and "soul." If such are to be sought to any degree, the former term probably denotes one's highest center of motivation, and for the Christian this would be quickened by the Holy Spirit. The latter term would denote the area of sensory experience.

This exhortation to unified thought and action has in view the goal of "contending" (GK *5254*) "for the faith of the gospel." Paul means here the objective faith (i.e., the body of truth) embodied in the Gospel message. "Contending" suggests their need to promote and protect the message of Christ, while at the same time implying that adversaries must be faced. Such work required joint effort, if we are to be victorious in the contest.

28 Paul does not want the Philippians to be terrified in any respect by their opponents. The noble character of their cause and the recognition that Christ is on their side should cause believers to avoid the unreasoning terror that prevents intelligent effort. Who were these opponents? Most likely the Jews, though it is not necessarily limited to them. Hostile Jews often dogged Paul's steps and caused trouble in the churches he founded (e.g., in Thessalonica: Ac 17:5; in Berea: Ac 17:13). In any case, it is virtually certain that these were external foes, not false teachers within the church. Whether Jewish or pagan enemies, they usually employed the same tactics, and the need for unity and courage among the believers was crucial.

Failure of the church to be intimidated by enemies was a token of the ultimate failure of God's enemies. The adversaries may not have recognized this, but it was nonetheless a "sign" that their attacks were futile and that the church would prevail. As a sign or token, it testified to two things: the ultimate destruction of the adversaries and the salvation of the believers. "And that by God" refers grammatically neither to "salvation" nor to "sign," but to the entire fact that believers have been granted courage from God to stand firm in their struggles and so are demonstrating their salvation.

29 The whole situation was part of God's gracious provision for those enlisted in the cause of Christ. The privileges enjoyed by Christians included the ability not only to believe in Christ initially at regeneration and subsequently throughout their Christian lives, but also to suffer for him. If we question the propriety of referring to suffering as a privilege and a gracious gift, we must remember that the NT regards suffering as God's means of achieving his gracious purposes both in his own Son (Heb 2:10) and in all believers (Jas 1:3–4; 1Pe 1:6–7).

30 In this matter of suffering, the Philippians were experiencing the same sort of "struggle" (GK *74*) Paul had endured throughout his ministry. They had seen some of Paul's sufferings when he was in Philippi (Ac 16:19–24). They had heard of others he had undergone more recently in Rome (from reports of travelers or other messengers, including those who conveyed the information about Epaphroditus, 2:26). The word "struggle," often used in an athletic sense, developed a metaphorical use for any kind of conflict. It is consistent with the thought of "antagonists" in v.28.

B. Exhortation to Unity and Humility Toward Those in the Church (2:1–11)

1 The following exhortation also concerns unity, but this time the focus is turned on problems within the church. To encourage the fulfillment of this injunction, Paul listed four incentives. All are stated as "if" clauses, but the condition is assumed to be true (the "if" becomes almost synonymous with "since"). (1) As Christians, the Philippians were in a vital union with Christ, and this placed obvious obligations on them. They were responsible to heed the orders of Christ as issued by him either directly during his ministry or through his apostles. (2) The comfort and encouragement provided by love should prompt the Philippians to desist from divisiveness in any form and to join hands in common action. (3) The fellowship produced by the Holy Spirit should stimulate the practical exercise of unity. They have been made one by the Spirit (cf. 1Co 12:13) and thus are partners with him and with each other. (4) The existence of tenderness and compassion among them would make the unity that was being called for the normal and expected thing.

"Encouragement" (GK 4155) means either "exhortation" or "consolation." To understand the term in this context as implying more than just comfort is consistent with other Pauline statements on unity. In Eph 4:1–3 the unity of the believers is made the subject of an exhortation. The translation "encouragement" can convey both ideas.

2–4 Paul exhorts the Philippians to make his joy full by "being like-minded" (lit., "minding the same thing"). He was already experiencing joy because of his associations with this church (1:3–4; 4:10), but one attitude that was still needed to make his joy "complete" was like-mindedness. Of course, this was not a command for unity at the expense of truth, for "the same thing" is also "the right thing."

Paul now elaborates on his enjoinder to maintain unity in their thought and action. By complying with the next four instructions, his readers would create a climate where true unity could flourish. (1) Believers should possess a mutual love. Inasmuch as all were indwelt by the same Spirit (v.1), love as a fruit of the Spirit (Gal 5:22) ought to be demonstrated in every life.

(2) Believers should set their minds on oneness "in spirit and purpose." This phrase repeats what was said in v.2 and reinforces the conclusion that there was a problem of disharmony within the congregation. It may be unfair to center the problem on Euodia and Syntyche (4:2), but they were at least involved.

(3) Believers should avoid "selfish ambition" (GK 2249) and "vain conceit" (GK 3029) and consider others above themselves (v.3). Paul himself had experienced adverse effects from selfish ambition among some unworthy preachers at Rome (1:17). Persons who seek to advance themselves usually enjoy glorying in their success. The Christian attitude should reveal itself in "humility" (GK 5425), a concept not highly regarded among the Greeks. Believers should be humble toward one another, mindful of their spiritual brotherhood and their ultimate subjection to Christ. In their exercise of humility, they should "consider others better than yourselves." This does not mean that we must have false or unrealistic views of our own gifts as compared with those of others. Rather, our consideration for others must precede concern for ourselves (Ro 12:10). This will go far toward removing their disharmony.

(4) Believers should be looking not only to their own interests but also to those of others (v.4). The self-centeredness that considers only one's own rights, plans, and interests must be replaced by a broader outlook that includes the interests of one's fellows Christians. "Not only . . . but also" indicates that believers should not neglect their own welfare or that of their families (1Ti 5:8) as they seek the good of others. Instead, Paul calls for a Christian concern that is wide enough to include others in its scope. When each member of the Christian community

exercises this mutual concern, problems of disunity quickly disappear.

5 The great example of humility is Christ Jesus. Although vv.5–11 contain one of the outstanding Christologies in the NT, they were written to illustrate the point of humility and selflessness. Another place where Paul incidentally makes a sublime statement about Christ in illustrating a practical point is Eph 5:25–27.

The literary form of this beautiful passage has led many to regard it as an early Christian hymn that Paul incorporated into his letter. But Paul himself was quite capable of a highly poetic style (cf. 1Co 13), and he may well have composed these exalted lines. Regardless of their precise origin, the passage provides a masterly statement of Christology and serves well the author's purpose of illustrating supreme condescension.

The exhortation comes first: "Your attitude should be the same as that of Christ Jesus." Here the Greek text could literally be rendered, "Keep thinking this [attitude] among you, which [attitude] was also in Christ Jesus." Believers cannot duplicate the precise ministry of Jesus but they can display the same attitude.

6 Christ's preincarnate status is then stated. Two assertions are made: He was "in very nature God" (lit., "in the form [GK 3671] of God"), and he did not regard his existing in a manner of "equality with God" as a prize "to be grasped" or held onto. The word "form" denotes the outward manifestation that corresponds to the essence (in contrast to the noun "appearance" [GK 5386; v.8], which refers to what is outward and perhaps temporary).

The participle "being" (in the sense of "existing") is in the present tense and states Christ's continuing condition. By saying that he was existing in the essential metaphysical form of God is tantamount to saying that he possessed the nature of God. The phrase is elaborated on by the words "equality with God." This does not mean the same as "the form of God," for one's essential nature can remain unchanged, though the manner in which that nature is expressed can vary greatly through changing times and circumstances.

The expression "something to be grasped" (GK 772) has been variously interpreted. Does it mean something that has been seized or something to be seized? This uncertainty has led to three possibilities: (1) The preincarnate Christ already possessed equality with the Father and resolved not to cling to it; (2) Christ had no need to grasp at equality with God, for he already possessed it; (3) Christ did not reach for his crowning prematurely, as Adam had, but was willing to wait till after his suffering. That the preexistent state is in view seems evident from the movement of the passage (see also 2Co 8:9). Inasmuch as Christ already existed in "the form of God," the mode of his existence as equal with God was hardly something totally future but must rather be something he divested himself of. Hence, view 3 above does not fit the context so well as view 1. View 2, though expressing a truth, does not provide an adequate basis for the statements that follow.

7–8 The description then moves to Christ's incarnate state. Two clauses carry the main thoughts: "[he] made himself nothing" and "he humbled himself." The first clause is literally "but himself he emptied" (GK 3033); the Greek word used here has lent its name to the so-called *kenosis* theories that probe the nature of Christ's "emptying" himself. Although the text does not directly state that he emptied himself "of something," such would be the natural understanding when this verb is used. Furthermore, the context has most assuredly prepared the reader for understanding that Christ divested himself of something.

The one who was existing in the form of God took on the form or "nature of a servant." The word "taking" does not imply an exchange, but rather an addition. The "form of God" could not be given up, for God cannot cease to be God; but our Lord could and did take on the very form of a lowly servant when he entered human life in his incarnation. This passage emphasizes his condescension and humble station. What an example our Lord provides of the spirit of humility (cf. 2:3–5)! The statement goes on to make it clear that Christ became part of humanity: "being made in human likeness." The word "likeness" (GK 3930) stresses similarity but leaves room for differences. Thus Paul implies that even though Christ became a genuine man, there were certain respects in which he was not absolutely like the other men. He may have had in mind the unique union of the divine and human natures in Jesus, or the absence of a sinful nature.

In sum, Christ did not empty himself of the form of God (i.e., his deity), but of his manner of existence as equal to God. Christ's action has been described as the laying aside during the Incarnation of the independent use of his divine attributes. This is consistent with other NT passages that reveal Jesus as using his divine powers and displaying his glories upon occasion (e.g., miracles, the Transfiguration), but always under the direction of the Father and the Spirit (Lk 4:14; Jn 5:19; 8:28; 14:10).

Externally, therefore, Christ appeared as a mere human being; outwardly considered, he was no different from other people. This was indeed an act of great condescension for one who possessed the form of God. But Christ's incomparable act did not end here; he further humbled himself by "becoming obedient to death." He was so committed to the Father's plan that he obeyed it even as far as death (Heb 5:8). Nor was this all, for it was no ordinary death, but the disgraceful death by crucifixion, a death not allowed for Roman citizens, and to Jews indicative of the curse of God (Dt 21:23; Gal 3:13).

9 The final movement of thought in this sublime illustration describes Christ's subsequent exaltation. The nature of this exaltation was God's elevating Christ to the highest position and granting him the name above all names. "Exalted ... to the highest place" (lit., "superexalted"; GK 5671) refers to the resurrection, ascension, and glorification of Jesus following his humiliating death, whereby all that he had laid aside was restored to him and much more besides. Implicit in this exaltation is the coming consummation mentioned in vv.10–11, when his triumph over sin and his lordship will be acknowledged by every being.

In view of the chronological pattern exhibited in this passage, the giving of "the name" must have been subsequent to the Cross. This would appear to be sufficient to rule out the identity of the name in view as being "Jesus." A more likely identification of "the name" is "Lord" (GK 3261), the equivalent of the OT "LORD" (Heb. "Yahweh"; GK 3378; cf. v.11). Christ's exaltation is expressly stated as manifesting his lordship in Ac 2:33–36. Another explanation takes "the name" in the sense of position, dignity, or office, similar to the OT use of that word (GK 9005; see that use elsewhere in the NT in Eph 1:21; Heb 1:4). There are also instances where "the name" is used alone as a reference to God or Christ (see Ac 5:41; 3Jn 7; cf. 2Sa 7:13; 1Ki 8:43–44).

10–11 The purpose of Christ's exaltation is that all beings might bow in acknowledgment of the name that belongs to Jesus and confess that "Jesus Christ is Lord." Because of what the name Jesus (i.e., "Savior"; see comment on Mt 1:21) represents, a time is coming when every knee will bow before him in recognition of his sovereignty. This statement is built on the wording of Isa 45:23 (cf. Ro 14:11; Rev 5:13). This universal acknowledgment will include angels and departed saints in heaven, people still living on earth, and the satanic hosts and lost humanity in hell. The phrases "in heaven," "on earth," and "under the earth" could possibly refer to all of creation, animate and inanimate (cf. Ro 8:19–22). However, the mention of "knee" (and "tongue") suggests that personal beings are in view here.

Submission will also be expressed by verbal confession. "Every" indicates a universal acknowledgment of Christ's sovereignty, even by his enemies. Paul does not imply by this a universal salvation, but means that every personal being will ultimately confess Christ's lordship, either with joyful faith or with resentment and despair.

This ultimate confession that "Jesus Christ is Lord" is apparently Paul's indication of the "name" granted Jesus at his exaltation following the Cross (v.9). That name with all the dignity and divine prerogatives this implies will eventually be recognized by every creature. Of course, the Son in his nature was always deity, but the exaltation following the Cross granted him the dignity of station commensurate with his nature and far superior to his humble state while on earth.

"To the glory of God the Father" is Paul's closing doxology to this remarkable Christology. He has never lost sight of the divine order and of the grand scheme in which the incarnation of Christ must be viewed. Recognition of Christ's lordship fulfills the purpose of the Father and so brings glory to God.

This picture of Christ's humiliation and subsequent exaltation was intended by Paul to encourage in his readers an attitude of Christlike humility (v.5). If they were to be identified as Christ's followers, they must demonstrate his characteristics. The appeal, however, was not only to a life of lowliness and hardship; it also contained the reminder that victory followed humiliation and that God's glory will ultimately prevail.

C. Exhortation to Work Out Their Salvation (2:12–18)

12 Paul now exhorts the Philippians to pursue their Christian progress without undue dependence on his presence. Perhaps he had noted a weakness along this line. Once before he had mentioned their need to be as diligent in his absence as they were when he was present with them (1:27). While the obedience he expects from them may be obedience to his commands, Paul ultimately wants them to obey the commands of God that he had taught them. They had always obeyed the commands of God implicit in the Gospel, beginning from the time when he first evangelized them, and it had been witnessed by him on all of his subsequent visits. But they must be just as careful to obey while he was away, especially if his circumstances should prevent a return.

Paul's specific exhortation is to "work out your salvation." The biblical concept of salvation needs to be understood in order to comprehend Paul's intent here. Salvation has many aspects, including a present one (see comment on 1:19). Regeneration initiates believers into a life with obligations, one of which is to obey Jesus our Lord. Hence, working out salvation does not mean "working for" salvation, but making salvation operational. Justification must be followed by sanctification, by which the new life in Christ is consciously appropriated and demonstrated. Moreover, the Christians in Philippi must not depend on Paul but must work out their *own* spiritual progress, because the same Lord who worked through Paul also worked in them (v.13).

"With fear and trembling" does not contradict the joyful spirit permeating this letter. Christian joy is the experience of every believer in God's will, but holy fear of God that trembles at the thought of sin is also the attitude of the careful Christian (Jas 4:8–10).

13 The Philippian Christians can carry out the exhortation of v.12 because God himself produces in believers both the desire to live righteously and the effective energy to do so. God does not demand of us what we cannot do. Furthermore, the provision from God takes into account our every need. It is not always enough to "will" something, for good intentions are not always carried out. Our wills must be energized by God himself.

14 Compliance with Paul's exhortation should be "without complaining or arguing." "Complaining" (GK *1198*) describes grumbling discontent in the congregation, and "arguing" (GK *1369*) depicts evil reasonings and disputes that usually follow. Are these complaints directed against God or against each other? Neither alternative is foreign to the context. On the one hand, this passage is influenced by Dt 32:5; and the example of Israel's complaining, which was chiefly against God, was used elsewhere by Paul to instruct the church (1Co 10:10). On the other hand, the problem of disunity in the congregation has already been noted in this letter (v.2), and more is to come (4:2). Perhaps the command is sufficiently general to cover both meanings.

Emphasis in the command falls on the word "everything" (lit., "all things"). Most Christians are able to do some things without complaint. But when we are exhorted to be doing "all things" with a joyful spirit, the difficulty arises. Yet the outworking of our

In Bible times, the central square of Philippi was the hub of commercial activity in Macedonia. Courtesy Bastiann Van Elderen.

Christian faith in daily life lays this responsibility on us.

15 The purpose of the exhortation to work out their salvation was that the readers might be pure and uncontaminated light-givers in the world. By regeneration they had already become children of God in nature and position. Now as they progressed in sanctification, they would become "children of God without fault," particularly as viewed by the world around them. By faithfully adhering to the word of God as contained in Scripture and taught by Paul, their lives would be free from anything blameworthy. Thus their witness would not be disfigured.

The apostle is mindful of their location within a corrupt society. Using OT language (Dt 32:5) he depicts humankind generally as "a crooked and depraved generation." Amid this moral blackness, the children of God should stand out as stars at midnight. Believers are the possessors of Christ, the Light of the world (Jn 8: 12), and so are now light-givers to the world (Mt 5:14). "You shine" states the present fact. They are not told to shine, but are reminded that they already do. The challenge was to let the light shine out unhindered (cf. Mt 5:16).

16 As luminaries in a world of spiritual darkness, they were to "hold out [GK 2091] the word of life." This word means either "hold fast" or "hold forth." Those who regard the clause about shining as parenthetical adopt the meaning "hold fast"—i.e., holding fast the word of life in contrast to a "crooked and depraved generation." On the other hand, the figure of "stars" supports the idea of "holding forth." Furthermore, this latter sense assumes the former, for those who hold out the word of life to others are understood to have first received it themselves. The word of life is, of course, the Gospel, which brings eternal life when it is received by faith (Jn 6:68).

Faithful living by the Philippians will provide Paul with added reason to "boast" (GK 3017) when he appears before Christ. "The day of Christ" is the time when Christ will return for his church and when believers will have their works inspected and rewarded (see comment on 1:6). Paul wants the basis of his boast at that time to be that his labors for the Philippians had not been useless. He hopes all his efforts to win them to Christ and to nurture their faith will be vindicated at Christ's judgment seat by the victorious presence of the Philippian believers.

17 The prospect of standing before Christ reminds Paul that it might be soon. By the vivid metaphor of a "drink offering," he explains that even though he was presently in a dangerous situation that could lead to a martyr's death, it was the climax of his ministry and a cause for rejoicing. Jewish religious practice included the use of wine poured out ceremonially in connection with certain sacrifices (Nu 15:1–10). Paul regarded his own life as such a sacrifice as he sought the spiritual advancement of those whom he had led to Christ (cf. 2Ti 4:6). "The sacrifice and service" employs only one article with two nouns and probably means "sacrificial service." By this phrase, Paul is thinking of the various Christian ministries that the Philippians performed as a spiritual sacrifice to God (4:18; Heb 13:15), springing from their faith. Thus they and Paul were priests together.

Paul rejoiced in his present labors and sufferings. He was willing to lay down his life, and the prospect of being with Christ and of having his ministry among the Philippians seen as successful filled him with joy. Enduring his present danger would demonstrate that he had learned something of the attitude of Christ (2:5). Furthermore, he also rejoiced with the Philippians as he contemplated his relation to their faith. He was its planter and nourisher, and thus their victories were his also. For this reason he could "rejoice with all of you."

18 Likewise the Philippians should display the same attitude as Paul. They must not wring their hands nor bewail their own trials and Paul's. They must learn to find real joy as they work out their salvation and learn to share Paul's attitude about his situation.

III. Two Messengers of Paul to the Philippians (2:19–30)

A. Timothy (2:19–24)

19 The somber note sounded in the previous two verses is balanced by the more optimistic tone that follows. Paul planned to send Timothy to Philippi with a report and hoped to come shortly himself. His hope was "in the Lord Jesus." Every believer is "in Christ," and this vital union should influence every thought and activity. Thus Paul loves in the Lord (1:8); grounds his confidence in the Lord (2:24); rejoices in the Lord (3:3; 4:10); and desires that others rejoice in Christ (1:26; 3:1), welcome Christian leaders in the Lord (2:29), and always stand firm in the Lord (4:1). It may be that Paul was uncertain of the outcome of his case at Rome and therefore the more obviously submitted all his plans and hopes to the lordship of Jesus.

Paul refers to Timothy, named in the opening of the letter, and to his proposed trip to Philippi with graciousness and delicacy. One might suppose that Paul would have explained that the purpose of the trip was to tell the Philippians about his situation. But he only hints at that idea by the word "also" (and by the clause "as soon as I see how things go with me" in v.23), because his main goal is to hear about them. The spiritual advancement of the churches was always uppermost to Paul.

Paul apparently expected Timothy not to remain at Philippi but to bring him word about the church immediately. Conceivably, they could have planned to meet at Ephesus after Paul's release. At least, they seem to have met together at Ephesus subsequent to this time (1Ti 1:3). This would require that before leaving for Philippi, Timothy knew with certainty the date of Paul's release. Otherwise, Timothy would have been expected to return to Paul at Rome before he left the city.

20 Paul's glowing testimony about Timothy was not to introduce his young associate, for he was already well known at Philippi (see comment on 1:1). It did serve, however, to avert possible disappointment that Paul himself could not come at once, and he indicated that he had the fullest confidence in his younger associate. Paul's phrase "no one else like him" compares Timothy with Paul's other available associates. In the matter of "a genuine interest in your welfare," no one that Paul might conceivably have sent had the same interest in the Philippians as did Timothy. How appropriate that two of the pastoral letters were later written to him as he exercised his pastoral concerns in another city.

21 These words must be understood in harmony with other statements in the letter. Paul had already noted that some among his acquaintances at Rome were more concerned with furthering their own interests (1:14–17), though his reference to them was a temperate one (1:18). Furthermore, Paul must have been on good terms with many of the brothers included in this verse, for he conveys their greetings in 4:21. Nevertheless, we must restrict Paul's reference here to some extent, for he would surely not include Epaphroditus, Luke, or Aristarchus as not seeking the interests of Christ. Most likely Paul is only referring to those around him who might conceivably have undertaken the trip to Philippi. He may have asked some of them, but they had refused in favor of their own pursuits. Luke and Aristarchus were probably away on other missions and so were unavailable (cf. no mention of them in 1:1).

22 The proven character of Timothy, however, put him in a class apart. By the thorough test of his repeated presence and ministry in Philippi, as well as by his reputation achieved elsewhere, the Philippian Christians knew him as a man of God. Paul also vouches for him on the basis of many years of personal experience. He and the younger Timothy had a father-son relationship. Together they had served Christ for the furtherance of the Gospel, beginning with Paul's second missionary journey more than ten years earlier (Ac 16:1–4).

23 Paul now gathers up all that he has just said about Timothy and emphasizes that he is the one to be sent to Philippi. He will not be the bearer of the letter, however, because Paul wants to retain him until he has more definite information about the outcome of his case. This implies that Paul thinks there will soon be some kind of legal decision regarding him. This letter will alert the Philippians to Timothy's coming and will also let them know the reason why he did not come with Epaphroditus. They will also know that when Timothy does come, he will be bringing word about the crucial developments in Paul's legal case.

24 Although the decision could go either way, Paul was still confident that release was imminent and that he would fulfill his wish to visit the Philippians (cf. comment on 1:25). This confidence in the Lord must be similar to that implied in 2:19—"I hope in the Lord

Jesus" (see comment on v.19). Everything we do should be consistent with, and submitted to, the Lord's will.

Evidence furnished by the pastoral letters supports the hypothesis of a release during which Paul did additional traveling in Crete, Asia Minor, Macedonia, and Achaia. There is good reason, therefore, to believe that Paul's hope was realized.

B. Epaphroditus (2:25–30)

25 The second of Paul's messengers to Philippi, and the one whose forthcoming trip was the immediate occasion for this letter, was Epaphroditus, mentioned only in this letter (2:25; 4:18). He had brought the Philippians' gift to Paul. He is identified by the apostle in a series of glowing terms. He was (1) "my brother," a sharer of spiritual life with Paul and so his brother in Christ; (2) a "fellow worker," a participant with Paul in the labors of the Gospel; (3) a "fellow soldier," a sharer of the dangers involved in standing firm for Christ and in proclaiming the Gospel.

(4) With respect to the Philippians, he had acted as their "messenger" (lit., "apostle"; GK 693), the duly appointed and commissioned delegate to convey the Philippians' gift to Paul. This Greek word has a broader use than the twelve apostles and is applied to Barnabas (Ac 14:14), Silas and Timothy (1Th 2:7; cf. 1:1), Andronicus and Junias (Ro 16:7), and James the Lord's brother (Gal 1:19; 1Co 15:7). (5) In this capacity Epaphroditus had served as their representative "to take care of" (GK 3313) Paul's needs, functioning officially in performing a sacred service to Paul. This word (a noun in Greek) often connotes a priestly sort of ministry. It is used of Christ's priestly ministry in the heavenly tabernacle (Heb 8:2) and of Paul's sacred service in evangelizing Gentiles and presenting them to God (Ro 15:16). Hence, its use here also has overtones of a priestly act, that of Epaphroditus's presenting to Paul the Philippians' offering, "an acceptable sacrifice, pleasing to God" (4:18).

26 The verb "longs for" (GK 2160) expresses Epaphroditus's intense desire. It had been used to describe Paul's own feelings toward the Philippians in 1:8. Elsewhere it designates the Spirit's strong yearning for the total allegiance of one's heart (Jas 4:5) and of a newborn baby's longing for milk (1Pe 2:2).

The addition of "distressed" (GK 86) to the mention of Epaphroditus's longings emphasizes the intensity of his feeling (cf. the use of this word to describe our Lord's emotions in Gethsemane; Mt 26:37; Mk 14:33). Epaphroditus had become deeply distressed when he learned that the Philippians knew of his serious illness. Conceivably some misunderstanding had arisen in Philippi, and word of it had gotten back to Rome. Perhaps there were rumors that he was a malingerer, or that he had been more of a burden than a help to Paul.

27 Paul therefore said that Epaphroditus had "indeed" been "ill" and had "almost died" as a result of his labors in the Lord's service, perhaps from the hazards or the exertions of the journey to Rome (v.30). The illness was so severe that Paul regarded his recovery as an intervention of God. By healing him, God was displaying his mercy both on Epaphroditus and on Paul. The restoration of health to the sick man spared Paul "sorrow upon sorrow." He felt keenly the misfortunes of his friends, and though he had been distressed over the illness of this courageous emissary, he was spared the additional sorrow that his death would have brought.

28 The expression "I have sent" refers to his present sending of Epaphroditus with this letter (by the time they receive the letter, the "sending" will be past). In view of the circumstances noted above, Paul was sending him more hastily than he would otherwise have done. If the serious illness and the apparent misunderstanding at Philippi had not occurred, Paul might have retained him longer, perhaps till the end of the trial. It was important, then, that this letter should accompany Epaphroditus, so that the Philippians would rejoice at his safe return. The return of the messenger to the church, along with the true explanation of what had happened, should bring a happy conclusion to the whole affair and satisfy both them and Epaphroditus himself. At the same time, Paul himself would benefit by being relieved from further anxiety, for knowing that his friends were relieved always brought a lessening of his painful concern over problems in the churches (cf. 2Co 12:28).

29 Paul therefore exhorted the Philippians to welcome Epaphroditus with joy as fellow

Christians should. He had fulfilled his mission with distinction and deserved an appropriate homecoming. Paul's words imply that more was involved in Epaphroditus's disturbed feelings than simple affectionate concern, otherwise no such urging from the apostle to "welcome him in the Lord" would have been necessary. Some sort of alienation had arisen. The church was to do more than refrain from criticism of Epaphroditus; they were to give him due recognition for his faithful and sacrificial service to Paul.

30 There were two reasons why Epaphroditus deserved a genuine welcome. First, he had been engaged in the work of Christ and had actually risked his life to accomplish it. Second, he had been trying by his labors to make up for the Philippians' absence from Paul, and so they owed him their gratitude. Epaphroditus's close call with death came about as a result of his sickness (v.27), not because of persecution or adverse judicial proceedings. Moreover, his ailment was directly due to his Christian labors on behalf of Paul. Inasmuch as 4:14–18 reveals that the Philippians had done more than other churches for the apostle, the lack of service mentioned here must be the lack of their physical presence with him (cf. 1Co 16:17). This Epaphroditus had supplied by his presence and personal care.

IV. Warning Against Judaizers and Antinomians (3:1–21)
A. The Judaizing Danger (3:1–16)

1 "Finally" seems to suggest that Paul is drawing his letter to a close. Inasmuch as over forty percent of the letter is yet to come, some assume that a combination of several letters makes up this letter and suggest that 3:1 is the conclusion of one of them. But Paul and other writers use this expression in a variety of ways. It is best to understand the meaning here in a nontechnical and natural way. A speaker may use the word "finally" as he passes the midpoint of an address, and will then continue on for a rather long time. This poses no real problem for the English listener, and even less for a Greek reader for whom the expression could also mean simply "furthermore" or "in addition" (cf. 1Th 4:1).

Paul's exhortation to "rejoice in the Lord" should be understood as belonging with what follows. The readers are to maintain the joyful spirit that has characterized this letter thus far, even though Paul now goes on to speak of some unpleasant matters. He repeats some of his former instructions, but this is "no trouble" to him, for it has in view the worthy goal of safeguarding them from entrapment in wrong doctrine.

How specifically should "the same things" be understood? Surely it does not refer to the command to rejoice, for this would not have been thought to be a troublesome task or a safeguard against something dangerous. Because there has been no earlier warning against Judaizers in this letter, some have referred "the same things" to prior correspondence with the Philippians. This is certainly possible, though little evidence exists to support it. If, however, Paul meant the words to refer to previous warnings against opponents generally, then 1:27–30 would be an earlier instance in this letter.

2 The verses that follow warrant the identification of these opponents with the Judaizers—those who dogged the trail of the apostles and endeavored to compel Gentile converts to submit to circumcision and other Jewish practices in order to be saved. Three epithets designate them. (1) "Dogs" denotes the wild, vicious, homeless animals that roamed the streets and attacked passersby. Used figuratively, it was always a term of reproach (cf. Dt 23:18; 1Sa 17:43; 24:14; Pr 26:11; Isa 56:10–11; Mt 7:6). Paul castigates the Judaizing teachers with the very term they probably used of others. (2) "Men who do evil" is literally "the evil workers." If the word *workers* is stressed, the epithet may emphasize their energetic labors and perhaps their concentration on performing deeds of law rather than trusting in God's grace for salvation. (3) By "mutilators of the flesh," Paul deliberately parodies the Judaizers' insistence on circumcision by sarcastically calling it mutilation. For those who had lost the significance of circumcision and insisted on it as a rite for Christians, it was nothing more than a mutilation of the flesh.

3 Paul follows the above warning with an explanation. Christians are the real "circumcision," not the Judaizers who insisted on the physical rite. He implies that they have received the circumcision of the heart (see Ro 2:25–29; Col 2:11)—a concept already referred to in the OT (Lev 26:41; Dt 10:16; 30:6;

Jer 4:4; Eze 44:7). The Judaizers misunderstood OT doctrine as well as Christian teaching. Elsewhere Paul equates this circumcision performed without hands with the believer's removal from spiritual death to spiritual life (Col 2:11, 13). Thus it is virtually synonymous with regeneration.

Just as Paul characterizes the Judaizing teachers by three terms in the previous verse, so here he explains the true circumcision by three descriptive clauses. (1) Such persons "worship by the Spirit of God," not by human traditions or some external rite. (2) They "glory in Christ Jesus" (cf. Jer 9:23–24; 1Co 1:31; 2Co 10:17). Satisfaction comes from recognizing that their hope is found in Christ alone, not through meticulous conformity to the external demands of the Mosaic law. They have understood that Christ's sacrifice has fulfilled the law for them. (3) They "put no confidence in the flesh." This states the negative aspect of the previous positive phrase. "Flesh" (GK 4922) refers to what a person is outside of Christ; Paul often uses the term in controversy with Judaizers (e.g., Ro 3:20; 7:18, 25; Gal 2:16; 3:3; 5:19, 24). He teaches that sinful humanity has no grounds for confidence before God, because no one is able to achieve righteousness before God on one's own. True believers, however, put all of their trust in Christ and so remove any grounds for human pride or boasting.

4 In stating that true believers put no confidence in the flesh, Paul has in mind the contrary teaching of those opponents who stressed the importance of conformity to Jewish practices. For the sake of argument, therefore, he temporarily adopts one of their attitudes ("confidence in the flesh") and shows that his rejection of certain Jewish "advantages" was not because he was jealous that he did not possess them. If any one of these opponents should claim an advantage because of his Jewish heritage and practices, Paul wanted it known that in such matters he could stand on equal footing with any Judaizer. He personally disavowed such as reasons for confidence before God because he had found them inadequate to provide the righteousness God requires (cf. vv.7–9).

5 Paul now enumerates some of his reasons for confidence in the flesh. First on the list is physical circumcision, perhaps because the Judaizers stressed it so much. Paul had been circumcised as a Jewish boy in accord with the instruction given to Abraham (Ge 17:12) and in the law (Lev 12:3). Furthermore, he was born of Israelite stock. He belonged to the tribe of Benjamin, a fact he proudly acknowledged on more than one occasion (Ac 13:21; Ro 11:1). This tribe alone had been faithful to the Davidic throne at the time of the division of the kingdom. It had given the nation its first king, after whom Paul had been named by his parents. By calling himself a "Hebrew of Hebrews," he suggests he was of pure Jewish ancestry from both parents and possibly that he knew both Hebrew and Aramaic, even though he had been born in the Diaspora (Ac 22:2–3). In addition, by his own choice he belonged to the most orthodox of the Jewish parties, the Pharisees. This party contained the most zealous supporters and interpreters of OT law, and Paul had studied under Gamaliel, its most celebrated teacher (Ac 22:3; cf. 5:34).

6 When measured for its zeal, Paul's pre-Christian life had been noted for promoting Judaism and condemning Christians. He had become the archpersecutor of the church, and his reputation had gone far beyond Jerusalem (Ac 9:13, 21; Gal 1:13–14). Judged by human standards in accord with the righteousness the law demands, he had been blameless. As an earnest Pharisee, he had paid meticulous attention to the external requirements of the Mosaic law, and no one could have charged him with failure to keep it.

7 Through his conversion on the Damascus road, Paul had learned to count such "advantages" as liabilities because of Christ. "Whatever" indicates that the previous listing was not exhaustive but illustrative. He once had regarded such things as "profit" (or "gains"; GK 3046) toward his goal of achieving righteousness by the law, but now he has come to the conviction that they were actually a detriment and did not provide him with true righteousness at all. By trusting in human performance, he had not only failed to make any progress toward the righteousness God requires but had also let his Jewish "advantages" drive him to persecute the church, which proclaimed the message of the righteousness of God that is received by faith.

8 "What is more" introduces a clause stressing that Paul's experience on the Damascus road had produced a strong and lasting impression. The merits of Christ counted for everything. Paul now broadens his thought from his Jewish advantages to include "all things" that might conceivably be a rival to his total trust in Christ. The "surpassing greatness" can be understood of Christ in an absolute sense, though it likely includes at least a sidelong glance at the list of supposed advantages he had once trusted in. Christ is far superior to them in every respect—so much so that Paul had cast them away as nothing but "rubbish."

For Paul, the knowledge of Christ Jesus as his Lord meant the intimate communion with Christ that began at his conversion and had been his experience all the years since then. It was not limited to the past (as v.10 shows), but was a growing relationship in which there was blessed enjoyment in the present and the challenge and excitement of increasing comprehension of Christ in personal fellowship. Although at regeneration a person receives Christ, this is only the beginning of one's discovery of what riches this entails. In Christ all the treasures of wisdom and knowledge are hidden (Col 2:3), but to search them out and appropriate them personally requires a lifetime.

9 Paul's desire to "be found in him" probably has an eschatological aspect. He wants the divine scrutiny he will undergo at Christ's return to reveal unquestionably that he had been in vital spiritual union with Jesus Christ. For this to be so, it could not be on the basis of a "righteousness" he could call "my own" (i.e., the kind of righteousness one might achieve through conformity to the Mosaic law). Such obedience might win the admiration of other people, but it could never achieve the absolute perfection God requires (Gal 3:10–11; Jas 2:10). In strong contrast, to be found in Christ implies a righteousness that has its source not in humans but in God, who has provided Jesus Christ, the "Righteous One" (Ac 3:14; 1Jn 2:1).

This latter righteousness is received by us "through faith" and thus we acquire it "by faith" or "on the basis of faith." It is God's provision freely offered to us in Christ (Ro 3:20–22). "Faith" is the opposite of human works; it is the reception of God's work by those who admit the futility of their own efforts to attain righteousness.

10 The phrase "to know Christ" resumes the thought of v.8 and explains in more detail what is involved in "knowing Christ Jesus." Paul wants to know experientially the power of Christ's resurrection. He is not thinking only of the divine power that raised Christ from the dead, but of the power of the resurrected Christ now operating in the believer's life. This power enables us to "live a new life" (Ro 6:4) because we have been "raised with Christ" (Eph 2:5–6; Col 3:1).

Closely associated in the apostle's thought is "the fellowship of sharing in his sufferings." No reference to Christ's expiatory sufferings is meant, for those were Christ's alone. But each believer, by identifying himself or herself with Christ, incurs a measure of Christ's afflictions (Col 1:24). These may be of varying kinds and degrees, both inward and external, as believers find themselves in a world that is hostile because of their allegiance to Christ. Paul has already expressed this thought in 1:29, where he regards suffering in some sense as an inevitable consequence of believing in Christ (cf. Mt 16:24).

"Becoming like him in his death" further elaborates the previous phrase. For believers to share Christ's sufferings involves such a complete identification with him that it can only be explained as a death to the former life (cf. Ro 6:4–11). One's union with Christ must be experientially demonstrated in a life of sanctification, which is intended to bring the believer's present state into ever-increasing conformity to Christ (Ro 8:29; 2Co 3:18; Php 3:21). Therefore, those who died with him and rose with him (Col 2:20; 3:1–3) must exhibit this truth by separating from their old life and continually walking in the power supplied by Christ's resurrection life.

11 The form of this statement poses a problem for interpreters, perhaps suggesting that, though Paul is hopeful of experiencing the resurrection, he has some doubt about it. This is difficult to harmonize with his strong affirmations of faith elsewhere (e.g., 1Co 15:1–34). Some have explained the expression as an indication of Paul's humility. But it is also possible to regard the clause as expressing sincere expectation rather than doubt.

"The resurrection from the dead" is not the usual NT expression for this event. Its use here suggests Paul is thinking not in terms of a general resurrection of the righteous and the wicked, but of believers only (cf. Rev 20:4–15). He is uncertain whether he will participate in the resurrection because he will have died by then, or whether he will receive his transformed body without dying because the Lord comes before his death (see 1Th 4:13–17).

12 Having stated that his conversion brought about a new assessment of his goals and gave him the overwhelming desire to know Christ ever more fully, Paul then explains how his present life is a pursuit in this new direction. But he does not want to be misunderstood as claiming that his conversion on the Damascus road has already brought him to his final goal. He has not yet received all he longs for, nor has he been brought to that perfection to which he has aspired. Perhaps there were those in Philippi who were claiming to have acquired already the consummation of spiritual blessings. But Paul knows that he must continue to pursue the purposes Christ had chosen him for. Spiritual progress is ever the imperative Christians must follow.

13 Paul now addresses the Philippians by the endearing title "brothers" and repeats the thought of v.12. He did not regard himself as having obtained the final knowledge of Christ and the fullest conformity to him. One thing, therefore, was the consuming passion of his Christian life. Using the metaphor of a footrace, Paul describes it as involving the continual forgetting of "what is behind" and the relentless centering of his energies and interests on the course that is ahead of him. "Forgetting" did not mean obliterating the memory of his past (cf. vv.5–7), but was a conscious refusal to let it absorb his attention and impede his progress. He never allowed his Jewish heritage nor his previous Christian attainments (vv.9–12) to obstruct his running of the race. No present attainment could lull him into thinking he already possessed all Christ desired for him.

14 Continuing the metaphor, Paul likens his Christian life to pressing onward to the goal so as to win the prize. In applying the figure, the goal and the prize are virtually identical, though viewed perhaps from different aspects. Paul's goal was the complete knowledge of Christ, both in the power of his resurrection and the fellowship of his sufferings (v.10). When the goal was reached, this prize would be fully his. The calling "heavenward" may relate to the summons to the winner to approach the elevated stand of the judge and receive the prize. The word "called" (GK 3104) is always used elsewhere by Paul to denote the effective call of God that brings people to salvation (1Co 1:26; 7:20; Eph 1:18; 4:1, 4; 2Th 1:11; 2Ti 1:9).

15 In concluding this section, Paul exhorts those who are "mature" (GK 5455; cf. 1Co 2:6; 14:20; Eph 4:13; Col 1:28; 4:12) to think in harmony with what he has just said, and he promises that those who think differently about minor points will be enlightened by God if their attitude is right. By "mature," Paul is referring to a certain level of spiritual growth and stability in contrast to infants. If the Philippian believers are lax in their pursuit of spiritual goals or erroneously suppose they have already arrived, they need to understand Paul's declaration. And if they generally agree but still differ on some isolated point, Paul is confident that God will lead them to the truth.

16 No one, however, must wait for God to reveal the truth on all points before one begins to give oneself to spiritual growth. Each believer should exercise fully the degree of maturity already possessed. "Live up to" (GK 5123) calls for Christians to maintain a consistent life in harmony with the understanding of God's truth they already have. Paul recognizes that Christians, though proceeding along the same path, may be at different stages of progress and should be faithful to as much of God's truth as they understand.

B. The Antinomian Danger (3:17–21)

17 In the early years of the church, believers needed practical guides for conduct. So Paul urged the Philippians to join together in imitating his conduct (see also 1Co 11:1). Such advice was not egotism, for Paul's emphasis was always strongly Christological (e.g., 1Co 11:1; Php 2:5–8). Furthermore, Paul here includes others in this model by urging his readers to take note of those who were living in conformity with "the pattern we gave you" (v.17)—i.e., the high standard outlined in vv.7–16. And by "we," Paul includes not only himself but Timothy and perhaps Epaphroditus. Hence, he was not claiming a unique superiority.

18 Who were these "enemies of the cross of Christ"? While some regard them as the Judaizers of v.2 (whose emphasis on legalism undermined the Cross), they are more likely antinomians, who went to the opposite extreme from the Judaizers and threw off all moral restraints. By their lawless lives, they too were enemies of the Cross and the new life that should issue from it.

It is not likely that these people were simply pagans, of whom nothing much better was to be expected. Rather, they were probably professing Christians, but ones whose lives were so profligate that it was clear to Paul that they had never been regenerated. Presumably, they were not members of the Philippian church (the character of this letter would have been different if "many" such people were in that congregation), but because there were such in the Christian world as a whole, they posed a danger to every church (cf. Ro 16:17–18; 2Pe 2:10–22). Paul had already warned of them, perhaps in former visits or in other letters, and felt real anguish when the churches were threatened with falseness of doctrine or life.

19 The ultimate end for such persons is "destruction" (GK 724), i.e., eternal loss. "Their god is their stomach" suggests sensualists who indulged various physical appetites without restraint (Ro 16:18; 1Co 6:13; Jude 11). By their indulgence, they actually bragged about what they ought to have been ashamed of (Eph 5:12). The final description characterizes these "enemies of the cross" as continually minding earthly things. Their whole attention focused on physical and material interests, rather than on spiritual things.

20 The "our" is emphatic here, stressing the distinction between true believers, whose essential relationships belong to the heavenly sphere, and the sensualists just discussed, who are exclusively concerned with earthly things. The Christian's "citizenship [GK 4487] is in heaven," and for each believer earthly things must at best be secondary. The Philippians would find this a most apt metaphor, for in a political sense they knew what it was to be citizens of a far-off city (even though most of them had probably never been to Rome), and they were proud of that status (Ac 16:12, 21; see comment on Php 1:27). On an immeasurably higher plane, believers belong to the "city . . . whose architect and builder is God" (Heb 11:10) or to the "Jerusalem that is above" (Gal 4:26), and are themselves "aliens and strangers on earth" (Heb 11:13; cf. 1Pe 2:11). As such, their eyes should be heavenward, anticipating the coming of their Savior, who is not a mere earthly emperor but the Lord Jesus Christ. An eager expectation of his return does much to protect believers from earthly, sensual enticements.

21 Christ at his return will "transform" (GK 3571) believers' mortal bodies, so that they will conform to the character of his resurrection body. The present body is described literally as "the body of lowliness," a description calling attention to its weakness and susceptibility to persecution, disease, sinful appetites, and death. At Christ's coming, however, the earthly, transient appearance will be changed, whether by resurrection of the dead or by rapture of the living (1Th 4:13–17), and believers will be transformed and will receive glorified bodies that will more adequately display their essential character as children of God and sharers of divine life in Christ (1Co 15:35–57). This will be accomplished by the same effective operation that will ultimately bring all things in the universe under the authority of Christ (cf. Eph 1:10).

V. Second Series of Exhortations (4:1–9)

A. Exhortation to Stand Firm in Unity (4:1–3)

1 This verse is another of Paul's subtle transitions, so skillfully blended as to make it difficult to decide whether it should be placed with what precedes or what follows. A good transition, however, fits both segments. Inasmuch as the following statements discuss the need for unity among certain individuals, it is appropriate to treat v.1 as a general exhortation to the whole church to stand firm in the manner Paul has just been outlining (especially 3:17–21). The same verb "stand firm" (GK 5112) was used also at the beginning of the first series of exhortations (1:27).

The reference to the Philippians as "brothers, you whom I love and long for," shows the strong feeling of intimacy the apostle felt toward these readers. Their description as Paul's "joy and crown" echoes his earlier words to another Macedonian church (1Th 2:19). The Philippians were his present joy as he received favorable reports of their spiritual growth, and their presence with Christ at his return would be his future crown when Christ comes to reward his servants (cf. 2:16).

2 The apostle turns from his general exhortation to an application of it. Two women, Euodia and Syntyche, are instructed to bring their attitudes into harmony. Paul does not indicate which one was in the wrong but knows that if the attitude of each would be formed "in the Lord," the disharmony would vanish. Repetition of "I plead" may indicate the need for separate admonitions because the rift between them had become so great. Paul's method of handling the problem suggests that it was not a doctrinal issue, but a clash of personalities.

3 At this point Paul seeks to enlist the aid of a third party, "yokefellow" (likely a proper name, "Syzygus"; GK 5187; see NIV note), whom he challenges to live up to his name and bring these women together. (Another Pauline play on a personal name occurs in Phm 10–11.) Inasmuch as Euodia and Syntyche had once worked side by side with Paul, they should be able to do so again. Perhaps they had been among the original group of converts at Philippi, for women had been Paul's first hearers there (Ac 16:13–15). Their Christian labors had been in conjunction with Clement and others of Paul's co-workers. Even though some of these names are not recorded in this letter, Paul knows that their service has not been forgotten, for their names are recorded in the Book of Life, the heavenly register of those who are saved (Rev 3:5; 17:8; 20:12, 15; 21:27; 22:19; cf. Lk 10:20; Heb 12:23). Paul's memory of these happy associations prompted his concern that the present disunity might be ended so that faithful Christian activity could proceed and prosper.

B. Exhortation to Maintain Various Christian Virtues (4:4–9)

4 From his previous exhortation to unity and from his attempt to correct a case of disunity, Paul proceeds to urge the church to maintain certain positive Christian virtues. First, believers must "rejoice in the Lord always" (repeated for emphasis, perhaps implying a question asked of Paul, "How can we rejoice, in view of our difficulties?"). In all the vicissitudes of the Christian life, whether in attacks from errorists, personality clashes among believers, persecution from the world, or threat of imminent death, Christians are to maintain a spirit of joy in the Lord. They are not immune to sorrow, nor should they be insensitive to the troubles of others; yet they should count God's will their highest joy and so be capable of knowing inner peace and joy in every circumstance (cf. 1Th 5:16–18).

5 Second, believers are to show "gentleness" (GK 2117) to all. No single word is adequate to translate this word. Involved is the willingness to yield one's personal rights and to show consideration and gentleness to others. It is easy to display this quality toward some persons, but Paul commands that it be shown toward all—Christian friends, unsaved persecutors, false teachers, anyone at all. Of course, truth may not be sacrificed, but a gentle spirit will do much to disarm an adversary.

As an encouragement, Paul now reminds his readers that "the Lord is near," a reference

When Paul came to Philippi on his second missionary journey, since it had no synagogue, he "went outside the city gate to the river" and "began to speak to the women who had gathered there" (Ac 16:13). Women played a prominent role in the church there. Courtesy Bastiaan Van Elderen.

to the Parousia (cf. 3:20–21; cf. Jas 5:8 for a similar connection between a longsuffering spirit and the Lord's coming). This statement is a reminder that at his arrival the Judge will settle all differences and bring the consummation that will make most of our human differences seem trifling.

6 Third, believers should be prayerful instead of "anxious" (GK *3534*). This verb can mean "to be concerned about" in a proper Christian sense (cf. 2:20), but here the meaning is clearly that of anxiety, fretfulness, or undue concern (cf. Mt 6:25–34). Paul is not calling for apathy or inaction, for as we make plans in the light of our circumstances, it is our Christian privilege to do so in full trust that our Father hears our prayers for what we need. The answer to anxiety is "prayer" (GK *4666*), a word that denotes the petitioner's attitude of mind as worshipful. "Petition" denotes prayers as expressions of need. "Thanksgiving" should accompany all Christian praying, as the supplicants acknowledge that whatever God sends is for their good. It may also include remembrance of previous blessings.

7 Paul attaches to this classic exhortation to pray the beautiful promise that when we turn from anxiety to prayer and thanksgiving, God will give us his own "peace." This peace is for those who are already at peace with God through justification by faith in Christ (Ro 5:1). This peace of God "transcends all understanding," for it is not only sufficient for us but far surpasses human comprehension. It acts as a sentry to guard our hearts and thoughts from all anxiety and despair.

8 Fourth, believers should keep on thinking and doing what is morally and spiritually excellent. This involves centering their minds on exalted things and then (v.9) putting into practice what they have learned from Paul's teaching and example.

Here (v.8) Paul sets forth in memorable words a veritable charter of virtues for Christian thought. "True" (GK *239*) has the sense of valid, reliable, and honest—the opposite of false. It characterizes God (Ro 3:4) and should also characterize believers. "Noble" (GK *4948*; cf. also 1Ti 3:8, 11; Tit 2:2) denotes a quality that makes people worthy of respect. "Right" (GK *1465*) refers to what is upright or just, conformable to God's standards and thus worthy of his approval. "Pure" (GK *54*) emphasizes moral purity and includes in some contexts the more restricted sense of "chaste." "Lovely" (GK *4713*) relates to what is pleasing, agreeable, or amiable. "Admirable" (GK *2368*) denotes what is praiseworthy, attractive, and true to the highest standards.

Suddenly Paul changes the sentence structure to conditional clauses, a rhetorical device that forces each reader to exercise his or her own discernment and choose what is "excellent" (GK *746*) and "praiseworthy" (GK *2047*). Paul knows that when we continually center our minds on such thoughts as these, we shall live like Christians.

9 Since Paul himself had been their teacher and example, what they had learned from him they were to keep on practicing. The four verbs in this verse form two pairs. The first pair, "learned" and "received," describes the Philippians' instruction by Paul, from whom they had been taught Christian doctrine and Christian living. The next pair, "heard" and "saw," depicts their personal observation of the apostle—both his speech and his conduct. In the early days of the church before the NT writings were written or widely circulated, the standards of Christian belief and behavior were largely taught by being embodied in the words and example of the apostles. Those who follow this apostolic guidance have the additional promise that God, who provides true peace (v.9; cf. v.7), will be with them.

VI. The Philippians' Gifts to Paul (4:10–20)

A. *The Recent Gift (4:10–14)*

10 As Paul begins to conclude his letter, he voices his joy over the Philippians' recent contribution to him. This is probably not his first note of thanks to them, for considerable time had elapsed since Epaphroditus had brought the gift and several contacts with the church at Philippi had already been made. Furthermore, it is doubtful that his expression of gratitude would have been left to the end of the letter. Paul retained a vivid memory of their generous act. "At last" should not be regarded as a rebuke, but merely as showing that communication had again occurred after a period of no contact. Paul makes it clear that the fault was not theirs but

came from a lack of opportunity; perhaps no messenger had been available. In addition, the apostle's own circumstances had been highly irregular in recent years, in part because of imprisonment and shipwreck. Now the demonstration of concern had bloomed again, like plants in the spring.

11–12 Paul hastens to make clear that though he undoubtedly had a need, it was not relief of this need that primarily concerned him. He had "learned to be content" with what God provided, irrespective of circumstances. It is significant that Paul had to "learn" this virtue; contentment is not natural to most of us.

In Stoic philosophy, "content" (GK *895*) described a person who accepted impassively whatever came. Circumstances that could not be changed were regarded as God's will, and fretting was useless. This philosophy fostered a self-sufficiency in which all the resources for coping with life were located within a person. In contrast, Paul locates his sufficiency in Christ, who provides strength for believers (cf. 2Co 12:7–10).

Paul truly understood what it was to be in want and "to have plenty." What he means by the latter we cannot tell; perhaps it was his earlier days as a rising figure in Judaism (Gal 1:14) or any of the times when he was not suffering privation (e.g., Ac 9:19, 28; 16:15, 33–34; 18:3; 21:8). He had learned how to trust God in every particular situation and in all situations as a whole.

13 Paul's outlook was no Stoic philosophy, however. He did not trace his resources to some inner fortitude that would enable him to take with equanimity whatever life brought him. Instead, his strength for "everything" lay in the One who continually empowered him. Although the name "Christ" does not appear in the Greek text, surely Paul has him in mind (cf. 1Ti 1:12). He was not desperately seeking a gift from the Philippians, for he knew that Christ would give him the strength for whatever circumstances were in store for him.

14 Nevertheless, the Philippians must not feel that their gift had been unnecessary. They had responded properly to his need, and Paul was truly grateful—not so much for what the gift did for him as for their willingness to share with him. They had accepted his affliction as their own and had done something about it.

B. The Previous Gifts (4:15–20)

15–16 In order to make it clear that he was not minimizing the Philippians' generosity toward him, Paul recalls some earlier demonstrations of their love for him. When the Gospel was first preached to them (approximately ten years before; Ac 16), they were the only church to contribute to him when he exited Macedonia (a better translation than "set out from"; GK *2002*). This gift he received while he was in Corinth (2Co 11:9). Then, as he mentions this gift, he also recalls two earlier instances of their generosity when he was in Thessalonica. Presumably these earlier gifts were small and thus in a different category from the one mentioned in v.15. This interpretation is also implied by 1Th 2:9; 2Th 3:7–8, which show that Paul earned his own living in Thessalonica. Paul does not mean that no other churches ever assisted him (cf. 2Co 11:8), but that on the specific occasion referred to here, no other church had come to his aid.

17 Paul's readers must not suppose that he is primarily concerned with their gift as such, but rather in the development of the grace of giving among them. Using business terminology, he says that he regards such displays as interest "credited to [their] account." Their spiritual growth was the fruit Paul desired, and to this end he directed his ministry.

18 The financial language continues as Paul says, "I have received full payment and even more." The gifts brought by Epaphroditus (2:25–30) had completely met his needs, and Paul considers this contribution a sacrificial offering to God, made to further the Lord's work by helping his servant (cf. Mt 25:40). "A fragrant offering" is used in Eph 5:2 of Christ's sacrificial offering of himself to God on our behalf, reflecting such passages as Lev 1:9, 13, 17; 2:12. Such offerings pleased God, because they came from obedient hearts.

19–20 In words that countless Christians have relied on as one of the great Scripture promises, Paul now reminds his benefactors that "my God" will do what he himself is in no position to do; namely, reimburse his benefactors. This assurance of the divine supply of the Philippians' needs implies that they had given so liberally that they actually left themselves in some real "need." Those who share generously with others, especially to advance the work of the Lord, are promised a divine supply of anything they might lack because of their generosity (Pr 11:25; 19:17; Mt 5:7).

"According to" conveys the thought that God's supply of the Philippians' need will not be merely from his great wealth but in some sense appropriate to or commensurate with it. The source of that supply is the heavenly glorious riches that Christ now enjoys. Small wonder that Paul closes this beautiful passage with a doxology. The glory of God's providential care must always be recognized by his children. Even the eternal ages yet to come will not be sufficient to exhaust the praises that belong to him.

Closing Salutation (4:21–23)

21 It is likely that the remaining words of the letter were written by Paul's own hand, after the pattern announced in Gal 6:11; Col 4:18; 2Th 3:17. He sends greetings to every believer at Philippi, to be conveyed to them no doubt by the leadership of the church to whom the letter was initially delivered. Paul's associates also send their greetings; they are to be distinguished from the resident Roman Christians who are mentioned in the next verse. These "brothers who are with me" include Timothy and perhaps Epaphroditus (1:1; 2:19–30), and possibly even some of those mentioned in 1:14. The inclusion of these greetings is a caution against interpreting 2:21 as an indictment of all Paul's associates except Timothy (see comment on 2:21).

22 "All the saints" refers to members of the church at Rome, from where Paul is writing. He also extends special greetings from "those who belong to Caesar's household." This expression denotes those engaged in imperial service, whether as slaves or freedmen, in Rome or elsewhere. Among them may have been some of the palace guard (1:13). The expression could refer to persons of considerable importance on the emperor's staff. Paul does not say why they were singled out for special mention. Perhaps some of these government servants had come from Philippi or had once been stationed at that Roman colony.

23 The concluding benediction is exactly the same as Phm 25 and similar to Gal 6:18. It invokes on the Philippian church the continuing favor of Christ to be with their spirits. The realization of this benediction would increase the harmony of the congregation by causing the spirit of each believer to cherish the grace of the Lord Jesus Christ and by bringing a joyous peace among them, fulfilling the apostle's opening wish (1:2).

Colossians

INTRODUCTION

1. Destination

Colosse was a small market town situated on the south bank of the Lycus River in the interior of the Roman province of Asia (an area included in modern Turkey). Located about a hundred miles east of Ephesus, its nearest neighbors were Laodicea and Hierapolis (both of these cities had communities of believers; cf. 2:1; 4:13). Colosse and Laodicea were probably evangelized during the time of Paul's extended ministry in Ephesus (Ac 19:10), though there is no record of it in Acts. All our information about the church must be found in this letter and in incidental allusions in the companion letter to Philemon.

2. Authorship

The authenticity of Colossians has been questioned, though today there is broad agreement that it is, as it purports to be (1:1; 4:18), from the hand of Paul. Evidence for this comes not only from within the letter but also from the witness of many early Christian writers. While the external testimony to Paul as the author of Colossians is not equal to that of some of his other letters, so far as we can determine, it was never doubted.

Pauline authorship was not seriously questioned until the mid-nineteenth century. Because of similarities with Ephesians, some scholars have accepted one of the two as genuine but not both, considering that one was dependent on the other. Others have denied the Pauline authorship of both Ephesians and Colossians because they thought both reflected second-century Gnosticism. But few today hold that the heresy opposed in Colossians was the fully developed gnostic systems of the second century. We have gained fresh knowledge of the bewildering variety of syncretistic religious movements of the Graeco-Roman world of the first century, and this has destroyed the earlier arguments.

In recent years doubts concerning the authenticity of Colossians have focused on *vocabulary, style,* and *doctrine.* (1) Vocabulary is no great problem, for the distinctive vocabulary is most apparent where Paul is dealing with the Colossian problem. Therefore, it is not unlikely that at least some of these words were borrowed from the errorists for purposes of refutation; naturally, then, they would not be used in other different contexts. Paul had new things to say in this letter and found new ways of saying them. (2) Regarding style, some of the unquestioned letters of Paul have passages that exhibit the same features of style found in Colossians. Where Colossians is stylistically distinct, it is bound up with the sustained note of thanksgiving that runs through the letter (especially ch. 1). (3) The doctrinal argument claims that this letter's teachings about Christ—especially the cosmic aspects of his redemptive work—are more fully developed than in other Pauline letters. Its overall Christology, it is sometimes argued, shows such a pronounced similarity to the Logos doctrine of John (Jn 1:1–18) that it betrays a post-Pauline date. But why could not two apostles share this exalted view of Christ's person and work? Moreover, this doctrine was not entirely new to Paul (cf. Ro 8:19-22; 1Co 8:6); it was only given greater prominence and a more systematic exposition in Colossians.

A strong argument *for* Pauline authorship is the relation of Colossians to Philemon. Both of these books, sent to the same town and in all likelihood conveyed by the same messenger, contain the names of Paul, Timothy, Onesimus, Archippus, Epaphras, Mark, Aristarchus, Demas, and Luke. The consensus of scholarly opinion is that Philemon is incontestably Pauline, and it is the feeling of many NT scholars that this carries over to Colossians.

3. Date and Place of Origin

Colossians was obviously written during an imprisonment of Paul (4:10, 18), but it

The site of Aphrodias in present-day Turkey is associated with the "God-fearers" of the early church. Aphrodias is near Colosse and was the site of an early Christian church.

contains no indication as to the place of imprisonment. Three options present themselves: Ephesus, Caesarea, and Rome (see introduction to Philippians for more on this). Whether Paul was ever imprisoned in Ephesus is only hypothetical; moreover, Luke was with Paul when Colossians was written (4:14), but he was not with the apostle during his Ephesian ministry. Regarding Caesarea, it is unlikely that such a small city would have been the center of such vigorous missionary activity as 4:3–4, 10–14 seems to suggest. The traditional theory, and the one most generally held, is that Paul was in Rome when Colossians was written (see also introduction to Ephesians). The letter should therefore be dated about A.D. 62, during Paul's first Roman imprisonment (cf. Ac 28:30–31). Perhaps it was written before Ephesians, but surely not much time separated the two.

4. Occasion

The immediate occasion for the writing of Colossians was the arrival of Epaphras (1:8) in Rome with disturbing news about the presence of heretical teaching at Colosse that was threatening the well-being of the church. This letter gives no direct account of the tenets of this strange teaching, and thus it is difficult to obtain a clear and consistent understanding of it. Yet from the many allusions to the heresy, we are able to sketch its leading features. (1) It professed to be a "philosophy," but Paul calls it a "hollow and deceptive philosophy" (2:8). (2) It placed much emphasis on ritual circumcision, dietary laws, and the observance of holy days (2:11, 14, 16–17). (3) Affirming the mediation of various supernatural powers in the creation of the world and the whole process of salvation, the false teaching insisted that these mysterious powers be placated and worshiped (2:15, 18–19). As a result of this, Christ was relegated to a relatively minor place in the Colossian system. (4) Some of the errorists were ascetic (2:20–23), teaching that the body is evil and must be treated as an enemy. (5) The advocates of this system claimed to be Christian teachers (cf. 2:3–10).

From these considerations we may conclude that the Colossian heresy was a syncretistic movement combining at least three separate elements: Judaism, paganism, and Christianity. (1) The insistence on legalism, ritualism, and the observance of holy days points to a Jewish element (though not a Pharisaic Judaism).

(2) The system's philosophical character, worship of angels, and perhaps ascetic tendencies point to a pagan element. This was probably an incipient form of what later became known as Gnosticism, a complex system that reached its zenith in the second century. This incipient Gnosticism was essentially a religio-philosophical attitude, not a well-defined system. It sought by its oriental myths and Greek philosophy to absorb any religion with which it came into contact. It lent itself to an air of exclusiveness, cultivating an "enlightened" elite for whom alone salvation was possible. Gnosticism, in all its forms, was characterized by belief in the evil of matter, in mediating beings, and in salvation through knowledge. Beginning with the assumption that all creation is evil, the Gnostics argued that God didn't create this world and that he has absolutely no contact with it. However, intellectual necessity did not permit them to break completely the bond between divinity and the material world. They therefore taught that God put forth from himself a series of emanations, called "aeons," each a little more distant from him and each having a little less of deity. At the end of this chain of intermediate beings there is an aeon possessing enough of deity to make a world but removed far enough from God that his creative activities could not compromise the perfect purity of God. The world, they argued, was the creation of this lesser power. These aeons were thought to inhabit the stars and rule human destiny. They therefore were to be placated and worshiped. Paul's references to "thrones," "powers," "rulers," "authorities" (1:16; 2:9, 15), and "the worship of angels" (2:18) are allusions to these supposed intermediate beings.

Belief in the inherent evil of matter made it impossible for the Gnostics to accept the real incarnation of God in Christ. Some of them explained it away by denying the actual humanity of Jesus, holding that he only seemed to be human. The body of Jesus, they taught, was an illusion. Other Gnostics explained away the incarnation by denying the real deity of Jesus. Both of these tendencies were perhaps present at Colosse in embryo form and both may be alluded to in the letter—for example, in the affirmation that "in Christ all the fullness of the Deity lives in bodily form" (2:9).

Belief that matter is evil also led to a distorted view of the Christian life. Some Gnostics turned to asceticism; they felt that they had to free themselves from the influence of matter (the body) by inflicting punishment on their bodies. Others turned to libertinism; they assumed an attitude of indifference to things physical and material, the idea being that only the soul is important and therefore the body may do what it pleases. Indications of both tendencies may be found in the Colossian letter, the former being opposed in 2:20ff. and the latter in 3:5ff.

Gnosticism—the word is related to *gnosis*, "knowledge" (GK *1194*)—taught that salvation is obtained not through faith but through knowledge. Such knowledge, however, was knowledge acquired through mystical experience, not intellectual apprehension. It was an occult knowledge, pervaded by the superstitions of astrology and magic.

(3) There was a "Christian" element in the Colossian error as well. While at its heart it was a combination of Judaism and paganism, it wore the mask of Christianity. It did not deny Christ, but it did dethrone him. It gave him a place, but not the supreme place. This Christian facade made the Colossian error all the more dangerous.

That Paul found it necessary to write this letter to the community of Christians at Colosse is evidence that the false teachers had made a strong impression on them and that the threat to the well-being of the church was real. There are indications, however, that the errorists had not achieved complete success (cf. 2:4, 8, 20). Paul therefore can express gratitude for the Colossian Christians and rejoice over the order within their ranks and in their continued fidelity to Christ (cf. 1:3ff.; 2:5).

5. Purpose and Theme

Paul's purpose in writing Colossians was threefold: (1) to express his personal interest in the church, (2) to warn them against reverting to their old pagan vices (cf. 3:5ff.), and (3) to refute the false teaching that was threatening the Colossian church. The last named was undoubtedly Paul's major concern as he made a plea for the fuller knowledge found in Christ. He confronted the false representation of knowledge by positively setting forth the exalted nature and unmatched glory of Christ.

Colossians therefore proclaims the absolute supremacy and sole sufficiency of Jesus Christ (cf. esp. 1:18; 2:9; 3:11). He is God's Son (1:14), the object of the Christian's faith (1:4), the Redeemer (1:14), the image of God (1:15), the Lord of creation (1:15), the head of the church (1:18), and reconciler of the universe (1:20). In him dwells the fullness of the Godhead (2:9), and under him every power and authority in the universe is subjected (2:10). He is the essence of the mystery of God (2:3), and in him all God's treasures of wisdom and knowledge lie hidden (2:3). He is the standard by which all religious teaching is to be measured (2:8) and the reality of the truth foreshadowed by the regulations and rituals of the old covenant (2:17). By his cross he conquered the cosmic powers of evil (2:15), and following his resurrection he was enthroned at the right hand of God (3:1). Our life now lies hidden with God in Christ, but one day both he and we will be gloriously manifested (3:3–4).

EXPOSITION

I. Introduction (1:1–14)

A. Salutation (1:1–2)

Paul follows the standard form of greeting of first-century letters but puts a distinctly Christian content into it. He names himself, with appropriate Christian expressions, as the author (v.1), identifies the readers (v.2a), and then expresses the characteristic greeting of grace and peace (v.2b).

1 In designating himself as "an apostle of Christ Jesus," Paul gives his authority for writing. At its deepest level, an apostle (GK 693) denotes an authorized spokesman for God, one commissioned and empowered to act as his representative. Such is the meaning of the word when applied to the Twelve (e.g., Lk 6:13) and to Paul (see also comment on Php 2:25).

Timothy, who was with Paul at the time of writing and is here identified as a "brother" of Paul, was named as a matter of courtesy. He appears to have had no part in the actual writing of the book (cf. 4:18).

2 In the OT, holiness is ascribed not only to persons (Lev 20:7; Dt 7:6; 2Ki 4:9; et al.), but also to places (Ex 29:31; Lev 6:16, 26; Dt 23:14; et al.) and things (Ex 28:2; 29:6; Nu 5:17; et al.). This suggests that the root idea in "holy" (GK 41) is not excellence of character but dedication, the state of being set apart for the work and worship of God. The word "faithful" (GK 4412) implies not only that the addressees are believers, but they are also loyal to Christ, a quality especially appropriate for a church under fire.

"Brothers," a term of affection used of Christians in every letter of Paul, calls attention to the intimacy of the fellowship of the Christian community. Despite their differences of culture, social status, and racial background, the Colossian believers are bound together by a common bond of love and thus constitute one spiritual family—all spiritually begotten by one Father. "In Christ" emphasizes the spiritual position of believers. They are united with Christ, joined to him as closely as limbs are joined to the body of which they are a part.

The greeting takes the form of a prayer for "grace and peace" to be given the readers. "Grace" (GK 5921) denotes the favor of God; Paul uses this word to express the essence of God's saving activity in Christ. In our thinking, "peace" (GK 1645) usually suggests the absence of conflict. The NT concept, however, is richer and broader. It denotes wholeness or soundness and includes such ideas as prosperity, contentedness, and good relations with others.

B. Prayer of Thanksgiving (1:3–8)

The content of this thanksgiving is determined by the condition of the church and by Paul's relationship to it through Epaphras. In these verses we may observe the circumstances and character of the apostle's thanksgiving (v.3) as well as the grounds and occasion for it (vv.4–8). This passage, which expresses the apostle's own gratitude, shows that what he enjoined upon others he himself practiced.

3 Paul addresses his thanksgiving to God, thus recognizing that he is the one ultimately responsible for the virtues and graces of his people and for the success of the Gospel—both of which are mentioned in the verses that follow. God is identified as "the Father of our Lord Jesus Christ." The God to whom we pray is the God whom Jesus Christ made known to us as our Father.

4–5 Verses 4–8 express the grounds and occasion of Paul's thanksgiving. The apostle specifically mentions three things, the first being the good report that had come to him of the well-being of the Colossian Christians. His reference to "hearing" about their spiritual condition is in keeping with the fact that he had not personally visited Colosse (cf. 1:9; 2:1). The source of this information was probably Epaphras (cf. v.8), though we must not rule out the possibility that Paul's reference includes other previous reports of the faith of the Colossians.

The triad of "faith" (v.4a), "love" (v.4b), and "hope" (v.5a) appears with some degree of frequency in Paul's writings (e.g., Ro 5:2–5; 1Co 13:13; 1Th 1:3; 5:8). "Faith" (GK 4411), which is commitment to or trust in another person, is defined as being anchored "in Jesus Christ." Theirs was a Christ-centered faith.

"Love" (GK 27) is the fruit of faith and the proof of its genuineness (cf. Gal 5:6; Jas 2:14ff.; 1Jn 3:14). It means caring love, the love that counts no sacrifice too great for the one loved (cf. the verb used in Jn 3:16.) The Colossians' love was expressed toward "all the saints," i.e., toward all God's people. Perhaps the apostle was contrasting the broad goodwill of the Colossian believers with the narrow exclusiveness of the heretical teachers.

"Hope" (GK 1828) is sometimes subjective (what a person feels; cf. Ro 5:2), sometimes objective (denoting what believers hope for; cf. Gal 5:5; 1Pe 1:3). Here it is the latter, referring to the glorious reward and future heavenly blessedness of God's people. This hope is securely "stored up" for the Colossians in heaven, like a treasure. Moreover, their knowledge of hope came from hearing "the word of truth," the Gospel that had come to them when Epaphras originally preached the Gospel to them and they were converted. That message seems to be contrasted tacitly with the more recent and heretical preaching of the Colossian errorists.

How does the word "hope" tie into this sentence? One possibility is that along with their faith and love, the Colossians' hope gives a reason for Paul to be grateful. It is also possible, as in the NIV, to interpret hope as a ground for, or an incentive to, faith and love. Whatever construction one chooses, hope is a part of the total experience of the Colossians that Paul thanks God for.

6 Paul is now led to develop the thought of the progress of the Gospel in the world. This is brought out in such a way as to suggest that this, as well as the report of the Colossians' welfare, was for Paul a basis for thankfulness. Two ideas are stressed. (1) The Gospel was a fruit-bearing power in the many places where it was preached throughout the ancient world. Perhaps Paul means that the ever-widening scope and deepening influence of the Gospel on its recipients was a mark of its authenticity. "Bearing fruit" suggests that the Gospel is like a living organism whose seed is in itself. "Growing" denotes the rapid spread of the Gospel. Thus these two terms speak of the inner working and the outward extension of the Gospel.

(2) The Gospel conveys the knowledge of "God's grace in all its truth." This phrase suggests that the "gospel" that had been recently introduced to the Colossians by the heretical teachers was a travesty. Their so-called "gospel" was not a message of divine grace and truth; it was a system of legal bondage and human traditions.

7–8 A third item in Paul's expression of thankfulness concerns the work of Epaphras, through whom the Colossians had been instructed in the Gospel. What we know about this man is found only in this passage (vv.4, 7, 9), in 4:12–13, and in Phm 23. He was a native of Colosse and had ministered not only in that city but also in Laodicea and Hierapolis. In Philemon he is described by Paul as his "fellow-prisoner in the cause of Christ Jesus."

We learn three things about Epaphras in vv.7–8. (1) He was Paul's "dear fellow servant." He was, like Paul, a slave of Jesus Christ, and Paul looked on him as a valued comrade in the work of the Lord. (2) He was "a faithful minister of Christ on our [Paul's] behalf." Epaphras appears to have preached in Paul's stead in establishing the work at Colosse. Perhaps Epaphras was himself a convert of Paul during the Ephesian ministry, and Paul had delegated him to take the Gospel to the Colossians. Yet as a "minister of Christ," Epaphras had acted not under the authority of Paul but under that of Paul's Lord. The Greek word "minister" (GK *1356*) here simply means "one who serves." (3) As a messenger from Colosse, Epaphras had communicated to Paul about the Colossians' love; the reference may be to the love they had for all the people of God (cf. v.4) or to the love they had for Paul. "In the Spirit" means that it was the Spirit of God who had awakened this love in Paul's readers. There were other matters not so favorable that Epaphras may have told Paul about the Colossians, but for the moment the apostle is concerned only with these positive features.

C. Prayer of Petition (1:9–14)

To the thanksgiving of vv.3–8, the apostle adds a fervent petition. He prays that the Colossians may be so filled with the knowledge of God's will (v.9) that they may be enabled to live worthily of the Lord, pleasing him in everything (v.10a). This worthy life involves fruitfulness in every good work (v.10b), growth in the knowledge of God (v.10c), patience and long-suffering (v.11), and gratitude to God for the blessings of redemption (vv.12–14).

9 The words "for this reason," referring back to vv.3–8, show that this petitionary prayer is Paul's response to the news that had come to him of the Colossians' experience in Christ. He was grateful for what had already happened to them and prays now for the further enrichment of their lives.

His prayer contains two requests. The first, and the one on which the rest of the prayer is based, is that God might fill the readers "with the knowledge of his will through all spiritual wisdom and understanding." The word "knowledge" (GK *2106*) is used in the NT only of moral and religious knowledge. It denotes thorough knowledge, i.e., a deep and accurate comprehension. Such knowledge of God's will is the foundation of all Christian character and conduct. Already here Paul may be touching on the fact that some in Colosse were failing to attain true knowledge by engaging in wild speculations of a philosophical wisdom.

The "will" of God in its broadest and most inclusive sense is the whole purpose of God as revealed in Christ. In this passage the term perhaps has special reference to God's intention for the conduct of the Christian life.

To be "filled" (GK *4444*) with the knowledge of the divine will suggests that such knowledge is to pervade all of one's being—thoughts, affections, purposes, and plans. There is an unusual emphasis on "fullness" in this letter. The recurrence of this idea suggests that the Colossian errorists claimed to offer a "fullness" of blessing and truth not found in the preaching of Epaphras. Paul answers by stressing the true fullness available only in Christ (cf. especially 2:9). We acquire knowledge of the will of God by "wisdom" and "understanding." These two words should be looked on as expressing a single thought, something like practical wisdom or clear discernment. The use of the two words gives completeness to the statement and thus deepens its impression on the reader.

10 Paul's second petition, built on and growing out of the request for knowledge of the divine will, is that the Colossians might "live a life worthy of the Lord"; living a worthy life is thus represented as a result of knowing God's desire for one's life. This suggests that knowledge of God's will is not imparted as an end in itself; it is given with a practical intent—so that one's conduct may be godly.

"Live a life" translates a single word (lit., "walk"; GK *4344*), one that is often used in Scripture to depict life in its outward expression (cf. 2:6; 3:7; 4:4; et al.). To live a life "worthy of the Lord" probably means to live a life that is commensurate with what the Lord has done for us. It may also suggest acting in conformity with our union with Christ and with his purpose for our lives. The ultimate aim of all this is to "please him [God] in every way." To "please" (GK *742*) suggests an attitude of mind that anticipates every wish. Believers want to do anything to meet the wishes of God; that is the surest path to our own highest development and gain.

Verses 10b–14 underline some of the constituent parts of the kind of life that is pleasing to the Lord. The leading ideas are expressed by four participles: "bearing fruit" (v.10b), "growing" (v.10c), "being strengthened" (v.11a), and "giving thanks" (v.12). (1) "Bearing fruit" (GK *2844*; cf. v.6) means that the Christian life is to exhibit continual fruitfulness (cf. Gal 5:22–23). The fruit itself consists in "every good work"—Paul lays great stress on good works in his letters (cf. Eph 2:10; Gal 5:5; Tit 1:16; 2:7, 14; 3:8, 15; et al.). In his discussion on good works, he represents them as the fruit, not the root, of a right relationship with God.

(2) The Christian should also experience continual personal spiritual enlargement, an idea expressed in the words "growing [GK 889] in the knowledge of God." The preposition *in* suggests that the knowledge of God is the sphere or realm in which spiritual growth takes place. It is possible, however, to translate the phrase as "growing *by* the knowledge of God." When rendered like this, the text affirms that the knowledge of God is the means by which the Christian grows. What rain and sunshine are to the nurture of plants, the knowledge of God is to the growth and maturing of the spiritual life.

11 (3) "Being strengthened with all power" is the next element in the life pleasing to God. Christians are engaged in moral conflict with the cosmic powers of a darkened world (cf. Eph 6:12), and nothing short of divine empowerment can enable them to stand. "Strengthened" (GK *1540*) translates the same root word used in Php 4:13: "I can do everything through him who gives me strength."

This empowerment is "according to his [God's] glorious might." That is to say, it is not proportioned simply to our need, but to God's abundant supply. "His glorious might" is literally translated "the might of his glory." We should probably retain this rendering and understand the thought to be the might of God's own manifested nature. In this interpretation "glory" stands for the revealed splendor or majesty of God—the sum total of his divine perfections.

The twofold issue of such empowerment is "endurance and patience." The first term (GK *5705*) denotes the opposite of cowardice and despondency; it is the capacity to see things through. "Patience" (GK *3429*) is the opposite of wrath or a spirit of revenge. It speaks of even-temperedness, the attitude that in spite of injury or insult does not retaliate.

It is debatable whether "joyfully" should be construed with "endurance and patience" or with "giving thanks." A distinctively Christian quality (cf. Gal 5:22; Php 1:18; 2:17; 3:1; et al.), joy is often associated in the NT with hardship and suffering.

12 (4) The crowning virtue of the worthy Christian life is "giving thanks." One reason for gratitude to God is that he has "qualified" believers "to share in the inheritance of the saints." In themselves believers have no fitness for sharing in the heritage of God's people. They can experience this only as God qualifies them for such a privilege. This God has done for the Colossians and does for any believer at the time of his or her conversion.

To "share in" the inheritance of the saints is to have a portion of the heritage belonging to God's people. There is an obvious allusion to the inheritance of ancient Israel in the Promised Land and the share of the inheritance each Israelite had. Christians, as the new people of God, also have an inheritance, and each believer has a share allotted to him or her.

"In the kingdom of light" seems to mark the inheritance as future and heavenly. But the following verse affirms that Christians have already been rescued from the dominion of darkness and are even now in the kingdom of God's Son. The kingdom of God is all around us—in our homes, our families, our businesses—in sum, in everything that makes up our lives.

13 The proof that God has qualified us for a share of the inheritance of the saints is that he has "rescued us from the dominion of darkness and brought us into the kingdom of the Son he loves." "Rescued" (GK *4861*) means to liberate, save, or deliver someone from something; that from which Christians have been rescued is a "dominion of darkness" (Jesus used the same phrase at the time of his arrest in Gethsemane; see Lk 22:53). "Darkness" in Scripture is symbolic of ignorance, falsehood, and sin (cf. Jn 3:19; Ro 13:12). But Paul probably had the Colossian heresy in mind, because the principalities and powers to which the false teachers urged Christians to pay homage are designated by him "the powers of this dark world" (Eph 6:12).

God's action in behalf of his people does not stop with deliverance from the authority of darkness. He has also "brought [them] into the kingdom of the Son he loves." "Brought" (GK *3496*) was a word used in reference to removing persons from one country and settling them as colonists and citizens in another country. This took place at the time of the Colossians' conversion. The "kingdom" (GK 993; see comment on Mk 1:15) is not to be interpreted as a future realm; it was for the Colossians a present reality (cf. Jn 3:3–5). Nor is the kingdom to be interpreted as an area designated on a map; it is the sovereign rule of the Lord Christ over human hearts. The expression "the Son he loves" is reminiscent of the words of the Father at the baptism and the transfiguration of Jesus (Mt 3:17; 17:5).

14 By virtue of union with Christ, redemption and forgiveness are ours. "Redemption" (GK 667), a term that speaks of a release brought about by the payment of a price, was used of the deliverance of slaves from bondage or of prisoners of war from captivity. "We have" teaches that the believer's redemption is a present possession. "Forgiveness" (lit., "a sending away"; GK 912) speaks of the removal of our sins from us, so that they are no longer barriers that separate us from God. By putting redemption and forgiveness in apposition to each other, Paul teaches that the central feature of redemption is the forgiveness of sins.

II. The Supremacy of Christ (1:15–23)

The most dangerous aspect of the Colossian errorists' teaching was its depreciation of the person of Jesus Christ. To them, Christ was not the triumphant Redeemer to whom all authority in heaven and on earth had been committed. At best he was only one of many spirit beings who bridged the space between God and humankind. This passage is part of Paul's answer to this heretical teaching. As one of several great Christological declarations in Paul (cf. 2:9–15; Eph 1:20–23; Php 2:5–11), it proclaims the unqualified supremacy of our Redeemer. The affirmations of this passage are all the more remarkable when we remember that they were written of One who only thirty years earlier had died on a Roman cross.

It is somewhat arbitrary to separate this passage from what precedes it. So imperceptibly does Paul move from prayer (vv.3–14) to exposition that it is difficult to know exactly where one leaves off and the other begins.

A. The Scope of Christ's Supremacy (1:15–18)

Three profound and sweeping statements concerning Christ are made, showing his relation to deity (v.15a), to creation (vv.15b–17), and to the church (v.18). In making these assertions, Paul refutes the Colossian errorists, in whose system angelic mediators usurped the place and function of Christ. His task in earlier letters (e.g., Romans and Galatians) had been to expound the importance of Christ for salvation; in the face of this new teaching at Colosse, he finds it necessary to affirm Christ's cosmic significance.

15 In regard to deity, Christ is "the image of the invisible God" (cf. 2Co 4:4). He is not the image of God in a material or physical sense. Nor should we, as some interpreters do, understand this as a reference to Christ's existence in the preincarnate state. The context strongly supports the view that Paul was thinking of Christ in his glorified state. To be sure, there is a very real sense in which Christ always has been, is, and always will be the "image" (GK 1635) of God. But that seems not to be the point here. The word expresses two ideas. One is likeness: Christ is the image of God in the sense that he is the exact likeness of God, like the image on a coin or the reflection in a mirror (cf. Heb 1:3). The other idea in "image" is manifestation: Christ is the image of God in the sense that the nature and being of God are perfectly revealed in him (cf. Jn 1:18). Therefore Paul can boldly say that we have "the light of the knowledge of the glory of God in the face of Christ" (2Co 4:6) and that believers, reflecting the Lord's glory, "are being transformed into his likeness with ever-increasing glory" (2Co 3:18). Paul's statement leaves no place for the vague emanations and shadowy abstractions so prominent in the gnostic system.

In relation to the universe, Christ is "the firstborn over all creation." "Firstborn" (GK 4758; see also v.18; Ro 8:29; Heb 1:6; Rev 1:15) may denote either priority in time or supremacy in rank. In the present passage, perhaps we should see both meanings. Christ is *before* all creation in time; he is also *over* it in rank and dignity. The major stress, however, seems to be on the idea of supremacy. Some see in the word an allusion to the ancient custom whereby the firstborn in a family was accorded rights and privileges not shared by the other offspring. He was his father's representative and heir, and to him the management of the household was committed. Following this line of interpretation, Christ is his Father's representative and heir and has the management of the divine household (all creation) committed to him. He is thus Lord over all God's creation.

16 The apostle now states the ground for Christ's dominion over creation: he is firstborn (Lord) over creation *because he made it*. To him it owes its unity, its meaning, indeed its very existence.

Three prepositional phrases define the creative activity of Christ: All things came to be "in [NIV, by] him" (v.16a), "through [NIV, by] him" (v.16b), and "for him" (v.16c). Creation was *in* him in the sense that it occurred within the sphere of his person and power. He was its conditioning cause, its originating center, its spiritual locality. Creation is *through* Christ in the sense that he was the mediating Agent through whom it actually came into being. The entire life of the universe is mediated from God through Christ (cf. Jn 1:3, 10). Creation is *for* Christ in the sense that he is the end for which all things exist, the goal toward whom all things were intended to move. They are meant to serve his will and to contribute to his glory.

"All things" denotes the totality of things in heaven and on earth, visible and invisible. The reference to "thrones," "powers," "rulers," and "authorities" is perhaps an allusion to the angelic hierarchy that figured so prominently in the Colossian heresy. Paul's mention of these things does not, of course, mean that he recognized the existence of a hierarchy of spirit beings, such as the errorists taught. His words do suggest, however, that whatever supernatural powers there may be, Christ is the One who made them and he is their Lord.

17 Verse 16 has stated the essential reason for Christ's lordship over creation, namely, that he is its creator. Verse 17 is a sort of summing up of the thought of vv.15–16. But in addition, it rounds out and completes the statement of Christ's relation to creation. "He is before all things, and in him all things hold together." That Christ is "before" all things means primarily that he is before all in time; yet the statement is general enough to include also the notion that he is above all in rank (cf. "firstborn over all creation" in v.15b). That all things "hold together" (GK *5319*) in Christ means that he is both the unifying principle and the personal sustainer of all creation. It springs from him and finds in him its common cohesion and center (cf. Heb 1:3).

18 Paul's third affirmation concerning Christ's supremacy relates to the new creation: "And he is the head of the body, the church" (v.18a; cf. 2:19; Eph 1:22–23; 4:15). To be the "head" (GK *3051*) of the church is to be its sovereign ruler. In the figure there may also be the suggestion that Christ is the source of the church's life, but this is not its primary significance. Christ, and no other person, is the chief and leader of the church. It is he who guides and governs it.

"Church" (GK *1711*), which means "assembly" or "congregation," is best interpreted here as a term embracing all the redeemed people of God. The mention of the church as "the body" of Christ suggests at least three things: (1) that the church is a living organism, composed of members joined vitally to one another, (2) that the church is the means by which Christ carries out his purposes and performs his work, and (3) that the union that exists between Christ and his people is most intimate and real. Together they constitute one living unit, each, in a sense, being incomplete without the other.

Verse 18b gives one ground or basis of Christ's headship over the church: "He is the beginning and the firstborn from among the dead." "Beginning" (GK *794*) may be interpreted in any one of three ways: (1) supremacy in rank, (2) precedence in time, or (3) creative initiative. There is, of course, truth in each of these, but it seems best to see in Paul's word the idea of creative initiative. In other words, Christ is the origin and source of the life of the church, the fount of its being.

"Firstborn" ((GK *4758*; cf. v.15) defines more precisely what Paul means by Christ as beginning. In v.15, this term pointed to Christ's relation to creation, and we concluded that it suggested both precedence in time and supremacy in rank. In the present passage the idea of precedence is the more prominent. Thus, Christ was the first to come from the dead in true resurrection life (i.e., never to die again, cf. 1Co 15:20). And because he was the first to be born from the dead, he possesses in himself the new and higher life that his people, by virtue of their union with him, now share. Thus he establishes his place as the beginning, the origin of the church's life.

"So that in everything he might have the supremacy" in one sense is a summary of all that Paul has affirmed from v.15 to this point, but syntactically it must be seen as expressing the purpose of the immediately preceding statement about Christ's being the beginning, the firstborn from the dead. He rose from the dead in order that his preeminence might become universal, extending both to the old creation and to the new. He had always been first, but by his resurrection he entered upon an even wider and more significant sovereignty (cf. Ac 2:26; Ro 1:4).

B. The Basis for Christ's Supremacy (1:19–23)

Paul has ascribed unique supremacy to Jesus Christ. He has affirmed him to be image of God, Lord over creation, Head of the church—indeed, preeminent in all things. These next verses now state the grounds (cf. "for" in v.19) on which such supremacy is affirmed. The last phrase of v.18 implies that Christ has unshared supremacy because God has decreed it. This section states this in different terms, but still puts it within the context of the divine will. Two things that God willed are specifically set forth, one having to do with the fullness of God in Christ (v.19), the other with the reconciling work of Christ (vv.20–23).

1. The fullness of God in Christ (1:19)

19 God has willed that in Christ "all fullness" should dwell. The word "fullness" (GK 4445) is one of the key words of this letter, but also one of the most difficult to interpret (cf. also 2:9; Eph 1:23; 3:19; 4:13; see comments on Col 1:9; 2:9). The word seems to have been in current use by the false teachers, and was possibly employed by them for the totality of supernatural powers that they believed controlled people's lives. But to Paul, the totality of divine powers and attributes exists only in Christ; nothing of deity is lacking in him (cf. 2:9 for a similar view).

According to the Colossian errorists, many spirit beings filled the space between God and the world as intermediaries, and any communication between God and the world had to pass through them. They probably included Christ among these supernatural powers, admitting that he was of heavenly origin and that God was in some sense present in him. He was, however, only one aspect of the divine nature and in himself was not sufficient for all the needs of humankind. Paul, in contrast, declares that Christ is not just one of many divine beings. He is the one and only Mediator between God and the world, and all, not part, of the attributes and activities of God are centered in him. "Dwell" (GK 2997) suggests permanent residence as opposed to temporary sojourn. Paul may be refuting a Colossian notion that the divine fullness had only a transient and incidental association with Christ. To Paul, it abides in him permanently.

2. The reconciling work of Christ (1:20–23)

20 The Father was pleased "to reconcile to himself all things" through Christ. This statement sustains a close connection with v.19. For one thing, "reconcile" (GK 639) is parallel with the word for "dwell" (v.19), both terms being grammatically dependent on the verb rendered "was pleased." That is, the Father willed that all fullness should dwell in Christ and that he would reconcile all things to himself through Christ. "Reconcile" suggests removing all enmity between God and the human race and effecting in humankind a condition of submission to, and harmony with, God (cf. Ro 5:10–11; 2Co 5:18–20; Eph 2:14–15). This reconciliation is on the widest possible scale—"all things." The "things in heaven" is an inclusive term, taking in everything not belonging to the "earth" (i.e., the starry heavens) "Things on earth . . . things in heaven" thus denotes everything in God's universe.

One must be careful not to interpret this verse in such a way as to make it contradict the clear teaching of other Scriptures. Admittedly, the statement might appear, on its surface, to indicate that eventually everything will be brought into a saving relationship with God. Such universalism, however, is contrary to those passages that affirm that apart from personal trust in Christ there is no salvation. Our Lord spoke of the impenitent as going away into "eternal punishment" (Mt 25:46). This statement refers, therefore, to the cosmic significance of Christ's work, the thought being similar to, but not identical with, that of Ro 8:19–22. There the general sense is that the disorder that has characterized creation will be done away and divine harmony restored. Here the main idea is that all things eventually are to be decisively subdued to God's will and made to serve his purposes.

21 Verse 20 has presented the general aspect of the reconciling work of Christ; vv. 21–23 show how this applies personally and specifically to the Colossians. Prior to their conversion to Christianity they had been "alienated" or estranged from God and were "enemies" (GK *2398*) in their minds. The latter word affirms the Colossians' hostility to God. This hostility, Paul explains, affected their "minds" (i.e., their thoughts and disposition) and was outwardly expressed in their wicked deeds.

22 God reconciled the Colossians "by Christ's physical body through death." The phrase "physical body" seems to emphasize (in contradiction to the views of the heretics) the reality of Christ's human body. To the errorists, reconciliation could be accomplished only by spiritual (angelic) beings; they attached little or no value to the work of Christ in a physical body. In opposition to this, Paul stressed the importance of Christ's body.

The result of Christ's reconciling work is the presentation of the Colossians as "holy in his sight, without blemish and free from accusation." Both the present and the future seem to be in view here. In reconciling believers, God brought them into his presence, no longer as stained by sin and bearing the burden of guilt, but as "holy" and "without blemish and free from accusation." That is their standing at the time of and by the death of Christ. But on the day of Christ's return, they will be officially presented as perfected in glory. In the meantime, they are progressing in holiness wrought in them by the Spirit of God.

"Holy" suggests consecration and dedication (see comment on v.2). "Without blemish" (GK *320*), which translates a technical sacrificial term (Lev 22:21), was used of animals that were without flaw and therefore worthy of being offered to God. The use of this word gives support to the view that in this statement Paul was not thinking about our personal conduct but about our position in Christ. There has never been, nor will there ever be, a Christian life that is without blemish in actual conduct. But Christians' identification with Christ is such that his righteousness and his standing before God are theirs (2Co 5:21; 1Jn 4:17).

"Free from accusation" likewise expresses a condition possible only because people are in Christ, covered by and sharing in the benefits of his death for them.

23 Those who emphasize the future aspects of v.22 explain v.23 as a warning against indolence and complacency. The Colossians will be thus presented to God only "if [they] continue in [their] faith, established and firm," and so forth. Those who emphasize v.22 as a statement of the believer's present condition contend that the words of v.23 are proof of a past (and continuing) experience, not a condition of what is future. Paul is simply stating the absolute accomplishment of salvation in the past sufferings of Christ. It is significant for both interpretations that the condition is stated in such a way as to express the apostle's confidence in his readers.

"Faith" (GK *4411*) here, as is usual in the NT, means one's personal faith, i.e., one's reliance on Christ. The words that follow "faith" explain what is involved in continuing in one's faith. "Established" suggests being founded securely, as on a rock. "Firm" depicts a steady and firm resolve. The "hope held out in the gospel" is in its fullest sense the expectation of ultimate, complete salvation that will belong to believers upon the return of their Lord. There may be an implicit contrast between the certainty of the Gospel and the delusive promises offered by the Colossian errorists.

In the closing words of v.23 Paul makes three statements to stress the importance of remaining true to the apostolic Gospel. (1) It is the message "that you heard." The reference is to the Gospel that had been initially preached to them by Epaphras (cf. 1:7) and was the instrument of their conversion. (2) It has been "proclaimed to every creature under heaven." The universality of the Gospel in all places of the Roman empire is a mark of its authenticity. Obviously there is an element of hyperbole in this statement. (3) Paul closes with the affirmation that he himself had "become a servant" of the Gospel. He does not designate himself in this fashion for the purpose of magnifying his office, but to impress on the Colossians that the Gospel heard by them from Epaphras and proclaimed in all the world was the same Gospel he had been preaching.

III. The Ministry of Paul (1:24-2:7)

This passage, which is somewhat parallel to Eph 3:1ff., comes as a sort of digression. Though decidedly autobiographical, it is not so much concerned with Paul the man as with the office he filled. In the course of his discussion, Paul mentions his suffering and its bearing on the Colossians (1:24), his commission to preach and its implications for them (1:25–29), and his personal interest in and concern for them (2:1–5). The passage closes with a direct appeal to the Colossians (2:6–7).

A. A Ministry of Suffering (1:24)

24 The interpretation of this verse is much disputed, but the general sense of it is clear. In it the apostle teaches that the sufferings he endured in the course of his work were in the interest of the Colossians, indeed, of the whole church; in that knowledge, he is able to rejoice (cf. Eph 3:13).

"Now" may be both temporal and transitional in force. In its temporal sense, the word indicates that Paul's joy and his suffering were both realities at the time of writing this letter. In its transitional sense, "now" shows that this paragraph is closely related to the thought of the preceding section. Looked at in this manner, the term is almost equivalent to "therefore" and shows that the thought of Christ's supremacy is a factor in Paul's ability to rejoice in the midst of suffering.

Three things are said in the verse about the sufferings of Paul. (1) They are for the sake of other people ("for you" and "for the sake of his [Christ's] body"). In both phrases "for" means "in the interest of." The first phrase alludes to the fact that Paul's imprisonment had come as a result of bringing the Gospel to the Gentiles, to which class the Colossians belonged. His sufferings, therefore, were for their sake in that they shared in the benefit of the ministry that brought on the sufferings. The second phrase affirms that the benefit of

The Colossian Heresy

Most scholars see in the letter to the Colossians evidence of a heretical group that was pressuring true believers there to adopt their teachings. Paul labels these teachings as "hollow and deceptive philosophy," based on "human traditions" (2:8). Judging from the content of this letter, the following appear to be the main tenets of the heretics and Paul's rebuttal to them.

Teaching of heresy	Paul's answer	Relevant texts
Emphasis on worship of angels, called "thrones," "rulers," "powers," and "authorities."	Christ created these powers and he rules over them; believers are delivered from their power.	1:13, 15–17; 2:9–10, 15, 18–19
Angels are intermediaries between God and human beings.	Christ is the only mediator we need.	1:13–23; 2:6, 9–10
Endorsed submission to the "basic principles of the world."	Christ rules over them, and Christians have died to them in Christ.	2:8, 20
Endorsed circumcision.	Believers undergo a form of circumcision in the death of Christ, experienced through baptism.	2:11–13
Endorsed special religious days and legalistic food rules.	Do not listen to such rules; believers have died to them and their power is cancelled.	2:14, 16–17, 20–23
Emphasis on a special, secret knowledge.	God fills all believers with his wisdom, knowledge, and understanding.	1:9–10, 28; 2:2–4, 22

Paul's sufferings extends not simply to those Colossians or even to the Gentile portion of the church; they in some sense have a bearing on the whole body of Christ. Indeed, his sufferings contribute even to our well-being, for had he not suffered imprisonment, this letter might never have been written, and we would have been deprived of its message.

(2) Paul's sufferings are identified with "Christ's afflictions." The words "I fill up in my flesh what is still lacking in regard to Christ's afflictions" have evoked a great amount of discussion. Many Roman Catholics, for instance, interpreting the "afflictions" of Christ as Christ's redemptive sufferings, have asserted that Christ's atonement is defective and that the sufferings of the saints are needed to supplement his work on our behalf. But whatever this verse means, we may be sure that Paul did not regard the death of Jesus as lacking in efficacy (cf. Col 2:11–15). That death was complete, once for all, and wholly adequate to meet our need.

The afflictions of Christ are undoubtedly those endured personally by him on earth, but the reference is to his ministerial afflictions, not his redemptive sufferings. "Afflictions" (GK 2568) is never employed in the NT of the sufferings of Christ on the cross; the reference, then, is to the tribulations our Lord endured in the course of his life and ministry. The sufferings his people endure are a continuation of what he endured, and in that sense they complete his afflictions. The church is built by acts of self-denial in Christ's servants; they continue the work he began.

The underlying principle is the believer's union with Christ. That union is so intimate—Christ the Head, his people the body—that he suffers when they suffer (cf. Isa 63:9). His personal sufferings are over, but his sufferings in his people continue (cf. 2Co 1:5; Php 3:10). Perhaps Paul was thinking of Christ's words to him on the Damascus road (Ac 9:4–5). "What is still lacking" is not an intimation of deficiency in Christ's own sufferings but a reference to what is yet lacking in Christ's suffering in Paul. In his experience as a prisoner, the apostle was filling up the sum or quota of suffering yet remaining for him to endure.

(3) They are the sphere of Paul's joy. The sufferings Paul endured for the Gospel seem never to have been to him a source of perplexity or of sadness. But his attitude had nothing in common with those ascetics of a later time who inflicted torture on themselves in the belief that they would thereby gain merit with God. Paul's joy was not in suffering as such, but in "what was suffered for you." That is to say, it was the distinctive character and circumstances of his sufferings that enabled him to find joy in the midst of them. He saw them as a necessary part of his ministry (see also Mt 5:12; Ac 5:41; Heb 10:34.)

B. A Ministry of Preaching (1:25–29)

A second feature of Paul's ministry was the proclamation of God's message. His statement concerning this is of great value to all who wish a better understanding of preaching. The thought revolves around four conceptions: Paul's appointment to the office of preacher (v.25a), the message he preached (vv.25b–28a), the method he employed (v.28b), and his ultimate aim (vv.28c–29).

25 Elsewhere Paul speaks of himself as a minister of the Gospel (v.23; Eph 3:7), of God (2Co 6:4), of Christ (2Co 11:23), and of a new covenant (2Co 3:6). Here he is the church's minister or "servant" (GK 1356; cf. 1:7, 23), and as such is bound to toil and suffer in whatever way the church's welfare requires.

Paul's appointment to his office was "by the commission God gave" him—lit., "according to the dispensation of God." The word translated "commission" (GK 3873) has a wide range of meanings; here it is perhaps best rendered by "stewardship" (cf. Lk 16:2–4). This rendering suggests that Paul conceived of the work to which God appointed him as both a high privilege and a sacred trust. He was a servant of the church, but in the deepest sense he was a steward of God (cf. 1Co 4:1).

The purpose of the apostle's stewardship was "to present the word of God in all its fullness." Some understand this to refer to the geographical extension of the Gospel (cf. Ro 15:19). But Paul probably means that his special ministry was to make clear the true nature of the Gospel as a divine provision intended for all.

26 The preceding verse has spoken of Paul's message as "the word of God," a general term that sums up the oral proclamation of the apostles. Verses 26–27 define the word of

God more specifically in terms of a "mystery" (GK *3696*), a word used in the NT of truth undiscoverable except by divine revelation (cf. 1Co 2:6ff.; 14:51); i.e., it denotes something that, though once a secret, has now been fully revealed in the Gospel. In Ephesians it is used six times—more often than in any other book of the NT: in 1:9, where it refers to the mystery of God's dealing with the world; in 3:3–9 (three times), where it has special reference to the inclusion of Gentiles in the privileges and blessings of the messianic salvation; in 5:22, where it speaks of the spiritual union of Christ and his church; and in 6:19, where it is practically equated with the Gospel. Here in Colossians the word occurs four times (1:26, 27; 2:2; 4:3).

Paul goes on to express two characteristics of this mystery: it was "hidden for ages and generations, but is now disclosed." "Ages" and "generations" are used together to refer to people living in former times. Now, however, "to the saints" (i.e., the people of God) the formerly hidden truth is "disclosed." Paul's expression here reflects an intense joy that the long silence has been broken.

27 God was pleased to reveal to his people how great is the glorious character of the gospel mystery. Paul's frequent use of "riches" (GK *4458*) suggests that Christ had made available an inexhaustible treasure of goodness (Ro 2:4), glory (Ro 9:23; Eph 1:18; 3:16; Php 4:19), wisdom (Ro 11:33), and grace (Eph 1:7; 2:7). "Among [lit., in] the Gentiles" defines the sphere in which the wealth of glory has been especially displayed. Paul seems to have been thinking of the wonder of the unfolding of the divine mystery in the conversion of pagan people and in their being drawn into the one body of Christ. The inner content of the mystery is defined as "Christ in you," a phrase that refers to an inner, subjective experience of the indwelling of Christ.

"Christ in you" is now declared to be "the hope of glory." "Hope" is joyous expectation or anticipation; "glory" is that which will belong to the Christian in the heavenly state (cf. 3:4; Ro 5:2; 8:17). The general truth is that Christ living in the believer is the ground for certainty of complete salvation (cf. Eph 1:13–14, where the Spirit is designated as "the deposit guaranteeing our inheritance"). In this letter Christ himself occupies the sphere that Paul elsewhere gives to the Spirit.

28 In v.25 Paul has defined his message as "the word of God." In vv.26–27 he has used the term "mystery." Here his message centers in the Christ who indwells believers. At the deepest level, therefore, the apostle conceived of his message not as a system or as a collection of rules and regulations, but as a living and glorious Person who is the fulfillment of the deepest hopes of humankind and the source of new life for all his people. "We" distinguishes Paul and his fellow preachers from the Colossian errorists. "Proclaim" (GK *2859*) suggests a solemn or public proclamation with authority. This term includes the idea of instruction and admonition.

"Admonishing" (GK *3805*) and "teaching" (GK *1438*) describe two attendant circumstances of Paul's preaching. The former word has to do with the will and emotions and connotes warning. Here it relates to non-Christians, the thought probably being that the apostle sought to awaken each of them to his or her need of Christ and to the necessity of repentance. The latter word, probably referring to a ministry for converts, stresses the importance of instruction in proclaiming the Word. "With all wisdom" seems to express the way the teaching was done.

"Everyone," stated twice for emphasis, shows that Paul's Gospel was not marred by the exclusiveness that characterized the false teachers. They believed the way of salvation to be so involved that it could be understood only by a select few who made up a sort of spiritual aristocracy. Unlike the errorists, Paul slighted no one. Every person was the object of his direct concern.

The aim of Paul's proclaiming, admonishing, and teaching was to "present everyone perfect in Christ." "Present" (GK *4225*) refers to being brought into God's presence at the return of Christ (cf. 1Th 2:19–20; 5:23); only then will God's work in the believer be complete. "Perfect" (GK *5455*) suggests attainment of the proper end of one's existence—maturity in faith and character (cf. Eph 4:13). Such maturity is possible "in Christ," i.e., by virtue of the believer's union with Christ.

29 Paul gave himself unstintingly to accomplishing this end. "Struggling" (GK *76*) is a term from the athletic arena, signifying intense exertion. This struggle is "according to his [God's] working." In other words, the struggle is carried on, not through Paul's own natural powers, but by the supernatural power at work in him. The entire statement shows that through faith in Christ we can link our life with a source of strength that enables us to rise above our natural limitations.

C. A Ministry of Intercession (2:1–5)

A third feature of Paul's ministry was his pastoral concern for those he served. The concern expressed in these verses arose from Paul's anxiety about the response of the Colossian Christians to the error being propagated by the false teachers (cf. Php 3:18). Anyone sharing Paul's exalted concept of Christ (cf. Col 1:15ff.) can never be indifferent to the inroads of error.

1 The metaphor of the arena is implicit in this verse as Paul again uses the word "struggling" (a Greek word built on the same root as "struggling" in 1:29; GK 74). He indicates how strenuously he was exerting himself with deep and earnest solicitude. The powers that wrestled with Paul for the ruin of his work were real and resolute; he therefore had to meet them full force in Christ. The particular struggle Paul had in mind appears to have been that of prayer. At the time he wrote these words he could not move beyond the walls of his "rented house" (Ac 28:30), being continuously held by the chain linking him to a Roman soldier. But even under these circumstances he could engage in the combat of prayer and so exert himself strenuously in behalf of his readers.

This brings before us an aspect of Paul's prayers that we often overlook—namely, that they sometimes involved him in a truly awesome conflict, an intense struggle of the soul. This agony in prayer was "for" (i.e., in behalf of) the Colossians. But it was also in behalf of "those at Laodicea and for all who have not met me personally." Laodicea was an important banking center in ancient times and is mentioned elsewhere in the NT only in 4:13, 15–16; Rev 3:14. The wording of v.1 seems to suggest that the Colossians and the Laodiceans were among those who had not met Paul personally.

2 Paul's concern for his readers was that "they may be encouraged in heart and united in love." The Greek word for "encouraged" (GK *4151*) means "to call to one's side," signifying such ideas as comfort, encouragement, and exhortation. The central thought here is being strengthened against the onslaught of error. "United" (GK *5204*) suggests being welded into a genuine unity. The Greek construction suggests that the means by which the strengthening takes place is the readers' being knit together in love.

One consequence of being encouraged and united is attaining "the full riches of complete understanding." Heart encouragement and being united in love bring an inward wealth that consists in full or assured understanding. This in turn brings a deep and full knowledge (see comment on 1:9) of Christ, who is "the mystery of God" (see comment on 1:26).

3 This Christ is now described as the One "in whom are hidden all the treasures of wisdom and knowledge." This statement contains two thoughts. (1) All the treasures of wisdom and knowledge are in Christ. The false teachers claimed to have, through their relation with a supposed hierarchy of supernatural beings, a higher knowledge than that possessed by ordinary believers. Against this, Paul argues that all wisdom and knowledge are in Christ and that their treasures are accessible to every believer. (2) The treasures of wisdom are in Christ in a hidden way. "Hidden" does not, however, mean that they are concealed but rather that they are laid up or stored away as a treasure.

4 Paul now expresses the reason for his anxious concern. His words in vv.1–3 have been written so that the Colossian errorists will not "deceive" (GK *4165*) the Christians in Colosse and lead them away from their convictions about Christ. "Deceive" implies leading astray by false reasoning; "fine-sounding arguments" has something of the same meaning, implying the attempt to convince someone by "fast talk."

5 Paul was no indifferent spectator of his readers' problems but had a sincere interest in them. Though not physically with them, he felt his spiritual oneness with them and rejoiced in their orderliness and in the firmness of their faith. "How orderly you are" contains a military term connoting the orderly array of a band of disciplined soldiers. "Firm" (GK *5106*) also belongs to military parlance and means solidity and compactness. If this is the imagery Paul intended, he sees the situation of the Colossians as being like that of an army under attack and affirms that their lines were unbroken, their discipline intact, and their "faith in [reliance on] Christ" unshaken.

D. A Ministry of Exhortation (2:6–7)

It seems best to take these two verses as a kind of summary appeal made in light of the preceding discussion—an appeal for the readers to remain true to Christ as Lord.

6 "So then" links Paul's appeal with what he has just said. The Colossians had received Christ as the Anointed of God ("Christ"), as the historic Savior ("Jesus"), and as the sovereign "Lord." Now Paul appeals to them to "continue to live [GK 4344] in him" in the same manner. He wants their present conduct to conform regularly to the doctrine taught them at the beginning, the doctrine they had committed themselves to at their conversion.

7 In this verse four participles describe the walk in Christ. The first two, "rooted [GK 4845] and built up [GK 2224] in him," go together. The first expression suggests a once-for-all experience, i.e., a being permanently rooted in Christ; the second one indicates a continual process. The Colossians have been "strengthened [GK 1011] in the faith"; i.e., their strength has been in the body of truth or the faith system that they learned when they first became Christians. The final phrase, "overflowing [GK 4355] with thankfulness," means that for believers thanksgiving is to be a continual, habitual thing. Paul may be implying that those who lack a deep sense of thankfulness to God are especially vulnerable to doubt and spiritual delusion.

IV. Warning Against Error (2:8–23)

The apostle now makes his most direct attack against the Colossian heresy. The entire passage bristles with exegetical difficulties and calls for closer attention to its wording and argument than any other part of this letter. Its tone is both admonitory and affirmative, but admonition is the prevailing note sounded throughout. The affirmations, which mainly concern Christ and his sufficiency (cf. vv.9–15), form the basis on which the warnings are issued and give point and power to them.

It is characteristic of Paul in Colossians to use the vocabulary of his opponents, though often in a different sense. Instances of this in the present passage may be "philosophy" (v.8), "fullness" (v.9), "Deity" (v.9), "powers and authorities" (v.15), "humility" (v.18), "disqualify" (v.18), and "self-imposed worship" (v.23).

A. The Error of False Philosophy (2:8–15)

1. The warning stated (2:8)

8 Paul first warns against the danger of being taken captive through a false philosophy. The singular "no one" suggests that Paul may have had a particular person in mind, perhaps the leader of the heretical teachers. The words translated "that no one takes you captive" point to a real, not a supposed, danger. "Takes captive" (GK 5194), a word regularly used of taking captives in war and leading them away as booty, depicts the false teachers as "people-stealers," wishing to entrap the Colossians and drag them away into spiritual enslavement.

"Through hollow and deceptive philosophy" expresses the means whereby the errorists were attempting to do this. This is the only occurrence of the word "philosophy" in the NT. It would be a mistake to conclude that Paul intended his statement to be a condemnation of all philosophy. Here, because of the reference to the Colossian error, it has a derogatory connotation.

Paul uses three descriptive phrases to characterize this "hollow and deceptive" system; each constitutes a reason for its rejection. (1) It was according to "human tradition." By "tradition" (GK 4142) Paul likely means the various pagan theories current in that day. He asserts that these, not divine revelation, were the bases of the "philosophy" of the Colossian errorists.

(2) It was a philosophy that depends on "the basic principles of this world." "Basic principles" (GK 5122) has a variety of meanings. Originally it denoted the letters of the alphabet, its root meaning being "things in a row." The term then came to be used of the elements ("ABC's") of learning (cf. Gal 4:3; Heb 5:12), of the physical elements of the world (cf. 2Pe 3:10), and of the elemental spirits or supernatural powers believed by many ancients to preside over and direct the heavenly bodies (cf. Gal 4:3). The sense in the

present passage may be either the elements of learning or the elemental spirits. If the former sense is intended, the statement means that the Colossian system was really only rudimentary instruction, the ABC's of the world—i.e., it was elementary rather than advanced. The rendering "elemental spirits" is, however, to be preferred. This philosophy probably had the elemental spirits of the universe as its subject matter. We know from 2:18, for example, that the Colossian heresy made much of the "worship of angels."

(3) It was a system not according to Christ. This is Paul's most telling criticism of the teaching at Colosse. The philosophy of the heretics did not accord with the truth as revealed in Christ. He is the standard by which all doctrine is to be measured, and any system, whatever its claims, must be rejected if it fails to conform to the revelation God has given us in him.

2. The warning justified (2:9-15)

Paul's warning rests on Christ's unshared supremacy (v.9) and his complete adequacy to meet human need (vv.10-15). Because of who he is and what we find in him, any system "not after Christ" must be wrong. The passage takes up the central phrase of 1:19 ("fullness") and draws out its consequences in relation to the Colossian heresy.

a. The full deity of Christ (2:9a)

9a Nearly every word in this statement is significant. "For," linking this and the following verses to v.8, shows that the warning in that verse rests on what is said here about Christ and his fullness. The phrase "in Christ" (see comment on 1:2) stresses that in Christ alone the fullness of deity dwells. "Lives" (GK 2997) suggests the idea of taking up permanent residence. The tense is present, stating a general truth and denoting continuous action. The full thought, then, is that in Christ the fullness of deity permanently resides, finding a settled home in him. The context suggests that the primary reference is to Christ in his present glorified state. "Fullness" (GK 4445; see comment on 1:19) is defined by the addition of "of the Deity" (GK 2540). This word is an abstract term, meaning not just divine qualities and attributes but the complete, inner essence of God that lives in Christ.

b. The real humanity of Christ (2:9b)

9b The preceding statement corresponds to the phrase in Jn 1:1, "the Word was God"; this present statement corresponds to Jn 1:14, "the Word became flesh." The fullness of deity dwells in Christ "in bodily form," i.e., in incarnate fashion. This fullness, to be sure, resided in the preincarnate Word, but not in bodily fashion.

c. The complete adequacy of Christ (2:10-15)

10 This statement crowns Paul's argument. Because Christ is fully God and really human, believers "are made full," i.e., share in his fullness; "in him" denotes our vital union with the Savior. In union with Christ, our every spiritual need is fully met. Possessing him, we possess all. There was no need, therefore, for the Colossians to turn to the "philosophy" of the errorists, the ritual of the Mosaic law, or the spirit-beings worshiped by the pagan world. All they needed was in Jesus Christ.

Paul goes on to affirm the all-sufficiency of Christ by stating that he is "the head over every power and authority." He is "the head" in the sense that he is the source of life for all that exists and sovereign Lord over it all (cf. 1:16, 18). Whatever powers there are in the universe, whatever ranks and orders of authority and government, they all owe their being to Christ and are under his lordship. It is important to observe that though Christ is here described as head, the powers and authorities are not called his body. That distinction is reserved for Christ's people.

11 Paul now expands on the idea of Christ's sufficiency. Our Lord has done three things for us: spiritual circumcision (vv.11-12), forgiveness of sins (vv.13-14), and victory over evil forces (v.15).

In union with Christ, believers have true "circumcision," i.e., they have found in him the reality symbolized by Mosaic circumcision. The Christian's "circumcision" is defined as "the putting off of the sinful nature." "Putting off" (GK 589) uses the picture of stripping off and casting away a piece of filthy clothing. The "sinful nature" (lit., "the body of the flesh") has been variously explained, but only two interpretations seem worthy of consideration. One understands "body" to be a reference to the physical body, "flesh" to be a description of the body as conditioned by our fallen nature. The other takes "body" to denote something like "mass" or sum total, "flesh" to denote our sinful nature (i.e., the entire carnal nature; cf. NIV).

The description of Christian circumcision as "not ... done by the hands of men" is obviously intended to contrast the Christian's "circumcision" with that required by the Mosaic law (and advocated also by the errorists of Colosse). The circumcision prescribed by Moses, which represented the cutting away of a man's uncleanness and was the outward sign of participation in Israel's covenant with God, was made with hands (i.e., was physical), and it affected an external organ of the body. The circumcision that the believer experiences in Christ is spiritual, and it relates not to an external organ but to one's inward being. In short, it is what elsewhere in Scripture is called "circumcision of the heart" (Ro 2:28; cf. Php 3:3)—something that took place at the time of conversion.

12 Paul gives a further explanation of spiritual circumcision: Christian baptism is the outward counterpart to that experience and as such is the means by which it is openly declared. The emphasis of the verse, however, is not on the analogy between circumcision and baptism; that concept is soon dismissed, and the thought shifts to that of baptism as symbolizing the believer's participation in the burial and resurrection of Christ (cf. Ro 6:3ff.).

Being "buried" and "raised" with Christ conveys the thought not simply of burying an old way of life and rising to a new kind of life but of sharing in the experience of Christ's own death and resurrection. That Paul did not think of baptism as actually effecting participation in that experience is made clear when he adds that the Colossians were raised through their "faith in the power of God." Baptism, then, is not a magic rite, but an act of obedience in which we confess our faith and symbolize the essence of our spiritual experience. Faith is the instrumental cause of that experience, and, apart from real faith, baptism is an empty, meaningless ceremony.

13–14 In the closing words of v.12 Paul mentioned God's raising Christ from the dead. Now he assures his readers that in Christ they share the resurrection experience. In Christ's case it was a literal bodily resurrection from the dead. In their case, the death was spiritual ("dead in your sins," "uncircumcision"), and the being make alive is also spiritual. Eventually, of course, believers will experience a bodily resurrection (see 1Co 15).

The NIV translation "dead in your sins and ... and in the uncircumcision of your sinful nature" suggests that "sins" and "uncircumcision" are the sphere in which death was manifested. It is perhaps better to follow ASV and read the text to mean dead *by reason of* trespasses and an uncircumcised (unregenerate or pagan) nature (cf. Ac 7:51).

The first part of v.13 affirms the readers' deadness through trespasses and their being made alive in union with Christ. The last part of this verse indicates that their being made alive involved the forgiveness of everything that had once alienated them from God. In other words, forgiveness and being made alive are two facets of the same act of divine grace.

Verse 14 vividly describes the attendant circumstances of forgiveness in Christ. One is the cancellation of "the written code." "Having canceled" (GK *1981*) should be translated "canceling out" (lit., "wiping out"; cf. Ac 3:19; Rev 3:5; 7:17; 21:4); it specifies the act by which the forgiveness was carried out. What is canceled is called "the written code," an expression used of any document written by hand. This can be understood as an official written indictment or as a self-acknowledged state of indebtedness (like an IOU); in any case, it refers is to the Mosaic law. God has blotted it out so that it no longer stands against us.

Paul uses three expressions to describe the law: (1) It was written with "regulations" (cf. Eph 2:15). (2) It was "against us" (i.e., God's law had a valid claim on us). It was (if we follow the imagery of a "bond") like a promissory note having our signature attached as evidence that we acknowledged its claim and our debt. (3) It "stood opposed to us." This suggests that because we could not meet the claims of the law, it was hostile toward us or was an obstacle in our way.

Verse 14a has asserted that this bond or indictment has been "canceled out"; v.14b now adds that God (or Christ) "took it away, nailing it to the cross." In other words, the bond (the Mosaic law) has been removed permanently, so that its claims against us can never again alienate us from God.

Paul's vivid metaphor of nailing the law to the cross has been variously explained. Some think it alludes to an ancient custom dictating that when decrees were nullified, a copy of the text should be nailed up in a public place. Others see here an allusion to the custom of hanging over the head of an executed person a copy of the charge on which he was condemned. When Jesus was crucified, the superscription nailed to his cross contained the words "The King of the Jews." Paul ignores the real superscription and imagines the law as nailed above the cross. That was, after all, the real reason why Christ was put to death—because of our sins against God's law. Still others understand the idea to be that the indictment was itself crucified.

To sum up, the great principle asserted in v.14 is the destruction of the law in and by the cross of Christ. The law, however, is viewed in a certain character (i.e., as a bond of indebtedness or as an instrument of condemnation).

15 The meaning of nearly every word of this verse is disputed. One of the key issues concerns the interpretation of "powers and authorities." The interpretation preferred here is that which sees these as hostile supernatural powers, i.e., as the hierarchy of spiritual forces that are in rebellion against God (see comment on 1:16; cf. 2:8; Eph 6:12). Paul affirms that Christ has "disarmed" (GK *588*) these forces of evil. He has stripped the powers and authorities just as a conquered antagonist was stripped of his weapons and armor and put to public shame.

Paul goes on to say that God (in Christ) "made a public spectacle of them." That is to say, he exposed them to public disgrace by exhibiting them to the universe as his captives. The added words, "triumphing over them by the cross," expand this idea. The picture, quite familiar in the Roman world, is that of a triumphant general leading a parade of victory. The conqueror, riding at the front in his chariot, leads his troops through the streets of the city. Behind them trails a wretched company of vanquished kings, officers, and soldiers—the spoils of battle. Christ, in this picture, is the conquering general; the powers and authorities are the vanquished enemy displayed as the spoils of battle before the entire universe (cf. 2Co 2:14). To the casual observer the cross appears to be only an instrument of death, the symbol of Christ's defeat; Paul sees it as Christ's chariot of victory.

B. The Error of Legalism (2:16–17)

16 The false teachers at Colosse laid down rigid restrictions with regard to eating and drinking and with regard to the observance of the religious calendar. "Therefore" shows that this and the following warnings grow out of what Paul says of Christ's complete sufficiency in vv.10–15. He is particularly thinking of Christ's removal of the law and his triumph over the forces of evil (vv.14–15). In light of what Christ did, the Colossians were to let no one "judge" their standing before God on the basis of their observance or nonobservance of the regulations of the Mosaic law. In such matters the principle of Christian liberty comes into play (cf. Gal 5:1). The Christians at Colosse should assert their Christian liberty in the face of the errorists' attempts to undermine it (though see also Ro 14:13–21; 1Co 8:7–13).

"What you eat or drink" is probably a reference to the dietary rules in the Mosaic law about clean and unclean food, though it could also refer to the peculiar ascetic tendencies of the Colossian heresy that may have required abstinence from such things as meat and wine. The reference to "Sabbath day" points clearly to the Jewish calendar, for only Jews kept the Sabbath. That being the case, "religious festival" and "New Moon celebration" undoubtedly point to the ritual calendar of the Jews. Paul's thought is that the Christian is freed from obligations of this kind (cf. v.14; Gal 4:9–11; 5:1). No one, therefore, should be permitted to make such things a test of piety or fellowship (cf. Ro 14:1ff.).

17 All such OT legal stipulations were but "a shadow [i.e., an anticipation] of the things that were to come." Therefore to cling to the prophetic shadow is to obscure the spiritual reality of which those things were a prefigurement. "The reality" or the substance belongs to Christ. In him, the things to come have appeared (on this issue, see also Heb 8:5; 10:1). These two verses are an earnest appeal for "Christian liberty." But we should also note that the "liberty" Paul means is the opposite of license and has nothing akin to the miserable individualism whose highest ambition is to do just what it likes. Paul's whole aim is for the fullest, deepest, and most watchful holiness. He wants his Colossian converts above all things to be holy and to live a life in submission to their Redeemer.

C. The Error of Angel Worship (2:18–19)

18 Paul's third warning brings before us two of the most puzzling verses in the NT. The expression "disqualify [GK 2857] you" has been rendered in many different ways. A technical meaning of the clause is "let no one act as umpire against you," i.e., give an adverse decision against you. Perhaps it is only a stronger and more picturesque way of saying, "Let no one judge you" (cf. v.16). The essential meaning is, "Let no one deny your claim to be Christians."

The person attempting to make such judgment is described as one "who delights in false humility and the worship of angels." The context suggests that someone was seeking to impose these things on the Colossians, and that this was the means by which he was attempting to disqualify them for their prize. "False humility" may be a technical term for fasting, since in the OT this was the usual way for one to humble oneself before God. Whether this be so or not, the word in this context appears to denote a mock humility. "Worship of angels" is an allusion to the deference the heretical teachers paid to the hierarchy of spirit-beings who, in their system, filled the whole universe. Perhaps the "humility" and the "worship of angels" were closely related. That is to say, the heretics probably insisted that their worship of angels, rather than appealing directly to the supreme God of all grace, was an expression of humility on their part.

We see a further indication of the method of the false teachers in the words "goes into great detail about what he has seen." The heretical teacher possibly took his stand on imaginary or alleged visions; he "harped" on those visions, claiming more than he could prove. Paul goes on to depict the heretical teacher as inflated with conceit. "His unspiritual [lit., fleshly] mind puffs him up with idle notions." That mind is one dominated by the unrenewed nature, without spiritual enlightenment.

19 The false teacher lacked vital contact with Jesus Christ. This is profoundly serious because it is from Christ as Head that "the whole body [the church], supported and held together by its ligaments and sinews, grows." Each believer is thought of here as forming a vital connection with Christ the Head. Thus joined to him, they all become the joints and ligaments by which the church is supplied with energy and life. The heretical teacher, without this contact with Christ, has cut himself off from the source of spiritual vitality for God's people and cannot possibly contribute to their growth.

D. The Error of Asceticism (2:20–23)

Paul's fourth and final warning is against asceticism—the imposition of man-made rules as a means of gaining favor with God. For ascetics the body was a thing to be buffeted and punished, to be treated like an enemy. They saw the body as evil and concluded that the way to holiness was to deny all the body's desires, refuse its appetites, and cut its needs down to an irreducible minimum. Asceticism was apparently a prominent feature of the Colossian heresy—one that could easily lead to the deprecation of marriage, the exaltation of virginity and monasticism, and the devising of endless means of self-torture. Paul condemns asceticism and urges the Colossians to reject it as a way of life.

1. The Christian's death to the world (2:20–22a)

20 When one becomes a Christian, one's connection with the world of legal and ascetic ordinances is severed. Asceticism, then, is not in keeping with the nature and circumstances of the new life in Christ. Believers at the time of their conversion have "died" to all the rules and requirements of asceticism. In the mention of dying and rising (3:1) with Christ, there may be an allusion to Christian baptism (see comments on 2:12). However, baptism only pictures the death of believers to an old way of life and their rising to a new life; the actual change is effected when they are joined to Christ by faith.

As they enter into fellowship with Christ, they are delivered from "the basic principles of this world." "Basic principles" has the same ambiguity that marks it elsewhere (see comment on 2:8). It can be understood as referring to the supernatural powers of evil, but the passage also yields an acceptable meaning if it is interpreted as in the NIV. At any rate, to order life by ascetic rules is to revert to an inferior state supposedly abandoned at the time of conversion. To die to "the basic principles of this world" is to have all connections with them severed, to be done with them, to be liberated from their authority once for all. "Submit to its rules" (GK *1505*) recalls v.14, where reference was made to the canceling out of the bond of ordinances against us. The Christian must not permit life to become a round of rules again.

21 The "rules" Paul had in mind are such decrees as "Do not handle! Do not taste! Do not touch!" The reference is to the dietary restrictions the errorists imposed as a means of attaining salvation. Some may have been re-enactments of the Mosaic law; others were doubtless prohibitions stemming from pagan asceticism. There is a descending order in the terms, the climax being reached in the last word—i.e., "Don't even touch."

22a Parenthetically, Paul adds that all such things are "destined to perish with use." Dietary restrictions have to do with things made to be used; and with their use they perish, for food ceases to be food once it is eaten. The underlying thought, then, is that the restrictive regulations of the Colossian heresy deal with matters that are temporary and unimportant. Christ, in fact, has made all food clean (Mk 7:19).

2. The human origin of ascetic restrictions (2:22b)

22b Such regulative prohibitions as "Do not handle! Do not taste! Do not touch!" are "based on human commands and teachings." The rules of the ascetic are, both in origin and in medium of communication, strictly human.

3. The ineffectiveness of ascetic restrictions (2:23)

23 Ascetic rules masquerade as wisdom. On the surface, they seem to be reasonable and wise. But this is only an appearance of wisdom. In reality these rules are expressions of "self-imposed worship" and spurious "humility." The first expression denotes worship which people choose for themselves without authorization from God. The context suggests that the errorists engaged in such "worship" (cf. v.18) in the hope that they would thereby acquire superior merit before God.

"Humility" (GK *5425*) must in this context refer to a mock humility (cf. v.18). The idea is that asceticism, while parading under the guise of humility, actually panders to human pride. "Harsh treatment of the body" is a reference to ascetic torturings of the body. "Lack any value in restraining sensual indulgence" translates a very difficult Greek construction. It suggests that the ascetics end up putting far more emphasis on the indulgence of the flesh than they ought to, and they are proud of it (cf. Gal 5:19–21).

To sum up, v.23 teaches that ascetic rules have the appearance of wisdom for many people in that they seem to be expressions of devotion to God, of humility, and of a commendable discipline of the body. Paul, however, declares that these regulations have nothing to do with real wisdom, and the worship and humility they seem to express are both spurious. His final appraisal is that asceticism is a dismal failure and not the way to spiritual victory. Christianity is not a religion of prescriptions but of a living relationship with Jesus Christ. This, of course, does not mean that once we are in Christ everything is permissible. That would amount to moral and spiritual anarchy, which is contrary to the very nature of the new life in Christ. It does mean that the controls of the Christian life spring from within and that genuine piety grows out of inward conviction generated by a consciousness of union with Christ. Indwelt by the Spirit, we walk by the Spirit and thus avoid carrying out the desires of the lower nature (Gal 5:16).

V. Appeal for Christian Living (3:1–4:6)

The apostle has refuted both the doctrinal and practical errors of the false teachers and, in the course of doing this, has given a profound exposition of the cosmic significance of Jesus Christ. In the present section, which is practical and ethical in its emphasis, he exhorts his readers to give outward expression in daily living to the deep experience that is theirs in Christ. The Christian life is a life "hidden with Christ in God," but it is still a life lived out on earth. Christians must therefore give attention not only to their inward experience with God but also to their outward relations with their fellow human beings.

A. The Root Principle of the Christian Life (3:1–4)

The opening verses of ch. 3 sustain close connection with the closing verses of ch. 2, where the apostle reminded the Colossians that ascetic regulations are of no real value in restraining the flesh. The only remedy for sinful passions is found in the believers' experience of union with Christ—a union by virtue of which the Christian dies to sin and to the world's way of thinking and doing. The opening verses of the third chapter, representing the positive counterpart of those verses, teach that this death with Christ involves also participation in his resurrection life. This releases into the believer's life a power that is more than adequate to resist the appetites and attitudes of the lower nature. These four verses, then, point to the believer's union with Christ as the root principle of the whole Christian life.

On the basis of this mystical but real experience with Christ, Paul urges the Colossians to seek heavenly things (v.1) and set their minds on them (v.2). As a further incentive, he reminds them that their lives are now securely hidden with Christ in God and thus belong to the invisible realm; they now live in a totally different sphere of being (v.3). Their lives, however, will not always be hidden in this way. When Christ appears, there will be a glorious manifestation of who they truly are (v.4).

1. Seeking the things above (3:1)

1 To set the heart on (lit., "seek"; GK 2426) things above is to desire and to strive for heavenly things. It is to see to it that one's interests are constantly centered in Christ, that one's attitudes, ambitions, and whole outlook on life are molded by Christ's relationship to the believer, and that one's allegiance to him takes precedence over all earthly allegiances. The description of Christ as "seated at the right hand of God" is another implied rejoinder to those who were seeking to diminish Christ's role as mediator, inasmuch as the right hand of God is a metaphor for the place of supreme privilege and divine authority.

2. Setting the mind on things above (3:2)

2 The NIV interprets the commands of vv.1–2 as essentially the same. There may, however, be a slight difference. Setting the heart on things above (v.1) is descriptive of one's aim for the practical pursuit of the Christian life. Setting the mind (v.2) on things above refers more to one's inner disposition. There is, of course, an intimate connection between the two.

To set the mind on (lit., "think on"; GK 5858) things above has the connotation of giving heavenly things a large place in one's thought life—seeing to it that the governing tendency of thought and will is toward God. This, of course, does not mean withdrawal from all the activities of this world to engage only in contemplation of eternity and heaven. The verses that follow make it quite clear that Paul expected Christians to maintain normal relationships in this world. But genuine Christians will see everything against the background of eternity.

"Earthly things" are not all evil, though some of them are. Even things harmless in themselves become harmful if permitted to take the place that should be reserved for the "things above." Here "earthly things" may be understood to include wealth, worldly honor, power, pleasures, and the like. To make such things the goal of life and the subject of preoccupation is unworthy of those who have been raised with Christ and look forward to sharing in his eternal glory.

3. The motivations for those actions (3:3–4)

3 One motive for seeking and setting the mind on the things above is the believer's union with Christ in death and in resurrection (2:20; 3:1). Verse 3 repeats and summarizes this theme. Since Christians have died with Christ, all that is alien to him should be alien to us. Death with Christ (2:20) is followed by resurrection with Christ (3:1), and so our lives are indeed "hidden with Christ in God." This suggests not only that our lives are secure, but also that they belong in a real and profound sense to the invisible spiritual realm. At the present time our connection with God and Christ is a matter of inner experience; one day it will come into full and open manifestation.

4 Another motivation to seeking and setting the mind on the things above is the prospect of the believer's future manifestation with Christ in glory. Christ is called our "life" because he is, quite literally, the essence of our lives. It is he who gives us life and nurtures it by his own continuing presence (cf. Ro 8:10).

"Appears" (GK *5746*), one of several terms that refer to the return of Christ, emphasizes the open display of Christ at his coming. When Christ is thus manifested, believers also "will appear with him in glory." Then the world that persecutes believers will be blinded with the dazzling glory of his return.

B. Guidelines for the Christian Life (3:5–4:6)

Having reminded his readers of their vital union with Christ and the power and encouragement this gives to holy living, Paul now shows in a practical way how this principle of union with Christ is to be applied in daily life. In short, he teaches that the Christian's experience in Christ calls not simply for regulating the old earthbound life but for digging out its roots and utterly destroying it. In this way the new life in Christ will have full control over the believer. The underlying thought is: Let the life that is in you by virtue of your union with Christ work itself out and express itself in all your thoughts, actions, and relationships.

1. Sins of the old life are to be abandoned (3:5–11)

Paul speaks forthrightly about the demands of the new life and our urgent need to repress all the degrading tendencies of the old nature. The three imperatives of the paragraph ("put to death" in v.5, "rid yourselves" in v.8, and "do not lie" in v.9) are the pegs on which the thought hangs.

a. Sins to be put to death (3:5–7)

5 In principle when we became Christians, we died with Christ (cf. 2:20; 3:3). Now we are charged to "put to death" (GK *3739*; lit., "to make dead") the old life in everyday practice. This verb suggests that we must not simply suppress or control evil acts and attitudes; rather, we are to wipe them out and completely exterminate the old way of life. The verb also suggests that we must do so in a vigorous, possibly painful act of personal determination (cf. the principle taught in Mt 18:8–9).

"Whatever belongs to your earthly nature" is defined by the list of sins placed in apposition with it in this verse. Paul is calling, then, not for the maiming of the physical body, but for the slaying of the evil passions, desires, and practices that root themselves in our bodies, make use of them, and attack us through them.

His catalog of sins is a grim one, and all of the sins, with the possible exception of the last, have to do with sexual vice. "Sexual immorality" translates the most general Greek word for illicit sexual activity (GK *4518*). "Impurity" (GK *174*), though sometimes used of physical impurity (Mt 23:27), here has a moral connotation. Including uncleanness in thought, word, and act, it has a wider reference than the previous word. "Lust" (GK *4079*) means uncontrolled desire and has a negative connotation. "Evil desires" is similar to lust, but is perhaps more general in meaning.

"Greed" (GK *4432*) suggests a desire to have more. It has a much wider significance than its English equivalent, denoting a ruthless desire for, and an intense seeking after, material things. Included in it is an entire disregard of the rights of others. This attitude is identified with "idolatry" because it puts self-interest and earthly things in the place of God.

6–7 Paul now mentions two factors that point out how improper it is for the sins listed in v.5 to exist in the lives of the Colossian believers. (1) Those sins incur "the wrath of God" (cf. Ro 1:18), a phrase that almost certainly refers to the eschatological wrath of God. "Is coming" (a present tense) may suggest that God's judgment on sin is already on the way, but more likely it depicts with vivid certainty that God's judgment will indeed someday fall on the disobedient. (2) Those sins characterized the pre-Christian experience of the Colossian believers (v.7). This kind of life belongs to the past, and Christians should be done with it. "Walk" (GK *4344*) calls attention to outward conduct; "lived" (GK *2409*), to the attitudes and feelings from which that conduct flows.

b. Sins to be put away (3:8)

8 Whereas the sins of v.5 had to do with impurity and covetousness, the catalog of v.8 concerns sins of attitude and speech. "But now" marks an emphatic contrast. The imagery in "rid yourselves" (GK 700) is that of putting off clothes—like stripping off from oneself a filthy garment. The believers in Colosse must shed the following sins from their lives.

The first three terms—"anger," "rage," "malice"—speak of sins of disposition. The first of these (GK 3973) may be the settled feeling of anger; the second (GK 2596), the sudden and passionate outburst of that feeling. "Malice" (GK 2798), a general term for badness, seems here to denote a vicious disposition, the spirit that prompts one to injure one's neighbor. "Slander" (GK 1060) denotes insulting and slanderous talk against one's fellowman. "Filthy language" (GK 155) may denote either filthy or abusive speech.

c. A sin to be discontinued (3:9a)

9a The sin of falsehood may be singled out because in it more frequently than in anything else we manifest ill-will toward our fellow human beings. Its being given separate treatment makes the condemnation of it more emphatic. The Greek construction used here suggests the translation "stop lying."

d. The reason: the new self (3:9b–11)

9b–10 Grammatically there is a strict connection between these verses and the prohibition against lying, though probably the "since" connects with the entire thought of vv.5–9a. The essence of it is that Christians have had a radical, life-changing experience in which they have put off the old self with its practices (i.e., habits or characteristic actions) and have put on the new self. The metaphor again is one of clothing. The "old self" is like a dirty, worn-out garment that is stripped from the body and thrown away. The "new self" (i.e., the regenerate self) is like a new suit of clothing that one puts on and wears. The picturesque language gives vivid expression to a great truth, but one must be careful not to press the imagery too far, for we are painfully aware that the old nature is ever with us.

The new self is described as "being renewed in knowledge." That is, the new self does not decay or grow old but by constant renewal takes on more and more of the image of its Creator. "Being renewed" (GK 363) expresses a continuous process of renewal. "Knowledge," the sphere of this process, denotes true knowledge (cf. 1:9).

11 The various groups mentioned reflect distinctions of national privilege ("Greek or Jew"), legal or ceremonial standing ("circumcised or uncircumcised"), culture ("barbarian, Scythian"), and social caste ("slave or free"). In the realm of the new self, where the image of God is truly reflected, these distinctions have no real significance (cf. Gal 3:28). Differences, to be sure, remain in the Christian community, but not in such a way as to be barriers to fellowship. To the extent that Christians do permit them to be barriers, they are acting out of character.

"Christ is all, and is in all" suggests that Christ is the great principle of unity. In him all differences merge, all distinctions are done away. Loyalty to Christ takes precedence over all earthly ties.

2. Virtues of the new life are to be cultivated (3:12–17)

a. Expressions of love (3:12–14)

12 Christians have already put on the new self (see comment on v.10). Now they must "clothe [them]selves" (GK 1907) with the garments that befit the new self. This verb should be compared with "put to death" (v.5) and "rid yourselves" (v.8). Those terms express the negative; this verse expresses the positive aspects of the Christian's reformation of character. The Greek verb suggests that this action should be undertaken with a sense of urgency.

Paul's appeal is based on this threefold fact: Christians are "chosen" of God, "holy" (set apart by and for God), and "dearly loved" by God. The three terms signify essentially the same great fact, but under different aspects. Used in the OT of Israel, they emphasize the favored position now enjoyed by Christians as the heirs of Israel's privileges.

Verse 12b contains five great Christian virtues: "compassion, kindness, humility, gentleness and patience." They point to those qualities of life which, if present in the community of believers, will reduce or eliminate, frictions. All of them are manifestations of love, mentioned in v.14 as the crowning virtue. "Compassion" (GK *5073* & *3880*) betokens pity and tenderness expressed toward the suffering and miserable. The word for "kindness" (GK *5983*) combines the ideas of goodness, kindliness, and graciousness. In Ro 11:22 it is contrasted with "severity," and in Gal 5:22 it is listed as a fruit of the Spirit. "Humility" (GK *5425*) and "gentleness" (GK *4559*), which are related terms, were not considered virtues by the pagan world. The NT, however, deepened and enriched their meanings and made them two of the noblest of Christian graces. Humility denotes a humble disposition (cf. Php 2:4–8). Gentleness is the opposite of pride and self-assertiveness and is the special mark of the one who has a delicate consideration for the rights and feelings of others. It is a characteristic of Christ (Mt 11:29), a fruit of the Spirit (Gal 5:23), and a distinctive trait of those who belong to Christ (Mt 5:5). "Patience" (GK *3429*) denotes the self-restraint that enables one to bear injury and insult without resorting to retaliation. It is an attribute of God (Ro 2:4) and a fruit of the Spirit (Gal 5:22).

13 Paul expands the idea of patience. Christians who are truly patient will willingly "bear with" (GK *462*) those whose faults or unpleasant traits are an irritant to them, and they will "forgive" (GK *5919*) those they have grievances against. "Forgive" is used in 2:13 of God's action toward us and has the sense of forgiving freely.

14 The final article in this description of Christian attire is "love" (*agape*, the distinctive Christian term for caring love; cf. 1Co 13; GK *27*). All the virtues listed in vv.12–13 are, on the highest level, manifestations of love; but love is larger than any one of them, indeed, larger than all of them combined. The mention of love as a separate "article of clothing" is therefore not superfluous.

b. The rule of peace (3:15)

15 Those who see this verse as a continuation of the appeal for loving concern (v.14) among Christians are inclined to interpret "peace" to mean peace among the members of the Christian community. Those who understand it as introducing a new idea interpret "peace" as inward "heart" peace in the midst of life's adversities. Perhaps we should not limit the word but should understand it as denoting peace in the broadest sense. It is the peace "of Christ" because it is the peace he gives—peace that comes by way of obedience to him (cf. Jn 14:27).

The word for "rule" (GK *1093*), an expressive term used only here in the NT, originally meant "to act as umpire." Scholars are not agreed whether in Paul's time the word retained the connotation of a contest or simply had the general sense of administering, ruling, or deciding (cf. also 2:18, where Paul used another form of it). Here it means that in all inner conflicts as well as in all disputes and differences among Christians, Christ's peace must give the final decision. We are to do nothing that would violate that peace.

The idea of being "thankful" (GK *2375*) is added not as an afterthought but because gratitude is intimately associated with peace. The main idea here is being grateful for the peace Christ bestows on us. Thankfulness for this peace becomes an incentive for preserving it. Perhaps the injunction should be taken in its broadest sense: Be thankful—both to God and to others. Such gratitude surely promotes peace and harmony within a fellowship.

c. The indwelling of Christ's word (3:16)

16 All the preceding appeals (with the possible exception of that in v.15) have to do largely with duties Christians owe one another. Verses 16–17 focus attention on matters that have to do more directly with one's personal life. Even here, however, the thought of our duty to others is not entirely absent.

"The word of Christ" probably refers to the Gospel, i.e., the message about Christ (though it could also refer to Christ's own teaching as recorded or remembered by his apostles). We must submit to the demands of the Christian message and let it become so deeply implanted within us that it controls all our thinking.

In the remainder of this verse, "with all wisdom" belongs with "teach" and "counsel." The thought is that under the influence of the word of Christ Christians are to do two things: (1) Making use of every kind of wisdom, they are to teach and admonish one another. (2) Using psalms, hymns, and spiritual songs, they are to sing with gratitude in their hearts to God.

No rigid distinctions should be made between "psalms," "hymns," and "spiritual

Songs in the New Testament

Paul encourages believers to sing "songs, hymns and spiritual songs" (Eph 5:19; Col 3:16). The OT, of course, has an entire book of songs (the Psalms). But the NT also contains songs that God's creatures sing in praise of their Maker and Redeemer. This chart lists these songs; those about which scholars are uncertain are listed in italics.

Songs in the Gospels	
The song of Mary	Lk 1:46–55
The song of Zechariah	Lk 1:68–79
The song of the angels at the birth of Jesus	Lk 2:14
The song of Simeon	Lk 2:29–31
The song of the crowds on Palm Sunday	Mt 21:9; Mk 11:9–10; Lk 19:31; Jn 12:13
Songs in NT Letters	
Doxology to God	Ro 11:33–36
Hymn of love	*1Co 13*
Wake-up song	Eph 5:14
Hymn to the human and divine Jesus	*Php 2:6–11*
Hymn to Jesus as supreme Lord	*Col 1:15–20*
Hymn on the life of Jesus	*1Ti 3:16*
Songs in Revelations	
Song of the four living creatures	Rev 4:8
Songs of the twenty-four elders	Rev 4:11; 11:17–18
Song of the four living creatures and the twenty-four elders	Rev 5:9–10
Songs of the many angels	Rev 5:12, 13; 7:12
Songs of the great multitude of saints	Rev 7:10; 19:1–3
Songs of the loud voice(s) in heaven	Rev 11:15; 12:10–12; 19:5
Songs of the seven angels (including the song of Moses and the song of the Lamb)	Rev 15:3–4, 6–8

songs." Paul is simply emphasizing the rich variety in Christian song. Essentially the three terms heighten the idea of joyousness called for in the passage. If any differences are made, "psalms" may be taken to refer to the OT psalter, "hymns" and "spiritual songs" to distinctly Christian compositions. The great periods of renewal in Christendom have always been accompanied by an outburst of hymnology. Christian hymns must express real emotion of the heart, adoration, and worship in a way that is worthy of our Savior.

d. The name of Christ (3:17)

17 Paul now gives us a kind of summary. There are various ways of interpreting "do it all in the name of the Lord Jesus." Some understand the meaning to be that everything a Christian does is to be undertaken *in dependence on the Lord*. Others think it means that everything a Christian does is to be done *in recognition of the authority of Jesus' name*. Still others take "in the name of the Lord Jesus" to mean "as followers of the Lord Jesus." This last interpretation reflects the thought that to act in the name of a person is to act as his representative. The last two interpretations are both acceptable, but the third is preferred. Paul is enunciating a general principle of Christian conduct, knowing that rules and regulations belong to a former dispensation and are not appropriate for the Christian life (see Gal 3:23–4:7). "Giving thanks" points to an essential accompaniment of acting in the name of the Lord Jesus—namely, that in everything we do we are to retain a sense of God's goodness and must thank him.

3. Family relationships are to be strengthened (3:18–4:1)

Several observations are in order as we approach this important paragraph. (1) We may see it as applying specifically to the general principle Paul set down in v.17. (2) The emphasis of the whole passage is on duties, not rights. (3) The duties are reciprocal—i.e., not all the rights are on one side and all the duties on the other. (4) The entire passage is remarkably similar to Eph 5:22–33, though it is much briefer. The chief difference is that in Ephesians, where Paul unfolds the Christian philosophy of marriage, he introduces a rather extended and beautiful statement about the church as the bride of Christ.

a. The wife's duty to the husband (3:18)

18 The one duty Paul enjoins on the wife is to "submit" (GK 5718), an attitude that recognizes the rights of authority. His main thought is that the wife is to defer to (i.e., be willing to take second place to) her husband. Yet we should never interpret this as if it implies that the husband may be a domestic despot, ruling his family with a rod of iron. It does imply, however, that the husband has an authority the wife must forgo exercising. In areas where one must yield—e.g., in the husband's choice of a profession or of a geographical location for doing his work—the primary submission devolves upon the wife.

Three things may be said about a wife's subjection to her husband. (1) The context shows that the wife's attitude is prompted and warranted by her husband's unselfish love. (2) The way in which Paul expresses this concept shows that the submission is to be voluntary. The wife's submission is never to be forced on her by a demanding husband; it is the deference that a loving wife, conscious that her home must have a head, gladly shows to a worthy and devoted husband. (3) Such submission is said to be "fitting in the Lord," i.e., it is becoming and proper not only in the natural order but also in the Christian order. This whole issue, then, is lifted to a new and higher level.

b. The husband's duties to the wife (3:19)

19 The ancient world was a man's world, and even among the Jews the wife was often little more than chattel. Paul's counsel in the present passage is in striking contrast to this. Husbands in that day often wielded an authority that others were bound to obey. While not openly challenging this assumption, Paul transforms it by the Christian principle of mutual love and deference.

Paul speaks of two responsibilities of the husband—one positive and the other negative. Positively, he urges husbands to "love [GK 26] your wives." This, of course, is their supreme duty. "Love" does not only denote affection or romantic attachment; it especially denotes caring love, a deliberate attitude of mind that concerns itself with the well-being of the one loved. Self-devotion, not self-satisfaction, is its dominant trait. Negatively, Paul urges husbands not to be "harsh" with their wives, using a word that suggests a surly, irritable attitude.

c. The duty of children to parents (3:20)

20 The one obligation Paul places on children is obedience to their parents. "Obey" (GK 5634) implies a readiness to hear and carry out orders; a child's ongoing responsibility is to listen to and carry out the instructions of his or her parents. Paul says two things about this obedience. (1) It is to be complete: "in everything." Paul, of course, sets this in a Christian context. He is dealing with the Christian home and presupposes Christian attitudes on the part of parents. (2) The obedience of children to their parents "pleases the Lord." In the Christian order, just as in the order under the law or in the natural realm, obedience to parents pleases God. The obedience of children is not, therefore, based on accidental factors, nor does it depend essentially on the parents' character. It is an obligation grounded in the very nature of the relationship between parents and children. It is a thing that is right in itself (see Eph 6:1–3). It is therefore especially pleasing to God

d. The duty of parents to children (3:21)

21 The specific mention of "fathers" suggests that the father as head of the household has a special responsibility for training the children. No slight toward the mother is intended, for Paul would surely have recognized her rights and the power of her influence in the home. In fact, "fathers" (GK 4252) occasionally has the broad meaning of "parents" (cf. Heb 11:23, where this word is used of the parents of Moses).

Fathers are not to "embitter" (GK 2241) their children. They must not challenge their children's resistance by an unreasonable exercise of authority. Firm discipline may be necessary, but it must always be administered in the right spirit. Parents should not give in to fault-finding, nor always be nagging their children.

The reason for this counsel is that "they will become discouraged" (GK 126). Parents can be so exacting, so demanding, or so severe that they create within their children the feeling that it is impossible for them to please. The Greek word used here has in it the idea of "losing heart" and suggests going about in a listless or sullen attitude. Paul may have had in mind the regimen of "don'ts" that loomed so large in the Colossian heresy.

e. The duty of slaves to masters (3:22–25)

22 Slavery, with all its attendant evils, was not only universally accepted in ancient times but also considered a fundamental institution, indispensable to civilized society. More than half the people seen on the streets of the great cities of the Roman world were slaves. And this was the status of the majority of "professional" people, such as teachers and doctors as well as menials and craftsmen. Slaves were people with few rights, mere property existing only for the comfort, convenience, and pleasure of their owners. Paul deals with their duty in the context of the family because slaves were considered a part of the household.

It is a matter of concern to some that neither Paul nor the other apostles denounced slavery and demanded its immediate overthrow. The apostles, however, were not social reformers; they were first and foremost heralds of the good news of salvation in Christ.

Then again, the church was a very small minority in the Roman world, and there was no hope that its stance on the matter of slavery would influence Roman policies. We should be careful to understand, though, that they did not condone slavery. Indeed, they announced the very principles (such as that of the complete spiritual equality of slaves and masters) that ultimately destroyed the institution of slavery.

The one duty Paul presses on slaves is complete obedience—i.e., "in everything." He was obviously thinking of the Christian household and thus did not have in mind carrying out orders contrary to the principles of the Gospel. Christian slaves were not, of course, to obey such orders; no matter what their position in life, the Christians' highest duty is to God, and all lesser duties must give way to this (cf. Ac 5:29). The latter part of the verse insists that obedience of slaves is to be sincere, ungrudging, and rooted in "reverence for the Lord."

23–24 Slaves must see their service as a service rendered not to human beings but to the Lord. This would transform the most menial responsibilities and give dignity to all of their work. They would thereby be reminded of the reward that would be theirs for serving faithfully in Christ's name. On "inheritance," see comment on 1:12.

25 This verse, set in contrast to the preceding ones, shows that wrong will be punished, because "there is no favoritism" with God. Doubtless Paul meant this as a warning to Christian slaves not to presume on their position before God and to think that he would overlook their misdeeds, even if they were acting unscrupulously because of being treated unfairly. In the parallel passage in Ephesians it is the master who is reminded that there is no partiality with God (Eph 6:9).

The entire passage about the duty of slaves (vv.22–25) may seem completely irrelevant to our day. It contains, however, this enduring principle: Christians, in whatever work they do, must see it as a service rendered to the Lord. This is what motivates them to give honest, faithful, ungrudging work in return for the pay they receive. Moreover, passages such as this impart a sense of dignity in work, regardless of how unimportant that work may seem to be.

f. The duty of masters to slaves (4:1)

1 Now Paul turns to the duty of masters toward their slaves in terms of dealing justly and equitably with them. Though in the Roman world slaves had few rights, Paul does not hesitate to teach that duty is not all on the side of slaves. Masters too have obligations. Paul's reason for their being completely fair with their slaves is a compelling one: "because you know that you also have a Master in heaven." It is to God that Christian masters are accountable for how they treat their slaves. Both master and slave alike bow before one Master, with whom there is no "favoritism."

4. Christian duties are to be faithfully performed (4:2–6)

The immediately preceding paragraph (3:18–4:1) consisted of a series of special appeals based on the several relationships in the Christian household. Now Paul returns to advice that applies to the entire church. Most of what he says relates to the personal devotional life (vv.2–5), but the section closes with an appeal for wise behavior toward non-Christians (vv.5–6). The injunctions given in this paragraph touch the two extremes of life—the hidden life of prayer, and the outward, busy life of the marketplace and the street.

a. The duty of prayer (4:2–4)

2 Here is a general appeal for prayerfulness. The word for "devote yourselves" (GK *4674*) is built on a root meaning "to be strong." It always connotes earnest adherence to a person or thing; here it implies persistence and fervor (cf. Ac 1:14; 2:46; 6:5; Ro 12:12). "Being watchful" (lit., "keeping awake"; GK *1213*) suggests constant spiritual alertness. So Christians must be watchful and active in prayer, alive in the fullest sense, never careless, mechanical, or dull and heavy (cf. Mt 26:41; Mk 14:38; 1Th 5:6; 1Pe 5:8). "Being thankful" refers to the spirit in which prayers should be offered (cf. Php 4:6).

3–4 Paul requests prayer for himself while being imprisoned in Rome. His concern was that he and his associates might have clear opportunities for witnessing and that Paul might make clear the great secret ("mystery"; cf. 1:26; 2:2 with Eph 1:9; 3:1) of redemption in Christ in a worthy manner. There was no selfish motive behind this prayer; Paul's consuming interest was for the advancement of the Gospel, not for his own blessing.

b. The duty of witnessing (4:5–6)

These verses, with their call for discreet behavior in an unbelieving society, may reflect the fact that charges of misconduct on the part of Christians were being circulated. Therefore the Colossian Christians should be all the more cautious, living in so exemplary a way as to give the lie to such slander. In reality, Paul makes two appeals—one having to do with how Christians are to live (v.5), the other relating how they are to speak (v.6). Careful attention to these matters will not only remove unfounded suspicions about Christians but also further the acceptance of the Gospel.

5 To "be wise in the way you act toward outsiders" is to show practical Christian wisdom in dealing with secular society. Paul's words imply that believers are to be cautious and tactful so as to avoid needlessly antagonizing or alienating their pagan neighbors. In a positive sense, these words also imply that believers should conduct themselves so that the way they live will attract, impress, and convict non-Christians and give the pagan community a favorable impression of the Gospel (see also 1Co 5:12–13; 1Th 4:12; 1Ti 3:7 for other passages where unbelievers are designated as "outsiders").

The verb in the statement "make the most [GK *1973*] of every opportunity" is a market word that means "to buy out" or "purchase completely." So Christians, as an expression of practical wisdom, must buy up and make the most of every opportunity for witnessing to the faith. "Opportunity" (GK *2789*) denotes either a specific point of time or a significant time, God's time. This latter meaning appears to be the preferred sense in the present passage.

6 Like his Lord and also like James the brother of the Lord, Paul knew how important the way Christians speak is (cf. Mt 12:36; Eph 4:24; Tit 2:8; Jas 3:1–12). Here he may well have had in mind the relation of the right kind of speech to witnessing. So their speech, he reminds the Colossians, must be always full of "grace" and "seasoned with salt." "Grace" (GK *5921*), a word that usually denotes divine favor, seems here to be used in the broader sense of "pleasantness," "attractiveness," "charm," and "winsomeness." These ideas are all implicit in the word.

"Seasoned with salt" may mean that Christian conversation is to be marked by purity and wholesomeness. Some, however, understand "salt" in the sense of that which gives taste or flavor. Among the ancient Greeks "salt" could designate the wit that gives zest and liveliness to conversation. The remainder of v.6 tells why we should cultivate this kind of speech: "so that you will know how to answer everyone." Conversation must be appropriate for each person to whom we speak.

VI. Conclusion (4:7–18)

The body of the letter, in which Paul has met head-on the false teachers threatening the church at Colosse, is complete. By a powerful exposition of the sovereign lordship and complete sufficiency of Jesus Christ, Paul has refuted their so-called "philosophy" with all its attendant errors (1:15–2:23); he has set forth the nature of the Christian life, calling attention to its springs of power, its heavenly aspirations, and its distinguishing characteristics (3:1–17); he has shown how the lofty principles of the Gospel must affect relationships within Christian households (3:18–4:2); and he has earnestly exhorted his readers to pray (4:2–4) and given them practical advice for living in the pagan world (4:5–6). Now all that remains are some personal matters.

A. Commendations (4:7–9)

7 These commendations, given to ensure their welcome by the Colossian church, concern two men, Tychicus (vv.7–8) and Onesimus (v.9). The former, described by Paul as "a dear brother" and "a faithful minister and fellow servant in the Lord," was probably the bearer of both this letter and the one we know as Ephesians (cf. Eph 6:21–22). He was a native of the province of Asia and was earlier selected to be one of the two delegates of the churches who were to accompany Paul on his last visit to Jerusalem, probably as a custodian of the offering that was given by the churches for the needy in Jerusalem (Ac 20:4; 24:17; Ro 15:25–26; 1Co 16:1; 2Co 8–9).

"Dear brother" shows that Tychicus was a much-loved fellow Christian. "Faithful minister [GK 1356]" may identify him as a loyal servant of Christ, but more likely the expression marks his relation to Paul (i.e., "trusted assistant"). Earlier Paul had used the same noun of Epaphras (1:7) and of himself (1:23). "Fellow servant" (GK 5281) speaks of Tychicus both as a slave of Christ and as a comrade with Paul (cf. 1:7, where Paul used this word to designate Epaphras).

8–9 Paul explains a twofold purpose he had in sending Tychicus to the Colossians: (1) "that you may know about our circumstances," and (2) "that he may encourage your hearts." Accompanying Tychicus was Onesimus, the runaway slave who in the providence of God had met Paul in Rome and had apparently been led to Christ by him (see introduction to Philemon). Paul is now sending Onesimus back to Colosse—with no mention of his past, but with the heartwarming phrase that he is now "one of you."

B. Greetings (4:10–15)

10–11 In vv.10–15 six persons join in sending greetings to the Colossian church. Three of them—Aristarchus, Mark, and Jesus Justus—were Jewish Christians. Aristarchus, a native of Thessalonica who had been arrested at the time of the riot in Ephesus (Ac 19:29), accompanied Paul to Jerusalem (Ac 20:4) and later on was with him on the journey from Caesarea to Rome (Ac 27:2). Here Paul calls him his "fellow prisoner." This term may be interpreted either literally or spiritually (i.e., literally in prison with Paul or one who, along with Paul, had been taken captive by Christ). Mark, called here "the cousin of Barnabas," wrote the gospel that bears his name. He appears in the NT with some frequency, and we know more about him than about any of the others mentioned in this passage (cf. Ac 12:12, 25; 13:13; 15:37–39; 1Pe 5:13). Of Jesus Justus we know nothing beyond the mention of his name here.

There is a note of pathos in Paul's remark about these three: "These are the only Jews among my fellow workers for the kingdom of God." Paul felt keenly his alienation from his countrymen (cf. Ro 9:3; Php 1:15–17). But these three, he adds, "have proved a comfort to me," perhaps in a particular time of crisis when they stood by Paul.

12 Epaphras, mentioned in 1:7 as the founder of the Colossian church and as Paul's representative, is here described as "one of you" (cf. v.9) and as "a servant of Christ Jesus."

Paul reminds the Colossians that Epaphras was continually "wrestling" (GK 76; cf. 1:29 for the same word) for them in his prayers. He was concerned that they stand firm, mature, and fully convinced in relation to everything God wills. Undoubtedly he had in mind the possibility of their wavering under the influence of the heretical teaching at Colosse.

13 Paul confirms Epaphras's anxiety for the Colossians and assures them that "he is working hard for [them] and for those at Laodicea and Hierapolis." The expression used here suggests heavy toil to the extent of pain. Epaphras undoubtedly had experienced much emotional distress in reference to the people at Colosse.

Laodicea and Hierapolis were cities near Colosse. The former, which lay ten miles downstream to the west of Colosse, was situated on a plateau to the south of the River Lycus. On the other side of the river, six miles north of Laodicea, was Hierapolis. Laodicea was a city of great wealth and boasted a medical school. The church there received the sternest denunciation of all the seven churches of Asia in the book of Revelation (Rev 3:14–22). The name Hierapolis (the name literally means "holy city") suggests the city owed its initial importance to religion. In 133 B.C., this entire district became the Roman province of Asia.

14 Luke and Demas are mentioned next; no descriptive phrase is used of Demas (cf. Phm 24; 2Ti 4:10). Of Luke, Paul says very little. Interestingly enough, however, much of what we know about him is derived from this casual reference. It is here that we learn that Luke was a physician, and the context (cf. v.11) suggests that he was a Gentile. The adjective "dear" confirms what is implied in Acts; namely, that Luke—assuming that he was author of Acts—was a trusted friend of Paul.

15 Greetings are given to the Christian "brothers" of Laodicea, to "Nympha," and to "the church in her house." The reference to the church in Nympha's "house" is significant. There were, of course, no church buildings in apostolic times, and in the NT, "church" always designates an assembly of believers, never the place where they met. The location of Nympha's "house-church" is uncertain, though the context implies that it was in the vicinity of Laodicea.

C. Instructions (4:16–17)

These final instructions relate to three matters: the Colossian letter (v.16a), the letter from Laodicea (v. 16b), and advice to Archippus (v.17).

16 After reading this letter, the Colossian Christians were to see to it that it was read also in the Laodicean church. Perhaps they first made a copy of it to keep for themselves and then sent the original to the Laodiceans. In return, the Colossians were to read "the letter from Laodicea." Most likely Paul wrote to the Laodicean church a letter that has not been preserved (cf. also 1Co 5:9 and comment on that verse).

17 Archippus, to whom Paul sends a special message, appears again in Phm 2. From the context there some think he was a member of Philemon's household, perhaps even Philemon's son. The present verse implies that he had some ministerial responsibility in the Colossian church, though Paul gives no definite information about it. Perhaps he was serving as pastor in the absence of Epaphras. Paul tells the Colossian church to instruct Archippus to "complete" the work assigned him. Whether this implies a degree of failure on the part of Archippus or is written only to indicate Paul's full support of this man, we do not know.

D. Benediction (4:18)

18 When a stenographer's services were used to write a letter (as perhaps was Paul's custom; cf. Ro 16:22), it was normally the stenographer's task to compose the final greeting. Apparently, however, Paul regularly wrote the benediction in his own hand (cf. 2Th 3:11). So here at the end of this letter, he took the stylus and signed the letter in his own hand. The letter ends as it began, with the simple but profound prayer: "Grace be with you."

1 Thessalonians

INTRODUCTION

1. Background

First Thessalonians is most likely the earliest of Paul's letters. One may see a special appropriateness in this because these five chapters reveal so much of Paul's mind and heart. They contain a number of his characteristic doctrinal emphases and show the depth of his feeling for the Christians in Thessalonica.

Having been hindered by divine intervention from going into Asia and Bithynia, Paul arrived at Troas, probably in the spring of A.D. 49 (Ac 16:6–8). From there he was directed in a vision to cross the Aegean Sea into Macedonia and to take the Gospel there for the first time (Ac 16:9). That he did (Ac 16:10–11) is one of the crucial events in history because through it the Gospel moved to the west, and the evangelization of Europe began. The first stop of the missionary party of Paul, Silas, Luke, and Timothy was Philippi. After a successful mission there (Ac 16:12–40), lasting about two months, Paul and Silas left under pressure from the city officials and went westward along the Egnatian Way toward Thessalonica, a major center about one hundred miles away. It must have been a painful journey because of what they had suffered while in prison at Philippi (Ac 16:22–24; 1Th 2:2).

At Thessalonica they found circumstances suitable for settling down to preach for a time. The city was of good size, perhaps with a population of 200,000. Its location was conducive to commerce, having a good natural harbor. The city attracted sufficient Jewish merchants of the dispersion to account for the presence of a well-established synagogue (Ac 17:1). It was a free city ruled by its own council of citizens and administered by five or six "politarchs" (Ac 17:6). Since 146 B.C. it had been the seat of Roman government for all Macedonia.

The presence of a synagogue in Thessalonica offered Paul an obvious place to begin (Ac 17:1–4). So he pursued his approach of proving from the OT that the Messiah must suffer and be raised and that Jesus is this Messiah. In the meantime, he followed his own trade of manufacturing the goat's-hair cloth that was a prominent part of the local economy (cf. Ac 18:3; 1Th 2:9; 2Th 3:8).

For three consecutive Sabbaths Paul spoke in the synagogue, but met with the usual Jewish resistance. After those three weeks he was forced to leave the synagogue, but was still able to continue his ministry in the city for some time. Several factors point to this as the correct interpretation of Ac 17:1–4. (1) Paul engaged in gainful employment at Thessalonica (1Th 2:9; 2Th 3:8); two to three weeks are not sufficient time for settling into a trade. Furthermore, Paul used his working as proof of his self-sacrifice for them, something he could hardly have done during a limited stay. (2) Upon his departure from Thessalonica, he left a thriving church. This church included many Gentiles fresh from heathen idolatry (1Th 1:9). They could not have been won through a synagogue ministry. (3) Before leaving, Paul had received at least two special gifts from Philippi, a hundred miles away (Php 4:16). It is difficult to crowd the necessary trips into two or three weeks.

A good number of Jews, God-fearing Gentiles, and prominent women responded to the synagogue phase, including Jason at whose home Paul stayed (Ac 17:4–9). Many Gentiles became Christians in the weeks following (1Th 1:9). After approximately three months, the Christian assembly was of considerable size, and the Jews became unbearably jealous. So they instigated riots to force the politarchs to rule against the Christians, whom they accused of upsetting society and opposing Caesar's decrees (Ac 17:5–9). Jason and several other Christians were brought in for a hearing. The city officials, however, stood firm under pressure and eventually let Jason and the others go. Though not personally involved in this incident, Paul, Silas, and perhaps Timothy knew it was time to leave so as to avoid bringing additional hardship on their brothers in Christ (Ac 17:10).

From Thessalonica they traveled west fifty miles to Berea. Here their synagogue ministry was favorably received for about seven weeks, and it might have continued even longer if adversaries from Thessalonica had not heard of their success and come to disrupt their preaching. At this point Paul departed to Athens, but since Silas and Timothy had not been so conspicuous, they were able to remain at Berea (Ac 17:11–15). He sent instructions to Silas and Timothy to join him at Athens (Ac 17:15), which they did (1Th 3:1). The two were then sent back to Macedonia; Timothy's responsibility was to encourage the Thessalonian Christians and bring back a report about them. Paul had become concerned about the converts there because he knew they were suffering persecution (1Th 3:1–5). Silas was probably sent on a similar mission to Philippi.

While the two men were away, Paul had a relatively fruitless ministry at Athens (Ac 17:16–34). Leaving there, he went to Corinth (about January, A.D. 50), where he enjoyed a spiritually prosperous eighteen-to-twenty-month ministry. In the spring of 50 (Ac 18:5; 1Th 3:6–7), Timothy returned to Paul in Corinth and reported on Thessalonica; it was so encouraging that Paul wrote 1 Thessalonians almost immediately.

2. Authorship and Date

Few have questioned Paul's authorship of 1 Thessalonians. Ancient testimony favors Paul. The canons of Marcion and Muratori have this letter among Paul's works. Irenaeus quotes it by name, and Tertullian and Clement of Alexandria acknowledge it as Pauline.

Paul's initial visit to Corinth probably terminated shortly after Gallio became proconsul in that city (Ac 18:11–18). An inscription at Delphi, dated early in A.D. 52, calls Gallio proconsul of Asia at the time (a term that began in the summer of 51). Paul's trial before this man appears to have come when he was new to the city, because the Jewish accusers tried to take advantage of his inexperience (Ac 18:12–13). Paul's departure from Corinth was therefore in the late summer or early fall of A.D. 51. Since he spent eighteen to twenty months in Corinth (Ac 18:11, 18), he arrived there from Athens in late A.D. 49 or early A.D. 50.

Timothy joined him from Thessalonica a few months later. After Paul's departure from the Thessalonian city, news about the Christians there had spread far and wide (1Th 1:8–9). Also, a number of converts to Christ had died (1Th 4:13). From the late summer of A.D. 49 till the spring of A.D. 50 is enough time for these things to have happened,. Hence, we may place Paul's writing of 1 Thessalonians some time in the spring of A.D. 50.

3. Occasion and Purpose

Elements of Timothy's report (1Th 3:6–7) undoubtedly prompted Paul to write 1 Thessalonians. The most significant of these included (1) encouraging words as to the spiritual stamina of the Thessalonian converts in the face of fierce opposition (3:6–10), (2) an alarming report of efforts to undermine Paul's reputation and question his sincerity (2:1–12, 17–20), (3) confusion and discouragement regarding the Lord's return and the part of the dead in it (4:13–5:11), and (4) areas of individual and community life that needed improvement (4:1–12; 5:12–22).

In response to Timothy's report, Paul wrote this letter (1) to express satisfaction and thanks to God for the healthy spiritual condition of the church (1:2–10), (2) to make a strong case against the false insinuations against himself and his associates (2:1–3:13), and (3) to suggest specific ways in which the already strong Christian behavior of the Thessalonians could be improved as they lived a life of holiness (4:1–5:24).

4. Theological Values

The two Thessalonian Epistles contribute much toward our understanding of Paul's theological outlook. In them he touches briefly on a number of themes: the doctrine of inspiration and authority of Scripture (1Th 2:13; 2Th 2:15; 3:6, 17); the doctrine of one true God (1Th 1:9) existing in three Persons (1Th 1:1, 5–6; 4:8; 5:19; 2Th 1:1–2; 2:13); the doctrine of Jesus Christ's deity (1Th 3:11–12; 2Th 2:16–17); the doctrine of salvation based on Christ's death (1Th 4:14; 5:9–10; 2Th 2:13–14) and the believer's union and identification with Christ (1Th 1:1; 5:5; 2Th 1:1); and the doctrine of sanctification as it relates to personal purity (1Th 4:3–8), love (1Th 4:9–10), vocational diligence (1Th 4:11–

12; 5:12–15; 2Th 3:6–15), motivation (1Th 5:16–18), and other areas. Also, by example, he teaches lessons on discipling (1Th 2:1–12, 1:7–20; 2Th 3:1–5) and prayer (1Th 3:11–13; 5:23–24; 2Th 1:11–12; 2:16–17; 3:5, 16).

By far the largest theological contribution of these letters lies in what they say about eschatology. Perhaps the best way to summarize this is to survey Paul's use of various terms and themes relating to the end time. "Coming" or "presence" (*parousia*; GK 4242) is the most frequent term, sometimes referring to an examination of Christians before the Father and Christ (1Th 2:19; 3:13; 5:23), sometimes to the moment of the Lord's meeting Christians in the air (1Th 4:15; 2Th 2:1), and sometimes to Christ's triumphant conquest of "the lawless one" (2Th 2:8). From all this the dead in Christ will not be excluded (1Th 4:13–18). "Revelation" (*apokalypsis*; GK 637) occurs only once (2Th 1:7) and spans the entire period beginning with the Lord's coming from heaven for the saints till his appearance on earth to put down those who do not know God and those who do not obey the Gospel of Christ. Between these two points is a time of God's "wrath" (GK 3973) on earth (1Th 1:10; 2:16; 5:9). This outworking of God's vengeance against earth's rebels (2Th 1:8) is the initial phase of the "day of the Lord" and may come at any moment (1Th 5:2–3). It will mean "trouble" or "tribulation" (GK 2568) to the unrepentant (2Th 1:6)—a "sudden destruction," comparable to a pregnant woman's labor pains, that will culminate in "eternal destruction" or separation from the returning Lord and his glory (1Th 5:3; 2Th 1:9). While suffering through the period of wrath, the rebels will unite in a great apostate movement (*apostasia*; GK 686) and support the rise of a great figure who advocates opposition to God's laws (2Th 2:3–4). They will be captivated by his deluding words and activities (2Th 2:9–11). His high point in opposing God will be the abomination "that makes desolate" (Da 12:11) in the rebuilt Jerusalem temple (2Th 2:4).

The "righteous judgment" of God (2Th 1:5) assures a devastating penalty against the ungodly, but it also guarantees that believers will be counted worthy of God's "kingdom" (GK 993; 2Th 1:5; cf. 1Th 5:24), find rest from hardships (2Th 1:7), and experience salvation and glory (1Th 1:10; 5:9; 2Th 1:7, 10, 12; 2:13–14). Hence, they have every reason to persevere because they anticipate a deliverer who at any moment may summon them to meet him in the air (1Th 1:10; 4:15–17; 5:4, 9; 2Th 1:4–10). But anticipation that the Lord will return soon does not release Christians from everyday responsibilities. On the contrary, they must continue working and providing for themselves (1Th 4:11–12; 5:14; 2Th 3:6–15).

EXPOSITION

I. Salutation (1:1)

1 This salutation follows the form Paul used in all his letters and is in the same style as that of other letters of his time. It contains three elements: the writer, the recipient, and the greeting or salutation proper.

(1) Three names are given as the writer: Paul, Silas, and Timothy. Obviously absent is the official title "apostle" that Paul used in all his other letters to churches except 2 Thessalonians and Philippians. A reasonable explanation for this is that no note of authority was necessary in these letters, for in Macedonia his apostolic position never seems to have been questioned. There was, of course, opposition to Paul in Thessalonica (1Th 2–3), but it never became overt as in other places and his opponents never specifically attacked his right to apostleship.

The second name is that of Silas (spelled "Silvanus")—Luke consistently uses "Silas" (e.g., Ac 15:22; 16:19; 17:4; 18:5); Paul always uses "Silvanus" (2Co 1:19; 2Th 1:1). This colleague of Paul was most likely a Jew by birth, a gifted prophet, and one highly esteemed among the Jerusalem Christians (Ac 15:22, 32). He was inclined toward the Hellenistic wing of Palestinian Christianity, as evidenced by his concurring with the Jerusalem Council's decision concerning Gentile believers (Ac 15:22–32), his being a Roman citizen (Ac 16:37), and his being chosen as Paul's fellow worker on the second missionary journey (Ac 15:40–18:6). As an associate in the founding of the Thessalonian church, he endured cruel beatings, imprisonment, and pursuit by an angry mob (Ac 16:23–25; 17:5). Silas was known for his reliability and his faithfulness in risking his life in the service of Christ (Ac 15:25–27). He eventually became associated with Peter, especially in the composition and sending of 1 Peter (1Pe 5:12).

Paul's third colleague at this time was Timothy. This young man, having helped in Philippi, had apparently remained behind when Paul left that city (Ac 16:40). His name is not included in the account of the founding of the Thessalonian church (Acts 17:1-10), but he presumably joined Paul and Silas at Thessalonica later (for more on him, see introduction to 1 Timothy).

(2) Paul next refers to the recipients of the letter. "Church" (*ekklesia*; GK *1711*) was applied to many types of public gatherings in the ancient Roman world, but after Pentecost it developed into a technical word for an assembly of believers in Christ. Literally, the word means "called out"; most likely something of this meaning is retained for the Christian "church" (Ac 15:14; Ro 9:24) as those "called out" from previous relationships in order to constitute a body with special relation to God (cf. 1Co 10:32). Sometimes *ekklesia* designates all Christendom and is a synonym for the body of Christ (Col 1:18, 24). At other times it is a particular assembly in a particular location (Ro 16:5; 1Co 16:19; Col 4:15). Finally, as here, it denotes all assemblies in a single city (Ro 16:1; 1Co 1:2).

This term is further defined as those "who are in God the Father and the Lord Jesus Christ." This phrase tells of the spiritual quality of the believers. This is not a pagan or nonreligious assembly, nor is it a Jewish assembly; it is distinctly "in Christ Jesus" (2:14). Being in union with the Father and Christ meant a new sphere of life, on an infinitely higher plane. It should not be overlooked that the deity of the Son is taught here. Combining "God the Father" and "the Lord Jesus Christ" under one preposition ("in") demonstrates Jesus' equality with the Father and consequently his deity.

(3) Finally comes the official greeting. "Grace" (GK *5921*) recalls the normal Greek greeting, and "peace" (GK *1645*) the normal Hebrew greeting. "Grace" highlights unmerited benefits given by God to the believer in Christ. Through grace the lost are saved from their sins in the eyes of a holy God by a transaction completely free of charge. But grace does not cease here; it continually issues in privileges, one of which is "peace"—a word that has a deep and rich meaning. Differences separating God from his creatures had for centuries worked against peaceful relationships, but with Christ's introduction of the fullness of grace (Jn 1:17), the ultimate basis for resolving this conflict and establishing harmony between God and humankind was laid. Because of this harmony, human beings can also enjoy inward wholeness and tranquility.

II. Thanksgiving for the Thessalonians (1:2-10)

A. The Manner of Giving Thanks—Praying (1:2)

2 It was Paul's practice to begin his letters by thanking God for his readers. Paul found much in the lives of the Thessalonians to be grateful for. In fact, he kept on being grateful (cf. "always"). Nor was he alone in gratitude. The pronoun "we" includes Silas and Timothy as sharing his appreciation.

By thanking God at the beginning of the letter, Paul lifts the thought above the human level. He is not trying to win the Thessalonians over by rhetorical flattery (cf. 2:5). On the contrary, he is sincerely giving the ultimate credit to the One from whom spiritual progress comes. When Christians realize their complete dependence on God and keep this in clear focus, then and only then are they capable of moving on to greater spiritual exploits.

"All of you" expresses Paul's desire not to exclude any of the Thessalonian believers. Every single one of them, no matter how obscure, had certain qualities worth thanking God for.

Paul then begins to elaborate on this idea of thanksgiving. The means used to express their thanks was prayer. As he prayed with Silas and Timothy, they remembered the Thessalonian believers one by one with gratitude for their spiritual progress and with intercession for their advancement in the Gospel.

B. The Circumstances of Giving Thanks—Remembering (1:3)

3 Whenever Paul and his colleagues recalled the threefold nature of the Thessalonians' progress, they could not stop thanking God. Of course, Paul does not mean that they thought of nothing but the Thessalonians.

He rather uses the hyperbolic "continually" to indicate their intense interest.

The words "before our God and Father" show the sincerity and genuineness of this remembrance in prayer. Some in the Thessalonian church had questioned Paul's motives in dealing with them. So at the very outset, he dispels this suspicion, and he confronts it more directly in chs. 2–3 (cf. 2:5, 10; 3:9).

The substance of what Paul and his colleagues remember about the Thessalonians is summed up in three words: "work," "labor," and "endurance." In turn, these three reflect three qualities of Christian character: "faith," "love," and "hope."

The exact nature of the "work [GK 2240] produced by faith" is a combination of direct missionary work (cf. 1:8), acts of goodness toward others (cf. 4:9–10), and loyalty to Christ in the face of severe persecution (1:6; 3:3–4, 8). "Faith" (GK 4411) indeed manifests itself on a broad front. For Paul to appreciate works is not surprising. Even in Romans, so notable for its repudiation of any system of justification by works (Ro 3:20–21, 28; 4:4–6), Paul finds occasion to speak of "work" as the essential fruit of the believing life (Ro 2:7; 13:3; 14:20; cf. 1Co 3:14; Eph 2:10; Tit 3:1). This emphasis aligns him with James regarding Christian living and the absolute necessity of works accompanying faith to prove its vitality (Jas 2:14–26). Indeed, wherever genuine faith is present, it works (Gal 5:6).

"Labor" (GK 3160) that is "prompted by love" approximates the meaning of "work" but with a connotation of extraordinary effort expended. Love as it is meant here does not stop with ordinary effort, but goes the second mile and even beyond for the sake of another. "Labor" is more distinctly spiritual service—beneficial efforts to help the sick and hungry and intense devotion to spreading the Gospel despite persecution (cf. 1Co 3:8; 15:10, 58; 2Co 10:15; Gal 4:11; Php 2:16). However it showed itself, one thing is certain: a great spirit of self-sacrifice was present, because this is inseparable from Christian "love" (GK 27).

The supreme example of such loving self-sacrifice comes from no less than God the Father (Jn 3:16; 1Jn 4:10) and his Son Jesus (Jn 13:34; 15:12). This is no mere emotional response prompted by the desirability of the person loved, though feeling certainly is not absent from it. It is ultimately traceable to the will of the one who loves, for he or she determines to love and does so regardless of the condition of the one loved. Such is God's love for us, and so must be the Christian's love for others, if "labor" is to result. Remembering this attainment of their readers, Paul and his helpers had additional cause for thanking God.

"Endurance" (GK 5705) is the third visible fruit that evoked thanksgiving. This is an aggressive and courageous Christian quality, excluding self-pity even when one encounters severe trials in living for Jesus Christ. Endurance accepts the seemingly dreary "blind alleys" of Christian experience with a spirit of persistent zeal. It rules out discouragement and goes forward no matter how hopeless the situation. Such endurance is possible only when one is "inspired by hope in our Lord Jesus Christ." "Hope" (GK 1828), especially in the certainty of the return of Jesus Christ, is the only adequate incentive for this heroic conduct. Confidence about the future braces the child of God to face all opposition while persevering and continuing in the spread of the Gospel. Jesus' return and the encouragement it brings to believers are major themes in both 1 and 2 Thessalonian (1Th 1:10; 3:13; 4:13–5:11; 5:23; 2Th 1:4, 7, 10; 2:16).

These three Christian virtues—faith, love, and hope—occupy a large place in early analyses of Christian responsibility (cf. 5:8; 1Co 13:13; Gal 5:5–6; Col 1:4–5; et al.). The expectation was that in every life faith would work (Gal 5:6; Jas 2:18), love would labor (Rev 2:2, 4), and hope would endure (Ro 5:2–4; 8:24–25).

C. The Cause for Giving Thanks—Knowing (1:4–10)

1. The impressions of the missionaries (1:4–5)

4–5 If v.2b supplies the manner of thanksgiving and v.3 the occasion, v.4 gives its ultimate cause. Intuitive knowledge of the Thessalonian believers' having been selected by God was the source of the missionaries' constant prayer of thanksgiving.

A touch of tenderness, the first of many in these two letters, punctuates Paul's acknowledgment of the election of the Thessalonians. "Brothers" denotes the spiritual brotherhood into which all disciples of the Lord Jesus have been inducted (cf. Mt 12:46–50; Mk 3:31–35; Lk 8:19–21). That this form of address, a partial carryover from Judaism (cf. Ac 2:29, 37; 3:17), became frequent in early Christianity is attested by twenty-eight occurrences in these two letters. This address is intensified when "loved by God" is added to it (cf. Ro 1:7; 2Th 2:13). The specific form in which this expression occurs here lays emphasis on the active exercise of God's love as already consummated and resulting in a fixed status of being loved.

Though God is identified as the agent in loving, the agent of choosing is not specifically named. But the obvious inference is that God "has chosen" (GK 1724) them. "Loved by God" is suitable assurance that he also chooses, since his love and election are inextricably bound together (Ro 11:28; cf. 11:5). This is God's sovereign choice of certain individuals, including the Thessalonian believers, prior to Adam's appearance on earth (cf. Eph 1:4). Some would locate God's choice of the Thessalonians at their conversion or thereafter by defining the elect as those who continue in faith and persevere in obedience. But Paul speaks of their election as a thing of the past, not as dependent on any human response. Knowledge of this prior choice by God was the root of Paul's thanksgiving.

Paul cannot leave unproved so direct a statement regarding election. So vv.5–10 give two grounds for the knowledge just asserted. The former of these relates to the experience of the missionaries themselves when they first presented the Gospel (v.5). They had sensed an unusual divine moving such as occurred only in special cases.

Instead of writing, "We came to you," the apostle puts the messengers in the background by saying, "Our gospel came to you." The message deserved foremost attention. Eight times in two letters "gospel" (GK 2295) is used to refer to the good news of salvation through Christ. Once the good news is unqualified by any modifier (2:4). Three times it is called "the gospel of God" (2:2, 8–9), God being the author of the Gospel. Twice it is "the gospel of Christ [or our Lord Jesus]" (1Th 3:2; 2Th 1:8), Christ being the topic of the Gospel message. The other two occurrences (1Th 1:5; 2Th 2:14) use "our gospel," meaning "the gospel we preach." Paul makes no claim to having originated the Gospel; he claims only to be a staunch proclaimer of the glad tidings from the Father concerning his Son.

The Gospel made its way to the Thessalonians through the missionaries in a fourfold manner. (1) It came "with words." This is obvious, since words are basic to intelligent communication. But the Gospel's coming was not "simply" in word; speaking was only a part of the whole picture. Their preaching contained three other ingredients essential to the outworking of God's elective purpose.

(2) The Gospel came "with power" (GK 1539). This verse primarily points to the inward power with which the speakers were filled as they gave the message, a power that might show itself in a variety of ways. This made the speakers aware of God's special involvement in the Gospel and its presentation.

(3) The spoken word is also personal, for the message came "with the Holy Spirit." This Person certainly was behind the power just named. Yet he is much greater and more versatile than the subjective power he produces. He is part of the Godhead and supplies a sense of divine reality to the spoken message.

(4) Growing out of the Spirit's special activity is "deep conviction [GK 4443]," which means that the preachers possessed perfect assurance as to the truth and effectiveness of their message. Such subjective certainty, sensed by Paul and his associates, served as a major ingredient of this first proof that these readers had been chosen by God.

"You know how we lived among you for your sake" draws on the Thessalonians' innate awareness of what Paul, Silas, and Timothy became while with them, so as to substantiate the sort of inner transformation God had wrought. Throughout the letter Paul carries his readers along with him by such expressions as "you know," which he uses as a precaution against those who might disagree (cf. 2:2, 5; 3:4). The quality of life shown by the missionaries had in itself been sufficient vindication of their sincerity and of the message they preached. Their attitudes were completely unselfish.

2. The effect on the Thessalonians (1:6–10)

The second proof of election lies in the effect of the Gospel on those evangelized (vv.6–10): (1) They "welcomed the message" and were converted. (2) They did so "in spite of severe suffering." (3) In difficult circumstances they had a joy that could only be "given by the Holy Spirit." (4) They rapidly became "imitators" of Paul and also the Lord. (5) They grew to a point of becoming a "model to all the believers in Macedonia and Achaia." Such a complete transformation happens only when God's elective purpose is at work in people.

a. Their transformation (1:6–7)

6–7 In v.6, Paul introduces a new point in his explanation of how he knew God had chosen the Thessalonians (cf. v.4). In a relatively short time they "became imitators" (GK 3629). Now their lifestyle was completely different from what it was before the Gospel came to them, because their conversion led them to imitate Paul and his companions. Paul repeatedly encouraged this wholesome following of examples (1Co 4:16; 11:1; Gal 4:12; Eph 5:1; Php 3:17; 4:9; 1Th 3:12; 2Th 3:7, 9). He did not hesitate to present himself as one to be copied, for he patterned his own life after Christ's (1Co 11:1). That is why he added "and of the Lord" here. The notion of imitating God and Christ applies to holiness (1Pe 1:15–16), love (Mt 5:43–48; Lk 6:36; Jn 13:34; 15:12), and suffering (Mt 16:24–25; Mk 10:38–39; Lk 14:27; Jn 15:18–20; 1Pe 2:18–21)—three areas touched upon later in this letter: holiness in 3:13; 4:3, 7; love in 3:12; 4:9–10; and suffering in 3:2–4.

Spiritual advance was possible for the Thessalonians only after they first "welcomed the message" preached by the missionaries. Even after their conversion, their response to the message was just as enthusiastic, though this response entailed "severe suffering." "Suffering" (or "tribulation"; GK 2568) plays a large part in these letters (1Th 1:6; 3:3–4, 7; 2Th 1:4, 6–7) because persecution was so common (Ac 17:5–9) and grew so intense as to be comparable to the bitter opposition by the Jews against the Lord Jesus and the Judean church (1Th 2:14–16). Christ's enemies would do anything to make life miserable for Christians. Yet instead of misery the Thessalonians displayed a "joy given by the Holy Spirit"; such a response defies natural explanation. The same One who gave Paul and his companions power for proclaiming the Gospel (v.5) dwelt within those who received the Gospel and transformed them.

The greatest attainment for these new Christians was becoming for others what Paul and his companions had been for them (v.7)—"a model" (GK 5596) to Christians throughout Greece. This word suggests an exact reproduction. Christians in Philippi, Berea, Athens, Corinth, and elsewhere in Macedonia and Achaia did well to look to Thessalonica.

b. Their witness (1:8–10)

8–10 In describing how the Thessalonians were a model Christian community and giving further proof of the effect of the Gospel on them, Paul gives another indication of their election (cf. v.4): a vigorous propagation of their faith. Their progress was remarkable in that what Paul and his companions had preached (v.5) and the Thessalonians had received (v.6), they were now sharing on the widest scale possible. "The word [NIV, "message"; GK 3364] of the Lord" is used extensively in Acts to describe the spreading Gospel message (Ac 8:25; 13:44, 48–49; 15:35–36; 16:32; 19:10, 20). Paul affirms that these converts played a substantial part in this ever-widening scope of Christian witness.

With Thessalonica as the starting point, the message "rang out" (v.8) like trumpets that keep on sounding. The range of their persistent testimony was ever increasing—"not only in Macedonia and Achaia ... everywhere." So impressed is Paul with how far the Gospel had progressed through the Thessalonians' faithful witness that he obviously indulges in a kind of hyperbole, for "everywhere" is clearly not worldwide in scope; e.g., in writing Romans some five years later, Paul said that Spain had not yet been evangelized (Ro 15:19–20, 24). Part of the Thessalonians' outreach stemmed from their location on the Egnatian Way and the Thermaic Gulf with access by sea to the whole Mediterranean world. But the largest factor was their diligence in communicating their faith to others. This was probably reported to Paul by Silas and Timothy on returning from Macedonia (Ac 18:5; 1Th 3:6).

So carried away with the Thessalonians' witness was Paul that he lengthened his sentence by adding, "Your faith in God has become known." News of this believing relationship constituted part of "the Lord's message" that had issued from them. So prominent was their witness that Paul and his companions did not need to speak of it, though Paul later did so (cf. 2Co 8:1–2).

Instead of Paul's telling others what had happened in Thessalonica, others were giving him a twofold report about this Macedonian city. They described how Paul, Silas, and Timothy had entered the city (cf. v.5), and how this church had turned to God from idols (v.9). Here Paul, who most often refers in a positive way to conversion as believing (cf. 1:7), uses a specific word for turning away from error and toward God (GK *2188*; cf. Ac 14:15; 26:18, 20; 2Co 3:16). His mention of "idols" shows the Thessalonians' Gentile origin, since idol worship did not dominate the Jews after the Babylonian exile. It also raises the question as to whether these are the same "God-fearing Greeks" (Ac 17:4) who were among Paul's original converts. Normally "God-fearers" had already separated themselves from idolatrous paganism because of their affiliation with a Jewish synagogue. Yet their release from past darkness may not have been total until secured by their relationship to God through Jesus Christ. Also, probably included in the Thessalonian church were additional Gentile converts who had no previous contact with Judaism.

Two purposes in the Thessalonians' turning to God are given: "to serve [GK *1526*] the living and true God" (v.9) and "to wait for his Son from heaven" (v.10). Service to God speaks of utter devotion and recognition of his rightful lordship over humankind. He alone is worthy of this, for he is "living," in contrast to lifeless idols, and he is "true," in contrast to counterfeit representations of himself.

The second purpose strikes a doctrinal note prominent throughout the remainder of the letter. In his second missionary journey Paul stressed eschatological events surrounding the return of Jesus Christ from the Father's right hand in heaven (cf. Ac 17:7, 31; 1Th 2:19; 3:13; 4:15; 5:2, 23; 2Th 2:1, 8). Early Christianity universally held that the resurrected and ascended Christ would return as King, and their expectancy of this event implied its nearness. For Paul to include himself and his readers among those to be rescued from the coming wrath (cf. "us," v.10) shows that they expected this to happen before their death. Had Jesus never been raised from the dead, he could never return; but since he had been raised, his future reappearance is guaranteed.

It is not some mystical spirit but the historical person "Jesus" who will return as rescuer of living Christians from the period of divine wrath at the close of the world's present age of grace. "Wrath" (GK *3973*) is frequently used in the NT as a technical term for the period just before Messiah's kingdom on earth, when God will afflict earth's inhabitants with an unparalleled series of physical torments because of their rejection of his will (Mt 3:7; 24:21; Lk 21:23; Rev 6:16–17). That wrath is pictured as already on its way and hence is quite near. Throughout the letter, the events of Jesus' coming are imminent (cf. 4:15, 17). The world was on the brink of being plunged into an unexpected time of trouble (cf. 5:2–3). Such was the outlook of early Christendom and such is always a proper Christian anticipation.

Rather than fearing this time, however, Christians find an incentive to persevere (cf. comment on 1:3), because for them it will mean rescue rather than doom. Not even the stepped-up persecution of Christ's followers that will mark this future period will touch them, for their deliverer will remove them from the scene of these dreadful happenings.

III. Vindication Before the Thessalonians (2:1–3:13)

A. Vindication Through Methods (2:1–12)

Having explained why he and his colleagues were thankful (1:2–10), Paul now takes up one of the main purposes for writing the letter—a lengthy vindication of their character and ministry (chs. 2–3). Chapter 2 expands on ch. 1—especially on 1:5–10, for 2:1–12 looks into Paul's coming to Thessalonica and his conduct there (cf. 1:5, 9a) and 2:13–16 turns attention to the Thessalonians' response (cf. 1:6–8, 9b–10). Yet ch. 2 does not just repeat the same ground. In ch. 1 Paul's coming and the peoples' response are intended to show a knowledge of election (1:4), whereas in ch. 2 the same themes establish Paul's defense against insinuations about his alleged ulterior motives.

1. Preaching, replete with power (2:1–2)

1–2 The identity of Paul's Thessalonian opponents is a difficult puzzle to piece together.

Most likely they were the Jews who were continuing adversaries of Paul, even after he left Thessalonica (cf. 2:14–16). They were so intent on destroying the work he had started that they persistently hurled accusations at him and labeled him another self-seeking religious propagandist. They distorted his teaching by accusing him of treason while he was still in the city (Ac 17:7). Subjected to a constant barrage of accusations, Thessalonian Christians easily began to question Paul's sincerity. There is no evidence of organized opposition within the church, yet Timothy apparently brought back news (3:6) that some uncertainty had arisen within it as to whether Paul's concern for it was genuine. This is not to say that his relations with the readers of the letter were no longer cordial (cf. 3:6), but symptoms of estrangement had appeared that could have led to an open rift unless treated immediately.

In light of this development, Paul again addresses his readers as "brothers" and reminds them of conditions throughout his initial visit. Special concern that his readers recall certain matters for themselves is evident in the recurrence of "you know" (vv.1–2, 5, 11; cf. vv.9–10 as well).

They are called to witness that Paul's initial "visit" to them "was not a failure." The word for "failure" (GK 3031) suggests "void of content" or "empty," especially since v.2 contrasts their boldness and earnestness in ministry. The opposite of an empty ministry is one in which no obstacle or threat is sufficient to deter the speaker of God's Gospel (v.2). In Philippi, Paul and Silas had been beaten and severely flogged; they had been put in prison with their feet in stocks (Ac 16:22–24) and cruelly mistreated because they had rescued a slave girl in the name of Jesus Christ. They had also been insulted by being arrested unjustly, stripped of their clothes, and treated like dangerous fugitives. Their Roman citizenship had been violated, and for this Paul demanded restitution (Ac 16:37). Still staggering from these injuries and indignities, the two came to Thessalonica. Under such conditions, most people would have refrained from repeating a message that had led to such violent treatment, but not these men. With God's help, they mustered sufficient courage to declare in this new city their Gospel from God.

Here in Thessalonica they again encountered "strong opposition [GK 74]"—a word that pictures an athlete's struggle to gain first place in a race or contest. Paul's conflict came from outward persecutions and dangers originated by his Jewish opponents (cf. Php 1:30). While Luke does not mention such opposition in Thessalonica (Ac 17:1–10), it is clear from this letter that such did come. In spite of it, however, Paul's inner help from God produced a continuing proclamation of the Gospel.

2. Preaching, removed from untruth (2:3–4)

3–4 Not only was the preaching of Paul and his companions filled with power and earnestness when they evangelized Thessalonica (vv.1–2), but wherever they went it was above suspicion of any kind (vv.3–4). The boldness just described was possible because God, who tests a person's motives, had approved their fitness to preach the Gospel.

"Appeal" (GK 4155) hints at the gently persuasive form of Paul's preaching, which always addressed the will in quest of a favorable decision, but included the intellect as well. Persuasion, however, can be of various types, both wholesome and otherwise. Paul and his fellow workers had apparently been accused of appealing on wrong grounds. The damage from this accusation he was quite anxious to repair.

First to be corrected was the claim that his appeal arose from "error" (GK 4415). Paul maintains that his message agreed perfectly with truth. He next answers his opponents in the matter of "impure motives" (GK 174), a word that has connotations of sexual impurity. Doubtless, Paul's enemies were attacking him on many fronts, including this sin so prevalent among traveling religious teachers. The apostle disclaims anything of this type as a motive for his missionary activities.

He further denies any attempt to use deceit so as to "trick" his listeners, even though he was accused of doing so on more occasions than this (cf. 2Co 4:2; 12:16). In seeking intelligent decisions from his hearers, he presented facts in their true light. The missionaries were so open and honest that an omniscient God had found them worthy "to be entrusted with the gospel" (v.4). To be "approved [GK 1507] by God" entails a process of testing, success in completing the tests, and a consequent state of endorsement by God. After calling Paul on the Damascus road, God subjected him to necessary rigors in order to demonstrate his capability for his assigned task. Having thus prepared him, he committed to him the Gospel message to proclaim among Gentiles. On the basis of this commission, the missionary team spoke wherever they went. They did nothing superficial just "to please men." Ultimately, they sought God's approbation (cf. 1Co 4:2–5). This kind of goal excluded anything hidden from the eyes of him "who tests our hearts." The scrutiny of a God who is able to sound the depths of every thought (cf. Ro 8:27) is Paul's ultimate court of appeal to prove his absolute sincerity.

3. Preaching, reinforced by godly concern (2:5–12)

Godly concern for his listeners underscores more forcefully than anything else the legitimacy of Paul's missionary methods. Starting with v.5, he explains how his general policy of vv.3–4 was applied in Thessalonica. He begins by denying allegations against his character (vv. 5–7a), and he then goes on to present the true picture (vv.7b–12).

a. Evidenced by the absence of lower motives (2:5–6)

5–6 In the first of three denials, Paul calls his readers to verify his complete abstinence from any type of "flattery" (GK *3135*)—the insidious practice of saying nice things in order to gain influence over others for selfish reasons. Paul wants them to confirm that he was never guilty of this practice.

Second, he denies putting on the kind of mask that "greed" (GK *4432*) would wear. The greed of which he was accused includes more than just avarice or love of money. It denotes self-seeking of all types, a quest for anything that brings self-satisfaction. It grows out of complete disinterest in the rights of others—an attitude foreign to Paul and his helpers. Only God can verify inner freedom from greed, so Paul calls on God as witness.

Third, Paul disavows the desire for "praise [GK *1518*] from men" (v.6). The world of Paul's time was filled with wandering philosophers, prophets of other religions, magicians, false prophets, and others seeking not only financial gain, but also the prestige of a good reputation. Divine approval (cf. v.4), not public esteem, was what motivated Paul and his companions.

Grammatically, it is best to see "as apostles of Christ we could have been a burden to you" as completing the sense of v.6, and it should begin with the word "although." The word "apostles" (GK *693*) is used here in its nontechnical sense (see comments on Ro 16:7; Gal 1:1), and the word "burden" (GK *983*) has primary reference to apostolic dignity. Paul, Silas, and Timothy could legitimately have claimed the dignity associated with their apostolic office. The important position of Paul and his colleagues as Christ's representatives earned for them the right to receive special respect, but they did not stand on this right. So this is further evidence that they were not prompted by lower motives.

b. Evidenced by the presence of higher motives (2:7–12)

7 Not only was the godly concern of Paul and his helpers proved by their freedom from lower motives (vv.5–6), but also by their higher motives (vv.7–12). The apostle now takes up a positive description that the Thessalonians were bound to agree with because of their own observations—"you remember" (v.9); "you are witnesses" (v.10); "you know" (v.11). When they were with these Macedonians, Paul and his helpers were gentle, not authoritarian (v.7). They demonstrated an utmost tenderness, comparable to that of a mother nursing her own children. The figure implies a special effort to protect one's children and to provide for their every need, even to the extent of great sacrifice.

8 The manner of gentle treatment involved a willingness to share with the Thessalonians both the Gospel of God and their own lives; that is how much they loved them. The missionaries constantly yearned for these people, so much so that they found it a continual delight to share their whole beings with them. "Lives" (GK *6034*) conveys more than just their physical lives; in the depths of their being they cared "because [the Thessalonians] had become so dear" to them.

9 Paul now recalls the long hours, day and night, of extreme toil and hardship by which he, Silas, and Timothy supported themselves while preaching. He takes the single item of self-support as evidence of his broader concern for the Thessalonians. "Toil" (GK *3160*;

cf. 1:3) emphasizes the fatigue they incurred in expending themselves, while "hardship" (GK *3677*) highlights external difficulties encountered in the process. As in 2Th 3:8, the combination describes the apostles' efforts at providing their own upkeep, an example much needed by some in Thessalonica (1Th 4:11–12; 5:14; 2Th 3:6–15). Paul's work was tentmaking (Ac 18:3), probably meaning the production of tent material from animal hair or skins. Part of a Jewish child's upbringing was learning a trade, and Paul was no exception to this. He did receive some financial help from the Philippian church while he was in Thessalonica (Php 4:15–16), but not enough to permit him to stop working. Apparently his wages were so low that he needed gifts to enable him to take some time off for preaching (Ac 18:5). Though missionary service includes the right to support from others (1Co 9:3ff.), Paul did not always use that right (cf. Ac 20:34–35; 1Co 4:12; 2Co 11:8).

By this "around-the-clock" diligence Paul lifted the burden of support from his converts. His central purpose was to give people the Gospel of God. From this nothing should detract, and making the Gospel "free of charge" (1Co 9:18) eliminated charges of selfish motives.

10 Paul appeals to the Thessalonians as witnesses of how both the missionaries' religious piety and moral conduct among them could not be faulted. God also is called to attest to whatever was hidden to human eyes. All this was for the sake of the believers.

11–12 A further comparison enlivens Paul's expression of concern. He changes his metaphor from a mother's tender care (v.7) to that of a father dealing with his children individually. Christians need fatherly teaching and advice as well as motherly care.

The fatherly treatment included encouragement, comfort, and urging. "Encouraging" (GK *4151*) can in some contexts signify a note of comfort, but here it has the hortatory flavor of "admonishing." "Comfort" (GK *4170*) is covered by the next verb. "Urging" (GK *3458*) adds a note of authority. These actions were more than mere requests. Their goal was a worthy lifestyle. "Live lives" represents the figure of "walking around" (GK *4344*), a common way of designating one's conduct. In reference to the Christian life, it relates primarily to the moral sphere. Conduct should be on the plane of God's standards.

God calls (GK *2813*) believers "into his kingdom and glory." This is an incentive to a high quality of life. Paul is looking back to the time when God first called his readers to salvation, a call that is always effectual. In one sense God's kingdom is already present (see comment on Mk 1:15), but ultimate realization of the messianic kingdom with its future glory is in view here (cf. Ac 17:7; 28:23). As frequently occurs in these two letters, those Paul is addressing are pointed to the bliss ahead as an incentive to godly living now. "Glory" is that unhindered manifestation of God's presence in which believers will share (Ro 5:2; 8:18).

B. Vindication Through Their Thanksgiving (2:13–16)

1. For the ready acceptance of the Word of God (2:13)

13 Having already thanked God in 1:2–3 for their progress, Paul now does so again by alluding to 1:5–10, which describes specifically how the Thessalonians so rapidly entered on a Christian way of life. Now he cites their ready acceptance of the word of God (cf. 1:6)—not in proof of their election as in ch. 1, but to show the reason for his sincere gratitude for them.

Because of the deep personal commitment that he and his helpers had to the work at Thessalonica, Paul could write, "We also thank God continually." "Also" connotes "on our part." The missionary team's reaction to the Thessalonians' ready response to the word was incessant thanksgiving. The spotlight now shifts from the evangelizers (vv 1–12) to those evangelized (vv.13–16).

The cause of thanksgiving having already been given in vv.1–12, the word "because" introduces the content of thanksgiving (the word for "because" should be translated "that"). Paul not only refers to an objective reception of the word of God, but also a subjective acceptance in their hearts. The latter, a wholehearted welcome, indicated their high estimate of God's word. They had heard the word preached by the missionaries, but ultimately it was the word of God that they heard. Here is indication of Paul's consciousness of his own divinely imparted authority (cf. 1Co 14:37). His preaching was not the outgrowth of personal philosophical meanderings, but was deeply rooted in a message given by God himself. What had been delivered to him through others (e.g., 1Co 11:23; 15:1, 3) and from the Lord directly (e.g., 1Th 4:15), he passed on to others. Such traditions were in turn taught to still others. Some teachings were put in written form and became part of the NT canon (cf. 2Ti 2:2; 2Pe 3:15–16).

Once received, this word of God becomes an active power operating continually in the believer's life. When it is at work in believers, there is a change in behavior and constant fruitfulness.

2. For their endurance under persecution (2:14–16)

14 The word "for" confirms the principal statement of v.13—their ready acceptance of God's word. Welcoming the word and enduring sufferings because of it often go together. The stature of the Thessalonians as "imitators" had already been established in the past (cf. 1:6). Deliberate imitation of sufferings for sufferings' sake is an unworthy Christian objective, but imitation of a Christian lifestyle is legitimate and desirable. Persecution inevitably arises when Christians pattern their lives after the Lord.

Paul tenderly reminds these brothers that they were not the first to be afflicted. "God's churches in Judea, which are in Christ Jesus" had been the first, and through faithful endurance they had become an example of what Jesus had predicted about the suffering entailed in discipleship. Apparently the way these earliest Jewish Christians handled themselves had become widely known, even before Luke wrote Acts (about A.D. 62). Paul's sympathy toward and harmony with Judean Christianity, whose bitter opponent he had been before conversion, are hereby assured, and the unity of all Christians, no matter what their ethnic background or geographical locality, underlies this description of their common experience in suffering. Hearty acceptance of God's message, which is so often accompanied by adversity, is the very thing that ensures one against falling away when adversity arises (cf. Mt 13:20–21; Lk 8:13).

Both the Thessalonian churches and the churches in Judea suffered persecution from fellow-countrymen. For the Thessalonians these were predominantly Gentiles, though Jews also had been instrumental in stirring up opposition in that city (Ac 17:5–9). For the Judean churches, opposition had come from those of a Jewish background, who were also strong advocates of the Jewish religion that Christianity so strongly threatened.

15–16 Mention of "the Jews" (v.14) furnishes Paul an occasion to digress slightly and deliver a violent criticism of this persecuting element among them. Such harsh language is markedly out of character for Paul as we know him from his other writings. He is renowned for his desire to see the salvation of his blood relatives (Ro 9:1–3; 10:1), regardless of how much he had suffered personally at their hands (2Co 11:24, 26). Exactly what provoked this sudden outburst cannot be known with certainty. An accumulation of hostile acts probably played a part. The writer had been chased out of Damascus (Ac 9:23–25) and Jerusalem (Ac 9:29–30) by his own people not long after his conversion. His message was rejected and his party driven out of Pisidian Antioch by them (Ac 13:45–46, 50). At Iconium the Jews poisoned people's minds against Paul and Barnabas and ultimately forced them out (Ac 14:2, 5–6). They made a special journey to Lystra to instigate an uprising that produced Paul's stoning and being left for dead (Ac 14:19). Jewish opposition continued to hound the missionary band into the second journey, specifically at Thessalonica, again producing Paul's exit (Ac 17:5, 10). Even now as Paul pens these words from Corinth, a united attack has been mounted against him by the city's Jewish residents (Ac 18:6, 12–13). Couple with this the present plight of the Thessalonian Christians (1Th 3:3), ultimately traceable to Jewish opponents, and it is no wonder that Paul uses the occasion to recount their consistent opposition to the Lord Jesus.

The acme of the Jews' opposition is their part in the death of the Lord Jesus. Hence, Paul places this crime first among their offenses (v.15). By persuasion of the Jewish leaders, the Roman authorities crucified Jesus (Jn 19:16; 1Co 2:8). Though joint responsibility was shared by Gentiles and Jews (Ac 4:27), at this point Paul lays guilt for the crime on Israel. It was the exalted Lord of glory against whom this heinous crime was committed.

In the NIV, "the prophets" (v.15) are grouped with "the Lord Jesus" as murder victims of the Jews. It is true that many OT prophets died in this way (cf. 1Ki 19:10; Mt 23:31, 35, 37; Lk 13:34; Ac 7:52; Ro 11:3). More important in this connection is Jesus' parable of the vineyard, in which killing some of the servants (i.e., prophets) was preliminary to killing the son (Mt 21:35–39; Mk 12:5–8). On the other hand, it seems better to connect "the prophets" with "us" in v.15 and translate this part of the verse, "drove out the prophets and us." If the parable of the vineyard furnishes a valid background, connecting "the prophets" with "the Lord Jesus" is unsatisfactory, for a chronological order is not observed and not all the servants in the parable are slain. Of greater import in this parable is the idea of the persecution of the servants. In fact, Luke's account (Lk 20:9–16) does not even mention killing the servants. And to list the prophets alongside Paul's missionary band furnishes an excellent reason for the past action in "drove ... out." Furthermore, it helps vindicate the missionaries by placing them alongside the honored OT prophets.

Paul concludes v.15 by listing two more characteristics of the Jewish antagonists. "They displease God and are hostile to all men." The former is clearly an understatement, since they were militantly opposed to God. Their zeal for God was not guided by knowledge (Ro 10:2). By opposing God's Messiah so strenuously, they became God's adversaries. This could not help but produce hostility to all people—a hostility not arising from a supposed racial superiority, but manifested in stubborn resistance to admitting Jesus' messiahship.

This is proved by their "effort to keep us from speaking to the Gentiles so that they may be saved" (v.16). The Jews were quite resistant to having Jesus' messiahship and saving work proclaimed among themselves (Ac 4:18–21; 5:27, 28, 40), but Paul's Gentile mission provoked even more indignation, for it implied God's forsaking of Israel (cf. Ac 13:46, 48–50; 17:4–5; cf. also Ro 11:11, 25). Thus they sought to eliminate preaching the message of salvation to the Gentiles. "They always heap up their sins to the limit" is the outcome of killing the Lord Jesus and all their subsequent adverse activity. The figure of "heap up ... to the limit" (GK 405) points to a well-defined limit of sin appointed by divine decree. After generations of repeated apostasies and rebellion, Israel had arrived at that point. The climax had come especially with rejection of the Messiah himself, and their already-fixed judgment was biding its time till its direct consequences were released.

"The wrath [GK 3973] of God" is none other than the eschatological wrath for which the whole world is destined just before Messiah's kingdom arrives (cf. 1:10). But then why does Paul speak of this wrath as happening in the past ("has come")? The best explanation comes from comparing the only other NT combinations of the expression "come upon" (Mt 12:28; Lk 11:20), where Jesus speaks of the kingdom's arrival in comparable terminology. The unique force of this verb connotes an arrival on the threshold of fulfillment, not the actual entrance into that experience. That is, the wrath that will precede Christ's kingdom has come before the Jews' full experience of that wrath. All prerequisites for unleashing this future torrent have been met. God has set conditions in readiness through the first coming and the rejection of Messiah by this people.

A time of trouble awaits Israel, just as it does the rest of the world, and the breaking forth of this time is portrayed as an imminent condemnation. As soon as human conditions in the progress of God's program warrant, the Jews with the rest of the non-Christian world will be plunged into this awful future turmoil. "At last" should probably be replaced by the NIV note "fully," the latter meaning that the issue is now settled. The determination cannot be reversed, the obstinate blindness of the Jewish people furnishing obvious proof of this.

C. Vindication Through Their Separation (2:17–3:13)

1. Desire to go to them (2:17–20)

17 Turning from his digression about the Jews, Paul continues to stress his deep feeling for the Thessalonians. He pictures himself in contrast to the persecutors just mentioned (2:14–16). The affectionate "brothers" prepares for heartfelt words about his leaving them—a painful experience because of a consuming attraction for them, like that of a child who has prematurely lost his parents. After only a brief absence, he wants to be with them. "We made every effort" conveys a depth of feeling amounting to zeal, a zeal heightened by separation. Added to this deep emotion already portrayed is his "intense longing."

Paul's warm words about his feelings for the Thessalonians may reflect rumors that he did not really care for them. Apparently some had said that he had no interest in coming back to them and that he had come the first time only to satisfy selfish ambition.

18 Therefore, as if he were not satisfied with his already-overwhelming expressions of his feeling for the Thessalonians, Paul proceeds to prove his longing to see them. It is his personal inclination and purpose. The tug on his heart is manifest in the words "certainly I, Paul." Though Timothy and Silas had already returned to Thessalonica, Paul's failure to do so did not come from lack of intention; he had attempted a visit several times.

What could hinder such intense desire? It must be nothing less than Satanic hindrance. The hindrance was probably not the demands of missionary work elsewhere, since it is not the enemy's purpose to encourage such work. Restraint by civil officials in Thessalonica and opposition from local Jews are other possibilities, but these would hardly be sufficient to prevent Paul's return. A more plausible identification of the hindrance might be his illness (cf. 2Co 12:7), even though this would require the "us" to refer only to Paul. The real existence of a personal and supernatural devil is incontrovertible. His present activity in opposing God is only a foretaste of heightened opposition to be launched in the future through his special human representative just prior to Jesus' personal return to earth (2Th 2:3–12).

19 Paul's rhetorical questions tie the Thessalonians into his anticipation of the Lord Jesus' coming and presence. They will bring him joy and be a victor's wreath for him to glory in at that future moment of truth. As always with Paul, this is a boasting or glorying in what God has done (cf. 1Co 1:31), not in personal accomplishment (Ro 3:27; 4:2; cf. 2Co 1:14; Php 2:16).

Interrupting his own question, he anticipates the answer: "Is it not you?" This is Paul's answer to those who said he did not care for the Thessalonian Christians. The future event Paul is looking toward is identical with the appearance of every Christian before the judgment seat of Christ (2Co 5:10), where our works will be evaluated. Because of his converts' spiritual attainments, Paul feels that this will be an occasion of joy and victory.

"When he comes" translates the literal meaning—"in [or at] his presence [or coming]." The noun is *parousia* (GK 4242), a word that in secular Greek sometimes meant a ruler's visit and in the NT applies to the return of Jesus Christ. The various facets of this future visit are defined by the contexts in which *parousia* appears. In this instance it is Jesus' examination of his servants subsequent to his coming for them (4:15–17) that is in view.

20 Finally, Paul declares that the Thessalonians are his "glory and joy." Not only will they be this when Christ returns; they are so right now. So he silences the insinuations about his lack of concern for his converts.

2. Sending Timothy to them (3:1–5)

Paul now sought another way to dull the pain of separation from his beloved Thessalonians: He sent Timothy, a valuable companion and effective servant, to serve in his place and bring back word about their afflictions and satanic temptation.

1 Paul gives as his reason for sending Timothy: "We could stand [GK 5095] it no longer." This verb has the metaphorical meaning of "hold out against." Paul was at this point unable to stand his ignorance of how his precious converts were faring in persecution. His personal trials meant far less to him than those for whom he suffered vicariously in Christ.

Paul's sincerity is therefore demonstrated by his willingness to do without his cherished co-worker Timothy and to remain alone in a strange city (Athens) dominated by pagan philosophy and animosity toward the Gospel (cf. Ac 17:16–34)—"we" here probably means Paul himself; cf. "I, Paul" in 2:18 and "I" in 3:5.

2 Some are troubled by the problem of harmonizing Timothy's movements with those recorded in Ac 17–18. But Luke does not write about everything in Paul's itinerary. In this case he omits the visit of Silas and Timothy to Athens. According to this verse, they came to Paul while he was in Athens and were sent back again to the Macedonian cities, Timothy going to Thessalonica (cf. v.1). With Silas's departure prior to or simultaneous with Timothy's, the apostle was subjected to an almost intolerable state of loneliness until their subsequent return when he was at Corinth (Ac 18:5; 1Th 3:6). And he was willing to endure this only for the sake of benefitting the Thessalonians and satisfying his thirst for news about them.

Timothy was valuable not only to Paul, but also to Christians more generally, for he was their "brother and God's fellow worker in spreading the gospel of Christ" (cf. Php 2:19–24). Timothy was a spiritual brother in the truest sense and an effective servant of God, and for Paul to choose him to go to Thessalonica demonstrates again his genuine concern for the Christians there.

Timothy's mission was "to strengthen and encourage" the Thessalonians in their "faith," as Paul himself usually did (Ac 14:22;

Paul remained in Athens while he sent Timothy and Titus back to Macedonia. This restored amphitheater in Athens is still in use.

15:32, 41; 18:23; Ro 1:11; 16:25; 1Th 3:13; 2Th 2:16–17; 3:3). Dependence on God in faith was their only recourse in adversity. They could remain faithful only as they let him supply inner strength (see also v.10).

3–4 Timothy told them not to be "unsettled by these trials." "Trials" (or "afflictions"; GK 2568) are the stiffest test of faith. Such is the inevitable lot of Christ's followers (e.g., Jn 16:33), just as it was for their Master (cf. Jn 15:18–16:4). These trials are not to be identified with the end-time tribulation just before Christ's *parousia*, which will mark the culmination of God's wrath against the ungodly (Mt 24:21; 1Th 2:16; 5:9; 2Th 1:6). Rather, they are part of the church's ongoing experience, as Paul indicates in v.4. Paul had already told them that trials are an inevitable part of Christian experience (3:3; cf. Ac 14:22); Timothy was to reinforce this message.

5 In this situation, Paul, speaking now only of himself at this point, was constrained to find out through Timothy the state of their faith. He knew that "the tempter" (i.e., Satan; cf. Mt 4:3) had been at work among them and that God permits the enemy this activity. What Paul did not know about the Thessalonians, however, was whether or not the tempter's solicitations had been successful, making his work and that of his colleagues "useless."

3. Delight over their progress (3:6–10)

Timothy finally returned from his Thessalonian mission with an opposite report from what Paul had feared. This cheering news greatly encouraged him and moved Paul to thanksgiving and prayer.

6 "Just now" shows that Timothy's arrival from Thessalonica immediately preceded the composition of the letter and probably provided its chief motivation. This arrival is the same as that in Ac 18:5, when Timothy and Silas came at approximately the same time. This substantiates the earlier conclusion that Paul was actually separated from both Timothy and Silas for a time (cf. 3:1). Doubtless he was refreshed by the return of his two associates, though by now he had moved from Athens to Corinth, where a new Christian fellowship had developed.

Timothy "brought good news" (GK 2294) about the Thessalonians. This verb is reserved almost exclusively for gospel preaching. That Paul places Timothy's report in this exalted category shows his high estimate of the Thessalonians. The report was both spiritual and personal. Spiritually, they had progressed in "faith"; their trust in God had been sufficient for their trials. Yet room for improvement remained (cf. v.10). Likewise their progress in "love" for others was uplifting news, though even here too there was room for growth (cf. 3:12; 4:9–10).

Timothy's report of the kindly feelings of the Thessalonians toward him ("pleasant memories," "long to see us") assured Paul that they had not written him off as an exploiter, disinterested in their welfare. They still maintained a warm spot for him, matching his own tender longing to see them (cf. 2:17; 3:10).

7–8 The report helped Paul in his adversity (cf. Ac 18:6, 9–10, 12–13). He was facing physical privations ("distress"; GK *340*) and suffering inflicted by his antagonists ("persecution"; GK *2568*). Like all Christians (3:3–4), he was called to suffer persecution (cf. 2Ti 3:12). It was their "faith" that encouraged him and the fact that they were "standing firm in the Lord." Since they were depending on God for help against impossible obstacles, Paul himself felt an additional incentive to do this in his own life (cf. Ro 1:12; 2Co 7:4, 13; Phm 7). Thus he felt rejuvenated—"for now we really live." He had been given a new lease on life.

9 The result was thanksgiving to God. Paul found words inadequate to express his appreciation for what had happened in their lives. The change in Paul's mood was radical; "all our distress and persecution" (v.7) has now become "all the joy we have" because of the steadfastness of the Thessalonians. His was no superficial happiness but heartfelt and sincere joy "in the presence of our God."

10 Along with his rejoicing, Paul prayed continually for the Thessalonians. "Night and day" does not mean once in the evening and once in the morning, nor that he did nothing else but pray. It rather points to the extreme frequency of his prayers, while "most earnestly" refers to the intensity of his prayers.

The thrust of Paul's petitions for the Thessalonians is twofold: that "we may see you" (cf. 2:18; 3:6) and "[may] supply what is lacking in your faith" (i.e., to correct, restore, and equip them in their faith). They had already been commended for "their work produced by faith" (1:3). Yet they had room for additional growth, and Paul felt his presence could foster it.

4. Seeking direction for them (3:11–13)

A transitional "now" introduces a related subject: Paul elaborates on his two petitions in v.10 for the Thessalonians. God is addressed indirectly in the third person, in keeping with a letter addressed to people (cf. 5:23; 2Th 2:16; 3:5, 16).

11 Paul recognizes the uselessness of personal efforts toward a revisit unless God "clears the way." At the moment, no return is possible (cf. 2:18), but he prays for the removal of the barriers. Two persons viewed as one (cf. Jn 10:30) possess power to open the way to Thessalonica once again; "our God and Father himself and our Lord Jesus" is the compound subject of a singular verb "may ... clear"—probably an indication of the unity of the Godhead. "Himself," the first word in this prayer, possibly refers to both Father and Son, once again implying the one essence of these two persons (cf. 2Th 2:16). The Father and Son eventually did grant this request, for Paul returned to Macedonia approximately five years later (Ac 19:21; 20:1; 1Co 16:5; 2Co 2:13) and in all likelihood made a point of visiting Thessalonica.

12 Paul's second petition pertains to "what is lacking" in their faith (cf. v.10), specifically the outworking of that faith in a growing "love." Since "Lord" refers to Jesus in vv. 11, 13 and likewise in all Paul's writings for the most part, it is best interpreted in this way here. Paul seeks the "increase" (GK *4429*) and "overflow" (GK *4355*) of the Thessalonians' love. Combined, these two words mean "increase to overflowing." Paul prays this not because they lacked love (4:9–10a), but because Christians must continually increase in selfless devotion to others.

In line with the consistent NT emphasis, the prime objects of love are fellow Christians ("each other"; cf. Jn 13:34–35; Ro 13:8; 1Th 4:9; 1Pe 1:22; 1Jn 3:11, 23). But love also reaches beyond the circle of Christians to all other people ("everyone else"). Jesus warned against a narrow conception of one's "neighbor" (Mt 5:43–48; Lk 10:25–37; cf. Mt 19:19;

22:39; Mk 12:31). Paul dares to set himself up as a standard of love to be emulated, a step he could take only because of his imitation of Jesus (see comment on 1:6), who is the ultimate standard (Jn 13:34; 15:12).

13 The goal of Paul's prayer for the Thessalonians is that the Lord will grant them inner strength to be "blameless" in holiness "in the presence of our God and Father" when the Lord Jesus returns. He looks forward to the time of final accounting. An overflow of love (v.12) is the only route to holy conduct in which no fault can be found (v.13). Unless love prevails, selfish motives inhibit ethical development by turning us toward ourselves and away from God and blameless living. The holiness of God is the ideal we must seek (cf. Lev 19:2; 1Pe 1:16).

The final accounting Paul alludes to will take place before "our God and Father," as "in the presence of" (GK 1869) a judge (Mt 25:32; 27:11; Lk 21:36; 2Co 5:10). Earlier Paul had made "our Lord Jesus" the judge at this scene (1Th 2:19). But this is no contradiction. The unity of the Father and Son, just seen in v.11, allows a joint judgeship. The judgment seat of Christ (2Co 5:10) is also the judgment seat of God (Ro 14:10), because Christ in his present session is with the Father on his heavenly throne (Rev 3:21; cf. Ro 8:34; Heb 1:3; 10:12). This hearing will take place at the *parousia* (GK 4242) of the Lord Jesus (see comment on 2:19). For the Thessalonians Paul prays for a favorable verdict at that time.

Others present at this reckoning will be "all his holy ones." In the NT, this phrase almost exclusively means redeemed human beings (except possibly Jude 14). The redeemed are elsewhere associated with Christ at his return (2Th 1:10). Since human beings are the objects of judgment and their holiness is what is in focus, we must identify "the holy ones" as other Christians joined with the Thessalonians before the judgment seat of God and Christ.

What relation does this event mentioned here bear to the predicted future wrath (1:10; 2:16; 5:9) and the meeting of the saints with the Lord in the air (4:15–17)? If it is Christ's coming prior to the period of God's final wrath, it is identifiable with the meeting of 4:15–17. This interpretation, however, encounters obstacles, for if "all his holy ones" refers to the redeemed, they cannot come *with* Christ until he has first come *for* them. To interpret "all his holy ones" as the spirits of the dead in Christ is not satisfactory, because some of those in Christ will not yet have died. Furthermore, the readers have not yet been assured that their dead would participate in the *parousia* (4:15).

But if this event refers to Christ's coming after God's final wrath, we encounter other difficulties—primarily a disregard for the contextual emphasis on the judgment of saints. By the time of his return to earth after the wrath, this reckoning will have already taken place in heaven, for 4:15–17 relates the judgment of God and Christ to Christ's return in the air before the wrath.

In resolving this difficulty, we must consider the scope of the word *parousia* as indicated in these letters (see the introduction). The complexity of this term demands that it include an extended visit by Christ as well as the arrival initiating that visit. This is provided for adequately in the rarer meaning of *parousia*, "presence" (cf. 1Co 16:17; 2Co 10:10; Php 2:12). Included in Christ's visit is an evaluation of the saints (cf. 2:19; 5:23), which is the aspect in view here in v.13. This judgment cannot be completely dissociated from Christ's coming in the air (4:15–17), because this advent marks its initiation. Yet it must be conceived of as a session in heaven in some measure separate from the arrival itself. At this juncture the degree to which Christians have attained a "blameless and holy" character will be divinely ascertained.

IV. Exhortation to the Thessalonians (4:1–5:22)

A. Exhortation Regarding Personal Needs (4:1–12)

1. Continual improvement (4:1–2)

1 Paul now urges the Thessalonians on to greater spiritual attainments outlined in 3:10–13. His exhortations, introduced by "finally," are logically based on more than 3:10–13. The drastic change to a new line of thought implies that all of chs. 2–3 are in view. "Finally" also shows that the series of admonitions launched here will be the final part of the letter. With Paul a final word may be brief (2Co 13:11; Php 4:8; 2Ti 4:8) or extended (Php 3:1; 2Th 3:1). "Brothers" again shows his tenderness in approaching delicate subjects.

The nature of Paul's appeal is conveyed in "ask" (GK 2263) and "urge" (GK 4151). The former word is a gentle, friendly request and the latter an authoritative apostolic plea—more than a request, but less than a command. The words "in the Lord Jesus" form the context of the exhortations that are to follow.

The Thessalonians had already been given instruction about how they must "live in order to please God." Paul again views the Christian life as a "walk" (GK 4344; see comment on 2:12). He might have immediately requested compliance with earlier instruction, but he first interrupts himself, lest he appear to be condemnatory. He gives credit where it is due, in this case recognizing the substantial progress that the Thessalonian Christians have already made (similarly 1:3, 6–10; 3:6, 8). Yet the realization of the ultimate goal of pleasing God and receiving his commendation entailed continual improvement (cf. 3:12; 4:10).

2 So Paul stimulates his converts' memory of what he and his companions had told them. He characterizes their previous ministry as a delivering of "instructions" (or "commands"; GK 4132). These were binding because they were given "by the authority of the Lord Jesus."

2. Sexual purity (4:3–8)

3 Christian holiness requires total abstinence from "sexual immorality" (GK 4518). This word requires a broad definition as including all types of sexual sins between male and female. A year or two earlier a Christian council in Jerusalem had ruled decisively on a related issue affecting Gentile Christians (cf. Ac 15:20). It is not clear whether the Thessalonians were guilty of such immorality, so common among the pagans (v.5). Though Paul may have had in mind the temptation to indulge in it, his strong words probably imply some overt transgressions. Pagan moral corruption looked upon fornication either indifferently or favorably. That the Thessalonians slipped into it after their conversion would not have been strange. While Paul had congratulated them on their faith (cf. 1:3), this does not mean that there was no occasional misbehavior, even this kind, within the church (cf. 1Co 1:4–9; 5:1–5; 6:12–20).

4 The positive side of holiness requires one to "learn to control his own body" (or "learn to live with his own wife"; cf. NIV note). The choice between these two options surrounds the word "body" (lit., "vessel"; GK 5007). It is highly probable that this word does mean "wife" (cf. 1Pe 3:7 for a somewhat parallel use). If so, the word translated "control" (GK 3227) means "acquire" or even "keep on acquiring" (i.e., "live with" in the sense of cultivating a wife's favor; cf. 1Co 7:2–5). A wholesome marriage was thus Paul's antidote for "sexual immorality." "Holy and honorable" describes the way to maintain the right kind of marriage, holiness being due God (4:3; cf. 3:13) and honor due the wife.

5 Those "who do not know God" (i.e., the "heathen" Gentiles; cf. Gal 4:8; 2Th 1:8; also Ps 79:6; Jer 10:25) know nothing of such holy and honorable behavior based on the law of Moses and the commands of Christ. Their guiding principle is "passionate lust." Once removed from that realm into the church of God (cf. 1Co 10:32), believers are obligated to maintain much higher standards.

6 Wronging and taking advantage of a "brother" (probably a Christian brother) are other violations of holiness. Paul is continuing here the matter of sexual transgression. To have relations with a woman outside marriage is not just a trespass against God's law. It also defrauds some fellow Christian who eventually will take, or has taken, this woman as his own wife—an especially heinous sin because the one robbed is a spiritual relative of the robber. Paul does not allude to the other simultaneous injustice, which is obvious—namely, that the woman herself is an object of cruel abuse in such a situation. This too is especially repulsive in a Christian setting.

A reason for complying with the standards set forth in vv.4–5 relates to the Lord Jesus' future punishment of "all such sins." Paul is speaking of the future judgment of Christians at the *parousia* (2:19; 3:13; 1Co 3:10–17)—a judgment to be carried out by Christ (Jn 5:22; 2Co 5:10) in association with God the Father (Ro 14:10; see comment on 1Th 3:13). Paul's initial expedition to Thessalonica had informed and solemnly warned them of these dire consequences. We do not know what prompted him to put in writing this admonition about judgment. Perhaps urgency required stern words.

7 Another reason for compliance is the nature of God's calling. As in 2:12, this is God's effectual call, mediated through gospel preaching (2Th 2:14). Believers called by God have been inducted into a holy life (cf. 3:13; 4:3–4). They now belong to a community with values different from those of "the heathen" (v.5).

8 A final reason for compliance with the standards set forth in vv.4–5 is that they are God-given. Therefore rejection of them means rejecting not a human being, but God, "who gives [us] his Holy Spirit"; the Spirit lives in us and is inseparable from the kind of holy living demanded in this paragraph (cf. Ro 8:1–17).

3. Filial love (4:9–10)

9–10 "Now about" is a frequent Pauline formula for introducing a new subject (4:13; 5:1; cf. 1Co 7:1, 25; 8:1; 12:1; 16:1, 12). Paul is now responding to a different element of Timothy's oral report about Thessalonica (1Th 3:6). In vv.9–10a he acknowledges their practical compliance with a responsibility to love each other. This "brotherly love" (GK 5789) presupposes the close ties within the spiritual family of God. Paul views further writing on the subject as superfluous in that they are "taught by God" through the indwelling Holy Spirit (v.8; cf. Jn 6:45) to so love. At conversion, believers become lifelong pupils as the Spirit bears inner witness to the love within the Christian family (cf. Ro 5:5; Gal 5:22). No external stimulus is necessary; mutual love among Christians is an inbred quality.

Proof of this inner instruction was visible in the Thessalonians' love for all Christians of their province. Any contacts they had with churches in Berea and Philippi are unknown except for the implications of these verses. Groups of believers had possibly sprung up in other parts of the province since the beginning of Paul's Macedonian mission (Ac 16:9–12). With some allowance for Paul's hyperbolic "all," it is safe to assume that a goodly proportion of the believers in the province had been touched by the Thessalonians' unselfish concern. Otherwise, the missionary zeal reflected in 1:8 lacks clear substantiation.

As exemplary as the Thessalonians had been (1:3; 3:6), however, further progress remained a goal for them (3:12). Paul repeats and particularizes v.1 in the expression, "we urge you, brothers, to do so more and more." More love is always possible for Christians because the ultimate example of Christ himself (Jn 13:34; 15:12) is infinite and can only be approached, never fully reached.

4. Individual independence (4:11–12)

These verses stand in close grammatical connection with v.10b. Yet the logical connection is not immediately obvious. From the subject of love, Paul changes to something quite different—namely, the importance of industry and individual responsibility in Christian living. The two are not completely unrelated. Nothing disrupts the peace of a Christian community more than the unwillingness of members to shoulder their part of the responsibility for it. To disturb tranquility violates the love that permeates a truly Christian community. More specifically, some members of the Thessalonian church appear to have taken advantage of the liberality of other Macedonian Christians (cf. 2Co 8:1–5) in accepting financial help while making no effort at self-support, a condition that later grew worse (2Th 3:6–15).

We do not know the reason for this idleness. But since these two letters are so strongly eschatological, it is probable that the condition stemmed from their misapplying truths about the Lord's return to their daily living. Christians must never evade their daily responsibilities under the pretense of preparing for Christ's return. To do so is to distort this great hope.

11 That restlessness may have been a problem for the Thessalonians is implied by Paul's exhortation—"make it your ambition to lead a quiet life." His exhortation to "mind your own business" implies that the meddlesome spirit that often goes with restlessness was troubling them. Busybodies were active (2Th 3:11) and needed a reprimand. But Paul means more than telling them to stay out of other people's affairs; he also wants them to keep their own affairs in order. A third exhortation, "work with your hands," suggests that idleness was likely a problem among the

Thessalonians. In a Greek culture that degraded manual labor, Christianity joined with Judaism in viewing work as an honorable pursuit. Most of the Thessalonian believers earned their living with their hands. Paul tells them to continue supporting themselves and thus avoid the pitfalls of idleness.

12 These exhortations find a twofold purpose. (1) The Thessalonians will "win the respect of outsiders," i.e., those who have no connection with Christ and hence are outside the family of God. Such people readily recognize proper conduct and are repelled by those who do not carry their share of social responsibility. (2) They will not "be dependent on anybody." Of course, independence in an absolute sense is neither possible nor even desirable. We must understand Paul's admonitions not to be dependent in the light of the situation described in this section.

B. Exhortation Regarding Eschatological Needs (4:13–5:11)

1. The dead in Christ (4:13–18)

Another issue raised by Timothy's report requires clarification: the part of the Christian dead in Christ's *parousia* (see comment on 2:19). Paul discusses this new subject in one of the classic NT passages on the Lord's return (vv.13–18). The Thessalonians' lack of knowledge concerning the part their fellow Christians who had died would have at the *parousia* led him to write this reassuring paragraph.

13 Paul's words "we do not want you to be ignorant" introduce his correction of false impressions (cf. Ro 11:25; 1Co 10:1; 12:1). The Thessalonians had concluded that "those who fall asleep" (GK *3121*) would miss the victory and glory of the Lord's return. Paul chooses this phrase in lieu of the "the dead" because of death's temporary nature for Christians (cf. 1Co 7:39; 11:30; 15:6, 18, 20, 51; cf. also Jn 11:11). "Sleep" is an appropriate term for deceased Christians because of their assured bodily resurrection—a doctrine Paul had previously taught the Thessalonians. That this sleep refers to the physical body and not to a person's spirit (i.e., "soul sleep") is clear for several reasons. (1) Death for Paul did not mean a state of unconscious repose, but a condition of consciously being with Christ (Php 1:23). (2) "Those who sleep" thus continue their relationship with Christ in heaven while their bodies are in the grave. (3) The essential issue in this section is not the intermediate state before bodily resurrection, but the part that those who are raised bodily will play in the *parousia*.

Paul wants to deliver his readers from the grief experienced by "the rest of men" (cf. "outsiders," v.12). Non-Christians sorrow out of pity for the departed who have entered an unknown realm. For Christians, however, there need be no sorrow on behalf of those who are dead. Grief on behalf of the living and the loss sustained when a loved one dies is legitimate for Christians (Php 2:27), but that kind of grief is not in view here. Those who have died are better off than those left behind and will be equal participants in future resurrection and the glory of Christ.

14 For Christians, relief from sorrow is related to what the future holds. Just as "Jesus died and rose again," so will "those who have fallen asleep in him" be raised when God brings them to heaven with Jesus at his *parousia*. The fact of Jesus' death and resurrection guarantees as its sequel the eventual resurrection of the dead in Christ (see also 1:10).

It is significant that Paul does not refer to Jesus' death as "sleep." The difference between Jesus' experience and that of believers is that he really endured actual separation from God for the world's sins. Because of his real death, Christian death has been transformed into sleep.

Though we might expect Paul to write "God will raise" instead of "God will bring with Jesus," he used the latter because of an unexpressed connection in his mind between the two ideas. Being brought with Jesus presupposes a rising from the dead as part of the process (v.16)—a teaching Paul had presented to the Thessalonians. Their ultimate anticipation is not just that of being raised, but that of being "with Jesus" (4:14; cf. 4:17; 5:10). The words "God will bring" further point to a continuing movement heavenward after the meeting in the air (v.17), until the arrival in the Father's presence (3:13; cf. Jn 14:2–3). A more detailed analysis of the process follows.

15–17 The authority that validates Paul's affirmation in v.14 is nothing less than "the Lord's own word" (cf. 1:8). Various attempts have been made to identify this source more specifically. Some say Jesus spoke the words while on earth, their substance being recorded later in such places as Mt 24:30–31 and Jn 6:39–40; 11:25–26. Similarities between 1Th 4:15–17 and the gospel accounts include a trumpet (Mt 24:31), a resurrection (Jn 11:25–26), and a gathering of the elect (Mt 21:31). Yet dissimilarities between it and the canonical sayings of Christ far outweigh the resemblances. For example, (1) in Matthew the Son of Man is coming on the clouds, in 1 Thessalonians ascending believers are in them; (2) in the former the angels gather, in the latter the Son does so personally; (3) in the former nothing is said about resurrection, while in the latter this is the main theme; (4) the former records nothing about the order of ascent, which is the principal lesson here in 1 Thessalonians. Distinctions between this and the Johannine passages are just as pronounced.

Other suggestions about the source also seem unlikely, such as a saying of Jesus not contained in the canonical gospels (cf. Ac 20:35). Because of its relevance to early Christian circumstances, such a saying of Jesus as important as this one would hardly have been passed over by the gospel writers. Nor is it likely that Paul was claiming this special authority for his own personal utterances.

The best solution is to see "the Lord's own word" as a direct revelation to the church through one of her prophets—Paul himself or possibly someone else. The NT prophet's function was to instruct and console believers (cf. v.18 with 1Co 14:31), utilizing predictions about the future in the process (Ac 11:27–28; 21:11). Since these elements are prominent here and since 1Co 15:51 classifies this subject as "mystery" revelation, which is a characteristic of prophetic utterances, this explanation of Paul's external authority is quite satisfactory. Nowhere in these letters are the addressees reminded of having heard this teaching previously, though they were fully informed about "the day of the Lord" (1Th 5:2). How they could have been uninformed about this detail of the *parousia* (v. 13) is not disclosed. Conceivably it was a special revelation to Paul as he was answering their question through Timothy. Whenever it came, it was now the privilege of the Thessalonians to know certain details about the role of departed believers in the *parousia*.

The first part of Paul's prophetic revelation in vv.15–17 tells what will not happen. Believers who are still alive at the *parousia* will not go to meet Christ before the dead in Christ do so (v.15). When Paul uses "we," he apparently places this event within his own lifetime. How then can it be explained that the *parousia* did not precede Paul's death? To theorize that Paul was mistaken and to consider biblical inspiration in the light of such errors is to ignore Paul's avoidance of date setting (5:1–2). In view of Jesus' own teaching about our not knowing the day or hour of his coming (Mt 24:36; cf. Ac 1:7), surely Paul would not limit it to his own life span.

There is some plausibility to seeing Paul as establishing two categories—those alive and those asleep. Since he did not fit into the latter, he had to place himself with the former. But this view fails to explain the emphasis in the Greek on the word "we" or tell us why Paul did not speak impersonally in the third person.

The best solution is to see Paul setting an example of expectancy for the church of all ages. Proper Christian anticipation includes the imminent return of Christ. His coming will be sudden and unexpected, an any-moment possibility. No divinely revealed prophecies remain to be fulfilled before that event. Without setting a date, Paul hoped that it would transpire in his own lifetime. While entertaining the possibility of his own death (2Ti 4:6–8) and not desiring to contravene Christ's teaching about delay (Mt 24:48; 25:5; Lk 19:11–27), Paul, along with all primitive Christianity, reckoned on the prospect of remaining alive until Christ returned (Ro 13:11; 1Co 7:26, 29; 10:11; 15:51–52; 16:22; Php 4:5)—a personal hope of his (2Co 5:1–4; Php 3:20–21; 1Ti 6:14; 2Ti 4:8; Tit 2:11–13). Had this not been the Thessalonians' outlook, their question regarding the dead in Christ and possible exclusion from the *parousia* would have been meaningless. They were thinking in terms of an imminent return, expecting to see it before their death. They were not anticipating an intervening period of messianic woes or birthpangs. Hence, Paul believed and taught his converts that the next event on the prophetic calendar for them was their being gathered to Christ.

This teaching about a future *parousia* that will be a cosmic and datable event in world history is as valid for the twentieth century as it was for the first. Just as God intervened in history through his Son's first coming, so he will do at his return.

The principal assertion of v.15, then, concerns those who are alive and anticipating Christ's momentary return and their relation to "those who have fallen asleep." The former group "will certainly not precede" the latter. This strong assertion alleviates the Thessalonians' apprehension about their dead.

The positive chronology of vv.16–17 supports this strong statement (cf. "for" at the beginning of v.16). "The Lord himself will come down from heaven," where he has been since ascending to the Father's right hand. In so doing, he will issue "a loud command" in order to awaken "those who have fallen asleep." Associated with the command will be "the voice of the archangel," probably Michael (Jude 9), and "the trumpet call" (cf. 1Co 15:52). Immediately thereafter, "the dead in Christ" will rise. Far from being excluded from the *parousia*, they will be main participants in the first act of the Lord's return. This word of comfort must have brought great relief to the Thessalonians, and it has certainly done so for innumerable Christians after them.

Only "after that" (v.17) will living Christians "be caught up" for the meeting with Christ. The interval separating these two groups will be infinitesimally small by human reckoning. Yet the dead in Christ will be the first to share in the glory of his visit. Then the living among whom Paul still hoped to be (cf. "we") will be suddenly snatched away ("caught up"; GK 773; cf. Ac 8:39; 2Co 12:2, 4; Rev 12:5). This term in Latin, *raptus*, is the source of the popular designation of this event as "the rapture." So sudden will it be that Paul likens it to a blinking of the eye (1Co 15:52). In this rapid sequence the living will undergo an immediate change from mortality to immortality (1Co 15:52–53), after which they will be insusceptible to death. Both resurrected and changed believers will ascend, be enshrouded in the clouds of the sky (cf. Ac 1:9), and "meet" the Lord somewhere in the interspace between earth and heaven ("air"; GK *113*).

The nature of this meeting deserves comment. Some feel that the technical force of the word "meet" (GK *561*) is relevant here—i.e., a visitor is formally met by a delegation of citizens and ceremonially escorted back into their city (cf. its use in Mt 25:6; Ac 28:15–16). On this basis, they contend that Christians go out to meet the Lord and return with him as he continues his advent to earth. But this is debatable. It should be emphasized that the saints are being snatched away rather than advancing on their own to meet the visitor. A meeting in the air is pointless unless they continue on to heaven with the Lord who has come out to meet them. Tradition stemming from Jesus' parting instructions fixes the immediate destination following the meeting as the Father's house, i.e., heaven (Jn 14:2–3).

The location is secondary, however, in light of the final outcome. To "be with the Lord forever" represents the fruition of a relationship begun at the new birth and far outweighs any other consideration of time and eternity.

18 With this word of assurance, Paul gives a basis for his converts to "encourage [GK *4151*] each other."

2. The day of the Lord (5:1–11)

a. The coming of the day (5:1–2)

1 With the perplexity about the dead in Christ resolved, Paul turns to a new subject, yet not one completely distinct from the previous one. The direct and affectionate address "brothers" marks the new discussion as an addition prompted by Timothy's report of the Thessalonians' situation. The nonarrival of the *parousia* had created another perplexity for them.

Despite their ignorance about the dead in Christ (4:13), they had received prior instruction regarding other eschatological matters. "We do not need to write to you" is Paul's attestation to this fact. "Times and dates" are well-known words describing the end times from two perspectives (cf. their use in Ac 1:7; 3:19–21). "Times" (GK *5989*) conceives more of elapsed time and hence a particular date when predictions will be fulfilled. "Dates" (GK *2789*; cf. Da 9:27, LXX; Mk 13:33; Eph 1:10; 1Ti 6:15; Heb 9:10; Rev 1:3; 22:10; et al.), while including some reference to extent of time, gives more attention to the character or quality of a given period, i.e., what signs will accompany the final events. During his first visit Paul had effectively communicated the basic features of precise times and accompanying circumstances of future events.

2 For this reason he could say to the Thessalonians, "You know very well" the features of "the day of the Lord." Their previous learning on this subject had been adequate and specific, including pertinent teachings of Christ (Mt 24:43; Lk 12:39).

The focus is on "the day of the Lord." This "day" (GK 2465) has multiple characteristics as described in the Bible. It is so associated with the ultimate overthrow of God's enemies (Isa 2:12) that it sometimes means "judgment" (1Co 4:3). It will be a day of national deliverance for Israel and a day of salvation (1Th 5:9), but it will also be a day when God's wrath puts extended pressure on his enemies (Isa 3:16–24; 13:9–11; Jer 30:7; Zep 1:14–18; 1Th 1:10; 2:16; et al.). By using "day of the Lord" terminology to describe the great tribulation, Christ includes the tribulation within its framework (cf. Mt 24:21 with Jer 30:7; Da 12:1; Joel 2:2). This time of trial at the outset of the earthly day of the Lord will not be brief, but comparable to a woman's labor before giving birth to a child (Isa 13:8; 26:17–19; 66:7ff.; Jer 30:7–8; Mic 4:9–10; Mt 24:8; 1Th 5:3). Growing human agony will be climaxed by Messiah's second coming to earth, a coming that will terminate this earthly turmoil through direct judgment. He cannot personally reappear on earth, however, until this preliminary period has run its course with Armageddon and other tribulation visitations (Rev 6–19). If Christ's triumphant return to earth (Rev 19.11–21) is part of the day of the Lord, as all admit, divine dealings preparatory to it must also be part of it.

But this earthly wrath does not pertain to those in Christ (v.9). They will meet Christ "in the air" and be separate from what God does with those on earth. The only way to hold that this meeting with Christ (i.e., the rapture) is an imminent prospect is to see it as simultaneous with the beginning of the divine judgment against earth. Only on that basis can both the Lord's personal coming and the "day's" coming be compared to a thief (cf. 2Pe 3:4, 10; Rev 3:3, 11; 16:15). They can arrive at any time (cf. 1:10), the "thief in the night" imagery marking the unexpectedness of both imminent events.

The Thessalonians had been instructed about these matters, though later they were to be deceived regarding them (2Th 2:1–2). Yet even with their present knowledge they had difficulty in applying the truths in a practical way while waiting for the day. So Paul seeks to alleviate this difficulty in the rest of this section.

b. Unbelievers and the day (5:3)

3 The surprise beginning of the day of the Lord has a twofold impact. For those who are not in Christ and therefore unprepared, the consequences will be far from cheerful. "People," "them," and "they" are identified only when v.4 contrasts them with the "brothers" who are the addressees. These "nonbrothers" compose an unbelieving world against whom the devastation of the coming day will be unleashed. Just as disaster overtakes the unsuspecting householder when set upon by a robber, so catastrophe will overcome the living who are spiritual outsiders.

Such people will be priding themselves on their secure lifestyles. "Peace" characterizes their inward repose, while "safety" reveals their freedom from outward interference. Yet when that tranquility seemingly reaches its peak, "destruction will come on them." "Destruction" (GK 3897) means utter and hopeless ruin, a loss of everything worthwhile, causing the victims to despair of life itself (Rev 9:6). Without being totally annihilated, they are assigned to wrath and denied the privileges of salvation (v.9).

Comparing the beginning of this period with a period of labor pains just before childbirth makes vivid the unexpectedness with which this day comes (cf. Isa 13:8–9; Jer 4:31; Hos 13:13; Mic 4:9). Pain is certainly involved in both (Isa 66:7) as are certainty and nearness, but "suddenly" points most prominently to the absence of any forewarning. Tribulation will become worldwide, rendering it impossible for non-Christians to escape.

c. Believers and the day (5:4–11)

4 In contrast to the non-Christians referred to in v.3 are the believers ("brothers") in Thessalonica. Continuing the figure of night (v.2), "darkness" (GK 5030) refers to the realm of wickedness and the darkened understanding and ignorance of impending doom that go with it. Such symbolical language occurs quite widely in biblical writings (cf. Dt 28:29; Job 19:8; Pss 11:2; 74:20; Isa 42:6–7; Jer 13:16; Mt 10:27; Jn 3:19; 8:12; Ro 13:12; Eph 5:8, 11; 1Jn 1:5–6; et al.). In reassuring his converts, Paul declares without qualification that believers in Christ belong to a realm different from that of the world. Thus they will not participate in "this day" of the Lord. It will not overtake them by surprise; their position in Christ guarantees their deliverance.

5 Paul's assertion that they are "all sons of the light and sons of the day" rules out living in darkness. "All" brings reassurance that none is excluded. The fainthearted may take heart as may those others who have been confused about the *parousia*.

To reinforce his point, Paul returns to the negative side. Putting light and day in inverse order, he excludes himself along with all Christians from the night of moral insensitivity. By a casual change from "you" to "we" he takes his place with his readers in accepting the exhortation of v.6. This dulls the edge of what would otherwise be a sharp rebuke. "The day" here has no reference to the eschatological day of the Lord, but is used metaphorically in association with spiritual light. Verse 5 guarantees the readers' participation in a spiritual environment entirely different from that of non-Christians.

6–7 Verse 5 provides a solid basis for the ethical behavior Paul now urges on the Thessalonians. Paul calls them to a lifestyle free from moral laxity. "Let us not sleep" represents the ethical insensitivity that besets people of the other realm. While it is impossible for the day of the Lord to catch Christians unprepared, it is possible for them to adopt the same lifestyle as those who will be caught unawares. Paul urges his readers not to let this happen.

Conduct in keeping with "the light" and "the day" also includes alertness. Inattention to spiritual priorities is utterly out of keeping for those who will not be subject to the coming day of wrath. Though the Thessalonians were, if anything, overly watchful to the point of neglecting other Christian responsibilities (4:11–12; 2Th 3:6–15), they were not to cease watching altogether.

Apparently being "self-controlled" (GK 3768) was a great need. This word denotes sobriety. To counteract what might become a state of wild alarm or panic, Paul urges self-control as a balance for vagaries arising from distorted views of the *parousia*. Undue eschatological excitement was a serious problem; spiritual sobriety was the cure.

To explain his exhortation in v.6, Paul appeals in v.7 to everyday experience. Sleep and drunkenness are most often associated with the night. So he illustrates his figurative use of "sleep" in v.6 by referring to the normal habit of sleep and uses "drunkenness" to point up his reference to sobriety.

8 Paul now resumes his exhortation but drops for the moment the need for alertness, speaking only of sobriety as a countermeasure against "spiritual" drunkenness. The idea of belonging to the realm of "spiritual" daylight goes back to vv.4–5 and becomes the motivation for self-controlled action. So Paul describes self-control in figurative language drawn from Isa 59:17 (cf. Eph 6:14–17). Though the breastplate and helmet were Roman military apparel, lexical similarity to the Isaiah passage points to the OT as the probable source for the reference to them here.

The relation of this soldierly figure of speech to sobriety has been a puzzle. Obviously soberness is a prerequisite to effective vigilance by a sentry on duty, though vigilance is covered in the earlier word on alertness (v.6). Intoxication prevents effective duty as a sentry, and this thought may supply the answer. To be armed against wild excitement with its disregard of normal Christian responsibilities requires soberness. Paul had earlier spoken of the need for calmness (4:11–12). The Thessalonians had already made significant progress in faith and love (1:3; 3:6), but additional improvement was still needed (3:10; 4:1, 10). So the breastplate of "faith and love" could furnish protection from the problems mentioned in 5:14. To these Paul added the indispensable helmet of the "hope of salvation" (cf. 1:10). These three (faith, love, and hope) strengthened them for their present trials and doubts. The Thessalonians could confidently anticipate a future deliverance not to be enjoyed by those in darkness (v.3), but assured to those in the realm of light (vv.4–5).

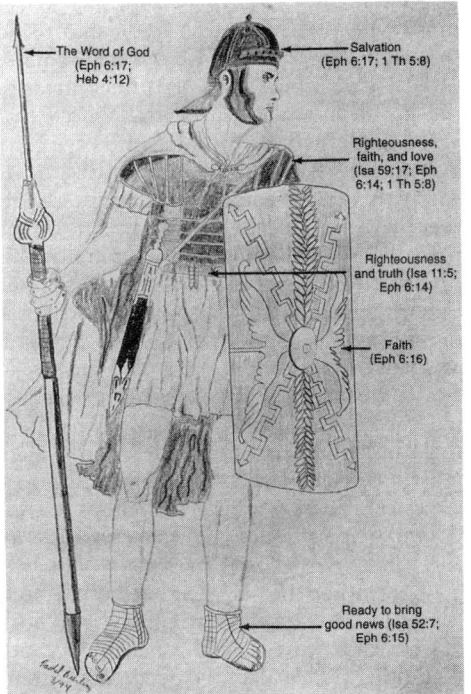

Paul used a fully dressed Roman soldier as a picture of the Christian warrior. Drawing by Rachel Bierling.

9 Paul now summarizes the reason for this guaranteed salvation. Negatively, "God did not appoint us to suffer wrath." Without question, this wrath is future and specific, being identified with the messianic era just prior to Christ's reappearance (1:10; 2:16) and with the sudden destruction mentioned in v.3. When God vents his anger against those who live on earth (Rev 6:16–17), the body of Christ will be in heaven as the result of the series of happenings outlined in 4:14–17. This is God's purpose.

The positive side of this purpose is that believers will "receive salvation through our Lord Jesus Christ." "Receive" (GK *4348*) here carries the idea of "possession" or "adoption." As Christians have been elected (1:4), they have also been adopted. For them to be possessed by God as his very own is synonymous with the future salvation to come "through our Lord Jesus Christ." In the certainty of this provision the Thessalonians could find relief from the frantic activity and panic that had been disturbing their tranquil anticipation of the future.

10 This verse is noteworthy. Here for the first time in Paul's writings, he states the specific means by which Jesus Christ procures our salvation: "He died for us"—though the death of Christ had undoubtedly been presented as the basis of all his teaching about salvation (cf. Ac 17:2–3). Though Paul's purpose here does not call for an extended discussion of that death, it is important in establishing the definite historical basis of our salvation. His death was "for us" or "on our behalf"—i.e., it was the sole condition whereby God procured as his peculiar possession a people destined for salvation when the rest of the world is plunged into the wrath of the future day.

"Awake [GK *1213*] or asleep [GK *2761*]" can be interpreted as metaphorical terms for the living and the dead. This would be consistent with Paul's discussion in 4:13–18 and match Jesus' use of "sleep" in raising Jairus's daughter (Mt 9:24). Yet this use of "asleep" is rare. It is better to take these two words in an ethical sense as in v.6. Since future salvation has been so fully provided by Christ's finished work, it cannot be cancelled by lack of readiness. Moral preparedness or unpreparedness does not affect the issue one way or the other; believers are secure in their salvation. Though this suggestion seems to nullify Paul's earlier exhortation to alertness (v.6), it must be acknowledged that this meaning is well established in other places in Scripture (Mt 24:42; 25:13; Mk 13:35, 37; Rev 3:3; 16:15).

But what about the seeming nullification of the exhortation of vv.6–8? This is a problem only if these exhortations are understood as relating just to watchfulness. We have not, however, found this to be the case. The Thessalonians were already watchful, and Paul warns them against extremes of overreaction. "Self-control" or "soberness" (vv.6, 8) serves as a complementary emphasis. Paul seeks to restore a proper balance between future anticipations and present obligations. In helping the Thessalonians, therefore, he had to calm their fears by convincing them of their participation in the *parousia* regardless of their degree of watchfulness. Every contingency has been met through the work done at Calvary by God himself. Christians need not fear missing the Lord's return, because they are "sons of the light and sons of the day" (vv.4–5). Their enjoyment of the future resurrection life in union with Christ is certain.

11 With such a guarantee, the Thessalonians are now equipped to "encourage one another and build each other up." As in 4:18, "encourage" (GK *4151*) has more a consolatory than a hortatory meaning. Here is an unconditional pledge to strengthen even the weakest in faith. These teachings can also "build ... up" (GK *3868*) Christians. This word was later to become one of Paul's favorite ways of writing about growth in the church (Eph 2:20–22; 4:12). An intellectual grasp of the provisions Paul has been describing leads to individual as well as collective growth of the body of Christ. Paul is quick to acknowledge progress along this line: "just as in fact you are doing." Yet he also looks forward to even greater attainments (cf. 4:1).

C. Exhortation Regarding Ecclesiastical Needs (5:12–22)

1. Responsibilities to the leaders (5:12–13)

12–13 No more effective way of carrying out mutual edification (v.11) can be found than Paul's closing exhortations for improvement within the assembly (vv.12–22). Heading the list are the exhortations regarding the proper attitude toward leaders (undoubtedly the elders and overseers, whose qualifications are described in more detail in 1Ti 3:1–2; 5:17; Tit 1:5). Paul requests ("we ask"; GK *2263*; cf. 4:1) that the Thessalonians "respect" (GK *3857*) those who "are over" (GK *4613*) them. This testifies to the presence of some form of church government in this early assembly; the leaders "stand over" the rest of the assembly in the Lord. Elsewhere "are over" bears the sense of "care for" (cf. Ro 12:6; 1Ti 3:4–5, 12; 5:17). Thus, Christian leaders must rule in such a way that the welfare of those ruled is uppermost in their minds (cf. Mt 20:26–28; 1Pe 5:2–3), though this element must not erode the authority of the office and the need to "respect" the office. The leaders were charged with guiding the congregation, and their decisions were binding (cf. Heb 13:17). It is important to note that this authority was not vested in one person.

In addition to caring leadership of the people, the leaders "work hard" among them—reminiscent of Paul and his colleagues with their unselfish toiling to support themselves while sharing the Gospel with the Thessalonians (2:9). It is appropriate for those who follow them in leadership to do the same. Thus they become local examples of how love works hard (1:3) in contrast to the problem group within the church that was doing practically nothing (4:11).

Finally, the leaders "admonish" (GK *3805*); this means correction administered either by word or deed. It implies blame on the part of the one admonished. Naturally, this process arouses resentment, since discipline is never pleasant. Still the apostle presents admonition as necessary for the congregation and requires respect for those who exercise it.

Another part of Paul's "request" regarding leadership is that the Thessalonians "hold them in highest regard in love" (v.13). They must hold these leaders in the highest possible esteem and give them wholehearted support in a spirit of love. No reservations are allowable.

Concluding the brief exhortation about leadership is a general command for both leaders and those led: "Live in peace with each other." That Paul included such a command shows that relations were not all they could have been. Perhaps there was trouble between the idle and those who were admonishing them. But no matter who was to blame, there had to be peaceful relations. Leaders were to guard against abusing their authority; idlers were not to disregard those over them in the Lord.

2. Responsibilities to all (5:14–15)

14 Paul now begins a new and stronger set of brief commands to all the Christians ("brothers"). "We urge" (GK *4151*) is more authoritative than Paul's previous "we ask" (5:12; cf. 4:1).

"Warn" (GK *3805*; cf. "admonish" in v.12) is an injunction to Christians in general, not just a limited few. The entire local body copes with practical situations by advising an errant believer. The only ones excused from the obligation to warn are those in need of warning, in this case described as "those who are idle" (GK *864*)—i.e., those who by their idleness are disorderly in conduct (cf. 2Th 3:6–7). A certain amount of unbecoming behavior had already appeared in the Thessalonian church (1Th 4:11–12).

"Encourage [GK *4170*; cf. "comfort" in 2:12] the timid" concerns a different need. Words of comfort to the fainthearted are also needed. In the light of ch. 4, those who needed comfort were both troubled over their friends who had died in Christ (4:13) and confused about what the *parousia* held for themselves (5:1–11). Within this letter Paul has given ample information for removing these misgivings.

"Help the weak" almost certainly relates to moral and spiritual debility. Whether it was weakness in shrinking from persecution (3:3–5), yielding to temptations to immorality (4:3–8), or something else cannot be precisely determined. It may well have been weakness in exercising full Christian liberty in doubtful matters (see Ro 14:1–15:6; 1Co 8–10). Whatever it was, the strong in faith were responsible to support those who were weak.

Summing up the previous three commands is a fourth general one: "Be patient [GK 3428] with everyone." This pictures the even-tempered response of one who is slow to anger. Dealing with the "idle," "the timid," and "the weak" requires this special disposition because they so often refuse to respond immediately to constructive counsel. Yet these are not the only ones requiring patient treatment. All Christians at one time or another provoke dissatisfaction through thoughtless or even intentionally hurtful acts. They too need patient treatment.

15 When tempers run short, the whole group has the responsibility for seeing that no member "pays back wrong for wrong." The natural tendency to retaliate and inflict injury for a wrong suffered must be strongly resisted, no matter what the injury. The Christian stand against retaliation crystallized very early, no doubt being formulated from principles established by Jesus in his Sermon on the Mount (see comments on Mt 5:38–42). Jesus emphatically set the tone for his followers in forbidding personal revenge altogether. Paul deals with this subject in more detail in Ro 12:17–21. Peter also shows the influence of this teaching (1Pe 2:19–23; 3:9). Nonretaliation for personal wrongs is perhaps the best evidence of personal Christian maturity.

Paul goes on to give a constructive alternative to retaliation: "Always try to be kind to each other and to everyone else." Eager expenditure of all one's energies is none too much in seeking to a be kind. Christians must diligently endeavor to produce what is intrinsically beneficial to others, whether other Christians ("each other") or unbelievers ("everyone else"). The seriousness of the abuse suffered is no issue. Some Thessalonians doubtless had been victims of unjustified harsh treatment, but regardless of this, a positive Christian response is the only suitable recourse. The welfare of the offender must be the prime objective.

3. Responsibilities to oneself (5:16–18)

16 Compliance with the social regulations of vv.12–15 is impossible apart from personal communion with God. So Paul turns to the believer's inner life. In the exhortation "Be joyful always," he voices a theme that is characteristic of the NT writings, beginning with Jesus' Sermon on the Mount (Mt 5: 11–12; see also Ac 5:41; 16:25; Php 1:18; 4:4). The uniqueness of Christian joy lies in its emergence under adverse circumstances. Paul states the paradox succinctly in 2Co 6:10: "sorrowful, yet always rejoicing" (cf. 2Co 12:10). The Thessalonian Christians had already suffered with joy (1Th 1:6) as had Paul himself (3:9). The challenge is for this joyful outlook to become constant. From a human perspective they had every reason not to be joyful—persecution from outsiders and friction among themselves. Yet in Christ they are to be more and more joyful.

17 Intimately related to constant joy is incessant prayer—the only way to cultivate a joyful attitude in times of trial. Uninterrupted communication with God keeps temporal and spiritual values in balance. "Continually" (GK 90; cf. 1:2–3; 2:13; Ro 1:9) does not mean nonstop praying. Rather, it implies constantly recurring prayer, growing out of a settled attitude of dependence on God. Whether words are uttered or not, lifting the heart to God while one is occupied with miscellaneous duties is the vital thing. Verbalized prayer will be spontaneous and will punctuate one's daily schedule, as it did Paul's writings (3:11–13; 2Th 2:16–17).

18 A final member of this triplet for personal development is "Give thanks in all circumstances." No combination of happenings can be termed "bad" for a Christian because of God's constant superintendence (Ro 8:28). We need to recognize that seeming aggravations are but a temporary part of a larger plan for our spiritual well-being. Out of this perspective we can always discern a cause for thanks. In fact, failure to do this is a symptom of unbelief (Ro 1:21).

"For this is God's will for you in Christ Jesus" justifies all three brief commands. Rejoicing, praying, and giving thanks do not exhaust God's will but are vital parts of it. "In Christ Jesus" is a significant qualification of God's will because only here can inner motives be touched. Paul's earlier rule, the Mosaic law, was strong on outward conformity, but was helpless to deal with human thoughts. It could not dictate an inner attitude even though it was a perfect expression of God's will. In union with Christ, together with an accompanying inward transformation (2Co 5:17), however, compliance with God's standards can extend to motives. These three commands penetrate the innermost recesses of human personality—the spring from which all outward obedience flows. The true victories in life are won by Christians who are joyful, prayerful, and thankful.

4. Responsibilities to public worship (5:19–22)

19 Paul now shifts from the personal life to communal worship (vv.19–22). "Do not put out the Spirit's fire" alludes to the Holy Spirit as a burning presence (cf. 2Ti 1:6). In particular, this is his impartation of specialized capabilities for ministry to people in the body of Christ. In his discussions of spiritual gifts elsewhere (Ro 12:6–8; 1Co 12:8–10, 28–30; Eph 4:11), Paul distinguishes eighteen such special abilities—half of which involve speaking publicly. When he commands, "Stop putting out the Spirit's fire" (lit. translation of v.19), he advocates stopping something already being practiced. Perhaps gifts other than prophecy (cf. v.20) had been abused, so that the more sober-minded leadership overreacted and prohibited Spirit manifestations altogether, with a resulting loss of spiritual benefit. Paul forbids such repression here. The proper course is to allow gifted people to share in a decent and orderly fashion what the Spirit can do through them for edifying of the body of Christ (1Co 14:12, 26, 40). Control is necessary, but overcontrol is detrimental. The leadership and the whole community must find the right balance.

20 Paul's next prohibition, "Do not treat prophecies with contempt," suggests that the Christians at Thessalonica, like those at Corinth (1Co 14:1), had underrated the gift of prophecy. This involved utterances of those who in their prophetic office proclaimed the will and command of God as well as predicted the future (Ac 11:28). Benefits from these utterances could build up a local church (1Co 14:3).

Apparently, however, certain "idle" brothers (v.14; cf. 4:11–12) had misused this gift by falsifying data regarding the Lord's return. This had soured the remainder of the flock against prophecy in general. Their tendency now was not to listen to any more prophetic messages, but to discount them in view of counterfeit utterances they had heard. Once again Paul warns against overreaction and urges the church to give prophecies their proper place in edifying its members (cf. v.11).

21 To balance the two prohibitions, Paul stipulates that all charismatic manifestations be tested with a view to accepting what is valid and disallowing what is not (vv.21–22). "Everything" is subject to the limitation of vv.19–20 (i.e., the exercise of spiritual gifts). The mere claim to inspiration is not a sufficient guarantee, because inspirations are known at times to come from below (1Co 12:2). The nature of the "test" (GK *1507*) is not specified, but suggestions are forthcoming from related passages. In 1Jn 4:1ff. (cf. 1Co 12:3), the test is theological in nature, having to do with a proper view of Jesus as the Christ and Lord. In 1Co 12:10; 14:29, discernment is a specific spiritual function in combination with the gift of prophecy; it consists of an ability to discern whether another's prophetic speech is genuinely inspired. But perhaps these two tests are too specialized for the present context, and preference should be given to a more general criterion of whether a positive contribution to the body's edification and mutual love has been made.

Testing like this will identify some spiritual activities as attractive and conducive to a growing love and to Christian power (5:11; 1Co 13; 14:3–5, 12, 26). These are genuine gifts and should be clung to tenaciously. Regarding "hold on to the good," Paul speaks of a determined tenacity to retain what is beneficial to the church (cf. Ro 12:9). The Thessalonian church had been remiss in this (vv.19–20).

22 Allowance must also be made for professed spiritual manifestations that do not contribute but rather detract from the development of the local body. Paul designates this category by "every kind of evil." That is, spiritual gifts could be of an "evil" (GK 4505) variety, falsely attributed to the Holy Spirit (2Th 2:9–10). Paul clearly intends here an antithesis with v.21: "Hold on to" (GK 2988; v.21) what the Spirit reveals as good, but "avoid" (lit., "hold yourselves free from"; GK 600) every kind of evil that tries to parade as a genuine representation of the Spirit. Only then can the body of Christ achieve maximum benefit in local worship.

V. Conclusion (5:23–28)

A. Petition for the Thessalonians (5:23–24)

23 Having concluded his assorted suggestions for practical improvement, Paul looks to God to grant these objectives in the light of the Lord's return (cf. 3:12–13). Sexual purity (4:3–8), brotherly love (4:9–10), personal independence (4:11–12), understanding the *parousia* (4:13–5:11), respect for leaders, love for other people, rejoicing, prayer, thankfulness, and concern for public worship (vv.12–22) are possible only through God. "I have simply told you all these things to do," Paul is saying, "but God alone has power to make your efforts a success."

Paul addresses God as the giver "of peace" (cf. 1Co 14:33), who has provided for a harmonious relationship between himself and humankind through Christ's death. At this point, in light of exhortations that imply at least a trace of disharmony (4:6, 10–12; 5:12–22), he invokes God's intervention as peacemaker.

Throughout the letter Paul has been concerned with sanctification (3:13; 4:3–4, 7–8). Now he prays that God will indeed "sanctify" (i.e., separate to himself; GK 39) his readers "through and through." This expression speaks of the ultimate maturity of Christian character. It presents the *qualitative* side of spiritual advance in its final perfection.

The *quantitative* objective of the prayer is in the word "whole" (GK 3908). Wholeness pertains to three parts of the human make-up, "spirit, soul and body." Paul petitions that this wholeness may be "kept" (or "preserved"; GK 5498) and that it may be "blameless at the coming of our Lord Jesus Christ."

The question arises as to how Paul conceives of the human being in the words "spirit, soul and body." Among the various explanations of this expression are these four: (1) Paul intends no systematic dissection of human personality. Instead, he uses a loose rhetorical expression emphasizing the totality of personality, reinforced by "through and through" and "whole" (cf. the comparable expression in Dt 6:5; Mk 12:30; Lk 10:27). (2) "Spirit" and "soul" are interchangeable, both referring to a person's immaterial substance. "Body" then completes the picture by referring to the material part: "your whole spirit (i.e., soul) and body." This sees the human being as dichotomous. (3) Others divide the last sentence of v.23 either into two independent parts or join "may your whole spirit" with the first part of the verse (both of these require adding words that are not in the Greek). (4) Paul saw a human being as a threefold substance, body, soul, and spirit.

Of the four options, this fourth one is by far the preferred interpretation, being generally recognized since the early fathers. The symmetrical arrangement of three nouns with their articles and their connection (in Greek) by means of two "ands" render this the most natural explanation. That Paul elsewhere does not make such a distinction is no argument against trichotomy. A trichotomous understanding of v.23 has so much to commend it that other interpretations cannot compete without summoning arguments from elsewhere. The difference between the material part ("body"; GK 5393) and the immaterial parts ("spirit"; GK 4460; and "soul"; GK 6034) is obvious in other places in Paul's writings (e.g., Ro 7:17–23; 1Co 2:14–15; 14:14; 15:44).

The "spirit" is the part that enables us to perceive the divine. Through this component we can know and communicate with God. This higher element, though damaged through the fall of Adam, is sufficiently intact to provide each individual a consciousness of God. The "soul" is the sphere of our will and emotions, the true center of personality, which gives us a self-consciousness that relates to the physical world through the body and to God through the spirit. The "body" is the physical side of the human person. This analysis of humankind had been Paul's training in the OT, though much unresolved mystery remains regarding the interrelationships between the different parts, including the body. How one affects the other is fully understood only by the Creator.

For such a composite creature Paul therefore prays, seeking an unblamable wholeness in the presence "of our Lord Jesus Christ" (cf. 2:19; 3:13).

24 To Paul, utterance of a prayer was not the end, but only the means to it. One who asks God for something can anticipate the fulfillment of that request because of God's character: "The one who calls you is faithful." He who issues an effectual call can be absolutely relied on to carry out his call (see comment on 2:12), including among other things the sanctification and preservation prayed for in v.23. Faithfulness is the characteristic of God that determines that he will do exactly as Paul has prayed. In his election of the Thessalonian church (1:4; 2:12), God had already determined to do so. This, however, did not render prayer for them superfluous, as human effort and application also have their place in carrying out the purposes of God.

B. Reciprocation by the Thessalonians (5:25–27)

25 Following his prayer, Paul offers his readers opportunity to reciprocate along three lines. First, he requests prayer for himself and his fellow missionaries. The scope of "brothers" presents two possibilities. On the one hand, Paul may be referring to the church leaders (cf. "all the brothers" in vv.26–27). But a strict distinction cannot be made between leaders and followers in vv.26–27. Moreover, vv.12–13 (which also have "brothers") address the congregation at large and even tend to exclude leadership. In each case where "brothers" is found earlier in the letter, the whole church is included. Hence, Paul probably follows his customary policy of requesting prayer from the total body, not just from a limited few (Ro 16:16; 1Co 16:20; 2Co 13:12).

Paul depended on his converts' spiritual support (Ro 15:30; Eph 6:19; Php 1:19; Col 4:3; 2Th 3:1; Phm 22). So now he asks for a continuing place in their prayers (v.17), similar to the place they have been given in his (vv.23–24).

26 A second closing request is for all the brothers to be greeted with "a holy kiss." Paul's usual "one another" (Ro 16:16; 1Co 16:20; 2Co 13:12; cf. 1Pe 5:14) is replaced this time by "all the brothers," an expression that may imply that the request is addressed to leaders only. This need not distinguish leaders from the rest of the assembly, however, as the letter will eventually find its way to all (v.27). In the meantime those receiving it first were to greet the rest with a holy kiss. This was not a kiss of respect as was used in ancient times to honor men of authority. Neither was it cultic as though copied from an ancient mystery religion. It most closely parallels the use of a kiss among members of the same family as a token of their close relationship. Christians have come into the family of God and have even closer ties than those of any human family (Mt 12:46–50). It was appropriate that a symbolic greeting be adopted. It was to be "holy," i.e., such as is becoming to saints; this may have involved the custom of men kissing men and women kissing women so as to forestall any suspicion of impropriety. A Jewish synagogue practice, it could easily have found its way into early Christian assemblies.

27 The third parting word is more than just a request. The formula "I charge you before the Lord" shows an unusual concern on Paul's part regarding the possibility of his letter's not being read. Invoking an oath and switching to the first person singular indicate his urgency. He may have feared that the contents of the letter might be limited to those interested in a particular issue (e.g., about those who had fallen asleep in Christ; 4:13–18). Perhaps he was aware that some were already at work attributing wrong teaching to his name and authority (2Th 2:2). Or he could have feared a breakdown in communications between the church's leadership and some of the communicants within the church (4:11–12; 5:12–13). Probably Paul sensed the far-reaching import of the teaching of the letter and its binding authority as part of a canon of Scripture (1Co 14:37). Whatever the case, this charge has implications of divine punishment for failure to comply. The first recipients of the letter, probably the church leaders, were bound under oath "to have this letter read to all the brothers."

Obviously it was to be read aloud, in line with the classical meaning of "read" (GK 336). With few people receiving a formal education, not all participants in Christian circles were able to read for themselves. The further limitation of insufficient copies and expense of writing materials prohibited distribution to all. The only solution was to give the letter a place in public worship alongside the OT Scripture, the consequence of which would eventually be ecclesiastical recognition of its authority as an inspired book.

C. Benediction (5:28)

28 This customary benediction was probably added in Paul's own handwriting (cf. 2Th 3:17–18). His distinctive farewell was always built around his favorite concept, "grace" (GK 5921), which replaced the farewell that was typically used in ancient letters (cf. Ac 15:29). This trait is distinctive in his letters whether his benediction is longer (2Co 13:14) or shorter (Col 4:18; 1Ti 6:21; 2Ti 4:22; Tit 3:15). The primacy of grace resulting from the saving work of "our Lord Jesus Christ" was a constant theme as the apostle sought the welfare of those whom he served (cf. 1:1).

2 Thessalonians

INTRODUCTION

1. Background

Paul's interest in his Thessalonian converts did not terminate with the dispatch of the first letter. His ministry was one of continual discipling of those he had won to Christ. This second letter was written only slightly later than 1 Thessalonians. Its background is therefore essentially the same (see introduction to 1 Thessalonians), with only slight additions. While he was still in Corinth, Paul received further word about this church's condition; this report prompted him to write 2 Thessalonians.

2. Authorship and Canonicity

The external evidence for the Pauline authorship of 2 Thessalonians is stronger than for 1 Thessalonians. Several of the Apostolic Fathers and some of the early church fathers clearly refer to it. In addition, the witnesses cited for 1 Thessalonians (see introduction) add their support to the Pauline authorship and early canonical recognition of 2 Thessalonians.

In spite of this, some scholars offer objections to Pauline authorship, mostly on internal grounds. (1) The objection most widely used finds in 2 Thessalonians an eschatology different from that of 1 Thessalonians, one that represents a Christian perspective that arose after the destruction of Jerusalem in A.D. 70. The principal difference cited is emphasis on certain signs prior to the *parousia* in 2 Thessalonians, in contrast to 1 Thessalonians' presentation of the event as something that may come at any moment. This commentary, however, will explain in detail why these two letters are not in conflict. A right understanding of the several phases of the *parousia* and of the meaning of 2Th 2:3 shows harmony between the two letters. Differing circumstances in Thessalonica called for emphasizing different aspects of end-time events.

(2) Paul's authorship is also questioned because of a supposed different view of the last judgment. The reversal of fates, with the persecutors receiving tribulation and the persecuted relief (2Th 1:5ff.), is not paralleled in Paul's acknowledged writings. This objection stereotypes Paul's thinking unreasonably to the point of prohibiting him from expressing his eschatology in added dimensions. Far from belonging to a later generation, vengeance in connection with the Lord's return is traceable to Jesus himself (Mt 24:15–22; 25:31–46; Lk 21:22) and to the OT (Isa 66:15). Paul simply developed it in 2 Thessalonians more than elsewhere (cf. also Ro 2:5–10).

(3) A third objection to its being post-Pauline is that it assigns divine attributes and functions to Christ. To some, the differences between the prayers of 1Th 3:11–13 and 2Th 2:16; 3:5 reveal that 2 Thessalonians could not have been written during Paul's lifetime. To affirm, however, that Paul never believed in the deity of Christ is precarious. Even 1 Thessalonians sees him as a source of divine grace (1:1; 5:28), as one to whom prayer is properly addressed (3:11–12), and as one to whom future accountability must be given (2:19). Both letters have a high view of Christ's person.

3. Date

If one accepts the accuracy of Acts 17–18, this letter must have been written during Paul's stay in Corinth, for Paul, Silas, and Timothy are not known to have been together after that. The conditions are still generally the same as those represented in 1 Thessalonians. That letter must have come earlier because its autobiographical portions leave no room for correspondence between Paul's departure from the city and the letter itself. A date shortly after 1 Thessalonians is most probable for the writing of 2 Thessalonians, perhaps late in the summer of A.D. 50.

4. Occasion and Purpose

Three main developments prompted the writing of 2 Thessalonians. (1) Persecution of Christians in Thessalonica had grown worse and was leaving victims at the point of despair. (2) A pseudo-Pauline letter and other false representations (see 2:2) were on the point of convincing believers that the end time was already present because of their increased suffering. (3) The nearness of Christ's return had been misused as a basis for shirking vocational responsibilities even more than at the time of 1 Thessalonians.

To meet the needs that occasioned this second letter, Paul pursued three broad purposes. (1) He provided an incentive for the Thessalonians to persevere a little longer by describing the reward and retribution issuing from the future judgment of God (1:3–10). (2) He clarified prominent events belonging to the day of the Lord to prove the falsity of claims that that day had already arrived (2:1–12). (3) He issued detailed instructions covering disciplinary steps the church was to take in correcting those who refused to work (3:6–15).

5. Theological Values

For the doctrines that are unique to 2 Thessalonians and those held in common with 1 Thessalonians, see the introduction to 1 Thessalonians.

EXPOSITION

I. Salutation (1:1–2)

1–2 After a period of several months, reports from Thessalonica about new conditions, especially some worsening problems, reached Paul while he and his missionary party were still in Corinth, leading him to write this second letter and to provide solutions.

The salutation is identical with that of the first letter (cf. comments on 1Th 1:1) except for two additions. The first is "our" in the expression "God our Father" (v.1). God is the Father of Christians. His being the Father of Jesus Christ is expressed elsewhere (e.g., 2Co 1:3; Eph 1:3; 1Pe 1:3).

The second addition is the phrase "from God the Father and the Lord Jesus Christ" in v.2. Identifying the sources of "grace and peace" occurs in all other Pauline superscriptions except 1Th 1:1. The words make explicit what is already implicit: God is ultimately the only source of grace and peace. Two persons of the Godhead are specified: the Father and the Son. To Paul, Jesus was Deity in the fullest sense. This is the only justification for placing his name beside the Father's as co-author of the unmerited favor and harmonious relationship pronounced in this greeting.

II. Assurance of Repayment at God's Righteous Judgment (1:3–12)

A. Thanksgiving for Present Perseverance (1:3–10)

1. Healthy development (1:3–5a)

3 As is his practice in every letter but Galatians, Paul begins his remarks by thanking God for the spiritual progress of his addressees. Here his appreciation is marked by a feature found nowhere else except later in this same letter (2:13)—that he was obligated (cf. "we ought"; GK 4053) to express gratitude for what God had done in their lives. His thanksgiving Paul conceived of as his duty to God. Paul felt an intense compulsion to give gratitude to God for what Christ had done and was doing in believers. His own post-conversion service was invested as a partial repayment for the personal debt he himself incurred when God gave him salvation (see Ro 1:14; 1Co 9:16–17).

"And rightly so" anticipates Paul's description of the readers' sterling performance amid persecutions and supplies a second reason for thanksgiving. Paul habitually gave credit where credit was due. The conduct of his readers "under fire" was so commendable that he could not refrain giving credit again.

So great was Paul's excitement over their progress that he gives some details: "because your faith is growing more and more, and the love every one of you has for each other is increasing." Faith and love comprehend the total Christian walk (cf. 1Co 16:13–14; 2Co 8:7; Gal 5:6; Eph 1:15; 3:17; 6:23; 1Th 3:6). The absence of "hope" from this combination is not overly significant. "Faith," an area commended in the first letter (see comment on 1Th 1:3), was something that needed improvement (cf. 1Th 3:10); apparently it had grown during his absence. "Love" too was a quality he had not only already commended them for (1Th 1:3; 4:9–10) but also prayed to increase (1Th 3:12). It is no wonder, then, to find him rejoicing over their growth in faith and love.

4 In further reference to this radical improvement Paul says, "among God's churches we boast [GK *1595*] about your perseverance and faith." Why this stress on the missionaries' boasting? Was Paul suggesting that those who establish a church normally do not brag about that church? Paul's intent here is probably to contrast the missionaries' boasting with the Thessalonians' self-evaluation. At least some of these Christians felt inferior because of failures (1Th 5:14) and so were not inclined to boast. Paul speaks to this discouragement when he says, "As far as we are concerned your progress has been tremendous, so much so that we boast about it to other churches." The churches to which Paul had boasted were probably more widespread than in the vicinity of Corinth. Churches everywhere had heard this report, either through letter or through personal contact with those visiting Paul in Corinth.

The boasting pertains to "your perseverance and faith in all the persecutions and trials you are enduring." "Perseverance" (GK *5705*) is the attitude that accepts trying circumstances without retarding progress (cf. also comment on "endurance" in 1Th 1:3). Accompanying the perseverance of the Thessalonians was their "faith" (GK *4411*) or, perhaps better, their "faithfulness" (cf. Ro 3:3; Gal 5:22). Their tenacious loyalty to Christ in spite of fierce adversity is what Paul finds so remarkable. "Persecutions" (GK *1501*) are sufferings incurred because of faith in Christ, while "trials" (GK *2568*) are troubles of any kind. The believers were "enduring" (GK *462*) these—but only for the time being; in God's plan such conditions were not to be permanent.

5a Instead of beginning a new paragraph, "all this is evidence that God's judgment is right" should probably be read with the end of v.4. The subject of Paul's boasting—i.e., their perseverance and faithfulness—is proof positive of God's righteous judgment. That he gives strength enough to face all the persecutions and trials victoriously shows that his "judgment is right." Withstanding present pressures demonstrates the rightness of God's future judgment. The phrase about righteous judgment here sets the tone for 1:5b–10, which describes what is to come.

2. Righteous judgment (1:5b–10)

a. Categorization of participants (1:5b–7a)

This section (vv.5b–10) expands on the reference to God's future righteous judgment in v.5a. Paul first describes what it will mean to victims of present persecution (v.5b). He then points out the fate of persecutors (v.6) and follows this with a second look at what will happen to the persecuted (v.7a).

5b Future reckoning assures a future recognition of the worthiness of those suffering for the sake of the kingdom of God. This recognition will not be self-earned but is graciously imparted by God as a result of their decision to believe in the Lord Jesus (1:3, 10; 2:13; 1Th 1:8), who himself earned the believer's forgiveness of sins and eternal life by dying a sacrificial death (1Th 5:10). The worthiness of the Thessalonian believers had already been established before persecutions came. Their firm stand in the face of persecutions (v.4) confirmed their relationship to God and was a pledge that their worthiness will be openly declared by God.

The Greek of v.5b has the word "also": "for which you also [untranslated in NIV] are suffering." That is, believers in Thessalonica were not the only ones suffering this kind of treatment; there were others, such as Paul, Silas, and Timothy (cf. Ac 17:5; 1Th 2:2; 2Th 3:2). With opposition behind them, all who are Christ's at his *parousia* (see comment on 1Th 2:19) will be welcomed into the messianic kingdom on the ground of their God-given worthiness.

6 On the other hand, those responsible for troubling Christians will be repaid proportionately for the suffering they have caused. This is only "just" (GK *1465*; translated "right" in v.5) in God's eyes; i.e., this future judgment is righteous. The antagonists will thus receive "trouble" (GK *2568*), a term not further defined at this point (cf. v.9). This word is often translated "tribulation." It is the present lot of Christians to undergo tribulation (v.4; 1Th 3:4). For the rest of the world, however, tribulation will be future and far greater in intensity (Mt 24:21; cf. Rev 3:10). In his first letter to this church, Paul described this period in relation to its source—God's wrath (1:10; 2:16; 5:9). But here he speaks of it from the standpoint of circumstances that engulf the victims. After the period of tribulation has passed, these troublers will be denied entrance into the messianic kingdom that welcomes the faithful followers of Christ (v.5; Mt 25:41, 46).

7a The other side of God's justice is full bestowal of rest on those who have been "troubled" (GK 2567), a reward awaiting Paul and his co-workers also. This will be the relief from tension and suffering that belongs to all who become Christ's disciples. Their rest and bliss in the future state (cf. Ac 3:19–20; Rev 14:13) are guaranteed by the justice of God. A sublime anticipation thus helps suffering Christians to maintain unwavering perseverance and faithfulness (cf. v.4).

Participants in God's righteous judgment, therefore, fall into these two classes: For the first class, the future holds a severe threat. Though their domination is tolerated for the present, at the proper time, the roles will be reversed. The second class, though under the heel of the other for the moment, will become the overcomers who will enjoy all privileges in God's kingdom.

b. Circumstances of fulfillment (1:7b)

7b "When the Lord Jesus is revealed" identifies the time of God's righteous judgment (see comments on vv.6–7a). As already suggested, the objects of Christ's revelation are twofold. (1) He will appear to those who are in Christ. It will be an appearance that means rest (1:7a) when he comes "from heaven" (cf. 1Th 4:16) to meet the dead and living in Christ in the air (1Th 4:17) and gather them to himself (2Th 2:1). This begins their unending fellowship with him (1Th 4:17; 5:10) and participation in his glory (2Th 1:10, 12). Paul hoped to be alive at this time (see comments on 1Th 4:15–17).

(2) The other group on whom God's righteous judgment and the revelation of the Lord Jesus will make their impact are their persecutors. The consequences for them will be prolonged and painful. Christ will begin by subjecting earth's rebels to a period of intense "trouble"—a time of human misery without parallel in the annals of history (Da 12:1; Mk 13:19). It will grow into a dominant factor during the time of "the rebellion ... and the man of lawlessness" (2:3). As the period runs its course, it will witness the abomination of desolation (2:4; cf. Da 9:27; 11:31, 36; 12:11; Mt 24:15) and the Satanic deception of an unbelieving world (2:9–10). This is the initial phase of God's vengeance against a world that persists in rebellion (cf. Lk 21:22; Rev 6:10; 19:2).

As the period draws to its close, the Lord Jesus will be revealed personally to culminate this vengeance with "everlasting destruction" and exclusion from the Lord's presence and glory (v.9). That time is a day of wrath and revelation of the righteous judgment of God (Ro 2:5; 1Th 1:10; 2:16; 5:9), just before the revelation of Christ's glory in the world.

Afflicted Christians, on the other hand, are offered the brightest anticipation. They look forward to the Lord Jesus' revelation from heaven and to the prospect of immediate rest. They will not be present for the apostasy (2:3), the rule of the lawless one (2:3–4) or his "counterfeit miracles, signs and wonders" (2:9), because their promised rest in heaven will have begun by then. With a hope like this there is ample reason to continue in faithfulness to the Lord.

The "blazing fire" of his coming recalls the glory of OT theophanies (Ex 3:2; 19:18; 24:17; Dt 5:4; Ps 18:12; Isa 30:27–30; Da 7:9–10). It will be a revelation of glory in which the saints will share (1:10, 12). The Lord Jesus will be accompanied by "his powerful angels," who will draw on his power for their part in the revelation.

Many have chosen to limit this "revelation" (GK 637) of Christ to a single event at the close of the tribulation. The role of "his powerful angels" favors this understanding in the light of Mt 24:30–31, 25:31. It is more persuasive, however, to explain revelation as a complex of events, including various phases of end-time happenings. The present context associates the word with Christ's coming for his own as well as his coming to deal with opponents. Since the primary thrust of vv.5–10 is to encourage suffering Christians, the meaning of this revelation for them should receive the emphasis. God's dealings with the rest of the world are included only to enhance the "relief" experienced by believers at the righteous judgment of God.

c. Consideration of repayment (1:8–10)

8 Two types of repayment to be meted out at the righteous judgment of God deserve consideration in light of the Christian's present trouble. One is toward the troublers (vv.8-9) and the other toward the troubled (v.10). "He will punish" (GK *1689*; lit., "render vengeance"—the word stem for "vengeance" is the same as that for "right" in v.5 and "just" in v.6) has no overtones of selfish vindictiveness or revenge, but proceeds from the justice of God to accomplish appropriate punishment for criminal offenses.

The recipients of God's avenging judgment will be in two groups. The first group is "those who do not know God." These people come from a Gentile background. They are "without God in the world" (Eph 2:12; cf. Gal 4:8; 1Th 4:5), being estranged from him (Ro 1:18-32). It is appropriate for Gentile persecutors at Thessalonica to be singled out in both letters (cf. 1Th 2:14) because of this church's history (Ac 17:5). Gentiles without any background in OT teaching about God are nonetheless culpable for their persecution of Christians.

The second group is those who "do not obey the Gospel of our Lord Jesus." These are those well-versed in OT Scriptures because of their Jewish backgrounds. Here Paul uses an apt description of unbelieving Jews (cf. Ro 10:3, 16). These are the persecutors against whom such strong feelings were evident in his first letter (1Th 2:14-16). Jews, like Gentiles, had been adamant in their opposition to Christians in Thessalonica and its vicinity (Ac 17:5, 13). Because of this, when the wrath of God makes itself felt at the revelation of the Lord Jesus, both classes of humanity will face dreaded agonies.

9 The most sobering experience of all will culminate God's righteous judgment against his enemies: "everlasting destruction [GK *3897*]," the price paid in return for the suffering inflicted on God's people. This does not refer to annihilation, which cannot be "everlasting." Just as endless life belongs to Christians, endless destruction belongs to those opposed to Christ (Mt 25:41, 46).

The consequences of permanent separation from God come out forcibly in the phrase "from the presence of the Lord." Banishment from the Lord's presence is what Jesus taught about punishment (Mt 7:23; 8:12; 22:13; 25:30; Lk 13:27). Words cannot adequately express the misery of this condition. On the other hand, those in Christ can anticipate the very opposite: "we will be with the Lord forever" (1Th 4:17).

The parallel phrase, "from the majesty of his power," likewise signifies separation from God and its anguish. Instead of enjoying God's glory or majesty, an uncrossable gulf will preclude access for those destined to everlasting punishment (cf. Lk 16:24-26).

10 Thankfully, another side of God's repayment remains, that of glorification. "On the day he comes" further defines "when the Lord Jesus is revealed" (v.7). It is composed of two distinct parts: "when he comes" and "in that day." "That day" is a frequent OT designation for the day of the Lord (cf. Isa 2:11, 17). Here it solemnly emphasizes a time coincident with "when he comes" (see also Mk 13:32; 14:25; Lk 21:34; 2Ti 1:12, 18, 4:8). Earlier Paul has disclosed how the day of the Lord will encompass in its initial stage a period of wrath and tribulation. The tribulation will be climaxed when Jesus Christ returns personally to judge and to inaugurate his reign on earth. In v.10, however, Paul has in view the very beginning of the day, before the wrath—the meeting of Christ with his saints in the air (1Th 4:17; 2Th 1:7a; 2:1). This is the moment of reward for those who have faithfully persevered in all their persecutions and trials (v.4).

The substance of their reward will be participation in the glory and marvel of the Lord's return. Our Lord intends to share his own glory and majesty "in [the midst of] his holy people and ... among all those who have believed." Here is a glorified assembly. Christ's glorification belongs to Christians also. The fact that we will be glorified constitutes more than sufficient incentive to endure life's present trials (cf. Ro 8:17-18; 9:23).

"Those who have believed" becomes very personal as Paul adds "because you believed our testimony to you." These words remind the troubled readers that they themselves will participate in the glory and amazement of that day. Enjoyment of the future glory of Christ's coming is the leading idea of the chapter and a prime incentive for faithfulness.

B. Prayer for Future Acceptance (1:11-12)

11 Not content with the certainty of coming glorification, Paul now prays for its realization. Human minds wrestle with the problem of praying for something already fixed in the unalterable purpose of God. Yet Paul has already done this in these letters (1Th 3:12–13; 5:23; cf. also Rev 22:20). It is God's pleasure for saints to cooperate with his ongoing program (Php 2:12–13).

The purpose of Paul's prayer is "that our God may count you worthy of his calling." This probably corresponds to their worthiness for the kingdom mentioned in v.5. No uncertainty of ultimate acceptance is implied in the prayer, for any uncertainty would undercut, not build, assurance for the fainthearted. On the other hand, certainty in the security of God's purposes does not diminish the need to keep on praying. Ultimate salvation rests on the sure foundation of God's faithfulness (1Th 5:24), but until its actual accomplishment, Paul continues praying for it.

"His calling" (GK *3104*) is usually regarded by Paul as a past decree (Ro 11:29; 1Co 1:26). To construe it like this here could imply the possibility of falling away from it. Yet such cannot happen to those already assured of a future worthiness (v.5) based solely on the grace of God (v.12). It is reassuring to know that God's call is made effective quite apart from human merit (cf. Gal 1:13–15; see comment on 1Th 2:12). Instead of limiting the call to what happened before the foundation of the world, the present emphasis on Christ's return (v.10) and the eschatological kingdom of God (v.5) argues for extending the scope of "calling" to include its future outworking at God's righteous judgment (v.5).

Paul's other prayer objective is for God to "fulfill every good purpose of yours and every act prompted by your faith." "Good[ness]" (GK *20*) is part of the fruit of the Spirit (Gal 5:22). Paul prays for the kind of desire that produces goodness—i.e., the active quality that constantly pursues what is right and beneficial for others. "Every act prompted by your faith" is what he had witnessed in them previously (cf. "work produced by faith," 1Th 1:3). What they had already attained was important, but room for growth was still there (cf. 1Th 3:10; 4:1). Realization of these objectives can come only by God's power.

12 Paul now states the purpose of his prayer—the glorification of Christ in the believers and they in him. This is an intermediate step toward the final recognition of the Lord's own worthiness and majesty and the saints' participation in these things with him. "Name" is a reference to the dignity, majesty, and power of the Lord's revealed character.

"In him" is a technical expression initiated by Jesus (Jn 15:4; 17:21); it was taken up by Paul and developed more completely (Ro 6:11, 23; 1Co 1:5; 2Co 13:4; et al.). The thought is that of reciprocity resting on the union of the Lord with his people. They are to share the future moment of glorification together.

Elsewhere Paul shows a continuing zeal to exclude merit from the salvation process (cf. Ro 4:16; 11:5–6; Eph 2:5, 8); so here also "grace" (GK *5921*) from both Father and Son (cf. 1:2) is the source of everything. We pray for such things as these and our prayers are answered in harmony with the working of God's grace.

III. Assurance of Noninvolvement in the Day of the Lord (2:1–17)

A. The False Claim (2:1–2)

1–2 The hortatory words "we ask you, brothers" (cf. 1Th 5:12) provides a transition from what Paul has been saying about the day of the Lord to an acute problem related to it. This problem has to do with the eschatological events he has just described in ch. 1. In the interest of truth about this vital hope, Paul must set down accurately certain features of "the day of the Lord" as a corrective to what some were falsely claiming.

He must explain what he means by "the coming of our Lord Jesus Christ and our being gathered to him" or else the solution to the problem cannot be grasped. "Being gathered" (GK *2191*) defines which part of the "coming" (*parousia*; GK *4242*) Paul has in mind. This is the great event he described more fully in 1Th 4:14–17—i.e., the gathering of those in Christ to meet him in the air en route to the Father in heaven. This begins the day of the Lord. The relationship that this happening bears to the tribulation phase of the day of the Lord so frequently mentioned in these letters is important. Some limit the *parousia* to a single event and insist that it comes after the tribulation. It is hardly possible, though, to explain the variety of relationships belonging to the *parousia* in these letters if it is understood only as a single event. Even the meaning of the word suggests a longer duration.

Another problem is encountered if the *parousia* that initiates the day of the Lord is considered as the single event of Christ's return to earth following the tribulation. If Paul had given oral or written instruction to this effect, the false claim that the day of the Lord was already present could hardly have alarmed these Christians. According to this scheme, the day of the Lord could not begin without Christ's personal reappearance. His continued absence was obvious to all.

Yet the claim was made and accepted to the extent that the church was troubled. This implies Paul had not taught that a one-phase *parousia* after the period of wrath would begin the day of the Lord. He had told them that the coming of the Lord to gather his saints into heaven would initiate both the tribulation and the day of the Lord. They were promised immediate "rest" (1:7) and glorification with Christ (1:10), not increased persecution.

The false instruction had, however, denied them an imminent "rest." They would first have to undergo the severe persecution of the tribulation and possibly even suffer martyrdom before Christ's coming, according to these misrepresentations. They were even told that their current suffering indicated the arrival of the expected tribulation. Paul speaks in 2:3–4, 8–12 of this future period in terms quite similar to those of Rev 13 and 17. The man of lawlessness has a number of affinities with the beasts of Revelation, enough to show that the two books describe the same period. Though 2 Thessalonians does not specifically mention the beast's war with the saints and their martyrdom, Rev 13:7, 10 declares it explicitly. If this is a possibility for the church, why did Paul at no point teach this kind of anticipation? The answer must lie in the removal of Christians (including the Thessalonian believers) from earth before this persecution. It is another group of God's people, following the church's translation, who must face the terror of this archenemy.

Despite their "persecutions and trials" (1:4) these Thessalonian Christians were not living in the day of the Lord, as they had been erroneously told. A right understanding of "being gathered to him" reveals that they could not be so enmeshed, because for them Christ's *parousia* will antedate the awful period to come. In fact, their "being gathered to him" would be the event that signals the day's beginning.

As their friend and brother, Paul respectfully requests ("we ask," v.1; cf. 1Th 4:1) them not to become "unsettled or alarmed" (v.2). This might easily happen if they were led to believe that somehow the glorious coming had passed them by. "Unsettled" (GK *4888*) means "to be shaken from your sensibleness [lit., mind]." Distorted teaching had "alarmed" (GK *2583*) them. Paul cautioned them against hastily adopting something other than the instruction he had previously given them (cf. v.15).

False teaching that purported to have come from Paul had reached them through three possible avenues. (1) One was the spiritual gift of "prophecy" (lit., "spirit," v.2; GK *4460*) or something like it (see also 1Th 5:19–20). Whatever the specific medium, the teaching was represented as having Paul's authority. (2) A second avenue was the spoken word ("report"; GK *3364*). Though this did not claim the direct inspiration of prophecy, it too was based on an allegedly Pauline foundation. (3) The same basis was claimed for a third medium of communication—"letter." Someone had misrepresented Paul's views in a letter bearing his name, a mistake he will rectify in any future correspondence (cf. 3:17–18). It is not clear whether the readers had been misguided through one or all three channels, but in any case Paul denounces them all.

The false teaching consisted in the claim that "the day of the Lord has already come" (lit., "is present"; GK *1931*). This word denotes actual presence. These readers who knew about the day (1Th 5:2) knew that its earlier phase would be a time of heightened persecution for the saints. Their suffering had already been so severe that someone tried to convince them that the period was already in progress, even though the Lord had not yet come to gather them to heaven. They knew of the time of trouble and the Lord's return to culminate it (1:7–9). They had been led to believe, however, that his coming for them would spare them the anguish of that hour (1Th 5:9). But here were people telling them, with Paul's apparent backing, that such a deliverance was not to be.

Therefore they were in great need of an authentic word from Paul assuring them that they had understood him correctly in his first letter. They needed to know that the *parousia* of Christ for his church would mark the beginning of the future day of trouble and consequently that the day had not yet arrived. To accomplish this, Paul proceeded to describe features, obviously not yet present, that would characterize the day's early stages.

B. The True Condition (2:3–12)

1. Defiance (yet to come) (2:3–4)

3 Paul supplements his request in v. 1 with a prohibition: "Don't let anyone deceive you in any way." Apparently those who willfully and maliciously troubled the Thessalonian believers had done this by deceiving anyone who would listen to them regarding the day of the Lord. Paul warns his readers not to be taken in by these speculations. He does not say what moved these promoters of error. Perhaps a misunderstanding of grace led them to teach that Christians must earn their part in the *parousia* by persevering through severe suffering. Whatever it was, Paul is determined to prove that his readers were not in the day of the Lord.

In the second part of this verse, the Greek sentence is not complete; it presupposes something to be added from the previous verse; i.e., "that day will not come" (lit., "that day is not present"). According to Paul's argument here, two conspicuous phenomena that will dominate the day's opening phase had not yet happened. That is, his readers had not missed the rapture (1Th 4:15–17) and were not in the day of the Lord (v.2) because two clear indicators of the earliest stage of this eschatological period had not yet appeared (cf. introduction to 1 Thessalonians).

Let us put it this way. Suppose the government of some country should announce, "In the near future on a date known only to us, Christianity will be suppressed. To mark the official beginning of this policy, on the appointed day the largest church in the country will be demolished and its pastor required to renounce Christianity publicly. Thereafter, all who admit they are Christians will be placed in jeopardy of imprisonment." At that time a foreigner might arrive in that country, having heard nothing more than that Christianity would be cruelly suppressed. He would doubtless find some Christians already experiencing certain hardships and, in his ignorance of the timing of the actual beginning of the policy of suppression, might assume that it was already in effect. A citizen who knew the details of the policy would have to tell him, "The period of suppression of Christianity is not yet present, because the largest church in the country has not yet been demolished and its pastor has not yet renounced Christianity publicly."

So far there is no logical problem. But some who have problems with the pretribulational view of the rapture ask, "How can the nonarrival of two events ('the rebellion' and the revealing of 'the man of lawlessness,' v.3) that initiate the day of the Lord, a period that will come after the believers have been raptured—how can the nonarrival of these events prove to the confused Thessalonian believers (who are to be raptured and thus will not be in the day of the Lord) that they are not actually in that day?" The answer still is that the absence of the phenomena demonstrates the nonpresence of the day of the Lord. Obviously, had "the rebellion" and the revealing of "the man of lawlessness" already taken place when Paul was writing this letter, then the teaching of the priority of the rapture to "the day of the Lord" would have been called into question. But here in ch. 2 Paul is not discussing the timing of the rapture. He is simply reassuring his readers that "the day of the Lord" had not come. Nor does he at any place in this context (vv.1–12) tell his readers that they will at some future time "see" the two initial phenomena of "the day of the Lord." Had he said that, there would indeed be a problem. But he did not speak of the Thessalonians' actually seeing the phenomena. He simply stressed the present nonarrival of the phenomena.

To sum up, let us return to the analogy of the newcomer to the country facing the suppression of Christianity. Suppose now that, arriving after the initial announcement, he is a short-term visitor due to leave before the official beginning of the anti-Christian policy. The answer to his confusion about being in the country with the policy already in effect would be corrected by his realizing that the largest church would have to be destroyed and its pastor publicly renounce Christianity before suppression of Christianity began. And this would be a valid answer, even though he would not be present when these things took place.

The troubled at Thessalonica could take heart in knowing they had not missed the gathering of those in Christ at the *parousia* (v.1). Their present persecutions were not identifiable with those to be inflicted by the man of lawlessness on a later group of saints after the eschatological day begins.

A closer look at the two phenomena accompanying the day of the Lord illuminates the characteristics of that day. "The rebellion" represents *apostasia* (GK *686*), from which the English word *apostasy* comes. This word points to a deliberate abandonment of a former professed position. Attempts to identify the apostasy with some past or present movement are futile because of its contextual association with the Lord Jesus' second advent (v.1). Other passages in Scripture likewise anticipate a defection of professing Christians (see Mt 24:11–12, 24; 1Ti 4:1ff.; 2Ti 3:1–5; 4:3–4; 2Pe 2:1–22; 3:3–6; Jude 17–18). After the rapture of those in Christ (1Th 4:17), all who are truly in him will be gone. Conditions will be ripe for people, especially those who call themselves Christians but are not really such, to turn their backs on God. Then their insincerity will demonstrate itself outwardly. This worldwide anti-God movement will be so universal as to earn for itself a special designation: "*the* apostasy"—i.e., the climax of the increasing apostate tendencies evident before the rapture of the church.

Following and in conjunction with the apostasy will come the unveiling of a mighty figure embodying everything opposed to God. His whereabouts before his unveiling are not given. He will be alive for years before his unveiling, but his dramatic public presentation will occur after the rebellion begins.

Paul characterizes this figure in three ways. (1) He is "the man of lawlessness"; i.e., he is the epitome of opposition to the laws of God. Satan so indwells and operates through him that his main delight will be in breaking God's righteous laws. (2) He is "the man doomed to destruction" (lit., "the son of perdition"). That is, he belongs to this class of people. The same expression describes Judas Iscariot (Jn 17:12), another member of this class.

4 (3) This individual "opposes and exalts himself over everything that is called God or is worshiped." His direct and determined opposition to the true God will be a leading feature of the continuing apostasy. It will be especially marked by removal of the symbolic articles from the Jerusalem temple. The man of lawlessness will occupy the holy precincts in order to accept and even demand worship that is due God alone. This evidently is a Jewish temple to be rebuilt in Jerusalem in the future. Dependence of these words on Da 9:26–27; 11:31, 36–37; 12:11 (cf. Mt 24:15; Mk 13:14) demands such a reference. There is no impressive evidence for understanding "temple" (GK *3724*) in a nonliteral sense. The well-known "abomination that causes desolation" (Mk 13:14) is sometimes regarded as a person and sometimes as an act of desecration by that person. The act of desecration to which this verse looks will transpire halfway through the seventieth prophetic week of Da 9:24–27, when the covenant made earlier with the Jewish people is broken. This will mark the climax of this lawless one's career. Historically, a foreshadowing of this blasphemous intrusion happened when Antiochus Epiphanes desecrated the temple in Jerusalem just before the Maccabean revolt.

The relationship of this portion of 2 Thessalonians to Christ's *parousia* confirms the impression that Paul must be referring to a single historical personage. Quests for such a person in the past and present have proved fruitless. Resemblances to Antiochus Epiphanes, Nero, Diocletian, one of the popes, and others may be admitted. But fulfillment of all details of the prophecy must await the future period of this man's prominence. "The man of lawlessness" will be a new historical figure whom Satan will energize to do his will in the world. As "man of God" in the OT regularly designates a divine prophet, the present "man of lawlessness" designates a false prophet, probably to be identified with the second beast of Rev 13:11ff. (cf. Rev 16:13; 19:20; 20:10). His primary function will be to preside over the religious apostasy in cooperation with the beast out of the sea (Rev 13:1ff.), who leads political opposition to God. As God's chief opponent in Jerusalem whose background is probably Jewish (cf. Da 11:36–37), the lawless one will give religious leadership to complement the dominance of his associate over governments of the world's nations.

The presence of such an apostasy and counterfeit god will not escape international observation. The nonpresence of these things when Paul wrote proves his thesis regarding the nonarrival of the day of the Lord.

2. Delay (presently in effect) (2:5–7)

5 A note of impatience may be detected in Paul's question. If the Thessalonian believers had recalled Paul's oral teaching, disturbing elements in the newly arisen false system could have been eliminated. Paul was certain about their previous familiarity with the substance of vv.3–4 because he had personally given them this information.

6 So he can declare, "You know what is holding him back." "Now" should be connected with "what is holding him back" rather than with "you know," to indicate that "holding back" is a present phenomenon. "What is holding ... back" (GK 2988) is a neuter title for this restraining force. The word recurs in the masculine in v.7, where it is translated "one who ... holds it back."

Proposed identifications of this phenomenon have been multiple. Because of inability to explain the neuter-masculine combination, such suggestions as the preaching of the Gospel, the Jewish state, the binding of Satan, the church, the Gentile world dominion, and human government are improbable as a referent for the restrainer. Moreover, to identify it with a supernatural force or person hostile to God is difficult because the restrainer is limiting Satan (vv.7–9), not cooperating with him. A popular understanding since early times has been that this is a reference to the Roman Empire (neuter) and its ruler (masculine). Paul had several times benefited from the intervention of the Roman government (Ac 17:6ff.; 18:6ff.). Though preferable to some other solutions, this explanation is disappointing in several ways. Paul nowhere else predicts the demise of the Roman Empire (cf. v.7). In addition, the Roman emperors sometimes precipitated anti-Christian activities rather than restrained them. Elimination of this solution is sealed when we remember that the Roman Empire has long since ceased to exist, and the appearance of Christ or the lawless one has yet to take place.

It is evident that the restrainer, to accomplish his mission, must have supernatural power to hold back a supernatural enemy (v.9). God and the outworking of his providence is the natural answer. Reference to God is favored by the restrainer's harmony with divine purpose and a divine timetable ("at the proper time," v.6). Yet to say that God is the restrainer is not quite enough to explain the variation in gender.

To one familiar with the Lord Jesus' Upper Room Discourse (Jn 13–17), as Paul undoubtedly was, fluctuation between neuter and masculine in reference to the Holy Spirit is common. Either gender is appropriate, depending on whether one thinks of natural agreement (masculine, because the Spirit is a person) or grammatical (neuter, because the noun *pneuma* [GK 4460] is neuter). This identification of the restrainer with deep roots in church history is most appealing. The special presence of the Spirit as the indweller of saints will terminate as abruptly at the *parousia* as it began at Pentecost. Once the body of Christ has been caught away to heaven, the Spirit's ministry will revert back to what he did for believers during the OT period. His function of restraining evil through the body of Christ (Jn 16:7–11; 1Jn 4:4) will cease similarly to the way he terminated his striving in the days of Noah (Ge 6:3). At that point the reins will be removed from lawlessness and the satanically inspired rebellion will begin. It appears that "what is holding back" was readily recognized at Thessalonica as a title for the Holy Spirit on whom the readers had come to depend in their personal attempts to combat lawlessness (1Th 1:6; 4:8; 5:19; 2Th 2:13).

God has a "proper time" for the lawless one's revelation, just as he does for the revelation of the Lord Jesus from heaven (1:7). No one knows that time, since it is part of the future day of the Lord (1Th 5:2; 2Th 2:2–3). Until the gathering of saints (2:1), the Spirit will continue his restraining work.

7 Further clarification ("for") is in order. The "secret power [lit., "mystery"; GK 3696] of lawlessness" was already evident in such things as their own persecutions (1:4), but lawlessness will be open when the rebellion arrives and the lawless one is unveiled (2:3, 8). The secrecy and limitation are attributable to "the one who now holds it back." Upon his removal, the rebellion will break out.

3. Deception and destruction (after the delay) (2:8–10)

Departure of the restrainer is the cue for the revelation (v.8) and coming (v.9) of the lawless one. That revelation, already mentioned in v.3 in conjunction with the rebellion and in v.6 as being delayed until the proper time by the restrainer's presence, is of satanic origin, though admittedly it can happen only by God's permission. Satan's present efforts to effect unhindered lawlessness are frustrated by divine restraint (v.7), but through cessation of the Spirit's indwelling ministry to the body of Christ, his lawless one will be granted a future interval to do his worst.

8 After this time has elapsed, the Lord Jesus will personally come to earth to "overthrow" (lit., "slay"; GK 359) the lawless one "with the breath of his mouth" and "destroy" (lit., "abolish"; GK 2934) him "by the splendor of his coming" (*parousia*; GK 4242). By putting the lawless one to death, the Lord will also bring to an end his program of deceiving the world. "The breath of his mouth" could be a figurative reference to a word spoken by Christ, but a literal sense is quite satisfactory. The breath of God is a fierce weapon according to the OT (Ex 15:8; 2Sa 22:16; Job 4:9; Ps 33:6; Isa 30:27–28). "The splendor [or "appearance"; GK 2211] of his coming" is his other means of conquest. The translation "appearance" is preferred, since in the Pastoral Letters this word is practically equivalent to *parousia* as a name for his coming (1Ti 6:14; 2Ti 1:10; 4:1, 8; Tit 2:13). This "appearance" phase of the *parousia* differs from the "gathering" phase (v.1). It concludes and climaxes the tribulation instead of beginning it. The visible presence of the Lord Jesus in the world will put an immediate stop to an accelerated diabolical program.

9–10a That Satan is the root of the lawless one's deception is explicit in a further elaboration. The word for "work" (GK 1918) is reserved for supernatural activities; i.e., a superhuman person will utilize supernatural means of "miracles, signs and wonders." These remarkable phenomena, which in the past were used so effectively in laying a foundation for the church (Ac 2:22, 43; 4:30; 5:12; 6:8; 7:36; 14:3; 15:12; Ro 15:19; 2Co 12:12; Heb 2:4), will be redirected to purposes of deceit. They will be "counterfeit" (GK 6022) in the sense that they produce false impressions, deluding people to the point of accepting the lie as truth (cf. v.11). The motivation of the lawless one is to deceive; it is the nature of unrighteousness to palm itself off as righteousness. "Those who are perishing" will be particularly vulnerable to trickery. Not only will they confuse unrighteousness with righteousness; they will also attribute deity to this lawless one (v.4).

10b Their blindness will be self-imposed because of a prior refusal to "love the truth and so be saved." They lack a positive committal to the Gospel. This is just as blamable as indifference or even antagonism toward the truth. The right choice could have brought them salvation and deliverance from the lawless one's devices, but they elected not to receive God's salvation.

4. Delusion and divine judgment (because of present recalcitrance) (2:11–12)

11 By covering again the same ground in vv.11–12 as in vv.9–10, Paul reemphasizes the fate of rejecters of the truth and adds more information about them. Already he has shown Satan's part in getting them to believe lies and bewildering them with deceitful measures, and he has shown their refusal to love the truth. Because they deliberately reject God, he himself will send them "a powerful delusion"; this is another way of referring to the lie (v.9) and deceit (v.10) already predicted. The end result is that they will "believe the lie." This is their only alternative because they have refused to love the truth (v.10). They will be completely defenseless against the false claims of the lawless one (v.4) and his perversion of the true Gospel. The satanic promise that deceived Eve (Ge 3:5) will find its ultimate fulfillment in the end-time master of deceit. They will mistake someone else and his lying promises for God and his truth.

12 The ultimate consequences for them will be condemnation. Failing to appropriate the truth of the Gospel, they willingly choose wickedness instead; they cannot blame circumstances. Retrospect will show their own wrongly directed personal delight to be the cause of God's adverse judgment against them (cf. 1:9). What an incentive this powerful passage is for non-Christians to turn to God before the rebellion and delusion arrive!

C. The Truth's Continuance (2:13–17)

1. Thanks for divine deliverance (2:13–14)

13 Paul is thankful that God chose some to believe the truth and to be delivered from delusion and divine judgment. He and his co-workers can rejoice in looking forward to salvation for themselves and their converts, an anticipation drastically different from the outlook for those awaiting perdition (cf. v.10). The salvation viewed from its human side in 1:3ff. is now seen as an undertaking of God.

For Paul to address these "brothers" as those "loved by the Lord" (cf. 1Th 1:4) is appropriate, because God chose them to be saved. "From the beginning" refers to their pretemporal election (cf. 1Th 1:4); Paul usually places God's prior choice of people to salvation (v.13) alongside their historical call (v.14; cf. Ro 8:30). This salvation entails present benefits and also future deliverance from the doom that will befall the lost at Christ's return (cf. 1:6, 8–9; 2:8–12). God's choice operates in the realm of belief in the truth and of the Spirit's sanctifying work. "Belief in the truth" is the means of the beginning and continuing relationships of salvation (cf. vv.10–12). The role of the Spirit in sanctification looms large for Paul (Ro 15:16; 1Co 6:11–12; 1Th 4:7–8) as it does for Peter (1Pe 1:2).

14 God has fulfilled his foreordained purpose by calling the chosen to this salvation "through our gospel." The good news of divine truth conveyed through Paul's preaching was the means whereby God called these Thessalonian converts at a particular point in time. What God purposed in eternity was carried out in history, so that they might share "in the glory of our Lord Jesus Christ." God's design was to make them adopted children who participate in Christ's glory at the *parousia* (coming; cf. 1:10, 12). They do not earn this status or in any other way acquire it for themselves. It is accomplished solely by God.

2. Call to doctrinal adherence (2:15)

15 "So then" turns the discussion to a practical responsibility derived from God's elective purpose (vv.13–14). Against a background of such an imminent world crisis as described in vv.1–10, the beneficiaries of God's saving work cannot afford to lapse into lethargy, but must respond with loyal steadfastness ("stand firm"; GK *5112*) and must keep a firm hold on the traditions ("teachings"; GK *1438*) taught them by Paul and his associates. A continuation in basic Christian doctrines would have alleviated the instability and alarm that prompted the writing of this letter (cf. v.2). Paul himself received Christian traditions subsequent to his conversion (cf. 1Co 15:3–5), and through divine revelation he had originated other traditions (1Th 4:15). These he had passed on to his converts both "by word of mouth" and "by letter" in his previous contacts with them. In light of their inclusion in God's saving purpose (vv.13–14), he commands them to remain unmovable and cling tenaciously to these doctrines.

3. Prayer for practical compliance (2:16–17)

16–17 As Paul closes ch. 2 with a prayer, he recognizes that he and his co-workers cannot in themselves make the appeal effective. Only God himself, who initially chose them (vv.13–14), can do that. Addressing his prayer to the first two persons of the Trinity, Paul names the Son before the Father (contra 1Th 3:11), probably in line with the Son's worthiness of equal honor with the Father and his special prominence in the chapter's emphasis on future salvation and glory. Yet the two persons are one God, as shown by several structural features in vv.16–17: (1) The pronoun "himself" is singular and probably should be understood as emphasizing both persons—"our Lord Jesus Christ and God our Father himself" (cf. 1Th 3:11). (2) "Loved us and . . . gave us" (v.16) represents two singular participles whose actions are applicable to both the Son and the Father. The singular number is explained by Paul's conception of the two persons as one God. (3) "Encourage and strengthen" (v.17) are likewise singular in number, though they express the action of a compound subject. This grammatical feature is attributable to the oneness of essence among the persons of the Godhead (cf. Jn 10:30). Paul conceived of Jesus Christ as God in the same full sense as he conceived of God the Father.

Paul notes that the Son and the Father will answer this prayer because they "loved us" and graciously "gave us eternal encouragement and good hope"; this is shown by the incarnation and death of Jesus Christ, which are often referred to in terms of God's loving and giving (Jn 3:16; Ro 5:5, 8; 8:35, 37; Gal 2:20; 1Jn 4:10). Because of God's love displayed in Christ, Paul's readers had a source of unending "encouragement" (GK *4155*) to offset their persecutions and accompanying doubts.

Paul prays that the encouragement provided in the crucifixion and resurrection of Christ may be appropriated inwardly and thereby give them strength for "every good deed and word." Disquiet regarding the coming of the Lord (v.2) was the need to be met. As God undertakes their cause, they can "stand firm and hold to the teachings" (v.15).

IV. Encouragement to Gainful Employment (3:1–15)

A. Prayerful Preparation for Encounter (3:1–5)

1. Prayer for Paul (3:1–2)

1 Eschatological matters were Paul's main concern in writing this letter. "Finally" indicates that these have in the main been dealt with. Yet an important and related matter needs to be discussed before the letter ends. Before discussing it, Paul makes one of his typical requests for prayer (cf. Ro 15:30–31; Eph 6:18–19; Col 4:3; 1Th 5:25; Phm 22). He desires the Gospel to "spread rapidly" (a picture of running) and "be honored" (a picture of triumph). As more people receive the good news, victories are being won and God is glorified. "Just as it was with you" recalls the amazing success of the message in Thessalonica (cf. 1Th 1:5–6, 8; 2:13). Paul wanted this repeated in other communities where he would preach Christ.

2 Again, Paul asked prayer for deliverance "from wicked and evil men." "Wicked" (GK *876*) labels them as capable of outrageous and harmful acts against others; "evil" (GK *4505*) speaks of persons not only themselves thoroughly corrupted but intent on corrupting others and drawing them into their own slide toward perdition. Who were they? The best suggestion ties these "wicked and evil men" to unbelieving Jews in Corinth where Paul was encountering opposition as he wrote (Ac 18:5–6, 12–13). As Paul wrote this second letter, he was facing a severe crisis in Corinth.

Evil people exist because "not everyone has faith." This understatement effectively highlights the large number of those who have not responded to the Gospel by believing in Christ. That the persecutors had had the opportunity to believe but had rejected it accounts for their vicious reaction against the message and those who preached it.

2. Prayer for the people (3:3–5)

3 In contrast with the widespread lack of faith among people (v.2) is the faithfulness of the Lord Jesus. He can be relied on to "strengthen [GK *5114*; cf. 2:17] and protect [GK *5875*]" Christians "from the evil one." Here is assurance of inner security and an outward protection from the author of evil whose activity is so prominent in these letters (1Th 2:18; 3:5; 2Th 2:9). Jesus' faithfulness provides a defense against even the touch of the enemy (cf. 1Jn 5:18).

4 The faithfulness of the Lord is supplemented by the faithfulness of his people. That is why Paul can add this verse—he has confidence in Christian people. Their union with Christ counteracts the weakness of sinful human nature. Paul and his co-workers can rely on the Thessalonian believers to do what they have been taught (cf. 1Th 4:2). By this favorable opinion, he paves the way for further instruction (cf. 3:6–15).

5 Paul realizes that the Lord's help is indispensable. His compliment in v.4 does not imply that they are self-sufficient. Therefore he requests the Lord to direct them into a fuller appreciation of God's love for them and of Christ's perseverance on their behalf. To comply with Paul's instructions to discipline the idle believers (vv.6–15) will be difficult. Thus the strongest possible motivation—recollection of God's love and Christ's endurance of suffering—will undergird that discipline.

B. Proper Solution for Idleness (3:6–15)

1. Previous instruction and example (3:6–10)

6 Now Paul comes to his command regarding the idle. That he invokes "the name of the Lord Jesus Christ" shows the urgency of the command. All those who remain idle are to be denied the privilege of associating with their fellow Christians. "Idle" (GK *865*) translates a word meaning "disorderly" (cf. 1Th 5:14). The disorder defined by the remainder of the paragraph is loafing, being remiss in daily work and conduct. This is contrary to the "teaching" that Paul had given them earlier (cf. 1Th 4:11–12; 5:14). No excuse could justify such misconduct. Paul therefore advocates the drastic discipline of keeping away from the "idle."

7–9 Paul himself was not idle. His readers could verify this claim ("you yourselves know," v.7; cf. 1Th 2:1; 3:3; 4:2; 5:2). In imitating Paul, they would be imitating the Lord himself (1Th 1:6) because Paul's life was so carefully patterned after his Lord's. He did not loaf at Thessalonica (v.7b), nor depend on others to supply him with free food (v.8a). He supported himself in spite of much fatigue ("laboring," v.8) and many obstacles ("toiling," v.8; cf. 1Th 2:9) in order to relieve the new Christians in Thessalonica of the burden of maintaining him.

Paul did not have to exert himself so tirelessly. As an apostle, he had "the right to such help" (v.9; cf. 1Co 9:4ff.; 1Th 2:7) from his converts. He decided, however, to forgo this privilege and leave an example for them to imitate.

10 Paul reinforced his example by this definite "rule." From a very early time denying food to the lazy was a traditional form of discipline in the church.

2. Renewed instruction (3:11–12)

11–12 Here the previously given rule (v.10) is repeated because of reports that the problem of loafing had recurred. People who came from Thessalonica to Corinth had reported this. Some of their number had stopped working, even since receiving the corrective of 1Th 4:11–12 and 5:14. They were using the extra time to interfere in other people's affairs.

"In the Lord Jesus Christ" Paul commanded such people to settle down and earn the bread they eat. He uses the common union of believers with Christ as ground for his appeal. He might well have addressed the idle ones pejoratively as "you loafers," but instead he tactfully refers to them as "such people," doubtless hoping to lead them back to earning their own food. Thus, order

The apostle Paul supported himself in his missionary activity by working in leather (possibly making tents out of leather). In Corinth he joined the leather business of Aquila and Priscilla (see Ac 18:1–3). Drawing by Rachel Bierling.

3. Corrective separation (3:13–15)

13–15 Paul now describes specifically how the Thessalonian Christians should deal with loafers who disobey his instructions. First, they are urged to keep on "doing what is right." "Tire" (GK *1591*) implies the possibility of their losing heart in struggling with their idle brothers. Exemplary conduct serves as a constant reprimand to wrongdoers and is an incentive for them to turn from their delinquency. Included in doing right is generosity toward those in need. Yet to keep on supporting those who have nothing because they refuse to work is wrong (v.10).

So the Thessalonians must deal firmly yet charitably with the mistakes of their fellow Christians. They were not to "associate" (GK *5264*) with anyone refusing to comply with the work ethic set out in this letter, so that they might be ashamed of their behavior. Such people were not to be expelled from the church like the sinning brother referred to in 1Co 5. In Corinth the offense was so flagrant as to bring disrepute on the whole church. In Thessalonica, however, the lapse was not yet so aggravated as to bring the reproach of the pagans on the church. The erring people were allowed to continue in the meetings, but probably were denied participation in such things as the love feast and the Lord's Supper. Certainly they were not to be given food, because this would make the community appear to condone the offense.

To sum up, any recalcitrant idler was not to be treated as an enemy, cut off from all contacts, but was allowed to continue in a brotherly status. So lines of communication were kept open for continued warnings about his behavior.

V. Conclusion (3:16–18)

A. Prayer for God's Peace and Presence (3:16)

16 "Now" (or perhaps more accurately "but") once again marks a transition from command and exhortation to prayer. The prayer recognizes that ultimately God alone can bring about compliance with what Paul has asked of his readers. "Yet without the Lord's help all your efforts will be in vain" is the thought behind this petition. "The Lord of peace" alone can make harmony among believers a reality. While this is, first and foremost, peace with God, it provides the ground for believers' peace with one another (Eph 2:14–18; cf. 1Th 5:23). "At all times" asks that there be no break in the flow of Christ's peace (cf. Jn 14:27; 16:33; Col 3:15); "in every way" asks that the prevalence of peace continue no matter what the outward circumstances. "The Lord be with all of you" requests what was previously guaranteed for Christians; his promise never to forsake his own provides assurance of this (Heb 13:5). Here is an instance of the cooperation of prayer in fulfilling what God's purpose predetermines (cf. 1:11–12).

B. Personalized Benediction (3:17–18)

17–18 Paul has been dictating to an amanuensis (a secretary) up to 3:17 (cf. Ro 16:22; 1Co 16:21; Col 4:18). At this point he takes the pen into his own hand to add a closing greeting. Though he undoubtedly did this frequently, he calls attention to it only here, in 1Co 16:21, and in Col 4:18. The greeting in his own hand, "which is the distinguishing mark" in all his letters (v. 17), includes the benediction of v.18. Apparently Paul followed this practice consistently, expecting churches where he had served to recall his distinctive handwriting. It was particularly needed in this letter as a deterrent against any attempt to forge a letter in his name (cf. 2:2).

Even when Paul did not call attention to it, a closing benediction came in his own hand. "The grace of our Lord Jesus Christ be with all of you" or a near equivalent is found at the close of all Paul's writings. The present benediction agrees verbatim with that of 1Th 5:28 except for the "all" added here. Significantly, no one was excluded from Paul's good wishes toward this church, not even those he had rebuked at various points.

1 Timothy

INTRODUCTION

The letters 1 Timothy, Titus, and 2 Timothy—probably written in that order and commonly called the Pastoral Letters—form a rather closely knit unity. They are somewhat distinct from Paul's other ten letters and share common problems of authorship and date. It is logical, then, to treat some of these issues together (see also introduction to Titus).

1. Authorship

All three Pastoral Letters begin with Paul's name. Many scholars have questioned, however, whether the apostle Paul really wrote these letters. We must investigate this subject at some length. Four arguments have been commonly raised against the Pauline authorship of these three letters.

a. Historical

According to some, the events in the Pastoral Letters do not fit into the account in Acts. For example, nowhere in Acts do we read about Paul preaching in Crete and leaving Titus there (Tit 1:5). Nor does his leaving Timothy at Ephesus fit into the Acts account. On these points all scholars agree.

But was Paul put to death at the end of his Roman imprisonment described in the closing verses of Acts? Most likely not. Rather, he was released from this imprisonment and made further journeys, during which he wrote 1 Timothy and Titus. It was during a later imprisonment that he wrote 2 Timothy.

There is considerable evidence for this position. Many of the church fathers testify to the accuracy of this history. The most definitive statement comes from Eusebius, who writes (A.D. 325):

> Paul is said, after having defended himself, to have set forth again upon the ministry of preaching, and to have entered the city [Rome] a second time, and to have ended his life by martyrdom. Whilst then a prisoner, he wrote the Second Letter to Timothy, in which he both mentions his first defence, and his impending death.

b. Ecclesiastical

In the Pastoral Letters we read about overseers, elders, and deacons. It is claimed by some scholars that this shows a more advanced church organization than existed during the lifetime of Paul.

But a careful reading of Tit 1:5–9 shows that "elders" (GK 4565) and "overseers" (GK 2176) are terms used interchangeably. In Php 1:1 (a letter that most accept as a genuine letter of Paul), the apostle addresses the "overseers and deacons" in the church at Philippi (see comments on Php 1:1). Furthermore, the situation a generation later was quite different (see the letters of Ignatius, c. A.D. 115). Here each local church had one overseer, several presbyters, and several deacons. The evidence is clear that the Pastoral Letters reflect the type of church organization known to Paul rather than a later type. Thus, a second-century date for the Pastorals seems unrealistic.

c. Doctrinal

A third argument against Pauline authorship is the claim that the doctrinal emphases of the Pastorals are different from those in Paul's earlier letters, especially the recurring use of the expression "sound doctrine" (2Ti 4:3; Tit 1:9; 2:1).

However, the later Jewish-Christian Gnostic heresy seems to have been present in an early form during Paul's lifetime, and Paul apparently combats it in the Pastorals. It is generally acknowledged today that Gnostic ideas had penetrated Judaism before the advent of Christianity. This fact makes it conceivable that Paul would use different words and concepts in answering those concerns. Paul also opposed Gnostic ideas in his letter to the Colossians (see introduction to Colossians).

d. Linguistic

The most serious argument against the genuineness of the Pastoral Letters is their difference in style and vocabulary from Paul's earlier writings. This is the main point stressed today by negative critics. One scholar, for example, found 175 words used nowhere else in the NT and 130 words not used elsewhere by Paul but shared by other NT writers. These statistics have carried great weight with many twentieth-century scholars.

But such numbers assume that we know everything about Paul's language and do not take into account differences of subject matter, of circumstances, and of addressees—all of which may lead to new words. An accurate statistical study of words requires far more than the limited number we have in the other letters of Paul for comparison.

In recent years several scholars have been suggesting that Luke was the amanuensis (secretary) who actually composed the Pastoral Letters under Paul's dictation. The careful student can discover a considerable number of significant Greek words that occur in both Luke-Acts and the Pastorals but nowhere else in the NT. Amanuenses were sometimes given considerable liberty in writing manuscripts, and we know that Paul was in the habit of using them for the actual writing of his letters (cf. Ro 16:22).

The position of this commentary is that Paul wrote these three letters.

2. Date and Place of Origin

The date of Paul's first Roman imprisonment was perhaps A.D. 59–61. The early church unanimously testifies that Paul was put to death by Emperor Nero, who committed suicide in June of A.D. 68. Since Paul asked Timothy to come to him "before winter" (2Ti 4:21), it is obvious that 2 Timothy was written no later than A.D. 67, though it may have been as early as 65. This means that 1 Timothy and Titus were written between 62 and 66. Paul was in Macedonia when he wrote 1 Timothy (see 1Ti 1:3).

3. Destination and Occasion

Timothy was at Ephesus when the apostle wrote him the first letter (1Ti 1:3). Presumably he was still there when Paul wrote the second letter.

These letters are called "pastoral" because they are addressed to pastors of churches to outline pastoral duties. Their responsibilities were twofold: to defend sound doctrine and maintain sound discipline. In 1 Timothy, Paul urges Timothy to stay in Ephesus to make sure that certain men do not teach false doctrines (1Ti 1:3). He goes on to deal with numerous problems that were arising in the church and gives advice as to how Timothy should handle them.

4. Summary of 1 Timothy

Paul begins by warning the young pastor against false teachers, who seem to be Judaizers (1:3–11). He thanks "Christ Jesus our Lord" for his amazing grace to him, "the worst of sinners" (1:12–20). Chapter 2 is taken up with instructions for public worship and ch. 3 with the qualifications of the overseers and deacons in the church. In ch. 4 Paul gives personal instructions to Timothy, again warning him against false teachers (4:1–5) and admonishing him to maintain sound doctrine and sound discipline (4:6–16). Chapter 5 deals mainly with the place of widows in the church (5:3–16) and the treatment of elders (5:17–20). The last chapter has instructions for slaves (6:1–2) and more warnings against false teachers (6:3–5) and the love of money (6:6–10). After a personal charge to Timothy (6:11–16), Paul gives special instructions to the rich (6:17–19).

5. Theological Values

Because both 1 and 2 Timothy were written primarily to an individual whom Paul loved dearly, they provide us with some valuable insights into his life and character. Yet, through Timothy, Paul was speaking to the church at Ephesus, and indeed the letter still speaks to the church of Jesus Christ today.

There is a strong OT background to these letters. This is reflected in the use of the phrase "God our Savior," which occurs five times in the Pastorals (1Ti 1:1; 2:3; Tit 1:3; 2:10; 3:4; see comment on 1Ti 1:1–2) and nowhere else in Paul's letters. But we also find in the Pastorals the typically Pauline emphasis on "our Savior, Christ Jesus" (2Ti 1:10), "Christ Jesus our Savior" (Tit 1:4), and "Jesus Christ our Savior" (Tit 3:6). The significant Pauline expression "in Christ" occurs seven times in 2 Timothy and twice in 1 Timothy.

Furthermore, the fact that salvation is through God's grace rather than our own good works is clearly asserted (2Ti 1:9; Tit 3:5). Closely allied to this is the teaching that eternal life comes by faith in Jesus Christ (1Ti 1:16).

More precisely than anywhere else it is stated: "For there is one God and one mediator between God and men, the man Christ Jesus" (1Ti 2:5). It is also declared that this Mediator gave himself "as a ransom for all men" (v.6). Here the doctrine of the atonement comes through clearly. By his coming, Christ "has destroyed death and has brought life and immortality to light through the gospel" (2Ti 1:10).

The divine inspiration of the Scriptures is stated in the Pastorals more forcefully than anywhere else in the NT: "All Scripture is God-breathed and is useful for teaching, rebuking, correcting and training in righteousness" (2Ti 3:16).

6. Special Problems

In most of Paul's letters he is concerned about the work of the Judaizers in hindering the progress of the Gospel. The mention of "myths and endless genealogies" (1:4) may refer to Judaistic or Gnostic emphases, or to both. But when Paul says that the troublemakers want to be "teachers of the law" (1:7), he is evidently talking about Judaizers (see also Tit 1:14).

There also seems to be a combination of Gnosticism and Judaism in those who "forbid people to marry and order them to abstain from certain foods" (4:3). The first of these prohibitions arose from a false asceticism, based on the Gnostic idea that all matter is evil.

Another troublesome topic concerned who should be enrolled as widows. Paul deals with this at some length and gives specific instructions about their qualifications (5:3–16).

EXPOSITION

I. Salutation (1:1–2)

1 In keeping with the custom of that day, every one of Paul's thirteen letters begins with his name. Born a Roman citizen (Ac 22:27–28), he had been given the Latin name "Paulus" in addition to his Jewish name Saul. At the beginning of his Gentile mission the apostle adopted the habit of using Paul (Ac 13:9).

Paul identifies himself as "an apostle" (GK 693). This word means "one sent on a mission." It was the title Jesus gave to his first twelve disciples (Lk 6:13). After the death of Judas Iscariot, Matthias was elected to take his place (Ac 1:23–26). Later the term was extended to take in Paul and Barnabas (Ac 14:14), the first two missionaries to the Gentile world. Paul's use of this word underscores the fact that he is writing with apostolic authority.

He was an apostle "of Christ Jesus." That is, Christ had commissioned and sent him as a missionary. It was not by his own choice but "by the command of God ... and of Christ Jesus." Paul was conscious of his divine call to the apostolic ministry. He had evidently expected to be a Jewish rabbi, but God had other plans for his life. Only the firm assurance of this could have carried him through all his hardships.

Why did Paul feel a need to mention his apostolic authority in writing to his two faithful colleagues, who never questioned his authority? The answer seems to be that he intended these letters to be read to local church congregations. He knew that both his recipients were being challenged by false teachers and he wanted to strengthen the hands of these two pastors.

The expression "God our Savior" occurs five times in the Pastorals and nowhere else in Paul's letters (see also 2:3; Tit 1:3; 2:10; 3:4). Elsewhere in the NT we find it only in Jude 25. A similar phrase, "God my Savior," occurs in Lk 1:47, in a hymn that is characterized largely by OT language. It is possible that Luke as the amanuensis may have had some influence on the apostle's language at this point (see introduction). It may be, too, that Nero's claim to the title "Savior of the world" caused Paul to assert emphatically that the only real Savior is God, the Supreme Being.

Another unique feature is the designation of Christ as "our hope" (see also Col 1:27). Jesus Christ is the only one in whom we may place our hope for this life and the life to come.

2 The letter is addressed to "Timothy my true son in the faith." Elsewhere Paul refers to him as "my son whom I love, who is faithful in the Lord" (1Co 4:17; see also Php 2:22). The word "true" (GK *1188*) means "genuine, true-born." Perhaps the thrust here is twofold: Timothy was a true believer and he was also a genuine convert of Paul's ministry.

We first meet Timothy in Ac 16:1–3. There we are told that on Paul's second missionary journey he found at Lystra a young disciple named Timothy, the son of a Jewish Christian mother and a Greek father. Paul was so impressed with the young man that he asked him to join the missionary party. It seems clear that Timothy had been converted under Paul's preaching at Lystra on the first missionary journey (about A.D. 47). He had matured so well as a Christian that only two years later (A.D. 49) he was ready to become an apprentice to the great apostle. He became one of Paul's most trusted helpers, so that the apostle could write, "I have no one else like him, who takes a genuine interest in your welfare" (Php 2:20). The life of Timothy is a constant challenge to every young Christian to imitate his devotion and faithfulness.

After the name of the writer (v.1) and the recipient (v.2a) comes the greeting (v.2b). In all ten of Paul's previous letters the greeting is twofold—"grace and peace." Here and in 2 Timothy it is "grace, mercy and peace," which come to us "from God the Father and Christ Jesus our Lord."

Two things may have suggested the addition of "mercy" (GK *1799*). One would be Timothy's frail health (see 5:23); as a loving father, the apostle wishes mercy for his son. The other would be the difficulties that Timothy was encountering at Ephesus; he was in need of God's mercy and help.

"Grace" (GK *5921*) is a favorite word with Paul, occurring nearly one hundred times in his letters. First meaning "gracefulness" and then "graciousness," it is used in the NT for the divine favor that God bestows freely on all who believe. "Peace" (GK *1645*) has always been the typical greeting of the East (*shalom*; GK 8934). It is one of God's best gifts to people. In a world of war, hate, and disharmony, this term is particularly significant. In Christ we have peace of heart and mind.

Paul's Fourth Missionary Journey

c. A.D. 62—68

It is clear from Ac 13:1—21:17 that Paul went on three missionary journeys. There is also reason to believe that he made a fourth journey after his release from the Roman imprisonment recorded in Ac 28. The conclusion that such a journey did indeed take place is based on: (1) Paul's declared intention to go to Spain (Ro 15:24, 28), (2) Eusebius's implication that Paul was released following his first Roman imprisonment (*Ecclesiastical History*, 2.22.2-3) and (3) statements in early Christian literature that he took the gospel as far as Spain (Clement of Rome, *Epistle to the Corinthians*, ch. 5; *Actus Petri Vercellenses*, chs. 1-3; Muratorian Canon, lines 34-39).

The places Paul may have visited after his release from prison are indicated by statements of intention in his earlier writings and by subsequent mention in the Pastoral Letters. The order of his travel cannot be determined with certainty, but the itinerary at the right seems likely.

© 1985 The Zondervan Corporation

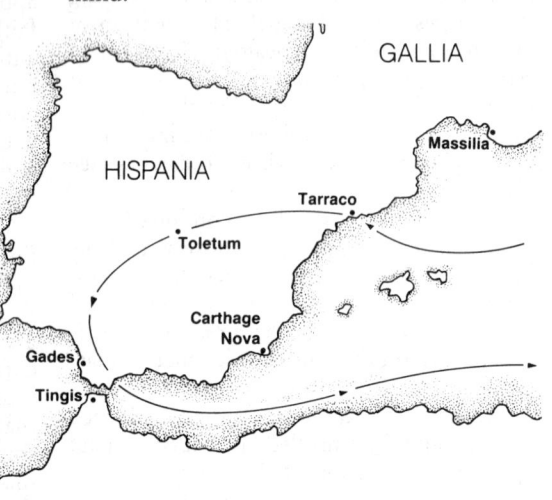

1. **Rome**—released from prison in A.D. 62
2. **Spain**—62-64 (Ro 15:24,28)
3. **Crete**—64-65 (Tit 1:5)
4. **Miletus**—65 (2Ti 4:20)
5. **Colosse**—66 (Phm 22)
6. **Ephesus**—66 (1Ti 1:3)
7. **Philippi**—66 (Php 2:23-24; 1Ti 1:3)
8. **Nicopolis**—66-67 (Tit 3:12)
9. **Rome**—67
10. **Martyrdom**—67/68

II. Timothy's Task at Ephesus (1:3–11)

1. Suppression of False Teachers (1:3–8)

3a When Paul went into Macedonia—at exactly what time we do not know—he urged Timothy to remain in Ephesus. As noted in the introduction, it appears that Paul was released from his first Roman imprisonment of two years (cf. Ac 28:30) and that he made another visit to Ephesus. There he discovered some conditions that needed extended attention. So he left Timothy as pastor of this important church.

3b–4a What was the problem that concerned Paul? We find the answer here in the purpose for which Timothy was to remain: "that you may command certain men not to teach false doctrines any longer nor to devote themselves to myths and endless genealogies." The church has always had false teachers—they appeared on the scene in the very first generation, within thirty-five years of the church's birth at Pentecost (A.D. 30–65).

What was the nature of these "false doctrines," and what is meant by "myths and endless genealogies"? There are two possible answers. (1) The reference could be to the vagaries of what became known as Gnosticism, with its endless genealogies of intermediary beings (aeons) between God and humankind. (2) But v.7 suggests that these were Jewish teachers, who were caught up in the mythological treatment of OT genealogies, and Tit 1:14 speaks of "Jewish myths." There is abundant evidence that both these features were found in the Judaism of that day.

4b Paul declares that such teachings "promote controversies rather than God's work— which is by faith." The word translated "work" (GK 3873) means "stewardship" or "dispensation." God's dispensation of truth does not produce whimsical fables but true faith.

5 The "goal" (GK 5465) of this instruction of Paul (and really, all of Paul's teaching and preaching can be included here) is "love" (GK 27). The highest goal of true religion is the unselfish love of full loyalty to God and boundless goodwill to our fellow human beings. This must be our ultimate goal in life.

This love comes "from a pure heart and a good conscience and a sincere faith." Our hearts must be cleansed from self-centered thoughts if we are going to obey the two greatest commandments enunciated by Jesus (Mt 22:37–40). Then we must maintain a good conscience if love is to function properly. And all this is based on "sincere" (lit., "unhypocritical"; GK 537) faith. All love comes from God, and it comes to us only as we are united to him by faith.

6 Unfortunately, some at Ephesus had "wandered away" (lit., "missed the mark"; GK 1762) from a sincere life of faith and had turned to "meaningless talk." They were doing much talking, but saying nothing of value.

7 Paul criticizes these would-be teachers of the Law heavily. His verdict was: "They do not know what they are talking about or what they so confidently affirm." Their self-confidence was empty pretense. They spoke many words, but had little substance.

8 Having identified the false teachers at Ephesus as self-appointed teachers of the Law of Moses, the apostle now points out the true purpose of that law: It is "good if one uses it properly [i.e., lawfully]."

2. The Purpose of the Law (1:9–11)

9a "Law" in this verse has no definite article and probably refers to law in general. The apostle indicates that the purpose of law is not to police good people but bad ones. In other words, we need law for the punishment of criminals and the protection of society.

The list that follows is typically Pauline (cf. Ro 1:24–32). It starts with more general terms, in three pairs: "lawbreakers and rebels, the ungodly and sinful, the unholy and irreligious." These represent attitudes or states of mind. "Lawbreakers" are those who ignore the law, and "rebels" are people who are insubordinate and refuse to be ruled. The word for "ungodly" means one who is deliberately guilty of irreverence. The adjective "irreligious" means having no sense of what is sacred—a common sin of secular society.

9b–10a The sins that follow covers the fifth to the ninth commandments. "Those who kill their fathers ... mothers" refers especially to dishonoring one's parents. For this outrageous violation of the fifth commandment the punishment of death was provided in the Mosaic Law (Ex 21:15). The fact that "murderers" (cf. the sixth commandment) immediately follows suggests that the sin of murder is also included in this sin concerning the "smiting" of one's parents.

Paul goes on to say that law was made "for adulterers and perverts" (the last term means "male homosexuals"; GK *780*; see also 1Co 6:9); both of these sins are against the seventh commandment. Despite its being condoned by some church leaders today, homosexual practices are categorically condemned in both the OT and NT. It is this particular sin that led to the destruction of Sodom and Gomorrah. It is widely recognized as one of the causes for the downfall of the Roman Empire, and its rapid increase today in Europe and North America poses a threat to the future of Western civilization.

"Slave traders" may also be translated "kidnappers" (GK *435*). Jewish rabbis specifically applied the eighth commandment about stealing to kidnapping—a crime that has greatly increased in the last few years.

Finally, "liars and perjurers" are both sins that relate to the ninth commandment about honesty and truth-telling.

10b–11 Lest he miss any other important item, Paul adds a general comment about any other sin that opposes "sound doctrine that conforms to the glorious gospel of the blessed God." "Sound" (GK *5617*) is one of the key words of the Pastoral Letters. It means "be in good health, to be healthy or sound." It refers to physical health in the Gospels, but an ethical, metaphorical usage as here is widely paralleled in Greek literature.

Does "sound" mean "healthy" or "healthful" (i.e., conducive to good health)? Really, both are included in the meaning. The Gospel is like healthy food, and the law is a sort of medicine that is only applied when one's moral nature is diseased.

"The glorious gospel of the blessed God" is the Gospel that displays God's glory, showing his moral character and perfections as they are exhibited in the person and work of Christ. Paul declares that this Gospel was "entrusted to me" (see 1Co 9:17; Gal 2:7; 1Th 2:4). It amazed him that God should have placed such trust in him—the one who had formerly opposed the Gospel and persecuted the church (cf. vv.12–14). The last clause of this paragraph is therefore a fitting introduction to the next section, in which he thanks God for choosing him.

III. Thanksgiving to God (1:12–17)

1. God's Abundant Grace (1:12–14)

12 Usually the thanksgiving in Paul's letters follows the salutation. But in this case the apostle has inserted between them a statement of his purpose in leaving Timothy at Ephesus. Now we find the familiar expression of thanks. In previous letters, thanksgiving was usually directed to God; here it is to "Christ Jesus our Lord." The lordship of Jesus finds increasing emphasis in Paul's later letters.

Christ has "given me strength" (lit., "empowered me"; GK *1904*). He did so because the Lord considered him "faithful" (GK *4412*), and he appointed Paul to his "service" (GK *1355*). This last word is often a technical word in the NT for Christian ministry.

13 Formerly Paul had been "a blasphemer," meaning that in his opposition to the Christian movement he cursed the name of Jesus. Now he realizes that this was blasphemy, because Jesus is divine. He was also "a persecutor" (see Ac 8:3; 9:1–2, 4–5; 22:4–5; 26:9–11; Gal 1:13). In his zeal to protect Judaism, the young Saul believed that he must destroy Christianity. Third and even worse, he was "a violent man" (GK *5616*); this word refers to insolence and extreme violence (cf. Ac 8:3).

In spite of these characteristics, Paul was "shown mercy" (GK *1796*) because he "acted in ignorance and unbelief." He was sincere in believing that he was serving God through his violence against the Christian movement. When brought later before the Sanhedrin in Jerusalem, he testified, "I have fulfilled my duty to God in all good conscience to this day" (Ac 23:1). This apparently included his pre-Christian life.

14 It was more than mercy that Paul received from God. He also received "the grace" of God poured out on him, "along with faith and love that are in Christ Jesus." This is another of the apostle's great triads. "Grace" provided his salvation, "faith" appropriated it, and "love" applied it.

2. The Worst of Sinners (1:15–17)

15–16 "Here is a trustworthy saying" is literally "faithful the word" (GK *4412* & *3364*);

this formula is found only in the Pastoral Letters (see 3:1; 4:9 2Ti 2:11; Tit 3:8). Here and in 4:9 we find the added words: "that deserves full acceptance." This repeated formula is always attached to a maxim relating to either doctrine or practice, on which full reliance can be placed. The saying here is "Christ Jesus came into the world to save sinners." This is the good news, the heart of the Gospel.

Paul claims that of all sinners he was "the worst"—lit., "first" or "chief." He felt this way because he had persecuted Christ's followers so vigorously. As far as morality was concerned, young Saul had been a strict Pharisee, living a life that was blameless before the law (Php 3:5–6). Yet in his case as chief sinner, Christ's "unlimited patience" had been displayed as an example to all who would believe in Jesus and thus receive eternal life. Paul's life was a powerful demonstration of what divine grace can do.

17 This verse is typical of Paul's habit of breaking out spontaneously into praise (see also 6:16; Ro 11:36; 16:27; Gal 1:5; Eph 3:21; Php 4:20; 2Ti 4:18).

IV. Timothy's Responsibility (1:18–20)

18–19 "Instruction" (GK *4132*) is the same word that is translated "command" in v.5. The aged apostle is giving his son in the faith a solemn charge "in keeping with the prophecies once made about you"—perhaps prophecies made at the time of Timothy's ordination or of his induction into missionary work (though this phrase can also be translated, "according to the prophecies leading me to you"—there may have been prophetic utterances that pointed Timothy's way into the ministry). Paul urges Timothy to "fight the good fight [a term from warfare], holding on to faith and a good conscience." Paul was concerned that he and his colleagues should have a good "conscience" (GK *5287*) always. Those who reject this "shipwreck" their faith.

20 Paul names two examples of those who have shipwrecked their faith: Hymenaeus and Alexander. The former is mentioned again as a heretical teacher in 2Ti 2:17; the latter is probably "Alexander the metalworker," who did Paul a great deal of harm (2Ti 4:14). The apostle had handed these two ringleaders "over to Satan to be taught not to blaspheme" (cf. 1Co 5:5, where this phrase indicates excommunication from the church). The purpose was to jolt the offenders to repentance, induced by the fearful thought of being turned over to Satan's control. Its purpose, therefore, is remedial, not punitive.

V. Worship and Conduct (2:1–3:16)

1. Prayer (2:1–7)

1 Paul now begins giving instructions for public worship. He was concerned that divine worship should be carried on in Ephesus most effectively and helpfully. So he says, "I urge" (GK *4151*; also translated "exhort"); it indicates the urgency of Paul's admonition. "First of all" emphasizes primacy in importance rather than in time. In other words, the most essential part of public worship is prayer.

The NT has seven different Greek nouns for prayer, four of which occur in this verse. (1) "Requests" (GK *1255*): This word basically carries the idea of desire or need. All true prayer begins in a sense of need and involves a deep desire, although it should never stop there. God wants us to bring our "requests" to him, and he always has a listening ear. (2) "Prayers" (GK *4666*): This word always signifies praying to God. It is used for both private and public prayers (here public). (3) "Intercession" (GK *1950*): This word was used in the sense of "conversation" and then of "petition." Perhaps it suggests the idea that prayer should be a conversation with God, but it also implied boldness of access to God's presence. We must come to God with full confidence and enter into close communion with him in a conversational atmosphere if we want to experience depth and richness in our prayer life. And only those who really commune with God in private can edify others in their public prayers. (4) "Thanksgiving" (GK *2374*): This word suggests that giving of thanks should always be a part of our praying. Thanking God for what he has done for us in the past strengthens our faith to believe that he will meet our needs in the future.

2 Prayers of these varied types are to be made "for everyone" (v.1), but especially "for kings and all those in authority." The term "king" applies both to the emperor at Rome and to lesser rulers. When one remembers that the Roman emperor when Paul wrote this letter was the cruel monster Nero—who later put Paul and Peter to death—one realizes that we should pray for our present rulers, no matter how unreasonable they may seem to be. Prayer for "all those in authority" in various levels of government should have a regular place in all public worship.

The purpose of this is logical and significant: "that we may live peaceful and quiet lives in all godliness and honesty." The fact that we are permitted to assemble peaceably for public worship is dependent on our rights under law—law as upheld and enforced by our legislators, administrators, and judicial leaders. We ought to pray for them, and also thank God for them.

"Peaceful" has the basic idea of restfulness not marred by outward disturbance; "quiet" suggests inner stillness that accompanies restfulness. The word for "godliness" (GK 2354) basically means "piety" or "reverence"; anyone who is irreverent is living an ungodly life. "Holiness" (GK 4949) suggests reverence, seriousness, and respectfulness (cf. also 3:4; Tit 2:7).

3–4 Such a life is "good" (GK 2819; also meaning "beautiful" or "excellent") and "pleases God our Savior" (see comment on 1:1). He "wants all men to be saved and to come to a knowledge of the truth." This statement accords well with Jn 3:16 and with the declaration in 2Co 5:14–15 that Christ died for all. Salvation has been provided for all, but only those who accept it are saved. "Knowledge" (GK 2106) means precise and accurate knowledge. Such knowledge of God's truth is both the root and fruit of salvation. Paul here sounds a frequent note of the Pastorals—true knowledge saves one from error.

5 This is one of the most significant verses of the NT. It declares first of all that "there is one God." This is a primary affirmation in the OT, in opposition to the polytheism of Paul's day. The fact that there is only one God (monotheism) is the basic premise of both Judaism and Christianity.

But then comes a difference, for Christianity goes on to assert that "there is one mediator between God and men, the man Christ Jesus." "Mediator" (GK 3542) occurs only once in LXX (Greek translation of the OT). Job was frustrated by the fact that God was not a man with whom he could converse. In despair he wished that there might be someone to arbitrate between himself and God (Job 9:33). Christ is the answer to this ancient cry for help. A "mediator" is someone who intervenes between two parties, either to make peace and restore friendship, or to form a covenant. In keeping with this, Christ by his death restored the harmony between God and human beings which sin had broken.

To be of any use, a bridge across a chasm or river must be anchored on both sides. Christ has closed the gap between deity and humanity. He has crossed the grand canyon, so deep and wide, between heaven and earth. He has bridged that which separated us from God. With one foot planted in eternity, he planted the other in time. He who was the eternal Son of God became the Son of Man. And across this bridge, we can come into the very presence of God, knowing that we are accepted because we have him as a Mediator.

6 This Christ "gave himself as a ransom for all men." The word "ransom" (GK 519; cf. also 3389) means that which is given in exchange for another as the price of redemption. In the first century it applied especially to the price paid to free a slave. So Christ paid the ransom to free us from the slavery of sin. Because of this we are rightfully his possession. Jesus gave his life as a ransom "for all men." The Greek word translated "for" means "on behalf of." Christ died on behalf of all people, but only those who accept his sacrifice are set free from the shackles of sin.

This message of Christ's redemptive death was the distinctive apostolic witness—"the testimony given in its proper time." Christ's sacrifice for sin took place at God's appointed hour.

7 For the purpose of giving this witness, Paul was "appointed" (lit., "placed"; GK 5502) as "a herald and an apostle." "Herald" (GK 3061) was used in Paul's day to designate a messenger vested with public authority, who conveyed the messages of public officials or who gave a public summons; in the NT it signifies the one who proclaims the divine word. Thus a "preacher" is someone who makes a public proclamation for the King of kings. He is not to air his own opinions or debate other people's ideas but to proclaim the Word of God. What a glorious privilege and what an awesome responsibility! On apostle, see comment on 1:1.

Paul adds, "I am telling the truth, I am not lying." This suggests that some of the church members at Ephesus were challenging his apostolic authority, as had happened at Corinth (2Co 10:10).

In addition, Paul was "a teacher of the true faith to the Gentiles." This was his special assignment from the Lord (Ac 9:15; Eph 3:2–8). Though he was "a Hebrew of the Hebrews" and brought up a strict Pharisee (Php 3:5), he had been born in Tarsus, one of the three main centers of Greek learning (after Athens and Alexandria), and was therefore suited to this assignment. The Christian leaders at Jerusalem agreed that he should evangelize the Gentiles (Gal 2:9).

2. Men (2:8)

8 Getting back specifically to the matter of public worship, the apostle wants "men everywhere to lift up holy hands in prayer, without anger or disputing." Lifting up one's hands in prayer is often mentioned in the OT (e.g., 1Ki 8:22; Pss 141:2; 143:6). It is a natural gesture, indicating earnest desire. The word "holy" here means devout, pious, and pleasing to God. Linked to lifting up holy hands is the idea of moral purity. We cannot pray effectively unless our lives are clean and committed to our Lord Jesus Christ. Nothing does more to alienate the mind from sincere prayer than an attitude of anger and a quarrelsome spirit.

3. Women (2:9–15)

9–10 In v.8 Paul desires that men pray; in v.9 he has some instructions for women and how they should conduct themselves in church services.

First, they are to "dress modestly." An expansion of the phrase used here is: "adorn themselves in modest clothes." This remains a much needed admonition today. "Decency" (GK 133) suggests a modesty that does not overstep the limits of womanly reserve. This should apply to both dress and deportment, although the rest of the verse suggests that the primary reference here is to one's clothing. Women are also to dress with "propriety" (GK 5408), a word that suggests good judgment. Paul hints at the snare of participating in the extreme forms of current fashions.

"Braided hair" means hair that is woven or braided (cf. 1Pe 3:3). The Christian woman is not to adorn herself with "gold or pearls or expensive clothes" so as to draw attention to herself. At worst, this is what the prostitutes did. At best, it shows pride and self-centeredness, both of which are contrary to the spirit of Christ. Such dress is especially unbecoming in church. Rather, Christian women are to adorn themselves "with good deeds, appropriate for women who profess to worship God." We must express our faith through good deeds. This thought is more dominant in the Pastoral Letters than in Paul's earlier letters—perhaps because the need for such emphasis was more apparent.

11–12 The teaching of these two verses is similar to that found in 1Co 14:33–35. There Paul tells the women that they are not allowed to talk out loud in the public services; here he says that they are to "learn in quietness and full submission." "Submission" (GK 5717) does not mean surrendering one's mind and conscience or abandoning one's private judgment. It does mean, however, that a woman must be submissive to her husband (cf. Tit 2:5)—though it may well have the wider application of submission to the officials and regulations of the church.

Paul goes on to say, "I do not permit a woman to teach or to have authority over a man." Some have said that the apostle's prohibition excludes women even from teaching Sunday school classes. But he is talking about public assemblies of the church. Paul speaks appreciatively of the fact that Timothy himself had been taught the right way by his godly mother and grandmother (2Ti 1:5; 3:15). He also writes to Titus that the older women are to train the younger (Tit 2:3–4). Women have always carried the major responsibility for teaching small children, in both home and church school. And what could we have done without them!

"Silent" (GK 2484) is exactly the same phrase that is rendered "in quietness" in v.11. This is an important Christian virtue. Paul was especially opposed to confusion in the public services of the church (1Co 14:33).

13–14 The apostle adds that the wife's role of submission to her husband is inherent in creation. Adam was created first, and then Eve (the story of Ge 2:21–23, where God made Eve from a rib taken from Adam). Many commentators have noted regarding this story that Eve was not made out of Adam's head to rule over him, nor out of his feet to be trampled upon by him, but out of his side to be equal with him and near his heart to be loved by him. This expresses perfectly the ideal of a happy married life. The husband who has this concept will usually find his wife eager to please him.

Paul makes one further point. It was the woman who was deceived by Satan and who disobeyed God (cf. Ge 3:1–6). Since she was so easily deceived, she should not be trusted as a teacher.

15 This verse is difficult to explain. Literally, the passage reads: "But she will be saved through the childbirth, if they continue in faith. . . ." The verb "save" (GK 5392) is used in the NT for both physical healing (mostly in the Gospels) and spiritual salvation (mostly in the letters). Perhaps it carries both connotations here. The wife may find both physical health and a higher spiritual state through the experience of bearing and rearing children.

Three interpretations of this verse have been suggested. (1) Since there is a definite article with "childbirth," some have suggested it refers to the birth of Christ, through whom salvation has come to the world. (2) Closely related to this is the interpretation that connects this statement with Ge 3:15. The seed of the woman would crush the serpent's head and bring salvation to humankind. (3) By begetting children and thus fulfilling the design God appointed for women, a woman will be saved from becoming a prey to the social evils of her day and will take her part in the local church. This third interpretation fits best with the context and the main emphasis of this letter.

4. Overseers (3:1–7)

Paul now gives the qualifications for overseers in the church (see also Tit 1:6–9).

1 "Sets his heart on" (GK 3977) means "aspires to." The word "overseer" (GK 2175) is based on a verb that means "to look upon," and so "to oversee, care for." The reference here is to the office of overseer in the church (elsewhere, an overseer is identical to an "elder"; see comment on Tit 1:6). Anyone who aspires to such a position "desires a noble task"—and, we might add, a place of heavy responsibility. One needs to be sure that such a desire is not an expression of pride, but rather that it reflects a deep commitment to the work of the church.

2 For the church organization that we know in the NT, it is apparent that churches had several overseers (see Ac 20:28; Php 1:1). The older translation of "overseer" (GK 2176) as "bishop" has led to misunderstanding, for the NT knows nothing of a single diocesan bishop, such as some contemporary churches have.

Paul lists fifteen specific qualifications of an "overseer" in vv.2–7. The first is that he must be "above reproach" (GK 455). This word describes someone against whom no charge of wrong doing can be brought. Because it stands at the head of his list, Paul suggests that an overseer should not be subject to criticism in any of the listed characteristics.

The second qualification is that he must be "the husband of but one wife" (cf. also v.12). While some have interpreted this as meaning "married only once," most commentators agree that it means monogamy—only one wife at one time—and that the overseer must be completely faithful to his wife.

The third qualification is "temperate" (GK 3767). In classical Greek this word meant "not mixed with wine"; in later writers it came to have the broader sense of "temperate" or "sober."

The fourth qualification of an overseer is "self-controlled" (GK 5409), a word that originally means "of sound mind." Thus it carried the sense of "self-controlled" or "sober-minded."

Fifth is "respectable" (GK 3177)—the same word as is translated "modestly" in 2:9. The basic meaning of the word is "orderly," but Greek writers used it in the sense of "respectable" or "honorable." That fits well here.

The sixth qualification is "hospitable" (GK 5811); this word means literally "loving strangers." Christians traveling in the first century avoided the public inns with their pagan atmosphere and food that had already been offered to idols (cf. 1Co 8). They would therefore seek out a Christian home in which to stop for the night. A valuable by-product was that believers from widely scattered areas would get to know each other, thus cementing lines of fellowship. So hospitality was an important Christian virtue in that day. Even in our modern hotel-motel age, it can have its place.

The seventh item is "able to teach" (GK *1434*). This implies not only a readiness to teach, but also having the spiritual power to do so, after the overseer has prayerfully reflected on God's Word and its practical application.

3 The eighth qualification for an overseer is that he must not be "given to drunkenness" (GK *4232*). Aristotle's use of this and related words suggests that it meant "tipsy" or "rowdy." It is a sad commentary on the culture of that day that such a warning would have to be given concerning church overseers.

Ninth on the list is "not violent" (GK *4438*); the person who drinks too much wine is apt to become involved in drunken brawls.

Paul now gives another positive quality: "gentle" (GK *2117*). This word is difficult to translate with one English word; gracious, kindly, forbearing, considerate, magnanimous, and genial are all included (cf. 2Co 10:1; Php 4:5).

The eleventh item is "not quarrelsome" (GK *285*). This word means "abstaining from fighting." Here it is used in the metaphorical sense of "not contentious." A contentious leader is a sad feature in any church.

Next is "not a lover of money" (GK *921*). The love of money (cf. 6:10) is one of the greatest dangers confronting every Christian worker. One who finds that he can make big money in part-time secular work is apt to be diverted from an effective ministry.

4–5 The final three stated qualifications are developed in greater length. The first concerns the relationship of an overseer to his family—he must be one who can "manage his own family well." His children must be obedient and respectful. This implies that the overseer would normally be a married man. Paul follows this up with the logical statement that if one cannot manage his own house, he should not be expected to take proper care of a local congregation. It is an argument from the lesser to the greater.

6 The overseer must not be "a recent convert" (GK *3745*), for there is the danger that such a person might "become conceited" (GK *5605*) or puffed up with pride. When this happens, the person will "fall under the same judgment as the devil." We believe that only God is uncreated, that he created all life, and that he pronounced everything he created as "good." Satan was therefore created by God as a good creature. At some time in history he fell, and the cause of his fall was pride. All proud people are subject to the same judgment as he is (see Rev 20:10).

7 The fifteenth and last qualification of an overseer is that he must "have a good reputation with outsiders." When a leader in the church has a bad reputation in the community, it often brings irreparable damage to the local congregation and indeed to the entire cause of Christ. Moreover, a church leader must have a good reputation "so that he will not fall into disgrace and into the devil's trap." Most commentators feel that this phrase means the trap that the devil lays for unsuspecting Christians (cf. a similar expression in 2Ti 2:26).

Paul's careful concern for the right choice of leaders in the church and the extensive qualifications listed here should serve as guidelines for those who are charged with the responsibility of such selection today.

5. Deacons (3:8–13)

8 Paul now moves to the qualification for "deacons." The word "deacon" (GK *1356*) often means "servant," and it is used that way many times in the Gospels. Specifically, it was used by various writers of that period for those who wait on tables. This leads us to Ac 6. The apostles as overseers of the church in Jerusalem did not have time to take care of the material needs of the poorer members, such as the widows (cf. Ac 6:2, where the verb form of this word is used). So the church chose seven men to assume this responsibility, while the apostles gave their attention to public "prayer and the ministry of the word" (v.4). Although the term *deacon* is not used in this connection, it would seem that these men were the forerunners of the deacons in the church. The term is first used in a technical sense in Php 1:1, and it probably means those who supervised material affairs of the church.

Paul says that the deacons, like the overseers, are to be "worthy of respect" (GK

4948; cf. 2:2; 3:4). This word combines the ideas of gravity and dignity.

Second, they are to be "sincere" (lit., "not double-tongued"; GK *1474*). This adjective has the idea of saying something twice, with the bad connotation of saying one thing to one person and something else to another.

The third qualification is "not indulging in much wine" (a longer and stronger expression than that found in v.3).

Next is "not pursuing dishonest gain" (GK *153*). This is understandable for people charged with handling money to give to the poor.

9 Fifth, deacons must have a grasp of "the deep truths [lit., "mystery"; GK *3696*] of the faith." "The faith" must be taken in an objective sense, referring to the truths of the Christian religion, rather than as subjective, having to do with one's personal faith in Christ. This letter has a strong emphasis on a pure "conscience" as well as a pure faith (cf. 1:5, 19). A "clear conscience" is one that has been cleansed by the blood of Christ (Heb. 10:22) and does not offend God or other people (Ac 24:16).

10 Deacons "must first be tested" (GK *1507*). This verb has three stages: (1) to test, (2) to prove by testing; and (3) to approve as the result of testing. Perhaps all three are in mind here. Before being accepted to serve as deacons, prospective deacons had to prove themselves beyond reproach before the community.

11 In the Greek language the same word is used for "woman" and "wife" (GK *1222*). Since this word is found here for "their wives," there are three possible interpretations as to what group Paul is talking about. (1) These women were the wives of the deacons, though the word "their" is missing in Greek. (2) Another possibility is that Paul is speaking of women in general; the context of vv.8–12 would seem to rule this out. (3) The third choice is a reference to deaconesses, of whom Phoebe (Ro 16:1) is an example. We know that there were deaconesses in the church in later centuries, but whether such an order existed in the first century is debatable.

We are inclined to favor the idea that the reference is to "their wives." Paul talks about the qualifications of the deacons in vv.8–10 and again in vv.12–13. It would seem natural to assume that he is talking about their wives in v.11. What he says that these women is that, whoever they are, they must, "in the same way" as the deacons, be "worthy of respect" (cf. v.8).

They are also not to be "malicious talkers" (GK *1333*), i.e., those who slander other people. This note was a needed warning in the early church and is still needed today.

On "temperate," see the comment on v.2. Both husbands and wives were have this virtue.

"Trustworthy in everything" is a comprehensive requirement. Church workers must not be lax in taking care of their assigned duties.

12 Now Paul returns to the specific qualifications of deacons. Like an overseer (v.2), a deacon must be the husband of one wife, and he must also "manage his children and his household well" (cf. v.4, where "household" [GK *3875*] is translated "family").

13 Those who serve well in their assigned duties in the church gain for themselves "an excellent standing." They should be able to maintain great respect in the eyes of the church as well as in God's sight. Likewise, "great assurance [GK *4244*]" relates to confidence both before God and before other people.

6. The Mystery of Godliness (3:14–16)

14–15 Paul was hoping to visit Timothy soon. But just in case he was delayed, he wants his young associate to know "how people ought to conduct themselves in God's household." The apostle's rules for church members and their leaders are what we find in chs. 2–3. God's "household" (GK *3875*) or "the church of the living God" has primary reference here to the local congregation, although the general church of Jesus Christ may also be in view.

This church is "the pillar and the foundation of the truth." "Pillar" (GK *5146*) and "foundation" (GK *1613*) both emphasize the certainty and firmness of "the truth" that is revealed in God's Word. Each local church must support and strengthen the truth by witnessing to the faith and by living exemplary lives.

16 The "mystery of godliness" is revealed in a Person, even Jesus Christ. The creedal hymn in this verse speaks particularly about the incarnate Christ. (1) The eternal Son of God, existing as pure spirit, was made visible in his incarnation, when he became a human being. (2) Christ's profound claims were vindicated by his miracles, climaxing in his resurrection; these were sure evidences that he was the sinless Son of God. (3) During his earthly ministry angels watched over him (Mt 4:11; Lk 22:43). (4) After Jesus' death and resurrection, the message of Christ (cf. 1Co 1:23) and of salvation in his name was proclaimed among the Gentile nations of the world. (5) People all over the world believed in Christ as they heard the preached message. (6) Finally, he "was taken up in glory"—a reference to his ascension in Acts 1:1–11. This was the climax of his earthly ministry. Preaching Christ means preaching his life, death, resurrection, and ascension as the glorified Lord.

VI. Special Instructions to Timothy (4:1–16)

1. False Asceticism (4:1–5)

1 Paul now gives instructions to Timothy on a variety of subjects, beginning with the matter of ascetic teachings (vv.1–5).

The Holy Spirit explicitly says that in later times some people will "abandon" (GK 923) the faith, i.e., become apostate. Instead of being led by the Holy Spirit, these apostates give their attention to deceiving spirits and the teaching of "demons" (i.e., evil spirits who are led by the devil). The expression "in later times" is not as strong as the phrase "in the last days" (2Ti 3:1); the conditions that Paul is discussing here evidently took place during his lifetime.

2 The apostle uses strong language in describing the teachers of the false doctrines he is about to mention. He declares that they are "hypocritical liars"; this implies that they know better, but they have deliberately forsaken the faith and teach falsehood. They are people whose consciences "have been seared as with a hot iron," so that they have become unfeeling about their willful wrongdoings.

3 Paul now mentions two of their false teachings: forbidding marriage and ordering people "to abstain from certain foods." This ascetic emphasis crept into the church in the first century and was widely felt in the second century under the influence of Gnosticism. The Gnostics taught that all matter is evil and that only spirit is good; thus all physical pleasure is sin.

What these false teachers forgot is that marriage is an institution that God established as the normal thing in human society (see Ge 2:24). The idea of abstaining from certain foods goes back, of course, to the Mosaic law. But Christ has freed us from the Law (Gal 5:1–6), so that we are no longer under its restrictions regarding certain kinds of food, "which God created to be received with thanksgiving by those who believe and who know the truth." Only those whose faith is weak avoid eating meat and restrict themselves to a vegetable diet (Ro 14:1–2). In spite of this, some still advocate and practice vegetarianism in the name of Christianity. Paul deals much more severely with this heresy in 1 Timothy than he did in Romans. Evidently the false teaching of asceticism was spreading in the church and the apostle struck out forcefully against it as a negation of our freedom in Christ.

4–5 The simple fact is that "everything God created is good" (echoing a statement made six times in Ge 1 [Ge 1:10, 12, 18, 21, 25, 31]). It is true that vegetarianism may have prevailed before the Flood (cf. Ge 2:9, 16), but God clearly told Noah that animals could also be eaten as food (Ge 9:3).

Paul then declares that "nothing is to be rejected if it is received with thanksgiving." This underscores the importance of "offering thanks" always before we eat, and this is reinforced by v.5: "because it is consecrated [GK 39] by the word of God and prayer." Food thus becomes "holy" to the eaters—not that they are inherently unclean, but some people's scruples or unthankfulness might make them unclean to them. "The word of God" suggests the use of Scripture phrases when saying a prayer at the table.

2. Superiority of the Spiritual (4:6–10)

6 Paul tells Timothy that if he calls the attention of the believers to these truths, he will be a good "minister" (lit., "servant"; GK 1356). To be "a good minister of Christ Jesus" should be the aim of every pastor today. Timothy had been trained or nurtured "in the truths of the faith." His earliest training was in Judaism, but he had been converted as a young man to Christianity (Ac 16:1–3). He had closely "followed" (GK *4158*) its teachings.

7–8 Timothy is to avoid "godless myths" and tall "tales" such as elderly women love to tell children. That is the way Paul describes the Jewish legends of his day (cf. Tit 1:14). Rather, Timothy is admonished to "train" (GK *1214*) himself to be godly. "Physical training" clearly refers to athletic discipline, and it does have some value, at least for life on this earth. But spiritual exercise is far more important, for it has value for eternity—"holding promise for both the present life and the life to come."

9–10 Again we find the formula, "This is a trustworthy saying that deserves full acceptance" (cf. comment on 1:15). In this case, it most likely refers to the preceding statement (v.8). "Labor" (GK *3159*) and "strive" (GK *76*) are both strong terms. The first means "grow weary" and implies working with effort; the second was used for competing in an athletic contest, implying "struggle." Just as athletes exert what seems to be their last ounce of energy to win a race, so Paul was giving the ministry all he had.

God is "the Savior of all men, and especially of those who believe." In what sense is he the Savior of *all* men? To interpret this in terms of universal salvation would be contrary to the whole tenor of Scripture. What Paul means is that God is potentially the Savior of all men because of Calvary, but actually the Savior of only those who believe.

3. Pastoral Duties (4:11–16)

11–12 Timothy must keep on commanding and teaching the things Paul has been writing about, exercising his authority as pastor. Moreover, he must conduct himself in such a way that no one will look down on him in a condescending way because of his young age. A person could be a "young man" until his fortieth year. Timothy was probably about thirty years old at this time.

On the positive side, he must be "an example" (GK *5596*). He is to present the proper image of the Christian and to be a pattern for other believers to follow. This is an awesome responsibility for those who enter the ministry. They must set an example in what they say, in how they live their lives, and in what they believe. The five nouns used at the end of this verse are vital constituents of all Christian living. Carelessness in any one of these areas can spell failure and even disaster.

13 Until Paul comes, Timothy is to devote himself "to the public reading of Scripture." The early church followed the example of the Jewish synagogue in publicly reading the Scriptures at every service. He is also to give himself to "preaching" (lit., "exhortation"; GK *4155*). Every pastor must not only read the Word of God to the people but also exhort them to obey it. The third important function of the pastoral ministry is "teaching" (GK *1436*). The people need instruction in Christian living, and the pastor should give it to them.

14 Furthermore, Paul advises his younger colleague not to neglect his gift (GK *5922*). This word, *charisma*, occurs sixteen times in Paul's letters and only once elsewhere in the NT (1Pe 4:10). It comes from *charis* ("grace"), and so means a free gift, especially an extraordinary working of the Holy Spirit in a person. "Neglect" (GK *288*) means to be careless about something; being careless about God's gifts is a sin.

The specific gift Paul has in mind was given to Timothy "through a prophetic message" when the elders of the church placed their hands on him. We are not told when or where this happened—perhaps at Ephesus, when Paul left Timothy there (cf. also 1:18; 2Ti 1:6).

When the Scriptures were read in either a synagogue or a church (4:13), the reading took place from a scroll.

15 "Be diligent" means "care for"; it was used frequently in the sense of "practice, cultivate, take pains with," though it is also possible for this phrase to mean "ponder these things." Timothy must also give himself completely to what Paul has been writing, so that everybody might see his "progress." Timothy was to make progress in his own spiritual life and in his effectiveness in the ministry.

16 The first thing that every Christian worker must watch is his or her own life—not only one's outward life but also one's inner thoughts and feelings. No matter how straight people may be in their doctrine or how effective they may be in their teaching, if there is a flaw in their inner or outer lives, it will ruin them. This is where many ministers have failed tragically. While watching over others, pastors must keep an eye on themselves.

To "persevere" (GK 2152) means to persist in doing something. Paul is instructing Timothy to keep on doing the things he has been writing about. By so doing, he will save both himself and his hearers. For a soul-winner to save others and lose his or her own soul is an unmitigated tragedy. To save one's own soul and have one's hearers lost is no less tragic.

VII. Special Groups in the Church (5:1–6:2)

1. The Older and the Younger (5:1–2)

1–2 "Exhort" (GK 4151) also means "encourage"; this verb carries through to the end of v.2. The young man Timothy should treat the older men with gentleness and kindness, as he would a father; he must treat the "younger men" as brothers and the "older women" as mothers. Fortunate is the young pastor who has godly "mothers in Israel" in the congregation. In relation to "younger women," a needed caution is added. They are to be treated as sisters—because the Christians are all one family in the Lord—but "with absolute purity." The pastor who does not heed this warning will soon be in trouble.

2. Widows (5:3–16)

3 "Give proper recognition to" (GK 5506) reflects a word that means first "price" and secondarily "honor" or "reverence." In view of the following context, it could possibly mean "give proper compensation to" widows in real need. Timothy is to look after widows who genuinely have no other means of support.

4 The case is different with a widow who has "children or grandchildren." In that case, they are to take care of her. "To put their religion into practice by caring for their own family" is literally "to show piety toward one's own household." In so doing they would be "repaying" (GK 625) those who brought them up. This is "pleasing" (GK 621) to God.

The Jewish synagogues gave careful attention to the care of their widows, and the early church followed that custom (Ac 6:1). This was due to the fact that in the culture of those days, a widow could not ordinarily find any employment and so would need financial support. Today, with insurance income, social security, and job opportunities, the situation is very different. But each church should still see to it that no widow in its congregation is left destitute. Christian love demands this, and it is especially appropriate in view of the NT concept that all believers are one in Christ, fellow members of the family of God. We should care for each other.

5 This verse gives the characteristics of a true Christian widow. She must be one who is "left all alone," i.e., she is childless. Such a woman puts her hope in God, for she has no earthly hopes. She continues in her supplications and her prayers night and day. One is reminded of the widow Anna, who was eighty-four years old. "She never left the temple but worshiped night and day, fasting and praying" (Lk 2:37).

6 In contrast with that picture is this statement: But the widow who lives luxuriously or self-indulgently "is dead even while she lives."

7–8 Timothy is to "give the people these instructions." The purpose of the instruction is that they may be not "open to blame" (lit., "irreproachable"; GK 455).

Paul goes on with strong words on this matter of caring for the needy. Those who do not "provide for" (lit., "think of beforehand"; GK 4629) their own relatives, especially those of their own immediate family, fall below the best heathen standard of family affection and are more blameworthy, for they have not followed what they have been taught about the supreme example of love in Jesus Christ.

9–10 Having defined a real widow as one bereft of all relatives to take care of her, Paul now restricts the matter further by saying that no widow under sixty years of age should be "put on the list." It seems evident that an official list of widows was kept by each church and that only these received material support.

Furthermore, she must have "been faithful to her husband" (lit., "the wife of one man"). This is the same sort of expression as is found in the qualifications for overseers (3:2) and deacons (3:12). As we noted there, this does not mean "only once married," especially since Paul goes on in v.14 to instruct younger widows to remarry.

To qualify for enrollment, a widow must also be well known for her good deeds, several of which are spelled out as essential if she were going to be supported by the church. The first is "bringing up children" (GK 5452). This would most naturally refer to her own children but could also include the care of orphans. The second is "showing hospitality" (lit., "welcoming strangers"; GK 3827). Next is "washing the feet of the saints"; this was an important courtesy whenever guests entered a house. The last two duties are "helping those in trouble and devoting herself to all kinds of good deeds."

11–12 Regarding the widows under sixty years of age, Paul instructs Timothy not to put them on the official list. Most of them will become restless against the limitations of Christian widowhood and will want to marry. If they do, they incur "judgment" (GK 3210), because they will have broken "their first pledge" (GK 4411), i.e., the solemn promise to be devoted only to Christ that they made when they joined the list of widows.

13 Another risk with younger widows is that "they get into the habit of being idle" or inactive. Instead of working, they go from house to house as "gossips [GK 5827] and busybodies [GK 4319]." That is, they pick up private matters and spread them abroad, and they meddle in things that do not concern them (cf. 1Th 3:11). The consequences of such meddling can be tragic.

14–15 In view of these dangers, Paul advises "younger widows to marry, to have children, to manage their homes," in order that they may "give the enemy no opportunity for slander." "Enemy" (GK 512) means "adversary." Most think that the reference here is to a human adversary, not to Satan (who is mentioned in v.15). "Slander" (GK 3367; cf. 1Pe 3:9) is a strong term meaning "abuse" or "railing." Paul fears that the unfortunate conduct of younger widows might bring serious reproach on the church. Some younger widows have already turned away to follow "Satan."

16 The female believer who has widows dependent on her "should help them," so that the church will be free to spend its time, money, and energy helping those who are truly needy widows (cf. v.3).

3. Elders (5:17–25)

17 Paul now addresses concerns about "elders" in the church (i.e., those who officially "direct the affairs of the church"). It was the responsibility of these earliest church officials (cf. Ac 14:23) to supervise the work of the local congregation.

Those who performed their functions well were worthy of "double honor [GK 5507]." Since this word was often used in the sense of a price paid for something, it has been suggested that here it might be translated "honorarium." But that raises the problem of "double"—double what was paid to the widows, or double what the other elders received? Perhaps we should allow both "honor" and "honorarium." Highest honor is to be given to "those whose work is preaching and teaching." Some have found here a distinction between ruling elders and teaching elders. But this is doubtful. Probably some elders gave themselves to preaching and teaching in addition to their regular duties—as was the case with Stephen and Philip as deacons (Ac 6–8).

18 This verse, as well as the preceding discussion of support for widows (vv.3–16), suggests definitely that the "double honor" for elders was to be a financial remuneration. Quoting Dt 25:4 (cf. 1Co 9:9) and Lk 10:7, Paul makes the point that a worker should receive compensation. As usual, Paul quotes the OT as "Scripture." But does the introductory formula, "For the Scripture says," apply also to the second quotation? Scholars are divided on this question, but if it does, this is probably the earliest instance of the Lord's words being quoted as Scripture.

19–20 Paul sounds a salutary warning that an "accusation" (GK *2990*; cf. Tit 1:6) concerning an individual elder was not to be "entertained" (lit., "received"; GK *4138*) as a charge against him unless it was supported by two or three witnesses. The last part of this verse is almost a verbal quotation from Dt 19:15 (cf. Dt 17:6; see also comment on 2Co 13:1). If there are any elders whose sins are substantiated, such offenders Timothy is to rebuke "publicly." Does this mean before the whole church or only before the other elders? The next clause seems to favor the latter: "so that the others [i.,e., the rest of the elders] may take warning."

21 The mention of "elect angels" in this charge is typical of Paul (cf. 3:16; 1Co 4:9). Timothy is solemnly charged to keep these instructions without showing any partiality. He is to do nothing out of favoritism. That is, he is not to permit his personal prejudices tip the scales of justice.

22 What is meant by "the laying on of hands"? While some commentators feel that the context favors the idea of laying hands of reconciliation on repentant fallen elders when they are received back into the church, most view this as a reference to ordination. In other words, this passage prohibits hasty ordination. That fits in well with the main discussion of this chapter. The laying on of hands in the Pastoral Letters seems to be regularly associated with ordination (cf. 4:14; 2Ti 1:7).

What about "Do not share in the sins of others"? Whenever Timothy ordained an elder, he became in a measure a surety for that person's character and thus was implicated in any sins the man might commit. So the young superintendent is warned, "Keep yourself pure"—primarily by being cautious about ordaining candidates, though the more general application to the whole of life may also be intended.

23 Apparently for medicinal purposes, Timothy is told not to restrict himself to drinking water but to "use a little wine because of your stomach and your frequent illnesses." The word for wine (GK *3885*) is sometimes used in LXX for unfermented grape juice. Furthermore, it is generally agreed that the wine of Jesus' day was usually rather weak and, especially among the Jews, often diluted with water. Moreover, safe drinking water was not always readily available in those eastern countries.

24–25 The sins of some people are clearly evident; these precede a person to judgment. The less obvious sins of others "trail behind them"—but finally catch up. Similarly, good deeds are clearly evident, "and even those that are not cannot be hidden." In the context about avoiding hasty ordination, Paul is saying that some people's sins are so evident that there is no question about rejecting them as candidates. Their sins precede them to judgment—first Timothy's judgment and finally divine judgment. The sins of others do not show up so soon but careful investigation will discover them. In the same way, the good deeds of qualified candidates will be easily seen. Those that seem less obvious will still appear on further search; they cannot be hidden.

4. Slaves (6:1–2)

1 Paul now has a word for servants or slaves. Their servitude is further emphasized by the phrase "under the yoke." About half the population of the Roman Empire in the first century was composed of slaves. This would undoubtedly have included Christian households (cf. the book of Philemon). Slaves are admonished to give full respect to their masters. Paul was always concerned that the conduct of Christians should be such as to bring glory to God and not bring reproach on his name and on the Gospel.

2 Not all Christian slaves had "believing masters." But those who did were not "to show less respect [GK *2969*] for them." Instead, they were to serve them even better, realizing that they were benefiting their brothers in Christ; their masters were "dear to them" (lit., "beloved"; GK *28*). This would give added incentive to their service.

The last sentence can be seen either as a specific instruction to Timothy about what to say to slaves, or else a general command regarding all that Paul has written to Timothy. Either makes good sense.

VIII. The Danger of the Love of Money (6:3–10)

3–5 A false teacher is someone who "teaches false doctrines" (i.e., doctrines other than the ones Timothy has been taught). Furthermore, he does not assent to "sound" (GK 5617) or healthy instruction, such as Paul has been writing in this letter.

Having defined the false teacher, Paul goes on to describe him in vv.4–5. Bluntly he declares that such a person "is conceited [GK 5605] and understands nothing." In spite of this ignorance, the false teacher has a morbid craving for endless "controversies and quarrels about words." The first of these two nouns (GK 2428) can mean the legitimate investigation of religious and theological problems, though here it indicates debates or disputes (cf. 2Ti 2:23; Tit 3:9). Even well-intentioned theological discussions sometimes have a tendency to degenerate into word-battles or exercises in semantics.

Five things are mentioned as the result of the disputes and arguments. The first two are "envy" (GK 5784) and "strife" (GK 2251; cf. also Ro 1:29; Gal 5:21). Envy always produces quarreling and strife. "Malicious talk" (GK 1060), when directed against God, means "blasphemy," but when directed against other people, as here, it means "abusive speech" or "slander." The fourth result is "evil suspicions."

The fifth result is spelled out at considerable length, comprising all of v.5. "Constant friction" refers to the continual wrangling that occurs between those whose minds are corrupt. In spite of whatever good intentions they may have, these men "have been robbed of the truth." They think that godliness is merely a way to make a lot of money.

6 Although "godliness" or "piety" should never be used as a means of securing financial gain, it is nevertheless true that "godliness with contentment is great gain." The word for "contentment" (GK 894) was used in classical Greek in a philosophical sense for a situation of life in which no aid or support is needed (also used in 2Co 9:8). But here it is used subjectively for a mind that is contented with its situation in life (cf. Php 4:11). Contentment is one of the greatest assets of life.

7–8 The reason we should be content is that "we brought nothing into the world, and we can take nothing out of it." That is, nothing in the entire world can add to the inner person. Thus, if we have food and clothing (and we may also include shelter here), we should be content with these things.

9 Those who are determined to become rich fall into temptation and "a trap" (GK 4075) and into many desires that are senseless and harm people. Wrong desires plunge people into "ruin [GK 3897] and destruction [GK 724]." Both words mean "destruction," but the second is stronger, implying eternal condemnation. The combination of these two words here suggests that Paul is speaking of destruction for time and eternity.

10 It is not money that is a root of all kinds of evil, but "the love of money" (GK 5794). Some people are always grasping at money. This is the curse of too much of modern living. Some Christians, unfortunately, have been trapped in this way and are led astray from the faith. In straying from the straight path, they have been caught in the thorn bushes and have "pierced themselves with many griefs." Some have questioned the validity of the first part of this verse. But this proverbial statement echoes what had already been said by both Greek and Jewish writers. There is no kind of evil to which the love of money may not lead people, once it starts to control their lives.

IX. Paul's Charge to Timothy (6:11–16)

11 In contrast to such people, Paul addresses Timothy as "man of God." This is a common designation for prophets in the OT (e.g., 1Sa 9:6; 1Ki 12:22; 13:1). There has been much discussion as to whether it carries that connotation here or is used as a general title for all Christians (cf. also 2Ti 3:17). In any case, it refers to someone who is in God's service, represents him, and speaks in his name. "Pursue" means "keep on making [these things] your lifelong pursuit." Paul then names six Christian virtues.

12 "Fight the good fight" (GK 76 & 74) is a phrase taken from the field of athletics, such as "contend in the gymnastic games." In the NT both words are used to describe the struggles of the Christian life (cf. 2Ti 4:7). The background of the words suggests exerting every ounce of energy to win.

Timothy is then told to take hold of the eternal life to which he was called when he made the good profession of faith. This probably refers to Timothy's confession of faith in Christ at his baptism, when "many witnesses" were no doubt present.

13–14 Typically, Paul appeals to God, who "gives life to everything," and to Christ Jesus, who himself made a good confession while testifying before Pontius Pilate. In their sight he solemnly charges Timothy to keep what he has been instructing him in a blameless way and without reproach (cf. 3:2).

There has been much discussion as to whether "without spot or blame" modifies "commandment" or "you." Elsewhere in the NT these adjectives are applied to persons, but here they are more closely attached to "commandment." Perhaps the best way is to try to combine the two ideas. If Timothy keeps himself unspotted and blameless, the commandment itself, so far as he is concerned, will be maintained flawless.

Timothy is to keep the commandment until the "appearing" (GK *2211*) of our Lord Jesus Christ. This word occurs five times in the Pastoral Letters (cf. 2Ti 1:10; 4:1, 8; Tit 2:13) and only once elsewhere in the NT (2Th 2:8; see comment on that verse). It is found in late Greek writers and in the inscriptions of that period for a visible manifestation of an invisible deity. It is also used frequently in the LXX for manifestations of God's glory. In 2Ti 1:10 it refers to the first coming of Christ; elsewhere (including this verse) it is used for the Second Coming.

15–16 God will "bring about" (lit., "display"; GK *1259*) this Second Coming "in his own time." The return of Christ will be God's final display to the world that Jesus is the Son of God and Savior (cf. the use of this same verb in Jn 2:18). "Time" (GK *2789*) means a fixed or definite time. In the NT it is often used in a prophetic sense for God's appointed time, especially in relation to the Second Coming and the future judgment.

The rest of vv.15–16 form a doxology, such as we often find in Paul's letters (cf. 1:17; 2Ti 4:18). Much of the language is derived from the OT. God is first described as "the blessed and only Ruler [GK *1541*]." The last word indicates a sovereign person, one who possesses power.

The next two titles, "King of kings and Lord of lords," are applied to Christ in Rev 17:14; 19:16. They are used for God in the OT (Dan 4:34 in LXX; cf. Dt 10:17; Ps 136:3). God alone is "immortal" (cf. 1Co 15:53–54), i.e., not subject to death. The idea of immortality is not clearly expressed in the OT. But the NT teaches that God alone has inherent immortality; ours is derived from him. It is in the resurrection that the true believer receives an immortal body (1Co 15:53), so that the whole person, body and soul, becomes immortal.

We are next told that God lives in light "unapproachable" (a word that other Jewish writers also apply to God). Paul adds that no person has ever seen God or can see him (cf. Ex 33:20; Jn 1:18). The doxology ends with the ascription: "To him be honor and might forever. Amen." It is typical of Paul to inject a doxology in the midst of a discussion (cf. 1:17; Ro 1:25; 11:36).

X. Closing Instructions (6:17–21)

1. Admonitions to the Wealthy (6:17–19)

17 Timothy is to command the wealthy not to be high-minded or proud. It is evident that in the wealthy city of Ephesus there were some church members who had money. Timothy is to warn them not to put their hope in "wealth, which is so uncertain." The uncertainty of wealth has been commented on from ancient times. It takes to itself wings and flies away (Pr 23:5). Even great fortunes have disappeared almost overnight (cf. the book of Job).

Instead, one should put one's hope in God (cf. Ps 52:7). He is the one who "richly provides us with everything for our enjoyment." Physical pleasure in itself is not sinful, but divinely ordained when sought within the structure of God's will.

18 The wealthy are to use their money "to do good" (GK *14*; cf. Ac 14:17) and are "to be rich in good deeds." Wealth imposes a heavy responsibility on its possessor. The greater our means for doing good, the greater our obligation. What an opportunity wealthy people have for benefiting the needy!

So the rich must be "generous [GK *2331*] and willing to share [GK *3127*]." This second word is related to the word *koinonia* (GK *3126*), meaning "fellowship, communion." Paul's use of this word suggests that wealthy

Christians should share their hearts as well as their money. This combination is what pleases God and imparts a double blessing to the recipient. Paul rejoiced that the generous Macedonians first gave themselves (2Co 8:1–5). It is easier to give money than to give ourselves, but love requires both.

19 By following these instructions the well-to-do will "lay up treasure . . . as a firm foundation for the coming age." This is in line with Jesus' teaching in Mt 6:19–21 about not storing up treasures on earth but storing them up in heaven. "For where your treasure is, there your heart will be also." In place of the uncertainty of earthly riches (v.17), Christians have a "firm foundation" (v.19) of treasure laid up in heaven. The purpose of this is that believers may take hold of "the life that is truly life," i.e., eternal life.

2. Admonition to Timothy (6:20–21a)

20–21a Paul concludes with a personal admonition to Timothy: "Guard what has been entrusted to your care" (cf. 2Ti 1:12, 14). Here the context suggests the sound doctrine that had been entrusted to Timothy, i.e., the revelation of Jesus Christ in all its fullness.

Timothy is to turn away from "godless chatter" or empty babbling. This is how Paul characterizes what the false teachers were saying (cf. 4:7; 6:3–5). The "opposing ideas" intimated here are likely rival teachings, such as those taught by Gnostics or Judaizers, in contrast to the truth of Christianity. This opposition consisted of "what is falsely called knowledge." We have already seen several times in this letter that Paul is combating the false teachings of Gnosticism—those who professed a superior knowledge and believed that salvation comes to those who have this secret, intellectual treasure (see also introduction to Colossians). This is the kind of false gospel that some have "professed" (GK 2040; cf. 2:10) and so have deviated from the sound doctrine of the Christian faith.

3. Farewell (6:21b)

In the closing benediction, "you" is plural, thus including the church along with Timothy.

The Old Testament in the New

NT Text	OT Text	Subject
1Ti 5:18	Dt 25:4	Not muzzling an ox

2 Timothy

INTRODUCTION

1. Authorship

See introduction to 1 Timothy.

2. Date and Place of Origin

See introduction to 1 Timothy. Paul was in prison in Rome, shortly before his death, when he wrote 2 Timothy. The date is thus sometime in A.D. 67.

3. Destination and Occasion

Timothy was at Ephesus when the apostle wrote him the first letter (1Ti 1:3). Presumably he was still there when Paul wrote this second letter. The occasion of this letter is stated rather fully. In prison at Rome, Paul is expecting execution. He longs to see his "son" Timothy (2Ti 1:4). He is getting cold in the dungeon and urges him to come before winter (4:21) and to bring the warm coat Paul left at Troas. Paul also wants the young pastor to bring Paul's books and parchments. perhaps to do some further reading and perhaps writing (4:13).

4. Summary of 2 Timothy

This second letter of Timothy is much more personal than 1 Timothy, written near the close of Paul's life. Paul talks directly to Timothy, urging him to maintain the spiritual glow (1:1–7) and to be a faithful partner of his in suffering for the Gospel (1:8–2:13). The apostle warns against the false teachers (2:14–19) and urges Timothy to be a noble servant of Christ (2:20–26). The third chapter contains a description of conditions in the last days (3:1–9). Then the aged apostle gives his final charge to his son in the faith (3:10–4:5) and his own testimony (4:6–8). The letter closes with personal remarks about his current situation (4:9–18) and the final greetings (4:19–21) and benediction (4:22).

5. Theological Values

See introduction to 1 Timothy.

EXPOSITION

I. Salutation (1:1–2)

1–2 This salutation is similar to the one found at the beginning of 1 Timothy (see comments on 1Ti 1:1). Paul adds something here: "according to the promise of life that is in Christ Jesus." All spiritual life comes to us only "in Christ." And the more fully and consciously we live in him, the richer that life becomes.

In his first letter Paul greeted Timothy as "my true son in the faith." Here it is "my dear [GK 28] son." Paul had a warm affection for his young convert and colleague. The actual greeting (v.2b) is exactly the same as that in 1 Timothy (see comments on 1Ti 1:2). Everything we have comes to us from God through Christ.

II. Thanksgiving (1:3–7)

A. Timothy's Heritage (1:3–5)

3 In contrast to his first letter, where Paul began by informing Timothy about his urgent task at Ephesus, even before his thanksgiving to God, Paul here follows his regular custom of having a thanksgiving right after the greeting. Paul was serving God "as my forefathers did." He greatly appreciated his religious heritage (cf. Ac 22:3; 24:14), and so today should all those who have been brought up in a Christian environment. The apostle served God with a clean or pure conscience (see the note on 1Ti 1:5.); Paul had maintained a clear conscience even in his earlier years (Ac 23:1).

"Night and day" Paul was "constantly" remembering Timothy in his prayers (cf. Ro 1:10; 1Th 1:2; 3:6). He must have had a large heart to carry such a loving concern for so many people.

4 "Long" (GK 2160) is a word expressing intense desire. Recalling Timothy's tears, probably when they last parted, Paul deeply longed to see his son in the faith, that he might be "filled with joy." In Paul's letters we see this man of God's real humanity. He was a stalwart soldier, but he had a tender heart.

5 Some external occasion, perhaps a message from Timothy, had brought his faith to Paul's remembrance. That faith was genuine and "sincere" (lit., "unhypocritical"; GK 537). As this verse testifies, Timothy had a godly mother and grandmother.

B. God's Gift to Timothy (1:6–7)

6 Because of his sincere faith and spiritual heritage, Timothy is urged to "fan into flame the gift [GK 5922] of God" that was given to him when Paul laid his hands on him (see comments on 1Ti 4:14). This would most naturally be taken as the time of Timothy's ordination. The tendency of fire is to go out and it must be stirred occasionally. This provides a spiritual metaphor of what believers must do with God's gifts to them.

7 Paul is fond of making a negative statement and then following it with three positive ideas (cf. Ro 14:17). God has *not* given us a spirit of "timidity" (GK 1261) or cowardice, but a spirit of "power" (GK 1539), of "love" (GK 27) and of "self-discipline" (GK 5406). The effective Christian worker must have the power of the Holy Spirit (cf. Ac 1:8). But that power must be expressed in a loving spirit, or it may do damage. And often the deciding factor between success and failure is the matter of self-discipline.

This is one of the several passages in these two letters that hint at Timothy's naturally timid nature. He had been brought up by his mother and grandmother, and now Paul was taking the place of a father to him.

III. Suffering for the Gospel (1:8–18)
A. Plea to Timothy (1:8)

8 In view of the spirit that has been divinely given to Timothy (cf. v.7), apparently Paul felt that his young colleague needed to have his courage strengthened. Thus he urges him not to be ashamed "to testify about our Lord," nor "of me his prisoner." The aged apostle was now a prisoner of the emperor (probably Nero) and was facing almost certain death. Timothy must not be so fearful as to be ashamed to visit Paul in prison. Instead, he is told to "join with me in suffering" (GK 5155) for the sake of Christ and the Gospel.

B. Paul's Testimony (1:9–12)

9 Paul's personal testimony begins with a confession that God saved him and called him "to a holy life." Paul typically says that believers are called to a life of holiness (see 1Th 4:7).

The next part of this verse picks up Paul's central theme in Romans—"not because of anything we have done but because of his own purpose and grace . . . given us in Christ Jesus." Grace (GK 5921) is central to his theology; only through grace can we be united with Christ. This grace was given to us long before we were born.

10 This hidden grace has now been "revealed" (GK 5746) to the human race "through the appearing [GK 2211] of our Savior, Jesus Christ." The word "appearing" normally refers to the second coming of Christ (see comments on 2Th 2:8; 1Ti 6:14; cf. also 2Ti 4:1, 8; Tit 2:13), but here it obviously refers to his first coming. At his first coming Christ "destroyed death" through his own death on the cross (cf. Heb 2:14). The preaching of the cross offers all people life and immortality; this is the good news Christ came to bring.

11 For the proclamation of this Gospel Paul was appointed "a herald and an apostle and a teacher." We find the same three functions, together with exactly the same introductory formula in 1Ti 2:7 (see comments on that verse).

12 Paul's appointment as a preacher of the Gospel had cost him much in "suffering" and persecution. But he was not ashamed, because he knew the Person in whom he believed, and he was persuaded that God was able to guard until the day of the Lord what was "entrusted to him" (see comments on 1Ti 6:20). That is, God would guard Paul's teaching, his apostolic work, his converts, and his life, even if there should be death.

C. Paul's Admonition (1:13–14)

13 What Timothy has heard from Paul he is to keep as the "pattern [GK 5721; cf. 1Ti 1:16] of sound teaching." But this was to be done "with faith and love in Christ Jesus." The only way to keep doctrine is to both live and proclaim it with faith and love.

14 Similar to what Paul has done (v.12), Timothy is to "guard the good deposit that was entrusted to" him. Paul had entrusted the Gospel to Timothy to preach and the doctrine to preserve. This goal could not be accomplished in one's own human strength, but only "with the help of the Holy Spirit who lives in us."

D. Paul Deserted (1:15)

15 "Asia" in the NT means the Roman province of Asia, at the west end of Asia Minor. It was made into a province by the Romans about 133 B.C., and Ephesus finally became its capital. On his third missionary journey Paul had spent three years in Ephesus (Ac 20:31), longer than anywhere else. While he was there, the preaching of the Gospel reached every part of the province (Ac 19:10). There is deep pathos, then, in this verse: "You know that everyone in the province of Asia has deserted me"—i.e., turned away from me. Paul singles out two men for special mention among the deserters, perhaps because they were well known to Timothy. But of "Phygelus and Hermogenes" we know nothing further.

When did the Christians of Asia turn away from Paul? Perhaps it was when he was arrested and taken to Rome for his second and final imprisonment. If so, one can understand the "tears" (v.4) Timothy shed at that time.

E. Paul Befriended (1:16–18)

16–18 In contrast to the attitudes and actions of the majority was the kindness of Onesiphorus. He had lived up to his name, which means "help-bringer." This man had often "refreshed" Paul and had not been ashamed of the apostle's chains, as the others had been. When he went to Rome, Onesiphorus had "searched hard" for Paul until he finally found him. There were many prisoners in Rome, and it was not an easy task to locate this particular one. Paul prays that mercy may be shown to Onesiphorus "on that day"—presumably the day of judgment. Then he adds that Timothy knew very well how this faithful Christian had often helped Paul when the latter was in Ephesus.

Those must have been lonely hours for the aged apostle in prison, facing almost certain death and forsaken by his friends. It is difficult for us to understand why God's servants who have given themselves in sacrificial service to others should suffer like this at the end. But Paul knew that the glory of the next life would repay it all.

IV. Three Symbols of the Christian (2:1–7)

A. Introduction (2:1–2)

1–2 After exhorting Timothy to "be strong in the grace that is in Christ Jesus," Paul sounds his frequent note in the Pastorals about preserving and transmitting the tradition of truth (cf. 1:13–14). As Paul had entrusted the Gospel to Timothy (1:14), so now Timothy must pass it on to "reliable men who will also be qualified to teach others."

B. The Soldier (2:3–4)

3 "Endure hardship" (GK *5155*) suggests pain and suffering as part of the Christian's lot in life (see comment on 1:8). That will inevitably happen as one engages in warfare against evil. So Timothy must be "a good soldier of Christ Jesus." Paul uses this figure for ministers of the Gospel (Php 2:25; Phm 2).

4 No one "serving as a soldier" gets entangled in the affairs of this life. The soldier must lay aside all secular pursuits, and the Christian minister must be willing to do the same. "His commanding officer" (lit., "the one who enrolled him as a soldier") is Jesus Christ. When Christ enrolls us as full-time soldiers in his army, we should seek to please him by giving ourselves to his service without distraction.

C. The Athlete (2:5)

5 In addition to military metaphors, Paul is also fond of athletic metaphors. The Christian, and especially the minister, must be spiritually a good athlete (see also comment on 1Ti 6:12). The goal of an athlete is to "receive the victor's crown" (cf. Heb 2:7, 9), the wreath given to the winner. But the winning athlete does not receive this crown unless he competes "according to the rules." Anyone who breaks the rules is disqualified.

D. The Farmer (2:6–7)

6–7 The Christian ministry can also be compared to farming. The pastor must sow the seed and cultivate the growing plants. One of Paul's main emphases here is on hard work and diligence, which he hopes will be a part of Timothy's pattern as pastor. Paul winds up this section by saying, "Reflect on what I am saying." If Timothy does this, he will understand what it is all about.

The three metaphors that Paul uses here—soldier, athlete, farmer—are also found together in 1Co 9:6, 24–27. The closest parallel between these two Scriptures is in the case of the athlete, who must go into strict training if he is going to win the prize. So Christians must have intense devotion and firm self-discipline if they are to win out for the Lord.

V. Suffering and Glory (2:8–13)

8 Now Paul urges Timothy to keep on remembering Jesus Christ. "Raised from the dead" emphasizes his deity; "descended from David," his humanity (cf. Ro 1:3–4). It is not the dead Christ that Timothy is to contemplate, but the risen living Lord. This is Paul's "gospel" (lit., "good news"; GK *2295*).

9 For preaching this Gospel, Paul is suffering like a chained criminal. But he rejoices that "God's word is not chained." The preacher is in prison, but the Word of God is still moving on and transforming lives.

10 Because of this, the apostle is patiently willing to "endure" (GK *5702*) everything for the sake of the "elect" (GK *1723*). God has set apart from among the rebellious human race those who are dear to himself; them he has made, through faith in Christ, citizens in his kingdom. The whole purpose of Paul's ministry was that people might "obtain the salvation that is in Christ Jesus," and the ultimate goal of this salvation is being with Christ in "eternal glory."

11–13 For "here is a trustworthy saying," see comment on 1Ti 1:15. In this case, the trustworthy saying is the following three verses, which may be an early Christian hymn. It is in the typical form of Hebrew poetic parallelism—four "if" clauses, each followed by a balancing conclusion. The first two are positive, the other two negative.

The implications of "if we died with [GK *5271*] him" is spelled out by Paul in Ro 6:3–6. It is only as we die with Christ, by identification with him in his death, that we can have spiritual life in him. "We will also live with him" does not refer to our future resurrection, but to our present life in Christ (cf. the parallel in Ro 6:8, 11). Right here and now we are to count ourselves "dead to sin but alive to God in Christ Jesus." The Pauline formula is "You have to die in order to live."

Paul goes with "if we endure, we will also reign with him." It is only as we keep on enduring to the end that we will be saved in time of persecution (Mt 10:22; cf. context).

The third proposition is negative: "If we disown him, he will also disown us." This is a serious warning: We cannot reject Christ without being rejected ourselves.

"If we are faithless" (GK *601*) is in the present tense, indicating a settled state of refusing to believe in Jesus and to obey him. But whatever we do, "he will remain faithful, for he cannot disown himself." God's faithfulness is eternal.

VI. Contrasts in the Church (2:14–26)

A. True and False Teachers (2:14–19)

14–15 In these two verses Paul challenges Timothy to be an approved workman. He is to "keep reminding" the believers of the things about which Paul has been writing. He is also to warn them before God against "quarreling about words" (GK *3362*; see comment on 1Ti 6:4). Fighting over mere words is a waste of time; "it is of no value" and only brings ruin to the listeners.

"Do your best" (GK *5079*) refers to a person being zealous or eager. Timothy must put forth every effort to be a Christian minister approved by God. When his work is inspected by God, he will then have no reason to feel ashamed. "Who correctly handles" (GK *3982*) suggests a plowman making a straight furrow in the soil. As Timothy teaches the Scriptures, he is to guide the word of truth along a straight path and not turn aside into the devious paths of deceiving interpretations.

16–18 In these three verses the apostle describes the heretical teachers. He warns Timothy to "avoid [GK *4325*] godless chatter" (cf. 1Ti 6:20), such as some were engaged in their godless myths and hair-splitting controversies (cf. 1Ti 4:7; 6:3–5). He says that their "teaching will spread like gangrene [GK *1121*]." This word was used by medical writers of that day to indicate a sore that eats into the flesh.

Hymenaeus is probably the man mentioned in 1Ti 1:20; nothing is known about Philetus. These two had "wandered away [GK *846*; see 1Ti 1:6; 6:21] from the truth." Their specific teaching was that the resurrection had already taken place, and thereby they were destroying the faith of some people. They were evidently explaining the resurrection in a spiritual sense, equating it with regeneration or the new birth. Paul gave an extended answer to this false teaching in 1Co 15.

19 The apostle now emphasizes the solid foundation of truth. He declares that in spite of the subversion, God's "solid foundation stands firm." This foundation is either Christ Jesus (see 1Co 3:11) and his apostles (see Eph 2:20; Rev 21:14) or, more widely, the church (see 1Ti 3:15), which stands firm in spite of the waywardness of some of its members. The foundation is "sealed" with two inscriptions, two mutually complementary aspects. The first is the objective fact of God's knowledge of those whom he has chosen; the second is the recognition in the consciousness of each individual of the relationship that he or she has with the Lord, together with his call to holiness (cf. 1:9).

B. Noble and Ignoble Vessels (2:20–21)

20–21 Having drawn at some length the contrast between true and false teachers (vv. 14–19), Paul now points up a second contrast—that between noble and ignoble vessels. Both will be found in the church. "In a large house," where a wealthy man lives, "there are not only articles of gold and silver, but also of wood and clay." Those that are gold certainly receive honor by the owner. Some less eminent articles are "of silver." But others are of "wood" (e.g., wooden bowls for holding flour) or "clay" (e.g., pottery). The latter two have a more mundane use.

We find the same two expressions in Ro 9:21. In the verses that follow there we find that the former vessels are "objects of [God's] mercy, whom he prepared in advance for glory" (v.23), whereas the latter are "objects of his wrath—prepared for destruction" (v.22). On the basis of this, as well as the context here in 2 Timothy, some scholars feel that the articles for ignoble purposes are the false teachers in the church (vv.16–18), who are destined for eternal destruction. In that case, "if a man cleanses himself from the latter" (v.21) means that Timothy must expel from the church the ignoble members.

Another interpretation is less drastic. It holds that in the local congregation are members who are prepared for "noble purposes" and others who are fitted for more menial tasks. Both have their place and function in the church. Verse 21 would then mean that the individual who cleanses himself from "the latter" (perhaps false teachings) will be "an instrument for noble purposes." He will be "made holy" (GK 39), will be "useful to the Master," and will be "prepared to do any good work."

Both of these interpretations seem valid. Since we cannot be sure which one Paul had in mind, we can make both applications.

C. The Kind and the Quarrelsome (2:22–26)

The last of the three "contrasts in the church" is that between kind people and quarrelsome people (vv.22–26). Unfortunately, both types are often in the visible, organized church.

22 Timothy was still a rather young man, probably in his early thirties, and so the aged apostle warns him: "Flee the evil desires of youth." The implication is that he must keep on fleeing youthful lusts and pursuing positive virtues instead. It is not enough to run away from wrong; we must run after what is good. This is the only way to escape temptations to evil (cf. Ro 12:21).

Timothy must pursue four things: "righteousness, faith, love and peace" (see also 1Ti 6:11). Although Timothy must purge the church of false teachers, he had to be careful to promote "love and peace" among the Christian believers committed to his care. "Faith" (GK 4411) may also be translated "faithfulness"; both ideas fit well here.

23 Paul goes on to instruct Timothy again to avoid and even refuse to get involved in senseless and ignorant "arguments" (GK 2428). If such questions are brought before Timothy, he should refuse to discuss them. Sometimes the wise pastor has to do this, because they only produce fights. These tend to divide the church and so destroy it.

24 "The Lord's servant"—i.e., every Christian, but particularly the pastor of a church—must not "quarrel." Rather, they must be "kind" (GK 2473) to everyone, "apt to teach" (cf. 1Ti 3:2), and "not resentful." Christians must have this sort of attitude toward those who oppose them.

25–26 At the same time, a good minister must "gently instruct" such people, in the hope that God will give them "repentance" (lit., "a change of heart"; GK *3567*), leading to a full "knowledge" (GK *2106*) of the truth, and that "they will come to their senses" and be set free from the snare of the devil.

VII. Characteristics of the Last Days (3:1–9)

A. Love of Money and Pleasure (3:1–5)

1 The expression "in the last days" comes from the OT (e.g., Isa 2:2; Mic 4:1). In Peter's quotation of Joel 2:28 on the day of Pentecost (Ac 2:17), it clearly refers to the whole messianic age, for he declared that the prophecy was being fulfilled that very day. Some insist that "in the last days" has the meaning here, but it seems more natural to take it as applying especially to the last days of this age, just before the Second Coming (as in 2Pe 3:3; Jude 18). This does not at all deny that these conditions have been and will be present throughout the church age. It is simply to say that the characteristics enumerated here will be more intensive and extensive as the end approaches. Paul declared that the last days will see troublesome and dangerous times.

2–4 In these three verses we find a list of no fewer than eighteen vices that will characterize people in the last days. These conditions have always existed in some measure but they have become more marked in recent decades. People will be selfish and greedy (cf. 1Ti 6:10), and they will be "boasters" or braggarts. They will also be "proud" (lit., "showing oneself above others"; GK *5662*). Originally used in a good sense in Greek literature for truly superior persons, this word soon took on the bad connotation that it always has in the NT; a person with this characteristic treats others with contempt.

"Abusive" (GK *1061*) means slanderous. And it may well be questioned whether children and young people were ever more "disobedient to their parents" than they are today.

"Ungrateful" (GK *940*; cf. Lk 6:35) is the opposite of being thankful. "Unholy" (GK *495*; cf. 1Ti 1:9) describes the person who has no fellowship with God and so is living a merely "secular" life. "Without love" (GK *845*; cf. Ro 1:31) means "without family affection." "Unforgiving" (GK *836*) originally indicated one who was irreconcilable.

"Slanderous" is *diaboloi* (GK *1333*). This usually occurs in the NT as word meaning "the devil." But the adjective connotes "prone to slander" or "accusing falsely."

"Without self-control" (GK *203*) has a wide sense, but it is especially applicable to no control regarding bodily lusts. It describes the weak person who is easily led into sin. "Brutal" means one who is savage and fierce. "Not lovers of the good" (GK *920*) is a word that is found nowhere else in the ancient Greek literature.

"Treacherous" is a noun meaning "traitor" or "betrayer"; it is used for Judas Iscariot (Lk 6:16). "Rash" describes one who is reckless. On "conceited," see comments on 1Ti 3:6; 6:4. "Lovers of pleasure [GK *5798*] rather than lovers of God [GK *5806*]" is a play on two similar Greek words. They describe those who put self in the place of God as the center of their affections.

5 Yet they are religious—"having a form of godliness but denying its power." Timothy is told to turn away from such hypocrites.

B. Depraved Living and Thinking (3:6–9)

6–7 In the first five verses of this chapter Paul has been pointing out the characteristics of the false teachers in their love for money and pleasure. Now he criticizes them for their depraved living and thinking. He says that they "worm their way into homes." "Gain control over" (lit., "take captive," as in war; GK *170*) may mean only "deceive." "Weak-willed women" (GK *1220*) are those who are overwhelmed with sins and "swayed by all kinds of evil desires." Such women become an easy prey for false teachers. Verse 7 suggests that these women wanted to pose as learned people, but actually they remained ignorant of the truth.

8–9 Jannes and Jambres are not mentioned in the OT, but there was a Jewish tradition that they were two of the Egyptian magicians who withstood Moses and Aaron. They are mentioned in an Aramaic paraphrase of Ex 7:11. Paul likens the false teachers at Ephesus to these ancient magicians. He describes them as men of utterly corrupted minds. As far as the faith is concerned, they are "rejected" (GK *99*); they cannot be trusted to teach the truth. But they will not get far. As in the case of Jannes and Jambres, their "folly" (GK *496*) will be clearly seen.

VIII. Persecution and Steadfastness (3:10–17)

A. All Christians Persecuted (3:10–13)

10–11 In sharp contrast to the above-mentioned people, Paul now addresses Timothy directly. "Know all about" (GK *4158*) means to follow closely; Timothy has been faithfully following the life of the apostle. He was familiar with Paul's "teaching" (GK *1436*), his "way of life" (GK *73*), God's "purpose" (GK *4606*; cf. 1:9) in him, his "faith" (GK *4411*), his "patience" (GK *3429*) shown toward his opponents, the constant, steadfast "love" (GK *27*) that God implanted in his heart, and his "endurance" (GK *5705*) or brave patience with which he handled the various hindrances and persecutions that happened to him.

In v.11 Paul adds two more things that Timothy knew about: "persecutions" and "sufferings." These things had happened throughout his missionary career (cf. 2Co 11:23–29), beginning in Pisidian Antioch, Iconium, and Lystra (Ac 13:50; 14:2, 5, 19)—cities in the Roman province of Galatia where Paul had founded churches on his first missionary journey. In Lystra, he was actually bombarded with stones and left for dead. Since Timothy was a young man in Lystra at that time and had evidently just been converted under Paul's ministry, he had poignant memories of this incident. But out of them all the Lord had delivered Paul, even reviving him from the stoning.

12–13 Paul was not alone in his sufferings. He declares that everyone who desires "to live a godly life in Christ Jesus will be persecuted." Meanwhile, "evil men and impostors will go from bad to worse"; such people have been deceived by false teachers, and they are now deceiving others.

B. The Adequacy of Scripture (3:14–17)

14–15 Rather than being led astray by these impostors, Timothy must continue in the teachings that he had learned and of which he had "become convinced." These Scriptural teachings he had learned from his grandmother Lois and his mother Eunice (1:5) right from the time he was a baby. Jewish children were customarily taught the law at an early age, and they had to commit parts of it to memory. "The holy Scriptures" renders "the sacred writings," i.e., what we now call the OT Scriptures, which were able to make him "wise" in preparation "for salvation through faith in Christ Jesus." They disciplined him in obedience to God and also pointed forward to the coming Messiah, through whom salvation by faith would become available.

16–17 "All Scripture is God-breathed." The adjective used here is *theopneustos* (GK *2535*), which is a combination of two other Greek words: *theos* ("God"; GK *2536*) and *pneo* ("breathe"; GK *4463*). This is one of the greatest texts in the NT describing the inspiration or the "God-breathed" aspect of the Bible. Another outstanding passage is 2Pe 1.21, which describes how divine inspiration took place (see comments on that verse).

Inspired Scripture is "useful" or "profitable" in various areas: "teaching" (GK *1436*) us Christian truths; "rebuking" (GK *1791*) or convicting us of sin; "correcting" (GK *2061*) us where we have gone wrong; "training" (GK *4082*) us in how to live both inwardly and outwardly in righteous living.

The purpose of all this is so that Christians will be completely ready to meet the demands of discipleship.

IX. Preach the Word (4:1–5)

1 Here Paul speaks of Christ Jesus as the one who will "judge the living and the dead"—a

Early Christians could expect persecution for their faith (cf. 3:10–13). Many (likely including Paul; cf. 4:6–7, 16–18) were persecuted under Nero in the Coliseum of Rome.

clause found in all the early creeds of the church (cf. 1Th 4:16–17). Using language reminiscent of a legal setting, Paul solemnly charges Timothy to be governed in his thinking, not just by the present life, but also by the coming judgment and the eternal kingdom of Christ.

2 The basic charge is: "Preach [GK 3062] the Word." Preachers are not to air their own opinions but to proclaim God's eternal, authoritative Word of truth as contained in the Scriptures. The minister has to be on duty constantly, ready for any emergency at any time. In addition to preaching the Word, Timothy is to "correct" (GK 1794) or reprove, "rebuke" (GK 2203) or admonish, and "encourage" (GK 4151) or comfort and exhort. That is, both the positive and the negative must be included. But preachers must do these things with great "patience" (GK 3429) and careful "instruction" (GK 1439).

3 Timothy is now warned that the time will come when people will not be able to tolerate "sound doctrine" (a key phrase in the Pastorals; cf. 1Ti 1:10; Tit 1:9; 2:1). Timothy's major task in Ephesus is to defend and proclaim doctrines in accord with the truth of God's Word (v.2). He must do this constantly, since the time will come when people will not listen to the truth. Instead, "to suit their own desires, they will gather around them" many teachers who will say what they want them to say, in order to gratify their self-willed hearts.

4 People like this will "turn away" (GK 695; cf. 1:15) their ears from the truth and will "turn aside" (GK 1762; see 1Ti 1:6; 5:15; 6:20; 2Ti 2:16–18) to senseless "myths" (see 1Ti 1:4; 4:7).

5 "Keep your head" (GK 3768) is from a verb that often means "be sober, abstain from wine." But in the NT (cf. 1Th 5:6, 8; 1Pe 1:13; 4:7; 5:8) it has the metaphorical sense of being self-controlled or self-possessed—Timothy is to keep his self-control under all circumstances. He is then again urged to "endure hardship" (GK 2802; cf. 2:3). He must do the work of an "evangelist" (cf. Ac 21:8; Eph 4:11), which means to announce the good news of salvation in Christ. This word may well refer to an itinerant preacher, but the established pastor must also be an evangelist, pointing sinners to Christ.

The summary of Paul's solemn charge to Timothy is this: "Discharge all the duties of your ministry." He is to fulfill his calling by packing his ministry to the full with the things Paul has been exhorting him to do in these two letters.

X. Paul's Final Testimony (4:6–8)

6 In Php 2:17 Paul wrote, "But even if I am being poured out like a drink offering on the sacrifice"; here he says, "For I am already being poured out as a drink offering." In both passages "I am being poured out like a drink offering" (GK 5064) presents the picture of a drink offering poured on the lamb of sacrifice just before it was burned on the altar (Nu 28:24). In the earlier letter, written during his first Roman imprisonment, Paul was expecting to be released soon and revisit Philippi (Php 2:24). But now the case is different. He is nearing the end of his second and final imprisonment at Rome. He is conscious that his fate is sealed, for he adds, "And the time has come for my departure." Paul was about ready to leave his physical body and forsake this earth for the presence of his Lord.

7 There are two ways of interpreting this verse. One is to assume that we have here three figures of speech: the first military, the second athletic, the third religious. But the three clauses of the verse may all be taken as related to athletics. The verb translated "fought" (GK 76) can have a military meaning (cf. Jn 18:36), but it can just as clearly relate to athletics (1Co 9:25). All in all, it seems more natural to understand Paul as speaking in the athletic sense in all of them (cf. especially 1Ti 6:12). If so, then we can paraphrase the verse like this: "I have competed well in the athletic contest [of life], I have finished the race, I have kept the rules"—not "fouled out" and so been disqualified from winning.

8 One of the main reasons for preferring the athletic interpretation in v.7 is that it fits in perfectly with v.8, where Paul says a "crown" (GK 5109) awaits him. The word for "crown" is not the one used for a royal crown but for the laurel wreath that was given to the winner of the Marathon race (cf. 1Co 9:25). The Lord, the righteous Judge (of the contest) was ready to "award" this prize to Paul at the end of the race, his victorious life. The same reward awaits all who run the Christian race successfully to the finish and long for "his appearing" (the Second Coming).

XI. Paul's Final Plea (4:9–13)

9 Paul had already said that he longed to see Timothy (1:4). Now he urges him to come speedily.

10 Verses 10-12 give the reasons for this: Paul was left almost alone. Demas, his trusted associate, had deserted him. During the apostle's first Roman imprisonment, he twice mentioned Demas as one of his fellow workers (Col 4:14; Phm 24). Some have tried to put a good construction on the reference to Demas here, suggesting that he had gone on a missionary errand to Thessalonica. But Paul uses the same verb for "deserted" (GK 1593) as in v.16. And we are told that Demas left "because he loved this world." He was not willing to pay the price of hardship and suffering that Paul was paying.

Crescens (mentioned only here) had gone to Galatia, and Titus to Dalmatia, presumably to do missionary work. The latter place was on the eastern shore of the Adriatic Sea, north of Macedonia.

11 "Only Luke is with me." There is pathos in these words. Luke was probably the one who acted as the apostle's secretary in the actual writing of this letter (see introduction). Perhaps Luke's own loneliness is also reflected here. He stayed with Paul to the end perhaps because the aged, ailing apostle needed the care of a doctor (Col 4:14) in his closing years and because Luke's deep personal devotion to Paul would lead him to stay right with him.

"Mark" had had a checkered career. We first meet him in Ac 12:12. When Peter was miraculously delivered from prison, he went to Mark's home. Barnabas and Paul took him to Antioch (Ac 12:25) and then took him with them as their assistant on the first missionary journey (13:5). But the young Mark left and returned to Jerusalem (13:13). Because of this, Paul refused to take him along on the second journey (15:36–40). Later Mark matured and was with Paul in his first Roman imprisonment (Col 4:10). Now the aging apostle gives his young associate his highest accolade: "Get Mark and bring him with you, because he is helpful to me in my ministry."

12 "Tychicus" was from the province of Asia and accompanied Paul on his last journey to Jerusalem (Ac 20:4). He was the bearer of the letters to the Colossians (Col 4:7–8) and to the Ephesians (Eph 6:21). In both places he is described as a "dear brother" and "faithful servant in the Lord." It is obvious that Paul had high regard for Tychicus. "I sent" may well mean "I am sending." If so, Tychicus was the bearer of this letter and was being sent by Paul to take Timothy's place as supervisor of the work at Ephesus. The apostle wanted his "dear son" (1:2) with him in the closing days of his life. We can only conjecture as to whether Timothy reached Paul before the latter's death.

13 It is evident that Timothy was not to go by ship directly to Rome from the large seaport of Ephesus, for he is requested to pick up the cloak Paul had left with Carpus at Troas. Nothing further is known about Carpus. The "cloak" was probably a traveling cloak with long sleeves, which would keep Paul warm while in prison.

Timothy was also to bring Paul's "scrolls," written documents probably made of papyrus. Paul especially wanted his "parchments," i.e., scrolls or codices written on animal skins. These may have been leather scrolls of OT books.

XII. Human Opposition and Divine Support (4:14–18)

14–15 We know nothing further about "Alexander," who is called a "metalworker." Alexander was a common name in the NT world. We do not know when, where, or in what way Alexander did Paul "a great deal of harm." One good guess is that he had been responsible for the apostle's arrest and imprisonment. Paul prophesies that the Lord Jesus "will repay" him. Paul warns Timothy to be on guard against this malicious enemy who "strongly opposed our message." This opposition may have included not only Paul's preaching but also his defense before the court (cf. v.16).

16 Paul now reflects on his first "defense" (GK 665), when no one came to his support but everyone deserted him. Older commentaries usually refer this to Paul's first Roman imprisonment (Ac 28:30), which resulted in his release. But most scholars today feel that the language here is too strong for that earlier event, when in accordance with Roman custom, he may have been automatically released without trial at the end of two years. Rather, the reference is to Paul's first hearing in court.

Paul's magnanimous Christian love is revealed in the last sentence of this verse: "May it not be held against them." He could and did forgive his deserters for their weakness in fearing to stand by him.

17 But he did not lack support. Triumphantly and gratefully he cries, "But the Lord stood at my side and gave me strength." The result was that the Gentiles in Caesar's court heard the Gospel, which thereby got wider publicity in Rome. When was Paul "delivered from the lion's mouth"? If we accept the reference to his first imprisonment, the answer seems simple. But was he threatened to the extent implied by this vivid figure? The only alternative would be that his first trial had seemed to go well for him, with perhaps a temporary reprieve. The "lion" would then be Nero. If so, it was this same emperor who later, according to the unanimous tradition of the early church, condemned him and put him to death.

18 "Rescue" and "delivered" (v.17) translate the same verb (GK *4861*; cf. also Mt 6:13, where it is used in the Lord's Prayer). Paul trusts that the Lord will bring him safely through anything that comes his way. "His heavenly kingdom" is probably identical to the phrase "the kingdom of heaven," found thirty-two times in Matthew, though the reference here is to the future kingdom in the eternal realm.

Paul is fond of breaking out into spontaneous praise now and then in his letters. One of his many doxologies occurs here: "To him [the Lord, i.e., Christ] be glory for ever and ever. Amen."

XIII. Closing Greetings, Farewell (4:19–22)

19 Priscilla and Aquila figured prominently in Paul's life. When he first arrived in Corinth—evidently short of funds and disappointed at the meager results of his ministry in Athens—he found both employment and lodging with Aquila and Priscilla. Like him, they were leather workers (Ac 18:2–3). When Paul left Corinth, this couple sailed across the Aegean with him to Ephesus and stayed there (Ac 18:18–19). They performed a useful function by instructing Apollos (v.26). From there they, and the church that met in their home, sent greetings to the Christians at Corinth (1Co 16:19). Later we find them back in Rome (Ro 16:3); Paul sent greetings to them there and referred (Ro 16:4) to an occasion when they had "risked their lives" for him. But now they are once more in Ephesus. In those days prosperous Jews traveled a great deal from city to city. In four of the six places where Priscilla and Aquila are mentioned, Priscilla's name comes first. Evidently she was the stronger character of the two. It may well be that their moves were due as much to her missionary concern as to her husband's trade.

The "household of Onesiphorus" is mentioned with great appreciation in 1:16–18 (see comments there).

20 When Paul wrote to Rome from Corinth, he sent greetings from "Erastus, who is the city's director of public works" (Ro 16:23). There was also an Erastus who, along with Timothy, was Paul's helper at Ephesus (Ac 19:22). We have no way, of course, of knowing whether these three passages refer to the same person. At any rate, "Erastus stayed in Corinth," possibly when Paul left there for the last time.

The apostle had "left Trophimus sick in Miletus" (near Ephesus). This man came from the province of Asia and was one of Paul's associates in carrying the offering from the Gentile churches to the poor saints at Jerusalem (Ac 20:4). There he became the cause, unintentionally, of Paul's being mobbed and arrested (Ac 21:29).

21–22 Paul is beginning to feel the cold and dampness in his prison cell. So now he speaks with fresh urgency: "Do your best [GK *5079*; cf. v.9] to get here before winter." If not, he will suffer desperately in the cold weather.

Finally, Paul sends greetings from four members of the church at Rome—Eubulus, Pudens, Linus, and Claudia—"and all the brothers." Church tradition says that Linus became the first bishop of Rome after the death of Peter and Paul. About the others, we have no certain knowledge.

Paul pronounces a personal benediction on Timothy ("your" in "your spirit" is singular), before concluding comprehensively with "Grace be with you all."

Titus

INTRODUCTION

As the shortest of the Pastoral Letters, Titus has often been overshadowed by the longer letters to Timothy. But it is rich in doctrinal and practical values and is worthy of study in its own right.

1. Authorship

The Pauline authorship of the letter was not questioned in the early church. Arguments against its authenticity are of modern origin. Its claim to Pauline authorship is here accepted without reserve (see introduction to 1 Timothy).

2. Recipient

The letter is addressed to "Titus, my true son in our common faith" (1:4). The appended identification marks a close and affectionate relation between Paul and Titus. He was probably a comparatively young man when Paul wrote to him (cf. 2:6–7). Scriptural references to Titus are surprisingly rare. Although he was closely connected with Paul, his name never occurs in Acts and, aside from the letter addressed to him, his name is found in only three Pauline letters (2Co 2:13; 7:6, 13–14; 8:6, 16, 23; 12:18; Gal. 2:1, 3; 2Ti 4:10).

Chronologically, the first mention of Titus is in Gal 2:1–3. When Paul went from Antioch to discuss "his" Gospel with the leaders in Jerusalem, he took along Titus, an uncircumcised young Greek, as a worthy specimen of the fruits of his ministry to the Gentiles. "My true son" (1:1) implies that he was Paul's convert, perhaps won during the ministry in Ac 11:25–26. At Jerusalem Paul's position that Gentile believers were not under the Mosaic law was vindicated when Titus was not compelled to be circumcised (Gal 2:3–5). Paul's selection of this young convert to test this crucial issue speaks well of his spiritual vitality.

We hear nothing further of Titus until the time of Paul's ministry at Ephesus on the third missionary journey. Perhaps Paul took him along to Ephesus from Antioch (Ac 18:22–19:1). He was an unnamed member of the group of assistants to Paul there (Ac 19:22; cf. 2Co 2:13; 7:6, 13–14). On three separate occasions Paul seems to have sent Titus to Corinth on important missions.

About a year before the writing of 2 Corinthians, Paul sent Titus to Corinth to enlist Corinthian participation in the collection for the Judean saints (1Co 16:1–4; 2Co 9:2; 12:18). Apparently shortly after writing 1 Corinthians, Paul again sent Titus to Corinth to help straighten out the tangled affairs in that church and to counter the work of Paul's opponents there. Plans called for a reunion at Troas where Paul was to engage in missionary work (2Co 2:12–13). The failure of Titus to return as planned caused Paul much anxiety. Terminating the inviting work at Troas, Paul went into Macedonia, hoping in this way to meet Titus sooner. Eventually Titus appeared in Macedonia with the good news that his difficult mission to Corinth had been successful (2Co 7:5–7). Paul rejoiced in this success and was encouraged by the personal joy of Titus at the response of the Corinthians (2Co 7:6–7, 13–15). Cheered by these developments, Paul wrote the second letter to the Corinthians and sent it back with Titus, instructing him also to complete the collection at Corinth (2Co 8:6–7, 16–22). Paul gave Titus and the two men sent with him (2Co 8:18–22) his strong recommendation (2Co 8:23–24), assuring any critical Corinthian that Titus could be fully trusted as one motivated by Paul's own spirit (2Cor 12:17–18).

When Paul came to Corinth for three months (Ac 20:2), the difficulties there had been resolved and the collection completed (cf. Ro 15:25–27). But Titus was no longer at Corinth when Paul wrote to the Romans, for his name does not appear among those of Paul's co-workers who sent greetings to the Roman saints (Ro 16:21–23). Nothing further is heard of Titus until the time of the Pastoral Letters.

When Paul wrote to Titus, he was working on the island of Crete (1:5). Their joint labors there were long enough for Paul to realize the deplorable conditions of the local churches. Apparently Titus had been working there for some time when Paul wrote. He informed Titus that as soon as a replacement arrived, he was to rejoin Paul at Nicopolis (3:12), a city in western Greece. Paul was formulating further plans for Titus.

We get a final fleeting glimpse of Titus in 2Ti 4:10, where Paul informed Timothy that Titus had gone to Dalmatia. This implies he had been with Paul during his second Roman imprisonment. Although the reason for the trip is not given, we may assume that he went there at the call of Christian duty.

These references to Titus reveal that he was a trustworthy, efficient, and valued young co-worker. He possessed a forceful personality, was resourceful, energetic, tactful, skillful in dealing with difficult situations, and effective in conciliating people.

3. Occasion and Purpose

The external occasion for the letter to Titus was the trip through Crete planned by Zenas and Apollos (3:13). They conveyed the letter to Titus. The internal occasion for writing was Paul's concern to strengthen the hand of Titus as his personal representative in Crete in carrying out a difficult assignment. Paul knew that Titus would face opposition (1:10–11; 2:15; 3:10). He aimed to encourage Titus and reinforce his authority in working among the churches in Crete. The letter would serve as written authorization for this task, proof to them that he was working in accordance with Paul's own instructions.

The origin of the Cretan churches is unknown. They had evidently been in existence for some time when Paul visited Crete. Their condition was discouraging. They were inadequately organized, so Titus was directed to appoint morally and doctrinally qualified elders in the various churches (1:6–9). In view of the operation of false teachers (1:10–16), this was essential.

The prevailing moral conditions in the churches were far from what they might be. The Christians were adversely influenced by the prevailing low moral standards in Crete. Perhaps the Gospel of the grace of God had been misinterpreted to mean that salvation was unrelated to daily conduct. Titus was urged to insist on the need for sound doctrine and a high level of moral and social conduct (2:1–10; 3:1–3). Christian behavior must be grounded in the basic truths of the Gospel (2:11–14; 3:4–8).

The letter also conveyed personal information for Titus. The instruction to join Paul at his winter quarters at Nicopolis after a replacement arrived (3:12) apprised Titus of the fact that Paul was formulating further plans for their joint labors.

4. Date and Place of Origin

The date assigned the letter depends on the reconstruction accepted for Paul's journeys following his release from the first Roman imprisonment, as well as the dating for that imprisonment, commonly accepted as A.D. 61–63, though it may have been as early as 59–61. Since this letter makes no mention of the Neronian persecution, which apparently began in October 64, it seems best to date it between the time of Paul's release and the commencement of that persecution. The journeys to the east indicated in 1 Timothy and Titus were apparently made as soon as he was released. The letter to Titus may have been written during the fall of A.D. 63, not long after Paul left Crete.

The place of origin can only be conjectured. The remark in 3:12 indicates that Paul had not yet reached Nicopolis. Any suggested place will depend on the reconstruction of Paul's movements following his release. A case can be made for Corinth.

5. Theological Value

The letter of Titus covers the same general ground as 1 Timothy but is more compact and less personal. Its greater part deals with ministerial duties and social relations, yet it contains no fewer than three summary passages that are theological gems (1:1–3; 2:11–14; 3:3–7). In 1 Timothy Paul stresses sound doctrine; in Titus he stresses worthy Christian conduct and insists that Christian conduct must be based on and regulated by Christian truth. Nowhere else does Paul more forcefully urge the essential connection between evangelical truth and the purest morality than in this brief letter. Here the basic truths of the Gospel are displayed in the abiding glory of their saving and sanctifying appeal. The regenerating work of the Holy

Spirit is the experiential basis for Christian conduct (3:3–7).

EXPOSITION

I. Salutation (1:1–4)

The salutation is remarkably long and weighty for such a brief letter. Only Romans has a longer salutation. It displays the usual three parts of an epistolary salutation of that day—writer, reader, greeting. Each part could be expanded according to the occasion and the writer's purpose.

A. The Writer (1:1–3)

1 The length of this salutation is due to the expansion of the first part, where Paul emphasizes his authoritative message. While this solemn self-identification was not needed by Titus, it effectively stressed the authoritative commission and message of the one for whom Titus acted in Crete. This letter was written to preserve and further that message, which was closely linked with godliness in daily life.

To his name Paul added two credentials. "A servant of God" occurs only here in Paul; elsewhere it is "servant of Jesus Christ" (Ro 1:1; Gal 1:10; Php 1:1). "Servant" (GK *1528*) is the common term for "slave" and its use implies Paul's acknowledged ownership by God and complete dependence on him. "Servant of God" was used of Moses (Jos 1:2) and the prophets (Jer 7:25; Am 3:7) to denote their use by God to accomplish his will. Paul is nothing less than God's agent. Furthermore, he is Jesus Christ's "apostle" (GK *693*), having been called, equipped, and sent forth as his authoritative messenger.

"For the faith of God's elect and the knowledge of the truth" describes his apostolic office. "For" as used in the NIV denotes purpose; Paul's mission was to promote Christian faith and knowledge. It can also be translated "according to," so that Paul's apostleship is in full accord with the faith and knowledge that God's elect have received. His apostleship is not regulated by their faith (cf. Gal 1:11–17) but is wholly in accord with it. The Cretan Christians needed to evaluate their faith by that fact.

"God's elect" (GK *1723*) are those who have responded to God's call through the Gospel. The expression embodies a true balance between the divine initiative and the human response. Although surrounded with mystery, the biblical teaching on election is for the benefit of believers and is intended as a practical truth. It assures faithful, struggling Christians that their salvation is all of God from beginning to end.

Christian faith is linked with the full apprehension of truth, the inner realization of divine reality as revealed in the Gospel. Faith is a heart response to the truth of the Gospel, but it must also possess the mind. God never intended his people to remain intellectually ignorant of the truth of the Gospel.

Christian truth has a moral aspect; it "leads to godliness." Conduct must be evaluated by the demands of godliness, that reverential attitude that leads to conduct pleasing to God. Those gripped by God's truth walk in harmony with such demands. There is an intimate connection between a vital possession of truth and genuine godliness—a lesson the Cretan church needed to learn.

2 The intended connection of v.2 is not quite certain. The NIV translators have added the words "a faith and knowledge" to make explicit their understanding of the connection—that the Christian life is grounded in the hope of eternal life. As with all of God's elect, Paul's life and service were firmly rooted in "hope" (GK *1828*), which eagerly and confidently awaits the realization of "eternal life"—life not only endless but having an eternal quality. Believers already possess eternal life (Jn 5:24), but its full and perfect realization awaits the return of the Prince of Life.

This hope is not a vague, pious aspiration but is sure because it is grounded in the absolute trustworthiness of God. The character of the God "who does not lie" (GK *950*) assures the fulfillment of his promise. This characterization places God in contrast with the notorious deceptiveness of the Cretans (1:12).

God promised this eternal life before the ages of time, begun at creation, started to roll (cf. 2Ti 1:9). This promise existed within the Godhead before he created the world. In other words, it is rooted in God's eternal purpose for humankind.

3 The reliability of the above-mentioned promise was demonstrated through the clear, public revelation it received in the preaching of the Gospel. "His word" is not the personal Christ, the Logos (cf. Jn 1:1), but rather the saving message of the Gospel. This message was made known "at his appointed season," the opportune time established by God in his eternal wisdom. All history was the preparation for that revelation. The historical appropriateness of the time is evident from the existence of the Roman peace that gave a favorable setting for the preaching of the Gospel and the development of Greek as the linguistic medium of its proclamation throughout the entire world.

The message was brought to the world "through the preaching entrusted to me." This refers, not to the act of preaching, but to the message that was heralded, the message of the Gospel. There is no substitute for that message, and Paul was writing so that its purity might be preserved on the island of Crete. That life-giving message was committed to Paul personally as a divine trust. He could never escape the wonder that this assignment should be given to him, unworthy as he was (1Co 15:9; Eph 3:8; 1Ti 1:11–13).

The assignment came to him "by the command of God our Savior." It is a vigorous assertion of his divine commission, underlining the authority behind this letter. The One who saves and preserves us is none other than God; we must personally appropriate and publicly confess him in this capacity. Paul's usage of "God our Savior" suggests that his reference here is to the Father. In the Pastorals the term is applied to both the Father (1Ti 1:1; 2:3; 4:10, Tit 1:3; 2:10; 3:4) and the Son (2Ti 1:10; Tit 1:4; 2:13; 3:6). As the ultimate source of all salvation, the designation is appropriately applied to the Father.

B. The Reader (1:4a)

The recipient is tersely described as "my true son in our common faith." This phrase reveals the intimate and endearing relationship between Paul and Titus; it also implies that Titus was Paul's convert. The adjective "true" (GK *1188*) means "legitimately born or genuine" and acknowledges that Titus was running true to his spiritual parentage and thus represented Paul's position. "Common" (GK *3123*) reaches farther than writer and reader to denote a faith mutually held by God's elect.

C. The Greeting (1:4b)

The greeting with "grace and peace" is Paul's usual greeting. "Grace" (GK *5921*) is the unmerited favor of God at work in the life of the believer, while "peace" (GK *1645*) is the resultant experience of harmony and well-being in the life of the reconciled. This double blessing comes "from God the Father and Christ Jesus our Savior." Since Paul viewed Father and Son as one source of blessing and the one object of every Christian aspiration, "from" is not repeated. "Our Savior," applied in v.3 to the Father, is here transferred to the Son; both are involved in bestowing the same salvation. "Our" again signifies the common testimony of believers.

II. Concerning Elders and Errorists in Crete (1:5–16)

The first major division, designed to further the welfare of the Cretan churches, falls into two parts. Verses 5–9 give instructions concerning church officials, whereas vv.10–16 deal with the needed refutation of false teachers in Crete. The presence of the false teachers made more imperative the appointment of qualified leaders.

A. The Appointment of Qualified Elders (1:5–9)

1. The duties of Titus in Crete (1:5)

5 "I left you in Crete" asserts the joint labors of Paul and Titus on that island for a brief time. Paul's labors there cannot be fitted into Ac 27:7–9 or before. The alternatives are to reject Pauline authorship of the Pastorals or to accept that the reference is to a time following his Ac 28 imprisonment. The latter alternative is probable scripturally and is asserted by tradition.

"Left" (GK *657*) implies that Titus was deliberately left behind in Crete to carry out a specific assignment. Before Paul's departure, the commission was orally delivered; now it is restated concisely in writing. Titus's task was comprehensive: to "straighten out what was left unfinished." "Straighten out" (GK *2114*) denotes that his task was personally to set things in order. "What was left unfinished" points to several serious defects that still needed Titus's attention. Organization was lacking (1:5), false teachers were unchecked (1:10–11; 3:10–11), and instruction in doctrine and conduct was needed

(2:1–10; 3:1–2). Paul had observed and had begun to correct these matters; Titus must now complete the work.

An initial duty was to "appoint elders" in each place where there was a group of believers. Such a plural leadership in the local congregation continued Paul's own earlier practice (Ac 14:23). Probably the congregation chose the elders with the encouragement of Titus, who in turn had the responsibility of formally appointing them to office. "As I directed you" recalls that this was in accord with his previous orders. In this way, Titus would carry out Paul's ideal for these congregations.

2. The qualifications of the elders (1:6–9)

This list of qualifications corresponds closely to that given in 1Ti 3:1–7, yet the differences indicate that it was realistically applied to a contemporary situation. The fact that no deacons are mentioned suggests that the organization of these churches was more primitive than at Ephesus.

6 "An elder must be blameless" marks the basic qualification, demanding an irreproachable reputation in the community. This demand is elaborated in what follows, which begins with two domestic qualifications. The precise implications of "the husband of but one wife" have been debated through the centuries (see comment on 1Ti 3:3). Most natural is the view that an elder must be the husband of only one living woman.

Since older men would be chosen for leadership, it is assumed that the elder would have children. The latter must share their father's Christian faith by having made a personal decision. Their remaining pagan would throw into question the father's ability to lead others to the faith. Moreover, the children must personally fulfill the ethical requirements of the Christian life. They must not be chargeable as being "wild" (self-indulgent and wasteful in their manner of life, like the prodigal son) or "disobedient" (refusing to bow to parental authority). An elder's inability to train and govern his children would also place in question his ability to train and govern the church.

7 The leader's true position and personal qualifications are given in vv.7–9. The switch in v.7 from "elder" (GK 4565) to "overseers" (GK 2176) shows that these two terms are interchangeable (cf. also Ac 20:17 and 20:28). Yet both these words have a different connotation. "Elder" implies the maturity and dignity of the man, while "overseer" indicates his work of overseeing God's flock.

Again Paul stresses that the overseer must be "blameless" (GK 441). This time the stress is on "it is necessary," because of the elder's position as being entrusted with "God's work" (lit., "God's steward"; GK 3874). A steward was the manager of a household or estate, appointed by and accountable to the owner. The picture of the steward embodies one of Paul's favorite concepts of the ministry (1Co 4:1–2; 9:17; Eph 3:2; Col 1:25). The Christian minister is not merely the servant of the church; he exercises his office under God's authority and is directly accountable to him. This high office makes high demands on the character of the man.

Five negative and six positive personal qualifications are listed in vv.7–8. The overseer must *not* be (1) "overbearing" (GK 881), arrogantly disregarding the interests of others in order to please himself; (2) "quick-tempered" (GK 3975), readily yielding to anger, for pastoral work demands much patience; (3) "given to drunkenness" (GK 4232); i.e., he must not be an alcoholic; (4) "violent" (GK 4438), ready to assail an opponent, either with fists or by bellicose behavior; (5) "pursuing dishonest gain" (GK 153), using his office to profit in an underhanded and shameful way. The laborer is worthy of his hire (cf. 1Ti 5:17–18), but he must not turn his office into a money-making business.

8 "Rather" introduces the contrasting positive qualifications. An overseer must be: (1) "hospitable" (lit., "lover of strangers"; GK 5811), ready to befriend and lodge traveling or fleeing believers; (2) "one who loves what is good" (GK 5787), an ally and zealous supporter of the good, including people as well as deeds and things; (3) "self-controlled" (GK 5409), in control of his mind and emotions so that he can act rationally and discreetly, a virtue much needed on Crete and one stressed in the Pastorals (cf. 1Ti 2:9, 15; 3:2; 2Ti 1:7; Tit 2:2, 4–6, 12); (4) "upright" (GK 1465), conforming his conduct to right standards; (5) "holy" (GK 4008), denoting his personal piety, an inner attitude of conforming to what is felt to be pleasing to God and consistent with religious practices; and (6) "disciplined" (GK *1604*), having the inner strength that enables him to control his bodily appetites and passions, a virtue listed in Gal 5:23 as one quality of the fruit of the Spirit. These last three characteristics may be viewed as looking toward others, God, and self, respectively.

9 Doctrinal fitness is also necessary. The overseer must be known to "hold firmly to the trustworthy message," clinging to it despite the winds of false teaching and open opposition. "Trustworthy" (GK *4412*) underlines that the Christian Gospel is perfectly reliable and completely worthy of one's confidence. Overseers must adhere to the Word "as it has been taught" and be in accord with the teaching of the apostles.

Unfaithfulness to the biblical revelation disqualifies people from leadership in God's church. On the other hand, doctrinal fidelity enables them to perform a twofold task: (1) They can appeal to others to adhere to and advance in their Christian faith. This can be done by proclaiming "sound doctrine"—teaching that is biblically correct and promotes spiritual health—in contrast to the unhealthy false teaching. (2) Their work also demands that they "refute those who oppose" the true Gospel and speak against it as the advocates of error. They must expose the errors of others and try to convince them that they are wrong.

B. The Refutation of False Teachers (1:10–16)

"For" introduces the justification for the requirement that elders must be able to expound and defend the truth (v.9). This is essential because of the false teachers described in vv.10–13a. Verses 13b–14 state the necessary action, while vv.15–16 present the evidence condemning these errorists.

1. The picture of the false teachers (1:10–13a)

10 "There are many rebellious people" is a general statement of the external danger facing the Cretan churches. These false teachers, most likely Cretans by birth, are apparently gnosticizing Judaists who as professed Christians seek to infiltrate the churches with their misguided teaching. They try to fasten onto Christianity various aspects of Judaism and to present the hybrid as a teaching containing higher philosophical insights.

Three terms describe these "many" false teachers: They are (1) "rebellious" (GK *538*), refusing to subordinate themselves to any authority and rejecting the demands of the Gospel on them; (2) "mere talkers" (GK *3468*), fluent and impressive in speech that accomplishes nothing constructive; and (3) "deceivers" (GK *5855*), those whose glib tongues exercise a fascination over the minds of their dupes and lead them astray. "Those

Qualifications for Elders/Overseers and Deacons

Self-controlled	ELDER	ITi 3:2; Tit 1:8	Temperate	ELDER	ITi 3:2; Tit 1:7
Hospitable	ELDER	ITi 3:2; Tit 1:8		DEACON	ITi 3:8
Able to teach	ELDER	ITi 3:2; 5:17; Tit 1:9	Respectable	ELDER	ITi 3:2
Not violent but gentle	ELDER	ITi 3:3; Tit 1:7		DEACON	ITi 3:8
Not quarrelsome	ELDER	ITi 3:3	Not given to drunkenness	ELDER	ITi 3:3; Tit 1:7
Not a lover of money	ELDER	ITi 3:3		DEACON	ITi 3:8
Not a recent convert	ELDER	ITi 3:6	Manages his own family well	ELDER	ITi 3:4
Has a good reputation with outsiders	ELDER	ITi 3:7		DEACON	ITi 3:12
Not overbearing	ELDER	Tit 1:7	Sees that his children obey him	ELDER	ITi 3:4-5; Tit 1:6
Not quick-tempered	ELDER	Tit 1:7		DEACON	ITi 3:12
Loves what is good	ELDER	Tit 1:8	Does not pursue dishonest gain	ELDER	Tit 1:7
Upright, holy	ELDER	Tit 1:8		DEACON	ITi 3:8
Disciplined	ELDER	Tit 1:8	Keeps hold of the deep truths	ELDER	Tit 1:9
Above reproach (blameless)	ELDER	ITi 3:2; Tit 1:6		DEACON	ITi 3:9
	DEACON	ITi 3:9	Sincere	DEACON	ITi 3:8
Husband of one wife	ELDER	ITi 3:2; Tit 1:6	Tested	DEACON	ITi 3:10
	DEACON	ITi 3:12			

© 1985 The Zondervan Corporation

of the circumcision group" were the most active offenders.

11 Paul demands that these people "be silenced" (GK *2187*)—a word that means "to close the mouth by means of a muzzle or gag." The offenders must be refused opportunity to spread their teachings in the churches; the term also includes silencing them by a logical refutation of their views.

Their suppression is necessary because of their seductive work. They belong to that class of people who are "ruining whole households," disturbing and turning upside down the faith of entire families. They achieve these disastrous results by teaching things that simply must not be presented as Christian truth.

"For the sake of dishonest gain" unveils their materialistic motives (cf. v.7), the desire to enrich themselves at the expense of the spiritual welfare of their victims.

12 These Cretan false teachers were all the more dangerous because of the known nature of the people on whom they preyed. As evidence, Paul quotes a line from Epimenides (a 6th-5th century B.C. Cretan poet and religious reformer). This man had intimate knowledge of his own people and was esteemed by them as a "prophet." Paul was willing to accept this evaluation in order to underline the authority of his own judgment. The quotation establishes the picture without exposing Paul to the charge of being anti-Cretan. It put the Cretans on the horns of a dilemma. They must either admit the truthfulness of his verdict concerning them or deny the charge and brand their own prophet a liar.

The triple charge that "Cretans are always liars, evil brutes, lazy gluttons" is supported by other writers. So notorious was their reputation for falsehood that the Greek word *kretizo* ("to Crete-ize") meant "to lie." "Evil brutes" stigmatizes them as having sunk to the level of beasts, unrestrained in their brutality. "Lazy gluttons" underlines their greed as idle sensualists who desired to be filled without exerting personal effort to earn an honest living.

13a Paul's own observations confirm the adverse judgment. Probably he had some unpleasant experiences on the island that verified the verdict.

2. The response to the situation (1:13b–14)

13b "Therefore" introduces the action demanded by this situation. Titus must continue to "rebuke them sharply," dealing pungently and incisively with the danger, like a surgeon cutting away cancerous tissue. "Rebuke" (GK *1794*) may be rendered "convict," effectively showing the error of the teaching that is being opposed. "Them" refers directly to the false teachers, who must obviously be dealt with whenever they seek to gain a hearing in the church. But it seems clear that the action demanded also includes those church members who were known to be receptive to the claims of the false teachers.

The positive result aimed at is "that they will be sound [lit., healthy; GK *5617*] in the faith," i.e., in the truth embodied in the Gospel they have personally accepted. Their personal spiritual health will be impaired if they feed on unhealthy doctrine.

14 As a result of this positive aim, the Cretan Christians will be led to a position where they "pay no attention to Jewish myths" (cf. 1Ti 1:4). These myths were seemingly speculative and fanciful inventions drawn from the OT records, such as are found in the apocryphal and pseudepigraphical writings of Judaism. The rejected teaching is further characterized as "the commands of those who reject the truth." These commands were evidently Jewish-Gnostic ritual observances that the false teachers sought to make binding on Christians (cf. 1Ti 4:3–6). They are to be spurned because they are merely unauthorized human commands of people who have rejected the truth. There is a close connection between false doctrine and evil character.

3. The condemnation of the false teachers (1:15–16)

15 The test of character condemns these false teachers. This is stated in the form of a double maxim. "To the pure, all things are pure" embodies a principle enunciated by Jesus himself in dealing with Jewish food laws (Mt 15:10–11; Mk 7:14–19; Lk 11:37–41) and forcefully impressed on Peter in his vision at Joppa (Ac 10:9–15, 28). These Cretan teachers apparently were engrossed in perpetuating ceremonial distinctions between the pure and the impure. They tended to lay emphasis on outward appearance and judged others on the basis of their own external criteria. Paul teaches that true purity lies not in adherence to nonmoral external rites and regulations but in the inner purity of the regenerated heart. Material things receive their moral character from the inner attitude of the user. This maxim does not, however, invalidate the revelation that certain things are morally wrong.

The converse of the principle carries the attack into enemy territory. Their attribution of impurity to nonmoral things reveals both their own inner state of corruption or defilement and their unbelief. A moral perversion has taken place in their whole being. Their "minds" have become polluted, and their conscience has lost its ability to make correct moral judgments, leaving them unable to make true distinctions between good and evil.

16 The false teachers also stand condemned by the test of conduct. They publicly confess that they are fully informed about God and stand in intimate relations with him (because of either their Jewish religious privilege or their Gnostic claim to an esoteric knowledge of God). But their vaunted claim is belied by their evil conduct. Moral quality of life is the determinative test of religious profession (1Jn 2:4) and by it true character is exposed. Three terms describe the corrupt and unbelieving. They are (1) "detestable" (GK *1008*) or loathsome, causing horror and disgust because of their hypocrisy; (2) "disobedient" (GK *579*), insubordinate to God's truth because of their willful adherence to their man-made rules and regulations; (3) "unfit for doing anything good," disqualified by their impurity from performing any morally good deed. They are like coins found, upon testing, to be spurious, utterly to be rejected as worthless.

III. Concerning the Natural Groups in the Congregations (2:1–15)

Chapter 2, concerned with the pastoral care of the Cretan Christians, is the second main division. Verses 1–10 give ethical instructions for the different groups in the congregations; vv.11–14 unfold the grace of God as the motivating power for Christian living; and v.15 summarizes the duty of Titus on Crete.

A. The Instructions for the Different Groups (2:1–10)

Paul here stresses the importance of building up the inner life of believers as the best antidote against error. Sound doctrine must lead to ethical conduct in the lives of all the groups in the congregations. Emphasis falls on the family groups, where the false teachers had apparently done their greatest damage (1:11).

1. The instructional duty of Titus (2:1)

1 The opening "you" contrasts Titus with the false teachers. He must show the difference by continuing to communicate orally "what is in accord with sound doctrine," i.e., teaching that promotes spiritual health and requires conduct consistent with the teaching professed. Correct doctrine must result in good behavior.

2. The instruction to different age groups (2:2–6)

2 The term "older men" (GK *4566*) denotes age, not office. The senior male members are named first as natural leaders. The value of their example will depend on their moral character. Four qualifications are insisted on; they must be (1) "temperate" (GK *3767*), basically meaning "abstaining from wine," but having a wider meaning, such as "clear-headed"; (2) "worthy of respect" (GK *4948*), revealing a personal dignity and seriousness of purpose that invite honor and respect; (3) "self-controlled" (GK *5409*), possessing self-mastery in thought and judgment (cf. 1:8); and (4) "sound in faith, in love and in endurance," revealing a Christian healthiness of heart and mind. In v.1 "sound" (GK *5617*) is applied to doctrine, here to character. "Faith" may be objective, as the doctrinal content of the faith professed, but the following two items suggest that it is subjective, their personal faith in the Lord. They must be mature in their exercise of genuine "love," not bitter and vindictive, and they must display active "endurance" (GK *5705*), that steadfast persistence that bravely bears the trials and afflictions of life.

3 "Likewise" indicates that the same kind of deportment is expected of the "older women," although the demands on them are related to their own station in life. The basic demand is that they "be reverent in the way they live." Their conduct must reveal that they regard life as sacred in all of its aspects.

Their reverential behavior requires that they "not be slanderers or addicted to much wine." As mature Christians, they must not be given to gossip, repeating vicious and unfounded charges against others, and must not overindulge in wine. The union of the two negatives suggests the close connection between a loose tongue and intoxicating drink.

Positively, the older women must "teach what is good." By personal word and example, they must teach what is morally good, noble, and attractive. The reference is not to public instruction, but to their teaching function in the home.

4 The training of the younger women is the duty, not of Titus, but the older women, qualified to do so by position and character. "Train" (GK 5405) means to school in the lessons of sobriety and self-control (cf. vv.2, 5). "Younger" suggests a reference to the newly married. Paul then lists seven characteristics that must be commended to such women (vv.4–5a). "To love their husbands and children" forms a pair of instructions. It means "devoted to husbands and devoted to children." Such domestic affection stands at the very heart of any Christian home.

5 "To be self-controlled [GK 5409] and pure [GK 54]" forms another pair. The former is a standing duty for all Christians (cf. 1:8; 2:2, 6); the latter denotes not only chastity in their sex life but also purity of heart and mind in all their conduct.

"To be busy at home, to be kind" designates a third pair. The first describes the many domestic activities of the housewife that she must willingly accept as part of her position as queen of the home. The devoted wife and mother finds her absorbing interest in the innumerable duties of the home (cf. Paul's condemnation of idleness in 1Ti 5:13–14). These demand unsparing self-giving and may subject her to the temptation to be irritable and harsh in her demands on members of her household. She must therefore cultivate the virtue of being "kind" (GK 19), i.e., benevolent, heartily doing what is good and beneficial to others.

The seventh item for a younger married woman stresses her acceptance of the established relationship between husband and wife as her Christian duty. "To be subject to" (GK 5718) suggests the voluntary acceptance of the headship of the husband (cf. Eph 5:22–24). In declaring the spiritual equality of the woman before God (Gal 3:28), Christianity immeasurably elevated her status but did not thereby abolish her functional position as the complement and support of her husband as the head of the home.

The concluding purpose clause apparently relates to all seven items. It is the first expression of Paul's strong sense of a religious purpose behind these ethical demands. If Christian wives ignore these demands and flout the role their culture demanded of good wives, the Gospel will be maligned, criticized, and discredited by non-Christians. Christianity will be judged especially by the impact that it has on the women. It therefore is the duty of the women to protect God's revelation from profanation by living discreet and wholesome lives. No lifestyle is justified that hinders the message of God's salvation in Christ.

6 The requirement for the young men is brief but comprehensive: self-control. As a young man, Titus must fittingly convey his instructions for the young women indirectly, but his age was an advantage in dealing directly with the young men. "Encourage" (GK 4151) is stronger than "teach" in v.1; it may be rendered "urge" or "admonish." Since young men are inclined to be somewhat impetuous and unrestrained in conduct, their basic need is to be "self-controlled" (GK 5404), cultivating balance and self-restraint in daily practice. It was a quality of which Paul found it necessary to remind the Cretan believers (1:8; 2:2, 4–5).

3. The personal example of Titus (2:7–8)

7 In concluding instructions to the different age groups, Paul reminds Titus that his own conduct must confirm his teaching. There is no word for "them" in the Greek, so that his example is not to be restricted to the young men. "In everything" underlines the comprehensiveness of the duty. It is expanded in what follows. "Doing what is good" places the initial stress on his conduct, reflecting his noble deeds. Personal example must precede effective teaching, but his "teaching" in its manner and content must be of the highest quality and must be characterized by "integrity" (GK 917) and "seriousness" (GK 4949).

The former stresses his purity of motive, revealing that he himself is uninfected by the evil conduct and erroneous views of the false teachers; the latter points to his outward dignity, reflecting the high moral tone and serious manner appropriate to his sacred task.

8 Titus must also demonstrate "soundness of speech that cannot be condemned." The content of his teaching and ordinary conversation must have two characteristics. (1) It must have "soundness" (GK 5617), conforming to healthful doctrine (cf. 1:9, 13; 2:1–2). (2) Such soundness will ensure that no critic will be able to point out anything in it justly open to censure or rebuke. Paul hints at the picture of a courtroom where the judge can find no basis for the accusation of the plaintiff.

Paul concludes his personal remarks to Titus with another purpose clause. The expression "those who oppose you" is apparently left intentionally vague to leave room for all types of critics. When the objections are examined, the anticipated result is that the critic "may be ashamed," i.e., made to look foolish because he is shown to have no case. An accusation of something morally "bad" or worthless "about us" (including Paul and Christians generally) will be found to be groundless.

4. The instructions to the slaves (2:9–10)

Paul's ethical instructions are now addressed to a distinct social group that overlaps groups divided by age and sex. Slaves formed a significant element in the apostolic churches and the welfare of the faith demanded that they too accept their spiritual responsibility as believers. Paul here makes no distinction between slaves who had Christian masters and those who did not (see comments on 1Ti 6:1–2).

9 Since the Greek has no opening command in v.9, we must substitute either "teach" from v.1 or, more likely, "encourage" from v. 6. The fundamental duty of slaves is voluntarily to accept subjection to their masters as a matter of principle to everything. "Masters" (GK 1305) denotes that as owners they had complete authority over their slaves. This command stresses the comprehensiveness of this duty, though a Christian slave could not submit when a pagan master demanded things contrary to Christian conscience.

In their voluntary subjection, slaves must "try to please" their masters. Instead of having a sullen disposition, they should aim to be well-pleasing. The word "please" (GK 2298) elsewhere refers to our relationship with God; it is the distinctive contribution of Christianity that slaves should govern their relations to their masters by this high principle.

Paul continues with three further phrases, two negative and one positive, that describe the slave-master relationship. The first is "not to talk back to them," i.e., not to dispute their commands and by deliberate resistance seek to thwart their will.

10 The second negative demand is "not to steal from them"—not underhandedly to divert to themselves part of anything their masters had not intended for them. Petty theft was common among slaves in Roman households. Employment in various trades and occupations offered slaves ample opportunity to resort to the various tricks of the trade for their own advantage.

Their positive duty is "to show that they can be fully trusted," demonstrating "good faith" in their whole relationship to their masters. They must not only be Christians but actively show this by proving themselves dependable in everything "good" or beneficial to their masters.

Such ethical conduct Paul again undergirds with a profound spiritual motive, "so that in every way they will make the teaching about God our Savior attractive." For a Christian there can be no higher motive. Slaves' acceptance of the teaching about "God our Savior" must find expression in their transformed conduct in every aspect of their lives. The very difficulty of their position would make such conduct a powerful recommendation of the Gospel, proving to the master the power of the Gospel.

B. The Foundation for Godly Living (2:11–14)

"For" begins Paul's masterly summary of Christian doctrine as the proper foundation for the ethical demands just made on the various groups and as an explanation for "God our Savior" in v.10. Christian conduct must be grounded in and motivated by Christian truth. The vitality of doctrinal profession must be demonstrated by transformed Christian conduct.

1. The manifestation of God's grace (2:11)

11 God's program of redemption is rooted in his "grace" (GK 5921), his free favor and spontaneous action toward needy sinners to deliver and transform them. This grace has been manifested as a historical reality in Christ's birth, life and ministry, atoning death, and resurrection. "Appeared" (GK 2210) conveys the image of grace suddenly breaking in on our moral darkness, like the rising sun (this verb is used of the sun in Ac 27:20).

The effect of the manifestation was redemptive, not destructive. The adjective rendered "that brings salvation" (GK 5403) asserts its saving efficacy; this salvation is available to all people, though its personal application is dependent on one's response of faith. Its universal scope justifies the application of its ethical demands to all classes of its professed recipients.

2. The training by God's grace (2:12)

12 Grace also goes to work in the lives of the saved. Grounded in God's nature, it makes ethical demands of Christians consistent with his nature. It instructs the believer in the things "in accord with sound doctrine" (2:1). The verb "teaches" (GK 4084) comprehends the entire training process—teaching, encouragement, correction, and discipline.

The negative pedagogical purpose of grace is to train us to renounce our past by saying "'No' to ungodliness and worldly passions." "Ungodliness" (GK 813) denotes the impiety and irreverence that characterizes the unsaved life; "worldly passions" are those cravings characteristic of the world in its estrangement from God. Such renunciation, standing at the beginning of a life of Christian victory, must be maintained in daily self-denial.

This negative work clears the field for its positive aim for believers: "to live self-controlled, upright and godly lives." Our entire course of life should be consistently characterized by the three stated qualities. They look in three directions, though sharp distinctions need not be pressed: (1) inward ("self-controlled"; GK 5407), already stipulated for different groups (1:8; 2:2,5) and now demanded of every believer; (2) outward ("upright"; GK 1469), faithfully fulfilling all the demands of truth and justice in our relations with others; (3) upward ("godly"; GK 2357), fully devoted to God in reverence and loving obedience.

Such a life is a possibility and a duty "in this present age" (Gal 1:4), which holds dangers for the believer (Ro 12:2; 2Ti 4:10) and stands in contrast to the anticipated future.

3. The expectation of Christ's return (2:13)

13 Those being trained by God's grace, having renounced their sinful past and living disciplined lives in the present, now "wait for" (GK 4657; cf. 1Th 1:9–10) the future. They anticipate "the blessed hope," the personal return of Christ who will consummate our bliss in eternal glory.

The Greek connects "blessed hope" and "glorious appearing" under one article, suggesting that the reference is to one event viewed from two aspects. For believers, it is indeed the blessed hope and the longed-for consummation of that hope. For Christ himself, this anticipated return will vindicate his character as the Lord of glory. "Glorious appearing" points to his present glorification in heaven. Now unrecognized and disregarded by the world, his glory at his return will be manifested in all its splendor.

Grammatically, the glory to be revealed relates either to Christ alone or to both the Father and Christ, but the former is to be preferred. (1) This is the most natural view, since both nouns are connected by one article as referring to one person. (2) The combination "god and savior" was familiar to the Hellenistic religions. (3) The added clause in v.14 refers to Christ alone, and it is most natural to take the entire preceding expression as its antecedent. (4) In the Pastorals the coming appearance is referred to Christ alone. (5) The adjective "great" of God is rather pointless but highly significant if applied to Christ. (6) This view is in full harmony with other passages such as Jn 20:28; Ro 9:5; Heb 1:8; and 2Pe 1:1. This view takes the statement as an explicit assertion of the deity of Christ.

4. The purpose of Christ's redemption (2:14)

14 From the future, Paul reverts to the historical work of Christ as Savior as the foundation for present sanctification. "Who gave himself for us" summarizes that work as voluntary, exhaustive, and substitutionary. His giving of himself was the grandest of all gifts. Because of our sinfulness, his atoning work had a dual aspect.

Its negative aspect was "to redeem us from all wickedness" (or "lawlessness"; GK *490*), our assertion of self-will in defiance of God's standard that is the essence of sin (1Jn 3:4). This expression stresses not our guilt as rebels but rather our deliverance from bondage to lawlessness through Christ's ransom. "From" indicates effective removal from that sphere and our deliverance from "all" aspects of its domination.

This negative work is the necessary prelude to the positive work of sanctification, "to purify for himself a people that are his very own." Behind "purify" (GK *2751*) is the moral defilement that the rebellion of humankind has produced. Sin makes us not only guilty but also unclean before a holy God. The blood-wrought cleansing (1Jn 1:7) enables us to be restored to fellowship with God as "a people that are his very own." Since we have been redeemed by his blood (1Pe 1:18–21), Christ wants us voluntarily to yield ourselves wholly to him. Such a surrender is our only reasonable response to divine mercy (Ro 12:1–2). "Eager to do what is good" delineates what this relationship involves. "Eager" (GK *2421*) means one who is "a zealot, an enthusiast"; for those who have been redeemed from the doom of sin and death and brought into a unique relationship with God, the true voluntary response is to be enthusiastic "to do what is good." He who eagerly awaits the return of the Savior will be eager also to further his cause by good works until he comes.

C. The Restatement of the Duty of Titus (2:15)

15 "Teach" looks back to 2:1, where the same word is used. As his central duty, Titus must continually present practical instructions to the various groups in their proper doctrinal setting. As part of his teaching he must "encourage" (GK *4151*) or exhort the hearers to appropriate and practice the instruction, and "rebuke" (GK *1794*) or convict those who are slack or fail to respond. He must perform these duties "with all authority," for the message is apostolic and authentic and its authority must be stressed. The Gospel must not be presented as an optional opinion to be accepted or rejected as its hearers may please. The minister's authority rests in the nature of his message; he is not raised above the truth but the truth above him.

As the apostolic representative in Crete, Titus must "not let anyone despise" him or belittle his message and authority. He must not permit his message and work to be disdainfully rejected. Since this letter would be read in the churches, the remark was intended as much for the Cretans as for Titus himself.

IV. Concerning Believers Among People Generally (3:1–11)

Having dealt with church leaders (ch. 1) and the conduct of believers as members of the Christian community (ch. 2), in this final section Paul insists that believers also have duties to the government and to the non-Christian world.

A. Their Obligations As Citizens (3:1–2)

1 Christians have a duty to government. "The people" refers to the members of the churches, not to all Cretans in general. "Remind" indicates that the duties now insisted on are not new to them; Titus must repeatedly press these duties upon their consciences. Early Christian preaching was never limited to the way of salvation but included instructions concerning the practical implications of that salvation for daily living. Paul wants believers to make a favorable impression on the non-Christian world.

The duty of believers is "to be subject to rulers and authorities." "To be subject" (GK *5718*) implies voluntary acceptance of this position of submission. "Rulers and authorities" signifies not the individual rulers but the various forms of human government (cf. also Ro 13:1–7; 1Pe 2:13–17); the known turbulence of the Cretans made such an instruction particularly appropriate here.

"To be obedient" (GK *4272*) states the result and visible demonstration of their attitude of submission. The context implies obedience to the particular demands of government, though the practice of obedience is not to be limited to these areas. It is assumed that the obedience demanded does not contradict explicit Christian duties.

As good citizens, believers must also "be ready to do whatever is good"—be prepared and willing to participate in activities that promote the welfare of the community. They must not stand coldly aloof from praiseworthy enterprises of government but show good public spirit, thus proving that Christianity is a constructive force in society.

2 Believers also have obligations to pagan neighbors. Negatively, they must "slander no one," i.e., abstain from hurling curses and vicious epithets at those offending or injuring them. The demand requires inner grace but is appropriate for followers of Christ, who did not revile when he was reviled (1Pe 2:23). Furthermore, they must be "peaceable" (lit., "nonfighting"; GK 285), refusing to engage in quarrels and conflicts. The Christian must not adopt the arts of the agitator.

Positively, Christians must be "considerate" (GK 2117) or gentle, not stubbornly insisting on their own rights but acting in courtesy and forbearance. Another positive duty is continually "to show true [lit., all] humility," an attitude of mind that is the opposite of self-assertiveness and harshness. Humility is not to be exhibited only in dealing with fellow believers but must be shown "toward all men," including those who are hostile and morally perverse. It is a difficult test of Christian character but one that effectively proves the genuineness of Christian profession.

B. The Motives for Such Godly Conduct (3:3–8)

The conduct required in vv.1–2 is undergirded by weighty reasons. Paul's masterly summary of evangelical teaching in these verses reminds his readers that such conduct is necessary and possible in view of God's transforming work in their own lives. He advances three supporting motives: their own pre-Christian past (v.3), the saving work of God in believers (vv.4–8a), and the necessary connection between Christian truth and conduct (v.8b).

1. The motive from our own past (3:3)

3 The remembrance of our own past should be a powerful motive for gentleness and consideration toward the unsaved. "We were," standing emphatically at the opening of the sentence, implies that what was once true of us is still true of the unsaved neighbor. The added "too" stresses that the condition described in retrospect applied to Paul and Titus as well as to the Cretan Christians; it is, in fact, true of all believers everywhere. It is salutary to remember our own past moral condition when dealing with the unsaved in their degradation.

The picture of our past is vividly and concisely drawn. We were "foolish" (GK 485)—without spiritual understanding and lacking discernment of spiritual realities because of the darkening effect of sin on the intellect (Eph 4:18). As outward evidence of our alienated condition, we were "disobedient"—willfully disregarding authority, refusing obedience to God's law, and fretting under human authority. "Deceived" pictures active straying from the true course by following false guides. By allowing our conduct to be dictated by a wide variety of personal "passions and pleasures," we inevitably became enslaved to them. Never finding true personal satisfaction in their pursuit, we lived our lives in the grip of the antisocial forces of "malice and envy," harboring an attitude of ill-will toward others and enviously begrudging others their good fortune. "Being hated" denotes being odious, repulsive, and disgusting to others. "Hating one another" marks the climax in the active operation of mutual antagonisms that hasten the dissolution of human society.

2. The motive from our present salvation (3:4–7)

"But" introduces the familiar Pauline contrast between what we once were and now are (cf. Ro 6:17–23; 1Co 6:9–11; Eph 2:2–13; 5:7–12; Col 1:21–22; 3:7–10). God's marvelous salvation, summarized here, must motivate our dealings with the unsaved.

a. The manifestation of salvation (3:4)

4 Our salvation roots in a definite historical event, "when the kindness and love of God our Savior appeared." "Appeared" (cf. 2:11) looks back to the salvation manifested in the incarnate Christ. The salvation embodied in him manifested two aspects of the nature of "God our Savior": (1) his "kindness" (GK 5983) that prompted him to bestow forgiveness and blessings; (2) his "love" (GK 5792) or affection for us that he displayed in spite of our sin and degradation. These two concepts are closely connected and form one whole. Through his action in Christ, God is now revealed as "our Savior." "Our" is strongly confessional and associates Paul with all those who have appropriated this Savior as their own (cf. Gal 2:20).

b. The basis of salvation (3:5a)

5a "He saved us" simply records the historic fact of his saving work in all who have accepted salvation in Christ. We now possess his salvation, although it is still incomplete, awaiting its consummation at Christ's return.

The basis of this experienced salvation is never due to personal merit but to God's sovereign grace. The negative clause repeats Paul's well-known denial of salvation by works (Ro 4:4–5; Gal 2:16–17; Eph 2:8–9). Our salvation did not arise out of works that we ourselves had performed in righteousness, for as sinners, we were not able to perform any righteous deeds. Positively, God saved us "because of his mercy" (GK 1799). In our wretchedness he graciously withheld deserved punishment and freely saved us.

c. The means of salvation (3:5b–6)

5b–6 God's salvation was mediated to us "through the washing of rebirth and renewal by the Holy Spirit." "Washing" (GK 3373) denotes an act that cleanses us from the defilement of sin. This washing is the means of our "rebirth" (GK 4098), the spiritual regeneration of the individual believer. Most commentators take the washing as a reference to water baptism. But if water baptism is the means that produces the spiritual rebirth, we then have the questionable teaching of a material agency as the indispensable means for producing a spiritual result (but cf. Mt 15:1–20; Ro 2:25–29; Gal 5:6). Thus the washing is properly a divine inner act, although the experience is symbolically pictured in Christian baptism. In the NT the inner experience is viewed as openly confessed before people in baptism.

The expression "through the washing of rebirth and renewal by the Holy Spirit" is open to two interpretations grammatically. (1) Both "rebirth" and "renewal" may be regarded as dependent on "washing" to form one concept. Then the washing of rebirth is further described as a renewal wrought by the Spirit. (2) The other view holds that the preposition "through" must be repeated with "renewal." This view sees two separate aspects of salvation, in which case the washing is viewed as producing an instantaneous change that ended the old life and began the new, while the work of renewal by the Spirit, beginning with the impartation of the new life, is a lifelong activity in the experience of the believer. In Ro 12:2 this renewal is viewed as a continuing process; in Eph 5:26–27 the act of cleansing of the church is followed by the work of sanctification until no spot or wrinkle remains. This process of renewal in the believer is the work of the Holy Spirit. He alone can produce a new nature that finds active expression in an entirely new manner of life.

"Whom he poured out on us generously" stresses that God has made ample provision for the development of this renewed life. "Poured out" (GK 1772) had its primary fulfillment at Pentecost, but "on us" marks the pouring out as individually experienced at conversion (Ro 5:5). The Spirit's work in each believer as a member of the body of Christ is a continuation of the Pentecostal outpouring. Every faulty or inadequate experience of renewal is always due to some human impediment, never to God's inadequate provision. "Through Jesus Christ our Savior" states the channel through which the Spirit's renewing presence was bestowed—a bestowal based on the finished work of Christ as Savior (Jn 7:38–39; 15:26; Ac 2:33). The "our" is again confessional. Our acceptance of Christ as Savior is the human condition for the bestowal of the Spirit. Note the Trinity in vv.5b–6: "the Holy Spirit," "he" (the Father), and "Jesus Christ." Each member of the divine Trinity has his own special function in the work of human redemption.

d. Its results (3:7)

7 "So that" here denotes not only purpose but also result; the aim of salvation has been accomplished. "Having been justified by his grace" records the result of salvation in our past. Sin had brought guilt and condemnation, but when we received Christ as our Savior, we were "justified" ("declared righteous"; GK 1467) and given a standing of acceptance before him. Justification is always the act of the Father, motivated by his grace, his free unmerited favor bestowed on the basis of Christ's perfect work. This condensed comment assumes knowledge of Paul's doctrine of justification.

The second stated result comprehends our present standing in relation to the future. "Might become heirs" denotes not just a future prospect but a present reality. As members of God's family, we now are heirs, but entrance upon our inheritance belongs to the future. Our standing as heirs is in full harmony with "the hope of eternal life" (cf. 1:2). Our present experience of salvation can give us only a tantalizing foretaste of the nature of our future inheritance.

3. The necessary connection between doctrine and conduct (3:8)

8a "This is a trustworthy saying" clearly looks back to the doctrinal statement in vv.4–7 as a unified whole and stamps it as worthy of full approval. Confined to the Pastoral Letters (see comment on 1Ti 1:15), this is the sole occurrence of this formula in Titus. Scholars generally accept the view that the writer is citing a hymn or confessional statement, but there is no agreement about the extent or exact contents of the assumed quotation. Whether it is a quotation or Paul's own composition, no nobler doctrinal statement is found in any Pauline letter.

8b It is Paul's definite intention that Titus, as his personal representative in Crete, continue insistently "to stress [GK 1331] these things" (i.e., the trustworthy truths contained in vv.4–7). Titus must stoutly and confidently affirm them. The orthodox preacher must proclaim his message with confidence and ringing certainty.

Such insistent preaching must aim at a definite result in the lives of believers. "Those who have trusted in God" pictures not only the believers' initial acceptance of these truths but also their present personal faith relationship to God. Because of this present relationship, they are obligated to "be careful to devote themselves to doing what is good." Again Paul emphasizes that the Gospel message of free forgiveness for sinners on the sole basis of faith must find expression in a life characterized by the performance of excellent deeds. The practice of good works is the logical outcome of a true apprehension of the grace of God.

Paul concludes with a summary evaluation of the instructions just given. "These things" could refer to his final demand that believers combine faith and practice, but more probably the reference is to the true teachings that Titus must insist on in his work in Crete. By their very nature they are "excellent" (GK 2819), i.e., good, attractive, and praiseworthy. They are also "profitable [GK 6068] for everyone," meaning that they have a beneficial impact on humankind. The beneficial effects of Christian ethical standards are not limited to believers only. A vital Christianity unites the beautiful and the profitable.

C. The Reaction to Spiritual Error (3:9–11)

9 "But" introduces the necessary reaction of Titus to matters contrary to the teaching insisted on in v.8. They are described as "foolish controversies and genealogies and arguments and quarrels about the law." The picture looks back to 1:10–16; "about the law" marks the Jewish coloring. The same sort of problems also existed at Ephesus (cf. 1Ti 1:3–7). They comprise various "foolish" or senseless inquiries, involving speculations about the OT genealogies, and resulted in sharp dissensions and open quarrels. All such matters Titus must "avoid" (GK 4325), i.e., deliberately shun and stand aloof from, because they produce no spiritual benefits and lead to no constructive results.

10 Paul now passes from these reprehensible opinions to their perverted advocates. The adjective "divisive" (GK 148) essentially characterizes what is a self-chosen opinion or viewpoint; because of their insistence on their opinions, devoid of a true scriptural basis, the dissidents stir up divisions. Those who persist in these opinions form heretical parties.

Any such person Titus must "warn" (GK 3804) or admonish by faithfully and lovingly pointing out the error. If a second effort to deal with him proves ineffective, let Titus "have nothing to do with him." Further efforts would not be a good stewardship of his time and energies and would give the offender an undeserved sense of importance.

11 Stubborn refusal of admonition will assure Titus that the person is "warped" (GK 1750), i.e., in a state of twisted perversion, wholly out of touch with truth. The passive voice seems to point to the satanic agency behind his condition. This person is also sinful, deliberately missing the divine standard by a persistent refusal to receive correction. It reveals an inner moral condition of being "self-condemned." That individual knows that in his deliberate refusal to abandon self-chosen views, he is wrong and stands condemned by his own better judgment.

V. Conclusion (3:12–15)

A. The Concluding Instructions (3:12–14)

12 Paul announces his plans for the future as they concern Titus. Another worker will be sent to replace Titus in Crete; the latter's assignment to Crete was not permanent. At the time of writing, however, neither the time nor the final selection of the replacement has been determined. Nothing further is known of Artemas. Tychicus was a trusted coworker who on several occasions appears as traveling with or for Paul (Ac 20:4; Eph 6:21–22; Col 4:7–8; 2Ti 4:12). As soon as a replacement arrives, Titus must proceed as quickly as possible to Nicopolis, apparently the city in Epirus on the west coast of Greece. Paul plans to spend the winter there, presumably making it a base of operation for work in Dalmatia. "There" shows that Paul is not yet there. The place of writing is unknown, but it may have been Corinth.

13 Zenas and Apollos are almost certainly the bearers of this letter. Zenas's name is Greek, but he may have been a convert from Judaism. If he was of Jewish origin, "lawyer" means that he had been an expert in the Mosaic law; if a Gentile, it means he had been a Roman jurist. Apollos is the well-known Alexandrian Jew who, having been fully instructed at Ephesus, effectively worked in the Corinthian church (Ac 18:24–28; 19:1; 1Co 1:12; 3:4–6; 4:6; 16:12). Their journey will take Zenas and Apollos through Crete, and Titus must diligently assist them by seeing that their further needs are supplied. Such generous material assistance for Christian workers on their journeys characterized the early church (Ac 15:3; Ro15:24; 1Co 16:6; 2Co 1:16; 3Jn 5–8).

14 Titus need not carry the burden alone. By appealing to the churches for further funds, he has an opportunity to train them in the practice of "doing what is good" (cf. 3:8). It will further the Gospel and develop their own Christian lives. This situation gives Paul a final opportunity to stress the theme that Christians must be characterized by the practice of noble deeds, thus assuring that their lives will not be "unproductive." Noble deeds are the fruit of the tree of salvation.

B. The Personal Greetings (3:15a)

15a All the workers with Paul join in sending their greetings. They are left unnamed, since Zenas and Apollos will orally identify them. Titus is to pass on these greetings to the believers in Crete, who are filled with affection for Paul and his assistants "in the faith." "Faith" probably refers to the sphere where their affection is operative.

C. The Closing Benediction (3:15b)

15b The "you" is plural, including all those to whom Titus is to convey Paul's greetings. It suggests that Paul expects the letter to be read in the various churches.

Philemon

INTRODUCTION

1. Authorship, Date, and Place of Origin

Few, if any, dispute that Philemon was written by the apostle Paul. Those who claim it is non-Pauline on the basis of its similarity in final greetings with Colossians are making an unwarranted conclusion concerning Colossians (see introduction to Colossians). This letter appeared early as a letter of Paul in the Muratorian Fragment and in Marcion's canon.

Those who hold that Colossians and Philemon were written at about the same time, while Paul was in prison at Rome, date it c. A.D. 58–60. If it was written from Ephesus (see introduction to Philippians), a date c. A.D. 56 would be likely. Since runaway slaves were apt to seek asylum almost anywhere, either Rome or Ephesus is possible. The question of date cannot be firmly settled.

2. Destination

The traditional view is that the letter was written to Philemon, a slave owner and resident of the Lycus Valley (most likely in Colosse) in Asia Minor. Some have suggested that this is the lost letter to the Laodiceans (Col 4:16), but it cannot be shown that Philemon was really a letter to the church rather than to an individual. Also addressed is Archippus (v.1), who is told in Col 4:17 to "complete the work," an instruction that may refer to Paul's request in behalf of Onesimus.

3. Occasion and Purpose

In this letter, Paul intercedes in behalf of Philemon's runaway slave, Onesimus. His suggestions for handling the matter are difficult to determine because of his obscure and deferential words. At a minimum he asks that Onesimus be reconciled to the household without harsh punishment. He also strongly hints that the slave would be useful to him in the work of evangelism. Nowhere does Paul openly state that Philemon should set Onesimus free. Nor is it necessary to assume that Onesimus would be freed if he were to join Paul in his missionary work.

Brief and intensely personal, the letter is addressed to one person, Philemon, but other interested parties are mentioned in the salutation. Apphia, his wife, would have had daily responsibility over the slaves of the household. Archippus, perhaps Philemon's son and possibly also a local pastor ("fellow soldier"), would look after the interests of the church, which is also mentioned in the salutation. No doubt the church at Colosse would find significant the reconciliation of a runaway slave on the intercession of no less a person than the apostle Paul.

Some of the events that led to the writing of the letter can be stated without qualification. On the other hand, many of the tantalizing details are lost to us. Onesimus came in contact with Paul while the latter was in prison, most likely in Rome, and was converted. Presumably the authorities in charge of Paul were unaware of the personal status of Onesimus. Paul intimates that he had robbed his master in some way, but oddly he does not mention the details.

The traditional interpretation has been that Paul sent Onesimus back with this letter and with Tychicus at the same time as the writing of the letter to the Colossians, to a city in the Lycus Valley. The names in the greetings at the end of both letters are similar—Epaphras, Mark, Demas, and Luke appear in both.

It seems possible, however, to understand that Philemon was composed at a time prior to Colossians. The evidence for this is striking. According to Col 4:7–9, Tychicus and Onesimus were returning to Colosse together and would "tell all that is happening here." It is usually assumed that this is the return of the runaway slave Onesimus. But if so, why is he described as a "faithful ... brother"? Paul usually reserved the word "faithful" (GK *4412*) for fellow workers who showed great determination and endurance in the work of the Gospel, not for people who have run away from and stolen from their master.

Furthermore, Phm 22 states clearly that Paul expects to be in Colosse soon. But in writing Colossians the apostle says, "Pray for us, too, that God may open a door for our message." If he had expected to be released from imprisonment soon, he would almost certainly have mentioned this to the Colossians as well.

Finally, Paul writes in Colossians that Onesimus is accompanying Tychicus, but Tychicus is nowhere mentioned in Philemon. That Tychicus accompanied Onesimus when the latter returned as a runaway is only an assumption.

4. Literary Form

The letter is unique in the Pauline corpus because it is a personal letter of commendation and recommendation. There are innumerable examples of similar letters, both pagan and Christian, from the Greco-Roman world. Among these, Philemon belongs to the kind of letter written to intercede for a delinquent slave. It begins with a salutation and is followed by expressions of thanks and petition, the principal subject matter, a conclusion, and greetings. Most of the Pauline letters follow this format, even when they are more like theological treatises.

5. Theological Values

Paul, Philemon, and Onesimus are persons in a real-life drama of profound social significance. Each has heard the claims of Christianity from totally different backgrounds. Paul was once a rigorous Jew of the Dispersion who advanced in Judaism beyond all his contemporaries. Philemon was a wealthy Asiatic Gentile. Onesimus was the most despicable of all creatures, a runaway slave. They find themselves united in the Gospel of Christ. Here is a living example of Paul's statement that "there is neither Jew nor Greek, slave nor free, male nor female, for you are all one in Christ Jesus" (Gal 3:28). It was in this oneness that Paul sought a solution to the problem presented by the relationship of Onesimus to Philemon.

Neither Paul nor the other authors of the NT ever call for the abolition of slavery. For a new religion to do so would have been suicidal in the ancient world. Paul's main concern is that Philemon not act out of obligation to the apostle; rather, he is to be motivated by the love of Christ within himself. Out of that should come more than mere reconciliation (v.21). Freedom of slaves, like all freedom, must come from the heart of Christ-inspired people. Under this compulsion, slavery will ultimately wilt and die. While all ethical behavior for Christians should arise out of love rather than regulation or constraint, yet it takes fully committed disciples to put it into practice.

EXPOSITION

I. Salutation (1–3)

1–3 The salutation is significant for its departures from Paul's other salutations. The letter is in the form of an ancient letter of commendation, and Paul's opening words are calculated to suggest that his appeal for Onesimus should be favorably received.

Paul is a "prisoner of Jesus Christ" and therefore suffers for the sake of the Gospel. His suffering is a mark of his apostleship, which in turn lends weight to any suggestion he might make. Furthermore, Timothy, a well-recognized young steward of the Gospel, joins him in the appeal. Finally, Paul not only greets Philemon, the owner of Onesimus, but also his wife Apphia. She is as much a party to the decision as her husband, because according to the custom of the time, she had day-to-day responsibility for the slaves.

As for Archippus and the church, Paul includes them in the salutation with good reason. Archippus, one of the leading figures in the community (perhaps a pastor), and the church will bring appropriate pressure to bear on Philemon should he fail to fulfill the great apostle's request. Philemon would have had to have been a very strong-minded individual to resist the plea of Paul and his protégé Timothy.

II. Thanksgiving and Prayer (4–7)

4–5 In both pagan and Christian letters of the first centuries of the Christian era, the salutation was often followed by an expression of thanksgiving and a prayer. Paul here tells when he gives thanks—"always ... in my prayers"—and also tells why he does so—

"because I hear about your love and faith" (cf. Ro 1:8–10; 1Th 1:2–11; Php 1:3–11; Col 1:3–8). The "you" in "I remember you" is singular, suggesting that the recipient of the letter is primarily Philemon.

6 At this point, Paul's prayer begins. It is not easy to translate, but he is most likely praying that Philemon's active participation in the faith will be made effective because of his understanding of God's goodness to both of them. As Paul repeatedly suggests, true knowledge of the faith precedes good works (cf. Col 1:9–10).

7 Paul has been repeatedly impressed by the expressions of Philemon's love; they have brought him much joy and comfort. This verse justifies Paul's expansive use of the phrases "full understanding" and "every good thing" in v.6. That is, he is praying for great Christian maturity in his brother. The implication is that this maturity will find expression in Philemon's treatment of Onesimus.

III. Plea for Onesimus (8–22)

The situation of both Paul and Onesimus is all-important to the understanding of this section of the letter. Paul's circumstances are just as significant as those of Onesimus—a fact often overlooked by commentators. Because he is in prison, he cannot do the things a free man might do to help the slave. He can do little more than write a letter asking for clemency for his new-found brother, and he can suggest that he hopes to visit the Lycus Valley soon to put additional pressure on Philemon. Under more usual circumstances, a free man could have assumed custody of a runaway slave after he had given guarantees of his return to the public officials, and he could have suggested that the slave be formally assigned to him for a time. This was not uncommon in the Greco-Roman world.

Onesimus's status was the lowest that one could reach in the ancient world. Because he was a runaway slave, he was protected by no laws and he was subject to all manner of abuse. Fugitive slaves usually went to large cities, remote parts of the Roman state, or into unsettled areas. Their capture and return was largely an informal arrangement between the owner and a provincial administrator. They were frequently beaten unmercifully or put to tasks in which their life expectancy was very short.

Paul must have put Philemon in a precarious position indeed. In pleading for forgiveness and restitution for Onesimus without a punishment that was obvious to all, he was confronting the social and economic order head-on. While he does not ask for manumission, even his request for clemency for Onesimus and hint of his assignment to Paul defied Roman tradition. By this plea Paul is also giving new dignity to the slave class.

8 Paul first reminds Philemon of his apostolic authority. "Bold" (GK 4244) has the idea of "freedom" or "boldness." Here it implies "right" or "authority"—hence, "I could be bold and order you." The suggestion of authority was probably enough, coupled as it was with the appeals to love, old age, and imprisonment in v.9.

9 Part of Paul's appeal is based on his being an "old man" (GK 4566), which usually implied authority (in antiquity, wisdom and authority were assumed to go with old age). Here, however, the stress is on the apostle's aged and feeble condition.

10 The imagery in this verse is very strong. The figure of the father and child was often used in Judaism as an illustration of the relationship of teacher and student or of leader and convert. Paul is here pleading on behalf of his spiritual son.

11–12 There is a double play on words here. "Onesimus" was a common slave name; it meant "useful" or "profitable." This is also the meaning of another Greek word *chrestos*, which appears here in *achrestos* ("useless"; GK 947) and *euchrestos* ("useful"; GK 2378). *Chrestos* in turn sounded much like *Christos* (the Greek word for "Christ"; GK 5986). An ancient reader would have thought this play on words much more clever and humorous than we would. That Paul uses it at the beginning of his plea for Onesimus shows us something of his exquisite sensitivity and tact. It is as if, realizing the radical nature of what he was about to ask of Philemon, Paul deliberately introduces this bit of humor.

In v.12, Paul again stresses how very dear to him Onesimus is. He is not simply the one "I am sending back"; he is "my very heart."

13 This is the culmination of the appeal. Onesimus has been serving in place of Philemon, already described as a man of great spiritual advancement (vv.6–7).

14 Paul has been speaking as an urbane, deferential, educated man of the classical world. But now, after he has cited a number of reasons for allowing Onesimus to remain with him, he goes further and urges Philemon to make his decision out of Christian love rather than obligation. How could Philemon refuse Paul's plea for him?

15 The contrast between "for a time" and "forever" shows Paul's conviction that the hand of God was at work in the whole situation. It also shows his tact: instead of bluntly referring to Onesimus as a runaway, he speaks of his temporary separation from Philemon as a prelude to permanent reunion with him.

16 In similar fashion he contrasts "slave" (GK *1528*)—a temporal and demeaning condition—with "brother" (GK *278*)—an eternal relationship in the Lord. The innate problem of the slavery of human beings troubled the ancients. In many of the ancient religions and in Greek and Roman law insofar as religion was concerned, Onesimus would have been treated as an equal. But Paul is claiming the enabling power of the *love of Christ* to break the economic and social barriers between people. Ancient pagan religions never claimed that they loved the gods or were loved by them as the motive for people to love one another. But to Paul, Philemon will love Onesimus all the more because of both long-standing human ties and their common faith.

Here, where Paul so sensitively suggests that Philemon take Onesimus back "no longer as a slave, but better than a slave" (cf. also v. 17), it almost seems as if emancipation is implied.

17 Now Paul uses a term from the business world. "Partner" (GK *3128*; related to the NT word "fellowship," GK *3126*) here has the sense of "business partner." No doubt Paul meant for the word to imply "fellowship" in the work of the risen Christ. Philemon is to "welcome" (GK *4689*) Onesimus as he would welcome Paul himself (this word always has a positive meaning).

18 The wonderfully gracious offer to assume the financial obligation of Onesimus is an altogether astonishing statement. We can only speculate how Paul came to have such warm feelings toward him. Yet we cannot be certain the slave had robbed his master, though this was a common act of runaway slaves. The loss may have been the result of the departure of a highly skilled slave from whose activities Philemon derived great income. In fact, slave prices in the Greco-Roman world were directly proportional to the skill and economic value of the slave. A common drudge brought only 500 denarii (a denarius was a laborer's ordinary daily wage), but skilled teachers, physicians, and actors were purchased for a hundred times as much.

Paul uses another accountant's word ("charge"; GK *1823*) to maintain the business imagery. Observe Paul's tact in not saying that Onesimus had stolen, but he leaves that possibility open by his use of "if he has done you any wrong and owes you anything."

19 The subject is still the indebtedness of Onesimus. Paul is now writing these words himself. As in our own society, handwritten statements of obligation carried great weight and legal validity. So Paul gives Philemon what amounts to a promissory note.

Then in v.19b he shifts abruptly to another thought—namely, "not to mention that you owe me your very self." In Paul's view, Philemon's spiritual indebtedness to him should easily cover all of Onesimus's wrongdoing. Again Paul's hint can hardly be missed: "I will repay it. Charge it to the bank of heaven." What Paul did for Onesimus reflects the infinitely greater intercession and redemptive act of Christ for us, who because of our sin are all indebted to God in a way we cannot ourselves repay.

20 Paul now expresses another wish, using the same word in "I do wish . . . some benefit" (GK *3949*) as is in the root of the name Onesimus. Paul then returns to the vocabulary of v.7, where he told Philemon that he had refreshed the hearts of many. How, then, can he do less than that for the apostle to the Gentiles? In its relationship to v.7 this sentence is an excellent example of literary reinforcement.

21 Paul has avoided giving any commands to Philemon (cf. v.8), but he nonetheless expects "obedience" (GK 5633). To what? Perhaps the love of Christ (cf. Eph 6:9). "Even more than I ask" may be an intimation that Paul would like Onesimus set free from enslavement. He has hinted that Onesimus be loaned to him (cf. v.13); only emancipation could be beyond that. Paul never directly assaults the social and economic institutions of his day. Yet he clearly perceives in Christianity an ethic that reaches beyond human social institutions.

22 Here the suggestion of an imminent visit lends more weight to Paul's hints and requests. The hope expressed in these words seems to imply that the apostle is nearby. He expects to be released soon and to see the outcome of his letter at first hand.

IV. Greetings and Benediction (23–25)

23–24 These five co-workers who send greetings to Philemon are also mentioned in Col 4:10–14 (Jesus Justus is a sixth coworker). The question remains as to why the same greetings were given in two letters that were sent at the same time. Some see the unity of the greetings as evidence that the letters were written at the same time to the same place, while Paul was in the company of the same co-workers. One should not discount the possibility, however, that Philemon preceded Colossians (see the introduction).

25 With his apostolic "grace" (GK 5921), Paul ends this brief but unusually beautiful letter in which he reveals so much of himself.

Hebrews

INTRODUCTION

This book is unlike any other in the NT, though not without resemblance to 1 John. In subject matter it is distinctive, and its picture of Jesus as our great High Priest is its own. It is not easy to see who wrote it, to whom it was written, or why. It lacks an epistolary opening but has an epistolary conclusion. The profundity of its thought gives it a significant place in the NT.

1. Literary Form

Though we usually call Hebrews a letter, important epistolary features are lacking for this book. But if we cannot straightforwardly label it a letter, there are at least indications that it was meant for a restricted circle of readers, not for the general public or even the general Christian public. The recipients are a group who ought to be teachers (5:12). The writer knows them and looks forward to visiting them (13:19, 23). He has a good opinion of them (6:9). He can ask for their prayers (13:18) and give them news of their mutual friend Timothy (13:23). The writer recalls "earlier days" (10:32) and remembers persecutions that his friends had endured (10:32; 12:4), their generosity to other believers (6:10), and their cheerful attitude when their property had been confiscated (10:32–34). He knows their present attitude toward their leaders (13:17). In the light of such statements, it is plain that the writer is addressing a definite, known group, and a small one at that (not many Christians would qualify for the position of teacher).

Moreover, the intended recipients were a group whose needs the writer knew. He wanted them to advance to the level of being teachers (5:12) and to avoid apostasy (6:4ff.). There is a homiletic air about much that he writes; so it is not surprising that many have considered the book a sermon—one the author had preached earlier or one he was now composing for the benefit of his friends. He himself calls his work "my word of exhortation" (13:22; cf. Ac 13:15). It has oratorical touches, and the style makes it not unlikely that a sermon stands behind it. But as we now have it, we may call it a letter, written to correct some specific erroneous tendencies the author sees in the recipients.

2. Recipients

The title "To the Hebrews" is in the oldest manuscripts, though this may be a later addition (we have no knowledge of any other title). If the title is accurate, then it follows that the letter was written to a group of Jews. However, it still remains to be determined whether they were Jewish Christians or non-Christian Jews. The traditional view is that the recipients were Christians from a Jewish background.

Yet some scholars argue for Gentile Christians rather than Jewish Christians. One significant passage for them is the author's appeal to basic Christian doctrines in ch. 6. The "elementary teachings" are listed as "repentance from acts that lead to death ... faith in God, instruction about baptisms, the laying on of hands, the resurrection of the dead, and eternal judgment" (6:1–2). But while Gentiles had to be taught these doctrines, it would also have been necessary to teach Jews elementary truths, such as that Jesus is the Christ and that God is present in the Holy Spirit.

From the first the OT was the Bible of both Gentile Christians and Jewish Christians. The church saw itself as the true Israel, as the heir of the promises of the OT. While the author makes a good deal of the Jewish priesthood and Jewish practices, it must be borne in mind that he does not take his information and symbolism from the temple that existed in the first century. Rather, he refers to the much earlier tabernacle, about which all the available information is in the OT.

The most persuasive argument for Jewish recipients is the way the book moves so consistently within the orbit of the OT Scriptures and Jewish liturgy. The writer has much to say about the worship of the tabernacle, the priests and the kind of sacrifices they offered, the covenant that meant so much to the Jews, and Jewish worthies like Abraham, Moses, Joshua, and a host of others mentioned in ch. 11. Topics like the sufferings of the Messiah and the replacement of the Levitical priesthood by a priesthood after the order of Melchizedek would interest Jews. The argument that Jesus is superior to Moses (3:1ff.) would have more weight with Jews than with anyone else.

Furthermore, if Gentiles were falling away from the faith, the OT would lose its authority for them. But it always remained authoritative for Jewish readers (whether Christians or not). One of the author's cogent arguments is that apostasy is pictured in the Israelites' rejecting Moses' leadership and their rebelling against God (3:16ff.), again suggesting a Jewish background.

On the whole, more can be said for Hebrews having been written for Jewish rather than Gentile Christians. It is hard to think that a writing that moves so much in the area of Jewish ritual was in the first instance intended for non-Jews, however readily they may have embraced the OT. While absolute certainty is impossible, the most likely possibility is a group of able Jewish Christians who were hesitant about cutting themselves off decisively from the Jewish religion (which was tolerated by the Romans) in favor of the Christian way (which was not).

There also seem to be more reasons for seeing the letter directed to Christians living in Rome than in any other place. The greeting "Those from Italy send you their greetings" (13:24) is most naturally understood of a group of Italian origin now living elsewhere and sending greetings back home. Also, there was more hesitation at Rome to regard this book as canonical than anywhere else, and a large factor in this hesitation was doubt that Paul wrote the letter. Presumably the Romans knew who wrote it, and they knew that the author was not Paul (see next section).

3. Authorship

The earliest reference to authorship is a statement of Clement of Alexandria that Paul wrote this work in Hebrew and that Luke translated it into Greek. When it was accepted as part of the NT, this was partly because contemporaries held Paul to be the author. This view, however, appears to rest on no reliable evidence but rather is a deduction from the facts that Paul was a prolific writer of letters and that Hebrews is a noble writing that must have had a distinguished author. But both the language and thought forms are unlike those of Paul. The Greek is polished; Paul's is rugged, though vigorous. This book moves in the context of Levitical symbolism, about which Paul elsewhere says nothing.

No early writer who cites the letter mentions its author. Nor does internal evidence help us much. The author was plainly a teacher, a second generation Christian (2:3). Its style is unlike that of any other NT document; consequently, we can only conjecture who the author was. Many suggestions have been made, of which the most prominent are Barnabas (he was a Levite, and this would account for the emphasis on Levitical ritual), Apollos (he was an eloquent man, who had "a thorough knowledge of the Scriptures"; Ac 18:24), and Priscilla (a male-dominated world would naturally have suppressed her name, though the masculine form of the Greek participle translated "to tell" in 11:32 would seem to eliminate her from consideration). In the end, however, we must agree that we have no certain evidence about the authorship of Hebrews. As Origen said, "Who wrote the letter, God only knows the truth."

4. The Use of the Old Testament in Hebrews

There are some interesting features of the author's use of the OT. To begin with, he uses the LXX (the Septuagint, the Greek translation of the OT) almost exclusively. Now and then he bases his argument on the LXX where that differs from the Hebrew (e.g., 10:5-7). The author's favorite sources are the Pentateuch and the Psalms. Twenty-three out of twenty-nine quotations come from these two sections of the OT. It is curious that there is so little from the Prophets, especially in view of the author's attitude toward the sacrifices. One would think he would have found much in the Prophets that was applicable to his purpose.

The author has an unusual method of citation; he almost always neglects the human author of his quotations (exceptions are 4:7; 9:19–20), though throughout the rest of the NT the human author is often noted. He normally ascribes the passage he quotes to

God, except, of course, where God is addressed, as in 2:6. Twice he attributes words in the OT to Christ (2:11–12; 10:5ff.) and twice to the Holy Spirit (3:7; 10:15). No other NT writer shares this way of quoting the OT. Elsewhere in the NT words from Scripture are usually ascribed to God only when God is the actual speaker. Thus the author emphasizes the divine authorship of the whole OT.

Moreover, the author sees Scripture as pointing to Jesus. What the ancient writings say is fulfilled in him. This means more than that specific prophecies are fulfilled in Jesus. Rather, the thrust of the entire OT is such that it leads inescapably to him. The author writes of Christianity as the final religion, not because he regards the faith of the OT as mistaken, but because he sees it as God's way of pointing us to Jesus. Judaism is not so much abrogated by Christianity as brought to its climax. The fuller meaning of the OT is to be seen in the person and work of Jesus. Only in Jesus are we able to discern its true meaning.

5. Date

The mention of Timothy (13:23) shows that the writing must be early, though since we know nothing about the dates of Timothy's birth and death, this reference only narrows our search to the second half of the first century. The words "you have not yet resisted to the point of shedding your blood" (12:4) points to a date before severe persecutions began, or at least before any lives of the recipients were lost. Once again we have an indication of an early date, but one we cannot narrowly tie down.

The principal indication of the date is that the letter says nothing about the destruction of the temple but leaves the impression that the Jewish sacrificial system, with its ministry of priests and all that that involved, was a continuing reality (cf. 9:6–9). The author is arguing that Judaism is superseded by Christianity and specifically that the sacrifices of the old system are of no avail now that the sacrifice of Jesus has been offered. It would have been a convincing climax had the author been able to point out that the temple and all that went with it had ceased to exist. The author's failure to mention this surely means that it had not yet occurred.

This seems about as far as we can go. A date before A.D. 70 is indicated, but how much before that we cannot say. Some passages in the letter gain in force if we think of a time not long before, when there was a compelling call to loyal Jews to cast in their lot with those fighting against Rome. So perhaps we should think of a date near or even during the war of A.D. 66–70.

EXPOSITION

I. Introduction (1:1–4)

The author begins with a magnificent introduction in which he brings out something of the greatness of Jesus and his saving work. He goes on to point out that Jesus is superior to the angels and thus leads into the first main section of the letter. In the Greek these four verses are a single, powerful sentence that shows the difference between the old revelation, which is fragmentary and spoken through prophets, and the new, which is complete and comes from one who has all the dignity of being Son of God.

1 It is significant that the subject of the first verb is "God," for God is constantly before the author (used sixty-eight times in the letter). Right at the beginning, then, we are confronted with the reality of God and the fact that he has been active. The first divine activity commented on is that God has spoken in a variety of ways. He spoke to Moses in the burning bush (Ex 3:2ff.), to Elijah in a still, small voice (1Ki 19:12ff.), to Isaiah in a vision in the temple (Isa 6:1ff.), to Hosea in his family circumstances (Hos 1:2), and to Amos in a basket of summer fruit (Am 8:1). God at times conveyed his message through visions and dreams, through angels, through Urim and Thummim, through symbols, through natural events, etc. He appeared in various locations, such as Ur of the Chaldees, Haran, Canaan, Egypt, and Babylon. Revelation was never monotonous activity that took place in the same way. God used variety.

The revelation the writer is speaking of has its roots deep "in the past" (GK *4093*). He is referring to what God did in days of old, in the time of "our forefathers." This expression is usually translated "fathers" and is normally used in the NT of the patriarchs, but here the contrast to "us" in v.2 shows that the term "forefathers" is a shorthand way of referring to OT believers in general. "Through [lit., in] the prophets" uses the Greek preposition *en*; this suggests that God was "in" the prophets as his interpreters. They were God's messengers, inspired by his Spirit. The construction used here is parallel to that in v.2: God was in Christ and before that he was in the prophets, using them as his voice. The "prophets" here probably means more than the canonical prophets and may include people like Abraham.

2 "In these last days" is more literally "on the last of these days"—an expression that often refers in some way to the days of the Messiah (e.g., Nu 24:14). Here it means that in Jesus the Messianic Age has appeared. Jesus is more than simply the last in a long line of prophets. He has inaugurated a new age altogether.

In Jesus there is both continuity and discontinuity. The continuity comes out when we are told that God "has spoken to us by his Son." The verb "spoken" (GK *3281*) is the same one used in v.1 of the prophets. The earlier revelation is continuous with the later revelation; the same God has spoken in both. The old prepares the way for the new, a truth that will be brought out again and again in this letter.

The discontinuity is seen in the reference to the Son. It is noteworthy that in the Greek there is no article with "Son" (i.e., there is nothing corresponding to NIV's "his"). In essence the writer is saying God has spoken "in one who has the quality of being Son." It is the Son's essential nature that is stressed. This stands in contrast to "the prophets" in the preceding verse. The consummation of the revelatory process took place when God spoke not in the prophets but in his very Son. Throughout the letter we shall often meet such thoughts, as the writer shows that in Jesus Christ we have such a divine person and such divine activity that there can be no going back from him.

This emphasis on the Son leads to a series of seven propositions about him. First, God "appointed" him "heir of all things." The verb "appointed" (GK *5502*) is somewhat unexpected. We should have anticipated that the Son would simply "be" heir. Perhaps there is a stress on the divine will as active. In the term "heir" (GK *3101*) there is no thought of entering into possession through the death of a testator. In the NT this word and its cognates are often used in a sense much like "get possession of," without reference to any specific way of acquiring the property in question. "Heir of all things," then, is a title of dignity and shows that Christ has the supreme place in all the mighty universe. His exaltation to the highest place in heaven after his work on earth was done did not mark some new dignity but his reentry to his rightful place (cf. Php 2:6–11).

The second truth about the Son is that "through" him God "made the universe." God is the Creator, but as is said elsewhere in the NT, he performed the work of creation through the Son (cf. Jn 1:3; 1Co 8:6; Col 1:16). "The universe" (lit., "the ages"; GK *172*) has a temporal sense. While the universe may well be in mind as that which was "made," it is the universe as the sum of the periods of time. This word may be hinting at the temporal nature of all things material.

3 The third proposition about the Son is that he is "the radiance of God's glory." The word translated "radiance" (GK *575*), meaning a shining forth because of brightness within, may also mean "reflection," a shining forth because of brightness from without. Jesus is thus spoken of either as the outshining of the brightness of God's glory, or as the reflection of that glory. In both cases we see the glory of God in Jesus, and we see it as it really is. "Glory" (GK *1518*), sometimes used of literal brightness (cf. Ac 22:11), is more commonly used in the NT of the radiance associated with God and with heavenly beings in general. It sometimes indicates the presence of God (e.g., Eze 1:28; 11:23), and, to the extent that human beings are able to apprehend it, the revelation of God's majesty.

"The exact representation of his being" is the fourth of the statements about the Son. "Exact representation" (GK *5917*) originally denoted an instrument for engraving and then a mark stamped on that instrument. Hence it came to be used of the impress of a die and of the impression on coins. It could also be used figuratively (e.g., of God as making us in his own image). Here the writer is saying that the Son is an exact representation of God. The word "being" (GK *5712*) suggests that the Son is such a revelation of the

Father that when we see Jesus, we see what God's real being is.

"Sustaining" (GK 5770), the fifth characteristic of the Son, does not picture Christ as holding up the universe like the Greek god Atlas, but as carrying it along and bearing it onward toward the fulfillment of the divine plan. The concept is dynamic, not static. "All things" is the totality, the universe considered as a whole. Nothing is excluded from the scope of the Son's sustaining activity. And he does this "by his powerful word." "Word" (GK 4839) is thought of as active and powerful—the same word that created the universe (11:3); "powerful" (GK 1539) is often used to describe literal physical power.

With the sixth statement about the Son (his having effected purification of sins), the author comes to what is for him the heart of the matter. The thing that gripped him most was that the very Son of God had come to deal with the problem of human sin. The author sees him as a priest, who offers up the sacrifice that really put sin away. The author has an unusual number of ways of referring to what Christ has done for us (e.g., see 2:17; 8:12; 9:15, 26, 28; 10:12, 17–18). From such passages it is clear that the author sees Jesus as having accomplished a many-sided salvation. Whatever had to be done about sin he has done.

The word "purification" (GK 2752) is most often used in the NT of ritual cleansing (e.g., Mk 1:44), but here it refers to the removal of sin (cf. also 2Pe 1:9) with its defiling aspect. Sin stains, but Christ has effected a complete cleansing of sin at Calvary. In this letter sin appears as the power that deceives people and leads them to destruction. Only the sacrifice of Jesus Christ could remove it. In him and him alone are sins really dealt with.

The seventh in the series of statements about the Son is that when his work of purification was ended, "he sat down at the right hand of the Majesty in heaven." Sitting is the posture of rest, and the right-hand position is the place of honor. Sitting at God's right hand, then, is a way of saying that Christ's saving work is done and that he is now in the place of highest honor. "Majesty" (GK 3448) means "greatness" and thus came to signify "majesty." Here it is obviously a title for God himself, who dwells in heaven (cf. Eph 4:10; Php 2:9).

4 "He became" is again somewhat unexpected (cf. "appointed," v.2). The writer has made some strong statements about the excellence of Christ's person, and so we should expect him to describe Christ as eternally superior to the angels rather than as "becoming" superior to them. But the writer says it this way because he was thinking of what the Son did in becoming human and putting away the sins of humanity. Of course, the Son was also eternally superior to the angels. That, however, is not what is in mind here. It was because he had put away sins that he sat down on the throne in the place of highest honor, and it is in this aspect that he is seen as greater than any angel.

"Superior" (usually rendered "better"; GK 3202) is one of the author's favorite words (see 6:9; 7:7, 19, 22; 8:6; 9:23; 10:34; 11:16, 35, 40; 12:24). This strong emphasis on what is "better" arises from the author's deep conviction that Jesus Christ is "better" and that he has accomplished something "better" than anyone or anything else.

Another word that appears frequently in this letter is "angel" (GK 34). While the term can be used of a human messenger (Lk 9:52), sometimes sent by God (Mk 1:2), in the overwhelming number of cases it means a spirit being from the other world. In many cases the idea of a messenger remains. Sometimes, however, the thought is simply that of beings intermediate between God and human beings. It also may be used of evil beings, but references to good angels are much more common.

In antiquity "the name" (GK 3950) meant much more than it does today. We use a name as little more than a distinguishing mark or label to differentiate one person from other people. But in the world of the NT the name concisely sums up all that a person is. One's whole character was somehow implied in the name. Opinions differ as to what is meant here by "the name." Some take this to mean that in his whole character and personality Christ was superior to any angel. Others think the reference is simply to the name "Son," which is a better name than "angel" because it denotes superiority in character and personality. Either interpretation is possible.

The word "superior" (GK 1427; a different word from earlier in v.4) as applied to "the name" has a derived sense, "excellent";

the name of the Son is "more excellent" than that of any angel. "Inherited" (GK *3099*) as used here denotes entering into possession of an inheritance without regard to the means. So here we should think of Christ as obtaining the more excellent name as the result of his atoning work. The main idea is that of an abiding possession in Christ's capacity as heir (see comments on v.2).

II. The Excellence of the Christ (1:5–3:6)

In the introduction the author has drawn attention to the excellence of the Christ; now he dwells on the point by emphasizing that Christ has a greater dignity than any other being—so great indeed that he must be classed with God rather than with human beings. Without weakening the doctrine of the Incarnation, this letter has as high a Christology as is conceivable. Nobody insists on the limitations of Jesus' human frame as does the writer of Hebrews. But he unites with this the thought that Jesus is exalted far above all creation.

A. Superior to Angels (1:5–14)

The discussion of the excellence of the Son begins with a series of seven quotations from the OT, five being from the Psalms, all of which stress the superiority of Christ to the angels.

5 The opening question, "For to which of the angels did God ever say," implies that Christ is to be seen in all the Scriptures because there is no explicit reference to him in the passage cited. In the OT angels are sometimes called "sons of God" (cf. NIV note on Job 1:6; 2:1); and the term was applied to Israel (Ex 4:22; Hos 11:1) and Solomon (2 Sa 7:14; 1 Ch 28:6). But none of the angels nor anyone else was ever singled out and given the kind of status this passage gives to Christ. The first quotation comes from Ps 2:7. Among the rabbis, the "Son" is variously identified as Aaron, David, the people of Israel in the messianic period, or the Messiah himself. Our writer is clearly taking the psalm as messianic and sees it as conferring great dignity on Jesus.

The second quotation comes from 2 Sa 7:14 (= 1 Ch 17:13). Though the words were originally used of Solomon, the writer of Hebrews applies them to the Messiah. There was a widespread expectation that the Messiah would be a descendant of David. The quotation points to the father-son relationship as the fundamental relationship between God and Christ. No angel can claim such a relationship. This and 12:9 are the only passages in Hebrews in which the term "Father" is applied to God.

6 This verse is the only place in the NT where "firstborn" (GK *4758*) is used absolutely of Christ. Elsewhere it is linked with Jesus' birth (Lk 2:7), many brothers (Ro 8:29), all creation (Col 1:15), or the church (Col 1:18; Rev 1:5), where it represents Christ in his relationship to others and gives the word a social significance. Here, however, it signifies that he has the status with God that a human firstborn son has with his father (cf. reference to "heir" in v.2). Christ is exalted and enthroned as sovereign over the inhabited world, including the angels.

The quotation is from the LXX of Dt 32:43; it is absent from our Hebrew text. The LXX reads "sons of God" where this quotation has "God's angels," but "angels" occurs later in the verse and again in a similar context in Ps 97:7. "All" shows that this is no small, hole-in-the-corner affair but one in which the worship of all heaven is offered to the Son. The one the angels worship is clearly superior by far to them.

7 The Hebrew of Ps 104:4 can mean either that God makes the winds his messengers and the flames his servants or that he makes his messengers (angels) into winds and his servants into flames. The LXX, which the author quotes, takes the latter view, though this does not suggest any downgrading of the angels. But if the angels are immeasurably superior to human beings, the Son is immeasurably superior to the angels. Whereas he has sonship, they are reducible to nothing more than the elemental forces of wind and fire. This passage also seems to imply that the angels are temporary in contrast to the Son, who is eternal.

8–9 The quotation here is from Ps 45:6–7, which refers to the Son, who is then addressed as "God." His royal state is brought out by the references to the "throne," "scepter," and "kingdom" and by his moral concern for the "righteousness" that is supreme where he reigns. This concern continues with his loving righteousness and hating "wickedness" (lit., "lawlessness"; GK *490*), which lead to the divine anointing. We should perhaps take the first occurrence of the word "God" in v.9 as another vocative: "Therefore, O God, your God has set you." Anointing was usually a rite of consecration to some sacred function (e.g., Ex 28:41; 1Sa 10:1; 1Ki 19:16). This is in view here as the Son is set above his companions, who are probably the "brothers" of 2:11.

10–12 The author next quotes from Ps 102:25–27 to bring out the Son's eternality and supremacy over creation. In the OT these words are applied to God. Here, however, they apply to Christ without qualification or any need for justification. Christ was God's agent in creation, the one who laid the earth's foundations and constructed heaven. All these will in due course perish, but not their Maker. The metaphor of clothing has a twofold reference: the created things will wear out (the process is slow but certain); and the Son deals with them as with clothing, rolling them up and changing them. He began the universe and he will finish it. Clearly the final transformation of all things is in mind (cf. Isa 66:22; Rev 6:14; 21:1)—their replacement by a totally new heaven and earth. But through it all the Son remains unchanged. Our years come to an end, but his will never do so.

13 The quotation from Ps 110:1 is introduced with a formula that stresses its inapplicability to angels (see comment on 1:4). This psalm is accepted by the NT writers as messianic. It is repeatedly applied to Christ; and apparently even Jesus' opponents accepted it as messianic (Mk 12:35–37), though, of course, they would not apply it to Jesus. Since the angels stand before God (Lk 1:19; Rev 8:2; cf. Da 7:10), it is a mark of superior dignity that the Son sits. And the statement that God discharges the task of a servant in preparing a footstool for the Son is a striking piece of imagery. The angels are God's servants. How great then is he whom God deigns to serve! To make the enemies a footstool means to subject them utterly. Consequently, God will render all Christ's enemies utterly powerless.

14 The angels are now contrasted with the Son of God. He sits in royal state; "all" of them, however, are no more than servants—servants of saved people. "Spirits" preserves their place of dignity, but their function is "to serve" (GK *1355*). The word used here is the usual NT term for the service Christians render to God and other people, but nowhere else is it used of the service angels render. "Inherit" (GK *3099*) is often used in the NT in senses other than the strict one of obtaining something by a will. It is used of possessing the earth (Mt 5:5), the kingdom of God (1Co 6:9–10), eternal life (Mk 10:17), the promises (Heb 6:12), incorruption (1Co 15:50), blessing (Heb 12:17), and a more excellent name (see comment on v.4).

"Salvation" (GK *5401*) is a general word, but among first-century Christians it was used of salvation in Christ, either in its present or, as here, future aspect. This word is used seven times in Hebrews, the most of any NT book, so the concept clearly matters to the author. His use of it here without qualification shows that it was already accepted by the readers as well as the author as a technical term for the salvation Christ brought.

B. Author of "Such a Great Salvation" (2:1–9)

The second step in the argument for Jesus' superiority shows him to be infinitely great because of the nature of the salvation he won. He who brought about a salvation that involved tasting death "for everyone" (v.9) cannot but be greater by far than any angel. The author precedes the development of this thought with a brief section in which he typically exhorts his readers to attend to what has been said (cf. also 3:7–11; 5:11–14).

1 "Therefore" most likely refers to the whole argument of 1:5–14. Since the Son is so far superior to the angels and his message is superior to theirs, we should "pay more careful attention" (GK *4668*) to it. This verb means not only to turn the mind to a thing but also to act upon what one perceives. Inaction in spiritual things is fatal. The author does not explain what he means by "what we have heard," but we need not doubt that the whole Christian Gospel is in mind. By the word "we" the author puts himself in the same class as his readers, i.e., dependent on others for the message. He was not one of the original disciples.

The danger is that we might "drift away" (GK *4184*). This verb is used of such things as a ring slipping off a finger; it is a vivid figure for the person who lets himself or herself drift away from the haven of the Gospel. One need not be violently opposed to the message to suffer loss; one need only drift away from it (see comment on v.3).

2 "Message" (Gk. *logos*; GK *3364*) means in the first place a word spoken (as opposed to a deed) and then a series of words or a statement. What the statement is varies with the context. It can mean a message from God, a revelation, and so the Christian Gospel (Ac 4:4; 8:4). The final revelation is, of course, Christ. He himself is "the Word" (Jn 1:1). In Hebrews the "word" is usually God's word (e.g., 2:2; 4:2, 12), though it can also be the writer's own word (5:11) or the word the Israelites did not wish to hear (12:19). Here in v.2 it is the divinely given law.

"By angels" is literally "through angels," which stresses the important truth that the law came from God. The OT does not speak of angels in connection with the giving of the law; but their presence is mentioned in other NT passages (Ac 7:53; Gal 3:19) and in the LXX of Dt 33:2. The author is appealing to this accepted view for his "how shall we?" argument (v.3). If the law came through angels, how much more should respect be given the message that came, not through angels, but through the Son! The law was "binding" (GK *1010*), i.e., fully valid. And it had provision for the proper punishment of wrongdoers so that every transgression was dealt with in the proper way.

3 The just penalties meted out under the law show that where God is concerned, strict standards apply. This makes it imperative that those to whom a great salvation is offered do something about the offer. The disaster that threatens is brought on by nothing more than mere neglect. It is not necessary to disobey any specific injunction. This is the first of a number of warnings to the readers not to surrender their Christian profession.

The writer is determined to guard against the possibility of losing salvation. This salvation is distinguished from the many other kinds of salvation offered in the ancient world by calling it "such a great salvation" and then by telling us three things about it (see comment on 1:14). In the first place, it was "announced by the Lord." The salvation originates with the Father. The author's use of "announced" (GK *3281*) makes a point of contact with the gospel of Luke, for there only does Jesus announce salvation (Lk 19:9; cf. also 1:69, 71, 77; 2:11).

The second point about salvation is that it "was confirmed to us by those who heard him." The author is here again appealing to the first hearers as those to whom the authentic Gospel was entrusted (cf. Lk 1:2). Any later preaching must agree with theirs. If it does not, then it will stand convicted of being an innovation instead of the genuine thing. For this writer, as for his readers, the message was "confirmed" (GK *1011*) by the original disciples. This verb is used as a legal technical term to designate properly guaranteed security; the certainty of the message is guaranteed to us, and there cannot be the slightest doubt about the genuineness of the offer of salvation.

4 The third and clinching point about our "great salvation" is that God himself has also "testified" to it. Preachers are not left to bear their witness alone. No less a one than God himself has shared in this. In John's gospel we have the bold thought that God has borne witness to Christ (Jn 5:37). Since anyone who bears witness commits himself by that very act, God has gone on record, so to speak, that he too is a witness to the great salvation of his Son.

Here, however, we have an even bolder thought: God has been pleased to commit himself through the original disciples. He gave the "signs" (GK *4956*) or miracles that attested their preaching. The Gospel is not a human creation, and the early hearers were not left in doubt as to its origin. They actually saw the miraculous way God attested it. Miracles were not pointless displays of power but they pointed beyond themselves to the message of salvation. "Wonders" (GK *5469*) emphasizes the marvelous aspect of the signs. They were such that no mere person could produce them, nor were they explicable on merely human premises. It is this wonder-producing aspect that comes spontaneously to mind when we think of miracles. "Miracles" (GK *1539*) is properly "mighty works" and is the term usually employed in the Synoptic Gospels. It brings out the truth that in Christ's miracles there is superhuman power. They prove something about the Gospel because they are not of human origin and thus show that the Gospel they attest is not human either.

It is not clear whether "gifts of the Holy Spirit" refers to gifts that the Holy Spirit gives (cf. 1Co 12:11) or the gift of the Holy Spirit himself (cf. Gal 3:5). Either way, there were manifestations of the Holy Spirit in believers, and the author sees these as confirming the Gospel. Most likely the author is speaking about God as giving people the gift (and the gifts) of the Holy Spirit. The supreme God does this as he wills.

5 Having looked at "such a great salvation" that Christ won for his own, the author goes on to the further point that the subjection of the world to the human race spoken of in Ps 8 is to be seen in Christ, not in humanity at large. "Not to angels" implies that the subjection was made to someone other than the angels. "The world" (GK *3876*) is a term that normally denotes the inhabited earth (a term used by both Greeks and Romans for the spheres of their earthly influence). It is unusual to have it employed of the Messianic Age.

6 A quotation from Ps 8:4–6 is introduced by the unusual verb "testified" (GK *1371*). Only here in the NT does it introduce a quotation from Scripture. More often the word means to "testify solemnly" and shows that the words following it are to be taken with full seriousness. The author tells us neither the place where the words are found nor who said them. Consistently he regards all that is in his Bible as coming from God and puts no emphasis on the human author. He quotes the passage exactly, and his whole letter shows that he was very familiar with the Psalms. His quotation is exact, with one line omitted.

The psalmist is concerned with both the insignificance and the greatness of the human race. There is, of course, no difference in meaning between "man" and "son of man" in this verse. The parallelism of Hebrew poetry requires that the two be taken in much the same sense; and in any case it is quite common in Hebrew idiom for "the son of" to denote quality, as, for example, "the son of strength" means "the strong man." So "son of man" means one who has the quality of being a human being (this is different from Jesus' self-title in the gospels, "Son of Man"). God is said to be "mindful of" (GK *3630*) and to "care for" (GK *2170*) people. "Mindful" has the sense of remembering with a view to helping. It includes total dedication to God, concern for the brethren, and true self-judgment (cf. 13:3). The psalmist goes on to ask what there is about humankind that the great God should stoop to help them.

7 Having asked the rhetorical questions that pinpoint human insignificance, the psalmist goes on to the greatness of human beings. God has given them an outstanding position, one but a little lower than that of the angels. The author follows the LXX here again (the Hebrew can mean "lower than God"). Human dignity, then, is such that human beings are placed in God's order of creation only a short way below the angels, and this seems to set them above all else in creation, an impression that the rest of the passage confirms. God "crowned him with glory and honor." "Glory" (GK *1518*) denotes brightness or splendor and is used of the splendor of God as well as of the glory of earthly potentates. "Honor" (GK *5507*) is frequently linked with "glory," and the combination stresses the supreme place of humankind in creation.

8 The dignity of a human being is further brought out by the fact that God has "put everything under his feet." The human race is supreme among the beings of this created world. "Under his feet" shows that humans have complete supremacy.

After completing the quotation, the writer goes on to draw out an important implication. In putting all things in subjection to humankind, God left nothing unsubjected. It is a picture of a divinely instituted order in which humanity is sovereign over all creation. A few commentators see "him" as referring in this place to Christ, to whom alone all things are rightly subjected. But grammatically there is no reason for this. The passage is describing the place of humankind in God's order, and we do not come to Christ's place until v.9. While in one sense everything is subject to Christ, there is another sense in which human beings have their rightful place of supremacy over the created order.

From this ideal picture the writer turns his attention to current reality. As things are now, we do not see the subjection of all things to human beings, but one day this subjection will be fully realized. While the human race has power and dignity, there are many limitations. It is part of the frustration of life that in every part of it there are the equivalents of the "thorns and thistles" (Ge 3:18) that make life so hard for the tiller of the soil. We all know what it is like to chafe under limitations while we glimpse the vision of what will someday be realized.

9 But if we do not see the fulfillment of this passage from Scripture in the way we might have expected, we do see a fulfillment in another way. We see it fulfilled in Jesus. He has gone through the experience of living out this earthly life, and he is now "crowned . . . with glory and honor" (the very words of the psalm) because of his saving work for humanity. The writer calls the Savior by his human name, Jesus—a usage we find nine times in this letter (here; 3:1; 4:14; 6:20; 7:22; 10:19; 12:2, 24; 13:12); on each occasion he seems to place emphasis on the humanity of our Lord. That Jesus was true man meant a good deal to the writer of Hebrews. We do not see the psalm fulfilled in the human race at large, but we do see it fulfilled in the man Jesus. He had a genuine incarnation because he "was made a little lower than the angels." But we do not now see him in this lowly place, for he is now crowned with glory and honor. He is in the place of supremacy that the psalmist envisaged. And he is there because of his saving work, "because he suffered death."

"So that" looks back to the reference to suffering rather than to "crowned"; the clause it introduces shows the purpose of the death of Jesus. This is one of several places in the NT where someone is said to "taste" (GK *1174*) death (also Mt 16:28; Mk 9:1; Lk 9:27; Jn 8:52). The verb means "to taste with the mouth," from which the metaphorical sense "come to know" develops. It means here that Jesus died, with all that that entails. By God's "grace" (GK *5921*), Christ's saving work was accomplished. Grace is one of the great Christian words, and it is not surprising to find it connected with the doctrine of the atonement here.

C. True Man (2:10–18)

The author has argued that Jesus was greater than the angels and that his greatness is to be seen in the salvation he obtained for us. But he lived on earth as an ordinary man. There was nothing about the Teacher from Nazareth to show that he was greater than the angels. Indeed, the reverse was true, for he had undergone humiliating sufferings, culminating in a felon's death. The author proceeds to show, however, that, far from this being an objection to his greatness, this was part of it. This was the way he would save us. He would be made like those he saves.

10 Usually we do not speak of things as being "fitting" for God, but here the word is appropriate. The way of salvation is not arbitrary but befitting the character of the God we know, the God "for whom and through whom everything exists" (i.e., he is the goal and the creator of all that is). The words show that the sufferings of Jesus did not take place by chance; they had their place in God's great eternal purpose. "Many sons" is an unusual expression for the total number of the saved. But sonship is important and so is the fact that the number of the saved will not be few. "Glory" points to the grand splendor of salvation.

Christ is "the author of their salvation." "Author" (GK *795*) can denote a leader, a ruler, or the originator or founder. Here the thought of origination is stressed, but the choice of word enables the writer to see Jesus as one who walked this earthly way before us as he established the way of salvation.

The idea of being made "perfect" (GK *5457*) is at first sight a startling one to apply to Jesus, but it is one the author repeats (he uses this verb nine times). He suggests that there is a perfection that results from actually having suffered and that this is different from the perfection of being ready to suffer. The bud may be perfect, but there is a difference between its perfection and that of the flower. There is, of course, no thought of perfecting what was morally imperfect; no imperfection is implied (cf. 4:15).

11 The writer now emphasizes the link between Jesus and those whom he saves. He "who makes men holy [GK *39*]" is, of course, Jesus. He makes them into God's people by his offering of himself (10:10). The passive, "those who are made holy" (coming from the same verb), puts some emphasis on the unity of Christ and his own. But the writer does not say they are one; he says they are "of the same family" (lit., "of one"). Since the thrust of the passage refers to earthly descent, this "one" is most likely Adam (as in Ac 17:26). The thought, then, is that Jesus is qualified to be our Priest and Savior because he shares our nature, i.e., because he is not some remote being but truly "one of us." He shares with us a descent from Adam; this enables him to call us "brothers."

Those who follow Christ are often called "brothers"; rarely, however, are they called *his* brothers in the NT. Indeed, sometimes the two are differentiated, as when Jesus says, "You have only one Master and you are all brothers" (Mt 23:8). Mostly Jesus' "brothers" refers to those in his immediate family (e.g., Mt 12:46–48; Lk 8:19–20; Jn 2:12), though occasionally the word is used in a spiritual sense when linking people to Christ (Mt 12:49–50; Mk 3:33–35; Lk 8:21; Ro 8:29). Thus this passage in Hebrews is not unparalleled. There is a sense in which Jesus is brother to all who call God "Father." That is why it is important to identify the "them" in "Jesus is not ashamed to call them brothers." It is not all people he calls brothers but only those who are sanctified.

12 The writer clarifies the point of spiritual brotherhood with an appeal to Ps 22, a psalm that was regarded as messianic in the early church. As he hung on the cross, Jesus quoted its opening words: "My God, my God, why have you forsaken me?" (Mk 15:34). And the words about dividing garments (Ps 22:18) are seen as fulfilled in what the soldiers did as they crucified Jesus (Jn 19:24). It was thus the most natural thing in the world for the writer of Hebrews to see Jesus as the speaker in this psalm.

He will declare his name to his brothers. In antiquity "name" generally stood for the whole character. So in this psalm the writer sees Jesus as saying that he will proclaim God's character as he has revealed himself, not simply that he will declare the name of God. The important thing in this quotation is that Jesus will do this "to [his] brothers." Jesus recognizes them as kin. The parallel statement in the next line reinforces the idea.

The word "congregation" (*ekklesia*; GK *1711*) can mean a properly summoned political group (Ac 19:39) or an assembly of almost any kind, including the rioting Ephesians (Ac 19:32, 41). But it is also used of the congregation of ancient Israel (Ac 7:38). In the NT it became the characteristic word for the "church," the gatherings of Christians. Now he who sings God's praises in the midst of God's people is by that very fact showing that he is one of them, their spokesman. The "brothers" are the church.

13 Two further citations from Scripture underscore the point—the first is from Isa 8:17, the second from Isa 8:18. The reason for the first passage is not obvious. The context in Isaiah, however, speaks of difficulties, and the thought may be that just as Isaiah had to trust God to see him through, so was it with Jesus. In this he was brother to all God's troubled saints. The second quotation continues the first, but it is introduced here with "and again he says," because it makes a new point. The author now sees believers as "the children [GK *4086*] God has given" Christ. This word is normally used of literal children, but this is the one place where it is used of "children" of Christ. These children are "given" by God as the disciples were given to Jesus (Jn 17:6).

All three quotations from the OT, then, place the speaker in the same group as God's children. The actual word "brothers" occurs only in the first, but they all locate Christ among people. He had a real community of nature with those he came to save.

14–15 The author now develops the thought of community of nature. Jesus shared "blood and flesh" (the proper order in Greek) with the children. He really came where they are, in order to nullify the power of the devil—who is described as the one "who holds the power of death." This raises a problem because it is God alone who controls the issues of life and death (Job 2:6; Lk 12:5). But it was through Adam's sin, brought about by the temptation of the devil, that death entered the world (Ge 2:17; 3:19; Ro 5:12). From this it is logical to assume that the devil exercises his power in the realm of death. But through his own death, Christ destroyed the power of the devil.

The author does not explain how Christ's death does this but contents himself with the fact that it does. In doing so, he stresses the note of victory that we find throughout the NT (e.g., 1Co 15:54–57). The defeat of the devil means the setting free of those he had held sway over, i.e., those who had been gripped by fear of death. Fear is an inhibiting and enslaving thing; and when people are gripped by the ultimate fear—the fear of death—they are in cruel bondage. In the first century this was very real. The philosophers urged people to be calm in the face of death, and some of them managed to do so. But to most people this brought no relief. One of the many wonderful things about the Christian Gospel is that it delivers men and women from the fear of death (cf. Rev 1:18). They are saved with a sure hope of life eternal, a life whose best lies beyond the grave.

16 The writer now makes a strong affirmation and appeals to information shared by the reader. There is a problem about the verb rendered "helps" (GK *2138*). It means "to take hold of for a purpose," "to take by the hand." The author does have in mind that Jesus came to rescue people (cf. v.17), but it is another question whether this is all contained in the verb. On the whole, it seems better to see this statement as pointing to the *fact* of the Incarnation rather than to its *purpose*. "Abraham's descendants" particularizes the manner of the Incarnation and makes it harder to see the meaning of the verb as "helps," for Jesus helps many more than Jews. But he did become incarnate as a Jew. He did not descend to the level of the angels and become one of them. He descended to the level of humankind and became a Jew.

17 The purpose of salvation involved a genuine incarnation. "He had to" means "he owed it" (GK *4053*; the verb can be used of financial debts). There is the sense of moral obligation here. The nature of the work Jesus came to accomplish demanded the Incarnation. This Incarnation was not aimless; it was for the specific purpose of Jesus' becoming a high priest, another way of saying that it was to save people. Our great High Priest is one who is first and foremost "merciful" (GK *1798*), and he is also "faithful" (GK *4412*). This latter adjective can refer to the faith that relies on someone or something or that on which one can rely, i.e., "relying" or "reliable." Jesus is, of course, both. But here the emphasis is on his relationship to God the Father, and so the first meaning is more probable (cf. Rev. 1:5; 3:14; 19:11).

Only in Hebrews is the term "high priest" applied to Jesus in the NT. This is the first example of its use, but the author does not explain it. He may want us to see Jesus as superior to all other priests. Or he may be using the term because he sees Jesus' saving work as fulfilling all that is signified by the ceremonies of the Day of Atonement, for which the high priest's ministry was indispensable.

"In service to God" (lit., "with respect to the things of God") shows where Christ's high priestly work is carried out. Some of the service of the high priest was directed toward the people, but this is not in view here. The service Christ was to render was in order "that he might make atonement for the sins of the people." "Make atonement" (GK *2661*) is better rendered "propitiate"; it relates to putting away the divine wrath (see NIV note). When people sin, they arouse the wrath of God (Ro 1:18) and become his enemies (Ro 5:10). One aspect of salvation deals with this wrath, and it is to this that the author is directing attention at this point. Christ saves us in a way that takes account of and appeases the divine wrath against every evil thing. "The people" means the people of God—those for whom Christ died.

18 The sufferings Jesus endured enable him to help others. Contrary to what might have been expected, he suffered—not only on the cross, but throughout his earthly life. Being what he is, temptation must have been far more distasteful for him than it is for us. "Tempted" (GK *4279*) sometimes means "tested," but the verb is more often used in the sense of "tempt." Jesus can help those who are tempted because he has perfect sympathy with them. He too was tempted and knows what temptation is. Only one who suffers can help in this way. Jesus went all the way for us. He was not only ready to suffer, but he actually did suffer.

D. Superior to Moses (3:1–6)

The author steadily develops his argument that Jesus is supremely great. He is greater than the angels (1:4), the author of a great salvation (2:3), and great enough to become human to accomplish it (2:9–18). Now he turns his attention to Moses, regarded by the Jews as the greatest person of all. They could even think of him as greater than angels. Perhaps then he was superior to Jesus? The writer does nothing to belittle Moses. Nor does he criticize him. He accepts Moses' greatness but shows that as great as he was, Jesus was greater by far.

1 The address "holy brothers" combines affection and consecration. These people are members of the Christian family and are dear

The "Greater-Thans" in Hebrews

One of the author's main points in Hebrews is that Jesus is *greater than* all those things associated with the Jewish religion and way of life. Sometimes he actually uses the word "greater than"; sometimes he does not. But in all cases the theme is clear.

Theme	Passage in Hebrews
Jesus is greater than the prophets	1:1–3
Jesus is greater than the angels	1:4–14; 2:5
Jesus is greater than Moses	3:1–6
Jesus is greater than Joshua	4:6–11
Jesus is greater than the high priest	5:1–10; 7:26–8:2
Jesus is greater than the Levitical priests	6:20–7:25
Jesus as the high priest after Melchizedek is greater than Abraham	7:1–10
Jesus' ministry is greater than the tabernacle ministry	8:3–6; 9:1–28
Jesus' new covenant is greater than the old covenant	8:7–13
Jesus' sacrifice is greater than OT sacrifices	10:1–14
Experiencing Jesus is greater than the experience on Mount Sinai	12:18–24

to the writer. They are also people who have been set apart for the service of God. The reference to "the heavenly calling" shows that the initiative of this service comes from God. "Therefore" links this section to the preceding. Because Christ has taken our nature and can help us, *therefore* we are invited to consider him in his capacities as apostle and high priest.

"Apostle" (GK *693*) is applied to Jesus only here in the NT, but the idea that God "sent" him with a mission is more frequent, especially in John. "High priest" emphasizes the sacrificial nature of that mission. Though "Jesus" is the most glorious of beings, his name draws attention to his humanity. It is as a human being that his work as apostle and high priest is accomplished.

2 The point could have been made that there were times when Moses was not as faithful as he might have been. But the writer makes no criticism of the man held in such honor by the Jews. He prefers to accept Moses as "faithful." Yet he sees Jesus' faithfulness as much more comprehensive. Moses was no more than part of the "house," but Jesus made the house. Again, Jesus as Son was over the house, whereas Moses was a servant in it. The "house," of course, is the household of God, the people of God. Moses was a member of that house and proved faithful there (see Nu 12:7). The adjective "all" may point to a concern both Moses and Jesus had for the whole house. Others, such as prophets, kings, or priests, dealt with restricted areas.

3 The first point of comparison pronounces Jesus as "worthy of greater honor than Moses" because he was builder of the house rather than part of it. "Honor" (lit., "glory"; GK *1518*) belonged to Moses, but his glory did not measure up to that of Christ. The one who makes a house is worthy of more honor than the house itself, glorious though it may be. Moses was at all times a member of the people of God, that and no more. He had great honor among the people, but there was no way for him to be any other than one of them. Not so Jesus! He was more. The author of Hebrews has just made the point that Jesus became true human and could truly call people "brothers." But that does not alter his conviction that Christ is also more than a man. He is the founder of the church, and the church was continuous with the OT people of God. The author will come back to this thought in v.6.

4 Parenthetically, this verse makes the point that God is over all—a fact that the author does not want us to lose sight of. So he uses the analogy that the very existence of a house is an argument for a builder. Thus everything that exists argues for God. At the same time, God cannot be put on a level with any builder of a house.

5 Having made his point that God transcends everyone, the writer returns to Moses. He repeats his statement that Moses was faithful in God's house (cf. v.2). Now he makes a further point: Whereas Moses was no more than a servant, Jesus was greater, for he was Son over the house. The thought is still that of Moses' faithfulness. There is no criticism of him, but his faithfulness consisted in his discharge of his role as servant.

The word for "servant" (GK 2544) is found only here in the NT. It denotes an honored servant, one who is far above a slave but is still a servant. The emphasis is on the subordinate, if honorable, capacity. The writer goes on to say that Moses' faithfulness did not relate to his own day only. He was "testifying to what would be said in the future"—implying that there would be revelations to others. This letter began with a reference to such revelations and to the importance of what God said (cf. 1.1; 2:3).

6 The name "Christ" (GK 5986) is used here for the first time in this letter, without the article (as in 9:11, 24). Here, where a name of dignity is called for, it is a proper name. Christ is contrasted with Moses "as a son over God's house." Moses was no more than a member—though a very distinguished member—of the house. He was essentially one with all the others. But Christ has an innate superiority. He is the Son and as such is "over" the household.

The author adds a most important explanation as to the composition of this house. One might easily suppose that he was referring to the Jews or at least to the Jews of the OT. They were, of course, in mind. But he is not thinking of the Jews as a race nor of a group of historical figures. He is thinking of the people of God. In OT days this had been the people Israel. But Israel had rejected the Son of God when he came, and now the people of God is the church. Perseverance is one of the marks of being a Christian. Without it we are not Christ's. The teaching about final perseverance implies that the saints are the people who persevere.

We must hold on to "our courage [GK 4244]." The word used here has the feeling of being quite at home when words flow freely and so means "confidence" or "courage." "The hope of which we boast [GK 3017]" brings out the truth that membership in God's household is something of which we may be proud. Instead of being ashamed of this gift, we should glory in it. "Boast" is connected with "hope" (GK 1828), a word that in the NT usually refers to the certainty that God will carry out his promises, especially those in the Gospel. The Christian looks forward eagerly, expecting God's triumph. To be God's house, then, means to persevere in quiet confidence, knowing that one has matter for pride in the Christian hope.

III. The Promised Rest (3:7–4:13)

The comparison between Christ and Moses leads to one between their followers. The writer uses the conduct of the Israelites as a means of challenging his readers to a closer walk with God. There was a promise in the OT that God's people would enter into rest. The writer sees this promise as fulfilled—not in anything in the OT—but in Christ. In drawing attention to this, he shows from another angle that Christ is God's final word to humankind (cf. 1:2).

A. Scriptural Basis (3:7–11)

The writer begins this section with a quotation from Ps 95:7–11. Israel did not walk in fellowship with God but disobeyed and provoked him. Therefore they did not enter his rest. Judaism is not the way of entry into God's promised rest.

7 The author's intent is to instruct his readers not to repeat the mistake the Israelites made. The quotation from Ps 95 is ascribed directly to the Holy Spirit (cf. 9:8; 10:15; Ac 28:25; the human author is mentioned in 4:7). The author is fond of the word "today," using it eight times. Here its prominent position gives it emphasis. Immediate action is imperative. The voice of God is sounding now. It must not be neglected.

8 To "harden" (GK *5020*) the heart is to disobey the voice of God and act in accordance with one's own desires. This is what Israel did in the wilderness. The psalmist refers to the incident when there was no water and the Israelites "put the Lord to the test" (Ex 17:1–7). In the LXX the place names "Massah" and "Meribah" are always translated by words such as "rebellion" and "testing." Through lack of faith and failure to appreciate God's purposes of grace, the people of Israel put him to the test.

9 The thought of "testing" God continues. The Israelites ought to have proceeded in faith. Since God had done so much for them, they should have trusted him where they could not see. Instead, they tested his works where they could see. This faithlessness was no passing phase but something that went on for forty years. Possibly when this letter to Hebrews was written, it was the fourth decade since Jesus' crucifixion. The Israelites had rejected God for forty years, and it was now nearly forty years since their descendants had rejected Jesus—a reason for serious concern.

10 We should not miss the reference to the anger of God. The Lord is not impassive or indifferent in the face of human sin. He is a "consuming fire" (12:29), and his inevitable reaction to sin is wrath. "Generation" refers to all the Israelites living at a particular time. They showed constancy in error, "always going astray." "Heart" (GK *2840*) as used in the Bible does not stand for the emotions as with us but for the whole inner being—thoughts, feelings, and will. Often the emphasis is on the mind. Thus the writer is stressing that Israel went wholly astray; their inner state was not right with God. The last line of the verse implies that if people really knew the ways of God, they would walk in them. But these people did not know. Their ignorance was culpable, not innocent. They were not blamed simply for not knowing but for not knowing things they ought to have known and acted on.

11 The seriousness with which God viewed Israel's sin is shown by the divine oath; this points to an unshakable determination. The form of the oath in the Hebrew, reflected in the LXX, is "If they shall enter"; i.e., "If they shall enter into my rest . . . then my name is not God!" The oath refers to the time when the spies had returned from their survey of the Promised Land (Nu 14:21ff.).

The psalmist has brought together two incidents in Israel's history to make the impressive point that the Israelites of old consistently provoked God. God swore the oath in his "anger" (lit., "wrath"; GK *3973*; a different word from "angry" in v.10). This word points to the passionate and settled opposition of God's holy nature to all that is evil and to his concern for what is right. God is not passive in the face of wrongdoing; he actively opposes it.

God did not allow the sinning Israelites to enter his rest. "Rest" (GK *2923*) must be taken in a spiritual sense; it points to a place of blessing where there is no more striving but only relaxation in the presence of God. The wilderness generation would have no part in the world to come; their disobedience had cut them off from this blessing.

B. Some Did Not Enter the Rest (3:12–19)

Having shown that Scripture looks for a rest for God's people, the author proceeds to show that Israel of old did not enter that rest. The implication is that it is still available for others. And there is also a warning here. When God opens up an opportunity, that does not necessarily mean that those who have that opportunity will take it.

12 The writer has a tender concern for every one of his readers. He exhorts them to beware lest any of them fall away. The "sinful, unbelieving heart" stands in marked contrast to the faithfulness ascribed to both Jesus and Moses (v.2). The author stresses the heinousness of this sin by speaking of it as turning away from or rebelling against "the living God" (cf. 9:14; 10:31; 12:22). The rebellion he warns against consists of departing from a living, dynamic person, not from some dead doctrine. Jews might retort that they served the same God as the Christians, so that they would not be departing from God if they went back to Judaism. But to reject God's highest revelation (Jesus Christ) is to depart from God, no matter how many preliminary revelations are retained. A true faith is impossible with such a rejection.

13 Contrariwise, the Hebrew Christians must encourage one another constantly and urgently. The author sees Christian fellowship as very important. It can build people up in the faith and form a strong bulwark against sin and apostasy (cf. 10:25; Mt 18:15–17). "Daily" means that encouragement should be habitual. "As long as it is called Today" adds a touch of urgency, for "Today" does not last forever. The aim of the swift action desired by the writer is that not a single one of his readers be "hardened" (GK 5020). This verb refers not only to "the heart" but is general. One's whole life may be hard, and in that case one is no candidate for spiritual progress. What hardens a person is "sin's deceitfulness." The readers were being tempted to go back to Judaism in the belief that by doing so they would be better off. But sin deceives those who think like this. Temporal and physical safety will be bought only at the price of spiritual disaster.

14 True believers "share in Christ" (cf. 1:9). The author here is stressing the privilege we have in being Christians. He suggests the two sides of a paradox appear in the phrases, "we have come" and "if we hold firmly." What God has done God has done. But it is important that believers hold firmly to what God has given them (cf. v.6). When the addressees first became believers, they had "confidence" (GK 5712); i.e., they had no doubts then, nor should they have any now. "Till the end" may point to the end of the age or the end of the believer's life.

15 The construction is uncertain. This verse may be taken with the preceding one (cf. NIV) or with what follows. Some link the words with v.13 and regard v.14 as a parenthesis: "Exhort one another while it is called Today ... while it is said...." The question is not an easy one, but it seems best to take things in order, as NIV does. The words, of course, have already been quoted (see comments on vv.7–8).

16 The author presses home his point by three questions that emphasize that the psalmist of Ps 95 is thinking about the people who were in a position of spiritual privilege and yet sinned grievously. The first question asks, "Who were they who heard and rebelled?" The verb "rebelled" (GK 4176) means "embitter" or "make angry," and is a strong expression for the rebellious attitude that characterized the Exodus generation.

The writer answers his question with another, this one phrased so as to expect a yes answer. "All those Moses led out of Egypt" is comprehensive, but that Joshua and Caleb are not mentioned does not invalidate the argument. The nation was characterized by unbelief, and the faithfulness of two men does not alter this. NIV says that Moses "led" the people out of Egypt; but, more literally, the author said that they "came out through Moses"—implying that they acted of their own volition and made a good start.

17 The second question refers to those with whom God was angry for forty years (see comments on vv.10–11). In the earlier treatment of the incident (vv.7–8), the forty years referred to testing God and seeing his works. Here it refers to the continuing wrath of God. This wrath was not something transitory and easily avoided. It lasted throughout the "desert" period, as the Israelites wandered in the Sinai wilderness. The question is phrased in such a way as to leave no doubt whatever that God was angry with the sinners in question. Their punishment is mentioned in words reminiscent of Nu 14:29, 32. Those who sinned against God had been destroyed, just as he had prophesied through Moses.

18 The third question refers to those to whom the oath was sworn (cf. v.11). Those who would not enter God's rest were "those who disobeyed" (GK 578). This verb usually means "disobey," though some accept the meaning "disbelieve" (cf. NIV note). This translation is possible since for the early Christians the supreme disobedience was refusing to believe the Gospel. God did much for these people. Yet in the end they went their own way and refused to obey him.

19 The depressing conclusion sums up what has gone before. The author does not say that they did not enter but that they "were not able to enter" the land of Canaan. Sin is self-defeating and prevents people from entering God's rest. This is not an arbitrary penalty imposed by a despotic God. It is the inevitable outcome of "unbelief." The warning to the people of the writer's day is clear. To slip back from their Christian profession into unbelief would be fatal.

C. Christians Enter the Rest (4:1–10)

The author argues that the purposes of God are not frustrated because Israel of old disobeyed him and failed to enter the rest he had promised his people. The promise remains. If ancient Israel did not enter God's rest, then someone else will; namely, the Christians. But this should not lead to complacency on their part. If the Israelites of an earlier day, with all their advantages, failed to enter the rest, Christians ought not to think there will be automatic acceptance for them. They must take care lest they, too, fail to enter the blessing.

1 "Let us be careful" is more strictly "let us fear"; the writer does not want his readers to grow complacent, for there is real danger. God's promises mean much to the writer. The particular promise in question "still stands." That is to say, though it has not been fulfilled, neither has it been revoked. In one sense, of course, there was a fulfillment, for the generation after the people who died in the wilderness entered Canaan. But throughout this section it is basic to the argument that physical entry into Canaan did not constitute the ultimate fulfillment of the promise. God had promised "rest" and that meant more than living in Canaan.

There is a problem about the word translated "be found" (GK *1506*). It can mean either "think" or "seem." If "think" is chosen, the writer is reassuring fearful Christians who thought they might miss out on the rest. If "seem" is chosen, these words constitute a soft warning to the readers to take care lest they miss the promised rest. A decision is not easy, but on the whole it seems that this second interpretation fits the context better. The author, then, is reminding his readers that there was a generation to whom the rest was promised and who missed it. They should beware lest they make the same mistake.

2 "We have had the gospel preached to us" (GK *2294*) uses the verb that became the technical term for preaching the Gospel (though the word can also mean simply "heard good news"). Israel of old, like Christians in the author's day, heard the Gospel. The first half of the verse makes it clear that on the score of hearing God's Good News, there was not much difference between the wilderness generation and the readers. The stress is on the readers. They have the message, and they must act on it, in contrast to the Israelites of old who did not.

"The message they heard" brought them no profit. The last part of this verse can be taken in either of two ways (see NIV note for the second option). The meaning is either "It [the word] was not mixed with faith in them that heard," or, "They were not united by faith with them that heard" (i.e., with real believers, men like Caleb and Joshua). The main thrust is plain enough: It is not enough to hear the message; it must be acted on in faith.

This is the writer's first use of "faith" (GK *4411*), a term he will employ frequently. This word means "faithfulness" as well as "faith," but the latter preponderates in the NT. Sometimes faith in God is meant and sometimes faith in Christ. In this letter it is often the former (see comment on 6:1). Here the term points to the right response to the Christian message—the attitude of trusting God wholeheartedly. The writer speaks of "those who heard" without specifying what it was they heard. But there can be no doubt that he is looking for a right response to what God had done and to what God had made known.

3 "We who have believed" (GK *4409*) once more stresses the necessity of faith. It is believers who enter God's rest, not members of physical Israel, and they do so through a right relationship to God, with an attitude of trust. Characteristically, the writer supports his position by an appeal to Scripture.

There is nothing in the Greek to correspond to "God" in "God has said." Yet this is a correct interpretation because the writer habitually regards God as the author of Scripture. The verb tense used in "has said" (GK *3306*) emphasizes permanence. What God has spoken stands. The quotation is from Ps 95:11 (already cited in 3:11; see comments). Its point appears to be that those to whom the promise was originally made could not enter the rest because of the divine oath. This does not mean any inadequacy on God's part, for he had completed his works from the time of Creation. God's rest was thus available from the time Creation was completed, and his "rest" was the rest he himself enjoyed. The earthly rest in Canaan was no more than a type or symbol of this.

4 The writer does not precisely locate his quotation (Ge 2:2) but contents himself with the general "somewhere." Nor does he say who the speaker is, though once again it must be God, the author of all Scripture. Locating a passage precisely was not easy when scrolls were used; and unless it was important, there was a tendency not to look it up. The important thing is that God said these words. The passage speaks of God as resting from his work on the seventh day.

It is worth noticing that in the creation story each of the first six days is marked by the refrain "And there was evening, and there was morning." However, this is lacking in the account of the seventh day. There we simply read that God rested from all his work. This does not mean that God entered a state of idleness, for there is a sense in which he is continually at work (Jn 5:17). But the completion of creation marks the end of a magnificent whole. There was nothing to add to what God had done, and he entered a rest from creating, a rest marked by the knowledge that everything that he had made was very good (Ge 1:31). So we should think of the rest as something like the satisfaction that comes from accomplishment, from the completion of a task.

5 The writer again adds Ps 95:11, which is central to his argument at this point. As here, he often uses "again" where a further quotation is added to a preceding one (e.g., 1:5; 2:13; 10:30). In this case, however, it does more than reinforce his idea; it introduces a second point in the argument. The first passage said that God rested (and by implication that the rest was open to those who would enter it); the second passage said that the Israelites did not enter that rest because God's judgment fell on them. So the way is prepared for later steps in the argument.

6–7 The argument moves along in logical sequence. Some will enter that rest because it is unthinkable that God's plan should fail of fulfillment. If God prepared a rest for humanity to enter into, then they will enter into it. Perhaps those originally invited will not do so, for there is often something conditional about God's promises. It is precisely the force of the present argument that nothing can stop the promises from being kept, but they must always be appropriated by faith. So if one does not approach the promises by faith, one does not obtain what God offers and the offer is made to others. Some, then, must enter God's rest, though the first recipients of the Good News (cf. v.2) did not.

The writer concentrates on two generations only: the wilderness generation and his contemporaries. There had been other generations who might have appropriated the promise. But the focus is on the first generation who set the pattern of unbelief and then on the writer's generation, who alone at that time had the opportunity of responding to God's invitation. The intervening generations were not germaine to his argument.

The reason the first group did not enter God's rest was "their disobedience" (GK 577). This word is always used in the NT of disobeying God, often with the thought of the Gospel in mind; so it comes close to the meaning disbelief (cf. v.11; Ro 11:30). Because the first generation had passed the opportunity by, God set another day. The idea that the wilderness generation was finally rejected was one the rabbis found hard to accept. Thus they expressed a conviction that somehow those Israelites would be saved. The author, however, has no such reservations about that generation. They disobeyed God and forfeited their place. Psalm 95 was written long after the Israelites in the desert had failed to use their opportunity and had perished. Its use of the term "Today" shows that the promise had never been claimed and was still open. The voice of God still called. A day of opportunity remained, even though the fate of the wilderness generation stood as an impressive witness to the possibility of spiritual disaster.

8 This sentence expresses a contrary-to-fact condition: "If Joshua had given them rest [as he did not], God would not have spoken later about another day [as he did]." The name "Joshua" is the Hebrew form of the Greek name "Jesus." "Joshua" is a good way of rendering the text, as it makes clear to the English reader who is in mind. The Greek text, however, says "Jesus"; and both the writer and his original readers would have been mindful of the connection with the name of Christ, even though the emphasis in the passage lies elsewhere. There had been a "Jesus" who could not lead his people into the rest of God, just as there was another "Jesus" who could.

9 This verse expresses the logical consequence of what precedes. The Greek word used for "Sabbath-rest" (GK *4878*) is most likely a word made up by the author. There were various kinds of "rest." There was, for example, the kind of rest Israel was to get in its own land when it had rest from wars (Dt 25:19). When the psalmist wrote Ps 95, he knew firsthand what this kind of rest in Palestine meant, and he was still looking for "rest." Thus rest from war is not the kind of rest that the author of Hebrews had in mind. Jesus spoke of quite another kind of rest—rest for the souls of people (Mt 11:28–30). This is nearer to what the author means. He links rest with the original Sabbath, with what God did when he finished Creation and what Christians are called into. This, then, is a highly original view. The author sees the rest as for "the people of God" (cf. 11:2; 1Pe 2:10). In the OT "the people of God" is the nation of Israel, but in the NT it signifies believers. The rest the author writes about is for such people. Those who shut themselves out by disobedience and unbelief cannot enter into it.

10 We now have a description of at least part of what the rest means. The writer reverts to the word for "rest" that he has been using earlier instead of the "Sabbath-rest" of v.9. To "enter God's rest" means for a believer to cease from one's own work, just as God ceased from his.

The main question that arises is whether the rest takes place here and now, or after death, as seen in Rev 14:13: "Blessed are the dead who die in the Lord . . . they will rest from their labor." It is best to see this rest as an experience in which they live here and now by faith, but the rest they know here is not the full story. That will be revealed in the hereafter. There is a sense in which to enter Christian salvation means to cease from one's works and to rest securely on what Christ has done. And there is a sense in which the works of the believer, works done in Christ, have about them that completeness and sense of fulfillment that may fitly be classed with the rest in question.

D. Exhortation to Enter the Rest (4:11–13)

The idea of the rest of God is not simply a piece of curious information not readily accessible to the rank and file of Christians. It is a spur to action. So the writer proceeds to exhort his readers to make that rest their own.

11 It is possible that this verse should be attached to the preceding paragraph, but it seems preferable to see it as introducing an exhortation based on the penetrating power of the Word of God. The writer includes himself with his readers in urging a quick and serious effort to enter the rest "so that no one will fall by following their example of disobedience." Paul refers to the same generation to hammer home a similar lesson, and he regards the wilderness happenings as types (1Co 10:1–12). These earlier people had perished. Let the readers beware!

12 "The word of God" means anything that God utters—particularly the word that came through Jesus Christ. "Living and active" shows that there is a dynamic quality about God's revelation. It does things. Specifically, it penetrates and, in this capacity, is likened to a "double-edged sword" (cf. Isa 49:2; Eph 6:17; Rev 1:16; 2:12; 19:15).

The Word of God is unique. No sword can penetrate as it can. We should not take the reference to "soul" and "spirit" as indicating a "dichotomist" over against a "trichotomist" view of a human being (but see comments on 1Th 5:23), nor the reference to "dividing" to indicate that the writer envisaged a sword as slipping between them. Nor should we think of the sword as splitting off "joints" and "marrow." What the author is saying is that God's Word can reach to the innermost recesses of our being. We must not think that we can bluff our way out of anything, for no secrets are hidden from God. We cannot keep our thoughts to ourselves. There may also be the thought that the whole of human nature, however we divide it, physical as well as nonmaterial, is open to God.

With "judges" we move to legal terminology. The Word of God passes judgment on our feelings and thoughts. Nothing evades the scope of this Word. What people hold as most secret they find subject to its scrutiny and judgment.

13 The same truth is now expressed in different imagery. This time the impossibility of hiding anything from God is illustrated by the thought of nakedness. "Nothing in all creation" (or "no created being") remains invisible to God. "Uncovered" (GK *1218*) here means that all things are truly naked before God. "Laid bare" (GK *5548*) is an unusual word, sometimes used of wrestlers who had a hold that involved gripping the neck and brought victory. So the term can mean "to prostrate" or "overthrow." Most scholars, however, think a meaning like "exposed" is required. Yet it is not easy to see how this meaning is to be obtained. It has been suggested that the wrestler exposed the face or neck of his foe by his grip. While this may be so, it entails reading something into the situation. Another suggestion is the bending back of the head of a sacrificial victim to expose the throat. Unfortunately, no example of the word used in this way is attested. In the end we must probably remain unsatisfied. Clearly the author is saying that no one can keep anything hidden from God, but the metaphor by which he brings out this truth is not clear.

The verse contains yet another difficulty, namely, the precise meaning of its closing words. The expression is used of accounting, and it seems likely that the translation "him to whom we must give account" is correct. Nothing is hidden from God, and in the end we must give account of ourselves to him. The combination makes a powerful reason for heeding the exhortation and entering into the rest by our obedience.

IV. A Great High Priest (4:14–5:11)

One of the major insights of this letter is that Jesus is our great High Priest. The author proceeds to reinforce his exhortation to enter the rest with a reminder of the character of our High Priest. Jesus is one with his people, and for them he offers the perfect sacrifice. This is seen largely in terms of the Day of Atonement ceremonies in which the role of the high priest (and not simply any priest) was central.

A. Our Confidence (4:14–16)

The first point is that Jesus knows our human condition. It is not something he has heard about, so to speak, but something he knows; for he, too, was human. We may approach him confidently because he knows our weakness.

14 Our confidence rests on Jesus. He is "a great high priest," a title that suggests his superiority to the Levitical priests. He has "gone through the heavens." The Jews sometimes thought of a plurality of heavens (cf. Paul's reference to "the third heaven" in 2Co 12:2 or other Jewish references to seven heavens). Jesus has gone right through to the supreme place. His greatness is further emphasized by the title "Son of God." All this is the basis for an exhortation to hold firmly to our profession.

15 Our High Priest has entered into our weakness and so can sympathize meaningfully with us. He "has been tempted . . . just as we are" may mean "in the same way as we are tempted" or "by reason of his likeness to us"; both are true. There is another ambiguity at the end of the verse where the Greek means "apart from sin." This may mean that Jesus was tempted just as we are except that we sin and he did not. But it may also mean that he had a knowledge of every kind of temptation except that which comes from actually having sinned. Perhaps the writer was not trying to differentiate between the two. At any rate his words can profitably be taken either way. The main point is that, though Jesus did not sin, we must not infer that life was easy for him. His sinlessness was, at least in part, an earned sinlessness as he gained victory after victory in the constant battle with temptation that life in this world entails. In fact, the Sinless One knows the force of temptation in a way that we who sin do not. We give in before the temptation has fully spent itself; only he who does not yield knows its full force.

16 Having this High Priest gives "confidence." So the writer exhorts his readers to approach God boldly. The word "us" does away with the mediation of earthly priests. We can approach God's "throne of grace" directly. This expression for God's throne points both to the sovereignty of God and to God's love to people. The rabbis sometimes spoke of a "throne of mercy" to which God goes from "the throne of judgment" when he spares people. The idea here is not dissimilar, all the more so since the writer goes on to speak of receiving "mercy" (GK *1799*). We need mercy because we have failed so often, and we need grace because service awaits us in which we need God's help. And help is what the writer says we get—the help that is appropriate to the time, i.e., "timely help."

Christians should not be tentative because they have the great High Priest in whom they can be confident. His successful traverse of the heavens points to his power to help, and his fellow-feeling with our weakness points to his sympathy with our needs. In the light of this, what can hold us back?

B. The Qualities Required in High Priests (5:1–4)

The author now directs his readers to the qualities required in the well-known institution of high priests, though he confines his attention to the Aaronic priesthood in the OT and does not consider contemporary Jewish priests who fell far short of the ideal. He shows that the necessary qualifications include oneness with the people, compassion, and appointment by God. Then the author goes on to show that Christ had all these qualifications.

1 The author proposes to explore something of the nature of high priesthood and begins by showing that it has both a humanward and a Godward reference. It is of the essence of priesthood that the priest has community of nature with those he represents. But his work is "in matters related to God," specifically in offering "gifts and sacrifices for sins." The writer is summarizing the priestly function of offering.

2 "Deal gently with" (GK 3584) is not easy to translate; it refers to taking the middle course between apathy and anger. A true high priest is not indifferent to moral lapses, but neither is he harsh. He "is able" to take this position only because he himself shares in the same "weakness" (GK 819) as the sinners on whom he has compassion. This word may denote physical or moral frailty, and the following words show that in the case of the usual run of high priests the latter is included. The earthly high priest is at one with his people in their need for atonement and forgiveness.

3 The high priest is required to make offerings for himself just as for his people. For the Day of Atonement it was prescribed that the high priest present a bull "for his own sin offering" (Lev 16:11). Only then was he able to minister on behalf of the people. In the matter of sins and of sacrifices the priest must regard himself in exactly the same way he regards the people. His case is identical with theirs.

4 The negative statement immediately refutes any thought that a man can take the initiative in being made high priest. It is an honor to be a high priest, and this can happen only by divine appointment; the appointment of Aaron sets the pattern (Ex 28:1–3). In point of fact, no other call to be high priest is recorded in Scripture, though we might reason that the call to Aaron was not simply personal but also included his family and descendants. At any rate, the Bible records disasters that befell those who took it upon themselves to perform high priestly duties, as in the cases of Korah (Nu 16), Saul (1Sa 13:8ff.), and Uzziah (2Ch 26:16ff.).

C. Christ's Qualifications as High Priest (5:5–11)

Having made clear what is required in high priests, the author shows that Christ has these qualifications. Moreover, Christ is both Priest and King, which goes beyond the view expressed in some Jewish writings that there will be two messiahs, one of Aaron and another of David. No other NT writer speaks of Jesus as a high priest. It is a highly original way of looking at him.

5–6 Christ has the qualification of being called by God. There is perhaps a hint at his obedience in the use of the term "the Christ" rather than the human name "Jesus." He who was God's own Christ did not take the glory on himself (cf. Jn 8:54). The writer cites two passages, the first being Ps 2:7 (cf. Heb 1:5). He will later argue that Jesus ministers in the heavenly sanctuary. Accordingly, it is important that Jesus be seen to be the Son, one who has rights in heaven.

The second citation is from Ps 110:4. The first verse of this psalm is often applied to Jesus (e.g., Heb 1:13), but this is the first time the Melchizedek passage is used in this way. The psalm says, "You are a priest forever," which is the first use of the term "priest" (GK 2636) in this letter (used fourteen times). The author uses it of priests generally (7:14; 8:4), of the Levitical priests (7:20, etc.), of

Melchizedek (7:1, 3), and of Christ (5:6; 7:11, 15, 17, 21; 10:21). When it is used of Christ, it seems to differ little from "high priest." It is a powerful way of bringing out certain aspects of Christ's saving work for the human race. All that a priest does in offering sacrifice for people Christ does. But whereas priests do it only symbolically, he really effects atonement.

"Forever" is another contrast. Other priests have their day and pass away. Not Christ! His priesthood abides. He has no successor (a fact that will be brought out later). He is a priest "of the same kind as Melchizedek" (a better translation than "of the order of Melchizedek," for there was no succession of priests from Melchizedek). Jesus was a priest of this kind—not like Aaron and his successors.

7 The author turns to the second qualification—Jesus' oneness with humankind. In realistic language he brings out the genuineness of Jesus' humanity. Commentators agree that the writer is referring to the agony in Gethsemane, though his language does not fit into any of our accounts. It seems that he may have had access to some unrecorded facts. It is also possible that he wants us to see that there were other incidents in Jesus' life that fit into this general pattern. "Prayers and petitions" points to dependence on God, who alone can save from death.

There are difficulties at the end of v.7. The word "heard" (GK *1653*) is usually taken to mean that the prayer was answered, not simply noted. Most interpreters agree. But they also contend that the prayer must have been answered in the terms in which it was asked. The problem, then, is that Jesus prayed, "Take this cup from me" (Mk 14:36); but he still died. Various solutions have been proposed. All in all, it seems best to remember that Jesus' prayer was not simply a petition that he should not die, because he immediately said, "Yet not what I will, but what you will." The important thing about answered prayer is that God does what brings about the end aimed at, not what corresponds exactly to the words of the petitioner. In this case the prayer was that the will of God be done, and this has precedence over the passing of the cup from Jesus. Since the cup had to be drunk, it was drunk! But the significant point is that the Son was strengthened to do the will of the Father.

8 We should take these words in the sense of "son though he was" rather than "although he was a son." It is the quality of sonship that is emphasized. Jesus' stature was such that one would not have expected him to suffer. But he did suffer, and in the process he learned obedience. This, startling though it is, does not mean that Jesus passed from disobedience to obedience. Rather, he learned obedience by actually obeying. There is a certain quality involved when one has performed a required action—a quality that is lacking when there is only a readiness to act. Innocence differs from virtue.

9 Here we must make a similar comment about Jesus' being "made perfect." This does not mean that he was imperfect and that out of his imperfection he became perfect. There is a perfection that results from having actually suffered; it is different from the perfection that is ready to suffer. "He became" indicates a change of relationship that follows the perfecting. The suffering that led to the perfecting did something—Jesus became "the source of eternal salvation." "Eternal" (GK *173*) means "pertaining to an age." Normally the word refers to the age to come and so means "without end," though it can also be used of what is without beginning or end (9:14) or simply of what is without beginning (Ro 16:25). It is used of what does not end in connection with redemption (Heb 9:12), covenant (13:20), judgment (6:2), and inheritance (9:15). Jesus will bring people a salvation that is eternal in its scope and efficacy, a salvation that brings them into the life of the world to come. It is a nice touch that he who learned to obey brought salvation to those who obey.

10 The writer has forcefully made his point that Jesus shared our human life. He was qualified to be high priest because of his common nature with us and his compassion. Now the writer returns to the thought that Jesus was made high priest by God. What is to become his characteristic designation throughout this letter is a title not given by people, nor assumed by himself, but conferred on him by God the Father.

11 Although NIV takes this to be the opening of a new paragraph, it seems better to take it as completing the preceding paragraph. The writer points out that there is a good deal that could be said about his subject. It is "hard to explain," not because of some defect in the writer or the intrinsic difficulty of the subject, but because of the slowness of the learners. This leads to a new train of thought that is pursued throughout ch. 6 (we come back to Melchizedek in ch. 7). "This" refers to the way Melchizedek prefigures Christ. "Are" should really be "have become"; it is an acquired state, not a natural one. "Slow" (GK *3821*) means "sluggish" or "slothful." His readers ought to have been in a different condition, but they had allowed themselves to get lazy.

V. The Danger of Apostasy (5:12–6:20)

Obviously the author was much concerned lest his readers slip back from their present state into something that amounts to a denial of Christianity. So he utters a strong warning about the dangers of apostasy. He wants his friends to be in no doubt about the seriousness of falling into it.

A. Failure to Progress in the Faith (5:12–14)

This little section is of special interest because it shows that the recipients of the letter were people of whom better things might have been expected. They should have been mature Christians. Since they had evidently been converted for quite some time, they ought to have made more progress in the faith than they in fact had. The author is troubled by their immaturity.

12 The readers had been Christians for long enough to qualify as teachers. This does not necessarily mean that the letter was written to a group of teachers, for the emphasis is on progress in the faith. Those addressed had failed to go on, though they had been believers long enough to know more. Christians who have really progressed in the faith ought to be able to instruct others (see 1Pe1 3:15; cf. Ro 2:21). But, far from this being the case, they still needed instruction, and that in elementary truths.

"Someone to teach you" stands over against "teachers" and points up the contrast. Their knowledge of the faith is minimal when it ought to have been advanced. "The elementary truths" renders an expression that is equivalent to our "ABC." It points to the real beginnings. The Greek actually means something like "the ABC of the beginning of the oracles of God." There can be no doubt as to the elementary nature of the teaching in question. But it is not quite clear what "God's word [lit., oracles; GK *3359*]" is. Quite possibly the OT is meant, though some think it is the entire Jewish system. Since the expression is quite general, it seems better to take it of all that God has spoken— i.e., the divine revelation in general.

The verse ends with another strong statement about the plight of the readers. "You need milk" renders an expression that literally means "you have become having need of milk," an expression in which "you have become" is important (cf. 5:11). Once again the writer is drawing attention to the fact that his readers have moved their position. Always in the Christian life, one either moves forward or slips back. It is almost impossible to stand still. These people had not advanced; so the result was that they had gone back and had "become" beginners. The contrast between milk and solid food is found elsewhere (cf. 1Co 3:2). "Milk" stands for elementary instruction in the Christian way; "solid food" is, of course, more advanced instruction, the kind of teaching beginners cannot make much of but which is invaluable to those who have made some progress. What is appropriate at the early stages of the Christian life may cease to be suitable as time goes on.

13 The author now explains his reference to milk and solid food. "Anyone" is inclusive; in other words, the author is saying, "This is the way it is." Christians occupied with elementary truths are spiritually still infants and must be treated as such. They are without experience in "the teaching about righteousness." It is uncertain what "righteousness" (GK *1466*) means, for it may be taken in more ways than one. Most likely it means the right conduct God expects believers to follow, but which the readers of this letter have not been following.

14 With "but" the author contrasts infants in v.13. Mature people (GK *5455*), who have "trained themselves," need solid food. The NT makes considerable use of metaphors from athletics, as our writer does here. Mature Christians constantly exercise themselves in spiritual perception, and the result is manifest. They can "distinguish good from evil" and, therefore, the implication runs, will not be in danger of doing the wrong thing to which the readers find themselves attracted. Lacking this perception, Christian service will always be immature and partial.

B. Exhortation to Progress (6:1–3)

Since the readers were still in need of milk, we anticipate that this is what the writer will provide. Instead, he says he will leave elementary things and go on to "maturity." We expect him to introduce this with "despite your condition" or the like. Instead, we get "therefore." The reason for this may lie in the nature of what he calls "the elementary teachings." Almost every item in his list had a place in an orthodox Jewish community. He may have felt that to concentrate on this area would be of no help to those slipping back into Judaism. Therefore he goes on to "solid food."

1 The writer links himself with his readers in his exhortation to leave elementary things behind and go forward. He sees "repentance from acts that lead to death" as basic. "Repentance" (GK 3567) was the first thing required in the preaching of John the Baptist, Jesus, and the apostles; and it remains basic. Repentance is "from dead works," a phrase that has been understood to mean legalistic adherence to Jewish ways (works that could never bring life) or genuinely evil actions (actions that belong to death and not life). The latter seems preferable. Linked with this is the positive attitude of "faith in God." Faith matters immensely to the author (see comment on 4:2). As used here it means more than a conviction that there is a God; it means trusting in that God in a personal relationship. And it is not so different from faith in Christ as some suggest, because it is basic Christian teaching that God was in Christ (cf. 2Co 5:19).

2 "Instruction" is in apposition to "foundation" and introduces a fresh group of subjects. "Baptisms" is a word usually used of purification ceremonies other than Christian baptism (9:10; Mk 7:4), and it is plural (which would be unusual for baptism). Thus it is likely that the word refers to something other than Christian baptism. There were such purification ceremonies, or lustrations, in the Jewish religion as in most other religions of the day. Sometimes there was confusion over ritual washings (Jn 3:25ff.; Ac 19:1–5). It would thus be one of the elementary items of instruction that converts be taught the right approach to the various "baptisms" they would encounter.

The "laying on of hands" was a widespread practice in antiquity. Among Christians, hands were laid on new converts (Ac 8:17), on Timothy by the presbyterate (1Ti 4:14), and on Timothy by Paul (2Ti 1:6). This action was sometimes associated with commissioning for ministry and sometimes with the beginnings of Christian service. It seems to have been connected with the gift of the Spirit at least on some occasions (e. g., Ac 8:17–19). It is Christian beginnings, perhaps with the thought of God's gift of the Holy Spirit, that are in mind here.

"The resurrection of the dead . . . and eternal judgment" were topics that went together and were important for Jews and Christians alike. They form a reminder that this life is not everything. We are responsible people, and one day we shall rise from the dead and give account of ourselves to God. This must have been of importance to new converts in a time when many people thought of death as the end of everything.

3 This verse expresses not only a resolute determination to go ahead on these lines but also a recognition that it is only with the help of God that this can be done. We should take these words as coming out of the author's realization that without divine aid the plan he was suggesting was impossible.

C. No Second Beginning (6:4–8)

The writer proceeds to underline the seriousness of apostasy from the Christian faith and, indeed, of any failure to make progress. He does this by pointing to the impossibility of making a second beginning. It is impossible for Christians to stand still. They either progress in the faith or slip back. And slipping back is serious; it can mean cutting oneself off from the blessings God offers. The writer is not questioning the perseverance of the saints. As he has done before, he is insisting that only those who continue in the Christian way are the saints.

4 This verse indicates the reasonableness of what follows: Had his readers really fallen away, there would be no point in talking to them. The word "enlightened" (GK 5894) affirms that those who are admitted to the Christian faith are brought to that light that is "the light of the world" (Jn 8:12; cf. 2Co 4:6; 2Pe 1:19). To abandon the Gospel would be to sin against the light they had received.

"The heavenly gift" is not closely defined. The thought is of God's good gift, and we cannot be more precise than this. The Holy Spirit is active among all believers and for that matter to some extent beyond the church, in his work of "common grace." It is clear that some activity of the Spirit is in mind. Yet once more our author does not define it closely.

5 The people in question have "tasted the goodness of the word of God." While some limit this to the Gospel, there seems to be no need to do this. Any word that God has spoken is a good gift to people, and those the writer has in mind here have come to hear something of God's word to the human race. They have also experienced something of "the powers of the coming age." The "age to come" is normally the Messianic Age; powers proper to the coming Messianic Age are in some sense realized now for God's people. "Powers" (GK *1539*) indicates that that age puts at people's disposal powers they do not have of themselves.

6 "If they fall away" clearly means "fall away from Christianity." The writer is envisaging people who have been numbered among the followers of Christ but now leave that company. Such cannot be brought back to repentance. The author does not say "cannot be forgiven" or "cannot be restored to salvation" or the like. It is *repentance* that is in mind, and the writer says that it is impossible for these people to repent. Most likely this refers to a repentance that means leaving the backsliding into which the person has fallen. Such a person cannot bring himself or herself to this repentance.

It is probable that we should take the verb rendered "are crucifying ... all over again" (GK *416*) simply as "crucifying." The author is saying that those who deny Christ in this way are really taking their stand among those who crucified Jesus. In heart and mind they make themselves one with those who put him to death on the cross at Calvary.

There has been much discussion of the significance of this passage. Some think that the author is speaking about genuine Christians who fall away and that he denies that they may ever come back. This view sets the writer of the letter in contradiction with other NT writers for whom it is clear that the perseverance of the saints is something that comes from God and not from our own best efforts (e.g., Jn 6:37; 10:27–29). Others think that the case is purely hypothetical. Because the writer does not say that this has ever happened, they infer that it never could really happen and that to put it this way makes the warning more impressive. But unless the writer is speaking of something that could really happen, it is not a warning about anything. Granted, he does not say that anyone has apostatized in this way; nevertheless, he surely means that someone could, and he does not want his readers to do so. A third possibility is that the writer is talking about what looks very much like the real thing but lacks something. The case of Simon Magus springs to mind. He is said to have believed, to have been baptized, and to have continued with Philip (Ac 8:13). Presumably he shared in the laying on of hands and the gift given by it. Yet after all this Peter could say to him, "Your heart is not right before God.... you are full of bitterness and captive to sin" (Ac 8:21–23). The writer is saying that when people have entered into the Christian experience far enough to know what it is all about and have then turned away, then, as far as they themselves are concerned, they are crucifying Christ. In that state they cannot repent.

7 This process is now illustrated from agriculture. Land drinks in rain and as a result brings forth a crop. The rain comes first. The land does not produce the crop of itself. The spiritual parallel should not be overlooked. The word translated "a crop" (GK *1083*) is a general term for herbage; it does not mean any specific crop. "Useful to those for whom it is farmed" means that the beneficiaries are people in general and not only those who actually work on the farm. This land, then, receives God's blessing.

8 We should not miss the point that this is the same land as in v.7. We should probably place a comma at the end of v. 7 and proceed thus: "but if it produces ...," or, "but when it produces...." The reference to producing "thorns and thistles" reminds us inevitably of the curse of Ge 3:17ff.—a curse on that very creation of which it had been said, "God saw all that he had made, and it was very good" (Ge 1:31). This land then, producing only what is worthless, awaits the curse. "Is in danger of being cursed" might give the impression that the land came close to being cursed but just escaped. The author seems rather to be saying that at the moment of which he speaks the curse has not yet fallen, certain though it is. Such a field in the end "will be burned." Some commentators think the writer knew little of agriculture, for the burning of the field was not a curse but rather a source of blessing as it got rid of the weeds and so prepared for a good crop. But whatever his knowledge of farming, he had a valid point. Land that produced nothing but weeds faced nothing but fire. The warning to professing Christians whose lives produce only the equivalent of weeds is plain.

D. Exhortation to Perseverance (6:9–12)

The preceding sections have contained salutary warnings about the dangers of apostasy. The readers have had it made clear to them that they must make progress along the Christian way or suffer disaster. There are no other possibilities. Now the writer indicates that he has confidence in his correspondents. He has felt it necessary to warn them, but he does not really think they will fall away. So he speaks encouragingly and warmly, at the same time using the occasion to exhort them to go forward.

9 For the only time in this letter the writer addresses the readers as "dear friends" (GK 28). He has a tender concern for his correspondents, even though he has had to say some critical things about them. "We are confident" carries a note of certainty ("we" is a plural of authorship and means "I"). He is sure that there are "better" things about them than the kind of disaster he has been speaking about (the writer is fond of the word "better"; see comment on 1:4). He does not say what these good things are better than, but it is clearly implied that it is the cursing and the like that he has been speaking of. He does not think that in the end they will be caught in the condemnation he has referred to. He goes on with "And having salvation." This unusual expression might mean "things that lead to salvation" or "things that follow from salvation." Perhaps we should leave it general as NIV: "things that accompany salvation."

10 This verse begins with the Greek word meaning "for" and introduces the grounds for his confidence—a confidence that rests basically on God's constancy. In a masterly understatement the writer refers to God as "not unjust." It is the character of God as the perfectly just judge of all that gives rise to the author's confidence. This God will not forget what the readers have done. The statement is not an intrusion of a doctrine of salvation by works. Rather, the Christian profession of the readers had been more than formal, and they had shown in changed lives what that profession meant. This, the writer is saying, would not go unnoticed with God. He adds, "And the love you have shown him." The following words show that it is deeds of kindness to people that are in mind. Such deeds, proceeding from loving hearts as they do, demonstrate that the doers have a real affection for God. Showing love to others is proof for a real love for God (cf. 1Jn 4:19–21). These Christians have served God's

The author of Hebrews pictures vibrant Christians as productive land. Notice the abundant dates on this date palm in Israel.

people in the past, and they continue with this kind of service.

11 "We want" (GK *2121*) refers to strong desire. The writer was passionately concerned for his friends (see v. 9), and we see it again in his desire for "each" of them. No one is excluded. He calls on them to show "this same diligence." The past had set a standard, and he looks for it to be maintained "to the very end," bringing before them the importance of perseverance. "In order to make your hope sure" renders a somewhat unusual expression (lit., "to the fullness [GK *4443*] of the hope"). This phrase suggests the full development of the hope. In these verses we have love (v. 10) and faith (v. 12) as well as hope. These three are often joined in the NT (Ro 5:2–5; 1 Cor 13:13; 1Th 1:3; 5:8; Heb 10:22–24; et al.). In the twentieth century we would easily think of faith and love. But hope? Clearly it had a greater significance for the early church than it has for us. Hope is important, for no movement ever grips the hearts of people if it does not give them hope.

12 The writer continues with the purpose behind his instruction: he does not want them to "become lazy." The readers are to "imitate" those who get the promises—"imitate" (GK *3629*) and not simply "follow." It is uncertain whether he is alluding to the great ones of the past (see ch. 11) or to outstanding contemporaries. Perhaps the present tense in "inherit" tips the scale in favor of those then living. The readers had good examples. "Faith" in God is important throughout this letter, and it is not surprising to have it included here as an important part of the Christian life. "Patience" (GK *3429*) points to a quality of being undismayed in difficulties. Faith has a steadfastness about it that sees it through whatever difficulties present themselves. The verb "inherit" (GK *3099*; see comment on 1:14) here means "to have sure possession of" without specifying the means.

E. God's Promise Is Sure (6:13–20)

Abraham is a splendid example of what the author has in mind. Though that patriarch had God's promise, he had to live for many years in patient expectation with nothing to go on except that God had promised. But that was enough. God is utterly reliable. What he has promised he will certainly perform. But we must wait patiently, for he does it all in his own good time, not in ours.

13 The author is fond of Abraham, whom he refers to ten times. He is the supreme example of one who continued to trust God and to obey him even though the circumstances were adverse and gave little support to faith. The NT often speaks of God's promise in connection with this man (Ac 3:25; 7:17; Ro 4:13; Gal 3:8, 14, 16, 18). His greatness and the frequency with which God's promise was linked with his name made him a natural example for the author. It is the fact of the promise rather than its content that the author appeals to—especially in that God confirmed it with an oath. The oath in itself implies delay in fulfilling the promise. If God had been about to fulfill it immediately, there would have been no place for an oath. So from the first Abraham was faced with the prospect of waiting in hope and faith. God swore the oath by himself, for there was no one greater to swear by—a point that is significant to the author.

14 The quotation is from Ge 22:17. "I will surely bless you" conveys the ideas of emphasis and certainty (the first of seven occurrences of "bless" [GK *2328*] in this letter). Sometimes it is used of people, meaning "to invoke blessings on." But where God is the subject, the meaning is "prosper." Here the blessing refers to Abraham's descendants who would form a great nation, possess the land, and in due course be the source of blessing to others.

15 "So" should not be taken too closely with "waiting patiently." It is not so much "waiting thus" as "thus [confident in God's promise], he waited patiently." Abraham was content to await God's time for the fulfillment of the promise. This meant real patience, because Isaac was not born till twenty-five years after the promise was first given (Ge 12:4; 21:5) and long after Sarah could have been expected to bear children. Abraham's grandchildren were not born for another sixty years (Ge 25:26), only fifteen years before his death (Ge 25:7). The complete fulfillment of the promise, of course, could not take place within his lifetime (a nation cannot be born so quickly). But enough happened for the writer to say, "Abraham received what was promised."

We should possibly also bear in mind Jn 8:56: "Abraham rejoiced at the thought of seeing my day; he saw it and was glad." In that sense Abraham did see the fuller working out of the promise. But the important thing in the present context is that Abraham had to be patient if he was to see anything in the way of fulfillment. He was patient and he did see it. So the readers are encouraged to be patient and await God's action. He does not go back on his promises; he is completely reliable. But he works in his own way and time, not ours.

16 The importance of the oath is now brought out. When one swears an oath, one makes a solemn affirmation of the truth of his or her words before a greater being, who presumably will punish any misuse of his name if a false statement is made. Thus an oath "puts an end to all argument." It is an authoritative word guaranteed by the highest authority.

17 We now turn from human oaths to the oath God swore to Abraham. God had no need to swear an oath. Nevertheless, he did it to make absolutely clear to his servant that his promise would be fulfilled. The operation of God's will is stressed and is further brought out by the reference to "the unchanging nature of his purpose." God's will does not change. He has his purpose and he works it out. That was what the oath said.

The word rendered "confirmed" (GK *3541*) has the idea of "stand as guarantor." God appears, so to speak, in two characters: the giver of the promise and then its guarantor. God is one of the parties of his promise. But with his oath, he puts himself on neutral ground and pledges the fulfillment of that promise. We should not miss the reference to "the heirs." The promise was not confined to Abraham or even to him and his immediate family. Since he was to have a mighty multitude of heirs, it was to all those who follow him, including not merely physical Israel but also his spiritual descendants (Gal 3:7). The readers of the letter must number themselves among those to whom the oath referred.

18 God's swearing the oath gave us "two unchangeable things," the promise and the oath. Once God had spoken, it was inconceivable that either should alter. It is impossible for God to lie. "So that" introduces the purpose God had in mind. This purpose may be as NIV has it, or we can understand it as "so that ... we who have fled may have strong encouragement to lay hold on the hope." The writer does not specify what we have "fled" from, but the context makes it clear that he is thinking of some aspect of life in a sinful world. So far from clinging to that, he and his readers "take hold of the hope offered." Once again we see the importance of hope, the very antithesis of the despair that might grip us if we saw no more than a sinful world. But we do see more. We look forward to the consummation of God's great work of salvation. The word translated "offered" (GK *4618*) pictures hope lying before us, spread out like some inviting prospect; and we are encouraged to go in to it.

19 While the metaphor of the anchor is widely used in antiquity, it occurs only here in the NT. A ship firmly anchored is safe from idle drifting. Its position and safety are sure. So hope is a stabilizing force for the Christian. "Soul" (GK *6034*) is a general word that probably means the "life" of a human being. The author is not saying simply that hope secures the "spiritual" aspect of a person; he is affirming that hope forms an anchor for the whole of life. Those with a living hope have a steadying anchor in all they do, giving them a solid footing and security.

And there is something more: hope "enters the inner sanctuary." The imagery takes us back to the tabernacle, with its "curtain" shutting off the Most Holy Place. That little room symbolized the very presence of God, but people were not allowed to enter it. But hope can, says the author. The Christian hope is not exhausted by what it sees of earthly possibilities. It reaches into the very presence of God.

20 We return to the imagery of the Day of Atonement, when the high priest entered the Most Holy Place on behalf of the people. Our forerunner, Jesus, has entered the holiest of all for us—something more than the Levitical high priest could do. Though he entered the Most Holy Place to make atonement on behalf of the people, at the end he and they were still outside. But to call Jesus our "forerunner" implies that we will follow in due course.

"On our behalf" indicates that Jesus did something for us. He not only showed the way but also atoned for us. So we come to the thought that he has become "a high priest forever, in the order of Melchizedek." The thought had been introduced in 5:6, and the author will now proceed to develop it.

VI. Melchizedek (7:1–28)

The writer has mentioned Melchizedek before and has spoken of Jesus as a priest of the Melchizedekian kind, but he has done no more than glance at the theme. Now he develops it. This is an understanding of Christ's work that is peculiar to this letter, and in the author's hands it is very effective. He uses it to show something of the uniqueness of Christ and of the greatness of the work he accomplished for humanity. For the Jews of his day, it would have been axiomatic that there was no priesthood other than the Aaronic. We are now shown that the Law itself proves that there is a higher priesthood than that.

A. The Greatness of Melchizedek (7:1–10)

The writer begins with a brief notice of the incident recorded about Melchizedek, namely his meeting with Abraham as the patriarch returned from the slaughter of the five kings (Ge 14:18–20; Melchizedek is mentioned again only in Ps 110:4). He draws attention to what is known of this man and reaches some important conclusions for Christians. He sees several reasons for regarding Melchizedek as superior: he received tithes from Abraham (and through him, from Levi, the ancestor of the Levitical priests); he blessed Abraham; he was "without beginning of days or end of life" (v.3); he "is declared to be living" (v.8, in contrast to the Aaronic priests who die).

1 The writer begins his explanation of the significance of Melchizedek by referring to Ge 14:17–20. Melchizedek is "king of Salem," which may mean "king of Jerusalem" ("Salem" is another name for Jerusalem in Ps 76:2). But it is curious that if the writer thought that Jerusalem was in fact where Melchizedek ministered, he does not mention the fact that Jesus suffered there (cf. 13:12). Perhaps he saw Salem as some other place; the LXX of Ge 33:18 seems to identify Shechem with Salem.

Melchizedek was not only a king but a "priest of God Most High." It was not uncommon for one person to combine the roles of priest and king in antiquity. It is, however, the special characteristics of this man rather than the dual offices that are noteworthy. The author ignores the fact that the king of Sodom, who had suffered defeat at the hands of the kings Abraham had just routed, went out to meet the triumphant patriarch, and that Melchizedek brought out bread and wine. Instead, he focuses on what will help him make the points he has in mind about the work of Christ. The first of them is that he "blessed him," a point to which he will return in v.7.

2 Abraham gave Melchizedek "a tenth of everything," i. e., of the spoils from the battle (cf. vv.4ff.). So far the author is simply identifying Melchizedek with his reference to the incident after the battle. Now he goes on to the significance of Melchizedek's name and title: "king of righteousness" and "king of Salem" respectively. The place name "Salem" comes from the same root as *shalom* (Hebrew for "peace"—GK 8934), and it may accordingly be translated in this way. This word means more than absence of war; it signifies the presence of positive blessing. In the NT "peace" (GK *1645*) means the result of Christ's work for us (cf. Ro 5:1). We are reminded of the promised Messiah as "Prince of Peace" (Isa 9:6; cf. also "righteousness" in v.7, another distinctive aspect of Christ's saving work).

3 The terms "without father" and "without mother" were often used for waifs of unknown parentage, for illegitimate children, for people who came from unimportant families, and sometimes for deities who were supposed to take their origin from one sex only. Some scholars hold that Melchizedek is viewed in the last mentioned way and is being pictured as an angelic being. But it seems more likely that the author is assuming that the silences of Scripture are as much due to inspiration as are its statements. When nothing is recorded of the parentage of this man, it need not be assumed that he had no parents but simply that the absence of the record is significant. Melchizedek is also "without genealogy." Taken together, the three aspects are striking, for in antiquity a priest's genealogy was considered all-important. After the Exile, certain priests whose genealogy could not be established "were excluded from the priesthood as unclean" (Ne 7:64). Moreover,

the priesthood of Melchizedek is without any end.

What was true of Melchizedek simply as a matter of record was true of Christ historically, but they also have significant spiritual dimensions in a fuller sense. The writer is, of course, speaking of the Son's eternal nature, not of his appearance in the Incarnation. He uses the official title of Jesus—"Son of God"—as in 4:14; 6:6; 10:29 (cf. 1:5; 5:5). Since the writer does not use this often, we may sense an emphasis on the high dignity of the Son of God. Moreover, it is the Son of God who is the standard, not the ancient priest-king. The writer says that Melchizedek is "made like" the Son of God, not that the Son of God is like Melchizedek. Thus it is not that Melchizedek sets the pattern and Jesus follows it. Rather, the record about Melchizedek is so arranged that it brings out certain truths that apply far more fully to Jesus than they do to Melchizedek.

4 The author proceeds to bring out the greatness of Melchizedek with an argument that the modern mind may find rather curious but which would have been compelling to his contemporaries. In the ancient world, it was generally recognized that there was an obligation to pay tithes to important religious functionaries. This implies a certain subjection on the part of those paying. So it was significant that Abraham paid to Melchizedek "a tenth of the plunder." From the spoils of victory an offering would often be made to the gods as a thanksgiving. Abraham gave a tenth of the very best to Melchizedek.

5–6a Here the meaning of the payment of the tithe is spelled out. Not only was such a payment widely customary, but the law required it to be made. The writer speaks of "the descendants of Levi who become priests" as "collecting a tenth from the people." In the law it was provided that the people were to pay tithes to the Levites (Nu 18:21, 24). But the Levites similarly paid tithes to the priests (Nu 18:26ff.); so it could well be said that the people paid tithes to the priests (and in the first century it seems that the priests themselves carried out the whole tithing operation).

The writer is strongly interested in "the law" (GK *3795*), which he mentions fourteen times. Here it means the law of Moses. The law required tithes to be taken from people of whom the priests were "brothers." There is a sense in which the priests had no inherent superiority, for they were related to those who gave tithes to them. They owed their ability to collect tithes to the provision made in the law and not to any natural superiority. But with Melchizedek it was different. He "did not trace his descent from Levi." Melchizedek was not simply one among a host of brothers. He was a solitary figure of grandeur. And he exacted tithes not simply from his brothers but from Abraham. His greatness stands out.

6b–7 Not only did Melchizedek exact tithes from Abraham, but he also blessed him. The giving of a blessing was a significant act in antiquity. As used here, it is an official pronouncement given by an authorized person. When that happens, there is no denying that it proceeds from a superior: "The lesser person is blessed by the greater."

In the Genesis account Melchizedek makes no claims, nor does Abraham concede anything in words. But both Abraham's giving of tithes and his receiving a blessing from Melchizedek implicitly acknowledge the superior place of Melchizedek. The situation is clear to all parties. The author is simply drawing attention to what the narrative clearly suggests about the superior status of Melchizedek. Even when Abraham is seen as the one "who had the promises," Melchizedek is superior.

8 In the Levitical system, those who receive tithes eventually die. But in the Melchizedek episode, tithes are received by one who is "living." Melchizedek is in strong contrast to the Aaronic priests. The writer does not say that Melchizedek lives on but that the testimony about him is that he lives. Once more he is emphasizing the silence of Scripture to bring out his point, for Scripture records nothing about the death of Melchizedek (v.3). This must be borne in mind when estimating the significance of the incident and the way the priest-king prefigures Christ.

9–10 The expression "one might even say" often introduces a statement that startles a reader and requires one to be careful against misinterpretation. The characteristic of Levi (and his descendants after him) was not that of paying but of receiving tithes. Of course, there is something of the "in-a-manner-of-speaking" about Levi's collecting of tithes, just as there is in his paying of them, because he collects them not in person but through his descendants. But the startling thing is that he should be said to pay tithes at all.

In other words, when Abraham paid Melchizedek a tithe, the author sees Levi as paying it, for "Levi was still in the body of his ancestor." This is a way of speaking we find here and there in the Bible when the ancestor includes the descendants. For example, it was said to Rebekah that not two children but "two nations are in your womb" (Ge 25:23). Levi and all subsequent priests were thus included in the payment of the tithe. The author wants his readers to be in no doubt about the superiority of Christ to any other priests, and he sees the mysterious figure of Melchizedek as powerfully illustrating this superiority.

B. The Royal Priesthood of Melchizedek and of Christ (7:11–14)

For the Jew there was an air of finality about the law; it was God's definitive word to his people. Also, the Jews felt that the Aaronic priesthood was superior to that of Melchizedek, for the law came later than Melchizedek and thus replaced all previous priesthoods. But the author points out that the priesthood of Melchizedek was spoken of in Ps 110, long after the giving of the law. That God spoke through David about the Melchizedekian priesthood while the Aaronic priesthood was still a going concern, shows that the priests of the line of Aaron could not accomplish what a priesthood truly aimed at. And because the priesthood and the law went together, a change in priesthood also meant a change in the law. The author sees it as significant that Jesus did not come from the priestly tribe of Levi but from the royal tribe of Judah. This fits in with the fact that Jesus' priesthood is of the order of Melchizedek and that he was king as well as priest.

11 Here "perfection" (GK 5459) means the condition in which people are acceptable to God. The work of the priests of the line of Levi aimed at bringing about this acceptability, but our author tells us that they failed. That the writer of Ps 110 speaks of another priest shows that the Levitical priests had not accomplished what they aimed at. The words in parentheses show that the law and the priesthood were closely connected.

We ought not to think of the law and the priesthood as two separate things that happened to be operative at the same time among the same people. The priesthood was the very basis of the law. Without that priesthood it would be impossible for the law to operate in its fullness. Thus the declaration by the psalmist (v.17) that there would be another priest was devastating. He looked for a priest "in the order of Melchizedek, not in the order of Aaron." The Aaronic priesthood was not succeeding and thus had to be replaced by a more effective priesthood.

12 The link between the priesthood and the law meant that a change in the one involved a change in the other. The author is speaking of a change from one kind of priesthood to another. Priesthood like that of Melchizedek differs fundamentally from that after the order of Aaron. Christ is not another Aaron; he replaces Aaron with a priesthood that is both different and better. And with the Aaronic priesthood went the law that had been erected with that priesthood as its basis. So the author says there must be a change of law.

13 The change in the law is seen in that Jesus did not belong to the tribe recognized by the law as the priestly tribe. His tribe was "different," which may mean no more than that it was another than the priestly tribe or that the tribe was of a different nature. It was a nonpriestly tribe. In fact, it was a royal tribe. From this tribe no one "has ever served at the altar," and Jesus has a permanent share in that tribe.

But what about David and Solomon, who were of the tribe of Judah and who offered sacrifices (2Sa 6:12–13, 17–18; 24:25; 1Ki 3:4; 8:62ff.)? Two things should be said about this. (1) It is possible that these kings did not do the actual ceremony. (It is unlikely that Solomon personally offered 22,000 oxen and 120,000 sheep.) David and Solomon may have "offered" in the sense that they provided the sacrificial victims, leaving priests to perform the liturgical function. (2) Even if these kings did sometimes perform the actual offering, this was occasional and not their regular function. The author's concern is the regular ministrations of a priest at the altar, which belonged to Aaron and his sons during the OT period.

14 "For" introduces the explanation of the preceding. The author calls Jesus "our Lord" (GK 3261) again only in 13:20 (a title usually reserved for the Father). His verb "descended" (GK 422) is unusual here. It means "rise" or "spring up," and it can be used of the rising of a star or of the springing up of a shoot from the roots of a plant. The author may have in mind the rising of a star or, more likely, the OT prophecies about the Messiah being a shoot from the root of David (see Isa 11:1; Jer 23:5). Here Jesus is said to come "from Judah," a tribe for which Moses had nothing to say about priests; the law did not envisage priests from any tribe other than Levi. That is what made a priesthood like Melchizedek's so unusual.

C. Christ's Priesthood Superior (7:15–28)

The author pursues his theme of the superiority of Christ—superior because of his life, the divine oath, the permanence of his priesthood, and his sacrifice.

1. Because of his life (7:15–19)

15 What it is that is "even more clear" is not said (there is nothing in the Greek equivalent to NIV's "what we have said"). Most likely the expression is meant to include both the ineffectiveness of the Levitical priesthood and the abrogation of the law. It is the appearance of a priest "like Melchizedek" that is the decisive factor.

16 This priest is distinguished by the quality of his life. "A regulation as to his ancestry" renders an expression that is literally "a law of a fleshly commandment." This phrase includes this new priest's ancestry, but it may well be wider including all that is "fleshly" about the law. Christ's priesthood is not based on this type of law, but it depends on "the power of an indestructible life." There is a special quality about the life of Christ. It does not end, nor can it end.

17 "For" introduces the clinching testimony of Scripture, giving the reason for the foregoing. It is quoted verbatim as in 5:6 (see comments) and establishes the special character of Christ's priesthood, because of no other priest could it be said that his life was "indestructible." Though it could be said that the Aaronic priesthood was "a priesthood that will continue for all generations" (Ex 40:15), no individual priest is "forever."

18 "Regulation" refers, as in v.16, to the whole law. The Levitical system in its entirety is "set aside" and annulled by Christ's coming and work. At the same time, there is a connection (implied by the word "former"). The Levitical system was not simply earlier in time; it also prepared the way for the coming of Christ. But it had to give way because it was "weak and useless." It could not give people strength to meet all the needs of life. It could not bring salvation.

19 The parenthesis underlines the defects of the law. The writer does not explain what he means by "made perfect" (see comments on 2:10), but clearly he has in mind something like "made fit for God." The law did not give people complete and lasting access to the presence of God. It had its merits, but it did not satisfy their deepest needs. For the writer's use of "better," see comments on 1:4; and for his use of "hope," see comments on 3:6; 6:11. The thought of what is "better" is characteristic of Hebrews, and "hope" is central to the Christian way. Law and Gospel stand in contrast. The Gospel is "better" because it enables people to "draw near to God." It was this that the old way could not bring about, but the new way can.

2. Because of the divine oath (7:20–22)

The argument is now developed with reference to the oath (cf. Ps 110:4) that established the Melchizedekian priesthood. There was no such oath when the Aaronic priesthood was set up, which means that this priesthood lacks the permanence so characteristic of the other priesthood. There was always something conditional about Aaron's priesthood.

20–21 The oath declares the purpose of God in an absolute fashion. It allows of no qualification on account of human weakness or sinfulness or anything else. So the writer contrasts the priesthood that has the security of the divine oath to that which lacked it. Christ is contrasted with the Levitical priests, and the importance of the oath is stressed. It was not simply that an oath was sworn at the same time as he was made priest but that the oath was the very essence of what was done. That is the point of the argument. Psalm 110 is quoted once more, this time beginning a little earlier to include the reference to the swearing of the oath and the assurance that the Lord will not change his mind. The new priesthood is permanent. There is no question of its ever being done away.

22 "Guarantee" (GK *1583*) brings before us an unusual idea. The old covenant was established with a mediator (Gal 3:19) but with no one to guarantee that the people would fulfill their undertaking. But Jesus stands as a continuing guarantor and that in two directions. He guarantees to the people that God will fulfill his covenant of forgiveness, and he guarantees to God that those who are in him are acceptable.

This is the writer's first use of the term "covenant" (GK *1347*), an important word he uses seventeen times. In nonbiblical Greek this word denotes a last will and testament, but in the LXX it is the normal rendering of the Hebrew *berit* ("covenant"; GK 1382). In the NT it usually means "covenant," though now and then the meaning "testament" is not out of mind (e.g., 9:16). There is something absolute about a will. One cannot dicker with the testator. And in like manner, humans cannot bargain with God; he lays down the terms.

3. Because of its permanence (7:23–25)

It matters to the author that Christ's life was different in quality from other lives. He has emphasized this in vv.15ff., and he comes back to it with the thought that the permanence of Christ's priesthood makes it superior to the Levitical priesthood. His life is such that there is no need and no place for a successor.

23–24 Once more the Levitical priests are set in contrast to Christ. They had to be numerous because like all people they died, and successors were needed to keep the priesthood functioning. The death of the Aaronic priests meant the cessation of their exercise of the high priesthood. But with Christ it is different. He remains forever and thus his priesthood never has to be continued by another. The word rendered "permanent" (GK *563*), found only here in the NT, is often understood to mean "without a successor," but this meaning is not justified. The word means "that cannot be transgressed," or, "inviolable, and so unchangeable." Christ lives through eternity, and his priesthood lives with him. The quality of his life means a quality of priesthood that cannot be matched by the Levitical priests.

25 From Christ's unchanging priesthood the author draws an important conclusion about the salvation Christ accomplishes. The verb "to save" (GK *5392*) is used absolutely, which means that Christ will save in the most comprehensive sense; he saves from all that humanity needs saving from. The expression rendered "completely" is an unusual one; it signifies that Christ's salvation is a complete deliverance, no matter what the need of the sinner. It may also have a temporal sense and mean "forever" or "always." The verb "is able" (GK *1538*) refers to power. Christ's inviolable and permanent priesthood means that he has the capacity (as others have not) of bringing a complete salvation to all who approach God through him.

The author then mentions that Christ lives "to intercede" (GK *1961*) for those who come to him (cf. Ro 8:34). He is supreme, and his very presence in heaven, seated at God's right hand, as the one who died for the human race and rose again is itself an intercession. We should not infer from this verse that our Lord has to maintain a kind of continuous liturgical action in heaven for our benefit.

4. Because of his better sacrifice (7:26–28)

This section is rounded off with a glowing description of Christ as our High Priest, better qualified than the Levitical priests, and as One who offered a better sacrifice than they did.

26 This verse (beginning in Greek with the word "for") gives the basis for the preceding verse. Because Christ is what he is, he intercedes as he does. "Meets our need" implies that even our human sense of the fitness of things is able to recognize Christ's suitability for his saving work.

"Holy" (GK *4008*) signifies the character involved in the separation of human beings from God. Christ is also "blameless" (GK *179*) and "pure" (GK *299*). "Pure" contains the thought of being undefiled, and there may be a contrast between the ritual purity that the Levitical high priest must be careful to maintain and the complete moral purity of Jesus.

There is probably another contrast in the words "set apart from sinners," for Jewish tradition prescribed that the Levitical high priest was required to leave his home seven days before the Day of Atonement and live in such a manner as to ensure that he avoided ritual defilement. But Jesus' separation was not ritual. While these words refer to his spotless character and his contrast with sinful human beings, it is more likely that they should be taken closely with the following. His work on earth is done. He has accomplished his sacrifice. He has been "exalted above the heavens." This makes him the perfect intercessor.

27 There is a problem in the reference to offering sacrifices "day after day" for, while there were daily sacrifices in the temple, the high priest was not required to offer them personally; and the sacrifices that did demand his personal action, those on the Day of Atonement, took place once a year, a fact the author well knows (9:7, 25; 10:1). Perhaps what he had in mind was that it was always possible for the high priest, as for anyone, to commit inadvertent sin, which required the offering of a sin offering (Lev 4:2–3), and that thus the high priest needed to offer daily (to ensure his own fitness for ministry). We should also bear in mind that Leviticus requires the high priest to offer the grain offering each day (Lev 6:19–23). This came to be regarded as expiatory.

Jesus stands in contrast to the earthly priests. He has no need to offer for his own sins because he has none (4:15). And he has no need to keep offering for the sins of the people, for his one sacrifice has perfectly accomplished this. Earthly priests were sinful people who had to provide for the putting away of their own sin before they were in a fit condition to do anything about the sins of the people. What they did for themselves they then proceeded to do for others. But Christ's offering is different. There is none for himself. And he offered "once for all" (GK 2384). There is an air of utter finality about this expression. Characteristically, the author introduces the thought of Christ's sacrifice but does not elaborate. He will return to the thought later and develop it.

28 Here the contrast between human beings with all their infirmities and the Son with his eternal perfection is further brought out.

"The law" brings us back to the law of Moses, the law of divine origin indeed, but the law that necessarily operates among people who are "weak" (GK 819). And when the law appoints high priests, they must be limited, for they are not made from some super race but from ordinary people, with all their human frailty.

"But" introduces the contrast; "the oath" makes all the difference. This oath, we are reminded, "came after the law" and so cannot be thought of as superseded by it. And the oath "appointed the Son." Actually Ps 110, which speaks of the oath, does not mention the Son, who is referred to in Ps 2:7. But the author sees both psalms as referring to Jesus (cf. 1:5); so he has no difficulty in applying terminology taken from the one to a situation relating to the other. And the Son "has been made perfect forever." He has been made perfect through those sufferings (2:10) that bring people to God.

VII. A New and Better Covenant (8:1–10:39)

Throughout the OT period the relationship of God's people to their God was characteristically viewed in terms of covenant, which was fundamental to their thinking and outlook. It is accordingly something radically new and daring to maintain that this whole system has been done away and replaced by a new covenant. Central to the new covenant is the death of Jesus, the sacrifice that established the new covenant. The demonstration of what all this means spells out the end of the Mosaic system.

A. Christ's "More Excellent" Ministry (8:1–7)

The author leads on from his treatment of the priesthood after the order of Melchizedek to emphasize that Christ's ministry far surpasses that of the Levitical priests. The readers of the letter would be familiar with this priesthood, and the writer makes it clear that Jesus has a ministry far excelling it.

1 In this opening verse the author picks out his principal "point" (GK 3049) and proceeds to develop it. We have, he says, a high priest who is so great that he took his seat at God's right hand. "The Majesty in heaven" is a reverent way of referring to God, and to be at his right hand is to be in the place of highest honor (see comment on 1:3). The posture of sitting suggests a completed work. "Heaven" can be used in a variety of ways, but here it clearly means the dwelling place of God.

2 Christ is one "who serves" (GK *3313*) in "the sanctuary" (lit., "the holy things"; GK *41*). The former word is actually a noun, used of one who performed a variety of forms of public service. In the Bible, it is confined to the service of God, whether by angels (1:7) or by people (Ro 15:16; Php 2:25). It can even include what is done by pagan officials (Ro 13:6). It speaks of Christ in his capacity as servant, which is striking, as it immediately follows the reference to his high place in heaven.

The "tabernacle" (GK *5008*) takes us back to the wilderness days. The word means no more than "tent" and could be used of tents that people lived in. But it was also used of the tent used for worship during the wilderness wanderings (e.g., Ex 27:21). That earthly tent corresponds to a heavenly reality, and it is in this heavenly reality that Christ's ministry is exercised. "True" (GK *240*) means authentic, insofar as the reality is possessed only by the archetype and not by its copies. This is further brought out with the statement that "the Lord" pitched the tabernacle, "not man." Sin is dealt with in the way and place determined by God.

3 Earlier, the author said that high priests are appointed to offer sacrifices (5:1). Now we see Christ as high priest ministering in the real tabernacle (v.2). Thus it is "necessary" that Christ have something to offer. As he has already indicated, the author has in mind the one offering made once for all (see 7:27), not a continuous offering always being made in heaven. Even though Christ is eternally High Priest, he is not eternally offering up a sacrifice. Characteristically, he does not say at this point what is offered; that subject he will explain more fully later (9:14).

4 We must be clear that Christ's priesthood is not one of this earth (even though his offering of himself took place here). There are divinely appointed earthly priests, but Jesus has no place among them. On earth he was a layman, who performed no priestly functions in any earthly sanctuary. Those functions were performed by the priests to whom God had entrusted them. Christ's priestly functions must obviously, then, be exercised elsewhere, in the true sanctuary in heaven.

5 The earthly priests serve in a sanctuary they value highly, though it is no more than "a copy and shadow of what is in heaven." There has been much discussion as to how "Platonic" this idea is. Some remind us that Plato thought of heavenly "ideas" as the archetypes of all things earthly; they argue that the author has used the idea of an earthly sanctuary as the imperfect actualization of a Platonic heavenly sanctuary. Much can be said for the idea that his language is that of the Alexandrian modification of Platonism. But this means only that he is using popular terminology. His main thought accords with the OT, though he has added to his thinking the idea that the earthly is imperfect and the heavenly is real. Inevitably the ministry of the Levitical priests was defective; they could serve only the "copy and shadow." So we are reminded of the Lord's words to Moses that he must make everything "according to the pattern shown [him] on the mountain" (Ex 25:40).

6 The ministry of priests in a sanctuary made according to the heavenly pattern is obviously one of great dignity. But the author's point is that Jesus' ministry in the heavenly archetype is of incomparably greater dignity and worth. He chooses to bring this out by using a comparison of the two covenants. Jesus is the mediator of a "superior" covenant. "Mediator" (GK *3542*) is a legal term for one who arbitrates between two parties. Christ mediates between people and God; it is he who establishes the new covenant (see comment on 7:22). This new covenant is better than the old because it is "founded on better promises"—it concentrates on spiritual things (e.g., the forgiveness of sins) and is unconditional in nature.

7 The author brings out the superiority of the new covenant by referring to the supersession of the old one. If there had been "nothing wrong" with the old covenant, there would have been no place for the new. That the new covenant has now been established is itself evidence that the old one was not adequate (cf. 7:11ff.). The old covenant was lacking not so much in what its terms spelled out as in the fact that it was weak and unable to

B. The Old Covenant Superseded (8:8–13)

This long quotation from Jer 31:31–34 makes the point that the old covenant under which Israel has had its religious experience is now superseded by a new covenant under which forgiveness of sins is brought about. As soon as he comes to the words about forgiveness, he breaks off his quotation.

8 The writer proceeds to show that a place was indeed sought for a new covenant. God found fault with the people of old, he reminds us, and this thought leads to the quotation from Jer 31:31–34. As usual, he suggests that what is found in Scripture was written by God (lit., it reads, "he . . . said"). "I will make" (GK 5334) is not the usual word for making a covenant but means something like "I will bring a new covenant to accomplishment." The author implies that the "covenant" (GK 1347; cf. comments on 7:22) is all of God. Human beings do not bargain with God and come to an acceptable compromise. Rather, God is the one who lays down the terms. Jeremiah looks for the unification of "the house of Israel" and "the house of Judah." They had long been separated when he wrote, but his vision was large enough to take in both and to look for the day when they would be one.

9 The new covenant is contrasted with the old one. Jeremiah does not say that God will simply patch up the old covenant and give it new life, but will make a completely new covenant, with four significant differences (see vv.10–12). But first the kindness and the love of God are brought out by the reference to taking the people "by the hand" to bring them out of Egypt. The metaphor is that of a father or mother taking a little child by the hand to lead him safely to the place where he is going (cf. Hos 11:1–4). Egypt had been a place of slavery. Yet God had brought Israel out of it to set up the old covenant. But the Israelites lacked perseverance. They refused to remain faithful and found that accordingly God was ranged against them.

10 From the failures of the past, Jeremiah turns his vision to the future. Again he sees a united people as he thinks of the covenant being made with "the house of Israel." It will be made "after that time," which clearly refers to the future, though he does not locate it with any precision. The repeated "declares the Lord" keeps before the reader the truth that a divine and not a human act is in mind. The first point is that the new covenant is inward and dynamic: it is written on the hearts and minds of the people. A defect in the old had been its outwardness. Although it had divinely given laws, it was written on tablets of stone (Ex 32:15–16). The people had not been able to live up to what they knew was the word from God. Jeremiah looked for a time when people would not simply obey an external code but would be so transformed that God's own laws would be written in their inmost beings. We should not distinguish too sharply between "minds" and "hearts" (note the poetic parallelism).

The second point in the new covenant is that there will be a close relationship between the God who will be "their God" and the people who, he says, will be "my people." There is nothing really new in the terms of this promise, for in connection with the old way it was said, "I will take you as my own people, and I will be your God" (Ex 6:7). But "I will be your God" acquires fuller meaning in the light of Jesus Christ. His life, death, resurrection, and ascension mean that God has acted decisively to save a people. The God who saves people in Christ is the God of his redeemed in a new and definitive way. And when people have been saved at the awful cost of Calvary, they are the people of God in a way never before known.

11 The third significant feature of the new covenant is that all who enter it will have knowledge of God; there will be no need for anyone to instruct his or her "neighbor" (lit., "citizen"; GK 4489). Jeremiah then moves from the wider relationship in the community to the narrower relationship in the family ("brother") and says that in neither case will there be the need for exhorting anyone to know God. For "from the least of them to the greatest," all will "know the Lord." There will always, of course, be the need for those who have advanced in the Christian way to pass on to others the benefit of their knowledge. But this knowledge of God will not be confined to a privileged few. Everyone in the new covenant will have his or her own intimate and personal knowledge of God.

12 The fourth significant thing about the new covenant is that in it sins are forgiven. "For" shows how important this point is: God's forgiveness is the *basis* of what has just been mentioned. It is because sins are really dealt with that the blessings enumerated earlier become possible. God's wrath no longer rests on sinners and God does not bear their sins in mind. They are completely forgotten, because of the once-for-all sacrifice of Jesus on the cross. Sin has been completely and finally dealt with.

13 The author picks out the word "new" (cf. v. 8; GK *2785*) and sees it as making his essential point. It implies that something else is "old" and that the old has to be replaced. When God speaks of a "new" covenant, then, it means that the old one is "obsolete" and ineffective, unable to meet people's needs. And that in turn means that it is close to disappearing. It is not something people should go back to with nostalgia.

The idea of the "new covenant" is not confined to this letter. It is implied in the narratives of the institution of the Lord's Supper in Mt 26:27–28; Mk 14:23–24, and it is explicit in Lk 22:20; 1Co 11:25. Paul also saw Christian ministers as "ministers of a new covenant" (2Co 3:6). The new covenant is thus one of the strands in the NT teaching about what Christ has done for us. While it emphasizes radical novelty, we should not overlook the fact that it also points to continuity. The new arrangement retains the term "covenant," and it is established on the basis of sacrifice. In other words, it fulfills the old covenant rather than stands in outright opposition to it.

C. The Old Sanctuary and Its Ritual (9:1–10)

The author now proceeds to bring out the superiority of the new covenant by pointing to the significance of the way of worship in the old one. He concentrates his attention not on the temple but on the long-vanished tabernacle, which would have had a wider appeal to Jews than the temple had. The temple was accessible only to those in Jerusalem; but wherever Jews were, their Scriptures told them all about the tabernacle. Furthermore, it was the synagogue rather than the temple that was the center of worship for most Jews. Thus, the tabernacle was held in greater esteem by many Jews. It is also significant that the account of the setting up of the old covenant in Ex 24 is followed by the description of the tabernacle in the next chapter. So when the author wants to show the greatness of the new covenant, he naturally draws attention to the ineffectiveness of the old as reflected in the way the tabernacle was set up and used.

1 The writer has no noun with his adjective "first," but NIV is certainly correct in inserting "covenant." The author is contrasting two whole ways of approach to God—the old covenant that has been superseded and the new one that Jesus has now established. The old one had been set up with a full set of regulations for worship, prescribed directly by God. Thus the new covenant, also established by God, is its fulfillment, not its contradiction.

The old way not only had regulations but also a sanctuary described as "earthly" (GK *3176*). This sanctuary belonged to this world in contrast to the heavenly sanctuary where Jesus ministers (v.11). The first covenant, then, was established with its due regulations for worship and its holy place of this earth where worship could be carried on. The author will go on to stress the "earthly" nature of it all.

2 The tabernacle was a tent with two compartments. The term rendered "was set up" (GK *2941*) is not the usual word for the pitching of a tent but has rather the meaning of "prepare." It may be used not only of the erection of a building but also of its furnishings and equipment. This is in mind here as is shown by the list of furnishings that follows. In the first tent there was "the lampstand," i.e., the seven-branched lampstand (Ex 25:31ff.; 37:17ff.). It also had "the table and the consecrated bread" (a hendiadys for "the table of the consecrated bread"). There were twelve loaves, each baked from two-tenths of an ephah of fine flour, arranged in two rows of six, pure frankincense being put with each row. Every Sabbath day Aaron had to set them up, and it was prescribed that they were to be eaten only by the priests (Lev 24:5–9). The loaves were called "the continual bread" (cf. Nu 4:7), a name that brings out the fact that there were always to be such loaves in the Holy Place, put on a table specially constructed for the purpose (Ex 25:23–30; 37:10–

HEBREWS 9

The Tabernacle Fulfilled in Jesus Christ

According to the writer to the Hebrews, the Old Testament tabernacle was a shadow pointing to the real thing, Jesus Christ (8:6; 9:23; 10:1). This chart depicts in detail how the various parts of the tabernacle are fulfilled in Jesus Christ.

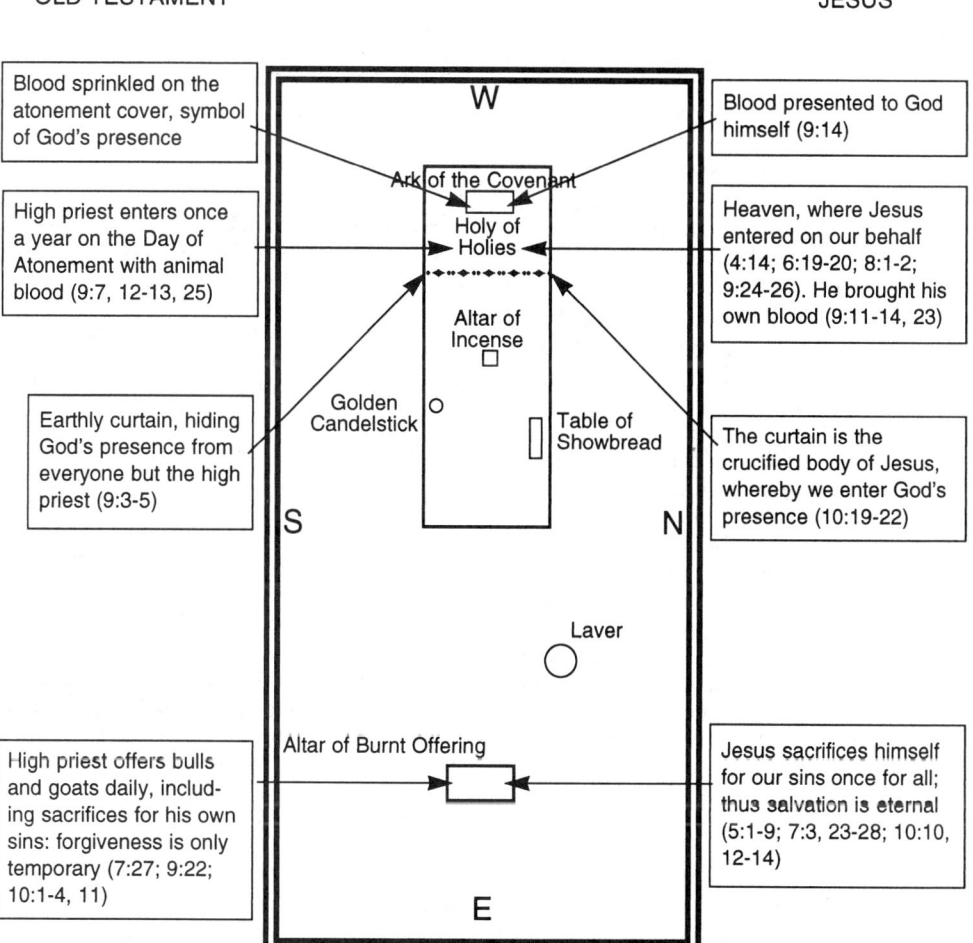

16). The tent in which these objects were placed was called "the Holy Place."

3 Then there was a "second curtain" (cf. Ex 26:31–33; 36:35–36; Lev 24:3); it is called the "second" to distinguish it from the curtain between the outer court and the Holy Place (Ex 26:36–37; 36:37–38). Behind this curtain was a tent called the "Most Holy Place," the very special place where God dwelt between the cherubim. As the author will presently emphasize, it was never to be entered by anyone other than the high priest, and by him only on the Day of Atonement.

4 The author now says some things about the furnishings of the Most Holy Place, beginning with the golden "altar of incense" (GK

2593). There is a problem in that the author seems to locate this altar inside the Most Holy Place, though its place was really "in front of the curtain" (Ex 30:6). Indeed, it had to be outside the Most Holy Place, for it was used daily (Ex 30:7–8). Most likely he has in mind the intimate connection of the incense altar with the Most Holy Place; it "belonged to the inner sanctuary" (1Ki 6:22), as is shown by its situation "in front of the curtain that is before the ark of the testimony— before the atonement cover [mercy seat] that is over the Testimony" (Ex 30:6). The writer does not say that this altar was "in" the Most Holy Place but only that Place "had" it. It is true that the same verb covers the ark that was undoubtedly inside the veil, but the indefinite term may be significant.

On the Day of Atonement, the high priest offered incense, using coals of fire from this altar, "so that he will not die" (Lev 16:12–13). The incense was indeed important.

There is no question that the "gold-covered ark of the covenant" was in the Most Holy Place of the tabernacle (Ex 25:10ff.; 26:33; 40:21). The ark contained "the golden jar of manna" (cf. Ex 16:33–34) and Aaron's rod that had budded (Nu 17:1–11). Neither of these is said in the OT to be "in" the ark; rather, they were "in front of" it (Ex 16:34; Nu 17:10). We are told in 1Ki 8:9 that in Solomon's temple there was nothing in the ark but the tablets of stone. But the author is not concerned with the temple. He is writing about the tabernacle, and it is possible that a different arrangement held there. Also in the ark were "the stone tablets of the covenant" (cf. Ex 25:16; 31:18; Dt 9:9ff.; 10:3ff.). They represented the permanent record of the terms of the old covenant and were kept in the most sacred place.

5 Above the ark were "the cherubim of the Glory." The exact form of these is not known, but most interpreters hold that they had bodies of animals; they were certainly winged (Ex 25:18–20; 37:7–9). Moreover, they were especially associated with the presence of God (Ps 80:1; 99:1), which is why they are here called the cherubim "of the Glory." They overshadowed the lid of the ark, which is here called "the place of atonement." The justification for this translation is that on the Day of Atonement this object was sprinkled with the blood of the sin offering, whereby sins were atoned for. Doubtless the writer would have been glad to dwell on the significance of all these objects. He points out, however, that it is not the time for him to do this. His argument proceeds on other lines.

6 From the sanctuary the author moves to the ritual, notably what was done on the Day of Atonement. He uses the limitations attached to the high priest's entry into the Most Holy Place to bring home the inferiority of the whole Levitical system. But he begins with the ministry of the lower priests. When the tabernacle system was established, the priests did their work in "the first tent" (NIV "outer room"). This included such things as burning incense (Ex 30:7–8), setting out the holy loaves (Lev 24:8–9), and trimming the lamps (Ex 27:20–21; Lev 24:3–4). There was a sharp distinction between the duties of the priests and those of the Levites (Nu 18:1–7).

7 "But" marks the contrast. We move from the priests to the high priest and from ministry in the Holy Place to that in the Most Holy Place. Into "the inner room" (i.e., "second tent," v.3) only the high priest might go and he "only once a year." The reference is to the ceremonies of the Day of Atonement (Lev 16). We should understand "once" to mean "on one day," because the high priest made two and perhaps even three entrances into the room beyond the curtain (see Lev 16:12–15).

To go into the Most Holy Place was dangerous; so the high priest had to safeguard himself by offering blood in the prescribed manner. His offering was "for himself and for the sins the people had committed in ignorance." Being a sinner himself, he had to atone for himself before he could minister on behalf of others. The sins "committed in ignorance" point to the truth that ignorance can be culpable. Sins of this kind do matter, and we should be on our guard against minimizing their seriousness.

8 The Holy Spirit used the pattern of the OT tabernacle to teach important truths. The limited access into the Most Holy Place was meant to bring home the fact that ordinary people had no direct access to the presence of God. Now, however, people do have such access through the finished work of Christ.

9 "This is an illustration [GK *4130*] for the present time." That is, the real meaning of the tabernacle can now be understood. The writer is contrasting the limited access that was all that could be obtained in OT days with the free access to the presence of God that Christ has made possible for his people. The trouble with the sacrificial offerings of the old covenant was that they could not "clear the conscience of the worshiper." The reference to "conscience" (GK *5287*) is significant. The ordinances of the old covenant had been external. They had not been able to come to grips with the real problem, that of the troubled conscience. This does not mean, of course, that OT saints never had a clear conscience, but they did not obtain it by the sacrifices as such.

10 The externality of the old way is brought out from another viewpoint. It concerned only matters like "food and drink and various ceremonial washings." There is no problem about the mention of food, for the OT had some strict food laws (Lev 11). But drink is not so prominent. Priests were to abstain from alcoholic drinks while engaged in their ministry (Lev 10:8–9), and there were limitations on the Nazirites (Nu 6:2–3). No one was allowed to drink from an unclean vessel (Lev 11:33–34). And, of course, there were libations accompanying some of the sacrifices (e.g., Nu 6:15, 17; 28:7–8), several ceremonial lustrations (such as those performed by the priests in their ministry; Ex 30:20), and a variety of washings for defiled people (Lev 15:4–27; 17:15–16; Nu 19:7–13). All such things the author dismisses as "external regulations." They have their place, but only "until the time of the new order." The new covenant Christ brought has replaced all the merely external regulations of the old way.

D. The Blood of Christ (9:11–14)

The argument moves to a further stage as the author turns specifically to what Christ has done. The sacrifices of the old covenant were ineffectual. In strong contrast Christ made an offering that secures a redemption valid for all eternity. In the sacrifices, a good deal pertained to the use of blood. So in accord with this, the author considers the significance of the blood of animals and that of Christ.

11–12 The author does not specifically explain what the "good things that are already here" are, but the expression is evidently a comprehensive way of summing up the blessings Christ has won for his people. The past tense in "came" points us to the Cross and all it means, though the author well knows that there is more to come than we now see. Yet the full realization of what this means is yet to come.

There is a difficult problem in the meaning of the "greater and more perfect tabernacle" (v.11) and with it the meaning of "through" (GK *1328*), which relates to this tabernacle. Also, this same Greek word (translated "by means of" in v. 12) relates negatively to the blood of animals and positively to the blood of Christ. Many commentators see a reference to heaven in "a greater and more perfect tabernacle"; others think of Christ's flesh, his glorified body, or his people (cf. 3:6). Some suggestions seem negated by the words "not man-made, that is to say, not a part of this creation" (v. 11). We should take notice of the similar expression in v.24, where the author says that it was by means of the heavenly sanctuary, and by means of Christ's own blood (not that of animals), that Christ entered the holiest of all, into the presence of God. This is an emphatic way of saying that he has won for his people an effective salvation and that this has nothing to do with earthly sacrifices.

Some suggest that Christ took his blood into heaven, implying that Christ's atoning work was not completed on the cross but that he still had to do some atoning act in heaven, just like the earthly high priest who took the blood into the Most Holy Place on the Day of Atonement. This is unwarranted. In this letter, what Christ did on the cross was final and needed no supplement. "Once for all" (GK *2384*) underlines the decisive character of his saving work. There can be no repetition. "Redemption" (GK *3391*) is the process of setting free by the payment of a ransom price, in this case the death of Jesus.

13 The author turns again to the Levitical sacrifices. In them he finds the power to effect an external purification, a cleansing from ritual defilement. He refers to the blood "of goats and bulls," which means much the same as that of "goats and calves" in v. 12. "The ashes of a heifer" point to the ceremony for purification described in Nu 19:1–10. A red heifer was killed, the carcass was burned, and the ashes used "in the water of cleansing; it is for purification from sin." When anyone was ceremonially unclean because of contact with a dead body or even by entering a tent where a dead body lay (Nu 19:14), he was made clean by the use of these ashes. The verb "sanctify" (GK 39), often used of the moral and spiritual process of "sanctification," here refers to a ritual matter. The Levitical system is not dismissed as useless. It had its values and was effective within its limits. But those limits were concerned with what is outward.

14 The "how much more" argument stresses the incomparable greatness of Christ and his work for us. "The blood of Christ" means Christ's death regarded as a sacrifice to God for sin. Atonement must be seen in the light of God's demand for uprightness in a world where people sin constantly. No view of atonement can be satisfactory that does not regard the divine demand. "Unblemished" (GK 320) is the word used technically of animals approved for sacrifice, animals without defect of any kind.

There is a problem in the way we should understand "the eternal Spirit." It may refer to the Holy Spirit, but the Holy Spirit is nowhere else referred to in this way. Thus many commentators prefer to see the "spirit" as Christ's own spirit. But perhaps we ought to see the "Servant of the Lord" imagery behind this whole passage, who is introduced in Isaiah with "I will put my Spirit on him" (Isa 42:1). Just as the prophet sees the Servant as accomplishing his entire ministry in the power of the divine Spirit, so we should see Christ as winning our salvation by a mighty act performed in the power of the Spirit of God. There is, in other words, an allusion to the Trinity here. Christ's own spirit was indeed involved in his voluntary sacrifice, but so is the divine Spirit. The writer seems to have chosen this unusual way of referring to the Holy Spirit to bring out the truth that there is an eternal aspect to Christ's saving work.

Christ, then, offered himself in sacrifice, the aim being "to cleanse our consciences." His saving work operates on quite a different level from that of the Levitical sacrifices. These latter were external and material, as the author repeatedly emphasizes. But Christ was concerned with the sins that trouble the human conscience (see comment on v.9). Thus, his sacrifice was directed to cleansing the conscience, something that the OT sacrifices could never do (cf. 10:2). This cleansing is "from acts that lead to death," and the final result of those purified by Christ is that they "serve the living God" (see comment on 3:12). The Christian way is positive, not negative.

E. The Mediator of a New Covenant (9:15–22)

Having introduced the thought of the death of Christ, the author proceeds to develop it. This death is the means of redeeming people from the plight in which they found themselves as the result of sin. It brings them an eternal inheritance. With a play on the double meaning of *diatheke* (both "a covenant" and "a last will and testament"; GK *1347*), the author brings out the necessity for the death of Christ just as the death of the testator is required if a will is to come into force.

15 "For this reason" may refer to the preceding: because Christ really cleanses us from dead works by his blood, he mediates the new covenant. But it is also possible that the words look forward: Christ mediates the new covenant so that the called might receive the inheritance. The passive voice in "those who are called" (GK *2813*) preserves the divine initiative, as does "promised" (GK *2039*). Both expressions remind us of the freeness of salvation and of God's will to bless his people. "Inheritance" (GK *3100*; see comment on 1:14) originally denoted a possession received through the will of someone who died; then it came to denote anything firmly possessed regardless of how it was obtained. "Eternal" (GK *173*) stresses that the believer's possession is no transitory affair. The salvation Christ won is forever.

Christ's death is viewed, then, as "a ransom" (GK *667*), the price paid to set free a slave or a prisoner or a person under sentence of death. While the idea of redemption was widespread in the ancient world, the word used here (the most common one in the NT) is rare—suggesting that the redemption Christians know is not simply another redemption among many. It is unique. And it system looks constantly for blood as the means of putting away sin and impurity.

F. The Perfect Sacrifice (9:23–28)

From the sanctuary and what is needed to purify it, the author turns to the sacrifice that perfectly cleanses, a sacrifice that was offered once and for all. That one sacrifice has effectively put away sin. And the author looks forward briefly to the time when our Lord will come back again, this time not to do anything in connection with sin but to bring final salvation.

23 "It was necessary" points to something more than expediency or the selection of one among a number of possible actions. There was no other way, because "without the shedding of blood there is no forgiveness" (v.22). This cannot be ignored as merely Jewish, for the Mosaic system was set up by divine command.

It is true, the author reasons, that the Mosaic system was concerned only with "the copies of the heavenly things"; it was taken up with the external. But the fact that God commanded that system to be set up means that there must be something analogous in it to the way true forgiveness of sin was brought about. Where atonement really matters—i.e., in the heavenly sphere—better sacrifices are needed than were provided under the old system.

There is a problem in understanding in what sense things in heaven—where God is (v.24)—need purification. Some deny outright that they need it, regarding the expression as a way of referring to God's people. After all, the author tells us repeatedly that it is people's consciences that need to be cleansed, that the needed cleansing is spiritual and not material. The difficulty with such interpretations is that, while what they say is true, "the heavenly things themselves" is a strange way of referring to men and women here on earth. Other commentators see here a reference to Satan's rebellion and think of that as somehow defiling heaven so that heaven itself needs cleansing. Still others think of purification as used here meaning not so much the removal of impurity as a process of consecration. Akin to that is the view that the earthly sanctuary needed cleansing, not so much because it was unclean, but because it was the place where sinners were restored. So with heaven.

On the whole, it seems best to recall that in the NT there are references to "the spiritual forces of evil in the heavenly realms" (Eph 6:12); the "rulers of this age" (1Co 2:8); the "powers" like "height" and "depth" (Ro 8:38–39), as well as "angels" and "demons." Such references seem to indicate wickedness beyond this earth. And when Christ performed his atoning work, he "disarmed the powers and authorities . . . triumphing over them by the cross" (Col 2:15). It was God's will "through him to reconcile to himself all things, whether things on earth or things in heaven, by making peace through his blood, shed on the cross" (Col 1:20). This strand of teaching is not prominent in Hebrews. Nevertheless, the language used here seems to accord with it better than with other views.

The author is fond of the word "better" (see comment on 1:4), but it is unexpected for him to use the plural "sacrifices" (GK 2602), since he is insistent that there was but one sacrifice and that Christ suffered "once for all" (v.26). Probably we should take "sacrifices" as the generic plural that lays down the principle fulfilled in the one sacrifice.

24 "For" introduces an explanation of what precedes. Christ's work for humankind was done where it really counted. We have already had the idea that Christ's ministry was not in a sanctuary that is "man-made" (v.11), and here we come back to it. Not in such sanctuaries can the atonement be made that really deals with sin. A "man-made" sanctuary is a "copy" (GK 531) of the true one. This word as used here means that the tabernacle is the shadow of the real thing; the earthly antitype points us to the heavenly reality, "the true one."

What Christ entered is "heaven itself," which is regarded as the true sanctuary. "Now" points to present activity. After his atoning work was done once for all, Christ now appears before God. We ourselves are not fit to stand before God and plead our case, and in any event we are on earth and not in God's heaven. But Christ is there in our stead and in his capacity as the one who died as a better sacrifice (v.23) for sins.

25 "Nor" carries on the negative idea at the beginning of v.24: "Christ did not enter a man-made sanctuary . . . nor did he . . . offer avails for those who sinned under the old covenant as well as for those who are embraced in the new covenant. The author insists that the sacrifices offered under the old covenant cannot take away sins. So it is left to Christ to offer the sacrifice that really effects what the old offerings pointed to.

16 The argument is not easy to follow in English because we have no single word that is the precise equivalent of *diatheke* (GK 1347). This Greek word is the normal word for a "last will and testament," but it was also used to refer to any "covenant" God makes with people. These are not the result of a process of negotiation in which God talks things over with people and they come to a mutually acceptable arrangement. God lays down the terms. The result is a covenant characterized by the same kind of finality we see in a testament. (One cannot dicker with a testator!) The author therefore moves easily from the idea of covenant to that of testament. It might help us follow him if we render the first clause in v. 15 as "he is the mediator of a new covenant, or testament." This gives two translations for the one Greek word but helps us retain something of the continuity of thought. The death of the testator is necessary for a will or testament to come into effect. The will may be perfectly valid, but it does not operate till death takes place.

17–18 The author uses a technical legal term to indicate that the will (*diatheke*) is "in force only" when a death occurs. "It never takes effect" is another legal term. Only the death of the testator brings the provisions of a will into force. From this the author reasons to the necessity for Christ's death, since he is bringing into force a new covenant (*diatheke*). It was not, so to speak, an option God happened to prefer. (The author later shows the same theme from the Law, that for sin to be forgiven blood had to be shed; i.e., Jesus had to die.)

19 When the first covenant was made (Ex 24), Moses did two things. First, he "proclaimed every commandment of the law to all the people." That is to say, he set out the terms and conditions of the covenant; he explained the requirements the covenant laid on the people, so they were left in no doubt as to what covenant membership demanded of them. Since they were now God's people, they had to obey God's laws.

Second, Moses performed certain ritual actions. In what follows the author includes some details not mentioned in Ex 24. There Moses threw blood on the altar and on the people and read the book to the people. But there is no mention of the water, scarlet wool, hyssop, or the sprinkling of the book. Water, scarlet cloth, and hyssop were used in the rite of cleansing healed lepers (Lev 14:4–6; cf. 49–51). Hyssop is mentioned also in connection with the Passover (Ex 12:22) and the cleansing rites associated with the ashes of the red heifer (Nu 19:6, 18; see also Ps 51:7). The sprinkled book was written by humans, and thus it had to be cleansed of any defilement conveyed to it.

20 "This is the blood of the covenant" (a quotation from Ex 24:8) is also reminiscent of the words used by Jesus at the Last Supper (Mk 14:24). The phrase "which God has commanded" is highly suitable in the case of a covenant where God lays down the terms. This is no negotiated instrument.

21 "In the same way" does not imply "at the same time," for when the covenant was made, the tabernacle had not been constructed. But the cleansing with blood that marked the solemn inauguration of the covenant marked also the solemn inauguration of the place of worship (according to Josephus, Aaron's garments, Aaron himself, and the tabernacle and its vessels were all sprinkled with blood). Under the old covenant sprinkling with blood was the accepted way of cleansing. Perhaps the dedication of the tabernacle should be seen as a kind of renewal of the covenant.

22 Cleansing, then, meant blood, though the qualification "*nearly* everything" shows that the author is well aware that there were exceptions. Thus the worshiper who was too poor to offer even little birds might instead make a cereal offering (Lev 5:11–13). Some purification could be effected with water (e.g., Lev 15:10), and there might be purification of metal objects by fire and "the water of impurity" (Nu 31:22–23). On one occasion gold made atonement for the warriors (Nu 31:50), while on another occasion incense atoned (Nu 16:46). But such ceremonies were all exceptional. As a whole the Levitical himself again and again." The author wants in this verse to repudiate the idea that Christ might have made an offering from time to time in the manner of the high priests. It was basic to their ministry to offer sacrifices repeatedly, just as it was basic to Christ's ministry that he did not do so. The reference here to entering "the Most Holy Place every year" shows that the sacrifices mainly in mind are those of the Day of Atonement.

The author clearly implies that only Christ's offering can put away sin. Even the sins of those who lived in old times were dealt with by Christ's one offering. If that offering had not been sufficient, Christ would have had to offer himself "again and again." Moreover, when the high priest entered the Most Holy Place, he did so "with blood that is not his own." The superiority of Christ's offering is also seen in that he does not press into service some external means, like the blood of some noncooperative, noncomprehending animal. He uses his own blood and with it makes the one sufficient offering.

26 Again the author emphasizes that there is no other way of dealing with sin than Christ's own offering of himself. If his one offering was not enough, he would have had to "suffer" (GK 4248) death over and over. The reference to "creation" carries the idea right back to the beginning.

"But now" introduces the real situation after the contrary-to-fact clause. Again the author emphasizes the decisive quality of Christ's sacrifice with the word "once for all" (GK 562). It matters a great deal to him that Christ made the definitive offering and that now that it has been made, there is no place for another. We should probably understand "the end of the ages" to mean "the climax of history." The first coming of Christ—and more particularly his offering of himself on the cross—ushered in the final state of affairs in human history. It is a common thought of the NT writers that God's decisive action in Christ has altered things radically. The Messianic Age has come—the age that all the preceding ages have led up to.

The purpose of Christ's coming was "to do away with sin," an expression that signifies the total annulment of sin. Sin is rendered completely inoperative by Christ's "sacrifice of himself." The self-offering of Christ is the decisive thing.

27 This phase of the argument is rounded off with a reference to the one death people die and the one death Christ died. There is a finality about both, but with very different consequences. Human beings are "destined to die once." This is not something within their control. A condition of life here on earth is that it ends in death. There is a finality about it that is not to be disputed. But it is not the complete and final end. Death is more serious than that because it is followed by "judgment." People are accountable, and after death they will render account to God.

28 "So" introduces a correspondence with the "just as" at the beginning of the previous verse. The passive "was sacrificed" is interesting because it is much more usual for the author to say that Christ offered himself (cf. v.26). Some see the thought here that Christ's enemies were in a sense responsible for his death, but it seems more likely that the passive voice hints at the divine purpose in that death. Once more we have the adverb "once-for-all" (GK 562) applied to the death of Christ.

"To bear sin" is a concept found in the NT only here and in 1Pe 2:24, but it is quite frequent in the OT, where it plainly means "to bear the penalty of sin." For example, the Israelites were condemned to wander in the wilderness for forty years as the penalty for their failure to go up into the land of Canaan: "For forty years—one year for each of the forty days you explored the land—you will suffer for your sins" (Nu 14:34; cf. Eze 18:20; et al.). Many see here an echo of the fourth Servant Song: "He will bear their iniquities" (Isa 53:11); "he bore the sin of many" (Isa 53:12). So the author is saying that Christ took upon himself the consequences of the sins of the many (cf. Mk 10:45).

But this is not the whole story. Christ will come back a second time, and then he will not be concerned with sin. In other words, sin was dealt with finally at his first coming, and there is nothing more that he needs to do. The second time he will come "to bring salvation." In one sense, salvation was brought about by Christ's death. But there is another sense in which it will be brought to its consummation when he returns. Nothing is said about unbelievers. At this point the writer is concerned only with those who are Christ's.

They "are waiting for" (GK *587*) him, eagerly looking for the Lord's coming.

G. The Law a Shadow (10:1–4)

The preceding sections have brought out the efficacy of the blood of Jesus as a prevailing sacrifice; now stress is laid on the once-for-all character of that sacrifice. First, the author contrasts the substance and the shadow. He sees the ancient system that meant so much to the Jews as no more than a shadowy affair. The real thing is in Christ. To leave Christ in favor of Judaism would be to forsake the substance for the shadow. The sacrificial system practiced by the Jews could not deal effectually with sin.

1 "The law" as used here stands for the whole OT, with particular reference to the sacrificial system. This is dismissed as no more than "a shadow" (GK *5014*; see comment on 8:5). It points to something unsubstantial in opposition to what is real. The law is a foreshadowing of what is to come. Perhaps those exegetes are right who see a metaphor from painting. The "shadow" then is the preliminary outline that an artist may make before he gets to his colors, and the "reality" (GK *1635*) is the finished portrait. Thus the law is no more than a preliminary sketch. It shows the shape of things to come, but the solid reality is not there. It is in Christ. The "good things that are coming" are not defined, but this general term is sufficient to show that the law pointed forward to something well worthwhile.

In the second half of this verse, the expression translated "endlessly" can go with what precedes it in the Greek (as NIV) or with what follows, meaning that the law can never bring worshipers to perfection "for all time." The latter interpretation is preferable. The author is saying, then, that the Levitical sacrifices continue year by year, but they are quite unable to bring the worshipers into a permanent or endless state of perfection. The yearly sacrifices mark another reference to the ceremonies of the Day of Atonement—ceremonies of which the author makes a good deal of use. "Can never" points to an inherent weakness of the old system: the animal sacrifices are quite unable to effect the putting away of sin. The yearly repetition repeats the failure. The same rites that were unavailing last year are all that the law can offer this year. There is an inbuilt limitation in animal sacrifice.

2 The rhetorical question here emphasizes the truth that the very continuity of the sacrifices witnesses to their ineffectiveness. Had the sacrifices really dealt with sins, the author reasons, the worshipers would have been cleansed and that would have been that. There would have been no need for repeating them (cf. 9:9). The necessity for repetition shows that the desired cleansing and atonement have not been effected. The translation "would no longer have felt guilty for their sins" obscures the reference made here to "conscience," noted so often in this letter (see also 9:9, 14; 10:22; 13:18). A really effectual atonement would mean the permanent removal of the worshipers' sins and eliminate the need for the annual Day of Atonement.

3 The author now contrasts false estimates of what sacrifices might do. "Reminder" (lit., "remembrance"; GK *390*) is a word that usually involves action. When people remember sins, they either repent (Dt 9:7) or persist in sin (Eze 23:19). When God remembers sin, he usually punishes it (1Ki 17:18; Rev 16:19); when he pardons, he no longer remembers sin (Ps 25:7). This verse uses an expression that recalls what Jesus said, "Do this in remembrance of me" (Lk 22:19), as he established a covenant in which the central thing is that God says, "[I] will remember their sins no more" (Jer 31:34). The Day of Atonement ceremonies each year reminded people of the fact that something had to be done about sin. But the ceremonies did no more than that.

4 The yearly ceremonies were ineffective because "it is impossible for the blood of bulls and goats to take away sins." The word "impossible" (GK *105*) is a strong one. There is no way forward through the blood of animals. "Take away" (GK *904*) is used of a literal taking off, as of Peter's cutting off the ear of the high priest's slave (Lk 22:50), or metaphorically as of the removal of reproach (Lk 1:25). It signifies the complete removal of sin so that it is no longer a factor in the situation. That is what is needed and that is what the sacrifices could not provide.

H. One Sacrifice for Sins (10:5–18)

Again the author rounds off and clinches his argument by appealing to Scripture as proof of the correctness of the position he has advocated. Animal sacrifices could not take away the sins of the people. But it was the will of God that sin be atoned for. Christ's perfect sacrifice of himself fulfills God's will as animal sacrifices could never do. This the author sees foretold in Ps 40. Then, as he goes on to bring out something of the utter finality of the offering of Christ, he returns to the quotation from Jeremiah he had used in ch. 8 to initiate his discussion of the new covenant. His argument up till now has been the negative one that the animal sacrifices of the old covenant were unavailing. Now he says positively that Christ's sacrifice, which established the new covenant, was effectual. It really put away sin.

5–7 "Therefore" introduces the next stage of the argument. Because the Levitical sacrifices were powerless to deal with sin, another provision had to be made. The writer then quotes from Ps 40:6–8, words that he sees as coming from Christ and as giving the reason for the Incarnation. The preexistence of Christ is assumed here. This psalm is not quoted elsewhere in the NT, and this reminds us once more that the writer of this letter has his own style of writing and his own way of viewing Holy Writ.

In the passage quoted, the LXX reads "a body you prepared for me," whereas the Hebrew has "ears you have dug for me." Most likely the LXX gives an interpretative translation of the original Hebrew. It may be expressing the view that the body is the instrument through which the divine command, received by the ear, is carried out. Or it may be taking a part of the body (the "ears") as meaning the whole body.

The words "sacrifice" and "offering" (v.5) are both general and might apply to any sacrificial offering, whereas the "burnt offerings" and the "sin offerings" (v.6) are both specific. The four terms taken together are probably meant as a summary of the main kinds of Levitical sacrifices under the old covenant.

The psalmist says that God did not "will" (NIV "desire"; GK 2527) or "take pleasure in" such offerings. This does not mean that the offerings were against God's will or that God was displeased with them. Rather, considered in themselves as a series of liturgical actions, the offerings did not bring God pleasure. They might have done so if they had been offered in the right spirit, by penitent people expressing their state of heart. But the thrust of the quotation emphasizes the importance of the will.

"Then" (v.7) means "in those circumstances" rather than "at that time." Since sacrifice as such did not avail before God, other action had to be taken. That action means that Christ came to do God's will. In his case, there was no question of a dumb animal being offered up quite irrespective of any desires it might have. He came specifically to do the will of the Father, and his sacrifice was the offering of one fully committed to doing that will.

The reference to the "scroll" (GK *1046*) is not completely clear, but probably the psalmist meant that he was fulfilling what was written in the law. The author of Hebrews sees the words as emphasizing that Christ came "to do" what was written in Scripture. The words that immediately follow in the psalm ("your law is within my heart") show what this expression implies. The author uses the word "will" (GK *2525*) five times, always of the will of God. It was important to him that what God wills is done. Christ came to do nothing other than the will of God.

8 It is not clear why the references to sacrifices are all plural here, while at least two of them ("sacrifice" and "offering" in v.5) are singular. Probably all we can say is that the plural makes it all very general. Multiply sacrifices and offerings how you will and characterize them how you will, God still takes no pleasure in them. Indeed, this is so even though the law requires them to be offered and the law is from God.

We should see this latter statement as another illustration of the attitude consistently maintained by the author that the OT system is divinely inspired but preliminary. He holds it to be effective but only within its own limited scope. The sacrifices were commanded in God's law and therefore must be offered. But they were not God's final will nor God's answer to the problem of sin. They were partial and they pointed the way to the final answer.

9 The words that Christ spoke through the psalmist about doing God's will are there for all time and express what Christ did. The verb "sets aside" (GK *359*) means "takes away" and is used sometimes in the sense of taking away by killing, i.e., murdering; it is therefore a strong word that points to the total abolition of the former way. By contrast the second way is "established" or "made firm." The way of the Levitical sacrifices and the way of the sacrifice of Christ are being set over against each other. These are not complementary systems that may exist side by side. The one excludes the other. No compromise is possible between them.

10 "By that will" may also be translated as "in that will." It may be that our author sees the sanctified as "in" the will of God. That will is large enough and deep enough to find a place for them all. We should point out a difference between the way this author uses the verb "made holy" (lit., "sanctify"; GK *39*) and the way Paul uses it. For the apostle, sanctification is a process whereby the believer grows progressively in Christian qualities and character. In Hebrews the same terminology is used of the process by which a person becomes a Christian and is therefore "set apart" for God. There is no contradiction between these two; both are necessary for the fully developed Christian life. But we must be on our guard lest we read this letter with Pauline terminology in mind. The sanctification meant here is one brought about by the death of Christ. It has to do with making people Christians by the offering of Christ's body on the cross, not with developing Christian character.

The offering of Jesus' body was made "once for all" (GK *2384*). It matters immensely that this one offering avails for all people at all times. This contrasts sharply with the sacrifices under the old covenant, as the author has been emphasizing. But it contrasts also with other religions. No other religion speaks of one great event that brings salvation through the centuries and through the world. This is the distinctive doctrine of Christianity.

11 The author now brings out the finality of Jesus' sacrifice from another angle as he considers once more the continuing activity of particularly the Levitical priests. He does not actually confine the continual activity to those priests, for he uses the quite general expression "every priest." A priest normally *stands* and ministers day by day, and keeps offering sacrifices that can never take sins away. Standing is the posture appropriate to priestly service, and in the tabernacle or temple the priests of Aaron's line never sat during the course of their ministry in the sanctuary.

The word translated "performs his religious duties" (GK *3310*) is related to the word "serves" in 8:2 (see comments). The Bible uses it only for service of a religious character. Here it clearly applies to all the services a priest performs. Yet despite all their religious activity, priests cannot deal with the basic problem—that of removing sin.

12 Jesus' work is contrasted to that of priests. He offered one sacrifice—just one alone. Then he "sat down." The author mentioned this before (e.g., 1:3; 8:1), but he put no emphasis on it. Now he stresses Jesus' posture, contrasting it to that of the Levitical priests, and the contrast brings out an important point for understanding the work of Christ. Levitical priests stand, for their work is never done but goes on. Christ sits, for his atoning work is done; there is nothing to be added to it.

Furthermore, to be seated at God's right hand is to be in the place of highest honor. Not even angels are said to have attained to this, for they stand in God's presence (Lk 1:19). When Jesus claimed this place for himself, the high priest tore his robe at what he regarded as blasphemy (Mk 14:62–63). The author is combining with the thought of a finished work the idea that our Lord is a being of the highest dignity and honor.

13 His work accomplished, the Lord now "waits" (GK *1683*). The author then quotes from Ps 110:1, with slight alterations to fit the grammatical context. The "enemies" are not defined, but the meaning appears to be that Christ rests until in God's good time all evil is overthrown. Other parts of the NT refer to God's enemies being defeated at the end time (notably Revelation), but this is not a feature in Hebrews; and we have no means of knowing precisely what enemies he has in mind. There is possibly a hint of warning to the readers—i.e., they should take care that they are not numbered among these enemies.

14 "Because" introduces the reason for the statement in v.13. Again the writer emphasizes that Christ has offered "one" offering that perfects the saints. So important is this for him that he comes back to this theme over and over. The writer does not say that Christ's sacrifice perfects the people but that Christ does this. His salvation is essentially personal. We have seen a number of times that the author is fond of the idea of making "perfect" (GK 5457). He applies it to Christ (see comment on 2:10) and also to his people. The process of salvation takes people who are far from perfect and makes them fit to be in God's presence forever. It is not temporary improvement that he is speaking of but improvement that is never ending.

As in v.10, the author uses the concept of sanctifying, or making holy (GK 39), to characterize the saved. The present tense in "those being made holy" poses a small problem. Some see it as timeless; others think of it as indicating a continuing process of adding to the number of the saved; still others claim that it refers to those who in the present are experiencing the process of being made holy. The last-mentioned view is not likely to be correct because, as we have noticed (see comment on v.10), the idea of sanctification as a continuing process does not seem to appear in Hebrews. But either of the other two views is possible. Those Christ saves are set apart forever for the service of God. The writer, then, is contemplating a "great salvation" (2:3), brought about by one magnificent offering that cannot and need not be repeated—an offering that is eternal in its efficacy and that makes perfect the people it sanctifies.

15–17 The writer consistently regards God as the author of Scripture and, as we have seen, ascribes to God words uttered by Moses and others. He does not often speak of the Holy Spirit as responsible for what is written (see also 3:7; 9:8); but this is consistent with the writer's general approach, and we should not be surprised at it here. The Spirit, he says, "testifies" (GK 3455), a word that implies that there is excellent testimony behind what he has been saying about Christ. Once more he quotes from Jer 31:31–34 (see Heb 8:8–12), citing enough of the passage to show that it is the "new covenant" passage he has in mind; he then goes straight to the words about forgiveness, omitting everything else that does not directly apply. The author therefore emphasizes the fact that Christ has established the new covenant and that he has done so by providing for the forgiveness of sins.

18 This short verse emphatically conveys the utter finality of Christ's offering and the sheer impossibility of anything further. Where sins have been effectively dealt with, there can be no additional offering for sin. The author sees this as established by Scripture, and this is consistent with his normal use of the OT. Since the new covenant has been established as a reality, the prophetic word allows no further sacrifice for sin.

I. The Sequel—The Right Way (10:19–25)

We have now concluded the solid doctrinal section that constitutes the main section of the letter. As Paul often does, the writer of Hebrews exhorts his readers on the basis of the doctrine he has made so clear. Because the great teachings he has set forth are true, it follows that those who profess them should live in a manner befitting them. There are resemblances between the exhortation in this paragraph and that in 4:14–16. But we must not forget that the intervening discussion has made clear what Christ's high priestly work has done for his people. On the basis of Christ's sacrifice, the writer exhorts his readers to make the utmost use of the blessing that has been won for them.

19 The address "brothers" is affectionate, and the writer exhorts them on the basis of the saving events. "Therefore" links the exhortation with all that has preceded it. These saving events give the Christian a new attitude toward the presence of God. Nadab and Abihu died while offering incense (Lev 10:2), and it had become the custom for the high priest not to linger in the Most Holy Place on the Day of Atonement lest people be terrified. But Christians approach God confidently, completely at home in the situation created by Christ's saving work. They enter "the Most Holy Place," which, of course, is no physical sanctuary but is, in truth, the presence of God. And they enter it "by the blood of Jesus," i.e., on the basis of his saving death.

20 The way to God is both "new" and "living." It is "new" (GK 4710) because what Jesus has done has created a completely new situation; it is "living" (GK 2409) because that way is indissolubly bound up with the living Lord Jesus. The writer does not say, as John does, that Jesus is "the way" (Jn 14:6), but this is close to his meaning. This is not the way of the dead animals of the old covenant; rather, it is the way of the living Lord. This way to God he "opened" (GK *1590*; this word is the same one used in 9:18 of putting into effect the old covenant with blood), which hints again at his sacrifice of himself. The "curtain" goes back once more to the imagery of the tabernacle, for it was through the curtain that hung before the Most Holy Place that the high priest passed into the very presence of God.

There is a problem as to whether we take "that is, his flesh" (NIV, "body"; GK *4922*) with "curtain," which is the more natural way of taking the Greek, or with "way." The difficulty in taking it with "curtain" is that it seems to make the flesh of Christ that which veils God from human beings. There is a sense, however, in which Christians have always recognized this, even if in another sense they see Christ's body as revealing God. As a well-known hymn puts it, "Veiled in flesh the Godhead see." The value of this way of looking at the imagery of the curtain is that it was by the rending of the veil—the flesh being torn on the cross—that the way to God was opened. The author is saying in his own way what the writers of the Synoptic Gospels said when they spoke of the curtain of the temple as being torn when Christ died (Mt 27:51; Mk 15:38; Lk 23:45). The "body" ("flesh") here is the correlate of the "blood" in v.19.

21 The term "great priest" is a literal rendering of the Hebrew title we know as "high priest" (see, e.g., Nu 35:25, 28; Zec 6:11). We have had references to Jesus as "a son over God's house" (3:6) and as a high priest. Now these two thoughts are brought together. The author does not forget Jesus' high place. He has taken a lowly place (cf. the reference to his flesh, v.20), and he has died to make a way to God for us. But this assumption of the role of a servant should not blind us to the fact that Jesus is "over" God's household. Once again we have the highest Christology combined with the recognition that Jesus rendered lowly service.

22 Now come three exhortations: "Let us draw near," "Let us hold unswervingly" (v.23), and "Let us consider" (v.24). The contemplation of what Christ has done should stir his people into action. First, we are to draw near to God "with a sincere heart." The "heart" (GK *2840*) stands for the whole of our inner life; and it is important that as God's people approach him, they be right inwardly. It is the "pure in heart" who see God (Mt 5:8). Furthermore, in view of what Christ has done for us, we should approach God in deep sincerity. The "full assurance of faith" stresses that it is only by trusting in Christ, who has performed for us the high priestly work that gives access to God, that we can draw near at all.

The references to the "sprinkled" hearts and the "washed" bodies should be taken together. The washing of the body with pure water is surely a reference to baptism. But the thing that distinguished Christian baptism from the multiplicity of lustrations that were practiced in the religions of the ancient world was that it was more than an outward rite cleansing the body from ritual defilement. Baptism is the outward sign of an inward cleansing, and it was the latter that was the more important. So here it is mentioned first. The sprinkling of the hearts signifies the effect of the blood of Christ on the inmost being. Christians are cleansed within by his shed blood (cf. the sprinkling of the priests, Ex 29:21; Lev 8:30).

23 The second exhortation is to "hold" (GK *2988*) fast to the profession of hope. The author has already used this verb in urging his readers to "hold on to" their confidence and their glorying in hope (3:6, 14). He also has told them to "hold firmly" (GK *3195*) to the confession (4:14). Now he wants them to retain a firm grasp on "the hope we profess." This is an unusual expression, and we might have expected "faith" rather than "hope." But there is point in referring to hope, which has already been described as an "anchor for the soul" (6:19). Christians can expect that the promises God has made will be fulfilled because behind them is a God in whom they can have full confidence. God can be thoroughly relied on. When he makes a promise, that promise will be infallibly kept.

24 The third exhortation is to "consider" (GK *2917*) one another. The author is speaking of a mutual activity, one in which believers encourage one another rather than one where leaders direct the rest. The word rendered "spur" (GK *4237*) is actually a noun, which usually has a meaning like "irritation" or "exasperation." It is unusual to have it used in a good sense, and the choice of the unusual word makes the exhortation more striking.

Christians are to spur one another to "love" (GK *27*). This is the characteristic NT term for a love that is not self-seeking, a love whose paradigm is the Cross (1Jn 4:10). This is a most important Christian obligation, and believers are to help one another attain it. It is interesting that this kind of love is thus a product of community activity, for it is a virtue that requires others for its exercise. One may practice faith or hope alone, but not love (see also comment on 6:11). The readers are to urge one another to "good deeds" as well as to love. The contemplation of the saving work of Christ leads on to good works in the lives of believers. The expression is left general, but the writer selects as especially important love and the gathering together of believers (v.25)—an interesting combination.

25 The exhortation in this verse belongs grammatically with v.24, rather than functions as an independent exhortation. Some believers were giving up "meeting together." We have no way of knowing who these abstainers were; we know no more than that the early church had its problems with people who stayed away from church. It was a dangerous practice for any early Christian to try to live without the support of the community. Perhaps these abstainers saw Christianity as just another religion to be patronized or left alone. They had missed the finality on which the author lays such stress.

The writer goes on to suggest that Christians ought to be exhorting one another, and all the more as they see "the Day" getting near. Most certainly this Day is the Day of Judgment. The main thing is that the writer is stressing the accountability of his readers. They must act toward their fellow believers as those who will give account of themselves to God.

J. The Sequel—the Wrong Way (10:26–31)

The issues are serious. While the writer continues to express confidence that his friends will do the right thing, he leaves them in no doubt as to the gravity of their situation and the terrible consequences of failing to respond to God's saving act in Christ. God is a God of love. But he is implacably opposed to all that is evil. Those who persist in wrong face judgment.

26 The writer clearly has apostasy in mind here. He is referring to people who "have received the knowledge of the truth," with "truth" (GK *237*) standing for the content of Christianity as the absolute truth. They know, then, what God has done in Christ. If they revert to an attitude of rejection and of continual sin, there remains no sacrifice for sins. Such people have rejected the sacrifice of Christ, and the author has earlier shown that there is no other. If they revert to the Jewish sacrificial system, they go back to sacrifices that cannot put away sin (v.4). The writer adopts no pose of superiority, but his "we" puts him in the same class as his readers.

27 Far from any sacrifice to put away the sins of the apostates, "only a fearful expectation of judgment" awaits such evil people. The precise nature of this expectation is not defined, and the fact that their fate is left indefinite makes the warning all the more impressive. "Fearful" (GK *5829*) conveys the idea of "frightening." The writer describes the judgment as "raging fire" (possibly borrowed from Isa 26:11). The word "enemies" (GK *5641*) shows that the apostates were not regarded as holding a neutral position. They have become the adversaries of God.

28–29 An argument from the greater to the lesser brings out the seriousness of the situation. To despise the law of Moses was a serious matter, but this is more serious still. The law of Moses was held by Jews to be divinely given: anyone who rejected it rejected God's direction. When this happened, no discretion was allowed: the person had to be executed. In a serious matter the charge had to be proved beyond doubt. Thus the testimony of one witness was not sufficient: there had to be two or three. But when there were the required witnesses to say what the person had done, justice took over. There was no place for mercy. He had to be executed (Dt 17:6; 19:15).

The writer invites the readers to work out for themselves how much more serious is the punishment of the one who apostatizes from

Christ. It must be more severe than under the old way because Jesus is greater than Moses (3:1ff.), and the new covenant is better than the old, founded on better promises (8:6) and established by a better sacrifice (9:23).

There are three counts in the indictment of those who are apostate. (1) They have "trampled the Son of God under foot." "To trample under foot" is a strong expression for disdain. It implies not only rejecting Christ but also despising him—him who is no less than "the Son of God."

(2) They take lightly the solemn shedding of covenant blood. "The blood of the covenant" is an expression used of the blood that established the old covenant (Ex 24:8; cf. Heb 9:20) and also of the blood of Jesus that established the new covenant (Mt 26:28; Mk 14:24; cf. also Lk 22:20; 1Co 11:25). The author regards it as a dreadful thing to take lightly the shedding of the blood of one who is so high and holy and whose blood moreover is the means of establishing the new covenant that alone can bring people near to God. The apostates regard that blood as "an unholy thing" (lit., "common"; GK *3123*); i.e., they treat the death of Jesus as just like the death of anyone else. The idea of "unholy" stands out all the more sharply when it is remembered that that blood has "sanctified" (GK *39*) them—i.e., set them apart for God through Christ's death. As elsewhere in this letter, sanctification refers to the initial act of being set apart for God, not progressive growth in grace (see comment on 10:10).

(3) The apostates have "insulted the Spirit of grace." The author does not often refer to the Holy Spirit, being occupied for the most part with the person and work of the Son. Nevertheless, he esteems the person of the Spirit highly. This phrase also implies that he saw the Spirit as a person, not an influence or a thing, for only a person can be insulted. In the NT there is a variety of ways of referring to the Spirit, but only here is he called "the Spirit of grace" (cf. Zec 12:10); the expression may mean "the gracious Spirit of God" or "the Spirit through whom God's grace is manifested." Willful sin is an insult to the Spirit, who brings the grace of God to us.

30 The expression "we know" reminds us of Paul, who is fond of appealing to his readers' understanding. The author calls God the One who spoke the words of Scripture to humankind. The first quotation here is from Dt 32:35 (also quoted in Ro 12:19). It mentions that vengeance is a divine prerogative; it is not for us to take it into our own hands. But the emphasis is on the certainty that the Lord will act. The wrongdoer cannot hope to go unpunished because avenging wrong is in the hands of none less than God. The second quotation (from Dt 32:36; see also Ps 135:14) leaves no doubt whatever about the Lord's intervention, for he is named and so is his activity.

The word "judge" (GK *3212*) may mean "give a favorable judgment" as well as "condemn." In both Dt 32:36 and Ps 135:14, it is deliverance that is in mind. But in the OT God does not vindicate his people if they have sinned. Vindication implies that they have been faithful in their service. But where they have not, that same principle of impartial judgment according to right demands that intervention bring punishment. This is what the author has in mind. That one claims to be a member of God's people does not exempt one from judgment. God judges all.

31 The sinner should not regard the judgment of God calmly. It is "a dreadful thing" (GK *5829*; cf. v.27) to fall into God's hands. David chose to fall into God's hands (2Sa 24:14; 1Ch 21:13). But David was a man of faith; he committed himself in trust to God, not other people. It is different with those who have rejected God's way. They must realize that they will one day fall into the hands of an all-powerful deity. Such a fate is a daunting prospect.

K. Choose the Right (10:32–39)

After a section containing stern warnings, the author expresses his confidence in his readers and encourages them to take the right way (cf. ch. 6). He reminds them of the early days of their Christian experience, when they had experienced some form of persecution and had come through it triumphantly. This should teach them that in Christ they had blessings of a kind they could never have had if they had given way to persecution.

32 The author does not class his friends among those who go back on their Christian profession. He begins by inviting them to contemplate the days just after they had become Christians. The verb translated "received the light" (GK *5894*) means the

The Christian community addressed in Hebrews had experienced persecution for their faith. Many Chrstians in the first centuries lived in the Catacombs because of persecution, where they painted biblical scenes—such as this scene of Samson with the jawbone of a donkey (Jdg 15).

enlightenment the Gospel brought. This had resulted in some form of persecution that the readers had endured in the right spirit. There should be no going back on that kind of perseverance now. "Contest" (GK *124*) is a word used of athletic competition. It became widely used of the Christian as a spiritual athlete and so points to the strenuous nature of Christian service. On this occasion, the athletic performance had been elicited by a period of suffering they had steadfastly endured.

33–34 This suffering is further explained. "Sometimes . . . at other times" is often taken to mean that the one group of people had two experiences. But it seems more likely that it means two groups: "Some of you . . . others of you." The first group had been subjected to verbal attack ("insult") and other forms of "persecution" (GK *2568*). The readers had been made a public spectacle by being exposed to insult and injury.

The second group had suffered by being associates of the former group. This is explained as sympathizing with prisoners. In the world of the first century the lot of prisoners was difficult. They were to be punished, not pampered. Little provision was made for them, and they were dependent on friends for their supplies. For Christians to visit prisoners was a meritorious act (Mt 25:36). But there was some risk, for the visitors became identified with the visited. Yet the readers of the letter had not shrunk from this. They had endured being lumped with the prisoners. Precisely which persecution is meant here we have no way of knowing.

In addition to identifying with prisoners, the readers had had the right attitude to property. There is a question whether the word rendered "confiscation" (GK *771*) means official action by which the state took over their goods, or whether it points rather to mob violence. On the whole, the latter seems more likely. The readers had taken this in the right spirit. It would not be a surprise if they endured all this with fortitude, but that they accepted it "joyfully" is another thing altogether. So firmly had their interest been fixed on heavenly possessions that they could take the loss of earthly goods with exhilaration.

The reason for their cheerful attitude is unclear; they knew they "themselves had a better and lasting possession" in Christ, or they "had themselves as a better and lasting possession" (similar to Lk 21:19). Whichever way we take it, the "possession" (GK *5638*; the word is singular) was both better and longer lasting. The possession in Christ cannot be stolen; it is an abiding possession.

35 "So" indicates that what precedes provides a reason for the conduct now suggested. "Throw away" (GK *610*) seems to convey the thought of a reckless rejection of what is valuable. Their earlier conduct showed that they knew the value of their possession in Christ; thus the writer can appeal to them not to discard it. As Christians they had a confidence that was based firmly on Christ's saving work, and that would be the height of folly to throw away. What they had endured for Christ's sake entitled them to a reward. Let them not throw it away. The NT does not reject the notion that Christians will receive rewards, though, of course, that is never the prime motive for service.

36 Christians "need [GK *5970*, a word denoting absolute necessity] to persevere"; Christianity is no flash in the pan. This leads to the thought that doing the will of God has its recompense. The author earlier spoke of Christ as doing the will of God (vv.7ff.). Now he makes the point that Christ's people must similarly be occupied in doing that will. As a result, they will "receive" God's promise. This safeguards against any doctrine of salvation by works. God's good gift is in mind, and it is secured, though not merited, by their persevering to the end.

37–38 Now the writer encourages his readers with passages in Scripture that point to the coming of God's Messiah in due course. The "very little while" (cf. Isa 26:20) points to a quite short period. The argument is that the readers ought not let the "very little while" rob them of their heavenly reward.

The author goes on to quote from Hab 2:3–4, which he interprets as referring to the coming of the Messiah (cf. Mt 11:3; 21:9; Jn 11:27). He reverses the order of the clauses from Habakkuk, finishing with the words about shrinking back; this enables him to apply them immediately to his readers. By using the LXX, the author is able to interpret Hab 2:3 as the prophet waiting for a deliverer to come. Christ will come in due course. In the meantime, the readers must patiently await him.

The words about the "righteous one" living by faith are used again in Ro 1:17; Gal 3:11. In those passages the emphasis is on what happens to those who have faith (they will be declared righteous), whereas here the author conveys the meaning that the person whom God accepts as righteous will live by faith. Paul is concerned with the way someone comes to be accepted by God, while the author here is concerned with the importance of holding fast to one's faith in the face of temptations to abandon it.

Mention of "faith" (GK *4411*) leads us into the most sustained treatment of this subject in the NT. The term is mentioned again in v.39 and then throughout ch. 11. The first point made is that faith and shrinking back are opposed to each other. The passage does not say from what the shrinking back is. In the context, however, it must relate to proceeding along the way of faith and salvation. The quotation from Habakkuk makes it clear that God is not at all pleased with those who draw back. It is important to go forward in the path of faith.

39 The chapter closes with a ringing affirmation of confidence in which the writer identifies himself with his readers. He takes no position of superiority but sees himself as one with them. He sees only two possibilities: drawing back and being destroyed, and persevering in faith to final salvation. The end result of shrinking back is to be "destroyed" (GK *724*). But that will not be the fate of his readers; they will go on in faith and be saved.

VIII. Faith (11:1–40)

The subject of faith is now continued in one of the classic treatments of the topic. In a passage of great eloquence and power, the author unfolds some of his thoughts on this most important subject for Christians. While he does not have the same warm personal faith in Jesus Christ that meant so much to Paul, what he says is both true and important in its own right. The writer does not contrast faith with works as Paul sometimes does, nor does he treat it as the means of receiving justification. Instead, he treats faith with reference to the future. It is that trust in God that enables believers to press on steadfastly whatever the future holds for them. They know that they can rely on God. So the writer's method is to select some of the great people in the history of God's people and to show briefly how faith motivated all of them and led them forward, no matter how difficult the circumstances. The result is a great passage that not only encouraged his readers but also has encouraged hosts of Christians through the ages.

A. The Meaning of Faith (11:1–3)

The chapter begins with some general observations on the nature of faith. They do not constitute a formal definition; rather, the writer is calling attention to some significant features of faith. Then he proceeds to show how faith works out in practice.

1 Faith is a present and continuing reality, not simply a virtue sometimes practiced in antiquity. It is a living thing, a way of life the writer wishes to see continued in the practice of his readers. Faith, he tells us, is a "being sure" (GK 5712) of things hoped for. The word used here sometimes has a subjective meaning, as NIV translates it (cf. also "confidence" in 3:14). But it may also be used more objectively ("substance"), though this does not seem to be what the writer is saying. There are realities for which we have no material evidence, though they are not the less real for that. Faith enables us to know that they exist and, while we have no certainty apart from faith, faith does give us genuine certainty. Faith is the basis, the substructure of all that the Christian life means, all that the Christian hopes for.

There is a further ambiguity about the word translated "certain" (GK 1793), which usually signifies a "proof" or "test." Some take it here as "test" and some see its legal use, while many prefer to understand it in much the same sense as the preceding expression (e.g., NIV). If we were to adopt the meaning "test," then the author is saying that faith, in addition to being the basis of all that we hope for, is that by which we test things unseen. We have no material way of assessing the significance of the immaterial. But Christians are not helpless. We have faith and by this we test all things. "What we do not see" excludes the entire range of visible phenomena which here stand for all things earthly. Faith extends beyond what we learn from our senses. Its tests are not those of the senses, which yield uncertainty.

2 "The ancients" (lit., "the elders"; GK 4565), a term that may be used of age or dignity, refers to the religious leaders of past days and means much the same as "the forefathers" in 1:1. These men had witness borne to them on account of their faith. As this chapter unfolds, the writer will go on to bring out some of that testimony and link the heroes of old specifically with faith. This chapter in Hebrews is distinguished from all others by its consistent and single-minded emphasis on faith.

3 "By faith" runs through the chapter with compelling emphasis. For the most part it is attached to the deeds of the great ones of previous generations. Here, however, the writer and his readers are involved in the "we." Faith is a present reality, not exclusively the property of past heroes. Faith gives us convictions about creation. Belief in the existence of the world is not faith, nor is it faith when people hold that the world was made out of some preexisting "stuff." But when we understand that it was the Word of God that produced all things, that is faith. The emphasis on God's word agrees with Ge 1, with its repeated "And God said." The point is emphasized with the explicit statement that the visible did not originate from the visible. For the author the visible universe is not sufficient to account for itself. But it is faith, not something material, that assures him that it originated with God. This world is God's world, and faith assures him that God originated it.

B. The Faith of the People Before the Flood (11:4–7)

The author proceeds to demonstrate the universality of faith in those whom God approves. He selects a number of men and women universally regarded among the Jews as especially outstanding. He begins by looking to remote antiquity and shows that faith was manifested in the lives of certain great people who lived before the Flood.

4 The first example of faith is Abel, who brought God a more acceptable sacrifice than did his brother Cain (Ge 4:3–7). Scripture never says there was anything inherently superior in Abel's offering. Some passages refer to Abel as being a righteous man (Mt 23:35; 1Jn 3:12), while the author of Hebrews insists on the importance of Abel's faith. Abel was right with God, and his offering was a demonstration of his faith.

The passive voice in "was commended" (lit., "it was testified"; GK *3455*) implies that God is the subject; he bore witness to Abel's offerings. This indicates the importance that the author attached to Abel's sacrifice offered in faith, for rarely is God said to have borne witness. The meaning may be either that on the basis of Abel's sacrifice God testified to his servant or that God bore witness about the gifts Abel offered. The author then stresses that Abel is not to be thought of as one long-since dead and of no present account. He is dead, but his faith is a living voice.

5 The NT refers to Enoch only in Lk 3:37, Jude 14, and here. The Hebrew OT says nothing of the manner of his departure from this life, only that God "took" him (Ge 5:24). But our author follows LXX in speaking of him as "transferred," which indicates that he did not die, a truth made explicit in the words "he did not experience death." God "had taken him away" (GK *3572*). On "was commended," see comment on previous verse. Testimony was borne to him, the content of the testimony being that he was "one who pleased God" (cf. Ge 5:22, 24).

6 Though the OT does not say that Enoch had faith, the author goes on to explain why he can speak of it so confidently. It is impossible to please God without faith, and Enoch pleased God. Therefore, it is clear that he must have had faith. The author lays it down with the greatest of emphasis that faith is absolutely necessary. He does not say simply that without faith it is difficult to please God; he says that without faith it is *impossible* (GK *105*) to please him! There is no substitute for faith. He goes on to lay down two things required in the worshiper. First, he must believe that God exists. This is basic. Without it there is no possibility of faith at all. But it is not enough of itself. After all, the demons can know that sort of faith (Jas 2:19). There must also be a conviction about God's moral character, belief "that he rewards those who earnestly seek him." Without that deep conviction, faith in the biblical sense is not a possibility.

7 Attention moves to Noah. He was "warned" (GK *5976*; a verb used frequently of divine communications) by God himself; he was not acting on a hunch or on merely human advice. The warning concerned events of which there was no present indication. At the time Noah received his message from God, there was no sign of the Flood and related events. His action was therefore motivated solely by faith, not by probability.

In the expression "holy fear" (GK *2326*), some put the emphasis on "holy" and some on "fear." While it is true that this word may convey the notion of fear, it does not do so here. The author is not telling us that Noah was a timid type but that he was a man of faith. He acted out of reverence for God and God's command and "built" an ark, in order "to save his family" (lit., "for the salvation of his house"). In the NT the noun "salvation" (GK *5401*) usually refers to salvation in Christ. Here, however, as in a few other places, it is the more general idea of salvation from danger—deliverance from disaster—that is in mind. "By his faith" (or possibly through the ark as the outward expression of faith) Noah's entire household was preserved during the Flood. His faith in action condemned the people of his day who failed to respond to the example of that godly man and presumably to the reasons he gave for his conduct. Noah undoubtedly told them why he was doing such an extraordinary thing as building an ark on dry land (cf. 2Pe 2:5). Upright conduct will always condemn wickedness (cf. Mt 12:41–42; Lk 11:31–32; 1Jn 3:12).

"The world" signifies the totality of humankind of that day who did not obey God. "Heir" (GK *3101*) is used in the sense of "possessor," not strictly of one who enters a possession as a result of a will. Here we have the author's one use of the term "righteousness" (GK *1466*) in the Pauline sense of the righteousness that is ours by faith. Noah was the first man to be called righteous (Ge 6:9). He was right with God because he took God at his word and acted on it.

C. The Faith of Abraham and Sarah (11:8–19)

The great progenitor of the Jewish people and his wife are now singled out as examples of faith. The Jews prided themselves on their descent from Abraham, and the great patriarch is mentioned a number of times in the NT as one who had faith and who acted on his faith (Ac 7:2–8; Ro 4:3; Gal 3:6; Jas 2:23).

In line with this the author gives more space to Abraham than to any other individual on his list. Abraham is an excellent example of what he has in mind, for his faith accepted God's promises and acted on them even though there was nothing to indicate that they would be fulfilled. This faith is seen in his acceptance of the promise of a child when Sarah was old and even more in his readiness to sacrifice that child—the one through whom the promise was to be fulfilled—when God commanded.

8 Abraham is mentioned ten times in Hebrews. The author shows a strong interest in this patriarch. He obeyed God's call the moment it came. His prompt obedience took him out to a region as yet unknown to him but which he would later receive "as his inheritance" (GK 3100). The last half of this verse is a classical statement of the obedience of faith. People like to know where they are going and to choose their way. But the way forward can be obscure. Abraham was one who could go out, knowing that it was right to do so, but not knowing where it would all lead. God told him to go "to the land that I will show you" (Ge 12:1). Yet it was not till some time after he reached Canaan that he was informed that this was the land God would give his descendants (Ge 12:7; later on Abraham himself was included in the same promise, Ge 13:15). To leave the certainties one knows and go out into what is quite unknown—relying on nothing other than the Word of God—is the essence of faith.

9 Paradoxically, when he got to "the promised land" of Canaan, Abraham lived in it, not as its owner, but as though "in a foreign country." This earthly Canaan was a foretaste of God's heavenly country (cf. v.10). He had no rights here. He and his household "lived" (GK 2997) "in tents," i.e., in temporary dwellings. Right to the end of his life the only piece of the country he owned was the field he purchased as Sarah's burial place (Ge 23). God "gave him no inheritance here, not even a foot of ground" (Ac 7:5).

Nor was it any better with Isaac and Jacob. They shared the same promises as the descendants through whom God's purpose would be worked out. But all their lifetimes they had no more share in Canaan than Abraham did. Toward the end of Jacob's life the clan went down to Egypt, and when they came back many years later, it was not as sojourners but as a mighty people who made the land their own. The lives of the three patriarchs thus cover the whole time of the temporary dwelling in the land.

10 The reason for Abraham's patient acceptance of his lot was his forward look in faith to "the city with foundations." To people in the first century, the city was the highest form of civilized society. Nothing served so well as the pattern for the ideal community. Since it is difficult to see God as the literal "architect and builder" of the earthly Jerusalem, the ultimate reference here is to "the heavenly Jerusalem" (cf. v.16; 12:22; 13:14; also Php 3:20; Rev 3:12; 21:10; et al.). The "foundations" are not anything literal (cf. Rev 21:19–20); the expression probably means that the city is well based—i.e., a city with permanent foundations. It is eternal, more lasting than earth's ephemeral edifices.

The city owes everything to God, who is its "architect [GK 5493] and builder [GK 1321]." The first of these words means a craftsman or designer. As applied to a city, it may point to what we would call a "city planner." The second word points to one who does the actual work. God built the city as well as designed it; it owes nothing to any inferior being. The thought of this verse shows clearly that more than Canaan was in Abraham's mind when he went out in faith. God is not the "architect and builder" of Canaan any more than he is of any other land.

11 This verse presents us with a difficult problem. On the face of it, the verse in Greek ascribes to Sarah an activity possible only to males, that she deposited seed for children. Two of the best suggested interpretations are: (1) To see the words "Sarah herself" as dative and not nominative. The meaning would then be "By faith he, together with Sarah herself, received power...." Abraham then had faith in connection with the birth of Isaac, and Sarah is linked with him. (2) To take the words about Sarah as a parenthesis, as NIV does. This translation also inserts "Abraham" into the text and makes the rest of the verse refer unambiguously to a male.

There is a further problem in that in Genesis Sarah was anything but an example of faith, for she laughed incredulously at the suggestion that she should bear a son in her old age (Ge 18:9ff.). The author appears to mean that, despite her initial skepticism, Sarah came to share Abraham's faith (otherwise she would not have cooperated with her husband to secure the birth of the boy). The aged couple lacked the physical ability to cause birth, but faith introduced them to the power that brought about the birth of Isaac. "Past age" draws attention to the area in which faith had to operate. On the human level, there was no hope, but for Abraham there was hope. He knew that God had made a promise and that he is "faithful" (GK *4412*) to his promises (cf. 10:23). Faithfulness to his word is a characteristic of God.

12 "And so" introduces the inevitable result. Because God promised and Abraham believed him, the consequence necessarily followed. The smallness of the beginning is brought out: Abraham was but "one man." Moreover, he was not one from whom a numerous progeny might be anticipated because he was "as good as dead" (an expression referring to his capacity for begetting offspring, not to his general state). By contrast his descendants would be as numerous as the stars in the sky or the sand on the seashore (cf. Ge 15:5; 22:17; Ex 32:13; Dt 1:10; 10:22). Both the stars and the sand were proverbial for multitude; so the general meaning is that Abraham's descendants would be too many to count. God's blessing is beyond human calculation.

13 The author breaks off his treatment of Abraham for a moment to engage in some general remarks about "all these people," i.e., those he has dealt with thus far. They died still exercising faith, without having possessed what was promised. "All" allows no exceptions; what is said applies to every one of them. They knew that God had promised certain blessings, but they did not receive them. We must be careful how we understand this, for the author has already said that Abraham "received what was promised" (6:15). Humanly speaking, when there was no hope of having a son, he saw Isaac born. God's promise to Abraham, however, meant far more than that; it is the fullness of the blessing that is in mind in v.13. The best that happened to the saints of old was that they had glimpses of what God had in store for them.

The patriarchs did no more than "see" the equivalent of the Promised Land (cf. Moses in Dt 3:26–28; 34:1–4). "See" can be used of various kinds of sight. Here it is plainly an operation of faith that is in mind, for the word points to an inner awareness of what the promises meant. In their attitude, the patriarchs showed that they knew themselves to be no more than "aliens and strangers [GK *4215*]." This latter term means those living in a country they do not belong to, i.e., resident aliens.

The combination "aliens and strangers" reminds us of Abraham's description of himself as "an alien and a stranger" (Ge 23:4) and Jacob's words to Pharaoh (Ge 47:9). The psalmist could also describe himself as "an alien, a stranger," and add, "as all my fathers were" (Ps 39:12). It is true that Isaac once sowed "crops" (Ge 26:12), and Jacob at one time "built a place for himself" (Ge 33:17). But neither really settled down in the land, and to the end of their lives they were pilgrims rather than residents. The author sees that it was faith that enabled all these great men of old to recognize their true position as citizens of heaven and thus as aliens everywhere on earth.

14–15 To acknowledge the things stated in v.13 has further implications; namely, that the kind of people spoken of are looking for "a country of their own." If they had regarded themselves only as earthlings, they would not have retained the vision of faith with their attention squarely fixed on what is beyond this earth. The patriarchs could have gone back to Mesopotamia, had they so chosen. There was nothing physical to stop them. But their attitude excluded the possibility.

The Bedouin still live in tents as nomads, just as Abraham did in the land to which God called him (vv.8–9).

When Abraham wanted a wife for Isaac, he wanted her to be from his homeland. But he did not go back there himself. Instead, he sent a servant to get the bride and said to him, "Make sure that you do not take my son back there" (Ge 24:6). After Jacob had spent twenty years in Mesopotamia, he still regarded Canaan as "my own homeland" (Ge 30:25); and he heard God say, "Go back to the land of your fathers" (Ge 31:3). Abraham buried Sarah in Canaan, not Mesopotamia, and in due course he was buried there himself (Ge 23:19; 25:9–10), as were Isaac (Ge 35:27–29) and Jacob (Ge 49:29–33; 50:13), Jacob being brought up from Egypt for the purpose. Joseph commanded that the same be done for him (Ge 50:24–26; cf. Ex 13:19; Jos 24:32). All these men wholeheartedly accepted God's word. Since they were not earthly minded, they set their hearts by faith on a heavenly home, and they did not go back to an earthly homeland.

16 "Instead" contrasts the actuality with what might have been. The people's longing was for the heavenly country. The adjective "heavenly" (GK 2230) connects country with God and with all it means to belong to God. So firm was their commitment to their heavenly calling that God was not ashamed of them. Indeed, he is spoken of again and again as "the God of Abraham, the God of Isaac, and the God of Jacob." Sometimes God uses these very words of himself (Ex 3:6, 15–16), and Jesus used the same expression to show the truth that the patriarchs are still alive (Mk 12:26–27). Not only is God not ashamed of those servants of his, but he honored their faith by preparing a city for them (see comments on v.10). The use of the past tense here should not be overlooked. It is not that God will one day prepare their city but that he has already done so.

17–18 The writer returns from the patriarchs in general (vv.13–16) to Abraham in particular. He now brings out something of the significance of the greatest trial that this great man had to endure: the sacrifice of his son Isaac. We are apt to see this as a conflict between Abraham's love for his son and his duty to God. But for the author the problem was Abraham's difficulty in reconciling the different revelations made to him. God had promised him a numerous posterity through Isaac; yet now he called on him to offer Isaac as a sacrifice. How, then, could the promise be fulfilled? Though he did not understand, Abraham knew how to obey. His faith told him that God would work out his purpose, even if he himself could not see how that could be. So he "offered Isaac as a sacrifice." That is, in will and purpose he did offer his son. He held nothing back. At the same time, however, God did not require him to slay his "one and only" (GK 3666) son. While it is true that Abraham had other sons (Ge 25:1–2, 5–6), he had no other born in the way Isaac was and bearing the kind of promises that were made about Isaac. Abraham's faith is highlighted here. He was not passive; he took the responsibility of being the man through whom God would work out his promise. Yet he was ready to offer the required sacrifice. His dilemma is brought out with the quotation of God's promise from Ge 21:12—a promise that was to be fulfilled in Isaac alone.

19 Now the author explains why Abraham, who believed that God was going to fulfill his promises through Isaac, was nevertheless ready to offer up his son. He "reasoned" (GK 3357) that God could raise the dead. This fits in with the Genesis narrative, for as Abraham went off with the boy to sacrifice him, he said to the servants, "Stay here with the donkey while I and the boy go over there. We will worship and then we will come back to you" (Ge 22:5).

"And figuratively speaking, he did receive Isaac back from death." Abraham had reconciled himself to the death of the son in whom he had thought the promises of God would be realized. To have Isaac alive was like getting someone back from the dead. Abraham's unswerving faith in God was vindicated.

D. The Faith of the Patriarchs (11:20–22)

What impresses the author about these patriarchs was that they had a faith that looked beyond death. It was when he thought he was near death that Isaac blessed Jacob and Esau (Ge 27:2, 4), Jacob blessed Joseph's sons, and Joseph gave instructions concerning himself after he died. With all three the significant thing was their firm conviction that death cannot frustrate God's purposes. Their faith, being stronger than death, in a way overcame death, for their words were fulfilled.

20 Just as Abraham acted in view of things to come, so did Isaac. He blessed his two sons in terms that looked into the distant future (Ge 27:27–29, 39–40). The author says nothing about Jacob's deception of his old father. Perhaps one might object that the words Isaac spoke to Jacob he thought he was speaking to Esau, so that what he said did not really apply and was not an example of soundly based faith. But Isaac quickly recognized that the blessing belonged to Jacob (Ge 27:33), and later he did bless Jacob with full knowledge of what he was doing (Ge 28:1–4). In any case, the author is not interested in such details; it is enough that both blessings concerned "their future." His concern is with the faith that undergirded the patriarch's blessing. On each occasion Isaac spoke out of a firm conviction that a blessing given in accordance with God's future purposes could not possibly fail. Fittingly, the sons are listed in the order in which they received the blessings, not that of their birth.

21 Jacob's claim for inclusion in the list rests on his blessing of his grandsons Ephraim and Manasseh (Ge 48). As with Isaac, the blessing went against the natural order of birth. In fact, when Jacob was dying, Joseph tried to have the major blessing given to Manasseh, the firstborn. But Jacob crossed his hands to pick out Ephraim as the greater. God is not bound by human rules like those that give pride and benefit of place to the firstborn. This incident, like the preceding one, again illustrates the theme of the patriarchal blessing with its fulfillment far distant. At the time the words were spoken, fulfillment could be known only by faith.

The author then adds a reference to a previous incident in which Jacob "worshiped as he leaned on the top of his staff" (see Ge 47:31). He speaks of Jacob as adopting a worshipful attitude as he blessed the sons of Joseph.

22 Joseph's faith, like that of the others, looked beyond death, though his words referred to nothing more than his burial arrangements. But the charge to carry his bones to Canaan (Ge 50:24–25; Ex 13:19; Jos 24:32) gives evidence of his deep conviction that in due course God would send the people back to that land. Joseph's wish to be buried in Canaan is all the more striking when we remember that, apart from his first seventeen years, he spent all his life in Egypt. But Canaan was the land for the people of God, so he wanted to be buried there. His speaking about the "exodus" of the Israelites from Egypt and his concern about the proper disposal of his bones reflect his high faith that in due course God would act.

E. The Faith of Moses (11:23–28)

No OT character ranked higher in popular Jewish estimation than Moses. He was the great lawgiver, and the law was central to Jewish life. Many astonishing feats were attributed to him in Jewish legends. Moses is highly honored in the NT, but the references to him there are more sober than Jewish tradition (e.g., Ac 7:20–44). The author has a just appreciation for the greatness of Moses but shows none of the extravagances so typical of the Judaism of his time. Both Christians and Jews honored Abraham and Moses; but whereas the Jews tended to put Moses in the higher place and to see Abraham as one who kept the law before Moses, the Christians preferred to put Abraham in the more exalted place and see Moses as one who followed in the steps of Abraham's faith. The author is certainly interested in the way Moses exercised faith, and he gives five instances of faith in connection with the great lawgiver.

23 Like the others in this chapter, Moses lived by faith. But the reference to him begins with the faith exercised when he was too young to know what was going on—the faith of his parents. In the account in Exodus the role of Moses' mother receives all the attention, his father not being mentioned. In the LXX, however, the plural verbs in Ex 2:2–3 show that both parents were involved. In any case, the mother could not have hidden the child without the father's agreement. So both parents were necessarily involved.

NIV says both parents hid Moses "because they saw he was no ordinary child." However, the Greek word that is used here means "beautiful" (GK *842*) or perhaps "well-pleasing"; the meaning appears to be that the child was so exceptionally beautiful that his parents believed that God had some special plan for him. The king's edict was for every male Hebrew child to be thrown into the Nile (Ex 1:22). Presumably anyone who disobeyed would be severely punished. But

Moses' parents were people of faith. They hid their beautiful baby for three months, trusting God rather than fearing Pharaoh.

24 Passing over the putting of the baby in the ark of bulrushes, the finding of the child by Pharaoh's daughter, and the rearing of Moses in Pharaoh's house, the author comes at once to Moses' faith as a grown man. Stephen tells us that Moses was about forty years old when the incident in this verse occurred (Ac 7:23); the author of Hebrews writes that the decision Moses reached was that of a mature man. In full knowledge of what he was doing, Moses "refused to be known as the son of Pharaoh's daughter," which must have seemed an act of folly by worldly standards. He had open to him a place of great prestige and could have lived comfortably among the Egyptian aristocracy. But he gave it all up.

25 Moses' decision involved the ready acceptance of oppression as he cast in his lot with God's people instead of with the pleasures he could have had at the court. He was fully committed to "the people of God." Moses is seen not as a revolutionary but as a man of faith deliberately aligning himself with God's own people, even though doing that meant ill treatment. "The pleasures of sin" implies that once he saw where God's call lay, it would have been sin for him to turn away from it and align himself with the Egyptians. There would have been pleasures, but they would have been enjoyed only at the expense of disobeying God. Moreover, they would have been purely temporary. Moses had a sense of true values.

26 Here the point made in v.25 is seen from another angle. While Moses knew what "the treasures of Egypt" were worth, he counted "the disgrace for the sake of Christ" as great riches. Most likely the author thought of Christ as identified in some way with the people of God in OT times (cf. 1Co 10:4). Isaiah could say of God, "In all their distress he too was distressed" (Isa 53:9). Similarly, Christ could be said to be involved with the people.

When Moses suffered, he suffered with Christ—the same Christ whom the writer is encouraging his readers to identify with. It no doubt carried great weight with them to realize that they were being called to participate in the same kind of experiences and attitudes the great Moses had. Moses looked forward to the "reward" (GK 3632). He was not deceived by the glitter of the Egyptian court and the security of worldly safety. History, of course, has vindicated him. The choice Moses made has resulted in his influence still being felt.

27 This verse poses a problem because Moses left Egypt on two occasions: he fled to Midian after he had slain the Egyptian oppressor (Ex 2:11–15), and he went out with the rest of the Israelites at the Exodus. There would be little doubt that the former is meant here were it not for the fact that it was fear that led Moses to flee to Midian after killing the Egyptian (Ex 2:14), whereas this verse says he did not fear "the king's anger." In spite of this problem, the author seems to have Moses' flight to Midian in mind for the following reasons: (1) The order of events. The Passover is mentioned in v.28; therefore, Moses' flight seems to have preceded this event. (2) "He" left Egypt seems a strange way of referring to the Exodus of an entire nation. (3) The Exodus was the result of Pharaoh's request (Ex 12:31–32), not his "anger."

The author goes on to give the reason for Moses' perseverance in a fine paradox: "He saw him who is invisible." The OT has a good deal to say about Moses' close relationship with God: "The Lord would speak to Moses face to face, as a man speaks with his friend" (Ex 33:11; cf. Nu 12:7–8). This close walk with God sustained Moses through all the difficult days.

28 The final example of faith in connection with Moses concerns the Passover. The verb "kept" (GK 4472) can also be translated "instituted." Whichever translation we prefer, the striking thing is Moses' provision for its continuance: "For the generations to come you shall celebrate it as a festival to the Lord—a lasting ordinance" (Ex 12: 14). The author of Hebrews adds a reference to "the sprinkling of blood" (cf. Ex 12:7), which is a further illustration of faith. Nothing in the previous experience of either Moses or the Israelites justified putting blood above the doors, but their faith was vindicated when "the destroyer of the firstborn" passed over them. Moses had nothing to go on but the conviction that God had directed him. Clearly, faith triumphed.

F. The Faith of the Exodus Generation (11:29–31)

The author moves naturally enough from Moses to those associated with him. For some reason he does not mention Joshua, nor does he recount any example of faith during the wanderings in the wilderness. Since the wilderness generation was not noteworthy for faith (though there were some conspicuous exceptions), their omission is understandable. But the omission of Joshua is puzzling. Perhaps we should think of him in connection with the destruction of Jericho.

29 Some of those who went out of Egypt with Moses were anything but shining examples of faith. But they must have had some faith to follow Moses through the sea, and it is on this that attention is focused. The crossing of the Red Sea is attributed to God (Ex 14:14) and to the east wind that God sent (Ex 14:21); but the author prefers to concentrate on the faith that enabled the people to respond to what God had done. That their faith and not merely their courage was important is shown by the fate of the Egyptians. The Egyptians were just as courageous as the Israelites, for they attempted to cross in the same way. But they lacked faith, and the result was disaster. Their fate shows that the faith of Moses and his followers was real and not just a formality.

30 That the falling of the walls of Jericho should be ascribed to faith is not surprising (see Jos 6:1–21). What else could account for it? The author does not say whose faith he discerned in the story, though it was probably that of both Joshua and those who followed him. The taking of Jericho is a striking example of the power of faith. Apart from the conviction that God would act, nothing could have been more pointless than the behavior of those warriors. Rather than attack, they simply walked around the city once a day for six days and then seven times on the seventh. But once more faith was vindicated, for the walls tumbled down.

31 Rahab the prostitute seems at first sight an unlikely example of faith. But she was highly regarded among both Jews and Christians. According to Jewish tradition, she married Joshua and became the ancestress of eight priests. Among Christians, she is mentioned favorably in Jas 2:25 and is listed in the genealogy of the Lord as the wife of Salmon (Mt 1:5). She came from outside Israel and was one who might not be expected to believe in the Lord, but she acted decisively out of her deep convictions. She put her life at risk, for she would undoubtedly have been destroyed by her countrymen had they known what she was doing. So Rahab did exercise a faith that might have been very costly (Jos 2:1–21). She is contrasted to the "disobedient" (GK 578), which appears to be a general term for those who do not walk in God's ways. Rahab "welcomed" the spies; she did not act in the spirit of a combatant but looked after the Lord's men. It is significant that a woman from an immoral background could become an example of faith.

G. The Faith of Other Servants of God (11:32–38)

From particular cases the author moves to generalities. To continue in such detail would require writing at great length, and the author has no time for that. On the other hand, there are many shining examples of faith, and it would be a pity not to notice them in some way. So the author names a few outstanding people of faith without detailing what their faith led them to do and then goes on to mention certain groups of the faithful.

32 With a neat rhetorical flourish, the author shows that his subject is far from exhausted. Not having time to go through all the ones on his list, he lists a half dozen faithful men: Gideon, Barak, Samson, Jephthah, David, and Samuel. The first four of these are mentioned only here in the NT. Samuel is mentioned only twice elsewhere in the NT. David, of course, is mentioned frequently. The reason for the order of these names is not clear. It is not chronological. If we arrange them in pairs, the second of the two in each case is the earlier in time. Samuel might well be placed last as heading up the prophets who came after him, but we can only guess at the reasons for the way the rest are placed.

The writer does not go into detail about these men. The OT indicates that each one battled against overwhelming odds so that, humanly speaking, there was little chance of his coming out on top. For people in such positions faith in God was not a formality. It meant definite trust when the odds seemed to be stacked against them. They set worthy examples for the readers in their difficult circumstances. It is true that in the first four, there were serious defects in their faith. Nevertheless, even imperfect and incomplete faith receives God's approval.

33 In the list of vv.33–34, there are three groups of three. We may see them as indicating: (1) the broad results of the believers' faith: material victory, moral success in government, spiritual reward; (2) forms of personal deliverance: from wild beasts, from physical forces, from human tyranny; (3) the attainment of personal gifts: strength, the exercise of strength, and the triumph of strength. In each case it is possible to see OT examples.

There are those who "conquered kingdoms" (as did Joshua and others) and "administered justice"; the reference seems to be to people like the judges. The next group may be, as in NIV, those who "gained what was promised," or those who obtained words of promise from God. Either way they were people of faith. In the OT a number of men can be said to have "shut the mouths of lions," notably Daniel (Da 6:17–22). David also was delivered from a lion (1Sa 17:34–37), and Benaiah killed one in a pit on a snowy day (1Ch 11:22; cf. also Samson, Jdg 14:5–6).

34 When he speaks of those who "quenched the fury of the flames," the writer probably has in mind the three Jews whom Nebuchadnezzar had cast into the furnace and who then emerged unharmed (Da 3:23–27). Those who "escaped the edge of the sword" may refer to people who ran away successfully when forced to flee, or to people who emerged unscathed from battle. Probably the writer is thinking of people like Elijah, who was not killed by Jezebel (1Ki 19:2ff.). The OT contains many examples of those "whose weakness was turned to strength," such as Gideon, who also "became powerful in battle and routed foreign armies." It might fairly be said that the typical deliverance of Israel in OT times came about when a small number of Israelites (like Gideon's three hundred [Jdg 7:7] or the tiny armies of Israel "like two little flocks of goats" [1Ki 20:27]) fought at God's direction against vastly superior forces and defeated them. It was God's power that prevailed; he made these puny forces strong enough to defeat mighty enemies.

35–36 A number of women in Scripture "received back their dead" as living: Elijah's hostess (1Ki 17:17–24), the Shunammite who befriended Elisha (2Ki 4:18–37), the son of the widow of Nain (Luke 7:11–14), Lazarus (Jn 11), and Dorcas, the friend of widows (Ac 9:36–41). Sometimes, however, faith worked in another way. Some accepted torture rather than release in order that "they might gain a better resurrection," i.e., be raised to the life of the age to come with God and not simply be restored to the life of this age. A "better resurrection" perhaps implies that all will be raised; it is better to endure suffering and even torture now in order that the resurrection may be joyous. Other forms of torture were severe mockery, floggings, chains, and imprisonment.

37 Stoning was a characteristic Jewish form of execution. Some people of faith suffered at the hands of their fellow-countrymen. To be "sawed in two" was a most unusual form of killing. According to tradition this was the way the prophet Isaiah was killed. The statement that some were put to death "by the sword" is important, lest it be deduced from v.34 that people of faith were inevitably safe from this fate. While God delivered some from it, his purpose for other believers was to be slain in this way. They trusted God and knew that, whether in life or death, all would ultimately be well.

From the various ways people of faith died, the writer turns to consider the hardships they had to endure in their lives. Their clothing had been the simplest. Apparently the prophets sometimes wore sheepskins (cf. Elijah's "garment of hair," 2Ki 1:8). The reference here is not, however, so much to a definite class (like the prophets) as it is to people of faith in general who were roughly clad. That they were "destitute" is in accord with this, for the author is speaking of those without earthly resources. Misery pressed on them as they were "persecuted and mistreated."

38 To all outward appearance, these people of faith were insignificant and unimportant. But in truth they were worth more than all the rest of humanity put together, though they lacked everything. Their description is rounded off with the reminder that they had no settled homes. They wandered in lonely places, and their shelters were "caves and holes in the ground." The heroes of the faith had no mansions; they cared for other things than their own comfort.

H. The Promise (11:39-40)

The author rounds off this section with a reminder of the great privilege Christians have. The giants of the faith had done great things for God in their times, and there is no question regarding God's approval of them. Nevertheless, they would not be "made perfect" apart from the humble followers of Jesus.

39 "These" refers to the preceding heroes of the faith; "all" omits none of them. God never forgets any of his faithful servants. All of them "were commended" (lit., "had witness borne to them"; GK *3455*) on account of their faith. The importance of faith, which has been stressed throughout the chapter, continues to the end. But for all the blessing God gave them, these heroes of the faith did not receive "the promise." Verse 33 tells us that they "gained what was promised." Indeed, Abraham was cited as an example of that as far back as 6:15. But here it is not a question of "the promises" but of "the promise." God made many promises to his people and kept them. But the ultimate blessing (which the author characteristically sees in terms of "promise") was not given under the old dispensation. God kept that until Jesus came.

40 God's plan provided for "something better for us." The precise nature of the blessing is left undefined. The important thing is not exactly what it is but that God has not imparted it prematurely. "Us" means "us Christians"; we who are Christ's have our place in God's plan. And that plan provides that the heroes of the faith throughout the ages should not "be made perfect" (GK *5457*) apart from Christians. Salvation is social; it concerns the whole people of God. We can experience it only as part of the whole people of God. As long as the believers in OT times were without those who are in Christ, it was impossible for them to experience the fullness of salvation. Furthermore, it is what Christ has done that opens the way into the very presence of God for them as well as for us. Only the work of Christ brings those of OT times and those of the new and living way alike into the presence of God.

IX. Christian Living (12:1-13:19)

The last main section of the letter is largely devoted to the practical business of living out the Christian faith.

A. Christ Our Example (12:1-3)

The writer begins by pointing to what Christ has done for us. In one of the great, moving passages of the NT, he points to the Cross as the stimulus that nerves Christ's people to serious and concentrated endeavor as they face the difficulties involved in living out their faith.

1 "We" links the writer to his readers. He is a competitor in the race as well as they and writes as one who is as much caught up in the contest as they are. The word "cloud" may be used of a mass of clouds in the sky, but it is also used of a throng of people. The witnesses are a vast host.

There is a question whether we should understand "witnesses" (GK *3459*) as those who have witnessed to the faith or those who are spectators witnessing the present generation of Christians. Normally the word is used in the former sense, and it is doubtful whether it ever means simply "a spectator." Still it is difficult to rid the word of this idea in 1Ti 6:12 (perhaps also in Heb 10:28), and the imagery of the present passage favors it. The writer pictures athletes in a footrace, running for the winning post and urged on by the crowd. Yet they are "surrounded," which makes it hard to think of them as looking to the "witnesses"—and all the more so since they are exhorted to keep their eyes on Jesus (v.2). Both ideas may be present. Perhaps we should think of something like a relay race where those who have finished their course and handed in their baton are watching and encouraging their successors.

With the great gallery of witnesses about us, it is important for us to run well. So we are exhorted to "throw off everything that hinders." "Hinders" (GK *3839*) is really a noun that means any kind of weight. It is sometimes used of superfluous bodily weight that the athlete sheds during training. Here, however, it seems to be the race rather than the training that is in view. Athletes carried nothing with them in a race (they ran naked), and the writer is suggesting that the Christian should "travel light." He is not referring to sin (see the next clause). Some things that are not wrong in themselves hinder us in putting forward our best effort. So the writer tells us to get rid of them.

Christians must also put off every "sin that so easily entangles." Sin forms a crippling hindrance to good running. We must lay aside all that can hinder us in our race and "run with perseverance." The author is not thinking of a short, sharp sprint but of a race that requires endurance and persistence—a long-distance race that demands sustained effort by the runner, who keeps on with great determination. That is what the heroes of faith did in their day, and it is that to which we are called.

2 We are to run this race with no eyes for any one or anything except Jesus. He is the one toward whom we run with undivided attention. The "author and perfecter of [the] faith" may mean that Jesus walked the way of faith first and brought it to completion. Or it may mean that he originated his people's faith and will bring it to its perfection. Both ideas may be involved, but since it is not easy to think of the faith by which Jesus lived as essentially the same as our own, the emphasis seems to fall on what he does in his followers. As the heroes of faith in ch. 11 are OT characters, the thought is that Jesus led all the people of faith, even from the earliest days.

The expression rendered "for the joy set before him" is problematic. The preposition translated "for" (GK 505) strictly means "in the place of." Accordingly, the meaning may be that in place of the joy he might have had, Jesus accepted the cross. The "joy" is then the heavenly bliss that the preincarnate Christ surrendered in order to take the way of the Cross. He replaced joy with the Cross. But this preposition sometimes has the meaning "for the sake of," which is preferable here. With this understanding of the term, Jesus went to the Cross because of the joy it would bring. He looked right through the Cross to the coming joy, the joy of bringing salvation to those whom he loves. For this joy, then, Jesus "endured the cross."

The "cross" is not as common a way of referring to the death of Jesus as we might have expected. This is the one occurrence of the word outside the gospels and Pauline letters. If one "scorns" a thing, one normally has nothing to do with it; but "scorning its shame" means rather that Jesus thought so little of the pain and shame involved that he refused to avoid it; instead, he endured it. Then, having completed his work of redemption, he "sat down at the right hand of the throne of God" (see comment on 1:3).

3 "Consider" (GK 382) is a word used in calculations. The readers are invited to "take account of" Jesus, the one who "endured" [GK 5702] opposition from sinful men." He was thus in the same kind of position the readers found themselves in, and he served as the example for them. They were not being called upon to put up with something their Master had not first endured. The two verbs "grow weary" (GK 2827) and "lose [GK 1725] heart" are sometimes used of runners who relax and collapse after they have passed the finishing post. The readers were still in the race. They must not give way prematurely, nor allow themselves to faint and collapse through weariness. Once again there is the call to perseverance in the face of hardship.

B. Discipline (12:4–11)

Suffering comes to all; it is part of life, but it is not easy to bear. Yet it is not quite so bad if it can be seen as meaningful. The author has just pointed out that Christ endured his suffering on the cross on account of the joy set before him. His suffering had meaning. Thus, for Christians all suffering is transformed. The writer points to the importance of discipline and proceeds to show that for Christians, suffering is rightly understood only when seen as God's fatherly discipline, correcting and directing us. Suffering is evidence, not that God does not love us, but that he does. We are God's children and are treated as such.

4 The "struggle [GK 497, retaining the imagery of athletic games] against sin" does not seem to refer to sin that the readers might be tempted to commit but to the sin of oppressors who were trying to terrorize them into abandoning their faith. Shedding blood does not normally accompany temptation, but it was a very real possibility for those facing persecution. Jesus had been killed, and many of those honored in ch. 11 had likewise been killed for their faithfulness to God. The words "not yet" show that there was real danger and that the readers must be ready for difficult days. But they had not had to die for their faith. They were evidently concerned at the prospect facing them, and he points out that their experience is not nearly so difficult as that of others.

5–6 They had forgotten an important point: Scripture links suffering and sonship, as Pr 3:11–12 shows. The address "My son" is normal for a writer of proverbs who assumes a superior but caring position. This author, however, sees a fuller meaning in these words than that, for they are words from God to his people. When God speaks of discipline and rebuke, it is sons whom he addresses. This warning is called "that word of encouragement." The certainty of suffering encourages believers rather than dismays them because they know that it is God's discipline for them. It seems not improbable that the words should perhaps be taken as a question: "Have you forgotten?"

The word for "discipline" (GK 4082) combines the thoughts of chastening and education. It points to sufferings that teach us something. In v.4 the striving was against sin, but somehow the hand of God was in it, too. No circumstances are beyond God's control, and there are none he cannot use to carry out his purpose. So believers are not to belittle the significance of their sufferings nor lose heart in the face of God's correction. God disciplines the people he loves, not those he is indifferent to. The readers should see the sufferings they were experiencing as a sign of God's love, as Scripture already assured them.

In the ancient world it was universally accepted that bringing up children involved disciplining them. The Roman father possessed absolute authority. When a child was born, he decided whether to keep or discard it. Throughout its life he could punish it as he chose. He could even execute a child and, while this was rarely done, the right to do it was there. Discipline was to be expected.

7 It is not as misery, accident, or the like that Christians should understand suffering but "as discipline." God uses it to teach important lessons; he "is treating you as sons." The author's rhetorical question appeals to the universality of fatherly discipline. It was unthinkable to the writer and his readers that a father would not discipline his children. Perhaps we should notice in passing that while the author clearly sees believers as children of God, he does not specifically call God a father (except in a quotation in 1:5; cf. also "the Father of our spirits," 12:9).

8 The hypothetical possibility of being without chastisement is looked at and a devastating conclusion drawn. It is the universal experience of children that life means discipline. If anyone does not receive discipline, then, the author says, that child is "illegitimate" (GK 3785). This word is used of one born of a slave or a concubine, or of illegitimate children in general. The point is that such children are not heirs, not members of the family. For them the father feels no responsibility. Their freedom from discipline is not evidence of a privileged position. Rather, the reverse is true.

9 The writer appeals to the practice and result of discipline exercised in the human family. He and his readers experienced discipline from their fathers, who are seen in their capacity as trainers of their children by punishing them when they go wrong. The effect of such paternal chastisement is to arouse respect, not resentment. How much more, then, should believers submit to God's discipline! "The Father of our spirits" means something like "our spiritual Father." The verb "live" (GK 2409) as used here probably refers to the life to come. When people accept life's sufferings as discipline from God's fatherly hand, they enter the life that alone is worthy of the name.

10 There is a difference in the quality of the discipline we have received from our earthly fathers and that which comes from God. They disciplined us "for a little while," i. e., the comparatively brief days of childhood; and they did their best (the phrase implies that they made mistakes). But God's discipline is always "for our good"; its aim is "that we may share in his holiness." The word "holiness" (GK 42) points to God's holy character. The aim of his chastisement of his people is to produce in them a character like his own.

11 At the time it takes place, chastisement is never a happy affair. On the contrary, sorrow goes with it. But while it does not "seem pleasant," it does produce a result the writer calls a "harvest of righteousness and peace." Suffering can easily render people irritable and impatient with one another's faults. Therefore, it is important that suffering be accepted in the right spirit in order to produce the right result. So the author goes on to speak of those who have been "trained" (GK *1214*; another athletic word) by it, meaning those who have continued to exercise themselves in godly discipline. It is not a matter of accepting a minor chastisement or two with good grace; it is the habit of life that is meant. When that is present, the peaceable fruit follows.

C. Exhortation to the Christian Life (12:12–17)

From the acceptance of life's discipline in general, the writer turns to the way this discipline is applied in Christian experience. It is important that God's people live as God's people. They are not to take their standards from the ungodly.

12 "Therefore" links this exhortation to what has gone before. Because of what they now know of God's loving discipline, they must put forward their best effort. The "hands" (not "arms" as NIV) are pictured as "limp" and thus useless. They accomplish nothing. The knees are "weak" (see Isa 35:3, from where the writer may have taken his imagery). "Strengthen" (GK *494*) presents the picture of someone whose hands and legs are for some reason out of action but are put right. The exhortation implies that the readers are acting as though they are spiritually paralyzed. They are urged to put things right and get moving.

13 A quotation from Pr 4:26 is added. The idea is to put the paths into better shape in order to facilitate travel, specifically for the lame. The writer is mindful of the fact that Christians belong together. They must have consideration for the weak among their members, i.e., the "lame"; they must not "be disabled" (lit., "be turned away"; GK *1762*). By caring for the defective members of the congregation, the stronger members can help them along the way and revitalize them.

14 The NT contains a number of exhortations to believers to be at "peace" (GK *1645*), either with one another or with people in general (cf. Mt 5:9; Mk 9:50; Ro 12:18). People are often selfish and abrasive, but this is not the way Christians should be. For them peace is imperative, and they must put forth "every effort" to attain it. Commentators differ as to whether "all men" is to be taken in its widest sense or whether the writer means "all fellow believers." Granted that it is especially important for Christians to live in harmony with one another, there seems to be no reason for taking "all" in anything other than its normal meaning. The readers should make every effort to live peaceably with all people. While the writer is especially interested in harmony in the Christian community, he has so worded his exhortation as to cover all relations, not only those among believers.

Coupled with peace is "to be holy" (lit., "holiness"; GK *40*). Holiness means being set apart for God. It is characteristic of believers to live differently from and separate from the world. Their standards are not the world's standards. Without this readiness to belong to God, no one will see God (cf. Mt 5:8).

15 The verb rendered "see to it" (GK *2174*) is an unusual one. It conveys the idea of oversight (the verb is connected with the noun we translate as "overseer"). In this context the thought is that believers must have care for one another. The writer speaks of three things in particular that the readers must avoid. (1) They must not come short of God's grace. Paul could speak of receiving God's grace in vain (2Co 6:1) and of falling from grace (Gal 5:4). Something like this is intended here. God is not niggardly in offering grace. Accordingly, it is important for people not to fail to make use of their opportunities.

(2) They must guard against the springing up of a "bitter root." This is a root that bears bitter fruit, a metaphor taken from the growth of plants. Such growth is slow, but what is in the plant will surely come out in time. So it is possible for a seed of bitterness to be sown in a community and, though nothing is immediately apparent, in due time the fruit will appear. It will certainly "cause trouble" and possibly poison a whole community. "Defile" (GK *3620*) often refers to ceremonial defilement (Jn 18:28), but it is also used of moral defilement. Bitterness defiles people and makes them unfit to stand before God.

16–17 (3) The final warning begins with a reference to the "sexually immoral" (GK *4521*), a warning that occurs frequently in Scripture. With this is coupled the warning not to be "godless" ("unhallowed" or "profane"; GK

1013) like Esau. Esau was not spiritually minded but rather taken up with the things of the here and now. This is apparent in the incident referred to, when Esau for a single meal bargained away "his inheritance rights as the oldest son" (cf. Ge 25:29–34). He could not recognize its true value. His insistence on the gratification of his immediate needs led him to overlook what was of infinitely greater worth, his rights as the firstborn. So with the apostates.

Continuing his reflection on Esau, the author appeals to knowledge common to his readers and himself. Nothing is known about Esau's change of mind other than what we read here. It appears that in due course Esau came to realize he had made a mistake. He wanted to go back but found he could not. There is often a finality about what we do. This is not a question of forgiveness. God's forgiveness is always open to the penitent. Esau could have come back to God. But he could not undo his act.

D. Mount Sinai and Mount Zion (12:18–24)

The writer proceeds to contrast the Jewish and Christian ways by contrasting the terrors associated with the giving of the law on Mount Sinai with the joys and the glory associated with Mount Zion. He sounds the note of warning that great privilege means great responsibility.

18–19 Though the word "mountain" is not in the original Greek, there is no doubt that the events on Sinai are in mind. The writer chooses to refer to what the mountain represented—the outward, the physical, and the material. The phenomena listed are all associated with the Sinai event (see Dt 4:11). Elsewhere they are linked with the presence of God: fire (Jdg 13:20; 1Ki 18:38), darkness (1Ki 8:12), and tempest (Na 1:3); the trumpet (v.19) is associated with the end time when God will manifest himself (Mt 24:31; 1Co 15:52; 1Th 4:16).

The trumpet is spoken of repeatedly in connection with Sinai (Ex 19:16, 19; 20:18), and on that occasion the people heard the voice of God (Dt 5:24). But the effect of it all was to terrify them, and they asked that they should hear God's voice no more (Ex 20:19; Dt 5:25–27). They were overcome with awe and wanted no further part in the wonderful events.

20 The fearfulness of the giving of the law on Sinai is brought out with reference to one of the commands laid on the people, namely, that neither humans nor animals should even touch the mountain under penalty of death (see Ex 19:13). The command that nothing touch it indicates the holiness and separateness of the mountain. Killing by stoning (or by arrows) was prescribed so that those taking part would not touch the mountain themselves.

21 This verse cites a further indication of the awesomeness of the experience at Mount Sinai. At the time of the giving of the law, Moses was the leader of the people. He was known as one who had an especially close relationship with God (Ex 33:11). Yet even he was terrified. The words quoted are not found in the Sinai narrative but do occur at the time of the golden calf (Dt 9:19). The author may have had access to a tradition that recorded these words on this occasion. Or he may be including Moses in the general fear spoken of in Ex 20:18. Or possibly he is taking words spoken on one occasion and applying them to another. At any rate, he is picturing an awe-inspiring occasion, one that affected all the people and terrified even Moses, the man of God.

22 "But" is a strong word that introduces a marked contrast. It is not a Sinai-type experience that has befallen Christians. They "have come" to Mount Zion. This is one of the hills on which the city of Jerusalem was built. It sometimes stands for that city (Mt 21:5) and stands here, of course, for that city as the home of God's people. It is also called "the heavenly Jerusalem" and "the city of the living God." Elsewhere in the NT there is the thought of the Jerusalem above (Gal 4:26, where again there is a contrast with Mount Sinai; cf. also Rev 3:12; 21:2, 10).

The author has already spoken of "the city with foundations, whose architect and builder is God" (11:10). He is bringing out the thought of the ideal, heavenly city. His mention of "the living God" (see comment on 3:12) emphasizes that this city is no static affair; it is the city of a vital, dynamic, living Being, one who is doing things. For angels at Sinai, see Dt 33:2; the heavenly city is certainly not deficient on this score.

The expression "joyful assembly" (GK *4108*) most likely belongs with angels rather than with the next verse. The word meant originally a national festive assembly to honor a god, then more generally any festal assembly.

23 "The church [GK *1711*] of the firstborn" is a difficult expression. Does it mean the angels just spoken of? They are not usually called a "church," but the word basically means "assembly" and so could be applied to angels. If it refers to people, it is not easy to see it as the church triumphant because that is the same as "the spirits of righteous men made perfect" at the end of the verse. Nor is it easier to see it of the church here and now, for (1) the readers would be included and would be "coming" to themselves, and (2) it would give a strange sequence—angels, the church on earth, God, the departed. Nor are angels normally described as having their "names ... written in heaven," whereas there are references to the recording of the names of the saved (e.g., Lk 10:20; Rev 21:27). Perhaps the best solution is to see a reference to the whole communion of saints, the church on earth and in heaven. Believers not only come to it but *into* it. This would follow naturally on the reference to angels, after which there is the thought of God as Judge.

In the next part of the sentence, then, the author is concerned with the Judge (i.e., God), who has rewarded "the spirits of righteous men." It is unusual to have the departed referred to as "spirits." It is probably used here to give emphasis to the spiritual nature of the new order that the righteous find themselves in. There is a sense in which they are not made perfect without Christians (11:40). But there is also a sense in which they have been brought to the end for which they were made.

24 The climax is reached with the reference to Jesus, seen here as "the mediator of a new covenant" (see comment on 8:6). The covenant involves "sprinkled blood" (cf. 9:19–22), which reminds us of the cost of the covenant. The idea of blood speaking is not common, and there is undoubtedly a reference to Ge 4:10, where Abel's blood cried from the ground for vengeance on his killer. But Jesus' blood speaks "a better word" than that. His blood opens up for us a way into the Most Holy Place (10:19), whereas Abel's blood sought to shut out the wicked person.

E. A Kingdom That Cannot Be Shaken (12:25–29)

Earthly, material things (i.e., things that can be "shaken") will not last forever. By contrast, God's kingdom is unshakable, and the author uses the contrast as an exhortation to right conduct. He has made it plain that God will not trifle with wrongdoing. The persistent sinner can count on severe judgment. God will bring all things present to an end. Accordingly, the readers should serve him faithfully.

25 Several times in this letter Judaism and Christianity have been contrasted, and here the contrast concerns the way God speaks. Some feel there is a contrast between Moses and Christ. This may be so, but the basic contrast is between the way God spoke of old and the way he now speaks. Israel of old "refused" him, which means that in their manner of life they rejected what God said and failed to live up to what he commanded (cf. Dt 5:29). This warning was "on earth" because it was connected with the revelation at Sinai. If, then, the Israelites of old did not escape the consequences of their refusal of a voice on earth, the readers ought not to expect to escape far worse consequences if they "turn away from him who warns us from heaven" (cf. 2:2–4).

26 The solemnity of Sinai is recalled. Repeatedly we are told that then the earth shook (Ex 19:18; Jdg 5:4–5; Pss 68:8; 77:18; 114:4, 7). The writer has already spoken of the awe-inspiring nature of what happened when the law was given. Now the reference to the shaking of the earth brings it all back. At the same time it enables him to go on to speak of a promise that involved a further shaking, the one recorded in Hag 2:6. The prophet looked forward to something much grander than Sinai, a day when God would shake "not only the earth but also the heavens." The reference to heaven and earth may hint at the concept of the new heaven and the new earth (Isa 66:22). At any rate, it points to the decisive intervention that God will make at the last time.

27 The writer picks out the expression "once more" to point out the decisive significance of the things of which he is writing. There is an air of finality about it all. "The removing" (GK *3557*) of what can be shaken will occur in the final day. This physical creation can be shaken, and it is set in contrast to what cannot be shaken—the things that really matter. The author does not go into detail about the precise nature of the ultimate rest. But whatever it may be, it will separate the things that last forever from those that do not. "So that" introduces a clause of purpose. It is God's will for this final differentiation to be made so that only what cannot be shaken will remain.

28 The "kingdom" is not a frequent subject in this letter (cf. 1:8; 11:33). This is in contrast to the Synoptic Gospels where the "kingdom" frequently occurs in the teaching of Jesus (see comment on Mk 1:15). But this passage shows that the author understood ultimate reality in terms of God's sovereignty, in contrast with earthly systems. They can be shaken and in due course will be shaken. Not so God's kingdom! The author does not simply say that it will not be shaken but that it *cannot* be shaken. The kingdom is something we "receive." It is not earned or created by believers; it is God's gift.

It is not quite certain how we should understand the expression "let us be thankful" (lit., "let us have grace [*charis*; GK *5921*]"). Since elsewhere in this letter *charis* signifies "grace," this phrase more likely means, "Let us hold on to God's grace." The writer appears to be saying that we must appropriate the grace God offers and not let it go, because only by grace can we serve as we should. "Worship" (GK *3302*) is a word that is used of service of various kinds. Whether the meaning is service in general or worship in particular, it must be done "with reverence and awe." The combination stresses the greatness of God and the lowly place his people should take in relation to him.

29 In an expression apparently taken from Dt 4:24, the writer emphasizes that God is not to be trifled with. We can be so taken up with the love and compassion of God that we overlook his implacable opposition to all evil. The wrath of God is not a popular subject today, but it looms large in biblical teaching. We overlook this wrath only at our peril.

F. Love (13:1–6)

The first twelve chapters of Hebrews form a closely knit argument. In ch. 13 we come to something of an appendix, dealing with a number of practical points. Christians are to be concerned for the needs of others. Christianity is faith in action and that means love at work. So the writer draws attention to something of what it means to live in love.

1 "Loving each other as brothers" (GK *5789*) is a most important virtue in the NT. Those who are linked in the common bond of having been saved by the death of Jesus cannot but have warm feelings toward one another (cf. Ro 12:10; 1Th 4:9; 1Pe 1:22; 2Pe 1:7; see also Ps 133:1).

2 To brotherly love the author adds "entertaining strangers" (lit., "love of strangers"; GK *5810*). Entertaining "angels without knowing it" reminds us of Abraham (Ge 18:1ff.) and Lot (Ge 19:1ff.). The writer is not advocating hospitality on the off chance that one might happen to receive an angel as guest but rather because God is pleased when believers are hospitable. Sometimes unexpectedly happy results follow acts of hospitality. Hospitality was highly esteemed in the ancient world, and it was certainly important for Christians. Accommodation at inns was expensive, and in many cases inns had a bad reputation. But as Christian preachers traveled around, believers gave them lodging and so facilitated their mission. Without that, the spread of the faith would have been much more difficult.

3 The writer turns his attention to prisoners. Guests may come unbidden, but prisoners must be actively sought out (see comment on 10:34). Some people withheld help from prisoners for fear of suffering a similar punishment. But Christians should have compassion on those in prison "as if you were their fellow prisoners." "If one part suffers, every part suffers with it," wrote Paul (1Co 12:26); there is something of the same thought here. Believers should feel so much for their friends in prison and for "those who are mistreated" that they become one with them. Compassion is an essential part of Christian living.

4 From love for the badly treated the author turns to love within the marriage bond. The opening expression implies an imperative: "Let marriage be held in honor." "By all" probably means "in all circumstances." Some ascetics held marriage in low esteem, but the author of Hebrews rejects this position.

"The marriage bed" is a euphemism for sexual intercourse. He considers the physical side of marriage important and "pure." Contrary to the views of some thinkers in the ancient world, there is nothing defiling about it. Over against honorable marriage he sets the "sexually immoral" (GK 4521) and the "adulterer" (GK 3659; a word used for a violation of the marriage bond).

All forms of sexual sin come under the judgment of God. This was a novel view to many in the first century. For them chastity was an unreasonable demand to make. It is one of the unrecognized miracles that Christians were able not only to make this demand but to make it stick. Sexual sinners are likely to go their way, careless of all others. But in the end they will be judged by none less than God.

5 Sins of impurity and "love of money" are linked elsewhere in the NT (e.g., 1Co 5:10–11; Eph 4:19; 5:3–5; 1Th 4:3–6). A covetous person pursues selfish aims, whether sexual or financial, without regard to the rights of others. So the writer warns against this sin and urges contentment with what one has. Covetousness is needless, for believers have the promise that God will never leave them nor forsake them. The origin of this quotation is not clear; the words do not correspond exactly to any OT passage, though there are several statements that are rather like it (e.g., Ge 28:15; Dt 31:6, 8; Jos 1:5; 1Ch 28:20; Isa 41:17). The words point to the complete reliability of God and his promises. God's people are secure no matter what comes, because he is with them.

6 Despondency is foreign to Christians. They can speak "with confidence" (GK 2509), i.e., with an attitude of courage and trust. "We" once more links the writer with his readers; he sees his lot as bound up with theirs. The quotation from Ps 118:6 has three points in this confidence. (1) The Lord is the psalmist's (and our) "helper." This carries on the argument of the previous verse, sharpening a little the thought of the assistance that the believer may count on. (2) There is the ringing declaration of confidence as the psalmist renounces fear. With the Helper at his side, there is no reason to "be afraid." (3) The rhetorical question underlies one's insignificance. The question is "What will man do to me?" not "What can man do to me?" The psalmist is not thinking theoretically but of what will happen. No one will succeed in anything he or she attempts to do against one who trusts in God.

G. Christian Leadership (13:7–8)

The concluding section of the letter contains a number of small, disconnected units. From love the writer passes to a few thoughts about Christian leaders. This is important, for there is not much in the NT about the way Christians should treat their leaders (there is more about how leaders should behave).

7 "Leaders" (GK 2451; cf. also vv.17, 24) is a general term, used of leaders of religious bodies as well as of princes, military commanders, etc. This makes it difficult to say precisely who these leaders were. They may have been "elders," but that word is not used of them and so we cannot be sure about this. They "spoke the word of God," so that one of their principal functions was preaching or teaching. The specific tense used may point to the original proclamation of the Gospel to these readers (cf. 2:3). "The word of God" is the totality of the Christian message, and the expression reminds the readers that this word is no human invention but one of divine origin.

The word translated "outcome" (GK 1676) may mean death, and thus it seems as though past leaders were in mind. They are held up as examples to be imitated; specifically, their faith is singled out. Faith is the important thing, and the readers were being tempted to unbelief in falling back from the Christian way. They should instead follow these good examples of faith.

8 In this profound and wonderfully succinct verse, the writer's thoughts turn again to Christ. Earthly leaders come and go, but one is always there. The full name "Jesus Christ" (cf. 10:10; 13:21) adds solemnity to this pronouncement. "Yesterday" refers not to Christ's preexistence or the Incarnation, but to the past as a whole; it is part of an expression taking up past, present, and future into an impressive statement of Christ's unchanging nature. The readers need not fear that Christ is different now or will ever be different from what he has been in the past. "Forever" takes the continuity as far into the future as it will go. No matter what ages lie ahead, Christ will be unchanged through them. Christian conduct is based on this certainty.

H. Christian Sacrifice (13:9–16)

The writer has put strong emphasis on the centrality of Christ's sacrifice and keeps this steadily in view as he approaches the end of his letter. He has some erroneous teaching in mind, but we cannot define it with precision. He and his readers both knew what it was; so there was no need for him to be specific. Whatever it was, the unchangeability of Christ should inspire them to refuse its curious diversities and novel teaching.

The writer again uses the ceremonies of the Day of Atonement as the basis for his argument. Some may have thought the Christian way impoverished, lacking the sacrifices that were central to religion in the ancient world. But Christians do have sacrifices—real ones, though they are spiritual and not material.

9 The writer warns against being carried away by "all kinds of strange teachings." Since this phrase points to a great variety of teaching, it is difficult to identify specifically what is in mind. "Strange" (GK 3828) means foreign to the Gospel. The readers should know better than to go after such teachings, for they have known the "grace" of God. The heart, as often, stands for the whole of the inner life; and this is sustained, not by anything material, such as food, but by grace. God is the source of a believer's strength as he or she lives out the Christian life.

Most religions of that day had food regulations, including the Jews; usually this meant that some foods were regarded as "unclean." So it seems likely that the author has in mind some sacrificial meal that the worshipers took to have beneficial effects. The author denies it. A Christian's real life is not sustained on the level of things to eat. It requires the grace of God.

10 Some see the "altar" as the communion table (from which Christians, but not others, eat). But this is an odd way of interpreting the passage in the light of the point just made. This would simply be substituting one material thing for another, and the whole argument would fall to the ground. Instead, the writer is saying that the cross is distinctive to the Christian way. It was on a cross that the Christian sacrifice was offered. Thus it may not improperly be spoken of as an "altar." In a Christian context the sacrifice must be on the cross, as the author has made abundantly clear in a number of places. "Those who minister at the tabernacle" are Jewish worshipers in general. Such people have no rights in the altar of the cross; the crucified Savior means nothing to them. The writer is again pointing his readers to the privilege Christians have and warning them against losing it.

11–12 The author moves from the general idea of serving the altar to a specific example, one most likely taken from the Day of Atonement ceremonies. On that Day the high priest brought the blood of the victims into the Most Holy Place (Lev 16:14–15), but the bodies of the animals were totally burned outside the Israelite camp (Lev 16:27). "And so" introduces an inference. The Day of Atonement typologically foreshadowed the atoning work of Jesus. The author apparently is reasoning that because the type (the sacrificial victim in Lev 16) involved an activity "outside the camp," there will be an equivalent with the antitype (Jesus). But the parallel is not complete, because in the case of the sin offerings the animal was actually killed inside the camp and only the carcass disposed of outside the camp. The human name "Jesus" brings before us the picture of the Man, suffering for us. His suffering was not aimless but was designed "to make his people holy" (GK 39). This verb means "to set aside for God"; and it is applied both to things used for ritual purposes and to people who are thus taken out of the circle of the merely worldly and brought into the number of the people of God.

This process was effected "through his own blood." This expression puts some emphasis on the fact that Christ did not need an external victim (as did the high priests) but brought about the sanctification in question by the sacrifice of himself. "Blood" clearly signifies "death," as is commonly the case in the Bible. "People" can mean people in general; but more characteristically it means "the people of God," a meaning that suits this passage. To make people holy, then, Jesus suffered "outside the gate." Though not stated elsewhere in the NT, this is implied in Jn 19:17; and, anyway, crucifixions normally took place outside cities.

13 This leads to an appeal to the readers to "go to him outside the camp." Christ is outside the camp of Judaism, and the readers are encouraged to go to him where he is. To remain within the camp of Judaism would be to be separated from him. Here there may be an allusion to Moses' pitching "the tent of meeting" outside the camp and to the people's going out to it (Ex 33:7). But in the case of Christ, there was a price to pay—that of sharing in the rejection he had undergone, "bearing the disgrace he bore." In 11:26 Moses was said to have accepted "disgrace for the sake of Christ." To align oneself with Christ is to subject oneself to scorn, reproach, and perhaps more. But consistently throughout this letter the writer has argued that it is well worth it. The Jews held that the way Christ died proved him to be accursed (Dt 21:23; Gal 3:13). The readers must be ready to stand with Christ who bore that curse for them.

14 The writer reinforces his appeal to go to Jesus by reminding Christians that they have no stake in any earthly city, Jewish or otherwise. For people with such an outlook it is no great matter to be "outside the camp." As in 11:10 (see comments), the "city" stands for the highest and best in community life, the heavenly city; it is not to be found "here" on earth. No earthly city is "enduring." But Christians are looking for a city to come. People love to look for earthly security, but the best earthly security is insecure. The readers should pursue that which is really lasting and strive for the abiding city, letting go of any earthly one.

15 The verse begins with an emphatic "through him." It is through Jesus and not the Jewish priests (or any other priests) that people "offer" (GK *429*) to God acceptable sacrifices. "Offer" is a technical word for the offering of sacrifices of animals and the like. The author uses it of the only sacrifices Christians offer—spiritual sacrifices (cf. Ro 12:1; Jas 1:27). So he urges them to offer "a sacrifice of praise," i.e., a sacrifice consisting of praise. This sacrifice is to be offered "continually." In systems like Judaism sacrifices were offered at set times, but for Christians praise goes up all the time. Since a loving God is working out his purposes all the time, there are no circumstances in which praise should not be offered (cf. 1Th 5:18). The sacrifice is further explained in an expression from Hos 14:2 (cf. Pr 18:20), "the fruit of lips that confess his name." In the light of the Cross, there is no room for sacrifices such as those the Jews offered. Now believers offer the sacrifice of praise and acknowledge Christ.

16 The writer gives two more examples of the sacrifices Christians offer. "To do good" (GK *2343*) is a general term, while "to share with others" (GK *3126*) is more specific. The latter signifies sharing with others such things as we have: money, goods, and, of course, those intangibles that make up "fellowship." Even though Christians had no animals to sacrifice, this did not mean they had nothing to offer. They had their sacrifices, and it is "with such sacrifices" that God is well pleased. Christ's suffering "outside the camp" has altered everything. Now God looks to people to take Christ's way. And that means they offer no animals but make their response to what Christ has done for them in praise, good deeds, and works of love and charity.

I. Christian Obedience (13:17)

The author is mindful of the responsibility of the Christian leaders to whom he has already referred (v.7). In due course they must give account to God for their flock. So he urges his readers to keep this in mind and not make things hard for their leaders.

17 The readers must obey their leaders. In v.7 the leaders were men who had died. Here, however, those alive and currently in positions of authority are meant. The reason for their submission is that the leaders "keep watch" (lit., "keep oneself awake"; GK *70*). The imagery is of the leaders keeping awake at nights in their concern for their people. "Over you" translates "for your souls [GK *6034*]." This word may be simply a periphrasis for "you," but it seems preferable to see it as a reference to one's spiritual life and spiritual well-being. The leaders are concerned for the deep needs of their people, not simply for what lies on the surface, because they must render "account." The writer pleads with the readers to act in such a way that keeping watch will be a thing of joy for the leaders (cf. Php 2:16; 1Th 2:20; 3Jn 4). The alternative is for them to do it as "a burden" (lit., "with groaning"; GK *5100*), which would be "of no advantage" for the readers.

J. Prayer (13:18–19)

A short appeal for prayer reveals both the writer's conviction that prayer is a powerful force and his hope that he will soon see his correspondents again.

18 The imperative "Pray" (GK *4667*) implies a continuous activity, one that they had already been doing. "Keep praying for us" is its force. It seems that the plural "us" is an epistolary plural, meaning "me" (cf. 5:11; 6:9, 11).

The writer has rebuked his readers from time to time; he has warned them of the dangers in their conduct and exhorted them. But he depends on them, too, and looks to them now to support him with their prayers. At the same time there is a problem arising from the way he puts his request. He says (literal translation), "Pray for us, for we are persuaded that we have a good conscience." Having a good conscience is a most unusual reason for requesting prayer. We could understand it if the writer spoke of his difficulties or the like. Lacking knowledge of the circumstances, we cannot be sure why he phrases it this way. Perhaps the readers have been accusing the writer of some fault. They may have attributed his absence from them to unworthy motives. The writer protests that he has a clear conscience and that this is a reason for asking for their fellowship in prayer.

The writer himself is not aware of having committed any sin. He goes on to affirm his determination ("desire" is too weak a translation for GK *2527*) "to live honorably in every way." He allows no exceptions but expresses wholeheartedness.

19 The author underlines the importance of the readers' doing as he asks. He "urges" (GK *4151*) them "strongly" or "more abundantly" (NIV "particularly"; GK *4359*). It seems as though he had at one time been a leader in the group, for he desired to "be restored" to them. What was preventing him from this restoration is not said, but evidently the obstacle was considerable. Some have suggested that he had been imprisoned for his faith. We know too little of the circumstances to rule this out, but there is nothing to indicate it. The language suggests that it was something outside the writer's control and that it needed a good deal of prayer.

X. Conclusion (13:20–25)

The writer has finished what he has to say. It remains for him only to round off his letter, and he does so with a magnificent doxology and a few greetings.

A. Doxology (13:20–21)

This doxology gathers up a number of the themes that have meant so much as the argument of the letter has unfolded: the blood, the eternal covenant, the lordship of Jesus, and the importance of doing his will. But it also introduces some things not yet dealt with. This is the only place in the letter, for example, where Jesus is seen as our Shepherd or where his resurrection is specifically referred to. The whole forms a superb doxology that has meant much to Christians throughout the centuries.

20 God is called "the God of peace" a number of times in the Pauline writings (Ro 15:33; 16:20; 2Co 13:11; Php 4:9; 1Th 5:23). "Peace" (GK *1645*) connotes the fullest prosperity of the whole man, taking up as it does the OT concept of the Hebrew *shalom* (GK *8934*; see comments on 7:2). Here it reminds us that all our prosperity is centered in God and that a well-rounded life depends on him. The expression is especially suitable in view of what the letter discloses of the condition of the readers. They have had to cope with some form of persecution and were still not free from opposition. They were tempted to leave Christianity and have had to be warned of the dangers of apostasy. They may have had doubts about who their true leaders were. It is well for them to be reminded that real peace is in God.

The doxology goes on to characterize God in terms of the Resurrection. In the NT, Jesus is occasionally said to have risen. It is, however, much more common in the NT for the Resurrection to be ascribed to God, as here. The one whom God brought up from the dead is now described as "the great Shepherd of the sheep" (see Isa 63:11; Jn 10:1–18; 1Pe 2:25; cf. also Mt 26:31; Mk 14:27). It is a piece of imagery that stresses the care of our Lord for his own, for sheep are helpless without their shepherd. But an aspect we in modern times sometimes miss is that the shepherd has absolute sovereignty over his flock (cf. Rev 2:27; 12:5; 19:15; in each case the verb rendered "rule" in NIV means "to shepherd"). The adjective "great" (GK *3489*) is used because Christ is not to be ranked with other shepherds. He stands out.

The Resurrection is linked with "the blood of the eternal covenant" (cf. Isa 55:3; Zec 9:11). It is interesting to see how the thought of covenant, one of the major themes of this letter, persists to the end. "Eternal" again brings out the point that this covenant will never be replaced by another as it replaced the old covenant. And it was established by "blood." The author never forgets that. For him the death of Jesus is central. At the same time, his linking it with the Resurrection shows that he did not have in mind a dead Christ but one who, though he shed his blood to establish the covenant, lives forever. The expression "our Lord Jesus" is unusual outside of Acts, where it occurs a number of times. It combines the lordship of Christ and his real humanity, two themes of continuing importance.

21 The prayer is that God will "equip" (GK *2936*) the readers "with everything good for doing his will." "Equip" in this context means to supply one with what one needs to live the Christian life. "Everything good" is comprehensive; the writer wants nothing to be lacking. Notice the emphasis on doing the will of God, a thought we have had before in this letter.

It is also interesting to notice the juxtaposition of "doing his will" and "may he work in us." From one point of view any deed is the deed of a human being, but from another it is God working in and through his servant. We should not overlook the significance of the word "us," by which the writer again links himself with his readers. He looks for God to do his perfect work in them and in him alike. He needs the grace of God as much as they do. He wants God to do in us "what is pleasing [GK *2298*] to him," a word that usually refers to people being acceptable to God. We can do what is acceptable only through Jesus Christ.

Whether "to whom" refers to the Father or to Christ poses a problem. Grammatically it could be either, and a good case can be made for either. Perhaps the writer himself was not making a sharp distinction.

The doxology concludes with "for ever and ever. Amen." It is curious that doxologies should include "Amen," as this one does, for the word was normally the response of a congregation. Perhaps initially a doxology was spoken by the leader of a congregation, and the people responded with their "Amen." In time the response was added to the doxology as being the normal thing. In any case, the "Amen" makes a satisfying close.

B. Final Exhortations (13:22–25)

The author now rounds off the whole letter with a final appeal and a brief section of greetings. The greetings show that the letter was being sent to a definite, known group of Christians with whom the author had ties.

22 "I urge" (GK *4151*) seems to mean something more like "I beg you." There is appeal in it, but also encouragement. The letter has had its share of rebukes and warnings, and the writer now softens the impact a little with this appeal and with the affectionate address "Brothers." He calls his letter the "word of exhortation" (cf. Ac 13:15, where this phrase clearly means a homily). So the point here may be that this letter is rather like a written sermon with lots of "exhortation" (GK *4155*).

The author goes on to say that he has written only briefly. This letter is short, considering the subject matter. Some of the subjects could have been dealt with at much greater length (cf. 11:32). There has been some straight speaking. So before he finishes, the writer adds this brief section inviting the readers to take it in the right spirit.

23 The writer is giving new information in this verse. Timothy is no doubt the companion of Paul (no other Timothy is known to us from those times), and he seems to have had some ties with both the readers and the writer. Otherwise we would expect a general expression instead of "our brother Timothy." It is not clear what "released" (GK *668*) means, for the word can refer to starting off on a journey (as in Ac 13:3; 28:25) or making other beginnings. It is possible that Timothy started on a journey or he had been released from some obligation. But it seems most likely that the term, used absolutely as it is here, means that he had been released from imprisonment. All that we can say for certain is that Timothy had left the place where he was. The writer now expects Timothy to come to where he is and hopes that then the two of them can go on to visit the readers. But evidently he intends moving fairly soon, whether or not Timothy comes.

24 For the third time in this chapter, the "leaders" come to our attention (see comment on v.7). That they are to be greeted by the recipients of the letter makes it clear that they were not the recipients and, furthermore, that the letter was not sent to the whole church. That greetings were to be sent shows that the recipients were on good terms with the leaders. The words "and all" may be significant—namely, there are no exceptions. "God's people" (lit., "the saints"; GK *41*) means those consecrated to God, set apart to do him service. The greeting from "those from Italy" can mean either Italians living abroad (cf. Ac 21:27) or living in their own country (cf. Ac 10:23).

25 The NT letters normally end with a prayer for "grace" for the recipients. Grace is a fitting note on which to end a letter like this one, so full of what God has done for people in Christ. The author then closes by praying sfor God's grace for all his friends. He omits no one from his concern or from God's.

The Old Testament in the New

NT Text	OT Text	Subject
Heb 1:5	Ps 2:7	You are my Son
Heb 1:5	2Sa 7:14; 1Ch 17:13	Father and son
Heb 1:6	Dt 32:43	Rejoice, O nations
Heb 1:7	Ps 104:4	Angels and winds
Heb 1:8	Ps 45:6–7	God's eternal throne
Heb 1:10–12	Ps 102:25–27	The unchangeable God
Heb 1:13	Ps 110:1	At God's right hand
Heb 2:6–8	Ps 8:4–6	Lower than the angels
Heb 2:12	Ps 22:22	Declaring God's name
Heb 2:13	Isa 8:17	Trust in God
Heb 2:13	Isa 8:18	God's children
Heb 3:2, 5	Nu 12:7	Faithful Moses
Heb 3:7–11, 15	Ps 95:7–11	No rest for the wicked
Heb 4:3, 5, 7	Ps 95:7–11	No rest for the wicked
Heb 4:4	Ge 2:2	God rested the seventh day
Heb 5:5	Ps 2:7	You are my Son
Heb 5:6	Ps 110:4	Melchizedek
Heb 6:14	Ge 22:17	God's oath to Abraham
Heb 7:17, 21	Ps 110:4	Melchizedek
Heb 8:5	Ex 25:40	Pattern of the tabernacle
Heb 8:8–12	Jer 31:31–34	The new covenant
Heb 9:20	Ex 24:8	The blood of the covenant
Heb 10:5–9	Ps 40:6–8	Offerings and obedience
Heb 10:16–17	Jer 31:33–34	The new covenant
Heb 10:28	Dt 17:6	Two or three witnesses
Heb 10:30	Dt 32:35	God avenges sins
Heb 10:30	Dt 32:36; Ps 135:14	God judges his people
Heb 10:37–38	Hab 2:3–4	Persevere in faith
Heb 11:18	Ge 21:12	God's choice of Isaac

The Old Testament in the New

NT Text	OT Text	Subject
Heb 12:5–6	Pr 3:11–12	Love and discipline
Heb 12:13	Pr 4:26	Level paths for your feet
Heb 12:15	Dt 29:18	No root of bitterness
Heb 12:20	Ex 19:12–13	Not touching the mountain
Heb 12:21	Dt 9:19	Moses' fear
Heb 12:26	Hag 2:6	One more shaking
Heb 12:29	Dt 4:24	God is a consuming fire
Heb 13:5	Dt 31:6	Faithfulness of God
Heb 13:6	Ps 118:6–7	The Lord is my helper

James

INTRODUCTION

1. Authorship

Even though this letter names its author, it does not specify his actual identity. James was a common name in the first century. There are in the NT four men called James. Of these, only two have ever been seriously suggested as possible authors of this letter. A few scholars have understood the writer to be James the son of Zebedee, one of the twelve apostles. Most scholars, however, have recognized that he was martyred too early (A.D. 44) to have written this letter (Ac 12:1–2).

Since at least the third century, the most prominent view has been that James, the Lord's brother (Mk 6:3), wrote the book. This was the belief of Origen (c. A.D. 185–253), Eusebius (c. 265–340), and Jerome (c. 340–420). The evidence of the letter itself favors this traditional view. The characteristics of this James as seen in Ac 21:11–25 and Gal 2:12, and the description of "James the Just" by Hegesippus, are in harmony with this letter's heavy emphasis on genuine religious practice and ethical conduct. The vocabulary of James's speech and letter in Ac 15:13–29 reveals significant similarity to this letter, and the authoritative tone of the letter (forty-six imperatives) agrees well with the authority exercised by James in Ac 15:13ff.; 21:18.

2. Date

If the Lord's brother is identified as author, the book must have originated prior to A.D. 62, when, according to Josephus, James was martyred. There are two general opinions as to when it was written. Some insist that the letter was written before A.D. 50; others argue for a date near the end of James's life, perhaps in the early sixties. If the earlier date is correct, James may have been the first NT book written.

Several considerations make it probable that James wrote between A.D. 45 and 50. (1) The Jewish orientation of the letter fits the earlier period more naturally than the later. That the author does not refer to Gentiles or related subjects may well point to the time in the history of the early church when Gentiles were only beginning to be reached with the Gospel. (2) The absence of any reference to the controversy concerning the Judaizers and their insistence on Gentile circumcision is best explained by the earlier date. (3) The close affinity of the teaching of James to that of the OT and Christ suggests a time before other NT letters were written. (4) The evidence of a simple church order favors the early date. The leaders are "teachers" (3:1) and "elders" (5:11). (5) Finally, the use of the Greek term *synagoge* (GK 5252; NIV, "meeting") to describe the church assembly or meeting place (2:2) points to the early period when Christianity was largely confined to Jewish circles.

3. Destination

The letter is addressed to "the twelve tribes scattered among the nations" (1:1). Although this is indefinite, it does reveal that the recipients were clearly Jewish. The description of their congregation or meeting place as a *synagoge* (2:2) also supports this interpretation. Moreover, the recipients were used to the Hebrew title "Lord Almighty" (5:4; lit., "Lord of hosts").

The author further limits his intended readership by statements that assume the recipients are Christians (see especially 2:1, where James assumes his readers are followers of Christ; see also 5:7–8, about the Lord's coming being near). It would seem, then, that the letter was addressed to Jewish believers in Jesus as Messiah.

The geographical location of these Jewish Christians is not specifically identified. They are merely described as "scattered among the nations" (1:1), which means they were not centered in one locality. Possibly they were the believers who were forced to leave Jerusalem during the persecution that followed Stephen's death. These Jewish Christians spread out over Judea and Samaria (Ac 8:1) and even as far as Phoenicia, Cyprus, and Syrian Antioch (Ac 11:19). James, the leading elder of the Jerusalem church, felt responsible for these former "parishioners" and attempted to instruct them somewhat as he would have done had they still been under his care in Jerusalem. The letter reveals his intimate knowledge of their circumstances and characteristics. And he writes with the note of authority expected of one who had been recognized as a spiritual leader in the Jerusalem church.

4. Occasion and Purpose

If we are correct that James wrote this letter to believers who had been dispersed from Jerusalem in the persecution following Stephen's death, the occasion for writing is fairly clear. These Jewish Christians no longer had contact with the apostles, nor was James among them to instruct and exhort them. Yet difficulties—perhaps persecutions—were confronting them (1:2–4); the ungodly rich were oppressing them (5:1–6); the religion of some was becoming a superficial formality (1:22–27; 2:14–26); discriminatory practices revealed a lack of love (2:1–13); and bitterness in speech (3:1–12) and attitude (3:13–4:3) marred their fellowship. Apparently reports of such problems among the scattered brothers had reached James in Jerusalem. In response, he wrote as pastor in absentia to urge his people to make the needed changes in their lives and in their corporate relationships.

5. Canonicity

The letter was not readily received into the collection of writings considered as authoritative Scripture. It was rejected by some as late as the time of Eusebius (c. 265–340). Few early Christian writers refer to it.

Such negative evidence could be taken as a basis for doubting the authority of the book, were it not that, after a period of questioning, the churches finally granted unanimous recognition to it as canonical. Furthermore, there are reasonable explanations for the late acceptance of the letter. Eusebius himself explained that denials of the book's canonicity came not because of any fault in the book itself, but merely because it had not been widely used. There are reasons why this condition existed, such as its untheological nature, its brevity, the question of James's identity, the fact that it was not written by one of the twelve apostles, and its general address (sent to no specific person or church).

In due time, such authorities as Eusebius and Jerome (c. 340–420) placed their stamp of approval on the book, and the Council of Carthage (397) recognized its canonicity. Ultimately, churches everywhere were reading it as authoritative Scripture.

6. Relation to Other Writings

Many attempts have been made to trace a connection between the letter of James and numerous biblical and extrabiblical writings. In two areas the literary relationships seem relatively well defined and significant. The similarity between this letter and the teachings of Jesus in the Sermon on the Mount has often been noted. A clear example of this almost verbal connection is seen between Jas 5:12 and the words of Jesus recorded in Mt 5:34–37. Other related statements include Jas 2:5 (Lk 6:20), Jas 3:10–12 (Mt 7:16–20), and Jas 3:18 (Mt 5:9). From such parallels we may conclude that James reflects the thoughts and often the very words of Christ.

Another possible literary relationship is between James and OT wisdom writings such as Proverbs. While this letter was not written in the same style as Proverbs, the two do have noteworthy affinities. For example, the pithy, proverbial style of James should be noted (1:8, 22; 4:17), as well as the juxtaposition of good and evil (3:13–18). Also, James's use of the word "wisdom" is significant (see 1:5; 3:13–17). The book of Proverbs abounds with references to wisdom, always viewing it as the kind of understanding that produces a sensible and an upright life. In Proverbs, as in James, wisdom has its source in God. James even quotes from Proverbs (see Jas 4:6 and Pr 3:34) and also alludes to it (cf. Jas 1:5 with Pr 2:6; 1:19 with Pr 29:20; 3:18 with Pr 11:30; 4:13–16 with Pr 27:1; 5:20 with Pr 10:12).

7. Theological Values

The letter of James is one of the least theological NT books. In fact, one of the reasons for the delay in canonical recognition of the letter was its lack of theological content. Having recognized this, however, one must hasten to insist that the book is not without theological value. The practical emphases of James rest on a solid theological foundation,

James and the Sayings of Jesus

James shows a remarkable familiarity with the words spoken by Jesus in the gospels, especially in the Sermon on the Mount (Mt 5–7). This chart depicts the many parallels between James and Jesus that scholars have noted—both parallels in words and in themes.

Theme	James	Gospels
Joy in persecution	1:2	Mt 5:11–12; Lk 6:22–23
A person's goal of being perfect and mature	1:4	Mt 5:48
Asking and receiving from God	1:5	Mt 7:7; Lk 11:19
Asking in faith and not doubting	1:6	Mt 21:21–22; Mk 11:22–24
Reversal of proud and humble	1:9–10; 4:6, 10	Mt 23:12; Lk 14:11; 18:14
Sun scorching plants and they wither	1:11	Mt 13:6; Mk 4:7
Blessings for perseverance under trial	1:12	Mt 5:11–12
God as the giver of gifts	1:17	Mt 7:11; Lk 11:13
Not only listen to, but do the Word of God	1:22; 2:14, 17	Mt 7:21–27; Lk 6:46–49
Compassion for those who are needy and hurting	1:27; 2:15	Mt 25:34–36
The poor to inherit the kingdom	2:5	Mt 5:3; Lk 6:20
"Love your neighbor as yourself"	2:8	Mt 22:39; Mk 12:31
Not breaking the least commandment	2:10	Mt 5:19
Judgment on those who show no mercy	2:13	Mt 18:23–34; 25:41–46
Through obedience becoming friends of God	2:23	Jn 15:13–15
Teachers judged more strictly	3:1	Mk 9:38, 40; Lk 20:45, 47
We are judged by what we say	3:2	Mt 12:37
What corrupts is what comes out of our mouths	3:6	Mt 15:11, 18; Mk 7:15, 20; Lk 6:45
Same source cannot produce good and evil	3:11–12	Mt 7:16–18; Lk 6:43–44
Peacemakers blessed by God	3:18	Mt 5:9
A (spiritually) adulterous people	4:4	Mt 12:39; Mk 8:38
Friendship with the world means enmity with God (or vice versa)	4:4	Jn 15:18–21
Laughter to be turned into mourning	4:6	Lk 6:25
Not judging others	4:11–12; 5:9	Mt 7:1–2
God can both save and destroy	4:12	Mt 10:28
Foolishness of planning the future apart from God	4:13–14	Lk 12:18–20
Punishment for those who know God's will but refuse to do it	4:17	Lk 12:47
Woe to the rich	5:1	Lk 6:24
Wealth removed by moth and corrosion	5:2–3	Mt 6:19–20
Self-indulgence with no concern for the poor	5:5	Lk 16:19–20, 25
Returning Judge is at the door	5:9	Mt 24:33; Mk 13:39
Persecution of prophets	5:10	Mt 5:10–12
Do not swear oaths	5:12	Mt 5:33–37
Restoring an erring brother or sister	5:19–29	Mt 18:15

which is often explicitly revealed and perhaps more often assumed or implied.

Three doctrines often surface. (1) The most prominent one is the doctrine of God. He is seen as being generous (1:5) and holy (1:13), the unchanging source of good (1:17). He is the one and only God (2:19), the Father of his people and the one in whose likeness people were created (3:9). Furthermore he is sovereign (4:15) and just (5:4), filled with pity and tender mercy (5:11).

(2) In keeping with the ethical nature of the letter is the repeated stress on the doctrine of sin. James views sin as universal (3:2), indwelling all persons (1:14–15) and resulting in death (1:15). It expresses itself in anger (1:20), moral filth (1:21), blasphemy (2:7), discrimination (2:9–11), bitterness and lust (4:1–3), intimate ties with the evil world (4:4), pride (4:6), and theft and oppression (5:4).

(3) The third prominent theological theme is eschatology. James sees the end time as the day of rewards (1:12), when God's kingdom will be introduced (2:5), the day of judgment will come (2:12; 3:1), and the Lord will return (5:7–8).

Several other doctrines receive limited mention: Christ as Lord (1:1; 2:1); regeneration (1:18); salvation (1:21); justification (2:21–25); and forgiveness of sins (5:15). James discusses the relation of saving faith and resultant good deeds (2:14–26).

EXPOSITION

I. Salutation (1:1)

1 James is most likely the brother of Jesus (see introduction). More specifically, since Jesus was virgin born, James was his half brother. In Acts this same James appears as the leader of the Jerusalem church (Ac 15:13ff.; 21:18). He describes himself as "a servant [GK *1528*] of God and of the Lord Jesus Christ." This word designates a slave, the rightful property of one's master, though it does not necessarily carry the degrading connotation attached to the word today. James was proud to belong—body and soul—to God and to Jesus Christ.

The letter is addressed to "the twelve tribes," a designation intended to identify the readers as Jews. They were not residents of Palestine but were "scattered among the nations" as part of the Jewish Dispersion. James's later designation of his readers as "believers in our glorious Lord Jesus Christ" (2:1) makes it clear that he means Christian Jews. It is probable that the recipients were the members of the Jerusalem church who had been driven out of Jerusalem at the time of Stephen's martyrdom (Ac 8:1, 4; 11:19–20). If so, James had formerly been their spiritual leader and he was writing them with rightful spiritual authority and with full knowledge of their needs.

II. Trials and Temptations (1:2–18)

1. The Testing of Faith (1:2–12)

2 In vv.2–4 James explains that trials are a reason for rejoicing because of the wholesome effects they produce. The word "trials" (GK *4280*) describes things that put a person to the test. They may be difficulties that come from without, such as persecution (see vv.2–4), or they may be inner moral tests, such as temptations to sin (see vv.13–18). An outward trial, rather than being a reason for unhappiness, can be a ground for "pure joy." And it is not merely the coming of a single trial that is described; James speaks of "trials of many kinds." "Face" (GK *4346*) suggests that one is surrounded by people, objects, or circumstances that try one's faith.

3 Why can trials be considered grounds for genuine rejoicing? If a person has truth faith, those trials are capable of developing "perseverance" (GK *5705*). This word denotes tenacity and stick-to-it-iveness. It is the quality that enables a person to stand on one's feet facing the storm. In struggling against difficulty and opposition, spiritual stamina is developed.

4 If perseverance is to "finish its work," faith must persist and not falter or give up. The goal in view is that believers "may be mature [GK *5455*] and complete [GK *3908*]." Perseverance in facing trials develops maturity of character and a balance of all the graces and strengths needed for the Christian life.

5 Verses 5–8 contain God's offer of help for those who are facing trials. The repetition of the word "lack" shows that James is still discussing the subject of trials. In v.4 he assures his readers that when perseverance has finished its work, the believer will lack none of the needed virtues and strengths. In v.5, however, James speaks of the period of testing before perseverance has completed its work. During such testing, if anyone lacks "wisdom" (GK 5053), he or she may have it by asking. People facing trials often do lack wisdom. What they need is not the speculative wisdom of a philosophical system, but the kind of wisdom that plays such a large part in the book of Proverbs (1:2–4; 2:10–15; 4:5–9). It is God-given understanding that enables a person to avoid the paths of wickedness and to live a life of righteousness. In this context wisdom is understanding the nature and purpose of trials and knowing how to meet them victoriously. Such wisdom is available to the one who will "ask God" for it, not once only, but repeatedly; the promise is that wisdom "will be given to him." It is God's practice to give "generously" and "without finding fault." He does not scold his children for asking or berate them for their deficiency.

6 Although nothing in God prevents him from giving wisdom to his people, a barrier may exist in them. When they ask, they "must believe and not doubt." Their faith must be more than mere acceptance of a creed. To believe is to be confident that God will give what is requested. The extent of faith that God looks for is emphasized by the words "not doubt" (GK 1359). "Doubt" describes one who is divided in the mind and who wavers between two opinions. One moment he voices the yes of faith; the next moment it is the no of disbelief. Such an attitude is graphically illustrated by "a wave of the sea." Completely lacking in stability, it is "blown and tossed by the wind." First there is the crest, then the trough. Instead, prayer that moves God to respond must be marked by the constancy of unwavering faith.

The reference to the sea is the first of James's illustrations from nature (see also 1:10–11, 17–18, 26; 3:3 5, 7, 11–12; 5:7, 17–18. As Jesus drew numerous illustrations from life around him, so James revealed his love for nature by his repeated use of it for illustrative purposes.

7–8 "That man" is a somewhat derogatory reference to the doubter, whom James has just compared to the tossing wave. Here he is further characterized as "double-minded" (lit., "double-souled"; GK 1500). It is as though one soul declares, "I believe," and the other in turn shouts, "I don't!" This sort of instability is not only apparent when the person prays, it marks "all he does." In one's personal life, business life, social life, as well as spiritual life, indecisiveness negates all effectiveness. A person like this will not "receive anything from the Lord."

But one may wonder how this man is different from the anguished father who cried, "I do believe; help me overcome my unbelief!" (Mk 9:24). This father was not oscillating between belief and unbelief. He desired to believe—and even asserted his belief—but because he felt keenly the inadequacy of his faith, he asked for help in believing. He was not facing both directions at the same time like the "double-minded man" of Jas 1:8. In spite of his conscious weakness, he had set his heart to believe. And Christ responded to his faith and healed his son (Mk 9:25–27). In response to this kind of faith, God will give wisdom to those who ask for it and enable them to persevere in times of trial.

9 Verses 9–11 appear to continue the same subject (cf. the continuation of the subject of persevering "under trial" in v.12). Trials erase any superficial distinctions that one may think separates the rich brother from the poor one.

"Brother" (GK 81) shows that James is referring to a believer. To describe the "circumstances" of this brother, the author uses the word "humble" (GK 5424), which has the basic meaning of "lowly," "insignificant," or "poor." In view of the contrast with the

James frequently uses metaphors from nature. These waves on the Mediterranean Sea (picture taken at Caesarea) remind him of the instability of a doubter (1:6).

"rich" in v.10, it is best to understand that the person in v.9 is one who is financially poor and thus "in humble circumstances." The "high position" in which such people are to take pride refers first of all to their position in Christ. In saving them, God lifts them up and gives them new dignity and worth. James also has in mind the privilege of "suffering disgrace for the Name [Jesus]" (Ac 5:41). To endure persecution for Christ's sake lifts believers to a position of honor that more than offsets their poverty.

10 The text does not explicitly state that "the one who is rich" is a believer, and for that reason some have insisted that he is unsaved. It would seem most natural, however, for James to omit the word "brother" in v.10 and assume that it would be carried over from v.9. The wealthy believer, then, is exhorted to glory "in his low position." Since the context deals with trials, the low position may describe the humbling experience of suffering persecution for Christ's sake. The very same treatment that exalts the poor and gives them a new sense of worth also humbles the rich. Suffering shows the rich that, instead of having a lasting lease on life on this earth, their lives are no more permanent than "a wild flower" (cf. Isa 40:6–8). Suffering and persecution reveal how tentative and short life really is.

11 The phenomenon James speaks of was a familiar one. Green grass and plants do not last long under the "scorching heat" of the Palestinian summer sun. More specifically, the reference may be to the sudden coming of a hot, searing wind known as the sirocco, which quickly withers and burns the vegetation. The withering of the plant and falling of its blossom are taken almost verbatim from Isa 40:7. It may be that the "beauty" of the blossom is suggestive of the fine clothes that the rich wear. As impressive and attractive as the garments may be, they soon fade and wear out. And, what is even more important, "the rich man" himself "will fade away, even while he goes about his business." Unexpectedly, in the midst of a busy life, the end comes. These are sobering thoughts that tend to reduce the rich to the level of human beings in general, just as the privilege of suffering for Christ lifts the poor person to a new plane of dignity and worth.

12 James concludes his discussion of the testing of faith with a promise of the reward to be given to the one who successfully stands the test. This verse is to be related to the preceding verses on the subject of trials (cf. the repetition of "trials" from v.2; "testing" and "perseverance" from v.3). The expression "Blessed is the man" reveals the author's familiarity with the language of the OT (cf. Pss 1:1; 32:2; 34:8; 84:12; Pr 8:34; Isa 56:2; Jer 17:7) and the beatitudes of Jesus (Mt 5:3–11). "Blessed" (GK *3421*) speaks of the distinctive religious joy that is a benefit of salvation. This word describes the enviable state of the person who does not give up when confronted with trying circumstances but remains strong in faith and devotion to God. "Stood the test" suggests the process of successfully testing precious metals and coins and their consequent approval as genuine. Perseverance under trial results in approval, and approval results in "the crown [GK *5109*] of life." Although "crown" may designate a kingly crown, it more often refers to the crown given to a victorious athlete—a wreath of laurel, oak, or even celery. For James, this word refers to the reward given to believers who are victorious in their struggles against trials. This life "that God has promised" is more than the eternal life given to every believer at the time of his or her salvation (Jn 5:24). Since it is a reward for an accomplishment subsequent to initial faith, it must refer to a still higher quality of life.

2. The Source of Temptation (1:13–18)

No one should assume that enticement to sin comes from God (v.13a); James then proceeds to give a series of reasons for his assertion (vv.13b–18).

13–14 The word "temptation" here is the same as "trials" in v.2 (see comment on v.2); here, however, it obviously means temptation (see the words "evil" in v.13; "evil desire" in v.14; "sin" in v.15). Temptation does not come from God because God himself cannot be successfully tempted by evil. His omnipotent, holy will fully resists any invitation to sin. Furthermore, in him there is not the slightest moral depravity to which temptation may appeal. Therefore, it is inconsistent to think that God could be the author of temptation.

Instead, the source of temptation lies within a person. One is tempted "by his own evil desire." James personifies a person's sinful desire and identifies it, rather than some external person or object, as the efficient cause of temptation. By one's own sinful nature a person is "dragged away and enticed." James pictures a person's "evil desire," first, as attracting his attention and persuading him to approach the forbidden thing and, second, as luring him by means of bait to yield to the temptation.

15 James changes his figure from a snare to conception and birth to describe the experience of yielding to sin. The genealogy of evil desire is traced for three generations, as it were. First, temptation comes (v.14); then desire, like a human mother, conceives and "gives birth to sin." Then sin, the child of evil desire, develops till it "is full-grown" and ready to produce its own offspring. When it conceives, it "gives birth to death." James is not suggesting that only when sin has reached its full development does it result in death. The penalty of sin of any kind or extent is spiritual death. The details of the illustration must not be pressed too far; the author's intention is simply to trace the results of temptation when one yields to it.

16 "Don't be deceived" normally introduces a significant statement (see 1Co 6:9; 15:33; Gal 6:7; cf. also 1Jn 3:7). The author warns against being deceived into thinking that God is the author of temptation. In fact, the specific Greek construction used here may imply that the addressees have been engaging in the practice being prohibited. In that case James would be saying, "Stop being deceived."

17 Here follows the significant statement that the prohibition of the previous verse was intended to introduce. Instead of sending temptation, God is the giver of "every good and perfect gift." The concept of God's goodness rules out the possibility that he would send an influence as destructive as temptation. His gifts are marked by kindness and helpfulness, not destructiveness. They are "perfect" (GK 5455), which in this context excludes any possibility of moral evil as coming from God.

Here God is designated as "the Father of the heavenly lights"—presumably the stars and planets. "Father" probably has a twofold significance, pointing to God as the creator of the lights and to his continuing sovereignty over them.

Unlike the "shifting shadows" that are caused by the sun, moon, and stars, God "does not change." With him there is no variation at all. The shadows cast by the sun are minimal at noon, but just before sunset they stretch out for yards across the landscape. God is not like that. He does not change. He is always the giver of good gifts, never a sadistic being who would entice his creatures to destroy themselves in sin.

18 James advances his final reason for denying that God is the author of temptation. Rather than acting destructively, God acts constructively. "He chose to give us birth." Seeing that this birth is "through the word of truth" (i.e., through the Gospel), this birth must be spiritual rather than natural. God accomplishes this action by his own deliberate choice. His purpose in regeneration is "that we might be a kind of firstfruits." The figure the author has in mind is drawn from such OT passages as Ex 34:22 and Lev 23:10. "Firstfruits" refers to the first portion of the harvest given to God, a foretaste of that which was to come. So it was that the early Christians were a preliminary indication of the great host of people who through subsequent centuries would be born again.

III. The Practice of the Word (1:19–27)

Verses 19–21 may seem at first glance to be an isolated section of miscellaneous exhortations. Further examination, however, reveals significant links to the preceding and following contexts. The term "word" (GK 3364) is found in vv.18, 21–25 and refers to the Scriptures, the Word of God. Verse 18 indicates that regeneration comes through the instrumentality of the Word; v.21 contains a call to receive the Word; and vv.22–25 discuss the doing of the Word. Thus vv.19–21 emphasize listening to and receiving the Word, while vv.22–25 stress the doing of the Word.

19 In vv.19–21a, James is attempting to clear the way for the reception of God's truth (v.21b). He begins by calling for the readers' attention: "Take note of this." The reception of the Word demands a readiness "to listen" (GK 201). Reluctance at this point will block the acceptance of truth. It also demands restrained speech. A continual talker cannot hear what anyone else is saying and by the same token will not hear when God speaks. Finally, the restraint of anger is demanded, for anger closes the mind to God's truth. A fiercely argumentative attitude is not conducive to the humble reception of truth.

20 "For" indicates that this verse gives the reasoning that lies behind the last exhortation. One's anger does not produce "the righteous life that God desires." An angry attitude is not the atmosphere in which righteousness flourishes. James stresses this from the positive side when he later says, "Peacemakers who sow in peace raise a harvest of righteousness" (3:18).

21 In further preparation for the reception of the Word, one must "get rid of all moral filth." The word translated "get rid of" (GK 700) was primarily used of taking off garments (cf. Heb 12:1, which speaks of throwing off any excessive weight to make ready for the race of faith). The "moral filth and the evil" that are so abundant must be stripped off like dirty clothes in preparation for "accept[ing] the word." The reception of truth must of necessity be marked by humility or meekness (GK 4559). This is not to be construed as spineless weakness. Instead, it is the quality of a strong man that makes him docile and submissive rather than haughty and rebellious. Only in such a spirit can one fully receive God's truth. That the Word is described as "planted in you" suggests that the readers were believers who already possessed the truth. The phrase "which can save you" simply describes the truth as saving truth. James is not calling for an initial acceptance of that message, but for a full appropriation of the truth as the Christian grows in spiritual understanding.

22 The author next discusses putting the Word into practice. It is not enough merely to "listen to the word" or, by the same token, merely to read it. Those who congratulate themselves on being hearers of the truth are deceiving themselves. If they assume that this is all that is needed to earn them a position of special favor with God, they are sadly mistaken. In reality, the responsibility of those who hear is far greater than that of those who have never heard. If they do not combine doing with hearing, they put themselves in a most vulnerable position. The call to "do what it says" lies at the center of all that James teaches and sums up the whole book: Put into practice what you profess to believe.

23–24 The author proceeds to explain why people should do more than merely listen to the truth, using the illustration of a man who "looks at his face in a mirror." "Looks at" (GK 2917) means careful observation; the man carefully studies his face and becomes thoroughly familiar with its features. Those who listen to the Word do so attentively and at length, so that they understand what they hear. They know what God expects them to do. Any failure to respond cannot be blamed on lack of understanding.

James further explains that upon going away, the man "immediately forgets what he looks like." For him it is "out of sight, out of mind." This is, of course, ludicrous, but no less ludicrous are believers who listen carefully to God's truth and do not remember to put into practice what they have heard. Listening to truth is not an end in itself any more than gazing at one's face in a mirror is an end in itself. The purpose of listening to truth is to act upon it. Theoretical knowledge of spiritual truth is never commended in Scripture. Knowledge is inseparably tied to experience. Believers gain knowledge through experience, and such knowledge is intended to affect subsequent experience.

25 In contrast to those who listen to the Word but do not do what it says, James now describes one who both listens and puts into practice what has been heard. "He will be blessed in what he does." The reason for this blessing is fourfold. (1) He "looks intently" (GK 4160) into God's truth, a verb that described John's act of stooping and peering into the tomb of Jesus (Jn 20:5). Here it is as though a person stoops over the Scripture, zealously searching for its message. (2) "He continues to do this." He is the blessed man of Ps 1 who meditates on God's law day and night. (3) He does not forget "what he has heard." (4) Most important, he puts the truth into practice.

James's term "the perfect law of liberty" (literal translation) deserves special attention. The word "law" (GK 3795) reveals his Jewish orientation and that of his readers. But he qualifies this word to make sure that his readers do not misunderstand, describing it as "perfect" (GK *5455*) and as characterized by "freedom" (GK *1800*). It is not merely the OT law, nor is it the Mosaic law perverted to become a legalistic system for earning salvation by good works. When James calls it the "perfect law," he has in mind the sum total of God's revealed truth—not merely the preliminary portion found in the OT, but also the final revelation made through Christ and his apostles that was soon to be inscripturated in the NT. Thus it is complete, in contrast to that which is preliminary and preparatory. Furthermore, it is a law that does not enslave. Instead, it is freely accepted and fulfilled with glad devotion under the enablement of the Spirit of God (Gal 5:22–23; see Jas 2:8, 12 for more on this concept of law).

26 Verses 26–27 point out three specific areas where truth should be put into practice. (1) The first is speech. James introduces a hypothetical case. The person involved "considers himself religious" (GK *2580*). This word describes a person who performs the external acts of religion, such as public worship, fasting, or giving to the needy, but he exerts no controlling restraint on his speech. Exactly how his speech offends is not indicated, whether it be by the cutting criticism of others, by uncleanness, by dishonesty, or by other ways. His uncontrolled tongue reveals that "his religion" is external sham. In living like this, "he deceives himself" (cf. v.22).

27 (2) The kind of "religion that God our Father accepts" is the kind that exerts a positive influence on one's life. This verse does not give us a definition of religion. Instead, it presents a concrete way of insisting that genuine religion is a life-changing force. One's religion should be more than external; it must spring from an inner spiritual reality that expresses itself in love to others and holiness before God. James then describes a specific example of love—the care of "orphans and widows." "Look after" (GK *2170*) also appears in Mt 25:36, 43 with reference to visiting the sick; it is not merely making a social call, but caring deeply for their needs. This is "faith expressing itself through love" (Gal 5:6).

(3) One whose religion is genuine will also avoid "being polluted by the world." "World" (GK *3180*) here describes the total system of evil that pervades every sphere of human existence and is set in opposition to God and to righteousness.

To summarize, vv.22–27 insist that a person's religion must consist of more than superficial acts. It is not enough to listen to the statement of spiritual truth (vv.22–25), nor is it sufficient to engage in formal religious activity (v.26). The person whose religious experience is genuine will put spiritual truth into practice, and one's life will be marked by love for others and holiness before God.

IV. The Condemnation of Partiality (2:1–13)

In 1:19–27 James has shown the importance of putting spiritual truth into practice. In each of the following sections he discusses at some length the application of the Word of truth to a specific aspect of life. In 2:1–13 he shows how partiality or discrimination violates the standard of God's truth.

1 James begins his discussion of partiality by a prohibition: "Don't show favoritism" (lit., "stop showing favoritism"). That the recipients of this letter were guilty of practicing discrimination is apparent from v.6. Partiality is inconsistent with faith "in our glorious Lord Jesus Christ." To say that practicing favoritism contradicts one's profession of faith is another way of saying that one's action does not measure up to the truth one professes to believe. The stress on Christ as "glorious" heightens the gross inconsistency of allowing favoritism and discrimination to be associated with faith in such an exalted person as Christ.

2 A hypothetical illustration follows: "Suppose a man comes into your meeting." The word translated "meeting" is *synagoge* (GK *5252*), which had primary reference to the Jewish synagogue. The term need not be taken literally, however, as an indication that the Jewish Christians were still meeting in synagogue buildings. Even after leaving the synagogue, Jewish Christians no doubt continued to refer to their church meeting as a *synagoge*.

James pictures two men entering this early assembly. The first one is "wearing a gold ring and fine clothes"—the clothing of a rich person or a dignitary. In sharp contrast are the "shabby [lit., filthy; GK *4865*] clothes" of the "poor man" (GK *4777*). Inasmuch as this poor man is in reality a beggar, it seems most natural that his clothes should be described as filthy.

3 The rich man is shown "special attention" (GK *2098*), a word that means "to look with favor on" someone and so to give assistance (cf. its use in Lk 9:38). This rich man is the object of solicitous attention as he is shown to "a good seat." In contrast, "the poor man" is abruptly told to "stand there," perhaps in the back of the assembly or in some other out-of-the-way place; his other alternative is to "sit on the floor by my feet" (lit., "sit by my footstool"). The contrast between the speaker who has a stool for his feet and the beggar who must sit on the floor heightens the discrimination.

4 The expressed condemnation of this practice is put in question form, but in a question that expects the readers to agree with the conclusion: "Have you not discriminated?" The practice illustrated in vv.2–3 rests on an unjustified distinction. The basis for showing favor is wrong. Those acting in this way "become judges with evil thoughts." Here the play on words in the Greek is not apparent in the English translation. The word translated "discriminated" (GK *1359*) is built on the same root as the word for "judges" (GK *3216*). In so judging between people, the readers had become unjust judges.

5 Verses 5–11 advance two arguments against the practice of favoritism. The first may be called the *social* argument (vv.5–7). The importance the author attaches to these arguments is seen in the imperative "Listen, my dear brothers." The early church was not drawn from the wealthy or ruling classes. It was largely made up of poorer people, those who were "poor in the eyes of the world" (cf. Mt 11:5; 1Co 1:26–29). By saying that the believers' poverty is poverty "in the eyes of the world," James suggests that they are not really poor. They are "rich in faith" and heirs of the kingdom. The aspect of the kingdom James has in mind is future. It is the eternal kingdom that Christ equated with eternal life (Mt 25:34, 46). The social snobbery of the world is short-sighted and superficial. And the favoritism James's readers practiced was based on this same shallow kind of evaluation.

James's concept of the blessed poor may be misunderstood. He does not say that all poor people are "rich in faith," nor does he exclude the rich from the ranks of the saved. Furthermore, God's choice of the poor must not be taken as based on any merit inherent in poverty. One reason God "has chosen those who are poor" may be seen in the account of the rich young ruler (Mk 10:17–27). There Jesus indicated that those who have riches find it exceedingly difficult to enter God's kingdom (vv.23–25), apparently because their wealth stands in the way. God blesses those who willingly recognize their spiritual bankruptcy (Mt 5:3). A second reason why God chooses the poor is explicitly stated in 1Co 1:26–29. God selects those who have nothing or are nothing in themselves "so that no one may boast before him" (v.29).

6–7 In sharp contrast to God's choice of the poor (v.5) is the way James's readers had treated them. God had chosen them, but they had "insulted" them! The incongruity of such treatment is dramatized by three pointed questions. (1) The rich are the ones "who are exploiting you" (GK *2872*), are they not? "Exploiting" is a strong term describing the brutal and tyrannical deprivation of one's rights (cf. its use in the LXX of Eze 22:29; Zec 7:10).

(2) Is it not the rich "who are dragging you into court?" The picture presented here is the act of forcibly dragging a person before a court of law (cf. Ac 16:19; 21:30)—perhaps being literally done by the rich themselves.

(3) The rich "are slandering [lit., blaspheming; GK *1059*] the noble name" of Christ, aren't they? They are speaking irreverently and disrespectfully of Deity. Christ's name is described as "noble," "excellent," or "honorable" (GK *2819*), a word that refers to what is kind or morally good. This "noble name" is the name of "him to whom you belong" (lit., "the noble name that was called upon you"). This expression clearly reveals its OT background (Dt 28:10; 2Ch 7:14; Am 9:12). A person was dedicated to God by calling God's name over him or her. That act indicated that the individual belonged to God. So Christians bear the worthy name of Christ as indication that they are his people. To show favoritism to those who blaspheme that wonderful name is the greatest incongruity of all.

8 James now proceeds to his *moral* argument in refutation of the practice of showing favoritism (vv.8–11). Here it is not a question of mere incongruity but of the rightness or wrongness of showing partiality. The commandment to love one's neighbor as oneself (Lev 19:18) is not described as the "royal" (GK 997) law simply because of its lofty character. Rather, it is because it is the supreme law to which all other laws governing human relationships are subordinate. It is the summation of all such laws (Mt 22:36–40). The one who keeps this supreme law is "doing right." The right course of action is to show favor to everyone, whether one is rich or poor. Love overlooks such superficial distinctions as wealth and quality of clothing. It shows kindness to a person in spite of any distasteful qualities he or she may have.

9 Whereas v.8 depicts the positive example of one who fully keeps the law, v.9 sets forth the negative example of one who breaks it. To "show favoritism" is not merely to be guilty of an insignificant fault or social impropriety; it is "sin." Such a conclusion is based on solid legal ground rather than general human opinion. Those engaging in partiality "are convicted by the law as lawbreakers." Having just cited the "royal law" in v.8, James says that anyone who shows favoritism breaks the supreme law of love for one's neighbor, the law that comprehends all laws governing one's relationships to one's fellow human beings.

10 "For" indicates that James is going to explain how an act of favoritism makes a person a "lawbreaker" (v.9). It is obvious that he has set up a hypothetical case when he speaks of someone who "keeps the whole law" except for "one point," for in 3:2 he insists that "we all stumble in many ways." However, for the sake of his argument, he imagines a person who "stumbles" (GK 4760) or sins at just one point. His reasoning is that to break one commandment makes a person "guilty of breaking" the whole law.

11 This verse also opens with "for," showing that the author is continuing his explanation. He does so with a simple illustration based on the unity of law. Although God's law has many facets, it is essentially one, being the expression of the character and will of God himself. To violate the law at any one point is not to violate one commandment only; it is to violate the will of God and to contradict the character of God. The same God who said, "Do not commit adultery," also said "Do not murder." It is also the same God who gave the royal law of love for one's neighbor. The person who breaks just one of these laws has "become a lawbreaker." Although only one commandment is broken, the entire law of God has been flouted. When viewed like this, an act of favoritism is far from insignificant.

12 The section (2:1–13) concludes with an urgent exhortation and a warning (vv.12–13). The commands "Speak and act" are stronger in the Greek text than in the English. Literally, James says, "So speak and so act." The double "so" serves to distribute the emphasis equally between the two verbs. James would have his readers continue to speak and act in light of the fact that they "are going to be judged." Since he is speaking to believers, the judgment to which he refers must be their judgment at "the judgment seat of Christ" (2Co 5:10). The standard of judgment will be "the law that gives freedom," not the enslaving legalistic system developed by some of the scribes and Pharisees. It is the royal law of love (v.8), which the believer is enabled to keep by the Holy Spirit (Gal 5:22–23).

13 The reason for responding to the exhortation of v.12 is that "judgment without mercy" will be the lot of the unmerciful. No doubt "mercy" is singled out because James has the poor man of v.2 in mind. Instead of the mercy the man needed, he received cruel discrimination—and that at the hands of professing Christians. The basic principle that underlies v.12a was stated by Christ himself in Mt 18:33: The recipient of mercy should likewise be merciful. Mercy should be the mark of the regenerated person. If it is present in the believer's life, he or she will have nothing to fear at the judgment. It is in this sense that "mercy triumphs over judgment." The believer will be able to smile triumphantly in the time of judgment (cf. also 1Jn 4:17).

V. The Relation of Faith and Action (2:14–26)

This section has sometimes been misunderstood as conflicting with Paul's doctrine of justification by faith alone. No less a scholar than Martin Luther thought he saw an inconsistency between the teachings of

James and Paul. However, careful study reveals that there is no disagreement between a Pauline statement like Eph 2:8–10 and the declaration of Jas 2:24.

The passage at hand (2:14–26) divides itself into three sections: the proposition (vv.16–17); the argument (vv.18–25); and the concluding statement (v.26). Here the author makes another application of the bedrock principle set forth in 1:19–27, that hearing must be accompanied by doing. This letter leaves no place for a religion that is mere mental acceptance of truth.

14 James first states his proposition in two questions, both of which declare that faith not accompanied by good deeds is of no saving value. The two questions set up the hypothetical case of a person who "claims to have" genuine saving faith. James does not say that the person actually has faith. The question "Can such faith save him?" is so structured in the Greek text that it expects a negative answer: "This faith [i.e., faith not accompanied by deeds] can't save him, can it?" Faith that saves requires faith that proves itself in the deeds it produces. These deeds do not earn merit before God; rather, genuine faith is a concomitant of regeneration and therefore affects the believer's behavior. Faith that does not issue in regenerate actions is superficial and spurious.

15–16 The proposition is now illustrated by a supposition bordering on the ludicrous. It is the case of a fellow-believer who is in dire need of clothes and food. The statement "Go, I wish you well" is a modern idiom used to represent James's "Go in peace" (a standard Hebrew farewell). The translation "keep warm and well fed" may be somewhat misleading in suggesting that the person is already warm and fed, which is not the case. The form of these two verbs either suggests that it is someone else's responsibility to clothe and feed the unfortunate person ("Be warmed and fed by someone else"), or it means, "Get yourself some warm clothes and some food," without defining the source. The preposterousness of such a command is no doubt intentional. "What good is it?" James asks. Its seeming concern for the welfare of the poor person is a worthless facade.

17 James states the proposition he intends to demonstrate in the following verses: "Faith ... not accompanied by action is dead." Action is the proper fruit of living faith. Because life is dynamic and productive, faith that lives will surely produce the fruit of good deeds. Therefore, if no deeds are forthcoming, it is proof that the professed faith is dead. James does not deny that it is faith. He simply indicates that it is not the right kind of faith. It is not living faith, nor can it save.

18 James next proceeds to develop the argument in support of his proposition. His first point is that deeds are necessary to prove that a person has faith. The problem of identifying the persons referred to by the pronouns "you" and "I" is not easily resolved. Perhaps it is best to paraphrase the quotation as follows: "One person has faith; another has deeds." The statement then becomes an assertion that faith and works are not necessarily related to each other and that it is possible to have either one without the other. To this assertion James responds with a challenge: "Show me your faith without deeds." He implies that faith cannot be demonstrated apart from action. It is an attitude of the inner person, and it can only be seen as it influences the actions of the one who possesses it. Mere profession of faith proves nothing as to its reality. Hence James declares, "I will show you my faith by what I do."

19 The second argument offered in support of the proposition stated in v.17 concerns the nature of saving faith. All faithful Jews believed the creed known as the Shema found in Dt 6:4: "Hear, O Israel: The LORD our God, the LORD is one." James commends his Jewish Christian readers for believing "that there is one God." This is "good!" But such acceptance of a creed is not enough to save a person. To prove his point, James declares that "even demons believe" the Shema. They know that there is but one God, and as a result they "shudder" (GK 5857) from fear. That the demons are afraid of God is evidence that their belief is a thorough conviction. However, their response is also evidence that their faith is not saving faith. Their belief has not brought them peace with God. Saving faith, then, is not mere intellectual acceptance of a theological proposition. It goes much deeper, involving one's whole inner being and expressing itself outwardly in a changed life.

20 James introduces the next argument in support of his proposition (v.17) with the question "Do you want evidence?" His manner of addressing his imagined opponent is blunt. The Greek adjective translated "foolish" (GK *3031*) means "empty." It refers to a deficiency that is intellectual, but in the theological and moral context of the NT the term also has a moral and spiritual flavor. So James addresses his opponent as one who has no comprehension of spiritual truth, one who does not see "that faith without deeds is useless [GK *734*]." In v.1, such faith is called "dead"; here it is described as something that does not work. The evidence he offers his opponent is found in vv.21–25 and consists of two OT examples—Abraham and Rahab.

21 The designation of Abraham as "our ancestor" (lit., "father"; GK *4252*) agrees with evidence found elsewhere in the letter (e.g., 1:1) that James wrote for a Jewish readership. "Considered righteous" (GK *1467*; can also be translated "justified") is a forensic term; it never refers to making a person subjectively righteous, but always describes the act of declaring a person righteous. To James, Abraham was declared righteous "for what he did." It was a pronouncement that found its source in Abraham's obedient offering of his son (Ge 22:1–14), as the following verses explain.

22 James now makes it clear that he is not talking about works as the sole source of Abraham's justification, as v.21 taken out of its context might lead one to believe. Instead, Abraham's "faith and his actions were working together." Faith and works are inseparable. It is not possible for one person to have valid faith without works and for another to have genuine works without faith, as James's opponent argued in v.18.

But this may sound as if Abraham's justification resulted from a mixture of faith and works, each being equally efficacious. If this is what James meant, he is in conflict with Paul, who insists that faith is the only means of justification. However, it is not necessary to take James's statement in this way. James, assuming that a person is justified by faith alone, declares that this justifying faith has a certain quality, a vitality that makes it the producer of good deeds. It is an action-producing faith, the same type of faith Paul described when he wrote about "faith expressing itself through love" (Gal 5:6). In this sense Abraham's faith was validated by his deeds. If there had been no good deeds following, faith would have been incomplete (v.22), dead (v.17), and useless (v.20). In this sense also Abraham was "considered righteous for what he did." If there had been no good deeds forthcoming, his faith would not have been genuine; and therefore it could not have been counted to him for righteousness.

23 "The scripture" that James considers "fulfilled" is Ge 15:6; the account of the offering of Isaac on the altar appears in Ge 22:1-14 (cf. v.21). Thirty years may have intervened between the events of these two chapters. In the former passage Abraham's faith was "credited to him as righteousness"; the obedient offering of Isaac in Ge 22 "fulfilled" that former statement. This should not be understood as the fulfillment of a prophecy. Rather, it is fulfillment in the sense of completion (cf. v.22). God's act of crediting Abraham with righteousness because of his faith was vindicated by his act of obedience in offering his son. James adds, as a parallel description of Abraham's standing with God, that "he was called God's friend" (see 2Ch 20:7; Isa 41:8). This is another way of saying that he was right with God. He acted as a friend of God should act and thus showed that he was in reality God's friend.

24 In this summary statement James assumes that a person is justified by faith but "not by faith alone." It is by faith *and* "by what he does." Taken by itself, this declaration may seem blatantly contradictory to such Pauline statements as Eph 2:8–9. If both passages are studied in context, however, the seeming contradiction disappears. James has indicated that deeds complete faith (v.22). Thus deeds are the evidence that saving faith is present in a person's life (v.18). He was combating a superficial faith that had no wholesome effect in the life of the professed believer. Paul, on the other hand, was combating legalism—the belief that one may earn saving merit before God by one's good deeds. Consequently he insisted that salvation is not by works but by faith alone. However, the following context in Eph 2:10 reveals that Paul did not depreciate good works. He declared, "We are God's workmanship, created in Christ Jesus to do good works." In Paul, therefore, as well as in James, good deeds are the product of genuine faith. In both writers faith that produces no good deeds is incapable of saving a person.

25 The second OT person cited as an example of genuine faith is "Rahab the prostitute." She too was "considered righteous for what she did." Although her faith was like that of Abraham, she was unlike the patriarch in almost every other way. She was a pagan, a woman, and a prostitute. Nevertheless, she chose to become identified with the people of Israel, a decision based on faith (cf. Jos 2:8–13; Heb 11:31). Far from being dead or worthless, her faith moved her to risk her life to protect the spies. As a result, she was declared righteous. James does not give approval to Rahab's former life; it is her living faith, seen against the background of her previous immorality, that he commends.

26 The argument of vv.18–25 concludes with a statement that cites the human body as an illustration. "The body without the spirit" is nothing but a corpse. "Faith without deeds" is as dead as a corpse and equally useless. James does not imply that deeds are the actual life principle that gives life to faith, but only that faith and deeds are inseparable.

VI. The Control of the Tongue (3:1–12)

In this section the author picks up a subject first mentioned in 1:19 and reiterated in 1:26. Genuine religion should exert a controlling influence over a person's tongue. James's treatment of the topic may be broken into three subdivisions: the weighty responsibility of teachers (vv.1–2); the powerful influence of the tongue (vv.3–6); and the perversity of the tongue (vv.7–12).

1 James's first concern in this passage has to do with those who desired to be "teachers" in the scattered Jewish Christian congregations (cf. 1Ti 1:7). It seems to have been a common practice for many of the readers to seek to become teachers. So James warns that they should stop becoming teachers in such large numbers. No doubt many who were not qualified by natural ability or spiritual gift were coveting the prestige of teaching. They are warned that teachers "will be judged more strictly." It is apparent from the words "we who teach" that James includes himself as a teacher. The judgment of teachers will be especially strict because greater responsibility rests on them. The reason for this is that the teacher's essential instrument, the tongue, has such great influence.

2 James gives the basis for what he has just said in v.1: The tongue is the most difficult member of the body to control. To say that "we all stumble" (GK 4760) is not merely to declare that everyone makes mistakes. This word is used figuratively to refer to acts of sin (cf. 2:10). Thus the author declares the universality of sin, even among believers. The person who "is never at fault" in his speech (i.e., never commits sins of speech) "is a perfect man." If anyone could be found who never sins with the tongue, that person would never sin in any other way, either. Since sins of the tongue are hardest to avoid, anyone who can control the tongue is surely able to "keep his whole body" from being used as an instrument of sin.

3 James illustrates the powerful influence of the tongue by the practice of putting "bits into the mouths of horses to make them obey us." A small bit "can turn the whole animal." So a person who controls the tongue can control his or her whole being.

4 The next illustration on the influence of the tongue is the rudder of a ship. Three factors made ships of that day difficult to control: they were "so large"; they were "driven by strong winds"; and they were "steered by a very small rudder." The rudder was a small blade on the end of a tiller, extending through a form of oarlock from the rear of the ship. Compared to the size of the vessel and the power of the gale, the rudder was but a minute part; yet it guided the ship "wherever the pilot want[ed] to go."

5 With the words "likewise the tongue," the application of the two preceding verses is introduced. Like bits (v.3) and rudders (v.4), the tongue also is a small item. Yet, also like them, it exerts a powerful influence. "It makes great boasts," and these are not empty claims. The tongue is able to sway multitudes. It can alter the destinies of nations. The destructive potential of the tongue is graphically pictured by a forest fire. Thousands of acres of valuable timber may be devastated by a "small spark." In the first two illustrations, animals and ships are controlled by small objects; in this last illustration, a huge forest is destroyed by a tiny spark. The tongue likewise can either control or destroy.

6 So, James says, "The tongue also is a fire." The inflammatory tongue has turned brother against brother, neighbor against neighbor, nation against nation. The tongue is also "a world of evil." It is as though all the wickedness in the whole world were wrapped up in that little piece of flesh. There are few sins people commit in which the tongue is not involved.

James describes the tongue's influence as both destructive and as corrupting the whole "person" (lit., "body"; GK 5393). Since the person resides in the body and uses the body as his or her instrument, James seems to use "body" to refer to the entire person. In reality, he is not referring to the tongue of flesh but to the intelligent, communicating mind that uses the tongue as its instrument. So the mind corrupts the whole person. But the corrupting influence of the tongue reaches out in widening circles, for it "sets the whole course of his life on fire." James is referring to the effect the tongue has on the whole of human existence. Finally, he traces the inflaming nature of the tongue back to its source. It is "set on fire by hell [GK *1147*]" (see comment on Mk 9:43–48); this is James's way of saying that it comes from the devil.

7 James shifts almost unnoticeably from discussing the power of the tongue (vv.3–6) to a discussion of its perversity (vv.7–12). According to vv.7–8, one's inability to tame the tongue shows the perversity of the tongue. At creation God gave human beings the dominion over the animals that they have exercised ever since (Ge 1:28). "All kinds" of creatures of land, sea, and air have been subdued by them. To emphasize the continuing aspect of that dominance over the animals, James uses both the present and the perfect tenses—"are being tamed and have been tamed."

8 But even though humanity has retained dominion over all kinds of animals, because of the fall they have lost dominion over themselves. When James says, "No man can tame the tongue," he is stating that no one by himself or herself can subdue the tongue. This is not to say that God cannot bring it under control, for the tongue of the regenerate person can be controlled by the indwelling Holy Spirit. In its natural state the tongue "is a restless evil," like a ferocious beast that will not be subdued. It is "full of deadly poison," like a serpent ready to inject venom into its victim.

9 Here James speaks of inconsistency as an aspect of the tongue's perversity (vv.9–12). We can use the same instrument to "praise our Lord and Father" and to "curse men." But praising God and cursing people is tantamount to praising and cursing the same person, for in v.9 James describes a human being as "made in God's likeness" (cf. Ge 1:26–27). Although marred by sin, that image is still very much a reality; and human intellect, emotion, and will show that people still bear God's likeness. Obviously, James is not referring to such curses as those that Paul invoked on anyone who perverts the Gospel (Gal 1:6–9). Instead, it is the cursing that grows out of bitterness and hatred that he speaks of.

10 Again, James stresses the inconsistency of the tongue in that it is the source of such direct opposites as "praise and cursing." He does not have only the unsaved in mind because he introduces his rebuke with the words "my brothers," the term used throughout the letter to address believers (1:2, 16, 19; 2:1, 5, 14; 3:1; et al.). Although believers have in the indwelling Holy Spirit the potential for controlling the tongue, they may not be appropriating this potential. Hence, James insists that "this should not be." The mouth should be used consistently to praise God and to express love and kindness to other people.

11 James again turns to nature for his illustrations. He asks, "Can both fresh water and salt water flow from the same spring?" The water is sweet (NIV "fresh"; GK *1184*) and bitter (NIV, "salt"; GK *4395*). The former describes fresh water that is good for drinking; the latter refers to water so brackish or even salty as to be unfit for drinking. James may have had the Dead Sea in mind.

12 James concludes his discussion of the tongue by going behind the physical organ to the real source of speech. He asks, "Can a fig tree bear olives?" A plant produces according to its nature, whether figs, grapes, or any other fruit. So with "a salt spring." It cannot "produce fresh water" because it is not a fresh water spring. Therefore, out of the mouth of a good person come good words, and out of the mouth of a sinful person come sinful words.

VII. Two Kinds of Wisdom (3:13–18)

This passage is a natural outgrowth of the discussion of the tongue. The six verses divide into three sections: an exhortation (v.13); earthly wisdom (vv.14–16); and wisdom from heaven (vv.17–18).

13 James addresses the person who is "wise [GK 5055] and understanding [GK 2184]." The former word was a technical term among the Jews for the teacher, the scribe, and the rabbi. James is still speaking to those who would be teachers (cf. 3:1); here it is not what they say that he is concerned with, but rather how they live. "Understanding" describes one who is an expert, who has special knowledge or training. Thus anyone who would be a teacher, who claims to be an expert with special understanding, is under obligation to "show it by his good life." He should possess "know how" and be skilled in applying God's truth to practical, everyday living.

The particular characteristic stressed in this verse is "humility that comes from wisdom." "Humility" (GK 4559) is perhaps better translated "gentleness," but even this does not adequately render the Greek word (see comment on 1:21). It is not a passive gentleness growing out of weakness or resignation; rather, it is an active attitude of deliberate acceptance. The word was used to describe a horse that had been broken and trained to submit to the bridle. So this gentleness is strength under control, the control of the Spirit of God (Gal 5:22–23). It is a gentleness that is characteristic of "wisdom" (GK 50 53; see comment on 1.5). James does not have in mind the Greek concept of speculative or theoretical wisdom but the Hebrew idea of practical wisdom that enables one to live a life of godliness.

14 The specific form of "if" used here suggests that some of James's readers were harboring "bitter envy and selfish ambition" in their hearts. "Selfish ambition" (GK 2249) is a self-seeking attitude bent on gaining advantage and prestige for oneself or one's group. This forceful term colors the word "envy" (GK 2419), so that it here means "selfish zeal." The word is often used to describe fanatical zeal for a cause (1Ki 19:10; Ps 69:9; Isa 9:7), in either a good or a bad sense. James makes it clear by the adjective "bitter" (GK 4395) that he is referring to a sinful zeal. Because this condition existed among his readers, he insists that they must "not boast about [bitter zeal and selfish ambition] or deny the truth." James's readers may have been priding themselves in their partisan defense of the truth—a defense that was to their own advantage and advancement. Through such bitter and partisan defense, they were in reality denying the very truth they were attempting to defend.

15 Though James refers to the attitude described in v.14 as "wisdom," he obviously does not mean that it is genuine wisdom. On the contrary, it is the wisdom claimed by the would-be teachers of v.14, whose lives contradict their claims. Such "wisdom" evaluates everything by worldly standards and makes personal gain life's highest goal. Yet even this spurious use of the term reflects the Hebrew concept of wisdom as practical rather than theoretical. God is the source of genuine wisdom (1:5; cf. Pr 2:6), but this pseudo-wisdom is not from him, because, as James declares, "such 'wisdom' does not come down from heaven." Instead, it is "earthly" in source as well as kind. It views life from the limited viewpoint of this world rather than from heaven's vantage point. Its mind is set on earthly things (Php 3:19). James also calls this wisdom "unspiritual" (GK 6035; cf. 1Co 2:14–15, where this word is contrasted with "spiritual," GK 4461). The "spiritual" person has received the Spirit of God (1Co 2:12), but the "unspiritual" person does not have the Spirit (Jude 19). Thus "wisdom" that is "unspiritual" characterizes unregenerate human nature. Furthermore, it is "of the devil."

16 The conjunction "for" indicates that bitter zeal and selfish ambition always result in "disorder and every evil practice." "Disorder" (GK 189) is a common word for anarchy and political turmoil (Luke uses it to refer to political uprisings in Lk 21:9). James is no doubt speaking of disturbance and turmoil in the church. The "evil practice" refers specifically to worthless activity, to deeds that are bad because they are good for nothing and cannot produce any real benefit. Selfish zeal and ambition, then, always tend to destroy spiritual life and work.

17 In contrast to the denial of v.15, James turns to a description of "the wisdom that comes from heaven." Its basic characteristic is "pure" (GK 54). The reference is not to sexual purity but to the absence of any sinful attitude or motive. It is the opposite of the self-seeking attitude of vv.14–16. From this inner quality flow the outward manifestations given in the rest of the verse.

James goes on to describe this wisdom as "peace-loving" (GK 1646), in contrast to the bitter spirit of competitiveness and selfish ambition described in v.14. Next, it is "considerate" (GK 2117). In the LXX this word is used mostly of God's disposition as King. He is gentle and kind, although in reality he has every reason to be stern and punitive toward people in their sin. God's people also are to be marked by this godlike quality, not insisting on their legal rights but exercising love's leniency instead.

Likewise, godly wisdom is "submissive" (GK 2340). This quality is the opposite of obstinacy and self-seeking; it is a readiness to yield. Furthermore, it is "full of mercy and good fruit." That is, it is compassionate and always ready to help those who are in need. It is "impartial" (GK 88), showing no favoritism, and discriminating against no one. Finally, this wisdom is "sincere" (lit., "without hypocrisy"; GK 537). Far from being theoretical and speculative, James's concept of wisdom is thoroughly practical. It is the understanding and attitude that result in true piety and godliness.

18 James concludes his discussion of "the wisdom that comes from heaven" by reiterating the second quality listed in v.17. To "raise a harvest of righteousness" demands a certain kind of climate. A crop of righteousness cannot be produced in the climate of bitterness and self-seeking. Righteousness will grow only in a climate of peace; thus it must be sown and cultivated by the "peacemakers." Such persons not only love peace and live in peace but also strive to create conditions of peace.

VIII. The Worldly Attitude (4:1–10)

In 3:14–16 James has discussed a philosophy of life that is characteristic of the unregenerate mind and is a major ingredient of worldliness. Now he examines this worldly attitude in greater detail. First he identifies the source of worldly antagonisms (vv.1–3); next, he reproves spiritual unfaithfulness (vv.4–6); finally, he pleads for submission to God (vv.7–10).

1 Instead of the climate of peace necessary for the production of righteousness (3:18), James's readers were living in an atmosphere of constant "fights and quarrels." These two nouns were normally used of national warfare, but they had also become common, forceful expressions for any kind of open antagonism. James answers his question about the cause of fights and quarrels with an answer with which he expects his reader to agree: "Don't they come from your desires [GK 2454]?" The Greek word for "desires" is the source of the English word "hedonism," the designation of the philosophy that views pleasure as the chief goal of life. James pictures these pleasures as residing within his readers as the overriding desires of their lives. Nothing will be allowed to stand in the way of their realization.

2 "You want something" (GK 2121) is not quite forceful enough to fit the context or to represent the Greek verb, which expresses anxious longing and eager desire. So strong is the desire that "you kill and covet." This last statement has aroused much discussion. First, it is difficult to believe that James's readers, whom he elsewhere addresses as Christians (2:1), were actually guilty of murder. Some, insisting that the word must be taken literally, say that James is not referring to any specific occurrences but is indicating what generally happens when people desire pleasure rather than God. This interpretation, however, does not do justice to the pointed accusation "*You* kill." In the context of "wars and battles," it seems best to take "you kill" as hyperbole for hatred (equivalent to murder in Mt 5:21–22; 1Jn 3:15). This also resolves the problem of seeming anticlimactic word order. To say "You hate and covet" is a much more natural order than to say "You murder and covet." James then repeats his assertion that, with all their consuming desire and bitter antagonism, his readers were not able to obtain what they wanted, because they were going after it in the wrong way. They did "not ask God" for it. They were lusting and fighting rather than praying.

3 Even when James's readers did ask God for things, they did "not receive" what they requested. Why? They asked "with wrong motives." Their purpose was to "spend" what they got for "pleasures" (same word as "desires" in v.1). The prodigal son exemplifies one who spent his money in this way (Lk 15:14). It was the desire of James's readers for pleasures that was battling within them for satisfaction (v.1) and even leading them to try to use prayer as a means of gratification. They wanted to gratify themselves rather than help others and please God.

4 Having identified the source of the bitter fighting as being the desire for pleasure, James next rebukes his readers for spiritual unfaithfulness. "Adulterous people" renders "adulteresses" (GK 3655). The people of God in the OT are considered the wife of the Lord (Jer 31:32), and in the NT, the bride of Christ (Eph 5:23–32). It is reasonable, therefore, to understand "adulteress" as a figure of speech for spiritual unfaithfulness. It is a blunt and shocking word, intended to jar the readers and awaken them to their true spiritual condition. The concept of spiritual adultery was no doubt taken from the OT (cf. Hos 2:2–5; 3:1–5; 9:1).

For believers, however, there are two possible objects for affection: the world and God, and these two are direct opposites. James uses "world" (GK 3180) to refer to the system of evil controlled by Satan. It includes all that is wicked and opposed to God on this earth. James is thinking especially of pleasures that lure people's hearts from God. By its very nature, "friendship with the world is hatred toward God." To have a warm, familiar attitude toward this evil world is to be on good terms with God's enemy. It is to adopt the world's set of values and to want what the world wants. The person who deliberately "chooses [GK 1089] to be a friend of the world becomes an enemy of God."

5 This verse is one of the most difficult in the letter. Various translations have been suggested, but there is good reason to believe that the first translation given in the NIV footnote for the last part of the verse is correct and fits the context better: "God jealously longs for the spirit that he made to live in us." Verse 4 indicates that believers who are friends of the world are guilty of spiritual adultery. Although their love and devotion belong to God, they have fallen in love with the world. It is natural, therefore, to expect v.5 (closely tied to v.4 by "or") to speak of God's jealous longing for his people's love, not the people's own envious spirit (cf. Ex 20:5; 34:14, which refer to God as jealously desiring the devotion of his people).

A second reason for preferring the NIV footnote rendering is that it more accurately represents the Greek text. The Greek words representing "envies" form an idiom meaning "jealously." Together with GK 2160 (translated "intensely"), it means "longs jealously for." In v.4 James has accused his readers of spiritual unfaithfulness. If they are not willing to accept this indictment, he asks in v.5 what they think about the OT passages dealing with God's jealous longing for his people. This is the significance of the introductory conjunction "or." Do they think Scripture speaks "without reason"? Of course they don't think this. Consequently, it is necessary to believe that friendship with the world is enmity toward God, and thus it is spiritual unfaithfulness.

6 The words "he gives us more grace" are taken from Pr 3:34, quoted later in this verse. The meaning of vv. 4–6 is that God has set a high standard for wholehearted love and devotion on the part of his people as they resist the appeal of the world, but he gives grace that is greater than the rigorous demand he has made. This assurance is documented from Proverbs, the point of which is in the second clause. The reference to "the humble" (GK 5424) constitutes the theme for vv.7–10, where James pleads for submission to God. They should be the people who willingly submit to God's desire for them rather than proudly insist on satisfying their own desires for pleasure (cf. vv.1–3).

7 James issues a series of ten commands in vv.7–10. In each one the specific Greek form used calls for immediate response. It is a pointed and forceful way to demand action. The command to "submit" (GK 5718) to God is the logical response to the quotation from Pr 3:34 (cf. "then," which has the inferential meaning of "therefore"). Since "God opposes the proud" but helps "the humble," believers should submit to him. Submission is not the same as obedience. Instead, it is the surrender of one's will, which in turn leads to obedience.

Rather than resisting God's will for us, we should "resist the devil." James appears to suggest that the spiritual unfaithfulness of v.4 was the result of the devil's influence. The promise "he will flee from you" gives assurance that, as powerful as he may be, Satan can be resisted.

8 The series of imperatives continues with the command to "come near to God." In setting their hearts on pleasure, James's readers had drifted away from God. Though still his people, they had become estranged from him. But the assurance that God will welcome them back accompanies the command to return. God jealously yearns for their devotion (v.5). The call to "wash your hands" is a command to make one's conduct pure. Similarly, the call to "purify your hearts" insists on purity of thoughts and motives. The eager quest for pleasure (vv.1–5) had resulted in sins of heart and hand. So James bluntly addresses them as "you sinners," a strong term, showing the extent of their involvement in worldly attitudes and actions. The designation "double-minded" is used somewhat differently than in 1:8. Here it describes the attempt of the readers to love God and the pleasures of the world at the same time.

9 Four of the ten imperatives of vv.7–10 occur in this verse, and all four are calls to repentance. "Grieve" (GK *5415*) is a strong word meaning "to be miserable or wretched." In contrast to the worldly pleasures they had sought so eagerly, James's readers are to repent in misery. They also are commanded to "mourn" (GK *4291*), a verb depicting passionate grief that cannot be hidden. Similar outward grief is called for in the verb "wail" (GK *3081*). In the past, when the readers had pursued pleasure, their lives had been marked by "laughter" and "joy"; but now they are to change their "laughter to mourning" and their "joy to gloom." Some have imagined that the attitude expressed in this verse is to be the constant characteristic of the Christian. Such an interpretation, however, overlooks the situation that gave rise to these commands. It was the burning desire for pleasures that led James to issue this powerful call to all-out repentance.

10 James now returns to the text quoted from the OT in v.6. God graciously gives aid to the humble; therefore "humble yourselves" (GK *5427*). Here the specific form of humbling is that of repentance for the sin of transferring affections from God to the pleasures of the world. However, the principle stated is much more comprehensive in its application. That God lifts up those who humble themselves is a consistent biblical principle (cf. Mt 23:12; Lk 14:11; 18:14; Php 2:5–11; 1Pe 5:6).

IX. Faultfinding (4:11–12)

11 The prohibition introducing this verse is more accurately translated "Do not speak against one another" rather than "Do not slander" (GK *2895*). To slander is to make false charges or misrepresentations that damage the reputation of another person; the verb used here, however, refers to any form of speaking against someone else. What is said may be true in its content but harsh and unkind in the manner of its presentation. The specific grammatical construction used here usually forbids the continuation of a practice already in progress. James's readers had fallen into the habit of criticizing one another, and so he says, "Stop speaking against one another."

The reason he gives is that the one who criticizes or judges a fellow-Christian "speaks against the law and judges it." The law referred to is probably the command of Lev 19:18: "Love your neighbor as yourself." To speak against your neighbor is to violate this law. Those who do so place themselves above the law and, by their actions, declare that law to be a bad or unnecessary statute. Rather than submitting to it and "keeping it," they pass judgment on its validity and set it aside.

12 In passing judgment, this critic of a fellow-Christian has usurped a position of authority that is reserved for God alone. God is the "one Lawgiver and Judge." Since he gave the law, he is qualified to judge those who are responsible to keep it. That he is "able to save and destroy" is proof that he is in a position to enforce the law, rewarding those who keep it and punishing those who violate it. "But you—who are you?" catches James's full force here. With shattering bluntness, he crushes any right his readers may have claimed to sit in judgment over others. This is not to rule out civil courts and judges, but it does root out the harsh, unkind, critical spirit that continually finds fault with others.

X. Arrogant Self-Sufficiency (4:13–17)

13 This section gives another example of the "wisdom" that characterizes the world (cf. 3:15). James addresses businessmen, probably Christians, since v.17 seems to suggest that the readers know that their practice is wrong. He begs them to pay careful attention to the seriousness of what follows. The form of the word "say" suggests that the situation under consideration was something that occurred frequently. Business travel in the first century was common, and Jews especially traveled widely for business purposes (cf. Aquila and Priscilla in Ac 18:2, 18; Ro 16:3; Lydia in Ac 16:14). Notice the well-laid plan: (1) "go to this or that city," (2) "spend a year there," (3) "carry on business," and (4) "make money." The starting time is arranged ("today or tomorrow"); the city has been selected; but God has no place in the plans.

14 No allowance is made for unforeseen circumstances. These businessmen are confident that they will be able to carry their plans through to completion. Thus James points out their fallacy. They "do not even know what will happen tomorrow," to say nothing about a year from now. They have been planning as if they know exactly what the future holds or even as if they can control the future. Not only is their knowledge limited, but their lives are uncertain. To point up the transitory nature of life, James employs another illustration from nature—"You are a mist." In the morning it covers the countryside; before noon it is gone. But some of James's readers had been planning as if they were going to be here forever!

15 Instead of saying v.13, the Christian businessman "ought to say, 'If it is the Lord's will.'" No Christian can live independently of God. For believers to leave God out of their plans is an arrogant assumption of self-sufficiency, a tacit declaration of independence from God. It also overlooks reality. Whether people recognize it or not, they "will live and do this or that" only "if it is the Lord's will." A study of the use of this conditional clause in the NT makes it clear that we are not to repeat it mechanically in connection with every statement of future plans. Paul, for example, employs it in Ac 18:21 and 1Co 4:19, but he does not use it in Ac 19:21; Ro 15:28; or 1Co 16:5, 8. Yet it is obvious that whether Paul explicitly stated it or not, he always conditioned his plans on the will of God.

16 Some of James's readers, however, rather than subjecting their plans to God's will, were making it their practice to "boast and brag." To make plans without considering God's plan is the same thing as arrogantly claiming to be in full command of the future. The word translated "brag" (GK 224) refers to proud confidence in one's own knowledge or cleverness (i.e., arrogance). The businessmen addressed by James were proud of their arrogant assumption that they could foresee and control the future. "Such boasting," says James, "is evil." It not only lacks the quality of being good, it is aggressively and viciously wicked.

17 Although this statement may apply to any number of situations, James intends it to refer to the immediately preceding context. Perhaps this is a maxim that means something like "You have been fully warned," as if James were saying, "Now that I have pointed the matter out to you, you have no excuse." Knowing what should be done obligates a person to do it.

XI. Denunciation of the Wicked Rich (5:1–6)

In these six verses James first declares the fact of coming judgment (v.1) and then lists the crimes against which this judgment will be meted out: hoarded wealth (vv.2–3); unpaid wages (v.4); luxury and self-indulgence (v.5); and the murder of innocent people (v.6).

There is good reason to believe that the persons referred to in this section are not believers. It might be argued that they are personally addressed in the same way as other groups (cf. 3:1; 4:13). Since the letter in general is written to Christians, it might be assumed that the rich of 5:1–6 are Christians just as the rich of 1:9–11 are. However, there are significant differences between 5:1–6 and the rest of the letter. These individuals are not addressed as "brothers" (cf. 1:2, 16, 19; et al.). Furthermore, they are not called on to repent and change their ways but only to "weep and wail" because of the judgment they are going to undergo. It is, therefore, more reasonable to understand this section as similar to OT prophetic declarations of coming judgment against pagan nations, which are interspersed among sections addressed to God's people (e.g., Isa 13–21, 23; Eze 25–32).

1 That this verse begins a new section is indicated by the repeated call for attention, "Now listen" (cf. 4:13). The rich are to "weep [GK *3081*] and wail (GK *3909*)." While the first word may describe audible weeping, the second term most certainly does. It is an onomatopoeic word that sounds like howling. In 4:9 James's readers are commanded to make themselves miserable in all-out repentance. But here in 5:1 the rich are told that God will send the miseries of judgment upon them.

2 The first crime charged against the wicked rich is that of hoarding various forms of wealth. They have so much wealth stored up that it "has rotted"; their clothes also are moth eaten. Wealth in those days consisted of both money and such commodities as grain, oil, and costly garments. Evidence that costly garments were stored as wealth and used as payment for services rendered occurs in such passages as 2Ki 5:5, 22; Mt 6:19. Thus what rotted were the commodities and what had been invaded by moths were the stored garments. There is no reason to take these happenings as figurative or as predictive of the future. The tragic fact was that the rich had hoarded so much food and clothing that it was going to waste. Their crime was uncontrolled greed that resulted in oppression of the poor (v.4).

3 An obvious form of wealth was "gold and silver," and this is said to have become "corroded." Since gold and silver do not rust or even corrode, James must refer to tarnished metal, the tarnish indicating how long the hoarded wealth had lain idle. He warns the rich, "Their corrosion will testify against you." It witnessed to the greed and selfishness of these wicked men, who had far more than they could ever use, while their workers were deprived of their wages. The idea that the corrosion will eat the flesh of the rich "like fire" is a graphic way of declaring that their greed will result in their own destruction, as if the corrosion that ate their riches actually will eat their very flesh.

James's statement that the rich had "hoarded wealth in the last days" shows that he had the future judgment in mind. The NT regards the whole period between Christ's first and second comings as the last time or "last days" (cf. Heb 1:1–2; 1Jn 2:18). In comparison with the preparatory days of the OT, this is the last period before Christ comes to set up his kingdom and to judge all people. It was even in the last hour, as it were, before Christ comes to judge, that the rich "hoarded wealth."

4 The second crime the rich are charged with is that they "failed to pay the workmen" who harvested their crops. Here James vividly pictures the unpaid wages, still in the possession of the unscrupulous rich farmers, as continually accusing them of their dishonesty. It was as though the very coins cried out the guilt. The harvesters complained about their treatment, and their complaints "reached the ears of the Lord Almighty." God heard their cries, as he always hears the voice of his suffering people (cf. Ex 3:7). The designation "the Lord Almighty" represents a Hebrew expression that means "Lord of hosts [GK *7372* & *4877*]" or "Lord of the armies." In 1Sa 17:45 this word refers to the armies of Israel, but in 2Ch 18:18 it refers to God's angels and in Dt 4:19 to all the stars. God is Lord of the armies of earth, of the angelic armies, and of all the starry host. He is almighty, and he will vindicate his suffering people in due time.

5 The third charge against the rich is that they have lived "in luxury [GK *5587*] and self-indulgence [GK *5059*]." These two words are synonyms, though there is a shade of difference between them. The first refers to a soft, enervating luxury that tends to demoralize; the second word describes extravagant and wasteful self-indulgence. Both have immoral associations. In their unrestrained indulgence, the rich had "fattened" themselves for "the day of slaughter"—a designation of the day of judgment (Jer 12:3). James uses graphic imagery to indicate that the rich are on the brink of judgment. They were like cattle completely unaware of their impending destruction.

6 The final crime of the wicked rich was that they had "murdered innocent men." In 2:6 the rich are accused of dragging believers into court; here they are charged with murder. This is not to be taken figuratively but literally. Examples are Christ, Stephen, James the son of Zebedee, and, later, the author himself.

By "innocent" (lit., "righteous"; GK *1465*) James has in mind that class of people known as "the righteous," i.e., believers, who came largely from the ranks of the poor (cf. 2:5–7). "Who were not opposing you" misses the bluntness of James's indictment. The Greek text abruptly declares, "He does not oppose you." The rich were guilty of attacking not merely a righteous person but a person who was defenseless or who refused to fight back.

XII. Miscellaneous Exhortations (5:7–20)

1. Concerning Patience (5:7–11)

This exhortation concerning patience is built around three illustrations: the farmer (vv.7–9); the prophets (v.10); and Job (v.11).

7 This exhortation is addressed to the "brothers," indicating that James is turning his attention from the unbelieving rich back to the believing Jewish Christians to whom the letter was sent. The word "then" suggests that the oppression of the righteous poor described in vv.1–6 is what gives rise to the message of vv.7–11. James has just warned the oppressing rich of coming judgment; now he encourages the oppressed poor to "be patient" (GK *3428*). This verb describes the attitude of self-restraint that does not try to get even for a wrong that has been done. It usually represents long-suffering patience toward persons rather than things. So James calls for a patience toward the rich oppressors that will last "until the Lord's coming." "Coming" (*parousia*; GK *4242*) was a common term used to describe the visit of a king to a city or province of his kingdom and thus depicts Christ as a royal personage.

The first illustration of patience is that of the farmer who waits patiently "for the fall and spring rains." In Palestine the early rains came in October and November soon after the grain was sown, and the latter rains came in April and May as the grain was maturing. Both rainy seasons were necessary for a successful crop. Knowing this, the farmer was willing to wait patiently until both rains came and provided the needed moisture.

8 With the words "You too, be patient," James applies the illustration of the patient farmer. In addition, he urges his readers to "stand firm" (lit., "strengthen your hearts"). This expression has the idea of providing solid support, of establishing a person, and thus of enabling one to stand unmoved by trouble. The reason given for standing firm is again that "the Lord's coming is near." The day when things will be set right is imminent. This confident expectation will make the faint heart strong.

9 The believers must be patient toward both outsiders who oppress them and insiders who irritate them. Christians are not to "grumble [GK *5100*] against each other." This verb, often meaning "sigh" or "groan," speaks of inner distress rather than open complaint. What is forbidden here is not the loud and bitter denunciation of others but the unexpressed feeling of bitterness or the smothered resentment that may express itself in a groan or a sigh. For them to continue that hateful practice would result in judgment. And the Judge is represented as "standing at the door," as if his hand is on the latch, ready to enter at any time.

10 The second illustration of patience is that of "the prophets who spoke in the name of the Lord." In their position as God's representatives, they experienced affliction and responded to it with long-suffering patience. Although James refers to "the prophets" as a group, Jeremiah certainly stands out as one who endured mistreatment with patience. He was put in the stocks (Jer 20:2), thrown into prison (32:2), and lowered into a miry dungeon (38:6); yet he persisted in his ministry without bitterness or recrimination. Such men constitute an "example" for believers who are oppressed and mistreated.

11 The third illustration is Job. "Those who have persevered" are considered blessed. No doubt James has in mind his words in 1:12, where he points out the enviable joy of the person who does not cave in under trial. In 5:7–10 the plea is for patience, for self-restraint that does not retaliate; but here in 5:11 he is referring to perseverance in difficult circumstances. It is significant that James speaks of Job's "perseverance" (GK *5705*), not his patience, for despite the popular phrase "the patience of Job," he hardly exemplified that quality (cf. Job 12:2; 13:3–4; 16:2). He was, however, an outstanding example of perseverance in the most trying situations (cf. Job 1:21–22; 2:10; 13:15; 19:25–27). His experience also was proof that "the Lord is full of compassion and mercy," as we see in "what the Lord finally brought about" for him: God gave him "twice as much as he had before" (Job 42:10–17). To sum up, in vv.7-11 James is urging his readers not to fight back but to exercise long-suffering patience toward the rich who oppress them; and he is calling for stout-hearted perseverance in the trying circumstances that confront them.

2. Concerning Oaths (5:12)

12 James next places special emphasis on the prohibition of oaths: "Above all . . . do not swear." As in v.9, the grammatical construction shows that the use of oaths was an existing practice that ought to be discontinued. James is echoing the words of Jesus in Mt 5:34–37, which forbid swearing altogether. It should be obvious that what is referred to in Matthew and James is the light, casual use of oaths in informal conversation—not formal oaths in such places as courts of law. God himself is said to have taken an oath (Ps 110:4), and Paul sometimes called God to witness (2Co 1:21; Gal 1:20). Rather than employing an oath to convince people that a statement is true, Christians should let their "'Yes' be yes," and their "'No,' no." That is, they should be honest in all their speech so that when they make an affirmation or denial, people will know it is unquestionably the truth. In the careless use of oaths people are in danger of taking God's name in vain, for which they will come under judgment (cf. Ex 20:7).

3. Concerning Prayer (5:13–18)

This passage on prayer falls into two sections. Verses 13–16 constitute a call for prayer in every circumstance of life; vv.17–18 illustrate the effectiveness of sincere prayer.

13 One circumstance that calls for prayer is the experience of being "in trouble" (GK 2802). When such an experience comes, Christians need patience. They are not to grumble in bitter disgust (v.9), nor are they to expresses themselves in oaths (v.12). Instead, they "should pray." Patience comes from God, and prayer is an effective way to obtain it. James also urges anyone who is in good spirits to "sing songs of praise." This too is prayer.

14 Sickness is another circumstance where prayer is needed, and concerning such prayer James gives detailed instructions. The sick person "should call for the elders of the church" (cf. Tit 1:5, 7; Ac 20:17, 28). In Ac 20:28 the elders are instructed to shepherd the church of God, i.e., to do the work of a pastor (cf. also 1Pe 5:1–4). Thus, the sick person is to call the pastors of the church "to pray over him and anoint him with oil." Prayer is the more significant of the two ministries performed by the elders, for the overall emphasis of the paragraph belongs on prayer. There are a number of reasons for understanding the application of oil as medicinal rather than sacramental. The word "anoint" (GK 230) is not the usual word for sacramental or ritualistic anointing. Furthermore, it is a well-documented fact that oil was one of the most common medicines of biblical times (see Isa 1:6; Lk 10:34). Josephus reports that during his last illness Herod the Great was given a bath in oil in hopes of effecting a cure. It is evident, then, that James is prescribing prayer and medicine.

15 The assurance is given that prayer "will make the sick person well." In the final analysis, this is what effects the healing. In answer to "the prayer offered in faith," God uses the medicine to cure the malady. The statement "the Lord will raise him up" means that the sick man will be enabled to get up from his sick bed. If it was sin that occasioned his sickness, "he will be forgiven." This suggests the possibility that, because of persistence in sin, God sent sickness as a disciplinary agent (cf. 1Co 11:30). The conditional "*if* he has sinned," however, makes it clear that not all sickness is the result of sin.

16 From the promise of v.15 James draws an inference. Since confession of sin and the prayer of faith bring healing, Christians should confess their "sins to each other and pray for each other." It is not merely the elders who are told to pray here, but Christians in general. If a person has sinned against a fellow-Christian, he or she should confess the sin to that person. This will no doubt result in mutual confession—"to each other." Then the two believers should "pray for each other." If the sin has caused sickness, healing will follow confession and prayer. James proceeds to add the assurance that prayer "is powerful and effective." The "righteous man" here referred to is the one whose sins have been confessed and forgiven. His prayer is fully able to secure results, such as healing of the sick.

17–18 James now offers illustrative proof that a righteous man's prayer is "powerful and effective." "Elijah," he says, "was a man just like us." He had no superhuman powers; he was by nature a human being and nothing more. However, when he prayed "that it would not rain ... it did not rain" (cf. 1Ki 17:1; 18:42–45). The explanation of his power in prayer is twofold: he was a righteous man, and "he prayed earnestly." So James assures his readers that such answers to prayer are within the reach of any believer. It is true that 1Ki 17–18 does not explicitly say that Elijah prayed, but this may be assumed from 17:1 and especially from 18:42. The three and one-half years is a round number based on 18:1.

4. Concerning the Wanderer (5:19–20)

19–20 It is clear from the words "my brothers" that James addresses this last exhortation to believers. It is also apparent that he speaks of the possibility that one of them may "wander from the truth." Verse 20 gives reason to believe that the truth from which the wanderer turns is the saving truth of the Gospel. James's purpose in these closing verses is to encourage Christians to make an effort to bring the wanderer back. Two worthy results of such an accomplishment are cited. First, it will "save him from death." That this cannot be physical death may be inferred from the literal translation of the Greek text: it "will save his soul from death"; thus, it would seem that spiritual death is in view. Since Scripture teaches that once a person is regenerated he or she can never be lost, it may be assumed that his hypothetical wanderer is not a genuine believer. He is one who has been among the believers and has made a profession of faith, but his profession has been superficial. To bring him to genuine faith in the truth saves his soul from eternal death and covers his "many sins"; the wanderer's sins will never be held against him again. As difficult as it may be to win such a person to saving faith, the eternal results make it infinitely worthwhile (see also Heb 6:4–8).

The Old Testament in the New

NT Text	*OT Text*	*Subject*
Jas 2:8	Lev 19:18	Love your neighbor as yourself
Jas 2:11	Ex 20:14; Dt 5:18	Seventh commandment
Jas 2:11	Ex 20:13; Dt 5:17	Sixth commandment
Jas 2:23	Ge 15:6	Faith in Abraham
Jas 4:6	Pr 3:34	Grace for the humble

1 Peter

INTRODUCTION

1. Simon Peter

According to the four gospels, Peter was the leader and spokesman for the early disciples (Mt 15:15; 18:21; Mk 1:36–37; 8:29; 9:5–6; Lk 12:41; Jn 6:68). His original name in Hebrew was "Simeon" (cf. Ac 15:14; 2Pe 1:1). The Greek name "Simon," however, is applied to Peter forty-nine times in the NT. A third name, "Cephas," is a Greek transliteration of the Aramaic word *kepa'* ("rock"), which means the same as "Peter" (Greek *Petros*, "rock"). The NT, therefore, has four names for Peter. The phrase "Simon who was known as Peter" (Ac 10:18) indicates that his new name (Peter) became his common designation.

Simon was one of the first disciples called into the service of Jesus (Mk 1:16–18). He was a fisherman from Bethsaida (Jn 1:44), in a portion of the Transjordan immediately east of Galilee. Peter had a home in Capernaum (Mk 1:21, 29), which was across the Jordan, about three miles west of Bethsaida, in Galilee. He was married (Mt 8:14; Mk 1:30; Lk 4:38) and took his wife on journeys to churches (1Co 9:5). His strong north-country accent marked him as a Galilean (Mk 14:70). Doubtless he was influenced by the preaching of John the Baptist; his brother Andrew was one of the Baptist's disciples (Jn 1:35–42).

Andrew introduced Peter to Jesus (Jn 1:42). Peter quickly became the leader of the twelve disciples, and his name stands first in lists of them in the Synoptics. Peter was one of the inner three disciples (along with James and John) closest to Jesus (Mk 5:37; 9:2; 14:33). His preaching in the early days of the church (Ac 1–10) shows his great ability. The risen Lord appeared especially to him (1Co 15:5) and gave him a special commission (Jn 21:15–19).

Peter's leadership in the early church is not matched by his literary output. The NT contains only two letters that bear his name. According to tradition, Mark became the interpreter of Peter and transmitted into writing the things preached by Peter (see introduction to Mark).

2. Authorship

This first letter claims to be from "Peter, an apostle of Jesus Christ" (1:1), who says he was "a witness of Christ's sufferings" (5:1). In addition, it states that he wrote it "with the help of Silas . . . a faithful brother" (5:12)—undoubtedly the "Silas" of Ac 15:22 and 1Th 1:1. Also, the "Mark" mentioned in 1Pe 5:13 appears to be the same man mentioned in Ac 12:12. These two references and the strong, early reception of the letter by the church led to the almost universal acceptance of this letter as from Peter.

Many modern scholars, however, have denied that this letter could have been written by the apostle Peter. The positive case for Peter's authorship, however, rests on these considerations: (1) The self-witness of the book is clear in claiming Peter as author. (2) The alternative of a pseudonymous letter by someone using Peter's name has serious credibility problems. (3) The church's early and strong reception of the letter as Peter's cannot be overlooked. (4) The letter reveals none of the telltale marks of a later writing in which the author ascribed his work to one of the apostles. (5) The letter makes good sense when taken at face value as by Peter; the content and tone are fully consistent with apostolic times.

3. Date and Place of Origin

First Clement 5:4-7 names Peter and Paul as victims of persecution. The common understanding is that the passage refers to the persecution by Nero at Rome, which began after the disastrous fire in the city of Rome on July 19, A.D. 64. First Peter is written from "Babylon" (5:13; most likely a code word for "Rome"; see comment on 5:13), probably shortly before Nero's great persecution—i.e., in A.D. 62–64.

1 PETER

4. Destination

This letter is addressed to "God's elect, strangers in the world, scattered throughout Pontus, Galatia, Cappadocia, Asia and Bithynia" (1:1—these are all places in northern Asia Minor or modern Turkey). Peter may have evangelized the northern region of Asia Minor while Paul founded churches in the southern and western areas of Asia Minor. Silas too may have ministered in these northern provinces. The churches were no doubt composed of Christians from both Jewish and Gentile backgrounds, though a majority of the Christians in this area had been converted out of paganism rather than out of Judaism (4:3-4; see comment). Jewish blindness to the Gospel was a common phenomenon (cf. Ac 4:17–18; 28:25–28; Ro 10–11; 2Co 3:13–15).

5. Occasion and Purpose

The tone of 1 Peter is a warm pastoral one, full of encouragement. The exhortations are addressed to Christians who are scattered over a wide area. They shared a common faith with Christians everywhere and faced common problems. Their basic problem was to live for God in the midst of a society ignorant of the true God. Because they were Christians, they were misunderstood and subjected to cruel treatment. Peter's pastoral purpose was to help these early believers see their temporary sufferings in the full light of the coming eternal glory. In the midst of all their discouragements, the sovereign God would keep them and enable them by faith to have joy. Jesus Christ by his patient suffering and glorious future destiny had given them the pattern to follow and also a living hope. Life in a pagan society was difficult and required humility and submission. The immediate future for the church was an increase in the conflict with the world (4:7–18). But God would provide the grace to enable the community of the faithful to grow into maturity. They must help one another and show loving concern lest the members of God's flock be injured (4:8, 10; 5:1–2).

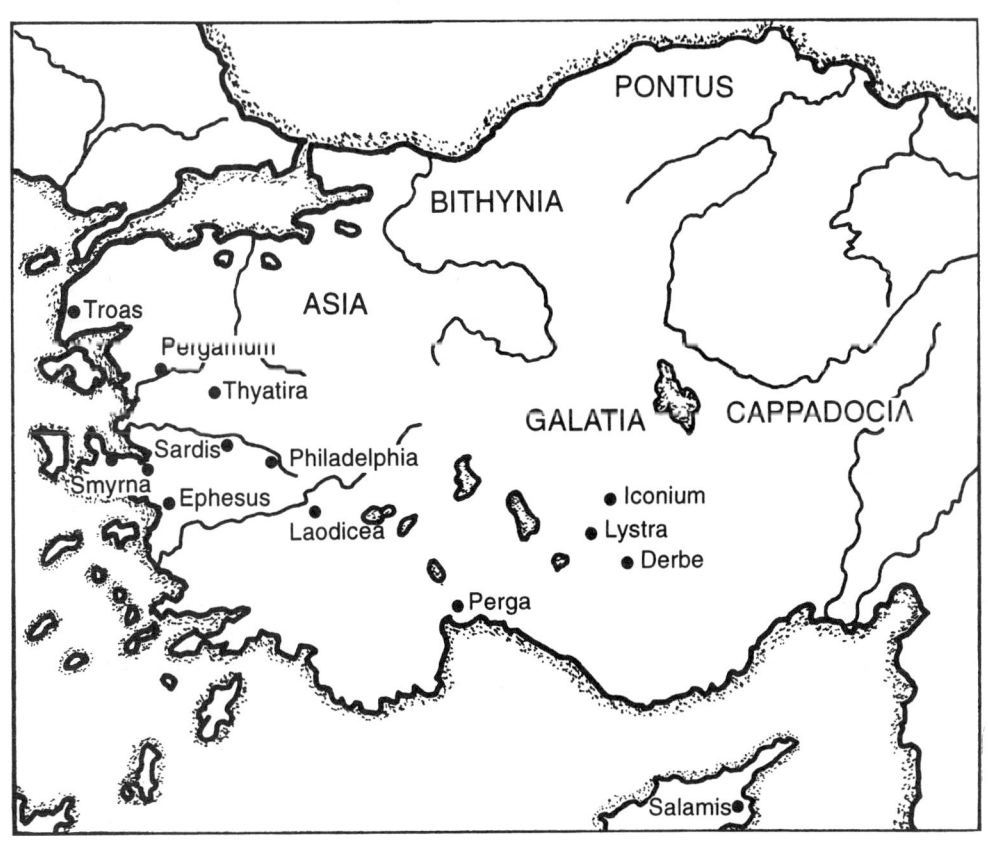

6. Literary Form

First Peter is a letter, written in the normal letter form of the NT world. Many scholars have worked to isolate or identify creedal or hymnic fragments in 1 Peter. It has been viewed as a sermon or homily, a paschal liturgy, or even an early Christian catechesis. The rhetorical and didactic nature of the letter may reflect the fact that it was intended to be read aloud to congregations (cf. Col 4:16; 1Th 5:27; Rev 1:3). This commentary takes the view that while Peter may have used material that existed in other forms, these materials now form a letter that is intelligible apart from the knowledge of previously existing forms.

7. Theological Values

Although it is not a theological treatise, 1 Peter abounds with valuable theological implications. It presupposes a biblical world view based on God's sovereignty. This is God's world; yet the devil "prowls around like a roaring lion looking for someone to devour" (5:8). People who live in this world are subject to evil desires, ignorance, false gods, and all forms of sinful living (1:14; 4:3–4). God allows people time to repent of their sins, but the time for repentance is limited. He is gracious (5:2, 10), but he is also a righteous and holy Judge, who will visit all people, living and dead, with their just deserts (1:17; 2:12, 23; 4:5–6, 17–19).

In common with the rest of the NT, 1 Peter presents a new perspective on the end times. With the coming of Jesus as Messiah, the age-old plan of God is on the way to its consummation (1:20). The writings of the prophets have found fulfillment in the death and resurrection of Jesus (1:11–12). Two major themes of prophetic teaching in 1 Peter are the messianic sufferings and the subsequent messianic glory. The first phase of the messianic times has already occurred! Jesus is the Suffering One who has died and has now been raised. The time is short, and Jesus must soon enter into his full glory. Already God has glorified him in heaven (1:21). All that remains is the final manifestation of the glorious Lord from heaven (1:7, 13; 4:13).

Christians are God's chosen people in an ignorant and rebellious world. In God's grace, the Triune God (1:2) is accomplishing in history a plan of redemption (1:20). The Father's role is extensive (1:1–3, 5, 15, 20–21; et al.) and is neither impersonal nor remote. The Spirit's participation in the salvation of humanity is also shown (1:2, 11–12; 4:14).

Peter regularly speaks of Jesus as "Jesus Christ," indicating his confession and that of the church (cf. Mt 16:16ff.). He also calls Jesus "Lord" (see 1:3; 2:13; 3:15) and recognizes the exaltation of Jesus (cf. Ac 2:36). He declares that the Spirit of Christ inspired the prophets (1:11); as the Messiah, he was "foreknown" before the creation of the world (1:20). Peter implies the deity of Christ (see comments on 2:3; 5:11). Jesus is also called "lamb" (1:19), "living Stone" (2:4), "Shepherd and Overseer of your souls" (2:25), and "Chief Shepherd" (5:4).

In his sufferings, Jesus fulfills the OT Scriptures in types and prophecies. He is the spotless Passover lamb of Exodus (1:16–21), the Suffering Servant of Isa 53 (2:24–25), and the scapegoat of Leviticus (2:24a). He carries away the sins of people, takes the punishment on himself, and provides a new life of righteousness. Not only is his death a substitutionary atonement (2:24), but it also provides a pattern for Christian living. Since Jesus was the Suffering Servant, his followers must suffer (2:21).

Peter emphasizes the godly life of submission and good deeds in the midst of suffering. By their noble deeds, Christians may glorify God in difficulties (2:12). The sovereign Lord sustains them in adversity and has all power (5:10–11). Thus faith, submission, and trust provide the basis for Christian living. With a distinctively pastoral tone and a strong emphasis on godly behavior in suffering, this letter is of great value for Christians today, who are still in a hostile world and many of whom in certain lands are suffering for Christ. A faithful witness to him can be costly, not only under repressive regimes but also in our more open society.

8. Canonicity

In his letter to the Philippians, Polycarp (c.70–150/166) unmistakably refers to 1 Peter. Following him, the Church Father Irenaeus, Clement of Alexandria, Tertullian, and Origen all attest Peter's authorship of the letter. It was accepted by the church because it universally recognized its worth and authority. No book of the NT has earlier, better, or stronger attestation.

EXPOSITION

I. Salutation (1:1–2)

1 Peter begins by using his name in its most common NT form (see introduction for more on his name). "An apostle [GK 693] of Jesus Christ" indicates the dignity and authority of someone selected by Jesus and given unique responsibilities of ministry in the establishment of the Christian church (Mt 16:18–19; Mk 1:16–17; 3:16; Jn 1:42; 21:15–19).

As is common in Greek letters of the NT era, the writer first identifies himself, then identifies the recipient, and finally gives a word of greeting. Peter designates those he is writing to as "God's elect" (GK 1723). In biblical teaching, election is a central theme and the foundation of spiritual blessing (cf. Dt 4:37; 7:6; 14:2; Ps 105:6, 43; Isa 15:4; Eph 1:4–5). No believer should ever feel threatened by the doctrine of election, because it is always presented in Scripture as the ground of comfort. So here the designation "elect" reminds the scattered Christians in danger of persecution that God's purposes for them are certain and gracious. "Strangers in the world" points to the fact that Christians are pilgrims who do not reside permanently on earth. They belong to the heavenly realm (cf. Eph 2:19; Php 3:20; Heb 11:13–16). The destination of the letter is "Pontus, Galatia, Cappadocia, Asia and Bithynia." These were the Roman provinces north of the Taurus Mountains in what is today Turkey.

2 Peter next announces some basic themes of his letter that will later be expanded and developed. He reminds his readers of their Triune faith and of the work of the Triune God. The "foreknowledge [GK 4590] of God" is more than God's simply knowing what will take place in the future, for it includes God's special relations with humankind even before creation (cf. 1:20; Am 3:2; Ac 2:23; Ro 8:29–30; 11:2). The "sanctifying" (GK 40) work of the Spirit is his operation of applying the work of redemption to Christians, purifying them and setting them to tasks of service. The goal of election and redemption is "obedience" (GK 5633) to Jesus Christ, who shed his blood on Calvary (cf. Ro 1:5). The salutation closes with the wish for the multiplication of God's "grace and peace" to the believers.

II. The Privileges and Responsibilities of Salvation (1:3–2:10)

The first major section of Peter's letter concerns "salvation" (GK 5401), the key term of this unit (see 1:5, 9–10: 2:2); it occurs nowhere else in the book. Its basic meaning is "deliverance, preservation, or salvation." The section closes with an OT quotation, as does the next major division (cf. 3:10–12).

A. God's Plan of Salvation (1:3–12)

1. The praise of God for salvation (1:3–9)

3–4 The nature of this salvation as a new birth according to the mercy of God evokes praise to God the Father, who is the source of salvation. The new birth is the work of the Holy Spirit (see Jn 3:3–8). The Christian has a "living hope" because Jesus has been raised by the Father (cf. Tit 2:13). This hope is further described in v.4 as an "inheritance [GK 3100] that can never perish, spoil or fade." The concept of inheritance is one of the major Bible themes and stresses family connection and gift (see Gal 3:18; cf. also Mt 5:5; 19: 29; 25:34; 1Pe 3:9). The inheritance "is kept" (GK 5498) or reserved in heaven by God for his people.

5 God's people are described as those who are being "shielded" (lit., "guarded"; GK 5864). This stresses the continued activity of God in their lives, while the phrase "through faith" stresses the believers' activity. The divine protection and the final salvation are only for believers. The salvation "ready to be revealed in the last time" looks at the final realization of what Christians already have and enjoy.

6 "In this" probably refers to anticipation of the future deliverance. As Christians long for their inheritance, they can "rejoice." Peter goes on to emphasize that their suffering is brief, for the present time, and necessary (cf. "have had to"). That Peter uses "trials" (GK 4280) instead of "persecutions" (GK 1501) or "tribulations" (GK 2568) is significant. He is thinking in terms of the broadest category of the pagans' attitude toward Christians rather than of specific actions.

7 When gold is refined, its impurities are removed by a fiery process. Though extremely durable, it belongs to the perishing world-order. Faith, which is more valuable than gold because it lasts longer and reaches beyond this temporal order, is purified in the tests of life. Gold, not faith, is presently highly valued by people. But God will set his stamp of approval on faith that has been tested and will show this when Christ is revealed. Then believers will openly share in the praise, glory, and honor of God.

8 Faith is directed toward Jesus Christ and produces love and joy in Christians. Without seeing Jesus (either because they were second-generation believers or because they were geographically removed), Peter's readers have come to love Jesus because they believe he loved them enough to die for them. Christians do not rejoice with inexpressible joy because of sufferings but because of the glorious expectation of their future with Christ.

9 "For you are receiving" gives the reason for the paradoxical joy, while stressing that the anticipated salvation is even now in the process of realization. The "goal" (GK 5465) or consummation of faith is "the salvation of your souls." No soul-and-body dichotomy of Greek thought is implied. The "soul" (GK 6034) is used in the Semitic biblical sense of "self" or "person." Therefore the thought of this section closes with the believers' total enjoyment in this present age of their future salvation.

2. The prophecy of salvation (1:10–12)

10–11 This salvation was the subject of the OT prophecies of the messianic sufferings and glories. The prophets not only spoke to the situation of their contemporaries, but they also spoke of the longed-for messianic times. In predicting the future, they did not always understand their utterances (the clearest example is Daniel and his visions [8:27; 12:8] and his study of other prophets [9:2ff.]). The prophets longed to see the messianic time and so searched into what they could know of it (cf. Lk 10:24).

The motivating force in prophecy is not the human will but the Holy Spirit of God (cf. 2Sa 23:2; 2Pe 1:21). The content of the prophecies embraced both the "sufferings" (GK 4077) and the "glories" (GK 1518) of Christ (cf. Lk 24:26). Both words are plural. The gospels list various aspects of the predicted sufferings of Christ—e.g., hatred by his people, betrayal by his friend, being forsaken by his flock, his scourging and crucifixion, etc. His glories include his transfiguration (2Pe 1:17), his resurrection (1:21), his glorious return, and his final reign.

12 Through revelation the prophets learned that some of their utterances related to future generations. Their writings contain both "near" and "far" aspects. Yet the prophets were often unable to understand the time significance of their prophecies or to understand fully the relation of the sufferings of the Messiah to his glory. The word translated "serving" (GK 1354) is significant, for it points to the fact that the writings of the OT are of service to the new community—the church. The unity of the OT and NT writings centers in Christ and his salvation. This message of salvation has come to humanity through people under the power of the Holy Spirit, who has come from heaven.

The last statement of v.12 is especially significant—"even angels long to look into these things." The Scriptures reveal that the angels have intense interest in human salvation. They observed Jesus in his early life (1Ti 3:16); they rejoice at the conversion of a sinner (Lk 15:10); they will rejoice in songs of praise at the completion of redemption (Rev 5:11–14). The expression to "long [GK 2121] to look" means "to stoop over to look" (cf. Lk 24:12; Jn 20:5, 11; Jas 1:25). It implies a willingness to exert or inconvenience oneself to obtain a better perspective. The specific tense used means continuous regard rather than a quick look. The Bible says nothing about salvation for angels. On the contrary, they learn about it from the church (Eph 3:10); and they serve the church (Heb 1:14).

B. The Lifestyle of Salvation (1:13–25)

1. A life of hope and holiness (1:13–16)

13 "Therefore" relates this section to the previous one, which gives the basis of the commands in these verses; the reception of salvation must result in a life of holiness, reverence, and love. Moreover, since the prophets and the angels take great interest in this salvation, how much more should Christians pay careful attention to its results! Peter here changes to the imperative, citing commands that give specific direction to his readers.

"Prepare your minds for action" presents the figure of a man gathering the folds of his long garment and tucking it into his belt so that he can move freely and quickly (cf. 1Ki 18:46: Jer 1:17; Lk 17:8). "Be self-controlled" (GK 3768) originally meant abstaining from excessive use of wine. In the NT its sense broadens to "live soberly"—a meaning that embraces sound judgment in all areas of life.

The main emphasis of v.13 is on putting one's hope wholly in the final consummation of the grace of God in Jesus Christ. At the present time, we enjoy only a beginning of that grace (cf. 1Jn 3:2–3). This longing for the unveiling of Jesus at his second coming permeates the NT (cf. Ac 1:11; Ro 11:26. 1Co 15:51; 1Th 4:13ff.; Heb 9:28; Jas 5:8; 2Pe 3:12–13; Rev 1:7; et al.)

14 The Christians' lifestyle is not to conform to the base desires that formerly dominated them and kept them from God. Christians must not allow the world to squeeze them into its sinful mold (cf. Ro 12:2). Peter exhorts Christians to control their desires rather than to be controlled by them. Formerly Christians were in ignorance; now they have come to know God and his will. They are to be "children of obedience"—an expression describing not only their quality but also their nature.

15–16 God is first described as the one who "called" (GK 2813) them. This verb implies the divine calling or what theologians term "efficacious grace." God is described as "holy" (GK 41). Holiness embraces purity and moral integrity. Those called to be God's children are to be like him; Peter reinforces this command by citing Leviticus (cf. 11:44–45; 19:2; 20:7) The basic idea of holiness in the Bible is that of separation from all that is profane. The developed sense of holiness includes various meanings translated into English as "purify," "sanctify," "separate from," "dedicate," etc. The simplest definition of holiness is that of conformity to God's commands and to his Son (cf. 1Jn 2:4–6).

2. A life of reverence before God (1:17–21)

17 This verse carries on the call to a lifestyle that is different from that of non-Christians. Peter reminds Christians that they invoke God as "Father" and that as his children (v.14) they should indeed call on him constantly in prayer. But God is Judge as well as Father, and those who call on his name must remember that he is impartial in judgment. Simply because some people call themselves Christians does not mean that all will be well for them in the Judgment. Sinners "will not stand in the judgment" (Ps 1:5–6); at the Last Judgment the unregenerate will be doomed. Those who have been saved by grace must walk in good works as the evidence of grace (Eph 2:10). They too will have their lives evaluated by God (Ro 14:10–12; 1Co 3:13–17; 2Co 5:10) and will receive according to what they have done. Yet justified persons cannot be condemned (Ro 8:1, 34); only the Lord who knows the hearts knows who the justified are.

Since judgment is certain, Christians must live in reverential awe of God—yet not in terror, for peace is one of their prerogatives (1Pe 1:2). The Christian life is a temporary stay on this earth (cf. comment on 1:1). So the brief time granted us should be used carefully.

18–19 The logic of this verse is "Live ... because you know!" That is, the Christian life is lived out of knowledge of the redemption that Christ has accomplished. What do Christians know? Peter reminds his readers of the cost of redemption, based on the value of the Person of the righteous Messiah himself.

The Greek word for "redeem" (GK 3390) goes back to the institution of slavery in ancient Rome. Any representative first-century church would have three kinds of members: slaves, freemen, and freed men. People became slaves in various ways—through war, bankruptcy, sale by themselves, sale by parents, or by birth. Slaves normally could look forward to freedom after a certain period of service and often after the payment of a price. Money to buy one's freedom could be earned by the slave in his spare time or by doing more than his owner required. Often the price would be provided by someone else, who purchased a person's freedom from servitude. A freed man was a person who formerly had been a slave but was now set free. Jesus also described his ministry in this picture taken from slavery (cf. Mk 10:45).

The redemption of Christians is from the "empty" (GK 3469) lifestyle of their ancestors. This implies Peter's readers had come from a pagan lifestyle rather than a Jewish one, for the NT stresses the emptiness of paganism (cf. Ro 1:21; Eph 4:17).

Verse 19 stresses the value of the purchase price of redemption and at the same time identifies the blood as that of a spotless lamb—the Messiah. When Israel was in bondage in Egypt, the Passover lamb was killed and its blood provided release from slavery and judgment. Because Jesus is without sin, he is unique and his life is of infinite value as the Sacrificial Lamb of the Passover (cf. Ex 12:46; Jn 19:36; 1Co 5:7).

20 Jesus "was chosen before the creation of the world." "Chosen" (lit., "known before"; GK *4589*) means more than "foresight," for why would Peter at this point make the obvious statement that God knew before about Jesus and his death? Rather, "chosen" connotes purpose (cf. Ro 11:2), giving the idea of predestination. That is, redemption was in God's plan before the time of creation (cf. Eph 1:3–4). And now this redemption has been "revealed" in Jesus of Nazareth "in these last times." With the coming of Jesus, the last age has come (cf., e.g., Ac 2:17; Heb 1:2; 9:26). Salvation in Christ, purposed from eternity, is now made plain, Peter tells his readers, "for your sake." He personalizes it so as to spur them to a life of response to God.

21 The section closes with a statement about the believers' faith in God. That faith comes through the work of Jesus because he is the one who reveals the Father (Jn 1:18) and because he is the means of reconciliation (2Co 5:19). Peter identifies the Father (v.17) as the God who raised Jesus and glorified him, with the result that believers have faith and hope in God. Jesus' resurrection is the foundation of our faith, and his glorification is the pledge of the hope of our new future (cf. Ro 8:17–30; 1Co 15:1–11; Heb 2:10).

3. A life of love (1:22–25)

22 In the third subdivision of this section on the Christian way of life, Peter adds to the command to be holy and to reverence God, the command to "love" (GK *26*). He also gives two reasons for Christians to love one another. The first is that they have "purified" (GK *49*) themselves, a word that is not common in the NT but denotes the moral purity that comes to Christians through the Gospel.

The means of this purification is "by obeying the truth" of the Gospel (cf. Ac 15:9; Ro 10:16; 2Th 1:8). The Good News carries with it a command to repent and believe. In the early church, this was commonly tied to baptism. Not that the church believed that baptism itself saved; rather, it was the focal point of decision (cf. Ac 2:38). Being purified from sin enables Christians to show genuine family love for God's children. Yet this love is not entirely a foregone conclusion, because it can be and is commanded.

This love is to be "from a pure heart" (see NIV note). So Peter exhorts Christians—because they are purified—to love fellow Christians purely and fervently. Love for non-Christians is not in view here, but of course it is also part of Christians' obligations (cf. Mt 5:44; Lk 6:27, 35). The NT teaches that there are different kinds of love and different emotions of love. Yet Christians are enabled to love all people with true Christian love—a self-sacrificing desire to meet the needs of others that finds expression in concrete acts (cf. 1Jn 3:14–18).

23 Peter now expresses the second reason for Christians to love others: "you have been born again." This phrase stresses the state into which Christians come at conversion. What is the "seed" that gives the new birth? Though some connect it with baptism and others with the seed of divine life, it is best explained as the life-giving message about Jesus' death and resurrection. That is, the new birth comes through the living and abiding word of God. By the "word" (GK *3364*), Peter probably means "God's self-revelation," which would include both his spoken and written message. God's word is living because it imparts life (cf. Ps 33:9; Isa 55:10–11; Heb 4:12). It endures because the God who speaks it is the eternal, faithful, powerful One who keeps his promises.

24 The quotation from Isa 40:6–8 supports the assertion of the character of God, with its stress on the abiding faithfulness of the Lord's statements. The quotation comes from Isaiah's so-called "Book of Comfort," his inspired messages to an exiled and oppressed people. How fitting the application is to pilgrim Christians (cf. 1Pe 1:1) in the light of their oppression by the pagan world! The theme of Isaiah's prophecy is the perishable nature of all flesh and the imperishable nature of the Word of God. To the exiles in Babylon, the message was that while human

"Are being built" (GK 3868) is descriptive of believers of all ages in history. When anyone comes to Christ, a new stone is added to the "spiritual" (GK 4461) house. The use of the word "spiritual" does not mean that what Peter is speaking of is less "real" than a material house or material sacrifices. Rather, the material sacrifices and temples that were shadows of the reality to come are now superseded. The OT spoke of the offerings of prayer, thanksgiving, praise, and repentance (Pss 50:14; 51:19; 107:22; 141:2) in addition to material sacrifices and offerings. The NT speaks of the offering of "faith" (Php 2:17), material gifts as "a fragrant offering" (Php 4:18), "your bodies as living sacrifices" (Ro 12:1), "a sacrifice of praise" (Heb 13:15), the conversion of the Gentiles as "an offering acceptable to God" (Ro 15:16), and Paul's coming death as "a drink offering" (2Ti 4:6).

The great new truth Peter states here is the revelation that "through Jesus Christ," i.e., through his work on the Cross, every Christian is part of a new priestly order. This truth of the "priesthood of all believers" was rediscovered and restressed during the Reformation. It means that all Christians have immediate access to God, that they serve God personally, that they minister to others, and that they have something to give. This does not mean, however, that each Christian has public gifts of preaching or teaching. In this verse Peter is stressing the reassuring fact that through Christ believers are able to worship and serve God in a manner pleasing to him.

6 Next Peter cites Scripture to support his teaching. The quotation of Isa 28:16 refers to God's foundation stone, carefully chosen and very costly, placed in position in Zion. The picture is from the building of a temple. At great cost and care the corner foundation stone was obtained, moved, and laid. Once in place, the rest of the building was determined. Isaiah uses this figure to encourage his people to build on the Lord himself, the one who is immovable and unchangeable. As Peter applies this, God has set Jesus forth in Jerusalem as the foundation of the new temple. Whoever builds on this foundation will be established and will never be ashamed (cf. 1Co 3:10; Eph 2:20).

7 "Now to you who believe, this stone is precious" literally reads, "For you, therefore,

This cornerstone of Pilate, found at Caesarea, was reused elsewhere after he was rejected as governor.

who believe [is] the honor [GK 5507]." The honor for Christians is linked to their union with Christ. Since Christ is honored by God, so will all who participate in Christ. But for unbelievers, two other "stone" citations from the OT are strong warnings. The first is from Ps 118:22, where the builders rejected a building block that later turned out to be the final stone (the capstone) in the building (cf. Mk 12:10–12). In the same way, Jesus, who was rejected by human beings, has been exalted by God.

8 The second warning is from Isa 8:14, where the disobedient are portrayed as stumbling over the stone. So Peter warns that those who refuse to believe in Jesus as Messiah stumble—"which is also what they were destined for." What is it that is "destined" (GK 5502)? The unbelief of these people or the stumbling that is the result of the unbelief? More likely the latter. Peter probably means to say that the appointment of God embraces both the setting forth of Christ and his work and the rejection by others. Peter's preaching in Ac 2:14–40 made the same emphasis (cf. esp. v.23). Scripture in other places teaches that human disobedience is within the plan of God (cf. Ro 11:8, 11, 30–32). Yet it must be recognized that though this is true, one does not become less blameworthy (cf. Ac 2:23). It is important to recognize also that human disobedience is not necessarily final or irretrievable. Paul says, "God has bound all men over to disobedience so that he may have mercy on them all" (Ro 11:32).

help is weak, God's promise of restoration will not fail.

25 Peter now applies Isaiah's words. Since Jesus is equivalent to the Lord in the OT, his utterances endure. So he stresses the specifically Christian application of the Isaiah prophecy. The reliable message about Jesus as proclaimed to Peter's readers gives life and transforms life so that Christians are able to love.

C. Growth in Salvation (2:1–10)

This section flows logically out of the previous section (cf. "therefore"). Peter uses a variety of images to describe the Christian life. He begins by speaking of "stripping off" habits like garments and then compares Christians to babies. Next he likens them to stones in the temple and finally to a chosen, priestly people.

1. Growth through the pure milk (2:1–3)

1 Peter's Christian readers have obeyed the truth of the Gospel and were purified (1:21). Therefore they must "rid" themselves (GK 700) of various pagan vices. He is probably reminding them of what was symbolized in their baptism, the focal point of their commitment to Christ, when they stripped off the old life and made a new beginning in repentance and faith. Vice lists such as this were common in the ancient world and in the NT (cf. Mk 7:21–22; Ro 1:29–31; 13:13; 1Co 5:10; Gal 5:19–20, 2Pe 2:10–14).

2 Peter's addressees were, in the main, new converts, i.e., "newborn." A major characteristic of a healthy new baby is its instinctive yearning for its mother's milk. Christians are to crave what is "pure" milk in contrast to the "deceit" (v.1) of the old life. The "spiritual milk" is probably a reference to the Word of God. Therefore the translation might be expanded to "crave the unadulterated spiritual milk of the word." Continuous nourishment from this "milk" causes the newborn to "grow up in [their] salvation." Salvation is the present possession of Christians as well as their future goal (cf. 1Pe 1:5, 9). After conversion, their lives should be marked by continuous growth (cf. 1Co 3:1–4; Heb 5:11–14). This growth comes from the teaching about Christ and God the Father that is at the core of God's Word.

3 The image of "tasting" the Lord goes back to Ps 34:8: "Taste and see that the LORD is good." Those who have come to taste the graciousness or goodness of the Lord should have a continuing appetite for spiritual food. In Ps 34 the reference is to Yahweh ("LORD"; GK 3378), Israel's God. In his writings, Peter applies the Greek word used to translate this title—i.e.,"Lord" (GK *3261*)—to Jesus. He thus implies the full deity of Christ.

2. Participation in the temple and priesthood (2:4–10)

a. Christ the Rock and the Christian living stones (2:4–8)

4 This section is connected to the previous one by the relative clause "As you come to him," by the continued use of Ps 34, and by the concept of Christians' finding in Christ great value. But the figure changes, for Peter now presents Christ as a rock or a stone. The "rock-stone" imagery is common in Scripture: see the stumbling stone of Isa 8:14, the foundation-stone of Isa 28:16, the parental rock of Isa 51:1–2, the rejected stone of Ps 118:22, the supernatural stone of Da 2:34, and the burdensome stone of Zec 12:3. "Rock/Stone" was an accepted messianic title among the Jews as well as among Christians.

"As you come to him" probably reflects "come to him" in v.5 of the Greek translation of Ps 34 (LXX). Christians have "come" to Christ in salvation, but their continual "coming" is also required. Jesus Christ is identified as the "living Stone," a word that refers to his stability as the risen Lord. God's raising of Jesus from the dead shows his value and God's choice of him. The "rejected" Christ is the rejection of Jesus by the Jewish nation (Mt 26:14–15; Ac 2:22–24; 3:13–15; 4:10–11), as well as the current rejection of him by the disobedient in every land.

5 Jesus' great prophecy to Peter (Mt 16:18–19) concerned Jesus' building of his church. Peter sees, in the coming of individuals to Jesus the Rock, the building of a new spiritual edifice. Solomon was amazed at the thought of God's gracious condescension in dwelling among his people and in a house (the temple) that Solomon built (1Ki 8:27). Now the localized manifestation of God's presence on earth is replaced by his indwelling of all believers (1Co 3:17; 6:19).

b. The nation of priests (2:9–10)

9 "But you" marks the contrast with the disobedient who were mentioned in vv.7–8. Peter applies to the church various terms originally spoken concerning Israel (cf. Ex 19:5–6; Dt 4:20; 7:6; Isa 43:20–21). But this does not mean that the church is Israel or even that the church replaces Israel in the plan of God. Romans 11 should help us to guard against that misinterpretation. Why then does Peter apply OT terminology to the church? He does so chiefly because of the conviction of the church that the OT writings are for it (2Ti 3:16) and that these writings speak of Jesus and his times. The functions that Israel was called into existence to perform in its day of grace the church now performs in a similar way. In the future, according to Paul, God will once again use Israel to bless the world (cf. Ro 11:13–16, 23–24).

The title "chosen people" (GK *1723* & *1169*) stresses God's loving initiative in bringing the church to himself. "Royal priesthood" (GK *994* & *2633*) may be understood as "a royal house" and "a body of priests." Both titles stress the dignity of the church because of its union with Christ. Jesus is King, and all in his "house" belong to a royal house. Calling the church "a body of priests" emphasizes its corporate role in worship, intercession, and ministry. "Holy nation" (GK *41* & *1620*) shows that God has "set apart" the church for his use. The title "a people [GK *3295*] belonging to God" stresses ownership (cf. Tit 2:14). "That you may declare the praises" gives the purpose of God's grace to people. "The praises" (GK *746*) often means his "self-declarations" or his manifestations to humankind. So then the church is to advertise the noble acts of God in history and thus make him known. Specifically, the Father ("him who called you"; cf. 1:15) is revealed by Jesus in his death and resurrection. Peter again reminds them of God's action in bringing them out of darkness into his marvelous light (cf. Ps 34:5: "Those who look to him are radiant"). Light-darkness is a common dualism in the Bible to contrast God-evil, good-bad, revelation-ignorance, new age-old age (e.g., Isa 8:21–9:2; Jn 1:4, 8–9; Eph 5:8; 1Jn 1:5–2:2).

10 Peter closes this section with another free use of the OT—this time the words of Hosea (Hos 1:6, 9–10; 2:23). In their original context they describe God's rejection of disobedient Israel, followed by future restoration to grace. Here Peter applies them to the salvation that has come to the Asian Christians. Once they were "not a people [GK *3295*]"—the special word used for Israel); now they are "the people of God."

III. Christian's Submission and God's Honor (2:11–3:12)

A. The Noble Life and God's Glory (2:11–12)

11 This next division of the letter deals with some practical implications of what it means to be God's people in a hostile world. Peter begins by reminding them of their position. He calls them "Dear friends" (lit., "beloved"; GK *28*) because they are bound together by Christ's love. Then he exhorts them as "foreigners and strangers." These titles are rich in content, going back to Abraham (cf. Ge 23:4; cf. also Ps 39:12; Heb 13:14, 1Pe 1:1, 17). Christians are only in the world, not of it, for their true destiny is the renewed earth in which righteousness will dwell. Therefore, they are not to derive their values from what is transitory. So Peter warns of "sinful desires."

The body's desires are not wrong or sinful in themselves, but sin perverts them; and the Christian is tempted to satisfy the bodily desires in ways contrary to God's will. "Which war against your soul" speaks of the warfare that is a mortal threat against the entire person (cf. comment on 1:9). Peter's exhortation means that Christians are not to participate in pagan immorality.

12 Instead, Christians are to have a "noble lifestyle" among the pagans. The purposes of the godly life of Christians are twofold. (1) As the pagans take careful notice of our good works, they will not slander us. (2) In the future they will glorify God. What kind of charges did non-Christians make in Peter's time? Some of the more common were disloyalty to the state or Caesar (Jn 19:12), upsetting trade or divination (Ac 16:16ff.; 19:23ff.), teaching that slaves are "free" (cf. 1Co 13:13; Gal 3:20), not participating in festivals because of "hatred of mankind" (cf. Col 2:16), holding "antisocial" values, and being "atheists" because they had no idols (cf. Ac 15:29).

The meaning of "on the day he visits us" is problematic. Does Peter mean "on the return of the Lord" or "on God's gracious visitation of salvation that may come to the non-Christian?" In favor of the latter is the word "see" (GK 2227), which suggests that the pagans will continuously observe the good works and perhaps God will grant them repentance unto life.

B. The Duty of Christian Submission (2:13–3:7)

1. The submission to civil authority (2:13–17)

13–14 "Submit yourselves" (GK 5718; cf. 2:13, 18; 3:1) is the key theme of this section of the letter. The word in general means to "subject oneself." Here it means acquiescence in the divinely willed order of society. The phrase "every authority instituted among men" is perhaps better translated as "every human creature." Peter's thought is that of Christians who do not seek their own interests but rather assume a voluntary submission of themselves to others. The reason for this submission is expressed in the phrase "because of the Lord." "The Lord" here means Christ in his divine lordship order as manifest in his creative activity (cf. Jn 1:1–4; Col 1:16; Heb 1:2).

Peter then mentions the rulers of the time. The "king" (GK 995) is the title used in the East for the emperor who had the "supreme authority" among people. The "governors" (GK 2450) are the legates, procurators, or proconsuls charged with carrying out the imperial will of punishing the disobedient and rewarding the good.

15 Peter is speaking of ordinary situations and not of persecutions (cf. Ac 4:18ff.; 5:18ff.) when he speaks of governors as commending the good. Later in this letter, he deals with the more difficult situation of governmental persecution of those who do good (3:14, 17; 4:1, 12–19). No government that consistently rewards evil and punishes good can long survive, because evil is ultimately self-destructive. It is God's will for Christians by their submission to the state authorities to "silence the ignorant talk of foolish men." The word "foolish" (GK 933) is a common biblical adjective for an obstinate sinner.

16 Christians are free because the service of God is freedom (cf. Jn 8:32; Ro 6:15; Gal 5:13)—freedom from bondage to sin, Satan, and selfish desires. Christians are not to misuse their freedom in Christ and invoke "freedom" as a covering for wickedness. Christ himself said, "I tell you the truth, everyone who sins is a slave to sin" (Jn 8:34). In the service of God, who is the source of joy, Christians experience perfect freedom, because Christ frees us from the bondage of sin.

17 Peter next sums up the social obligation of Christian in four succinct commands. (1) "Show proper respect to [lit., honor; GK 5506] everyone." Peter instructs us to recognize the value of each person in his or her place as a creature of God. (2) "Love the brotherhood." Special love is due to others within the family of believers because they are brothers and sisters. (3) "Fear God." (4) "Honor the king." God is to be feared, but the emperor was only to be honored. Christ taught, "Do not be afraid of those who kill the body but cannot kill the soul. Rather, be afraid of the one [i.e., God] who can destroy both soul and body in hell" (Mt 10:28). Normally duties to God and Caesar do not conflict, and Christians can obey both (Mt 22:15–21); but in special cases their higher loyalty is clear: "We must obey God rather than men!" (Ac 5:29).

2. The submission of slave to master (2:18–25)

a. The submission of household slaves (2:18–20)

18 It is difficult for twentieth-century Christians to understand the slavery of the ancient world. During the time of the NT writings, slavery was not as bad as that practiced in America before the Civil War. Ancient slaves had fairly normal marital lives. Often people sold themselves into slavery (for a period of time) as a way to get ahead in the world. Nevertheless the lot of a slave could be very hard if the master was unkind. Here "slaves" (GK 3860) means "house-servants"—i.e., domestic slaves. Their Christian duty was submission and loyalty to their master, even if he was harsh.

19 Peter motivates this latter clause. "For it," he writes, "is commendable"—i.e., a "grace" (GK 5921). It is an attractive quality in the sight of God when because of conscience (or perhaps "consciousness" of God) a Christian slave puts up with pain as he suffers unjustly.

20 To endure a well-deserved "beating" (lit., "strike with the fist"; cf. Mk 14:65) is nothing extraordinary. However, it is "commendable" in the sight of God to do good and to endure suffering. The commendable thing is not the suffering as such but being so committed to God's will that devotion to him overrides personal comfort.

b. The example of Christ's submission (2:21–25)

21 Peter's exhortation for Christians to be submissive now receives a christological foundation. Christians are "called" (GK 2813) to suffer. The "calling" is God's grace that brings them to salvation (cf. comment on 1:15) and includes the divine ordination in all aspects of their life (Ro 8:28–30), "because Christ also suffered for you." The sufferings of Christ referred to here are exemplary as well as expiatory on behalf of Christians. "Leaving you an example [GK 5681]" shows that Christ is the pattern for believers to copy in their lives. Just as in his life Christ suffered unjustly for doing God's will, so Christian slaves may have this calling. Servants are to follow their Master's tracks (cf. Mt 10:38; Mk 8:34; Jn 13:15).

22–23 The preeminent OT passage on the suffering of the Messiah is Isaiah's fourth Servant Song (Isa 52:13–53:12). Peter quotes Isa 53:9 to stress the submission of the innocent Sufferer. Other echoes of Isa 53 sound in the next verses: 53:12 in v.24a; 53:5 in v.24b; 53:6 in v.25. Throughout his earthly ministry, Jesus was reviled (cf. Mt 11:19; 26:67; 27:30, 39–44; Mk 3:22). In all these situations, he was ever the patient sufferer who was able to control his tongue. He committed his case to the heavenly Judge whom he trusted to give a just judgment.

24–25 Peter explores the sufferings of the Messiah more deeply. He has stated that Christ was patient and innocent. Moreover, his sufferings for us are indeed expiatory and substitutionary. He did no sin (v.22) and he "bore our sins" (v.24; cf. Jn 1:29). The exact figure of bearing sins is not clear. It may be a reference to the scapegoat (Lev 16), to other Levitical sacrifices (cf. Lev 14:20; Isa 53:12), or to the basic ideas involved in the sacrificial system. The location of the expiatory offering was "in his body on the tree" (cf. Dt 21:23; Gal 3:13; Col 1:22). The purpose of Christ's death on the cross is to produce new life in the believer. By means of it all those who come to him end their old life and begin a new one devoted to righteousness (cf. Ro 6:1–14, 18–19; 2Co 5:14–15; Gal 2:20; 6:14).

"By his wounds you have been healed" is Peter's application of this precious truth from Isaiah to Christian slaves who had received lashes unjustly. Formerly they were straying sheep (Isa 53:6; Lk 15:3–7) but now they "have returned" to Jesus, the "Shepherd and Overseer of your souls" (cf. Jn 10).

3. The submission of Christian wives (3:1–6)

1 "In the same way" in both v.1 and v.7 points back to 2:13. Christian wives are not to be submissive like slaves; rather, the principle of Christian subjection to God's will relates to every class and every situation. Rules for wives occur in other locations in the NT (Eph 5:22; Col 3:18; 1Ti 2:9–15; Tit 2:4–5).

The phrase translated "so that" introduces the purpose of the command. Here an evangelistic motivation is added to the general necessity of the divine order. As the Gospel was proclaimed, it was always possible for a wife to be converted before her husband. In such a situation where the man is disobedient to the Gospel message, he may be "won over" (GK 3045) for the faith without a word by the way his wife lives.

2 The husband will then observe purity of life lived in the "fear" (NIV, "reverence"; GK 5832) of God. Note might be taken here of the mother of Augustine, who eventually led her husband to accept Christ.

3–4 The divinely intended manner of life for wives is inward, not outward. Human beings constantly make superficial value judgments (see 1Sa 16:7). Many have taken Peter's words to be an absolute prohibition of any outward adornment. But Peter's emphasis is not on prohibition but on a proper sense of values.

The "inner self" is the "hidden person of the heart," or the character of a person. In biblical psychology the "heart" (GK 2840) is the central psychological term and refers to the faculty where a human being relates to God and makes basic decisions (cf. Pr 3:5;

4:23; 21:1). The Christian woman is to cultivate an inner disposition ("spirit"; GK 4460) of a "gentle" (lit., meek"; GK 4558; applied to Christ in Mt 11:29) and quiet sort that is imperishable or "unfading." Today, when the world's values governed by materialism, self-assertion, and sex obsession are seeping into the church, Peter's words need to be taken seriously (cf. Isa 3:16–24).

5–6 Next Peter turns to the OT in support of his exhortation—first broadly and then from the example of Sarah. The major characterization of these women who were "holy" because they were set apart to God was their hope in God. They trusted the promises of God and longed for the messianic salvation (cf. 1:3, 13, 3:15; Heb 11:13). In so doing, they were habitually adorning themselves with an inner beauty.

The great model of womanly submission is Sarah, whose respect and obedience to Abraham extended to her speech—she "called him her master." Such terminology was not uncommon in the ancient world (cf. Ge 18:12). Peter does not hesitate to apply Sarah's example to his readers: "You are her daughters if you do what is right." The norm for wifely conduct should be submission to God and devotion to the development of Christian character. Moreover, wives are "not [to] give way to fear"; their submissive trust in the living God will keep them from undue apprehension.

4. The obligation of Christian husbands (3:7)

7 Peter's instructions for the Christian husband are brief, probably because the family normally followed the husband's religious choice. Yet the husband too needed instruction concerning the care of his wife. "In the same way" does not refer back to subjection to the wife (v.1) but rather to the husband doing in the relationship of marriage everything possible to foster the spiritual life of the home. A harsh or unthinking Christian husband can be a hindrance to the family's spiritual growth. The woman is called the "weaker partner" (lit., "vessel"; GK 5007); but this is not to be taken morally, spiritually, or intellectually. It simply means that the woman has less physical strength. The husband must recognize this difference and take it into account. "As you live with" probably refers to sexual intercourse in addition to the broader aspects of living together. The husband is to show his wife "respect" (lit., "honor"; GK 5507) and not despise her physical weakness.

Men are also to remember that women are coheirs of "the gracious gift of life." The sexual function and sexual distinctions are only for this age. Women will have an equal share in the new age; and even now in the life of the new age, they experience the grace of God equally with men (cf. Gal 3:28). Men must also remember that selfishness and egotism in the marriage relationship will mar their relationship with God.

C. The Call to Righteous Living (3:8–12)

8 Peter brings his treatment of the duties of Christians, considered in various groupings, to a close with general practical advice for the whole community. Here he gives several imperatives for Christians' getting along together. The five virtues in v.8 have many illustrations in the life of Jesus and parallels in the other letters. They are normative qualities every person united to Christ should manifest. On "harmony," see Ro 12:16; Php 1:27; 2:2; on "be sympathetic," see Ro 12:15; 1Co 12:26; on "love as brothers," see 1Th 4:9–10; for "be compassionate," see Christ's example in Mt 11:29; and concerning "humble," see Christ's example as set forth in Php 2:5–11.

9 Peter goes on to give his readers a basic imperative for dealing with those who are hostile to them, turning to Christ as the pattern to follow. The natural response to hostility is retaliation. But Jesus in his teaching (Mt 5:44) and in his practice responded to hostility with grace (Lk 23:34; 1Pe 2:21–22). What does it mean to "bless" (GK 2328) our enemies? It means "to speak well [of someone]." The word includes friendly disposition toward one's enemies, but it goes beyond this to active prayer and intercession (cf. Ac 7:60; 1Co 4:12). The great desire of Christians must not be revenge but for God to grant the gift of repentance to those who do not know him. The phrase "because to this" probably means that the calling of Christians to grace should make them gracious to others.

10–12 Peter now reinforces his teaching of non-retaliation by going to Ps 34:12–16, which he has already alluded to in 2:3. In the psalm, the "life" and the "good days" refer to earthly life and joys. Peter's use of these terms is not limited to this life but goes beyond it to our final salvation. Yet it is still true in this age that being gracious to others may lead to longer life and better days. On the contrary, a life of evil and strife may be shortened and marred (cf. Pr 13:15).

Christians should desire life in its goodness. Therefore, they must guard their ways and their tongues. Most important, they are to overcome evil with good (cf. Ro 12:21). Since peace between people is elusive and hard to achieve, Christians must actively seek and pursue it. The fear of the Lord provides a rationale for godly living and a warning to the wicked. Our facial organs (vv.10–11) speak of our personal relationship with God. The "eye" of the Lord over the righteous reminds us of his providential care for his people (cf. Ex 2:25), and his "ear" is open to our cries for help in prayer (cf. Ex 3:7). The "face" of the Lord is an expression for "God's countenance"; here it relates to his anger against evildoers.

IV. The Suffering and Persecution of Christians (3:13–5:11)

Peter's major emphasis in this letter is on Christian conduct under persecution. Especially in this section, this is his chief concern.

A. The Blessing of Suffering for Righteousness (3:13–17)

13 While suffering and unjust treatment have been in the background (1:6–7; 2:12, 15, 19ff.; 3:9), now they come to the fore. If Christians have the zeal for good that Ps 34 speaks of, who will do them harm? The "harm" Peter alludes to must be understood in the light of Paul's rhetorical question "If God is for us, who can be against us?" (Ro 8:31) and his reference to Christians as being like "sheep to be slaughtered" and yet being "more than conquerors" (Ro 8:36–37).

14–16 The expression "But even if you should suffer" points to the fact that suffering is not the expected outcome of zeal for doing good, though it can and does happen. The suffering in view results from righteousness—i.e., from the kind of life that conforms to God's standard. If this should happen to his readers, they are "blessed" (GK *3421*). This blessedness or happiness is the certainty that comes from belonging to God and his kingdom with the promises of future vindication (cf. Mt 5:3–10).

Verses 14b–15 are built on Isa 8:12b–13, where the prophet admonishes the godly in Israel not to fear the impending invasion as do the unbelievers. Instead, godly reverence is to be their concern (cf. Mt 10:28). Thus Peter admonishes his readers not to be afraid of other people but acknowledge "Christ as Lord." This passage is important for Peter's Christology, for here again he ascribes to Christ the OT name for the Lord (see comment on 2:3). Peter's readers are to acknowledge in their "hearts" (see comment on 3:3–4) Christ as the Holy One. When the center of a person's life is rightly related to God, he or she is able to respond properly to the vicissitudes of life.

One of the distinguishing marks of Christians is their possession of "hope" (GK *1828*; cf. 1:3, 21; Ro 4:18; Eph 2:12; Tit 2:13). Christian hope is so real and distinctive that non-Christians are puzzled about it and ask for a "reason" (GK *3364*). The type of questioning could be either official interrogations by the governmental authorities (cf. Ac 25:16; 26:2; 2Ti 4:16) or informal questioning.

Christians should respond with care. "Gentleness" (GK *4559*) is the quality that trusts God to do the work of changing attitudes (cf. 2Ti 2:24–25; cf. also Pr 15:1); "respect" (GK *5832*) is reverential awe of God (cf. 1:17; 2:17; 3:2). The "clear conscience" relates to the liberty and boldness that come from living before God in purity (cf. Ac 24:16; 1Ti 1:19). So in the case in which non-Christians slander believers the statement of the truth may shame them into silence (cf. Lk 13:17).

17 It is better to suffer for doing good than for doing evil. Suffering is a just recompense for doing evil. But if one does good and still suffers, there is no disgrace—if one's conscience is clear before God—for that person can have confidence that such suffering was not caused by sin. There must be a providential reason for it—perhaps to prick the conscience of some and bring them to salvation. Or suffering may be a necessary prelude to glorification (cf. Php 2:6–11).

B. The Pattern of Christ's Suffering and Exaltation (3:18–22)

This section contains some of the most difficult exegetical problems in the NT. We should give a brief overview of the three major types of interpretations before giving our exposition of the passage, These may be easily differentiated if the following questions are kept in one's mind: (1) Who are the "spirits" to whom Christ made a proclamation? (2) When did Christ make this proclamation? (3) What was its content?

(1) The first group sees Christ going down to the realm of the dead and preaching to Noah's contemporaries during the interval between his crucifixion and resurrection. His message is interpreted as an offer of salvation to the spirits, as the announcement of condemnation, or as the announcement of good tidings to those already saved.

(2) The second group views the preexistent Christ as preaching in the time of Noah to Noah's sinful generation.

(3) The third group sees Christ as proclaiming to the fallen angels his victory on the cross. This victorious proclamation took place perhaps during the three days in a literal descent into hell, but more likely it occurred during his exaltation. Our exposition develops and defends this third position.

18 The main purpose of vv.18–22 is fairly clear. "For Christ died" suggests that the example of Christ's experience through suffering into victory gives assurance that those joined to him will share the same destiny. "For Christ died for sins once for all" stresses the definitive and final work of Jesus in salvation (cf. Ro 6:10). "For sins" is a phrase describing the reason for his death (cf. Ro 4:25; 1Co 15:3; Gal 1:4; Heb 10:12). "The righteous for the unrighteous" points to Jesus as the Righteous Servant of Isa 53 (cf. Ac 3:13f.), who suffered in the place of the sinners (cf. Isa 53:5–6, 11–12) and thus died a substitutionary death. The purpose of his death is "to bring you to God" (cf. Ro 5:2, where a similar concept is taught).

He was "put to death in the body but made alive by the Spirit" can also be translated, "put to death in flesh, but made alive in spirit." Behind the NIV translation stand a number of problems. Paul's antithesis is between the Greek words for "flesh" (here "body"; GK 4922) and "spirit" (GK 4460). These two words do not refer to two "parts" of Christ (i.e., his body and his soul), nor does the "spirit" refer to the Holy Spirit or Christ's human spirit. Rather, "flesh" refers to Christ in his human sphere of life and "spirit" refers to Christ in his resurrected sphere of life (cf. Ro 1:3–4; 1Ti 3:16). If this view is adopted, the exegesis makes good sense.

19 "Through whom" can also mean "in which." If the reference in v.18 is to two different states of Christ, then v.19 says in which state he went and preached: the state of resurrection. To whom did Christ preach? The "spirits" are best understood as fallen angels. Jesus, then, in his resurrection "goes" to the place of angelic confinement. Since this is in another realm, we cannot locate it spatially. However, there does not seem to be good evidence for seeing here a literal "descent into hell."

What did he preach? The content of the proclamation is not stated, but Peter uses "preached" (GK *3062*) rather than "proclaim good news" (GK *2294*; cf. 4:6), because Christ did not announce the Gospel to the fallen angels. The thought of salvation for angels is foreign to the NT (Heb 2:16), including Peter (cf. comment on 1:12). The announcement is of Christ's victory and of their doom that has come through his death on the cross and his resurrection.

To sum up, the thought of vv.18–19 may be paraphrased as follows: "He was put to death in the human sphere of existence but was made alive in the resurrection sphere of existence, in which state of existence he made a proclamation of his victory to the fallen angels." As for the pastoral significance of these verses, it is one of comfort because through suffering Christians go on to victory. Those who oppose Christians will be defeated (Col 2:15; 2Th 1:6–8).

20 These fallen angels are now identified as those who were disobedient at the time of Noah. This connects with the rebellion of Ge 6:1–4 (see also 2Pe 2:4; Jude 6). Peter makes a connection between the disobedience of the spirits and the Flood-judgment. The Flood-judgment is a warning to humanity of God's coming final judgment on the disobedient world (cf. Mt 24:37–41; 2Pe 3:3–7). The ark that saved a few through water portrays the salvation now available in Christ.

21 Although the parallel between the OT deliverance of Noah's family and NT salvation through Christ is not precise in every detail, Peter says that the water of the Flood-judgment portrays the water of baptism.

Baptism is the counterpart of what is represented in the Flood, even the "fulfillment" of the OT deliverance from judgment. How does baptism "save" (GK 5392)? Peter says it does not concern an external washing from filth but relates to the "conscience" (GK 5287). In the proclamation of the Gospel, salvation from sin and its punishment is announced through Jesus' death and resurrection. The announcement of the penalty for sin stirs the conscience and the Spirit brings conviction (Jn 16:8–11; Acts 2:37–38; 13:37–41).

"The pledge of a good conscience toward God" renders a difficult expression in Greek. The thought appears to be as follows: The conviction of sin by the Spirit in the human mind calls for a response of faith or commitment to Christ and his work. This is concretely and "contractually" done in the act of baptism. Saving faith is expressed in baptism (cf. Ac 2:38–39). Salvation comes to people because Christ has risen from the dead.

22 Not only has Christ been raised from the dead, but in his victory he "has gone" into heaven to the place of power and authority (cf. Ps 110:1; Ro 8:34). "With angels, authorities and powers" now under him, he is the supreme Lord. Therefore, the oppressed Christians in Asia Minor to whom Peter is writing need not fear anyone. Psalm 110:1 speaks of Messiah sitting at God's right hand "until I [God] make your enemies a footstool for your feet." So now even the fallen angels are subject to Jesus the Messiah (cf. Ro 8:38–39; 1 Cor 15:24ff.).

C. Death to the Old Life (4:1–6)

1 "Suffered in his body" may be more literally translated "suffered in the flesh" (see comment on 3:18); this is a reference to Jesus' death. The thought appears to be this: Since Christ suffered to the extent of death in the realm of fleshly existence, Christians are to arm themselves with the same attitude that guided Christ.

"He who has suffered in his body is done with sin" is best taken as a proverbial expression and is linked in thought to Ro 6:7 (though it is also possible to refer this statement to Christ and the finality of his work against sin). By their union with Christ, Christians must understand that their conversion is a death to sin. Thus they are "done with sin."

2 Peter gives a twofold purpose for Christians' arming themselves with Christ's attitude as expressed in v.1. First, one "does not live the rest of his earthly [lit., in the flesh] life for evil human desires." One's life after conversion is not to be lived according to human passions, but the ruling principle is the will of God. Christ himself did God's will (Jn 8:29; cf. 4:34; 5:30; 6:38–40; 7:16–17), and he taught his disciples to pray, "Your will be done" (Mt 6:10).

3 The counsel of pagans is now contrasted with God's will. This verse clearly supports the position that the recipients of the letter had, before their conversion, been pagans. The "detestable idolatry" (or "illicit idolatries") distinguished the Jews from their pagan neighbors. The other items listed (cf. comment on 2:1) are the common excesses of drink, sex, and wild parties found among the non-Christians then (and now).

4–5 The Christian lifestyle of sober, godly living condemns the values of pagan society. Pagans will respond with astonishment when Christians refuse to plunge into the "flood of dissipation" (cf. the prodigal son's "wild living" in Lk 15:13), for they expect Christians to "plunge with them" into the pleasures of the satisfaction of the flesh. Peter's denial is at once a warning and a judgment on the life lived in such a fashion. The pagan amazement will often turn to hatred and evil speaking (cf. Jn 3:19–21).

Christians are supported in their stand against the ungodly life by the truth of the coming judgment. In both OT and NT, God is the Judge. Yet the NT also shows that the Father has given judgment into Jesus' hands (Jn 5:22–23). This judgment is near (4:7); it will be universal, for it will embrace all the living and the dead. In it unbelievers will have to give an account of their lives and will not be able to withstand the divine scrutiny (cf. Ps 1:5–6).

6 The interpretation of this verse is often linked to 3:19, but the vocabulary of the text and its context differ. There are four main interpretations of the "dead" in this passage (cf. comment on 3:18–22). (1) Christ, while in his three-day death, went and preached salvation to all the dead, offering salvation to those who lived in pre-Christian times. (2) Christ, while in his three-day death, went and preached salvation to the just of OT times.

(3) The apostles and others on this earth preached the Gospel to those who were spiritually dead. (4) The dead are Christians, who had the Gospel preached to them and who then died (or were put to death). Our interpretation falls in line with this fourth option.

"For this is the reason" points ahead to the rest of the sentence rather than looks back to vv.1–5. The coming judgment will not only bring sinners into account (v.5) but will also reverse the judgments of human beings (v.6). The Good News had been proclaimed to those (Christians) who are now dead. Even though pagans might condemn Christians and put them to death in the realm of the flesh, yet in God's judgment there will be a reversal. Christians will live in a new realm, the spiritual realm.

D. The Life for God's Glory (4:7–11)

7 As is common in the NT, the final salvation of Christians is set before them to stimulate their faith and to encourage them in difficulty. "The end of all things" has now drawn near. All is in readiness. "Therefore" introduces the ethical implications of this realization. Jesus taught responsible living in the light of his return (cf. Lk 12:35–43; 17:26–27). Christians must not give way to "eschatological frenzy" but practice self-control and be active in prayer. (Peter himself had set a negative example in his failure to watch and pray in the Garden [Mt 26:40–41].)

8 "Above all" reminds us of the primacy of *agape*, "love" (GK *26* & *27*) among fellow Christians. This love is to be "eager" or "earnest" (NIV "deeply"; GK *1756*). Such love can be commanded because it is not primarily an emotion but a decision of the will leading to action. The reason for us to show love is that "love covers over a multitude of sins." This quotation from Pr 10:12 does not mean that our love covers or atones for our sins. In the proverb the meaning is that love does not "stir up" or broadcast sins. So the major idea is that love suffers in silence and bears all things (1Co 13:5–7). Christians forgive faults in others because they know the forgiving grace of God in their own lives.

9 "Hospitality" (GK *5811*) between Christians was an important, concrete expression of love in a world without our modern inns and hotels. This virtue was required of the overseers and widows (1Ti 3:2; 5:10; Tit 1:8) and is commanded for us all (Mt 25:35ff.; Ro 12:13; 3Jn 5–8). Hospitality is to be "without grumbling"—a phrase that connotes the difficulty of carrying out this command. In certain cultures that are strongly family-orientated, the bringing of strangers into a house may be somewhat shocking. Yet Christians overcome these conventions because God's love has made them into a single great family.

10–11 Hospitality is not a one-way virtue; all believers are in some way capable of ministering to others. Every Christian has a gift (Ro 12:6–8; 1Co 12:12–31) that he or she has received from God, presumably from the indwelling of the Holy Spirit at the time of regeneration. That the Holy Spirit can take "natural" talents and abilities and redirect them for Christ was most dramatically shown in Paul's ministry. Believers should not only view themselves as gifted but also as "serving" (GK *1354*) others and as "administering" (GK *3313*) the grace of God. One of the long-standing misconceptions in church practice is the idea that only one person is to "minister" in the local church. The biblical principle is that all can and should minister in various ways.

Peter puts these manifestations of grace in two broad categories: "speaking" (GK *3281*) and "serving" (GK *1354*). The former covers all forms of oral service—teaching, preaching, prophecy, perhaps even tongues. "The very words [GK *3359*] of God" are utterances from God's mouth. So what one says must be as God says it (cf. 2Co 5:20; 1Th 2:13). As for service, it is to be empowered "with the strength God provides," which means by dependence on God's help by the Spirit (cf. Eph 3:16). The purpose of mutual Christian service is that through Jesus Christ God will be glorified. Serving fellow Christians does glorify God because people will praise him for his grace that comes to them through Jesus and through his followers.

Peter adds a doxology—something that is not uncommon in Christian letters at various places besides the end (cf. Ro 11:33–36; Eph 3:20–21). God possesses all glory (cf. Isa 6:1ff.) and all power (cf. Isa 46:9–10). The "Amen" signifies assent—"So it is!"

E. Consolations in Suffering (4:12–19)

12 "Dear friends" (see comment on 2:11) marks the beginning of a new section, which (with 5:1–14) makes a fitting climax to the letter's argument. Suffering is not to be regarded as something foreign to Christian experience but rather as a refining test. Peter has already mentioned the necessity of faith being refined through suffering and testing (1:6–7). Here the idea of refining is found in the word "painful" (lit., "burning"; GK *4796*), a word used in the refining of metals. Jesus himself said, "If the world hates you, keep in mind that it hated me first" (Jn 15:18; cf. 1Jn 3:13). In the light of Jesus' experience and teaching, his followers should expect troubles, but troubles should encourage them (cf. Jn 16:33).

13 In contrast to the usual response of sorrow and shock to suffering and persecution, Christians should rejoice because they are participating in Christ's sufferings (see also Ro 8:17; 2Co 1:5–7; Php 3:10). The apostles themselves rejoiced because they had been counted worthy of suffering disgrace for the name of Christ (Ac 5:41; 16:22–25). Christian rejoicing rests on the fact that just as we share in Christ's suffering, so we will share in his glory with great joy. The prospect of Christ's full manifestation in all his glory fills believers with joy and comfort.

14 Here we have a fulfillment of the Lord's own promises to his disciples when he said, "Blessed are you when people insult you, persecute you and falsely say all kinds of evil against you because of me. Rejoice and be glad" (Mt 5:11–12). In Matthew the cause for happiness is the reward in heaven; here it is the possession of the messianic Spirit. This verse is based on Isa 11:2 (perhaps also Ps 89:50–51). One of God's great characteristics is his glory (Ac 7:2; Eph 1:17), and in Jesus his glory is revealed (Jn 1:14, 18).

The Spirit of the Father and of the Son now rests on and in every believer. The martyrdom of Stephen illustrates this. He is described as "a man full of faith and of the Holy Spirit" (Ac 6:5; cf. v.8). In his defense his face was like that of an angel (Ac 6:15), and he saw the "glory of God" (7:55).

15 The blessing of the Spirit promised to those who suffer is not universal, for not all who suffer are sharing in Christ's sufferings. Much suffering is the punishment or consequence of sin. If they suffer, it should be because of their union with Jesus, not with evil. Christians must make a clear break with sin (4:1–3; cf. Ro 6:1ff.; 1Co 6:9–11). The sins mentioned here characterize a pagan, not a Christian, lifestyle. Yet it is possible for Christians to fall in times of weakness.

16 But to suffer as a "Christian" (GK *5985*) is no shame. The title "Christian," which is now so common, was just coming into use when Peter wrote. At first Christians were known as "Jews," "disciples," "believers," "the Lord's disciples," and those "who belonged to the Way" (cf. Ac 1:15; 2:44; 6:1; 9:1–2). It was not until the church took root in Antioch that the word "Christians" for believers began to be used (see comment on Ac 11:26). Peter's injunction not to feel shame to suffer as a Christian recalls his own shame at his betrayal of Jesus (Mk 14:66–72). "That you bear that *name*" probably refers to the name "Christian."

17–18 Paul said, "We must go through many hardships to enter the kingdom of God" (Ac 14:22). Before the full unfolding of the messianic kingdom, there are to be judgments. In the Prophets, mention is made of judgment coming first upon the people of God (Eze 9:6; Zec 13:7–9; Mal 3:1–5) before coming upon the nations. Here in 1 Peter the idea seems to be that the coming of the Lord in his eschatological judgment has, as a harbinger, a beginning of "birth pains" that will purify believers (cf. 1:7). (This judgment is not, of course, a punishment for the believers' sins, which were laid on Jesus.) Now if the preliminary judgment (Christian suffering) is already taking place, the final doom on the disobedient is certain to follow shortly. Peter cites Pr 11:31 (in LXX) to reinforce this thought. The righteous are barely saved. The rest come far short, and only a great disaster awaits them.

19 The conclusion to this section is that the Christians who are suffering according to the divine will (1:6; 3:17) are to "commit [GK *4192*] themselves" to God. In his seventh word from the Cross, Jesus used this verb in committing his Spirit to God (Lk 23:46). Peter describes God as the "faithful Creator." The combination of these two words reminds believers of God's love and power in the midst of trials so that they will not doubt his interest or ability. The continuation in good works is a concrete sign of the faith that is the essence of being a Christian (cf. 2:15, 20; 3:6, 17).

F. The Shepherd's Suffering Flock (5:1–4)

1 The "elders" (GK *4565*) are the leaders of the local congregations. The institution of a group of older and wiser men providing direction and rule goes back to the early days of Israel as a people. This was done both nationally and locally. Thus there were "elders" of the Sanhedrin in Jerusalem as well as "elders" of local synagogues. The institution of eldership was adopted by the Jerusalem church (Ac 11:30; 21:18), and Paul and Barnabas applied it to the local congregations they founded on their missionary journeys (Ac 14:23; 1Ti 3:1–7; Tit 1:5ff.). Peter, therefore, addresses the elders because of their vital role in the life of the congregation.

In the Greek, this verse begins with "therefore." Because of suffering and persecution, the need of pastoral leadership was important for the local churches. The early church utilized more people than the church today does (see comment on 4:10; cf. Eph 4:12) and so put spiritual leadership in the hands of a plurality.

The basis of Peter's exhortation to the elders is threefold: (1) He is their fellow elder. In Jn 21:15–19, Jesus charged Peter with the care of his sheep. (2) He is a witness (GK *3459*) of Christ's sufferings. It is possible Peter is referring here to the sufferings of Jesus that he had seen, though the stress is on the testimony (or witness) he gives to those sufferings (cf. Lk 24:45–48; Ac 1:8). (3) He is a sharer of the coming glory. It is notable that Peter does not issue commands as an apostle (much less as a "pope") but speaks as a fellow elder (cf. also John in 2Jn 1; 3Jn 1).

2–3 Peter's instruction is to "be shepherds of God's flock [GK *4480*]." The comparison of God's people to a flock of sheep and the Lord to a shepherd is prominent in Scripture (see, for example, Ge 48:15; Pss 23; 100:3; Isa 53:6–7; Lk 15:3–7; Jn 10:1–16). The verb "to shepherd" (GK *4477*) occurs in Christ's command to Peter (Jn 21:16) and in Paul's charge to the Ephesian elders (Ac 20:28). Its meaning embraces protecting, leading, guiding, feeding, etc. Peter reminds the elders that the flock is God's and that they are responsible for its loving care. "Serving as overseers" (GK *2174*) reveals the interchangeability of the terms "bishop" ("overseer") and "elder" (see comment on Tit 1:7). The latter denotes the dignity of the office; the former denotes its function—"to oversee."

Peter's exhortation to the elders to be shepherds is followed by three contrasting statements that tell how this responsibility should be carried out and how not carried out. The positive statements are "serving as overseers ... because you are willing ... eager to serve." These words remind us of what Paul wrote to Timothy in 1Ti 3:1. Regarding the negative statements, (1) since the responsibilities of the office of elder are great and since elders will be required to give account of their work (Heb 13:17), no one should be forced into this position ("not because you must"). God will work in their lives and make them willing to do his will. The motivation of elders should be divine, not human. (2) Nor should the motivation be financial, though elders were evidently paid in the early church and handled the finances of congregations (cf. 1Co 9:7–11; 1Ti 5:17). Not money but enthusiasm and zeal for God and his work must motivate elders. (3) They are not to be "lords" over "those entrusted to" them. Probably in each congregation, individual elders had portions of the congregation for which they were particularly responsible. Elders should endeavor to be patterns for Christ's sheep.

4 Those elders who are faithful will receive a "crown of glory that does not fade away." The "crown" (GK *5109*) could be a garland or wreath made of leaves or of gold. In Christ's suffering it was ironically made of thorns (Mt 27:29). The unfading "crown of glory" makes a striking contrast to the use of withered parsley used for the crown at the Isthmian games. The glorification will take place at the manifestation of the True Shepherd or Chief Shepherd (cf. Ro 8:17ff.; 1Jn 3:2).

G. Humility and Watchfulness in Suffering (5:5–9)

5 "Young men" most likely refers to young men in general. The women are not mentioned because their activity in the churches was limited in Peter's time. "In the same way" indicates a new unit of instruction (cf. 3:1, 7). The exhortation to submission is not limited to a few, but all Christians are to manifest this quality.

"Clothe yourselves" (GK *1599*) is a rare word that refers to a slave putting on an apron before serving. So Christians are to imitate their Lord, who girded himself and served (Jn 13:4–17). The reason for humility is based on Pr 3:34 (cf. Jas 4:6) that states God's provision of grace to the submissive and God's continuing opposition to the proud.

6 Christians should, therefore, "humble" (GK *5427*) themselves under God's "mighty hand." In the OT, God's hand symbolized discipline (Ex 3:19; 6:1; Job 30:21; Ps 32:4) and deliverance (Dt 9:26; Eze 20:34). Both meanings are appropriate in view of the sufferings of the Asian Christians. Once more Peter ties his exhortation to humility to the end times. The "due time" is the time God has set for Christ's appearing. Thus the whole destiny of Christians—whether it is suffering or glory—is God-ordained.

7 Peter then exhorts believers to "cast all your anxiety" on the Lord. He does not say what the anxiety is; perhaps he had persecution in mind. The application of his exhortation embraces all the difficulties believers who want to live godly in a fallen world must face. The "casting" entails an act of the will and should be done prayerfully and in obedience to Jesus' teaching about anxiety (Mt 6:25–34). "He cares for you" means that God is not indifferent to our sufferings. This conception of God's concern for human affliction is one of the peculiar treasures of the Judeo-Christian faith; though Greek philosophy at its highest could formulate a doctrine of God's perfect goodness, it could not even imagine his active concern for humankind. The Incarnation reveals a caring God, and Christ's teaching about his heavenly Father stresses his intimate concern for his children (Mt 10:29–31).

8–9 Belief in the sovereignty of God and in his fatherly concern for us (vv.6–7) does not permit us to sit back and do nothing. We are to "work out [our] salvation" because "it is God who works in [us]" (Php 2:12–13). So here Peter warns his flock of the danger of making the fact of God's sovereign care an excuse for inactivity. "Be sober, be watchful" perhaps reflects Peter's own experience in which Satan had "sifted" him (Lk 22:31) and he had failed to "watch" (Mt 26:38; Mk 14:34). God's sovereignty does not preclude peril to the Christian life.

Peter calls Satan "your enemy the devil" and likens him to a lion in search of prey. The word "enemy" (GK *508*) meant an opponent in a lawsuit (cf. Job 1:6ff.; Zec 3:1; Rev 12:10). "Devil" (GK *1333*) is the Greek translation of the Hebrew "Satan" (1Ch 21:1; Job 2:1; GK 8477), which means "slanderer." According to Scripture, he has great power on earth, "being the prince of this world" (Jn 14:30) and "the ruler of the kingdom of the air" (Eph 2:2). But God has limited his activity. Through his captive subjects (Eph 2:2; 2Ti 2:25–26), the devil attempted to destroy the infant church by persecution.

The Christian response to satanic opposition is not panic or flight but firm resistance in faith (v.9). "Resist" (GK *468*) is the same word as that found in Eph 6:11–13 and Jas 4:7 in contexts of struggle against hostile spiritual forces. This implies a common "resist-the-devil" formula in the early church. "In the faith" is not so much "the Christian faith" or "your faithfulness" but rather "your positive faith and trust in God."

Support in the struggle also comes from realizing that the sufferings of the Asian Christians were not unique (cf. 1Co 10:13). The same kinds of sufferings are afflicting "your brothers," whereby Peter stresses the solidarity of the Christian body. All who are in union with Christ may expect suffering (Jn 15:18–20; 16:33), and the whole body is joined together in suffering (1Co 12:26). The "world" (GK *3180*) is that orderly system under Satan that is opposed to God and his Messiah (cf. Ps 2).

H. The Sustaining Grace of God (5:10–11)

10–11 Peter now contrasts satanic opposition to God's purpose and enablement. For Christians, God has as his gracious purpose bringing his children himself to share in his glory (cf. Ps 73:23–24; Jn 17:22, 24; Ro 8:30). "Called" (GK *2813*) in the Pauline and Petrine writings stresses God's sovereign working. The eternal glory contrasts with the temporal trials Christians suffer. "Restore you and make you strong, firm and steadfast" translates four verbs that emphatically promise divine aid.

With a brief doxology, Peter closes the main part of his letter by ascribing power to Christ. This ascription of a doxology to Jesus reveals his dignity and deity.

V. Final Words (5:12–14)

A. Silas's Role in Writing the Letter (5:12)

12 Silas is undoubtedly the same person as the one mentioned in Ac 15:22–33; 15:40–18:5; 1Th 1:1; 2Th 1:1. He was one of the leading men in the early church. What help he gave Peter in writing this letter is uncertain. If he was the writing secretary (amanuensis), it would have been normal for him to have a significant part in writing, perhaps even using his own words to convey Peter's message.

Peter says this letter is brief, and he characterizes it as exhortation and testimony. The reference to "encouraging" (GK *4151*) reminds us of the commands for ethical living he has given his readers, while the reference to "testifying" (GK *2148*) stresses the reliability of what he has borne witness to. His final exhortation, "Stand fast in it," relates to the "grace of God," which no Christian earns or merits but which all Christians are obligated to abide in.

B. The Greeting From Rome (5:13)

13 Who is "she" whom Peter calls "chosen together with you"? Who is the Mark referred to? What and where is Babylon? "She" could be Peter's wife (Mk 1:30; 1Co 9:5), and "Mark" his own son. Most, however, think "she" refers to the church (GK *1711*, a Greek word that is feminine; cf. 2Jn 1, 13) and "Mark" to John Mark (cf. Ac 12:12, 25; 15:36–39). Strong early tradition links John Mark with Peter and his gospel (see introduction to Mark). "Babylon" could be (1) in Mesopotamia, (2) a town in Egypt, or (3) a cryptic reference to Rome. The last view is best because (1) according to early church tradition Peter was in Rome; (2) there is no evidence for Peter's having been in Egypt or Mesopotamia; and (3) the reference may be cryptic because of persecution, or it may be an allusion to the "exile" of God's people (cf. 1:1) on the pattern of the exile of ancient Israel in Babylon.

C. A Final Exhortation and a Prayerful Wish (5:14)

14 The formal kiss was common among early Christians as an expression of love in the church. From the third century A.D., the sexes were separated in the practice of the "kiss of love." But we do not know how old the practice of the formal kiss was. Peter ends his letter with a wish that all his readers who are believers—i.e., who are "in Christ"—may have God's peace. Such a wish is also a prayer. "Peace" (GK *1645*) reflects the common Hebrew blessing "*Shalom*" (GK *8934*). Peter begins (1:2) and ends this letter with peace.

The Old Testament in the New

NT Text	OT Text	Subject
Pe 1:16	Lev 11:44–45	Holiness commanded
Pe 1:24–25	Isa 40:6–8	Eternity of the word
Pe 2:6	Isa 28:16	Trust in the cornerstone
Pe 2:7	Ps 118:22–23	Rejected cornerstone
Pe 2:8	Isa 8:14	A stone on which people stumble
Pe 2:9	Isa 43:21	Declaring God's praise
Pe 2:10	Hos 1:6, 9	Not God's people
Pe 2:10	Hos 2:23	Now God's people
Pe 2:22	Isa 53:9	Sinless servant
Pe 2:24	Isa 53:4	Taking out infirmities
Pe 2:25	Isa 53:6	Like sheep gone astray
Pe 3:10–12	Ps 34:12–16	Turn from evil
Pe 3:14–15	Isa 8:12–13	Do not fear
Pe 4:8	Pr 10:12	Love covers sin
Pe 4:18	Pr 11:31	Receiving due reward
Pe 5:5	Pr 3:34	Grace for the humble

2 Peter

INTRODUCTION

1. Authorship and Canonicity

Among the books of the NT, none has been more disputed as to canonicity and authorship than 2 Peter. There is no assured reference to it in early Christian writings till Origen (c.185–c.254), who accepted Peter as the author. Doubt about it persisted into the fourth century. But already in the early third century, a papyrus manuscript of a portion of the NT contains this letter along with 1 Peter and Jude and enjoins a blessing on its readers; in fact, 2 Peter receives more elaborate support than the other two. This letter was eventually admitted to the canon and, despite widespread questioning of its Petrine authorship, it still speaks with the authority of Scripture.

Canonicity and authorship, though not synonymous, are often related. In the early church, one of the main reasons for accepting a book as authoritative was its apostolic authorship or authorization. The canonicity of 2 Peter was questioned primarily because of doubts about its Petrine authorship. These doubts reappeared at the time of the Reformation. Today they are widespread among contemporary scholars.

Various arguments have been used against Peter as the author. Eusebius and Jerome give us the first two: (1) No long line of tradition for accepting 2 Peter could be traced to their day. (2) Its style is different from that of 1 Peter, which was strongly accepted by the church as Petrine. The next two arguments also stem from the ancient church: (3) Peter's name was used in connection with some Gnostic literature. (4) Knowledge of 2 Peter was geographically limited.

In addition, modern scholars have added these arguments: (5) Petrine authorship is unlikely because this letter seems so dependent on the letter of Jude. (6) Its conceptual and rhetorical language is too Hellenistic for a Galilean fisherman. (7) The problem of the delay of the Second Coming is a second-century one. (8) The collection of Paul's letters referred to in 3:15–16 was made in the second century.

In analyzing these claims, we should note that no single argument is conclusive enough to rule out its apostolic authorship. (1) Because of the letter's brevity, governmental persecutions of the early church, and communication problems in the ancient world, the lack of a long tradition for 2 Peter is hardly surprising. If the letter had been sent to an area not in the main travel routes or one that suffered sudden persecutions, normal circulation patterns may have been hindered.

(2) The style does differ from that of 1 Peter, but this may be explained by the use of a different amanuensis (see comment on 1Pe 5:12). If 1 Peter was written by Peter with the assistance of Silas, 2 Peter could either be in Peter's own style or in his style with the assistance of a different amanuensis. Moreover, stylistic arguments are hard to evaluate because the criteria for the identity and distinctiveness of writers are not settled.

The work of the Spirit in inspiration may well extend to the amanuensis who in certain cases may even be termed a coauthor. The stylistic differences in the Pastoral Letters have long been recognized. In 2Ti 4.11, Paul says, "Only Luke is with me." Perhaps Luke served as Paul's amanuensis. So the Pastorals would have a different style from other letters of Paul. Yet their authority would not be inferior because the superintendence of the Spirit would be over Luke as well as over Paul. The same factors may apply to Peter's letters. Furthermore, some scholars have concluded that the linguistic differences between 1 and 2 Peter have been exaggerated.

(3) It is true that the appearance of Peter's name on certain Gnostic writings led to some hesitation in the acceptance of 2 Peter by the early church. But that the early church accepted 2 Peter in spite of the circulation of such spurious works shows that it recognized a difference in character between the

two letters and the other works bearing his name.

(4) The literary dependence of 2 Peter on Jude is not conclusively settled (see below, Special Problem). But even if Peter quoted or used a substantial part of Jude's letter, this precludes neither Peter's authorship of the second letter nor its inspiration. For scholars to accept Mark's priority and Matthew's use of Mark is compatible with a high view of biblical inspiration and authority.

(5) In answer to the claim that the language of the letter is too Hellenistic for a man of Peter's background, we may reply that the extent of Hellenistic influence Peter had in his life is not known. He lived about five miles from the region of the Greek league of ten cities known as Decapolis. We do not know whether he was bilingual or how much he learned between the Resurrection and his martyrdom.

(6) The problem of the delay of the Second Coming was most certainly a first-century problem as well as a second-century one (see Jn 21:20–23; Mt 25:1–13; Ac 1:6–11; 2Th 2:1–4; Heb 9:28; these are all NT books universally acknowledged as first century).

(7) The reference in 3:15–16 to Paul's letters need not mean a complete corpus of his letters but only those known to the writer of these verses. The collecting of Paul's letters would have begun as soon as a church or some influential person recognized their value. Paul's instruction about exchanging letters (cf. Col 4:16) and their public reading (1Th 5:27) would have facilitated the collection of his letters. That Luke or Timothy were traveling companions of Paul makes them likely collectors of his writings.

(8) The common assumption that writing under a prominent person's name was an established convention is by no means well-established. Many clearly pseudonymous writings are from the Gnostics, an early Christian heresy that was trying to claim apostolic sanction for its teachings, and none of them was ever considered a candidate for the NT canon. Furthermore, Tertullian states that the presbyter who wrote *The Acts of Paul and Thecla* was deposed for doing so.

(9) On a more positive note, the book clearly claims to have been written by the apostle Peter (1:1). It recalls how the Lord spoke to Peter about his imminent death (1:14) and refers to Peter's presence as an eyewitness at Jesus' transfiguration (1:16–18). It claims to be his second letter (3:1), a claim most commentators interpret as referring back to 1 Peter, and says that Paul is his "beloved brother" (3:15). Such indications of apostolic authorship are not easily set aside. Either 2 Peter is a genuine work of Simon Peter the apostle or it is an unreliable forgery.

(10) Finally, the quality of its teaching should not be underestimated. In contrast to the Petrine apocrypha, one does not detect false notes in reading 2 Peter. The book rings true. The author's zeal for truth (1:12), his rejection of clever fables (1:16), and his concern for righteousness (2:7–9) are impressive.

As mentioned above, authorship and canonicity were closely related in the ancient church's decisions about canonicity. Seven NT books—Hebrews, James, Jude, 2 Peter, 2 and 3 John, and Revelation—were recognized as canonical only after a certain amount of discussion. The other twenty books had almost universal early acknowledgment. But many other books were known and widely circulated in the early church. Some were highly regarded (e.g., The Shepherd of Hermas) but were never recognized by the church as Scripture. By the time of Cyril of Jerusalem (c. 315–86), 2 Peter was considered canonical; and Cyril's acceptance of it as well as its acceptance by Athanasius, Augustine, and Jerome settled the issue for the early church. These leaders acknowledged 2 Peter to be Scripture because the evidence, both internal and external, showed its solid worth.

2. Date

From 3:15–16 it is clear that the letter could not have been written until a good number of the Pauline letters had been written and gathered together. This means that the earliest possible date would be A.D. 60. If the reference in 3:1 ("Dear friends, this is now my second letter to you") refers to 1 Peter (though this is not entirely certain; cf. comments at 3:1), then the earliest possible date for 2 Peter would be about 63–64, i.e., shortly after the time of the writing of 1 Peter. The latest possible date (if its apostolic authorship is accepted) is shortly before his death (cf. 1:12–15) or about A.D. 64–68. Some evangelical writers favor a posthumous publication of this letter by one of Peter's followers (i.e., about A.D. 80–90).

3. Place of Origin

Rome is a favorite choice for where the letter was written from because Peter is known to have been there. But since he traveled widely (Palestine, Asia Minor, Corinth [?], and Rome), it is impossible to determine for sure where 2 Peter was written.

4. Destination

The only clues to the destination are in the letter itself. It is addressed "to those who through the righteousness of our God and Savior Jesus Christ have received a faith as precious as ours" (1:1). This contrasts with the provinces in Asia Minor mentioned in 1Pe 1:1 and may imply that 2 Peter was written to Christians in various places. In 3:1 the writer says, "Dear friends, this is now my second letter to you." If this refers to 1 Peter, then the letter is addressed to Christians in Pontus, Galatia, Cappadocia, Asia, and Bithynia. But if 3:1 refers to a lost letter of Peter's (cf. 1Co 5:9; Col 4:16b for probable lost letters of Paul), then we have no firm information about the destination of 2 Peter. From the warnings in the letter concerning the false teachers (2:1–20), it seems that their vices were more typical of Gentiles than Jews.

5. Occasion and Content

The occasion for writing 2 Peter may be inferred from its contents. The immediate occasion was the author's knowledge that his time was short and that God's people were facing many dangers (1:13–14; 2:1–3). Just as sheep are prone to wander, so Christians are prone to forget the basic truths of the faith. The gift of exhortation in the church was a means of correcting this tendency (cf. Ro 12:8). Peter himself mentions this need in his first letter (5:1, 12). 2 Peter reminds us of the basis for Christian faith (cf. 1:12–13). Faith in Jesus as Messiah is not grounded on myths or clever stories (1:16); it is based on sure revelation from God (1:16–21). The Christian's personal faith should not be static but ever growing. Continual growth in the Christian graces gives a certainty of election to the believer (1:8–10).

Christians must beware of false teachers (2:1–22) who deny the imminent return of the Lord (3:3–4) and live immoral and greedy lives. These teachers are clever and claim scriptural support from Paul's letters for their views of liberty, but they pervert the letters and are headed for damnation (3:15–16). The church is to be alert to error and growing in the grace and knowledge of Christ (3:17–18).

6. Special Problem

There are so many similarities between 2 Peter and Jude that some kind of dependence seems necessary. The common material almost entirely relates to the description and denunciation of false teachers. The majority view is that 2 Peter is dependent on Jude. Some scholars use this apparent dependence on Jude to deny Peter was the author. But the use of Jude by the author of 2 Peter would pose a problem for Petrine authorship of the letter only if (1) the dependence of 2 Peter on Jude were conclusively proved, (2) the composition of Jude were definitely dated later than A.D. 64, or (3) it could be shown that an apostle such as Peter would not have used so much material from another writer.

In answer to these concerns, (1) the dependence of 2 Peter on Jude is not a certainty. Some scholars have argued the contrary—that Jude is dependent on 2 Peter. It is also possible that both letters used a common source. (2) The date of Jude is not fixed by any firm internal or external data, and it may have been written by A.D. 60. In that case Peter could have used Jude. (3) Peter seems to have used a certain amount of catechetical material in 1 Peter (see introduction to 1 Peter), and there is no reason not to think that he may have done so here. In any case, whatever position is adopted does not necessarily affect the authenticity, authorship, or inspiration of these letters.

EXPOSITION

I. Salutation and Blessing (1:1–4)

1 The author identifies himself as "Simon Peter." The best Greek manuscripts spell it in the Hebraic form *Symeon* (a name that goes back to the second son of Jacob and Leah; also used in Ac 15:14). This detail supports the Petrine authorship of the letter, for a pseudonymous author would probably have used the more common spelling. This disciple also had the nickname, "Cephas" (i.e., "Rock" or "Peter"; see the introduction to 1 Peter).

Peter gives a twofold identification of himself: "a servant and apostle of Jesus Christ." As a "servant" (lit., "slave"; GK *1528*), he belongs to Jesus by right of purchase (see 1Pe 1:18–19; cf. 1Co 6:19–20) and must obey his commands and do his will. The "servant" has status by virtue of the Lord he serves. As an "apostle" (GK *693*), Peter has an authoritative commission and speaks God's words.

Those whom Peter is addressing are described only in general terms that can apply to any Christian. The letter itself, however, contains specific clues concerning the people Peter is writing to. A relationship of some duration between author and recipients is implied by 1:12–15. From 3:15 we learn that Paul also wrote to them. In 3:1 Peter says, "This is now my second letter to you." Many scholars believe that this reference is to 1 Peter. If so, the recipients of 2 Peter are clearly identified in 1Pe 1:1 (but see comment on 3:1). If "second letter" does not refer to 1 Peter, we know practically nothing about those to whom 2 Peter was addressed.

The recipients are described as possessing "a faith as precious as ours." Is this "faith" the objective faith or body of truth committed to an individual? Or should we take it in a subjective sense of one's ability to trust God? The latter is the better choice, for (1) the article is omitted in the Greek (when faith is clearly objective, e.g., Jude 3, 20, the article is often present), and (2) the only other use of "faith" in this letter (1:5) is most likely subjective in sense. It is also possible that Peter combines both objective and subjective senses of faith. The faith of those to whom he is writing is "as precious [lit., equally privileged; GK *2700*] as ours"—i.e., every Christian has the same heavenly Father, the same prospect of glory, and thus equal access to God (Ro 5:2).

The statement that those the letter is addressed to "have received" their faith clearly implies that faith (whether objective, subjective, or both) is a gift of God. God's bestowal of faith is through his "righteousness" (GK *1466*) or, better, "justice." This word is often used and developed by Paul (e.g., "justification by faith" as the theme of Romans; cf. Ro 1:1–16). But here it means "justice," either in the sense of the impartiality of God's justice in giving all believers an equally privileged faith or in the sense of God's granting of salvation being compatible with his justice.

The grammar of the phrase "of our God and Savior Jesus Christ" leaves little doubt that in these words Peter is calling Jesus Christ both God and Savior.

2 The first seven words of this verse are identical with 1 Peter 1:2b (see comment there), but here the words "through the knowledge of God and of Jesus our Lord" are added. As in other NT letters, the basic theme of the letter is quickly sounded. For 2 Peter it is the "knowledge" (*epignosis*; GK *2106*) of God (cf. vv.3, 8; 2:20); a related verb (GK *2105*) occurs twice in 2:21. Another related word meaning "knowledge" (*gnosis*; GK *1194*) occurs at 1:5, 6; 3:18; and its companion verb "to know" (GK *1182*) occurs at 1:20 and 3:3. This makes a total of eleven occurrences of these related words in this short letter. The knowledge of God is a central biblical theme (cf. Jer 9:23–24; Jn 17:3), but it was also claimed by the false teachers of the apostolic and postapostolic times. As Paul warned in Tit 1:16, "They claim to know God, but by their actions they deny him." Later a developed "Gnosticism" became a great challenge to the Christian church.

3 The grammar of this verse connects it more closely with v.2 than the NIV indicates; it shows the way in which the multiplication of the knowledge of God takes place—through the divine power given to us. God has called believers "by his own glory [GK *1518*] and goodness [GK *746*]"—i.e., God in salvation reveals his splendor and his moral excellence, and these are means he uses to effect conversions. In bringing people to the knowledge of himself, God's divine power supplies them with everything they need for life and godliness. Probably what is in view is the work of the Spirit of God in believers, providing them with gifts and enabling them to use these gifts.

4 "Through these" refers to God's "glory and goodness" or more generally to his salvation mediated through the Incarnation. So when Jesus Christ came in his first advent, God made certain promises ("very great and precious") of the new Messianic Age (cf. 3:9, 13) to be brought in when Christ returned. These promises enable Christians to "participate in the divine nature."

How does this participation come about? In at least two ways. (1) The promises themselves have a purifying effect on the believer's life (cf. 1Jn 3:3). (2) Conversion entails a definite break with "the corruption ... caused by evil desires." In coming to know God through Christ, believers escape the corruption of sin; and Christ renews and restores the image of God in them.

II. The Essential Christian Virtues (1:5–15)

A. The Efforts for Christian Fruitfulness (1:5–9)

5 Because of the new birth and the promises associated with it, Christians participate in the divine nature (v.4). But the new birth does not rule out human activity. Sanctification is a work of God in which believers cooperate. This is why the Bible gives ethical imperatives based on dogmatic indicatives (cf. Ro 6:11–14; 12:1–2; Php 2:12–13; 1Pe 1:13–21); this principle is in accord with biblical statements of how God works (cf. Ro 8:13b; Php 2:13). So Peter urgently calls for a progressive, active Christianity. It is by faith alone that we are saved through grace, but this saving faith does not continue by itself (Eph 2:8–10). Peter's chain of eight virtues (vv.5–7) starts with "faith" and ends in "love" (cf. 1Ti 1:5).

Christians are told to "make every effort to add to [their] faith." In NT times the word "add" (GK 2220) was used of making a rich or lavish provision. To make every "effort" (GK 5082) requires both zeal and seriousness in the pursuit of holiness. "Goodness" (GK 746) is an attribute of Christ himself (1:3) and therefore is to be sought by his people. It is excellence of achievement or mastery in a specific field—in this case virtue or moral excellence (cf. Php 4:8; 1Pe 2:9). The "knowledge" (GK 1194) that is to be added to faith is the advance into the will of God. The false teachers (eventually known as the Gnostics) claimed a superior knowledge. The apostles stressed that it was necessary for those who know God to live a godly life (cf. 1Jn 2:3–4; 5:18) and that Christ taught them the will of the Father (Jn 15:15).

6 The next virtue in Peter's chain is "self-control" (GK 1602). The concept of self-control played a great role in the philosophical ethics of classical Greece and Hellenism. But in NT ethical discussions it is not generally used, perhaps because the normal biblical emphasis is on God at work in us by the Spirit rather than on human self-mastery. Self-control is the exact opposite of the excesses (2:3, 14) of the false teachers and the sexual abuses in the pagan world. The NT concept of self-control is instructive. Paul uses the verb "to control oneself" of the unmarried (1Co 7:9; cf. Ac 24:25) and of his own self-discipline for the Gospel (1Co 9:25). In the only other use of the noun besides 2Pe 1:6, Paul lists it as one facet of the fruit of the Spirit (Gal 5:23). So while the biblical ethic does include "self-control," it sees it as the manifestation of the Spirit's work in believers, resulting in the human activity Paul speaks of in Ro 8:13.

Following self-control is "perseverance" or "patience" (GK 5705). This virtue views time with God's eyes (3:8) while waiting for Christ's return and for the punishment of sin. Perseverance is the ability to continue in the faith and resist the pressures of the world system (cf. Lk 8:15; Ro 5:3; Heb 12:2). "Godliness" (GK 2354) is piety or devotion to the person of God.

7 "Brotherly kindness" (GK 5789) and "love" (*agape*; GK 27) complete the list. The knowledge of God issues into love for other believers (1Jn 4:7–20). Brotherly kindness denotes the warmth of affection that should characterize the fellowship of believers, and love is the queen of the virtues (cf. 1Co 13), denoting self-sacrificing action in behalf of another. This love flows from God who is himself love (1Jn 4:8) and who reaches out to the world (Jn 3:16; 1Jn 3:16). Godly people who participate in the divine nature must abound in love.

8 The "knowledge" of God is the beginning, the continuance, and the goal of the Christian life (cf. Php 3:10). If Christians possess in ever-increasing measure the eight virtues just listed, they will not be "ineffective and unproductive" (like the false teachers described in ch. 2). Progressive growth in the Christian graces is a sign of spiritual vitality and prevents sloth and unfruitfulness (Mt 13:22; Jn 15:1–7).

9 Not to have these virtues is to be "nearsighted and blind." In the NT "blind" (GK 5603) is commonly used in a metaphorical as well as a literal sense (cf. Jn 9:39–41). Spiritual blindness can come from being spiritually "nearsighted" (GK 3697). Such a defect of vision leads one to forgetfulness of cleansing from old sins. Perhaps Peter had in mind those who turn away from their commitment at baptism.

B. The Confirmation of Election (1:10–11)

10 In view of the dangers spoken of in v.9 and the possibility of a fruitful knowledge of God (v.8), Peter exhorts Christians "to make [their] calling and election sure." "Sure" (GK 1010) is a word used of confirming something, as in the legal terminology of validating a will. So a Christian by growing in grace becomes assured of having been called and elected by God. Some prefer a corporate sense of election here (cf. 1Pe 1:1). In favor of this view is the fact that "calling" (GK 3104) and "election" (GK 1724) are bound together by a single Greek article and that the word "calling" can have a general application (cf. Mt 22:14). Nevertheless, in the Pauline letters calling and election are normally used in a particular sense (cf. Ro 8:28–30). People respond in faith to God's gracious working. Likewise Peter's emphasis here is on human response. Many see Paul's influence on Peter (cf. comment on 3:15).

If Christians are continually advancing in the virtues mentioned in vv.5–7, they will never "stumble" or "fall." Some have argued that "the loss of salvation" is in view here, but the meaning of "suffer a reverse or misfortune" fits the context well. Strong warnings about unfaithfulness to Christ and emphasis on the necessity of perseverance are common in the letters of Paul (e.g., Col 1:22–23; 2Ti 2:12–13).

11 Eschatology provides a motivation for ethics. Present difficulties are easier to go through because of bright prospects for the future, when "the kingdom of our Lord and Savior Jesus Christ" will be inaugurated. In one sense, Christians are already in the kingdom (Col 1:13). Yet, as Paul and Barnabas said, "We must go through many hardships to enter the kingdom of God" (Ac 14:22). The kingdom is seen as temporally limited in 1Co 15:24 and Rev 20:1–6, but in this verse, Peter speaks of it as "the eternal kingdom." The diversity of statements about the kingdom in the Bible reflects the many facets of the rule of the triune God over humanity (both saved and lost) and also over angels (both fallen and unfallen) (cf. Pss 22:28; 145:11–13; Da 4:35; Ac 17:24).

Jesus Christ is now the Lord (Ac 2:36), and as such he rules. In his coming to earth, his rule or kingdom will be visibly manifested and imposed (Mt 13:40–43; see comment on Mk 1:15). This will mark the end of this age and inaugurate the earthly messianic phase of the kingdom (Rev 20:1–6), which will last for a thousand years. Yet the kingdom does not end, for God's reign is eternal (Rev 11:15), and the mediatorial kingdom becomes the eternal kingdom of the triune God. Here, then, Peter looks to the future aspects of the kingdom of Jesus Christ that believers enter at death or at the imposition of that kingdom.

The future for Christians who diligently pursue holiness is very bright. They will "receive a rich welcome." They will not barely make it into the kingdom or "be saved . . . only as one escaping through the flames" (1Co 3:15); but each one will receive the Lord's "Well done, good and faithful servant!" (Mt 25:21). Peter's words in this verse may allude to the honors paid to winners of the Olympic games. When a winner came back to his hometown, he would be welcomed by a special entrance built in the town or city wall in his honor.

C. The Need for Reminders (1:12–15)

12 Truth needs to be repeated. The future hope is indeed well known to Christians. Yet to "remind" them of it and to exhort them regarding its application to life and service are essential. "So" links what Peter now says about reminding his readers with his statements about the need for possessing Christian virtues in increasing measure (v.8), participating in the divine nature (v.4), and the eschatological hope (v.11). He knows that they have a settled conviction of "the truth [they] now have." This statement implies a relatively fixed body of truth (cf. Jude 3), which goes all the way back to the body of recognizable apostolic truth (Ac 2:42).

"Firmly established" (GK 5114) picks up the exhortation of Jesus to Simon Peter to "strengthen" (GK 5114) his brothers (Lk

22:32). Knowing apostolic truth leads to spiritual strength; those who have received this teaching are established. But this does not obviate the need for warnings of spiritual pitfalls, exhortations to pursue truth, and prayer for divine strengthening (1Pe 5:10).

13–14 That Peter knows that he will not always live in "the tent of this body" underlines what he has been saying. The word "tent" (GK *5013*; cf. *5008*) was used of a body either living or dead (see 2Co 5:1, 4). Although it is possible that Peter was influenced by Paul's usage, it is also possible that they shared a common linguistic and conceptual heritage. Peter knows that he will soon die and refers to a special revelation Jesus gave him (possibly Jn 21:18–19, where Jesus spoke of a violent death for Peter).

For Christians death should hold no terrors; it is like putting off old clothes or like exiting from old age. According to Paul, to die is to "be with Christ" (Php 1:23) in a new way. So in view of his approaching death, Peter wants "to refresh [his readers'] memory"—"refresh" (GK *1444*) means "to wake up" or "arouse."

15 "And I will make every effort" (GK *5079*) recalls words used in vv.5, 10. Peter then uses an educational term, wanting to do something so that his readers "remember" the basic truths after his death. Much discussion has centered around this sentence and the nature of what Peter is promising. He may be referring to the written form of his teaching or perhaps even to the gospel of Mark. In any case, he intends to continue his ministry with all diligence until his death so as to strengthen the church.

III. Christ's Divine Majesty (1:16–21)

A. Attested by Apostolic Eyewitnesses (1:16–18)

16 Here Peter links himself with the other apostles ("we"—cf. comment on v.18) in certifying that their message is based on their own eyewitness experience of Jesus and on the hearing of God's attestation of him. Peter denies that they have followed "cleverly invented stories" (lit., "myths"; GK *3680*)—the words refer to fables about the gods. The NT always uses this word in a negative sense and in contrast to the truth of the Gospel (see 1Ti 1:4; 4:7; 2Ti 4:4; Tit 1:14). It is likely that the false teachers claimed that the Incarnation, Resurrection, and coming kingdom that the apostles spoke about were only fabricated stories. These teachers may have been men like Hymenaeus and Philetus, who said that "the resurrection has already taken place" (2Ti 2:17–18). Apparently they denied a future aspect of eschatology or else reinterpreted it so that it lost its intended meaning.

Peter's specific point was the second coming of Jesus. He sees his preaching of the Second Coming as based on his eyewitness observation of the transfiguration of Jesus (cf. vv.17–18 with Mt 16:28–17:5). When Jesus returns, the kingdom will be visibly inaugurated in power. The dead will be raised, and judgment will occur. The "power" (GK *1539*) he will then manifest embraces destruction of the lawless one (2Th 2:8) and his hosts (Rev 19:11–16), calling out the dead by his voice (Jn 5:28), the final judgment (Jn 5:27), and the consummation of the kingdom (Rev 11:15–18).

"Eyewitness" (GK *2228*) seems to be a favorite term used by the false teachers, and Peter uses their own vocabulary against them (a verb form related to this word is used in 1Pe 2:12; 3:2).

17–18 These verses explain how and when Peter was an eyewitness of the majesty of Jesus Christ. God the Father gave honor and glory to Jesus. The "honor" is the public acknowledgment of his sonship (cf. Ps 2:6–7; Mt 3:17; Lk 3:22), and the "glory" is the transfiguration of the humiliated Son into his glorious splendor. On the Mount of Transfiguration, Jesus' face "shone like the sun," his clothes "became as white as the light" (Mt 17:1–9; Mk 9:2–10; Lk 9:28–36), and a unique voice sounded from a bright cloud that covered them and said, "This is my Son, whom I love; with him I am well pleased." The scene showed Jesus as Messiah and was a preview of his glory as King.

Peter emphatically says, "We [i.e., Peter, James, and John] heard this voice that came from heaven," while they were with Jesus "on the sacred mountain." It was the Transfiguration that transformed the mountain from a common one into a "sacred" (GK *41*) one. As for the place of the Transfiguration, Mount Hermon (over nine thousand feet high and near Caesarea Philippi, where the event that preceded the Transfiguration took place) is the most likely choice (see comment on Mk 9:2).

B. Attested by Divinely Originated Prophecy (1:19–21)

19 By saying "And we have the word of the prophets made more certain [GK *1010*]," Peter indicates that the OT prophets spoke of the same things he did and that their words are made more certain because the Transfiguration was a foreview of their fulfillment. The Scriptures, in other words, confirm the apostolic witness. Peter is making an obvious comparison between the OT prophecies (which were accepted as God's reliable word) and the apostles' testimony or that of the Voice at the Transfiguration.

After affirming the reliability of the OT Scriptures, Peter exhorts his readers to continue to pay careful attention to the prophetic message. He compares it to "light shining in a dark place" (cf. Ps 119:105). The "dark place" is the whole world, which has turned from God the Light to darkness (cf. Isa 9:2; Eph 6:12; Jn 3:19). Christians are to ponder and keep the word of God "until the day dawns." The "day" is the day of the Second Coming (cf. Ro 13:12). The "morning star" is a reference to the Messiah (see Nu 24:17; cf. also Lk 1:78; Rev 22:16).

The phrase "rises in your hearts" is difficult. The best interpretation sees "in your hearts" as the subjective result of Christ's actual coming. When he comes, an illuminating transformation will take place in the hearts of believers.

20 Peter continues his exhortation with the expression "above all." The primary thing to be known is that the prophetic Scriptures did not come into being through the prophet's "own interpretation [GK *2146*]" (lit., "of one's own unloosing"). What exactly does Peter mean by this expression? There are three major views. (1) No prophecy is to be interpreted by any individual in an arbitrary way—so either the church must interpret prophecy, the interpretation must be that intended by the Holy Spirit, or the individual's interpretation is not to be "private" but according to the analogy of faith. (2) "No prophecy of Scripture came about by the prophet's own interpretation"—i.e., no prophecy originated through the interpretation of the prophet himself. (3) The word translated "interpretation" does not mean interpretation but refers to the origination of Scripture. The sense of the verse is probably that of the first view. This fits well with the problem of the false teachers' distorting Paul's writings and other Scripture mentioned at 3:16, and the next verse clarifies that the prophecy originated with the Holy Spirit.

21 Each prophecy originated in God, not in the will of a human being. No prophet wrote his own private ideas. This verse is notable for the light it sheds on how Scripture was produced. Peter's statement "men spoke from God" implies the dual authorship of Scripture—a teaching also implied in the OT (see 2Sa 23:2; Jer 1:7, 9). The human prophets spoke, but God so worked in them that what they said was his word. It was not through a process of dictation or through a state of ecstasy that the writers of Scripture spoke but through the control of the Spirit of God—"as they were carried along by the Holy Spirit."

IV. False Prophets and Teachers (2:1–22)

A. Warning Against False Teachers (2:1–3)

1 Although Israel ("the people" [GK *3295*], a common designation for Israel) had a notable succession of true prophets, she was often plagued by false or lying prophets (cf. Dt 13:1–5; 18:20; 1Ki 18:19; 22:6ff.; Jer 5:31; 23:9–18). Likewise, the church must expect false teachers to come in (cf. Ac 20:29), who "secretly introduce" or smuggle in their doctrines. Similar warnings occur in Gal 2:4 concerning the entrance of false brothers into a Christian gathering, and in 2Co 11:13–15 concerning Satan's masqueraders. The "destructive heresies" are teachings that lead to darkness and damnation. The focal point of their error was Christological; they denied "the sovereign Lord who bought them." The "sovereign Lord" (GK *1305*) is Christ (cf. Jude 4).

"Who bought them" is a difficult phrase. It seems to some to raise questions about the doctrine of the perseverance of the saints (i.e., eternal security), for here it appears that persons bought by Christ are lost. Various solutions have been advanced. (1) Some suggest that "the sovereign Lord who bought them" refers to the God of the Exodus rather than to Jesus Christ. This requires understanding the antecedent of "them" to be "the people"

Passages Indicating the Inspiration of Scripture

Many passages in both the OT and NT demonstrate that the Bible is the inspired Word of God. This chart compiles the major passages that support this important Christian doctrine.

The Bible Writers Write About Themselves	
Moses spoke and wrote what God told him	Ex 19:3; 34:33–36; Dt 18:18
David spoke and wrote as led by the Spirit of God	2Sa 23:2; cf. Mt 22:43
The prophets spoke and wrote what the Lord told them	Isa 7:7; Jer 1:9; 2:1; Eze 7:1; Hos 4:1; Am 1:3; 3:1; Ob 1; etc.
Jesus promised to speak to the disciples by his Spirit	Jn 14:25–26; 16:13–15
Paul wrote and spoke as the Spirit directed him	1Co 2:11–13; 14:37; Gal 1:8–9; 1Th 2:13
John wrote and spoke what God showed him and said to him	Rev 1:1–2, 10–11; 2:7, 11, 19, 29; etc.

The Bible Writers About Other Bible Writers	
"All Scripture is God-breathed"	2Ti 3:16
Prophets spoke and wrote "as they were carried along by the Holy Spirit"	2Pe 1:20–21
To Jesus, the authority of Scripture extends to the smallest letters	Mt 5:20–21; Lk 16:17
To Jesus, the Scriptures cannot be broken	Jn 10:34–35
To Jesus, what the Scriptures said, "God said"	Mt 15:4
To Jesus, David spoke "by the Holy Spirit"	Mk 12:36
To the early Christians, "the Holy Spirit" spoke in the Scriptures	Ac 4:25–26
To Paul, "the Holy Spirit" or "God" spoke through the prophets	Ac 28:25; Ro 9:25; 2Co 6:1–2; Eph 4:8
To the writer to the Hebrews, "God spoke … through the prophets"	Heb 1:1
To the writer to the Hebrews, the Scriptures are "God" speaking or "the Holy Spirit" speaking to us	Heb 1:6–13; 3:7; 4:3; 8:8
To Peter, the process of inspiration applies equally to Paul's writings	2Pe 3:15–16

in the first part of the sentence. While this is grammatically possible, it is unlikely because of the distance between the pronoun and its antecedent. The natural sense of the verse is that "they" (the false teachers) deny the Lord who bought them (the false teachers).

(2) Others suggest that the false teachers were redeemed but fell away or lost their salvation. But to many Christians, the idea that a redeemed person can lose his or her salvation contradicts clear passages that state the contrary (e.g., Jn 10:28–29; Ro 8:28–39). Moreover, v.2 says nothing about the application of redemption to the false teachers or their appropriation of it.

(3) Others take the word "bought" (lit., "redeem"; GK 60) in the sense of "temporal deliverance"—i.e., the word is not used here of one's personal salvation.

(4) Still others argue that Peter is speaking not in terms of the reality of the false teachers' faith but in terms of their profession. They *profess* to be those who have been bought by the blood of Christ, but they are lying.

In my judgment, v.1 asserts that Christ "bought" the false teachers, but this does not necessarily mean that they were saved. Salvation in the NT sense does not occur until the benefits of Christ's work are applied to the individual by the regeneration of the Spirit and belief in the truth. In other words, Christ crucified is the atoning sacrifice for the sins of the whole world (1Jn 2:2). Yet the wrath of God is on all sinners (Jn 3:36; Eph 2:3) until the work of the Cross is applied specifically to those who believe.

"Bringing swift destruction [GK 724] on themselves" refers to the everlasting state of torment and death. It will be "swift" because it will descend on them suddenly, either at their death or at the return of the Lord.

2 The false teachers will be popular with many followers. John speaks of the same phenomenon when, speaking of the false prophets who do not acknowledge that Jesus is from God, he says, "The world listens to them" (1Jn 4:5). Moreover, Peter says that the many adherents of the false teachers will follow "their shameful ways" (i.e., "vices," "sexual debaucheries"; GK *816*; cf. 1Pe 4:3; 2Pe 2:7, 18). Their disciples will be like the false teachers and, bringing their sexual immorality into the churches, will cause "the way of truth" to be defamed. "The way" (GK *3847*) was a common early name for the Christian faith (cf. Ac 9:2; 19:9, 23; 22:4; 24:14, 22). Such ungodly conduct brings reproach on the name of God or Christ (cf. Ro 2:23–24; 1Ti 6:1; Tit 2:5). It is also important to understand that the Christian faith is "the way *of truth*"—the "way" of life that responds to and is determined by the "truth." True doctrine must issue in true living (see comment on 1:5).

3 Christian teachers have the right to financial support (cf. 1Co 9:1–14; Gal 6:6; 1Ti 5:17–18), but their motivation in the ministry should not be mercenary. For false teachers, however, religion will be commercialized; they will "exploit" people. With fabricated stories they will fleece the sheep. In the light of the commercialism of religious cults today, Peter's warning is clear enough. But the popularity and prosperity of the errorists will certainly come to an end. Their judgment and doom have been announced long ago (cf. Ps 1:5–6). "Destruction" (GK *724*; cf. v.1) is now personified as "not sleeping."

B. Three Examples of Previous Judgments (2:4–10a)

In the Greek, vv.4–9 form a single sentence. The "if" clause is extended by the use of three examples of divine judgment; the conclusion of this conditional sentence is delayed until v.9. The cumulative examples of the first part of the sentence make the main point (v.9) stand out with force and emphasis.

4 The first example of divine judgment is that which came upon the fallen "angels." If angels are judged, then certainly human beings will also be judged. Of which judgment of angels does Peter speak? The most common and best interpretation relates the judgment Peter speaks of with the mention of angels in Ge 6:1–4, where "sons of God" apparently means "fallen angels" (cf. Job 1:6; 2:1; 38:7). (1) This interpretation was common in Jewish literature. (2) The three examples (angels, Flood, and cities of the plain) all come one after another in the early chapters of Genesis. (3) The angels referred to here in 2 Peter are confined to "gloomy dungeons." Apparently some fallen angels are free to plague human beings as demons while others are imprisoned. The connection with Ge 6:1–4 provides a reason for this phenomenon.

Peter uses the verb *tartaroo* (lit., "to hold captive in Tartarus"; GK 5434) to tell where the sinning angels were sent. "Tartarus," considered by the Greeks as a place under the earth that was lower than Hades where divine punishment was meted out, was also regarded this way in nonbiblical Jewish literature. The usual translation of this verb as "sent them to hell" (so NIV) only approximates the idea of a special place of confinement until the final judgment. Though "gloomy dungeons" may be correct, "chains of darkness" is an equally possible translation (cf. Jude 6).

5 Peter's second example is the Flood. He has referred to this in his first letter (1Pe 3:18–22) and will do so again in the next chapter of this one (3:6). With Noah seven others were saved (his wife, his three sons, and his three daughters-in-law). They were guarded or protected by God during the Flood that wiped out the ungodly pre-Flood civilization. Noah was a "preacher [GK 3061] of righteousness." This could refer to his preaching activity not recorded in the OT or to the fact that his lifestyle condemned sin and proclaimed righteousness to his contemporaries (Ge 6:9).

6 The third example of judgment is the destruction of the cities of Sodom and Gomorrah. According to Ge 19:24–28, "the LORD rained down burning sulfur on Sodom and Gomorrah—from the LORD out of heaven." Peter says God "condemned" them "by burning them to ashes" (GK 5491). This rare word means either "reduce to ashes" or "cover with ashes"; it was used at the time of Vesuvius's volcanic eruption and Lycophron's "being overwhelmed with ashes." Thus God may have used a volcano to destroy the wicked cities. This total destruction is an "example" (GK 5682) to the ungodly of the things that are going to happen to them.

7–8 In the midst of God's judgment of the cities of the plain, he delivered Lot, whom Peter calls "righteous." This is puzzling because in Genesis Lot is hardly notable for his righteousness. He seems worldly and weak and had to be dragged out of Sodom (Ge 19:16). Yet Abraham's intercession in Ge 18:16–33 may imply that Lot was righteous. Furthermore, Peter may have inferred Lot's righteousness from his deliverance from the destruction of Sodom and from his being "tormented" and "distressed by the filthy lives" of his fellow citizens. The contemporary application is plain. To what extent are Christians who are living today in a godless society "tormented" by what they see?

9 Peter now states the main point. It is one of abiding comfort: "The Lord knows how to rescue godly men from trials." Suffering Christians anywhere and at any time can find consolation in the fact that their Lord knows all about their plight. Moreover, "the Lord knows how . . . to hold the unrighteous for the day of judgment, *while continuing their punishment*" (italics mine). Immediate judgment of sinners is only the beginning. Temporal judgments, death, and "being in torment" in Hades (Lk 16:23) do not exhaust the divine wrath. A great Judgment is yet future (Rev 20:11–15), followed by the "second death" of fire (Rev 20:14).

10a God's wrath is especially certain to fall on the false teachers of Peter's day. He characterizes them as "those who follow the corrupt desire of the sinful nature"—a reference to sexual profligacy. They also "despise authority." "Authority" (GK 3262) may refer to the rejection of angelic powers (cf. Eph 1:21; Col 1:16), but more likely it refers to their rejection of the rule of the Lord (GK 3261) Jesus Christ over them.

C. The Insolence and Wantonness of the False Teachers (2:10b–16)

10b The false teachers are "bold and arrogant"—i.e., presumptuous and self-willed. They respect no one, and nothing restrains them. "They are not afraid to slander celestial beings"—probably referring to fallen angels. As to when they slandered or what kind of slander was involved, one can only surmise. Perhaps the false teachers were accused of being in league with Satan, and their reply was to disparage and mock him (cf. Jude 8–9).

11 In contrast to these audacious errorists, angels themselves, even though they are stronger and more powerful (cf. Rev 12:7–8), do not indict the celestial beings (perhaps the fallen angels of v.4) in the presence of the Lord.

12 The false teachers act like irrational animals without the restraint that angels and righteous people have. They may claim a special knowledge, but they blaspheme out of their ignorance. Like wild beasts who are slaves to their instincts and are born to be slaughtered, they too are destined for total destruction.

13 "They will be paid back with harm for the harm they have done" preserves a word play in Greek that is quite characteristic of Peter's style in this letter. The errorists suffer harm as a wage of injury. Normally one thinks of carousing as a nighttime activity (1Th 5:7), perhaps because of the shame involved. But these people carouse in broad daylight. Peter sees them as "feasting together" with the recipients of his letter. Perhaps he has in mind the love feasts or communal meals of the church. They also revel in their deceptions.

14 In the Greek text vv.12–16 form one sentence. So the vivid phrase "with eyes full of adultery" (meaning to desire every woman they see) implies that the false teachers desired to turn church gatherings into times of dissipation. Their eyes unceasingly looked for sin. They "seduce" (or "lure"; GK *1284*) "unstable" persons, i.e., those with no foundation to their lives. In 1:12 of this letter Peter has spoken of his readers as being "firmly established in the truth," and in 3:16–17 he will warn them of "unstable people" and of the danger of falling "from [their] secure position" (similar Greek words are used here).

Deep within these false teachers are thoughts of "greed" (GK *4432*) and avarice. Of them Peter exclaims, "An accursed brood!" (lit., "children of a curse"), meaning that God's curse is on them.

15–16 The false teachers resemble Balaam, the son of Beor, in that Balaam loved money and was willing to pursue it instead of obeying God (Nu 22:5–24:25). Balaam also taught immorality (Nu 31:16; Rev 2:14). So the false teachers have left the biblical way and have gone into Balaam's error—mercenary greed and sexual impurity. As Balaam went to curse the children of Israel for money (if he could), "he was rebuked for his wrongdoing by a donkey—a beast without speech." Actually, according to the account in Nu 22:27–35, the rebuke is twofold: first from the donkey, then from the angel of the Lord. Ironically the mute animal had more spiritual perception than the prophet! The utterance "restrained" the prophet's insanity.

D. The Impotence of Their Teaching (2:17–22)

17 Whatever else may be said about this chapter, it is a powerful piece of writing that gains momentum as it reaches its climax. In vivid words, Peter goes on to describe the false teachers as "springs without water." Christ provides "a spring of water welling up to eternal life" (Jn 4:13–14), and from those who believe in him flow streams of living water (Jn 7:37–38). But the false teachers give nothing because they have nothing to give. They are "mists driven by a storm," a metaphor of their instability. The "blackest darkness . . . reserved for them" may refer to hell.

18 These heretics use sensual propaganda to "ensnare [or entice; GK *1284*; cf. v.14] people who are just escaping from those who live in error." In other words, they take for their targets new converts to Christianity from paganism.

19 They promise "freedom," perhaps from any law or restraint of the flesh. Paul ran into similar error—"Everything is permissible for me" (1Co 6:12–13)—among false teachers in Corinth and possibly in Galatia (cf. Gal 5:14). Yet, Peter says, the very ones who speak of freedom are "slaves of depravity—for a man is a slave to whatever has mastered him." To this the best parallel is Jesus' word: "Everyone who sins is a slave to sin" (Jn 8:34; cf. Ro 6:16). So though the false teachers talk of religion and freedom, they do not know the Son; for as Jesus said, "If the Son sets you free, you will be free indeed" (Jn 8:36).

20 Of whom is Peter speaking in vv.20–22 i. e., who does the pronoun "they" refer to? Does it refer (1) to the false teachers of v. 19, (2) to the unstable people of v.18 or (3) more generally to both but particularly to the false teachers? In my opinion, it refers basically to false teachers because (1) proximity makes the false teachers (spoken of in v.19) the normal antecedent of "they," (2) v. 19 and v.20 are connected by the word "for" (untranslated in NIV), (3) "mastered" in v.19 has the same verbal root as "overcome" in v.20, and (4) the teachers are the main subject of the whole chapter.

Verse 20 mentions the possibility of reverting to the old paganism after having "escaped the corruptions of the world" through knowing Jesus Christ as Lord and Savior. Is it possible, then, for Christians to lose their salvation? Many would answer affirmatively on the basis of this and similar texts (e.g., Heb 6:4–6; 10:26). But this verse asserts only that false teachers who have for a time escaped from worldly corruption through knowing Christ and then turn away from the light of the Christian faith are worse off than they were before knowing Christ. It uses no terminology affirming that they were Christians in reality (e.g., "children of God," "born again," "regenerate," "redeemed"). The NT makes a distinction between those who are in the churches and those who are regenerate (cf. 2Co 13:5; 2Ti 2:18–19; 1Jn 3:7–8; 2:19). So when Peter says, "They are worse off at the end than they were at the beginning," the reference is to a lost apostate.

21 Peter now underlines the seriousness of apostasy. The "sacred commandment that was passed on to them" evidently refers to the authoritative, apostolic message of the Christian faith (cf. 1Co 15:3). It is the entire Christian message with an emphasis on the ethical demands of our Lord.

22 Peter concludes his strong denunciation of the false teachers by citing two proverbs. The first is a biblical one (Pr 26:11); the second is extrabiblical. Both dogs and pigs were considered vile by the Jews. Jesus also used the designations "dogs" and "pigs" in speaking of those opposed to God and his Word (cf. Mt 7:6). So the false teachers are unclean and return to the pagan corruption. The "dog [that] returns to its vomit" or the sow that "is washed" portrays the person who has a religious profession or outward change without a regenerating inner change that affects his or her nature. Such persons soon revert to their true nature.

V. The Promise of the Lord's Coming (3:1–18)

A. The Certainty of the Day of the Lord (3:1–10)

1 "Dear friends" (lit., "beloved"; GK *28*) is repeated in vv.8, 14, and 17 in this chapter (see also 1Pe 2:11; 4:1). "This is now my second letter to you." Does this refer to 1 Peter? Most commentators say yes. But this is not certain because (1) it has not been established that the recipients of the two letters are the same; (2) 1:12, 16 may imply a personal ministry to the recipients of this second letter that 1 Peter gives no indication of; (3) the description of the two letters ("both of them as reminders") here does not fit 1 Peter very well; and (4) other letters of apostles have not been preserved (cf. 1Co 5:9; Col 4:16). None of these points is in itself very strong; yet taken together and when coupled with the lack of use of 1 Peter in 2 Peter, they raise a doubt that leaves the question open.

"As reminders to stimulate you" is almost identical with "to refresh your memory" in 1:13. "To wholesome thinking" (lit. "to pure minds") reflects the author's goal to maintain in his readers a pure disposition.

2 The "words spoken in the past" are the prophetic oracles with special reference here to the day of the Lord. The "command" is a way of referring to the moral demands of the Christian faith (see comment on 2:21) and primarily to the command of love. These prophecies and commands were given to the early Christians by the NT prophets and apostles (cf. Eph 2:20).

3 Peter next states a primary thing to be remembered from the prophetic and apostolic deposit: the appearance of scoffers in the last days, who deny biblical truths and live in an ungodly way (cf. Da 7:25; 11:36–39; Mt 24:3–5, 11, 23–26; 1Ti 4:1ff.; 2Ti 3:1–7; Jude 17–18). The "last days" are the days that come between the first coming of the Messiah and his second coming. The "scoffers" are the false teachers of ch. 2 who deny a future eschatology.

4 Part of the early church proclamation was the announcement of the return of Jesus to complete the work of salvation and to punish the wicked (e.g., Mt 24:3ff.; Jn 14:1–3; Ac 1:11; 17:31; Ro 13:11; 1Co 15:23; 1Th 4:13–5:11; 2Th 1:7–10; Heb 9:28; Rev 1:7). The false teachers ask, "Where is this 'coming' he promised?" Mocking the faith of Christians, they support their own position by claiming, "Ever since our fathers died, everything goes on as it has since the beginning of creation." "Our fathers" most likely means the OT fathers (see Jn 6:31; Ac 3:13; Ro 9:5; Heb 1:1). "Died" (lit., "fell asleep"; GK *3121*) is a lovely metaphor for the death of believers (cf. Ac 7:60; 1Th 4:13–14). The argument of the false teachers is essentially a naturalistic one—a kind of uniformitarianism that rules out any divine intervention in history.

5–6 But they "deliberately [lit., willingly; GK *2527*] forget" the great Flood, when God intervened in history by destroying the world. What they forget is not only the Flood but also God's prior activity by his word—the existence of the heavens and the watery formation of the earth (Ge 1:2–10). It seems unlikely that Peter is seeking to affirm that water was the basic material of creation. He does not use the verb "create" but says that the earth "was formed [GK *5319*] out of water and with water." In Genesis the sky separates the waters from the waters by the word of God, and the land appears out of the water by the same word.

At the beginning of v.6, the phrase "by these waters" (lit., "through these") probably refers to both water and the word as the agents used by God for destroying the former world (v.6), just as word and fire will be the destructive agents in the future (v.7). "The world of that time" obviously means that the inhabitants of the earth were destroyed (the world itself was not destroyed).

7 Peter's reference to a future conflagration to destroy the present cosmos is highly unusual. The OT speaks of fire in the day of the Lord (Ps 97:3; Isa 66:15–16; Da 7:9–10; Mic 1:4; Mal 4:1). And Mt 3:11–12 speaks of the future baptism of fire by the Messiah in which he will destroy the "chaff" (cf. 2Th 1:7). Peter argues that just as in the past God purged the then-existing world by his word and by waters, so in the future he will purge the world by his word and by fire. Whether this will take place before the Millennium or after, Peter does not say. Matthew 3:11–12 supports the former, while the sequence of Rev 20–21 puts the new heaven and new earth after the thousand years (cf. 2Pe 3:13).

8 Peter's second argument against the false teachers' scoffing at the "delay" of the Lord's coming stems from Ps 90:4: "For a thousand years in your sight are like a day that has just gone by, or like a watch in night." They have overlooked God's time perspective. The admonition "Do not forget" is addressed to believers and uses the same word that is used in v.5 of the false teachers' deliberate forgetfulness. Christians must be careful lest the propaganda of the scoffers distort their thinking.

9 The third argument against the scoffers grows out of the second one. God's delay is gracious; it is not caused by inability or indifference. The scoffers argued that God was slow to keep his promise of the new age, and evidently some Christians were influenced by this thinking. God's time plan is influenced by his being "patient" (GK *3428*), an attribute of God prominent in Scripture (cf. Ex 34:6; Nu 14:18; Ps 86:15; Jer 15:15; Ro 2:4; 9:22). In Ro 9:22 Paul says that God "bore with great patience the objects of his wrath." Here in v.9 that patience is directed "to you."

With whom is God patient and whom does he desire to come to repentance? This verse has been a battleground between Arminian and Calvinistic interpreters. Some of the latter argue that it is not God's will that everyone without exception should repent. Thus Peter is simply saying that Christ will not return until all of the elect have repented and been saved. This view, if rigorously applied, is incompatible with premillennialism, whose adherents normally teach that some will be saved during the millennial period following Christ's return.

Calvin himself showed moderation and exegetical wisdom, when he suggested that God's love toward the human race is so wonderful that he wants all of them to be saved, and he is prepared to bestow salvation on the lost. Thus the "you" is addressed to humankind and "not wanting" is used of his will of desire, not of his will of decree (cf. Eze 18:23; 1Ti 2:4).

10 Peter's fourth argument against the false teachers reaffirms the early church's teaching that the day of the Lord will come suddenly. Jesus taught that his coming would be as unexpected as the coming of a thief (Mt 24:42–44), an analogy often repeated in the NT (cf. Lk 12:39; 1Th 5:2; Rev 3:3; 16:15). The "Lord" in these texts is Jesus in his exaltation and should be so understood here. In that catastrophic day "the heavens will disappear" with a loud noise made by something passing swiftly through the air. The sky will recede "like a scroll, rolling up" (Rev 6:14), and the earth and sky will flee from the presence of God (Rev 20:11).

"The elements" (GK *5122*) could be the basic materials that make up the world; those commonly thought of in NT times were air, earth, fire, and water. But it is also possible that Peter is looking at three realms (the heavens, that of the heavenly bodies, and the earth), and that the "the elements" refers to "heavenly bodies," those mentioned in other eschatological passages (Joel 2:10; Mk 13:24–26; Rev 6:12–13). The phrase "the earth and everything in it" probably refers to all human products that will be destroyed.

B. The Ethical Implications of the Day of the Lord (3:11–16)

11 Peter now makes the impending disintegration of the universe the ground for a personal challenge to his readers. In view of what is in store for the world, Peter asks his readers, "What kind of people ought you to be?" Since the day of the Lord will soon come to punish the wicked and reward the righteous, believers should live "holy and godly lives." Holiness entails separation from evil and dedication to God; godliness relates to piety and worship.

12 Another element of godly living is expectation of the future day. Peter relates this to the idea of "speed[ing] its coming." But how can Christians hasten what God will do? Peter would probably answer by saying that prayer (Mt 6:10) and preaching (Mt 24:14) are the two principal means to bring people to repentance and thus to hasten the day (cf. Mt 24:14). To the crowd that gathered after the healing of the lame beggar at the Beautiful Gate in Jerusalem Peter proclaimed, "Repent . . . so that your sins may be wiped out, that times of refreshing may come from the Lord, and that he may send the Christ" (Ac 3:19–20). Peter again describes this coming as a fiery disintegration of the very heavens (cf. comment on v.10); the "elements" probably refers again to the "celestial bodies" on fire.

13 Through his prophets God promised righteousness. Jeremiah sees the Righteous One bringing in righteousness, and his name is "The LORD Our Righteousness" (Jer 23:5–7; 33:16; cf. Ps 9:8; Isa 11:4–5; 45:8; Da 9:24). This promise of righteousness will be fulfilled ultimately in the new heavens and the new earth of which Isaiah spoke (Isa 65:17–25) and which Peter refers to here. John also saw "a new heaven and a new earth" in which there was nothing impure (Rev 21:1, 8, 27).

14 Since there will be perfect righteousness in the new heaven and new earth and since all will appear before Christ, Christians must now be righteous in their lives. "Make every effort" (GK *5079*) is a favorite word of Peter's (cf. 1:10, 15; also the related noun in 1:5). Christians are to make intense efforts to be morally pure—"spotless" (GK *834*) and "blameless" (GK *318*) like Christ. These two words occur in reverse order in 1Pe 1:19, where they refer to Jesus. In 2Pe 2:13 Peter has called the false teachers "blots and blemishes" (the opposite of these two words). Believers should also aim to live so as to be found having the "peace" that results from their efforts to please the Lord. In Rev 2:16, the risen Christ warns the church to repent or he will "fight against them with the sword of his mouth." Those who are "found at peace with him" have put out of their lives the things he hates.

15–16 Again Peter stresses the purpose of the Lord's "patience" (GK *3429*), that it is designed for salvation. Some confuse the divine patience with slackness. But Christians should esteem it as "salvation."

"Just as our dear brother Paul also wrote you" is significant in the light of Paul's rebuke of Peter (Gal 2:11–14). Peter had recognized the ministry of Paul and Barnabas to the Gentiles. What had Paul written to the recipients of 2 Peter? We cannot answer that question. Nor is it necessary to do so in view of Peter's general statement: "He [Paul] writes the same way in all his letters." In Ro 2:4 Paul says that "God's kindness leads you toward repentance." Peter goes on to affirm that Paul's letters contain "some things that are hard to understand." The difficulty in Paul's letters stems from the profundity of the God-given wisdom they contain. Apparently false teachers were seeking to use Pauline support for their opposition to Peter. Paul's letters contain things—e.g., slogans and arguments—that can be given meanings far beyond what Paul intended.

The unlearned (NIV, "ignorant"; GK *276*) are those who have not learned the apostolic teaching (Ac 2:42), nor have they been taught by the Father (Jn 6:45). They are "unstable" because they are without a foundation (cf. comment on 2:14). They "distort" the things in Paul's letters as they do the "other Scriptures." Like Satan, the false teachers and their followers can quote Scripture out of context for their purpose (cf. Mt 4:6). Does Peter's expression "the other Scriptures" imply that Paul's writings were already considered Scripture by this time (c. A.D. 64)? This is the normal understanding of the Greek. That Paul's writings should be considered "Scripture"—i.e., authoritative writing—is not surprising, for from the moment of composition they had the authority of commands of the Lord through his apostle (Ro 1:1; 1Co 14:37; Gal 1:1).

Twisting the Scriptures leads to "destruction" (GK 724; cf. comments on 2:1, 3) because it is the rejection of God's way and the setting up of one's own way in opposition to God (cf. Ro 8:7). In a time when the Christian church is plagued by heretical cults and false teaching, Peter's warning about the irresponsible use of Scripture is important. Correct exegesis must be a continuing concern of the church.

C. The Need to Guard Against Error and to Grow in Grace (3:17–18)

17–18 With the word "therefore" and an affectionate reference to his readers (see comment on 3:1), Peter begins his conclusion. These two verses touch on the main themes of the letter and summarize its contents. First, there is the reminder for his readers to watch out lest the false teachers lead them astray. Second, there is the exhortation to grow in Christ. The dominant motivation for writing this letter was Peter's love and concern for the flock (cf. the repeated use of "dear friends"). Since he has told the believers beforehand about the false teachers, they are able to be on guard.

The "lawless men" (GK 118) will attempt by their error to shift the believers off their spiritual foundation. The word translated "secure position" (GK 5113) occurs only here in the NT, but the related verb and adjective are important in Peter's life (cf. Lk 22:32 of Jesus' command to Peter) and also in this letter (see comments on 2:14; 3:16–17). The Christians' guarding against false teachers includes (1) prior knowledge of their activities, (2) warning against their immoral lives (ch. 2; cf. Mt 7:16), (3) reminders of the historicity of the apostolic message (1:16–18), (4) the prophetic teaching of the past (1:19; 3:1–2), and (5) the warning of judgment (e.g., the Flood).

Now Peter speaks positively: "But grow in the grace and knowledge of our Lord and Savior Jesus Christ." In 1:3–11 he has already stressed the necessity for progress in Christian living. If Christians do not keep moving forward, they will regress or fall back. As Paul says, Christians never in this life attain all there is in Christ; so their goal is to know Christ in a fuller, more intimate way (Php 3:10–13; cf. Eph 1:17).

The closing doxology is notable for its direct ascription of "glory" (GK 1518) to Christ. For a Jew who has learned the great words in Isa 42:8—"I am the LORD; that is my name! I will not give my glory to another"—this doxology is a clear confession of Christ (cf. Jn 5:23: "that all may honor the Son just as they honor the Father"). This supreme honor belongs to Jesus Christ today ("now") and "forever." So Peter finally points his readers to the new age, "the day of the Lord," when Christ will be manifested in all his glory.

The Old Testament in the New

NT Text	OT Text	Subject
2Pe 2:22	Pr 26:11	Dog returns to vomit
2Pe 3:13	Isa 65:17	New heavens and new earth

1 John

INTRODUCTION

The letters of John are foundational to what is known in the NT as Johannine Christianity. Even as his gospel account is distinct from the others in content, structure, and theological emphasis, so John's letters differ in style and content from the other NT letters. These letters are not concerned with the problem of institutionalizing the Christian Movement, nor do they fit easily into any historical reconstruction of the growth and development of the Christian church in the world.

If John's letters address the problem of heresy, they do so in unconventional terms. They insist that true Christian faith requires knowing that Jesus the Christ came in human flesh, lived a human life, and died in the flesh. But the evidence of that faith is measured more by the genuineness of one's Christian lifestyle, rather than by what one "knows." The knowledge that God is light is tested by whether one walks in that light and obeys God's commands. The knowledge that God is righteous is tested by whether one lives righteously as befits one born of God. The knowledge that God is love is tested by whether one loves fellow believers even as one loves God. The single but radical requirement for love and obedience in these letters recalls the simplicity of Jesus' own teaching and the response he required of those who would follow him. These letters have a special place preserved for them in the life and devotion of the church.

1. Background

Establishing the background for the three letters of John is at best speculative. Whereas for Paul's letters we have the book of Acts with its treatment of the origin of the church, the conversion of the apostle, and a record of his subsequent journeys to provide background for understanding his letters, we have nothing similar for the Johannine material. While Paul's letters fairly bristle with historical allusions that we can readily identify from other sources, those of John contain almost no references to known persons or places. Nonetheless, traditions relating to the origin of these writings did develop in the church. And since there are no alternatives, it is these traditions that have been largely responsible for providing the historical background for interpreting these letters. These traditions have connected them and the fourth gospel with the apostle John (see "Authorship"), recognized Asia as the place of their publication, and identified Cerinthianism as the heresy troubling the churches addressed.

Asia as the place of the letter's publication finds support from two lines of tradition. Irenaeus (c. A.D. 175–200) stated explicitly that John wrote his material while living at Ephesus in Asia. The earliest-known references to 1 John are by church leaders from Asia. Polycarp of Smyrna (mid-second century) appears to have been depending on 1 John when he asserted that whoever does not confess that Jesus Christ has come in the flesh is antichrist. He also urges a return to the message handed down from the beginning (cf. 1Jn 1:1, 3). Moreover, comparison of the problems presented in 1 John with the more complete description of the heresies of the second century provides additional support for Asia as the place where 1 John originated.

The tradition identifying Cerinthus as the opponent of 1 John also depends on Irenaeus. He preserved a description from Polycarp of an encounter between the apostle and Cerinthus in a public bathhouse, which John hurriedly left so that he would not have to bathe in the same place with such an enemy of the truth. Irenaeus also described in some detail the heresy of Cerinthus. Cerinthus, he said, denied the virgin birth of Jesus. After his baptism, Christ descended on Jesus in the form of a dove from God in heaven, and he began his ministry of preaching and miracles. Christ departed from Jesus on the cross, and it was only Jesus who suffered and rose again.

It is not absolutely certain, however, that Cerinthus was the opponent of John or that the heresy in view in the letter resulted from a Gnostic theological movement that had infiltrated the church. First John itself strongly suggests that the heresy arose *within* the church and was propagated by respected and able teachers in the community who had defected from the true faith and fellowship (2:19). Indeed, the seriousness of the situation probably derived from the fact that past leaders had become "false prophets," teaching untruths and becoming embodiments of Antichrist. That they were able to lead the community astray (2:26; 3:7) gives strong support to the idea they were secessionists, not intruders. Moreover, it is clear that the views expressed in 1 John also differed from Cerinthus in significant ways. There is no reflection, for example, of Cerinthus's distinctions between the supreme God and the series of divine emanations proceeding downward to the aeon who was Christ and who created the material universe. Furthermore, the false teachers in 1 John appear to draw theological conclusions that have no parallels in Cerinthian Gnosticism. The espousal of sinlessness (1:8, 10), their claim to know God through inspiration (2:4; 4:1–3), their loss of "fellowship" with God (1:6), and their life in the light (2:9) seem to be independent of Cerinthus's teaching. The attempt to identify the false teachers with Cerinthus or his followers is therefore dubious.

Alternate suggestions for the identity of the false teachers have lacked scholarly consensus. Perhaps the best suggestion is the one that sees the root of the problem in the confrontation of Christianity with the evangelistic and pietistic religious movements developing especially in Asia. When missionaries of the Christian faith first came into contact with the representatives of these movements, they undoubtedly received, at least initially, a warm welcome. Their willingness to accept any new religious movement made sure that they were prepared to adopt Christianity, just as they had already tried to adopt Judaism. Since the Johannine community was already reflecting some of the language of this religious world, they were presumably unusually successful in their missionary effort among such persons. But these converts inevitably brought philosophical and religious verbiage with them into the community that required an extensive theological response by the teachers. The gospel of John may in itself represent not only a missionary document for these persons but a response to the questions raised by the converts. Inevitably, however, a significant number of the faithful proved vulnerable to a pagan reinterpretation that borrowed from Christian categories.

In his first letter John seems to recognize this pull and seeks to help those trying not to fall back into non-Christian speculation. On the other hand, the community inevitably contained some enthusiastic but ill-informed converts to Christianity, who were eager to reinterpret their new-found faith. The false teachers who previously had been in the community and had then departed, proving that they had not really belonged to the community, may well have been representatives of such a movement. They would be presenting themselves as preserving the best of both traditions.

The false teachers' motive, at least at first, may have been prompted only by the desire to translate the Gospel into the terms of another culture. Their enthusiasm likely blinded them to the fact that their reinterpretation would ultimately lead to the dissolution of what was central to the Christian faith: Jesus as the Son of God through whose death the bonds of sin had finally been destroyed. If this reconstruction is valid, it helps explain why these new "false teachers" had such a strong position in the community. Originally they had belonged to those who were most involved in the missionary activity of the community. That they no longer were true to the faith and were to be classed as antichrists would certainly be hard for some to accept.

2. Occasion and Purpose

It is clear from the internal evidence of 1 John that a developing schism within the Christian community led to its writing. The difficulty had already reached a point where some members, including teachers, had separated themselves from the others and were in the process of setting up their own community (2:19). Although the breach was complete, the dissidents continued to keep in touch with the rest of the membership and were actively trying to entice them to join the new group (2:26). The breach of fellowship also led to a breach in understanding the faith. What earlier may have been hypothetical questions now became tenets of the rival community, identified in John's letters primarily by what the false teachers denied. They denied: Jesus as the Christ, the Son of God (2:22; 5:1, 5); the coming of Christ in the flesh (4:2; 2Jn 7); the authority of Jesus' commands (2:4); their own sinfulness (1:8, 10); salvation through the work of Christ (2:2); the absolute demand that believers love one another (2:9); righteous conduct as a requirement of fellowship with God (1:6; 2:29; 3:6, 10); the responsibility to live as Jesus had lived (2:4, 6: 3:7); the nature of the company of believers as a community of fellowship with the Father, with his Son, and with one another (1:3; 2:11); and the authority of the writer of the letters as the proclaimer of the message that had been from the beginning (1:5; 3Jn 10).

It is harder to reconstruct the points at which the false teachers agreed with the community of faith. Apparently they believed that God is light (1:5); that the truth of the Gospel released them from the power of sin (1:8); that the Christ is a philosophical concept (though they denied his existence in the flesh; 4:2); that they had a mission to the world (2Jn 10); that they have been anointed of the Spirit (2:27); and that the devil is an anti-God (3:8–10; 4:2–3).

The writer responded to the false teachers by recognizing them as a supreme danger threatening the very life and faith of the community. What was called for was a positive reaffirmation of the cardinal doctrines of the faith that had been from the beginning and a clear and explicit exposure of the heresies the dissidents were promoting. He also sensed the need for reassuring the faithful. So he gave his letter a strong pastoral flavor. Its contents are marked by strong affirmations and words of encouragement for theChristian community—namely, that the nature of the fellowship is one of love and righteousness (1:3, 7); that its origin is from the beginning (1:1); that in the community there is genuine forgiveness of sins (1:9) and a walk of obedience not unlike Jesus' own example (2:6); that walking in the light is living in love (2:10); that members of the community will not be ashamed at Jesus' coming (2:28); and that they may have complete confidence in his answering their prayers (3:22). Warnings are addressed to the community against the seduction of the world (2:15), against the present antichrist, (2:18), and against false spirits and false prophets (3:22; 4:1–2). Reminders to the members of their anointing (2:20) as being sufficient to enable them to remain in God (4:13) are provided, as well as promises that belong to them as the children of God (3:1). Jesus Christ as the epitome and example of love to the community becomes a critical theme (3:16–18), just as the proclamations that God himself is love (4:16), that love derives from him, and that the Christian life is lived in him (4:12–13) are also critical themes. Again and again the letter returns to the primary confession that Jesus is the Christ, the one who has come in the flesh and has overcome the world. He is the true God and eternal life (5:20).

3. Structure

John follows a somewhat structured approach in this letter without being bound by it. He is quite willing to depart from the structure in order to allow room for the introduction of divergent themes as well as overlapping ones. As the exposition will show, the writer of the letter deals with the problems raised by the schismatic actions of the "false teachers." He does this within the context of a general exposition that focuses on the nature and life of the community of God. His deepest concern is pastoral. He desires to reassure, protect, alert, and teach the faithful members about their life together as the people of God. To accomplish this he shows that "from the beginning" the basis of the believing community is Jesus Christ. He is the one through whom fellowship with the Father and with the members of the community becomes possible. This fellowship is further defined as life in him and as eternal life.

John goes on to assert that the fellowship of believers draws its character from God, who is light, righteousness, and love. It is these attributes of God, shown by Jesus our example, that in turn become criteria for the standard of conduct expected of the children of God. Obedience to him thus becomes a primary obligation of the community.

The writer also makes clear that the fellowship is exclusive. It consists of those born of God who are committed to obedience to his Son's commands and example; who confess Jesus as the Christ, the incarnate Son of

The Gospel of John and the First Letter of John

There is a remarkable similarity of language and theme between the gospel of John and the first letter of John. The following chart outlines where these parallels are.

Theme	1 John	Gospel of John
Word was from the beginning and became flesh, and we saw it	1:1; 2:14	1:1–2, 14
We could touch the "Word of life"	1:1	20:27, 29
The Word was "the life"	1:2; 5:20	1:4; 11:25; 14:6
The Word was "with the Father"	1:2	1:1, 18
We must testify to the Word	1:2	15:27
Complete joy available through Christ	1:4	3:29; 16:24; 17:13
Light from God dispels darkness	1:5–7	1:4–5; 3:19–21
Life through the blood of God's Son	1:7	6:53–56
The word has no place in unbelievers	1:10	5:38
Jesus as the atoning sacrifice for the sin of the world	2:2; 3:5; 4:10	1:29; 3:16–17; 11:51
Loving God involves obeying his commands	2:3, 5; 3:22; 5:2–3	14:15, 21; 15:10
Jesus as our example	2:6	13:15
Jesus' command to love one another	2:7; 3:11, 23; 4:7, 11	13:34; 15:12, 17
Jesus as the true shining light	2:8	1:9; 8:12; 9:5
Walking in darkness and stumbling	2:11	11:9–10; 12:35
Word of God living in us	2:14	5:38
Those who do not have the love of God in them	2:15	5:42
Knowledge gained through the Holy Spirit	2:20, 27	14:16
Knowing the truth	2:21	8:32
Knowing the Father involves knowing the Son	2:23	8:19; 14:7
Remaining in the Father and the Son	2:24, 27; 3:24	15:4
God's love that makes us his children	3:1–2	1:12; 3:16
Those who do not know God	3:1	15:21; 16:3
The Son of God is sinless	3:5	8:46

God; and who depend on him for forgiveness and for overcoming the evil one. So he provides tests by which the false teachers can be exposed and the faithful members of the community reinforced in their own confidence that they truly are the children of God. Over and over he stresses the fact that the test of true faith and practice for those born of God is to love one's fellow believer. This becomes the final test for walking in the light, living in truth and righteousness, and loving God.

4. Authorship and Date

The author of 1 John never identifies himself in the letter. Apparently his identity was so well known to his "children" that he knew they would recognize him by what he wrote. We do get an ambiguous clue in 2 John and 3 John when he uses the title "elder" to address them. The fourth gospel is likewise unidentified as to authorship except that in the epilogue there is the enigmatic statement about "the disciple whom Jesus loved" (21:20; cf. 13:23): "This is the disciple who testifies to these things and who wrote them down" (21:24). For those who recognize common authorship for the gospel of John and John's letters, it is possible through a process of elimination to identify the "beloved" disciple as John the son of Zebedee (see introduction to John).

External evidence for John's authorship is preserved in the writings of Irenaeus, who

Theme	1 John	Gospel of John
The devil has been sinning from the beginning	3:8	8:44
Being born of God	3:9; 4:7; 5:1, 4, 18	1:13; 3:3, 6
Hatred from the world	3:13	15:18–19; 17:14
Crossing from death to life	3:14	5:24
Jesus laid down his life for us	3:16	10:11
Laying down our lives for others	3:16	15:13
Truth is found in the Son of God	3:19	14:6; 18:37
God knows all things	3:21	21:17
Receiving from God what we ask	3:22; 5:14–15	14:13–14; 15:7, 16; 16:23
The command to believe in God's Son	3:23	6:29
Jesus has come in the flesh	4:2	1:14
Overcoming the world	4:4; 5:4–5	16:33
The world loves those of the world	4:5	15:19
Those who are not from God do not listen to him	4:6	8:47
The Spirit of truth	4:6; 5:6	14:17; 15:26; 16:13
God sent his one and only Son so we can live	4:9, 14; 5:11–12	1:18; 3:16–17, 36; 20:31
No one has seen God	4:12, 20	1:18
Jesus is the Savior of the world	4:14	3:17; 4:42; 12:47
We are in God and God is in us	4:16	15:4–5; 17:21
Jesus and the water and the blood	5:6–8	19:34–35
Human testimony and divine testimony	5:9–10	5:32–37; 8:14–17
How to know we have eternal life	5:13	20:30–31
Believing on the name of God's Son	5:13	1:12
Satan as the prince of this world	5:19	12:31; 14:30
Knowing the true God	5:20	17:3
Jesus as true God	5:20	1:1; 20:28

quotes copiously from 1 John and attributes this letter to John. The Muratorian Canon (c. A.D. 200) assumes that 1 John and John's gospel have a common origin and that they have been received as such by the church.

The date for the letters of John is at best problematic. It depends largely on our ability to reconstruct the history of the Johannine community. This community may have begun about the same time as the church at Antioch. Persecution may have finally driven the leaders from Jerusalem, and John may have gathered with some of the Samaritan converts along with the former followers of the Baptist. They probably located somewhere in southern Palestine and continued their mission to the Jews.

Sometime before A.D. 70, perhaps as a result of increased hostility from the Jews, the Johannine community migrated to Asia Minor and initiated what became a very successful mission to those Gentiles whose religious orientation was in the direction of "higher paganism." The need for a gospel that would double as a missionary document for these converts became evident, and the gospel of John was thus published somewhere around A.D. 70–80. It expresses its own purpose clearly: "These are written that you may believe that Jesus is the Christ, the Son of God, and that by believing you may have life in his name" (Jn 20:31).

The heretical developments discussed earlier took place during the next ten years and finally resulted in the secession of some members of the community in order to found a rival one. John's first letter was written in response to this crisis around 80–90. That it was written to reassure the faithful is clear from its author's own testimony: "I write these things to you who believe in the name of the Son of God so that you may know that you have eternal life" (5:13). The letter is addressed to a single community but probably was meant to circulate throughout the geographical area where John's churches had been established.

John's second and third letters are brief ones written to member churches in other places. These churches also appear in danger of problems created by the secessionists. So the two letters were apparently written in anticipation of these problems.

The perspective of 1 John is clearly reflected in 2 John. Writing soon after 1 John, "the elder" (v.1) addresses the community that has been faithful to "the truth" (i.e., the Gospel) as he has proclaimed it (v.4). He warns, however, against traveling missionaries whom he expects to visit this locality soon (v.10). Evidently they will present themselves as emissaries of the secessionists and continue to spread their false teaching (v.7). The elder warns the church neither to extend hospitality to such emissaries nor even to welcome them into the community (v.11).

The background of 3 John is more obscure, despite its personal references. It seems best to consider that the situation was the same for 3 John as for 1 and 2 John. If so, still another community is addressed—a community in which there appear to be several groups of Christians in "house" churches as well as one larger group or church led by Diotrephes (v.9). The smaller house churches, one led by Gaius and another apparently led by Demetrius, have remained faithful to the elder. They remain "in the truth" and "in love." They have received missionaries from the elder's faithful community and have shown them the proper hospitality (vv.5–8). But the elder complains against Diotrephes, the description of whom shows that he has been affected by the secessionists. He "gossips" maliciously against the elder and refuses to receive his message. He even goes so far as to throw out of the church anyone who welcomes the faithful "brothers" from the elder's community (v.10).

There would appear to be an interval of time between 2 John and 3 John. The situation has grown decidedly worse in the place where Gaius ministers than in that where the "chosen lady" is. Probably one would do well to think of an interval of a year or more between the two letters (c. A.D. 90).

EXPOSITION

I. Preface (1:1–4)

The first four verses represent a single sentence in Greek. The main verb and subject, "we proclaim" (GK 550), do not actually appear until v.3; instead John opens with the object of the verb, which consists of four relative clauses—"That which was from the beginning, which we have heard, which we have seen with our eyes, which we have looked at"—and is followed by a parenthesis in v.2 enlarging on "the Word of life." Only then are the subject and main verb introduced, with a restatement of the object, "what we have seen and heard." Two purpose clauses conclude the preface: "that you also may have fellowship with us" and "to make our joy complete."

What confronts us here is the intensity of the author's feeling as he reflects on the nature of the Christian message in the light of its very beginnings. Although the events that the message is founded on occurred many years earlier, the immensity of their implication and the abiding mystery they represent retain the power to overwhelm his thinking and extend his literary skills as he witnesses to them. This first paragraph could be described as the author's language of ecstasy.

1 The reader is clearly pointed back to Jn 1:1—"In the beginning was the Word"—and from there to Ge 1:1—"In the beginning God"—with this difference: The Gospel deals with the "personal word" of God's eternity and his entrance into time. The letter centers on the life heard and in turn proclaimed (cf. Ac 5:20; Php 2:16). This message is from the beginning because it is of God. It precedes creation, time, and history. But in God the message of life also draws near to humanity and finds its culmination in Jesus. In him the Word of life becomes incarnated, manifested, and hence can be seen, touched, and even handled.

The author's stress is twofold. He states what has always been true about the Gospel. His witness, unlike that of his opponents, represented neither innovation nor afterthought. Moreover, his witness was based on the immediate evidence of the senses. It is not a fabricated tale.

The use of the pronoun "we" assures the reader that the message is being proclaimed by those who had heard the Gospel with their own ears and who had touched him with their own hands (perhaps a reference to the Resurrection appearances—Lk 24:39; Jn 20:24–29). Already the writer is mounting his polemic against the heretics who denied that Christ had a human body.

2 Because this is the nub of John's argument, he takes pains to restate it: The life to which he bears witness, the life that was with the Father, is precisely the life manifested in the historical person of Jesus. That is why John can say he has seen it, can bear personal witness to it, and can make an apostolic declaration concerning it. The three verbs "seen," "testify," and "proclaim" present personal experience, responsible affirmation, and authoritative announcement. The phrase "eternal life" underscores the divine character of the life described, not its length.

3 This verse introduces the purpose of the letter: "that you also may have fellowship with us. And our fellowship is with the Father and with his Son, Jesus Christ." The Greek word rendered "fellowship" (*koinonia*; GK 3126) occurs here and in v.6. It is not easy to translate. Suggestions are "fellowship," "communion," "participation," "share a common life," and "partnership." Its root word means "common" or "shared" as opposed to "one's own" (*koinos*; GK 3123). The Greeks used this word group to describe partners in business, joint owners of a piece of property, or shareholders in a common enterprise. In the NT it refers to Christians who share a common faith (Phm 6), who share possessions (Ac 2:44; 4:32), or who are partners in the Gospel (Php 1:5).

Koinonia and other words in that word group occur over sixty times in the NT in reference to the supernatural life that Christians share. This supernatural life is disclosed in the incarnate Christ. It is the eternal life that comes from the Father and becomes the life shared individually and corporately by the company of believers. Oneness with God is what causes the oneness of faith. That the words "fellowship with us" precede in the text the words "fellowship is with the Father and with his Son, Jesus Christ" may be significant. There can be no fellowship with the Father or with the Son that is not based on apostolic witness. So John stresses "fellowship with us" as having priority in time.

4 The author links his concern for his readers to his own standing as an apostolic witness. Their obedience will result in the completion of "joy" (GK 5915) in him, and therefore also in them and in the whole fellowship. This joy is mentioned in his gospel: "I have told you this so that my joy may be in you and that your joy may be complete" (Jn 15:11; cf. also 16:22–24; 17:13).

Clearly this joy is inseparable from the salvation that is present in the Son, but it is directly bound up with the person of the Son, who is himself present in the fellowship. Joy is a gift of the Father, even as the Son is a gift of the Father; it is present wherever the fellowship truly appears. But joy can never be perfectly known or fully complete because the fellowship itself, though real, is imperfectly realized. The present joy in the fellowship is a token of the ultimate expression of joy, which depends on the final revelation of the Son. In John's gospel, this final revelation required Jesus' "going away" so that he may "come again" (cf. Jn 16:16).

II. Requirements for Fellowship With God Who Is Light (1:5–2:28)

A. Walking in the Light (1:5–2:2)

If the readers are to have fellowship with the Father and with the Son (v.3), they must understand what makes this possible. They must know who God is in himself and, consequently, who they are in themselves as creatures of God. So the author first describes the moral character of God in terms of light (v.5) and then goes on to deny three claims made by those who falsely boast of their knowledge and fellowship with God: (1) that moral behavior is a matter of indifference in one's relationship to God (v.6); (2) that immoral conduct does not issue in sin for one who knows God (v.8); and (3) that the knowledge of God removes sin as even a possibility in the life of the believer (v. 10). True evidences for fellowship with God or walking in the light are: (1) fellowship with one another (v.7), followed by cleansing in the blood of Christ; (2) confession of sin, (v. 9) which brings both forgiveness and cleansing; and (3) confidence that if we sin we have Jesus Christ as an advocate and sacrifice for our sins (2:2).

5 John begins his exposition by referring to the message heard from Jesus. His allusion is probably not to a specific word of Jesus but to Jesus himself as the Son in whose life and death the Father manifested himself. As in vv.1–4, in contrast to the false teachers he opposes, the author shows the authority that lies behind his own apostolic witness.

The message that "God is light" needs to be compared with declarations elsewhere by John that "God is spirit" (Jn 4:24) and "God is love" (1Jn 4:8). All three stress the immateriality of God and the "Godness" of God—i.e., God in his essence. Light emphasizes especially the splendor and glory of God, the truthfulness of God, and his purity.

Certain OT ideas dominate the Christian concept of "light" as a description of God. Light stresses the self-communicative nature of God and the action of God for human beings and for their salvation. The psalmist catches this with such utterances as "In your light we see light" (Ps 36:9) or "The Lord is my light and my salvation" (Ps 27:1). John expounds this in vv.5–7 (cf. Jn 1:9). Light also accents God's empowering activity in our lives. God as light not only shines downward for our salvation but enables us to walk in the light. Jesus said, "I am the light of the world. Whoever follows me will never walk in darkness, but will have the light of life" (Jn 8:12; cf. also 12:35). John encourages his readers to walk in the light (v.7; cf. Eph 5:8–14). Light, then, is the presence of God's grace.

God's light also has the character of a demand. That is certainly the meaning here in vv.5-6. If people turn from the light or love darkness rather than light, it is because their deeds are evil (Jn 3:19–21). In the world of first-century religious thought, the word "light" described ultimate realities. But there the weight was on the metaphysical implications. John is far removed from that type of speculation. He is concerned with the goodness of God and also the goodness of the human race.

The latter part of v.5 is a negative corollary emphasizing the statement that God is light. As darkness has no place in God, so all that is of the darkness is excluded from having fellowship with God. This idea stands out as the author now discusses the behavior pattern of his opponents.

6 John introduces the first of three tests of Christian faith by the clause "If we claim." He uses this device to refer to false claims made by the false teachers. The first claim—to have fellowship with God and yet to walk in darkness—probably belongs to early Gnostics who, as John describes them, have no love for one another (v.7), hate their brothers (2:9, 11), claim sinlessness (v.8), and deny that Jesus came in the flesh (2:22). To "walk in the darkness" is the same as "abiding" in darkness or "living in darkness"—i.e., allowing darkness to define one's life. In the final part of the verse, the author indicates that the test of truth is not one's belief—though that is not excluded—but one's action, deeds, and conduct. Speaking the truth is only one part of doing the truth, and not the most important part.

It must not be assumed that the opponents agreed with the author's claim that they walked in darkness. Far from it! They claimed to walk in the light while they practiced the deeds of darkness. This is what made their actions so pernicious. Inevitably they began to call their "darkness" light and to claim righteousness without doing righteousness. In such situations, the author says, we lie and do not live by the truth.

7 The positive test of knowing God is to live (lit., "walk"; GK *4344*) in the light as he himself is in the light. John thus reiterates the fact that light is God's sphere. It is his nature, and he wills that it should become ours.

One consequence of obeying the command to walk in the light is having fellowship with one another. The author is combating the heresy that boasts of knowledge of and communion with God but neglects fellowship with other Christians. True fellowship with God comes through other people; fellowship with them is the proof of fellowship with God.

A second consequence of walking in the light is that the blood of Jesus keeps on cleansing us from every defilement due to sin. The language reminds us of the sacrificial system of the OT, as well as of the interpretation of Christ's death given us in the letter to the Hebrews. Without Christ's ongoing cleansing, enduring fellowship would be impossible, for the guilt resulting from sin destroys fellowship. The results of that cleansing are forgiveness, restoration, and the reestablishment of love. John's use of the singular "sin" reminds us that the emphasis is not on specific sinful acts but on the work of God in Christ that meets and deals with the sin principle itself.

8 The second false claim by John's opponents is that a Christian has no sin. The opponents probably did not claim that they had never committed wrongful acts, but they denied that the sin principle had lasting power over them or even had a presence in them, at least in those who had attained superior spiritual enlightenment. They were, after all, already perfect and free from guilt. It is not surprising that Gnostics, whether Christian or otherwise, should have denied sin. No human being, ancient or modern, wishes to understand existence under that rubric.

Others in John's community may have argued, like some in Corinth, that sin was a matter of the flesh and had nothing to do with the spirit, or that since they possessed the spirit, they were beyond the categories of good and evil and therefore moral principles no longer applied to them.

Whatever the shape of the argument, and regardless of whether it is an affirmation from the ancient world or a modern restatement, it remains true that whenever the principle of sin is denied as an ongoing reality, there follows a denial of responsibility for individual actions. Gossip, defiling of persons, hatred of the brethren, jealousy, and boasting become sanctioned as non-sins; walking in the light is denied; and the fellowship to which we are called is never permitted to exist. Furthermore, when the sin principle is denied, truth as an principle of life cannot exist in us. As a result, in God's name, we make his presence and power an impossibility.

9 John now confronts us with our second definite test of obedience. Walking in the light is demonstrated not by the denial of sin but by confessing it and abandoning it. This action links us to God's mercy. Those who confess their sins and condemn them are linked to God. And we can confess our "sins" to God and before other people fearlessly and in confidence because God is both faithful and just.

The plural "sins" makes clear that we affirm our sinfulness by confessing our sins. The forgiveness that comes is related to God's faithfulness and justice. God is faithful in himself, i.e., to his own nature (cf. 2Ti 2:13), and faithful to his promises (cf. Ro 3:25; 1Co 10:13; Heb 10:23; 11:11). Everywhere he promises forgiveness to his children (e.g., Jer 31:34; Mic 7:19–20). And in keeping this promise, God reveals his faithfulness and justice.

The force of God's being "just" (GK *1465*) points to the Cross, to the covenant, to God's rule over us, and to the attributes of God from which forgiveness flows. And certainly God's mercy must not be set against his justice. The phrase "he is faithful and just" includes all those things. It is a corollary of the fact that God is light and love.

The verb used for "forgive" (GK *918*) has at its roots the idea of the "cancellation of debts" or the "dismissal of charges." The verb used for "purifies" (GK *2751*) pictures an act of cleansing from the pollution of sin so that a new life of holiness may begin. Sinners are perceived as cleansed from moral imperfections and from the injustices that separate them from God.

10 This verse gives the third and final false claim: "If we claim we have not sinned." But is this a different assertion from the one in v.8 or just a restatement of the same issue with an even more dramatic conclusion: "We make him [God] out to be a liar and his word has no place in our lives"?

In favor of the former possibility is the change in the verbal construction from "we have no sin" to "we have not sinned." The latter statement is more inclusive. The persons involved could be saying, "Whatever is true about the sin principle in others, we as Gnostic believers have transcended it all. We do not sin! We have not sinned! Sin has gained no foothold in us." Probably both statements had their adherents among the Gnostic believers. Some may have said it one way, some the other. Some may have claimed that through their "knowledge" derived from the Christian proclamation they were removed from the possibility of sin. Others may have boasted that they had entered a sinless state through "knowledge" before the Gospel had even come to them.

This latter statement, in other words, is far more blatant and defiant. It makes a mockery of the Gospel. It states that the reason God acted in grace and mercy toward us for the sake of our sins is false, that God first deceived us about ourselves and then becomes himself the Deceiver. The statement "his word has no place in our lives" means that the word proclaimed, the tradition received, and the witness from the OT Scriptures have no place in the heart and conscience of those who deny their sin. Consequently the possibility of hearing a redemptive word is also denied, and one can neither live by the Word nor receive forgiveness offered by God.

2:1 As John resumes his discourse on sin and forgiveness, we see a striking change of mood. Whereas earlier he was focusing on his opponents and their false teaching, now he speaks about these things as they affect his followers. The note of endearment—"my dear children"—in no way minimizes the seriousness of the discussion. Lest any conclude from his previous statements that sin must be considered inevitable in the life of the believer and not a matter of urgent concern since God forgives sins through Christ, John hastens to add, "I write this to you so that you will not sin." There is no question at all in his mind that sin and obedience to God are irreconcilable. Sin is the enemy. It removes the believer from the light, prevents fellowship with God, and destroys fellowship with the children of light. The principle of sin as the power of darkness must be excluded from the believer's life, and individual acts of sin must be resisted. Where failure occurs, the sin must be confessed before the body and the Lord and then abandoned. And always the intent of the believer remains the same—not to commit sin!

If any of his children should fail and commit sin, the author is anxious that they neither deceive themselves about it nor lie about their action and give up walking in the light. The answer to lapsing into sin is the forgiveness of God made available through Jesus Christ. He has been designated the believer's advocate, the counsel "who speaks . . . in our defense." His worthiness to perform this function rests on the fact that even as God is righteous (1:9), so he too merits the title "The Righteous One."

2 Our advocate does not maintain our innocence but confesses our guilt. Then he enters his plea before the Father on our behalf as the one who has made "the atoning sacrifice [GK 2662] for our sins" (this word also occurs in 4:10; cf. also Lk 18:13; Ro 3:25; Heb 2:17; 9:5). And his sacrifice is not only for our sins, "but also for the sins of the whole world." This statement asserts two things: Christ's sacrifice is sufficient for all, and it is necessary for all.

B. Obeying His Commands (2:3–11)

The first section (1:1–2:2) dealt with fellowship, primarily fellowship with God. Three false claims made by the opponents were denied (vv.6, 8, 10), and each false claim was used as an occasion for the presentation of what are true evidences of living in fellowship with God. The second section (2:3–11) is concerned with knowledge of God. Again the false claims to knowledge by the opponents are stated first, this time introduced by the clause "he who says" (cf. vv.4, 6, 9). Each of these claims is again denied and the evidence of the true knowledge of God is set forth: obeying his commands (v.5), walking in his likeness (v.6), and loving one's brother (v.10).

3 There appears to be a break in subject matter with what precedes as the author now turns to the topic of knowing God. For him to know God is, however, a natural corollary to the idea of walking in the light and of having fellowship with God. It is simply another way of speaking of the reality of God. In this instance the language probably is a response to the opponents for whom knowledge (*gnosis*; *GK 1194*) was a key term. To these "Gnostic" opponents, knowledge of God came through "mystical insights" or by a "direct vision of God." At the same time, they were uninterested in moral conduct and unconcerned about human behavior.

For the Hebrew or Christian mind, however, knowledge of God cannot be separated from the experience of righteousness. Consequently there is no greater claim one can make in knowing God than to obey him. "We can be sure we know him," the author says, "if we obey his commands." For John, therefore, the test of knowledge of God is moral conduct (cf. also Tit 1:16). There is no knowledge of God that does not also keep his commandments.

4 Now the author addresses his opponents who claim that they know God but at the same time break his commandments. Since he considers knowledge of God practical and experiential, to claim to know God and at the same time to disobey his commandments is to lie and be devoid of all truth.

5 Next John states the positive side of knowledge. The one who "obeys his word" (a more comprehensive way of speaking of the Gospel, including both promises and commandments) finds God's love "made complete" (GK 5457) in him. True knowledge of God does not end with speculative ideas, as for the Gnostics, but with obedience to the moral law and with the presence of God's love in the believer. "Made complete" carries with it the idea of continuous growth and development; it describes both state and process. As obedience is practiced, so God's love matures in us.

6 "To live in him" (either the Father or the Son, but in the context the Father is more likely) introduces another way the opponents described their relationship to God. What they claimed by this experience we do not know; probably they boasted of mystical experiences, visions of the light, and the like. What they did not claim was any seriousness to live in a godly manner. The author's comment is direct and forceful: "Whoever claims to live in him must walk [i.e., live] as Jesus did." Relationship to God requires moral behavior worthy of God. And as the revelation of God in Christ is accepted as the high point of divine self-disclosure, so the human life of Jesus becomes the measuring stick of true moral and ethical behavior. The author is not claiming that the walk of Jesus can be perfectly imitated but that there is a divine imperative—which must be taken seriously—for believers to live according to the way Jesus lived.

7 The affectionate term "dear friends" (lit., "beloved"; GK 28) reminds us that the author is looking in two directions at once: (1) He is setting forth tests that will expose the false teachings and claims of his opponents. (2) He is providing tests by which his own spiritual children will know they are walking in the light.

In addition, John may be dealing with a serious charge against his own teaching. His opponents may have claimed that he has in fact distorted the Gospel by adding to it. For them the knowledge of God available in the Gospel was itself the end of the religious quest. To John, however, the Gospel is fulfilled in the knowledge of God that is revealed in Jesus, and this in turn requires obedience to his commands and results in a new relationship with God expressed in a life of love. The point of view reflects Jesus' words as recorded in Jn 13:34. The new command that John speaks of here in v.7 sums up what it means to "walk in the light" and to "walk as Jesus did." Thus it stands at the heart of the Gospel. Moreover, what John was proclaiming was not "a new command but an old one" they had had "since the beginning." So he denies that there ever was "a message" that did not have this command at its heart.

8 In view of v. 7, how can the author assert that this command is also at the same time "a new command"? Its newness lies at the point of its realization and fulfillment. Jesus lived a life of divine love, and he extended this life to his disciples as a new command to be fulfilled in their lives (Jn 15:12ff.). After Jesus' death and resurrection, they discovered that as they obeyed his commands, his promise did indeed find fulfillment. What had been true in Jesus' own life now became part of the reality of their lives. They too began to know what it was to "love." Just as Luke (Ac 2) and Paul (2Co 5:17) wrote about the experience of this realized new life in the present, John expresses the realized fulfillment by simply saying that "the darkness is passing and the true light is already shining" (cf. Eph 5:8–14; 1Th 5:4–8).

9 This verse brings us to the third false claim that the author denies. Whereas obedience to the new command leads to love among the Christian community, among the opponents who claim to "be in the light" there is hate. This hate for one's fellow believer shows that the light they follow is nothing but darkness.

How does John understand hate? His answer lies primarily in what one does. Hate is the absence of the deeds of love. To walk in the light is to love one's brother, and God's love will express itself in concrete actions. If these are missing, it is not because love can be neutral or can exist unexpressed. Love unexpressed is not love at all. When it is absent, hate is present.

In this instance, hate is the failure to deny oneself, the unwillingness to lay down one's life for a brother (Jn 15:13). One considers one's own plight first (1Co 13:5); disregards the robbed and afflicted (Lk 10:30–37); despises the little ones (Mt 18:10); withholds the cup of cold water from the thirsty (Mt 25:42); and makes no effort to welcome the stranger, clothe the naked, or help the sick (Mt 25:43). Whenever a brother has need and one does not help him, then one has, in fact, hated his brother.

Does the word "brother" (GK *81*) refer here to one's neighbor or to one who belongs to the community of faith? In this instance it probably refers to a member of the community of faith. It is not that John lacks concern for those outside the faith: rather, in this letter he has the community of believers in view. Moreover, if believers cannot love their fellow believers, it is doubtful that they can truly love their neighbors.

10 The author now gives us a positive test of living in the light. Unlike his opponents, his concern is with deeds, not claims. "Whoever loves," he says, is "in the light." Conversely, the one who does not live "in the light" will not manifest God's love.

The uncertain antecedents of the Greek pronouns leads to some ambiguity in the rest of the sentence. In view of the author's aim, he is probably saying that the one who loves and abides in the light will never cause the offense the opponents do.

11 Now the author picks up the concept of "darkness" from v.9 and gives it a final elaboration and conclusion. One who "hates his brother" is not simply "in the darkness" but is condemned to spend his life in darkness. Though he has eyes, he can see nothing. And the darkness so blinds his eyes that he has no idea "where he is going." Life is a search, but for him it is without direction. He never knows whether he is closer to or farther from his destination. The only certainty is that he is without hope of reaching it. So hate destroys any window for light from God. To live without loving one's brother means to deny oneself the presence of God and the reality of fellowship with the community of faith.

C. Knowing the Father and Abiding Forever (2:12–17)

The first part of the letter (1:5–2:11) involved untrue assertions made by the author's Gnostic–type opponents and provided "tests" for exposing the false claims as well as for assuring those who walked in the light. The next section is in two parts. The first (2:12–14) contrasts the position of believers who walk in the light with that of the Gnostics who walk in darkness. The second part (2:15-17) warns believers not to fall into the trap of worldliness, as the false teachers did.

The first section is rhythmical, almost lyrical. Two sets of three statements introduced by the words "I write" and "I have written," or "I wrote" (NIV does not bring out this distinction), are addressed in turn to "children," "fathers," and "young men." We do not know why the author changes tenses, nor do we know the significance of the various forms of address. Possibly John intends to address his entire congregation from two standpoints—that of chronological age ("children," "young men," "fathers") and that of spiritual age (novices in the faith, those whose faith is vigorous and who are responsible for the work of the Gospel, and those whose knowledge and experience in the faith are the foundation on which the community exists).

12 "Dear children" (GK *5448*) is the author's favorite term for the congregation of believers as a whole. Under this rubric he offers the most basic and universal words of assurance he can give: "Your sins have been forgiven on account of his name." They have confessed their sins (1:9) and, on account of the name of Jesus (cf. Ac 4:12), or by faith in his name (3:23; 5:13), or by faith in him (5:1, 5)—the meaning is the same—they have received forgiveness through the covenant of his blood (1:7). In this knowledge they may stand firm. Because they are forgiven, they may also have fellowship with God and true knowledge of him (v.13c).

13a "Fathers" is an unusual form of address for senior members of a congregation. According to Jewish custom, it would refer to those who had responsibility for authority. Many times it is used to refer to the leaders of the past, such as the patriarchs, etc. If it refers to members of the congregation who were mature both in years and in faith, it was indeed a solemn designation, one implying they had responsibility in the community of believers. The secondary address to the "fathers" in v.14a is particularly appropriate to older members of the community. It stresses the historic origins of the faith and the growth of the personal knowledge of Christ that comes only with experience.

The pronoun "him" is ambiguous, and while it could refer to God, it is more likely here to refer to Christ. In any case, it looks back to 1:1–3, where both God and Christ are equally represented, and it reminds the readers that they have come to know Jesus as the One who is and who was from the beginning. The idea of knowing God reflects a special interest of the prophets (see Isa 9:1–9; 52:6; Jer 31:34).

13b The description of the community as "young men" who "are strong" (v.14b) and "have overcome" adds a new dimension. Believers are to see themselves as not only in conflict with the enemy but as having perceived the victory in Christ's name and by his power. The victory obviously was gained through Christ's death, and now his followers have the task under his leadership of establishing his reign over the world and "the evil one" (v.14b—a reference to the devil; see 3:12; 5:18; cf. Jn 17:15; Eph 6:16; 2Th 3:3). This victory does not promise that believers will be removed from the heat and peril of the battlefield. But it does assure them that if they are faithful they will overcome the devil. As Christ has been victorious over Satan, so they too may commit themselves to the conflict without fear of defeat (cf. Jn 16:33; Ro 8:31–39; Col 2:15; 1Jn 3:8).

13c This time the "children" are addressed by a different word (GK 4086). While the word in v.12 emphasizes the relationship of the dependence, the word used here stresses the immaturity of the child and the need to be under instruction or direction. As children who are under teachers in the faith, John's readers have come to know God as the Father. Second only to forgiveness in importance for the new community of faith is the relationship to God as Father that comes through the Gospel of Jesus Christ.

14 After referring again to the "fathers" (see comment on v.13a), the author concludes by addressing the young men as those in whom "the word of God lives." They were indeed "strong" (GK 2708) as the children of faith, but the author reminds them that their strength ultimately depends on one fact alone—the Word of God abiding or living in them.

15 Having assured the believers of their position before God—i.e., their sins are forgiven, they know the Father, and they have overcome the evil one—John moves to application. He warns them not to love the world and gives two reasons: Love for the world precludes love for the Father, and the investment of love in the world is without meaning because the world is passing away (v.17). The love of the world versus the love of the Father provides yet another "test" of walking in the light.

"World" (GK 3180) occurs six times in vv.15–17. It obviously means something quite different here than in Jn 3:16. There the Father's love of the world is apparently based on his having willed the world into existence. It is his creation; he created it to be good, beautiful, and worthy of giving glory to him. Likewise those who live in the world are his creatures, whom he loves; even in their desperate state of living in darkness and the shadow of death, he remains constant in desiring to rescue them from eternal death. Here, however, the world is presented as the evil system under the grip of the devil (cf. 1Jn 5:19; Jn 12:31; 14:30).

Love also means something different in this passage. Here it is not the selfless love for one's brother (cf. 2:10) but the love that entices by an evil desire or a forbidden appetite (Jn 3:19; 12:43). It is the world's ability to seduce believers, to draw them away from love of the Father, that concerns John.

16 What love for the world or worldliness entails is now spelled out by John in a memorable triad: "the cravings of sinful man, the lust of his eyes and the boasting of what he has and does." The phrase "the cravings of sinful man" (lit., "the desire of the flesh [GK 4922]") describes the principle of worldliness from which love of the world flows. "Flesh" refers to a selfish outlook that pursues its own ends, independent of God and independent of one's fellowman. The "flesh" not only becomes the basis for rebellion against God and for despising his law but also connotes all that is materialistic, egocentric, exploitative, and selfish. It is at the root of racism, sexism, love of injustice, despising the poor, neglecting the weak and helpless, and every unrighteous practice.

The "lust of the eyes" can refer especially to sexual lust, but can also mean everything that entices the eyes. It is a tendency to be captivated by outward show, and especially indicates greed and a desire for things aroused by seeing them (cf. Eve in Ge 3; Achan in Jos 7; David in 2Sa 11).

The key term in the third phrase is "pride" (NIV, "boasting"; GK 224); it occurs only here and in Jas 4:16 (cf. GK 225 in Ro 1:30; 2Ti 3:2). It describes a pretentious hypocrite who glories in himself or in his possessions. If one's public image means more than the glory of God or the well-being of one's fellow human beings, such pretentiousness of life has become a form of idol-worship. "Pride of life" will be reflected in whatever status symbol is important to me or seems to define my identity. When I define myself to others in terms of my honorary degrees, the reputation of the church I serve, my annual income, the size of my library, my expensive car or house, and if in doing this I misrepresent the truth and in my boasting show myself to be only a pompous fool who has deceived no one, then I have succumbed to the pride of life.

17 All the vanity of this evil world with its devices is passing away. It has already begun to putrefy. It is a corpse not yet buried. But the person who really does the will of God has the breath of eternal life.

D. Warnings Against Antichrists (2:18–28)

In the first three sections of his letter, the author has been directly presenting his followers with "tests" by which they could know they were truly in union with the Father. At the same time, he was dealing with his opponents by showing that they failed each of these tests of discipleship. In this section he reverses his method. He is no longer using indirection against his opponents, but now confronts them and their teaching by openly labeling them for what they are: antichrists (vv.18–19). He exposes their method: they lie and deny Jesus as Christ (vv.20, 23).

He teaches his followers how to cope with this: they are to remain in what they were taught (vv.24–26). Finally, he assures his followers of their power to overcome: "His anointing teaches you" (vv.27–28).

18 The reference to the transitoriness of the world in v.17 provides the link to what has preceded. One sign of the end of this transitory world is the appearance of false teaching and of the Antichrist. What the apostles warned of is now being fulfilled. The spirit of "antichrist" (GK 532) is present in the world, evidenced by the many "antichrists" who have already appeared. This is no surprise, however, but only further confirmation that the company of believers are living in the last hour.

The term "last hour" occurs only here in the NT. Like the similar terms "the last days" and "the last times," it owes much to OT expectations (cf. Joel 2:28; Mic 4:1) and to later Jewish ideas. Jesus called the present age an evil age and looked forward to the age to come, which would be ushered in by God's own intervention. The NT writers thought of the "last days" in two ways. (1) Theologically, they connected this period to the new age associated with the coming of Jesus. In the gospel of John this new age is designated by the statement "the hour is come" and is marked by Jesus' death and resurrection (Jn 4:23; 5:25). In Acts the new age is referred to as the "days to come" and is signaled by the pouring forth of the Spirit (Ac 2:17) and salvation through calling on the name of the Lord (Ac 2:21). But the NT writers did not believe this new age had completely come. They recognized it as being present provisionally in Christ and in the Holy Spirit. But because of this dawning of the new age, they saw the present age as already doomed and passing away.

(2) Eschatologically, the term "last days" designates the last days before Christ's return (cf. 2Ti 3:1ff.; 2Pe 3:3). In the gospel of John, the last day refers to the last resurrection and judgment (cf. Jn 6:39–40, 44, 54; 11:24; 12:48).

Should the term "last hour" here be understood theologically or eschatologically? More likely the former. Since the Greek literally translates "it is *a* last hour," the term seems to describe the general character of the period rather than its specific time in history.

In addition, the words used here involve no chronological or temporal assertions. Also, in his gospel, John uses "hour" (GK *6052*) theologically to indicate the fulfillment of time—the time of redemption and salvation (Jn 2:4; 4:21; 7:30; 8:20; 12:23).

19 The departure of the opponents may have had a greater effect on the congregation than the reason for it. The early church obviously had severe debates, with significant differences of opinion being expressed. Yet as far as we know, no one thought that "separation from the congregation" was an option for anyone professing faith in Jesus. Departure, like Judas's going out from the community of disciples, pointed to betrayal, denial of faith, and separation from God's grace. That is why John acknowledges that those false teachers, whom he now designates as antichrists, had been regular members of the congregation. "They went out from us," he says, but hastens to add, "they did not really belong to us." Like Judas, they had been nominal members of the community and had never truly shared its fellowship.

John goes on to teach the significance and abiding nature of life in the community. "If they had belonged to us, they would have remained with us." Those who have actually been a part of the divine life will without fail persevere in the community. But in order that the true nature of the false teachers might be exposed, "they went out from us," so that the community might know that "none of them belonged to us" (cf. Mt 24:24).

Expulsion from the Christian community for misdeeds was and is a serious act, and hopefully it lasts only long enough to allow for repentance and restoration (cf. 1Co 5:2–5; 2Co 2:5–11). The case at hand is unique; the departure of the opponents was not expulsion or excommunication but a voluntary departure. It shows that they were never truly members of the community.

20 The author now returns to the heretical claims of his opponents. They probably claimed superior knowledge because they had received an exclusive ritual anointing that gave them knowledge. Their attitude may have been similar to that of the later "Gnostic" sect known as Naassenes, who claimed a special sacrament of anointing. John combats his opponents' claim by reminding his readers: "But you have an anointing from the Holy One, and all of you know [because all of you received it] the truth." This is probably an allusion to the coming of the Holy Spirit as prophesied by Jesus in John's gospel: "But when he, the Spirit of truth, comes, he will guide you into all truth" (Jn 16:13; cf. also 14:17; 15:26). The early Christians connected this with their baptism. Although "anointing" is used only infrequently in the NT, both Luke and Paul do use it with reference to the Holy Spirit (Lk 4:18; Ac 10:38; 2Co 1:21–22).

The messengers of God proclaimed the Gospel, but God himself by his Spirit taught the heart, from which true knowledge was then manifested. When this divine teaching was truly recognized, Christians were genuinely protected against false teaching or unbelief (cf. 1Th 4:9; Ro 15:14).

21 Lest there be any doubt among the faithful as to John's perception of their understanding and orthodoxy, he says that he has not written because they did not know the truth—he himself is not providing any new information or teaching—but because they know it so certainly. They know the character of truth, and therefore they know that "no lie comes from truth." John aims his remarks precisely at the innate knowledge of the Gospel that he knows his followers possess. Lies cannot come from God. The antichrists and their followers, the false teachers, are liars. So they do not come—in fact, they cannot come—from God, who is the truth.

22 "Who is the liar?" v.22 asks and then rhetorically answers by pointing to those antichrists who promulgate the particularly pernicious falsehood that Jesus is not the Christ. This falsehood should not be linked to the Jewish opponents who denied that Jesus was the Messiah but rather to the Gnostic opponents who denied that Christ came in the flesh (see also 4:2–3; 2 Jn 7).

The exact kind of Gnostic denial in view is uncertain. It probably included the ideas that the true Christ, who was preexistent, merely appeared in human form to bring eternal life, that his human existence was without real significance, and that his human presence was not essential to his true being. The revelations he brought came not through any of his actions as Jesus of Nazareth or through any events connected to his life—especially not through his sufferings or his death on the cross. To the opponents, eternal life came in Jesus' divine glory as the preexistent and eternal Christ.

Obviously such a denial of Jesus' humanity struck at the very heart of the Incarnation. By denying Jesus' true sonship, these opponents of John denied the Father as well. Because they denied Jesus' human life, they rejected the community of love he established. Most likely the false teachers mocked the commands of Jesus as taught by the apostles. Little wonder that John designates them "antichrists." They rejected Jesus. They rejected their own sinfulness and need of forgiveness (1:8–10), the life of love (2:4, 6, 8), and their "fellowship" with the Father and the Son (1:1–4, 6–7).

23 The statement "No one who denies the Son has the Father; whoever acknowledges the Son has the Father also" makes clear the singular dependence of the Christian faith on the reality of God available through the Son. Those who claim they have a Father but exclude the Son have neither the Father nor the Son. Consequently, when Jesus is acknowledged as the Son and as the eternal Christ, the Father has also truly been lifted up, known and honored, confessed and possessed. John is not talking here about having a creed but about possessing a person by accepting or acknowledging our relationship to him. So also we deny God by denying him his proper relationship with us.

24 At this point John shifts his attention to his readers. They, in contrast to the antichrists, are exhorted to make certain that what they heard "from the beginning"—i.e., the true apostolic declaration concerning Jesus as Son and Christ—"remains" (GK *3531*) in them. If it does, they may be assured that they will also "remain" in the Son and in the Father. The use of "remain" gives weight to the warning. The word of the Gospel must not only be heard but be given a vital place in one's life. The message must continue to be active in the lives of all who have heard it. They must reflect on it and let it affect their lives.

While John's exhortation here is clearly to faithfulness to the Word, it is also an exhortation with an assured promise of fulfillment. Where the Word abides, there also the Son and Father abide in intimate fellowship. The Word is not the goal of the fellowship but rather a means to the goal of fellowship. The listing of the Son before the Father may emphasize the fact that access to the Father becomes possible only through the Son (Jn 10:10; 17:2; 20:31).

25 What is promised in the Gospel is the everlasting knowledge of Father and Son (Jn 17:3). It is a promise the community has already received. Eternal life has begun, but its eschatological fulfillment is also promised. What dimension this fellowship with the Son and the Father will assume in the "life to come" is yet unknown (3:2). But the hope is certain. All that is now known about it is only a foretaste of the glory that will be revealed.

26–27 The author concludes his attack on the false teachers with a warning and a word of encouragement for his followers. He has identified the heretical beliefs of those who have deserted the community of believers (v.22). He has properly labeled his opponents antichrists (v.18) and has described them as "those trying to lead you astray" (cf. 4:6; 2Jn 7). This description is more significant because it reveals the actual intent of those who have deserted the community. Not only have they forsaken the true faith, but they intend to lead many of the faithful astray. Their aim is to assume leadership over the community. They are enemies who are not content to spread new teaching but "invaders" and "deceivers" who seek to win the whole community over to their position.

Against their threat, John once more expresses his supreme confidence in the power of the divine anointing. The Son's gift of the Spirit, who accompanied the apostolic word "from the beginning," abides in them (cf. Jn 14:16). If they abide in the teaching and in the anointing, they need neither new teaching nor new teachers. Since they have received their "teaching" from the Son through those who were his witnesses from the beginning and have his "anointing," they have in fact no need for anyone more to teach them, not even John himself. Does he think of this letter as further "teaching"? Probably not. He is simply reminding them to keep to the teaching they received from the beginning. Any teaching in the church should only be what was received from the beginning (cf. Gal 1:6; 1Ti 6:3; 2Ti 1:13; 4:3–5; Tit 1:9; 2Pe 3:2).

The last part of v.27 summarizes the threefold reason to trust the anointing already received from Jesus (2:20). (1) His anointing teaches all things necessary for them to know concerning the Word of Life. He does not advance the idea, perhaps favored by some of his opponents, that the Spirit will add new revelation to what has already been given. (2) This anointing is "real, not counterfeit" (cf. Jn 15:26; 16:3)—a reference to the gnosticizing opponents who claim as the source of their teaching a special anointing not commonly received by the company of believers. But the test of the anointing is its fidelity to that which is from the beginning. Since the opponents' teaching fails precisely at this point, their anointing is exposed as false. (3) The community has in its history experienced the teaching from the anointing—i.e., they have known the confirming work of the Spirit in their lives. The Gospel has taken root in them and has brought forth its fruit (cf. 2:12–14). Therefore, John concludes with his most important word to them: "Remain [abide] in him [Christ]."

28 This verse makes the transition from concern about false teachers to concern for the children of God. It joins the admonition developed in the previous paragraph to the "confidence" (GK *4244*) and unashamedness that should belong to God's children when Christ appears. "Confidence" is one of John's favorite words to describe the freedom and boldness that belong to the Christian before God in prayer (3:21; 5:14; cf. Heb 4:16; 10:19) and at Christ's coming.

"Coming" (*parousia*; GK *4242*; see comment on 1Th 2:19) occurs only here in 1 John and not at all in John's gospel. Combined with "when he appears," this is a technical term referring to Jesus' second coming in visible splendor, a teaching that the author held in common with other early Christians. Historically this word was used to describe the festivities attendant on a monarch's arriving for a state visit. The early Christians anticipated the Lord's return as being no less joyous and majestic.

III. Requirements for Fellowship With God Who Is Righteous (2:29–4:6)

The dominant theme of this second main division of the letter is to provide assurance that even as the believers "continue in Jesus," they can know they are the children of God. The "tests" for knowing this are: (1) doing what is right (2:29–3:10), (2) loving one another (3:11–24), and (3) testing the spirits (4:1–6). Obedience will guarantee confidence before Jesus at his coming (2:28) and before God in prayer (3:21).

A. Doing What Is Right (2:29–3:10)

John begins this section with a promise of future likeness to Jesus (2:29–3:3) and follows it by a warning that a life of sin is not compatible with a life of fellowship with God but evidences the presence of the devil. Christ came to destroy the devil's work, prominent in which is hatred of one's fellow believer.

29 There is a clear break in thought and a new topic—"tests for knowing the children of God"—introduced here. Attention naturally focuses on the Father (3:1) and the significance of being "born of him." Since John never speaks of being "born of Jesus," it makes more sense to conclude that the subject from the beginning of v.29 is the Father and that John depends on his readers to get the meaning from the total context.

Neither God's righteousness nor that of the Son is disputed between John and his opponents (cf. 1:5; 2:1, 20; 3:7) but rather the significance of this righteousness. For John, to be born of God and to become his child means to accept as the standard for Christian conduct the Father's righteousness as revealed through the Son (2:6; 3:7; cf. Mt 5:48). Therefore, one must keep Jesus' commands, especially the command to love, which also becomes the test for distinguishing who are truly born of God. Those who do his righteous will should know that they have been born of him. Righteous conduct is not a condition for rebirth but a consequence of it.

On the other hand, John's opponents, who presumably also claimed rebirth, apparently thought of it not in ethical or moral terms but in terms of nature. They may have said that because they possessed the divine nature they could not sin (1:8) and were consequently removed from any obligation to the commandments (2:3–4). For them the proof that they were born of God lay in their new teaching, which freed them from commandments; in their knowledge, which enabled them to reject Christ's coming in the flesh; and in their exclusivism, which allowed them to hate their brothers (3:17–20), forsake the community (2:19), and deny the commandment to love (3:10).

From the tone of the letter, we conclude that the denial of the necessity to keep the commandments had not yet led to flagrant immoral conduct among the dissidents but that the implications of their theological method were seen by John as allowing—if not encouraging—that possibility.

3:1 The phrase "born of him [God]" (2:29) leads the author to marvel at the wonder of God's redemptive activity. See how great the gift of his love really is! Why, he has identified us as being his very own children! And this is exactly what we have become through his acts. Clearly the author means to encourage his readers by reminding them of the lavishness of God's grace and love—qualities that are missing from his opponents' lives. They fail to recognize God's love and feel no obligation to express it. But apart from love, there would have been no children of God.

Because believers are children of God, John warns them that the world is unable to recognize them or relate to them. That should not surprise them because neither did the world recognize God. The failure of the world to know God is one of the basic themes of the gospel of John (5:37; 7:28; 16:3). Those who belong to the world live in darkness. They cannot come to the light but must inevitably hate it.

The author wants his readers to know that approval by the world is to be feared, not desired. To be hated by the world may be unpleasant, but ultimately it should reassure the members of the community of faith that they are loved by God, which is far more important than the world's hatred.

2 Though they are now God's children, the unveiling of their identity or the complete revelation of their nature still lies in the future (probably only at the last time). John does not encourage speculation in these matters. His concern is to reiterate the "tradition" from which the promise comes. He (Jesus) will appear. We will see him as he truly is; his full glory will be revealed (cf. Jn 17:1, 5, 24). And we will become like him. That the author is once more presenting the teaching shared in the church "from the beginning" seems clear from its similarity to Paul's teaching in Ro 8:29; 1Co 15:49; 2Co 3:18; Col 3:4.

3 All who have their hope in Jesus—i.e., their hope of being like him (3:2) when he appears (2:28)—will also be committed to keeping themselves from sin. They will put away every defilement; they will aim to be like him in purity and righteousness. Once more we have the pattern of the incarnate Jesus being held up as an example to believers (cf. 2:6; 3:7, 16; 4:17). Those who claim likeness to him must be conformed to his earthly life, even as they wait for his coming. To live in sin or disobedience to his commands is to abandon any hope in him. It is the pure in heart who will see God (cf. Mt 5:8).

4 Here John uses two words to describe sin: "sin" (GK *281*) and "lawlessness" (GK *490*). In both OT and NT, these two words are used frequently as synonyms (cf. Pss 32:1; 51:3; Ro 4:7; Heb 10:17). In John's community, however, they were used apparently with different meanings. The former word was used to describe transgression of the law, the breaking of God's commandments. The latter defined sin as rebellion against God and was connected with Satan's rebellion against God (cf. Mt 7:22; 24:11–13; 2Co 6:14–16; 2Th 2:1–12). Apparently the false teachers and John agreed that "lawlessness" was incompatible with being born of God. What they did not agree on was that sin, defined as transgression of the moral law, was "lawlessness." Indeed, as those "born of God" they claimed themselves "morally" to be without sin or guilt. Either they believed that they were by nature incapable of violating the law or that sinful deeds done in the flesh were of no concern to God.

John decries such thinking. That his opponents hate their brothers (2:11) shows that their claim to sinlessness is a lie, and their failure to love stems from their lawlessness. Lawlessness, in turn, shows that they do not belong to God but to the devil (3:10). They are part of the evil soon to be revealed (2:18).

5 In this verse John turns again to the teaching received "from the beginning" and raises two additional arguments against sin as a principle of life. (1) Not only is sin lawlessness (v.4), but Jesus appeared in history in order to remove it (cf. Jn 1:29; Heb 9:26). (2) Jesus himself lived a sinless life (cf. 2:1;

3:3; 2Co 5:21). In this latter statement the author probably is looking in two directions. Because Jesus was sinless, the devil had no hold on him (cf. John 14:30), so that Jesus was able to destroy the works of the devil (3:8). In addition, Jesus' sinlessness reveals the kind of lifestyle required for those who abide in him. John uses the present tense to emphasize that sinlessness is characteristic of Jesus' eternal nature. He was sinless in his preexistence, in his life in the flesh, and in his eternal position as Son.

6 This verse seems to contradict 1:8, 10. However, as we have reconstructed the situation (see comment on 3:4), the author simultaneously faced two different problems with these precursors of Gnosticism. There were those who apparently claimed to be sinless by nature; i.e., they were unable to sin because they were "born of God." There were others who claimed a standing with God apart from a life of righteousness. They believed that the commandments had no authority over them and taught that it was a matter of indifference to God whether they sinned or not. Therefore they could hate their brothers without guilt or concern.

In opposition to the latter opponents, the author states that those who "live" in the "sinless one" will, like him, live a life of righteousness. They commit themselves not to sin. And if they sin, they will confess it as lawlessness and abandon it.

John acknowledges that the life of righteousness is possible only in Christ. By "living" in him, in his "sinlessness," one can expect conformity to his righteousness. On the other hand, those who continue to sin make it certain that they have never had their eyes opened spiritually to see him, nor have they ever known him (cf. Jn 5:37–38; 8:19; 14:7, 9; 3Jn 11).

7 The warning "do not let anyone lead you astray" appears to have been directed against the false teachers in the community. The author, by using the address "dear children" (see comment on 2:1), places his own position in the community on the line.

8 There is clearly a progression in the author's thought on sin in this section. He begins with the "sinfulness" of sin—i.e., "it is lawlessness," or rebellion against God (v.4). Next he shows its incompatibility with Christ (v.5) and its incompatibility for anyone who lives in Christ (v.6). Now he shows the diabolic nature of sin—its source is the devil, who "has been sinning from the beginning" (v.8). That the Son of God appeared "to destroy the devil's work" is an elaboration of what John said in v.5.

John sees the enmity of God against the devil as absolute. It lies at the heart of God's commitment to rescue the human race from the devil's clutches. God will destroy the devil and all his works, including those children of the devil who accept sinning as a way of life. The statement "the devil has been sinning from the beginning" probably refers to the Genesis account of the Fall and includes an identification of the devil with the serpent. He was, from the beginning, evil (cf. Jn 8:44). Therefore, the very being of those like the false teachers derives from the devil. His desires become their desires. Like him they become liars and seducers. Those who continue in sin become children of the devil (v.10).

9 John summarizes what he has said. In v.6 he stated that no one who "lives in him" can practice a life of sin. Here he adds that "no one who is born of God" or has "God's seed" in him can "continue to sin." Both elements are necessary for understanding John's theology of community. Believers must "live" in him. The Father in turn must live in the believers (3:24; 4:12; cf. Jn 14:20; 17:21–23). If we do live in him, "we are removed" from life under the dominion of Satan. And if he lives in us, then our life will be his life in us and we will live even as he lived.

10 This verse reveals the heart of the entire section and furnishes a transition to the next one. John is not concerned with a theoretical consideration of the nature of sinfulness or the possibility of sinlessness but the issue of the community. How are the children (community) of God to be recognized and how are the children (community) of the devil to be discerned?

"Anyone who does not do what is right is not a child of God." And what is the "right" he does not do? He "does not love his brother." "Love for one's brother" is the true test of righteous behavior. This requirement of love helps explain the absolute requirement that those who are born of God "cannot go on sinning" (vv.6, 9). For if God is love, and if he lives in us and we in him, then love for fellow believers will occur as an expression of righteousness without exception.

The author, then, is not stressing absolute moral conformity or "sinless perfection" but the one requirement by which all other requirements are measured—love for one's fellow Christian. For this there is no substitute, its violation allows for no excuse, its application permits no compromise. Here there are no gray areas, no third possibilities. We either love our fellow believers and prove we are God's children, or we do not love them and prove we belong to the devil.

B. Loving One Another (3:11–24)

As the knowledge of God is tested by conduct (1:5–2:11), so being "born of God" (2:29) is tested by righteous action and love of fellow believers. The command to love fellow believers was first introduced in 2:9–11 as a test of whether one was walking in light, i.e., had true knowledge. Here it is the sum of the new life in God. In the former instance it was leveled as a charge against the heretics. Here it is addressed to the community of faith for encouragement and admonition. Most likely the disregard for love by the heretics had caused a lessening of an emphasis on love within the Christian community. The author presents the case for love first by the negative example of Cain (vv.12–15), contrasted with the positive example of Jesus (v.16).

11 The admonition that "we should love one another" is highlighted by the return to the critical formula, "This is the message you heard from the beginning," an almost identical reminiscence of 1:1, 5 (see comments). The command to "love one another" has its origin in the nature of God. The entire goal and aim of the Gospel is to create and strengthen love.

12 The mention of Cain points back to 3:8 and reminds us that hatred is also from the beginning. The choice between the children of God and the children of the devil, between hatred and love or life and death, stems from the earliest moment of human existence. It also points to Jn 8:37–47, where some Jewish opponents of Jesus had exhibited the same kind of hatred toward Jesus that Cain expressed toward Abel (Jn 8:59). There Jesus labels his enemies as people who "belong to your father, the devil . . . [who was] a murderer from the beginning" (Jn 8:42).

The sequence of thought in this section is significant. It is not that Cain by murdering his brother became the child of the devil; but, being a child of the devil, his actions were evil and culminated in the murder of his brother. The reason why he "murdered" (lit., "butchered"; GK *5377*) him was that his brother's acts were righteous. Righteousness draws hatred from the devil and hatred from the children of the devil. Darkness cannot tolerate light; immorality, morality; hatred, love; or greed, sacrifice. This is the only direct reference to the OT in this letter.

13 The hatred of the "world" (GK *3180*) for the community of faith must not surprise the believers. The author does not say that the world always hates believers; it did not always hate Jesus. But whenever the community of faith acts so as to expose the greed, avarice, hatred, and wickedness of the world, it must expect rejection; and if it should go so far as to interfere with its evil practices, as Jesus did in the temple, it may expect suffering and brutal death (cf. Jn 15:18–19, 25; 17:14).

"Brothers" (GK *81*) occurs only here in 1 John as an address. At this most critical point, the author steps past his relationship to them as "little children" (see comment on 2:1) and openly proclaims them his peers. Perhaps they have already experienced persecution with him. Or perhaps he knows that if they receive his letter and obey it, persecution will soon come because they have identified themselves with him rather than with his opponents.

14 John looks back to v.10 and answers the question: How do we know those who have been "born of God"? or, Who are the children of God? "We know that we have passed from death to life, because we love our brothers" (cf. Jn 5:24). This conviction is not based on self-judgment or self-justification but on the certainty that love is the basis for life in the believing community. This is a self-test by which each person can examine himself or herself. Love will not, of course, cause one's passage to spiritual life but will give evidence of it. Conversely, to be unable to love means that a person is without spiritual life and remains in death.

15 Here John links hatred with murder (cf. Mt 5:21–22). In the heart there is no difference; to hate is to despise, and murder is the fulfillment of that attitude. Cain, by murdering his brother, was cut off from the covenant community. So no murderer is within the community, nor anyone who "hates his brother." Such a person has no life of God and no fellowship with the faithful.

16 The test of true love is identified as willingness to sacrifice one's life for one's brother. The demonstrative "this" that begins the statement points backward to the negative example of Cain and forward to the positive example of Christ. Love is used absolutely and its reference point is Christ's death. The demand for love thus arises from his command, and the meaning of love is found in his example.

"We know" suggests that the knowledge that is involved belongs to events of Jesus Christ, which they heard from the beginning (cf. 1:1; 3:11). "Love" (*agape*; GK 27) cannot be derived from some intuitive grasp of an idea but is known in the historical event in which Jesus Christ laid down his life for us (cf. Jn 10:11). His sacrificial death thus distinguishes *agape* love from all other loves by its costliness, its unconditional acceptance of another, and its accomplishment.

The personal commitment of Christ is expressed in the words of Jn 15:12–13 (cf. 13:1): "Love each other as I have loved you. Greater love has no one than this, that one lay down his life for his friends." Its accomplishment as a "for us" kind of love is reflected in Jesus' work. It is clear that Jesus understood his death as an effectual, accomplishing act for giving us eternal life (Jn 10:28); it was the only method open to him to fulfill his Father's will (cf. Jn 10:11–18, 27–30; 15:9–18; 17:19). Since *agape* love is grounded in Jesus' death for us, knowledge of it can be received only where his "death" is appropriated into our experience.

The dramatic conclusion we are irresistibly led to is this: "And we ought to lay down our lives for our brothers." We are to do this not simply because that is what Jesus did, but because that is what Jesus revealed to be the demand of *agape* love. Love is denial of self for another's gain.

17 Again John's penchant for providing practical "tests" of the validity of one's faith comes to the fore. How can we know whether we would sacrifice our life for a fellow believer? We can know by being compassionate toward such a one in his or her present need. If we are unable or unwilling to sacrifice material advantage for the sake of our fellow believers, we know that the love of God is not in us. What are the conditions for our involvement? If we are in a position to see with our own eyes someone's need (as, for example, the good Samaritan did) and can offer help, then we cannot do otherwise than act. To withhold help in such a situation is to shut off compassionate action and to deny the presence of God's love in our own heart.

18 Turning back to "little children" (see comment on v.13), John admonishes with the tone of a spiritual father pleading for the heartfelt response of his children. Love requires more than idle talk or exalted theology. It demands simple acts, which anyone can see, in order to meet the needs of brothers and sisters in distress. Any expression of love that fails here is not only empty but blasphemous (cf. Jas 2:15; 1Co 13:1).

19–20 John began this section (2:29–4:6) by addressing the question, How may we be confident and unashamed at Christ's coming? (cf. 2:28). The answer, expressed in the phrases "continue in Jesus" and "doing what is right" (2:29; 3:7, 10), is tested by our love for our fellow believers. Now the author addresses the question of assurance—i.e., confidence before God. How may "we know that we belong to the truth" (3:19) and how do we deal with our own condemning hearts (3:20–21)? The anxious note in the first part of the question should probably be attributed at least in part to the unrelenting attack of opponents on the "teaching" and "beliefs" of the Christian community. The whole section, however, may also simply be explaining the nature of "fellowship" with the Father (1:3).

This passage allows several translations and interpretations. (1) "This" (v.19) may be taken to point backward to the absolute demand of love introduced in 3:14ff. If we know that we love truly, with actions and not mere words, that knowledge will not only assure us "that we belong to the truth" but will also act to "set our hearts at rest in his presence whenever our hearts condemn us." (2) It is also possible to put a period after "presence" and to read v.20 as follows: "If our hearts should condemn us, God is greater than our hearts, and he knows everything." (3) The best option is to see the "this" in v.19 as pointing both backward and forward. In other words, there are two ways we know that we "belong to the truth": (a) because we love in deed (vv.14ff.), and (b) because God himself assures us that we belong to the truth—he "is greater than our hearts, and he knows everything" (v.20b).

What is stressed is *agape* love, which is always expressed first in deeds and is reassuring evidence that we are of God. Why our hearts should condemn us is not discussed by the author. Apparently it is not important. His readers, like all others, know how easily the conscience can render us ineffective. Doubt, guilt, and failure are never far from any of us. Sometimes our misgivings are the result of our own actions or inactions. Sometimes it is the "accuser" who seizes our weaknesses and shortcomings and so elevates them that we wonder whether we can really be in the truth. What then can we do? We can remember that God understands everything. His word and his truth are greater than our feelings or our conscience. We may rest ourselves in his love for us and live in that love and by that love. We will not excuse ourselves of any sin, but neither will we needlessly accuse ourselves (cf. 1Co 4:3–5).

21 Christians are called to fellowship with God (1:3; 2:24). But if they are guilt-ridden and conscience-stricken, rather than seeking that fellowship or enjoying it, they will flee the presence of God and will not dare seek answers to prayer that he alone can provide. On the other hand, those who have his peace in their hearts will have "confidence" (GK *4244*) not only at his appearing but in the ordinary here-and-now relationship to the Father.

22 The fruit of this boldness is God's own openness to his children. He never withholds any good thing from those who ask. The author does not give the basis for his assurance, but his words "because we obey his commands and do what pleases him" point directly to Jesus' own words in Jn 8:28–29. As one who always did his Father's will, Jesus knew that his Father heard him (Jn 11:42). Jesus also gave similar assurances to his disciples (Jn 16:26–27).

23 This verse specifies what command it is that the children must obey in order to receive whatever they ask of him (v.22). It is "to believe [GK *4409*] in the name of his Son, Jesus Christ, and to love one another." The idea of believing, which occurs here for the first time in this letter, will be seen more and more as the issue between John and the "false teachers." They do not love—that is clear—but the reason for that is that God's love is not in them, since they have not truly believed in Jesus Christ, the Son of God. To believe in Jesus Christ means in this context to believe the Gospel about Jesus—that he is God's Son, that he came to save men and women from their sins, and that by believing in him they can have eternal life (Jn 3:16–18). Joining belief and love in a single command shows how inextricably connected the two are in John's mind. Belief comes first because it is the basis for love (cf. Jn 3:16), but love is the only expression of true faith.

The end of this command—"to love one another as he commanded us"—recalls Jesus' own command in Jn 13:34; 15:12, 17. John's practice of not distinguishing the subjects of verbs such as "he commanded" is characteristic both of his writing and of his theology. God the Father is revealed in Christ Jesus. To see the Son is to see the Father; to know the Father is to know the Son. The deeds of the one are the deeds of the other. So completely are their wills joined that it is many times a matter of indifference as to which one is in view.

24 In this summary verse the author states for the first time the mutual reciprocity involved in "living" in God. Obedience issues in the perfection of the "fellowship" between God and us. We "live" in him; he "lives" in us. We come to our "fellowship" with the Father through the "fellowship" the Son has with the Father (Jn 14:20; 17:21–23). The Son also enters into fellowship with us (Jn 15:4–5); and through him we have fellowship with the Father and with one another, just as the sign of our fellowship with the Father and with the Son is our love for them (cf. Jn 17:23–26).

The latter part of v.24 characteristically furnishes a transition to the next section. The evidence that we abide in him is our obedience to his commands. The evidence that he abides in us is the presence of his Spirit, whom he gave to us (cf. Ro 5:5; 8:14–16).

This is the first mention of the Spirit in 1 John. The author presupposes knowledge about the Spirit in his readers and applies it to the problem at hand—distinguishing the true Spirit from false spirits (4:1–3) and receiving the Spirit's witness (5:6–7). Referring to the Spirit as the one "he gave us" is not an appeal to their existential experience of the Spirit but to their knowledge of the Gospel as it had come to them from the eyewitnesses. The Father's giving or the Son's sending the Spirit to the disciples (Jn 14–16; 20:22) was a well-known event in the church (cf. Ac 1–2; Ro 8; Gal 4:6).

C. Warning Against the False Spirits (4:1–6)

This passage parallels 2:18–27, where the author warned against the presence of antichrists among those who had "gone out" from them. Now he has a second warning, this time against the "spirit" of antichrist, who even now inspires the false prophets (v.1). The false spirit can be detected because he will deny that Jesus Christ came in the flesh (v.3). The community of faith will overcome the false prophets because believers belong to God, and the Spirit in them is greater than the false spirit (v.4). The world listens to the false prophets (v.5) but the children of God listen to the apostolic declaration. Belief of the Gospel is the true test of the Holy Spirit's presence and work (v.6).

1 The opponents not only lay claim to God but boast of their inspiration by the "spirit" (GK 4460). Likely they gave evidence of their inspiration through "prophetic utterings" and perhaps even other signs, such as ecstasies and glossolalia. Such "signs" were present in the religious milieu of the Greeks and Romans and most persons took them seriously. That they sometimes caused special problems in the early church is attested by Paul (cf. 1Co 12:3; 14; 1Th 5:21). John's warning here is not against those who pretend to have the Spirit's presence but against genuine evil spirits' inspiring of false prophets. Outwardly these people were no less inspired than members of the faithful community. They were zealous in proclamation (cf. 2Jn 7) and may have been even more successful than the faithful community in making converts from the world (4:5). Likely John saw in them the fulfillment of Jesus' warnings (cf. Mk 13:22) against false prophets in the "end times" (cf. 2:18). His readers needed some test to discern the presence of false prophets.

2 The test itself appears to hinge on the words "that Jesus Christ has come in the flesh." The false prophets may well have believed that Christ was the Savior of the world, but they denied the connection between the divine Christ and Jesus of Nazareth. At least they clearly denied that "the Christ" ever had come "in the flesh." The clause "that Jesus Christ has come" reflects the author's clear view of the preexistence of the Son, who came from the Father and from the moment of his historical birth was Jesus Christ in the flesh.

How does this confession give evidence of the Spirit? For John, as for Paul, the truth of the Christian Gospel is hidden from the world (cf. 1Co 2:7–16). Only because there is a divine intervention and the darkness is removed can the light of the Gospel be recognized (cf. 4:6).

3 Here a negative confession gives the counterpart of that in v.2, and the source of this denial is seen as "the spirit of the antichrist." John reminds his followers that Jesus had warned that the Antichrist would come. It is now John's painful duty to announce that in the false teachers (cf. 2:18ff.) the spirit of antichrist is already present. By this the community was warned that the conflict between the false teachers and John was not a "leadership" or "personality" one. The Gospel itself was at stake. The struggle they were facing was not against flesh and blood but against principalities and powers (Eph 6:12). Hence, whatever success the opponents had had within the community resulted from satanic inspiration.

4 Once again the author addresses the community with "dear children" (see comment on 2:1). They have overcome the false prophets, because they resisted their teaching (v.5). Thus they are "from God"—i.e., "born of him" (2:29)—and the one who is in them is "greater than the one who is in the world" (v.4). The false teachers do not have the Spirit of Christ living in them because "living" involves "fellowship," which is possible between God and his children only by the Holy Spirit. The false teachers are without this

Biblical Evidence for the Trinity

According to the Bible, there is only one God (Dt 6:4; Isa 45:21; 1Ti 2:5; Jas 2:19). But this one God has revealed himself in three person: the Father, the Son, and the Holy Spirit. The word used to express this doctrine is "Trinity"—"tri-unity," "three-in-oneness." While this word is not used in the Bible, it adequately expresses biblical teaching. There is little difficulty acknowledging the Father as God. Regarding the deity of Jesus the Son, see the chart on "Passages Indicating the Deity of Christ" on p. 000. As to the Holy Spirit being specifically called God, see Lk 1:32, 35 and Act 5:3–4.

Hints in the OT of the Trinity	
God speaks of himself as "us" rather than "me"	Ge 1:26–27; 3:22; 11:7; Isa 6:8
God promises to send someone who is God	Isa 7:14; 9:6
The "angel of the LORD" speaks as if he is the Lord	Ge 16:10; 22:15–17; Ex 3:6; 23:20–23; Jdg 6:14

The Trinity in the NT	
Father, Son, and Holy Spirit have one name	Mt 28:19
Father, Son, and Holy Spirit were present at Jesus' baptism	Mt 3:16–17; Lk 3:21–22
The Spirit is sent by the Father through the Son	Jn 15:26
The Spirit testifies that we are God's children and co-heirs with Christ	Ro 8:16–17; Gal 4:4–6
One Spirit, one Lord Jesus, and one God	1Co 12:4–6
A blessing from Father, Son, and Holy Spirit	2Co 13:14
Chosen by the Father, sprinkled with Jesus' blood, and sanctified by the Spirit	1Pe 1:2
The Spirit testifies that Jesus came from the Father	1Jn 4:2
Other places in the NT where Father, Son, and Holy Spirit appear together	Ro 5:5–6; 1Th 1:2–5; 2Th 2:13; Tit 3:4–6; Jude 20–21
Holiness is ascribed to Father, Son, and Holy Spirit	Jn 17:11; Ro 1:4; 1Co 1:30
Eternity is ascribed to Father, Son, and Holy Spirit	1Ti 1:17; Heb 1:2–3, 8; 9:14
Father, Son, and Holy Spirit each know everything	Mt 6:8, 32; Jn 2:24–25; 1Co 2:10–11
Father, Son, and Holy Spirit are each all-powerful	Ps 135:5–7; Mt 28:18; Ro 15:13, 17; 1Co 15:24–27
Father, Son, and Holy Spirit are each everywhere present	Ps 139:7–10; Jer 23:24; Mt 28:20
Father, Son, and Holy Spirit all involved in creation	Ge 1:1–2; Ps 104:30; Jn 1:3
Father, Son, and Holy Spirit all involved in giving spiritual life	Eze 37:14; Jn 10:10; Eph 2:4–5
Father, Son, and Holy Spirit all involved in miracles	1Ki 18:38; Mt 4:23–24; Ro 15:19
Father, Son, and Holy Spirit all involved in teaching	Ps 71:17; Isa 48:17; Jn 13:13; 14:26
Father, Son, and Holy Spirit all experience grief because of sin	Ge 6:6; Lk 19:41–44; Eph 4:30

fellowship. Therefore they do not love because they do not know love. The antichrist can be "in the world" and evil spirits can be "in the false teachers," but "living in God" is possible only for the children of God.

5 In contrast to the "dear children" who "are from God" are the false teachers who "are from the world." The false teachers are successful "in the world" because their thinking is accommodated to the world's beliefs. Naturally the world hears such teachers gladly. The term "world" (GK *3180*) is probably to be understood in two ways: as a system of thought antithetical to Christian belief and as a description of those members of the community who were led astray by the false teachers. That some members of the community were easily persuaded to forsake the truth of the Gospel should not bewilder the faithful. Although these members appeared to belong to the community, their willingness to hear and follow the false teachers showed their true colors.

6 The author repeats the description of the true followers as "we [who] are from God." The "we" includes all the faithful but has particular reference to the true teachers. Whoever has knowledge of God through fellowship with him by loving him and abiding in him and his Word "listens to us" (cf. Jn 8:47; 10:4–5; 18:37), for the teachers proclaim the word heard "from the beginning" (cf. 1Jn 1:1). Thus a second test for discerning the presence of the Spirit of God has been added to the one developed in v.2. When people confess that Jesus came in the flesh, then the "Spirit of truth" has been present and active. When people deny the Gospel and will not confess that Jesus Christ has come in the flesh, then "the spirit of falsehood" has been at work.

IV. Requirements for Fellowship With God Who Is Love (4:7–5:12)

The third main division of the letter has as its major thesis an analysis of love. Love of one's brother was first introduced as a test of living in God who is light (2:9–11). The command to love received an even more significant treatment as a test of being born of God (3:10–24). Here love of fellow believers finds its most complete representation in the Father's own being and activity.

A. Brotherly Love (4:7–12)

7 The address "dear friends" (lit., "beloved"; cf. 2:7; 4:1) and the imperative force of the verb make clear that the author is speaking primarily to the community itself. His intention is to provide final assurance that the community's commitment to mutual love is the explicit requirement of the Gospel as revealed in God himself. Love for one's brother "comes from God." It is evidence of our being "born of God" that is as important as righteous behavior is (2:29). It is not a virtue innate in us nor is it learned behavior. It is "from God." He is the originator—the giver of love. Furthermore, whoever truly loves "his brother" not only is born of God (2:28; 3:24) but also "knows God."

8 Conversely, whoever does not love does not "know" God at all, for God in his very nature is love. To the statements, then, that God is light (1:5) and God is righteous (2:29), John adds the supreme statement "God is love [GK *27*]" (4:8, 16). Love here is not to be understood as one of God's many activities; rather, every activity of his is loving activity. Since this is true of God, our failure to love can only mean that we have no true knowledge of God, we have not really been born of him, and we do not have his nature.

9 The simple but profound statement "God is love" is explained by what God did. "He sent his one and only Son into the world" (cf. Jn 3:16–17). The author makes clear that the love he speaks of involves concrete actions. God's love required him to send his Son. God's love in us requires deeds by which we show our love for one another. The purpose of God's act is "that we might live through him." Death is our present condition (cf. 3:14); God intended that we might find life in him so that we might live in love as he works in and through us.

10 The author now distinguishes *agape* love from any love claimed by the false teachers. It is not that "we loved God" (3:17; 4:20), as his opponents claimed, but that "he loved us." *Agape* love can be given to God only when it has first been received from God. It exists only as response to his initial love for us. Moreover, God's love for us defines what true love requires—the commitment to sacrifice one's most beloved possession for another's gain. So for God, love required that he send "his Son as an atoning sacrifice [see comment on 2:2] for our sins."

The difference in understanding between John and the false teachers is never greater than in their understanding of love. The false teachers claimed to love God but understood love not in Christian terms but in those of Greek philosophy. Love in the Hellenistic world became a mystical craving for union with the eternal. Two things derive from this understanding of love. First, love for God as expressed by the false teachers becomes primarily an exercise in self-gratification. Second, one can never attribute love to God and say, for example, that God loves us. God as the Absolute is always passionless and unmoved, according to them.

11 The author continues to show that the true nature of love is unselfish and sacrificial. In 3:16 he appealed to Jesus, who laid down his life for believers, as the example for them to follow. Now he directs attention to God's own example: "Since God so loved us, we also ought to love one another." The nature of John's argument is not deductive but analogical. Just as God's children must be holy because he is holy (cf. Lev 11:44–45; 1Pe 1;15ff.) and merciful because he is merciful (Lk 6:36), so they must love because he loves. We must be like him.

12 Here most commentators see a reference to the false teachers who may have claimed "visions" of God—visions through which their own knowledge was mediated to them. John's response is the blanket rejection: "No one has ever seen God." But the conclusion he moves toward is different from that expected from the gospel of John. Instead of saying, "God the only Son, who is at the Father's side, has made him known" (Jn 1:18), he turns rather to love: "If we love each other," we know that God is present with us. As God was once present in his Son, so now he is present through the community of faith. And it is in this community that love has its ultimate fulfillment. With this conclusion, we can begin to understand a little better John's urgent concern for the "fellowship" of the community of believers. It was not an optional "blessing" or "fruit" of belief that so deeply concerned him but the basic question of God's presence and manifestation in the world through a community that has a love originating in him.

B. Living in God and Living in Love (4:13–16)

In v.12 the author linked living in God to loving one another. In 3:24 he linked living with God to obeying his commands. There, as here, the primary evidence for this relationship with God is the Holy Spirit. And it is the Spirit who enables us to testify that "the Father has sent his Son to be the Savior of the world" (4:14; cf. 4:2). Whoever confesses this also knows that God is present in them and that they live "in God" (v.15). Those who know they live in God know also that they live in his love (v.16).

13 Reciprocal abiding (2:24; 4:13, 15—God in us, we in God) is the final expression of fellowship with God. It is possible only through the gift of his Spirit, by whom the relationship with the Father and with the Son is sealed eternally (cf. Eph 1:13–14). Reciprocal abiding makes possible God's love for us and our love for him. It is also the reason we can love one another.

14 To whom does the "we" refer in the statement "we have seen and testify"? It certainly refers to all those, especially the apostles, who had direct knowledge of Jesus' earthly life; but it probably ought not to be limited to them. It is the Spirit working in them and in us who permits us to "see" in the historic event of Jesus' death God's act for our salvation. Although "no one has ever seen God" (v.12) at any time, we do "see" (GK *2517*) by faith that the cross of Christ was for our sins and for our salvation. We do "see" in Jesus our own Savior and Lord. We do "see" in the fellowship of faith the presence of his love. And because his Spirit in us gives us this "seeing" experience, we are commissioned to bear witness to the event (cf. Jn 15:26). Therefore, since there is such a close connection between seeing and testifying and the gift of the Holy Spirit, it is likely that the author meant his words to include his readers and to be applied to all Christians throughout history.

15 John goes on to state that "anyone" who "acknowledges" (lit., "confesses"; GK *3933*) God's act in his Son is included in the divine fellowship in which the Father is in the believers and the believers in the Father. Initially John connected the fellowship with obedience to the command to love one another (3:24). Then he showed its dependence on the gift of the Spirit (4:13). Here he shows that the fellowship is built on Jesus, who must be acknowledged as being one with the Father (2:23), as the one who came in the flesh (4:2), and as the Son of God who was sent "to be the Savior of the world" (4:14–15).

16 The same combination of knowing and believing is found in Peter's confession of Jesus in Jn 6:69, except that there the order of "believe" and "know" is reversed. The fact is that faith may lead to knowledge and knowledge may lead to faith. Here knowledge of God's love necessarily precedes the ability to "rely" on that love. The sequence of thought is this: First, we must know and rely on the fact that God loves us. Second, we come to realize through relying on his love (or having faith in his Son—the meaning is the same) that in his very nature God is love. Third, we discover that to live in God means to live in love. The fellowship we have with the Father and with the Son (1:3) is perceived as nothing other than a fellowship of love.

C. Love Displaces Fear (4:17–18)

17 The perfection or completeness of love brings "confidence" (GK *4244*), confidence relating especially to the time of judgment (cf. 2:28), though John probably believed that it was the mark of a believer in every relationship to God (cf. 3:21; 5:14). He may have introduced the judgment theme in the context of the commandment to love because Jesus himself made this command so specific and established love as the basis for judgment. Not to love, therefore, is to disobey Jesus and to spurn the Father's own love in sending Jesus. To live in love, however, is to live in God, and this results in complete confidence for prayer and judgment.

The meaning of "because in this world, we are like him" is uncertain. In view of the context, it is best to understand these words to mean that just as Jesus "abides" in the love of the Father (cf. Jn 15:10), an abiding that already marked his earthly existence and gave him "confidence" before God in the face of temptation, trial, and death, so "in this world" we also may abide in the Father's love and share in that same confidence.

18 The other side of confidence is "fear" (GK *5832*). If we truly abide in the Father's love, we will be without fear. That "perfect love drives out fear" should be taken as a Christian truism as well as an allusion to the fear of God in judgment. Love and fear are incompatible. They cannot coexist. For the Christian love is first an experience of the Father's love for us. That "love" is so powerful and life changing that when we know it, we are forever removed from the "fear" of God.

The fear spoken of here is not to be confused with reverence for God. Reverence will only deepen through the experience of God's love. The experience of the holiness of God's love makes us desire to be even more obedient to his commands. But it also removes us from the power of fear. Whatever may take place in this world cannot nullify the power of his love or separate us from it. Similarly, if we experience fear in any portion of our lives, to that extent we deny God's love and fail to trust him.

D. Love Summarized (4:19–21)

19 In summarizing the command to love one's brother, John begins with his most important truth. Love must never be conceived of as a "natural" experience of the natural man. There is a "natural" love, but it must not be confused with divine love (*agape*; GK *27*). The love John speaks of originates with the Father, became manifest in and through the Son, and now characterizes the life of the children of God. He thus begins this summary by saying, "We love." The love with which we love is not our own. It is always God's love or Jesus' love in us. But because we abide in the Father and in the Son, the love becomes also our own love. It is not that God reveals his love apart from us or in spite of us, but that he invites us to love even as he loves. So we return to him his own love and love him with the gift of his love. So also we love our fellow believers with the love God has loved us with.

20 The confidence we have in knowing that God loves us delivers us from fear but not from responsible action. In fact, God's love for us and in us sets us free to love our brother and sister even as God loves them. To fail this test of love proves that one's claim to love God is a lie—just as the previous claims to have fellowship with God while walking in darkness (1:6), to know him while disobeying his commands (2:4), or to possess the Father while denying his Son were lies (2:22–23). John has a double sense in "liar." A liar does not speak the truth in that what he claims is false, and his actions show that he has divorced himself from the reality of God.

The second part of the verse is problematic. It most likely means that if one fails the test of loving a visible brother, such a one makes it certain that he or she does not love the invisible God; this proves that such a person has no true love at all.

21 The final warrant of the life of love is obedience to the teaching of Christ. He gave the command that "whoever loves God must also love his brother" (cf. Mk 12:30–31; also Jn 13:34). John makes clear that obedience expresses itself in a single command. Love for God and love for neighbor are inseparable. The one is not possible apart from the other. Those who love God cannot refuse love to the image of God that meets them in their fellow believers. We are to love our neighbors in God, and God in our neighbors; this is what remaining in his love means.

E. Love for the Father and Faith in the Son (5:1–5)

The author now focuses on the relationship of the three fundamental elements so important to him in the knowledge of God: faith, love, and obedience. "To believe, have faith" (GK *4409*), first introduced at 3:23, becomes the primary term in this section. In John, faith requires not only that something is held true, but that someone has entered into one's life. A commitment has been made and a relationship established that one can then only "confess" (cf. 3:23; 4:2, 4, 15).

1 The argument parallels 4:19. Even as we love only because God first loved us, so also our belief is possible only because we have first been "born of God." The author is not addressing the question of incorporation into the family of God but is rather looking only at its result. "Believing" in Jesus is a direct consequence of our "having been born" of God and therefore becomes a test or proof of that birth. From this the author moves to a truism from nature: whoever loves one's progenitor will also love those similarly born, even one's brothers and sisters.

2 This statement troubles commentators because it reverses what is expected. One anticipates a conclusion like this: "And this is how we know that we love God: by loving his children and obeying his commands." Instead the author concludes: "This is how we know that we love the children of God: by loving God and carrying out his commands." Even as one cannot love God without loving his children, so also it is impossible to truly love the children of God without loving God also. Those who claim to love their brothers and not God have not truly recognized their brothers as those born of God and have not offered them the true love that comes from the Father. The author cannot really talk of loving God, however, without also linking his words to obedience to his commands.

3 The connection between love for God and obedience is meant to protect us against thinking of love for God as "emotional feelings" about God. *Agape* love requires action. In respect to humankind, it means willingness to lay down one's life. In respect to God, it means a life of willing obedience, a filial relationship with God, and service on behalf of God. It requires laying down one's life as being one's own possession and taking up a new life in response to a Lord and Master.

John now qualifies what he has just said by adding, "And his commands are not burdensome." To the natural man the will of God is strange; the requirement for righteousness, foreign and hard. Even the law of love is a burden. But when God enters into us and we trust God's Son, then his yoke becomes gentle and the burden light (cf. Mt 11:30). We who have been born of God have within us a desire and a yearning for the Father. Seeking and hungering after righteousness becomes our joy (Mt 5:6). Living the life of love becomes our delight. The commands of God bring us the freedom and the liberty we so ardently long for.

4 "Everyone [lit., everything] born of God overcomes the world." Our being born of God is God's act on our behalf, through which he moves to overcome the world. What is in view is the supernatural act by which human beings are being translated out of the kingdom of death into the kingdom of life through the Son.

The victory that overcomes the world is now identified with "our faith." It is best to interpret this statement as referring to a past event; John is emphasizing that the victory he

5 Observe the progression of thought in what John says about how victory over the world is gained. It begins with the new birth (v.4a). It moves on to the believer's experience and act of faith (v.4b). It culminates in the confession that "Jesus is the Son of God." Victory requires the whole process. It assures us that we too can love God and the children of God and that we too can obey his commands (v.3). Belief, love, and obedience are all the marks of the new birth. And the life lived in the new birth is not a burden but a life of celebration. This was the experience of the apostles and of the early church. Paul's cry that "in all these things we are more than conquerors" (Ro 8:37) echoed throughout the Roman world. Whereas at first the victories were thought of in terms of alien powers on the outside, Christian consciousness soon perceived that the victory included the internal enemies that confront the conscience, assail Christian beliefs and standards, corrupt the soul, and negate the life of love and obedience to God.

The confession with which the victory is linked is again the confession that "Jesus is the Son of God" (cf. 2:2–4:15). This is where the author began; it is also where he will end. Every single tenet of belief in God and of knowledge about him depends on obedient confession and commitment that Jesus is the eternal life that was with the Father (1:2). He is the Son of God. This confession has in view the false teachers who acknowledge Christ the Redeemer but deny his true humanity. Verse 5 makes the transition to the final exposition regarding the Son and provides the base on which the final section develops: the witness of the Father to the Son.

F. The Spirit, the Water, and the Blood (5:6–12)

6a Jesus, the Son of God (v.5) and the Christ (v.1), came not just by water, but "by water and blood." This enigmatic statement has given rise in the church to many interpretations. Augustine linked the reference to Jn 19:34, where the piercing of Jesus' side produced water and blood. Calvin and Luther connected it to Jn 4 and 6 and saw in it a reference to the sacraments. Most commentators today see the "water" as referring to Jesus' baptism and the "blood" to his death on the cross. Even though John's gospel does not describe the water baptism of Jesus, the Johannine community could not have been ignorant of it.

The purpose of the statement seems clear. The author once more affirms that it is the historical Jesus who is the Christ, the Son of God. Although the false teachers may have acknowledged Christ as the Savior, the divine Son of God, they denied his true human existence. Like Cerinthus, they probably held that the Christ came on the man Jesus at his baptism and remained till the time of the Crucifixion. In this way they could deny that the Christ had ever been truly human and subject to suffering and death. John rightly regards this as a denial of the redemptive activity of God. It was the Son of God who came into the world. It was this same divine Son who was baptized and received the Spirit. It was the Son who, with the Father's approval and in fulfillment of the Father's intention, shed his blood on the cross to redeem humanity. God would not be involved in human redemption apart from the Christ's true humanity, suffering, and dying. Water and blood become, therefore, the key words of the true understanding of the Incarnation.

Once the author had arrived at his primary understanding, he likely saw in the incident of Jn 19:34 a divine confirmation of it. He may also have seen the reference to the water in Jn 4:10, 14 and to drinking his blood in Jn 6:53 as confirmation. But these flow from the facts that are the historic base for them all. Jesus, the Son of God, came through the water of baptism. He came also through the Cross. This coming by water and blood is the basis of our salvation.

6b "And it is the Spirit who testifies" (cf. Jn 14:26; 15:26; 16:8, 12), because the Spirit, as ultimate truth, is the only one capable of so bearing witness (cf. 1Jn 3:24; 4:13). One cannot receive the witness concerning the Son of God by oneself. There are no human categories available through which one can understand it. God's redemptive act in Christ is not a bit of data humankind can deduce for itself by analogical reasoning. Like the Resurrection, it can only be announced. And this time it is not made known by angels (cf. Lk 24:6) but by the Spirit of God.

The Spirit bore witness historically in Jesus' baptism by coming down from heaven as a dove and remaining on him (Jn 1:32). At Jesus' death on the cross, the "blood and water" that flowed from his side bore witness and led to the following statement: "The man who saw it has given testimony, and his testimony is true. He knows that he tells the truth, and he testifies so that you also may believe" (Jn 19:35). But here in v.6 the present tense of the verb indicates that John wants to show that the Spirit continues in his witness to the community of believers.

7–8 "For there are three that testify: the Spirit, the water and the blood." Does the author mean that the Spirit still witnesses through the biblical Word in which Jesus' baptism and death are recounted, or that the Spirit gives witness to the community of the efficacy of the historic baptism and death through the rites of water baptism and communion? Probably the author is pointing to the former as having priority but not so as to exclude the latter. The biblical word confirms the prophetic word that the Spirit prophesied (cf. 2Pe 1:20–21).

But how does the Spirit give witness in the living voice of prophecy? Presumably he does it inwardly and supernaturally. The Spirit opens eyes and ears to perceive what God is declaring through his proclaimed word (cf. 1Co 12:3). He does not declare his own words, but through inward conviction he confirms the proclamation as being indeed the truth (cf. Ac 5:32). The Spirit provides what humanity is unable to acquire for itself. This witness of the Spirit accompanies every presentation of the word. The text contained in the NIV footnote made its way into the KJV through the Latin Vulgate. Most scholars agree that it is a later, though orthodox, addition to the text and is not part of John's reiginal letter.

9 The divine witness is not limited to the Spirit but includes the witness of the Father. His witness is greater than the authenticated witness of a human being because of the nature of the one who gives it and of its greater trustworthiness (cf. Jn 5:36–37; 1Jn 3:20). It was his voice that confirmed that Jesus' "passion" was an act in which God would glorify himself (Jn 12:28–30). So also it is God's own voice that is being heard again in the threefold witness.

10a Here the fact that the incarnate and crucified Jesus is God's own Son is clearly set forth. Those who believe this testimony receive the Father's own witness in their hearts that they are right to trust in Christ. Faith itself is God's own gift to the believer to lay hold of the Father. "Believing" becomes a "receiving," and the work of God in Christ results in forgiveness of sins and inward establishment of the love of God. Faith in the Son immediately becomes faith in the Father (cf. 2:23).

10b The gravity of receiving this witness is now demonstrated by the corollary: "Anyone who does not believe [the witness borne by] God [about the Son] has made him out to be a liar." To receive the Son is to receive the Father. To deny the Son is to deny the Father. John, then, cannot allow that one can profess belief in God, as did his opponents, and yet reject God's own testimony to his Son. Such rejection cannot be excused on the basis of ignorance. Rather, it is deliberate unbelief, the character of which in the end impugns the very being and character of God. If Jesus is not God's own Son in the flesh, then God is no longer the truth. He is the liar.

11–12 That Jesus is God's Son is established by God's own witness from the time of Jesus' baptism up to and including his suffering and death. It is a testimony given through the Spirit and confirmed in the heart of those who believe in the Son. The consequence of accepting this testimony from God is the fulfillment of the promise John made in 1:2 to bear witness and to testify to that "eternal life" that was with the Father and has now appeared to us in the Son. Eternal life (which is nothing less than fellowship with the Father, with the Son, and with his people) is present in his Son. Those who have the Son have this life. Those who are without the Son are without life. It is not an idea or a system of belief or even a fact that is the ultimate object of faith; it is a Person. That Person is Jesus Christ. He is to live in us (3:24). His love is to abide and be made complete in us (4:12). We are to live in him (4:13). And this is life eternal.

V. Concluding Remarks (5:13–21)

13 This verse makes the transition from the main argument to the epilogue. It reminds us of Jn 20:31, where the author said he had written his gospel so that his readers might believe in Jesus and receive eternal life in his name. This first letter of John is addressed to those who have accepted this belief but still need assurance that through this name they have indeed received eternal life. So the author refers six times in vv.15–20 (in addition to v.13) to what we believers *know* (GK *3857*).

The false teachers present a different "knowledge" as well as a different lifestyle. The author counters with a series of tests by which the believers can evaluate the false teachers' claims and practices. Walking in the light, obeying his commands, loving one's brother, being steadfast in the community of faith, doing what is right—these serve as tests of whether the life that is from God has been received. When it has been received, it is only because God's witness to his own Son as the source of that life has been accepted and believed. On this basis, we can expect God to hear us in prayer, free us from the presence and power of sin, and forgive our transgressions. Those who know these things know also that they have received eternal life.

14 The "confidence" (GK *4244*) we have in our life with Christ belongs not only in the future time of his coming (2:28) and of judgment (4:17) but also in the present and especially in the fellowship of prayer. We know that we have access to him (3:21) and that "he hears us." "Hearing" does not mean simply to be listened to but to be heard favorably (cf. Jn 11:41–42). The expectation is, of course, linked to the qualifying clause, "if we ask according to his will" (cf. Mt 6:10; Mk 14:36).

It is not any prayer that is answered but the confident prayer of the disciple who is in fellowship with the Father, who asks in Jesus' name (Jn 14:13; 15:16), who "remains" in him (Jn 15:7), and who obeys his commands (1Jn 3:22). This is not meant to dampen the expectation we may have in prayer, but the condition for addressing God is to know he will hear and act. Prayer becomes not only a time for petitioning but of yielding one's life to the will and work of God. Prayer made in these circumstances is always heard because it is God's will that is being done and his intention for humankind that is being met.

15 John now states that the "confidence" (v.14) for approaching God and asking him anything is absolute. A paraphrase of the text is as follows: "Since we know that he hears us whenever we ask in his will, we may also know with equal certainty that we possess the requests we have made the moment we have prayed."

That our petition is answered is not dependent on whether or not we have personally observed the answer. Some answers to prayer are recognized immediately, others later, and some are not recognized in our lifetime. But this is not the author's point. When we pray as Jesus prayed, in full accord with the Father's will, we can know that we have our requests because God has made them his own and his will must be done. What is required of us is simply the faith to believe that this is so and that his will will be done on earth as it is in heaven, and then decide to live accordingly. The author is exalting faith in the will of God and its relation to our privilege to pray. He is echoing Jesus' own words in Mk 11:24.

16a The author turns from confidence in prayer to the ministry of prayer. Although he does not give the basis for his statement, what he says about intercessory prayer follows logically from what he has been teaching. If love requires the willingness to lay down one's life for a member of the community (3:16), then certainly it follows that if one sees a brother commit sin, such a person must intercede for him in prayer. Not to pray for him would be as much a betrayal of God's love as to withhold material aid from him (3:17). Moreover, when we pray for a brother or a sister who commits sin, we can know that such a prayer is "according to his [God's] will" because Christ is the atoning sacrifice for sins (2:2); and if we confess our sins, he is committed to forgive us (1:9).

But why should a brother need such intercession? Why does he not pray for himself and make his own confession? We can only speculate as to John's answer. Perhaps again it is a matter of assurance. The brother may need to be forgiven through intercessory prayer as an expression of the community's forgiveness. Because the sin was presumably committed after entrance into the Christian community, the need to confess the sin to another and to have received assurance of forgiveness may have had special significance. Also, there might be an allusion here to Jesus' words in Jn 20:23.

16b The author comments that intercession is not required if it involves a "sin that leads to death." This is puzzling. We do not know exactly what the author has in mind. Judaism distinguished between deliberate sins—sins of open rebellion against God that were punishable by death—and inadvertent sins that can be atoned for (Lev 4; Nu 15:22, 29). First-century Judaism retained this pattern. In the Johannine community some such distinction was presumably made, hence the limitation "sin that leads to death." Why does he make such an exception? Presumably because he is speaking of spiritually efficacious prayer—prayer that will lead to eternal life. Such prayer can be made only for those who are rooted in God's life and love.

Who specifically is excluded from efficacious prayer? The text offers no clues. The sin mentioned might refer to the blasphemy against the Holy Spirit (Mk 3:29). But the content of the letter may point to the suggestion that John has in mind the sin of false teaching. For life to be given to those who deny Jesus Christ, hate their brothers, and refuse the witness of God would be a contradiction. Since such persons deny the mercy of God, prayer for them would appear to be limited to asking for their repentance and conversion to God's truth.

17 Earlier John defined sin as "lawlessness" (3:4). Now he adds "unrighteousness" (NIV, "wrongdoing"; GK 94). Possibly some in the community, knowing that God's children were not to sin (3:9–10), attempted to deal with the problem of Christians' sinning by limiting sin to deliberate or lawless acts. If so, John will have none of it. *All* wrongdoing is sin, even when done by the children of God. But not all sin results in death. John aims first at honesty (cf. 1:8) and only then at resolution. Sin is not dealt with by denial but by confession and by community intercession (v.16). Where this intercession occurs, the divine life of God is present and fellowship with God occurs. Within this life and fellowship, the blood of Jesus Christ purifies believers from all sin (1:7).

18 John concludes by stating three certainties that characterize his position over against the false teachers: (1) We know that anyone born of God does not continue in sin (v.18). (2) We know that we are the children of God (v.19). (3) We know that the Son of God has come and has given us certain, definite knowledge about himself (v.20). John has never wavered from the priority of the ethical requirement, nor does he do so now. Christians must not walk in darkness (1:7). They must not hate their fellow believers (2:10). They must not live a life of sin (3:6).

However noble the sentiments expressed by the false teachers, the test of the truth of God is conduct. A sinful life is totally incompatible with the life received from God. John is not unaware of the difficulties involved in living the new life or of the quality of the opposition from the evil one. He knows the wiles of the evil one and expects them. Nonetheless, he has been adamant in his confidence that the evil one need not prevail, because of the presence of the power of God in the believer.

Already John has shown that if those who live in God do not sin (3:6), no one born of God and possessing the divine life of God will fall victim to the life of sin (3:9). To this he now adds that the Son of God himself (i.e., "the one who was born of God") will keep him safe from the evil one (see comment on 2:13b). The phrase "keeps safe" (GK *5498*) recalls Jesus' words in Jn 17:12, 15.

19 The second affirmation builds on the first one (v.18), but emphasizes the positive consequence: "We know that we are children of God." The author now openly identifies himself with the community of faith and stresses the personal quality of the relationships involved in fellowship (cf. 1:3) with the Father. We know we "belong to him." And how is this known? It is not by boastful claims, like those made by the false teachers, but on the basis of the "tests of eternal life" that are substantiated by life and action. As we exhibit the marks of God's family, we demonstrate that we belong to the Father. In contrast to the true community that belongs to God (cf. Jn 8:47) is the rest of the world, which lies under the control of the evil one (cf. 2:15–17). Clearly there is no middle ground for the author. To be born of God is to be safe from the power of the evil one. Not to be born of God is to be wholly under the power of the evil one.

20 John's third and final affirmation is in fact the summary of the letter. It affirms the point of dispute with the false teachers. Christian faith has to do with Jesus Christ. He is the "Word of life" (1:1), "the eternal life" (v.2), which was with the Father and through the Incarnation came into human history. By his coming, we can know the true God and have fellowship with him. But the false teachers said that this relationship was apart from the Son. Fellowship with God as they taught it came through divine "knowledge" of the subject. From the beginning John denied this teaching. The reality of God can be known only through apprehending the reality that is in the Son. This comes through revelation that is grounded in the facts of history. It requires that we know Jesus Christ as God's Son and that we live our lives entirely in him. We know by this experiential life in the Son that we are also in the Father and that the Son is indeed the true God, the author of eternal life.

"He" in v.20b is translates "this one"; grammatically it most naturally refers to Jesus Christ (though some refer it to God as "him who is true"). Here at the climax of the letter John ascribes full deity to Jesus. After all, this is the crux of his argument and the basis for his statement that he who is in Jesus is in the Father. For Jesus Christ as the author of eternal life, see v.11; also Jn 11:25; 14:6.

21 John closes on an affectionate note and with a final admonition. "Dear children" (cf. 3:7; 4:4) reminds his readers of his genuine commitment to them. The exhortation "keep yourselves from idols" at first glance seems out of place. Idolatry has not so much as been mentioned in the letter. Although the warning may be understood as a general admonition to avoid any contact with paganism, it is more likely that the warning represents a final characterization of the "heresy" represented by the false teachers. False teaching is ultimately "apostasy from the true faith." To follow after it is to become nothing better than an idol worshiper, especially if it is a matter of the truth of one's conception of God. The author is blunt. The false teachers propose not the worship of the true God, made known in his Son Jesus, but a false god—an idol they have invented.

2 John

INTRODUCTION

For comments on the background, purpose, authorship, and date of this letter, see the introduction to 1 John.

EXPOSITION

I. Introduction (1–3)

The introduction is a normal epistolary salutation. The author is identified as "the elder" (cf. 3Jn l); the recipients are identified as "the chosen lady and her children"; and an appropriate Christian greeting is extended (v.3).

1 "Elder" (GK *4565*) can mean an old man, a senior person deserving respect, or a senior official of a local church (cf. Ac 11:30; 14:23; 1Ti 5:17). The author of this brief letter must have been so well known and established to those he was writing to that the title "elder" immediately identified him. That he assumes authority over them, though he is obviously not a member of their church, suggests that he was more than a local pastor. He probably held an influential position (like that of a bishop) in the region where his readers lived. That "the elder" was also the writer of the first letter and that he was the apostle John is a valid inference (see the introduction to 1 John).

The designation of the letter's addressee raises questions. "Chosen lady" in Greek is *Eclecta Kyria* (GK *1723* & *3257*). From ancient times opinion has been divided as to whether this letter was addressed to an anonymous noble lady named "Eclecta" or "Kyria," or to a Christian community metaphorically identified as "the chosen lady and her children"; those differences continue yet today.

While a strict interpretation supports an individual person as the addressee, the context supports an enigmatic reference to a Christian community. Such a veiled allusion may have been a device for shielding the identity of the community from adverse action by public officials who opposed the Christian community. If the letter fell into unfriendly hands, it would seem to be nothing more than a private message to a friend. The greetings extended to them from the children of her "chosen sister" (v.13) would be understood as being from the members of the community of "the elder." The statement "whom I love in the truth—and not I only, but also all who know the truth" seems more appropriate as a reference to a church than to an individual.

The linking of "truth" (GK *237*) and "love" (GK *26*) is of great importance. Because John's readers are in the truth—i.e., they know Jesus as the Christ, the Father's Son—they are also the recipients of God's love as it is known and manifested in the community of faith. And the love received by the community comes from all who know the truth. The author is speaking in clear contrast to the heretics. They do not have the truth, nor do they know what it means to be in the community of love.

2 John goes on to explain why the community of love can be so inclusive. Love relates to the truth, which lives in us and will be with us forever. Truth, for him, is more than what is objectively known. It is that which indwells believers, permeating their whole existence. Because it is the truth of God, it has no temporal limitation. Love and truth are not passing sentiments, nor are they dependent on depths of emotional feeling or the strength of one's personal commitment. Love and truth originate in God. Like him, they endure without changing, and their splendor never fades.

3 At the time John's letters were written, the salutation of a letter ended with a greeting. Most of the NT letters follow this custom but give it a special Christian character, such as "grace and peace to you" (Ro 1:7; cf. 1Pe 1:2) or "grace, mercy and peace from God the Father and Christ Jesus our Lord" (1Ti 1:2).

According to tradition, the apostle John served as the pastor of Ephesus in his latter years. Although during his time there were no specific church buildings, the Christians at Ephesus eventually built a huge basillica, whose remains are still visible.

Here, however, John adds a significant variation to this custom. Rather than wishing or praying that God may grant us peace, he turns it into a promise that God's mercy and grace will be ours if we truly remain in his truth and love. In the next section, "truth" and "love" continue to be the chief topic.

II. A Formal Word of Instruction (4–11)

A. An Exhortation (4–6)

4 The author continues to follow the custom of his time by expressing his pleasure in writing to his readers. Like other Christian writers, John relates this note of "joy" to their spiritual state, for they are faithful to the truth.

The force of "some" in v.4 is disputed. Some think that the elder had met only some members of the community, and it is to them he refers here. It seems more likely, however, that news of the church had been brought to the elder and that part of this news was that the church had suffered division as a consequence of the work of the heretics. But John rejoices that some of the children remained true to the faith that he had delivered to them and that he had just referred to in v.2. The next clause—"just as the Father commanded us"—seems to relate to "the truth" they heard "from the beginning" (v.5). The commandment received from the Father is explained in v.5 as the commandment of love and in v.7 as belief in the Son (cf. 1Jn 3:23).

5 Clearly for John the commandment of love has precedence here, just as it does in 1Jn 4:21. It is not that love precedes truth or belief but that love offers the clearest test of the truthfulness of the confession and the sincerity of the obedience given to God's commands. Belief may be feigned and confession only of the lips, but love is harder to counterfeit. The elder is not requiring something new but that which has been the supreme and final word "from the beginning." Love for one another is what the Father required (1Jn 4:7), the Son manifested (1Jn 3:16), and the Spirit makes available through life in him (1Jn 4:13–15).

6 Four times in vv.4–6 the author uses the noun "command" (GK *1953*). This is his way of making clear that what he is saying is a direct expression of God's will. And how does one know that one is fulfilling that will? The test of love is obedience to God's commands, and the test of obedience is whether one "walks in love." The argument is intentionally circular. Love of God must result in obedience to the Word of God or it is not true love, like God's gift in Jesus Christ. Jesus' own love was manifested by his obedience even to death. Love of God can finally be expressed only in action and truth (1Jn 3:18). Do we love our brother and sister? Are we prepared to die for them? Obedience that does not lead to the life of love in which we love one another even to death is not obedience offered to God. Not to love means to remain in darkness (1Jn 2:11) and in death (1Jn 3:14). Hatred of one's brother is obedience to and gratification of one's own evil nature (cf. 1Jn 3:12) and has nothing to do with God.

B. A Warning (7–11)

7 This verse is reminiscent of 1Jn 2:18, 27; 4:1–3. The "deceivers" (GK *4418*) are those who have left the believing community for the world. It is unlikely that those who went out were members of the "lady's" community. More likely they were members of the original community of the elder. Nonetheless, they may have been known to the community here addressed and were therefore a risk to that community also. What distinguishes them is their unwillingness to acknowledge that Jesus Christ has come in the flesh. Curiously the tense is changed from the past tense, "has come in the flesh" (1Jn 4:2), to the present participle, "as coming in the flesh." It would be possible, therefore, to interpret this as a reference to Jesus' return in the flesh (cf. 1Jn 2:28; 3:2). But since we know of no controversy in this area, this seems unlikely. John's intention is to say something beyond what he said in 1Jn 4:2. What the present tense emphasizes is the timeless character of the event (cf. Jn 3:31; 6:14; 11:27). It is not simply an event in history but an "abiding truth," defining the union between humanity and deity that is present in Jesus' person. This union is not limited to Jesus' historical manifestation but remains true of him as the one at the right hand of the Father.

8 In this verse, some manuscripts read, "Watch out that you do not lose what *you* have worked for," while others have, "Watch out that you do not lose what *we* have worked for." It is difficult to ascertain which one John actually wrote, though "we" seems preferable (cf. Gal 4:11, 19). As messengers of Christ, the apostles could not help but feel completely involved in the lives of their charges (cf. Php 2:16). Whether or not they actually planted all the churches under their wings is beside the point. Though Paul did not establish the Christian communities in Rome and Colosse, he accepted full responsibility for them and wrote to them. Similarly, as one in charge of the message that was "from the beginning," all of John's labors were directed to the maintenance of the truth that Jesus Christ has come in the flesh. If anyone failed to continue in this message, in a real sense John's apostolic mission had failed. That the reader would lose was self-evident, but so would the community of faith and John himself (i.e., "we").

"Rewarded fully" suggests that John envisions two possibilities. In this verse John addresses one situation, in which a reader is partially deceived and so loses some of his reward for faithfulness and perseverance. One receives according to his or her work. (For more on the concept of "rewards," see Mt 5:12; Jn 4:36; 1Co 3:8; Rev 11:18; 22:12.)

9 John's second possibility is a more radical departure from the faith: "Anyone who goes too far" (better than NIV's "Anyone who runs ahead"). The situation here implies not a loss of reward but of God himself, the loss or nonattainment of eternal life as promised in 1Jn 2:25.

The "teaching of Christ" can be construed as teaching about Christ or as the teaching that Christ himself did. The first option would be referring to the teaching that Jesus Christ has indeed come in the flesh. It is of little importance, however, which alternative is accepted, because the author holds equally to both positions. For Jesus Christ to be acknowledged as the one come in the flesh is fundamental to the faith, and for us to love one another (as taught by Jesus) is equally fundamental. To confess the former requires the latter. To have the Father and the Son is to have precisely what the false teachers have lost. To give up the Son is to lose the Father (cf. Jn 5:23; 14:6–7).

10–11 The last warning extended to the reader is both the most objective and the most final. "If anyone comes to you and does not bring this teaching, do not take him into your house or welcome him." The author is not certain what will happen in the lady's community. Probably he expects that the false teachers will soon arrive with their pernicious propaganda. If so, the situation is dangerous. They must not be shown hospitality, as if they were brothers in the faith. They are deceivers, and thus it would be a mockery of the Father and a sin against Christ to give those who deny the Son and hate fellow believers any place of respect within the community of faith. To do so means becoming a partaker in their unbelief and hatred of the truth.

This statement is all the more remarkable since it comes from the "apostle of love." Moreover, the command to extend hospitality is deeply rooted in the tradition (Ro 12:13; 1Ti 3:2; 5:3–10; Tit 1:8; Heb 13:2; 1Pet 4:8–10). It was an absolute demand that brothers in Christ be supported, fed, and housed by the local congregations they visited. Nevertheless, the elder invokes a higher principle here. False prophets, antichrists, and deceivers are not to share in the provision of hospitality. Even the Christian greetings that might be given ever so casually are forbidden in the case of the false teachers. One cannot serve God and mammon simultaneously (Mt 6:24). One cannot be a partner of God and a partner of the devil (1Co 10:20).

Clearly the elder's words are an offense to some today and are not considered worthy of the church. Admittedly great care should be exercised before applying such a radical withholding of hospitality from anyone. For the elder it was applied only to those who were committed to destroying the faith of the community. The issue involved more than disagreements in interpretation or personal misunderstandings among members of the body of Christ. It was clearly defined unbelief, and it involved active and aggressive promotion of perversions of truth and practice that struck at the heart of Christianity.

But ought not persons who had gone so far astray be dealt with all the more in love? Do they not require even more by way of grace, mercy, and forgiveness of Christ? At the personal level, Christians should always be prepared to turn the other cheek and seek tirelessly to be reconciled with others. But only those whose own faith is secure and whose understanding beyond corruption can do this. Unfortunately, the community of the elect lady was not yet in this position. It was not mature enough to deal with such deadly deviations; in fact, it was more likely that it might be destroyed by them. The responsibility of parents may furnish an analogy. Parents must discriminate as to whom even among their relatives they entertain in their home. Some relatives might be of such questionable character as to menace the moral, spiritual, and physical welfare of the children. Such relatives must be excluded. Parents must balance their concern for their relatives with their responsibility for their children. It is important to note that John does not suggest that the elect lady and her children deal with the false teachers in hatred or retaliate against them. Instead, he counsels that the false teachers be kept at a distance lest their heresy destroy the young church.

We today can only be grateful that the infant church took heresy regarding the person of Christ seriously. Christianity stands or falls with its Christology. From the human point of view, if John and other apostolic leaders had tolerated the "antichrists" who denied the basic truth of the Incarnation, the church might never have survived. We today benefit from the spiritual discernment and moral courage of John and others like him.

III. Conclusion (12–13)

12–13 The letter closes with a normal wish. The elder acknowledges that there is much more he might say, but he recognizes that it will be more effective if he were to say it in person (suggested by the phrase "face to face"). When the community of believers enjoys fellowship in Christ, one of the results of their fellowship is the "joy" of the Lord.

The "children" who sent "their greetings" were doubtless members of the elder's community who understood the plight of the community of the chosen lady; they wished to share John's concern to strengthen the bonds of love that unite all saints.

3 John

INTRODUCTION

For comments on the background, purpose, authorship, and date of this letter, see the introduction to 1 John.

EXPOSITION

I. Salutation (1)

Third John is a genuine letter written by "the elder" to a man named Gaius in another community. Although the letter is highly personal, it is also clearly official; the elder expresses thoughts that are meant to be shared with other members of the community. Concern for the situation in the church is the occasion for writing. The letter implies that Gaius was in an especially influential position and commends and supports him.

1 The "elder" (cf. comment on 2Jn 1; also the introduction to 1 John) addresses Gaius as "my dear friend"; his warm affection for Gaius permeates the letter. Although the name "Gaius" occurs elsewhere in the NT (cf. Ac 19:29; 20:4; Ro 16:23; 1Co 1:14) and is common enough in the literature of the time, his identity, aside from what is said of him in this letter, is unknown to us. He may have been a member of the church Diotrephes appears to have headed. But whether he held any official position in it is uncertain. Regarding "in the truth," see comment on 2Jn 1.

II. Personal Words to Gaius (2–4)

2 John's wishing good health to Gaius does not mean that Gaius was ill. This expression was a conventional one, and though it does not rule out the possibility of particular concern for Gaius's health, it does not necessitate it. John commends him by praying that things will be as well for his physical health as they have proved to be for his spiritual health. Implied in this verse is a tribute to the wholesome state of Gaius's spiritual life. Of how many Christians could their physical health be equated with their spiritual health? But the elder knew his man!

3 Behind this verse we see the flow of Christians between the early churches. This flow may have been occasioned in some instances by a change in personal circumstances and in others because of opposition and persecution. However, it may have been more intentional than this and may have represented, particularly among the Johannine churches, a commitment to live as a fellowship of Christians deeply concerned for one another.

Traveling missionaries and evangelists probably swelled the ranks of those who moved back and forth. Yet it is too much to read into the term "brothers" an exclusive reference to them. There was obviously a lively flow of persons between the church where Gaius was a member and the elder's community. Moreover, these men appear to be reporting to the elder as a normal and expected activity. They tell him about Gaius's faithfulness to Christian truth as well as about his sincerity and faithfulness in his daily living. In vv.5–8 the elder specifies the conduct he has in mind. Nowhere in this letter, however, does he refer to the theological issue before the church.

4 John now comments on his reaction to Gaius's stand for the truth. There is no more important news he can receive, no greater joy he can experience, than that his own "children" (i.e., his own converts to the faith) are living in faithfulness "to the truth." The word "children" could, of course, designate any for whom John feels pastoral responsibility (cf. 1Jn 2:13a).

III. Commendation for Gaius's Hospitality (5–8)

5 The writer's warm feeling shines through again as he for the third time addresses Gaius as his "dear friend" (cf. vv. 1–2). Now he commends him for his hospitality to Christian brothers who came from the elder to visit the church, even though they were at the

time unknown to Gaius. Likely Gaius's actions were in contrast to what others in his church did, and he may have incurred their displeasure. Although hospitality was required of all Christians (Mt 10:10; Ro 12:13; 1Ti 3:2; 5:10; Heb 13:2), it was sometimes necessary to refuse it (2Jn 10).

6 Part of what the traveling brothers had reported to the elder was the wholehearted way—involving, perhaps, risk to his standing in the community—in which Gaius had entertained them. On returning, they had testified to this before the whole church, and this increased the elder's pride in "his son in the faith." He had not only entertained the traveling brothers but had shown them *agape* love.

It seems that these brothers had again returned to Gaius, perhaps carrying letters from the elder; and they again needed Christian hospitality. The admonition to send them on their way "in a manner worthy of God" shows the supreme importance assigned to hospitality. The phrase probably means that the traveling brothers were to be recognized as servants of God and supported as such. In such instances, Christians were to provide hospitality as if the Lord himself were being welcomed (cf. Jn 13:20; Gal 4:1–15; Heb 13:2).

7 That they went out "for the sake of the Name" (i.e., Jesus Christ; cf. Ac 5:41) shows that they were missionaries. The sending body is either the elder's community or a company of believers known to the elder and Gaius. That they could receive nothing from pagans shows how strongly the Johannine church depended on Jesus' word in Mk 6:8, 10. Furthermore, common sense would also make them refuse support from pagans. We do know that wandering preachers and missionaries of pagan deities were common in the Roman world.

It was difficult enough accepting gifts from the church, as Paul showed, let alone taking help from unbelievers (cf. 1Co 9:14–18; 2Co 12:16–18; 1Th 2:6–9). Although Paul acknowledged the right of the traveling missionaries to be supported by the church (1Co 9:14), he was well aware of the risks this entailed. Nonetheless, for the mature Christian community such support was encouraged and gladly received (cf. Php 4:10–18). For both the giver and the receiver there was a blessing to be received. In the Johannine community such support was certainly a part of the sacrifice one Christian owed another. Even a Christian's life was not beyond the limit love required (1Jn 3:16–17).

8 Whether this call "to show hospitality" (GK 5696) is based on the principle that by their support church members are fellow laborers with missionaries in proclaiming the Gospel (cf 2Co 8:23; Col 4:11) or whether such support guarantees participation in the truth is not clear. In the Johannine community, *koinonia* (i.e., "fellowship"; cf. 1Jn 1:3–4) required the former, while obedience to the commands of Christ demanded the latter. The author could be deliberately ambiguous, desiring both alternatives.

IV. Complaints Against Diotrephes (9–10)

9 This paragraph brings us to the nub of the problem that the elder is writing about. He had already addressed a letter to the church through its leader Diotrephes. That letter is lost, perhaps destroyed by Diotrephes himself. Its contents are not, however difficult to imagine. On the basis of 3 John, we can surmise that he had written the church asking them to extend hospitality to the traveling missionaries he had sent out. It may also have included a request for support that would speed them on their way. Diotrephes chose to thwart John's intention by suppressing the letter or else opposing the request before the congregation. He also had threatened the expulsion of any in the church who were considering offering hospitality to the elder's emissaries. In fact, some may already have been forced out of the church.

Why Diotrephes was opposing the elder is not clear. The elder's statement that Diotrephes "loves to be first" could simply reflect personal rivalry. Or it could reflect an inflated and dictatorial ego. John's prominence in the community was obviously longstanding. Diotrephes may have been troubled by John's continued influence over the church he was leading. If Diotrephes was a younger man, the elder's age may have been a problem. That there was a deeper split, perhaps involving theological differences, is not supported by the text.

10 The elder has commended Gaius for his faithfulness to the truth and for living his according to the truth. Does this indicate that John suspected Diotrephes of wavering in opposition to the false teachers in the area? Does the statement that he "will have nothing to do with us" and that he is "gossiping maliciously about us" and "refuses to welcome the brothers" indicate that he is not really committed to the commandment of love? If so, Diotrephes had as yet shown no theological deviation regarding the person of Christ. If he had, we can, in view of John's other actions, be quite certain that he would have exposed Diotrephes and pronounced judgment on him. But quite apart from doctrinal deviation, the opposition of Diotrephes would have the effect of weakening the elder's position in the community and making the work of the false teachers that much easier.

Another cause for the problem may have been that John expanded the activity of the missionary emissaries in order to stem the tide of false teaching flooding the area. The presence of these missionaries would have been an effective deterrent to schism and would have strengthened his hand in dealing with this threat to the Gospel. But those actions may have been resented by Diotrephes as eroding the local autonomy of the churches. The "malicious gossip" referred to may have been that the elder was using the presence of false teachers as a pretext for establishing his own authority more completely over the churches.

Exactly how Gaius fits into all this is unclear. Perhaps he was the leader of another local church in the area, close enough so that he can be considered a member of the same church but far enough away so that he did not know all that was going on. It is difficult to place Gaius in the same location as Diotrephes, for why would John be telling Gaius about what Diotrephes is doing when presumably Gaius would already know about it firsthand?

It is important to note that the elder does not object that Diotrephes has authority, but he does object to its misuse to the detriment of the truth. The real conflict is not, as some contend, between two types of church organization. It is between two levels of commitment to the work of God: Diotrephes is more interested in furthering his own position than in furthering the work of God.

Exactly how John intended to deal with Diotrephes is unclear. His statement that he "will call attention to what he [Diotrephes] is doing" suggests that John planned to confront Diotrephes, perhaps personally, and expose his conduct before the whole church, unless he completely repented. There seems to be an implication that Diotrephes's misdeeds were not yet fully known to the congregation; and perhaps it was the elder's hope that once they were revealed, the church would either censure or expel Diotrephes from his position.

How are we to explain the sharp words and drastic response on the part of the "apostle of love"? Do they not represent a contradiction to his teaching? More probably they represent the response of one who sensed that the very nature of the Gospel was threatened by such hypocritical conduct on the part of one of its ministers. Diotrephes's actions against John were reprehensible by any standard; but they were even more so on the part of one who probably had been of the fellowship of the elders, who knew the message of love that had been received, and who had pledged to live a life according to the commandment given by the Son of God. For such a leader of the church to give way to personal pique and selfish ambition was unthinkable.

Furthermore, Diotrephes's wickedness spread beyond the vicious innuendos and lies directed against John. It extended to those wholly innocent of wrongdoing. The missionary "brothers," who ought to have benefited from Diotrephes as they served in the Gospel's cause, were denied the welcome due them as members of the household of faith. Because they came from the elder, they suffered the consequences of guilt by association. Furthermore, Diotrephes actually cast out of his congregation those whose conscience required them to extend hospitality to the brethren.

Such contradiction to the Gospel by word and deed could not be condoned, and indeed it was not. It was no longer Diotrephes who was on trial for his action but John and all those who believed as he did. Silence on their part in the face of such total rejection of the truth and the life of the Gospel would have been as hypocritical as Diotrephes's earlier action.

It was no pleasant experience that awaited the elder, but "truth" without "love" is no truth at all. Diotrephes was condemned not because he violated sound teaching regarding the person and nature of Jesus Christ but because his "life" was a contradiction to the truth of the Gospel.

V. Exhortation and Endorsement of Demetrius (11–12)

11 That the elder admonishes Gaius not to "imitate what is evil but what is good" need not imply that he fears for Gaius's character. It is rather for his encouragement in continuing to do good. He may have expected Diotrephes and his supporters to exert intense pressure on Gaius to give up his support of the elder and his missionaries. In that event, Gaius would have no option but to take his stand on principle. To give in to pressure against one's convictions is to submit to evil. Whatever its source or whoever its advocates, evil can never be reconciled to God. Even to contemplate giving in to evil means that loyalty to God's revealed will in Scripture is jeopardized.

Why does the elder appeal to those who "imitate"? Because it is the nature of God's revelation that truth (vv.1, 3), love (v.6), and righteousness (v.11) have been modeled first in Jesus Christ and then by those who are faithful to his commandments. We do not have innately a dependable standard by which to judge ourselves. We must always measure our understanding and actions by God himself, for whom love, truth, and righteousness are absolute attributes. In Christ these same attributes have become available to all who love God and desire to obey his commands. To show them forth in our lives proves that we are "from God." All goodness proceeds from him; our perseverance in goodness demonstrates that in Jesus Christ we have seen God.

12 The elder now commends Demetrius, of whom we know no more than what is said of him here. For some reason John felt it important for Gaius to know and trust him. Apparently he was also one of John's supporters. He may have been the bearer of this letter or a traveling missionary. John honors him with a threefold tribute: (1) He "is well spoken of by everyone." (2) He is well spoken of "by the truth itself." (3) The elder also "speaks well of him." This strong backing of Demetrius leads us to think he had been given a special mission that required unusual trust, but one that the elder did not choose to describe here. What does John mean that "the truth" speaks well of Demetrius? It is the truth of the Gospel in Demetrius's life that the elder is referring to. Like Gaius, Demetrius is "walking in the truth." His life matches his confession. In Pauline terms, he manifests the fruit of the Spirit. In John's terms, he lives the life of love. The clause "and you know that our testimony is true" reminds us of Jn 21:24.

VI. Personal Remarks and Farewell Greetings (13–15)

13–14 John's statement that he wished to write more is characteristic of him (cf. Jn 20:30; 2Jn 12). Also characteristic is his expressed desire to see Gaius soon and talk with him "face to face" (cf. comment on 2Jn 12).

15 The closing word again bears the mark of the warm relationship existing between John and Gaius. John extends "peace" (GK *1645*) to him, knowing that his situation may become very difficult in the days ahead. He also reminds him that all who are with John are also Gaius's friends. Then he concludes by asking Gaius to greet his friends in the church. This last remark supports the assumption that the elder's real desire is that Gaius will in fact share this letter with the members of the church.

Jude

INTRODUCTION

1. Authorship

The first verse identifies the author of this letter as "Jude, a servant of Jesus Christ and a brother of James." "James" (Gk., "Jacob"; GK *2610*) was a popular name among the Jews in NT times because of its patriarchal connection. Likewise popular was "Jude" (Gk., "Judah," the name of Jacob's fourth son and founder of the tribe of Judah; GK *2683*). The name gained added luster from Judas Maccabaeus, a national hero of the Jews, who led the revolt against Antiochus Epiphanes in the second century B.C. But the perfidy of Judas Iscariot seems to have led practically all major English versions to use the form "Jude" rather than "Judas" in translating this letter.

Can the author of this letter be identified with any certainty among the number of men in the NT named Judas? The link of Jude with James in v.1 provides the best clue for identifying him. After the martyrdom of James the son of Zebedee under Herod Agrippa I (c. A.D. 44; cf. Ac 12:2), the only James who is well enough known in the early church that the unspecified use of his name would be generally recognizable was James of Jerusalem. Paul called him "James, the Lord's brother" (Gal 1:19). Later he became known as "James the Just."

If the James of v.1 can be so identified, Jude was the brother of the leader of the Jerusalem church (Ac 12:17; 15:13; 21:18; 1Co 15:7; Gal 1:19; 2:9, 12) and the half-brother of Jesus of Nazareth (Mt 13:55; Mk 6:3). If this is who he is, he did not believe in the messiahship of Jesus until after the Resurrection (Jn 7:5; cf. Ac 1:14). This probably explains the humility with which Jude introduces himself in v.1 as a "servant" (or slave) of Jesus.

Modern objections to the authorship of the letter by a half-brother of Jesus include the fact that its language seems very Hellenistic for an author who grew up in Galilee. The vocabulary abounds in ornate and rare words (thirteen not found elsewhere in the NT). Yet it is unreasonable to dogmatize about what facility in the Greek language and literature or what knowledge of Jewish apocalyptic writings (see comments on vv.9, 14) the half-brother of Jesus might have had. Greek was the lingua franca of the Mediterranean world, and the presence of the Decapolis to the east and south of the Sea of Galilee provided ample opportunity for Greek influence on nearby Nazareth. It is certainly possible that Jesus and others in his family spoke Greek fluently.

2. Date

The letter is so short that it contains little to help fix its date of composition other than the points mentioned above and inferences that can be drawn from the heresy the author opposes. It was likely written between A.D. 40 and 80. If this letter was used by Peter in 2 Peter (cf. introduction to 2 Peter), the writing would have to be sometime prior to Peter's death or before A.D. 65. All things considered, the letter is best dated about 60 to 65.

3. Canonicity

If 2 Peter utilized Jude and if Peter wrote 2 Peter (both positions are disputed), then 2 Peter is the oldest witness to Jude, and its "apostolic" character or canonicity is, in principle, settled at a very early date. The Muratorian Canon (c. A.D. 200) states that a letter of Jude was accepted in the church. Tertullian, Clement of Alexandria, and Origen (late second- and early third-century Christian writers) all knew the book. On the other hand, there were doubts about the letter. Those who spoke against it objected to its use of noncanonical writings and noted also the limited number of citations of the letter in the literature of the early church. These doubts were overcome, and the worth of the book was recognized by the church. Since about A.D. 400 little objection to its canonicity has been voiced.

4. Destination

Since the address is so general—"To those who have been called, who are loved by God the Father and kept by Jesus Christ" (v.1)—it is quite possible that the author intended the letter to be circulated to a number of churches. Against this are the internal indications that the author knows the conditions within the church or churches to whom he writes (v.4). It is possible, however, that Jude itinerated and thus knew the dangers affecting the churches of a region or a circuit of churches within a region (perhaps Asia Minor, Syrian Antioch, or Palestine).

5. Purpose

Jude had wanted to write on the subject of the church's teaching ("the salvation we share," v.3). But he found it necessary instead to warn his readers concerning innovators who were smuggling false teaching into the churches. Likely, these teachers had an itinerant ministry in imitation of the apostles. Both Paul (cf. Galatians, Colossians) and John (cf. 1 and 2 John) faced the problem of false teachers who promoted a different gospel and erroneous instruction.

Jude's purpose is to give a strong denunciation of the errorists. He evidently hopes that by his concise but vigorous exposure of them, the church will see the danger of their error and be alert to the coming judgment on it. Jude also wants to reassure the church by showing that the coming of such scoffers was part of the content of apostolic prophecy. In his last paragraphs, he calls the Christians to exercise their faith within the received common instruction. He also praises God as the one who is able to keep both the church and individuals from falling. Christians may have confidence that the God who began a good work of salvation within them (Php 1:6) will keep them (v.1) and finally bring them safely into his glorious presence (v.24).

Though this book is often neglected by Christians, the church today needs to listen to Jude's contribution to biblical revelation. The emphasis on a "fixed" core of truth known as "the faith" needs to be pondered. Jesus is God's Word to humankind (cf. Ro 6:17; Heb 1:1–4). God is righteous and true, and he hates sin and error. Contemporary culture is becoming indifferent to the question of truth. Christians have found truth in Jesus (Eph 4:21). Jude warns of the dangers in the mixture of error with this truth. Thus his eloquent tract for maintaining the purity and truth of the Christian faith is needed in view of the relativity and syncretism so common today. While it must be granted that some Christians have been and are still intolerantly dogmatic about relatively minor theological issues, there is also the great danger of accepting uncritically all teaching or positions as valid and thus compromising God's once-and-for-all self-disclosure in Jesus.

6. Special Problems

At least two special problems confront the student of Jude: the identity of the heretics and the relation of Jude to 2 Peter. For a discussion of the second issue, see the introduction to 2 Peter.

Regarding the first problem, it would appear that the heresy has something to do with emerging Gnosticism. In general, the Gnostic worldview was hostile toward the world and all worldly ties. From this perspective, it branched into ascetic and libertine divisions. For the libertine Gnostic the idea of "thou shalt" or "thou shalt not" does not come from God (who is absolutely transmundane) but from the Archons (or the demiurges) who are related to this world. Salvation involves the intentional violation of the rules of the Archons. In some systems, the Gnostics despaired of this world to such an extent that body and soul were meaningless. Only the spirit would transcend this universe to reach the unknown God.

Against this kind of thinking, Jude's strong polemic becomes understandable. The heretics were antinomian; they did not observe Christian moral instruction. Though the false teachers spoke about the *pneuma* ("spirit") and claimed to be spiritual, they were really *psychikoi* ("psychic" or "unspiritual") and did not have "the Spirit" (v.19). Their lives gave evidence of bondage to the world, not liberation from it (v.8). Their rejection of Jesus (v.4), their blaspheming of angels (v.8, 10), and their complaining and cynicism (v.16) all fit libertine Gnosticism.

The ultimate threat of this Gnostic faith to Christianity lay in its denial of God's revelation in Christ. To follow the Gnostic path led to a radical rejection of all God's Word to humanity and to a substitution of a different salvation. The means of salvation became an esoteric teaching, not that which freed the whole person (body, soul, spirit) from the bondage of sin. This world was negated and the knowledge of the one, true God hidden. Jude's vehement opposition to this kind of error was justified in the light of the significant issues that were involved.

EXPOSITION

I. The Salutation (1–2)

1 This brief letter begins with the customary self-identification of the author. He is "Jude"—most likely the one who was the half-brother of Jesus (see the introduction). Modestly he calls himself a "servant" (lit., "slave"; GK *1528*) of Jesus Christ; as such he belongs to him. Jude's calling himself a servant implies that what he is about to write is what his Master wants him to say. He also calls himself "a brother of James," the half-brother of Jesus who wrote the letter of James and became the head of the church in Jerusalem (see the introduction).

The readers are "the called" (GK *3105*), which in Pauline theology stresses the sovereign activity of God's grace in summoning to salvation. This term is almost synonymous with "Christian." They are "loved by God the Father." The Father, who is love (1Jn 4:16), has set his love on his people (cf. Dt 7:6–8). Moreover, they are "kept [GK *5498*] by Jesus Christ." Since there is no word for "by" in the Greek text, it can also be translated "kept for Jesus Christ" (see NIV note); i.e., God the Father preserves Christians for his Son (cf. vv.24–25; Jn 17:15).

2 "Mercy, peace and love be yours in abundance" is typical of the greeting, or prayer, that stood at the head of ancient letters. Jude omits the word "grace," which is used in the salutations of practically all other NT letters. Perhaps his reference to these three words is a way of showing facets of God's grace to humankind. All three describe what God does for us. "Mercy" is his compassion, "peace" is his gift of quiet confidence in the work of Jesus, and "love" is his generosity in granting us his favors and meeting our needs.

II. The Reason for the Letter (3–4)

3 Jude tells his "dear friends" (lit., "beloved"; GK *28*) how he came to write this letter. He wanted to write a positive statement of the Christian faith. Whether he was actively engaged in writing or only in the process of thinking about it is not clear. "The salvation we share" is that which all Christians now participate in, though elsewhere in the NT salvation is spoken of as future (cf. 1Pe 1:5). Both are true. Christians have been saved (Tit 3:5), they now possess salvation (Jude 3; cf. Heb 6:9), and they long for Christ who "will appear a second time . . . to bring salvation to those who are waiting for him" (Heb 9:28).

By saying "I felt I had to write," Jude explains that a compelling obligation to the people of God prompted him to change his focus for their spiritual good. His letter is now intended to exhort the readers to struggle for "the faith that was once for all entrusted to the saints." "Contend" (GK *2043*; related to *74–76*) basically refers to the intense effort in a wrestling match (cf. 1Co 9:25). The specific form here shows that the Christian struggle is to be continuous. "The faith" (GK *4411*) is the body of truth that very early in the church's history took on a definite form (cf. Ac 2:42; Ro 6:17; Gal 1:23). Without doubt, the form of the faith as a body of recognized truth became clearer as time passed. Jude stresses that this faith has been entrusted "once for all" (GK *562*) to the "saints" (GK *41*)—the ones set apart by God for himself. Basically the Christian faith cannot be changed; its foundation truths are not negotiable (see also Gal 1:6–9; 2Jn 9).

4 Jude now explains the reasons why he was compelled to write. Ungodly men had "secretly slipped in" among the believers (cf. Gal 2:4), whose condemnation "was written about long ago." This phrase could refer to God's writing down from eternity the destiny (i.e., reprobation) of the wicked, but more likely it refers to previously written predictions about the doom of the apostates.

After stating the destiny of these men, Jude describes them as "ungodly" or "impious" (GK *815*), a term often used of notorious sinners. This general word is made more specific by the two charges that follow. (1) They "change the grace of our God into a license for immorality." Evidently their understanding of grace and perhaps of the forgiveness of sins led them to feel free to indulge in all forms of sexual depravity (cf. comment on 2Pe 2:2). (2) They "deny Jesus Christ our only Sovereign and Lord" (cf. 2Pe 2:1). Exactly how they denied Jesus Christ, Jude does not say. Certainly they denied him by immoral living that ran counter to his commands. Perhaps they also denied him in teaching a Christology that denied either his full humanity or his full deity. However, the word translated "Sovereign" (GK *1305*) is commonly used of the Father (Lk 2:29; Ac 4:24), and the word "only" makes it difficult to apply this word to Jesus. Thus this phrase can also be translated, "the only Sovereign [the Father] and our Lord Jesus Christ." If this is adopted, then the error of the godless men was moral rather than theological (cf. Tit 1:16).

III. The Warning Against the False Teachers (5–16)

A. Examples of God's Judgment in History (5–7)

5 As Peter did in 2Pe 1:12, Jude states that his readers already know what he is about to say but that he will remind them of it. So he gives them three examples of the Lord's judgments: on the unbelievers at the time of the Exodus, on the fallen angels, and on Sodom and Gomorrah. In each instance the objects of judgment are notable rebels against the Lord.

The first example is that of Israel, who experienced the great display of God's grace in the Exodus, saw and heard his revelation at Sinai, and received his care in the wilderness; yet a number of them disbelieved and rebelled. Obviously this is not an instance of people being saved and then losing their salvation. Jude describes the rebels as "those who did not believe." The Israelites were physically delivered from bondage, not by their faith as a nation, but by God's covenant love and mercy. The warning in this judgment is against unbelief and rebellion.

6 The second example is of the fallen angels. The most likely reference here is to the angels ("sons of God," cf. Ge 6:4; Job 1:6; 2:1) who came to earth and mingled with women. This interpretation is expounded in the pseudepigraphical book of Enoch, from which Jude quotes in v.14 (also commonly quoted in the intertestamental literature and the early church fathers). These angels "did not keep their positions of authority." The implication is that God assigned angels stipulated responsibilities and a set place. But because of their rebellion, God has reserved them in darkness and in eternal chains awaiting final judgment. Apparently some fallen angels are in bondage while others are unbound and active among people as demons.

7 The third example of judgment is Sodom and Gomorrah. In v.7 the NIV is so concise that it slides over a particular nuance that is apparent in a more literal translation: "Just as Sodom and Gomorrah and the surrounding cities, which practiced immorality in the same way as these and lusted after different flesh, stand out as an example, undergoing as they do a punishment of everlasting fire." The key factors are "these" (referring to the "angels" in v. 6) and the words "different flesh." Thus the sin of Sodom and Gomorrah was seeking union with "different flesh" in a way similar to what the "sons of God" did in Ge 6:2 when they mingled with "the daughters of men."

Normally angels do not marry, nor do they have substantial bodies, though at times they have assumed bodies or appeared in a bodily form as divine messengers (Ge 19:1ff.; Zec 1:9ff.; Mt 28:2ff.; Acts 1:10–11; et al.). In Ge 19 angelic messengers in the form of men visited Sodom, and the men of the city, motivated by their homosexuality and supposing the messengers to be men, desired them. Thus they "went after different flesh." God destroyed the cities of the plain by raining fire and burning sulfur from heaven on the cities (Ge 19:24).

B. The Description and Doom of the False Teachers (8–13)

8 Jude now links the examples of God's judgment (vv.5–7) to the false teachers, whom he calls "dreamers" (GK *1965*). Though this word might refer to pretensions of prophecy, it more likely refers to their carnal sin that leads them to live in a dream world. "In the very same way" points back to the sins of Sodom and Gomorrah (v.7). The false teachers pollute "their own bodies" (lit., "flesh"; GK *4922*) in various forms of sexual excess, doubtless including homosexuality. Their rejection of authority implies that they repudiated Jesus as Lord over their lives. Their third sin is that they "slander celestial beings." How and why, Jude does not say. Perhaps their materialistic and fleshy bent led them to deny all spiritual forces—good or evil.

9 The false teachers should have learned from the example of the powerful archangel Michael (see Rev 12:7; cf. Da 10:13, 21; 12:1; 1Th 4:16). Jewish literature tells of a struggle over Moses' body. One writing in particular, the apocryphal Assumption of Moses, refers to the devil claiming the right to Moses' body because of his sin of murder (Ex 2:12) or because he (the devil) considered himself the lord of the earth. Yet in spite of Michael's power and dignity, he dared not bring a "slanderous accusation" against the devil but referred the dispute to the sovereignty of God. So if he, a mighty archangel, had respect for celestial powers, Jude says, how much more should the mere human false teachers do so!

10 "Yet these men" connotes contempt. They, unlike Michael, presume to speak evil against what they know nothing about (cf. v.19, where Jude explains that they do not have the Spirit). These "dreamers" do have knowledge, but only on the instinctual level of animal passion. So like "unreasoning animals," they are destroyed (by God) through the things they practice.

11 Again Jude turns to the OT—this time for another triad of examples. Because of their coming judgment, he pronounces "woe" on the false teachers, just as Jesus did on the scribes and Pharisees (Mt 23:13, 15–16, 23, 25, 27, 29). (1) The false teachers have "taken the way of Cain." Cain's way was the religion of his own works without faith (Heb 11:4) and led to the hatred and murder of his brother (1Jn 3:12–13). Like Cain, these men belong to the evil one, manufacture religion, and kill the souls of other people by error.

(2) They have abandoned themselves to Balaam's error (cf. comments on 2Pe 2:15–16). Balaam was the prototype of all greedy religionists who lead God's people into false religion and immorality (cf. Nu 31:16–19). The false teachers were wholly consumed by their love of money.

(3) "They have been destroyed in Korah's rebellion." The OT tells of the drastic punishment inflicted on Korah, Dathan, Abiram, and 250 other rebels against Moses' authority (Nu 16:1–35). So, with a bold disregard of anachronism, Jude includes them in the destruction meted out there. It is a striking way of saying that their doom is certain and settled.

12–13 Now, with burning eloquence, Jude piles figure upon figure (six of them in all) to describe the errorists. (1) The false teachers are "blemishes [GK 5069] at your love feasts." The word translated "blemishes" can also be translated "hidden rocks." "Hidden rocks" connotes the danger of shipwreck of the faith (cf. 1Ti 1:19); "spots" or "blemishes" parallels 2Pe 2:13 and connotes defilement. The "love feasts" (GK 27) were meals in which the early church ate together and observed the Lord's Supper. "Eating with you" has the idea of sumptuous eating and is better translated "feasting with you." "Without the slightest qualm" (lit., "without fear"; GK 925) means that the false teachers do not recognize the terror of the Lord against those who mock his Son's death shown in the Supper (cf. 1Co 11:27–32; Heb 10:26–31).

(2) The false teachers are "shepherds who feed only themselves"—a figure that points to all the biblical warnings against the false shepherds who care nothing for the flock (e.g., Eze 34:8; Jn 10:12–13).

(3) They are like clouds that promise rain but are "blown along by the wind" and are "without rain." Consequently, the false teachers are devoid of refreshment, promise, and performance.

(4) They are like fruit trees in late autumn, long past the harvest, bearing no fruit. Furthermore, they are trees not only fruitless but also uprooted—thus "twice dead."

(5) Next is the metaphor of the restless sea (v.13). For modern people, the sea is often a thing of beauty; to ancient people, it was a terror (cf. Isa 57:20; also Rev 21:1, with its promise of no more sea). The errorists are busy, restless, and untamed. Their product is like the foam or scum at the seashore.

(6) The last metaphor ("wandering stars") is from astronomy. The reference here could be to meteors, shooting stars, comets, or planets; planets is the most likely meaning, for the ancients called them "wandering stars" because of their movements. An unpredictable star provides no guidance for navigation; so false teachers are useless and untrustworthy. Their doom is the eternal

C. Enoch's Prophecy of the Coming Judgment (14–16)

14 Enoch, who "walked with God; then he was no more, because God took him away" (Ge 5:21), is not specifically called "the seventh from Adam" in the OT. But in Ge 5 and 1Ch 1:1–3, he is the seventh in order (counting Adam as the first). Jude here quotes the book of Enoch, the longest of the surviving Jewish pseudepigraphical writings and a work highly respected by many Jews and Christians. Those who wonder about the propriety of Jude's quotation of a noncanonical book should note that he does not call it Scripture. Paul also quoted approvingly from noncanonical writers (see Ac 17:28; 1Co 15:33; Tit 1:12). Enoch's prophecy does not give any startling new information but is simply a general description of the return of the Lord in judgment (cf. Dt 33:2; Da 7:10–14; Zec 14:3; Mt 25:31).

15–16 The stress is on two words, each used four times: "all" (GK *4246*) and "ungodly" (GK *813–815*; cf. v.4). Jude finds Enoch's prophecy a good summary of the universal divine judgment on the impious and all their deeds.

Verse 16 completes Jude's denunciation of the false teachers as "grumblers" (GK *1199*). In 1Co 10:10 Paul uses the related verb (GK *1197*) of the rebels in the wilderness (cf. Ex 16–17; Nu 14–17). Jude also calls the false teachers "faultfinders" (GK *3523*), a term that underlines their critical attitude and habitual complaining. "They follow their own evil desires" might be translated "they live by their passions." "They boast about themselves" is can be rendered "and their mouth speaks haughty [or bombastic] words," which reminds one of Antiochus Epiphanes (cf. Da 7:8–11; 11:36). "Flatter others for their own advantage" reinforces Jude's stress on the venality of the false teachers.

IV. The Exhortations to the Believers (17–23)

17–18 "But, dear friends" makes the transition from the burning denunciation in vv. 8–16 to the preparation of the believers for their necessary struggles. They must remember (cf. v.5; 2Pe 1:12–15) the previously spoken words of the apostles. The apostles (the Twelve plus Paul) must have had a wide ministry of which we have little knowledge, and their preaching was part of the oral deposit of faith for the early churches. One of their prophecies was a prediction of mockers in the last days who would live ungodly lives. So the church must be vigilant and prepare itself for action, for that time is at hand and the ungodly mockers are already on the scene. The "last time" (Greek has singular) is the age of messianic salvation and judgment that culminates in the judgments of the Second Advent.

19 Again Jude returns to his triadic pattern of describing the false teachers. (1) They are "men who divide you" (GK *626*). This rare word may mean that "they made distinctions," perhaps as the later Gnostics divided Christians by classifying them into groups of initiates ("spiritual ones") and lesser ones. (2) Furthermore, they are men "who follow mere natural instincts" (lit., "psychic" or "unspiritual"; GK *6035*). This word was likely used by the Gnostics to slander the orthodox when in fact the false teachers themselves were living on the natural level. Jude turns the word against them. The church today is still plagued by false teachers claiming superior knowledge and experience; yet their lives are often worse than those of the average pagan. (3) Finally, Jude says that they "do not have the Spirit" (i.e., the Holy Spirit), in spite of all their vaunted claims and teaching.

20–21 The repetition (cf. v.17) of "dear friends" (lit., "beloved"; GK *28*) personalizes the message and redirects attention back from his opponents to the believers. Now he gives them a fourfold exhortation for their spiritual profit.

(1) Christians are to be "build [themselves] up" (GK *2224*) in their "most holy faith." In the NT "the faith" is the orthodox body of truth and practice from the apostles (see comment on v.3). It is "most holy" because the Spirit gave it concerning God's "holy servant Jesus" (Ac 4:27, 30). Christians build themselves by having fellowship with the Lord and his people, by continuing in the Gospel and in the Word of God, and by worshiping—especially by remembering the Lord at his table.

(2) Christians are to be praying (GK *4667*) "in the Holy Spirit" (cf. Ro 8:26–27; Gal 4:6;

Eph 6:18). Because all believers have the Spirit, they are to pray according to the Spirit's will (set forth in the written Word and made known by inner promptings) to accomplish God's work by God's power.

(3) Christians are to "keep [themselves] in God's love" (v.21; cf. vv.1–2). The realm of God's love is in Jesus Christ; those who depart from Christ depart from the love of God. Those who reject the commands of Jesus reject his love (cf. Jn 15:10).

(4) Christians are to keep their attention fixed on the "mercy of our Lord Jesus Christ [that brings them] to eternal life." True eschatology keeps present reality in focus. The mention of mercy reminds Christians that salvation is never a matter of good works and that only in Christ is our hope of salvation (cf. comment on v.3). "Eternal life" in this verse refers to the future aspects of the presently enjoyed salvation.

22–23 Three groups are mentioned here and an instruction is given for each one. (1) The first command is to show mercy to those who are doubting (or hesitating). The teaching and example of the false teachers have caused them to be uncertain about the truth of Christianity. They must be dealt with patiently and mercifully by showing them Christian love. (2) The next group needs to be dealt with directly and vigorously. Salvation is God's work, and here Christians are portrayed as God's instruments for snatching brands out of the fire (cf. Zec 3:3). Jude pictures a person slipping into the eternal fire but being rescued from error by the grace and truth of God. (3) The final group of people appears to be deep in the immorality of the false teachers. Their very clothing is "stained by corrupted flesh." Perhaps the figure is that their depravity has made them infectious. Christians are to show mercy as in the first case, but now they are do so "with fear," lest the infection spread to them. Yet even here God's wondrous grace can exchange the excrement-covered garments (cf. Zec 3:3) for festive garments of righteousness. For no one, not even the most defiled sinner, is beyond salvation through faith in Christ's redeeming work.

V. The Doxology (24–25)

24 Jude's message of warning and doom may have depressed and discouraged his readers. Beset by so much false teaching and immorality, how can Christians ever reach heaven? The answer lies only in the power of God. So this doxology, surely one of the greatest in the NT, reminds us of God's ability to bring every one of his own safely to himself. God "is able to keep [us] from falling" (or "stumbling"; GK 720). Furthermore, he is able "to present [us] before his glorious presence without fault [GK 320, used of Christ as a faultless lamb in 1Pe 1:19; see comment]." "With great joy" is the response of Christians for their completed salvation.

25 "To the only God our Savior" points to the monotheistic nature of the faith by showing that the Father is the Savior as well as the Son. Whatever the false teachers may say, there is only one God and Savior. To "God our Savior ... through Jesus Christ our Lord" belong four attributes: (1) "glory" (GK 1518), a word with many associations and connotations difficult to capture in a few words—perhaps "radiance" or "moral splendor" comes close to its meaning; (2) "majesty" (GK 3488), which refers to God's greatness and transcendence; (3) "power" (GK 3197); and (4) "authority" (GK 2026)—the last two words stress his might and the freedom of action God enjoys as Creator. The solemn time notation "before all ages, now and forevermore" indicates that these attributes of God suffer no change and that therefore his divine plan will surely be carried out. Salvation is completely secure because God's own purpose stands and because he is able to do all that he wills (Isa 46:9–10).

The Old Testament in the New

NT Text	OT Text	Subject
Jude 9	Zec 3:2	Rebuking Satan

Revelation

INTRODUCTION

1. General Nature and Historical Background

The book of Revelation fascinates as well as perplexes the modern reader. For the present generation, it is the most obscure and controversial book in the Bible. Yet those who study it with care agree that it is a unique source of Christian teaching and one of timeless relevance. It may well be that with the exception of the Gospels, this book is the most profound and moving teaching on Christian doctrine and discipleship found anywhere in Scripture. It differs in kind from the other NT writings, not in doctrine but in literary genre and subject matter. It is a book of prophecy (1:3; 22:7, 18–19) that involves both warning and consolation. In communicating its message, the Lord uses symbol and vision.

Why did the Lord use a method that seemingly makes his message so obscure? The answer is twofold. (1) The language and imagery were not so strange to first-century readers as they are to many today. Faced with the apocalyptic style of the book, the modern reader who knows little about biblical literature and its parallels is like a person who, though unfamiliar with stocks and bonds, tries to understand the Dow-Jones reports. In other words, familiarity with the prophetic books of the OT (especially Daniel and Ezekiel), apocalyptic literature current during the first century, the Dead Sea Scrolls, and other such literature will help the reader grasp the message of the Apocalypse.

(2) The subject matter, with its glimpses into the future and even into heaven itself, required the kind of language John used. Only through symbolism and imagery can we gain some understanding of the things the Lord was unveiling through the writer John. In fact, the evocative description of unseen realities carries a poignancy and clarity unattainable by any other method. For example, "evil" is an abstract term, but a woman "drunk with the blood of the saints" graphically sets forth the concrete and more terrible aspect of this reality. Such language can trigger all sorts of ideas, associations, and mystical responses that the straight prose found in much of the NT cannot attain.

The letters to the seven churches in the Roman province of Asia (modern Turkey) specifically locate the recipients of the book and give some broad indication of the historical situation. Some of the churches were experiencing persecution (2:10, 13). From this it has been customary to assume that persecution was quite intense and widespread. Revelation is then viewed as a "tract for the times" document, warning Christians against emperor worship and encouraging them to be faithful to Christ even to death. Recent studies, however, question how intense or widespread the persecution was, even under Domitian. Thus the primary occasion for the writing of the book must be sought elsewhere than about the persecution of that time.

The letters to the churches imply that five of the seven had serious problems, particularly with disloyalty to Christ. This may indicate that the major thrust of Revelation is not sociopolitical but theological. John is more concerned with countering the heresy that was creeping into the churches toward the close of the first century than in addressing the political situation.

Revelation is also commonly viewed as belonging to the body of nonbiblical Jewish writings known as "apocalyptic" literature. The name for this type of literature is derived from the Greek word *apokalypsis*, meaning "revelation" (GK *637*; cf. 1:1). The extrabiblical apocalyptic books were written in the period from 200 B.C. to A.D. 200. Usually scholars stress the similarities of the Apocalypse of John to these noncanonical books—similarities such as the use of symbolism and vision, the mention of angelic mediators of the revelation, the bizarre images, the new heavens and earth, etc.

Although numerous similarities do exist, John's writing also has some clear differences from these writings. (1) Unlike other apocalyptic books, Revelation clearly claims to be a book of prophecy (1:3; 22:7, 10, 18–19), the effect of which is to identify the message, as in the OT prophetic tradition, with the Word of God (1:2; 19:9). The Jewish apocalyptists used the literary form of prophecy to trace the course of history from ancient times down to their own day. John does not follow this method. He clearly places himself in the contemporary world of the first century and speaks of the future consummation in much the same way as Ezekiel and Jeremiah did. (2) While extrabiblical apocalypses are clearly pseudonymous, the last book of the NT is plainly attributed to John. (3) Many of the noncanonical apocalyptic works blame the immediate plight of God's people, not on their unfaithfulness, but on the pervasive presence of evil in the world. While Revelation does not lack encouragement to the faithful, it also strongly urges the churches to repent.

(4) Finally, and importantly, these apocalypses are pessimistic concerning the outcome of God's present activity in the world; and for hope they look wholly to the eschatological end, when God will once again intervene and defeat the evil in the world. Though Revelation is often read in this manner, there are great differences, for it describes the climactic event in history as already completed—in the victory of the slain Lamb (ch. 5). At the present time, the Lamb's victory is being worked out in the obedient suffering of his followers (12:11; 15:2). Their deaths are seen in Revelation as a part of the victory over evil that God is already effecting in the world. This partial victory through the suffering of the saints is combined with the hope of the final unambiguous victory of God at the end of history. By viewing history in this way, the book makes clear that the source of Christian hope is not in history itself but relates to a transcendent future. For John, there is no gradual progress of righteousness in history. Therefore, any identification of revelation with the writings of the other apocalyptists must be severely qualified.

John was no doubt familiar with the Jewish apocalyptists of the intertestamental period, and in some instances there seems to be a direct allusion to them (cf. comment on 2:7). But the relation is in general superficial. Only twice does an interpreting angel explain a vision (chs. 7 and 17), a feature constantly present in the other kind of apocalyptic writing. In no case does John depend on the assumed knowledge of the Jewish apocalyptists for clarity of meaning. On the other hand, he is everywhere dependent on the OT canonical books, especially those where symbol and vision play a dominant role. Although throughout the commentary occasional references to noncanonical apocalyptic literature appear, they are given only as aids in understanding the background of John's writing.

G. E. Ladd's suggestion that we create a category called "Prophetic-Apocalyptic" to distinguish canonical materials from the late Jewish apocalyptic literature has much merit. Thus, in his view, the beast of chs. 13 and 17 is historical Rome, but it is far larger than the ancient city and is also the future Antichrist. The references to the persecution of Christians likewise go far beyond the known historical situation of John's day. Evil at the hands of Rome is realized eschatology.

Much more important than the late Jewish apocalyptic sources is the debt John owes to the eschatological teaching of Jesus, such as the Olivet Discourse (Mt 24–25; Mk 13; Lk 21). The parallelism is striking and certainly not accidental. In the commentary, these connections are dealt with in more detail (see comment on 6:1). These passages form the ultimate source of his understanding of the future and his interpretation of the OT.

2. Unity

The question of the unity of Revelation is a relative one. Almost all scholars recognize a pervading unity of thought in the majority of the material. The evidence that allegedly argues against a single author revolves around a number of internal difficulties, falling into four categories: (1) the presence of doublets (the same scene or vision described twice); (2) sequence problems—i.e., persons or things introduced seemingly for the first time when in fact they had already been mentioned; (3) seeming misplaced verses and larger sections; and (4) distinctive content within certain sections that does not fit the rest of the book. In each case, however, there are satisfying alternative explanations. In fact, the difficulties just named stem more from the reader's presuppositions than from the text itself. We are more likely to discover the author's original intent if we approach Revelation with the assumption of its literary integrity than if we attempt at every turn to judge it by modern Western mentality.

Without belaboring the argument, we may affirm that the book everywhere displays both the literary and conceptual unity to be expected from a single author. This does not eliminate certain difficult hermeneutical problems nor preclude the presence of omissions or interpolations encountered in the extant manuscripts of the book. Nor does the view of single authorship preclude that John, in expressing in written form the revelation given to him by Christ, used various sources, whether oral or written. Yet, under the guidance of the Holy Spirit, who is of course the primary author, John has everywhere made these materials his own and involved them with a thoroughly Christian orientation and content.

3. Authorship and Canonicity

The question of the authorship of Revelation is linked with that of the authorship of the Gospel of John and the Johannine letters. Most second- and third-century witnesses ascribe Revelation to John the apostle, the son of Zebedee. Not until Dionysius, the distinguished bishop of Alexandria and student of Origen (d. c. 264), was any voice raised within the church against John as the author. He questioned its apostolic origin because the advocates of an earthly eschatological hope ("Chiliasts"), whom he opposed, appealed to Rev 20. Dionysius based his arguments on comparisons between 1 John and the Gospel of John at points where these differ from Revelation: for example, John and 1 John do not name their author but Revelation does; no reference to Revelation appears in John and 1 John and vice versa; and the Greek of Revelation is faulty and entirely different from that of John and 1 John. Not until Athanasius of Alexandria (d. 373) was the book accepted in the East.

In the West, however, the story was different. From at least the middle of the second century, the book held its own, being widely accepted and listed in all the principal canon enumerations. The Reformation period witnessed a renewal of the earlier questions concerning its apostolic authorship and canonical status. Thus Luther, offended by the contents of Revelation, declared that he regarded it as "neither apostolic nor prophetic." Many modern scholars believe that the John who wrote Revelation is not the same as the author of the Gospel and the three letters. They cite as the chief obstacle the barbarous Greek style of Revelation as compared to that of the other writings of John. However, despite the linguistic problem, a number of other scholars have been convinced of the similarities between Revelation and the other Johannine books. A third group of scholars simply leaves the issue open.

From the internal evidence, the following things can be said about the author with some confidence. (1) He calls himself John (1:4, 9; 22:8). This is not likely a pseudonym but instead the name of a well-known person among the Asian churches. Other than the apostle, John the Baptist, and John Mark, the only John we know about is the disputed "John, the presbyter" that Papias spoke about. (2) This John identifies himself as a prophet (1:3; 22:6–10, 18–19) who was in exile because of his prophetic witness (1:9). As such, he speaks to the churches with great authority. (3) His use of the OT and Targums makes it virtually certain that he was a Palestinian Jew, steeped in the temple and synagogue ritual. He may also have been a priest.

To sum up, the question of authorship is problematic. On the one hand, the language and grammatical style are incompatible with the Gospel and the letters; on the other hand, in imagery, literary forms, liturgical framework, and symbolism, there are notable similarities. Early and widespread testimony attributes the book to the apostle John, and no convincing argument has been advanced against this view. Finally, regardless of the problem of authorship, the church universal has come to acknowledge Revelation as divinely authoritative, inspired Scripture.

4. Date

Only two suggested dates for Revelation have received serious support. An early date, shortly after the reign of Nero (A.D. 54–68), is supported by references in the book to the persecution of Christians, the imperial cult (ch. 13), and the temple (ch. 11), which was destroyed in A.D. 70. The alternate and more generally accepted date rests primarily on the early witness of Irenaeus (c. 185), who stated that the apostle John wrote Revelation at the close of Domitian's reign (A.D. 81–96). Both views appeal to the book's witness to persecution because of refusal to comply with emperor worship. On the other hand, if the persecution referred to in the book is anticipatory, and if the exegesis that sees references to the succession of the emperors (ch. 17) and enforced emperor worship (ch. 13) is questionable, then no substantial argument can be advanced for either date. The question as to when Revelation was written is best left open.

5. Purpose

As a prophet, John is called to separate true belief from false—to expose the failures of the congregations in Asia. He desires to encourage authentic Christian discipleship by explaining Christian suffering and martyrdom in the light of how Jesus' death brought victory over evil. John wants to show that the martyrs would be vindicated (cf. 2:13). He discloses the end both of evil and of those who follow the beast (19:20–21; 20:10, 15), and he describes the ultimate issue of the Lamb's victory and of those who follow him. John is centrally concerned with God's saving purpose and its implementation by Jesus. He writes to the church universal in every age so that they too might join him in confirming this witness of Jesus (1:9; 22:16). Sadly, because of the overemphasis on either the symbolic or the literal and because of theological problems, the church has often been deprived of the valuable practical thrust of this book as through it God seeks to lead us into authentic Christian discipleship.

6. Theological Problems

From earliest times, certain theological emphases in Revelation have been cited as objections to the whole book or to certain parts that are considered unworthy and sub-Christian. Among these are (1) its eschatological view of history, which includes an earthly Millennium (ch. 20); (2) the cry for vengeance in 6:10; and (3) its overuse of visions and symbols. That is, Revelation is alleged to be sub-Christian in its Christology, eschatology, and doctrine of God—all three of which are thought to obscure or to contradict outright the central message of the NT. While none of the above problems should be glossed over, it is becoming apparent that prior commitment to a certain viewpoint on these three areas, rather than some intrinsic incompatibility of John's ideas with the central NT message, often determines the negative judgments passed on Revelation.

7. Interpretative Schemes

Four ways of understanding Rev 4–22 have emerged throughout history. In our day, additional views have developed by combining elements from these four traditions.

a. Futurist

This view is that, with the exception of chs. 1–3, all the visions in Revelation relate to a period immediately preceding and following the second advent of Christ at the end of the age. Therefore, the seals, trumpets, and bowls refer to events still in the future; the beasts of chs. 13 and 17 are identified with the future Antichrist, who will appear at the last moment in world history and will be defeated by Christ in his second coming to judge the world and to establish his earthly millennial kingdom.

Variations of this view were held by some of its earliest expositors, such as Justin Martyr (d. 165), Irenaeus (d. c. 195), and Hippolytus (d. 236). This futurist approach has enjoyed a revival of no small proportion since the nineteenth century and is widely held among evangelicals today. The chief problem with it is that it seems to make all but the first three chapters of Revelation irrelevant to the contemporary church. This objection is pressed more strongly when adherents to the futurist view affirm, as many do today, that the church will be removed from the earth before the events described in 6:1ff. occur.

b. Historicist

As the word implies, this view centers on history and its continuity as seen in Revelation. It started with Joachim of Floris (d. 1202). He assigned a day-year value to the 1,260 days of the Apocalypse. In his scheme, the book was a prophecy of the events of Western history from the times of the apostles (in some varieties, from the Creation) until Joachim's own time. A short time after his death, the Franciscans considered themselves the true Christians of John's vision. They interpreted Babylon not only as pagan Rome

Interpretations of Revelation

	1-3	**4-19**	**20-22**
Preterist	Historic churches	Symbolic of contemporary conditions	Symbolic of heaven and victory
Idealist	Historic churches	Symbolic of conflict of good and evil	Victory of good
Historicist	Historic churches	Symbolic of events of history: fall of rome, Mohammedanism, papacy, Reformation	Final judgment, millennium (?), eternal state
Futurist	Historic churches and/or seven stages of church history	Future tribulation; concentrated judgments on apostate church and on antichrist; coming of Christ	Millennial kingdom; judgment of wicked dead; eternal state

Theological Perspectives on Revelation

	1-3	**4-19**	**20-22**
Postmillennial	Historic churches	Generally historicist	Victory of Christianity over the world
Amillennial	Historic churches	Generally historicist	Coming of Christ; judgment; eternal state
Premillennial	Historic churches representative of historical stages	Generally futurist	Literal millennial reign; judgment of great white throne; New Jerusalem
Apocalytic	Historic churches	Generally preterist	Symbolic of heaven and victory

Taken from *Chronological and Background Charts of the New Testament* by Wayne House. Copyright© 1978 by The Zondervan Corporation. Used by permission.

but also as papal Rome. In the various schemes that developed as this method was applied to history, one element became common: the Antichrist and Babylon were connected with Rome and the papacy. Later, Luther, Calvin, and other Reformers came to adopt this view. That this approach does not enjoy much favor today is largely because of the lack of consensus as to the historical identification it entails.

c. Preterist

According to this view, Revelation relates to what happened in the time of the author; it is a contemporary and imminent historical document. Thus the main contents of chs. 4–22 are viewed as describing events wholly limited to John's own time. This approach identifies the book with the Jewish apocalyptic method of producing "tracts for the times" to encourage faithfulness during intense persecution. The beasts of ch. 13 are identified respectively as imperial Rome and the imperial priesthood. This is the view held by a majority of contemporary scholars, not a few of whom are identified with the liberal interpretation of Christianity. As a system, it did not appear till 1614, when a Spanish Jesuit named Alcasar developed its main lines. A variation of this are those who see the events as imminent but not yet realized when John wrote.

d. Idealist

This method of interpreting Revelation sees it as being basically poetic, symbolic, and spiritual in nature. Thus Revelation does not predict any specific historical events at all; on the contrary, it sets forth timeless truths concerning the battle between good and evil that continues throughout the church age. As a system of interpretation, it is more recent than the three other schools and somewhat more difficult to distinguish from the earlier allegorizing approaches of the Alexandrians (e.g., Origen). In general, the idealist view is marked by its refusal to identify any of the images with specific future events, whether in the history of the church or with regard to the end of all things. Undoubtedly, the book does reflect the great timeless realities of the battle between God and Satan and of divine judgment, and it sees history as being ultimately in the hand of the Creator. But certainly it also depicts the consummation of this battle and the triumph of Christ in history through his coming in glory.

Which view is the right one? Since there have been evangelicals who have held to each of the four views, the issue is not that of orthodoxy but of interpretation. In recent years many expositors have combined the stronger elements of the different views. The history of the interpretation of Revelation should teach us to be open to fresh approaches to it, even when this attitude goes contrary to the prevailing interpretations. Nothing short of the careful exegesis of the text uninhibited by prior dogmatic conclusions is required for a full understanding of the Apocalypse.

This commentary will pay close attention to the historical situation of first-century Christianity in its Judeo-Greco-Roman world setting. I do not, however, take the position that this emphasis necessarily leads to the conclusion that John's language and visions describe the political entities of imperial Rome or the imperial priesthood. Thus the preterist and to a lesser extent the preterist-futurist's views are misled. On the other hand, I believe that John is describing the final judgment and the physical, bodily return of Christ to the world. This means that in every age Revelation continues to encourage the church in persecution as well as to warn the church of the beast's satanically energized, multifaceted deception. Its language describes the deeper realities of the conflict of Christ's sovereignty with satanic power rather than the mere temporary historical-political entities, whether past (such as Rome) or future.

8. Use of the Old Testament

While Revelation does not have a single direct quotation from the OT, there are hundreds of places where John alludes in one way or another to the OT Scriptures. The OT he uses is primarily Semitic rather than Greek, agreeing often with Aramaic Targums and occasionally with other Jewish interpretations. From the Prophets, John refers frequently to Isaiah, Jeremiah, Ezekiel, and Daniel. John also refers repeatedly to the Psalms, Exodus, and Deuteronomy. Especially important are his christological reinterpretations of OT passages. He does not simply use the OT in its pre-Christian sense but often recasts its images and visions. While there is an unmistakable continuity in Revelation with the older revelation, the new emerges from the old as a distinct entity.

9. Structure

The main contents of Revelation are given in terms of a series of sevens, some explicit, some implied: seven churches (chs. 2–3); seven seals (chs. 6–7); seven trumpets (chs. 8–11); seven signs (chs. 12–15); seven bowls (chs. 16–18); seven last things (chs. 19–22). It is also possible to divide the contents around four key visions: (1) the vision of the Son of man among the seven churches (chs. 1–3); (2) the vision of the seven-sealed scroll, the seven trumpets, the seven signs, and the seven bowls (4:1–19:10); (3) the vision of the return of Christ and the consummation of this age (19:11–20:15); and (4) the vision of the new heaven and new earth (chs. 21–22).

EXPOSITION

I. Introduction (1:1–8)

A. Prologue (1:1–3)

The Prologue contains a description of the nature of the book, a reference to the author, and a statement that the book was meant for congregational reading.

1 The book is called the "revelation of Jesus Christ." "Revelation" (*apokalypsis*; GK *637*) means to expose in full view what was formerly hidden, veiled, or secret. In the NT this word occurs exclusively in the religious sense of a divine disclosure. It may refer either some to present or future aspect of God's will (Lk 2:32; Ro 16:25; Eph 3:5) or to persons (Ro 8:19) or especially to the future unveiling of Jesus Christ at his return in glory (2Th 1:7; 1Pe 1:7, 13). In the only occurrence of this word in John's writings, the meaning is not primarily the appearing or revealing of Christ—though certainly the book does this—but rather the disclosure of "what must soon take place."

The content of the book comes from its author, Jesus Christ. Yet even Christ is not the final author but a mediator, for he receives the revelation from God the Father ("which God gave him to show"). John is the human instrument for communicating what he has seen by the agency of Christ's messenger or angel (cf. 22:6, 8, 16). Through John the revelation is to be made known to the servants of God who comprise the churches (cf. 22:16). Thus there are five links in the chain of authorship: God, Christ, his angel, his servant John, and the servants in the churches.

"What must soon take place" implies that the revelation concerns events that are future (cf. Da 2:28–29, 45; Mk 13:7; Rev 4:1; 22:6). But in what sense can we understand that the events will arise "soon" (GK *5443*)? From the preterist point of view (see the introduction), all will take place in John's day. But we do not need to follow this interpretation of the book. In eschatology and apocalyptic literature, the future is *always* viewed as imminent without the necessity of intervening time (cf. Lk 18:8). "Soon" does not, in other words, preclude delays or intervening events, as Revelation itself suggests. In ch. 6 we hear the cry of the martyred saints: "How long, Sovereign Lord, holy and true, until you . . . avenge our blood?" They are told to "wait a little longer" (vv.10–11). Therefore, "soonness" means imminency in eschatological terms. The church in every age has always lived with the expectancy of the consummation of all things in its day. Imminency describes an event possible any day, impossible no day.

Two more focal points of the book are introduced by the words "by sending his angel to his servant John." (1) They introduce us to the significance of angels in the worship of God, in the revelation of God's Word, and in the execution of his judgments in the earth. John refers to angels sixty-seven times. (2) The word "servant" (GK *1528*) is important. All of God's people are known in Revelation as his servants, described as such at least eleven times (e.g., 2:20; 7:3; 22:3). John is one servant selected to receive this revelation and communicate it to other servants of God. "Servant," used throughout the NT to describe those who are designated as the special representatives of the Lord Christ himself, becomes a beautiful title of honor for God's people.

2 Two elements in the book are of chief importance: "The word of God and the testimony of Jesus Christ." In referring to his visions as the "word of God," John emphasizes his continuity with the prophets in the OT as well as the apostles in the NT (see 1:9; 3:8, 10; 6:9; 12:11; 17:17; 19:9; 20:4). In 19:13 Jesus is himself identified with the name "the Word of God." Here, in ch. 1, the reference is not directly to Christ but to the promises and acts of God revealed in this book that are realized through Jesus, the Word of God incarnate (cf. Jn 1:1–2; 1Jn 1:1). The church needs to be reminded that this book is the very Word of God to us. While John's literary activity is evident throughout, he claims that what he presents he actually "saw" in divinely disclosed visions. And in the book God himself bears witness to the readers that these things are not the product of John's own mind (1:1–2; 21:5; 22:6; cf. 2Pe 1:21).

"Testimony" (GK *3456*) can mean "witness," "validation," or "verification" (cf. 1:9; 6:9; 12:11, 17; 19:10; 20:4; 22:16–20). While "the testimony of Jesus" can mean John's own testimony about Jesus, here it means the testimony that Jesus himself gives. John testifies both to the Word of God received in the visions and to the validation of his message from Jesus himself.

3 "The one who reads" reflects the early form of worship where a reader read the Scriptures aloud on the Lord's Day. "Those who hear" are the people of the congregation who listen to the reading. "This prophecy" is John's way of describing his writing and refers to the entire book of Revelation (10:11; 19:10; 22:7, 9–10, 18). Prophecy involves not only future events but also the ethical and spiritual exhortations and warnings contained in the writing. Thus John immediately sets off his writing from the late Jewish apocalyptic literature (which did not issue from the prophets) and puts himself on a par with the OT prophets.

The twofold benediction "blessed" (GK 3421), pronounced on the reader and the congregation, emphasizes the importance of the message in that they will be hearing not only the word of John the prophet but the inspired word of Christ (see other beatitudes in 14:13; 16:15; 19:9; 20:6; 22:7, 14). John wrote in anticipation of the full and immediate recognition of his message as worthy to be read in the churches as the Word of God coming from Christ. In the ancient Jewish synagogue tradition in which John was raised, no such blessing was promised on anyone who recited a mere human teaching, even if from a rabbi, while one who read a biblical text was worthy to receive a divine blessing.

All must listen carefully and "take to heart what is written" because "the time [GK 2789] is near," the season for the fulfillment of the return of Christ (v.7; cf. Lk 11:28, 21:8) and for all that is written in this book (cf. 22:10). The season for Christ's return is always imminent—now as it has been from the days of his ascension (Jn 21:22; Ac 1:11).

A comparison of the Prologue (1:1–3) with the Epilogue (22:7–21) shows that John has followed throughout Revelation a deliberate literary pattern. This should alert us to the possibility that the entire book was designed to be heard and interpreted as a single unit, and every part should fit into the message of the book as a whole. This should not in any way detract from the fact that John claims to have seen real visions ("saw," v.2), which we may assume were arranged by John in their particular literary form for purposes of communication.

B. Greetings and Doxology (1:4–8)

John now addresses the recipients of his book: "To the seven churches in the province of Asia" (cf. v. 11; 2:1–3:22). Almost immediately he introduces an expanded form of the Christian trinitarian greeting that merges into a doxology to Christ (vv.5b–6) and is followed by a staccato exclamation calling attention to the return of Christ to the world (v.7). The Father concludes the greeting with assurances of his divine sovereignty.

4 The epistolary form of address immediately distinguishes this book from all other Jewish apocalyptic works. John writes to actual, historical churches, addressing them in the same way the NT letters are addressed. These churches actually existed in the Roman province of Asia (the western part of present-day Turkey). But why did John address these churches and only these seven churches? There were other churches in Asia at the close of the first century. The NT itself refers to congregations at Troas (Ac 20:5–12), Colosse (Col 1:2), and Hierapolis (Col 4:13).

At present it is difficult to say why the Lord selected just these seven churches. Some have suggested that these churches were prophetic of the church ages throughout history. Yet there is no reason from the text itself to hold this view. The churches are simply representative churches found in every age. Seven churches were chosen and were placed in this order because seven was simply the number of completeness, and here it rounds out the literary pattern of the other sevens in the book. These seven churches contained typical or representative qualities of both obedience and disobedience that are a constant reminder throughout every age to all churches (cf. 2:7, 11, 17, 29; 3:6, 13, 22; esp. 2:23). As for the order of their mention (1:11), it is the natural ancient travel circuit beginning at Ephesus and arriving finally at Laodicea (consult a map of the area).

"Grace and peace" are the usual greetings in NT letters: "grace" (GK 5921) represents a traditional Greek greeting, and "peace" (GK 1645; cf. 8934) represents a traditional Hebrew greeting. The source of blessing is described by employing an elaborate triadic formula for the Trinity:

"From him who is, and who was, and who is to come," i.e., the Father;

"From the seven spirits before his throne," i.e., the Holy Spirit;

"From Jesus Christ," i.e., the Son (v.5).

Similarly there follows a threefold reference to the identity and function of Christ: "the faithful witness, the firstborn from the dead, and the ruler of the kings of the earth";

and three indications of his saving work: "who loves us and has freed us from our sins ... and has made us to be a kingdom and priests."

The descriptive name of the Father occurs nowhere else except in Revelation (4:8; cf. 11:17; 16:5). It is generally understood as a paraphrase for the divine name represented throughout the OT by the Hebrew tetragrammaton YHWH (see comment on Ex 3:14; cf. also Isa 41:4, where the Lord is described as the one "who is to come"). The complete combination of these three tenses occurs in a Palestinian Targum on Dt 32:39. The force of the name has been widely discussed. In 1:8 and 4:8 it is parallel with the divine name "Lord God, the Almighty." The tenses indicate that the same God is eternally present with his covenant people to sustain and encourage them through all the experiences of their lives.

"And from the seven spirits before his throne" seems clearly to focus on the Holy Spirit. But why "seven spirits"? Some understand John to mean the "sevenfold spirit" in his fullness (see NIV note). Borrowing from the imagery of Zec 4, where the ancient prophet sees a lampstand with seven bowls supplied with oil from two nearby olive trees, John seems to connect the church ("lampstands" [v.20]) to the ministry of the Holy Spirit (3:1; 4:5; 5:6). The "seven spirits" represent the activity of the risen Christ through the Holy Spirit in and to the seven churches. This figure brings great encouragement to the churches, for it is "'not by might nor by power, but by my Spirit,' says the LORD Almighty" (Zec 4.6), that the churches serve God. Yet the figure is also a sobering one because the history of each church (chs. 2–3) is an unfolding of that church's response to the Holy Spirit—"He who has an ear, let him hear what the Spirit says to the churches" (2:7, 11, et al.).

5 Finally, greetings come from the Son— "from Jesus Christ." John immediately adds three descriptive epithets about Christ and a burst of doxology to him. (1) He is the "faithful witness." His credibility is proved by his earthly life of obedience in the past; it is proved in the present by his witness to the true condition of the churches; and it will be proved in the future by the consummation of all things in him. In the past he was loyal to the point of death (cf. Jn 7:7; 18:37; Php 2:8; 1Ti 6: 13), as was his servant Antipas (2:13). That Christ was a reliable witness to God's kingdom and salvation—even to the point of suffering death at the hands of the religious-political establishment of his day—is an encouragement to his servants who also are expected to be loyal to him, even to their death (2:10).

(2) The fact that he is "the firstborn from the dead" brings further encouragement. As Christ gave his life in faithfulness to the Father's calling, so the Father has raised Christ from the dead, pledging him as the first of a great company who will follow (cf. 7:13–14). John nowhere else refers to Christ as the "firstborn" (GK 4758), though Paul uses it in Ro 8:29; Col 1:15, 18 (cf. also Heb 1:6). In Col 1:18, this same expression is associated with words of supreme authority or origin such as "head," "beginning," and "supremacy." In Col 1:15 Paul refers to Christ as the "firstborn over all creation," meaning that he is the source, ruler, or origin of all creation (see comment on that verse). So for Christ to be the "firstborn" of the dead signifies not merely that he was first in time to be raised from the dead but also that he was first in importance, having supreme authority over the dead (cf. 1:18).

(3) "The ruler of the kings of the earth" virtually connects John's thought with Ps 89. Christ's rulership of the world is a key theme of John (11:15; 17:15; 19:16). Who are the "kings of the earth"? John could mean emperors such as Nero and Domitian, territorial rulers such as Pilate and Herod, and their successors. In that case John was affirming that even though Jesus is not physically present and the earthly monarchs appear to rule, in reality it is he, not they, who rules over all (6:15; 17:2). Another approach holds that Jesus rules over the defeated foes of believers, e.g., Satan, the dragon, sin, and death (1:18). A third possibility sees believers as "the kings of the earth" (2:26–27; 3:21; cf. 11:6); in the immediate context John refers to Christ's redeeming activity, and in v.6 he refers to believers as a "kingdom." All three ideas are true; so it is difficult to decide which was uppermost in John's mind. We should be careful, however, not to read into the term "king" our own power concepts but to allow the biblical images to predominate.

The mention of the person and offices of Christ leads John to a burst of praise to his Savior: "To him who loves us ... be glory and power." In the present, Christ is loving us. Through all the immediate distresses, persecutions, and even banishment, John is convinced that believers are experiencing Christ's continual care. Moreover, in the past Christ's love was unmistakably revealed in his atoning death, by which he purchased our release from the captivity of sin. Christ's kingly power is chiefly revealed in his ability to transform individual lives through his "blood" (i.e., his death; cf. 5:9; 7:14). Through his death on the cross, he defeated the devil; those who follow Christ in the battle against the devil share his victory (12:11).

6 This transformation simultaneously involves the induction of blood-freed sinners into Christ's "kingdom" and priesthood. Of Israel it was said that they would be a "kingdom of priests and a holy nation" (Ex 19:6; cf. Isa 61:6). As Israel of old was redeemed through the Red Sea and was called to be a kingdom under God and a nation of priests to serve him, so John sees the Christian community as the continuation of the OT people of God, redeemed by Christ's blood and made heirs of his future kingly rule on the earth (5:10; 20:6). Furthermore, all believers are called to be priests in the sense of offering spiritual sacrifices and praise to God (Heb 13:15; 1Pe 2:5). While John sees the church as a kingdom, this does not mean that it is identical with the kingdom of God. Nor do the new people of God replace the ancient Jewish people in the purpose of God (cf. Ro 11:28–29).

7 What Christ will do in the future is summed up in the dramatic cry: "Look, he is coming"—a clear reference to his return (22:7, 12, 20). The preceding affirmation of Christ's rulership over the earth's kings and the Christians' share in the messianic kingdom leads to tension between the believers' actual present condition of oppression and suffering and what seems to be implied in their royal and priestly status. So the divine promise of Christ's return is given by the Father, and the response of the prophet and congregation follows in the words "So shall it be! Amen." Or we might think of Christ as saying, "So shall it be!" and the prophet and the congregation responding, "Amen" (cf. 22:20). The promise combines Da 7:13 with Zec 12:10. Daniel 7 provides a key focus for John throughout the whole book (there are no fewer than thirty-one allusions to it).

Christ's coming will be supernatural ("with the clouds") and in some manner open and known to all ("every eye"), even to those who put him to death. "Those who pierced him" might be those historically responsible for his death (e.g., Pilate, Annas, and Caiaphas) and the Jewish leaders of the Sanhedrin who pronounced him guilty. Yet, when he comes, there will be mourning among "all the peoples of the earth." From the NT point of view, Pilate, Annas, Caiaphas, and the others were acting as representatives for all humankind in crucifying Jesus. Thus the mourning mentioned here is probably that which results from the judgment Christ brings upon "all the peoples of the earth."

8 Such a stupendous promise requires more than the prophet's own signature or even Christ's "Amen." God himself speaks and, with his own signature, vouches for the truthfulness of the coming of Christ. Of the many names of God that reveal his character and memorialize his deeds, there are four strong ones in this verse. (1) "Alpha and Omega" are the first and last letters of the Greek alphabet. Their mention here is similar to the "First" and "Last" in v.17 and is further heightened by the "Beginning" and the "End" in 21:6 and 22:13. Only this book refers to God as the "Alpha and the Omega." (2) He is the absolute source of all creation and history, and nothing lies outside him. Thus he is the "Lord God" of all. (3) He is the one "who is, and who was, and who is to come" (see comment on v.4). (4) He is continually present to his people as the "Almighty" (lit., "the one who has his hand on everything"; GK *4120*; cf. 4:8; 11:17; 15:3; 16:7, 14; 19:6, 15; 21:22; 2Co 6:18).

II. Vision of the Son of Man Among the Seven Churches of Asia (1:9–3:22)

A. The Son of Man Among the Lampstands (1:9–20)

1. Introduction and voice (1:9–11)

9 This verse begins a third introduction in which the author again identifies himself as John and adds significant information about where and when the visions took place together with their divinely appointed destination. John stresses his intimate identification with the Asian Christians and the reason for his presence on Patmos.

Patmos lies about thirty-seven miles west-southwest of Miletus, in the Icarian Sea. Consisting mainly of volcanic hills and rocky ground, it is about ten miles long and six miles wide at the north end; it was used for Roman penal purposes. It was "because of the word of God and the testimony of Jesus" that John was on Patmos (cf. 1:2; 6:9; 20:4). He was not there to preach that Word but because of religious-political opposition to his Christian faith.

John sees his plight as part of God's design and says he is a partner with the Asian Christians in three things. (1) Both share with Christ and one another the "suffering" (GK 2568) or agony that comes because of faithfulness to Christ as the only true Lord and God (Jn 16:33; Ac 14:22; Col 1:24; 2Ti 3:12). (2) They also share with Christ in his "kingdom" (i.e., his power and rule; GK 993). In one sense they already reign (1:6), though through suffering. Yet, in another sense, they will reign with Christ in the eschatological manifestation of his kingdom (20:4, 6; 22:5). (3) The present hidden rule of Christ and his followers is manifested through their "patient endurance" (GK 5705). As they look beyond their immediate distresses and put full confidence in Christ, they share now in his royal dignity and power. Whether those distresses were imprisonment, ostracism, slander, economic discrimination, hostility, disruption of the churches by false prophets, and the constant threat of death from mob violence or judicial action, believers are to realize their present kingship with Christ in their faithful endurance. Such endurance produces conflict with the powers of the world, and it calls for long-suffering as the mark of Christ's kingship in their lives (2:2, 19; 3:10; 13:10; 14:12; cf. Lk 8:15; 21:19; Ro 2:7; Col 1:11; et al.). Christ uses suffering to test and purify the loyalty of his servants. His strength is revealed through their weakness (2Co 12:9).

10 "I was in the Spirit" describes John's experience on Patmos. The words imply being transported into the world of prophetic visions by the Spirit of God (4:2; 17:3; 21:10; cf. Eze 3:12, 14; 37:1; Ac 22:17). At least the first vision—if not this whole book—was revealed on "the Lord's [GK 3258] Day." Since this is the only place in the NT where this expression is used, its identification is difficult. Some feel that John was transported into the great future day of the Lord, but John nowhere uses the common expression "the day of the Lord." Most commentators, both ancient and modern, have taken the expression to mean Sunday, the first day of the week. This usage occurs early in the apostolic fathers. Tendencies toward recognizing Sunday as a day designated by Christ to celebrate his redemption occur even earlier in the NT (Ac 20:7; 1Co 16:2). Such a reference would bind the exiled apostle to the worshiping churches in Asia through his longing to be with them on Sunday. More specifically, John may have had an Easter Sunday in mind.

11 The "voice" (GK 5889) John heard could be Christ's or, more likely, that of the angel who appears frequently to John (4:1; 5:2). What John sees (both visions and words), he is to write down in a papyrus scroll and send to the seven Asian churches (v.4). This writing would include the substance of the whole book, not just the first vision.

2. The sight of the vision (1:12–20)

Certain important literary features of John's first vision are noted. (1) Beginning with v.12, the vision extends as a unit through ch. 3. The quotation that begins in v.17 is not closed till the end of ch. 3.

(2) This introductory section (1:12–20) can be divided into two sections—the sevenfold features in the description of the glorified Christ (vv.12–16) and the address to John (vv.17–20).

(3) In this symbolic picture the glorified Lord is seen in his inner reality that transcends his outward appearance. The sword coming out of his mouth (v.16) alerts us to this. In words drawn almost entirely from imagery used in Daniel, Ezekiel, and Isaiah of God's majesty and power, John uses hyperbole to describe the indescribable reality of the glorified Christ. These same poetic phrases reappear in the letters to the churches in chs. 2–3 as well as throughout the rest of the book (see 14:2; 19:6, 12, 15).

(4) The words of Christ substantiate his absolute authority to address the churches, and the vision (vv.12–16) leads to John's

transformed understanding of Jesus as the Lord of all through his death and resurrection (vv.17–18).

12 For the OT tabernacle, Moses constructed a seven-branched lampstand (Ex 25:31ff.). Subsequently this lampstand symbolized Israel. Another golden seven-branched lampstand appears in a vision of Zechariah; it was fed by seven pipes and was explained to him as the "eyes of the LORD, which range through the earth" (Zec 4:10). Thus the lampstand relates directly to the Lord himself. Since other allusions to Zechariah's vision of the lampstand appear in the Revelation—e.g., "seven eyes, which are the seven spirits of God" (Rev 5:6) and the "two witnesses" that are "the two olive trees" (11:3-4), it is logical to assume here a connection with that vision as well.

But there are problems in any strict identification. In v.20 Christ tells John that the "seven lampstands are the seven churches," and in 2:5 that it is possible to lose one's place as a lampstand through a failure to repent. Thus, the imagery represents the individual churches scattered among the nations—churches that bear the light of the divine revelation of the gospel of Christ to the world (Mt 5:14). If Zechariah's imagery was in John's mind, it might mean that the churches, which correspond to the people of God today, are light bearers only because of their intimate connection with Christ, the source of the light, through the power of the Holy Spirit (1:4b; 3:1; 4:5; 5:6).

13 Evidently the words "someone 'like a son of man'" are to be understood in connection with Da 7:13 as a reference to the heavenly Messiah who is also human. Jesus preferred the title "Son of Man" for himself throughout his earthly ministry, though he did not deny, on occasion, the appropriate use of "Son of God" as well (Jn 10:36; cf. Mk 14:61). Both titles are nearly identical terms for the Messiah. The early church, however, rarely used the title "Son of Man" for Jesus, except when there was some special connection between the suffering of believers and Christ's suffering and glory (e.g., Ac 7:56; Rev 14:14).

"Dressed in a robe" begins the sevenfold description of the Son of Man. This vision creates an impression of the whole rather than of particular abstract concepts. John saw Christ as the divine Son of God in the fullest sense of that term. He also saw him as fulfilling the OT descriptions of the coming Messiah by using terms drawn from the OT imagery of divine wisdom, power, steadfastness, and penetrating vision. The long robe and golden sash were worn by the priests in the OT (Ex 28:4) and may here signify Christ as the great High Priest to the churches in fulfillment of the OT Aaronic priesthood, or, less specifically, it may indicate his dignity and divine authority (Eze 9:2, 11).

14 In an apparent allusion to Daniel, Christ's head and hair are described as "white like wool, as white as snow" (Da 7:9; cf. 10:5). For John, the same functions of ruler and judge ascribed to the "Ancient of Days" in Daniel's vision relate to Jesus. In Eastern countries, white hair commands respect and indicates the wisdom of years. This part of the vision may have shown John something of the deity and wisdom of Christ (cf. Col. 2:3). Christ's eyes were like a "blazing fire," a detail not found in Da 7 but occurring in Da 10:6. This simile is repeated in the letter to Thyatira (2:18) and in the vision of Christ's triumphant return and defeat of his enemies (19:12). It may portray either his penetrating scrutiny or fierce judgment.

15 The Son of Man's feet appeared like shining bronze (cf. 2:18), as if it were fired to white heat in a kiln (cf. a similar figure of glowing metal in Eze 1:13, 27; 8:2; Da 10:6). In both Ezekiel and Daniel the brightness of shining metal like fire is one of the symbols connected with the appearance of the glory of God. This image may represent Christ's triumphant judgment (i.e., his trampling down) of unbelievers.

"His voice ... like the sound of rushing [lit., many; GK *4498*] waters" (cf. 14:2; 19:6) describes the glory and majesty of God in a way similar to that which Ezekiel heard (Eze 1:24; 43:2). Anyone who has heard the awe-inspiring sound of a Niagara or Victoria Falls cannot but appreciate this image of God's power and sovereignty (Ps 93:4).

16 "In his right hand he held seven stars." The right hand is the place of power and safety, and the "seven stars" Christ held in it are identified with the seven angels of the seven churches in Asia (v.20). This is the only detail in the vision that is identified. The seven angels are those to whom the letters to the seven churches are addressed (chs. 2–3). Stars are associated in the OT and in Revelation with angels (Job 38:7; Rev 9:1) or faithful witnesses to God (Da 12:3). The letter to Ephesus includes in its introduction a reference to the seven stars (2:1), and in 3:1 they are associated closely with the "seven spirits of God."

John sees a "sharp double-edged sword" going forth from the mouth of Christ. The metaphor of a sword coming from the mouth is important for three reasons: (1) John refers to this characteristic of Christ several times (1:16; 2:12, 16; 19:15, 21); (2) he uses a rare word for "sword" (GK 4855), one found only once outside Revelation (Lk 2:35); and (3) there is no scriptural parallel to the expression except in Isa 11:4, where it is said that the Messiah will "strike the earth with the rod of his mouth" and "with the breath of his lips he will slay the wicked."

The sword is both a weapon and a symbol of war, oppression, and political authority. But John intends a startling difference in the function of this sword, since it proceeds from the mouth of Christ rather than being wielded in his hand. Christ will overtake the Nicolaitans at Pergamum and make war with them by the sword of his mouth (2:12, 16). He will strike down the rebellious at his coming with such a sword (19:15, 21). The figure points definitely to divine judgment, but not to the type of power wielded by the nations. Christ conquers the world through his death and resurrection, and the sword is his faithful witness to God's saving purposes. The weapons of his followers are loyalty, truthfulness, and righteousness (19:8, 14).

Finally, the face of Christ is likened to "the sun shining in all its brilliance." This is a simile of Christ's divine glory, preeminence, and victory (Mt 13:43; 17:2; cf. Rev 10:1).

17–18 These verses identify Christ to John and connect the vision of the glorified Christ (vv. 13–16) with his existence in history. The vision is seen in the light of the Eternal One who identifies himself in these verses. "I fell at his feet as though dead" indicates that John saw a supernatural being and was stricken with trembling and fear, as had prophets before him (Eze 1:28; Da 8:17; 10:9). Immediately Christ placed his hand on John and assured him that he would not die: "Do not be afraid" (cf. 2:10; 19:10, 22:8; cf. Mt 17:6–7).

The title "the First and the Last," which belongs to God in Isa 44:6 and 48:12 (where it means that he alone is God, the absolute Lord of history and the Creator), shows that in John's Christology, Christ is identified with the Deity.

Christ is also "the Living One" in that he, like God, never changes. Probably this expression is a further elaboration of what it means to be "the First and the Last," i.e., he alone of all the gods can speak and act in the world (Jos 3:10; 1Sa 17:26; Ps 42:2; Rev 7:2). These divine qualities of his person are now linked to his earthly existence in first-century Palestine—"I was dead, and behold I am alive for ever and ever!" John's view of Jesus and his kingdom revolves around the Cross and the Resurrection, i.e., around atonement theology—an interpretation that sets the tone for all the visions that follow.

It was through Jesus' suffering, death, and resurrection that he won the right to have the "keys of death and Hades." Keys grant the holder access to interiors and their contents, and in ancient times the wearing of large keys was a mark of status in the community (cf. 3:7; 9:1; 20:1; 21:25). "Hades" (GK 87) translates the Hebrew term *Sheol* ("death" or "grave"; GK 8619) almost everywhere in the LXX. In the NT the word has a twofold usage: in some cases it denotes the place of all the departed dead (Ac 2:27, 31); in others, it refers to the place of the departed wicked (Lk 16:23; Rev 20:13–14). Since Christ alone has conquered death and has himself come out of Hades, he alone can determine who will enter death and Hades and who will come out of them. He has the "keys." For the Christian, death can only be seen as the servant of Christ.

19 John is told to "write, therefore, what you have seen." This verse faces us with an important exegetical problem concerning the sense of the words and the relationship of the three clauses: "what you have seen, what is now and what will take place later." Does Christ give John a chronological outline as a key to the visions in the book? Many think he does. If so, are there three divisions: "seen," "now," and "later"? Or are there two: "seen," i.e., "now" and "later"? In the latter case, where does the chronological break take place in the book? For others, v.19 simply gives a general statement of the contents of all the visions throughout the book as containing a mixture of the "now" and the "later."

While no general agreement prevails, the key to the problem may lie in the middle term "what is now" (lit., "which [things] are"). There are two possibilities. (1) The verb can be taken temporally ("now"), as NIV has done. This would refer to things that were present in John's day, e.g., matters discussed in the letters to the churches (chs. 2–3). (2) The verb can be taken in the sense of "what things mean." This explanation agrees with John's usage of the verb "to be" throughout the book (cf. v.20; 4:5; 5:6, 8; 7:14; 17:12, 15). "What they are [mean]" is then immediately given in the next verse, i.e., the explanation of the mystery of the lamps and stars.

Most commentators understand the phrase "what you have seen" as referring to the first vision (1:12–16); but it may refer to the whole book as the expression "what you see" in v.11 does. In this case the translation could be either "what you saw, both the things that are and the things that will occur afterward," or "what you saw, both what it means and what will occur afterward." "What will take place later" clearly refers to the future, but to the future of what? Some have taken the similar but not identical phrase in 4:1 to mean the same as here and have rendered it "what shall take place after these present things," i.e., after the things relating to the seven churches (chs. 2–3). This results in either the historicist view of chs. 4–22 or the futurist view of them. But if the future is simply the future visions given to John after this initial vision, then the statement has little significance in indicating chronological sequence in the book. While v.19 may provide a helpful key to the book's plan, on careful analysis it by no means gives us a clear key to it.

In my understanding, John is being told here to write down a description of the vision of Christ that he has just seen, what it means, and what he will see afterward—i.e., not the end-time things, but the things revealed later to him. Whether these other things are wholly future, wholly present, or both future and present depends on the content of the vision.

20 The first vision is called a "mystery" (GK 3696). In the NT a "mystery" is something formerly secret but now revealed or identified (cf. John's identification of the "mystery" of the harlot in ch. 17 as the "great city" that rules over the kings of the earth).

The seven stars represent the "angels of the seven churches." Who are these angels? There is no totally satisfactory answer to this question. "Angels" (GK 34) occurs sixty-seven times in Revelation, and in every other instance it refers to heavenly messengers, though occasionally in the NT it can mean a human messenger (Lk 7:24; 9:52; Jas 2:25). A strong objection to the human messenger sense here is the fact that the word is not used that way anywhere else in apocalyptic literature. John's reference should thus be understood as the heavenly messengers who have been entrusted by Christ with responsibility over the churches and yet who are so closely identified with them that the letters are addressed at the same time to these "messengers" and to the congregation (cf. the plural form in 2:10, 13, 23–24).

Whatever may be the correct identification of the angels, the emphasis rests on Christ's immediate presence and communication through the Spirit to the churches (cf. the link of "stars" in 3:1 with the seven spirits of God). In some sense, the reference to angels in the churches shows that the churches are more than a gathering of mere individuals or a social institution; they have a corporate and heavenly character (cf. 1Co 11:10; Eph 3:10; Heb 1:14). That the "seven lampstands are the seven churches" not only shows that the churches are the earthly counterpart of the stars but links the vision of Christ with his authority to rule and judge his churches.

B. The Letters to the Seven Churches (2:1–3:22)

The letters are more in the nature of messages than letters. Each message to an individual church was apparently also intended for the other six churches (2:7, 11, 17, etc., esp. 2:23). By reading and comparing the similar components of the letters, one may gain a fuller insight into the messages. Each message generally follows a common literary plan consisting of seven parts:

(1) The addressee is first given in a set pattern: "To the angel of the church in Ephesus

write," etc. (for the location of these seven churches, see map at 1Pe 1).

(2) Then the speaker is mentioned; in each case some part of the great vision of Christ in 1:12–20 is repeated; e.g., "him who holds the seven stars in his right hand and walks among the seven golden lampstands" (2:1). This identification is preceded with the significant declaration "These are the words of him"—a declaration strongly reminiscent of the OT formula for introducing the words of God to Israel.

(3) Next, the knowledge of the speaker is given. His is a divine knowledge. He knows intimately the works of the churches and the reality of their loyalty to him, despite outward appearances. Each congregation's total life is measured against the standard of Christ's life and the works they have embraced. The churches have varying degrees of positive and negative things said about them. The enemy of the churches is Satan, who seeks to undermine the churches' loyalty to Christ (2:10, 24).

(4) Following his assessment of the accomplishments of the churches, the speaker pronounces his verdict on their condition in such words as "You have forsaken your first love" (2:4), or "You are dead" (3:1). Two letters contain no unfavorable verdict (Smyrna, Philadelphia) and two no word of commendation (Sardis, Laodicea); yet since all seven letters would be sent to each church together with the entire book of Revelation (cf. 1:11), we may assume that Christ intended all the churches to hear words of both commendation and blame. In the letters all derelictions are viewed as forms of inner betrayals of a prior relationship to Christ. Each congregation is responsible as a congregation for its individual members and for its leaders; each leader and each individual believer is at the same time fully responsible for himself and for the congregation. This responsibility especially involves the problem of self-deception concerning good and evil, the true and the false, in situations where they are easily confused. The evil appears under the cloak of good; the good appears as apparent evil. Christ's verdict sets before each church the true criteria for leading it out of self-deception into the truth.

(5) To correct or alert each congregation, Jesus issues a penetrating command. These commands further expose the exact nature of the self-deception involved. We are mistaken if we believe that the churches readily identified the heretics and heresies involved in Christ's descriptions. Because they were deceptions, they would not easily be identified; thus, there is the use of OT figures such as Balaam, Jezebel, etc., to alert the churches to the deceptiveness of the error. The greater the evil, the more deceptive the cloak. The thrust of the commands is not in the direction of consolation for persecuted churches. It is rather the opposite—namely, that John, like Jesus, was concerned to bring not peace but a sword.

(6) Each letter contains the general exhortation "he who has an ear, let him hear what the Spirit says to the churches" (e.g., 2:7); only its position in the letter is variable. The words of the Spirit are the words of Christ (cf. 19:10). The commands of Christ in the letters, being somewhat ambiguous, require the individual and the congregation to listen also to the Spirit's voice if they are truly to realize the victory he considers appropriate for them. The exhortations provide warnings about apathy as well as words of challenge and encouragement. By the Spirit's continual relevance these words transcend time limitation and speak to all the churches in every generation.

(7) Finally, each letter contains a victor's promise of reward. These promises are often the most metaphorical and symbolic portions of the letters and thus in some cases present interpretative difficulties. Each is eschatological and is correlated with chs. 21–22. For example, "the right to eat from the tree of life" (2:7) is parallel to "the tree of life" in 22:2; protection from "the second death" (2:11) finds its counterpart in "no more death" (21:4), etc. Furthermore, the promises are echoes of Ge 2–3: what was lost originally by Adam in Eden is more than regained in Christ. The expression "I will give" or "I will make" identifies Christ as the absolute source of every gift. We should probably understand the multiple promises as different facets that combine to make up one great promise to believers: wherever Christ is, there will the overcomers be. Who are these "overcomers"? Certainly it is those who are fully loyal to Christ as his true disciples. One should compare those who do not overcome in 21:8 with those referred to in the letters, e.g., the "cowardly" (2:10, 13), the "sexually

immoral" (2:14, 20), the "idolaters" (2:14, 20), and the "liars" (2:2, 9, 20; 3:9).

1. To Ephesus (2:1–7)

The church at Ephesus is addressed in the first letter. Ephesus was a crossroads of civilization. Politically, it had become the de facto capital of the province of Asia; it was known as "Supreme Metropolis of Asia." The Roman governor resided there. It was a "free" city, i.e., self-governed. Located on the western coast of Asia Minor at the convergence of three great highways, Ephesus was the trade center of the area.

Religiously, Ephesus was the center for the worship of the fertility "bee" goddess known to the Greeks as "Artemis" or to the Romans as "Diana" (Ac 19:23ff.). The temple with its statue of Artemis was one of the wonders of the ancient world. Thousands of priests and priestesses were involved in her service, many of which were dedicated to cult prostitution. The temple also served as a great bank for kings and merchants, as well as an asylum for fleeing criminals. To what extent the temple phenomena contributed to the general moral deterioration of the population cannot be assessed, but one of Ephesus's own citizens, the philosopher Heraclitus, said that the inhabitants of the city lived lives of terrible uncleanness. The church at Ephesus was probably founded jointly by Aquila, Priscilla, and (later) Paul (Ac 18:18–19; 19:1–10). Because the Ephesians were cosmopolitan and transient and because the city had a history of cultural-political change, these factors may have influenced the apostasy of the congregation at Ephesus from its first love (cf. 2:4).

1 The speaker identifies himself by a reference to the vision of ch. 1: "Him who holds the seven stars in his right hand" (cf. 1:16). These words strike both a note of reassurance, signaling Christ's strong protection, and control of the church. On the other hand, there is a note of warning in the description of Christ as the one who "walks [travels] among the seven golden lampstands," since he may journey to Ephesus to remove their lampstand (2:5).

2–3 The speaker's knowledge includes awareness of their activity, of their discernment of evil, and of their patient suffering. Their "deeds," their "hard work" (GK *3160*), and their "perseverance" (GK *5705*) are

Persecution of the Christians at Ephesus began in Ac 20, when a riot was instigated by Demetrius and the silversmiths, whose business was making images of the goddess Artemis (her temple stands in the foreground). But by the late first century the Ephesians had lost their first love.

underlined by the phrase "you have ... endured hardships for my name, and have not grown weary" (v.3). The Ephesian Christians did not lack serious activity, even to the point of suffering for Christ's name. Paul attributes the same threefold activity to the Thessalonians and there adds to each quality its motivating source: "faith," "love," and "hope" (1Th 1:3).

Christ also knows that doctrinal discrimination accompanies the toil and patience of the Ephesians: they "cannot tolerate wicked men." These were not the pagans in Ephesus but false brethren who "claim to be apostles but are not." It is not easy, however, to determine precisely who these people were, what they taught, or how the church tested them. An "apostle" (GK 693) is one who is sent as a representative of another and bears the full authority of the sender. The word is applied first in the NT to the original circle of the Twelve (Mk 3:14; Ac 1:2, 26), who had a special place historically in the foundation of the church (Eph 2:20; Rev 21:14). But the NT further broadens this original circle to include others such as Paul (Gal 1:1), Barnabas (Ac 14:14), James the brother of Jesus (Gal 1:19), and still others (cf. Ro 16:7). The name was applied to those who were authentically and specially called by Christ to be his authoritative spokesmen.

Miracles were the signs of apostolic authority (2Co 12:12; Heb 2:4), but miracles may also accompany false prophets (Mk 13:22; 2Th 2:9; 2Ti 3:8; Rev 13:13–14). Thus it was necessary to "test the spirits to see whether they are from God" (1Jn 4:1). Beyond their denial of Jesus as Lord, such apostles also sought selfish advantage through their claims (2Co 11:5, 13; 12:11).

As to whether the authoritative function of apostles continued after the first century, the writings of the Apostolic Fathers are instructive. In no case do their references to apostles relate to any recognized apostles other than those associated with the NT. They apparently understood the special apostolic function to have ceased with the end of the apostolic era.

About fifteen years after John's writing of Revelation, Ignatius wrote to the church of Ephesus and commended them for refusing to give a home to any heresy. Thyatira had failed (2:20ff.), but the Ephesians had won the victory over false teachers. They had heeded Paul's earlier warning (Ac 20:28–30).

4 The speaker's verdict shows, on the other hand, that however much had been gained at Ephesus by resisting the false apostles, not all was well there. They had "forsaken" or "let go" (GK 918) their "first love." This was a serious defect. If uncorrected, it would result in their loss of light-bearing (v.5). The majority of commentators take the first love to refer to the original Christian love the Ephesians had for one another. Paul's exhortation to the Ephesian elders to "help the weak" (Ac 20:35) and the warm commendation he gives them in their early years for their fervent love of one another (Eph 1:15) may lend support to this view. Other commentators, however, see the "first love" as a reference to their inner devotion to Christ that characterized their earlier commitment, like the love of a newly wedded bride for her husband (cf. Eph 5:22ff.). This interpretation is supported by the fact that the letters to the other churches reveal problems of inner betrayal to Christ as subjects of his complaint. Neither view necessarily eliminates the other. Loving devotion to Christ can be lost in the midst of active service, and certainly no amount of orthodoxy can be a substitute for a failure to love one another. "First" (GK 4755) love suggests that they still loved, but with a quality and intensity unlike that of their initial love.

5 The speaker's command further exposes the problem and offers a way to correct the fault. The imperatives are instructive: "Remember ... repent ... do." The Ephesians are to reflect on their earlier works of fervent love, to ponder how far they have fallen from their former devotion and enthusiasm, to humbly "repent" (GK 3566) before God, and to do their former works motivated by love. These imperatives are all part of a single action designed to keep the Ephesians from the judgment of Christ, which would effectively remove them as his representatives in the world.

How many churches today stand at this same crossroads? Do we sense the importance to Christ of not only honoring his name by our true confession but also of reflecting his life by our loving relationship to others? This threat of loss of light bearing applies equally to the other four churches to whom a similar exhortation to "repent" is given (Pergamum, Thyatira, Sardis, and Laodicea).

6 Christ adds a further commendation concerning the Ephesians' hatred of the practices of the Nicolaitans (cf. 2:15)—a hatred directed at the practices of these people, not the people themselves (cf. Ps 139:21). It is difficult to determine exactly who the Nicolaitans were and what they taught. Etymologically the name means "to conquer the people." Did they call themselves by this name, or is it a derogatory title Christ applied to them? The close association of the name with the Balaamites in vv.14–15 (see comments) may suggest either identity with this group or similarity to their teachings.

Information about the Nicolaitans is limited, ambiguous, and based on John's references here in Revelation. Irenaeus claims that John wrote his Gospel to thwart the teaching of the Gnostic Cerinthus whose error was similar to the earlier offshoot of the same kind of teaching known as Nicolaitanism. Eusebius mentions that the Nicolaitans lasted only a short time. Seeing the sect as a heresy would agree with the references in vv.14, 20, which warn against mixing Christian faith with idolatry and cult prostitution. The Nicolaitans claimed to have insight into the divine or, more probably, into the demonic. They lived immoral lives, which allowed them to become part of the syncretism of pagan society and to participate in the Roman civil religion. Others understand the Nicolaitans as Christians who still showed devotion to the emperor by burning incense to his image.

7 On the general exhortation and the meaning of "overcomes" (GK *3771*), see introductory comments on 2:1–3:22. The overcomer is promised access to the "tree of life, which is in the paradise of God." The "tree of life" is first mentioned in Ge 2:9 as one of the many trees given to Adam and Eve for food and was off-limits after their fall into sin (Ge 3:22, 24). It is last mentioned in Rev 22:2, 19, where it conveys symbolically the truth of eternal life. Those at Ephesus who truly follow Christ in deep devotion and thus experience the real victory of Christ will share the gift of eternal life that he alone gives.

Rabbinic and Jewish apocalyptic works mention that the glorious age of the Messiah would be a restoration to Edenic conditions before the Fall (see also Isa 51:3; Eze 36:35; cf. Eze 28:13; 31:8–9). Jewish thought joined the concepts of the renewed city of God, the tree of life, and the paradise of God. "Paradise" (GK *4137*) is a Persian loan word meaning "a park" or "a garden." The LXX uses it to translate the Hebrew expression the "garden" of Eden (Ge 2:8–10). John seems to reinterpret the Jewish idea of Paradise. Jesus Christ is the restorer of the lost Paradise (22:1–4, 14), and he gives access to the tree of life. Paradise means to be in fellowship with him rather than the idea of a hidden paradise with its fantastic sensual delights.

2. To Smyrna (2:8–11)

Smyrna lay forty miles almost due north of Ephesus. The city was exceptionally beautiful and large and ranked with Ephesus and Pergamum as "First of Asia." Known as the birthplace of Homer, it was also an important seaport that commanded the mouth of the Hermus River. Smyrna was a wealthy city where learning, especially in the sciences and medicine, flourished. It repeatedly sided with Rome in different periods of her history, and thus earned special privileges as a free city.

Smyrna was also a center of the emperor worship, having won the privilege from the Roman Senate in A.D. 23 (over eleven other cities) of building the first temple in honor of Tiberius. Under Domitian (A.D. 81–96) emperor worship became compulsory for every Roman citizen on threat of death. Such an act was probably considered more as an expression of political loyalty than religious worship, and all a citizen had to do was burn a pinch of incense and say "Caesar is Lord." Yet most Christians, with their confession "Jesus is Lord" (cf. Ro 10:9), refused to do this. Perhaps nowhere was life for a Christian more perilous than in this city of zealous emperor worship. There was a modern–day parallel to this predicament when the Japanese occupied Korea in 1937–40 and ordered Christians to worship at their Shinto shrines. Many Christians refused and were imprisoned and tortured. Concerning the founding of the Smyrna church, we have no information other than in this letter.

8 The speaker identifies himself as "him who is the First and the Last, who died and came to life again" (cf. comments on 1:17–18). The

"First and Last" might remind those suffering persecution and rejection from their countrymen (vv.9–10) that the one they belonged to is the Lord of history and the Creator. He is in control regardless of appearances of evil. This term may allude by contrast to Smyrna's claim to be the "first" of Asia in beauty and emperor loyalty, whereas Christians at Smyrna were concerned with him who was truly first in everything.

He who is "the First and the Last" is also the one "who died and came to life again." To a congregation where imprisonment and death impended, the prisoner who died and came back to life again was offering the crown of life and protection from the second death (vv.8, 10–11).

9 The speaker's knowledge is threefold: (1) He knows their "afflictions" (GK 2568—a word translated "persecution" in v.10). (2) He knows their "poverty" (GK 4775). This can only mean material poverty because the speaker (Christ) immediately adds, "Yet you are rich" (toward God). Why was this church so poor in such a prosperous city? We do not know. Perhaps the high esteem of emperor worship in the city produced economic sanctions against Christians who refused to participate. Sometimes, even today, a Christian's loyalty to the Lord entails economic loss (cf. 3:17). (3) The risen Lord also knows "the slander of those who say they are Jews and are not, but are a synagogue of Satan." Trouble arose from the Jewish community. Certain Jews used malicious untruths to incite persecution of the impoverished saints in Smyrna. Even though these men claimed descent from Abraham, they were not his true descendants because they did not have faith in Christ, the "Seed" of Abraham (Gal 3:16, 29). These hostile Jews probably viewed the Jewish Christians at Smyrna as heretics of the worst sort.

"But are of the synagogue of Satan" reveals for the first time in Revelation the ultimate source of the persecution of Christians—"Satan" (GK 4928). Many further references to this archenemy of the followers of Christ are found throughout the book (2:13; 3:9; 9:11; 12:9–10, 12; 13:4; 20:2, 7, 10). In fact, he is one of the principal actors in the apocalyptic drama. While Satan is the author of persecution and wicked men are his instruments, God remains sovereign in that he gives "the crown of life" to those who are "faithful, even to the point of death" (v.10). "Synagogue of Satan" refers, then, to certain Jews in ancient Smyrna who, motivated by Satan, slandered the church there.

10 The speaker's command immediately follows since no word of verdict or fault is spoken of. The prospect of further and imminent suffering may have made the believers at Smyrna fearful: "Do not be afraid [lit., Stop being afraid] of what you are about to suffer." The risen Christ reveals that some of them will be imprisoned by the devil in order to test them, and they will have ten days of persecution. Who will do this—whether Jew or pagan—is not stated. The testing will show where their true loyalty lies. For a faithful and suffering church, Christ offers further trial and suffering. The "ten days" may be ten actual days, or it may be an expression for an indeterminate but short period of time (cf. Ne 4:12; Da 1:12). In the Roman world, prison was usually not punitive but a prelude to trial and execution; hence the words "Be faithful, even to the point of death."

For those who would face martyrdom out of loyalty to Christ, there was to be a "crown of life" given by Christ himself. People at Smyrna were familiar with the term "the crown of Smyrna," which no doubt alluded to the beautiful skyline formed around the city by the hill Pagos and the public buildings on its sloping sides. The "crown" usually referred to a garland of flowers worn chiefly in the worship of the pagan gods. Faithful servants of the city appeared on coins with laurel wreaths on their heads. As the patriots of Smyrna were faithful to Rome and to their crown city, so Christ's people are to be faithful unto death to him who will give them the imperishable crown of life (Jas 1:12; 1Pe 5:4).

11 For those who overcome, the promise is that they "will not be hurt at all by the second death." Death was a real possibility for these believers. But greater than the fear of physical death should be the fear of God's eternal judgment (Lk 12:4–5). The "second death" is a well-known Targumic expression for the death that the wicked die in the world to come. Even though death was the outcome of Adam's sin, in Christ there is a complete reversal for the human race (Ge 2:16–17; Ro 5:15ff.). Since the messianic believers at

Smyrna were under attack by some in the Jewish community, it was reassuring indeed to hear the Lord himself say that his followers would not be harmed by the second death—i.e., the lake of fire (20:14; 21:8).

3. To Pergamum (2:12–17)

The inland city of Pergamum lay about sixty-five miles north of Smyrna along the fertile valley of the Caicus River. Pergamum held the official honor of being the provincial capital of Roman Asia, though this honor was in fact also claimed by Ephesus and Smyrna. Among its notable features were its beauty and wealth, its library of nearly two hundred thousand volumes, its famous sculpture, its temples to various gods, the three temples to the emperor cult, its great altar to Zeus, and its many palaces. The two main religions seem to have been the worship of Dionysus, the god of the royal kings (symbolized by the bull), and Asclepius, the savior god of healing (represented by the snake). The city got its name from its invention of vellum (Greek, *pergamene*, "from Pergamum"), a writing material made from animal skins.

12 The speaker identifies himself as "him who has the sharp, double-edged sword" (cf. comment on 1:16; cf. Isa 49:2). In dealing with the Pergamum congregation, divided by deceptive teaching, the risen Lord will use this sword to fight against the Balaamites and the Nicolaitans (v.16). It is interesting that Pergamum was a city to which Rome had given the rare power of capital punishment, symbolized by the sword. The Christians in Pergamum were thus reminded that though they lived under almost unlimited law, they were citizens of another kingdom—that of him who needs no other sword than that of his mouth.

13 The speaker's knowledge is searching: he knows that they live in a hostile and difficult place—"where Satan has his throne." This certainly refers to Pergamum as a center for the worship of pagan gods, especially the emperor cult. The first temple in the empire established in honor of Augustus was built in A.D. 29 at Pergamum, because it was the administrative capital of Asia. It was also an idolatrous center; and to declare oneself in that place a Christian who worships the one true God and Savior, Jesus Christ, would certainly provoke hostility.

Furthermore, the risen Lord knew their loyalty to him in all that he is revealed to be ("my name"), even when "Antipas, my faithful witness . . . was put to death in [their] city." Nothing further is known about Antipas. The proximity of the name "Satan" before and after Antipas in v.13 makes it virtually certain that his death was instigated by the enmity of pagans in Pergamum. He may have been the first or most notable of martyrs. Christ pays this hero of the faith a noble tribute: "faithful witness"—words that John applies to Christ himself in 1:5. Satan tries to undermine loyalty to Christ by persecution; Christ strengthens that loyalty by commending those who are true to him and by exposing those who are deceitful.

14–15 The speaker's verdict reveals that the church in Pergamum was divided. Some had followed Antipas and did not deny Christ's name or his faith (v.13). Others held to the teachings and practices of the Balaamites and Nicolaitans that Christ hates (2:6). Since "Balaam" can mean to "conquer the people" (i.e., the same meaning as "Nicolaitans") and since they are mentioned together in this letter, both groups may be closely related. The deadly effects of the error are described as "eating food sacrificed to idols and committing sexual immorality" (cf. "Jezebel" in v.20).

The OT names Balaam and Jezebel serve to alert the church community to the insidious nature of the teaching that was not until now recognized as overtly evil. Since Satan's chief method is deception, his devices are not

A great altar to Zeus stood out prominently in Pergamum. This city also boasted being an official center of emperor worship.

known until they are clearly pointed out. Christ exposes error here by identifying the false teaching in Pergamum with clear-cut evil such as that of Balaam and Jezebel. Balaam, who found he could not curse the Israelites (Nu 22–24), devised a plan whereby the daughters of the Moabites seduced the Israelite men and led them to sacrifice to their god Baal-peor and worship him (Nu 25:1ff.; 31:16; cf. 2Pe 2:15; Jude 11). So through Balaam's deception, God's judgment fell on Israel because of fornication and idolatry. What Satan could not accomplish at Smyrna or Pergamum through intimidation, suffering, and death from outside the church, he achieved from within through unconscious subversion.

The combination of "food sacrificed to idols" with "sexual immorality" may refer to the common practice of participating in the sacrificial meal of the pagan gods (cf. 1Co 10:19–22) and indulging in sexual intercourse with temple priestesses. It is entirely possible that some Christians at Pergamum were still participating in the holiday festivities and saw no wrong in indulging in the "harmless" table in the temples and the sexual excitement everyone else was enjoying (cf. 1Jn 5:21). This is the more normal way to understand the term "sexual immorality," though some feel that the term refers to spiritual unfaithfulness and apostasy from Christ (cf. Isa 1:21; Eze 23:37).

16 The speaker's command includes both a call to the whole congregation to "repent" and a special threat to the heretical members if they do not repent. Since those who did not indulge in these things tolerated the practices of other church members, they, along with the guilty, needed to repent. If those at Pergamum will not heed the word of Christ's warning, that word from his mouth will become a "sword" to fight against the disloyal. The words "I will soon come to you" is a coming "against" the congregation in judgment (cf. v.5), not a reference to Christ's second coming.

17 The promise to the overcomer includes three symbols: "hidden manna," "a white stone," and "a new name." The "hidden manna" is reminiscent of the manna hidden in the ark of the covenant by Moses (Ex 16:33–34; Heb 9:4). Since Moses' pot of manna was designed to remind the Israelites of God's grace and faithfulness in the desert (Ps 78:24), there may be a similar thought here. Apocalyptic Jewish teaching, however, saw in the messianic era the restoration of the hidden wilderness manna. Those at Pergamum who refused the banquets of the pagan gods will receive the manna of his great banquet of eternal life in the kingdom (Jn 6:47–48).

The "white stone" is a puzzle and has received various interpretations. It seems best to link the stone to the thought of the manna and see it as an allusion to an invitation that entitled its bearer to attend one of the pagan banquets.

The "new name ... known only to him who receives it" is either the name of Christ himself, now hidden from the world but to be revealed in the future as the most powerful of names (3:12; 14:1), or the believer's new name or changed character through redemption (Isa 62:2; 65:15). In an ancient Egyptian text, the goddess Isis plotted to learn the secret name of the supreme god Re to gain his hidden power for herself. The one who knew the hidden name would receive the power and status of the god who revealed it. Hence the name was jealously guarded by the god. This background fits the context here: to Christians tempted to compromise their loyalty to Christ to gain the favor of the pagan gods, Christ generously offers himself and the power of his name so that those who have faith in him may overcome.

4. To Thyatira (2:18–29)

On the inland route about forty-five miles due east of Pergamum was the city of Thyatira. Although not a great city, it was nevertheless important through commerce in wool, linen, apparel, dyed stuffs, leatherwork, tanning, and excellent bronze-work. Associated with its commerce was an extensive trade guild or labor union network, which must have played a prominent role in the social, political, economic, and religious life of the city. Each guild had its own patron deity, feasts, and seasonal festivities that included sexual revelries. Religiously, the city was unimportant. According to Acts, Lydia came from the Jewish settlement at Thyatira (Ac 16:14). She was a distributor of garments made of the purple dye substance known as "Turkey red" and no doubt a member of the dyers' guild.

18 The speaker of this fourth letter, the longest of the seven, identifies himself as "the Son of God, whose eyes are like blazing fire and whose feet are like burnished bronze" (cf. comments on 1:14–15). The expression "Son of God" appears only here in this book. It is a designation for the Messiah and is almost equivalent to the more frequently used title "Son of Man"; it probably anticipates the quotation from the messianic Ps 2 in v.27, which implies the term. But the name might also have captured the attention of those who were enticed by the emperor cult into calling Caesar "the son of God." That Christ's eyes are here described as blazing fire might be an allusion to the sun god, Apollo, worshiped at Thyatira. More likely, however, it refers to Christ's penetrating discernment of the false prophetess Jezebel (v.23). His feet, which are like burnished bronze, would no doubt have special significance to the bronze-workers at Thyatira.

19 The speaker's knowledge of the Thyatirans' works is essentially twofold: he knows their "love" and their "faith" (i.e., their "faithfulness"; GK *4411*). Their love manifests itself in "service" and their faithfulness in "perseverance" during trial. Their present state reflects outstanding progress, but there is a perilous flaw in the church there.

20 The speaker's verdict reveals that the congregation had allowed a woman prophetess (a false one, according to Christ's assessment) to remain in the church and to continue to teach the saints to indulge in "sexual immorality" and to "eat food sacrificed to idols." The genuine gift of prophecy was highly respected in the early church. Along with apostles, teachers, and elders, prophets were often elevated to leadership (1Co 12:28; Eph 4:11). Women also received the gift of prophecy from the Holy Spirit (Lk 2:36; Ac 21:9; 1Co 11:5). Prophets generally brought direct revelation from God in the form of teaching as well as occasional predictions of the future (Ac 11:27). Tests for a true prophet were available but often difficult to apply.

This supposedly Christian woman at Thyatira had claimed to be a "prophetess" and was presumably elevated to prominence in the church because of her unusual gifts. But only a small minority saw through her pious deception (v.24); the rest either followed her or ignored her views without objecting to her presence. In order to expose her true character, she is labeled "Jezebel"— the name of the Canaanite wife of King Ahab. She had not only led Ahab to worship Baal but had managed to promulgate her idolatry throughout all Israel (1Ki 16:31–33; 2Ki 9:22).

We must not, however, press the similarity too far. As this wicked and deceptive woman in the OT led Israel astray and persecuted the true prophets of God, so this woman at Thyatira was enticing the servants of God to abandon their exclusive loyalty to Christ. Her teaching was no doubt similar to that of the Nicolaitans and Balaamites at Ephesus and Pergamum. While most commentators prefer to see the "sexual immorality" as spiritual adultery (i.e., idolatry), the possibility of cultic fornication should not be ruled out (see comments on v.14). The distinction between the woman and those who follow her (v.22) may argue against the view that she is symbolic of a group in the church, unless the "woman" represents the false prophets and her "children" are those who follow the teaching (cf. 2Jn 1).

21–22 Christ's verdict continues with his strongest accusation directed against, not Jezebel's perversion, serious as that is, nor even against her successful deception of fellow Christians, but against her refusal to repent. Although Christ has dealt with her over a period of time, she will not change her ways or her thinking. The Lord, therefore, will judge Jezebel by two swift acts. She will be "cast" (lit., "hurled"; GK *965*) into a bed, and her children will be put to death. The "bed" or "couch" (GK *3109*) can mean a bed used for resting, for guild-banqueting, or for sickness. On a bed she sinned, and on a bed she will suffer; and those who committed adultery with her will also suffer intensely.

As in the case of Jezebel, Christ's strongest threat to the offenders is not in regard to their sin, but to their reluctance to repent. The Lord is walking among his churches. He judges evil; but he also offers deliverance to those who have fallen, if they repent and stop doing Jezebel's deeds.

23 For those who follow Jezebel ("her children") and refuse to repent, a fatal judgment will be meted out by the Lord Christ: "I will strike her children dead" (perhaps an idiom denoting "pestilence"; cf. 6:8). Whatever the exact nature of the judgment, it is announced beforehand by Christ so that when it occurs, not just Thyatira but "all the churches will know that I am he who searches hearts and minds," since they too will read the same letter and will later hear of the historical outcome. OT references ascribe omniscience to God alone (Ps 7:9; Pr 24:12; Jer 17:10). "Hearts" (GK *2840*) represents the moral center of the life, while "minds" (lit., "kidneys"; GK *3752*) represents the totality of the feelings, thoughts, and desires traced back to one's deepest inner life. Nothing in our thoughts or desires is hidden from Christ's penetrating gaze (Heb 4:12–13). Our only safety from judgment is in repentance. The risen Lord does not stop with searching hearts and minds but brings recompense according to deeds: for faithfulness, reward; for unfaithfulness, judgment.

24–25 Christ's only command to the church at Thyatira was probably for the minority who had sufficient insight to penetrate Jezebel's deception. They are simply to "hold on to what you have" (i.e., their insight into Jezebel's teaching and evil deeds) till Christ returns (v.25). This small group may have been nearer his standard than any other group mentioned in Revelation because they could discriminate between authentic and spurious worship.

The reference to "Satan's so-called deep secrets" is ambiguous (cf. "the deep things of God" in 1Co 2:10). This is probably an actual phrase that Jezebel used. But how could she lure Christians by using such a term? The reasoning of some in the early church (the Nicolaitans) might have gone something like this: The only effective way to confront Satan is to enter into his strongholds; the real nature of sin can only be learned by experience, and therefore only those who have really experienced sin can truly appreciate grace. So by experiencing the depths of paganism ("the deep secrets of Satan"), one will be better equipped to serve Christ or be an example of freedom to one's fellow believers (cf. 1Co 8:9–11). Thus the sin of Jezebel was deadly serious because of the depths of its deception. Only a few perceived where the teaching was leading.

"Until I come" is the first of several references to the second coming of Christ in these letters (cf. 1:7).

26–27 The promise to the overcomers is twofold: "authority over nations" and the gift of "the morning star." It contains one important modification of the regular overcomer's formula. Added to the words "to him who overcomes" is "and does my will to the end" (lit., "who keeps my works until the end"). It reminds us of Jesus' statement in his great eschatological discourse, that "he who stands firm to the end will be saved" (Mt 24:13; cf. also Col 1:23). Proof of authentic trust in Jesus is steadfastness of faith and continuance in God's will till Christ returns or death comes.

The first promise is a fulfillment of Ps 2, which is messianic and tells how the Father gave the Messiah the rule over the nations of the world. This psalm plays an important part in this book in thinking about Christ (11:18; 12:5; 19:15). The coming reign of the Messiah over the world is to be shared with his disciples (1:6; 3:21; 20:6; 1Co 6:2). The overcomers will participate with Christ in fulfilling the promise of Ps 2:9. There is a paradox in the combination of the mild word "rule" (lit., "to shepherd"; GK *4477*) with the harsh words "with an iron scepter; he will dash them to pieces like pottery" (cf. comments on 19:11ff.). The prospect of such a reversal of their experience of oppression and persecution would be a constant encouragement for suffering Christians.

28 Second, the overcomers in Thyatira are promised "the morning star." Some link this expression to Christ himself as in 22:16; believers receive Christ as their very life. Or it may refer to the Resurrection in the sense that the morning star rises over the darkness of this world's persecution and offers victory over it. Perhaps a combination of the two thoughts is intended. The promise of Christ's return is like the "morning star" (2Pe 1:19).

29 In this fourth letter and in the next three, this general exhortation comes at the very end, while in the first three letters it precedes the promise (cf. comments on 2:1–3:22).

5. To Sardis (3:1–6)

Sardis was about thirty miles south of Thyatira. It enjoyed prominence as a commercially prosperous and militarily strategic city throughout its history. The city's topography was notable for the acropolis, the temple of Artemis, and the necropolis. (1) The acropolis rose about eight hundred feet above the north section of Sardis and was virtually impregnable because of its nearly vertical rock walls (except on the south side); it became a refuge for the inhabitants in time of siege. Only twice in the history of Sardis (in the sixth and fourth centuries B.C.) was its fortress ever captured, though attacks on it were frequent. (2) The temple to Artemis equaled in size the famous temple of Artemis in Ephesus, though it was never finished. (3) The impressive necropolis, or cemetery, of "a thousand hills" was so named because of the hundreds of burial mounds visible on the skyline seven miles from Sardis.

Sardis retained its wealth into the first two centuries A.D. But its political brilliance as the capital city of Asia for Persia lay in the past. In A.D. 26, Sardis begged the Roman Senate to grant it the coveted honor of building a temple to Caesar, but that distinction went to Smyrna. The luxurious living of the Sardians led to moral decadence. Sardis was a city of peace—not the peace won through battle, but the peace of lethargy and past dreams. A great woolen industry flourished at Sardis, and this may account for Christ's reference to clothing (v.4).

1 The speaker identifies himself as "him who holds the seven spirits of God and the seven stars" (cf. comments on 1:4, 16, 20; 2:1). Christ is the one who controls the seven spirits of God. If the Sardian church is strong, it is because Christ has sent his Spirit to encourage and quicken the Sardian believers; if they are dead like Sardis, it is because in judgment he has withdrawn his Spirit from them. Yet the faithful minority at Sardis (v.4) can count on the divine power of Christ to sustain them, give life, and mobilize them to do his will even though the majority are dead.

The speaker's knowledge of the church in Sardis reveals their true condition. He knows their "deeds." This may allude to their past accomplishments, which gave them their reputation of being alive, but more likely it refers to their present deeds, which were not those Christ sought from them (cf. v.2). He also knows that though they claim to be a healthy Christian church, in reality they are "dead."

How does a church die? Why does Christ use this expression for Sardis, even though the churches in Thyatira and Laodicea also had serious problems? Sardis had had significant fame as a royal city, but now it was nothing. The citizens were living off past fame. Apparently the same spirit had affected the church. Their loyalty and service to Christ were in the past; now they were nothing. Perhaps they had so made peace with the surrounding society that the offense of the Cross had ceased, and they were no longer in jeopardy of life or vulnerable to suffering. Further facts emerge when we consider the series of commands in vv.2–3. Death was a special preoccupation of the Sardians, as witnessed by the impressive necropolis. What had been a part of the pagan rites had also crept into the church, but through deception. The Sardian church was for the most part a duped church.

2 The command "Wake up!" (lit., "Be watchful"; GK *1213*) is a call to reverse their attitudes radically. The congregation must be alerted to the seriousness of the situation. Their complacency led them to give up their identification with Christ and their mission for him. The situation is dire but not totally hopeless. Immediate steps must be taken to "strengthen [GK *5114*] what remains." Some persons and things are salvageable if quick and decisive action is taken. Otherwise, death will follow.

The Sardians' deeds are in danger of judgment because Christ has not found them "complete [GK *4444*] in the sight of my God." Though this could refer to incompleteness in the number of their deeds, more likely it describes the quality of their deeds—they do not measure up to the standard Christ sets. In the other letters, works acceptable to Christ are love, faithfulness, perseverance, keeping Christ's words, and not denying his name.

3 Like those in Ephesus, the Sardians must remember what they "have received and heard." What they "received" was the apostolic tradition of the gospel; what they "heard" probably were the teachings of the apostles and prophets who brought the gospel to them. Unlike the church at Philadelphia (v.8), the Sardians were not holding to the word of Christ. For them repentance was the only way out of certain and final death. So they were to repent by restoring the gospel and the apostolic doctrine to its authority over their lives. This would mean they would once more start to "obey" (lit., "keep"; GK 5498) the truth of Christ's word. Today's church needs to hear this challenge to take the word of Christ seriously. If the church at Sardis does not repent, Christ will come to them in judgment "as a thief"—i.e., by surprise. This phrase should probably not be taken as referring to the Second Coming but to Christ's opposing them in judgment (cf. his threat to the church in Ephesus in 2:5).

4 While the majority had departed from faithful obedience to Christ, a few at Sardis remained true. Here an allusion to the woolen industry at Sardis intensifies the image of soiled and defiled garments. Those with soiled garments were removed from the public lists of citizens in Sardis. In the pagan religions it was forbidden to approach the gods in garments that were soiled or stained. Soiling seems to be a symbol for mingling with pagan life and thus defiling the purity of one's relation to Christ (14:4; 1Co 8:7; 2Co 7:1; 11:2; Jude 23). To "walk with Christ" symbolizes salvation and fellowship with him—something the others at Sardis had forfeited through their sin (1Jn 1:6–7). "White" garments are symbolic of the righteousness, victory, and glory of God (Rev 3:18; 6:11; 7:9, 13–14; 19:14). This passage shows that not all faithful Christians were martyrs, nor can we make emperor worship the sole source of the problems of the early Christians. Ironically, the Sardians were occupied with their outward appearance, but they were not concerned with inner purity toward Christ and their outward moral life in a pagan society.

5 The overcomer's promise is threefold and grows out of the reference to white clothing. (1) "Like" the faithful Sardian Christians who will receive white clothes from Christ, the others who overcome the stains of pagan society will similarly be dressed in white.

(2) The pure relationship to Christ is permanently guaranteed: "I will never erase his name from the book of life." In ancient cities the names of citizens were recorded in a register till their death; then their names were marked out of that book. This same idea appears in the OT (Ex 32:32–33; Ps 69:28; Isa 4:3). From the idea of being recorded in God's book of the living (or the righteous) comes the sense of belonging to God's eternal kingdom or possessing eternal life (Da 12:1; Lk 10:20; Php 4:3; Heb 12:23; Rev 13:8; 20:15; et al.). For Christ to say that he will never "blot out [the overcomer's] name from the book of life" is the strongest affirmation that death can never separate us from Christ and the life he offers (Ro 8:38–39). A person enrolled in the book of life by faith remains in it by faithfulness and can be erased only by disloyalty. There is some evidence that one's name could be removed from the city register before death if one were convicted of a crime. In the first century, Christians who were loyal to Christ were under constant threat of being branded political and social rebels and then stripped of their citizenship. But Christ offers them an eternal, safe citizenship in his everlasting kingdom if they remain loyal to him.

(3) Finally, to the overcomer Christ promises to "acknowledge his name before [the] Father and his angels." "Acknowledge" (GK 3933) is a strong word for confession before the courts. It is Christ's confession of our name before the Father and his angels (implying our fellowship with him) that assures our heavenly citizenship (Mt 10:32; Lk 12:8).

What ultimately counts, then, is not our acceptance by this world's societies but that our relationship to Christ is genuine and hence will merit his approbation in the coming kingdom.

6 Again, the general exhortation comes last (see comments on 2:1–3:22; 2:29).

6. To Philadelphia (3:7–13)

About twenty-five miles southeast of Sardis, along the Hermus River valley, lay the important high plateau city of Philadelphia. A main highway that ran through the city connected Smyrna (about a hundred miles due west) to northwest Asia, Phrygia, and the east. Furthermore, the imperial post road of the first century A.D., which came from Rome, passed through this valley and Philadelphia on the way to the east. So situated, Philadelphia became a strong fortress city. To the northeast was a great vine-growing district, which, along with textile and leather industries, contributed greatly to the city's prosperity.

Philadelphia was established by King Attalus II (159–138 B.C.), who was given the epithet "Philadelphus" ("brother lover") because of his love for his brother. The city disseminated Greco-Asiatic culture and language in the eastern part of Lydia and in Phrygia. Its success is attested by the fact that the Lydian language ceased to be spoken in Lydia by A.D. 19 and Greek took over, though the same cannot be said for the Phrygians.

The whole region was earthquake prone. In A.D. 17 an earthquake that destroyed Sardis and ten other cities also destroyed Philadelphia. Consequently, many people preferred to live in the rural area surrounding the city. The fear of earthquakes caused those who continued to live in the city to leave it at the slightest sign of a tremor. After the devastating earthquake, Tiberius came to the peoples' aid and had the city rebuilt. In gratitude the citizens renamed it Neocaesarea ("New Caesar"), though it also kept the name Philadelphia. Since wine was one of the city's important industries, some have assumed that the worship of Dionysus was a chief pagan cult.

Although nothing is known about the origin of the Philadelphian church, it has had a long history of faithfulness to the Lord. Long after all the surrounding country had succumbed to Muslim control under Turkey, Philadelphia held out as a Christian populace till 1392.

7 The letter to the church in Philadelphia begins with the speaker's identifying himself as "him who is holy and true, who holds the key of David. What he opens, no one can shut; and what he shuts, no one can open." Each of these identifications calls attention to Jesus as the true Messiah. "Holy and true" relates to God himself and describes aspects of his presence among us (cf. 6:10; cf. Hos 11:9; Jn 14:6). Holiness is the attribute of God whereby we sense the presence of the "Wholly Other," and truth means that he is wholly trustworthy and reliable in his words and actions. For this congregation whom Christ has commends, these titles would bring encouragement, despite their "little strength" (v.8), to go on in their faithfulness.

The reference to the "key of David" alludes to Isa 22:20ff. and the incident of transferring the post of secretary of state in Judah from the unfaithful Shebna to the faithful Eliakim. The "key" (GK *3090*) signifies the power of the keys that were normally held by the king himself, unless delegated to another. The use of the name "David" points to Christ as the Messiah, who alone determines who will participate in his kingdom and who will be turned away. This may allude to the false claims of certain Jews at Philadelphia who argued that they, not the heretical Nazarenes, would inherit the kingdom of David (v.9) and thus excluded the followers of Jesus. But the true Messiah, Jesus, will exclude them instead!

8 Here the knowledge of the speaker and his verdict blend together in untarnished praise as in the letter to Smyrna. An awkward part of this verse is the interjection, "See, I have placed before you an open door that no one can shut." Since Christ has absolute authority from the Father, he has opened a door for the Philadelphians that even their enemies cannot close. But an open door to what? It most likely refers to Christ's opening the door to his kingdom for those who love him, thus reinforcing the statement in v.7. What became a serious problem at Sardis (v.3) was not the case with the Philadelphian congregation, for the risen Christ said, "You have kept my word." They had been faithful to the Gospel and the apostles' teaching even during the trial of their faith—they "have not denied my name."

9 Those opposing the witness of the congregation are called "those who are of the synagogue of Satan, who claim to be Jews though they are not, but are liars." These words are like those spoken to the church in Smyrna (cf. comment on 2:9). A "synagogue of Satan" appears to describe a Jewish element that vehemently denied Jesus as the Messiah and that actively persecuted others who made this claim. In the view of Jews like John and Paul, a true Jew is one who has found forgiveness and life in Jesus the Messiah, while a false Jew is one who rejects those who believe in Jesus and openly persecutes them; such a one is an antichrist (1Jn 2:22). But Christ will make those who have persecuted the followers of Jesus as heretics "acknowledge" (lit., "know"; GK *1182*) that God is indeed with the church in Philadelphia and that they are not heretics but are God's people.

We catch a glimpse here of the ever-widening gap between Judaism and Christianity toward the end of the first century. The church is the true people of God, loved by Christ, and in a real sense inheritors of the covenant promises in the OT made to the people of God (Isa 43:4; 45:14; 49:23; 60:14).

In these OT passages it is the Gentiles, or heathen nations, who bow before Israel and acknowledge that God is with them. In this letter Christ reverses these roles: his followers are now the people of God and Jewish unbelievers are the pagans who come and acknowledge the love of the Messiah for the church! There is, however, no indication as to when such acknowledgment will come. Underlying this verse is the truth Paul expressed in Php 2:10–11: "At the name of Jesus every knee should bow ... and every tongue confess that Jesus Christ is Lord, to the glory of God the Father." Some will do this joyfully and some remorsefully (cf. Rev 6:12–17).

10 This is another promise given the church in Philadelphia. Though not part of the promise to the overcomers in Philadelphia (v.12), like the special promises to Smyrna and Sardis (2:10; 3:4), it may be taken as a promise to all the churches. The words "since you have kept my command to endure patiently" (lit., "kept the word of my patience") refer to the condition under which the promise is valid. Some translate the phrase as in NIV, inferring that the "word of my patience" means the command of Christ to endure suffering until he returns (Lk 21:19; cf. Heb 10:36). Others translate it as "the word enjoining Christ's patient endurance," which would refer to an apostolic teaching (such as Paul's) encouraging Christians to endure the contrariness of a sinful world after the pattern of Christ's own endurance (2Th 3:5; cf. Heb 12:3). Either is possible, though the Greek text slightly favors the latter.

Related to the promise, "I will also keep you from the hour of trial that is going to come upon the whole world to test those who live on the earth" are two problems: the identification of the "hour of trial" and the sense of the phrase "keep you from the hour of trial." Both involve the ongoing debate among evangelicals over the Tribulation-Rapture question.

We can dismiss the view that the "hour of trial" refers to some general or personal distress that will come only upon the Philadelphian community and from which that church will be delivered. Not only does the Lord refer to "the whole world," but the phrase "those who live on the earth" is repeated in Revelation a number of times and refers not to believers but to unbelievers who are the objects of God's wrath (6:10; 8:13; 11:10; 12:12; 13:8, 12, 14; cf. Isa 24; Jer 13:12–14). According to many interpreters, the "hour of trial" is best understood as the time known to the Jews as the "messianic woes," a time of intense trouble to fall on the world before the coming of Christ and known as the eschatological "day of the Lord" or the "Great Tribulation" (Da 12:1, Joel 2:31; Mk 13:14; 2Th 2:1–12; Rev 14:7). This "hour of trial," then, will be the one described in great detail in the following chapters of this book.

If that is the proper meaning of "hour of trial," what does promise mean, "I will also keep you from the hour of trial"? There are two possibilities. (1) Some, comparing the expression "keep from" in Jn 17:15, argue that the sense is preservation while *in* the trial (to be kept from evil or the evil one does not mean to be removed from his presence but simply to be kept from his harmful power). Thus, the universal church will experience preservation from harm in the trial of persecution and suffering and will not be raptured till the end of the period (cf. 1Th 4:13ff.).

(2) Other writers object to this interpretation: (a) The "hour of trial" is a judgment from God on the unbelieving inhabitants of the world, not a form of persecution. (b) It is not true that the saints of the Tribulation period are exempt from harm during this period; a great group of them will be martyred (6:9–11; 7:9–14, etc.). (c) In the Gospel of John, preservation is from the devil; in Revelation, from a time period—the "hour" of trial.

In our opinion, we must identify "the hour of trial" as the wrath of God, deliverance from which is promised to every one of Christ's overcomers. The key phrase is "to keep from" (GK 5498 & 608; synonymous with "to keep out of," GK 5498 & 1666). This latter phrase is used in the LXX of Pr 7:5, where the wise man talks about delivering a man from contact with or the presence of the harlot. In Jas 1:27 the same expression means to be kept from the pollution of the world. In both instances the sense is that of exemption from something. Can one, then, be exempt from the "hour of trial" that will try the whole world by famines, earthquakes, wars, floods, etc., and still be present on the earth? Yes, but removal is one possible method of protection. The above discussion shows that v.10 does not settle the question of the time of the Rapture in relation to the Tribulation. Rather, it remains ambiguous. One might be on the earth and yet be exempt from the "hour of trial" if the "hour of trial" is directed only at the unbelievers in the world while the believers are divinely immune from the specific type of trial (God's wrath) aimed at the rebellious on the earth. In any event, we have here a marvelous promise of Christ to protect those who have kept his word by their loving obedience.

11 Here the words of Christ "I am coming soon" (cf. 22:7, 12, 20) are not a threat of judgment but a promise of Christ's second coming, such as the promise the faithful Christians in Thyatira received (2:25). The testing that faced the Philadelphians was not the same as that facing the unbelieving earth dwellers (v.10). Loyal disciples must face one type of conflict, the world with its earth dwellers quite another. Some such conflict is envisioned when Christ says, "Hold on to what you have, so that no one will take your crown." They had kept his word and had not denied his name in the face of persecution. Either Satan or other people could rob them of their crown by diverting them from exclusive loyalty to Jesus (on crown, see comment on 2:10).

12 The promise to the overcomer is again twofold and related to the experience and memory of the inhabitants of the city. (1) Christ will make the overcomer a "pillar in the temple of my God." As has already been noted, Philadelphia was constantly threatened with earthquakes. Often the only parts of a city left standing after a severe quake were the huge stone temple columns. Christ promises to set believers in his temple (the future kingdom?) in such a secure fashion that no disturbance can ever force them out. (2) A faithful municipal servant or a distinguished priest was sometimes honored by having a special pillar added to one of the temples and inscribed with his name. This may well be the sense of the second promise, "I will write on him the name of my God and the name of the city of my God, the new Jerusalem, ... and ... my new name." The inscribed name signifies identification and ownership. To those who have little influence because of being ostracized, Christ promises recognition in his kingdom worthy of the most noble hero of any society.

Remembering in days past the changes of name that their city received (e.g., Neocaesarea; see comment on vv.7–13), the Philadelphians would be impressed that God himself (not the emperor) had chosen to identify himself with them and to ensure their citizenship in the New Jerusalem (cf. 21:2ff.; Eze 48:35). Christ's "new name" could be either the unknown name that he alone knows, or the new name of Christ given to the believer through redemption (cf. Isa 62:2; 65:15).

13 The general exhortation follows the promise (see comments on 2:1–3:22)

7. To Laodicea (3:14–22)

Laodicea was about forty-five miles southeast of Philadelphia and about one hundred miles due east of Ephesus. Along with Colosse and Hierapolis, it was one of the cities in the fertile Lycus valley. The great Roman road stretching to the inland of Asia from the coast at Ephesus ran straight through its center, making Laodicea an important center of trade and communication. In addition, its wealth came from the production of a fine quality of famous glossy black wool. The city also had a huge banking industry. So wealthy was Laodicea that after a great earthquake in A.D. 17, the people refused imperial help in rebuilding the city, choosing rather to do it entirely by themselves.

Laodicea had a famous school of medicine; and a special ointment known as "Phrygian powder," famous for its cure of eye defects, was either manufactured or distributed there, as were ear ointments. Near the temple of the special god associated with healing (Men Karou) was a market for trading all sorts of goods. Zeus, the supreme god, was also worshiped in the city.

Laodicea is difficult to describe because no one thing stands out. It was a city with a people who had learned to compromise and accommodate themselves to the needs and wishes of others; they did not zealously stand for anything. For all its wealth, the city had poor water. A six-mile-long aqueduct brought Laodicea its supply of water from the south. The water came either from hot springs and was cooled to lukewarm or came from a cooler source and warmed up in the aqueduct on the way.

14 The speaker identifies himself by a threefold affirmation: "The Amen, the faithful and true witness, the ruler of God's creation." "Amen" means the acknowledgment of that which is sure and valid. It is a word of human response to the divine verity or action (cf. 2Co 1:20). Jesus is the "Amen" in the sense that he is the perfect human response of obedience and suffering to the divine promises (cf. Isa 65:16); he is the "faithful and true witness" (cf. comments on 1:5, 9; 2:13).

The "ruler" (GK 794; also means "source," "origin") further amplifies the Amen statement. Paul used this word in Col 1:18 to describe Christ as the source or origin of all creation (cf. Pr 8:22; John 1:3), no doubt to correct a heresy. Since Colosse was a neighboring city of Laodicea, it is not improbable that the same heresy was affecting the sister church at Laodicea. When Christ addresses a church that is failing in loyalty and obedience, he is to them the "Amen" of God in faithfulness and in true witness, and he is the only one who has absolute power over the world because he is the source of all creation (1:17; 2:8; 22:13).

15–16 Sadly, the speaker's knowledge reveals an unqualified condemnation of the Laodicean church—a verdict that is the exact opposite of the church's own evaluation (v.17). Their deeds were "neither cold nor hot." This expression may refer to their lack of zeal (v.19) or their uselessness, for Christ says, "I wish you were either one or the other" (lit., "either cold or hot"). There is good reason not to understand this expression as if Christ meant, "I wish you were either spiritually cold (i.e., unsaved or hostile) or spiritually hot (i.e., alive and fervent)." It is inconceivable that Christ would wish that people were spiritually cold in this sense. Furthermore, the application of "hot" and "cold" to spiritual temperature, though familiar to us, would have been foreign to first-century Christians. The two adjectives in "neither hot nor cold" should be understood together as equivalent to "lukewarmness" (v.16). That is to say, they were useless to Christ because they were complacent, self-satisfied, and indifferent to the real issues of faith in him and of discipleship.

"I am about to spit you out of my mouth" alludes to the "lukewarm" water that was a part of the situation in Laodicea (see comment on 3:14–22). "Cold" could refer to the useful cool water located at Colosse, less than ten miles away. "Hot" would remind the Laodiceans of the beneficial "hot springs" to the north of Hierapolis. Christ detests their attitude of compromise, one that seeks easy accommodation and peace at any cost. With such a condition, he must deal harshly. To be a Christian means to be useful to Christ.

17 The deeper problem in the Laodicean church was not simply their indifference. It was their ignorance of their real condition: "You say, 'I am rich; I have acquired wealth and do not need a thing.'" This indictment is related to the general condition of the populace at large—rich in material possessions and self-sufficient. The spirit of the surrounding culture had crept into the congregation and had paralyzed their spiritual life. But did they claim to be materially rich or spiritually rich? Most likely both were involved; the Laodiceans probably interpreted their material wealth as a blessing from God and thus were self-deceived as to their true spiritual state.

Christ's revelation of the Laodiceans' actual situation shatters their illusions and calls them to repentance: "But you do not realize that you are wretched, pitiful, poor, blind and naked." Note the contrast with Jesus' evaluation of the church at Smyrna, "I know ... your poverty—yet you are rich!" (2:9). Probably the first two characteristics—"wretched" (GK 5417) and "pitiful" (GK 1795)—are to be linked together, while the latter three explain this twofold condition in more detail (cf. v.18). To be "wretched" physically describes life when everything one owns has been destroyed or plundered by war. Here it refers to the Laodiceans' spiritual destitution and pitiableness before God.

The people at Laodicea knew what lukewarm meant. In nearby Pamukale, hot pools and lukewarm pools are still being used.

"Poor, blind and naked" refers to the three sources of their miserable condition (see comment on v.18). "Lukewarmness," then, does not refer to the laxity of Christians but the condition of not really knowing Christ as Savior and Lord and thus being useless to him.

18 The commands of Christ correspond exactly to the self-deceptions of the Laodiceans. Gold, a source of the wealth of the city, was to be bought from Christ and to become the spiritually poverty-stricken's true wealth. Their shameful nakedness was to be clothed, not by purchasing the sleek, black wool of Laodicea, but by buying from Christ the white clothing that alone can cover shameful nakedness (16:15). For those who were blind to their true condition, the "Phrygian powder" was useless (cf. comment on v.14). The three figures together point to the Laodiceans' need of authentic salvation through Christ.

19 Even though the state of a church verges on disaster, all is not lost if there are those in it who will receive Christ's loving rebuke and come back to him. Christ's statement "I rebuke and discipline" speaks of his love (Pr 3:12; 1Co 11:32; Heb 12:6). He spits out those he does not love and "rebukes" (GK *1794*) and "disciplines" (GK *4084*) those who hear his voice. The difference between the expelled and the disciplined lies in their response: "So be earnest [lit., zealous; GK *2418*] and repent." The Laodiceans' repentance would come from a rekindling of their loyalty to Christ.

20 To those who hear the words of rebuke, Christ extends an invitation to dine with him. This figure represents Christ standing at the door to the hearts of the members of the congregation at Laodicea. Christ will come and have fellowship with all those who hear his voice of rebuke and thus prove themselves as Christ's friends by zeal and repentance. The "eating" (GK *1268*) refers to the main meal of the day, which in Oriental fashion was a significant occasion for having intimate fellowship with the closest of friends. It is through the Holy Spirit that Christ and the Father come to have fellowship with us (Jn 14:23).

While most commentators have taken this invitation as addressed to lapsed, half-hearted Christians, the terminology and context (v.18) suggest that these Laodiceans were for the most part mere professing Christians who lacked authentic conversion to Christ in the first place, which is the essential prerequisite for true discipleship. Verse 20 is, therefore, more evangelistic than admonitory. Those who find in it an allusion to the Lord's Supper may be right.

21–22 The promise to the overcomers concerns the sharing in Christ's future reign in the eschatological kingdom. Such a reign with Christ has already been referred to earlier in the book (1:6, 9; 2:26–27) and appears later on (5:10; 20:4–6). The kingdom reign is also a theme in other NT writings (Lk 22:28–30; Ro 8:17; 2Ti 2:12). As Christ overcame through his suffering and death (Jn 16:33) and entered into the highest honor God could bestow—that of being seated at his "right hand" of sovereignty (Mk 16:19; Ac 2:22ff.; Rev 22:1)—so believers who suffer with Christ even to the point of death will share in the honor of Christ's exalted position. The distinction between the Father's throne and Christ's throne differentiates aspects of God's program in history (1Co 15:24–28). Christ is reigning now, for there is a sense in which the messianic kingdom of God was inaugurated in Christ's earthly ministry, death, and resurrection. But the promise here foresees a final earthly consummation of the kingdom when Christ returns.

On the closing exhortation, see comment on 2:1–3:22.

III. Vision of the Seven–Sealed Scroll, the Seven Trumpets, the Seven Signs, and the Seven Bowls (4:1–19:10)

In view of the elaborate use of imagery and visions from 4:1 through the end of Revelation and the question of how this material relates to chs. 1–3, it is not surprising that commentators differ widely. One problem is that of interpretation: What do the imagery and visions mean? Another problem involves chronology: When do the things spoken of occur? Furthermore, how does John use his frequent OT images? Does he interpret them in exact accordance with their OT sources, or does he freely reinterpret these images and figures? What is symbolic and what is literal? Answers to such questions will determine the interpreter's approach. Since few of these questions are capable of dogmatic answers,

A. The Seven-Sealed Scroll (4:1–8:1)

Chapters 4–5 form one vision of two parts—the throne (ch. 4) and the Lamb and the scroll (ch. 5). In actuality, the breaking of all seven seals (6:1–8:1) together with the throne vision (chs. 4–5) form a single, continuous vision and should not be separated. The throne pictures should be viewed as dominating the entire seven-seal vision (4:1–8:1).

1. Preparatory: the throne, the scroll, and the Lamb (4:1–5:14)

a. The throne (4:1–11)

1 Seeing a "door standing open in heaven," John is told to "come up here" (cf. Eze 1:1). He receives a new view of God's majesty and power (throne) so that he can understand the events on earth that relate to the seven-seal vision (cf. 1Ki 22:19). For the first time in Revelation, the reader is introduced to the frequent interchange between heaven and earth found in the remainder of the book. What happens on earth has its heavenly counterpart.

Chapter 4 focuses on the throne vision that provides the setting for the dramatic action of the slain Lamb in ch. 5. There is a connection between this throne vision and the vision of the glorified Christ in 1:11–16. We are told that John heard the same voice speaking to him that he "had first heard speaking ... like a trumpet" (cf. 1:10). The words of the messenger relate to what has just transpired: "I will show you what must take place after this"—after the time of the historical churches in Asia (cf. 1:19).

There is no good reason for seeing the invitation for John to come up into the opened heaven as a symbol of the rapture of the church. Some have so interpreted it and have inferred that the absence of the word "church" (GK *1711*) from Revelation till 22:16 and the continued references to the "saints" indicate that at this point the church departs from the earth. But the word "church" or "churches" always stands in Revelation for the historic seven churches in Asia and not for the universal body of Christ. Since 4:1–22:15 concerns the believing community as a whole, it would be inappropriate to find the narrower term "church" in this section (cf. 3Jn 6, 9–10).

Finally, it is significant that the visions that continue to the end of the book refer to the throne, the book, the crowns, the four living creatures, the twenty-four elders, and the victory of the Lamb. In all this, the central focus appears to be the five hymns of praise that begin in 4:8 and continue through ch. 5.

2–3 Chapter 4 is above all a vision of the royal throne of God. The prophet ascends "in the Spirit" to see the source of all that will happen on earth (cf. 1:10). It will all be an expression of the throne's purpose; nothing happens in the past, present, or future apart from God's intention. Whatever authority is given to an angel or to a horseman is given by God. The throne symbolizes God's majesty and power. Yet his majestic transcendence is fully safeguarded—John does not attempt to describe the "someone sitting on" the throne (cf. 1Ki 22:19; 2Ch 18:18; Ps 47:8; Isa 6:1ff.; Eze 1:26–28).

The minerals "jasper" and "carnelian" portray the supernatural splendor of God while the "rainbow, resembling an emerald," conveys the impression of God's encircling brilliance (cf. Eze 1:27–28). But we need not find symbolism in each element of the vision; it is enough to allow the imagery to create the impression of transcendent glory. Whether John intends God's judgment to be part of the symbolism of the throne vision (cf. Ps 9:4, 7) is not clear. What is unmistakably clear is that all—whether elders, angels, lamps, sea of glass, or living creatures—centers on the throne and the one who sits on it, "who lives for ever and ever" (v.9).

4 Next John sees "twenty-four elders." It would be helpful if we could ask an interpreting angel, "Who are the elders?" (see also 4:9–11; 5:5–14; 7:11–17; 11:16–18; 12:10–12; 14:3; 19:4). There are at least thirteen different views of their identity, ranging from the twenty-four ruling stars (or judges) in the heavens to a simple figure of wholeness and fullness. The elders are always associated with the "four living creatures" (4:6ff.) and engage in acts of worship of God and the Lamb. While not entirely ruling out the elders' possible representative or symbolic significance, the arguments of those who interpret the elders as a class of heavenly spirit-beings belonging to the general class of angels and living creatures seem more compelling. From this viewpoint, the "angels," the "twenty-four elders," and "the four living creatures" all designate actual supernatural beings involved with the purpose of God on earth and his worship in heaven. They are always distinguished from the "saints" (5:8; 11:17–18; 19:1–4).

In the Bible "twelve" appears to be the number of divine government—twelve months in a lunar year, twelve tribes of Israel, twelve apostles, twelve gates in the New Jerusalem, twelve angels at each gate, twelve foundations, twelve thousand sealed from each tribe, etc. Multiples of twelve—such as twenty-four, etc.—probably have a similar significance. "Thrones" are related to the heavenly powers in Col 1:16. In Revelation "white" clothing generally belongs to the saints but relates to angelic beings elsewhere in the NT (e.g., Jn 20:12). While the "crowns of gold" (cf. 4:10; 9:7; 14:14) are likewise usually related to the redeemed, here they refer to the royal dignity of those so closely associated with the throne of God (cf. 1Ki 22:19; Ps 89:7).

5 "Flashes of lightning, rumblings and peals of thunder" coming from the throne symbolize God's awesome presence and the vindication of the saints and occur with slight variation three more times in Revelation (8:5; 11:19; 16:18; cf. Ex 19:16; Eze 1:13; Ps 18:13–15). On the expression "seven blazing lamps," see comment on 1:4 (cf. Eze 1:13).

6–8 "A sea of glass, clear as crystal" adds to the magnificence of the scene (15:2). Its mirrorlike reflecting quality could symbolize the fact that before the sight of God all is revealed: "Everything is uncovered and laid bare before the eyes of him to whom we must give account" (Heb 4:13).

The "four living creatures" (cf. 5:6, 8, 14; 6:1ff.; 7:11; 14:3; 15:7; 19:4) should be linked with Isaiah's seraphim and Ezekiel's cherubim (cf. Isa 6:3; Eze 1:5–25; 10:1–22). They, like the elders and angels, are heavenly creatures of the highest order involved with the worship and government of God. "Covered with eyes" may give the impression of their exceeding knowledge of God, while the faces of a "lion," "ox," "man," and a "flying eagle" suggest qualities that belong to God, such as royal power, strength, spirituality, and swiftness of action. Each of the creatures mentioned is the chief of its species. Together they embody the reflection of God's nature as the fullness of life and power. Their six wings (cf. Isa 6:2) give the impression of unlimited mobility in fulfilling God's commands. Their position "in the center, around the throne" suggests that one might be before and one behind the throne with one on either side.

The four living creatures ceaselessly proclaim the holiness of God in a hymn: "Holy, holy, holy" (GK *41*; cf. Isa 6:3). In Hebrew, the double repetition of a word adds emphasis, while the rare threefold repetition designates the superlative and calls attention to the infinite holiness of God—the quality of God felt by creatures in his presence as awesomeness or fearfulness (Ps 111:9). The living creatures celebrate God's holiness and power as manifested in his past, present, and future activity. Such holiness cannot tolerate the presence of evil (21:27). For the titles of God in the rest of the hymn, see comments on 1:4, 8.

This hymn is the first not only of the five sung by the heavenly choirs in chs. 4–5 but also of a number of other hymns in Revelation (4:11; 5:9–10, 12, 13; 7:12, 15–17; 11:15, 17–18; 12:10–12; 15:3–4; 16:5–7; 18:2–8; 19:2–6). These hymns relate to the interpretation of the visions and provide a clue to the literary structure of Revelation. In the sequence of chs. 4–5, the first two hymns are addressed to God, the next two to the Lamb, and the last one to both. There is also a gradual enlargement in the size of the choirs. The internal movement builds as the last hymn is sung by "every creature in heaven and on earth and under the earth" to "him who sits on the throne and to the Lamb" (5:13).

9–11 The second hymn is sung by the twenty-four elders. When the living creatures confess the truth of God's holy deeds, the response of the highest order of God's heavenly creatures is to relinquish their crowns of honor before the feet of him who alone is "worthy" of "glory and honor and power" because he alone (no man, not even the emperor) is the source and stay of every created thing (Pss 33:6–9; 102:25; 136:5ff.). The expression "by your will they were created and have their being" (v.11) describes

b. The scroll and the Lamb (5:1–14)

This chapter is part of the vision that begins at 4:1 and continues through the opening of the seven seals (6:1–8:1; cf. comment on 4:1–8:1). Its center of gravity lies in the three hymns (vv.9, 12, 13) addressed to the Lamb. They beautifully combine the worship of the Lamb (hymns 1 and 2) with the worship of the one who sits on the throne (hymn 3, addressed to both God and the Lamb). The movement of the whole scene focuses on the slain Lamb as he takes the scroll from the hand of the one on the throne. The actions of all other participants are described in terms of worship directed to the Lamb and the one on the throne. The culminating emphasis is on the worthiness of the Lamb to receive worship because of his death.

1 John sees "in the right hand of him who sat on the throne a scroll [GK *1046*] with writing on both sides and sealed with seven seals." A problem arises regarding the phrase "with writing on both sides." In ancient times, papyrus rolls were used for public and private documents. Usually the writing was on one side only—the inside part, arranged in vertical columns. Occasionally a scroll was written on both sides; such double-sided writing was for private, nonsalable use in contrast to the usual scrolls written on only one side, which were sold. In the context of ch. 5, a double-sided scroll would signify a scroll full of words. A scroll could be opened only after all the seals were broken.

Scrolls, or folded sheets, were sealed with wax blobs impressed with a signet ring to protect the contents or to guarantee the integrity of the writing. Only the owner could open the seals and disclose the contents. Original documents were usually sealed; copies were not. Sealed documents were kept hidden while unsealed copies were made public (Rev 22:10).

As to the identity and significance of the scroll, there are a number of different views. (1) Ancient Roman wills were sealed with six seals, each of which bore a different name of the sealer and could only be opened by him. This has led some to identify the scroll as the testament of God concerning the promise of the inheritance of his future kingdom. (2) Others find the scroll containing, like Ezekiel's scroll, "words of lament and mourning and woe" (Eze 2:9–10) and depicting the future judgment of the world. (3) Still others find the significance to be the progressive unfolding of the history of the world. As each successive seal is opened, the further contents of the book are revealed. It is the "title-deed" (cf. Jer 32:10–14) to creation that was forfeited by sin in Genesis. By his redeeming death Christ has won the authority to reclaim the earth. (4) A more recent study finds the scroll to be the OT Torah (Law).

Each of these views has merit and may provide elements of truth for the background of the striking imagery in these chapters. Yet each view is vulnerable to criticism. Only from Revelation itself can the content and nature of the scroll be determined. Since the seals hinder the opening of the scroll until they are all broken, we may assume that the seals are preparatory to the opening of the scroll and the disclosure of its contents. This means that the seals have the effect of hiding the contents of the scroll until all are broken (Isa 29:11).

The following internal evidence relating to the contents of the scroll may be noted: (1) Just prior to the opening of the seventh seal, we read, "For the great day of their [i.e., of the One sitting on the throne and the Lamb] wrath has come, and who can stand?" (6:17). (2) When the seventh seal is opened (8:1–5), no immediate events follow on earth—except for the earthquake—as in the first six seals, unless the opening of the seventh seal includes among its events the blowing of the seven trumpets of judgment (8:6–11:15). This appears to be precisely the case. (3) The seventh trumpet likewise is not immediately followed by any specific events on earth (11:15ff.), except for an earthquake and a hailstorm (11:19). But just before the sounding of that trumpet, we read, "The second woe has passed; the third woe is coming soon" (11:14). When the seven angels prepare to pour out "the seven last plagues," symbolized by the bowls, we read that with these bowls "God's wrath is completed" (15:1, 7). Thus it seems reasonable to identify the content of the seventh trumpet with the seven bowls of judgment (chs. 16–19).

Furthermore, frequent references to the events of the seals, trumpets, and bowls appear throughout the remaining visions in

Revelation (cf. 19:19ff.; 20:4; 21:9), indicating that the content of the seven-sealed scroll ultimately includes the unfolding of the consummation of the mystery of all things, the goal or end of all history, for both the conquerors and the worshipers of the beast. In 10:7 we are told that in the days of the sounding of the seventh trumpet, "the mystery of God will be accomplished, just as he announced to his servants the prophets." From this it may be concluded that the scroll contains the unveiling of "the mystery of God" that OT prophets foretold (cf. comment on 10:7). Thus the "seals" conceal the mystery, which only Christ can disclose (Da 12:9; Rev 10:4), of how God's judgment and his kingdom will come. In 11:15, when the final trumpet sounds, heavenly voices say, "The kingdom of the world has become the kingdom of our Lord and of his Christ," indicating that the scroll also contains the announcement of the inheritance of Christ and the saints who will reign with him (5:10).

In conclusion, then, the scroll is not only about judgment or about the inheritance of the kingdom. Rather, it contains the announcement of the consummation of all history—how things will ultimately end for all people: judgment for the world and the final reward of the saints (11:18). Christ alone, as the Messiah, is the executor of the purposes of God and the heir of the inheritance of the world. He obtained this by his substitutionary and propitiatory death on the cross (5:9).

2–4 A mighty angel shouts out a challenge for anyone to come forth who is "worthy" (GK 545) to open the great scroll and its seals. All creation in heaven and earth and under the earth stood motionless and speechless. No one had the authority and virtue for such a task. If the scroll contains both the revelation and the carrying out of the final drama of history, then John's despair can be appreciated. In this vision, the execution of events on earth is ascribed to the Lamb. As the seals are broken and the roll opened, salvation history unfolds until history culminates in the kingdom reign of the Messiah over the whole earth. History, then, has its center in Jesus Christ and its goal in his triumphant reign over all the powers of the world.

5 John's sorrow is assuaged. One of the elders announces that there is one who has "triumphed" (GK *3771*; same word as "overcome" in 2:7; 3:21; et al.) because of his death (v.9). Two figurative titles are linked together of the one who is worthy: "the Lion of the tribe of Judah" and "the Root of David." Both are familiar OT messianic titles (Ge 49:9–10; cf. Isa 11:1, 10; Jer 23:5; 33:5; Rev 22:16). Jewish apocalyptic literature used the figure of a lion to designate the conquering Messiah who would destroy Rome. John's understanding of the role and function of the Messiah is both similar to and different from the Jewish understanding of the Messiah.

6 As John looked to see the mighty Lion (the conquering warrior-Messiah from the Root of David), he saw instead the striking figure of a "Lamb" as if it had been slaughtered, standing in the center of the throne court. This new figure portrays sacrificial death and links the Messiah to the OT passover lamb (Ex 12:5–6; Isa 53:7; Jn 1:29, 36; Ac 8:32; 1Co 5:7; 1Pe 1:19). Here John joins the OT royal Davidic Messiah with the Suffering Servant of Isaiah (Isa 42–53). Both prophetic themes come together in Jesus of Nazareth, the true Messiah. "As if it had been slain" (lit., "with its throat cut"; GK *5377*) could refer to the "marks of death" that the living Lamb still bore or to his appearance "as if being led to the slaughter," i.e., "marked out for death." The "lamb" metaphor dominates John's thought in the rest of the book (e.g., 6:1ff.; 7:9ff.; 12:11; 13:8; 21:9).

John notices that the Lamb is also the ruler who bears the signs of the fullness of divine omnipotence, dominion, and omniscience ("seven horns and seven eyes"). The "eyes" are more explicitly identified as the "seven spirits of God sent out into all the earth," probably a symbolic reference to the divine Holy Spirit who is sent forth by Christ into the world (1:4; 4:5; cf. a similar view of the Spirit in Jn 14:26; 15:26; 16:7–15).

7 Next the Lamb acts: "He came and took the scroll." Thus, symbolically, the one on the throne authorizes the slain messianic King to execute his plan for the redemption of the world because in and through him, God is at work in history for the salvation of humanity. This dramatic act of seizing the scroll is not itself the act of victory referred to in v.6 and later in v.9. Rather, Christ's victorious death on the cross is the basis of his authority to redeem the world by taking and opening the seven-sealed scroll.

8 The Lamb's act calls forth three hymns of praise (vv.9, 12, 13) from the living creatures and elders. John sees them fall down in worship before the Lamb as they had earlier done before the one on the throne (4:10), thus acknowledging the deity of the Lamb. They have "harps," which are the "lyres" used for the older psalmody (e.g., Pss 33:2; 98:5) but will now be used for the "new song" of praise to the Lamb (v.9; 15:2–3).

The "bowls full of incense" represent the "prayers of the saints" (8:3-4). Prayer (GK 4666) in this scene is not praise but petition. Why do the saints on earth petition God? In 6:10 the martyrs are seen as calling to God for his judgment on those who killed them, and in 8:3–4 the prayers of the saints are immediately connected with the trumpets of God's judgment. These prayers, then, are evidently for God's vindication of the martyred saints. And since v.10 refers to the coming kingdom, it may be that the prayers are petitions for God to judge the world and to extend his kingdom throughout the earth (Lk 18:7–8). "Saints" (GK 41) is simply the normal term for the rank and file of Christians, i.e., those set apart for God's purposes (2Co 1:1; Php 1:1; Rev 11:18; 13:7, 19; 19:8; 22:21).

9 The three hymns interpret the symbolism of the scroll and the Lamb. The number of singers increases from twenty-eight in v.8 to every creature in all creation in v.13. The first two hymns are songs of praise to the Lamb, whereas the last is praise to both the one on the throne and the Lamb (v.13). The first hymn (vv.9–10) is called a "new" song because there was never any like it before in heaven (cf. comment on 14:3).

"You are worthy" (lit., "equal to," "deserving"; GK 545) refers to the qualifications of this person who alone has won the right to take the scroll and open its seals. His worthiness for this task was won by his loving sacrifice on the cross—a direct reference to the earthly death of the human Jesus of Nazareth. Like other NT writers, John views the death of Jesus as a redeeming death.

The death of Jesus broke the stranglehold of the "powers and authorities" over the creation and produced a great victory of liberation for humankind (Col 2:15). It is this victory, obtained through suffering and death, that entitles Christ to execute the unfolding of the mystery of God's consummation of history. The centrality of the Cross and its meaning as a redemptive act comes repeatedly to the fore and should dominate our understanding throughout Revelation (1:5; 5:12; 7:14; 12:11; 13:8; 14:4; 15:3; 19:7, 21:9, 23; 22:3; et al.). Jesus' death secured a salvation universally applied to all classes and peoples of the earth (cf. 7:9).

10 The Lamb's right to open the scroll rests also on his having made the ransomed into a "kingdom" (GK 993) and his making them "priests" (GK 2636) to serve God in praise (cf. Heb 13:15–16). Christians "will reign on the earth" with Christ because they have been given kingly authority through his death (1:6; 20:4–6). While not excluding the present reign of believers, the reference to "the earth" is best taken to refer to the future eschatological kingdom reign of Christ.

11–12 Now John sees a new feature in the vision: "thousands upon thousands, and ten thousand times ten thousand" angels surrounding the throne (cf. Daniel's vision of the countless multitude before the Ancient of Days; Da 7:10). The imagery suggests the infinite honor and power of the One who is at the center of it all. The angels shout out their song of praise to the Lamb who was slain (cf. Heb 1:6). Their sevenfold shout rings out like the sound from a huge bell—"power ... wealth ... wisdom ... strength ... honor ... glory ... praise." All these are intrinsic qualities of Christ, except the last, which is the expression of the creatures' worship. Elsewhere the same qualities are ascribed to God himself (v.13; 7:12).

13–14 Finally, far beyond the precincts of the throne, there arises an expression of praise and worth from the whole created universe to the One on the throne and to the Lamb. John beautifully blends the worship of the Father (ch. 4) and the worship of the Son (5:8–12) together. In appropriate response, the living beings utter their "Amen" (cf. comment on 3:14), and the elders fall down in worship.

2. Opening of the first six seals (6:1–17)

1 The opening of the seals continues the vision begun in chs. 4–5. Now the scene shifts to events on earth. Before the exposition of each of the seals, it will be helpful to consider their overall meaning. As we have already seen (cf. comment on 5:1), the scroll itself involves the rest of Revelation and has to do with the consummation of the mystery of all things, the goal of history for both the overcomers and the beast worshipers. But what do the seals have to do with this mystery? Are the events of the seals representative and simultaneous world happenings that occur during the church age, or do they occur sequentially? Are they part of the final drama or merely preparatory to it? One thing is certain: the Lamb has the scroll and he himself opens the seals.

With the opening of the fifth seal, the martyrs cry out, "How long ... until you judge the inhabitants of the earth?" and are told to wait "a little longer" (vv.10–11). And when the sixth seal is opened, judgment appears imminent (v.17); this seems to indicate a time progression in the seals. The writer of this commentary tentatively suggests that the seals represent events preparatory to the final consummation. Whether these events come just before the end or represent conditions that prevail throughout the period preceding the end is a more difficult question.

The seals closely parallel the signs of the approaching end times spoken of in Jesus' Olivet Discourse (Mt 24:1–35; Mk 13:1–37; Lk 21:5–33). In these passages the events of the last days fall into three periods: (1) the period of false Christs, wars, famines, pestilences, earthquakes, and death, called "the beginning of birth pains" (Mt 24:8); (2) the period of the Great Tribulation (Mt 24:21; NIV, "great distress"; and, (3) finally, the period "immediately after the distress of those days," when the sun, moon, and stars will be affected and Christ will return (Mt 24:29–30). This parallel to major parts of Revelation is too striking to be ignored. Thus, the seals correspond to the "beginning of birth pains." The events are similar to those occurring under the trumpets (8:2–11:19) and bowls (15:1–16:21), but they should not be confused with those later and more severe judgments. In the eschatological reckoning of time (cf. comment on 1:1), the events immediately preceding the end can stretch out over the whole age of the church, from John's time until now, and can still be viewed as "next" (4:1) in the sense that the "last days" began in the first century and are still continuing (cf. 1Jn 2:18).

The first four seals are distinct from the next two in that they describe four horses of different colors with four riders who are given different powers over the earth. Background for this imagery reflects Zec 1:8ff. and 6:1–8. In Zechariah's visions the horsemen and chariots are divine instruments of judgment on the enemies of God's people, while the colors represent geographical points of the compass. This may also be the best interpretation of the horses and their riders here, where each is sent by Christ through the instrumentality of the living creatures. The emphatic "Come!" (vv.1, 3, 5, 7) should not be viewed as addressed either to John or to Christ but to the horsemen.

2 The identification of the first rider seated on a white horse has given interpreters great difficulty. The main difficulty is whether the rider on the white horse represents Christ and the victory of the gospel or the Antichrist and the forces of evil. In favor of the first identification is the striking similarity of this rider to the portrayal of Christ in 19:11–16, the symbolism of white throughout Revelation always being associated with righteousness and Christ (e.g., 1:14; 2:17; 3:4–5, 18; 4:4; et al.), and the references in the Olivet Discourse to the preaching of the gospel throughout the world before the end.

Support for the identification of the white horse with the Antichrist and his forces is the parallelism with the other three horses, which are instruments of judgment. The references in 19:11–16 to the rider on the white horse as "Faithful and True" and as one who judges and makes war with justice stands in contrast to the rider in 6:2, who is not faithful or true and who wages war for unjust conquest. Moreover, the Lamb opens the seals and would not be one of the riders, nor would it be proper to have an angelic being call forth Christ. Again, a "bow" would most naturally be connected with the enemy of God's people (Eze 39:3). Finally, Jesus himself shows that the first events mentioned are the rise of "false Christs and false prophets" (Mt 24:24).

It must be admitted that the problem of the identity of the rider on the white horse may be solved either way. The evidence, however, seems to favor slightly the second solution, which identifies the white horse with the Antichrist and his forces that seek to conquer the followers of Christ. John sensed that these persecutions were already present in his day and that they would culminate in a final, more severe form (1Jn 2:18; Rev 13:7).

Each of the first four seals, then, represents conflict directed at Christians to test them and to sift out false disciples (v.10). This interpretation need not necessarily eliminate the fact that the seals may also refer to judgments on humankind in general. Yet since the fifth seal stresses the cry of the martyred Christians, probably the thought of Christian persecution belongs also in the first four seals. Each of them unleashes events that separate false belief from true. The destruction of Jerusalem is a case in point (Lk 21:20ff.). The white horse goes forth to conquer, and as he does so, judgment falls on the unbelief of Israel (Lk 21:22–23), while at the same time there is a testing of believers to separate the chaff from the wheat (cf. Lk 21:12–19).

The "bow" suggests forces opposed to Christians (cf. Gog in Eze 39:3). A "crown" (GK 5109) refers to victorious conquest (cf. Rev 19:12). "He was given" is the formula for the sovereign permission to carry out acts that, from a human viewpoint, seem contrary to God's character but nevertheless accomplish his will (cf. 13:5, 7, 15). Thus the rider on the white horse may also point to the attacks of the false Jews (2:9; 3:9) and to the affront to Christians from pagan religionists and the persecutions from Rome, as well as to all future, limited victories over the church by Satan (cf. 2:13; 12:17).

While v.2 would be sobering for first-century believers, at the same time it would encourage them, provided they understood that the Lamb had permitted their testing and suffering. So they could trust that in the midst of seeming defeat from their enemies, he would ultimately be the victor (17:14).

3–4 The second horseman is war and bloodshed. He rides on a "fiery red steed," whose color symbolizes slaughter (2Ki 3:22–23). Therefore, he is given the "large sword" because the number of those he kills is so great (cf. 13:10, 14). John might have thought of Nero's slaughter of Christians, the martyrdom of Antipas (2:13), or perhaps those slain under Domitian's persecutions (cf. Mt 10:34; 24:9).

5–6 The third horseman is poverty and famine. He rides on a "black horse" and symbolizes the effects of war and bloodshed: sorrow, mourning, and desolation (Isa 50:3; Jer 4:28; La 5:10). In the rider's hand there is a "pair of scales." A voice is heard interpreting its significance in economic terms: "a quart of wheat ... and three quarts of barley for a day's wage." This amount suggests food prices much higher than normal and implies inflation and famine (Mt 24:7). A quart of wheat would supply an average person one day's sustenance. Barley was used by the poor to mix with the wheat. The expression "Do not damage the oil and wine" is less clear. Some view oil and wine as luxuries not necessary for survival, and the rich would have them while the poor were starving (cf. Pr 21:17). Others take them as showing the extent of the famine, since a drought affecting the grain may not be severe enough to hurt the vines and olive trees. Oil and wine are staple foods in the East, both in dearth and in prosperity (e.g., Dt 7:13; Hos 2:8, 22). So in this view the third seal brings poverty and partial, though not severe, famine. There is an increasing intensity in the three cycles of judgment.

7–8 The fourth seal reveals a rider on a "pale horse." "Pale" (GK 5952) denotes a yellowish green or the paleness of a sick person in contrast to a healthy appearance. This cadaverous color blends well with the name of the rider—"Death." It probably refers to the death brought by pestilence, or plague, which often follows famine (cf. Jer 14:12; Eze 5:17, 11:71, Lk 21:11). "Hades [cf. comment on 1:18] was following close behind him [Death]." But how? On foot? On the back of the same horse? On a separate horse? Scripture does not say. The growth of intensity in the judgments goes from the sword (human violence), to famine, to plague, and now to the wild beasts of the earth.

9–11 The fifth seal changes the metaphor of horsemen and discloses a scene of martyred saints under the altar crying out for justice upon those who killed them. They are told to wait a little longer until their fellow servants are also killed. Who are these martyrs (cf. 13:15, "all who refused to worship the image of the beast [were] killed"; 8:24, "all who have been killed on the earth"; 20:4, "those who had been beheaded"? The question arises as to why the martyrs alone receive so much attention rather than all suffering or persecuted Christians. Perhaps John is referring to all those who faithfully follow Christ as forming a group that may be characterized as "the slain of the Lord." They may or may not actually suffer physical death for Christ, but they have (like John) so identified themselves with the slain Lamb that they have in effect already offered up their lives "because of the word of God and the testimony they had maintained" (cf. 1:2, 9).

John says that he saw the "souls" (GK 6034) of those slain (v.9). This is generally understood to mean the disembodied souls of these saints. However, the word "soul" has various meanings and probably stands here for the actual persons who were killed. John sees them as persons who are very much alive, even though they have been killed by the beast. "Under the altar" sets the scene as occurring in the temple of heaven. This is most likely the golden altar of incense (see 8:3, 5; 9:13) that stood in the tabernacle either in or before the Most Holy Place (Ex 30:1ff.; Heb 9:4). The other references in Revelation to "altar" also seem to refer to this altar of incense (11:1; 14:18; 16:7). In accord with this sense, the prayers of the saints would be for God's vindication of the martyrs of Christ (cf. Lk 18:7–8).

The martyred address God as "Sovereign Lord" (GK 1305). This term implies "ownership" and is used elsewhere in the NT to denote slave masters (1Ti 6:1; 1Pe 2:18), God (Lk 2:29; Ac 4:24), or Jesus Christ (2Pe 2:1; Jude 4). (On the phrase "holy and true," see comment on 3:7.) The martyrs cry for God's vengeance on evildoers. The word "avenge" (GK 1688) relates everywhere in Scriptures to the idea of punishment or retribution. These saints follow the teaching of Paul in Ro 12:19 about leaving vengeance to the Lord. Though believers are forbidden to take revenge, God will vindicate his elect by punishing those who killed them (Lk 18:7–8; 2Th 1:8).

The martyrs were each given a "white robe" as an evidence of their righteousness and victory before the Judge of all the earth, who will speedily avenge their deaths. The wait of a "little longer" is in God's estimate but a fleeting moment, though for us it may stretch out for ages (cf. 12:12; 20:3; cf. Ps 90:4). The expression "until the number of their fellow servants ... was completed" means either that the number of the martyred or their companions on earth who will be killed will be completed, or that their fellow servants on earth will fulfill their Christian calling, which will involve martyrdom. In any event, what constitutes the essence of Christian discipleship in John's eyes should not be overlooked: every believer should be prepared for martyrdom.

12–14 The sixth seal is broken by the Lamb, and John witnesses certain eschatological signs heralding the imminent, final day of the Lord so often described in Scripture (e.g., Isa 2:10, 19, 21; 13:10; Jer 4:29; Joel 2:31; 3:15; Zep 1:14–18; Mt 24:29; et al.). The signs are threefold: (1) the great earthquake and its storm affecting the sun and moon, (2) the stars falling, and (3) the terror on earth (vv.15–17). It is difficult to know how literally the whole description should be taken. Some of the events are described from the standpoint of ancient cosmology—e.g., the falling of the stars to earth like figs from a shaken tree, the sky rolling up like a scroll, and the firmament suspended like a roof over the earth being shaken by the great earthquake.

The scene, whether taken literally or figuratively, is one of catastrophe and distress for the inhabitants of the earth. As later biblical authors seized on the earlier imagery of the theophany on Sinai to describe appearances of God to his people (e.g., Hab 3:3ff.), so John utilizes the imagery of the OT to describe this terrible visitation of God's final judgment on the earth. Just as we might describe a chaotic situation by saying "all hell broke loose" (though not intending to be taken in a strictly literal sense), so the biblical writers use the language of cosmic turmoil to describe the condition of the world when God comes to judge the earth (v.17). "Earthquakes" are mentioned in 8:5; 11:13, 19; 16:18 and sun, moon, and/or stellar disturbances in 8:12; 9:2; 16:8. Of course, physical phenomena may accompany the final judgment.

15–17 These verses record the terror of all classes of people at these events and at the wrath of God and the Lamb. "The kings of the earth, the princes [dignitaries], the generals" describe the powerful; "the rich, the mighty" describe the affluent and the heroes; finally, John refers to political distinctions of the widest kind—"every slave and every free man." Since all kinds of people are included, we cannot say that God's wrath is directed only at the powerful, at the rich, or at false Christians. His judgment will fall on all who refuse to repent and instead worship demons and idols and persecute Christ's followers (9:20–21; 16:6, 9).

The plea of people for the rocks and mountains to fall on them (v.16) occurs in OT contexts of God's judgment (Isa 2:19, 21; Hos 10:8). It expresses the desire to be buried under the falling mountains and hills so as to escape the pains and terrors of the judgment. Jesus said that the inhabitants of Jerusalem would cry out in this way when God's judgment fell on the city, in A.D. 70 (Lk 23:30).

The "wrath" (GK 3973) of the Lamb is not only a new metaphor but a paradoxical one. Lambs are usually gentle. But this Lamb shows "wrath" against those who have refused his grace (cf. Jn 5:27). Henceforth in Revelation the wrath of God and of the Lamb is a continuing theme and is described under the figures of the trumpets and bowls (11:18; 14:7, 10, 19; 15:1, 7; 16:1, 19; 19:15). Moreover, God's wrath is a present historical reality as well as an eschatological judgment (cf. Ro 1:18ff.; 2:5). So great is the day of destruction that they cry out, "Who can stand?" (cf. Joel 2:11; Na 1:6; Mal 3:2).

3. First Interlude (7:1–17)

Indications that ch. 7 is a true interlude are both the change in tone from the subject matter referred to in the sixth seal and the delay until 8:1 in opening the seventh seal. Two main subjects may be distinguished in this chapter. John first sees the angels who will unleash destruction on the earth restrained until the 144,000 servants of God from every tribe of Israel are sealed (vv.1–8). Then he sees an innumerable multitude clothed in white standing before the throne of God, identified as those who have come out of the "great tribulation" (vv.9–17). This chapter, one of the most difficult and yet most important in the book, probably functions both prospectively and retrospectively. Its principal exegetical difficulty centers around the identification of the 144,000 and of the innumerable multitude. Is the reference to the tribes of Israel symbolic, representative, or literal? What is the "great tribulation" (v.14)? Are those described in vv.9–17 martyrs?

a. The 144,000 Israelites (7:1–8)

1–3 The "four angels" at "the four corners of the earth" hold "the four winds of the earth" from blowing on the earth until the servants of God are sealed on their foreheads. The expression "the four corners of the earth" was used in antiquity among the Near-Eastern nations much as we use "the four points of the compass." Since nowhere in Revelation do we read of the four winds actually blowing, they may be taken as representing the earthly catastrophes that occur under the trumpets and bowls.

Another angel comes from the "east" (possibly from Jerusalem, to emphasize its mission of salvation?) and calls to the four others not to release their destruction until the servants of God have a "seal" (GK 5382) on their foreheads. Such a seal indicates ownership by God and the Lamb (14:1). It also offers protection or security for the bearers (cf. 9:4, where the demonic forces are told to harm "only those people who did not have the seal of God on their foreheads").

We can better understand the "seal" if we examine what John sees regarding the "mark" (GK 5916) of the beast (13:16–17). Those who have the mark are not only identified as beast worshipers but they have become the objects of God's irreversible wrath (14:9, 11). This implies, by contrast, that those who have "the seal of God" are God worshipers and are the objects of his abiding grace. In 16:2, the bowl of God's wrath seems directed exclusively toward those who have the mark of the beast, thus excluding those with the seal of God (cf. 16:6). Furthermore, those having the mark of the beast are deluded by the beast (19:20), whereas the sealed of God are apparently not deceived. Finally, a martyred group is seen just prior to their resurrection and thousand-year reign with Christ and are described as not having the mark of the beast or worshiping him (20:4).

In the light of these passages, we may say that the "sealed" are the people of God and that their sealing must be related to their salvation (cf. Paul's use of "sealed" in 2Co 1:22; Eph 1:13; 4:30). Elsewhere, the sealed are described as those "who had been redeemed from the earth" (14:3–4; cf. Ro 8:23; Jas 1:18). In fact, "baptism" was considered a "seal" of salvation in the early church. While the seal may not protect the sealed against harm inflicted by human agency (13:7; 20:4), they are protected from the divine plagues (16:2). As for OT background, Eze 9:4–7 seems primary. In this passage, a divine messenger with stylus in hand was to go through the apostate Jerusalem of Ezekiel's day and put a mark upon the foreheads of those who deplored the faithless idolatry of the Israelites. Those so marked were the faithful and true servants of God; they would be spared the divine slaughtering of the rebellious inhabitants of the city.

The sealing language would have the effect of assuring God's people of his special concern and plan for them. Even when facing persecution and martyrdom at the hand of the beast, they can be certain that no plague from God will touch them but that they will be in his presence forever because they are his very own possession (cf. 3:10). Therefore, the seal on the forehead is a divine mark of ownership, the presence of the Holy Spirit (cf. 2Co 1:22; Eph 1:13; 4:30). Consequently, those thus sealed must be Christians and not unconverted Jews or Gentiles.

4 John next gives the number of those sealed—144,000—and their identification: "From all the tribes of Israel." There are two principal views regarding the identification of this group: (1) The number and the tribal identifications are taken literally and refer to 144,000 Jewish Christians who are sealed (to protect them from destruction) during the time of the Great Tribulation. (2) John uses the language of the new Israel and thus refers the 144,000 to the completed church composed of Jew and Gentile.

In support of the first view is the normal usage of "Israel" in the NT as referring to the physical descendants of Jacob (Gal 6:16 is too uncertain to be conclusive). There is no unambiguous identification of the church with Israel until A.D. 160, and even then the term "Israel of God" is not used for the church. Reference to the twelve tribes (vv.5–8) would most naturally be understood to refer to the ancient historic Israel and not to the church. Thus, John is symbolically describing the beginning of what Paul foretold in Ro 11:25–29 as the salvation of "all Israel."

In support of the second view is the fact that the NT identifies the followers of Christ as "Abraham's seed" (Gal 3:29), as "the true circumcision" (Php 3:3) and as the "Israel of God" (Gal 6:16, though disputed). John himself has already made a distinction between the true Jew and the false (cf. Rev 2:9; 3:9); that could imply that here in ch. 7 he intends also to designate the church as the true Israel. Additional support is found if there is a unity between the first and second groups in ch. 7, groups that otherwise must be treated as different and unconnected.

Without discussing at length this disputed issue, we agree that those who argue that the term "Israel" in other NT books refers exclusively to Jews are in our opinion correct. Strict exegesis, however, must also ask whether the author of Revelation wishes the term to have this same more restricted usage or whether he in fact uses it differently. It is plausible that the usage of the term "Jew" among Christians had undergone a historic development from the earlier days when Paul wrote Romans (A.D. 56) until Revelation was written toward the close of the century. Paul himself made a distinction between the true, spiritual Jew and the physical descendants of Abraham (Ro 2:28–29; 9:8). Only those Jews who recognized Jesus as Messiah could rightly be called "Israel" (Ro 9:6), though the term might be used with qualifications to refer to the historic descendants of Jacob ("Israel after the flesh" [lit. tr. of 1Co 10:18]). Peter likewise described the church (Jew and Gentile) in terms drawn from the OT that historically describe the true people of God among the Jewish descendants ("holy priesthood . . . chosen people . . . royal priesthood . . . holy nation" [1Pe 2:4, 9]). Moreover, Gentiles who received Jesus as the Messiah and Lord were considered "Abraham's seed" (Gal 3:29) and the true "circumcision" (Php 3:3).

Already in Revelation the distinction has been made between Jews who were Jews in name only and not true Jews because they did not acknowledge Jesus as Lord (2:9; 3:9). Also, John uses the OT image of the people of Israel as a "kingdom" and "priests" to God for the followers of Jesus (1:6). Similarly, many promises to the victors in the churches of Asia (chs. 2–3) are fulfillments of OT promises given to the true people of Israel. In Christ's rebuke to the churches, we have the OT imagery of "Balaam" and "Jezebel" describing error that had influenced not the OT Israel but the NT church. In 21:9–12, the church is called the "bride, the wife of the Lamb"; she is identified with the

New Jerusalem, and on its twelve gates are inscribed the "names of the twelve tribes of Israel." Even in the Gospel of John, Jesus is the "true vine," which many commentators understand to be an allusion to the vine that decorated the temple entrance and stood as a symbol for Israel (cf. Isa 5:1ff. with Jn 15:1ff.). Jesus is thus claiming to be the true Israel and his followers are the branches, who are related to the true Israel (cf. Ro 11:17–24).

This usage is evident in the NT itself; the only question is whether John takes the final step in Revelation and, in the context of a largely Gentile church, uses the OT terminology to speak of the church. It is entirely possible that when the church actually separated itself from Israel (as seems apparent in Revelation), it could appropriate to itself the name "Israel." Other Jewish sectarian groups (such as at Qumran) also restricted the name "Israel" to their group and denied its use to other Jews. Thus in John's mind the followers of Jesus (14:4) are undoubtedly the true servants of God, the Israel of God (cf. Jn 11:51–52).

The identification of the 144,000 with the whole elect people of God, including both Jews and Gentiles, does not negate Paul's teaching to the effect that the majority of the Jews themselves will one day be brought back into a relationship of salvation before God. John simply is not dealing with Paul's emphasis at this point in Revelation (but cf. 11:2–3).

The number 144,000 is obviously obtained by combining 12,000 for each of the twelve tribes of Israel (vv.5–8). Earlier (cf. 4:4), twenty-four (a multiple of twelve) served as a symbolic number. The "thousand" multiple appears again later, in relation to the size of the Holy City: "He measured the city with the rod and found it to be 12,000 stadia in length, and as wide and high as it is long" (21:16). Thus, 12,000 is symbolic of completeness and perfection. Even the wall is "144 cubits" (i.e., twelve times twelve; v.17). The tree of life bearing "twelve crops of fruit, yielding its fruit every month" (i.e., twelve months; 22:2) further supports the view that John intends the number twelve to be taken symbolically. By 144,000, he signifies the sealing of the total number of God's servants who will face the Great Tribulation.

Those who are sealed come from "all the tribes of Israel," and this emphasizes even more the universality and comprehensiveness of the Christian gospel. Whereas in first-century Judaism there were many sects with exclusive tribal claims to being the "true Israel," for the followers of Jesus all such sectarianism is broken down and all groups, regardless of race, culture, religious background, or geographical location, are accepted before God (7:9; 14:4). There is an exclusivism in Revelation, but it is based on loyalty to Christ.

5–8 John goes even further. He enumerates each of the twelve tribes and their number: "From the tribe of Judah 12,000 were sealed," etc. Why was it necessary to provide this detailed enumeration? And why the particular tribal selection? In answering these difficult questions, some facts about the list should be noted. John places Judah first, evidently to emphasize the priority of the messianic King who came from the tribe of Judah (5:5; cf. Heb 7:13–14). Nowhere in the tribal listings of the OT except in the space arrangement of the wilderness camp (Nu 2:3ff.) does Judah come first. This exception may itself be linked with the messianic expectation through Judah (Ge 49:10; 1Ch 5:2). John's priority of Judah is comparable to the emphasis placed in Judaism on the tribe of Levi (the priestly tribe). It is significant that John includes Levi among the other tribes, and thus gives no special place to the Levitical order; he places Levi in the comparatively unimportant eighth place.

The particular order and names of the tribes as given here by John are unique. The OT has no fewer than twenty variant lists of the tribes, and these lists include anywhere from ten to thirteen tribes, though the number twelve is predominant (cf. Ge 49; Dt 33; Eze 48). The grouping of twelve may be a way of expressing the corporate identity of the elect people of God as a whole and may be maintained—even artificially at times—to preserve this identity (cf. the "twelfth" apostle chosen when Judas fell [Ac 1:25–26]). John omits Dan (which elsewhere is always included) and Ephraim. In order to maintain the ideal number twelve with these omissions, he must list both Joseph and Manasseh as tribes. This is peculiar because the tribe of Joseph is always mentioned in the other lists by either including Joseph and excluding his two sons, Ephraim and Manasseh (Ge 49), or vice versa (Eze 48). Moreover, only when the Levitical priesthood gained more prominence was the tribe of Levi omitted from the lists and replaced by the two sons of Joseph.

Various efforts have been made to solve the enigma of John's list and especially to explain the absence of the tribe of Dan. While no solution is completely satisfactory, the early church held that the Antichrist would arise from the tribe of Dan (this belief may in fact be a pre-Christian Jewish tradition). Furthermore, Dan was associated in the OT with idolatry (Jdg 18:18–19; 1Ki 12:29–30). This may be the clue. If John sought to expose Christian idolatry and beast worship in his day by excluding Dan from the list of those sealed, it may also be possible to explain, on the same basis, why Manasseh and Joseph were chosen to fill up the sacred number rather than Manasseh and Ephraim, for in the OT Ephraim was also explicitly identified with idolatry (Hos 4:17).

If idolatry is the reason for omitting Dan and Ephraim, the readjustment of the list to include Joseph and Manasseh to complete the twelve can be understood. Since Dan will be reckoned first in the tribal listing of the restored eschatological Jewish community (Eze 48) and John's list puts Judah first, it may be that John's listing describes the church, not ethnic Israel.

It is important to note that John does not equate the 144,000 with everyone in the tribes. Rather, his repeated use of the preposition "from" (lit., "out of"; GK *1666*) in vv.4–8 implies that the sealed were an elect group chosen *out of* the tribes. If John had the actual Jewish Israel in view, this use of "from" would indicate an election from the whole nation. On the other hand, if he intended to imply something about the church, his language might indicate God's selecting the true church out "from" the professing church. This thought has already been mentioned (cf. 2:14ff., 20ff.; 3:16ff.) and is supported by Eze 9:4–7, where the seal distinguished the true servants of God from the false ones among the professing people of God. Paul states the same thought: "Nevertheless, God's solid foundation stands firm, sealed with this inscription: 'The Lord knows those who are his,' and 'Everyone who confesses the name of the Lord must turn away from wickedness'" (2Ti 2:19).

The description of the judgments under the sixth seal (6:12ff.) ends with the question, "The great day of their wrath has come, and who can stand?" (6:17). John answers this question by implying that only the true servants of God, who are divinely sealed, can be protected from the wrath of God and the Lamb.

b. The great white-robed multitude (7:9–17)

John now sees a great multitude from every nation and cultural background, standing before the throne of God and clothed in white robes. They are identified by the angel as those "who have come out of the great tribulation" (v.14). Again, the question is that of identity. Are they the Gentiles who are saved in the Tribulation in contrast to the Jews in vv.1–8? Presumably not, because they are described as coming from every nation and tribe and language, and this would mean both Jews and Gentiles. Are they martyrs who have given their lives in the Great Tribulation and have been slain by the beast? If martyrs, are they the rest of those to be killed referred to when the fifth seal is opened (6:11)? Are they the complete group of martyrs? Or do they represent the whole company of the redeemed in Christ as seen in glory?

Although there is no direct evidence that the great multitude are martyrs, there are some indications of this: (1) they are seen in heaven "before the throne" (v.9) and "in his temple" (v.15); (2) they are described as those "who have come out of the great tribulation" (v.14). Thus it is assumed that, since they have died in the Great Tribulation, they have most likely been martyred because the Tribulation will be a time of great killing of the saints (17:6; 18:24, 19:2; 20:4; et al.). The multitude would then not be the whole company of the martyred throughout history but only those who were victims of the beast persecution during the Great Tribulation. The group is then those future martyrs referred to under the fifth seal as those "who were to be killed as they had been" (6:11). They cannot be seen as the whole redeemed church, unless all Christians are to be identified with the martyrs.

The identification of this second group is related to the identification of the first one (vv.1–8). Some argue that the two groups must be different since the first is numbered, the second innumerable; the first is limited to Jews, the second refers to every nation. These objections are not serious if we recall that in vv.1–8, (1) the number of the sealed was symbolic and not literal, and (2) the delineation of the Twelve Tribes was seen as John's deliberate attempt to universalize the election of God. Thus what some have seen as contrasts may actually be designed to complement each other and show the continuity of the first group with the second. Furthermore, we should bear in mind that John does not see any group at all in vv.1–8 but merely hears the number of the sealed, whereas in vv.9–17 he actually sees a group and describes what he sees and hears. Therefore, the unity of both groups can be maintained and vv.9–17 understood as the interpretative key to the 144,000. John's vision then leaps ahead to a scene in heaven after the Great Tribulation has run its course and views the glorified Tribulation saints as being in God's presence, at rest from their trial and serving him continually.

Two variations of the more literal Jewish identity of those in vv.1–8 and the relationship of this first group to the second (vv.9–17) are popular today. (1) Some see the 144,000 as a select group of Jews who will be converted to Jesus shortly after the rapture of the church to heaven. These Jewish evangelists will preach the gospel to the world during the Tribulation, resulting in a great multitude of Gentiles being converted to Christ. (2) Others, accepting a posttribulational view of the church's rapture, understand the 144,000 as a literal Jewish remnant preserved physically through the Tribulation and converted immediately after the Rapture. They will be the people who will constitute the beginning of the restored Jewish Davidic Kingdom at the inception of the millennial reign of Christ on the earth.

There are three different types of "tribulation" (GK 2568), and it is important to distinguish between them. (1) There is tribulation that is inseparable from Christian life in the world (Jn 16:33; Ac 14:22; Ro 5:3; 2Ti 2:11–12; 1Pe 4:12; Rev 1:9; 2:10; et al.). All Christians during all ages participate in tribulation; they share in the continuing sufferings of Christ (Col 1:24).

(2) The Bible also speaks of an intense tribulation that will come on the final generation of Christians and climax all previous persecutions (see Da 12:1; Mt 24:21; 2Th 2:3ff.). In Revelation this more intense persecution is mentioned in 7:14; 11:7–10; 13:7; 16:6; possibly the events under the fifth seal should be included here (6:9–11). This future tribulation is distinguished from previous persecutions of the church in its intensity, in its immediate connection with Christ's second coming, and in the presence of Antichrist during it.

(3) Scripture also speaks of a future time of God's intense wrath on unbelievers. Revelation refers to this as "the great day of their wrath" (6:17) and "the hour of trial that is going to come upon the whole world to test those who live on the earth" (3:10). Such wrath from God comes especially under the trumpets and bowls (8:2ff.; 16:1ff.). Probably drawing on the teaching of Jesus in the Olivet Discourse (Mt 24), Paul refers to this punitive action of God in 2Th 1:6–10. While for Christians the Great Tribulation may be concurrent with a portion of the period of God's wrath on the rebellious, the final and more intense judgment of God seems to follow the Great Tribulation itself and is directly connected with the coming of Christ (Mt 24:29; Rev 6:12ff.; 19:11ff.).

9 "A great multitude ... from every nation, tribe, people and language" might well describe the crowds common to the agora or the quay of a seaport in first-century Asia. Similar fourfold descriptions of the members of the Christian community or of the inhabitants of the world occur in 5:9; 11:9; 13:7; 14:6; 17:15. "Standing before the throne and in front of the Lamb" signifies their position of acceptance and honor as God's true servants (cf. v.15) and reminds us of the continuity of this vision with the earlier vision of the throne and the Lamb (chs. 4–5). This group seems to complete the full circle of participants before the throne begun in ch. 4.

Their "white robes" impress John and are an important feature of the vision (vv.9, 13–14). We cannot fail to connect them with the white robes given the martyrs under the fifth seal (6:11). The white robes symbolize salvation and victory (v.10), and their possessors obtained them by "[washing] their robes and [making] them white in the blood of the Lamb" (v.14). This implies that they were true recipients of Christ's redemption in contrast to others who, though professing belief in Christ, were not genuine overcomers (cf. 3:5–6, 18). "The blood of the Lamb" connotes here more than the profound reference to the sacrificial death of Jesus (5:9); it also suggests faithful witness in following Jesus in his death (2:13; 12:11).

"Palm branches" are referred to only one other time in the NT (Jn 12:13), where they are connected with the Passover. Moses provided that palms should be used at the Feast of Tabernacles (Lev 23:40). Later they were used on other Jewish festal occasions (1 Macc 13:51; 2 Macc 10:7). Jewish coins of the period 140 B.C. to A.D. 70 frequently contain palms and some have the inscription "the redemption of Zion." Palms were emblems of victory. In Jn 12 they denote the triumph of Christ, while here in Revelation the reference is to the victory of the servants of Christ.

10 In accord with the literary symmetry of chs. 4–7, this group also expresses their worship of the King and the Lamb. Their praise to God is for his "salvation" (GK *5401*), not their own accomplishments. Since this same word is associated with the final manifestation of God's power and kingdom (12:10; 19:1), here it may also denote God's final victory over sin and the principalities of this world that crucified Christ and that kill his true disciples (cf. Isa 49:8; 2Co 6:2).

11–12 Finally, the angelic hosts (cf. 5:12–13) respond to the cry of the redeemed (v.10) with "Amen" and voice their praise and worship of God for the salvation given to humanity (cf. Lk 15:10).

13–14 After the manner of the OT apocalyptic passages, the interpreting angel asks concerning the white-robed throng, "Who are they, and where did they come from?" (cf. Da 7:15–16; Zec 1:9, 19; 4:1–6). Here and in 5:5 are the only references in Revelation to an elder speaking individually, a fact that supports the view that the elders in Revelation are angels and not a symbolic group representing the church. The reference to the washed robes should be viewed in relation to 3:4, where soiled clothes represent defection from Christ through unbelief and worship of false gods (cf. 21:8). On the "great tribulation," see comments on 7:9–17.

15 This and the following verses describe the activity and condition of the true servants of God in their future and eternal relation to the Lamb. This scene is one of the most beautiful in the Bible. In it those who have washed their robes in the blood of the Lamb are described as being before the throne of God without fear or tremor, fully accepted by the divine Majesty. What are they doing? Theirs is no state of passivity but of continual service of God in praise and worship.

The reference to the "temple" (GK *3724*) of God raises the question whether the scene describes the final state of the saints or an intermediate state, since 21:22 tells us that the New Jerusalem has no temple. However, the language used in vv.15–17 (esp. v.17) seems to depict the same condition as that of the saints in chs. 21–22 (cf. 21:3–4, 6; 22:1). Since v.15 relates to worship, it would be appropriate to refer to the presence of God and the Lamb as "in" the temple. In 21:22, however, the future existence of the people of God is described as a city; and in that glorious city, unlike the pagan cities of the present world, there will be no special temple in which to worship God because God himself and the Lamb will be present everywhere.

To "spread his tent [GK *5012*] over them" calls to mind the Shekinah presence in the OT tabernacle or temple (Ex 40:34–38; 1Ki 8:10–11; cf. Eze 10:4, 18–19) and later in Jesus (Jn 1:14) and also the idea of a permanent heavenly dwelling (Rev 21:3). Never again will these people endure torment. They have the supreme protection of the living God himself.

16 The condition described here contrasts to the earthly experience of those who suffered much for their faith (cf. Heb. 11:37–38). For them, starvation, thirst, and the burning desert are forever past. There may be allusion here to Isa 49:10, which places the time of relief from such distresses in the days of Messiah's kingdom. There may also be an allusion to what the four horsemen bring (6:1–8; cf. Mt 24:7).

17 We now have a beautiful pastoral figure—that of the Lamb shepherding his people (cf. Jn 10:1–8; Heb 13:20; 1Pe 2:25). It is not through some perfect environment but through the continual ministry of the Lamb that their sufferings are forever assuaged. Whereas on earth their enemies may have tormented them, now the Lamb guides them: "He will lead them to springs of living water." In contrast to the burning thirst they

```
Seals    1 2 3 4 5 6 7                              Second
         Trumpets  1 2 3 4 5 6 7                    Coming
                   Bowls    1 2 3 4 5 6 7
```
Fig 1

```
Seals  1      2     3    4    5    6    7 Second
           Trumpets 1  2  3  4  5  6  7 Coming
                    Bowls 1  2  3  4  5  6  7
```
Fig. 2

```
Seals  1  2   3   4   5   6   7            Second
              Trumpets 1 2 3 4 5 6 7       Coming
                              Bowls 1234567
```
Fig. 3

What is the relationship among the seals, trumpets, and bowls? Many scholars consider them to be sequential, just as they appear in the book (see Fig. 1). Others hold that these three all conclude at precisely the same point in time, so that each group of seven steps back from the end of the preceding sequence (see Fig. 2). Still others read the seven trumpets as describing the missing judgments of the seventh seal, and the seven bowls as describing the missing judgments of the seventh trumpet (see Fig. 3). These charts are taken by permission from *The NIV Compact Bible Commentary* by John Sailhamer (Zondervan, 1994).

experienced in their tribulation, now they will enjoy the refreshing waters of life. Thus in the future life the saints will not know stagnation, boredom, or satiation (Ps 23:1–2; Jer 2:13; Eze 47:1–12; Zec 14:8).

Finally, even the sorrowful memory of the pain and suffering of the former days will be mercifully removed by the Father: "God will wipe away every tear from their eyes" (cf. 21:4). Tribulation produces tears. Like a tenderhearted, devoted mother, God will wipe each tear from their eyes with the eternal consolations of glory itself. Never again will they cry out because of pain or suffering.

4. Opening of the seventh seal (8:1)

1 After the long interlude of ch. 7, the sequence of the opening of the seals is resumed by the opening of the final or seventh seal. This action provides both a conclusion to the seals and a preparation for the seven trumpets. The praises ordinarily heard uninterruptedly in heaven (4:8) now cease in order to allow the prayers of the suffering, persecuted saints on earth for deliverance and justice to be heard (6:10; 8:4; cf. Lk 18:2–8). Most interpreters, however, understand the silence to refer to the awesome silence before the great storm of God's wrath on the earth. A kind of Sabbath pause might be thought of here.

B. The Seven Trumpets (8:2–11:19)

1. Preparatory: the angel and the golden censer (8:2–5)

2–4 While the seven seals were opened by the Lamb himself, the judgments of the seven trumpets and the seven bowls (15:1) are executed by seven angels. Before the trumpet judgments are executed, another angel enacts a symbolic scene in heaven. He takes a golden censer filled with incense and offers the incense on the altar in behalf of the prayers of all God's people. Earlier, John mentioned the altar that was near God's presence (6:9). A strong assurance is here given to the suffering followers of Christ that their prayers for vindication are not forgotten because God will speedily vindicate them from their enemies' assaults. So close is the altar to God that the incense cloud of the saints' prayers rises into his presence and cannot escape his notice (cf. Ps 141:2).

5 The censer or firepan is now used to take some of the burning coals from the altar and cast them to the earth. Symbolically, this represents the answer to the prayers of the saints through the visitation on earth of

God's righteous judgments. God next appears on earth in a theophany. The language, reminiscent of Sinai with its thunder, lightning, and earthquake, indicates that God has come to vindicate his saints (Ex 19:16–19; Rev 4:5; 11:19; 16:18).

2. Sounding of the first six trumpets (8:6–9:21)

6 Two questions confront the interpreter at this point: (1) What is the relationship of the trumpets to the preceding seals and the following bowls? (2) Are the events described symbolic or literal?

In answer to the first question, there are two options: either the series are parallel and simultaneous or they are sequential. It is not possible to decide with certainty for either view, for each contains elements of truth. This commentary has already argued for the chronological priority of the first five seals to the events of the trumpets and bowls (see comment on 6:1). But the sixth seal seems to take us into the period of the outpouring of God's wrath that is enacted in the trumpet and bowl judgments (6:12–17).

The sequential factors are as follows: (1) There is a rise in the intensity of the judgments (only a part of earth and humankind is affected in the trumpets, but all are affected under the bowls). (2) There is a difference in sequence and content of the events described in each series. (3) The reference to those not sealed in 9:4 (fifth trumpet) presupposes the sealing of 7:1–8. (4) The explicit statement in 8:12 implies a sequence between seals and trumpets—"When he opened the seventh seal ... I saw the seven angels ... to them were given seven trumpets." (5) The bowl judgments are directly called the "last plagues" because with them God's wrath is "completed" (15:1), implying the prior trumpet judgments. When the seventh bowl is poured out, the words "It is done" are spoken (16:17).

On the other hand, there are parallelisms. The sixth-seventh seal (6:12ff.), the seventh trumpet (11:15ff.), and the seventh bowl (16:17ff.) all seem to depict events associated with the second coming of Christ. This last event parallelism may indicate that all these series (seals, trumpets, bowls) are parallel in their entirety or that there is a partial recapitulation or overlap in the three series. The text seems to demand some type of sequential understanding and hence rules out a complete parallelism.

The main question is whether the parallelism indicates that the events described under the sixth-seventh seal, seventh trumpet, and seventh bowl are identical or merely similar and hence really sequential. Here the following points are relevant: (1) The sixth seal brings us into the period of God's wrath on the beast worshipers but does not actually advance beyond that event to refer to the coming of Christ (6:12–17). (2) The seventh seal introduces the trumpet judgments, which run their course, and the seventh trumpet seems to bring us into the kingdom of Christ (11:15–18). (3) The seventh bowl likewise brings us to the consummation and return of Christ, that is, if we keep in mind that the incident of Babylon's destruction is an elaboration of events under the seventh bowl (16:17ff.; 19:11ff.).

But are all three series parallel in their last events or only parallel in the last trumpet and last bowl? It seems apparent that the "third woe" (9:12; 11:14) is never fulfilled by the seventh trumpet, unless the content of the seventh trumpet is the seven bowls, which is also the "third woe." This is another way of saying that there is some limited recapitulation or overlap with the seventh seal and the first trumpets and in the seventh trumpet with the first bowls. This might be called a telescopic view of the seals, bowls, and trumpets. Further support for this view is also found in observing that interludes come between the sixth and seventh seals and between the sixth and seventh trumpets but not between the sixth and seventh bowls, which would be expected if the trumpets were strictly parallel to the bowls.

The second problem concerns the literalness of the events described under each trumpet. The important but hard question is not literal versus nonliteral but what John intended. Some things may need to be understood more literally and others symbolically. For example, the reference to the army of 200 million (9:16–19) can hardly be literal (cf. comment on 9:16). Either the number is figurative or the army refers to demonic powers rather than human soldiers. It is also difficult to handle literally the reference to the eagle that speaks human words (8:13). While there is no way to settle this problem finally, this exposition will attempt to steer between a literal approach and a totally symbolic one.

As in the seals, there is a discernible literary pattern in the unfolding of the trumpets. The first four trumpets are separated from the last three, which are called "woes" (8:13; 9:12; 11:14), and are generally reminiscent of the plagues in Exodus. While John refers in 15:3 to the Song of Moses (Ex 15:1–18), he does not follow out the plague parallelism precisely, and the connections should not always be pressed.

Shofar "trumpets" (GK 4894; made of a ram's horn) were used in Jewish life as signaling instruments. They sounded alarms for war or danger as well as for peace and announced the new moon, the beginning of the Sabbath, or the death of a notable. Trumpets were also used to throw enemies into panic (Jdg 7:19–20). Their use as eschatological signals of the day of the Lord or the return of Christ is well established in the OT and NT (Isa 27:13; Joel 2:1; Zep 1:16; Mt 24:31; 1Co 15:52; 1Th 4:16).

7 *The first trumpet.* Hail and fire remind one of the fourth plague of the Exodus (Ex 9:23–26), with added intensity suggested by the reference to hail and fire mixed with blood (cf. Eze 38:22). A "third" refers to a relative fraction of the total and should not be construed as a specific amount (cf. Eze 5:2; Zec 13:8–9).

8–9 *The second trumpet.* A huge blazing mass like a mountain is thrown into the sea and turns part of iy into blood. This suggests the first plague, when the Nile was turned blood red and the fish were destroyed (Ex 7:20–21; cf. Zep 1:3). Reference to the destruction of ships shows the intense turbulence of the sea.

10–11 *The third trumpet.* John next sees a huge fiery star fall on the rivers and springs of water and turn a part of these fresh-water supplies into very bitter water. The star's name is "Wormwood," which refers to the bitter herb *Artemesia absinthium* found in the Near East and mentioned elsewhere in the Bible (Jer 9:15; 23:15; La 3:15, 19; Am 5:7). It is not clear whether John intended the star to be understood as an angel as in 9:1 and in 1:20. Here is the first reference in the plagues to the loss of human life (cf. 9:15, 20). This plague, aimed at the fresh water, is a counterpart of the preceding one, which was aimed at the sea.

12 *The fourth trumpet.* The heavens are struck with partial darkness, reminiscent of the ninth plague (Ex 10:21–23). The references to "a third of . . ." refer to a partial impairment of the ordinary light from these bodies. In the OT the darkening of the heavens appears in connection with the theophany of God in judgment (cf. Isa 13:10; Eze 32:7–8; Joel 2:10; 3:15; cf. Mt 24:29). An unusual darkness also attended the crucifixion of Christ (Mt 27:45).

13 Before the last three trumpets sound, John hears a flying eagle call out "woe" (GK 4026) three times. His cry announces the especially grievous nature of the last three plagues, which kill a third part of the population of the earth (9:18). Two of the woes are identified with the fifth and sixth trumpets (9:12; 11:14). (See the comments on 8:6, which argue that the third woe should be seen as the seven bowl judgments in 16:1ff.) The "inhabitants of the earth" distinguishes the Christ rejecters of the world from the true, faithful followers of the Lamb (cf. comment on 3:10). A flying "eagle" announces these words. This must be taken symbolically. In Revelation there are two other references to eagles (4:7; 12:14). Since 4:7 relates to the description of one of the four living beings, it may be that John intends the eagle mentioned here to have the same significance.

9:1–11 *The fifth trumpet: The first woe.* John now focuses attention on the fifth and sixth trumpets (first and second woes) by giving more than twice the space to their description than he does to the previous four trumpets together. The fifth trumpet releases locusts from the Abyss. For five months these locusts torment the inhabitants of the earth who do not have the seal of God. John sees a "star" that has fallen to the earth. Since this star is given a key to open the Abyss, it is reasonable to understand it as being a symbolic reference to an angel. This is supported by v.11, where "the angel of the Abyss" is mentioned and named "Abaddon," as well as 20:1, where reference is also made to "an angel coming down" who has the key to the Abyss, where Satan is thrown.

The "Abyss" (GK 12) is also referred to in 11:7 and 17:8 as the place from which the beast arises. This word refers to the underworld as (1) a prison for certain demons (Lk 8:31; cf. 2Pe 2:4; Jude 6) and (2) the realm of the dead (Ro 10:7). When the Abyss is opened, huge billows of smoke pour out, darken the sky, and release horselike locusts on the earth.

Locust plagues are one of the severest plagues of humankind. The imagery of locusts, appearing like armies, advancing like a cloud, darkening the heavens, and sounding like the rattle of chariots, goes back to Joel's vision of the locust army that came on Israel as a judgment from God (Joel 1:6; 2:4–10). But the locusts of the Apocalypse inflict agony like scorpion stings (vv.3, 5, 10). This, together with the fact that they do not eat grass (v.4), shows that these locusts are something other than ordinary earthly insects. Indeed, they have the special task of inflicting a nonfatal injury only on the beast worshipers, who do not have the seal of God on their foreheads (v.4; cf. comment on 7:3). This may imply that these locust-like creatures are not simply instruments of a physical plague (as in Moses' or Joel's day or under the first four trumpets) but are demonic forces out of the Abyss from whom the true people of God are protected (cf. John's use of frogs to represent demonic powers in 16:13). The five months of agony (vv.5, 10) may refer to the life span of the locust (i.e., spring and summer). So severe is the torment they inflict that their victims will seek death (cf. Job 3:21; Jer 8:3; Hos 10:8).

John describes the locusts as an army of mounted troops ready for the attack (v.7). The heads of the locusts resemble horses' heads. John does not say that the locusts had crowns of gold on their heads but that they wore "something like crowns of gold" on their heads. This may refer to the yellow green of their breasts. This, combined with their resemblance to human faces, suggests something unnatural, hence demonic. The comparison of their "hair" with that of women may refer to the locusts' long antennae, while their lionlike teeth suggest the terrible devastation they can bring (cf. Joel 1:6–7). The "breastplates of iron" refers to their scales, which appeared as a cuirass of metal plates across the chest and long flexible bonds of steel over the shoulders. Their sound was like the rushing of war chariots into battle (v.9; cf. Joel 2:5).

This description creates an image of the fearful onslaught of demonic powers in the last days. Therefore, their leader is called "Abaddon" (GK 11 & 13) in Hebrew and "Apollyon" (GK 661) in Greek. The Hebrew term means "destruction" or "ruin" (cf. Job 26:6; Pr 27:20) and more often "the place of ruin" in Sheol (cf. Job 26:6; Pr 15:11; 27:20), "death" (cf. Job 28:22), or "the grave" (cf. Ps 88:11). The Greek term means "exterminator" or "destroyer" and does not occur elsewhere in the Bible. Some understand Apollyon as a separate angel entrusted with authority over the Abyss. Why John names the king of the Abyss in both Hebrew and Greek is open to question. Perhaps his readers' background in Hebrew, on which John's names and thoughts seem to turn (cf. 16:16), was so slender that an additional help here and there was necessary. This stylistic trait of giving information in bilingual terms is peculiar to Revelation and John's Gospel (see Jn 6:1; 19:13, 17, 20; 20:16).

12 This verse is transitional, indicating that the "first woe" (fifth trumpet) is finished and two woes are yet to come (presumably the sixth and seventh trumpets; cf. 8:13 with 11:14). There may be in this verse a resumption of the eagle's words (cf. 8:13).

13–19 *The sixth trumpet: The second woe.* Here we find a description of disasters that reach to the death of a third of humankind (vv.15, 18; cf. 8:7). "Four angels," the instruments of God's judgment, are held at the river Euphrates, whence traditionally the enemies of God's ancient people advanced on the land of Israel (Jer 2:18; 13:4–5; 51:63; Rev 16:12) and which was recognized as its northeastern extremity (Ge 15:18). John makes use of the ancient geographical terms to depict the fearful character of the coming judgment of God on a rebellious world. While the language is drawn from historical-political events of the OT, it describes realities that far transcend a local geographical event. God's dealings are not accidental but planned, and they happen at a precise moment in time. By a reference to the "golden altar" of incense, the release of these angels is again connected with the prayers of God's saints for vindication (6:9; 8:3).

At v.16 a mounted army of some 200 million horses and riders is rather abruptly introduced. While some argue for a literal human army here, several factors point to their identity as demonic forces. First, the horsemen are not in themselves important but wear brightly colored breastplates of fiery red, dark blue, and sulfurous yellow, more suggestive of supernatural than natural riders. More important are the horses, which not only have heads resembling lions but are, rather than their riders, the instruments of death by the three plagues of fire, smoke, and sulfur that come from their mouths. Furthermore, these horses have tails like snakes that are able to kill (vv.17–19), unlike the locusts' scorpionlike tails that do not inflict death but only injury (v.5). Finally, an army of 200 million could not be conscripted, supported, and moved to the Middle East without totally disrupting all societal needs and capabilities. Thus it seems better to understand the vast numbers and description of the horses as indicating demonic hordes. Such large numbers do occasionally indicate angelic hosts elsewhere in Scripture (Ps 68:17; Rev 5:11; cf. 2Ki 2:11–12; 6:17). This would not eliminate the possibility of human armies of manageable size also being involved. But the emphasis here (vv.16–19) is on their fully demonic character, utterly cruel and determined, showing no mercy to man, woman, or child. These demons might also be manifest in pestilences, epidemic diseases, or misfortunes as well as in armies. Such would explain the use of "plagues'" to describe these hordes (vv.18, 20; cf. 11:6; 16:9, 21).

20–21 God's first purpose for the plagues is judgment on the human race for their willful choice of idolatry and the corrupt practices that go with it (v.21). John had earlier called the churches to "repent" of their faithless tendencies lest they too share in God's judgment (2:5, 16, 21–22; 3:19). In these verses we see the end result of refusing to turn to God. This stubbornness leads to worship of demons as well as worship of cultic objects made by human hands (gold, silver, bronze, stone, and wood; cf. Pss 115:4–7; 135:17; Jer 10:1–16; Da 5:23). "Demons" may mean either pagan deities (Dt 32:17; Ps 106:37) or malign spirits (1Co 10:20–21; 1Ti 4:1). John no doubt shared Paul's concept of demons as evil spirits (Rev 16:14; 18:2). Hence, there is a twofold evil in idol worship: it robs the true God of his glory (Ro 1:23) and it leads to consorting with evil spirits.

This demonic corruption is manifest in the inhuman acts of those who have given up God for idols—acts of murder, sexual immorality, and thefts (cf. Ro 1:24, 28–31). In general, these are violations of the ten commandments. "Magic arts" (GK 5760) means "a practice of sorceries" or "witchcraft" (cf. Ex 7:11; 9:11; Gal 5:20; Rev 21:8; 22:15); usually drugs were involved.

God's second purpose revealed in the agonizing plagues described in chs. 8–9 is to bring societies to repentance (cf. 16:9, 11). God is not willing that any person should suffer his judgment but that all should repent and turn to him (Lk 13:3, 5; 2Pe 3:9). But when God's works and words are persistently rejected, only judgment remains (Eph 5:6; Heb 10:26–31).

3. Second interlude (10:1–11:14)

a. The little book (10:1–11)

1–4 As in the seals, the sequence of the sixth and seventh trumpets is interrupted to provide additional information bearing on the previous events and to prepare the reader for further developments. The author sees a mighty angel (possibly Michael, "the great prince" of Da 12:1), whom he describes in such dazzling terms that some have wrongly identified him with Christ. The voice that speaks in vv.4, 8 could, however, be that of Jesus.

The angel has in his hand a small scroll (v.2)—not to be confused with the Lamb's scroll of chs. 5–7 but connected with the symbolic scroll of Ezekiel (Eze 2:9–3:3; cf. Jer 15:15–17). This prophet was told to "eat" the scroll, just as John is told to eat the scroll given him (vv.9–10). Such an action symbolized the reception of the Word of God into one's innermost being as a necessary prerequisite to proclaim it with confidence. John could see the words on the scroll because it "lay open" in the angel's hand. The angel standing on both land and sea symbolizes that the prophetic message is for the whole world.

When the angel shouted (v.3), seven thunders spoke, and John proceeded to write down their words. But he is interrupted and is commanded, "Seal up what the seven thunders have said and do not write it down" (v.4). Conceivably, this might have been another series of sevens. Either the seven thunders were intended for John's own illumination and were not essential to the main vision of the seven trumpets, or the reference is designed to strike a note of mystery with reference to God's revelatory activities (cf. 2Co 12:4). As the visible portion of an iceberg is only a small part of the iceberg, so God's disclosures reveal only part of his total being and purposes.

5–7 The angel's action of raising his right hand to heaven doubtless alludes to the Jewish oath-swearing procedure (Dt 32:40; Da 12:7). He swears that "there will be no more delay" (v.6). Clearly there is some type of progression in the seals, trumpets, and bowls that nears its conclusion as the seventh trumpet is about to sound (v.7). When the seventh trumpet is finally sounded, there is an announcement that "the kingdom of the world has become the kingdom of our Lord and of his Christ" and that the time has come to judge the dead, to reward the saints, and to destroy the earth destroyers (11:15, 18). These events are recorded in the remaining chapters of the book, which include the seven bowl judgments and the new heavens and the new earth. Thus, here in 10:7 it is announced that "the mystery of God" is accomplished. That mystery is his purposes for humanity and the world as revealed to both OT and NT prophets.

The way the NIV translates v.7 suggests that the consummation comes before the blowing of the seventh trumpet: "when the seventh angel is about to sound his trumpet...." While this is grammatically possible, it is also possible to render the expression "about to sound" as "when he shall sound." Thus understood, the meaning is that during the time of the sound of the seventh trumpet, when the angel sounds, the final purposes of God will be completed. This rendering clarifies the statement in 11:14, "The second woe has passed: the third woe is coming soon," a statement made just before the seventh trumpet sounds. Hence, the seventh trumpet will reveal the final judgments of the bowls and the final establishment of God's rule on the earth.

8–11 John, like Ezekiel, is now commanded to take the prophetic scroll and eat it. The scroll tasted "as sweet as honey" but was bitter to the stomach. Receiving the Word of God is a great joy; but since the Word is an oracle of judgment, it results in the unpleasant experience of proclaiming a message of wrath and woe (cf. Jer 15:16, 19). The symbolic act of eating the scroll might also mean that the prophetic message was mixed with joy and comfort as well as gloom. The sweetness should not be taken to refer to the joy of proclaiming a message of wrath, for to all God's prophets this was a sorrowful, bitter task (Jer 9:1).

The chief import of ch. 10 seems to be a confirmation of John's prophetic call, as v.11 indicates: "You must prophesy again about many peoples, nations, languages and kings." This prophesying should not be understood as merely a recapitulation in greater detail of the previous visions but a further progression of the events connected with the end. John uses the word "kings" instead of "tribes" (as in 5:9; 7:9; 13:7; 14:6); this may anticipate the emphasis on the kings of the earth found in 17:9–12 and elsewhere.

b. The two witnesses (11:1–14)

Some have considered this chapter one of the most difficult to interpret in the book of Revelation. In it John refers to the temple, the Holy City, and the two prophets who are killed by the beast and after three and one-half days are resurrected and ascend to heaven. Does John intend all this to be understood literally—namely, the literal temple in Jerusalem; two people prophesying for 1,260 days, who are killed by the Antichrist, raised from the dead, and ascend to heaven; a great earthquake that kills seven thousand people and the survivors of which glorify God? Or does he intend all or part of these as symbols representing something? Most commentators take at least part of these things as symbolic. Furthermore, how does this section (11:1–13) relate to the total context (10:1–11:19)?

While details of interpretation vary, there are but two main approaches to the chapter: (1) the temple, altar, worshipers, and Holy City have something to do with the Jewish people and their place in the plan of God; or (2) John is here referring to the Christian church. As in ch. 7, John's references to particular Jewish entities create the chief source of the problem.

At the outset, it may be helpful to state why the Jewish view is less preferable. This approach has two slightly different aspects.

Dispensational commentators generally understand the "temple" and the "city" to refer to a rebuilt temple in Jerusalem. While some elements may be symbolic, the main import of the passage depicts a future protection of the nation of Israel prior to her spiritual regeneration. The Antichrist (beast) will permit the rebuilding of the temple in Jerusalem and the restoration of Jewish worship for three and a half years; then he will break his covenant and trample down a part of the temple and the Holy City until Christ returns to deliver the Jewish people (cf. Da 9:27).

Others have argued for a modified Jewish view. To them, John is prophetically predicting the preservation and ultimate salvation of the Jewish people, similar to Paul in Ro 11:26. This group believes that the temple and the city of Jerusalem are not the literal Jewish restored temple or the city located in Palestine. Rather, they represent, on the one hand, the believing Jewish remnant (temple, altar, and worshipers) and, on the other hand, the Jewish people or nation as a whole who are now under Gentile oppression (outer court and city). Both Jewish views suffer from their inability to relate this chapter to the context of ch. 10, to the parallelism in the seal interlude (ch. 7), to the ministry and significance of the two witnesses, or to the further chapters in Revelation (esp. chs. 12–13). Therefore, it is better to understand John as referring in ch. 11 to the whole Christian community.

1 John is given a "reed" (GK 2812), long and straight like a "rod" and thus suitable for measuring a large building or area (cf. Eze 40:5). Its purpose is to "measure the temple of God and the altar." Most agree that the principal OT passage in John's mind was Ezekiel's lengthy description of the measuring of the future kingdom temple (Eze 40:3–48:35). Since interpreters are confused about what Ezekiel's vision means, the ambiguity extends also to John's description. Measuring with a reed or line may have various metaphorical meanings. It may refer to the promise of restoration and rebuilding, with emphasis on extension or enlargement (Jer 31:39; Zec 1:16). It may also be done to mark out something for destruction (2Sa 8:2; 2Ki 21:13; Isa 28:17; La 2:8; Am 7:7–9). In Eze 40:2ff., this latter sense would be inappropriate. But what does John's measuring mean?

Since John is told in v.2 not to measure the outer court but to leave it for the nations to overrun, it seems that here in ch. 11 the measuring means that the temple of God, the altar, and the worshipers are to be secured for blessing and preserved from spiritual harm or defilement. In 21:15–17, John similarly depicts the angel's measuring of the heavenly city (with a golden rod), apparently to mark off the city and its inhabitants from harm and defilement (21:24, 27). As a parallel to the sealing of 7:1–8, the measuring does not symbolize preservation from physical harm but the prophetic guarantee that none of the faithful worshipers of Jesus as the Messiah will perish, even though they suffer physical destruction at the hand of the beast (13:7).

In Eze 43:10, the prophet is told to "describe the temple to the people of Israel, that they may be ashamed of their sins." The purpose of the elaborate description and temple measurement there is to indicate the glory and holiness of God in Israel's midst and convict them of their defilement of his sanctuary (43:12). Likewise, John's prophetic ministry calls for a clear separation between those who are holy and those who have defiled themselves with the idolatry of the beast.

John is to measure "the temple of God." There are two Greek words used in the NT for temple. *Hieron* (GK 2639) is a broad term that refers to the whole structure of Herod's temple, including courts, colonnades, etc. (e.g., Mt 4:5; Jn 2:14). *Naos* (GK 3724) is narrower and refers to the sanctuary or inner house where only the priests were allowed (Mt 23:35; 27:51; always in Revelation). While the distinction between the two words is not always maintained, in this context (11:1) it may be appropriate since the next verse mentions the outer precinct as a separate entity.

Does John mean here the heavenly temple often mentioned in Revelation (cf. 11:19; 15:5, 8; 16:17), or does he refer to the Christian community, as in 3:12: "Him who overcomes I will make a pillar in the temple of my God"? *Naos* always refers to the Jerusalem temple in the Gospels with the single exception of John's Gospel, where it refers to Jesus' own body (Jn 2:19–21; cf. Rev 21:22). Outside the Gospels it refers either to pagan shrines (Ac 17:24; 19:24) or, in Paul's letters, metaphorically to the physical bodies of

Christians or to the church of God (1Co 3:16; 6:19; 2Co 6:16; Eph 2:21; most likely also 2Th 2:4). Since John refers to the "outer court" in v.2, it is likely that he has in mind not the heavenly temple of God but an earthly one, and likely also, symbolically, the covenant people. To take the temple in this verse as representing the church in the Great Tribulation is not without problems, but this seems the best view.

The "altar" (GK 2603) would then refer to the huge stone altar of sacrifice in the court of the priests, and the expression "the worshipers" would most naturally indicate the priests and others in the three inner courts (the court of the priests, the court of Israel, the court of the women). These represent symbolically the true servants of God and the measuring symbolizes their recognition and acceptance by God in the same manner as the numbering in ch. 7. The writer of Hebrews likewise speaks of an "altar" that Christians eat from, but that Jewish priests who serve in the temple are not qualified to eat from (Heb 13:10). By this language he speaks of the once-for-all sacrifice of Christ on the cross utilizing the background of the temple images, as does John.

2 As the "outer court" in the Jerusalem temple was frequented by a mixed group including Gentiles and unbelievers, so in John's mind the earthly temple or community of God may involve a part where those who are impure or unfaithful will be (21:8; 22:15). The effect of not measuring this part of the temple is to exclude those in it from spiritual security and God's blessing. So in measuring the temple, Ezekiel is instructed to exclude from the sanctuary "the foreigners uncircumcised in heart and flesh" (Eze 44:5–9)—i.e., pagans who do not worship the true God and whose presence would desecrate the sanctuary. Previously, John has shown concern over those who were associated with the local churches but were not true worshipers of Christ (cf. 2:14–16, 20–25; 3:1–5, 16). When the great test comes, they will join the ranks of the beast and reveal their true colors.

On the other hand, it may be better to understand the desecration of the outer court as a symbolic reference to the victory of the beast over the saints (described in v.7). Thus by using two slightly different images, the "temple-altar-worshipers" and the "outer court-holy city," John is viewing the church under different aspects. Though the Gentiles (pagans) are permitted to touch the "outer court" and to trample on the "holy city" for a limited time ("42 months"), they are not able to destroy the church because the "inner sanctuary" is measured or protected in keeping with Christ's earlier word in Mt 16:18.

Since John says the outer court will be "given to the Gentiles," it is important to establish the best translation of "Gentiles" (*ethnos*; GK 1620). (1) In some NT contexts, this word may have the more general sense of "nations," describing the various ethnic or national groups among humankind (e.g., Mt 24:9, 14; Lk 24:47; Ro 1:5; 15:11). (2) In other contexts, it denotes "Gentiles" in contrast to the Jewish people (e.g., Mt 4:15; 10:5; Lk 2:32; Ac 10:45; Ro 11:11). In many cases the broader sense may shade off into the narrower, producing ambiguity. (3) But there is a third use of *ethnos*. Just as the Jews referred to all other peoples outside the covenant as "Gentiles," so there gradually developed a similar Christian usage of the term that saw all peoples who were outside of Christ as *ethnos*, including unbelieving Jews (1Co 5:1; 12:2; 1Th 4:5; 1Pe 2:12; 3Jn 7; cf. our word "pagan" or "heathen"). When the sixteen cases of *ethnos* in Revelation are examined, not once is "Gentiles" appropriate. Everywhere they are the peoples of the earth, either in rebellion against God (11:18; 14:8; 19:15; 20:3) or redeemed and under the rule of Christ (2:26; 21:24, 26; 22:2). There is no good reason why John does not intend the same sense in 11:2.

To sum up, "given to the Gentiles" refers to the defiling agencies that will trample down the outer court of the church, leading to defection from Christ or physical destruction, though all the while the inner sanctuary of the true believers will not be defiled by idolatry. This spiritual preservation of true believers will be accomplished by John's prophetic ministry, which distinguishes loyalty to Christ from the deception of the beast.

The nations will "trample on the holy city for 42 months." What is "the holy city"? The more literal viewpoint sees it as the earthly city of Jerusalem. Support for this is found in (1) the OT's use (Ne 11:1; Isa 48:2; 52:1; Da 9:24) and Matthew's use of "holy city" for Jerusalem (Mt 4:5; 27:53), (2) the proximity of the term "the holy city" to the temple reference (v.1), and (3) the mention in v.8 of the "great city ... where also their Lord was crucified."

Since Jerusalem was destroyed in A.D. 70, and since Revelation was presumably written about 95, these interpreters hold two views about the meaning of this reference to the city. Some believe it to refer to a rebuilt Jerusalem and temple during the future Tribulation period. Others see it as merely a symbolic reference to the Jewish people without any special implication of a literal city or temple. But if John does in fact differentiate here between believing Jews (inner court) and the nation as a whole (outer court), this would be the only place in the book where he does so. Furthermore, such a reference at this point in the context of chs. 10–11 would be abrupt and unconnected with the main themes in these chapters—the nature of the prophetic ministry and the great trial awaiting Christians.

Far more in keeping with the emphasis of the whole book, and of these chapters in particular, is the view that "the holy city," like the temple, refers to the church. The consistent usage of the expression "holy city" means the community of those faithful to Jesus Christ, composed of believing Jews and Gentiles (21:2, 10; 22:19; cf. 3:12; 20:9). It should also be noted that the name Jerusalem nowhere appears in ch. 1, though a circumlocution for it in v.8 ("where also their Lord was crucified") is prefaced with the word "figuratively" (see comment on v.8). While the vision of the future Holy City (chs. 21–22) describes the condition of the city when she has completed her great ordeal and is finally delivered from the great deceiver, the present reference is to God's people as they must first endure the trampling of the pagan nations for "42 months."

Does the trampling (GK 4251) indicate defilement and apostasy, or does it instead mean persecution? This word can metaphorically mean either of these. Two factors favor the latter sense. The time of the trampling is "42 months," which is the exact time John attributes to the reign of the beast (13:5–7). Furthermore, in Daniel's prophecy the trampling of the sanctuary and host of God's people by Antiochus Epiphanes (Da 8:10, 13) is clearly a persecution of the people of God.

But what of the term "42 months"? This exact expression occurs in the Bible only here and in 13:5, where it refers to the time of the authority of the beast. Mention is also made of a period of 1,260 days (i.e., 42 months of 30 days each) in 11:3 and 12:6. In 12:14 a similar length of time is referred to as "a time, times [i.e., two times] and half a time." All these expressions equal a three-and-one-half-year period. In Revelation, "42 months" refers to the period of oppression of the Holy City and the time of the authority of the beast (11:2; 13:5). The "1,260 days" is the period the two witnesses prophesy and the time the woman is protected from the dragon's reach (11:3; 12:6). "Time, times and half a time" seems to be used synonymously for the 1,260 days during which the woman will be protected in the desert (12:14). We cannot assume that because these periods are equal, they are identical. On the other hand, the three different expressions may well be literary variations for the same period.

Daniel is generally taken to be the origin of the terms. In Da 9:27 a week is spoken of ("seven," NIV), and the context makes it clear that this is a week of years, i.e., seven years. Further, the week is divided in half—i.e., three and a half years for each division. These half weeks of years are spoken of in Da 7:25 as "a time, times and half a time." Both early Jewish and Christian interpreters referred this to the period of the reign of the Antichrist. In Da 12:7 the identical expression refers to the period "when the power of the holy people has been finally broken"; in 12:11 the equivalent period expressed in days (1,290) refers to the time of the "abomination" and defilement of the temple. Whether or not these references refer to the second-century B.C. activities of Antiochus Epiphanes must be left to the exegetes of Daniel; but it is known that the Jews and later the Christians believed that these events at least foreshadow, if not predict, the last years of world history under the Antichrist. Thus John would have a ready tool to use in this imagery for setting forth his revelation of the last days.

Some commentators suggest that the first three and a half years is the period of the preaching of the two witnesses, while the second half of the week is the time of bitter trial when Antichrist reigns supreme. Others believe the expressions are synchronous and thus refer to the identical period. With some reservations, the former view is preferable.

The 1,260-day period of protected prophesying by the two witnesses (11:3–6) synchronizes with the period of the woman in the desert (12:6, 14). When the death of the witnesses occurs (11:7), there follows the forty-two-month murderous reign of the beast (13:5, 7, 15), which synchronizes with the trampling down of the Holy City (11:2). This twofold division seems to be also supported by Jesus' Olivet Discourse, where he speaks of the "beginning of birth pains" (Mt 24:8) and then of the period of "great distress" shortly before his second coming (Mt 24:21).

Finally, are the two periods of three and a half years symbolic or do they indicate calendar years? Not all will agree, but a symbolic sense that involves a real period but understands the numbers to describe the kind of period rather than its length is in keeping with John's use of numbers elsewhere (cf. 2:10; 4:4; 7:4). Hence, if we follow the twofold division of Daniel's seventieth week of seven years, the preaching of the two witnesses occupies the first half, while the second half is the time of trial when the beast reigns supreme, and during which time the fearful events of chs. 13–19 take place. This explanation must, however, remain tentative.

3 Perhaps a greater diversity of interpretation surrounds these two personages than even the temple in the previous verses. They are called "two witnesses" (v.3), "two prophets" (v.10), and, more figuratively, "two olive trees and the two lampstands who stand before the Lord of the earth" (v.4). Interpretative suggestions are: two historic figures such as Moses and Elijah (already taught in Jewish tradition) or the apostles Peter and Paul, the church in its witness, Christian martyrs, all the prophets, and the two groups of the Jewish believers and Gentile believers in the church.

Since opinion varies so greatly at this point, it may be wise not to be dogmatic about any one view. Perhaps the best view is the one which sees the two witnesses as representing those in the church who are specially called, like John, to bear a prophetic witness to Christ during the whole age of the church. They also represent those prophets who will be martyred by the beast. Indications that they represent many individuals and not just two are: (1) they are never seen as individuals but do everything together—they prophesy together, suffer together, are killed together, are raised together, and ascend together—and all this is hardly possible for two individuals; (2) the beast makes war on them (v.7), which is strange if they are merely two individuals; (3) people throughout the whole world view their ignominious deaths (v.9)—something unlikely if only two individuals are involved; (4) their description as two "lamps" is applied in chs. 1–2 to local churches comprised of many individuals. They are "clothed in sackcloth" because they are prophets (cf. Isa 20:2; Zec 13:4) who call for repentance and humility (Jer 6:26; 49:3; Mt 11:21); this was the most suitable garb for times of distress, grief, danger, crisis, and self-humbling.

4 The reference to the "two olive trees and the two lampstands" is an allusion to Joshua and Zerubbabel in Zechariah's vision, who were also said "to serve the Lord of all the earth" (Zec 4:1–6a, 10b–14). The import of Zechariah's vision was to strengthen these two leaders by reminding them of God's resources and to vindicate them in the eyes of the community as they pursued their God-given tasks. Thus John's message is that the witnesses to Christ who cause the church to fulfill her mission to burn as bright lights to the world will not be quenched (cf. Rev 1:20; 2:5).

Why there should be two olive trees and two lampstands has been variously answered. Some suggest that "two" is the number of required legal witnesses (Nu 35:30; Dt 19:15; cf. Mt 18:16; Lk 10:1–24); others, that two represents the priestly and kingly aspects of the church or the Jewish and Gentile components. Perhaps the dualism was suggested to John by the two olive trees from Zechariah and the two great prophets of the OT who were connected with the coming of the Messiah in Jewish thought, i.e., Moses and Elijah (v.6; cf. Mt 17:3–4). What Joshua (the high priest) and Zerubbabel (the prince) were to the older community and temple, Jesus Christ is to the new community. He is both anointed Priest and King, and his church reflects this character especially in its Christian prophets (1:6; 5:10; 20:6).

5 Here the prophets' divine protection from their enemies is described in terms reminiscent of the former prophets' protection by God (2Ki 1:10; Jer 5:14). Fire is understood symbolically as judgment from God; and since it proceeds from the witnesses' mouths, we understand that their message of judgment will eventually be fulfilled by God's power (Ge 19:23–24; 2Sa 22:9; Ps 97:3). Their Lord gives them immunity from destruction until they complete their confirmation of God's saving deed in Christ. This assures the people of God that no matter how many chosen saints are oppressed and killed, God's witness to Christ will continue until his purposes are fulfilled.

6 The words "power to shut up the sky ... and power to turn the waters into blood" clearly allude to the ministries of the prophets Elijah and Moses (1Ki 17:1 and Ex 7:17–21). There is, however, no need for the literal reappearing of these two if it is understood that the two witnesses come in the same spirit and function as their predecessors. Thus Luke interprets the significance of John the Baptist as a ministry in the "spirit and power of Elijah" (Lk 1:17). The author of Revelation is simply describing the vocation of certain Christian prophets, indicating that some follow in the same tradition as the former prophets of Israel. According to Lk 4:25 and Jas 5:17, Elijah's prophecy shut up the heaven for "three and a half years," a curious foreshadowing, perhaps, of the span of time that these prophets witness (i.e., 1,260 days [v.3]).

7 When they finish their witness, the witnesses are killed by the beast from the Abyss. This is the first reference to the "beast" (GK 2563) in the book. The abruptness with which it is introduced seems not only to presuppose some knowledge of the beast but also to anticipate what is said of him in chs 13 and 17. Only here and in 17:8 is the beast described as coming "up from the Abyss" (cf. 9:1), showing his demonic origin. He attacks the prophets (lit., "makes war with them"; cf. 9:7; 12:7, 17; 13:7; 16:14; 19:19; 20:8). This attack possibly reflects Da 7:21 and is again described in 12:17 and 13:7. This is the second and final phase of the dragon's persecution of the Christian prophets and saints.

8 John mentions the place of the attack on the witnesses and of their death: "The street of the great city, which is figuratively called Sodom and Egypt, where also their Lord was crucified." This verse is both full of meaning and difficult to interpret. At first glance, John seems to be referring to the actual city of Jerusalem, where Christ died. Yet his terminology implies more than this. The city is called the "great city," a designation that refers to Babylon throughout the rest of the book (16:19; 17:18; 18:10, 16, 18–19, 21). Moreover, John's use of the word "city" (cf. 3:12) is symbolic. In fact, there are really only two cities in this book, the city of God and the city of Satan, which is later referred to as Babylon. A city may be a metaphor for the total life of a community of people (cf. Heb 11:10; 12:22; 13:14).

Here the "great city" is clearly more than merely Jerusalem, for John says it is "figuratively called Sodom and Egypt." "Figuratively" (GK 4462) means "spiritually, in a spiritual manner, full of the divine Spirit." Elsewhere in the NT, this word characterizes that which pertains to the Spirit in contrast to the flesh (1Co 2:14–15; Eph 1:3; 5:19; Col 3:16; 1Pe 2:5; et al.). Thus the spiritually discerning will catch the significance of the threefold designation of this city. It is called "Sodom," which connotes rebellion against God, the rejection of God's servants, moral degradation, and the awfulness of divine judgment (cf. Eze 16:49). In Isaiah's day the rebellious rulers of Jerusalem were called the rulers of Sodom (Isa 1:10; cf. Eze 16:46). The second designation is "Egypt." Egypt is a country, not a city. It is virtually certain that by John's day, Egypt had become a symbolic name for anti-theocratic world kingdoms that enslaved Israel. The third designation is "the great city ... where also their Lord was crucified" (cf. Mt 23:28–31, 37–38; Lk 13:33ff.; 21:20–24).

If, as most commentators believe, John also has Rome in mind in mentioning the "great city," then there are at least five places all seen by John as one—Babylon, Sodom, Egypt, Jerusalem, and Rome. This one city has become, in the eyes of the spiritually discerning, all places opposed to God and the witness of his servants. Wherever God is opposed and his servants harassed and killed, there is the "great city," the transhistorical city of Satan, the great mother of prostitutes (cf. 17:1ff.). What can happen to God's witnesses in any place is what has already happened to their Lord in Jerusalem.

9–10 People from every nation—Jew and Gentile—will "gloat over" their corpses and refuse them the dignity of burial. To have a dead body lie in view of all was the worst humiliation a person could suffer (Ps 79:3). Furthermore, the pagan world will celebrate the destruction of the witnesses and the victory over them by exchanging gifts, a common custom in the Near East (Ne 8:10, 12; Est 9:19, 22). Thus the beast will silence the witness of the church to the glee of the beast-worshiping world. The time of their silence corresponds in days to the time of their witness in years. It denotes only a brief time of triumph for the beast.

11–12 The witnesses now experience a resurrection and an ascension to heaven following their three-and-one-half-day death. It is generally held that John had Ezekiel's vision of the restoration of the dry bones in mind (Eze 37:5, 10–12). Just as interpretations of Ezekiel's vision vary, so interpretations of vv.11–12 vary. Some hold that the dry bones vision refers to the spiritual quickening of the nation of Israel. Others understand the descriptions to refer to the physical resurrection of the dead. If the two witnesses represent the witness of the church, then physical resurrection and ascension could be in mind. The summons "Come up here," followed by "they went up to heaven in a cloud," perhaps points to the Rapture (1Th 4:16–17).

On the other hand, John may be using the figure of physical resurrection to represent the church's victory over the death blow of the beast. In Ro 11:15 Paul uses the figure of resurrection symbolically to depict a great spiritual revival among the Jews in a future day. Here in v.12 the reference to the "cloud" (GK *3749*) is significant. Normally, the "cloud" depicts God's power, presence, and glory; this is the only instance in the book where strictly human figures are associated with a cloud. These two witnesses share in Christ's resurrection, and the cloud is a sign of heaven's acceptance of their earthly career. Even their enemies see them, just as they will see Christ when he returns with the clouds (1:7). The events of Christ's return and the ascension of the witnesses seem to be simultaneous. Thus in the two witnesses, John has symbolized the model of all true prophets, taking as a central clue the story of Jesus' appearance in Jerusalem and describing the common vocation of appearing in the holy city (or temple) in such a way that reaction to their work separates the worshipers of God from the unbelievers.

13 The earthquake is God's further sign of the vindication of his servants (cf. 6:12). But unlike the earthquake under the sixth seal, this one produces what appears to be repentance: "The survivors . . . gave glory to the God of heaven." The opposite response in 16:9, "they refused to repent and glorify him," seems to confirm that v.13 here speaks of genuine repentance (cf. 14:7; 15:4). Since the death, resurrection, and ascension of the two witnesses is worldwide in scope (vv.9–10), we may infer that the earthquake is also symbolic of a world-wide event. Even in the midst of judgment, God is active in the world to save those who repent. If there is such hope in the terrible time of final judgment, how much more now! God has not abandoned the human race. Neither should we!

14 All the events from 9:13 to 11:14 fall under the sixth trumpet and are called the second "woe" (see comments on 8:13; 9:12). Since further judgments are mentioned in this chapter, it is natural to see at the sounding of the seventh trumpet (vv.15–19) the third woe taking place. Its nature is described in the bowl judgments (16:11ff.). Apparently the third woe will come without further delay. Indeed, the seventh trumpet (v.15) brings us to the final scenes of God's unfolding mystery (10:7).

4. Sounding of the seventh trumpet (11:15–19)

15 The seventh trumpet sounds, and in heaven loud voices proclaim the final triumph of God and Christ over the world. The theme is the kingdom of God and of Christ—a dual kingdom eternal in its duration. The "kingdom" (GK *993*) is a main theme of the entire book of Revelation (1:6, 9; 5:10: 11:17; 12:10: 19:6; 20:4; 22:5). This kingdom involves the millennial kingdom and its blending into the eternal kingdom (chs. 20–22). The image suggests the transference of the world empire, once dominated by a usurping power, that has now at length passed into the hands of its true owner and king. The present rulers are Satan, the beast, and the false prophet. The announcement of the reign of the king occurs here, but the final breaking of the enemies' hold over the world does not occur till the return of Christ (19:11ff.).

Verses 15–18 are reminiscent of Ps 2. The opening portion of this psalm describes the pagan nations and kings set in opposition to God and his Anointed One. Then there follows the establishment of the Son in Zion as the Sovereign of the world and an appeal to the world rulers to put their trust in the Son before his wrath burns. John does not distinguish here between the millennial kingdom of Christ and the eternal kingdom of the Father (but cf. 3:21) as Paul does (1Co 15:24–28). This should be viewed as a difference merely of detail and emphasis, not of basic theology. In John's view this world becomes the arena for the manifestation of God's kingdom. While at this point the emphasis is on the future visible establishment of God's kingdom, that same kingdom is in some real sense now present; and John is participating in it (see 1:9).

16–17 As the other features in these verses are anticipatory, so the expression "have begun to reign" looks forward to the millennial reign depicted in ch. 20. Significantly, the title of God found earlier in the book, "who is, and who was, and who is to come" (1:8; 4:8), now is "who is and who was." He has now come! God has taken over the power of the world from Satan (Lk 4:6).

18 This passage contains a synopsis of the remaining chapters of Revelation. The nations opposed to God and incited by the fury of the dragon (12:12) have brought wrath on God's people (Ps 2:1–3). For this, God has brought his wrath on the nations (14:7; 16:1ff., 18:20, 19.19b, 20.11–15). The time (GK 2789) has now come for three further events: the judgment of the dead (20:11–15); the final rewarding of the righteous (21:1–4; 22:3–5); and the final destruction of the destroyers of the earth (Babylon, the beast, the false prophet, and the dragon; 19:2, 11; 20:10).

In Revelation three groups of persons receive rewards: (1) God's "servants the prophets" (cf. 18:20; 22:9); (2) the "saints" (perhaps the martyrs; cf. 5:8; 8:3–4; 13:7, 10; 16:6; 18:20, 24; or simply believers in every age, cf. 19:8; 20:9); and (3) "those who reverence [God's] name" (cf. 14:7; 15:4). In whatever way these groups are denoted, it is important to note that in Revelation the prophets are specially singled out (16:6; 18:20, 24; 22:6, 9).

19 In the heavenly temple John sees the ark of God's covenant. In the OT the ark was the chest that God directed Moses to make and place within the holiest room of the tabernacle sanctuary (Ex 25:10–22). He was directed to put in the ark the two tablets of the Decalogue—the documentary basis of God's redemptive covenant with Israel (Ex 34:28–29). Presumably the ark was destroyed when Nebuchadnezzar burned the temple in 586 B.C., for there was no ark in the second temple. Although the way into the Most Holy Place was barred under the old covenant to all except the high priest, now full and immediate access for all, along with a perfect redemption, has been secured by Christ's death (Heb 9:11–12; 10:19–22).

In v.19 the kingdom of God is seen retrospectively as having fully come. Yet its coming will be elaborated in chs. 20–22. Prospectively, this sight of the ark prepares us for the following chapters, which concern the faithfulness of God to his covenant people. As the ark was the sign to Israel of God's loyal love throughout their desert journeys and battles, so this sign of the new covenant will assure the followers of Christ of his loyal love through their severe trial and attacks by the beast. "Flashes of lightning, rumblings, peals of thunder" represent God's presence and vindication of his people (cf. comment on 6:12; 8:5).

C. The Seven Signs (12:1–14:20)

This section is what might be called a Book of Signs. While no signs (cf. comments on 12:1) appear in chs. 1–11, at least seven signs are mentioned in chs. 12–19 (cf. the seven signs in Jn 1–11). Three are in heaven (12:1, 3; 15:1); four on earth (13:13–14; 16:14; 19:20). Only one is a sign of good (12:1); the others are omens of evil or judgment from God. They explain and amplify previous material (e.g., the beast in 11:7 is more fully described in ch. 13) and also advance the drama to its final acts.

This intermediary section (chs. 12–14), preceding the final bowl judgments (15:1ff.), picks up and develops the theme of the persecution of God's people (see 3:10; 6:9–11; 7:14; 11:7–10). Chapter 12 gives us a glimpse into the dynamics of the persecution of God's people under the symbolism of the dragon who wages war on the woman and her children (v.17). Chapter 13 continues the same theme by telling of the persecution of the saints by the dragon-energized beasts. The section closes with the scene of the redeemed 144,000 on Mount Zion who are triumphant over the beast (14:1–5) and of the final hour of judgment on the beast worshipers (14:6–20).

1. The woman and the dragon (12:1–17)

In this chapter are three main figures: the woman, the child, and the dragon. There are also three scenes: the birth of the child (vv.1–6), the expulsion of the dragon (vv.7–12), and the dragon's attack on the woman and her children (vv.13–17).

1 John sees a dazzling sight—a pregnant woman, "clothed with the sun, with the moon under her feet," and wearing a victor's "crown" (GK *5109*; cf. 2:10; 3:11; 4:4, 10; 6:2; 9:7; 14:14) of twelve stars. John calls the sight a great "sign" (GK *4956*). This shows that the woman is more than a mere woman. She signifies something. Generally John uses "sign" to refer to something miraculous that points to a deeper spiritual significance (Jn 2:11, 18, et al.; Rev 12:1, 3; 13:13–14; 15:1; 16:14; 19:20).

The basic plot of the story was familiar in the myths and legends of the ancient world. A usurper doomed to be killed by a yet unborn prince plots to succeed to the throne by killing the royal seed at birth. The prince is miraculously snatched from his clutches and hidden away until he is old enough to kill the usurper and claim his kingdom. These stories were probably known to both John and his Asian readers.

While it is easy to point to parallels between the earlier myths and Rev 12, the differences are striking enough to eliminate the possibility that John merely borrowed pagan myths. Certainly John, who is so anti-pagan throughout his writings, would not draw on pagan mythology for his messages. Did he draw more directly on OT parallels? Some cite Ge 37:9–11, where the heavenly bodies of sun, moon, and eleven stars are associated together in Joseph's vision, though there are enough differences to maintain that it is unlikely that John intended his readers to see Ge 37 in this chapter.

Others see a more conscious parallelism between the story and the activities of the emperor Domitian around 83 A.D. After the death of his ten-year-old son, Domitian immediately proclaimed the boy a god and his mother, the mother of god. Some coins of this period show the mother Domitia as the mother of the gods standing with the scepter and diadem of the queen of heaven. Another coin shows the mother with the child before her. In his left hand is the scepter of world dominions, and with his right hand he is blessing the world. Still another coin shows the dead child sitting on the globe of heaven, playing with seven stars, which represent the seven planets, symbolic of his heavenly dominion over the world. On a fourth coin he represents the imperial Zeus child, who has been exalted to be lord of the stars and who will usher in the age of universal salvation. Such parallel imagery is hardly accidental. But whereas the coinage of Domitian glorifies the son of Domitia as the lord of heaven and savior of the world, Rev 12 presents Jesus Christ, the Lord of heaven and earth, as the One who will rule all nations with a rod of iron (v.5). John, as it were, demythologizes the Domitian myth by presenting Christ as the true and ascended Lord of heaven, the coming Ruler and Savior of the world.

The Dead Sea Scrolls have a story about the birth of the Messiah through the suffering messianic community, using imagery taken from the OT (see Isa 9:6–7; 26:17; 66:7; Mic 5:2). Elsewhere in the OT, the image of a woman is often associated with Israel, Zion, or Jerusalem (Isa 54:1–6; Jer 3:20; Eze 16:8–14; Hos 2:19–20). This background seems to provide a much closer link to the intended significance of ch. 12 than any other proposed parallels. In any case, while there does seem to be in ch. 12 a blending of elements from OT concepts, Jewish materials, ancient

John saw a dazzling pregnant woman being attacked by a ferocious dragon. Drawing by Rachel Bierling.

mythical stories, and possibly the Domitian child myth, John here reinterprets these older stories and presents a distinctively Christian view of history.

Who then is the woman? While it is not impossible that she is an actual woman, such as Mary, the evidence shows that she, like the woman in ch. 17, has symbolic significance. At the center of ch. 12 is the persecution of the woman by the dragon, who is definitely identified as Satan (v.9). This central theme renders it virtually certain that the woman could not refer to a single individual (cf. the persecution of the "rest of her offspring"; v.17).

Some identify the woman exclusively with the Jewish people, the nation of Israel. This view seems supported by the reference to the woman giving birth to the Messiah or "male child" (v.5); the twelve stars would refer to the twelve tribes (Ge 37:9–11). But there are internal problems with this view. The dragon's persecution of the woman after the Messiah's birth could hardly refer to the devil's attack on the nation as a whole but could apply only to the believing part of the people. The whole intent of the passage is to explain the persecution of the believing community, not the persecution of the nation of Israel as a whole.

Since the context indicates that the woman under attack represents a continuous entity from the birth of Christ until at least John's day or longer, her identity in the author's mind must be the believing covenant-messianic community. This group would include the early messianic community, which under John the Baptist's ministry was separated from the larger Jewish community to be the people prepared for the Lord (Mk 1.2–3). Later this group merged into the new community of Christ's disciples called the church, or less appropriately, the new Israel, composed of both Jews and Gentiles. John does not at this point seem to distinguish between the earlier almost totally Jewish community and the one present in his day. Their continuity in identity is so strong that whatever ethnic or other differences they have does not affect his single image representing one entity.

The woman's dazzling appearance like the sun relates her to the glory and brilliance of her Lord (1:16) as well as to her own light-bearing quality (1:20). With the moon under her feet signifying her permanence (Pss 72:5; 89:37; cf. Mt 16:18) and a crown of twelve stars on her head indicating her elect identity (cf. comments on 7:4ff.), she appears in her true heavenly and glorious character despite her seemingly fragile earthly history (vv.13–16). The church viewed as a woman is found elsewhere in the NT (cf. 2Co 11:2; Eph 5:25–27, 32; 2Jn 1, 5, 13).

2 The woman is in the throes of childbirth. The emphasis on her pain and suffering, both physically and spiritually, signifies the suffering of the faithful messianic community as a prelude to the coming of the Messiah himself and the new age (Isa 26:17; 66:7–8; Mic 4:10; 5:3). The "birth" itself does not necessarily refer to the actual physical birth of Christ but denotes the travail of the community from which the Messiah has arisen.

3 The second "sign" now appears. It likewise is a heavenly sign and introduces us to the second character, the ultimate antagonist of the woman. The "dragon" is clearly identified with the "ancient serpent called the devil, or Satan" (v.9; cf. 20:2–3). His description as an "enormous red dragon" symbolically suggests his fierce power and murderous nature. He is further described as having "seven heads and ten horns and seven crowns on his heads." Except for the exchange of the crowns from the heads to the horns, the same description is used for the beast from the sea in ch. 13 and the beast of ch. 17. It is a picture of the fullness of evil in all its hideous strength (cf. the monsters in Ps 74:13–14; Isa 27:1, 51:9–10; Da 7:7, 8:10). The diadem crowns on the heads may indicate fullness of royal power (13:1; 19:12).

4 So great is the dragon's power that his tail can even sweep away a large number of the stars and cast them down to the ground (for "a third," see comment on 8:7). This probably represents the dragon's power, not over some of the angels (sometimes called stars), but over the saints of God (cf. Da 8:10, 24). Satan has placed himself before the woman, thus expecting certain victory over the messianic child. Through this figure the church shows her awareness that Satan is always threatening the purposes of God. Although the attack of Herod against the children of Bethlehem and many incidents during the life of Jesus (cf. Lk 4:28–39) must also be included, the greatest attempt to devour the child must certainly be the Crucifixion.

5 This verse records the first element of the story. The messianic child comes, finishes his mission, is delivered from the dragon, and is enthroned in heaven. John again refers to the destiny of the child by alluding again to Ps 2:9: "Who will rule all the nations with an iron scepter" (Rev 2:27; 19:15). Some exegetes, using passages such as Da 7:13–14, 27 (which seems to fuse the individual son of man with the people of God) and Rev 1:5–6; 2:26–27; 11:15 (which alternates between the rule of Christ and the rule of the saints), see a collective identity in the birth of the male child. It is, however, difficult to see how the child as well as the woman could be a group of believers. Through Christ's resurrection and ascension, the dragon's attempt to destroy God's purposes through the Messiah have been decisively defeated.

6 What is this flight into the desert? Is it a symbolic or an actual historic event? Among those who take it literally, some have understood the reference as the escape of the early Jerusalem Christians to Pella in A.D. 66 to escape the Roman destruction of Jerusalem. Pella continued to be an important Christian center even after many returned to Jerusalem in 135. Others refer the event to the future, when a portion of the Jewish people will be preserved through the Tribulation period to await Christ's return.

Most commentators, however, understand the desert to mean the place of safety, discipline, and testing. This view is preferable because of the highly symbolic nature of the whole chapter, the symbolic use of "desert" in 17:3, and the parallelism to the Exodus where the children of Israel fled from Pharaoh. All are agreed that the reference here to the flight of the woman is anticipatory of vv.13ff. The intervening verses show why the dragon is persecuting the woman (vv.7–12). For a discussion of the 1,260 days, see comments on 11:2.

7 All agree that the section beginning with this verse, which describes the battle in heaven between Michael and the dragon (vv.7–12), provides the explanation as to why the dragon has turned on the woman and caused her to flee into the desert for protection (vv.6, 13ff.). The account is in two parts:

(1) the battle in heaven between Michael and his angels and the dragon and his angels, which results in the ejection of Satan from heaven to the earth (vv.7–9), and (2) the heavenly hymn of victory (vv.10–12).

As elsewhere in the book, the narrative material can be interpreted only in the light of the hymns. This principle is especially important in vv.7–9, where the victory takes place in heaven as the result of Michael's defeat of the dragon. Were this the only thing told us about the "war in heaven," it might be concluded that the dragon's defeat was unrelated to Jesus Christ. But the interpretative hymn (vv. 10–12) says that it was in fact the blood of Christ that dealt the actual death blow to the dragon and enabled the saints to triumph (v.8; cf. 5:9). Does this not suggest that the redeeming work of Christ is here depicted by the cosmic battle of Michael and the dragon, as it is elsewhere seen as a loosing from sin (1:5), as a washing of our garments (7:14), and as a purchasing to God (5:9)? The time of the dragon's defeat and ejection from heaven must therefore be connected with the incarnation, ministry, death, and resurrection of Jesus (v.13; Lk 10:18; Jn 12:31). Christ has appeared in order to destroy the works of the devil (Mt 12:28–29; Ac 10:38; 2Ti 1:10; 1Jn 3:8).

Early Jewish belief held the view that Michael would cast Satan from heaven as the first of the last-time struggles to establish the kingdom of God on earth. John, in contrast, sees this event as already having taken place through Jesus Christ's appearance and work. Only the final, permanent blow of Satan's ejection from earth remains (20:10). The fact that the battle first takes place in heaven between Michael, the guardian of God's people (Da 10:13, 21; 12:1; Jude 9), and the dragon shows that evil is cosmic in dimension and that events on earth are first decided in heaven. The single intent of the passage is to assure those who meet satanic evil on earth that it is really a defeated power, however contrary it might seem to human experience.

8–9 The triumph of the archangel results in the ejection of the dragon and his angels from heaven to earth. Apparently, prior to this event Satan had access to the heavens and continually assailed the loyalty of the saints (Job 1:9–11; Zec 3:1); but now, together with his angels, he has been cast out (cf. Lk 10:18).

Whatever appears to be the earthly situation for God's people now, the victory has already been won. When the battle grows fiercer and darker for the church, it is but the sign of the last futile attempt of the dragon to exercise his power before the kingdom of Christ comes (v.12). The "ancient serpent" who tempted Eve with lies about God (Ge 3:1ff.) is in John's mind the "devil" or "Satan." He is also the one who "leads the whole world astray." His power lies in deception, and by his lies the whole world is deceived about God (2:20; 13:14; 18:23; 19:20; 20:3, 8, 10; 2Jn 7; cf. Ro 1:25).

10 This anonymous hymn, which interprets the great battle of the preceding verses, has three stanzas: the first (v.10) focuses on the victorious inauguration of God's kingdom and Christ's kingly authority; the second (v.11) calls attention to the earthly victory of the saints as they confirm the victory of Christ by their own identification with Jesus in his witness and death; the third (v.12) announces the martyrs' victory and the final woe to the earth because of the devil's ejection and impending demise.

In the first stanza (v.10), the triumph of Christ is described as the arrival of three divine realities in history: God's "salvation" or victory (7:10; 19:1), God's "power," and God's "kingdom." This last reality is further identified as Christ's assumption of his "authority." The historic event of Christ's life, death, and resurrection has challenged the dominion of Satan and provoked the crisis of history. At the time of Christ's death on earth, Satan was being defeated in heaven by Michael.

In times past, Satan's chief role as adversary was directed toward accusing God's people of disobedience to God. The justice of these accusations was recognized by God, and therefore Satan's presence in heaven was tolerated. But now the presence of the crucified Savior in God's presence provides the required satisfaction of God's justice regarding our sins (1Jn 2:1–2; 4:10). Thus, Satan's accusations are no longer valid and he is cast out. What strong consolation this provides for God's faltering people!

11 This second stanza is both a statement and an appeal. It announces that the followers of the Lamb also become victors over the dragon because they participate in the "blood of the Lamb," the weapon that defeated Satan, and because they have confirmed their loyalty to the Lamb by their witness even to death. The blood of the martyrs, rather than signaling the triumph of Satan, shows instead that they have gained the victory over the dragon by their acceptance of Jesus' cross and their obedient suffering with him. This is one of John's chief themes (1:9; 6:9; 14:12; 20:4).

Verses 12 and 17 lead to the conclusion that only a portion of the martyrs is in view (cf. 6:11). Thus this hymn of victory also becomes an appeal to the rest of the saints to confirm their testimony to Christ, even if doing so means death. This seems to suggest that in some mysterious sense the sufferings of the people of God are linked to the sufferings of Jesus in his triumph over Satan and evil (Jn 12:31; Ro 16:20; Col 1:24). Since the martyrs have gotten the victory over the dragon because of the cross of Jesus, they are now free even to give up their lives in loyalty to their Redeemer (Jn 12:25; Rev 15:2).

12 Satan has failed. Therefore, the heavens and all who are in them should be glad. But Satan does not accept defeat without a bitter struggle. His final death throes are directed exclusively toward "the earth and the sea." Therefore their inhabitants will mourn, for the devil will now redouble his wrathful effort in one last futile attempt to make the most of an opportunity that he knows will be brief (three and one-half years; cf. vv.6, 14).

13–14 The narrative is resumed after the flight of the woman into the desert (v. 6). Why? Because she is under attack from the defeated but still vicious dragon (vv.7–12). No longer able to attack the male child who is in heaven or to accuse the saints because of the victory of Jesus on the cross, the devil now pursues the woman, who flees into the desert. The word "pursue" (GK *1503*) was no doubt carefully chosen by John because it is also the NT word for "persecute" (e.g., Mt 5:10). Since the woman has already given birth to the child, the time of this pursuit by the dragon is subsequent to the earthly career of Jesus.

The reference to eagle's wings again introduces imagery from Exodus on the pursuit of Israel by the dragon in the person of Pharaoh: "You yourselves have seen what I did to Egypt, and how I carried you on eagles' wings and brought you to myself" (Ex 19:4). As God's people were delivered from the enemy by their journey into the desert, so God's present people will be preserved miraculously from destruction (cf. Dt 32:10–12; Isa 40:31).

15–16 The serpent spews a floodlike river of water out of his mouth to engulf and drown the woman. The water imagery symbolizes destruction by an enemy (Pss 32:6; 69:1–2; 124:2–5; Na 1:8) or calamity (Ps 18:4). As the desert earth absorbs the torrent, so the covenant people will be helped by God and preserved from utter destruction (Isa 26:20; 42:15; 43:2; 50:2). Just as the ancient Egyptians of old were swallowed by the earth (see Ex 15:12), so the messianic community will be delivered by God's power.

17 This attack of Satan against "the rest" of the woman's offspring seems to involve the final attempt to destroy the messianic people of God. Having failed in previous attempts to eliminate them as a whole, the dragon now strikes at individuals who "obey God's commandments and hold to the testimony of Jesus." To "make war" is the identical expression used of the beast's attack on the two witnesses in 11:7 and on the saints in 13:7. There is good reason to correlate the three groups and to indicate their common identity under different figures.

Those attacked are called "the rest of her [the woman's] offspring." Some identify this group as Gentile Christians in distinction from the Jewish mother church. Others identify the mother as the nation of Israel and see the "rest" as the believing remnant in the Jewish nation who turn to Christ. Still others have suggested that the woman represents the believing community as the universal church composed of both Jews and Gentiles, whereas the "offspring" of the woman represents individuals of the community (Jews and Gentiles) who suffer persecution and martyrdom from the dragon. The close identification of the seed of the woman as first of all Jesus and then also those who have become his brothers and sisters through faith agrees with other NT teaching (Mt 25:40; Heb 2:11–12). While Satan cannot prevail against the Christian community itself, he can wage war on certain of its members who are called on to witness to their Lord by obedience even unto death (cf. Mt 16:18; Rev 11:7; 13:7, 15).

The church, then, is paradoxically both invulnerable (the woman) and vulnerable (her children; cf. Lk 21:16–18).

2. The two beasts (13:1–18)

This chapter forms part of the theme of the persecution of God's people that John began to develop in ch. 12. Turning from the inner dynamics of the struggle, ch. 13 shifts to the earthly instruments of this assault—namely, the two dragon-energized beasts. In the context of ch. 12, we may assume that the beast-related activities constitute the way the dragon carries out his final attempts to wage war on the seed of the woman (12:17). A contest is going on to seduce the whole world—even the followers of Jesus—to worship the beast. John emphasizes three things about the first beast: (1) the conspiracy of the dragon with it (vv.2–4); (2) the universal success of this partnership in deceiving the whole world to worship them (vv.3–4, 8); and (3) the partnership that will succeed in a temporary defeat of the saints of God, thus accomplishing the greatest blasphemy of God (vv6–7a).

Finally, not being able to seduce all the earth alone, the conspirators summon yet a third figure to their aid—the beast from the earth. He must remain loyal to his associates and at the same time be sufficiently similar to the Lamb to entice even the followers of Jesus. He must be able to perform miraculous signs much as the two witnesses did (vv.11ff.; cf. 13:13 with 11:5). As the battle progresses, the dragon's deception becomes more and more subtle. Thus the readers are called to discern the criteria that will enable them to separate the lamblike beast from the Lamb himself (13:11 with 14:1).

Two basic problems confront the reader, which have led students of the book to different understandings of this chapter: (1) The identification of the beast and his associate—are they personal or some other entity? (2) The time of the beast's rule—is it past, continuous, or still future? In seeking some satisfactory answers to these questions, it may be helpful to first set forth the facts about the beast. He (1) rises from the sea (v.1); (2) resembles the dragon (v.1); (3) has composite animal features (v.2); (4) is empowered by the dragon (v.2); (5) has one head wounded to death but healed (vv.3–4, 7b–8); (6) blasphemes God and God's people for forty-two months (vv.5–6); (7) makes war against the saints and kills them (vv.7a, 15); and (8) gives to those who follow him his "mark," which is either his name or his number, 666 (vv.16–18).

There are no fewer than a dozen further references in Revelation to the beast (11:7; 14:9, 11; 15:2; 16:2, 10, 13; 19:19–20; 20:4, 10), excluding the nine references to the scarlet-colored beast in ch. 17, which should probably be included. Among these references, 11:7 indicates that the beast rises from the Abyss, 19:19 refers to a coalition of the beast with the "kings of the earth," and 19:20 describes his final end in the lake of fire.

The history of the interpretation of ch. 13 is extensive. As early as the second century, two different understandings of the Antichrist appeared. Some early interpreters took the position that the Antichrist would be a person, a world deceiver who would reign for the last half of Daniel's seventieth week (Da 7:25). To Irenaeus (d. c. 202), the first one who discusses extensively the Antichrist, he is to be an unrighteous king from the tribe of Dan, the little horn of Da 7:8, who will reign over the earth during the last three and one-half years of Daniel's seventieth "week" (Da 9:27). To him, the Antichrist is the first beast of Rev 13 and the "man of lawlessness" of 2Th 2:3–4, who will exalt himself in the Jerusalem temple. Tertullian saw the docetic teachers of his day as the forerunners of a future Antichrist, who would come with counterfeit signs and wonders to mislead those who have not believed the truth but have delighted in wickedness (2Th 2:9–12). Many contemporary interpreters also follow a similar line of thinking. In its favor is the more literal reading of 2Th 2.1–10 and the natural understanding of the Antichrist as the personal counterpart to the personal Christ.

On the other hand, from the earliest times some interpreters have understood the Antichrist as a present threat of heresy, depending more on the concept found in the letters of John (1Jn 2:18, 22; 4:3; 2Jn 7). Thus Polycarp (d. 155) understood the Antichrist as the docetic heresies of his time. Many of the Reformers identified the beast with the institution of the papacy. Many modern commentators also adopt the theological heresy interpretation of the Antichrist. In its favor are the references to the Antichrist in the letters of John and the advantage of seeing the beast as an ever-present threat to the church rather than a figure of the last days. This view also argues that 2Th 2 need not be understood as referring to a single future individual. This issue is difficult to settle with any finality. However, I will develop ch. 13 more in accord with the theological heresy view, while recognizing that Tertullian's position is consistent with my position and that the personal future Antichrist view has strong support (see also the comments on v.11).

Many modern interpreters agree that the "wounded head" (v.3) refers to the Nero redivivus legend. Toward the end of his reign Nero became extremely unpopular among Roman citizens. He was finally repudiated by the praetorian guard and by the Senate, fled from Rome, and hid in the suburbs. Having been warned that soldiers were closing in on him, he cut his own throat with a sword. After his death, however, a rumor spread that he was not actually dead but was living in Parthia, from where he would return to regain his throne. On the basis of this rumor, several impostors arose who assumed the name of Nero in the effort to exploit the legend. At a later stage in the legend, Nero became invested with supernatural status. His return from the abyss with hordes of demons was an omen of the "last days."

This Neronic interpretation presupposes an identification in John's mind between the sea beast and the Roman Empire, a view espoused in our day by both preterist and preterist-futurist interpreters of Revelation. This in turn usually assumes that Rev 17 identifies the seven heads of the beast as the successive emperors of the Roman Empire. Yet a question concerning the reliability of this whole Neronic approach must be raised, for the Nero redivivus legend does not fit either the facts of history or the text of Rev 13 and 17 (see comments on 17:8–9).

Various considerations call the Nero myth into question. Irenaeus, for example, never refers either to a Domitian persecution as the background for John's thought or to any Nero-myth interpretation, even though he is attempting to refute the identification of the number 666 with any Roman emperor. Likewise, rabbinic exegesis up to the first century A.D. identified the fourth beast of Da 7 as Edom-equals-Rome. Since the beast of Rev 13 is a composite that unites all the features of the four beasts of Da 7, it therefore cannot be identified exclusively with Rome. An attempt will be made in this exposition to demonstrate that the Rome hypothesis is untenable. This leaves the question open as to whether John sees the Antichrist (or beast) as a person or some more encompassing entity.

1a Most modern translations include v.1a as the concluding verse of ch. 12 because they adopt manuscripts that read "he [i.e., the dragon] stood" rather than KJV's "I stood." If "he stood" is the correct reading, the sense would be that the dragon, who has now turned his rage on the children of the woman (12:17), stands on the seashore to summon his next instrument, the beast from the sea. But if the text reads "I stood," the sense is that John receives a new vision (cf. 10:1).

1b–2 The beast (GK 2563) has already been described in 11:7 as rising from the "Abyss" (cf. 17:8). Thus the sea may symbolize the Abyss, the source of demonic powers that are opposed to God (cf. 9:1; 20:1–3). This view agrees with the OT images of the sea as the origin of the satanic sea monsters—the dragon, Leviathan, and Rahab (Job 26:12–13; Pss 74:1:13–14; 87:4; 89:10; Isa 27:1; 51:9; cf. also Eze 32:6–8). The ancient Hebrews demythologized the sea-monster myths to depict the victory of the Lord of Israel over the demonic forces of evil that had sought in several ways to destroy God's people. Similarly, John later foresees the day of Christ's victory when there will "no longer [be] any sea."

John describes the beast in words similar to those he used in 12:3 of the dragon, the only difference being in the matter of the crowns. Any attempt to identify the heads or horns as separate kings, kingdoms, etc., should be resisted. It may be argued that John's beast from the sea should be connected to Leviathan, Rahab, and the dragon in the above-cited OT texts. While these refer to political powers, such as Egypt and Assyria, that were threatening Israel, to the OT writer, these nations were inseparably identified with the archetypal reality of the satanic, idolatrous systems represented by the seven-headed monster. Thus the beast represented, not the political power, but the system of evil that found expression in the political entity. The reason this point is so important is that it helps us see that the beast itself is not to be identified in its description with any one historical expression or with any one institutional aspect of its manifestation. It may appear now as Sodom, Egypt, Rome, or even Jerusalem, and it may manifest itself as a political power, an economic power, a religious power, or a heresy (1Jn 2:18, 22; 4:3)

In John's mind, the chief enemy is diabolical deception; his description therefore has theological overtones, not political ones. This interpretation does not exclude the possibility that there will be a final climactic appearance of the beast in history in a person, in a political or religious economic system, or in a final totalitarian culture combining all these. The point is that the beast cannot be limited to either the past or the future.

John further states that this beast had "on each head a blasphemous name" (cf. vv.5–6; 17:3). Arrogance and blasphemy also characterize the "little horn" of Daniel's fourth beast (Da 7:8, 11, 20, 25) and the willful king of Da 11:36. John alludes to the vision of Daniel but completely transforms it.

In keeping with the Rome hypothesis, many identified the blasphemous names with titles of the emperor (e.g., "Savior" and "Lord"). But was this in John's mind? In 2:9 he refers to the blasphemy "of those who say they are Jews and are not," a reference to the fact that some Jews at Smyrna had spoken against the lawful messianic claims of Jesus. They may also have charged the Christians with disloyalty to the empire and thus sided with the pagan officials in persecuting them. Could these Jews also be part of the blasphemous names? In v.6 the blasphemies are directed against God and are further defined: "to blaspheme God, by blaspheming his name, his temple, those who dwell in heaven" (my translation). Thus the beast challenges the sovereignty and majesty of God by denying the first commandment: "You shall have no other gods before me" (Ex 20:3). In other words, whatever person or system cooperates with Satan by exalting itself against God's sovereignty and by setting itself up to destroy the followers of Jesus, or entices them to become followers of Satan through deception, idolatry, blasphemy, and spiritual adultery, embodies the beast of Rev 13.

The description John gives of the beast from the sea does not describe a mere human political entity such as Rome. Rather, it describes in archetypal language the hideous, satanic system of deception and idolatry that may at any time express itself in human systems of various kinds. Yet at the same time John also seems to be saying that this blasphemous, blaspheming, and blasphemy-producing reality will have a final and, for the saints, utterly devastating manifestation.

3 The beast has a fatal wound, but the wound is healed. This results in great, world-wide influence, acceptance, and worship of both the beast and the dragon. This verse is important and requires careful exegesis because of the widespread Nero redivivus viewpoint that is read into the wounded head (see comment on 13:1–18). There are a number of features of John's description that are inconsistent with both the Nero redivivus and the Roman Empire interpretations.

(1) It should be observed that the wounded "head" of v.3 is elsewhere in the chapter a wound of the whole beast (vv.12, 14). A wound inflicted in a former and rejected emperor is not a wound inflicted on the whole empire. If the reference is to Nero, it is difficult to see how his self-inflicted wound could have hurt the whole empire or how the healing of his throat enhanced the authority of the beast or the dragon's war against the saints.

(2) The fatal wound must be carefully examined. "Wound" (GK *4435*) everywhere else in Revelation means "plague," in fact, a divinely inflicted judgment (9:18, 20; 11:6; 15:1ff.; 16:9, 21; et al.). Elsewhere in the NT the word is used of "beatings" or official "floggings" (Lk 10:30; 12:48; Ac 16:23, 33; 2Co 6:5; 11:23). In 13:14 we find that the beast was wounded "by the sword" (GK *3479*), which supposedly refers to Nero's dagger. But elsewhere in Revelation, "sword" (a) refers symbolically to the divine judgment of the Messiah (1:16; 2:12, 16; 19:15, 21); (b) is the sword of the rider on the red horse and equals divine judgment (6:4, 8); and (c) is a sword used as a weapon against the saints of God (13:10). We are, then, nearer to John's mind if we see the sword, not as referring to an emperor's death, but as the symbol of God's wrath that had struck a death blow to the authority of the beast (and the dragon), yet which had been deceptively covered up or restored (for a probable antecedent, see Isa 27:1).

(3) The correct identification, therefore, of the beast's enemy will enable us to understand what event John had in mind in the death blow. Everywhere in the book the only sufficient conqueror of the beast and the dragon is the slain Lamb, together with his faithful saints (12:11; 19:19–21). Moreover, what dealt this death blow to the dragon and the beast is Jesus' life, especially the crucifixion, resurrection, and exaltation (1:5; 5:9; 12:11; cf. Lk 10:17–24; 11:14–22; Jn 12:31–33; Col 2:15; also Ge 3:13ff.). That event is the mortal wound of the beast.

The same paradox found in ch. 12 appears here in ch. 13. While the dragon is defeated and cast out of heaven through the blood of Jesus (cf. 12:11), he still has time and ability to wage a relentless war against the people of God (12:13ff.). Similarly, the beast has been dealt a fatal blow by the cross of Christ and still has time and ability to wage war against the saints. He appears to be alive and in full command of the scene; his blasphemies increase. What the sea beast cannot accomplish, he commissions the earth beast to do (vv.11ff.). All three—the dragon, the sea beast, and the earth beast—are in collusion to effect the same end: deception that leads the world to worship the dragon and the sea beast and the destruction of all who oppose them.

(4) It is this description that leads to a final reason why identifying the beast exclusively with any one historical personage or empire is probably incorrect. In John's description of the beast, there are numerous parallels with Jesus that should alert us to the fact that John is seeking to establish, not a historical identification, but a theological characterization: Both wielded swords (2:12, 16; 13:10); both had followers on whose foreheads were inscribed their names (13.16–14.1), both had horns (5:6; 13:1); both were slain (5:12; 13:3, 8); both had arisen to new life and authority (1:18; 11:15–16; 13:3–4); and both were given (by different authorities) power over every nation, tribe, people, and tongue, and over the kings of the earth (1:5; 7:9; 13:7; 17:12). The beast described here is the great theological counterpart to all that Christ represents. Therefore, it is easy to understand why many in the history of the church have identified the beast with a future, personal *Anti*christ.

While the references in the Johannine literature may be taken as supporting the view that the Antichrist is manifested in multiple persons and was a reality present in John's day (1Jn 2:18, 22; 4:3; 2Jn 7), Paul's description in such personal terms of the coming "man of lawlessness" (2Th 2:3–4, 8–9) has led the majority of ancient and modern interpreters to adopt the viewpoint that it is a personal Antichrist. It is not necessary to understand Paul's apocalyptic language as describing a personal Antichrist. Moreover, John says that in the false teachers "the antichrist" was actually present (2Jn 7).

But the question must remain open as to whether John in the Apocalypse points to a single archenemy of the church—whether past or future—or to a transhistorical reality with many human manifestations in history. Thus the imagery would function similarly with regard to the image of the woman of ch. 12 or the harlot of ch. 17. If such is the case, this does not mean that John would have denied the earthly historical manifestations of this satanic reality; but it would prevent us from limiting the imagery merely to the Roman Empire or to any other single future political entity.

4 The goal of the dragon and the beast in their conspiracy is to promote the idolatrous worship of themselves—a perversion further enhanced by the earth beast (vv.12, 15). The means of deception varies because not all humankind is deceived in the same way. People follow and worship the beast because he is apparently invincible: "Who can make war against him?" His only real enemy seems to be the saints of Jesus, whom he effectively destroys (2:10, 13; 12:11; 13:15). But little does he realize that in the death of the saints the triumph of God appears. As they die, they do so in identification with the slain Lamb who through the Cross has decisively conquered the dragon by inflicting on him a truly fatal wound. "Who is like the beast?" echoes in parody similar references to God himself (Ex 15:11; Mic 7:18).

5–6 (See comments on v.1.) The period of the beast's authority is given as "forty-two months," the same period already referred to in 11:2-3; 12:6, 13 (see comments at 11:2).

7 As elsewhere in the Apocalypse, to "make war" does not mean to wage a military campaign but refers to hostility against and destruction of God's people in whatever manner and through whatever means the beast may choose (see 2:16; 11:7; 12:7, 17; 16:14; 17:14; 19:11, 19; 20:8; 2Co 10:4). "To conquer" them refers not to the subversion of their faith but to the destruction of their physical lives (cf. Mt 10:28). Their apparent defeat by the beast and his victory turn out in reality to be the victory of the saints and the defeat of the beast (15:2). Messiahlike universal dominion was given the beast by the dragon (Lk 4:4–7; 1Jn 5:19).

8 John further identifies the worshipers of the beast as "all whose names have not been written in the book of life belonging to the Lamb" (see comment on 3:5; cf. 17:8; 20:12, 15; 21:27). This contrast further emphasizes the theological nature of the description of the beast. The beast from the earth represents the idolatrous system of worship instigated by the dragon to deceive humankind into breaking the first commandment.

A debatable issue is whether the words "from the creation of the world" (also 17:8) belong grammatically with "have not been written" or with "that was slain." In other words, is it the Lamb who was slain from the creation of the world, or is it the names that were not recorded in the book of life from the creation of the world? In Greek, either interpretation is grammatically acceptable. But 17:8 implies that the word order in the Greek favors the latter view and suggests that John is deliberately providing a complementary thought to 17:8. In the former instance, the emphasis rests on the decree in eternity to elect the Son as the redeeming agent for humanity's salvation (13:8; 1Pe 1:20); in the latter, stress lies on God's eternal foreknowledge of a company of people who would participate in the elect Son's redeeming work (17:8). In any event, these words cannot be pressed to prove eternal individual election to salvation or damnation, since 3:5 implies that failure of appropriate human response removes one's name from the book of life. This verse distinguishes clearly between the followers of the beast and those of the slain Lamb. It also calls for faithful commitment and clear discernment of error on the part of the Lamb's people.

9–10 These verses are both important and difficult. This is the only occurrence in Revelation, apart from chs. 2–3, of the words "he who has an ear, let him hear." John calls special attention to the need for obedience to the exhortation in v.10b. Most contend that the language of v.10 alludes to Jer 15:2; 43:11, where the prophet describes the certainty of divine judgment that will come upon the rebels in Israel—they will suffer captivity, famine, disease, and death from the sword. Yet it is difficult to see how Jeremiah's words are appropriate here in this context of an exhortation for believers to be faithful. John's meaning must be different—namely, that as the rebels in Jeremiah's day would certainly encounter the divine judgment, so the faithful to Christ are assured that their captivity and martyrdom are in God's will.

No completely satisfying resolution of the problems in v.10 is available. Since the difficult part (10a) is both preceded by (v.9) and followed by (v.10b) appeals to obedience and loyalty, it seems best to stay with the sense of obedient faithfulness. The day of persecution for Christians is at hand, and they will have to suffer. In calmly undergoing this final tribulation they must manifest endurance and faithfulness (cf. Php 1:28). John, in other words, seems to call believers here to passive resistance against their enemies. Yet this resistance, which may result in captivity and even martyrdom, contributes to the eventual defeat of evil.

11 John sees another beast, rising from the earth. This second beast completes the triumvirate of evil—the dragon, the sea beast, and the land beast. This beast is subservient to the beast from the sea and seems utterly dedicated to promoting not himself but the wounded beast from the sea. Elsewhere the land beast is called the "false prophet" (16:13; 19:20; 20:10). As with the first beast, identification is a problem. That this beast comes from the land rather than the sea may simply indicate his diversity from the first, while other references stress their collusion.

A survey of the history of interpretation reveals in general, as with the first beast, two main lines: either the beast represents a power or a movement, or it describes a human being allied with the Antichrist at the close of the age. Early Christian interpreters, who identify the first beast not with Rome but with a personal Antichrist, find in the second beast the "armor-bearer" of the first, who employs the demonic forces to work magic and deceive the inhabitants of the earth. Many of the Reformers, drawing on earlier traditions, were led to identify this beast with the papacy or specific popes. In other words, they saw the beast as a present threat and not some entity awaiting a yet future manifestation. Most modern commentators, following the Nero redivivus view of the first beast, identify this beast as the priesthood of the imperial cultus. Others would extend the symbolism to all ages and see in the second beast persecuting power, pagan or Christian, and would call special attention to the Roman papacy, though by no means limiting it to this priesthood.

While recognizing that no view is without problems, the following discussion takes the position that the land beast is John's way of describing the false prophets of the Olivet Discourse (Mt 24:24; Mk 13:22). This identification is consistent with the previously stated view of the sea beast as describing not just a specific political reality but the worldwide anti-God system of Satan and its manifestation in periodic, historical human antichrists. The land beast is the antithesis to the true prophets of Christ symbolized by the two witnesses in ch. 11. If the thought of a nonpersonal antichrist and false prophet seems to contradict the verse that describes them as being cast alive into the lake of fire (19:20), consider that "death" and "Hades" (nonpersons) are also thrown into the lake of fire (20:14).

The "two horns like a lamb" seems to highlight the beast's imitative role relative to the true Lamb in the rest of the book (e.g., 5:6ff.; 13:8; 14:1). Could the two horns be in contrast to the two witnesses in ch. 11? Since one of the primary characteristics of this second beast is his deceptive activities (v.14; 19:20), his appearance as a lamb would contribute to the confusion over the beast's true identity. If the land beast represents satanic false teaching and false prophets, their evil is intensified because of its deceptive similarity to the truth. Even though the beast is like the Lamb, in reality he is evil because "he [speaks] like a dragon," i.e., he teaches heresy. Jesus gave such a twofold description of false prophets in the Sermon on the Mount: "Watch out for false prophets. They come to you in sheep's clothing, but inwardly they are ferocious wolves" (Mt 7:15). On the other hand, the lamblikeness may simply be a reference to the beast's gentle outward manner in contrast to his true identity as a fierce dragon.

12 The activity of the land beast is repeatedly described as that of promoting the first beast's worship (v.14). Could this be the kind of activity referred to in the reference to the false prophets in Pergamum and Thyatira, who seduce the servants of God to idolatry (2:14–15, 20, 24)? The phrase "on his behalf" (GK *1967*) is perhaps better translated "before him"; the land beast does not merely exercise his authority as the sea beast's representative but stands "before him." One who stands "before" someone else is ready to do that person's bidding. The same preposition is used of the two witnesses in 11:4: "These are the two olive trees and the two lampstands that stand before [GK *1967*] the Lord of the earth." As the antitheses of the two witnesses, the false prophets derive their authority and ministry from the first beast.

13 One of the strategies the land beast uses to deceive people into following the first beast is the performance of "miraculous signs" (GK *4956*; see comment on 12:1). The ability of the Satan-inspired prophets to perform deceiving miracles is attested elsewhere in Revelation and in other parts of the Bible (16:14; 19:20; Dt 13:1–5; Mt 7:22; 24:24; Mk 13:22; 2Th 2:9). Distinguishing between the true and false prophets has always been difficult but not impossible. The followers of Jesus must be constantly alert to discern the spirits (1Jn 4:1–3).

The "fire ... from heaven" may allude to the fire that the prophet Elijah called down from heaven (1Ki 18:38) or to the fire coming out of the mouths of the two witnesses (Rev 11:5). John seems to intend a deliberate contrast between the true witnesses' use of fire and its use by the false prophets (11:5; cf. Lk 9:54). Fire also represents the true word of God and the Holy Spirit's witness (such as at Pentecost; Ac 2:3). The false fire would then be a reference to pseudo-charismatic gifts that create a counterfeit church community whose allegiance is to the Antichrist. In any case, the reference to fire from heaven indicates that no mighty deed is too hard for these false prophets, because they derive their power from the Antichrist and the dragon. Christ's true servants must not be deceived by even spectacular miracles that the false prophets may perform. Such miracles in themselves are no evidence of the Holy Spirit.

14a Here more must be involved than the deceptions of the imperial priesthood. The quality of the miracles deceives those who follow the beast—namely, "the inhabitants of the earth." "Deceive" (GK *4414*) is John's term for the activity of false teachers who lead people to worship gods other than the true God (2:20; 12:9; 18:23; 19:20; 20:3, 8, 10; cf. 1Jn 2:26; 3:7; 4:6; also Mt 24:11, 24).

14b–15 The second beast orders the setting up of an "image" (GK *1635*) of the first beast. Elsewhere, the worship of the first beast, his "image," and his "mark" are inseparable (14:9, 11; 15:2; 16:2; 19:20; 20:4). An "image" of something is not a mere copy but partakes in its reality and in fact constitutes its reality. Those interpreters who follow the Roman-emperor exegesis identify the image with the statue of Caesar and refer the "breath" and speaking of the image to the magic and ventriloquism of the imperial priests. But as has been argued earlier (see comments on vv.1, 11), serious questions can be raised against such an exegesis of John's language, which is much more theologically descriptive than the Roman hypothesis allows. This is not to deny that the imperial worship could be included as one form of the beast worship. But the reality described is much larger and far more transhistorical than the mere worship of a bust of Caesar. John, however, would not deny that these realities have their historical manifestations, for in every age the beast kills those who will not worship his image. In terms reminiscent of the great golden image Nebuchadnezzar made and commanded every person to worship on the threat of death (Da 3:1–11), John describes the world-wide system of idolatry represented by the first beast and the false prophet(s) who promotes it. It is a system that produces a breach of the first two commandments (Ex 20:3–5).

In speaking about giving "breath" (GK *4460*) to the image, John implies the activity of the false prophets in reviving idolatrous worship, giving it the appearance of vitality, reality, and power. Curiously, the two witnesses were also said to receive "breath" (GK *4460*; 11:11). This idolatrous satanic system has the power of death over those who worship the true God and the Lamb. The same "image" tried to kill Daniel and his friends, killed many of the prophets of God, crucified the Lord Jesus, and put to death Stephen (Ac

7:60), James the apostle (Ac 12:1–2), and Antipas (Rev 2:13). Thus John demonstrates to his followers the apparent healing of his wounded head. To limit the image to the bust of Caesar or to some future statue or ventriloquistic device constricts John's deeper meaning and eliminates the present significance of his language. All throughout history there have been those who have sought worship for themselves instead of for the Lord Jesus Christ. A contemporary example is Sun Myung Moon, who calls himself the "Lord of the Second Advent." Many are being deceived into following him and his teaching.

16 The immediate effect of the worship of the beast involves receiving a "mark" (GK 5916) on the right hand or forehead. By comparing the other passages where the beast, image, mark, and name of the beast are mentioned, it seems clear that the mark is an equivalent expression to the "name of the beast" (v.17; 14:11; also 14:9; 15:2; 16:2; 19:20; 20:4), which is also the "number of his name" (v.17; 15:2). The Greek word "mark" usually refers to a work of art such as a carved image of a god (Ac 17:29), a written inscription, an impress "seal" of the emperor, or a "brand" on camels indicating ownership. But such a mark was never placed on a person, let alone on the "right hand" or on the "forehead." Thus, the "mark" is not a literal impress seal or mark of identification, but it is John's way of symbolically describing authentic ownership and loyalty. Those who worship the beast have his brand of ownership on them, just as the followers of Jesus have the brand of God's possession on them (see also comments on 7:1–3).

17 Those having the "mark" can "buy or sell," those without it cannot. This statement apparently refers to some sort of socioeconomic sanctions that would, of course, affect the social and economic condition of Christians in the world. Earlier, John alluded to certain such conditions. Smyrna was a greatly persecuted church and was "poor" (2:9); Philadelphia was of "little strength" (3:8); those faithful to Christ in the Great Tribulation are seen in heaven as never again hungering (7:16), while the great harlot grows rich and wallows in luxury (18:3). Other NT writers also hint at socioeconomic sanctions practiced against Christians (Ro 15:26, Heb 10:34).

18 In v.17, John indicates that the "mark" is the name of the beast or the number of his name. He now reveals the number of the beast: "His number is 666." The list of conjectures concerning the meaning of the number is almost as long as the list of commentators on Revelation. Taking their cue from the words "let him calculate the number of the beast," most of these interpreters have tried to play the ancient Hebrew game of *gematria*. Ancient languages, including Hebrew and Greek, use standard letters from their alphabets as numerical signs. For example, an alpha in Greek (an aleph in Hebrew) can represent the number one, a beta the number two, an iota and beta together, the number twelve, etc. A series of letters could form a word and at the same time indicate a number. Gematria took many forms and consisted in trying to guess the word from the number or trying to connect one word with another that had the same numerical value. Some Jews loved to find mysterious connections between words, based on the same numerical value. For example, the Hebrew word *nahash* ("serpent") has the same numerical value as the Hebrew word *mashiah* ("Messiah"). From this it was argued that one of the names of the Messiah was "serpent" (cf. Moses' lifting up the "serpent" in the desert; Nu 21; Jn 3:14).

Thus it is not difficult to understand why most commentators have understood John's words "Let him calculate the number.... His number is 666" to be an invitation to the reader to play gematria and discover the identity of the beast. Irenaeus (d. c. 202) mentions that many names of contemporary persons and entities were being offered in his day as solutions to this number mystery, though he himself cautioned against the practice and believed that the name of the Antichrist was deliberately concealed because he did not exist in John's day. The name would be secret till the time of his future appearance in the world. He expressly refutes the attempt of many in his day to identify the name with any of the Roman emperors and warns the church against endless speculations.

Irenaeus's fear was not misplaced, for endless speculation is just what has happened in the history of the interpretation of v.18. One of the most popular interpretations is a Hebrew rendition of "Neron Caesar," which equals 666, thus linking this beast with the

Nero redivivus legend (see comments on 13:1–18); more recently this understanding has been seriously challenged. All proposed solutions based on gematria seem unsatisfactory. If John was seeking to show believers how to penetrate the deception of the beast as well as to contrast the beast and his followers with the Lamb and his followers (14:1ff.), he has clearly failed—that is, if he intends for us to play the gematria game.

Several exegetical factors, however, argue strongly for another sense of John's words. In the first place, nowhere does John use gematria as a method. Everywhere, however, he gives symbolic significance to numbers (e.g., seven churches, seals, trumpets, bowls; twenty-four elders; 144,000 sealed; 144,000 cubits for the New Jerusalem, etc.). Furthermore, in 15:2 the victors have triumphed over three enemies: the beast, his image, and the number of his name, which suggests a symbolic significance connected with idolatry and blasphemy rather than victory over a mere puzzle solution of correctly identifying someone's name.

John seeks to give "wisdom" (GK 5053) and "insight" (GK 3808) to believers as to the true identity of their enemy. A similar use of these two words occurs in 17:9, where John calls attention to the identity of the beast ridden by the harlot. What he seems to be asking for in both cases is divine discernment, not mathematical ingenuity! Believers need to penetrate the deception of the beast. John's reference to his number will help them to recognize his true character and identity.

The statement "it is man's number" further identifies the kind of number the beast represents. Does John mean that the beast is a man, that he has a human name? In 21:17 John uses similar words for the angel: "by man's measurement, which the angel was using." The statement is difficult. How can the measure be both "man's" and at the same time of an "angel"? John seems to be calling attention to some inner meaning in the number of the size of the height of the wall in respect to the size of the city. The meaning perhaps is a mild polemic against first-century tendencies to venerate angels unduly by stating that both human beings and angels can understand and enter the future city (see comments on 21:15–21). In any case, the statement "it is man's number" alerts the reader to some hidden meaning in 666. From this it may be concluded that the number of the beast is linked to humanity. Why would it be necessary for John to emphasize this relationship unless he assumed that his readers might have understood the beast to be otherworldly without any connection to humanity? Might it be, then, that the statement signifies that the satanic beast, the great enemy of the church, manifests itself in human form? Thus, as 21:17 links the angelic and the human, so here the satanic is joined with the human.

Finally, how are we to understand 666? The best way is to return to one of the most ancient interpretations, that of Irenaeus. This church father proposed (while still holding to a personal Antichrist) that the number indicates that the beast is the sum of all apostate power, a concentrate of six thousand years of unrighteousness, wickedness, deception, and false prophecy. To him, the digit six indicates the recapitulations of that prophecy that occurred at the beginning, during the intermediate periods, and which will take place at the end. The significance of the name of the beast is abundantly clear elsewhere in Revelation (12:3; 13:1–6; 14:11; 17:3ff.). Wherever there is blasphemy, there the beast's name is found. The number 666 is the heaping up of the number 6, which indicates the apex of incompleteness and demonic parody, in contrast to the perfection that is symbolized by the number 7. This interpretation of 666 as a symbolic number referring to the unholy trinity of evil or to the human imperfect imitation of God rather than a cipher of a name

The number 666 has been found scribbled by worshipers of Satan on walls, doors, windows, etc. Courtesy Bill Reisman.

has been held by a long line of conservative commentators.

3. The Lamb and the 144,000 (14:1–5)

The two previous chapters have prepared Christians for the reality that as the end draws near, they will be harassed and sacrificed like sheep. This section shows that their sacrifice is not meaningless. A glance back at ch. 7 reminds us that there the 144,000 were merely sealed; here, however, they are seen as already delivered. When the floods have passed, Mount Zion appears high above the waters; the Lamb is on the throne of glory, surrounded by the triumphant songs of his own; the gracious presence of God fills the universe.

John now answers two pressing questions: What becomes of those who refuse to receive the mark of the beast and are killed (vv.1–5)? What happens to the beast and his servants (vv.6–20)?

1 The Lamb standing on Mount Zion is contrasted to the dragon standing on the shifting sands of the seashore (13:1). Although the rapid movement mood of the previous chapters gives way to one of victorious rest (vv.1–5, 13), activity continues because the battle between the dragon and the woman (cf. 12:11) is still going on. Immediately the question arises whether the 144,000 here are the same as those in ch. 7. The only reason for possibly viewing them differently in ch. 7 is that here they are described as "firstfruits" and "pure," who "did not defile themselves with women" (v.4). The two-group viewpoint has been defended especially by some Roman Catholic exegetes, though this is by no means unanimous among them.

The problem of the location of the 144,000 is more complex. "Mount Zion" may refer to the hilly area in southeast Jerusalem, the temple mount, the whole city of Jerusalem, or the whole land of Judah and the Israelite nation (see ZPEB, 5:1063–65). In the prophetic tradition, Zion came to symbolize the place where the Messiah would gather to himself a great company of the redeemed (Ps 48:1ff.; Isa 24:23; Joel 2:32; Ob 17, 21; Mic 4:1, 7; Zec 14:10). In Jewish apocalyptic literature, Zion can symbolize the strength and security that belong to the people of God.

In the seven NT references to Zion, five occur in OT quotations. The other two (here and Heb 12:22–23) imply a connection between Mount Zion and the church. Some, by connecting the reference in Hebrews to the one here, have argued for the heavenly location of the 144,000. Others view Mount Zion as the earthly seat of the messianic or millennial kingdom. Whether this Mount Zion has any connection (as to locality) with ancient and historical Zion, John does not say. At any rate, that the 144,000 are singing "before the throne" (v.3) is not an objection to seeing them as the earthly Zion; it is not the redeemed who are singing but the angelic harpists.

The 144,000 have on their foreheads the names of the Father and the Lamb, showing that they belong to God, not the beast. In 7:3ff., the elect group has the seal of God on their foreheads, linking them to this group in ch. 14, while the further description that "they follow the Lamb" (v.4) may show their connection with the second group in 7:9ff. (see esp. 7:17). One of the most beautiful and assuring promises in the whole book is that God's servants will have his name on their foreheads (cf. 3:12; 22:4).

This chapter advances the drama a step further than ch. 7. While the members of the multitude are the same, the circumstances in which they are seen have altered. In ch. 7 the whole company of God's people are sealed (7:1–8), readied for the satanic onslaught, and then a company (a martyred portion?) are seen in heaven serving before the throne of God (7:9ff.). In ch. 14, the whole body of the redeemed is seen (resurrected?) with the Lamb in the earthly eschatological kingdom. The repetition of the reference to the 144,000 may also be a liturgical phenomenon, a chief characteristic of the book.

The background of the scene (vv.1–5) may reflect John's reinterpretation of Ps 2, which he had alluded to elsewhere and which describes the battle between the rebellious nations and God, with God suppressing the revolt by enthroning his Son on Mount Zion. John, however, does not see the warrior-king the writer of Ps 2 hoped for, but he sees the Lamb and those who repeated his victory over the enemy by their submission (his name on their forehead). Psalm 76 may also be part of the background, where Zion is the symbol of the defeat of God's enemies and the salvation of his people.

2 The "sound" (GK 5889) John hears is probably a "voice," as in 1:15. It is important to recognize that this voice is not that of the redeemed; it is a loud angelic chorus (cf. 5:11), sounding like "the roar of rushing waters," like "a loud peal of thunder," and like "harpists playing their harps" (1:15; 5:8; 6:1; 19:1, 6; cf. comment on 5:8). Again the scene is liturgical, emphasizing the connection between the earthly victory and the heavenly throne.

3 This "new song" should be related to the "new song" in 5:9, also sung by the angelic choirs. It is the song of redemption and vindication. What was seen in ch. 5 as secured for the redeemed by Christ's death (i.e., that "they will reign on the earth" [v.10]) has now been realized on Mount Zion. In the one further reference to a song in Revelation, the redeemed "victors" sing "the song of Moses... and the song of the Lamb" (15:3), which may also relate to the new song of chs. 5 and 14 (see comment on 15:3). This heavenly example of worship may help us understand and appreciate Paul's references to songs inspired by the Spirit and sung in the first-century congregations (Eph 5:19; Col 3:16). Also instructive are the OT references to a "new song" (Pss 33:3; 40:3; 96:1; 144:9; 149:1; Isa 42:10). A new song, resulting from some mighty deed of God, comes from a fresh impulse of gratitude and joy in the heart. The angels sing a new song because now the victors themselves have become victorious. We are reminded again of the Passover motif (Ex 15:1ff.).

While the angels sing, only the 144,000 can "learn" (GK 3443) the new song, for they alone of earth's inhabitants have experienced God's mighty deed of victory over the beast through their ordeal of suffering and death. The word "learn" may also mean "hear deeply" in this context; in the Gospel of John, this word is used in the sense of a deep listening to divine revelation that results in learning (Jn 6:45). The 144,000 who were "redeemed" (GK 60) "from the earth" or "from among men" (v.4) must be the same as those "purchased" (GK 60) from all the earth's peoples in 5:9 and those sealed in 7:4–8, who have washed their garments in the blood of the Lamb (7:14ff).

4 John's most difficult statement about this group is that they did "not defile themselves with women." Does he mean that this group consists only of men who had never married? Or should it be understood as referring to spiritual apostasy or cult prostitution? It is unlikely that "defile" (GK 3662) refers merely to sexual intercourse since nowhere in Scripture does intercourse within marriage constitute sinful defilement (cf. Heb 13:4). On the other hand, the word "defiled" is found elsewhere in Jewish literature in connection with the promiscuous intercourse practiced by the Gentiles that defiled them but from which the Jews have separated themselves. Therefore, the words can refer only to adultery or fornication; and this fact, in turn, establishes "pure" as the meaning of *parthenoi* (lit., "virgins"; GK 4221). In addition, we can relate the reference to purity to the defilement of idolatry. John seems to use "defile" this way elsewhere of cult prostitution (3:4; cf. 2:14, 20, 22).

The group as a whole has remained faithful to Christ; "they follow the Lamb wherever he goes" in obedient discipleship. They are purchased by Christ's blood and offered to God as a holy and pure sacrifice of firstfruits. Surely this symbolically implies that the bride of Christ must be pure from idolatry. Paul, likewise, uses this figure: "I promised you to one husband, to Christ, so that I might present you as a pure virgin to him" (2Co 11:2–3).

Those spoken of in v.3 are "firstfruits" (GK 569) presented to God. This word can have two meanings. (1) It may designate the initial ingathering of the farmer, after which more follows. So it may mean a pledge or down payment with more to follow. This seems to be its meaning in Ro 8:23; 11:16? (cf. 1Co 15:20; 16:15). (2) In the usual OT sense and alternate NT use, "firstfruits" means simply an offering to God in the sense of being separated to him and sanctified (wholly consecrated), where no later addition is made, because the firstfruits constitutes the whole (see "sacred contributions" in Nu 5:9; see also Dt 18:4; 26:2; Jer 2:3; Jas 1:18). That this is John's intended sense is evident from the expression "offered as firstfruits to God."

5 The "lie" that brings "blame" refers to the blasphemy of the beast worshipers who deny the Father and the Son and ascribe vitality to the beast by believing his heresies and worshiping his image (21:27; 22:15; see also

Jn 8:44–45; Ro 1:25; 2Th 2:9–11; 1Jn 2:4, 21–22, 27).

4. The harvest of the earth (14:6–20)

This section forms a transition from the scene of the saints' final triumph (14:1–5) to the seven bowls (16:1ff.), which depict the final judgments on the enemies of the Lamb. As such, it forms a consoling counterpart to the first vision by assuring the 144,000 that God will judge the beast, his followers, and his world-wide system—Babylon.

6–7 The first angel announces that there is still hope, for even at this crucial moment in history God is seeking to reclaim the beast followers by issuing a message appealing to the people of the world at this time of judgment to "fear God ... and worship him." That this appeal is called a "gospel" (GK 2295) has raised a question. How is it good news? The intent of the gospel message is that people should fear God and worship him. John is perhaps showing the final fulfillment of Mk 13:10. Moreover, we must never forget that the announcement of divine judgment can never be separated from the proclamation of God's mercy. The gospel is "eternal" because it announces eternal life (Jn 3:16).

The reference to the coming of the hour of judgment supports the view that there is chronological progression in Revelation and that not everything described by John is simultaneous (see comment at 15:1). This is the first reference in the book to the "judgment [GK 3213] of God" (16:7; 18:10; 19:2), though the "wrath" of God, which appears to be a synonymous term (v.19), has been mentioned earlier (6:16–17; 11:18; 14:8, 10; 15:1; cf. 16:1, 19; 18:3; 19:15).

8 In anticipation of a more extended description in chs. 17–18, the fall of Babylon, the great anti-God system of idolatry, is announced. The actual fall does not occur until the final bowl judgment (16:19). There may be in 11:8 a previous allusion to Babylon as the "great city" (cf. 17:18).

9–12 The explicit reference to the certain judgment of the beast worshipers links this section to ch. 13. Through an OT figure of eschatological judgment, unmixed wine (not diluted with water) in the cup of God's wrath (Ps 75:8; Jer 25:15) and "burning sulfur" (Isa 30:33; 34:8–10; cf. Ge 19:24; Rev 19:20; 20:10; 21:8), John describes God's judgment inflicted on those who refuse his truth and worship a lie (Ro 1:18, 25). For those who drink Babylon's cup (v.8), the Lord will give his own cup of wrath.

The reference to "torment" (GK 989; cf. 9:5; 11:10; 12:2; 20:10) has troubled some commentators since this torment takes place "in the presence ... of the Lamb." The view that some recalcitrant individuals will suffer eternal deprivation seems repugnant to Christian sensitivity, but John's imagery conveys a sense of finality and sober reality. It is not clear whether this imagery points only to permanency and irreversibility of God's punitive justice or also includes the consciousness of eternal deprivation (cf. 20:10; Jn 5:28–29). Preaching about hell, of course, should never be used as a terror tactic by the church but should always be presented in such a way as to show that God's mercy is the final goal. Yet when all is said and done, the question is not whether the doctrine of hell is detestable but whether it is true. It does have the full support of Scripture and of our Lord (Mt 25:46; Ro 2:3–9; 2Th 1:6–9).

The worshipers of the beast will be unable to rest day and night, in contrast with the saints who will "rest" from their labor (v.13). While the beast worshipers had their time of rest, and while the saints were persecuted and martyred, in the final time of judgment God will reverse their roles (7:15ff.; cf. 2Th 1:6–7).

The great test for Christians is whether through patient endurance they will remain loyal to Jesus and not fall prey to the deception of the beasts (see comment on 13:10). They do this by paying serious attention to God's Word and their faithfulness to Christ Jesus (1:3; 2:26; 3:8, 10; 22:7, 9; cf. Php 1:28–30).

13 A fourth voice comes from heaven (an angel's or Christ's?), pronounces a beatitude, and evokes the Spirit's response. This is the second beatitude in Revelation (cf. comment on 1:3). Its general import is clear. But how are the words "from now on" to be understood? Do they mean that from the time of the vision's fulfillment onward (i.e., the judgment of idolaters and the 144,000 with the Lord on Mount Zion) the dead will be blessed in a more complete manner? Or do they refer to the time of John's writing onward? While either interpretation is grammatically possible, the preceding verse, which implies an exhortation to Christians in John's day, favors the latter view. John expects the imminent intensification of persecution associated with the beast, and this beatitude indicates that those who remain loyal to Jesus will be blessed indeed.

Apart from 22:17, this is the only place in Revelation where the Spirit speaks directly (cf. Ac 13:2; Heb 3:7; 10:15). The beatitude is no doubt intended to emphasize the reality of the martyrs' future. Their blessedness consists in "rest" (GK 399) from the onslaught of the dragon and his beasts and the assurance that their toils (GK 3160; cf. 2:2) for Christ's name will not be in vain but will be remembered by the Lord himself after their death (Heb 6:10; cf. 1Ti 5:24–25).

14–16 After a brief pause to encourage the faithfulness of the saints, John returns to the theme of divine judgment on the world. He does this by first describing the judgment in terms of a harvest (vv.14–20) and then by the seven bowl plagues (chs. 15–16). John sees a white cloud and seated on it one resembling a human being ("a son of man"). He has a crown of gold and a sharp sickle, the main instrument of harvest. John clearly wishes to highlight this exalted human figure and his role in the final judgment. The question of the identity of the "son of man" is not unlike the problem of the identity of the rider of the white horse (6:1). The same words "like a son of man" are used of Jesus in 1:13. But some have noted the close association of the one "seated on the cloud" with the words "another angel" in v. 15 and with "another angel ... too" in v.17, the one who has a sharp sickle—implying that the former figure with the sickle was also an angel. Further, if the figure on the cloud is Jesus, how can we account for an angel giving a command to him to reap the earth (v.15)?

Though there are difficulties, there can be little question that the divine figure seated on the cloud must be associated, through Da 7:13–14, with the person of the Messiah under the title "a son of man." Indeed, it is quite appropriate for John to use the term "Son of Man," since in the Gospels that term is most frequently associated with the Messiah's suffering and the glory of the Second Advent as well as with his right to judge the world (Mt 26:64; Jn 5:27; see comment on Mk 8:31). Both themes are present in the context of Revelation. The imagery of Da 7, frequently used in this book, links the suffering people of God ("the saints") to the Son of Man who sits in judgment over the kingdoms of the world. It should, of course, be remembered that this is a highly symbolic description of the final judgment.

The harvest is a typical OT figure used for divine judgment (Hos 6:11; Joel 3:13), especially on Babylon (Jer 51:33). Jesus also likens the final judgment to the harvest of the earth (Mt 13:30, 39). He may use the instrumentality of angels or human beings, but it is his prerogative to put in the sickle. While this reaping may be the gathering of his elect from the earth (cf. Mt 9:37–38; Jn 4:35–38; et al.), the context favors taking the harvest to be a reference not to salvation but to judgment.

17–20 "Another" angel here has no more necessary connection with the Son of Man than "another" angel in v.15; it may simply mean another of the same kind of angel mentioned in the succession of personages in the book (cf. 14:6, where no other angel is involved except the one mentioned). This angel (v.17) will gather the vintage of the earth. He is associated with the angel from the altar who has authority over its fire. Though opinion about the identification of the altar is divided, it seems to be the incense altar, and the fire is symbolic of God's vindication of his martyred people (cf. 8:3–5 and comments on 6:9–11).

The divine final judgment is presented in three images: the unmixed wine in the cup (v.10), the grain harvest (vv.14–16), and the vintage harvest (vv.17–20). These are best understood as three metaphors describing different views of the same reality, i.e., the divine judgment. Again the OT provides the background for this imagery of divine judgment (Isa 63:1–6; La 1:15; Joel 3:13; cf. Rev 19:13, 15). The reference to the "great winepress of God's wrath" in v.19 should clarify the imagery and leave no doubt that it denotes God's judgment on the rebellious world.

The final verse (v.20) is gruesome: blood flows up to the horses' bridles for a distance of about 1,600 stadia (200 miles). Once again the source of the imagery is Isa 63:1–6, heightened by John's hyperbole. A similar apocalyptic image for the final judgment on idolaters occurs in the pre-Christian book of Enoch, where the righteous will slay the wicked. Here in Revelation the judgment is not the task of human vengeance but belongs exclusively to the Son of Man and his angelic reapers (cf. Ro 12:19–21). The symbolism is that of a head-on battle, a great defeat of the enemy, a sea of spilled blood. To go beyond this to find a symbolic meaning of the 1,600 stadia or to link the scene to some geographic location (cf. 16:4–6) is pure speculation.

The term "outside the city" requires explanation. It may refer merely to ancient warfare when a besieging army was slaughtered at the city walls, and the blood flowed outside the city. Some think John may have had an actual city in mind and have suggested Jerusalem because of the OT predictions of a final battle to be fought near the city (Da 11:45; Joel 3:12; Zec 14:4; but cf. Rev 16:16—"Armageddon" is not near Jerusalem). On the other hand, John's symbolic use of "city" in every other reference favors taking the word symbolically here. In Revelation there are in essence only two cities: the city of God, which is the camp of the saints, and the city of Satan, Babylon, which is made up of the followers of the beast. There is no way to be really sure of the identity of the city, nor is its identity important. It is sufficient to take it as the same city that was persecuted by the pagans (11:2) and is seen in 20:9, i.e., the community of the saints.

D. The Seven Bowls (15:1–19:10)

It is difficult to know where the divisions should fall in these further visions. Since the last series of sevens in Revelation includes the fall of Babylon under the seventh bowl (16:19), it has seemed appropriate to include the extensive description of the city's fall under the bowl-series division.

Chapter 15, a sort of celestial interlude before the final judgment, prepares for the execution of the bowl series (ch. 16), while chs. 17–18 elaborate the fall of Babylon. What has already been anticipated under the three figures of the divine final judgment—the cup of wine (14:10), the harvest of the earth (14:14–16), and the vintage (14:17–20) is now further described under the symbolism of the seven bowls. In typical Hebrew fashion, each cycle repeats in new ways the former events and adds fresh details.

It is clear that in these final judgments only the unbelieving world is involved; therefore, they are punitive plagues (16:2). Yet even in these last plagues, God is concerned with effecting repentance, though none abandon their idolatry (16:9, 11). Are the faithful still on earth? Presumably not, for 15:2 locates the whole company of conquerors before the throne.

The inclusive series of bowl judgments constitute the "third woe" announced in 11:14 as "coming soon" (see comment on 11:14). Since the first two woes occur under the fifth and sixth trumpets, it is reasonable to see the third woe, which involved seven plagues, as unfolding during the sounding of the seventh trumpet, when the mystery of God will be finished (10:7). The actual woe events were delayed till John could give important background material concerning not only the inhabitants of the earth but also the church herself, her glory and shame, her faithfulness and apostasy (12:1–14:20). These last plagues take place "immediately after the distress of those days" referred to by Jesus in the Olivet Discourse and may well be the fulfillment of his apocalyptic words in Mt 24:29. Significantly, the next event that follows this judgment, the coming of the Son of Man in the clouds (Mt 24:30–31), is the same event John describes following the bowl judgments (19:11).

1. Preparatory: The seven angels with the seven last plagues (15:1–8)

Chapter 15 is tied closely to ch. 16, for both deal with the seven last plagues of God's wrath. One is preparatory and interpretative, the other descriptive. Chapter 15 is oriented to the OT account of the Exodus. It has two main visions: the first portrays the victors who have emerged triumphant from the great ordeal (vv.2–4); the second relates the appearance from the heavenly temple of seven angels clothed in white and gold and holding the seven bowls of the last plagues (vv.5–8).

1 This verse forms a superscription to chs. 15–16. The final manifestation of the wrath of God takes the form of seven angels of judgment and is called a "sign" (GK *4956*), the third identified heavenly "sign" (cf. the woman and dragon at 12:1, 3). The adjective "marvelous" (GK *2515*; cf. v.3) is added because John understood the seven angels to represent that God's wrath is completed (GK *5464*)—i.e., the "last" (GK *2274*) plagues—and they are awesome as well as final in character. While these plagues may be the finale to the whole historical panorama of God's judgments, it is exegetically preferable to find a connection of them with other events related in Revelation. As has already been argued, the first reference to the final judgment is found in 6:17: "For the great day of their wrath has come, and who can stand?" After the interlude of the sealing of the saints from spiritual harm (ch. 7), the seven trumpets are sounded (8:1ff.). The sixth one involves three plagues that kill a third of the human race (9:18). The third woe (11:14) includes the bowl judgments or the "last" plagues. Thus the trumpets begin the final wrath of God that is finished in the seven bowls.

2 As in 14:1ff., John again focuses his attention on a scene that contrasts sharply with the coming judgment, an indication of his pastoral concern. He sees before the throne the likeness of a sea of glass shot through with fire (cf. 4:6). It is a scene of worship, and its imagery is suitable for depicting the majesty and brilliance of God, which the sea of glass is reflecting in a virtual symphony of color. Firmly planted "beside" (or "on") the sea are those who were "victorious over the beast." They are the same ones who are seen throughout Revelation as having won out over the idolatrous beasts through their faithful testimony to Christ, even to the extent of martyrdom (e.g., 2:7, 11, 26; 12:11; 21:7; cf. 3:21; 5:5). They are the 144,000, the elect of God (7:4; 14:1), the completed company of martyrs (6:11), those who did not have "the number of his name" (see comment on 13:17). Suddenly in this dazzling scene the sound of harps and singing is heard.

3–4 The song sung by the redeemed is the "song of Moses, the servant of God and the song of the Lamb"—a single song as vv.3–4 show. The Song of Moses is in Ex 15:1–18. It celebrated the victory of the Lord in the defeat of the Egyptians at the Red Sea. In the ancient synagogue it was sung in the afternoon service of each Sabbath to celebrate God's sovereign rule over the universe, of which the redemption from Egypt reminded the Jew. As the deliverance from Egypt, with its plagues of judgment on Israel's enemies, became for the Jew a signpost of God's just rule over the world, so God's final judgment and the deliverance of the followers of the Lamb bring forth from the victors over the beast exuberant songs of praise to God for his righteous acts in history.

Each line in vv.3–4 picks up phrases from the Psalms and Prophets. Compare the following OT words with vv.3–4: "Then Moses and the Israelites sang this song" (Ex 15:1); "your works are wonderful" (Ps 139:14); "Lord God Almighty" (Am 4:13); "all his ways are just. A faithful God . . . upright and just is he" (Dt 32:4); "who shall not revere you, O King of the nations" (Jer 10:7); "they will bring glory to your name" (Ps 86:9), etc. John may or may not have heard the victors over the beast singing these actual words. But it was revealed to him that they were praising God for his mighty deliverance and for judgment on their enemies.

5–8 A second and still more impressive scene follows. The door to the temple in heaven is again opened (cf. 11:19), and the seven angels dressed in white and gold come out of the temple. In a dignified manner, one of the living creatures gives a bowl to each of the seven messengers. The bowls (GK *5786*) are the vessels used in the temple ministry, especially for offerings and incense (5:8). It was probably a ritual bowl used for collecting the blood of the sacrifices (Ex 27:3). Golden bowls seem to be always associated with the temple (e.g., 1Ki 1:50; 2Ki 12:13; 25:15).

The "smoke" (GK *2837*) that filled the temple refers to the Shekinah cloud first associated with the tabernacle and then with the temple (see comment on 7:15). It symbolizes God's special presence and the One who is the source of the judgments (Ex 40:34ff.; 1Ki 8:10–11; Eze 11:23; 44:4). His awesome presence in the temple until the plagues are finished (16:17) prohibits even angels from entering it (cf. Isa 6:4; Hab 2:20).

2. Pouring out of the seven bowls (16:1–21)

1 This chapter describes the "third woe" (see comment on 15:1–19:10) in the form of the outpouring of seven bowl judgments. They occur in rapid succession with only a brief pause for a dialogue between the third angel and the altar, accentuating the justice of God's punishments (vv.5–7). This rapid succession is probably due to John's desire to give a telescopic view of the first six bowls and then hasten on to the seventh, where the far more detailed judgment on Babylon occurs. Again, seven symbolizes fullness, this time fullness of judgment (cf. Lev 26:21). The striking parallelism between the order of these plagues and those of the trumpets (8:2–9:21), though clearly not identical in every detail, has led many to conclude that the two series are the same. The similarity, however, may be merely literary.

Each plague in both series (the trumpets and the bowls) is reminiscent of the plagues on Egypt before the Exodus. The first four of each cover the traditional divisions of nature: earth, sea, rivers, and sky. But in each of the bowls, unlike the trumpets, the plague on nature is related to the suffering of humankind. Furthermore, each bowl plague seems to be total in its effect ("every living thing ... died" [v.3]), whereas under the trumpets only a part is affected ("a third of the living creatures ... died" [8:9]). Therefore, it seems better to understand the trumpets and bowls as separate judgments. The final three plagues are social and spiritual in their effect and shift from nature to humanity. These descriptions should probably not be taken literally; the important point is that they depict God's sure and righteous judgment that will one day be actually done in this world.

2 The *first bowl* has no strict counterpart in the trumpets but recalls the sixth plague of boils under Moses (Ex 9:10–11). As the antagonists of Moses were affected by the boils, so the enemies of Christ who worship the beast will be struck by this plague.

3 The *second bowl* turns the sea into polluted blood (see comment on 8:8). Ge 1:21 is reversed; all marine life dies (cf. Ex 7:17–21).

4 The *third bowl* affects the fresh waters of the earth, which are essential to human life. They too become polluted as blood (cf. Ex 7:17–21).

5–7 Here the reference to blood calls forth the dialogue between the angel and the altar concerning the logic of the plagues. The blood that sinners drink is just requital for their shedding of the blood of the saints (15:1–4) and prophets (11:3–13; cf. 17:6; 18:20). With blood, God vindicates the blood of the martyrs of Jesus. People must choose whether to drink the blood of saints or to wear robes dipped in the blood of the Lamb.

8–9 The *fourth bowl* increases the intensity of the sun's heat; it is the exact opposite of the fourth trumpet, which produced a plague of darkness (cf. 8:12). The earth dwellers, instead of repenting of their deeds and acknowledging the Creator (the only act that could even now turn away God's wrath), curse (lit., "blaspheme"; GK *1059*) God for sending them agonizing pain (vv.11, 21). Yet their problem goes beyond the awful physical pain and is moral and spiritual (cf. Isa 52:5; Ro 1:25; 2:24).

10–11 The *fifth bowl* plunges the kingdom of the beast into darkness. This is not a reference to the fall of the Roman Empire or Caesar worship, though John's words would include this level of meaning. In 2:13, John used the word "throne" to designate the stronghold of Satan at Pergamum. Thus "the throne of the beast" symbolizes the seat of the world-wide dominion of the great satanic system of idolatry (the Abyss? cf. 20:1). This system is plunged into spiritual darkness or disruption, bringing chaos on all who sought life and meaning in it. This bowl plague, while similar to the fifth trumpet, strikes at the very seat of satanic authority over the world; and the darkness is moral and spiritual rather than physical (cf. 21:25; 22:5; Jn 8:12; 12:35–36, 46; 1Jn 1:5–7; 2:8–10). Again the terrible refrain is repeated: "But they refused to repent of what they had done."

12–16 The *sixth bowl* is specifically aimed at drying up the Euphrates River and so will allow the demonically inspired kings from the East to gather at Armageddon where God himself will enter into battle with them. The reference to the Euphrates in the sixth trumpet is a striking parallel to the sixth bowl plague (9:14). Thus many identify the two series as different aspects of the same plagues. But while the sixth trumpet releases demonic hordes to inflict death on the earth dwellers, the sixth bowl effects the assembling of the rulers (kings) from the East to meet the Lord God Almighty in battle.

The Euphrates was not only the location of Babylon, the great anti-God throne, but the place from which the evil hordes would invade Israel (see comment on 9:14). Thus, by mentioning the Euphrates by name, John is suggesting that the unseen rulers of this world are being prepared to enter into a final and fatal battle with the Sovereign of the universe. It is a warfare of a primordial and eschatological order, more descriptive of contemporary actualities than political history. Thus John is not describing the invasion of the Parthian hordes advancing on Rome or any future political invasion of Israel. How could such political groups be involved in the battle of the great day of God Almighty? Instead, in terms reminiscent of the ancient battles of Israel, John describes the final defeat of the forces of evil, represented by the kings from the East.

Further confirmation that these Eastern kings represent the combined forces of evil in the world is John's reference to the three froglike evil (lit., "unclean"; GK *176*; see NIV note) spirits that proceed out of the mouths of the dragon, the beast, and the false prophet (frogs were considered unclean animals by the Jews; cf. Lev 11:10, 41). To the Egyptian, the frog was the symbol of the goddess Heqt, a goddess of resurrection and fertility. But to a Jewish mind, such gods were "demons" (v.14), Satan's emissaries, and inseparable from idolatry (9:20; 18:2; 1Co 10:20–21). These demons produce miraculous signs like the false prophet (13:13–14), and this connects their activity to the deception of the earth's kings. Since these demons come from the "mouths" of the figures, lying and deceptive words are implied (contrast the sword from Christ's mouth that is equal to his word of truth). These kings are summoned to the battle of the great day of God Almighty. Under the sixth bowl, the kings are only gathered. Not until the seventh bowl do the confrontation and defeat actually occur (19:19–21).

Somewhat abruptly, but not inappropriately, a warning is issued. Those who worship and serve the Lamb must be constantly vigilant lest their loyalty to him be diverted through the satanic deception (cf. Mt 24:43ff.; 1Th 5:2, 4). The Parousia (second coming) of Christ is here connected with the judgment of Armageddon and the fall of Babylon. After John has described the latter in more detail (chs. 17–18), he describes the vision of the return of Jesus (19:11–16). In v.15 the third of the seven beatitudes is pronounced (cf. 1:3; 14:13; 19:9; 20:6; 22:7, 14).

Similar to the exhortation given to those in the churches at Sardis (3:2–4) and Laodicea (3:18), the warning about Jesus' coming "like a thief" implies a need for alertness to the deception of idolatry and disloyalty to Jesus. Like a guard who watches by night, the true Christian will remain steadfast and prepared. One need not relate this warning only to the end time as in the context, since the appeal for the steadfast loyalty of Christians is relevant at any time. Such appeals, however, are associated in the Gospels with the return of Christ (Mk 13:32–37).

Many modern interpreters identify "Armageddon" with the Galilean fortified city of Megiddo and believe that a literal military battle will be fought in the latter days in that vicinity. While this sense is not impossible, it is better to take the name as being symbolic. In Hebrew *har* means hill or mountain, while *megiddon* could mean Megiddo, a Canaanite stronghold in the Jezreel Plain later captured by the Israelites (Jos 12:21; Jdg 5:19). Megiddo, however, is only a tell (an artificial mound—only seventy feet high in John's day), not a hill or mountain, though the fact that over two hundred battles have been fought in this vicinity makes this site an appropriate symbol for the final battle against evil. Neither can it mean Mount Carmel near Megiddo, for such a designation is never used and would be totally obscure to the residents of Asia to whom John writes. Therefore it is better to understand the term symbolically in the same manner as "in Hebrew" in 9:11 alerts us to the symbolic significance of the name of the angel of the Abyss.

An argument from language yields the same conclusion. *Magedon* can be derived from the secondary sense of the Hebrew verb *gadad*, which means "to gather in troops or bands." A simple way in Hebrew to make a noun from a verb is to prefix a *ma* to the verbal form. Thus we have *maged*, "a place of gathering in troops," and the suffix *o*, meaning "his," yielding "his place of gathering in troops." This is almost equivalent to the expressions in vv.14, 16—"to gather them [the kings] for the battle on the great day of God Almighty"—and would allude to the prophetic expectation of the gathering of the nations for judgment (Joel 3:2, 12). In any case, the name is symbolic and probably does not refer to any geographical location, in Palestine or elsewhere; rather, it describes the final

In Hebrew *har* means hill or mountain, while *megiddon* may mean Megiddo, which was a Canaanite stronghold in the Jezreel Plain. This picture shows the valley in front of the hill of Megiddo, where (according to some) the Battle of Armageddon will take place.

confrontation where God will meet the forces of evil in their final defeat. It does, however, refer to a real point in history and to real persons who will encounter God's just sentence.

17–21 The *seventh bowl* is poured out into the air. Nothing further is said about the "air"; rather, John is concerned with the loud voice that cries out, "It is done," or, "It has come to pass." With this bowl, the eschatological wrath of God is completed (cf. 6:17; 21:6; Jn 19:30). Flashes of lightning, peals of thunder, and a severe earthquake occur (cf. 4:5; 8:5; 11:19). These eschatological signs symbolize the destruction of the anti-God forces throughout the world (cf. Heb 12:27). So great is the earthquake of God's judgment that it reaches the strongholds of organized evil represented by the cities of the pagans. Even the great city Babylon, which seduced all the earth's kings and inhabitants (17:2), now comes under final sentence (see comment on 11:8).

The judgment of Babylon will occupy John's attention in chs. 17–18. While the catastrophe is described in geophysical terms (islands and mountains disappearing, huge hailstones accompanying a gigantic storm), there is a question whether John intends the destruction to be merely natural or even politico-historical entities or exclusively of the unseen powers of evil. Like the Egyptian plague of hail that further hardened Pharaoh's heart, this plague of hail falls on the unrepentant to no avail; they curse God for sending his judgment on them (cf. Ex 9:24). By such language John describes the rising pitch of God's wrath on the rebellious powers of the earth. His words should not be politicized as if he spoke merely of Rome or of some impending historical crisis for the church. He is speaking of the great realities of the end, when God puts down all his enemies.

3. The harlot and the beast (17:1–18)

In an important sense, the interpretation of this chapter controls the interpretation of the whole book of Revelation. For many exegetes, Babylon represents the city of Rome, and the beast stands for the Roman Empire. The seven hills (v.9) are the seven selected dynasties of Roman emperors from Augustus to Domitian. The ten kings are heads of lesser and restless states, eager to escape their enslavement to the colonizing power. John's prediction of the fall of Babylon is his announcement of the impending dissolution of the Roman Empire in all its aspects. For such a view there is considerable evidence. Babylon was a term used by both Jews and Christians for Rome (2 Baruch 11:1; 1Pe 5:13). Rome was a great city (v.18), a city set on seven hills (v.9), and by the time of Domitian (A.D. 85), it was notorious for persecuting and killing the saints (v.6).

Yet there is evidence that casts doubt on this exegesis and impels us to look for a more adequate understanding of John's intention. Babylon cannot be confined to Rome or to any other historical city, past or future; it has multiple equivalents (cf. 11:8). The details John describes do not neatly fit any past historical city, such as Babylon, Rome, Tyre, or Jerusalem. Babylon is found wherever there is satanic deception. It can be seen in any of these classic manifestations from the past or in modern times—e.g., Nazi Germany, Soviet Russia, Mao's China, Saddam Hussein's Iraq, British colonialism, or even in aspects of American life. Babylon is defined more by dominant idolatries than geographic boundaries, and is best understood here as the archetypal head of all worldly resistance to God. It is a symbol of satanic deception and power, a divine mystery that can never be wholly reduced to empirical earthly institutions. It represents the total culture of the world apart from God, while the divine system is depicted by the New Jerusalem. Rome itself is only one manifestation.

Chapters 17–18 form one continuous unit dealing with the judgment on Babylon. John first describes the nature of the harlot and the beast she rides (ch. 17); then he describes her momentous fall in terms drawn from the OT descriptions of the fall of great cities (ch. 18). The woman is identified as the great city (17:18). From internal evidence in Revelation, the identity of Babylon the woman (ch. 17) with Babylon the great city (ch. 18) is so unmistakable that it would be inappropriate to make them different entities. These two chapters form an extended appendix to the seventh bowl, where the judgment on Babylon was mentioned (16:19). They also expand the earlier references to this city (11:8; 14:8) and look forward by way of contrast to the eternal Holy City (chs. 21–22).

Chapter 17 may be divided into the vision of the great harlot (vv.1–6) and the interpretation of the vision (vv.7–18).

1 "One of the seven angels" connects this vision with the preceding bowl judgments, showing that it is a further expansion or appendix of the final bowl action.

John sees a great prostitute (GK *4520*) established on many waters. This verse forms a superscription for the chapter. The relationship between prostitution (GK *4518*) and idolatry has already been discussed (see comments on 2:14, 20). The prevalence of cult prostitution throughout the ancient world makes this figure appropriate for idolatrous worship (cf. comments on "abominable things" in 17:4 and "magic spell" in 18:23). In the OT, the same figure of a harlot city is used of Nineveh (Na 3:4), of Tyre (Isa 23:16–17), and of idolatrous Jerusalem (Eze 16:15ff.). The best background for understanding the language of the chapter is not the history of the Roman Empire or the pagan gods but the descriptions of Jerusalem as the harlot in Eze 16 and 23 and Babylon as the harlot in Jer 51.

Amazingly, the harlot-city societies mentioned in Scripture have certain common characteristics that are also reflected in John's description of the great Babylon. Royal dignity and splendor combined with prosperity, overabundance, and luxury (Jer 51:13; Eze 16:13, 49; Na 2:9; cf. Rev 18:3, 7, 16–17); self-trust or boastfulness (Isa 14:12–14; Jer 50:31; Eze 16:15, 50, 56; 27:3; 28:5; cf. Rev 18:7); power and violence, especially against God's people (Jer 51:35, 49; Eze 23:37; Na 3:1–3; cf. Rev 18:10, 24); oppression and injustice (Isa 14:4; Eze 16:49; 28:18; cf. Rev 18:5, 20); and idolatry (Jer 51:47; Eze 16:17, 36; 23:7, 30, 49; Na 1:14; cf. Rev 17:4–5; 18:3; 19:2) are all here. Wherever and whenever these characteristics have been manifested historically, there is the appearance of Babylon.

The great prostitute "sits on many waters." This goes back to Jeremiah's oracle against historical Babylon, situated along the waterways of the Euphrates, with many canals around the city, greatly multiplying its wealth by trade (Jer 51:13). This description has a deeper significance, as is explained in v.15 with "peoples, multitudes, nations and languages"—figurative for the vast influence of the prostitute on the peoples of the world.

2 Earth's kings and inhabitants "committed adultery" with the prostitute. This language goes back to references to the harlot cities of the past (e.g., Jer 51:7) and means that the peoples of the world have become drunk with abundance, power, pride, violence, and especially false worship. "Kings of the earth" may describe simply the rulers in contrast to the rest of the people.

3 John is carried in the Spirit (see comment on 1:10; cf. 4:2; 21:10) into a "desert," where he again sees ancient Babylon (Isa 14:23; 21:1; cf. Rev 18:2; see comment on 12:6) as a prostitute seated on "a scarlet beast"—scarlet, presumably, because the color symbolizes the beast's blasphemy in contrast to the white-horse rider and those dressed in white, who are faithful and true (19:8, 11, 14). Since this beast is a seven-headed monster, there is no cogent reason against identifying it with the first beast in ch. 13, which is also inseparable from the seven-headed dragon of ch. 12.

4 Dressed in queenly attire (Eze 16:13; cf. Rev 18:7), the woman rides the beast, swinging in her hand a golden cup full of her idolatrous abominations and wickedness. Note the contrast—beauty and gross wickedness. Her costly and attractive attire suggests the prostitute's outward beauty and attraction (Jer 4:30). The golden cup filled with wine alludes to Jeremiah's description of Babylon's world-wide influence in idolatry (Jer 51:7). Her cup is filled with "abominable things" (GK *1007*)—things most frequently associated with idolatry, which was abhorrent to Jews and Christians alike (21:27). Jesus used this word to refer to Daniel's "abomination that causes desolation" standing in the temple (Mk 13:14 cf. Da 9:27; 11:31; 12:11). "Filth" (lit., "uncleannesses"; GK *176*) is associated in the NT with evil (unclean) spirits (e.g., Mt 10:1; 12:43) and with idolatry (2Co 6:17), perhaps with cult prostitution (Eph 5:5).

5 The woman has a title written on her forehead, showing that in spite of all her royal glamour she is nothing but a prostitute. It was customary for Roman prostitutes to wear their names in the fillet that encircled their brows.

The first word in the woman's title is "MYSTERY" (GK *3696*; cf. 1:20; 10:7; 17:7). It seems best to see this word as a prefix to the actual name—i.e., "She has a name written on her forehead, which is a mystery, 'Babylon....'" Elsewhere in Revelation John uses "mystery" as a word denoting a divine mystery or allegory that is now revealed (cf. also comment on 11:8).

No doubt the specific mystery is that this prostitute is the mother of all earth's idolatrous prostitutes. She is the reservoir or the womb that bears all individual cases of historical resistance to God's will on earth; she is the unholy antithesis to the woman who weds the Lamb (19:7–8) and to the New Jerusalem (21:2–3). That is in part why she cannot be any particular historical city (see comment on 17:1–18). While at its beginning Babel was associated with resisting and defying God (Ge 11:1–11), it is probably the epoch of the Babylonian captivity of Israel that indelibly etched the proud, idolatrous, and repressive nature of Babylon on the memories of God's people and thus provided the symbolic image that could be applied to the further manifestations of the mother prostitute.

6 This mother prostitute is also the source of the shed blood of the followers of Jesus (cf. 2:13), the martyrs referred to throughout the book (6:9; 7:9ff.; 13:8; 18:24). Though there is no direct reference here to Rome or Jerusalem, early Christian readers would understand that whenever they were threatened with death by any temporal power—whether political, religious, or both—they were in reality facing the blood-thirsty mother prostitute God was about to judge and destroy once for all. To be drunk with blood was a familiar figure in the ancient world for the lust for violence.

7 Verses 7–18 contain an extended interpretation of the vision that parallels the method used in apocalyptic sections in OT prophecy (cf. Zec 1:8ff., etc.; Rev 7:9ff). First the beast is described and identified (vv.7–8), then the seven heads (vv.9–11), the ten horns (vv.12–14), the waters (v.15), and finally the woman (v.18). John's astonishment over the arresting figure of the woman on the beast is quickly subdued by the interpreting angel's announcement that John will be shown the

1205

explanation of the divine mystery of the symbolic imagery of woman and beast.

8 Much difficulty in interpreting this section has resulted from incorrectly applying John's words either to the Roman emperor succession (the seven heads), to the Nero redivivus myth (see comments on 13:1–18), or to a succession of world empires. None of these views is satisfactory. John's description is theological, not political. He describes a reality behind earth's sovereigns, not the successive manifestations in history.

The beast is the monster from the Abyss—i.e., the satanic incarnation of idolatrous power that is mentioned in 11:7 and described in 13:1ff., and whose destruction is seen in 19:19–20. John is told that the beast "once was, now is not, and will come up out of the Abyss." This seems clearly to be a paraphrase of the earlier idea of the sword-wounded beast who was healed (13:3, 14); the language is similar, the astonishment of the world's inhabitants is identical, and the threefold emphasis on this spectacular feature is repeated (13:3, 12, 14; 17:8 bis, 11).

The play here on the tenses "was . . . is not . . . will come" refers to a three-stage history of the beast that requires a mind with wisdom to understand. That John's beast "is not" refers to his defeat by the Lamb on Calvary (cf. Jn 12:31–32). To those who worship only the Father and the Son, all other gods are nothing or nonexistent (1Co 8:4–6). Satan once had unchallenged power over the earth ("was," cf. Lk 4:6; Heb 2:14–15). Yet he is given a "little time" to oppose God and his people (12:12c; 13:5; 20:3b) before his final sentencing to "destruction" (v.11; cf. Mt 7:13; Jn 17:12; Ro 9:22; 2Th 2:3). It is this apparent revival of Satan's power and authority over the world after his mortal wound (Ge 3:15) that causes the deceived of earth to follow him.

There is a subtle change from the way the first reference to the beast is stated (v.8a) to that of the second (v.8b). Whereas the first instance reveals to believers his satanic origin ("out of the Abyss") and his final destruction, the second simply states an unbeliever's view—how that "he once was, now is not, and yet will come." This twofold viewpoint is paralleled in vv.9–11, where one of the kings "is" (v.10) and an eighth king "is" (v.11); yet the beast "is not" (v.11). There seems to be an intentional double-talk whereby the author identifies theologically the nature of the power that supports the profligate woman.

John uses a present tense for the beast's coming up out of the Abyss (cf. 11:7), suggesting a continuing aspect of his character, similar to the use of the present tense to describe the New Jerusalem descending from heaven (cf. 3:12; 21:2, 10). The beast's going into perdition may likewise indicate one of his continuing characteristics. There is also a possible parallelism in the expression "once was, now is not, and yet will come" with the divine attributes described in the phrase "who is, and who was, and who is to come" (1:8). On the meaning of the "book of life," see comment on 3:5 (cf. 13:8).

9 This and the following verses form the key of the Roman emperor view of the Apocalypse. Most scholars consider the seven hills to refer to the seven hills of Rome and the seven kings to seven successive emperors of that nation. Yet there is good reason to doubt that this is the interpretation John intended. In the first place, the seven hills belong to the monster, not the woman. It is the woman (i.e., the city [v.18]) who sits upon (i.e., has mastery over) the seven heads (or seven hills) of the monster. If the woman is the city of Rome, it is obvious that she did not exercise mastery over seven successive Roman emperors that are also seven traditional hills of Rome. Also, how could the seven hills of Rome have any real importance to the diabolical nature of the beast or the woman? Finally, nowhere in the NT is Rome described as the enemy of the church.

This interpretation also explains the meaning of John's call "for a mind with wisdom." The call for divine "wisdom" (GK 5053) requires theological and symbolical discernment, not mere geographical or numerical insight (cf. comment on 13:18).

In the seven other instances in Revelation of the word translated "hills" here (GK 4001), it is always rendered "mountain." Mountains allegorically refer to world powers in the Prophets (Isa 2:2; Jer 51:25; Da 2:35; Zec 4:7). It seems better, then, to interpret the seven mountains as a reference to the seven heads or kings, which describe not the city but the beast. In addition, the expression "they are also seven kings" requires strict identification of the seven mountains with seven kings.

John's use of numbers elsewhere in the book likewise argues against the Roman Empire identification. He has already shown a disposition for their symbolic significance—e.g., seven churches, seals, trumpets, bowls, and thunders; twenty-four elders; 144,000 sealed, etc. By his use of seven, he indicates completeness or wholeness. The seven heads of the beast symbolize fullness of blasphemy and evil.

10 If the seven heads symbolically represent the full source of evil power and blasphemy, why, then, does John talk about five fallen heads or kings, one existing head or king, and one yet to come? Does this not fit the view of dynastic successions to the imperial throne? To be sure, there have been many attempts to fit the date of Revelation (the then contemporary king would be he who "is") into the emperor lists of the first century. But immediately there are admitted problems. Where do we begin—with Julius Caesar or Caesar Augustus? Are we to count all emperors or just those who fostered emperor worship? Are we to exclude Galba, Otho, and Vitellius who had short, rival reigns? If so, how can they be excluded except on an arbitrary basis? A careful examination of the historic materials yields no satisfactory solution. If Revelation were written under Nero, there would be too few emperors; if under Domitian, too many. The original readers would have had no more information on these emperor successions than we do. Furthermore, how could the eighth emperor who is identified as the beast also be one of the seven (v.11)?

Recognizing these problems, others have sought different solutions to John's five-one-one succession of kings. Since the word "king" (GK 995) may also represent kingdoms, some have suggested an interpretation that takes the five-one-one to refer to successive world kingdoms that have oppressed the people of God: Egypt, Assyria, Babylon, Persia, Greece (five fallen), Rome (one is), and a future world kingdom. While this solves some of the emperor succession problems, it too must admit arbitrary omissions, such as the devastating persecution of the people of God under the Seleucids of Syria, especially Antiochus IV Epiphanes. This view also suffers in not respecting the symbolic significance of John's use of seven throughout the book. Also, how can these kings (kingdoms) survive the destruction of the harlot and be pictured as mourning over her demise (18:9)? And what sense can be made of the fact that the seventh king (kingdom), usually identified with Antichrist, is separate from the eighth one, which is clearly identified with the beast (vv.10b-11)?

A convincing interpretation of the seven kings must do justice to three considerations: (1) Since the heads belong to the beast, the interpretation must relate their significance to this beast, not to Babylon. (2) Since the primary imagery of kingship in Revelation is a feature of the power conflict between the Lamb and the beast and between those who share the rule of these two enemies (cf. 17:14; 19:19), the kind of sovereignty expressed in v.10 must be the true antithesis to the kind of sovereignty exercised by Christ and his followers. (3) Since the kings are closely related to the seven mountains and to the prostitute, the nature of the relationship between these must be clarified by the interpretation. If we can see that the seven heads do not represent a quantitative measure but show qualitatively the fullness of evil power residing in the beast, then the falling of five heads conveys the message of a significant victory over the beast. The image of a sovereignty falling is better related to God's judgment on a power than to a succession of kings (kingdoms) (cf. Jer 50:32; 51:8, 49; Rev 14:8; 18:2).

The imagery of the seven heads presented in 12:3 and 13:1 must be restudied. An ancient seal showing a seven-headed chaos monster being slain well illustrates John's imagery here. In that ancient scene, the seven-headed monster is being slain by a progressive killing of its seven heads. Four of the heads are dead, killed apparently by the spear of a divine figure who is attacking the monster. His defeat seems imminent. Yet the chaos monster is still active because three heads still live. Similarly, John's message is that five of the monster's seven heads are already defeated by the power of the Lamb's death and by the identification in that death of the martyrs of Jesus (12:11). One head is now active, thus showing the reality of the beast's contemporary agents who afflict the saints; and one head remains, indicating that the battle will soon be over but not with the defeat of the contemporary evil agents. This last manifestation of the beast's blasphemous power will be short—"he must remain for a little while." This statement seems to go with the function of the ten horns (kings) who for "one hour" (v. 12) will rule with the beast. The seventh king (head) represents the final short display of satanic evil before the divine blow falls on the beast (cf. 12:12c; 20:3c).

11 This verse presents all interpreters with a real difficulty. One interpretation refers the language to the Nero redivivus myth (see comments on 13:1–18)—namely, that a revived Nero will be the reincarnation of the evil genius of the whole Roman Empire. Furthermore, among futurist interpreters there is no agreement as to whether the seventh or the eighth king is the Antichrist. It must be admitted that any king (kingdom) succession hypothesis founders on v.11. On the other hand, if John has in mind qualitative identification and not quantitative, a theological rather than historical or political sense, the passage may yield further insight into the mystery of the beast.

First, we note the strange (to us) manner in which the sequence of seven kings gives way to the eighth, which is really the whole beast. This pattern of seven-to-eight-equals-one was familiar to the early church. The eighth day was the day of the resurrection of Christ, Sunday. It was also the beginning of a new week. The seventh day, the Jewish Sabbath, is held over, to be replaced by the first of a new series, namely Sunday. In fact, the whole theme of the Apocalypse is integrally related to this idea. Sunday is the day of the Resurrection. Revelation deals with one week, extending from Christ's resurrection to the general resurrection, when death is destroyed.

Each of the series of sevens in the book, except for the seven churches, follows a pattern of the seventh in the series becoming the first of a new series; thus seven to eight equals one. The eighth was the day of the Messiah, the day of the new age and the sign of the victory over the forces of evil. But does this provide a key to interpret the symbolism of the chaos monster? Of the three stages of the beast—was, is not, will come—only the last is related to his coming "up out of the Abyss" (v.8). These words appear to be the equivalent of the beast's healed wound (plague) mentioned in 13:3, 14. While, on the one hand, Christ has killed the monster by his death (Ge 3:15; Rev 12:7–9) and for believers he "is not" (has no power), yet, on the other hand, the beast still has life ("one is" [v.10]) and will attempt one final battle against the Lamb and his followers ("the other has not yet come . . . he must remain for a little while"). In order to recruit as many as possible for his side of the war, the beast will imitate the resurrection of Christ (he "is an eighth king" [v.11]) and will give the appearance that he is alive and in control of the world (cf. Lk 4:5–7). But John quickly adds, for the pastoral comfort of God's people, that the beast belongs to the seven, i.e., qualitatively not numerically (as if he were a former king revived); he is in reality not a new beginning of life (such as the resurrected Christ) but a part of the seven-headed monster that has been slain by Christ and, therefore, he goes "to his destruction." While this imagery may seem to us to be unnecessarily obscure, it reveals the true mystery of the beast in a fashion that exposes the dynamics of satanic deception so that every Christian may be forearmed.

12–14 Here John seems to allude to Da 7:7, 24. The ten horns are usually understood as either native rulers of Roman provinces or to governors of Palestine. Others see in them a ten-nation confederacy of the future revived Roman Empire. There are good reasons for abandoning these explanations. In the first place, the number ten should—like most of John's numbers—be understood symbolically. Ten symbolizes a repeated number of times or an indefinite number. It is perhaps another number like seven, indicating fullness (Ne 4:12; Da 1:12; Rev 2:10). Thus the number should not be understood as referring specifically to ten kings (kingdoms) but as indicating the multiplicity of sovereignties in confederacy that enhance the power of the beast.

Second, since these kings enter into a power conflict with the Lamb and his followers (v.14), the kind of sovereignty they exercise must be the true antithesis of the kind of sovereignty the Lamb and his followers exercise. These rulers as well as the beast with which they are allied can be no other than the principalities and powers, the rulers of the darkness of this world, the spiritual forces of evil in the heavenly realms that Paul describes as the true enemies of Jesus' followers (Eph 6:12). To be sure, they use earthly instruments, but their reality is far greater than any specific historical equivalents. These "kings" embody the fullness of Satan's attack against the Lamb in the great final showdown. They are the "kings from the east" (16:12–14, 16), and they are the "kings of the earth" who ally themselves with the beast in the final confrontation with the Lamb (19:19–21).

Finally, there is a link between v.12 and v.11. The ten kings are said to receive authority for "one hour" along with the beast. This corresponds to the "little while" of the seventh king. From the viewpoint of the saints, who will be greatly persecuted, this promise of brevity brings comfort. These kings have "one purpose": they agree to oppose the Lamb. But the Lamb will overcome them because he is Lord of lords and King of kings (cf. Dt 10:17; Da 2:47; Rev 19:16). He conquers by his death, and those who are with him also aid in the defeat of the beast by their loyalty to the Lamb even to death (cf. 5:5, 9; 12:11).

15 On first reading, this verse seems out of place. However, closer examination shows that v.16 also refers to the prostitute and the horns. Verse 15 teaches that the influence of the idolatrous satanic system of Babylon is universal (cf. vv.1–2) and embraces all peoples, from the humblest to the kings of the earth.

16–17 On these verses the Roman hypothesis (empire and city) breaks down, for in that view the emperors (the beast and its heads) turn against the city or empire and destroy her. What is being taught by the attack on the prostitute is that in the final judgment the kingdom of Satan will be divided against itself. The references to the prostitute being hated by her former lovers, stripped naked, and burned with fire are reminiscent of the OT prophets' descriptions of the divine judgment falling on the harlot cities of Jerusalem and Tyre (e.g., Eze 16:39–40; 23:25–27; 28:18). The description of the punishment of convicted prostitutes who are priests' daughters (cf. Lev 21:9) is combined with the picture of judgment against rebellious cities (18:8).

In the declaration "God has put it into their hearts to accomplish his purpose," there is another indication of God's use of the forces of evil as instruments of his own purposes of judgment (Jer 25:9–14; cf. Lk 20:18). Nothing will distract them from their united effort to destroy the prostitute until God's purposes given through the prophets are fulfilled (cf. 10:7; 11:18).

18 The "woman" and "the great city" are one. Yet this city is not just a historical one; it is the *great* city, the *mother* city, the archetype of every evil system opposed to God in history (see comments on 17:1–18). Her kingdom holds sway over the powers of the earth. The cities in Revelation are communities, of which there are only two: the city of God, the New Jerusalem (3:12; 21:2, 10; 22:2ff.), and the city of Satan, Babylon the Great (11:8; 14:8; 16:19; 18:4, 20; et al.). The meaning cannot be confined to any earthly cities. Instead, John describes the real transhistorical system of satanic evil that infuses them all.

4. The fall of Babylon the Great (18:1–24)

This chapter contains a full description of the previously announced "punishment" (lit., "judgment"; GK *3210*) of the prostitute (17:1). It is important not to separate this chapter from the portrayal of the prostitute in ch. 17, for there is no warrant in making the prostitute different from the city in ch. 18 (cf. 17:18). Under the imagery of the destruction of the great commercial city, John describes the final overthrow of the great prostitute, Babylon. We stress again that he is not writing a literal description of the fall of an earthly city; rather, he describes God's judgment on the great satanic system of evil that has corrupted the earth's history. Drawing especially from the OT accounts of the destruction of the ancient harlot cities of Babylon (Isa 13:21; 47:7–9; Jer 50–51) and Tyre (Eze 26–27), John composes a great threnody that has some of the most beautifully cadenced language in the whole book. He combines the song of triumph and the wailing strains of lamentation into a noble funeral dirge (cf. 2Sa 1:17–27; Isa 14:4–21; Lamentations).

First, there is a kind of prelude in which the whole judgment is proclaimed (vv. 1–3). Then comes a call for the people of God to separate themselves from the city because the divine plagues are about to descend upon her in recompense for her crimes (vv.4–8). The main movement that expresses the laments for the city's fall is divided into three parts: (1) the lament of the kings of the earth (vv.9–10), then (2) the lament of the merchants who traded with her (vv. 11–17), and (3) the lament of the sea captains who became rich from the cargoes they took to the city (vv. 18–20). The finale sounds the death knell of the city because she deceived the nations and killed God's people (vv.21–24).

1–3 So magnificent is the event about to be enacted that a dazzling angel of glory bears the divine news. Perhaps we can associate this glory with the Shekinah glory that, in Ezekiel's vision, departed from the temple because of Israelite harlotry (Eze 11:23) but later returned to the restored temple (Eze 43:2).

In words similar to those of the prophets who encouraged the people of God as they faced ancient Babylon, the angel announces that Babylon the Great, Mother of all the earthly prostitute cities, has fallen (cf. Isa 21:9; 23:17; Jer 51:8 with Rev 14:8; 18:2), using words reminiscent of the judgment announced against ancient Babylon (Isa 13:19–22; 34:11; Jer 50:39). "Demons" (GK *1228*) are associated elsewhere with idolatry (see comments on 9:20 and 16:14). The "haunt" (GK *5871*) is a watchtower; the evil spirits, watching over fallen Babylon like night birds or harpies waiting for their prey, build their nests in the broken towers that rise from the ashes of the city. She who was a great city has become a desert.

The prostitute city will be judged because of her surfeit of fornication (v.3). The thought of 17:2 is expanded as we hear echoes of the judgments on ancient Tyre and Babylon. One of the great sins of Babylon was her luxury (cf. 18:7, 9). Because wealth may lead to pride, the prophets and John view surfeit as a manifestation of Babylon (Rev 18:7; cf. Eze 28:4–5, 16–18).

4–8 "Come out of her, my people" forms the burden of Jeremiah's refrain concerning Babylon (Jer 50:8; 51:6–9; cf. Isa 48:20; 52:11; 2Co 6:17). Even in its OT setting, this was no mere warning to leave the actual city of Babylon, much less here in Revelation. John is burdened to exhort the churches to shun the charms and ensnarements of the queen prostitute (v.7) as her qualities are manifest in the world they live in. Wherever there are idolatry, prostitution, self-glorification, self-sufficiency, pride, complacency, reliance on luxury and wealth, avoidance of suffering, violence against life (v.24), there is Babylon. Christians are to separate themselves ideologically and physically from all the forms of Babylon (chs. 2–3). If they refuse, they will "share in her sins" and in the divine judgments. This warning is addressed to professing Christians who were being seduced by Satan through the wiles of the prostitute to abandon their loyalty to Jesus. If this occurred, Christ would be forced by their decision to blot out their names from the book of life and to include them in the plagues designed for Babylon when she is judged (cf. 3:5).

God will not forget her crimes, which are multiplied to the height of heaven (v.5; cf. Ge 18:20–21; Jer 51:9). Her punishment will fit her crimes (v.6; cf. Ps 137:8; Jer 50:15, 29; Mt 7:2). This OT principle of lex talionis is never enjoined on God's people in the NT but, as here, is reserved for God alone (Mt 5:38–42; Ro 12:17–21). "Mix her a double portion from her own cup" (cf. Ex 22:4, 7, 9; Isa 40:2) reflects both the ideas of the severity of God's judgment on those who refuse to repent and the truth that God's wrath is related to the outworking of sin (cf. Ro 1:24–32).

Babylon's threefold web of sin is described as satiety ("luxury"), pride ("boasts, I sit as a queen"), and avoidance of suffering ("I will never mourn"). These three may be interrelated. Luxury leads to boastful self-sufficiency (Eze 28:5), while the desire to avoid suffering leads to the dishonest pursuit of luxury (Eze 28:18). "I sit as a queen" echoes Isaiah's description of judgment on Babylon (Isa 47:7ff.) and Ezekiel's description of Tyre (Eze 27:3). As she avoided grief through her satiety, her punishment therefore is "mourning and famine." Like ancient Babylon, this queen of prostitutes will become unloved and barren (Isa 47:9). In spite of her many charms (v.23c), she will be powerless to avert her destruction (v.8). The words "consumed by fire" (cf. 17:16) may refer to the destruction of a city (cf. vv.9, 18) or to the OT punishment for prostitution if the woman is a priest's daughter (Lev 21:9). As strong as "Babylon the Great" is, the Lord God is stronger and will judge her.

9–19 Even quick reading of Eze 27 shows that John has in mind Ezekiel's lamentation over the fall of ancient Tyre. Those who entered into fornication with the great mother prostitute wail over her destruction. John describes the end of the great symbol of evil, Babylon the Great.

First, the kings of the earth cry out their dirge (vv. 9–10). There is a connection between their adultery with Babylon and their sharing of her luxury, as if sharing her luxury was part of their adultery (cf. Eze 26:16; 27:30–35). So great is the heat and smoke of her burning that they must stand "far off" (v.10). Though ultimately the kings are all the heavenly powers that rule in the affairs of earthly kings and kingdoms (see comments on 17:10, 14; cf. 1Co 2:6, 8), here they are the princes who bewail the collapse of the last great city of humankind under Satan's rule. The lament "Woe! Woe, O great city" (cf. 8:13; 9:12; 11:14; 12:12) is repeated three times in this part of the threnody over Babylon and reflects pain at the suddenness of her downfall (cf. vv.8, 17) and the emptiness of their own existence apart from her.

The merchants wail (vv.11–17). They have most to lose because Babylon the Great was built on luxury. The lists that follow are inventories of exotic items reminiscent of the great Oriental marketplaces. In v.13 "bodies and souls of men" requires special mention: "Bodies" (GK 5393) is a Greek idiom for slaves, while "souls" (GK 6034) means essentially persons. Thus the whole expression means "slaves, that is, human beings." The refrain (v.16) also shows the blending of the prostitute image of ch. 17 ("dressed in fine linen," etc.; cf. 17:4) and the city image of ch. 18 ("O great city").

Finally, in vv.17–19 the sea captains and sailors add their lament because they too suffer irreparable loss because of the city's burning (cf. Eze 27:28). This language is more appropriate to Tyre as a great port city than to the inland city Rome (it had Ostia as its port). But again, John did not intend to describe any one city but the great harlot city, the archetype of all evil cities.

20 The threefold lament is balanced by a song of heavenly jubilation. Babylon has also persecuted the church of Jesus (saints, apostles, prophets). Regarding "apostles," John may have had in mind Herod's martyrdom of James (Ac 12:1–2) or Rome's killing of Peter and Paul (cf. v.24). The picture of Babylon cannot, however, be confined to the political activity of Rome. Therefore, John attributes the deaths of the martyrs to Babylon the Great. It is she who has killed Jesus (11:7–8) and Stephen by the hands of unbelieving Jews (Ac 7:57–60) and the martyr Antipas by the hands of pagan cultists (2:13; cf. Mt 23:34–37).

21–24 The final lament over the fall of Babylon, spoken by an angel, is poignant and beautiful. A mighty angel picks up a huge stone like a giant millstone (four to five feet in diameter, one foot thick, and weighing thousands of pounds) and flings it into the sea. One quick gesture becomes a parable of the whole judgment on Babylon the Great! Suddenly she is gone forever (cf. Jer 51:64; Eze 26:21), leaving only melancholy behind.

All nations were "led astray" (GK 4414) by her "magic spell" (GK 5758), a word previously used in conjunction with "murders," "fornicators," and "thefts" (see comment on 9:21). An element of drugging is involved that results in fatal poisoning. With her deceit, Babylon had charmed the nations (cf. Na 3:4).

In the final verse, the great sin of Babylon is cited. She has martyred the prophets and followers of Jesus. John has already mentioned this blood-guiltiness (17:6; cf. 19:2). Elsewhere the death of martyrs is attributed to "the inhabitants of the earth" (6:10), the "beast that comes up from the Abyss" (11:7, 13:7), and the "beast, coming out of the earth" (13:15). In the OT, the city of Jerusalem (Eze 24:6, 9; cf. Mt 23:37) and Babylon (Jer 51:35) are called cities of bloodshed. In v.24 "the blood ... of all who have been killed on the earth" refers to all those who have been martyred because of their loyalty to the true God. Once again, in John's mind, Babylon the Great encompasses all the persecution against the servants of God until his words are fulfilled (cf. 17:17).

5. Thanksgiving for the destruction of Babylon (19:1–5)

In stark contrast to the laments of Babylon's consorts, the heavenly choirs burst forth in a great liturgy of celebration to God.

In vv.1–5, we hear four shouts of praise for the fall of Babylon. First, there is the sound of a great multitude praising God for his condemnation of the prostitute (vv.1–2). Then they shout out in celebration of the city's eternal destruction (v.3). Following this, we hear in antiphonal response the voices of the twenty-four elders and the four living creatures (v.4). Finally, a voice from the throne calls on all the servants of God to praise him (v.5).

1–2 The English word "Hallelujah" (GK 252) transliterates a Greek word, which in turn transliterates the Hebrew *hallelu yah*, meaning "Praise the LORD!" This transliteration occurs only here in the NT (vv.1, 3, 4, 6), but in the LXX it is a frequent title for certain of the psalms (Pss 111: 1; 112:1; 113:1; et al.). This phenomenon clearly illustrates the connection of the early church's liturgical worship with the synagogue and temple worship of the first century. These praise psalms formed an important part of Jewish festival celebrations.

The Hallel is the name especially applied to Pss 113–118 (also called "The Hallel of Egypt" because of the references in them to the Exodus). They had a special role in the Feast of Passover. Most Jewish sources associate the Hallel with the destruction of the wicked, exactly as this passage in Revelation does. These psalms were what Jesus and the disciples sang after the Passover-Eucharist celebration, before going out to the Mount of Olives the night before his death (Mt 26:30). This close connection between the Hallel, Passover Lamb, and the death of Jesus no doubt explains why all the early church liturgies incorporated the Hallel into the Easter and Easter Week liturgies, which celebrate the gospel of redemption from sin, Satan, and death in the victorious triumph of Christ, our Passover. Two texts in the great Hallel (Pss 113:1; 115:13) are unmistakably cited in 19:5.

The theme of "salvation" (GK 5401) has already been sounded in Revelation in connection with victory or divine justice (7:10; 12:10). God has indeed vindicated the injustice visited on his servants by meting out true justice on the great prostitute, Babylon. She deserves the sentence because she corrupted the earth (cf. 11:18; Jer 51:25) and killed the saints of God (cf. 18:24).

3 The second Hallel supplements the first one. Babylon's permanent end is celebrated in words reminiscent of ancient Babylon's judgment (Isa 34:10).

4 In response to the heavenly Hallels, the twenty-four elders cry out, "Amen, Hallelujah" (cf. comments on 1:7 regarding "Amen" and on 4:4 regarding the elders).

5 This final praise is spoken by a single voice from the throne (cf. 16:17). The voice is probably neither that of God nor of Christ because of the words "*our* Lord God Almighty reigns" (v.6). "Praise our God, all you his servants" reflects Ps 113:1; "you who fear him, both small and great" reflects Ps 115:13 (cf. Ps 135:1, 20). All socio-economic distinctions are transcended in the united worship of the church (cf. 11:18; 13:16; 19:18; 20:12).

6. Thanksgiving for the marriage of the Lamb (19:6–10)

6–8 Finally, the cycle of praise is completed with the reverberating sounds of another great multitude. If the multitude in v.1 was angelic, then this one would most certainly be the great redeemed throngs (cf. 7:9). They utter the final Hallel in words reminiscent of the great kingship psalms (93:1; 97:1; 99:1). It is also the prelude to Pss 95–99, which are messianic, and has as its theme the eternal sovereignty of God who will conquer all his enemies. "Reigns" (GK 996) may better be rendered "has begun to reign."

There is also rejoicing because the "wedding of the Lamb has come, and his bride has made herself ready" (v.7). This is John's way of giving us a glimmer of the next great vision at the close of the former one (cf. 21:2, 9). Contrast the prostitute and her immoral lovers in the preceding chapters with the Lamb and his chaste bride ("fine linen, bright and clean").

The bride is the heavenly city, the New Jerusalem (21:2, 9), which is the symbol of the church, the bride of Christ, the community of those redeemed by Christ's blood. The wedding imagery was for the Jews a familiar image of the kingdom of God. Jesus used wedding and banquet imagery in his parables of the kingdom (Mt 22:2ff.; 25:1–13; Lk 14:15–24). The OT used this figure for the bride of Israel (Eze 16:1ff.; Hos 2:19), and NT writers applied it to the church (2Co 11:2; Eph 5:25ff.). Heaven's rejoicing has signaled the defeat of all God's enemies. The time of betrothal has ended. Now it is the time for the church to enter into her full experience of salvation and glory with her beloved spouse, Christ. The fuller revelation of the realization of this union is described in chs. 21–22.

The church's garments are white linen—in marked contrast to the purple and scarlet clothing of the great mother of prostitutes (17:4; 18:16). Linen was an expensive cloth used to make the garments worn by priests and royalty. It has two qualities: brightness and cleanness (cf. 16:6). "Bright" (GK *3287*) is the color of radiant whiteness that depicts glorification (cf. Mt 13:43). "Clean" (GK *2754*) reflects purity, loyalty, and faithfulness, the character of the New Jerusalem (21:18, 21).

An explanatory interjection, probably added by John, states that "fine linen stands for the righteous acts of the saints." These "righteous acts" (GK *1468*) do not imply any kind of meritorious works that would bring salvation. Rather, there is a delicate balance between grace and obedient response to it. The bride is "given" the garments, but she "has made herself ready" for the wedding by faithfulness and loyalty to Christ (cf. 3:4–5, 18). In the parable of the man without a wedding garment, the garment he lacked was probably a clean one supplied by the host but either refused or soiled through his carelessness. The clean garment probably symbolizes repentance and obedient response to Christ (see comment on 12:11). Thus John contrasts the faithful disciples of Jesus, who have been true to God, with those who were seduced by the beast and the prostitute.

9–10 This beatitude is the fourth of seven (1:3; 14:13; 16:15; 20:6; 22:7, 14) in Revelation. Each one has a subtle contrast to those who are not loyal followers of the Lamb. The word "invited" (lit., "called"; GK *2813*) is used in the NT of the call to salvation (e.g., Mt 9:13; Ro 8:30; 9:24; 1Co 1:9; 2Th 2:14), though it may also mean "invited," with no connotation of election (cf. Mt 22:3, 8; Lk 14:16; Jn 2:2). A wedding supper began toward evening on the wedding day, lasted for many days, and was a time of great jubilation. Here in Revelation, the wedding is the beginning of the earthly kingdom of God, the bride is the church in all her purity, and the invited guests are both the bride and the people who have committed themselves to Jesus.

To assure John and his readers of the certainty of the end of the great prostitute and the announcement of the wedding supper of the Lamb, the angel adds, "These are the true words of God" (cf. 1:2; 17:17; 21:5). A similar sentence later seems to give the same assurance for the whole book (22:6).

John, who was himself a prophet and who had received clear revelation about idolatry, now falls prey to this temptation (cf. also 22:8). Whether John included these references to his own failure because he knew of the tendency toward angel worship in the churches of Asia is not clear. Be that as it may, we need to recognize how easy it is to fall into idolatry. Whenever Christians give anyone or anything other than God control of their lives, they have broken the first commandment. The "testimony of Jesus" is Jesus' own testimony that he bore in his life and teaching and especially in his death (see comments on 1:2, 9; cf. 6:9; 12:11; 14:12; 20:4). Those who hold to or proclaim this testimony are Christian prophets. Thus "the testimony of Jesus is the spirit of prophecy." The words spoken by the Christian prophets come from the Spirit of God, who is the Spirit of the risen Jesus.

IV. Vision of the Return of Christ and the Consummation of This Age (19:11–20:15)

A. The Rider on the White Horse and the Defeat of the Beast (19:11–21)

This new vision is introduced by the words "I saw heaven standing open." Earlier John had seen a door standing open in heaven (4:1), the temple in heaven standing open (11:19), and now, in preparation for a revelation of God's sovereignty, he sees heaven itself flung wide open (cf. Eze 1:1). In one sense, this vision, which depicts the return of Christ and the overthrow of the beast, may be viewed as the climax of the previous section (vv.1–10) or as the first of a final series of seven last things: the return of Christ; the destruction of the beast; the binding of Satan; the Millennium; the destruction of Satan; the last judgment; and the new heaven, new earth, and New Jerusalem.

For the most part, all interpreters have seen in vv.11–16 a description of the Second

Coming of Christ—an event to which the NT bears a frequent and unified witness. As for the features of this event, they are variously understood by interpreters.

11 The great vision that begins here reminds us of the first vision of the book (1:12ff.), though its function is entirely different. The whole scene looks alternately to the OT and to the previous references in Revelation to Christ, especially in the seven letters (chs. 2–3). A white horse with a rider has appeared at 6:1 (see comment). Both white horses represent conquest or victory, but with that the similarity ends. The rider here is "faithful and true" (cf. 1:5; 3:7, 14), in contrast to the forces of Antichrist with their empty promises and lies. Christ will keep his word to the churches. In contrast to those who pervert justice and wage unjust war, John says of Christ, "With justice he judges and makes war [GK *4482*]," an allusion to the messianic character described in Isa 11:3ff. The questions in 13:4, "Who is like the beast? Who can make war [GK *4482*] against him?" anticipate the answer that Christ alone can do this, while in 17:14 the beast and the ten kings "make war" (GK *4482*) against the Lamb.

Though John uses OT language descriptive of a warrior-Messiah, he does not depict Christ as a great military warrior battling against earth's sovereigns. The close proximity in v.11 of "justice" and "war" shows us that the kind of warfare Christ engages in is more the execution of "justice" (lit., "righteousness"; GK *1466*) than a military conflict. He who is the faithful and true witness will judge the rebellious nations.

12 The reference to the blazing eyes connects this vision with that of 1:14 (cf. 2:18). On his head are not just seven crowns (12:3), or ten (13:1), but "many crowns" of royalty (GK *1343*). Perhaps they signify that the royal power to rule the world has now passed to Christ by virtue of the victory of his followers (11:15).

So great is Christ's power that his name is known only by himself. Knowledge of a name is in antiquity associated with the power of the god. When a name becomes known, then the power is shared with those to whom the disclosure is made (cf. comment on 2:17). But since two names of Christ are revealed in this vision—"the Word of God" (v.13) and "KING OF KINGS AND LORD OF LORDS" (v.16)—it may be concluded that the exclusive power of Christ over all creation is now to be shared with his faithful followers (3:21; 5:10; 22:5). On the other hand, the secret name may be one that will not be revealed till Christ's return.

13 The imagery in this verse has traditionally been related to Isa 63:1–6, a passage understood messianically by the Jews and one that John has used in portraying God's wrath in 14:9–11, 17–19. Isaiah pictures a mighty warrior-Messiah who slaughters his enemies. Their life-blood splashes on his clothing as he tramples them down in his anger, just as the juice of grapes splashes on the wine-treader in the winepress. But is Christ's blood-dipped robe red from his enemies' blood or from his own blood? There are good reasons for accepting the latter. If the blood is his enemies', how is it that Christ comes from heaven with his robe already dipped in blood before any battle is mentioned? Moreover, the blood mentioned in connection with Christ in the Apocalypse is always his own life-blood (1:5; 5:6, 9; 7:14; 12:11). The word "dipped" (GK *970*) does not fit the imagery of Isa 63:2; but it does fit that used in Revelation of believers' garments being washed thoroughly in Christ's blood (7:14; 22:14). Finally, the sword with which Christ strikes down the nations comes from his mouth and is not in his hand (v.15); this too is incompatible with battle imagery.

Applying the expression "the Word of God" to Jesus in a personal sense is peculiar to the Johannine writings (Jn 1:1, 14; cf. 1Jn 1:1). In Revelation "the Word of God" refers to the revelation of God's purpose (1:2; 17:17; 19:9). It is also the message and lifestyle for which the saints suffer oppression and even death (1:9; 6:9; 20:4). The adjectives "true and faithful," applied to Christ, are likewise identified with the Word of God (19:9; 21:5; 22:6; cf. 1:5; 3:14; 19:11). Thus Jesus in his earthly life bore reliable and consistent witness in all his words and actions to the purposes of God and was completely obedient in doing this. In him the will of God found full expression. The Word of God and the person of Christ are one.

14 This verse seems somewhat parenthetical because it does not refer directly to Christ's person or his actions. The armies of heaven mounted on white horses may be angelic hosts, since both OT and NT speak of the armies of heaven as angels (Pss 103:21; 148:2; Lk 2:13; Ac 7:42). Furthermore, the NT also associates the coming of Christ with angels (e.g., Mt 13:41; 16:27; 24:30–31). On the other hand, this may not be John's meaning. These soldiers, like their leader, are riding white horses of victory—something hardly true of angels. Their clothing of bright and clean linen is identical to the bride's attire (cf. v.8). Thus human victors probably accompany Christ, either all of them (resurrected and raptured [1Th 4:16–17]) or the company of the martyrs. In 17:14, John writes that the Lamb will overcome the beast and the ten kings "because he is Lord of lords and King of kings—*and with him will be his called, chosen and faithful followers*" (italics added; cf. 15:1–2).

15 There are three OT allusions to the warrior-Messiah in this verse: he strikes down the nations (Isa 11:3ff.); he rules them with an iron rod (Ps 2:9; see comments on 2:27); he tramples out the winepress of God's wrath (Isa 63:1–6; see comment on v.13; also on 14:17ff.). In the first allusion, there are significant changes in imagery. Here the Lamb-Messiah does not wield a sword in his hand, but his sword comes from his mouth (cf. comments on 1:16 and 2:16). This has no OT parallel and cannot be accidental, since John emphasizes it so much (1:16; 2:12, 16; 19:15, 21). Christ conquers by the power of his word, the instrument of both his judgment and his salvation (Mt 12:37; Jn 12:48).

16 This third name of Christ, which all can read, is displayed on that most exposed part of his cloak, the part that covers the thigh, where it cannot escape notice. The name has already appeared attached to the Lamb (17:14). He is the absolute Lord and King, full of the divine power and authority.

17–18 This section brings us to the anticipated confrontation between the beast and his soldiers and the Lamb (vv.17–21; cf. 16:12–16; 17:14; see comment on 19:11–21). First, there is the summons to the vultures to come to God's great supper and gorge themselves on the slain corpses of the battlefield—a horrible picture of human carnage. The language is borrowed from Eze 39:17ff., which describes the eschatological overthrow of Gog. It may be unnecessary to press the literalness of the description. This battlefield language is designed to indicate that a great victory is about to occur.

19–21 The contrast between the assembling of the beast's might with his kings and their soldiers and the ease by which he is defeated and captured highlight the beast's powerlessness before his mighty conqueror. The "kings of the earth" refer to the ten horns (kings) of the beast, which is another way of describing the beast's power (see comments on 17:12–14). Both the beast and the false prophet (13:1ff.) are seized and thrown into the lake of fire. Their followers fall before the sword (i.e., the word) of Christ. No battle is fought; only the arrangement of the foes and the defeat of the beast is described. John may be indicating that the battle has already been fought and won. In ch. 5 the Lamb had won the victory by his death (5:5, 9). Further, in the battle in heaven, Satan was cast out and defeated by the blood of the Lamb and the word of his followers' testimony (12:7–9, 11).

There thus seems to be only one actual battle described in Revelation (ch. 12), and these further scenes may be understood as more judicial in character than as literal battles. Because of John's christological reinterpretation, no great final military battle will actually be fought, for the decisive battle has already been won at the Cross. These armies and the beast, who destroy the earth (11:18) are the satanic principalities of the world and have been positionally defeated at the Cross (Jn 12:31; 16:11; Col 2:15). But they will be stripped of all power at Christ's return—though John did not deny that Satan and his evil powers promulgate great evil and deception in the world in the present age (cf. Eph 2:2; 1Th 3:5; 1Pe 5:8–9; Rev 2:10), allying themselves with their human puppets to harass Christians. Yet he is a deposed ruler who is now under the sovereign authority of Christ but who for a "little time" is allowed to continue his evil until God's purposes are finished. In the defeat of the beast, his kings, and their armies, John shows us the ultimate and swift downfall of these evil powers by the King of kings and Lord of lords. They have met their Master in this final confrontation. On the "lake of fire," see comment on 20:14.

REVELATION 19

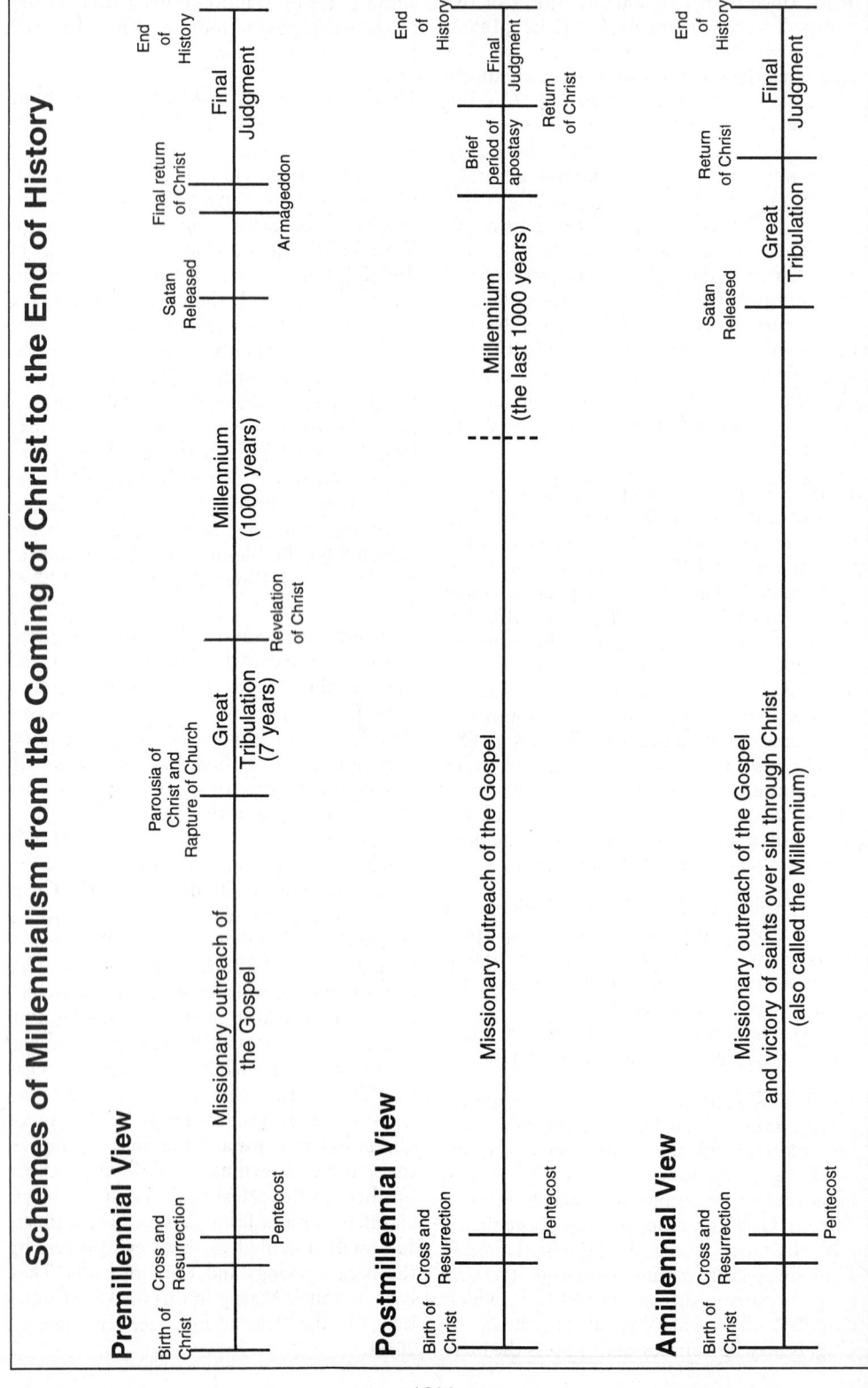

B. Binding of Satan and the Millennium (20:1–6)

This passage on the Millennium is a constant source of insurmountable difficulty for the exegete. The Millennium itself is one of the most controversial questions of eschatology (the doctrine of the last things). While the OT and later Jewish literature point forward to a time when the kingdom of God will be manifest in the world, nowhere is the time of the reign of the Messiah stated to be a thousand years.

My exegesis of the passage leads me to a premillennial interpretation. It should be recognized, however, that there are problems with this view of 20:1–6, just as there are problems with other views of this difficult portion of the book; responsible Christian scholars vary in its interpretation according to their convictions and presuppositions.

For the moment the question of the duration of the reign of Christ (which is equal to the duration of the binding of Satan) may be delayed. The main problem concerns whether the reference to a Millennium indicates an earthly historical reign of peace that will manifest itself at the close of this present age or the whole passage symbolizes some present experience of Christians or some future nonhistorical reality.

The ancient church down to the time of Augustine (354–430) (though not without minor exceptions) unquestionably held to the teaching of an earthly, historical reign of peace that was to follow the defeat of Antichrist and the physical resurrection of the saints but precede both the judgment and the new creation. To be sure, there were various positions as to the material nature of the Millennium (see comments on v.4), but the true conception of the thousand years was a balance between the worldly aspects of the kingdom and its spiritual aspects as a reign with Christ.

The break with this earlier position came with the views of the late fourth-century interpreter Tyconius, who developed a view of the Millennium based on the recapitulation method of interpretation of Origen. He viewed Revelation as containing a number of different visions that repeated basic themes throughout the book. Though his original work is not available, his exegesis of the Apocalypse can be largely reconstructed through Augustine, as well as Tyconius's many Roman Catholic followers. In ch. 20, he interpreted the thousand years in nonliteral terms and understood it as the church age, the time between the first and second advents of Christ. Tyconius interpreted the first resurrection as the resurrection of the soul from spiritual death to the new life, while the second resurrection was the resurrection of the body at the end of history. The binding of Satan had already taken place in that the devil cannot seduce the church during the present age. Moreover, the reign of the saints and their "thrones of judgment" had already begun in the church and its rulers. Augustine adopted this same view against the expectation of a literal millennial kingdom for a thousand years. This interpretation is the first main option in modern nonmillennial (or amillennial) interpretations of Rev 20.

Augustine's approach, however, was not to remain unchallenged. Joachim of Floris (c. 1135–1202) saw in Revelation a prophecy of the events of Western history from the time of Christ till the end. He thought the Millennium was still future in his time but soon to begin. The Franciscans, who followed Joachim, identified Babylon with ecclesiastical Rome and the Antichrist with the papacy. The Reformers followed suit.

During Reformation times, still another type of interpretation developed, expounded by a Jesuit scholar named Ribera (1537–91). He held that almost all the events described in Revelation are future and apply to the end times rather than to the history of the world or contemporary Rome and the papacy. He still, however, held to Augustine's view of the Millennium as the period between the first and second advents of Christ. But at one important point he changed Augustine's view. Instead of the Millennium taking place on earth between the advents, Ribera saw it as taking place in heaven. It is a reward for faithfulness. When the saints at any time in history are martyred, they do not perish but live and reign with Christ in heaven in the intermediate state before the final resurrection. This is the second main option today for amillennialists. John's basic message in ch. 20, according to this viewpoint, is pastoral. If Christians face the prospect of suffering death for Jesus, they should be encouraged because if they are killed, they will go to reign with him in heaven.

The Augustinian view of Rev 20 and its variant espoused by Joachim cannot be harmonized with a serious exegesis of this chapter on two important counts. (1) It founders on the statements concerning the binding of Satan (vv.1–3); (2) it must handle in an absurd fashion the statements about the coming to life of the martyrs, which cannot be exegetically understood as anything other than physical resurrection without seriously tampering with the sense of the words (cf. discussion on vv.1–4). While it is popular among certain amillennialists to view vv.1–6 as a symbolic description of the reward to be granted the martyrs on their entrance into heaven, this variation of the Augustinian exegesis, while removing the criticism that the passage refers to the present rule of Christ in the church age, fails to deal seriously with the binding of Satan and other details of the text.

There is yet another view that, though not free of problems, does more justice to the book of Revelation as a whole and to the exegesis of ch. 20 in particular. This view rejects both the Augustinian interpretation that the Millennium is the rule of Christ during this dispensation and the variant of Joachim that locates the resurrection and the reign of the martyrs in heaven for an interim period before their bodily resurrection and the return of Christ. It likewise rejects the variation of Augustine's view known as postmillennialism, which teaches that the forces of Antichrist will gradually be put down and the gospel will permeate and transform the world into an interim of the reign of peace before the return of Christ.

Any view of the Millennium must account for how the reality of the divine kingdom of God has actually invaded history in Jesus Christ. The view espoused in this commentary argues that the Millennium is in history and on the earth as an eschatological reality. Much in the same manner as the kingdom of God was present in the life and ministry of Jesus—present, yet still future—so the Millennium is at once the final historical event of this age *and* the beginning of the eschatological kingdom of Christ in eternity. Christ's lordship is the larger concept, which begins now and extends into eternity. The thousand-year reign, on the other hand, belongs temporally as the final act of Christ's lordship, the act that begins with his return.

This view is called the "end-historical" view. It follows the same chronological sequence as the early church's position, i.e., Parousia—defeat of Antichrist—binding of Satan—resurrection—Millennium—the release of Satan—final judgment—new heavens and earth. It differs slightly from earlier millennialism in viewing the Millennium as an end-historical event that at the same time is the beginning of the eternal reign of Christ and the saints.

The problem as to the limits of the description of the Millennium in chs. 20–22 is a more difficult question. Some expositors believe that 21:9–22:5, 14–15 belong with 20:1–10 as a further description of the millennial reign, whereas 21:1–5 refers to the eternal state, which follows the final judgment of the dead. This approach attempts to harmonize a literal understanding of certain statements in 21:9ff. with the assumed conditions during the eternal state. References to "nations" and "kings" seem to describe an earthly kingdom better than the eternal condition (21:24, 26); references to leaves "healing" the nations (22:2) seem more likely to describe an imperfect condition than the perfected eternal state; and the blessing pronounced on those who come and eat the tree of life and a curse resting on those outside the city (22:14–15) suggest the thousand years rather than the eternal state when the wicked are in the lake of fire.

Admittedly, this solution has the advantage of giving more descriptive content to the millennial reign, but it suffers from two serious criticisms. (1) Though it rightly assigns 21:1–5 to the postmillennial New Jerusalem in the context of the new heaven and earth, it arbitrarily assigns 21:9ff. to the millennial New Jerusalem without the slightest hint from the text. Thus, there is an eternal state New Jerusalem followed immediately by a millennial New Jerusalem, both bearing the same title. This is hardly plausible. (2) This view strongly argues for historical progression in 19:11–20:15: Parousia—defeat of Antichrist—binding of Satan—the first resurrection—Millennium—the release of Satan—last judgment—new heavens and earth—and then argues for recapitulation in 21:9ff.

It seems best, therefore, to regard the sequence begun at 19:11 as running chronologically through 22:6, thus placing all the material in 21:1ff. after the Millennium. At this point, a suggestion is offered. If the Millennium is a true eschatological, historical event like the person, ministry, and resurrection of Jesus, may not 21:1ff. be viewed as the full manifestation of the kingdom of God, a partial manifestation of which will be realized in the thousand-year reign of Christ and the saints, during which time Christ will defeat all his enemies, including death (1Co 15:23–28)? Some of the same conditions described in 21:1ff. would then, at least in part, characterize the Millennium.

Finally, why the Millennium? There are at least four answers to this question: (1) During the Millennium, Christ will openly manifest his kingdom in world history; it will provide an actual demonstration of the truthfulness of the divine witness borne by Christ and his followers during his life on earth. It will be a time of the fulfillment of all God's covenant promises to his people.

(2) The Millennium will reveal that humanity's rebellion against God lies deep in one's own heart, not in the devil's deception. Even when Satan is bound and righteousness prevails in the world, some people will still rebel against God. The final release of Satan will openly draw out this hidden evil.

(3) The release of Satan after the Millennium shows the invulnerability of the city of God and the extent of the authority of Christ, since the devil is immediately defeated and cast into the lake of fire forever.

(4) The Millennium will serve as a long period required to do the "house-cleaning" needed after the preceding ages of sin.

1–3 These verses are integrally related to 19:20–21. After the destruction of the beast and his followers and of the false prophet, Satan (the dragon, the ancient serpent) is dealt with. He is thrown into the Abyss to be imprisoned there for a thousand years (the third last thing; see comment on 19:11–21). The Abyss is the demonic abode (see comment on 9:1; cf. 11:7). The angel's mission is to restrain Satan from deceiving the nations—hence the key, the chain, and the violent casting into the Abyss. That this whole action is not a recapitulation of earlier descriptions of Satan is evident from a number of points. In 12:9, Satan is "hurled" out of heaven "to the earth," where he goes forth with great fury to work his deception and persecute God's people (13:14; 18:23c). But in 20:1–3, the situation is different. Here Satan is cast out of the earth into a place where he is kept from "deceiving the nations." The former period of Satan's restriction to earth is described as a "short time" (12:9, 12), while the time here (20:1–3) of his binding is a thousand years. In the earlier references to Satan, he is active on the earth (2:10, 13; 12:17; 16:13, cf. 1Pe 5:8); here he is tightly sealed in "prison" (v.7; GK 5871). The binding of Satan removes his deceptive activity among "the nations," a term never used to describe the redeemed community (until ch. 21, after Satan's permanent end).

From at least the time of Victorinus (d. c. 303), some have interpreted the binding of Satan as the work of Christ in the lives of believers. Thus Satan is "bound" for believers since he no longer deceives them, but he is still "loose" for unbelievers who are deceived. This explanation, however, does not take seriously the language of the Abyss and the prison in which Satan is confined, nor does it account for the releasing of Satan after the thousand years. The binding of spirits or angels is mentioned in Isa 24:21–23; Jude 6, as well as in Jewish literature. In all these references there is no question of the spirits being bound in some respects and not in others; it signifies a complete removal as to a prison, usually in the depths of the underworld.

In only one NT reference is there a question as to the limited binding of Satan. In Mk 3:27 Jesus refers in his parable to the strong man first being bound before his goods can be plundered. The reference is to Satan's being bound by Christ and specifically relates either to the temptation of Jesus or to Jesus' exorcisms. In any case, the binding of Satan by the ministry of Jesus did not totally immobilize the devil but struck him a vital blow. But does the reference in Mark provide a true analogy for the binding of Satan in 20:1–3, as Augustine claimed? A careful examination of this verse and Rev 20:1–3 leads to the conclusion that the two passages are not teaching the same truth. There is a sense in which, according to the Gospel account, Satan is in the process of being bound by the activity of Christ and the kingdom of God; but this is clearly an event different from the total consigning of Satan to the Abyss.

Finally, it may be noted that the thousand-year binding of Satan is concurrent with and inseparable from the thousand-year reign of the resurrected martyrs. For a thousand years on this earth, within history, the activity of Satan leading humankind into false worship and active rebellion against God and his people will be totally curbed under the authority of Christ in his kingdom. If that reign is yet future, the binding is future. If the binding refers to an earthly situation—which it clearly does—the thousand-year reign most naturally refers to an earthly situation.

4–6 The fourth last thing (see comment on 19:11–21) is the thousand-year reign of Christ on the earth. John gives us no picture of life in the Millennium in these verses; they contain only a statement about who will participate in it. He sees thrones, and judges sitting on them. The scene is usually connected with Daniel's vision of the Son of Man (Da 7:9, 22, 27). There, justice was done for the saints by the Ancient of Days, and they began their kingdom reign. If that thought is found here, those who sit on the thrones are the angelic court. On the other hand, those on the thrones may be the resurrected martyrs who exercise judgment and rule during the Millennium. This possible reinterpretation of Daniel seems preferable in the light of other NT teaching as well as of Revelation itself (cf. Lk 22:30; 1Co 6:2; Rev 2:26). They who were once judged by earth's courts to be worthy of death are now the judges of the earth under Christ.

A more difficult question concerns the identity of those who will rule with Christ. They are the "beheaded" (with an axe) martyrs who have previously occupied John's attention (cf. 6:9). The cause of their death is attributed to their faithful witness to Jesus and the word of God (see comment on 1:9; cf. 6:9; 12:11). The reference to "souls" (GK 6034) recalls 6:9, where this word is used of the slain witnesses under the altar. It describes those who have lost their bodily life but are nevertheless still alive in God's sight. This term prepares us for their coming to (bodily) life again at the first resurrection. It is a mistake to take this word to imply a later spiritual resurrection or rebirth of the soul.

These martyrs are also those who did not worship the beast or his image or receive his mark on them (cf. 13:1ff.; 15:2); in a word, they are the followers of the Lamb. At this point, NIV omits a very important term. Between the description of those beheaded and the description concerning the beast worship in v.4 are two Greek words meaning "and who." This construction is capable of bearing two different meanings. It could simply introduce a further qualifying phrase to the identification of the martyrs (so NIV). But it may also be understood to introduce a second group. There are (1) those who were beheaded for their witness and (2) "also those who" did not worship the beast (see NASB). This immediately alleviates a thorny problem, i.e., why only the martyrs should live and reign with Christ. Usually in Revelation the specific relative pronoun "who" used here refers to the preceding group and adds some further detail (2:24; 9:4; 17:12); but in one other reference, the phrase so introduced singles out a special class or group from the more general group in the preceding statement (1:7). Thus the "and who" clause introduces a special class of the beheaded, i.e., those who were beheaded because they did not worship the beast, etc. In any case, it seems that John has only the beheaded in mind (cf. 14:13).

But this presents a problem because John has elsewhere indicated that the kingdom reign will be shared by every believer who overcomes (2:26–28; 3:12, 21) and is purchased by Christ's blood (5:10). Also, in 1Co 6:2–3, Paul clearly speaks of all believers—not just martyrs—exercising judgment in the future. Unless only those beheaded by the beast will reign in the Millennium, another explanation is demanded. There are two possible approaches. (1) The pastoral approach explains John's reference to only the martyrs as a piece of special encouragement to them, while not implying that others would be left out. (2) The other view, with which I am more comfortable (see comment on 6:9), sees the martyrs as representing the whole church that is faithful to Jesus, whether or not they have actually been killed. They constitute a group that can in truth be described as those who "did not love their lives so much as to shrink from death" (12:11). As such, the term "martyrs" is a synonym for overcomers (chs. 2-3). Thus John could count himself in this group, though he may never have suffered death by the axe of the beast. In 2:11 those who during persecution are faithful to Christ even to the point of death are promised escape from the second death, which in 20:6 is promised to those who share in the first resurrection, i.e., the beheaded (v.4). In fact, several other promises to overcomers in the letters to the seven churches find their fulfillment in ch. 20 (cf. 2:11 with 20:6; 2:26–27 with 20:4; 3:5 with 20:12, 15; 3:21 with 20:4).

The martyrs "came to life" (GK 2409). The interpretation of these words is crucial to the whole passage. Since Augustine, the majority of interpreters have taken the words to refer to new birth (a spiritual resurrection) or to the triumph of the church. This construes the historical event of physical resurrection in a symbolic way. Others, rightly, chastened by a more serious exegesis of the text, hold that the language teaches bodily resurrection but that the whole section (20:1–10) is not to be taken as predicting events within history but is apocalyptic language, figurative of the consolation and reward promised the martyrs. The verb "came to life" is used in v.4 of the martyrs and also in v.5 of the "rest of the dead." When the context is that of bodily death, this NT verb connotes physical resurrection (Jn 11:25; Ac 1:3; 9:41), even though the normal word is "raise up" (GK 1586). More importantly, Revelation clearly uses "live" for the resurrection of Christ (1:18; 2:8) and also curiously for the sea beast (13:14). John plainly says in 20:5 that this is the first "resurrection" (GK 414). The word "resurrection," which occurs over forty times in the NT, is used almost exclusively of physical resurrection (Lk 2:34 is the only exception). There is no indication that John has departed from this usage.

Why does John call this the "first" (GK 4755) resurrection? This word clearly implies the first in a series of two or more. John does not directly refer to a second resurrection, though a second resurrection is inferred both from the use of "first" and from the expression "the rest of the dead did not come to life until the thousand years were ended" (v.5). Some early interpreters connect John's first resurrection with the "resurrection of the just" (Lk 14:14). From at least the time of Augustine, the first resurrection was understood as a regeneration of the soul and the second resurrection as the general physical, bodily resurrection of just and unjust. It must, however, be insisted that it is quite weak exegesis to make the first resurrection spiritual and the second one physical, unless the text itself clearly indicates this change, which it does not.

Another response would be to understand "the rest of the dead" who lived not until the close of the thousand years to be all the faithful except the martyrs, plus the entire body of unbelievers. This view, in our opinion, runs aground on the fact that John clearly seems to tie exclusion from the second death with those who are part of the first resurrection, thus strongly implying that those who participate in the second resurrection are destined for the second death. Therefore, we may understand the first resurrection as being the raising to physical life of all the dead in Christ (cf. Jn 5:29; 1Co 15:12ff.; 1Th 4:13ff.). For those who participate in this resurrection, "the second death [the lake of fire (20:14)] has no power over them" (v.6). Therefore, they are "blessed and holy" (the fifth beatitude; see comment on 1:3) and shall be priests of God and Christ for the thousand years. On the other hand, those over whom the second death will have power must be "the rest of the dead" (v.5), who will be participants in the second resurrection, who will "rise to be condemned" (Jn 5:29; cf. Ac 24:15).

The only NT place other than 2:11 and 20:6 that mentions the second death refers to exclusion from physical resurrection (v.14). Likewise, the Palestinian Targum on Dt 33:6 reads: "Let Reuben live in this world and not die in the second death in which death the wicked die in the world to come." Here the second death means exclusion from the resurrection. Not to die the second death, then, means to rise again to eternal life.

What now may be said as to the length of the kingdom reign? Nowhere in other literature is the kingdom reign of the Messiah specified as a thousand years. Thus parallels to John's use of a thousand years must be sought elsewhere. It seems that the earliest traditions in Asia relate the thousand years to Adam's paradisiacal time span. The Book of Jubilees, for example, attempts to justify the correctness of Ge 2:17, that Adam died "on the day" that he ate of the forbidden fruit. According to Ge 5:5, his sin caused him to die at 930 years of age, "seventy years before attaining a thousand years, for one thousand years are as one day [Ps 90:4] in heaven." Thus Adam died before completing one day (a thousand years). Some believe that this is the origin of John's use of the thousand years.

Later, the thousand years began to be associated with the Jewish cosmic-week framework in which the history of the world is viewed as lasting a week of millennia, or seven thousand years. The last day millennium is the Sabbath-rest millennium, followed by the eighth day of the age to come. This idea was then linked interpretatively but inappropriately to 2Pe 3:8.

Is the thousand years symbolic of a perfect human life-span or some ideal kingdom environment on the earth? In the first place, the number symbolisms of John in Revelation should not be used to argue against an earthly kingdom. It might be said that the number is symbolic of a perfect period of time of whatever length. The essence of premillennialism is in its insistence that the reign will be on earth, not in heaven, for a period of time before the final judgment and the new heavens and earth. For example, we may rightly understand the 1,260 days (42 months) of earlier chapters as a symbolic number, but it still refers to an actual historical period of whatever length during which the beast will destroy the saints. In any case, it is not of primary importance whether the years are 365-day years or symbolic of a shorter or longer period of bliss enjoyed by believers as they reign with Christ on earth (cf. 5:10 with 11:15; 22:5).

C. The Release and End of Satan (20:7–10)

7–10 The fifth last thing (see comment on 19:11–21) is the defeat of Satan. In v.3 the release of Satan after the Millennium was anticipated: "He must [GK *1256*] be set free for a short time." Why "must" he once again be released? The answer is so that he can "deceive the nations" throughout the world and lead them into conflict against "God's people." But why should God allow this? Certainly if a human being alone were prophetically writing the history of the world, he or she would not bring the archdeceiver back after the glorious reign of Christ in vv.1–6. But God's thoughts and ways are not ours (Isa 55:8). Ezekiel's vision of Gog brought out of the land of Magog seems to be clearly in John's mind (Eze 38–39). Gog refers to the prince of a host of pagan invaders from the North, especially the Scythian hordes from the distant land of Magog. Here in Rev 20, however, the names are symbolic of the final enemies of Christ duped by Satan into attacking the community of the saints. The change in meaning has occurred historically through the frequent use in rabbinic circles of the expression "Gog and Magog" to refer to the rebellious nations spoken of in Ps 2.

If the beast and his armies are already destroyed (19:19ff.), who are these rebellious nations? It may be that the beast and his armies in the earlier context refer to the demonic powers and those in 20:7ff. to human nations in rebellion—not an unlikely solution (see comments on 19:19ff.)—or it may be that not all the people in the world will participate in the beast's armies and thus those mentioned here in v.8 refer to other people who during the millennial reign defected in their hearts from the Messiah. In any case, this section shows something of the deep, complex nature of evil. The fundamental source of rebellion against God does not lie in our environment or with the devil but springs up from deep within a person's own heart. The return of Satan will demonstrate this in the most dramatic manner once for all. The temporal reign of Christ will not be fulfilled till this final challenge to his kingdom occurs and he demonstrates the power of his victory at the Cross and puts down all his enemies (1Co 15:25).

The gathered army, which is extensive and world-wide, advances and in siege fashion encircles the "camp of God's people, the city he loves." Most commentators take the expressions "camp" and "city" as different metaphors for God's people. "Camp" (GK *4213*) in the NT refers to either a military camp or the camp of Israel (Ac 21:34, 37; 22:24; Heb 11:34; 13:11, 13). It reminds us of the pilgrim character of the people of God even at the end of the Millennium, as long as evil is active in God's creation. The "city he loves" presents more difficulty. Following standard Jewish eschatology, many understand this as a reference to the physically restored and spiritually renewed city of Jerusalem. On the other hand, John may have intended to refer merely to the community of the redeemed without any specific geographical location in mind. This would be in harmony with his previous references to the city elsewhere in the book (cf. comments on 3:12; 11:2, 8). There are only two cities or kingdoms in the Apocalypse: the city of Satan, where the beast and harlot are central, and the city of God, where God and the Lamb are central. This city, then, is the kingdom of God in its millennial manifestation; it is the same city that appears in its final, most glorious form in the last chapters (21–22). Wherever God dwells among his people, there the city of God is (21:2–3).

The swiftness and finality of the divine judgment (v.9) emphasize the reality of the victory of Christ at the Cross. The fire imagery may reflect Ezekiel's vision of the destruction of Gog (Eze 38:22; 39:6). It is God, not the saints, who destroys the enemy (cf. comment on 19:19). The devil is now dealt the long-awaited final and fatal blow (Ge 3:15; Jn 12:31). The "lake of fire" imagery is probably related to the teaching of Jesus about hell (see Mt 5:22; 7:19; 10:28; 13:49–50; see comment on Mk 9:48). This figure intensifies the idea of the permanency of judgment (cf. comment on 14:11; also 19:20; 20:11–15; 21:8). That the beast and false prophet are already there does not argue for their individuality, since later "death" and "Hades," nonpersonal entities, are personified and cast into the same lake of fire (v.14).

D. Great White Throne Judgment (20:11–15)

11–15 John describes in vivid pictures the sixth last thing (see comment on 19:11–21), the final judgment of humankind. Unlike many of the vivid, imaginative paintings based on this vision, here John describes a strange, unearthly scene. Heaven and earth flee from the unidentified figure who sits on the majestic white throne. The language of poetic imagery captures the fading character of everything of the world (1Jn 2:17). Now the only reality is God seated on the throne of judgment, before whom all must appear (Heb 9:27). His verdict alone is holy and righteous (the symbolism of "white"). Since vv.11–12 make use of the theophany of Da 7:9–10, the one seated on the throne is presumably God himself; but since 22:1, 3 mention the throne of God and of the Lamb, it may well be that here Jesus shares in the judgment (Jn 5:27). God has kept the last judgment in his own hands. This vision declares that even though it may have seemed that earth's course of history ran contrary to his holy will, no single day or hour in the world's drama has ever detracted from the absolute sovereignty of God.

But who are "the dead" (vv.12–13)? Earlier in the chapter, John has mentioned the "rest of the dead" who are not resurrected till the thousand years are completed (v.5). While no resurrection is mentioned in vv.11–15, the dead are probably those who did not participate in the first resurrection. Since the second death has no power over those who were raised in the first resurrection (v.6), only the enemies of God now stand before this throne (Jn 5:24).

A moment of tension arrives. The books are opened. It is sobering to ponder that in God's sight nothing is forgotten; all will give an account of their actions (v.13). Divine judgment always proceeds on the basis of human deeds (Mt 25:41ff.; Ro 2:6; 2Co 5:10; Heb 4:12–13), recorded in the "books" (v.12). John is probably alluding to Da 7:10. We are not told whether these books contain both good and evil works or only the latter. John is more concerned about another book, the book of life, which alone seems to be decisive (vv.12, 15; cf. 3:5; 13:8; 17:8; 21:27). How can judgment by works and eternal life given by grace be harmonized? There is no conflict. Works are the unmistakable evidence of the loyalty of the heart; they express either belief or unbelief, faithfulness or unfaithfulness. The judgment will reveal whether or not one's loyalties were with God and the Lamb or with God's enemies. John's theology of faith and its inseparable relation to works is the same as Jesus' and Paul's (Jn 5:29; Ro 2:6ff.). This judgment is not a balancing of good works over bad works. Those who have their names in the Lamb's book of life will also have records of righteous deeds. The opposite will also be true. The imagery reflects the delicate balance between grace and obedience (cf. comments on 19:6–8).

Three broad places are mentioned as containing the dead: the sea, death, and Hades (v.13). The sea represents the place of unburied bodies while death and Hades represent the reality of dying and the condition entered on at death (cf. 1:18; 6:8).

The imagery suggests release of the bodies and persons from their places of confinement following death; i.e., it portrays resurrection. They rise to receive sentence (Jn 5:29b). Death and Hades are personified (cf. 6:8) and are cast into the lake of fire, to be permanently destroyed (cf. 19:20; 20:10). This not only fulfills Paul's cry concerning the last enemy, death, which will be defeated by the victorious kingdom of Christ (1Co 15:26), but also signals the earth's new condition in 21:4.

In the final scene in this dark and fearful passage (v.15), it is clear from the specific Greek form of "if" that John uses that some people will be thrown into the lake of fire. We might paraphrase the verse: "If anyone's name was not found written in the book of life, and I assume there were such, he was thrown into the lake of fire." When taken seriously, this final note evaporates all theories of universalism.

V. Vision of the New Heaven and the New Earth and the New Jerusalem (21:1–22:5)

The seventh last thing (see comment on 19:11–21) is the vision of the new heavens, the new earth, and the New Jerusalem. Countless productions of art and music have through the ages been inspired by this vision. Cathedral architecture has been influenced by its imagery. John discloses a theology in stone and gold as pure as glass and color. Archetypal images abound. The church is called the bride (21:2). Completeness is implied in the number twelve and its multiples (21:12–14, 16–17, 21) and fullness in the cubical dimension of the city (21:16). Colorful jewels abound, as do references to light and the glory of God (21:11, 18–21, 23, 25; 22:5). There is the "river of the water of life" (22:1) and the "tree of life" (22:2). The "sea" is gone (21:1).

Most of John's imagery in this chapter reflects the New Jerusalem vision of Isa 60 and 66 and the new temple vision of Eze 40–48. The multiple OT promises converging in his mind suggest that he viewed the New Jerusalem as the fulfillment of all these strands of prophecy. There are also allusions to Ge 1—the absence of death and suffering, the dwelling of God with people as in Eden, the tree of life, the removal of the curse, etc. Creation is restored to its pristine character.

The connection of this vision with the promises to the overcomers in the letters to the seven churches (chs. 2–3) is significant. For example, to the overcomers at Ephesus was granted the right to the tree of life (2:7; cf. 22:2); to Thyatira, the right to rule the nations (2:26; cf. 22:5); to Philadelphia, the name of the city of my God, the New Jerusalem (3:12; cf. 21:2, 9ff.). In a sense, a strand from every major section of this book appears in chs. 21–22. Unique in John's theology is the Lamb's centrality in the city and the absence of a temple in the New Jerusalem.

In other NT passages, the kingdom reality of the age to come has already appeared in history in the life of Jesus and also in the presence of the Holy Spirit in the church. But the reality is now present only in a promissory way, not in actual fulfillment. Therefore, while the Jerusalem that is from above has present implications for believers (Gal 4:25–31), they are nevertheless, like Abraham, "looking forward to the city with foundations" (Heb 11:10; 13:14). In this sense, the medieval synthesis that made the church on earth and the kingdom synonymous and built its cathedrals to depict that notion was misdirected. John's vision in chs. 21–22 is one of eschatological promise, future in its realization, totally dependent on God's power to create it, yet having present implications for the life of the church in this age.

A. The New Jerusalem Introduced (21:1–8)

1 The new heavens and earth were foreseen by Isaiah (Isa 65:17) as a part of his vision of the renewed Jerusalem. John's picture of the final age to come focuses not on a platonic ideal heaven or distant paradise but on the reality of a new earth and heaven. God originally created the earth and heaven to be our permanent home. But sin and death entered the world and transformed the earth into a place of rebellion and alienation; it became enemy-occupied territory. But God has been working in salvation history to effect a total reversal of this evil consequence and to liberate earth and heaven from bondage to sin, corruption, and death (cf. v.4; Ro 8:21). John's emphasis on heaven and earth is not primarily cosmological but moral and spiritual (cf. also 2Pe 3:13).

The Greek word for "new" (GK 2785) means new in quality rather than new in time. That it is a "new" heaven and earth and not a second heaven and earth suggests something of an endless succession of new heavens and earth. It is the newness of the endless eschatological ages (2:17; 3: 12; 5:9; cf. Eph 2:7).

What makes the new heaven and earth "new" is above all the reality that now "the dwelling of God is with men.... They will be his people, and God himself will be with them and be their God" (v.3). The heaven and earth are new because of the presence of a new community of people who are loyal to God and the Lamb in contrast to the former community of idolaters.

The sea—the source of the satanic beast (13:1) and the place of the dead (20:13)—will be gone. Again, John's emphasis is not geographic but moral and spiritual. The sea serves as an archetype with connotations of evil (cf. comment on 13:1). Thus, no trace of evil in any form will be present in the new creation.

2–4 The Holy City, the New Jerusalem, occupies John's vision for the remainder of the book. First, he sees the city "coming down out of heaven from God"—a phrase used three times (3:12; 21:2, 10) in an apparent spatial reference. But the city never seems to come down; it is always in the process of descending from heaven. Therefore, the expression stresses the idea that the city is a gift of God, forever bearing the marks of his creation.

Second, John calls the city a "bride" (GK 3813; cf. 21:9, 22:17; cf. also 19:7–8, where a different word was used). The purity and devotedness of the bride are reflected in her attire. The multiple imagery is needed to portray the tremendous reality of the city. A bride-city captures something of God's personal relationship to his people (the bride) as well as something of their life in communion with him and one another (a city, with its social connotations).

The subtitle of the Holy City, "the new Jerusalem," raises a question. The "old" Jerusalem was also called the "holy city" and a "bride" (Isa 52:1; 61:10). Since the Jerusalem from above is the "new" Jerusalem, we may suppose that it is connected in some manner with the old one so that the new is the old one renewed. The old Jerusalem was marred by sin and disobedience. In it was the blood of prophets and apostles. Still worse, it became a manifestation of Babylon the Great when it crucified the Lord of glory (11:8). But the old city always involved more than the mere inhabitants and their daily lives. It represented the covenant community of God's people, the hope for the kingdom of God on earth. Thus the OT looked forward to a renewed Jerusalem, rebuilt and transformed into a glorious habitation of God and his people. But the prophets also saw something else. They saw a new heaven and new earth and a Jerusalem connected with this reality. Thus it is not altogether clear precisely what the relationship is between the old and the new, the earthly, restored Jerusalem of the prophets and the Jerusalem associated with the new heaven and earth (cf. Gal 4:25-31; Heb 11:10; 12:22; 13:14).

The key to the puzzle must be understood with due respect for the old city. Any exegesis, therefore, that completely rejects any connection with the old city cannot take seriously the name "new" Jerusalem, which presupposes the old. To speak of the heavenly Jerusalem does not deny an earthly city, as some suggest, but stresses its superiority and affirms the eschatological nature of Jewish hope—a hope that could not be fulfilled by the earthly Jerusalem but which John sees realized in the Holy City of the future. This city is the church in its future glorified existence. It is the final realization of the kingdom of God.

God's "dwelling" (GK 5008) among his people (v.3) is a fulfillment of Lev 26:11–13, a promise given to the old Jerusalem but forfeited because of apostasy. As a backdrop for the scene, consider Ge 3, when humanity lost their fellowship with God (cf. Ex 25:8; Eze 37:26–27). Thus the holy Jerusalem is not only humanity's eternal home but the city where God will place his own name forever. God's presence will blot out the things of the former creation. In a touching metaphor of motherly love, John says that God "will wipe away every tear from their eyes" (cf. 7:17; Isa 25:8). These tears have come from sin's distortion of God's purposes for the human race. God now has defeated the enemy of humankind and liberated his people and his creation.

5 For the second time in the book, God himself speaks (cf. 1:8). From his throne comes the assurance that the One who created the first heaven and earth will indeed make "everything new." This confirms that God's power will be revealed and his redemptive purposes fulfilled. Since these words are God's words (cf. 19:9; 22:6), it is important that this vision of the new heaven and the New Jerusalem be proclaimed to the churches.

6–8 Using the same word that declared the judgment of the world finished, God proclaims that he has completed his new creation: "It is done" (cf. 16:17). The names of God, "the Alpha and the Omega, the Beginning and the End," emphasize his absolute control over the world as well as his creatorship of everything (cf. comment on 1:8; see 22:13).

To those who thirst for him, God offers the "water of life" without cost (cf. 7:17; 22:1, 17; Jn 7:37–39; Ro 3:24). Here salvation is beautifully depicted by the image of drinking at the spring of life. Twice in chs. 21–22, God invites those who sense their need and are drawn toward him to come. John knows that the visions of God's glory among his people, proclaimed as the Word of God, will create a thirst to participate in the reality of this glory. Nothing is required except to come and drink.

Those who respond to this invitation and remain loyal to Christ as overcomers (see comments on 2:7, 11, et al.) will inherit all the new things of the city of God. They will be God's children, and he will be their Father. This is the essence of salvation—unending, intimate relationship with God himself (cf. Jn 17:3). For John this is really what the heavenly city is all about.

Before John shows us the city, however, he must first confront us with a choice. This choice must be made because there are two cities: the city of God and the city of Babylon, each with its inhabitants and its destiny. Those who drink from salvation's springs supplied by God himself are true followers of Christ. The "cowardly" are those who fear persecution arising from faith in Christ. Not having steadfast endurance, they are devoid of faith (Mt 8:26; Mk 4:40; cf. Mt 13:20–21). Thus they are linked by John to the "unbelieving" and "vile." They are called "murderers" because they are guilty of the death of the saints (17:6; 18:24). The "sexually immoral, those who practice magic arts, the idolaters and all liars" are those associated with idolatrous practices (cf. 9:21; 18:23; 21:27; 22:15; contrast 14:5). By their own choice, Babylon is their eternal home.

B. The New Jerusalem Described (21:9–22:5)

For reasons why this section does not describe the millennial kingdom of ch. 20, see comments on 20:1–6. John first describes the gates and the walls of the city (vv.9–14). Then the angel measures the city, and John cites the precious stones in the twelve foundations (vv. 15–21). Finally, he describes various aspects of the life of the city (21:22–22:5).

9–10 Here the parallelism with 17:1 is clearly deliberate. The bride, the wife of the Lamb, contrasts with the great prostitute, the archetypal image for the great system of satanic evil. The bride is pure and faithful to God and the Lamb, whereas the prostitute is a mockery. To see the prostitute, John was taken to the desert; now he is elevated by the Spirit to the highest pinnacle of the earth to witness the exalted New Jerusalem (cf. 1:10; 4:2; 17:3). As his vision will be a reinterpretation of Ezekiel's temple prophecy (Eze 40–48), like the former prophet, he is taken to a high mountain (Eze 40:2). For the moment, the author drops the bridal metaphor and in magnificent imagery describes the church in glory as a city with a lofty wall, splendid gates, and jeweled foundations.

11–14 In John's description of the city, precious stones, brilliant colors, and the effulgence of light abound. The problem of the literalness of the city has received much attention. If the city is the bride and the bride the glorified community of God's people in their eternal life, there is little question that John's descriptions are primarily symbolic of that glorified life. This in no way diminishes the reality behind the imagery. In the most suitable language available to John, much of it drawn from the OT, he shows us something of the reality of the eschatological kingdom of God in its glorified existence.

Its appearance is all glorious, "with the glory of God" (v.11; cf. Eze 43:4). The city has a "brilliance" (GK 5891) given it by God's presence that appears as crystal-clear jasper (Isa 60:1–2, 19; Rev 21:23). "Jasper" is mentioned three times in ch. 21 (vv.11, 18–19; cf. 4:3). This is an opaque quartz mineral and occurs in various colors, commonly red, brown, green, and yellow, rarely blue and black, and seldom white.

The wall is high, its height symbolizing the greatness of this city as well as its impregnability against those described in 21:8, 27. The twelve gates are distributed three on each of the four walls. These may be like the triple gates that can now be seen in the excavated wall of the old Jerusalem (see also v.21). What impresses John about the gates are their angel guards and the inscribed names of the twelve tribes of Israel. The presence of angels proclaims that this is God's city, while the twelve tribes emphasize the complete election of God (cf. comment on 7:4). Here is a deliberate allusion to Ezekiel's eschatological Jerusalem on whose gates the names of the twelve tribes appear (Eze 48:30–34). Ezekiel 48:35 says, "The name of the city from that time on will be: THE LORD IS THERE" (cf. Rev 21:3; 22:3–4).

Like the gates, the twelve foundations of the wall have twelve names written on them—in this case, the names of the twelve apostles of the Lamb. Foundations of ancient cities usually consisted of extensions of the rows of huge stones that made up the wall, down to the bedrock. Jerusalem's first-century walls and foundation stones have recently been excavated. Huge stones, some of which are about five feet wide, four feet high, and thirty feet long, weighing eighty to one hundred tons each going deep into the ground, have been found.

Here John stresses the names of the twelve apostles on the foundations (see also vv.19–21). Theologically, it is significant that he brings together the twelve tribes and the twelve apostles of the Lamb and yet differentiates them. This is not unlike what Matthew and Luke tell us that Jesus said (Mt 19:28; Lk 22:30). The earlier symbolic use of twelve (see comment on 7:4), representing completeness, implies that it is unnecessary for us to know precisely which twelve apostles are there. Judas fell and was replaced by Matthias (Ac 1:21–26), but Paul also was a prominent apostle. Furthermore, the number "twelve" is sometimes used to refer to the elect group when all twelve are not in view (Jn 20:24 has ten; 1Co 15:5 has eleven; cf. Lk 9:12). The apostles represent the church, the elect community built on the foundation of the gospel of Jesus Christ, the slain Lamb. The dual election here depicted admittedly entails some difficulty in identifying the twelve tribes in 7:4ff. with the church (see comments at 7:1ff.).

15–21 The angel measures the city with a golden measuring rod (see comment on 11:1). The act of measuring signifies securing something for blessing. Ezekiel's elaborate description of the future temple and its measuring was to show the glory and holiness of God in Israel's midst (Eze 43:12). The measuring reveals the perfection, fulfillment, or completion of all God's purposes for his elect bride. Thus the city is revealed as a perfect cube of twelve thousand stadia (12x1000 [about 1,400 miles]). The wall is 144 cubits (about 200 ft.) thick (12x12). These dimensions should not be interpreted as providing architectural information about the city. Rather, we should think of them as theologically symbolic of the fulfillment of all God's promises. The New Jerusalem symbolizes the paradox of the completeness of infinity in God. The cube reminds us of the dimensions of the Most Holy Place in the tabernacle (10x10 cubits [15x15 ft.]) and in the temple (20x20 cubits [30x30 ft.]). John adds that the measurement was both human and divine (v.17). In some sense both the human and the divine will intersect in the Holy City.

In vv.18–21, John describes in more detail the priceless materials of the city with its foundations and gates (cf. Isa 54:11–15). The symbolism is not meant to give the impression of wealth and luxury but to point to the glory and holiness of God. The wall of jasper points to the glory of God (4:2–3; see comment on 21:11), while the fabric of the city is pure gold—as clear as glass (v.21). Such imagery portrays the purity of the bride and her splendor in mirroring the glory of God (cf. Eph 5:27).

The foundation stones are made of twelve precious stones. Here the imagery may reflect three possible sources: (1) the high priest's breastplate (Ex 28:17–20), (2) the jewels on the dress of the king of Tyre (Eze 28:13), or (3) the signs of the zodiac. The second one, though referring to only nine stones, suggests the splendor of ancient royalty and might be appropriate as a symbol for the glorious kingdom reign in the Holy City. Yet there is something inappropriate about taking this pagan king as symbolic of the future kingdom. Others prefer the first option—that of the high priest's breastplate.

But while the twelve stones are perhaps the same, the order of their mention is different. This leaves the third option. According to Philo and Josephus, Israel associated these same stones with the signs of the zodiac, and their tribal standards each bore a sign of the zodiac. If we begin with Judah, the tribe of Christ (7:5), the sign is Aries, the Ram, which has the amethyst as its stone. The last sign is Pisces, the fishes, which has jasper as its stone. So the first zodiacal sign agrees with the twelfth foundation and the last zodiacal sign with the first foundation. In fact, the whole list agrees with John's, though in reverse order. This may be a significant device to show John's disapproval of pagan cults.

The gates are twelve great pearls. Though pearls are not mentioned in the OT, some rabbinic texts refer to gates for Jerusalem hewn out of jewels about forty-five feet square. As for the one main street of the Holy City, it is like the fabric of the city itself, of pure gold, clear as glass.

22–27 John turns from this beautiful description of the city to the life within it. In antiquity every notable city had at least one central temple. The New Jerusalem not only differs in this respect from ancient cities but also from all Jewish speculation about a rebuilt temple and the restoration of the ark of the covenant. Illuminated by the overflowing radiance of the presence of the glory of God, the Holy City no longer needs a temple (GK 3724). Yet paradoxically it has a temple, for the Lord God Almighty and the Lamb are its temple (v.22). And in another sense, the entire city is a temple, since it is patterned after the Most Holy Place (v.16). In his glorious vision, John sees the fulfillment of these hopes in the total presence of God with his purified people, while the Lamb, the sign of the new covenant, is the fulfillment of the restoration of the ark of the covenant (see comment on 11:19; cf. Jn 4:21, 23). In the new city, where there is no longer any uncleanness, no actual temple is needed. In fulfillment of Isa 60:19–20, there will be no further need for any natural or artificial lighting because the glory of God will dim the most powerful earthly light into paleness (cf. Zec 14:7). In the earthly tabernacle and temple, there was, to be sure, artificial lighting (the seven-branched lampstand); yet the Most Holy Place had no such lighting because of the light of God's own presence.

Verses 24–26 present a remarkable picture of "the nations" and "the kings of the earth" entering the city and bringing their "splendor" (GK *1518*) into it. John receives a vision of social life, bustling with activity. Elsewhere in Revelation, the "nations" (GK *1620*) are the pagan, rebellious peoples of the world who trample the Holy City (cf. comments on 11:2; 11:18) and have become drunk with the wine of Babylon, the mother of prostitutes (18:3, 23); they will be destroyed by the second coming of Christ (19:15). But here they stand for the peoples of earth who are the servants of Christ, the redeemed nations who follow the Lamb and have resisted the beast and Babylon (1:5; 15:3; 19:16; 2:26; 5:9; 7:9: 12:5). This latter group, described figuratively here, have part in the activity in the Holy City, the kingdom of God.

Life in the age to come will certainly involve continuing activities and relationships that contribute to the glory of the Holy City throughout eternity. Instead of the nations bringing their precious possessions to the harlot city, the redeemed nations will bring these offerings to the throne of God (cf. Isa 60:3ff.). So certain is its perpetual light and security that the gates will never be shut for fear of evil (v.25; cf. Isa 60:11).

One thing is absolutely certain. Nothing impure (lit., "common"; GK *3123*) will ever enter the city's gates (v.27); by this word John means no ceremonial impurity (cf. 21:8; 22:15). Only those can enter whose names are in "the Lamb's book of life" and who thus belong to him through redemption (cf. 3:5; 20:12, 15). This should not be taken as implying that in the New Jerusalem there will still be unsaved roaming around outside the city who may now and then enter it by repenting. Instead, John warns present readers that the only way to participate in the future city is to turn one's total loyalties to the Lamb now (cf. 21:7).

C. The River of Life and the Tree of Life (22:1–5)

1–5 This section continues the description of the Holy City begun in 21:9, but now with the emphasis on its inner life. John returns to his archetypal images from Ge 1–3 and Eze 40ff. Here Paradise is regained. As in the OT imagery of the age to come, metaphors of water and light abound (cf. Isa 12:3; Zec 14:7–8). "The river of the water of life" recalls Eze 47:1ff. (cf. Joel 3:18) and the pastoral scene of Rev 7:17. In both Testaments water is frequently associated with the salvation of God and the life-imparting and cleansing ministry of the Holy Spirit (Isa 44:3; cf. Jn 3:5; 4:13–14; 7:37–39; 13:10; 19:34; Tit 3:5). In the new city of God the pure water does not issue from the temple as in Eze 47 but comes from "the throne of God," since this whole city is a Most Holy Place with God at its center. Life from God streams unceasingly through the new world.

"The tree of life" spreads all along the great street of the city (v.2). What was once forfeited by our first parents in Eden and denied to their succeeding posterity is now fully restored (cf. Ge 3:22–24). In Ezekiel's vision there are multiple trees on each side of the river that bear fruit monthly (Eze 47:12). Thus, the tree John speaks of may be a collective word for Ezekiel's trees. So abundant is its vitality that it bears a crop of fruit each month! Its leaves produce healing for the nations. The imagery of abundant fruit and medicinal leaves should be understood as symbolic of the far-reaching effects of the death of Christ in the redeemed community, the Holy City. So powerful is the salvation of God that the effects of sin are completely overcome. The eternal life God gives the redeemed community will be perpetually available, will sustain them, and will cure eternally the effects of every former sin.

Thus the curse pronounced in Eden is removed (v.3; cf. Ge 3:17). This may mean that no one who is cursed because of idolatry will be in the city (v.15). Instead of Babylon and its servants occupying the earth, the throne of God will be central and his servants will serve him (cf. 2:13). Wherever the throne is in sight, the priestly service of the saints will be perpetual (cf. 1:6). Here our true liturgy is fulfilled (cf. Ro 12:1). John emphasizes God and the Lamb (21:22–23; 22:1, 3). They share the same glory, the same throne, the same temple significance. The high Christology of John's vision is everywhere evident even though stated in functional terms.

With no restrictions such as those that pertain to Moses (Ex 33:20, 23) or the high priests (Heb 9:7), the redeemed will be in Christ's presence, beholding perpetually his glory (cf. Ps 17:15; Mt 5:8; 1Co 13:12; 2Co 3:18; 1Jn 3:2). Eternal life is perfect communion, worship, the vision of God, light, and victory. Concerning the name on their foreheads, see comment on 14:1.

A final burst of light engulfs the whole scene, and an announcement that the saints "will reign for ever and ever" fulfills the first promise of the book (1:6; cf. 5:10; 20:4 6; see esp. 11:15). The logical sequence as well as the inner relationship of the words "his servants will serve" (v.3) and "they will reign" (v.5) have deep implications for the whole nature of God's kingdom in contrast to that of the satanic Babylon. Surely it is fitting for such a book of prophecy as Revelation to close around the throne, with God's servants both worshiping and ruling.

VI. Conclusion (22:6–21)

With consummate art, the notes of the introit (1:1–8) are sounded again in the conclusion. So the book ends with the voices of the angel, Jesus, the Spirit, the bride, and, finally, John (v.20). The book is a seamless garment. There are three major emphases in the conclusion: confirmation of the genuineness of the prophecy (vv.6–7, 16, 18–19); the imminence of Jesus' coming (vv.7, 12, 20); the warning against idolatry and the invitation to enter the city (vv.11–12, 15, 17–19).

6 A word of assurance similar to that in 19:9 and 21:5 provides the transition from the glorious vision of the Holy City to the final words of the book. An angel declares that it is "the Lord, the God of the spirits of the prophets," the one from whom prophets like John receive their message, that assures the readers of the speedy fulfillment of all that has been revealed (cf. 1:1; 10:6–7).

7 This first declaration of the imminent coming of Jesus is Jesus' own response to the yearnings of the church (cf. comments on 1:7; 2:25; 3:11). This is the sixth beatitude in Revelation; and, like the first one (1:3), it is directed toward those who "keep" (i.e., "obey"; GK *5498*) the words of the prophecy (cf. vv.18–19).

8–9 The "I, John" is reminiscent of 1:4, 9. His confession that he "heard and saw these things" and the repetition of the prohibition (19:10) against John's worshiping the angel serve a purpose. No believer, not even one of great spiritual stature as John, is beyond the subtle temptation to worship what is good itself in place of God, who alone is to be worshiped.

10–11 These verses stand in contrast to the command given Daniel to seal up his book (8:26; 12:4, 9–10). John's message cannot be concealed because the contents of the vision are needed immediately by the churches. On the sealing metaphor, see comment on 7:3.

Verse 11 appears to be fatalistic. Yet on further reflection, the exhortation stresses the imminency of Jesus' return and the need for immediate choices. It echoes the aphorism: As now, so always. Far from being an encouragement to remain apathetic, it is evangelistic in spirit. It may also allude to the great ordeal John viewed as imminent. For the unfaithful and wicked, this appeal would be a deep confirmation of their choice, whereas for the faithful, it would alert them to the necessity of guarding themselves against apostasy (cf. Jude 20–21). There is no reason to take this passage as teaching the irreversibility of human choices. Repentance is always a live option while a person is alive. After death, however, there remains only judgment (Heb 9:27).

12–13 This second of three announcements of the imminent return of Jesus in this chapter (cf. vv.7, 20) is associated with the truth of rewards and judgment based on deeds (cf. comment on 20:12; also 11:18). On the terms Alpha and Omega, etc., see comments on 1:8, 17.

14 The seventh and last beatitude in Revelation is evangelistic in emphasis (cf. 21:6; 22:11, 17). Strands of the earlier imagery are blended in it. In 7:14 the washing of the robes indicates willing identification with Jesus in his death. It also carries the thought of martyrdom during the great ordeal for the saints (cf. 6:11). Thus it symbolizes a salvation that involves obedience and discipleship, since it is integrally related to the tree of life (cf. comment on 22:2) and the gates of the city (cf. 21:25).

15 John has already made it clear that no idolaters can ever enter the city but only those whose names are in the Lamb's book of life (cf. comments on 21:8, 27). Such are "the dogs"—those who "practice magic arts...," i.e., those who rebel against the rule of God (on "dog," cf. Dt 23:18; Mt 15:26; Php 3:2–3).

No doubt such people will not be admitted through the gates of the Holy City but will be in the lake of fire (20:15). But the problem involves what appears to be their present exclusion from the city at the time of John's writing. Are they "outside" now? As has been previously argued, the city is future and is not to be identified with the present historical church (see comments on 21:1–22:21; 21:2). Only in an eschatological sense can it be maintained that the new city exists in the present. Since the fulfillment of v.14 lies in the future, the time of v.15 is also most naturally future. The word "outside" is simply a figure that agrees with the whole imagery of the Holy City. It means exclusion. To be outside the city means to be in the lake of fire.

16 As in 1:8, 17–20, Christ addresses John and the churches directly (the "you" is plural). Here Christ's words authenticate the whole book of Revelation ("this testimony") as being a message to the churches. Therefore, any method of interpreting Revelation that blunts the application of this message in its entirety to the present church disregards these words of Christ. He is the Messiah of Israel, "the Root and the Offspring of David" (cf. Isa 11:1; see comment on Rev 5:5), and the fulfillment of the "Star" promise to the overcomers at Thyatira (see comment on 2:28).

17 The first two sentences are not an evangelistic appeal but express the yearning of the Holy Spirit and the "bride" (the whole church, cf. 21:9) for the return of Christ. In v.20 John gives us the Lord Jesus' answer: "Yes, I am coming soon." The members of the local congregations in John's time join in the invitation for Christ to return. Then, any in the congregations who are not yet followers of Jesus are invited to come and take the water of life as a free gift (cf. Ro 3:24; Rev 21:6). On "the water of life," cf. 21:6; 22:1; see also comment on v.20).

18–19 These verses should not be taken as a warning against adding anything to the Bible. They are primarily a strong warning to false prophets not to alter the sense of John's prophecy in this book, either textually or in its moral and theological teaching (cf. 1Co 16:22). So severe is the danger he is warning against that John says that those who teach contrary to the message of Revelation will not only forfeit any right to salvation in the Holy City but will have visited on them the divine judgments ("plagues") inflicted on the beast worshipers.

20 This is the third affirmation in ch. 22 of Jesus' imminent return and perhaps the response to the longing cry in v.17. John responds to the Lord Jesus' declaration by saying, "Amen. Come, Lord Jesus." These fervent words were part of the liturgy of the early church. They were a prayer used at the close of the meal in the eucharistic liturgy (*Didache* 10.6). As Jesus appeared to his disciples alive on the first day of the week, so he was expected to be present in the Spirit at every first-day Eucharist celebration and to appear again at the end, which is often represented by the picture of a messianic meal. The expression "Come, Lord Jesus" is equivalent to the Aramaic *marana' 'atah* (i.e., Maranatha; cf. 1Co 16:22, "Come, O Lord"). So in closing the book of Revelation, John alludes to ch. 1, with its reference to the Lord's Day (1:10).

21 A conclusion such as this is wholly appropriate for this prophetic message addressed to the ancient church and, indeed, to the whole body of Christ. The benediction is reminiscent of Paul's usual practice (cf. the final verses in his letters). Nothing less than God's grace is required for us to be overcomers and triumphantly enter the Holy City of God, where we shall reign with him forever and ever.

The Old Testament in the New

NT Text	OT Text	Subject
Rev 1:7	Zec 12:10	Looking on one pierced
Rev 1:13	Da 7:13	Coming Son of Man
Rev 1:13–15	Da 10:5–6	Vision of a man
Rev 1:15	Eze 43:2	Voice of rushing waters
Rev 2:27	Ps 2:9	Ruling the nations
Rev 4:6–8	Eze 1:4–10	Four living creatures
Rev 4:8	Isa 6:3	Holy, holy, holy
Rev 5:6	Zec 4:10	Seven eyes of God
Rev 6:2–8	Zech 6:1–6	Four different-colored horses
Rev 6:8	Eze 14:21	Four dreadful judgments
Rev 7:3	Eze 9:4	A mark on the forehead
Rev 7:16	Isa 49:10	Eternal blessings
Rev 7:17	Isa 25:8	God wipes away tears
Rev 10:4	Da 12:4	Sealed words
Rev 10:9–10	Eze 3:1–3	Eating a scroll
Rev 11:1	Eze 40:3	Measuring the temple
Rev 11:4	Zec 4:1–2	Lampstand and olive trees
Rev 11:15	Da 7:27	An everlasting kingdom
Rev 12:14	Da 7:25; 12:7	Three times and a half
Rev 13:1–2	Da 7:3–7	Beasts from the sea
Rev 13:6	Da 11:36	Blaspheming God
Rev 13:7	Da 7:21	War against the saints
Rev 14:14	Da 7:13	Coming Son of Man
Rev 17:12	Da 7:24	Ten horns as ten kings
Rev 18:13–19	Eze 27:27–32	Destruction of a sinful city
Rev 19:15	Ps 2:9	Ruling the nations
Rev 19:17–21	Eze 39:17–20	Food for the birds

The Old Testament in the New

NT Text	OT Text	Subject
Rev 20:8–9	Eze 38:1–39; 16	Gog and Magog
Rev 20:12	Da 7:10	Court books being opened
Rev 21:4	Isa 25:8	God wipes away tears
Rev 21:7	1Ch 17:13	Father and son
Rev 21:10	Eze 40:1–2	Vision of new Jerusalem
Rev 21:12–13	Eze 48:30–35	Twelve gates of the city
Rev 22:1–2	Eze 47:1, 12	Flowing waters and fruit trees

Index of Goodrick/Kohlenberger Numbers

Greek Words

GK No.	Page(s)	GK No.	Page(s)
11	1172	146	740
12	1171	148	933
13	1172	149	773
14	907	153	900, 923
19	89, 545, 565, 927	155	835
20	596, 741, 879	170	914
24	174	172	582, 635, 757, 943
26	29, 373, 741, 778, 838, 1046, 1056, 1110	173	116, 297, 305, 961, 980
27	29, 233, 586, 638, 643, 702, 736, 767, 791, 816, 836, 847, 893, 910, 915, 989, 1056, 1065, 1097, 1101, 1122	174	774, 834, 851
		176	163, 227, 627, 740, 1202, 1205
		179	972
28	223, 274, 905, 909, 965, 1049, 1073, 1087, 1120, 1123	189	1031
		199	243
34	85, 410, 944, 1138	201	67, 170, 245, 1022
39	31, 251, 358, 493, 609, 623, 627, 778, 871, 901, 913, 949, 980, 986, 987, 990, 1010	203	914
		214	762
		219	517
40	1005, 1043	224	1035, 1090
41	130, 318, 524, 582, 617, 623, 627, 752, 752, 789, 815, 974, 1014, 1045, 1049, 1067, 1120, 1156, 1159	225	1090
		230	1038
		237	326, 714, 772, 783, 989, 1110
42	1004	239	809
49	1046	240	974
54	809, 927, 1032	247	189
60	1070, 1196	248	654
70	1011	252	1212
73	915	276	1075
74	404, 795, 826, 851, 906	278	938
76	825, 842, 902, 906, 916	279	544
80	1096	281	556, 679, 753, 756, 1094
81	27, 369, 383, 663, 1020, 1088	283	44, 148, 544
86	802	285	899, 931
87	57, 267, 1137	288	902
88	1032	297	26, 666
90	869	299	972
94	527, 1108	303	300
96	623	318	1075
99	529, 914	320	752, 822, 980, 1124
105	984, 994	337	73
113	864	340	628, 858
118	1076	353	656
124	991	357	252
126	839	359	884, 986
133	897	363	835
135	120, 654	368	753
145	794	373	618

1233

INDEX

GK No.	Page(s)	GK No.	Page(s)
377	783	*636*	527, 614
382	1003	*637*	696, 711, 755, 845, 877, 1125, 1131
390	984	*639*	761, 821
391	772	*640*	401
397	639	*648*	614
399	58, 1198	*652*	1091
405	855	*657*	922
414	220, 476, 1221	*660*	52, 272, 305
416	964	*661*	1172
422	971	*665*	790, 917
424	217	*666*	623
429	1011	*667*	753, 773, 819, 980
435	894	*668*	1013
437	656	*686*	845, 882
441	923	*690*	159, 160, 358, 576
455	898, 903	*691*	625
462	836, 876	*693*	47, 160, 385, 459, 523, 601, 609, 632, 663, 708, 751, 802, 815, 852, 891, 921, 952, 1043, 1064, 1141
468	28, 1059		
476	615		
482	776	*695*	916
485	720, 931	*700*	835, 1023, 1047
490	930, 945, 1094	*710*	388
492	804	*720*	1124
494	1005	*724*	807, 906, 992, 1070, 1076
495	914	*734*	1028
496	530, 538, 915	*740*	476
497	1003	*742*	817
505	1003	*746*	809, 1049, 1064, 1065
508	1059	*766*	243, 280
512	904	*768*	300
519	896	*771*	991
531	982	*772*	797
532	1090	*773*	864
537	893, 910, 1032	*774*	622
538	924	*775*	676, 754
540	304	*780*	894
545	49, 1158, 1159	*788*	32, 316
547	766	*794*	755, 783, 820, 1153
550	1082	*795*	949
561	864	*801*	157
562	983, 1120	*807*	757
563	972	*813*	527, 929, 1123
565	121	*814*	1123
569	564, 600, 651, 1196	*815*	544, 1120, 1123
575	943	*816*	740, 1070
577	957	*819*	564, 697, 700, 960, 973
578	955, 1000	*820*	591
579	926	*822*	544, 591, 633
587	984	*825*	488
588	830	*832*	656
589	828	*834*	1075
600	194, 871	*836*	914
601	912	*842*	998
605	781	*845*	914
608	1151	*846*	912
610	992	*861*	776
621	903	*864*	868
625	589, 903	*865*	886
626	1123	*876*	886
635	401, 1123	*881*	923

INDEX

GK No.	Page(s)	GK No.	Page(s)
889	818	*1192*	710, 794
894	906	*1194*	643, 814, 1064, 1065, 1086
895	810	*1197*	1123
898	210	*1198*	799
904	984	*1201*	404
912	457, 753, 819	*1207*	670
917	927	*1208*	71, 611
918	753, 1085, 1141	*1213*	257, 840, 867, 1148
920	914	*1214*	902, 1005
921	899	*1218*	959
923	238, 901	*1220*	914
925	1122	*1222*	647, 900
929	738	*1228*	227, 1210
933	694, 776, 1050	*1255*	895
940	914	*1256*	79, 187, 209, 228, 260, 284, 384, 1222
947	937	*1259*	907
950	921	*1261*	910
965	1146	*1268*	1154
967	767	*1283*	226
970	1214	*1284*	1072
975	525	*1305*	406, 928, 1068, 1121, 1162
983	744, 852	*1312*	84
987	105	*1313*	79
989	1197	*1321*	995
993	16, 141, 362, 381, 620, 623, 740, 819, 845, 1135, 1159, 1180	*1322*	474
		1328	979
994	1049	*1331*	933
995	362, 1050, 1207	*1333*	19, 224, 900, 914, 1059
996	1212	*1343*	1214
997	1026	*1347*	120, 193, 568, 724, 972, 975, 980, 981
1002	594	*1354*	92, 414, 1044, 1056
1007	109, 188, 835, 1205	*1355*	414, 585, 640, 769, 894, 946
1008	926	*1356*	414, 589, 595, 599, 763, 789, 817, 824, 841, 899, 901
1010	947, 1066, 1068		
1011	666, 827, 947	*1359*	1020, 1025
1012	790	*1363*	476, 480
1013	1006	*1369*	799
1037	677	*1371*	948
1046	985, 1157	*1379*	101
1059	124, 255, 457, 480, 1025, 1201	*1427*	944
1060	62, 124, 417, 835, 906	*1433*	666
1061	914	*1434*	899
1063	187, 631	*1436*	585, 902, 915, 915
1083	964	*1437*	99, 103, 769
1089	1033	*1438*	711, 825, 885
1093	836	*1439*	397, 916
1111	630	*1443*	388
1119	1123	*1444*	1067
1121	912	*1465*	148, 545, 809, 876, 1037, 1085
1147	173, 1030	*1466*	18, 23, 27, 354, 457, 526, 536, 537, 538, 554, 593, 679, 721, 772, 784, 962, 944, 1064, 1214
1155	56, 82, 111, 276		
1161	9		
1164	7	*1467*	457, 531, 537, 623, 717, 718, 932, 1028
1169	478, 1049	*1468*	548, 717, 1213
1174	610, 949	*1469*	717, 929
1181	297	*1470*	717
1182	112, 326, 331, 373, 730, 1064, 1150	*1472*	513
1184	1030	*1474*	900
1185	387, 442, 641	*1491*	133
1188	892, 922	*1496*	740

1235

INDEX

GK No.	Page(s)	GK No.	Page(s)
1500	1020	1756	1056
1501	876, 1043	1762	893, 916, 1005
1503	586, 645, 1185	1763	781
1505	832	1772	544, 932
1506	278, 956	1791	915
1507	640, 775, 851, 870, 900	1793	993
1509	544	1794	353, 775, 916, 925, 930, 1154
1512	1168	1795	1153
1514	1148	1796	569, 585, 894
1518	208, 313, 358, 423, 537, 636, 637, 671, 687, 852, 943, 948, 952, 1044, 1064, 1076, 1124, 1228	1798	951
		1799	215, 569, 757, 892, 932, 959
		1800	1024
1519	236, 321, 344, 354, 356	1823	938
1526	738, 850	1827	736
1528	114, 523, 710, 789, 921, 938, 1019, 1064, 1120, 1131	1828	542, 544, 596, 736, 767, 816, 847, 921, 953, 1053
1530	627	1839	335
1538	972	1869	859
1539	241, 525, 621, 645, 699, 755, 848, 910, 944, 947, 964, 1067	1877	660
		1904	894
1540	818	1907	783
1541	907	1918	755, 884
1543	591	1920	640
1559	1036	1931	880
1562	394, 537	1950	895
1581	16	1953	1111
1583	972	1961	972
1586	776, 1221	1965	1121
1590	988	1967	1192
1591	674, 888	1973	723, 776, 840
1593	917	1975	709
1595	876	1981	829
1599	1058	1987	557
1602	742, 1065	2002	810
1604	924	2007	298
1609	327	2016	244
1613	900	2026	241, 280, 633, 637, 755, 783, 1124
1620	61, 1049, 1176, 1228	2039	396, 980
1630	740	2040	908
1635	637, 673, 819, 984, 1192	2043	1120
1645	24, 218, 287, 355, 543, 594, 663, 708, 741, 752, 790, 815, 846, 892, 922, 968, 1005, 1012, 1060, 1117, 1132	2047	809
		2061	915
		2091	800
1646	1032	2098	1025
1648	248	2103	305, 675
1651	332, 358	2105	1064
1653	961	2106	817, 896, 914, 1064
1666	340, 1151, 1166	2114	922
1676	1009	2117	808, 899, 931, 1032
1683	986	2121	966, 1032, 1044
1688	1162	2138	951
1689	878	2146	1068
1711	5, 78, 388, 409, 493, 609, 766, 820, 846, 950, 1007, 1060, 1155	2148	1060
		2152	903
1721	60, 244, 752	2157	252
1723	99, 110, 188, 269, 912, 921, 1043, 1049, 1110	2160	802, 909, 1033
		2170	216, 948, 1024
1724	848, 1066	2173	214
1725	1003	2174	1005, 1058
1750	933	2175	898

INDEX

GK No.	Page(s)	GK No.	Page(s)
2176	461, 789, 889, 898, 923	*2450*	1050
2184	1031	*2451*	1009
2187	925	*2454*	1032
2188	850	*2465*	617, 865
2191	879	*2473*	913
2203	916	*2484*	897
2210	929	*2488*	579
2211	884, 907, 910	*2505*	673
2213	776	*2509*	1009
2220	1065	*2515*	1200
2224	761, 827, 1123	*2517*	1102
2227	1050	*2525*	32, 708, 753, 985
2228	1067	*2527*	985, 1012, 1074
2230	997	*2529*	616
2240	741, 759, 847	*2535*	915
2241	839	*2536*	915
2245	19	*2540*	828
2247	109, 188	*2544*	953
2249	740, 796, 1031	*2563*	1188
2251	740, 906	*2565*	673
2263	355, 860, 868	*2567*	877
2274	1200	*2568*	109, 824, 845, 849, 857, 858, 876, 876,
2288	784		991, 1043, 1135, 1143, 1167
2294	222, 226, 764, 857, 956, 1054	*2579*	654
2295	21, 139, 848, 912, 1197	*2580*	1024
2296	769	*2581*	669
2298	928, 1013	*2583*	880
2305	60, 223	*2593*	978
2306	753	*2596*	740, 773, 835
2317	141	*2602*	774, 982
2326	994	*2603*	1176
2328	115, 288, 966, 1052	*2610*	1118
2329	216, 752	*2627*	132
2330	688	*2633*	1049
2331	907	*2636*	960, 1159
2336	428	*2639*	1175
2340	1032	*2652*	10
2343	1011	*2661*	951
2351	52	*2662*	1086
2354	896, 1065	*2663*	538
2356	438	*2671*	153
2357	929	*2683*	1118
2368	809	*2700*	1064
2373	193, 278, 609	*2707*	712
2374	895	*2708*	1089
2375	836	*2709*	755
2378	937	*2751*	778, 930, 1085
2380	669	*2752*	944
2384	973, 979, 986	*2754*	24, 351, 1213
2389	211	*2761*	867
2397	740	*2767*	623
2398	545, 822	*2779*	132
2409	834, 987, 1004, 1221	*2785*	670, 976, 1224
2418	1154	*2786*	556
2419	692, 740, 1031	*2789*	43, 382, 626, 745, 753, 840, 864, 907,
2420	645, 732		1132, 1181
2421	150, 930	*2798*	773, 835
2428	906, 913	*2802*	916, 1038
2433	58	*2812*	1175
2437	297, 339, 410, 560, 673	*2813*	21, 541, 853, 980, 1045, 1051, 1059, 1213

INDEX

GK No.	Page(s)	GK No.	Page(s)
2819	896, 933, 1025	*3176*	976
2820	671	*3177*	898
2827	1003	*3179*	783
2837	1200	*3180*	84, 297, 352, 541, 757, 1024, 1033, 1059, 1089, 1096, 1101
2840	33, 62, 101, 238, 755, 790, 954, 988, 1051, 1147	*3186*	165
2843	37, 741	*3195*	988
2844	817	*3196*	501
2857	831	*3197*	755, 1124
2859	825	*3202*	475, 944
2872	1025	*3203*	101
2890	548	*3210*	904, 1209
2895	1034	*3212*	35, 233, 533, 593, 990
2903	679	*3213*	27, 61, 339, 354, 1197
2906	218	*3215*	622
2907	25, 594	*3216*	1025
2917	988, 1023	*3221*	53, 69
2923	954	*3227*	48, 860
2934	761, 884	*3231*	759
2936	1013	*3232*	563, 679
2938	769	*3257*	1110
2941	976	*3258*	1135
2969	905	*3261*	4, 131, 178, 185, 229, 248, 264, 385, 393, 431, 439, 472, 480, 508, 524, 575, 640, 798, 971, 1047, 1071
2981	676		
2988	871, 883, 988		
2990	905	*3262*	755, 1071
2994	211	*3269*	740
2997	821, 828, 995	*3281*	777, 943, 947, 1056
2999	762	*3287*	1213
3016	617, 691	*3295*	10, 212, 222, 273, 277, 282, 399, 464, 1049, 1049, 1068
3017	794, 800, 953		
3029	796	*3301*	582
3031	851, 1028	*3302*	1008
3033	797	*3306*	956
3043	654	*3310*	986
3045	85, 1051	*3313*	802, 974, 1056
3046	804	*3320*	143
3049	973	*3334*	95
3051	820	*3356*	654, 710
3060	377	*3357*	540, 553, 997
3061	896, 1071	*3359*	534, 962, 1056
3062	916, 1054	*3362*	912
3081	1034, 1036	*3364*	210, 210, 296, 380, 481, 773, 849, 880, 894, 947, 1022, 1046, 1053
3082	398		
3090	79, 1150	*3367*	904
3099	23, 945, 946, 966	*3373*	778, 932
3100	493, 774, 980, 995, 1043	*3383*	660
3101	943, 994	*3389*	92, 177, 896
3103	754	*3390*	1045
3104	755, 806, 879, 1066	*3391*	216, 979
3105	565, 612, 1120	*3395*	79
3109	1146	*3407*	11
3121	424, 650, 862, 1073	*3411*	133
3123	922, 990, 1083, 1228	*3412*	232, 317, 435
3126	397, 635, 684, 702, 907, 938, 1011, 1083	*3421*	22, 215, 232, 1021, 1053, 1132
3127	907	*3422*	540, 731
3128	938	*3425*	636
3135	852	*3426*	396, 790
3159	902	*3428*	869, 1037, 1074
3160	847, 852, 1140, 1198	*3429*	530, 741, 767, 818, 836, 915, 916, 966,

INDEX

GK No.	Page(s)	GK No.	Page(s)
	1075	3767	898, 926
3440	266	3768	866, 916, 1045
3443	1196	3771	1142, 1158
3448	944	3777	654
3455	312, 987, 994, 1002	3783	527, 763
3456	297, 312, 1131	3785	1004
3457	50, 613	3791	229
3458	853	3795	481, 535, 539, 555, 558, 718, 738, 969, 1023
3459	288, 381, 1002, 1058		
3468	924	3804	781, 933
3469	1045	3805	596, 825, 868
3479	1189	3808	615, 1194
3488	1124	3813	225
3489	109, 1013	3821	962
3494	740	3827	904
3496	818	3828	761, 1010
3508	628	3839	1002
3523	1123	3842	354
3531	1092	3847	431, 1070
3532	627	3857	326, 868, 1107
3533	696	3860	1050
3534	809	3864	656
3541	967	3867	51
3542	896, 974	3868	493, 868, 1048
3546	760	3869	594, 616
3556	773	3873	753, 762, 824, 893
3557	1007	3874	618, 923
3565	81, 170, 583	3875	106, 900
3566	16, 394, 1141	3876	948
3567	17, 221, 683, 914, 963	3880	582, 664, 836
3571	807	3885	905
3572	709, 994	3897	865, 878, 906
3584	960	3899	73
3620	1005	3904	635
3625	84	3908	871, 1019
3629	636, 849, 966	3909	1036
3630	948	3930	797
3631	262	3933	243, 575, 1102, 1149
3632	999	3943	57
3635	24	3949	938
3655	1033	3950	349, 355, 357, 400, 621, 944
3657	88	3965	696
3659	1009	3973	307, 588, 773, 835, 845, 850, 855, 954, 1163
3662	1196		
3666	298, 997	3975	923
3671	797	3977	898
3677	853	3982	912
3680	1067	3988	278
3696	65, 152, 238, 580, 603, 613, 618, 643, 645, 654, 753, 825, 883, 900, 1138, 1205	4001	1206
		4008	923, 972
		4009	772
3697	1066	4011	669
3702	612	4017	673
3704	113	4022	153
3724	617, 624, 681, 762, 882, 1168, 1175, 1228	4026	57, 104, 1171
3739	834	4051	589
3740	673	4052	32
3745	899	4053	562, 589, 875, 951
3749	81, 1180	4063	221, 280, 282
3752	1147	4075	906

1239

INDEX

GK No.	Page(s)	GK No.	Page(s)
4077	1044	*4348*	867
4079	834	*4355*	753, 827, 858
4080	619, 726	*4359*	1012
4082	915, 1004	*4376*	78
4084	929, 1154	*4377*	78
4086	84, 950, 1089	*4395*	1030, 1031
4090	61, 406	*4409*	293, 298, 427, 457, 534, 616, 956, 1098, 1104
4093	942		
4094	552	*4411*	457, 526, 536, 540, 583, 592, 613, 641, 643, 718, 736, 742, 758, 784, 816, 822, 847, 876, 904, 913, 915, 956, 992, 1120, 1146
4098	932		
4108	1006		
4114	886		
4120	1134	*4412*	610, 815, 894, 924, 935, 951
4126	725	*4414*	276, 1192, 1211
4130	111, 152, 979	*4415*	851
4132	860, 895	*4418*	1112
4137	283, 1142	*4428*	858
4138	905	*4431*	622
4140	50, 83, 116, 119, 172, 198, 249, 566, 639	*4432*	772, 774, 834, 852, 1072
4142	162, 827	*4435*	1189
4151	664, 679, 766, 826, 853, 860, 864, 868, 895, 903, 916, 927, 930, 1012, 1013, 1060	*4436*	459
		4438	899, 923
		4443	848, 966
4155	585, 686, 796, 851, 886, 902, 1013	*4444*	5, 14, 25, 106, 226, 235, 247, 487, 738, 776, 817, 1148
4156	346		
4157	548	*4445*	579, 756, 821, 828
4158	902, 915	*4446*	101, 184, 590
4160	1023	*4458*	825
4161	639, 711	*4460*	305, 387, 561, 614, 621, 682, 739, 795, 871, 880, 883, 1052, 1054, 1099, 1192
4165	826		
4170	853, 868		
4176	955	*4461*	557, 615, 634, 743, 752, 1031, 1048
4183	548, 753, 756	*4462*	1179
4184	946	*4463*	915
4192	1057	*4472*	216, 999
4213	1222	*4477*	1058, 1147
4215	996	*4478*	769
4221	10, 213, 628, 1196	*4480*	1058
4225	779, 825	*4482*	1214
4230	761	*4486*	498, 760
4232	899, 923	*4487*	807
4237	989	*4488*	795
4242	108, 651, 845, 856, 859, 879, 884, 1037, 1093	*4489*	975
		4498	93, 177, 667, 1136
4244	764, 785, 793, 900, 937, 953, 1093, 1098, 1103, 1107	*4505*	871, 886
		4514	711
4246	133, 1123	*4518*	88, 620, 740, 774, 834, 860, 1204
4247	621	*4520*	1204
4248	983	*4521*	1005, 1009
4251	1177	*4539*	122, 194, 639
4252	103, 251, 839, 1028	*4558*	23, 58, 1052
4272	930	*4559*	742, 767, 836, 1023, 1031, 1053
4279	19, 224, 951	*4565*	461, 889, 923, 993, 1058, 1110
4280	32, 122, 252, 635, 1019, 1043	*4566*	926, 937
4287	343	*4589*	565, 1046
4291	1034	*4590*	1043
4319	904	*4598*	754
4325	912, 933	*4606*	764, 915
4344	561, 757, 817, 827, 834, 853, 860, 1084	*4613*	585, 868
4346	1019	*4618*	967

1240

INDEX

GK No.	Page(s)	GK No.	Page(s)
4629	903	*5013*	1067
4633	565	*5014*	984
4639	296, 676	*5020*	954, 955
4643	543, 761	*5023*	602
4657	929	*5030*	865
4666	398, 809, 895, 1159	*5053*	611, 611, 753, 764, 1031, 1194, 1206
4667	1012, 1123	*5055*	604, 617, 1031
4668	946	*5064*	916
4670	104	*5066*	476
4674	397, 840	*5069*	1122
4682	593, 631	*5072*	250
4683	680	*5073*	836
4686	12, 38, 46, 132, 133, 440	*5079*	767, 912, 918, 1067, 1075
4689	938	*5082*	1065
4705	1019	*5083*	165
4710	987	*5090*	106
4713	809	*5095*	856
4714	774	*5100*	675, 1011, 1037
4721	782	*5106*	826
4735	585	*5109*	916, 1021, 1058, 1161, 1182
4736	645	*5112*	807, 885
4737	321	*5113*	1076
4755	1141, 1221	*5114*	1066
4758	819, 820, 945, 1133	*5116*	747
4760	1026, 1029	*5122*	728, 827, 1075
4775	1143	*5123*	806
4777	23, 1024	*5146*	900
4796	1057	*5150*	600
4800	578	*5154*	757
4801	771	*5155*	910, 911
4839	944	*5169*	763
4845	827	*5187*	808
4855	1137	*5188*	757
4861	32, 818, 918	*5194*	827
4865	1024	*5204*	826
4871	498	*5210*	532
4877	1036	*5212*	763, 775
4878	958	*5230*	247
4881	183, 402	*5252*	1016, 1024
4888	880	*5254*	795
4894	1171	*5264*	622, 888
4920	615	*5271*	912
4922	555, 560, 621, 654, 682, 738, 739, 757, 988, 1054, 1089, 1121	*5274*	762
		5281	841
4928	1143	*5283*	757
4935	508	*5284*	187, 403
4936	445	*5287*	532, 589, 672, 895, 979, 1055
4948	809, 900, 926	*5304*	763
4949	896, 927	*5306*	424
4956	62, 77, 110, 313, 597, 611, 699, 947, 1182, 1192, 1199	*5309*	794
		5319	820, 1074
4957	418, 418	*5334*	975
4958	218, 226, 327, 371	*5343*	452
4966	774	*5362*	763
4997	193	*5364*	670
4998	80, 593, 612, 737	*5377*	1096, 1158
5007	673, 860, 1052	*5381*	666, 754
5008	81, 974, 1067, 1225	*5382*	754, 1163
5011	675	*5386*	797
5012	298	*5388*	642

1241

INDEX

GK No.	Page(s)	GK No.	Page(s)
5392	10, 90, 129, 157, 209, 268, 272, 404, 898, 972, 1055	5678	334
5393	552, 582, 642, 653, 871, 1030, 1211	5681	1051
5400	209	5682	1071
5401	209, 216, 217, 404, 410, 526, 793, 946, 994, 1043, 1168, 1212	5694	255
5403	929	5695	30, 74, 162
5404	927	5696	1115
5405	927	5702	644, 912, 1003
5406	910	5705	544, 818, 847, 876, 915, 926, 1037, 1065, 1135, 1140
5407	929	5712	943, 955, 993
5408	897	5717	897
5409	898, 923, 926, 927	5718	588, 647, 756, 777, 838, 927, 930, 1033, 1050
5415	1034	5721	910
5417	1153	5735	644
5419	114	5738	305, 524, 340
5424	58, 683, 796, 1020, 1033	5746	372, 910
5425	767, 832, 836	5757	5, 229, 411
5427	84, 1034, 1059	5758	740, 1211
5434	1071	5760	1173
5435	335, 457	5767	666
5443	1131	5770	944
5448	344, 1088	5771	635
5452	904	5784	740, 906
5455	30, 613, 644, 646, 806, 825, 962, 1019, 1022, 1024	5785	654
		5786	1200
5457	949, 987, 1002, 1087	5787	923
5459	970	5789	586, 861, 1008, 1065
5464	235, 365, 644, 1200	5792	931
5465	574, 635, 644, 652, 893, 1044	5794	906
5469	597, 699, 947	5797	373
5491	1071	5798	914
5493	995	5799	656
5498	357, 871, 1043, 1108, 1120, 1149, 1151, 1151, 1229	5806	914
		5810	586, 1008
5502	896, 943, 1048	5811	898, 923, 1056
5506	780, 903, 1050	5827	904
5507	586, 904, 948, 1048, 1052	5828	44, 215
5528	622	5829	989
5548	959	5832	677, 1051, 1103
5553	1020	5845	744
5587	1036	5850	760
5596	547, 554, 849, 902	5855	924
5603	1066	5857	1027
5605	899, 906	5858	833
5616	894	5860	753
5617	894, 906, 925, 926, 928	5861	49, 113
5625	563	5864	1043
5626	24, 333	5871	1210, 1219
5633	548, 939, 1043	5875	886
5634	838	5881	630
5638	992	5882	757
5641	989	5889	431, 1135, 1196
5642	545	5890	323
5647	834	5891	1226
5650	755	5894	764, 963, 990
5655	766	5915	741, 1083
5662	914	5916	1163, 1193
5671	798	5917	943
5677	210, 618	5919	725, 836

INDEX

GK No.	Page(s)	GK No.	Page(s)
5921	493, 539, 547, 578, 663, 665, 684, 702, 708, 752, 753, 757, 768, 790, 815, 840, 846, 879, 892, 910, 922, 929, 939, 949, 1008, 1050, 1132	*6057*	94, 180
		6068	933
			Hebrew Words
		253	10
5922	394, 547, 585, 626, 640, 902, 910	1382	972
5952	1161	2876	45
5970	992	3051	710
5976	994	3359	565
5982	774	3378	341, 672, 798, 1047
5983	741, 758, 836, 931	5431	167
5985	446, 1057	6625	10
5986	163, 299, 392, 937, 953	6872	174
5987	666	7372	1036
5989	382, 864	8082	781
5992	525	8120	387
6022	884	8477	1059
6034	169, 331, 339, 795, 852, 871, 967, 1011, 1044, 1162, 1211, 1220	8619	267, 1137
		8642	418
6035	1031	8934	157, 287, 663, 708, 852, 892, 968, 1012, 1060
6047	108		
6052	280, 302	9005	798

BUILD YOUR CORE REFERENCE LIBRARY

The more you read your Bible, the more you'll want to establish a personal library of core reference works to help you get the most out of your scriptural studies. Five types of reference books are all that you'll require to meet your three basic needs of Bible study.

Five Types of Books

1. Bible Handbook / Bible Companion
2. Bible Concordance
3. Topical Bible
4. Bible Dictionary
5. Bible Commentary

For Three Basic Needs

1. For an OVERVIEW of the Bible (Handbook/Companion)
2. To FIND something in the Bible (Concordance and Topical Bible)
3. To UNDERSTAND something in the Bible (Dictionary and Commentary)

Depending on your personal interests and the kinds of questions for which you want to find answers, you'll soon want more information. Expand your library to include an encyclopedia of Bible words, who's who of the Bible, Bible atlas, survey or history of the Bible, Bible encyclopedia, and other works. These are available in print or CD-ROM editions from Zondervan Publishing House.

Zondervan*Reference* is committed to publishing outstanding books and software that help you better understand the Bible. Our contemporary reference tools and time-tested classics contain the most reliable and accessible evangelical scholarship supporting the NIV and traditional Bible translations. Depend on Zondervan*Reference* when you want to know more about the Bible.

GRAND RAPIDS, MICHIGAN 49530 USA
WWW.ZONDERVAN.COM

PREMIER REFERENCE SERIES

The Zondervan NIV Premier Reference Series is the award-winning library of choice for readers who insist upon the best when it comes to thoroughness of evangelical scholarship and excellence in hardcover quality. Based on the most widely acclaimed contemporary Bible translation, the New International Version, this series consists of the *Zondervan NIV Exhaustive Concordance, Zondervan NIV Nave's Topical Bible, Zondervan NIV Bible Commentary* (OT and NT volumes), *Zondervan NIV Matthew Henry Commentary,* and *Zondervan NIV Atlas of the Bible.*

Zondervan NIV Nave's Topical Bible
0-310-57950-3

This is the most extensive revision and expansion of the 19th century *Nave's Topical Bible* ever published. It is

- Revised for greater usefulness, accessibility, and accuracy
- Expanded to include references to many current issues
- Fully adapted to the best-selling contemporary translation of the Bible, the New International Version.

The Silver Medallion Award-winning *Zondervan NIV Nave's Topical Bible* proves you can improve on a classic. Its many new features make this the most complete, useful, and accessible topical Bible ever produced—an ideal companion to the *Zondervan NIV Exhaustive Concordance.*

- Keyed to the Goodrick/Kohlenberger numbering system
- Related words listed in article headings to assist in further concordance study
- New, revised, and/or expanded articles on contemporary issues such as abortion, drug abuse, homosexuality, ecology, and discipleship
- Archaic terms from the King James Version (such as unicorn) cross-referenced with contemporary language
- Articles combined whenever appropriate
- Long articles subdivided for easier reference and access
- Personal names and place names accompanied by their meanings
- A bibliography of Bible dictionaries, expository dictionaries of Bible words, and dictionaries of archaeology, ethics, and theology included for further study

In addition to the hardcover print edition of the *Zondervan NIV Nave's Topical Bible,* it is also included in *The NIV Study Bible Basic Library* CD-ROM and *The NIV Study Bible Complete Library* CD-ROM.

Available at your local Christian bookstore

Zondervan NIV Atlas of the Bible
0-310-25160-5

For quick reference and detailed study, the *Zondervan NIV Atlas of the Bible* is the most comprehensive Bible atlas available. This Gold Medallion Award winner is distinguished in several ways:

- The Geographical Section presents the physical geography of the lands of the biblical world, from Egypt to Mesopotamia. The Israel/Jordan region especially is highlighted. The *Atlas* divides the area into twenty-three natural regions and discusses their role in biblical times and such physical features as distances, topography, climate, natural lines of communication, soil types, agricultural uses, and major sources of water.
- The Historical Section presents in detail the flow of biblical history in its geographical context and shows how geography influenced the course of biblical history. Each chapter in this section begins with a chronological chart for the period under discussion, allowing you to see at a glance how the history of Israel fits into the history of the Ancient Near East as a whole.
- A separate section on Jerusalem traces the history and development of the city that is at the center of much of biblical history.
- The Disciplines of Historical Geography chapter shows you how the actual sites of ancient cities are rediscovered—an often complex process that stirs the imagination with the excitement of highly specialized detective work.
- An outstanding feature is the Gazetteer. This is an exhaustive place-name index that gives the exact geographical location for each name with the pages and maps on which the name is found in the *Atlas*. It also gives a brief biblical/historical summary for each name, with Scripture references, and the modern-day name in Hebrew and/or Arabic.

Available at your local Christian bookstore

Zondervan NIV Matthew Henry Commentary

0-310-26040-X

Matthew Henry's commentary remains one of the best-loved and most widely used biblical commentaries, three hundred years after it was first published. But the modern reader often cannot fully appreciate the power and wisdom of Matthew Henry's insights. His writing was often wordy, and he used many terms and expressions that have changed in meaning since his day.

This one-volume edition of Matthew Henry's commentary overcomes both problems through these outstanding features:

- The careful condensation retains the essential content of Matthew Henry's incomparable devotional commentary
- The precise replacement of readily misunderstood words with modern ones updates Matthew Henry's vocabulary without changing his personal style
- The meticulous adaptation of Matthew Henry's commentary to the New International Version makes it fully compatible with today's best-loved Bible translation.

The fresh, contemporary language captures anew the practical wisdom and spiritual insights that have made this commentary a highly valued Bible study resource and devotional guide.

Available at your local Christian bookstore

Zondervan NIV Exhaustive Concordance

0-310-22997-9

A concordance is the one integral Bible study tool that absolutely must match the Bible translation you're using. Among concordances based on the New International Version, only the *Zondervan NIV Exhaustive Concordance* provides an exhaustive indexing of every appearance of every word in the NIV Bible. It gives complete access to every word of the NIV text as well as to the Hebrew, Aramaic, and Greek from which the NIV was translated. Feature for feature, this Gold Medallion Award-winning volume is by far the finest, most thorough NIV-based concordance available.

SPECIAL FEATURES:

- Complete alphabetical listings for every word in the NIV.
- NEW to the second edition: Thorough dictionary-indexes define every Hebrew, Aramaic, and Greek word in the Bible, including the possible meaning of every proper name. The dictionary-indexes also supply an exhaustive listing of every NIV translation for a given word, and show all related words in the original languages. Frequency counts are given for each original language word and each of its English translations.
- Special index of articles, conjunctions, particles, prepositions, and pronouns.
- All references listed in biblical order.
- All words cross-referenced to spelling variations and variant forms.
- More than 2,000 key words from the KJV cross-referenced to their NIV equivalents.
- Each word heading lists total number of occurrences in the NIV.
- Special typefaces indicate the word or words used in the NIV translation for all Hebrew, Aramaic, and Greek terms.
- Unique numbering system developed by Goodrick and Kohlenberger (G/K) eliminates the inherent gaps, flaws, and inaccuracies of the old Strong's numbering system.
- Special indexes allow for easy cross-referencing between the G/K numbering system for those using reference books keyed to the outdated Strong's numbers.

Available at your local Christian bookstore

Zondervan's Understand the Bible Reference Series

This 6-volume hardcover series supplies readers of today's most popular modern Bible translation, the New International Version, with scholarly, economical, and uncompromisingly evangelical study tools. Recommend these books to your friends who want complete, accessible reference tools at a thrifty price.

New International Bible Commentary
F.F. Bruce, General Editor
0-310-22020-3

With twenty-eight introductory articles and numerous maps and charts, this Gold Medallion Award-winning one-volume commentary is an analytical exposition of the Bible by 43 outstanding scholars, such as Carl Armerding and Walter L. Liefeld.

New International Bible Dictionary
J. D. Douglas and Merrill C. Tenney
0-310-33190-0

Based on the NIV, this comprehensive, Silver Medallion Award-winning Bible dictionary is crossed referenced to the KJV and contains a complete Scripture index, more than 5,400 entries and more than 1,000 illustrations, maps, charts, tables, and photographs.

New International Bible Concordance
John R. Kohlenberger III and Edward W. Goodrick
0-310-22902-2

Keyed to the NIV, the number one contemporary Bible translation, this Silver Medallion Award-winning concordance features every biblical reference to over 12,800 words; indexed alphabetically. If you read the NIV, you need a NIV-based concordance.

New International Encyclopedia of Bible Words
Lawrence O. Richards
0-310-22912-X

Based on the NIV and NASB, with cross-references to the KJV, this Silver Medallion Award-winning book helps you to easily understand the original, rich meanings of the key words used in the Bible. It includes the G/K numbering system, topical index, Scripture index, and index of Hebrew and Greek words. No knowledge of Hebrew or Greek is required.

New International Encyclopedia of Bible Characters
Paul D. Gardner, Editor
0-310-24007-7

This is an exhaustive ready reference of every person named in the Bible, from Aaron to Zurishaddai. With entries based on the NIV, this easy-to-use volume will help pastors, teachers, students, and lay people identify and understand the importance of every person in the Bible.

New International Encyclopedia of Bible Difficulties
Gleason L. Archer
0-310-24146-4

This extensive encyclopedia addresses, in the order in which they appear in Scripture, the problems and questions, which are raised in the biblical text against the doctrine of inerrancy, including a full index. It is intended for everyone, from scholars and students to layperson—for all who are troubled by apparent contradictions in the Bible.

Available at your local Christian or College Bookstore

NIV COMPACT REFERENCE SERIES

This portable softcover series sits handsomely on your desk or bookshelf, ready to quickly and authoritatively answer your Bible study questions. These inexpensive books are perfect for the student, Bible study leader, or anyone wanting mobility in their Bible reference library.

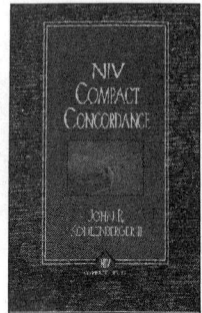

NIV Compact Concordance

John R. Kohlenberger III
0-310-22872-7

This is a streamlined adaptation of the Gold Medallion Award-winning *Zondervan NIV Exhaustive Concordance*. It features more than half the vocabulary of the NIV translation and 70,000 biblical references. The words represent those most significant for general biblical knowledge, theology, and spiritual development.

NIV Compact Bible Commentary

John H. Sailhamer
0-310-22868-9

This book explains the Bible book by book, but unlike other commentaries, it begins with the Bible as a whole, then shows how all its books fit into the grand picture. Instead of a verse-by-verse exposition, it unlocks the meanings of larger sections of Scripture.

NIV Compact Nave's Topical Bible

John R. Kohlenberger III
0-310-22869-7

This expansion on the original *Nave's Topical Bible* offers quick and easy access to more than 7,000 subjects in the Bible. It contains all the Bible references of the full-length Silver Medallion Award-winning *Zondervan NIV Nave's Topical Bible*, with the biblical text eliminated to save space.

NIV Compact Dictionary of the Bible

J. D. Douglas
0-310-22873-5

A Bible dictionary, topical index, and survey all rolled into one, this is a careful condensation of the Silver Medallion Award-winning *New International Bible Dictionary*, complete with maps, charts, illustrations, and photographs. This concise book helps you clear up the who, where, when, why, and how of the Bible.

Available at your local Christian bookstore

OTHER BOOKS BY JOHN KOHLENBERGER III

The Exhaustive Concordance to the Greek New Testament

0-310-41030-4

An exhaustive index to every Greek word in the New Testament, UBS4, with context lines in Greek. Coauthored with Edward W. Goodrick.

The Greek New Testament UBS4 with NIV and NRSV

0-310-41400-8

The only parallel New Testament with the Greek text, as well as the NIV and NRSV.

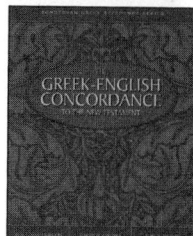

The Greek-English Concordance to the New Testament

0-310-40220-4

Presents in alphabetical order every word in the Greek New Testament along with, in English, the passages in which the word occurs. Unlike the older *Englishman's Greek Concordance to the New Testament*, it is exhaustive and contains many new features. Coauthored with Edward W. Goodrick.

The Hebrew-English Concordance to the Old Testament

0-310-20839-4

The most complete concordance showing the relationships of Hebrew words to the NIV Bible translation. A companion volume to *The Greek-English Concordance to the New Testament*. Coauthored with James A. Swanson.

The NRSV Concordance: Unabridged

0-310-53910-2

Provides easy access to every word and its reference in the NRSV and includes an index to alternate and "literal" translations found in the footnotes of the NRSV. Also features a phrase concordance and topical index.

Available at your local Christian bookstore

We want to hear from you. Please send your comments about this book to us in care of zreview@zondervan.com. Thank you.

GRAND RAPIDS, MICHIGAN 49530 USA
WWW.ZONDERVAN.COM